MOON HANDBOOKS®

NORTHERN CALIFORNIA

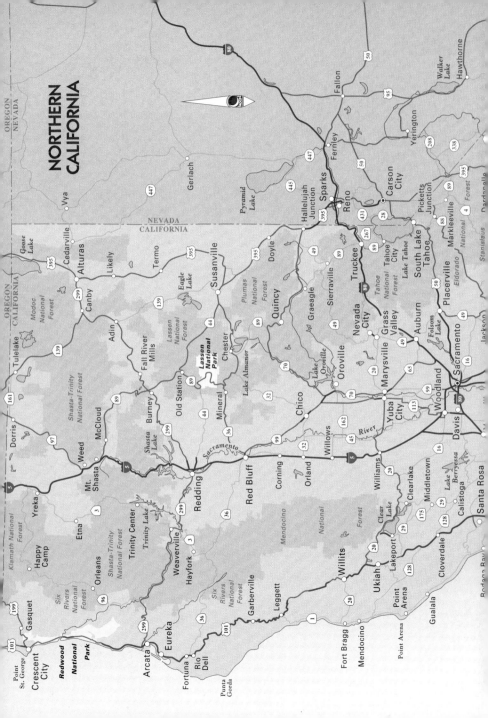

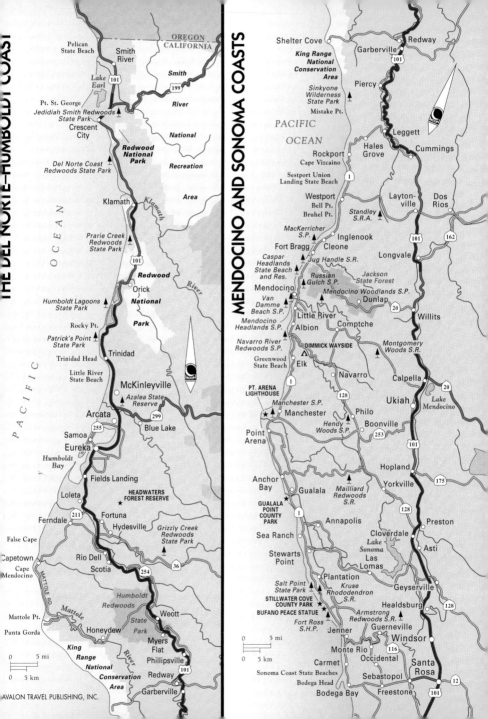

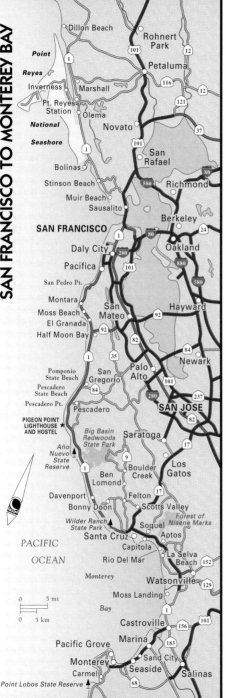
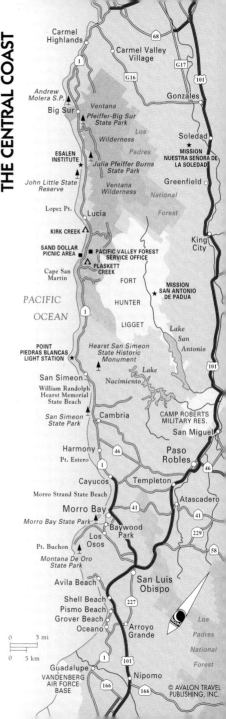

LAKE TAHOE AND VICINITY

To Graeagle, Portola, and Quincy
To Loyalton
Sierraville
To Susanville
Sparks
To Elko and Winnemucca
Tahoe National Forest
Jackson Meadow Res.
Independence Lake
Stampede Res.
Boca Res.
Verdi
Reno
Mt.
Rose
Fordyce Lake
Soda Springs
TAHOE DONNER
BOREAL
Truckee
Mt.
Rose
Wilderness
MT. ROSE
DIAMOND PEAK
Washoe Lake
Virginia City
To Fallon
Cisco Grove
SODA SPRINGS
ROYAL GORGE
SUGAR BOWL
DONNER SKI RANCH
Donner Memorial State Park
NORTHSTAR-AT-TAHOE
Kings Beach
Incline Village
Carson City
SQUAW VALLEY USA
Tahoe City
Lake Tahoe-Nevada State Park
Tahoe National Forest
Granite Chief
ALPINE MEADOWS
Wilderness
GRANLIBAKKEN
Lake
Tahoe
Glenbrook
French Meadows Reservoir
Homewood
HOMEWOOD
Sugar Pine Point State Park
D.L. Bliss State Park
Zephyr Cove
Hell Hole Res.
Meeks Bay
Loon Lake
Eldorado
Desolation Wilderness
Emerald Bay State Park
Stateline
South Lake Tahoe
Minden
Gardnerville
National
Camp Richardson
HEAVENLY
ICE HOUSE RD.
Union Valley Res.
Ice House Res.
Fallen Leaf Lake
Fallen Leaf
LAKE TAHOE AIRPORT
Lake Valley State Recreation Area/ Washoe Meadows State Park
Lake Aloha
Echo Lake
Meyers
Pollock Pines
Strawberry
SIERRA-AT-TAHOE
Picketts Junction
NEVADA CALIFORNIA
Riverton
Jenkinson Lake
MORMON EMIGRANT TRAIL
Carson Pass
SORENSEN'S RESORT
Markleeville
Topaz Lake
Placerville and Sacramento
KIRKWOOD
Caples Lake
Grover Hot Springs State Park
Topaz Lake
NORTH-SOUTH RD.
Silver Lake
IRON MOUNTAIN
Monitor Pass
Topaz
To Jackson
Bear River Res.
Mokelumne
Wilderness
Ebbets Pass
Coleville
Stanislaus
BEAR VALLEY
Lake Alpine
Carson
Iceberg
Walker
Salt Springs Res.
Spicer Meadows Res.
Wilderness
National
COTTAGE SPRINGS
Forest
Dorrington
Donnell Lake
Dardanelle
Sonora Pass
To Bridgeport
To Angels Camp
Calaveras Big Trees State Park
To Sonora
KENNEDY MEADOWS
To Loyalton
To Susanville

MOON

5 mi
5 km

AVALON TRAVEL PUBLISHING, INC.

Hearst Castle, San Simeon

MOON HANDBOOKS®

NORTHERN CALIFORNIA

FOURTH EDITION

KIM WEIR

AVALON
TRAVEL

MAPS

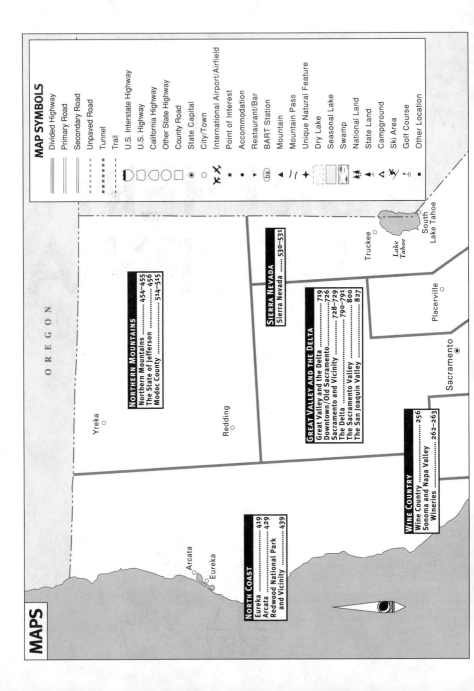

O R E G O N

MAP SYMBOLS

▦	Divided Highway
◫	Primary Road
▭	Secondary Road
▭	Unpaved Road
▪▪▪	Tunnel
┅	Trail
⬭	U.S. Interstate Highway
⬯	U.S. Highway
⬮	California Highway
⬭	Other State Highway
▢	County Road
◉	State Capital
○	City/Town
✈	International Airport/Airfield
★	Point of Interest
•	Accommodation
✕	Restaurant/Bar
ⓑⓐ	BART Station
◀	Mountain
)(	Mountain Pass
✦	Unique Natural Feature
▨	Dry Lake
▨	Seasonal Lake
≋	Swamp
▲	National Land
▲	State Land
⌂	Campground
⚡	Ski Area
⛳	Golf Course
▪	Other Location

Yreka ○

Redding ○

Truckee ○

Lake Tahoe

South Lake Tahoe

Placerville ○

Sacramento ◉

Arcata ○

Eureka ○

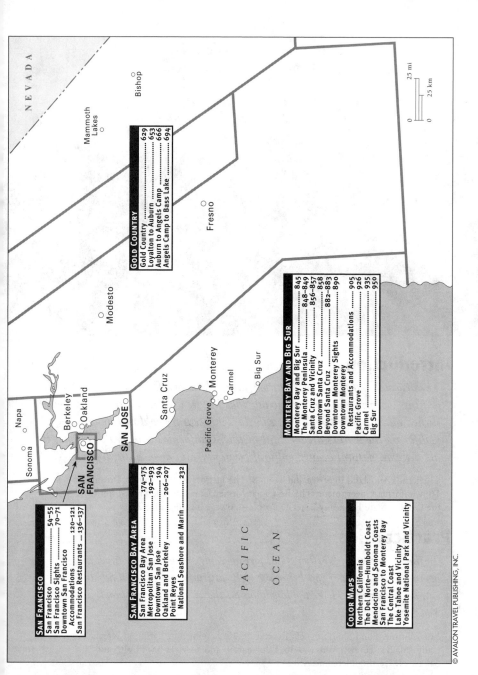

© AVALON TRAVEL PUBLISHING, INC.

Contents

San Francisco .... .52

Prominent at the edge of the continent, San Francisco is also at the cutting edge of California's ongoing social revolutions. Beloved for its restaurants, cable cars, magnificent museums, storied hotels, bookstores, and wild bars, the city is eccentric yet sanguine—happily situated at the epicenter of Northern California culture.

San Francisco Bay Area 173

Vast in its endless urbanism, from Berkeley and Oakland to Silicon Valley, the San Francisco Bay Area also has wildness and surprising wayside pleasures: Sleep in a lighthouse, watch whales from Point Reyes, hike Mt. Diablo, or picnic at the annual TarantulaFest.

Wine Country .... .254

The inland valleys of Napa, Sonoma, Mendocino, and Lake Counties have become known as California's wine country, though only a small amount of California wine is produced here. Quality, not quantity, is the point. Honoring appetite has led to the region's deepening appreciation for fine wines and fresh, well-prepared foods.

North Coast 359

Here's a California too few celebrate, where surreal seastacks and craggy coastal formations point the way to deep, dramatic forests. Hike the Lost Coast. See where The Birds *was filmed. Buy local art in Mendocino and Eureka. Or commune with redwoods and Roosevelt elk.*

Northern Mountains and Modoc 453

It's been only 60-some years since this part of California tried to secede as the state of Jefferson. The spirit of secession survives, but these days many roads are paved— making it that much easier to visit Lassen Volcanic National Park and spectacular sister volcano Mt. Shasta.

Sierra Nevada 529

No one says it better than 19th-century naturalist John Muir: Smitten by "sunbursts of morning among the icy peaks," he dubbed the Range of Light "the most divinely beautiful of all the mountain chains." With world-class hiking, skiing, and scenery, from famed Lake Tahoe and Yosemite to magical Mono Lake, the Sierra Nevada still has it all.

Gold Country 628

*California's mythic gold became real in 1848 when
gold was found at Sutter's Mill on the American River.
The astounding history of the gold rush is celebrated
today in the dozens of Wild West towns it created,
from charmed Nevada City and Sutter Creek to
Volcano, Angels Camp, Murphys, and Columbia.*

Great Valley and the Delta 717

California's capital city is also at the center of the state's agricultural heartland, where the two central river valleys merge into the vast Sacramento–San Joaquin Delta. Sacramento serves up great restaurants and sparkles with unpretentious museums and amusements. Head north, south, and west for agricultural vistas, slow-paced farm towns, and impressive wildlife reserves.

Monterey Bay and Big Sur 844

Sometimes veiled by what Robert Louis Stevenson called its "vast, wet, melancholy fogs," Monterey Bay is a natural wonder, one of the world's richest ecosystems. The surrounding cities—Santa Cruz, Monterey, Salinas, Pacific Grove, and Carmel—have their own charms. Just south is the spectacular, soaring highway along Big Sur.

Kim Weir

Kim Weir was born in Southern California but raised in far Northern California. For a time, Kim's father operated a beer distributorship, a weekend job that required rattling around the foothills and mountains of Northern California in a Falstaff delivery van. Some of the author's earliest summer adventures involved washboarding with her dad down back roads, the stench of stale beer rising from flats of empties. Kim has happily explored California byways ever since—typically without the beer.

Since childhood Kim has struggled with herself over the relative merits of travel and books, as well as the challenges of hitching the two together. Take her first trip to the Grand Canyon. Upon arrival her parents insisted that the 11-year-old put away James Michener long enough to at least get out and take a good look at that #!^%#$*&!! hole in the ground. Kim did better than that, though. She walked all the way down into the canyon that day—and back up—toting copies of *The Source*, *Gone with the Wind*, and other tomes in her knapsack as useful ballast against the wind.

Kim's love of California, travel, and books finally came together in 1990 with the publication of the colorful *Moon Handbooks Northern California*. Other books soon followed, including *Moon Handbooks Southern California*, *Moon Handbooks Coastal California*, *Moon Handbooks California*, and *Moon Handbooks Monterey & Carmel*.

Among other worthwhile pursuits, Kim has worked as an editor at Scholars Press and as communications director for the Faculty Association of California Community Colleges (FACCC). She holds a degree in environmental studies and analysis from CSU Chico and is now pursuing her MFA in Creative Writing. She is also an active member of the Society of American Travel Writers (SATW).

Introduction

California is a myth—a myth in the sense of a traditional tale told to impart truth and wisdom, and in the fanciful sense of some extravagant storybook fiction. Californians happen to like the quirky character of the state they're in. Whether or not they realize it, California as myth is exactly why they're here—because in California, even contradictions mean nothing. In California, almost everything is true and untrue at the same time. In California, people can pick and choose from among the choices offered—as if in a supermarket—or create their own truth. Attracted to this endless sense of creative possibilities—California's most universal creed, the source of the ingenuity and inventiveness the state is so famous for—people here are only too happy to shed the yoke of tradition, and traditional expectations, that kept them in harness elsewhere.

Californians tend to think life itself is a California invention, but "lifestyle" definitely is: people come to California to have one. Coming to California, novelist Stanley Elkin observes, "is a choice one makes, a blow one strikes for hope. No one ever wakes up one day and says, 'I must move to Missouri.' No one chooses to find happiness in Oklahoma or Connecticut." And according to historian Kevin Starr, "California isn't a place—it's a need." Once arrived in California, according to the myth, the only

Napa Valley

reason to carry around the baggage of one's previous life is because one chooses to.

But it would be naive to assume that this natural expansiveness, this permission to be here now, is somehow new in California. It may be literally as old as the hills. Native peoples, the first and original laid-back Californians, understood this. Busy with the day-to-day necessities of survival, they nonetheless held the place in awe and managed to honor the untouchable earth spirits responsible for creation. The last remembered line of an ancient Ohlone dancing song—"dancing on the brink of the world"—somehow says it all about California.

As a place, California is still a metaphor, for Shakespeare's "thick-coming fancies" as well as for those awesome mysteries that can't be taken in by the five senses. People come here to sort it all out, to somehow grasp it, to transform themselves and the facts of their lives—by joining in the dance.

CALIFORNIA AS EUROPEAN MYTH

Native peoples had many explanations for how the land and life in California came to be, almost as many stories as there were villages. But it's a stranger-than-fiction fact that California as a concept was concocted in Europe, by a Spanish soldier turned romance writer.

The rocky-shored island paradise of California, according to the 1510 fictional *Las Sergas de Esplandían* by Garcí Ordóñez de Montalvo, overflowed with gold, gems, and pearls, was inhabited by griffins and other wild beasts, and "peopled by black women, with no men among them, for they lived in the fashion of Amazons" under the great Queen Calafia's rule. With such fantastic images seared into the European imagination, it's no wonder that Cortés and his crew attached the name California to their later territorial claims from Baja California north to Alaska.

THE MYTH OF NORTHERN AND SOUTHERN CALIFORNIA

While California is still a destination of the imagination and a rich land indeed, its true wealth is (and always was) its breathtaking beauty, its cultural creativity, and its democratic dreams.

The primary political fact of life here is that California is one state. Technically indisputable, this fact is nonetheless widely disputed. Californians themselves generally view the state as two distinct entities: Northern California, centered in sophisticated San Francisco, and the continuous sprawl of Southern California south of the Tehachapi Mountains, its freeways spreading out from its Los Angeles heart like the spokes of a bent and broken wheel.

According to the myth that successfully populated Southern California, simple, neighborly, nature-oriented living amid sunny gardens and citrus groves would save civilization from the mass-production mind-set of industrialism—almost shocking to contemplate now, when one sees what's become of that idea. Yet this is also the land of the American dream made manifest, where the sun always shines—on the degenerate and deserving alike, the ultimate in California-style social democracy—and where even the desert itself is no limitation since, thanks to the wonders of modern engineering, water can be imported from elsewhere. In the newer Southern California myth, style is more important than substance and image is everything, cultural truths shaped in large part by Hollywood and the movies. Life itself is defined by humanity—by an artificial environment of pavement and plastic technologies manufactured by human need and vanity, by the worship of physical beauty in human form, and by the relentless search for the ultimate in hedonistic diversion and novelty. An engineered Eden ruled by Midwestern social and political mores, Southern California worships everything new—from new beliefs and ideas and commercially viable images transmitted via its own film and media industries to art and innovation for their own sakes—and rarely questions the intrinsic value of cosmetic change. The main moral question in the southstate is not "Is it important?" or "Is it right?" but: "Is it new?"

Northern California's mythic soul is represented by nature in all its contradictions—the rugged outdoors in tandem with the rugged individualist struggling for survival, the simple beauty of humanity in nature as well as more complicated relationships that result from humanity's attempts to change and control nature's inherent wildness. The collective and personal histories of Northern California suggest secessionism, rebellion, and the high-technology innovations largely responsible for today's global culture. Northern California is also about human awareness in nature, and a modern consciousness seemingly sprung fully formed from nature worship: holistic health and get-in-touch-with-yourself psychological trends; mandatory physical fitness, as if to be ready at a moment's notice to embark upon ever more challenging outdoor adventures; natural foods and a regionally focused appreciation for fresh produce and fine wines. Life in Northern California is defined by outdoor-oriented, socially responsible narcissism—and symbolized by an upwardly mobile young professional couple nudging their new, gas-guzzling four-wheel drive onto well-engineered highways leading out of the city and into the wilderness.

Yet in many ways the two ends of the state are becoming one. Despite regional chauvinism, southstate-style growth, with all its attendant problems, is fast becoming a fact of life in the north; within several decades, almost as many people will live in Northern California as in Southern. In all parts of the state, growth is moving away from major cities and into the suburbs—a fact that is influencing political trends as well. Northern California, traditionally more liberal than Southern California, is becoming more Republican, while the southstate's increasing concerns over health and environmental issues are liberalizing urban political trends. And though Northern California politicians tend to openly oppose any increased water shipments to Southern California (unless their districts are paid well for private water sales), most are much quieter about supporting water engineering feats designed to meet the needs of the northstate's own suburban growth.

Californians themselves still see most statewide social, political, and "style" differences in terms of north versus south regionalism. The time-honored historical issue of politically splitting California into two separate states—an idea now at least rhetorically quite popular in the rural north, though the state's first secessionism arose in the south—still comes up regularly. But the actual facts about modern-day California suggest a different reality. Life here is, and will be continue to be, defined by the conflicting cultures of minority-dominated urban areas, more conservative Sun Belt suburbs created by "white flight," and declining, truly rural resource-based communities.

CALIFORNIA AS "FIRST IN THE NATION"

California's most obvious "first" is its population. Half of the people living in the West, the fastest-growing region of the nation, live in California. Number one in the nation now—with almost 36 million people—California's population at current growth rates will be nearly 40 million by the year 2005, nearly 50 million by 2030 (some say 2020 or 2025), and 60 million by 2040. Or more. The state has been growing so rapidly during the past decade, largely because of legal and illegal immigration, that demographers can't keep up (After the 2000 census, for instance, state head-counters added another million to the feds' estimate). Keeping tabs on Californians has been complicated further by their increasing migration, in recent years, to other states; more than 2.2 million left between 1995 and 2000.

The sheer heft of California humanity makes it first in the nation in immigration (both legal and illegal), first in bomb threats and investigations, first in firearm-related violent crime, and first in prison budgets. Largely because of Southern California population pressures, California also ranks shockingly high for endangered and threatened species. Yet California boasts more Nobel Prize laureates than any other state, more engineers and scientists, and more research labs, colleges, and universities.

California is also number one in construction-related business contracts and leads the nation in number of millionaires, though it no longer tops the nation's lists for livable cities or average personal incomes-and in fact falls behind the rest of the nation in the latter category. Despite the crush of its urban population, California usually makes more money in agriculture than any other state, and produces—and consumes—most of the country's wine.

The land has its own firsts-and-bests, since California boasts the highest point in the contiguous U.S. (Mt. Whitney) and the lowest (Death Valley). California is also home to the world's largest living thing, the Sequoia big tree; the world's tallest, the coast redwood; and the world's oldest. The state's bristlecone pine has long been considered life's old-timer, an honor now claimed by a nondescript creosote bush, still flourishing after 11,000 years. Depending upon how one defines individuality, however, two of the latter records may fall. One particular subterranean fungus in Michigan, sprouting multiple mushrooms, spans at least 37 acres, is estimated to weigh 220,000 pounds, and may have been alive since the end of the last Ice Age.

Common wisdom in the U.S. holds that "as California goes, so goes the nation." As with most California legends, there is at least some truth to this. California is quite often the national trendsetter, from fads and fashions in political or social beliefs to styles in cars and clothes. In its endless pursuit of style, California searches for its identity, for some explanation of itself. California is constantly inventing and reinventing its own mythology. Yet California was among the last states in the U.S. to emerge from the latest recession, and few states so far are following California's lead in eliminating affirmative action programs and attempting to withhold public services from immigrants.

The Free Speech Movement, the philosophical foundation supporting both civil rights and anti-Vietnam War activism, took root in California. But so did the New Republicanism (best represented by Richard Nixon and Ronald Reagan), a reactionary trend toward social control that arose at least as an indirect result. California is usually first in the nation for new religious and spiritual trends, too, from New Age consciousness to televangelism.

California is the birthplace of the motel, the climate-controlled shopping mall, suburban sprawl, and a lifestyle almost entirely dependent upon cars and elaborately engineered highway and freeway systems. But California is also first in the nation in car thefts and in marijuana cultivation. It's home to the back-to-the-land culture and spawning ground for the philosophy of bioregionalism, too, decrying all things homogenized, unnatural, unnecessarily imported, and plastic. For every action in California, there is also a reaction.

CONTEMPORARY CALIFORNIA FACTS AND FANCY

Among common misconceptions about the state is the one the rest of the world tenaciously clings to—that everyone in California is laid-back, liberal, blond, rich, and well educated.

California as Laid-Back

California may be casual, but it's not exactly relaxed. Despite the precedents set by native peoples and early Californios (those of Spanish descent born in the pre-U.S. period), most of the state's modern residents are hardly content to live in leisure. In their frantic rush to accumulate, to stay in style, to just keep up with the state's sophisticated survival code and incredible rate of change, Californians tend to be tense and harried. And now that Californians have remembered— and reminded the rest of the world—that rest and relaxation are necessary for a well-rounded life, people here pursue recreation with as much determination as any other goal. Just sitting around doing nothing isn't against the law in California, but it's definitely déclassé.

California as Liberal

If people in California aren't particularly laid-back, they aren't particularly liberal either. After all, California created both Richard Nixon and Ronald Reagan. The truth is, California has never committed itself to any particular political party. Democratic legislators still predominate in California's Senate and Assembly—a surprise in 1996, considering the general Republican drift elsewhere—and Democrats, after losing ground

ON JOHN MUIR'S TRAIL

I could give up this life
of children and fuss
because there's still a John Muir
trail I retreated down
that insane sixties summer I was
trapped between boy and man.

I would carry my life
again in the green canvas pack
and hike Muir's high granite trail
from lake to barely-touched lake,
lonely and learning to live
in someone else's world.

I should step from this mirror
of my responsibly-shaved face
to face John Muir's white-bearded
stare at the camera. It says:
he blazed his own mountain way
away from family and Martinez farm
with abandon.

—*Gary Thompson*

in 1994, regained strength in the U.S. House of Representatives in 1996. Some blame former Republican governor Pete Wilson, described by national columnist Anthony Lewis as "the premier gutter politician of our day," since Wilson's reactionary anti-immigrant reelection campaign of 1994 and his activist anti-affirmative action stance in 1996 made Latino citizens—and other voters—angry enough to vote Democratic in a big way. Perhaps it was only fitting that Fresno's Cruz Bustamante, the first Latino speaker of the state Assembly, took office in 1996. Subsequently, there was a rapid decline in the Republicans' recent race-baiting politicking—but not enough to slow the statewide decline in Republican influence.

In November 1998, California elected a Democratic governor, Gray Davis, by a whopping 20-point margin, though the state has supported only Republicans in that office since the departure of "Governor Moonbeam," Jerry Brown, in the late 1970s. And Cruz Bustamante was elected

lieutenant governor, the first Latino in the 20th century elected to statewide office. In the same election, the previously ascendant Christian conservatives in the Republican Party lost big—and the state also elected its first Green Party candidate, Audie Bock, to the state Assembly.

Yet even in 1992, when Republicans otherwise dominated state politics, California was first in the nation to elect women—both Democrats, Barbara Boxer and Dianne Feinstein—to fill its two U.S. Senate seats, outdoing all other states, cities, and municipalities in paying homage to "the year of the woman." (Ten years later, in a trickle-up effect, U.S. House Democrats enthusiastically elected veteran San Franciscan politician Nancy Pelosi to lead their party.) And California overwhelmingly supported Gov. Bill Clinton, a Democrat, in the 1992 presidential election. President Clinton's support, though still a majority, was substantially less in the 1996 election. Yet the Democrats' previous declines and Republican dominance on the national level have diminished the state's traditional political clout in the U.S., at least in the short term, because of the loss of key committee chairs and committee rankings once held by California Democrats.

The tattered terms of Governor Gray Davis, beset by a manufactured energy crisis and fiscal fallout from the dotcom bomb, didn't bode well for the Democrats. Republicans seem equally ill-prepared to manage the massive scale of problems now facing California, though Governor Arnold has promised to tackle California's perennially pressing issues: education, energy, and the economy.

Occasional flamboyant public figures and long-standing double-edged jokes about the land of "fruits and nuts" aside, predicting the direction in which political winds will blow here is difficult. Until recently, pollsters detected a steady trend toward increasing identification with the Republican party among the state's voting-age population. Generally speaking, the political labels of Democrat and Republican mean little in California. People here tend to vote on the basis of enlightened economic interest, personal values, and "political personality."

But if the New Republicanism is quite comfortable in California, so is the orthodoxy of no orthodoxy. Values, political and social, are discarded as easily as last year's fashions. (Californians don't oppose tradition so much as they can't find the time for it.) The state's legendary liberalness is based on the fact that, like social voyeurs, Californians tolerate—some would say encourage—strangeness in others. Rooted in the state's rough-and-tumble gold rush history, this attitude is almost mandatory today, considering California's phenomenal cultural and ethnic diversity.

California as Blond

Despite the barrage of media and movie images suggesting that all Californians are blond and tan and live at the beach, not much could be further from the truth. Though Caucasians or "Anglos" predominate ethnically, California's population has represented almost every spot on the globe

COURTESY OF SAN JOSE CONVENTION AND VISITORS BUREAU

Despite cultural myths to the contrary, not everyone in California is blond, tan, and living at the beach.

since the days of the gold rush. More than 240 identified cultures or ethnicities have been identified in California. Blacks, Asians, and those of Latino descent have the highest numbers among the state's diverse minority populations. Already, California's collective "minority" populations have become the majority. This has long been true in major cities, including Los Angeles, East Los Angeles, Fresno, Oakland, and San Francisco, and in many public school classrooms.

California's Asian population, now representing almost 11 percent of the total, will grow slightly. Its Latino population, now approximately 32.4 percent, will increase to 50 percent by the year 2040 (some say this demographic event will occur much sooner). Blacks in California will remain at a fairly stable population level, demographers project, about seven percent of the population, as will Native Americans at around one percent.

No matter what color they started out, people in paradise have been getting a bit gray; throughout the 1980s, retirees were California's fastest-growing age group. But just as it seemed the Golden State's stereotypical golden glow of youth was on the wane came the news that the population is actually getting younger, helped along by the arrival of five million preschoolers since 1990. And that trend underscores the others. According to the most recent U.S. census—already inadequate for keeping pace with the state's fast-changing face—10.6 percent of the population is 65 and over, while 27.3 percent is under 18, for a median age of 33.

California as Rich

Though California is the richest state in the union, with a bustling economy of nation-state status and an average per-capita personal income of $22,000, the gap between the very rich and the very poor is staggering—and shocking to first-time visitors in major urban areas, since the despair of homelessness and poverty is very visible on city streets.

The news in 1995 that the U.S. is now the most economically stratified of all industrialized nations—with the top 20 percent of the population controlling 80 percent of the nation's wealth—barely raised an eyebrow in California. Neither did the word in 1996 from the Public Policy Institute of California that, with the state's economy once again booming, California has the largest gap between rich and poor in the world because of precipitous declines in wages and income among the working poor. That income gap is still growing in 2000, with the widest income disparities in Los Angeles.

Interpretations of U.S. census data suggest that California is becoming two states—or at least two states of mind. One California is educated, satisfied, and safe. The other is young, uneducated, immigrant (many do not speak English), restless, and impoverished. The ranks of the upper-income professional class (household income $50,000 or above) increased 15 percent between 1990 and 2000, to 48 percent—a phenomenon partly attributed to greater numbers of working women. (It's also striking to note that 18 percent of all U.S. households with an annual income of $150,000 or more are in California.) During that same decade, the state's middle-income households shrank from 33 percent to 26.6 percent, and the number of low-income households also declined, from 34 percent to 25.5 percent. But the numbers of the actual poor increased, from 12.5 percent to 14.2 percent.

Contradicting the skid row-alcoholic image of street life, nearly one-third of the homeless in California are under age 18. But almost more disturbing is California's unseen poverty. Not counting those who are turned away because there isn't enough to go around, more than two million people—almost one in every 10 Californians—regularly require food from public and private charitable organizations just to survive; on any given day in the Golden State, half a million people stand in line to get a free meal at a soup kitchen or commodity pantry. Minors, again, are California's largest class of hungry people. More than one in every four children in the Golden State live in poverty.

California as Well Educated

California has long been committed to providing educational opportunity to all citizens—a commitment expressed in once-generous public school funding as well as public financing for the nine (soon 10) campuses of the prestigious University of California, 23 California State University (CSU) campuses (CSU recently acquired the Maritime Academy), and the 106 independent California Community College (CCC) campuses. But because of the obvious educational impacts of increased immigration—80 separate languages are spoken at Los Angeles schools, at least 40 at Hollywood High alone—and the unofficial reality of socially segregated schools, uneven early educational opportunities are a fact of life even in well-intentioned California. Until recently the situation has been steadily worsening, with California spending $900 less per public school student than the national average; ranked 40th in per-pupil spending; and burdened with the nation's highest student-teacher ratios. Faced with a projected 18 percent enrollment increase in elementary and high schools by 2006, California has lately turned its attention to improving public schools—both with increased levels of funding and increased performance testing. The state's entrenched economic crisis, however, threatens that recent progress.

Previous declines in public school performance, coupled with increasingly stringent entrance requirements at both University of California and California State University campuses, have led critics such as former Senator Tom Hayden of Santa Monica to suggest that California's current public education policies are creating a "de facto educational apartheid." Though California's two-year community colleges are providing more four-year college preparation courses and are increasingly encouraging students to transfer to state universities, most minority groups in California are vastly underrepresented even in public universities.

The state's budget crisis in the early 1990s meant significant cuts in public financial support for education; fees at public universities (California educators and legislators never say "tuition") have increased rapidly. Student fees jumped 40 percent at the University of California in 1992 alone, for example. Fees at CSU have also increased radically since 1990; CSU trustees plan to increase undergraduate student fees until they reach at least $2,500 annually, or about one-third the per-student education cost. The state's current budget crisis suggests far worse news still to come. Yet even with the general public financing a diminishing share of the cost of each student's college education, there still isn't enough opportunity to go around. Just to keep pace with current and anticipated demand early in the coming century, the University of California needs three new campuses, the California State University system needs five, and the California Community Colleges need 28. According to a gloomy 1996 report by the nonprofit RAND think tank in Santa Monica, all three levels of California public higher education will be in deep financial crisis yet challenged to absorb a record 2.3 million potential students by 2010.

Overall trends in education, economics, and employment patterns suggest that California is evolving into a two-tiered society dominated by an affluent and well-educated Anglo-Asian "overclass." Those who make up the underclass and who compete for relatively low-paying service jobs will increasingly be immigrants or the functionally illiterate. According to Bill Honig, former state superintendent of public instruction, about 60 percent of California's public school students leave school without being able to read well enough to compete in California's increasingly complex, technology-oriented job market.

The Land: An Island in Space and Time

California's isolated, sometimes isolationist human history has been shaped more by the land itself than by any other fact. That even early European explorers conceived of the territory as an island is a fitting irony, since in many ways—particularly geographically, but also in the evolutionary development of plant and animal life—California was, and still is, an island in both space and time.

The third-largest state in the nation, California spans 10 degrees of latitude. With a meandering 1,264-mile-long coastline, the state's western boundary is formed by the Pacific Ocean. Along most of California's great length, just landward from the sea, are the rumpled and eroded mountains known collectively as the Coast Ranges.

But even more impressive in California's 158,693-square-mile territory is the Sierra Nevada range, which curves like a 500-mile-long spine along the state's central-eastern edge. Inland from the Coast Ranges and to the north of California's great central valley are the state's northernmost mountains, including the many distinct, wayward ranges of the Klamaths—mountains many geologists believe were originally a northwesterly extension of the Sierra Nevada. Just east of the Klamath Mountains is the southern extension of the volcanic Cascade Range, which includes Mt. Shasta and Lassen Peak.

This great partial ring of mountains around California's heartland (with ragged eastern peaks reaching elevations of 14,000 feet and higher) as well as the vast primeval forests that once almost suffocated lower slopes, have always influenced the state's major weather patterns—and have also created a nearly impenetrable natural barrier for otherwise freely migrating plant and animal species, including human beings.

But if sky-high rugged rocks, thickets of forest, and rain-swollen rivers blocked migration to the north and east, physical barriers of a more barren nature have also slowed movement into California. To the south, the dry chaparral of the east-west Transverse Ranges and the northwest/southeast-trending Peninsular Ranges impeded northern and inland movement for most life forms. The most enduring impediment, however, is California's great southeastern expanse of desert—including both the Mojave and Colorado Deserts—and the associated desert mountains and high-desert plateaus. Here, only the strong and well-adapted survive.

EARTHQUAKES, VOLCANOES, AND CRUSTY PLATES

Perched along the Pacific Ring of Fire, California is known for its violent volcanic nature and for its

© ROBERT HOLMES/CALTOUR

Mt. Shasta is in the southern part of the volcanic Cascade Range.

earthquakes. Native peoples have always explained the fiery, earth-shaking temperament of the land quite clearly, in a variety of myths and legends, but the theory of plate tectonics is now the most widely accepted scientific creation story. According to this theory, the earth's crust is divided into 20 or so major solid rock (or lithospheric) "plates" upon which both land and sea ride. The interactions of these plates are ultimately responsible for all earth movement, from continental drift and landform creation to volcanic explosions and earthquakes.

Most of California teeters on the western edge of the vast North American Plate. The adjacent Pacific Plate, which first collided with what is now California about 250 million years ago, grinds slowly but steadily northward along a line more or less defined by the famous San Andreas Fault (responsible for the massive 1906 San Francisco earthquake and fire as well as the more recent shake-up in 1989). Plate movement itself is usually imperceptible: at the rate things are going, within 10 million years Los Angeles will slide north to become San Francisco's next-door neighbor. But the steady friction and tension generated between the two plates sometimes creates special events. Every

so often sudden, jolting slippage occurs between the North American and Pacific Plates in California—either along the San Andreas or some other fault line near the plate border—and one of the state's famous earthquakes occurs. Though most don't amount to much, an average of 15,000 earthquakes occur in California every year.

A still newer theory augments the plate tectonics creation story, suggesting a much more fluid local landscape—that California and the rest of the West literally "go with the flow," in particular the movement of hot, molten rock beneath the earth's crust. "Flow" theory explains the appearance of earthquake faults where they shouldn't be, scientists say, and also explains certain deformations in the continental crust. According to calculations published in the May 1996 edition of the journal *Nature,* the Sierra Nevada currently flows at the rate of one inch every three years.

CALIFORNIA CREATION: WHEN WORLDS COLLIDE

In ancient times, some geologists say, the American Southwest was connected to Antarctica.

This theory, presented in 1991 by researchers at the University of California at Davis and the University of Texas, suggests that 500–700 million years ago a "seam" connected the two continents; Antarctica's Transatlantic Mountains were contiguous with the western edge of the Sierra Nevada, parts of Idaho, and the Canadian Rockies. The geological similarities between the now far-flung rock formations are unmistakable. Yet at that time the North American continent was missing California. Some geologists theorize that California came along later; certain rock formations now found south of the equator match those of California's Coast Range.

Wherever its raw materials originally came from, California as land was created by the direct collision, starting about 250 million years ago, of the eastward-moving Pacific Plate and the underwater western edge of the North American Plate—like all continents, something like a floating raft of lighter rocks (primarily granite) attached to the heavier, black basalt of the earth's mantle. At first impact, pressure between the two plates scraped up and then buckled offshore oceanic sediments into undulating ridges of rock, and an eventual California shoreline began to build.

But the Pacific Plate, unable to follow its previous forward path against such North American resistance, continued on its way by first plunging downward, creating a trough that soon began filling with oceanic basalts, mud, and eroded sediments from what is now Nevada. Sinking (or subducting) still farther beneath the North American Plate, some of these trench sediments slipped into the hot core (or athenosphere) beneath the earth's lithosphere and melted—transformed by heat into the embryonic granitic backbone of the Sierra Nevada and other metamorphic mountains that slowly intruded upward from the inner earth.

Approximately 140 million years ago, the northern section of what would later be the Sierra Nevada started to shift westward along the east-west tectonic fault line known as the Mendocino Fracture, the genesis of the Klamath Mountains. The Pacific Ocean, sloshing into the area just north of the infantile Sierra Nevada, brought with it the sediments that would create California's northeastern Modoc Plateau—a high-plains landscape later transformed by volcanic basalt flows and "floods."

About 60 million years ago, California's modern-day Sierra Nevada was a misshapen series of eroded ridges and troughs sitting on the newly risen edge of the continent. The violent forces generated by continuing plate confrontation, including sporadic volcanism and large-scale faulting, pushed the state's mountains slowly higher. Remaining ocean sediments later rose to create first the Coast Ranges, as offshore islands about 25 to 30 million years ago, and eventually an impressive, 450-mile-long inland sea, which, once filled with sediment, gradually evolved into the marshy tule wetlands recognizable today as California's fertile central valley.

Though California's creation has never ceased—with the land transformed even today by volcanic activity, earthquake shifts, and erosion—the landscape as we know it came fairly recently. According to the widely accepted view, about 10–16 million years ago the Sierra Nevada stood tall enough (approximately 2,000 feet above sea level) to start changing the continent's weather patterns: blocking the moisture-laden winds that had previously swept inland and desiccating the once-lush Great Basin. Then, one million years ago, the Sierra Nevada and other fault-block ranges "suddenly" rose to near their current height. By 800,000 years ago, the mountains had taken on their general modern shape—but fire was giving way to ice. During the million-year glaciation period, particularly the last stage from 100,000 to 30,000 years ago, these and other California landforms were subsequently carved and polished smooth by slow-moving sheets of ice. Vestigial glaciers remain in some areas of the Sierra Nevada and elsewhere.

A "countercultural" view of Sierra Nevada creation is emerging, however. According to this theory, based on research done in the southern Sierra Nevada, the range reached its zenith about 70 million years ago—massive mountains, as tall as the Andes, looming large during the last days of the dinosaurs. The height of the Sierra Nevada, once reaching 13,000 feet, has been declining ever since—a loss of about a quarter-inch in the course of a single person's lifetime—because erosion has proceeded faster than the forces of ongoing creation.

Though vegetation typical of the late ice age has largely vanished and mastodons, saber-toothed cats, and other exotic animals no longer stalk the land, the face of the California landscape since those bygone days has been transformed most radically by the impact of humanity—primarily in the past century and a half. Building dams and "channeling" wild rivers to exploit water, the state's most essential natural resource; harvesting state-sized forests of old-growth trees; hunting animals, to the edge of extinction and beyond, for fur and pelts; digging for, and stripping the land of, gold and other mineral wealth; clearing the land for crops and houses and industrial parks: all this has changed California forever.

FROM FIRE TO ICE: THE CALIFORNIA CLIMATE

California's much-ballyhooed "Mediterranean" climate is at least partially a myth. Because of extremes in landforms, in addition to various microclimatic effects, there are radical climatic differences within the state—sometimes even within a limited geographic area. But California as a whole does share most of the classic characteristics of Mediterranean climates: abundant sunny days year-round, a cool-weather coast, dry summers, and rainy winters. California, in fact, is the only region in North America where summer drought and rainy winters are typical.

Between the coast and the mountains immediately inland, where most of the state's people live, temperatures—though cooler in the north and warmer to the south—are fairly mild and uniform year-round. Because of the state's latitudinal gradation, rain also falls in accordance with this north-south shift: an average of 74 inches falls annually in Crescent City, 19–22 inches in San Francisco, and less than 10 inches in San Diego. When warm, moist ocean air blows inland over the cool California Current circulating clockwise above the equator, seasonal fog is typical along the California coast. Summer, in

other words, is often cooler along the coast than autumn. (Just ask those shivering tourists who arrive in San Francisco every June wearing Bermuda shorts and sandals.)

Inland, where the marine air influence often literally evaporates, temperature extremes are typical. The clear, dry days of summer are often hot, particularly in the central valley and the deserts. (With occasional freak temperatures above 130° Fahrenheit, Death Valley is aptly named.) In winter, substantial precipitation arrives in Northern California—especially in the northwest "rain belt" and in the northern Sierra Nevada—with major storms expected from October to May. California's northern mountains "collect" most Pacific Ocean moisture as rain; in the High Sierra, the average winter snowpack is between 300 and 400 inches. Wrung out like sponges by the time they pass over the Sierra Nevada and other inland mountains, clouds have little rain or snow for the eastern-slope rain-shadow.

Since the 1970s, California's climate patterns have been increasingly atypical—which may be normal, or may be early local indications of global warming. The reason no one knows for sure is because the state's "average" weather patterns were largely defined between the 1930s and the 1970s, a period of unusually stable weather conditions, it now appears. Complicating the question further is new scientific research suggesting that California climate has been characterized, since ancient times, by alternating cycles of very wet and very dry weather—200- to 500-year cycles. Epic droughts have been traced to the Middle Ages, and just 300 years ago California experienced a drought lasting 80–100 years. California's last century and a half, it turns out, represents one of the wettest periods in the past 2,500 years.

The increasing scientific consensus is that global warming is indeed having a major impact on California weather. Researchers at the University of California at Santa Cruz conclude that the state most likely will see warmer temperatures and a smaller snowpack during the next 50 years. Temperature increases could range as high as 15 degrees for the Sierra Nevada and five to six degrees for coastal Los Angeles. In addition, rising sea levels may erode the state's coastline and increase salinity in the critical Sacramento–San Joaquin Delta, degrading much of the state's drinking water. Since the late 1970s, El Niño "events" have increased noticeably, bringing warmer offshore waters and heavy storms in California and the Southwest. But in other years—drought times for California—"La Niña" occurs, with colder offshore waters and storms tracking into the Pacific Northwest. Being whipsawed between periods of torrential rains and flooding (yet subnormal snowpack) and devastating drought seems to be California's future—a future almost certain to feature disrupted water supplies, even without a 100-year drought.

CALIFORNIA FLORA: BLOOMING AT THE BRINK

"In California," observed writer Joaquin Miller, "things name themselves, or rather Nature names them, and that name is visibly written on the face of things and every man may understand who can read." When explorers and settlers first stumbled upon California's living natural wonders, they didn't "read" landforms or indigenous plants

and animals in the same way native peoples did, but they were quite busy nonetheless attaching new names (and eventually Latin terminology) to everything in sight. From the most delicate ephemeral wildflowers to California's two types of towering redwoods, from butterflies and birds to pronghorns, bighorn sheep, and the various subspecies of grizzly bear, the unusual and unique nature of most of the territory's life forms was astonishing. California's geographical isolation—as well as its dramatic extremes in landforms and localized climates—was (and still is) largely responsible for the phenomenal natural divergence and diversity found here.

Former President Ronald Reagan, while still governor of California and embroiled in a battle over expanding redwood parks, unwittingly expressed the old-and-in-the-way attitude about the state's resources with his now-famous gaffe, widely quoted as: "If you've seen one redwood, you've seen 'em all." (What Reagan actually said was: "A tree is a tree—how many more do you need to look at?") But his philosophy, however expressed, is the key to understanding what has happened to California's trees, other native flora, and animal species.

© ROBERT HOLMES/CALTOUR

flowers along the coast at Point Reyes National Seashore

Even today, the variation in California's native plantlife is amazing. Nearly 5,200 species of plants are at home in the Golden State—symbolized by the orange glow of the California poppy—and more than 30 percent of these trees, shrubs, wildflowers, and grasses are endemic. (By comparison, only 13 percent of plantlife in the northeastern U.S., and one percent of flora in the British Isles, are endemic species.) In fact, California has greater species diversity than the combined totals of the central and northeastern U.S. and adjacent Canada—an area almost 10 times greater in size.

But to state that so many plant species survive in California is not to say that they thrive. The economic and physical impacts of settlement have greatly stressed the state's vegetative wealth since the days of the gold rush, when the first full-scale assaults on California forests, wetlands, grasslands, and riparian and oak woodlands were launched. The rate of exploitation of the state's 380 distinct natural communities has been relentless ever since. Half of the state's natural terrestrial environments and 40 percent of its aquatic communities are endangered, rare, or threatened. Human settlement has eliminated 85 percent of old-growth redwoods, 91 percent of the state's wetlands, and 99 percent of its grasslands.

Some of the state's most notable natural attractions are its unique trees—entire forests nearly toppled at the edge of extinction. California's *Sequoiadendron giganteum,* or giant sequoia, grows only in limited surviving stands in the Sierra Nevada—saved as much by the brittleness of its wood as by the public outcry of John Muir and other enlightened 19th-century voices. But the state's remaining virgin forests of *Sequoia sempervirens,* the "ever-living" coast redwoods, are still threatened by clearcutting, a practice that also eliminates the habitat of other species. The same conservation-versus-economic expediency argument also rages over the fate of the few remaining old-growth outposts of other popular timber trees. And decades of fire suppression, logging, grazing, and recreational development in California's vast forests of ponderosa pines, combined with increasing air pollution and the state's recent drought, have led to insect infestations, tree disease, and death—and a tinder-dry,

fuel-rich landscape more vulnerable than ever to uncontrollable fires. Even trees without notable economic value are threatened by compromises imposed by civilization. Among these are the ancient bristlecone pines near the California-Nevada border—the oldest living things on earth, some individuals more than 4,000 years old—now threatened by Los Angeles smog, and the gnarled yet graceful valley oak. An "indicator plant" for the state's most fertile loamy soils, even the grizzled veteran oaks not plowed under by agriculture or subdivision development are now failing to reproduce successfully. The Bush administration's 2002 decision to allow U.S. Forest Service managers to revise long-term, ecosystem-based plans for individual forests means that California's remaining forests are even more vulnerable to the ax.

And while the disappearance of trees is easily observed even by human eyes, other rare and unusual plants found only in California disappear, or bloom at the brink of extinction, with little apparent public concern. A subtle but perfectly adapted native perennial grass, for example, or an ephemeral herb with a spring blossom so tiny most people don't even notice it, are equally endangered by humankind's long-standing laissez-faire attitude toward the world we share with all life.

Only fairly recently, with so much of natural California already gone for good, have public attitudes begun to change. No matter what Ronald Reagan says, and despite the very real economic tradeoffs sometimes involved, most Californians—and usually the state's voters—strongly support conservation, preservation, and park expansion proposals whenever these issues arise. Yet urban and suburban sprawl and commercial development continue unabated throughout California, with little evidence that the general public connects its personal and political choices with a sense of shared responsibility for the state's continued environmental decline.

CALIFORNIA FAUNA: A LONELY HOWL IN THE WILDERNESS

The Golden State's native wildlife is also quite diverse and unique. Of the 748 known species

© ROBERT HOLMES/CALTOUR

hoary marmot, Yosemite National Park

of vertebrate animals in California, 38 percent of freshwater fish, 29 percent of amphibians, and nine percent of mammals are endemic species; invertebrate variation is equally impressive. But with the disappearance of quite specific natural habitats, many of these animals are also endangered or threatened. Nearly six out of 10 fish species native to California are now extinct, and one in five of the state's land bird species is endangered.

One notable exception is the intelligent and endlessly adaptable coyote, which—rather than be shoved out of its traditional territory even by suburban housing subdivisions—seems quite willing to put up with human incursions, so long as there are garbage cans to forage in, swimming pools to drink from, and adequate alleys of escape. Yet even the coyote's lonely late-night howl is like a cry for help in an unfriendly wilderness.

The rapid slide toward extinction among California's wild things is perhaps best symbolized by the grizzly bear, which once roamed from the mountains to the sea, though the wolf, too, has long since vanished from the landscape. The last wild wolf in California was killed in Lassen County in 1924. The Sierra Nevada bighorn

sheep, the San Joaquin kit fox, the desert tortoise, and the California condor—most surviving birds maintained now as part of a zoo-based captive breeding program—are among many species now endangered. Upward of 550 bird species have been recorded in California, and more than half of these breed here. But the vast flocks of migratory birds (so abundant they once darkened the midday sky) have been thinned out considerably, here and elsewhere, by the demise of native wetlands and by toxins. The 12 million ducks that traditionally migrated along the California flyway recently are now estimated to number two million (and shrinking).

The fate of the state's once-fabled fisheries is equally instructive. With 90 percent of salmon spawning grounds now gone because of the damming of rivers and streams, California's commitment to compensatory measures—fish hatcheries and ladders, for example—somehow misses the point. Now that humans are in charge of natural selection, the fish themselves are no longer wild, no longer stream-smart; many can't even find their way back to the fisheries where they hatched out (in sterile stainless steel trays). California's once-fabled

INTRODUCTION

OVER CALIFORNIA

Audubon would die
or kill every bird he ever saw
to be up here, goose-eyed,
looking down over California.

We're following the flyway
south, out of season, battling
head winds, angling cross-valley
and bayward, to root

(not nest) at the home-opener.
If this were an Audubon spring
we'd have crashed long ago,
sent back to earth by flocks

of northbound waterfowl
blackening the sky, fouling the prop.
But in our age, only a few
late skeins stitch the air going home.

After years of drought, water's
what we notice of earth:
the smooth-flowing leveed Sacramento
we follow, man-made ponds

near mansion ranch homes. A refuge
at Colusa and Graylodge, but few
other wetlands or marshes
to beckon flocks down from long flights.

The plane yaws west at the Buttes
as if guided by natural law,
still on course and on time
for the bay and the ballgame—

baseball, Audubon
just missed out on, though we guess
he would've cheered a few teams:
Cardinals, Blue Jays, Baltimore Orioles.

—*Gary Thompson (for Richard Collins)*

marine fisheries are also in dire straits because of the combined effects of overfishing, pollution, and habitat degradation, a subject of only very recent political concern. Rockfish species in particular have been so heavily harvested by both commerical and sporting interests that a fishing moratorium has been imposed along the entire state's coast.

However, some California animals almost wiped out by hunters, habitat elimination, and contamination are starting out on the comeback trail. Included among these are native elk and the antelope-like pronghorn populations, each numbering near 500,000 before European and American settlement. Also recovering in California is the native population of desert bighorn sheep. Among marine mammals almost hunted into oblivion but now thriving in California's offshore ocean environments are the northern elephant seal and the sea otter. And in 1994 the

California gray whale was removed from the federal endangered species list—the first marine creature ever "delisted"—because its current population of 21,000 or so is as high, historically speaking, as it ever was.

Until recently, California's predators—always relatively fewer in number, pouncing from the top of the food chain—fared almost as poorly as their prey, preyed upon themselves by farmers, ranchers, loggers, and hunters. Though the grand grizzly hasn't been seen in California for more than a century, California's black bear is still around—though increasingly tracked and hunted by timber interests (for the damage the bears inflict on seedling trees) and poachers out to make a fast buck on gall bladders popular in Asian pharmacology. Of California's native wildcats, only the mountain lion and the spotted, smaller bobcat survive. The last of the state's jaguars was hunted down near Palm Springs in 1860.

The History of the Golden Dream

Europeans generally get credit for having "discovered" America, including the mythic land of California. But a dusty travel log tucked away in Chinese archives in Shenshi Province, discovered in the 19th century by an American missionary, suggests that the Chinese discovered California—in about 217 B.C. According to this saga, a storm-tossed Chinese ship—misdirected by its own compass, apparently rendered nonfunctional after a cockroach got wedged under the needle—sailed stubbornly for 100 days in the direction of what was supposed to be mainland China. (The navigator, Hee-li, reportedly ignored the protests of his crew, who pointed out that the sun was setting on the wrong horizon.) Stepping out into towering forests surrounding an almost endless inlet at the edge of the endless ocean, these unwitting adventurers reported meetings with red-skinned peoples—and giant red-barked trees.

Conventional continental settlement theory holds that the first true immigrants to the North American continent also came from Asia—crossing a broad plain across the Bering Strait, a "bridge" that existed until the end of the ice age. Archaeologists agree that the earliest Americans arrived more than 11,500 years ago, more or less in synch with geologists' belief that the Bering bridge disappeared about 14,000 years ago. Circumstantial support for this conclusion has also come from striking similarities—in blood type, teeth, and language—existing between early Americans and Asians, particularly the northern Chinese. But recent discoveries have thrown all previous American migration theories into doubt.

In 1986, French scientists working in Brazil discovered an ancient rock shelter containing stone tools, other artifacts, and charcoal that was at first carbon-dated at approximately 32,000 years old. (A subsequent announcement, that the discovery was actually more than 45,000 years old, shocked archaeologists and was widely discredited.) Then in 1989 University of California at Berkeley linguist Johanne Nichols took a systematic look at Native American languages. She found 150 languages families in North and South America and, knowing that languages take a long time to develop, suggested that humans had lived on the two continents for the last 30,000 to 40,000 years. Wall paintings suggest that cave art developed in the Americas at about the same time it did in Europe, Asia, and Africa. Preliminary evidence of very early human habitation (possibly as long ago as 33,000 years) has also been found in Chile. Subsequent Chilean finds at Monte Verde, dated authoritatively to 10,900 to 11,200 years ago, were announced in 1997—setting off a flurry of searches for still earlier sites of human habitation.

So the question is: if migration to the Americas was via the Bering Strait, and so long ago, why hasn't any similar evidence been discovered in North America? The mummified, mat-wrapped body of an elderly man discovered in 1940 in Spirit Cave near Fallon, Nevada, has subsequently been dated as 9,415 years old—making this the only Paleonoid (more than 8,500 years old) ever found in North America; the body was particularly well preserved by the desert climate. And a human skull dated as 9,800 years old has been discovered on Canada's Prince of Wales Island. But both of these finds are thought to bolster the Bering Straits land bridge theory—as does the Monte Verde discovery in Chile, if the first American arrivals were fishing people who worked their way down the continental coastline to settle, first, in South America. Some suggest that signs of earlier human habitation in North America have been erased by climatic factors, or by glaciation. But no one really knows. One thing is certain: most archaeologists would rather be buried alive in a dig than be forced to dust off and reexamine the previously discredited "Thor Heyerdahl theory" of American settlement: that the first immigrants sailed across the Pacific, landed in South America, and then migrated northward.

CALIFORNIA'S FIRST PEOPLE

However and whenever they first arrived in California, the territory's first immigrants gradually created civilizations quite appropriate to the land they had landed in. "Tribes" like those typical elsewhere in North America did not exist in California, primarily because the political unity necessary for survival elsewhere was largely irrelevant here. Populations of California native peoples are better understood as ethnic or kinship or community groups united by common experience and shared territory.

Though no census takers were abroad in the land at the time, the presettlement population (about 500 groups speaking 130 dialects) of what is now California is estimated at about 250,000—a density four to eight times greater than early people living anywhere else in the United States. Before their almost overnight decimation—from settlement, and attendant disease, cultural disintegration, and violence—California's native peoples found the living fairly easy. The cornucopia of fish, birds, and game, in addition to almost endlessly edible plantlife, meant that hunting and gathering was not the strict struggle for survival it was elsewhere on the continent. Since abundance in all things was the rule, at least in nondesert areas, trade between tribal groups (for nonlocal favorite foods such as acorns, pine nuts, or seafood and for nonlocal woods or other prized items) was not uncommon. Plants and animals of the natural world were respected by native peoples as kindred spirits, and a deep nature mysticism was the underlying philosophy of most religious traditions and associated myths and legends.

Most California peoples were essentially nonviolent, engaging in war or armed conflict only for revenge; bows and arrows, spears, and harpoons were used in hunting. The development of basketry, in general the highest art of native populations, was also quite pragmatic; baskets of specific shapes and sizes were used to gather and to store foods and for cooking in. Homes, boats, and clothing were made of the most appropriate local materials, from slabs of redwood bark and animal hides to tule reeds.

Time was not particularly important to California's first immigrants. No one kept track of passing years, and most groups didn't even have a word for "year." They paid attention, however, to the passage of the moons and seasons—the natural rhythm of life. Many native peoples were seminomadic, moving in summer into cooler mountain regions where game, roots, and berries were most abundant, and then meandering down into the foothills and valleys in autumn to collect acorns, the staff of life for most tribes, and to take shelter from winter storms.

But there was nowhere to hide from the whirling clouds of change that started sweeping into California with the arrival of early explorers and missionaries, or from the foreign flood that came when the myth of California gold became a reality. Some native peoples went out fighting: the 19th-century Modoc War was one of the last major Indian wars in the United States. And others just waited until the end of their world arrived. Most famous in this category was Ishi, the "last wild man in America" and believed to be the last of his people, captured in an Oroville slaughterhouse corral in 1911. Working as a janitor as a ward of the University of California until his death five years later from tuberculosis, Ishi walked from the Stone Age into the industrial age with dignity and without fear.

FOREIGNERS PLANT THEIR FLAGS

The first of California's official explorers were the Spanish. Though Hernán Cortés discovered a land he called California in 1535, Juan Rodríguez Cabrillo—actually a Portuguese, João Rodrigues Cabrilho—first sailed the coast of Alta California ("upper," as opposed to "lower" or Baja California, which then included all of Mexico) and rode at anchor off its shores.

But the first European to actually set foot on California soil was the English pirate Sir Francis Drake, who in 1579 came ashore somewhere along the coast (exactly where is still disputed, though popular opinion suggests Point Reyes) and whose maps—like others of the day—reflected his belief that the territory was indeed an island. Upon his return to England, Drake's story of discovery served primarily to stimulate Spain's territorial appetites. Though Sebastián Vizcaíno entered Monterey Bay in 1602 (18 years before the Pilgrims arrived at Plymouth), it wasn't until

© ROBERT HOLMES/CALTOUR

Mission San Francisco Solano in the city of Sonoma

if the Russians' agricultural and other enterprises hadn't ultimately failed. And enterprising Americans, at first just a few fur trappers and traders, were soon in the neighborhood.

As things happened, the challenge to Spain's authority came from its own transplanted population. Inspired by the news in 1822 that an independent government had been formed in Baja California's Mexico City, young California-born Spanish ("Californios") and independence-seeking resident Spaniards declared Alta California part of the new Mexican empire. By March 1825, when California proper officially became a territory of the Republic of Mexico, the new leadership had already achieved several goals, including secularizing the missions and "freeing" the associated native neophytes (not officially achieved until 1833), which in practice meant that most became servants elsewhere. The Californios also established an independent military and judiciary, opened the territory's ports to trade, and levied taxes.

During the short period of Mexican rule, the American presence was already prominent. Since even Spain regularly failed to send supply ships, Yankee traders were always welcome in California. In no time at all, Americans had organized and dominated the territory's business sector, established successful ranches and farms, married into local families, and become prominent citizens. California, as a possible political conquest, was becoming increasingly attractive to the United States.

Gen. John C. Frémont, officially on a scientific expedition but perhaps acting under secret orders from Washington (Frémont would never say), had been stirring things up in California since 1844—engaging in a few skirmishes with the locals or provoking conflicts between Californios and American citizens in California. Though the U.S. declared war on Mexico on May 13, 1846, Frémont and his men apparently were unaware of that turn of events and took over the town of Sonoma for a short time in mid-June, raising the secessionist flag of the independent—but very short-lived—Bear Flag Republic.

With Californios never mustering much resistance to the American warriors, Commodore John C. Sloat sailed unchallenged into Monterey

1746 that even the Spanish realized California wasn't an island. It wasn't until 1769 and 1770 that San Francisco Bay was discovered by Gaspar de Portolá and the settlements of San Diego and Monterey were founded.

Though the Spanish failed to find California's mythical gold, between 1769 and 1823 they did manage to establish 21 missions (sometimes with associated presidios) along El Camino Real or "The Royal Road" from San Diego to Sonoma. And from these busy mission ranch outposts, maintained by the free labor of "heathen" natives, Spain grew and manufactured great wealth.

But even at its zenith, Spain's supremacy in California was tenuous. The territory was vast and relatively unpopulated. Even massive land grants—a practice continued under later Mexican rule—did little to allay colonial fears of successful outside incursions. Russian imperialism, spreading east into Siberia and Central Asia, and then to Alaska and an 1812 outpost at Fort Ross on the north coast, seemed a clear and present danger—and perhaps actually would have been,

Bay on July 7, 1848, raised the Stars and Stripes above the Custom House in town, and claimed California for the United States. Within two days, the flag flew in both San Francisco and Sonoma, but it took some time to end the statewide skirmishes. It took even longer for official Americanization—and statehood—to proceed. The state constitution established, among other things, California as a "free" state (but only to prevent the unfair use of slave labor in the mines). This upset the balance of congressional power in the nation's anti-slavery conflict and indirectly precipitated the Civil War. Written in Monterey, the new state's constitution was adopted in October 1849 and ratified by voters in November.

GOLD IN THEM THAR HILLS

California's legendary gold was real, as it turned out. And the Americans found it—but quite by accident. The day James Marshall, who was building a lumber mill on the American River for John Sutter, discovered flecks of shiny yellow metal in the mill's tailrace seemed otherwise quite ordinary. But that day, January 24, 1848, changed everything—in California and in the world.

As fortune seekers worldwide succumbed to gold fever and swarmed into the Sierra Nevada foothills in 1849, modern-day California began creating itself. In the no-holds-barred search for personal freedom and material satisfaction (better yet, unlimited wealth), something even then recognizable as California's human character was also taking shape: the belief that anything is possible, for anyone, no matter what one's previous circumstances would suggest. Almost everyone wanted to entertain that belief. (Karl Marx was of the opinion that the California gold rush was directly responsible for delaying the Russian revolution.) New gold dreamers—all colors and creeds—came to California, by land and by sea, to take a chance on themselves and their luck. The luckiest ones, though, were the merchants and businesspeople who cashed in on California's dream by mining the miners.

Because of the discovery of gold, California skipped the economically exploitive U.S. territorial phase typical of other western states. With almost endless, indisputable capital at hand, Californians thumbed their noses at the Eastern financial establishment almost from the start: they could exploit the wealth of the far West themselves. And exploit it they did—mining not only the earth, but also the state's forests, fields, and water wealth. Wild California would never again be the same.

Almost overnight, "civilized" California became an economic sensation. The state was essentially admitted to the union on its own terms—because California was quite willing to go its own way and remain an independent entity otherwise. The city of San Francisco grew from a sleepy enclave of 500 souls to a hectic, hell-bent business and financial center of more than 25,000 within two years. Other cities built on a foundation of prosperous trade included the inland supply port of Sacramento. Agriculture, at first important for feeding the state's mushrooming population of fortune hunters, soon became a de facto gold mine in its own right. Commerce expanded even more rapidly with the completion of the California-initiated transcontinental railroad and with the advent of other early communications breakthroughs such as the telegraph. California's dreams of prosperity became self-fulfilling prophecies. And as California went, so went the nation.

SOUTHERN CALIFORNIA'S GOLDEN AGE

There was gold in Southern California, too—and it was actually discovered first, at Placerita Canyon not far north of Mission San Fernando. But the subsequent discovery at Sutter's Mill soon dwarfed Southern California's gold rush-era mining finds. The bonanza here came from inflated beef prices and otherwise supplying the booming northstate gold fields. The boom went bust in the mid-1850s, and depression came to California. Only the arrival of the railroads awakened Southern California from its social and economic slumber. Lured by well-promoted tales and photographs of the salubrious sunny climate—a place where oranges grew in people's backyards, where even roses bloomed in winter—migrants arrived by the trainloads, particularly from the Midwest, throughout the 1880s. Soon agriculture, with orchards and fields of crops stretching to every horizon, became Southern California's economic strength. Real estate developments and grand hotels, often built on land owned by the railroad barons, soon boomed as well. In the late 1800s oil was discovered throughout the greater Los Angeles basin, creating still more regional wealth.

As a land with little annual rainfall, its vast underground aquifers already well on the way to depletion because of agricultural irrigation and urban use, by the early 1900s Los Angeles was quickly running out of water. Yet the inventiveness of self-taught water engineer William Mulholland, soon an international celebrity, eliminated any prospect of enforced limits on growth. When the floodgates of the famed Los Angeles Aqueduct first opened, to great public acclaim, in 1913, Southern California had made its first monumental step toward eliminating the very idea of limits. Mulholland's engineering miracle, which successfully tapped into Owens Valley water supplies that originated 250 miles to the north, also tapped into the southstate's social imagination. In no time at all the "desert" was in full bloom, landscaped with lush lawns, ferns, roses, and palm trees and populated by happy, healthy families frolicking in the sunshine.

That image, translated to the world's imagination via Hollywood's movie industry in the 1920s and subsequent years, essentially created the Southern California of today. Massive growth followed World War II, when Los Angeles began to create itself as an industrial and technological superpower—one soon beset by traffic, pollution, and social problems befitting its size.

Yet for all its current challenges Southern California is still a surprisingly optimistic place. For every problem there is a solution, according to traditional southstate thinking.

DREAMING THE NEW GOLDEN DREAM

California as the land of opportunity—always a magnet for innovation, never particularly respectful of stifling and stodgy tradition—has dictated terms to the rest of the country throughout

its modern history. Even with the gradual arrival of what the rest of the world could finally recognize as civilization, which included the predictable phenomenon of personal wealth translated into political power, California's commitment to prosperity and change—sometimes for its own sake—has never waned.

From the founding of the Automobile Club of Southern California in 1900 to the construction of Yosemite's Hetch Hetchy Dam (to slake San Francisco thirst) in 1923; from the establishment of the first Hollywood movie studio in 1911 to the 1927 transmission, from San Francisco, of the first television picture; from the completion in 1940 of the world's first freeway to the opening of Disneyland in 1955; from the 1960s' Free Speech Movement, the rise of Black Power in the wake of the Watts riots in 1965, and the successes of César E. Chávez's United Farm Workers Union to the Beat poets, San Francisco's Summer of Love, and the oozing up of New Age consciousness; from California's rise as leader in the development of nuclear weapons and defense technology to the creation of the microchip and personal computer: California history is a chronicle of incredible change, a relentless double-time march into the new.

"All that is constant about the California of my childhood," writes Sacramento native Joan Didion in an essay from *Slouching Towards Bethlehem,* "is the rate at which it disappears."

CALIFORNIA GOVERNMENT: THE BEST THAT MONEY CAN BUY

California's political structure is quite confusing, with thousands of tax-levying governmental units—including special districts, 58 county governments, and hundreds of cities both large and small—and a variety of overlapping jurisdictions. Based on the federal principle of one person, one vote and designed with separate executive, judicial, and legislative (Assembly and Senate) branches, the game of state-level California government is often quite lively, almost a high form of entertainment for those who understand the rules. The use and abuse of public resources is the ultimate goal of power-brokering in the Golden State, affecting statewide and local economies as well as the private sector and creating (or abandoning) commitments to social justice and various human rights issues many Californians still hold dear.

The popularity of unusually affable, charismatic, and highly visible California politicians, from Ronald Reagan to Jerry Brown, would suggest that Golden State politics generally takes place in the entertainment arena. Nothing could be further from the truth. Though Californians are committed to the concept of public initiatives and referenda on major issues—politicians be damned, basically—most decisions affecting life in California are still made in the time-honored behind-the-scenes tradition of U.S. politics, with backroom deal-making conducted something like a poker game. In order to know the score, you must know the players and what cards they hold.

Those in the know contend that the California Legislature, considered the best state-level legislative body in the nation as recently as 1971, has steadily been careening downhill, in terms of effectiveness and ethics, ever since—largely because of "juice," or the influence of lobbyists and special interest money. According to veteran *Sacramento Bee* political reporter and columnist Dan Walters: "Votes are bought, sold, and rented by the hour with an arrogant casualness. There are one-man, one-vote retail sales as well as wholesale transactions that party leaders negotiate for blocs of votes."

Though from some perspectives California voters—and nonvoters—are largely responsible for the seemingly insoluble problems the state now faces, polls indicate that Californians increasingly distrust their politicians. From his years observing the species from the 19th-century Washington, D.C., press gallery, Mark Twain offered this fitting summary, a quote from a fictitious newspaper account in his novel, *The Gilded Age:* "We are now reminded of a note we received from the notorious burglar Murphy, in which he finds fault with a statement of ours that he had served one term in the penitentiary and one in the U.S. Senate. He says, 'The latter statement is untrue and does me great injustice.'"

Given California voters' current penchant for taking matters into their own hands, no matter how disastrously, it came as no surprise in 1992 when California became one of the first states in the nation to pass a "term limitations" law, restricting its Assembly members to maximum six-year terms in office and limiting the terms of governor, state senators, and other constitutional officers to eight years. Another initiative, put before the voters in 1990 as Proposition 140, cut the Legislature's operating budget by $70 million, about 38 percent. It has been upheld as constitutional by the state supreme court.

THE GLITTER OF THE GOLDEN STATE ECONOMY

If the lure of gold brought pioneers to California, the rich land, its seemingly endless resources, and the state's almost anarchistic "anything goes" philosophy kept them here. The Golden State has essentially become a nation-state—an economic superpower, the the fifth-largest (or sixth or seventh, depending on the comparison data) economy in the world. A major international player in the game of Pacific Rim commerce, California's cry is usually "free trade," in contrast to the philosophy of high-tariff trade protectionism typically so strong elsewhere in the United States. And with so much financial clout, California is often the tail that wags the dog of U.S. domestic and foreign economic and political policy. No one ever says it out loud, but California could easily secede from the union, only too happy to compete as an independent entity in the world market. This seems especially true in the early 21st century, given the state's booming export traffic to both Japan and Mexico.

Though industry of every sort thrives in California, until recently agriculture has been the state's economic mainstay. ("The whole place stank of orange blossoms," observed H.L. Mencken on a Golden State visit.) Though most Southern California citrus groves have long since been paved over for parking lots and shopping malls—those disturbed by California's proclivity for bulldozing the past in the name of progress have coined a verb for it: "to californicate"—

INTRODUCTION

agriculture in pockets of Southern California and in Northern California is still going strong. Because of the large size and concentrated ownership of farm and ranch lands, helped along by public subsidies of irrigation engineering projects, agriculture in California has always been agribusiness. In its role as agricultural nation-state, California produces more food than 90 percent of the world's nations, a $25 billion annual business. But with farmers caught between rising production costs and declining crop prices due to global competition, some state economists say that food production can no longer be regarded as the profitable business it once was. And population increases continue to put pressure on limited water resources as well as productive farmland.

The economic spirit of the northstate, suggested philosopher George Santayana in a 1910 Berkeley speech, is best summed up by the immense presence of nature in Northern California—nature in tandem with engineering and technology. Now that the roughshod, rough-and-tumble days of man against nature are no longer widely condoned, Californians increasingly expect technology to respect nature's standards. In Northern California particularly, but increasingly in Southern California, information is the cleanest industry of all. It seems no coincidence that both the microchip and the personal computer were born here.

Yet California, northern and southern, is industrious in all ways. Travel and tourism is a major industry—now promoted, in good budget years, at least, since California has started to lose ground in the tourist sweeps to other Western states—with annual revenues in the $52 billion range. Growth itself is a growth industry in California, with all aspects of the construction trade generating an average $30 billion in business annually. Revenues generated by California's top 100 privately held companies—including Bechtel Group, Hughes Aircraft, USA Petroleum (and other oil companies), Twentieth-Century Fox Films (and other media giants), Purex Industries, Denny's Inc., Raley's, both the AAA-affiliated Automobile Club of Southern California and the California State Automobile Associa-

tion, and a long string of agricultural cooperatives as well as health- and life-insurance companies—approach $100 billion annually.

A U.S. capital of finance and commerce, the state is also the world's high-technology headquarters. Helped along by state-supported University of California labs and research facilities, California has long been a leader in the aerospace and weapons development industries. Including military bases and research, testing, and surveillance sites, about 80 outposts of nuclear weaponry are—or were—based in California; recent federal cuts in defense spending have slowed business considerably.

THE PEOPLE— ALWAYS ON THE MOVE

Everyone is moving to California and vicinity, it seems. According to *American Demographics,* the geographic center of the U.S. population moves 58 feet farther west and 29 feet to the south every year. (Recent bad times in California slowed that trend temporarily, as nearly one million Californians left to find jobs elsewhere, but that loss has been overshadowed by increased immigration.) Be that as it may, some people consider Californians among the most obnoxious people on earth, and this is not necessarily a new phenomenon.

To some, the state is a kind of cultural purgatory, settled (in the words of Willard Huntington Wright) by "yokels from the Middle West who were nourished by rural pieties and superstitions." Others consider, and have always considered, Californians as somehow inherently unstable. "Insanity, as might be expected, is fearfully prevalent in California," Dr. Henry Gibbons stated before San Francisco's local medical society in 1857. "It grows directly out of the excited mental condition of our population, to which the common use of alcoholic drink is a powerful adjunct." The general outside observation today is that if Californians aren't talking about themselves—and about accomplishing their latest career, financial, fitness, or psychospiritual goals—they talk about California. New Englander Inez

Hayes Irwin defined those afflicted with California in her 1921 book *Californiacs:*

> *The Californiac is unable to talk about anything but California, except when he interrupts himself to knock every other place on the face of the earth. He looks with pity on anybody born outside of California, and he believes that no one who has ever seen California willingly lives elsewhere. He himself often lives elsewhere, but he never admits that it is from choice.*

There may be more than a shred of truth in this, even today; pollsters say one out of every four Californians would rather live elsewhere—for the most part, either in Hawaii or Oregon. But many who live and work in California are not native Californians. This is almost as true today as it ever was; at least one-third of contemporary Californians were born somewhere else. Somehow, California's amazing cultural and ethnic diversity is the source of both its social stability and its self-renewal.

Perhaps because of misleading portrayals of California's past, in the media and the movies as well as the history books, a common misconception is that the impact and importance of California's ethnic populations is relatively recent, a post-World War II phenomenon. But many peoples and many races have made significant contributions to California culture and economic development since the days of the gold rush—and since the decimation of native populations.

Blacks and Latinos, despite attempts (official and otherwise) to prevent them from dreaming the California dream, were among the first to arrive in the gold fields. The Chinese, who also arrived early to join the ranks of the state's most industrious citizens, were relentlessly persecuted despite their willingness to do work others considered impossible—including the unimaginable engineering feat of chiseling a route over the forbidding Sierra Nevada for the nation's first transcontinental railroad. And when the state's boom-bust beginnings gave way to other possibilities, including farming, ranching, and small business enterprises, California's minorities stayed—helping, despite the realities of subtle discrimination and sometimes overt racism, to create the psychological pluralism characteristic of California society today.

Practicalities

California is crowded—both with people trying to live the dream on a permanent basis and with those who come to visit, to re-create themselves on the standard two-week vacation plan. Summer, when school's out, is generally when the Golden State is most crowded, though this pattern is changing rapidly now that year-round schools and off-season travel are becoming common. Another trend: "mini-vacations," with workaholic Californians and other Westerners opting for one- to several-day respites spread throughout the year rather than traditional once-a-year holidays. It was once a truism that great bargains, in accommodations and transport particularly, were widely available during California's nonsummer travel season. Given changing travel patterns, this is no longer entirely true. Early spring and autumn are among the best times to tour the Northern California coastline, for example. And winter is "peak season" at Lake Tahoe, Mammoth Lakes, and other ski and winter-sport areas—as well as in Palm Springs. Yet winter travel can be less expensive.

Official holidays, especially during the warm-weather travel season and the Thanksgiving-Christmas–New Year holiday season, are often the most congested and popular (read: more

Pacific Grove bike trail, Monterey Peninsula

expensive) times to travel or stay in California. Yet this is not always true; great holiday-season bargains in accommodations are sometimes available at swank hotels that primarily cater to businesspeople. Though most tourist destinations are usually jumping, banks and many businesses close on the following major holidays: New Year's Day (January 1); Martin Luther King Jr. Day (the third Monday in January); Presidents' Day (the third Monday in February); Memorial Day (the last Monday in May); Independence Day (July 4); Labor Day (the first Monday in September); Veterans Day (November 11); Thanksgiving (the fourth Thursday in November); and Christmas (December 25). California's newest state holiday is César E. Chávez Day, in honor of the late leader of the United Farm Workers (UFW), signed into law in August 2000 and celebrated each year on the Friday or Monday closest to March 31, Chávez's birthday. In honor of the nation's most famous Latino civil rights leader, all state offices close but banks and other businesses may not.

Spontaneous travel, or following one's whims wherever they may lead, was once feasible in California. Unfortunately, given the immense popularity of particular destinations, those days are long gone. Particularly for those traveling on the cheap and for travelers with special needs or specific desires, some of the surprises encountered during impulsive adventuring may be unpleasant. If the availability of specific types of lodgings (including campgrounds) or eateries, or if transport details, prices, hours, and other factors are important for a pleasant trip, the best bet is calling ahead to check details and/or to make reservations. (Everything changes rapidly in California.) For a good overview of what to see and do in advance of a planned trip, including practical suggestions beyond those in this guide, also contact the chambers of commerce and/or visitor centers listed. Other good sources for local and regional information are bookstores, libraries, sporting goods and outdoor supply stores, and local, state, and federal government offices.

PRACTICALITIES

Entertainment and Shopping

Not even the sky's the limit on entertainment in California. From air shows to harvest fairs and rodeos, from symphony to opera, from rock 'n' roll to avant-garde clubs and theater, from strip shows (male and female) to ringside seats at ladies' mud-wrestling contests, from high-stakes bingo games to horse racing—anything goes in the Golden State. Most communities offer a wide variety of special, often quite unusual, annual events; many of these are listed by region or city elsewhere in this guide.

Most stores are open during standard business hours (weekdays 8 A.M.–5 P.M. or 9 A.M.–5 P.M.) and often longer, sometimes seven days a week, because of the trend toward two-income families and ever-reduced leisure time. This trend is particularly noticeable in cities, where shops and department stores are often open until

9 P.M. or later, and where many grocery stores are open 24 hours.

Shopping malls—almost self-sustaining cities in California, with everything from clothing and major appliances to restaurants and entertainment—are the standard California trend, but cities large and small with viable downtown shopping districts often offer greater variety and uniqueness in goods and services. Also particularly popular in California are flea markets and arts-and-crafts fairs, the former usually held on weekends, the latter best for handcrafted items and often associated with the Thanksgiving-through-Christmas shopping season and/or festivals and special events. California assesses a 7.25 percent state sales tax on all nonfood items sold in the state, and many municipalities levy additional sales tax.

Recreation

With its tremendous natural diversity, recreationally California offers something for just about everyone. Popular spring-summer-fall activities include hiking and backpacking; all water sports, from pleasure boating and water-skiing to sailing, windsurfing, kayaking, and swimming; white-water rafting, canoeing, and kayaking; mountain and rock-climbing; even hang gliding and hunting. In most years, winter activities popular in Northern California can also be enjoyed in Southern California, at least to a certain extent. These include both Alpine and Nordic skiing, snowshoe hiking, sledding and tobogganing, and just plain snow play. Also high on the "most popular" list of outdoor California sports: bicycling, walking and running; coastal diversions from beachcombing to surfing; and the increasingly popular statewide diversion, bird-watching. The most likely places to enjoy these and other outdoor activities are mentioned throughout this book.

And where do people go to re-create themselves in the great outdoors? To Northern California's vast public playgrounds—to the rugged coast and almost endless local, regional, and state parks as well as national parks and forest lands. In Southern California, where wide-open spaces are all but gone, outdoor recreation still centers on local beaches, some nice local and regional parks as well as state parks and beaches, national forests—and the vast expanse of the state's deserts. For more information on the national parks, national forests, and other state- and federally owned lands (including Bureau of Land Management wilderness areas) mentioned in this book, contact each directly.

NATIONAL PARKS INFORMATION AND FEES

For those planning to travel extensively in national parks in California and elsewhere in the U.S., a one-year Golden Eagle Passport provides unlimited park access (not counting camping fees) for the holder and family, for the new price of $50. Though the Golden Eagle pass has recently doubled in price, it can still be worth it in California, where fees at certain national parks have recently increased; admission to Death Valley is now $10 (for up to a one-week stay) and Yosemite is $20. Those age 62 or older qualify for the $10 Golden Age Passport, which provides free lifetime access to national parks, monuments, and recreation areas, and a 50 percent discount on RV fees. Disabled travelers are eligible for the $10 Golden Access Passport, with the same privileges. You can buy all three special passes at individual national parks or obtain them in advance, along with visitor information, from: **U.S. National Park Service,** National Public Inquiries Office, U.S. Department of the Interior, 1849 C St., P.O. Box 37127, Washington, DC 20013, www.nps.gov. For regional national parks information covering California, Nevada, and Arizona, contact: **Pacific West Region U.S. National Park Service,** One Jackson Center, 1111 Jackson St., Ste. 700, Oakland, CA 94607, 510/817-1300, or see the website: www.nps.gov/pwro.

Campgrounds in some national parks in California—including Sequoia–Kings Canyon and Whiskeytown National Recreation Area, along with Southern California parks including Channel Islands, Death Valley, and Joshua Tree—can be reserved (with MasterCard or Visa) through the **National Park Reservation Service,** website: reservations.nps.gov, or by calling 800/365-2267 (365-CAMP) at least eight weeks in advance. The total cost includes both the actual camping fee plus a $8–9 reservations fee. From California, call 7 A.M.–7 P.M. (10 A.M.–10 P.M. Eastern time). If you're heading to **Yosemite,** make campground reservations via the Internet (see address above) or by calling 800/436-7275 (436-PARK). And to cancel your reservations, call 800/388-2733. To make national park camping reservations from outside the U.S., call 619/452-8787.

To support the protection of U.S. national parks and their natural heritage, contact the nonprofit **National Parks and Conservation As-**

PRACTICALITIES

© ROBERT HOLMES/CALTOUR

tunnel view, Yosemite National Park

sociation (NPCA), 1300 19th St. N.W., Ste. 300, Washington, DC 20036, 800/628-7275, ext. 213, or 202/223-6722, www.npca.org. Both as a public service and fundraiser, the NPCA sells sweatshirts, T-shirts, and books about national park history. You can also sign up for tours and keep abreast of regional conservation events.

NATIONAL FORESTS AND OTHER FEDERAL LANDS

For general information about U.S. national forests, including wilderness areas and campgrounds, contact: **U.S. Forest Service,** U.S. Department of Agriculture, Publications, P.O. Box 96090, Washington, DC 20090, 202/205-8333. For a wealth of information via the Internet, try www.fs.fed.us. For information specifically concerning national forests and wilderness areas in California, and for maps, contact: **U.S. Forest Service, Pacific Southwest Region,** 1323 Club Drive, Vallejo, CA 94592, 707/562-8737, www.fs.fed.us/r5. Additional California regional offices are mentioned elsewhere in this guide.

Some U.S. Forest Service and Army Corps of Engineers campgrounds in California can be re-

served through ReserveAmerica's **National Recreation Reservation Service** (with MasterCard or Visa) at the website: www.reserveusa.com, or call 877/444-6777 (TDD: 877/833-6777), a service available 5 A.M.–9 P.M. (8 A.M.–midnight Eastern time) from April 1 through Labor Day and otherwise 7 A.M.–4 P.M. (10 A.M.–7 P.M. Eastern time). From outside the U.S., call 518/885-3639. Reservations for individual campsites can be made up to eight months in advance, and for group camps up to 360 days in advance. Along with the actual costs of camping, expect to pay a per-reservation service fee of $8–9 for individual campsites (more for group sites). In addition to its first-come, first-camped campgrounds, in some areas the U.S. Forest Service offers the opportunity for "dispersed camping," meaning that you can set up minimal-impact campsites in various undeveloped areas. For detailed current recreation, camping, and other information, contact specific national forests mentioned elsewhere in this book.

Anyone planning to camp extensively in national forest campgrounds should consider buying U.S. Forest Service "camp stamps" (at national forest headquarters or at ranger district

COASTWALKING: THE CALIFORNIA COASTAL TRAIL

Californians love their Pacific Ocean coastline. Love of the coast has inspired fierce battles over the years concerning just what does, and what does not, belong there. Among the things most Californians would agree belong along the coast are hiking trails—the reason for the existence of the nonprofit educational group **Coastwalk,** which sponsors group walks along the **California Coastal Trail** to introduce people to the wonders of the coast.

The California Coastal Trail seems to be an idea whose time has come. Now a Millennium Legacy Trail, honored at special White House ceremony in October 1999 that recognized 50 unique trails in the U.S., Washington, D.C., Puerto Rico, and the Virgin Islands, in March 2000 the California Coastal Trail also received a special $10,000 Millennium Trails Grant from American Express.

Yet in some places, the trail is still just an idea. It doesn't yet exist everywhere along the California coastline—and changing that fact is the other primary purpose of this unique organization. That's why members of Coastwalk set out in June of 2003 to walk the entire length of California's coastline—and its coastal trail-to-be—pointing out various "missing links" along the way, from Sea Ranch in Sonoma County to David Geffen's beachfront Malibu estate. Since 1983, Coastwalk's mission has been to establish a border-to-border California Coastal Trail as well as preserve the coastal environment.

You can join the coastwalking club. Guided four- to six-day Coastwalk trips, typically covering 5–10 miles each day, include in the far north the Del Norte coastline, Redwood National Park in Humboldt County, the rugged Medocino shoreline, and Sonoma and Marin Counties. Always popular, too, is the eight-day Lost Coast Backpack in Humboldt and Mendocino Counties. In central California, coastwalks are offered near San Francisco Bay, along the San Mateo and Santa Cruz coasts, in Monterey and San Luis Obispo Counties, and along the Ventura coast. Southern California coastwalks cover Los Angeles (the Santa Monica Mountains) and Catalina Island, Orange County, and San Diego County.

Accommodations, arranged by Coastwalk as part of the trip, include state park campgrounds and hostels with hot showers. "Chuckwagon" dinners, prepared by volunteers, are also provided; bring your own supplies for breakfast and lunch. All gear—you'll be encouraged to travel light—is shuttled from site to site each night, so you need carry only the essentials as you walk: water bottle, lunch, camera, and jacket. Daily coastwalk fees are $50 adults, $25 full-time students, and $18 children ages 12 and under—all in all a very reasonable price for a unique vacation.

For more information and to join Coastwalk— volunteers are always needed—contact Richard Nichols, Coastwalk, 7207 Bodega Ave. (across from the Sebastopol Library at Bodega Ave. and High St.), Sebastopol, CA 95472, 707/829-6689, www.coastwalk.org. The California coastal trail's website is www.californiacoastaltrail.org.

---

stations) in denominations of 50 cents, $1, $2, $3, $5, and $10. These prepaid camping coupons amount to a 15 percent discount on the going rate. (Many national forest campgrounds are first-come, first-camped; without a reserved campsite, even camp stamps won't guarantee one.) Senior adults, disabled people, and those with national Golden Age and Golden Access recreation passports pay only half the standard fee at any campground and can buy camp stamps at half the regular rate as well.

For wannabe archaeologists, the U.S. Forest Service offers the opportunity to volunteer on archaeological digs through its **Passport in Time** program—certainly one way to make up for stingy federal budgets. To receive the project's newsletter, which announces upcoming projects in various national forests, contact: Passport in Time Clearinghouse, P.O. Box 31315, Tucson, AZ 85751, 800/281-9176 or 520/722-2716, www.passportintime.com.

Some Northern California public lands and vast expanses of Southern California are managed by the **U.S. Bureau of Land Management** (BLM). For general information, contact: U.S. Bureau of Land Management, Office of Public

Affairs, 1849 C St. NW, LS 406, Washington, DC 20240, 202/452-5125, fax 202/452-5124, www.blm.gov. For information specifically related to California, contact: **California BLM,** 2800 Cottage Way, Ste. W1824, Sacramento, CA 95825, 916/978-4400, www.ca.blm.gov. If you plan to camp on BLM lands, be sure to request a current *California Visitor Map,* which includes campgrounds and other features; the BLM also allows "dispersed camping" in some areas (ask for details). For detailed information on all 69 of the BLM's new desert wildernesses in California, contact the BLM's **California Desert District Office,** 22835 Calle San Juan de Los Lagos, Moreno Valley, CA 92553, 909/697-5200, www.ca.blm.gov/cdd.

For information on national wildlife reserves and other protected federal lands, contact: **U.S. Fish and Wildlife Service,** Division of Refuges, Arlington Square, 4401 N. Fairfax Dr., Room 670, Arlington, VA 22203, 800/344-9453 or 703/358-1744, www.fws.gov.

STATE PARKS

California's 275 beloved state parks, which include beaches, wilderness areas, and historic homes, have recently been going through bad times—the unfortunate result of increasing public use combined with budget cuts.

Day-use fees for admission to California state parks now range from $3 to $5 per vehicle ($1 less for seniors), with extra fees charged for extra vehicles and other circumstances. In highly congested areas, state parks charge no day-use fee but do charge a parking fee—making it more attractive to park elsewhere and walk or take a bus. For information on special assistance available for individuals with disabilities or other special needs, contact individual parks—which make every effort to be accommodating, in most cases.

Annual passes (nontransferable), which you can buy at most state parks and at the State Parks Store in Sacramento (see below), are $67 for day use. Golden Bear passes, for seniors age 62 and older with limited incomes and for certain others who receive public assistance, are $5 per year and allow day-use access to all state parks and

off-road vehicle areas except Hearst/San Simeon, Sutter's Fort, and the California State Railroad Museum. For details on income eligibility and other requirements, call 916/653-4000. "Limited use" Golden Bear passes, for seniors age 62 and older, allow free parking at state parks during the nonpeak park season (usually Labor Day through Memorial Day) and are $10 per year; they can be purchased in person at most state parks. Senior discounts for state park day use ($1 off) and camping ($2 off, but only if the discount is requested while making reservations) are also offered. Special state park discounts and passes are also offered for the disabled and disabled veterans/POWs (prisoners of war). For more information, contact state park headquarters (see below).

Detailed information about California's state parks, beaches, and recreation areas is scattered throughout this guide. To obtain a complete parks listing, including available facilities, campground reservation forms, and other information, contact: **California State Parks,** Public Information, P.O. Box 942896, Sacramento, CA 94296, 800/777-0369 or 916/653-6995 (recorded, with an endless multiple-choice menu), www.parks.ca.gov.

State park publications include the *Official Guide to California State Parks* map and facilities listing, which includes all campgrounds, available free with admission to most state parks but available by mail, at last report, for $2; send check or money order to the attention of the Publications Section. Also available, and free: a complete parks and recreation publications list (which includes a mail order form). Other publications include the annual magazines *Events and Programs at California State Parks,* chock-full of educational and entertaining things to do, and *California Escapes,* a reasonably detailed regional rundown on all state parks.

For information about the state parks' Junior Ranger Program—many parks offer individual programs emphasizing both the state's natural and cultural heritage—call individual state parks. For general information, call 916/653-8959. Also available through the state parks department is an annually updated "Sno-Park" guide to parking without penalty while cross-country skiing or otherwise playing in the snow; for a current Sno-Park listing, write in care of the program at the state parks' address listed above or call 916/324-1222 (automated hotline). Sno-Park permits (required) cost $5 per day or $25 for the entire season, Nov. 1–May 30; you can also buy them at REI and other sporting goods stores and at any AAA office in California. Another winter-season resource, free to AAA members, is the annual *Winter Sports Guide* for California, which lists prices and other current information for all downhill and cross-country ski areas.

California state parks offer excellent campgrounds. In addition to developed "family" campsites, which usually include a table, fire ring or outdoor stove, plus running water, flush toilets, and hot showers (RV hookups, if available, are extra), some state campgrounds also offer more primitive "walk-in" or environmental campgrounds and very simple hiker-biker campsites. Group campgrounds are also available (and reservable) at many state parks. If you plan to camp over the Memorial or Labor Day weekends, or the July 4th holiday, be sure to make reservations as early as possible.

Make campground reservations at California state parks (with MasterCard or Visa) through **ReserveAmerica,** website: www.reserveamerica.com, or call 800/444-7275 (444-PARK) weekdays 8 A.M.–5 P.M. For TDD reservations, call 800/274-7275 (274-PARK). And to cancel state park campground reservations, from the U.S. call 800/695-2269. To make reservations from Canada or elsewhere outside the U.S., call 619/638-5883. As in other camping situations, before calling to make reservations, know the park and campground name, how you'll be camping (tent or RV), how many nights, and how many people and vehicles. In addition to the actual camping fee, which can vary from $10 for more primitive or "environmental" campsites (without showers and/or flush toilets) to $8–13 for developed campsites, there is a $3–4 peak-season surcharge, a $4 "premium site" fee, and a $7.50 reservations fee. Sites with hookups cost $6 more. You can make camping reservations up to seven months in advance. (Be ad-

vised: popular coastal and other prime destinations often sell out for summer on "opening day"—seven months in advance—for reservations.) Certain campsites, including some primitive environmental and hiker/biker sites (now just $2) can be reserved only through the relevant state park.

To support the state's park system, contact the nonprofit **California State Parks Foundation,** 800 College Ave., P.O. Box 548, Kentfield, CA 94914, 800/963-7275 or 415/258-9975, fax 415/258-9930, www.calparks.org. Through memberships and contributions, the foundation has financed about $100 million in park preservation and improvement projects in the past several decades. Volunteers are welcome to contribute sweat equity, too.

OTHER RECREATION RESOURCES

For general information and fishing and hunting regulations, usually also available at sporting goods stores and bait shops where licenses and permits are sold, call the **California Department of Fish and Game** in Sacramento at 916/653-7664 or 916/445-0411; for license information or to purchase licenses online, call 916/227-2244, www.dfg.ca.gov. For additional sportfishing information, call 800/275-3474 (800-ASK-FISH).

For environmental and recreational netheads, the California Resources Agency's CERES website: ceres.ca.gov (aka the California Environmental Resources Evaluation System) offers an immense amount of additional information, from reports and updates on rare and endangered species to current boating regulations. The database is composed of federal, state, regional, and local agency information as well as a multitude of data and details from state and national environmental organizations—from REINAS, or the Real-time Environmental Information Network and Analysis System at the University of California at Santa Cruz, The Nature Conservancy, and NASA's Imaging Radar Home Page. Check it out.

Worth it for inveterate wildlife voyeurs is the *California Wildlife Viewing Guide* (Falcon Press), produced in conjunction with 15 state, federal, and local agencies in addition to Ducks Unlimited and the Wetlands Action Alliance. About 200 wildlife viewing sites are listed—most of these in Northern California. Look for the *California Wildlife Viewing Guide* at local bookstores, or order a copy by calling 800/582-2665. With the sale of each book, $1 is contributed to California Watchable Wildlife Project nature tourism programs.

To support California's beleaguered native plantlife, join, volunteer with, and otherwise contribute to the **California Native Plant Soci-** ety (CNPS), 1722 J St., Ste. 17, Sacramento, CA 95814, 916/447-2677, fax 916/447-2727, www.cnps.org. In various areas of the state, local CNPS chapters sponsor plant and habitat restoration projects. The organization also publishes some excellent books. Groups including the **Sierra Club, Audubon Society,** and **The Nature Conservancy** also sponsor hikes, backpack trips, bird-watching treks, backcountry excursions, and volunteer "working weekends" in all areas of California; call local or regional contact numbers (in the telephone book) or watch local newspapers for activity announcements.

PRACTICALITIES

Staying and Eating in Northern California

CAMPING

Because of many recent years of drought, and painful lessons learned about extreme fire danger near suburban and urban areas, all California national forests, most national parks, and many state parks now ban all backcountry fires—with the exception of controlled burns (under park supervision), increasingly used to thin understory vegetation to prevent uncontrollable wildfires. Some areas even prohibit portable campstoves, so be sure to check current conditions and all camping and hiking or backpacking regulations before setting out.

To increase your odds of landing a campsite where and when you want one, make reservations (if reservations are accepted). For details on reserving campsites at both national and state parks in California, see relevant listings under Recreation, immediately above, and listings for specific parks elsewhere in this book. Without reservations, seek out "low-profile" campgrounds during the peak camping season— summer as well as spring and fall weekends in most parts of California, late fall through early spring in Southern California desert areas—or plan for off-season camping. Some areas also offer undeveloped, environmental, or dispersed "open camping" not requiring reservations; contact relevant jurisdictions above for information and regulations.

Private campgrounds are also available throughout California, some of these included in the current *Campbook for California and Nevada,* available at no charge to members of the American Automobile Association (AAA), which lists (by city or locale) a wide variety of private, state, and federal campgrounds. Far more comprehensive is Tom Stienstra's *Foghorn Outdoors California Camping,* available in most California bookstores. Or contact **California Travel Parks Association,** 530/823-1076, fax 530/823-5883, www.campgrounds.com/ctpa, which features a great online campground directory. Request a complimentary copy of the association's annual *California RV and Campground Guide* from any member campground, or order one by mail—send $4 if you live in the U.S., $7 if outside the U.S.—by writing to: ESG Mail Service, P.O. Box 5578, Auburn, CA 95604.

Two Internet sites worth visiting for campground information are FreeCampgrounds.com, to track down free sites, and Campsites411.com, which lists campgrounds throughout the United States, including California.

HOSTELS

Among the best bargains around, for travelers of all ages, are the **Hostelling International-USA** (HI-USA) scattered throughout California—in major urban areas, at various scenic spots along the coast, and in other appealing locations. Most are listed separately throughout this guide, but the list continually expands (and contracts); the annual Hostelling International *Hostelling North America* guide, available free with membership (or for $6.95 plus tax at most hostels), includes updated listings. Most affiliated hostels offer separate dormitory-style accommodations for men and women (and private couple or family rooms, if available), communal kitchens or low-cost food service, and/or other common facilities. Some provide storage lockers, loaner bikes, even hot tubs. At most hostels, the maximum stay is three nights; most are also closed during the day, which forces hostelers to get out and about and see the sights. Fees are typically $10–16 ($25–30 in big cities) for HI members, usually several dollars more for nonmembers. Since most hostels are quite popular, especially during summer, reservations—usually secured with one night's advance payment—are essential. Contact individual hostels for details (or see listings elsewhere in this book), since reservation requirements vary. Guests are expected to bring sleeping bags, sleepsacks, or sheets, though sheets or sleepsacks are sometimes available; mattresses, pillows, and blankets are provided.

For membership details and more information about hostelling in the U.S. and abroad, contact: **Hostelling International USA,** 8401 Colesville Rd., Ste. 600, Silver Springs, MD 20910, 301/495-1240, fax 301/495-6697, www.hiayh.org. For more information on Northern California hostels, contact the **HI Golden Gate Council,** 425 Divisadero St., Ste. 307, San Francisco, CA 94117, 415/863-1444 or 415/701-1320, fax 415/863-3865, www.norcalhostels.org, and the **HI Central California Council,** P.O. Box 2538, Monterey, CA 93942, 831/899-1252, fax 831/465-1553, http://westernhostels.org/centralcalifornia.

You'll find other reputable hostels in California, some independent and some affiliated with other hostel "chains" or umbrella organizations (such as the Banana Bungalow group, now well represented in Southern California). For current comprehensive U.S. listings of these private hostels, contact: **BakPak Travelers Guide,** 670 West End Ave., Ste. 1B, New York, NY 10025,/fax 718/504-5099, http:// bakpakguide.com, and **Hostel Handbook of the U.S. and Canada,** c/o Jim Williams, 722 St. Nicholas Ave., New York, NY 10031. Copies of both these guides are also usually available at affiliated hostels.

Particularly in urban areas, the **Young Men's Christian Association** (YMCA) often offers housing, showers, and other facilities for young men (over age 18 only in some areas, if unaccompanied by parent or guardian), sometimes also for women and families. **Young Women's Christian Association** (YWCA) institutions offer housing for women only. Life being what it is these days, though, many of these institutions are primarily shelters for the destitute and the homeless; don't steal their beds unless absolutely necessary. For more information, contact: **YMCA Guest Room Reservations,** 224 E. 47th St., New York, NY 10017, 212/308-2899 (Mon.–Fri. 9 A.M.–5 P.M. Eastern time), or contact local YMCA outposts. Another low-cost alternative in summer is on-campus housing at state colleges and universities; for current information, contact individual campuses (the student housing office) in areas you'll be visiting. For seniors, the **Elderhostel** program, www.elderhostel.org, links up the perennially curious with bargain study programs and accommodations not only in California but worldwide.

MOTELS AND HOTELS

California, the spiritual home of highway and freeway living, is also the birthplace of the motel, the word a contraction for "motor hotels." Motels have been here longer than anywhere else, so they've had plenty of time to clone themselves. As a general precaution, when checking into a truly cheap motel, ask to see the room before signing in (and paying); some places look much more appealing from the outside than from the inside. Midrange and high-priced motels and hotels are generally okay, however. In addition to the standard California sales tax, many cities and counties—particularly near major tourism destinations—add a "bed tax" of 5–18 percent (or higher). To find out the actual price you'll be paying, ask before making reservations or signing in. Unless otherwise stated, rates listed in this guide do not include state sales tax or local bed taxes.

Predictably reliable on the cheaper end of the accommodations scale, though there can be considerable variation in quality and service from place to place, are a variety of budget chains fairly common throughout California. Particularly popular is **Motel 6,** a perennial budget favorite. To receive a copy of the current motel directory, from the U.S. and Canada call 800/466-8356, which is also Motel 6's central reservations service, or try the website at www.motel6.com. (To make central reservations from outside the U.S., call 817/355-5502; reserve by fax from Europe and the United Kingdom at 32-2-753-5858.) You can also make reservations, by phone or fax, at individual motels, some listed elsewhere in this book. Other inexpensive to moderately priced motels are often found clustered in the general vicinity of Motel 6, these including **Comfort Inn,** 800/228-5150, www.comfortinn.com; **Days Inn,** 800/329-7466, www.daysinn.com; **Econo Lodge,** 800/553-2666, www.econolodge.com; **Rodeway Inn,** 800/228-2000, www.rodewayinn.com; and **Super 8 Motels,** 800/800-8000, www.super8.com. You can also pick up a current accommodations directory at any affiliated motel.

You'll find endless other motel and hotel chains in California, most of these more expensive—but not always, given seasonal bargain rates and special discounts offered to seniors, AAA members, and other groups. "Kids stay free," free breakfast for families, and other special promotions can also make more expensive accommodations competitive. Always reliable for quality, but with considerable variation in price and level of luxury, are **Best Western** motel and hotel affiliates, 877/237-8802 in the U.S., www.bestwesterncalifornia.com. Each is independently owned and managed, and some are listed in this guide. Though the gold rush is over, the West's amenities rush is in full swing. There are many upmarket hotels and chains in California, with the **Four Seasons,** www.fshr.com, and **Ritz-Carlton,** www.ritzcarlton.com, hotel and resort chains at the top of most people's "all-time favorite" lists of places to stay if money is no object.

For members of the American Automobile Association (AAA), the current *Tourbook for California and Nevada* (free) includes an impressive number of rated motels, hotels, and resorts, from inexpensive to top of the line, sometimes also recommended restaurants, for nearly every community and city in both Southern and Northern California. Nationwide, AAA members can also benefit from the association's reservations service, 800/272-2155; with one call, you can also request tour books and attractions information for any destination. Other travel groups or associations offer good deals and useful services, too.

Even if you don't belong to a special group or association, you can still benefit from "bulk-buying" power, particularly in large cities—which is a special boon if you're making last-minute plans or are otherwise having little luck on your own. Various room brokers or "consolidators" buy up blocks of rooms from hoteliers at greatly discounted rates and then broker them through their own reservations services. Sometimes, brokers still have bargain-priced rooms available—at rates 40–65 percent below standard rack rates—when popular hotels are otherwise sold out. Lately, though, in an attempt to outbid brokers, hotel chains are touting prices equal to or lower than those offered by brokers. Consequently, prices shift rapidly and no one source has the corner on cheap rates. You'll have the best luck by checking all relevant sources-brokers as well as hotels' websites and reception desks.

That said, for hotel deals try **Hotel Discounts,** 800/715-7666, www.hoteldiscount.com. Particularly helpful for online reservations is the discounted **USA Hotel Guide,** 888/729-7705, www.usahotelguide.com. For other bargain hotel prices in San Francisco, Los Angeles, San Diego, and sometimes also Santa Barbara and Palm Springs, contact **Hotel Reservations Network,** 800/364-0801, www.180096hotel.com, and **Room Exchange,** 800/846-7000, www.hotelrooms.com. If you're willing to bid for a hotel bargain, try **Revelex,** www.revelex.com. Other popular websites for hotel booking include **hotels.com, quikbook.com,** and **1800USAHotels.com.** Two general-purpose broker sites, which handle accommodations as well as transportation and other travel-related bookings, are **expedia.com** and **travelocity.com.** You can download hotel coupons at **www.roomsaver.com.**

BED-AND-BREAKFASTS

Another hot trend, particularly in Northern California, is the bed-and-breakfast phenomenon. Many bed-and-breakfast guides and listings are available in bookstores, and some recommended B&Bs are listed in this book. Unlike the European tradition, with bed-and-breakfasts a low-cost yet comfortable lodging alternative, in California these inns are actually a burgeoning small-business phenomenon—usually quite pricey, in the $100–150-plus range (occasionally less expensive), often more of a "special weekend getaway" for exhausted city people than a mainstream accommodations option. In some areas, though, where motel and hotel rooms are on the high end, bed-and-breakfasts can be quite competitive.

For more information on what's available in all parts of California, including private home stays, contact **California Association of Bed and Breakfast Inns,** 2715 Porter St., Soquel, CA 95073, 831/462-9191, fax 831/462-0402, www.cabbi.com. This group also maintains a search engine at www.innaccess.com that lists all bed-and-breakfasts in the state. **International Bed and Breakfast Pages,** P.O. Box 50594, Denton, TX 76206, www.ibbp.com, claims to include every bed-and-breakfast in the world. It can help with information gathering but doesn't make reservations.

CALIFORNIA CUISINE

One of the best things about traveling in California is the food: they don't call the Golden

WATCHING THE CALIFORNIA GRAYS

A close-up view of the California gray whale, the state's official (and largest) mammal, is a life-changing experience. As those dark, massive, white-barnacled heads shoot up out of the ocean to suck air, spray with the force of a firehose blasts skyward from blowholes. Watch the annual migration of the gray whale all along the California coast—from "whale vistas" on land or by boat.

Despite the fascination they hold for Californians, little is yet known about the gray whale. Once endangered by whaling—as so many whale species still are—the grays are now swimming steadily along the comeback trail. Categorized as baleen whales—which dine on plankton and other small aquatic animals sifted through hundreds of fringed, hornlike baleen plates—gray whales were once land mammals that went back to sea. In the process of evolution, they traded their fore and hind legs for fins and tail flukes. Despite their fishlike appearance, these are true mammals: warm-blooded, air-breathing creatures who nourish their young with milk.

Adult gray whales weigh 20–40 tons, not counting a few hundred pounds of parasitic barnacles. Calves weigh in at a hefty 1,500 pounds at birth and can expect to live for 30–60 years. They feed almost endlessly from April to October in the arctic seas between Alaska and Siberia, sucking up sediment and edible creatures on the bottom of shallow seas, then squeezing the excess water and silt out their baleen filters. Fat and sassy with an extra 6–12 inches of blubber on board, early in October they head south on their 6,000-mile journey to the warmer waters of Baja in Mexico.

Pregnant females leave first, traveling alone or in small groups. Larger groups make up the rear guard, with the older males and nonpregnant females engaging in highly competitive courtship and mating rituals along the way—quite a show for human voyeurs. The rear guard becomes the frontline on the way home: males, newly pregnant females, and young gray whales head north from February to June. Cows and calves migrate later, between March and July.

State the land of fruits and nuts for nothing. In agricultural and rural areas, local "farm trails" or winery guides are often available—ask at local chambers of commerce and visitor centers—and following the seasonal produce trails offers visitors the unique pleasure of gathering (sometimes picking their own) fresh fruits, nuts, and vegetables direct from the growers.

This fresher, direct-to-you produce phenomenon is also quite common in most urban areas, where regular farmers markets are *the* place to go for fresh, organic, often exotic local produce and farm products. Many of the most popular California farmers markets are listed elsewhere in this book—but ask around wherever you are, since new ones pop up constantly. For a reasonably comprehensive current listing of California Certified Farmers Markets (meaning certified as locally grown), contact: **California Federation of Certified Farmers Markets,** P.O. Box 1813, Davis, CA 95617, 707/756-1695, http://ca-farmersmarkets.com.

Threaded with freeways and accessible on-ramp, off-ramp commercial strips, particularly in urban areas, California has more than its fair share of fast-food eateries and all-night quik-stop outlets. (Since they're so easy to find, few are listed in this guide.) Most cities and communities also have locally popular cafés and fairly inexpensive restaurants worth seeking out; many are listed here, but also ask around. Genuinely inexpensive eateries often refuse to take credit cards, so always bring some cash along just in case.

The northstate is also famous for its "California cuisine," which once typically meant consuming tastebud-tantalizing, very expensive food in very small portions—almost a cliché—while oohing and aahing over the presentation throughout the meal. But the fiscally frugal early 1990s restrained most of California's excesses, and even the best restaurants offer less-pretentious menus and slimmed-down prices. The region's culinary creativity is quite real, and worth pursuing (sans pretense) in many areas. Talented chefs, who have migrated throughout the region from Los Angeles and San Francisco as well as from France and Italy, usually prefer locally grown produce, dairy products, meats, and herbs and spices as basic ingredients. To really "do" the cuisine scene, wash it all down with some fine California wine.

© ROBERT HOLMES/CALTOUR

Variety and abundance of fresh produce are the norm in California.

Foreign Travelers

VISAS

A foreign visitor to the U.S. is required to carry a current passport and a visitor's visa plus proof of intent to leave (usually a return airplane ticket is adequate; find passport information at the **Bureau of Consular Affairs** http://travel.state.gov). Also, it's wise to carry proof of one's citizenship, such as a driver's license and/or birth certificate. To be on the safe side, photocopy your legal documents and carry the photocopies separately from the originals. To obtain a U.S. visa (most visitors qualify for a B-2 or "pleasure tourist" visa, valid for up to six months), contact the nearest U.S. embassy or consulate. Should you lose the Form I-94 (proof of arrival/departure) attached to your visa, contact the nearest local U.S. **Immigration and Naturalization Service** (INS) office. Contact the INS also for a visa extension (good for a maximum of six months). To work or study in the U.S., special visas are required; contact the nearest U.S. embassy or consulate for current information. To replace a passport lost while in the U.S., contact the nearest embassy for your country. Canadian citizens entering the U.S. from Canada or Mexico do not need either a passport or visa, nor do Mexican citizens possessing a Form I-186. (Canadians under age 18 do need to carry written consent from a parent or guardian.)

TIME AND MEASUREMENTS

California, within the Pacific time zone (two hours behind Chicago, three hours behind New York) is on daylight saving time (a helps-with-harvest agricultural holdover), which means clocks are set ahead one hour from the first Sunday in April until the last Sunday in October. Without this seasonal time adjustment, when it's noon in California, it's 10 A.M. in Hawaii, 8 P.M. in London, midnight in Moscow, and 4 A.M. (the next day) in Hong Kong.

Despite persistent efforts to wean Americans from the old ways, California and the rest of the union still abide by the British system of weights and measures (see measurements chart in the back of this book). Electrical outlets in California (and the rest of the U.S.) carry current at 117 volts, 60 cycles (Hertz) A.C.; foreign electrical appliances require a converter and plug adapter.

BANKS AND CURRENCY EXCHANGE

Standard business hours in California (holidays excepted) are Mon.–Fri. 9 A.M.–5 P.M., though many businesses open at 8 A.M. or 10 A.M. and/or stay open until 6 P.M. or later. Traditional banking hours—10 A.M. until 3 P.M.—are not necessarily the rule in California these days. Particularly in cities, banks may open at 9 A.M. and stay open until 5 or 6 P.M., and may offer extended walk-up or drive-up window hours. Many banks and savings and loans also offer Saturday hours (usually 9 A.M.–1 P.M.) as well as 24-hour automated teller machine (ATM) service; you'll even find ATMs at most theme parks and, increasingly, inside most grocery stores. Before traveling in California, contact your bank for a list of California branches or affiliated institutions.

For the most part, traveling in California is expensive. Depending on your plans, figure out how much money you'll need—then bring more. Most banks will not cash checks (or issue cash via ATMs) for anyone without an account (or an account with some affiliated institution). Major credit cards (especially Visa and MasterCard) are almost universally accepted in California, except at inexpensive motels and restaurants. Credit cards have become a travel essential, since they are often mandatory for buying airline tickets, renting cars, or as a "security deposit" on bicycle, outdoor equipment, and other rentals. The safest way to bring cash is by carrying traveler's checks. American Express traveler's checks are the most widely recognized and accepted.

Domestic (U.S.) travelers who run short of money, and who are without credit lines on their credit cards, can ask family or friends to send a postal money order (buyable and cashable at any U.S. Postal Service post office); ask your bank to wire money to an affiliated California bank (probably for a slight fee); or have money wired office-to-office via Western Union, 800/325-6000 (800/225-5227 for credit-card money transfers; 800/325-4045 for assistance in Spanish). Use the local phone book to find Western Union offices. In each case, the surcharge depends upon the amount sent.

International travelers should avoid the necessity of wiring for money if at all possible. With a Visa, MasterCard, or American Express card, cash advances are easily available; get details about affiliated U.S. banks before leaving home, however. If you must arrange for cash to be sent from home, a cable transfer from your bank (check on corresponding California banks before leaving), a Western Union money wire, or a bank draft or international money order are all possible. Make sure you (and your sender) know the accurate address for the recipient bank, to avoid obvious nightmarish complications. In a pinch, consulates may intervene and request money from home (or your home bank) at your request—deducting their cost from funds received.

MAIL AND COMMUNICATIONS

Even without a full-fledged post office, most outback California communities have at least some official outpost of the U.S. Postal Service, usually open weekdays 8 A.M.–5 P.M., for sending letters and packages and for receiving general delivery mail. At last report, basic postal rates within the U.S., which may soon increase, were 23 cents for postcards, 37 cents for letter mail (the first ounce). Rates for international mail from the U.S. were 60 cents for postcards, 80 cents for letters (the first ounce), except to Canada and Mexico, which cost 60 cents. The postal code for any address in California is CA. For mail sent and received within the U.S., knowing and using the relevant five- or nine-digit zip code is important. Mail can be directed to any particular post office c/o "General Delivery," but the correct address and zip code for the post office receiving such mail is important—especially in

cities, where there are multiple post offices. (For zip codes and associated post office information, refer to the local phone book, call 800/238-3150, or go to www.usps.com.) To claim general delivery mail, current photo identification is required; unclaimed mail will be returned to the sender after languishing for two to four weeks. At larger post offices, **International Express Mail** is available, with delivery to major world cities in 48–72 hours.

Telephone communication is easy in California; always carry change in your pocket in case you need to make an emergency call. Keep in mind, though, that with the proliferation of cell phones, old-fashioned pay phones are fast disappearing from the landscape. Local calls are often free (or inexpensive) from many motel and hotel rooms, but long-distance calls will cost you. Some hotels add a per-call surcharge even to direct-dialed or credit card calls, however, due and payable when you check out. And the anything-goes aspect of deregulation has also resulted in a spate of for-profit "telephone companies" that generate most of their income through exorbitant rates charged through the hotels, motels, and miscellaneous pay telephones they serve. Using your own long distance carrier (usually with a personal phone card) is typically a better deal. If in doubt about what long-distance services are available on a given phone system, what rates they charge, and whether a hotel or motel surcharge will be added to your bill, ask *before* making your phone call(s). Collect and person-to-person operator-assisted calls are usually more expensive than direct-dial and telephone company (such as AT&T or Sprint) credit-card calls, but in some cases they could save you a bundle.

Telephone communication in California has been further complicated, almost overnight, by a mushrooming number of area codes, those three-digit parenthetical regional prefixes preceding seven-digit local telephone numbers. This chaotic change in California, as elsewhere, is directly related to the proliferating numbers of people, phones, fax machines, pagers, and online computer connections. Between about 1990 and 2000, every telephone area code in

California has "split" (usually into two, the previous code plus a new one) at least once, and some more than once. There have also been "overlays," or the addition of a new area code to the mix of existing ones. This book has made every effort to keep up with area code changes, and has noted upcoming changes that were known at the time of publication. But during the useful life of this guide, it's likely that a few new area codes will present themselves nonetheless, or that area codes and/or phone numbers associated with areas outside this book's immediate scope will change. So—when in doubt, call the local operator and check it out.

Information and Services

Visitors can receive free California travel-planning information by writing the **California Division of Tourism,** P.O. Box 1499, Dept. 61, Sacramento, CA 95812-1499, or by calling 800/862-2543. Or try the website: www.visitcalifornia.com. California's tourism office publishes a veritable gold rush of useful travel information, including the annual *California Official State Visitors Guide* and *California Celebrations.* Particularly useful for outdoor enthusiasts is the new 16-page *California Outdoor Recreation* guide. CalTour also maintains its own **California Recreation** website: www.californiarecreation.com. The quarterly *California Travel Ideas* magazine is distributed free at agricultural inspection stations at the state's borders. For travel industry professionals, the *California Travel and Incentive Planner's Guide* is also available. Most of these California tourism publications, in addition to regional and local publications, are also available at the various roadside volunteer-staffed **California Welcome Centers,** a burgeoning trend. The first official welcome center was unveiled in 1995 in Kingsburg, in the San Joaquin Valley, and the next four—in Rohnert Park, just south of Santa Rosa; in Anderson, just south of Redding; in Oakhurst in the gold country, on the way to Yosemite National Park; and at Pier 39 on San Francisco's Fisherman's Wharf—were also in Northern California. There are others in Northern California, too, including the fairly new one in Arcata, and several in Southern California. Eventually the network will include virtually all areas of California; watch for signs announcing new welcome centers along major highways and freeways.

Most major cities and visitor destinations in California also have very good visitor information bureaus and visitor centers, listed elsewhere in this book. Many offer accommodations reservations and other services; some offer information and maps in foreign languages. Chambers of commerce can be useful, too. In less populated areas, chambers of commerce are something of a hit-or-miss proposition, since office hours may be minimal; the best bet is calling ahead for information. Asking locals—people at gas stations, cafés, grocery stores, and official government outposts—is often the best way to get information about where to go, why, when, and how. Slick city magazines, good daily newspapers, and California-style weekly news and entertainment tabloids are other good sources of information.

ACCESS FOR THE DISABLED

Well worth checking out is **Access Northern California,** 1427 Grant St., Berkeley, CA 94703, 510/524-2026, which publishes its own guidebook, **Access San Francisco,** and also offers a very useful website: www.accessnca.com. Similarly helpful in the southstate is **Accessible San Diego,** P.O Box 124526, San Diego, CA 92112-4526, 858/279 0704, www.accessandiego.org, which publishes a helpful San Diego area guidebook. Useful in a more general sense is **Access-Able Travel Source,** P.O. Box 1796, Wheat Ridge, CO 80034, 303/232-2979, fax 303/239-8486, www.access-able.com, which also manages the Travelin' Talk Network at www.travelintalk.net, an international network of disabled people available "to help travelers in any way they can." Membership is only $19.95, a bargain by any standard, since by joining up you suddenly have a vast network of allies in otherwise strange places who are all too happy to tell you what's what. Also particularly useful is the **Society for Accessible Travel & Hospitality** (SATH), P.O. Box 382, Owatonna, MN 55060, 507/451-5005, www.sath.org, dedicated to making barrier-free travel a reality. Primarily an educational group, SATH provides useful travel tips and consumer travel information on its website and in *Open World* magazine.

For current information about the Americans with Disabilities Act, which spells out U.S. laws regarding accessibility at public and other buildings, see www.usdoj.gov/crt/ada. Information specific to accommodations and transportation for the disabled is also available. Before plotting transportation logistics, get a free copy of *Access Amtrak,* a booklet published by Amtrak that lists its accessible services; call 800/872-7245 for details. Also helpful is *The Disabled Driver's Mobility Guide* put out by the American Automobile Association (AAA) and available by calling 800/637-2122.

Flying Wheels Travel, 800/535-6790, www.flyingwheelstravel.com, is a travel agency that specializes in independent vacations for the disabled. **1-888-Inn-Seek,** an online search engine, lists wheelchair-accessible bed-and-breakfasts. Access it either via phone, 888/466-7355, or online at www.1-888-Inn-Seek.com.

Mobility International USA, P.O. Box 10767, Eugene, OR 97440, and TDD 541/343-1284, fax 541/343-6812, www.miusa.org, provides two-way international leadership exchanges. Disabled people who want to go to Europe to study theater, for example, or British citizens who want to come to California for Elderhostel programs—anything beyond traditional leisure travel—should call here first. The individual annual membership fee is $25 for individuals, $35 for organizations.

SENIOR CITIZENS

Senior adults can benefit from a great many bargains and discounts. A good source of information is the *Travel Tips for Older Americans* pamphlet published by the U.S. Government Printing Office, 202/275-3648, www

.gpo.gov, available for $1.25. (Order it online at the website: www.pueblo.gsa.gov/travel.) The federal government's Golden Age Passport offers free admission to national parks and monuments and half-price discounts for federal campsites and other recreational services; state parks also offer senior discounts. (For detailed information, see appropriate recreation listings under Recreation, above.) Discounts are also frequently offered to seniors at major tourist attractions and sights as well as for many arts, cultural, and entertainment destinations and events in Southern California. Another benefit of experience is eligibility for the international **Elderhostel** program, 11 Avenue de Lafayette, Boston, MA 02111, 877/426-8056 or 617/426-7788, www.elderhostel.org, which offers a variety of fairly reasonable one-week residential programs in California.

For information on travel discounts, trip planning, tours, and other membership benefits of the U.S.'s largest senior citizen organization, contact the **American Association of Retired Persons** (AARP), 601 E St. NW, Washington, DC 20049, 800/424-3410, fax 501/451-1685, www.aarp.org. Despite the name, anyone age 50 and older—retired or not—is eligible for membership. Other membership-benefit programs for seniors include **Senior Citizens America,** 8403 Colesville Rd., Ste. 1200, Silver Springs, MD 20910, 301/578-8800, fax 301/578-8999.

RECOMMENDED MAPS

The best all-around maps for general California travel, either in the city or out in the countryside, are those produced by the **American Automobile Association,** which is regionally organized as the California State Automobile Association (CSAA) in Northern and Central California, and as the Automobile Club of Southern California in the southstate. The AAA maps are available at any local AAA office, and the price is right (free, but for members only). In addition to its California state map and Southern California map, AAA provides urban maps for most major cities, plus regional maps with at least some backcountry routes marked (these latter

DUCK THE BUDGET BLUES

Heads up, California travelers. Present and future circumstances have become decidedly uncertain as a direct result of California's ongoing budget crisis. When will state parks be open, and how much is admission? Public libraries? Will there be lifeguards at public pools and beaches? Will mass transit trains and buses run on time—or run at all? Will there be adequate police and fire protection? Every effort was made to corral current details, but it's likely that circumstances have changed. For the sake of a pleasant and fruitful visit *please* call ahead to verify essential details.

maps don't necessarily show the entire picture, however; when in doubt about unusual routes, ask locally before setting out). For more information about AAA membership and services in Northern California, contact the **California State Automobile Association;** the main office address is 150 Van Ness Ave., P.O. Box 429186, San Francisco, CA 94102, 415/565-2012 or 415/565-2468, www.csaa.org, but there are also regional offices throughout the northstate. Members can also order maps, tour books, and other services online. If you'll also be visiting Southern California, the AAA affiliate there is the **Automobile Club of Southern California,** 2601 S. Figueroa St., Los Angeles, CA 90007, 213/741-3686, www.aaa-calif.com. For AAA membership information, from anywhere in the U.S. call 800/222-4357, or try www.aaa.com.

The best maps money can buy, excellent for general and very detailed travel in California, are the **Thomas Bros. Maps,** typically referred to as "Thomas guides." For the big picture, particularly useful is the *California Road Atlas & Driver's Guide,* but various other, very detailed spiral-bound book-style maps in the Thomas guide street atlas series—San Francisco, Monterey County, Los Angeles, Orange County, San Diego—are the standard block-by-block references, continually updated since 1915. Thomas guides are available at any decent travel-oriented bookstore, or contact the company directly. In

Southern California, you'll find a major Thomas Bros. Maps store at 521 W. Sixth St., Los Angeles, CA 90017, 888/277-6277 or 213/627-4018; the map factory and other store is in Orange County, at 17731 Cowan in Irvine, 800/899-6277 or 949/863-1984, fax 949/852-9189. In Northern California, stop by Thomas Bros. Maps, 595 Market St., San Francisco, CA 94105, 800/969-3072 or 415/543-8020. Or order any map by calling, from anywhere in California, 800/899-6277—or by trying, from anywhere in the world, www.thomas.com.

When it comes to backcountry travel—where maps quickly become either your best friend or archenemy—the going isn't nearly as easy. U.S. Geological Survey quadrangle maps in most cases are reliable for showing the contours of the terrain, but U.S. Forest Service and wilderness maps—supposedly the maps of record for finding one's way through the woods and the wilds—are often woefully out of date, with new and old logging roads (as well as disappearing or changed trail routes) confusing the situation considerably. In California, losing oneself in the wilderness is a very real, literal possibility. In addition to topo maps (carry a compass to orient yourself by landforms if all else fails) and official U.S. maps, backcountry travelers would be wise to invest in privately published guidebooks and current route or trail guides for wilderness areas; the Sierra Club and Wilderness Press publish both. Before setting out, compare all available maps and other information to spot any possible route discrepancies, then ask national forest or parks personnel for clarification. If you're lucky, you'll find someone who knows what's going on where you want to go.

Aside from well-stocked outdoor stores, the primary California source for quad maps is: **U.S. Geological Survey,** 345 Middlefield Rd., Menlo Park, CA 94025, 650/853-8300 (ask for the mapping division); an index and catalog of published California maps is available upon request. Or try the USGS website: info.er.usgs.gov, or call 888/275-8747. Also contact the U.S. Forest Service and U.S. National Park Service (see Playing Here: Outdoor Recreation, above). The best bet for wilderness maps and guides is **Wilder-**

ness Press, 1200 Fifth St., Berkeley, CA 94710, 510/558-1666 or 800/443-7227 (for orders), www.wildernesspress.com. Most Wilderness Press titles are available in California bookstores.

Not necessarily practical for travelers are the beautiful yet utilitarian maps produced by **Raven Maps & Images,** 34 N. Central, P.O. Box 850, Medford, OR 97501, 541/773-1436, or (for credit-card orders) 800/237-0798, www.ravenmaps.com. These beauties are big, and—unless you buy one for the wall and one for the road—you'll never want to fold them. Based on U.S. Geological Survey maps, these shaded relief maps are "computer-enhanced" for a three-dimensional topographical feel and incredible clarity—perfect for planning outdoor adventures. Raven's *California* map measures 42 by 64 inches, and *Yosemite and the Central Sierra* is 34 by 37 inches. Wonderful for any California-lover's wall is the three-dimensional, five-color *California, Nevada, and the Pacific Ocean Floor* digital landform map, which offers three aerial oblique views: now, five million years ago, and five million years in the future. Fabulous. All Raven maps are printed in fade-resistant inks on fine quality 70-pound paper and are also available in vinyl laminated versions suitable for framing.

CONDUCT AND CUSTOMS

Smoking is a major social sin in California, often against the law in public buildings and on public transport, with regulations particularly stringent in urban areas. People sometimes get violent over other people's smoking, so smokers need to be respectful of others' "space" and smoke outdoors when possible. Smoking has been banned outright in California restaurants and bars, and smoking is not allowed on public airplane flights, though nervous fliers can usually smoke somewhere inside—or outside—airline terminals. Many bed-and-breakfasts in California are either entirely nonsmoking or restrict smoking to decks, porches, or dens; if this is an issue, inquire by calling ahead. Hotels and motels, most commonly in major urban areas or popular tourist destinations, increasingly offer nonsmoking rooms (or entire floors). Ask in advance.

The legal age for buying and drinking alcohol in California is 21. Though Californians tend to (as they say) "party hearty," public drunkenness is not well tolerated. Drunken driving—which means operating an automobile (even a bicycle, technically) while under the influence—is definitely against the law. California is increasingly no-nonsense about the use of illegal drugs, too, from marijuana to cocaine, crack, and heroin. Doing time in local jails or state prisons is not the best way to do California.

English is the official language in California, and even English-speaking visitors from other countries have little trouble understanding California's "dialect" once they acclimate to the accents and slang expressions. (Californians tend to be very creative in their language.) When unsure what someone means by some peculiar phrase, ask for a translation into standard English. Particularly in urban areas, many languages are commonly spoken, and—even in English—the accents are many. You can usually obtain at least some foreign-language brochures, maps, and other information from city visitor centers and popular tourist destinations. (If this is a major concern, inquire in advance.)

Californians are generally casual, in dress as well as etiquette. If any standard applies in most situations, it's common courtesy—still in style, generally speaking, even in California. Though "anything goes" just about anywhere, elegant restaurants usually require appropriately dressy attire for women, jacket and tie for men. (Shirts and shoes—pants or skirt too, usually—are required in any California restaurant.)

By law, public buildings in California are wheelchair-accessible, or at least partially so. The same is true of most major hotels and tourist attractions, which may offer both rooms and restrooms with complete wheelchair accessibility; some also have wheelchairs, walkers, and other mobility aids available for temporary use. Even national and state parks, increasingly, are attempting to make some sights and campgrounds more accessible for those with physical disabilities; to make special arrangements, inquire in advance. But private buildings, from restaurants to bed-and-breakfasts, may not be so accommodating. Those with special needs should definitely ask specific questions in advance.

TIPPING

For services rendered in the service trade, a tip is usually expected. Some say the word is derived from the Latin *stips,* for stipend or gift. Some say it's an 18th-century English acronym for "to ensure promptness," though "to ensure personal service" seems more to the point in these times. In expensive restaurants or for large groups, an automatic tip or gratuity may be included in the bill—an accepted practice in many countries but a source of irritation for many U.S. diners, who would prefer to personally evaluate the quality of service received. Otherwise, 15–20 percent of the before-tax total tab is the standard gratuity, and 10 percent the minimal acknowledgment, for those in the service trade—waitresses and waiters, barbers, hairdressers, and taxi drivers. In fine-dining circumstances, wine stewards should be acknowledged personally, at the rate of $2–5 per bottle, and the maitre d' as well, with $5 or $10. In very casual buffet-style joints, leave $1 each for the people who clear the dishes and pour your coffee after the meal. In bars, leave $1 per drink, or 15 percent of the bill if you run a tab. At airports, tip skycaps $1 per bag (more if they transport your baggage any distance); tip more generously for extra assistance, such as helping wheelchair passengers or mothers with infants and small children to their gates.

At hotels, a desk clerk or concierge does not require a tip unless that person fulfills a specific request, such as snagging tickets for a sold-out concert or theater performance, in which case generosity is certainly appropriate. For baggage handlers curbside, $1 tip is adequate; a tip of at least $1 per bag is appropriate for bell staff transporting luggage from the lobby to your room or from your room to the lobby. For valet parking, tip the attendant $2–3. Tip the hotel doorman if he helps with baggage or hails a cab for you. And tip swimming pool or health club personnel as appropriate for extra personal service. Unless one stays in a hotel or motel for several days, the standard practice is not to tip the housekeeper, though you can if you wish; some guests leave $1–2 each morning for the housekeeper and $1 each evening for turn-down service.

BASIC SERVICES

Except for some very lonely areas, even backwater areas of California aren't particularly primitive. Gasoline, at least basic groceries, laundries of some sort, even video and DVD rentals are available just about anywhere. Outback areas are not likely to have parts for exotic sports cars, however, or 24-hour pharmacies, hospitals, and garages, or natural foods stores or full-service supermarkets, so you should take care of any special needs or problems before leaving the cities. It's often (though not always) cheaper to stock up on most supplies, including outdoor equipment and groceries, in urban areas.

Health and Safety

MEDICAL CARE AND GENERAL HEALTH

In most places in California, call 911 in any emergency; in medical emergencies, life support personnel and ambulances will be dispatched. To make sure health care services will be readily provided, health insurance coverage is almost mandatory; carry proof of coverage while traveling in California. In urban areas and in many rural areas, 24-hour walk-in health care services are readily available, though hospital emergency rooms are the place to go in case of life-threatening circumstances.

To avoid most health and medical problems, use common sense. Eat sensibly, avoid unsafe drinking water, bring along any necessary prescription pills—and pack an extra pair of glasses or contacts, just in case. Sunglasses, especially for those unaccustomed to sunshine, as well as sunscreen and a broad-brimmed hat can help prevent sunburn, sunstroke, and heat prostration. Drink plenty of liquids, too, especially when exercising and/or in hot weather.

No vaccinations are usually necessary for traveling in California, though here as elsewhere very young children and seniors should obtain vaccinations against annually variable forms of the flu virus; exposure, especially in crowded urban areas and during the winter disease season, is a likelihood.

As in other areas of the United States and the world, the AIDS (Acquired Immune Deficiency Syndrome) virus and other sexually transmitted diseases are a concern. In mythic "anything goes" California, avoiding promiscuous or unprotected sex is the best way to avoid the danger of contracting the AIDS virus and venereal disease—though AIDS is also transmitted via shared drug needles and contaminated blood transfusions. (All medical blood supplies in California are screened for evidence of the virus.) Sexually speaking, "safe sex" is the preventive key phrase, under any circumstances beyond the strictly monogamous. This means always using condoms in sexual intercourse; oral sex only with some sort of barrier precaution; and no sharing sex toys.

CITY SAFETY

Though California's wilderness once posed a major threat to human survival, in most respects the backcountry is safer than the urban jungle of modern cities. Tourism officials don't talk about it much, but crimes against persons and property are a reality in California (though the state's overall crime rate has dropped sharply in recent years). To avoid harm, bring along your street-smarts. The best overall personal crime prevention includes carrying only small amounts of cash (inconspicuously, in a money belt or against-the-body money pouch); labeling (and locking) all luggage; keeping valuables under lock and key (and, in automobiles, out of sight); being aware of people and events, and knowing where you are, at all times; and avoiding dangerous, lonely, and unlighted areas after daylight, particularly late at night and when traveling alone. If you're not sure what neighborhoods are considered dangerous

or unsafe, ask locals or hotel or motel personnel—or at the police station, if necessary.

Women traveling alone—not generally advisable, because of the unfortunate fact of misogyny in the modern world—need to take special care to avoid harm. For any independent traveler, self-defense classes (and/or a training course for carrying and using Mace) might be a worthwhile investment, if only to increase one's sense of personal power in case of a confrontation with criminals. Being assertive and confident, and acting as if you know where you are going (even when you don't), are also among the best deterrents to predators. Carry enough money for a phone call—or bus or taxi ride—and a whistle. When in doubt, don't hesitate to use it, and to yell and scream for help.

OUTDOOR SAFETY

The most basic rule is, know what you're doing and where you're going. Next most basic: whatever you do—from swimming or surfing to hiking and backpacking—don't do it alone. For any outdoor activity, be prepared. Check with local park or national forest service officials on weather, trail, and general conditions before setting out. Correct, properly functioning equipment is as important in backpacking as it is in hang gliding, mountain climbing, mountain biking, and sailing. (When in doubt, check it out.)

Among the basics to bring along for almost any outdoor activity: a hat, sunscreen, and lip balm (to protect against the sun in summer, against heat loss, reflective sun, and the elements in winter); a whistle, compass, and mylar "space blanket" in case you become lost or stranded; insect repellent; a butane lighter or waterproof matches; a multipurpose Swiss Army-type knife; nylon rope; a flashlight; and a basic first-aid kit (including bandages, ointments and salves, antiseptics, pain relievers such as aspirin, and any necessary prescription medicines). Hikers, backpackers, and other outdoor adventurers should bring plenty of water—or water purification tablets or pump-style water purifiers for long trips—at least minimal fishing gear, good hiking shoes or boots, extra socks

© ROBERT HOLMES/CALTOUR

and shoelaces, "layerable" clothing adequate for all temperatures, and a waterproof poncho or large plastic garbage bag. (Even if thunderstorms are unlikely, any sort of packable and wearable plastic bag can keep you dry until you reach shelter.) The necessity for other outdoor equipment, from campstoves to sleeping bags and tents, depends on where you'll be going and what you'll be doing.

Poison Oak

Poison oak (actually a shrublike sumac) is a perennial trailside hazard, especially in lowland foothill areas and mixed forests; it exudes oily chemicals that cause a strong allergic reaction in many people, even with only brief contact. (Always be careful what you're burning around the campfire, too; smoke from poison oak, when inhaled, can inflame the lungs and create a life-threatening situation in no time flat.) The best way to avoid the painful, itchy, often long-lasting rashes associated with poison oak is to avoid contact with the plant—in all seasons—and to immediately wash one's skin or clothes if you even suspect a brush with it. (Its leaves a bright, glossy green in spring and summer, red or yellow in fall, poison oak can be a problem even in win-

ter—when this mean-spirited deciduous shrub loses its leaves.) Learn to identify it during any time of year.

Once afflicted with poison oak, never scratch, because the oozing sores just spread the rash. Very good new products on the market include Tecnu's **Poison Oak-n-Ivy Armor** "pre-exposure lotion," produced by Tec Laboratories, Inc., of Albany, Oregon, 800/482-4464 (800-ITCH-ING). Apply it before potential exposure to protect yourself. Another excellent product, quite helpful if you do tangle with poison oak, is Tecnu's **Poison Oak-n-Ivy Cleanser,** the idea being to get the toxic oils off your skin as soon as possible, within hours of initial exposure or just after the rash appears. The cleanser—which smells suspiciously like kerosene—also helps eliminate the itching, remarkably well. (But do *not* apply after oozing begins.) Various drying, cortisone-based lotions, oatmeal baths, and other treatments can help control discomfort if the rash progresses to the oozing stage, but the rash itself goes away only in its own good time.

Lyme Disease and Ticks

Even if you favor shorts for summer hiking, you had better plan on long pants, long-sleeved shirts, even insect repellent. The weather may be mild, but there's an increasing risk—particularly in California coastal and foothill areas, as in other states—that you'll contract Lyme disease, transmitted by ticks that thrive in moist lowland climates.

A new ailment on the West Coast, Lyme disease is named after the place of its 1975 discovery in Old Lyme, Connecticut. Already the most common vector-transmitted disease in the nation, Lyme is caused by spirochetes transmitted through blood, urine, and other body fluids. Research indicates it has often been wrongly diagnosed; sufferers were thought to have afflictions such as rheumatoid arthritis. Temporary paralysis, arthritic pains in the hands or arm and leg joints, swollen hands, fever, fatigue, nausea, headaches, swollen glands, and heart palpitations are among the typical symptoms. Sometimes an unusually circular red rash appears first, between three and 30 days after the tick bite. Untreated, Lyme disease can mean a lifetime of suffering, even danger to unborn children. Treatment, once Lyme disease is discovered through blood tests, is simple and 100 percent effective if recognized early: tetracycline and other drugs halt the arthritic degeneration and most symptoms. Long-delayed treatment, even with extremely high doses of antibiotics, is only about 50 percent effective.

Outdoor prudence, coupled with an awareness of possible Lyme symptoms even months later, are the watchwords when it comes to Lyme disease. Take precautions against tick bite: the sooner ticks are found and removed, the better your chances of avoiding the disease. Tuck your pants into your boots, wear long-sleeved shirts, and use insect repellent around all clothing openings as well as on your neck and all exposed skin. Run a full-body "tick check" daily, especially checking hidden areas such as the hair and scalp. Consider leaving dogs at home if heading for Lyme country; ticks they pick up can spread the disease through your human family.

Use gloves and tweezers to remove ticks from yourself or your animals—never crush the critters with your fingers!—and wash your hands and the bitten area afterward. Better yet, smother imbedded ticks with petroleum jelly first; deprived of oxygen, they start to pull out of the skin in about a half hour, making it easy to pluck them off without tearing them in two and leaving the head imbedded.

Getting Here and Around

BY CAR

This being California, almost everyone gets around by car. Urban freeway driving in California, because of congestion and Californians' no-nonsense get-on-with-it driving styles, can inspire panic even in nonlocal native drivers. It doesn't help that California's aging highways are ranked worst in the nation in terms of condition and upkeep. If this is a problem, plan your trip to skirt the worst congestion—by taking back roads and older highways, if possible, or by trying neighborhood routes—but only if you know something about the neighborhoods. Alternatively, plan to arrive in San Francisco, other Bay Area destinations, Sacramento, and anywhere in Southern California well after the day's peak freeway commute traffic, usually any time after 7 or 8 P.M.

A good investment for anyone traveling for any length of time in California is a membership in the American Automobile Association (see above) since—among many other benefits, including excellent maps and trip-planning assistance—a AAA card entitles the bearer to no-cost emergency roadside service, including five gallons of free gas and at least limited towing, if necessary.

Gasoline in California is typically more expensive than elsewhere in the U.S., up to 40 cents per gallon more, only in part because of California's new cleaner-burning "reformulated" fuels, the world's cleanest gasoline. The effect of using the new gasoline is roughly equivalent to the effect of taking 3.5 million cars off the road on any given day—or sucking about three million pounds of toxins and particulate matter out of the air. The clean fuels are designed to reduce vehicle

PRACTICALITIES

CALIFORNIA ON WHEELS

California's public officials, at least in urban areas, continue to make every effort to offer viable alternatives to automobile travel, but Golden State residents and their cars are almost inseparable. Part of the Western myth, after all, is the freedom to move, to go anywhere at the drop of a ten-gallon hat. Given the state's vast size and the great distances between destinations—and despite at least nominal awareness about the evils of air pollution, global warming, and excess energy consumption—California's love affair with wheels is a basic fact of life.

So, what's a visitor to do?

Those who arrive by air and prefer to travel by public transportation can reach most areas of California—with careful advance planning—by train and/or bus. (See relevant regional chapters for specific information.) Travelers can also tour by bicycle, an option most feasible for the very fit and flexible, requiring conscientious back-roads route mapping and careful planning.

Most people who arrive without their own wheels, however, soon choose to rent some, either a car or, for longer trips to more obscure destinations, a recreational vehicle. Major national car rental agencies are well represented at San Francisco, Oakland, and Sacramento International Airports, where most fly-ins first arrive. Lower-cost statewide and local agencies are also abundant and usually reliable. Smaller regional airports usually also offer car rentals. Consult the telephone directory yellow pages for a complete listing, and also consult chambers of commerce and visitor bureaus. (If in doubt about a given com-

pany, contact local visitor bureaus and chambers of commerce.) If you'll be arriving in summer, during the holidays, or at other peak travel times, reserve rental vehicles well in advance.

Flat rate (daily or weekly) and unlimited mileage rentals are generally the best deal, since a California-style day trip can easily pass the 300-mile mark. When planning a trip or trips to outlying areas, it is usually much less expensive to start from—and return your rental vehicle to—agencies located in major urban areas. Renting a car in a small, remote city with the idea of ending your adventure back in San Francisco or Oakland may make perfect sense; but the associated "drop-off fee"—essentially an inconvenience penalty imposed by the rental company, concerned about getting that car back in their shop—can range to $500 and more, a definite drawback. Recreational vehicles (RVs), including four-wheel drives and pickup trucks with campers, are substantially more expensive to rent than cars and are usually available only through specialized agencies and RV sales dealers.

California vehicle rentals are relatively expensive. Once comfortable with one's vehicle and familiar with California driving customs and laws, a special bonus for European and other international travelers is the price of gasoline—still remarkably inexpensive in the U.S., averaging $1.50 to $2 per gallon. Though this fact of life may change, for the time being, at least, travel by car remains cheaper here (at least in terms of personal finances) than almost anywhere else in the world.

emissions and improve air quality, which seems to be working, but a new concern is that clean fuel residues (particularly from the additive MTBE) are polluting California's water. Though MTBE will soon be banned, the Golden State's pollution solutions are, clearly, ideas that still need work.

To check on current **California road conditions** before setting out—always a good idea in a state with so much ongoing road construction and such variable regional weather—call **Caltrans** (California Department of Transportation) from anywhere in California at 800/427-7623, and from outside California at 916/445-7623.

The road-condition phone numbers are accessible from touch-tone and pay phones as well as cellular phones. Or check road conditions for your entire trip via real-time travel maps available on the Caltrans website: www.dot.ca.gov/traffic.

Though every municipality has its own peculiar laws about everything from parking to skateboarding or roller skating on sidewalks, there are basic rules everyone is expected to know and follow—especially drivers. Get a complete set of regulations from the state motor vehicles department, which has an office in all major cities and many medium-sized ones. Or contact **Cali-**

fornia Department of Motor Vehicles, 2415 First Ave., P.O. Box 942869, Sacramento, CA 94269, www.dmv.ca.gov. Foreign visitors planning to drive should obtain an **International Driver's License** before leaving home (they're not available here); licensed U.S. drivers from other states can legally drive in California for 30 consecutive days without having to obtain a California driver's license. Disabled travelers heading for California can get special handicapped-space parking permits, good for 90 days, by requesting applications in advance from the DMV and having them signed by their doctors (there is an application fee). If you'll be renting a car, ask the rental car agency to forward a form to you when you make reservations.

Among driving rules, the most basic is observing the posted speed limit. Though many California drivers ignore any and all speed limits, it's at their own peril should the California Highway Patrol be anywhere in the vicinity. The statewide speed limit for open highway driving varies, typically posted as somewhere between 55 and 70 miles per hour; freeway speeds can vary at different points along the same route. Speed limits for cities and residential neighborhoods are substantially slower. Another avoidable traffic ticket is *not* indulging in what is colloquially known as the "California stop," slowing down and then rolling right through intersections without first making a complete stop.

Once arrived at your destination, pay attention to parking notices, tow-away warnings, and curb color: red means no parking under any circumstances; yellow means limited stops only (usually for freight delivery); green means very limited parking; and blue means parking for the disabled only. In hilly areas of California—and most necessarily in San Francisco—always turn your front wheels into the curb (to keep your car from becoming a rollaway runaway) and set the emergency brake.

Driving while under the influence of alcohol or drugs is a very serious offense in California—aside from being a danger to one's own health and safety, not to mention those of innocent fellow drivers and pedestrians. Don't drink (or do drugs) and drive.

Rental Cars

Renting a car—or a recreational vehicle—in California usually won't come cheap. Rates have been accelerating, so to speak, in recent years, especially when consumers put the kibosh on mileage caps. Turns out people really liked the idea of unlimited "free" mileage. So now the average car rental price is just above $60 a day (lower for subcompacts, higher for roadhogs). Still, bargains are sometimes available through small local agencies, though rates can vary, from city to city and company to company, by as much as 80 percent. It definitely pays to comparison shop for car rentals. Among national agencies, National and Alamo often offer the lowest prices. But in many cases, with weekly rentals and various group-association (AAA, AARP, etc.) and credit-card discounts ranging from 10–40 percent, you'll usually do just as well with other major rental car agencies. According to the *Consumer Reports* June 1996 national reader quality survey, **Hertz, Avis,** and **National** were rated highest by customers for clean cars, quick and courteous service, and speedy checkout.

Beware the increasingly intense pressure, once you arrive to pick up your rental car, to persuade you to buy additional insurance coverage. In some companies, rental car agents receive a commission for every insurance policy they sell, needed or not, which is why the person on the other side of the counter is so motivated (sometimes pushy and downright intimidating). Feel free to complain to management if you dislike such treatment—and to take your business elsewhere. This highly touted insurance coverage is coverage you probably don't need, from collision damage waivers—now outlawed in some states, but not in California—to liability insurance, which you probably don't need unless you have no car insurance at all (in which case it's illegal to drive in California). Some people do carry additional rental-car collision or liability insurance on their personal insurance policies—talk to your agent about this—but even that is already covered, at least domestically, if you pay for your rental car with a gold or platinum MasterCard or Visa. The same is true for American Express for domestic travelers, though American Express recently rescinded such coverage on overseas car rentals; it's possible that Visa and MasterCard will soon follow suit. (Check your personal insurance and credit-card coverage before dealing with the rental car agencies.) And bring personal proof of car insurance, though you'll rarely be asked for it. In short—buyer beware.

For current information on options and prices for rental cars in Northern California, Southern California, and elsewhere in the U.S., contact **Alamo,** 800/462-5266, www.alamo.com.; **Avis,** 800/831-2847, www.avis.com; **Budget,** worldwide 800/527-0700, www.budget.com; **Dollar,** 800/800-3665, www.dollar.com; **Enterprise,** 800/736-8222, www.enterprise.com; **Hertz,** worldwide 800/654-3131, www.hertz.com; **National,** 800/227-7368, www.nationalcar.com; and **Thrifty,** 800/847-4389, www.thrifty.com. You can also make rental car arrangements online otherwise, through virtual travel agencies and reservations systems such as **Travelocity,** www.travelocity.com, and **The Trip,** www.thetrip.com.

Though some rental agencies also handle recreational vehicle (RV) rentals, travelers may be able to get better deals by renting directly from local RV dealers. For suggestions, contact area visitor bureaus—and consult the local telephone book.

BY AIRPLANE

Following the September 11, 2001, terrorist attacks, airport security measures are now strictly enforced. For travelers, this means extra time for air travel. To reduce the chances of delays of problems, keep in mind the following. A couple of days before your flight, contact your travel agent or the airline for an update on departure time, ID requirements, and luggage rules. Don't bring wrapped gifts. Pack any instruments capable of puncturing or cutting (such as nail files, knives, scissors, box cutters, etc.) in your checked luggage. Arrive two hours early to ensure you'll have time to check your luggage and get through security inspections before your flight.

Airfares change and bargains come and go so quickly in competitive California that the best way to keep abreast of the situation is through a travel agent. Or via the Internet, where major U.S. airlines regularly offer great deals—discounts of up to 90 percent (typically not *quite* that good). Popular home pages include **American Airlines,** www.aa.com; **Continental,** www.flycontinental.com; **Delta,** www.delta-air.com; **Northwest,** www.nwa.com; **TWA,** www.twa.com; **United,** www.ual.com; and **US Airways,** www.usairways.com. Also look up the people's favorite, **Southwest,** at www.southwest.com. Have your credit card handy. To find additional websites, know your computer—or call any airline's "800" number and ask.

Online travel brokers offer cheap fares as well. A recent Consumer Reports study concluded that **Expedia,** www.expedia.com, **Travelocity,** www.travelocity.com, and airlines-owned **Orbitz,** www.orbitz.com offer the best ratio of low fares to viable itineraries (such as single-carrier flights and fewer connecting flights and lengthy layovers). However, the smaller online brokers often advertise the lowest-though generally nonrefundable-fares. Among these, **Cheap Tickets,** www.cheaptickets.com, **One Travel,** www.onetravel.com, and **TravelNow,** www.travelnow.com are reputable. **Travelzoo,** www.travelzoo.com, searches the 20 major airline websites for the deep-discounted fares and posts them, so you don't have to spend hours looking for the best deals. **Hotwire,** www.hotwire.com, offers airline tickets at a 40 percent discount (though with limited consumer routing control), with hotel rooms and rental car discounts added to the mix in late 2000. For possibly great deals on last-minute departures, try **Savvio,** www.savvio.com.

Another good information source for domestic and international flight fares: the travel advertisements in the weekend travel sections of major urban newspapers. Super Saver fares (booked well in advance) can save fliers up to 30–70 percent and more. Peak travel times in and out of California being the summer and the midwinter holiday season, book flights well in advance for June–August and December travel. The best bargains in airfares are usually available from January to early May.

Bargain airfares are often available for international travelers, especially in spring and autumn. Charter flights are also good bargains, the only disadvantage usually being inflexible departure and return-flight dates. Most flights from Europe to the U.S. arrive in New York; from there, other transcontinental travel options are available. Reduced-fare flights on major airlines from Europe abound.

Keep in mind, too, if you're flying, that airlines are getting increasingly strict about how much baggage you're allowed to bring with you. They mean business with those prominent "sizer boxes" now on display in every airport. Only two pieces of carry-on luggage are allowed on most carriers—some now allow only one—and each must fit in the box. Most airlines allow three pieces of luggage total per passenger. (Fortunately for parents, diaper bags, fold-up strollers, and—at least sometimes—infant carrier seats don't count.) So if you are philosophically opposed to the concept of traveling light, bring two massive suitcases—and check them through—in addition to your carry-on. Some airlines, including American, charge extra for more than two checked bags per person. Contact each airline directly for current baggage guidelines.

BY TRAIN

An unusually enjoyable way to travel the length of the West Coast to California, or to arrive here after a trip west over the Sierra Nevada or across the great desert, is by train. Within Northern California, travel along the coast on Amtrak's immensely popular and recently spiffed up **Coast Starlight,** which now features more comfortable tilt-back seats, a parlor car with library and games, and California-style fare in its dining cars. (From the south, the two-way route continues north to Oakland, across the bay from San Francisco, and eventually continues all the way to Seattle.) If you'll eventually arrive in Southern California, from grand Union Station near downtown L.A. you can head east to New Orleans on the **Sunset Limited,** to San Antonio on the **Texas Eagle,** and to Chicago on the **Desert Wind** and the **Southwest Chief.** Regional trains operated by Amtrak within California include the **Pacific Surfliner** (formerly the San Diegans) along the state's central and south coasts, and the **San**

EURAIL-STYLE TRAIN PASSES

Amtrak now sells passes for unlimited train travel in the Golden State. For $159 ($80 for children 2–15), the **California Rail Pass** allows holders to board, on any seven days during a 21-day period, *Capitol* trains between Sacramento and the Bay Area; other local trains such as the *Pacific Surfliner* between San Diego and San Luis Obispo; and the California portions of the *Coast Starlight* route that runs between Los Angeles and Seattle. The price includes any available Thruway bus routes to connecting trains.

Similar five-in-seven-days passes are available for Southern California as far north as San Luis Obispo, and for Northern California as far south as Santa Barbara. These cost $99 for adults, $50 for children. All three passes are available from travel agents or Amtrak, 800/872-7245. For more information, visit either of the company's two websites: www.amtrak.com or www.amtrakwest.com.

PRACTICALITIES

Joaquins connecting Sacramento with the greater San Francisco Bay Area.

For **Amtrak** train travel routes (including some jogs between cities in California by Amtrak bus), current price information, and reservations, contact a travel agent or call Amtrak at 800/872-7245 (USA RAIL), www.amtrak.com or amtrakwest.com. For the hearing impaired, Amtrak's TTY number is 800/523-6590 or 91.

BY BUS

Most destinations in California are reachable by bus, either by major carrier, by "alternative" carrier, or in various combinations of long-distance and local bus lines. And if you can't get *exactly* where you want to go by bus, you can usually get close.

Greyhound is the universal bus service. Obtain a current U.S. route map by mail (see below), but check with local Greyhound offices for more detailed local route information and for information about "casino service" to Reno and other local specials. Greyhound offers discounts for senior adults and disabled travelers, and children under age 12 ride free when accompanied by a fare-paying adult (one child per adult, half fare for additional children). The **Ameripass** offers unlimited travel with on-off stops for various periods of time, but it is usually more economical for long-distance trips with few stopovers. International travelers should inquire about the **International Ameripass.** For more information, in the U.S. contact Greyhound Bus Lines, Inc., at 800/232-9424, or www.greyhound.com.

Then there are alternative bus options, most notably **Green Tortoise,** the hippest trip on wheels for budget travelers, combining long-distance travel with communal sightseeing. Sign on for a westbound cross-country tour to get to California, an eastbound trip to get away—seeing some of the most spectacular sights in the U.S. along the languid, looping way. As the motto emblazoned on the back of the bus says: "Arrive inspired, not dog tired." Unlike your typical bus ride, on Green Tortoise trips you bring your sleeping bag—the buses are converted sleeping coaches, and the booths and couches convert into beds come nightfall. And you won't need to stop for meals, since healthy gourmet fare (at a cost of about $10 a day) is usually included in the freight; sometimes the food charge is optional, meaning you can bring your own. But

Green Tortoise also offers a weekly three-day **California Coast Tour,** with departures from both Los Angeles and San Francisco, making it easy—and fairly entertaining—to get from one end of the state to the other. From San Francisco, you can also get to Southern California on the Green Tortoise **Death Valley National Park** tour; dropoffs can be arranged in either Bakersfield or Mojave, and Greyhound can get you to Los Angeles. For more information, contact: Green Tortoise Adventure Travel, 494 Broadway, San Francisco, CA 94133, 415/956-7500 or, from anywhere in the U.S. and Canada, 800/867-8647, www.greentortoise.com.

BY BICYCLE

Many parts of California are not much fun for cyclists. Let's face it: cities are car country. Cycling on public roadways here usually means frightening car traffic; brightly colored bicycle clothing and accessories, reflective tape, good lights, and other safety precautions are mandatory. And always wear a helmet. Only the brave would pick this part of the world—or at least the urban part of this world—for bicycle touring, though some do, most wisely with help from books such as *Bicy-*

cling the Pacific Coast (The Mountaineers) by Tom Kirkendall and Vicky Spring. Yet there are less congested areas, and good local bike paths here and there, for more timid recreational bikers; rental bike shops abound, particularly in beach areas. For those who hanker after a little two-wheel backroads sightseeing, many areas aong the central and north coasts, throughout the Sonoma and Napa County "wine countries," and in the Sierra Nevada foothills, are still sublime. Southern California has bicycling possibilities, too, including paved beachfront bike paths and reasonably untraveled backcountry routes.

Various good regional cycling guides are available, though serious local bike shops—those frequented by cycling enthusiasts, not just sales outlets—and bike clubs are probably the best local information sources for local and regional rides as well as special cycling events. For upcoming events, other germane information, and referrals on good publications, contact: **California Association of Bicycling Organizations** (CABO), P.O. Box 26864, Dublin, CA 94568, www.cabobike.com. The **Adventure Cycling Association,** P.O. Box 8308, Missoula, MT 59807, 406/721-1776 or 800/755-2453, www.adv cycling.org, is a nonprofit national organization that researches long-distance bike routes and organizes tours for members. Its maps, guidebooks, route suggestions, and *Cyclist's Yellow Pages* can be helpful. For mountain biking information via the Internet, also try the **International Mountain Bicycling Association** at www.imba.com.

PRACTICALITIES

San Francisco

"When I was a child growing up in Salinas we called San Francisco 'The City,'" California native John Steinbeck once observed. "Of course it was the only city we knew but I still think of it as The City as does everyone else who has ever associated with it."

San Francisco is The City, a distinction it wears with detached certitude. San Francisco has been The City since the days of the gold rush, when the world rushed in through the Golden Gate in a frenzied pursuit of both actual and alchemical riches. It remained The City forever after: when San Francisco started, however reluctantly, to conceive of itself as a civilized place; when San Francisco fell down and incinerated itself in the great earthquake of 1906; when San Francisco flew up from its ashes, fully fledged, after reinventing itself; and when San Francisco set about reinventing almost everything else with its rolling social revolutions. Among those the world noticed this century, the Beatniks or "Beats" of the 1940s and '50s publicly shook the suburbs of American complacency, the 1960s and San Francisco's Summer of Love caused a social quake, part of the chaos of new consciousness that quickly changed the shape of everything, and the 1990s dot-com revolution transformed the way the entire world works.

Of its many attributes, perhaps most striking is The City's ability, still, to be all things to all people—and to simultaneously contradict itself and its own truths. San Francisco is a point of beginning. Depending upon where one starts, it is also the ultimate place to arrive. San Francisco is a comedy. And San Francisco is tragedy.

As writer Richard Rodriguez observes: "San Francisco has taken some heightened pleasure from the circus of final things. . . . San Francisco can support both comic and tragic conclusions because the city is geographically *in extremis*, a metaphor for the farthest flung possibility, a metaphor for the end of the line." But even that depends upon point of view. As Rodriguez also points out, "To speak of San Francisco as land's end is to read the map from one direction only—as Europeans would read or as the East Coast has always read it." To the people living on these hills before California's colonialization, before the gold rush, even before there was a San Francisco, the land they lived on represented the center, surrounded on three sides by water. To Mexicans extending their territorial reach, it was north. To Russian fur hunters escaping the frigid shores of Alaska, it was south. And to its many generations of Asian immigrants, surely San Francisco represented the Far East.

The precise place The City occupies in the world's imagination is irrelevant to compass points. If San Francisco is anywhere specific, it is certainly at the edge: the cutting edge of cultural combinations, the gilt edge of international commerce, the razor's edge of raw reality. And life on the edge is rarely boring.

THE LAND

Imagine San Francisco before its bridges were built: a captive city, stranded on an unstable, stubbed toe of a peninsula, one by turns twitching under the storm-driven assault of wind and water, then chilled by bone-cold fog.

The city and county of San Francisco—the two are one, duality in unity—sit on their own appendage of California earth, a political conglomeration totaling 46.4 square miles. Creating San Francisco's western edge is the Pacific Ocean, its waters cooled by strong Alaskan currents, its rough offshore rocks offering treachery to unwary sea travelers. On its eastern edge is

San Francisco Bay, one of the world's most impressive natural harbors, with deep protected waters and 496 square miles of surface area. (As vast as it is, these days the bay is only 75 percent of its pre–gold rush size, since its shoreline has been filled in and extended to create more land.) Connecting the two sides, and creating San Francisco's rough-and-tumble northern edge, is the three-mile-long strait known as the Golden Gate. Straddled by the world-renowned Golden Gate Bridge, this mile-wide river of sea water cuts the widest gap in the rounded Coast Ranges for a thousand miles, yet is so small that its landforms almost hide the bay that balloons inland.

Spaniards named what is now considered San Francisco Las Lomitas, or "little hills," for the landscape's most notable feature. Perhaps to create a romantic comparison with Rome, popular local mythology holds that The City was built on seven hills—Lone Mountain, Mt. Davidson, Nob Hill, Russian Hill, Telegraph Hill, and the two Twin Peaks, none higher than 1,000 feet in elevation. There are actually more than 40 hills in San Francisco, all part and parcel of California's Coast Ranges, which run north and south along the state's coastline, sheltering inland valleys from the fog and winds that regularly visit San Francisco.

City on a Fault Line

The City has been shaped as much by natural forces as by historical happenstance. Its most spectacular event involved both. More than any other occurence, San Francisco's 1906 earthquake—estimated now to have registered 8.25 on the Richter scale—woke up residents, and the world, to the fact that The City was built on very shaky ground. California's famous, 650-mile-long San Andreas Fault, as it is now known, slips just seaward of San Francisco. In the jargon of tectonic plate theory, The City sits on the North American Plate, a huge slab of earth floating on the planet's molten core, along the San Andreas earthquake fault line. Just west is the Pacific Plate. When earth-shaking pressure builds, sooner or later something has to give. In San Francisco, as elsewhere in California, a rumble and a roar and split-second motion announces an earthquake—and the fact that an interlocking

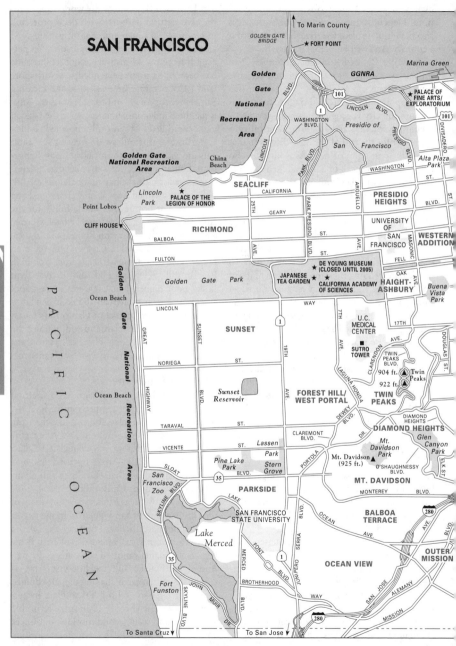

SAN FRANCISCO

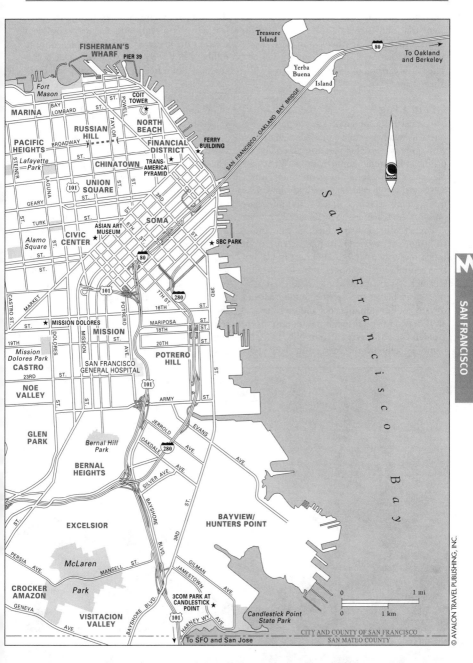

section of the earth's crust has separated, a movement that may or may not be visible on the earth's surface. San Francisco's most recent major quake, on October 17, 1989, reminded us that The City's earthquake history is far from a finished chapter.

City in a Fog

San Francisco's second most famous physical feature is its weather—mild and Mediterranean but with quite perverse fog patterns, especially surprising to first-time summer visitors. When people expect sunny skies and warm temperatures, San Francisco offers instead gray and white mists, moist clouds seemingly filled with knife-sharp points of ice when driven by the wind.

Poets traditionally call forth all nine muses to honor the mysteries of fog. Scientists are much more succinct. Summer heat in California's central valley regions creates a low-pressure weather system, while cooler ocean temperatures create higher atmospheric pressure. Moving toward equilibrium, the cool and moist coastal air is drawn inland through the "mouth" of the Golden Gate and over adjacent hills, like a behemoth's belly breath. Then, as the land cools,

the mists evaporate. So even during the peak fog months of July and August, wool-coat weather dissipates by midafternoon—only to roll back in shortly after sundown. Due to microclimates created by hills, certain San Francisco neighborhoods—like the Mission District, Noe Valley, and Potrero Hill—may be quite sunny and warm when the rest of the city still shivers in the fog.

Weather

The coast's strong high-pressure system tends to moderate San Francisco weather year-round: expect average daytime temperatures of 54–65° F in summer, 48–59° F in winter. (Usually reliable is the adage that for every 10 miles you travel inland from the city, temperatures will increase by 10 degrees.) September and October are the warmest months, with balmy days near 70 degrees. The local weather pattern also prevents major rainstorms from May through October. Despite the water-rich imagery associated with the San Francisco Bay Area, the region is actually semiarid, with annual (nondrought) rainfall averaging 19–20 inches. Snow is a very rare phenomenon in the region.

© DAVID GROENINGER

the infamous San Francisco fog

HISTORY AND CULTURE

At its most basic, the recorded history of San Francisco is a story of conquest and curiosity. The region's original inhabitants, however, were generally content with the abundant riches the land provided quite naturally. Descendants of mysterious nomads who first crossed the Bering Strait from Asia to the North American continent some 20,000 or more years ago, California's native peoples were culturally distinct. The language groups—"tribes" doesn't serve to describe California Indians—living north of the Golden Gate were classified by anthropologists as the Coast Wiwok people. Though the barren and desolate site of San Francisco attracted few residents, the dominant native population throughout the greater Bay Area was called Costanoan ("coast people") or Ohlone by the Spanish, though the people called themselves Ramaytush.

In precolonial days, the region was the most densely populated on the continent north of Mexico, with a population of 10,000 people living in 30 or more permanent villages. Though each village considered itself unique, separated from others by customs and local dialect, the Ohlone intermarried and traded with other tribes and shared many cultural characteristics. Though dependent on shellfish as a dietary staple, the Ohlone also migrated inland in summer and fall to hunt game, fish, and collect acorns, which were valued throughout California for making bread and mush. Thousands of years of undisturbed cultural success created a gentle, gracious, unwarlike society—a culture that quickly passed away with the arrival of California's explorers and colonizers.

Early Explorations

Discoveries of dusty manuscripts, ancient stone anchors, and old coins now suggest that Chinese ships were the first foreign vessels to explore California's coastline, arriving centuries before Columbus bumbled into the new world. The Portuguese explorer Juan Cabrillo (João Cabrilho) was the coast's first official surveyor, though on his 1542 voyage he failed to discover the Golden Gate and the spectacular bay behind it. In 1579 the English pirate Sir Francis Drake took the first foreign step onto California soil, quite possibly near San Francisco, and claimed the land for Queen Elizabeth I. (Where exactly Drake landed is a subject of ongoing controversy and confusion. For a further discussion, see Point Reyes National Seashore.) And even Drake failed to see the Golden Gate and its precious natural harbor, perhaps due to the subtle subterfuge of landforms and fog.

The Arrival of Outsiders

In 1769, some 200 years after Drake, a Spanish scouting party led by Gaspar de Portolá discovered San Francisco Bay by accident while searching for Monterey Bay farther south. After Monterey was secured, Capt. Juan Bautista de Anza was assigned the task of colonizing this new territorial prize. With 35 families plus a lieutenant and a Franciscan priest, de Anza set out on a grueling trip from Sonora, Mexico, arriving on the peninsula's tip on June 27, 1776, just one week before the American Revolution. The first order of business was establishing a military fortress, the Presidio, at the present site of Fort Mason. And the second was establishing a church and mission outpost, about one mile south, on the shores of a small lake or lagoon named in honor of Nuestra Señora de los Dolores (Our Lady of Sorrows). Though the mission church was dedicated to Saint Francis of Assisi, it became known as Mission Dolores—and the name "San Francisco" was instead attached to the spectacular bay and the eventual city that grew up on its shores.

Though Spain, then Mexico, officially secured the California territory, underscoring ownership by means of vast government land grants to retired military and civilian families, the colonial claim was somewhat tenuous. By the 1830s, Americans were already the predominant residents of the settlement at Yerba Buena Cove (at the foot of what is now Telegraph Hill), the earliest version of San Francisco. Yerba Buena was first a trading post established by William Anthony Richardson, an Englishman who married the Presidio commandant's daughter. In the early 1800s, Russian fur hunters established themselves just north along the coast, at the settlement of Fort Ross. They sailed south to trade.

English, French, and American trading ships were also regular visitors. By the 1840s, Yankees were arriving by both land and sea in ever greater numbers, spurred on by the nation's expansionist mood and the political dogma of "Manifest Destiny!" The official annexation of the California territory to the United States, when it came in mid-1846, was almost anticlimactic. After the 13-man force at the Presidio surrendered peacefully to the Americans, the citizens quickly changed the name of Yerba Buena to that of the bay, San Francisco—a shrewd business move, intended to attract still more trade.

The Gold Rush

Events of early 1848 made the name change all but irrelevant. San Francisco could hardly help attracting more business, and more businesses of every stripe, once word arrived that gold had been discovered on the American River in the foothills east of Sacramento. Before the gold rush, San Francisco was a sleepy port town with a population of 800, but within months it swelled to a city of nearly 25,000, as gold seekers arrived by the shipload from all over the globe. Those who arrived early and lit out for the goldfields in 1848 had the best opportunity to harvest California gold. Most of the fortune hunters, however, arrived in '49, thus the term "forty-niners" to describe this phenomenal human migration.

As cosmopolitan as the overnight city of San Francisco was, with its surprisingly well-educated, liberal, and (not so surprisingly) young population, it was hardly civilized. By 1849 the ratio of men to women was about 10 to one, and saloons, gambling halls, and the notorious red-light district—known as the Barbary Coast—were the social mainstays of this rootless, risk-taking population. Though early San Francisco was primarily a tent city, fire was a constant scourge. The city started to build itself then burned to the ground six times by 1852, when San Francisco was recognized as the fourth largest port of entry in the United States. And though eccentricty and bad behavior were widely tolerated, unrestrained gang crime and murder became so commonplace that businessmen formed Committees of Vigilance to create some semblance of social order—by taking the law into their own hands and jailing, hanging, and running undesirables out of town.

More Barbarians and Big Spenders

By the late 1850s, the sources for most of California's surface gold had been picked clean. Ongoing harvesting of the state's most precious metal had become a corporate affair, an economic change made possible by the development of new technologies. The days of individualistic gold fever had subsided, and fortune hunters who remained in California turned their efforts to more long-lasting development of wealth, often in agriculture and business.

The city, though temporarily slowed by the economic depression that arrived with the end of the gold rush, was the most businesslike of them all. A recognizable city and a major financial center, no sooner had San Francisco calmed down and turned its attentions to nurturing civic pride than another boom arrived—this time silver, discovered in the Nevada territory's Comstock Lode. Silver mining required capital, heavy equipment, and organized mining technology; this was a strictly corporate raid on the earth's riches, with San Francisco and its bankers, businesses, and citizenry the main beneficiaries. Led by the silver rush "Bonanza Kings," the city's nouveau riche built themselves a residential empire atop Nob Hill and set about creating more cultured institutions.

Confident California, led by San Francisco, believed the future held nothing but greater growth, greater wealth. That was certainly the case for the "Big Four," Sacramento businessmen who financed Theodore Judah's dream of a transcontinental railroad, a development almost everyone believed would lead to an extended boom in the state's economy. (For more on the state's railroading history, see the Sacramento chapter.) Soon at home atop Nob Hill with the city's other nabobs, Charles Crocker, Mark Hopkins, Collis Huntington, and Leland Stanford also set out to establish some political machinery—the Southern Pacific Railway—to generate power and influence to match their wealth.

Bad Times and Bigotry

But the transcontinental railroad did little to help California, or San Francisco, at least initially. As naysayers had predicted, the ease of shipping goods by rail all but destroyed California's neophyte industrial base, since the state was soon glutted with lower-cost manufactured goods from the East Coast. A drought in 1869—a major setback for agricultural production—and an 1871 stock market crash made matters that much worse.

Legions of the unemployed, which included terminated railroad workers all over the West, rose up in rage throughout the 1870s and 1880s. They attacked not those who had enriched themselves at the expense of the general populace but "outsiders," specifically the Chinese who had labored long and hard at many a thankless task since the days of the gold rush. Mob violence and the torching of businesses and entire Chinese communities, in San Francisco and elsewhere, wasn't enough to satisfy such open racist hatred. Politicians too bowed to anti-Chinese sentiment, passing a series of discriminatory laws that forbade the Chinese from owning land, voting, and testifying in court, and levying a special tax against Chinese shrimp fishermen.

A near-final bigoted blow was the federal government's 1882 Oriental Exclusion Act, which essentially ended legal Asian immigration until it was repealed during World War II. (For more information, see Angel Island State Park.) San Francisco's Chinese community, for the most part working men denied the opportunity to reunite with their families, was further damaged by the Geary Act of 1892, which declared that all Chinese had to carry proper identification or face deportation. The failure of American society to support traditional Chinese culture led to rampant crime, gambling, and prostitution—acceptable diversions of the day for bachelors—and a lawless reign of terror by competing tongs who fought to control the profits. Only the gradual Americanization of the Chinese, which minimized tong influence, and the disastrous events during the spring of 1906 could change the reality of Chinatown. But the year 1906 changed everything in San Francisco.

Earthquake and Fire

By the early 1900s, San Francisco had entered its "gilded age," a complacent period when the city was busy enjoying its new cosmopolitan status. San Francisco had become the largest and finest city west of Chicago. The rich happily compounded their wealth in downtown highrises and at home on Nob Hill and in other resplendent neighborhoods. The expanding middle class built rows of new Victorian homes, "painted ladies" that writer Tom Wolfe would later call "those endless staggers of bay windows," on hills far removed from the low life of the Barbary Coast, Chinatown, and the newest red-light district, The Tenderloin. But the working classes still smoldered in squalid tenements south of Market Street. Corruption ruled, politically, during the heyday of the "paint eaters"—politicians so greedy they'd even eat the paint off buildings. The cynical reporter and writer Ambrose Bierce, sniffing at the status quo, called San Francisco the "moral penal colony of the world." But the city's famous graft trials, a public political circus that resulted in 3,000 indictments but shockingly little jail time, came later.

Whatever was going on in the city, legal and otherwise, came to an abrupt halt on the morning of April 18, 1906, when a massive earthquake hit. Now estimated to have registered 8.25 on the Richter scale, the quake created huge fissures in the ground, broke water and gas mains all over the city, and caused chimneys and other unstable construction to come tumbling down. The better neighborhoods, including the city's Victorian row houses, suffered little damage. Downtown, however, was devastated. City Hall, a shoddy construction job allowed by scamming politicians and their contractor cohorts, crumbled into nothing. Though a central hospital also fell, burying doctors, nurses, and patients alike, the overall death toll from the earthquake itself was fairly small. Sadly for San Francisco, one of the fatalities was the city fire chief, whose foresight might have prevented the conflagration soon to follow.

More than 50 fires started that morning alone, racing through the low-rent neighborhoods south of Market, then into downtown, raging out of control. The flames were unchecked for four

WALKING ON WATER ACROSS THAT GOLDEN GATE

Nothing is as San Francisco as the astounding **Golden Gate Bridge,** a bright, red-orange fairy pathway up into the fog, a double-necked lyre plucked by the wind to send its surreal song spiraling skyward. The bridge stands today as testimony to the vision of political madmen and poets, almost always the progenitors of major achievements. San Francisco's own **Emperor Norton**—a gold rush–era British merchant originally known as Joshua A. Norton, who went bankrupt in the land of instant wealth but soon reinvented himself as "Norton I, Emperor of the United States and Protector of Mexico"—was the first lunatic to suggest that the vast, turbulent, and troublesome waters of the Golden Gate could be spanned by a bridge. The poet and engineer **Joseph Baermann Strauss,** a titan of a man barely five feet tall, seconded the insanity, and in 1917 he left Chicago for San Francisco, plans and models in hand, to start the 13-year lobbying campaign.

All practical doubts aside, San Francisco at large was aghast at the idea of defacing the natural majesty of the Golden Gate with a manmade monument; more than 2,000 lawsuits were filed in an effort to stop bridge construction. California's love of progress won out in the end, however, and construction of the graceful bridge, designed by architect Irwin F. Morrow, began in 1933. As Strauss himself remarked later: "It took two decades and 200 million words to convince the people that the bridge was feasible; then only four years and $35 million to put the concrete and steel together."

Building the Golden Gate Bridge was no simple task, rather, an accomplishment akin to a magical feat. Some 80,000 miles of wire were spun into the bridge's suspension cables, a sufficient length to encircle the earth (at the equator) three times, and enough concrete to create a very wide sidewalk between the country's west and east coasts was poured into the anchoring piers. Sinking the southern support pier offshore was a particular challenge, with 60-mile-per-hour tidal surges and 15-foot swells at times threatening to upend the (seasick) workers' floating trestle. Once the art-deco towers were in place, the *real* fun began—those acrobats in overalls, most earning less than $1 an hour, working in empty space to span the gap. Safety was a serious issue with Strauss and his assistant, Clifford Paine. Due to their diligence, 19 men fell but landed in safety nets instead of in the morgue, earning them honorary membership in the "Halfway to Hell Club." But just weeks before construction was completed, a scaffolding collapsed, its jagged edges tearing through the safety net and taking nine men down with it.

When the Golden Gate Bridge was finished in 1937, the world was astonished. Some 200,000 people walked across the virgin roadbed that day, just to introduce themselves to this gracious steel wonder. At that time, the bridge was the world's longest and

days, burning through downtown, parts of the Mission District, and also demolishing Chinatown, North Beach, Nob Hill, Telegraph Hill, and Russian Hill. The mansions along the eastern edge of Van Ness were dynamited to create an impromptu firebreak, finally stopping the firestorm.

When it was all over, the official tally of dead or missing stood at 674, though more recent research suggests the death toll was more than 3,000, since the Chinese weren't counted. The entire city center was destroyed, along with three-fourths of the city's businesses and residences. With half of its 450,000 population now homeless, San Francisco was a tent city once again. But it was an optimistic tent city, bolstered by relief and rebuilding funds sent from around the world. As reconstruction began, San Francisco also set out to clean house politically.

Modern Times

By 1912, with San Francisco more or less back on its feet, Mayor James "Sunny Jim" Rolph, who always sported a fresh flower in his lapel, seemed to symbolize the city's new era. Rolph presided over the construction of some of San Francisco's finest public statements about itself. These included the new city hall and Civic Center, as well as the 1915 world's fair and the Panama-Pacific International Exposition, a spectacular 600-acre temporary city designed by Bernard Maybeck to

tallest suspension structure—with a single-span, between-towers distance of 4,200 feet—and boasted the highest high-rises west of New York's Empire State Building. Its total length was 1.7 miles, and its 746-foot-tall towers were equivalent in total height to 65-story buildings. Even now, the bridge's grace is much more than aesthetic. As a suspension bridge, the Golden Gate moves with the action of the immediate neighborhood. It has rarely been closed for reasons of safety or necessary repairs, though it *was* closed, in 1960, so French President Charles de Gaulle could make a solo crossing. Even in treacherous winds, the bridge can safely sway as much as 28 feet in either direction, though standing on a slightly swinging bridge of such monstrous dimensions is an indescribably odd sensation.

Perhaps the best thing about the Golden Gate Bridge, even after all these years, is that people can still enjoy it, up close and very personally. Though the bridge toll is $5 per car (heading south), for pedestrians it's a free trip either way, although Golden Gate bridge officials hope that the views will inspire visitors to make voluntary contributions to donation boxes on the bridge. Pedestrians may access the sidewalk daily 6 A.M.–6 P.M. (sunrise to sunset, with specific hours adjusted seasonally for daylight savings time). The hike is ambitious, about two miles one-way. For those who don't suffer from vertigo, this is an inspiring and invigorating experience, as close to walking on water as most of us will ever get. (But it's not necessarily a life-enhancing experience for the seriously depressed or suicidal. The lure of the leap has proved too tempting for more than 900 people.) Parking is available at either end of the bridge.

Though the Golden Gate Bridge is the Bay Area's most royal span, credit for San Francisco's propulsion into the modern world of commerce and crazy traffic actually goes to the **Bay Bridge** spanning San Francisco Bay between downtown San Francisco and Oakland. Completed in 1936, and built atop piers sunk into the deepest deeps ever bridged, the Bay Bridge cost $80 million to complete, at that time the most expensive structure ever built. And in recent history, the Bay Bridge has made front-page and nightly news headlines. The whole world watched in horror when part of the bridge collapsed amid the torqued tensions of the 1989 earthquake, a pre-rush-hour event. There were deaths and injuries, but fewer casualties than if the quake had come during peak commuter traffic. Despite the quake, the bridge still remained structurally sound, and the more critically necessary repairs have been made. Work is already underway on a new eastern span of the Bay Bridge, which is budgeted for $2.6 billion, though in the end it could cost much more. Also in progress is a huge and complex project to demolish the existing double-deck western section of the bridge in San Francisco and replace it with stronger side-by-side roadways.

reflect the "mortality of grandeur and the vanity of human wishes." Though the exposition was intended to celebrate the opening of the Panama Canal, it was San Francisco's grand announcement to the world that it had not only survived but thrived in the aftermath of its earlier earthquake and fire.

During the Great Depression, San Francisco continued to defy the commonplace, dancing at the edge of unreal expectations. Two seemingly impossible spans, the Golden Gate Bridge and the Bay Bridge, were built in the 1930s. San Francisco also built the world's largest man-made island, Treasure Island, which hosted the Golden Gate International Exposition and "Magic City" in 1939 before becoming a U.S. Navy facility. (The Navy abandoned ship in the late 1990s and ceded the island to the city of San Francisco; the city will redevelop the island, after first completing earthquake stabilization. Meanwhile renovated buildings provide private housing as well as homeless assistance. The island is also a venue for occasional concerts and a regular flea market.)

No matter how spectacular its statements to the world, San Francisco had trouble at home. The 1929 stock market crash and the onset of the Depression reignited long-simmering labor strife, especially in the city's port. Four longshoremen competed for every available job along the waterfront, and members of the company-controlled

SUSAN SNYDER

SAN FRANCISCO

mention anti-Vietnam War protests and the rise of the Black Panther Party. Since then, San Francisco has managed to make its place at, or near, the forefront of almost every change in social awareness, from women's rights to gay pride. And in the 1980s and '90s, San Franciscans went all out for unabashed consumerism. The dot-com boom met up with baby-boomer enthusiasms in the city's South of Market area, creating a new wave of high-tech style. But there are other styles, other trends. You name it, San Francisco probably has it.

Tourism

Tourism is the city's top industry these days, though even the tourist trade has been more difficult since September 11, 2001. It's not difficult to understand San Francisco's appeal. The city offers almost everything, from striking scenery and sophisticated shopping to fine hotels and restaurants. Even budget travelers can arrive, and stay, with exceptional ease, at least compared to elsewhere in California. And the city's multiethnic cultural, artistic, and entertainment attractions are among its most undervalued treasures.

Downtown San Francisco, which serves as the city's corporate and financial headquarters as well as tourist central, is a world of skyscraping office towers and imposed isolation. Surely it's no accident that the city's homeless live here. But the most authentic spirits of San Francisco live elsewhere, out in the neighborhoods. So do get out—out past the panhandlers and the polished glass buildings, past the pretty shops and the prettier shoppers—to see San Francisco.

Even out in the neighborhoods, though, San Franciscans have started to suspect that things aren't quite as wonderful as they once were. Their beloved city suffers from the same problems as other major cities, from staggering demands on urban services to worsening traffic problems and astronomical housing costs.

But at last report—and despite some notable historical lapses—the city's deepest traditions, liberalism and tolerance, are still going strong. And freedom is still the city's unofficial rallying cry.

Longshoremen's Association demanded kickbacks for jobs that were offered. Harry Bridges reorganized the International Longshoremen's Association, and backed by the Teamsters Union, his pro-union strike successfully closed down the waterfront. On "Bloody Thursday," July 5, 1934, 800 strikers battled with National Guard troops called in to quell a riot started by union busters. Two men were shot and killed by police, another 100 were injured, and the subsequent all-city strike—the largest general strike in U.S. history—ultimately involved most city businesses as well as the waterfront unions. More so than elsewhere on the West Coast, labor unions are still strong in San Francisco.

Other social and philosophical revolutions, for iconoclasts and oddballs alike, either got their start in San Francisco or received abundant support once arrived here. First came the 1950s-era Beatniks or "Beats"—poets, freethinkers, and jazz aficionados rebelling against the suburbanization of the American mind. The Beats were followed in short order by the 1960s, the Summer of Love, psychedelics, and rock groups like the legendary Grateful Dead. More substantial, in the '60s, the Free Speech Movement heated up across the bay in Berkeley, not to

Orientation and Tours

San Francisco is a walking city par excellence. With enough time and inclination, exploring the hills, stairways, and odd little neighborhood nooks and crannies is the most rewarding way to get to know one's way around. Helpful for getting started are the free neighborhood walking-tour pamphlets (Pacific Heights, Union Square, Chinatown, Fisherman's Wharf, the Barbary Coast Trail, and more) available at the Convention & Visitors Bureau Information Center downstairs at Hallidie Plaza (Powell and Market Streets), 415/391-2000. Also helpful: books such as Adah Bakalinsky's *Stairway Walks in San Francisco,* Rand Richards's **Historic Walks in San Francisco,** and Gail Todd's **Lunchtime Walks in San Francisco.**

Even with substantially less time, there are excellent options. A variety of local nonprofit organizations offer free or low-cost walking tours. Commercial tours—many unusual—are also available, most ranging in price from $20 to $50 per person, more for all-day tours.

FREE AND INEXPENSIVE WALKING TOURS

Gold rush–era San Francisco is the theme behind the city's **Barbary Coast Trail,** www.barbarycoasttrail.com, a four-mile self-guided walking tour from Mission St. to Aquatic Park, marked by 150 bronze plaques embedded in the sidewalk along the way. Among the 20 historic sites en route are the oldest Asian temple in North America, the western terminus of the Pony Express, and the Hyde Street historic ships. Two different guides to the trail are sold at the Hallidie Plaza visitor information center (Powell and Market).

City Guides walking tours offered by Friends of the San Francisco Public Library, headquartered at the main San Francisco Public Library (Larkin and Grove), include many worthwhile neighborhood prowls. Call 415/557-4266 for a recorded schedule of upcoming walks (what, where, and when) or try www.sfcityguides.com. Most walks include local architecture, culture,

and history, though the emphasis—Art Deco Marina, Pacific Heights Mansions, Cityscapes and Roof Mansions, the Gold Rush City, Landmark Victorians of Alamo Square, Haight-Ashbury, Mission Murals, Japantown—can be surprising. City Guides tours are free, but donations are definitely appreciated.

Pacific Heights Walks are sponsored by the **Foundation for San Francisco's Architectural Heritage,** headquartered in the historic Haas-Lilienthal House at 2007 Franklin St. (between Washington and Jackson), 415/441-3000 (office) or 415/441-3004 (recorded information), and offer a look at the exteriors of splendid pre–World War I mansions in eastern Pacific Heights. The **San Francisco Museum & Historical Society,** 415/775-1111, www.sfhistory.org, offers free historical tours and architectural walks conducted by Charles A. Fracchia, and includes details on these and other local heritage tours on its website.

Friends of Recreation and Parks, headquartered at McLaren Lodge in Golden Gate Park, Stanyan and Fell Streets, 415/263-0991 (for upcoming hike schedule), offers guided flora, fauna, and history walks through the park May–Oct., Sat. and Sun. at 11 A.M. and 2 P.M. Group tours are also available.

Precita Eyes Mural Arts Center, at 2981 24th St. (at Harrison), 415/285-2287, www.precitaeyes.org, offers fascinating two-hour mural walks through the Mission District on Saturday and Sunday starting at 11 A.M. and 1:30 P.M. Admission is $12 adults, $8 seniors/students, $2 youths 18 and under. Call for information on the center's many other tours. In addition to its self-guided Mission murals tour, the **Mexican Museum,** 415/202-9700, sponsors docent-led tours of San Francisco's Diego Rivera murals. The **Chinese Culture Center,** inside the Holiday Inn at 750 Kearny (between Clay and Washington), 415/986-1822, offers both a culinary and a cultural heritage walking tour of Chinatown.

The San Francisco Symphony Volunteer

Council, San Francisco Opera Guild, and San Francisco Ballet Auxiliary combine their services to offer a walking tour of the three **San Francisco Performing Arts Center** facilities: Davies Symphony Hall, the War Memorial Opera House, and Herbst Theatre. The tour takes about an hour and 15 minutes; costs $5 adults, $3 seniors/students; and is offered every Monday, hourly from 10 A.M.–2 P.M. Purchase your ticket at the Davies Symphony Hall box office (main foyer) 10 minutes before tour time. For more information, call 415/552-8338.

COMMERCIAL WALKING TOURS

Helen's Walk Tours, 510/524-4544 or 888/808-6505, offers entertaining walking tours, with a personal touch provided by personable Helen Rendon, tour guide and part-time actress. Tour groups usually meet "under the clock" at the St. Francis Hotel (Helen's the one with the wonderfully dramatic hat) before setting off on an entertaining two-hour tour of Victorian Mansions, North Beach (want to know where Marilyn Monroe married Joe DiMaggio?), or Chinatown. Other options: combine parts of two tours into a half-day Grand Tour, or, if enough time and in-

terested people are available, request other neighborhood tours. Make reservations for any tour at least one day in advance.

Dashiell Hammett Literary Tours, 510/287-9540, www.donherron.com, are led by Don Herron, author of *The Literary World of San Francisco and its Environs.* The half-day tours prowl downtown streets and alleys, on the trail of both the writer and his detective story hero, Sam Spade. They're usually offered Sundays in May and October, and other literary themes can be arranged. You can't make reservations; just show up or call to schedule a tour.

The personable Jay Gifford leads a **Victorian Home Walk Tour** (including a scenic bus trolley ride) through Cow Hollow and Pacific Heights, exploring distinctive Queen Anne, Edwardian, and Italianate architecture in the neighborhoods. You'll see the interior of a Queen Anne and the locations used for *Mrs. Doubtfire* and *Party of Five.* While also enjoying spectacular views of the city, bay, and gardens, you'll learn to differentiate architectural styles. Tours meet at 11 A.M. daily in the lobby of the St. Francis Hotel on Union Square and last about two and a half hours. For reservations and information, call 415/252-9485 or visit www.victorianwalk.com.

Hob Nob Tours, 650/851-1123, www.hob-nobtours.com, offers an absolutely scandalous historical walking tour of Nob Hill—one that lets guests in on lurid tales of high-society assignations and assassinations as well as the complex histories of the silver kings, the "Big Four" railroad barons, and opulent mansions, hotels, and other buildings and sights. The tour is $30 per person and includes a cable car ride up Nob Hill, appreciation of Huntington Park, and a tour of California's first cathedral. Optional (and extra): a full buffet breakfast at the Ritz Carleton ($25), a two-course luncheon at the Huntington Hotel's Big Four restaurant ($20), or high tea at the Renaissance Stanford Court Hotel ($20). Reservations are required. Tours start at the Fairmont Hotel lobby (Mason and California) at 9:30 A.M. and 1:30 P.M., respectively.

Cruisin' the Castro, historical tours of San Francisco's gay mecca, 415/550-8110, www.webcastro.com/castrotour, are led by local historian Trevor Hailey and offer unique insight into how San Francisco's gay community has shaped the city's political, social, and cultural development. Everyone is welcome; reservations are required. Tours are offered Tues.–Sat., starting at 10 A.M. at Harvey Milk Plaza, continuing through the community's galleries, shops, and cultural sights, then ending at the Names Project (original home of the AIDS Memorial Quilt) around 2 P.M. Brunch included.

San Francisco's coffeehouse culture is the focus of popular **Javawalk,** 415/673-9255, www.javawalk.com, a two-hour stroll through North Beach haunts on Saturdays at 10 A.M., $20 per person (kids half price). Group rates available. Tours begin near the Chinatown arch in front of The Sak, 334 Grant Avenue. "Javagirl" Elaine Sosa also offers a **North Beach Beat** tour that concludes with three-course lunch, $35.

CULINARY WALKING TOURS

No matter where else you walk off to, don't overlook San Francisco's fabulous food tours—most of which focus on Chinatown. **Wok Wiz Chinatown Walking Tours,** 654 Commercial St. (between Montgomery and Kearny), 415/981-8989, www.wokwiz.com, are a local institution. Reservations required. The small-group Wok Wiz culinary and historical adventures are led by founder Shirley Fong-Torres, her husband Bernie Carver, and other tour leaders, starting at 10 A.M. at the Wok Wiz Tours and Cooking Center and ending at 1:15 P.M. after a marvelous dim sum lunch (optional). Stops along the way include: Portsmouth Square; a Chinese temple; herb, pastry, and tea shops (where the traditional tea ceremony is shared); a Chinese open-air market; and a brush-paint artist's studio. Along with taking in the sights along Chinatown's main streets and back alleys, visitors receive a fairly comprehensive history lesson about the Chinese in California, and particularly in San Francisco. Wok Wiz also offers an "I Can't Believe I Ate My Way Through Chinatown!" tour, with an exclusive emphasis on Chinese foods and food preparation, and a shorter "Walk and Wok" shopping tour and hands-on cooking class. (Special group tours can also be arranged.) Serious food aficionados will probably recognize Fong-Torres, well known for her articles, books, and Chinese cooking television appearances. She is also the author of several books, including *San Francisco Chinatown: A Walking Tour, In the Chinese Kitchen,* and the *Wok Wiz Cookbook.*

Combining two cross-cultural tidbits of folk wisdom—"You never age at the dinner table" (Italian) and "To eat is greater than heaven" (Chinese)—**Ruby Tom's Glorious Food Culinary Walk Tours,** 415/441-5637, stroll through both North Beach and Chinatown, separately or on the same tour. Special walking tours include North Beach Bakeries (an early morning slice of life), North Beach Nightbeat (complete with cabaret, theater, or jazz entertainment), and Lanterns of Chinatown (a stroll under the night-lit red lanterns followed by a hosted banquet). A graduate of the California Culinary Academy, Ruby Tom is an award-winning chef herself. She conducted and organized the first professional chefs exchange between the People's Republic of China and the city of San Francisco. **All About Chinatown Tours,** 100 Waverly Place, 415/982-8839, www.allaboutchinatown.com, conducted

SAN FRANCISCO

FERRY BUILDING FOOD FEST

The 1903 beaux-arts Ferry Building designed by A. Page Brown, with its sky-scraping clocktower, is still a standout along the Embarcadero—and one of the city's most significant historic buildings. (The late *San Francisco Chronicle* columnist Herb Caen once observed that without the Ferry Building Tower, San Francisco would be like a birthday cake without a candle.) An enduring symbol of the days when ferries were almost the only way to get to San Francisco, the building survived the 1906 earthquake with nary a tremble, and still stood tall following the construction of both the Golden Gate and Bay Bridges. The Ferry Building is certain to survive gentrification too: Fresh from a painstaking renovation, this grand bayside building of brick arches and steel trusses debuted again in 2003 as the city's foremost food palace.

That's right. Just like the rest of San Francisco, at the new, improved Ferry Building it's all about hale, hearty, and happenin' food.

The building's vast interior, naturally lit by a skylight that extends the length of two football fields, is now home to a bumper crop of sophisticated food-related shops, restaurants, and related enterprises. In addition to specialty produce, meat, seafood, and sweets shops, the Ferry Building boasts the only other Bay Area outlet of Berkeley's famed **Acme Bread,** a **Cowgirl Creamery Artisan Cheese Shop,** and the **Miette** patisserie.

Stop into **Book Passage** for an impressive selection of books (about food and other topics) then settle into **Peet's Coffee & Tea** or **Imperial Tea Court** to dip into them. For something more substantial, try St. Helena–based **Taylors Refresher** for a grain-fed beef burger or fish taco; 25-seat

Hog Island Oyster Company oyster bar; **Marketbar** Mediterranean bistro; and **Lulu Petite** and very North Beach **Mastrelli's Delis.** Flagship of San Francisco's very chic Vietnamese **Slanted Door** restaurant family is here, too, in a spectacular setting overlooking San Francisco Bay.

Still, the Ferry Building's dominant food-related presence is the **Ferry Plaza Farmers Market,** sponsored by the nonprofit Center for Urban Education about Sustainable Agriculture (CUESA) and fast becoming the Embarcadero's (if not the city's) most enjoyable street scene.

One day soon the herb, produce, and flower vendors in the open-air arcades in front, facing the Embarcadero, will be open for business every day. At last report, though, farmers markets were scheduled Tues. 10 A.M.–2 P.M., Thurs. 3–7 P.M., and Sat. 8 A.M.–2 P.M., year-round. (On Saturday, the largest market, the rear plaza, is used as well.) Also offered is a special Garden Market, Sunday 8 A.M.–2 P.M., selling everything from vegetable starts to houseplants. With a permanent facility, CUESA also hosts conferences, classes, workshops, and exhibits about sustainable agriculture and other food and agriculture issues.

For more farmers market information, contact Ferry Plaza Farmers Market, 415/353-5650, www.ferryplazafarmersmarket.com. For more information about the Ferry Building and its businesses, contact **Ferry Building Marketplace,** One Ferry Bldg., 415/693-0996, www.ferrybuildingmarketplace.com. The Ferry Building looms large along the Embarcadero at the foot of Market Street. It is accessible by ferry, MUNI, and BART; the historic trolley cars (Line F Market) stop right out front.

by San Francisco native Linda Lee, also walk visitors through Chinatown's past and present; tours include a traditional Chinese lunch or dinner. Call for reservations and current schedule.

Over on the spaghetti-eating side of Columbus, *Chronicle* food writer GraceAnn Walden leads the **Mangia North Beach!** tour through the neighborhood's best trattorias, delis, and bakeries. Along the way, you'll pick up cooking tips, sample Italian cheeses, and learn some local history. The four-hour tour concludes with a mul-

ticourse lunch. Tours begin Sat. at 10 A.M.; for reservations, call 415/927-3933 or check www.sfnorthbeach.com/gawtour.

TOURS BY LAND

A Day in Nature, 1490 Sacramento St. (between Hyde and Leavenworth), 415/673-0548, www.adayinnature.com, offers personalized half-day or full-day naturalist-guided tours (groups of just one to four people) of North Bay destinations like the Marin Headlands, Muir Woods, and the Napa Valley wine country, complete with gourmet picnic.

Gray Line, 415/558-9400 or 800/826-0202, www.grayline.com, is the city's largest tour operator, commandeering an impressive fleet of standard-brand buses and red, London-style double-deckers. The company offers a variety of narrated tours touching on the basics, in San Francisco proper and beyond. Unlike most other companies, Gray Line offers its city tour in multiple languages: Japanese, Korean, German, French, Italian, and Spanish. Much more personal is the **Great Pacific Tour Company,** 518 Octavia St. (at Hayes), 415/626-4499, www.greatpacifictour.com, which runs 13-passenger minivans on four different tours: half-day city or Marin County trips plus full-day Monterey Peninsula and Napa/Sonoma wine country tours (foreign-language tours available). **Tower Tours,** 77 Jefferson (at Pier 43), 415/434-8687, is affiliated with Blue & Gold Fleet and offers tours of the city, Marin, Alcatraz, the wine country, Monterey Peninsula, and Yosemite; all tours leave from their office at Fisherman's Wharf. **Quality Tours,** 5003 Palmetto Ave., Pacifica, 650/994-5054, www.qualitytours.com, does a San Francisco architecture tour and a "whole enchilada" tour in a luxury seven-passenger Chevy suburban. **Three Babes and a Bus Nightclub Tours,** 415/552-CLUB or 800/414-0158, www.threebabes.com, caters to visiting night owls, who hop the bus and party at the city's hottest nightspots with the charming hostesses.

Many firms create personalized, special-interest tours with reasonable advance notice; contact the Convention & Visitors Bureau for a complete listing.

Though both are better known for their ferry tours, both the Blue & Gold Fleet and the Red & White Fleet (see below) also offer land tours to various Northern California attractions.

TOURS BY SEA

The **Blue & Gold Fleet** is based at Piers 39 and 41, 415/705-8200 (business office), 415/773-1188 (recorded schedule), or 415/705-5555 (information

and advance ticket purchase), www.blueandgoldfleet.com. Blue & Gold offers a narrated year-round (weather permitting) **Golden Gate Bay Cruise** that leaves from Pier 39, passes under the Golden Gate Bridge, cruises by Sausalito and Angel Island, and loops back around Alcatraz. The trip takes about an hour. Fare: $19 adults, $15 seniors over 62 and youths 12–18, $9 children 5–11. The justifiably popular **Alcatraz Tour** takes you out to the infamous former prison (see Touring the Real Rock for more information). Fare is $13.25 adults with a self-guided audio tour, or $9.25 adults without the audio. Day-use fee on the rock is $1. (Also available is an evening "Alcatraz After Hours" tour, $20.75 adults, which includes a narrated guided tour.) Blue & Gold ferries also can take you to **Sausalito, Tiburon, Oakland, Alameda, Vallejo,** and **Angel Island.**

The **Red & White Fleet,** at Pier 43, 415/447-0597 or 800/229-2784 (in California), www.redandwhite.com, offers one-hour, multilingual Bay Cruise tours that loop out under the Golden Gate and return past Sausalito, Angel Island, and Alcatraz ($19 adults, $15 seniors/youths, $11 kids 5–11, not including the $1 day-use fee). Other offerings include weekend Blues Cruises in summer and a variety of land tours in Northern California.

Hornblower Cruises and Events, 415/788-8866, www.hornblower.com, docks at Pier 33 and elsewhere around the bay. The company offers big-boat on-the-bay dining adventures, from extravagant nightly dinner dances and weekday lunches to Saturday and Sunday champagne brunch. Occasional special events, from whodunit murder mystery dinners to jazz cocktail cruises, can be especially fun. And Hornblower's Monte Carlo Cruises feature casual Las Vegas-style casino gaming tables (proceeds go to charity) on dinner cruises aboard the M/V *Monte Carlo.*

Oceanic Society Expeditions, based at Fort Mason, 415/474-3385, www.oceanic-society.org, offers a variety of seagoing natural history trips, including winter whale-watching excursions, usually late Dec.–May (about $50 per person), and Farallon Islands nature trips, June–Nov. (about $70 per person). Reservations are required. Oceanic Society trips are multifaceted. For example, only

SUSAN SNYDER

Ferries offer a lovely introduction to the City by the Bay.

scientific researchers and trusted volunteers are allowed on the cold granite Farallon Islands, but the Society's excursion to the islands takes you as close as most people ever get. The Farallons, 27 miles from the Golden Gate, are a national wildlife refuge within the Gulf of the Farallones National Marine Sanctuary, which itself is part of UNESCO's Central California Coast Biosphere Reserve. The nutrient-rich coastal waters around the islands are vital to the world's fisheries, to the health of sea mammal populations, and to the success of the breeding seabird colonies here. Some quarter million birds breed here, among them tufted puffins and rhinoceros auklets (bring a hat). The Oceanic Society trip to the islands takes about six and a half hours, shoving off at 9:30 A.M. (Sat., Sun., and select Fri.) from the San Francisco Yacht Harbor on Marina Green. The 63-foot Oceanic Society boat carries 46 passengers and a naturalist. Contact the nonprofit Oceanic Society for other excursion options.

SELF-GUIDED TOURS

If you have a car, taking the city's **49 Mile Scenic Drive** is a good way to personally experience the entirety of San Francisco. The route is a bit tricky to follow, though, so be sure to follow the map and directions provided by the Convention & Visitors Bureau—and never try this particular exploration during rush hours or peak weekend commute times.

With enough time, design your own tour or tours, starting with the neighborhood and district information included in this chapter. Or, using a variety of special-interest books and other resources, design a tour based on a particular theme—such as "literary haunts," "bars throughout history" (best as a walking tour), "stairway tours," "musical high notes," "theatrical highlights," or even "steepest streets."

The **Steepest Streets Tour** is a particular thrill for courageous drivers and/or suicidal cyclists. (However you do this one, take it slow and easy.) As far as vertical grade is concerned, those all-time tourist favorites—Mason St. down Nob Hill, and Hyde St. to Aquatic Park—don't even register in San Francisco's top 10. According to the city's Bureau of Engineering, **Filbert Street** between Leavenworth and Hyde, and **22nd Street** between Church and Vicksburg are the city's most hair-raising roadways, sharing a 31.5

percent grade. Coming in a close second: **Jones** between Union and Filbert (29 percent, plus a 26 percent thrill between Green and Union). So a good way to start this side trip is by shooting down Filbert (a one-way, with the 1100 block a special thrill), then straight up intersecting Jones. It's a scream. For more cheap thrills, try: **Duboce** between Buena Vista and Alpine (a 27.9 percent grade), and between Divisadero and Alpine, then Castro and Divisadero (each 25 percent); **Webster** between Vallejo and Broadway (26 percent); **Jones** between Pine and California (24.8 percent); and **Fillmore** between Vallejo and Broadway (24 percent). Whether or not you travel all

these streets, you'll soon understand why hard-driving local cabbies burn out—their brakes, that is—every 2,000 miles or so.

A worthy variation is the **Most Twisted Streets Tour,** starting with one-way **Lombard Street** between Hyde and Leavenworth, a route touted as "The World's Crookedest Street," with eight turns within a distance of 412 feet. But San Francisco's truly most twisted is **Vermont Street** between 20th and 22nd Streets, which has six fender-grinding turns within a distance of 270 feet. Better for panoramic views in all directions is **Twin Peaks Boulevard,** with 11 curves and six about-face turns in its one-mile descent.

Seeing Downtown

In other times, San Francisco neighborhoods and districts had such distinct ethnic and cultural or functional identities that they served as separate cities within a city. It wasn't uncommon for people to be born and grow up, to work, to raise families, and to die in their own insular neighborhoods, absolutely unfamiliar with the rest of San Francisco.

For the most part, those days are long past. Since its inception, the city has transformed itself, beginning as a sleepy mission town, then a lawless gold-rush capital that gradually gained respectability and recognition as the West Coast's most sophisticated cultural and trade center. The process continues. The city's neighborhoods continue to reinvent themselves, and California's accelerated economic and social mobility also erase old boundaries. Just where one part of town ends and another begins is a favorite San Francisco topic of disagreement.

For more information about major attractions, see Delights and Diversions below. For complete practical information, including how to get around town and where to stay and eat, see the concluding sections of this chapter.

Defining Downtown

In San Francisco, "downtown" is a general reference to the city's hustle-bustle heart. Knowing just where it starts and ends is largely irrelevant, so

long as you understand that it includes Union Square, much of Market St., and the Civic Center government and arts buildings. The Financial District and the Waterfront are also included. Six or seven blocks directly west of the Civic Center is the Alamo Square Historic District, one among other enclaves of gentrified Victorian neighborhoods in the otherwise down-and-out Western Addition, which also includes Japantown. Though purists will no doubt quibble, for reasons of proximity these are included with downtown. And while more "uptown" parts of the South of Market Area (SoMa) are essentially downtown too, as are Nob Hill and Chinatown, those areas are covered in more depth elsewhere below.

AROUND UNION SQUARE

Named after Civil War–era rallies held here in support of Union forces (California eventually spurned the Confederacy), San Francisco's Union Square is the oasis at the center of the city's premier shopping district and also parking central for downtown shoppers, since the square also serves as the roof of the multilevel parking garage directly below—the world's first underground parking garage, in fact. (Other garages within walking distance include the Sutter-Stockton Garage to the north, the Ellis-O'Farrell Garage two blocks

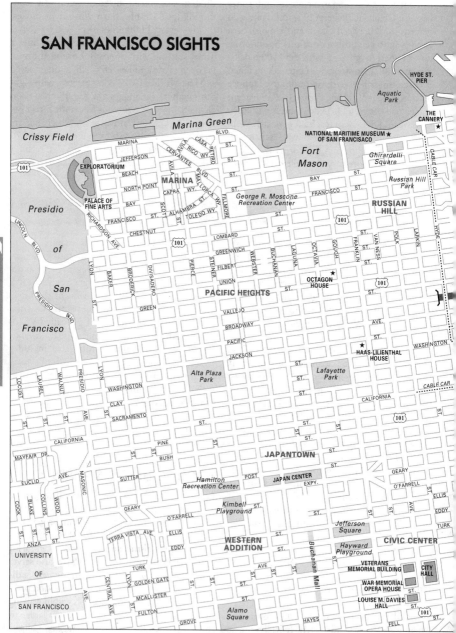

SAN FRANCISCO SIGHTS

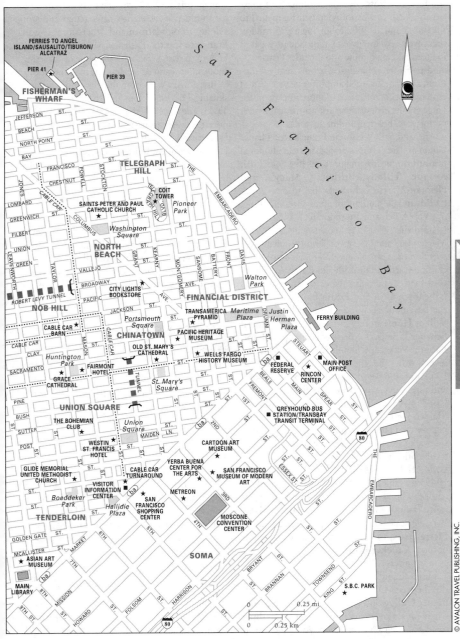

FERRIES TO ANGEL
ISLAND/SAUSALITO/TIBURON/
ALCATRAZ
PIER 41
PIER 39

FISHERMAN'S
WHARF

San Francisco Bay

JEFFERSON ST.
BEACH
NORTH POINT ST.
BAY

FRANCISCO
CHESTNUT
STOCKTON
POWELL

TELEGRAPH
HILL

THE EMBARCADERO

COIT
TOWER
SAINTS PETER AND PAUL
CATHOLIC CHURCH
Pioneer
Park

LOMBARD
GREENWICH
FILBERT
UNION
GREEN
Washington
Square

CABLE CAR
COLUMBUS

NORTH
BEACH

VALLEJO
BROADWAY
CITY LIGHTS
BOOKSTORE
PACIFIC

ROBERT LEVY TUNNEL

NOB HILL

JACKSON

GRANT ST.
KEARNY
MONTGOMERY AVE.
SANSOME
BATTERY
FRONT
DAVIS

Walton
Park

FINANCIAL DISTRICT

CABLE CAR
BARN

CHINATOWN

Portsmouth
Square

TRANSAMERICA
PYRAMID

Maritime
Plaza

Justin
Herman
Plaza

FERRY BUILDING

CABLE CAR
CLAY
SACRAMENTO

MASON

PACIFIC HERITAGE
MUSEUM

OLD ST. MARY'S
CATHEDRAL

Huntington
Park
FAIRMONT
HOTEL
GRACE
CATHEDRAL

WELLS FARGO
HISTORY MUSEUM

STEUART

FEDERAL
RESERVE
RINCON
CENTER

MAIN POST
OFFICE

TUNNEL

St. Mary's
Square

BEALE
MAIN
SPEAR

PINE

FREMONT
1ST

UNION SQUARE

BUSH
SUTTER
THE BOHEMIAN
CLUB
Union
Square
MAIDEN

GREYHOUND BUS
STATION/TRANSBAY
TRANSIT TERMINAL

80

POST
WESTIN
ST. FRANCIS
HOTEL
MAIDEN LN.
2ND

CARTOON ART
MUSEUM

GLIDE MEMORIAL
UNITED METHODIST
CHURCH
CABLE CAR
TURNAROUND
YERBA BUENA
CENTER FOR
THE ARTS

SAN FRANCISCO
MUSEUM OF MODERN
ART

ESSEX ST.

VISITOR
INFORMATION
CENTER
METREON
3RD

Boeddeker
Park
SAN
FRANCISCO
SHOPPING
CENTER

Hallidie
Plaza

MOSCONE
CONVENTION
CENTER

TENDERLOIN

GOLDEN GATE
MCALLISTER
MARKET
6TH
5TH
4TH

SOMA

ASIAN ART
MUSEUM

BRYANT
BRANNAN

THE EMBARCADERO

MAIN
LIBRARY

7TH
MISSION
FOLSOM
HARRISON

TOWNSEND
KING

S.B.C. PARK

9TH ST.
HOWARD

80

0   0.25 mi

0   0.25 km

SAN FRANCISCO

south, and, across Market, the huge and inexpensive Fifth & Mission Garage.) Reopened to the public in late 2002 following a $25 million makeover, new, improved Union Square is paved in green and tan granite and includes Canary Island palm trees, pavilions, arbors, light sculptures, an orchestra-sized amphitheater, a café and espresso stop, and a discount theater ticket outlet. Large granite pedestals are custom-made for street performers. Be there and be square.

The landmark **Westin St. Francis Hotel** flanks Union Square on the west, its bar a time-honored retreat from nearby major stores like **Saks Fifth Avenue, Tiffany, Burberry, Macy's,** and **Neiman-Marcus** (which also has its own popular **Rotunda** restaurant for après-shop dropping; open for lunch and afternoon tea).

Immediately east of Union Square along Post, Maiden Ln., and Geary, you'll find an unabashed selection of expensive and fashionable stores, including **Cartier, Dunhill,** and Euro-hip **Wilkes Bashford,** to more mainstream options such as **NikeTown USA** and **Eddie Bauer.** (Down in the basement at Wilkes Bashford is his new **Wilkes Home** store. Across Sutter is wobderful **Scheuer Linens.**) Or dress yourself up at **Ralph Lauren, Versace, Chanel, Escada, Gucci,** and several other designer emporiums. **Gumps** at 135 Post is the elegant specialist in one-of-a-kind and rare wares, where even the furniture is art. Don't miss a stroll down traffic-free, two-block **Maiden Lane,** a onetime red-light district stretching between Stockton and Kearny, chock-full of sidewalk cafés and shops. Here stands the spectacular brick V.C. Morris Building, now home to **Folk Art International Gallery.** Designed in 1949 by Frank Lloyd Wright, with its spiral interior this building is an obvious prototype for his more famous Guggenheim Museum in New York. Upscale houseware shops—**Sur La Table, Pierre Deux,** and **Christofle**—share the neighboorood. **Crocker Galleria,** at Post and Montgomery, offers still more shopping.

Heading south from Union Square on Stockton, between O'Farrell and Market, you'll pass **Planet Hollywood** and the **Virgin Megastore,** where music lovers can find just about anything to add to their CD collection. At Market St. is bargain-priced **Old Navy,** as well as a cheap thrill for shoppers—the eight-story circular escalator ride up to **Nordstrom** and other stores at **San Francisco Centre,** Fifth and Market, which was built in the late 1980s with the hope of attracting suburbanites and squeezing out the homeless.

Just down a ways from the theater district and skirting The Tenderloin at 561 Geary (between Taylor and Jones) is the odd **Blue Lamp** bar—note the blue lamp, a classic of neo-neon art. Once just a hard-drinkers' dive, now the Blue Lamp is a campy, hipsters', hard-drinkers' dive, most interesting late at night when the neighborhood gets a bit scary. But the real reason to come here is live music, just-starting band badness. A few blocks farther downtown, near Union Square at 333 Geary (between Powell and Mason), is another world entirely—**Lefty O'Doul's,** a hofbrau-style deli and old-time bar stuffed to the ceiling with baseball memorabilia. Lefty was a local hero, a big leaguer who came back to manage the minor-league San Francisco Seals before the Giants came to town.

THE TENDERLOIN

Stretching between Union Square and the Civic Center is The Tenderloin, definitely a poor choice for a casual stroll by tourists and other innocents. A down-and-out pocket of poverty pocked these days by the city signposts of human misery—drug dealing, prostitution, pornography, and violent crime—the densely populated Tenderloin earned its name around the turn of the century, when police assigned to patrol its mean streets received additional hazard pay—and, some say, substantial protection money and kickbacks. (The extra cash allowed them to dine on the choicest cuts of meat.) The Tenderloin's historic boundaries are Post, Market, Van Ness, and Powell. In reality, however, the city's designated theater district (with accompanying cafés and nightspots), many newly gentrified hotels, even the St. Francis Hotel and most Civic Center attractions fall within this no-man's land, which is especially a no-woman's land. More realistic, better-safe-than-sorry boundaries are Larkin, Mason, O'Farrell, and

Market, with an extra caution also for some streets south of Market (especially Sixth) as far as Howard. As a general rule, perimeters are safer than core areas, but since this is San Francisco's highest crime area, with rape, mugging, and other assaults at an all-time high, for tenderfeet no part of The Tenderloin is considered safe—even during daylight hours. Ask local shopkeepers and restaurant or hotel personnel about the safety of specific destinations, if in doubt, and travel in groups when you do venture any distance into The Tenderloin.

But the area has its beauty, too, often most apparent through the celebrations and ministries of the Reverend Cecil Williams and congregation at the renowned **Glide Memorial United Methodist Church,** which rises up at 330 Ellis (at Taylor), 415/674-6000, www.glide.org. Glide sponsors children's assistance and other community programs, from basic survival and AIDS care to the Computers and You program, which helps the economically disadvantaged learn computer skills. The Glide Ensemble choir sings an uplifting mix of gospel, freedom songs, and rock at its celebrations, held each Sunday at 9 and 11 A.M. Lines begin forming at the Taylor Street entrance 40 minutes before each celebration, plan on arriving early to get a seat. And feel free to contribute generously, and often. Surging hunger and homelessness in the new millennium make it hard for even Glide to keep up with community needs.

Yet some neighborhoods are cleaning up considerably, the indirect influence of commercial redevelopment and the influx of large numbers of Asian immigrants, many from Cambodia, Laos, and Vietnam. The annual **Tet Festival** celebrates the Vietnamese New Year. The Tenderloin also supports a small but growing arts community, as the 'Loin is one of the few remaining pockets of affordable housing in San Francisco. Among the neighborhood's many bars, the **Edinburgh Castle** at 950 Geary (between Polk and Larkin), 415/885-4074, stands out, drawing an interesting crowd of Scottish expatriates and young urbanites. The pub specializes in single malt Scotch, lager, fish 'n' chips,, and literary events, including several signings by Irvine Welsh, author of *Trainspotting*.

MARKET STREET AND THE FINANCIAL DISTRICT

The Financial District features San Francisco's tallest, most phallic buildings, perhaps suggesting something profound about the global capitalist thrust. When rolling into town on the river of traffic, via the Golden Gate Bridge or, especially, Oakland's Bay Bridge, this compact concentration of law offices, insurance buildings, investment companies, banks, brokerages, and high-brow businesses rises up from the sparkling waters like some fantastic illusion, the greenback-packed Emerald City of the West Coast. Even if wandering on foot and temporarily lost, to get back downtown one merely looks up and heads off toward the big buildings.

The actual boundaries of the Financial District, built upon what was once water (Yerba Buena Cove), are rather vague, dependent upon both personal opinion and that constant urban flux of form and function. In general, the district includes the entire area from the north side of Market St. to the Montgomery St. corridor, north to the Jackson Square Historic District. Market Street is anchored near the bay by the concrete square of **Justin Herman Plaza** and its either-loved-or-hated **Vaillancourt Fountain,** said to be a parody of the now-demolished freeway it once faced.

Embarcadero Center

Above and behind the plaza is the astounding and Orwellian Embarcadero Center complex, the high-class heart of the Golden Gateway redevelopment project. Here is the somewhat surreal **Hyatt Regency Hotel,** noted for its 17-story indoor atrium and bizarre keyboard-like exterior, as well as the **Park Hyatt Hotel.** But the main focus is the center's four-part shopping complex, **Embarcadero One** through **Embarcadero Four,** stretching along four city blocks between Clay and Sacramento. Inside, maps and information kiosks can help the disoriented. For a hands-on lesson in the **World of Economics,** including the chance to pretend you're president of the U.S. or head of the Fed, stop by the lobby of the **Federal Reserve Bank,** 101 Market (at Spear), 415/974-2000, open weekdays 9 A.M.–4:30 P.M., to play with the computer games and displays. **Robert Frost Plaza,** at the intersection of Market and California, is a reminder that New England's poet was a San Francisco homeboy.

Heading up California St., stop at the **Bank of California** building at 400 California (between Sansome and Battery), 415/445-0200, for a tour through its basement **Museum of the Money of the American West,** everything from gold nuggets and U.S. Mint mementos to dueling pistols. The **Wells Fargo History Museum,** inside Wells Fargo Bank at 420 Montgomery (near California), 415/396-2619, features an old Concord Stagecoach; a re-created early Wells Fargo office; samples of gold, gold scales, and gold-mining tools; and a hands-on telegraph exhibit, complete with telegraph key and Morse code books. It's open Mon.–Fri. 9 A.M.–5 P.M.; admission free. **Bank of America** at California and Kearny also has historical exhibits. In the 1905 **Merchants Exchange** building at California and Montgomery, the bygone boat-business days are

remembered with ship models, now located on the third and eighth floors, and William Coulter marine murals along the bank's back wall. Mercantile action has entered a new era at the **Pacific Stock Exchange,** the former "temple of capitalism" at Pine and Sansome since 1930, which closed its doors in 2002 and transferred equity trading activities to its fully electronic Archipelago Exchange (ArcaEx).

People were outraged over the architecture of the **Transamerica Pyramid** at Montgomery and Washington, the city's tallest building, when it was completed in 1972. But now everyone has adjusted to its strange winged-spire architecture. Until recently it was possible to ride up to the 27th floor, to the "viewing area," for breathtaking sunny-day views of Coit Tower, the Golden Gate Bridge, and Alcatraz. These days, you'll get only as far as the lobby and the popular **Virtual Observation Deck,** with its four monitors connected to cameras mounted at the very tip of the Pyramid's spire. What's fun here is the chance to zoom, tilt, and pan the cameras for some fairly unusual views. The Transamerica lobby is open weekdays from 9 A.M.–6 P.M. Back down on the ground, head for Transamerica Center's **Redwood Park** on Friday lunch hours in summer for "Music in the Park" concerts.

Designated these days as the **Jackson Square Historical District,** the section of town stretching into North Beach across Washington St. was once called the Barbary Coast, famous since the gold rush as the world's most depraved human hellhole. Pacific St. was the main thoroughfare, a stretch of bad-boy bawdy houses, saloons, dance halls, and worse—like the "cowyards," where hundreds of prostitutes performed onstage with animals or in narrow cribs stacked as high as four stories. Words like "Mickey Finn," "Shanghaied," and "hoodlum" were coined here. Local moral wrath couldn't stop the barbarity of the Barbary Coast—and even the earthquake of 1906 spared the area, much to everyone's astonishment. Somewhat settled down by the Roaring '20s, when it was known as the International Settlement, the Barbary Coast didn't shed its barbarians entirely until the 1950s. Today it's quite tame, an oddly gentrified collection of quaint brick buildings.

SUSAN SNYDER

the Transamerica Building, once outrageous, now a landmark

ON THE WATERFRONT

San Francisco's waterfront stretches some six miles along the wide, seawall-straddling **Embarcadero,** which runs from Fisherman's Wharf in the north to China Basin south of the Bay Bridge. Remnants of bygone booming port days, the docks and wharfs here are today devoted as much to tourism as to maritime commerce. The area is much improved, aesthetically, now that the elevated, view-blocking Embarcadero Freeway is gone (it was razed after being damaged in the 1989 earthquake). Today the Embarcadero is lined with nonnative Canary Island palm trees—a landscaping strategy that initially irked some botanical purists who dismissed the trees as being "too L.A."

Just south of Broadway is the city's only new pier since the 1930s; 845-foot-long **Pier 7** is an elegant public-access promenade for dawdlers and fisherfolk, complete with iron-and-wood benches, iron railings, and flanking colonnades of lampposts, the better for taking in the nighttime skyline. At the foot of Market St. is the **Ferry Building,** completed in 1898. Formerly the city's transportation center, the Ferry Building today is largely office space. But the building still features

its 661-foot arcaded facade, triumphal entrance arch, and temple-style clocktower echoing the Giralda tower of Spain's Seville cathedral. During commute hours, the area bustles with suits disembarking ferries from Marin. Hop one of the high-speed boats to Sausalito for lunch and you'll get there in about half an hour. Boats leave frequently daily, with extended hours in summer.

Across from the updated 1889 Audiffred Building at 1 Mission is city-within-the-city **Rincon Center,** incorporating the former Rincon Annex Post Office, which was saved for its classic New Deal mural art. Note, too, the **36,075-pound brass propeller** from a World War II tanker at 100 Spear St., introducing the waterfront exhibits inside.

The **Waterfront Promenade** stretches from the San Francisco Maritime National Historic Park at the foot of Hyde St. all the way along the bay to the new Giants ballpark. The promenade, built in stages over the last few years, replaces the waterfront's old piers 14 through 22. Named **Herb Caen Way** (complete with the dot-dot-dot) in 1996, for the late *San Francisco Chronicle* columnist, the seawall walkway features grand views of the bay. It's a favorite spot for

M

SAN FRANCISCO

SUSAN SNYDER

SBC Park sits right on the waterfront, and offers sweeping views of the bay and city skyline.

midday runners and office brownbaggers; literary types enjoy the brass poem plaques embedded in the sidewalk.

A very long block south of Rincon Center is **Hills Plaza,** a fairly new commercial-and-apartment development with a garden plaza, incorporating the shell of the old Hills Brothers Coffee building. Farther south along the Embarcadero are more new developments also housing restaurants, including **Bayside Village** and the world-renowned drug rehabilitation program **Delancey Street.** Beyond, in China Basin, is **South Beach Marina Pier,** a public fishing pier with a good skyline view of the South Beach Marina.

Rising up at the foot of Second St. is the hugely popular **SBC Park** (formerly Pacific Bell Park), www.sfgiants.com, which replaced 3Com Park (better known by its original name—Candlestick Park) as the home of the San Francisco Giants in 2000. SBC Park sits right on the waterfront, seats 42,000 fans, and offers sweeping views of the bay and the city skyline. Designed by Hellmuth, Obata & Kassabaum architect Joe Spear, the fellow responsible for Coors Field in Denver and Camden Yards in Baltimore, the park combines the feel of an old-time ballpark with modern amenities. If you go, keep in mind that the popular games have 40,000 fans trying to drive and find parking downtown, and leaving the city by car takes two to three hours in traffic. Smart fans may find public transportation a better option, and in any case the ballpark is a fairly short walk from downtown.

Another corporate namesake is near SBC Park at the new Mission Bay campus of the **University of California, San Francisco.** Campus centerpiece is five-story, 435,000-square-foot **Genentech Hall,** one of 20 buildings planned here to lure biotech and drug companies. The campus will also include housing for students and staff, a campus community center, and parking.

CIVIC CENTER AND VICINITY

Smack dab in the center of the sleaze zone is San Francisco's major hub of government, the Civic Center, built on the onetime site of the Yerba Buena Cemetery. (See cautions mentioned under

THE NEW ASIAN

San Francisco's venerable Asian Art Museum is now at home in one of its equally venerable buildings—both newly polished cultural stars in the city's revitalized Civic Center. A main attraction at the Civic Center since its early 2003 opening, the "new Asian"—officially known, now, as the **Asian Art Museum—Chong-Moon Lee Center for Asian Art and Culture**—has successfully relocated from the M. H. de Young Museum in Golden Gate Park to the city's restyled 1917 beaux arts Main Library.

The old library's $160.5 million renovation—brainchild of renowned Italian architect Gae Aulenti, particularly adept in "adaptive reuse" techniques—left the dignified exterior intact yet radically transformed the once somber interiors into well-lighted, spacious galleries. And there's so much more space, about 75 percent more than the museum enjoyed in its wing at the de Young: some 29,000 square feet for the permanent collection, another 8,500 square feet for changing exhibits, enhanced at every turn with state-of-the-art interpretive exhibits and displays.

At the heart of the new Asian is an indoor sky-lit court that incorporates the library's prominent entrance and grand staircase, a dramatic focus for the museum's enlightened central space. The museum's overall "flow" encourages visitors to circulate through, above, and around the central court; a glass-enclosed escalator leads to upper floors, including a new second floor. Reworked interior walls allow art lovers to peer into galleries from a multitude of perspectives. Still, significant architectural history remains from architect George Kelham's original library design, including the interior's painted ceilings, skylights, great hall, stone floors, molded plasters, light fixtures, and inscriptions.

The Tenderloin above, which also apply to almost any section of downtown Market St. after dark.) A sublime example of America's beaux arts architecture, the 1915 **San Francisco City Hall,** 401 Van Ness (at Polk), 415/554-4904, www.ci.sf.ca.us/cityhall, was inspired by a Parisian church, complete with dome and majestic staircase. Renaissance-style sculptures state the city's dreams—the not necessarily incongruous collection of Wisdom, the Arts, Learning, Truth, Industry, and Labor over the Van Ness Ave. entrance, and Commerce, Navigation, California Wealth, and San Francisco above the doors on Polk Street. After sustaining severe damage in the 1989 earthquake, the building was repaired and meticulously refurbished, and its interior stylishly redone, on the watch of equally stylish Mayor Willie Brown, a project with a price tag of several hundred million dollars. Former state senator Quentin Kopp, never a Brown fan, has called this the "Taj Mahal" of public works projects. Decide for yourself whether that's true; free 45-minute tours are available daily.

The **War Memorial Opera House,** 301 Van Ness (at Grove), 415/861-4008, www.sfopera.com, is the classical venue for the San Francisco Ballet Company as well as the San Francisco Opera, the place for society folk to see and be seen during the September to December opera season. Twin to the opera house, connected by extravagant iron gates, is the **Veterans Building/Herbst Theatre,** home to the **San Francisco Arts Commission Gallery,** 415/554-6080, as well as **San Francisco Performing Arts Library & Museum,** 415/255-4800. The theatre hosts the noted **City Arts & Lectures** series, 415/392-4400, www.cityarts.net. The modern **Louise M. Davies Symphony Hall** at Van Ness and Grove, which features North America's largest concert hall organ, is the permanent venue for the **San Francisco Symphony,** www.sfsymphony.org, 415/864-6000.

The **Asian Art Museum,** at 200 Larkin St., 415/581-3500, www.asianart.org, reopened on March 20, 2003, the Spring Equinox, after the $160.5-million "adaptive reuse" of the city's former Main Library. The 1917 beaux arts–style building is recognized as one of San Francisco's most important historic structures, and the

For all its new wonders, the true heart of the Asian Art Museum—the first museum in the U.S. dedicated solely to Asian art—is its permanent collection, an exquisite introduction to all major Asian cultures. Built from the renowned art collection of onetime Olympic athlete and Chicago millionaire Avery Brundage and his wife, Elizabeth, the museum now includes more than 13,000 art works representing 40 nations and 6,000 years of history. From the bronze *Seated Buddha,* dated A.D. 338, the oldest known Chinese image of Buddha in existence, to the gilt bronze *White Tara* from Nepal, from illuminated Iranian manuscripts to exquisite Thai gilded-lacquer panels and Japanese bamboo baskets—this is the West's most spectacular Asian art collection.

The new Asian also features a café, a store, and expanded educational facilities, which include three classrooms and a ground-floor resource center, allowing visitors to watch videos and listen to recordings.

Completion of the new Asian represents the final phase of San Francisco's 10-year renovation of its French neoclassical Civic Center complex, one of the nation's outstanding examples of the "City Beautiful" movement inspired by the Chicago World's Fair of 1893.

The Asian Art Museum is open Tues.–Sun. 10 A.M.–5 P.M., with extended evening hours every Thursday until 9 P.M. Museum admission, which includes a complimentary audio tour of the museum's galleries, is $10 adults, $7 seniors, $6 youths ages 12–17, free for children under 12. For more information, contact the Asian Art Museum at 200 Larkin St., 415/581-3500, www.asianart.org.

13,000 objects in the museum's permanent collection represent countries and cultures across Asia—which is why the "new Asian" is expected to be the premier arts institution of its kind. Meanwhile, San Francisco's **New Main Library,** 100 Larkin (at Grove), 415/557-4400, is worth a browse, especially for the free Internet access offered at computer stations throughout the library. Free volunteer-led City Guides tours are headquartered here, 415/557-4266, schedules available at www.cityguides.org, and some depart from here. **Civic Center Plaza,** across Polk from the library, is home to many of the area's homeless, and also forms the garden roof for the underground **Brooks Hall** exhibit center and parking garage. **United Nations Plaza** stretches between Market St. and the Federal Building at McAllister (between Seventh and Eighth), commemorating the U.N.'s charter meeting in 1945 at the War Memorial Opera House. On Wednesday and Sunday the plaza reflects the multi-cultural face of San Francisco, bustling with buyers and sellers of fish, Asian greens, unusual fruits, mushrooms, and vegetables at the **Heart of the City Farmer's Market.**

Across Market St., technically in SoMa but allied in spirit with the Civic Center, is the stunningly refurbished former San Francisco Post Office and **U.S. Courthouse,** at Seventh and Mission. This gorgeous 1905 granite masterpiece, full of marble and mosaic floors and ceilings, was damaged in the 1989 earthquake but it's now back and better than ever after a $91-million earthquake retrofit and rehabilitation. The post office is gone, replaced by an atrium, but the courts are back in session here. The third-floor courtroom is particularly impressive.

On Sunday mornings, the solemn sound of jazz emanates from **St. John's African Orthodox Church,** which lost its lease on a storefront in the Western addition and currently operates as a guest of St. Paulus Lutheran Church at 930 Gough Street(at Turk), 415/673-3572. The tiny ministry devoted to celebrating the life of St. **John Coltrane,** and services are part celebration and part jam session. Lack of funds has delayed plans to renovate a space in the traditionally African-American Hunter's point area, so until then check for updates at www.saintjohn-coltrane.org In addition to the area's many cafés, restaurants, and nightspots, the **California Culinary Academy,** 625 Polk St. (at Turk), 415/771-3500 or 800/229-2433, is noted for its 16-month chef's training course in Italian, French, and nouvelle cuisine. For the curious, the academy is also an exceptionally good place to eat wonderful food at reasonable prices. The academy operates a bakery and café, the basement **Tavern on the Tenderloin** buffet, 415/771-3536, and the somewhat more formal **Careme Room,** 415/771-3535, a glass-walled dining hall where you can watch what goes on in the kitchen. Call for hours and reservation policies, which vary.

WESTERN ADDITION

These central city blocks west of Van Ness Ave. and south of Pacific Heights are certainly diverse. Settled in turn by Jewish, Japanese, and African Americans, the neighborhood's historical associations are with the Fillmore's jazz and blues bars, which hosted greats like John Coltrane and Billie Holiday in the 1950s and '60s.

The area is remarkable architecturally because so many of its 19th-century Victorians survived the 1906 earthquake, though some subsequently declined into subdivided apartments or were knocked down by the wrecking ball of redevelopment. The Western Addition's remaining Victorian enclaves are rapidly becoming gentrified. The most notable—and most photographed— example is Steiner St. facing **Alamo Square** (other pretty "painted ladies" with facelifts stretch for several blocks in all directions), though countrylike **Cottage Row** just east of Fillmore St. between Sutter and Bush is equally enchanting.

Today most of the Western Addition is home to working-class families, though the area south of Geary, considered "The Fillmore," was long composed almost exclusively of heavy-crime, low-income housing projects. Many of those boxy projects have been demolished, and redevelopment here is generally improving the aesthetics of the neighborhood.

The Western Addition's intriguing shops, restaurants, and cultural attractions reflect the neighborhood's roots. For an exceptional selection of African-American literature, Malcolm X marks the spot at **Marcus Books,** 1712 Fillmore (at Post), 415/346-4222, which also hosts occasional readings. Fancy dressing like a member of Run DMC? You'll find the country's biggest selections of Adidas clothing as well as vintage and retro wear at **Harput's,** 1527 Fillmore (between Ellis and Geary), 415/923-9300. **Jack's Record Cellar,** 254 Scott St. (at Page), 415/431-3047, is the perfect place to browse through obscure jazz and blues records.

Fillmore Street also creates the western border of **Japantown,** or Nihonmachi, an area encompassing the neighborhoods north of Geary, south of Pine, and stretching east to Octavia. This very American variation on Japanese community includes the old-style, open-air **Buchanan Mall** between Post and Sutter, and the more modern and ambitious **Japan Center,** a three-block-long concrete mall on Geary between Fillmore and Laguna. It's inaccessibly ugly from the outside,

in the American tradition, but offers intriguing attractions inside, like karaoke bars and the **Kabuki Hot Springs,** 415/922-6000, a communal bathhouse on the ground floor.

Lined with boutiques selling clothing from independent labels, sidewalk restaurants, bookstores, and one-of-a-kind furniture stores, **Hayes Street** between Gough and Webster is an oasis of funky charm. Stroll the 300 and 400 blocks of Hayes for ornate and imported items. Browse **Worldware,** 336 Hayes Street, 415/487-9030, for home decor; **Richard Hilkert, Bookseller,** 333 Hayes, 415/863-3339, for an independent selection of books; and **Zeitgeist** at 437 Hayes St. (between Gough and Octavia), 415/864-0185, for vintage timepieces from top manufacturers like Longines and Rolex. Farther up the street you'll find high fashion for feet at **Gimme Shoes,** 416 Hayes (at Gough), 415/864-0691, and **Bulo Women,** at 418 Hayes Street, 415/255-4939, with the matching **Bulo Men** at 437-A Hayes Street, 415/864-3244.

Seeing Other Neighborhoods

NOB HILL

Snide San Franciscans say "Snob Hill" when referring to cable car-crisscrossed Nob Hill. The official neighborhood name is purported to be short for "Nabob Hill," a reference to this high-rent district's nouveau riche roots. Robert Louis Stevenson called it the "hill of palaces," referring to the grand late-1800s mansions of San Francisco's economic elite, California's railroad barons most prominent among them. Known colloquially as the "Big Four," Charles Crocker, Mark Hopkins, Collis Huntington, and Leland Stanford were accompanied by two of the "Irish Big Four" or "Bonanza Kings" (James Fair and James Flood, Nevada silver lords) as they made their acquisitive economic and cultural march into San Francisco and across the rest of California.

Of the original homes of these magnates, only one stands today—James Flood's bearish, square Connecticut brownstone, now the exclusive **Pacific-Union Club** (the "P-U," in local vernacular)

at 1000 California Street. The rest of the collection was demolished by the great earthquake and fire of 1906. But some of the city's finest hotels, not to mention an exquisite Protestant place of worship, have taken their place around rather formal **Huntington Park.** Huntington's central memorial status atop Nob Hill is appropriate enough, since skinflint Collis P. Huntington was the brains of the Big Four gang and his comparatively simple home once stood here.

Facing the square from the corner of California and Taylor is the charming, surprisingly unique red-brick **Huntington Hotel** and its exceptional **Big Four** bar and restaurant. The **Mark Hopkins Hotel** ("the Mark," as it's known around town) was built on the spot of Hopkins' original ornate Victorian, at 1 Nob Hill (corner of California and Mason). Take the elevator up to the **Top of the Mark,** the bar with a view that inspired the city's song, "I Left My Heart in San Francisco," and perhaps its singer, Tony Bennett, as well. Straight across the street, facing

SAN FRANCISCO

Mason between California and Sacramento, is the famed **Fairmont Hotel,** an architectural extravaganza built "atop Nob Hill" by James Fair's daughter Tessie (the lobby recognizable to American TV addicts as the one in the short-lived series *Hotel*). Inside, the Tiki-inspired **Tonga Room** is straight out of *Hawaii Five-O.* Kick back, enjoy a frozen cocktail, and soak in the strange ambience. Simulated rainstorms interrupt the tropical calm every half hour.

The **Stanford Court Hotel** at California and Powell, one of the world's finest, occupies the land where Leland Stanford's mansion once stood. For an artistic rendering of local nabobery, stop for a peek at the Stanford's lobby murals.

The **Bohemian Club** on the corner of Taylor and Post is a social club started by some of California's true bohemians, from Jack London, Joaquin Miller, and John Muir to Ambrose Bierce, Ina Coolbrith, and George Sterling. Though for old-time's sake some artists are invited to join, these days this very exclusive all-male club has a rank and file composed primarily of businessmen, financiers, and politicians. In July each year, these modern American bohemians retreat to the Russian River and their equally private Bohemian Grove all-male enclave for a week of fun and frolic.

Grace Cathedral

At the former site of Charles Crocker's mansion is Grace Cathedral, facing Huntington Park from Taylor St., an explosion of medieval Gothic enthusiasm inspired by the Notre Dame in Paris. Since the lot *was* cleared for construction by a very California earthquake, Grace Cathedral is built not of carefully crafted stone but steel-reinforced concrete.

Most famous here, architecturally, are the cathedral doors, cast from Lorenzo Ghiberti's Gates of Paradise from the Cathedral Baptistry in Florence, Italy. The glowing rose window is circa 1970 and comes from Chartres. Also from Chartres: Grace Cathedral's spiritual **Labyrinth,** a roll-up replica of an archetypal meditative journey in the Christian tradition. Since Grace is a "house of prayer for all people," anyone can walk the Labyrinth's three-fold path, just part of the

cathedral's multifaceted **Veriditas** program. The indoor Labyrinth is open to the public during church hours, 8 A.M.–5 P.M. every day. The outdoor Labyrinth, outlined in stone, is an ancient Hopi/Cretan/Celtic design open 24 hours. Music is another major attraction at Grace Cathedral, from the choral evensongs to pipe organ, carillon, and chamber music concerts. Mother church for California's Episcopal Diocese, Grace Cathedral hosts endless unusual events, including St. Francis Day on October 6, which honors St. Francis of Assisi—the city's patron saint—and the interconnectedness of all creation. At this celebration all God's creatures, large and small—from elephants and police horses to dressed-up housepets, not to mention the women walking on stilts—show up to be blessed. For more information about Grace Cathedral's current calendar of odd and exhilarating events, call 415/749-6300 or see www.gracecathedral.org. And while you're in the neighborhood, take a peek into the modern **California Masonic Memorial Temple** at 1111 California, with its tiny scale model of King Solomon's Temple and colorful mosaic monument to Freemasonry.

Cable Car Barn

Not just material wealth and spiritual high spirits are flaunted atop Nob Hill. Technical innovation is, too, and quite rightly, since this is where Andrew Hallidie launched the inaugural run of his famous cable cars, straight down Clay Street. A free stop at the **Cable Car Barn,** 1201 Mason (at Washington), 415/474-1887, open daily 10 A.M.–5 P.M. (until 6 P.M. during the summer), tells the story. No temple to tourist somnambulism, this is powerhouse central for the entire cable car system, energized solely by the kinetic energy of the cables. Electric motors turn the giant sheaves (pulleys) to whip the (underground) looped steel cables around town and power the cars. The idea is at once complex and simple. Feeding cable around corners is a bit tricky; to see how it works, hike down to a basement window and observe. But the "drive" mechanism is straightforward. Each cable car has two operators, someone working the grip, the other the brake. To "power up," heading uphill, the car's "grip" slides through the slot in the street to grab onto the cable, and the cable does the rest. Heading downhill, resisting gravity, the brake gets quite a workout. Also here: a display of historic cable cars and a gift shop.

CHINATOWN

The best time to explore Chinatown is at the crack of dawn, when crowded neighborhoods and narrow alleys explode into hustle and bustle, and when the scents, sounds, and sometimes surreal colors compete with the energy of sunrise. Due to the realities of gold rush-era life and, later, the Chinese Exclusion Act of 1882, this very American variation on a Cantonese market town was for too long an isolated, almost all-male frontier enclave with the predictable vices—a trend reversed only in the 1960s, when more relaxed immigration laws allowed the possibility of families and children. The ambitious and the educated have already moved on to the suburbs, so Chinatown today—outside of Harlem in New York, the country's most densely populated neighborhood—is home to the elderly poor and immigrants who can't speak English. It's still the largest community of Chinese anywhere outside China. And it's still a cultural and spiritual home for expanding Chinese communities in the Bay Area and beyond. Even those who have left come back, if only for a great meal and a Chinese-language movie.

To get oriented, keep in mind that Stockton St. is the main thoroughfare. Grant Ave., however, is where most tourists start, perhaps enticed away from Grant's endless upscale shops and galleries by the somewhat garish green-tiled Chinatown Gate at Bush, a 1969 gift from the Republic of China. As you wander north, notice the street-sign calligraphy, the red-painted, dragon-wrapped lampposts, and the increasingly unusual roofscapes. Grant goes the distance between Market St. and modern-day Pier 39. This happens to be San Francisco's oldest street and was little more than a rutted path in 1834, when it was dubbed Calle de la Fundación (Foundation St. or "street

SAN FRANCISCO

The Chinatown Gate was a gift from the Republic of China.

of the founding") by the ragtag residents of the Yerba Buena pueblo. By the mid-19th century the street's name had been changed to Dupont, in honor of an American admiral—a change that also recognized the abrupt changing of California's political guard. But by the end of the 1800s "Du Pon Gai" had become so synonymous with unsavory activities that downtown merchants decided on another name change, this time borrowing a bit of prestige from Ulysses S. Grant, the nation's 18th president and the Civil War's conquering general. Despite the color on Grant, the in-between streets (Sacramento, Clay, Washington, Jackson, and Pacific) and the fascinating interconnecting alleys between them represent the heart of Chinatown.

Since traffic is horrendous, parking all but impossible, and many streets almost too narrow to navigate even sans vehicle, walking is the best way to see the sights. If you haven't time to wander aimlessly, taking a guided tour is the best way to get to know the neighborhood.

Seeing and Doing Chinatown

At the corner of Grant and California is **Old Saint Mary's Cathedral,** the city's Catholic cathedral from the early 1850s to 1891, still standing even after a gutting by fire in 1906. On Saint Mary's clock tower is sound maternal advice for any age: "Son, Observe the time and fly from evil." (Saint Mary has a square, too, a restful stop just east and south of California St., where there's a Bufano sculpture of Dr. Sun Yat-sen, the Republic of China's founder.) Also at the Grant/California intersection is the **Ma-Tsu Temple of the United States of America,** with shrines to Buddha and other popular deities.

Packed with restaurants and tourist shops, Grant Ave. between California and Broadway is always bustling. Of particular interest is the unusual and aptly named **Li Po Bar** at 916 Grant, a former opium den and watering hole honoring the memory of China's notoriously romantic poet, a wine-loving warrior who drowned while embracing the moon—a moon mirage, as it turned out, reflected up from a river.

The **Chinese Historical Society of America,** 965 Clay (between Stockton and Powell), 415/ 391-1188, www.chsa.org, is the nation's only museum specifically dedicated to preserving Chinese-American history. Chinese contributions to California culture are particularly emphasized. Some unusual artifacts in the museum's huge collection: gold-rush paraphernalia, including a "tiger fork" from Weaverville's tong war, and an old handwritten copy of Chinatown's phone book. Open Tues.–Fri. 11 A.M.–4 P.M., Sat. and Sun. 12–4 P.M., closed Mondays and major holidays. Admission is $3 adults, $2 students and senior citizens, $1 for children 6–17, and free for children under 5.

The **Pacific Heritage Museum,** 608 Commercial (between Montgomery and Kearny, Sacramento and Clay), 415/399-1124, is housed in the city's renovated brick 1875 U.S. Mint building. The museum features free rotating exhibits of Asian art and other treasures; open Tues.–Sat. 10 A.M.–4 P.M. To place it all in the larger context of California's Wild West history, head around the corner to the **Wells Fargo History Museum,** 420 Montgomery, 415/396-2619, open weekdays 9 A.M.–5 P.M.

Portsmouth Square—people still say "square," though technically it's been a plaza since the 1920s—on Kearny between Clay and Washington is Chinatown's backyard. Here you'll get an astounding look at everyday local life, from the city's omnipresent panhandlers to early-morning tai chi to all-male afternoons of checkers, *go*, and gossip—life's lasting entertainments for Chinatown's aging bachelors. Across Kearny on the third floor of the Financial District Holiday Inn is the **Chinese Culture Center,** 750 Kearny (between Clay and Washington), 415/986-1822, which has a small gallery and gift shop but otherwise caters mostly to meeting the needs of the local community.

The further actions and attractions of Chinatown's heart are increasingly subtle, from the Washington St. herb and herbalist shops to Ross Alley's garment factories and its fortune cookie company, where you can buy some instant fortune, fresh off the press—keeping in mind, of course, that fortune cookies are an all-American invention. Intriguing, at 743 Washington, is the oldest Asian-style building in the neighborhood, the three-tiered 1909 "temple" once home to the Chinatown Telephone Exchange, now the **Bank of Canton.** But even **Bank of America,** at 701 Grant, is dressed in keeping with its cultural surroundings, with benevolent gold dragons on its columns and doors, and some 60 dragons on its facade. Also putting on the dog is **Citibank** at 845 Grant, guarded by grimacing temple dogs.

Both Jackson and Washington Streets are best bets for finding small and authentic neighborhood restaurants. **Stockton Street,** especially between Broadway and Sacramento and especially on a Saturday afternoon, is where Chinatown shops. Between Sacramento and Washington, **Waverly Place** is referred to as the "street of painted balconies," for fairly obvious reasons. There are three temples here, open to respectful visitors (donations appreciated, picture-taking usually not). **Norras Temple** at 109 Waverly (at Clay) is affiliated with the Buddhist Association of America, lion dancing and all, while the fourth-floor **Tien Hau Temple** at 123 Waverly primarily honors the Queen of Heaven, she who protects sojourners and seafarers as well as writers, actors, and prostitutes. The **Jeng Sen Buddhism and Taoism Association,** 146 Waverly, perhaps offers the best general introduction to Chinese religious tolerance, with a brief printed explanation (in English) of both belief systems.

For a delightfully detailed and intimate self-guided tour through the neighborhood, bring along a copy of Shirley Fong-Torres's *San Francisco Chinatown: A Walking Tour,* which includes some rarely recognized sights, such as the **Cameron House,** 920 Sacramento (between Powell and Stockton), a youth center named in honor of Donaldina Cameron (1869-1968), who helped young Chinese slave girls escape poverty and prostitution. Fong-Torres's marvelous and readable guide to San Francisco's Chinese community also covers history, cultural beliefs, festivals, religion and philosophy, herbal medicine (doctors and pharmacists are now licensed for these traditional practices by the state of California), and Chinese tea. It includes a very good introduction to Chinese food—from ingredients, cookware, and techniques to menus and restaurant recommendations.

Shopping

To a greater extent than, say, Oakland's Chinatown, most shops here are aware of—and cater to—the tourist trade. But once you have some idea what you're looking for, bargains are available. Along Grant Ave., a definite must for gourmet cooks and other kitchen habitués is the **Wok Shop,** 718 Grant (between Sacramento and Clay), 415/989-3797, the specialized one-stop shopping trip for anything essential to Chinese cooking (and other types of cooking as well). The **Ten Ren Tea Company,** 949 Grant (at Jackson), 415/362-0656 or 800/543-2885, features more than 50 varieties of teas, the prices dependent on quality and (for blends) content. There's a private area in back where you can arrange for instruction in the fine art of a proper tea ceremony. (Notice, on the wall, a photo of former president George Bush, who didn't quite get it right when he tried it.) For unusual gifts, silk shirts, high-quality linens and such, **Far East Fashions,** 953 Grant (between Washington and Jackson), 415/362-0986 or 415/362-8171, is a good choice.

Finally, musicians and nonmusicians alike shouldn't miss Clara Hsu's **Clarion Music Center,** 816 Sacramento St. (at Waverly Place), 415/391-1317, a treasure trove of African drums, Chinese gongs, Tibetan singing bowls, Indian sitars, Native American flutes, Bolivian panpipes, Australian didjeridoos, and other exotic instruments from every corner of the world. The store also offers lessons, workshops, and concerts to promote awareness of world musical culture. Open Mon.–Fri. 11 A.M.–6 P.M., Sat. 9 A.M.–5 P.M.

NORTH BEACH AND VICINITY

For one thing, there isn't any beach in North Beach. In the 1870s, the arm of San Francisco Bay that gave the neighborhood its name was filled in, creating more land for the growing city. And though beatniks and bohemians once brought a measure of fame to this Italian-American quarter of the city, they're all gone now, priced out of the neighborhood.

Quite a number of American poets and writers grubbed out some kind of start here: Gregory Corso, Lawrence Ferlinghetti, Allen Ginsberg,

Bob Kaufman, Jack Kerouac, Gary Snyder, Kenneth Rexroth. By the 1940s, North Beach as "New Bohemia" was a local reality. It became a long-running national myth.

Otherwise sound-asleep America of the 1950s secretly loved the idea of the alienated, manic "beat generation," a phrase coined by Jack Kerouac in *On the Road*. The Beats seemed to be everything no one else was allowed to be—mostly, free. Free to drink coffee or cheap wine and talk all day; free to indulge in art, music, poetry, prose, and more sensual thrills just about any time; free to be angry and scruffy and lost in the forbidden fog of marijuana while bopping along to be-bop. But Allen Ginsberg's raging *Howl and Other Poems,* published by Ferlinghetti and City Lights, brought the wolf of censorship—an ungrateful growl that began with the seizure of in-bound books by U.S. Customs and got louder when city police filed obscenity charges. The national notoriety of an extended trial, and Ginsberg's ultimate literary acquittal, brought busloads of Gray Line tourists. And the Beats moved on, though some of the cultural institutions they founded are still going strong.

Nowadays, North Beach is almost choking on its abundance—of eateries, coffeehouses, tourist traps, and shops. Forget trying to find a parking place; public transit is the best way to get around.

Adding to neighborhood stresses and strains—and to the high costs of surviving—is the influx of Asian business and the monumental increase in Hong Kong-money property investment, both marching into North Beach from Chinatown. Old and new neighborhood residents tend to ignore each other as much as possible, in that great American melting-pot tradition. (Before the Italians called North Beach their home turf, the Irish did. And before the Irish lived here, Chileans did. In all fairness, Fisherman's Wharf was Chinese before the Italians moved in. And of course Native Americans inhabited the entire state before the Spanish, the Mexicans, the Russians, and the Americans.) Like the city itself, life here makes for a fascinating sociology experiment.

What with territorial incursions from Chinatown, the historical boundaries of North Beach increasingly clash with the actual. Basically, the entire valley between Russian Hill and Telegraph Hill is properly considered North Beach. The northern boundary stopped just short of Fisherman's Wharf, now pushed back by rampant commercial development, and Broadway was the southern boundary—a thoroughfare and area sometimes referred to as the "Marco Polo Zone" because it once represented the official end of Chinatown and the beginning of San Francisco's Little Italy. The neighborhood's spine is diagonally running Columbus Ave., which begins at the Transamerica Pyramid at the edge of the Financial District and ends at The Cannery near Fisherman's Wharf. Columbus Avenue between Filbert and Broadway is the still-beating Italian heart of modern North Beach.

Seeing and Doing North Beach

Piazza-like **Washington Square,** between Powell and Stockton, Union and Filbert, is the centerpiece of North Beach, though, as the late *San Francisco Chronicle* columnist Herb Caen once pointed out, it "isn't on Washington St., isn't a square (it's five-sided) and doesn't contain a statue of Washington but of Benjamin Franklin." (In terms of cultural consistency, this also explains the statue of Robert Louis Stevenson in Chinatown's Portsmouth Square.) There's a time capsule beneath old Ben; when the original treasures (mostly temperance tracts on the evils of alcohol) were unearthed in 1979, they were replaced with 20th-century cultural values, including a bottle of wine, a pair of Levi's, and a poem by Lawrence Ferlinghetti. In keeping with more modern times Washington Square also features a statue dedicated to the city's firemen, yet another contribution by eccentric little old Lillie Hitchcock Coit, Coit Tower's namesake. **Saints Peter and Paul Catholic Church** fronts the square at 666 Filbert, its twin towers lighting up the whole neighborhood come nightfall. Noted for its rococo interior and accompanying graphic statuary of injured saints and souls burning in hell, the Saints also offers daily mass in Italian and (on Sunday) in Chinese.

Two blocks northeast of Washington Square is the **North Beach Playground,** where bocce ball is still the neighborhood game of choice, just as

October's **Columbus Day Parade** and accompanying festivities still make the biggest North Beach party. Just two blocks west of the square are the stairs leading to the top of **Telegraph Hill,** identifiable by **Coit Tower,** Lillie Coit's most heartfelt memorial to the firefighters. (More on that below.)

For an overview of the area's history, stop by the free **North Beach Museum,** 1435 Stockton St. (near Green, on the mezzanine of Bayview Bank), 415/626-7070, open Mon.–Thurs. 9 A.M.–5 P.M. and Friday until 6 P.M., which displays a great collection of old North Beach photos and artifacts in occasionally changing exhibits.

The North Beach "experience" is the neighborhood itself—the coffeehouses, the restaurants, the intriguing and odd little shops. No visit is complete without a stop at Lawrence Ferlinghetti's **City Lights Bookstore,** 261 Columbus (between Broadway and Pacific), 415/362-8193, on the neighborhood's most literary alley. City Lights is the nation's first all-paperback bookstore and a rambling ode to the best of the small presses; its poetry and other literary programs still feed the souls of those who need more nourishment than what commercial bestsellers can offer. A superb small museum, **Lyle Tuttle's Tattoo Museum and Shop,** is a few blocks up the way at 841 Columbus, 415/775-4991.

You can shop till you drop in this part of town. And much of what you'll find has something to do with food. For Italian ceramics, **Biordi Italian Imports,** 412 Columbus (near Vallejo), 415/392-8096, has a fabulous selection of art intended for the table (but almost too beautiful to use). For a price—and just about everything is pricey—the folks here will ship your treasures, too.

While you're wandering, you can easily put together a picnic for a timeout in Washington Square. The landmark Italian delicatessen **Liguria Bakery,** 1700 Stockton (at Filbert), 415/421-3786, which opened in 1911, is the place to stop for traditionally prepared focaccia, and nothing but. Head to **Molinari's,** 373 Columbus (between Broadway and Green), 415/421-2337, for cheeses, sausages, and savory salads, or to the Italian and French **Victoria Pastry Co.,** 1362 Stockton St. (at Vallejo), 415/781-2015, for cookies, cakes, and unbelievable pastries. Other good bakery stops nearby include the **Italian French Baking Co. of San Francisco,** 1501 Grant (at Union), 415/421-3796, known for its French bread. If you didn't load up on reading material at City Lights—for after you stuff yourself but before falling asleep in the square—stop by **Cavalli Italian Book Store,** 1441 Stockton (between Vallejo and Green), 415/421-4219, for Italian newspapers, magazines, and books.

Bohemian Hangouts

Caffe Greco, 423 Columbus (between Vallejo and Green), 415/397-6261, is regarded as the most European of the neighborhood's Eurostyle coffeehouses. But for that classic beatnik bonhomie, head to what was once the heart of New Bohemia, the surviving **Caffe Trieste,** 609 Vallejo (at Grant), 415/982-2605. Drop by anytime for opera and Italian folk songs on the jukebox, or come on Saturday afternoon for jazz, opera, or other concerts. Also-been-there-forever **Vesuvio Cafe,** 255 Columbus Ave. (at Broadway), 415/362-3370, across Kerouac Alley from the City Lights bookstore (look for the mural with volcanoes and peace symbols), is most appreciated for its upstairs balcony section, historically a magnet for working and wannabe writers (and everyone else, too). It was a favorite haunt of Ginsberg and Kerouac, as well as an in-town favorite for Welsh poet Dylan Thomas. And Francis Ford Coppola reportedly sat down at a back table to work on *The Godfather.* A painting depicts *Homo beatnikus,* and there's even an advertisement for a do-it-yourself beatnik makeover (kit including sunglasses, a black beret, and poem).

Another righteous place to hide is **Tosca,** 242 Columbus (between Broadway and Pacific), 415/391-1244, a late-night landmark with gaudy walls and comfortable Naugahyde booths where the hissing of the espresso machine competes with Puccini on the jukebox. Writers of all varieties still migrate here, sometimes to play pool in back. But you must behave yourself: Bob Dylan and Allen Ginsberg got thrown out of here for being unruly. **Cafe Malvina,** 1600 Stockton (at Union), 415/391-1290, is a good bet, too, especially for early-morning pastries with your coffee.

POETIC AMUSEMENTS

There's probably only one thing better than reading a good poem in a quiet room by yourself. And that's listening to an impassioned poet reading a poem out loud in a small coffee-scented café full of attentive writers, lawyers, bikers, teachers, computer programmers, divinity students, musicians, secretaries, drug addicts, cooks, and assorted oddball others who all love poetry and are hanging onto every word being juggled by the poet behind the microphone. The only thing better than *that* is to read your own poems at an open-mike poetry reading.

One of the wonderful things about San Francisco and vicinity is that this kind of poetic melee takes place in some café, club, or bookstore almost every night, for those who know where to look. No one revels in the right to free speech like Bay Area denizens, and open poetry readings are as popular as stand-up comedy in many cafés and clubs, with sign-up lists at the door. Bring your own poetry, or just kick back and listen to some amazing musings.

The following suggested venues will get you started. Since schedules for local poetic license programs do change, it's prudent to call or otherwise check it out before setting out. Current open readings and other events are listed in the monthly tabloid *Poetry Flash*, 510/525-5476, www.poetryflash.org, the Bay Area's definitive poetry review and literary calendar, available free at many bookstores and cafés.

—*Ed Aust*

Open-Mic Poetry Readings in San Francisco
BrainWash Cafe and Laundromat, 1122 Folsom St., 415/864-3842
Keane's 3300 Club, 3300 Mission St. (at 29th), 415/826-6886
Paradise Lounge, 1501 Folsom St. (at 11th), 415/861-6906

In the East Bay
Diesel—A Bookstore, 5433 College Ave. (between Lawton and Hudson), Oakland, 510/653-9965
La Val's Pizza and Subterranean Theatre, 1834 Euclid Ave. (at Hearst), Berkeley, 510/843-5617
Starry Plough, 3101 Shattuck Ave., Berkeley, 510/841-2082

Serious social history students should also peek into the **Condor Cafe,** 300 Columbus (at Broadway), 415/781-8222, the onetime Condor Club made famous by stripper Carol Doda and her silicone-enhanced mammaries, now a run-of-the-mill sports bar. Still, the place offers a memory of the neighborhood's sleazier heyday. Other neighborhood perversion palaces, survivors of the same peep-show mentality, are becoming fewer and farther between, and in any event aren't all that interesting.

Nightlife

Opened in 1931, **Bimbo's 365 Club,** 1025 Columbus (between Chestnut and Francisco), 415/474-0365, retains its old-time supper club atmosphere. Bimbo's hosts live music most nights, and if you get there early you can settle into one of the plush red booths lining the stage. The crowd varies according to the band. A fairly inexpensive hot spot, on the site of an old Barbary Coast saloon, is the **San Francisco Brewing Company,** 155 Columbus (between Jackson and Pacific), 415/434-3344, known for its hearty home brews. **The Saloon,** 1232 Grant (at Columbus), 415/989-7666, across from Caffe Trieste at Grant and Fresno Alley, is the city's oldest pub, circa 1861. It's a bit scruffy, but still hosts what's happening after all these years (stiff drinks and blues bands, mostly). **Specs 12 Adler Museum Cafe,** across from Vesuvio at 12 Adler Place (off Columbus, between Broadway and Pacific), 415/421-4112, open daily after 4:30 or 5 P.M., is also a treasure trove-cum-watering hole of eclectic seafaring and literary clutter.

Perhaps destined for a long-lasting run is

Beach Blanket Babylon at **Club Fugazi,** 678 Green St. (at Powell), 415/421-4222, song-and-dance slapstick of a very contemporary high-camp cabaret style, where even favorite Broadway tunes end up brutally (and hilariously) twisted. Thematic and seasonal changes, like the Christmas revue, make this babbling Babylon worthy of return visits—especially to see what they'll create next in the way of 50-pound decorative headdresses.

TELEGRAPH HILL AND COIT TOWER

The best way to get to Telegraph Hill—whether just for the view, to appreciate the city's hanging gardens, or to visit Coit Tower—is to climb the hill yourself, starting up the very steep stairs at Kearny and Filbert or ascending more gradually from the east, via either the Greenwich or Filbert steps. Following Telegraph Hill Blvd. as it winds its way from Lombard, from the west, is troublesome for drivers. Parking up top is scarce; especially on weekends you might sit for hours while you wait—just to park, mind you. A reasonable alternative is taking the #39-Coit bus from Fisherman's Wharf.

Lillie Hitchcock Coit had a fetish for firemen. As a child, she was saved from a fire that claimed two of her playmates. As a teenager, she spent much of her time with members of San Francisco's all-volunteer Knickerbocker Engine Company No. 5, usually tagging along on fire calls and eventually becoming the team's official mascot; she was even allowed to play poker and smoke cigars with the boys. Started in 1929, financed by a Coit bequest, and completed in 1933, Coit Tower was to be a lasting memorial to the firemen. Some people say its shape resembles the nozzle of a firehose, others suggest more sexual symbolism, but the official story is that the design by Arthur Brown was intended to look "equally artistic" from any direction. Coit Tower was closed to the public for many years, due to damage caused by vandalism and water leakage. After a major interior renovation, the tower is now open in all its original glory, so come decide for yourself what the tower sym-

bolizes. Or just come for the view. From atop the 180-foot tower, which gets extra lift from its site on top of Telegraph Hill, you get a magnificent 360-degree view of the entire Bay Area. Coin-op telescopes allow you to get an even closer look. Coit Tower, 415/362-0808, is open daily 10 A.M.–6 P.M., until 9 P.M. in summer. Admission is free, technically, but there is a charge for the elevator ride to the top: $3.75 adults, $2.50 seniors, $1.50 children ages 6–12.

Another reason to visit Coit Tower is to appreciate the marvelous Depression-era Social Realist interior mural art in the lobby, recently restored and as striking as ever. (At last report, seven of the 27 total frescoes, those on the second floor and along the narrow stairway, weren't available for general public viewing, since quarters are so close that scrapes from handbags and shoes are almost inevitable. You can see these murals on the Saturday guided tour.) Even in liberal San Francisco, many of these murals have been controversial, depicting as they do the drudgery,

SUSAN SNYDER

Whatever its symbolism, Coit Tower offers great views and houses a striking collection of Depression-era frescoes.

SAN FRANCISCO

sometimes despair, behind the idyllic facade of modern California life—particularly as seen in the lives of the state's agricultural and industrial workforce. Financed through Franklin Roosevelt's New Deal-era Public Works Art Project, some 25 local artists set out in 1934 to paint Coit Tower's interior with frescoes, the same year that Diego Rivera's revolutionary renderings of Lenin and other un-American icons created such a scandal at New York's Rockefeller Center that the great Mexican painter's work was destroyed.

In tandem with tensions produced by a serious local dock worker's strike, some in San Francisco almost exploded when it was discovered that the new art in Coit Tower wasn't entirely politically benign, that some of it suggested less than total support for pro-capitalist ideology. In various scenes, one person is carrying *Das Kapital* by Karl Marx, and another is reading a copy of the Communist-party *Daily Worker;* grim-faced "militant unemployed" march forward into the future; women wash clothes by hand within sight of Shasta Dam; slogans oppose both hunger and fascism; and a chauffeured limousine is clearly contrasted with a Model T Ford in Steinbeck's Joad-family style. Even a hammer and sickle made it onto the walls. Unlike New York, even after an outraged vigilante committee threatened to chisel away Coit Tower's artistic offenses, San Francisco ultimately allowed it all to stay—everything, that is, except the hammer and sickle.

Another Telegraph Hill delight: the intimate gardens along the eastern steps. The **Filbert Steps** stairway gardens are lined with trees, ivy, and garden flowers, with a few terraces and benches nearby. Below Montgomery St., the Filbert stairway becomes a bit doddering—unpainted tired wood that leads to enchanting Napier Ln., one of San Francisco's last wooden-plank streets and a Victorian survivor of the city's 1906 devastation. (Below Napier, the stairway continues on to Sansome Street.) The brick-paved **Greenwich Steps** wander down to the cliff-hanging Julius' Castle restaurant, then continue down to the right, appearing to be private stairs to the side yard, weaving past flower gardens and old houses to reach Sansome. If you go up one way, be sure to come down the other.

RUSSIAN HILL

Also one of San Francisco's rarer pleasures is a stroll around Russian Hill, named for the belief that Russian sea otter hunters picked this place to bury their dead. One of the city's early bohemian neighborhoods and a preferred haunt for writers and other connoisseurs of quiet beauty, Russian Hill today is an enclave of the wealthy. But anyone can wander the neighborhood. If you come from North Beach, head up—it's definitely up—Vallejo St., where the sidewalks and the street eventually give way to stairs. Take a break at **Ina Coolbrith Park** at Taylor, named in honor of California's first poet laureate, a woman remarkable for many accomplishments. A member of one of Jim Beckwourth's westward wagon trains, she was the first American child to enter California by wagon. After an unhappy marriage, Coolbrith came to San Francisco, where she wrote poetry and created California's early literary circle. Many men fell in love with her, the ranks of the hopelessly smitten including Ambrose Bierce, Bret Harte, and Mark Twain. (She refused to marry any of them.) Librarian for both the Bohemian Club and the Oakland Free Library, at the latter Coolbrith took 12-year-old Jack London under her wing; her tutelage and reading suggestions were London's only formal education. Up past the confusion of lanes at Russian Hill's first summit is **Florence Street,** which heads south, and still more stairs, these leading down to Broadway (the original Broadway, which shows why the city eventually burrowed a new Broadway under the hill). Coolbrith's last home on Russian Hill still stands at 1067 Broadway.

To see the second summit—technically the park at Greenwich and Hyde—and some of the reasons why TV and movie chase scenes are frequently filmed here, wander west and climb aboard the Hyde-Powell cable car. Worth exploration on the way up: Green St., Macondray Ln. just north of Jones (which eventually takes you down to Taylor Street), and **Filbert Street,** San Francisco's steepest driveable hill, a 31.5-degree grade. (To test that thesis yourself, go very slowly.) Just over the summit, as you stare straight toward Fisherman's Wharf, is another wonder of road engineering: the one-block stretch of Lombard St. between Hyde and Leavenworth, known as the **Crookedest Street in the World.** People do drive down this snake-shaped cobblestone path, a major tourist draw, but it's much more pleasant as a walk.

FISHERMAN'S WHARF

San Francisco's fishing industry and other port-related businesses were once integral to the city's cultural and economic life. Fisherman's Wharf, which extends from Pier 39 to the municipal pier just past Aquatic Park, was originally the focus of this waterfront commerce. Early on, Chinese fishermen pulled ashore their catch here, to be followed in time by Italian fishermen who took over the territory. After World War II, however, the city's fishing industry declined dramatically, the result of both accelerated pollution of San Francisco Bay and decades of overfishing. Today, Fisherman's Wharf has largely become a carnival-style diversion for tourists. Nevertheless, beyond the shopping centers, arcade amusements, and oddball museums, a small fishing fleet struggles to survive.

Pier 39

At Beach St. and Embarcadero, Pier 39 offers schlock par excellence. If you don't mind jostling with the schools of tourists like some sort of biped sardine, you're sure to find *something* here that interests you. But this place really isn't about San Francisco—it's about shopping and otherwise spending your vacation wad. And you could have done that at home.

Unusual stores include the **Disney Store,** selling licensed Disney merchandise; the **Warner Bros. Studio Store,** offering meep-meeps, cwazy wabbits, and the like; the **NFL Shop,** hawking official 49er jerseys and other pigskin paraphernalia; the **College Shop,** selling campus items from schools across the country; and **The Sunken Treasure Museum Store,** displaying artifacts collected by Fisher on his shipwreck dives.

Great fun is the new **San Francisco Carousel,** $2 per ride, handcrafted in Italy and painstak-

ingly hand-painted to depict famous San Francisco landmarks, from the Golden Gate Bridge and Coit Tower to Pier 39's ever-popular California sea lions. At **Turbo Ride Simulation Theatre,** 415/392-8313, you'll be thrown around in your spastic, hydraulically controlled seat in perfect time with what's happening on the big screen before you; think armchair Indiana Jones (and three similar adventure scenarios). Open daily. Summer hours are Sun.–Thurs. 10 A.M.–9:30 P.M., Friday 10 A.M.–11 P.M.; Sat. 10 A.M.–midnight. The rest of the year, it's open Sun.–Thurs. 10:30 A.M.–8:30 P.M., Fri.–Sat. 10 A.M.–10 P.M. Admission is $9 general, $6 seniors/children under 12. And at **Aquarium of the Bay,** 415/623-5300, you can travel through a 300-foot-long acrylic tube on a moving walkway, looking out on schools of glittering anchovies, stingrays, leopard sharks, and other sea creatures swimming through the 700,000-gallon Pier 39 Aquarium. Aquarium of the Bay is open daily 10 A.M.–6 P.M.; extended summer hours. Admission is $12.95 adults, $6.50 seniors, $6.50 children 3–11.

No, you won't lack for attractions to take your money at Pier 39. But for free you can spend time watching the lolling **sea lions** out on the docks, a fairly recent invasion force. The docks once served as a marina full of pleasure boats—until the sea lions started making themselves at home. It turned out to be a futile effort trying to chase them off, so the powers that be decided to abandon the marina idea and let the pinnipeds (up to 600 of them in the peak Jan.–Feb. herring season) have their way, becoming a full-time tourist attraction. Score: Sea Lions 1, Yachties 0.

Most shops at the pier are open daily 10:30 A.M.–8:30 P.M. Hours are longer in summer. For more information, call 415/981-7437, or look up www.pier39.com online. Also here are the **Blue & Gold Fleet** ferries to Alcatraz and elsewhere around the bay.

Along Jefferson Street

A culinary treat on the Wharf, especially in December or at other times during the mid-November-to-June season, is fresh **Dungeness crab.** You can pick out your own, live or already cooked, from the vendor stands, or head for any of the more famous Italian-style seafood restaurants here: **Alioto's, Franciscan Restaurant, Sabella's,** or the excellent and locally favored **Scoma's,** hidden slightly away from the tourist hordes on Pier 47 (near the intersection of Jones and Jefferson), 415/771-4383.

If you're in the mood for still more entertainment, Fisherman's Wharf offers a wacky variety. **Musée Méchanique,** on Pier 45 at Jefferson, 415/346-2000, is a delightful and dusty collection of penny arcade amusements (most cost a quarter)—from nickelodeons and coin-eating music boxes to fortune-telling machines. Open Mon.–Fri. 11 A.M.–7 P.M., Fri.–Sat. 10 A.M.– 8 P.M. Admission free. **Ripley's** *Believe It Or Not!* **Museum,** 175 Jefferson St. (near Taylor), 415/771-6188, features both bizarre and beautiful items—including a two-headed cow, a shrunken head, and other grotesqueries—collected during Robert L. Ripley's global travels. Open Sun.–Thurs. 10 A.M.–10 P.M., Fri.–Sat. 10 A.M.–midnight. Admission $10.95 adults, $8.95 seniors, and $7.95 children. And the **Wax Museum at Fisherman's Wharf** is back, 145 Jefferson, 800/439-4305, www.waxmuseum.com, open weekdays 10 A.M.–9 P.M. and weekends 9 A.M.–11 P.M., $12.95 adults, $6.95 children. Stars waxing eloquent here include Robin Williams, Keanu Reeves, Ricky Martin, and an all-American Britney Spears.

Around Ghirardelli Square

You can also shop till you drop at elegant **Ghirardelli Square,** 900 North Point (Beach and Larkin), 415/775-5500, a complex of 50-plus shops and restaurants where you can get one of the best hot fudge sundaes anywhere, or **The Cannery,** 2801 Leavenworth (at Beach), 415/ 771-3112, another huge theme shopping center, this one offering outdoor street artist performances as well as the **Museum of the City of San Francisco,** 415/928-0289; and **Cobb's Comedy Club,** 415/928-4320. Beer and wine lovers will be intoxicated at The Cannery just checking out the offerings of **The Wine Cellar** 415/673-0400, with daily wine tastings 11 A.M.– 7 P.M., and **Jack's Cannery Bar,** 415/931-6400, a restaurant and bar featuring 110 different beers

on tap. Time-honored for imports and the occasional bargain is the nearby **Cost Plus,** 2552 Taylor (at North Point).

Quieter, less commercial pleasures are also available along Fisherman's Wharf—a stroll through **Aquatic Park** perhaps, or fishing out on **Municipal Pier.**

San Francisco Maritime National Historical Park

Historic ships and a first-rate maritime museum make up the core of this national park on the west end of Fisherman's Wharf. To get oriented, first stop by the park's **National Maritime Museum of San Francisco** in Aquatic Park at Beach and Polk, 415/561-7100, open daily 10 A.M.–5 P.M., free admission. The double-decker building itself looks like an art deco ocean liner. Washed ashore inside are some excellent displays, from model ships and figureheads to historic photos and exhibits on fishing boats, ferries, and demonstrations of the sailor's arts. The newest permanent exhibit is the interactive *Sparks, Waves & Wizards: Communication at Sea,* which tracks maritime communications history from semaphore to satellite and includes a walk-in re-creation of a radio room on a 1943 Victory ship. The affiliated **J. Porter Shaw Library,** 415/556-9870, housed along with the park's administrative offices west of Fisherman's Wharf in Building E at Fort Mason (a reasonable walk away along a bike/pedestrian path), preserves most of the Bay Area's documented boat history, including oral histories, logbooks, photographs, and shipbuilding plans.

Not easy to miss at the foot of Hyde St. are the **Hyde Street Pier Historic Ships,** 415/561-7100, an always-in-progress collection that is also part of the national park. Admission $5 adults, free for visitors under 17. Here you can clamber across the decks and crawl through the colorfully cluttered holds of some of America's most historic ships.

The Hyde Street fleet's flagship is the three-masted 1886 schooner *Balclutha,* a veteran of twice-annual trips between California and the British Isles via Cape Horn. Others include the sidewheel *Eureka* (the world's largest passenger ferry in her day, built to ferry trains), the 1915 steam schooner *Wapama,* the oceangoing tugboat *Hercules,* the British-built, gold rush-era paddlewheel tug *Eppleton Hall,* the scow schooner *Alma,* and the three-masted lumber schooner *C.A. Thayer.* Also among the collection, but berthed at Pier 45, is the **U.S.S. Pampanito,** 415/775-1943, a tight-quarters Balao-class World War II submarine that destroyed or damaged many Japanese vessels and also participated in the tragic sinking of the Japanese *Kachidoki Maru* and *Rayuyo Maru,* which were carrying Australian and British prisoners of war.

Tagging along on a ranger-led tour (complete with "living history" adventures in summer) is the best way to get your feet wet at this national park. Call for tour schedule (guided tours are usually offered daily). But self-guided tours are available anytime the pier is open, which is daily 9:30 A.M.–6 P.M. year-round (until 8 P.M. in summer); open for all major holidays. Special activities give you the chance to sing sea chanteys, raise sails, watch the crews "lay aloft," or participate in the Dead Horse Ceremony—wherein the crowds heave a horse doll overboard and shout "May the sharks have his body, and the devil have his soul!"

SS Jeremiah O'Brien

Berthed at Pier 45, this massive 441-foot-long World War II Liberty Ship made 11 crossings from England to the beaches of Normandy to support the Allied invasion. It even returned to Normandy for the 50th anniversary of D-Day. The ship is still powered by its original engines. In fact, the engine-room scenes in the movie *Titanic* were filmed here.

The historic ship is open for self-guided tours year-round, daily 10 A.M.–5 P.M.; admission is $8 adults, $6 seniors/military, $4 children 6–12, children under 6 free. In addition, the ship makes several day-long cruises each year; rates start at around $100 per person. For more information or for cruise schedule and reservations, call 415/544-0100.

MARINA DISTRICT, COW HOLLOW, AND PACIFIC HEIGHTS

The neat pastel homes of the respectable **Marina District,** tucked in between Fort Mason and the Presidio, disguise the fact that the entire area is essentially unstable. Built on landfill,

the Palace of Fine Arts

COCKTAIL TIME

Sometimes you just need to cast out those sturdy shoes and the sightseeing parka to join what used to be known as the "jet set" to toast the high life. The following establishments offer a sample of that old San Francisco sparkle.

The revamped classic **Redwood Room,** 495 Geary St. (at Taylor) at the Clift Hotel, 415/775-4700, in the heart of the theater district and just two blocks from bustling Union Square, is something to behold. The Redwood Room is such a sentimental favorite that Save the Redwood Room kept its collective eye on Studio 54 and Royalton hotel king Ian Shrager's renovations, careful that the makeover did not include stripping the walls hewn of 2,000-foot redwood trees. As a concession, the walls remain, and the hunting lodge decor was updated with plasma-screen portraits that move subtly over time, elevating the idea to a highly stylized level of perfection. The crowd of fashion victims occupying chairs and couches ranging from leather numbers to velvet smoking chairs somehow enhances the overall effect, although drinks here are not cheap—a straight shot will set you back $9.

The **Tonga Room** at 950 Mason St. (between California and Sacramento), 415/772-5278, opened its exotic doors in 1945 inside the Fairmont Hotel to bring the Pacific Islander theme to San Francisco. Polynesian decor and thatch-roofed huts surround a deep blue lake, where simulated tropical rainstorms hit every half-hour. The lethal Bora Bora Horror tops the list of intriguing frozen cocktails, combining rum, banana liqueur, and Grand Marnier with a huge slice of pineapple. Rum also features in the Hurricane, Lava Bowl, and the Zombie. Happy hour offers the most eco-nomical visit possible. Normally pricey drinks cost $6, and you can graze on a buffet of edible treats (egg rolls, pot stickers, and dim sum) while listening to the house band's forgettable elevator music.

The drinkery at the **Top of the Mark,** 999 California St. (at Mason), 415/392-3434, is the city's most famous view lounge, an ideal place to take friends and dazzle them with the lights of San Francisco. Large windows offer a panorama of San Francisco's landmarks, from the Sutro Tower to the Transamerica Pyramid and the Golden Gate Bridge. There's live music every night, and given the ritzy setting, a $5–10 cover charge doesn't seem all that steep. Classic cocktails—Manhattans, sidecars, and Martinis—are the libations of choice. The bar food is upscale and excellently prepared, with selections ranging from a Mediterranean platter to Beluga caviar.

The word "cocktail" practically whispers from behind the ruby red silk curtains at the glamorous **Starlight Room** at 450 Powell St. (between Post and Sutter), 415/395-8595, perched on the 21st floor of the 1928 Sir Francis Drake Hotel. Polished mahogany fixtures, luxurious furnishings, and a 360-degree view of the city make the Starlight Room one of the nicest cocktail experiences going. The spacious bar, mahogany dance floor, and live music by Harry Denton's Starlight Orchestra, draw an upbeat crowd of young and old couples dressed to the nines for a night out on the town. Light supper options range from pan-roasted crab cakes to oysters on the half-shell. All of this dazzle is surprisingly affordable, with a small evening cover charge and cocktails $7–10.

—*Pat Reilly*

in an area once largely bay marsh, the Mediterranean-style Marina was previously the 63-acre site of the Panama-Pacific International Exposition of 1915—San Francisco's statement to the world that it had been reborn from the ashes of the 1906 earthquake and fire. So it was ironic, and fitting, that the fireboat *Phoenix* extinguished many of the fires that blazed here following the 1989 earthquake, which caused disproportionately heavy damage in this district.

The Marina's main attractions are those that surround it—primarily the neighborhood stretch of San Francisco's astounding shoreline Golden Gate National Recreation Area, which includes the **Fort Mason** complex of galleries, museums, theaters, and nonprofit cultural and conservation organizations. (For more information on the park and its many facets, see Golden Gate National Recreation Area below.) If you're in the neighborhood and find yourself near the yacht harbor, do wander out to see (and hear) the park's wonderful **Wave Organ** just east of the yacht club on Bay Street. Built of pieces from an old graveyard, the pipes are powered by sea magic. (The siren song is loudest at high tide.) Then wander west toward the Golden Gate Bridge on the **Golden Gate Promenade,** which meanders the three-plus miles from Aquatic Park and along the Marina Green—popular with kite fliers, well-dressed dog walkers, and the area's many exercise freaks—to Civil War-era **Fort Point.** (Be prepared for wind and fog.) The truly ambitious can take a hike across the bridge itself, an awesome experience.

Exhausted by nature, retreat to more sheltered attractions near the Presidio, including the remnants of the spectacular Panama-Pacific International Exhibition of 1915, the Bernard Maybeck-designed **Palace of Fine Arts,** and the indescribable **Exploratorium** inside, fun for children of all ages and a first-rate science museum (see The Presidio and Fort Point for more area information).

Separating the Marina District from high-flying Pacific Heights is the low-lying neighborhood of **Cow Hollow,** a onetime dairy farm community now noted for its chic **Union Street** shopping district—an almost endless string of bars, cafés, coffeehouses, bookstores, and boutiques stretching between Van Ness and Steiner. Not to be outdone, the Marina boasts its own version: **Chestnut Street.** Other chic areas have included upper **Fillmore Street** near the Heights (and near the still-surviving 1960s icon, the **Fillmore** concert hall, at Geary and Fillmore), and outer **Sacramento Street** near Presidio Avenue. (Who knows where the next trendy block will crop up? The fashion fates are fickle.) **Pacific Heights** proper is the hilltop home pasture for the city's well-shod blue bloods. Its striking streets, Victorian homes, and general architectural wealth are well worth a stroll (for personal guidance, see Walking Tours, under Delights and Diversions, below). Especially noteworthy here is the **Haas-Lilienthal House,** 2007 Franklin (at Jackson), 415/441-3004, a handsome and huge Queen Anne Victorian featured on A&E's America's Castles' *Castles by the Bay,* a survivor of the 1906 earthquake and the city's only fully furnished Victorian open for regular public tours.

Tours are usually conducted Wed., Sat., and Sun.; call for times. Admission is $5 adults, $3 seniors and children.

In the Cow Hollow neighborhood, don't miss the unusual 1861 **Octagon House,** 2645 Gough (at Union), 415/441-7512, owned by the National Society of Colonial Dames of America; it's now restored and fully furnished in colonial and federal period antiques. Open only on the second and fourth Thursday and the second Sunday of each month from noon–3 P.M.(closed in January and on holidays). Call to request special tour times. Donations greatly appreciated.

Exploratorium: Sophisticated Child's Play

Scientific American considers this the "best science museum in the world." Good Housekeeping says it's the "number one science museum in the U.S." It's definitely worth spending some time here. Inside the Palace of Fine Arts, 3601 Lyon St. (at Bay), 415/397-5673, www.exploratorium.edu, the Exploratorium is billed as a museum of science, art, and human perception, and is ostensibly designed for children. But this is no mass-marketed media assault on the senses, no mindless theatrical homage to simple fantasy. The truth is, adults also adore the Exploratorium, a wonderfully intelligent playground built around the mysterious natural laws of the universe.

The Exploratorium was founded in 1969 by physicist and educator Dr. Frank Oppenheimer, the original "Explainer" (as opposed to "teacher"), whose research career was abruptly ended during the blacklisting McCarthy era. Brother of J. Robert Oppenheimer (father of the atomic bomb), Frank Oppenheimer's scientific legacy was nonetheless abundant.

"Explaining science and technology without props," said Oppenheimer, "is like attempting to tell what it is like to swim without ever letting a person near the water." The Exploratorium was the original interactive science museum and influenced the establishment of hundreds of other such museums in the U.S. and abroad. Its 650-some three-dimensional exhibits delve into 13 broad subject areas: animal behavior, language, vision, sound and hearing, touch, heat and temperature, electricity, light, color, motion, patterns, waves and resonance, and weather. Everything can be experienced—from a touch-sensitive plant that shrinks from a child's probing hand, to strategically angled mirrors that create infinite reflections of the viewer; from tactile computerized fingerpainting to the wave-activated voice of the San Francisco Bay, as brought to you by the "Wave Organ." The extra special **Tactile Dome,** 415/561-0362 (reservations recommended), provides a pitch-black environment in which your vision is of no use, but your sense of touch gets a real workout.

Stock up on educational toys, games, experiments, and oddities at the Exploratorium Store. Especially worth purchasing, for teachers and brave parents alike, is the Exploratorium Science Snackbook, which includes instructions on building home or classroom versions of more than 100 Exploratorium exhibits.

The Exploratorium is open in summer daily 10 A.M.–6 P.M. (Wednesday until 9 P.M.). The rest of the year, hours are Tues.–Sun. 10 A.M.–5 P.M. (Wednesday until 9 P.M.). On the first Wednesday of each month, admission is free. Otherwise it's $10 adults, $7.50 seniors/students with ID, $6 youths 6–17, and children 4 and under free. Admission to the Tactile Dome is $14 per person, which includes museum admission.

THE AVENUES
Richmond District and Vicinity

Originally called San Francisco's Great Sand Waste, then the city's cemetery district (before the bones were dug up and shipped south to Colma in 1914), today the Richmond District is a middle-class ethnic sandwich built upon Golden Gate Park and topped by Lincoln Park and the Presidio. White Russians were the first residents, fleeing Russia after the 1917 revolution, but just about everyone else followed. A stroll down **Clement Street,** past its multiethnic eateries and shops, should bring you up to speed on the subject of cultural diversity.

The area between Arguello and Park Presidio, colloquially called "New Chinatown," is noted for its good, largely untouristed Asian eateries and shops. Russian-Americans still park themselves on the playground benches at pretty **Mountain Lake Park** near the Presidio. And the gold-painted onion domes of the Russian Orthodox **Russian Holy Virgin Cathedral of the Church in Exile,** 6210 Geary Blvd., along with the Byzantine-Roman Jewish Reform **Temple Emanu-El** at Arguello and Lake (technically in Pacific Heights), offer inspiring architectural reminders of earlier days.

Highlights of the Richmond District include the **University of San Francisco** atop Lone Mountain, an institution founded by the Jesuits in 1855, complete with spectacular **St. Ignatius** church, and the **Neptune Society Columbarium,** 1 Loraine Ct. (just off Anza near Stanyan), 415/221-1838 or 415/752-7891, the final resting place of old San Francisco families including the newspaper Hearsts and department store Magnins. With its ornate neoclassical and copper-roofed rotunda, the Columbarium offers astounding acoustics, best appreciated from the upper floors. The building is open to the public weekdays 9 A.M.–5 P.M., weekends 10 A.M.–2 P.M.

Seacliff, an exclusive seaside neighborhood nestled between the Presidio and Lincoln Park, is the once-rural community where famed California photographer **Ansel Adams** was raised. West of Seacliff, **Land's End** is the city's most rugged coastline, reached via footpath from Lincoln Park and the Golden Gate National Recreation Area. **China Beach,** just below Seacliff, was probably named for Chinese immigrants trying to evade Angel Island internment by jumping ship, all a result of the Exclusion Act in effect from the 1880s to World War II. During the Civil War, this was the westernmost point of the nation's antislavery "Underground Railroad." You can swim here—facilities include a lifeguard station plus changing rooms, showers, restrooms—but the water's brisk. Northeast is **Baker Beach,** considered the city's best nude beach.

California Palace of the Legion of Honor

The area's main attraction, though, just beyond Lincoln Park's Municipal Golf Course, is the **California Palace of the Legion of Honor,** on

THE CITYPASS

The money-saving CityPass provides admission to six of San Francisco's top attractions—California Academy of Sciences/Steinhart Aquarium, California Palace of the Legion of Honor, the Exploratorium, Museum of Modern Art, Muni and Cable Car 7-Day Passport, and a San Francisco Bay Cruise—for a price, at last report, half of what the individual admissions would cost: $34.95 adults, $25.75 youths 12–17. It's good for seven days and is available at any of the participating attractions, any of the city's visitor information centers, or at www.citypass.com.

Legion of Honor Drive (enter off 34th and Clement), 415/750-3600 (office) or 415/863-3330 (visitor hot line), www.famsf.org. Established by French-born Alma de Bretteville Spreckels, wife of the city's sugar king, this handsome hilltop palace was built in honor of American soldiers killed in France during World War I. It's a 1920 French neoclassic, from the colonnades and triumphal arch to the outdoor equestrian bronzes. Intentionally incongruous, placed out near the parking lot in an otherwise serene setting, is George Segal's testimony to the depths of human terror and terrorism: the barbed wire and barely living bodies of *The Holocaust.* Also here are some original bronze castings from Rodin, including *The Thinker* and *The Shades* outdoors, just part of the Legion's collection of more than 70 Rodin originals. Inside, the permanent collection was originally exclusively French, but now includes the M.H. de Young Museum's European collection—an awesome eight-century sweep from El Greco, Rembrandt, and Rubens to Renoir, Cézanne, Degas, Monet, and Manet. Take a docent-led tour for a deeper appreciation of other features, including the Legion's period rooms.

Special events include films, lectures, and painting and music programs, the latter including Rodin Gallery pipe organ concerts as well as chamber music, jazz, and historical instrument concerts in the Florence Gould Theater. The Legion of Honor also features a pleasant

café and a gift shop. Museum hours are Tues.–Sun. 9:30 A.M.–5 P.M., and until 8:45 P.M. on the first Saturday of every month. Admission is $8 adults, $6 seniors, $5 youths 12–17, free for children under 12 and free for everyone on the second Wednesday of each month. Admission may be higher during some visiting exhibitions.

The fit and fresh-air loving can get here on foot along the meandering **Coastal Trail**—follow it north from the Cliff House or south from the Golden Gate Bridge.

Sunset District

Most of San Francisco's neighborhoods are residential, streets of private retreat that aren't all that exciting except to those who live there. The Sunset District, stretching to the sea from south of Golden Gate Park, is one example, the southern section of the city's "Avenues." In summertime, the fog here at the edge of the continent is usually unrelenting, so visitors often shiver and shuffle off, muttering that in a place called "Sunset" one should be able to see it. (To appreciate the neighborhood name, come anytime *but* summer.) The golden gates, both the city and national parks, offer delights and diversions at the fringe. For beach access and often gray-day seaside recreation, from surfing and surf fishing to cycling, walking, and jogging (there's a paved path), follow the **Great Highway** south from Cliff House and stop anywhere along the way.

Stanyan Street, at the edge of the Haight and east of Golden Gate Park, offers odd and attractive shops, as does the stretch of **Ninth Avenue** near Irving and Judah. Just south of the park at its eastern edge is the **University of California at San Francisco Medical Center** atop Mt. Sutro, the small eucalyptus forest here reached via cobblestone Edgewood Ave. or, for the exercise, the Farnsworth Steps. From here, look down on the colorful Haight or north for a bird's-eye view of the **Richmond District,** the rest of the city's Avenues. **Stern Grove,** at Sloat Blvd. and 19th Ave., is a wooded valley beloved for its Sunday concerts.

Other good stops in the area include large **Lake Merced** just south, accessible via Skyline Blvd. (Hwy. 35) or Lake Merced Blvd., once a tidal lagoon. These days it's a freshwater lake popular for canoeing, kayaking, nonmotorized boating (rent boats at the Boat House on Harding), fishing (largemouth bass and trout), or just getting some fresh air.

The Lake Merced area offers one of the newer sections of the **Bay Area Ridge Trail,** a hiking route (signed with blue markers at major turning points and intersections) that one day will total 400 miles and connect 75 parks on ridgelines surrounding the San Francisco Bay. For more information, contact the **Bay Area Ridge Trail Council,** 1007 General Kennedy Avenue, Suite 3, San Francisco, CA 94129, 415/561-2695, www.ridgetrail.org. Farther south still is **Fort Funston,** a onetime military installation on barren cliffs, a favorite spot for hang gliders and a good place to take Fido for an outing (dogs can be off-leash along most of the beach here). East of Lake Merced are **San Francisco State University,** one of the state university system's best—noted for its **Sutro Library** and **American Poetry Archives**—and the residential **Ingleside,** home to a 26-foot-tall sundial, built as the focal point of the upper-income Ingleside Terraces community in 1913.

San Francisco Zoo

Located between Lake Merced and Ocean Beach, the San Francisco Zoo, 1 Zoo Rd. (Sloat Blvd. At 45th Ave.), 415/753-7061, www.sfzoo.org, isn't considered one of the best zoos in the country, but it has all the animal attractions expected of a major facility, including the Primate Discovery Center and Gorilla World, one of the largest naturalistic gorilla exhibits in the zoo world. The Lion House is home to majestic African lions and highly endangered Siberian and Sumatran tigers (Mealtime for the big cats, 2 P.M. every day except Monday, is quite a viewing treat). Other attractions include The Koala Station, based on an Australian outback station and home to six koalas, the Lemur Forest, which mimics their old-growth forest habitat in Madagascar, and Penguin Island, fashioned after the Patagonian coast of South America, and the setting for a colony of 40 Magellanic penguins. There's also a children's petting zoo, where children can feed the goats, sheep, and Highland cow, and a gorgeous old-fashioned miniature steam train ($2), and nice open spaces for play and picnics. Open daily 10 A.M.–5 P.M.; admission is $10 adults, $7 seniors/youth 12–17, $4 children 3–11, and free on the first Wednesday of every month.

HAIGHT-ASHBURY

Aging hippies, random hipsters, and the hopelessly curious of all ages are still attracted to San Francisco's Haight-Ashbury, once a commercial district for adjacent Golden Gate Park and a solid family neighborhood in the vicinity of Haight Street. The Golden Gate's block-wide Panhandle (which certainly resembles one on a map) was intended as the park's carriage entrance, helped along toward the desired ambience by neighboring Victorian-age Queen Annes. Once abandoned by the middle class, however, Haight-Ashbury declined into the cheap-rent paradise surrounded by parklands that became "Hashbury," "hippies," and headquarters for the 1967 Summer of Love.

Drawn here by the drum song of the coming-of-age Aquarian Age, some 200,000 young people lived in subdivided Victorian crash pads, on the streets, and in the parks that summer, culturally recognizable by long hair, scruffy jeans, tie-dyed T-shirts, granny glasses, peace signs, beads, and the flowers-in-your-hair style of flowing skirts and velvet dresses. Essential, too, at that time: underground newspapers and unrestrained radio, black-lights and psychedelia, incense, anything that came from India (like gurus), acid and mescaline, hashish, waterpipes, marijuana and multicolored rolling papers, harmonicas, tambourines, guitars, and bongo drums. A Volkswagen van was helpful, too, so loads of people could caravan off to anti–Vietnam War rallies, to wherever it was the Grateful Dead or Jefferson Airplane were playing (for free, usually), or to Fillmore West and Winterland, where Bill Graham staged so many concerts. It was all fairly innocent, at first, an innocence that didn't last. By late 1967, cultural predators had arrived: the tourists, the national media, and serious drug pushers and pimps. Love proved to be fragile. Most true believers headed back to the land, and Haight-Ashbury became increasingly violent and dangerous, especially for the young runaways who arrived (and still arrive) to stake a misguided claim for personal freedom.

"The Haight" today is considerably cleaner, its Victorian neighborhoods spruced up but not exactly gentrified. The classic Haight-Ashbury head shops are long gone, runaway hippies replaced by runaway punks panhandling for quarters (or worse). But Haight St. and vicinity is still hip, still socially and politically aware, still worth a stroll. The parkside Upper Haight stretch has more than its share of funky cafés, coffee shops, oddball bars and clubs, boutiques, and secondhand stores. If this all seems stodgy, amble on down to the Lower Haight in the Western Addition, an area fast becoming the city's new avant-garde district.

Seeing and Doing Haight-Ashbury

Aside from the commercial versions, there are a few significant countercultural sights in the Upper Haight, like the old Victorian **Dead House** at 710 Ashbury (near Waller), where the Grateful Dead lived and played their still-living music (and possibly where the term "deadheads" first emerged for the Dead's fanatic fans), and the **Jefferson Airplane's** old pad at 2400 Fulton (on the eastern edge of Golden Gate Park at Willard). Definitely worth a stop, for organic juice and granola, art to meditate by, and New Age computer networking, is **The Red Victorian** at 1665 Haight (near Belvedere), 415/864-1978, www.redvic.com, also a fascinating bed-and-breakfast complex that successfully honors The Haight's original innocence. Do climb on up the steep paths into nearby **Buena Vista Park,** a shocking tangle of anarchistically enchanted forest, just for the through-the-trees views.

Otherwise, the scene here is wherever you can find it. **Bound Together,** 1369 Haight St. (at Masonic), 415/431-8355, is a collective bookstore featuring a somewhat anarchistic collection: books on leftist politics, conspiracy theories, the occult, and sexuality. **Pipe Dreams,** 1376 Haight (at Masonic), 415/431-3553, is one place to go for Grateful Dead memorabilia and quaint drug paraphernalia, like water pipes and "bongs," but **Distractions,** 1552 Haight (between Clayton and

Ashbury), 415/252-8751, is truest to the form; in addition to the Dead selection, you can also snoop through head shop supplies, an ample variety of Tarot cards, and Guatemalan clothing imports.

Style is another Haight St. specialty. Though secondhand clothing stores here tend to feature higher prices than elsewhere, three of the best are **Wasteland,** 1660 Haight (at Belvedere), 415/863-3150; the **Buffalo Exchange,** 1555 Haight (between Clayton and Ashbury), 415/431-7733; and **Aardvarks,** 1501 Haight (at Ashbury), 415/621-3141. For old-style music bargains—and actual albums, including a thousand hard-to-find ones—head to **Recycled Records,** 1377 Haight (at Masonic), 415/626-4075. For thousands of used CDs and tapes, try **Amoeba Music,** housed in a former bowling alley at 1855 Haight (between Stanyan and Shrader), 415/831-1200.

Shops of interest in the Lower Haight include: **Zebra Records,** 475 Haight (near Webster), 415/626-9145, a DJ supply store that's the place to find cutting-edge hip hop, acid jazz, and Latin House; the **Naked Eye,** 533 Haight (between Fillmore and Steiner), 415/864-2985, which specializes in impossible-to-find videos; and **Compound Records,** 597 Haight (at Steiner), 415/626-7855, which specializes in DJ gear and drum and bass records. Well respected in the neighborhood for organic personal decoration is **Love and Haight,** 252 Fillmore (between Haight and Waller), 415/861-9206. Shop the Lower Haight, too, for stylish used clothing stores with good pickings, low prices, and zero crowds.

Nightlife

In the 1980s and '90s, the Haight was known as a rock nightspot, but the Haight's pulse has slowed considerably in the last 20 years. The I-Beam, Kennel Club, and Nightbreak are no more, gone along with the street's ability to attract big talent. In their place, the Haight's comfortable bars make great hideouts from elbow-to-elbow crowds found elsewhere.

A laid-back bar popular with young and old is **The Gold Cane,** 1569 Haight St. (between Ashbury and Clayton), 415/626-1112, serving the cheapest drinks in town. More typical of modern Haight is the **Trophy Room,** 1811

Haight (between Shrader and Stanyan), 415/752-2971, full of self-styled hippies and punks as well as unusual combinations of leather jackets, long hair, and tattoos. **Martin Macks,** 1568 Haight (between Ashbury and Clayton), 415/864-0124, is cleaner, quieter, and a bit more upscale than the usual Haight bar scene, with at least 16 imported beers on tap. Retro-swing bars are still quite popular in San Francisco, and **Club Deluxe,** 1511 Haight (at Ashbury), 415/552-6949, is one of the best.

Wilder by far are the bars and clubs in the Lower Haight. No matter what the weather, **Mad Dog in the Fog,** 530 Haight (between Fillmore and Steiner), 415/626-7279, is packed every night, the very mixed clientele attracted by the English pub-style dart boards as much as the live music. Across the street, serious drinking is the main agenda at the loud and boisterous **Toronado,** 547 Haight (between Fillmore and Webster), 415/863-2276. **Nickie's Haight Street BBQ,** 460 Haight (between Fillmore and Webster), 415/621-6508, serves barbecue by day, red-hot DJed dance music by night—everything from hip-hop and salsa to world beat and the music of Islam. (And the bar jumps, too.) Quieter and perhaps a tad too self-conscious for this very natural neighborhood is the **Noc Noc,** 557 Haight (between Fillmore and Steiner), 415/861-5811, a cavelike, romantically gloomy environment simultaneously inspired by *The Flintstones* cartoons and *Star Trek* reruns. For genuine cultural inspiration, though, that now-gone mural of former president George Bush shooting up at The Kennel Club was a classic.

MISSION DISTRICT

Vibrant and culturally electric, the Mission District is one of San Francisco's most exciting neighborhoods. The fact that most tourists never discover the area's pleasures is a sad commentary on our times. To the same extent people fear that which seems foreign in America—a nation created by foreigners—they miss out on the experience of life as it is. And the country becomes even more hell-bent on mandating social homogenization despite ideals and rhetoric to the contrary.

On any given day in the Mission District, especially if it's sunny, the neighborhood is busy with the business of life. The largely Hispanic population—Colombian, Guatemalan, Mexican, Nicaraguan, Peruvian, Panamanian, Puerto Rican, Salvadorean—crowds the streets and congregates on corners. Whether Mission residents are out strolling with their children or shopping in the many bakeries, produce stores, and meat markets, the community's cultural energy is unmatched by any other city neighborhood—with the possible exception of Chinatown early in the morning. This remains true now that gentrification has arrived even in the Mission.

Before the arrival of the Spanish, the Bay Area's Ohlone people (they called themselves Ramaytush) established their largest settlement here in the sheltered expanse later known as Mission Valley. Largely uninhabited until the 1860s, the valley attracted a large number of Irish immigrants and became one of the city's first suburbs. Most of the Mission District was spared the total devastation otherwise characteristic in the fiery aftermath of the 1906 earthquake, so some of San Francisco's finest Victorians are still area standouts.

Even with onrushing gentrification, the Mission's ungentrified modern attitude has created a haven for artists, writers, social activists, and politicos. The Latino arts scene is among the city's most powerful and original. This is one of San Francisco's newest New Bohemias, a cultural crazy quilt where artists and assorted oddballs are not only tolerated but encouraged. Symbolic of this new symbiosis is the **826 Valencia Writing Project** headquartered at McSweeney's literary journal and pirate supply store at 826 Valencia St., a project undertaken by Dave Eggers (author of *A Heartbreaking Work of Staggering Genius*) and other area writers to tutor and otherwise support literacy and constructive risk-taking in the neighborhod's at-risk kids. Businesses catering to this emerging consciousness are also becoming prominent along Valencia St., already considered home by the city's lesbian community.

Technically, the Mission District extends south from near the Civic Center to the vicinity of Cesar Chavez (Army). Dolores or Church St. (or thereabouts) marks the western edge, Alabama St. the eastern. Mission Street, the main thoroughfare (BART stations at 16th and 24th), is lined with discount stores and pawnshops. Main commercial areas include 16th St. between Mission and Dolores, 24th St. between Valencia and York, and Valencia St.—the bohemian center of social life, lined with coffeehouses, bars, bookstores, performance art venues, and establishments serving the lesbian and women's community. For the latest word on feminist and lesbian art shows, readings, performances, and other events, stop by the nonprofit **Women's Building,** 3543 18th St. (just off Valencia), 415/431-1180.

Mission Dolores

With the Mission District's return to a predominantly Hispanic ethnic attitude, a visit to the city's oldest structure seems especially fitting. Completed in 1791, Mission San Francisco de Asis at Dolores and 16th Streets, 415/621-8203, is open daily 9 A.M.–4:30 P.M. A donation of $2 or more is appreciated. (The best time to arrive, to avoid busloads of tourists and the crush of schoolchildren studying California history, is be-

fore 10 A.M.) This is the sixth mission established in California by the Franciscan fathers. Founded earlier, in 1776, the modest chapel and outbuildings came to be known as Mission Dolores, the name derived from a nearby lagoon and creek, Arroyo de Nuestra Señora de los Dolores, or "stream of our lady of sorrows."

And how apt the new shingle proved to be, in many ways. In the peaceful cemetery within the mission's walled compound is the "Grotto of Lourdes," the unmarked grave of more than 5,000 Ohlone and others among the native workforce. Most died of measles and other introduced diseases in the early 1800s, the rest from other varieties of devastation. After California became a state, the first U.S. Indian agent came to town to take a census of the Native American population. It was an easy count, since there was only one, a man named Pedro Alcantara who was still grieving for a missing son. Near the grotto are the vine-entwined tombstones of pioneers and prominent citizens, like California's first governor under Mexican rule, Don Luis Antonio Arguello, and San Francisco's first mayor, Don Francisco de Haro.

The sturdy mission chapel—the small humble structure, not the soaring basilica adjacent—survived the 1906 earthquake due largely to its four-foot-thick adobe walls. Inside, the painted ceilings are an artistic echo of the Ohlone, whose original designs were painted with vegetable dyes. And the simple altar offers stark contrast to the grandeur next door. For a peek at the collection of mission artifacts and memorabilia, visit the small museum.

Murals

The entire Mission District is vividly alive, with aromas and sounds competing everywhere with color. And nothing in the Mission District is quite as colorful as its mural art. More than 200 murals dot the neighborhood, ranging from brilliantly colored homages to work, families, and spiritual flight to boldly political attacks on the status quo.

Start with some **"BART art,"** at the 24th St. station, where Michael Rios' columns of humanoids lift up the rails. Another, particularly impressive set, is eight blocks down, off 24th St. on the fences and garage doors along **Balmy**

SUSAN SNYDER

Mission Dolores, the city's oldest structure

SAN FRANCISCO

Alley, and also at **Flynn Elementary School** at Precita and Harrison. At 14th and Natoma is a mural honoring Frida Kahlo, artist and wife of Diego Rivera.

Walking tours of the neighborhood murals (with well-informed guides) are led by the **Precita Eyes Mural Arts Center,** a charming gallery at 2981 24th St. (at Harrison), 415/285-2287, www.precitaeyes.org. The tours are offered every Saturday and Sunday at 11 A.M. and 1:30 P.M.; $12 general, $5 seniors, $2 youths 18 and under. Call for information on the center's many other tours.

Other good art stops in the area include the nonprofit **Galeria de la Raza,** 2857 24th St. (at Bryant), 415/826-8009, www.galeriadelaraza.org, featuring some exciting, straight-ahead political art attacks; the affiliated **Studio 24** gift shop adjacent, with everything from books and clothing to religious icons and Day of the Dead dolls; and the **Mission Cultural Center for Latino Arts,** 2868 Mission (near BART between 24th and 25th Streets), 415/821-1155, www.missionculturalcenter.org, a community cultural and sociopolitical center that can supply you with more information on area artworks.

Potrero Hill

East of the Mission District proper and southeast of the SoMa scene is gentrifying (at least on the north side) Noe Valley-like Potrero Hill, known for its roller-coaster road rides (a favorite spot for filming TV and movie chase scenes) and the world-famous **Anchor Brewing Company** microbrewery, 1705 Mariposa St. (at 17th), 415/863-8350, makers of Anchor Steam beer. Join a free weekday tour and see how San Francisco's famous beer is brewed. If you drive to Potrero Hill, detour to the "Poor Man's Lombard" at 20th and Vermont, which has earned the dubious honor of being the city's second twistiest street. This snakelike thoroughfare is not festooned with well-landscaped sidewalks and flowerbeds, but instead an odd assortment of abandoned furniture, beer bottles, and trash. Not yet socially transformed is the south side of the hill, which is close to **Bayview-Hunters Point;** these once-industrialized neighborhoods

were left behind when World War II-era shipbuilding ceased and are now ravaged by poverty, drugs, and violence. Railroad buffs, please note: the Hunters Point Naval Shipyard is home to the **Golden Gate Railroad Museum,** 415/822-8728, www.ggrm.org, where (for a fee) you can drive your own full-size steam or diesel locomotive. Museum open weekends 10 A.M.–5 P.M., otherwise by appointment only.

Shopping

For the most part Noe Valley's 24th St. is laid-back and boutiquey, a rare combination in San Francisco. Finds—and affordable by San Francisco standards—include **A Girl and Her Dog,** 3932 24th St., 415/643-0346, for stylish, comfortable SoMa-style styles; friendly, youthful **Ambiance,** 3985 24th St., 415/647-7144; and been-there-forever **Joshua Simon,** 3915 24th St., 415/821-1068, for quality and comfort. For glorious adornments, peruse the **Gallery of Jewels,** 4089 24th St., 415/285-0626, which offers exquisite jewelry, many pieces by local designers. For the latest retrowear trends, try **Guys and Dolls,** 3789 24th St., 415/285-7174.

Clothes Contact, 473 Valencia (just north of 16th), 415/621-3212, sells fashionable vintage clothing for $8 per pound. (Consumer alert: those big suede jackets in the back weigh more than you might imagine.) Worth poking into, too, is the **Community Thrift Store,** 623-625 Valencia (between 17th and 18th), 415/861-4910, a fundraising venture for the gay and lesbian Tavern Guild. It's an expansive, inexpensive, and well-organized place, with a book selection rivaling most used bookstores. (The motto here is "out of the closet, into the store.") Cooperatively run **Modern Times Bookstore,** 888 Valencia (between 19th and 20th), 415/282-9246, is the source for progressive, radical, and Third World literature, magazines, and tapes.

If you're down on your luck, head up to **Lady Luck Candle Shop,** 311 Valencia (at 14th), 415/621-0358, a small store selling some pretty big juju, everything from high-test magic candles and religious potions (like St. John the Conqueror Spray) to Lucky Mojo Oil and Hold Your Man essential oil. **Good Vibrations,** 1210 Valencia (at 23rd), 415/974-8980, home of the vibrator museum, is a clean, user-friendly, liberated shop where women (and some men) come for adult toys, and to peruse the selection of in-print erotica, including history and literature.

More common in the Mission District are neighborhood-style antique and secondhand stores of every stripe. Bargains abound, without the inflated prices typical of trendier, more tourist-traveled areas.

Nightlife

The Roxie, 3117 16th St. (at Valencia), 415/863-1087, www.roxie.com, is the neighborhood's renowned repertory film venue, with a full schedule of eclectic and foreign films as well as special programs, including live audience interviews with filmmakers. Most of the Mission's coffeehouses, bars, and clubs are equally entertaining. For good

coffee and Ethiopian food (including some vegetarian selections), head to **Cafe Ethiopia,** 878 Valencia St. (at 20th), 415/285-2728.

The Mission District may seem to have a bar on every block, but some are more appealing than others. Scoring high marks on the cool-o-meter is the **Latin-American Club** (aka "the Latin"), 3286 22nd St. (between Mission and Valencia), 415/647-2732. The Latin has a truly neighborhood vibe, funky but comfortable clubhouse atmosphere and good people-watching. Just across the way and favored by local musicians is the **Make-Out Room,** 3225 22nd (between Mission and Valencia), 415/647-2888. Easy to miss from the outside, the small, windowless storefront entrance is painted all black (look for the bar's flickering sign out front). Inside, the dark bar extends back to a pool table and a small stage covered with red velvet curtains.

AN OPEN-MINDED GUIDE TO NIGHTCLUBBING IN SAN FRANCISCO

First, ask the basic questions: Who am I? What am I doing here? Where do I belong? To go nightclubbing in San Francisco, at least *ask* the questions. The answers don't really matter; your political, social, sexual, and musical preferences will be matched somewhere. Hip-hop, disco, new wave, house, fusion, industrial, world beat—whatever it is you're into, it's out there, just part of the creative carnival world of San Francisco nightclubbing. Everything goes, especially cultural taboos, leaving only freewheeling imaginations and an unadulterated desire to do one thing and only one thing—dance with total abandon. In the city, heteros, gays, lesbians, blacks, whites, Asians, and Latinos all writhe together, unified in a place where all prejudice drops away: the dance floor.

The hottest dance clubs come and go considerably faster than the Muni buses do, so the key to finding the hippest, most happening spot is to ask around. Ask people who look like they should know, such as young fashion junkies working in trendy clothing shops, used-record stores, or other abodes of pretentious cool.

Throbbing together with hundreds of other euphorics, experiencing ecstasy en masse, may be the

closest we'll ever really get to living in one united world. Still, San Francisco nightclub virgins tend to avoid their initiation, somehow intimidated by the frenzied cosmic collision of electrifying lights, thumping dance tunes, and sweat-drenched bodies. But be not afraid. There are answers to even the three most common worries:

Worry: I can't dance. *Answer:* It wouldn't matter even if you could. The dance floors are so crowded, at best it's possible only to bounce up and down.

Worry: I'm straight (or gay) and the crowd seems to be predominantly gay (or straight). *Answer:* Since the limits of gender and sexuality are hopelessly blurred in San Francisco, and since nobody would care even if they weren't, just dump your angst and dance.

Worry: I'm afraid I'll look like a fool (feel out of place, be outclassed, fall down, throw up, whatever). *Answer:* As we said, nobody cares. You're totally anonymous, being one of more than 776,733 people in town. And no matter what you do, nobody will notice, since narcissism in San Francisco's clubs is at least as deep as the Grand Canyon.

—*Tim Moriarty*

Shot straight from the glittering heart of NYC (the original site is in Manhattan's East Village), the **Beauty Bar,** 2299 Mission (at 19th), 415/285-0323, offers an odd and intoxicating mix of cocktails and 1950s beauty parlor ambience. The walls are pink, the chrome blow-dryers sparkle, and the crowd is a mix of Mission trendsetters and fashion victims. Specialty drinks are named after beauty products, like the Aqua Net made with blue curaçao and the Prell made with crème de menthe. Come on a weeknight and you may even score a complimentary manicure with your cocktail. A neon sign outside **Doc's Clock,** 2575 Mission (at 21st), 415/824-3627, announces it's "Cocktail Time," but the vibe down here is more relaxed, and flannel shirts outnumber silver pants 10 to 1.

Up on 16th St., **Doctor Bombay's,** 3192 16th St. (at Guerrero), 415/431-5255, is dim and diminutive, the clientele quite happy to talk the night away while downing the good doctor's award-winning specialty drink, the melon-flavored Pixie Piss. Across the street is **Dalva,** 3121 16th St. (at Valencia), 415/252-7740, another Mission favorite. A handsome mahogany bar and an assortment of wooden tables make this a great place to settle in. Weekday happy "hour" runs from 4 to 7 P.M., and it's best on weekdays as the small room gets packed later in the week. **Esta Noche,** 3079 16th (between Mission and Valencia), 415/861-5757, is the red-hot Latino answer to the almost-all-white gay bars in the Castro.

La Rondalla, 901 Valencia (at 20th), 415/647-7474, is the most festive bar around, what with the year-round Christmas lights, smoke-stained tinsel, and revolving overhead disco ball. (Good traditional Mexican food is served in the restaurant.) Down at the foot of Mission St., hole-in-the-wall **El Rio,** 3158 Mission St. (at Cesar Chavez), 415/282-3325, sports a big welcome sign outside announcing this is "Your Dive," and indeed the feeling here is warm yet slightly seedy. The outdoor deck, shuffleboard set-up, and pool tables make it an excellent warm-weather hangout. Next door is **Roccapulco,** 3140 Mission (at Cesar Chavez), 415/648-6611, a supper club where you can dine and dance salsa to live Latino bands.

Live, new theater is the specialty of **The Marsh,** 1062 Valencia St. (near 22nd), 415/826-5750, www.themarsh.com. A neighborhood classic, the Marsh isn't glitzy, fashionable, or expensive (tickets usually cost $7–15). But it has heart. The performers (and audiences) here are serious about art. Experimentation is de rigueur, meaning you're never at risk of encountering formula productions. You won't need your tux here, and your applause will be well-deserved gold to the performers, some of whom may go on to fame and fortune. Definitely check it out.

CASTRO STREET AND VICINITY

The very idea is enough to make America's righteous religious right explode in an apoplectic fit, but the simple truth is that San Francisco's Castro St. is one of the safest neighborhoods in the entire city—and that's not just a reference to sex practices.

This tight-knit, well-established community of lesbian women and gay men represents roughly 15 percent of the city's population and 35 percent of its registered voters. Nationally and internationally, the Castro District epitomizes out-of-the-closet living. (There's nothing in this world like the Castro's Gay Freedom Day Parade—usually headed by hundreds of women on motorcycles, the famous Dykes on Bikes—and no neighborhood throws a better street party.) People here are committed to protecting their own and creating safe neighborhoods. What this means, for visitors straight or gay, is that there is a response—people get out of their cars, or rush out of restaurants, clubs, and apartment buildings—at the slightest sign that something is amiss.

Who ever would have guessed that a serious revival of community values in the U.S. would start in the Castro?

Actually, there have been many indications. And there are many reasons. The developing cultural and political influence of the Castro District became apparent in 1977, when openly gay Harvey Milk was elected to the San Francisco Board of Supervisors. But genuine acceptance seemed distant—never more so than in 1978, when both Milk and Mayor George Moscone were assassinated by conservative political rival Dan White, who had resigned his board seat and wanted it back. (White's "diminished capacity" defense argument, which claimed that his habitual consumption of high-sugar junk food had altered his brain chemistry—the "Twinkie" defense—became a national scandal but ultimately proved successful. He was sentenced to a seven-year prison term.)

The community's tragedies kept on coming, hitting even closer to home. Somewhat notorious in its adolescence as a safe haven for freestyle lifestyles, including casual human relationships and quickie sex, the Castro District was devastated by the initial impact of the AIDS epidemic. (With younger gays that history seems determined to repeat itself.) The community has been stricken to the center of its soul by the tragic human consequences of an undiscriminating virus. But otherwise meaningless human loss has served only to strengthen the community's humanity. Just as, after Milk's assassination, greater numbers of community activists came forward to serve in positions of political influence, Castro District organizations like the Shanti Project, Open Hand, and the Names Project extended both heart and hand to end the suffering. And fierce, in-your-face activists from groups like Act Up, Queer Nation, and Bad Cop No Donut have taken the message to the nation's streets.

So, while Castro District community values are strong and getting stronger, the ambience is not exactly apple-pie Americana. People with pierced body parts (some easily visible, some not) and dressed in motorcycle jackets still stroll in and out of leather bars. Its shops also can be somewhat unusual, like **Does Your Mother Know,** a seriously homoerotic greeting card shop on 18th St. near Castro.

Seeing and Doing the Castro

The neighborhood's business district, both avant-garde and gentrified Victorian, is small, stretching for three blocks along Castro St. between Market and 19th, and a short distance in each direction from 18th and Castro. This area is all included, geographically, in what was once recognizable as **Eureka Valley.** (Parking can be a problem, once you've arrived, so take the Muni Metro and climb off at the Castro St. Station.) Some people also in-clude the gentrifying **Noe Valley** (with its up-scale 24th St. shopping district) in the general Castro stream of consciousness, but the technical dividing line is near the crest of Castro St. at 22nd Street. Keep driving on Upper Market St., and you'll wind up into the city's geographic center. Though the ascent is actually easier from Haight-Ashbury (from Twin Peaks Blvd. just off 17th—see a good road map), either way you'll arrive at or near the top of **Twin Peaks,** with its terraced neighborhoods, astounding views, and some of the city's best stairway walks. More challenging is the short but steep hike to the top of Corona Heights Park (at Roosevelt), also noted for the very good **Josephine D. Randall Junior Museum,** 199 Museum Way (at Roosevelt), 415/554-9600, www.randallmuseum.org, a youth-oriented natural sciences, arts, and activities center open Tues.–Sat. 10 A.M.–5 P.M. Admission free; donations welcome.

Down below, **A Different Light,** 489 Castro St. (between Market and 18th Streets), 415/431-0891, is the city's best gay and lesbian bookstore, with literature by and for. Readings and other events are occasionally offered; call for current information. Truly classic and quite traditional is the handsome and authentic art deco **Castro Theater,** 429 Castro (at Market), 415/621-6120, built in 1923. San Francisco's only true movie palace, the Castro is still a favorite city venue for classic movies and film festivals. Another highlight is the massive house Wurlitzer organ, which can make seeing a film at the Castro a truly exhilarating experience. **Cliff's Variety,** 479 Castro (at 18th), 415/431-5365, is another classic, a wonderfully old-fashioned hardware store where you can buy almost anything, from power saws to Play-doh.1

Nightlife

Many of San Francisco's 200-plus gay bars are in the Castro District. Those in the know say the best way to find just the scene you're looking for is to wander. **The Cafe,** 2367 Market St. (between 17th and 18th), 415/861-3846, is the Castro's best lesbian bar, also attracting many gay boys and some straights. From its balcony overlooking Market and Castro, you can get a good overview of the whole Castro scene below. Also featured: an indoor patio, pool tables, and a spacious dance floor. DJs spin a loud mix of techno and house with a few '70s and '80s remixes for a crowd that often packs the floor by 11 P.M.

Over at **The Mint,** 1942 Market St. (near Guerrero), 415/626-4726, sing yourself silly with many of the city's top Karaoke singers. Now home to a mixed crowd, including a fair number of office workers letting off steam, this is in fact the oldest gay bar in continuous operation in the Castro, circa 1968. Another neighborhood mainstay, **Twin Peaks Tavern,** at 410 Castro St. (at 17th St.), 415/864-9470, is home away from home for a mainly 40-plus, gay white male crowd. The bar has a light and airy atmosphere, with large windows overlooking the street, good for people-watching and conversation.

Just up the street at 18th and Castro, **Midnight Sun,** 4067 18th St., 415/861-4186, is named for the glow of its TV screens. This is the place for happy-hour renditions of the latest episodes of *Queer As Folk, Will and Grace,* or *Sex and the City.* Hip and unpretentious, **The Pilsner Inn,** 225 Church St. (between Market and 15th St.), 415/621-7058, has a punky soundtrack and barkeeps busy pouring a selection of European ales.

A onetime speakeasy, **Cafe du Nord,** 2170 Market (between Church and Sanchez), 415/861-5016, is underground, quite literally, in the basement of the Swedish American building. Descend the stairs into a nightspot with the look of a classic supper club: deep red walls and mahogany fixtures. Alternative and swing music make this place popular with a diverse crowd, not to mention excellent cocktails, a good dinner menu, and only moderate pretense. DuNord also hosts **Girl66,** a dance club for women, once a month, making this and the Café the only places in the Castro where a significant number of girls regularly congregate.

SOUTH OF MARKET (SoMa)

Known by old-timers as "south of the slot," a reference to a neighborhood sans cable cars, San Francisco's South of Market area was a working- and middle-class residential area—until all its homes were incinerated in the firestorm following the great earthquake of 1906. Rebuilt early in the century with warehouses, factories, train yards, and port businesses at **China Basin,** these days the area has gone trendy. In the style of New York's SoHo (South of Houston), this semi-industrial stretch of the city now goes by the moniker "SoMa."

As is usually the case, the vanguard of gentrification was the artistic community: the dancers, musicians, sculptors, photographers, painters, and graphic designers who require low rents and room to create. Rehabilitating old warehouses and industrial sheds here into studios and performance spaces solved all but strictly creative problems. Then came the attractively inexpensive factory outlet stores, followed by eclectic cafés and nightclubs. The Yerba Buena Gardens redevelopment project sealed the neighborhood's fate, bringing big-time tourist attractions including the **Moscone Convention Center** (newly expanded with the addition of Moscone West at Fourth and Howard), the San Francisco Museum of Modern Art, the Yerba Buena Center for the Arts, and The Rooftop at Yerba Buena Gardens, a multifacility arts and entertainment complex.

Coming soon to a site on Mission near Yerba Buena is the new **Mexican Museum** facility, expected to open in 2004. (The museum has been located at Fort Mason; for contact information, see that section.) Designed by internationally acclaimed architect Ricardo Legorreta, the new, seven-story Mexican Museum will provide some 63,000 square feet of exhibit and activity space. Legorreta's other Bay Area projects include the Tech Museum of Innovation and the Children's Discovery Museum, both in San Jose.

Now the city's destination for the young, sleek, and wealthy, the 30-story **W San Francisco,** towers over Third and Howard. Sony's futuristic **Metreon** holds down Fourth and Mission. Even near the once-abandoned waterfront just south of the traditional Financial District boundaries, avant-garde construction like **Number One Market Street,** which incorporates the old Southern Pacific Building, and **Rincon Center,** which encompasses the preserved Depression-era mural art of the Rincon Annex Post Office, have added a new look to once down-and-out areas. More massive highrises are on the way, and land values are shooting up in areas previously dominated by longshoremen's flophouses and garment factories. The starving artists have long since moved on to the Lower Haight and the Mission District, and in SoMa, the strictly eccentric is now becoming more self-consciously so.

San Francisco Museum of Modern Art

SoMa's transformation is largely due to the arrival of the San Francisco Museum of Modern Art (SFMOMA), 151 Third St. (between Mission and Howard), 415/357-4000, www.sfmoma.org, a modern building designed by Swiss architect Mario Botta that many consider to be a work of art in itself. Love it or hate it, you're not likely to miss the soaring cylindrical skylight and assertive red brick of the $60-million structure rising above the gritty streets south of Market.

The museum's heavy hitters include pieces that any museum in the country would kill for: de Kooning's intense *Woman*, and Henri Matisse's masterpiece *Femme au Chapeau*. Also featured in the permanent collection: works by Piet Mondrian, Georgia O'Keeffe, Pablo Picasso, Salvador Dali, Marcel DuChamp, and some outstanding paintings by Jackson Pollock. Mexican painters Frida Kahlo and her husband, Diego Rivera, are represented, as are the works of many Californian artists, including assembler Bruce Connor and sculptor Bruce Arneson. The museum also hosts blockbuster temporary exhibitions showcasing world-renowned individual artists, such as an amazing Paul Klee retrospective in 2002. And if you don't know the difference between a Klee and a Kahlo, fear not; the new **Koret Visitor Edcation Center** presents exhibits, films, and lectures, often related to the main exhibit. There's a hip little café, the **Cafe Museo,** 415/357-4500, serving fresh, healthful, "artistic" sandwiches, salads and pizzas, and boxed lunches to go, and the **SFMOMA Museum Store,** well stocked with pricey coffee-table books and postcards.

The Museum of Modern Art is open 11 A.M.–6 P.M. daily except Wednesday. Additionally, it's open until 9 P.M. on Thursday, and open 10 A.M.–6 P.M. in summer (Memorial Day through Labor Day). The museum is closed Wednesdays and the following public holidays: Thanksgiving, Christmas, and New Year's Day. Admission is $10 adults, $7 seniors, and $ 6 students with ID (children under 12 free). Admission is free for everyone on the first Tuesday of each month, and half-price Thursday 6–9 P.M. Admission charge is sometimes higher during special exhibitions.

Yerba Buena Center for the Arts

Opposite the museum on the west side of Third St. is the Yerba Buena Center for the Arts, 701 Mission St. (at Third), 415/978-2700 or 415/978-2787 (ticket office), www.yerbabuenaarts.org, a gallery and theater complex devoted to showcasing the works of experimental, marginalized, and emerging artists. The YBC hosts varied exhibitions including pop culture classics such as Fantastic! The Art of Comics and Illusions, examining the work of artists showcased in the seminal publication RAW, including Dan Clowes *(Eightball),* Lynda Barry *(Cruddy),* and Art Spiegelman *(Maus),* and screenings of *Surf Trip* and *Star Wars.* A five-acre downtown park surrounds the complex, where a waterfall is dedicated to the memory of Martin Luther King Jr. with the words: "We will not be satisfied until 'justice rolls down like a river and righteousness like a mighty stream.'" Amen. The Center for the Arts galleries are open 11 A.M.–5 P.M. daily except Monday (until 8 P.M. on the first Thursday of each month). Admission is $6 adults, $3 seniors/students; children 12 and under free. Everyone gets in free all day on the first Tuesday of every month.

The Rooftop at Yerba Buena Gardens

Cleverly built atop the Moscone Center along Fourth, Howard, and Folsom Streets, this park-cum-entertainment complex is the youth destination at Yerba Buena Gardens. Rooftop attractions include a 1906 Charles Looff carousel, a full-size indoor ice rink with city-skyline views, a bowling alley, and **Zeum,** 415/820-3349, an interactive art and technology center for children ages 8–18. Hours are Wed.–Sun. 11 A.M.–5 P.M., and admission is $7 adults, $6 seniors and students, $5 youths ages 5–18. The **Ice Skating Center,** 415/777-3727, is open for public skating daily, 1–5 P.M. Admission is $6.50 adults, $4.50 seniors, and $5.00 children ($2.50 skate rental). The **Bowling Alley,** 415/820-3540, is open Sun.–Thurs. 10 A.M.–10 P.M., Fri.–Sat. 10 A.M.–midnight, with Black Lite bowling from 9 P.M.–midnight. Prices are $4 per game for adults, $2.50 per game for children 12 and under.

Metreon

Anchoring the corner of Fourth and Mission Streets like a sleek spacecraft, the block-long, four-story-tall **Metreon** is the latest icon of pop culture to land in San Francisco's SoMa district. The Sony Entertainment-sponsored mall features a 15-screen cinema complex, the biggest IMAX theater in North America (tied with Sony's IMAX theatre in New York), and trendy shopping options including a Sony Style store and Playstation, where you can test drive the latest titles at the videogame bar, or quiz the super user "game tenders" on staff.

Interactive exhibits include **Where the Wild Things Are,** based on Maurice Sendak's magical children's book; **Portal One,** a futuristic gaming area; and **Action Theatre,** a triple-screen theatre dedicated to screening Japanese anime, animated entertainment, and action features. The mall's food court features offshoots of several popular local restaurants: LongLife Noodle Co., Buckhorn, Sanraku, and Firewood Café, gathered under the umbrella "A Taste of San Francisco." For admission prices, hours, and other current information, call Metreon at 415/369-6000, or check www.metreon.com.

Other SoMa Sights

An awesome neighborhood presence is the 1874 granite Greek revival **Old U.S. Mint** building at Fifth and Mission, vacant since 1998 and in need of restoration. At last report the nonprofit **San Francisco Museum and Historical Society** had been given the go-ahead to rehabilitate the building for a new civic museum, retail space, and a new visitor center for the San Francisco Convention & Visitors Bureau—projects de-

CLEAN UP YOUR ACT AT BRAINWASH

No doubt the cleanest scene among SoMa's hot spots is BrainWash at 1122 Folsom, 415/861-FOOD, 415/431-WASH, or www.brainwash.com, a combination café, performance space, nightclub, and laundromat in a reformed warehouse. The brainchild of UC Berkeley and Free Speech Movement alumna Susan Schindler, BrainWash ain't heavy, just semi-industrial, from the beamed ceilings and neon to the concrete floor. The decor here includes café tables corralled by steel office chairs with original decoupaged artwork on the seats. (Admit it—haven't you always wanted to sit on Albert Einstein's face?) BrainWash also features a small counter/bar area, and bathrooms for either "Readers" (lined with *Dirty Laundry Comics* wallpaper) or "Writers" (with walls and ceiling of green chalkboard, chalk provided for generating brainwashable graffiti). Since literary urges know no boundaries in terms of gender, of course both are open to both basic sexes. And others.

The small café at BrainWash offers quick, simple fare—salads, burgers, pizza, and decent sandwiches (vegetarian and otherwise)—plus pastries and decadent pies, cakes, and cookies. Try a BrainWash Brownie, either double chocolate or double espresso. There's liquid espresso, of course, plus cappuccinos and lattes, fresh unfiltered fruit or carrot juice, teas, beer, and wine.

Behind the café (and glass wall) is the BrainWash washhouse, a high-tech herd of washers and dryers ($1.50 per load for a regular wash load, $3.50 for a jumbo washer, and a quarter for 10 minutes of dryer time). Ask about the Laundromat's wash-and-fold and dry-cleaning services. The whole shebang here is open daily 7 A.M.–11 P.M. "Last call" for washers is 9:30 P.M. nightly. Call ahead to make sure, but most nights Brainwash offers free live music, comedy, and spoken word events, television nights available otherwise. BrainWash also sponsors community events, and the place can be rented for private parties.

So come on down, almost anytime, for some Clorox and croissants.

pendent on successful financing. The San Francisco Mint was established in 1854 to safeguard gold and silver mined in the West, which may help explain the Old Mint's resemblance to both temple and fortress. The oldest stone building in San Francisco, the Old Mint was also the first and largest federal building in the West when it opened in 1874. The building is listed on the National Register of Historic Places, designed by Architect Alfred B. Mullet, who also designed both the U.S. Treasury building and the Old Executive Office Building in Washington, D.C.

The **Cartoon Art Museum,** 814 Mission (between Fourth and Fifth Streets), 415/227-8666, www.cartoonart.org, chronicles the history of the in-print giggle, from cartoon sketches and finished art to toys and videos. Open Tues.–Sun. 11 A.M.–5 P.M., closed Mondays and major holidays. Admission is $6 adults, $3 seniors/students, $2 children. The first Tuesday of every month is "Pay what you wish day."

The **California Historical Society Museum,** 678 Mission St. (between Second and Third Streets), 415/357-1848, www.californiahistoricalsociety.org, displays rare historical photographs and includes exhibits on early California movers and shakers (both human and geologic), Western art of California, and frontier manuscripts. The museum bookstore features a great selection of books by California authors. The museum and bookstore are open Tues.–Sat. 11 A.M.–5 P.M. Admission is $3 adults, and $1 for seniors and children. Actually closer to the waterfront and Financial District, the **Telephone Pioneers Communications Museum,** 140 New Montgomery (at Natoma), 415/542-0182, offers electronic miscellany and telephone memorabilia dating to the 1870s. Open Tues.–Thurs. only 10 A.M.–2 P.M.

Shopping

Shop-and-drop types, please note: serious bargains are available throughout SoMa's garment district. The garment industry is the city's largest, doing a wholesale business of $5 billion annually. Most of the manufacturing factories are between Second and 11th Streets, and many have off-price retail outlets for their own wares. But you won't necessarily shop in comfort, since some

don't have dressing rooms and others are as jam-packed as the post office at tax time. Major merchandise marts, mostly for wholesalers, are clustered along Kansas and Townsend Streets. Some retail discount outlets for clothing, jewelry, and accessories are here, too, also along Brannan St. between Third and Sixth Streets. If at all possible, come any day but Saturday, and always be careful where you park. The parking cops are serious about ticketing violators. Some of the best places have to be hunted down. **Esprit Direct,** 499 Illinois (at 16th), 415/957-2540, is a warehouse-sized store offering discounts on San Francisco's hippest women's and children's wear. (Try lunch—weekdays only—at **42 Degrees,** tucked behind the outlet at 235 16th St., 415/777-5558.) Anchoring the neighborhood at the border of South Park, **Jeremy's** 2 South Park (at Second), 415/882-4929, sells hip designer clothes for one-third or more off retail. Consumer alert: because some of the items are returns, be sure to check garments for snags or other signs of wear before buying. **Harper Greer,** 580 Fourth St. (between Bryant and Brannan), 415/543-4066, offers wholesale-priced fashions for women size 14 and larger.

Since shopping outlets open, close, and change names or locations at a remarkable rate, pick up a copy of *Bargain Hunting in the Bay Area* by Sally Socolich, updated annually, or consult the "Style" section of the Sunday *San Francisco Chronicle,* which lists discount centers and factory outlets in SoMa and elsewhere around town.

Nightlife

Many SoMa restaurants (see Eating in San Francisco below) do double-duty as bars and club venues. You won't go far before finding something going on. The classic for people who wear ties even after work is **Julie's Supper Club,** 1123 Folsom (at Seventh), 415/861-0707. The **M&M Tavern,** 198 Fifth St. (at Howard), 415/362-6386, is a genuine institution, the place to find most of the *Chronicle* staff, even during the day.

Catch touring and local rock bands at **Slim's,** 333 11th St. (between Folsom and Harrison), 415/522-0333, the cutting edge for indie rockers; pretty steep cover.

Artistically and genetically expansive, in a punkish sort of way, is the **DNA Lounge,** 375 11th St. (between Harrison and Folsom), 415/626-1409, serving up dancing nightly after 9 P.M., cover on weekends.

Since SoMa in the 1970s was a nighttime playground for the bad-boys-in-black-leather set, the gay bar scene here is still going strong. The original gay bar is **The Stud,** 399 Ninth St. (at Harrison), 415/252-7883, formerly a leather bar, now a dance bar. But the hottest younger-set gay nightclub in the neighborhood, some say in the entire city, is the **Endup** ("you always end up at the Endup"), 401 Sixth St. (at Harrison), 415/357-0827, famous for serious dancing—"hot bodies," too, according to an informed source—and, for cooling down, its large outdoor deck.

Other SoMa clubs to explore (if you dare) include: **Cherry Bar,** 917 Folsom (between Fifth and Sixth), 415/974-1585, a mostly lesbian girl bar with excellent drink specials; **Holy Cow,** 1535 Folsom (between 11th and 12th), 415/621-6087; the **Hotel Utah Saloon,** 500 Fourth St. (at Bryant), 415/546-6300, featuring eclectic live music; and the dance club **1015 Folsom,** 1015 Folsom (at Sixth), 415/431-1200.

GOLDEN GATE NATIONAL RECREATION AREA

One of San Francisco's unexpected treasures, the Golden Gate National Recreation Area (GGNRA) starts in the south along Sweeney Ridge near Pacifica, then jumps north to a narrow coastal strip of land adjacent to Hwy. 1, taking in Thornton Beach, Fort Funston, the Cliff House, and other milestones before it pauses at the pilings of the Golden Gate Bridge. The GGNRA also includes Alcatraz Island, one of the nation's most infamous prison sites, and state-administered Angel Island, "Ellis Island of the West" to the Chinese and other immigrant groups. In the mid-1990s, the historic Presidio—1,480 acres of forest, coastal bluffs, military outposts, and residences adjacent to the Golden Gate Bridge—was converted from military to domestic purposes and formally included in the GGNRA. Vast tracts of the southern and western Marin County head-

lands, north of the bridge, are also included within GGNRA boundaries, making this park a true urban wonder. Much of the credit for creating the GGNRA, the world's largest urban park, goes to the late congressman Phillip Burton. Established in 1972, the recreation area as currently envisioned includes more than 36,000 acres in a cooperative patchwork of land holdings exceeding 114 square miles. The GGNRA is also the most popular of the national parks, drawing more than 20 million visitors each year.

One major attraction of the GGNRA is the opportunity for hiking—both **urban hiking** on the San Francisco side, and **wilderness hiking** throughout the Marin Headlands. Get oriented to the recreation area's trails at any visitor center (see below), look up the National Park Service website at www.nps.gov/prsf, or sign on for any of the GGNRA's excellent guided hikes and explorations. The schedule changes constantly, depending upon the season and other factors, but the following outings represent a sample of what's available on the San Francisco end of the Golden Gate Bridge: the Sutro Heights Walk, the Presidio's Mountain Lake to Fort Point Hike and Main Post Historical Walk, and the Point of the Sea Wolves Walk. National Park Service rangers also lead other guided tours through the Presidio, including a Natural History of the Presidio hike. A particularly spectacular section of the GGNRA's trail system is the 2.5-mile trek from the St. Francis Yacht Club to Fort Point and the Golden Gate Bridge. This walk is part of the still-in-progress **San Francisco Bay Trail,** a 450-mile shoreline trail system that will one day ring the entire bay and traverse nine Bay Area counties. Ambitious hikers can follow the GGNRA's **Coastal Trail** from San Francisco to Point Reyes National Seashore in Marin County. Once on the north side of the Golden Gate, possibilities for long hikes and backpacking trips are almost endless.

Special GGNRA events include such worthy offerings as a Story of the Golden Gate Bridge tour, a Family Fun at Muir Woods theater workshop, and presentations at the reserve's several former defense installations, including: Women on Military Posts, and Songs and Sounds of the Civil War (at Fort Point); Seacoast Defense (at

Baker Beach); and Rockets to Rangers (at Nike Site 88 on the Marin Headlands).

San Francisco–Side GGNRA Sights

The GGNRA includes the beaches and coastal bluffs along San Francisco's entire western edge (and both south and north), as well as seaside trails and walking and running paths along the new highway and seawall between Sloat Blvd. and the western border of Golden Gate Park.

The original Cliff House near Seal Rocks was one of San Francisco's first tourist lures, its original diversions a bit on the licentious side. That version, converted by Adolph Sutro into a family-style resort, burned to the ground in 1894 and was soon replaced by a splendid Victorian palace and an adjacent bathhouse, also fire victims. Ruins of the old **Sutro Baths** are still visible among the rocks just north. Aptly named **Seal Rocks** offshore attract vocal sea lions.

The current **Cliff House,** across the highway from Sutro Heights Park, dates from 1908 and still attracts locals and tourists alike. The views are spectacular, which explains the success of the building's Cliff House Restaurant, 415/386-3330, as well as the building's Phineas T. Barnacle pub-style deli and the Ben Butler Room bar. The GGNRA **Cliff House Visitor Center,** 415/239-2366, is a good stop for information, free or low-cost publications and maps, and books. Open daily 10 A.M.–5 P.M. A $14 million makeover of Cliff House began in 2003, to remove old facades and additions and to add a new building with a grand lobby, two-story "view" dining room, and observation deck. Renovation will also add elevators, to provide wheelchair access, and repair the beloved **Camera Obscura & Hologram Gallery** located just below the Cliff House. The **Musée Méchanique** collection of antique penny arcade amusements has been relocated to Fisherman's Wharf but may return to Cliff House at some point in the future.

Wandering northward from Cliff House, Point Lobos Ave. and then El Camino del Mar lead to San Francisco's **Point Lobos,** the city's westernmost point. There's an overlook, to take in the view. Nearby is the USS *San Francisco* Memorial, the bridge of the city's namesake ship, lost during WWII, now preserved on a clifftop. Also nearby is **Fort Miley,** 415/556-8371, which features a 4-H "adventure ropes" course. But the most spectacular thing in sight (on a clear day) is the postcard-pretty Golden Gate Bridge. You can even get there from here, on foot, via the **Coastal Trail,** a wonderful city hike that skirts Lincoln Park and the California Palace of the Legion of Honor before passing through the Seacliff neighborhood then flanking the Presidio. From Fort Point at the foot of the Golden Gate, the truly intrepid can keep on trekking—straight north across the bridge to Marin County, or east past the yacht harbors to Fort Mason and the overwhelming attractions of Fisherman's Wharf.

For some slower sightseeing, backtrack to the Presidio's hiking trails and other attractions. The GGNRA's **Presidio Visitor Center,** 102 Montgomery St. (that's a *different* Montgomery St. than the one downtown), 415/561-4323, can point you in the right direction. It's open year-round, daily 9 A.M.–5 P.M.

Or spend time exploring the coast. At low tide, the fleet of foot can beach walk (and climb) from the Golden Gate Bridge to **Baker Beach** and farther (looking back at the bridge for a seagull's-eye view). Though many flock here precisely because it is a de facto nude beach, the very naked sunbathers at Baker Beach usually hide out in the rock-secluded coves beyond the family-oriented stretch of public sand. Near Baker Beach is the miniature **Battery Lowell A. Chamberlain** "museum," a historic gun hold, home to the six-inch disappearing rifle. Weapons aficionados will want to explore more thoroughly the multitude of gun batteries farther north along the trail, near Fort Point.

Information

For information on the GGNRA included elsewhere in this chapter, see also Touring the Real Rock, The Presidio and Fort Point, and Fort Mason immediately below, and The Avenues, above. For more information on the Marin County sections of the GGNRA, see Point Reyes National Seashore and Angel Island State Park in the following chapter.

TOURING THE REAL ROCK

Visiting Alcatraz is like touring the dark side of the American dream, like peering into democracy's private demon hold. At Alcatraz, freedom is a fantasy. If crime is a universal option—and everyone behind bars at Alcatraz exercised it—then all who once inhabited this desolate island prison were certainly equal. Yet all who once lived on the Rock were also equal in other ways—in their utter isolation, in their human desperation, in their hopelessness.

Former prison guard Frank Heaney, born and raised in Berkeley, is now a consultant for the Blue & Gold Fleet's exclusive Alcatraz tour. When he started work as a correctional officer at age 21, Heaney found himself standing guard over some of America's most notorious felons, including George "Machine Gun" Kelly, Alvin "Creepy" Karpis, and Robert "The Birdman of Alcatraz" Stroud. Heaney soon realized that the terrifying reality of prison life was a far cry from Hollywood's James Cagney version.

The job was psychologically demanding, yet often boring. There was terror in the air, too. Inmates vowed—and attempted—to "break him." But he ignored both death threats and too-friendly comments on his youthful appeal. Guards were prohibited from conversing with the inmates—one more aspect of the criminals' endless isolation—but Heaney eventually got to know Machine Gun Kelly, whom he remembers as articulate and intellectual, "more like a bank president than a bank robber." Creepy Karpis, Ma Barker's right-hand man and the only man ever personally arrested by FBI Director J. Edgar Hoover, was little more than a braggart. And though the Birdman was considered seriously psychotic and spent most of his 54 prison years in solitary confinement, Heaney found him to be "untrustworthy" but rational and extremely intelligent. Many of Heaney's favorite stories are collected in his book *Inside the Walls of Alcatraz*, published by Bull Publishing and available at Pier 39 and the National Park Store gift shop.

Others who remember the Rock, both guards and inmates, are included on the **Alcatraz Cellhouse Tour,** an "inside" audio journey through prison history provided by the Golden Gate National Park Association and offered along with Blue & Gold Fleet tours to Alcatraz.

Among them is Jim Quillen, former inmate, who on the day we visit is here in person. He leans against the rusted iron doors of Cell Block A. His pained eyes scan the pocked walls and empty cells, each barely adequate as an open-air closet. Quillen spent the best years of his life on Alcatraz. "Ten years and one day," he says in a soft voice. "The tourists see the architecture, the history—all I see are ghosts. I can point to the exact spots where my friends have killed themselves, been murdered, gone completely insane."

For current information about GGNRA features and activities, contact: **Golden Gate National Recreation Area,** Fort Mason, Building 201, 415/556-0560, www.nps.gov/goga. To check on local conditions, events, and programs, you can also call the GGNRA's other visitor centers: **Cliff House,** 415/556-8642; **Fort Point,** 415/556-1693; **Marin Headlands,** 415/331-1540; **Muir Woods,** 415/388-2596; and **Presidio,** 415/561-4323.

To receive a subscription to the quarterly park newsletter and calendar of GGNRA events, join the nonprofit **Golden Gate National Parks Association,** same Fort Mason address, 415/561-3000, an organization that actively supports educational programs as well as park conservation and improvement. Basic annual membership includes five or six members-only events—such as tours of Presidio architecture, moonlight hikes to the Pt. Bonita Lighthouse, or candlelight after-hours tours of Fort Point.

Useful publications and guidebooks published by the Golden Gate National Parks Association, available at GGNRA visitor center bookstores and

That's the main reason to visit Alcatraz—to explore this lonely, hard, wind-whipped island of exile. The ghosts here need human companionship.

There is plenty else to do, too, including the ranger-guided walk around the island, courtesy of the Golden Gate National Recreation Area (GGNRA), and poking one's nose into other buildings, other times. National park personnel also offer lectures and occasional special programs. Or take an **Evening on Alcatraz** tour, to see the sun set on the city from the island. For current information, contact the GGNRA at 415/561-4700 or www.nps.gov/goga, stop by the **GGNRA Visitors Center** at Fort Funston in San Francisco, 415/239-2366, or contact the nonprofit, education-oriented Golden Gate National Park Association, 415/561-3000. (For more information about the recreation area in general, see that section elsewhere in this chapter and also Point Reyes National Seashore.)

If you're coming to Alcatraz, contact the **Blue & Gold Fleet,** Pier 41, Fisherman's Wharf, 415/705-8200, www.blueandgoldfleet.com, for general information. To make charge-by-phone ticket reservations—advisable, well in advance, since the tour is quite popular, attracting more than one million people each year—call 415/705-5555, or make reservations through the website. At last report, roundtrip fare with audio was $15.50 per adult, $10.25 per child, plus a $2.25-per-ticket reservation surcharge if you reserve your ticket by phone/Internet; there's also a $1 day-use fee in addition to the ferry price. (Be sure to be there 30 minutes early, since no refunds or exchanges are allowed if you miss the boat.) The entire audio-guided walking tour takes more than two hours, so be sure to allow yourself adequate time. (The audiotape is available in English, Japanese, German, French, Italian, and Spanish.) If at all possible, try to get booked on one of the early tours, so you can see the cellblocks and Alcatraz Island in solitude, before the rest of humanity arrives. Pack a picnic (though snacks and beverages are available), and bring all the camera and video equipment you can carry; no holds barred on photography. Wear good walking shoes, as well as warm clothes (layers best), since it can be brutally cold on Alcatraz in the fog or when the wind whips up.

In the past, the island's ruggedness made it difficult to impossible for those with limited mobility, with moderate to strenuous climbing and limited access for wheelchairs and strollers. Now wheelchair users and others with limited mobility who can't "do" the Alcatraz tour on foot can take SEAT (Sustainable Easy Access Transport) up the 12 percent grade hill one-quarter mile to the prison. Contact the Blue & Gold Fleet information line for details.

If you're not coming to Alcatraz in the immediate future, you can still take a comprehensive virtual tour, on the web at www.nps.gov/alcatraz/tours.

—*Tim Moriarty and Kim Weir*

elsewhere (such as the National Park Store on Pier 39 at Fisherman's Wharf), include the comprehensive 100-page *Park Guide,* plus *Alcatraz: Island of Change; Fort Point: Sentry at the Golden Gate;* and *Muir Woods: Redwood Refuge.* Also widely available is *The Official Map and Guide to the Presidio,* a detailed multicolored map jam-packed with historical and other information.

For a set of maps of the entire San Francisco Bay Trail ($10.95) or detailed maps of specific trail sections ($1.50 each), contact the **San Francisco Bay Trail Project,** c/o the Association of

Bay Area Governments, 510/464-7900, or order the maps online at www.abag.org. About 215 of the Bay Trail's 450 total miles of trails are completed, with planning and/or construction of the rest underway. Call the Association to volunteer trail-building labor or materials, to help with fundraising, or to lead guided walks along sections of the Bay Trail.

Also of interest to area hikers: the **Bay Area Ridge Trail,** a 400-mile ridgetop route that one day will skirt the entire bay, connecting 75 parks. For information, contact the **Bay Area Ridge**

Trail Council, 26 O'Farrell St., 415/391-9300, www.ridgetrail.org.

FORT MASON

Headquarters for the Golden Gate National Recreation Area, Fort Mason is also home to **Fort Mason Center,** a surprisingly contemporary complex of onetime military storage buildings at Marina Blvd. and Buchanan St., now hosting a variety of nonprofit arts, humanities, educational, environmental, and recreational organizations and associations.

Since the 1970s, this shoreline wasteland has been transformed into an innovative multicultural community events center—perhaps the country's premier model of the impossible, successfully accomplished. Several pavilions and the Conference Center host larger group events, though smaller galleries, theaters, and offices predominate. The variety of rotating art exhibits, independent theater performances, poetry readings, lectures and workshops, and special-interest classes offered here is truly staggering.

Expansion plans include the establishment of a marine ecology center, another theater, more ex-

SUSAN SNYDER

Fort Mason: a locus for the arts

hibit space, and another good-food-great-view restaurant. All in all, it's not surprising that Fort Mason has been studied by the Presidio's national park transition team, and even by other nations, as a supreme example of how urban eyesores can be transformed into national treasures.

Museums

The **San Francisco African American Historical & Cultural Society,** in Building C, Room 165, 415/441-0640, is a cultural and resource center featuring a library, museum (small admission), speaker's bureau, and monthly lecture series. Open Wed.–Sun. noon–5 P.M.

The **Mexican Museum,** Building D, 415/202-9700 or 415/441-0404, www.mexicanmuseum .org, is devoted exclusively to exhibitions of, and educational programs about, Mexican-American and Mexican art. Its permanent collection includes 9,000 items from five periods, including pre-Hispanic and contemporary Mexican art, and rotating exhibits attract much public attention. The changing exhibits typically focus on one particular artist or on a theme, such as *100 Years of Chroma Art Calendars.* Open Wed.–Sun. 11 A.M.–5 P.M.; admission $4 adults, $3 students and seniors. The museum plans to move downtown to the Yerba Buena Center in 2004, so call or check the website before setting out.

Exhibits at the **Museo ItaloAmericano,** in Building C, 415/673-2200, foster an appreciation of Italian art and culture. Open Wed.–Sun. noon–5 P.M. Small admission.

Definitely worth a detour is the **San Francisco Craft & Folk Art Museum,** Building A-North, 415/775-0990, www.sfcraftandfolk.org, which features rotating exhibits of American and international folk art. Open Tues.–Fri. and Sun. 11 A.M.–5 P.M.; Sat. 10 A.M.–5 P.M. Free on Saturday, 10 A.M.–noon, otherwise there's a small admission fee.

In addition to any free hours listed above, all of the museums at the center are free (and open until 7 P.M.) on the first Wednesday of every month.

Performing Arts

Fort Mason Center's 440-seat **Cowell Theater,** 415/441-3400, is a performance space that hosts events ranging from the acclaimed Solo Mio Festival and the New Pickle Circus to guest speakers such as Spalding Gray and unusual video, musical, and theatrical presentations. Among its showstoppers is the **Magic Theatre,** Building D, 415/441-8001 (business office) or 415/441-8822 (box office), which is internationally recognized as an outstanding American playwrights' theater, performing original plays by the likes of Sam Shepard and Michael McClure as well as innovative new writers.

Other Fort Mason performing arts groups include the **Performing Arts Workshop,** Building C, 415/673-2634, and the **Young Performers' Theatre,** Building C, 415/346-5550, both for young people. The **Blue Bear School of American Music,** Building D, 415/673-3600, offers lessons and workshops in rock, pop, jazz, blues, and other genres. **Bay Area Theatresports** (BATS) is an improv comedy group that performs at the **Bayfront Theater,** Building B, 415/474-8935, and **World Arts West,** Building D, 415/474-3914, promotes and produces world music and dance festivals.

Visual Arts

The **Fort Mason Art Campus** of the City College of San Francisco, Building B, 415/561-1840, is the place for instruction in fine arts and crafts. Works of students and faculty are showcased at the **Coffee Gallery,** in the Building B lobby, 415/561-1840. The 10-and-under set should head to the **San Francisco Children's Art Center,** Building C, 415/771-0292. One of the most intriguing galleries here is the **San Francisco Museum of Modern Art Artist's Gallery,** Building A-North, 415/441-4777, representing more than 1,300 artists and offering, in addition to rotating exhibits, the opportunity to rent as well as buy works on display.

Environmental Organizations

The **Endangered Species Project,** Building E, 415/921-3140, works to protect wildlife and habitat and to prevent illegal poaching and trade of endangered animals. The **Fund for Animals,** Building C, 415/474-4020, is an animal-rights organization. The **Oceanic Society,** Building E,

415/441-1106, offers environmental education programs including whale-watching trips, cruises to the Farallon Islands, and coral-reef and rainforest expeditions. The **Resource Renewal Institute,** Building D, 415/928-3774, promotes integrated environmental planning—"Green Plans"—at every level of government, both domestically and internationally. The **Tuolumne River Preservation Trust,** Building C, 415/292-3531, focuses its efforts on protecting and preserving the Tuolumne River watershed.

Greens Restaurant

No one will ever starve here, since one of the country's best vegetarian restaurants, the San Francisco Zen Center's **Greens,** is in Building A-North, 415/771-6222. It's open Tues.–Sat. for lunch, Mon.–Sat. for dinner and late-evening desserts, Sunday for brunch. The restaurant also offers **Greens-To-Go** take-out lunches Tues.–Sun.; call 415/771-6330.

Information and Services

Book Bay Bookstore, Building C-South, 415/771-1076, is run by friends of the San Francisco Public Library. Book sales are regularly held to benefit the city's public-library system.

For more complete information on Fort Mason, including a copy of the monthly *Fort Mason Calendar of Events,* contact the **Fort Mason Foundation,** Building A, Fort Mason Center, 415/441-3400, www.fortmason.org, open daily 9 A.M.–5 P.M. To order tickets for any Fort Mason events, call the **Fort Mason box office** at 415/345-7575.

GOLDEN GATE PARK

Yet another of San Francisco's impossible dreams successfully accomplished, Golden Gate Park was once a vast expanse of sand dunes. A wasteland by urban, and urbane, standards, locals got the idea that it could be a park—and a grand park, to rival the Bois de Boulogne in Paris. Frederick Law Olmsted, who designed New York's Central Park, was asked to build it. He took one look and scoffed, saying essentially that it couldn't be done. Olmsted was wrong, as it turned out, and

THE PRESIDIO AND FORT POINT

In 1994 San Francisco's **Presidio,** both national historic landmark and historic military installation, passed from the Sixth Army Command to the National Park Service, creating a new national park with 1,446 acres and some spectacular features—not the least of which are its wraparound views.

The Presidio lies directly south of the Golden Gate Bridge along the northwest tip of the San Francisco Peninsula, bordered by the Marina and Pacific Heights districts to the east and Richmond and Presidio Heights to the south. To the west and north, a coastal strip of the Golden Gate National Recreation Area frames the Presidio, which boasts some 70 miles of paths and trails of its own winding along cliffs and through eucalyptus groves and coastal flora. The 1,600 buildings here, most of them eclectic blends of Victorian and Spanish-revival styles, housed the U.S. Army beginning in 1847.

Founded by the Spanish in 1776 as one of two original settlements in San Francisco, the Presidio had a militaristic history even then, for the area commands a strategic view of San Francisco Bay and the Pacific Ocean. The Spanish garrison ruled the peninsula for the first 50 years of the city's history, chasing off Russian whalers and trappers by means of the two cannons now guarding the entrance to the Officer's Club. After 1847, when Americans took over, the Presidio became a staging center for the Indian wars, a never-used outpost during the Civil War, and more recently, head-quarters for the Sixth Army Command, which fought in the Pacific during World War II.

Though much of the Presidio looks as it has in the past, change is definitely underway; the park is required to be financially self-sufficient by 2013. To that end, the overall approach is to fill the Presidio's houses, barracks, warehouses, and other buildings with paying customers—tenants whose rents will finance renovations and ongoing maintenance. Limited new construction will be allowed, though open space will increase overall.

Some new construction has enthralled the public, in fact, despite vocal opposition to private use of public lands. A case in point is filmmaker George Lucas's $300 million, 23-acre **Letterman Digital Arts Center,** now being built where the Letterman Hospital and associated research center once stood. The Lucasfilm Ltd. enterprise will house all of Lucas's 2,500 employees and all of his movie production companies, including Industrial Light & Magic. An onsite coffee bar and restaurant, open to the public, are included in development plans.

Most of the Presidio is completely open to the public, however, and visitors may drive around and admire the neat-as-a-pin streets with their white, two-story wood Victorians and faultless lawns or trace the base's history at the **Visitor's Center** located on the Parade Grounds, 415/561-4323, www.nps.gov/prsf. Pick up a map there showing the Presidio's hiking trails, including a six-mile historic walk and two ecology trails, and ask about scheduled events and activities. Open

eventually he had the grace to admit it. William Hammond Hall, designer and chief engineer, and Scottish gardener John McLaren, the park's green-thumbed godfather, achieved the unlikely with more than a bit of West Coast ingenuity. Hall constructed a behemoth breakwater on the 1,000-acre park's west end, to block the stinging sea winds and salt spray, and started anchoring the sand by planting barley, then nitrogen-fixing lupine, then grasses. Careful grading and berming, helped along in time by windrows, further deflected the fierceness of ocean-blown storms.

"Uncle John" McLaren, Hall's successor, set about re-creating the land on a deeper level. He trucked in humus and manure to further transform sand into soil, and got busy planting more than one million trees. And that was just the beginning. In and around walkways, benches, and major park features, there were shrubs to plant, flowerbeds to establish, and pristine lawns to nurture. McLaren kept at it for some 55 years, dedicating his life to creating a park for the everlasting enjoyment of the citizenry. He bravely did battle with politicians, often beating them at their own games, to nurture and preserve "his" park for posterity. He fought with groundskeepers who tried

daily 9 A.M.–5 P.M., closed major holidays, admission free. For those bone-chilling days when the wind and fog flow through the Golden Gate, stop by the welcoming **Warming Hut** at the western end of Crissy Field, 415/561-3040, a onetime Army warehouse that's been refashioned into a café and bookstore (closed Tues. and Wed.).

Ranger-led GGNRA guided tours include the **Bay Area Ridge Trail Hike,** an exploratory lesson in the San Francisco Peninsula's geology, geography, and plant and animal life, which circumnavigates the Presidio; **Presidio Main Post Historical Walks;** and the **Ecological Restoration of the Waterfront** hike along the Crissy Field tidal marsh.

More businesslike in design but in many respects more interesting than the Presidio, **Fort Point** off Lincoln Blvd. is nestled directly underneath the southern tip of the Golden Gate Bridge and worth donning a few extra layers to visit. Officially the Fort Point National Historic Site since 1968, the quadrangular redbrick behemoth was modeled after South Carolina's Fort Sumter and completed in 1861 to guard the bay during the Civil War. However, the fort was never given the chance to test its mettle, as a grass-roots plot hatched by Confederate sympathizers in San Francisco to undermine the Yankee cause died for lack of funds and manpower, and the more palpable threat that the Confederate cruiser *Shenandoah* would blast its way into the bay was foiled by the war ending before the ship ever arrived.

Nonetheless, military strategists had the right idea situating the fort on the site of the old Spanish adobe-brick outpost of Castillo de San Joaquin, and through the years the fort-that-could was used as a garrison and general catchall for the Presidio, including a stint during World War I as barracks for unmarried officers. During the 1930s, when the Golden Gate Bridge was in its design phase, the fort narrowly missed being scrapped but was saved by the bridge's chief design engineer, Joseph B. Strauss, who considered the fort's demolition a waste of good masonry and designed the somewhat triumphal arch that now soars above it.

Fort Point these days enjoys a useful retirement as a historical museum, open Fri.–Sun. 10 A.M.–5 P.M., admission free. (Be aware, however, that Fort Point is closed when the nation is on orange or red security alert.) While the wind howls in the girders overhead, park rangers clad in Civil War regalia (many wearing long johns underneath) lead fort history tours through the park's honeycomb of corridors, staircases, and gun ports. Cannon muster is solemnly observed with a Napoleon 12-pounder field cannon. A fairly recent addition is the excellent exhibit and tribute to black American soldiers. At the bookstore, pick up some Confederate money and other military memorabilia. For more information about tours and special events, call Fort Point at 415/556-1693.

—*Taran March*

to keep people off the lush lawns, and he attempted to hide despised-on-principle statues and other graven images with bushes and shrubs. In the end he lost this last battle; after McLaren died, the city erected a statue in his honor.

McLaren's Legacy

Much of the park's appeal is its astounding array of natural attractions. The botanic diversity alone, much of it exotic, somehow reflects San Francisco's multicultural consciousness—also transplanted from elsewhere, also now as natural as the sun, the moon, the salt winds, and the tides.

The dramatic **Victorian Conservatory of Flowers,** 415/641-7978, www.conservatoryof-flowers.org, is a prim and proper presence on John F. Kennedy Drive at the eastern end of the park. Reopened in 2003 after extensive repairs, the conservatory was imported from Europe in crates and originally assembled between 1876 and 1883. It showcases a jungle of tropical plants under its soaring dome, including rare orchids, and also offers seasonal botanic displays.

The 55-acre **Strybing Arboretum and Botanical Gardens,** Ninth Ave. at Lincoln Way, 415/661-1316, www.strybing.org, features more than

7,000 different species, including many exotic and rare plants. Noted here is the collection of Australian and New Zealand plant life, along with exotics from Africa, the Americas, and Asia. Several gardens are landscaped by theme, such as the Mexican Cloud Forest and the California Redwood Grove. The serene Japanese Moon-Viewing Garden is a worthy respite when the Japanese Tea Garden is choked with tourists. The Biblical Garden is a representation of plants mentioned in the Bible or thought to have grown in the eastern Mediterranean Basin during biblical times. Quite a delight, too, is the Fragrance Garden—a collection of culinary and medicinal herbs easily appreciated by aroma and texture, labeled also in Braille. Any plant lover will enjoy time spent in the small store. The arboretum is open weekdays 8 A.M.–4:30 P.M., weekends 10 A.M.–5 P.M.; admission is free, donations appreciated. Guided tours are offered on weekday afternoons and twice a day on weekends; call for tour times and meeting places. Next door is the **San Francisco County Fair Building,** site of the annual

"fair"—in San Francisco, it's a flower show only—and home to the **Helen Crocker Russell Library,** 415/661-1316 ext. 303, containing some 18,000 volumes on horticulture and plants.

The **Japanese Tea Garden** on Tea Garden Dr. (just east of Stow Lake, between JFK and Martin Luther King Jr. Drives), 415/752-4227 (admission information) or 415/752-1171 (gift shop), is a striking and enduring attraction, started (and maintained until the family's World War II internment) by full-time Japanese gardener Maokota Hagiwara and his family. Both a lovingly landscaped garden and tea house concession—the Hagiwaras invented the fortune cookie, first served here, though Chinatown later claimed this innovation as an old-country tradition—the Tea Garden is so popular that to enjoy even a few moments of the intended serenity, visitors should arrive early on a weekday morning or come on a rainy day. The large bronze *Buddha Who Sits Through Sun and Rain Without Shelter,* cast in Japan in 1790, will surely welcome an off-day visitor. The Japanese Tea Garden is most enchanting in April, when the cherry trees are in bloom. Open daily Mar.–Dec. 8:30 A.M.–6 P.M., Jan.–Feb. 8:30 A.M.–dusk. The tea house is open 10 A.M.–5:15 P.M. Admission is $3.50 adults, $1.25 seniors and children 6–12.

Also especially notable for spring floral color in Golden Gate Park: the **Queen Wilhelmina Tulip Garden** on the park's western edge, near the restored (northern) **Dutch Windmill,** and the **John McLaren Rhododendron Dell** near the Conservatory of Flowers. The very English **Shakespeare Garden,** beyond the Academy of Sciences, is unusual any time of year, since all the plants and flowers here are those mentioned in the Bard's works. Poignant and sobering is the expansive **National AIDS Memorial Grove,** www.aidsmemorial.org, at the east end of the park between Middle Drive East and Bowling Green Drive. Regardless of whether or not you personally know anyone with AIDS, this is a good place to wander among the groves of redwoods and dogwoods, quietly contemplating the fragility of life and your place in it. The grove is maintained by volunteers; to volunteer, or for more information, call 415/750-8340.

The Japanese Tea Garden beckons those in search of serenity.

The stately **M. H. de Young Memorial Museum,** 75 Tea Garden Dr. (at Ninth Ave.), 415/750-3600, www.thinker.org, built in 1894 for the Midwinter International Exposition in honor of *Chronicle* newspaper publisher M. H. de Young, was seriously damaged in the 1989 earthquake, and a new, $135 million de Young is scheduled to open in 2005. (Until then highlights of the museum's fine collection of American art, including many 20th-century realist paintings, are on display at the Palace of the Legion of Honor.) Designed by Swiss architects Jacques Herzog and Pierre de Meuron, acclaimed for the Tate Modern in London and the Dominus Winery in the Napa Valley, the new de Young will be constructed of light colored natural materials—copper, wood, and glass—and will open to the surrounding park environment thanks to "ribbons" of windows that reflect the landscape, offer panoramic park vistas, and allow park visitors to preview museum art from the outside looking in. The new landscape design by Walter Hood will include a large public plaza with palm trees at the museum's front entrance and a "garden of enchantment" to the east. For an interactive tour of the new de Young, visit the website.

California Academy of Sciences

At home on the park's Music Concourse (between Martin Luther King Jr. and John F. Kennedy Drives), 415/750-7145, www.calacademy.org, the California Academy of Sciences is a multifaceted scientific institution, the oldest in the West, founded in 1853 to survey and study the vast resources of California and vicinity. In the academy's courtyard, note the intertwining whales in the fountain. These were sculpted by Robert Howard and originally served as the centerpiece of the San Francisco Building during the Golden Gate International Exposition of 1939-40.

Natural History Museum: Dioramas and exhibits include **Wild California,** the **African Hall** (with a surprisingly realistic waterhole), and **Life Through Time,** which offers a 3.5 billion-year journey into the speculative experience of early life on earth. At the **Hohfeld Earth & Space Hall,** the neon solar system tells the story of the universe and the natural forces that have

shaped—and still shape—the earth. Especially popular with children is **Earthquake,** a "you are there" experience that simulates the city's famous 1906 and 1989 earthquakes. The **Wattis Hall of Human Cultures** specializes in anthropology and features one of the broadest Native American museum collections in Northern California, with an emphasis on cultures in both North America and South America. The **Far Side of Science Gallery** includes 159 original Gary Larson cartoons, offering a hilarious perspective on humanity's scientific research. The **Gem and Mineral Hall** contains some real gems, like a 1,350-pound quartz crystal from Arkansas.

Morrison Planetarium: The Morrison's trippy Skyvision sky shows—famously slow-moving, realistic, and "immersive" simulations projected onto the 65-foot dome—recently included such themes as *Stars Over San Francisco* and *Above Earth.* But the Morrison's one-of-a-kind "star projector" and the worlds it created ended in late 2003 when one of the world's oldest planetariums, went dark for rebuilding. When the Morrison reopens in 2008, expect it to dazzle the crowds with more contemporary, whiz-bang special effects. Perhaps other things will remain, such as the associated Earth & Space Hall and its moon rock, meteorite, and other exhibits. At last report admission (over and above Academy admission) was $2.50 adults, $1.25 seniors/youths, free for children under 6. For more information, call 415/750-7141.

Steinhart Aquarium: The oldest aquarium in North America, the 1923 Steinhart Aquarium allows visitors to commune with the world's most diverse live fish collection, including representatives of around 600 different species (including fish, marine invertebrates, and other sea life). The stunning glass-walled, 100,000-gallon Fish Roundabout here puts visitors right in the swim of things, as if they were standing in the center of the open ocean; it's especially fun at feeding time (daily at 2 P.M.). Altogether there are 189 exhibits here, but some of the most dramatic include Sharks of the Tropics; the Penguin Environment, featuring an entire breeding colony of black-footed penguins; and The Swamp, featuring tropical critters like alligators, crocodiles, snakes, lizards, and frogs. Fun for some hands-on wet and wild exploring is California Tidepool.

The Academy of Sciences, 415/221-5100 or 415/750-7145 (24-hour recorded information), is open daily 10 A.M.–5 P.M. (9 A.M.–6 P.M. from Memorial Day weekend through Labor Day). Admission is free the first Wednesday of the month (when hours are extended until 8:45 P.M.), otherwise $8.50 adults; $5.50 youths 12–17, seniors, and students with ID; and $2 children 4–11.

Activities, Events, and Information

Kennedy Drive from 19th Ave. to Stanyan is closed to automobile traffic every Sunday; enjoy a walk, bike ride, or rollerblade. Equipment can be rented at **Lincoln Cyclery,** 772 Stanyan St., 415/221-2415, and other businesses on Stanyan, Fulton, and Haight Streets.

Friends of Recreation and Parks, 415/750-5105, www.frp.org, offers free guided tours throughout the park May–Oct. But even more active sports fans won't be disappointed. Golden Gate Park action includes archery, baseball and basketball, boating and rowing, fly-casting, football, horseback riding and horseshoes, lawn bowling, model yacht sailing—there's a special lake for just that purpose—plus polo, roller skating, soccer, and tennis. In addition to the exceptional Children's Playground, there are two other kiddie play areas. Free **Golden Gate Band Concerts** are offered at 2 P.M. on Sunday and holidays at the park's Music Concourse. The **Midsummer Music Festival** in Stern Grove, Sloat Blvd. at 19th Ave., is another fun, and free, park program. Scheduled on consecutive Sundays from mid-June through August, it's quite popular, so come as early as possible. (For exact dates and program information, call the park office, listed below.) A variety of other special events are regularly scheduled in Golden Gate Park, including **A la Carte, a la Park,** San

Francisco's "largest outdoor dining event." This gala gourmet fest, with themed pavilions, showcases the wares of Bay Area restaurants and Sonoma County wineries, the talents of celebrity chefs, and a wide variety of entertainment. It's a benefit for the San Francisco Shakespeare Festival, which offers an annual schedule of free public performances in August. A la Carte, a la Park is usually scheduled in late summer, over the three-day Labor Day weekend. Call 415/458-1988 for information.

To save money on visits to multiple park attractions, purchase a **Culture Pass** for $10 at the park office in ivy-covered **McLaren Lodge,** 501 Stanyan (at Fulton, on the park's east side), 415/831-2700, open weekdays 8 A.M.–5 P.M., which offers free tours of the park, events and activities, and maps. The park's official website is www.parks.sfgov.org.

There's also a park visitor center downstairs in the 1925 Willis Polk–designed **Beach Chalet** at Ocean Beach, 1000 Great Highway, with Depression-era murals, mosaics, and wood carvings commissioned by the Works Progress Administration (WPA). Upstairs is the **Beach Chalet Brewery & Restaurant,** 415/386.8439, www.beachchalet.com. Light meals and snacks are available at other concessions, including the Academy of Sciences and the **Japanese Tea Garden Teahouse** (fortune cookies and tea). There is also great choice in restaurants near the intersection of Ninth Ave. and Irving, or along Haight and Stanyan Streets.

To reach the museums and tea garden via public transportation, board a westbound #5-Fulton bus on Market St., climbing off at Fulton and Eighth Avenue. After 6 P.M. and on Sunday and holidays, take #38-Geary to Geary and Park Presidio. Call 415/673-MUNI or check www.sfmuni.com for other routes and schedule information.

Staying in San Francisco

San Francisco is an expensive city, for the most part. A first-time visitor's first impression might be that no one is welcome here unless they show up in a Rolls Royce. What elsewhere would be considered rather high rent is charged for the "standard" room, two persons, one bed, in peak summer season. (Many hotels offer off-season and weekend deals; always ask about specials before booking.) Most also have higher-priced suites, and if you feel the need to drop $500 or $1,000 (or more) per night on a suite, you'll find plenty of places in town that will be more than happy to accommodate you. If you can afford these prices ("tariffs," actually), you'll not be disappointed. And some of the city's four- and five-star hotels also rank among its most historic, survivors of the great 1906 earthquake and fire.

That said, a little looking uncovers accommodation options suitable for the rest of us. San Francisco offers three hostels affiliated with Hostelling International, in addition to other hostels and inexpensive options. Other than the hostels, some dirt-cheap fleabags can be found, but they're often in seedy areas; budget travelers with city savvy, street smarts, and well-honed self-preservation skills might consider these establishments, but women traveling solo should avoid them. (In the context of truly low-budget accommodations, "European-style" generally means "the bathrooms are in the hallway.")

City-style motels offer another world of possibilities. Some reasonably priced ones are scattered throughout the city, though Lombard St. (west of Van Ness) is the place to go for overwhelming concentrations of motel choice. The city also supports a wide variety of bed-and-breakfast inns, with ambiences ranging from Haight-Ashbury-style funk to very proper Victoriana.

In general, San Francisco offers great choices in the midrange hotel market, including a number of "boutique" hotels. Many of these attractive and intimate hotels—old-timers and aging grand dames now renovated and redecorated for the modern carriage trade—are well located, near visitor attractions and public transit. Lack of convenient off-street parking is rarely a drawback, since most offer some sort of valet parking arrangement. Very good to exceptional restaurants—and room service—are often associated with boutique hotels. When travel is slow, most notably in winter, off-season and package deals can make these small hotels (and others) genuine bargains. Do check around before signing in. Also check at the visitors center on Market St., since some establishments offer special coupons and other seasonal inducements. Many boutique and fine hotels also offer substantial discounts to business travelers and to members of major "travel-interested" groups, including the American Automobile Association (AAA) and the American Association of Retired People (AARP). The visitor center is located at Benjamin Swig Pavilion on the lower level of Hallidie Plaza at Market and Powell Streets. Open weekdays 9 A.M.–5 P.M., Sat. and Sun. until 3 P.M., 415/391-2000. Or see the visitors bureau website, www.sfvisitor.org. You can also call 415/391-2001 24 hours a day for a recorded message listing daily events and activities.

Reservation Services

If you're unable to make an accommodations choice well in advance, or if you'd rather let someone else do the detail work, contact a local reservations service.

San Francisco Reservations, 510/628-4450, or 800/677-1550, www.hotelres.com, offers a no-fee reservations service for more than 200 hotels, most of these in San Francisco, and keeps current on discounts, specials, and packages. The company offers preferred rates for business travelers at some of the city's finest hotels, including many of the boutiques. With one call, you can also take advantage of their free best-deal car rental reservations service. Reservation lines are open daily 7 A.M.–11 P.M.

Places to Stay, 650/392-1705, or 866/826-3850, www.placestostay.com, is a Bay Area-based online reservation service, with over 150 properties in the San Francisco Bay Area and elsewhere. The

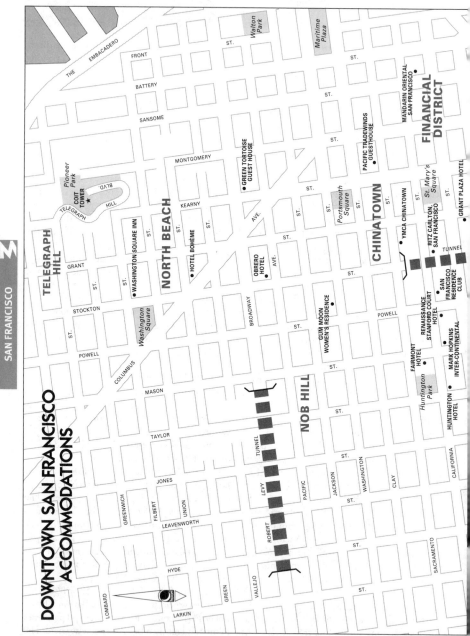

DOWNTOWN SAN FRANCISCO ACCOMMODATIONS

TELEGRAPH HILL

NORTH BEACH

CHINATOWN

FINANCIAL DISTRICT

NOB HILL

Pioneer Park

COIT TOWER

Washington Square

Portsmouth Square

St. Mary's Square

Huntington Park

Walton Park

Maritime Plaza

• WASHINGTON SQUARE INN
• HOTEL BOHÈME
• OBRERO HOTEL
• GREEN TORTOISE GUEST HOUSE
• GUM MOON WOMEN'S RESIDENCE
• PACIFIC TRADEWINDS GUESTHOUSE
• YMCA CHINATOWN
• RITZ-CARLTON, SAN FRANCISCO
• SAN FRANCISCO RESIDENCE CLUB
• RENAISSANCE STANFORD COURT HOTEL
• FAIRMONT HOTEL
• MARK HOPKINS INTER-CONTINENTAL
• HUNTINGTON HOTEL
• MANDARIN ORIENTAL SAN FRANCISCO
• GRANT PLAZA HOTEL

THE EMBACADERO
FRONT
BATTERY
SANSOME
MONTGOMERY
KEARNY
GRANT
STOCKTON
POWELL
COLUMBUS
MASON
TAYLOR
JONES
LEAVENWORTH
HYDE
LARKIN

BLVD.
HILL
TELEGRAPH

BROADWAY

POWELL

GREENWICH
FILBERT
UNION
GREEN
VALLEJO
LOMBARD

PACIFIC
JACKSON
WASHINGTON
CLAY
SACRAMENTO
CALIFORNIA

TUNNEL
LEVY
ROBERT
TUNNEL

ST.

SAN FRANCISCO

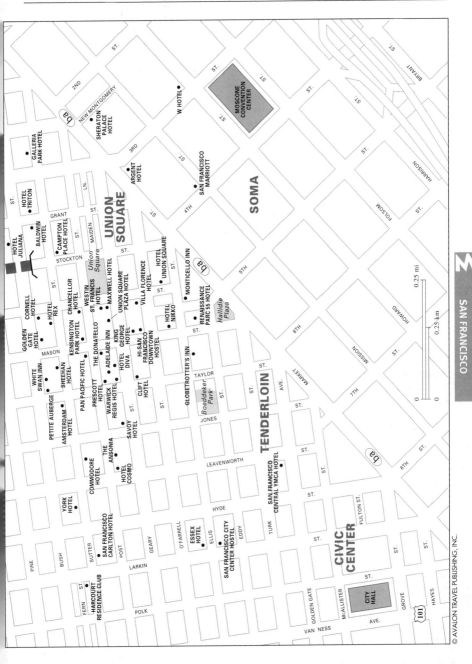

© AVALON TRAVEL PUBLISHING, INC.

company is a clearinghouse for hotel bookings, and offers competitive prices on the city's midrange and luxury hotels. The service is free, but prepayment is required at the time of booking, and cancellation fees may apply.

Bed and Breakfast San Francisco, 415/899-0060 or 800/452-8249, www.bbsf.com, offers referrals to a wide range of California bed-and-breakfasts—everything from houseboat and home stays to impressive Victorians and country-style inns—especially in San Francisco, the Napa-Sonoma wine country, and the Monterey Peninsula.

HOSTELS AND OTHER CHEAP SLEEPS: UNDER $50

San Francisco is full of shoestring-priced hostels renting dorm-style bunks for around $18–28 per person per night. Many also have higher-priced private rooms for around $35–48. Some hostels are open to everybody; others, as noted below, are open only to international travelers. Most have group kitchen facilities, laundry facilities, and helpful staff to give you hot tips on seeing the city.

Hostelling International

The Hostelling International **San Francisco City Center Hostel** is the city's newest, opened since late 2002 and centrally located at 685 Ellis St. (between Larkin and Hyde Sts.), 415/474-5721 or 800/909-4776 #62, fax 415/776-0775, www.norcalhostels.org. Just a stroll away from the new Asian Art Museum and Civic Center performance arts venues as well as Union Square, the theater district, and Chinatown, this seven-story 1927 hotel has been beautifully restored. The hostel, once the Atherton Hotel, features 75 rooms, each designed for two to five people, each with a private bathroom. The 12 private rooms feature either a double bed or two twin beds; 62 dormitory-style rooms, both single-gender and coed, feature four or five beds. Linen and towels are provided. A fully stocked shared kitchen, great common areas, 24-hour building access, on-site Internet kiosks, daily activities and excursions, luggage storage and lockers, bike

storage, valet parking, and a full-time housekeeping staff are some of the pluses. Price is another—$22–25 per person for a dorm stay, $66–69 per private room. Make reservations—essential in summer—by mail, phone, fax, or online (at least 48 hours in advance) and confirm with a major credit card (Visa, Mastercard).

Near all the downtown and theater district hubbub is the 285-bed HI-USA **San Francisco Downtown Hostel,** 312 Mason St. (between Geary and O'Farrell), 415/788-5604 or 800/909-4776 #02, fax 415/788-3023, www.norcalhostels.org, another good choice for budget travelers, $22–25 per person for dorm stays. This hotel-style hostel, once the Hotel Virginia, offers double and triple rooms—most share a bathroom—and amenities from kitchen to baggage storage and vending machines. Laundry facilities are nearby. The desk is essentially open for check-in 24 hours; no lockout, no curfew, no chores. Family rooms available. Groups welcome, by reservation only, and reservations for summer stays are essential for everyone and should be made at least 30 days in advance. Reserve online or by mail, phone, or fax with Visa or MasterCard. Rates include linens, but bring your own towel. Ask about the best nearby parking.

The HI-USA **San Francisco Fisherman's Wharf Hostel** is just west of the wharf at Fort Mason, Bldg. 240, 415/771-7277, fax 415/771-1468, www.norcalhostels.org, $21–23 per person. It's a local institution—located on a hill overlooking the bay and occupying part of the city's urban national park, the Golden Gate National Recreation Area. Close to the "Bikecentennial" bike route, Marina Green, and the cultural attractions of the Fort Mason complex, the hostel is within an easy stroll of Fisherman's Wharf and Ghirardelli Square, as well as Chinatown and downtown (you could take the cable car).

The hostel itself is one of HI-USA's largest—and finest—offering a total of 160 beds in clean rooms; one chore a day expected. Popular with all age groups and families, amenities include lots of lounge space, a big kitchen, plenty of food storage, laundry facilities, and pay lockers for baggage. No lockout or curfew. Family rooms are available, as is parking, and it's wheelchair accessible. The ride board here is helpful for travelers without wheels. Guests can also participate in hostel-sponsored hikes, tours, and bike rides. Reservations are essential for groups and advisable for others—especially in summer, when this place is jumping. Rates include linen and free breakfast; 14-day maximum, no minimum stay. Reservations accepted by mail, phone, fax, or online at least 48 hours in advance; confirm with a major credit card (Visa, Mastercard).

Other Hostels

The excellent **Green Tortoise Guest House,** 494 Broadway, 415/834-1000, fax 415/956-4900, www.greentortoise.com, sits on the corner of Broadway and Kearny, where Chinatown runs into North Beach. It offers a kitchen, laundry, sauna, free internet access, and complimentary breakfast. No curfew. Rates: single/double $48, triple $56, and quads $58.

The **Interclub Globe Hostel,** 10 Hallam Place (south of Market near the Greyhound station, just off Folsom), 415/431-0540, is a fairly large, lively place located in the heart of SOMA with clean four-bed hotel rooms, a private sundeck, community lounge, pool table, café, and laundry room. The Globe is specifically for foreign guests, usually students, but these can also include Americans who present passports with stamps verifying their own international travels. Open 24 hours, no curfew. Dorm beds $19 per person, singles/doubles $47. Also in the area and strictly for international travelers ("operated by students for students" and affiliated with the American Association of International Hostels) are two other SoMa budget outposts: the **European Guest House,** 761 Minna (between Eighth and Ninth Streets), 415/861-6634, with $18-per-person dorm stays and $40 private rooms, and the affiliated **San Francisco International Student Center,** 1188 Folsom (near BrainWash), 415/487-1463 or 415/255-8800, both offering dorm-style accommodations ($15 per person) and basic amenities.

North of Market, the **Globetrotter's Inn,** 225 Ellis St. (at Mason, one block west of Powell), 415/346-5786 (or 415/673-4048 to reach guests), offers $15 dorm beds and $27 private rooms (per person). In the Chinatown area, the lively **Pacific Tradewinds Guest House,** 680 Sacramento St., 415/433-7970 or 800/486-7975, www.sanfranciscohostel.org, is in a prime spot near the Transamerica Pyramid. Widely regarded as the friendliest hostel in the city, the Pacific offers eight-bed rooms or larger dorm rooms for $18–20 per person per night, $108–120 per week; rates include free tea and coffee all day, use of a fully equipped kitchen, Internet access, free maps, laundry service, fax service, and long-term storage. The cozy lounge is a nice place to relax and chat with fellow travelers. No curfew.

Boardinghouses

A good budget bet in the Mission District is the **San Francisco International Guest House,** 2976 23rd St. (at Harrison), 415/641-1411, an uncrowded Victorian popular with Europeans. Accommodations include two- to four-bed dorm rooms, as well as four couples rooms (all $15 per person); five day minimum stay. It's geared toward longer-term stays and usually full. Also a good choice for a longer visit is the **Harcourt Residence Club,** 1105 Larkin, 415/673-7720, where a stay includes two meals a day, Sunday brunch, and access to TV. Unlike most other residence hotels, this one attracts international students—a younger clientele. Weekly rates: $175–275 per person. Inexpensive in Chinatown for women only is the **Gum Moon Women's Residence,** 940 Washington (at Stockton), 415/421-8827. Singles and doubles $22–26, weekly rate for singles and doubles $88/105.

The large **San Francisco Central YMCA Hotel,** 220 Golden Gate Ave. (at Leavenworth), 415/885-0460, www.centralymcasf.org, is in an unappealing area two blocks north of Market at Leavenworth, with adequate rooms for women and men (double locks on all doors), plus a pool, gym, and the city's only indoor track—a plus for runners, since you won't want to run through the neighborhood (for fun, anyway). Room rates include continental breakfast: dorm beds (summer only) $23.50, singles $39, doubles $56, triples $82.50. Hostel beds are also available, for travelers only. Another "Y" option closer to downtown is the men-only **YMCA Chinatown,** 855 Sacramento St. (between Stockton and Grant), 415/576-9622, singles $35–38.

SOME HIP SAN FRANCISCO STAYS

Every city has its style, reflected in how things appear, of course, but mostly in how they feel. The following establishments offer just a sample of that inimitable San Francisco attitude.

The Phoenix Inn at 601 Eddy St. (at Larkin), 415/776-1380 or 800/248-9466, www.the-phoenixhotel.com, is more than just a 1950s motel resurrected with flamingo pink and turquoise paint. It's a subtle see-and-be-seen art scene, first attracting rock 'n' roll stars and now attracting almost everybody—*the* place in San Francisco to spy on members of the cultural elite. This is, for example, the only place Sonic Youth ever stays in San Francisco. Just-plain-famous folks like Keanu Reaves and Courtney Love can also be spied from time to time. Like the trendy, on-site restaurant, **Buddha**, even the heated swimming pool here is famous, due to its Francis Forlenza mural, *My Fifteen Minutes—Tumbling Waves,* the center of a big state-sponsored stink over whether it violated health and safety codes (since public pool bottoms are supposed to be white). "That's how it is up at the corner of Eddy and Larkin, where the limos are always parkin'," according to the inn's complimentary *Phoenix Fun Book,* a cartoon-style coloring book history illustrated by *Bay Guardian* artist Lloyd Dangle. (Also as a service for guests, the Phoenix sporadically publishes its own hippest-of-the-hip guide to San Francisco, *Beyond Fisherman's Wharf.*)

Accommodations at the Phoenix—the inn named for the city's mythic ability to rise from its own ashes, as after the fiery 1906 earthquake—are glass-fronted, uncluttered, pool-facing '50s motel rooms upscaled to ultramodern, yet not particularly ostentatious, with handmade bamboo furniture, tropical plants, and original local art on the walls. Phoenix services include complimentary continental breakfast (room service also available), a guest library that offers made-in-San Francisco movies (plus a film library with 20 "band on the road" films)—and a complete massage service, including Swedish, Esalen, Shiatsu, even poolside massage. In addition to concierge services, the Phoenix also offers blackout curtains, an on-call voice doctor (for lead vocalists with scratchy throats), and free VIP passes to SoMa's underground dance clubs. Regular rates: $50–100 midweek, $100–150 weekends, and $150–250 for each of the three suites, including the Tour Manager Suites. Ask about deals, including the "special winter rate" for regular customers (subject to availability), with the fourth night free.

Awesomely hip, too, is the playful **Hotel Triton** on Grant, in the heart of the city's downtown gallery district. The onetime Beverly Plaza Hotel just across from the Chinatown Gateway has been reimagined and reinvented by Bill Klimpton, the man who started the boutique hotel trend in town in 1980. The Triton's artsy ambience is startling and entertaining, boldly announcing itself in the lobby with sculpted purple, teal, and gold columns; odd tassle-headed, gold brocade "dervish" chairs; and mythic Neptunian imagery on the walls. Rooms are comfortable and contemporary, with custom-designed

The **San Francisco Residence Club,** 861 California St. (at Powell), 415/421-2220, www.sfresclub.com, is a European style pension on Nob Hill. Rates include full breakfast and dinner, and there's a comfortable lounge and garden dining area. Daily rates start at $55 per person, weekly rates at $370.

BUDGET HOTELS: $50–100

Perhaps the epitome of San Francisco's casual, low-cost European-style stays is the **Adelaide Inn,** 5 Isadora Duncan Ct. (in the theater district, off Taylor between Geary and Post), 415/441-2261. Reservations are advisable for the 18 rooms with shared baths. Rates include continental breakfast. Also in the area, **The Ansonia,** 711 Post, 415/673-2670, is a real find. This small hotel has a friendly staff, comfortable lobby, nice rooms, a laundry, and breakfast and dinner (except on Sunday). Student monthly rates available.

Close to Union Square, the **Gates Hotel,** 140 Ellis (at Cyril Magnin), 415/781-0430, www.gateshotel.com, features basic rooms. A budget

geometric mahogany furniture, sponge-painted or diamond-patterned walls, original artwork by Chris Kidd, and unusual tilework in the bathrooms. Each guest room reflects one of three basic configurations: a king-size bed with camelback upholstered headboards, similar double beds, or oversized daybeds that double as a couch. Imaginative guest suites include the kaleidoscopic J. Garcia suite, furnished with swirls of colorful fabrics and a self-portrait of Jerry next to the bed. All rooms include soundproof windows, same-day valet/laundry service, room service, color TV with remote (also cable and movie channels), in-room fax, voice mail, and two-line phones with long cords and dataports. Basic rates: $150–250 for deluxe rooms and suites. A nice feature of this and other Klimpton-owned hotels, too, is the fully stocked honor bar—unusual in that items are quite reasonably priced. For more information or reservations, contact Hotel Triton, 342 Grant Ave., 415/394-0500 or 800/800-1299, www.hotel-tritonsf.com.

Affordable style is apparent and available at other small San Francisco hotels, including Klimpton's Prescott Hotel, home to Wolfgang Puck's Postrio Restaurant. But there's nothing else in town quite like Haight-Ashbury's **Red Victorian Bed and Breakfast Inn,** a genuine blast from San Francisco's past. This 1904 survivor is red, all right, and it's a bed-and-breakfast—but except for the architecture, it's not very Victorian. The style is early-to-late Summer of Love. Downstairs is the Peace Arts Bazaar, a New Age shopper's paradise.

(Peace Arts also offers a coffee house, computer networking services, meditation room, and gallery of meditative art with calligraphic paintings to help you program yourself, subliminally and otherwise, with proper consciousness.) Everything is casual and *very* cool—just two blocks from Golden Gate Park and its many attractions.

Upstairs, the Red Victorian's 18 guest rooms range from modest to decadent, with sinks in all rooms; some have private baths, others share. (If you stay in a room that shares the Aquarium Bathroom, you'll be able to answer the question: "What happens to the goldfish when you flush the toilet?") The Summer of Love Room features genuine '60s posters on the walls and a tie-dyed canopy over the bed. The Peace Room has an unusual skylight, though the Skylight Room beats the band for exotica. Or get back to nature in the Japanese Tea Garden Room, the Conservatory, or the Redwood Forest Room. Expanded continental breakfast (with granola and fresh bakery selections) and afternoon popcorn hour are included in the rates, which range from $50–100 shared bath and $100–150 private bath to $150–250 for suites (with specials if you stay over three days, two-night minimum on weekends). Spanish, German, and French spoken. No smoking, no TVs, no pets, and leave your angst on the sidewalk. Well-behaved children under parental supervision are welcome. Make reservations for a summer stay well in advance. For more information, contact: The Red Victorian Bed and Breakfast Inn, 1665 Haight St., 415/864-1978, www.redvic.com.

SAN FRANCISCO

gem in the Chinatown area, the **Obrero Hotel,** 1208 Stockton, 415/989-3960, offers just a dozen cheery bed-and-breakfast rooms with bathrooms down the hall. Full breakfast included. Another best bet is the **Grant Plaza Hotel,** 465 Grant Ave. (between Pine and Bush), 415/434-3883 or 800/472-6899, where amenities include private baths with hair dryers, telephones with voice mail, and color TV. Group rates available. Unpretentious and reasonably priced (private bathrooms) is the **Union Square Plaza Hotel,** 432 Geary (between Powell and Mason), 415/776-7585.

A few blocks north of the Civic Center between Hyde and Larkin, in a borderline bad neighborhood, is the justifiably popular **Essex Hotel,** 684 Ellis St., 415/474-4664 or 800/443-7739 in California, 800/453-7739 from elsewhere in the country. The hotel offers small rooms with private baths and telephones; some have TV. Free coffee. It's especially popular in summer—when rates are slightly higher—with foreign tourists, particularly Germans. Weekly rates, too.

Noteworthy for its comfort, antiques, and fresh flowers is the small **Golden Gate Hotel,**

775 Bush St. (between Powell and Mason), 415/392-3702 or 800/835-1118, www.goldengatehotel.com. Sixteen of the rooms have private bath; the other seven, with shared bath, are less expensive. Rates include complimentary breakfast and afternoon tea.

Located right across from the Chinatown gate just off Union Square, the bright and comfortable **Baldwin Hotel,** 321 Grant Ave. (between Sutter and Bush), 415/781-2220 or 800/622-5394, www.baldwinhotel.com, offers comfortable guest rooms with TV and telephones with modem hookups. Weekly rates available.

BOUTIQUE HOTELS: $100–150

Styled after a 1920s luxury liner, the **Commodore Hotel,** 825 Sutter St., 415/923-6800 or 800/338-6848, www.thecommodorehotel.com, is a fun place to stay downtown. All of the rooms are spacious, with modern bathrooms and data ports on the phones. Downstairs, the **Titanic Café** serves California-style breakfast and lunch, and the Commodore's **Red Room** is a plush cocktail lounge decorated with rich red velvets, pearlized vinyl, and red tile. Other stylish Joie de Vivre hotels near Union Square include the **Hotel Bijou** and the **Andrews Hotel;** for details, see www.jdvhospitality.com.

Between the theater district and Nob Hill is the onetime Amsterdam Hotel, now **USA Hostels San Francisco,** 749 Taylor St. (between Bush and Sutter), 415/673-3277 or 800/637-3444, www.usahostels.com, with clean, comfortable, spacious private rooms, all with queen bed, TV, and private marble-tiled bathrooms. Four-bed dorms also have private baths. The hostel includes a complete kitchen, lounge, two large patios, laundry facilities, Internet access, and complimentary all-you-can-eat pancake and waffle breakfast. (Dinner is $4.) Dorm beds are $14–21, private rooms $35–54.

Near Union Square, the **Sheehan Hotel,** 620 Sutter St. (at Mason), 415/775-6500 or 800/848-1529 in the U.S. and Canada, www.sheehanhotel.com, is a real find—a surprisingly elegant take on economical downtown accommodations. Rooms have cable TV and phones; some have private baths, others have European-style shared baths (these the bargains). Other facilities include an Olympic-size lap pool, a fitness and exercise room, and a downstairs tearoom and wine bar. The hotel is close to shopping, art, BART, and other public transportation. Discount parking is available. Rates include continental breakfast, and children under 12 stay free with parent(s).

Quite charming and quite French, between Union Square and Nob Hill, is the **Cornell Hotel,** 715 Bush St. (at Powell), 415/421-3154 or 800/232-9698, www.cornellhotel.com, where rates include breakfast; all rooms are nonsmoking. Another best bet, and a bargain for the quality, is the **Chancellor Hotel,** 433 Powell (on Union Square), 415/362-2004 or 800/428-4748, www.chancellorhotel.com, offering elegant rooms within walking distance of just about everything. (Or hop the cable car.)

BOUTIQUE HOTELS: $150–250

San Francisco's bouquet of European-style boutique hotels is becoming so large that it's impossible to fit the flowers in any one container. In addition to those mentioned above, the following sampling offers an idea of the wide variety available. Most of the city's intimate and stylish small hotels are included in the annual San Francisco Convention & Visitors Bureau Lodging Guide, listed among all other accommodations options, by area, and not otherwise distinguished from more mainstream hostelries. Two clues to spotting a possible "boutique": the number of rooms (usually 75 to 150, rarely over 200) and prices (for a double room) over $100.

Near Union Square and Nob Hill

The 111-room **Hotel Diva,** 440 Geary (between Mason and Taylor, right across from the Curran and Geary Theaters), 415/885-0200 or 800/553-1900, www.hoteldiva.com, is a chrome-faced contemporary Italian classic, awarded "Best Hotel Design" honors by *Interiors* magazine. Special features include a complete business center—with computers, wireless Internet, and high-speed access, you name it—daily newspaper, complimentary breakfast delivered to your door, meeting facilities, a 24-hour fitness center, and maid service twice a day.

Cable cars roll right by the six-floor **Hotel Union Square,** 114 Powell St., 415/397-3000 or 800/553-1900, www.hotelunionsquare.com, one of the city's original boutiques, with an art deco lobby and 131 boldly decorated, stylishly contemporary rooms blending with the building's old-brick San Francisco soul. Multiple amenities, including continental breakfast and on-site parking. Wonderful rooftop suites with gardens.

The onetime Elks Lodge #3 is now the 87-room **Kensington Park Hotel,** 450 Post St., 415/788-6400 or 800/553-1900, www.kensingtonparkhotel.com, just steps from Union Square. Its parlor lobby still sports the original hand-painted Gothic ceiling and warm Queen Anne floral decor. Guests enjoy all the amenities, including financial district limo service, a fitness center, complimentary continental breakfast, and afternoon tea and sherry. Inquire about hotel/theater packages, since Theatre On The Square is also located here, along with **Farallon** restaurant.

The century-old **King George Hotel,** 334 Mason (at Geary), 415/781-5050 or 800/288-6005, www.kinggeorge.com, is a cozy and charming stop near Geary St. theaters and Union Square. Breakfast and afternoon tea served daily in the traditional English **Windsor Tearoom.** Ask about seasonal discounts and other specials, with doubles as low as $85.

Fairly reasonable, near the theater scene, and très retro is artsy yet relaxed **Hotel Cosmo** (formerly the Bedford), 761 Post St., 415/673-6040 or 800/252-7466, www.hotel-cosmo.com, a 17-story 1929 hotel featuring refurbished art deco–style guest rooms as well as more Victorian rooms in florals and pastels. The basics here include in-room coffee, hairdryers, iron, and ironing board. Also appreciate the rotating local art on exhibit. Another good choice in the vicinity is the stylish art deco **Maxwell Hotel,** 386 Geary, 415/986-2000, or 888/734-6299. Specials can go as low as $109 Also close to the theaters is the wonderful 1913 **Savoy Hotel,** 580 Geary, 415/441-2700 or 800/227-4223, www.thesavoyhotel.com, a taste of French provincial with period engravings, imported furnishings, and goose down featherbeds and pillows. Amenities include complimentary afternoon sherry and tea.

Closer to Nob Hill and Chinatown is the nine-floor **Hotel Juliana,** 590 Bush St., 415/392-2540 or 866/325-9457, www.julianahotel.com, offering deals in the off-season. The 107 rooms and suites have in-room coffee makers, hair dryers, and irons and ironing boards. Stylish lobby. Other amenities include complimentary evening wine, morning limo service to the Financial District (just a few blocks away), and the on-site **Malisa** restaurant, serving "nuevo" French-Latin American bistro fare.

Also within an easy stroll of Nob Hill: the elegant art deco **York Hotel,** 940 Sutter St., 415/885-6800 or 800/808-9675 in the U.S. and Canada, www.yorkhotel.com, used as the setting for Alfred Hitchcock's *Vertigo.* The York offers the usual three-star comforts, including limousine service and complimentary breakfast.

The **Villa Florence Hotel,** 225 Powell St., 415/397-7700 or 866/823-4669, www.villaflorence.com, features a 16th-century Tuscany/Italian Renaissance theme, and American-style European ambience. The colorful and comfortable guest rooms feature soundproofed walls and windows—a good idea above the cable cars and so close to Union Square—as well as in-room coffeemakers and all basic amenities. The hotel has a beauty salon and features the adjacent (and outstanding) NorCal-NorItal **Kuleto's Restaurant** and antipasto bar, 415/397-7720.

For an all-American historical theme, consider the **Monticello Inn,** 127 Ellis (between Powell and Cyril Magnin), 415/392-8800 or 866/778-6169, www.monticelloinn.com. Its cool colonial-style lobby features Chippendale reproductions and a wood-burning fireplace. Rooms feature early-American decor, soundproofed walls and windows, refrigerators, honor bars, phones with data ports and voice mail, and other amenities. Complimentary continental breakfast is served in the lobby. The inn's adjacent **Puccini & Pinetti,** 415/392-5500, is a highly regarded Cal-Italian restaurant well patronized by theatergoers.

Between Union Square and Nob Hill is **Hotel Rex,** 562 Sutter (between Powell and Mason), 415/433-4434 or 800/433-4434,

CITY-STYLE BED-AND-BREAKFASTS

San Francisco's bed-and-breakfast inns can be an intimate alternative to the city's large hotels. Most B&Bs are restored historic houses with eight to 20 rooms, priced in the $150–250 range (for two); a few offer at least some rooms for under $100. Many of the city's bed-and-breakfasts offer standard hotel services—concierge, bellman, valet/laundry, and room service.

The **Chateau Tivoli** townhouse, 1057 Steiner St., 415/776-5462 or 800/228-1647, www.chateau-tivoli.com, is an 1892 Queen Anne landmark with an astounding visual presence. "Colorful" just doesn't do justice as a description of this Alamo Square painted lady. The Tivoli's eccentric exterior architectural style is electrified by 18 historic colors of paint, plus gold leaf. Painstaking restoration is apparent inside, too, from the very Victorian, period-furnished parlors to exquisite, individually decorated guest rooms, each reflecting at least a portion of the city's unusual social history. (Imagine, under one roof: Enrico Caruso, Aimee Crocker, Isadora Duncan, Joaquin Miller, Jack London, opera singer Luisa Tettrazini, and Mark Twain. Somehow, it is imaginable, since the mansion was once the residence of the city's pre-earthquake Tivoli Opera.)

Chateau Tivoli offers nine rooms and suites, all but two rooms with private baths, two with fireplaces.

Onetime home to Archbishop Patrick Riordan, the **Archbishop's Mansion,** 1000 Fulton St. (at Steiner), 415/563-7872 or 800/543-5820, www.thearchbishopsmansion.com, is also exquisitely restored, offering comfortable rooms and suites in a French Victorian mood. Some rooms have fireplaces and in-room spas, and all have phones and TVs. Continental breakfast.

Near Alamo Square, the **Grove Inn,** 890 Grove St., 415/929-0780 or 800/829-0780, www.grove-inn.com, is a restored Italianate Victorian inn with 19 rooms (some share baths). Off-street parking available for a small fee. Complimentary breakfast.

Close to the Civic Center arts scene is the **Inn San Francisco,** 943 S. Van Ness Ave., 415/641-0188 or 800/359-0913, www.innsf.com, a huge, renovated 1872 Italianate Victorian with 21 guest rooms, double parlors, and a sun deck. The five bargain rooms here share two bathrooms, but most rooms feature private baths. All include TVs, radios, telephones, and refrigerators; some have hot tubs or in-room spa tubs; and two also have fireplaces and balconies.

www.jdvhospitality.com,, furnished in 1930s style and "dedicated to the arts and literary world," refurbished and reopened in February 2003. Rates include a complimentary evening glass of wine. Doubles $175–219. Also reasonable by boutique hotel standards is the **San Francisco Carlton Hotel,** 1075 Sutter (at Larkin), 415/673-0242 or 800/922-7586, www.carltonhotel.com, placed on Condé Nast Traveler's 1999 Gold List and offering 165 comfortable rooms with Queen Anne-style chairs and pleasant decor, as well as the on-site Oak Room Grille.

Among other well-regarded small hostelries in the vicinity of Union Square is the wheelchair-accessible, 80-room **Warwick Regis Hotel,** 490 Geary St., 415/928-7900 or 800/203-3232 in the U.S. and Canada, www.warwicksf.com, furnished with French and English Louis XVI antiques and offering exceptional service. Ameni-

ties include hair dryers and small refrigerators in every room, plus cable TV, complimentary morning newspaper, and on-site café and bar. Also exceptional is **The Donatello,** 501 Post St. (at Mason, a block west of Union Square), 415/441-7100 or 800/301-0217 in the U.S. and Canada, www.thedonatello.com, noteworthy for its four-star amenities and its restaurant, **Zingari** (415/885-8850).

Moving into San Francisco's trend-setting strata, the gleeful **Hotel Triton,** 342 Grant Ave., 415/394-0500 or 800/800-1299, www.hoteltriton.com, is still the talk of the town—and other towns as well—attracting celebrities galore as well as comparisons to New York's Paramount and Royalton Hotels. For more information, see Some Hip San Francisco Stays.

Other Areas

North of Market at the edge of the Financial

The **Alamo Square Inn,** 719 Scott St., 415/922-2055 or 800/345-9888, www.alamoinn.com, is another neighborhood possibility, offering rooms and suites in an 1895 Queen Anne and an 1896 Tudor Revival.

Petite Auberge, 863 Bush St. (near Nob Hill and Union Square), 415/928-6000 or 800/365-3004, www.foursisters.com, is an elegant French country inn right downtown, featuring Pierre Deux fabrics, terra-cotta tile, oak furniture, and lace curtains. All 26 guest rooms have private bathrooms; 16 have fireplaces. The "Petite Suite" has its own entrance and deck, a king-size bed, fireplace, and Jacuzzi. Two doors down is the affiliated **White Swan Inn,** 845 Bush, 415/775-1755 or 800/999-9570, www.foursisters.com, with parlor, library, and 26 rooms (private baths, fireplaces, wet bars) decorated with English-style decor, from the mahogany antiques and rich fabrics to floral-print wallpapers. Both inns serve full breakfast (with the morning paper), afternoon tea, and homemade cookies, and provide little amenities like thick terry bathrobes. All rooms have TVs and telephones.

Close to the Presidio and Fort Mason in Cow Hollow is the **Edward II Inn,** 3155 Scott St. (at Lombard), 415/922-3000 or 800/473-2846, www.edwardii.com, an English-style country hotel and pub offering 24 rooms and six suites, all with color TVs and phones, some with shared bathrooms. The suites have in-room whirlpool baths. A complimentary continental breakfast is served.

Peaceful and pleasant amid the hubbub of North Beach is the stylish and artsy 15-room **Hotel Bohème,** 444 Columbus Ave., 415/433-9111, www.hotelboheme.com, offering continental charm all the way to breakfast, which is served either indoors or out on the patio. On-site restaurant, too. Also in North Beach is the French country **Washington Square Inn,** 1660 Stockton St., 415/981-4220 or 800/388-0220, www.wsisf.com, featuring 15 rooms (most with private baths), continental breakfast, and afternoon tea.

Not a B&B per se, but providing as intimate a lodging experience as you'll get, **Dockside Boat & Bed,** Pier 39, 415/392-5526 or 800/436-2574, www.boatandbed.com, contracts a stable of luxury yachts, both motor and sail, on which guests can spend the night and view city lights from the boat deck.

District is the **Galleria Park Hotel,** 191 Sutter (between Montgomery and Kearny), 415/781-3060 or 866/756-3036, www.galleriapark.com, its striking art nouveau lobby with crystal skylight still somehow overshadowed by the curvaceous, equally original sculpted fireplace. Amenities include attractive rooms with soundproofed windows and walls, meeting facilities, on-site parking, a rooftop park and jogging track, and athletic club access. Dine at adjacent **Perry's** restaurant.

The Embarcadero YMCA south of Market near the Ferry Building now shares the waterfront building with the **Harbor Court Hotel,** 165 Steuart St. (at Mission), 415/882-1300 or 866/792-6283, www.harborcourthotel.com, a fairly phenomenal transformation at the edge of the financial district and a perfect setup for business travelers. The building's Florentine exterior has been beautifully preserved, as have the building's original arches, columns, and vaulted ceilings. Inside, the theme is oversized, Old World creature comfort. The plush rooms are rich with amenities, including TV, radio, direct-dial phones with extra-long cords, and complimentary beverages. The penthouse features a Louis XVI-style bed and 18-foot ceilings. Business travelers will appreciate the hotel's business center, financial district limo service, and same-day valet laundry service. And to work off the stress of that business meeting, head right next door to the renovated multilevel YMCA, where recreational facilities include basketball courts, aerobics classes, an Olympic-size pool, whirlpool, steam room, dry sauna, and even stationary bicycles with a view. Rates include complimentary continental breakfast and valet parking. Affiliated **Ozumo Restaurant** is a full service Japanese restaurant, with a sushi bar, grill, and sake lounge.

Adjacent and also worthwhile is the **Hotel Griffon,** 155 Steuart St. (at Mission), 415/495-2100 or

800/321-2201 in the U.S. and Canada, www
.hotelgriffon.com, with amenities like continental
breakfast, complimentary morning newspaper,
and a fitness center.

Near Civic Center cultural attractions is the exceptional small **Inn at the Opera,** 333 Fulton,
415/863-8400 or 800/325-2708, www.innathe-
opera.com, featuring complimentary breakfast
and morning newspaper, in-room cookies and
apples, free shoeshine service, available limousine service, and an excellent on-site restaurant,
Ovation. The guest list often includes big-name
theater people.

A stylish option in the Marina District is Joie de
Vivre's **Hotel Del Sol,** 3100 Webster St., 415/921-
5520 or 877/433-5765, www.jdvhospitality.com,
a onetime motel redone in the sunny colors of a
day at the beach. Abundant amenities, including
continental breakfast served out by the pool and
free kites, beach balls, and sunglasses for kiddos.

TOP OF THE LINE HOTELS: $250 AND UP

In addition to the fine hotels mentioned above,
San Francisco offers an impressive selection of
large, four- and five-star superdeluxe hotels. The
air in these establishments is rarefied indeed.
(Sometimes the airs, too.) Many, however, do
offer seasonal specials. Business-oriented hotels
often feature lower weekend rates.

The Ritz

Peek into **The Ritz-Carlton, San Francisco,** 600
Stockton (between California and Pine), 415/296-
7465 or 800/241-3333, www.ritzcarlton.com, to see
what a great facelift an old lady can get for $140
million. Quite impressive. And many consider the
hotel's Dining Room at The Ritz-Carlton among
the city's finest eateries. Rooms start at $325. For
more information, see Puttin' on the Ritz.

PUTTIN' ON THE RITZ

Serious visiting fans of San Francisco, at least
those with serious cash, tend to equate their
long-running romance with a stay on Nob Hill,
home base for most of the city's ritzier hotels. And
what could be ritzier than the Ritz?

The Ritz-Carlton, San Francisco, 600 Stockton
St. (at California)., 415/296-7465 or 800/241-
3333, www.ritzcarlton.com, is a local landmark,
San Francisco's finest remaining example of neoclassical architecture. At the Financial District's former western edge, and hailed in 1909 as a "temple
of commerce," until 1973 the building served as
West Coast headquarters for the Metropolitan Life
Insurance Company. Expanded and revised five
times since, San Francisco's Ritz has been open for
business as a hotel only since 1991. After painstaking restoration (four years and $140 million worth),
this nine-story grand dame still offers some odd
architectural homage to its past. Witness the terra-
cotta tableau over the entrance: the angelic allegor-
ical figure ("Insurance") is protecting the American
family. (Ponder the meaning of the lion's heads and
winged hourglasses on your own.)

The Ritz offers a total of 336 rooms and suites,
most with grand views. Amenities on the top two
floors ("The Ritz-Carlton Club") include private
lounge, continuous complimentary meals, and
Dom Perignon and Beluga caviar every evening. All
rooms, however, feature Italian marble bathrooms,
in-room safes, and every modern comfort, plus
access to the fitness center (indoor swimming pool,
whirlpool, training room, separate men's and
women's steam rooms and saunas, massage, and
more). Services include the usual long list plus
morning newspaper, childcare, video library, car
rental, and multilingual staff. Rates run $325–425
for rooms, $525–3,500 for suites. (The Ritz-Carl-
ton's "Summer Escape" package, when available, includes a deluxe guest room, continental breakfast,
valet parking, and unlimited use of the fitness center.) The Ritz-Carlton also provides full conference facilities. **The Terrace** restaurant here offers the
city's only alfresco dining in a hotel setting—like
eating breakfast, lunch, or dinner on someone else's
well-tended garden patio. (Come on Sunday for
brunch and jazz.) Adjacent, indoors, is the somewhat casual **Lobby Lounge.** More formal, serving neoclassical cuisine, is **The Dining Room.**

The Palace

Equally awesome—and another popular destination these days for City Guides and other walking tours—is that grande dame of San Francisco hostelries, the renovated and resplendent 1909 **Sheraton Palace Hotel,** 2 New Montgomery St. (downtown at Market), 415/512-1111 or 800/325-3589, www.sfpalace.com. Wander in, under the metal grillwork awning at the New Montgomery entrance, across the polished marble sunburst on the foyer floor, and sit a spell in the lobby to appreciate the more subtle aspects of the hotel's $150 million renovation. Then mosey into the central **Garden Court** restaurant. The wonderful lighting here is provided, during the day, by the (cleaned and restored) 1800s atrium skylight, one of the world's largest leaded-glass creations; some 70,000 panes of glass arch over the entire room. It's a best bet for Sunday brunch. Note, too, the 10 (yes, 10) 700-pound crystal chandeliers. The **Pied Piper Bar,** with its famous Maxfield Parrish mural, is a Palace fixture, and adjoins **Maxfield's** restaurant. Tours of the hotel are available; call for schedules and information.

In addition to plush accommodations (rooms still have high ceilings), the Palace offers complete conference and meeting facilities, a business center, and a rooftop fitness center. The swimming pool up there, under a modern vaulted skylight, is especially enjoyable at sunset; spa services include a poolside whirlpool and dry sauna. Rooms start at $300.

The St. Francis

Another beloved San Francisco institution is the **Westin St. Francis Hotel,** 335 Powell St. (between Post and Geary, directly across from Union Square), 415/397-7000 or 888/625-5144 in the U.S. and Canada, www.starwood.com/westin, a recently restored landmark recognized by the National Trust for Historic Preservation as one of the Historic Hotels of America. When the first St. Francis opened in 1849 at Clay and Dupont (Grant), it was considered the only hostelry at which ladies were safe, and was also celebrated as the first "to introduce bedsheets to the city." But San Francisco's finest was destroyed by fire four years later. By the early 1900s, reincarnation was

imminent when a group of local businessmen declared their intention to rebuild the St. Francis as "a caravansary worthy of standing at the threshold of the Occident, representative of California hospitality." No expense was spared on the stylish 12-story hotel overlooking Union Square—partially opened but still under construction when the April 18, 1906, earthquake and fire hit town. Damaged but not destroyed, the restored St. Francis opened in November 1907; over the entrance was an electrically lighted image of a phoenix rising from the city's ashes. Successfully resurrected, the elegant and innovative hotel attracted royalty, international political and military leaders, theatrical stars, and literati.

But even simpler folk have long been informed, entertained, and welcomed by the St. Francis. People keep an eye on the number of unfurled flags in front of the St. Francis, for example, knowing that these herald the nationalities of visiting dignitaries. And every long-time

The Westin St. Francis boasts five restaurants, a ballroom, and shopping arcade.

San Franciscan knows that any shiny old coins in their pockets most likely came from the St. Francis; the hotel's long-standing practice of washing coins—to prevent them from soiling ladies' white gloves—continues to this day. Meeting friends "under the Clock" means the Magneta Clock in the hotel's Powell St. lobby; this "master clock" from Saxony has been a fixture since the early 1900s.

After additions and grand renovations, the St. Francis today offers 1,200 luxury guest rooms and suites (request a suite brochure if you hanker to stay in the General MacArthur suite, the Queen Elizabeth II suite, or the Ron and Nancy Reagan suite), plus fitness and full meeting and conference facilities, a 1,500-square-foot ballroom, five restaurants (including elegant Victor's atop the St. Francis Tower), shopping arcade, valet parking. Rooms start at $249, suites at $650.

Others Downtown

The idea of Ian Schrager, king of New York's Studio 54 and Royalton Hotel, revamping the classic **Clift Hotel** in collaboration with designer Phillippe Stark raised eyebrows among WASPy San Franciscans. Brows furrowed, too, at the thought of renovating the hotel's famous art-deco **Redwood Room** bar, its walls hewn from 2,000-foot redwood trees. Yet the result is an intoxicating combination of old-school luxury and faux-Tinseltown irony. The Redwood Room's walls are intact, now paired with witty modern touches—Ostrich-stamped leather pillows on the chairs, a dramatic curved glass bar, and plasma screen monitors on the walls. The nuevo opulence carries over to the old French Room, now Schraeger's **Asia de Cuba,** a dimly lit Latin restaurant with intimate booths and kitschy artwork. Guest rooms are fairly subdued, featuring lavender walls and orange furnishings. Rooms at the Clift, 495 Geary St. (at Taylor), 415/775-4700 or 800/652-5438, www.clifthotel.com, start at $195, suites at $295.

The city has more classical class, of course. The four-star **Prescott Hotel,** 545 Post St. (between Taylor and Mason), 415/563-0303 or 866/271-3632, www.prescotthotel.com, elegantly combines uptown style with the feel of a British men's club. Rooms and suites come complete with paisley motif, overstuffed furniture, and every imaginable amenity—from honor bar and terry robes to shoe shines and evening wine and cheeses. Not to mention room service courtesy of Wolfgang Puck's downstairs **Postrio** restaurant, 415/776.7825, where hotel guests also receive preferred dining reservations (if rooms are also reserved well in advance). Services for guests on the Club Level include express check-in (and checkout), continental breakfast, hors d'oeuvres from Postrio, personal concierge service, and even stationary bicycles and rowers delivered to your room on request.

Quite refined, too, with the feel of a fine residential hotel, is **Campton Place Hotel,** 340 Stockton St. (just north of Union Square), 415/781-5555 or 800/235-4300, www.camptonplace.com, which regularly shows up near the top of U.S. "best of" hotel and restaurant lists. The hotel has all the amenities, including the acclaimed **Campton Place Restaurant,** serving impeccable contemporary American cuisine (415/955-5555). Rooms start at $195, suites at $450.

Also within easy reach of downtown doings is the sleek, modern, four-star **Pan Pacific Hotel,** 500 Post St. (at Mason, one block west of Union Square), 415/771-8600, 800/327-8585 or 800/223-5652, www.panpac.com. The business-oriented Pan Pacific offers three phones with call waiting in each room, personal computers delivered to your room upon request, notary public and business services, and Rolls Royce shuttle service to the Financial District. It's also luxurious; bathrooms, for example, feature floor-to-ceiling Breccia marble, artwork, a mini-screen TV, and a telephone. Specials start at $209, and some include breakfast in your room or at the third-floor **Pacific** restaurant (California-fusion cuisine), 415/929-2087.

Other worthy downtown possibilities include the contemporary Japanese-style **Hotel Nikko,** 222 Mason, 415/394-1111 or 800/645-5687, www.nikkohotels.com, which boasts a glass-enclosed rooftop pool, and the 1,000-room **Renaissance Parc 55 Hotel,** 55 Cyril Magnin St. (Market at Fifth), 415/392-8000 or 800/468-

3571, www.renaissancehotels.com. The exquisite **Mandarin Oriental San Francisco,** 222 Sansome, 415/276-9888 or 800/622-0404, www.mandarin-oriental.com, is housed in the top 11 floors of the financial district's California First Interstate Building. The 160 rooms boast great views (even from the bathrooms) and all the amenities. Another plus is **Silks** restaurant, 415/986-2020. The **Hyatt Regency San Francisco,** 5 Embarcadero Center (Market and California), 415/788-1234 or 800/233-1234, www.hyatt.com, is famous for its 17-story lobby, atrium, and rotating rooftop restaurant, **The Equinox,** 415/291-6619. There are Hyatts all over San Francisco, including the nearby **Park Hyatt** on Battery—home of the outstanding **Park Grill,** 415/296-2933—plus those at Union Square, Fisherman's Wharf, and out at the airport in Burlingame; a call can reserve a room at any and all.

Other comfortable hotel choices near the financial district and the booming new media companies south of Market include the superstylish, granite-faced **W Hotel,** 181 Third St. (at Howard), 415/777-5300 or 877/946-8357 or 888/625-5144 in the U.S. and Canada, www.starwood.com/whotels,, which is as sleek as its next-door neighbor, the San Francisco Museum of Modern Art. This business-oriented hotel also offers boutique touches: plush down comforters and Aveda bath products in all rooms. Downstairs, the **XYZ** restaurant and bar, 415/817-7836, serves creative fusion cuisine to a crowd of wannabe supermodels. Also in the area: the **San Francisco Marriott,** 55 Fourth St., 415/896-1600 or 800/228-9290, www.marriott.com, located south of Market and just north of the Moscone Convention Center, and the nearby **Argent Hotel,** 50 Third St. (at Market), 415/974-6400 or 888/238-0302, www.argenthotel.com.

Nob Hill

Some of the city's finest hotels cluster atop Nob Hill. Since judgment always depends upon personal taste, despite official ratings it's all but impossible to say which is "the best." Take your pick.

Across from Grace Cathedral and Huntington Park, the **Huntington Hotel,** 1075 California St. (at Taylor), 415/474-5400 or 800/227-4683., www.huntingtonhotel.com, is the last surviving family-owned fine hotel in the neighborhood. It's a beauty, a destination in and of itself. Every room and suite (onetime residential apartments) has been individually designed and decorated, and every service is a personal gesture. Stop in just to appreciate the elegant lobby. Dark and clubby, and open daily for breakfast, lunch, and dinner, the **Big Four Restaurant** off the lobby pays pleasant homage to the good ol' days of Wild West railroad barons—and often serves wild game entrées along with tamer continental contemporary cuisine. Relax at the **Nob Hill Spa** adjacent to the hotel. Guest rooms start at $315 for two, suites at $490.

Top-of-the-line, too, is the romantic, turn-of-the-20th-century **Fairmont Hotel,** 950 Mason St. (at California), 415/772-5000 or 800/257-7544 for reservations, www.fairmont.com, recognizable to as the setting for the fictional San Francisco hotel the "St. Gregory" in the 1980s TV series *Hotel.* The Fairmont offers 596 rooms (small to large) and suites, all expected amenities, and several on-site restaurants. Locally loved, are the hotel's **Laurel Court,** for steak and seafood (also open for breakfast), and the fantastically kitschy Tiki-inspired **Tonga Room,** which specializes in Chinese and Polynesian cuisine and features a simulated tropical rainstorm every half hour. The Fairmont also offers full conference and business facilities (20 meeting rooms) and the **Club One at Nob Hill Health Club** (extra fee) for fitness enthusiasts. Rooms start at $199, suites at $550. The five-star **Renaissance Stanford Court Hotel,** 905 California St. (at Powell), 415/989-3500 or 800/468-3571, www.marriott.com, boasts a 120-foot-long, sepia-toned lobby mural honoring San Francisco's historic diversity. On the west wall, for example, are panels depicting the hotel's predecessor, the original Leland Stanford Mansion, with railroad barons and other wealthy Nob Hill nabobs on one side, Victorian-era African Americans on the other. Other panels depict the long-running economic exploitation of California places and peoples, from Russian whaling and fur trading, redwood logging, and the California gold rush (with Native Americans and the

AHOY, ARGONAUTS

The notably nautical decor of the new Klimpton **Argonaut Hotel,** launched as a new Fisherman's Wharf hotel in August 2003, acknowledges the 1849 argonauts who sailed through the Golden Gate to seek their fortunes in the California goldfields. San Francisco Maritime National Historic Park's 252-room hotel as well as (in the hotel lobby) the park's new visitor center are open daily 9:30 A.M.–7 P.M. Rooms offer all the modern amenities, and some feature the building's venerable brick walls, timbers, steel warehouse doors, or large porthole-style windows. Rates are $200–300, with discounted rates dropping as low as $129. The kid-friendly, pet-friendly, fully accessible Argonaut Hotel is located inside the park, 495 Jefferson St. (at Hyde), 415/563-2800 or 800/790-1415, www.argonauthotel.com. Adjacent is the hotel's **Blue Mermaid Chowder House and Bar.**

Chinese looking on) to the 1906 earthquake and fire framed by the construction of the transcontinental railroad and California's Latinization, as represented by Mission Dolores. Stop in and see it; this is indeed the story of Northern California, if perhaps a bit romanticized.

The hotel itself is romantic, recognized by the National Trust for Historic Preservation as one of the Historic Hotels of America. The Stanford Court features a decidedly European ambience, from the carriage entrance (with beaux arts fountain and stained-glass dome) to guest rooms decked out in 19th-century artwork, antiques, and reproductions (not to mention modern comforts like heated towel racks in the marble bathrooms and dictionaries on the writing desks). Opulent touches in the lobby include Baccarat chandeliers, Carrara marble floor, oriental carpets, original artwork, and an 1806 antique grandfather clock once owned by Napoleon Bonaparte. Guest services include complimentary stretch limo service, both for business and pleasure. Rooms start at $235, suites at $775. Even if you don't stay, consider a meal (breakfast, lunch, and dinner daily, plus weekend brunch) at the hotel's Mediterranean-inspired restaurant, **Fournou's Ovens,** 415/989-1910 for reservations, considered one of San Francisco's best.

Don't forget the Mark Hopkins Hotel, now the **Mark Hopkins Inter-Continental,** 1 Nob Hill (California and Mason), 415/392-3434 or 800/327-0200, www.san-francisco.interconti.com,, another refined Old California old-timer. Hobnobbing with the best of them atop Nob Hill,

the Mark Hopkins features 380 elegant guest rooms and suites (many with great views) and all the amenities, not to mention the fabled **Top of the Mark** sky room, still San Francisco's favorite sky-high romantic bar scene. The French-California **Nob Hill Restaurant** is open daily for breakfast, lunch, and dinner. Rooms start at $290.

Other Areas

Two blocks from Pier 39 at Fisherman's Wharf, the **Tuscan Inn,** 425 North Point, 415/561-1100 or 800/648-4626, www.tuscaninn.com, a Best Western reinvented by hotelier Bill Kimpton. The hotel features an Italianate lobby with fireplace, a central garden court, and 221 rooms and suites with modern amenities. Rates include morning coffee, tea, and biscotti, and a daily wine hour by the lobby fireplace. Rooms start at $249. Just off the lobby is a convenient Italian trattoria, **Cafe Pescatore,** specializing in fresh fish and seafood, pastas, and pizzas (baked in a wood-burning oven) at lunch and dinner. Open for breakfast also.

In Pacific Heights, west of Van Ness and south of Lombard, the **Sherman House,** 2160 Green St. (between Fillmore and Webster), 415/563-3600, www.theshermanhouse.com, is among the city's finest small, exclusive hotels. Once the mansion of Leander Sherman, it now attracts inordinate percentages of celebrities and stars, who come for the privacy and personal service. The ambience here, including the intimate dining room, exudes 19th-century French opulence. Rooms start at $460, suites at $775.

Eating in San Francisco

San Franciscans love to eat. For a true San Franciscan, eating—and eating well—competes for first place among life's purest pleasures, right up there with the arts, exercising, and earning money. (There may be a few others.) Finding new and novel neighborhood eateries, and knowing which among the many fine dining establishments are currently at the top of the trendsetters' culinary A-list, are points of pride for long-time residents. Fortunately, San Franciscans also enjoy sharing information and opinions—including their restaurant preferences. So the best way to find out where to eat, and why, is simply to ask. The following listings should help fine-food aficionados get started, and will certainly keep everyone else from starving.

UNION SQUARE AND NOB HILL

A well-kept secret, perhaps downtown's best breakfast spot, is **Dottie's True Blue Cafe,** 522 Jones St. (between O'Farrell and Geary), 415/885-2767, a genuine all-American coffee shop serving every imaginable American standard plus new cuisine, such as (at lunch) grilled eggplant sandwiches. Open daily for breakfast and lunch only, 7 A.M.–3 P.M.

Another area classic, if for other reasons, is **John's Grill,** 63 Ellis (just off Powell), 415/986-3274 or 415/986-0069, with a neat neon sign outside and *Maltese Falcon* memorabilia just about everywhere inside. (In the book, this is where Sam Spade ate his lamb chops.) Named a National Literary Landmark by the Friends of Libraries, USA, this informal eatery ode to Dashiell Hammett serves good continental-style American fare, plus large helpings of Hammett hero worship, especially upstairs in Hammett's Den and the Maltese Falcon Room. Open Mon.–Sat. for lunch and dinner; Sunday for dinner only. Live jazz nightly.

For excellent seafood, dive into the French provincial **Brasserie Savoy** at the Savoy Hotel, 580 Geary St. (at Jones), 415/441-2700, open for breakfast (until noon), dinner, and late supper.

Gallic stodgy? *Mais, non!* How about a "Lobster Martini?" Or a fish soup described as "haunting" by one local food writer (perhaps she had one too many Lobster Martinis?).

Farallon, 450 Post (near Powell), 415/956-6969, might be *the* place in town for seafood. And the unique Pat Kuleto-designed interior might make you feel like you're under the sea, in an octopus's garden, perhaps. Look for such intriguing specialties as truffled mashed potatoes with crab and sea urchin sauce, or ginger-steamed salmon. Open for lunch Mon.–Sat. and for dinner nightly.

Two blocks from Union Square, **Puccini & Pinetti,** 129 Ellis (at Cyril Magnin), 415/392-5500, is a beautifully designed Cal-Italian restaurant popular with theater crowds. Menu highlights include bruschetta with arugula and roasted garlic, smoked salmon pizzas, and risotto with charred leeks and wild mushrooms. Prices are surprisingly reasonable—most entrées run $10–15. Open for lunch and dinner.

Worth searching for downtown is **Cafe Claude,** 7 Claude Ln. (between Grant and Kearny, Bush and Sutter, just off Bush), 415/392-3505, an uncanny incarnation of a genuine French café, from the paper table covers to the café au lait served in bowls. Good food, plus live jazz four nights a week.

A good choice downtown for pasta is **Kuleto's,** 221 Powell St., 415/397-7720, a comfortable trattoria-style Italian restaurant and bar at the Villa Florence Hotel. It's popular for power lunching and dinner, and it's also open for peaceful, pleasant breakfasts.

Better yet, though, is **Zingari Ristorante,** 501 Post St. (at Mason, in the Donatello hotel), 415/885-8850, justifiably famous for its Northern Italian regional dishes. Dining rooms are small and intimate, and dressing up is de rigueur—putting on a show as good as, or better than, almost anything else in the neighborhood.

People should at least pop into Wolfgang Puck's **Postrio,** 545 Post St. (at Mason, inside the Prescott Hotel), 415/776-7825, to appreciate

SAN FRANCISCO

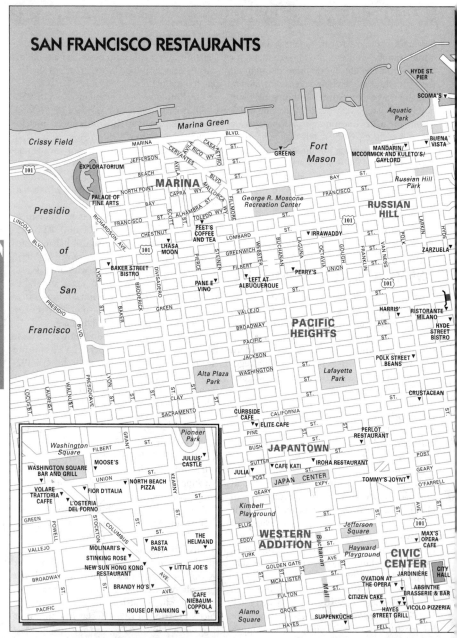

SAN FRANCISCO RESTAURANTS

HYDE ST. PIER

SCOMA'S ▾

Aquatic Park

Crissy Field

Marina Green

BLVD.

GREENS ▾

Fort Mason

BUENA VISTA ▾

MANDARIN/ ▾
MCCORMICK AND KULETO'S/
GAYLORD

Presidio

of

San

Francisco

EXPLORATORIUM

PALACE OF FINE ARTS

MARINA

PEET'S COFFEE AND TEA ▾

LHASA MOON ▾

BAKER STREET BISTRO ▾

PANE E VINO ▾

LEFT AT ALBUQUERQUE ▾

IRRAWADDY ▾

PERRY'S ▾

Russian Hill Park

RUSSIAN HILL

ZARZUELA ▾

PACIFIC HEIGHTS

HARRIS' ▾

RISTORANTE MILANO ▾

HYDE STREET BISTRO ▾

Alta Plaza Park

Lafayette Park

POLK STREET BEANS ▾

CRUSTACEAN ▾

CURBSIDE CAFE ▾
ELITE CAFE ▾

PERLOT RESTAURANT ▾

JAPANTOWN

CAFE KATI ▾

IROHA RESTAURANT ▾

TOMMY'S JOYNT ▾

Kimbell Playground

Jefferson Square

MAX'S OPERA CAFE ▾

WESTERN ADDITION

Hayward Playground

CIVIC CENTER

CITY HALL

JARDINIÈRE ▾

Alamo Square

OVATION AT THE OPERA ▾

CITIZEN CAKE ▾

SUPPENKÜCHE ▾

HAYES STREET GRILL ▾

ABSINTHE BRASSERIE & BAR ▾

VICOLO PIZZERIA ▾

Pioneer Park

Washington Square

WASHINGTON SQUARE BAR AND GRILL ▾

MOOSE'S ▾

JULIUS' CASTLE ▾

VOLARE TRATTORIA CAFFE ▾

L'OSTERIA DEL FORNO ▾

FIOR D'ITALIA ▾

NORTH BEACH PIZZA ▾

JULIA ▾

MOLINARI'S ▾

STINKING ROSE ▾

NEW SUN HONG KONG RESTAURANT ▾

BRANDY HO'S ▾

BASTA PASTA ▾

THE HELMAND ▾

LITTLE JOE'S ▾

CAFE NIEBAUM-COPPOLA ▾

HOUSE OF NANKING ▾

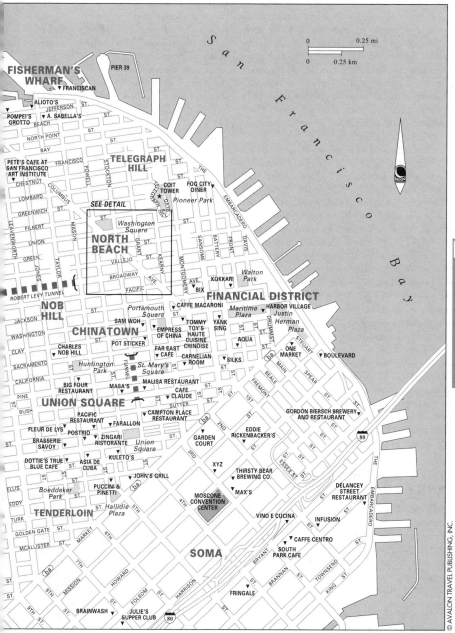

the exquisite ribbon-patterned dining room designs by Pat Kuleto. The food here is exceptional, with most entrées representing Puck's interpretations of San Francisco classics. Since the restaurant is open for breakfast, lunch, and dinner, try Hangtown fry and some house-made pastries at breakfast, perhaps a pizza fresh from the woodburning oven or Dungeness crab with spicy curry risotto at lunch. Dinner is an adventure. Great desserts. Make reservations well in advance, or hope for a cancellation.

Famous among local foodies, not to mention its long-standing national and international fan club, is **Masa's,** 648 Bush St. (at the Hotel Vintage Court), 415/989-7154, one of the city's finest dinner restaurants and considered by many to be the best French restaurant in the United States. Masa's serves French cuisine with a fresh California regional touch and a Spanish aesthetic. Reservations accepted three weeks in advance. Very expensive.

Fleur de Lys, 777 Sutter (between Jones and Taylor), 415/673-7779, is another local legend—a fine French restaurant that also transcends the traditional. Nothing is too heavy or overdone. Expensive. Open Mon.–Sat. for dinner. Reservations.

On Nob Hill, **Charles Nob Hill,** 1250 Jones St. (at Clay), 415/771-5400, is a neighborhood French restaurant featuring specialties like Hudson Valley foie gras and Sonoma duck. Open for dinner Tues.-Sat. Some of the city's finest hotels, on Nob Hill and elsewhere, also serve some of the city's finest food.

THE FINANCIAL DISTRICT AND EMBARCADERO

Still a haute spot for young refugees from the Financial District is the casual **Gordon Biersch Brewery and Restaurant,** 2 Harrison St., 415/243-8246, along the Embarcadero in the shadow of the Bay Bridge. The German-style lagers here are certainly a draw—three styles (Pilsner to Bavarian dark) are created on the premises—as is the surprisingly good food, which is far from the usual brewpub grub. Open from 11 A.M. daily. (Gordon Biersch also has

outposts in Palo Alto, San Jose, Pasadena, San Diego, and elsewhere.)

Also on the Embarcadero, **Boulevard,** 1 Mission St. (at Steuart), 415/543-6084, is a Franco-American bistro serving American classics—ribs, pork chops, mashed 'taters—in an art nouveau atmosphere. Nice views. Open for lunch weekdays and dinner nightly. Also overlooking the Embarcadero is **One Market,** 1 Market St., 415/777-5577, a sleek haven for the expense-account set featuring the best of seasonal fresh California ingredients in its upscale American specialties. Extensive wine list. Open for lunch weekdays and dinner Mon.-Sat.

In the seafood swim of things, **Aqua,** 252 California St.(between Front and Battery), 415/956-9662, is making a global splash among well-heeled foodies. Signature creations include basil-grilled lobster, lobster potato gnocchi, and black-mussel soufflé. Open weekdays for lunch, Mon.-Sat. for dinner. **Jeanty at Jack's,** 615 Sacramento St. (at Montgomery), 415/693-0941, brings Philippe Jeanty's wonderful brasserie fare to one of San Francisco's classic restaurants, 1864-vintage Jack's—from cassoulet to and coq au vin to steak frites.

At **Delancey Street Restaurant,** 600 Embarcadero (at Brannan), 415/512-5179, the restaurant staff is comprised of Delancey's drug, alcohol, and crime rehabilitees. The daily changing menu at this radical chic, sociopolitically progressive place is ethnic American—everything from matzo ball soup to pot roast. And there's a great view of Alcatraz from the outdoor dining area. Open for lunch, afternoon tea, and dinner.

A half-sibling to SoMa's Fringale, homey **Piperade** at 1015 Battery St. (near Green), 415/391-2555, serves a contemporary interpretation of chef Gerald Hirigoyen's Basque roots—everything from pork daube and steamed Pacific snapper to the restaurant's namesake *piperade,* a stew of thin-sliced Serrano ham, bell peppers, tomatoes, and garlic. Wonderful desserts.

On the 52nd floor of the Bank of America building, the **Carnelian Room,** 555 California St. (between Kearny and Montgomery), 415/433-7500, is the closest you'll get to dining in an airplane above the city. The menu is up-

SUSAN SNYDER

scale American, with specialties including Dungeness crab cakes, rack of lamb, and Grand Marnier soufflé. **Yank Sing,** 101 Spear St. (at Mission, inside the Rincon Center), 415/957-9300, is popular with the Financial District crowd and noteworthy for the shrimp dumplings in the shapes of goldfish and rabbits. (There's another Yank Sing at 49 Stevenson St. between First and Second Sts., 415/541-4949.) A good choice for Cantonese food is Hong Kong-style **Harbor Village,** 4 Embarcadero Center (at the corner of Clay and Drumm), 415/781-8833, serving everything from dim sum to Imperial banquets. Open daily for lunch and dinner.

CIVIC CENTER AND VICINITY

Tommy's Joynt, 1101 Geary (at Van Ness), 415/775-4216, is a neighborhood institution—a hofbrau-style bar and grill boasting bright paint, a bizarre bunch of bric-a-brac, beers from just about everywhere, and a noteworthy pastrami sandwich. Farther north along Polk Gulch (roughly paralleling fairly level Polk St., from Post to Broadway) are abundant cafés, coffeehouses, and avant-garde junque and clothing shops. Worthwhile eateries include **Polk Street Beans,** 1733 Polk (at Clay), 415/776-9292, a funky Eurostyle coffeehouse serving good soups and sandwiches. Pitching itself to the neighborhood's more theatrical standards is **Max's Opera Cafe,** 601 Van Ness (at Golden Gate), 415/771-7300, Like Max's enterprises elsewhere, you can count on being served huge helpings of tantalizing all-American standards. At least at dinner, you can also count on the wait staff bursting into song—maybe opera, maybe a Broadway show tune. Open daily for lunch and dinner, until late (1 A.M.) on Friday and Saturday nights for the post-theater crowds.

Tucked inside the Inn at the Opera, **Ovation at the Opera,** 333 Fulton St. (between Gough and Franklin), 415/305-8842 or 415/553-8100, is a class act noted as much for its romantic charms as its fine French-Continental cuisine—a fitting finale for opera fans who have plenty of cash left to fan (this place is on the expensive side). Open nightly for dinner (until 10:30 or 11 P.M. Fri. and Sat. nights).

Also by the Opera House is the elegant and superlative **Jardinière,** 300 Grove St. (at Franklin), 415/861-5555, a French-Californian restaurant created by the city's top restaurant designer and one of its top chefs, serving very stylish comfort food. Open for lunch weekdays and for dinner nightly (late-night menu available after 10:30 P.M.).

Nearby, in Hayes Valley, are a number of great choices, including the **Hayes Street Grill,** 320 Hayes (at Franklin), 415/863-5545, a busy bistro serving some of the best seafood in town. Open weekdays for lunch, Mon.-Sat. for dinner. For something simpler, also right behind Davies Hall is **Vicolo Pizzeria,** 201 Ivy St. (at Franklin), 415/863-2382, where favorites include the corn-meal-crust pizzas. The **Absinthe Brasserie & Bar,** 398 Hayes (at Gough), 415/551-1590, is a great little French bistro famous for its weekend brunches. Wonderful for lunch and dinner and absolutely wicked for its cakes, cookies, chocolates, and other sweet treats is **Citizen Cake** café and patisserie, 399 Grove (at Gough), 415/861-2228. A bit farther on but a best bet for gourmet German—really—is casual **Suppenküche,** 601 Hayes (at Laguna), 415/252-9289.

Sometimes more like a moveable feast for fashion, judging from all the suits and suited skirts, the **Zuni Cafe,** 1658 Market (at Gough), 415/552-2522, is an immensely popular restaurant and watering hole noted for its Italian-French country fare and Southwestern ambience. Expensive.

At Chelsea Square, **Crustacean,** 1475 Polk St. (at California), 415/776-2722, is another one of those cutting-edge eateries enjoyable for ambience as well as actual eats. This place serves exceptional Euro-Asian cuisine (specialty: roast crab) and looks like a fantasy home to those particularly crunchy critters, with underwater murals and giant seahorses, not to mention handblown glass fixtures and a 17-foot wave sculpture. Open for dinners only, nightly after 5 P.M.; valet parking, full bar, extensive wine list. Reservations preferred.

Near Japan Center, **Cafe Kati,** 1963 Sutter (near Fillmore), 415/775-7313, is a well-regarded neighborhood place serving wonderfully inventive food (expensive). **Iroha Restaurant,** 1728 Buchanan (at Post), 415/922-0321, is a great inexpensive stop for noodles and Japanese standards.

A serious foodie destination, homey, pricey **Julia,** 2101 Sutter (at Steiner), 415/441-2101, offers chef Julia McClaskey and her specialty pot roast, chile verde, king salmon with green curry sauce, and grilled dolmas on couscous salad.

CHINATOWN

To find the best restaurants in Chinatown, go where the Chinese go. Some of these places may look a bit shabby, at least on the outside, and may not take reservations—or credit cards. But since the prices at small family-run enterprises are remarkably low, don't fret about leaving that plastic at home.

Very popular, and always packed, the **House of Nanking,** 919 Kearny (between Jackson and Columbus), 415/421-1429, has a great location at the foot of Chinatown on the North Beach border. At this tiny restaurant, diners often sit elbow to elbow, but the excellent food and reasonable prices make it well worth the wait.

For spicy Mandarin and the best pot stickers in town, try the **Pot Sticker,** 150 Waverly Place, 415/397-9985, open daily for lunch and dinner. Another Hunan hot spot is **Brandy Ho's,** 217 Columbus (at Pacific), 415/788-7527, open daily from noon to midnight.

A great choice for Cantonese, the **Far East Cafe,** 631 Grant Ave. (between Sacramento and California), 415/982-3245, is a dark place lit by Chinese lanterns. Another possibility is the tiny turn-of-the-century **Hang Ah Tea Room,** 1 Pagoda Place (off Sacramento St.), 415/982-5686, specializing in Cantonese entrées and lunchtime dim sum. Inexpensive and locally infamous, due largely to the rude waiter routine of Edsel Ford Wong (now deceased), is three-story **Sam Woh,** 813 Washington St. (at Grant), 415/982-0596, where you can get good noodles, jook (rice gruel), and Chinese-style doughnuts (for dunking in your gruel).

Once one of San Francisco's destination restaurants, the **Empress of China,** 838 Grant Ave. (between Washington and Clay), 415/434-1345, hasn't changed much since the Nixon administration, though it still attracts large crowds of tourists and young people looking for a campy dining experience. The ground floor lobby is worth a look for its forgotten celebrities; Eric Estrada, Jerry Hall, Englebert Humperdinck, and

Raymond "Perry Mason" Burr all beam from the walls. The top floor dining room is splendid, with peacock feathers curling up against beautifully ornate furnishings, and amazing views of Coit Tower and Telegraph Hill. It's been a long time since anyone came here for the food, a relic of old-style Chinese-American cuisine featuring chow mein, fried won tons, and egg rolls. Stick to the basic menu items, and this place is a kick for the atmosphere.

Great Eastern Restaurant, 649 Jackson (between Grant and Kearny), 415/986-2500, is a relaxed family-style place serving good food at great prices. A best bet here is the fixed-price seafood banquet.

JACKSON SQUARE, NORTH BEACH, AND RUSSIAN HILL
Jackson Square
Seductively combining upscale American cuisine with an exotic 1940s-style film noir atmosphere, **Bix,** 56 Gold St., 415/433-6300, is a high-toned supper club complete with richly detailed fixtures and a dramatic mahogany bar, hidden away in a narrow alley between Jackson and Pacific, Montgomery and Sansome. Traditional dishes such as grilled pork chops and buttery mashed potatoes are prepared with fresh local ingredients. You'll want to get dolled up and bring a date; classic cocktails are de riguer, of course. At Kearny and Columbus, you'll find movie-magnate-turned-winemaker Francis Ford Coppola's **Café Niebaum-Coppola,** 916 Kearny St., 415/291-1700, which offers an Italian menu and a good wine bar (serving, among other selections, Coppola's own vintages). At last report, contemporary American **Moose's,** 1652 Stockton St. (near Filbert), 415/989-7800, boasted chef Jeffrey Amber, previously of XYZ, and served impressive entrées such as lobster with globe squash, pork chops with cabbage and figs, and pan-seared duck breast with quinoa pilaf.

One of the country's best Greek restaurants is **Kokkari,** 200 Jackson St. (at Front), 415/981-0983. Open weekdays for lunch and Mon.-Sat. for dinner. While in the Montgomery-Washington Tower, **Tommy Toy's Haute Cuisine Chinoise,** 655 Montgomery St. (between Washington and Clay), 415/397-4888, serves up classical Chinese cuisine with traditional French touches, called "Frenchinoise" by Tommy Toy himself. The restaurant itself is impressive enough; it's patterned after the reading room of the Empress Dowager of the Ching Dynasty, and the rich decor includes priceless Asian art and antiques. Open for dinner nightly and for lunch on weekdays; reservations always advisable.

North Beach
Farther north in North Beach proper, you'll find an almost endless selection of cafés and restaurants. Historically, this is the perfect out-of-the-way area to eat, drink good coffee, or just while away the hours. These days, North Beach is a somewhat odd blend of San Francisco's Beat-era bohemian nostalgia, new-world Asian attitudes, and other ethnic culinary accents. An example of the "new" North Beach: the **New Sun Hong Kong Restaurant,** 606 Broadway (at the cultural convergence of Grant, Broadway, and Columbus), 415/956-3338. Outside, marking the building, is a three-story-tall mural depicting the North Beach jazz tradition. But this is a very Chinatown eatery, open from early morning to late at night and specializing in hot pots and earthy, homey, San Francisco-style Chinese fare.

Also here are some of old San Francisco's most traditional traditions. The **Washington Square Bar and Grill,** also affectionately known as "The Washbag," is back at 1707 Powell St. (at Union), 415/982-8123, following a brief flirtation with its dot-com identity as the Cobalt Tavern. The Washbag, one of Herb Caen's haunts, may once again become a social stopoff for the city's cognoscenti. The venerable **Fior D'Italia,** 601 Union St. (at Stockton), 415/986-1886, established in 1886, is legendary for its ambience—including the Tony Bennett Room and the Godfather Room—and its historic ability to attract highbrow Italians from around the globe.

"Follow your nose" to the **Stinking Rose,** 325 Columbus (between Broadway and Vallejo), 415/781-7673, an exceptionally popular Italian restaurant where all the food is heavily doused in

FIOR d' ITALIA
Est. 1886
Oldest
Italian Restaurant

SUSAN SNYDER

garlic. For exceptional food with a more elevated perspective, a dress-up restaurant on Telegraph Hill is appropriately romantic: **Julius' Castle,** 1541 Montgomery St. (north of Union), 415/392-2222, for French and Italian, and beautiful views of the city. Not that far away (along the Embarcadero), renowned for its fine food and flair, is the one and only **Fog City Diner,** 1300 Battery St. (at Lombard), 415/982-2000. Though this is the original gourmet grazing pasture, Fog City has its imitators around the world.

But the real North Beach is elsewhere. For genuine neighborhood tradition, head to stand-up **Molinari's,** 373 Columbus (between Broadway and Green), 415/421-2337, a fixture since 1907. It's a good deli stop for fresh pastas, homemade sauces, hearty sandwiches, and tasty sweet treats.

"Rain or shine, there's always a line" at very–San Francisco **Little Joe's,** 523 Broadway (between Kearny and Columbus), 415/433-4343, a boisterous bistro where the Italian food is authentic, the atmosphere happy, and everyone hale and hearty. The open kitchen is another main attraction. For faster service, belly up to a counter stool and watch the chefs at work. Classic, too, especially with the lots-of-food-for-little-money set, is the casual **Basta Pasta,** 1268 Grant Ave., 415/434-2248, featuring veal, fresh fish, and perfect calzones fresh out of the wood-burning oven.

Volare Trattoria Caffe, 561 Columbus (between Union and Green), 415/362-2774, offers superb Sicilian cuisine—try the exceptional calimari in tomato-garlic sauce. Owner Giovanni Zocca plants himself outside on Friday and Saturday nights and sings the restaurant's theme tune, "Volare, volare, volare, ho ho ho." Just up the street is **L'Osteria del Forno,** 519 Columbus, 415/982-1124, a tiny storefront trattoria with six tables. This place is a great budget bet for its wonderful Italian flatbread sandwiches.

For pizza, the place to go is **North Beach Pizza,** 1499 Grant (at Union), 415/433-2444, where there's always a line, and it's always worth standing in. Heading down toward the Financial District, **Caffe Macaroni,** 59 Columbus (between Washington and Jackson), 415/956-9737, is also a true blue—well, red, white, and green—pasta house in the Tuscany tradition: intimate, aromatic, and friendly.

A CUPPA AT CAFÉ COPPOLA

Try something downright cinematic for your next cuppa—Café Niebaum-Coppola in North Beach, 916 Kearny St. (at Columbus Ave.), 415/291-1700, www.cafecoppola.com, movie director Francis Ford Coppola's latest commercial venture. This one, a European style bistro conveniently located on the ground floor of Coppola's American Zoetrope film production company, extends his wine-and-food empire into fairly sophisticated yet rustic culinary territory. The very Italian wood-fired pizzas are the main attraction, some named after various family members. The wine bar features Niebaum-Coppola wines from Coppola's Napa Valley winery. Here as there, sample an exuberant supply of merchandise. There's another Café Niebaum-Coppola in Palo Alto at 473 University Ave. (at Cowper St.), 650/752-0350.

Exceptional for Afghan fare is **The Helmand,** 430 Broadway (between Keany and Montgomery), 415/362-0641. Here linguistics majors can enjoy ordering such dishes as *dwopiaza, bowlani,* and *sabzi challow.* Most entrées are oriented around lamb and beef, but vegetarian entrées are available and are separated out on the menu, making for easy selection.

Russian Hill

Zarzuela, 2000 Hyde St. (at Union, right on the Hyde/Powell cable-car route), 415/346-0800, offers its eponymous signature dish—a seafood stew—and other Spanish delicacies, including paella and assorted tapas. Open for dinner Tues.-Sat. Another neighborhood possibility is the **Hyde Street Bistro,** 1521 Hyde St. (between Jackson and Pacific), 415/292-4415, one of those sophisticated little places where San Franciscans hide out during tourist season. It's quiet, not too trendy, and serves good French cuisine. Appreciate the breadsticks.

Ristorante Milano, 1448 Pacific Ave. (between Hyde and Larkin), 415/673-2961, is a happy, hopping little Italian restaurant with pas-

tas—do try the lasagna—fresh fish, and sometimes surprising specials.

Not far away and a real deal for foodies who don't care one whit about the frills is **Pete's Cafe at San Francisco Art Institute,** 800 Chestnut St. (at Jones), 415/749-4567, where you can get a great lunch for $5 or less, along with one of the city's best bay views. The atmosphere is arty and existential, with paper plates and plastic utensils just to remind you that this is for students. Everything is fresh and wholesome: Southwestern black bean/vegetable stew, white bean and escarole soup, even house-roasted turkey sandwiches. Good breakfasts, too. Open in summer Mon.–Fri. 9 A.M.–4 P.M., and during the school year Mon.–Fri. 8 A.M.–9 P.M., Sat. 9 A.M.–2 P.M. (hours can vary; it's best to call ahead).

FISHERMAN'S WHARF AND GHIRARDELLI SQUARE

Fisherman's Wharf is both tourist central and seafood central. Most locals wouldn't be caught dead eating at one of the Wharf's many seafood restaurants—but that doesn't mean the food isn't good here. Pick of the litter is probably **Scoma's,** on Pier 47 (walk down the pier from the intersection of Jefferson and Jones Streets), 415/771-4383. It's just off the beaten path (on the lightly pummeled path) and therefore a tad quieter and more relaxing than the others—or at least it seems so. The others would include: **A. Sabella's,** 2766 Taylor St. (at Jefferson), 415/771-4416; **Alioto's,** 8 Fisherman's Wharf (at Jefferson), 415/673-0183; the **Franciscan,** Pier 43, The Embarcadero, 415/362-7733; **Pompei's Grotto,** 340 Jefferson St. (near Jones), 415/776-9265; and a large number of places at Pier 39. You can get a decent bowl of clam chowder and a slab of sourdough bread at any of them.

Ghirardelli Square, 900 North Point (at Larkin), though technically part of the same Fisherman's Wharf tourist area, houses some fine restaurants patronized by locals even in broad daylight. The fourth floor **Mandarin,** 415/673-8812, was the city's first truly palatial Chinese restaurant and the first to serve up spicy Szechuan

THE SAN FRANCISCO FOOD? SOURDOUGH BREAD

As mentioned elsewhere, if only in passing, San Francisco has a long roster of culinary inventions—from the all-American Chinese fortune cookie (invented in the Japanese Tea Garden) and Italian fish stew, or cioppino, to hangtown fry and peach melba. But nothing is more San Francisco in the food department than sourdough French bread, a much-loved local specialty. Dating from gold rush days, when yeasts and shortenings were scarce, breads were leavened by fermented "starters" of flour, water, and other live ingredients, this bacteria-enhanced souring ingredient then added in small amounts to bread dough. With each new batch of bread, some dough was pinched and put aside as the next generation of leavening. And on and on, down through time. Since sourdough-bread connoisseurs believe that a good starter, and the bread line it creates, can only improve with age, a bakery's most prized asset is its own unique variety. It's no surprise, then, that during the great San Francisco earthquake and fire of 1906, many of the city's bakers risked their lives to rescue their starters. Such heroic acts are directly responsible for the time-honored tastes of the city's best breads.

and Hunan dishes. The food here is still great. Stop by at lunch for off-the-menu dim sum (including green onion pie, spring rolls with yellow chives, and sesame shrimp rolls), served 11:30 A.M.–3:30 P.M. daily, or come later for dinner. You won't go wrong for seafood at second floor **McCormick and Kuleto's,** 415/929-1730, which features its own Crab Cake Lounge and 30 to 50 fresh specialties every day. Another much-loved Ghirardelli Square eatery is the third floor **Gaylord,** 415/771-8822, serving astounding Northern Indian specialties with a side of East Indies decor.

Elsewhere in the area, the Victorian-style **Buena Vista,** 2675 Hyde St. (at Beach), 415/474-5044, is notorious as the tourist bar that introduced Irish coffee. It's a great spot to share a table for breakfast or light lunch, and the waterfront views are almost free.

PACIFIC HEIGHTS, THE FILLMORE, AND THE MARINA DISTRICT

Perhaps San Francisco's most famous, most fabulous vegetarian restaurant is **Greens,** at Building A, Fort Mason (enter at Buchanan and Marina), 415/771-6222, where the hearty fare proves for all time that meat is an unnecessary ingredient for fine dining—and where the views are plenty ap-

petizing, too. Open for lunch and dinner Tues.-Sat., and for brunch on Sunday; reservations always advised. The bakery counter is open Tues.–Sun. from 10 A.M.–mid- or late afternoon.

Left at Albuquerque, 2140 Union St. (at Fillmore in Cow Hollow), 415/749-6700, offers Southwestern ambience and an energetic, dining-and-drinking clientele. Modern-day Malcolm Lowrys could spend the rest of their tormented days here, sampling from among 100-plus types of tequila. (Stick with the 100 percent blue-agave reposados.) Good food, too. Open daily for lunch and dinner.

For coffee and tasty pastries, an outpost of that Berkeley intellectual original **Peet's Coffee and Tea** is at 2156 Chestnut (between Pierce and Steiner), 415/931-8302. **Pane e Vino,** 3011 Steiner St. (at Union), 415/346-2111, is a justifiably popular neighborhood trattoria that's unpretentious and unwavering in its dedication to serving up grand, deceptively simple pastas. If you tire of privacy, head over to **Perry's,** 1944 Union (between Buchanan and Laguna), 415/922-9022, one of the city's ultimate see-and-be-seen scenes and a great burger stop.

Named for the winding river that irrigates Burma's fertile plains, **Irrawaddy,** 1769 Lombard St. (between Octavia and Laguna), 415/931-2830, is well-regarded for its Burmese cuisine. **Curbside Cafe,** 2417 California, 415/929-9030, specializes in flavorful delights from all over—France, Morocco, Mexico, and the Caribbean (the crab cakes are justifiably famous). **Lhasa Moon,** 2420 Lombard (at Scott), 415/674-9898, offers excellent, authentic Tibetan cuisine Thurs.–Fri. for lunch, and Tues.–Sun. for dinner.

Elite Cafe, 2049 Fillmore (between Pine and California), 415/346-8668, is a clubby pub serving Cajun and Creole food in a dark, handsome room. It's somehow appropriate to the neighborhood. **Baker Street Bistro,** 2953 Baker St., 415/931-1475, is on the quiet end of Baker near Lombard. Warm atmosphere and hearty fare are what make this a popular local's place. Tasty meals are classic Paris bistro: Sonoma rabbit in a light Dijon sauce, steak frites, and crispy chicken. The prix-fixe menu is a bargain at $15.

Close to Japantown and adjacent to the Majestic Hotel (a onetime family mansion), the **Perlot Restaurant,** 1500 Sutter St. (at Gough), 415/441-1100, is a perfect place to go for a romantic tête-a- tête. The setting radiates old-world charm: ornate Edwardian decor, pale green and apricot decor with potted palms. It's sedate, yet far from stuffy, serving plentiful breakfasts on weekdays and brunch on weekends. Listen to a live classical pianist Fri.-Sat. nights and at Sunday brunch. Lunch is served Tues.–Fri., dinner nightly. Reservations are wise.

East of Pacific Heights, where Hwy. 101 surface-streets its way through the city en route to the Golden Gate Bridge, is **Harris',** 2100 Van Ness Ave. (at Pacific), 415/673-1888, the city's best steakhouse, and unabashedly so. This is the place to come for a martini and a steak: T-bones, ribeyes, and filet mignon all star on a beefy menu. Open for dinner daily.

THE RICHMOND, SEACLIFF, THE SUNSET

A fixture in the midst of the Golden Gate National Recreation Area and a favorite hangout at the edge of the continent, the current incarnation of the **Cliff House,** 1090 Point Lobos Ave. (at Upper Great Hwy.), 415/386-3330, is also a decent place to eat. Sunsets are superb, the seafood sublime. As close to fancy as it gets here is **Up-**stairs at the **Cliff House,** an Old San Francisco-style dining room. Decidedly more casual at this cliff-hanging complex are both the **Seafood and Beverage Company** and the **Phineas T. Barnacle** pub. Come to the **Terrace Room** for Sunday brunch.

Heading south down the beachfront, on the opposite side of Great Hwy. is the **Beach Chalet Brewery and Restaurant,** 1000 Great Hwy. (between Fulton and Lincoln), 415/386-8439. This delightful renovation, upstairs (above the Golden Gate Park visitor center) in the old 1925 Willis Polk–designed building, features wall-to-wall windows looking out on the surf (a great spot to watch the sunset) as well as creative California cuisine and a long list of house-made microbrews. The atmosphere is casual—don't come in your bathing suit, but you won't need the dinner jacket—and the service is friendly. Open daily for lunch and dinner.

Moving inland, exceptional ethnic fare is a specialty of Richmond District restaurants. The 100-plus eateries lining Clement St.—among them Asian, South American, Mexican, Italian, and even Russian restaurants and delis—are representative of the district's culinary and cultural mix.

Notable in the city's "new Chinatown," the modern **Fountain Court,** 354 Clement St. (at Fifth Ave.), 415/668-1100, is a wonderful, inexpensive stop for northern-style dim sum and other Shanghai specialties. One of the few San Francisco restaurants serving spicy, sweet Singapore-style fare is **Straits Cafe,** 3300 Geary (at Parker), 415/668-1783, a light, airy, white-walled rendition complete with interior palm trees. For delicious (and cheap) Taiwanese food, head to the **Taiwan Restaurant,** 445 Clement (at Sixth), 415/387-1789, which serves great dumplings.

Good for Indonesian fare is **Jakarta,** 615 Balboa St. (between Seventh and Eighth Avenues), 415/387-5225, another airy and bright place featuring an extensive menu of unusually well-done dishes, plus an eye-catching array of artifacts, musical instruments, and shadow puppets. Some say that the romantic **Khan Toke Thai House,** 5937 Geary (at 23rd Ave.), 415/668-6654, is San Francisco's best Southeast Asian restaurant (and a good deal). Open daily for dinner only, reservations accepted. Another reliable neighborhood choice is **Bangkok Cafe,** 2845 Geary (at Collins), 415/346-8821.

For the whole Moroccan experience, including a belly dancer on some nights, try **El Mansour,** 3121 Clement (near 32nd Ave.), 415/751-2312. A bit more grand, **Kasra Persian & Mediterranean Cuisine,** 349 Clement (at Fifth Ave.), 415/752-1101, is a very good choice for all kinds of shish kabobs.

Unpretentious, welcoming **Café Riggio,** 4112 Geary (between Fifth and Sixth Aves.), 415/221-2114, is much appreciated for its antipasti, world-class calamari, and homemade cannoli for dessert. **Clement Street Bar & Grill,** 708 Clement (at Eighth Ave.), 415/386-2200, serves a mostly American menu featuring vegetarian fare, grilled seafood, and California-style pastas. Farther up Geary toward the beach, **Bill's Place,** 2315 Clement (between 24th and 25th Aves.), 415/221-5262, is an eclectic burger joint with presidential portraits on the walls and a Japanese-style garden. The culinary creations here are named in honor of local celebrities. Guess what you get when you order a Carol Doda burger: two beefy patties with an olive sticking out smack dab in the middle of each. **Tia Margarita,** 300 19th Ave. (at Clement), 415/752-9274, is a long-running family café serving American-style Mexican food.

Things are more than a bit gentrified in Presidio Heights. Just a few blocks south of the Presidio is the **Magic Flute Garden Ristorante,** 3673 Sacramento (between Locust and Spruce), 415/922-1225, which offers Italian and other continental specialties in a sunny French country atmosphere.

Out at the edge of the Sunset District, assemble everything for a memorable picnic from the delis and shops along Taraval. Or check out the diverse ethnic neighborhood eateries. People from all over travel out to the Sunset for **Thanh Long,** 4101 Judah (at 46th Ave.), 415/665-1146, for its signature whole roasted crabs. Thanh Long shares owners with popular Crustacean restaurant, and their French, Vietnamese and Chinese influenced menu also features wonderful garlic noodles and seafood soup. **Brother's Pizza,** 3627 Taraval (near 46th Ave.), 415/753-6004, isn't

much to look at, but the pizzas (try the pesto special), pastas, and calzone overcome that first impression in a big hurry. **El Toreador Fonda Mejicana,** 50 W. Portal (between Ulloa and Vicente), 415/566-2673, is a homey place serving traditional Central and Southern Mexican food. Just down the way on the buzzing West Portal retail strip, **Cafe for All Seasons,** 150 W. Portal (between Vicente and 14th Ave.), 415/665-0900, is a popular stop for hungry shoppers. The California-American menu emphasizes light pastas, grilled fish, and big salads.

HAIGHT-ASHBURY AND VICINITY

On any afternoon, most of the restaurants and cafés lining the Haight will be filled to the gills with young hipsters chowing down on brunch specials or self-medicating with food to cure party-related hangovers.

Campy as all get out, what with those murals and all, **Cha Cha Cha,** 1805 Haight St. (at Shrader), 415/386-5758, is just a hop or skip from Golden Gate Park. A hip Caribbean restaurant, it features unforgettable entrées such as grilled chicken paillard in mustard sauce, shrimp in spicy Cajun sauce, and New Zealand mussels in marinara. It's one of the most popular places around, so it's sometimes hard to find a place to park yourself.

Love the Haight: you can fill up at hippie-ish prices (cheap!) at several places that serve all-day breakfasts or pizza by the slice. For monstrously generous omelettes and a hearty side of potatoes, slide on into **All You Knead,** 1466 Haight (between Ashbury and Masonic), 415/552-4550. You'll get just that. The Haight is always popular for pizza, try **Fat Slice** at 1535 Haight St. (at Ashbury), 415/552-4200, and **Cybelle's,** 203 Parnassus (at Stanyan), 415/665-8088. When East Coast transplants get homesick, they escape to **Escape from New York Pizza,** 1737 Haight (between Cole and Shrader), 415/668-5577. (There's another Escape at 508 Castro, at 18th, 415/252-1515.)

In the Haight's heyday, **Magnolia Pub & Brewery,** 1398 Haight (at Masonic), 415/864-7468, was occupied by the Drugstore Café and later by Magnolia Thunderpussy's, a way-cool dessert-delivery business. The place has retained much of its bohemian charm with colorful murals and sweeping psychedelic signs out front. The menu offers a twist on traditional pub fare—mussels steamed in India Pale Ale, mushroom risotto cakes, along with regular old burgers and house-cut fries. The formidable house-made beer list includes Pale Ales, Porters, and more offbeat selections like the Old Thunderpussy Barleywine, a tribute to the brewpub's most famous tenant.

The strip referred to as "the lower Haight" is an avant-garde enclave sandwiched between the Western Addition and Market Street, with nary a tourist attraction in sight. Without the homeless, runaways, and drug dealers notable in the upper Haight, this several-block area bounded by Webster and Divisadero has become a fairly happy haven for artists and low-end wannabes, as well as the cafés, bars, and restaurants they inhabit. (Great people-watching.) **Kate's Kitchen,** 471 Haight (at Fillmore) 415/626-3984, is a small storefront diner where the emphasis is on down-home American food like buttermilk pancakes and scallion-cheese biscuits. A bit more boisterous, with sunny-day sidewalk tables, is the **Horse Shoe Coffee House,** 566 Haight (between Fillmore and Steiner), 415/626-8852, which also offers high-octane coffee and Internet access.

Most of the neighborhood's bars serve fairly decent food during the day and into the evening; try **Mad Dog in the Fog,** 530 Haight (between Steiner and Fillmore), 415/626-7279, a rowdy English-style pub, or just across the street, painfully hip **Noc Noc,** 557 Haight, 415/861-5811. In the spirit of the neighborhood, customers at the **Toronado,** 547 Haight, 415/863-2276, often duck next door to **Rosamunde Sausage Grill,** 545 Haight, 415/437-6851, for a German sausage-stuffed bun to accompany their beer (the Toronado has more than 40 on tap).

THE MISSION DISTRICT AND THE CASTRO

The Mission District is known for its open-air markets. One of the best is **La Victoria Mexican Bakery & Grocery,** 2937 24th St. (at Al-

abama), 415/642-7120. Buy some homemade tamales, fruit, and a few *churros* (Mexican sugar-dipped doughnuts) and have a feast at the children's park (between Bryant and York on 24th) while studying the murals. Other ethnic bakeries worth poking into for impromptu picnic fixings include **Pan Lido Salvadoreno,** 3147 22nd St. (at Capp), 415/282-3350, and **Pan Lido Bakery,** 5216 Mission (at Niagra), 415/333-2140. An ethnic change-up, serving great sandwiches, is **Lucca Ravioli Company,** 1100 Valencia (at 22nd St.), 415/647-5581. For superb bread and French-inspired pastries—from perfect croissants to cookies and lemon tarts—the place is **Tartine,** 600 Guerrero St. (near 18th St.), 415/487-2600.

Among the Mission's inexpensive neighborhood joints is the justifiably famous **Taqueria Can-Cun,** 2288 Mission (at 19th), 415/252-9560, which serves jumbo-size veggie burritos, handmade tortilla chips, and scorching salsa. There are two other locations: 10 blocks south at 3211 Mission (nearCesar Chavez), 415/550-1414, and at Sixth and Market, 415/864-6773. **Fina Estampa,** 2374 Mission St. (between 19th and 20th), 415/824-4437, is a nondescript Peruvian outpost featuring exceptional seafood, chicken, and beef entrées (humongous portions) and good service (there's another one at 1100 Van Ness (at Geary), 415/440-6364). At **La Rondalla,** 901 Valencia (at 20th), 415/647-7474, mariachi bands play while you eat. At **Pancho Villa Taqueria,** 3071 16th (between Mission and Valencia), 415/864-8840, you'll be hard-pressed to find anything over seven bucks. And the portions are huge, including the grand dinner plates of grilled shrimp. Across the street from the murals at the Mission Cultural Center, **La Taqueria,** 2889 Mission (at 25th), 415/285-7117, is one of the most popular taquerias in the neighborhood. The staff don't use rice in the burritos, so you get more meat for your buck—their carne asada and carnitas rate among the city's best. At **Los Jarritos,** 901 S. Van Ness Ave. (at 20th), 415/648-8383, the "little jars" add color to an already colorful menu of Jalisco specialties.

The line between the Mission and Castro Districts, like distinct geographical and sociopolitical divisions elsewhere in the city, is often blurred.

Yet the Mission is becoming *the* foodie destination, despite the fact that parking is such a challenge. **Destino,** 1815 Market St. (between Valencia and Guerrero), 415/552-4451, has an almost religious South American feel what with all the candles, wood-and-amber walls, and heavy oak chairs. The food here measures up to the cultural interpretation: the ceviche and empanadas pair nicely with wines from Chile, Argentina, Spain, and California. The place for inspired Peruvian is modest, citrus-splashed **Limon,** 3316 17th St. (between Mission and Valencia), 415/252-0918, serving some 20 flavorful selections—everything from bouillabaisse and *tamal criollo* to exceptional pork chops. **Platanos,** 598 Guerrero (at 18th St.), 415/252-9281, is another understated hotspot, serving excellent *pupusas* and enchiladas Centro Americana as appetizers and entrées including mole *poblano,* chiles rellenos, and a paella made with coconut milk.

Popular with young foodies is casual, festive **Luna Park,** 694 Valencia (at 18th St.), 415/553-8584, where people's favorites range from hunter's pie and grilled chicken to house-made Graham crackers for the make-your-own S'mores. Superchic **Foreign Cinema,** 2534 Mission St. (between 21st and 22nd Sts.), 415/648-7600, keeps an internationally intellectual atmosphere by beaming foreign films on a wall in the outdoor courtyard. The restaurant is a happy marriage between Berkeley's Chez Panisse and Zuni Café, with a distinct Mission district spin. People flock from all over the city, so make a reservation or be prepared to wait.

One more stop along the Mission's restaurant row (Valencia between 16th and 24th Streets) is the lively and colorful tapas bar **Ramblas,** 557 Valencia (at 16th), 415/565-0207, the place to go for a social evening of grazing on small plates of Paella Las Ramblas and classic tortilla espanola while knocking back the fruity house sangria. A few blocks down, a no less pleasant Vietnamese alternative is **Saigon Saigon,** 1132 Valencia (at 22nd), 415/206-9635, serving an astounding array of authentic dishes, from majestic rolls and barbecued quail to Buddha's delight (vegetarian). Open for lunch on weekdays, for dinner nightly.

In a neighborhood saturated with tapas bars, **Esperpento,** 3295 22nd St. (at Valencia), 415/282-8867, stands out as a great place for delectable Catalonian entrées, as well as tasty and sophisticated Spanish finger foods. Fairly inexpensive. Open Mon.-Sat. for lunch and dinner.

A neighborhood classic in the retro diner genre is **Boogaloos,** 3296 22nd St. (at Valencia), 415/824-4088, famous for huge breakfasts, slacker crowds, and its signature dish, the Temple o' Spuds. **Cafe Ethiopia,** 878 Valencia (at 20th), 415/285-2728, offers all the usual espresso drinks plus Ethiopian cuisine, including poultry, beef, and vegetarian dishes from mild to spicy hot. Hugely popular and excellent value for the money, **Ti Couz,** 3108 16th St. (at Valencia), 415/252-7373, specializes in crepes—stuffed with everything from spinach to salmon to berries. Meanwhile, denizens of the Mission have discovered that the filling Indian and Pakistani food at **Pakwan,** 3182 16th St. (between Valencia and Guerrero), 415/255-2440, is perfectly suited for sustenance between bars. Flavorful curries, tandooris and daals are the main attractions. There's no table service (you order at a counter), and no alcohol.

For real cheap eats in the Castro, head to **Hot 'n' Hunky,** 4039 18th St.(at Castro), 415/621-6365, for locally famous burgers and renowned French fries, not to mention excessive neon and Marilyn Monroe memorabilia. Very Castro is **Cafe Flore,** 2298 Market St. (at Noe), 415/621-8579, a popular gay hangout and café serving up omelettes and crepes, salads and good sandwiches, and current information about what's going on in the neighborhood. (Great for people-watching, especially out on the plant-populated patio.)

Missed by most tourists but popular for brunch is the **Bagdad Cafe,** 2295 Market St. (at 16th), 415/621-4434, offering a healthy take on American-style fare, plus great salads. Nearby, and wonderful for succulent seafood, is the **Anchor Oyster Bar,** 579 Castro (between 18th and 19th), 415/431-3990.

It's Tops, 1801 Market (at McCoppin), 415/431-6395, looks like a classic American greasy spoon—the decor hasn't changed since 1945—but the surprise is just how good the pancakes and other breakfast selections are. **Sparky's 24-Hour Diner,** 242 Church St. (between Market and 15th), 415/626-8666, got lost somewhere in the 1950s, style-wise, but the breakfast omelettes, burgers, and salads are certainly up to modern expectations.

The atmosphere at suave, contemporary **2223 Market** (at Noe), 415/431-0692, is cozy, and the food is down-home American. Excellent garlic mashed potatoes and onion rings.

Beyond the Mission and Castro—but not that far—is upstairs-downstairs **Chenery Park** in Glen Park/Noe Valley, 683 Chenery St. (near Diamond), 415/337-8537, a restaurant that draws foodies from all over and specializes in homey yet stylish Americana. Chenery Park's changing menu of comfort foods includes such things as pot roast with root vegetables; baked macaroni and cheese; seafood gumbo with scallops, shrimp, and catfish; and braised lamb shank with red wine and polenta.

SOUTH OF MARKET (SoMa)

San Francisco's answer to New York City's SoHo, the South of Market area, or SoMa, is geographically a large neighborhood, extending from Market Street to China Basin, and Hwy. 101 to the Bay. The new money is here, and new businesses spring up every month, though many areas of the neighborhood are still considered unsafe, especially after dark. Reality here ranges from streetpeople chic to chichi restaurants and clubs. The row of nightclubs around 11th Street has survived since the 1980s, but business owners have done their demographic homework, so SoMa has seen a steady growth of trendy new restaurants.

The burgers at **Eddie Rickenbacker's,** 133 Second St. (between Mission and Minna), 415/543-3498, are considered by connoisseurs to be close to the best, though other good bets at Eddie's include the salads, soups, and fish dishes.

Head toward the bay down second to reach the delightful South Park neighborhood, home to photo studios and shops serving the multimedia and advertising industries, as well as trendy coffeehouses, restaurants, and the block-square greensward of South Park itself (bordered by Bryant and Brannan, Second and Third). A crowd that appears to have walked off the pages of *Dwell* magazine is energized by South Park's **Infusion,** 555 Second St. (at Brannan), 415/543-2282, a busy, chic restaurant beloved for its innovative, spicy menu and fruit-infused vodka drinks. Inside leafy South Park, crowded and noisy **Caffe Centro,** 102 South Park, 415/882-1500, packs in a lively multimedia crowd for breakfast and lunch. The lures: excellent coffee, panini sandwiches, and soup, along with consistently good Franco-style salads (including a classic Nicoise). On sunny days order at the To-Go window and dine alfresco in the park on one of the benches, or better yet, on the lawn. Straight across the park is the smart and locally-favored **South Park Cafe,** 108 South Park, 415/495-7275, a little pocket of Paris in the city, with a zinc-topped bar, sidewalk seating, and an international selection of newspapers hanging from wooden rods. The menu features bistro classics such as grilled steak with frites, mussels in white wine sauce, or leg of lamb with couscous, and wonderful desserts.

After exploring Moscone Center and Yerba Buena Gardens, drop in for a cold one at **Thirsty Bear Brewing Co.,** 661 Howard (between Second and Third), 415/974-0905, where you can enjoy one of the seven house-made microbrews and outstanding Spanish and Catalan dishes. Marked by the huge tomato hanging outside, no-fuss **Vino e Cucina,** 489 Third St. (at Bryant), 415/543-6962, offers fine Italian cuisine, including pastas, pizzas, and unusual specials. Down two blocks, **Max's,** 311 Third St. (between Folsom and Howard), 415/546-6297, has a lighthearted New-York diner atmosphere and heavyweight portions of deli sandwiches, burgers, and gigantic breakfasts. The décor and food remain true to diner tradition, with a few "Californian" concessions (salads). Exceptional **Fringale,** 570 Fourth St. (between Bryant and Brannan), 415/543-0573, is a bright and contemporary French/American bistro serving excellent food at remarkably reasonable prices—a place well worth looking for.

Continuing southwest through the district, you'll find good and pretty cheap, fast-as-your-laundry-cycle fare at **BrainWash,** 1122 Folsom (between Seventh and Eighth), 415/861-3663 (see Clean Up Your Act at BrainWash). It's by one of the area's sociocultural flagships, **Julie's Supper Club,** 1123 Folsom (between Seventh and Eighth), 415/861-0707, a restaurant and nightclub/bar known for its combination of space-age-meets-the-1950s supper-club style and Old West saloon atmosphere. Not to mention the famous martinis. For spice and great atmosphere, **India Garden,** 1261 Folsom (at Ninth), 415/626-2798, is well worth poking into for wonderful nans (flatbreads) and *kulchas* baked in a tandoor oven.

It's another trendy Asian-Californian fusion restaurant. Or maybe its not. What's certain is that **Asia SF,** 201 Ninth St. (at Howard), 415/255-2742, is as much a nightclub as a restaurant. There's a DJ every night of the week, and the cocktails are as famous as the waitstaff of beautiful and talented gender illusionists. And, surprisingly, the kitchen staff take their job seriously—turning out well-respected fusion cui-sine (try the noodle dishes). At the bar, the girls command your attention on the half-hour; they climb atop the colossal structure then kick it up to pop hits. This is one of the most "San Francisco" places going. Bring an open mind and your go-go boots.

If you're on a tight budget, you won't go wrong at **Manora's Thai Cuisine,** 1600 Folsom (at 12th), 415/861-6224, which serves deliciously spicy Thai food at bargain prices. The menu features well-prepared seafood and curries. Night owls like to come here before hitting the nearby clubs.

Over in China Basin the industrial-chic hotspot (great view of the railroad tracks) is **42 Degrees,** 235 16th St. (behind the Esprit Outlet at Illinois, along the waterfront in China Basin), 415/777-5558, serving "nouvelle Mediterranean" food. The menu offers cuisine from southern France, Italy, Spain, and Greece—all regions at 42° north latitude. This is still one of the trendiest spots around, so sometimes you wait awhile.

Arts and Entertainment

A selection of entertaining bars, nightclubs, and other worthy diversions is included under sight-seeing sections above, which are organized by neighborhood. To keep abreast of the ever-changing arts and entertainment scene, consult local newspapers, especially the calendar sections of the *Bay Guardian* and other local weeklies, and the pink Datebook section of the Sunday *Chronicle.*

PERFORMING ARTS

San Francisco's performing arts scene offers everything from the classics to the contemporary, kitschy, and downright crazed. Find out what's going on by picking up local publications or calling the San Francisco Convention & Visitors Bureau information hotlines (see Useful Information, below). Tickets for major events and performances are available through the relevant box offices, mentioned below.

Low-income art lovers, or those deciding to "do" the town on a last-minute whim, aren't nec-essarily out of luck. **TIX Bay Area,** on Stockton St. at Union Square, 415/433-7827, www.theatrebayarea.org, offers day-of-performance tickets to local shows at half price. Payment is cash only, no credit card reservations. Along with being a full-service BASS ticket outlet, TIX also handles advance full-price tickets to many Bay Area events. Open Tues.–Sat. noon–7:30 P.M., closed Mondays. You can get a catalog for ordering advance tickets at half price by calling **TIX by Mail** at 415/430-1140. To charge arts and entertainment tickets by phone or to listen to recorded calendar listings, call Tickets.com 415/478-2277. Another helpful information source: KUSF 90.3 FM's **Alternative Music and Entertainment News (AMEN)** information line, 415/221-2636.

Other ticket box offices include: **City Box Office,** 415/392-4400, **Ticketfinder,** 650/756-1414, 800/523-1515, or www.ticketfinder.com, and **St. Francis Theatre and Sports Tickets,** a service of the Westin St. Francis Hotel, 415/362-3500, www.premiertickets.com.

Dance and Musical Productions

One of the nation's oldest classical dance companies, the **San Francisco Ballet** has been called "a truly national ballet company" by the *New York Times*. The ballet troupe's regular season, with performances in the Civic Center's War Memorial Opera House, runs Feb.–May, though holiday season performances of the *The Nutcracker* are a long-running San Francisco tradition. For tickets, call 415/865-2000 or order tickets online at www.sfballet.org. The opera house also hosts visiting performances by The Joffrey Ballet and The Kirov Ballet, among others.

The smaller **Herbst Theatre** inside the War Memorial Veteran Building, 401 Van Ness Ave. (at McAllister), 415/621-6600, hosts smaller dance and musical productions, including performances by the San Francisco Chamber Symphony and the San Francisco Early Music Society.

The **San Francisco Opera** season runs Sept.–Dec., offering a total of 10 productions with big-name stars. Since this is the heart of the San Francisco social scene, tickets are expensive and hard to come by; call 415/864-3330. Generally more accessible is the **San Francisco Symphony,** which offers a Sept.–June regular season in Louise M. Davies Hall downtown in the Civic Center, plus July pops concerts. For tickets, call 415/864-6000; a limited number of discount tickets go on sale two hours before performances at the box office (cash only). Davies Hall is also a venue for other performances, including some programs of the West's only major independent music conservatory, the **San Francisco Conservatory of Music**—call 415/759-3475 for tickets.

Theater

Wherever you find it, pick up a copy of *Callboard* magazine, for its current and comprehensive show schedules, or check its website at www.theatrebayarea.org For Broadway shows, the **Curran Theatre,** 445 Geary (between Mason and Taylor), 415/551-2000 (information), 415/478-2277 (BASS) for tickets, is the long-running standard. The **Golden Gate Theatre** at Sixth and Market, the **Orpheum** at Eighth and Market, and the **Marines Memorial Theatre** at

Sutter and Mason are other popular mainstream venues for comedies, musicals, and revues; call 415/551-2000 for all three theaters. The award-winning **Lamplighters Music Theatre,** 415/227-4797, specializes in Gilbert and Sullivan musicals and schedules three productions a year (in August, October, and January) at the Yerba Buena Center, 415/978-2787, and at other locations around the bay.

The repertory **American Conservatory Theater** (ACT), 415/834-3200 or 415/749-2228 (box office), performs its big-name-headliner contemporary comedies and dramas in the venerable **Geary Theatre,** 415 Geary (at Mason). Union Square's theater district is also where you'll find **Theatre on the Square,** 450 Post (between Powell and Mason), 415/433-9500.

San Francisco is also home to a number of small, innovative theaters and theater troupes, including the Magic Theatre, Cowell Theater, and Young Performers' Theatre at Fort Mason and the Asian American Theatre in the Richmond District, mentioned in more detail under Fort Mason and The Avenues, respectively. The **Actors Theatre of San Francisco,** 533 Sutter (between Powell and Mason), 415/296-9179, usually offers unusual plays. **Theatre Rhinoceros,** 2926 16th St. (between Mission and S. Van Ness), 415/861-5079, is America's oldest gay and lesbian theater company, est. 1978.

The long-running **Eureka Theatre Company,** 215 Jackson (between Front and Battery), 415/788-7469 (box office and information), is noted for its provocative, politically astute presentations. **Intersection for the Arts,** 446 Valencia St. (between 15th and 16th), 415/626-2787 (administration) or 415/626-3311 (box office), the city's oldest alternative arts center, presents everything from experimental dramas to performance and visual art and dance. onetime "new talent" like Robin Williams, Whoopi Goldberg, and Sam Shepard are all Intersection alumni.

Mimes, Circuses, and Cabaret

Worth seeing whenever the group is in town is the much-loved, always arresting, and far from silent **San Francisco Mime Troupe,** 855 Treat Ave. (between 21st and 22nd), 415/285-1717, a

SAN FRANCISCO

SAN FRANCISCO ON STAGE

Geary Street near both Mason and Taylor is the official center of the theater district, and the 400 block of Geary serves as the epicenter of the mainstream theater scene. These days the concentration of upscale Union Square hotels roughly demarcates the theater district boundaries. With so many fine theaters scattered throughout the city, it's something of a New York affectation to insist on that designation downtown. But San Francisco, a city that has loved its dramatic song and dance since gold rush days, definitely insists. Poetry readings, lectures, opera, and Shakespeare were integral to the 1800s arts scene. Superstar entertainers of the era made their mark here, from spider-dancer Lola Montez and her child protégé Lotta Crabtree to actress Lillie Langtry, opera star Luisa Tetrazzini, actress Helena Modjeska, and actor Edwin Booth. Today, out-of-towners flock to big spectacular shows like the Andrew Lloyd-Webber musicals and evergreens such as the zany musical revue *Beach Blanket Babylon*. Luckily, the best shows are often less crowded. Most shows begin at 8 P.M., and the majority of theaters are closed on Monday.

Theater Information

Finding information on what's going on in the theater is not a difficult task. Listings are printed in the *San Francisco Bay Guardian,* the *SF Weekly,* and the Sunday edition of the *San Francisco Chronicle.* Or check out the arts online at **TheatreMania,** www.theatremania.com. And pick up a copy of **Callboard** for its current and comprehensive show schedules.

Getting Tickets

Theater tickets can be purchased in advance or for half price on the day of the performance at **TIX Bay Area,** on Powell St. at Union Square, 415/433-7827, www.theatrebayarea.org. Payment is cash only, no credit card reservations. A full-service Ticketmaster outlet as well, TIX also handles advance full-price tickets to many Bay Area events (open Tues.–Thurs. 11 A.M.–6 P.M., Fri.–Sat. 11 A.M.–7 P.M., Sun. 11 A.M.–3 P.M.). You can get a catalog for ordering advance tickets at half price by calling **TIX by Mail,** at 415/433-1235. Order full-price tickets in advance with a service charge from Ticketmaster, 415/421-8497 or 800/755-4000, www.ticketmaster.com.

decades-old institution true to the classic Greek and Roman tradition of theatrical farce—politically sophisticated street theater noted for its complex simplicity. In addition to boasting actor Peter Coyote and the late rock impressario Bill Graham as organizational alumni, and inspiring the establishment of onetime troupe member Luis Valdez's El Teatro Campesino, the Mime Troupe was repeatedly banned and arrested in its formative years. In 1966, the state Senate Un-American Activities Committee charged the group with the crime of making lewd performances, the same year troupe members were arrested in North Beach for singing Christmas carols without a permit. In l987, the Mime Troupe won a special Tony Award for Excellence in Regional Theater; it has also garnered several Obies and the highly prized San Francisco Bay Area Media Alliance Golden Gadfly Award.

A tad more family-oriented, "the kind of circus

parents might want their kids to run away to," according to NPR's Jane Pauley, is the **Pickle Family Circus,** another exceptional city-based theater troupe, which performs at Fort Mason's Cowell Theatre, 415/441-3400.

Bizarre cabaret-style *Beach Blanket Babylon,* playing at **Club Fugazi,** 678 Green St. (between Powell and Columbus) in North Beach, 415/421-4222, is the longest-running musical revue in theatrical history. The story line is always evolving. Snow White, who seems to be seeking love in all the wrong places, encounters characters who strut straight off the front pages of the tabloids.

Eclectic" is the word used most often to describe the **Audium,** 1616 Bush St. (at Franklin), 415/771-1616 or www.audium.org, perhaps the ultimate performance of sound, certainly the only place like this in the world. Some 169 speakers in the sloping walls, coupled with the suspended ceiling and floating floor, all create an

Other ticket box offices include: **City Box Office,** 415/392-4400, www.cityboxoffice.com; **Ticketfinder,** 650/756-1414 or 800/523-1515, www.ticketfinder.com; and **Premier Tickets,** 415/346-7222, www.premiertickets.com.

Theater District Venues

For Broadway shows, the **Curran Theatre,** 445 Geary (between Mason and Taylor), 415/551-2000, is the long-running standard. The repertory **American Conservatory Theater** (ACT), 415/834-3200 or 415/749-2228 (box office), performs its big-name-headliner contemporary comedies and dramas in the venerable **Geary Theatre,** 415 Geary (at Mason).

Other neighborhood venues include the **Golden Gate Theatre,** 1 Taylor (at Golden Gate), 415/551-2000, and the **Marines Memorial Theatre,** 609 Sutter (at Mason), 415/551-2000. Both are good bets for off-Broadway shows. Unusual small theaters include the **Plush Room Cabaret,** inside the York Hotel at 940 Sutter (at Leavenworth), 415/885-6800.

Performance Spaces Elsewhere

San Francisco is also home to a number of small, innovative theaters and theater troupes, including the **Magic Theatre, Cowell Theater,** and **Young Performers Theatre** at Fort Mason, and the **Asian American Theatre** in the Richmond District, mentioned in more detail in The Avenues section of this chapter. The **Actors Theatre of San Francisco,** 533 Sutter (between Powell and Mason), 415/296-9179, usually offers unusual plays. **Theatre Rhinoceros,** 2926 16th St. (between Mission and S. Van Ness), 415/861-5079, is America's oldest gay and lesbian theater company, est. 1978.

The long-running **Eureka Theatre Company,** 215 Jackson (between Front and Battery), 415/788-7469, is noted for its provocative, politically astute presentations. **Intersection for the Arts,** 446 Valencia St. (between 15th and 16th), 415/626-2787 (administration) or 415/626-3311 (box office), the city's oldest alternative arts center, presents everything from experimental dramas to performance and visual art and dance. Onetime "new talent" like Robin Williams, Whoopi Goldberg, and Sam Shepard are all Intersection alumni.

unmatched aural experience. Regular performances are on Friday and Saturday nights at 8:30 P.M.; tickets ($12) go on sale at 8 P.M. at the box office, or buy in advance at Tix in Union Square. Children under age 12 not allowed.

ART GALLERIES AND STUDIOS

The downtown area, especially near Union Square and along lower Grant Ave., is rich with art galleries and arts-related specialty shops. The free *San Francisco Arts Monthly,* www.sfarts.org, available around town and at the visitor information center downtown, includes a complete current listing of special gallery tours, exhibits, and art showrooms. Very useful, too, is *The San Francisco Bay Area Gallery Guide,* 415/921-1600, which details goings-on at galleries large and small, and provides information about current shows at major Bay Area museums.

San Francisco's Real Food Company delis and stores—at 3060 Fillmore St., 2140 Polk St., 3939 24th St., and elsewhere in the Bay Area—are the most predictable places to pick up free **San Francisco Open Studios** artists' listings, detailed maps, and resource directories. Or stop by Bay Area bookstores, art supply stores, and selected galleries. The Open Studios concept offers direct-to-you fine arts, plus an opportunity to meet the artists and often see how and where they work. The Bay Area's Open Studios experience, sponsored by local businesses, offers regularly scheduled open-studio days, usually scheduled on consecutive Saturdays and Sundays from October to mid-November. On these days, more than 500 local artists open their studios or personally share their work with the public. You can come just to schmooze, but these working artists will eat better if you buy. For more information, call 415/861-9838 or see www.sfopenstudios.com.

FILM

The **San Francisco International Film Festival,** 415/929-5000 (office) or 415/931-3456 (recorded information), Northern California's longest-running film festival, is scheduled annually, usually from late April into May. This cinematic celebration typically includes 60 or more films from dozens of countries. Call for current program and price information. The city has all sorts of noteworthy festivities focused on film, including the **Lesbian & Gay Film Festival,** usually held at the Castro Theater in late June.

Classic theaters in the neighborhoods, these most likely to host foreign, revival, and other film festivals, include the 1922 **Castro Theater,** 429 Castro St. (near Market), 415/621-6120, where you get live Wurlitzer music during interludes, Hollywood classics, contemporary films, and clever double bills; and the hip **Roxie,** 3117 16th St. (near Valencia), 415/863-1087, www.roxie.com, specializing in independent, oddball, and trendy films, and sometimes showing silent flicks accompanied by organ. At the Haight's **Red Victorian Movie House,** 1727 Haight St., 415/668-3994, count on art films, revivals, interesting foreign fare—and California-casual couch-like benches for comfort.

Hole-in-the-wall **Artists' Television Access (ATA),** 992 Valencia, 415/824-3890, offers truly underground, experimental, and radical political films from unknown, independent filmmakers. Other good movie theater bets: the **Metreon** at 101 Fourth St. (at Mission), 415/369-6000; the **AMC 1000,** 1000 Van Ness Ave., 415/931-9800; and the **Embarcadero Center Cinema** at Embarcadero One, 415/352-8010.

COMEDY AND BILLIARD CLUBS

Bay Area Theatresports (BATS), 415/474-8935, schedules performances in Fort Mason's Bayfront Theater. Their hilarious, improvisational shows are often team efforts, with the "scripts" for instant plays, movies, and musicals created from audience suggestions.

The hottest yuckspot in town, some say, is **Cobb's Comedy Club** at The Cannery on Fisherman's Wharf, 2801 Leavenworth (at Beach), 415/928-4320. Another stand-up venue is **Punchline Comedy Club,** 444 Battery (between Washington and Clay), 415/397-7573.

Located inside the Rincon Center, **Chalkers Billiard Club,** 101 Spear St. (at Mission), 415/512-0450, has the feel of a clubby pub with its dark polished wood, pristine pool tables, and workers unwinding after the 9-to-5 grind at nearby Financial District offices. Also gentrified and comfortable even for absolute beginners is **The Great Entertainer,** 975 Bryant (between Seventh and Eighth), 415/861-8833, once a paint warehouse, now the West Coast's largest pool hall. Most of the tables in the 28,000-square-foot hall are nine feet long. Private suites are available. Also here: snooker, shuffleboard, and Ping-Pong (table tennis) tables.

SPECTATOR AND TEAM SPORTS

The **San Francisco Giants** major-league baseball team plays ball on the bay at the city's 42,000-seat SBC Park on the Embarcadero, 415/468-3700, www.sfgiants.com. (To betray the city's baseball heritage, zip across the bay to the Oakland Coliseum and the Oakland A's games, 510/430-8020, www.oaklandathletics.com.) Still at home at 3Com Park—once known as Candlestick Park—are the **San Francisco 49ers,** NFL footballers made famous by their numerous Super Bowl victories. For 49er tickets and information, call 415/656-4900 or check www.sf49ers.com.

San Franciscans are big on participatory sports. Some of the city's most eclectic competitive events reflect this fact, including the famous **Bay to Breakers** race in May, 415/808-5000 or www.baytobreakers.com, which attracts 100,000-plus runners, joggers, and walkers, most wearing quite creative costumes—and occasionally nothing at all. It's a phenomenon that must be experienced to be believed. (Request registration forms well in advance.)

San Francisco's outdoor and other recreational opportunities seem limited only by one's imagination (and income): hot-air ballooning, beachcombing, bicycling, bird-watching, boating, bowling, camping, canoeing, kayaking, hang-gliding, hiking, horseshoes, fishing, golf, tennis, sailing, swimming, surfing, parasailing, rowing, rock climbing, running, windsurfing. Golden Gate National Recreational Area and Golden Gate Park are major community recreation resources.

For a current rundown on sports events and recreational opportunities, or for information on specific activities, consult the helpful folks at the San Francisco Convention & Visitors Bureau.

EVENTS

Even more kaleidoscopic than the city's arts scene, San Francisco events include an almost endless combination of the appropriate, inappropriate, absurd, inspired, and sublime. Well-known among these are the spectacular Chinese New Year Parade, the Gay Pride Parade, the Folsom Street Fair, and the eccentric Bay to Breakers road race. For a fairly complete listing, consult local newspapers or see the San Francisco Convention & Visitor's Bureau website, www.sfvisitor.org. Museums, theaters, neighborhood groups, and other cultural institutions usually offer their own annual events calendars.

January/February

In January or February, Chinatown comes to life with the **Chinese New Year Parade,** 415/982-3000, www.chineseparade.com, when celebratory Asian spirits prevail on the streets of Chinatown. The vibrant nighttime parade features elaborate floats, Chinese acrobats, stilt walkers, lion dancers, capped by the appearance of a 200-foot Golden Dragon ("Gum Lung") festooned with colored lights.

On February 14, let your animal passions run wild at the San Francisco Zoo's **Valentine's Day Sex Tour.** The special narrated Safari Train tour will tell you everything you always wanted to know about sex in the animal kingdom. Horny rhinos? Gay wallabees? Lesbian penguins? Why, it's all true. The tour is followed by a champagne, crepes, and truffles reception where you'll have the chance to get up close and personal with a variety of animals. Reservations required and, because of the risque sub-

ject matter, age 21 and over only. For more information, call 415/753-7165.

March

Expect everything to be Irish and/or green at the United Irish Societies' **St. Patrick's Day Parade,** 415/675-9885, www.uissf.org, celebrated for the last 150 years the Sunday before or after March 17, when it often rains (bring an umbrella). The day starts with a special Mass at St. Patrick's Church, at Fourth and Mission. At noon marching bands, political activists, and Celtic dancers begin winding their way through downtown to the Civic Center; the parade officially ends with a gathering at Justin Herman Plaza. For St. Paddie's Day diehards, the party lasts all weekend at Irish bars around the city.

Later in March, quite is the event is the **San Francisco International Asian American Film Festival,** 415/863-7428, www.naatanet.org, a showcase for Asian films from both sides of the Pacific Ocean.

April

Wavy Gravy once walked a plastic fish at the **St. Stupid's Day Parade,** www.saintstupid.com, a day for San Francisco to celebrate its tradition of anything goes, which falls, not coincidentally, on April Fool's Day (April 1). The demonstration/march/celebration starts at the Transamerica Pyramid, the "pointy building" downtown, and weaves its way down Market Street. Prankster participants carry banners like "Do Not Read This Sign," and "I Voted for Bush. (Twice.)" That's stupid, all right.

Health and healing are the focus of the annual **New Living Expo** at the Concourse Exhibition Center, 415/382-8300, www.newageexpo.com, which in previous years featured workshops and lectures by Julia Butterfly Hill, Shakti Gawain, John Gray, and Rodney Yee, as well as a marketplace offering all manner of New Age products and services.

Held over two weekends, Japantown's **Cherry Blossom Festival,** 415/563-2313, showcases traditional Japanese arts with martial arts demonstrations, tea ceremonies, taiko drumming, and other unique cultural festivities. Outdoor life comes back to the bay with a bang as both **base-ball season** and **yachting season** start up again. The latter's **Opening Day on the Bay** is quite the sight.

May

In late April or early May, the San Francisco Film Society presents the two week **San Francisco International Film Festival,** 415/561-5000 or 415/931-3456 (recorded information), www .sfiff.org. The program of approximately 200 new features, documentaries, and shorts offers films from around the world, many of which lack commercial distribution. Past audiences have been the first to see new films by Jean-Luc Godard and Woody Allen. Screenings take place at the Kabuki 8, the Castro, the Pacific Film Archives in Berkeley, and other venues around the Bay Area.

The Mission District hosts two major events in May: the **Cinco de Mayo Parade and Festival,** a two-day party (with plenty of mariachi music and *folklorico* costumes and dancers) scheduled as close to May 5 as possible, and late May's **Carnaval San Francisco,** featuring an uninhibited parade with samba bands, dancers, floats, and hundreds of thousands of revelers. For more information on both, contact the **Mission Economic and Cultural Association,** 415/282-3334, www.medasf.org. In mid-May the whole city turns out for the world's largest footrace, the **Bay to Breakers,** 415/808-5000 or www.baytobreakers.com, when some 100,000 participants, many decked out in hilarious and/or scandalous costumes, hoof it from the Embarcadero out to Ocean Beach. Don't miss this wild, wacky, and wonderfully San Franciscan event.

June

The Haight celebrates its long-gone Summer of Love in June with the **Haight Street Fair,** 415/661-8025. Among the arts, crafts, and other wares, you can probably count on plenty of tie-dyed items, prism-cut glass, and other hippie-style creations. But by summer everyone's in a street-party mood, so June also features the **North Beach Festival,** 415/989-6426, and the **Union Street Art Festival,** 415/441-7055. Also in June are the long-running **Ethnic Dance Fes-**tival, 415/392-4400, www.worldartswest.org, at the Palace of Fine Arts. The **San Francisco International Lesbian and Gay Film Festival,** 415/703-8650, www.frameline.org, is the longest-running independent gay film festival in the country. Usually also late in June, coinciding with the film festival, is the annual **Lesbian-Gay-Bisexual-Transgender Pride Parade and Celebration,** 415/864-3733 or www.sf-pride.org, one huge gay-pride party usually led by Dykes on Bikes and including cross-dressing cowboys (or girls), gay bands and majorettes, cheerleaders, and everyone and everything else. Show up, too, for the start of Golden Gate Park's **Stern Grove Midsummer Music Festival,** 415/252-6253, www.sterngrove.org, which offers concerts in the grove on Sundays at 2 P.M. (The festival ends in late August.)

July

In inimitable American style, **Independence Day** (July 4) is celebrated in San Francisco with costumes—prizes for Most Original Uncle Sam and Best Symbol of America—ethnic food, multicultural entertainment, comics, and nighttime fireworks at Crissy Field. In mid-July, San Francisco's cable car operators compete in the annual **Cable Car Bell-Ringing Championship,** 415/923-6217. Also in July: **Jazz and All That Art on Fillmore,** on Fillmore between Post and Jackson, 415/346-9162, celebrating the cultural and musical heritage of what was once a largely black neighborhood; the **Midsummer Mozart Festival,** 415/292-9620 or www.midsummermozart .org; and the **San Francisco Symphony Pops Concerts,** 415/864-6000. Golden Gate Park's annual **Stern Grove Festival,** www.sterngrove .org, is a free series of R&B, jazz, and world concerts playing through September.

August/September

Hot in August are **Comedy Celebration Day** in Golden Gate Park, 415/777-7120; Fort Mason's **ACC Craft Fair,** 415/896-5060; and the **San Francisco Butoh Festival,** an ethnic dance fest at Fort Mason, 415/441-3687. Or head to Japantown for the **Nihonmachi Street Fair,** 415/771-9861, www.nihonmachistreetfair.org. In late August comes the big **A la Carte, A la Park** food and brewfest to Golden Gate Park, 415/478-2277.

Labor Day weekend brings the popular **San Francisco Shakespeare Festival,** 415/422-2222, www.sfshakes.org, with free performances offered in Golden Gate Park and other parks around the Bay Area through October. In mid-September, look for Chinatown's **Autumn Moon Festival,** 415/982-6306, a large street fair with arts, crafts, lion dances and live music. Also in September: the annual **Bay Area Robot Olympics** at the Exploratorium, 415/563-7337; **Opera in the Park,** 415/864-3330; and the **San Francisco Blues Festival** at Fort Mason, 415/826-6837 or www.sfblues.com, which draws legendary blues artists. Toward the end of the month the **Folsom Street Fair,** 415/861-3247, www.folsomstreetfair.com, unleashes the bondage crowd for an all-day parade of men (and some women) in chaps, biker hats, and restraints.

October

Bless your pet at Grace Cathedral's **St. Francis Day service.** During **Fleet Week,** the U.S. Navy lowers the plank for the public and also welcomes ships from around the world. A major cultural blowout around Columbus Day is the **Italian Heritage Parade and Festival** on Fisherman's Wharf and in North Beach, 415/989-2220. Also scheduled in October: the **Castro Street Fair,** 415/467-3354 or www.castrostreetfair.org, which attracts large crowds from the gay community; Fort Mason's **San Francisco Fall Antiques Show,** 415/546-6661; and the annual **San Francisco Jazz Festival,** 415/398-5655, www.sfjazz.org, showcasing established and up-and-coming jazz performers. To finish off the month in absolutely absurd style, on a weekend near Halloween head for the **Exotic Erotic Ball,** 415/567-BALL, www.exoticeroticball.com. Alternatively, the best **Halloween** drag and costume show is the Castro's bash, 415/826-1401, actually held in the Civic Center.

November/December

On November 2, the Mission District celebrates the Aztec/Spanish tradition of Dia de los Muertos

BIG AND BIGGER: THE NEW BLOOMIES

Downtown's oft-discussed Bloomingdale's is finally becoming a reality. Essentially two malls under one roof with a total of 1.5 million square feet, the new shopping center will include the second-largest store in the Bloomingdale's chain as well as the interconnected San Francisco Centre and Nordstrom. When the project opens to the public in 2006, it will be the largest urban shopping center west of the Mississippi River.

The new conjoined shopping center complex will extend from Market to Mission Sts., between Fourth and Fifth—strategically located between Union Square and Yerba Buena Gardens—with interconnecting walkways on five levels. The project will incorporate elements of the historic 19th-century Emporium, particularly its ornate dome—destined to offer more shops as well as charm from yesteryear.

or **Day of the Dead,** 415/821-1155, www.dayofthedeadsf.org, with a festival of art, music, and dance in honor of dead friends and relatives. Other November events include the **San Francisco International Auto Show** at Moscone Center, 415/331-4406, where auto manufacturers unveil new models and high-tech concept cars to the public; **Tree Lighting** at Pier 39, 415/981-7437, www.pier39.com; and the start of holiday festivities all over town.

Most December events reflect seasonal traditions. The major traditional arts performances are quite popular, so get tickets well in advance. The **San Francisco Ballet** performs *The Nutcracker,* 415/865-2000, and the **American Conservatory Theater** presents *A Christmas Carol,* 415/749-2228, a traditional holiday favorite.

SHOPPING

Whether the addiction is neighborhood boutique hopping or spending days in major-league malls, San Francisco is a shopper's paradise. To seek something specific, study the visitors bureau's current *San Francisco Book* for mainstream shopping destinations. To pursue shopping as social

SUSAN SNYDER

It's not hard to spend big money when shopping in Union Square.

SAN FRANCISCO

exploration, wander the city's neighborhood commercial districts. (Be sure to take advantage of museum and arts-venue gift shops, which usually feature an unusual array of merchandise. Secondhand and thrift shops can also be surprising. Some suggestions are included under the neighborhood sightseeing sections of this chapter.) To shop for one's consumer identity—covering as much ground, and as many shops, as possible without having any particular result in mind—visit the city's mall-like marketplaces.

The uptown **Union Square** area is an upscale shoppers delight. Major San Francisco shopping palaces include the nine-story **San Francisco Shopping Centre,** 415/495-5656, a few blocks from Union Square at Fifth and Market, astonishing for its marble and granite elegance as well as its spiral escalators and retractable atrium skylight. Also in the neighborhood are **Macy's** overlooking Union Square at 170 O'Farrell St., 415/397-3333; **Neiman-Marcus** across the way at 150 Stockton St., 415/362-3900; and a branch of the New York based retailer **Sak's Fifth Avenue** at 384 Post St., 415/986-4300. Another major downtown commercial attraction is the **Embarcadero Center,** 415/772-0500, designed by John

C. Portman, Jr., an eight-block complex (between Clay and Sacramento, Drumm and Battery) with three plaza-style levels and four main buildings plus the Hyatt Regency and Park Hyatt hotels, not to mention five office towers.

Blocks from Union Square, Sony's futuristic **Metreon** complex at Fourth and Mission, 415/369-6000, features four levels of entertainment and shopping options, including a PlayStation game store, Moebius comic and action figure shop, MicrosoftSF computer emporium, and Wild Things, with Maurice Sendak books and toys for children.

The three-square-block **Japan Center,** 1625 Post St. (at Laguna), 415/922-6776, in the Western Addition's Japantown, designed by Minoru Yamasaki, adds up to about five acres of galleries, shops, restaurants, theaters, hotels, and convention facilities. **Chinatown** is famous for its ethnic commercial attractions, and adjacent **North Beach** also has its share.

But **Fisherman's Wharf,** along the northeastern waterfront, is becoming shopping central. Most famous of the shopping destinations on the Wharf is 45-acre, carnival-crazy **Pier 39,** 415/981-7437, www.pier39.com, with more than 100 shops and endless family amusements. A close second is one-time chocolate factory **Ghirardelli Square,** 900 North Point (at Beach), 415/775-5500, with stylish shops and restaurants, and some great views. **The Cannery,** 2801 Leavenworth (at Beach), 415/771-3112, one block east of the Hyde St. cable car turnaround, is a brick-and-ivy behemoth. Once the world's largest fruit cannery, the building is now home to collected cafés, restaurants, shops, galleries, and a comedy club.

The **Anchorage Shopping Center,** 2800 Leavenworth (bounded by Jefferson, Beach, and Jones), 415/673-7762, is a contemporary, nautical-flavored plaza with daily entertainment and some unusual shops (e.g., Magnet Kingdom and Perfumania). The **Stonestown Galleria,** 415/759-2626, on Hwy. 1 at Winston Dr. near San Francisco State University and Lake Merced, offers all sorts of sophistication—and the luxury, in San Francisco, of free parking.

Information and Services

The clearinghouse for current visitor information is the **San Francisco Convention & Visitors Bureau,** 900 Market St. (at Powell, downstairs—below street level—outside the BART station at Hallidie Plaza), P.O. Box 429097, San Francisco, CA 94142-9097, 415/391-2000, www.sfvisitor.org. Here you can pick up official visitor pamphlets, maps, booklets, and brochures about local businesses, including current accommodations bargains and various coupon offers. Multilingual staffers are available to answer questions. The Visitor Information Center is open for walk-ins weekdays 9 A.M.–5 P.M., Sat.–Sun. 9 A.M.–3 P.M.; closed major holidays.

If you can't make it to the Visitor Information Center or are planning your trip in advance and need information, you have a couple of options. To find out what's going on in town, from entertainment and arts attractions to major professional sports events, you can call the city's free, 24-hour visitor hot line, available in five languages. To get the news in English, call 415/391-2001; in French, 415/391-2003; in German, 415/391-2004; in Japanese, 415/391-2101; and in Spanish, 415/391-2122. The information is updated weekly. You can also write to the SFCVB to request current information on accommodations, events, and other travel planning particulars. For $3 postage and handling, you can get a copy of the SFCVB's semiannual *The San Francisco Book,* which contains thorough information about sights, activities, arts, entertainment, recreation, shopping venues, and restaurants, as well as a detailed map. (And

then some.) If you'll be in town awhile, it's worth the money to request in advance.

The state of California operates the **California Welcome Center & Internet Café @ Pier 39** in the Pier 39 shopping center at Fisherman's Wharf, 415/956-3491, www.weblightningcafe.com, open daily 9 A.M.–8 P.M. The center offers a number of travel-related services for the greater San Francisco Bay Area and California's northern coast—from free tourist information, itinerary planning, hotel reservations, and special discounts to stamps and phone cards. The Internet Café features 30 high-speed, dedicated T-1 stations with email access, low cost Internet phones, and digital camera rentals. Espresso and coffee drinks, teas, deli sandwiches, salads, and pastries are served daily. The Café also has a great view overlooking the Marina.

PUBLICATIONS

Available free at hotels, restaurants, and some shops around town is the small, magazine-style *Key: This Week San Francisco,* which is chock-full of the usual information and has a thorough and current arts, entertainment, and events section. Though focused primarily for permanent Bay Area residents, *San Francisco* magazine also offers regular food and entertainment columns, plus in-depth feature articles about the real world of San Francisco and environs.

Where: San Francisco is a slick, free magazine full of useful information on accommodations, dining, shopping, and nightlife. It's available at the

Hallidie Square visitor center and elsewhere around town. You can also order a subscription by contacting: Where Magazine, 74 New Montgomery St., Ste. 320, San Francisco, CA 94105, 415/546-6101, or online at www.wheremagazine.com.

Even more real: the **San Francisco Bay Guardian,** www.sfbg.com, and **SF Weekly,** www.sfweekly.com, popular tabloid newspapers available free almost everywhere around town. The Guardian's motto (with a hat tip to Wilbur Storey and the 1861 *Chicago Times,* as interpreted by Editor/Publisher Bruce Brugmann), "It is a newspaper's duty to print the news and raise hell," is certainly comforting in these times and also generates some decent news/feature reading, along with comprehensive arts, entertainment, and events listings. The Guardian also publishes insider guides to the city with some of the same punchy, irreverent writing. The *Weekly* also offers what's-happening coverage and—to its everlasting credit—Rob Brezsny's *Free Will Astrology* column. Way to go. Excellent for alternative media info online is the **San Francisco Bay Artea Independent Media Center,** sf.indymedia.org.

While roaming the city, look for other special-interest and neighborhood-scope publications. The **San Francisco Bay Times** is a fairly substantive gay and lesbian biweekly. For comprehensive events information, pick up a copy of the **Bay Area Reporter.** Widely read throughout the Sunset and Richmond Districts is **The Beacon.** Other popular papers include the award-winning, hell-raising, **Street Sheet,** published by the Coalition on Homelessness in San Francisco and distributed by the homeless on San Francisco's streets; the **New Mission News;** and the **Noe Valley Voice.**

The city's major daily, **San Francisco Chronicle,** www.sfgate.com, is universally available at newsstands and in coin-op vending racks. The **San Francisco Examiner,** www.examiner.com, formerly the city's scrappy afternoon/evening paper, continues (at least for a while) only as a free daily paper available at city newsstands and retail stores. In 2000 the Hearst Corporation purchased the *Chronicle,* and planned to sell or close the city's competing daily *Examiner* if no buyer could be found. The purchase was complicated by antitrust concerns. The two papers had been linked in a federally regulated operating agreement since the 1960s, and any deal that led to a one-paper town would have been blocked. The sale was finally approved when the well-connected Fang family purchased the *Examiner,* in a deal that included a three-year, $66 million subsidy from Hearst. Yet the new owners laid off almost its entire staff in 2003, creating, finally, a one-newspaper town. The *Chronicle* was never considered a top major-city newspaper, but after being sold to Hearst it has shown an increased interest in publishing better, tougher coverage of local politics—perhaps because all of the *Examiner*'s reporters and editors immediately went to work for the *Chronicle.* The *Chronicle*'s humongous Sunday newspaper, once published in conjunction with the *Examiner,* is still popular for its *Datebook* section, sometimes called The Pink, packed with readable reviews, letters from sometimes demanding or demented Bay Area readers, and the most comprehensive listings of everything going on.

San Francisco's major non-English and ethnic newspapers include **Asian Week,** the **Irish Herald,** and the African-American community's **Sun Reporter.**

Bookstores and Libraries

San Francisco is a well-read city, judging solely from the number of booksellers here. Perhaps most famous is that bohemian bookshop of lore in North Beach, **City Lights,** 261 Columbus Ave. (at Broadway), 415/362-8193, founded in 1953 by Lawrence Ferlinghetti and Peter Martin. The small press and poetry sections here are especially impressive. Also well worth a stop is **A Clean, Well Lighted Place for Books,** 601 Van Ness Ave. (between Golden Gate and Turk), 415/441-6670.

For European books and magazines, head over to the **European Book Company,** 925 Larkin (between Geary and Post), 415/474-0626, offering a selection of books in French, German, and Spanish, as well as a good travel section including English-language titles.

At Union Square, you'll find a four-story outpost of **Borders Books and Music,** 400 Post (at Powell), 415/399-1633 (books) or

SUSAN SNYDER

Don't miss a visit here.

415/399-0522 (music). The store stocks more than 200,000 titles, and has its own coffee shop on the second floor, and the fourth floor is devoted to CDs. Open Mon.–Thurs. 9 A.M.–11 P.M., Fri.-Sat. 9 A.M.–midnight, Sunday 9 A.M.–9 P.M.

Probably the best downtown San Francisco stop for travel and maps is the Financial District's **Rand McNally Map and Travel Store,** 595 Market St. (at Second), 415/777-3131. Worthwhile elsewhere is **Get Lost—Travel Books, Maps, and Gear,** 1825 Market St. (at Guerrero), 415/437-0529, www.getlostbooks.com, which offers travel guides, travel literature, luggage and travel accessories, maps, atlases, and author events. It's open Mon.–Fri. 10 A.M.–7 P.M., Sat. 10 A.M.–6 P.M., Sunday 11 A.M.–5 P.M.

Just off Union Square, **Brick Row Bookshop,** 49 Geary, 415/398-0414, specializes in antiquarian books, with a wide assortment of 18th- and 19th-century British and American literature.

Some unusual specialty or neighborhood bookstores include pulp-fiction bookseller **Kayo Books,** downtown at 814 Post (between Hyde and Leavenworth), 415/749-0554; the **San Francisco Mystery Book Store,** 4175 24th St. (between Castro

and Diamond, in Noe Valley), 415/282-7444; and **Marcus Book Store,** 1712 Fillmore St. (at Post, in the Western Addition), 415/346-4222, specializing in African-American books. Foreign-language book specialists include: **Kinokuniya,** 1581 Webster St. (at Fillmore in the Japan Center), 415/567-7625; **Russian Books,** 332 Balboa (Richmond District), 415/668-4723; and **Znanie Bookstore,** 5237 Geary (at 11th Ave.), 415/752-7555, also in the Richmond and also specializing in Russian titles.

Bookstores are also covered in individual districts above. Keep in mind, too, that museums and other major sites sometimes offer impressive selections of books and gifts.

If you don't feel obliged to buy what you need to read, the controversial yet technologically state-of-the-art **San Francisco Main Library,** downtown at 100 Larkin (at Grove), 415/557-4400, is a good place to start becoming familiar with the local library system. Main library special collections include the Art and Music Center; the San Francisco History Center; the African American Collection; and the James C Hormel Gay and Lesbian Center. Services include Internet access, copiers, fax machines, word processors, and a good cafeteria. The Main Library also offers free, special events.

A complete listing of neighborhood branch libraries is offered in the white pages of the local phone book, under "Government Pages—SF City & County—Libraries."

Consulates, Passports, and Visas

San Francisco is home to some 70 foreign consulates, from Argentina, Botswana, and Brazil to Indonesia, Malta, the Philippines, and what was once Yugoslavia. For a complete listing, contact the San Francisco Convention & Visitors Bureau (above). The **Australian Consulate** is downtown at 625 Market St., Ste. 200, 415/536-1970(in emergencies:888/239-3501); the **British Consulate** is at 1 Sansome St. (at Sutter), Ste. 850, 415/617-1300(emergencies: 800/434-5308); and the **Canadian Consulate** is at 50 Fremont St., Ste. 2100, 415/834-3180. The **French Consulate** is at 540 Bush St., 415/397-4330 (emergencies: 415/515-3600); the **German Consulate** is at 1960 Jackson St., 415/775-1061 (emergencies: 415/730-2924); and the **Hong Kong Economic and Trade Office,** essentially the Chinese consulate here, is at 130 Montgomery, 415/835-9300. The **Irish Consulate** is at 44 Montgomery St., Ste. 3830, 415/392-4214; the **Italian Consulate** is at 2590 Webster St., 415/931-4924 (emergencies: 415/999-0094); and the **Japanese Consulate** is at 50 Fremont St., Ste. 2300, 415/777-3533. The **Mexican Consulate** is at 870 Market St., Ste. 528, 415/392-5554; the **New Zealand Consulate** is at 1 Maritime Plaza, 415/399-1255; and the **Spanish Consulate** is at 1405 Sutter St., 415/922-2995.

For passports and visas, go to the **U.S. Department of State Passport Agency,** 95 Hawthorne St. (at Folsom), 415/538-2700; open weekdays 9 A.M.–4 P.M. For customs information and inquiries, contact the **U.S. Customs Service,** 555 Battery St., 415/782-9210, open weekdays 8 A.M.–4:30 P.M.

For help in locating a foreign-language translator, or for information about San Francisco's foreign-language schools, contact the Convention & Visitors Bureau, which maintains a current listing of member public and private schools.

Post Offices, Banks, Currency Exchanges

San Francisco's main post office is the Rincon Annex, 180 Steuart St. (just off the Embarcadero, south of Market), 415/896-0762,. It's open weekdays 7 A.M.–6 P.M., Sat. 9 A.M.–2 P.M. For help in figuring out local zip code assignments, and for general information and current postal rates, call 800/275-8777 or log on to www.usps.gov. Regional post offices are also scattered throughout San Francisco neighborhoods. Some branches are open extended hours, such as 7 A.M.–6 P.M. weekdays, or with limited services some Saturday hours, and some have after-hours open lobbies, so customers can purchase stamps via vending machines. Public mailboxes, for posting stamped mail, are available in every area. Stamps are also for sale in major hotels (usually in the gift shop) and in major grocery stores.

Branches of major national and international banks are available in San Francisco; most offer ATM facilities, often accessible through various member systems, though most banks charge a $1 to $2 service fee unless you have an account with them. Getting mugged while banking is another potential disadvantage of getting cash from an automated teller. Always be aware of who is nearby and what they're doing; if possible, have a companion or two with you. If the situation doesn't feel "right," move to another location—or do your banking inside.

Most currency exchange outlets are either downtown or at the San Francisco International Airport (SFO). **Bank of America Foreign Currency Services,** 345 Montgomery St., 415/622-2451, is open Mon.–Fri. 9 A.M.–6 P.M. Another possibility is the Bank of America at the Powell St. cable car turnaround, 1 Powell (at Market), 415/622-4498 (same hours). **Thomas Cook Currency Services, Inc.,** 75 Geary, 415/362-3453 or 800/287-7362, is open weekdays 9 A.M.–5 P.M., Sat. 10 A.M.–4 P.M. To exchange currency at the airport, head for the International Terminal, where **Bank of America,** 650/615-4700, offers currency exchange for both in- and out-bound travelers daily 7 A.M.–11 P.M.

For members, the **American Express Travel Agency** at 455 Market (at First), 415/536-2600, is another possibility for check cashing, traveler's-check transactions, and currency exchange. In Northern California, the American Automobile Association (AAA) is known as the California State Automobile Association (CSAA), and the San Francisco office is near the Civic Center at 150 Van Ness Ave., 415/565-2012, www.csaa .com. The CSAA office is open weekdays for all member inquiries and almost endless services, including no-fee traveler's checks, free maps and travel information, and travel agency services.

San Francisco's major hotels, and most of the midrange boutique hotels, have a fax number and fax facilities; some offer other communications services. For telex and telegrams, you can pop into one of the many **Western Union** branches throughout the city.

Special Travel Information

For current **weather information** or to find out when the next fog bank is rolling in, call the free TellMe interactive phone service, 800/555-8355, for a summary of San Francisco weather, news, travel, sports, stock news, and entertainment happenings. For current San Francisco **time**, call that old-time favorite POPCORN (767-8900). For current **road conditions** anywhere in California, call 800/427-7623 or see the CalTrans website, www.dot.ca.gov/hq/roadinfo/.

The **International Diplomacy Council** is at 312 Sutter St., Ste. 402 (between Grant and Kearny downtown in the financial district), 415/986-1388, www.diplomacy.org. This nonprofit organization promotes international understanding and friendship; foreign visitors are welcome to visit headquarters and to participate in the Meet Americans at Home program.

On the third floor of the Chinatown Holiday Inn, the **Chinese Culture Center,** 750 Kearny (at Washington), 415/986-1822, www.c-c-c.org, is the community clearinghouse for Chinese educational and cultural programs, including classes, lectures, workshops, and current events—from the arts and upcoming performances to festivals. Check out the gallery here for shows of Chinese art and artifacts; open Tues.–Sun. 10 A.M.–4 P.M. While Japan Center or Japantown in its entirety is the center of Japanese-American cultural life, the **Japanese Cultural and Community Center** is here, too, at 1840 Sutter St. (between Buchanan and Laguna), 415/567-5505, www.jcccnc.org.

The **Alliance Française de San Francisco,** 1345 Bush St. (between Polk and Larkin), 415/775-7755, www.afsf.com, is an international cultural center committed to promoting French culture and language. The center's facilities include a café, library, school, theater, and satellite television services. In the Richmond District, the **Booker T. Washington Community Service Center,** 800 Presidio Ave. (between Post and Sutter St.), 415/928-6596, sponsors a variety of educational, recreational, scouting, and sports activities of specific interest to the black community. **La Raza Information and Translation Center,** 474 Valencia (near 16th in the Mission District), 415/863-0764, is useful for Latino community information. The **Jewish Community Information and Referral Service,** 121 Steuart St. (between Mission and Howard), 415/777-4545, www.sfjcf.org, offers information on just about everything Jewish, from synagogue locations to special-interest community events. For **Senior Citizen's Information and Referrals,** call 415/626-1033 or stop by the office at 25 Van Ness Ave. (at Market).

The **Women's Building of the Bay Area,** 3543 18th St. (in the Mission District, just off Valencia), 415/431-1180, www.womensbuilding.org, serves as the region's central clearinghouse for feminist and lesbian arts, entertainment, and other information. This is the place to contact for a variety of nonprofit women's services (and for advice about where to go for others). Berkeley's **Pacific Center for Human Growth,** 2712 Telegraph Ave., 510/548-8283, www.pacificcenter.org, provides information about everything from local gay and lesbian clubs to current community events, in addition to its counseling service.

An invaluable regional resource for visitors in wheelchairs and those who are otherwise physically challenged is **Access Northern California,** 1427 Grant St., Berkeley, CA 94703, 510/524-2026, www.accessnca.com, which describes its work as "ramping the way to accessible travel." Their *Access San Francisco* travel guide is available through the Convention & Visitors Bureau. For special assistance and information on the city's disabled services, contact San Francisco's disability coordinator at the **Mayor's Office of Community Development,** 25 Van Ness Ave., Ste. 700, 415/252-3100, and the helpful local **Easter Seals Bay Area,** 180 Grand Ave., Ste. 300, 510/835-2131, www.esba.org. For the ins and outs of disabled access to local public transit, request a copy of the *Muni Access Guide* from Muni Accessible Services Program, 415/923-6142 weekdays or 415/673-6864 anytime, or visit the Rider Information section of Muni's website, www.sfmuni.com.

Weather

San Francisco's weather can upset even the best-laid plans for a frolic in the summertime California sun. For one thing, there may not be any sun. In summer, when most visitors arrive, San Francisco is enjoying its citywide natural air-conditioning system, called "fog." When California's inland areas are basting in blast-furnace heat, people here might be wearing a down jacket to go walking on the beach. (Sometimes it does get hot—and "hot" by San Francisco standards refers to anything above 80° F) Especially during the summer, weather extremes even in the course of a single day are normal, so pack accordingly. Bring warm clothing (at least one sweater or jacket for cool mornings and evenings), in addition to the optimist's choice of shorts and sandals, and plan to dress in layers so you'll be prepared for anything. The weather in late spring and early autumn is usually sublime—balmy, often fog-free—so at those times you should bring two pairs of shorts (but don't forget that sweater, just in case). It rarely rains May–Oct.; raingear is prudent at other times.

Access and Other Services

Modern buildings in San Francisco and most public-transit facilities are required by law to provide access to people in wheelchairs and those with other physical limitations; hotels, restaurants, and entertainment venues housed in historic facilities have a staff member who can help with access to their building and events.

All of San Francisco's (and California's) public buildings and restaurants are nonsmoking. Most motels and hotels have nonsmoking rooms, and many have entire floors of nonsmoking rooms and suites.

Unless otherwise stated on a restaurant menu, restaurants do not include a gratuity in the bill. The standard tip for the wait staff is 15 percent to 20 percent of the total tab, and the average tip for taxi drivers is 15 percent. It's customary to tip airport baggage handlers and hotel porters ($1 or more per bag, one way), parking valets, and other service staff. When in doubt about how much to tip, just ask someone.

HEALTH AND SAFETY

San Francisco is a reasonably safe city. Definitely unsafe areas, especially at night, include The Tenderloin, some areas south of Market St. (Sixth and Seventh Sts.), parts of the Western Addition, and parts of the Mission District (including, at night, BART stops). For the most part, drug-related gang violence is confined to severely impoverished areas. The increased number of homeless people and panhandlers, particularly notable downtown, is distressing, certainly, but most of these people are harmless lost souls.

If you're driving, be observant and look around before entering and returning to parking lots. When you get in your car, be sure to lock the doors immediately. Though rare, over the years there have been highly publicized cases involving carjacking.

If your own vehicle isn't safe, keep in mind that no place is absolutely safe. Sadly, in general it still holds true that female travelers are safest if they confine themselves to main thoroughfares. As elsewhere in America, women are particularly vulnerable to assaults of every kind. At night, women traveling solo, or even with a friend or two, should stick to bustling, yuppie-happy areas like Fisherman's Wharf and Union Street. The definitely street-savvy, though, can get around fairly well in SoMa and other nightlife areas, especially in groups or by keeping to streets with plenty of benign human traffic. (You can usually tell by looking.)

In any emergency, get to a telephone and dial 911—the universal emergency number in California. Depending upon the emergency, police, fire, and/or ambulance personnel will be dispatched. Runaways can call home free, anytime, no questions asked, by dialing the **California Youth Crisis Line,** 800/843-5200. Other 24-hour crisis and emergency hot lines include: the St. Vincent de Paul Society's **Helpline,** 772-HELP; **Rape Crisis** (operated by Women Against Rape, or WAR), 415/647-7273, the number to call in the event of any violent assault; **Suicide Prevention,** 415/781-0500; **Drug Line,** 415/834-1144 or 415/362-3400; **Alcoholics Anonymous,** 415/621-1326; **Narcotics Anonymous,** 415/621-8600; and **Poison Control,** 800/876-4766.

The **San Francisco Police Department** (general information line: 415/553-0123) sponsors several Japanese-style kobans—police mini-station neighborhood kiosks—where you can get law-enforcement assistance if you're lucky enough to be nearby when they're open. The Hallidie Plaza Koban is in the tourist-thick cable-car zone at Market and Powell; open Tues.-Sat. 10 A.M.–6 P.M. The Chinatown Koban is on Grant between Washington and Jackson; open daily 1–9 P.M. The Japantown Koban is at Post and Buchanan; open Mon.–Fri. 11 A.M.–7 P.M.

San Francisco General Hospital, 1001 Potrero Ave. (at 22nd St., on Potrero Hill), 415/206-8000 (911 or 415/206-8111 for emergencies), provides 24-hour medical emergency and trauma care services. Another possibility is **UCSF Medical Center,** 505 Parnassus Ave. (at Third Ave.), 415/476-1000. (The UCSF dental clinic is at 707 Parnassus, 415/476-1891 or 415/476-5814 for emergencies.) Convenient for most visitors is **Saint Francis Memorial Hospital** on Nob Hill, 900 Hyde St.(between Bush and Pine), 415/353-6000, which offers no-appointment-needed clinic and urgent-care medical services as well as a **Center for Sports Medicine,** 415/353-6400, and a physician referral service, 415/353-6566.

For nonemergency referrals, call the **San Francisco Medical Society,** 415/561-0853, or the **San Francisco Dental Society,** 415/421-1435.

Getting Here and Around

GETTING HERE

At least on pleasure trips, Californians and other Westerners typically drive into San Francisco. The city is reached from the north via Hwy. 101 across the fabled Golden Gate Bridge ($5 toll to get into the city, no cost to get out); from the east via I-80 from Oakland/Berkeley across the increasingly choked-with-traffic Bay Bridge ($2 toll to get into the city, no cost to get out); and from the south (from the coast or from San Jose and other South Bay/peninsula communities) via Hwy. 1, Hwy. 101, or I-280/19th Avenue. Whichever way you come and go, avoid peak morning (7–9 A.M.) and afternoon/evening (4–6 P.M.) rush hours, unless you qualify for the carpool lane (driver plus two or more passengers, or driver plus one passenger in a two-seat vehicle). Carpools don't have to pay tolls during commute hours, and you'll be able to whiz through the backup at the bridge. The Bay Area's traffic congestion is truly horrendous.

Airports

About 15 miles south of the city via Hwy. 101, **San Francisco International Airport** (SFO), 650/876-2377 (general information) or 650/877-0227 (parking information), www.flysfo.com, perches on a point of land at the edge of the bay. (That's one of the thrills here: taking off and landing just above the water.) Travel time from downtown is 40 minutes during peak commute hours, and 20 to 25 minutes at other times. Each of the terminals—Terminal 1, Terminal 2, and Terminal 3—has two levels, the lower for arrivals, the upper for departures. San Francisco's state-of-the-art International Terminal, built in 2000, is the largest international terminal in the U.S. More than 40 major scheduled carriers (and smaller ones, including air charters) serve SFO.

San Francisco International has its quirks. For one thing, its odd horseshoe shape often makes for a long walk for transferring passengers; the "people movers" help somewhat, but people seem to avoid the second-floor intraterminal bus. (In all fairness, though, since SFO is primarily an origin/destination airport, for most travelers this isn't a problem.) For another, with such a high volume of air traffic—an average of 1,000 flights per day—delays are all too common, especially when fog rolls in and stays.

People complain, too, that facilities always seems to be under major construction, as the airport continues with a multi-billion-dollar expansion. And in the wake of the 2001 terrorist attacks, increased security measures have made for a lengthier check-in process and possible delays. Airlines and governments have added their own new regulations, so check directly with your travel agent or airline for specifics. The following general tips may help expedite the process: Plan on arriving two hours prior to your scheduled flight, bring proper identification and a printout of your E-ticket, and limit carry-on baggage to two pieces—one personal bag (briefcase or purse) and one carry-on. Again, check with your airline before departure, as some carriers seem to take perverse pleasure in making regulations increasingly complicated.

Information booths are located in the lower (arrivals) level of all terminals, open daily 8 A.M.–midnight. Traveler's Aid Society booths can be found on the upper (departures) level and are open daily 9 A.M.–9 P.M. ATMs are located in all terminals. Weary travelers can take a shower after a long-haul flight Mon.-Sat. 8 A.M.–5 P.M. at **Hairport,** in the International Terminal to right of the security checkpoint for G gates. Hairport offers valet services, a hair salon, and massage. There is a medical clinic on the lower floor of Terminal 2. Other airport facilities include outposts of popular San Francisco restaurants (Harry Denton's in the International Terminal, the North Beach Deli in Terminal 1, among others), and shops including the California Product Shop (where you can get some wine and smoked fish or crab to go with that sourdough bread you're packing) and several bookstores, which prominently features titles by Bay Area and California writers.

Due to its excellent service record and relatively lower volume, many travelers prefer flying into and out of efficient, well-run **Oakland** **International Airport** just across the bay, 510/577-4000, www.oaklandairport.com. It's fairly easy to reach from downtown San Francisco. Travel time by car or shuttle is 30 minutes (depending on traffic), or take BART from downtown to the airport.

Airport Taxi and Shuttles

If flying into and out of SFO, avoid driving if at all possible; parking and curbside access are limited. Airport shuttles abound, however, and are fairly inexpensive and generally reliable. The airport offers a hot line, 800/736-2008, for information on ground transportation. Operators are available weekdays 7:30 A.M.–5 P.M. Most companies offer at-your-door pick-up service if you're heading to the airport (advance reservations usually required) and—coming from the airport—both taxis and shuttles take you right where you're going. **Taxis** operate on the airport's lower level. A taxi from the airport to downtown San Francisco will cost $30 to $35, plus tip. The usual one-way fare for shuttles, depending upon the company, is around $15 per person for most SFO/San Francisco hotel service. Inquire about prices for other shuttle destinations.

The blue-and-gold **SuperShuttle** fleet has some 100 vans coming and going all the time, 415/558-8500, www.supershuttle.com. When you arrive at SFO, the company's shuttle vans to the city (no reservation needed) are available at the outer island on the upper level of all terminals. To arrange a trip to the airport, call and make your pick-up reservation at least a day in advance. (And be ready when the shuttle arrives—they're usually on time.) Group, convention, and charter shuttles are also available, and you can pay on board with a major credit card. (Exact fare depends on where you start and end.)

SFO Airporter, 650/624-0500, www.sfairporter.com, offers nonstop runs every 20 minutes between the airport and the Financial District or Union Square. No reservations are required in either direction. **City Express Shuttle** in Oakland, 510/638-8830, offers daily shuttle service between the city of San Francisco and Oakland International Airport. **Bayporter Express, Inc.,** 415/656-2929 or 415/467-1800, or 800/287-

6783 (from inside the airport), specializes in shuttle service between most Bay Area suburban communities and SFO, and offers hourly door-to-door service between any location in San Francisco and the Oakland Airport. **Marin Airporter** in Larkspur, 415/461-4222, provides service every half hour from various Marin communities to SFO daily, 4:30 A.M.–11 P.M., and from SFO to Marin County daily, 5:30 A.M.–midnight.

BART and Trains

The ride to the airport will surely get easier. The **Bay Area Rapid Transit (BART),** 650/992-2278, www.bart.gov, extension to SFO was launched in June 2003, connecting travelers to a network of stations around the bay, including several along Market Street in San Francisco near Union Square and the Financial District. The extension adds 8.7 miles of track to the existing system and new stations in San Francisco, San Bruno, Millbrae, plus a station at the International Terminal inside the airport. The one-way fare from SFO to the Powell Street near Union Square will cost around $5, and take just 30 minutes, making it an attractive alternative to the shuttles.

Of course BART is more than just a fancy airport shuttle; primarily, it's a high-speed train and subway system connecting San Francisco to the East Bay. Yet BART can also take passengers across the bay (actually, *under* the bay) to and from the **Amtrak** station at Oakland's Jack London Square for train connections both north and south. For details call Amtrak, 510/238-4306 or 800/USA-RAIL, or see www.amtrak.com. Amtrak does have a ticket office/waiting room in San Francisco, inside The Agricultural Building at the foot of Market St., 101 Embarcadero (at Mission), Ste. 118, open daily 5:45 A.M.–10 P.M. The only staffed station in San Francisco, Amtrak services include ticket sales, checked baggage, and package express. Buses carry passengers between San Francisco Amtrak stops and trains departing and arriving across the bay at the Emeryville Station, located at 5855 Landgegan St., just off Powell.

Primarily a regional commuter service, **CalTrain,** 800/660-4287 within Northern California, www.caltrain.com, runs south from downtown to Palo Alto, Stanford, Mountain View, Sunnyvale,

Santa Clara, San Jose, Morgan Hill, and Gilroy, among other stops. The San Francisco CalTrain depot is at Fourth and Townsend Streets. A $64.5-million expansion is underway, to accommodate CalTrain's "baby bullet" express commuter trains.

Buses

San Mateo County Transit (SamTrans), 800/660-4287, www.samtrans.com, offers extensive peninsula public transit, including express and regular buses from SFO to San Francisco. It's cheap, too ($2.20 to $3). Buses leave the airport every 30 minutes from very early morning to just after midnight; call for exact schedule. The express buses takes just 35 minutes to reach the Transbay Terminal near downtown San Francisco but limit passengers to carry-on luggage only, so heavily laden travelers will have to take one of the regular buses—a 55-minute ride to the city.

The **Transbay Terminal,** 425 Mission St. (just south of Market St. between First and Fremont), 800/231-2222, is the city's regional transportation hub. An information center on the second floor has displays, maps, and fee-free phone lines for relevant transit systems. Bus companies based here include **Greyhound,** 415/495-1569, www.greyhound.com, with buses coming and going at all hours; **Golden Gate Transit,** 415/455-2000, www.goldengatetransit.org, offering buses to and from Marin County and vicinity; **AC Transit,** 415/817-1717, www.actransit.org, which serves the East Bay; and **San Mateo County Transit** (SamTrans), 800/660-4287, www.samtrans.org, which runs as far south as Palo Alto.

Ferries

Since the city is surrounded on three sides by water, ferry travel is an unusual (and unusually practical) San Francisco travel option. Before the construction of the Golden Gate Bridge in 1937, it was the only way to travel to the city from the North and East Bay areas. Nowadays, the ferries function both as viable commuter and tourist transit services. (See Orientation and Tours for more about ferry tours and other oceangoing entertainment.)

SAN FRANCISCO

The **Blue & Gold Fleet,** 415/773-1188 (recorded schedule) or 415/705-5555 (reservations and information), www.blueandgoldfleet.com, based at Fisherman's Wharf, Piers 39 and 41, offers roundtrip service daily between San Francisco (either the Ferry Building or Pier 41) and Oakland (Jack London Square), Alameda (Gateway Center), Sausalito, Tiburon, Angel Island, and Vallejo (via high-speed catamaran). During baseball season, Blue & Gold also offers ferry service from Oakland and Sausalito to a launch near Pac Bell Park. Return ferries depart about 20 minutes after the end of the game. The company also offers bay cruises, tours of Alcatraz, an "Island Hop" tour to both Alcatraz and Angel Island, and various land tours (Muir Woods, Yosemite, Monterey/Carmel, Wine Country).

Golden Gate Transit Ferries, headquartered in the Ferry Building at the foot of Market St., 415/923-2000, www.goldengateferry.org, specializes in runs to and from Sausalito (adults $5) and more frequent large-ferry (725-passenger capacity) trips to and from Larkspur. Family rates available, and disabled pasengers and seniors (over age 65) travel at half fare.

Red & White Fleet at Fisherman's Wharf, Pier 43, 415/673-2900or 877/855-5506, www.redandwhite.com, offers bay cruises and various land tours, as well as a commuter run to Richmond.

GETTING AROUND

San Francisco drivers are among the craziest in California. Whether they're actually demented, just distracted, insanely rude, or perhaps intentionally driving to a different drummer, walkers beware. The white lines of a pedestrian crosswalk seem to serve as sights, making people easier targets. Even drivers must adopt a heads-up attitude. In many areas, streets are narrow and/or incredibly steep; if you're driving a stick (manual) transmission, make sure you're well versed in hill-starts. Finding a parking place requires psychic skills. So, while many people drive into and out of the Bay Area's big little city, if at all possible many use public transit to get around town.

But some people really want to drive in San Francisco. Others don't want to, but need to, due to the demands of their schedules. A possible compromise: if you have a car but can't stand the thought of driving it through the urban jungle yourself, hire a driver. You can hire a chauffeur, and even arrange private sightseeing tours and other outings, through companies like **WeDriveU, Inc.,** 60 E. Third Ave. in San Mateo, 650/579-5800 or 800/773-7483. Other local limousine companies may be willing to hire-out just a city-savvy driver; call and ask.

Though those maniacal bicycle delivery folks somehow manage to daredevil their way through downtown traffic—note their bandages, despite protective armor—for normal people, cycling is a no-go proposition downtown and along heavy-traffic thoroughfares. Bring a bike to enjoy the Golden Gate National Recreation Area and other local parks, though it may be easier to rent one. Rental outlets around Golden Gate Park include **Avenue Cyclery,** 756 Stanyan, 415/387-3155, and other businesses on Stanyan, Fulton and Haight Streets. In Golden Gate Park, you can rent a bike, Rollerblades, or a pedal-powered surrey at **Golden Gate Park Bike & Skate,** 3038 Fulton (between Sixth and Seventh Aves.), 415/668-1117.

Car Rental Agencies

Some of the least expensive car rental agencies have the most imaginative names. Near the airport in South San Francisco, **Bob Leech's Auto Rental** 435 S. Airport Blvd., 650/583-3844, specializes in new Toyotas, from $30 per day with 150 fee-free miles. (You must carry a valid major credit card and be at least 23 years old; call for a ride from the airport.) Downtown, family-owned **Reliable Rent-A-Car,** 349 Mason, 415/928-4414, rents new cars with free pick-up and return for a starting rate of $29 per day ("any car, any time"). That all-American innovation, **Rent-A-Wreck,** 2955 Third St., 415/282-6293, rents out midsize used cars for around $29 per day with 150 free miles, or $159 per week with 700 free miles.

The more well-known national car rental agencies have desks at the airport, as well as at other locations. Their rates are usually higher than those of the independents and vary by vehicle make and model, length of rental, day of the week (sometimes season), and total mileage. Special coupon savings or substantial discounts through credit card company or other group affiliations can lower the cost considerably. If price really matters, check around. Consult the telephone book for all local locations of the companies listed below.

Agencies with offices downtown include: **Avis Rent-A-Car,** 675 Post St., 415/885-5011 or 800/831-2847; **Budget Rent-A-Car,** 321 Mason, 415/928-7864, or 800/763-2999; **Dollar Rent-A-Car,** 364 O'Farrell (opposite the Hilton Hotel), 415/771-5301 or 800/800-4000; **Enterprise,** 1133 Van Ness Ave., 415/441-3369 or 800/736-8222; **Hertz,** 433 Mason, 415/771-2200 or 800/654-3131; and **Thrifty Rent-A-Car,** 520 Mason (at Post), 415/788-8111 or 800/367-2277.

For a transportation thrill, all you wannabe easy riders can rent a BMW or Harley-Davidson motorcycle from **Dubbelju Tours & Service,** 271 Clara St., 415/495-2774. Rates start at $99 a day and include insurance, 100 free miles, and road service. Weekly and winter rates available. Open Mon.–Fri. 9 A.M.–noon and 4–6 P.M., Sat. 9 A.M.–noon, or by appointment. German spoken.

Parking Regulations and Curb Colors

If you're driving, it pays to know the local parking regulations as well as rules of the road. It'll cost you if you don't.

Curbing your wheels is the law when parking on San Francisco's hilly streets. What this means: turn your wheels toward the street when parked facing uphill (so your car will roll into the curb if your brakes and/or transmission don't hold), and turn them toward the curb when facing downhill.

Also, pay close attention to painted curb colors; the city parking cops take violations seriously. Red curbs mean absolutely no stopping or parking. Yellow means loading zone (for vehicles with commercial plates only), half-hour time limit; yellow-and-black means loading zone for trucks with commercial plates only from 7 A.M.–6 P.M., half-hour limit; and green-yellow-and-black means taxi zone. Green indicates a 10-minute parking limit for any vehicle from 9 A.M.–6 P.M.,

and white means five minutes only, effective during the operating hours of the adjacent business. As elsewhere in the state, blue indicates parking reserved for vehicles with a California disabled placard or plate displayed. Pay attention, too, to posted street-cleaning parking limits, to time-limited parking lanes (open at rush hour to commuter traffic), and avoid even a quick-park at bus stops or in front of fire hydrants. Any violation will cost $25 to $275 (fire lane), and the police can tow your car—which will cost you $140 or so (plus daily impound fees) to retrieve.

Parking and Parking Garages

If you're driving, you'll need to park. You also need to find parking, all but impossible in North Beach, the Haight, and other popular neighborhoods. San Franciscans have their pet parking theories and other wily tricks. Some even consider the challenge of finding parking a sport, or at least a game of chance. But it's not so fun for visitors, who usually find it challenging enough just to find their way around. It's wise to park your car (and leave it parked, to the extent possible), then get around by public transit. Valet parking is available (for a price, usually at least $15 per day) at major and midsize hotels, and at or near major attractions, including shopping districts.

Call ahead to inquire about availability, rates, and hours at major public parking garages, which include: **Fisherman's Wharf,** 665 Beach (at Hyde), 415/673-5197; **Fifth and Mission Garage,** 833 Mission St. (between Fourth and

TAKING A TAXI

Taxis from SFO to San Francisco cost around $30–35 (plus tip, usually 15 percent). Standard San Francisco taxi fare, which also applies to around-town trips, was at press time $2.85 for the first mile, $2.25 per additional mile. Among the 24-hour taxi companies available, these are recommended.
DeSoto Cab Co., 415/970-1300
Luxor Cab, 415/282-4141
Veteran's Taxicab Company, 415/552-1300
Yellow Cab, 415/626-2345

Fifth Sts.), 415/982-8522; **Downtown,** Mason and Ellis, 415/771-1400 (ask for the garage); **Moscone Center,** 255 Third St. (at Howard), 415/777-2782; **Chinatown,** 733 Kearny (underground, near Portsmith Square), 415/982-6353; and **Union Street,** 1550 Union, 415/673-5728. For general information on city-owned garages, call 415/554-9805.

And good luck.

Public Transportation: Muni

The city's multifaceted San Francisco Municipal Railway, or Muni, 415/673-MUNI weekdays 7 A.M.–5 P.M., Sat.–Sun. 9 A.M.–5 P.M., www.sfmuni.com, is still the locals' public transit mainstay. One of the nation's oldest publicly owned transportation systems, Muni is far from feeble, managing to move almost 250 million people each year. Yet even small glitches can wreak havoc when so many people depend on the system; heated criticism regularly crops up on local talk-radio shows and in the Letters to the Editor sections of local newspapers.

The city's buses, light-rail electric subway-and-surface streetcars, electric trolleys, and world-renowned cable cars are all provided by Muni. It costs $3 to ride the cable car. (It's odd that people stand in long lines at the Powell and Market turnaround, since it actually makes much more sense—no waiting, unless there's absolutely no space available—to grab on at Union Square or other spots en route.) Otherwise, regular Muni fare is $1.25 ($0.35 for seniors and youths, children under 5 free), exact coins required, and includes free transfers valid for two changes of vehicle in any direction within a two-hour period. If you'll be making lots of trips around town, pick up a multitrip discount Muni Passport (which includes cable car transit), available for sale at the Muni office, the Convention & Visitors Bureau information center downtown, Union Square's TIX box office, the City Hall information booth, and the Cable Car Museum. A one-day pass costs $6, a three-day pass $10, a seven-day pass $15, and a monthly pass $45.

Muni route information is published in the local telephone book yellow pages, or call for route verification (phone number listed above). Better yet, for a thorough orientation, check out one of the various Muni publications, most of which are available online or wherever Muni Passports are sold (and usually at the Transbay Terminal). A good overview and introduction is provided (free) by the *Muni Access Guide* pamphlet and the useful, seasonally updated *TimeTables,* which list current route and time information for all Muni transit. Especially useful for travelers is Muni's *Tours of Discovery* brochure, which lists popular destinations and possible tours with suggested transit routes (including travel time) and optional transfers and side trips. But the best all-around guide, easy to carry in pocket or purse, is the official annual *Muni Street & Transit Map* ($2), available at bookstores and grocery stores in addition to the usual outlets. The Muni map explains and illustrates major routes, access points, frequency of service, and also shows BART and Muni Metro subway stops, along with the CalTrain route into San Francisco. As a city map, it's a good investment, too.

San Francisco's Muni buses are powered by internal-combustion engines, and each is identified by a number and an area or street name (such as #7 Haight or #29 Sunset). Similarly numbered local trolleys or streetcars are actually electrically operated buses, drawing power from overhead lines, and are most notable downtown and along the steepest routes. The Muni Metro refers to this five-line system of streetcars, often strung together into trains of up to four cars, that run underground along Market St. and radiate out into the neighborhoods. Metro routes are identified by letters in conjunction with point of destination (J-Church, K-Ingleside, L-Taraval, M-Oceanview, and N-Judah). Muni Metro's streetcars also include an international fleet of vintage streetcars, the F-Market Line, which starts at the Embarcadero and runs along Market St. to and from Castro St.; the F-Line also runs to Fisherman's Wharf. Another landmark line of historic streetcars, the E-Embarcadero, which will run from Mission Bay to Fort Mason, is coming one day soon. For more info, call 415/956-0472 or see www.streetcar.org.

Cable Cars

With or without those Rice-a-Roni ads, Muni's cable cars are a genuine San Francisco treat. (Don't allow yourself to be herded onto one of those rubber-tired motorized facsimiles that tend to cluster at Union Square, Fisherman's Wharf, and elsewhere. They are not cable cars, just lures for confused tourists.) San Francisco's cable cars are a national historic landmark, a system called "Hallidie's Folly" in honor of inventor Andrew S. Hallidie when these antiques made their debut on August 2, 1873. The only vehicles of their kind in the world, cable cars were created with the city's challenging vertical grades in mind. They are "powered" by an underground cable in perpetual motion, and by each car's grip-and-release mechanism. Even though maximum speed is about nine mph, that can seem plenty fast when the car snaps around an S-curve. (They aren't kidding when they advise riders to hold onto their seats.) After a complete system overhaul in the early 1980s, 26 "single-enders" now moan and groan along the two Powell St. routes, and 11 "double-enders" make the "swoop loop" along California Street. (New cars are occasionally added to the city's collection.) To get a vivid education in

how cable cars work, visit the reconstructed Cable Car Barn and Museum.

BART

The Bay Area's 104-mile **Bay Area Rapid Transit** (BART) system, headquartered in Oakland, 510/464-6000 or 650/992-2278 (transit information), www.bart.gov, calls itself "the tourist attraction that gets people to the other tourist attractions." Fair enough. Heck, it is pretty thrilling to zip across to Oakland and Berkeley *underwater* in the Transbay Tube. An idea seemingly sprung from Jules Verne, the concept had been proposed at various times since 1911—and emerged once again in 1947, when a joint U.S. Army-Navy review board proposed such a transit link to prevent traffic congestion on the Bay Bridge. The rest, as they say, is transportation history. And as far as it goes—which is not nearly far enough—BART is a good get-around alternative for people who would rather not drive. In San Francisco it's a convenient link from downtown to the Mission District. (When the BART-SFO extension is completed, travelers will be able to board BART inside the International Terminal at the San Francisco Airport for a fast

SUSAN SNYDER

one of the more traditional ways to climb—and descend—the city's steep streets

and convenient ride to downtown San Francisco and other stops around the bay.) From Oakland/Berkeley, lines extend north to Richmond, south to Fremont, and east to Pittsburg or Pleasanton. BART Express buses extend transit service to other East Bay communities

Helpful publications include the annual *All About BART* (with fares, travel times, and other details), and the *BART & Buses* BART guide to connections with the bus system. BART trains operate Mon.–Fri. 4 A.M.–midnight, Sat. 6 A.M.–midnight, and Sun. 8 A.M.–midnight. Exact fare depends upon your destination, but one-way fares vary from $1.15 to the maximum fare for the longest trip (about 53 miles) of $6.90. Tickets are dispensed at machines based at each station. (Change machines, for coins or dollar bills, are nearby.) Various discounts are available, for students and seniors as well as the disabled. If you don't have a current BART map, you can get your bearings at each station's color-keyed wall maps, which show destinations and routes.

San Francisco Bay Area

"Everything in life is somewhere else, and you get there in a car," writer E. B. White once observed. And so it is, for the most part, once outside San Francisco with one's sights set on the wilds, scrambling through the urban and suburban fringe surrounding the bay. Worth exploring in its almost endless urbanism, the Bay Area also has its own wildness and wayside pleasures. As White also said: "I would feel more optimistic about a bright future for man if he spent less time proving that he can outwit Nature and more time tasting her sweetness and respecting her seniority." The San Francisco Bay Area offers ample opportunity for both.

Pigeon Point Lighthouse in Half Moon Bay

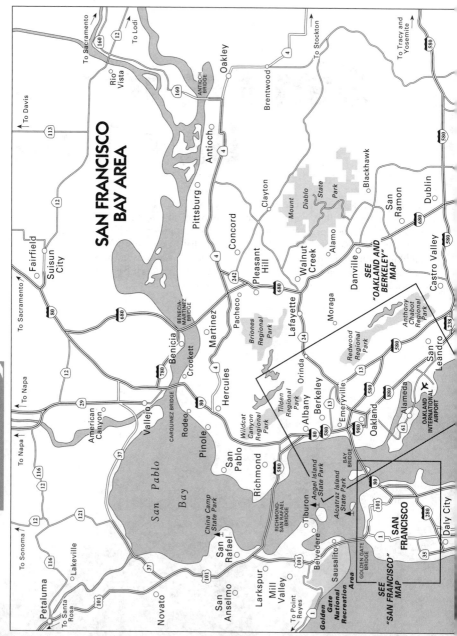

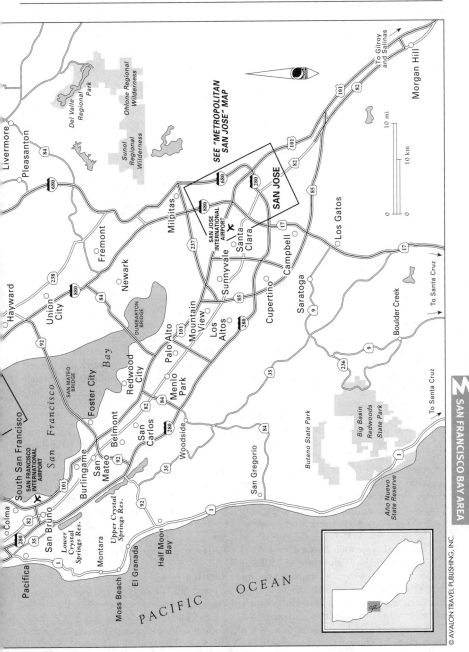

SEE "METROPOLITAN SAN JOSE" MAP

To Gilroy and Salinas

Morgan Hill

SAN JOSE

Los Gatos

To Santa Cruz

Del Valle Regional Park

Ohlone Regional Wilderness

Sunol Regional Wilderness

Livermore

Pleasanton

Milpitas

SAN JOSE INTERNATIONAL AIRPORT

Santa Clara

Campbell

Saratoga

Boulder Creek

To Santa Cruz

Fremont

Newark

Sunnyvale

Cupertino

237

Hayward

Union City

DUMBARTON BRIDGE

Mountain View

Los Altos

To Santa Cruz

Palo Alto

Menlo Park

Redwood City

Bay

San Francisco

SAN MATEO BRIDGE

Foster City

Belmont

San Carlos

Woodside

San Gregorio

Butano State Park

Big Basin Redwoods State Park

Año Nuevo State Reserve

South San Francisco

SAN FRANCISCO INTERNATIONAL AIRPORT

Burlingame

San Mateo

Half Moon Bay

El Granada

Moss Beach

Colma

San Bruno

Lower Crystal Springs Res.

Upper Crystal Springs Res.

Montara

Pacifica

PACIFIC OCEAN

10 mi

10 km

The Peninsula

Sticking out into the Golden Gate like an aristocratic nose is the city and county of San Francisco, the northern tip of the San Francisco Peninsula. South of the city along the San Mateo County coastline is **Daly City,** its hillside neighborhoods almost immediately recognizable as the inspiration for Malvina Reynolds's "Little Boxes" lyrics: "And they're all made out of ticky tacky and they all look just the same." Smaller communities, including **Pacifica** and **Half Moon Bay,** pop up alongside the string of state beaches that continue down the coast as far as the northern elephant seal refuge at Año Nuevo. Just inland from the coast near San Andreas Lake is Sweeney Ridge, a small nugget among the parks collected into the Bay Area's Golden Gate National Recreation Area.

South of the city along the shores of San Francisco Bay are **Brisbane** (which merges with Daly City) and undeveloped San Bruno Mountain County Park. Continuing south, you'll pass a stretch of the San Francisco Bay National Wildlife Refuge and a slew of bayside communities stretching into Santa Clara County. A bit farther is the heart of high-tech Silicon Valley, its suburbs spreading out like printed circuits from hard-driving **San Jose.**

South from San Francisco along the peninsula's inland spine is **Colma,** an incorporated city inside Daly City where the dead outnumber the living by more than 2,000 to one, due to Colma's cemetery industry. Among the city of the dead's most famous residents are gunfighter Wyatt Earp, riveted-blue-jeans creator Levi Strauss, sculptor Benjamin Bufano, and baseball batting champ Lefty O'Doul (whose gravestone lists his statistics and this comment: "He was here at a good time and had a good time while he was here.")

After the onetime dairy town of **Millbrae** comes down-to-the-bayshore **Burlingame** (the West's first community dedicated to the country club lifestyle) and very highbrow Hillsborough, founded in 1851 by a deserter from the British Navy, just north of **San Mateo.** San Mateo spreads into **Belmont,** which collides with San

Carlos and the outskirts of **Redwood City,** named for its brisk business, historically, as a redwood-lumber port. **Atherton,** nearby **Menlo Park,** and economically depressed **East Palo Alto** all stand in the intellectual shadow of **Palo Alto,** home of California's prestigious Stanford University and the contentious Hoover Institution.

SAN MATEO COASTLINE: FROM PACIFICA SOUTH

The unstable wave-whipped coast south of San Francisco is all buff-colored bluffs and sandy beaches faced with rough rocks. Often foggy in summer, the coastline in winter is crowded with bird- and whalewatchers. But from late summer into autumn, the weather is usually good and the crowds mimimal, making this the perfect time for a superb escape. Though wetsuit-clad surfers brave the snarling swells even in gale-force winds, swimming is dangerous even on serene sunny days due to treacherous undertows. Many of the region's beaches are officially accessible as state beaches or local beach parks; others are state-owned and undeveloped, or privately owned. Almost 20 miles of this 51-mile-long coastline are included as part of the San Mateo Coast State Beaches, starting with Daly City's **Thornton Beach** (popular for fishing and picnicking) in the north and ending with tiny **Bean Hollow State Beach** just north of Año Nuevo in the south. Though campgrounds are available inland, seaside public camping is possible only at Half Moon Bay State Beach, 650/726-8820. For more information, call **San Mateo State Beaches,** 650/726-8819. For more information on public-transit access to the San Mateo coast, call Sam-Trans at 650/508-6219 or 800/660-4287.

Pacifica

The self-proclaimed Fog Capital of California, Pacifica is sometimes a dreary place. But the locals make up for the opaque skies with *attitude.* Come here in late September for the annual **Pacific Coast Fog Fest,** which features a Fog Calling Contest (almost everyone's a winner), the Phileas Fogg Balloon Races, high-octane alcoholic "fogcutters" (if drinking, *don't* drive off into the fog), plus a fog fashion show. When the weather's sunny, the town offers superb coastal views. And good food abounds here—fog or shine. For more information on the town or the Fog Fest, call the **Pacifica Chamber of Commerce** at 650/355-4122.

At **Sharp Park State Beach** along Beach Blvd. (reached from Hwy. 1 via Paloma Ave., Clarendon Rd., or streets in between) is the **Pacifica Pier,** popular for fishing and winter whale-watching. Migrating gray whales are attracted to the abundant plankton at the end of the community's sewage outfall pipe (the treatment plant is the building with the Spanish arches). Some old salts here say the great grays swim so close to the pier you can smell the fish on their breath.

Farther south is sort-of-secluded **Rockaway Beach,** a striking black-sand beach in a small rectangular cove where the coast has backed away from the rocky bluffs. Hotels and restaurants cluster beyond the rock-reinforced parking lot.

South from Pacifica

Long and narrow **Montara State Beach** offers hiking and rock-and-sand beachcombing. The state's tiny **Gray Whale Cove Beach** a.k.a. Devil's Slide here is a concession-operated clothing-optional beach, open for all-over tans only to those 18 and over; for information, call 650/726-8819. Just south of Montara proper is the cypress-strewn **Moss Beach** area, named for the delicate sea mosses that drape shoreline rocks at low tide.

Best for exploration Nov.–Jan. are the 30 acres of tidepools at the **James V. Fitzgerald Marine Reserve** (open daily from sunrise to sunset), which stretches south from Montara Point to Pillar Point and Princeton-by-the-Sea. At high tide, the Fitzgerald Reserve looks like any old sandy beach with a low shelf of black rocks emerging along the shore, but when the ocean rolls back, these broad rock terraces and their impressive tidepools are exposed. For area state park information, call 415/330-6300; for information on low-tide prime time at the Fitzgerald Reserve, call 650/728-3584; for more about

docent-led guided tours of the reserve, call Coyote Point Museum, 650/342-7755.

Nearby, along Hwy. 1 in Montara, are **McNee Ranch State Park** and Montara Mountain, with hiking trails and great views of the Pacific. Next south is **El Granada,** an unremarkable town except for the remarkable music showcased by the **Bach Dancing & Dynamite Society,** 311 Mirada Rd. (technically in Miramar), 650/726-4143, www .bachddsoc.org, the longest-running venue for jazz greats in the Bay Area. Begun in 1958 when jazz fanatic Pete Douglas started letting jazz musicians hang out at his house and jam, public concerts blast off every Sunday (except around Christmas and New Year's) in a baroque beatnik beachhouse. The family lives downstairs; upstairs at "the Bach" is the concert hall and deck, though guests are free to amble down to the beach and back at all times. Admission isn't charged, but a contribution of $20–25 or so is the usual going rate for Sunday concerts. The Dancing & Dynamite Society has become so popular that Friday night candlelight dinner concerts cosponsored by local businesses or other supporters are also offered (reservations and advance payment required). For a fee, anyone can join the society and receive a newsletter and calendar of coming attractions.

Practicalities

Inexpensive and incredibly pleasant for a coast overnight is **HI Point Montara Lighthouse Hostel,** on Hwy. 1 at 16th St., Montara, 650/728-7177, www.norcalhostels.org. It's quite popular, so reservations (by mail or phone with credit card) are advisable. Dorm-style bunks, and couple and family rooms are available in the wheelchair-accessible annex. Under $50. Also, motels—not many are inexpensive—pop up here and there along the coast.

The charming **Goose and Turrets Bed and Breakfast,** 835 George St., Montara, 650/728-5451, is a huge 1908 Italian-style seaside villa that dates back to the Bay Area's early bohemian days, when the adventurous and/or artistic rode the Ocean Shore Railroad from San Francisco to the arts colony and beach here. The five guest rooms are just part of the pleasure of this 6,000-square-foot home, which features great windows on its

FLYING HIGH: HILLER AVIATION MUSEUM

Flying high in San Carlos since it opened in 1998 is the Hiller Aviation Museum, 601 Sklyway Rd., 650/654-0200, www.hiller.org, "where inspiration takes flight." Inspiration for the museum's 27,600-square-foot main gallery exhibits, documenting Bay Area contributions to flight history, reaches back to 1869 and leaps ahead 100 years. Among local dreamers who literally soared was Santa Clara University professor John Montgomery, who surveyed San Jose from his homemade glider in 1903. And in 1869, Frederick Marriott's football-shaped "aeroplane" rose over San Mateo County. The walking tour is amazingly educational. Then visit the restoration shop to see history literally being resurrected, and the museum shop—one of the largest collections of aviation toys, books, flight wear, models, and memorabilia anywhere (also available online). The museum is open daily 10 A.M.–5 P.M. Admission is $8 adults, $5 seniors and youths, free for children under 8.

west wall. All rooms have private bathrooms and little luxuries; three rooms have fireplaces, German down comforters, and English towel warmers. French spoken; email the Goose and Turrets at rhmgt@montara.com, and find them on the web at www.goose.montara.com. Breakfast is a four-course feast; tea and treats are served in the afternoon. Standard rooms are $100–150.

The English-style **Seal Cove Inn,** 221 Cypress Ave., Moss Beach, 650/728-4114, is another find—an elegant and romantic inn overlooking the Fitzgerald Marine Reserve. The 10 guest rooms here each feature a wood-burning fireplace, refrigerator, TV, and ocean views; some have a private deck. For small group meetings, there's even a conference room. Rooms $150–250, suites $250 and up.

Traditional for a meal in Moss Beach is the old **Moss Beach Distillery** in Moss Beach, 140 Beach Way (at Ocean), 650/728-5595, now a romantic cliffside restaurant, very good for seafood, ribs, lamb, and veal. Open for lunch and dinner. **Barbara's Fish Trap,** 281 Capis-

trano Rd. in Princeton-by-the-Sea, 650/728-7049, open daily for lunch and dinner, offers great Half Moon Bay views, fishnet kitsch decor, and fish selections that are a cut above the usual. Try the garlic prawns. Head for **Mezza Luna,** 459 Prospect Way, 650/728-8108, for authentic, relaxed Italian. **Café Gibraltar** at 425 Alhambra Ave. in El Granada, 650/560-9039, is just about everyone's favorite Mediterranean, serving everything from flatbread pizzas to polenta with mushrooms and lamb shank slow-braised with North African spices.

HALF MOON BAY

Known until the turn of the 20th century as Spanishtown, Half Moon Bay was a farm community settled by Italians and Portuguese, and specializing in artichokes and Brussels sprouts. Down and out during the early 1900s, things picked up during Prohibition when the area became a safe harbor for Canadian rumrunners. Fast becoming a fashionable Bay Area residential suburb, Half Moon Bay is famous for its pumpkins and offers a rustic Main St. with shops, restaurants, and inns, plus pseudo-Cape Cod cluster developments along Highway 1. In 1999, Half Moon Bay's commercial ship-to-shore radiotelegraph station, the nation's last, tapped out its final Morse code transmission. Just a few miles south of Half Moon Bay off Pillar Point and legendary among extreme surfers is **Mavericks,** home of the world's baddest wave. When surf's up here, during wild winter storms, Mavericks creates mean and icy 35-foot waves—mean enough to break bones and boards.

Nearby **Burleigh Murray Ranch State Park** is still largely undeveloped, but the former 1,300-acre dairy ranch is now open to the public for day use. You can take a hike up the old ranch road, which winds up through sycamores and alders along Mill Creek. About a mile from the trailhead is the ranch's most notable feature, the only known example of an English bank barn in California. This century-old structure relied on simple but ingenious design, utilizing slope ("bank") and gravity to feed livestock most efficiently. Especially for those who can't remember even the

Half Moon Bay is famous for its pumpkins and Art & Pumpkin Festival.

basics of farm life, other outbuildings also deserve a peek. To get here, turn east on Higgins-Purisima Rd. from Hwy. 1 just south of Half Moon Bay. It's about two miles to the parking area (marked, on the left).

A Portuguese **Chamarita** parade and barbecue are held here seven weeks after Easter. Over the July 4th weekend, the community's **Coastside County Fair and Rodeo** takes place. Half Moon Bay's **Great Pumpkin Weigh-Off** in early October awards the prize to the largest pumpkins grown on the West Coast, an event followed by the annual **Art & Pumpkin Festival,** featuring everything from pumpkin-carving and pie-eating contests to haunted house. For a complete list of area events and other information, contact the **Half Moon Bay/Coastside Chamber of Commerce,** 520 Kelly Ave., 650/726-8380, www.halfmoonbaychamber.org.

Staying in Half Moon Bay

At **Half Moon Bay State Beach** campground (open year-round, hot showers and all), reservations are usually required Mar.–Oct. to guarantee a tent or RV campsite. Unreserved space is often available on nonweekend autumn days. For reservations, contact **ReserveAmerica,** 800/444-7275, www.reserveamerica.com.

Motels in Half Moon Bay tend to be on the pricey side. A nice midrange choice is **Harbor View Inn,** 51 Alhambra Ave. (four miles north of town in El Granada), 650/726-2329. Midweek/off-season rates $50–100, weekend/summer rates $100–150. The upscale **Half Moon Bay Lodge,** 2400 S. Hwy. 1 (about 2.5 miles south of the Hwy. 92 junction), 650/726-9000, has a pool, Jacuzzi, fitness center, some rooms with fireplaces and some with golf course views. Rooms and suites $150–250.

The in thing in Half Moon Bay is inns, many of which offer reduced midweek rates. Much loved is the **Mill Rose Inn** bed-and-breakfast, 615 Mill St. in "old town," 650/726-8750, or 800/900-7673, a romantic Victorian with frills like fireplaces, a spa, English gardens, and excellent breakfasts. Midweek room rates $150–250, weekend room rates and suites $250 and up. Another local favorite is the restored **San Benito House** country inn, 356 Main St., 650/726-3425, www.sanbenitohouse.com, with 12 rooms on the upper floor (three share a divided bath), plus a sauna, redwood deck with flowers and firepit, and a downstairs restaurant and saloon. Street and deck side rooms $100–150. The **Old Thyme Inn,** 779 Main St., 650/726-1616 or 800/720-4277, www.oldthymeinn.com, has some rooms with two-person whirlpools. For special occasions or extra privacy, book the Garden Suite, which features a private entrance. The atmosphere here is very English, in a casually elegant style. Rooms are individually decorated, and some feature fireplaces and/or in-room whirlpool tubs. Especially delightful for gardeners is the herb garden here, boasting more than 80 varieties (true aficionados are allowed to take cuttings). Expect such treats as homemade scones and marmalade, or possibly even French cherry flan. Standard rooms $150–250, deluxe rooms and suites $250 and up.

Another historic local favorite is the **Zaballa House,** 324 Main St. (right next door to the San Benito House), 650/726-9123. It's Half Moon Bay's oldest surviving building (circa 1859) and now features nine standard guest rooms and three private-entrance suites, all with private bath. Several rooms have two-person whirlpool tubs and/or fireplaces. Ask about the "resident ghost" in Room 6. Rates $100–150.

The contemporary **Cypress Inn,** 407 Mirada Rd. (three miles north of Hwy. 92, just off Hwy. 1; exit at Medio Ave.), Miramar, 650/726-6002 or 800/832-3224, www.cypressinn.com, is right on the beach and just a few doors down from the Bach Dynamite & Dancing Society. The inn's motto is "in celebration of nature and folk art," and the distinctive rooms—each with an ocean view and private deck, fireplace, and luxurious private bath—do live up to it, whether you stay in the Rain, Wind, Sea, Sky, Star, Sun, or Moon rooms. For a special treat, head up into the Clouds (the penthouse). Gourmet breakfasts, afternoon tea, winetasting, and hors d'oeuvres included. Massage is available by appointment. $250 and up. North of Half Moon Bay, **Pillar Point Inn** 380 Capistrano Rd., El Granada, 650/728-7377 or 800/400-8281, www.pillarpoint.com, overlooks the harbor in Princeton-by-the-Sea. All rooms have fireplaces and other modern amenities. Rates $150–250.

A lot of people are still plenty upset by the hugeness of its presence on this low-key stretch of coastline—don't the rich people already have everything else?—yet the **Ritz Carlton Half Moon Bay Resort** arrived in 2001. What you get is what you expect from Ritz Carlton, starting with accommodations inspired by swank 19th-century seaside resorts—only these rooms and suites include every imaginable luxury, down to the laptop-compatible in-room safes. The resort also features the fine-dining **Navio** restaurant, the more casual **Conservatory** restaurant/bar, complete with telescopes for spying on the ocean; the stylish **Salon** tearoom; full fitness and spa facilities; and 36 holes of "view" golf. And if you have to ask how much all that costs, you definitely can't afford it. For more information, contact the resort at 650/712-7000, www.ritzcarlton.com.

Eating in Half Moon Bay

The **Half Moon Bay Bakery,** 514 Main, 650/726-4841, is also a stop on the local historic walking tour. The bakery still uses its original 19th-century brick oven and offers sandwiches, salads, and pastries over the counter. Other popular eateries include wonderful **Pasta Moon** café, 315 Main St., 650/726-5125; and the **San Benito House** restaurant inside the hotel, 356 Main (at Mill), 650/726-3425, noted for its French and Northern Italian country cuisine at dinner. Open Thurs.–Sun. for dinner only. Call for reservations. Simpler but excellent lunches (including sandwich selections on homemade breads) also served at the hotel's Garden Deli Café.

FROM SAN GREGORIO SOUTH

On the coast just west of tiny San Gregorio is **San Gregorio State Beach,** with the area's characteristic bluffs, a mile-long sandy beach, and a sandbar at the mouth of San Gregorio Creek. San Gregorio proper is little more than a spot in the road, but the back-roads route via Stage Rd. from here to Pescadero is pastoral and peaceful.

Inland Pescadero ("Fishing Place") was named for the creek's once-teeming trout, not for any fishing traditions on the part of the town's Portuguese settlers. Both **Pomponio** and **Pescadero State Beaches** offer small estuaries for same-named

PARADISE FOUND:
HIKING THE PENINSULA RESERVOIRS

In August 2003 the city of San Francisco initiated regular guided hikes deep into the suburban paradise of the San Francisco Peninsula Watershed—23,000 acres of pristine nature, home to the largest populations of rare, threatened, and endangered animals in the Bay Area. The 10-mile **Fifield-Cahill Ridge Trail**, which eventually connects to the Golden Gate National Recreation Area's Sweeney Ridge Trail in San Bruno, saunters past the lower Crystal Springs and San Andreas Reservoirs. Previously a major "missing link" of the in-progress 425-mile Bay Area Ridge Trail, this new trail (graveled road) starts at the Skyline Quarry (west of the Skyline Blvd./Hwy. 92 junction) in San Mateo. Access is strictly limited, however, with three groups of no more than 20 people allowed into the watershed three times per week.

For more information about the Fifield-Cahill Rudge Trail and to make reservations, contact the **San Francisco Public Utilities Commission,** 1155 Market St., 415/554-3289, www.sfwater.org. Map, trail, and natural history information is available online, along with current reservation details. For more information about other great Bay Area hikes, bike rides, and equestrian events, contact the **Bay Area Ridge Trail Council,** 415/561-2595, www.ridgetrail.org.

---

creeks. The 584-acre **Pescadero Marsh Natural Preserve** is a successful blue heron rookery, as well as a feeding and nesting area for more than 200 other bird species. (To birdwatch—best in winter—park at **Pescadero State Beach** near the bridge and walk via the Sequoia Audubon Trail, which starts below the bridge.) Rocky-shored **Bean Hollow State Beach,** a half-mile hike in, is better for tidepooling than beachcombing, though it has picnic tables and a short stretch of sand.

For a longer coast walk, head south to the **Año Nuevo** reserve. (Año Nuevo Point was named by Vizcaíno and crew shortly after New Year's Day in 1602.) The rare northern elephant seals who clamber ashore here are an item only in winter and spring, but stop here any time of year for a picnic and a stroll along Año Nuevo's three-mile-long beach.

Staying Along the Coast

Affordable—and quite appealing in a back-to-basics style—are the two lighthouse hostels offered in California by Hostelling International (HI), both located on the coast north of Santa Cruz.

Closest to Santa Cruz is the **Pigeon Point Lighthouse Hostel,** 210 Pigeon Point Rd. (at Hwy. 1) in Pescadero, 650/879-0633 (for phonetree reservations, call 800/909-4776 #73), www.pigeonpointlighthouse.org—*the* inexpensive place to stay while visiting the elephant seals.

Named after the clipper ship *Carrier Pigeon,* one of many notorious shipwrecks off the coastal shoals here, the 1872 lighthouse is now automated but still impressive with its Fresnel lens and distinctive 10-second flash pattern. Lighthouse tours (40 minutes) are offered by state park staff every weekend year-round, and also on Fridays in summer; rain cancels. Small fee. For tour reservations, call 650/879-2120.

The hostel itself is made up of four former family residences for the U.S. Coast Guard— basic male or female bunkrooms, plus some spartan couples' and family rooms. The old Fog Signal Building is now a rec room; there's also a hot tub perched on rocky cliffs above surging surf. Fabulous sunset views, wonderful tidepools. Rates: under $50. Extra charge for couples'/family rooms and for linen rental (if you don't bring your own sleep sack or sleeping bag). Get groceries in Pescadero and prepare meals in the well-equipped communal kitchens, or ask for local restaurant suggestions. For information and/or to check in, the hostel office is open 7:30–9:30 A.M. and 4:30–9:30 P.M. only. Very popular, so reserve well in advance.

Farther north, beyond Half Moon Bay between Montara and Moss Beach, is picturesque **Point Montara Lighthouse Hostel,** 16th St. at Hwy. 1 in Montara, 650/728-7177 (for phonetree reservations, call 800/909-4776 #64), www.norcalhostels.org. Point Montara is popular with bicyclists, and it's also accessible via bus from the Bay Area. The 1875 lighthouse itself is no longer in operation, and the Fog Signal Building here is now a roomy woodstove-heated community room. Hostel facilities include kitchens, dining rooms, laundry, bunkrooms, and couples' and family quarters. Volleyball court, outdoor hot tub, and bicycle rentals are also available. Open to travelers of all ages. Popular, so reserve in advance. Under $50. Ask at the office for restaurant recommendations.

If the hostels are full, the campground at **Butano State Park,** 650/879-2040, probably will be too—at least on Fridays, Saturdays, and holidays May–September. Campsites do not have showers or running water. Reached from Pescadero via Cloverdale Rd. (or from near Gazos Beach via Gazos Creek Rd.), the park offers 21 family campsites, 19 walk-in sites, and a handful of backcountry trail camps. During the high season, reserve main campsites through **ReserveAmerica,** 800/444-7275, www.reserveamerica.com. The rest of the year, it's usually first-come, first-camped.

Unusual in the nature getaway category is **Costanoa Coastal Lodge and Camp** on the coast near Pescadero. In addition to its sophisticated 40-room lodge, deluxe traditional cabins, luxurious "camp bathroom" comfort stations, and gourmet-grub General Store, Costanoa also offers the nation's first "boutique camping resort." Though some RV and pitch-your-own-tent campsites are available, most of the camping provided is tent camping—in 1930s-style canvas "safari tents," complete with skylights, that range from economy to luxury. Deluxe canvas cabins feature queen-size beds, heated mattress pads, nightstands with reading lamps, and Adirondack chairs for taking in the great outdoors. And nature *is* the main attraction. Costanoa itself, near Año Nuevo State Reserve, is linked to four nearby state parks—30,000 acres of hiking trails. Other possible adventures here include mountain biking, sea kayaking, tidepooling, whale-watching, elephant seal observation, and bird-watching. For more information, contact: Costanoa, 2001 Rossi Rd. (at Hwy. 1) in Pescadero, 650/879-

1100 or 800/738-7477 for reservations, www.costanoa.com. Pitch-your-own-tent camping is under $50. RV camping and most canvas cabins: $50–100. Deluxe canvas cabins: $100–150. Regular cabins and lodge rooms: $150–250.

Hard to beat for an overnight in Pescadero are the six cottages at **Estancia del Mar,** 460 Pigeon Point Rd., 650/879-1500, estanciadm@aol.com. Located 500 yards from the surf, each attractive cottage sleeps four and includes custom-tiled bathroom, fully equipped kitchen, wood-burning stove, and stereo/CD player/radio and VCR. Linens and towels are provided. Kids and pets welcome. Rates $150–250, with multinight discounts.

Another option is the Spanish-style **Rancho San Gregorio** bed-and-breakfast, 5086 La Honda Rd., San Gregorio, 650/747-0810, a best bet featuring just four attractive rooms (three have woodstoves; all have private baths). Many of the veggies and fruits served at breakfast are home-grown. Great hiking nearby. Rates: $100–150. Or head south along the coast. About nine miles north of Santa Cruz, the **New Davenport Bed and Breakfast Inn,** 31 Davenport Ave. (Hwy. 1), 831/425-1818 or 800/870-1817, www.davenportinn.com, is a colorful ocean-view hideaway (rooms above the restaurant) with artist owners and beach access. Rates: $100–150.

Eating Along the Coast

In Pescadero, down-home **Duarte's Tavern,** 202 Stage Rd., 650/879-0464, is most noted for its artichoke soup and delicious olallieberry pie, not to mention the ever-changing fresh fish specials scrawled across the menu chalkboard. Open daily for breakfast, lunch, and dinner; reservations wise (especially in summer) for dinner and Sunday brunch. Near Pescadero is **Phipps Ranch,** where berries, dried beans, baby lettuce, squash, and other local produce are available in season. (San Mateo County's *Coastside Harvest Trails* map lists other regional produce stands.)

Down the coast toward Santa Cruz, the **New Davenport Cash Store & Restaurant,** 831/426-4122, is a store, arts and crafts gallery, and inexpensive eatery with healthy food (whole grains, salads, soups) in the Americanized Mexican tradition. Great desserts. Bed-and-breakfast rooms upstairs.

OTHER SAN MATEO PARKS: NORTH

San Bruno Mountain County Park exists because the lupine-loving mission blue butterflies were wiped out elsewhere in the Bay Area. Their last remaining habitat (on one east-facing slope) is now protected from development. San Bruno is a great almost-in-the-city hiking park also fine for picnics. Its trails are most enjoyable during the spring wildflower bloom, but the views are fabulous on any unfoggy day. Bay Area Mountain Watch offers free group walks to prime butterfly-viewing spots and ancient Native American village sites.

To get here from San Francisco, head south on the Bayshore Freeway (Hwy. 101), take the Cow Palace-Brisbane exit, and follow Bayshore Blvd. past Geneva Ave. to Guadalupe Road. Turn right at Guadalupe and climb to the saddle, then turn left at the park sign and follow Radio Rd. uphill all the way; park near the telecommunications towers. For more information about San Bruno Mountain and other county parks, contact: **San Mateo County Parks and Recreation,** 455 County Center, Redwood City, 650/363-4020.

Down the bayshore, **Coyote Point County Park,** 1701 Coyote Point Dr., 650/573-2592, is popular for fishing, sailboarding, swimming, and picnicking. Entrance fee. The park is also home to the **Coyote Point Museum for Environmental Education,** 1651 Coyote Point Dr., 650/342-7755, www.coyoteptmuseum.org, one of the best environmental science centers in the Bay Area. The museum houses superb educational displays, including a bay ecosystems exhibit and interpretive wildlife habitats with over 50 rescued, non-releasable animals native to California, including river otters, foxes, red-legged frogs, and burrowing owls. Special events are scheduled year-round. Open Tues.–Sat. 10 A.M.–5 P.M., Sunday noon–5 P.M.; admission $6 adults, $4 seniors and youth 13–17, $2 children 3–12, free children 2 and under. If you've got some time and bikes on board, start from Coyote Point or the parking lot near the San Mateo Fishing Pier (at the eastern end of Hillsdale Blvd.) to explore the eight-mile **Bayfront Path,** a paved bicycling and walking trail that heads south along the bay, meanders through area sloughs, then loops back to (and through) Foster City and Marina Lagoon. Leave early to avoid afternoon winds, and pack a picnic if you'll be making a day of it. For a map of this and other bikeways in the area, call the **San Mateo Department of Public Works,** 650/363-4100. To the northwest, where Skyline Blvd. branches off from scenic I-280, is **Junipero Serra County Park,** 1801 Crystal Springs Ave., San Bruno, 650/589-5708, with hiking and nature trails, playgrounds, picnicking, and great views.

Sweeney Ridge, just east of Hwy. 1 near Pacifica, and south of Sharp County Park, is a fairly new segment of the Bay Area's extensive Golden Gate National Recreation Area. The ridge offers great hiking and 360-degree views of San Francisco Bay and the Pacific—the same vantage point that Gaspar de Portolá stumbled upon during his expedition to find Monterey Bay in 1769. From the Pacific coast side, the GGNRA trailhead up to Sweeney Ridge is near the Shelldance Bromeliad Nursery at 2000 Cabrillo Hwy. (Hwy. 1), on the left facing the hill. From the east, hike in from the trailhead just off Sneath Ln. from Skyline Boulevard. (However you arrive, wear good hiking boots or shoes and bring a sweater or jacket.) For more information, call the GGNRA information line at 650/556-0560.

Narrow San Andreas Lake and Crystal Springs Reservoir mark the route taken by the discouraged Gaspar de Portolá expedition of 1769 (which he described as "that small company of persons, or rather say skeletons, who had been spared by scurvy, hunger, and thirst"). The lakes also mark the route of the San Andreas Fault. Due to chain-link fences and the hum of the freeway, modern-day adventurers will be disappointed with a hike along the San Andreas Trail, but the connecting Crystal Springs Riding and Hiking Trail to the south is worthwhile. Recent plans to expand public access, with guided hikes deep into the watershed, were dashed in early 2003 due to terrorism concerns. Other access may also be curtailed.

Worth it, too, is a moment of reverent reflection at the **Pulgas Water Temple** at the reservoir's south end just off Canada Rd. (closed through early 2004 for planned water system improvements), a monument to the elusive and liquid god of California progress. This circular Greek-style classic designed by architect Willis Polk marks the spot where the once-wild waters from behind Hetch Hetchy Dam in Yosemite are taken into custody by the San Francisco Water Department, originally established by gold-rush czar William Bourn in the 1860s as part of his Spring Valley Water Works. The old company is also enshrined here, near the two major reservoirs it built to provide water for up-and-coming San Francisco.

Also off Canada Rd. is Bourn's 17-acre **Filoli Mansion,** one of several mansions he built as temples to his wealth. This one was named from a condensation of his personal motto: FIght, LOve, LIfe. Filoli posed as a Shanghai mansion in *The Joy Luck Club,* was Warren Beatty's home in *Heaven Can Wait,* and was the Georgian mansion seen in the opening scenes of the *Dynasty* TV series. Also a creation of San Francisco architect Willis Polk, the mansion is filled with priceless furnishings from around the world. Almost more impressive, though, are Bourn's acres of formal gardens—at their best on a sunny spring day. The mansion and grounds are open mid-February through mid-October, 10 A.M.–3 P.M.; admission $10 adult, $5 students, $1 children 7–12, children under 7 free. Self-guided tours of the mansion and its 17 acres of gardens are permitted from 10 A.M.–2:30 P.M. Guided tours are offered by Friends of Filoli and are available with advance reservations. For more information about tours and to make reservations, call 650/364-2880.

South of Lower Crystal Springs Reservoir are two distinct parks connected via trails. **Huddart County Park,** 1100 Kings Mountain Rd., Woodside, 650/851-0326, comprises almost 1,000 acres of cool canyons with second-growth redwoods, Douglas firs, and foothill oaks. It offers a short trail system with ties to the Crystal Springs Trail to the north and the Skyline Trail to the south. The Skyline Trail leads two miles to **Wunderlich County Park,** 4040 Woodside Rd.,

Woodside, 650/851-0326, which has its own 25-mile trail system. To get to Huddart, take Hwy. 84 west to Kings Mountain Rd. in Woodside (stop off at the historic Woodside Store) and continue along Kings Mountain for two miles. From Wunderlich, the Skyline Trail continues south to the hamlet of Sky Londa. Across the Junipero Serra Freeway (I-280) is **Edgewood County Park and Natural Preserve,** Edgewood Rd. at Old Stage Rd., 650/368-6283, a wonderful patch of open space threaded with trails and bright with blossoming wildflowers from spring into summer.

OTHER SAN MATEO PARKS: SOUTH

Five miles inland from Año Nuevo State Reserve is **Butano State Park,** 650/879-2040, which offers 30 miles of excellent if strenuous hikes among redwoods, plus picnicking, camping, and summer campfire programs. Another worthy redwoods destination is **San Mateo Memorial County Park,** 9500 Pescadero Rd. (eight miles east of Pescadero), 650/879-0238, which features a nature museum, 200-foot-tall virgin trees, creek swimming, camping, and trails connecting with surrounding local and state parks. Adjacent **Pescadero Creek County Park** (same address and phone) includes the steelhead trout stream's upper watersheds—6,000 acres of excellent hiking. (The Old Haul Rd. and Pomponio Trails link Pescadero to nearby Memorial and Portola Parks.)

Just to the north outside La Honda (though the entrance is off Pescadero Rd.) is 867-acre **Sam McDonald County Park** (same address and phone as San Mateo Memorial and Pescadero Creek Parks), offering rolling grasslands and redwoods, trails interconnecting with Pescadero Park, and a Sierra Club hiker's hut for overnights (to reserve, call the Loma Prieta chapter of the Sierra Club at 650/390-8411). To the southeast via Alpine Rd. and Portola State Park Rd. is La Honda's **Portola State Park,** 650/948-9098, comprised of rugged redwood terrain between Butano and Skyline Ridges. Here you'll find backcountry hiking, a short nature trail, a museum and visitor center, picnicking, and year-round camping. Campsite reservations are usually necessary Apr.-Sept.; call **ReserveAmerica** at 800/444-7275 (reserve the trail camp through park headquarters).

The **Midpeninsula Regional Open Space District,** 330 Distel Circle, Los Altos, 650/691-1200, administers other parkland in San Mateo and Santa Clara Counties—primarily preserves and limited-use areas perfect for hikers seeking even more seclusion. Among these: Purisima Creek Redwoods, southeast of Half Moon Bay; Mount El Sereno, south of Saratoga; the Long Ridge Preserve near Big Basin; and the rugged chaparral Sierra Azul-Limekiln Canyon Area

near Lexington Reservoir. Contact the district's office for more information and maps.

For detailed information about regional sights, restaurants, and lodging, contact any of the following chambers of commerce: the **San Mateo County Convention and Visitors Bureau,** 111 Anza Blvd., Ste. 410, Burlingame, CA 94010, 650/348-7600; the **Burlingame Chamber of Commerce,** 290 California Dr., Burlingame, 650/344-1735; the **San Carlos Chamber of Commerce,** 1500 Laurel St., San Carlos, 650/593-1068; and the **Belmont Chamber of Commerce,** 1070 Sixth Ave., Ste. 102, Belmont, 650/595-8696.

Palo Alto

Characteristic of the San Francisco region, most Peninsula and South Bay communities offer up culture in surprising, usually delightful ways. In Palo Alto, hometown of Stanford University, cultural creativity is concentrated and always accessible—making this a choice destination when climbing down out of the hills. This is the place, after all, where the Silicon Valley computer revolution started—where, in the 1930s, Bill Hewlett and Dave Packard, founders of modern-day Hewlett-Packard, started their spare-time tinkering with electronic bells, whistles, and other gadgetry in a garage on Addison Avenue. (Their first creation was the audio oscillator, a sound-enhancing system first used by Walt Disney in *Fantasia,* which catapulted the inventive duo into the corporate big leagues.)

The northernmost city in Santa Clara County, Palo Alto is not a typical tourist destination, which is in itself a major attraction for those tired of prepackaged community charm. For more information, including a current listing of member restaurants and accommodations, contact the **Palo Alto Chamber of Commerce,** 325 Forest Ave., 650/324-3121, www.paloaltochamber.com. For local public transportation options, depending upon which way you're heading, contact: **Caltrain** (Caltrans), which serves the peninsula and San Francisco, 800/660-4287, www.caltrain.com; **San Mateo County Tran-**

sit (SamTrans), 650/508-6219 or 650/508-6200 or 800/660-4287, www.samtrans.com; or **Santa Clara Valley Transportation Authority (VTA),** 408/321-2300, www.vta.org.

STANFORD UNIVERSITY

Once known as The Farm, the 9,000-acre campus of modern-day Stanford University was formerly Leland Stanford's Palo Alto stock farm, his spacious spread for thoroughbred racehorses. Some people now refer to Stanford as The Idea Farm, since this is the place that spawned birth-control pills, gene splicing, heart transplants, the IQ test, the laser, the microprocessor, music synthesizers, and napalm—among other breakthroughs of the civilized world. Royalties from on-campus inventiveness earn private Stanford University millions of dollars each year.

Though Stanford has a renowned medical school, a respected law school, and top-drawer departments in the sciences, most famous here is the Hoover Institution on War, Revolution, and Peace, which started out in 1919 to delineate and demonstrate "the evils of Karl Marx" with an original collection of five million World War I-related documents contributed by 40 governments. Though less stridently since the fall of the Berlin Wall and the rise of the Bushies, critics of the Hoover Institution, both on-campus and off, suggest that the organization has become too ideological—tainting Stanford University's otherwise legitimate claims to intellectual objectivity—to stay on campus in the hallowed Hoover Tower and should establish headquarters elsewhere.

Next most famous on campus: the run-amok Stanford University Marching Band, a self-perpetuating autocracy still blamed by embarrassed alumni for "the Play" in 1982, when winning Stanford lost The Big Game to arch nemesis UC Berkeley across the bay with just four seconds remaining. When not getting trampled by football players for being in the wrong place at the wrong time, the Stanford band never marches (members say they don't know how) but instead swarms onto the field during half time and jostles into formations like Gumby's head, Ronald Reagan's nose, Jimmy Carter's hemorrhoids, the Death Star from Star Wars, a spotted owl (Stanford vs. Oregon), and more mundane symbols like chainsaws and computers.

Seeing and Doing Stanford

The sprawling Spanish-style campus, designed by famed landscape architect Frederick Law Olmsted (designer of New York City's Central Park), is much too large to tour on foot; use a bike or the free Marguerite Shuttle. A good place to start is the campus quadrangle, where between-class undergraduate students mill around (some perhaps still proudly wearing T-shirts announcing the student body's unofficial motto: Work, Study, Get Rich). Before arriving, get a campus map and other Internet information at www.stanford.edu; once arrived, try the Visitor Information booth (below). For special event tickets, call 650/725-2787.

For a fairly comprehensive one-hour general campus walking tour, contact **Stanford University Visitor Information Services,** 650/723-2560, in the Memorial Auditorium in front of the Hoover Tower. The student-guided tours are offered daily, except holidays and quarter breaks. (Tours leave from the Serra St. quadrangle entrance.) For a tour of the **Hoover Observation Tower and Archives** (small fee), call 650/723-2053. Finely focused tours of the **Stanford Lin-**

ear Accelerator Center,** home of the quark, are led by graduate students; call 650/926-3300 for information and appointments. For unguided good times, try the hiking trails through the campus's wooded west end—or, for bird-watching, head out to the **Baylands Nature Preserve** outside Palo Alto at the end of Embarcadero Rd., 650/329-2506.

Iris & B. Gerald Cantor Center for the Visual Arts, formerly the Stanford Art Museum, Museum Way and Lomita Dr., 650/723-4177, www.stanford.edu/dept/ccva, reopened in 1999 after the Loma Prieta Earthquake closed the museum for 10 years of restoration and repair damage. New wings have been added to the seismically restored original 1890s building, for a total of 27 galleries. The museum's exhibits range from ancient to contemporary times and roam the globe, from the ancient Mediterranean to Africa, America, Asia, and Oceania. The Cantor center is also home to the world's second largest collection of Rodin works, after only the Musée Rodin in Paris. Outside in the sculpture garden are *The Gates of Hell, Adam and Eve,* and 18 others, and inside are two Rodin galleries. The museum is open Wed.–Sun. 11 A.M.–5 P.M. (until 8 P.M. on Thursday). Admission is free. The museum's very cool **Cool Café,** 650/725-4758, is a best bet for tasty organic lunch.

That brawling bad boy of American letters is showcased in the Stanford Library's **Charles D. Field Collection of Ernest Hemingway,** which includes first editions, translations, stories and poems, published and unpublished letters, and galley proofs. (While a student at Stanford, another American literary lion—double-dropout **John Steinbeck**—got a "C" in freshman English. He later said college was a waste of time.)

OTHER AREA SIGHTS

Palo Alto-Stanford (PASt) Heritage, 650/299-8878, offers guided one-hour walking tours of Palo Alto, either downtown or "Professorville." Both areas are included on the National Register of Historic Districts. Usually departing on Saturdays at 10 or 11 A.M., the downtown tour covers Ramona St. and architectural gems like

William Weeks's Cardinal Hotel and Birge Clark's shops, plus Spanish colonial revival courtyards by Pedro de Lemos. The 1932 U.S. post office at 380 Hamilton was the first to sidestep the formal federal style. Professorville describes the collection of historic homes bordered by Addison, Cowper, Embarcadero, and Emerson, characterized by brown shingle-style houses built between the 1890s and 1920s. A standout is Bernard Maybeck's Sunbonnet House at 1061 Bryant.

Other Palo Alto community attractions include the **Palo Alto Art Center,** 1313 Newell Rd., 650/329-2366, a de facto art museum with child- and family-oriented features as well as rotating exhibits and performances, and the **Junior Museum and Zoo,** 1451 Middlefield Rd., 650/329-2111, the nation's first children's museum, this one emphasizing science and the arts. More children's "firsts" here: the **Children's Theatre,** 1305 Middlefield Rd., 650/463-4970, a theatrical arts program started in 1932 with youngsters doing it all, from the writing and staging to lighting, sound, and set design, and the nearby public **Children's Library,** 1276 Harriet St., 650/329-2134, which includes 18,000 books plus an adjacent "Secret Garden," a favorite for storytellers.

It's also fun to just stroll around downtown. Especially along University and Hamilton Avenues, notice the town's nine surreal outdoor murals by Greg Brown. Some of Palo Alto's best attractions are its bookstores, from **Megabooks,** 444 University Ave., 650/326-4730 (good used books) to the **Stanford Bookstore** just down the street at 135 University, 650/614-0280. **Bell's Books,** 536 Emerson, 650/323-7822, is a Palo Alto classic—a time-honored book emporium stacked floor to ceiling with both new and used volumes. Near Palo Alto, Menlo Park is home to the West Coast lifestyle-establishing institution of *Sunset* magazine, 80 Willow Rd. (at Middlefield), 650/324-5479. The gorgeous gardens at *Sunset* are open to the public weekdays 9 A.M.–4:30 P.M. Also in Menlo Park is the **U.S. Geological Survey map center,** 345 Middlefield Rd., 650/329-4390. For earthquake information, call the survey office at 650/329-4025 or visit their website at quake.usgs.gov.

STAYING IN PALO ALTO

Southwest of town in Los Altos Hills is the wonderful **HI-USA Hidden Villa Ranch Hostel,** 26870 Moody Rd., 650/949-8648, www.norcalhostels.org, a woodsy and rustic ranch-style cabin setup on 1,600 acres but open only Sept.–May. Dorm beds under $25 and private rooms under $50. (Popular, so call ahead.) Also available—and not that far for those with a car— is the **HI-USA Sanborn Park Hostel** in Saratoga (see San Jose and Vicinity).

Though some distance away, in Burlingame north of Palo Alto, unusual and unusually enjoyable is a stay at the tranquil **Mercy Center,** 2300 Adeline Ave., 650/340-7474, an ecumenical retreat run by the Sisters of Mercy. Individuals can stay in rooms ($50–100) when space is available. Silence is the rule. The center is popular for group retreats, so call ahead to check current rates and make reservations.

In Palo Alto proper, ever-faithful **Motel 6,** 4301 El Camino Real, 650/949-0833, www .motel6.com, is almost always full—call well in advance for reservations. This one is pricey by Motel 6 standards, rates of $50–100. Other motels abound along El Camino Real. The **Country Inn Motel,** 4345 El Camino Real, 650/948-9154, is among the most reasonable ($50–100), though there's also the **Coronet Motel,** 2455 El Camino Real, 650/326-1081 ($50–100), and the very nice **Sky Ranch Inn,** 4234 El Camino Real (across from the Hyatt), 650/493-7221 ($50–100). The **Hyatt Rickeys,** 4219 El Camino Real, 650/493-8000 or 800/532-1496, www .hyatt.com, has all the usual Hyatt amenities. Weeknight rates of $150–250. (Rooms are cheapest on Friday and Saturday nights, with weekend specials between $100–150.) A better bargain, usually, is **Creekside Inn,** 3400 El Camino Real, 650/493-2411 or 800/492-7335, www.creekside-inn.com. Rates $100–150.

Top-drawer accommodations close to campus include the **Sheraton Palo Alto,** 625 El Camino Real, 650/328-2800 or 800/325-3535, www.starwood.com ($150–250), and **Stanford Terrace Inn,** 531 Stanford Ave., 650/857-0333, www.stanfordterraceinn.com ($150–250). The exquisite **Garden Court Hotel** is downtown at 520 Cowper St., 650/322-9000, www.gardencourt.com. Rates $250 and up.

Homier and usually more reasonable is **Cowper Inn** bed-and-breakfast, 705 Cowper St., 650/327-4475, www.cowperinn.com, which offers 14 rooms in a turn-of-the-century Victorian within walking distance of downtown and the university. Nice continental breakfast. Two rooms with shared bath ($50–100; others $150–250). Quite reasonable, too, is **Hotel California,** a bed-and-breakfast establishment at 2431 Ash St., 650/322-7666, www.hotelcalifornia.com. Rates $50–100. The **Victorian on Lytton,** 555 Lytton Ave., 650/322-8555, www.victorianonlytton.com, is an elegant Victorian, circa 1895, with an English country garden, 10 guest rooms, in-room continental breakfast service, and afternoon tea and cookies, port, and sherry. Room rates $150–250. Also serving up a taste of history, minus most of the frills, is downtown Palo Alto's historic **Cardinal Hotel,** 235 Hamilton Ave., 650/323-5101, www.cardinalhotel.com, with rooms with shared or private bath. Even if you don't stay, do stop by for a look—noting in particular the automobile included in the exterior terra-cotta, a very unusual artistic flourish. Rates vary widely, from $50–100 shared bath, $100–150 standard and deluxe rooms, to $150–250 suites.

For more information about accommodations and restaurants in the greater Palo Alto area, contact either the **Menlo Park Chamber of Commerce,** 1100 Merrill St., Menlo Park, 650/325-2818, www.menloparkchamber.com, or the **Los Altos Chamber of Commerce,** 321 University Ave., Los Altos, 650/948-1455, www.losaltoschamber.org.

EATING IN PALO ALTO
Inexpensive Student-Style Fare

The University Ave. area offers a generous choice in fairly cheap eats. For gourmet pizza, including thick and thin crusts and dozens of topping choices, head to **Pizza A Go Go,** 220 University Ave., 650/322-8100, where you can even buy by the slice. Open daily for delivery

and pick up only. Chili pepper lights brighten **Andale Taqueria,** 209 University, 650/323-2939, which specializes in California-fresh Mexican: mesquite-grilled chicken, low-fat black beans and fresh tamales.

A little farther afield is one of two local **Hobee's,** 4224 El Camino Real, 650/856-6124, locally famous for its coffeecake, omelettes, burgers, sandwiches, and such. No reservations, so prepare to wait. (The other Hobee's is at the Town & Country Village shopping center on El Camino Real, 650/327-4111.) In Mountain View, **Frankie, Johnnie, and Luigi Too,** 939 W. El Camino Real, 650/967-5384, is popular for pizza. An American classic already, if a bit pricey, is the **Peninsula Fountain & Grill** at the Stanford Shopping Center, 180 El Camino Real, 650/327-3141, the place for all-day breakfast, burgers, big-deal malts, and blue-plate specials.

More Expensive Fare

Spago Palo Alto, 265 Lytton Ave., 650/833-1000, is the Northern California outpost of Wolfgang Puck's celebrated L.A. eatery. Look for the same intriguing approach—anything from gourmet minipizzas to Chinese-style duck. Open for lunch weekdays only and for dinner daily. For an interesting Victorian-Industrial ambience and excellent Mediterranean-influenced cuisine, try **Zibibbo,** 430 Kipling Ave., 650/328-6722, which sports a wood-fired grill and lots of alfresco seating. New Orleans Cajun and Creole cookin' is the specialty at **Nola,** 535 Ramona St. (between University and Hamilton), 650/328-2722, open weekdays for lunch, nightly for dinner.

Here as elsewhere, **Il Fornaio,** 520 Cowper St. (inside the Garden Court Hotel), 650/853-3888, is a chic California-style franchise born at a baker's school in Milan and noted for its good breakfasts and Northern Italian specialties. Always a good bet for a bit of that Northern Italian ambience is the venerable **Osteria,** 247 Hamilton Ave., 650/328-5700, one of the area's best trattorias. **L'Amie Donia,** 530 Bryant St., 650/323-7614, serves outstanding rustic French-American cuisine from an open kitchen where you can watch the action. Open Tues.–Sat. for dinner.

A well-kept local secret is **Bistro Elan,** 448 California Ave., 650/327-0284.

Astounding portions of good American food are served with a song (at least at dinner) at the local outpost of **Max's Opera Cafe,** in the Stanford Shopping Center (180 El Camino Real), 650/323-6297. (In nice weather, head for a patio table.) A prime stop for meat eaters is **MacArthur Park,** 27 University Ave., 650/321-9990, where oak- and mesquite-grilled meats, fowl, and fish are served in a historic building. **Gordon Biersch Brewery,** 640 Emerson St., 650/323-7723, is a brewery/restaurant ("brewpub" doesn't quite fit) serving ethnically interesting variations on the California cuisine theme. Good for French food is New Orleans–style **Chantilly II,** 3001 El Camino Real, 650/321-4080. For elegant and upscale California cuisine with a Vietnamese flair, head for Los Altos and **Beausejour,** 170 State St., 650/948-1382.

Surrounding communities also offer some excellent fine-dining choices. In Mountain View, **Amber India,** in the Olive Tree Shopping Center at 2290 El Camino Real, 650/968-7511, ranks as one of the Bay Area's best Indian restaurants, well worth the wait. Open for lunch and dinner daily. **Chef Chu's,** 1067 N. San Antonio Rd. (at El Camino Real) in Los Altos, 650/948-2696, serves Chinese food, with Mandarin cuisine a specialty. Very organic, in the innovative California cuisine category, is the amusingly translated **Flea Street Cafe,** 3607 Alameda de las Pulgas (near Santa Cruz Ave.) in Menlo Park, 650/854-1226, open for dinner Tues.–Sun., and worth a special trip for Sunday brunch. For Thai food, also in Menlo Park is **Siam Garden,** 1143 Crane St. (between Oak Grove and Santa Cruz Ave.), 650/853-1143. **Carpaccio,** 1120 Crane, 650/322-1211, is Northern Italian, in a California kind of way, from the exceptional entrées right down to the oak-oven pizzas.

EVENTS AND ENTERTAINMENT

For a university town, Palo Alto is somewhat straight-laced—more spit-polished than scruffy—but there's life here nonetheless. Pick up the free local *Palo Alto Weekly* around town for its calendar section and reviews of upcoming events. Another good source of information, particularly for university events, is the *Stanford Daily,* which lists events daily and provides a comprehensive look at what's coming up in its "Friday Daily" section. Even better for what's happening is the supplement *Intermission* a weekly pullout entertainment section.

In May, the **Palo Alto Film Festival** showcases the work of Bay Area filmmakers. Local **TheatreWorks,** 650/463-1950 (administration) or 650/903-6000 (box office), is one of the Bay Area's best repertory theater companies, with performances usually staged in the **Mountain View Center for the Performing Arts,** 500 Castro, 650/903-6000. Though movie theaters abound, particularly enjoyable are the offbeat flicks shown at **Stanford Theatre,** 221 University Ave., 650/324-3700, a nonprofit enterprise dedicated to the memory of Hollywood's "golden age." The theater is famous for its classics double features. (Come early or stay late to appreciate a performance on the "Mighty Wurlitzer" pipe organ.)

Being a college town, Palo Alto and environs has its fair share of bars and nightclubs. Catch touring bands at **The Edge,** 260 S. California Ave., 650/289-0222, a nightclub with a massive sound system and a rockin' crowd. Dance nights are also popular, good drink specials before 10 P.M. More traditional, for those on the prowl, is Menlo Park's **British Banker's Club,** 1090 El Camino Real, 650/327-8769, a convincing Edwardian bar with 25-foot ceilings, stained glass, and library books.

San Jose and Vicinity

Once thickly forested in oaks, the vast Santa Clara Valley was quickly converted to farmland by the early settlers. Even within recent memory, the valley was one continuous orchard of almonds, apples, apricots, peaches, cherries, pears, and prunes where blossom snow fell from February into April. Now unofficially known as Silicon Valley—in honor of the computer chip and its attendant industry—these fertile soils today grow houses, office buildings, and shopping malls—all tied together by frightening freeways.

Sunny San Jose, more or less in the middle of it all, though aptly described as "all edges in search of a center," is the biggest city in Northern California. Though such a sprawling suburban enclave doesn't feel like a city, it is—with lively, sophisticated arts and entertainment and other attractions. San Jose, in fact, was California's first city—not counting mission settlements and other early outposts of empire—and was the state's first capital following American territorial occupation. What is now **San Jose State University** was California's first normal school, the only one in the state for many years.

Though others in the Bay Area taunt San Jose for its all-too-contemporary concrete and its apparent lack of community, the area has many merits—one being a good sense of humor. While Palo Alto enshrines the memory of Ernest Hemingway, and Oakland honors its native-born Gertrude Stein, San Jose honors the badly written novel. Launched by professor Scott Rice, San Jose State University's Bulwer-Lytton ("It was a dark and stormy night . . . ") Fiction Contest attracts 10,000 or more entries each year for its Worst Possible Opening Sentence competition. Among earlier entries: "She was like the driven snow beneath the galoshes of my lust" (Larry Bennett, Chicago) and "We'd made it through yet another nuclear winter and the lawn had just trapped and eaten its first robin" (Kyle J. Spiller, Garden Grove). The contest's 2002 Detective Award winner, Matthew Chambers of Hambleton, West Virginia, won with this opening line: "Chief Inspector Blancharde knew that this murder would be easy to solve—despite the fact that the clever killer had apparently dismembered his victim, run the corpse through a chipper-shredder with some Columbian beans to throw off the police dogs, and had run the mix through the industrial-sized coffee maker in the diner owned by Joseph Tilby (the apparent murder victim)—if only he could figure out who would want a hot cup of Joe." For an anthology of the best of the contest's worst writing, look for Penguin's *It Was a Dark and Stormy Night: The Final Conflict*.

DOWNTOWN SAN JOSE

Tired of being mocked for years as the city without a heart, San Jose is determined to obtain both heart and soul. Typical of the Bay Area gentrification trend, the city's decrepit downtown—more or less defined as the plaza area near San Carlos and Market Streets—is being swept clean of derelicts and the otherwise down-and-out. Nowadays, new office buildings, hotels, and cleaned-up urban shopping and residential neighborhoods are taking the place of flophouses and run-down liquor stores.

As a friendly destination for families and businessfolk alike, the new downtown San Jose is astounding. The unofficial and striking centerpiece is the towering 541-room **Fairmont Hotel,** part of the city's Silicon Valley Financial Complex, which also includes a 17-story office tower, an apartment complex, and a retail pavilion. Market Street's **Plaza de César Chávez,** the original center of the Pueblo of San Jose, is almost like the Fairmont's private front lawn, with walkways, benches, and a dancing-water fountain. Not far away, at Market St. and Viola Ave., is the city's downtown **San Jose McEnery Convention Center,** a 425,000-square-foot, $140 million project that augments existing convention facilities and the **Center for Performing Arts.** Other hotels surrounding the Convention Center—including the Crowne Plaza San Jose, the San Jose Hilton and Towers, and the refurbished historic Hotel De Anza and Hyatt Sainte Claire—help make the area attractive to conventioneers. Families and other travelers will enjoy downtown's variety of museums—including the **Tech Museum of Innovation,** the **Children's Discovery Museum of San Jose,** and the **San Jose Museum of Art.** Nearby **San Jose State University,** between E. San Fernando and E. San Salvador Streets at S. Fourth St., is home to the unique **Center for Beethoven Studies and Museum.** Not far away is San Jose's artsy **SoFA** neighborhood, a blend of galleries, small theaters, and coffee joints located in the South of First (Street) Area.

Still under development these days is **Guadalupe River Park,** a three-mile stretch of parks, gardens, jogging trails, and recreational facilities that will one day connect directly to San Jose International Airport. The park runs by downtown's **HP Pavillion** (formerly the San Jose Arena) a major sports facility that is home to the immensely popular National Hockey League team, the San Jose Sharks. Next to the Arena, on Arena Green, is a carousel featuring several custom-designed animals (including a shark for the hockey team).

To make it easy to get around once you've arrived in central San Jose, the downtown transit mall is a centralized stop for public buses—including the vintage trolleys that ply an around-downtown route—and a light rail system that runs all the way to Great America.

San Jose Museum of Art

Tucked in next to the restored St. Joseph Cathedral right downtown on the plaza, the San Jose Museum of Art, 110 S. Market St. (at San Fernando St.), 408/271-6840 or 408/294-2787 (recorded information), www.sjmusart.org, is a sparkling touch of tradition hitched to the avant-garde art world. The striking dark Romanesque main building, built in 1892 as a post office, later became the San Jose City Library. Since 1971, it has been San Jose's public home for the arts. The ultramodern, 45,000-square-foot, $14 million annex was added in 1991, when the museum took a giant step into the big-time art world. It's now able to attract major traveling exhibits, concentrating on contemporary and culturally diverse regional, national, and inter-

national visual arts. The museum's permanent collection emphasizes modern and American paintings, sculpture, drawings, and photographs. It includes works by David Best, Richard Diebenkorn, Sam Francis, Rupert Garcia, Robert Hudson, Nathan Oliveira, and many others.

The museum also sponsors an active public education program—from art classes, lectures, and symposia to art and art history instruction in the public schools—and features a fine book and gift shop. Museum hours are Tues.–Sun. 11 A.M.–5 P.M. (until 10 P.M. on Friday). It may be open at other times as well, for special events. The book/gift shop is open Tues.–Sun. 11 A.M.–5 P.M., (until 8 P.M. on Friday). Admission to the museum is free for everyone, every day. Free guided docent tours are offered daily at 12:30 and 2:30 P.M., Fridays at 6:30 P.M., and are also scheduled at other times. Spanish- and Vietnamese-speaking docents are available, as are free audiotape tours in English, Spanish, and Vietnamese.

Tech Museum of Innovation

People visiting San Jose often ask how to find Silicon Valley, that mythic destination where California has worked its high-tech, silicon-chip magic since the 1960s. The exact directions are difficult to give. Silicon Valley is a phenomenon, more than any precise place—though that "place," to the extent it can be located on a map, is indeed here, in the general vicinity of the Santa Clara Valley. If one really wants to see the result of computer-related creativity, entrepreneurial drive, innovation, unrelenting competitiveness, and massive amounts of venture capital, one can easily find Silicon Valley. The facile facelessness of the area's contemporary industrial parks is as much a part of San Jose's integrated circuitry as its freeway system.

A better place to "see" Silicon Valley, in the end, is at the community's technology museum. Everyone knows a purported "children's museum" is a smashing success when grown-ups practically knock each other over trying to get their hands on the exhibits. San Jose's exciting Tech Museum of Innovation, 201 S. Market St. (at Park), 408/795-6100 or 408/294-8324, www.thetech.org, is just that kind of place.

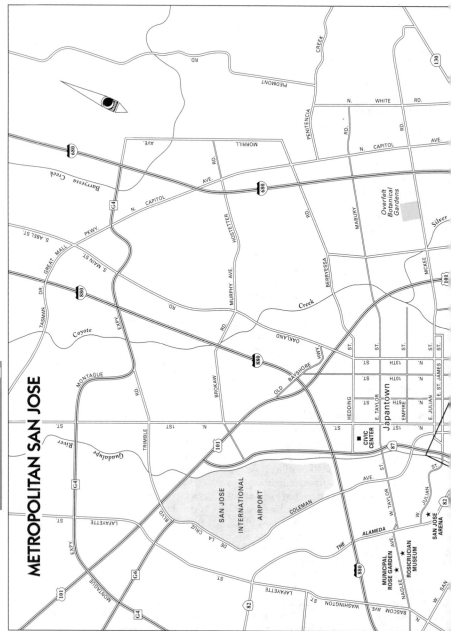

SAN FRANCISCO BAY AREA

METROPOLITAN SAN JOSE

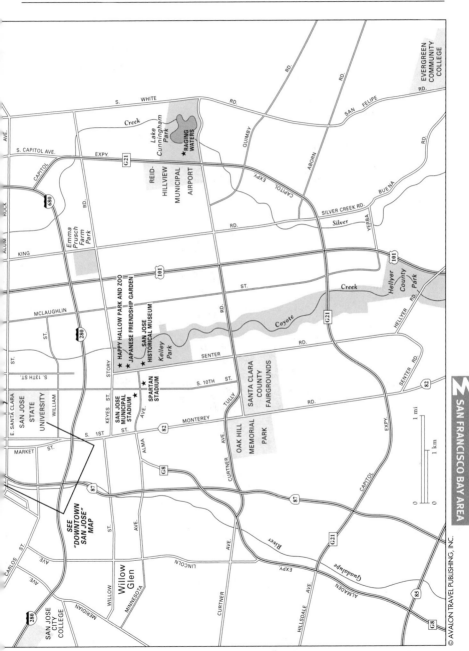

EVERGREEN COMMUNITY COLLEGE

S. WHITE

RD.

Creek

Lake Cunningham Park

RAGING WATERS

SAN FELIPE

QUIMBY

ABORN

BUENA

S. CAPITOL AVE.

EXPY.

G21

REID-HILLVIEW MUNICIPAL AIRPORT

CAPITOL EXPY

SILVER CREEK RD.

Silver

YERBA

AVE.

CAPITOL

680

RD.

Emma Prusch Farm Park

Hellyer County Park

101

ROCK

ALUM

KING

Creek

HELLYER RD.

101

MCLAUGHLIN

ST.

280

STORY

ST.

HAPPY HALLOW PARK AND ZOO

JAPANESE FRIENDSHIP GARDEN

SAN JOSE HISTORICAL MUSEUM

Coyote

G21

SENTER RD.

ST.

S. 13TH ST.

Kelley Park

SENTER

82

E. SANTA CLARA

SAN JOSE STATE UNIVERSITY

KEYES ST.

SPARTAN STADIUM

S. 10TH

ST.

WILLIAM

SAN JOSE MUNICIPAL STADIUM

AVE.

TULLY

SANTA CLARA COUNTY FAIRGROUNDS

RD.

MARKET

ST.

S. 1ST

ST.

82

MONTEREY

OAK HILL MEMORIAL PARK

1 mi

1 km

CURTNER

ALMA

G8

SEE "DOWNTOWN SAN JOSE" MAP

87

AVE.

CAPITOL EXPY

0

87

CARLOS

ST.

AVE.

Willow Glen

WILLOW

River

LINCOLN

Guadalupe

G21

EXPY

85

280

MERIDIAN

SAN JOSE CITY COLLEGE

MINNESOTA

CURTNER

AVE.

ALMADEN

HILLSDALE

AVE.

G8

N SAN FRANCISCO BAY AREA

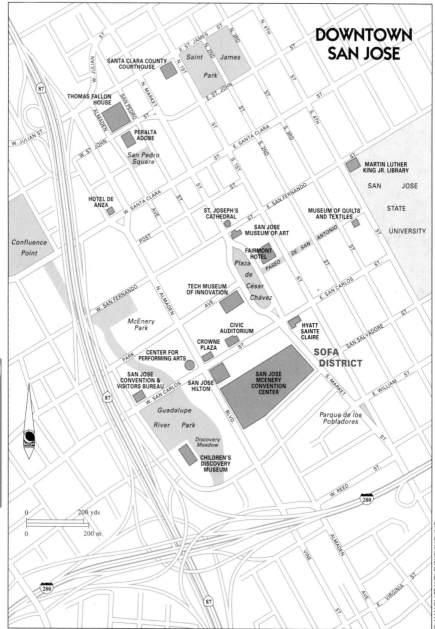

DOWNTOWN SAN JOSE

Santa Clara County Courthouse
Thomas Fallon House
Peralta Adobe
San Pedro Square
Saint James Park
Hotel de Anza
Confluence Point
St. Joseph's Cathedral
San Jose Museum of Art
Museum of Quilts and Textiles
Martin Luther King Jr. Library
San Jose State University
Fairmont Hotel
Plaza de César Chávez
Tech Museum of Innovation
McEnery Park
Civic Auditorium
Hyatt Sainte Claire
SOFA District
Crowne Plaza
Center for Performing Arts
San Jose Convention & Visitors Bureau
San Jose Hilton
San Jose McEnery Convention Center
Parque de los Pobladores
Guadalupe River Park
Discovery Meadow
Children's Discovery Museum

0   200 yds
0   200 m.

SAN FRANCISCO BAY AREA

© AVALON TRAVEL PUBLISHING, INC.

The museum's new 132,000-square-foot building houses five galleries—Innovation, Exploration, Communication, Life Tech, and "Center of the Edge"—all filled with interactive exhibits. You can design a roller coaster, pilot a robot sub, experience a simulated earthquake, look at an ultrasound image of your hand, or experience the huge, wrap-around Hackworth IMAX Dome Theater and its 14,000-watt sound system. This is without a doubt the Mother of All Interactive Museums.

The gift shop is also entertaining, stocking an impressive selection of educational toys and oddities, like jewelry made with real chips and light-emitting diodes. The Tech Museum is open daily 10 A.M.–6 P.M. in summer, and Tues.–Sun. (and Monday holidays) 10 A.M.–5 P.M. the rest of the year; closed on Easter, Thanksgiving, Christmas, and New Year's Day. Admission to either the galleries or the IMAX theater is $9 general, $8 seniors, $7 kids 3–12. Combination tickets good for both cost $16/$15/$13, respectively. Discounts available for groups of 12 or more.

To "help fight scientific illiteracy," which is the purpose of the Tech Museum, become a Tech Member. For membership information, call 408/795-6107.

Children's Discovery Museum

The concept is enough to terrorize parents and babysitters, but the fact is, there are no rules at the Children's Discovery Museum of San Jose, a shocking purple presence in the southern section of Guadalupe River Park. Open since 1990, this is a learning and discovery center for children, families, and schools, based on the premise that children need a place where they can be children without undue interference. Three particular themes—connections, community, and creativity—drive the action here. Children can run the lights and sirens on police cars, for example, and clamber all over firetrucks, or slide down a culvert to "Underground," to explore sewers and termite colonies. They can write letters and send them anywhere in the museum via the U.S. Post Office, or experiment with pneumatic tubes, telecommunications devices, and ham radio. They can try their hand at bank-

---

DO NOT COLLECT $200

Buy Boardwalk or go to jail (Do Not Pass Go, Do Not Collect $200) at the world's largest permanent **Outdoor Monopoly Board,** part of a "game garden" open for play in Guadalupe River Park. Monopoly here includes 930 square feet of granite and oversized player markers, including a thimble and that trademark top hat. (Bring your own tails.) Game "rent," $300 and up, is prohibitive for the casual tourist but might be feasible for an office party or family reunion. For information, call Friends of San Jose Beautiful, 408/995-6487, www.monopolyinthepark.com.

---

ing, play doctor or dentist, and move water with pumps and valves. Always popular are the "Step into the Past" exhibit, where kids can sit on a porch swing and do chores the old-fashioned way: with a grinding wheel, carpet beater, and a washboard, and the Postal Annex, a behind-the-scenes look at the postal service. In good weather, adventures and games are often available outside, too. And the museum offers a full calendar of special events year-round.

The Children's Discovery Museum is close to downtown at 180 Woz Way, which can be reached via the Guadalupe Parkway (Hwy. 87) between I-280 and Hwy. 101, then Auzerais Street. Call 408/298-5437 for current hours and special activities. The museum's regular hours are Tues.–Sat. 10 A.M.–5 P.M., Sunday noon–5 P.M. Admission is $7 adults, $6 seniors, $7 children (infants age 1 and younger free).

San Jose Museum of Quilts and Textiles

Unusual downtown is the San Jose Museum of Quilts and Textiles, 110 Paseo de San Antonio, 408/971-0323, www.sjquiltmuseum.org, which features galleries of historic and contemporary samples of the fabric arts, in addition to special rotating shows by individual artists. The museum is open Tues.–Sun. 10 A.M.–5 P.M. (Thursday until 8 P.M.); admission is $4 general, $3 seniors and students, under age 13 free, and free for everyone on the first Thursday of each month.

MORE SAN JOSE ADVENTURES

Winchester Mystery House

Though somewhat expensive for voyeuristic time travel, at least once in a lifetime everyone should visit the beautifully bizarre **Winchester Mystery House,** 525 S. Winchester Blvd. (west of downtown, at Hwy. 17 and I-280), 408/247-2101, www.winchestermysteryhouse.com. A six-acre monument to one woman's obsession, built up from eight rooms by Sarah L. Winchester and now a state historic monument, this labyrinth of crooked corridors, doors opening into space, and stairs leading nowhere includes 40 stairways, some 2,000 doors and trapdoors in strange places, and 10,000 or so windows. (Though only 160 rooms survive, 750 interconnecting chambers once testified to Winchester's industriousness.)

A sudden widow and heir to the Winchester firearms fortune, the lady of the house was convinced by a medium that she was cursed by her "blood money" and the spirits of all those shot by Winchester rifles, but that she would never die as long as she kept up her construction work. So Sarah Winchester spent $5.5 million of the family fortune to create and re-create her Gothic Victorian, working feverishly for 38 years straight. But death eventually came knocking on her door anyway, and the around-the-clock racket of workers' hammers and saws finally ceased.

At least, that's the official version of the story, the one that draws the crowds to this amazing mansion. But others, including her personal attorney, recall Sarah Winchester as quite sane, a clearheaded businesswoman who actively managed her vast holdings and estate. According to a 1923 *San Jose Mercury News* interview with Roy F. Leib, Winchester reconstructed the house "due to her desire to provide accommodations for her many relatives who she thought would come to California to visit her." And she stopped work on the house long before her death; according to Leib's records, she hired no more carpenters after the 1906 earthquake. The wild stories about Winchester's eccentricities, Leib suggested, grew out of her extreme reclusiveness, which may have been related to severe arthritis and limb deformities.

Beautifully bizarre, the Winchester Mystery House is a must-see.

In any event, the lady of the house was quite a woman. People tend to focus on Sarah Winchester's craziness, but—once here—it's hard not to be impressed by her creativity and craft as an impromptu architect.

The estate is open daily except Christmas. In summer, it opens at 9 A.M., with the last tour departing at 7 P.M.; reduced hours the rest of the year. The Estate Tour costs $17.95 general, $14.95 seniors, $11.95 children ages 6–12. The Behind the Scenes Tour costs $14.95 adults, $13.95 seniors. A combined tour costs $24.95 general, $21.95 seniors. Children under 12 are not permitted on the Behind the Scenes or combined tours.

Rosicrucian Museum

A very worthwhile destination and San Jose's most popular tourist attraction is the Rosicrucian Egyptian Museum, 1342 Naglee Ave. (at Park Ave.), 408/947-3635, www.egyptianmuseum.org, a temple of possibilities (in the California tradition) set up in a parklike setting open to all. The Egyptian Museum includes outdoor statuary and the largest collection of Assyrian, Babylonian, and Egyptian artifacts in the western U.S.: amulets and charms, mummies, musical instruments, a life-sized walk-through replica of a pyramid tomb (guided tours every half hour), and other artifacts in the mystical mode. Also here is the **Rosicrucian Planetarium,** built in 1936, which has been closed for major repairs; call to inquire about its reopening date.

The museum is open Tues.–Fri. 10 A.M.–5 P.M., Sat.–Sun. 11 A.M.–6 P.M., closed major holidays. Museum admission is $9 adults, $75 seniors and students (with ID), $5 children ages 5–10, free for children under age 5.

Kelley Park and San Jose Historical Museum

One of a string of parks developed (and being developed) along San Jose's past-trashed Guadalupe River is 156-acre Kelley Park, 635 Phelan Ave., 408/297-0778, which offers some special pleasures, including the **Japanese Friendship Garden,** 1500 Senter Rd., 408/277-2757, six acres of serenity created around small lakes complete with koi, strong-swimming ornamental carp representing the male principle.

Also well worth some time here is the open-air San Jose Historical Museum, 1600 Senter Rd., 408/287-2290, a full-scale village of historic buildings and replicas. Next to A.P. Giannini's first Bank of Italy (now Bank of America) branch office and looming above all else is a half-scale reconstruction of one of old San Jose's "Eiffel Towers." After a priest at St. Ignatius College invented arc lighting in 1881, San Jose latched onto the idea and constructed four 327-foot-tall light towers to illuminate the entire downtown district. The system worked—so well, in fact, that the entire sky was lit up at night and surrounding farmers complained that their livestock couldn't sleep and became confused and crotchety. But, way off in Paris, Alexander Eiffel heard about the towers' design and found his way to San Jose to study them.

In addition to historic homes, hotels, businesses, and fundraising concessions, the 16-acre outdoor museum also includes a Trolley Barn, where in-progress restoration of the city's trolleys can be observed, also the starting point for short trolley rides around "downtown." Inside the elegant Pacific Hotel, displays document the history and culture of the area's native Ohlone people. Fascinating, too, is the new replica of the 1888 Ng Shing Gung Chinese Temple, or the "Temple of Five Sages," once located at Taylor and Sixth Streets (the site of today's Fairmont Hotel) and central to San Jose's Chinatown. Original temple furnishings and other displays tell the story of the Chinese in Santa Clara Valley. Representing a more recent historical era, the 1927 Associated Gasoline Station is a classic. For a deeper sense of life in the Santa Clara Valley prior to freeways and suburban development, stop by the Stevens Ranch Fruit Barn and take in the "Passing Farms: Enduring Values" exhibit.

The museum is open Tues.–Sun. noon–5 P.M. Admission is $6 general, $5 seniors, and $4 children 6–17, children 5 and under free. Tours are available every day but Monday. Ask about membership in the nonprofit San Jose Historical Museum Association, which supports the preservation of Santa Clara Valley's heritage.

At the opposite end of Kelley Park is **Happy Hollow Park and Zoo,** 1300 Senter Rd., 408/277-3000, great fun for the kiddos with more than 150 animals, as well as playgrounds and rides. Small admission fee.

Kelley Park and all of its attractions are managed and maintained by History San Jose. They maintain a well-designed website at www.serve.com/sjhistory/ where you'll find a map of the park, information on current events, and driving directions. There are two nominal-cost public parking lots off Senter Rd. between Phelan and Keyes/Story Roads.

Peralta Adobe and Fallon House

Two historic buildings make up this minipark at San Pedro and W. St. John Streets, 408/993-8182. The Peralta Adobe was built in 1797 and is the city's oldest surviving building. The Fallon House is an 1855 Victorian that was home to early San Jose mayor Thomas Fallon. Each is furnished in the style of its period. Guided tours are offered Tues.–Sun. noon–3:30 P.M.; $6 adults, $5 seniors, $4 children 6–17.

ADVENTURES NEAR SAN JOSE

Well worth a look-see in nearby Milpitas is the unique, free **Wall of Garbage Recycling Museum** at the Browning-Ferris Recyclery, 1601 Dixon Landing Rd., 408/262-1401. (Take the Dixon Landing Rd. West exit from I-880 and follow the garbage trucks.) The 100-foot-long, 20-foot-high "wall" represents the amount of trash discarded by the entire United States every second, by Santa Clara County in three minutes, and by one person in about six years—empty beer cans, half-eaten food, disposable diapers, plastic foam cups and containers, egg cartons, plastic bags, paint thinner cans, old shoes, and broken toys and appliances. This museum is about as real as they get. (Despite the overwhelming odds, the garbage on display is not malodorous, since it's all been sterilized or preserved.) Other museum displays show how metals can be separated for recycling by an electromagnet; how garbage dumps can produce methane gas; and other aspects of refuse recycling. Children, and sometimes adults, especially appreciate the recycling trivia shared by the museum—including the fact that every recycled can saves enough energy to power a TV set for three years, and that the average car interior contains 60 pounds of recycled paper. The Recyclery is open Mon.–Sat. 7:30 A.M.–3:30 P.M. Free (guided tours available).

If the kids are overly distressed by life in the real world, perhaps they can be distracted for a time by the waterslides and pools at **Raging Waters** at Lake Cunningham Regional Park east of I-680 on Tully Rd. off Capitol Expressway. The 14-acre theme park has more than 30 waterslides in a tropical atmosphere. Admission is $25.99 general, $19.99 children under 48 inches tall, $15.99 seniors over 50; $3 off after 3 P.M., under 2 free. Call 408/238-9900 for more information or visit www.rwsplash.com.

Alviso Environmental Education Center

Just north of San Jose proper is tiny Alviso, an officially nonexistent city of 1,600 or so (plus chickens and stray dogs) technically incorporated into San Jose but actually at home on 11 square miles of bayside swampland. Fairly new here is the Environmental Education Center of the Don Edwards San Francisco Bay National Wildlife Refuge (at the southern tip of the bay and reached via Hwy. 237, then Taylor St. and Grand Blvd.), 408/262-5513, a solar-powered building plus trail complex dedicated to educating the public about the bay environment. The building itself is designed for classroom use, but the self-guided Alviso Slough Trail is available for marsh exploration and bird-watching. For more information, contact the refuge at 1 Marshlands Rd. in Fremont, 510/792-0222, desfbay.fws.gov.

Ames Research Center and Great America

Two miles and a time warp away is NASA's space-age Ames Research Center at Mountain View's Moffett Field, 650/604-6497, www.arc.nasa.gov. Facilities include the world's largest wind tunnel and—more modern and certainly appropriate to Silicon Valley—computer-simulated aircraft-safety test facilities. Tours were not available at press time, call for current schedules. Ames Visitor's Center is free and open to the public weekdays 8:00 A.M.–4:30 P.M., closed weekends and Federal holidays.

Several miles north of San Jose (via Hwy. 101) in Santa Clara is **Paramount's Great America,** 408/988-1776 (recorded information), www.pgathrills.com, one of the nation's largest family-style amusement parks, with more than 100 rides—some considerably more thrilling than the traditional roller coaster—plus kiddie diversions of all types, live entertainment, shops, and restaurants. Attractions at this 100-acre complex include eight roller coasters (among them Vortex—a stand-up coaster-Stealth, where riders "fly" hanging from shoulder and knee harnesses, and Invertigo), KidZville for the younger set, and the IMAX Pictorium Theater (extra charge). Open daily from Memorial Day weekend to Labor Day, otherwise weekends only from late March through May and early September to mid-October. Admission is $45.99 general, $39.99 seniors, $33.99 children ages 3–6 or under 48 inches tall. Group rates and season passes are available; ask about ticket specials. Parking is $10 per vehicle.

Santa Clara is also home to well-respected Santa Clara University, on the site of the original but long-gone Mission Santa Clara.

Los Gatos and Saratoga Sights

Nearby Los Gatos and Saratoga are picturesque upscale communities tucked into the forested hills west of San Jose. Both of these onetime logging towns are now noted for their turn-of-the-century architecture and sophisticated downtown shopping districts. In Los Gatos, particularly worthwhile are the **Forbes Mill History Museum,** 75 Church St. (off Main), 408/395-7375, and, for movie buffs, the **Los Gatos Cinema,** 41 N. Santa Cruz Ave., 408/395-0203, which runs many foreign and art films. Stop for some good joe and baked goods at the **Los Gatos Coffee Roasting Company** at 101 W. Main, 408/354-3263, to fortify yourself before heading on to Saratoga—because if you go to Saratoga, you might as well go hiking in the redwoods. Unusual gardens seem to be the signature of Saratoga, an affluent foothill town southwest of San Jose and the starting point for the very scenic Hwy. 9 route up to Saratoga Gap and Skyline Blvd., then on past undeveloped Castle Rock State Park and the backdoor entrance to Big Basin Redwoods.

Saratoga's **Hakone Japanese Gardens** city park, nearby at 21000 Big Basin Way, 408/741-4994, is considered the finest of its type outside Japan, a 17th-century-style Zen garden: monochromatic, simple, and symbolically powerful. Open daily 12:30–4:30 P.M. Parking fee $5 per car, except on the first Tuesday of each month.

Still in Saratoga, **Villa Montalvo,** 15400 Montalvo Rd., 408/961-5800, www.villamontalvo.org, is a monument to wealth, one of California's last ostentatious country estates. Built for onetime U.S. senator and three-time San Francisco mayor James Phelan, patron of artists and writers, the villa is now an artists-in-residence hall plus gallery, book shop, and gift shop surrounded by terraced gardens with nearby arboretum and bird sanctuary. Various concerts and other cultural events are offered regularly at the villa gallery and in the onetime carriage house (now a theater). The 175-acre arboretum is open weekdays 8 A.M.–5 P.M., weekends and holidays 9 A.M.–5 P.M.; admission is free.

Lick Observatory and Fremont Peak State Park

On the western peak of Mount Hamilton to the east of San Jose and reached from downtown via Hwy. 130 (the Alum Rock Ave. extension of E. Santa Clara St., which connects with adventurous Mt. Hamilton Rd.) is **Lick Observatory,** 408/274-5061, www.ucolick.org, which has been casting its 36-inch telescopic eye skyward since 1888. The telescope was named for its eccentric gold rush-millionaire benefactor James Lick, who was convinced there was life on the moon. At the time that it was dedicated as part of UC Berkeley's research facilities, the Lick telescope was the world's most powerful and the only one on the planet staffed permanently. Nowadays, the Lick Observatory is administered by UC Santa Cruz, and additional telescopes (including the 120-inch Shane Telescope, built in the 1950s and one of the world's most productive) have been added to this mountaintop astronomy enclave.

Excepting major holidays, the observatory opens to the public Mon.–Fri. 12:30–5 P.M., Sat.–Sun. 10 A.M.–5 P.M. Fifteen-minute tours are offered every half hour, starting half an hour after opening and ending at 4:30 P.M. From spring through fall, free stargazing programs are conducted one or two nights a week (usually Friday and/or Saturday); for reservations (required far in advance), call the UCSC box office at 831/459-2159. Also ask about concerts and other special events at the observatory.

Also fun for astronomy buffs—considerably farther away, at **Fremont Peak State Park** south of San Juan Bautista—is the 30-inch homemade Kevin Medlock telescope, available to the public for the actual eyes-on experience of stargazing on most new-moon or quarter-moon Saturday nights, Mar.–Oct., weather permitting. No reservations required. Call 831/623-2465 for information. Medlock, a mechanical engineer at the

BRONCHO BILLY RIDES AGAIN

Notable in the city of Fremont is historic Niles Main Street, a district that by its very existence commemorates the East Bay's Wild West—and its pioneering cinematic past. The prolific Essanay Film Company produced silent films in what was then the community of Niles and in nearby Niles Canyon from 1912 to 1916. These 16 mm movies starred Broncho Billy, Wallace Berry, Charlie Chaplin, Chester Conklin, and Ben Turpin, among others. During the annual Niles **Broncho Billy Silent Film Festival,** rare films starring Broncho Billy, Charlie Chaplin, and other silent-screen stars are shown. For more information about Niles, its silent movie era, and community events, contact the **Niles Main Street Association,** 37457 Niles Blvd., Fremont, 510/742-9868, www.niles.org.

Lawrence Berkeley Laboratory, scrounged up the necessary materials ($2,000 worth) for this project, an amazing accomplishment in itself.

Mission San Jose

Well north of San Jose via I-680, then Mission Blvd. (Hwy. 238) is beautiful Mission San Jose at Mission and Washington Boulevards in Fremont, 510/657-1797, open daily 10 A.M.–5 P.M. for self-guided tours (slide shows on the hour, in the museum). Painstakingly restored at a cost of $5 million, then reopened to the public in 1985, Mission San Jose was once the center of a great cattle-ranching enterprise—a successful Spanish outpost noted also for its Ohlone Indian orchestra. Very evocative, worth a stop. Wheelchair accessible and free, though donations are appreciated. Group tours available by advance reservation.

Hiking

South of downtown San Jose is **Almaden Quicksilver County Park,** 21785 Almaden Rd., 408/268-8220. The old New Almaden Mine here was once the largest U.S. mercury mine. These days, there's a small museum open Fri.–Sun. as well as 23 miles of old mining roads now converted to trails. No dogs allowed. For more in-

formation on Almaden and other county parks, call 408/358-3741. Off Alum Rock Ave. (Hwy. 130) is **Joseph D. Grant County Park,** 18405 Mt. Hamilton Rd., 408/274-6121, a former cattle ranch now offering camping and heavenly hiking, with 40 miles of trails—especially enjoyable in spring when wildflowers are in bloom.

Southeast of San Jose and reached via Hwy. 101 and E. Dunne Ave. (follow it to the end) is undeveloped **Henry W. Coe State Park,** Northern California's largest state park, famous for its tarantulas. (Come to the **TarantulaFest** and Barbecue in early October, where the park's own band—The Tarantulas—is part of the fun.) The park also includes 87,000 acres of oak woodlands and pines, wildflowers, spectacular views, and the best spring and fall backpacking in the Bay Area. The Pine Ridge Museum here is also worthwhile. Family campsites and backpacking campsites (no showers or hookups) are available by reservation through ReserveAmerica, 800/444-7275 or www.reserveamerica.com; $7 per night, or $2 per night per person for the backcountry sites. Day-use fee: $4. For more information, contact Henry W. Coe State Park, 408/779-2728 or www.coepark.org.

West of Saratoga in Cupertino, **Stevens Creek County Park,** 11401 Stevens Canyon Rd., 408/867-3654, includes a popular recreation lake as well as picnicking and hiking trails that interconnect with the Fremont Older Open Space Preserve to the east and adjacent Pichetti Ranch to the west. The **Sanborn-Skyline County Park** southwest of Saratoga and Los Gatos along Skyline Blvd. offers some walk-in camping, hikes, and a tie-in (at the park's north end) to the Skyline-to-the-Sea Trail, which slips down through Castle Rock State Park, then follows Hwy. 9 into Big Basin Redwoods State Park before reaching the Pacific Ocean. Also here: the AYH Sanborn Park Hostel (see below).

STAYING IN SAN JOSE

Under $100

Best bet on the low-cost end is out a ways: the **HI-USA Sanborn Park Hostel,** 15808 Sanborn Rd. in Saratoga, 408/741-0166, www.sanbornparkhostel.org, featuring the wonderful old redwood Welchhurst hunting lodge, listed on the National Register of Historic Places, and surrounding cabins. A plush place by hostel standards, Sanborn Park Hostel offers a fireplace-cozy lounge, dining room, and modern kitchen complete with three refrigerators, range, and microwave. Family room available. Under $50. Popular in summer, reservations advised.

Close to downtown San Jose, rooms at **San Jose State University** are available in summer, 408/924-6180; under $50. **Motel 6,** 2560 Fontaine Rd. (off Hwy. 101, the Bayshore Freeway), 408/270-3131, is fairly close to everything; $50–100. There's another Motel 6 near the airport, reasonably accessible to downtown, at 2081 N. First St., 408/436-8180 ($50–100), and a third in Campbell at 1240 Camden Ave., 408/371-8870 ($50–100). For reservations at any Motel 6, call 800/466-8356 or check the website: www.motel6.com.

Also off the Bayshore is the **Best Western Gateway Inn,** 2585 Seaboard Ave., 408/435-8800 or 800/437-8855, www.bestwestern.com; $50–100. Downtown is the **Ramada Limited,** 455 S. Second St. (east off Hwy. 82), 408/298-3500 or 800/350-1113, www.ramada.com, with sauna, whirlpool, pool; $50–100. The **Best Western San Jose Lodge** is at 1440 N. First St., 408/453-7750 or 800/528-1234, www.bestwestern.com; $50–100. For more low and moderately priced accommodations choices, and/or suggestions on places to stay in a specific area of San Jose and vicinity, contact local visitors bureaus (see above).

Downtown Hotels

An immense presence towering over San Jose's newly redeveloped downtown plaza, the **Fairmont Hotel,** 170 S. Market St., 408/998-1900 or 800/527-4727, www.fairmont.com, is a 541-room study in elegance and sophistication. San Jose's Fairmont, part of the world-class luxury chain, features comfortable rooms and every imaginable amenity, and is central to just about everything. There's a 58-foot rooftop pool on the Cabana Level with restaurant service and a complete fitness center below—exercise room with treadmills and stairclimbers, both men's

COURTESY OF SAN JOSE CONVENTION AND VISITORS BUREAU

San Jose's Fairmont Hotel is the unofficial centerpiece of downtown redevelopment.

and women's saunas, steam rooms, and massage. Restaurants here include the excellent **Grill on the Alley,** serving steaks, chops, and seafood (reservations suggested); **Pagoda** for Cantonese cuisine; and the more casual, all-American **Fountain Restaurant.** Underground valet parking. Rates $150–250, suites $250 and up.

The queen of San Jose's original hotels, the historic **Sainte Claire,** now the Hyatt Sainte Claire, 302 S. Market St. (at San Carlos St. downtown), 408/885-1234 or 800/492-8822, www .sainteclaire.hyatt.com, has been immaculately restored into a state-of-the-art luxury hotel with every amenity and fine European-style service. This relatively small hotel has 170 rooms, including 18 suites, and offers services such as in-room safes and valet parking. Especially attractive is the newly restored interior courtyard, with exceptional Spanish tile work, circa 1927, by local artist Albert Solon. The Sainte Claire is also home to an outpost of **Il Fornaio** restaurant, noted for its Northern Italian specialties and wonderful

SAN FRANCISCO BAY AREA

bakery items. Rates $100–150, deluxe rooms and suites $150–250.

Another long-time local beauty, the 1931 art deco **Hotel De Anza,** 233 W. Santa Clara St., 408/286-1000 or 800/843-3700, www.hotel-deanza.com, has also recently been redone—a national historic landmark and a 10-story study in elegance with a deco-esque bar, the **Hedley Club,** and Northern Italian restaurant, **La Pastaia** (408/286-8686). Standard and deluxe rooms $150–250, suites $250 and up

The 17-story **San Jose Hilton and Towers** nearby at 300 Almaden Blvd., 408/287-2100 or 800/445-8667, www.hilton.com, is next to the convention center. Amenities here include health club, spa, private pool, restaurant, and bar. Standard and deluxe rooms $150–250, suites $250 and up. Also in the neighborhood: **Crowne Plaza—Downtown San Jose,** 282 Almaden Blvd., 408/998-0400 or 800/465-4329, www.six-continentshotels.com, with all the usual amenities and pool. Standard rooms $100–150, deluxe rooms $150–250

Out near the airport are some other top-of-the-line choices, including the French provincial **Radisson Plaza Hotel,** 1471 N. Fourth St., 408/452-0200 or 800/333-3333, www.radisson.com, with some great weekend bargain rates ($100–150); the **Doubletree San Jose,** 2050 Gateway Place, 408/453-4000 or 800/222-8733, www.doubletree.com ($100–150); and the **Hyatt San Jose,** 1740 N. First St., 408/993-1234 or 800/233-1234, www.hyatt.com ($100–150).

Inns and Bed-and-Breakfasts

One of Saratoga's hidden attractions is the **Inn at Saratoga,** 20645 Fourth St., 408/867-5020 or 800/338-5020 for reservations, www.innat-saratoga.com. This exclusive, romantic European-style retreat is a Bay Area favorite. The inn's 46 guest rooms and suites, some with double whirlpool baths, all overlook Saratoga Creek. Rates $250 and up. Special retreat packages with a welcome gift, continental breakfast, afternoon refreshments, and access to the Los Gatos Athletic Club (exercise facilities, pool, spa, the works) are available.

Back in San Jose, the **Hensley House,** 456 N. Third St. (at Hensley), 408/298-3537 or 800/498-3537, www.hensleyhouse.com, is a statuesque 1884 Queen Anne Victorian with elegant dark wood decor, crystal chandeliers, and 10 comfortable guest rooms with queen-size beds and private bathrooms. Wonderful gourmet breakfast. Most room rates $150–250.

To commune with the memory of Maxfield Parrish, stroll through English gardens, and feast on real (and real good) food, plan on a stay at the **Briar Rose,** 897 E. Jackson St., 408/279-5999 or 877/724-5999, www.briar-rose.com, an 1875 farmhouse-style Victorian with six rooms, full breakfast. Room rates $100–150.

EATING IN SAN JOSE
Inexpensive Fare

A shining star in San Jose's small downtown Japantown district, lively **Gombei** 193 E. Jackson St. (Jackson and Fifth St.), 408/279-4311, is well worth seeking out, for the specials and noodle dishes as much as the ambience. Open for lunch and dinner, closed Sunday. Also downtown and a bit more expensive is **Thepthai,** 23 N. Market (between Santa Clara and St. John), 408/292-7515, open daily at lunch and dinner for Thai specialties, especially good for fried tofu dishes. Another option for Thai food is the **House of Siam,** 55 S. Market St. (at Post), 408/279-5668.

A place worth hunting for, if you've got the time, is unpretentious **Chez Sovan,** next to a gas station at 923 Old Oakland Rd. (13th St. and Oakland), 408/287-7619, a decrepit diner-style joint serving exceptional Cambodian fare, open weekdays for lunch only.

Otherwise, central San Jose holds plenty of inexpensive choices. (With a small appetite, some of the places listed below, under Pricier Fare, may also fit into the budget category.) For the real McCoy in Mexican food, head for **Tacos al Pastor,** 400 S. Bascom Ave., 408/275-1619. **Original Joe's,** 301 S. First St., 408/292-7030, is famous for its "Joe's Special" sandwich of scrambled eggs, spinach, and ground beef, but most of what you'll find on the menu is Italian American. The **Red Sea,** 684 N. First St., 408/993-1990, serves Ethiopian food.

Pricier Fare

Brewpub fans: **Gordon Biersch Brewery Restaurant** is an upscale place in an alley downtown between First and Second Streets, 33 E. San Fernando St., 408/294-6785, where in good weather you can quaff a few of the namesake German-style brews out on the patio. The food's not bad, either. (Gordon Biersch also has outposts in Palo Alto, San Francisco, and beyond.) Some people prefer the area's other notable brewpub, boisterous **Tied House Cafe and Brewery of San Jose,** 65 N. San Pedro St., 408/295-2739, with eight beers on tap and an American-style pubhouse menu. (Vegetarian dishes, too.) Chic for sushi and such is **California Sushi and Grill,** 1 E. San Fernando, 408/297-1847.

The city's most genuine steak house and rib joint is **Henry's World Famous Hi-Life,** 301 W. St. John St. (at Almaden Blvd.), 408/295-5414, a no-frills thrill from the Formica tables and paper placemats to the rhythm and blues on the jukebox. For German food, try **Teske's Germania,** 255 N. First St., 408/292-0291.

Eulipia, 374 S. First St. (between San Salvador and San Carlos), 408/280-6161, is chic yet casual, one of the South Bay's best for California cuisine at lunch and dinner. Glamorous and expensive, just the place for foodies if someone else is buying, is **A.P. Stump's,** 163 W. Santa Clara St., 408/292-9928, for California-style New American—from pizza with Dungeness crab, asparagus, braised fennel, fresh basil, and parmesan cheese sauce to Tandoori-style "rosie chicken," spiced basmati rice, sautéed tat soi, and a trio of chutneys. Menu changes daily. Great wine list, spectacular desserts. Longtime local legend **Paolo's** is now home downtown at 333 W. San Carlos St., 408/294-2558, across from the Center for Performing Arts, and noted for its contemporary turn on Italian classics. Open for lunch weekdays, for dinner nightly except Sunday. Also good for upscale Italian fare is **Bella Mia,** 58 S. First St. downtown, 408/280-1993.

San Jose suffers no shortage of fine French restaurants. Inside an old hotel overlooking a creek, **La Forêt,** 21747 Bertram Rd., 408/997-3458, is an exceptional French restaurant specializing in seafood and wild game entrées.

Another good choices for French cuisine is **Le Papillon,** 410 Saratoga Ave. (at Kiely Blvd.), 408/296-3730, open for lunch weekdays and for dinner daily. For other top-of-the-line choices, consider also the best hotels. But the general consensus is that the area's best restaurant is another local institution. In the four-star category, **Emile's,** 545 S. Second St., 408/289-1960, is famous for its very expensive Swiss and French fare and classically romantic ambience.

Surrounding communities, including Campbell, Santa Clara, and upscale Saratoga, also have their culinary claims to fame. In Saratoga, for example, top fine-dining selections include the **Plumed Horse,** 14555 Big Basin Way, 408/867-4711, for French country; the exceptional French **Le Mouton Noir,** 14560 Big Basin Way, 408/867-7017, housed in a classy Victorian; and **Gervais Restaurant Français,** 14560 Big Basin Way, 408/275-8631, open for lunch Tues.–Fri. and for dinner Tues.–Sat. for superb classic French cuisine. Casual and contemporary in nearby Los Gatos: **Cats Restaurant,** 17533 Santa Cruz Hwy., 408/354-4020, a roadhouse with good dinners Tues.–Sun. and live music Fri.–Sat. For current regional restaurant reviews, pick up a Friday edition of the *San Jose Mercury News.*

INFORMATION AND TRANSPORTATION

For more information about food and lodgings in the San Jose area, as well as area wineries and other diversions, contact the excellent **San Jose Convention & Visitors Bureau,** downtown at 125 S. Market St., Ste. 300, San Jose, 408/295-9600, 800/726-5673, www.sanjose.org. The visitors bureau also sponsors three Visitor Information Centers, one in the lobby of the San Jose McEnery Convention Center (408/977-0900), the others inside Terminal C and the new Terminal A at the San Jose International Airport.

In addition to brochures and listings of major area attractions, the visitors bureau also offers a useful annual *Travel & Meeting Planner* and the *Official Visitors Guide to San Jose* (both free). Also available here: the *San Jose History Walk* brochure, the *Historic Trolley Rider's*

Guide, the *Downtown Public Art and Gallery Guide,* and the Santa Clara Valley Wine Growers Association brochure. To get a sense of the depth and breadth of the local multicultural arts, entertainment, and community celebration scene, also request a current calendar of events—there's always something going on. For current San Jose events, call the **FYI Events Line** at 408/295-2265.

For information about nearby communities, contact the **Santa Clara Chamber of Commerce/Convention and Visitors Bureau,** 1850 Warburton Ave. in Santa Clara, 408/244-9660 or 408/244-8244, www.santaclara.org; the **Saratoga Chamber of Commerce,** 14485 Big Basin Way in Saratoga, 408/867-0753, www.saratogachamber.org; and the **Los Gatos Chamber of Commerce,** 349 N. Santa Cruz Ave., Los Gatos, 408/354-9300, www.losgatosweb.com.

As befits the megalopolis it has become, the San Jose area is fairly serious about its public transportation. In addition to the downtown historic trolleys (summers only) and the light rail transit system that runs from South San Jose/Almaden to North San Jose and Santa Clara, the local **Santa Clara Valley Transportation Authority (VTA),** 408/321-2300 or 800/894-9908, www.vta.org, also operates a fleet of mass transit buses that travel all over San Jose and connect with other public transportation. The trolleys are primarily a downtown district convenience and entertainment, running along light rail tracks in the immediate vicinity of downtown attractions. Visitors can get farther on the commuter-oriented light rail—to Great America, and even to the San Jose International Airport from downtown. Buses and/or CalTrain and Amtrak connections can get you almost anywhere.

Get oriented to local public transit with a system map and a variety of other easily available

publications, including the *Bus and Light Rail Rider's Guide,* the *Light Rail Schedule,* and the *Guide to Park and Ride.* Try the visitors bureau, which usually carries most of them, or stop by the **Transportation Information Center** downtown at 2 N. First St. (at Santa Clara St.), open Mon.–Fri. 8 A.M.–6 P.M., Sat. 9 A.M.–3 P.M. Otherwise, for information on bus and light rail operations, including fares and schedules, call 408/321-2300 between 5:30 A.M. and 8 P.M. weekdays, 7:30 A.M.–4 P.M. Saturdays and holidays. (From the 415 or 650 area codes, call 800/894-9908.) Information is posted on the Transportation Information Center's website: www.511.org. For information on **AC Transit** bus connections to Fremont, call 510/839-2882; call 510/441-2278 for information on **BART** mass transit service connections in Fremont. For **SamTrans** bus service information, in San Mateo County up the peninsula, call 415/817-1717 or 800/660-4287, www.samtrans.org.

Train transportation to and from the area, already a very viable option due to Amtrak's new routes through San Jose, will be even better now that the the historic **Cahill Street Station,** an Italian Renaissance Revival building circa 1935, has been restored and refurbished as a full-fledged transit center. The station is currently used by both Amtrak, Altamont Commuter Express (ACE) commuter rail service, and the 47-mile Caltrain, a freeway-commuter train service between San Jose and San Francisco. For information on **Caltrain** service, call 650/508-6455 or 800/660-4287 or visit Caltrain's website: www.511.org/Caltrain. For Altamont Commuter Express (ACE) service, call 800/411-7245, www.acerail.com. For **Amtrak** route and schedule information, call 800/872-7245, www.amtrak.com, and see also the transportation information included in the Great Valley chapter under Sacramento and Vicinity.

Oakland

Since the job description requires them to say what needs to be said, writers tend to offend. Gertrude Stein, for example, apparently insulted her hometown until the end of time when she described Oakland with the statement "There is no there there"—most likely a lament for the city she no longer recognized. But Oakland later proved Stein wrong by erecting a sculpture to *There,* right downtown on City Square at 13th and Broadway where everyone can see it.

Long bad-rapped as crime-riddled and somehow inherently less deserving than adjacent Berkeley or San Francisco across the bay, Oakland has come a long way, with a booming economy, downtown redevelopment and neighborhood gentrification, and both a thriving port industry and waterfront district to prove it. In many ways, Oakland has become one with Berkeley, with some neighborhoods defined most strongly by shared cultural associations. And the city has become a respectable neighbor to San Francisco, that relationship integrated by accessibility. But Oakland still struggles with its own contradictions. It was the birthplace of the Black Power movement but also home base for the Hell's Angels. It's home to the World Series–winning Oakland A's but also home to one of the most troubled public school systems in the nation. The class distinctions here are obvious; Oakland houses its immigrants and low-income residents in the flatlands while those with money and power live up in the hills. There's definitely a there here, for those who can afford it.

The city was shaken to its roots by the October 1989 Bay Area earthquake, which collapsed a section of the Bay Bridge and flattened a double-decker section of the Nimitz Freeway (I-880) in the flatlands. No sooner had the city made peace with that disaster than another struck; in October 1991, wildfires raged through the Oakland hills, killing 22 people, torching entire neighborhoods at a cost of some $2 billion, and stripping hills of the luxuriant growth so typical of the area. Though wildflowers and other sturdy survivors sprang back to life with the next spring's rains, these naked neighborhoods have been slow to rebuild. Times have been tough in many areas of Oakland.

And yet, Oakland abides. Blessed with fair weather year-round, excellent health-care services, a generally robust economy, and a good public transportation system, Oakland ranked eighth in *Money* magazine's 2002 survey of the best U.S. places to live. Even political life here seems destined to wake up: in 1999, new urban visionary and former California governor Jerry Brown was sworn in as Oakland's mayor, and in 2002 won a second term by a landslide.

SEEING AND DOING OAKLAND
Oakland Museum of California
On Lake Merritt's harbor side is the jewel of downtown Oakland, the renowned Oakland Museum of California, 1000 Oak St. (at 10th, one block from the Lake Merritt BART Station), 510/238-2200 or 888/625-6873. Designed by Kevin Roche, John Dinkeloo, and Associates and something like a walled garden complex, the museum is actually three separate museums under one roof; galleries are arranged so the roof of one becomes the terrace of another. The Oakland Museum creatively examines California art, history, and the natural sciences, suggesting how all are interrelated. Altogether, this is probably the finest regional museum in the country.

The first stop is actually a stroll through the "Walk Across California" exhibit in the first-floor Hall of California Ecology, which displays the state's eight major life zones in varying levels of detail in a west-to-east "walk" across the state. For warm-ups, spend a few minutes at the massive relief map (with push-button "table of contents" overlays) and watch the astounding five-minute John Korty film, *California Fast Flight,* for ground-level views of the state.

If the Smithsonian Institution is the nation's attic, then the Oakland Museum's Cowell Hall of California History is California's. The happy historical clutter on the second floor includes the whimsical 20th-century "Story of California: A

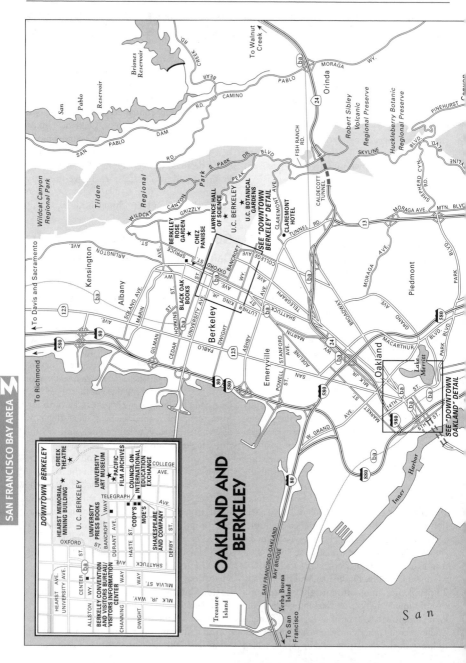

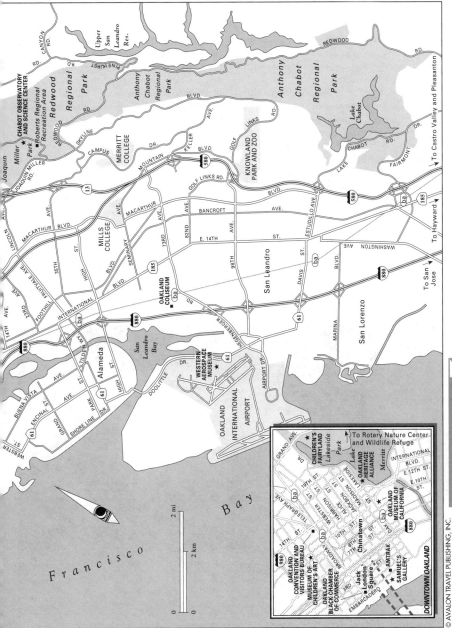

SAN FRANCISCO BAY AREA

© AVALON TRAVEL PUBLISHING, INC.

People and Their Dreams," displaying everything from old automobiles and Apple computers to Mickey Mouse memorabilia and Country Joe McDonald's guitar. The museum's third level, devoted to California art and artists, offers a chronological collection of paintings, photography, pottery, and other artistic endeavors. The museum's central courtyard includes multilevel lawns and a sculpture garden.

The museum is open Wed.–Sat. 10 A.M.–5 P.M. (until 9 P.M. on the first Friday of every month), Sunday noon–5 P.M.; admission is $6 adults, $4 seniors and students, free on the second Sunday of every month. Parking is available beneath the museum. Call or check the museum's website, www.museumca.org, for current information on special exhibits.

Downtown and the Waterfront

Water seems to be Oakland's most prominent natural feature. Right downtown, wishbone-shaped **Lake Merritt** is an unusual urban lake—actually an enclosed saltwater tidal basin. Merritt's **Lakeside Park** includes delightful gardens (spec-

tacular chrysanthemums in the fall); the **Rotary Nature Center and Wildlife Refuge,** 552 Bellevue Ave. (at Perkins), 510/238-3739, a fine nature center and bird sanctuary featuring Buckminster Fuller's first public geodesic dome (now a flight cage); and **Children's Fairyland,** the original inspiration for all the world's theme parks (including Disneyland). Well-heeled hopeless romantics will want to avail themselves of **Gondola Servizio,** 510/663-6603, www.gondolaservizio.com, a company offering gondola rides on the lake (from $55 per couple). Or, stroll down the trail through Channel Park on the lake's bayside, an area noted for its decent city-style bird-watching. Despite the beads remaining in its 1925 necklace of lights and its relative proximity to downtown, Lake Merritt is not safe to stroll at night.

Preservation Park, 13th St. at Martin Luther King Jr. Way (near the City Center), 510/874-7580, is worth a wander for lovers of Victoriana. A re-creation of a 19th-century Oakland neighborhood, the park is home for 16 old Victorians that had been slated for demolition. The

There are all kinds of recreational opportunities on downtown Oakland's Lake Merritt.

old homes are being developed as office space for nonprofit organizations and small businesses.

For some architectural appreciation and a close-up look at old and new Oakland, take a walking tour with the **Oakland Heritage Alliance,** 1418 Lakeside Dr., 510/763-9218. The organization offers various Oakland tours, including a Black Panther Legacy tour conducted by the Huey Newton Foundation, for a small fee—call for a descriptive brochure and to make reservations.

On the waterfront where Jack London once toted cargo is **Jack London Square,** a collection of shops and restaurants the twice-defeated Socialist candidate for Oakland mayor probably would have ignored. Still, it's a mystery why anyone would prefer San Francisco's Pier 39, for example, considering the quality of these shops and businesses housed in a former warehouse district. (Take a peek into Jack London's

OAKLAND FLOATS THAT FLYING BOAT

The Western Aerospace Museum just off Doolitte Ave. at Oakland International Airport's North Field is housed in a hangar built in 1940 by the Boeing School of Aeronautics, used to train aircraft mechanics for the U.S. Army Air Corps and U.S. Navy during World War II. In addition to the 24 historic aircraft on display, museum exhibits address topics such as Early Oakland Aviation, African-American Aviation, Women Pilots, Jimmy Doolittle, the 8th Air Force, the Eagle Squadron, Aerial Photography, and Space.

The museum's most spectacular display is the last remaining Short Solent 4-Engine Flying Boat, built in 1946 as an upgraded version of the famous World War II-era British Sunderland. Designed to take off and land only in the water, the Flying Boat is almost 90 feet long and its tail section is 37 feet above the ground. Also exhibited is a sister ship to the airplane Amelia Earhart was flying when she disappeared over the Pacific Ocean after taking off from North Field in 1937. For more information, contact the **Western Aerospace Museum,** 8260 Boeing St., Bldg. 621 at North Field, Oakland Airport, 510/638-7100.

Yukon Cabin and maybe quaff a couple at the classic **Heinhold's First & Last Chance Saloon,** 56 Jack London Square, 510/839-6761.) **Samuel's Gallery,** 70 Franklin St., 510/452-2059, boasts one of the nation's largest collections of African American posters, original prints, cards, and graphics.

In summer, Jack London Square (at the foot of Alice St. and Broadway) is the launch point for free tours of the thriving Port of Oakland; for reservations and information, call 510/627-1188. It's also home port (at the foot of Broadway) for the **Jack London Water Taxi,** 510/839-7572, which can putt you over to Alameda or just take you on a cruise around the estuary. Other good port-activity vantage points include the foot of Clay St. and Portview Park at the end of Seventh Street. Or head seaward by car over the Bay Bridge to Treasure Island, created to accommodate the 1939 Golden Gate International Exposition and later used as a naval base.

At last report still an Oakland attraction, though it was seeking new funding, the **Presidential Yacht Potomac,** Franklin Delano Roosevelt's "Floating White House," is a 165-foot-long national historical landmark and floating museum parked at the FDR Pier (Clay St. at Embarcadero). To find out if tours are available, call 510/627-1215 or see the website: www.USSPotomac.org.

More Sights

A walk up 10th St. from the Oakland Museum leads straight into thriving **Chinatown** (though "Asiatown" is actually more accurate) east of Broadway, its wide streets packed with authentic restaurants and shops but surprisingly few tourist traps. Aside from regional parks offering hiking and recreation (see below), the park in Oakland is **Knowland Park and Zoo,** 9777 Golf Links Rd. (off I-580, at 98th St.), 510/632-9523, www.oaklandzoo.org; admission $7.50 general, $4.50 seniors and children 2–14, plus $3 per auto. With more time to nose around, visit the campuses of **California College of Arts and Crafts,** 5212 Broadway (at College), 510/594-3600, one of the oldest art colleges in the nation, and well-respected **Mills College,** 5000 MacArthur Blvd., 510/430-2255, the only independent all-women's college west of the Mississippi. Many of the buildings at Mills were designed by famed architect Julia Morgan.

The **Western Aerospace Museum,** 8260 Boeing St. (off Earheart Rd., North Field, Oakland International Airport), 510/638-7100, offers exhibits of aircraft, aviation artifacts, and historical photos with a local emphasis. Open Wed.–Sun. 10 A.M.–4 P.M.; admission $7 general, $6 seniors, $3 kids 12 and under. The **Museum of Children's Art (MOCHA),** 538 Ninth St. (between Washington and Clay), 510/465-8770, is a gallery and studio for young prodigies and wannabes. Open Mon.–Sat. 10 A.M.–6 P.M., Sunday noon–5 P.M.

The **African-American Museum and Library at Oakland,** 659 14th St. (at Martin Luther King), 510/637-0200, houses some 20,000 photos and more than 200 original manuscripts relating to the African-American community in Northern California since 1850. The museum is open Tues.–Sun. noon–5:30 P.M.

Outdoors: Into the Hills

In the hills behind Oakland is large **Anthony Chabot Regional Park,** most noted for large Lake Chabot, a peaceful and popular spot for fishing and boating (rentals only). No swimming is allowed, since it's classified as an emergency local water supply. On weekends Apr.–Sept., take the *Lake Chabot Queen* ferry (small fee) to points around the lake. Other attractions include picnic areas, archery and rifle ranges, and a golf course. The vast backyard of this 4,700-acre park holds some hidden attractions, including a blue heron rookery and remnants of an old Chinese village. You can also camp here: 73 eucalyptus-shaded sites above Lake Chabot (including 35 walk-in sites), hot showers, flush toilets, group camping also available; $22 for RV camping, $16 for tenting. To get here, take Castro Valley Blvd. east off I-580, then turn north onto Lake Chabot Boulevard. To reserve camping and picnic sites, call 510/562-2267.

Adjacent to Chabot Park on the north, mushroom-shaped **Redwood Regional Park** offers 1,800 acres of redwood serenity and forest meadows and creeks—wonderful hiking. To get here,

take Hwy. 13 to the Redwood Rd. exit, then take Redwood uphill beyond Skyline for two miles to the main entrance.

West of Redwood Regional Park, smaller **Joaquin Miller Park** was named for the irascible writer who once lived on 80 acres here and hoped to establish an artists' colony. At the park's entrance, on the corner of Sanborn Dr. and Joaquin Miller Rd., you can see Miller's small home, The Abbey. Here he wrote his masterwork, "Columbus," which was equated with the Gettysburg Address before the poet's literary reputation was eclipsed by the passage of time. You can tip your hat to the house, but you can't go in. Farther up Sanborn is a ranger station where you can appreciate a small display about Joaquin Miller and pick up a park brochure and map. The most lasting homage to the poet are the redwood trees here, planted by Miller and now integral to the park, which is said to be the world's only urban redwood forest. (Along with whiskey, women, and poetry, trees were a passion of Joaquin Miller's.)

Joaquin Miller Park also houses the huge, 80-some-thousand-square-foot **Chabot Observatory and Science Center,** 10000 Skyline Blvd., 510/336-7300, www.chabotspace.org, which is affiliated with both NASA and the Smithsonian institution. It boasts several large telescopes, a 270-seat planetarium, a Challenger Center space mission simulation, a MegaDome theater for large-format films, and three exhibition halls hosting permanent and traveling exhibits focusing on the natural and physical sciences. Other facilities at the park include picnic grounds and an amphitheater. Admission is $8 adult, $5.50 senior and youth 4–12, free for children under 3, and free the first Wednesday of every month. To get here from Hwy. 13, take the Joaquin Miller Rd. exit.

Nearly surrounded by Redwood and Joaquin Miller Parks is lush **Roberts Regional Recreation Area** off Skyline Blvd., which offers more hiking among the redwoods, as well as picnicking, baseball and volleyball, an outdoor dance floor, and a heated swimming pool equipped with a hoist to assist the disabled in and out of the water.

Just north of this multipark complex, in the hills behind Piedmont, are the wild surprises of **Huckleberry Botanic Regional Preserve.** Though the eucalyptus and logged-over redwoods here testify to the area's disturbance over time, most of the shrubs in this rare-plant community are natives—thriving in the park's unusually protective microclimate. Spring comes early every year, attracting hummingbirds, and autumn comes early too, with still more birds flocking in to harvest berries and nuts. The preserve's narrow path can be almost invisible amid the thickets, yet offers some scenic overviews in spots; more views are gained by looping back on the East Bay Skyline National Trail.

Farther north is **Robert Sibley Volcanic Regional Preserve,** actually the remnants of what was once the East Bay's dominant volcano. Exploring otherwise unimpressive Round Top Peak here is a favorite pastime for amateur and professional geologists alike. To find out why, follow the self-guided trail.

For more information about regional parks here and in nearby Berkeley, contact the East Bay Regional Park District office at 510/635-0135, www.ebparks.org.

Bayshore Parks

A few areas along San Francisco and San Pablo Bays offer some respite from modern reality. In Alameda, **Crab Cove Marine Reserve,** McKay near Central, 510/521-6887, offers a nice beach and a visitor center with marine biology exhibits. And while you're in the area, head out to the former Alameda Naval Air Station to view the **USS** *Hornet,* Pier 3, Alameda Point, 510/521-8448, a World War II–era aircraft carrier now serving as a museum. Hours are Mon., Weds.–Sun. 10 A.M.–5 P.M. (closed Tuesdays); admission $12 adults, $10 seniors/students, $5 youth 5–18, free for children 4 and under.

Along the eastern edge of the South Bay, the **Don Edwards San Francisco Bay National Wildlife Refuge,** 1 Marshlands Rd., Fremont, 510/792-0222, usually yields good bird-watching throughout its protected marshes and mudflats. The refuge was renamed in recognition of Congressman Don Edwards' 25-year effort to protect sensitive wetlands in southern San Francisco Bay. Trailheads are located at Alviso (see Adventures near San Jose, above), at nearby Coyote

Hills Regional Park, and at the visitors center at the end of the Newark Slough (reached via Thornton Rd.) parallel to the Dumbarton Bridge toll plaza. The refuge is open for day use only (free).

In the midst of semi-industrial Fremont is an unusual Victorian-era farm park, the only one of its kind in the northstate. **Ardenwood Historical Farm,** 34600 Ardenwood Blvd. (off Hwy. 84), 510/796-0663, is a 200-acre remnant of a major mid-1800s ranch. The highlight here is historic Patterson House mansion, which has been restored by the East Bay Regional Park District to its original, upper-class ambience and features picket fences, period furnishings, and period-clothed character actors. Small admission fee. To get here: from I-880 take the Hwy. 84 (Decoto Rd./Dumbarton Bridge) exit, then exit at Newark Blvd. and follow Ardenwood/Newark north to the park's entrance.

The bulk of the land once encompassed by the old ranch now makes up nearby **Coyote Hills Regional Park,** noted for its own living-history program—one that re-creates the daily life of the Ohlone people who lived in these salt-marsh grasslands ("Old Ways" workshops are also offered). For more information on ranger-led tours to area shell mounds and other archaeological sights, including a reconstructed Ohlone village, stop by the Coyote Hills Visitor Center, 8000 Patterson Rd. in Fremont, open daily 10 A.M.–5 P.M., or call 510/795-9385. Coyote Hills Regional Park is also a good place to start a creekside trek along the Alameda Creek Bicycle Path, the longest (12 mile) paved bike trail in the East Bay. Pick up trail and park maps at the visitor center.

Farther north, undeveloped **Hayward Regional Shoreline** (in two separate sections along the bay just north of Hwy. 92) is not particularly appealing—but will be one day, because this is the largest salt-marsh restoration project underway on the West Coast. Though it's much more difficult to reestablish what was so easily destroyed through diking and other diversions of nature, the birds are already coming back.

North of San Pablo and jutting into San Pablo Bay is 2,000-acre **Point Pinole Regional Shoreline,** an area once dedicated to manufacturing dynamite—which explains why there has been no development here—and now an amazement: several miles of pristine bay frontage and salt marshes sheltering rare birds, meadows, and peace.

STAYING IN OAKLAND

Though San Francisco offers a wider range of accommodations options, Oakland has its share of nice digs; for a complete listing, contact the **Oakland Convention and Visitors Bureau,** 510/839-9000, www.oaklandcvb.com, or the **Oakland Chamber of Commerce,** 475 14th St., 510/874-4800. Camping at Lake Chabot is always an option (see above).

Best Western Inn at The Square, 233 Broadway (near the entrance to Jack London Square), 510/452-4565 or 800/780-7234, www.bestwestern.com, offers a pool, sauna, and parking garage. Room rates $100–150. Just north of Jack London Square is **Waterfront Plaza Hotel,** 10 Washington St., 510/836-3800 or 800/729-3638, www.waterfrontplaza.com. Rates $150–250.

Hampton Inn, 8465 Enterprise Way (a few miles south of downtown, off I-880 and Hegenberger Rd.), 510/632-8900 or 800/426-7866, www.hamptoninn.com, offers the usual amenities plus whirlpool and airport transportation; $100–150. The **Marriott Oakland,** 1001 Broadway, 510/451-4000 or 800/228-9290, www.marriott.com, is near the Convention Center and has rooms with a view. Rates $150–250.

Special Stays

The **Washington Inn,** 495 10th St. (between Broadway and Washington, just across from the Oakland Convention Center), 510/452-1776, www.thewashingtoninn.com, is an intimate 1913 hotel restored to its turn-of-the-century self, yet with all the modern amenities, including a business center for corporate roadies and a great little bar and restaurant downstairs. Good value in the $150–250 price category. Also appealing in downtown Oakland is the 1927 art deco **Clarion Suites—Lake Merritt Hotel,** 1800 Madison, 510/832-2300 or 800/933-4683, www.lakemerritthotel.com, which has been restored to its original elegance. The deluxe and apartment-style suites feature modern amenities like in-room coffee makers, microwaves, and dataport phone connections, not to mention the plush appointments. Aside from basic business services, the Lake Merritt offers complimentary limo service to the downtown financial district in the A.M., after continental breakfast downstairs. If at all possible, get a room facing the lake. Given all the amenities and service, the rates constitute a great bayside bargain. Room rates $150–250, suites $250 and up.

Quite special in Oakland is the fabled **Claremont Resort and Spa,** 41 Tunnel Rd. (in the hills at Ashby and Domingo Avenues), 510/843-3000, 800/551-7266 or www.claremontresort.com. The elegant white-as-a-handkerchief grand dame is built in the 1915 chateau style, offering well-manicured grounds and luxury accommodations with all the frills: heated pools, saunas, whirlpools, 10 tennis courts, and—for an extra charge—a health club, massage, steam room, and restaurant. People often come just for the pampering offered by the Claremont's exceptional spa. Rooms and suites $250 and up.

Also unique in the vicinity of Oakland is the nonprofit **East Brother Light Station Bed and Breakfast,** 510/233-2385, www.ebls.org, which sits on a tiny island just north of the I-580 Richmond–San Rafael Bridge. The charming Victorian lighthouse, with four lighthouse guest rooms and another in the fog signal building, is accessible only by boat and also offers dinner and breakfast Thurs.–Sunday. Definitely different; reservations necessary well in advance. Rooms $250 and up.

In Alameda, bed-and-breakfast choices include the **Garratt Mansion,** 900 Union St., 510/521-4779, www.garrattmansion.com ($100–150), and **Webster House,** 1238 Versailles Ave., 510/523-9697, an 1854 Gothic revival and the oldest house on the island. Rates include afternoon tea for two and a full breakfast. Rates $100–150. If you're heading south, consider **Lord Bradley's Inn,** 43344 Mission Blvd. in Fremont, 510/490-0520 or 877/567-3272, www.lordbradleysinn.com, an Early California-style B&B adjacent to Mission San Jose. Good value: rooms and suites $100–150.

EATING IN OAKLAND

Chinatown

For exotic food supplies, head to Oakland's Chinatown, centered between Clay and Webster, and Seventh and Ninth Streets; everything here is generally cheaper than in San Francisco. Come on Friday mornings, 8 A.M.–2 P.M., for the **Old Oakland Certified Farmers Market,** Ninth and Broadway, 510/745-7100, Alameda County's largest. Other farmers' markets in town include **Grand Lake Certified Farmers Market,** Sat. 10 A.M.–2 P.M. at Grand Ave. and Lake Park Way, 800/897-3276. Otherwise, **G.B. Ratto & Company International Grocers,** 821 Washington (at Ninth), 510/832-6503, features an appetizing and eclectic collection of predominantly Italian wines and foods, from barrels of smoked fish to exotic cheeses and salamis and open crates of imported pastas, as well as an unpretentious restaurant serving lunch (sandwiches, salads, daily specials) and, on Friday nights, dining and opera singing; call ahead for reservations.

Some of the most reasonable restaurants around are either in Chinatown or nearby. Among these, **Jade Villa,** 800 Broadway (at Eighth St.), 510/839-1688, serves varied and very good dim sum during the day, Cantonese fare at night. **Pho 84,** 354 17th St., 510/832-1338, is an Asian-style stop serving rich beef broth with noodles (and just about anything else you choose to add), chicken or crab combination soups, and daily specials. The tidy **Phnom Penh House** 251 Eighth St., 510/893-3825, serves wonderful yet inexpensive Cambodian food. **Le Cheval** 1007 Clay St. (at 10th St.), 510/763-8495, serves inexpensive yet refined Vietnamese food; excellent orange-flavor spicy beef or chicken. This place can be very crowded on weekends.

Inexpensive

Bright blue **Mama's Royal Cafe,** 4012 Broadway, 510/547-7600, is a true neighborhood restaurant with an astounding breakfast menu. Over in Rockridge, **Isobune,** 5897 College Ave., 510/601-1424, offers diners the opportunity to sit at the bar and pick from sushi floating by on little boats. For award-winning Chicago-style pizza, try **Zachary's,** 5801 College Ave., 510/655-6385. Reservations or a wait in line are usually necessary.

Zza's Trattoria, 552 Grand Ave., 510/839-9124, is always packed and always cheerful. The daunting line streaming down the sidewalk is testimony to the popularity of the pizzas and exceptional yet inexpensive entrées here. Another pizza hot spot is **Pizza Rustica,** 5422 College Ave., 510/654-1601, serving pizzas traditional-style as well as California-style (with cornbread crusts), and specializing in the exotic—like Cuban and Thai pizzas. The **Rockridge Cafe,** 5492 College Ave., 510/653-1567, is an all-American hip diner beset by fans at breakfast, lunch, and dinner; it's great for burgers (on whole wheat buns) and real food of all persuasions. **Asmara,** 5020 Telegraph, 510/547-5100, is the place to go for East African fare.

At Jack London Square, **Everett & Jones,** 126 Broadway (at Second), 510/336-7021, serves up some mean barbecue, along with plentiful rations of blues and beer.

Expensive

For "Louisiana Fancyfine" food, head to the visually astounding and somehow spiritually supercharged **Gingerbread House,** 741 Fifth St., 510/444-7373, a chocolate-brown building dressed up like a fairy tale from the bayou and serving up Cajun/Creole specialties like iron pot jambalaya, cherry duck, sautéed quail, and catfish étouffée. Reservations essential.

Oliveto, 5655 College Ave., 510/547-5356, specializes in creative Mediterranean fare, especially Northern Italian. It's the ultimate in authentic; the café is more relaxed. Open for lunch weekdays and for dinner daily. The homey **Bay Wolf Cafe & Restaurant,** in a dignified Victorian at 3853 Piedmont, 510/655-6004, in that sense resembles Berkeley's Chez Panisse and is known for its fine Mediterranean-style dishes and California cuisine, served here long before anyone thought to call it that. Reservations wise. Très French is **Trio Bistro,** 542 Grand Ave. (near Lake Merritt), 510/444-8746.

Worth seeking out in Emeryville is **Bucci's,**

6121 Hollis (between 59th and 61st), 510/547-4725, which has an upscale brick-and-glass warehouse ambience and very good Cal-Italian fare.

ENTERTAINMENT

If you're around during baseball season (Apr.–Sept.), head to the Oakland Coliseum to take in an **Oakland A's baseball** game; call 510/638-0500 for information and tickets. You can also visit the Athletics' official website at www.oaklandathletics.com. Or, from October to April, take in a **Golden State Warriors basketball** game; call 510/986-2222 for information, or 510/762-2277 for tickets. At **Golden Gate Fields Racetrack,** 1100 Eastshore Hwy. in Albany, 510/559-7300, thoroughbred races take place Nov.–Jan. and Apr.–June, and pari-mutuel wagering is offered on races at other tracks year-round.

For other happenings and events, pick up local newspapers—including the *Bay Guardian* and the *Express,* both of which feature comprehensive calendar listings and worthwhile arts and entertainment coverage.

Oakland is famous for its nightclubs; jazz and blues are the town's mainstays but also popular are the reggae and salsa scenes. **Kimball's Carnival** 522 Second St. in Jack London Square, 510/444-6979, has 6,000 square feet of dance floor and hosts live salsa, blues, R&B and Latin Jazz bands most nights. Call for current performances and reservations. **Yoshi's,** 510 Embarcadero West in Jack London Square, 510/238-9200, combines a Japanese restaurant with eclectic jazz. For information on other blues venues and special events, contact the **Bay Area Blues Society,** 510/836-2227.

If Oakland proper is having a sleepy night, head west to adjacent Emeryville, in the shadow of the Bay Bridge. Neighborhood diversions here include **Kimball's East,** 5800 Shellmound St., 510/658-2555, a venue for quality jazz, salsa, Latin jazz, and R&B performers; the acoustics are excellent, and Kimball's restaurant is a good place to start the evening. The eclectic lineup of performers that has graced Kimball's East include Eartha Kitt, Chaka Khan, and Herbie Hancock. Or head to **Oaks Club**

Room, 4097 San Pablo Ave., 510/653-4456, a 24-hour card club (Pai Gow, Hold-Em, Pan, Low-Ball) with hofbrau and grill.

Oakland's traditional performing-arts groups include the **Oakland Ballet,** 510/452-9288, which usually performs in the astounding 1931 art deco **Paramount Theatre of the Arts,** 2025 Broadway, 510/893-2300. Also well worth: the **Oakland Lyric Opera** (not to be confused with the defunct Oakland Opera), 510/836-6772, and the **Oakland Symphony,** 510/444-0801.

Movie buffs, head to the restored Egyptian-style art-deco **Grand Lake Theatre,** 3200 Grand Ave., 510/452-3556. On weekends, the theater presents live organ music. The Paramount Theatre of the Arts (see above) also hosts regular film series; call for current information.

For an inexpensive thrill anytime, have a drink atop Oakland's world at the **Marriott Oakland,** downtown at 1001 Broadway, where it costs nothing extra to drink in the nighttime views of San Francisco across the bay.

For more detailed arts and events information, contact the **City of Oakland, Visitor Marketing,** 510/238-2935, or try the city's website: http://oaklandnet.com.

EVENTS

February, Black History Month, would be a particularly good time to sign on for **The Black Panther Legacy Tour,** offered the last Saturday of each month year-round, noon–2:30 P.M. The Dr. Huey P. Newton Foundation offers a guided historical tour of 18 Oakland sites that were significant to the Black Panther Party. Tour fee is $20 adults, $15 children 14 and under. For information, call 510/986-0660. Also see what's showing at the monthly **Black Filmmakers Hall of Fame,** 510/465-0804, www.blackfilmmakershall.org.

Come in mid-May for the **Annual Wildflower Show** at the Oakland Museum, 510/238-2200, which offers a very full year-round calendar of events as well as changing exhibits. The annual **Open Studios** tour of East Bay artists studios is scheduled in early June; for details, call 510/763-4361. Also come in June for

Oakland's Dunsmuir House hosts events year round.

Walk in the Wild fundraiser with over 60 Bay Area wineries, restaurants and breweries at the Oakland Zoo in Knowland Park, 510/632-9525. Popular in July: the **Annual Scottish Highland Games Festival** at Dunsmuir House & Gardens, 510/615-5555.

Not to be missed in September: **Blues and Art on the Bay** and the **Oakland Blues and Heritage Festival,** both held at deFremery Park in West Oakland, 510/836-2227. In mid-September, visit the **Fall Boat Show** at Jack London Square, 510/814-6000. The free **Community Dance Day** in October, 510/451-1230, includes celebrations of African dance, jazz, hip hop, and the samba. The **Annual Black Cowboys Parade and Festival,** 510/531-7583, celebrates the considerable contributions of the black cowboy in America.

From just after Thanksgiving to early January, don't miss the mile-long holiday **ZooLights at the Oakland Zoo,** in Knowland Park, 510/632-9525—a "megawatt menagerie" of some 90 characters created from 90,000 lights. December events include the **Annual Lighted Yacht Parade** at Jack London Square, and the ongoing **Christmas at Dunsmuir** traditions at historic Dunsmuir House,

510/615-5555. All month, the **Oakland Ballet** performs the *Nutcracker* at the Paramount.

INFORMATION AND TRANSPORTATION

The **Oakland Convention and Visitors Bureau,** 475 14th St., Ste. 120, 510/839-9000, www.oaklandcvb.com, publishes the slick annual *Destination Oakland,* a fairly comprehensive listing of where to go, eat, and sleep; it's also helpful with other information. Walk-in **visitor centers** are located in Jack London Square at Broadway and Embarcadero (in the same building with Barnes & Noble), at the **Oakland City Store,** 14th and Broadway, and at the **Oakland Black Chamber Convention & Visitor Center,** 117 Broadway, 510/444-5741.

The main traffic artery between San Francisco and Oakland is I-80 over the San Francisco–Oakland Bay Bridge. The bridge is nightmarishly crowded most of the time, as are all of the highways surrounding either end of the span. To avoid the traffic, use public transit. Oakland is well served by **Bay Area Rapid Transit (BART),**

510/465-2278, www.bart.org, the high-speed intercity train system that runs 4 A.M.–midnight; fare depending upon destination. Call for fare and connecting bus service information; fare charts are also posted at each BART station.

If BART doesn't do it, try **AC Transit** buses, 510/817-1717 or 510/891-4777, which operate in and around Oakland daily; routes are covered every six to eight minutes during peak hours (6–9 A.M. and 4–6 P.M.), every 15 minutes between "peaks," and every 30–40 minutes after 6 P.M.

If the idea of driving or commuting across the Bay Bridge in bumper-to-bumper traffic doesn't thrill you, consider taking a ferry to San Francisco and back. The City of Alameda's **Alameda-Oakland Ferry** provides service from Jack London Square and Alameda to San Francisco's Ferry Building and Pier 41; for schedules and information, call 510/522-3300 or check www.eastbayferry.com.

Travelers can also get to and from Oakland via **Greyhound,** 2103 San Pablo Ave. (at 21st St.), 510/834-3213, www.greyhound.com, though the depot north of downtown is in a questionably safe neighborhood; doors are open 5:30 A.M.–midnight. **Amtrak** is in Jack London Square at 245 Second St., 510/238-4306 or 800/872-7245 for general information and reservations; if you're coming into Oakland via Amtrak and aiming for Oakland International Airport, get off at the Richmond train station (which is adjacent to BART), then take BART to the Coliseum Station and catch the airport shuttle. BART buses leave the Fremont Line's Coliseum BART Station for the airport south of town

every 10 minutes; call 510/465-2278 or check www.bart.org for information.

Now there's even more of the Bay Area to see from the train window. Oakland is connected to the state's capital via Amtrak **Capitol** trains, a system initiated by Amtrak but now managed by the Capitol Corridor Joint Powers Authority and operated by the Bay Area Rapid Transit District. Each day, six trains connect Oakland and Emeryville with Sacramento, passing through Richmond, Martinez, Fairfield, and Davis on the way. From Oakland, "feeder" bus links continue on to destinations including San Francisco, Hayward, Fremont, and San Jose. Call 800/872-7245—or check the website, www.amtrakcapitols.com—to verify current schedule and fare information. Fares were still remarkably reasonable, at last report, at $30 roundtrip for the Oakland-Sacramento trip. For more information on Amtrak's "Capitol Corridor" train service, write to the Capitol Corridor Joint Powers Authority, 1000 Broadway, Suite 604, Oakland, CA 94607. Make advance reservations through Amtrak or your travel agent—or take your chance on a space-available trip; Amtrak station agents accept cash and major credit cards.

Oakland International Airport at Doolittle and Airport Dr. on the bay south of Oakland, 510/563-3300, www.flyoakland.com, is efficient, well run, and preferred by many over San Francisco International due to its usually on-time flights. To reach downtown San Francisco or North Bay counties from the Oakland airport, take the BART bus directly from the airport to San Francisco, or hop on the **Oakland–Alameda County Airporter,** 510/444-4404.

Berkeley

Berkeley is too casually dismissed as "Berserkley" or the "People's Republic of Berkeley," epithets deriding fairly recent historical trends. Berkeley, after all, was named for evangelist Bishop Berkeley of Ireland, who crossed the great waters to save wild America from itself with the cry: "Westward, the course of empire takes its way." The course of empire in Berkeley, however, veered off to the left. That trend began in the 1930s, was sparked anew in the '60s with Mario Savio and the Free Speech Movement, and ignited during years of anti-Vietnam War protests and activism on behalf of minorities, women, the politically downtrodden worldwide, and the beleaguered environment. Still the star at the city's center, the prestigious University of California at Berkeley has become the somewhat reluctant mother ship in the ever-expanding universe of ideas swirling around it.

SEEING AND DOING BERKELEY

The University of California

There are other respected campuses in the University of California system, yet UC Berkeley—by virtue of its history and preeminence—is the one often referred to simply as "Cal." Despite town-gown tensions, most everything in Berkeley radiates from the Frederick Law Olmsted–designed campus. Before wandering around this sprawling 1,232-acre institution, get oriented at the **visitors information center** in University Hall Room 101, 2200 University Ave. (at Oxford St.), 510/642-5215. The center offers maps and pamphlets for self-guided tours in addition to other information. Or take a guided tour, also offered through the visitors center.

Many earlier buildings were part of a beaux-arts ensemble designed by John Galen Howard and financed by William Randolph Hearst. A total of 25 UC Berkeley buildings are included on the National Register of Historic Places, including the spectacular Hearst Memorial Mining Building, recently refurbished and reopened; Sather Tower or the "Campanile," inspired by

the campanile of San Marco in Venice; the Doe Memorial Library; and the Greek Theatre.

Behind Sather Gate is Sproul Plaza, where Mario Savio and others spoke out against university policies in the 1964 genesis of the Free Speech Movement. Fronting the plaza is Sather Tower, which holds 61 fully chromatic carillon bells that are usually played weekdays just before 8 A.M., at noon, and at 6 P.M.; the bells can be heard from almost anywhere on campus. (To watch the bell players at work, take a ride to the top; $2.)

To soak up some of the university's powerfully impersonal seriousness, spend time in any of its 25 libraries, a total information collection second only in size and prestige to Harvard's. The **Bancroft Library**, 510/642-3781 or 510/642-6481, is the most immediately impressive; its stacks are open to the public, and its excellent exhibits change frequently. Also worth a stop: the **UC Earth Sciences Building,** home of the Berkeley Seismographic Station, the Museum of Paleontology (510/642-1821), and the Museum of Geology (510/642-3993); and the **Phoebe Apperson Hearst Museum of Anthropology** in Kroeber Hall, once known as the Lowie Museum of Anthropology (510/643-7648), which boasts the finest collection of anthropological artifacts in the western United States, including many of A.L. Kroeber's contributions.

Another on-campus monument to the memory of William Randolph Hearst and clan is the **Hearst Memorial Mining Building.** Also donated by Hearst: UC's gorgeous outdoor **Greek Theatre,** 510/642-0527. The **University Art Museum,** 2626 Bancroft Way, 510/642-0808, also runs the **Pacific Film Archives,** 2625 Durant Ave., 510/642-1412 (office) or 510/642-5249 (tickets), a cinema collection with screenings of oldies but goodies. The films are presented on campus at the PFA theater, Bancroft at Bowditch (tickets available at the theater box office).

Modest **Le Conte Hall** on campus has been the birthplace of some of the university's most striking achievements: physical and nuclear science breakthroughs that have changed the course of history.

UC Berkeley, birthplace of free speech and the bomb

The university was already internationally renowned as a leader in the field of physics by 1939, when Ernest Lawrence won the Nobel Prize for inventing the cyclotron. By 1941, as a result of cyclotron experiments by Glenn Seaborg and others, plutonium had been discovered. In that same year, Lawrence, Edward Teller, and J. Robert Oppenheimer began planning the development of the atomic bomb, at the behest of the U.S. government. For development and testing, that project was transferred from Berkeley to New Mexico—the world saw the result in 1945 when the first A-bombs were dropped on Nagasaki and Hiroshima—the swan song of World War II and the birth of our brave new world.

The exceptional **Lawrence Hall of Science** on Centennial Dr. (at Grizzly Peak), 510/642-5132 or 510/642-5133, pays postmodern homage. A top contender for the title of Northern California's best science museum, Lawrence Hall holds hands-on exhibits (and the opportunity to try some freestyle physics experiments in the Wizard's Lab) and includes Holt Planetarium. Outside, hands-on exhibits include a 60-foot model of a DNA molecule. Open daily 10 A.M.–5 P.M. Admission is $8 general, $6 seniors, $4 children 3–6. Nearby, on UC's eastern fringe, is the Strawberry Canyon **UC Botanical Garden,** 200 Centennial Dr. (above Memorial Stadium), 510/643-2755. The garden's 30 acres of native plants and exotics include some 17,000 species, one of the world's biggest and best botanic collections. Open daily 9 A.M.–7 P.M. in summer, 9 A.M.–5 P.M. the rest of the year. Small admission, free on Thursday. Free guided tours are offered on weekends. Pleasant picnicking. Across the way is the university's **Mather Redwood Grove,** open daily.

More Sights

Berkeley's northside, with its burgeoning bookstores and high-tech trendiness, attracts mostly the university crowd these days. More famous during its Free Speech heyday and later anti-war riots is the Telegraph Ave. and Durant area south of the university. From Dwight Way to Bancroft, it's one busy blur of bookstores, boutiques, cheap clothing shops, record shops, ethnic restaurants, and fast-food stops—plus street people and street vendors, Berkeley's version of a year-round carnival. One wag has called Telegraph Ave. "a theme park with no theme"—an astute observation about much of California.

Since the area has also been inundated on weekends by bored teenagers and the drug dealers and other unsavories who prey upon them, cleaning up the area has become a new community rallying cry. The notorious **People's Park,** on Haste just off Telegraph, is owned by the university but hasn't yet been repossessed from the homeless. A rallying point for community self-determination since the 1960s and '70s, today the area is primarily a refuge for dealers and lost souls. The park seems destined to have no genuine purpose in the community—which may, after all, be its purpose. Among the incredible numbers of bookstores in the area, **Cody's,** 2454 Telegraph (at Haste), 510/845-7852, has been a haven for poetry (readings once a week) and prose since the days of the Beats.

Bookstores are almost as necessary to maintaining community consciousness as coffee. Older hipsters may remember **Moe's,** 2476 Telegraph, 510/849-2087, from the film *The Graduate.* The store holds four floors of used books, including antiquarian and art sections. Literature and art lovers should also meander through **Shakespeare and Company,** 2499 Telegraph, 510/841-8916, and, if you're in the Gourmet Ghetto, **Black Oak Books,** 1491 Shattuck, 510/486-0698 or 510/486-0699, where they actually hope you'll sit down and start reading. Popular contemporary authors, from Ursula K. Le Guin and Toni Morrison to Salman Rushdie, are often on the guest lecture circuit here. **University Press Books,** 2430 Bancroft Way, 510/548-0585, carries the largest selection of university press regional titles in the West.

Outdoors
Back up in the Berkeley Hills, **Tilden Regional Park** and adjacent **Wildcat Canyon Regional Park** are the area's major parks. The trend at Tilden over the years has been toward recreational development, so this is the place for getting away from it all city-style: swimming in Lake Anza and sunning on the artificial beach; picnicking with family and friends; stopping off at Little Farm and riding the miniature train, merry-go-round, and ponies with the kiddies; or playing tennis or 18 holes at the golf course.

Tilden Park's popular **Native Plant Botanic Garden** (not to be confused with the university's), 510/841-8732, shelters 1,500 varieties of native California plants and wildflowers. Open 10 A.M.–5 P.M. daily, with free tours offered on weekends June–Aug. The park's Environmental Education Center, 510/525-2233, is a good stop for trail brochures and other park information, as well as the starting point for a self-guided nature walk around little Jewel Lake on the Wildcat border. Though Tilden has some trails, for full-tilt hiking, Wildcat Canyon is preferable—no paved roads and not many hikers or runners on its fire roads, which contour through grazing lands and foothill forests.

Right in town on the southeast side of the university is **Claremont Canyon Regional Preserve,** consisting of 200 steep, secluded acres suitable for deer-path wandering. **Indian Rock Park** on Indian Rock Ave. at Shattuck is popular with practicing rock climbers. But for just smelling the roses, stop by **Berkeley Rose Garden** on Euclid Ave. at Eunice, 510/644-6530, open May–Sept.

STAYING IN BERKELEY
Since Berkeley residents have a hard time both finding a place to live then affording it once they do, visitors shouldn't complain. If none of the following places suit you, pick up a more complete list of local accommodations at the visitors bureau (information below).

Hotels and Motels
A good deal on the cheap end, for men only (age 18 and older), is the **YMCA,** 2001 Allston Way (at Milvia), 510/848-6800. Singles under $50, doubles $50–100.

Golden Bear Motel, 1620 San Pablo Ave., 510/525-6770, is quite nice and quite reasonable; $50–100. **Berkeley Ramada Inn** is at 920 University Ave., 510/849-1121; $50–100. **Hotel**

Durant, 2600 Durant Ave., 510/845-8981 or 800/238-7268, www.hoteldurant.com, is just a block from the university; pay parking, but airport transportation is provided; $100–150. Close to campus, too, is the stunning pink **Flamingo Motel,** 1761 University Ave., 510/841-4242, a 1950s-style wonder with the basics plus in-room coffee; $50–100. If you want to get away from it all, or be near the water, consider the Berkeley **Marina Radisson,** 200 Marina Blvd. (take the University Ave. exit and head west), 510/548-7920, www.radisson.com, where some rooms have a view. Standard rooms $100–150, view rooms $150–250.

The **French Hotel,** 1538 Shattuck Ave., 510/548-9930, is right across the street from Chez Panisse, smack dab in the center of Berkeley's food lover's zone—a consideration if you become too satiated to move. This small European-style hotel sits right above its own café, a popular coffee-and-pastries hangout, so the wonderful aroma of freshly ground coffee wafts right up the stairs. (Room service is available, but you can also go downstairs for some latte and join the Berkeleyites out on the sidewalk.) Rooms are airy and contemporary, and complimentary continental breakfast is a genuine pleasure. But once you park your stuff, parking your car can be a problem; ask the concierge for suggestions. Room rates $100–150.

Inns and Bed-and-Breakfasts

For a comfortable stay in Berkeley's brown-shingled neighborhoods, residential style, try **Garden Cottage B&B,** 1822 Virginia St., 510/649-8938, www.gardencottage.net, just three blocks from Shattuck Ave. and "Gourmet Ghetto" specialty shops, cafés, and restaurants, yet quite quiet. The cottage features a full-size bed and sofabed with a private bathroom, and amenities include a continental breakfast featuring organic fruits and baked goods. Rates $100–150. An expanding local institution is **Gramma's Rose Garden Inn,** 2740 Telegraph Ave., 510/549-2145 or 800/992-9005, www.rosegardeninn.com, now offering a total of 40 rooms in two huge old homes—a turn-of-the-20th-century Tudor-style mansion and the Victorian next door—plus a cottage, carriage house, and garden house. English gardens in back.

Rooms in the Fay House have striking stained-glass windows and pristine hardwood floors; those in the carriage and garden houses have fireplaces. Guests can expect a basket of apples in their room. Coffee, tea and cookies are available all day; full buffet breakfast with eggs, bacon, fresh pastries, and fruit are served in the morning. Everything has been freshly painted, wallpapered, and carpeted, with new amenities added. Rooms are $100–150, suites $150–250.

Julia Morgan's Moorish "little castle" is the 1927 **Berkeley City Club,** 2315 Durant Ave. (between Ellsworth and Dana), 510/848-7800, www.berkeleycityclub.com, originally a posh women's club with grand public areas. The pool, fitness facilities, and on-site restaurant are open only to club members and bed-and-breakfast guests. The 40 guest rooms here are fairly small and modestly appointed, with private bathrooms. Rooms $100–150, suites $150–250, buffet breakfast included.

EATING IN BERKELEY

The Shattuck Ave. and Walnut St. area between Rose and Virginia is known as Berkeley's Gourmet Ghetto (or Gourmet Gulch) in wry recognition of the fine delis, food shops, gelato stops, and upscale restaurants so prominent here—a phenomenon started by the internationally renowned Chez Panisse. The entire neighborhood offers poor parking possibilities but wonderful opportunities for trend-watching. And the trend has spread far beyond its original geographical limits—onto University and San Pablo Avenues, along Fourth St., even onto Telegraph Ave.—hence the far-flung listings below. For truly inexpensive food, head south toward Telegraph, though bargains can be found in and around the fringes of Berkeley's Gourmet Ghetto.

Student Fare

The **Blue Nile,** 2525 Telegraph, 510/540-6777, offers good Ethiopian food, both vegetarian and meat entrées. **Blondie's Pizza,** 2340 Telegraph, 510/548-1129, is a local institution for good pizza available by the slice. **Juan's Place,** 941 Carleton St. (near Ninth), 510/845-6904, serves shockingly generous portions of authentic Mexican standards. **Mario's La Fiesta,** 2444 Telegraph, 510/540-9123, also serves great inexpensive Mexican food (and has lines inside and out at rush hours).

For authentic Chicago-style pizza, head to **Zachary's Chicago Pizza,** 1853 Solano, 510/525-5950 (there's another at 5801 College Ave. in Oakland, 510/655-6385). Great for inexpensive real food in West Berkeley, from apple-cornmeal pancakes to hearty sandwiches, is **Westside Bakery Cafe,** 2570 Ninth St., 510/845-4852, open daily for breakfast and lunch. Good for lunch anytime is **Panini,** 2115 Allston Way (at Shattuck, in Trumpet Vine Court), 510/849-0405, which offers fresh gourmet everything in sometimes exotic combinations.

The **Berkeley Thai House,** 2511 Channing Way (near Telegraph), 510/843-7352, has reasonable choices at lunch and dinner. **Long Life Vegi House,** 2129 University Ave. (at Shattuck), 510/845-6072, serves vegetarian Chinese food (even potstickers) and brown rice. **Pasand Madras,** 2286 Shattuck (at Bancroft), 510/549-2559, serves excellent Indian food, with dinners as cheap as $5. **Party Sushi,** 1776 Shattuck Ave. (at Francisco), 510/841-1776, is great for exotic California-style sushi. Near Rockridge, **La. Bayou,** 3278 Adeline, 510/594-9302, is worth checking out for its heaping portions of down-home Cajun and Creole cuisine at low prices, open Tues.–Sat. for lunch and dinner.

For burgers, the place is cash-only **Barney's,** located in San Francisco and Oakland as well as its two Berkeley locations: 1600 Shattuck Ave., 510/849-2827, and 1591 Solano Ave., 510/526-8185. And don't skip the fries.

Coffee Stops

Coffeehouses and coffee stops are popular in Berkeley. **Peet's Coffee & Tea,** 2124 Vine St. (at Walnut, a block off Shattuck), 510/841-0564, is a much-loved local institution, with caffeine addicts buzzing like bees outside on the sidewalk. (Peet's has several other locations around town and elsewhere in the Bay Area and Northern California.) Peet's fans will be happy to know they can order fresh coffee and teas direct, from anywhere in California at least, by calling 800/999-2132. Or try the website: www.peets .com. The neighborhood classic, though, is **Caffe Mediterraneum,** 2475 Telegraph, 510/549-1128. Among Berkeley's other coffee house hangouts: very hip **Cafe Milano,** 2522 Bancroft, 510/644-3100, and **Espresso Roma,** 2960 College Ave. (at Ashby), 510/644-3773, a see-and-be-seen stop for the intelligentsia.

Gourmet Ghetto

Along Shattuck, the true heart of Berkeley's upscale Gourmet Ghetto, is **Chez Panisse,** 1517 Shattuck, 510/548-5525 for dinner reservations, 510/548-5049 for café information. Alice Waters's excellent and expensive but relaxed restaurant in a wood-frame house was the unassuming epicenter of California's culinary earthquake. Dinners (downstairs) are fixed-price, with a daily changing menu; reservations a must. Café fare is served upstairs from the central open kitchen with brick ovens—little pizzas and other simple fare in an amiable atmosphere. Open for dinner Mon.–Sat. Très French—and that's still cool in Berkeley—is **Bistro Liaison,** 1849 Shattuck, 510/849-2155.

Cesar, 1515 Shattuck, 510/883-0222, is an upscale gourmet tapas bar with a casual country ambience; the big, family-style tables encourage you to strike up a conversation with your fellow diners, perhaps over a glass of sangria. Open daily from 4 P.M. **Poulet,** 1685 Shattuck, 510/845-5932, is famous for its chicken specialties and organic and low-cholesterol chicken choices. Another worthy stop on Shattuck's gourmet trail is the collectively run **Cheese Board,** 1512 Shattuck, 510/549-3055, which specializes in handmade bread, cheese, and gourmet pizza. A little farther up the street, next to Black Oak Books, **Saul's Restaurant & Deli,** 1475 Shattuck, 510/848-3354, serves fresh bagels, lox, and deli sandwiches.

Hopkins Street

Gourmet grazing is also available along Hopkins St., between Monterey and McGee, where you'll find **Made To Order,** 1576 Hopkins, 510/524-7552, a neighborhood deli with handmade sausages and at least 30 kinds of olive oil; and **Magnani Poultry,** 1586 Hopkins, 510/528-6370, where you'll find those famous free-range chickens and even more unusual fowl, as well as rabbits. For fresh fish, almost next door is **Monterey Fish Co.,** 1582 Hopkins, 510/525-5600. The **Monterey Market,** 1550 Hopkins, 510/526-6042, carries some organically grown local and exotic produce. And don't even walk down this street unless you stop at **Hopkins Street Bakery,** 1584 Hopkins, 510/526-8188, noted for its widely varied and unusual breads as well as decadent sweet treats. Chocolate cookie lovers, pick up a dozen Freak Outs.

Fourth and Gilman Streets

Locally mythic is **O Chamé,** 1830 Fourth St., 510/841-8783, a Japanese-style wayside inn with a rustic interior. The fare here reflects Taiwanese Buddhist-Taoist culinary influences, as well as Japan's Kansei and Kaiseki cuisine. The fixed-price menu at dinner allows patrons to choose delicacies from various categories. For lunch, select an entrée—or buy a bento box lunch from the cart outside. Microbrews, both Japanese and American, are served. Open Mon.–Sat. for lunch and dinner. Nearby, contemporary, meaty **Cafe Rouge,** 1782 Fourth St., 510/525-1440, offers rotisserie chicken, steaks, oysters, and more—all with French and Italian finesse. Open for lunch daily and for dinner Tues.–Sun. For that red vinyl-and-white-Formica ambience, complete with jukebox, try **Bette's Oceanview Diner,** 1807-A Fourth St., 510/644-3230, which serves thick milkshakes and other all-American standards.

At **Lalime's Cafe,** 1329 Gilman St., 510/527-9838, the nightly changing menu may include chicken, beef, pork, and fresh fish, but people have been known to make a meal of the appetizer selections alone. Down the street, **Pyramid Brewery & Alehouse,** 901 Gilman, 510/528-9880, is the large brewing concern's Berkeley brewpub, though "pub" seems a drastic understatement for the cavernous "nouveau-warehouse" brewery/restaurant. Good beer, and gourmet pub grub. Open for lunch and dinner daily.

Other Neighborhoods

Rick & Ann's, 2922 Domingo Ave. (between Claremont and Ashby), 510/649-8538, is very Berkeley for breakfast, a best bet for all-American comfort food at dinner. Family-friendly too. Foodies flock to **Cafe Fanny,** 1603 San Pablo Ave., 510/524-5447, another of Alice Waters's progeny, wonderful for breakfast and simple stand-up lunches. The casual layout includes just a counter and a bench or two. Next door is another Alice Waters enterprise, the **Acme Bread Company,** 1601 San Pablo, which makes the best bread around. Popular for burgers and simple suppers is **Christopher's Nothing Fancy Cafe,** 1019 San Pablo Ave., 510/526-1185.

For good Thai food, head to **Plearn Thai Cuisine,** 2050 University Ave., 510/841-2148, or **Siam,** 1181 University, 510/548-3278. **Kensington Circus,** 389 Colusa, 510/524-8814, is a pub known for its hearty fish-and-chip suppers. Tiny **À La Carte,** 1453 Dwight Way (in west Berkeley), 510/548-2322, used to serve traditional French fare to a dwindling number of diners in this low- to middle income neighborhood. Reborn as a down-home Creole restaurant, this place is hopping again. Open Wed.–Sun. for dinner; reservations recommended. **Rivoli,** 1539 Solano, 510/526-2542, is a Mediterranean favorite for its rustic cuisine, bright atmosphere, and good service. Open for dinner daily.

ARTS AND ENTERTAINMENT

Count on the **University Art Museum,** 2626 Bancroft (on campus), 510/642-0808, for some unusual, and unusually brave, special exhibits. Also noteworthy in Berkeley is the **Judah L. Magnes Museum,** 2911 Russell St. (at Pine), 510/549-6950, the West's largest Jewish cultural museum, with a Holocaust exhibit in addition to modern Jewish art and special exhibits. The lovely redwood and fir **Julia Morgan Theater,** 2640 College Ave., 510/845-8542, considered its namesake's masterpiece, is a prime venue for local productions, including jazz, kids' shows, and chamber music. Best known for nonuniversity theater, one of the state's finest repertory companies is the **Berkeley Repertory Theater,** 510/647-2949. For the latest in dance, plays, and performance art by black artists, find out what's playing with the **Black Repertory Group,** 3201 Adeline, 510/652-2120. **UC Theater,** 2036 University, 510/843-6267, shows nightly changing revival films, and count on the **Pacific Film Archives,** 2625 Durant, 510/642-1412, for classics as well as avant-garde and underground movies.

Call the Berkeley Convention & Visitors Bureau at 510/549-7040 or 800/847-4823 for an update on current events and activities. For information about local galleries and current arts and entertainment events on campus and off, pick up the UC Berkeley *Daily Californian,* www.daily-cal.org, student paper, the free weekly *Express* (usually available in book and record shops), www.eastbayexpress.com, and the slick and reliable *East Bay Monthly* magazine, 510/658-9811.

Definitely different is sake tasting at **Takara Sake USA,** 708 Addison, 510/540-8250, which brews exceptional sake from Sacramento Valley rice and Sierra Nevada water; open to visitors noon–6 P.M. daily. During the afternoon at least, before the place becomes standing-room-only, the **Triple Rock Brewery and Alehouse,** 1920 Shattuck, 510/843-2739, is a hotspot for beer lovers. Shuffleboard out back, roof garden. Less fratty is **Bison Brewery,** 2598 Telegraph, 510/841-7734, which experiments with the genre. Ales are handcrafted and exotic—the list includes sagebrush ale, gingerbread porter, and a spicy coriander-infused golden ale, as well as hard teas.

Ashkenaz, 1317 San Pablo, 510/525-5054, is a folk-dance cooperative with folk, reggae, and world beat, while **Freight and Salvage,** 1111 Addison St., 510/548-1761, is the Euro-style folkie hangout. For blues, head to **Blake's** downstairs at 2367 Telegraph, 510/848-0886. The **Starry Plough,** 3101 Shattuck Ave., 510/841-2082, is an Irish-style pub with darts, a good selection of beers, and live music most nights.

Since every day in Berkeley is an event, organized activities per se aren't really the point here. One significant Berkeley event, though, is the **California Shakespeare Festival,** formerly the Berkeley Shakespeare Festival, usually held out-

The Bay Bridge, viewed here from Yerba Buena Island, links Berkeley and Oakland to San Francisco.

© KIM WEIR

doors in Orinda from late May through mid-October (dress warmly). For information, call the festival at 510/548-9666 (box office) or 548-3422 (administration), or visit www.calshakes.org.

INFORMATION AND TRANSPORTATION

For basic Berkeley information, contact the **Berkeley Convention and Visitors Bureau,** 2015 Center St., 510/549-7040 or 800/847-4823, www .berkeleycvb.com, though budget travelers will find the **Council Travel Berkeley,** 2387 Telegraph Ave., 510/848-8604, much more helpful. AC Transit buses and BART serve the community, though Oakland is closest and most convenient for Amtrak and Greyhound travelers. For more transit information, see Oakland, above. For other information and options on public transportation, cycling, and otherwise just getting around, contact **Berkeley TRIP,** 2033 Center St., 510/644-7665. There are ride boards in the Student Union building on the UC Berkeley campus.

East Bay Outback

The eastern expanse of the Bay Area is best known for its Berkeley-Oakland metropolis and surrounding suburban communities. But natural areas in the East Bay's outback offer snippets of silence and serenity in the midst of suburban sprawl, and an occasional glimpse of life as it once was in these hilly former farmlands. Many of the East Bay's treasures are collected into the East Bay Regional Park District, which includes some 60,000 acres of parklands.

For brochures, maps, and other information about the major East Bay parks—including current information on the system's ever-expanding interconnected trail system—call the district office at 510/635-0135 or try the website: www.ebparks.org; for picnicking and camping reservations, call 510/636-1684. For help in figuring out public transit routes to parks, call Bay Area Rapid Transit (BART), 510/464-6000, and AC Transit, 510/817-1717 or 510/891-4777, www.bart.gov.

A beautifully written "personal guide" to the East Bay's regional parks, the perfect hiking companion, is *The East Bay Out* by Malcolm Margolin, published by Heyday Books. It's currently out of print, but readily available at used bookstores around the Bay Area.

EAST BAY PARKS

Briones Regional Park

More than 5,000 semi-wilderness acres between Lafayette and Martinez, Briones Regional Park offers wonderful hiking up hillsides, down valleys, and across meadows, past everything from wildflowers and waterfalls to valley oaks and vistas of the bay and Mt. Diablo. When temperatures and leaves fall and autumn winds whisk away the haze, you can even see the Sierra Nevada from the Briones Crest Trail. Grazing cattle and deer are fairly abundant year-round, but in the spring newts are more noticeable. Included in the park are the John Muir Nature Area, small lakes, 45 miles of trails, and an archery range. Day-use is $4.

To get there from Lafayette, take Happy Valley Rd. north from Hwy. 24 and turn right on Bear Creek Rd., or, farther east, take Pleasant Hill Rd. north from Hwy. 24 (access off Pleasant Hill Road). From Martinez, take Alhambra Valley Rd. south from Hwy. 4 and turn left on Reliez Valley Road.

Las Trampas Regional Wilderness

More than 3,000 acres of wilderness just west of Danville—home to mountain lions, wildcats, skunks, foxes, weasels, and golden eagles—Las Trampas Regional Wilderness offers heavenly hikes and great views, particularly from Las Trampas Ridge. The developed Little Hills Ranch area near the park's entrance offers picnic areas, a swimming pool, playground, stables (horse rentals available; call 925/838-7546), and a stocked fishing hole. To get here: from I-680 south of Danville, take Crow Canyon Rd., then Bollinger Canyon Rd. into the park. For more information, contact the park at 18012 Bollinger Canyon Rd. in San Ramon, 925/837-3145.

Mt. Diablo State Park

When early explorers and settlers first started groping toward California's great bay, they set their course by Mt. Diablo's conical presence, and the peak itself was the base point for the U.S. government's first territorial surveys in 1851. Then—and on a clear day now, usually after a winter storm—views from Mt. Diablo (elevation 3,849 feet) are spectacular: the Farallon Islands to the west, Lassen Peak to the north, even (with binoculars) Half Dome in Yosemite to the southeast. Mythic home of Eagle and Coyote to the Miwok, the mountain has rugged terrain and wicked winds that led settlers to believe it was haunted. According to a tale told to the state legislature by Mariano Vallejo in 1850, the mountain's name resulted from some linguistic confusion; local native people believed that their victory over Spanish troops in an early 1800s skirmish was due to assistance from the mountain's "spirit," which the Spanish incorrectly translated as "devil" (*diablo*).

Mt. Diablo State Park is a wonder, one which some half-million people enjoy each year. Peak experiences here include the view from the summit, the Mitchell Canyon hike to the summit (the park has a total of 50 miles of trails), rock climbing, fabulous spring wildflower displays, and Fossil Ridge (don't touch). Mountain bikers may ride unpaved roads to the west of North Gate and South Gate Roads. A wonderful visitor center occupies the beautiful 1939 stone Summit Building built by the WPA.

Diablo is open daily 8 A.M.–sunset, when both gates close. The day-use fee is $4, but when area fire danger is extremely high, the park may be closed for all uses. Three year-round campgrounds with water and flush toilets (some showers) are often available on a first-come basis, but can be reserved in advance ($12–15 per night) through ReserveAmerica, 800/444-7275, www .reserveamerica.com. Remote walk-in environmental campgrounds are available only Oct.–May due to high fire danger; bring your own water. No alcohol is permitted in Mt. Diablo State Park (due to drunk-driving incidents and other disasters). For more information, contact: Mt. Diablo State Park, 96 Mitchell Canyon Rd. in Clayton, 925/837-2525 (information) or 925/837-0904, www.mdia.org.

Black Diamond Mines Regional Preserve

One way to beat the heat in summer is by heading underground for a stroll through the cool sandstone caverns deep within the six-level Hazel-Atlas Mine—part of the former Mount Diablo coal-mining district (the state's largest) and later, prime underground fields for harvesting high-grade silica sand. Included as part of the Black Diamond Mines Regional Preserve, the mine is open for two-hour tours ($3 per person) by advance reservations only. For safety reasons, children under age 7 are not allowed. To contemplate the generally short life spans of miners—too often killed in cave-ins, explosions, or by silicosis—wander through the nearby Rose Hill Cemetery. Visit the underground Greathouse Visitor Center from March through November, open weekends only 10 A.M.–4:30 P.M. On weekends

and holidays, $4 parking fee. Camp at Stewartville Backpack Camp, $5 per night (two-night limit). For more information about the park and its naturalist programs, contact the park at 5175 Somersville Rd. in Antioch, 925/757-2620. For camping reservations, call 510/636-1684. To get here: from Hwy. 4 in Antioch, head six miles south via Somersville Road.

Morgan Territory Regional Preserve

A fascinating feature on these remote eastern ridgetops beyond Mt. Diablo, as elsewhere throughout the East Bay (on Mission Peak in Fremont, near Vollmer Peak in Tilden Park, and on Round Top Peak in the Oakland Hills), are squat stone walls with no traceable history. Someone obviously went to considerable trouble to build them, hauling large stones up the mountainside, but the walls have no apparent practical value and follow no known property lines. Rumor has it that they predate the Spanish and even native populations, and were possibly built by early Chinese explorers as astronomical markers.

Even today, the park's 4,147 acres are mysterious, remote, quiet, and almost inaccessible due to the wild one-lane road winding up the mountain. For those looking for solitude, here it is. Also here: a few picnic tables (pack out your trash), rusting farm equipment, and fruit trees from the land's onetime ranch status. For more information, contact the park at 9401 Morgan Territory Rd. in Livermore, 925/757-2620. To get here: from I-580 north of Livermore, head north on N. Livermore Ave. to the end, turn left onto Manning Rd., then turn right at Morgan Territory Road.

Other Regional Parks

Ohlone Regional Wilderness encompasses some 7,000 acres of wild high ridges on the south end of Alameda County, accessible only via the Sunol Regional Wilderness to the west or the Del Valle Regional Recreation Area to the north. Backpackers generally have the place to themselves, following old roads over ridges and through meadowlands, then camping at one of several backcountry sites. The peak experience here is a day hike (starting 10 miles in from either entrance) to the top of Rose Peak—a brutal climb for heavily laden backpackers. Rewards from the summit include top-of-the-world views of the Santa Clara Valley, San Francisco Bay, and Mt. Diablo. Overnight camping along the Ohlone Wilderness Trail is allowed by reservation; call 510/636-1684.

For more information about the Ohlone Wilderness, contact **Sunol Regional Wilderness,** 925/862-2244, which also features oak woods and remoteness alongside developed family picnic facilities and camping. Parking is $4; family tent camping is $12; reserve campsites by calling 510/636-1684. To get here: from the I-680/Hwy. 84 interchange take Calaveras Rd. to Geary Rd. and continue to the end.

Del Valle Regional Recreation Area, 925/373-0332, is popular for swimming and windsurfing on Lake Del Valle, as well as picnicking and camping around the shore. Particularly worthwhile is a spring hike to Murietta Falls, a fairly rugged 12.5-mile roundtrip (pack a lunch and carry water, plenty of it); park at the south end of the reservoir, where the trail begins as an old fire road. Access to Del Valle is via Arroyo Dr., south of Hwy. 84 in Livermore.

OUTBACK COMMUNITIES
San Pablo Bay

Along the shores of San Pablo Bay are the salt marshes, mudflats, and open waters of the **San Pablo Bay National Wildlife Refuge,** a winter refueling stop for migrating shorebirds and waterfowl, also permanent home to two endangered species: the California clapper rail and the salt marsh harvest mouse. Largely undeveloped but accessible—under certain conditions—for boaters and hunters, the only easy access for the general public is at **Tubbs Island,** originally acquired by The Nature Conservancy. To get here, park (well off the road) along Hwy. 37 just east of its intersection with Hwy. 121 (and just east of Tolay Creek) and walk. It's almost three miles (one-way) to these marsh ponds and nature trails on the northern edge of San Pablo Bay. Open during daylight hours only, no restrooms available, bring your own drinking water. Come in January for the huge—and hugely popular—annual **Northern San Francisco Bay Flyway Festival.** For more information about the reserve, contact the San Pablo Bay NWR office in Building 505 on Mare Island, 707/562-3000.

ASK MR. JELLY BELLY

A particularly sweet treat in Fairfield is the tour of the Herman Goelitz Candy Company and adjacent **Jelly Belly Visitors Center,** where the phrase "bean counter" takes on immense new meaning—especially just before Easter, when the factory here produces more than a million jelly beans every hour. These aren't just any jelly beans. Former President Ronald Reagan made them internationally famous, when he started to eat Jelly Belly beans to help kick his pipe-smoking habit. And a Jelly Belly was the first jelly bean in space. These are the original "gourmet jelly beans." The company boasts 50 flavors on its regular roster—buttered popcorn, root beer, pink bubble gum, buttered toast, jalapeño, and many fruit flavors among them—and produces many more for its seasonal lists.

Jelly Belly is always experimenting with new possibilities, these known as "rookies," which each get a one-year tryout.

At the end of the factory tour, you'll probably meet up with a few rookies. But first you'll follow the **Jelly Belly Candy Trail,** looking down on the production floor to see how the beans are made. You'll also find out how the company comes up with all those flavors. You'll even get to sample the merchandise. There's a fully stocked Jelly Belly store and a Jelly Belly restaurant.

Free tours are offered several times daily (except major holidays) though the factory may be closed the day before or after a holiday. For current information, call 707/428-2838 or 800/522-3267. Take a virtual Jelly Belly tour on www.jellybelly.com. Mr. Jelly Belly will happily answer all your questions.

JUSTIN MARLER

view of Mt. Diablo from Tilden Regional Park

Vallejo

Vallejo sprawls across the spot where the Napa River flows into San Pablo Bay, near now-closed Mare Island Naval Shipyard. (The shipyard is now open for tours.) Begin an exploration of Vallejo's rich history at the **Vallejo Naval &**

TOURING ST. PETER'S

The spectacular interdenominational **St. Peter's Chapel** at the Mare Island Shipyard is the oldest naval chapel in the United States, built in 1900. All of the chapel's 29 stained-glass windows were designed by Tiffany Studios; this is the largest "collection" of Tiffany stained glass in the West. Tours of once-secret Mare Island, closed for military use by the federal government in 1996, include St. Peter's Chapel, the mansions along Officer's Row, and the historic stone drydock. For details, contact the **Mare Island Historic Park Foundation,** 328 Seawind Dr. in Vallejo, 707/557-1538, www.mareislandhpf.org.

Historical Museum, in the city's old city hall at 734 Marin St., 707/643-0077 www.vallejomuseum.org, open Tues.–Sat. 10 A.M.–4:30 P.M. The museum includes two floors of exhibits about Vallejo and Mare Island, including a working World War II–era submarine periscope. Small admission.

Vallejo is also home to **Six Flags Marine World,** a big-time theme park next to the Solano County Fairgrounds. A popular venue for family-style fun, Marine World features some 30 rides—including Boomerang, Hammerhead Shark, Kong, Roar, and Voodoo—and 35 marine and land animal exhibits. Among the most intriguing experiences are the tamest, including strolls through the fluttering **Lorikeet Aviary** and the glassed-in **Butterfly Habitat.** Trained-animal performances and other shows round out the action here. Marine World is open daily in summer, weekends only in fall and spring, and is closed entirely Nov.–Feb.; call or see the website for current days and hours. At last report, admission was $43.99 adults, $34.99 seniors, and $26.99 children (under 48 inches

SAN FRANCISCO BAY AREA

tall). There's a parking fee, too. For more information, contact: Six Flags Marine World, Marine World Parkway, Vallejo, CA 94589, 707/644-4000, www.sixflags.com. For more information about Vallejo and vicinity, contact: **Vallejo Chamber of Commerce,** 2 Florida St. 707/644-5551, www.vallejochamber.com.

Northeast of Vallejo and north of Suisun Bay is **Fairfield** and adjacent Travis Air Force Base with its **Travis Air Force Base Heritage Center Museum,** 707/424-5605, www.travis.af.mil/, open 9 A.M.–4 P.M. Mon.–Sat., an impressive indoor-outdoor collection of old aircraft—including a handmade 1912 wooden biplane, cargo planes, jet fighters, and bombers.

Benicia

Just north of the Benicia-Martinez Bridge via I-780 lies Benicia, the onetime capital of California. The town is proud of its "firsts," though some seem stretched in significance. Benicia had the state's first chamber of commerce, law school, fire department, and public school (so far, so good)—but also the first steamboat built by Americans in California, the first railroad ferry west of the Mississippi, and the first recorded marriage in Solano County.

Back in the good ol' days of early settlement, Benicia, named by General Mariano Vallejo after his wife, was a warren of militarty barracks, tanneries, and whorehouses. Get oriented at the restored **Benicia Depot,** now a visitor center, then take a quick tour of the town's historic architecture (most buildings aren't open to the public). Stop at the restored **Benicia Capitol State Historic Park,** 115 W. G St. (at First St.), 707/745-3385, which preserves the 1852 brick building that housed the California Senate, Assembly, and Treasury for 13 months in 1853-54. Also part of the park is the 1850s Fischer-Hanlon House next door, which holds Victorian-era furnishings and displays of period clothing. Admission to the park is free.

Benicia's **Camel Barn Museum,** 2024 Camel Rd. (in the town's onetime military arsenal complex, now an industrial park), 707/745-5435, is named for a short-lived 1860s experiment—using camels to transport military supplies across the Southwest. The cranky creatures were once stabled here,

but the barn is now home to local memorabilia. Open Wed.–Sun. 1–4 P.M.; small admission.

The **Benicia Fire Museum,** 900 E. Second St. (at E. J St.), 707/745-1688, holds displays of rare firefighting equipment and a collection of historical photos. It's open on the first three Sundays of each month, noon–4 P.M., or by appointment.

Benicia proper is experiencing an art-community boom and overall revitalization, with interesting cafés and shops popping up everywhere. Try breakfast, lunch, or dinner at Benicia's **Union Hotel,** 401 First St., 707/746-0105, noted for its creative (and fairly reasonable) California-style cuisine and nice hotel rooms. Just northwest of town along the strait (off I-780) is **Benicia State Recreation Area,** 707/648-1911, popular for fishing, hiking, and picnicking. Day-use fee is $2 per vehicle.

Martinez

Martinez, on the other end of the Benicia bridge, was settled by Italian fishing families and is historic home to both the martini and New York Yankee baseball great Joe DiMaggio. A modern-day attraction is the **John Muir House National Historic Site,** 4202 Alhambra Ave., 925/228-8860, www.nps.gov/jomu, which preserves the naturalist's 1882 Victorian home and grounds. Home to Muir and his wife during the last 24 years of his life, this is where he did most of his conservation writing. In addition to becoming an astute businessman, orchardist, inventor, pioneer of factory automation, patron of the arts, and magazine editor, the indefatigable Scot explored California and Alaska, established the U.S. Forest Service and five national parks, and co-founded the Sierra Club.

The house holds many of Muir's books and writings, along with exhibits chronicling his amazing influence. In mid-December, come for Christmas carols and Victorian tea. Also on the grounds is the **Martinez Adobe,** the 1844 home of Don Vincente Martinez, part of the old Rancho Las Juntas. Muir House is open Wed.–Sun. (except major holidays) 10 A.M.–5 P.M.; small admission. Well worth a stop across the way is the spectacular California-related shop **California Collectible Books,** 3503 Alhambra Ave., 925/229-4878.

AT JOHN MUIR'S GRAVE

I want to remember stumbling
across fresh-turned clods in the peach orchard
he would have planted a few years later . . .
but that's memory; these are words.

I walked to the isolated plot
where John Muir is buried
with the rest of his family.
An ornate fence kept me out.

His stone is simple,
factual with dates and place.
A bit of laurel,
alive and carved, befits the man

All beneath his loved and noted
incense cedar, a scraggly tree
often milled to pencils
for making words, for making words.

—Gary Thompson

Also in the area is the **Carquinez Strait Regional Shoreline Park,** a 969-acre tract good for bird-watching, biking, and hiking. It's reached via Hwy. 4 (from I-80), then McEwen Rd. and Carquinez Scenic Drive. After a short hike down to Port Costa, backtrack to 344-acre **Martinez Regional Shoreline Park,** on N. Court St. (north of Ferry St.), for more views and usually fresh air (and wind). The park has a marina, fishing pier, playground and ball fields, a picnic area, par course, and numerous other recreation facilities. For more information on regional parks, call East Bay Regional Parks headquarter, 510/562-7275, or see the website: www.ebparks.org

Crockett

Crockett is most famous for the C&H sugar refinery here, but it's also something of an artsy-industrial enclave, like a smokestack-style Sausalito. Under the Carquinez Bridge, on the pilings, is **Nantucket Restaurant,** 501 Port St., 510/787-2233, a good seafood place with views of the bridge's underbelly and the nearby sugar refinery.

Danville

Eugene Gladstone O'Neill, winner of four Pulitzer Prizes and the only Nobel Prize–winning playwright from the U.S., is considered the modern architect of American theater. O'Neill lived in the far eastern reaches of the San Francisco Bay Area, in the hills above Danville, from 1937 to1944. Worthwhile these days is a stop at **Eugene O'Neill's Tao House National Historic Site,** a two-story Spanish-style home and national historic landmark where O'Neill wrote some of his last plays, including *The Iceman Cometh, Long Day's Journey into Night,* and *A Moon for the Misbegotten.* Reopened in 2003 after a seismic retrofit, the museum offers two tours per day Wed.–Sun., with buses leaving from downtown Danville. Every spring, in the restored barn, the acclaimed **Playwright's Theatre** performs works by O'Neill and playwrights he influenced. Call 925/838-0249 for more information and advance reservations (required) or see the website: www.nps.gov/euon. For more information about the writer's life and works, explore the **Eugene O'Neill Foundation** website: www.eoneill.com.

Also in Danville, the opulent **Blackhawk Automotive Museum,** 3700 Blackhawk Plaza Circle, 925/736-2277, www.blackhawkmuseum.org, is a showcase for a $100 million collection of classic cars, including the 1924 torpedo-shaped Tulipwood Hispano Suiza built for Andre Dubonnet of French aperitif fame; Clark Gable's 1935 Deusenberg convertible; and Rudolph Valentino's 1926 Isotta Fraschini. The ground floor of the museum boasts an **Automotive Art Gallery.** Open Wed.–Sun. 10 A.M.–5 P.M.; admission is $8 adults, $5 seniors and students, free for children 6 and under. Free guided tours offered weekends at 2 P.M. To get here: from I-680, exit at Crow Canyon Rd. 10 miles south of Walnut Creek, head east to Camino Tassajara, then turn right and look for the sign—and the mall.

If you get hungry out here in the hinterlands, the expensive, shiny, and automobile-oriented **Blackhawk Grille,** 3540 Blackhawk Plaza Circle (at the other end of the mall), 925/736-4295, serves exceptional and eclectic food. Other good choices in the area, generally less pricey: **Bridges,** 44 Church St., 925/820-7200, with an impressive

JOHN MUIR'S MOUNTAIN DAYS

Come in August for the month-long **Mountain Days: The John Muir Musical** produced at the John Muir Amphitheater on the Martinez waterfront by Concord's Willow Theatre, 925/798-1300, www.willowstheatre.org for information and to order tickets. In just a few years the production has become such a sensation that development of the new John Muir Festival Center (along the waterfront, at the foot of Ferry St.) is now underway. The new complex will encompass the 1,100-seat amphitheater, a 500-seat year-round indoor theater, an education center, and offices of the Martinez Historical Society, which will be housed in the 1877 train depot along with the center's administrative and support services.

East-West menu, and inexpensive **La Ultima** in downtown Danville, 455 Hartz Ave., 925/838-9705, serving genuine New Mexican specialties rarely found in California.

Livermore Valley

Pleasanton seems to be the face of California's future: corporate business parks mixed with backyard barbecues. But the surrounding hills provide some great hiking opportunities, particularly at 1,800-acre **Pleasanton Hills Regional Park** (exit I-680 at Sunol Blvd., head west on Castlewood Dr., then north on Foothill Road). If you're exploring the area and need a snazzy place to stay, try **Evergreen,** 9104 Longview Dr., 925/426-0901, www.evergreen-inn.com, a contemporary B&B up in the hills. Each of the four rooms has a private bath, telephone, TV, and refrigerator. Rates $150–250 (one room is $135).

Livermore is home of **Lawrence Livermore National Laboratory,** 7000 East Ave. (follow the signs), 925/423-3272 (visitor center), 925/422-4599 (public affairs), or 925/422-1100 (main operator), which was developing the X-ray laser for the U.S. "Star Wars" defense system before the world changed. The visitor center here is open to the public daily, with scientific displays and videos of atomic test sites and the lab's underground linear accelerator. Tours of the top-secret research and development facilities are not available. One thing no one here will probably discuss is the fact that this is a Superfund toxic waste site (with a 50-year cleanup time frame) and that lab employees have a melanoma cancer rate about five times the national average.

If the lab gives you the willies, you can stop to pray at the town's lovingly handcrafted **Hindu Shiva-Vishnu Temple,** 1232 Arrowhead Ave., 925/449-6255. Unique because it combines the stylistic traditions of both northern and southern India, the temple is an architectural anachronism here amid Livermore's tract homes.

The surrounding Livermore Valley, home of the Livermore Rodeo every June, is noted for its wineries—some of the oldest in the state. The historic Cresta Blanca vineyard has been resurrected as **Wente Vineyards,** 5050 Arroyo Rd., 925/456-2450, which offers a restaurant open daily for lunch and dinner. Also in the neighborhood: **Concannon Vineyards,** 4590 Tesla Rd., 925/456-2505; award-winning **Fenestra Winery,** 83 E. Vallecitos Rd., 925/447-5246, which offers winetasting on weekends from noon–5 P.M.; and the traditional **Wente Estate Winery,** 5565 Tesla Rd., 925/456-2300, where picnicking is possible on the grounds. For more area winery information, contact the **Livermore Valley Winegrowers Association,** 1984 Railroad Ave. in Livermore, 925/447-9463, www.livermorewine.com.

A wine-related stop in the area is **Ravenswood Historic Site,** 2647 Arroyo Rd. (south of Superior), 925/373-5708, an early winery estate open to the public only on the second Sunday of each month for free guided tours given by costumed docents. Two Victorian homes preside over 33 acres of apple orchards and vineyards; one of the old Vics is filled with period furniture and functions as a museum.

Beyond Livermore on the way to Tracy via I-580 is the Altamont Pass area, open foothill grazing land best known for the thousands of wind turbines in its power-generating "wind farms."

Point Reyes National Seashore

Some 65,000 acres of fog-shrouded lagoons, lowland marshes, sandy beaches, coastal dunes, and ridgetop forests, Point Reyes National Seashore also features windy headlands and steep, unstable, colorful cliffs, populations of tule elk and grazing cattle, and a wonderful lighthouse all too popular for winter whale-watching. A dramatically dislocated triangular wedge of land with its apex jutting out into the Pacific Ocean, Point Reyes is also land in motion: this is earthquake country. Separated from mainland Marin County by slit-like Tomales Bay, the Point Reyes Peninsula is also sliced off at about the same spot by the San Andreas Fault. When that fault shook loose in 1906—instantly thrusting the peninsula 16 feet farther north—the city of San Francisco came tumbling down.

Geologists were long baffled by the fact that the craggy granite outcroppings of Point Reyes were identical to rock formations in the Tehachapi Mountains some 310 miles south. But the theory of plate tectonics and continental drift provided the answer. The Point Reyes Peninsula rides high on the eastern edge of the Pacific Plate, which moves about three inches to the northwest each year, grinding against the slower-moving North American Plate. The two meet in the high-stress, many-faulted rift zone of the Olema Valley, an undefined line "visible" in landforms and weather patterns. In summer, for example, fog may chill the coastal headlands and beaches while the sun shines east of Inverness Ridge.

Seasonally, dogs are specifically restricted at Point Reyes—and people must also restrain themselves—because the northern elephant seals have returned to area beaches and established a breeding colony. To protect the elephant seals during the winter breeding and pupping season, some beaches are temporarily closed. Only leashed dogs are allowed on North Beach, Kehoe Beach, and the southern part of Limantour Beach. Contact the park office for current details.

To be fully informed about what's going on in and around Point Reyes while visiting, contact the park. A good free companion is the quarterly tabloid *Coastal Traveler,* published by the area's Pulitzer Prize-winning *Point Reyes Light* newspaper and available at area shops and businesses. For advance or additional information, contact the **West Marin Chamber of Commerce** in Point Reyes Station, 415/663-9232, www.pointreyes.org.

SEEING AND DOING POINT REYES

Get oriented at the park's barnlike **Bear Valley Visitor Center,** 415/464-5100, just off Bear Valley Rd. (off Hwy. 1 near Olema), which, in addition to natural history and fine arts exhibits, includes a seismograph for monitoring the earth's movements. Near the picnic tables at the visitor center is the short **Earthquake Trail** loop (wheelchair accessible), which demonstrates the San Andreas seismic drama, from sag ponds and shifts in natural boundary lines to the old Shafter Ranch barn, a corner of which slid off its foundations during the 1906 San Francisco earthquake. Also near the Bear Valley Visitor Center are the short, self-guided **Woodpecker Nature Trail;** the **Morgan Horse Ranch,** where the Park Service breeds and trains its mounts; and **Kule Loklo,** an architectural re-creation of a Coast Miwok community. (When Sir Francis Drake purportedly arrived at Point Reyes in the late 1500s, he found more than 100 such villages on the peninsula.) The best time to see Kule Loklo is during July's Annual Native American Celebration, when this outdoor exhibit, complete with sweathouse, thatched and redwood bark dwellings, and dancing lodge, comes to life with Miwok basketmakers, wood- and stonecarvers, and native singing and dancing.

Limantour Estero near Drakes Estero and Drakes Beach is great for bird-watching; **McClures Beach** is best for tidepooling; and both **North Beach** and **South Beach** north of Point Reyes proper offer good beachcombing but treacherous swimming. Protected **Drakes Beach** and **Limantour Beach** along the crescent of Drakes Bay are safe for swimming.

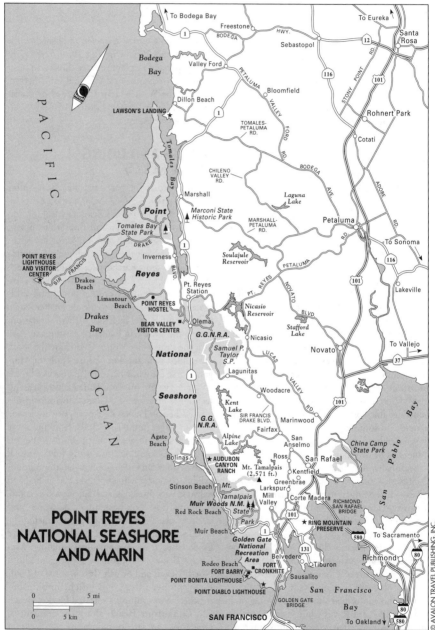

To Bodega Bay

Freestone
BODEGA
Bodega

To Eureka

Santa
Rosa

HWY.

Sebastopol

12

Bodega
Bay

Valley Ford

Bloomfield

116

Rohnert Park

Dillon Beach

PETALUMA

VALLEY

FORD

Cotati

LAWSON'S LANDING

TOMALES-
PETALUMA
RD.

BODEGA

101

AVE.

STONY POINT RD.

ADOBE

RD.

CHILENO
VALLEY
RD.

Marshall

Laguna
Lake

Petaluma

To Sonoma

Point

Marconi State
Historic Park

MARSHALL-
PETALUMA
RD.

PETALUMA

116

Tomales Bay
State Park

DRAKE

Inverness

BLVD.

Soulajule
Reservoir

PT. REYES

NOVATO

101

Lakeville

POINT REYES
LIGHTHOUSE
AND VISITOR
CENTER

Reyes

SIR FRANCIS

Drakes
Beach

Pt. Reyes
Station

Nicasio
Reservoir

BLVD.

To Vallejo

Limantour
Beach

POINT REYES
HOSTEL

Olema

Stafford
Lake

Drakes
Bay

BEAR VALLEY
VISITOR CENTER

G.G.N.R.A.

Nicasio

Novato

37

National

Samuel P.
Taylor
S.P.

LUCAS

1

Lagunitas

Woodacre

101

Seashore

Kent
Lake

SIR FRANCIS
DRAKE BLVD.

VALLEY

RD.

G.G.
N.R.A.

Marinwood

Fairfax

Agate
Beach

Alpine
Lake

San
Anselmo

China Camp
State Park

San
Pablo
Bay

Bolinas

AUDUBON
CANYON
RANCH

Ross

San Rafael

Stinson Beach

Mt. Tamalpais
(2,571 ft.)

Kentfield

Mt.
Tamalpais
State

Greenbrae

Larkspur

RICHMOND-
SAN RAFAEL
BRIDGE

Muir Woods N.M.

Red Rock Beach

Mill
Valley

Corte Madera

Park

101

POINT REYES
NATIONAL SEASHORE
AND MARIN

Muir Beach

Golden Gate
National
Recreation
Area

RING MOUNTAIN
PRESERVE

580

To Sacramento

131

Belvedere

Richmond

80

Rodeo Beach
FORT BARRY
POINT BONITA LIGHTHOUSE

FORT
CRONKHITE

Tiburon

Sausalito

San Francisco

80

POINT DIABLO LIGHTHOUSE

GOLDEN GATE
BRIDGE

Bay

580

SAN FRANCISCO

To Oakland

PACIFIC

OCEAN

Tomales Bay

0   5 mi

0   5 km

© AVALON TRAVEL PUBLISHING, INC.

For astounding views when the fog lifts above the ship graveyard offshore, head out to Point Reyes proper and the **Point Reyes Lighthouse and Visitor Center,** 415/669-1534 (open daily 9 A.M.–4:30 P.M. during whale-watching season, more limited hours at other times). Restoration of the Point Reyes Lighthouse is ongoing through early 2004; call ahead for more information. The Chimney Rock Trail is wonderful for spring and summer wildflowers and, if you head west, is also a roundabout way to reach the lighthouse. On all Point Reyes hikes, carry water, wear proper walking shoes, and dress for sudden, unpredictable weather changes.

To experience the sound and fury of Coast Creek hurling itself into the Pacific via the "sea tunnel" at the **Arch Rock Overlook,** dress warmly, wear raingear and slip-proof shoes, and come (via the popular Bear Valley Trail) during a storm. For safety's sake, stay well back from the spectacle, and don't attempt to walk through the tunnel under any circumstances—though people often do in calm weather.

To make the most of a full moon at Point Reyes, head to the **Wildcat Beach Overlook** via the Bear Valley Trail from the visitor center, then south via the Coast Trail to the area overlooking the beach, **Alamere Falls** (most spectacular after heavy rains), and the southern stretch of Drakes Bay. An alternate route to Alamere Falls, about one mile south of Wildcat Camp, is via the Palomarin Trail from Bolinas or the Five Brooks Trail. For the best panoramic vista of Drakes Bay, take the Bear Valley, Sky, then Woodward Valley Trails to the bay (alternatively, take the Coast Trail from Coast Camp to the Woodward Valley Trail), then climb up the small hill overlooking the bay, just northwest of the trail.

The **Randall Spur Trail,** created by the Civilian Conservation Corps, connects the Bolinas Ridge Trail with the various Inverness Ridge and Olema Valley trails—making Point Reyes's southern stretches more accessible for day hikers. Worth a stop on the way to the Palomarin trailhead in south Point Reyes is the **Point Reyes Bird Observatory,** 415/868-1221, www.prbo.org, established in 1965 as the first bird observatory in the country. Though it's a full-fledged research facility,

Bear Valley Trail

the Palomarin observatory is open to the public, with bird walks, educational classes (call ahead for information), interpretive exhibits, and a nature trail. Field biology internships are also available. To get here by car, take the unmarked turnoff to Bolinas (near highway marker 17.00 at the north end of Bolinas Lagoon), continue two miles or so to Mesa Rd., then turn right and continue four miles to the observatory's bird-banding station.

These days, visitors can also horse around in Point Reyes, thanks to guided tours offered by **Five Brooks Ranch,** 415/663-1570, www.fivebrooks.com. The two-hour Fir Top Trail Ride is $50 per person, though one-hour and six-hours ride, overnight pack trips, and brief pony rides for the kids are also available.

Whale-Watching

Whale-watching, particularly fine from the lighthouse, is immensely popular at Point Reyes and best from about Christmas through January, when whales pass from one to five miles offshore. (Come on a weekday to avoid the crowds.) A hundred or more whale sightings per day is fairly typical here, though a 307-step descent to the lighthouse must be negotiated first. (Remember, what goes down must come back up.) You'll also get good views from the platform at the top of the stairs. The parking lot at the Point Reyes Lighthouse is fairly small, so in peak season—late December through April—whalewatchers park at Drakes Beach near the park entrance and take a shuttle bus to the lighthouse and Chimney Rock; the fee is $4 general, kids 12 and under free. National Park Service naturalists provide whale facts and whale-watching tips in January 10 A.M.–4 P.M. daily, both at the lighthouse and the small information center near the viewing platform. For more information about Point Reyes whale-watching, including the complete shuttle schedule and special naturalist programs, call the Bear Valley Visitor Center at 415/464-5100 or see the park's website. The lighthouse is open to the public for self-guided and ranger-led tours Thurs.–Mon. 10 A.M.–4:30 P.M. (closed in the event of high winds), as is the visitor center.

Not far from the lighthouse is the **Point Reyes Historic Lifeboat Station,** established in 1889 with a "surfcar" (like a tiny submarine) pulled through the surf on a cable, hand-pulled surf-boats, and a Lyle gun and breeches buoy. The facility is open infrequently and is available for educational programs on marine biology and maritime history. For more information, call 415/464-5100.

Information

For information about Point Reyes, including current trail maps, and to obtain permits for camping and backpacking, stop by any of the park's three visitor centers: the main **Bear Valley Visitor Center** at the park's Bear Valley entrance, 415/464-5100, open year-round Mon.–Fri. 9 A.M.–5 P.M., weekends 8 A.M.–5 P.M.; **Kenneth C. Patrick Visitor Center** at Drakes Beach, 415/669-1250, open weekends and holidays all year, 10 A.M.–5 P.M., and Fri.–Tues. 10 A.M.–5 P.M. in summer; and **Point Reyes Lighthouse Visitor Center** at the end of Sir Francis Drake Blvd., 415/669-1534, open year-round Thurs.–Mon., 10 A.M.–4:30 P.M. Or contact Point Reyes National Seashore, 415/464-5100, www.nps.gov/pore.

There isn't any car camping at Point Reyes, but hike-in family campgrounds are available; camping on the west side of Tomales Bay is boat-in only. Family campsites are $12 per night, group camps $25–35; for more details see the park's website. Call 415/663-8054 on weekdays for advance reservations and permit information.

For information about the year-round schedule of excellent classes and field seminars held at Point Reyes (most offered for credit through Dominican College, some offered cooperatively through the Elderhostel program), contact **Point Reyes Field Seminars,** 415/663-1200, www.ptreyes.org, and ask for the current seminar catalog.

A very good guidebook to the area is *Point Reyes—Secret Places & Magic Moments* by Phil Arnot. Also by Arnot (and Elvira Monroe): *Exploring Point Reyes: A Guide to Point Reyes National Seashore.*

For information about what's going on in Point Reyes and surrounding communities, pick up a copy of the Pulitzer Prize-winning *Point Reyes Light,* which made a name for itself with investigative reporting on the area's former Synanon cult. For information about area practicalities, see Staying in Western Marin and Eating Well in Western Marin below.

THE FARALLON ISLANDS

Visible from Point Reyes on a clear day are the Farallon Islands to the southwest. Protected as the Farallon National Wildlife Refuge, the largest seabird rookery south of Alaska, these islands are one of the five most ecologically productive marine environments on earth and now part of an international UNESCO Biosphere Reserve. Some 948 square nautical miles of ocean from Bodega Head to Rocky Point are included in the Gulf of the Farallones National Marine Sanctuary. These rugged granite islands 27 miles west of San Francisco are actually the above-sea-level presence of the Farallones Escarpment, which parallels the coast from the tip of Point Reyes to south of the Golden Gate. The natural but rare phenomenon of upwelling around the islands, with warm offshore winds drawing cold, nutrient-rich ocean water to the surface in spring, creates the phenomenal algae and plankton populations that support the feeding frenzies and breeding successes of animals farther up the food chain.

But during recent centuries, life has been almost undone at the Farallones. In the 1800s, "eggers" exploited the rookeries here to provide miners and San Franciscans with fresh eggs at breakfast. The islands have also survived assaults from sealers, whalers, gill netters, bombers, ocean oil slicks, and radioactive waste dumping.

In the summer, more than 250,000 breeding birds—from tufted puffins and petrels to auklets and murres—consider the Farallones home. Seals (including the once-almost-extinct northern elephant seal) and sea lions also breed here, and gray and humpback whales as well as northern fur seals are often spotted in the area. The nonprofit, member-supported **Point Reyes Bird Observatory,** 4990 Shoreline Hwy. (Hwy. 1) in Stinson Beach, 415/868-1221, staffs a scientific study center at the Farallones (in addition to its center at Point Reyes), but otherwise people are not allowed on the islands—though the **Oceanic Society,** 415/474-3385, www.oceanic-society.org, sponsors one-day educational expeditions around the Farallon Islands June–Nov. and during the winter whale-watching season. (Bring binoculars.) The public is welcome, however, at the **Point Reyes Bird Observatory's Palomarin Field Station,** 415/868-0655, at the end of Mesa Rd. near Bolinas, to observe bird banding. The station is open daily May–Nov. and on Wed., Sat., and Sun. the rest of the year; call for hours and to make reservations for groups of five or more people.

For more information about the Farallon Islands and the surrounding marine sanctuary, contact the **Farallones Marine Sanctuary Association** headquartered at the Presidio in San Francisco, 415/561-6622, www.farallones.org.

GOLDEN GATE NATIONAL RECREATION AREA AND VICINITY

Beginning immediately adjacent to Point Reyes near Olema is the Golden Gate National Recreation Area (GGNRA), which wraps itself around various state and local parks inland, then extends southeast across the Marin Headlands and the Golden Gate Bridge to include the Presidio and a thin coastal strip running south to Fort

JANE MUSSER

The Marin Headlands are often cloaked in a shroud of fog.

Funston. The GGNRA also includes two notable tourist attractions in San Francisco Bay: Angel Island and Alcatraz. Most notable is the dramatic natural beauty of the Marin Headlands—sea-chiseled chilly cliffs, protected valleys, and grassy wind-combed hills rich with wildlife and wildflowers, all opening out to the bay and the Pacific Ocean. Protected at first by the Nature Conservancy until coming under national management in 1972, the vast Marin Headlands feature trails for days of good hiking and backpacking (stop by headquarters for a current trail map). Backcountry and group camps are scattered across the area.

Aside from the GGNRA's natural beauty, here also is historic scenery, from the 1877 Point Bonita Lighthouse to four military installations—Forts Barry, Cronkhite, Baker, and Funston—that protected the Bay Area beginning in the 1870s and continuing through World War II. The last U.S. Army post in the Bay Area was closed in late 2002 when Fort Baker was transferred by the military to the National Park Service.

For more information about the GGNRA,

SAN FRANCISCO BAY AREA

including trail maps, events calendars, and backcountry camping details, stop at the **Marin Headlands Visitor Center** at Fort Barry, in the historic Fort Barry Chapel at Field and Bunker Rds., 415/331-1540, open daily 9:30 A.M.– 4:30 P.M., or the **Muir Woods Visitor Center** at Muir Woods, 415/388-7368, open daily 8 A.M.–sunset. The Golden Gate National Recreation Area offers two hike-in and two walk-in campgrounds in the Marin Headlands; inquire here for details and to make reservations (required). If you're still in San Francisco, get GGNRA information at: **Pacific West Information Center,** Bldg. 201 at Fort Mason, 415/561-4700, open Mon.–Fri. 8:30 A.M.– 4:30 P.M.; the **Cliff House Visitor Center,** 415/556-8642, open daily 10 A.M.–5 P.M.; the **Fort Point Bookstore,** 415/556-1693, open only Fri.–Sun. 10 A.M.–5 P.M.; and the **William Penn Mott Jr. Visitor Center** at the Presidio,

415/561-4323, open daily 9 A.M.–5 P.M. Or see the park website: www.nps.gov/goga.

Several guidebooks published by the nonprofit Golden Gate National Parks Conservancy, 415/ 561-3000 or 415/657-2757, www.parksconservancy.org, are well worth buying—including the 96-page *Guide to the Golden Gate National Parks* ($9.95), which covers every feature of the recreation area.

Point Bonita Lighthouse

The Point Bonita Lighthouse (call 415/331-1540 for hours and tour information) was one of the first lighthouses ever built on the West Coast and is still operating. Technically, though, this isn't really a lighthouse—there's no house, just the French-import 1855 Fresnel lens and protective glass, walls, and roof, with gargoyle-like American eagles guarding the light. Getting here is as thrilling as being here—meandering along the

HYSTERICAL HISTORICAL HOAX: SIR FRANCIS DRAKE MYSTERY SOLVED

The mystery behind one of the West's best historical hoaxes has finally been revealed. As it turns out, all along the joke was on a famed UC Berkeley professor—thanks to those merrily besotted pranksters of E Clampus Vitus, who in the 1930s cleverly faked "proof" that British privateer Sir Francis Drake came ashore north of San Francisco.

Historians agree that Drake explored coastal California. Tired of pursuing Spanish ships around the world, he beached the *Pelican* (later known as the *Golden Hinde*) and came ashore at "a fit and convenient harbour" somewhere in California in June 1579. Naming the land Nova Albion, here he made repairs, rested his tired crew, and claimed the area for Queen Elizabeth I with "a plate of brasse, fast nailed to a great and firme post." This much most historians agree on. The rest of the story has always been contentious, at best. Indeed, the desire to discover the truth about Drake's California adventure certainly created the context for a grand hoax.

Where exactly did Drake land? Since the main estuary at Point Reyes is named after Drake, as is the bay, the simple answer is that he came ashore here,

some 20 nautical miles north of San Francisco. But some contend that Drake actually landed at Bolinas Lagoon or explored San Francisco Bay and landed near Point San Quentin or Novato, near an old Olompali village site where a 1567 English silver sixpence was discovered in 1974. A more recent quest for remnants of Drake's visitation centers on Bodega Bay. Others say he stumbled ashore on Goleta Beach near Santa Barbara, where five cast-iron British cannons similar to those missing from the *Golden Hinde* were unearthed in the 1980s. But 70 pieces of antique Ming porcelain found near Point Reyes is proof enough, say true believers of the Point Reyes theory, since four chests of Chinese porcelain, which Drake stole from the Spanish, never arrived in England. Unbelievers counter that the porcelain washed ashore instead from the wreckage of the *San Agustin* off Drakes Bay.

In the midst of decades of speculation remained the mystery of a brass plate found on a beach near Point San Quentin in 1936. Was it genuine, or a clever forgery? Eminent UC Berkeley historian Herbert Bolton, who died in 1953, declared it to be authentic "beyond all reasonable doubt" and con-

half-mile footpath to the rocky point through hand-dug tunnels and across the swaying footbridge, in the middle of nowhere yet in full view of San Francisco. Especially enjoyable are the sunset and full-moon tours conducted by GGNRA rangers. At last report the lighthousehouse was open to tours (free) Sat.–Mon. 12:30–3:30 P.M.

To get to the lighthouse, follow the signs to Fort Baker/Fort Cronkhite/Fort Barry from Alexander Ave. just off the north end of the Golden Gate Bridge, then turn left at Field Rd. and continue, following the signs. (For seaside barbecues, head to the picnic area at Battery Wallace near Point Bonita.) For more information about American lighthouses, contact the **U.S. Lighthouse Society,** 244 Kearny in San Francisco, 415/362-7255 or website: www.uslhs.org.

Fort Barry

Just north of Point Bonita, Fort Barry includes an intact 1950s missile launch site and underground bunkers not usually open to the public; one of the bunkers is still home to a Nike Hercules missile. The **Nike Missile Site** is open for self-guided tours Wed.–Fri. 12:30–3:30 P.M., and you can come out for a free guided tour of all areas of the site the first Sunday of the month 12:30–3:30 P.M. For information, call 415/331-1453.

Also at Fort Barry: Hostelling International's marvelous **Marin Headlands Hostel,** Bldg. 941, 415/331-2777, www.norcalhostels.org; the **Headlands Center for the Arts,** Bldg. 144, 415/331-2787, www.headlands.org, which explores the relationship of art and the environment (studio space for artists is provided, and public programs include lectures, installations, exhibits, and performances); and the **Marin Headlands Visitor Center,** 415/331-1540, open to the public 9:30 A.M.–4:30 P.M. daily and offering

sidered it "one of the world's long-lost treasures." After years of controversy, in 1977 the British Museum declared the corroded placard an "undoubted fake" despite the Olde English ring of its language, and metallurgists said the plate was no more than 100 years old. But who would undertake such an elaborate hoax, and why? For years, no one knew.

In February 2003, four historians revealed the truth—or, as much of the truth as will likely ever emerge—in a heavily footnoted article in the California Historical Society's *California History* magazine. The "plate of brasse" discovered at San Quentin was just a practical joke played on Bolton by several of his colleagues, who (like Bolton) were members of the Ancient and Honorable Order of E Clampus Vitus, an organization that variously describes itself as a historical drinking society or a drinking historical society and is still known for its prankster tendencies. Bolton had long searched for Drake's plaque, proof that the explorer had come ashore at Point Reyes, so his friends decided to find it for him. They purchased a brass plate in an Alameda ship chandlery and carefully covered it with Elizabethan writing. Before they dumped it off at Point

Reyes in the early 1930s, they also marked the back of the plate with transparent fluorescent paint—spelling out the letters "ECV," for E Clampus Vitus.

Yet when the plate was discovered, to Bolton's delight, the "ECV" lettering escaped his attention, and everyone else's. The "inside joke" went public, in a big way—even a second fake brass plate, with an announcement by a Miwok "Great Hi-oh" failed to shake Bolton's certainty—so the friendly conspirators ultimately decided to keep their silence.

Mystery lingers, though. What became of Drake's journal, which supposedly documented his California sojourn as well as his discovery of the Northwest Passage? What happened to the gold, gems, and silver Drake stole from the Spanish ship *Cacafuego* and others, estimated in today's currency values as worth $50 million? Some say no treasure was buried along the California coast, that Drake would have jettisoned cannons, china, and other goods instead to lighten his ship's load. Drake, they say, took all his loot back to England, where he and his crew became millionaires, and the queen retired some of the national debt and started the East India Company. Others, however, are still looking.

SAN FRANCISCO BAY AREA

hands-on natural science exhibits, and educational and historical displays.

Fort Cronkhite

Just north of the Visitor Center is Fort Cronkhite, home of the **California Marine Mammal Center,** 1065 Fort Cronkhite (just above Cronkhite Beach), Sausalito, 415/289-7325, www.marine-mammalcenter.org. Established in 1975, this hospital for wild animals returns its "patients," once fit, to their native marine environments. The center, with more than 400 active volunteers and popular hands-on environmental education programs for children, is open to the public daily 10 A.M.–4 P.M. Wheelchair accessible. New members and financial contributions always welcome.

Hawk Hill

For views of the Golden Gate Bridge, San Francisco Bay, and the San Francisco skyline—not to mention exceptional birding opportunities—head to Hawk Hill (abandoned Battery 129, reached via Conzelman Rd.) on the north side of the Golden Gate above the bridge. Come in the fall (with binoculars and fog-worthy clothing) to appreciate the incredible numbers of birds of prey congregating here—100 or more each day representing 20-plus species. In spring, bring your kite—or keep watching. With any luck at all, Hawk Hill's Moby Vulture will still be flying. Any time of year, this is a great vantage point for watching huge cargo ships and other vessels make their way through the Golden Gate. For more information about the fall hawk migration, contact the **Golden Gate Raptor Observatory,** 415/331-0730, www.ggro.org.

Other Marin GGNRA Sights

The hands-on **Bay Area Discovery Museum** at East Fort Baker, 415/487-4398, www.badm.org, is designed for children ages 2–12 and their families. It offers a great variety of special programs year-round—"In the Dream Time" children's art workshops, for example. Open Tues.–Fri. 9 A.M.–4 P.M., Sat.–Sun. 10 A.M.–5 P.M., $7 admission for adults and children, 1 and under free. Two miles north of Muir Beach is the **Slide**

Ranch demonstration farm and family-oriented environmental education center, 2025 Hwy. 1, 415/381-6155, www.slideranch.org, which offers special events (such as "Family Farm Day") year-round. Reservations are required for all events.

Alcatraz: "The Rock"

Part of the GGNRA is infamous Alcatraz, one-time military outpost, then island prison and federal hellhole—"The Rock"—for hard-core criminals. Among the notorious bad guys incarcerated here were mobsters Al Capone, "Machine Gun" Kelley, and Mickey Cohen, not to mention Robert Stroud, the "Birdman of Alcatraz"—who, despite the romance of his popular myth, never kept birds on The Rock. Closed in the 1960s, then occupied for two years by Native Americans who hoped to reacquire the property for a cultural heritage center, Alcatraz Island and its prison facilities are now open for tours; see Touring the Real Rock in the San Francisco chapter. Ferries operated by the Blue & Gold Fleet at San Francisco's Pier 39, 415/773-1188 (recorded schedule) or 415/705-5555 (information and advance ticket purchase), www.blueandgold-fleet.com, shuttle visitors out to The Rock and back. Blue and Gold also offers a unique one-day **Island Hop Tour** of Alcatraz and Angel Island State Park together. For general information, contact the Alcatraz Visitor Center, 415/705-1042, www.nps.gov/alcatraz.

Tomales Bay State Park

Among the half-moon beaches and secret coves along the steep cliffs and shores of Tomales Bay are those protected within fragments of Tomales Bay State Park. One section is just north of Inverness, via Pierce Point Rd. off Sir Francis Drake Blvd., and others are scattered along Hwy. 1 north of Point Reyes Station on the east side of the bay. One of the prime picnic spots at Tomales Bay is **Heart's Desire Beach,** popular for family picnicking and swimming, and usually empty on weekdays (parking $4 per vehicle). The warm, usually sunny, and surf-free inland beaches here are the main attraction, but hiking the forested eastern slope of Inverness Ridge is also worth it—especially in early spring, when trees, young ferns, and wildflowers burst forth from their winter dormancy. Unique is the park's fine virgin forest of Bishop pines. Walk-in campsites are available. For views and a great hiking trail, get directions to Inverness Ridge from Tomales Bay State Park personnel. The southern grasslands section of Tomales Bay, now included in the GGNRA after the federal purchase of the 250-acre Martinelli Ranch, is prime turf for hiking (best in March for wildflowers) and bird-watching. The trailhead and parking area is just off Hwy. 1, about 1.5 miles north of Point Reyes Station. For more information about the park, contact Tomales Bay State Park in Inverness, 415/669-1140.

Along the eastern edge of Tomales Bay, the **Marconi Conference Center,** 18500 Hwy. 1 in Marshall, 415/663-9020, www.marconiconference.org, occupies the 1914 Marconi Hotel once owned by Guglielmo Marconi, inventor of the wireless. This onetime communications center facility—taken over by the U.S. Navy during World War I, later operated by RCA, and more recently home to the much-praised then pilloried Synanon alcohol and drug abuse program—is now a state-owned conference center operated on the model of Asilomar on the Monterey Peninsula.

Samuel P. Taylor State Park

East of Point Reyes National Seashore and hemmed in by the Golden Gate National Recreation Area is Samuel P. Taylor State Park, 2,600 acres of redwoods, mixed forests, and upcountry chaparral reached via Sir Francis Drake Boulevard. The park offers an extensive hiking and horseback trail system, a paved bicycle path running east-west, family campsites, group camps, no-frills camping (including hiker/biker camps), picnicking, and swimming. Day use is $4. To reserve family campsites ($11–14), contact ReserveAmerica, 800/444-7275, www.reserveamerica.com. For more information, contact Samuel P. Taylor State Park in Lagunitas, 415/488-9897.

East of Samuel Taylor near Nicasio is the vast Skywalker Ranch owned by Lucasfilms and George Lucas, film- and mythmaker in the tradition of mythologist Joseph Campbell and his Hero With a Thousand Faces. The public is not welcome. (And for the record, Lucas Valley Rd., connecting Nicasio and Marinwood, was named long before Lucas bought property here.) Lucasfilms is now in the process of moving to new headquarters at San Francisco's Presidio.

JANE MUSSER

SAN FRANCISCO BAY AREA

campground at Samuel P. Taylor State Park

Bolinas Lagoon and Audubon Canyon Ranch

Well worth a visit is the Bolinas Lagoon, as serene as a Japanese nature print, especially in spring, when only the breeze or an occasional waterfowl fracas ruffles the glassy blue smoothness of this long mirror of water surrounded by a crescent-moon sandspit. Reflected above is wooded Bolinas Ridge, the northwestern extension of Mt. Tamalpais. In autumn, the lagoon is much busier, temporary home to thousands of waterfowl migrating south along the Pacific Flyway as well as the salmon offshore waiting for a ferocious winter storm to break open a pathway through the sandbars blocking their migratory path. At minus tide any time of year, the surf side of the sandspit offers good beachcombing.

Facing out into the Bolinas Lagoon several miles north of Stinson Beach is the Audubon Canyon Ranch, a protected canyon offering a safe haven and rookery for great blue herons and common egrets in particular, though more than 50 other species of water birds arrive here each year. By quietly climbing up the canyon slopes during the Mar.–July nesting season, visitors can look down into egret and heron nests high atop the redwoods in Schwartz Grove and observe the day-to-day life of parent birds and their young. Eight miles of self-guided hiking trails lead to other discoveries; picnic facilities also available.

The old dairy barn here serves as ranch headquarters and bookstore/visitor center. The ranch is wheelchair accessible and generally open to the public mid-March through mid-July only on weekends and holidays, 10 A.M.–4 P.M. Admission is free, though donations are greatly appreciated. Large groups can make tour arrangements for weekdays, though the ranch is always closed Mondays. For more information, contact: Audubon Canyon Ranch, 4900 Shoreline Hwy. (Hwy. 1) in Stinson Beach, 415/868-9244, www.egret.org.

Mt. Tamalpais State Park

Though the park also stretches downslope to the sea, take in the views of Marin County, San Francisco Bay, and the Pacific Ocean from the highest points of Mt. Tamalpais. This long-loved mountain isn't particularly tall (elevation 2,600 feet), but even when foggy mists swirl everywhere below, the sun usually shines atop Mt. Tam. And the state park here has it all: redwoods and ferns, hillsides thick with wildflowers, 200 miles of hiking trails with spectacular views (plus access to Muir Woods), beaches and headlands, also camping and picnicking. The best way to get here is via Hwy. 1, then via the Panoramic Hwy., winding up past Pan Toll Ranger Station and park headquarters (stop for information and a map) to near the summit. From the parking lot, it's a quarter-mile hike up a steep dirt road to the fire lookout on top of Mt. Tam.

The best way to explore Mt. Tamalpais is on foot. Take the loop trail around the top. For the more ambitious, head downslope to the sea and the busy public beaches at Stinson Beach, still noted for its annual **Dipsea Race** held in June, a tradition since 1904. Rugged cross-country runners cross the still more rugged terrain from Mill Valley to the sea at Stinson Beach; the last stretch down the footpath is known as the Dipsea Trail. Or hike into the park from Marin Municipal Water District lands on the east (for information, call the Sky Oaks Ranger Station in Fairfax, 415/945-1181) and head upslope, via the Cataract Trail from just off Bolinas Rd. outside of Fairfax and past Alpine Lake—something of a steep climb but worth it for the waterfalls, most dramatic in winter and early spring but sublime for pool-sitting in summer.

Via the Matt Davis Trail, or the Bootjack Camp or Pan Toll Ranger Station routes, hike to the charming old (1904) **West Point Inn,** 1000 Panoramic Hwy., 415/388-9955, for a glass of lemonade and a rest in the porch shade. (Accommodations available; see below.) Four miles away is the **Tourist Club,** 30 Ridge Ave., 415/388-9987, a 1912 chalet where overnight stays are available only to members and their families, but hikers arriving via the Sun, Redwood, or Panoramic Trails can get snacks, cold imported beer, sodas, and juices. Open daily, great views of Muir Woods from the deck. More accessible for a picnic or snack stop (bring your own) is Mt. Tam's Greek-style **Mountain Theater,** also known as the Cushing Memorial Theater, a 3,750-seat outdoor amphitheater on Ridgecrest Blvd. built from natural stone by the Civilian Conservation Corps. Rousing performances of the *Mountain Play* have been produced here each spring since 1913.

Mt. Tamalpais State Park is open daily from 7 A.M.–sunset. Day use (parking) is $4. Limited primitive camping ($7–10) and rustic cabins ($27) are available (see Staying in Western Marin, below). Make reservations for both through ReserveAmerica, 800/444-7275, www.reserveamerica.com. For more information, contact park headquarters at 801 Panoramic Hwy. in Mill Valley, 415/388-2070. For current information on Mt. Tam's Mountain Theater productions, contact the **Mountain Play Association,** 177 E. Blithedale in Mill Valley, 415/383-1100, www.mountainplay.org.

Muir Woods National Monument

Muir Woods is peaceful and serene but quite a popular place—not necessarily the best destination for getting away from them all. Lush redwood canyon country surrounds Redwood Creek within the boundaries of Mt. Tamalpais State Park, with a short trail system meandering alongside the stream, up to the ridgetops, and into the monument's main Cathedral and Bohemian redwood groves. For an easy, introductory stroll, the Muir Woods Nature Trail wanders through the flatlands, identifying the characteristic trees and shrubs. Fascinating at Muir Woods, the first national monument in the U.S., are the dawn redwood from China and the park's albino redwood, the shoots from this freak of nature completely chlorophyll-free. But to avoid the crowds imported in all those tour buses clogging the parking lot, get away from the visitor center and the trails near the parking lot. Muir Woods is open daily 8 A.M.–sunset, $3 day-use fee, no picnicking or camping. No dogs. For more information, contact the Muir Woods Visitor Center in Mill Valley, 415/388-7368, www.nps.gov/muwo, or call 415/388-2595 (recorded information) or 415/388-2596.

STAYING IN WESTERN MARIN

Camping

So popular that each has a four-day limit, the four primitive walk-in campgrounds at Point Reyes National Seashore are perfect for backpackers, since each is within an easy day's hike of the main trailhead and each other. Call 415/663-8054 for information and telephone reservations weekdays 9 A.M.–2 P.M.; permits required. Reservations can also be made in-person at Bear Valley Visitor's Center (on Bear Valley Rd. just west of Olema), 415/464-5100. Stop, too, for maps and wilderness permits.

Popular Coast Camp is most easily accessible from the parking lot at the end of Limantour Rd. and makes a good base for exploring the Limantour Estero and Sculptured Beach. Wildcat Camp is a group camp popular with Boy Scouts and others in Point Reyes's lake district (best swimming in Bass and Crystal Lakes). Glen Camp is tucked into the hills between Wildcat Camp and Bear Valley, and Sky Camp, perched on the western slopes of Mt. Wittenberg, looks down over Drakes Bay and Point Reyes.

Other area camping options include the backpack and group camps of GGNRA, 415/331-1540; the state campground at Samuel P. Taylor State Park, 415/488-9897; and the 18 primitive campsites plus backpack camps and group camp at Mount Tamalpais State Park, 415/388-2070.

Hostel

Best bet for noncamping budget travelers is **HI Point Reyes Hostel** on Limantour Rd. in Point Reyes Station, 415/663-8811 or 800/909-4776 #61, www.norcalhostels.org. Pluses here include the well-equipped kitchen (get food on the way) and all that beach. Advance reservations advisable. To get here: from Point Reyes Station, take Seashore west from Hwy. 1, then follow Bear Valley Rd. to Limantour Rd. and continue on Limantour for six miles. Dorm rooms under $16 per person. For information on getting to Point Reyes on public transit, call the hostel or Golden Gate Transit, 415/923-2000. The hostel's office hours are 7:30–10 A.M. and 4:30–9:30 P.M. daily; no check-in after 9:30 P.M. Considerably closer to urban Marin but also an excellent choice is the Marin Headlands hostel within the Golden Gate National Recreation Area. For information, see Staying in Eastern Marin, below.

Cabins and Retreats

The state's quite reasonable **Steep Ravine Environmental Cabins** on Rocky Point in Mount Tamalpais State Park, looking out to sea from near Stinson Beach, are small redwood-rustic homes-away-from-home with just the basics: platform beds (bring your own sleeping bag and pad), woodstoves, separate restrooms with pit toilets. But such a deal: $27 per cabin per night (each sleeps five) and an almost-private beach below in a spectacularly romantic setting. Before the state wrested custody of these marvelous cabins from the powerful Bay Area politicians and other clout-encumbered citizens who held long-term leases, photographer Dorothea Lange wrote about staying here in *To a Cabin,* co-authored by Margaretta K. Mitchell. Even the walk down to the bottom of Steep Ravine Canyon is inspiring, Lange noted, with "room for only those in need of sea and sky and infinity." One cabin (there are only 10) is wheelchair accessible; none have electricity, but they do have outside running water. Bring your own provisions. To reserve, contact ReserveAmerica, 800/444-7275, or make reservations online at www.reserveamerica.com.

Also notable and inexpensive in the area is the historic, rustic **West Point Inn,** built in 1904 as a traveler's stop for the Mill Valley/Mt. Tamalpais Railway. One of the five rustic cabins is wheelchair accessible, and there is a single-use restroom in the main lodge featuring a roll-in shower. Lodge rooms are coziest in winter months. Travelers with disabilities can drive in on an access road, but otherwise this is strictly a hike-in experience. (Bring your own food. Lodge cooking facilities available.) Rates are $30 per person. For more information and reservations, contact: West Point Inn, 1000 Panoramic Highway in Mill Valley, 415/388-9955.

Zen but not quite inexpensive is the San Francisco Zen Center's **Green Gulch Farm** or Green Dragon Temple near Muir Beach, where guests stay in the octagonal Lindisfarne Guest House. Rates are $75–105 per person or $125–155 for two, vegetarian meals included. Private Hope Cottage is available for private retreats, $200. For more information, call 415/383-3134 or see the website: www.sfzc.com/ggfindex.htm.

Inns

Even those without wheels can explore the seaward coast of Marin County in comfort and fine style—by hiking or walking the whole way from the Golden Gate Bridge with little more than a day pack and staying along the bay at a combination of hostels, campgrounds, hotels and motels, and the area's very nice bed-and-breakfast inns. (How far to go each day and where to stay depends upon time and money available.) For area lodging referrals and information, contact **Point Reyes Lodging,** 415/663-1872 or 800/539-1872, www.ptreyes.com; or **Inns of Marin,** 415/663-2000 or www.innsofmarin.com.

Especially for fans of the grand ol' days of the Arts and Crafts movement and invigorating wilderness lodges and, the most romantic place around is **Manka's Inverness Lodge** on Argyle St. up on the hill in Inverness, 415/669-1034, www.mankas.com, famous for its "honest beds" and fabulous food. The lodge's four upstairs and four annex rooms—not to mention both the amazing Fishing Cabin and Manka's Cabin—serve up luxurious rustic charms. Room rates are $150–250 and $250 and up, higher on weekends (wonderful breakfasts included) and $100 more during certain holiday periods, due to exceptionally popular Thanksgiving–Christmas food fests. (Don't miss the restaurant here.) Cabins are $395 and up. Except for midwinter weekdays, make reservations *way* in advance.

The classic Craftsman **Ten Inverness Way,** 10 Inverness Way (on the town's block-long main street), 415/669-1648, www.teninvernessway.com, is comfortable and cozy. Rooms feature excellent beds, handmade quilts, and private baths; there's a stone fireplace in the living room, wonderful full breakfast, private hot tub. Standard rooms $100–150, deluxe rooms slightly higher.

In a woodsy canyon just outside town, welcoming **Blackthorne Inn,** 266 Vallejo Ave. in Inverness Park, 415/663-8621, www.blackthorneinn.com, offers appealing furnishings in four-level "treehouse" accommodations with decks. Good buffet breakfast, great stone fireplace in the living room, fabulous setting. Hot tub available. The peak experience here is a stay in the Eagle's Nest, the aptly named octagonal, glass-walled room at the top of the stairs. Rates start at $225; most are $250 and up.

Also in Inverness Park is **Holly Tree Inn & Cottages,** 3 Silverhills Rd., 415/663-1554, www.hollytreeinn.com, which offers four charming rooms in the inn, plus a cottage on the premises (all $150–250), as well as the off-site **Sea Star Cottage** and **Vision Cottage** (both $250 and up).

Up on Inverness Ridge is **The Ark,** 415/663-9338 or 800/808-9338, www.rosemarybb.com, a very appealing cabin built from mostly recycled materials featuring bedroom, sleeping loft, woodstove, and fully equipped kitchen. Rates $150–250. Other cottages (all are "green") include the woodsy, two-room **Rosemary Cottage,** which has a cathedral ceiling, great light and windows, antiques, oriental rugs, well-equipped kitchen, woodstove, and garden hot tub ($150–250); and **Fir Tree Cottage,** a spacious two-bedroom house perfect for families or two couples ($250 and up). Near Tomales Bay, **Marsh Cottage,** "a bed with a view" at 12642 Sir Francis Drake Blvd., 415/669-7168, www.marshcottage.com, features a fireplace and yes, a view, plus kitchen with make-your-own-breakfast supplies. Rates $150–250 per night, weekly rates available.

Olema offers a number of good choices. These include the **Olema Inn,** 10000 Sir Francis Drake Blvd. (at Hwy. 1), 415/663-9559, a onetime stage stop and World War II–era barracks now decked out in classic American furnishings (wonderful restaurant downstairs), and **An English Oak** on Bear Valley Rd. at Hwy. 1, 415/663-1777, www.anenglishoak.com, a bed-and-breakfast with with three cheery rooms and spacious separate cottage. Rates at both are $100–150.

For nostalgia with all the modern amenities

(try to get a room away from the highway), the 1988 **Point Reyes Seashore Lodge,** 10021 Hwy. 1 (in Olema), 415/663-9000, www.pointreyesseashore.com, is an elegant re-creation of a turn-of-the-20th-century country lodge, a three-story weather-beaten cedar building with three two-story suites,18 rooms, and two private cabins, all with down comforters, telephones, and private baths, many with whirlpool tubs and fireplaces, most with a private deck or patio. Continental breakfast. Most rooms $150–250 (some are $135), suites $250 and up.

The restored 1885 **Olema Druids Hall** 9870 Hwy. 1, 415/663-8727 or toll free 866/554-4255, www.olemadruids.com, was originally built as a meeting hall for the Ancient Order of Druids (AAOD), a fraternal organization established in England in the late 1700s and in New York in 1830. The hall features expansive rooms and unique architectural details, three large guest rooms plus a master suite in the main house, and a separate cottage on the grounds. Rooms feature radiant-heated hardwood floors, down comforters, cable TV and VCRs; rates include complimentary continental breakfast. Rooms are $150–250, cottage $250 and up. Downstairs is the "store," Vita Collage, a commercial amalgamation of old and new.

The place to stay in Bolinas is **White House Inn,** 118 Kale Rd., 415/868-0279, www.thomaswhitehouseinn.com, a New England–style inn with two guest rooms sharing two bathrooms in the hall; continental breakfast. Rates $100–150.

The original 1912 **Mountain Home Inn** restaurant, 810 Panoramic Hwy. (on Mount Tamalpais) in Mill Valley, 415/381-9000, www.mtnhomeinn.com, has been transformed into an elegant and striking three-story hotel with upstairs restaurant and bar. Fabulous views. Some of the rooms have fireplaces or Jacuzzis. Rates include breakfast. Standard rooms $150–250, deluxe rooms $250 and up.

When Sir Francis Drake steered the *Pelican* to shore near here in 1579, he claimed everything in sight on behalf of Elizabeth I, Queen of England. For a taste of more modern true Brit on your way down from Mount Tam, stop at the **Pelican Inn,** 10 Pacific Way (Hwy. 1 at Muir

Beach Rd.) in Muir Beach, 415/383-6000, www.pelicaninn.com. This is a very British Tudor-style country inn, a replica of a 16th-century farmhouse, where guests sit out on the lawn with pint of bitter in hand on sunny days or, when the fog rolls in, warm up around the bar's fireplace with some afternoon tea or mulled cider or wine. Hearty pub fare includes meat pies, stews, burgers, homemade breads, various dinner entrées. Restaurant and pub open 11 A.M.–11 P.M. daily. Not authentically old (built in 1979), the Pelican is still authentic: the leaded-glass windows and brass trinkets, even the oak bar and refectory tables come from England. There's usually a months-long waiting list for the seven rooms here, which offer very appealing period charm (no phones or TVs). Rates are $150–250 and $250 and up.

EATING IN WESTERN MARIN

Inverness and Vicinity

After a relaxed afternoon spent reading in **Jack Mason Museum and Inverness Public Library** on Park Ave. (open limited hours, 415/669-1288 or 415/669-1099), head out Sir Francis Drake Blvd. from Inverness to **Johnson's Oyster Company,** 415/669-1149, for a tour and some farm-fresh oysters. Open Tues.–Sun. 8 A.M.–4:30 P.M.; free admission. **Barnaby's by the Bay,** 12938 Sir Francis Drake (at the Golden Hinde Inn just north of Inverness), 415/669-1114, open for lunch and dinner (closed Tuesday and Wednesday), has daily pasta and fresh fish specials, barbecued oysters, clam chowder, and crab cioppino.

Back in Inverness, try one of the town's two popular restaurants. At **Vladimir's Czechoslovak Restaurant & Bar,** 12785 Sir Francis Drake, 415/669-1021, expect good Eastern European food in an authentically boisterous atmosphere. (Yell across the room if you want dessert; that's what everyone else does.) The exceptional **Manka's** at Manka's Inverness Lodge on Argyle St., 415/669-1034, is a destination in its own right. Manka's serves sophisticated American-style dinners Thurs.–Sun. nights, carefully prepared from neighborhood produce, seafood, fish, fowl, livestock, and game.

Marshall, Point Reyes Station, and Olema

Popular in Marshall, along the east side of Tomales Bay north of Point Reyes Station via Hwy. 1, is **Tony's Seafood,** 18863 Hwy. 1, 415/663-1107. The food's quite fresh: they clean the crabs and oysters right out front.

Famous for its Pulitzer Prize–winning newspaper, the not-yet-too-yuppie cow town of Point Reyes Station is also noted for the mooing clock atop the sheriff's substation at Fourth and C. The bovine bellow, a technical creation of Lucasfilm staff, actually emanates—like clockwork, at noon and 6 P.M.—from loudspeakers atop the Old Western Saloon at Second and Main Sts. For "udderly divine" bakery items, from French pastries, bran muffins, and scones to cookies, stop by **Bovine Bakery,** 11315 Hwy. 1 (Main St.), 415/663-9420. The **Station House Cafe,** 11180 Main (at Third St.), 415/663-1515, is the local hot spot, a cheerful country café serving breakfast, lunch, and dinner daily but particularly wonderful for breakfast, especially on foggy or rainy days.

Both a good restaurant and lodging stop, the **Olema Inn,** at Hwy. 1 and Sir Francis Drake Blvd. in Olema, 415/663-9559, is a grandmotherly kind of place serving basic good food and soups as well as California-style cuisine. Open for dinner Fri.–Sat. at 6 P.M. and for lunch and dinner during the summer. For plain ol' American food, head for **Olema Farmhouse,** 10005 Hwy. 1 in Olema, 415/663-1264: good burgers and hefty sandwiches, daily fresh fish specials.

Bolinas

Bolinas is noted for the locals' Bolinas Border Patrol, an unofficial group dedicated to keeping outsiders out by taking down road signs. Once *in* Bolinas, however long that may take you, the gravel beach here is clean and usually uncrowded. The colorfully painted **Bolinas People's Store,** 14 Wharf Rd., 415/868-1433, is a good stop for snacks and picnic fixings. **The Coast Cafe,** 46 Wharf Rd., 415/868-9984, is comfortable and cozy on a foggy or rainy day. (At lunch, try the fish and chips, made with fresh local halibut or salmon.) When you're ready for a casual pint of Anchor Steam, belly up to the bar at **Smiley's Schooner Saloon,** 41 Wharf Rd., 415/868-1311, a classic dive bar that's as local as it gets. Mind your manners and have some fun.

Eastern Marin and Vicinity

Though the marshlands and open areas fringing the northern and eastern portions of San Pablo Bay could almost be included, the San Francisco Bay's northernmost boundary is actually Marin County. More than just the structural anchor for the other side of San Francisco's Golden Gate Bridge, eastern Marin has somehow become the psychological center for "the good life" Californians pursue with such trendsetting abandon. This pursuit costs money, of course, but there's plenty of that in Marin County, which boasts one of the highest per-capita income levels in the nation. Jaguars, Porsches, and more exotic automobiles are among Marin folks' favored means of transport, and BMWs are so common here that the late *San Francisco Chronicle* columnist Herb Caen long referred to them as Boring Marin Wagons. Marin County is also a liberal enclave, with a mere 29 percent registered Republicans—which means it's also the target of political bombast. In 2002, former president George H. W. Bush outraged Marin County residents when he called suspected terrorist John Walker Lindh "a misguided Marin County hot tubber." After protests poured in from irate Marinites, the president issued an apology: "I apologize. I am chastened and will never use the word 'Marin County' and 'hot tub' in the same sentence again."

Jokes about Marin County change, but other things stay the same. The weather here is unusually pleasant, mild in both summer and winter. Also, Marin au naturel is incredibly diverse. From Mill Valley west to the Bolinas Lagoon near Point Reyes, seven different ecological communities are typical: chaparral, grassland, coastal scrub, broadleaf forest, redwood and mixed evergreen forest, salt marsh, and beach strand. Almost one-third of the county is public parkland—national, state, and local.

SEEING AND DOING EASTERN MARIN

Sausalito

Sausalito is a community by land and by sea, a hillside hamlet far surpassed in eccentricity by the highly creative hodgepodge of houseboaters also anchored here. Though, for a time, mysterious midnight throbbings from the deep kept Sausalito's houseboat community awake night after summer night—with some locals even speculating that these nocturnal noises came from a top-secret CIA weapon being tested underwater in Richardson Bay—it eventually turned out that the racket was simply due to romance. Singing toadfish have become to Sausalito what swallows are to Capistrano, migrating into Richardson Bay from the shallows each summer for their annual mating song—comparable, collectively, to the sound of a squadron of low-flying B-17 bombers. People here have adapted to this almost indescribable language of love, and now welcome these bulging-eyed, bubble-lipped lovers back to the bay every year with their **Humming Toadfish Festival,** a celebration conducted by kazoo-playing residents dressed up as sea monsters and clowns. Come over Labor Day weekend for the famed **Sausalito Art Festival,** www.sausali-toartfestival.org.

Aside from the pleasures of just being here—and exploring the nearby **Golden Gate National Recreation Area** (see above)—stop in Sausalito at the U.S. Army Corps of Engineers' **San Francisco Bay Model,** 2100 Bridgeway, 415/332-3870 (recording) or 415/332-3871 (office), a working 1.5-acre facsimile of the Bay and Delta built by the Corps to study currents, tides, salinity, and other natural features. We should all be grateful that the ever-industrious Corps realized it couldn't build a better bay even with access to all the bulldozers, landfill, and riprap in the world and settled, instead, for just making a toy version. Interpretive audio tours are available in English, Russian, German, Japanese, French, and Spanish. Guided group tours (10 or more people) can be arranged by calling 415/332-3871 at least four weeks in advance. Open in summer Tues.–Fri. 9 A.M.–4 P.M., weekends and holidays 10 A.M.–5 P.M.; the rest of the year, Tues.–Sat. 9 A.M.–4 P.M. Free. Get out and sample the bay on various boats and charters, particularly intriguing among them the 18th century–style *Hawaiian Chieftan,* 415/331-3214, www.hawaiianchieftan.com, with lunch sails offered from late April through December, $70 adults, $35 children. Sailing in the same fleet is the brigantine *Irving Johnson.* Saturday "adventure," Sunday brunch, and sunset sails are also offered.

Also in town, among Sausalito's armada of houseboat residents and bayside shops, is **Heath Ceramics Outlet,** 400 Gate 5 Rd., 415/332-3732, open Mon.–Sat. 10 A.M.–5 P.M. and Sun. noon–5 P.M., a wonderful array of seconds and overstocks for fine dishware fans.

Sausalito (or San Francisco, from Crissy Field via the Golden Gate Bridge) is a perfect place to start a serious Bay Area **bike tour.** For a 20-mile trip, head north along the paved bike path (Bay Trail), following the green "bike route" signs along the left arm of Richardson Bay to fairly new Bayfront Park in Mill Valley. Continue north to (busy and narrow) E. Blithedale Ave., and follow it east two miles or so to less-busy Tiburon Boulevard. From that thoroughfare, jog south along the bay on Greenwood Cove Rd., picking up the two-mile Tiburon Bike Path at its end. To make it a complete circle, take a ferry from Tiburon past Angel Island and Alcatraz to Fisherman's Wharf in San Francisco. From here, head back via the Bay Trail, up the grade (fairly steep) to the Golden Gate Bridge and over the bay, then back into Sausalito via the Bridgeway Bike Path.

Easier bike trips from Sausalito include the several-mile trip into Mill Valley, via the bike path past the houseboats and mudflats and marshes to Bayfront Park (picnic tables and benches available). Then backtrack to Miller Ave. and roll into town, right into the midst of a pleas-

ant plaza-style shopping district. To get to Tiburon, from Bayfront Park follow the route described above.

For more information about Sausalito attractions and practicalities, contact: **Sausalito Chamber of Commerce,** 10 Liberty Ship Way, Bay 2, Ste. 250 in Sausalito, 415/331-7262 or 415/332-0505 (visitor information), www.sausalito.org, open weekdays 9 A.M.–5 P.M.

Mill Valley

Mill Valley is another affluent North Bay bedroom community, this one rooted on the eastern slope of Mount Tamalpais. This is the lovely town that fuels so many of the Marin County stereotypes. The big event here every autumn is the **Mill Valley Film Festival,** the biggest little film festival outside Telluride, Colorado, with screenings of local, American independent, international, avante-garde, and various premiere films. For more information about the festival, contact the festival office at 38 Miller Ave., 415/383-5256. For information on other Marin art events, contact the **Marin Arts Council** in San Rafael, 415/499-8350, www.marinarts.org.

Just north of Mill Valley is **Corte Madera,** where a must-do destination for travelers is always the independent **Book Passage** bookstore in the Marketplace shopping center, 51 Tamal Vista Blvd., 415/927-0960, www.bookpassage.com, famous for its travel book section but well-stocked with mysteries, kids' books, fiction, nonfiction, you name it. Book Passage has also become a local destination thanks to its "author event" series, where in any given week you might get to hear talks by T.C. Boyle, Arianna Huffington, and Pico Iyer. There's a café here, too.

Tiburon

Tiburon ("shark" in Spanish), once a ramshackle railroad town, is an affluent bayside community most noted for the Audubon Society's 900-acre **Tiburon Audubon Center and Sanctuary,** 376 Greenwood Beach Rd. (in the Belvedere Cove tidal baylands), 415/388-2524. Wonderful for bird-watching and nature walks, also picnicking (pack out your trash); day-use fee $2. The wooded 24-acre **Tiburon Uplands Nature Pre-**

serve, south of Paradise Beach Park on Paradise Dr., 415/499-6387, includes a natural history loop trail and great bay views from higher ground. Absolutely spectacular for spring wildflowers, though, are the few acres surrounding the 19th-century Gothic church at **Old St. Hilary's Historic Preserve,** 201 Esperanza (at Mar West), 415/435-1853, open to the public Wed. and Sun. 1–4 P.M. Apr.–Oct., otherwise by appointment only. FYI, nearby Belvedere is one of the nation's 10 most expensive outposts of suburbia.

For more information about Tiburon attractions and practicalities, contact: **Tiburon Peninsula Chamber of Commerce,** 96-B Main St. in Tiburon, 415/435-5633, www.tiburonchamber.org.

Nature Preserves

Inland on the Tiburon Peninsula near Corte Madera is the **Ring Mountain Preserve,** another Nature Conservancy success story. A protected tract of native California grasslands around a 600-foot-tall hill known for its unusual serpentine soils and rare endemic plants, geological peculiarities, and Native American petroglyphs, Ring Mountain is known particularly for the rare Tiburon mariposa lilies—they grow nowhere else—that now thrive here, in a population estimated at 32,000 plants. To get to Ring Mountain, take the Paradise Dr. exit from Hwy. 101, then continue east to the preserve's entrance, 1.75 miles down the road. For more information, contact Marin County Open Space, 3501 Civic Center Dr., Room 415 in San Rafael, 415/499-6387. Also in Marin is the **Spindrift Point Preserve** near Sausalito; for more information, call the Nature Conservancy at 415/777-0487.

San Rafael

San Rafael is Marin's biggest little city and the county seat, a Modesto-like community where scenes from George Lucas's *American Graffiti* were shot (on Fourth St., restaurant row). San Rafael is known for its downtown mansion district; for the 1947 replica of the **Mission San Rafael** (second to last in California's mission chain), 1104 Fifth Ave., open daily 11 A.M.–

4 P.M.; and most of all for the **Marin Civic Center** just off Hwy. 101, Frank Lloyd Wright's last major architectural accomplishment. The center, home to the county's administrative complex and quite the tour de force, exemplifies Wright's obsession with the idea that all things are (or should become) circular. Surrounded by 140 acres of lovingly groomed grounds, the county fair is held here on the fourth weekend of every July. The **Marin Civic Center/Marin County Certified Farmers Market,** 800/897-3276, takes place here Thursday and Sunday 8 A.M.–1 P.M., year-round, rain or shine. Docent-led civic center tours are available, but call 415/499-6646 at least several days in advance. The center is wheelchair accessible, open weekdays 8 A.M.–5 P.M. excepting legal holidays.

Another San Rafael attraction is the 11-acre **Guide Dogs for the Blind** campus, 350 Los Ranchitos Rd. (off N. San Pedro Rd.), 415/499-4000, where German shepherds, labradors, and golden retrievers are trained to "see" for their human companions. Monthly "graduations," which include tours and demonstrations of guide dog selective obedience work, are open to the public. Altogether it's a moving experience, especially when the 4-H children who raised these dogs to their pretraining age of 15 or 16 months show up to say goodbye, as the graduates depart with their new owners.

For more information about the area, contact the **San Rafael Chamber of Commerce,** 817 Mission Ave. in San Rafael, 415/454-4163, www.sanrafael.org, open weekdays 9 A.M.–5 P.M.

Nearby Greenbrae is neighbor to **San Quentin State Prison,** home since the mid-1800s to sociopaths and other criminals, though more than 100 union members and organizers of the Industrial Workers of the World were also imprisoned here after World War I. San Quentin's disciplinary dungeons were closed in 1935. The new museum here and the Boot Hill prison cemetery—posthumous home now to a veritable Who's Who of Very Bad Guys—are open for (very popular) public visits.

Stop by the prison gift shop at San Quentin's entrance for inmate-made arts and crafts—from San Quentin T-shirts and hats to belt buckles,

SUSAN SNYDER

Mission San Rafael is the second to the last in California's mission chain.

rings and other jewelry, artwork, and novelties. Head on through the entrance to visit the **California State Prison Museum,** housing artifacts, memorabilia, historical photographs, and records documenting the prison's history. For hours and information on both, call 415/454-1460.

China Camp State Park

After the gold rush, many of California's Chinese turned to fishing as a way to make ends meet. Chinese fishing camps were common all along the northstate's coast, and 30 or more flourished on the more remote edges of San Francisco Bay. The Chinese were quite successful at plying their trade in the state's waters—so successful that by the 1900s enforcement of anti-Chinese, anti-bag netting fishing laws essentially killed these Asian communities. Partially restored China Camp, once the Bay Area's largest Chinese shrimp center, is the last of these old fishing villages. The community, where John Wayne's *Blood Alley* was filmed, survives now as a memory complete with history museum, renovated buildings, and rebuilt rickety piers. The only actual survivor is **Frank Quan's bait and sandwich shop,** which serves up fresh bay shrimp when avail-

able (put in your order early, especially on weekends). The park's 1,600 acres of oak forest, grasslands, and salt marshes also offer hiking, picnicking, and walk-in developed family campsites (carry in your equipment and supplies), $12–15 per night. Hiker-biker campsites also available. Reserve through ReserveAmerica, 800/444-7275 or www.reserveamerica.com.

Hiking trails at China Camp include the Shoreline Trail, which starts near the historic district and heads across Point San Pedro Rd., then forks—the left path leading to a view, the right path onward to the northwest, through the grasslands and chaparral. Good views all the way. Backtrack and you've walked an easy four miles. Or, from the entrance to Back Ranch Meadows Campground outside the park, take the Bayview Trail and climb up a ravine to an access road, returning by the Back Ranch Meadows Trail, more than three miles altogether.

China Camp State Park is open daily, 8 A.M.–sunset; day-use fee is $4. The museum is open daily 10 A.M.–5 P.M. year-round. To get here, take the San Pedro Rd. exit from Hwy. 101 and continue for several miles past the Marin Civic Center. For more information, contact: China Camp State Park in San Rafael, 415/456-0766.

Novato

Two museums in Novato are worth a stop: **Novato History Museum,** 815 De Long Ave., 415/897-4320, a monument to the town's pioneer past, open Wed.–Thurs. and Sat. noon–4 P.M. (free), and **Marin Museum of the American Indian** and park at 2200 Novato Blvd., 415/897-4064, www.marinindian.com, a small but fascinating place with friendly staff and hands-on exhibits and other displays about Coast Miwok, Pomo, and other cultures. Open Tues.–Fri. 10 A.M.–3 P.M., Sat.–Sun. noon–4 P.M., closed Monday. Admission $5 adults, children under 12 free.

Just north of Novato is **Olompali State Historic Park,** 415/892-3383, a 700-acre ranch with broad historic significance. At one time it was a major Miwok trading village, a fact archaeological finds have verified. Sir Francis Drake and his men may have passed through, since a silver sixpence circa 1567 was discovered here. A Bear Flag Revolt skirmish occurred at the Olompali Adobe in the mid-1800s. Olompali's tenure as a ranch is obvious, given the weathered barns and the Victorian home of the onetime ranch manager. Restoration and park development are still under way, but the public is welcome to stop for a picnic and a hike to the top of Burdell Mountain, offering some good views of San Pablo Bay. Olompali is open daily 10 A.M.–5 P.M. Day-use fee: $2. To learn more about Olompali's fantastic history, pick up a copy of **_Olompali in the Beginning_** by June Gardener. Getting here is easy from the north; from Hwy. 101, just take the marked exit (north of Novato proper). From the south via Hwy. 101, exit at San Antonio Rd. and head west, then backtrack to the park on Hwy. 101.

Angel Island State Park

Still sometimes called the "Ellis Island of the West," at the turn of the century Angel Island was the door through which Asian immigrants passed on their way to America. Japanese and other "enemy aliens" were imprisoned here during World War II, when the island's facilities served as a detention center. Explore the West Garrison

Civil War barracks and buildings at the 1863 site of Camp Reynolds—built and occupied by Union troops determined to foil the Confederacy's plans to invade the bay and then the gold country. Among the buildings, the largest surviving collection of Civil War structures in the nation, note the cannons still aimed to sea (but never used in the war because Confederate troops never showed up). On weekends, volunteers in the park's living history program—with the help of apparently willing visitors—fire off the cannons, just in case the South rises again.

Though most visitors never get past the sun and sand at Ayala Cove (where spring through fall the Cove Cafe offers lunch, coffee, and beer), also worth a stop are the 1899 Chinese Immigration Center, quarantine central for new Asian arrivals, and World War II-era Fort McDowell on the island's east side near the Civil War battlements. Often sunny in summer when the rest of the Bay Area is shivering in the fog, outdoorsy types consider Angel Island's hiking trails its chief attraction. (The eucalyptus trees being felled on Angel Island are nonnatives first planted in the 1860s and now being removed so natural vegetation can be reintroduced.) On a clear day, the view from the top of Angel Island's Mount Livermore is spectacular—with three bridges and almost the entire Bay Area seemingly within reach.

Park day use is $4. Maps are available in peak season, $1. Hiking and biking are popular; bring your own bike and helmet or, at least in peak season, rent them at Ayala Cove. Motorized island tram tours are offered daily April through October, on weekends only in March and November; call for details. Tours of Angel Island's historic sites are offered on weekends in peak season, and can be arranged for other times. For unbeatable scenery (and sometimes brisk winds), try a simple picnic atop Mount Livermore. Picnic sites are scattered elsewhere, and group sites (fee) are also available. There's even a reservable baseball diamond, at Fort McDowell. The intrepid can camp on Angel Island, which features nine hike-in environmental campsites, $7–10. For reservations contact ReserveAmerica, 800/444-7275, www.reserveamerica.com. (Campstove or charcoal cooking

Angel Island used to be known as the Ellis Island of the West.

© ROBERT HOLMES/CALTOUR

only—no fires.) If you're coming, pack light, since you'll have to manage the load on the ferry and pack it all into camp, up to a two-mike hike.

The **Tiburon–Angel Island State Park Ferry,** berthed at the pier on Main St. in Tiburon, 415/435-2131, is available to island-bound hikers, bikers, and backpackers daily during summer (and often into autumn, weather permitting), but only on weekends during the rest of the year. The **Blue and Gold Fleet,** 415/773-1188, offers Angel Island runs from San Francisco's Pier 41. Blue and Gold also offers "Island Hop" Angel Island and Alcatraz tours, departing from San Francisco. You can also get here on the **Alameda-Oakland Ferry,** 415/705-5555, and the **Vallejo Baylink Ferry,** 707/643-3779. To find all regional ferry schedules and fares online, see the regional transit website: www.511.org. **Sea Trek,** 415/488-1000, offers kayak tours. For current information on tram tours, call 415/897-0715.

For more park information, contact the **Angel Island Association,** 415/435-3522, www.angelisland.org, **Angel Island State Park headquarters** in Tiburon, 415/435-1915; and the **park ranger station,** 415/435-5390.

RECREATION
Tours

In addition to the North Bay's astounding coastal access opportunities, particularly in western Marin County, there are also many ways to enjoy San Francisco Bay. In San Francisco, both **Blue and Gold Fleet,** 415/773-1188, and **Red and White Fleet,** 415/673-2900, offer bay ferry tours. Or design your own tours using the bay's ferry system. Blue and Gold's San Francisco–based ferries offer regular commuter service connecting Fisherman's Wharf and PacBell Park to Sausalito, Tiburon, Vallejo, Angel Island, and Alcatraz. The Golden Gate Bridge District's fun triple-decker **Golden Gate Ferries,** 415/923-2000, come complete with indoor and outdoor seating and full bars, and connect the San Francisco's historic Ferry Building with both Larkspur and Sausalito, with departures about once each hour on weekdays (early morning through evening), less frequently on weekends. Golden Gate ferries feature special events, including the popular roundtrip "Lunch for the Office Bunch" mid-day runs from San Francisco to Sausalito and back with live lunchtime jazz or rhythm and blues, on selected Fridays from early June through early October. Other "tourable" ferries include the **Alameda-Oakland Ferry,** 415/705-5555, and the **Vallejo Baylink Ferry,** 707/643-3779. For all current regional ferry schedules and fares, see the regional transit website: www.511.org.

For very special sightseeing beyond San Francisco Bay, a responsible nonprofit organization offering guided whale-watching boat tours and other nautical expeditions is the **Oceanic Society** based at Fort Mason in San Francisco, 415/474-3385, www.oceanic-society.org, with local whale-watching trips and Farallon Islands tours. Advance reservations are required. The organization considers these tours part of their public education work on behalf of whales, and some trips support ongoing whale research. Whale-watching boats leave from either Half Moon Bay (three-hour trip) or San Francisco (six and a half hours) and head out to the migration paths near the Farallon Islands.

Water Sports

Weather and wave conditions permitting, dedicated kayakers, rowers, sailors, whaleboaters, and windsurfers are as at home on the bay as the ferries and big ships. **Sea Trek** in Sausalito at Schoonmaker Point, 415/488-1000 or 415/332-4465, www.seatrekkayak.com, is a big-league kayaking center offering something for everyone: classes for all skill levels (beginners' classes, two-hour classes to improve basic skills, day-long "Open Bay" classes and family instruction also available), kayak rentals, guided day trips, and overnight camping excursions. **Open Water Rowing Center,** 85 Liberty Ship Way in Sausalito near Sea Trek, 415/332-1091, www.owrc.com, requires equipment renters to have previous experience or certification, or to take their two-hour beginners' or intermediate class before setting out for serious adventures to Tiburon, Angel Island, Alcatraz, or out through the Golden Gate.

Quite special is **Environmental Traveling Companions** in San Francisco, 415/474-7662, www.ectrips.org, with its kayaking program (and other outings) for the physically disabled, including overnight kayak-camping on Angel Island. To rent sailboards for windsurfing, head for Sausalito. A variety of companies rent sailboards and offer lessons.

STAYING IN EASTERN MARIN

Best bet for budget travelers in eastern Marin County is the **HI-USA Marin Headlands Hostel,** in Bldg. 941 at Fort Barry, 415/331-2777 or 800/909-4776 #168, www.norcalhostels.org—definitely urban enough (just five minutes from the Golden Gate Bridge) but also remote, 103 beds in early-20th-century buildings at a park-like abandoned fort complex. Basic dorm-style accommodations with hot showers preedominate, but family rooms are available by advance reservation. Facilities also include a great kitchen, dining room, common room with fireplace, even laundry facilities, game room, tennis court, and bike storage. Quite popular in summer and on good-weather weekends, so reservations advised; $18 per person for a dorm bed, extra fee for linen rental (or bring a sleeping bag). To get here: if coming from San Francisco, take the Alexander Ave. exit just north of the Golden Gate Bridge (southbound, take the second Sausalito exit) then follow the signs into GGNRA and on to the hostel.

A former Sausalito fort will offer considerably more luxurious accommodations one day soon, when the Golden Gate National Recreation Area unveils its conversion of Fort Baker officers quarters into a 156-room retreat and conference center. Stay tuned.

The Spanish-style **Hotel Sausalito,** 16 El Portal (at Bridgeway), 415/332-0700 or 888/442-0700, www.hotelsausalito.com, offers 16 Victorian-style rooms and continental breakfast. Room rates $150–250, suites $250 and up. Practically next door and right on the water is the **Inn Above Tide,** 30 El Portal, 415/332-9535 or 800/893-8433, www.innabovetide.com, a luxurious boutique hotel with just 30 rooms. Great views of the city and bay. Rooms and suites $250 and up. Another possibility is Sausalito's mythic **Casa Madrona,** 801 Bridgeway Blvd., 415/332-0502 or 888/367-7625, website: casamadrona .rockresorts.com, both its historic (vintage 1885) and modern sections built into the hillside and connected by quaint pathways. Newer rooms are plusher, generally speaking, but all are unique and inviting; some have spectacular views of the bay and some have fireplaces. The cottages are the epitome of privacy. Buffet breakfast. Rooms and suites are $250 and up, though specials can be dramatic. Perched on the hillside above town is another Sausalito charmer, the Bay Area's beloved **Alta Mira Hotel,** 125 Bulkley Ave., 415/332-1350, 30 rooms with a view in a magnificent Spanish-Colonial inn, also separate cottages. Rates $100–150.

Other more urban North Bay accommodations include the fun and funky 1910 Victorian **Panama Hotel,** 4 Bayview St. in San Rafael, 415/457-3993 or toll free 800/899-3993, www.panamahotel.com, with bed-and-breakfast-style rooms with ($100–150) or without private baths ($50–100), continental breakfast. Suites and bungalow are $150–250. Also in San Rafael: **San Rafael Inn** motel at 865 Francisco Blvd. E, 415/454-9470 (under $100); **Four Points by Sheraton,** 1010 Northgate Dr., 415/479-8800, www.starwood.com ($100–150); and **Embassy Suites,** 101 McInnis Pkwy. (near the Civic Center), 415/499-9222 or 800/362-2779, www.embassysuites.com ($150–250).

EATING IN EASTERN MARIN

San Rafael is a good place to start your culinary explorations. At the Civic Center in San Rafael is the **Marin County Certified Farmers Market** at the Civic Center, Hwy. 101 and San Pedro, 800/897-3276, held year-round on Thurs. and Sun. 8 A.M.–1 P.M. The **Rice Table,** 1617 Fourth St., 415/456-1808, serves a 14-dish traditional Indonesian *risttafel*—appetizers, main dishes, and *pisang goreng* (banana fritters) for dessert—for about $17 per person (two-person minimum); a smaller five-course feast, separate entrées, and vegetarian fare (call ahead for details) are also available. Open Wed.–Sun. for dinner. The long-time local standard for Thai food is **The Thai House,** 534 Fourth St., 415/454-2626, open Mon.–Sat. for lunch and dinner, though **Royal Thai,** 610 Third St., 415/485-1074, also gets raves. For Chinese, you can't go wrong at **China Dynasty,** 1335 Fourth St., 415/457-3288.

Still in San Rafael, for very good Afghani fare, try **Bamyan Afghan Cuisine,** 227 Third St., 415/453-8809, open for lunch weekdays, for dinner nightly. For the real thing, Mexican-style, head to the superb **Las Camelias,** 912 Lincoln Ave. (between Third and Fourth Streets), 415/453-5850. Also in San Rafael, locals swear by the **Seafood Peddler & Oyster Bar,** 100 Yacht Club Dr., 415/460-6669, which serves exceptional fresh fish—from East and West Coasts. Outdoor and waterfront dining with a boat dock. And some say **Il Davide,** 901 A St., 415/454-8080, has the best Italian food in the county. Don't miss the outrageous tiramisu.

In San Anselmo, Mediterranean cuisine extraordinaire is the specialty of **Insalata's,** 120 Sir Francis Drake, 415/457-7700, considered one of the North Bay's best restaurants. Look for such delectables as couscous, braised lamb shank, and an assortment of tapas. Open for lunch and dinner daily. For outstanding New American cuisine in Fairfax near San Anselmo, try **Ross Valley Brewing Company,** 765 Center Blvd., 415/485-1005, a brewery and restaurant voted one of the Top 50 Restaurants in the Bay Area by the *San Francisco Chronicle* Magazine. Menu highlights include organic Bloomsdale spinach salad, herb-roasted Sonoma chicken, and a half-pound Black Angus burger. Their beers are good, too, especially the Belgian-style St. Marks Ale.

Truly unique in Larkspur and all the rage in the Bay Area these days is **Roxanne's,** 320 Magnolia Ave. (at King), 415/924-5004. Raw food—exceptionally prepared and appealing—is the deal here. Roxanne's mission is "serving the community at the intersection of sensual flavors, healthy lifestyle, and sustainability." The restaurant's "living foods" cuisine avoids all grains, cheeses, and meat products; ingredients are organic and exceedingly fresh. In cooking, nothing is heated to a temperature above 118 degrees, since the belief here is that anything higher destroys essential enzymes. What you do get—pad thai made with coconut noodles, say, or lasagna terrine—is surprisingly tasty, and served forth in an environmentally friendly atmosphere, right down to the unbleached organic cotton tablecloths. Organic wine list. Fixed-price menu (expensive).

In a beautiful Victorian north of Corte Madera in Larkspur, the **Lark Creek Inn,** 234 Magnolia Ave., 415/924-7766, is considered one of the state's best restaurants, with hearty Americana like Yankee pot roast as well as California continental-style mixed grill, seafood, and other specialties. For more casual fare, consider the **Marin Brewing Company,** 1809 Larkspur Landing Circle, 415/461-4677, beloved for its microbrewery ales as well as its pizzas, calzones, and salads. Live music on weekends. Farther north, in Kentfield, the place for breakfast or lunch is the **Half Day Cafe,** 848 College Ave. (across from the college), 415/459-0291, serving omelettes, good sandwiches, and just about everything else. Open daily.

In Mill Valley, the **Cactus Cafe,** 393 Miller Ave., 415/388-8226, is a locally loved hole-in-the-wall serving inexpensive Mexican food—the real thing, quite good. **Jennie Low's Chinese Cuisine,** 38 Miller, 415/388-8868, serves a decent lunch beginning at 11:30 A.M., also open for dinner.

Still big news in Mill Valley these days is the refurbished and revitalized **Buckeye Roadhouse,** 15 Shoreline Hwy. (at the Stinson Beach-Mill Valley exit from Hwy. 101), 415/331-2600, brought to you by the folks behind the Fog City Diner and Mustard's. The roadhouse is part of a very hip social scene (especially in the bar), with contemporary and quite good American fare served up in the cavernous dining room of this hybrid diner/hunting lodge. Try Sunday brunch, lunch Mon.–Sat., or dinner any night.

Mill Valley's **Da Angelo Restaurant,** 22 Miller Ave., 415/388-2000, is up there among the Bay Area's best authentic Italian restaurants, serving excellent food—like linguine with fresh mussels in marinara sauce, homemade tortellini in chicken broth, and meat specialties including carpaccio—for reasonable prices.

Fred's Place, 1917 Bridgeway in Sausalito, 415/332-4575, is a surprising local institution, a no-frills coffee shop where 500 or more people compete all day for Fred's 30 seats. Serving unpretentious food à la American grill—with an excellent Monterey Jack omelette and other standards plus Polish sausage and bratwurst, fresh-squeezed orange juice—Fred's is the place, for millionaires and houseboaters alike. People even wait outside in the rain to get in. Open only for breakfast and lunch, weekdays 6:30 A.M.–2:30 P.M., weekends 7 A.M.–3 P.M., no checks or credit cards.

But the **Casa Madrona Hotel** restaurant, 801 Bridgeway in Sausalito, 415/331-5888, offers the best food around for dinner Friday, Saturday, and Sunday, Marin-style California cuisine using only the freshest available ingredients. For fine fare away from the tourist throngs, try tiny **Sushi Ran,** 107 Caledonia St., Sausalito, 415/332-3620. For great views, alfresco dining, and a full menu of margaritas, consider popular **Margaritaville,** 1200 Bridgeway, 415/331-3226, offering casual atmosphere and great California-style Mexican food daily for lunch and dinner (if you like it hot, try the exquisite Camarones à la Diabla). Other popular Sausalito restaurants include the **Spinnaker,** 100 Spinnaker, 415/332-1500, and **Horizons,** 558 Bridgeway, 415/331-3232—both upscale, on-the-water places specializing in great seafood.

In Tiburon, **Sam's Anchor Cafe,** 27 Main St., 415/435-4527, is the traditional bayside eatery and bar scene for yachting types, open daily for breakfast, lunch, and dinner. Tiburon has an almost endless string of moderate to expensive bayside restaurants stretched out along Main. Nothing beats **Guaymas,** 5 Main St., 415/435-6300, with upscale and imaginative Mexican food, but you can try **Servino Ristorante Italiano,** 114 Main, 415/435-2676, serving decent pastas and fresh fish specials.

Wine Country

California wine is big business. California's vineyards occupy more than 500,000 acres of land, and in 2002 produced 463 million gallons of wine—about 95 percent of the total wine production in the U.S. The annual impact of the wine industry on the state's economy is estimated to be $14 billion. According to the Wine Institute, if viewed as a separate country California would be the world's fourth largest wine producer, after France, Italy, and Spain.

The inland valleys of Napa, Sonoma, Mendocino, and Lake Counties have become known as California's wine country—this despite the fact that a fairly small percentage of California wines are produced in this region. Quality, not quantity, is the point here, an area home to some of the state's (and the world's) finest small wineries.

Yet California's small-is-beautiful wine country secret has definitely been shared. More than five million visitors each year squeeze through the Napa Valley alone. On summer weekends (on weekends generally) and during the "crush," or the September and October harvest, wine tasting traffic is bumper-to-bumper. The foothills and valleys, cooled by north coastal weather patterns yet usually fog-free, snap to life with lush greenery in spring when the vines and foothill trees leaf out. By late fall, most of the summer's tourists have evaporated, though the sweet harvest heat still hangs in the air and the vineyards flame with autumn colors. This is the best time to come, particularly on weekdays. Whenever you arrive, stick to back-road

ballooning over the Napa Valley

routes (and destinations) whenever possible to avoid the worst of the wine-country crush.

FIRST AND LASTING IMPRESSIONS

For many, a first-time trip to the wine country is overwhelming. Particularly in the Napa Valley, the first impression is one of pleasure-seeking pretension: too few people have too much money and all arrive at the same place (at almost the same time) to spend it on themselves. Others just come to watch, satisfied to partake vicariously of the region's various indulgences. Yet these first impressions aren't lasting. California's wine country is actually dedicated, consciously and otherwise, to an appreciation of the appetites—and to an understanding of how we human beings go about satisfying them.

"Bottled Poetry" and other Appreciations

Writer Robert Louis Stevenson hinted at modern wine-country trends in his *Silverado Squatters* when he described the 19th-century Schramsberg wines as "bottled poetry." Closer to the modern-day mark, though, is Sonoma Valley resident M.F.K. Fisher, food writer extraordinaire, who died in June 1992. Fisher was America's finest prose writer according to W.H. Auden, and "poet of the appetites" to John Updike. More than anyone else, Mary Frances Kennedy Fisher is responsible (in America) for newly nonpuritanical and unaffected attitudes about the pure pleasures of good regional foods and wines. That she settled in California's wine country is no accident.

Indulgence and Overindulgence

Notably, but not exclusively, American is the blurred line between indulgence and overindulgence, particularly as applied to alcohol and other mood-altering drugs. When the appearance of pleasure is actually a self-administered remedy of "spirits" to alleviate personal spiritual pain, addiction shows up, the shadow side of the pleasure principle. Alcohol abuse and alcoholism aren't more prevalent in the wine country than

elsewhere in California, but the opportunities for their more open expression are almost endless.

Perhaps it's also no coincidence that the phenomenally successful adventure novelist Jack London, whose alcohol-related death at age 40 shocked the world, lived here with his second wife, Charmian, for many otherwise charmed (if compulsive) years on their Glen Ellen ranch north of Sonoma. He lived by following the boldly defiant creed:

I would rather be ashes than dust! I would rather that my spark should burn out in a brilliant blaze than it should be stifled by dry rot. I would rather be a superb meteor, every atom of me in magnificent glow, than a sleepy and permanent planet. The proper function of man is to live, not to exist. I shall not waste my days trying to prolong them. I shall use my time.

London also died by his personal creed. A noted barroom orator and people's philosopher who wrote of his struggles with alcohol, he died officially of gastrointestinal uremic poisoning in 1916. Whether his death was actually due to a morphine overdose is still disputed by his biographers.

BRIEF HISTORY OF WINE

The Golden State has a venerable winemaking history. Franciscan missionary Father Junípero Serra planted the first known vineyard in San Diego in 1769, and viticulture soon spread throughout California, with the establishment of successive Spanish missions to the north along the coast. The state's first wines were produced for sacramental and daily table use. In the early 1800s pioneering winemakers established new vineyards, from European cuttings, in Los Angeles and Orange County.

After the California gold rush began in 1849, immigration and settlement boomed in Northern California and winemaking became a growing northstate industry—soon a much improved one, thanks to Count Agoston Haraszty, who brought cuttings back to California on his frequent trips to Europe. Shortly after the completion of the transcontinental railroad in 1869,

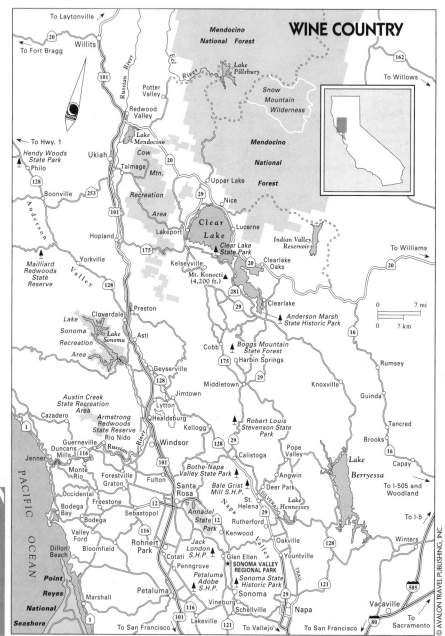

WINE COUNTRY

THE GROWLING OF THE BEAR FLAG REPUBLIC

Mexican fears of Russian territorial incursions weren't put to rest by the 1823 establishment of California's last missionary outpost, Mission San Francisco Solano de Sonoma, in what was then Mexico's far northern territory. So General Mariano Vallejo was sent to Sonoma to found a frontier pueblo for Alta California. Due to hostilities with Native American populations, Vallejo failed to establish colonies at both Santa Rosa and Petaluma. His third try, the town of Sonoma, was laid out near the mission in 1835. Troops rode out to subdue northern natives on many occasions, but General Vallejo further secured the town through his alliance and friendship with the chief of the Suisun, baptized "Solano."

Peace reigned until June 14, 1846, when a scruffy band of armed gringos rode into town and took over. Taking orders from Captain (later General) John C. Frémont, these Yankee trappers had camped out near Marysville on a "scientific expedition" while awaiting the opportunity to conquer California (or at least acquire some large tracts of land). Fearing expulsion by Mexican authorities, the ragtag revolutionaries decided to launch their own war for acquisition and independence, unaware that the U.S. had already declared war against Mexico in May.

There was no battle. Frémont and his freedom fighters met with Vallejo, who peacefully surrendered after offering the Americans some wine. The whole town surrendered, seemingly amused. To justify their theft of the township with a greater purpose, the Americans declared California a new republic, and quickly fashioned an appropriate banner and ran it up the flagpole in the plaza. (Almost no one saluted.) The banner of the Bear Flag Republic flew over Sonoma for just a few weeks, though, before U.S. Navy Commodore John Sloat sailed into Monterey Bay and on July 9 raised the American flag over the Alta California capital, ending Frémont's dream of an independent western republic.

As for Vallejo, after two months' imprisonment at Sutter's Fort, he went on to become the district's first state senator, and later Sonoma's mayor. Though Vallejo owned more than 175,000 acres of California lands at one time, his holdings shrank to a mere five acres by the time he died in 1890. But he wasn't bitter, despite the wild swings in his fate and fortune. "I had my day," he said, "and it was a proud one."

California wines were on their way to connoisseurs in the eastern U.S. and Europe—and on their way to international recognition. That recognition arrived generously, in 1890, when more than half the California wines entered in the Paris Exhibition won gold medals.

California's winemaking success soon faltered, however, due to vineyard infestations of phylloxera and, in 1919, Prohibition, which banned the production and sales of alcohol. Following the repeal of Prohibition in 1933, California's winemaking industry began to rebuild.

Almost an Overnight Sensation

Local winemaking got its local start in Sonoma, where Franciscan fathers planted the first grapes; their bottled efforts were fairly foul, by most accounts. The locally recognized Hungarian "father of the wine industry," Agoston Haraszthy, soon followed suit, planting European varieties at his Buena Vista Winery. Samuele Sebastiani started what became a family empire nearby. In Napa Valley, one of the first California areas settled by American farmers, early settlers planted grapevines taken as cuttings from mission vineyards at Sonoma and San Rafael. Charles Krug was the region's wine pioneer: Riesling grapes were introduced in 1861, the start of the flourishing, sophisticated local viticulture that has made Napa Valley the spiritual center of the country's growing wine industry.

Since the 1970s, wineries in Napa, Sonoma, and Mendocino Counties have gained almost overnight renown—largely due to the world's surprise in 1976 when Stags' Leap Winery's finest beat Mouton Rothschild in a Paris competition.

WINE COUNTRY

California wines had definitely arrived by 1985, when Quail Ridge Vineyard's 1981 chardonnay was served to Prince Charles and Lady Di at a White House banquet. As international wine awards have become almost commonplace vineyard acreage has expanded, with grapevines climbing higher into hillside oak woodlands.

With California's wine renaissance well underway, even Californians focused first on the small, innovative wineries of Napa and Sonoma Counties. Yet California's wine country now extends throughout various "appellations of origin." Of the 124 U.S. regions officially recognized as distinct American Viticultural Areas (AVAs) by the regulatory U.S. Bureau of Alcohol, Tobacco and Firearms, 70 of these are in California. California wines now regularly dominate *Wine Spectator* magazine's list of the world's top10 wines. In 2002, for example, four Napa-Sonoma wines made the list—all cabernet sauvignons, from Chateau St. Jean, Duckhorn, Pine Ridge, and Whitehall Lane wineries—as compared to three wines each from France and Italy.

Trouble in Vintners' Paradise

Life in even the Napa-Sonoma-Mendocino wine country hasn't been one long harvest festival, however. Recent troubles have included plague and pestilence, first in the form of the root louse phylloxera, which has forced growers to replant thousands of acres of prime vineyards in the past 15 years, followed by unwelcome appearances of the glassy-winged sharpshooter—the wine industry's biggest pest—spreading the fatal vine malady known as Pierce's disease, which has ravaged swaths of vineyards ever since it brought all Southern California wine grape growing to a halt in 1883, and more recently devastated grape growers in the late 1990s.

Environmentalists might point to ecological principles to explain increasing vineyard disease; so many acres planted to any single crop, or monoculture, generally leads to ecosystem imbalance and increased vulnerabilities. But environmentalists are too busy protesting the increase in vineyard acreage, period—particularly the intrusion of vineyards and wineries onto area hillsides and into native oak woodlands. Vineyard opponents worry about soil erosion, pesticides, water pollution, and wildlife habitat destruction. Some vineyardists say they must plant grapes on the hillsides, since there's nowhere else for new

WINE COUNTRY BOAT CRUISES

You can't actually *do* Napa Valley and Sonoma wineries by cruise ship, of course—but you can get there by boat from San Francisco, certainly a memorable way to launch a wine country group adventure. The 102-passenger *Spirit of Endeavour* offers two fall and spring small-ship cruises from San Francisco, the four-day/three-night **Culture of the Vine Cruise** and the five-day/four-night **Behind the Scenes Cruise.** The four-day trip departs from San Francisco, spends the next two days sightseeing and wine tasting in the Napa Valley, Sonoma Valley, and Carneros before the return trip to San Francisco. The five-day trip includes the same basic itinerary with an additional mid-trip excursion back to San Francisco and Sausalito for sightseeing and an overnight stay. Wineries visited each year change, but tend to include those not typically open for drop-in tastings and tours.

Four-day cruises start at $699–799 per person, double occupancy, and five-day cruises start at $1,050 per person, but more generous staterooms—with double beds, sofa, TV/VCR, and in-room refrigerator—and suites cost considerably more. For current details or to book a trip, call **Cruise West** in Seattle at 800/580-0072, www.cruisewest.com.

Or consider **American Safari Cruises,** 888/862-8881, www.amsafari.com, luxurious *Safari Quest* cruises the Petaluma and Napa Rivers in search of good times and fine wine at smaller, boutique wineries. The cruise ship can only get you to the general neighborhood of the Napa Valley, Carneros, and Sonoma Valley wineries, of course; tours, tastings, and special winemaker events require van transportation.

plantings to go, but others say hillside vineyards will never be profitable, considering the exhorbitant costs involved.

Some residents—including James Conaway, in *The Far Side of Eden: New Money, Old Land, and the Battle for Napa Valley*—argue that conspicuous wealth and new residents' desires to build an ostentatious "in-your-face mansion and an in-nature's-face vineyard" threaten to turn California's wine country into a spectacle.

Perhaps the spectacle will be self-limiting. Recent economic challenges, at least in some quarters, suggest that the party's over, or at least slowing down. The critical and financial success showered upon California's upmarket winemakers in the 1970s and 1980s encouraged many others to get into the game. By 2003 there were 500,000 acres of California vineyards—more than double the acreage of just 10 years earlier—and quality wine grape prices were plummeting, due to oversupply, at the same time demand for fine wines was also heading south. Very good California grapes were finding their way into very good, very cheap wines, like the now infamous "Two Buck Chuck" produced by Charles Shaw—so consumers got a price break while the fortunes of many growers and winemakers declined. Bankruptcies as well as forced winery sales and relentless corporate consolidations are thinning the ranks.

CONSCIOUS WINE-TASTING

Though there *are* other things to do, tasting superior wines—and finding out how they're made—is where the action is for most wine country visitors. In preparation for wine tasting, *don't* feel obliged to memorize lines like "rich, bold, unassuming," "light but perspicacious," and "flushed with heroic tonalities." Despite first impressions, pretense is passé; an honest personal response is all that's required. (To get up to speed on the sensory awareness skills and wine knowledge necessary for informed appreciation, buy a copy of Dr. Marian Baldy's *The University Wine Course,* an excellent self-tutorial available through the Wine Appreciation Guild in San Francisco, 800/231-9463, www.wineappreciation.com.) Courtesy, however, is never out of style. Since the wine-country crush has become overwhelming, most wineries now charge a tasting fee (sometimes only for premium varietals) or offer wine tasting only after tours. And because still too many people come, some wineries also require advance reservations even for tasting. Keep in mind, too, that small, independent wineries are often family operations: tasting rooms and tours tend to shut down when everyone's out in the fields or busy in the wineries. So, always call before going.

For the sake of lasting wine art appreciation, beginners should start at the established larger wineries—many give excellent educational and informational tours—before venturing into the small winery avant-garde. Focus on one variety of wine or wine grape while tasting, or start with a white, proceed on to a rosé or red wine, then finish with a dessert wine. Do ask questions whenever possible, particularly at smaller wineries where hands-on experience *creates* the experience. People here love what they do and (generally) like to talk about it.

While wine tasting, be selective about stops—plan your destinations in advance, and try to visit only a handful of wineries each day—and, if traveling by car, choose a nondrinking designated driver in advance. Tasting rooms are dangerously close together as you head north on Hwy. 29 through the Napa Valley, so the unwary can easily be seeing double before getting as far as St. Helena. A popular way to explore the valley is by bus-the Yountville Shuttle and St. Helena Shuttle operate between wineries and restaurants in upvalley towns while several companies, including **California Wine Tours,** 800/294-6386, www.californiawinetours.com, will do the driving-on chartered winery tours. Drunk driving is not only dangerous, it's illegal—a serious offense in California.

Napa and Vicinity

A cozy 35 miles long and framed by rounded rolling hills, the Napa Valley is the nation's most famous vineyard and winery region. Though the town of Napa is more prosaic than Sonoma, the valley itself has seasonally changing charm, hill-hugging vineyards, world-renowned wineries, and famous spas—experiences available even to budget travelers, though even the middle class is increasingly challenged to afford a Napa Valley visit. Disappointed refugees from the California gold fields helped build the city of Napa, working in lumber mills, orchards, and on cattle ranches. Napa in the 1850s was already a rowdy town of hotels, saloons, and money. But the "silver rush" of the late 1870s brought more of all these, plus mine shafts throughout the county. The hottest currency nowadays? Wine and rumors of wine, tourists and rumors of tourists.

For more information on California wines and winemaking, contact the **Wine Institute of California,** 425 Market St., Ste. 1000 in San Francisco, 415/512-0151, www.wineinstitute.org. For information about the Napa Valley appellation and its wines and wineries, contact the **Napa Valley Vintners Association,** 707/942-9775 or 800/358-5476, www.napavintners.com. Information on attractions and practical details concerning the entire Napa Valley is available from the **Napa Valley Conference and Visitors Bureau,** 1310 Napa Town Center in Napa, 707/226-7459, www.napavalley.com. For information about Napa and the immediate vicinity, contact the **Napa Chamber of Commerce,** 1556 First St., 707/226-7455, www.napachamber.org, open weekdays 8:30 A.M.–5 P.M., which offers free maps, information on wineries and other places of interest, suggested bike routes and picnic stops, and current brochures on lodging, restaurants, and recreation. Be sure to pick up a copy of the **"Napa Yolano" Harvest Trails** guide to Napa, Yolo, and Solano County u-pick farms, ranches, and other rural attractions—Napa's answer to Sonoma County Farm Trails. Also ask about the free historic **Downtown Napa Trolley,** which visitors can use going to and from down-town B&Bs and shops, restaurants, and Copia. The *Napa Valley Guide,* usually available here, features good regional information. The free, widely available *Wine Country This Week* is a good winery information source, as is *The Vine* magazine, another free publication.

SEEING AND DOING NAPA

Most Napa wineries aren't *in* Napa but are farther north, scattered among smaller, more picturesque Napa Valley towns. Napa itself is the valley's city, with more than half of the valley's 100,000-plus population concentrated here. It's also more down-to-earth and oddly less "Napa-like" than its northern neighbors. Yet it is well on its way to becoming a permanent upscale bedroom community for San Francisco and the Bay Area—and an unabashed anchor for the fleets of wine tasters sloshing northward.

Napa's small town identity lives on, however, in older, shaded Victorian neighborhoods. Napa, in fact, boasts more Victorians than any California city north of San Francisco. One good place to appreciate them is downtown in the **Fuller Park Historic District,** roughly bounded by the Napa River and Pine, Jefferson, Third, Fourth, and Division Streets; tour the area in more detail with an assist from the local walking tour brochure. A marvelous example of Queen Anne Victoriana is the elegant 1893 La Belle Epoque bed-and-breakfast in Napa's **Calistoga Avenue Historic District** of Napa. Definitely stop to appreciate the newly restored 1880 Italianate **Napa Valley Opera House,** 1030 Main St., 707/226-7372, www.nvoh.org, which sat empty and dark from 1914 until the 1970s, when concerned citizens saved it and other downtown treasures from the wrecking ball. In 1997 the grand façade was restored and Robert and Margrit Mondavi put up a $2.2 million challenge grant in support of the subsequent $14 million renovation. In 2000 a downstairs café theatre opened. The main landmark theater reopened in fall 2003 with many of its historic features restored, though the original hard wooden benches were replaced by plush seats. These days there's a full calendar of dance, music, and theatrical events, from an elegant a cappella *Early Music* concert from the Scholars of London to *MacHomer: The Simpsons Do MacBeth.*

Downtown Napa also has its share of intriguing shops (lots of antique stores) and galleries, including the **Napa County Historical Society Museum and Gallery,** 1219 First St. (in the library building downtown), 707/224-1739, open Tuesday and Thursday noon–4 P.M. Napa's downtown **post office** is at 1351 Second Street. **Bookends Book Store,** 1014 Coombs St. (downtown near First), 707/224-1077, has books, magazines, and U.S. Geological Survey topo maps. Another good local bookshop (new and used) is **Copperfield's,** 1303 First St., 707/252-8002. Stop by the **Salvation Army** thrift shop, 1326 Main St., 707/224-8220, for good secondhand clothes—keeping in mind that bargain hunting in rich people's backyards is almost always rewarding. To power up for further shopping and wine tasting, stop by the "ABC"—**Alexis Baking Company**—not far away at 1517 Third St., 707/258-1827, for a good cup of coffee and a piece of cake.

Copia

The high life is still going strong these days at Napa's $55 million Copia, opened in 2001 at the edge of downtown on a 13-acre site along the Napa River. Brainchild of Robert Mondavi, the Napa Valley's visionary winemaker, this unique museum—the first in the world devoted exclusively to food and wine—is dedicated to "the American passion for living well," in Mondavi's words, and to elevating America's cultural image worldwide. Copia combines the arts traditions of museum, performing arts venue, cooking and wine education center, and public gardens with the personal pleasures of fine dining, wine tasting, and shopping. Wine education programs address topics such as The ABCs of Starting a Wine Cellar and Touring the Wine Country. More than 200 cooking classes are offered each year by master chefs. The **Wine Spectator Tasting Bar** features wines from all 50 states and several countries, on a rotating basis.

Adjacent is the California-style French **Julia's Kitchen,** Copia's signature eatery, named for chef Julia Child and featuring indoor/outdoor seating for 150, and the **American Market Café.** The 80,000-square-foot building designed by Polshek Partnership Architects is surrounded by seven acres of gardens—an orchard, vineyards, and seasonal plantings of herbs, fruits, vegetables, and flowers—inspired by the 16th-century kitchen gardens at Château de Villandry, a castle in France's Loire Valley. The grounds also include a 500-seat outdoor amphitheater for live music and theater performances.

Copia, 500 First St., 707/259-1600, www .copia.org, is open in spring and summer Monday, Tuesday and Thursday, 10 A.M.–5 P.M., Fri.–Sun. 10 A.M. 9 P.M. (closed Wednesday); in fall and winter Thurs.–Mon. 10 A.M.–5 P.M. (closed Tues. and Wed.). Admission is $12.50 adults, $10 youths (13–17), and seniors, $7.50 children. Admission includes a free garden tour, offered daily at 10:15 A.M. and 2 P.M.

Napa Valley Wine Train

Popular with tourists, though not necessarily with the upvalley towns that host its visits, is the Napa Valley Wine Train, which rolls along 18 miles of railroad from Napa to St. Helena, paralleling Hwy. 29. Passengers ride in luxuriously renovated vintage Pullman cars that feature plush touches such as burnished mahogany woodwork, overstuffed chairs, and marble-and-brass bathrooms. The basic Wine Train tour includes food (brunch, lunch, or dinner—all cooked up fresh onboard) and costs $60–80 plus gratuity. There's also a package that includes lunch at Domaine Chandon. In addition to an array of fine wines, full cocktail service is available. Trains run daily, and a full calendar of special events is offered. For information and reservations (required), contact the Napa Valley Wine Train, 1275 McKinstry St. (First and Soscol) in Napa, 707/253-2111 or 800/427-4124 (in California), www.winetrain.com.

Lake Berryessa

One of the state's big reservoirs and the county's eastern "escape" route since 1957 when the Monticello Dam was completed, Lake Berryessa is

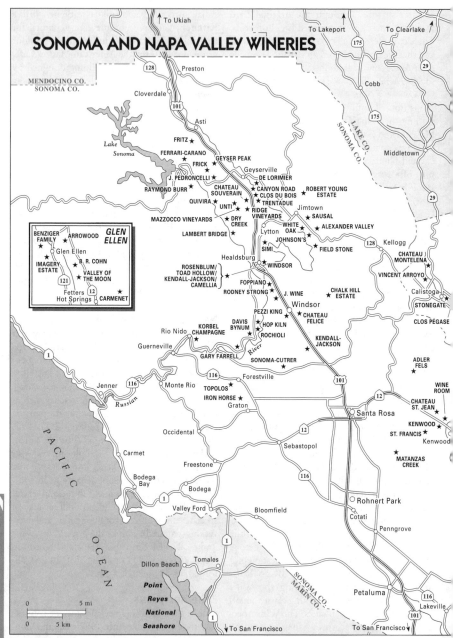

SONOMA AND NAPA VALLEY WINERIES

To Ukiah
To Lakeport
To Clearlake
175
29

Preston
128
Cobb

MENDOCINO CO.
SONOMA CO.

Cloverdale

175

Asti
101

Lake
Sonoma

FRITZ ★
FERRARI-CARANO ★
FRICK ★
J. PEDRONCELLI ★
RAYMOND BURR ★

GEYSER PEAK ★
Geyserville
DE LORIMIER ★
CHATEAU
SOUVERAIN ★
CANYON ROAD ★
CLOS DU BOIS ★
TRENTADUE ★
QUIVIRA ★
UNTI ★
RIDGE
VINEYARDS ★
MAZZOCCO VINEYARDS ★
DRY
CREEK ★
LAMBERT BRIDGE ★

Middletown

29

ROBERT YOUNG
ESTATE ★

Jimtown
SAUSAL ★
WHITE
OAK ★
ALEXANDER VALLEY ★
Lytton
JOHNSON'S ★
SIMI ★
FIELD STONE ★

128
Kellogg

CHATEAU
MONTELENA ★

VINCENT ARROYO ★

Calistoga

STONEGATE ★

CLOS PÉGASE ★

GLEN ELLEN

BENZIGER
FAMILY ★
ARROWOOD ★
Glen Ellen
IMAGERY
ESTATE ★
B. R. COHN ★
VALLEY OF
THE VALLEY
MOON ★
121
Fetters
Hot Springs
12
CARMENET ★

Healdsburg
ROSENBLUM/
TOAD HOLLOW/
KENDALL-JACKSON/
CAMELLIA ★
WINDSOR ★
FOPPIANO ★
RODNEY STRONG ★
J. WINE ★
CHALK HILL
ESTATE ★

Windsor
PEZZI KING ★
CHATEAU
FELICE ★
DAVIS
BYNUM ★
HOP KILN ★
ROCHIOLI ★
KENDALL-
JACKSON ★

Rio Nido
KORBEL
CHAMPAGNE ★
Guerneville
GARY FARRELL ★
SONOMA-CUTRER ★

ADLER
FELS ★

Jenner
116
Monte Rio
Russian
River
116
Forestville
TOPOLOS ★
IRON HORSE ★
Graton

101
12
Santa Rosa

WINE
ROOM ★
CHATEAU
ST. JEAN ★
KENWOOD ★
ST. FRANCIS ★
Kenwood

Occidental
12
Sebastopol
MATANZAS
CREEK ★

Carmet

Freestone
116

Bodega
Bay
Bodega
Rohnert Park
Cotati
Penngrove

1
Valley Ford
Bloomfield

1

Tomales
Dillon Beach

SONOMA CO.
MARIN CO.

Petaluma
116
Lakeville
101

**Point
Reyes
National
Seashore**

0   5 mi

0   5 km

PACIFIC   OCEAN

To San Francisco
To San Francisco

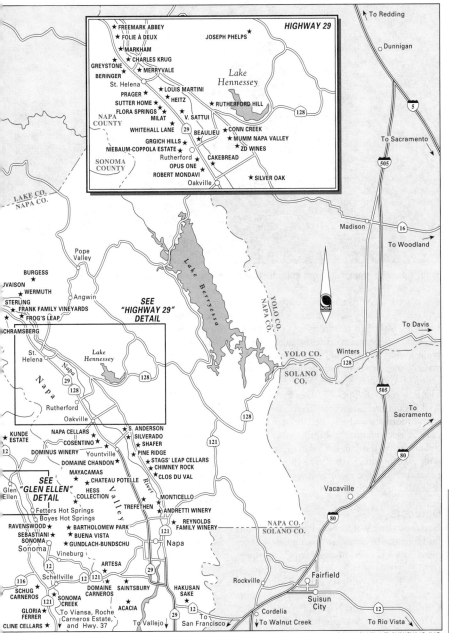

© ROBERT HOLMES/CALTOUR

Enjoy fine wine along with your gourmet lunch or dinner on the Napa Valley Wine Train.

one place to avoid the wine-country crunch—arid oak foothills in summer, gorgeous greenery in spring—though it, too, is also popular on weekends. Berryessa has the usual lake action, from good trout fishing, swimming, sailing, water-skiing, even houseboating, to private campgrounds. Camp at **Spanish Flat** (call Spanish Flat Resort at 707/966-7700), or **Putah Creek** (call Putah Creek Resort at 707/966-0794). For more information about the lake, call the Bureau of Reclamation at 707/966-2111. **Lake Solano** below the dam is a Solano County park with 90 campsites ($18 RVs, $15 tents)—and peace and quiet (no motorboats); call 530) 795-2990 for information.

Outdoors

Napa's **Skyline Wilderness Park,** 2201 Imola (at Fourth), 707/252-0481, is a great place for picnicking and offers hiking, biking, and equestrian trails as well as camping ($15 tents, $25–27 RV sites with hookups). Commercial horseback rides are offered in season by **Sonoma Cattle Company and Napa Valley Trail Rides,** 707/255-2900, www.napasonomatrailrides.com, headquartered here. Or plan a hike to the large

grove of rare Sargent cypress in the obscure **Cedar Roughs** area west of Rancho Monticello on Lake Berryessa. No public trail or road leads to the area; to find it, contact the local field office (see above).

WINERIES

In the Napa Valley dry French-type wines are the specialty, while the hot San Joaquin Valley produces sweet, bulk wines from the state's largest vineyard acreages. The area near Napa is coolest, known for delicate pinot noir, riesling, and chardonnay grapes. North of Yountville grow world-class cabernet sauvignon and chardonnay grapes. Farther north, near Calistoga, petite sirah and chenin blanc varieties flourish—though chenin blanc is fast disappearing from the landscape, done in by the popularity of chardonnay and white zinfandel. Merlot, pinot blanc, white zinfandel, and sauvignon blanc are also produced regionally. Here and elsewhere in California, wine grape growers and winemakers are becoming bolder and more creative, and as a result unexpected varietals can be expected almost anywhere.

NAPA VALLEY EVENTS

Spring in the Napa Valley means fields of blooming wild mustard—and the annual **Napa Valley Mustard Festival,** an imaginative calendar of events stretching from late January or early February through March. The Mustard Festival celebrates mustard—and the arts, culture, cuisine, and agriculture of the Napa Valley—and entertains visitors, but also supports the community. Proceeds from the festival help fund local nonprofit organizations, such as the Napa Valley Museum, the Sharpsteen Museum, Dreamweavers Theatre, and music and drama programs in local high schools. The grand opening event usually has a French theme: past celebrations kicked off with Mustard Magic—Une Soirée Française at the Culinary Institute of America at Greystone, where the Grand Cask Room became a gallery and theater with trapeze artists dangling from the ceilings, accompanied by live opera, and the three-story atrium a Parisian café. The signature two-day Napa Valley Mustard Festival Marketplace in mid-March, now held at Copia, features mustards from around the world, cooking demonstrations, arts and crafts, children's events, and live music on three stages. For current information or to become a sponsor, contact the Napa Valley Mustard Festival, 707/259-9020, www.mustardfestival.org. Always integral to the festival is February's **Savor St. Helena,** featuring fine food and wine tastings.

Almost all the valley's wineries also get into the act for the **Napa Valley Wine Auction,** usually held in St. Helena each year in June—the party of the year, and a rich people's wine-bidding bash on behalf of charity. In 1985, for example, Du Pont heirs paid $21,000 for the first case of "California Cognac," double-distilled Remy-Martin/Schramsberg Vineyards brandy; in 2003 the total winning bid for the "Bidder's Brand" lot was $1 million. Offbeat and unhyped sweetheart wines can be reasonable, though bidding paddles (necessary to get in the door) cost plenty. Surrounding celebrations throughout the valley—themed parties and concerts at almost every winery, black-tie dinners, and a week full of related events—add up to the party of the year for just about everyone else. In 2003 the auction raised $6.57 million for local charities. For information, contact the Napa Valley Vintners Association, 707/942-9775 or 800/358-5476, www.napavintners.com.

But something is always happening on the winery scene. In addition to events mentioned elsewhere below, consider the Napa Valley's very big big-band, folk, classical, and jazz concerts at the **Robert Mondavi Winery** in Oakville—always hot acts. Mondavi also sponsors other events throughout the year, including fine art shows at its Vineyard Room Gallery and the Great Chefs series of culinary education and indulgences. For more information and advance reservations for the Mondavi Sunday-evening Summer Festival Series concerts (tickets go on sale in May) call 888/766-6328 or 888/769-5299; for Great Chefs events, call 707/968-2100; for events at the Vineyard Gallery, call 707/968-2213.

Domaine Chandon, 1 California Dr. in Yountville, 707/944-2280, usually offers live music during its July 4th and Bastille Day (July 14) celebrations, in addition to its summer and fall concert calendar. Various performances are also hosted at **Charles Krug Winery,** 2800 Main St. in St. Helena, 707/967-2200, and elsewhere.

In November and December, come for **Carols in the Caves,** 707/224-4222, David Auerbach's intriguing acoustical folk music holiday events staged in wine caves throughout both the Napa and Sonoma Valleys. Immensely popular, so reserve well in advance.

Not all the local action centers on wineries. The **Napa County Fair** at the county fairgrounds in Calistoga, 707/942-5111, usually takes place over the July 4th weekend, with main events including the sheepdog trials, livestock exhibits, a pulling contest for horses, sprint-car racing, and amusement rides.

For current calendars of upcoming Napa Valley events—from food and wine events and cat, dog, and horse shows to cribbage tournaments, crab feeds, and crafts fairs—contact the local chambers of commerce or visitors bureaus listed by community.

NAPA VALLEY BICYCLE TOURING

Napa County's back roads are paved and rural. If it weren't for the treacherous traffic, cycling through the Napa Valley would be the only way to go. Bicyclists brave enough to pedal into the wine country, avoid hair-raising Hwy. 29 (Napa Valley's wine spine) and opt instead for the generally safer **Silverado Trail** up the east side of the valley from Napa to Calistoga. (In peak season, though, and particularly on busy weekends, even this route can be frightening.) Other good rides include the back roads threading through the Pope Valley/Lake Berryessa area (avoid on weekends, when Bay Area boaters take over the roads) and the killer hills into Sonoma County from the valley's west side. Carneros is another popular destination. Still a good guide for route planning is *Cyclists' Route Atlas: A Guide to Yolo, Solano, Napa and Lake Counties* by Randall Gray Braun, currently out of print but widely available in used bookstores.

To take yourself on an impromptu tour, rent bikes at **Napa Valley Bike Tours and Rentals,** 1988 Wise Dr. in Napa, 707/255-3377 or 800/707-2453, www.napavalleybiketours.com, which also offers some great guided day trips, or at **St. Helena Cyclery,** 1156 Main St. in St. Helena, 707/963-7736, www.sthelenacyclery.com.

Sophisticated, fairly pricey guided wine country bike tours are offered by the Bay Area's popular **Backroads,** 800/462-2848, www.backroads.com; they're rated among the world's top 50 tours by *Bicycling* magazine. Offered 10 months of the year, Backroads tours include inn-to-inn tours as well as less expensive camping options. Contact the valley's visitors bureau for other suggested regional bike-tour companies.

Also near Napa (just south and west, north of San Pablo Bay) is Los Carneros, the Napa-Sonoma Carneros AVA, an area defined by the Carneros Hwy.; for details, see the Carneros section elsewhere in this chapter.

Silverado Trail

Escape the crush by avoiding Hwy. 29 as much as possible. Instead, head up the **Silverado Trail** from Napa to Calistoga on the valley's east side. (Cut across the valley to Hwy. 29 and westside wineries via several main crossroads.)

Near Napa on the Silverado Trail is **Reynolds Family Winery,** 3266 Silverado Trail, 707/258-2558, www.reynoldsfamilywinery.com, specializes in handcrafted cabernet sauvignon and pinot noir. Open for retail sales 10 A.M.–4 P.M. daily (tasting and tours by appointment only). A bit farther north, turn left on Oak Knoll Ave. to reach a couple of other good tasting options. Founded by racecar driver Mario Andretti in 1994, **Andretti Winery,** 4162 Big Ranch Road (off Oak Knoll), 707/261-1714, www.andrettiwinery.com, is open for tasting daily 10 A.M.–5 P.M.; call about tours, lunches, and dinners. **Monticello Cellars,** 4242 Big Ranch Rd. (off Oak Knoll), 707/253-

2802 or 800/743-6668, offers tasting and picnicking daily 10 A.M.–4:30 P.M., tours twice daily. The immense three-story redwood winery at **Trefethen Vineyards,** 1160 Oak Knoll Ave., 707/255-7700, www.trefethen.com, produces five premium varietals; open for tasting daily 10 A.M.–4:30 P.M., tours by appointment.

Back on Silverado Trail, north of the Big Ranch turnoff (in the hilly Stags' Leap district), is the **Clos du Val Wine Company,** 5330 Silverado Trail, 707/259-2220 or 800/993-9463, www.closduval.com. Included on *Wine & Spirits* magazine's 2003 Winery of the Year list, Clos du Val's classic wines include cabernet sauvignon, merlot, and chardonnay. Open daily 10 A.M.–5 P.M. for tasting ($5 fee) and shady picnic. Tours are offered by appointment only; call 707/259-2225 or 800/820-1972. Next door is recently expanded **Chimney Rock Winery,** 5350 Silverado Trail, 707/257-2641 or 800/257-2641, www.chimneyrock.com (tasting daily 10 A.M.–5 P.M., tours by appointment only), which makes cabernet sauvignon, cabernet franc, and fume blanc. A bit farther north (about six miles north of Napa) is famed **Stags' Leap Winery,** 5766 Silverado Trail, 707/944-1303 or 800/640-5327, www.stagsleapwinery.com, noted for its "rock soft" cabernet sauvignon and also proud purveyor of merlot, syrah, petite syrah, viognier, and chardonnay. Call for current tasting and tour information.

Continuing north up Silverado Trail from Stags' Leap, you'll pass several other worthy wineries. Surrounded by pine trees and the steep hillsides of the Stags' Leap district, **Pine Ridge Winery,** 5901 Silverado Trail, 707/253-7500 (administration) or 800/575-9777 (tours and tasting), is an especially interesting winery for visitors. The grounds are dotted with pine trees, picnic tables, and barbeque pits. After wine tasting, explore the Cabernet Caves that extend out from the tasting room. Open daily 10:30 A.M.–4:30 P.M. for tasting and picnicking. Tours featuring barrel tasting are available by appointment-daily at 10 A.M., 12 P.M., and 2 P.M. **Silverado Vineyards,** 6121 Silverado Trail, 707/257-1770 or 800/997-1770, www.silveradovineyards.com, is known for its chardonnay, cabernet, and herb-scented sauvignon blanc, among other varietals; tasting is offered daily 10:30 A.M.–5 P.M. in the visitor center (tours by appointment). Nearby is **Shafer Vineyards,** 6154 Silverado Trail, 707/944-2877, www.shafervineyards.com, noted for its cabernet sauvignon. Shafer is open for retail sale Mon.–Fri., 9 A.M.–4 P.M., for tasting and tours (and subsequent sales) by appointment only, at least 4–6 weeks in advance. Closed weekends.

Mayacamas Mountains

Well worth the adventurous side trip is **Mayacamas Vineyards,** 1155 Lokoya Rd., 707/224-4030, www.mayacamas.com, which has been here atop Mt. Veeder since 1941. Mayacamas is so *period,* in fact, that it was selected as a 1940s location for the film *A Walk in the Clouds.* Low-tech and intriguing, Mayacamas makes some excellent wines—rich, earthy chardonnay that ages exceptionally well, cabernet sauvignon, some zinfandel and pinot noir—and the original 1889 stone winery is still used for winemaking. Closed weekends. Tasting and tours only by appointment.

The remote, stone **Hess Collection Winery** in the Mayacamas hills just west of Napa, 4411 Redwood Rd., 707/255-1144, www.hesscollection.com, is noted for its chardonnay and cabernet

sauvignon. But many people also come for the collection itself—very abstract contemporary American and European art dramatically showcased as part of the self-guided tour. The remodeled Christian Brothers winery also includes a small theater for watching a short slide show about growing grapes here on Mt. Veeder. Open daily 10 A.M.–4 P.M. for tasting and self-guided tours.

STAYING IN AND NEAR NAPA

Camping is one honorable strategy that permits the unmonied to stay awhile in the wine country. During most months of the year it's also one of the best ways to take full advantage of the wonderful climate. Both **Lake Berryessa** to the east and **Bothe–Napa Valley State Park** to the north, between Calistoga and St. Helena, offer public campsites. **Skyline Wilderness Park** is another option. (For all three, see listings elsewhere.) In a pinch, camp at the far-from-elegant **Napa Valley Exposition,** 575 Third St., 707/253-4900 ($20 a night, self-contained RVs only).

There are very few inexpensive lodgings. One of them is the **Napa Valley Budget Inn,** 3380 Solano Ave. (formerly Motel 6, north of Napa proper via the Redwood Rd. exit off Hwy. 29), 707/257-6111 or 877/872-6272. The **Discovery Inn,** 500 Silverado Trail (near Soscol), 707/253-0892, offers 15 clean units with small kitchens and TV. Rates at both are usually $50–150. Often you're money ahead (and more comfortable to boot) with a small or otherwise bargain room at more expensive hotels or B&Bs, such as the **John Muir Inn,** 1998 Trower Ave., 707/257-7220 or 800/522-8999, where amenities include in-room coffee, cable TV, continental breakfast, and access to the mineral pool and spa. Suites have a king-sized bed, double sleeper sofa, in-room spa, and wet bar/refrigerator. Winter/midweek rates are $100–150, and summer/weekend rates $150–250. Other possibilities include the **Best Western Inn at the Vines,** the **Napa Valley Marriott** (fresh from a $20 million renovation, and now offering the onsite Amadeus Spa & Salon), the **Embassy Suites Napa Valley,** and the **Silverado Resort** several miles east of town.

UP, UP, AND AWAY

An 18th-century diversion of the French aristocracy, hot air ballooning somehow seems appropriate here, though local residents and many wineries alike have long since tired of the sight and sound of ballooners in the skies. For most people, this is an expensive airborne experience, at about $180 an hour and up. Reservations are required.

Napa Valley Balloons Inc., 707/944-0228 or 800/253-2224 (in Northern California), www.napavalleyballoons.com, offers dawn balloon trips launched from the Napa Valley Grill, followed by brunch and sparkling wines. Also well known among local high-but-slow floaters are a trio of affiliated companies headquartered at the Vintage 1870 complex (6525 Washington) in Yountville: **Balloon Aviation of Napa Valley,** 707/252-7067 or 800/367-6272; **Adventures Aloft,** 707/944-4408 or 800/944-4408; and **Above the West Hot Air Ballooning,** 707/944-8638 or 800/627-2759, which is the most expensive but for its base rate offers either complimentary shuttle service from San Francisco or a trip guaranteed at just four passengers. All three of these companies make single flights instead of multiple hops, offer preflight coffee and pastries and postflight champagne, and have the same website: www.nvaloft.com. In Rutherford, the **Bonaventura Balloon Company,** 707/944-2822, www.bonaventuraballoons.com, is headquartered at the Rancho Caymus Inn; ask about the "Stay and Fly" package.

"New" and quite special in downtown Napa is the historic **Napa River Inn,** 500 Main St., 707/251-8500 or 877/251-8500, www.napariverinn.com, a plush boutique hotel anchoring the redevelopment of the historic **Napa Mill** and Hatt buildings as an entertainment, dining, and shopping complex. Included on the National Trust for Historic Preservation's impressive hotel roster, the Napa River Inn features 65 striking, stylish rooms and one suite, with all the comforts. Many rooms have fireplaces, balconies, and river views, $200–400 in summer, breakfast and wine tasting included. The historic suite

is $500. In season you can take a gondola ride then sit down to an exceptional meal—at excellent country French **Angèle,** at grand and global **Celadon,** and at the very good **Napa General Store** café and wine bar. For dessert or breakfast pastries, the place is **Sweetie Pies Bakery.**

Bed-and-Breakfasts

Putting its grand old homes to good use, Napa has many bed-and-breakfasts, none particularly inexpensive. The **Blue Violet Mansion,** 443 Brown St., 707/253-2583 or 800/959-2583, www.bluevioletmansion.com, a striking 1886 Queen Anne Victorian with antiques, a heated pool on the one-acre grounds, and vintage Napa atmosphere. It offers 17 rooms with trompe l'oeil touches, gorgeous antiques, and private baths; depending on the room, additional amenities include balconies, in-room spas, and gas fireplaces. Rates include full breakfast and refreshments (picnic baskets and dinner also available), $150–400. Also presiding over an acre of gardens is stately, stylish **Churchill Manor,** 485 Brown St., 707/253-7733, www.churchillmanor.com, a three-story Second Empire mansion built in 1889 and offering 10 guest rooms (some with fireplaces, one with spa, all with private bath) and full breakfast. Rates are $150–250. Accessible **Candlelight Inn,** 1045 Easum Dr. (west of Hwy. 29 off First St.), 707/257-3717, www.candlelightinn.com, is a 1929 English Tudor tucked into verdant, one-acre grounds. Candlelight offers 10 rooms (all with private bath), a large swimming pool, full gourmet breakfast, and evening wine, sherry, and hors d'oeuvres. Rates: $100–300.

A favorite among wine tasters is **La Belle Époque,** 1386 Calistoga Ave., 707/257-2161 or 800/238-8070, www.labelleepoque.com, is an 1893 Queen Anne Victorian with many-gabled dormers and period antiques, vintage and contemporary stained glass—and a wine tasting room and cellar. All six guest rooms have private baths, several have fireplaces. Rates include full breakfast, wine tasting, and appetizers. From here it's a short walk to the Wine Train and the local opera house. Rates are $200–300, lower in winter. Two suites in the Buckley House, $300–350, are also available.

A notable Napa landmark is the grand brick 1902 **Beazley House,** 1910 First St., 707/257-1649 or 800/559-1649, www.beasleyhouse.com, Napa's first bed-and-breakfast, with 11 guest rooms. All have private baths, six feature fireplaces, and five have whirlpools. Rooms are $150–250, and include full breakfast, tea and cookies. Secluded Carriage House rooms, many with private gardens, are $250 and up.

Other good choices include the **Arbor Guest House,** 1436 G St., 707/252-8144, www.arborguesthouse.com, $100–250; the 1899 Queen Anne Victorian **Napa Inn,** 1137 Warren St., 707/257-1444 or 800/435-1144, www.napainn .com, $150–250; and the striking **Cedar Gables Inn,** 486 Coombs St., 800/309-7969, www .cedargablesinn.com. Refreshingly free of lace and Victorian airs is the 1903 Queen Anne **1801 First,** 1801 First St., 707/224-3739 or 800/518-0146, www.the1801inn.com, rates $200–350.

A pleasant change-up, too, is **La Residence Country Inn,** 4066 St. Helena Hwy. (two miles north of Napa), 707/253-0337, which has grown from a bed-and-breakfast into a luxurious yet casual country inn. La Residence offers 20 rooms (most with private bath) in an 1870 Gothic Revival farmhouse and French-style barn. Full breakfast, pool, and hot tub, too. Standard rooms $150–250, deluxe rooms $250 and up.

EATING IN NAPA

Doing the farm trails here is a good way to gather up the freshest, best food available; the inexpensive prices are only incidental. Or time your visit to take advantage of the local farmers markets. The **Napa Chef's Certified Farmers Market** is held May–Aug. Fri. evenings, 4–8 P.M., at First and Main Sts. The **Napa Downtown Certified Farmers Market** is held May–Oct. Tues. 7:30 A.M.–noon, at 500 First St. in the Copia parking lot. For information on both, call 707/252-7142.

Well worth seeking out is the casual, whimsical **Foothill Café,** in a shopping center at 2766 Old Sonoma Rd. (west of Hwy. 29), 707/252-6178, where hearty vegetarian, seafood, poultry, and meat selections (try the baby-back ribs) star at dinner.

There are many choices downtown. The new Napa Mill complex on Main offers a range of good restaurants, from the casual **Napa General Store,** 540 Main St., 707/259-0762, the place for wood-fired pizzas, pulled-pork sandwiches, and Chinese chicken salad plus good coffee, beer, and wine. Before you sit down for a bite overlooking the river, peruse some 100 kinds of cheese and other upscale stuff. Nearby is relaxed, indoor-outdoor **Celadon,** in the onetime Hatt Market at 500 Main, 707/254-9690, which serves Mediterranean-style New American, from fish sandwiches to Moroccan braised lamb. Open weekdays from lunch through dinner; Sat. and Sun. for dinner only. The charming and expensive **Angèle** bistro, in a onetime boathouse at 540 Main St., 707/252-8115, serves entrées such as pan-roasted duck breast and mushroom risotto with Reggiano parmesan. Ask to sit out on the large patio, weather permitting.

Still talk of the town for foodies is the exceptional yet fun **Bistro Don Giovanni,** 4110 St. Helena Hwy. (Hwy. 29 just north of Napa), 707/224-3300, brought to you by the folks behind Scala Bistro at San Francisco's Sir Francis Drake Hotel. Expect a daily-changing menu of Italian bistro fare with the occasional French accent—spicy prawns and goat cheese pizza, pesto and ricotta cheese ravioli with lemon cream sauce, or grilled double cut pork chops—whether served forth from the wood-fired pizza oven or mesquite grill. Open for lunch and dinner daily. Two popular downtown trattorias include **Tuscany,** 1005 First St. (at Main), 707/258-1000, for classic Northern Italian dishes cooked in an open kitchen, and **Uva Trattoria Italiana,** 1040 Clinton St. (at Main St.), 707/255-6646, a lively destination featuring Southern Italian specialties and bar seating with a small plates menu.

Housed in a historic stone building and big brother to Celadon, **Cole's Chop House,** 1122 Main St., 707/224-6328, is the place to go for steak in the valley. Cole's beef is USDA certified prime Angus, aged for three weeks and outstanding, though you'll also find salmon and other selections on the menu (and at least one vegetarian option). Everything is true-blue traditionalist at Cole's—right down to the appetizers, oysters on the half-shell and lobster bisque. Another downtown hotspot is **ZuZu,** 829 Main, 707/224-8555, serving great Spanish-style tapas, specialties from South and Central America, and desserts—all ingredients organic, seasonal, and locally grown.

YOUNTVILLE AND VICINITY

George Yount built the first house in the valley—a fortified log cabin—and planted the valley's first vineyard in the 1830s. But Yountville's humble beginnings are none too apparent these days. Yountville has gone—and is still going—yupscale. Plenty of high-end restaurants and hotels grace the main drag, Washington Street, and area vineyards include heavy-hitters such as Domaine Chandon, Dominus, Cosentino, and S. Anderson Winery.

The modern **Napa Valley Museum,** chronicles the history of winemaking in the area. The **Veterans Home of California** here, now run by the state, first opened its doors in 1884, started by veterans of the Mexican War and members of the Grand Army of the Republic. The doors are still open—a huge, somehow disturbing human warehouse. If you have time, spend some here. The attached **Armistice Chapel Museum,** 707/944-4919, is stuffed with military memorabilia, some items on loan from San Francisco's Presidio Army Museum.

For most people, though, the town's main event is browsing through the tony clothing, jewelry, and art and antique shops. A good place to start is the **Vintage 1870** complex, 6525 Washington St. (on the former Groezinger Wine Estate), 707/944-2451, open daily 10 A.M.–5:30 P.M. and chock-full of specialty shops and restaurants, including the **Vintage 1870 Wine Cellar,** 707/944-9070, offering a great selection of wines (including sherries and ports), beers, and cigars. Also here is the **Blue Heron Gallery,** 707/944-2044. After doing the town, try a simple picnic in **Yountville City Park** at Washington and Lincoln. Nearby is the fascinating cemetery where George Yount and other valley pioneers are buried. For information, contact the **Yountville Chamber of Commerce,** 6516 Yount St., 707/944-0904, www.yountville.com.

Napa Valley Museum

Yountville's modernist, 40,000-square-foot Napa Valley Museum at 55 Presidents Circle (off California Dr. at the entrance to the Veterans Home), 707/944-0500, www.napavalleymuseum.org, offers an alternative to all-day shopping and wine tasting—including the "industry gallery," changing exhibits on the art, culture, and land of Napa Valley, and a permanent, high-tech interactive exhibit, California Wine: The Science of an Art, which takes you through a year in the winemaking process.

The museum is open daily except Tuesday 10 A.M.–5 P.M. (until 8 P.M. on the first Thursday of every month). Admission is $4.50 adults, $3.50 seniors/students, and $2.50 children 7–17. Free for everyone 5–8 P.M. on the first Thursday of every month.

Wineries

Domaine Chandon is the valley's most famous bubbly facility, just west of Hwy. 29 at 1 California Dr., 707/944-2280, www.chandon.com. Owned by France's Moet-Hennessey cognac and champagne producers (the Dom Perignon people), Domaine Chandon was founded here in 1973, a pioneer in Napa Valley and Carneros sparkling wines. These days Carneros varietals, including pinot noir, pinot meunier, and chardonnay, are also produced. The winery is striking architecturally, sporting fieldstone walls with barrel-arched vaulted roofs over terraced stair steps. Inside you'll find a champagne museum and a fine, fairly expensive restaurant with a seasonally changing menu, including a seven-course tasting menu paired with Domaine Chandon wines. (Call 800/736-2892 for reservations.) The visitor center, tasting room, and retail shop are open daily 10 A.M.–6 P.M. Complimentary tours are offered on weekdays at 11 A.M., 2 P.M., and 5 P.M., on weekends every hour from 11 A.M. to 5 P.M.

Still a big buzz in Yountville is the stark, surreal **Dominus Estate Winery,** 2570 Napa Nook Rd. (paralleling Hwy. 29), 707/944-8954, www.dominusestate.com, noted for its modernist architecture. Designed by Swiss architects Jacques Herzog and Pierre de Meuron, their first project in the U.S., Dominus was commissioned after the team won

NAPA VALLEY "TERROIR"

Here they come, the "terroirists," those wine aficionados determined to discover the unique environmental characteristics—created by geography, geology, soil characteristics, and climate—responsible for the distinct personality of wines made from particular grapes. Terroirists also celebrate the great diversity expressed by wines within a given appellation. And few appellations are as diverse as the Napa Valley, which to date boasts 14 sub-appellations and 140 different soil types.

Notions of "terroir," from the French, first determine which areas are good for grape growing in general, which areas produce excellence in particular varietals, and then which environmental factors will create further distinctiveness—in aroma, flavor, texture, color, acidity and wine "personality"—an ever-changing balance along several continuums. Far from being an exact science, terroir is in many ways an experimental process. Wines made from particular grapes are influenced as much by the winemaker as by terroir, after all, and attributes can be more confused in wines that blend grapes from different vineyards.

Be that as it may, careful tasters may associate certain characteristics with grapes and wines from various parts of the Napa Valley—and terroirists in tasting rooms and on various winery tours will tell you all about it.

---

the competition to design London's new Tate Gallery of Modern Art. Minimalist but deceptively simple, the basalt stone of the low-slung building's façade is held in place by a wire-mesh frame supported by vertical pipes attached to the steel frame—something like the gabions used as retaining walls along European roadways. As a result, both light and air filter into the building, and from inside you can also see out into the world. Napa Valley visitors, intrigued by what they've heard and then by what they see, stop for tastings and tours—but none are offered, or will be, since this is strictly a production facility. (Architects, some at the winery say, have been the most determined trespassers.) You can look at the building from the road, but please, do not trespass.

Cosentino Winery, 7415 St. Helena Hwy. (next to Mustard's Grill), 707/944-1220, www.cosentinowinery.com, is a local innovator, known for its small, distinctive grape selections and a "micro" approach to winemaking. Open daily 10 A.M.–5:30 P.M. for tasting ($5 fee), no appointment necessary. Just north (technically in Oakville) is **Napa Cellars,** 7481 St. Helena Hwy. 707/944-2565 or 800/535-6400, open for sales and tastings ($5 fee, refundable with wine purchase) daily 10 A.M.–5:30 P.M. and for tours by appointment.

Across the valley, **S. Anderson Winery** 1473 Yountville Cross Rd. (near the Silverado Trail),

707/944-8642 or 800/428-2259, www.sandersonvineyard.com, is a small family-owned producer of sparkling wines, also identified as **Cliff Lede Vineyards,** for the sale of non-sparkling varietals. The facility itself is a fascination; its 18-foot-high wine-aging caves tunnel into a rhyolite hillside and boast peaked ceilings, cobblestone floors, and a stage. Special wine tastings and concerts are held in the caves. Open daily 10 A.M.–5 P.M.; public tours are offered twice daily at 10:30 A.M. and 2:30 P.M. (private tours by appointment).

Staying in Yountville

Once a bordello, **Maison Fleurie,** 6529 Yount St., 707/944-2056 or 800/788-0369, www.foursisters.com, is now a fine bed-and-breakfast offering a total of 13 rooms (six with fireplace, all with private bath) in a luxuriously restyled 1873 brick-and-fieldstone lodge and two other ivy-covered buildings). All rooms are furnished in French country style; amenities include a pool, whirlpool, and full breakfast. Bikes are available for touring local wineries or attractions in Yountville. Rates are $100–300.

The recently renovated **Vintage Inn,** 6541 Washington St., 707/944-1112, www.vintageinn.com, is a first-rate place for a grape escape. All rooms have wood-burning fireplaces, whirlpool baths, and wine bars. Most also have either a balcony or patio, not to mention other cushy wine-country comforts. Many of the upstairs rooms have very high ceilings. A canal runs through the grounds, which also feature a heated pool and spas situated here and there. Rates include a champagne-and-pastry breakfast and afternoon tea. The hotel has a private limo you can hire, and a honeymoon package is available. Rates are $250 and up, lower in winter. The neighboring (and sister) **Villagio Inn & Spa,** 6481 Washington, 707/944-8877 or 800/351-1133, www .villagio.com, is Yountville's own Tuscany, with its clustered village style, sunny, earthy colors, and every comfort—from the oversized sunken bathtubs, plush robes, and down comforters to the romantic fireplaces. Rates start at $250.

Eating in Yountville

Foodies work full-time at getting into the exceptional (and exceptionally expensive) **French Laundry,** 6640 Washington St., 707/944-2380, at home in a charming old ivy-covered 1890s stone house, a onetime laundry. This particular laundry is awash in accolades, at the top of the wine-country charts in both price and quality for fixed-price French. But given the number of great casual Napa Valley and Sonoma restaurants, why bother with all the bother? If you must, however, reservations are accepted up to two months in advance. Four-course lunch is served Fri.–Sun., and there's a choice of a five- or seven-course tasting menu at dinner, including vegetarian options. A new neighborhood star, cheek-kissin' cousin to the French Laundry, is the more affordable Parisian-style **Bouchon** bistro, 6534 Washington, 707/944-8037, complete with shellfish bar and serving menu items such as sautéed gnocchi, pan-roasted trout, lamb medallions, and lemon tarts for dessert. Great wine list. Attention picnickers: Load up on sandwiches, breads, macaroons, and wonderful pastries at the next-door **Bouchon Bakery.**

A Yountville classic is casual **Bistro Jeanty,** 6510

Washington, 707/944-0103, like a French farmhouse overflowing with antique cooking tools and other country color. The ever-changing menu might include home-smoked trout and potato salad, coq au vin, steak frites, cassoulet, and crêpes Suzette. Open daily for lunch and dinner.

Good restaurants cluster along Washington Street. Locals also stream into **Gordon's Café & Wine Bar,** 6770 Washington St., 707/944-8246, located in a onetime stage stop and country store (notice the Market sign still on the wall) for muffins and eggs benedict at breakfast, and French-inspired soups, salads and sandwiches at lunch. A fixed-price, three-course dinner is served only on Friday nights—very special, and *very* popular, accompanied by an impressive selection of superb Napa wines at retail prices. Reservations essential. Another local favorite is **Hurley's,** 6518 Washington, 707/944-2345, serving a wonderful grilled salmon and prawn salad, great sandwiches, and signature dishes such as blue-nose sea bass in red wine sauce. Open for lunch and dinner daily.

The original **Ristorante Piatti,** 6480 Washington St., 707/944-2070, chain staked a claim with filling portions of pastas and wood-fired pizzas and easygoing ambiance that's a nice alternative to higher-priced eateries. Daily specials often include variations on grilled chicken, rabbit, and risotto. (There's another Piatti in Sonoma.) Open daily for lunch and dinner.

Cindy Pawlcyn's famed foodie mecca, **Mustards Grill,** 7399 St. Helena Hwy., 707/944-2424, opened as a "gourmet truck stop" in 1983. Mustards' innovative and well-prepared comfort food—onion rings with house-made tomato-apple ketchup, wild mushroom tamales, gardener's pie with potato parmesan crust—starred local produce and products yet was (and is) quite affordable. Great desserts, such as warm chocolate hazelnut tart and lemon-lime pie. Full bar, extensive wine list, microbrews. Open daily for lunch and dinner.

St. Helena and Vicinity

The next town to speak of upvalley, small St. Helena is surrounded by historic vineyards and wineries. Increasingly, the town is an elite enclave catering to the monied minions from the city, though the area was originally settled by German, Italian, and Swiss farm families. If possible, park on the east side of the highway—so you don't have to try to cross it—then, to get oriented, stop by the **St. Helena Chamber of Commerce** office on the main drag, 1010 Main St., Ste. A, 707/963-4456 or 800/799-6456, www.sthelena.com. Ideally, *leave* your car parked and avoid the local traffic snarls by renting leisure bikes ($7 an hour, $30 a day) or touring bikes ($50 a day) at **St. Helena Cyclery,** 1156 Main St., 707/963-7736, www.sthelenacyclery.com, where the staff will happily recommend local tour routes (open daily).

SEEING AND DOING ST. HELENA

Like Yountville, St. Helena is becoming a hoity-toity shopping mecca, and few utilitarian farm-town businesses still survive. **On the Vine** 1234 Main Street, 707/963-2209, specializes in natural clothing, hand-painted silk scarves, and jewelry, and other functional and decorative items. **Main Street Books,** 1315 Main St., 707/963-1338, carries both fiction and nonfiction, and provides a children's book corner. A further stroll down Main St. in either direction leads visitors through the heart of St. Helena's high-priced, tasteful consumerism. Factory outlet malls are all the rage among bargain hunters, appearing in the form of the **St. Helena Premium Outlets** on Hwy 29 two miles north of downtown, 707/963-7782, includes bargains on Donna Karan, Coach, Movado, Tumi, and more; open Mon.–Sun. 10 A.M.–6 P.M. (In case you missed it, there's another, larger Premium Outlets center in Napa.) But St. Helena's newest trendy shop-spot is the **Dean and Deluca** market at 607 S. St. Helena Highway, 707/967-9980, offering a fantastic array of produce, bread, cheeses, and California wines—a terrific (though pricey) stop for wine country picnic supplies. If nothing else is going on come nightfall—(and, due to local preference, nightlife here is quiet—take in a movie at the local **Cameo Cinema,** 1340 Main St., 707/963-9779.

Silverado Museum

Well worth a visit is the world-renowned Silverado Museum collection of Robert Louis Stevenson memorabilia, housed in its own wing at the St. Helena Public Library Center, 1490 Library Ln., 707/963-3757, www.silveradomuseum.org, open daily noon–4 P.M. except Mondays and holidays. Stevenson's honeymoon story is the stuff of true romance. He met his bride-to-be (Fanny Osbourne, a married American woman) at an artists' colony in France, fell in love with her, then left his Scotland home for California in hot pursuit. Critically ill and poverty-stricken—living briefly in Monterey, San Francisco, and Oakland while awaiting Fanny's divorce—Stevenson managed to survive until his marriage to Fanny in May 1880. Too poor to afford the $10 a week for room and board in Calistoga, the two honeymooned in an abandoned bunkhouse at the Old Silverado Mine on Mt. St. Helena above the Napa Valley. Almost overnight, Robert Louis Stevenson regained his health, won his parents' approval of his new marriage, and returned to Scotland with his beloved Fanny to write his masterworks *(Treasure Island* and *The Strange Case of Dr. Jekyll and Mr. Hyde* among them).

On display at this red-carpeted "jewel box" museum—which offers something for everyone—are more than 8,000 items related to Stevenson's life and literary career: first editions and variant editions of almost all his works, more than 100 books from his library in Samoa, original manuscripts and letters, as well as paintings, photographs, sculptures, and drawings. The collection here includes some of the first words he ever wrote, in the form of childhood letters, as well as his last written words. Also here: his wedding ring, his work desk, and the lead soldiers he played with as a boy. The Silverado Library is free, though voluntary contributions to the library's Vailima Foundation are always welcome.

Next door in the public library, the fine **Napa Valley Wine Library,** 1492 Library Ln. (at Adams St.), 707/963-5244, www.napawinelibrary.org, shelves 3,000 or so wine-related books, journals, and magazines—one of the largest collections of libation literature on the West Coast. Wine-appreciation seminars, wine tastings, and other events are regularly scheduled, primarily during summer months.

Bale Grist Mill State Historic Park

Dr. Edward T. Bale (a surgeon originally from London who became General Vallejo's medical officer and his nephew by marriage) owned a substantial portion of the Napa Valley in the 1830s, due to Vallejo's largesse. A physician with a sense of humor, Bale named his spread Carne Humana Rancho—perhaps to suggest that we are all grist for the mill of life. Bale himself was ground up early, at the age of 38. But in 1846, he built a small state-of-the-art flour mill—powered by a 20-foot waterwheel—on Mill Creek just north of modern-day St. Helena. The original grist for the mill was locally grown wheat, but later corn was ground into highly prized cornmeal.

The wooden waterwheel (today's massive 36-footer a 19th-century improvement) and three-story mill were first restored in the 1920s, at a cost of nearly $1 million; a 10-year restoration project to reachieve the mill's fully operational 1850 status was completed in 1988. The massive millstones inside are impressive just to look at, and though flume water to power the wheel now comes from a pipe and recirculating pump, the mill is capable of grinding five to six tons of grain daily. Lucky visitors may get to see the whole works in operation.

The park is a few miles north of St. Helena on Hwy. 29. No admission. To get to the waterwheel and millworks—open for tours on weekends only—follow the shaded, paved path downhill from the parking lot—a good stretch for car-cramped legs. Ramps make the area wheelchair accessible. Better yet, hike in on the mile-long History Trail from Bothe–Napa Valley State Park.

Bothe–Napa Valley State Park

This is not exactly wilderness, but it's the only place to really camp in the valley. Bothe-Napa Valley's 100 acres of pleasant wooded valley and Coast Ranges ridgetops stretch from four miles north of St. Helena to three miles south of Calistoga. Hiking is a major attraction. You can walk here from Bale Grist (see above). You can even hike to the park from **Sugarloaf Ridge State Park** near Santa Rosa on the California Riding and Hiking Trail—sometimes a hot trek in summer but usually tolerable. Guided hikes and campfire programs are offered in summer. From spring into fall, **Triple Creek Horse Outfit,** 707/933-1600, www.triplecreekhorseoutfit.com, offers small-group 1.5-hour rides (for either novice or experienced riders) along Ritchey Creek, $50 per person. Reservations required. Triple Creek also offers rides "over the mountains" in Sonoma County's Jack London and Sugarloaf Ridge State Parks.

Included within the park's boundaries are the foundation ruins of Napa Valley's first church and a pioneer cemetery with Donner Party gravestones. Near the cemetery (and the speeding highway traffic) are a pleasant maple-shaded picnic area, a group camp, and (a rarity in state parks) a swimming pool, complete with dressing rooms and showers. The pool is open mid-June through Labor Day, noon–6 P.M., lifeguard on duty (small admission).

The longest Bothe-Napa hike (almost four miles one way) combines an easy lowland stroll along **Ritchey Canyon Trail** (an old fern-fringed, redwood-shaded roadbed paralleling Ritchey Creek) with a moderate hike up **Upper Ritchey Canyon Trail** and past a waterfall. (Continue from here to reach Sonoma County.) The easy mile-long **Redwood Trail** offers early-spring access to blooming redwood orchids under a canopy of second-growth trees. For glimpses of the Napa Valley below, head up more strenuous **Coyote Peak Trail.** The **History Trail** leads from the picnic area past the cemetery and church ruins, up the ridge, and down into Mill Creek and to the historic **Bale Grist Mill.**

Park day use is $4 per car. **Ritchey Creek Campground** features 40 fairly private family campsites tucked into wooded thickets. Each site comes equipped with a table, food locker, and barbecue stove ($13–16 per site). Restrooms have laundry tubs, flush toilets, drinking fountains, and hot showers. No RV hookups here, but a dump station is available. The park also has 10 walk-in (tents only) campsites, one reserved for hikers and bikers. Camping reservations are wise in spring, summer, and fall; Memorial Day to Labor Day is prime time. For camping reservations, contact ReserveAmerica at 800/444-7275, www.reserveamerica.com. For more information contact Bothe–Napa Valley State Park, 3801 St. Helena Hwy. N., 707/942-4575.

WINERIES

In the tourist sweeps, the biggest St. Helena wineries are Beringer and Charles Krug. At **Beringer Vineyards,** 2000 Main St. (Hwy. 29), 707/963-7115 (main office), 707/963-4812 (retail sales and tours), and 866/244-1581 (orders), www.beringer.com, the famous wine-aging caves were hand-dug in 1876 by Chinese laborers hired by Frederick and Jacob Beringer. Open for business ever since, Beringer is the oldest Napa Valley winery in continuous operation. The wines here have earned their accolades, and pop up among *Wine Spectator*'s Top 100 Wines more often than any other winery. Beringer's strikingly ornate 17-room Victorian **Rhine House,** listed on the National Register of Historic Places, is a study in stained glass and oak paneling surrounded by lovely gardens. Thirty-minute tours of the winery—which include a peek into the wine caves—end at Rhine House, where a good time is had by all tasting award-winning wines. (It's a mob scene here in summer; to avoid the crowds, head up to Beringer's Reserve Room on the second floor of Rhine House, where generous samples of better wines are poured.) Open daily 10 A.M.–6 P.M. from late May through October, until 5 P.M. otherwise, with historical tours departing every half-hour. Closed on major holidays. Group tours by appointment only.

At the Charles Krug Home Ranch, the **Charles Krug Winery,** 2800 Main St. (Hwy. 29), 707/963-5057 or 800/682-5784, www

.charleskrug.com, was founded in 1861, making it the valley's oldest working winery. Now owned by Robert Mondavi's brother, Peter Mondavi, the winery is noted for its consistently good California cabernets—among the best anywhere. Krug also offers quite popular tours, which were suspended recently while the winery was being retrofitted. The regular free 45-minute facility tour covering everything from the ancient 30,000-gallon redwood aging tanks to a review of new computer-assisted winemaking technology, followed by a 15-minute tasting session (no charge, no reservations required). The "select tasting" option, possible in addition to the tour, offers visitors eight premium wines (including vintage reserve cabernets) for leisurely tasting, no reservations needed. Call for other tour information. Tasting room—the first established in the Napa Valley—is open daily 10:30 A.M.–5 P.M. Note the redwood tasting bars, built from 19th-century aging casks.

The beautiful, three-story stone structure on the north end of town is the famed former 1888 **Christian Brothers' Greystone Winery,** now the Napa Valley campus of the **Culinary Institute of America** (CIA), 2555 Main St., 707/967-1100 or 800/333-9242, www.ciachef.edu. Foodies, stop by for a superlative lunch or dinner at the **Wine Spectator Greystone Restaurant** on the first floor of the original winery, 707/967-1010, serving "cuisine de terroir" to complement regional wines; reservations are usually essential. While you're here, wander through the museum of winemaking memorabilia (open daily 10 A.M.–6 P.M.), which includes a collection of unique corkscrews.

At home midway between Calistoga and St. Helena is historic **Schramsberg Vineyards,** 1400 Schramsberg Rd., 707/942-4558, www.schramsberg.com, established in 1862 by Jacob Schram, five miles north of St. Helena off Hwy. 29. This was the first hillside winery in Napa Valley and was immortalized by Robert Louis Stevenson in his *Silverado Squatters* (". . . and the wine is bottled poetry"). Jacob Schram was one of the first to successfully export American wines to Europe. So it should have come as no surprise when Schramsberg produced the "California champagne" President Nixon took along on his first trip to China in 1971. And how appropriate: part of Schramsberg's secret of success is its collection of underground wine caves, dug by Chinese workers out of volcanic tufa deposits. The original Victorian home and old underground cellars, tucked into oaks and madrones, have been carefully preserved, but most visitors pay more attention to the wines. A beautiful peach-colored Cuvée de Gamay and a Cuvée de Pinot are among Schramsberg's prestigious specialties, though other winemakers make equally impressive sparklers. Very difficult to get into; tours are by appointment only, and tastings ($20) are not offered without a tour. For tour reservations call 707/942-2414.

Oakville Area

Most famous of all is the landmark **Robert Mondavi Winery,** 7801 St. Helena Hwy. in Oakville, 707/259-9463 or 888/766-6328, www.mondavi.com. Centerpiece of the winery is Cliff May's California mission-style building, with the famous arch and tower pictured on the winery's labels. Robert Mondavi boasts decent wines, a never-ending schedule of marquee entertainment, and the best free tour available for the untutored. Drop by early or call first for reservations; tours are limited and fill up fast, especially in summer. Open year-round daily 9 A.M.–5 P.M., with the exception of Easter, Thanksgiving, Christmas, and New Year's Day. A partnership venture between Robert Mondavi and the Baroness Philippine de Rothschild is adjacent **Opus One** winery, 707/944-9442, www.opusonewinery.com, The building itself resembles this Franco-American duet, a partnership between New World and Old World—redwood and stainless steel combined with the aesthetics of cream-colored limestone. According to architect Scott Johnson, Opus One is "introverted, like a jewel box." Introverted or not, the partnership has produced very expensive progeny. It's even expensive to taste here ($25). North of Mondavi, exceptional and relaxed **Cakebread Cellars,** 8300 St. Helena Hwy., 707/963-5221, www.cakebread.com, is noted for cabernet sauvignon, sauvignon blanc, chardonnay, syrah, and special wines like Vin de Porche, everything housed in a striking, abstract barn. Open daily (except holidays) 10 A.M.–4 P.M. for tastings ($5 and

ZEN OF ZIN

Just where California's historic zinfandel hailed from has long been a mystery. Because of its similarities to Italy's primitivo, some of the wine's aficionados were convinced that the wine's roots would be traced back to the Mediterranean. Yet zinfandel, the robust wine associated with California winemaking since the gold rush, originated in the Balkans. Research by Carole Meredith, a grape geneticist at UC Davis, confirmed early in the new millennium that the zinfandel grape is genetically identical to the obscure Croatian black grape crljenak (pronounced "cheer-ya-knock") recently discovered along the Dalmatian coast. Meredith believes the grape may have grown there for 1,000 years, and that crljenak is indigenous to the Balkans because the area is the center of its genetic diversity, a fact proven by the large number of closely related grapes in the same area.

Among unanswered questions are zinfandel's parentage, a matter Meredith will pursue, and just how the globetrotting grape got to California, a question best left to the historians. Some believe zinfandel came to California after Croatian grapevines from the imperial nursery in Vienna were imported to Long Island in 1829; a Boston nurseryman was selling vines identified as "zenfendel" by 1831. According to one dispersal theory, descendants of these imported vines were carried to California during the gold rush by New Englanders. Others think the grapevines were imported by Croatians enticed to California during the gold rush.

$10 options). Good 1.5-hour tours are free, typically offered at 10:30 A.M. and 2 P.M., but reservations are required; call 707/963-5222 to schedule. Special tour/tastings (not free) include the Library Classics Tour and the Wine-Food Tasting Experience.

East of Oakville **Silver Oak Cellars,** 915 Oakville Cross Rd., 800/273-8809, www.silveroak.com, produces only cabernet sauvignon, aged five years before release, and lives by the motto: "Life is a cabernet." Silver Oak is open for wine sales and tasting ($10) Mon.–Sat. 9 A.M.–

4 P.M., and for tours by advance appointment only, weekdays at 1:30 P.M. **Rudd Winery,** 500 Oakville Cross Rd. (on the valley's east side), 707/944-8577, www.ruddwines.com, which offers tours and tastings together ($20) by appointment only, daily at 10:30 A.M. and 2:30 P.M. West of Oakville up the hill on Mt. Veeder is **Chateau Potelle Winery,** 3875 Mt. Veeder Rd. (off Oakville Grade), 707/255-9440, www.chateaupotelle.com, a noted producer of zinfandel and cabernet sauvignon, open fall and winter Thurs.–Mon. 11 A.M.–5 P.M., daily 11 A.M.–6 P.M. starting in mid-April. Chateau Potelle wines were served at the first President George Bush's inaugural dinner.

Rutherford Area

Vine-covered **Beaulieu Vineyard** (BV), 1960 St. Helena Hwy. S, 707/967-5200 (main number) and 707/967-5230 or 800/373-5896 (visitor center), www.beaulieuvineyard.com, an old family winery founded by Georges de Latour in 1900, survived Prohibition by producing altar wines. Beaulieu is known for being an early pioneer in developing premium chardonnay and pinot noir vineyards in the Carneros district; BV is also credited with making cabernet sauvignon "king of the California wines." Open daily 10 A.M.–5 P.M. (excellent guided tour and tasting). Continuing north, **Grgich Hills,** 1829 St. Helena Hwy., 707/963-2784 or 800/532-3057, www.grgich.com, offers some of the valley's finest chardonnay and zinfandel. Open daily 9:30 A.M.–4:30 P.M. for tastings, for tours by appointment only.

A hot destination among moviegoers is the **Niebaum-Coppola Estate Winery,** now headquartered at 1991 St. Helena Hwy., 707/963-9099, www.niebaum-coppola.com, the former chateau of the Inglenook Winery, acquired along with the vineyards in 1994. But the daring filmmaker and screenwriter Francis Ford Coppola (*The Godfather, Apocalypse Now,* and Bram Stoker's *Dracula,* among many others) and his wife have been making wine at their original Napa Valley estate (adjacent) for years. Tastings—cabernet sauvignon, cabernet franc, pinot noir, merlot, syrah, zinfandel, and more—are offered daily, and don't miss the museum in the Inglenook Chateau, where Coppola's and Inglenook's histories are on display. Shopping is another main attraction, what with the wine, books, movie-themed gifts, sweatshirts, T-shirts, even F.F. Coppola's own line of pastas, vinegars, olive oils, candies, and cigars. Keep an eye out for copies of another Coppola enterprise, the literary magazine *Zoetrope*. Tours of the chateau, the vineyards, and the Rubicon red wine process are offered regularly; call 707/968-1161 to confirm times and make reservations.

East of Rutherford, Rutherford Cross Road leads to more wine tasting. **Frog's Leap,** 8815 Conn Creek Rd., 707/963-4704 or 800/959-4704, www.frogsleap.com, seemingly an amphibious takeoff on Stags' Leap Winery, was founded in 1981 in a spot along Mill Creek known as Frog Farm. The winery produces organically grown premium chardonnay, cabernet sauvignon, sauvignon blanc, and zinfandel varietals, as well as, ahem, Leapfrögmilch. The winery is very small and open for retail sales Mon.–Sat. 10 A.M.–4 P.M., tours and tastings by appointment only.

Continue on to Silverado Trail and turn north (left) to reach the well-known **Rutherford Hill Winery,** 200 Rutherford Hill Rd. (at Silverado Trail), 707/963-1871 (office) or 707/963-7194 (visitor center), www.rutherfordhill.com. The winery looks like an old-fashioned hay barn perched on the hill—but there's nothing really "country" here except the straw-colored white wines and flowery picnic grounds. Noted for its award-winning merlot, cabernet sauvignon, sauvignon blanc, and several other varietals, Rutherford Hill's wine-aging caves are quite spectacular, the tunnels and cross-tunnels capable of storing 6,500 small oak barrels. (Some of these caves, like most throughout the region, were dug by Alf Burtleson using a Welsh coal-mining machine with carbide teeth.) Open daily 10 A.M.–5 P.M. for tastings and public picnicking, with cave tours offered three times daily, at 11:30 A.M. and 1:30 and 3:30 P.M.

Head south on Silverado Trail to find several other wineries. Small **Conn Creek Winery,** 8711 Silverado Trail, 707/963-9100, www.conncreek.com, is low-key and lovely, producing cabernet franc, cabernet sauvignon, merlot, and and its

Bordeaux-style Anthology red wine blend. Wine tasting offered daily 10 A.M.–4 P.M. ($5), closed on major holidays, tours by appointment only. Also worth a stop is **Mumm Cuvée Napa,** 8445 Silverado Trail, 707/967-7700 or 800/686-6272, www.mummcuveenapa.com, acclaimed for its sparkling wines and open daily for tasting ($5–12) and free tours 10 A.M.–5 P.M. (last tour at 3 P.M.). Private 1.5-hour tours with tastings ($10–20) are also offered. Of special note here are the two galleries, one of which features a permanent exhibit of Ansel Adams photographs. **ZD Wines,** 8383 Silverado Trail, 707/963-5188 or 800/487-7757, www.zdwines.com, makes fine pinot noir, merlot, cabernet sauvignon, and chardonnay. Open daily 10 A.M.–4:30 P.M. for tasting, $5–10.

South of St. Helena

Among the closest wineries to town, **Merryvale Vineyards,** 1000 Main St. (next to Tra Vigne), 707/963-7777, www.merryvale.com, is noted for its award-winning wines, antique cask collection, and bocce ball court. Merryvale offers a very worthwhile two-hour wine seminar ($15) on weekends, 10:30 A.M., call ahead for reservations; on the fourth weekend of every month the seminar focuses on wine and food pairing. Tasting room open daily 10 A.M.–6:30 P.M.

Heading south from St. Helena toward Rutherford on Hwy. 29, every driveway seems to lead to a different winery. Just south of town is **Louis Martini Winery,** 254 St. Helena Hwy. S (Hwy. 29), 707/963-2736 or 800/321-9463, www.louismartini.com, the family legacy of three generations. The refurbished tasting room is open daily 10:30 A.M.–4:30 P.M. for tastings, tours, and picnicking. Across the street is **Sutter Home Winery,** 277 St. Helena Hwy. S, 707/963-3104, www.sutterhome.com, famous for its white zinfandel and chardonnay. The tasting room is open daily 10 A.M.–5 P.M. offering complimentary tastings and self-guided garden tours. Next door, off the highway, small, family-owned **Prager Winery and Port Works,** 1281 Lewelling Ln., 707/963-7678 or 800/969-7678, www.pragerport.com, is open daily 10:30 A.M.–4:30 P.M. for tasting, tours only by appointment.

Prager also offers bed-and-breakfast accommodations at the winery.

Continuing south, the small family-owned **V. Sattui Winery,** White Ln. at Hwy. 29 (1.5 miles south of St. Helena), 707/963-7774 or 800/799-2337, www.vsattui.com, is as renowned for its fabulous setting and tasting room (stone-and-beam construction) as it is for its award-winning wines, sold directly to consumers. Also here: a Eurostyle deli stocking some 200 local and imported cheeses, and a pleasant three-acre picnic area. Open daily 8 A.M.–5:30 P.M., for tours by appointment. Founded in 1961, the family-owned **Heitz Wine Cellars,** 436 St. Helena Hwy. S. (Hwy. 29), 707/963-3542, www.heitzcellar.com, rose to world renown with its Martha's Vineyard cabernet sauvignon. Heitz now makes Napa Valley, Bella Oaks Vineyard, and Trailside Vineyard cabernets as well, along with chardonnay, zinfandel, and grignolino. The tasting room, housed in what was the original winery, is open daily 11 A.M.–4:30 P.M. Tours of the winery, 500 Taplin Rd., are by appointment only. **Flora Springs Wine Company,** 677 St. Helena Hwy. S., 707/963-5711 or 800/913-1118, www.florasprings.com, specializes in estate-grown chardonnay, sauvignon blanc, cabernet sauvignon, and merlot. The winery's tasting room and visitor center is open Mon.–Sat. 10 A.M.–5 P.M.; tasting is $5 ($8 for premium wines), and winery tours are only by appointment. Just south, a family enterprise well worth a stop is **Milat Vineyards,** 1091 St. Helena Hwy. S, 707/963-0758 or 800/546-4528, www.milat.com, open daily 10 A.M.–6 P.M., which offer estate-grown St. Helena wines including cabernet sauvignon, pinot noir, merlot, chenin blanc, and chardonnay. Accommodations are available in cottages on the vineyard property. Just north, family-operated **Whitehall Lane Winery,** 1563 St. Helena Hwy. S., 707/963-9454 or 800/963-9454, www.whitehalllane.com, a consistent *Wine & Spirits* magazine Winery of the Year. The modern redwood winery produces winning Rutherford and St. Helena varietals, including cabernet sauvignon, merlot, and up-and-coming chardonnay and sauvignon blanc, and welcomes visitors in its friendly tasting room. Open daily 11 A.M.–6 P.M. (tours by appointment).

North of St. Helena

North of St. Helena, you'll find yet more tasting opportunities. **Markham Vineyards,** 2812 St. Helena Hwy. N. (in the 1876 St. Helena Cooperative Winery building), 707/963-5292, www.markhamvineyards.com, is open daily 10 A.M.–5 P.M. for tasting of its premium cabernet sauvignon, merlot, sauvignon blanc, and chardonnay. Tours are offered by appointment, only to trade and corporate groups. **Freemark Abbey Winery,** 3022 St. Helena Hwy. N. (two miles north of St. Helena on Hwy. 29), 707/963-9694 or 800/963-9698, www.freemarkabbey.com, occupies an 1895 building filled with new winery technology. The specialties here are chardonnay, riesling, and cabernet sauvignon—including the prestigious Cabernet Bosché. Open daily 10 A.M.–5 P.M., tours by appointment.

A favorite for those with a similarly peculiar sense of humor is **Folie à Deux,** 3070 St. Helena Hwy. N., 707/963-1160 or 800/473-4454, www.folieadeux.com. Two psychiatrists started this "shared fantasy or delusion," believing that people are crazy to go into the wine business, but also believing that wine and life go together. Share their fantasy and taste the award-winning zins and cabs and Menage à Trois red and white blends. Open daily 10 A.M.–5 P.M. for tasting, with public picnicking. Cave tours and barrel tasting by appointment only.

East of St. Helena

Across the valley, getting into **Joseph Phelps Vineyards,** 200 Taplin Rd. (off Silverado Trail), 707/963-2745, www.jpvwines.com, takes some work, though it is worth the effort. Spectacular cabernet sauvignon and Rhône-style varietals and blends. Open for retail sales Mon.–Sat. 9 A.M.–5 P.M., Sun. 10 A.M.–4 P.M. (tours, tasting, and picnicking by appointment).

In the Deer Park area, **Burgess Cellars,** 1108 Deer Park Rd., 707/963-4766 or 800/752-9463, www.burgesscellars.com, is another rare old stone and woodframe winery, this one also producing premium varietals—cabernet franc, cabernet sauvignon, zinfandel, syrah, and chardonnay—and serving up some sumptuous valley views as well. Open for retail sales 10 A.M.–4 P.M. daily, for tasting and tours by appointment only.

STAYING IN AND NEAR ST. HELENA

Inns, B&Bs, and Hotels

In general, there's not much room at the inn in St. Helena for people without *money,* though well-located camping with hot showers is available at Bothe–Napa Valley State Park (see listing above). A great deal a few miles outside town is the venerable **White Sulphur Springs Inn & Spa,** 3100 White Sulphur Springs Rd., 707/963-8588 or 800/593-8873 (spa: 707/967-8366 or 707/967-8396), www.whitesulphursprings.com, which offers rustic cottages and small hotel rooms with no frills—just trails, meadows, trees, hammocks, and lounge chairs. No phones, no TVs. Rooms in the carriage house share baths down the hall, European-style, and are $85–100. Hotel rooms are $115–140, cottages $150–210.

Fairly pricey bed-and-breakfast establishments are the rule in and around St. Helena. Greater St. Helena offers a lengthy list of B&Bs—contact the chamber of commerce for a current listing—but local options include the **Ambrose Bierce House,** 1515 Main St., 707/963-3003, www.ambrosebiercehouse.com, the crotchety cynic's former residence, an 1870 Victorian with three guest rooms, all with private bath, $200–300. A surprise, though, and a particularly good deal in winter is **El Bonita Motel,** 195 Main St. (on the south end of town), 707/963-3216 or 800/541-3284, www.elbonita.com. Once a darker (and cheaper) 1950s motel, now the El Bonita is all spruced up. Some rooms are smallish (and the walls are thinnish), but all come with TV, phone, alarm clock, wall heaters, window air-conditioners, microwaves, refrigerators, and in-room coffee; some rooms have whirlpool baths. Rates rise and fall seasonally, with rooms $100–200 and suites $150–300. An updated version of 19th-century St. Helena is presented by the landmark 1888 **Hotel St. Helena,** 1309 Main St., 707/963-4388 or 888/478-4355, www.hotelsthelena.com, an 18-room inn that feels as much like a B&B as a hotel. The rooms

WINE COUNTRY

are all furnished with antiques, and most have private baths. Rates include continental breakfast in the lobby. Midweek rates are $100–150, weekend $150–250, and suites $250 and up.

Exceptional among uptown contemporary hotels is the English Tudor–style **Harvest Inn,** 1 Main St. in downtown St. Helena, 707/963-9463 or 800/950-8466, www.harvestinn.com, tucked into acres of gardens and featuring 54 luxurious rooms and cottages graced with antiques; many have wood-burning fireplaces. Endless amenities include in-room refrigerators, wetbars, vanities, and patios or balconies. Rental bikes available. Rates are $250 and up, but winter rates are more affordable.

South of St. Helena, the **Rancho Caymus Inn,** 1140 Rutherford Rd. (one block east of Hwy. 29) in Rutherford, 707/963-1777 or 800/845-1777, www.ranchocaymus.com, is a fine Old California–style hotel, its 26 suites a marvel of skilled craftsmanship, from the adobe walls and fireplaces (wood-burning), hand-thrown pottery sinks, and hand-hewn beams and furnishings to south-of-the-border wall hangings and evocative stained glass. Rates: $250 and up.

Auberge du Soleil

This 33-acre elite but relaxed retreat among the olive trees on Rutherford Hill above the Silverado Trail evokes the sunny south of France, from the village-clustered cottages on the terraced hillside to the panoramic valley views. Each of the 11 rough-walled two-story cottages features four large rooms and suites, each with a private entrance, private terrace with French doors, and plenty of privacy. The basics include tiled floors, fireplaces, large and luxurious bathrooms with every imaginable amenity, and refrigerators stocked with wine, cheese, and snacks. Rates: $250 and up—way up, to $2,500 per night for an 1,800-square-foot cottage.

Other facilities at Auberge du Soleil include a multi-million dollar spa with swimming pool with Jacuzzi, sauna, massage room, well-supplied exercise room, and three tennis courts. The Auberge Spa offers several hotel and spa getaway packages. If the tab for an overnight here would put a serious dent in the monthly budget, don't

let that keep you from a marvelous meal at the exceptional on-site restaurant. Lunch and dinner served daily, though a dinner is very expensive. Many opt to have a glass of wine and an appetizer on the deck, where you can enjoy the lovely view of surrounding vineyards.

For more information or to make reservations, contact: Auberge du Soleil, 180 Rutherford Hill Rd., 707/963-1211 or 800/348-5406, www .aubergedusoleil.com.

Meadowood Napa Valley Resort

Also tops for hotel-style resort luxury in St. Helena is the 256-acre **Meadowood Napa Valley Resort,** which looks out on St. Helena and vicinity from just above the Silverado Trail. Guest rooms and suites inside the gray New Englandesque mansions and lodges are scattered around the wooded grounds along with tennis courts, two croquet lawns, a nine-hole golf course, lap pool, and complete spa facilities. Rates are $250 and up. Nonguests with reservations can enjoy the two excellent on-site restaurants—the **Restaurant at Meadowood,** for fine dining overlooking the golf course, and the more casual **The Grill at Meadowood,** for its breakfast, lunch, and Sunday brunch. For more information or to make reservations, contact Meadowood Resort, 900 Meadowood Ln., 707/963-3646 or 800/458-8080, www.meadowood.com.

EATING IN ST. HELENA
The Basics

For the absolutely freshest local produce, show up for the **St. Helena–Napa Valley Certified Farmers Market,** 707/252-2105, held May–Oct. every Fri. 7:30 A.M.–11:30 A.M. at St. Helena Hwy. (Hwy. 29) and Grayson-Crane Park. The **Model Bakery** in St. Helena, 1357 Main St., 707/963-8192, is a must-do destination—one of the best bakeries anywhere, specializing in European country-style breads and still using its 1920s brick-and-sand ovens (without thermostats). The Model Bakery is noted for its sourdough bread—the starter is made from wine grapes—as well as seeded whole-wheat sourdough, walnut, and black olive breads, not to mention pizzas and pastries. **Guigni's Deli,** 1227 Main St., 707/963-3421, is a local institution making hefty sandwiches for about $5 (including salad). It's a good, unpretentious place for putting picnic fixings together. In bad picnic weather, you can even eat in the back. Sunny **Sunshine Foods,** 1115 Main St., 707/963-7070, is the place to stop for just about anything else.

South of St. Helena and Rutherford in Oakville, the famed **Oakville Grocery Co.,** 7856 St. Helena Hwy., 707/944-8802, is actually an upscale deli featuring items like country hams, salmon jerky, pâtés, truffles, imported caviar and cheeses, and an endless array of curds, butters, chutneys, and marmalades. Not to mention decadent desserts, pastries, and premium wines and beers. Or get picnic supplies at **Napa Valley Olive Oil Manufacturing Company,** hidden away at 835 Charter Oak Ave. south of town (at Allison Avenue), a real find for wonderful sausages, cheeses, and other reasonably priced, authentic Italian deli fare, even extra-virgin California olive oil. Picnic tables, too. Call 707/963-4173 for hours and directions.

Good and Affordable

Surprisingly good food is almost everywhere around town, so poke around to see what's new. For a casual meal, try a longstanding St. Helena original—the 1950s-style drive-up **Taylor's Automatic Refresher,** 933 Main St., 707/963-3486, a burger-and-fries stand originally opened here by Lloyd Taylor in 1949. Now owned by the folks behind Palisades Market in Calistoga, Taylor's has outstanding and unusual milkshakes (vanilla as well as white pistachio), onion rings, and shady picnic tables out back. But this is no ordinary fast-food establishment. You can also get fish tacos, fish and chips with halibut, ahi burgers (with wasabi mayo and pickled ginger), and wine—plus Taylor's accepts American Express. Open daily 11 A.M.–9 P.M. Another St. Helena classic is **Gillwood's Cafe,** 1313 Main St., 707/963-1788, a locals-friendly, sit-down restaurant and bakery famous for its herb rolls and omelettes, serving breakfast until 3 P.M.

Big burritos, guacamole with big chunks of avocado, and melt-in-your mouth carnitas keep locals (and fancy food-weary tourists) happy at **Villa Corona** 1138 Main St., 707/257-8685, a family-run place serving straight-up Mexican food. The place has a walk-up order counter and a comforting, homey atmosphere. For something stylish yet family-friendly and casual, head for **Tomatina** inside the Inn at Southbridge, 1020 Main St., 707/967-9999, where the self-serve menu runs to pasta, imaginative pizza, and *piadine,* or open-faced flatbread sandwiches. Open daily for lunch and dinner.

High style yet homey and not all that expensive, **Cindy's Backstreet Kitchen,** 1327 Railroad Ave. (between Hunt and Adams), 707/963-1200, is Cindy Pawlcyn's latest Napa Valley venture—eclectic American comfort foods in the Buckeye Roadhouse-Fog City Diner-Mustards Grill tradition. Signature dishes like meatloaf, Backstreet fry, and spring chicken pie share the menu with some surprises, like the rabbit tostada and the duck burger with sweet and savory shiitake ketchup. There are some grand desserts, too, including the amazing campfire pie—guaranteed to remind you of summertime s'mores. Full bar.

Also noteworthy for fine food without the usual Napa Valley fuss is the **Market** bistro, 1347 Main St. (between Spring and Adam), 707/963-3799, with most entrées under $15. At lunch and dinner look for home-style classics such as macaroni and cheese, roasted portabello sandwich, thick pork chop with house-made applesauce, and buttermilk fried chicken with mashed potatoes and cornbread. There are uptown options, too, such as sautéed Alaskan halibut with Meyer lemon vinaigrette. Comfort desserts, too, and an exceptional wine list. Open Wed.–Mon for lunch, Wed.–Sun. for dinner.

Haute and Hautest

Finding fine food—to accompany the area's fine wines—seems to be a favorite pastime in and around St. Helena. Reservations at the region's best restaurants are mandatory. **Tra Vigne,** 1050 Charter Oak Ave., 707/963-4444, offers a stunningly serene setting and fine California-style Italian fare in the Napa Valley style but the Tuscany tradition: simple sauces, fresh and hearty food, just about everything house-made. Some people make a meal out of the appetizers or pastas and pizzas. Great desserts. All this in a refurbished old stone building with sky-high ceilings and a relaxed, breezy atmosphere, refreshingly unaffected. Open daily for lunch and dinner. For something lighter or less expensive at lunch—or to grab something delicious to go—try **Cantinetta Tra Vigne** in front, 707/963-8888.

At home in a historic and romantic fieldstone building is **Terra,** 1345 Railroad Ave., 707/963-8931, serving a changing menu of Northern Italian/Southern French with an Asian accent. Entrées might include grilled Maine lobster with saffron risotto and broiled sake-marinated Alaskan black cod and shrimp dumplings. No one was surprised when chef Hiro Sone was named 2003 Best California Chef by the James Beard Foundation. Open Wed.–Mon. for dinner only.

Joaquim Splichal, of L.A.'s famed Patina restaurant and its various Pinot siblings, has arrived in the Napa Valley. Splichal's festive French bistro-style **Pinot Blanc,** 641 Main St., 707/963-6191, serves both hearty fare and lighter selections, either in the dining room or out on the vine-covered patio. The intimate surroundings make for great atmosphere, though sit outside if at all possible. Open for lunch and dinner daily.

Don't leave town before trying out the Culinary Institute of America's **Wine Spectator**

Restaurant at Greystone, at home on the first story of the historic onetime Greystone Chateau north of town, 2555 Main St. (at Deer Park), 707/967-1010. The menu changes constantly, for starters as well as full lunches or dinners, according to the season, and much of the produce comes from the restaurant's own terrace gardens. Delightful New American food, from Dungeness crab salad to fresh quail, is served from a large open kitchen. Weather permitting, enjoy your meal on one of the outdoor terraces—or by an open fire. Greystone has beautiful surroundings both inside and out. Open daily in summer for lunch (call for off-season days and times) and daily year-round for dinner. Full bar. Reservations essential in summer.

The ultimate in destination dining, though, is the fabulous French **La Toque,** 1140 Rutherford Cross Rd. just south of St. Helena in Rutherford, 707/963-9770, understated and sophisticated, the dining room warmed by candlelight and, much of the year, by a huge stone fireplace. La Toque serves an ever-changing menu with entrées such as roasted Oregon quail with port and green peppercorns and wild Atlantic striped bass with lobster cabernet sauce At last report the prix-fixe menu was $98. During the holiday season La Toque also offers several different truffle menus. Open Wed.–Sun. for dinner, reservations essential.

Calistoga and Vicinity

Despite the Napa Valley's hectic hubbub, there's something fun and funky about Calistoga. It's genuinely *hot,* for one thing, built atop a boiling underground river. Industrious Sam Brannan officially laid out the town in 1859 on the site of the natives' Colaynomo, or "oven place." Brannan's dream was to make the area the "Saratoga of California." So his original hotel and 20 cottages were christened "Calistoga"—an awkward combination of the state's name and the well-known resort spa in New York. The spas here are still going strong—along with area wineries, downtown shops, galleries and restaurants. Yet during much of the year Calistoga still feels far

removed from the madding crowds. For more information, contact the **Calistoga Chamber of Commerce,** 1458 Lincoln Ave. #9 (in the back of the Depot building), 707/942-6333, www.calistogachamber.com.

SEEING AND DOING CALISTOGA

The main stop nowadays (besides the spas and nearby wineries) is **Sharpsteen Museum** and the adjacent **Sam Brannan Cottage,** 1311 Washington St., 707/942-5911, www.sharpsteen-museum.org. The modern brick museum, next to

© KIM WEIR

Sam Brannan Cottage

public restrooms and the senior center, features a well-designed diorama of 1865 Calistoga plus antique dolls, clothing, and quilts. The cottage itself is furnished in wealthy San Franciscan, circa late 1800s. Open daily 11 A.M.–4 P.M., $3 donation requested; docent-guided tours can be arranged. In the mood for classical ruins and Renaissance art but can't afford the airfare to Italy? Special tours of Calistoga's marvelous (and marvelously amusing) **Villa Ca'Toga,** home of the artist and noted muralist Carlo Machiori, featuring trompe l'oeil murals and floors, are offered on Saturday mornings May–Oct., $20 per person (no children under 12, no pets). Tour tickets and art can be purchased at the **Ca'Toga Galleria D'Arte,** near downtown at 1206 Cedar St., 707/942-3900, www.catoga.com, open daily except Tuesday and Wednesday.

Downtown at 1458 Lincoln, California's oldest surviving railroad depot has been converted into the **Calistoga Depot,** 1458 Lincoln Ave, Calistoga with shops, a café, and the chamber of commerce office. Some good galleries and shops are scattered elsewhere throughout Calistoga. Also in the area: production facilities for well-known mineral waters, including Calistoga, Crystal Geyser, and Napa Valley Spring Water.

Well worth a stop in Calistoga is the **Evans Designs Gallery,** 1421 Lincoln Ave., 707/942-0453, the world's leading producer of raku pottery, open daily 10 A.M.–6 P.M. Evans also offers unique glass pieces. Overruns, seconds, and prototypes are for sale at the studio outlet here, where prices are 40–90 percent lower than retail—such a deal. **Hurd Beeswax Candles,** 1255 Lincoln Ave., 707/942-7410 or 800/977-7211, www.hurdbeeswaxcandles.com, is a retail store with a demonstration beehive and small candle workshop where you can see how handmade candles are made. To make your own organic beeswax candles, Hurd sells sheets of honeycomb, intriguing wax blends, and other candle-making supplies.

Spas

Bathe in a volcano—or at least the bubbling springs and murky mud generated by one. The combinations available for curing yourself of whatever ails you are almost endless, but the basic routine is this: a soak in a mud bath usually followed by a mineral bath and whirlpool (with or without steam bath and blanket sweat), finished with a massage. Some new twists: herbal facials, herbal wraps, eucalyptus steams, and Japanese-style enzyme baths (heat-generating tubs full of cedar, bran, and fiber).

Nance's Hot Springs, 1614 Lincoln, 707/942-6211, is a good place to take the mud cure. The basic program includes hot springs mineral bath, steam bath, black volcanic mud bath, and blanket sweat; extra for massage. (Nance's is also a clean and fresh downtown motel with nice mountain views). Sam Brannan's original resort site is now completely renovated at nearby **Indian Springs Spa and Hot Springs Resort,** 1712 Lincoln, 707/942-4913, which boasts a huge 1913 geyser-heated mineral swimming pool. The spa menu includes mud baths (100 percent volcanic ash) with mineral bath, eucalyptus steam, and blanket wrap (all about one hour), with half-hour massage extra. Reservations are necessary for **Dr. Wilkinson's Hot Springs,** 1507 Lincoln, 707/942-4102 for reservations, www.drwilkinson.com, which offers a bathhouse, no-nonsense complete physical therapy package, and 1950s-style accommodations ($150–250). **Calistoga Spa Hot Springs,** 1006 Washington, 707/942-6269, www.calistogaspa.com, is family-oriented, with use of outdoor mineral pools, mud baths, and massage extra.

Housed in an old bank building, **Lincoln Avenue Spa,** 1339 Lincoln, 707/942-5296, www .lincolnavenuespa.com, offers a mineral Jacuzzi, acupressure face lifts, herbal facials, manicures and pedicures, mud wraps, and massage. Open daily 9 A.M.–9 P.M. At **Lavender Hill Spa,** 1015 Foothill Blvd. (Hwy. 29), 707/942-4495, or 800/528-4772, www.lavenderhillspa.com, you can get a unique type of low-viscosity mud bath ("like a sango bath without the salicyl"), an herbal facial, herbal blanket wrap, massage, acupressure, or reflexology. Bathhouses are designed for couples, and the massage is about the best around. Open daily 9 A.M.–9 P.M. The **Golden Haven Spa,** 1713 Lake St., 707/942-6793, www.goldenhaven.com, is open daily 8 A.M.–9 P.M. and also offers accommodations, some with kitchenettes ($50–250).

Wineries

On the way to Calistoga from St. Helena is the historic weathered-wood-and-old-stone **Frank Family Vineyards,** formerly the famed Hanns Kornell Champagne Cellars, at 1091 Larkmead Ln. (east of Hwy. 29, north of St. Helena), 707/942-0859 or 800/574-9463, which still makes fine sparkling wines, including blanc noir, brut, and rouge, as well as chardonnay, cabernet, sangiovese, and zinfandel. Open daily 10 A.M.–5 P.M. for tasting, tours, and sales.

Several wineries lie along Dunaweal Ln., which intersects Hwy. 29 just south of Calistoga. **Stonegate Winery,** 1183 Dunaweal Ln., 707/942-6500 or toll free 800/946-6500, www.stonegatewinery.com, is a small winery with a big reputation for its premium cabernet sauvignon, sauvignon blanc, and chardonnay. Open daily 10:30 A.M.–4 P.M. for tasting and sales (tours by appointment only). Stop at Seagram's **Sterling Vineyards,** 1111 Dunaweal Ln., 707/942-3344 or 800/726-6136, www.sterlingvineyards.com, for a gondola-car ride up to this majestic, modern, monastic-style Martin Waterfield palace ($10 adults, $5 under 21, toddlers free). Great valley views. Open for tasting and tours (self-guided with visual aids) daily 10:30 A.M.–4:30 P.M., and picnicking May–Oct. Nearby, Bacchus is the big guy at the postmodern terra-cotta **Clos Pégase Winery,** 1060 Dunaweal Lane, 707/942-4981, www.clospegase.com, designed by architect Michael Graves and conceived as a tribute to mythology, art, and wine. Clos Pé-

gase produces cabernet sauvignon, sauvignon blanc, chardonnay, and merlot. Big attractions here are the underground wine caves, a unique art gallery, and the occasional "Wine in Art" slide show. Open daily 10:30 A.M.–5 P.M. for tasting (fee), with guided tours at 11 A.M. and 2 P.M.

Continuing on to Silverado Trail from Dunaweal, you'll find **Cuvaison,** 4550 Silverado Trail, 707/942-6266 or 707/942-2468 (tasting room), www.cuvaison.com, another of the region's elite small wineries. Here wine lovers find some of the best cabernet, chardonnay, merlot, and zinfandel produced anywhere. Open daily 10 A.M.–5 P.M. for tastings ($8), sales, and picnicking (tours by appointment). South down the Silverado Trail from Cuvaison is small **Wermuth Winery,** 3942 Silverado Trail, 707/942-5924, open weekends 11 A.M.–5 P.M. (irregular hours on weekdays, so call first).

Heading north from Dunaweal on the Silverado Trail leads to **Vincent Arroyo Winery,** 2361 Greenwood Ave., 707/942-6995, www.vincentarroyowinery.com, open weekdays 9 A.M.–4:30 P.M., weekends starting at 10 A.M. (tours by appointment), and **Chateau Montelena,** 1429 Tubbs Ln., 707/942-5105, www.montelena.com, open daily 9:30 A.M.–4 P.M. for tasting ($10 fee). Chateau Montelena is noted for its cabernet

WAY-COOL CAVE MUSIC

A Napa-Sonoma wine country phenomenon since 1986, David Auerbach, "the Improvisator," brings his rare musical instruments into the wine caves—from Celtic harp, hammered dulcimer, and psaltery to concertinas, flutes, panpipes, drums, and steel pans—every holiday season for the unique and amazingly popular **Carols in the Caves** concerts. "Cave music" is an adventure in acoustics—as much about silence as it is surprising resonance, reverberation, and echo. Demand is so high for the Improvisator's unique performances that the season keeps expanding, and now includes seasonal and drum concerts as well as a new Halloween show. For current information, contact Carols in the Caves, 707/224-4222, www.cavemusic.net.

sauvignon, which has appeared on White House menus, *and* its intriguing medieval French chateau surrounded by Chinese gardens. Somehow it's all very American. Extensive tours ($25) are offered, 9:30 A.M. and 1:30 P.M. Mar.–Oct., just 1:30 P.M. in winter.

Small, family-owned, and fun **Hans Fahden Vineyards,** 4855 Petrified Forest Rd., 707/942-6760, www.hansfahden.com, is noted for its estate grown cabernet sauvignon. In addition to wine tours and tasting, pack a picnic and head for the Monet Garden. Dinners and special events hosted in the wine caves are locally popular.

Then, if Napa Valley's wineries still haven't quenched that vineyard thirst, head northwest on Hwy. 128 through the mountains above Calistoga into the Alexander Valley area near Healdsburg—such a pleasant, peaceful contrast that you'll wonder why you spent so much time in the Napa Valley. The Field Stone Winery, Alexander Valley Vineyards, and Johnson's Alexander Valley all produce fine wines. For more information, see Healdsburg and Vicinity below.

Old Faithful and Petrified Forest

Northwest of town is California's **Old Faithful Geyser,** 1299 Tubbs Ln., 707/942-6463, www.oldfaithfulgeyser.com, one of just three in the world that erupt on schedule. Lately, Old Faithful has been erupting about every 13 minutes for about 60–90 seconds a shot. That's much more frequently than the 25-year average of about once every 30–45 minutes; the blast once lasted four minutes. Geologists think these and other irregularities indicate seismic changes within the earth. The blasts of hot water and steam shoot up 75–100 feet into the air, creating rainbows if the sun is right. Open daily year-round, 9 A.M.–6 P.M. in summer and 9 A.M.–5 P.M. the rest of the year. Admission is $8 general, $7 seniors, $3 kids 6–12.

Turn west off Hwy. 29 onto Petrified Forest Rd. (just north of downtown Calistoga) to take the back-roads route to Santa Rosa. About five miles down this road is the **Petrified Forest,** 4100 Petrified Forest Rd., 707/942-6667, www.petrifiedforest.org, a California historic landmark of volcano-flattened, fossilized remains

of ancient redwoods along a quarter-mile, wheelchair-accessible trail, with fossils in the small museum. Picnicking possible. Open daily 10 A.M.–6 P.M. in summer, until 5 P.M. in winter. Admission is $5 adults, $3 kids.

Robert Louis Stevenson State Park

Twisting north up Mt. St. Helena like a corkscrew, Hwy. 29 out of Calistoga leads to an easy-to-miss sign at the pass marking essentially undeveloped 5,000-acre Robert Louis Stevenson State Park (about seven miles out of Calistoga, with parking pullouts on both sides of the road). Particularly pleasant in spring and fall, the open mixed woodland offers good hiking and freestyle picnicking (no dogs, no camping, no fires) and blissful quiet. Stevenson honeymooned on the cheap in the old bunkhouse here in 1880 with his American bride. There's a monument on the site of the old Silverado Mine, already abandoned when the couple spent two happy months here. Stevenson wrote parts of *Silverado Squatters* while here and generated notes for some of his later, greater works. He called Mt. St. Helena (the 4,500-foot peak named after a visiting Russian princess) "the Mont Blanc of the Coast Ranges," and, some say, modeled *Treasure Island* scenes from his impressions.

Most of the trail to the summit follows an abandoned roadbed, but it's well worth the five-mile effort for panoramic views of the Sonoma and Napa Valleys, San Francisco to the south, and even (on rare clear and cool smogless days) mighty Mt. Shasta far to the northeast. The park was recently expanded by 588 acres to include a nearby ridge known as the Palisades, a peregrine falcon nesting habitat, thanks to the Napa County Land Trust. A hiking trail links the area below the Palisades to Table Rock and the old Oat Hill Mine Road. Naturalist-led hikes are occasionally offered. For information, call 707/942-4575.

STAYING IN CALISTOGA

It's first-come, first-camped at the **Napa County Fairgrounds,** 1435 Oak St., 707/942-5111, offering fairly cool campsites with electricity and hot showers Rates: tens sites $10, RV hookup $22–25. In town is the friendly landmark **Calistoga Inn,** 1250 Lincoln Ave., 707/942-4101, www.calistogainn.com, a clean and cozy old hotel with genuine nicks in the down-home furniture. Rates include continental breakfast. In the grand old European style, bathrooms and showers are down the hall. Rooms are $75 midweek (ask about the half-price winter special), $100 on weekends. Also affordable are the restyled motor court-style **Carlin Country Cottages,** just a few blocks from the action at 1623 Lake St., 707/942-9102 or 800/734-4624, www.carlincottages.com. Rates are $89–135 for studios, $105–150 for a one-bedroom cottage, and $150–205 for two bedrooms (sleeps up to four). All have a kitchen or kitchenette and private bathroom, air-conditioning, phones, and cable TV. Onsite amenities include an outdoor mineral pool and Jacuzzi.

Otherwise, the cheapest lodging choices are well out of town. A great deal is **Triple S Ranch,** 4600 Mountain Home Ranch Rd., 707/942-6730, a collection of tiny, rustic redwood cabins open Apr.–Dec. Rates: $50–100. The restaurant here is popular with locals, good food for a good price. (To get there from Calistoga, head west on Petrified Forest Rd., then north on Mountain Home Ranch Rd.) **Mountain Home Ranch,** 3400 Mountain Home Ranch Rd., 707/942-6616, www.mtnhomeranch.com, has a lake, creek, pools, and accommodations ranging from rustic cabins to deluxe cottages. Rates: $50–150. Another rarefied rustic possibility is the **Mayacamas Ranch,** 3975 Mountain Home Ranch Rd., 707/942-5127, www.mayacamasranch.com, atop the Mayacamas Mountains on 80 acres of foothill woodlands, with a huge redwood lodge, swimming pool, spring-fed lake, and hot tub. Guests can choose A-frame sleeping cabins, cottages, or high-beamed motel rooms. Popular for group retreats and weddings, individual rooms and cabins are available for $150–250.

Even if you're not doing the spa scene, you can stay at the historic **Indian Springs Resort,** 1712 Lincoln Ave. (between Brannan St. and Wappo Ave.), 707/942-4913, www.indianspringscalistoga.com, where the family-friendly cottages with kitchens are a main attraction—

along with the marvelous swimming pool, fed by natural hot springs (open only to hotel and spa guests). Rates: $250 and up. Or try **Nance's Hot Springs,** 1614 Lincoln, 707/942-6211, www.nanceshotsprings.com, where some rooms have kitchens and rates include use of the hot mineral spa. Midweek rates are $50–100, weekends and holidays $100–150.

Bed-and-Breakfasts

Calistoga boasts a dozen or more bed-and-breakfasts. The art-deco **Mount View Hotel,** 1457 Lincoln Ave., 707/942-6877 or 800/816-6877, www.mountviewhotel.com, is a beautifully restored 1917 hotel-style bed-and-breakfast with Jacuzzi, pool, and spa facilities. Accommodation options include 20 guest rooms (all with private bath), nine suites, and three cottages (each with private patio and Jacuzzi). Continental breakfast is delivered to your room, and the excellent on-site **Catahoula** restaurant, 707/942-2275, serves fare inspired by the Louisiana bayou. Rates: $150–250.

Among the area's other historic offerings, the restored Greek Revival **Brannan Cottage Inn,** 109 Wapoo Ave. (near downtown), 707/942-4200, www.brannancottageinn.com, is one of the original Sam Brannan guesthouses. It offers two suites and four guest rooms, all with private entrances, private baths, and queen beds. Full breakfast. Rates are $100–150. Also included on the National Register of Historic Places is **The Elms,** 1300 Cedar St., 707/942-9476 or 888/399-3567, www.theelms.com, an 1871 home in the French Second Empire style, with six rooms plus a carriage house (all with private bath), afternoon wine and cheese, and full breakfast. Rates are $150–250.

Quite special is small **Scott Courtyard,** 1443 Second St., 707/942-0948 or 800/942-1515, www.scottcourtyard.com, featuring three suites—two with an interconnecting living area, perfect for couples traveling together—and three bungalows, all with unique 1940s and 1950s decor, private bathrooms, and private entrances. Rooms are cheerful and inviting, featuring amenities including in-room coffee makers, refrigerators, irons, and hair dryers; half have wood-burning fireplaces and kitchens. Scott Courtyard also includes a pool, hot tub, art studio, and gardens, and a sunny central bistro-style social area. Generous buffet-style breakfast, afternoon wine and cheese. Rates: $150–250.

The 16 luxurious bed-and-breakfast cabins at the **Cottage Grove Inn,** 1711 Lincoln Ave., 707/942-8400 or 800/942-1515, www.cottagegrove.com, just about have it all, starting with soundproofing, recycled hardwood floors, tasteful decor, wood-burning fireplaces, vaulted ceilings, and front porches with their own white wicker rockers. Creature comforts include the deep two-person Jacuzzi tub, stereo system with CD, cable TV and VCR, refrigerator, wetbar, in-room coffee maker, and phone with modem jack. Not to mention cozy down comforters and pillows, an ironing board and iron, and dressing robes. Expanded continental breakfast, afternoon wine and cheese. Rates: $250 and up. Inquire at the local chamber of commerce for a more complete listing of accommodation options.

EATING IN CALISTOGA

Almost everything is on Lincoln Ave., Calistoga's main drag. **Nicola's Delicatessen,** 1359 Lincoln Ave., 707/942-6272, is open daily 7 A.M.–5 P.M. and makes a good stop for inexpensive breakfast, lunch, or picnic fixings. Another picnic put-together possibility is the stylish **Palisades Market,** 1506 Lincoln, 707/942-9549, stocked with the best regional fare. **Pacifico,** 1237 Lincoln, 707/942-4400, offers a wide-ranging Mexican menu (try the mole del pueblo). If barbecue suits your fancy, head to the **Smokehouse Cafe,** 1458 Lincoln Ave. (in the Depot building), 707/942-6060, which does a fine breakfast and lunch, too, but specializes in finger-lickin' hickory- or mesquite-smoked pork or beef ribs smothered in a choice of barbecue sauces. Brave vegetarians can attempt the smoked barbecue tofu plate.

Hipper by far than most local restaurants is the relaxed **Calistoga Inn,** 1250 Lincoln Ave., 707/942-4101, home of the **Napa Valley Brewing Company** pub, serving its own lagers and ales, and a spicy contemporary menu—like grilled gulf prawns with red-curry Thai sauce, or a home-smoked turkey sandwich with double-cream jack cheese on rye. Meals are served outside (in season) on a relaxed backyard patio.

WINE COUNTRY SAFARI

Here's something you won't see on every wine country tour—a herd of zebras and Saharan desert antelopes. Not a zoo or animal park, **Safari West** is a 400-acre private wildlife sanctuary dedicated to conserving and propagating African plains species in particular. Its endangered-species breeding programs have earned Safari West membership in the American Zoo and Aquarium Association, a rare feat for a private enterprise.

Though animal protection is the primary emphasis here, visitors are welcome—by appointment only—on naturalist-guided small-group jeep tours through the sanctuary. Guests are invited to dress for the experience (comfortable walking shoes, sun hat, and sunscreen) and to bring their cameras, because the photo ops are close to unbelievable on this 2.5-hour trip. Fees are $58 adults, $28 children. Sunset, twilight, photo, and holiday safaris, as well as a group safari/trek (walking during second half),

winter-only walking tours, "wild child nights," and guided hikes are also available.

Since late August 1999, **The Tent Camp at Safari West** has also welcomed guests at its safari-style accommodations—canvas tents with hardwood floors, king-size beds, and separate bathrooms (with showers)—up close to the animals. A guest cottage and lodge, both with private kitchen and bath facilities, are also available. Rates are $225–325 (tent cabins) and $300–400 (cottage), continental breakfast included, with a two-night minimum stay on weekends. Weekly rates are available, but also ask about special packages. For lunch and dinner, dine at the **Savannah Café.**

For more information and tour reservations, contact Safari West, 3115 Porter Creek Rd. between Santa Rosa and Calistoga, 707/579-2551 or 800/616-2695, www.safariwest.com. Ask for directions when you make your tour reservations.

The **All Seasons Market and Cafe,** 1400 Lincoln, 707/942-9111, is something of a wine country destination these days—boasting one of the most impressive, and reasonably priced, wine lists anywhere. California-style wine country fare (changing menu) is served at lunch and dinner. Beloved locally is the **Wappo Bar & Bistro,** 1226-B Washington St. (near Lincoln), 707/942-4712, named for local Native Americans. The style, though, is craftsman-like, and the fare is an eclectic regional take on global cuisine—everything from duck carnitas, chiles rellenos with walnut-pomegranate sauce, and

Moroccan lamb stew to chicken pot pie. Open Wed.–Mon. for lunch and dinner.

Also quite enticing is the **Catahoula Restaurant** at the Mount View Hotel, 1457 Lincoln Ave., 707/942-2275, rather cheekishly named after Louisiana's state dog. Yet Catahoula definitely fits a place serving up creative interpretations of dishes from Louisiana and the Deep South, from oyster Bienville cakes and pan-fried catfish to pizza with andouille sausage and crayfish. Try the brown-butter fruit tarts for dessert. Open for lunch and dinner Wed.–Mon., dinner daily in summer (reservations recommended, especially at dinner).

Lake County

Suffocated by the sophisticated air of the wine country? Too mellowed by Mendocino? Lake County has the cure. The area supported various world-class health spas from the late 1800s through the early 1900s, but now it's a friendly, frumpy, working people's resort and retirement area, as familiar as an old sneaker. Things are inexpensive in the tiny towns around Clear Lake, there are no parking meters, and nobody seems to mind the noise that comes packaged as children. People have been coming here for a long, *long* time. The Clear Lake Basin is one of California's oldest known areas of human habitation: petroglyphs and artifacts found here in recent years date back 10,000 years or more.

Besides the area's hot springs and mineral springs, Lake County is famous for its Bartlett pears. The county's first pear tree was planted in 1854 near Upper Lake. Today there are 1,350 pear orchards in Lake County, number two in the nation for total pear production.

Lately there have been signs that the unpretentious charms of Clear Lake may soon be supplanted. If marketeers have their way—consultants hired early in the new millennium by county supervisors—Clear Lake will be getting a makeover soon, starting with hauling away some of the region's rusty mobile homes and other eyesores. There might even be a name change. Lake Konocti, anyone? Or perhaps Konocti Hills? Can gated subdivisions and golf courses be far behind?

Historic Clear Lake

Pomo peoples lived throughout the Clear Lake Basin, an area naturally rich with game, fish, nuts, and berries. The medicinal value of the hot springs and mineral baths along with abundant hunting spawned a Native American type of tourism: outsiders paid with shells, woodpecker scalps, and fur pelts for the privilege of bathing at Clear Lake. Russian fur trappers entered the region in 1811, but no real conflict occurred until Spanish-American rule. Salvador Vallejo's troops made "pacification raids" near Clear Lake in 1836, killing many Pomos. Children and young men and women were sold as slaves. Surviving natives escaped smallpox, but many were felled by respiratory diseases. Vallejo cattle were driven into the valley to graze, but continuing Indian conflict provoked the land's sale to Americans. Small-scale war with natives came after still crueler treatment at the hands of American settlers, that uprising crushed by U.S. troops from Benicia who slaughtered hundreds of Pomos in the Bloody Island Massacre. But the gold rush and the rapid arrival of still more settlers led to the near decimation of native peoples. Today very few Pomo people live in the area.

TO CLEAR LAKE

The trip from the Napa Valley to Clear Lake via narrow Hwy. 29 (the old Calistoga-Lakeport stage route) is slow but beautiful. Thickly forested hillsides hug the old road, soft green in spring, hazy with blazing color in fall. The only settlement of any size in Loconomi Valley along the way to Clear Lake is **Middletown,** aptly named, since it's exactly halfway between Calistoga and Lower Lake. At the **Calpine Geothermal Visitor Center** at 15500 Central Park Rd. (at Pine) in Middletown, 707/987-4270 or 866/439-7377, www.geysers.com, you can take a free guided bus tour of the nearby geothermal power district, Thurs.–Mon. at 10 A.M., noon, and 2 P.M. Advance reservations required.

Harbin Hot Springs

Close to Middletown is the historic Harbin Hot Springs Retreat Center, 707/987-2477 or 800/622-2477 (reservations only), www.harbin.org, now operated as a nonprofit retreat and workshop center. Once a sacred place for native Pomo people, these days you can sign up for massage, watsu, yoga, and more. Otherwise camp here and do the baths for a very reasonable fee plus membership ($10 trial membership). Or stay in lodge or dorm rooms, or private cottages. Call for details. To get to Harbin from Middletown, take Barnes St. to Big Canyon Rd. (turn right), then turn left outside town onto Harbin Springs Rd. and drive to the end.

Wineries

In the early 1900s, Lake County had almost 40 noted wineries. Among the area's wine pioneers was Seranus C. Hastings, founder of the Hastings School of Law. More famous, though, was the notoriously beautiful and independent British actress Lillie Langtry, who left her husband and came here to raise thoroughbred horses and make Bordeaux wines on her 4,200-acre ranch. **Guenoc & Langtry Estate Vineyards and Winery,** 21000 Butts Canyon Rd. (just east of town), 707/987-2385, www.guenoc.com, was once owned by Langtry—friend of Oscar Wilde, mistress of the Prince of Wales (later King Edward VII), and the state's first celebrity winemaker. The award-winning premium winery welcomes visitors 11:30 A.M.–5 P.M. daily. On special occasions, Langtry's house is open to the public

for group tours—call in advance to arrange a visit—and her likeness is included on every Guenoc wine label.

Though Clear Lake hasn't seriously accommodated itself to the tasting-and-tours set, there are other worthy wineries in the area. **Steele and Shooting Star Wines,** 4350 Thomas Dr. (at Hwy. 29, halfway between Lakeport and Kelseyville), 707/279-9475, www.steelewines.com, was founded by former (and founding) Kendall-Jackson winemaker Jed Steele, previously winemaker at Edmeades. The impressive list—zinfandel, cabernet franc, syrah, pinot noir, chardonnay—goes "beyond the terroir." Steele is open weekdays Mon.–Fri. 11 A.M.–5 P.M. most of the year, also Sat. 8 A.M.–5 P.M. in summer. Tours are available only by appointment. Steele makes a chardonnay cuvée, but the new place for sparkling wines is the one-time Stuermer Winery south of Lower Lake, now **Ployez Winery,** 11171 Hwy. 29, 707/994-2106 or 707/263-8300, www.ployezwines.com, open daily 11 A.M.–5 P.M.

AT CLEAR LAKE

Not only is Clear Lake 19.5 miles long and the largest natural lake completely within the state's borders (Tahoe sloshes over into Nevada), it may also be the oldest lake on the North American continent. Researchers have discovered lake sediments at least 450,000 years old, and some perhaps two million years old. The waters of Clear Lake once flowed west to the Pacific, but the earth's upheavals redirected the outflow east from the Cache Creek gap into the Sacramento River. The dam at Cache Creek is a relatively new addition, raising the lake's summer water level by seven feet. The mythic guardian of Clear Lake, Mt. Konocti is a prominent volcanic peak, technically "active," connected to the lake via an underground passage. At the lake's giant Soda Springs, sulphurous hydrogen bubbles up from the reefs below.

Every so often, huge dead carp line the lakeshore—not a pretty sight, and a powerful stench. But Fish and Game folks say this is a natural phenomenon attributed to "pre-spawning stress syndrome" and unseasonable heat. "Clear" Lake sometimes turns pea-soup green and smelly in late summer and fall, due to algae bloom. At last report the county had an "algae buster" squad to round up the errant floating plant colonies, in bad years, using an algae skimmer designed by Ed Headrick (Frisbee inventor and former local resident). Not so natural, though, are high levels of mercury in the lake's fish. The fishing in Clear Lake is remarkably good, though—so good, in fact, that Cal Bass, U.S. Bass, Western Bass, and other professional bass fishing organizations have designated Clear Lake as the nation's number-one bass lake, based on numbers of fish caught.

Anderson Marsh State Historic Park

Lower Lake proper is little more than a seedy stretch of commercial zoning. But just north of the Hwy. 29/Hwy. 53 junction is Anderson Marsh State Historic Park, a seemingly nonde-script 900 acres rich with tules, rare birds, and the remains of ancient villages. The area was inhabited at least 10,000 years ago by gatherers and hunters, then by various Pomo peoples and their descendants during the past 5,000 years. The marsh areas here and at nearby Borax Lake— considered one of the most important archaeo-logical sites on the Pacific coast—suggest a very different ancient California near the end of the Ice Age: cooler, wetter, and a land of endless lakes in-habited by fierce predators (the agile short-faced bear, saber-toothed cats, the dire wolf) and their prey. Abundant obsidian from Mt. Konocti's oc-casional eruptions made toolmaking (and hunt-ing) here easy.

The historic and restored **John Still Anderson Ranch House** on the highway serves as a small discovery museum, the world's smallest jail, and headquarters for the park—and for ar-chaeology field schools at work here on pro-jects. Beyond the house are the marshes, which in summer seem more like a prairie, with its willow thickets, dry grasses, dried mud, and shy rat-tlesnakes overshadowed in places by gracefully gnarled valley oaks. This is also the 35-acre dig site known as Lake-589. At the other end of the ridge is a reconstructed model Pomo vil-

LA LOOSE CABOOSE, ANYONE?

In an attractive parklike setting along the shores of Clear Lake is the **Featherbed Railroad Co.,** with nine brightly painted, individually deco-rated cabooses now doing duty as bed-and-break-fast rooms. Most elegant is Casa Blanca, with abundant art deco details, and most romantic is The Lovers, also known as the honeymoon ca-boose. La Loose Caboose sports the bordello look, from mirrored ceilings to the black velvet painting imported from Nevada's Mustang Ranch. The red, white, and blue Casey Jones features the largest amount of train memora-bilia. Most have a Jacuzzi tub for two—rather prominently featured, right in the middle of the room. Rates are $100–200. For more informa-tion, contact the Featherbed Railroad Co., 2870 Lakeshore Blvd. in Nice, 707/274-8378 or 800/966-6322, www.featherbedrailroad.com.

lage, including a ceremonial roundhouse where the Elem people celebrate the Big Head Dance. Hiking trails follow Cache Creek and thread elsewhere throughout the area.

Come in April for **Heron Days,** a celebra-tion of the lake's great blue herons and fundraiser for the Rodman Slough heron rookery; some heron nesting sites are here. (Guided walks and kayak tours of Rodman Ranch are also offered; for current details, call the Lake County Land Trust, 707/995-1398, or inquire at the Lake County Visitor Center, 800/525-3743.) In Au-gust is the annual **Blackberry Festival** here, a two-day living history celebration beloved for its blackberry pancakes, blackberry pie, candle-making and butter-churning demonstrations, fiddle contest, and more. Proceeds support stu-dent scholarships. For more information, contact Anderson Marsh State Historic Park in Lower Lake, 707/994-0688.

Clear Lake State Park

Clear Lake State Park is 500 acres of oaks, cot-tonwoods, and lakeshore at the foot of Mt. Konocti. Primarily a camping park, hiking, pic-nicking, swimming, sunbathing, and boating are also popular here. The **Indian Nature Trail** is an easy walk starting near the park's entrance, offering a brief appreciation of the medicinal plants central to Pomo and Lile'ek cultures. (To learn more, visit the museum in Lakeport.) The longer **Dorn Nature Trail** near the lake climbs up through chaparral and oak scrub for a lake view. For years people have boated out to **Soda Baths** from Soda Bay—no facilities, no restrictions, no fees, no address, no phone, just private, natural mineral baths, situated on the island beyond the soda springs themselves. The baths were closed by the BLM following a death from toxic gas concentrations in 2000; the Bureau of Land Management closed the area until a more permeable retaining wall could be built. In any event, ask at the park before using the baths.

The park's year-round campsites (four campgrounds) include hot showers. Camping is $12–16, with a 15-day summer limit; reservations are necessary Mar.–Oct. To reserve campsites, contact **ReserveAmerica,** 800/444-7275, www.reserveamerica.com. For more information contact Clear Lake State Park, 5300 Soda Bay Rd. in Kelseyville, 707/279-4293. To get here, from Kelseyville follow convoluted Soda Bay Road east four miles.

Museums

The charming 1871 **Lake County Courthouse** in Lakeport at 255 Main St. (between Second and Third), 707/263-4555, is a state historic landmark housing a museum *and* superior court. The small but surprisingly fine Lake County Museum includes a display of Pomo basketry—work by the world's finest basketmakers—along with elegant ceremonial clothing, fish and bird traps, grinding stones, thousands of stone tools, and more. Open Wed.–Sat 11 A.M.–4 P.M. The two-story **Lower Lake Historical Schoolhouse and Museum,** 16435 Morgan Valley Road, 707/995-3565, is the county's newest museum, open Wed.–Sat. 11 A.M.–3 P.M., was built in 1877 from local lumber and bricks. On the second floor is a large auditorium and stage. In use as a grammar school until 1935, schoolhouse museum exhibits include pioneer artifacts and geology display from the Homestake Mining Company.

PRACTICALITIES

Everybody knows that **Konocti Harbor Resort,** 8727 Soda Bay Rd. in Kelseyville, is the place to go for hot entertainment—the likes of Merle Haggard, Lyle Lovett, Charlie Musselwhite, Pam Tillis, Eddie Money, and the Robert Cray Band—because the **Joe Mazzola Classic Concert Showroom,** a dinner theater-style venue, is America's top small concert house. Also here is the 5,000-seat **Konocti Field Amphitheater,** for summer open-air concerts, every seat within 200 feet of the stage. For information and tickets, call 800/660-5253.

There's always something going on. Come for the **Pear Blossom Square Dance Festival** in April, held at the county fairgrounds in Lakeport, and on July 4 don't miss the **Clearlake International Worm Races.** In mid-August, there's a **Blackberry Festival** at Lower Lake's Anderson Marsh State Park, and in September more fruit—the **Pear Festival** in Kelseyville. Other area events include regular **bass fishing tournaments** and occasional **boat races and water-ski contests** at Lakeport.

For more information about the area, contact: the **Lake County Visitor Information Center,** 6110 E. Hwy. 20 in Lucerne, 707/274-5652 or 800/525-3743, www.lakecounty.com; the **Lakeport Regional Chamber of Commerce,** 875 Lakeport Blvd. in Lakeport, 707/263-5092 or 866/525-3767, www.lakeportchamber.com; or the **Clearlake Chamber of Commerce,** 4700 Golf St. in Clearlake, 707/994-3600, www.clearlakechamber.com. For information about local art events and exhibits, contact **Lake County Arts Council & Main St. Gallery,** 325 N. Main St. in Lakeport, 707/263-6658 or 707/263-6659, www.lakecountyartscouncil.com.

Camp at **Clear Lake State Park** on the lake near Kelseyville (bring mosquito repellent), at various public campgrounds in Mendocino National Forest, or—if heading westward—at pretty **Lake Mendocino** near Redwood Valley on Hwy. 20. Otherwise the coolest thing about Clear Lake is the chance to stay at old-time vacation cabins. The seven lakefront housekeeping cabins at **Blue Fish Cove,** 10573 E. Highway 20 in

Clear Lake Oaks, 707/998-1769, www.blue-fishcove.com, sleep at least four and come with large, fully equipped kitchens (except #6), private baths, towels and bedding, and TV. Several have a deck or patio and outdoor barbecue; some units can be combined. Summer rates are $50–150 (starting at $55, topping out at $110), or $350–600 weekly; winter rates (Oct. through Feb.) are $45 and up. Onsite hot tub and pier, too. Such a deal. The renovated **Gingerbread Cottages,** 4057 E Hwy. 20 in Nice, 707/274-0200, www.gingerbreadcottages.com, are more romantic bed-and-breakfast cottages with kitchenettes and abundant amenities, $100–200. Ask at local chambers for other possibilities, including B&Bs and motels.

Roadside cafés and fast-food eateries abound. Popular for steak and seafood is **Howard's Grotto** restaurant in Clearlake, 14732 Lakeshore Dr., 707/995-9800. Another possibility is unpretentious **Kathie's Inn,** 14677 Lakeshore Dr., 707/994-9933. **Anthony's** in Lakeport at 2509 Lakeshore Blvd., 707/263-4905, is noted for its Italian and American specialties, good early-bird specials. Open for lunch and dinner weekdays (closed Wednesday), for dinner only Saturday and Sunday nights. Reservations suggested. For pasta and seafood, try **Park Place,** right next to Library Park in downtown Lakeport, 50 Third St., 707/263-0444.

EAST AND NORTH OF CLEAR LAKE

Indian Valley Reservoir

Twenty-two miles east of Clearlake Oaks on Hwy. 20 is the Walker Ridge Rd. turnoff to Indian Valley Reservoir, a quiet place for fishing, warm-water swimming, and camping in the foothills. Bush monkeyflowers, western wallflowers, and hound's tongue bloom along the road in spring. (You can also reach the reservoir via northward-winding Bartlett Springs Road between Lucerne and Nice.) For boating information, call the marina, 530/662-0607. For other information, contact the U.S. Bureau of Land Management **Ukiah Field Office,** 2550 N. State St. in Ukiah, 707/468-4000, www.ca.blm.gov/ukiah.

Lake Pillsbury and Snow Mountain Wilderness

Good for camping and recreation is the Lake Pillsbury reservoir in the Mendocino National Forest's Eel River watershed, with plenty of room for boating, fishing, and swimming; 115 campsites. Head up Elk Mountain Rd. from Upper Lake, or Potter Valley Road if you're coming from the west. Pitch your tent at **Oak Flat, Pogie Point,** or **Sunset Campgrounds,** or picnic at **Squaw Creek. Mendocino National Forest** includes almost 900,000 acres of forest land, extending north of Clear Lake to boundaries with the Six Rivers and Shasta-Trinity National Forests. You'll need a forest map to get around—and second sight to anticipate logging trucks and such on narrow, unpaved, sometimes dusty and steep roads (many closed by mud or snow in winter; check with rangers on road conditions). The 37,000-acre Snow Mountain Wilderness is just east of Lake Pillsbury (wilderness permit required). Twin-peaked Snow Mountain itself is the southernmost peak in the northern Coast Ranges, the last outpost for a wide variety of mountainous plants—but far from the last time you'll see poison oak. The wilderness offers great backpacking, with 52 miles of ridge trails. The best time for hiking is late spring and early summer.

For current information about both, including maps and trail conditions, contact the Mendocino National Forest's **Upper Lake Ranger District** office, 10025 Elk Mountain Rd. in Upper Lake, 707/275-2361, www.fs.fed.us/r5/mendocino.

Sonoma Valley

According to the native Miwok, when they walked at night through the valley between the Mayacamas and Sonoma Mountains, the moon rose seven times—thus the name Sonoma, or many moons. Dubbed the "Valley of the Moon" by Jack London, a romantic but off-key translation popularized by his semi-autobiographical 1913 novel *Valley of the Moon* and subsequent 1914 film, the narrow 17-mile-long Sonoma Valley is as rich in history as it is in natural beauty and agricultural wealth. Often called "the cradle of California history," Sonoma has been ruled by many flags—English, Russian, Spanish, Mexican, and of course, the U.S. Stars and Stripes—and much colonial fervor. But no other ruling power was quite as colorful as the Bear Flaggers, a seedy band of several dozen American freelance landgrabbers.

The land is still the primary local focus, and these days it's grabbed up most frequently for vineyards and wineries. In additional to excellent wines, estate-made olive oils, tapenades, and exotic mustards are other culinary claims to fame. From the historic town of Sonoma, fine wine estates, fruit and nut orchards, and livestock and poultry farms scatter out in all directions.

SEEING AND DOING SONOMA

Picturesque Sonoma, protected from progress by strict zoning laws, gracefully withstands the troops of tourists massing in the plaza for their wine country assault in spring, summer, and fall. So with the area's increasingly sophisticated food and wine scene, Sonoma still feels a little bit country. A California-style Spanish town built around an eight-acre central plaza, Sonoma's center is surrounded by carefully preserved old adobes and historic buildings, stately trees, rose gardens, and picnic tables. Many of the superb stone buildings here were crafted by Italian masons. The trees alone comprise a California botanical native garden, including some of the state's most impressive species—Monterey pine and cypress, coast redwood, giant sequoia, California live oak, California bay laurel, foothill pine, and sycamore.

The **Sonoma Valley Visitors Bureau,** 453 First St. E. (in the old Carnegie Library building on the plaza), 707/996-1090, www.sonomavalley.com, offers the free ***Sonoma Valley Visitors Guide***—a complete listing of sights, galleries, wineries, events, accommodations, and restaurants, also available elsewhere around town—and abundant free brochures and flyers. If you didn't find it elsewhere, pick up a copy of *Sonoma County Farm Trails,* the invaluable guide to local produce and farm products. The visitors bureau also helps arrange accommodations. Very helpful staff, worth a stop. There are public restrooms out back, too. If you start your Sonoma visit farther south, there is a second visitors center adjacent to the Viansa Winery on Hwy. 121. Both are open daily 9 A.M.–5 P.M., often later in summer.

Sonoma State Historic Park

This spread-out collection of historic buildings includes the Sonoma Mission itself (properly known as Mission San Francisco Solano de Sonoma); the Sonoma Barracks; the remnants of Vallejo's La Casa Grande; the Blue Wing and Toscano Hotels; and Lachryma Montis ("Mountain Tears"), Vallejo's adobe-insulated Gothic retirement home just outside town. Pick up basic information and a walking tour guide at park headquarters, 363 Third St. W., 707/938-1519. A small fee covers admission to all historic attractions open to the public (10 A.M.–5 P.M. daily, except Thanksgiving and Christmas). The fee here also covers admittance to uncrowded **Petaluma Adobe State Historic Park,** west of town in Petaluma, where Vallejo's ranch headquarters still stands. For details, see Petaluma below.

Sonoma Mission, on the corner of E. Spain St. and First St. E, was an upstart enterprise founded in 1823 by Father José Altimira, who didn't bother to ask his superiors for permission. The Russians at Fort Ross on the coast apparently weren't threatened by the mission's presence: they sent bells and other gifts in honor of its dedication. Now a

© ROBERT HOLMES/CALTOUR

The Sonoma Barracks building dates from the mid-1830s.

museum with a restored chapel (Vallejo built the church for the pueblo in 1840) and adjacent padres' quarters (constructed in 1825, the oldest building in town), the mission also houses historic exhibits, displays on adobe-building techniques and restoration, and mission art. The impressive and unrestored **Blue Wing Inn** across the street at 217 E. Spain St., built in the 1840s, was the first hotel north of San Francisco.

The two-story adobe and redwood **Sonoma Barracks** building dates from the mid-1830s, when it provided troop housing and headquarters for Mexico's far northern frontier and later headquarters for the boisterous Bear Flaggers. In 1860, Vallejo started his winery here, next door to his home. Now a state-run history museum with exhibits on Sonoma-area Native Americans, Sonoma's rancho era, and the early U.S. years, the dusty courtyard and corral—complete with fowl underfoot—add even more historic authenticity. **La Casa Grande,** Mariano Vallejo's first home in Sonoma, stood near the barracks. The main house was destroyed by fire in 1867, but the servants' wing still stands in the dooryard of the **Toscano Hotel.**

Just as California moved from a Mexican to an American national identity, Vallejo modified his house style in later years. Named "Mountain Tears" by Vallejo (after nearby natural hot and cold springs), this seemingly un-Spanish two-story New England mansion at the end of the tree-lined lane was built in 1851—the wooden walls wisely layered over adobe brick, traditionally appreciated for its insulating qualities. **Lachryma Montis,** at W. Spain St. and Third St. W., is finely furnished with many of the general's family belongings, as if waiting for Vallejo himself to return. The grounds, too, are unusual, planted with prickly pear cacti, magnolia trees, even some of Vallejo's original grape vines. The white cast-iron fountains in front and back are part of the original garden decor of Vallejo's 17-acre homesite. Inquire at park headquarters about upcoming special events, such as the Sonoma City Opera's open-air summer presentations of historical operas.

Other Sights and Shops

Start at the plaza—the largest in California, intended as the center of community life—for a

CALIFORNIA'S FIRST AND FINAL FLAG

William Todd, a nephew of Mary Todd Lincoln, designed the flag that flew over Sonoma for less than a month in 1846 on behalf of the Bear Flag Republic. The grizzly bear became the primary symbol—reverse psychological warfare, since the rowdy Americans were nicknamed *osos* (bears) by the Mexicans. Like the republic's one star, the grizzly was drawn with blackberry juice; so clumsy was the original artwork that the flat-faced bear was initially mistaken for a pig. A strip of red flannel was stitched along the bottom, below the words "California Republic." The same basic (but artistically improved) design, with a red star in the upper corner, was officially adopted as the state's flag in 1911. Charred fragments of the original flag (destroyed by fire in San Francisco's 1906 earthquake) are still on display in the Sonoma Mission museum.

shop in town, though Chuck Williams's upscale housewares company did get its start here, as a combination hardware-kitchenware store. For intriguing kitchen items these days, try **Sign of the Bear** on the plaza at 435 First St. W., 707/996-3722. **Reader's Books,** at 127 and 130 Napa St. E., 707/939-1779, where you'll find both used and new and may also luck into a great reading or other author event. At the **Plaza Book Shop,** 40 W. Spain St., 707/996-8474, rare books mingle with more used books. For très Sonoma clothing, stop into **Bear Moon Clothing Co.,** 117 E. Napa St., 707/935-3392, or **Viva Sonoma,** across the way at 180 E. Napa, 707/939-1904. **Pardon My Garden,** 112 E. Napa St., 707/939-9282, offers stylish garden accessories and decor. Rockhounds, birddog fascinating **Sonoma Rock & Mineral Gallery,** 414 First St. E., Ste. G, 707/996-7200. Best bet for one-stop wine shopping is the **Wine Exchange of Sonoma,** 452 First St. E., 707/938-1794.

downtown walking tour. Shady green and inviting today, the plaza was a dusty, barren piece of ground in Sonoma's early years, trampled by Vallejo's marching troops and littered with animal skeletons left over from communal feasts. (The town still "burns the bull" here, though more stylishly, during the annual Ox Roast in early June.) The small duck pond adds fuss and flutter to the spacious gardens and picnic grounds, and the bronze **Bear Flag Republic sculpture** to the northeast is a reminder of the region's short-lived political independence. The impressive stone **Sonoma City Hall** and courthouse in the center of the plaza is post-Spanish, added by Americans in 1906. The **Swiss Hotel** near the Toscano Hotel was built by Mariano Vallejo's brother Salvador and now houses the Swiss Hotel restaurant. Down First Street is the 1846 **Jacob Leese House,** home of California's military governor (and Vallejo's brother-in-law) in 1849.

Need to slow down to the speed of Sonoma? The **Sonoma Spa on the Plaza,** 457 First St. W., 707/939-8770, offers facials, mud baths, herbal wraps, and massage (open daily 9 A.M.– 9 P.M., walk-in appointments okay). Search high and low but you won't find a Williams-Sonoma

WINERIES

Sonoma County boasts 11 American Viticultural Areas (AVAs). As a result, here it's quite OK to be a "terroirist." Terroir describes the vineyard-specific environmental factors (soil, slope direction, elevation, climate, etc.) that affect the characteristics of particular wines. Increasingly, where grapes are grown, and how, is every bit as important as what happens in the winemaking process. The astonishing diversity between—and within—Sonoma County AVAs makes distinctive terroir a visitor draw. Within the Sonoma Mountain AVA, higher slopes are cool, lower slopes are warm; cabernet sauvignon predominate on the east side, pinot noir on the west. The birthplace of modern California viticulture, Sonoma Valley successfully supports many varietals.

Near Sonoma

Napa Valley gets the glory these days, but California's wine industry was born in Sonoma. The local mission planted the state's first vineyards in 1824. Part of the Sonoma Mission's original vineyards are living history at **Sebastiani Vineyards and Winery,** 389 Fourth St. E, 707/938-5532

Sonoma's historic Buena Vista Winery

have had a happier ending if he'd only stayed in Sonoma County, where his new winery was beginning to thrive. But after he was acquitted of all charges he moved to Nicaragua and was eaten by a crocodile. No lasting bad karma here, though. The striking stone **Buena Vista Winery,** a mile east of town at 18000 Old Winery Rd., 707/938-1266 or 800/926-1266, www.buenavistawinery.com, open daily 10:30 A.M.–4:30 P.M., is the Hungarian's original winery and a state historic landmark. Though the winery is now owned by a muiltinational and its focal point these days is its Carneros estate, stone cellars here (some tunnels collapsed during the 1906 earthquake) are the oldest in California and are also the headquarters for the only wine brotherhood in the U.S., the Knights of the Vine. Take the free self-guided tour, which emphasizes the life and times of Haraszthy, or sign on for the $15 heritage tour that explores winery history and a demonstration vineyard and also includes a private tasting (11 A.M. and 2 P.M.; call 707/265-1472 for reservations). Otherwise there's a $5 tasting fee; lift a glass of Green Hungarian to toast the count, then hike up to the art gallery on the second floor of the original winery press house. Additional fee for Haywood Estate wines. Buena Vista's picnic grounds are quite inviting—and free.

Noted for its merlot and other fine wines is the prestigious but small **Gundlach-Bundschu Winery,** 2000 Denmark St., 707/938-5277 (tasting room: 707/939-3015), www.gunbun.com, a family-run operation since the mid-1800s yet the kind of place you're more likely to hear vintage rock than classical music. The winery's 400-acre Rhinefarm Vineyards were originally established in 1858 by Jacob Gundlach and Charles Bundschu. Tasting is offered daily 11 A.M.–4:30 P.M.; estate and specialty wines available free of charge, fee for library wines, when available. Guided tours are offered regularly on weekends, by request on weekdays. Outdoor picnicking (free) at various winery locales. The winery also sponsors a fun Shakespeare series ("Sandlot Shakespeare"), the Midsummer Mozart Festival, and the GunBun Summer Fun Film Fest (such as *This Is Spinal Tap* to accompany a zin release and barbecue), and all sorts of other fab events—

or 800/888-5532, www.sebastiani.com, open daily 10 A.M.–5 P.M. for tours, tasting ($5 fee), and sales. Sonoma County wines include cabernet sauvignon, merlot, chardonnay, zinfandel, and pinot noir, with wines from specific vineyards and appellations also offered. The winery was one of the few open during Prohibition, producing altar wine and a potent "wine tonic" patent medicine. The "new" tasting room unearthed 1904 Samuele Sebastiani stonework and other lost winery history, as a result of earthquake retrofitting. In addition to the wines, there's a large collection of oak barrel carvings.

Green Hungarian is bottled in the Sonoma Valley (as elsewhere) in honor of "Count" Agoston Haraszthy, who fled San Francisco in 1857 after being accused of embezzling gold from the U.S. Mint. The aristocratic Austrian-Hungarian immigrant convinced California's governor to send him to Europe in 1861 to collect vinifera vines. He returned with 100,000 or so, which he distributed throughout the area. The count's story might

from shoot positioning seminars to the Wine of the Moment Club Holiday Open House. Take a short hike to the top of Towle's Hill for the view of San Francisco and San Pablo Bays. **Bartholomew Park Winery,** located at the former site of the Hacienda winery, two miles east of town at 1000 Vineyard Ln., 707/935-9511, www.bartholomewparkwinery.com, was founded in 1994 by the Bundschu family, so it comes as no surprise that "Bart Park" emphasizes handmade, single-vineyard wines—cabernets, merlots, pinots, and chardonnays—and wine education. (Come in September and October to experience "punch-down.") Once owned by Frank Bartholomew, journalist and later president of United Press International (UPI), the vineyard and winery here (Count Haraszthy's's original Buena Vista) were resurrected by the Bartholomews after World War II. The historic winery and gardens have since been restored. The **Museum of Wine** here displays vintage winemaking equipment, period clothing, and local history—including Pomo Indians, Agoston Haraszthy, and Kate Johnson and her 2,000 angora cats, whose Victorian castle became a work farm for "wayward women." Open 11 A.M.–4:30 P.M. daily (except Thanksgiving, Christmas, New Year's Day, and Easter) for tasting, self-guided tours, and picnicking.

At **Carmenet Vineyard,** 1700 Moon Mountain Dr., 707/996-5870, www.carmenetwinery.com, the aging caves are large, with room for stacking wine barrels as well as daily hand-racking and washing. Specialties here are cabernet sauvignon, sauvignon blanc, chardonnay, cabernet franc, merlot, zinfandel—wines made using traditional French techniques, including malolactic fermentation, barrel aging, and cellaring. Tours by appointment only.

Well worth visiting near Sonoma is very hip **Ravenswood,** 18701 Gehricke Rd., 707/938-1960 (tasting room: 707/933-2332 or 888/669-4679), www.ravenswood-wine.com, now associated with Constellation Brands/Franciscan Estates and much appreciated for its zinfandel ("Zinfomania") but still dedicated to handcrafted wines ("no wimpy wines") including cabernet franc, merlot, petite sirah, and Gewürz-

traminer. Open 10 A.M.–4:30 P.M. daily except Easter, Thanksgiving, Christmas, and New Year's Day. One tour is offered daily at 10:30 A.M., by reservation only. The fee is $4 for tasting and/or tour. Picnicking is free. Cool merchandise here, too—some of it particularly popular with Edgar Allan Poe fans.

Glen Ellen Area

Prominent in the tiny Somona Mountain AVA, the 85-acre **Benziger Family Winery,** 1883 London Ranch Rd., 707/935-4085 or 888/490-2739, www.benziger.com, offers a tractor-drawn tram vineyard tour—quite informative, covering subjects such as root grafts, covercrops, trellising, terracing, and crushing. French biodynamic viticulture is the emphasis for "vineyard designate" wines here. Tram tours are offered daily (call for current information), and a self-guided tour of the demonstration vineyard is available, too. Open for tastings—sauvignon blanc, fume blanc, chardonnay, pinot noir, zinfandel, syrah, merlot, cabernet sauvignon, cabernet franc, and more—in everyone's favorite tasting room, open daily 10 A.M.–5 P.M. Picnic in the cedars.

In early 1999, the Benziger clan closed its innovative Sonoma Mountain Brewery about 10 minutes north of Sonoma, and decided to move production of its Imagery Series wines to that location. These days **Imagery Estate Winery,** 14355 Hwy. 12, 707/935-4500, www.imagery-winery.com, describes itself as a "coalescence of the arts"—a mouthful, yes, but one well worth savoring, as it turns out. Imagery's wines attract considerable attention, as when Anthony Dias Blue of *Bon Appetit* declared Imagery's Ash Creek cabernet sauvignon one of the year's 10 best. The onsite **Imagery Gallery** is the world's largest collection of original wine label art, the works commissioned from renowned artists—the likes of Robert Stackhouse, Gladys Nilsson, Yuriko Yamaguchi, Kurt Kemp, and Willy Weeks—as Imagery labels. Open daily for art appreciation, tasting, and wine sales 10 A.M.–4:30 P.M. Nearby **Arrowood Winery,** overlooking the Sonoma Valley at 14347 Sonoma Hwy., 707/938-5170 or 800/938-5170, www.arrowoodvineyards.com, specializes in Sonoma County "sub-appellations," producing excellent high-end wines made from prestigious area vineyards. Open daily 10 A.M.–4:30 P.M. for tasting (fee). Tours are offered daily. Come at noon for the history tour ($10), no reservation necessary. The guided "grape to glass" vineyard and cellar tour ($25) is offered at 2:30 P.M., by advance reservation.

The **B.R. Cohn Winery,** 15000 Sonoma Hwy., 707/938-4064 or 800/330-4064, www.br-cohn.com, is owned by *the* Bruce Cohn, manager of the Doobie Brothers—so you can bet the annual **B.R. Cohn Charity Fall Music Festival** at the amphitheater here rocks. The winery's none too shabby either, acclaimed for its cabernet sauvignon, merlot, and chardonnay. The operation is also noteworthy for its gourmet vinegars and olive oil—certified organic French picholine olive oil pressed from the 1875 olive trees here. Come in winter for special events (mostly on weekends) anchoring the **Sonoma Valley Olive Festival**—olive oil tastings, olive oil cooking demonstrations by gourmet Bay Area chefs, and more. Proceeds benefit local charities. The winery's new tasting room is installed in the estate's refurbished original house, once a Wells Fargo stage stop. The previous tasting room has been transformed into a viewing kitchen, for visiting guest chefs. The B.R. Cohn Winery is open daily 10 A.M.–5 P.M. for tasting, guided tours, and picnicking.

Or try the white zinfandel at award-winning **Valley of the Moon Winery,** 777 Madrone Rd. (four miles west of Hwy. 12, near Arnold Dr.), 707/996-6941, www.valleyofthemoonwinery.com. Established on part of General Mariano Vallejo's original land grant. Founded by General "Fighting Joe" Hooker and including part of Senator George Hearst's 19th-century Madrone Vineyards, Valley of the Moon has been spectacularly "rebuilt" to retain its old-stone soul, and is open 10 A.M.–5 P.M. daily. For those on a budget—and all these "tastes" do add up—note that here, the first four tastings here are free.

Kenwood Area

Taste buds still willing, visit famed **Chateau St. Jean,** 8555 Sonoma Hwy. (Hwy. 12), 707/833-4134 or 877478-5326 (wine orders), www.chateaustjean.com, still the only winery to garner five wines in a single *Wine Spectator* Top 100 rating, among endless other accolades. Not only that, it's so pretty here. Everything is arranged around the 1920s chateau, which sits at the heart of this wooded 250-acre estate, all of it thoroughly renovated and upgraded since St. Jean went corporate—a small fish swallowed by successively larger fish, including Berringer then Foster's Brewing Group of Australia. Open for tastings—try one of the justly famous single-vineyard chardonnays—sales, and self-guided tours daily 10 A.M.–5 P.M. The fee for sampling mainstream wines, $10–25 for Reserve Room tastings held in the chateau. The swank visitors center includes an impressive Sonoma County-focused charcuterie, the stuff of grand picnics.

Stop at the **Wine Room,** 9575 Sonoma Hwy. (Hwy. 12, at Warm Springs Rd.), 707/833-6131, open 11 A.M.–4 P.M. daily, to taste wines produced by local vintners including Adler Fels, Moondance, and the Smothers Brothers' award-winning Remick Ridge Winery. For more information, see www.the-wine-room.com and www.smothersbrothers.com. The excellent **Kenwood Vineyards** across the way, 9592 Sonoma Hwy., 707/833-5891, www.kenwoodvineyards.com, has exclusive rights to Jack London's vineyards, and bottles several special wines in his honor each year. According to *The Wine Journal,* among its other accomplishments Kenwood consistently produces one of California's best sauvignon blancs. Open daily 10 A.M.–4:30 P.M. for tasting, with the first four tastes free. On weekends, enjoy food and wine pairings.

The **Kunde Estate Winery,** 10155 Sonoma Hwy., 707/833-5501, www.kunde.com, features a half mile of hillside aging caves, dug with the same technological expertise that brought you BART. Cave tours are offered frequently Fri.–Sun., otherwise by appointment. Open daily 11 A.M.–5 P.M. for tours (call for details), sales, and tastings of its chardonnay and unusual viognier, made from a French grape. If you're lucky, Kunde may even have some of its immensely popular zinfandel, produced from ancient vines (more than a century old). The tasting room is open daily 10:30 A.M.–4:30 P.M.

for wine tasting ($5 fee for estate wines, $10 for reserve wines).

Also worth time in the neighborhood is **St. Francis Vineyards & Winery,** the new visitors center (located about a mile west of the original) at 100 Pythian Rd., (off Sonoma Hwy.), 707/833-4666 or 800/543-7713, www.stfranciswine.com, open 10 A.M.–5 P.M. daily (except New Year's Day, Easter, Thanksgiving, Christmas Eve, and Christmas) for tours and tasting. Any four wines served in the main tasting room can be tasted for $5, while there's a $20 fee for single-vineyard wines offered in the reserve room. Tours are offered, by reservation, for groups of 10 or more.

Also technically in Santa Rosa but overlooking the Sonoma Valley from its perch in the Mayacamas Mountains is the excellent, acclaimed **Adler Fels Winery,** popping up like a Tudor-style village in the woods at 5325 Corrick Ln., 707/539-3123, www.adlerfels.com. Adler Fels is known for its chardonnay, sauvignon blanc, and Mélange à Deux sparkling wine. Open for tours, tasting, and sales daily, but only by appointment. Otherwise, taste Adler Fels at the Wine Room, mentioned above.

Closer still to Santa Rosa is the **Matanzas Creek Winery,** 6097 Bennett Valley Rd., 707/528-6464 or 800/590-6464, www.matanzascreek.com, known for its merlot, chardonnay, and sauvignon blanc. Matanzas Creek also grows lavender—and lots of it—and estate-grown lavender products are available here. Open daily 10 A.M.–4:30 P.M. for tasting and sales. Winery tours are offered by appointment, but you can take a self-guided tour of the gardens at your lesiure.

STAYING IN SONOMA
Camping, Motels, and Hotels

Forget about camping in Sonoma. Not far north is **Sugarloaf Ridge State Park,** 2605 Adobe Canyon Rd. (above Kenwood), 707/833-5712, which offers RV and tent camping, as well as good hiking (see listing below for more information). The county's **Spring Lake Park** in Santa Rosa offers open space, swimming, and campsites with flush toilets, showers, and electrical outlets for $23 ($16 plus reservation fee). For reservations call 707/565-

2267 and see www.sonoma-county.org. If headed toward the Napa Valley, consider camping at **Lake Berryessa** or **Bothe–Napa Valley State Park.**

Lower-rent accommodations are scarce. Quite stylish and surprisingly affordable is the thoroughly renovated **Sonoma Creek Inn,** 239 Boyes Blvd., 707/939-9463 or 888/712-1289, www.sonomacreekinn.com, a charming throwback to motor hotels of the 1930s with a warm, folk-art feel. Contemporary rooms feature original art, colorful tilework trim, and colorful handmade accessories. Amenities include refrigerator, in-room coffee and tea, color TV with cable, telephone with dataport, and spacious bathrooms. Many rooms feature patios or decks. Rates are in the $100–200 range (starting at $89) June–Oct., and drop as low as $69 in the off season. Such a deal. Also a good bet among motels is the family-owned **El Pueblo Inn,** 896 W. Napa St., 707/996-3651 or 800/900-8844 in California, www.elpuebloinn.com, which is well located (about a mile from the plaza) and features comfy rooms with refrigerators and other amenities, garden, pool, and spa. Rates start at $115. The contemporary **Best Western Sonoma Valley Inn,** near the plaza at 550 Second St. W., 707/938-9200 or 800/334-5784, www.sonomavalleyinn.com, has it all also—from pool, whirlpool, and fitness center to fireplaces (in most rooms), in-room coffee and refrigerators, hair dryers, and complimentary continental breakfast. Pets are welcome. Friday night offers wine tastings. Most rooms are $150–350.

The historic **Sonoma Hotel,** on the plaza at 110 W. Spain St., 707/996-2996 or 800/468-6016, www.sonomahotel.com, offers very tasteful yet small rooms upstairs from the Girl & the Fig restaurant. According to local lore, Maya Angelou wrote *Gather Together in My Name* while staying here. Most rooms are $100–200, suites $200–250, slightly less in the off season.

Also a deal by local standards and right downtown is the elegantly restored yet unfussy 1843 **El Dorado Hotel,** 405 First St. W., 707/996-3030 or 800/289-3031, www.hoteleldorado.com, onetime home of Don Salvador Vallejo. Even the Bear Flaggers once took refuge here. The 26 tile-floored

WINE COUNTRY

rooms feature private baths, balconies with French doors, contemporary four-poster beds with down comforters. Two wheelchair-accessible bungalows are also available. Other pluses include courtyard, heated lap pool, complimentary bottle of wine, continental breakfast, and the wonderful on-site **Piatti Ristorante** (707/996-2351). Rates are $150–200, as low as $135 in winter.

Bed-and-Breakfasts

The town offers a number of B&B-style "cottages," most family operated, many quite inviting for a close-in stay. Most of these and other area bed-and-breakfasts require a two-night minimum stay on weekends. Contact the visitors bureau for a fairly comprehensive current listing; the bureau also offers an online lodging availability service. Or see what's available through the **Bed & Breakfast Association of Sonoma Valley,** 707/938-9513, www.sonomabb.com.

Convenient, charming, and relaxed **Thistle Dew Inn,** 171 W. Spain St., 707/938-2909 or 800/382-7895, www.thistledew.com, offers six rooms and suites in two historic houses (1869 and 1905) with arts and crafts decor, queen beds, private baths. Four rooms have fireplaces, three have two-person Jacuzzi tubs. Scrumptious full breakfast, complimentary hors d'oeuvres, a garden spa, and use of bicycles. Best yet: There's no two-night minimum on weekends, though there is a $20 surcharge for a one-night weekend stay.

Rooms and suites are $150–300. The 1870 Greek revival **Victorian Garden Inn** farmhouse at 316 E. Napa St. (near the plaza), 707/996-5339 or 800/543-5339, victoriangardeninn.com, has just five possible rooms (three with private entrance) and offers an expanded continental breakfast and swimming pool. Marvelous garden. Rates start at $129, with most rooms$150–300.

The special **Sonoma Chalet,** 18935 Fifth St. W., 707/938-3129 or 800/938-3129, www.sonomachalet.com, offers relaxed country charms quite close to town, and features a suite and three rooms in a chalet-style farmhouse (two share a bath and living room) plus three outlying cottages with private baths and a fireplace or woodstove. Amenities include a hot tub and expanded continental breakfast. Rooms are $100–150, the suite and cottages are $150–250.

Also definitely different is **Ramekins,** 450 W. Spain St., 707/933-0452, www.ramekins.com, where the six rooms (all feature private baths) are upstairs, above the cooking school of the same name. Everything is so enticingly food-themed—the staircase features asparagus-spear spindles—that you'll be grateful that there are so many restaurants in and near the Sonoma Plaza. (The General's Daughter restaurant is right next door.) Continental breakfast. Rates are $150–250, with slightly lower off-season rates.

An impressive newcomer is Four Sisters' **Inn at Sonoma,** two blocks from the plaza at 630

SONOMA VALLEY CYCLING

Though Napa Valley is touted as the area's bicycling mecca, Sonoma County is better in many respects—not nearly as trammeled (yet) with treacherous traffic and offering many more back-country routes. Far better for cyclists than Hwy. 12, for example, is the parallel Arnold Dr.–Bennett Valley Rd. route through the Sonoma Valley toward Santa Rosa. An excellent casual cyclist's guide to the region (including Sonoma and the Sonoma Valley) is *Sonoma County Bike Trails* by Phyllis L. Neumann, available in many local shops and bookstores, featuring 29 good rides from easy to challenging. (If you'll be wandering farther afield,

Neumann is also the author of *Marin County Bike Trails.*) Area visitor bureaus can offer suggestions about where to rent bikes.

In Sonoma proper, where many people start their wine country adventure, rent bikes at **Sonoma Valley Cyclery,** 20093 Broadway, 707/935-3377, www.sonomavalleycyclery.com, which offers 21-speed mountain bikes with rear racks and travel bags and hybrid bikes. Helmets are supplied as needed, though many riders bring their own. Rates are $6 per hour or $25 per day. By prior arrangement, customized self-guided tours, complete with packed lunch, are also offered. Open daily.

Broadway, 707/939-1340 or 888/568-9818, www.foursisters.com, the style here a luxurious yet casual interpretation of California "country" in subtle stripes, florals, and plaids. All 19 rooms feature private bathrooms, a fireplace, and abundant amenities; most have a deck. A stay includes a full, memorable breakfast, afternoon teas, and complimentary wine and hors d'oeuvres. Rates are $150–250. At least two dozen bed-and-breakfast inns are scattered throughout the Sonoma Valley, some in Kenwood, Glen Ellen, and Santa Rosa. Some of these are listed elsewhere below.

Spa Resorts

The public hot springs are long gone at Boyes Hot Springs, but the old hotel still stands. The peachy-pink **Fairmont Sonoma Mission Inn & Spa,** 18140 Sonoma Hwy., 707/938-9000, 800/257-7544, or 866/540-4502, www.sonomamissioninn.com, is definitely in the pink these days, following its purchase by Fairmont Hotels and a $50 million makeover. Even before the restyling, this was among the best spas in the world. And what's not to like? Swank Sonoma Mission Inn facilities—"10 acres of pure indulgence"—include a luxury hotel, exceptional restaurants, and an incredible 27,000-square-foot spa offering Roman baths, individual baths and whirlpools, herbal steam, and everything from aromatherapy, shiatsu massage, and "watsu" (floating massage, like shiatsu) to seaweed or herbal body wraps. Even the inn's swimming pool is filled with mineral water. Other active diversions include hiking, yoga, exercise classes, and tennis. Low-fat, organic fare is available at on-site **Santé** restaurant, or try the upscale diner **Big 3.** Rates start at $250.

Sonoma's magnificent **MacArthur Place Inn & Spa** is the town's celebrity magnet, a onetime Victorian ranch transformed into a downtown inn with 64 rooms and suites and seven acres of lush, art-filled gardens. Every imaginable luxury is on offer, from the fresh interpretations of Victorian country style and original art to the exclusive grape seed–based bath products. The small onsite spa and fitness center offers massage, wraps, and facials; pool and whirlpool are adjacent. Still, the privacy and peace of the gardens are the main attractions here. In addition to the grand rooms and great food, of course. Stylish **Saddles,** one of the country's best steakhouses, is installed in the estate's original barn. Martini bar, too. Rooms start at $275, suites at $375. For more information or inn reservations, contact MacArthur Place at 29 E. MacArthur St., 707/938-2929 or 800/ 722-1866, www.macarthurplace.com.

Marriott Renaissance Hotels' **Lodge at Sonoma,** 1325 Broadway, 707/935-6600, www .thelodgeatsonoma.com, is right across from Traintown, if a mini-train ride is on the family schedule. This Mediterranean village–like hotel includes a small garden area, pool, onsite restaurant and lounge, and full fitness and **Raindance Spa** facilities. Summer rates start at $200–250.

EATING IN SONOMA
Food to Go

The best food is the simplest. With a current *Sonoma County Farm Trails* brochure and map in hand (available here at local shops and the visitors bureau, or try www.farmtrails.org), or by visiting one of the popular local farmers' markets, hunting down local produce in season is easy as fresh Sonoma County apple pie. The **Sonoma Certified Farmers Market** is held Friday year-round, 9 A.M.–noon, at the Depot Museum parking lot, First and Spain Streets. The **Sonoma Tuesday CFM,** held Apr.–Oct. Tues. 5:30–8:30 P.M., takes place at Sonoma Plaza (at Napa Street). For information on both markets, call 707/538-7023. The **Cherry Tree Country Store,** 1901 Fremont Dr., 707/938-3480, is a combination fruit stand/deli with wonderful black cherry cider. Delis abound. For upscale Italian deli fare brought to you by the Viansa Winery folks, head for **Cucina Viansa,** on the plaza at 400 First St. E. (at Spain), 707/935-5656, where you can pack your picnic basket with delectable specialty meats, cheeses, rotisserie specials, pasta salads, condiments, and Viansa wine (tastings offered). Since the grill was added, you can even plan a sit-down lunch or dinner. And how about a Jewish-Italian deli? Then **Follini & Eichenbaum,** 19100 Arnold, Ste. A (at Grove), 707/996-3287, is just the place.

Or combine a walking tour with the pleasure of putting together a homegrown picnic. An excellent cheese stop on the way up the hill and off the usual tourist track is the **Vella Cheese Company,** 315 Second St. E., 707/938-3232, www.vellacheese.com. Vella has been in the cheese business since 1931, much of that time in this same sturdy stone building. World famous for its sweet, nutty-tasting "dry" jack cheeses, Vella also makes garlic, onion, and jalapeño jack varieties, tasty raw milk cheddar, and an Oregon bleu cheese. The usual visitor draw is the **Sonoma Cheese Factory,** 2 W. Spain St., 707/996-1000, known for its well-distributed Sonoma Jack cheeses—including garlic, pepper, and pesto jack—yet Sonoma also makes cheddar, havarti, teleme, and reduced-fat cheeses. Take a peek at the cheese makers, try some homemade salads or good basic sandwiches, and browse through the awesome array of deli and gourmet items while you wait. The **Sonoma Sausage Company,** 414 First St. E., 707/938-1215, a favorite of chef Julia Child. There are more than two dozen possibilities, from chicken-spinach-feta to southwestern salsa, but made all are made in the Old World European style.

For bread—next stop—everyone around here will tell you that family-run **Artisan Bakers,** across the street from the public library at 750 W. Napa St., 707/939-1765, www.artisanbakers.com, makes some of the finest breads and other bakery items you'll find anywhere, consistent winners at the Sonoma County Harvest Fair. But when founder Craig Ponsford baked the American Baking Team baguette that won the World Cup of Baking in Paris in 1996, and coaches the Bay Area team of American bakers that won the contest outright in 1999, suddenly the whole world knew the way to Sonoma. Artisan Bakers products are sold at retail outlets throughout the Bay Area and are served in many restaurants, but Sonoma is mecca—the bakery and original storefront. Everyone has a favorite bread, the ciabatta or "slipper bread," for some, the sour country walnut or dry jack sourdough for others, and there are endless other delights, from date pecan muffins and banana nut teacakes to biscotti, bread pudding, coconut macaroons, fruit pies, and lemon bars. Simple lunch fare—quiche, pizzas, sandwiches—is available, too. Open Mon.–Sat. 6:30 A.M.–3 P.M., Sun. 7 A.M.–2 P.M.

Restaurants

You've arrived in foodie paradise, most of it much more fun (less stuffy and self-absorbed) than Napa Valley. Some are locals' favorites, like **Murphy's Irish Pub,** 464 First St. E., in Ste. F of Place de Pyrenees Alley, 707/935-0660, serving Sonoma Mountain Amber along with great Irish beer, fish and chips, shepherd's pie, and full-tilt ambience—including occasional literary events and live music four nights.

Plan to relax and enjoy yourself at intimate, arty, and inviting **Café La Haye,** 140 E. Napa St., 707/935-5994, which serves hearty, fresh fare including specialty risottos, grilled seafood, and grilled pork chops with mustard vinaigrette and sweet potatoes. "Very Sonoma," from the fresh local produce and seasonal fruits to the Vella dry jack cheese and Artisan Bakers breads. Open Tues.–Sat. for dinner, Sun. for brunch. Reservations recommended.

The Girl & the Fig, downstairs in the Sonoma Hotel, 110 W. Spain St., 707/938-3634, serves passionate and fun French bistro fare, from quiche Lorraine and grilled cheese or crabcake sandwiches to pork chops with fried green tomatoes. And how about a caramel nut tart for dessert? Wine list emphasizes Rhône varietals. Open daily for lunch and dinner, 11:30 A.M.–10 P.M.; a simplified late-night menu is served until 11 P.M. on Fri. and Sat. nights.

Delightful downtown for rustic Italian and a long-running favorite is romantic, quite reasonable **Della Santini's,** 133 E. Napa St. (near First), 707/935-0576, with a wonderful outdoor patio. You won't go wrong with the marvelous gnocchi, other house-made pastas, spit-roasted meats, or wonderful pastries. Open daily for lunch and dinner. Just the place for tequila connoisseurs, **Maya** on the plaza at 101 E. Napa St., 707/935-3500, is the place for stylish Yucatan fare—from grand nachos and spit-roasted spice-rubbed chicken to prawns diablo. Margarita worshipers tend to congregate near Maya's "temple of tequila" to contemplate the merits of various tequilas. Tastings available, along with Mexican and other beers.

Among foodie favorites, **Sonoma Meritâge Restaurant & Oyster Bar** near the plaza at 522 Broadway, 707/938-9430, is about the only place around that serves breakfast—such things as vegetarian frittatas, Canadian bacon and egg sandwiches, pecan waffles, and orange brandy French toast stuffed with mascarpone cheese. Otherwise, delectable Southern French and Northern Italian is spoken here—vegetarian and vegan selections as well as well-prepared meats and game. Daily changing menu. Open Wed.–Sun. for breakfast (brunch on weekends until 3 P.M.) and Wed.–Mon. for lunch and dinner.

Welcoming in the American bistro style is family-owned **Deuce,** at home in a charming 1890 house at 691 Broadway, 707/933-3823, where Sonoma Valley meats, produce, vegetables, fruits, and fine wines star in seasonally changing fare—from heirloom tomato and baby spinach salads to eggplant parmesan and filet mignon. And do try that strawberry shortcake, when available. Lunch entrées are $9–14, dinner $15–22. A very reasonable bar menu is also served. Outdoor patio dining, full bar, great Sonoma County wine list.

For a fresh, Northern California take on Portuguese, the place is dinner-only **La Salette,** 18625 Hwy. 12 (near Siesta Way), 707/938-1927, where the daily seafood specials, pork stew, and roasted Petaluma duck are usually worth a try. Open Wed.–Sun. 5–9 P.M.

Get a leg up on the steakhouse of your dreams at **Saddles,** the earthy yet elegant dining room at the MacArthur Place Inn that's gained national acclaim. The beef here is corn-fed USDA prime, mesquite grilled, from burgers and baby back ribs to ribeye and filet mignon. The toppings are to yodel for, whteher you choose the cabernet demi-glace, caramelized onions, or peppercorn sauce. Grilled chicken, pork, and lamb are also on order, along with intriguing starters, including red cornmeal haystack onions rings. Generous sides include five kinds of potatoes, classic creamed spinach. You'll find Saddles at 29 MacArthur Place, 707/933-3191. Patio or "barn" dining available. Full bar. Reservations strongly advised.

The **General's Daughter,** 400 W. Spain St., 707/938-4004, is among Sonoma's finest restaurants. Housed in the 1864 Victorian home General Mariano Vallejo built for his daughter Natalia, the General's Daughter serves everything from ahi tostadas with avocado and salsa to grilled game hens. At Sunday brunch, savor such things as the applewood-smoked bacon and jack cheese omelette, Canadian bacon Benedict, or homemade cinnamon and raisin bread French toast. Nice Sonoma County wine list. Open Mon.–Sat. for lunch, Sun. for brunch, and dinner nightly.

ARTS AND ENTERTAINMENT

While exploring downtown Sonoma, stop by the local historical society's **Depot Park Historical Museum,** 270 First St. W., 707/938-1762, for a look at annually changing local heritage exhibits as well as permanent displays on the short-lived Bear Flag Republic, local railroad history, and more. Open Wed.–Sun. 1–4:30 P.M.; donations always appreciated. Ask here, or at the visitors bureau, about historical walking tours.

Also well worth a stop is the free **Sonoma Valley Museum of Art,** just south of the plaza in a onetime furniture store at 551 Broadway, 707/939-7862, www.svma.org, open Thurs.–Sun. 11 A.M.–5 P.M. Rotating exhibits range from juried regional art competitions and student-curated art exhibits to fascinating arts and crafts by Mexican and Latin American artists, such as 2003's *Colors of the Earth: Latin American Masterworks.* The area's migrant workers are acknowledged during the annual Day of the Dead (Dia de Los Muertos) ceremonies in late October and early November, when local Latino families install colorful altars honoring the dead.

A mile south of the plaza, the miniature **Sonoma Traintown Railroad,** 20264 Broadway, 707/938-3912, www.traintown.com, is a quarter-scale model railroad featuring a replica of the 1875 diamond-stack Baldwin Mogel 2-6-0 locomotive and other fascinations. Take the 20-minute ride through the Lilliputian landscape. Climb aboard at the station and clocktower,

VINTAGE SONOMA SKIES

Worth some time, especially for fans of historic flight, is the **Pacific Coast Air Museum,** at the Charles M. Schulz Airport, 2330 Airport Blvd., Santa Rosa, 707/575-7900, pacificcoastairmuseum.org. This nonprofit group acquires, restores, operates, and displays some classics, particularly World War II warbirds. During WWII the airport here was an airfield offering pilot training for P-38 Lightnings and P-39 Airacobras. The collection here includes more than a dozen restored planes (and counting), including an F14-A Tomcat, F-4C Phantom II, HU-16E Albatross, and C-118 Liftmaster. Museum exhibits emphasize local flight history, aviation personalities, cut-away engine displays, and things you just don't see every day, such as the gyrocopter. The museum is open Tues. and Thurs. 10 A.M.–2 P.M. and on Sat. and Sun. 10 A.M.– 4 P.M., suggested donation $5 (age 12 and under free), and also sponsors a wide variety of special events and activities. Come in late August for the **Wings Over Wine Country Airshow.**

To actually tour Sonoma County skies, head for the Sonoma Valley Airport ("Schellville") and the **Vintage Aircraft Co.,** 23982 Arnold Dr. (about six miles north of the Hwy. 37/121 intersection), 707/938-2444, www.vintageaircraft.com. Vintage offers rides in 1940 Boeing PT-17 Stearman biplanes and a North American SNJ-4 Texan "Warbird," planes originally built to train pilots for the U.S. Army Air Corps and the Navy during World War II. Scenic tours above Sonoma County are a specialty; aerobatic and kamikaze rides are the "e-ticket rides," considerably more exciting. Prices for Stearman rides start at $130; for the Warbird, $250. (Closed Tues.) Currently being restored at Vintage is a Curtiss P-40N, made famous by the Flying Tigers.

And while you're out in Schellville, see what else you can see. There are some 150 antique and classic aircraft hangared at the 77-acre airport.

---

modeled after Oakland's 16th Street Depot, and see the sights; the route includes five bridges and two tunnels, one 140 feet long. Also here are a Ferris wheel, carousel, petting zoo, gift shop, snack stand, and picnic facilities. Open daily 10 A.M.–5 P.M. in summer, just Fri.–Sun. otherwise (closed Thanksgiving and Christmas). Adults $4, children $3.50 (babes-in-arms free), amusement rides extra.

For live music, there are some promising venues in town. Appropriately enough, the **Vaquero** restaurant at 144 W. Napa St., 707/996-1440, offers sometimes great live music on weekends (Thurs.–Sat. nights), from bluegrass to the blues, and family-friendly fare ("for cowpokes of all ages") on Wednesday nights.

Racing fans migrate to the **Infineon Raceway** (previously Sears Point International Raceway) south of Sonoma at 29355 Arnold Dr. (junction of Highways 37 and 121), 800/870-7223, www.infineonraceway.com, which definitely offers life in the fast lane. The Grand Prix of Sonoma, NASCAR Winston Cup, and other professional stockcar, drag, kart, and motorcycle racing are scheduled spring through fall.

EVENTS

For reasonably comprehensive calendars of area events, try both the Sonoma Valley and Sonoma County Wineries Association websites, www.sonomavalley.com and www.sonomawine.com, respectively. The winter **Sonoma Valley Olive Festival** kicks off in December with the **Blessing of the Olives** at the Sonoma Mission and the **Feast of the Olives.** Olive tastings, olive press tours, olive arts and entertainment, delectable dinners, celebrations of the martini, and other events continue through February, culminating with the grand Artisans Market weekend in Sonoma Plaza. Come in March for the annual **Heart of the Valley Barrel Tasting,** www.heartofthevalley.com, a charity fundraiser featuring offerings from 20-plus Sonoma Valley wineries.

Anytime's a good time to take in a movie at the historic, single-screen **Sebastiani Theatre** at 476 First St. E., 707/996-2020, which screens both indie and mainstream movies. Expect special films and other events at the Sebastiani (and elsewhere in the valley) during the April **Sonoma**

Valley Film Festival, www.cinemaepicuria.org, celebrating "independent filmmaking that captures the richness of the human experience"—including the pleasures of the palate. The festival is so well seasoned with food and wine events that it's become known as Cinema Epicuria.

In May (and again in October) **Sonoma State Historic Park** and nearby **Petaluma Adobe State Historic Park** hold "living history" weekends, when park employees and volunteers (practically the whole town) dress in period costumes to re-create the 1840s spirit of Spanish ranchos. Vintage cars become the stars—along with gourmet food and wine—at the **Vintage Race Car Festival,** an annual benefit event held in late May or early June and featuring Gundlach-Bundschu, Glen Ellen, Ravenswood, Buena Vista, and other Sonoma Valley wineries. The parade starts at Infineon Raceway and continues on to Sebastiani Cask Cellars.

That celebratory spirit continues into June, when Sonoma honors the Bear Flag era with and its **Annual Ox Roast** old-fashioned picnic and barbecue in the plaza. Local society is more visible at the late June **Red & White Ball** dinner and dance on the plaza, when folks dress up in the colors of the wine (the more outrageous the get-up the better) and party quite heartily. The **Fourth of July,** a day that also commemorates the consecration of the local mission, is another seriously eccentric local holiday. A wacky parade around Sonoma Plaza—starring the Sonoma Town Band, which also clowns around as The Other Town Band—starts at 10 A.M., and the day soon runneth over with wine, food, art, and live music, capped off by fireworks at the Field of Dreams. Wackier still—kind of a biker/cowboy version of patriotic celebration—and staged in Kenwood just upvalley every July 4th for several decades and counting—are the annual **World Championship Pillow Fights,** in which pairs of combatants straddle a wet pole stretched across a massive mud pit then proceed to pound each other senseless with oversized wet pillows until one contestant falls into the mud. Yeehaw!

In mid-July the Sonoma County Wineries Association sponsors the **Sonoma County Showcase of Wine and Food,** 707/586-3795 or 800/939-7666, www.sonomawine.com, which includes a **Taste of Sonoma County,** appellation tours, celebrity chefs, barrel auction, entertainment, and golf tournament. Though this is usually a countywide celebration, some events are located in and near Sonoma. Also starting mid-month (extending into August) is the **Wine Country Film Festival,** 707/935-3456, www.winecountryfilmfest.com. Huge in Sonoma come late July or early August is the annual **Sonoma Salute to the Arts,** "Northern California's ultra-premium showcase of the winemaking, culinary, visual, performing, and literary arts," sponsored by the Sonoma Valley Arts Alliance. This long-weekend art celebration usually kicks off with a Friday night gala at the Buena Vista Winery and continues with two days of food, wine, and art in Sonoma Plaza and a Saturday night auction and dinner at Chateau St. Jean. For more information and tickets, call 707/938-1133 or see www.salutetothearts.com.

The town's *big* event, the **Sonoma County Wine Showcase and Auction,** is held in late August or early September (usually over Labor Day weekend) at various Sonoma venues and throughout the county. The benefit auction attracts primarily trade people and costs a fortune for a bidder's paddle, offering players an entrée into the best parties and an informal industry hotline into the hot local wine gossip. For more information, contact the Sonoma Valley Vintners & Growers Alliance, 707/935-0803, www.sonomavalleywine.com. To support the longest-running wine festival around—over a century now and counting—come to the **Valley of the Moon Vintage Festival,** 707/996-2109, www.sonomavinfest.com, complete with fireman's water fight, parade, and grape stomp plus food, wine tasting, live music, and art. Worth the trip in October is the **ARTrails Open Studio Tour,** 707/579-ARTS, www.artrails.org, featuring more than 100 artists working in many media.

Area wineries offer their own very full events calendars, including the wonderful **Sonoma Valley Shakespeare Festival** held outdoors at the Gundlach-Bundschu Winery, weekends from mid-July through September; the **Catalan Festival** at Gloria Ferrer in mid-July; the annual

Shakespeare at Buena Vista theater festival (with the Avalon Players) on weekends from mid-July through mid-September; and the October **Wine Games Carnival** at Chateau St. Jean.

JACK LONDON STATE HISTORIC PARK

When Jack London first saw the soft primeval forests sprawling up the sides of Sonoma Mountain in 1905, he knew this was his new home. The canyons and grassy hills separated by streams and natural springs, the mixture of redwoods, firs, live oaks, and madrones all spoke to him. This was his escape from city life, which he called "the man-trap." So here, at his beloved Beauty Ranch, Jack London lived with his second wife Charmian for 11 years, "anchoring good and solid, and anchoring for keeps," except for a two-year sail through the South Seas.

Once out of the city, London became a hardworking, forward-looking farmer—eventually expanding his holdings from 130 to 1,400 acres. He raised horses, cattle, and pigs, and grew innovative and unusual crops, a passion shared by his Santa Rosa contemporary and friend, "Mr. Arbor Day," horticulturist Luther Burbank. London also wrote here, voluminously. He sometimes scrawled away for 19 hours straight.

The Londons' former ranch, until recently an 840-acre state historic park near Glen Ellen, is a must-do destination—a strangely silent monument to one person's grand spirit. The park was expanded substantially in 2002, when 600 acres of state land were added to the park for open space preservation and multiuse public trails, instead of being sold to clamoring wine grape growers. To get to the park, take London Ranch Road (up the hill from Arnold Drive at the curve in "downtown" Glen Ellen) then follow the signs. The park is open daily 9:30 A.M.–5 (until 7 P.M. in summer), and the park's museum, in the House of Happy Walls on the park's east end, is open daily 10 A.M.–5 P.M. The London Cottage—where Jack London lived and wrote from 1911 until his death in 1916—is undergoing restoration and is at the west end of the park, open weekends and holidays only, 10 A.M.–2 P.M. Fortunately for future visitors, restoration of Beauty Ranch is still underway. Contributions are welcomed. No camping is allowed in the park, and the day-use fee is $5 per car. Docent-guided tours are available. For more information, contact Jack London State Historic Park, 2400 London Ranch Rd. in Glen Ellen, 707/938-5216.

House of Happy Walls

The park's once-overflowing museum collection has been slimmed down substantially. At home in the two-story stone House of Happy Walls, which Charmian London built from 1919–22, the museum is still well worth the short hike uphill from the main parking lot. The impressive collection of rejection slips should comfort any writer (as will the meticulously worked page proofs), and much of London's correspondence is hilarious. In addition to the Londons' array of South Pacific paraphernalia, Jack London's study—too neat for a working writer—is quite evocative. A well-done display on his social life

JACK LONDON

A phenomenally successful and prolific author (the first writer ever to earn $1 million with his pen), Jack London (1876–1916) completed more than 50 books and hundreds of short stories and articles between 1900 and 1916.

Colorful and controversial, Jack London was just as celebrated for his other activities: socialist lecturer, political activist, barroom orator, war correspondent, world traveler, sailor, and outdoorsman.

Part of London's public appeal was the essential contradiction he represented: the rugged individualist in search of universal justice. The illegitimate Irish son of an astrologer, primarily self-educated through public libraries (his formal schooling ended at age 14 when he went to work in the factories of West Oakland), Jack London became a founding member of the original Bay Area Bohemian Club (then an artists' club, now an elite social clique).

Jack London's redwood-and-stone Wolf House burned to the ground before the Londons could move in.

and socialist political adventures and polemics (London ran twice, on the Socialist ticket, for mayor of Oakland) is upstairs.

Wolf House

It's an easy half-mile downhill walk to the still-standing rock ruins of the Londons' dream home, Wolf House, a magnificent 15,000-square-foot mansion of carefully carved maroon lava and natural unpeeled redwood logs on an earthquake-proof concrete slab. Built with double-thick concrete walls to make it fireproof, it was long speculated that Wolf House was burned to the ground by unknown arsonists, just before the Londons planned to move in. Scientists studying the ruins in 1995 concluded that the fire was started by rags soaked in linseed oil, which may have combusted spontaneously in the August heat.

"Beauty Ranch" Trail and Beyond

Take the Beauty Ranch Trail through the other side of the park to see what remains of London's experimental farm, which raised Shire draft horses

and grew for feed the spineless cacti developed by London's friend, Luther Burbank. The circular, stone **Pig Palace** is London's original design. Tucked among vineyards on the rolling gold and green hills is the simple white wood-frame **London Cottage** where Jack and Charmian lived and worked, and where Jack died (open to visitors on weekends). Adjacent are the ruins of the old winery (severely damaged by the 1906 earthquake) where the Londons' many guests usually stayed. Trails lead beyond Beauty Ranch to London's **Lake and Bathhouse** and to the summit of **Sonoma Mountain.**

London Ranch Horseback Rides

"I am a sailor on horseback!" Jack London once proclaimed. "Watch my dust!" Though elsewhere horseback rides seem like a mere tourist diversion, at Jack London State Park the trip is a real treat—and an opportunity to see parts of London's ranch just as he and Charmian did (though hikers can cover the same terrain for free, of course). **Triple Creek Horse Outfit,** 707/933-1600, www.triplecreekhorseoutfit.com, offers guided small group rides (for either novice or experienced riders) through the park's hinterlands, past London's vineyards, his onetime irrigation lake and bathhouse, abandoned ranch buildings, London's disappointing experimental forest of eucalyptus—even up the steep slopes of Sonoma Mountain. One- to three-hour rides are available—$40–70—as are special lunch, winery-tour, and private rides. Reservations required. Triple Creek also offers rides in nearby Sugarloaf Ridge (see below) and Bothe–Napa Valley State Parks.

GLEN ELLEN AND KENWOOD

The **Jack London Bookstore,** 14300 Arnold Dr., 707/996-2888, has new and used copies of the writer's works, including first editions. The bookstore also maintains the **Jack London Research Center** and foundation, www.jacklondonfdn.org, featuring London memorabilia and sponsoring an annual writing contest for high school students and a Jack London birthday dinner and book auction. Also see www.jacklondon.com. London fans, please note: In 2000 scholar Carl Bernatovech's complete collection of Jack London first-edition books, original magazine articles, papers, letters, and movie memorabilia was donated to the Sonoma State University library in Rohnert Park (south side of Santa Rosa) and is available to scholars and other serious researchers. A comparable treasure trove of London material (original manuscripts and letters) is collected at the Huntington Library in Southern California.

Still, not everything in and around tiny Glen Ellen revolves around memories of Jack London. The equally adventurous octogenarian, globetrotting gourmet, and prolific prose writer M.F.K. Fisher, considered by most to be the ultimate food writer in the English language, lived (and wrote) just outside town. The author of *Serve It Forth* and *How to Cook a Wolf*, among many other books, Fisher believed that writers are born, not created. Once, when asked by a young girl why "so-and-so's" books were best-sellers but she was barely known, she reportedly replied: "Because he is an author, and I am a writer." To honor Fisher, be sure to enjoy a meal in the area—either in a good local restaurant (see below) or by serving forth an impromptu picnic.

Though Jack London's spread can't be beat for picnics, the large oak-forested **Sonoma Valley Regional Park,** 13630 Sonoma Hwy. (off the highway next to the forestry station), is pleasant, too (picnic area and portapotty near trailhead). Plus there's a one-acre dog park, if Fido needs a romp. The park is open sunrise to sunset, day-use fee $3. Or head for Kenwood and **Morton's Warm Springs,** 1651 Warm Springs Rd., 707/833-5511, a family-style place, featuring two large pools and a wading pool for toddlers. Pools are flushed and "refreshed" nightly. Good for picnics, too. Open May–Sept. Fee.

Adjacent to Sonoma Valley Park is the **Bouverie Audubon Preserve** in Stuart Creek Canyon, noted for its bird-watching, impressive populations of red-bellied California newts, some 350 species of flowering plants. The best wildflowers are in April. Guided walks are offered only Sept.–May, on certain Saturdays; space is limited, so visitors are selected by lottery. For details call 707/938-4554 or see www.egret.org.

Dedicated gardeners will want to visit the 61-acre **Quarryhill Botanical Garden,** www.quarryhillbg.org, dedicated to propagating rare and unusual "wild source" plants from Asia. Docent-led tours for individuals are offered (by appointment only) May–Oct. on the third Saturday of the month. No clipping or cutting allowed. For reservations call 707/996-3802.

The **Olive Press** in Glen Ellen's Jack London Village at 14301 Arnold Dr., 707/939-8900 or 800/965-4839, www.theolivepress.com, offers tasting and sales of California estate-grown, extra-virgin olive oils and olive-themed gifts.

Eating in Glen Ellen and Kenwood

Convenient to both Santa Rosa and Sonoma, Glen Ellen has become Sonoma County's secret Gourmet Gulch. The **Cellar Cat Café,** in Jack London Village, 14301 Arnold Dr., 707/933-1465, is the cat's meow for French bistro fare in these parts, serving lots of veggie options, most everything pretty darned organic. Open Tues.–Sun. for lunch and dinner. The Cat is also a way-cool nightclub, too, serving up great live music. The Girl & the Fig has a sister here in Glen Ellen, bright, cheery **The Fig Café & Wine Bar,** 13690 Arnold Dr., 707/938-2130, open Thurs.–Mon. for dinner. Start with marinated olives, pork and pistachio paté, or fig and arugula salad, continue with hearty chicken stew or braised pot roast, and top it off with fresh fruit coppler and vanilla ice cream.

For a romantic yet relaxed dinner, try the nearby **Glen Ellen Inn** restaurant, 13670 Arnold Dr., 707/996-6409, as warm and inviting indoors as it is refreshing outdoors on the deck. Start with figs in a blanket—mission figs, spinach, and walnuts with goat cheese wrapped in a crepe—or Dungeness crab potstickers and taste on, through the filet mignon crusted with walnuts and bleu cheese to the cinnamon-pecan bread pudding or house-made peanut butter ice cream.

Once a funky roadside diner, the **Kenwood Restaurant & Bar** across from the Kunde Estate Winery at 9900 Sonoma Hwy. (Hwy. 12), 707/833-6326, is now a bright, city-style surprise for lunch and dinner. The great California-style country French fare—gazpacho and salads to roast duck, pork tenderloin, and prawns simmered in saffron Pernod sauce—is accompanied by good country views. The very reasonable deli-like **Cafe Citti,** 9049 Sonoma Hwy., 707/833-2690, is an Italian-style trattoria that specializes in focaccia sandwiches, house-made pastas, and rotisserie chicken stuffed with garlic and rosemary. Open daily for breakfast, lunch, and early dinner.

Staying in Glen Ellen and Kenwood

After a relaxing meal at the Glen Ellen Inn, you may also want to stay there. Earthy yet elegant "secret" creekside cottages alongside the creek offer the essential elements for romance, from fireplaces to large steamer showers and two-person Jacuzzi tubs. Winter rates are a real deal, too, $100–150. Otherwise on peak-season weekends, rates are $200–250. For more information, call 707/996-6409 or see www.glenelleninn.com. It's also hard to beat Glen Ellen for accommodations. Another of the wine country's best-kept secrets, the New Orleans-style **Beltane Ranch,** 11775 Sonoma Hwy., 707/996-6501, www.beltaneranch.com, is a bed-and-breakfast once owned by Mammy Pleasant, a former slave who in the 1800s shook up some in San Francisco with her antiracist voodoo. The five farmhouse rooms and charming private cottage here feature private baths and outside entrances. Full country breakfast. The 1,600-acre estate offers hiking trails, birding, and a private tennis court. Rooms are $100–200, the cottage is $220.

The elegant and stylish **Gaige House Inn,** 13540 Arnold Dr., 707/935-0237 or 800/935-0237, www.gaigehouseinn.com, is a wine country showplace, not the prim Victorian it first appears to be. Expect all the comforts, with contemporary "plantation" and Indonesian flair. Breakfasts are absolutely spectacular, a delight for even dedicated foodies. Room rates start at $250; suites and cottages are $295–595.

Once a landmark antique store, the **Kenwood Inn & Spa,** 10400 Sonoma Hwy., 707/833-1293 or 800/353-6966, www.kenwoodinn.com, is now a luxurious, romantic Italian-style villa with 30 elegant suites, all with a fireplace, feather bed, and private bath. Swimming pools, Jacuzzi, full-service spa. Full breakast. Rates start at $375.

Sugarloaf Ridge State Park

It's several steep and narrow miles via Adobe Canyon Rd.—mud or rockslides may close the road in winter—up to Sugarloaf Ridge State Park, a fine 2,700-acre wine-country park in the Mayacamas Mountains, headwaters of Sonoma Creek. Camping is available, and the park also invites hiking, horseback riding, fishing, and rock climbing. In summer, days are hot, the vegetation is tinder dry, and Sonoma Creek dribbles into dust. But in spring, the air is cool, the hillsides are green and thick with wildflowers, and trout swim up the creek's seasonal 25-foot waterfall, below the campground. On any clear day, the views from the park's ridgetops are worth the hike. Twenty-five miles of trails lace the park, which is connected via **Goodspeed Trail** to **Hood Mountain Regional Park,** 707/527-2041, open for day use only on weekends and holidays, closed during the fire season. Starting from the campground on the meadow, Sugarloaf's **Creekside Nature Trail** introduces native vegetation and area landforms. The park also features one of the largest public viewing telescopes, the 40-inch scope at the **Ferguson Observatory,** which can be rented (with the group campsite) for private parties.

Triple Creek Horse Outfit, 707/933-1600, www.triplecreekhorseoutfit.com, offers small group rides (for either novice or experienced riders) through Sugarloaf. One- to three-hour rides are available—$40–70—as well as special two-hour moonlight rides ($60). Reservations required. Triple Creek also offers rides in nearby Jack London and Bothe–Napa Valley State Parks.

The turnoff to Sugarloaf Ridge is about seven miles east of Santa Rosa via Hwy. 12, or—on winter or spring weekends and holidays only—hike in from Hood Mountain. The campground has flush toilets but no showers ($12–15), reservations usually required late Mar.–Oct. Hiker and biker campsites are also available. Day-use fee: $4 per car. Trail map available at the entrance or at the visitor center near the campground. For more information, contact: Sugarloaf Ridge State Park, 2605 Adobe Canyon Rd. in Kenwood, 707/833-5712. For camping reservations, call ReserveAmerica at 800/444-7275 or see www.reserveamerica.com.

Carneros

Taking in the southern reaches of both Sonoma and Napa Valleys is a distinct, and increasingly distinctive, wine area—the relatively uncrowded Carneros appellation. Generally defined by Hwy. 12/121—renamed the Carneros Highway in 1992, the only U.S. highway named after an American Viticultural Area—this was once sheep grazing land (*los carneros* is Spanish for "the sheep"), though it was vineyard country before that. September, October, and early November are the most pleasant times to visit, weather wise, and with any luck at all the bumper-to-bumper traffic on the way into Napa will also have eased up.

Carneros is one of the state's oldest wine regions. The unique climate here, often windy or foggy and cold, but moderated by proximity to San Pablo Bay, provides a longer growing season perfect for persnickety pinot noir grapes. For that reason, the Napa-Sonoma Carneros AVA is known for its rich, sweet pinot noir wines. Chardonnay also does exceptionally well here, as do sparkling wines. In fact, most of California's top sparkling-wine makers are either located here or buy their grapes here. Still, fitting traditional viticulture to the region has been a challenge for growers. With demand for the region's grapes much greater than supply, most Carneros wines are on the pricey side.

WINERIES

Southern Napa County boasts an impressive roster of Carneros wineries, but Sonoma County's is equally prestigious. From downtown Sonoma, it's a fairly short, straight shot south on Broadway to reach the Carneros region. Ravenswood and Buena Vista wines qualify those Sonoma wineries for the Carneros appellation.

The historic start for a Carneros tour is the **Schug Carneros Estate Winery,** 602 Bonneau Rd., 707/939-9363 or 800/966-9365, www .schugwinery.com. Schug was among the first contemporary wineries to use Carneros grapes, and pinot noir in particular. Pinot noirs and chardonnays are the specialties here, wines with

a distinctively French Burgundian character. Open daily 10 A.M.–5 P.M.

It soon becomes clear that the Spanish have returned to Sonoma County. About six miles north of Infineon Raceway are the **Gloria Ferrer Champagne Caves,** 23555 Carneros Hwy. (Hwy. 121), 707/996-7256 or 707/933-1917 (tasting room), www.gloriaferrer.com. This is the American winemaking arm of Barcelona's 600-year-old Ferrer family enterprise, Freixenet S.A.—the world's largest producer of *méthode champenoise* sparkling wines (called *cava* in Spain, after the aging caves). While the "caves" here at Gloria Ferrer are not much to explore, the champagnery itself is as elegant in its genteel, understated way as the Napa Valley's Domaine Chandon is opulent—a Mediterranean-style villa with a terrace and "Hall of Tasters" for wine tasting (fee for the wines, snacks provided free). Tasting available daily 10:30 A.M.–5:30 P.M., tours usually offered at noon, 2 P.M., and 4 P.M. daily. For a taste of Spain's Catalonia, come in late July for Gloria Ferrer's huge **Catalan Festival,** with flamenco and circle dancing (*sardana*), guitar, *gegants,* tapas, cooking demonstrations, wines, and more—typically an early sellout, tickets around $30.

A bit farther south on the opposite side of the highway, the **Viansa Winery and Italian Marketplace,** 25200 Hwy. 121, 707/935-4700 or 800/995-4740, www.viansa.com, occupies a hilltop perch overlooking the Carneros region, a popular destination (watch out for those tour buses). Founded by Sam and Vicki Sebastiani, on less busy days the Mediterranean-inspired grounds feel like a Tuscan villa, a perfect place for a picnic. Inside the tasting room, you'll find one of the valley's best selections of delectable finger foods—olives, cheeses, crackers, pestos, etc.—for sale or sample. But be careful; after you try, you'll *want* to buy. Open daily 10 A.M.–5 P.M. Also note that Viansa is a wildlife refuge, thanks to the 90-acre restored wetlands here—an effort that won the winery a National Wetlands Award in 1995. Even novice bird-watchers can identify migrating winter waterfowl from the winery's

WINE AND WETLANDS

Sonoma County is as good a place as any to start a bird-watching tour of California, since the county is on the Pacific Flyway "flight path" for migratory birds, which pass overhead year-round.

South of the town of Sonoma and created by Sam and Vicki Sebastiani and their Viansa Winery are the **Viansa Winery Wetlands,** a 90-acre waterfowl preserve that is the seasonal home to some one million ducks, shorebirds, and golden eagles each year; 156 species have been identified here. During peak migration periods more than 10,000 birds per day feed and refuel at Viansa. The wetlands—once a hayfield—also now host a thriving and diverse array of wildlife and grasses. The Viansa Wetlands can be viewed from the winery's hilltop; visitors who desire a closer look can take a tour, offered February through May, weather permitting. Wetlands tours include a guided walk, informal talk on the history of the Carneros AVA, video presentation on current preservation efforts, and wine tasting. For more information, contact the Viansa Winery on Hwy. 121, 707/935-4700 or 800/995-4740, www.viansa.com.

The cool, foggy Carneros region borders the 40,000-acre **Napa-Sonoma Marsh** near San Pablo Bay. The marsh itself is getting new attention these days, thanks to the efforts of Acacia Vineyard & Winery, working in conjunction with the California Dept. of Fish and Game to restore the 13,000-acre Napa-Sonoma Marshes Wildlife Area. Proceeds from the winery's **Acacia Marsh Chardonnay** ($15), sold exclusively at the winery, go into the nonprofit Wines for Wildlife fund. Acacia employees have built a comfy wildlife-viewing blind and also planted trees and wild rosebushes at the end of Buchlui Road (off Las Amigas Road, close to the marshes' public entry near Napa). Work on needed restoration projects continues. For more information contact **Acacia Winery,** 2750 Las Amigas Rd. in Napa, 707/226-9991, www.acaciawinery.com, open by appointment Mon.–Sat. 10 A.M.–4:30 P.M. and Sun. noon–4:30 P.M.

terrace; January, February, and March are the best months to try. For more information, see Wine and Wetlands elsewhere in this chapter.

Nearby **Cline Cellars,** 24737 Arnold Dr. (Hwy. 121), 707/935-4310 or 800/546-2070, www.clinecellars.com, got its start in Oakley, in the Sacramento–San Joaquin Delta. The old-vine wines are handcrafted in the style of Fred Cline's maternal grandfather, Valeriano Jacuzzi, who with his brothers founded the famous pump and spa company. Cline's intriguing wines include Ancient Vines Mourvèdre, viognier, several zinfandels, Oakley red and white wine blends, and Carneros syrah. The grounds here are particularly inviting, from the 1850s farmhouse tasting room and deli/gift shop to the old rock-walled ponds, wood-plank bathhouse, and 5,000 blooming roses. Open daily 10 A.M.–6 P.M. for tasting (fee only for reserve wines), sales, and picnicking in the eucalyptus grove. Tours are offered at 11 A.M., 1 P.M., and 3 P.M.

Other wineries near Sonoma featuring Los

Carneros wines include the onetime site of the Sonoma Rodeo, **Sonoma Creek Winery,** 23355 Millerick Rd., 707/938-3031, www.sonoma-creek.com, which also offers a rental guesthouse, and the **Roche Carneros Estate Winery,** One Carneros Hwy. (Hwy. 121; previously 28700 Arnold Dr.), 707/935-7115 or 800/825-9475, www.rochewinery.com, which produces pinot noir, chardonnay, merlot, cabernet, zinfandel, and other wines. Roche—the white barn at the top of the hill—sells its wines only through its futures program, and here at the winery.

Then it's on to Napa's Carneros wineries. In the heart of the district is elegant **Domaine Carneros,** 1240 Duhig Rd. (four miles southwest of Napa just off Hwy. 121/12), 707/257-0101, www.domaine.com, which produces *méthode-champenoise* sparkling wine from Carneros grapes. Established in 1987 and considered a regional landmark, Domaine Carneros is architecturally inspired by the historic 18th-century Champagne residence of its founding Taittinger family, as in Champagne Taittinger of Reims, France. Climb the grand front stairs to the chateau, which houses the visitor center. Built into a hillside next to the main winery building is the new, 23,500-square-foot pinot noir building, with the largest solar electrical system of any U.S. winery. Taste wines and enjoy complimentary hors d'oeuvres either in the Louis XV salon or out on the ultimate "view" terrace. Most affordable, at $18 per bottle, is the new Carneros Avant-Garde Pinot Noir. Open daily 10 A.M.–6 P.M. for tours and tasting.

Make the leap from traditional European to cutting-edge contemporary style by heading east then north on Old Sonoma Hwy. to **Artesa Vineyards & Winery,** 1345 Henry Rd. in Napa, 707/224-1668 or 707/254-2140 (tasting room), www.artesawinery.com. As striking as the wine is the avant-garde architecture and art, including outdoor fountains and sculpture garden, at what was originally a sparkling wine venture by Spain's Codorniu clan. The focus now is on four varietals—chardonnay, pinot noir, merlot, and cabernet sauvignon—and various versions of each handcrafted varietal, involving a number of appellations, are produced here, in addition to changing "unique" wines. In addition to tasting wines and sampling the views, both the Carneros and winemaking museums are worth some time. Open daily 10 A.M.–5 P.M.

South of Carneros Hwy. (Hwy. 121/12) is **Saintsbury Vineyards,** 1500 Los Carneros Ave., 707/252-0592, www.saintsbury.com, noted for its Garnet pinot noir and more full-bodied Carneros, Reserve, and Brown Ranch pinot as well as chardonnay. New wines include pinot gris and vin gris ("Vincent Vin Gris"). The office is open Mon.–Fri. 9 A.M.–5 P.M. for retail sales, but tasting is by appointment only. Nearby **Etude Wines,** 1250 Cuttings Wharf Rd., 707/257-5300, www.etudewines.com, is famed for its Carneros pinot noir.

"Exclusive" has long been the word for **Acacia Winery,** 2750 Las Amigas Rd., 707/226-9991, www.acaciawinery.com, with its winning pinot noir and chardonnay. These days "environmentally responsible" also fits, thanks to Acacia's ongoing efforts to restore the Napa-Sonoma Marshes

and expand wildlife habitat. Be sure to buy a bottle or two of Acacia Marsh Chardonnay, sold only at the winery, to support wetlands restoration. The tasting room is open Mon.–Sat. 10 A.M.–4:30 P.M. and Sun. noon–4:30 P.M., but appointments are required. Also nearby are **Bouchaine Vineyards,** 1075 Buchli Station Rd., 707/252-9065 or 800/654-9463, www.bouchaine.com, which produces pinot noir and chardonnay as well as the affordable Buchli Station ("BS for short") pinot/chardonnay blend, open daily for tasting and sales 10:30 A.M.–4 P.M. (tours by appointment); and **Casa Carneros,** 1159 Bayview Ave., 707/257-8713, www.casacarneros.com, which offers merlot and pinot noir.

Definitely different in the Napa Valley neighborhood but not otherwise associated with the Carneros AVA is **Hakusan Sake Gardens,** 1 Executive Way (southern junction of Hwy. 12 and Hwy. 29; enter from N. Kelly Rd.), 707/258-6160 or 800/425-8726, www.hakusan.com, open for sake tasting and sales daily 10 A.M.–5 P.M.

For more information about Carneros wines and wineries, contact: the **Carneros Quality Alliance,** 707/938-5906, www.carneros.org.

STAYING IN CARNEROS

Los Carneros is quite close to both Napa and Sonoma, so it's convenient to stay and eat in both towns, then venture out to explore the region on day trips. Yet you can stay—and eat—in Carneros. Join local growers and ranchers in their natural environment at **Matthew's Schellville Grill,** south of Sonoma at 22900 Broadway, 707/996-5151, just the place for breakfast omelettes and frittatas or burgers and sandwiches at lunch. Come on Friday and Saturday nights, 6–9 P.M., for the "Dinner of Dreams." Particularly convenient to Carneros is **Starwae Inn,** "A Place for Art and Leisure," at 21490 Broadway in Sonoma, 707/938-1374 or 800/793-4792, www.starwae.com, where rooms and suites are $150–200 and the cottage is $325.

A definite sign that times are changing came in 2003, with the opening of the new **Carneros Inn,** 4048 Carneros Hwy. (Hwy. 121/12), 707/254-7003, www.thecarnerosinn.com, a lux-

A GARDEN OF MODERN ART

The 200-acre **di Rosa Art and Nature Preserve,** 5200 Carneros Hwy. (Hwy. 12/121), 707/226-5991, www.dirosapreserve.org, at home in a onetime winery right across the road from Domaine Carneros, is a fascinating destination on the Napa end of the Carneros region. This 40-year-old labor of love by Rene di Rosa and his late wife Veronica, open to the public since 1997, blends art into the landscape in surprising ways.

The motto of the eclectic collection here is: "Divinely regional, superbly parochial, wondrously provincial—an absolute native glory." And so it is. More than 2,000 works by emerging Northern California artists, most of them from Davis, Sacramento, and the San Francisco Bay Area, have the run of the place—having taken over the winery building, multiple galleries, and the large meadow and lake. A wooden horse pulls a cart, cows inhabit the lake, sheep guard the dam, and a rooster hangs from a tree—but the only living, breathing animals in the collection are the peacocks. A vehicle that once belonged to di Rosa's mother, refashioned with horse head and saddle and otherwise surprisingly redecorated, is among several reimagined car mosaics on display. If you expect the label on each work to explain what you're looking at, you're out of luck—no labels here, because di Rosa wants people to look at the *art.*

So, come and look—at the Robert Arneson bust at the door in the main gallery, Ray Beldner's *Nature Remains,* David Best's *Ghost Rider,* the Mark Di Suvero, the Robert Hudson, the Viola Frey, and all the others. The di Rosa Preserve is open for tours (two-plus hours) year-round, and are conducted rain or shine. Call for tour times and reservations (required). The cost is $12 per person. At last report Tuesday evening tours were offered July–Sept., too, along with other special tours.

---

ury residential development and resort. Dozens and dozens of "elegant cottages" (cherrywood floors, wood-burning fireplaces, large-panel flat screen TVs, heated private patios, etc.) are surrounded by newly planted vineyards and come with extras like full spa services, bocce ball courts, and the new **Boon Fly Café & Wine Bar.** Rates start at $325 and climb to $1,200 per night.

Petaluma

You can't always tell a town by its freeway. Petaluma, for example, is hometown America. Though inspired by the mores of Modesto, *American Graffiti* was filmed here, as were *Peggy Sue Got Married* and the forgettable *Howard the Duck* (not to mention *Basic Instinct.*) Petaluma means "beautiful view" (or by some accounts, "flat back," a reference to local Miwok people). Once promoted as the World's Egg Basket, the area still has plenty of chicken ranches and once even had a Chicken Pharmacy downtown, which dispensed poultry medicines. Dairy farming is another major area industry, as are its 30-plus antique shops.

Get oriented at the **Petaluma Visitors Center,** 800 Baywood Dr., Ste. A, 707/769-0429 or 877/273-8258, www.visitpetaluma.com. To get there, take the Washington Street exit off Hwy. 101, go west on Washington and turn left (south) on Lakeville; Baywood intersects Lakeville. Free parking is available downtown in the city garage at Keller and Western, as well as along the riverfront on Water Street.

SEEING AND DOING PETALUMA

Petaluma is noted for its historic downtown district; through some quirk of fate, the 1906 earthquake that torched San Francisco and flattened other towns completed spared Petaluma, so a great number of the town's Victorian buildings still stand. Some 65 local buildings are listed on the National Register of Historic Places; the local walking tour takes you past many of them. To get the whole story stop by the **Petaluma Historical Library and Museum** inside the stunning stone

WINE COUNTRY

SUSAN SNYDER

downtown Petaluma

Carnegie Library building, 20 Fourth St., 707/778-4398, www.petalumamuseum.com, which features the largest freestanding leaded glass dome in Northern California. Open Wed.–Sat. 10 A.M.–4 P.M., Sun. noon–3 P.M. Many of Petaluma's historic buildings are on or near the Petaluma River, in the town's redeveloped **historic district**—homes, shops, restaurants, and more, described by the good walking-tour brochure available at the visitors center. The antique shops alone might keep you here all day. Free **guided walking tours**—docents dress in Victorian attire—are offered May–Oct., departing from the museum on Saturday (and sometimes on Sunday) mornings at 10:30 A.M. Call the visitor center for details.

Petaluma is also something of a garden spot, home to an incredible number of prime gardener destinations—including the rose-lover's nine-acre **Garden Valley Ranch**, 498 Pepper St., 707/795-0919, www.gardenvalley.com, which offers some 8,000 rose bushes, a one-acre fragrance garden, nursery, and gift shop (self-guided and group tours available). Also in fine petal are the **Petaluma Rose Company**, 581 Gossage Ave., 707/769-8862, www.petrose.com, with more than 400 varieties of roses and, every fall, a bare-

root rose catalog, and the **Rose Garden Nursery and Sprinkler Store**, 2040 Petaluma Blvd. N, 707/763-4173, which also sells roses and unusual perennials. Other notable gardener draws include the **North Coast Native Nursery**, 2710 Chileno Valley Rd., 707/769-1213, www.northcoastnativenursery.com, and **Cottage Garden Growers of Petaluma**, 4049 Petaluma Blvd., 707/778-8025, with hundreds of perennial varieties, dozens of different types of clematis, old and new roses, ornamental grasses, and drought-tolerant plants on its three acres of flagstone terraces.

The **Butter and Egg Days Parade** (including the Cutest Chick in Town contest) comes to town the last weekend in April, followed in June by the **Riverfront Arts & Garden Weekend** and the **Sonoma-Marin Fair** at the Petaluma Fairgrounds with its fun **Ugly Dog Contest** (especially fun for people who believe that pets resemble their people). Come in August for the **Summer Music Festival** in the historic Cinnabar Theater and the **Petaluma Waterfront Jazz Festival.** In September, look for **Art in the Park** in downtown's Walnut Park and, later in the month, the **Petaluma Poetry Walk.** Don't miss the **World Wristwrestling Championships,** held here in October. Among the multitude of holiday events, enjoy the **Victorian Fantasy of Lights** in late November and the **Holiday Lighted Boat Parade** in mid-December.

For live jazz, drop by **Zebulon's Lounge,** 21 Fourth St., 707/769-7948, www.zebulonslounge .com. Also see what's happening at the **Cinnabar Theater,** in a onetime schoolhouse ar 3333 Petaluma Blvd. N, 707/763-8920, www.cinnabartheater.org, and the jazz/blues/rock **McNear's Mystic Theater & Music Hall,** adjacent to the dining hall and saloon (a must-do destination for Irish everywhere, come St. Paddy's Day) at 21 Petaluma Blvd., 707/765-6665, www.mcnears.com. Head east via Hwy. 116 to Petaluma Adobe State Historic Park, or drive to the Sonoma coast via Petaluma–Valley Ford Rd. along eucalyptus-lined country lanes through coastal farmlands.

Petaluma Adobe State Historic Park

Due east of town on the way to Sonoma is Petaluma Adobe State Historic Park. The park's centerpiece is Vallejo's Casa Grande, a huge two-story adobe hacienda that was once headquarters for the old Rancho Petaluma. The site, atop a low hill, is almost as stark today as it was in its prime; the landscape was intentionally left barren, the better to spy potential interlopers. Vallejo's "big house" was originally a quadrangle, with a traditional interior courtyard and massive front gates. Only a U-shaped section remains, protected then as now by a wide redwood veranda and overhanging roof. The park's special events include **Sheep Shearing Day** in mid-April, weekend **Living History Days** in mid-May and October—with an 1840s atmosphere, authentic period costumes, and demonstrations of blacksmithing, bread baking, and candlemaking—and the similar **Old Adobe Fiesta** in August, which includes adobe-brick making. Shaded picnic areas. Petaluma Adobe State Historic Park is at 3325 Adobe Rd. off Hwy. 116, 707/762-4871, and is open daily (except major holidays) 10 A.M.–5 P.M.

STAYING IN PETALUMA

Delightfully different in Petaluma is the **Métro Hôtel and Café,** an eclectic yet inspired outpost of Eurostyle at 508 Petaluma Blvd. S, 707/773-4900, www.metrolodging.com, with rooms starting at $79. The **Old Palms,** 2 Liberty St., 707/658-2554, www.oldpalms.com, offers exquisite Victorian style, from the floral wallpapers and antiques to authentic clawfoot tubs (private bathrooms). The **Cavanagh Inn,** 10 Keller St., 707/765-4657 or 888/765-4658, www.cavanaghinn.com, offers a total of seven bed-and-breakfast rooms in a 1912 Craftsman cottage and a 1902 Georgian revival mansion; two rooms share a bath, one has a whirlpool tub. Amenities include a VCR and assorted movies, as well as a full breakfast. Rates at both are $100–200. Beyond Petaluma proper is refreshingly rural **Chileno Valley Ranch Bed & Breakfast,** a lovingly restored 1850s Italianate Victorian on a cattle ranch at 5105 Chileno Valley Rd., 707/765-6664 or 877/280-6664, www .chilenobnb.com. The four lovely and large rooms and the private Creamery Cottage (out by the barn) are $150–200.

EATING IN PETALUMA

Get it fresh, get it local. Show up on Sat. 2–5 P.M. May–Oct. for the **Petaluma Certified Farmers Market,** 707/762-0344, held in Walnut Park, Fourth and D Sts., 707/762-0344. Stop at **Marin French Cheese Co.,** one of California's most venerable cheesemakers, 7500 Red Hill Rd., 707/762-6001, for wonderful local Camembert. A fairly complete listing of area delis, food shops, and restaurants is included in the free *Petaluma Visitors Guide,* but just to get you started: **Whole Foods Market & Deli** at 621 E. Washington St., 707/762-9352, is good for a healthy bite at lunch. **Dempsey's Restaurant & Brewery** in the Golden Eagle Center at 50 E. Washington, 707/765-9694, is a microbrewery features excellent beer and food; everything is homemade, down to the hand-cut fries and bar snacks like spicy nuts and jerky. Grab a table outside, overlooking the Petaluma River. For family-friendly Mexican, try **Velasco's,** 190 Kentucky St. (near Washington), 707/773-0882.

A grand choice at breakfast or lunch (closed Tues.) is the tiny **Water Street Bistro,** facing Water Street from 100 Petaluma Blvd. N. (at

Western), 707/763-9563, and serving up organic coffee, buttermilk waffles, and other inexpensive yet delectable fare created by one of the chefs at Sonoma's famed Babette's. Weather permitting, sit out on the riverfront terrace. And if you like Sonoma's cheery and stylish **The Girl &the Fig** bistro, you'll probably also like the one here, across the turning basin at 222 Weller St., 707/769-0123. A long-running local favorite for country French is bustling **De Schmire**, 304 Bodega Ave., 707/762-1901, serving dinner nightly.

The outdoor patio at the Sheraton Hotel's **Jellyfish**, 745 Baywood, 707/283-2888, offers views of the marina along with savory Californian,

Mediterranean, and Asian fusion, prepared from Sonoma County's best. Open daily for breakfast, lunch, and dinner. Sophisticated **Hiro's**, 107 Petaluma Blvd. N., 707/763-2300, serves marvelous Japanese. Open Tues.–Sat. for lunch, Tues.–Sun. for dinner.

If you'll be driving to Point Reyes or out to the Sonoma County coast, consider **Washoe House**, at the corner of Roblar and Stony Point Roads, 707/795-4544, California's oldest roadhouse, still open for lunch and dinner daily—a good place to pull over for steaks, prime rib, chicken in a basket, even buffalo burgers. Great homemade pie.

Santa Rosa and Vicinity

A sprawling Bay Area bedroom community and one of the fastest-growing towns in Northern California, Santa Rosa, with its suburban malls and housing developments, is fast spreading into rich Sonoma County farmlands. The most prominent citizen historically was horticulturalist Luther Burbank; California celebrates Arbor Day on his birthday, March 7. But Robert "Believe It or Not!" Ripley was a local boy who also made good, as was famed *Peanuts* cartoonist Charles Schulz, a long-time local still revered by the citizenry (he died February 2000) for contributing the local ice-skating rink and Snoopy's more recent paradise, the Charles M. Schulz Museum. A thrill for Alfred Hitchcock fans is the fact that the chilling 1942 *Shadow of a Doubt* was filmed here, largely at the house still standing on McDonald Avenue. Santa Rosa's Old Courthouse Square, the Carnegie library building, and the Railroad Square depot are also recognizable.

Immediately south of Santa Rosa are Rohnert Park and Cotati, once part of Sheriff Thomas Page's 1847 Rancho Cotate land grant—named after local Miwok chief Kotate, whose clan greeted the area's first Spanish settlers. Cotati now is a haven for **Sonoma State University** students. Notable is the town square, Cotati Plaza, a state historic landmark. Both the square and its outer hub are laid out hexagonally; the six streets on the outer hexagon were named for Page's six sons.

Old Redwood Hwy. south of the hub offers an array of inexpensive and ethnic restaurants.

SEEING AND DOING SANTA ROSA
Downtown

Santa Rosa looks so thoroughly modern (i.e., ordinary) to the casual observer that it's tempting to assume there's nothing much worth seeing. Not so. Though Santa Rosa lost most of its would-have-been historic heart to the 1906 San Francisco earthquake, head downtown to experience Santa Rosa's true character—much disguised but definitely *there,* at least where the renovation wrecking balls were held back.

Railroad Square, west of Hwy. 101 along Third, Fourth, and Fifth Streets downtown, is now part of a restored 1920s-vintage district with worthy shops, cafés, restaurants, and concentrated nightlife. For antiques, don't miss **Whistlestop Antiques** at 130 Fourth St., 707/542-9474, www.whistelstopantiques.net, and other treasures. Thrift and vintage shopping is also good, with neighborhood opportunities including the **Assistance League's New to You Shop,** 5 W. Sixth St., 707/546-9484; **Hot Couture Vintage Fashions,** 101 Third St., 707/528-7247; **Sacks on the Square,** 116 Fourth St., 707/541-7227, "upscale resale" benefiting the

Railroad Square near downtown Santa Rosa

Sonoma County AIDS Network; and the **Welfare League Shop,** 126 Fourth, 707/542-7480.

The depot here in **Depot Park,** built of locally quarried stone, was among the few local buildings still standing in 1906 when aftershocks from the big quake subsided. Yes, this is the train station in *Shadow of a Doubt.* These days it houses a **California Welcome Center** for convenient visitor information, sponsored by the **Santa Rosa Convention & Visitor Bureau,** as well as the **Northwestern Pacific Rail Museum.** Another nearby quake survivor is the graceful **Hotel La Rose.**

Luther Burbank Home and Gardens

Visit the Luther Burbank Home and Memorial Gardens on Santa Rosa Ave. at Sonoma Ave., 707/524-5445, a registered national, state, and city historic monument where the gardens (free) are open year-round, daily 8 A.M.–dusk. Self-guided audio garden tours, with MP3 players, are offered spring through fall, Tues.–Sun. 10 A.M.–3 P.M. ($3 per person). Also take a trip through the Burbank Cottage. In Burbank's dining room, the 1946 edition of the Webster's dictionary may be opened to the word burbank, a verb meaning: "to modify and improve plant

life." Outside is Luther Burbank's greenhouse—his beloved tools still inside, along with changing exhibits—where he burbanked his way to fame if not fortune. Many of his most impressive accomplishments, from the Shasta daisy to the plumcot, are cultivated and on display in the gardens. The "plant wizard" is buried just a few steps away from the greenhouse, originally planted beneath a large cedar of Lebanon. That tree has since passed on as well, though a descendant guards the gardens' entrance. The Carriage House Museum and gift shop are also worth some time. Guided tours include the house, carriage house, gardens, and greenhouse, and are offered from April through October Tues.–Sun. 10 A.M.–3:30 P.M. The fee is $4 adults, $3 seniors and youths, free for children under 12. In May Santa Rosa hosts its **Rose Festival** here. Come in December for the annual **Holiday Open House.**

Church of One Tree

Right across from the Burbank Gardens in Julliard Park is the Church of One Tree, an unusual Gothic church—70-foot spire and all—built entirely from 78,000 board feet of lumber

LUTHER BURBANK

An astoundingly successful, self-taught horticulturist, Luther Burbank (1849–1926) was also quite pragmatic. His primary aim in 50 years of work was producing improved varieties of cultivated plants. Joaquin Miller wrote that Burbank was "the man who helped God make the earth more beautiful." And he did, with the help of Santa Rosa Valley's rich soils and mild climate. More modest, Burbank himself said: "I firmly believe, from what I have seen, that this is the chosen place of the earth, as far as nature is concerned."

Have you ever admired a showy bank of Shasta daisies or giant calla lillies? Ever bitten into a Santa Rosa plum, tried plumcots, or been grateful for stoneless prunes? These are just a few of the 800 or so "new creations" spawned at the Burbank Experimental Gardens in Santa Rosa and in Se-bastopol, whose alumni also include the Burbank cherry, gold plums, Burbank potatoes, asparagus, edible and thornless cacti, paradox walnuts, and countless other fruits, nuts, vegetables, trees, flowers, and grasses.

A calm and colorful but controversial figure and a student of Charles Darwin, Burbank openly advocated eugenics and outraged the general population with his heterodox religious views. Luther Burbank's long work days were often interrupted by visitors: his good friend Jack London, William Jennings Bryan, Thomas Edison, Henry Ford, Helen Keller, John Muir, and King Albert and Queen Elizabeth of Belgium. Others (via some 10,000 personal visits per year plus 2,000 letters each week) sought his advice on everything from marigolds and mulch to mysticism.

contributed by a single coast redwood felled near Guerneville in 1875. Robert L. Ripley made the onetime First Baptist Church famous in his syndicated *Believe It or Not!* cartoon strip. Julliard Park also makes a nice place for a picnic.

Luther Burbank Center for the Arts

Santa Rosa boasts a striking temple to the arts. The huge, nonprofit Luther Burbank Center for the Arts, 50 Mark West Springs Rd. (at Hwy. 101), 707/527-7006 or 707/546-3600, www .lbc.net, is home to four theaters, seven performing companies—from the **Actor's Theatre** and **Santa Rosa Players** to the **Santa Rosa Symphony**—as well as the **Sonoma Museum of Visual Art,** 707/527-0297, where the exhibits change with the seasons (small fee). Main gallery exhibits of paintings, photographs, and other arts are open Wed.–Sat. 10 A.M.–4 P.M. and Sun. 1–4 P.M.; atrium and passageway galleries and outdoor exhibits are open daily 9 A.M.–9 P.M.

For more information about area arts, contact the **Cultural Arts Council of Sonoma County** downtown at 529 Fifth St., 707/579-2787, www.sonomaarts.org.

Museums

The building housing the **Sonoma County Mu-seum,** 425 Seventh St., 707/579-1500, www .sonomacountymuseum.com, was once Santa Rosa's post office. This 1,700-ton Renaissance revival building was moved to its present site, from deeper downtown, in 1979—a slow trip, just 25 feet per day on railroad ties and rollers. The museum features changing exhibits on local history, culture, and the arts, as well as a full calendar of literary and community events. Open limited hours, small fee. The **Jesse Peter Memorial Museum** at Santa Rosa Junior College, 1501 Mendocino Ave., 707/527-4479, features rotating exhibits of local interest, particularly Native American art and artifacts.

Spring Lake and Lake Ralphine Parks

Both Spring Lake and Howarth Parks adjoin Annadel State Park. Spring Lake is a 320-acre county park at 5585 Newanga Ave. just east of Santa Rosa proper, with picnic sites, a 75-acre swimming and sailing lagoon, fishing, walking trails, and bike paths. One of the best things about Spring Lake, though, is camping, practically right in town—31 campsites plus group camp, hot showers but no hookups. The camping season is daily May–Sept., weekends only otherwise. Campsites are $16 for the first vehicle (or for walk-ins), reservation fee $7; call 707/565- 2267,

YOU'RE A GOOD MAN, SPARKY SCHULZ

Charlie Brown, Snoopy, Woodstock, and all the rest of the *Peanuts* gang are darned happy to have a permanent new home at Santa Rosa's contemporary **Charles M. Schulz Museum,** which commemorates the life and work of cartoonist Charles Monroe "Sparky" Schulz, a longtime, low-key Santa Rosa resident until his death in 2000. Despite his comfortable, very local life, Schulz was internationally celebrated—more widely syndicated than any other cartoonist, and the only newspaper comic artist ever honored with a retrospective show at the Louvre in Paris.

Cartoonish ideas aside, this is no Disneyland. Designed by C. David Robinson Architects, the stunning 27,000-square-foot building features graceful, spacious galleries—the emphasis here is on the art—plus classroom space, a research center, and a 100-seat auditorium. Permanent exhibits include the 1951 **Charles M. Schulz Wall Mural,** including early versions of Snoopy and Charlie Brown, from the family's onetime residence in Colorado Springs; the astonishing **tile mural** by Japanese artist Yoshiteru Otani, composed of 3,588 comic strips; and Otani's massive wooden *Morphing Snoopy Sculpture,* which shows how Sparky's childhod pet Spike ultimately became Snoopy. And remember Christo's *Running Fence,* miles and miles of environmental art that brought fame to the Sonoma and Marin coastlines in the late 1970s? At the time Sparky Schulz celebrated the artist's feat in one of his comic strips, by artistically wrapping Snoopy's doghouse. In late 2003 Christo returned the honor by installing his permanent *Wrapped Snoopy House* in the museum's main gallery, which also displays many original *Peanuts* comic strips. Changing first-floor exhibits include the likes of *Cartoonists Who Influenced Charles Schulz, From Elzie Segar to Frank Wing—A Legacy Continued* and *Tom Everhart: Under the Influence.* Second-story exhibits are dedicated to Schulz's life, a re-creation of his cartoon studio among them. In front of the museum is the whimsical **Snoopy Labyrinth,** shaped like Snoopy's head and more than 50 feet square.

As you might imagine, the museum store here is a dandy, selling everything from plush Snoopys and Lucy and Charlie Brown baseball jersey–style T-shirts to the "Speak Softly and Carry a Beagle" T-shirt commemorating the current museum traveling exhibit. Not to mention the books—including *Snoopy's Guide to the Writing Life*—videos, posters, and stationery. While it's true that product sales from Schulz's creative empire have made him the second-richest deceased celebrity, behind only Elvis Presley at last report, *Peanuts* fans wouldn't have it any other way.

The museum is open most weekdays (closed Tues.) noon–5:30 P.M., and on weekends 10 A.M.–5:30 P.M. The museum is closed on major holidays—New Year's Day, Easter, July 4, Thanksgiving Day, and both December 24 and 25. Admission is $8 adult, $5 seniors and youths. For more information, contact the Charles M. Schulz Museum, 2301 Hardies Ln. (at W. Steele), 707/579-4452, www.schulzmuseum.org. Also see www.snoopy.com, www.snoopystore.com, and www.peanutscollectorclub.com.

There's more *Peanuts*-related amusement in the immediate neighborhood. If you're pretty slick on skates, take a few spins at the **Redwood Empire Ice Arena,** "Snoopy's Home Ice" at 1667 W. Steele Ln., 707/546-7147, www.snoopyshomeice.com, the impressive local ice palace and **Warm Puppy** coffee shop. In December, come for **Snoopy on Ice.** Adjacent to the ice arena is **Snoopy's Gallery and Gift Shop,** 707/546-3385 or 800/959-3385, www.snoopygift.com, open daily 10 A.M.–6 P.M.

Mon.–Fri. 10 A.M.–3 P.M. On Nov. 1, callers can reserve campsites for the following year. Seven-day summer limit. To get to the campsites from Santa Rosa, head east on Hwy. 12 to Hoen Ave., turn left on Summerfield Rd., then right onto Newanga. Abundant picnic areas. Park day use is $4 when the lagoon is open for swimming, otherwise $3. Spring Lake's hands-on **Environmental Discovery Center** on Violetti Road, open in summer Wed.–Fri. 10 A.M.–5 P.M. and noon–5 P.M., otherwise Wed.–Sun. noon–5 P.M., offers nature encounters of all stripes—from nature trails and the storytelling cavern to the "technology tent." There are six miles of paved walking trails as well as equestrian trails. From Spring Lake, you can hike into adjacent Annadel State Park via the Spring Creek Trail. For more park information, call 707/539-8092.

Lake Ralphine is a small sailing pond in **Howarth Park** just west of Spring Lake Park on Montgomery Drive, an area connected by bike path to adjacent Spring Lake. You can stop here for a picnic and swim, or go rowing on the lake in summer (no camping). Tennis courts, too. Diversions for the young and young-at-heart include a miniature steam train, pony rides, an animal farm, merry-go-round, roller coaster, and frontier village. Rent paddleboats, rowboats, and sailboats. For information, call 707/543-3282.

STAYING IN SANTA ROSA

Camp at **Spring Lake** or farther east at **Sugarloaf Ridge State Park** (see separate listings above). Quite reasonable among motels is the **Sandman Motel,** 3421 Cleveland Ave., 707/544-8570, which has a large heated pool, Jacuzzi, and amenities including inroom coffee, irons, ironing boards, and hair dryers. Rates are $50–100. Look for other relatively inexpensive motels downtown along Santa Rosa Avenue or north along Mendocino Avenue. (actually an extension of Santa Rosa Avenue, north of Sonoma Avenue).

The classic downtown stay is the 1907 cobblestone **Hotel La Rose** and associated carriage house, 308 Wilson St. (on Railroad Square), 707/579-3200 or 800/527-6738, www.hotel-larose.com, associated with Historic Hotels of America. With English country-house atmosphere and all the modern comforts—from two-line phones with dataports and voicemail and high-speed wireless Internet to marble and brass bathrooms—a stay here somewhere merges Old and New World sensibilities. Most rooms are $100–200, suites $150–250, but do ask about specials. While exploring the hotel—**Josef's** French restaurant is downstairs—note that the hotel staircase originated in San Francisco, at the Cable Car Barn.

New at Railroad Square is **Vineyard Creek Hotel, Spa & Conference Center,** 170 Railroad St., 707/636-7100 or 888/920-0008, www.vineyardcreek.com, sister hotel to The Heathman in Portland, Oregon. Rooms are contemporary and colorful, with in-room coffeemakers, refrigerators, and all the modern comforts for $150–250. The onsite country

TIPTOE THROUGH THE TIDY TIPS?

Near Cotati is the onetime Nature Conservancy **Fairfield Osborn Preserve,** now owned and protected by Sonoma State University. This isolated foothill area on volcanic Sonoma Mountain—the rocks 300 feet below the surface are still warm, they say—is a fascinating oak woodland ecological patchwork of vernal pools, ponds, streamside riparian habitat, mixed evergreens, chaparral, and freshwater marshes and seeps. The reserve boasts incredible spring wildflowers, and California fuchsias bloom here in autumn. Note that poison oak abounds and sudden oak death (SOD) has been discovered here, so when visiting *stay on the trail* and adopt appropriate preventive measures. The preserve is open to the public for docent-led hikes at 10 A.M. on Saturdays in spring and fall, at other times only by special arrangement. To get there, take E. Cotati Ave. to Petaluma Hill Rd. and turn right, then make a left at Roberts Road. From Roberts, Lichau Rd. leads to the preserve (narrow road, blind curves). Get more information and specific instructions when you call the Fairfield Osborn Preserve, 6543 Lichau Rd. in Penngrove, 707/795-5069, for permission to visit.

French **Seafood Brasserie** (707/636-7388) serves a seasonally changing menu comprised of local products and produce—all quite good, from the lemon poppy seed pancakes to the fish and chips and ribeye steak. Onsite spa and fitness facilities. Also worth some serious appreciation is the hotel's sculpture garden, a collection of works by Sonoma County artists.

Absolutely luxurious north of Santa Rosa proper is the **Vintners Inn,** 4350 Barnes Rd., 707/575-7350 or 800/421-2584, www.vintnersinn.com, an upscale place with modern amenities, Mediterranean atmosphere, trailing ivy, and tall trees planted amid 92 acres of the Ferrari-Carano Vineyards. All 44 spacious rooms and junior suites are furnished in a country-French style, and most have fireplaces. Expect all the comforts, from plush bathrobes, hair dryers, and irons, to in-room safe deposit box and refrigerator. Suites feature large bathrooms with Jacuzzi tub and separate shower, 32-inch TV with CD and VCR player, two-line phones with data ports. Rooms are $200–300, suites $300–400, full breakfast buffet included. Amenities include a spa, gorgeous grounds, and concierge service. Next door is John Ash & Co. restaurant, one of the county's finest, open for lunch, dinner, and Sunday brunch—and available to hotel guests for room service.

EATING IN SANTA ROSA

Farmers Markets

Best and cheapest is stocking up on the basics—bread and cheese from Sonoma, Santa Rosa Valley fruits and veggies, perhaps some bakery items from Sebastopol's Village Bakery—then just picnicking around. To find your own fresh local produce, pick up a current copy of the *Sonoma County Farm Trails* map and brochure at area visitor centers or see www.farmtrails.org. By happy coincidence, most Farm Trails stops are near Sebastopol and Forestville, west of Santa Rosa. Or do the region's farmers markets. Santa Rosa alone hosts four, three hosted year-round. The **Santa Rosa Original Saturday Certified Farmers Market** is held year-round at the Veterans Building parking lot, 1351 Maple just

north of Bennett Valley Rd./Hwy. 12 (near Brookwood), 8:30 A.M.–noon; the **Original Wednesday CFM** is held midweek at the same time and place. For information on both, call 707/522-8629. There's also the **Saturday Oakmont CFM** in the bank parking lot at White Oak and Oakmont (southwest of Hwy. 12) on Sat. 9 A.M.–noon (call 707/538-7023 for details) and the **Downtown CFM** held at Fourth and B downtown, May–Aug., on Wed. night 5–8:30 P.M. (707/524-2123).

Otherwise, food purists can stock up at **Organic Groceries and Community Market** on the way to Forestville at 2841 Guerneville Rd., 707/528-3663, one of the largest natural food stores in the northstate, offering organic *everything* in bulk, and **Pacific Market,** at the onetime Town & Country Market, 1465 Town & Country Dr. (north of Pacific Avenue and Bryden Lane), 707/546-3663.

Basics Downtown

A real treat for beer lovers is downtown's **Third Street Ale Works,** 610 Third St., 707/523-3060, an extremely well-designed brewpub that produces a fine repertoire of ales, happy "Hoppy Hour" dart and pool players (weekdays 4–6 P.M.), and a full calendar of special events, including benefits for the Surfrider Foundation. Do try award-winning "brewster" Denise Jones's **Blarney Sisters' Dry Irish Stout** and **Bodega Head IPA,** and the lower alcohol **"Drunken Weasel" Dunkelweizen.** Specialty brews include **Goat Rock Doppelbock** and **Winter Wassail.** Third Street offers a full menu of classy pub fare as well, from the southwestern-style Roadhouse Chili to the Sourdough Hippie and Cheesy Rider sandwiches. In pleasant weather, sit outside on the courtyard patio and people-watch. Open daily 11:30 A.M.–midnight.

The award-winning **Russian River Brewing Company,** 707/545-2337, www.russianriverbrewing.com, previously affiliated with Korbel, was set to open its new production facility and brewpub downtown by late 2003. So check it out. Who wouldn't love a brewpub that actually served a beer named after Pliny the Elder? Not to mention Damnation, Redemption, Salvation, and Temptation.

Kids wanna have fun, too, and a good place to take them to breakfast and lunch is the cozy brick **Omelette Express,** 112 Fourth St., 707/525-1690, where making omelettes has become an art. Choose from 30 or so fillings and either whole wheat or white sourdough bread or toast. Also sandwiches and salads. Another locally popular choice for sandwiches and such (including a nice selection of meatless options) and house-made soups, quiches, and more is cheerful, clean **Arrigoni's Deli & Café,** 701 Fourth St. (at D), 707/545-1297. Breakfast, served until 10:30 A.M., includes chicken apple sausage omelettes and buttermilk pancakes. Espresso bar, some 50 bottled beers, and wine. Open Mon.–Fri. 7 A.M.–4:30 P.M., Sat. 8 A.M.–3:30 P.M.

Upscale Food Downtown

Probably still talk of the town downtown is relative newcomer **Syrah,** 205 Fifth St. (at Davis), 707/568-4002, "brilliantly innovative" and serving California-style French—from chicken pot pie and delectable crab cakes to a garden veggie frittata and meatier entrées. Open Tues.–Sat. for lunch and dinner, reservations a must. Stock up on wine at **Petite Syrah,** the little wine shop next door.

One of Santa Rosa's best kept secrets, though, is very Sonoma County **Café Lolo,** 620 Fifth St. (between D St. and Mendocino Ave.), 707/576-7822, where the ever-changing menu of high-style comfort foods includes such things as Laura Chenel goat cheese and wild mushroom fritters; lobster, fennel, and applewood smoked bacon ragout with corn crepes and creme fraiche; and grilled beef tenderloin with roasted garlic mashed potatoes and crispy fried onions. Catering offered too.

For uptown Asian, from the house-made potstickers and walnut prawns to General Toa's chicken, everybody's favorite is **Gary Chu's,** across the street at 611 Fifth St., 707/526-5840. Executive lunch ($7–8) is offered 11:30 A.M.–3 P.M. daily and features more than a dozen choices, including pineapple sesame pork, snow pea beef, and "sautéed happy family" (meaning seafood family, we think).

A consistent local winner of the *Wine Spec-*

tator Award of Excellence yet kid-friendly too is **Mixx,** on Railroad Square at 135 Fourth St., 707/573-1344, which serves an inventive, Sonoma County-based "California" menu that mixes it all up—Mediterranean standards with Indian, Southwestern, and other influences. How 'bout basil fettuccine with smoked chicken, or grilled Cajun prawns? Good sandwiches, fresh seafood, pastas, and house-made desserts round out the menu. Saturday brunch includes such things as vegetarian eggs Benedict, brioche French toast, and a house-made Italian sausage omelette with peppers, mushrooms, and dry Jack cheese. Reservations advisable. Open Mon.–Fri. for lunch, Sat. for brunch (10 A.M.–2 P.M.), and Mon.–Sat. for dinner.

La Gare, in Railroad Square, 208 Wilson St., 707/528-4355, is also a legend in Santa Rosa—and beyond—recognized as one of the area's best restaurants, quite romantic. Known for its French-Swiss cuisine, decadent desserts, and charming white-linen atmosphere, La Gare fare includes fresh baked filet of salmon, New York steak with classic peppercorn and brandy cream

WINE COUNTRY

ANNADEL STATE PARK

A good cure for the Santa Rosa shopping mall syndrome is a day hike through Annadel State Park, 5,000 acres of small canyons, rolling foothills, woodlands, grassland meadows, and marshland (also poison oak) on the city's eastern edge. No camping, but good hiking; some trails also accommodate mountain bikers and equestrians. Most of the trail ascents here—except Steve's S Trail—are gradual. Bring drinking water. No dogs are allowed on the trails. To beat the heat, come in spring or fall. Small **Lake Il-sanjo,** less than a half mile from the parking lot, is popular with fisherpeople (black bass, bluegill). More than 130 bird species have been spotted, primarily near **Ledson Marsh** along Bennet Ridge. In spring, appreciate the wild-flowers: wild iris, lupine, shooting stars, poppies, buttercups, goldfields. *Don't* pick the delicate white fritillaria—it's endangered.

Annadel State Park is open daily from an hour before sunrise to an hour after sunset. To get to Annadel from Santa Rosa or from the Sonoma Valley area, head south on Los Alamos Rd., turn right on Melita Rd., then take a quick left onto Montgomery Dr. and left again on Channel Dr., which leads to the park office and the parking lot beyond. From Spring Lake, take Montgomery Dr. east. For more information, call 707/539-3911 or 707/938-1519. Trail map available at the park office, or online at www.parks.sonoma.net.

---

sauce, roasted chicken in light garlic herb sauce, and braised duck with orange sauce—everything quite reasonable.

Beyond Downtown

Wonderful on the way to Guerneville is the very reasonable, roadhouse-style **Zazu,** the reincarnation of the popular Willowside Café, at 3535 Guerneville Rd. (at Willowside), 707/523-4814, where the copper-topped tables all but overflow with well-prepared fare. The menu changes seasonally yet also daily, depending on what's freshest. In fall expect such things as beer battered popcorn shrimp with three deeping sauces, in winter spicy tomato soup with Bellwether Farm's grilled cheese sandwich, in spring Zazu-cured duck prosciutto with melon and basil, and in summer poppyseed crusted softshell crab with ruby grapefruit, avocado, and poppyseed dressing. Don't miss dessert, like the Zazu "nutter butters," peanut-shaped cookies you dip in chocolate fondue, and peach and almond crostata with buttermilk ice cream. Open Wed.–Sun. from 5:30 P.M. for dinner.

Relaxed **Willi's Wine Bar,** 4404 Old Redwood Hwy. (near River Rd.), 707/526-3096, is a stylish newcomer, serving dozens of different small plates at lunch and dinner—everything from lobster gnocci with white corn and smoked bacon to grilled Hog Island oysters with pancetta glaze. Open Wed.–Mon. from 11:30 A.M. (from 5 P.M. on Sun., for dinner only).

The acclaimed **John Ash & Company** sits amid the Ferrari-Carano Vineyards at the Vintners Inn, 4330 Barnes Rd., 707/527-7687. The romantic setting certainly stimulates the appetite, and the menu helps, too—featuring California's best, served with imaginative French flair. Delights include black mission fig pizza (with prosciutto, cambozola, and caramelized onions), curried sweet potato raviolis, duck spring rolls, and roasted pork chop with gingered applesauce. Reservations required.

In fall 2003 the acclaimed Lisa Hemenway's Bistro was sold to Kendall-Jackson executive chef Randy Lewis and partner James McDevitt and suddenly became Latin-flavored **Popina,** 714 Village Court, 707/526-5111. At first report Lewis and McDevitt planned to serve great food without the fuss and white tablecloths. Check it out. A bit more formal but every bit as worthy, the onetime Mistral is now the innovative New American **Sassafras Restaurant & Wine Bar,** named for the spicy American laurel and spicing up the Santa Rosa Business Park at 1229 N. Dutton Ave. (north of W. College), 707/578-7600. Small plates include thin-crusted pizza with shrimp and cilantro pesto and bay scallop and corn chowder, large plates, hickory-smoked Willie Bird turkey club sandwiches, olive oil poached halibut, barbecued quail with hominy cakes, and cowboy steak with onion rings. Kid's menu, too. Full bar. Open for lunch weekdays 11:30–5:50 P.M., for dinner nightly at 5:30 P.M.

INFORMATION

To find out what's going on while you're in town, check out the *Santa Rosa Press-Democrat,* www.pressdemocrat.com, the daily newspaper, or the *North Bay Bohemian,* www.bohemian.com, originally the *Sonoma County Independent.* For area information online, try www.sterba.com. Otherwise, the best place to start is the **Santa Rosa Convention & Visitors Bureau,** 9 Fourth St., 707/577-8674, www.visitsantarosa.com, which publishes its own visitor guide to Santa Rosa and Sonoma County.

Just south of Santa Rosa in Rohnert Park is the **Sonoma County Wineries Association visitor center,** 5000 Roberts Lake Rd., 707/586-3795, www.sonomawine.com. To get there, take the Country Club Dr. exit from Hwy. 101. In addition to detailed Sonoma County winery information and tastings (offered 11 A.M.–4 P.M.), the visitor center, open 9 A.M.–5 P.M. daily (except major holidays), offers other area visitor information. Also here: a demonstration winery and educational exhibits. The website includes a complete roster of member wineries—some have their own websites—and a comprehensive calendar of upcoming events. Sharing space with the wine association is the **Rohnert Park Chamber of Commerce,** 707/584-1415, www.rpchamber.org. For other area information stop by the **Cotati Chamber of Commerce,** next to city hall at 216 E. School St., 707/795-5508, www.cotati.org.

To receive a complimentary preplanning guide to Sonoma County, contact the **Sonoma County Tourism Program,** www.sonomacounty.com, a fairly comprehensive online guide; you can also requests a printed guide.

GETTING AROUND

Sonoma County Transit, 355 W. Robles Ave., 707/576-7433 or 800/345-7433 (in Sonoma County), www.sctransit.com, goes just about everywhere—to Sebastopol, Guerneville, and the lower Russian River, even Jenner and Gualala—except on major holidays. Base fare is $1 adult, $.80 students, and $.50 seniors, ranging to $2.60. Best for getting around this spread-out town, though, is **Santa Rosa Transit,** 707/534-3925, www.511.org.

Conveniently straddling Hwy. 101, Santa Rosa is well served by buses. From the **Greyhound** depot at 435 Santa Rosa Ave., 707/545-6495, www.greyhound.com, daily buses run north and south to major urban destinations and also connect to Calistoga, Sonoma, and Sebastopol. Also call **Golden Gate Transit,** 707/541-2000, www.511.org, for a current schedule and stops. This bus line runs to Sebastopol and also to Rohnert Park/Cotati, but its mainline local links are to and from Petaluma, to and from the Bay Area's Transbay Terminal, and a one-way connection to San Francisco.

Seven miles north of town, the **Charles M. Schulz Sonoma County Airport,** 2200 Airport Blvd., 707/524-7240, www.sonomacountyairport.com, with limited runways, is used primarily by private pilots, though in late 2003 the Board of Supervisors was negotiating with a small airline. The **Sonoma County Airport Express,** 707/837-8700 or 800/327-2024, www.airportexpressinc.com, provides shuttle services to and from various local pickup points and both SFO and Oakland Airports, $24 one-way.

In January 2003 a new regional transit district, **Sonoma Marin Area Rail Transit,** www.sonomamarintrain.org, was established to one day provide public train transit between the Marin County ferry station and Cloverdale in northern Sonoma County and the San Francisco Bay Area. Check the website for project progress.

Sebastopol and Vicinity

Perched on Sonoma County's "Gold Ridge" and famous for its early-ripening, reddish-yellow Gravensteins, Sebastopol was once part of the original Analy Township. An early Irish settler, inspired by the British and French siege of the Russian seaport of Sebastopol, named the California town when one of two feuding local residents barricaded himself inside a store. Remnants of **Gold Ridge Farm,** Luther Burbank's 1885 experimental farm at 7781 Bodega Ave., include the Burbank cottage now listed on the National Register of Historic Places and a reconstructed barn with attached greenhouse. Take a self-guided tour year-round. The **Western Sonoma County Historical Society,** 707/829-6711,www.wschs-grf.pon.net, offers docent-guided tours April through October (by appointment) and also propagates various Burbank plant varieties (visit the Shasta Daisy Garden) to sell, spring through fall, Wednesday 9 A.M.–noon. The annual open house is held in April, during the town's Apple Blossom Festival. For more area history, stop by the society's **West County Museum,** inside the restored 1917 Petaluma and Santa Rosa Electric Railway Depot at 261 S. Main St., open Thurs.–Sun. 1–4 P.M.

Ives Memorial Park (duck pond, playground, picnic areas, public swimming pool nearby) next to the Veterans' Memorial Building on High Street is at the center of Sebastopol's April **Apple Blossom Festival,** which includes the crowning of the Apple Blossom Queen, an Apple Juice Run, parade, apple pie-baking contests, good homemade foods, country music, and arts and crafts. To the west **Ragle Ranch Park** is where the Sonoma County Farm Trails' **Gravenstein Apple Fair** is held every August at the beginning of harvest season. Just south of town at 1200 Hwy. 116 is the **Enmanji Buddhist Temple,** 707/823-2252, which was originally brought over from Japan for the Chicago World's Fair in 1933. Show up in July for the **Teriyaki Chicken Barbecue** and **Japanese Bon Dancing Festival.** The **Sebastopol Center for the Arts,** 6821 Laguna Park Way, 707/829-4797, offers visual arts exhibits as well as literary and performance arts. Come on the first Thursday of every month for the local gallery **ArtWalk** downtown and related events.

Increasingly sophisticated Sebastopol—this is a "nuclear free zone"—offers shops galore downtown, selling New Age edginess as well as wine country chic. Gravenstein Hwy. S from Bodega Hwy. to Hwy. 101 is an eight-mile antique row. If you have time for only one stop, try the **Antique Society,** offering more than 125 dealers in a 20,000-square-foot facility at 2661 Gravenstein Hwy. S, 707/829-1733, www.antiquesociety.com, open daily 10 A.M.–5 P.M.

Traffic congestion is a growing problem for fast-growing Sebastopol. Highway 116 heads northwest from here through Forestville and Guerneville—a scenic drive—and also southeast to Cotati, a good route for avoiding Santa Rosa's own traffic problems. The Luther Burbank Memorial Hwy. (Hwy. 12) connects Sebastopol to Santa Rosa but becomes the Bodega Hwy. as you head west to Freestone, Bodega, and Bodega Bay—more traffic trouble in both directions.

For more information about the area and its attractions and events, contact the **Sebastopol Chamber of Commerce,** 265 S. Main, 707/823-3032 or 877/828-4748, www.sebastopol.org. The office is open weekdays during business hours, and also on Saturday in summer.

APPLE FARMS

A rare treat is a trip to Sebastopol during apple harvest in early August. Gravensteins, the best all-purpose apples anywhere, ripen from late July into September and just don't keep—which explains all the apple-processing plants in the area. (In the U.S., you can't get these red or green beauties beyond the Bay Area.) **Twin Hill Ranch,** 1689 Pleasant Hill Rd., 707/823-2815, www.twinhillranch.com, has a playground and some tolerant animals to amuse the children while adults load up on fresh apples (40 varieties are grown here, but the Gravensteins ripen first) and apple cider, apple pie, homemade apple bread, and apple oatmeal cookies. The fruit stand at **Walker Apple Ranch,** 10955 Upp Rd. (at the end of a half-mile dirt road), 707/823-4310, offered 27 apple varieties at last count. Open daily 10 A.M.–5 P.M. Aug–mid-Nov. If the sight of all those apples makes you think of Mom and apple pie, stop in at **Mom's Apple Pie,** 4550 Gravenstein Hwy. N. (toward Forestville), 707/823-8330. Mom bakes apple and other assorted pies fresh daily and sells them—by the pie or by the slice.

Kozlowski Farms, 5566 Gravenstein Hwy. (Hwy. 116) in nearby Forestville, 707/887-1587 or 800/473-2767, www.kozlowskifarms.com, is the place to load up on jams and jellies, dessert sauces (like red raspberry fudge), vinegars, and more. At the end of your apple adventures, consider tossing back some hard (fermented) cider. Yes, that's the kind that gives you a buzz. The place to give it a try is **Ace in the Hole Pub and Cidery** back toward Sebastopol at 3100 Gravenstein Hwy. N. (at Graton Road), 707/829-1101, www.acecider.com, where apple-pear, apple-berry, and apple-honey ciders are also available. For a complete listing and map of the area's fruit, nut, and vegetable (even fresh goat cheese) vendors, pick up the current *Sonoma County Farm Trails* brochure at the chamber office or see www.farmtrails.org.

GARDENS AND NURSERIES

Luther Burbank would be pleased that a deep appreciation of horticulture still abides in the area. **Vintage Gardens,** 2833 Gravenstein Hwy. S., 707/829-2035, www.vintagegardens.com, open Thurs.–Mon. 9 A.M.–5 P.M., offers antique and rare roses—more than 3,000 varieties—and an impressive collection of hydrangeas. At the same address is **Apple Art Espalier,** www.appleart.com, which also artfully espaliers fig, pear, pomegranate, persimmon, and ornamental trees, as well as **California Carnivores,** "the strange and beautiful world of carnivorous plants," 707/824-0433, www.californiacarnivores.com, offering the most extensive collection in the U.S. Open Thurs.–Mon. 10 A.M.–4 P.M.

Wayward Gardens, 1296 Tilton Rd., 707/829-8225, www.waywardgardens.com, is "your source of flora for fauna," which means the emphasis

here is on creating "habitat gardens" and otherwise making the garden more hospitable for butterflies, birds, and other creatures. Open weekends only, 10 A.M.–5 P.M., and weekdays by appointment. For azaleas and rhododendrons, the place is **Sonoma Horticultural Nursery,** 3970 Azalea Ave., 707/823-6832, open Thurs.–Mon. 9 A.M.–5 P.M. most of the year but daily during the Mar.–May bloom season. **Pic-a-Lily Gardens,** 2401 Schaeffer Rd., 707/823-3799, www.picalily.com, offers specialty daylilies. For organic gardening "putting by" supplies, the place is **Harmony Farm Supply and Nursery,** 3244 Hwy. 116 N, 707/823-9125, www.harmonyfarm.com.

Open to visitors only by appointment, **Bamboo Sourcery,** 666 Wagnon Rd., 707/823-5866, www.bamboosourcery.com, is a demonstration garden boasting hundreds of bamboo varieties. Also open only by appointment is **Japanese Maples by Momiji Nursery,** 2765 Stony Point Rd., 707/528-2917, www.momijinursery.com, which propagates its own trees from some 200 cultivars (and counting).

Worth the slightly longer drive is the **Occidental Arts & Ecology Center,** 15290 Coleman Valley Rd., 707/874-1557, www.oaec.org, a nonprofit, biointensive organic farm and orchards. The Mother Garden here, an open-pollinated, heirloom, and rare plant and seed collection, offers three open-house plant sales (two in spring, one in fall) every year, everything California Certified Organic. Note: When the sales are on, traffic backs up forever. The mythic **Western Hills Rare Plants Nursery** and display garden nearby, 16250 Coleman Valley Rd., 707/8744-3731, is open on weekends 10 A.M.–4 P.M. or by appointment. Closed December and January. The **Wishing Well Nursery,** 306 Bohemian Hwy. in Freestone, 707/823-3710, offers an endless selection of fuchsias. And dig those eight-foot Bernard Maybeck goddesses.

WEST OF SEBASTOPOL

Heading out toward the coast and Bodega Bay on Hwy. 12, first there's **Freestone,** a peach of a place. Unusual here is a Japanese-style spa called **Osmosis,** 209 Bohemian Hwy., 707/823-8231, where you can relax in an enzyme bath. Don't miss local **Wild Flour Bread,** 140 Bohemian Hwy., 707/874-2938, which bakes a variety of hearty breads and other goodies in a wood-fired brick oven (no electric utensils allowed) on the premises. The luscious loaves are expensive, but worth every penny. Open Fri.–Mon. from 8:30 A.M. until the bread runs out.

Continuing north on the Bohemian Highway from Freestone, you'll soon come to **Occidental,** a bigger burg than Freestone and home of the **Union Hotel,** 3703 Main St., 707/874-3555, where locals go to linger over a bowl of minestrone and a glass of red wine. Intriguing local shops include the **Leapin' Lizards Fun Store,** for kids of all ages. The place to stay is the striking **Inn at Occidental** (see below). Note: There's no gas in town, so fill up before you come out here.

Continuing west from Freestone leads to **Bodega.** Not to be confused with much-larger Bodega Bay, Bodega isn't quite on the coast. Though Alfred Hitchcock did film some scenes from *The Birds* here, Bodega is a peaceful little spot with few distractions.

STAYING IN SEBASTOPOL

A good choice is the comfortable motel-style **Sebastopol Inn,** 6751 Sebastopol Ave. 707/829-2500 or 888/544-9400, www.sebastopolinn.com, conveniently located directly behind the historic Gravenstein Railroad Station thereby incorporating it. Most rooms are $100–150, balcony rooms and suites $150–200. Inside the train barn and refurbished railcars are the Sebastopol Inn Day Spa, hip Victorian-style Coffee Catz coffeehouse and live music venue, very cool Appellations Wine Bar, and other local attractions. The location is unbeatable, within walking distance of downtown and the jogging/bike path that parallels Hwy. 12 toward Santa Rosa.

Farther away from the action are area bed-and-breakfasts. The lovingly restored 1897 **Vine Hill Inn** farmhouse, 3949 Vine Hill Rd., 707/823-8832, www.vine-hill-inn.com, features four uniquely decorated second-floor guest rooms, each with private bath, some with Jacuzzi tubs, others with private decks. Ask at the chamber for a more complete local B&B list. West of Sebastopol in Occidental is the eclectic yet upmarket **Inn at Occidental,** 3657 Church St., 707/874-1047 or 800/522-6324, www.innatoccidental.com, every room an adventure in folk-art style. Wonderful breakfasts. Room rates start at $195; the Sonoma Cottage guesthouse is $560–600.

EATING IN SEBASTOPOL

Show up Apr.–Dec. for the **Sebastopol Certified Farmers Market,** 707/522-9305, held on Sunday, 10 A.M.–1:30 P.M., at the New Town Plaza (at Petaluma and McKinley). For bread and other fine baked goods—cakes, cookies, and more—stop by the acclaimed **Village Bakery,** 7225 Healdsburg Ave., 707/829-8101, with its organic extra-sour sourdough, seeded sourdough, and potato and onion ciabatta. For natural foods and other quality groceries, try **Fiesta Market & Deli,** 550 Gravenstein Hwy. N, 707/823-9735, www.fiestamkt.com.

Coffee Catz, 6761 Sebastopol Ave. (Hwy. 12, two blocks east of downtown in the Gravenstein Station building), 707/829-6600, is a hangout for artists, writers, and other creative types—so enjoy the poetry readings, live entertainment, and original art along with your java. Light meals served, too. A big hit with the natural foods crowd is the vegetarian **East West Bakery Cafe,** 128 N. Main St., 707/829-2822, which serves good pancakes at breakfast, fresh salads and sandwiches, and well-prepared dinners for under $10. **Lucy's Café,** 110 N. Main, 707/829-9713, is another healthy choice.

One of Sonoma County's best restaurants these days and everybody's favorite for French is the very reasonable **K&L Bistro,** 119 S. Main, 707/823-6614. Even the mac and cheese will make you weep. The bistro has branched out a bit, too, with its **Appellations Wine Bar,** in Gravenstein Station at 6761 Sebastopol Ave., 707/829-7791, where many wines are $3 per glass, pizza for two is $7. Excellent **Stella's Café,** at the onetime home of Mom's Apple Pie, 4550 Gravenstein Hwy. N. (Mom's moved next door), 707/823-6637, is upscale yet homey and rustic, still a hot local dinner ticket; the changing menu accents what's local, seasonal, and best. For dessert, head for **Screaming Mimi's,** 6902 Sebastopol Ave., 707/823-5902, for handmade ice cream.

The two-block spot in the road outside Sebastopol now gussied-up as old-timey Graton features two notable restaurants. The **Willow Wood Market,** 9020 Graton Rd., 707/823-0233, feels like an old country store, and does offer some eclectic shopping. But Willow Wood is actually a restaurant and relaxed locals' hangout, boasting art on the walls and poetry readings during slower months. On weekends and in the summer foodies from the city tend to crowd the place, beloved for its breakfasts, hearty sand-

wiches liked Black Forest ham with brie, and some of the world's best polenta dishes. Come any other time to get a real feel for the place. Open Mon.–Thurs. 8 A.M.–9.P.M., weekends until 9:30 P.M. No reservations taken. Brought to you by the same folks in December 2002 and right across the street is the **Underwood Bar & Bistro,** 9113 Graton Rd. (at Edison), 707/823-7023, considerably more "San Francisco," with a tapas and small-plates menu (great oysters) and entrées ranging from grilled burgers and fish stew to roasted duck breast. Excellent warm chocolate torte. Open Tues.–Thurs. 4 P.M.–midnight, Friday and Saturday 4 P.M.–2 A.M.

Russian River

When the area was more renowned for apples than wines and wineries, most people thought of the Russian River as that cluster of rustic redwood-cloistered resort villages stretching from Guerneville west along Hwy. 116 to Jenner-by-the-Sea, about an hour-and-a-half drive north from San Francisco. Once a popular resort area for well-to-do City folk, the Russian River's recreational appeal dried up as faster transportation and better roads took people elsewhere. Lured by low rents and the area's spiritual aura, back-to-the-landers started arriving in the late 1960s. Some long-time locals still sniff at the hippies. The newest waves of Russian River immigrants are the relatively affluent, urban refugees bringing more urbane ways and much-needed money to renovate and revitalize the area.

Today's colorful cultural mix, including venture capitalists, loggers, gays, sheep ranchers, farmers, hippies, and retirees, is surprisingly simpatico despite occasional outbreaks of intolerance. For all their apparent differences, people who manage to survive here share some common traits: they're good-humored, self-sufficient, and stubborn. After the devastating winter floods that regularly inundate the area, for example, locals accept the raging river's most recent rampage and set out, as a community, to make things right.

These days it's clearly a mistake to view the Russian River as strictly a Guerneville-to-Jenner

phenomenon. The river's headwaters are far to the north, just southeast of Willits, though the Russian is not much of a river until it reaches Cloverdale. Roughly paralleling Hwy. 101 inland, this slow, sidewinding waterway—called Shabaikai or Misallaako ("Long Snake") by Native Americans, and Slavianka ("Charming One") by early Russian fur traders—slithered into San Francisco Bay long before there were people around to notice. The river changed to its modern course over the eons and now flows west to Jenner. The Russian uncoils slowly through Sonoma County's northern wine country, and multiple small wineries cluster like grapes along its northern stretch. To find them, explore the Alexander Valley, Dry Creek Valley, Russian River Valley, Chalk Hill, and Green Hill appellations. For details see Healdsburg and Vicinity below.

GUERNEVILLE TO JENNER

Strictly as a matter of survival—this *is* a resort area—people here generally tolerate tourists and tourist-related traffic tedium, but don't push your luck with gratuitous rubbernecking. To get off the road for a while, take a fun spring or fall canoe trip down the river with **Burke's Canoe Trips,** 8600 River Rd. (at Mirabel Rd.) in Forestville, 707/887-1222, www.burkescanoetrips.com, advance reservations advised. The best months are

April and September. One-day self-directed canoe trips (no guide), including courtesy shuttle service back to Burke's from their private beach in Guerneville, cost $45 per canoe. Longer trips (up to five days) are also offered. Burke's also offers camping, picnicking, bath facilities, and fishing.

But the Pacific Ocean is so close—and the rolling coastal hills both north and south of Jenner so wide open and wonderful—that once here, in summer, it's hard to resist heading west for a negative ion recharge. In winter, Guerneville and other lower river towns are often shrouded in ghostly white and bone-chilling fog for days, sometimes weeks at a time, and a special quiet—one transcending the mere absence of tourists—descends.

For more information about the area, contact the **Russian River Chamber of Commerce,** 16209 First St. in Guerneville, 707/869-9000 or 800/823-8800, www.russianriver.com, for a fairly complete listing of river-area lodgings, restaurants, and upcoming events. The chamber has a complete business directory of gay-oriented establishments, available for reference.

Guerneville

Don't say "Gurneyville." The name's GURNville—and any other pronunciation will peg you straight away as a tourist. George Guerne (*his* name's pronounced "gurney," so of course you're confused) founded the town after building the first sawmill here in 1865. This is the big city in these parts, home to most of the area's resorts, restaurants, and bars. It becomes recreation central in summer for swimming, tubing, canoeing, and river rafting. It's easy to walk the entire town. The area's main **post office** is in downtown Guerneville at 14060 Mill St., 707/869-2167. Stop off at **King's Fishing & Kayak,** 16258 Main St. in downtown Guerneville, 707/869-2156, for current fishing information and other sporting supplies. The chamber can suggest other kayak and outdoor adventure companies. But don't miss the **Pee Wee Golf Course** in Guerneville, something you won't find everywhere.

The **Russian River Rodeo** is held here in June, as is the big **Russian River Blues Festival** at Johnson's Beach. The biggest deal of all, though, is the **Russian River Jazz Festival** in September—quite the event, featuring big-name talent from everywhere. For current information and advance tickets, contact the local chamber office. **Halloween** is big, too, at least a weeklong celebration.

Armstrong Redwoods State Reserve

A small, 805-acre redwood reserve with first- and second-growth *Sequoia sempervirens,* Armstrong Redwoods State Reserve is a study of nature's moods in various shades of green, peaceful for picnics and hikes right outside Guerneville. (Day-use is free for those who walk or bike in, otherwise $4 per car.) The reserve itself includes a self-guided nature trail and the 2,000-seat outdoor Redwood Forest Theatre, a grand place to contemplate the fact that all the world's a stage.

Beyond Armstrong to the north, reaching up into the surrounding mountains, is the adjacent **Austin Creek State Recreation Area,** 5,683 backwoods acres of steep trails shinnying up from Armstrong Redwoods to sunny ridgetops of chaparral and oak woodlands, past small streams and freshwater springs. Getting to Austin Creek's sky-high **Redwood Lake Campground** (primitive tent camping, fishing in the artificial lake, hiking) is itself an adventure. The climb is a hair-raising 2.5-mile turn of the corkscrew up a steep, twisting, threadlike road (RVs strongly discouraged). Notice the huge madrones. Austin Creek also has an equestrian camping area plus—a rarity outside the Sierra Nevada and Northern Mountains—a pack station. **Armstrong Woods Pack Station,** 707/887-2939, www.redwoodhorses.com, is as noted for its camp cuisine as for its well-trained horses. It offers half-day, full-day, and overnight to three-day rides for experienced riders.

For information about both the reserve and the recreation area, contact: Armstrong Redwoods State Reserve, 17000 Armstrong Woods Rd. in Guerneville, 707/869-2015 or 707/865-2391 (district office). First-come, first-served campsites at Austin Creek cost $12; walk-in and hike-in sites cost $7 and require a special permit.

Monte Rio

Monte Rio is a gracefully sagging old resort town, with a big faded Vacation Wonderland sign stretching across the highway near **Fern's**

THE BOHEMIAN GROVE

Monte Rio's real claim to fame is the infamous Bohemian Grove on the south side of the river, the all-male elite enclave where the rich and powerful come to play. These 2,700 acres of virgin redwoods—the largest remaining stand in the Russian River region—are enjoyed exclusively by members and guests of San Francisco's Bohemian Club, founded (an irony only in retrospect) by anarchist-socialist journalist types like Ambrose Bierce and Jack London.

Once each year, during their two-week Annual Summer Encampment, 1,500 or so Bohemians and guests get together in this luxurious grown-up summer camp "to celebrate the spirit of Bohemia." According to local lore, what that amounts to is getting drunk, urinating on trees, and staging silly skits and plays. The traditional summer encampment—which President Herbert Hoover once called the "the greatest men's party on earth"—was held for the first time in 1869. Bohemian Grove guests include U.S. presidents and cabinet members, members of Congress, captains of industry and finance, plus diplomats and foreign dignitaries. Past encampment guests have reportedly included former President George H. W. Bush, President George W. Bush, former House Speaker Newt Gingrich, Secretary of State Colin Powell, and Dow Chemical chairman Frank Popoff.

According to encampment rules, Bohemian Club members and guests *never* discuss business or politics, and *never* make deals. (Each summer's Lakeside Talks, however, sometimes come awfully close to being "private" public policy talks.) It's difficult to verify these official facts, however. Double chain-link fences, guardposts, and highly sensitive security systems provide ample protection from riffraff. Unless invited, no one—and never a woman—gets inside the

Grocery, almost the last stop for bait, booze, gas, and groceries before reaching the Pacific Ocean. Beach access is good near the bridge, with plenty of parking. On the July 4th weekend, Monte Rio has its traditional **Water Carnival Parade, Annual Fireman's Barbecue,** and the **Big Rocky Games** down at the beach. From Monte Rio, take the Bohemian Hwy. to Camp Meeker and vicinity, or take the back way (via Moscow Road) to Duncans Mills a few miles farther west. For more area information, contact the **Monte Rio Chamber of Commerce,** 707/865-1533, www.monterio.org.

Cazadero

Because of its geography, Cazadero is wetter (with an average of 80–100 inches of rain per year) and greener than anywhere else in the county. Banana slugs grow well here, too. The main road to Cazadero is excellent, and locals drive these eight miles up from Hwy. 116 along Austin Creek *fast.* The town itself has a general store, sometimes a café, even a post office. But the real fun starts outside town. Beyond Cazadero, the road becomes a twisting one-lane

backcountry route (via Fort Ross Road) to historic Fort Ross farther north along the Sonoma County coast. Even more challenging is the backdoor trip from here through Kruse Rhododendron State Reserve. To get there, take King Ridge Road, then the even more obscure (dirt, still unmarked at last report) Hauser Bridge Road, then turn right at Seaview. Talk to locals about road conditions before setting out, and gas up before going.

Duncans Mills

Most of the redwood used to build San Francisco was shipped south from Duncans Mills and Duncan Landing. A lumber-loading depot during the region's redwood-harvesting heyday—the original mills were constructed in 1860—Duncans Mills is now a newly built old-looking collection of buildings and businesses: crafts and gift shops, galleries, two very good restaurants (Blue Heron and Cape Fear), a coffee house-cum-kayak-rental shop, candy store, barber shop, and Wine & Cheese Tasting of Sonoma County (just what it sounds like). The barn-red **Duncans Mills General Store** has been in business

compound. But judging from the very visible, very professional imported prostitutes doing a brief, brisk local business during the week, each year at least some from inside manage to "jump the river" and get out.

At the right time in July, during the Bohemian Grove encampment, it's an astoundingly absurd sight: caravans of Rolls-Royces and black stretch limos jockeying for highway position among the ranks of one-eyed VWs and battered Ramblers. Most Bohos (a favorite local epithet) step down from their private Lear jets at the airport in Santa Rosa, then travel to the Grove under the cover of darkness, to avoid unnecessary visibility. The real bigwigs usually arrive by helicopter.

Among Russian River residents, there's at least begrudging acceptance of these ruling-class Bohemians, since locals do work at the Grove as waiters, carpenters, and repairmen. But there is also resentment, if rarely expressed openly. On the Russian River, for example, there are no hospitals or emergency health-care facilities, but the Bohemian Grove has a fully staffed emergency hospital and cardiac care unit—open year-round yet rarely used—completely off-limits to the community. In the event of a heart attack or drowning accident, for residents it's a half-hour ambulance ride to Santa Rosa.

In the recent past, outside-the-gates "people's encampments" like the Bohemian Grove Action Network kept 24-hour vigils when the Bohos came to town, with banners ("See You in Hell!"), placards, and arrests for civil disobedience in protest of the incestuous relationship of business and government. But some years, all's quiet on the Bohemian front. Except for the limos and prostitutes, it's hard to know when the party's going on.

---

forever and is one of this spot-in-the-road's only original buildings, though no longer the quirky *real* general store it was. There's a small railroad museum at the reconstructed **Depot** south of the highway (open daily).

This stretch of the Russian River is good for steelhead in winter. The bridge on Moscow Rd. marks the inland limits of tidewater flow. The been-there-forever **Casini Ranch Family Campground** is nearby at 22855 Moscow Rd., 707/865-2255 or 800/451-8400. For more information on Duncans Mills, call the **Christopher Queen Gallery** at 707/865-1318, which also offers stunning representational art of early and contemporary California, much of it regional. Come to Duncans Mills in June for the annual weekend-long **Festival of Art & Wine** (formerly held in nearby Jenner), a full day of arts, crafts, ethnic food, and great music—everything from jazz to bebop and blues—to benefit the **Stewards of Slavianka,** the docent group that protects the seals at the river's mouth (see the Sonoma Coast chapter) and otherwise serves state parks in both Sonmna and Mendocino Counties.

STAYING ALONG THE RUSSIAN RIVER

Camping

For public camping, climb up to **Austin Creek State Recreation Area** near Armstrong Redwoods, a few miles outside Guerneville ($7–12 per night), 707/869-2015, or try either Bodega Dunes or Wrights Beach Campgrounds, south from Jenner among the Sonoma Coast State Beaches (for both, reservations are suggested year-round; call ReserveAmerica at 800/444-7275 or see www.reserveamerica.com. Safest for coastal swimming is the **Doran County Beach Campground** in Bodega Bay. Good choices north along the coast include Fort Ross and Salt Point State Parks. (For more information on nearby coastal camping, see The Sonoma Coast in the North Coast chapter.) The private **Faerie Ring Campgrounds,** 16747 Armstrong Woods Rd. in Guerneville, 707/869-2746, is right outside Armstrong Redwoods and open year-round for both tents (mostly) and RVs. Faerie Ring features coin-op showers, a family area, and an adults-only area ($20–25 for two people, $5 each additional person, $3 kid, $2 dog). Also private, 210-acre **Schoolhouse Canyon Campground** ($23–25 for two) is four miles east of Guerneville at 12600 River Rd., 707/869-2311, and offers a mile of river access. Or camp downriver at **Casini Ranch,** $20–27 (see Duncans Mills above).

Inns and Bed-and-Breakfasts

Rustic resorts have long been a local mainstay. **Fern Grove Cottages** in Guerneville, 16650 Hwy. 116, 707/869-8105, www.ferngrove.com, is a local classic, with attractive, comfy cabins (studios as well as one- or two-bedroom units) with private baths and a deck or patio. Some have kitchens, two person spa tubs, wood-burning stoves. There's a pool, too, and generous continental breakfast. Pets allowed by prior arrangement. Studios start at $79; one-bedroom cabins, $109; and two-bedroom cabins, $159. The local chamber can suggest other options.

The **Village Inn** overlooking the river in Monte Rio, 20822 River Blvd., 707/865-2304 or 800/303-2303, www.villageinn-ca.com, is where some of the scenes in Bing Crosby's *Holiday Inn* were filmed, according to local lore, though that won't be immediately obvious today. What is clear is that the once funky-and-hip old hotel rooms have been jazzed-up considerably—and they're all still pretty cool. Four rooms are in the main hotel building, seven in the associated lodge. All have private baths and abundant amenities, including cable TV and VCR (free videos), mini refrigerator, microwave, hair dryer, and an iron and ironing board. Many have a river view, too, the "deluxe" rooms offering the most deluxe view. Most rates are $100–200, lower in winter. Ask about specials, too. Another reason to stay here is the good onsite restaurant (outdoor dining, weather permitting).

The Russian River showplace is the **Applewood Inn** bed-and-breakfast, 13555 Hwy. 116 in Guerneville, 707/869-9093 or 800/555-8509, www.applewoodinn.com. Three Mediterranean-style villas surround a garden courtyard and offer a total of 19 rooms. All are quite comfortable and elegant, and feature private baths, fine Italian linens, down comforters and pillows, thick terrycloth robes, hair dryer, cable TV, phones, and radio/CD player. Some feature a private patio or deck, wood-burning fireplace, and Jacuzzi. Rates start at around $200. Heated pool, afternoon wine, concierge service. Full gourmet breakfast—and you can wander through the inn's bountiful gardens to see where many of the fruits, vegetables, and herbs come from. Applewood also features the Applewood Restaurant and affiliated La Buona Forchetta cooking school.

The showplace down the road in Forestville is the farmhouse-style **Farmhouse Inn,** 7871 River Rd., 707/887-3300 or 800/464-6642, www.farmhouseinn.com, with eight sophisticated yet welcoming cabins and all the comforts—from "rain" showerheads, double-jetted tubs, and VCR/CD players to personal saunas, fireplaces, and refrigerators. Onsite spa services, too. The acclaimed restaurant (see below) is reason enough for a special occasion stay. High-season weekend rates start at $200, lower on weekdays and in winter.

Gay-Friendly Resorts

Catering to gays and lesbians but "straight-friendly," the 1920s-vintage, adults-only **Highlands Resort,** 14000 Woodland Dr. in Guerneville, 707/869-0333, www.highlandsresort.com, offers cabins, rooms, and amenities including a swimsuits-optional pool and hot tub. Tent camping (with shower facilities) also offered. Rates are $50–150. Cabins with private bathrooms start at $70; two-room cabins with kitchenettes are $100–150. A room in a small cabin with shared bathroom is $45. Winter rates are still lower, most cabins $50–100 (no winter camping). Short walk to town. **Fife's Guest Ranch,** 16467 River Rd. (also close to town, just west of Safeway), 707/869-0656, www.fifes.com, is another large gay-oriented resort, 15 acres featuring cabins (circa 1905) and tent camping along the river. Onsite Roadhouse Restaurant and Bunkhouse Dance Club. High-season cabin rates start at around $100, $85 (or less) in winter. Ask at the chamber office for other possibilities.

EATING ALONG THE RUSSIAN RIVER

The simple **River Inn** on Main Street as you roll into town (next to the theater in downtown

Guerneville), 707/869-0481, is a lively, homey-looking café with cheery yellow Formica tables, well-stuffed Naugahyde booths, and a café counter with spin-around stools. The café serves surprisingly good basic American food and offers an incredible number of choices on the menu.

West of town in Monte Rio is the very popular 1906-vintage **Village Inn** hotel restaurant, on the river at 20822 River Blvd., 707/865-2304, *the* breakfast spot. At lunch and dinner, expect pastas, steaks, chicken, and fish. Patio dining overlooking the river, weather permitting. The relaxed yet sophisticated **Blue Heron Inn,** 25300 Steelhead Blvd., near the post office in Duncans Mills, 707/865-9135, is noted for its innovative, very good vegetarian fare. Come for a serene Sunday brunch on the banks of the Russian River, or stop in to appreciate the striking rosewood bar in the tiny lounge. People go some distance to find **Cape Fear** across the road, 25191 Hwy. 116 (Main Street), 707/865-9246, just for the Cajun seafood and Caribbean jerk chicken. Just down the road in Jenner, where the Russian River flows into the Pacific Ocean, are more great choices; see the Sonoma Coast for details.

The fine dining destination these days is back toward Forestville, the **Farmhouse Inn Restaurant,** 7871 River Rd. (at Wohler Road), 707/887-3300, a lovingly restored Victorian farmhouse that pays spectacular homage to the finest Sonoma County foods and Russian River Valley wines—definitely an excellent choice for a night on the town. The menu changes daily (call for current specifics) but might include Jerusalem artichoke or curried cauliflower and apple soup; parmesan flan with spring asparagus; a Laura Chenel goat cheese souffle; or a Niman Ranch pork chop glazed with passionfruit and habañero chili. Inpressive, largely Californian wine list. Open for dinner Thurs.–Sun. from 5:30 P.M., Otherwise the place to get a reservation is "California-Provençal" **Applewood Restaurant** at the Applewood Inn on Hwy. 116 in Guerneville, 707/869-9093. The seasonally changing menu might include local king salmon roasted with potato-olive oil puree and Maine lobster poached in lobster butter with little lobster tortellini. The restaurant's wine list has received *Wine Spectator* magazine's Award of Excellence every year since 1998. Open Thurs.–Sat. for dinner.

There are a number of great restaurants in and around Sebastopol, including Zazu on Guerneville Rd. (heading back toward Santa Rosa) and still more choices in and near Healdsburg; for details, see listings above and below. Quite close to Guerneville in the "great food" category is fairly casual yet charming **Topolos Russian River Vineyards Restaurant** at the winery in Forestville, 5700 Gravenstein Hwy. N, 707/887-1562, serving Californian with a definite Greek accent—choices such as *tiropitas,* quiche Lorraine, and *spanakopita* for lunch, *moussaka* (ground lamb or vegetarian style), chicken Saltimboca, and prawns Santorini for dinner.

Healdsburg and Vicinity

Though most people head to Napa or Sonoma for wine-country tastings and tours, an increasingly popular destination in Sonoma County is Healdsburg, the urban convergence of three well-known wine regions or American Viticultural Areas: the Alexander, Dry Creek, and Russian River Valleys. (The Russian River Valley AVA also includes two sub-appellations—Chalk Hill, designating the area southeast of Healdsburg with notably chalky soils, and Green Valley, noted for its apple and pear orchards, an area stretching north from Graton and Forestville to the Russian River.) The back-road routes connecting Healdsburg to the lower Russian River area are worthy detours. Both Eastside and Westside Roads twist through rolling Russian River vineyard country—watch for slow tractors and trucks, especially during harvest season—then turn into River Road, which leads west to Forestville and then Guerneville. Even more thrilling is narrow Sweetwater Springs Rd., which shoots up over the ridge from Westside Rd., then drops down to Armstrong Woods Rd. just north of Guerneville near the park. Other back roads in the vicinity of

Healdsburg area are well worth a wander. Explore the listings below to find them.

SEEING AND DOING HEALDSBURG

Even visitors here will tell you, with some pride, that Healdsburg is still relaxed and "real," still untrammeled by the wine-hungry hordes that have already overrun the Napa Valley—the parts not walled-off as private estates—and all but usurped Sonoma's serenity. Judging from the sudden jump in trendy restaurants and high-priced hostelries, Healdsburg has already been discovered by the style-conscious. Get here for a visit while you still can.

A onetime trading post founded by Harmon Heald, downtown Healdsburg is built around a Spanish-style plaza. Shaded by citrus trees, palms, and redwoods, **Healdsburg Plaza** is "community central"—home to summer concerts and celebrations, pleasant for picnics, and surrounded by upscale shops and shoppers. The **Healdsburg Inn on the Plaza** in The Kruse Building features the only existing original second story on the plaza, since that building survived the 1906 earth-

quake. The **Gobbi Building** is one of three remaining structures in Healdsburg with cast iron fronts, the iron columns cast at the McCormick Foundry in San Francisco. The exceptional **Healdsburg Museum**, a block east of the plaza at 221 Matheson, 707/431-3325, www.healdsburgmuseum.org, is housed in the 1911 Carnegie library, a neoclassical Greek revival building designed by Petaluma architect Brainerd Jones. The museum, open Tues.–Sun. 11 A.M. 4 P.M., features newly renovated permanent exhibits on northern Sonoma County history and agriculture as well as changing exhibits.

Then there are wines and rumors of wines. Unique in Healdsburg is the **Sonoma County Wine Library** in the Healdsburg Regional Library, 139 Piper St. (at Center), 707/433-3772. This special collection of wine and winery information includes the thousand-volume Vintner's Club Library of San Francisco. To appreciate some of the wine library's dedicated work, see www.winefiles.org, an attempt to make its clipping files and wine industry database available online. Wine connoisseurs, the **Russian River Wine Company,** 132 Plaza St., 707/433-0490, stocks top vintages from more than 60 small area wineries, includ-

shopping in downtown Healdsburg

ing some hard-to-find labels. The town otherwise overfloweth with tasting rooms (see below).

Not everything concerns wines and vines: In season, stop by **Trees of Antiquity,** 4395 Westside Rd., 707/433-6420, www.treesofantiquity.com, for flavorful apples and other heirloom fruit and nut trees (even bareroot, in season) so you can grow your own. Most are California Certified Organic. The place for an art-house movie as well as thoughtful new releases is the **Raven Theater and Film Center,** 115 North St. and 415 Center St., 707/433-5448, www.raventheater.com. At last report the restored art deco theater on North Street was being managed as the Healdsburg Performing Arts Theater, and the four-theater Center Street facility directly behind it had become the local cinema. The city-run **Healdsburg Veterans Memorial Beach** along the Russian River south of town at 13839 Old Redwood Hwy., 707/433-1625, offers swimming (lifeguards are provided in summer), grassy lawns, and picnicking—at least one small solution to the persistent problem of public river access along this stretch. The day-use fee is $4 in summer—come early—and otherwise $3.

Events

Area events tend to toast the grape. Many are sponsored by regional winery associations, such as the Fourth of July **Reds, Whites, and Blends** event sponsored by the Alexander Valley Winegrowers, and the March **Crab and Fennel Fest** sponsored by the Russian River Valley Winegrowers. Winemaker dinners, food and wine pairings, benefit tastings—you name it and relate it to wine, it's probably happening somewhere around here. There are other events, too, of course, including the **Healdsburg Country Fair and Twilight Parade** in late May. Come in June for the **Healdsburg Jazz Festival.** Huge in summer, from early June to mid-September, is the **Rodney Strong Vineyards Summer Concert Series,** serving up jazz, food, and wine in an intimate outdoor theater. Show up in September for the **Beer Tasting & Food Festival.**

For more information about the area, contact the **Healdsburg Area Chamber of Commerce & Visitors Bureau,** 217 Healdsburg Ave., 707/433-

6935 or 800/648-9922 (in California), www .healdsburg.org, which offers free winery and *Farm Trails* produce maps, plus current information about events, accommodations, and food.

Windsor

People tend to blast right past Windsor on the way to and from Healdsburg and Mendocino County, though the town's new **Windsor Town Green** may soon change that. A 4.5-acre splash of lawn, trees, arbors, fountains, even a children's playground, the green is central to Windsor's redevelopment, connecting the old downtown district with government offices and hosting community festivals and other town get-togethers. And business is on the way: The prestigious **Pezzi King Winery Tasting Room** was scheduled to open near the green in early 2004. (To get to the green and Windsor's old downtown district, exit Hwy. 101 at the Central Windsor exit and continue west.) Come to the **Windsor Farmers Market,** held at the town green mid-Apr.–mid-Dec. Sun. 10 A.M.–1 P.M. Even the market is ambitious: In October 2003 Windsor entered the *Guinness Book of World Records* by baking the world's largest pumpkin pie—more than six feet across. Other reasons to linger in Windsor include the **Sonoma County Hot Air Balloon Classic,** www.schabc.org, usually held in late June. For more information about the Windsor area, just south, contact the **Windsor Chamber of Commerce & Visitor Center,** 8499 Old Redwood Hwy., Ste. 202., 707/838-7285, www.windsorchamber.com.

WINERIES

Healdsburg

It's appropriate that the tasting rooms and wineries in and near town represent all the appellations that converge in Healdsburg. You can sample many wines without leaving town. Award-winning **Windsor Vineyards,** now owned by Australia's Foster's Brewing Group, sells its wines directly to consumers only, a notable Internet and direct-marketing success story, but the winery offers tastings in downtown Healdsburg at 308-B Center St., 800/204-9463, www.windsorvineyards.com. Open

RUSSIAN RIVER ROADIES

The best way to explore northern Sonoma County wineries is to become a roadie—to head out on the Russian River Wine Road. This "road," conveniently charted out as a foldable map and as a website, includes more than 100 wineries and reaches north to Cloverdale, sashays south to Windsor and Santa Rosa, then rolls west to Sebastopol and Guerneville.

Various winery events connect the region's wineries even more effectively—year-round. In January, for example, **Winter Wineland** is the weekend before the Super Bowl—two days of tasting, tours, and talks with winemakers. The free annual **Barrel Tasting Weekend** is scheduled for the the first weekend in March, followed in short order by **Passport Weekend** in April and **A Taste of the Valley** in June.

Roadies also participate in the Sonoma County Wineries Association's July **Sonoma Country Showcase & Wine Auction,** and the Russian River Winegrowers Association's three-day August **Grape to Glass** event—exclusive vineyard and winery tours and tastings offered to the public only once a year. They then hit the road again for the **Sonoma County Harvest Fair** in October and **A Wine & Food Affair** in November.

For a current regional wine guide, which will lead the way throughout northern Sonoma County wine country, pick up the free **Russian River Wine Road** map and brochure at local chamber of commerce offices, stop by the wine road office at 139 Healdsburg Ave. in Healdsburg, call 707/433-4335 or 800/723-6336, or see www.wineroad.com. The online winery database offers fairly comprehensive winery information, too, which can help in planning your visit.

---

weekdays 10 A.M.–5 P.M., weekends until 6 P.M. New **Rosenblum Cellars** next to the Oakville Grocery, 250 Center St., 707/431-1169, shares space with the **Andy Katz Gallery,** the vintner's art merging with the visual arts. Open daily noon–5 P.M., until 6 P.M. on weekends. The **Gallo of Sonoma,** tasting room, 320 Center St., 707/433-2458, is open daily year-round except major holidays, Sun.–Wed. 11 A.M.–5 P.M., Thurs.–Sat. until 7 P.M. The stylish, contemporary **Kendall-Jackson** tasting room on the square, 337 Healdsburg Ave., 707/433-7102, www.kj.com, emphasizes high-end and estate-grown wines. There's a $2 tasting fee, $10 for premium wines. Open daily 10 A.M.–5 P.M. Le Faux Frog, anyone? The fun **Toad Hollow Vineyards** tasting room, near Willi's Seafood Bar in the Healdsburg Courtyard Building, 409A Healdsburg Ave., 707/431-8667, www.toad-hollow.com, is open daily 10 A.M.–5 P.M. and serves tastes of chardonnay, merlot, pinot noir, and zinfandel. Celebrated **Camellia Cellars,** noted for sangiovese and zinfandel, also has a tasting room on the plaza, in the Old Roma Station at 57 Front St., 707/433-1290, www.camelliacellars.com, open daily 11 A.M.–6 P.M.

Heading south from Healdsburg on the Old Redwood Hwy. (Healdsburg Avenue) leads to some significant stops. First stop is the 1896 **Foppiano Vineyards** winery, 12707 Old Redwood Hwy., 707/433-7272, www.foppiano.com, one of California's oldest family-owned wineries, open for complimentary tasting and picnicking daily 10 A.M.–4:30 P.M. Self-guided tour, vineyard stroll. Renowned for its petite sirah, the Foppiano label also graces merlot, pinot noir, cabernet sauvignon, and zinfandel; Fox Mountain is the label for Foppiano white wine, Riverside Vineyards for value wines.

Founder Rodney Strong of **Rodney Strong Vineyards,** 11455 Old Redwood Hwy., 707/431-1533 or 800/678-4763, www.rodneystrong.com, was a pioneer in modern California winemaking and crowned Winemaker of the Year by the *Los Angeles Times* way back in 1983. Now owned by Klein Family Vineyards, today the company is the granddaddy of the Russian River Valley appellation, producing a full complement of high-end wines, including cabernet sauvignon, pinot noir, zinfandel, merlot, chardonnay, and sauvignon blanc. The snazzy new Rodney Strong Hospitality Center, the result of a careful remodel, is open for free tastings (fee for reserve wines) and self-guided tours 10 A.M.–5 P.M. daily. Informative guided tours are offered at 11 A.M. and 3 P.M.

Pleasant picnicking. Sharing the parking lot with Rodney Strong is the **J Wine Company** just south, 11447 Old Redwood Hwy., 797/431-5400 or 888/594-6326, www.jwine.com, founded in 1986 by Judy Jordan and specializing in sparkling brut and fine pinot noirs. For $3–8 for a flight of wines and caviar, cheese, and other delicacies, you'll learn a lot about the arcane details of the fizzy wine bizz.

Russian River Valley

Stretching from just southwest of Headsburg south to the Windsor and Santa Rosa areas and west to Guerneville and Sebastopol, the Russian River Valley appellation also includes the Green Valley and Chalk Hill appellations. The wineries below are organized as if visitors will be meandering toward Healdsburg from the Lower Russian River. If you'll be starting from Healdsburg (or Santa Rosa) instead, study the map then work your way backward through this list.

The Russian River Valley grape-growing area near Forestville and Sebastopol, the Green Valley AVA (actually a sub-appellation) is noted for its fine pinot noir, chardonnay, and sparkling wines, wine grapes especially rich and balanced because of the cool and steady climate. Family-owned **Topolos Russian River Vineyards and Restaurant,** 5700 Gravenstein Hwy. N (Hwy. 116 one mile south of Forestville, on the way to Sebastopol), 707/887-1575, www.topolos.net, is famous for its fruity, full-bodied Sonoma County Old Vine Zinfandel and other specialty, single-vineyard zins—including "Eco Zin," made from Lodi-grown California Certified Organic grapes, and a zinfandel port. In addition to a few white wines Topolos produces an impressive roster of other reds, including a Russian River Valley pinot noir, petite sirahs, syrahs, Alicante Bouschets (made from the "Bootlegger's Grape"), and Sonoma County Riserva, a Bordeaux-style blend of cabernet sauvignon and merlot. In addition to its fine varietals, Topolos offers a very good Greek continental restaurant. The winery tasting room is open daily 11 A.M.–5:30 P.M. **Iron Horse Vineyards,** not far south at 9786 Ross Station Rd., 707/887-1507, www.ironhorsevineyards.com, has been named Sparkling Winery of The Year by

Wine & Spirits magazine, several years running. Family-owned Iron Horse produces cuvées for top restaurants and its sparkling wines have long been served at U.S. summits and other events of state, but Iron Horse is most famous to date for its wedding cuvée. And if you can't find a bottle of the 2002 Good Luck Cuvée, don't kick up a fuss. It will come around again in 2014, the next Chinese Year of the Horse. Open daily for tasting 10 A.M.–3:30 P.M., for tours by appointment.

North of the Russian River just outside Guerneville is imposing **Korbel Champagne Cellars,** dominating the big vineyard-hugging curve on River Road a few miles east of Rio Nido. The vine-covered red brick 1886 Korbel Champagne Cellars is well worth a stop for tastes of Korbel champagne and wines or a snifter of brandy. Bohemian immigrants, the three brothers Korbel started out in the 1860s as loggers. Soon Anton and Joseph Korbel began planting vines between the massive redwood stumps on the rich bottomland along the river. The rest, as the winery here still testifies, is history. The Korbels sold the operation in 1954, but the old family estate still stands, as attractive as ever. As America's largest premium champagne producer—sparkling wines are made by the classic, traditional *méthode champenoise*—Korbel is no secret. This was the only champagne poured during the past five presidential inaugurations. Another reason to stop by, though, is to taste Korbel's table wines, sold only here, and brandies. On the grounds are the winery and tasting room, a restored brandy tower, a gourmet deli, a wine museum, and a hillside garden boasting more than 250 time-honored rose varieties, coral bells, and violets. Peaceful picnicking. Open May–Sept., daily 10 A.M.–5 P.M. (shorter hours in winter); tours and tastings are offered hourly. For more information, contact: Korbel Champagne Cellars, 13250 River Rd. in Guerneville, 707/824-7000, www.korbel.com.

For many years, people picked up winemaker Gary Farrell's pinot noir wherever they were lucky enough to find it. Early on Farrell, who emigrated from Australia's Yarra Valley region, was long ago dubbed "the crown prince of pinot noir" by California wine critics, yet the prince had no castle, primarily working out of other wineries to produce his magic elixir. These days you can come by the winery itself for tasting and sales. The main focus at the modern, well-equipped **Gary Farrell Winery,** 10701 Westside Rd. on the back-road route to Healdsburg, 707/473-2900 or 707/473-2909, www.garyfarrell.com, is still pinot noir, but Farrell also makes merlot, a red meritage, a Dry Creek Valley old-vine zinfandel, sauvignon blanc, and chardonnay. In peak season the tasting room is open to the public daily 11 A.M.–4 P.M. (except holidays). A combination tour and tasting, by appointment only, is offered daily at 10 A.M. Reservations required for group visits. Acclaimed **Porter Creek Vineyards,** 8735 Westside Rd., 707/433-6321, produces outstanding pinot noirs, carignane, syrah, chardonnay, and sauvignon blanc.

Before he got his own castle and hilltop view, Gary Farrell was winemaker at nearby family-owned **Davis Bynum Winery,** 8075 Westside Rd., 707/433-5852 or 800/826-1073, www.davis-bynum.com, now noted for its organic wines. Davis Bynum produces small quantities of some winning wines, including a still acclaimed pinot noir, zinfandel, merlot, cabernet sauvignon, and cabernet franc Tasting room (free tastings) open daily 10 A.M.–5 P.M. Also in the same general neighborhood is **Rochioli Vineyards and Winery,** 6192 Westside Rd., 707/433-2305, open daily 10 A.M.–5 P.M., a family-owned enterprise growing grapes here since the 1930s.

Farther along the road to Healdsburg is remote **Hop Kiln Winery,** 6050 Westside Rd., 707/433-6491, www.hopkilnwinery.com, award-winning, well respected, known for its rustic Old World wines—quite reasonably priced. Particularly attention-getting in recent years has been Hop Kiln's A Thousand Flowers, a blend of estate-grown gewürztraminer, chardonnay, and riesling. Hop Kiln's meticulously restored 1905 stone hop-drying "barn" houses the working winery, with winetasting in the more typical barn adjacent. And if the setting seems eerily familiar, keep in mind that the 1978 movie *Magic of Lassie,* with Jimmy Stewart and Mickey Rooney, was filmed here. These days Hop Kiln offers nice views of the vineyards, pond, and picnic area.

Small deli, too. Open for tasting and sales 10 A.M.–5 P.M. daily (closed major holidays), tours by appointment only.

On *Wine & Spirits* magazine's 2003 Winery of the Year list is the **Kendall-Jackson Wine Center** south of the river at 5007 Fulton Rd., 707/571-8100 or 800/769-3649, www.kj.com, where the charming chateau offers both wine tasting and a gift shop. Award-winning Kendall-Jackson wines, exclusively coastal (here they call them "true coastal wines"), include reds—cabernet sauvignon, merlot, pinot noir, syrah, and zinfandel—and whites, including chardonnay, muscat canelli, riesling, sauvignon blanc, zinfandel, and viognier. The tasting fee is $2, $10 for premium wines.

Kendall-Jackson also demonstrates that California agriculture includes horticulture, and that the sensory awareness required for wine appreciation can also celebrate gardens. The **Kendall-Jackson Aromatic Gardens** are designed to illustrate, via the senses, wine appreciation lingo. The Red Wine Sensory Garden, for example, is associated with the cabernet family of wines and includes plantings of cherry, black currant, blackberry, tobacco, mint, bell pepper, and oregano. Illustrating the floral varietals such as gewürztraminer. The White Wine Sensory Garden includes honeysuckle, jasmine, lilac, rose, pineapple sage, apricot, pear, grapefruit, nectarine, and lime. Four international gardens—French, Italian, South American, and Asian—feature herbs and plants associated with particular regional cuisines.

The **Kendall-Jackson Wine Center** is open daily 10 A.M.–5 P.M. Garden tours are offered daily at 11 A.M., 1 P.M., and 3 P.M. (weather permitting). Private tours and tastings are available by appointment. There's also a Kendall-Jackson tasting room on the square in Healdsburg.

The "chalk" in the Chalk Hill sub-appellation, located south of Healdsburg and east of Windsor, refers to the soil's characteristic white volcanic ash. Possible Chalk Hill stops—each open only by appointment—include the high-end **Chalk Hill Estate Vineyards & Winery,** 10300 Chalk Hill Rd., 707/838-4306, www.chalkhill.com, noted for its handcrafted chardonnay but also sauvignon blanc, pinot gris, semillon, cabernet sauvignon, and merlot. Also highly regarded is **Chateau Felice,** 10603 Chalk Hill Rd., 707/836-9011, www.chateaufelice.com.

For more information about the area's wineries, wines, and upcoming events, contact **Russian River Valley Winegrowers,** headquartered at Saralee's Vineyard, 3351 Slusser Rd. in Windsor, 707/521-2534, www.rrvw.org.

Dry Creek Valley

Dry Creek Valley is 16 miles long and two miles wide. Grape growing got its start here in the 1870s, when disillusioned refugees of the California gold fields settled here and began cultivating red gold. Some of these old vines are still producing. A recognized appellation since 1983, the valley's most recognized wines are zinfandel and sauvignon blanc yet cabernet sauvignon, merlot, chardonnay, and chenin blanc are rising stars. For more information about the region's wines, wineries, and events, contact **Winegrowers of Dry Creek Valley,** 707/433-3031, www.wdcv.com.

Jog south a short distance along Westside Road to visit the southern outposts of Dry Creek Valley, then backtrack and head north on W. Dry Creek Road before looping back on Dry Creek Road—the text below follows this route—or launch the same adventure in reverse. You won't find much commercial bricabrac in the Dry Creek Valley, thanks to serious agricultural zoning laws. The creaky old 1881 landmark **Dry Creek General Store,** 3495 Dry Creek Rd., 707/433-4171, was recently purchased by a member of the Gallo clan yet at last report was still a good place for great sandwiches, gourmet picnic finxings, and wine. Open Mon.–Thurs. 7 A.M.–7 P.M., Fri.–Sun. until 9 P.M.

The award-winning **Lambert Bridge Winery,** 4085 W. Dry Creek Rd., 707/431-9600, www.lambertbridge.com, resembles an old barn but is actually contemporary in all respects, including the view of the winemaking process from the tasting room. Open for tasting—sauvignon blanc, chardonnay, viogner, zinfandel, merlot, old vine cuvée—daily 10:30 A.M.–4:30 P.M. **Quivira Vineyards,** 4900 W. Dry Creek Rd., 707/431-8333 or 800/292-8339, www.quivirawine.com, is noted for its varietal wines, including zinfandel, petite sirah, sauvignon blanc, and Rhône varietals. Open daily 11 A.M.–5 P.M. for complimentary tasting, tours only by appointment. Picnic area available. Quivira's spacious new tasting room, with its tall arched ceiling and natural cork floor, looks out across the vineyards to Mt. St. Helena.

Raymond Burr Vineyards, 8339 W. Dry Creek Rd., 707/433-4365 or 888/900-0024, www.raymondburrvineyards.com, owned by actors Raymond Burr and Robert Benevides, wins awards with its estate-grown cabernet sauvignon, cabernet franc, and chardonnay. The tasting room is open by appointment only, 11 A.M.–5 P.M. daily. But don't miss the orchids; nursery tours are offered by appointment, on weekends only (call for details).

Just east from Dry Creek Road, about a mile northwest of Geyserville, is the family-owned **J. Pedroncelli Winery & Vineyards,** 1220 Canyon Rd., 707/857-3531 or 800/836-3894, www.pedroncelli.com, which sold grapes to home winemakers during Prohibition and later specialized in producing bulk wines. The winery now offers award-winning Alexander Valley and Dry Creek Valley premium varietals, with tasting and sales daily 10 A.M.–5 P.M. Nearby is small **Frick Winery and Tasting House,** tucked away at 23072 Walling Rd. in Geyserville, 707/857-3205, www.frickwinery.com, offering grand views and complex wines—viognier, syrah, cinsaut, merlot—which you sample inside the original homestead at a clear heart redwood bar. Tasting house open weekends noon–4:30 P.M.

Farther north along Dry Creek Road the **Ferrari-Carano Vineyards and Winery,** 8761 Dry Creek Rd., 707/433-6700 or 800/831-0381, www.ferrari-carano.com, is brought to you by the same folks behind the landmark El Dorado Hotel-Casino in Reno, the Don Carano family. At the center of this stunning and serene place is the overwhelming Villa Fiore, the tasting center—a virtual Florentine estate surrounded by five acres of gardens, streams, waterfalls, and ponds. Open 10 A.M.–5 P.M. daily for tasting and sales. The tasting fee is $3. Winery tours are offered Mon.–Sat. at 10 A.M., by advance reservation only.

Tiny, highly regarded **Unti Vineyards,** 4202

Dry Creek Rd., 707/433-5590, www.untivine-yards.com, grows syrah, sangiovese, and zinfandel and also produces grenache rosé, grenache rouge, and petite sirah. Open for sales and tasting by appointment only.

The ivy-covered stone winery at **Dry Creek Vineyard,** 3770 Lambert Bridge Rd. (four miles north of Healdsburg, just off Dry Creek Road), 707/433-1000, www.drycreekvineyard.com, is known for its fumé blanc, zinfandel, and meritage, everything produced in very limited quantities. And dig those sailboat labels. Pleasant picnic grounds, kids welcome. Open daily 10:30 A.M.–4:30 P.M. for tasting and tours. Nearby (just north) is celebrated Pezzi King Winery, 3805 Lambert Bridge Rd., www.pezziking.com, which alas no longer offers tastings here at the winery though it does host special events. For tastings and sales, head for the new tasting room in Windsor, on the Windsor Town Green.

Mazzocco Vineyards, 1400 Lytton Springs Rd., 707/431-8159 or 800/501-8466, www.mazzocco.com, is open daily for tastings (picnicking too) 10 A.M.–4:30 P.M. and known for its cabernet sauvignon, merlot, zinfandel, and chardonnay. A real treat: a vertical tasting of Mazzocco's famous Matrix wines. **Ridge Vineyards,** once the Lytton Springs Winery, 650 Lytton Springs Rd. (three miles north of Healdsburg off Hwy. 101), 707/433-7721, www.ridgewine.com, doesn't offer picnic facilities, doesn't sell food, and doesn't do weddings. But it is a 2003 Winery of the Year—one of just ten in the world—according to *Wine & Spirits* magazine and does produce a fine zinfandel. Open 11 A.M.–4 P.M. daily (except holidays) for tasting and sales; regular tastings are free.

Alexander Valley

Formally recognized as the Alexander Valley AVA in 1984, the valley is 20 miles long and up to seven miles wide, stretching from Healdsburg to Geyserville. The appellation is known for cabernet sauvignon, merlot, zinfandel, and Chardonnay; up-and-coming varietals include viognier, pinot blanc, shiraz, and sangiovese. For more information about the area's wines, wineries, and upcoming events, contact **Alexander Valley Winegrowers,** 58 W. North St. in Healdsburg, 707/431-2894, www.alexandervalley.org.

To tour Alexander Valley Vineyards starting from Healdsburg, it makes sense to go either north or south then loop back toward town. The following loop heads north before turning south; reverse the route by starting at the bottom of this section. Whichever way you go, always a worthy stop along the way is homey and hip **Jimtown Store,** 6706 Hwy. 128 (north of Alexander Valley Road), 707/433-1212, www.jimtown.com, which serves up house-made soups, chilis, sandwiches and other deli fare (like Jimtown's own fig and olive spread) along with wines by the glass, espresso, and homestyle desserts. There's an outdoor patio here, but box lunches (and suppers) are also available. Eclectic goods for sale, too, from old-time candies and toys to gift items. Open daily 7 A.M.–5 P.M., opening on weekends at 7:30 A.M. Another good stop is the **Chateau Souverain Café**; for details, see winery listing below

Just north of town, the 1876 handhewn stone and modernized **Simi Winery,** 16275 Healdsburg Ave., 800/746-4880, www.simiwinery.com, which once specialized in bulk wines. But now—like most Napa-Sonoma establishments—it produces premium wines, from both the Alexander and Russian River Valleys, these available for sampling in the redwood-and-stone tasting room. Open daily 10 A.M.–4:30 P.M., guided tours available. It's a wonderful spot for picnics.

Among the region's best is **Chateau Souverain,** a jog north then across the freeway at 400 Souverain Rd. (Hwy. 101 at Independence Lane), 707/433-3141, 707/433-8281 or 888/809-4637, www.chateausouverain.com. The winery's twin buildings, chateau-like yet designed to resemble Sonoma County's traditional hop-drying kilns, sit atop a knoll overlooking the Alexander Valley and are visible from just a few miles north of Healdsburg. In addition to its fine wines—chardonnay, cabernet sauvignon, sauvignon blanc, merlot—Souverain offers chamber music and jazz concerts during the summer months, other special events, and a great bistro. Open for tasting and sales daily 10 A.M.–5 P.M. The very good **Café at the Winery,** 707/433-3141, serves up vineyard views, California-style fare, and fine

Souverain wines. For lunch, try the caesar salad with Vella dry jack with either chicken or shrimp or the slow braised pork sandwich with an apple-zinfandel barbecue sauce, for dinner, sautéed salmon with watercress pesto or truffled polenta with grilled portobello mushrooms, Fontanella cheese, and roasted root veggies. Open for lunch daily 11:30 A.M.–2:30 P.M., with an "al fresco" menu served 2:30–5 P.M. Dinner is served Fri.–Sun. only, reservations recommended.

On the other side of the freeway are three intriguing stops. Look for the stone lions to find award-winning **Trentadue Winery,** 19170 Old Redwood Hwy., 707/433-3104 or 888/332-3032, www.trentadue.com, is open daily 10 A.M.–5 P.M. Trentadue varietals include carignane, zinfandel, sangiovese, merlot, petite sirah, and cabernet sauvignon, though there are several blends, including Old Patch Red and a red LaStoria meritage. Gourmet food and gift shop, too. Nearby **Clos du Bois,** 19410 Geyserville Ave., 707/857-3100 or 800/222-3189, www.closdubois.com, has won so many awards since its inception in 1974 for its various fine varietal and vineyard-designated wines that even most of the winery's fans have stopped counting. Now an Allied Domecq subsidiary, Clos du Bois produces four tiers of high-end wines, from its Classics line of seven Sonoma County varietals and Appellation Reserve (predominantly Alexander Valley) and Vineyard Designate series to its "best of the best" Winemaker's Reserve cabernet sauvignon, merlot, and malbec wines. Ask about the J. Garcia Wines, Sonoma County varietals featuring label art by Jerry Garcia of the Grateful Dead. Open daily 10 A.M.–4:30 P.M. for tasting ($5 per tasting which can be shared, for up to seven wines), logo wineglass included. No tours, but snacks and other goodies are available along with "view" picnicking.

A onetime bulk winery, the 1888-vintage **Canyon Road Winery** adjacent at 19550 Geyserville Ave., 707/857-3417, www.canyonroad-winery.com, has sold its wines to high-end hotels such as the Four Seasons and Ritz-Carlton chains. Now a subsidiary of Peak Wines International (Jim Beam), it sells respectable varietals to the general public—some available only here, including the "Big River Ranch" Alexander Valley

cabernet. Ask about the new J. Garcia wines, Sonoma County varietals that feature label art by Jerry Garcia of the Grateful Dead. Open for tasting and sales only, 10 A.M.–5 P.M. daily. To continue a Peak International tour, head for **Geyser Peak Winery,** farther north at 22281 Chianti Rd. (off Canyon Rd., west of Hwy. 101), 707/857-9463 or 800/255-9463, www.geyserpeakwinery.com, open for tasting daily 10 A.M.–5 P.M.

A must-do destination east of Geyserville and the Russian River is the time-honored, family-owned **Robert Young Estate Winery,** east of Hwy. 128 at 4950 Red Winery Rd. (off Geysers Road), 707/431-4811, www.ryew.com, the original old barn recently replaced by a state-of-the-art winery and wine caves. Visitors are welcome by appointment, Wed.–Sat. 10 A.M.–4:30 P.M. and Sun. 12:30–4 P.M., to taste the chardonnay and Scion Bordeaux Blend (fee).

Rolling south along the river's east side, **de Lorimier Vineyards and Winery,** 2001 Hwy. 128, 707/857-2000 or 800/546-7718, www.delorimierwinery.com, is open daily 10 A.M.–4:30 P.M. for tasting and sales of its sauvignon blanc, chardonnay, merlot, with an emphasis on various handcrafted estate-grown blends—including its famed red Mosaic and Spectrum Reserve sauvignon blanc.

Imagine what it's like to live in the midst of the ongoing Napa-Sonoma cultural wars farther south at the pioneering **Murphy-Goode Estate Winery,** 4001 Hwy. 128, 707/431-7644 or 800/499-7644 (wine sales only), www.murphy-goodewinery.com, where the winery is "our life," not "a lifestyle." Stop for a taste, 10:30 A.M.–4:30 P.M. daily, to appreciate Murphy-Goode's estate-grown and reserve cabernet sauvignon, merlot, pinot noir, Liar's Dice and Snake Eyes zinfandels, Wild Card claret, chardonnay, and sauvignon blanc.

Striking **Stryker Sonoma Winery & Vineyards,** 5110 Hwy. 128, 707/433-1944 or 800/433-1944, www.strykersonoma.com, is open to the public for tasting and picnicking Thurs.–Sun. 10:30 A.M.–5 P.M. (Mon.–Wed. by appointment only). Taste the award-winning cabernet sauvignon, zinfandel, merlot, sangiovese, Russian River Valley gewürztraminer, Alexander Valley semillon, and chardonnay. In 2003 Stryker wines were available only at the winery or online.

Past the Jimtown store and the big curve is small, family-owned **Sausal Winery,** 7370 Hwy. 128, 707/433-2285 or 800/500-2285 (orders only), www.sausalwinery.com, is open for tasting and picnicking daily 10 A.M.–4 P.M. (closed major holidays), tours by appointment only. Blends are genuine bargains, such as the $7 Sausal Blanc and the $12 Cellar Cats Red, but there are other surprises here, including the Century Vine Zinfandel. Just south and across the road from Sausal is acclaimed **White Oak Vineyards,** 7505 Hwy. 128, 707/433-8429, www.whiteoakwinery.com, with a gorgeous new facility serving winning merlots, zinfandel, syrah, and famed sauvignon blanc and chardonnay, open daily for tasting and sales 10 A.M.–5 P.M. (private tours and tastings by appointment). Just down the road is historic **Johnson's Alexander Valley Wines,** a small premium winery at 8333 Hwy. 128, 707/433-2319, noted for its chardonnay and riesling and the occasional zinfandel, cabernet, and pinot noir, open daily 10 A.M.–5 P.M. for tasting. The 1924 Robert Morton pipe organ actually gets played, by the way, during periodic silent movies.

Across the street is historic **Alexander Valley Vineyards** on the old Cyrus Alexander place, the appellation's namesake homestead at 8644 Hwy. 128, 707/433-7209 or 800/888-7209, www.avvwine.com, known for its award-winning, estate-bottled, reasonably priced varietal wines—including the New Gewürz, a very good chardonnay, cabernet sauvignons, cabernet franc, pinot noir, syrah, and ever-popular Sin Zin. Do try Cyrus, a limited-production proprietary red. The inviting tasting room is open daily 10 A.M.–5 P.M. (closed major holidays) Picnic facilities available. Very informative guided tours of the wine caves are offered by appointment.

The aptly named **Field Stone Winery,** 10075 Hwy. 128 (near the Chalk Hill Rd. intersection), 707/433-7266, www.fieldstonewinery.com, has a striking yet deceptively simple facade. Literally a back-to-the-land bunker of concrete faced with fieldstone and sliced into this Anderson Valley hillside, Field Stone as a winery is actually contemporary and complex. Noted for its spring

cabernet, petite sirah, rosé of petite sirah, viognier, and other fine wines—how about some Convivio Heavenly White?—Field Stone sponsors winemaker dinners and other special events. Wine tasting daily 10 A.M.–4:30 P.M., tours by appointment only.

STAYING IN HEALDSBURG

To camp, head to Lake Sonoma (see listing below) or the **Dutcher Creek RV Park and Campground,** not far north of Healdsburg at 230 Theresa Dr. (exit at Dutcher Creek and head west), 707/894-4829, both RV and tent sites available ($12–25). There's also the **Cloverdale Wine Country KOA,** 707/894-3337 or 800/562-4042 (reservations), complete with swimming pool and hot tub, $32–48 for tents or RVs. Otherwise, finding cheap sleeps in these parts is increasingly difficult. For the basics plus indoor pool, sauna, spa, and roomy outdoor picnic area, the place is the family-owned **L&M Motel** just a few blocks from downtown at 70 Healdsburg Ave., 707/433-6528, www.landmmotel.com. Rates start at $50–100. The vaguely Spanish-style **Best Western Dry Creek Inn** on the north end of town at 198 Dry Creek Rd., 707/433-0300 or 800/222-5784, www.drycreekinn.com, features in-room conveniences from hair dryers to refrigerators plus pool, whirlpool, and a "welcome" bottle of wine. Rates start at $50–100, and kids under 16 stay free.

Contemporary and Cool

Newest kid on the block downtown is stylish, $21 million **Hotel Healdsburg,** 25 Matheson St., 707/431-2800 or 800/889-7188, www.hotel-healdsburg.com, already included in *Travel & Leisure*'s 2003 "top 100" list of U.S. and Canadian hotels. Modern and minimalist, open since 2001, this full-service luxury hotel is a country inn with urban style. From the stark yet warm lobby to the 55 simple yet elegant rooms and suites with all the comforts, less is more here. Bathrooms feature walk-in showers and six-foot soaking tubs, and rooms have French doors and patios, wooden floors and exotic rugs, understated furnishings, luxury linens. Having the exceptional **Dry Creek Kitchen** restaurant on-site—launched by chef Charlie Palmer, owner of New York's acclaimed Aureole—along with the grappa and espresso bars, and the 60-foot swimming pool, means that those with means really don't ever need to leave. Rates start at $250–300, but check for specials (such as stay two days, get a third free).

If you're in the mood for a high-end, slightly decadent yet artsy escape, **Duchamp Hotel,** 421 Foss St. (off North, just west of Healdsburg Ave.), 707/431-1300 or 800/431-9341, www.duchamphotel.com, is hip as all get out, just the place. Named for the surrealist Marcel Duchamp and very contemporary, the hotel's cottages and villas offer their own eccentricities, like Man Ray's neon lips and those twin Marilyns smiling down from Warhol's walls. Otherwise expect all the comforts, from oversized spa shower, fireplace, minibar, and all the latest electronics to exercise mats and king-size bed with down comforters and pillows. And if you insist on working, there's a modem hookup too. Rates are $225 and up, higher on weekends.

At **Belle de Jour Inn,** on a hilltop across from Simi Winery at 16276 Healdsburg Ave., 707/431-9777, www.belledejourinn.com, the décor is country floral but with sophisticated contemporary touches. Surrounded by gorgeous grounds, gardens, and wildlife habitat, rooms at Belle de Jour feature king- or queen-size beds, comfortable sitting areas, private baths (some with two-person Jacuzzis), gas fireplaces, ceiling fans, and central heat and air. Little luxuries include fresh flowers, plush robes, hair dryers, refrigerators, and CD/tape players. Full country breakfast. Rooms are $200–300. The second-floor Carriage House suite, with vaulted ceiling and stained glass window, four-poster king bed, and Jacuzzi for two, is $335.

Very Victorian

Old Healdsburg is very Victorian, heavy on the lace. Many area bed-and-breakfasts and hotels require two- or three-night minimum stays on weekends. Downtown is the wonderful Victorian **Healdsburg Inn on the Plaza,** 110 Matheson St., 707/433-6991 or 800/431-8663, www.healdsburginn.com, a bed-and-breakfast with 10 rooms (several with fireplace) attractively furnished in antiques. And then there's all that food. A full breakfast buffet is served on weekdays, champagne brunch on weekends; wine tasting is offered in the afternoon, dessert wine and chocolates after 8 P.M. There's a guest fridge stocked with water and drinks and also a bottomless cookie jar. High-season weekend and holidays rates are $250–300, fall/winter midweek rates are $150–250.

The new Victorian in town is the luxurious and historic **Honor Mansion,** 14891 Grove St., 707/433-4277 or 800/554-4667, www.honormansion.com. This 1883 Italianate Victorian features five rooms in the house (some with fireplaces and decks); five luxury suites; the Squire's Cottage out back near the koi pond; and the Plaza Cottage back toward the plaza. There's also a lap pool. Romantic luxury is the theme here, from the exquisite décor—fine European linens, featherbeds, and fresh flowers—to every imaginable amenity. Fabulous breakfasts, evening sherry, a 24-hour espresso/cappuccino machine, tea, biscuits, and cookies are on hand. Gift shop, too. Most rooms are $200–300, suites and cottage $300–500.

The elegant **Calderwood, A Victorian Inn,** 25 W. Grant St., 707/431-1110 or 800/600-5444, www.calderwoodinn.com, is a 1902 Queen Anne Victorian set on one-acre grounds landscaped with rose gardens, fountains, and koi ponds. Inside, each of the six attractive rooms has a private bath and a queen bed with down comforter. Striking Victorian décor and antiques throughout. Rates are $150–250. Another best bet is the charming **Haydon Street Inn,** 321 Haydon St., 707/433-5228 or 800/528-3703, www.haydon.com, particularly the large upstairs rooms in the Victorian Cottage out back. Great country breakfasts. Rates are surprisingly reasonable, four rooms $100–150, four others $150–200. The **Raford House Bed and Breakfast Inn,** 10630 Wohler Rd., 707887-9573 or 800/887-9503, www.rafordhouse.com, features six rooms in a grand 1889 Victorian farmhouse, surrounded by vineyards and orchards. Rates are $100–200. The grand winery views are priceless.

The grand **Madrona Manor,** 1001 Westside Rd., 707/433-4231 or 800/258-4003, www .madronamanor.com, is a wine country institution, a venerable three-story 1881 Victorian mansion with 18 rooms and five suites (many with fireplaces but free of TV and electronics), five welcoming common rooms, acres and acres of gardens, and pool. Full breakfast, fantastic onsite restaurant. Rates begin at $175 but generally are $200–450. Special events include Jazz on the Veranda (May–Oct.), winemaker's dinners, and holiday season Thanksgiving and Dickens Dinners.

EATING IN HEALDSBURG

There are two farmers markets in season, The **Healdsburg Saturday Certified Farmers Market** is held at W. North and Vine Streets May–Dec. 9 A.M.–noon, and the **Healdsburg Tuesday CFM** is held June–Oct. 4–6:30 P.M. at the Healdsburg Plaza. For more information, call 707/431-1956. **Anstead's Marketplace & Deli,** a local institution now located two blocks north of the plaza at 428 Center St., 707/431-0530, is renowned for local produce, though you'll also find grand sandwiches and everything else needed for a fine picnic. Not to mention the organic smoothies. Open weekdays 11 A.M.– 7 P.M., weekends until 6 P.M. The hip **Flying Goat Coffee,** 324 Center St., 707/433-9081, serves the best fresh-roasted, along with great pastries and café fare. Open weekdays 7 A.M.– 6 P.M., weekends from 8 A.M.

For simple bakery specialties and snacks approaching perfection, try the full-service **Downtown Bakery and Creamery** on the plaza at 308-A Center St., 707/431-2719, an enterprise launched by pastry chef Lindsey Shere of Berkeley's Chez Panisse and her daughters. Nothing fancy, but everything is excellent, from the fresh-baked breads (try the sourdough French and the sourdough wheat-rye), light pastries, and sticky buns to *real* ice cream milkshakes, sundaes, and housemade ice creams and sorbets. Sonoma County and organics ingredients are used whenever possible. Lunch items include sandwiches and pizzas. Open weekdays 6 A.M.–5:30 P.M., Saturday 7 A.M.–5:30 P.M., Sunday 7 A.M.–4 P.M. Also a de-

lightful surprise is outstanding **Costeaux French Bakery & Café,** 417 Healdsburg Ave., 707/433-1913, where you'll have to buy at least one loaf of the whole-wheat walnut-rosemary bread and the award-winning sourdough. Desserts are amazing, from the caramel macadamia nut tart to triple chocolate mousse. Outdoor patio, bistro fare at breakfast and lunch, box lunches. Open Tues.–Sat. 6:30 A.M.–5 P.M., Sun. until 4 P.M.

If there's still plenty in your purse, further plump up your picnic basket at the **Oakville Grocery,** located in the onetime city hall at 124 Matheson St., 707/433-3200. This "grocery," third in the chain started in St. Helena, combines a surprising gourmet retail array—jams, olives, mustards, chutneys, cheeses, and more— with café and sandwich bar, pizzeria, rotisserie, and kitchen. Wine, too. Shaded outdoor patio. Open Sun.–Wed. 9 A.M.–7 P.M., Thurs.–Sat. 9 A.M.–8:30 P.M.

A great little lunch stop—the initial impression here is "little"—is casual **Ravenette,** a lunch-only fledgling in the Ravenous family (see below), open Wed.–Sun. only, annexed to the Raven Theater at 117 North St., 707/431-1770. Microbrew fans, hunt down the **Bear Republic Brewing Co.,** 345 Healdsburg Ave., 707/433-2337, "home of the best IPA in the USA."

Dining Destinations

A great local restaurant, still largely unsung, is exuberant **Ravenous,** which got its start in a Raven Theater annex (now the lunch-only Ravenette) and is at home these days in a charming house at 420 Center St., 707/431-1302, open Wed.–Sun. for lunch and dinner (garden dining available). The menu changes twice weekly. You'll soon be ravenous for the grand American bistro fare, from the smoked salmon and caviar and quesadillas with roast duck and summer salsa to pork tenderloin scaloppini in a wine, mushroom, and sage sauce. Desert might be house-made gingerbread with pears, ice cream, and caramel sauce, Asian pear and huckleberry cobbler with vanilla ice cream, or decadent chocolate crème pie.

Trendier restaurants come and go, but **Bistro Ralph,** 109 Plaza St. E, 707/433-1380, is a keeper—still one of the best restaurants in

Sonoma County. The menu at this all-American bistro changes constantly, ranging from Szechuan pepper calamari and duck breast with baked pears and rosemary potatoes to spring lamb stew. Expect salads and stylish sandwiches at lunch. Beer and wine only. Open for lunch Mon.–Sat., for dinner nightly. The place to get a good wood-fired pizza is at Ralph's related **Felix & Louie's,** 106 Matheson St., 707/433-6999, open daily from lunch until 10:30 P.M.

Healdsburg's nationally acclaimed high-end dining destination is likely to garner star billing for quite some time. The **Dry Creek Kitchen,** 317 Healdsburg Ave., 707/431-0330, one of numerous siblings to celebrity chef Charlie Palmer's Aureole in New York, makes the most of Sonomy County's bounty, from the spice-crusted roast beef on toasted focaccia to orecchiette pasta with house-made sausage. Open for lunch and dinner daily, indoor and outdoor seating. Full bar, great wine list. Reservations advised.

Zin Restaurant & Wine Bar, a block north of the plaza at 334 Center St., 707/473-0946, serves up an impressive roster of zinfandels—the wine list has won the *Wine Spectator*'s Award for Excellence—and such things as ribs with zin BBQ sauce, cioppino, and blue-plate specials. Seasonally changing menu. Also adding a bit of avant-garde style is **Manzanita,** 336 Healdsburg Ave., 707/433-8111, serving an eclectic seasonally changing menu with wood-fired pizzas and selections such as potato gnocchi with asparagus and truffled cheese. If you get the chance, try the apple-rhubarb crisp with vanilla ice cream. Open Wed.–Sun. for dinner.

Tastings Restaurant & Wine Bar, tucked away in a parking lot behind a bank at 505 Healdsburg Ave.,707/433-3936, is lauded for its New American tasting menu—from house-made ricotta gnocchi to skewered seafood. Good wine list, great pineapple upside-down cake. Open Fri.–Mon. for dinner only. Speaking of tastings: Culinary cousin of Willi's Wine Bar in Santa Rosa, **Willi's Seafood & Raw Bar,** featuring a serious selection of seafood small plates, oyster bar, and a Sonoma County wine list, is just off the plaza in the Healdsburg Courtyard Building at 409 Healdsburg Ave., 707/433-9191.

A worthy destination south of town in Windsor is marvelous **Mirepoix,** 275 Windsor River Rd., 707/838-0162, where the daily changing menu might feature grilled herb roasted organic chicken breast, braised pork loin with goat cheddar gratin, and grilled New York steak with lobster johnny cakes. Also consider **Langley's on the Green,** 610 McClelland Dr., 707/837-7984.

Or stay in Healdsburg and honor longstanding tradition. A Geyserville institution since the 1930s, **Catelli's the Rex** is now at home in Healdsburg, 241 Healdsburg Ave., 707/433-6000, still the white-tablecloth favorite of deeply rooted locals. For lunch try the brie lamb burger or roasted eggplant sandwich; for dinner, brandied filet tips, Dungeness crab ravioli, smoked chicken and cheese tortellini in marsala cream sauce, or fresh pan-seared king salmon with risotto. Full bar, award-winning Sonoma County wine list. Open Tues.–Fri. for lunch, Tues.–Sun. for dinner. Reservations wise.

GEYSERVILLE AND VICINITY

The tiny town of Geyserville lies at the heart of the Alexander Valley at the foot of Geyser Peak. Geyserville hosts a **Fall Color Tour** on the last Sunday in October—a good time to enjoy the autumn blaze of red, gold, and russet grape leaves. But Geyserville's hot even when the temperature cools. Since the 1960s geothermal plants have tapped into The Geysers, the underground steam fields stretchng east from here into Lake County, to spin turbines and produce electricity, a renewable energy source. This energy motherlode is running out of steam these days, because power has been overproduced. Attempts to "recharge" steam fields with treated wastewater seem to be working. Yet these massive water injections have also greatly increased area earthquakes, especially just east in Anderson Springs. Whether things are shaking here or not, you'll find most of the town on Hwy. 128, which is Geyserville Avenue, the main drag.

Definitely different for accommodations is the 10-acre **Isis Oasis Lodge and Cultural Center,** 20889 Geyserville Ave., 707/857-3524 or 800/679-7387, www.isisoasis.org, a lush 10-acre oasis centered on the Temple of Isis, a legally recognized church. Accommodations here range from the B&B-style Retreat House, The Lodge—Egyptian-motif rooms share baths, one for men and one for women—and the Isis Suite to various "alternative" options, including the enchanted cottage, a remodeled water tower, pyramid, tipi, and several yurts. (Pets are welcome in alternative lodgings.) Isis Oasis facilities also include a pool, sauna, hot tub, swan pond, aviary, and enclave of ocelots. Call for details.

Bed-and-breakfasters, try Geyserville's "Hope Houses," the associated **Hope-Merrill House** and **Hope-Bosworth House,** 21253 Geyserville Ave., 707/857-3356 or 800/825-4233, www.hope-inns.com, exceptional all-redwood Victorians. The grand, beautifully restored Hope-Merrill is an Eastlake Stick with Bruce Bradbury wallpapers, striking rooms with antiques and private baths, formal gardens. Hope-Bosworth across the street is a Queen Anne Craftsman built by Geyserville pioneer George Bosworth. A stay at either comes with heated pool and full country breakfast. Most rooms are $150–200, though some are as low as $124. Inquire about specials

Geyserville's excellent **Santi** restaurant, at the original site of Catelli's the Rex, 21047 Geyserville Ave., 707/857-1790, is a stylish California version of a tavern in the Italian countryside, from the authentic pastas to Open for lunch Thurs.–Sat, dinner Tues.–Sun. nights. Nearby, the **Hoffman House Wine Country Deli,** 21712 Geyserville Ave., 707/857-3264, serves deli sandwiches, soups, and salads. For slow-cooked ribs, try the **Geyserville Smokehouse,** in a onetime general store at 21021 Geyserville Ave., 707/857-4600, open for lunch and dinner daily.

For more information about Geyserville and vicinity, contact the **Geyserville Chamber of Commerce,** 21060 Geyserville Ave., 707/857-3745, www.geyservillecc.com.

Lake Sonoma

A mammoth recreation area created by the U.S. Army Corps of Engineers, Lake Sonoma offers swimming, fishing, boating, camping, and 40 miles of hiking and horseback trails over the wooded grasslands. Wildlife bounds; particularly notable are peregrine falcons. Lake Sonoma's

construction was controversial; the flooding of popular hot springs, sacred Native American sites, and rugged scenic valleys led to court battles and public protests in the 1970s. But Sonoma County voters really wanted a lake, and approved the construction of Warm Springs Dam in two separate elections. Near the dam are a fish hatchery and a visitor center/museum emphasizing Native American culture, the area's early history, and natural history.

For secluded camping, hike, ride, or boat in to primitive lakeside campgrounds equipped with tables and portable restrooms ($10). Or car camp at first-come, first-camped **Liberty Glen** developed campsites (both individual and group), which offer flush toilets and hot showers ($16). Various other "primitive" campgrounds are near the lake. All campsites are available only by reservation. Reserve five days or more in advance through the National Recreation Reservation Service, 877/444-6777, www.reserveusa.com. For more lake information, contact: **Lake Sonoma Recreation Area,** 3333 Skaggs Springs Rd. in Geyserville, 707/433-9483. For boating conditions and information, contact: **Lake Sonoma Resort and Marina,** 100 Marina Dr., 707/433-2200.

CLOVERDALE

Surrounded by oak-dotted foothills and usually free of summer's chilly coastal fog, Cloverdale was once an infamous traffic bottleneck on Hwy. 101, where local police made a killing on speeders trying to zip through town. But now the freeway has been rerouted to the east, and travelers on 101 can bypass Cloverdale altogether. Tourist revenues may or may not be down as a result, but the townfolk can once again hear birds sing. And Cloverdale is sprucing up its downtown, so much more to look at without all the big-rig traffic. On the north side of town begins back roads Hwy. 128, a winding route that wends through the **Anderson Valley** on the way to the Mendocino coast.

Seeing and Doing Cloverdale

Cloverdale's name fit better a century ago, when it was a stagestop and the landscape was still thick with redwood forests, carpeted with cloverlike trillium. The area then became orange-growing country, but vineyards are fast becoming the rage. The town's older residential streets are wide, shaded by maples and fragrant eucalyptus. The town hosts its annual **Citrus Fair** in February, an event started in 1893. The new **North Coast Wine & Visitor Center** at the Cloverdale Chamber of Commerce, 105 N. Cloverdale Blvd., 707/894-9060, is the place to stop for visitor information. The **Gould-Shaw House Museum,** 215 N. Cloverdale Blvd., 707/894-2067, www.cloverdalehistoricalsociety.org, is a worthwhile stop. Housed in the old brick Isaac E. Shaw home, the museum is loaded with local historical bric-a-brac, with one room displayed as an old California general store (free, but donations are appreciated).

Winter white-water rafting, canoeing, and kayaking are particularly good on the Russian River north of Cloverdale. Near the convergence of Pieta Creek, **Squaw Rock** looms overhead, old bedrock from the sea now designated as a historic landmark. As the story goes, a jilted Native American woman grabbed a large rock and jumped from here onto her lover with his new woman below, crushing them like grapes.

Practicalities

There are some decent, fairly inexpensive motels in town. The national historic landmark is the **Vintage Towers Inn,** 302 N. Main St., 707/894-4535 or 888/886-9377, www.vintagetowers.com, now a bed-and-breakfast. Some suites have "towers," and all rooms have private baths and air-conditioning. Rates include full gourmet breakfast. Sonoma airport pickup available. Tower rooms are $150–200, others are $100–150. The **Shelford House,** 29955 River Rd., 707/894-5956 or 800/833-6479, www.shelford.com, is a country Victorian circa 1885. Altogether there are seven rooms (private baths) that come with full breakfast, hot tub, deck, pool, and loaner bikes. Floral rooms in the Victorian are $100–150; in the carriage house, $150–250.

The 1940s-vintage **Owl Cafe,** 485 S. Cloverdale Blvd., 707/894-8967, is the place for road-food standards—huge breakfasts, homemade soup, good bread, fish and chips, chicken and steak,

prime rib and potatoes. Open 7 A.M.–8:30 or 9:30 P.M. daily. And everyone loves the **World Famous Hamburger Ranch and Pasta Farm,** up on the hill north of downtown at 31195 N. Redwood Hwy., 707/894-5616, for more than half a century just about the best in Sonoma County for all-American burgers and fries. Fresh pastas and blues, too, not to mention brews from the Anderson Valley Brewing Company. Open daily for breakfast, lunch, and dinner.

HOPLAND

If you continue north on Hwy. 101 instead of heading out to the coast, you'll soon come to tiny Hopland. Named for the brewery hops once raised throughout the area—a trend stopped in its tracks by plant disease—Hopland returned to tradition in the 1980s by opening the first brew-pub in California since Prohibition. The **Hopland Brewery,** 13351 Hwy. 101 S., 707/744-1015 or 707/744-1361, www.mendobrew.com, was once the Hop Vine Saloon. The Hopland brewery taproom is owned and operated by the Mendocino Brewing Company, maker of (among others) Red Tail Ale—one of the state's original microbrews and still among the best. Though the main brewery facility is now in Ukiah, this one features a Beer Garden out back, a big patio draped with trellised hops and furnished with long tables—a super place to spend some time in the sun, enjoying good brew. The restaurant here closed in October 2003—goodbye, Red Tail Chili!—but you can still sit down for a meal here, ordering from the menus of nearby establishments only too happy to rush it right over. The taproom and gift shop are open Thurs.–Mon. 11 A.M.–8 P.M.

Otherwise, this four-block-long Mendocino County town celebrates the grape, a truth reflected in all the wine shops front and center here—from **Brutocao Cellars** at the onetime Hopland High School, 13500 Hwy. 101 S., 707/744-166, complete with regulation-size bocce ball courts (there's another tasting room in Philo) and the onsite **Crushed Grape Restaurant,** to **Domaine St. Gregory, Jepson** wine and brandies, and **McDowell Wine & Mercantile.** The **Wine Reserve** specializes in personalized wine selection. Then there's **Zemolini's Wine & Coffee Bar,** 13420 Hwy. 101 S., 707/744-9463, which also serves live music. Definitely a Hopland classic, the **Blue-bird Café,** 13340 Hwy. 101 S, 707/744-1633, still boasts its original fixtures, sign, and exterior clock. The appealing 1890 **Hopland Inn** (previously the Thatcher Inn) in town at 13401 Hwy. 101 S., 707/744-1890 or 800/266-1891, www .hoplandinn.com, is a striking and fully restored 23-room Victorian bed-and-breakfast. Rooms feature shockingly high ceilings, period details, private bath, and little luxuries including hair dryers and ironing boards. Direct dial phones and air-conditioning, too. Full breakfast, nice on-site restaurant. A pool, garden patio, and library round out the amenities. Rates are $100–150. A pleasant overnight alternative is the **Bed and Breakfast at Valley Oaks** at nearby Fetzer Vineyards (see below).

Beyond the surrounding vineyards, pastures, and rolling hills, Hopland's attractions include the **Real Goods Solar Living Center,** just south of town at 13771 Hwy. 101 S, 707/744-2017, www.solarliving.org, is a 12-acre offshoot of **Gaiam Real Goods,** www.realgoods.com. Started as a service primarily for off-the-gridders, the center has grown exponentially. At this big new center (built of straw bales) see the latest in solar technologies and wind- and water-powered generators; study an impressive array of environmentally friendly products; consider the possibilities of biodiesel; wander the grounds, past ponds and fountains and "living shade structures"; meander through the gardens; or just hang out and picnic. Real Goods is a theme park for alternative energy and sustainable living, classroom as much as sales outlet. An impressive roster of workshops and events also offered. Open daily except Thanksgiving and Christmas, free. Tours ($1) are offered Fri.–Sun. at 11 A.M. and 3 P.M.

Wineries

Hopland's hop fields have been replaced with vineyards. The **Fetzer Vineyards** Food & Wine Center at Valley Oaks, 13601 Eastside Rd. (three-quarters of a mile east of Hopland off Hwy. 175), 707/744-1250 or 800/846-8637, www.fetzer .com, is open daily 9 A.M.–5 P.M. The complex offers wine tastings, vineyard tours, a "wine library" offering select tastings and sales of wines available nowhere else, a café/deli, picnic grounds by the lake, and a five-acre, wheelchair-accessible organic garden (actually seven "theme" gardens in one). In summer delightful garden and vineyard tours are offered Fri.–Sun. at 9:30 A.M. and 11:30 A.M. and 1:30 P.M.; the schedule varies otherwise, so call for current information. Also here is the very nice **Fetzer Inn at Valley Oaks Ranch,** 707/744-7600 or 800/846-8637, a 10-room B&B. High-season rates start at $140. In addition to its high-end premium wines, Fetzger also produces Emeril wines. Fetzer also produces organic wines—try the North Coast Cabernet Sauvignon—and by 2010 all the vineyards here will be certified organic.

Other wineries near Hopland include **McDowell Valley Vineyards,** on Hwy. 175 (between Old Toll and Ukiah Boonville Roads) is one of the "Rhône Rangers," wineries specializing in California-grown Rhône varietals, including syrah, grenache, viognier, marsanne, and roussanne. McDowell Valley's syrahs are consistently rated "best buys" by *Wine Spectator* magazine. The 2001 **Seabiscuit Syrah** was a recent hit. To taste and buy, head for the tasting room in Hopland (see above). The **Milano Winery,** where the tasting room is at home in an old hop kiln at 14594 Hwy. 101 S (near Mountain House Rd.), 707/744-1396, www.milanowinery.com, specializes in cabernet sauvignon and dessert wines; new are carignan, port, late harvest zinfandel, syrah, and cabernet-syrah. A big hit during California's 2003 recall madness was Milano's **Recall Red** table wine, with the amusing "no clowns" label—carefully politically correct, suitable for donkeys as well as elephants. (At last report there was also a recall white.) Open daily for tasting, for tours only by appointment. **Duncan Peak Vineyards,** 14500 Mountain House Rd., 925/283-3632, www.duncanpeak.com, makes just one wine—a lovely cabernet sauvignon, of which only 500 cases are produced each year. Tasting and tours only by appointment. **McNab Ridge Winery,** between Hopland and Ukiah at 2350 McNab Ranch Rd., 707/462-2423, www.mc-nabridge.com, brought to you by the enterprising

Parducci winemaking family (no longer associated with Parducci Winery), offers cabernet, merlot, petite sirah, a nice meritage, even a "mendotage" and "pinotage." Tasting by appointment only.

For more information on regional wineries and suggested winery and driving tours, contact: **Mendocino Wineries Alliance,** 707/468-9886, www.mendowine.com. Major area wine events include the annual June **Mendocino Wine Affair,** with food and wine pairings, cooking demonstrations, and wine auctions, and the twice-yearly **Hopland Passport** winemaker tour.

Anderson Valley and Ukiah

Traveling northwestward from Cloverdale into the Anderson Valley via Hwy. 128 is an enjoyable if slow and snaking roadtrip. Between Cloverdale and Boonville, Mailliard Redwoods (named for conservationist John Ward Mailliard) is a serene spot for a picnic and a hike, with 242 acres of old- and second-growth redwoods and the headwaters of the Garcia River (no fishing). To get here, about 17 miles northwest of Cloverdale head west on Fish Rock Rd. from Hwy. 128 and continue for 3.5 miles. The gravel road continues all the way to Hwy. 1 near Anchor Bay. For more reserve information, call 707/937-5804.

BOONVILLE

Some places have profound personality yet go to some lengths to disguise that fact from passersby. One of these places is Boonville, de facto capital of Anderson Valley. Among other things, this insular but culturally engaged community long ago created its own language. People in this individualistic coastal valley also have a tendency to choose up sides and turn against each other from time to time—a trend established during the Civil War when the northern part of the valley allied itself with the Union cause and the south went Confederate.

Fascinating, almost frightening, in the tiny Anderson Valley is the opportunity to see what outside capital and the winemaking boom can do—and have done elsewhere, both more and less noticeably—to usurp earlier notions of community. Though change is constant, especially in California, in many ways the Anderson Valley offers a look at the relationship between colonizers and the colonized. Now that urban refugees and retirees threaten to supplant the winemaking

community, one wonders if California will ever stop consuming itself.

Still, some traditions hold steady. Among the best here is Boonville's annual mid-September **Mendocino County Fair and Apple Show,** 707/895-3011, www.mendocountyfair.com, one of the last completely noncommercial, family-oriented county fairs in America and an incredibly good time. Attractions include Anderson Valley apples and other local produce; home canning, knitting, and quilting competitions; 4-H and FFA livestock; a sheep dog trial and team penning; live bluegrass and BJ's Puppet Truck; and (at least in some years) the All Alaskan Racing Pigs. On a Sunday in mid-July, there's an equally traditional **Woolgrower's Barbecue and Sheep Dog Trials** at the fairgrounds. For a look at still more tangible artifacts of the Anderson Valley's fast-fading traditions, stop by the free **Anderson Valley Historical Museum,** 12430 Hwy. 128, in the one-room schoolhouse just northwest of Boonville, 707/895-3207. Open Fri.–Sun. 11 A.M.–4 P.M. in summer, 1–4 P.M. in winter, or whenever the American flags are flying.

For more information on the Anderson Valley area contact the **Anderson Valley Chamber of Commerce,** 707/895-2379, www.andersonvalleychamber.com, and the **Mendocino County Alliance,** 866/466-3636, www.gomendo.com.

Anderson Valley Advertiser

One of the most fascinating things about this area is its newspaper, the *Anderson Valley Advertiser.* Despite the tame name, it's not at all what people expect in such a place. Instead of one of those smarmy small-town shoppers filled with good news and happy talk, this paper is well written and wild, dedicated to "fanning the

WINE COUNTRY

BOONTLING: A SLIB OF LOREY

Until recently, the friendly people here in Boonville regularly spoke Boontling, a creative local dialect combining English, Scottish-Irish, Spanish, French, Pomo, and spontaneous, often hilarious words with strictly local significance. This private community language, locals say, was originally created by people now in their "codgiehood" (old-timers) to "shark the bright lighters" (confuse outsiders) and befuddle children—a word game started by men toiling for endless hours in the hop fields. Outsiders still get confused. Local kids learn some of the lingo in school, but at last report, the number of locals fluent in Boontling—all well into their codgiehood—was down to three.

Bright lighters, by the way, are people from the city. A *walter levy* is a telephone, because Walter was the first person in town to have one. A more modern variation, *buckey walter* (pay phone), refers to the old-time nickel phone call and the Indian head, or "buck," on the nickel's face. There's a buckey walter, so labeled, right outside the Horn of Zeese (coffee) café in town. Another sign in downtown Boonville—and a sign of the times, over a realtor's office—is a facsimile of a clock with the phrase *A teem ta hig, a teem ta shay,* meaning: "A time to buy, a time to sell."

A *featherleg,* in Boontling, is a cocky, arrogant person (because everyone knows banty roosters have feathers down their legs). *Shovel tooth* means "doctor," because the valley's physician had buck teeth. A *jeffer* is a big fire, since old Jeff built a huge fireplace into his house. A *madge* is a house of ill-repute (in honor of Madge, who ran one of the best in Ukiah).

Burlappin' is a very active sexual verb (there are others in Boontling) referring to the time a shop clerk was caught in the act atop a pile of burlap sacks in the storeroom. *Skrage* means "to make love." *Charlie-ball* is a verb meaning "to embarrass," a direct reference to a local Pomo who was easily embarrassed.

But the ongoing creativity behind Boontling's evolution (and the community's insularity) started to get confused after World War I, with the coming of roads, telephones, and other inroads of civilization. To pick up whatever is left of the language, tutor yourself with the animated, sometimes outrageous, and impeccably written *Anderson Valley Advertiser* or the local language dictionary, *A Slib of Lorey.* The Anderson Valley Brewing Company, now headquartered just south of Boonville, also offers a decent primer and Boontling literacy test on its website.

---

flames of discontent." Notorious *AVA* editor and publisher Bruce Anderson is California's chief outlaw journalist, in the tradition of Mark Twain and Ambrose Bierce, raging without restraint at the world within his vision. To subscribe, contact: *Anderson Valley Advertiser,* 12451 Anderson Valley Way, Boonville, CA 95415, 707/895-3016, www.theava.com.

PARKS

Just outside Philo, 845-acre **Hendy Woods State Park** includes two virgin groves of enormous redwoods: 80-acre Big Hendy Grove, with a nature trail, and smaller Little Hendy Grove. There's a fallen redwood stump here that was once home to a man known to locals as the Hendy Woods Hermit. Besides redwoods, you'll find Douglas fir,

California bay, and wildflowers. The Navarro River is a peaceful stream in summer—poor for swimming, though wading is a possibility, good for kayaking and canoeing—and a raging torrent in winter. Most of the park is on the valley floor. Good camping is available at either **Azalea** or **Wildcat Campgrounds.** Reserve one of the 92 campsites ($11–14) through ReserveAmerica, 800/444-7275, www.reserveamerica.com. Day-use fee (picnicking, hiking) is $4. The park is eight miles northwest of Boonville, on Philo-Greenwood Road a half-mile south of Hwy. 128. For more information about Hendy Woods, call 707/895-3141 or 707/937-5804.

On the way to the Mendocino coast via Hwy. 128, beyond the vineyards and the apple orchards travelers are suddenly back in the redwoods. **Navarro Redwoods State Park** creates a magnificent 11-mile corridor of second-growth redwoods. In late winter and spring, canoeing, kayaking, and fishing are main attractions, in summer, swimming and picnicking. Camp at **Paul M. Dimmick Campground** (first-come, first-camped), six miles east of the Hwy. 1 junction, or at **Navarro Beach Campground** on the Pacific Ocean, at the mouth of the Navarro River; the access road is located on the south side of the Navarro River Bridge. For more park information, call 707/895-3141 or 707/937-5804.

In addition, there are two county parks in the valley. **Indian Creek County Park,** one mile east of Philo, five miles northwest of Boonville on the highway, is a pleasant place for picnicking or a short walk (the entrance is obscure, just south of Indian Creek Bridge). It's also a well-kept secret for camping, with a handful of sites (most along the creek).Even more remote is **Faulkner County Park,** two miles west of Boonville via snakelike Mountain View Road, which also offers a few tent sites. For more information, call Mendocino County Parks in Ukiah at 707/463-4267.

APPLE FARMS

For apples and other fresh local produce, if at all possible first see what's available at the **Boonville Certified Farmers Market,** held May–Oct. on Saturday, 10 A.M.–noon, in the parking lot at the Boonville Hotel. For information, call 707/964-6340. If you miss the market, find fresh local produce at the **Boont Berry Farm Store** (see Eating in Anderson Valley below). Popular for apples, peaches, pears, cherries, berries, and other local produce in season is the family-run **Gowan's Oak Tree** roadside produce stand 2.5 miles north of Philo at 6350 Hwy. 128, 707/895-3353. The **Bates & Schmitt Apple Farm** at 18501 Greenwood Rd. in Philo, 707/895-2461 or 707/895-2333, grows some 60 types of apples, longtime favorites as well as heirloom varieties, including Ashmead's Kernel, English Russett, Cox Orange Pippin, King of Tompkins County, Pink Pearl, Splendour, and Swaar. The family enterprise, no longer associated with the famed French Laundry restaurant in the Napa Valley, also produce jams, jellies, and

chutney (such as Prune, Plum, Onion & Mustard Seed) as well as juices and ciders.

WINERIES

Grapes have officially overtaken timber as Mendocino County's leading agricultural product, though many Mendocino County residents contend that marijuana is still the area's top cash crop—by far. It's impossible to make an accurate economic comparison, of course, since one crop is legal and the other still not. The Anderson Valley, ideal for pinot noir, riesling, gewürztraminer and other Northern European-style varietals, demonstrates how quickly vineyards and wineries can take root and dominate regional agriculture. Ongoing water wars (vineyards require much more water than sheep grazing) and related environmental concerns may slow the conversion to vineyards and wineries. Given the rates that escapees from the Bay Area are settling in the area, ridgetop vanity mansions may supplant them both.

Pacific Echo Cellars, 8501 Hwy. 128, 800/824-7754, was previously Scharffenberger Cellars, but John Scharffenberger moved on to make wine in Ukiah and gourmet chocolates in South San Francisco. The Echo still produces sparkling wines in the *méthode champenoise,* including brut, brut rosé, blanc de blancs, and crémant. Open daily 11 A.M.–5 P.M. If you missed **Brutocao Cellars** in Hopland you can try again at 7000 Hwy. 128, 707/895-2152, www.brutocaocellars.com.

The tasting room for **Navarro Vineyards,** 5601 Hwy. 128 near Philo, 707/895-3686 or 800/537-9463, www.navarrowine.com, is open daily 10 A.M.–5 P.M. (until 6 P.M. in summer). Navarro produces an excellent estate-bottled gewürztraminer, as well as chardonnay, pinot noir, and an *edelzwicker* table wine. Non-alcoholic grape juice, too. Picnic facilities are available outside the striking redwood tasting room. Remote **Greenwood Ridge Vineyards and Winery** on the ridge between Philo and Elk has been designated by *Wine & Spirits* magazine as one of the top 30 wineries in the U.S.—several times. The winery offers a more accessible tasting room at 5501 Hwy. 128 in Philo,

707/895-2002, www.greenwoodridge.com, open daily 10 A.M.–6 P.M. in summer, until 5 P.M. otherwise. Greenwood Ridge is home to the annual **California Wine Tasting Championships,** along with chocolate and cheese tasting championships and winery tours, an event held on the last weekend in July. Otherwise winery tours are offered only by appointment.

At **Edmeades Estate Winery Tasting Room,** 5500 Hwy. 128, 707/895-3009, now owned by Kendall-Jackson, wines are made with all native yeasts, including chardonnay, an outstanding gewürztraminer, zinfandel, and pinot noir. **Lazy Creek Vineyards,** 4741 Hwy. 128, 707/895-3623, www.lazycreekvineyards.com, offers only three wines, at last report, but they're very good ones. Tastings are offered by appointment, but you can drop in when the gate's open.

Roederer Estate wines, 4501 Hwy. 128, 707/895-2288, www.roedererestate.net, is the biggest winery operation in the area, owned by one of the top champagne producers in France. The three estate-grown champagne wines produced here—brut, brut rosé, and a cuvée—have often beaten the French competition. Open for tasting ($3 fee) and sales daily 11 A.M.–5 P.M. (tours by appointment only).

The oldest continuing winemaking establishment (here since 1971) and perhaps most famous is **Husch Vineyards Winery,** 4400 Hwy. 128, 800/554-8724, www.huschvineyards.com, open daily 10 A.M.–5 P.M. In its "unadorned rustic" tasting room, sample what the fine varietal wines Husch produces from its estate-grown grapes. Husch's 1983 estate-bottled gewürztraminer was one of several California wines taken to China in 1984 by President Reagan and served in Beijing at a state dinner honoring Zhao Ziyang. Of the 14 Husch varietals, only six are distributed nationally and a number are available only here.

Don't miss **Handley Cellars Winery,** 3151 Hwy. 128, 707/895-3876 or 800/733-3151, www.handleycellars.com; open daily 11 A.M.–6 P.M. in summer, until 5 P.M. in winter. Winemaker Milla Handley is the great-great-granddaughter of Henry Weinhard, mythic American beermeister. The winery displays wonderfully eclectic artifacts and folk art. Come on the first weekend of every month for Handley's "Culinary Adventures" program, which pairs Handley wine with a particular Asian, African, or New World cuisine. While you're in the neighborhood, stop at small **Christine Woods Vineyards,** next door at 3155 Hwy. 128, 707/895-2115, www.christinewoods.com, also open daily 11 A.M.–6 P.M., the only valley winery to make all of its wines from estate-grown grapes.

For more information about area wineries, contact **Anderson Valley Winegrowers Association,** 707/895-9463, www.avwines.com.

ANDERSON VALLEY BREWING COMPANY

Twice ranked among the world's top 10 breweries, the Anderson Valley Brewing Company started out in the basement of the Buckhorn Saloon. With its large new facility and growing prestige, these days AVBC is also a bastion of local cultural tradition—if the commercial use of boontling, the imaginative Anderson Valley lingo developed here in more isolated times, qualifies as cultural preservation. Stop by and sample **Hop Ottin' IPA** and **Poleeko Gold Pale Ale,** or maybe **Deep Enders Dark** porter. Tours of Anderson Valley Brewing Company, just south of Boonville at 17700 Hwy. 253 (Ukiah-Boonville Rd.), 707/895-2337 or 800/207-2337, www.avbc.com, are offered daily (except holidays) at 1:30 and 4 P.M. (Dig those big black shires.) Come to the fairgrounds in April for the **Legendary Boonville Beer Festival.**

STAYING IN THE ANDERSON VALLEY

Camp at Hendy Redwoods or Navarro River Redwoods or local county parks mentioned above (Parks Northwest of Boonville), or at Manchester State Beach or other nearby coastal campgrounds (see The North Coast chapter).

Always quite special is a stay at very hip **Boonville Hotel,** on Hwy. 128 in "downtown" Boonville (at Lambert), 707/895-2210, www.boonvillehotel.com. The hotel offers six rooms and two suites upstairs—furnished with simple

© KIM WEIR

the Boonville Hotel

handmade furniture crafted by local artisans—
and two pricier and private creekside cottages,
both wheelchair accessible and "child and pet
friendly." No phones or TVs. Continental breakfast. Rates are $100–250. The outstanding restau-
rant here (full bar too) is open every day but
Tuesday most of the year, making it that much
harder to think about leaving. The Boonville Hotel
is usually closed the first two weeks in January.

Do you and Fido really need to get away from
it all? Then 320-acre **Sheep Dung Estates** in
Yorkville, 707/894-5322, www.sheepdung.com,
is just the place—five solar-powered studio cabins
(one has its own guest cottage), most situated at
the end of its own private drive. There are few
electrical gadgets or other distractions but endless
views—and a pond! Kids are welcome, too, so
there's plenty of room for the entire family to
roam. Each cabin has a queen-sized bed, small
kitchen, shower and/or bathtub, covered porch,
wood-burning stove, and Weber grill. In the summer, stretch out in the hammock. Rates are
$100–200 per night, with a two- or three-night
minimum. Three more dog- and kid-friendly
cabins are available at 550-acre **The Other Place,**
$175–300, along with **Haiku House** at 800-acre
Long Valley Ranch, $175–400.

Highland Ranch off Philo Greenwood Road,
707/895-3600 www.highlandranch.com, offers
eight charming cabins with wood-burning fireplace, redwood deck, rocking chairs, and no TV,
though there are plenty of good books to read.
Rates include lodging and marvelous meals (and
beverages, including Anderson Valley Wines)
served in the big ranchhouse kitchen. Also included are horseback riding, hiking, mountain
biking, skeet shooting, fishing, swimming, and
other fun. Immensely popular, especially in summer, so reserve well in advance. At last report
the tariff was $285 per day adults, $190 per day
child (under age 12) but check the website for
current rates.

There aren't any potters anymore at the **Philo
Pottery Inn,** 8550 Hwy. 128, 707/895-3069,
www.philopotteryinn.com, but the 1888-vin-
tage farmhouse (once a Wells Fargo stage stop) is
"country" without too many frills. There are four
guest rooms (the two upstairs share a bath) and a
private cottage. Full country breakfast, complimentary wine, homemade goodies. Stroll in
nearby Hendy Woods, quite spectacular. Rates are
$100–200 (lower in winter).

EATING IN THE ANDERSON VALLEY

Even if local produce pickin's are abundant (see
Anderson Valley Apples above), don't miss the
Boont Berry Farm Store in Boonville, 13981
Hwy. 128, 707/895-3576, an amazing, sophisticated market. The casual, crowded-aisle general
store atmosphere can't disguise the thoughtful
choices behind the selections of local and organic
produce and other products, including an excellent variety of regional wines. The full deli here has
learn-to-speak-Boontling coffee mugs on the
counter. Try the chicken and avocado sandwich.

The **Boonville Hotel,** on Hwy. 128 in the
center of Boonville, 707/895-2210, serves simple,
superb, and reasonably priced meals. At dinners,
expect California-style interpretations—such
things as roast pork loin with red chile sauce,
chicken breast with salsa fresca, and pizzas with
local goat cheese. Much of the fresh produce
served here is from the hotel's own two-acre organic garden. The restaurant is open Wed.–Sun.
for lunch and dinner (call ahead for current
schedule). Reservations are advised at dinner.
Usually closed the first two weeks in January.

Across the street is Boonville's relaxed **Buckhorn Saloon,** 14081 Hwy. 128, 707/895-3368,
open daily for lunch and dinner, and popular
with locals because it's been here forever. The

original Buckhorn stood here from 1873 to the 1960s, pouring forth beer and good cheer. When it was rebuilt in 1987, it was to serve as a brewpub—and the new home of the Boonville Beer, also known as the Anderson Valley Brewing Company. The brewsters have moved on—AVBC is now situated at the junction of Hwys. 128 and 253, just south of downtown—but you can still enjoy Boonville's own famous beers here, along with Red Seal, Sierra Nevada Pale Ale, and other brews on tap. Or try some local wines. Open for lunch and dinner daily, from 11 A.M., often closed Tues.–Wed. in winter. Relatively new in Philo, for good, authentic, and reasonably priced Mexican, is **Libby's,** 8651 Hwy. 128, 707/895-2646, where Janie's Place used to be. Open Tues.–Fri. for lunch and dinner, on weekends for breakfast too.

UKIAH

Back on Hwy. 101, Ukiah is a sprawling old lumber town in the center of the inland Yokayo Valley. This rowdy and rough-edged place is populated by just plain folks: rednecks, redwood loggers, even redwood-loving tree huggers. The most interesting thing about Ukiah is its name: "haiku" spelled backward, but derived from the Pomo word Yu Haia, meaning either "south" or "deep." The town isn't particularly backward. Come in late June for the annual **Taste of Downtown,** early July for the **All American Fourth of July,** the second weekend in August for the **Redwood Empire Fair,** and September for the **Fabulous Flashback Car Show.** Truly unusual is the yule season **Truckers Light Parade** in December, when big rigs all decked out with Christmas lights parade through town after dark.

In summer, a side trip to the farm country of **Potter Valley**—where the headwaters of the Eel River's middle fork and the Russian's east fork trickle forth—is worth it, as much for the fresh produce as the pastoral scenery. Head up East Side Road toward "downtown" Potter Valley and stop at roadside produce stands for fresh corn, berries, melons, and other fruits and vegetables. There's a heck of a farm-town **Spring Festival** there over Memorial Day weekend, with still more good food. Wherever or whatever you eat,

try some local wines or a bottle of locally famous Mendocino Mineral Water—the "living waters" popular with Pomo natives—bottled over the hills to the west in Comptche. Mendocino Mineral Water is said to be salt-free but four times richer in dissolved minerals than other well-known waters, including Calistoga and Perrier. Another local choice: Vichy Springs Mineral Water. For more information about the area, contact the **Greater Ukiah Chamber of Commerce** is at 200 S. School St., 707/462-4705, www.ukiahchamber.com.

Seeing and Doing Ukiah and Vicinity

Moore's Flour Mill & Bakery, also a deli at 1550 S. State St., 707/462-6550, still uses century-old waterwheel-powered grindstones (tours available). Local history is otherwise collected at the **Held-Poage Memorial Home and Research Library** at Perkins and Dora Streets, 707/462-6969, and at the amazing **Grace Hudson Museum and Sun House,** 431 S. Main St,. 707/467-2836. For more about the Grace Hudson legacy, see Sun House and Grace Hudson. The **Pomo Cultural Center,** 707/485-8285, on a bluff overlooking **Lake Mendocino** resembles an Indian roundhouse and offers natural history exhibits, audio and video histories of the Pomo Indians, and an indoor-outdoor amphitheater for campfire ceremonies, tribal dances and other demonstrations.

Fourteen miles northwest of Ukiah on Orr Springs Rd. is ecologically rare and significant **Montgomery Woods State Reserve,** more than 1,100 acres of undeveloped redwoods on Big River and Montgomery Creek. The walk-in park features trails, trees, and marvelous seven-foot-tall woodwardia ferns. There's privacy too—a long, winding road keeps most people away—which is probably a good thing, since this is also the home of the world's tallest tree, the Mendocino Tree, one redwood among many here topping 350 feet. The Mendocino Tree is *not* identified, for its own safety. You'll have to guess. For other park information, call 707/937-5804.

Hot Springs and Mineral Baths

Secluded **Orr Hot Springs Resort,** 13201 Orr Springs Rd., 707/462-6277, historically acces-

GRACE AND JOHN HUDSON'S SUN HOUSE

Sometimes the most amazing people and things turn up in the most unlikely places. Unconventional Grace Carpenter Hudson and her physician-turned-ethnologist husband John lived in Ukiah in a modest custom redwood home they affectionately called Sun House. She was nationally recognized for her striking, sensitive paintings of Pomo Indians; he was a scholar and collector of Native Americana. Their former home is now part of the city of Ukiah's extraordinary museum complex honoring the contributions of both.

The large **Grace Hudson Museum** and gallery at 431 S. Main St., 707/467-2836, www.gracehudsonmuseum.org, has gotten considerably larger with completion of the new, 2,400-square-foot Ivan B. and Elvira Hart addition. The museum exhibits an impressive collection of Grace Hudson's paintings and John Hudson's artifacts, although only selected works—including some fine and rare examples of intricate and delicate Pomo basketry, essentially a lost art—are on display at any one time. Exhibitions change frequently, and occasionally an extensive show of items from the collection is shown. In addition to the museum's permanent collection, special exhibits of local artists are also featured.

It is astounding that Ukiah hosts such a rare and valuable collection. But the quality of the museum itself is still more astonishing. Just being in the Grace Hudson Museum creates a powerful awareness of the cycle of birth and rebirth that speaks to the truth at the heart of this place. An impressive accomplishment.

Adjacent **Sun House** (note the Hopi sun symbol over the entrance) and the museum are open Wed.–Sat. 10 A.M.–4:30 P.M., Sun. noon–4:30 P.M. (closed on major holidays). Suggested donation: $2 per person, $5 families. Docent-led tours of Sun House are available Wed.–Sun. noon–3 P.M. on the hour.

---

sible only by stagecoach, is still remote. It's well worth staying once you arrive. Orr's is a "clothing optional" hot springs resort—but almost no one opts for clothes here. Facilities include a large redwood hot tub, four private hot tubs (Victorian porcelain), plus a tile-inlaid natural rock mineral pool (cool), steam room, dry sauna, large mineral water swimming pool, and massage room. Overnight accommodations are available in private rooms or cottages or a communal sleeping loft. Or you can tent camp or car camp. The day-use fee is $20 per person ($12 on Monday).

Now a state historical landmark, once host to last century's literary lions and U.S. presidents, the restored **Vichy Hot Springs Resort & Inn** mineral baths are at 2605 Vichy Springs Rd., 707/462-9515, www.vichysprings.com. The day-use fee ($35 per person) covers all-day use of the mineral baths, Olympic-sized swimming pool (summer only), hot pool, and hiking trails on the 700-acre property. If two hours in the baths will suffice, the tariff is just $23.) Full access to the facilities and full breakfast come with an overnight stay here, in either motel-style rooms or private cabins ($150 and up for two). Massage and facials are also available at this wonderful, low-key retreat.

Wineries

Near Ukiah are some fairly well-known Mendocino County wineries and some up-and-comers. **Parducci Wine Cellars,** 501 Parducci Rd. (a few miles north of town), 707/463-5357 or 888/362-9463, www.parducci.com, has been in business since 1931. Its modern-day emphasis is on producing good-value premium varietals from Mendocino County grapes. Open for tasting and picnicking daily 10 A.M.–5 P.M. (Sunday until 4 P.M.). Some say the hand-distilled brandy produced by the Franco-American partnership of Ansley Coale and Hubert **Germain-Robin** is the country's best, and a challenge to the finest French cognacs. The distillery is at 3001 S. State St. #35, 707/462-3221 or 800/782-8145, www.germain-robin.com, open Mon.–Fri. 9 A.M.–3 P.M. There are a number of up-and-coming small wineries north of Ukiah in Redwood Valley. For more information, contact **Mendocino Winegrowers Alliance,** 707/468-9886, www.mendowine.com.

Camping

Camp at nearby **Lake Mendocino,** created in 1958 when construction of Coyote Dam blocked the Russian River's east fork. The lake has 300-plus family campsites, four group camps, and plenty of picnicking. It's a popular spot for swimming, fishing, and water-skiing. Also here is a Pomo cultural center with an impressive basketry display. For information, contact: Lake Mendocino/Park Manager, 1160 Lake Mendocino Dr., 707/462-7581, or the visitor center on Marina Dr., 707/485-8285. For campsite reservations—at **Bushay Campground** ($18–20), **Chekaka Campground** ($10), or **Kyen Campground** ($18–20), also a day-use area—call 877/444-6777 or see www.reserveusa.com.

Another place to camp is **Cow Mountain,** some 60,000 acres of BLM land east of Ukiah, most easily reached by the north fork of Mill Creek Road off Hwy. 20 on the way to Lakeport. Chaparral at lower elevations gives way to oaks, pines, and firs. Cow Mountain roads are narrow and steep, so trailers or RVs are a no-go. But the camping is easy: four campgrounds with water and pit toilets, plus unimproved camping areas and free trailside camping. (The area is popular with hunters, so either stay away during deer season or wear day-glo orange.) Pick up a map-leaflet at the Ukiah **BLM** office, 2550 N. State St., 707/468-4000. For information on campgrounds in nearby areas of **Mendocino National Forest,** some managed by PG&E, contact the **Upper Lake Ranger Station** near Clear Lake, 10025 Elk Mountain Rd., 707/275-2361, or see www.fs.fed .us/r5/mendocino. In **Potter Valley,** a small PG&E campground flanks Trout Creek near the Eel River. From Hwy. 20, head north on Potter Valley Rd., turn onto Eel River Road, then continue to the bridge over the Eel. The campground is about two miles east of Van Arsdale Reservoir, run by the Army Corps of Engineers.

Practicalities

There are motels along S. State Street. More elegant is the Queen Anne **Sanford House,** 306 S. Pine, 707/462-1653, www.sanfordhouse.com, with five rooms (all with queen bed and private bath) in a 1904 Victorian with a loungeable front porch, colorful garden, koi pond, and full gourmet breakfast. Rates are $75–125 single, $250 double. Another possibility is the 700-acre **Vichy Hot Springs Resort & Inn** outside town at 2605 Vichy Springs Rd., 707/462-9515, www.vichy-springs.com, with three cottage rooms and 12 rooms in the main 1854 early California house. Amenities include a full breakfast, good hiking and mountain biking, and the resort's mineral baths, pool, and hot pool. Rates are $150–300.

Ukiah has two farmers markets, both held

A SAGELY CITY OF TEN THOUSAND BUDDHAS

The tiny Mendocino County town of Talmage has become a world center for Buddhist study. The Sagely City of Ten Thousand Buddhas put up its shingle at the onetime site of Mendocino State Hospital in the mid-1970s and has since settled in quite comfortably. The Tudor-style complex and well-landscaped grounds became seminary, monastery, and home for 250–500 Buddhist monks and nuns. Visitors are welcome to stop by and wander the grounds (visitor check-in just beyond the massive golden gate). There seem to be at least 10,000 golden Buddhas in the temple, which is open to visitors, as is the vegetarian restaurant (perfect for a very good lunch). The program of prayer, meditation, and low-key study—including the grade school and high school here—is now becoming more academic. New is the **Dharma Realm Buddhist University,** a fully accredited four-year liberal arts college dedicated to Buddhist behavior standards and practices. Also here are the **Developing Virtue Secondary School** and the **Instilling Goodness Elementary School.** With its purpose of offering Buddhist education in the West, the school is sponsored by the largely Asian, million-member Dharma Realm Buddhist Association. For more information, contact the Sagely City of Ten Thousand Buddhas, 707/462-0939, www.drba.org.

June–Oct.—the **Ukiah Certified Farmers Market** on Sat. 7:30 A.M.–1 P.M., at the Longs Plaza parking lot, Orchard and Perkins, and the **Ukiah Tuesday CFM,** 3–6 P.M., at School and Clay Streets. For information on either, call 707/964-6340. To get healthy food for the road otherwise, try **Ukiah Natural Foods,** 721 S. State St. (enter from Gobbi, across from Safeway), 707/462-4778.

For hot dogs, the place is **Ellie's Mutt Hut & Vegetarian Café,** 732 S. State St., 707/468-5376, where you can also get omelettes, tofu dinners, and fruit smoothies. Vegetarian quiche is just one possibility at **Schat's Courthouse Bakery** and café, across from the courthouse at 113 W. Perkins St., 707/462-1670, where lunch might keep you going for the rest of the day. Alkso next to the courthouse is the **Ukiah Brewing Co.,** 102 S. State St., 707/468-5898, the first-ever certified organic brewpub, serving both organic vegetarian and meateater fare—veggie burgers to fish and chips. Brews include Pilsner Ukiah, Yokayo Gold ale, and Coops Stout. Cheesecake lovers, don't miss Mendocino County's famous **Cheesecake Momma,** 200 Henry St., 707/462-2253, now a successful wholesale operation with a little shop inside the warehouse.

NORTH OF UKIAH

Continuing north from Ukiah on Hwy. 101, you'll cross Ridgewood Summit, the divide that effectively separates red wine from redwood. With the last of the vineyards behind you, you're on the road to the land of *Sequoia sempervirens,* or coast redwoods, tallest trees in the world. At Leggett, coastal Hwy. 1 reaches its end at a T junction with Hwy. 101. (See The North Coast chapter for coverage of Hwy. 1 and of Hwy. 101 north of Leggett.) Between Ukiah and Leggett—on the north side of Ridgewood Summit—are some worthwhile stops.

Willits: Seabiscuit's Stomping Grounds

Winsome little Willits is a friendly frontier town among the ranches and railroads of Little Lake Valley north of Ukiah, a slice of life whittled from the Old West. The famed bandit Black Bart used to love it here, according to local lore. In more recent history this was Seabiscuit country, where the hit 2003 feature film *Seabiscuit* (based on the best-selling book) had its world debut as a benefit for the Frank Howard Memorial Hospital. Howard Hospital was built by Charles Howard, Seabiscuit's owner, in honor of the young son tragically killed in an accident at the family's nearby Ridgewood Ranch. For more on the Seabiscuit story, see Seabiscuit Wins Again.

Willits is most itself during its popular **Frontier Days** celebration for July 4th, a week filled with a rodeo—the oldest continuous rodeo in California, they say—and horse show, parade, carnival, barbecue, breakfasts, dances, and whatever else people can think of. Besides the horse shows, rodeos, and other regular town hoedowns, the best thing about this place is the **Willits Station** train depot, 299 E. Commercial St., the eastern terminus of the old Union Lumber Company logging line and (until recently) also the California Western Railroad's Skunk Train from Fort Bragg. The station itself is a little dowdy these days, but it was—and is—an astounding architectural achievement, carefully crafted from clear heart redwood. The next best thing in Willits is the marvelous **Mendocino County Museum,** 400 E. Commercial St., 707/459-2736, www.co.mendocino.ca.us/museum, with its impressive collection of Pomo artifacts, handmade quilts, and hop industry and pioneer chronicles. Of late, Seabiscuit has been an impressive exhibit.; the Wreck of the *Frolic,* a Gold Rush–era Baltimore clipper ship that went down off the Mendocino coast, was another recent focus. A major ongoing museum project is the Redwood Empire Railroad History Project, which will include an educational complex adjacent to the museum. The county museum also sponsors local historical walking tours, as museum fundraisers; call for current information. The museum is open Wed.–Sun. 10 A.M.–4:30 P.M. Free, though donations would certainly be appreciated.

Traffic is all but choking Willits these days; but is the new four-lane bypass proposed by Caltrans a feasible solution? Many locals are wary of building an urban-size freeway here. In the meantime: Highway 101 on the south side of town is motel row, where you'll find a number of

SEABISCUIT WINS AGAIN

Superstars need to get away from their adoring public, a fact every bit as true in the 1930s as it is today. For Seabiscuit, the superstar racehorse whose story was recently retold in Laura Hillenbrand's best-selling book *Seabiscuit* and adapted for the silver screen, Charles Howard's 17,000 acre Ridgewood Ranch in Willits was the place to get away from it all. Seabiscuit retired to the ranch pemanently in 1940, following his final victory at the Santa Anita Handicap. When he won the $100,000 purse at Santa Anita, he broke the world moneymaking record for thoroughbred racing. Even after Seabiscuit retired, his fans made the pilgrimage to Willits to see him and pay their respects. When the horse died in 1947, he was buried at the ranch.

Ridgewood Ranch is considerably smaller these days, reduced to 5,000 acres, and is now owned by Christ's Church of the Golden Rule. But Seabiscuit fans keep coming. Private tours of the horse's retirement barn and the Howard family's Craftsman-style ranch house are hot tickets. And the return of Seabiscuit's fame may mean the preservation, in perpetuity, of the grand old racehorses's stomping grounds. The Mendocino Land Trust hopes to buy a conservation easement to protect the property from development, and provide public access.

For current information about touring Ridgewood Ranch and visiting Seabiscuit's home, contact the Willits Chamber of Commerce, 239 S. Main St., 707/459-7910, www.willits.org.

---

motels and fast-food restaurants. The **Willits Thursday Certified Farmers Market** is held May–Oct., 3–6 P.M., at the city park at State and Commercial Streets. Downtown, the restaurant of choice is the casual but current **Purple Thistle** restaurant, 50 S. Main St., 707/459-4750, friendly successor to Tsunami, which serves great organic fare, Cajun-style fresh fish and seafood, even Harris Ranch steaks. Good microbrews and fine wines are available. Open for lunch weekdays, for dinner nightly.

For more information about what's going on in and around Willits, contact the **Willits Chamber of Commerce,** 239 S. Main St., 707/459-7910, www.willits.org.

At Willits, Hwy. 20 takes off west from Hwy. 101 and slithers up and over the Coast Range (excellent panoramic views from the ridgetop turnout) to Fort Bragg, covered in The North Coast chapter.

West of Laytonville

Admiral William Standley State Recreation Area, halfway to the coast on Branscomb Rd., 14 miles west of Laytonville, is a small, 45-acre park along the south fork of the Eel, with an impressive stand of coastal redwoods. It's undeveloped and perfect for picnicking, hiking, and fishing for salmon and steelhead. The rough, unpaved road continues to the coast. For more information, call 707/247-3318.

Nearby, the 8,000-acre **Heath and Marjorie Angelo Coast Range Reserve,** a unit of the California Coast Ranges Biosphere Reserve, was established in 1959 on the south fork of the Eel River and is now managed by the University of California Natural Reserve System. The hilly and mountainous preserve includes pristine Douglas fir forests on the Elder Creek watershed, some California bay, oaks, knobcone pines, redwoods, and meadows with incredibly diverse wildflowers. River otters are plentiful. Day-use only, no camping or motor vehicles allowed—you park at the edge and walk in. For directions and maps, contact Angelo Preserve headquarters, 42101 Wilderness Rd. in Branscomb, 707/984-6653.

North Coast

Fog created California's north coast, and still defines it. Fog is everywhere, endless, eternal, *there*. Even on blazing, almost blinding days of sunshine when the veil lifts, the fog is still present somehow, because life here has been made by it. Stands of sky-scraping coast redwoods need fog to live. So do many other native north coast plants, uniquely adapted to uniformly damp conditions. The visual obscurity characteristic of the coast also benefits animals, providing a consistent, year-round supply of drinking water and, for creatures vulnerable to predators, additional protective cover.

Fog even seems to have political consequences. As elsewhere in the northstate, the secessionist spirit is alive and well on the north coast, but the fog makes it seem fuzzy, and the urge is taken less seriously here than it is elsewhere. When, in the mid-1970s, for example, some Mendocino County citizens banded together to form their own state (they called it Northern California), the response from Sacramento was off-the-cuff and casual: "The county's departure, if it ever goes, would scarcely be noticed, at least not until the fog lifted."

People often find fog disquieting, depressing. Some almost fear it. If only momentarily, in fog we become spatially and spiritually bewildered. Our vision seems vague; we hear things. We fall prey to illusions; we hallucinate: trees walk, rocks

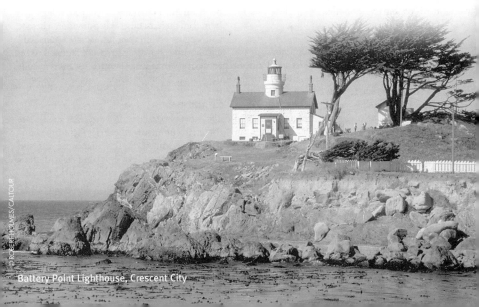

Battery Point Lighthouse, Crescent City

smile, birds talk, rivers laugh, the ocean sings, someone unseen brushes our cheek. All of a sudden, we don't know where we are and haven't the foggiest notion where we're going. Life as we know it has changed. We have changed.

Dense coastal fog occurs along this cool-weather coast, according to meteorologists, as a result of shoreward breezes carrying warm, moist oceanic air over colder offshore waters. The air's moisture condenses into fog, which rolls in over the coastal mountains in cloudlike waves. As the marine air moves inland and is warmed by the sun, it reabsorbs its own moisture and the fog dissipates.

But science doesn't really explain fog at all—not fog as change, as creator, as fashioner of fantastic forms, as shape-shifting summoner of strange sounds, or protector of the primeval purpose. Fog, in the mythic sense, is magic.

THE LAND

California's northern coastline has few sandy beaches, even fewer natural harbors. Land's end is rugged and inhospitable, with surging surf and treacherous undertows. Because of this—and because of zero-visibility coastal fog—shipwrecks are part of the region's lore. Bits and pieces of hundreds of ships have washed up on these unsympathetic shores.

Offshore west of Eureka, some 4,000 feet below the surface, is a formation known as the Mendocino Ridge. In 1994, researchers from Oregon State University discovered 100 miles of extensive beach deposits near the now-sunken ridge, which itself is a feature of the Mendocino Fault Zone. (The meeting here of the Pacific and Gorda tectonic plates with the North American continent creates the Mendocino Triple Junction—one of the most active earthquake zones in the world.) These scientists now speculate that when the ridge was young, some three to five million years ago, it had risen as a 200-mile-long east-west "fold" of islands offshore from what is now San Francisco. These islands profoundly changed the regions' climate—deflecting the cool California Current to the west, and allowing warm, subtropical waters from Mexico to surge north along the coast—before receding. This,

researchers say, would explain evidence that California's coastal climate was once quite warm—a trend that ended rather abruptly about three million years ago.

The region's major features on land are the Coast Ranges, consecutive ridges angling north to Eureka, where they meet up with the westward edge of the Klamath Mountains. Geologically, the Coast Ranges (with few peaks higher than 8,000 feet) are composed of once-oceanic, uplifted, and relatively "soft" Franciscan Complex sedimentary rock. The deep soils covering the bedrock were produced over eons by humidity (gentle but constant enough to crumble rock) and, augmented by forest humus, are generally protected from erosion by the ancient forests themselves. The thick coastal soil gives these mountains their gently rounded shape. When saturated with water, and especially when atop typically weathered bedrock, coastal hillsides have a tendency to slide. Landslides are even more common in areas where extensive logging or other removal of natural vegetation occurs, since intact native plant communities make good use of soil moisture.

Federal Wild and Scenic River status has finally been extended to the north coast's Eel, Klamath, Smith, and Trinity Rivers, protecting them from dam projects, other water-diversion schemes, and logging within their immediate watersheds. The Smith is now protected as a national recreation area. Other major north coast rivers include the Garcia, Mad, Navarro, Noyo, and Russian.

Climate

The north coast has a Mediterranean climate cooled in summer by the arctic California Current. Heavy rainfall, 80–160 inches per year, and winter's endless overcast days compete with thick fog the rest of the year for the annual let's-make-a-gray-day award. The sun is most likely to make its chilly appearance during early spring, but September usually brings balmy weather. Often at the end of February, "false spring" comes and stays for a week or more. North coastal temperatures are moderate year-round, but can *feel* cold anytime, due to bone-chilling fog and moist air whisked ashore by steady ocean breezes.

STANDING ON SHAKY GROUND

Because of the gale-force winds driving storms against the western edge of California for half the year, most north coast settlements are in more protected inland valleys. But some of these areas, including those near the Eel, Garcia, and Mad Rivers, parallel major northwesterly earthquake fault zones. As it turns out, even the redwoods, those gentle giants of the north coast, stand on shaky ground. The seismically active San Andreas Fault (responsible for San Francisco's devastating earthquake and fire in 1906 and again in 1989) runs north from the Bay Area on the seaward side of the mountains before veering back out to sea at Point Arena. Other faults related to the 1992 Eureka-area quake cluster farther north.

According to recent geologic speculations, a massive earthquake is likely somewhere along the Pacific Northwest's offshore Cascadia subduction zone within the next 50–150 years. Such a quake, expected to register as high as 9.5 on the "energy magnitude" scale (considered more accurate than the Richter scale for major quakes), could occur anywhere from Vancouver Island in British Columbia to Mendocino in California. Such an event would be more powerful than any earthquake the San Andreas Fault could generate, much more powerful than any quake ever measured in the mainland U.S., and roughly equal in destructive force to Chile's 1960 earthquake (the 20th century's most devastating).

Before arriving at this ominous conclusion, Humboldt State University geologists studied the Little Salmon Fault near Eureka. Their preliminary findings, announced in 1987 at the annual meeting of the Geological Society of America, suggest that the fault slipped 30–33 feet in separate earthquakes occurring roughly every 500 years during the past half-million years—suggesting quakes of "awesome, incomprehensible" power.

A rarity along the southern Sonoma County coast but nonetheless widely observed is an off-shore floating mirage resembling Oz's Emerald City, with towers, minarets, the whole show. This strange-but-true phenomenon is vaguely attributed to "climatic conditions." Also rare is the earthquake-related weather phenomenon of tsunamis, or giant coast-crushing waves. Radiocarbon dating of Native American cultural remains (which happen to coincide with dates of major Cascadia earthquakes) suggest that ancient tsunamis were so powerful they tossed canoes into the tops of trees. The most recent tsunami came in 1964, when a 13-foot wave generated by an 8.5-magnitude earthquake in Alaska smashed ashore in Crescent City on the Northern California coast, killing 11 people and destroying much of the town.

FLORA AND FAUNA
Trees to Trillium
In one of his more famous gaffes as governor of California, Ronald Reagan reportedly once cut redwood trees with the old saw, "If you've seen one, you've seen 'em all." (Reagan was misquoted, actually. What he said was, "A tree is a tree—how many more do you need to look at?") Despite Reagan's opinion on the subject, the north coast is noted for its deep, dark, and devastatingly beautiful forests of tall coastal redwoods, or *Sequoia sempervirens*—sadly, a tree most often appreciated as construction timber for suburban sun decks. Another regional tree with commercial value is the Douglas fir, *Pseudotsuga menziesii,* faster growing than redwood so often replanted by foresters on clearcut lands. Still another is the yew, whose bark contains components that have been used to treat breast cancer.

Yews, Sitka spruces, cedars, and lowland firs reach to the coast. Maples, sycamores, and alders add contrast and color in mixed streamside forests. Foothill woodlands—scattered oaks and conifers in a sea of grasses and spring wildflowers—are common north of San Francisco. Introduced groves of Australian eucalyptus trees—planted now primarily as windbreaks, though at one time intended as timber trees—are common along the Sonoma County coast, inland, and up into Mendocino County.

Coastal shrublands have no true chaparral but share some of the same species: fragrant California laurel (bay) trees, scrub oak, dogwood, ceanothus, and purple sage. The least favorite shrub here, as elsewhere in California, is poison oak, usually found in shaded areas. Among the most beautiful coastal "shrubs"—sometimes growing to tree size—are the native rhododendron species, both the western azalea and the California rose bay.

Red elderberries, blackberries, salmonberries, raspberries, huckleberries, and gooseberries all grow wild along the north coast. Wildflowers are abundant, primarily in spring. Unusual are the creeping beach primroses, beach peas, and sea rockets on beaches and sandy dunes. Beneath redwoods grow delicate fairy lanterns, oxalis, and trillium.

Oceangoing Animals

California gray whales are a stunning presence, offshore, during their annual migrations. Among other ocean animals are sea otters or "sea beavers" (see Monterey Bay Area for more information), fun to watch. The large (1,200-2,000 pounds) northern sea lion can be spotted along rugged far northern shores, but more common is the barking California sea lion. Coastal tidepools harbor clams, crabs, mussels, starfish, sand dollars, jellyfish, sponges, squids, sea anemones, and small octopi. (Look but don't touch: eager collectors and the just plain curious have almost wiped out tidepool communities.)

For those who enjoy eating mussels—steamed in butter, herbs, white wine, or even fried—find them on rocky sea coasts. People pry them off underwater rocks with tire irons, pickaxes, even screwdrivers. Keep these bivalves alive in buckets of cool, fresh seawater until you're ready to eat 'em. But *no* mussel collecting is allowed during the annual "red tide" (roughly May–Oct., but variable from year to year), when tiny red plankton proliferate. These plankton are fine food for mussels and other bivalves but are toxic to humans. (The red tide is less of a problem for clams, but to be on the safe side, just eat the white meat during the annual mussel quarantine.)

North coast salmon, steelhead, and American shad are all anadromous, living in the sea but returning to freshwater streams to reproduce.

Land-loving Animals

On land, deer are common mammals, found everywhere along the coast and inland. Protected colonies of Roosevelt elk can be seen far to the north in Redwood National Park. Smaller mammals include dusky-footed woodrats and nocturnal "pack rats," which nest in trees and rarely travel more than 50 feet in any direction. More common are gregarious California gray squirrels, black-tailed jack rabbits, raccoons, and skunks. Aquatic land mammals include muskrats or "marsh rabbits" and the vegetarian beaver.

Here, as elsewhere in California, gray foxes are common; characteristically clever red foxes are less so. From more remote areas, particularly at dusk or dawn, comes the lonely howl of coyotes. Bobcats (truly "wildcats" when cornered) are fairly abundant but rarely seen, though mating squalls can be heard in midwinter. Very rare are mountain lions, which usually discover people before anyone discovers them. Black bears, found even at sea level though they range up into higher elevations, usually won't attack humans unless frightened or protecting their cubs.

A common nonnative Californian along the coast is the nocturnal opossum, the only native U.S. marsupial. Also nonnative, and preferring the cover of night for their ferocious forays through the world, are wild pigs—an aggressive cross between domesticated and imported wild European hogs.

A surprising variety of birds can be spotted along the shore: gulls, terns, cormorants, egrets, godwits, and the endangered brown pelican. Mallards, pintails, widgeons, shovelers, and coots are common waterfowl, though Canada geese, snow geese, sandhill cranes, and other species fly by during fall and winter migrations. Great blue herons are nearly as common along inland rivers as they are near the sea. If unseen, mourning doves can still be heard (a soft cooing), usually near water or in farm country. Families of California quail scurry across paths and quiet roadways, sadly oblivious to the dangers of traffic.

Great horned owls, keen-eyed nocturnal hunters with characteristic tufted "ears," usually live in wooded, hilly, or mountainous countryside. Their evening cries are eerie. The magnificent ravens, which seem to dominate the terrain as well as the native mythology of the Pacific Northwest, are quite territorial, preferring to live inland at higher foothill and mountain elevations. The American kestrel or sparrow hawk can often be spotted in open woodlands and meadows or near grazing lands. More common is the red-tailed hawk, usually seen perched on telephone poles, power lines, or fences along the road—getting a good view of the countryside before snaring rabbits, ground squirrels, or field mice (though they're not above picking up an occasional roadkill). Speaking of roadkill: Least appreciated among the birds of prey are the common redheaded turkey vultures.

In rugged coastal canyons are some (but not many) golden eagles, a threatened species wrongly accused by ranchers and tale-spinners of attacking deer and livestock. Even rarer are endangered bald eagles, usually found near water—remote lakes, marshes, large rivers—primarily in inaccessible river canyons.

HISTORY

A Portuguese sailor first sighted Cape Mendocino in 1543, but explorers avoided setting foot on the foreboding, darkly forested coastline due to the lack of natural harbors. According to some historians, Sir Francis Drake dropped anchor at Point Reyes in 1579, that landing most likely pivotal in convincing the Spanish to extend their mission chain from Mexico up the California coast to Sonoma.

But after Drake's "discovery" of the north coast, it took nearly three centuries for substantial settlement to occur. Misery was the common experience of early explorers. The intrepid Jedediah Smith nearly starved while trailblazing through the redwoods, called "a miserable forest prison" by other unlucky adventurers. The Russians arrived on California's north coast in the early 1800s to slaughter sea otters for fashionable fur coats and hats. Their Fort Ross complex on the coast north of the Russian River (now a fine state historic park) was built entirely of redwood. After the otters were all but obliterated, the Russians departed. So desperate for building ma-

| YUROK TIME |

I like time before Darwin
and von Humboldt. I like Yurok
time, for example, when Umai
(a lonely girl) could sing herself
across the ocean into the world-
beyond-the-world

to visit the sunset and find
Laksis (Shining One), her nightly friend.
I like names without Latin:
seagull rather than *Larinae,*
stories without explanations,
a song for no reason,

a journey through the horizon
to unknowns without fear or shadow.
I like the sun going down
just now, a moment of gold
spraying out, a stunned instant when words
go back before books.

—Gary Thompson

terials and furniture was Sacramento's founder John Sutter that he traveled all the way up the coast to Fort Ross, purchasing (and dismantling) entire buildings for the lumber and carting off rooms full of Fort Ross furnishings and tools.

With the California gold rush of 1849 and the sudden onslaught of prospectors throughout the territory came new exploratory determination. The first settlements in California's far north, including the coastal towns of Eureka and Trinidad, started out as mining pack stations for inland gold mines. Then came redwood logging, a particularly hazardous undertaking in the early days, from felling to loading finished lumber onto schooners anchored off the rocky shoreline. (Most of the original logging towns and lumber "ports" have long since vanished.) Tourism had a respectable early start, too, particularly with the advent of drive-thru redwood trees and take-home knickknacks.

Now that the "harvesting" of the region's vast virgin redwood forests is all but complete, tourism will increasingly become a mainstay. Redwoods in isolated protected groves, a few redwood state parks, and Redwood National Park, not to mention the spectacular coastline, offer ample opportunity for increased tourism.

The Economy

Depending upon the year, who's running for office, and whom you talk to, illicit marijuana growing pumps somewhere between $110 and $600 million into the north coast's economy each year. According to NORML, the National Organization for the Reform of Marijuana Laws, California leads the nation in pot production with an annual crop estimated at $2.55 billion. Traditionally, though, the lumber business has been the reigning industry, booming and busting along with construction and the dollar. Fluctuations in demand mean frequent unemployment and localized economic depressions.

Agriculture—sheep and cattle ranching, dairy farming, and commercial fishing—is less important overall, but dominant in certain areas. Recreation and tourism, especially "green" tourism, along with related small businesses and service industries, are growing in importance. Locals tend to view these inevitable incursions of "outsiders" as both a blessing and curse. There's begrudging gratitude for the money visitors spend yet at times also thinly disguised disgust for the urban manners and mores, not to mention increasing development and higher prices, that come with it.

The Sonoma Coast

Northern California beaches are different from the gentler, kinder sandy beaches of the southstate. The coast here is wild. In stark contrast to the softly rounded hillsides landward, the Sonoma County coast presents a dramatically rugged face and an aggressive personality: undertows, swirling offshore eddies, riptides, and deadly "sleeper" or "rogue" waves. It pays to pay attention along the Sonoma coast. Since 1950, more than 70 people have been killed here by sleepers, waves that come out of nowhere to wallop the unaware, then drag them into the surf and out to sea.

October is generally the worst month of the year for dangerous surf, but it is also one of the best months to visit; in September and October the summertime shroud of fog usually lifts and the sea sparkles. Except on weekends, by autumn most Bay Area and tourist traffic has dried up like the area's seasonal streams, and it's possible to be alone with the wild things.

BODEGA BAY AND VICINITY

Alfred Hitchcock considered this quaint coastal fishing village and the inland town of Bodega perfect for filming *The Birds,* with its rather ominous suggestion that one day nature will avenge itself. But people come to Bodega Bay and vicinity to avoid thinking about such things. They come to explore the headlands, to whalewatch, to kayak, to beachcomb and tidepool, to catch and eat seafood (including local Dungeness crab), to peek into the increasing numbers of galleries and gift shops, and to *relax*. Bodega Bay's **Fisherman's Festival and Blessing of the Fleet** in April attracts upward of 25,000 people for a Mardi Gras-style boat parade, kite-flying championships, bathtub and foot races, art shows, and a barbecue. Ochlophobes, steer clear. Or come in late August for the **Bodega Bay Seafood, Art & Wine Festival,** a benefit for the Chanslor Wetlands Wildlife Project (see www.sonomawetlands.org) showcasing seafood entrées, wine and microbrew tasting, entertainment, "recycled art," and children's crafts.

Just wandering through town and along the harbor is fascinating. While keeping an eye on the sky for any sign of feathered terrorists, watch the chartered "party boats" and fishing fleet at the harbor; at six each evening, the daily catch arrives at the Tides Wharf. Bodega, just inland, is where visitors go to reimagine scenes from Hitchcock's movie, most particularly **St. Teresa of Avila Church** and **Potter Schoolhouse.**

Most people don't know, though, that Hitchcock's story was based on actual events of August 18, 1961, though they occurred in Capitola,

© ROBERT HOLMES/CALTOUR

St. Teresa of Avila Church

Rio Del Mar, and other towns on Monterey Bay, farther south. That night, tens of thousands of crazed shearwaters slammed into doors, windows, and hapless people; the next morning these birds, both dead and dying, stank of anchovies. In 1995, researchers at the Institute of Marine Sciences at UC Santa Cruz suggested that a lethal "bloom" of a natural toxin produced by algae—domoic acid—present in Monterey Bay anchovies was probably responsible for the birds' bizarre behavior. Toxic amounts of domoic acid cause amnesia, brain damage, and dementia.

Near Bodega Bay and stretching north to Jenner are the slivers of collectively managed **Sonoma Coast State Beaches,** which include **Bodega Head** and **Bodega Dunes** near the bay itself. Inland are a variety of small spots-in-the-road, some little more than a restaurant or boarded-up gas station at a crossroads, all connected to Bodega Bay by scenic roller-coaster roads. Not far south of town in Marin County is **Dillon Beach,** known for its tidepools. Keep going south via Hwy. 1 to the sensational **Point Reyes National Seashore.**

For more information on Bodega Bay and environs, stop by the **Bodega Bay Area Visitor In-**

formation Center, 860 Hwy. 1 (next to Texaco), 707/875-3866, www.bodegabay.com. The visitor center is open Mon.–Thurs. 10 A.M.–6 P.M., Fri. and Sat. until 8 P.M., and Sunday 11 A.M.–7.P.M., closed on major holidays.

Children's Bell Tower

Other than the beautiful landscape, one of the few sights in Bodega Bay is the Children's Bell Tower, next to the Community Center on the west side of Hwy. 1, about a mile and a half north of the visitor center. The monument was inspired by a heart-rending story. In 1994, seven-year-old Nicholas Green of Bodega Bay was shot and killed while traveling with his family in Italy. His parents, Maggie and Reg Green, decided to donate Nicholas's organs to needy Italian recipients—a decision all but unheard of in Italy, and one that moved Italians and Americans alike. Bay Area sculptor Bruce Hasson conceived and designed the bell tower as a memorial to Nicholas and the courage of his parents. Donated bells of all types—130 in all—came in from all over Italy. The centerpiece bell was cast by the Marinelli foundry, which has made bells for the papacy for 1,000 years; this bell is inscribed with the names of Nicholas and the seven Italians who were given a second chance at life thanks to the donation. In the words of Nicholas's father, when the memorial was dedicated in 1996, "We've tried to create a place of pilgrimage, a place where any parent can come for solace or inspiration, a place that reminds us of the fragility and preciousness of young life. . . ."

Recreation

All popular along and near the Bodega Bay coast: bird-watching, collecting driftwood, tidepooling, surf and rock fishing, hiking, bicycling the area's strikingly scenic backroads, sea kayaking, and whale-watching. Best yet, all these activities are free.

For good swimmers, free-diving for abalone (use of scuba gear for the purpose is illegal) is a special treat. Diving season is April 1 through the end of June, then August 1 through November, assuming the abalone population is adequate for harvest. Abalone divers are required to get a California fishing license with an additional abalone stamp and carry a shell gauge (minimum size is seven inches across at the shell's broadest point) and a legal abalone iron; they

can take no more than four abalone. According to new information about these creatures' lifestyles, abalone move toward the shore in winter, farther out to sea in summer. So it's no wonder that "shore picking" at low tide is dismal.

Staying in and near Bodega Bay

Camp at Bodega Dunes just north of the harbor, at smaller Wrights Beach on the way to Jenner, or at primitive Willow Creek Campground near Goat Rock. (For more information on these state park campgrounds, see Sonoma Coast State Beaches below). **Doran Beach County Park** to the south has first-come, first-camped primitive outdoor accommodations. Day-use fee is $3. Camping is $16 per night ($14 for county residents) for the first vehicle and $5 per additional vehicle, plus $1 per dog. No RV hookups. For information, call the park at. 707/875-3540, or call regional park headquarters at 707/527-2041. For reservations, call 707/565-2267. Another possibility is the private, full-service **Bodega Bay RV Park,** 2001 Hwy. 1, 707/875-3701 or 800/201-6864, www.bodegabayrvpark.com, $25–31.

In town, the hotspot is the fairly pricey **Bodega Bay Lodge & Spa,** 103 Hwy. 1 (off the highway

Bodega Harbor

SUSAN SNYDER

SUSAN SNYDER

Bodega Bay Lodge & Spa

at Doran Beach Rd.), 707/875-3525 or 800/368-2468, www.woodsidehotels.com, which offers full luxury amenities, including an ocean-view pool, spa, fitness center, and exceptional The Duck Club restaurant. Rooms and suites are $250 and up on weekends and holidays. It's also adjacent to the **Bodega Harbour Golf Links,** 21301 Heron Dr., 707/875-3538, an 18-hole Scottish links-style course designed by Robert Trent Jones Jr.

Another possibility is the **Inn at the Tides,** 800 Hwy. 1, 707/875-2751 or 800/541-7788, www .innatthetides.com, $150–250. Rates include full amenities (pool, sauna, whirlpool, TV and movies, and many rooms with fireplaces), great views, and continental breakfast. The Inn at the Tides also features a casual in-house restaurant—see below—and the very good Sonoma-style continental **Bay View** restaurant, and sponsors a **Dinner with the Winemaker** series of monthly dinners and wine-tastings. Also nice is the **Bodega Coast Inn,** 521 Hwy. 1, 707/875-2217 or 800/346-6999, www.bodegacoastinn.com, with rates $150–250. Much more affordable: old-fashioned, 14-room **Bodega Harbor Inn,** 1345 Bodega Ave., 707/875-3594, with rates $50–100. Cottages and houses are also available.

For spa services and pampering, head south six miles to plush **Sonoma Coast Villa,** 16702 Hwy. 1 (two miles north of Valley Ford), 707/876-9818 or 888/404-2255, www.scvilla.com. In-dulgences include massage, a seaweed mud body mask, or an herbal body wrap. Enjoy a Mediter-ranean-inspired dinner, featuring fresh local pro-duce (some right from the Villa's own organic garden) and the fine Sonoma County wines. Other amenities include a swimming pool and Jacuzzi, pool table, putting green, wood-burning fireplaces, beautiful Italian slate floors, stocked re-frigerators (Sonoma county wines, soft drinks), organic in-room coffee, and unique furnishings throughout. Rooms and suites are $250 and up (some lower), including full country breakfast.

The inviting **Chanslor Guest Ranch,** 2660 Hwy. 1 (near Bodega Dunes, just north of Bodega Bay), 707/875-2721, www.chanslor-ranch.com, is a working horse ranch that also boards people. Rooms feature quilts and homey comforts. Rates are $100–150 and include con-tinental breakfast. Horseback riding is extra; for details, call 707/875-3333.

Farther north is the coastal town of Jenner, near the mouth of the Russian River. **Jenner**

Inn & Cottages, 707/865-2377 or 800/732-2377, www.jennerinn.com, offers quite pleasing and private rooms and cottages—various buildings, all overlooking the ocean, the river, or both. In addition to unique features, many offer wood-burning fireplaces and/or Jacuzzis. All have private sundecks. Find something for every price range, too, with rooms as low as $88 and cottages as high as $378 (the Osprey house), though most accommodations are $150–250 or $250 and up. Breakfast is served at the inn's **Mystic Isle Café,** also open to the public. Massage and yoga classes available. Ask about packages, some quite intriguing.

Eating in Bodega Bay

Get fresh fish and chips, even hot seafood to go, at popular **Lucas Wharf Deli and Fish Market,** 595 Hwy. 1 (on the pier at the harbor), 707/875-3562. Or pick up a delicious seafood sandwich and microbrew, and take it out to one of the benches and tables overlooking a working dock. The adjacent sit-down **Lucas Wharf Restaurant and Bar,** 707/875-3522, is open for lunch and dinner daily and is known for its pastas and steaks as well as seafood. Great clam chowder, fisherman's stew, and sourdough bread. A bit more spiffy (and a *lot* more pricey) is the recently renovated **The Tides Wharf Restaurant,** 835 Hwy.

1 (just north of Lucas Wharf), 707/875-3652, which also overlooks the bay (and has its own dock and video arcade) and was featured as a backdrop in *The Birds.* The Tides is popular for breakfast, and you can count on fresh seafood at lunch and dinner. Open daily; there's a fresh fish market and bait shop here, too. For fine dining, head for **The Duck Club** at the Bodega Bay Lodge, 103 Hwy. 1, 707/875-3525, famous for its Sonoma County cuisine—everything from Petaluma duck with orange sauce and Hagemann Ranch filet mignon to grilled Pacific salmon with sweet mustard glaze. Open daily for breakfast and dinner (picnic lunch available).

The **Breakers Cafe,** 1400 Hwy. 1, 707/875-2513, is a good choice for breakfast (waffles, Benedicts, omelettes, breakfast burritos), lunch (good sandwiches like portobello mushroom or cold shrimp and crab), and dinner (pastas, soups, salads, steaks). The wholesome **Sandpiper Dockside Café & Restaurant,** 1410 Bay Flat Rd. (take Eastshore Dr. off Hwy. 1 and go straight at the stop sign), 707/875-2278, is a casual locals' place open daily for breakfast, lunch, and dinner.

To drive somewhere in order to totally enjoy sitting down again, head south on Hwy. 1 to Valley Ford, the town made famous by Christo's *Running Fence.* The frumpy white frame building

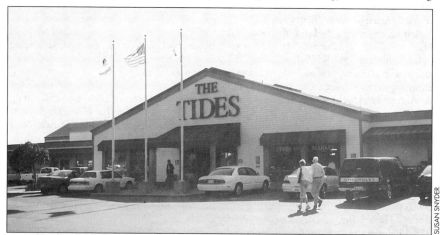

SUSAN SNYDER

The Tides Wharf Restaurant

is **Dinucci's,** 14485 Valley Ford Rd., 707/876-3260, a fantastically fun watering hole and dinner house. Study the massive rosewood bar inside, shipped around Cape Horn, while waiting for a table (folks are allowed to linger over meals). The walls in the bar are almost papered in decades-old political posters, old newspaper clippings, and an eclectic collection of lighthearted local memorabilia. The dim barroom lighting reflects off the hundreds of abalone shells decorating the ceiling. Dinucci's boisterous family-style dining room has close-together, sometimes shared (it's either that or keep waiting) checkerboard-clothed tables and a very friendly serving staff. Dinner starts with antipasto, a vat of very good homemade minestrone, fresh bread, and salad, followed by seafood or pasta entrées and desserts. For $15 or so, after eating here people can barely walk to their cars.

If you're heading north, try to be hungry when you get to Jenner. Just on the south side of the Russian River Bridge in Bridgehaven is **Sizzling Tandoor,** 9960 Hwy. 1 (at Willow Creek Rd.), 707/865-0625, where you can dine on superb Indian food at tables inside or out. Open for lunch and dinner daily. The traditional big night out in Jenner proper includes dinner and drinks at **River's End Inn & Restaurant,** 11048 Hwy. 1, 707/865-2484.

SONOMA COAST STATE BEACHES

Most of the spectacular 13 miles of coastline between Bodega Bay and Jenner is owned by the state. The collective Sonoma Coast State Beaches are composed of pointy-headed offshore rock formations or "sea stacks," natural arches, and a series of secluded beaches and small coves with terrific tidepools. Don't even think about swimming here, since the cold water, heavy surf, undertows, and sleeper waves all add up to danger. Never turn your back to the ocean. But for beachcombing, ocean fishing, a stroll, or a jog—well away from the water—these beaches are just about perfect. Rangers offer weekend whale-watching programs from mid-December through mid-April.

Bodega Head and Vicinity

Hulking Bodega Head to the north, protecting Bodega Bay from the heavy seas, is a visible chunk of the Pacific plate and the bulwark for the area's state beaches. Good whale-watching from here. Nearby is the University of California at Davis's **Bodega Marine Lab,** 2099 Westside Rd., 707/875-2211, www.bml.ucdavis.edu, a marine biology research center open to the public every Friday 2–4 P.M. for tours and at other times, in winter, for its special seminar series. Hike on and around the head on well-worn footpaths, or head out for an invigorating walk via hiking trails to **Bodega Dunes.** Five miles of hiking and horseback riding trails twist through the dunes themselves (access at the north end of the bay, via W. Bay Road). To get to Bodega Head, take Westside Rd. and follow the signs past **Westside Park.**

Doran County Park, on the south side of the bay, 707/875-3540, looks bleak, but its windswept beaches and dunes provide safe harbor for diverse wildlife and hardy plants. Due to the protected beaches, this is the only safe place to swim for many coastal miles. Good clamming, too. There's an excellent boardwalk, allowing people with physical disabilities to get close to the ocean. Day-use fee $3. Or visit the water-filled sump once destined for the nuclear age (called "hole in the head" and "the world's most expensive duckpond" by amused locals). With Hitchcock's nature-vengeance theme in mind, we can only shudder at what might have been if PG&E had built its proposed nuclear power plant here, just four miles from the San Andreas Fault.

Other Beach Areas

Sprinkled like garnish between the rocks and coastal bluffs from Bodega Bay north to Jenner are a variety of public beaches, including Miwok, Coleman, Arched Rock, Carmet, and Marshall Gulch. North of Bodega Bay, first among the state beaches is **Salmon Creek Beach,** part of which becomes a lagoon when sand shuts the creek's mouth. (If you must swim, try the lagoon here.) No dogs are allowed on Salmon Creek Beach, to protect nesting areas of the threatened snowy plover. **Schoolhouse** and **Portuguese Beaches,** best for rock fishing and surf fishing, are stunning sandy beaches surrounded by rocky headlands. Plan a picture-perfect picnic near **Rock Point** on the headland (tables available). There's picnicking and camping at **Wright's Beach,** but also danger; **Duncans Landing,** just south, is most famous for **Death Rock;** a former offshore lumber-loading spot during the redwood harvesting heyday. Today it's one of the most dangerous spots along the Sonoma coast, due to "sleeper" waves that snatch people off the shore. The area is now fenced, and clearly marked as off limits. Believe it. Heads up anyway, though, since rogue waves have reached as far as the parking lot. Farther north is **Shell Beach,** best for beachcombing and seaside strolls, with some tremendous tidepools and good fishing.

It's a spectacularly snaky road from Hwy. 1 down to dramatic Goat Rock, popular **Goat Rock Beach** just north, and the dunes just east. The craggy goat itself is an impressive promontory but illegal to climb around on: more than a dozen people have drowned in recent years, swept off the rocks by surging surf.

On Goat Rock Beach, near Jenner at the mouth of the Russian River, a large population of harbor seals has established itself, attracting considerable human attention. (No dogs are allowed on Goat Rock Beach, because of the seals and other wildlife, but Fido is permitted on Blind Beach south of Goat Rock.) Unlike sea lions, which amble along on flippers, harbor seals wriggle like inchworms until in the water, where their mobility instantly improves. On weekends, volunteer naturalists (members of Stewards of Slavianka) are here to answer questions, lend binoculars for a close-up look, and protect the seals from unleashed dogs and too-curious tourists. When panicked, harbor seals will protect themselves by biting. Some carry diseases difficult to treat in humans—which is why sailors of old used to cut off a limb if it was seal-bitten.

Harbor seal "pupping season" starts in March and continues into June. During these months, seals and their young become vulnerable to more predators, since they give birth on land. Some worry that Jenner's large seal colony will attract other enthusiastic observers, like sharks and killer whales. Not known to attack humans

(though no one will guarantee that), killer whales also consider harbor seals a delicacy. To avoid predators, harbor seals swim upriver as far as Monte Rio while fishing for their own prey: salmon and steelhead.

For a great hike, take the three-mile **Dr. David Joseph Trail,** starting at the Pomo Canyon Campground just off Willow Creek Rd., south of the mouth of the Russian River (see below). The route threads through the redwoods into the ferns, then on through the oak woodlands and grassland scrub down to the Pacific ocean at Shell Beach.

Four miles north of Jenner is the **Vista Trail,** which allows people in wheelchairs to come very close to the edge of a dramatic cliff for some fabulous views.

Practicalities

Along this stretch are plentiful pulloffs for parking cars, with access to beach trails and spectacular views. The day-use fee for the Sonoma Coast State Beaches is $4. Camp at **Wright's Beach,** with 27 developed campsites just back from the beach, $13–16; restrooms and some campsites are wheelchair accessible. Or try **Bodega Dunes,** a half mile south of Salmon Creek, with 98 developed sites secluded among the cypress-dotted dunes, hot showers, an RV sanitation station, and a campfire center, $16–20. (Wright's Beach campers may take hot showers at Bodega Dunes.) Developed Sonoma Coast campsites are reservable in advance through ReserveAmerica, 800/444-7275, www.reserveamerica.com. Primitive walk-in camping is available Apr.–Nov. at 11-site **Willow Creek Campground** along the banks of the Russian River (first-come, first-camped, $10); no dogs. Register at the trailhead, up Willow Creek Rd. (turn right at the Sizzling Tandoor restaurant). The walk-in **Pomo Canyon Campground** (also $10) is reached via the same route. About five minutes after turning off Hwy. 1, you'll reach the gravel parking lot marked Pomo Canyon Campground. From here, two trails run into the redwoods to the 20 walk-in sites, which feature a picnic table, fire grill, and leveled tent site.

The **Jenner Visitor Center,** 707/865-9433 or 707/869-9177, offering books, current infor-

EARLY BODEGA BAY

Though Cabrillo and his crew were probably the first Europeans to spot the area, the Spanish lieutenant Don Juan Francisco de la Bodega y Cuadra anchored the *Sonora* off Bodega Head in October 1775 and named it after himself—breaking with the more modest tradition of using saints' names corresponding to the day of discovery. Ivan Kuskov, an agent of the powerful Russian-American Fur Company, arrived in Bodega Bay from Sitka, Alaska, in 1809. He and his company grew wheat inland, hunted sea otters, then returned to Alaska with full cargo holds. Two years later, they built three settlements—Port Rumiantsov on the bay, and the towns of Bodega and Kuskov inland—before the construction of Fort Ross began farther north. American settlers first arrived in 1835, increasing after the Russians left in the 1840s. Bodega Harbor was a bustling seaport by the 1860s, though large oceangoing vessels haven't anchored here for more than a century.

mation, and wraparound views from the deck, is staffed by volunteers and open spring through October. Or contact park headquarters at the **Salmon Creek Ranger Station,** 3095 Hwy. 1 (just north of Bodega Bay), 707/875-2603.

FORT ROSS STATE HISTORIC PARK

A large village of the Kashia Pomo people once stood here. After the Russian-American Fur Company (Czar Alexander I and President James Madison were both company officers) established its fur-trapping settlements at Bodega Bay, the firm turned its attention northward to what, in the spring of 1812, became **Fort Ross,** imperial Russia's farthest outpost. Here the Russians grew grains and vegetables to supply Alaskan colonists as well as Californios, manufactured a wide variety of products, and trapped sea otters to satisfy the voracious demand for fine furs. With pelts priced at $700 each, no trapping technique went untried. One of the most effective: grabbing a sea otter pup and using its distress calls to lure otherwise wary adults into range.

The Russians' success here and elsewhere in California led to the virtual extinction of the sea otter. Combined with devastating agricultural losses (due to greedy gophers), this brought serious economic problems to the region. Commercial shipbuilding was attempted but also failed. The Russians got out from under this morass only by leaving, after selling Fort Ross and all its

contents to John Sutter. Sutter (who agreed to the $30,000 price but never made a payment) carried off most of the equipment, furnishings, tools, and whatever else he could use to improve his own fort. Sutter's empire building eventually required James Marshall to head up the American River to build a sawmill. Marshall's discovery of gold led to Sutter's instant ruin but also to the almost overnight Americanization of California.

The First Fort

The weathered redwood fortress perched on these lonely headlands, surrounded by gloomy cypress groves, was home to Russian traders and trappers for 40 years. The original 14-foot-high stockade featured corner lookouts and 40 cannons. Inside the compound were barracks, a jail, the commandant's house, warehouses, and workshops. At the fort and just outside its walls, the industrious Russians and their work crews produced household goods plus saddles, bridles, even 200-ton ships and prefabricated houses.

Perhaps due to the Russian Orthodox belief that only God is perfect, the fort was constructed with no right angles. Its Greek Orthodox chapel was the only building here destroyed by the 1906 San Francisco earthquake. It was rebuilt, then lost again to arson in 1970, though it's since been reconstructed from the original blueprints (fetched from Moscow). Outside the stockade was a bustling town of Aleut hunters' redwood huts, with a windmill and various outbuildings and shops. When the Russians at Fort Ross finally

© ROBERT HOLMES/CALTOUR

the Greek Orthodox Church at Fort Ross

The park's boundaries also encompass a beach, the ridgetop redwoods behind the fort, and other lands to the north and east. Thanks to the Coastwalk organization, hiking access (including a handicapped-accessible trail) has been added to the Black Ranch Park area south of the fort. Ask at the visitor center for current hiking information.

Practicalities

For more information, call Fort Ross at 707/847-3286 or 707/865-2391. Just 12 miles north of Jenner along Hwy. 1, the park is open 10 A.M.–4:30 P.M. daily (except major holidays). Day-use is $4 per car, seniors $3. Autophobes, get here via **Mendocino Transit** buses daily from the north, 707/462-1422.

On **Living History Day** in July or August, the colony here suddenly comes back to life circa 1836. History buffs can have fun questioning repertory company volunteers to see if they know their stuff.

For those who want to rough it, first-come, first-served primitive camping ($10) is possible at **Fort Ross Reef State Campground,** tucked into a ravine just south of the fort (20 campsites, no dogs); call for more information. Those who want to "smooth it" can instead try **Fort Ross Lodge,** 20705 Hwy. 1, 707/847-3333 or 800/968-4537, www.fortrosslodge.com, which offers all modern amenities and some great ocean views. Most rooms are $50–100 and $100–150, but those with private hot tub or Jacuzzi are $150–250.

prepared to leave their failed American empire, the Pomo held a mourning ceremony to mark their departure—a testament to the visitors' amicable long-term relations with the native peoples.

The Reconstructed Fort

A good place to start exploring Fort Ross is at its million-dollar **visitor center** and museum, which includes a good introductory slide program (shown throughout the day in the auditorium), as well as Pomo artifacts and basketry, other historic displays, period furnishings, and a gift shop. The free **audio tour** of the fort is itself entertaining (balalaika music, hymns, and Princess Helena Rotchev—namesake of Mt. St. Helena near Calistoga—playing Mozart on the piano).

The fort's only remaining original building (now restored) is the commandant's quarters. Other reconstructed buildings include the barracks—furnished as if Russians would sail up and bed down any minute—an artisans' center, and the armory.

TIMBER COVE TO SEA RANCH

Hard to miss even in the fog, the landmark eight-story **Benjamin Bufano *Peace* sculpture** looms over Timber Cove. Once a "doghole port" for lumber schooners, like most craggy north coast indentations, Timber Cove is now a haven for the reasonably affluent. But ordinary people can stop for a look at Bufano's last, unfinished work. From the hotel parking lot, walk seaward and look up into the the face of *Peace,* reigning over land and sea. The **Timber Cove Inn,** 21780 N. Hwy. 1, 707/847-3231 or 800/987-8319, www.timber-coveinn.com. offers fairly luxurious lodgings on a 26-acre point jutting out into the Pacific. Some rooms have private hot tubs, some have lofts, and most have fireplaces. Rates go as low as $78 and as high as $390, but most rooms are $100–150 and $150–250.

Salt Point State Park

This 6,000-acre park is most often compared to Point Lobos on the Monterey Peninsula, thanks to its dramatic outcroppings, tidepools and coves (this is one of the state's first official underwater preserves), wave-sculpted sandstone, lonely wind-whipped headlands, and highlands including a pygmy forest of stunted cypress, pines, and redwoods.

Though most people visit only the seaward side of the park—to dive or to examine the park's honeycombed *tafoni* rock (sculpted sandstone)—the best real hiking is across the road within the park's inland extension (pick up a map to the park when you enter).

Among Salt Point's other attractions are the dunes and several old Pomo village sites. In season, berrying, fishing, and mushrooming are favorite activities. Park rangers lead hikes and sponsor other occasional programs on weekends, and are also available to answer questions during the seasonal migration of the gray whales. The platform at Sentinal Rock is a great perch for whale-watching.

Among its other superlatives, Salt Point is also prime for camping—both tent and RV sites are $12—especially the ocean-view campsites at Gerstle Cove, though Woodside Campground offers more shelter from offshore winds. Make reservations, at least during the summer high season, through ReserveAmerica, 800/444-7275, www.reserveamerica.com. Salt Point also has hike-in/bike-in ($2) and environmental ($10) campsites as well as a group camp ($90). Pleasant picnicking here, too. Day-use fee $4 per car, $3 seniors. For more information, call Salt Point at 707/847-3221. For current dive conditions and information, call 707/847-3222.

Kruse Rhododendron Reserve

Adjoining Salt Point State Park, the seasonally astounding Kruse Rhododendron Reserve is an almost-natural wonder. Nowhere else on earth does *Rhododendron californicum* grow to such heights and in such profusion, in such perfect harmony—under a canopy of redwoods. Here at the 317-acre preserve, unplanted and uncultivated native rhododendrons up to 30 feet tall thrive in well-lit yet cool second-growth groves of coast redwood, Douglas fir, tan oak, and madrone. (Lumbermen downed the virgin forest, unintentionally benefitting the rhododendrons, which need cool, moist conditions but more sunshine than denser stands of redwoods offer.) The dominant shrub is the *Rhododendron macrophyllum,* or California rosebay, common throughout the Pacific Northwest. Also here is the *Rhododendron occidentale,* or western azalea, with its cream-colored flowers.

Most people say the best time to cruise into Kruse is in April or May, when the rhododendrons' spectacular pink bloom is at its finest. (Peak blooming time varies from year to year, so call ahead for current guestimates.) Another sublime time to come is a bit earlier in spring (between sweet-smelling rainstorms), when the rhododendron buds just start to show color and the tiny woods orchids, violets, and trilliums still bloom among the Irish-green ferns and mossy redwood stumps. But come anytime; the song of each season has its own magic note.

To get here from Hwy. 1, head east a short distance via Kruse Ranch Road. Coming in via the backwoods route from Cazadero is an adventure in itself, especially if the necessary signs have been taken down (again) by locals. To try it, better call ahead first for precise directions. Facilities at the preserve are appropriately minimal but include five miles of hiking trails, picnic tables, and outhouses. For bloom predictions, preserve conditions, and other information, call the reserve at 707/847-3222.

Stewarts Point

Heading north from Salt Point, stop at the weatherbeaten **Stewarts Point Store,** just to appreciate the 120-plus years of tradition the Richardson family has stuffed into every nook and cranny. You can buy almost anything, from canned goods and fresh vegetables to rubber boots and camp lanterns—and if they don't have it, they'll order it.

Not for sale are items creating the store's ambience: the abalone shells and stuffed fish hanging from the ceiling, horse collars, oxen yoke, turn-of-the-century fish traps, and an 1888 Studebaker baby buggy.

Big news in Stewarts Point in 1996 was the completion of the 144-acre **Odiyan Buddhist Center,** the largest Tibetan Buddhist center in the Western hemisphere. Not a tourist attraction and largely hidden from view, the cultivated center of these 1,100 acres on Tin Barn Rd. includes six copper-domed major temples, a 113-foot gold stupa (a traditional monument to enlightenment), four libraries of sacred texts, 800 prayer flags, 1,242 prayer wheels, 200,000 clay offerings, 6,000 rose bushes, and 200,000 new trees. The center is the brainchild of exiled Tibetan lama Tarthang Tulku, founder of the Nyingma Institute in Berkeley and both Dharma Publishing and Dharma Press. The main building, the three-tiered Odiyan Temple, resembles a three-dimensional mandala—symbolizing balance and order. Tours are usually available, but you can visit online at www.odiyan.org.

Sea Ranch

Almost since its inception, controversy has been the middle name of this 5,200-acre sheep ranch-cum-exclusive vacation home subdivision. No one could have imagined the ranch's significance in finally resolving long-fought battles over California coastal access and coastal protection. Sea Ranch hosted the first skirmishes in California's ongoing war over access to public beaches, battles that ended with the establishment of the California Coastal Commission.

From the start Sea Ranch architects got rave reviews for their simple, boxlike, high-priced condominiums and homes, which emulate weather-beaten local barns. The much-applauded cluster development design allowed "open space" for the aesthetic well-being of residents and passersby alike, but provided no way to get to the 10 miles of state-owned coastline without trespassing.

In 1972, Proposition 20 theoretically opened access, but the *reality* of beach access through Sea Ranch was achieved only in late 1985, when four of the six public trails across the property were ceremoniously, officially dedicated. But here, the public-access victory is only partial; Sea Ranch charges a day-use fee. So make it worth your while. From the access at Walk-On Beach, you can link up with the Bluff Top Trail that winds along the wild coastline to Gualala Point Regional Park some miles to the north.

There are other attractions. On the northern edge of the spread is the gnomish stone and stained-glass **Sea Ranch Chapel** designed by noted architect James Hubbell. Inside it's serene as a redwood forest. From the outside, the cedar-roofed chapel looks like an abstract artist's interpretation of a mushroom, perhaps a wave, maybe even a UFO from the Ice Age. What is it? Nice for meditation or prayer, if the door's unlocked.

Those who salivate over Sea Ranch and can afford the rates might consider an overnight stay (or maybe just a meal) at the 20-room **Sea Ranch Lodge,** 60 Seawalk Dr., 707/785-2371 or 800/732-7262, www.searanchlodge.com. Its pretty and plush accommodations look out over the Pacific, and some rooms have fireplaces and private hot tubs. Other amenities include pools, saunas, and an 18-hole links-style golf course (707/785-2468). Dine in the stylish Sea Ranch Lodge Restaurant or get simple breakfast or lunch at the Smokehouse Grill at the golf course. Rooms are $150–250 and $250 and up, though ask about specials. Vacation home rentals are also available.

The Southern Mendocino Coast

The Gualala River forms the boundary between Sonoma and Mendocino Counties. Travelers heading north will find that most of the Bay Area weekenders have by now tailed off, leaving Mendocino County's stretch of coast highway for the locals and long-haul travelers. It's a little greener (and wetter) here than in Sonoma County, but the crescent coves and pocket beaches you appreciated along the wild Sonoma Coast continue north across the county line, one after the next, like a string of pearls.

Beachcombers and hikers, to get properly oriented along the Mendocino coast, a travel essential is Bob Lorentzen's *The Hiker's Hip Pocket Guide to the Mendocino Coast,* which keys off the white milepost markers along Hwy. 1 from the Gualala River north. The book provides abundant information about undeveloped public lands along the southern Mendocino coast, such as the state's Schooner Gulch and Whiskey Shoals Beach. Also worthwhile to carry anywhere along the coast, though a bit unwieldy, is the *California Coastal Resource Guide* by the California Coastal Commission, published by the University of California Press.

GUALALA AND VICINITY

Though people in the area generally say whatever they please, Gualala is supposedly pronounced Wah-LA-la, the word itself Spanish for the Pomos' *wala'li* or "meeting place of the waters." Crossing the Gualala River means crossing into Mendocino County. On the way to Gualala from Sea Ranch is **Del Mar Landing,** an ecological reserve of virgin coastline with rugged offshore rocks, tidepools, and harbor seals. Get there on the trail running south from Gualala Point Regional Park, a "gift" from Sea Ranch developers, or via Sea Ranch trails. The Gualala area is also known as the north coast's "banana belt," due to its relatively temperate, fog-free climate. At its heart is secluded Anchor Bay, just north of Gualala, enormously popular with rumrunners during Prohibition.

If you're not just blasting through town, stop off at the **Gualala Arts Center** galleries and studios, 46501 Hwy. 1, 707/884-1138, www.gualalaarts .org, to see what's up. Since 1961 Gualala Arts has served up a year-round menu of art, music, and theater. Come on Labor Day weekend (and the following weekend) for the annual **Studio Discovery Tour.** The center's **Dolphin Gallery** downtown is open daily 10 A.M.–4 P.M., and also serves as the **Gualala Visitors' Center.** For more area information, contact the **Redwood Coast Chamber of Commerce,** 707/884-1080 or 800/ 778-5252, www.redwoodcoastchamber.com.

Staying in Gualala and Anchor Bay

Community life in this old lumber town always centered on the 1903 Gualala Hotel, where loggers and locals pounded a few after work, and where haute cuisine applied to spaghetti and steak and just about anything else served hot. Those days are gone, here and elsewhere, though it seems likely that the Gualala Hotel will remain a community draw. Along with new owners came serious efforts to rescue the hotel from dry rot and general decline—just in time for the hotel's centennial. Still a work in progress, the new, improved Gualala boasts new paint and new attitude, along with guest rooms gussied-up in old-fashioned style. Rates are quite reasonable; rooms with shared bathrooms are $50–100, with private baths $100–150. The dining room is pretty spiffy, too, whther you choose charbroiled burgers on foccacia bread or pan-seared local salmon. Lunch is served Tues.–Fri., dinner Tues.–Sun., brunch on weekends. On Mondays, when the restaurant's closed, sample the saloon's café menu. For information or reservations, contact the **Gualala Hotel,** 39301 S. Hwy. 1, 707/884-3441, www.thegualalahotel.com.

North of town is the **Old Milano Hotel,** 38300 S. Hwy. 1, 707/884-3256, www.oldmilanohotel.com, with five charming guest cottages and one genuine caboose. Cottages are each unique, rich with Victorian antiques, queen-size featherbeds, and stained glass; most offer an ocean view, Jacuzzi, or two-person shower. The caboose has a woodstove, terrace, and observation cupola. Rates are $150–250, including full breakfast and use of the ocean-view hot tub.

A stay at the **Whale Watch Inn,** 35100 S. Hwy. 1, 707/884-3667 or 800/942/5342, www.whale-watch.com, is just this side of coastal condo heaven. Perched on the cliffs overlooking Anchor Bay (north of Gualala), the Whale Watch is the kind of place where decadence and decency both reign and Debussy pours out over the intercom. The 18 romantic, sometimes surprisingly formal retreats are collected in five separate buildings. Rooms and suites offer stunning views and amenities such as fireplaces, fresh flowers, decks, and whirlpool tubs; some have kitchens. Attendants bring breakfast to the door. Rates are $150–250 and $250 and up.

Just up the road is the **North Coast Country Inn,** 34591 S. Hwy. 1, 707/884-4537 or 800/959-4537, www.northcoastcountryinn.com, a onetime sheep ranch offering six hillside cottages rich in redwood, antiques, handmade quilts, wood-burning fireplaces, and other homey touches—not to mention the privacy and ocean views. All have private baths, some feature kitchens, Jacuzzis, or private decks. The grounds include gazebo, deck, and a private hillside hot tub. Full breakfast. Rates are $150–250.

There are motels, too. Most rooms at the homey **Gualala Country Inn** on Center St. (at Hwy. 1) in Gualala, 707/884-4343 or 800/564-4466, www.gualala.com, are $100–150, a few slightly higher. The contemporary **Breakers Inn** on the bluffs, 39300 S. Hwy. 1, 707/884-3200 or 800/273-2537, www.breakersinn.com, features abundant amenities, including large private decks overlooking the sea. Most rooms are $150–250, "garden view" rooms lower. Spa rooms are $250 and up. Check out mid-week and off-season specials.

Campers, head to **Gualala Point Regional Park** just south of town, 707/785-2377 or 707/527-2041, which offers coastal access and camping ($16 per night, no hookups). The park day-use fee is $3. Call 707/565-2267 for reservations. For more amenities, try privately operated **Gualala River Redwood Park,** 46001 Gualala Rd., 707/

884-3533, www.gualalapark.com, in the redwoods on the north beach of the Gualala River, one mile east of town off Old Stage Road. The campground's 120 sites offer full hookups for $34–40 a night. Amenities include coin-op showers and restrooms. Abalone divers favor **Anchor Bay Campground,** down in a beachfront gulch just north of Anchor Bay village, 707/884-4222, www.abcamp.com. The small campground fills up often in spring and summer; reservations are accepted up to one year in advance. Rates start at $27 per night. Electrical hookups are extra; hot showers available. The campground also offers (for a small fee) access to Fish Rock Beach.

Eating in Gualala and Anchor Bay

If you're not eating at St. Orres (below), the fine-dining restaurant of choice in Gualala these days is the **Oceansong Pacific Grille,** next to the Breakers Inn at 39350 S. Hwy. 1, 707/884-1041, overlooking both beach and river. Since the kitchen has been under the direction of Swiss chef René Fueg, the restaurant has earned rave reviews from foodie magazines and locals alike. Seafood is one specialty, but you'll also find steaks, pastas, rack of lamb, and other entrées. For "downhome gourmet," try **The Food Company** just north of town at Robinsons Reef Rd., 707/884-1800, a combination café, deli, and bakery serving up fresh, wholesome fare. Sit outside on the sunporch or in the garden area, or pack your goodies to go. Open daily for breakfast, lunch, and dinner. To stock up on fresh local produce for the road, plan to arrive for the **Gualala Certified Farmers Market,** held May–Oct. on Sat., 3–5 P.M., at the Gualala Community Center, Hwy. 1 at Center Street. In Anchor Bay, services include a market and wine shop, as well as the **Fish Rock Cafe,** 707/884-1639, serving burgers, soups, salads, sandwiches (including veggie varieties), and Northern California microbrews. The café is open for lunch and dinner daily.

The **Pangaea Café,** which first brought culinary note to Point Arena, is now at home in Gualala, 39165 S. Hwy. 1, 707/884-9669, arty and elegant and serving "eclectic" global, local, and organic cuisine. What that means varies from night to night, but might include temptations such as mahimahi with Lebanese couscous tabouleh, lentils, greens, and a cumin-scented lemon tahini sauce. Outrageous. Pangaea uses organically grown produce, bakes its own bread in a wood-fired oven, makes its sausage, and smokes its meats. The wine list highlights wines made from sustainably farmed grapes. Open for dinner only, Wed.–Sun. 5:30–9 P.M. Reservations recommended.

St. Orres

Continuing north from Gualala, you'll soon come upon a local landmark—the ornate onion-domed inn and restaurant of St. Orres, 36601 S. Hwy. 1, 707/884-3303 or 707/884-3335 (restaurant), www.saintorres.com. Some rock 'n' roll-literate wits refer to a sit-down dinner here as "sitting in the dacha of the bay." Dazzling in all its Russian-style redwood and stained-glass glory, St. Orres is also a great place to stay. For peace, quiet, and total relaxation, nothing beats an overnight in one of the handcrafted redwood cabins (some rather rustic) scattered through the forest, or in one of the eight European-style hotel rooms (shared bathrooms). Hotel rooms are $50–100, cottages $100–150 and $150–250, full breakfast included.

Even if they don't stay here, people come from miles around to eat at St. Orres, known for its creative French-style fare. The fixed-price dinners ($40, not including appetizers or desserts) feature such things as a salad of greens and edible flowers from the garden, cold strawberry soup, puff pastry with goat cheese and prosciutto, venison with blackberries, wild boar, Sonoma County quail, salmon and very fresh seafood in season, eggplant terrine, and grilled vegetable tart. Wonderful desserts, and good wines (beer and wine only). No credit cards. Before dinner, sit outside and watch the sun set. Reservations are a must, a month or more in advance.

POINT ARENA

Farther north is remote Point Arena, "discovered" by Capt. George Vancouver in 1792. Another good spot for whale-watching, Point Arena was the busiest port between San Francisco and Eureka in the 1870s. When the local pier was wiped out by rogue waves in 1983, the already depressed local fishing and logging economy took yet another dive. But today Point Arena has a new pier—folks can fish here without a license—and a new economic boon: the sea urchin harvest, to satisfy the Japanese taste for *uni.* In winter, come watch for whales. Or check out a movie at the art house **Arena Cinema,** 214 Main St., 707/882-3456.

Point Arena Lighthouse

A monument to the area's historically impressive ship graveyard, the Coast Guard's six-story, automated 380,000-candlepower lighthouse north of town is open to visitors (limited hours, small donation requested). Built in 1908, this lighthouse was the first in the U.S. constructed of steel-reinforced concrete; it replaced the original brick tower that had come tumbling down two years earlier. The adjacent **museum** tells tales of the hapless ships that floated their last here. Tours of the light tower and museum are offered daily, $4 adults, $1 children; call for current hours.

St. Orres

© ROBERT HOLMES/CALTOUR

To help protect the lighthouse and preserve public access (no government support has been available), local volunteer lighthouse keepers maintain and rent out "vacation rental homes" (furnished three-bedroom, two-bathroom U.S. government-issue houses abandoned by the Coast Guard)—a good deal for families, with fully stocked kitchens, cozy wood-burning stoves, satellite TV, VCR, and stunning ocean views. Rates are $170–300.

For more information and reservations, contact **Point Arena Lighthouse Keepers, Inc.,** 45500 Lighthouse Rd., 707/882-2777 or 877/725-4448 (reservations only), www.pointarenalighthouse.com.

Practicalities

If you don't stay at the lighthouse cottages mentioned above, consider the **Coast Guard House Historic Inn** at Arena Cove, 707/882-2442 or 800/524-9320, www.coastguardhouse.com, originally an outpost of the U.S. Life-Saving Service, precursor to the Coast Guard. This 1901 Cape Cod features six guest rooms (two share a bath), a cottage, and a boathouse. Queen or double beds, expanded continental breakfast. Most rooms are $100–150, cottages and other rooms $150–250.

For a superb five-course Italian meal and charming personal service, make reservations most Friday, Saturday, or Sunday nights at the already legendary **Victorian Gardens,** an elegant farmhouse in nearby Manchester, 14409 S. Hwy. 1, 707/882-3606, one of the hottest dining destinations in Northern California. Stylish, very comfortable bed-and-breakfast rooms are available, too, $150–250.

TO MENDOCINO
Manchester State Park

This 5,272-acre park just north of Point Arena and the burg of Manchester is foggy in summer and cold in winter, but it presents dedicated beachcombers with a long stretch of sandy shore and dunes dotted with driftwood. Five miles of beaches stretch south to Pt. Arena. A lagoon offers good birding, and excellent salmon and steelhead fishing in both Brush and Alder Creeks. Also interesting here is the opportunity

for some walk-in environmental camping, about a mile past the parking area. (Making an overnight even more thrilling is the knowledge that here at Manchester is where the San Andreas Fault plunges into the sea.) Once here, it's first-come, first-camped, with an opportunity to personally experience those predictable summer northeasterlies as they whistle through your tent. Group camp, too. For more information about Manchester and a camping map, contact the Mendocino state parks office, 707/937-5804, or call the park directly at 707/882-2463. More private and protected is the **KOA** campground at 44300 Kinney Ln. (adjacent to the park office), 707/882-2375. Campsites start at $26; cabins and cottages also available.

Elk (aka Greenwood)

The tiny town of Elk perches on the coastal bluffs farther north. Elk was once a lumber-loading port known as Greenwood, hence **Greenwood Creek Beach State Park** across from the store, with good picnicking among the bluff pines. The park is also a popular push-off point for sea kayakers. If you're just passing through and looking for a bite to eat, note that the nondescript store beside the highway—the **Elk Store,** 6101 Hwy. 1, 707/877-3411—whips up great deli sandwiches, and also carries gourmet cheeses and an impressive selection of wines and microbrews. In addition to the restaurants mentioned below, **Queenie's Roadhouse Café,** installed in a restored garage circa 1901, 6061 S. Hwy. 1, 707/877-3285, is open for breakfast and lunch; closed Tuesday. The all-redwood Craftsman-style 1916 **Harbor House,** 5600 S. Hwy. 1, 707/877-3203 or 800/720-7474, www.theharborhouse-inn.com, is a sophisticated bed-and-breakfast noted for its stylish, classic accommodations (six elegant rooms and four luxurious cabins, recently refurbished) and fine dining (recipient of *Wine Spectator*'s Award of Excellence). Rates, $250 and up, typically include full breakfast and fabulous four-course dinner plus private access to a strip of beach. Off-season rates for some rooms can dip as low as $95–125 (breakfast-only) and $145–175 (with dinner). Dinners emphasize Sonoma County seafood, meats, poultry, and produce, à la Tuscany or Provence. Open for dinner daily, at least most of the year. Beer and wine. No credit cards. Limited seating, advance reservations required—and be sure to request a window table.

Another area institution, now under new ownership, is the **Elk Cove Inn,** 6300 S. Hwy. 1, 707/877-3321 or 800/275-2967, www.elk-coveinn.com, where you get a spectacular view of the cove below from the inn's romantic gazebo. The Elk Cove Inn offers seven fine rooms in the main 1883 Victorian, plus four ocean-view cottages overlooking the cove. Fairly new at the Elk Cove Inn—and truly spectacular, just the thing for an extra-special weekend— are its four ocean-view luxury suites, housed in the new Craftsman-style annex. These sophisticated suites are certainly a fitting tribute to the era of craftsmanship, with a keen sense of style and every imaginable comfort, down to the fireplaces, Jacuzzi tubs, California king beds with both down and regular comforters, and mini-kitchens complete with microwave, small fridge, and coffee/cappucino maker. Floors in the bathroom feature heated floor tiles. Newer still are the day spa facilities. Inn rates include full breakfast, served in a delightful, cheerful, ocean-view breakfast room with intimate tables. Room are $150–250 (Swallow's Nest $130), and cottages and luxury suites are $250 and up (most $300–350). Inquire about off-season and midweek specials (particularly mid-week stays in winter). The Elk Cove Inn also boasts a beer and wine bar—and a cocktail bar,

including a menu of 23 different martinis. Dig those Z-shaped glasses.

More relaxed but equally charming are the seven cottages at **Griffin House at Greenwood Cove,** 5910 S. Hwy. 1, 707/877-3422, www .griffinn.com. The "house" is now **Bridget Dolan's Irish Pub & Dinner House,** serving pub grub, soups and salads, Gaelic garlic bread, and hearty main dishes such as Irish stew, bangers and mash, and "very, very veg" specials. Out back are the flower gardens and cozy 1920s cottages; three feature sun decks and ocean views, and all have private baths (most with clawfoot tubs) and woodstoves. A hearty full breakfast is served in your room. Most cottages are $100–150, even in the high season—such a deal—and two are $150–250.

The **Greenwood Pier Inn,** 5928 S. Hwy. 1, 707/877-9997 or 707/877-3423, fax 707/877-3439, www.greenwoodpierinn.com, features eclectic cottages and cottage rooms perched at the edge of the cliffs above the sea, surrounded by cottage-gardenlike grounds. Most accommodations feature wood-burning fireplaces or wood-stoves, and some also have in-room spa tubs; two rooms are pet-friendly. Continental breakfast is delivered to your room. (If you must have TV or a telephone, head for the main house.) Other amenities include the cliffside hot tub, in-room massage and facials (extra), and the on-site **Greenwood Pier Café,** noted for its house-baked breads and fresh garden veggies and herbs. Most rates are $150–250; one room is $130, two cottages are $250 and up.

Mendocino and the Coast

People just love Mendocino. They love it for a variety of reasons. Some are smitten by the town's Cape Cod architecture, admittedly a bit odd on the California side of the continent. The seaside saltbox look of the 19th-century wood-frame homes here, explained by the fact that the original settlers were predominantly lumbermen from Maine, is one of the reasons the entire town is included on the National Register of Historic Places. Others love Mendocino for its openly

artistic attitude. Of course, almost everyone loves the town's spectacular setting at the mouth of Big River—and at the edge of one of the most sublime coastlines in California.

Everybody loves Mendocino—and as a result, people tend to love Mendocino to death, at least in summer. Not even 1,000 people live here, yet the community is usually clogged with people, pets, and parked cars. Mendocino-area rental homes are inhabited in summer and at other

NORTH COAST

© ROBERT HOLMES/CALTOUR

Hwy. 1 in Mendocino

"peak" times, but in the dead of winter, locals can barely find a neighbor to talk to. Besides, almost no one who actually *lives* here (or lived here) can afford to now. Exactly when it was that things started to change for the worse—well, that depends on whom you talk to.

The Arts and "Culture Vultures"

In the 1950s, when nearby forests had been logged over and the lumbermill was gone, and the once bad and bawdy doghole port of Mendocino City was fading fast, the artists arrived. Living out the idea of making this coastal backwater home were prominent San Francisco painters like Dorr Bothwell, Emmy Lou Packard, and Bill Zacha, who in 1959 founded the still-strong Mendocino Art Center. Soon all the arts were in full bloom on these blustery bluffs, and the town had come alive. But even back then, as *Johnny Belinda* film crews rolled through Mendocino streets and James Dean showed up for the filming of *East of Eden,* oldtimers and retirees could see what was coming. The town's possibilities could very well destroy it.

In the decades since, the costs of living and doing business in Mendocino have gotten so high that most of Mendocino's artists have long

since crawled out of town with their creative tails between their legs—pushed out, locals say, by the more affluent "culture vultures" who consume other people's creativity. Though many fine artists, craftspeople, performers, and writers work throughout Mendocino County, most art, crafts, and consumables sold in Mendocino shops are imported from elsewhere. Even finding a local place to park is nearly impossible in Mendocino, a town too beautiful for its own good.

Mendocino at Its Best

Thankfully, in postage-stamp-size Mendocino, cars are an unnecessary headache. You can stroll from one end of town to the other and back again—twice—without breaking a sweat. So leave your car parked at the village lodging of choice. If you're staying elsewhere, take the bus. Or hike here, or ride a bike. Mendocino is at its best when seen on foot or from the seat of a bike. Note, however, that street addresses in Mendocino can be either three digits or five digits, all in the same block. Fortunately, the town is small and beautiful. So just find the street you need by name and wander along it until you find what you're looking for.

To stroll the streets of Mendocino or explore the headlands at the moodiest, most renewing time, come when most people don't—in November or January. This is the season when Mendocino is still itself, and seems to slip back to a time before this New Englandesque village was even an idea. A sense of that self blasts in from the bleak headlands, come winter, blowing rural reality back into town. In winter you can meet the community—the fishermen, fourth-generation loggers, first-generation marijuana farmers, apple and sheep ranchers, artists and craftspeople, even city-fleeing innkeepers and shopkeepers as they, too, come out of hiding.

The Mendocino Coast: Greater Mendocino

Given Mendocino's proximity to, and dependence on, a number of nearby coastal communities, any visit to Mendocino also includes the coastline for about 10 miles in either direction. The Mendocino Coast business, arts, and entertainment communities are so intertwined that they share a single visitors bureau.

Not counting Garberville, **Fort Bragg** north of Mendocino is the last community of any size before Eureka. Mendocino's working-class sister city to the north was named after a fort built there in 1855 for protection against hostile natives. Fort Bragg is now unpretentious home to working (and unemployed) loggers and millworkers, an active fishing fleet, and many of Mendocino's working artists and much of their work. This friendly town offers an array of relatively urban services and amenities not found in smaller Mendocino. Just north of Fort Bragg is tiny **Cleone,** and at the south end of Fort Bragg is **Noyo Harbor,** with its bustling fishing fleet. Approximately halfway between Mendocino and Fort Bragg lies the little hamlet of **Caspar,** which makes Mendocino look like the big city.

Just a few miles south of Mendocino, near Van Damme State Park, is **Little River,** a burg boasting its own post office but most famous for the long-running Little River Inn that stands tall by the highway. A bit farther south is **Albion,** a miniscule coastal hamlet straddling the mouth of the Albion River—a natural harbor supporting a small fishing fleet. From just south of Albion and inland via Hwy. 128 is the attractive Anderson Valley and Boonville (for more information, see the Wine Country chapter).

SEEING AND DOING MENDOCINO
Historic Buildings

Start your Mendocino explorations at the state park's **Ford House interpretive center,** near the public restrooms on the seaward side of Main, 707/937-5397. The center features a model of Mendocino as it looked in 1890, historical photos, exhibits on lumbering and the Pomo Indians, wildflower displays, local art, lots of brochures, free apple cider, and a store selling books and postcards. It's open year-round, daily 11 A.M.–4 P.M. (longer hours if volunteers are available).

Across the street, sedately settled into its old-fashioned gardens, is the 1861 **Kelley House** (entrance around the front at 45007 Albion), 707/937-5791, now housing the Mendocino region's historical society museum, library, and bookstore. In addition to taking in the exhibits of pioneer artifacts and historical photos, sign up for a guided walking tour of Mendocino (nominal fee) with **Mendocino Historical Research, Inc.,** mendocinohistory.org, which maintains and operates Kelley House as a historical research facility. The museum is open daily 1–4 P.M. June–Sept. (small admission), otherwise Fri.–Mon. only.

Also of historical interest, one of Mendocino's earliest buildings (1852), is the **Temple of Kwan Tai joss house,** a half block west of Kasten on Albion (between Kasten and Woodward), 707/937-5123, open to the public by appointment only. While you're out and about, also drop by **Crown Hall,** 45285 Ukiah St. (toward the west end), to see what's going on. The intimate theater hosts everything from local comedy troupes and community plays to big-name touring bands.

Mendocino Art Center

When you're ready to head off around town, a good first destination is the nonprofit Mendocino Art Center, 45200 Little Lake Rd. (between

Williams and Kasten), 707/937-5818 www.mendocinoartcenter.com, open daily 10 A.M.–5 P.M. This place is a wonder—a genuine *center* for countywide arts awareness and artistic expression. The organization sponsors apprenticeships in ceramics, textiles, and weaving, as well as fine arts programs; maintains an art library and a satellite center in Fort Bragg; and sponsors countless events. Whatever artistic endeavor is happening in Mendocino County, someone at the center knows about it.

Check out **The Main Gallery** and both the **Abramson** and **Nichols Gallery** here for exhibits of member artists plus special fine arts and crafts shows, and the gift shop. The center also houses three large studios, with the emphasis on textiles and fiber arts, ceramics, and fine arts, respectively. With extra time, sample the **Zacha Commemorative Sculpture Garden.** Since the belief here is that art should be accessible to everyone, the art center sponsors weekend art classes Sept.–June, and in summer offers three-week workshops. The center's **Schoeni Theatre** is home for the Mendocino Theatre Company. Very reasonable (shared) accommodations with kitchenettes are available in center-sponsored apartments; if that's not feasible, the art center staff will help with other arrangements.

Art Galleries

The number of art galleries in and around Mendocino is staggering. Some seem strictly oriented to the tourist trade while others are more sophisticated.

If you like the idea of supporting local artists, a good place to start is the **Artists' Co-op of Mendocino,** upstairs in the Sussex Building, 45270 Main St., 707/937-2217, showcasing the work of its owner-artists. A veritable fine furniture and woodworking emporium in town is the three-story **Highlight Gallery,** 45052 Main, 707/937-3132, which also displays handwoven textiles. The famed **William Zimmer Gallery,** Ukiah and Kasten, 707/937-5121, offers a large, eclectic collection of highly imaginative, contemporary fine arts and crafts, aesthetic homage to Mendocino Art Center founder Bill Zimmer. **Panache Gallery,** 10400 Kasten, 707/937-1234,

has that, of course, but specializes in fine art, art glass, bronze, and wood, include works from Mendocino Coast Furnituremakers Association members (there's a second store location on Main, 707/937-0947). The intriguing **Partner's Gallery at Glendeven,** on the grounds of Glendeven Inn just south of the town, 8205 N. Hwy. 1, 707/937-3525, features changing exhibits by "partners" as well as guest artists.

Shopping and Entertainment

Despite its small size, Mendocino is stuffed with shops and stores, enough to keep shopping addicts happy for an entire weekend. **Alphonso's Mercantile,** 520 Main St. (between Kasten and Osborne), is a classical music store and smokeshop (even though Alphonso doesn't smoke anymore) with a million-dollar view of the coast. If you forgot to pack some summer reading, plan to spend some quality time at the **Gallery Bookshop & Bookwinkle's Children's Books** at Main and Kasten Streets, 707/937-2215, www.gallery-books.com, a truly impresssive independent bookstore. Just plain fun: **Out of This World** at 45100 Main, 707/937-3335, a megacollection of telescopes, microscopes, and binoculars.

Mendocino Village

© ROBERT HOLMES / CALTOUR

Also fascinating and very Mendocino is **Mendosa's Merchandise and Market,** 10501 Lansing (at Little Lake), 707/937-0563 and 707/937-5879, one of those rare *real* hardware stores long gone from most California communities, accompanied by a decent local grocery. Quite the contrast but equally wonderful (with its "food for people, not for profit" slogan) is the collectively run **Corners of the Mouth** natural food store, 45015 Ukiah (between Ford and Lansing), 707/937-5345.

Venerable **Dick's Place,** 45080 Main St., 707/937-5643, with few concessions to the changing times, is still Mendocino's real bar. Inside, the locals drink beer, plug the jukebox (lots of good Patsy Cline), and play darts. Outside, the bar's sign, a 1950s-style martini glass grandfathered in despite local anti-neon ordinances, is visible from miles away through the regularly dense coastal fog. Next door, definitely a sign of changing times, is the **Fetzer Wine Tasting Room,** 45070 Main St., 707/937-6190, open daily 10 A.M.–6 P.M.

SEEING AND DOING FORT BRAGG

Mendocino Coast Botanical Gardens

The nonprofit 47-acre Mendocino Coast Botanical Gardens, 18220 N. Hwy. 1 (two miles south of downtown), 707/964-4352, www.gardenbythesea.org, features native plant communities as well as formal plantings of rhododendrons, azaleas, fuchsias, and other regional favorites. Also here—in addition to some smashing views of the crashing coast—are a native plant nursery, picnic tables, the fine **Gardens Grill** restaurant, and summertime music concerts. A year-round calendar of special events and workshops are offered, too, from bird-watching tours to organic gardening classes. Wheelchair accessible. The gardens are open daily 9 A.M.–5 P.M. Mar.–Oct., and 9 A.M.–4 P.M. the rest of the year (closed Thanksgiving, Christmas, and the second Saturday in September). Admission is $6 general, $5 seniors (60 and up), $3 youths ages 13–17), and $1 children ages 6–12.

Historic Fort Bragg

For the local version of redwood logging history, as told through photos, artifacts, and tree-mining memorabilia, stop by the **Guest House Museum,** 343 N. Main St., 707/964-4251, in an attractive 1892 redwood mansion that was once used as a guest house for friends and customers of local Union Pacific Lumber execs. Open Wed.–Sun. 11 A.M.–3 P.M., small admission. The only remaining **fort building** from the original Fort Bragg stands a block east of the Guest House on Franklin Street.

Public tours of Georgia Pacific's Fort Bragg mill are no longer offered, but you can explore the **Georgia Pacific Tree Nursery,** 90 W. Redwood Ave., 707/961-3209, where you'll have the opportunity to commune with four million seedlings, take a stroll along the nature trail, and picnic—all for free. It's open daily 8 A.M.–4 P.M. Apr.–Oct. After November 1, the youngsters here take root in nearby forests, and a new nursery population takes their place.

Noyo Harbor

Fort Bragg's tiny fishing port lies at the south end of town, at the mouth of the Noyo River. It's a safe harbor for fisherfolk during stormy seas and shelters several fish restaurants popular with tourists, but fairly ho-hum in terms of cuisine and ambience. Don't miss Noyo's **Salmon Barbecue** festivities every July. It's a must-attend event for delicious fresh salmon and an intimate encounter with the local populace. Good folks, good food, big tradition.

Other Attractions

People think first of Mendocino when they think of art galleries, but Fort Bragg has at least as many—and more of the "working artist" variety. Not to be missed is the nonprofit **Northcoast Artists Collaborative Gallery,** 362 N. Main St., 707/964-8266, with everything from wearable art (weavings and handpainted silk scarves) and handcrafted jewelry to original art, prints, pottery, photographs, and greeting cards made by member artists. A very impressive enterprise. Fort Bragg's **Gallery District**—between Main and Franklin, and Redwood and Fir—so while you're in the area, see what else looks interesting. North Franklin St. between Laurel and Redwood boasts a number of **antique shops.**

Unique in Fort Bragg is **Adirondack Design,** 350 Cypress St., 707/964-4940 or 888/643-3003 (orders only), www.adirondackdesign.com. Founded by a group known as Parents and Friends, Inc., Adirondack Design provides jobs and services for the area's developmentally disabled adults. And what a job this crew does—crafting a high-quality line of redwood garden furniture and accessories, everything from Adirondack chairs, loveseats, rockers, and swings to garden benches and planters, cold frames, and a charming "bird chalet." Adirondack even produces a small footbridge.

RECREATION

Mendocino Headlands State Park

Start exploring the area's spectacular state parks in Mendocino proper. About the only reason there aren't shopping malls or condos and resort hotels between the town of Mendocino and its sea-stacked sandstone coast was the political creativity of William Penn Mott, the state's former director of Parks and Recreation. Mott quietly acquired the land for what is now Mendocino Headlands State Park by trading Boise Cascade some equally valuable timberlands in nearby Jackson State Forest.

The headlands and beach are subtle, more a monument to sand sculpture than an all-out ode to hard rock. The impressive stacks here and elsewhere are all that remain of sandstone headlands after eons of ocean erosion. Curving seaward around the town from Big River to the northern end of Heeser Dr., the park includes a three-mile hiking trail, a small beach along the mouth of Big River (trailheads and parking on Hwy. 1, just north of the bridge), sandstone bluffs, the area's notorious wave tunnels, offshore islands and narrows, and good tidepools. *The* peak experience from the headlands is whale-watching. (Whether watching the waves or whales, stand back from the bluff's edge. Sandstone is notoriously unstable, and the ragged rocks and wicked waves below are at best indifferent to human welfare.) For a

map and more information, get oriented at Ford House, 707/937-5397, or call the state parks' Mendocino District Headquarters, 707/937-5804. You can easily walk here from town—it's just an invigorating and spectacular stroll away. Pick up the path at the west end of Main Street.

Van Damme State Park

This small state park just south of Mendocino is not famous but, despite the considerable competition, is one of the finer things about this stretch of the coast. The excellent and convenient camping here midway between Mendocino and Albion is secondary. Van Damme State Park is an 1,831-acre, five-mile-long preserve around Little River's watershed, pointing out to sea. Squeezed into a lush ravine of second-growth mixed redwood forest, Van Damme's pride is its **Fern Canyon Trail,** a 2.5-mile hiking and bicycling trail weaving across Little River through red alders, redwoods, ferns—western sword ferns, deer ferns, bird's foot ferns, and five-finger ferns, among others—and past mossy rocks, pools, and streamside herds of horsetails. A 1.5-mile trail offers a self-guided tour of the coho salmon's life cycle.

Though the Fern Canyon Trail is easy, the going gets tougher at the east end as the path climbs the canyon and connects with the loop trail to Van Damme's **Pygmy Forest,** a gnarly thicket bonsaied by nature. What makes the pygmy forest pygmy? Beneath the thin layer of darker topsoil underfoot is *podzol* (Russian for "colored soil")—albino-gray soil as acidic as vinegar. Iron and other elements leached from the podzol collect below in a reddish hardpan layer impossible for tree roots (even moisture, for that matter) to penetrate. Similar fairy forests are common throughout coastal shelf plant communities between Salt Point State Park and Fort Bragg, an area sometimes referred to as the Mendocino White Plains. It is possible to drive most of the way to this green grove of miniatures via Airport Rd. just south of the park, and the forest is wheelchair accessible. A short self-guided discovery trail here loops through dwarfed Bolander pine (a coastal relative of the Sierra Nevada's looming lodgepole), Bishop pine, Mendocino pygmy cypress (found only between Anchor Bay

ROLL IT ON, BIG RIVER

Eight miles of Mendocino's Big River estuary, 50 miles of the river and its tributaries, 1,500 acres of coastal wetlands, and nearly 6,000 acres of surrounding watershed are now protected as **Big River State Park,** thanks to the relentless fundraising of the Mendocino Land Trust and additional funds from state and federal agencies. California's longest remaining undeveloped estuary, the new Big River park is bounded on the north by Jackson State Forest and Mendocino Woodlands State Park; its southern boundary is near Comptche-Ukiah Rd., connecting in places with Van Damme State Park and other nature reserves.

Named not for its own size but the trees that shade it, Big River is a prime salmon spawning estuary and essential wildlife habitat. It provides the last piece of a 74,000-acre public-lands jigsaw, an effective wildlife corridor extending inland as well as along the coast. Big River alone provides protected habitat for 27 endangered, threatened, or "special concern" species, including the northern spotted owl, California brown pelican, and bald eagle. The river is a natural nursery for threatened anadromous fish species, including Coho salmon, steelhead, and Pacific lamprey.

Big River visitor facilities are scarce; no camping is allowed, and the only restrooms are located at Big River's beach area. Hikers (dogs on leash only), equestrians, canoers, and kayakers will still find the essentials here: land, water, and that big coastal sky.

The Big River Trail (Big River Haul Road) begins on the river's north side and meanders alongside its course, into Mendocino Woodlands State Park; more than 100 miles of public trails link the park to adjacent areas. Exploring by kayak or canoe is immensely popular. If you're not packing your own, call **Catch-a-Canoe & Bicycles Too** at the Stanford Inn, 707/937-0273.

For more information, call Mendocino State Parks, 707/937-5804, or stop by the Ford House visitor center in Mendocino, open year-round 11 A.M.–4 P.M. daily, 9 A.M.–5 P.M. in summer. For details on the Big River story, see the land trust's website, www.mendocinolandtrust.org.

---

and Fort Bragg), and dwarf manzanita. Also noteworthy are the spring-blooming rhododendrons, which love acidic soils and here dwarf the trees.

Van Damme's tiny beach is a popular launch point for scuba divers and is usually safe for swimming, though no lifeguards are on duty. (The 1996 addition of Spring Ranch added more beach, and some spectacular tidepools.) The redwood-sheltered campground area is protected from winds but not its own popularity. Plan on making reservations April 1-mid-October. A small group camp is also available.

After breakfast, stop by the visitor center and **museum** in the impressive Depression-era Civilian Conservation Corps rec hall built from handsplit timbers. Inside you'll find an overview of the area's cultural, economic, and natural history. Or take the short **Bog Trail** loop from the visitor center to see (and smell) the skunk cabbage and other marsh-loving life. For more information, including details on kayaking tours, call the state parks' Mendocino District Headquarters, 707/937-5804. Reserve camp-sites ($13–16) in advance through ReserveAmerica, 800/444-7275, www.reserveamerica.com. The park's day-use fee is $4.

Russian Gulch State Park

Just north of Mendocino on the site of another days-past doghole port, Russian Gulch State Park is 1,200 acres of diverse redwood forests in a canyon thick with rhododendrons, azaleas, berry bushes, and ferns; coastal headlands painted in spring with wildflowers; and a broad bay with tidepools and sandy beach, perfect for scuba diving. Especially fabulous during a strong spring storm is the flower-lined cauldron of **Devil's Punch Bowl** in the middle of a meadow on the northern headlands. A portion of this 200-foot wave tunnel collapsed, forming an inland blowhole, but the devil's brew won't blast through unless the sea bubbles and boils.

Russian Gulch is a peaceable kingdom, though, perfect for bird-watching (osprey, red-tailed hawks, ravens, seabirds, shorebirds, and songbirds), whale-watching, even watching steelhead in their spawning waters. Rock fishing is popular around the bay, as is ocean salmon fishing and angling for rainbows in the creek (no fishing for spawning steelhead in fall or winter).

After a picnic on the headlands, take a half-day hike upcanyon. Make it a nine-mile loop by combining the southern trails to reach 36-foot **Russian Gulch Falls** (best in spring), then loop back to camp on the North Trail. (One of these trail links, the five-mile **Canyon Trail,** is also designated as a biking trail.) The far northern **Boundary Trail** is for hikers and horsebackers, running from the horse camp on the eastern edge of the park to the campground.

Camping at Russian Gulch is itself an attraction, with 30 family campsites ($13–16) tucked into the forested canyon; amenities include barbecue grills, picnic tables, food lockers, hot showers, and restrooms with laundry tubs. The separate group camp accommodates about 40 people ($67). This close to the coast, campers often sleep under a blanket of fog, so come prepared for wet conditions. Reserve campsites in advance through ReserveAmerica, 800/444-7275, www.reserve-america.com. For more information, contact the Mendocino District Headquarters (located here, open Mon.–Fri. 8 A.M.–4:30 P.M.), 707/937-5804. The day-use fee is $4.

Caspar Headlands and Point Cabrillo Light Station

About two miles north of Russian Gulch, reached via Pt. Cabrillo Dr., are the spectacular Caspar Headlands, hemmed in by housing. Miles of state beaches are open to the public, though, from sunrise to sunset—perfect for whale-watching. The headlands are accessible only by permit (free, available at Russian Gulch). A particular point of interest is the historic 300-acre **Point Cabrillo Light Station and Preserve,** the preserve open daily to pedestrians (no dogs) 9 A.M.–sunset, the light station and gift shop open weekends 11 A.M.–4 P.M. Thanks to the restoration efforts of dedicated volunteers, in 1999 the light station's 20th-century technology was replaced by that of the19th century—and the original third-order Fresnel lens once

again casts its light seaward. It's about a half-mile walk to the lighthouse along the access road, from the entrance gate; paved parking is available off Pt. Cabrillo Dr., 9 A.M.–6 P.M. Guided 1.5-mile walks are offered every Sunday at 11 A.M., starting at the parking lot. Come in March for the **Whale Festival at Point Cabrillo Light Station.** Handicapped access parking is available at the lighthouse, in front of area residences.

For details about headlands access, call 707/937-5804. For information on guided walks, whale-watching weekends, and special events, call 707/937-0816 or see www.pointcabrillo.org.

Jug Handle State Reserve

For serious naturalists, the "ecological staircase" hike at this reserve just north of Caspar is well worth a few hours of wandering. The staircase itself is a series of uplifted marine terraces, each 100 feet higher than the last, crafted by nature. The fascination here is the *change* associated with each step up the earth ladder, expressed by distinctive plants that also slowly change the environment.

The first terrace was a sand and gravel beach in its infancy, some 100,000 years ago, and is now home to salt-tolerant and wind-resistant wildflowers. (Underwater just offshore is an embryonic new terrace in the very slow process of being born from the sea.) A conifer forest of Sitka spruce, Bishop pine, fir, and hemlock dominates the second terrace, redwoods and Douglas fir the third. Jug Handle is an example of Mendocino's amazing ecological place in the scheme of things, since the area is essentially a biological borderline for many tree species. Metaphorically speaking, Alaska meets Mexico when Sitka spruce and Bishop pine grow side by side. The phenomenon of the hardpan-hampered Mendocino pygmy forest starts on the third step, transitioning back into old-dune pine forests, then more pygmy forest on the fourth step. At the top of the stairs on the final half-million-year-old step, are more pygmy trees, these giving ground to redwoods.

The only way to get to the staircase trail is by heading west from the parking lot to Jug Handle Bay, then east again on the trails as marked, hiking under the highway. (Call for trail conditions before setting out.) The day-use fee is $4. For

© KIM WEIR

tree at Jug Handle State Reserve

more information about Jug Handle, contact the Mendocino District Headquarters at Russian Gulch State Park, 707/937-5804.

Jackson State Forest

Bordering Jug Handle Reserve on the east is this 46,000-acre demonstration forest named after Jacob Green Jackson, founder of the Caspar Lumber Company. Extending east along the South Fork of the Noyo River and Hwy. 20, the Jackson Forest (logged since the 1850s) has picnic and camping areas, and almost unlimited trails for biking, hiking, and horseback riding. The forest is accessible at various points east off Hwy. 1 and along Hwy. 20; a forest map is necessary to get around. **Forests Forever** and other citizens groups are now actively challenging logging here, promoting restoration plans. For more forest information (and a map), contact the **California Department of Forestry** office in Forth Bragg, 802 N. Main St., 707/964-5674.

Mendocino Woodlands State Park and Outdoor Center

Entwined with Jackson State Forest about nine miles east of Mendocino is this woodsy 1930s camp facility—actually three separate facilities and some 200 separate buildings constructed of wood and stone by federal Works Progress Administration and Civilian Conservation Corps workers. Available for group retreats, each of the three rustic camps includes a well-equipped kitchen, a dining hall complete with stone fireplace, cabins, and spacious bathroom and shower facilities with both hot and cold running water. For

more information about this National Historic Landmark, contact the nonprofit **Mendocino Woodlands Camp Association,** 707/937-5755, www.mendocinowoodlands.org.

Directly south of Jackson State Forest and Mendocino Woodlands is the region's newest reserve, **Big River State Park.** See Roll It On, Big River for information.

MacKerricher State Park

This gorgeous stretch of ocean and forested coastal prairie starts three miles north of Fort Bragg and continues northward for seven miles. Down on the beach, you can stroll for hours past white-sand beaches, black-sand beaches, remote dunes, sheer cliffs and headlands, offshore islands, pounding surf, rocky outcroppings, and abundant tidepools. Or you can stay up atop the low bluff paralleling the shore, where you'll revel in great ocean views and, in spring, an abundance of delicate, butterfly-speckled wildflowers—baby blue eyes, sea pinks, buttercups, and wild iris.

The park's usage is de facto separated into two areas: the tourist area (crowded) and the locals' areas (desolate). Tourist usage centers around the park's little **Lake Cleone,** a fishable freshwater lagoon near the campground and picnic area with a wheelchair-accessible boardwalk; waterfowl from Mono Lake often winter at the lake. Nearby are a picturesque crescent beach pounded by a thundering shore break, and the **Laguna Point** day-use area (wheelchair accessible), a popular place for watching whales offshore and harbor seals onshore. (Another good local spot for whale-watching is **Todd's Point,** south of the Noyo Bridge, then west on Ocean View). That's the tourist's MacKerricher. Not bad. And most visitors to the park don't venture far from it.

Which leaves the locals and savvy passersby to enjoy in blissful, meditative solitude the extensive areas to the south and north, which are connected to the lake/campground area by the eight-mile-long **Old Haul Road.** Once used by logging trucks, the now-abandoned haul road parallels the shore from **Pudding Creek Beach** in the south to **Ten Mile River** in the north. Only a short stretch of the road is open to vehicles, so it's a great path for bicyclists and joggers. North of the campground area, the asphalt road gradually deteriorates until it gets buried completely by the deserted and exquisitely lovely Ten Mile Dunes; if you venture up the coast this far, you'll likely have it all to yourself. South of the campground, the road passes a few vacation homes and a gravel plant before ending up just past a parking lot and a phalanx of beachfront tourist motels. (If you wander far enough south, you'll end up at Fort Bragg's **Glass Beach** just north of town, where if you're lucky you might find a Japanese fishing float or an occasional something from a shipwreck.) Either way, you'll get magnificent ocean views and plenty of solitude.

The fine campgrounds at MacKerricher are woven into open woods of beach, Monterey, and Bishop pines. Campsites are abundant ($13–16, no hookups), with the usual amenities. It's a popular place, so reservations are wise; call ReserveAmerica, 800/444-7275, www.reserveamericausa.com. No day-use fee. For more information, call MacKerricher directly at 707/964-9112 or Mendocino District Headquarters, 707/937-5804.

Water Sports

For sightseeing afloat practically in Mendocino, catch a canoe (or kayak) from among the **Catch-a-Canoe & Bicycles Too!** fleet, at the Stanford Inn by the Sea (on the south bank of Big River), 44850 Comptche-Ukiah Rd., www.stanfordinn.com, 707/937-0273 or 800/331-8884. Birders especially will enjoy the serene estuarine tour of Big River. Catch a Canoe also rents bicycles and can offer tips on the best area rides. **Noyo-Pacific Outfitters** in Fort Bragg, 32400 N. Harbor Dr., 707/961-0559, www.noyopacific.com, offers guided kayaking trips, guided abalone diving, and kayak and dive rentals. **Lost Coast Adventures,** 707/937-2434, offers Sea-Cave Tours at Van Damme State Park in sit-on-top ocean kayaks. At last report **free, ranger-guided canoe trips** (for age 6 and older) were still offered in summer at **Navarro River Redwoods State Park** south of Mendocino. For details, call 707/937-5804.

Other Recreation

Ricochet Ridge Ranch, 24201 N. Hwy. 1, located north of Fort Bragg in Cleone, across the highway from the entrance to MacKerricher State Park, 707/964-7669 or 888/873-5777, www.horse-vacation.com, offers horseback rides along the beach at MacKerricher, as well as other rides (English/Western) by advance arrangement. **Back Kountry Trailrides,** about 14 miles east of Fort Bragg, 707/964-2700, www.bktrailrides.com, offers guided rides along redwood trails. Contact **Mendocino Village Carriage** on Little Lake Rd. in Mendocino, 707/937-4753 or 800/399-1454, for a tamer horsey experience—a carriage ride through town. For a guided llama trip, contact **Lodging and Llamas,** 18301 Old Coast Hwy., 707/964-7191, www.lodgingandllamas.com.

Near Fort Bragg, MacKerricher's Haul Rd. is a cycle path par excellence. Rent mountain bikes, 10-speeds, and two-seaters at **Fort Bragg Cyclery,** 579 S. Franklin St., 707/964-3509.

Just south of Mendocino is the historic **Little River Inn,** 7751 N. Hwy. 1, 707/937-5667, www.littleriverinn.com, with a regulation nine-hole golf course and lighted tennis courts.

STAYING IN AND NEAR MENDOCINO

The battle of the bed-and-breakfasts in and around Mendocino is just one aspect of the continuing local war over commercial and residential development. The conversion of homes to bed-and-breakfast establishments means fewer housing options for people who live here, but a moratorium on B&Bs may mean higher prices for visitor accommodations; the new Brewery Gulch Inn received the last "Mendocino village" bed-and-breakfast expansion permit allowed under the California Environmental Quality Act (CEQA). Most people here agree on one thing: only developers want to see large-scale housing or recreation developments in the area.

Avoid contributing to the problem altogether by camping. There are almost endless choices among the state parks nearby, and some very enjoyable, very reasonable alternatives inland along

Hwy. 128 toward Ukiah (see Anderson Valley in the Wine Country chapter). More than 2,000 commercial guest rooms are available in and around Mendocino, but that doesn't mean there's room at the inn (or motel) for spontaneous travelers. Usually people can find last-minute lodgings of some sort in Fort Bragg, though the general rule here is plan ahead or risk sleeping in your car or nestled up against your bicycle in the cold fog.

To stay in style in Mendocino, there are some great places to choose from; the region is renowned for its bed-and-breakfast inns. Advance reservations are absolutely necessary at most places on most weekends and during summer, preferably at least one month in advance (longer for greater choice). Most bed-and-breakfasts require a two-night minimum stay on weekends (three-night for holiday weekends) and an advance deposit. In the off season (winter and early spring) and at other low-demand times, many inns offer three-nights-for-the-price-of-two and other attractive specials, particularly midweek.

A number of the inns listed below, in both Mendocino and Fort Bragg, are members of the **Mendocino Coast Innkeepers Association,** 707/964-6725, and if one inn is full, it's possible that another can be accommodating. (Request a current brochure for full information.) **Mendocino Coast Reservations,** in Mendocino at 1000 Main St., 707/937-5033 or 800/262-7801, www.mendocinovacations.com, offers 60 or so fully furnished rentals by the weekend, week, or month, from cottages and cabins to homes and family reunion-sized retreats—"Fido-friendly" and "child-friendly" listings included. Mendocino Coast's "vacation stretch" policy gives you a third night free.

Mendocino Hotel

The grand 1878 **Mendocino Hotel & Garden Suites,** 45080 Main St., 707/937-0511 or 800/548-0513, www.mendocinohotel.com, started out as the town's Temperance House, a sober oasis in a wilderness of saloons and pool halls. Later, Mendocino's grand dame slid from grace and did time as a bordello. These days the Mendocino Hotel has settled back into her Victorian graces. All 51 meticulous rooms and

suites—24 Victorian rooms and two suites in the historic building, and 25 one- and two-story garden rooms and suites—are furnished in American and European antiques; many have fireplaces or wood-burning stoves and views of Mendocino Bay or the one-acre gardens, plus such not-like-home little luxuries as heated towel racks, fresh flowers from someone else's garden, and chocolate truffles on the pillow at bedtime. The hotel's parlor (note the 18th-century sculpted steel fireplace) is infused with informal Victorian coziness, more casual than the crystal-studded dining room. "European-style" Victorian rooms have in-room washbasins and shared baths (across the hall; bathrobes provided), $50–100; Victorian rooms with private bath are $100–150. Garden rooms are $150–250, suites $250 and up. Inquire about off-season specials, which can be quite attractive.

Bed-and-Breakfasts

Selecting "the best" bed-and-breakfasts in an area like Mendocino is like asking parents which of their children they love best. A new star in town, and amazingly elegant even for Mendocino, is **The Whitegate Inn,** 499 Howard St., 707/937-4892 or 800/531-7282, www.whitegateinn.com. This classic Victorian itself served as a star vehicle—in the classic *The Russians Are Coming* as well as Julia Roberts's *Dying Young* and Bette Davis's *Strangers.* But visitors don't stay strangers for long, once they step past that white gate and succumb to the Whitegate's charms—particularly if exquisite style and gourmet breakfasts served on bone china add up to the perfect escape. The entire inn, including the seven guest rooms, is impeccably decorated in French, Italian, and Victorian antiques. Amenities include fireplaces, European featherbeds and toiletries, down comforters, TVs, and clock radios—not to mention fresh-baked cookies and bedtime chocolates. Breakfast is also a sumptuous experience, with specialties such as pecan-and-date pancakes, eggs Florentine, and—everyone's favorite—caramel apple French toast. But don't forget to smell the roses, and all the other flowers in the spectacular cottage garden. Rates are $150–250 and $250 and up. Ask about midwinter specials.

The charming **MacCallum House,** 45020 Albion St., 707/937-0289 or 800/609-0492, www.maccallumhouse.com, is the town's most venerable bed-and-breakfast. This 1882 Victorian and its barn rooms and garden cottages, lovingly restored, still have a friendly quilts-and-steamer-trunk feel—like a fantasy weekend visit to Grandma's farm, if Grandma had some sense of style. MacCallum House features a total of 19 rooms—those recently remodeled feature sauna, hot tub, or jetted spa tub—and all have private baths. Six rooms are in the main house, some of these named after members of the MacCallum family; the master bedroom features a fabulous mahogany sleigh bed. Another six are in the barn, including the very special Upper Barn Loft. Of the seven cottages, the Gazebo Playhouse is most affordable, and the updated Greenhouse Cottage is wheelchair accessible. The spectacularly redone three-story Water Tower features a glass floor, to view the original hand-dug well (still producing water). A king and a queen bed plus pullout sofa, two-person Jacuzzi, sauna, fireplace, ocean view—you name it, it's here. MacCallum rates, including full gourmet breakfast, are $100–300 (Gazebo Playhouse, $120; Upper Barn Loft, $265; Water Tower, $295), but ask about specials. Children and pets (in some rooms) are welcome. Also on the premises are the excellent **MacCallum House Restaurant** and the **Grey Whale Bar & Café,** 707/937-5763, owned and overseen by Chef Alan Kantor, a graduate of the Culinary Institute of America. Both serve regional cuisine (seasonally changing menu), including fresh seafood and shellfish, meats and poultry, organic produce, and north coast wines, and both are open from 5:30 P.M. nightly. And don't miss the house-made ice creams. Reservations highly recommended.

The fine **Joshua Grindle Inn,** Mendocino's first bed-and-breakfast, 44800 Little Lake Rd., 707/937-4143 or 800/474-6353, www.joshgrin.com, is a New England country-style inn with 10 exquisite rooms furnished with Early Americana. The historic main building, surrounded with stunning cypress, was built in 1879 by local banker Joshua Grindle. All have private bathrooms; most feature wood-burning fireplaces or woodstoves; and some have deep soak tubs or other special features. Particularly inviting, for a little extra privacy, are the two large rooms in the converted water tower out back (there's also a small room, $130) and the two "saltbox cottage" rooms. Rates include a delicious full breakfast. Rates are $150–250, but ask about the inn's various specials, including Bed, Breakfast & Beaujolais; A Rub and a Tub; Mendocino Golf Special; and festival-related Winemaker's Dinner Packages. Joshua Grindle also offers an ocean-view guesthouse, located near the Point Cabrillo Light Station, north of Russian Gulch.

The 1878 **c.o. Packard House,** a striking carpenter's gothic Victorian on Mendocino's "executive row," across from the Mendocino Art Center at 45170 Little Lake Rd., 707/937-2677 or 888/453-2677, www.packardhouse.com, was once home to the town's chemist. The chemistry these days is notably stylish. All four rooms and the Maxwell Jarvis Suite boast sumptuous bed linens, jet-massage spa tubs (some with separate showers), TV/VCR, CD players, phones, and appealing French furniture. The suite features a living room, kitchenette, fold-away twin bed, and bedroom with an antique painted French bed. Rates for all are $150–250.

The **Blue Heron Inn,** 10390 Kasten St., 707/937-4323, www.theblueheron.com, is a small charmer, a New England–style home just a half-block from the ocean. Two of the inn's stylish yet simple, cozy upstairs rooms share a bath, $95 and $105; the other has a private bath, $115. Great ocean views from the deck. Downstairs is the popular **Moosse Café,** open for lunch (brunch on Sunday) and dinner daily.

The **John Dougherty House Bed & Breakfast,** 571 Ukiah St., 707/937-5266 or 800/486-2104, www.jdhouse.com, is a Mendocino classic. This 1867 Saltbox, surrounded by cottage gardens and filled with Early American antiques, is included on the town's historic house tour. Its two light, airy suites and several other rooms offer fabulous views. All six rooms (plus suites) have private baths, and some feature spa tubs and woodstoves. Two charming cabins are available. Bountiful hot breakfast. Rates are $150–250, with one room $135, another $145.

For something both contemporary and "country," try the blue-and-white **Agate Cove Inn,** just north of downtown at 11201 N. Lansing St., 707/937-0551 or 800/527-3111, www.agatecove.com. Agate Cove offers two rooms in an 1860s farmhouse (built by Mathias Brinzing, founder of Mendocino's first brewery) and a cluster of eight cottages, all on an acre and a half of beautifully landscaped grounds. Most rooms feature fireplaces, ocean views, and featherbeds; and; all have private baths, country decor, Scandia down comforters, hair dryers, TV/VCR, CD players, and irons with ironing boards. Enjoy a fabulous full country breakfast (cooked on an antique woodstove) of omelettes or other entrées with country sausage or ham, homebaked breads, jams and jellies, and coffee or tea. Rates are $150–250, with one room $119, two $269. The **Sea Rock Bed and Breakfast Inn,** 11101 Lansing St., 707/937-0926 or 800/906-0926, www .searock.com, is also a collection of country cottages and guest rooms, most of these with Franklin fireplaces; a few have kitchens, and all have private bath, queen bed, cable TV, and VCR. Breakfast buffet served in the lobby. Rooms are $150–250, suites $250 and up.

The **Headlands Inn,** at the corner of Albion and Howard Streets, 707/937-4431, www.headlandsinn.com, is a fully restored 1868 Victorian saltbox with seven rooms, each with antiques, private bath, and fireplace. In-room extras include fresh flowers, fruit, and a city newspaper. Two parlors, an English-style garden, and complimentary full breakfast, afternoon tea, and refreshments round out the amenities. Most rooms are $150–250, some lower.

The **Mendocino Village Inn Bed and Breakfast,** 44860 Main, 707/937-0246 or 800/882-7029, www.mendocinoinn.com, is a New England–style Victorian circa 1882, with 10 guest rooms (two attic rooms share a bath), many with fireplaces or woodstoves. Full breakfast. Rates are $100–150 and $150–250. Guests also have full spa privileges at the affiliated and adjacent **Sweetwater Spa & Inn,** 44840 Main St., 707/937-4076 or 800/300-4140, www.sweetwaterspa.com, which offers water tower rooms and cottages, rooms in an 1870 Victorian elsewhere in the village, and accommodations south of Mendocino in Little River. All accommodations except one have private baths; most have woodstoves or fireplaces, many are pet-friendly. Some have hot tubs. Most rates are $150–250 (one room $295); most Little River rooms are $50–100 (one room $130).

Stanford Inn by the Sea

How organic can you get? To find out, head for the comfortably luxurious yet outdoorsy Stanford Inn by the Sea (known in a previous incarnation as the Big River Lodge), 44850 Comptche-Ukiah Rd. (at Hwy. 1, on the south bank of Big River), 707/937-5615 or 800/331-8884, www .stanfordinn.com. This is an elegant, friendly lodge with vast gardens. But here, the working certified organic garden and farm—Big River Nurseries—dominate the setting. The swimming pool, sauna, and spa are enclosed in one of the farm's greenhouses. The on-site **Ravens** restaurant is strictly (and deliciously) vegetarian and/or vegan, even serving organic wines. The inn may be organic, but it's not overly fussy—pets are welcome (and also pampered), for a fee, and "guest-friendly" dogs, cats, llamas, and swans are available for those who arrive petless. The Stanford Inn also provides exercise facilities and complimentary mountain bikes; canoe and kayak rentals are available.

The 33 guest rooms and suites are inviting and outdoorsy, paneled in pine and redwood, and decked out with big four-poster or sleigh beds and decent reading lights. Each features a wood-burning fireplace or Irish Waterford stove, as well as houseplants and original local art. Amenities include in-room coffee makers and refrigerators, TV with cable and Cinemax, and stereos with CD players (on-site CD library, or bring your own). Rates are $250 and up, complimentary gourmet breakfast included; one-bedroom suites start at $320, two-bedroom suites, $630. But ask about the Stanford Inn's Health Kick and other special packages. **Catch a Canoe & Bicycles Too,** 707/937-0273, is also based here, for kayak, canoe, and outrigger rentals (and sales), lessons, and guided trips. Mountain bikes, too.

STAYING OUTSIDE MENDOCINO

Little River and Albion B&Bs

Heading north, the **Brewery Gulch Inn,** 9350 N. Hwy. 1, 707/937-4752 or 800/578-4454, www .brewerygulchinn.com, is a Mendocino phenom these days. The original pre-Victorian farmhouse has been supplanted by a dazzling new inn showcasing old-growth redwood felled in the mid-1800s but only recently fished up from the bottom of Big River as sodden, mineralized "eco-salvage" or "guiltless redwood." The new, red-wood shake-sided Brewery Gulch Inn is elegant in its simplicity and craftsmanship. From the spectacular Great Room, with its soaring ceilings and skylights, immense glass-and-steel fireplace, and dramatic views of Smugglers's Cove to exquisite Arts and Crafts period–inspired furnishings and quietly luxurious guest rooms—every painstaking detail attests to the Brewery Gulch Inn's emphasis on quality. Rooms feature striking hardwood furniture, leather chairs fronting gas fireplaces, luxury linens, down comforters, TVs with DVDs, CD players, and dataports. Most have private decks, all have ocean views. Private bathrooms, with granite vanities and redwood cabinetry, come with terry bathrobes, hair dryers, quality toiletries, and tub-shower combinations; some have Jacuzzi or large soaking tubs. One room has been designed for disabled access. Most rates are $150–250, ranging as high as $295 (lower off-season rates Nov.–Mar.). And here, the idea of fashioning something new from the old applies to the land itself, since this is the site of Mendocino's first real farm and a perfect microclimate for vegetables, fruit trees, and roses. A veritable farm once again, thanks to proprietor Dr. Arky Ciancutti and his green thumb, both inn and 10-acre homestead have met standards of the California Organic Foods Act of 1990.

Or head south. Rachel Binah is a creative cook and caterer also noted for her **Rachel's Inn,** 8200 N. Hwy. 1, 707/937-0088 or 800/347-9252, www.rachelsinn.com, with five rooms in the Victorian farmhouse and four suites in the adjacent barn. Just north of Van Damme State Park, the inn abuts an undeveloped strip of the park just two miles south of Mendocino. Each room has its own bathroom, a big bed, fresh flowers and personal amenities, plus individual charm: a view of the ocean or gardens, a balcony, or a fireplace. If you rent all or a combination of rooms for a casual conference or family gathering, special dinners can be arranged. Any day of the week, a good full breakfast is served in the dining room. Most rates are $150–250, with one room $145, another $135. New at Rachel's are two charming cabins—Parkside Cottage on the inn grounds, $285, and the Little River Cottage near the inn, $300–350.

Across the highway is **Glendeven,** 8221 N. Hwy. 1, 707/937-0083 or 800/822-4536, www .glendeven.com, part inn, part art gallery, the latter featuring quilted paper and other textile works, abstract art, and handcrafted furniture. It has been declared one of the 10 best inns in the U.S. by *Country Inns* magazine. Glendeven's charms start with the New England Federalist farmhouse, continue into the secluded and luxurious Carriage House, and also the Stevenscroft annex. Many rooms and suites feature fireplaces and ocean views—not to mention exquisite antiques and linens, every imaginable amenity, and sumptuous breakfast. Most rooms are $150–250 (above $200), one is $185. La Bella Vista, a two-bedroom rental house, is available for $275–380 per night.

South of Mendocino are several other options. Notable among them is **Cypress Cove** on Chapman Point, 45200 Chapman Dr., 707/937-1456 or 800/942-6300, www.cypresscove.com—quite the place to get away from it all. The property's two luxury suites look out on Mendocino and the bay. Amenities include queen beds, fireplaces, and two-person Jacuzzi tubs. Among the plush extras: in-room coffee, tea, brandy, chocolate, fresh flowers, and bathrobes. One suite has a full kitchen, the other a kitchenette. High-season rates (May–Oct.) are $250 and up, lower in the off-season.

In Little River, **The Inn at Schoolhouse Creek,** 7051 N. Hwy. 1, 707/937-5525 or 800/ 731-5525, www.schoolhousecreek.com, features a variety of restored 1930s country-style garden cottages looking downslope to the ocean. All have fireplaces, private baths, and TVs and VCRs; some have kitchens. Rates for cottages and suites are $150–250, including full breakfast, access to the welcoming lodge (books, games, and breakfast), and a chance to jump into that hot tub. The inn also offers attractive, motel-like rooms for $130; one has two queen beds. Be sure to ask about winter specials.

Farther south on the highway is the beautiful **Albion River Inn,** 3790 N. Hwy. 1 in Albion, 707/937-1919 or 800/479-7944, www.albionriverinn.com, offering 22 rooms in New England–style blufftop cottages, each one unique. Fireplaces, decks, and ocean views are par for the course here, and the inn's elegant gourmet restaurant draws visitors north from San Francisco, locals south from Mendocino and Fort Bragg—and raves from the likes of *Bon Appetit* and *Wine Spectator.* Rates include full breakfast, wine, coffee and tea, and morning newspaper. Standard rooms are $150–250, and "tub for two" and spa tub rooms are $250 and up.

The unusually charismatic **Fensalden Inn,** seven miles south of Mendocino and then inland, at 33810 Navarro Ridge Rd. in Albion, 707/937-4042 or 800/959-3850, www.fensalden.com, is a restored two-story stage station circa 1880, still straddling the ridgetop among open fields and forests. The eight charming rooms feature exquisite antiques; all have fireplaces. For the more rustically inclined, there's the weather-beaten, fully modern Bungalow beyond the inn, in a meadow. Hors d'oeuvres, wine, and full breakfast are complimentary. All rooms are under $200; one is $125, another $135 (lower in winter). The Bungalow is $225.

Little River Inn

In "downtown" Little River, the classic stay is the family-owned Little River Inn, just south of Van Damme State Park at 7751 N. Hwy. 1, 707/937-5942 or 888/466-5683, www.littleriverinn.com, originally just one rambling Victorian mansion built by lumberman Silas Coombs in the area's characteristic Maine style. (To get the whole story, buy a copy of *The Finn, the Twin, and the Inn: A History of the Little River Inn and Its Families.*) The Little River Inn has grown over the years. In addition to its classic fireplace cottages and updated lodging annex, it also includes fairly new romantic luxury suites just up the hill—complete with gigantic Jacuzzi tubs, wood-burning fireplaces, view decks and patios, and every imaginable amenity. The old inn itself is still a slice of Victorian gingerbread. Upstairs are several small and affordable rooms—and really the best, in terms of period charm: quilt-padded attic accommodations illuminated by tiny seaward-spying dome windows. The Little River Inn is a wonderful place, all the way around.

Tucked in behind appealing, locally loved **Ole's Whale Watch Bar**—from which, according to local lore, actor James Dean was once tossed for putting his feet up on a table—is the Little River Inn's **Garden Dining Room.** The restaurant serves great food, including simple and excellent white-tablecloth breakfasts with Ole's famous Swedish hotcakes, absolutely perfect eggs, and fresh-squeezed orange or grapefruit juice. The inn's restaurant is just about the only room in sight without an ocean view, but it does feature many windows—these opening out into lush and inviting gardens. If you arrive when the restaurant's closed, Ole's has a good bar menu. And great ocean views.

The inn also offers an **18-hole golf course**—the only one on the Mendocino Coast—and **lighted tennis courts.** For tee times, call 707/937-5667. In addition to full meeting and small-conference facilities, a recent arrival is **The Third Court Day Spa,** with a full menu of men's and women's body and facial massages, skin treatments, and hair and nail care. For spa reservations, call 707/937-3099.

The three antique rooms upstairs in the main lodge are $110. Most rooms and suites are in the $150–250 range, including the older, motel-style units, both with and without wood-burning fireplaces or woodstoves, and most of the spacious, contemporary suites up the hill that feature wood-burning fireplaces and two-person Jacuzzi tubs ($235–255 in the high season). They all offer fabulous ocean views. Luxury suites, with outdoor decks and hot tubs in addition to indoor Jacuzzi tubs and other luxuries, are available offsite, $250 and up, along with two cottages. White Cottage ($255 per night) features dramatics views, and Llama Cottage ($220) offers gardens, forest—and llamas. All accommodations are lower in the off season. Inquire about specials and packages. Two-night minimum stay on weekends, three-night on holiday weekends.

Heritage House

South of Little River proper, the Heritage House, 5200 N. Hwy. 1, 707/937-5885 or 800/235-5885, was once a safe harbor for notorious gangster Baby Face Nelson, though things are quite civilized and serene these days. Heritage House itself is an old Maine-style farmhouse (now the inn's dining room, kitchen, and office) and the center of a large complex of antique-rich luxury cottages and suites—the best ones looking out to sea. Rates $150–250. Another major attraction is the exceptional yet reasonably relaxed **Heritage House Restaurant**, with its stunning domed dining room, open nightly for dinner—except when the entire establishment is shut down in winter, usually from Thanksgiving through Christmas and again January 2 to President's Day in February. The gardens (and garden shop) at Heritage House are also quite impressive.

Fort Bragg Motels and Lodges

Mendocino has most of the bed-and-breakfasts, but Fort Bragg has the motels—in general the most reasonable accommodations option around besides camping. Most places have cheaper off-season rates, from November through March or April. Pick up a current listing of area motels at the chamber office.

Fisherfolk, you can stay in and near Noyo Harbor. **Harbor Lite Lodge,** 120 N. Harbor Dr., 707/964-0221 or 800/643-2700, www.harborlitelodge.com, overlooks Noyo Harbor from just off the highway. Most rooms (including view rooms) are $50–100, fireplaces extra. The **Anchor Lodge** in Noyo (office in The Wharf Restaurant), 780 N. Harbor Dr., 707/964-4283, www.wharf-restaurant.com, has 19 rooms, some right on the river, some with kitchens. Standard rooms are $50–100, apartment units $100–150. Pleasant **Surf Motel** is at 1220 S. Main St. (at Ocean View Dr., south of the Noyo River Bridge), 707/964-5361 or 800/339-5361, www.surfmotelfortbragg.com, with rooms $50–100. Across the way (on the ocean side) and open since 2001 is the 43-room **Emerald Dolphin Inn,** 1211 S.

Main St., 707/964-6699 or 866/964-6699, www.emeralddolphin.com. Most rooms and suites are $50–100 or $100–150, though ask about specials and discounts. Pets welcome in certain rooms ($10 extra).

You'll find a cluster of places on the beach side of the highway, just north of town past the Pudding Creek trestle. These places provide easy access to the Haul Road and beach, and all offer rooms in the $50–100 and $100–150 range. The very friendly **Beachcomber Motel,** 1111 N. Main St., 707/964-2402 or 800/400-7873, www.thebeachcombermotel.com ($50–100 and $100–150), sometimes welcomes pets. Shockingly urban, in such a remote setting, are the condo-like **Surf 'n Sand Lodge,** 1131 N. Main (Hwy. 1), 707/964-9383 or 800/964-0184, www.surfsandlodge.com, and across the highway, the **Beach House Inn,** 100 Pudding Creek Rd., 707/961-1700 or 888/559-9992, www.beachinn.com. Rates rangs $50–150.

Fort Bragg B&Bs

The boxy, weathered, clear-heart redwood **Grey Whale Inn,** 615 Main St., 707/964-0640 or 800/382-7244, www.greywhaleinn.com, was once the community hospital. If you're one of those people who don't think they like bed-and-breakfasts—under any circumstances—this place could be the cure for what ails you. The two-story whale of an inn offers peace and privacy, very wide hallways, 14 individually decorated rooms and suites (some quite large) with myriad amenities, a basement pool table and rec room, fireplace, and an award-winning breakfast buffet of hot dish, cereals, coffeecakes, fresh fruits and juices, yogurt or cheese, and good coffee. (And if you don't feel too sociable in the morning, load up a tray in the breakfast room and take breakfast back to bed with you.) A truly exceptional stay—and some of the rooms are quite affordable. All rooms are under $200. Four are under $125, including Fern Creek, a two-room suite with a queen bed, a twin, and a mini-kitchen. Another plus: from here it's an easy walk to downtown shops and galleries, Glass Beach, and area restaurants.

For fans of Victoriana, a particularly inviting local bed-and-breakfast is the 1886 **Weller House Inn,** 524 Stewart St., 707/964-4415 or 877/893-

5537, www.wellerhouse.com—the only Mendocino Coast inn listed on the National Register of Historic Places. The seven Victorian guest rooms all have private baths; some have fireplaces or woodstoves, Jacuzzi tubs, or clawfoot bathtubs. "Very full" breakfast is served in the 900-square-foot ballroom, completely paneled in exquisite old redwood. All rooms are $100–150, several slightly higher on weekends.

The newly restored 1892 **Old Coast Hotel,** 101 N. Franklin St., 707/961-4488 or 888/468-3550, www.oldcoasthotel.com, is another great choice, a painstakingly restored Victorian hotel with decorative tin ceilings, polished oak floors, and granite fireplaces—a historic restoration recognized in 1997 with the mayor's award. The hotel's 16 rooms are "European style," but with private bathrooms, cozy quilts, and unique decor. Most rooms are $50–100, some slightly higher. And hey, sports fans: this may be the place for a getaway weekend. The handsome sports-themed bar and grill downstairs serves up regional microbrews and plenty of sports, from four TV sets. Restaurant fare is quite good, from award-winning clam chowder to peppercorn steak.

The two-story **Noyo River Lodge,** 500 Casa del Noyo Dr., 707/964-8045 or 800/628-1126, www.noyolodge.com, is a redwood Craftsman-style mansion (circa 1868) on a hill with harbor and ocean views, rooms and suites with private baths (some with fireplaces), a restaurant and lounge, big soaking tubs, skylights, and gardens. All rooms are under $200.

South of Fort Bragg and just north of Caspar, across from the state park, is **Annie's Jughandle Beach B&B,** 32980 Gibney Lane (at Hwy. 1), 707/964-1415 or 800/964-9957, www.jughandle.com, with five rooms featuring private baths and fireplaces, as well as a hot tub, ocean views, and excellent breakfasts. Rates range $100–250 (oceanview rooms on the high end), including "Mendocino magic," Cajun-style gourmet breakfast.

EATING IN MENDOCINO

Basics

For the **Mendocino Certified Farmers Market,** which runs May through Oct., show up on Friday, noon–2 P.M., at Howard and Main Streets. Otherwise stock up on natural foods, for here or to go, at **Corners of the Mouth,** 45015 Ukiah St., 707/937-5345, and get general groceries at **Mendosa's,** 10501 Lansing St., 707/937-5879. For gourmet goodies, bakery goods, and take-out, stop by **Tote Fete,** 10450 Lansing, 707/937-3383. Wander over to **Café Beaujolais** (see below) for fresh-baked bread.

For a hefty slice of pizza or quiche, a bowl of homemade soup, or just a good danish and a café latte, head for the **Mendocino Bakery,** 10483 Lansing, 707/937-0836. It's the locals' coffee-house of choice and offers outdoor seating when the weather's nice. Open 7:30 A.M.–7 P.M. weekdays, 8:00 A.M.–7 P.M. weekends. The **Mendo Juice Joint,** on Ukiah a half block east of Lansing, 707/937-4033, specializes in fresh juices, smoothies, and healthy snacks.

Mendo Burgers, 10483 Lansing, 707/937-1111, is open 11 A.M.–7:30 P.M. and serves beef, turkey, fish, and veggie burgers, as well as ice cream. Also balm for that sweet tooth are the definitely decadent chocolates at **Mendocino Chocolate Company,** also at 10483 Lansing, 707/937-1107. The **Mendocino Cookie Company,** at home in the old Union Lumber Company building, 301 N. Main, 707/964-0282, serves up more than a dozen delectable varieties, from peanut butter chocolate chip and white chocolate almond to Grandma Daisy's shortbread.

Simple and Good

Herbivorous visitors will be right at home at **Lu's Kitchen,** 45013 Ukiah St., 707/937-4939, which serves "organic cross-cultural vegetarian cuisine" in a casual atmosphere. Garden seating and take-out, too. Look for salads, quesadillas, and burritos in the $4–7 range. Closed in January, part of Feb., and in heavy rain.

One of the best views in town is from the big deck at the **Mendocino Café,** 10451 Lansing St., 707/937-2422 or 707/937-6141, which has a great menu of Pacific Rim–inspired cuisine (try the Thai burrito) and a good beer selection. Another place for great views—but in a slightly more upscale atmosphere—is the **Bay View Cafe,** 45040 Main St. (upstairs), 707/937-4197, which serves south-of-the-border specialties and enjoys unobstructed views of the coast from its second-story bay windows.

Cafe Beaujolais

No one should come anywhere near Mendocino without planning to eat at least one meal at the noted Cafe Beaujolais, 961 Ukiah St., 707/937-5614, now under new ownership. The fresh-flower decor inside and on the deck of this old house is as refreshingly simple and fine as the food itself. Johnny Carson, Julia Child, Robert Redford, the food writer Elizabeth David, and food critics from the *New York Times* eat here when they're in town. But since Margaret Fox, once a baker in the back room of the Mendocino Hotel, first opened the café's doors more than a decade ago, it's been a people's place. Despite its fame, it still is—though some still haven't gotten over the fact that Cafe Beaujolais is no longer open for breakfast. (Beaujolais' famous blackberry jam, cashew granola, waffle mix, Panforte di Mendocino, and other take-home treats are available here and at various gift shops.)

Cafe Beaujolais begins with carefully selected ingredients—organic produce (visit the gardens here) as well as fresh local fish and seafood as well as chemical-free meat, poultry, and eggs from free-range, humanely raised animals. Dinner is a fixed-price French-and-California-cuisine affair featuring such things as local smoked salmon and roast duck with a purée of apples and turnips, still more decadent desserts, and an almost endless and excellent California wine list. Cafe Beaujolais is open for dinner nightly 5:45–9 P.M., though the restaurant is closed from late November through January. Reservations are necessary. Bring cash or personal checks; no credit cards accepted. The restaurant's bakery, called The Brickery, produces breads and pizzas from a wood-fired brick oven. Drop by for loves of country sourdough, Austrian sunflower bread, olive rosemary focaccia, and other signature breads daily, 11 A.M.–4 or 5 P.M.

Other Worthy Restaurants

Neighbor to Cafe Beaujolais is **955 Ukiah St.,** 707/937-1955, difficult to find in the fog despite its numerically straightforward attitude. (The entrance is 100 feet off the street around a few corners.) The dining room is a former art studio. Dinners feature entrées including excellent fresh seafood—say, lightly smoked salmon, prawns, ling cod, and mahi mahi with tomatoes, roasted garlic, and basil, mixed with fettuccine—leg of lamb stew, peppercorn steak, unforgettable breadsticks, and Navarro and Husch wines from the Anderson Valley. For dessert, don't miss the bread pudding with huckleberry compote. No credit cards. Open Wed.–Sun. from 6 P.M. Also quite good in town is the **MacCallum House Restaurant,** 45020 Albion, 707/937-5763, open nightly for dinner (see bed-and-breakfast listing above for more information), and the **Moosse Café,** 390 Kasten St., 707/937-4323, featuring an eclectic menu of north coast fare—and sumptuous chocolate desserts. Open for lunch and dinner daily, and brunch on Sunday.

For prime rib, steaks, and seafood in a Victorian setting, consider the crystal-and-Oriental-carpet ambience of the **Mendocino Hotel,** 45080 Main St., 707/937-0511. At the hotel's more casual Garden Court restaurant and bar, the ceiling is almost one immense skylight—to keep the interior garden going. With that in mind, enjoy the salads and other greens with gusto. Open daily for breakfast, lunch, and dinner. For fine vegetarian meals, try **Ravens** restaurant at the **Stanford Inn,** Hwy. 1 and Comptche-Ukiah Rd., 707/937-5615.

EATING OUTSIDE MENDOCINO

Little River and Albion

You can always find a great meal at the grand white Victorian **Little River Inn,** looming up next to the highway south of Mendocino, 707/937-5942, which is famous for its Swedish hotcakes and other breakfasts and brunches but also offers fine American-classic dinners emphasizing steak and seafood. Another Little River classic, a tad fancier, is **The Restaurant at Stevenswood** at Stevenswood Lodge, 8211 N. Hwy. 1, 707/937-2810, where dinner specialties range from herb-crusted lamb loin and prime dry-aged New York steak to pine nut–crusted salmon filet served with grilled parmesan polenta.

At the elegant **Ledford House,** 3000 N. Hwy. 1 (south of "downtown" Albion), 707/937-0282, even vegetarians can try the excellent soups because none are made with meat bases. Entrées include pasta picks like ravioli stuffed with ricotta cheese in sorrel cream sauce, and some definitely nonstandard seafood and meat specialties. The nearby **Albion River Inn,** 3790 N. Hwy. 1, 707/937-1919, serves up spectacular views, an outstanding wine list, and hearty California fusion, from grilled ginger-lime prawns to oven-roasted quail.

Another area dining destination is the **Heritage House Restaurant,** 5200 Hwy. 1 south of Little River, 707/937-5885, with a striking dining room, views, and an impressive seasonally changing menu.

Fort Bragg Basics

Finding a meal in Fort Bragg is usually a more relaxed task than in Mendocino, with less confusion from the madding crowds. Most restaurants are casual. For farm-fresh everything, show up for the **Fort Bragg Certified Farmers Market,** held May–Oct. on Wed. 3:30–6 P.M., at Laurel and Franklin. Call 707/964-6340 for details. The place for just-off-the-boat ingredients if you're cooking your own seafood is **Capt. Bobino's Mendocino Fresh Seafood** in Noyo Harbor at 32440 N. Harbor Dr., 707/964-9297. For something different to take home as a memento, stop by Carol Hall's **Hot Pepper Jelly Company,** 330 N. Main, 707/961-1899 or 866/737-7379, www.hotpepperjelly.com, an inviting shop that sells intriguing jams and jellies, fruit syrups, mustards, herb vinegars, and unusual food-related gift items.

For a sweet treat, head for the **Mendocino Chocolate Company,** two blocks away at 542 N. Main, 707/964-8800 or 800/722-1107 (for orders), www.mendocino-chocolate.com, which serves up everything from edible seashells and Mendocino toffee to an amazing array of truffles and chews—including Fort Bragg 2x4s (peanut butter-flavored fudge "veneered" with dark chocolate) and Mr. Peanut Coastal Clusters. Though this is headquarters, there's another company outlet in Mendocino. Another possibility is **Cowlicks Ice Cream Café,** 250-B N. Main,

707/962-9271, or sample dessert at any number of wonderful local restaurants. **Headlands Coffee House,** 120 E. Laurel St., 707/964-1987, an artsy place famous for its "hot java and cool jazz," is not at all shabby for dessert either; sample the Cafe Beaujolais Amazon Chocolate Cake. Headlands serves espresso, coffee drinks galore, fountain items, and a selection of soups, salads, and hearty, inexpensive entrées along with an interesting crowd of locals. At breakfast, try the Belgian waffle with fruit and yogurt.

Fort Bragg Breakfast and Lunch

In addition to local coffeehouses, a perennial favorite for breakfast is venerable **Egghead Omelettes of Oz,** 326 N. Main St., 707/964-5005, a cheerful diner with booths, the whole place decorated in a Wizard of Oz theme. (Follow the Yellow Brick Road through the kitchen to the restrooms out back.) Equally unforgettable, on the menu, are fried potatoes and omelettes with endless combinations for fillings, including avocado and crab. Good sandwiches at lunch. Open daily 7 A.M.–2 P.M. For organic everything—vegetarian fare in particular but also free-range chicken, seafood, and organic wines and beers—try **Cafe One,** 753 N. Main, 707/964-3309, open daily for breakfast and lunch, and (at last report) on Friday and Saturday in summer for dinner.

At lunch, locals line up for the Dagwood-style sandwiches at **David's Deli,** 450 S. Franklin St., 707/964-1946, but breakfast here is pretty special, too. For a unique atmosphere, head just south of town to the Mendocino Coast Botanical Gardens, where you can dine with garden views at the **Gardens Grill,** 18220 N. Hwy. 1, 707/964-7474. It's open for lunch Mon.–Sat., for dinner Thurs.-Sat., and for Sunday brunch.

Fort Bragg American-Style and Special

A Fort Bragg favorite is hip **Mendo Bistro,** 301 Main (at Redwood, upstairs in the Company Store), 707/964-4974, where the great food and reasonable prices share star billing. Here, you can pick a meat or seafood entrée and a style of preparation, then get it served just the way you like it for $8–15. Or choose from a half-dozen wonderful house-made pastas for $12, or entrées—such things as from free range–chicken pot pie to potato-crusted Alaskan halibut with roasted peppers, olives, and pesto—for $14–15. The monthly changing menu showcases the freshest possible ingredients. It really is affordable to eat here—so long as you don't carried away with the knock-out appetizers, including Mendo Bistro's award-winning crab cakes.

Otherwise, for a special dinner folks head to the **Rendezvous Inn & Restaurant,** just down the street from the Grey Whale Inn at 647 N. Main St., 707/964-8142 or 800/491-8142. This gorgeous homey bungalow with warm wood interiors serves marvelous crab cakes, jambalaya, vegetarian pasta and "beggar's purses," civet of venison, and other unusual entrées, starting from the freshest local ingredients. Open Wed.–Sun. for dinner. Upstairs are several guest rooms, each with private bath ($50–100, slightly higher in summer).

In a little less rarified atmosphere, good food is also available at **North Coast Brewing Co. Taproom and Restaurant,** 444 N. Main, 707/964-3400, a brewpub and grill pouring award-winning handmade ales to accompany pub grub (including Route 66 chili), pastas, steaks, seafood, and Cajun-inspired dishes. On a sunny day, the outside beer garden—a genuine garden, quite appealing—can't be beat. Beer lovers take note: North Coast is among the finest of North American micro-breweries, consistently producing brews that always satisfy and frequently astonish even the pickiest connoisseurs. All the offerings are outstanding, but don't miss the unique Belgian-style Pranqster or the positively evil Rasputin imperial stout. Open noon–11 P.M. daily except Monday. Across the street (at 455 N. Main) is the brewery itself, 707/964-2739, www.ncoast-brewing.com, offering free tours on weekdays, along with some memorable memorabilia and gift items.

A good choice for families is **The Restaurant,** 418 N. Main St., 707/964-9800, where the California-style fare might include delectable entrées such as poached halibut, calamari, scallops, shrimp, steak, and quail. Open for lunch and dinner (call for current schedule) and Sunday brunch. Children's menu. Reservations wise. The sports-themed restaurant at the restored **Old Coast Hotel,** 101 N. Franklin, 707/961-4488, is another possibility, with a steak and seafood menu. Open for lunch and dinner daily.

Fort Bragg Seafood

Well-prepared seafood abounds at the area's finer restaurants, but Fort Bragg's favorite fancy seafood restaurant, open for dinner only, is **The Cliff House,** just south of the Harbor Bridge, 1011 S. Main St., 707/961-0255. Overlooking the jetty and the harbor, The Cliff House serves wonderful seafood, steak, and pastas—try the smoked salmon ravioli—along with specialties including chicken mushroom Dijon and pepper steak. On Friday and Saturday night, prime rib is also on the menu.

The place for seafood with a view in Noyo Harbor is tiny, unpretentious **Sharon's by the Sea** at 32096 N. Harbor Dr., 707/962-0680, open daily for fish tacos, fish and chips, and snapper piccata at lunch, and northern Italian dinner specialties such as cioppino, linguini alla vongole, shrimp scampi, and spinach torta. Angle for a seat out on the deck to take in the sunset.

Otherwise, the harbor is where the tourists go for fish. That said, **The Wharf,** 780 N. Harbor Dr., 707/964-4283, serves a creamy clam chowder and crispy-outside, tender-inside fried clams, and the prime rib sandwich is nothing to throw a crabpot at. Dinner specialties include seafood and steak. The specialty at the plastic-tableclothed **Cap'n Flint's,** 32250 N. Harbor, 707/964-9447, is shrimp won tons with cream cheese filling.

Ethnic Options

Yes, Fort Bragg has ethnic food, and most of it is pretty darned good. **Viraporn's,** on S. Main St. at Chestnut (across the street from PayLess), 707/964-7931, serves great Thai food, while **Samraat,** 546 S. Main, 707/964-0386, specializes in the tastes of India. Both of these restaurants, humble as they may appear from the outside, are worth seeking out.

Just north of town in Cleone, the legendary **Purple Rose,** 24300 N. Hwy. 1, 707/964-6507, prepares locally famous Mexican food in a bright, spacious, and casual atmosphere. The veggie burrito here is a work of culinary art. Open Wed.–Sun. for dinner. (Within walking distance from the campgrounds at MacKerricher State Park, the Purple Rose makes the perfect break from roasted weenies and marshmallows.) Mexican fare is also available in town at **El Sombrero,** 223 N. Franklin, 707/964-5780, and down in Noyo Harbor at **El Mexicano,** 701 N. Harbor Dr., 707/964-7164, which serves up authentic Mexican, down to the fresh-daily tortillas.

For Italian, everyone's favorite is **D'Aurelio's,** 438 S. Franklin St., 707/964-4227, which offers outstanding pizzas, calzones, and the like in a comfortable, casual atmosphere. Another possibility is **Bernillo's,** 220 E. Redwood Ave., 707/964-9314.

ARTS AND ENTERTAINMENT

For most people, just being here along the Mendocino coast is entertainment enough. But if that's too quiet, consider the **Caspar Inn** between Mendocino and Fort Bragg, 707/964-

5565, www.casparinn.com, "home of the blues in Caspar, California" and a venerable roadhouse—the last classic roadhouse in California. This boisterous tavern adheres to tradition, too, with packed houses dancing to big-name blues and touring bands. If the nightlife is the right life for you, even on vacation, keep in mind that the Caspar Inn includes 10 rooms upstairs (shared baths down the hall), $60 including show admission, as well as **La Playa** Mexican restaurant.

On the first Friday evening of the month, don't miss Fort Bragg's **First Friday,** when arts galleries and shops keep later hours, 5–8 P.M., during open receptions with wine and hors d'oeuvres. Festivities include coffeehouse concerts, street theater, and other surprises. Similar **Second Saturday** events are held 5–8 P.M. in Mendocino's galleries (you guessed it) on the second Saturday of every month, with more universal participation April through September. For the latest on this and other art events, stop by the Mendocino Art Center (see Seeing and Doing Mendocino above) or contact the **Arts Council of Mendocino County,**

MOVIE-MAD MENDOCINO

Mendocino and the Mendocino Headlands have hosted countless movie crews, including the 1943 swashbuckling romance *Frenchman's Creek*—based on a Daphne du Maurier novel and starring Joan Fontaine, Arturo de Cordova, and Basil Rathbone—which took that year's Academy Award for Best Art Direction. In 1948 *Johnny Belinda* rolled into town. Jane Wyman, who played the tragic part of a deaf girl living on the Nova Scotia coast, left Mendocino to pick up an Oscar, later in the year, for Best Actress. But by the time film production ended, Jane Wyman and then-husband Ronald Reagan were in divorce court. "I think I'll name Johnny Belinda co-respondent," Reagan said.

In 1955 Mendocino's movie was Elia Kazan's version of *East of Eden,* the very-California John Steinbeck telling of the Cain and Abel story, starring James Dean as Caleb "Cal" Trask (Cain), the tragic loner, and Rochard Davolos as their father's favored son, Aron. Scenes from *Rebel Without a Cause* were also shot here. In 1966 the Cold War comedy *The Russians Are Coming! The Russians Are Coming!* rowed ashore, starring Alan Arkin in his first major role. In the 1970s came *The Summer of '42,* Herman Raucher's coming-of-age tale. The annual trysting place for Alan Alda and Ellen Burstyn in 1978's *Same Time, Next Year* was just south along the coast at Heritage House in Little River.

The popular 1980s TV series *Murder She Wrote* was also filmed largely in and around Mendocino; the house at 45110 Little Lake Street, now a bed-and-breakfast, was Jessica Fletcher's home in Cabot Cove, and Fort Bragg's Noyo Harbor starred as Cabot Cove's fishing harbor. Other movies made along the Mendocino Coast include *Overboard, Cujo, Forever Young, The Majestic, The Fog, Racing with the Moon, Slither, Island of the Blue Dolphins,* and *Humanoids from the Deep.*

14125 Hwy. 128 in Boonville, 707/895-3680 or 888/278-3773 (hotline), www.artsmendocino.org, an umbrella for some 30 nonprofit arts groups that maintains a comprehensive calendar of events.

At home in Mendocino is the **Mendocino Theatre Company,** 45200 Little Lake Rd., 707/937-4477, which typically begins its performance season in the tiny Helen Schoeni Theatre every March. An eclectic mix of one-night or short-run acts—anything from local school plays to comedy troupes to touring world-beat bands—are presented at Mendocino's **Crown Hall,** 45285 Ukiah St. (down at the west end), a delightfully intimate venue with reasonably good acoustics as well. Mendocino's **Opera Fresca,** 707/937-3646 or 888/826-7372, www.operafresca.com, has adopted Mendocino College's Center Theatre in Ukiah as its main stage, but is headquartered in Mendocino and does offer performances along the coast.

Fort Bragg is also quite theatrical. The **Gloriana Opera Company,** 721 N. Franklin St., 707/964-7469, www.gloriana.org, offers a six-week run in summer and special events throughout the year. The **Footlighters Little Theatre,** 248 E. Laurel St., 707/964-3806, performs Gay Nineties melodrama from Memorial Day through Labor Day. Fort Bragg is also home to the fine **Symphony of the Redwoods,** 707/964-0898. During its September to May season the orchestra plays three or four concert "sets," the first performance of each on Saturday night in Fort Bragg, the second on Sunday afternoon some 60 miles south along the coast at the Gualala Arts Center. The symphony also offers its **Opus Chamber Music Series** on Sunday afternoons in Mendocino's Preston Hall and performs at other events and venues, including the mid-July Mendocino Music Festival. The symphony and both area opera companies are working to renovate the 1914 redwood **Eagles Hall,** 210 N. Corry St. (at Alder), into a snazzy performance venue.

Events

Definitely hot in the chill of winter: **Mendocino Crab & Wine Days,** held from late January into February and featuring endless creativity in culinary and wine pairings. Down the coast, come February, is the annual **Gualala Chocolate Festival.**

Everyone celebrates the return of the California gray whale. The **Mendocino Whale Festival,** on the first weekend in March, celebrates the annual cetacean migration with wine and clam-chowder tastings, art exhibits, music and concerts, and other special events. The **Fort Bragg Whale Festival,** held the third weekend in March, happily coincides with the arrival of spring. Festivities include chowder tasting and beer tasting (the latter courtesy of Fort Bragg's own North Coast Brewing Company), a "whale run," doll show, car show, lighthouse tours, and more. On both weekends, **whale-watching tours** are offered from Noyo Harbor, and **whale-watch talks** are offered at area state parks. The **Whale Festival at Pt. Cabrillo Light Station,** held every weekend in March, also coincides with both festivals.

In April or May, come to Fort Bragg for the **John Drucker Memorial Rhododendron Show**—the granddaddy of all juried rhodie shows, with more thqn 700 entries. On the first weekend in May, Mendocino's **Annual Historic House & Building Tour** offers a self-guided tour of the town's historic treasures. In late May, Fort Bragg puts on its impressive annual **Memorial Day Quilt Show.** The annual **Mendocino Coast Garden Tour** in mid-June, sponsored by the Mendocino Art Center, includes some of the most spectacular gardens in and near Mendocino.

On or around July 4th, Fort Bragg hosts the **World's Largest Salmon Barbecue** down at Noyo Harbor. All proceeds support the Hollow Tree Creek Hatchery in Noyo Harbor. And Mendocino holds its old-fashioned **Fourth of July Celebration & Parade.** Starting in mid-July, Mendocino hosts the noted, two-week **Mendocino Music Festival,** 707/937-2044, www.mendocinomusic.com. At this gala event, held in a 600-seat tent set up next to the Ford House, the local Symphony of the Redwoods joins with talented players from Bay Area orchestras to perform classical works that might include symphonies, opera, and chamber music as well as the possibility of jazz, Big Band and show tunes, celtic harp, and other surprises. At

Greenwood Ridge Vineyards in the Anderson Valley, come in late July for the annual **California Wine Tasting Championships.**

Usually held in July or August is the Mendocino Art Center's **Summer Arts & Crafts Fair.** In August is the Mendocino Coast Botanical Gardens' **Art in the Gardens** event and the Gualala **Art in the Redwoods Festival.** Fort Bragg's biggest party every year is **Paul Bunyan Days,** held over Labor Day weekend and offering a logging competition, parade, and crafts fair. The following September weekend, the **Winesong!** wine tasting and auction takes place at the Mendocino Coast Botanical Gardens.

Come in November for the mushrooming **Mendocino Coast Mushroom Festival,** which started out as a simple display and lectures held at Mendocino's Ford House and now extends over two weeks. Regional restaurants and wineries celebrate Mendocino's edible fungi with "wild" meals and special mushroom walks. Come on Thanksgiving weekend for the **Thanksgiving Art Festival** at the Mendocino Art Center and, down the coast, the **Gualala Arts Studio Tour.**

December brings the Mendocino Coast's **Candlelight Inn Tours,** three consecutive nights when area inns dress up grandly for the holidays and host visitors for tours and refreshments; all proceeds support Big Brothers/Big Sisters of Mendocino County. In Fort Bragg, the yuletide spirit extends to special programs by the Symphony of the Redwoods, the Gloriana Theater Company, and the **Holiday Gift Show** at the restored Union Lumber Company Store, not to mention the **Hometown Christmas & Lighted Truck Parade** early in the month. This particular community party includes music, tree lighting, and truck lighting—a yuletide parade of logging trucks and big rigs all lit up for the holidays.

INFORMATION AND SERVICES

The **Fort Bragg–Mendocino Coast Chamber of Commerce,** 332 N. Main St. in Fort Bragg, 707/961-6300, www.mendocinocoast2.com, is an incredible resource. It's open Mon.–Fri. 9 A.M.–5 P.M., Sat. 9 A.M.–3 P.M. (closed Sun.). Among the free literature published by the chamber is the annually updated *Mendocino Coast* brochure and map, walking tours, and shopping guides. Also available here and elsewhere is the free annual *Mendocino Visitor* tabloid, the coast guide to state parks, the *Guide to the Recreational Trails of Mendocino County,* and local arts publications.

For books on the region—and just plain great books—plan to spend some quality time in **Gallery Bookshop & Bookwinkle's Children's Books** in Mendocino at Main and Kasten Sts., 707/937-2215, www.gallerybooks.com, a truly impressive independent bookstore.

The **Fort Bragg post office** is at 203 N. Franklin, 707/964-2302, open weekdays 8:30 A.M.–5 P.M. The **Mendocino post office** is at 10500 Ford St., 707/937-5282, open weekdays 8:30 A.M.–4:30 P.M. The **Mendocino Coast District Hospital,** 700 River Dr. in Fort Bragg, 707/961-1234, offers 24-hour emergency services.

GETTING AROUND

The **Mendocino Transit Authority** (MTA), based in Ukiah, 707/462-1422, www.mcn.org/a/mta, runs a daily north coast route (#60, The Coaster) between the Navarro River (Hwy. 1 and Hwy. 128 junction) and Fort Bragg on weekdays. Bus #65 (the "CC Rider") runs from Mendocino to Fort Bragg then on to Willits, Ukiah, and Santa Rosa. There's also a weekly route along the coast one bus each weekday between Ukiah and Gualala via the Navarro River bridge. At the bridge, you can transfer to or from the smaller vans of Fort Bragg's **Mendocino Stage,** 707/964-0167, www.mendostage.com, which run weekdays between Fort Bragg and Navarro, with stops in Mendocino and offers "custom" passenger service. The MTA also makes roundtrips between Point Arena and Santa Rosa. Connect with **Greyhound** in Ukiah.

Near Little River, a few miles inland from the coast, is the **Little River Airport,** 707/937-5129, the closest airfield to Mendocino. Private pilots flying into the airport can get a ride into Little River or Mendocino by calling Mendocino Stage.

Getting to Willits—or Westport

Fort Bragg is a major highway junction. From here, Hwy. 20 heads east through the forest and over the coastal mountains on a winding route to **Willits,** on Hwy. 101. There travelers can turn north (and continue further on into this chapter), or turn south and head back toward the wine country. Drive carefully along Hwy. 20, especially in wet weather.

Travelers heading north from Fort Bragg can also continue up scenic Hwy. 1. This route hugs the coast past the small coastal town of Westport and past easily missed Usal Rd.—the southern access road to Sinkyone Wilderness. For more on the Sinkyone Wilderness, see The Lost (and Found) Coast section of this chapter. Eventually, Hwy. 1 is forced inland by the King Range and joins Hwy. 101 at **Leggett.**

Blink-and-you-miss-it **Westport** anchors itself around a couple of 90-degree bends in the highway, along a lonely and pristine stretch of coast near Westport–Union Landing State Beach. You have to slow down for the turns anyway, so pull over and explore. You may decide to stay awhile. It's not a bad base camp for travelers heading north to the Sinkyone Wilderness. Farther north, tiny Rockport is closer to the Usal Rd. turnoff to Sinkyone, but it's up a gulch away from the sea and not as developed as Westport.

The **DeHaven Valley Farm,** 39247 N. Hwy. 1, Westport, 707/961-1660 or 877/334-2836, www.dehaven-valley-farm.com, is a large 1885-vintage Victorian farmhouse with a total of eight "view" rooms and cottages (two share a bath, five have fireplaces), serving full breakfast (dinner available in their restaurant). Most rooms are $50–100 (one is $119), and the four studio/cottage units are $100–150. Urbane accommodations are available at the cozy **Howard Creek Ranch** bed-and-breakfast, 40501 N. Hwy. 1 (near the south end of Usal Rd., north of Westport), 707/964-6725, www.howardcreekranch.com, a New England–style farmhouse and outlying cabins on 40 acres. Most of the 14 rooms, suites, and cabins (including one built around a boat) have private baths. Amenities include gorgeous gardens, a pool, sauna, and wood-heated hot tub. Full, hearty breakfast. Rates range $75–160.

The Lost (and Found) Coast

Dust off the backpack, get new laces for those hiking boots. This is the place. California's isolated "Lost Coast," virtually uninhabited and more remote than any other stretch of coastline in the Lower 48, has been found. Here steep mountains soar like bald eagles—their domes tufted with chaparral, a few redwoods tucked behind the ears—and sink their grassy, rock-knuckled talons into the surf raging on black-sand beaches. Local people, of course, snort over the very idea that this splendid stretch of unfriendly coast was ever lost in the first place, even if area highways were intentionally routed away from it. *They* knew it was here. And others have known, too, for at least 3,000 years.

Finding a Lost Culture

Much of the Lost Coast is included in two major public preserves: the **King Range National Conservation Area** in Humboldt County, and the **Sinkyone Wilderness State Park** in Mendocino County. Central to the decade-long battle over expanding the Sinkyone Wilderness, which since 1987 has doubled to include 17 more miles of Mendocino coast, was the fate of 75-acre Sally Bell Grove along Little Jackass Creek. The prolonged political skirmish between former property owner Georgia-Pacific (which planned to clearcut the area) and various private and public agencies focused first on the value of these thousand-year-old trees to posterity. But the war was also over preserving reminders of a lost culture.

Archaeologists believe that a site in the middle of Sally Bell was occupied by proto-Yukian people 3,000 to 8,000 years ago. Chipped-stone tools, stonecutting implements, milling tools, the remains of two houses, and charcoal from long-ago campfires have been discovered at the site. Since those ancient days, for at least 2,500 years up until a century ago, the Sinkyone and

Mattole peoples lived permanently along this vast seaside stretch, though other groups came here seasonally when the valleys inland roasted in 100-degree heat. The living was easy, with abundant seafood a dietary staple.

The beaches fringing the King Range were sacred to the Mattole. Descendants talk about the legendary wreck of a Spanish ship along the coast from which the Mattole retrieved triangular gold coins for their children to play with. The coins were lost, however, when their caves along the coast collapsed after the 1906 earthquake. Ancient shell mounds or middens (protected by the Archaeological Resources Protection Act) still dot the seashore. Archaeologists with the U.S. Bureau of Land Management are active throughout the area each summer, and volunteers can occasionally join in on digs. More intriguing, though, is work now underway to establish the nation's first Native American-owned wilderness park, on uplands adjacent to Sinkyone, as a retreat for reestablishing traditional culture. For details, see the callout on the intertribal Sinkyone Wilderness State Park.

Getting Here (and Not Getting Lost)

Visiting the Lost Coast requires first getting there, something of a challenge. Roads here are not for the faint of heart nor for those with unreliable vehicles. Unpaved roads are rough and rugged even under the best weather conditions; some wags refer to driving the area as "car hiking." Though Lost Coast road signs usually disappear as fast as they go up (the locals' way of sending a message), existing signs that state Steep Grade—Narrow Road: Campers and Trailers Not Advised roughly translate as "Prepare to drive off the end of the earth, then dive blindly into a fogbank."

From Humboldt Redwoods State Park, take Bull Creek Rd. west through the park and over the rugged mountains down to Honeydew. There turn north on Mattole Rd. and continue north to Petrolia, near the north end of the King Range National Conservation Area. Lost Coast hikers "going the distance" south along the King Range beaches to Shelter Cove often start outside Petrolia, near the squat old lighthouse (reached via Lighthouse Road). Arrange a shuttle system, with

pickup at Shelter Cove, to keep it a one-way trip (paid shuttle services are available).

The easiest path to the sea is steep, narrow, and serpentine Shelter Cove Rd., which ends up at the hamlet of Shelter Cove, roughly midway down the Lost Coast; from Garberville, take Frontage Rd. one mile to Redway, and go west 26 miles on Briceland/Shelter Cove Road. Off of this road, you can turn north on wild Wilder Ridge Rd., which connects with Mattole Rd. near Honeydew, or turn south on either Briceland Rd. or Chemise Mountain Rd. to reach Sinkyone Wilderness (the last nine miles are unpaved, 4WD-only in winter and never suitable for RVs or trailers). At Four Corners junction, you can take Bear Harbor Rd. down to the ocean at Needle Rock and Bear Harbor, or head south on Usal Rd., which eventually joins Hwy. 1.

From the south, reach Sinkyone Wilderness via Usal Rd., which turns north off Hwy. 1 a few miles north of Rockport (watch carefully—it's easy to miss, especially heading north).

Practicalities

The Lost Coast isn't nearly as "lost" as it once was. Expect company along the coast and on the trails, especially during the peak summer and fall seasons. September and October, when the weather is typically mild and fog-free, are often ideal. It's rainy and very wet here from late October to April; the area receives 100 to 200 inches of rain annually. The land itself is unstable, with landslides common during the rainy season. Fog is common much of the rest of the year. So in any season, come prepared to get wet. But dress in layers, since in mid-summer it can also get quite warm—in the 80s to 90s—and windy as well.

Mountain bikers will be in heaven here, provided they have strong legs, since "what goes down, must come up." To hike or backpack the Lost Coast, bring proper shoes. For coastwalking (often through sand but also over rocks), lightweight but sturdy shoes with good ankle support and nonslip tread are best. For hiking the inland backcountry—more grassland than forest due to the thin mountain soil, but also supporting chaparral, mixed stands of conifers and oaks, and omnipresent poison oak—heavy-duty hiking boots are wise. Also bring current maps of the area since hikers here are on their own, sometimes (though not always) trekking for days without meeting another human soul. You may meet up with bears, however, which is why **bear canisters** (hard-sided, bear-proof storage containers) are required for backcountry camping; canisters are available for rent at local BLM offices and elsewhere (see King Range listing, below). Ticks and rattlesnakes can also be problematic here, and if you're planning to hike the beach, bring a tide table (some sections are impassable at high tides). Given the area's remoteness and rugged road conditions, come with a full tank of gas and bring adequate emergency supplies, food, and drinking water.

Other useful items include the Wilderness Press *Trails of the Lost Coast* map, featuring the roads and trails of both the King Range and Sinkyone Wilderness; the BLM map of the area, *King Range National Conservation Area Recreation Guide* (available at BLM offices); and the very enjoyable *An Everyday History of Somewhere* by Ray Raphael (Real Books), available from local bookstores.

To make your hike or backpack a one-way adventure, **King Range Outfitters,** 707/786-9637, will pack your gear in on mules—and will also accompany and accommodate equestrians (bring your own horse or mule). Or sign on with a shuttle service such as **Lost Coast Trail Transport Service** in Whitethorn, 707/986-9909, or the **Shelter Cove RV Campground, Market, and Deli** in Shelter Cove, 707/986-7474. If you'd rather sightsee from sea, whale-watching charters along the Lost Coast can be arranged through **King Salmon Charters** in Eureka, 707/441-1075.

KING RANGE NATIONAL CONSERVATION AREA

The northern reaches of the Lost Coast stretch 35 miles from south of the Mattole River to Whale Gulch. Much of the BLM's King Range National Conservation Area, a total of about 60,000 acres of rugged coastal mountains jutting up at 45-degree angles from rocky headlands, is being considered for federal wilderness protection. Despite the fact that most beaches are already closed to motorized vehicles, rebel offroaders are becoming a problem.

Most people come here to "beach backpack," hiking north to south in deference to prevailing winds. The trailhead begins near the mouth of the Mattole River. Get there from Mattole Rd. near Petrolia via Lighthouse Rd., then head south on foot. After about three miles, you'll come to the red-nippled relic of the Punta Gorda light station; the rocks nearby harbor a seabird colony and a rookery for Steller's sea lions. It's possible to continue hiking all the way south to Shelter Cove, a two- or three-day trip one-way (five days roundtrip), but a longer trek for those heading on to Sinkyone.

The trail saunters along miles of sandy beaches, around some tremendous tidepools, and up onto headlands to bypass craggy coves where streams flow to the sea. In wintry weather, this makes for quite the wild walk (check conditions before setting out); in any season, watch for rattlesnakes on rocks or draped over driftwood. Between self-protective downward glances, look around to appreciate some of the impressive shipwrecks scattered along the way. Also just offshore (in proper season) are gray whales, killer whales, porpoises, and harbor seals. Inland, forming an almost animate wall of resistance, are the mountains, their severity thinly disguised by redwoods and Douglas fir, forest meadows, chaparral scrub, and spring wildflowers. Make camp on high ground well back from the restless ocean, and always adhere to the backpacker's credo: if you pack it in, pack it out.

The 16-mile **King's Crest Trail** starts near Horse Mountain Camp and offers spectacular ocean views on rare sunny days, as does the **Chemise Mountain Trail.** Another fine inland hike is the **Buck Creek Trail** from Saddle Mountain, a challenging near-vertical descent through the fog to the beach. (Before taking the challenge, consider the comments scratched by survivors into the government's signs: "It's a real mother both ways" and "This hill will kill you.") Four primitive BLM campgrounds dot the King Range along both main access roads. It's five miles from Four Corners via Chemise Mountain Rd. to **Wailaki Camp,** picnic tables and 16 campsites on Bear Creek's south fork. (From Wailaki Camp, it's a steep 3.5-mile scramble down to the wooden bench below, another half-mile to the mouth of Chemise Creek and the beach.) A bit farther is **Nadelos Camp,** with 14 sites. The smaller **Tolkan** and the very pretty, very private **Horse Mountain Camp** are on King Ranch Road.

The camping fee for the various campgrounds is $5–8 per night, and the day-use fee is $1 per day. Permits are required for building fires and using campstoves in the backcountry. All organized groups also need BLM permits. For more information, contact: **King Range Project Office** in Whitethorn, located .25 miles west of the Whitethorn Post Office on Shelter Cove Rd., 707/986-5400; the U.S. Bureau of Land Management's **Arcata Field Office,** 1695 Heindon Rd.707/825-2300, www.ca.blm.gov/arcata; and the **BLM Ukiah Field Office,** 2550 N. State St., 707/468-4000.

Rent bear canisters (required) locally for $5 each at the above offices, and also at the Shelter Cove RV Campground, Market, and Deli and the Petrolia Store. Canisters have a 600 cubic inch capacity and can hold no more than three days' worth of food, trash, and toiletries (soap, toothpaste, sunscreen) for one person. A $75 credit card deposit is also required for each canister.

SINKYONE WILDERNESS STATE PARK

Sinking into Sinkyone is like blinking away all known life in order to finally *see*. Named for the Sinkyone people, who refused to abandon their traditional culture and hire on elsewhere as day laborers, this place somehow still honors that indomitable spirit.

More rugged than even the King Range, at Sinkyone Wilderness State Park jagged peaks plunge into untouched tidepools where sea lions and seals play. Unafraid here, wildlife sputters, flutters, or leaps forth at every opportunity. The land seems lusher, greener, with dark virgin forests of redwoods and mixed conifers, rich grassland meadows, waterfalls, fern grottos. The one thing

trekkers won't find (yet) among these 7,367 wild acres is a vast trail system. Many miles of the coast are accessible to hikers, and much of the rest of the 40-mile main trail system includes a north/south trail and some logging roads. The trail system connects with trails in the King Range National Conservation Area around the Wailaki area, but you can't reach Sinkyone from Shelter Cove by hiking south along the coast.

Sinkyone Wilderness State Park is always open for day use. The park also offers limited camping at more than 22 scattered and primitive environmental campsites, rarely full. To get oriented, stop by the park's **visitor center** at **Needle Rock Ranch House,** named for an impressive sea stack offshore just beyond the black-sand beach. (Take shelter in the cottage in bad weather—rooms here are now available for rent—otherwise camp under alders and firs nearby.) **Jones Beach** features a secluded cove and an acre of eucalyptus trees at an abandoned homestead (steep trail). Easier to get to is **Stream Side Camp,** two campsites in a wooded creekside glen, with a third perched atop a nearby knoll (with great ocean views, fog permitting). Farther inland is **Low Bridge Camp,** by a stream 1.5 miles from the visitor center.

Beautifully rugged **Bear Harbor** in the Orchard Creek meadow was once a lumber port serving northern Mendocino and southern Humboldt counties. All that's left of the nine-mile-long railroad spur that served the area from the mid-1880s until 1906 is a short rusted section of narrow-gauge track. Fuchsias cascade over the small stone dam. In late summer, harvest a few apples from the homestead's abandoned orchard before the deer do.

Energized after the beach trails with no place else to go, hike unpaved Usal Rd., which runs north to south and passes through Bear Harbor. Most cars can't make it past the gully in the road just over a mile south of Bear Harbor, but it's an easy walk from there to Bear Harbor campsites (excellent beach also). Other camp possibilities include a secluded seaside campground at Usal Creek, and two backpackers' camps at Jackass and Little Jackass Creeks.

Campsites are first-come, first-camped ($10 May–Sept., $7 Oct.–Apr.), and the day-use fee is

$2 per car. Solitude seekers, please note that Sinkyone is particularly crowded on summer holiday weekends. For more information, contact **Sinkyone Wilderness State Park** in Whitethorn, 707/986-7711 (recorded). You can also pick up a park map at the **Humboldt Redwoods State Park Visitor Center** on the Avenue of the Giants in Weott, north of Garberville.

LOST (AND FOUND) TOWNS

People in **Briceland** once made a living as bark peelers. There was a plant here built for the purpose of extracting tannic acid from the bark of the tan oak. The spot called **Whitethorn** near the headwaters of the Mattole River was once a busy stage station, then a loud lumber camp with five working sawmills. East of Honeydew is old **Ettersburg**, now posted as **Divorce Flat** and first homesteaded in 1894 by apple grower Alfter Etter.

Honeydew was named for the sweet-tasting aphid dew beneath cottonwoods down by the river. There's a gas station/general store/post office in Honeydew, usually but not necessarily open during the day. Head-turning from here, though, are the roadside views of King Peak and its rugged range. Perfect for picnicking is the **A.W. Way County Park** in the Mattole River Valley, loveliest in spring when the wild irises bloom. Day use is $2, campsites $12. For a roof over your head, **Mattole River Organic Farms' Country Cabins,** three miles outside Honeydew at 42354 Mattole Rd., 707/629-3445 or 800/845-4607, iansigman@hotmail.com, offers housekeeping cottages on a bluff overlooking the river. Rates are $50–100, depending on sleeping arrangements and options. All have kitchens with gas stoves, apartment refrigerators, pots, pans, and all the basics. By the way, all equipment on the farm operates on politically correct fuel—biodiesel.

Fishing is good on the Mattole River between Honeydew and eucalyptus-sheltered **Petrolia,** named for California's first commercial oil well, drilled three miles east of here in the 1860s. Just south of downtown Petrolia is a great place to eat—the **Hideaway** bar and grill, 451 Conklin Creek Rd. (at the Mattole River bridge), 707/629-3533. It doesn't look like much from the outside,

but inside the locals gather for convivial conversation over glasses of Sierra Nevada Pale Ale on tap. The food is good, too. Petrolia also has a well-stocked general store, a gas station, and the deluxe, country-style **Lost Inn** in "downtown" Petrolia, 707/629-3394, actually a huge two-room suite in the front section of the family home (private entrance through a trellised opening and a private yard and garden). Inside you'll find a queen bed and a futon sleeper couch, a kitchenette, and a large glassed-in front porch perfect for capturing winter sun. An adjoining bedroom can also be rented—a perfect set-up for two couples traveling together. Guests enjoy fresh fruit and vegetables in season. Well-behaved pets are okay on the porch. Rates, including full breakfast, are $50–100. For a cabin stay, the place is **Windchime Cabins** (previously Ziganti's), 707/629-3582, with one studio cabin for $75 (two nights $125, three nights $175) and a two-bedroom cabin that sleeps four for $95 (two nights $135, three nights $195). Veggie garden onsite as well as equine overnight facilities (pipe fencing), $20 per horse per night with advance reservations.

Farther north, past the Mattole River lagoon and the road leading to the abandoned Punta Gorda Lighthouse, past the automated light tower atop Cape Ridge (built to replace the 16-sided pyramid tower built there in 1868), and past Cape Mendocino and Scottish-looking farm country lies the very Victorian town of Ferndale, just south of Eureka. As you come down to town, you'll get a great aerial view of the Eel River delta.

The big city on this lost side of the world, though, is **Shelter Cove,** a privately owned enclave within the King Range National Conservation Area once home to the Sinkyone and a major collecting point for the Pomos' clamshell money. Today, this is the place for soaking up some wilderness within range of humanity, for whale-watching, beachcombing, skin diving, and sport fishing. Stop by the **Shelter Cove RV Campground, Market, and Deli,** 492 Machi Rd., 707/986-7474, for current local information. Shuttle service to the Mattole Beach trailhead ($125) is also available. **Mario's,** at the marina, 707/986-1199, is open nightly for dinner and Fri.–Sun. for lunch. Declared one of the

ALMOST LOST LAND:
THE INTERTRIBAL SINKYONE WILDERNESS PARK

A side note to the expansion of **Sinkyone Wilderness State Park** is how it got expanded, an intriguing tale of life in the modern world. At the end of a complex series of events beginning in the mid-1970s—which included at times almost violent confrontations between logging company employees and protesters—the San Francisco–based Trust for Public Land in 1986 successfully negotiated with Georgia-Pacific to buy 7,100 acres of land appraised at $10.2 million. Seventeen miles of coastline (and 2,900 acres) were deeded by the Trust to the state park system; today the California Coastal Trail runs through it. The state contributed $2.8 million to the pot, but the public received land valued at $5.5 million. Another player in the game, the Save-the-Redwoods League, contributed $1 million and received protective custody of 400 acres of virgin redwoods, including the 75-acre Sally Bell Grove.

In addition, the California Coastal Conservancy lent $1.1 million to the Trust for Public Land to help develop a land-management and marketing plan for timber harvesting and other activities on the remaining 3,900 acres—that plan to be jointly developed by the Coastal Conservancy, interested environmental groups, the Mendocino County Board of Supervisors, and the International Woodworkers Union.

In a particularly unique twist, Native Americans also participated. By 1996—after some contentious public hearings—it was decided that they would have their own park. Working with the Trust for Public Land and the Coastal Conservancy to establish the first American Indian-owned wilderness park, a consortium of some 11 tribal groups finally gained approval for establishing the 3,900-acre Intertribal Sinkyone Wilderness Park—the first in the United States to be managed "in traditional ways"—in the uplands of tan oak, second-growth Douglas fir and redwood, and scrubby ceanothus, coyote bush, and berries adjacent to the Sinkyone State Wilderness Park.

A key element of the land-management plan requires the restoration of habitats damaged by logging, though limited logging—to guarantee a sustainable, mature forest—will be allowed. Unusual, though, will be the reestablishment of traditional Native American culture. Though no one will be allowed to live permanently in the intertribal wilderness, plans call for the construction of four villages—built only of traditional materials, in traditional ways—that will be available for rituals, retreats, and other cultural activities. Native groups from around the U.S. and the world are particularly interested in this project—seeing in it a possible model for cultural preservation that can be adopted elsewhere.

For current information about the Intertribal Sinkyone Wilderness Park, contact the nonprofit **Intertribal Sinkyone Wilderness Council,** 707/463-6745.

nation's premier fly-in dining destinations by *Private Pilot* magazine, the remote **Cove Restaurant** at 10 Seal Crt., 707/986-1197—is open Thurs.–Sun. for lunch and dinner. From well-prepared steaks and burgers to fresh fish and shellfish, just about everything's great. Luxury rooms and suites at the **Oceanfront Inn and Lighthouse,** 26 Seal Crt., 707/986-7002, are $100–150 and higher. The expanded coveside **Shelter Cove Motor Inn,** 205 Wave Dr., 707/986-7521 or 888/570-9676, offers rooms with abundant amenities (microwaves, refrigerators, coffee makers, hairdryers); some have Jacuzzi tubs, fireplaces, and Internet access. Rates $50–150. The **Shelter Cove Beachcomber Inn,** close to the store and overlooking the campground at 412 Machi Rd., 707/986-7551 or 800/718-4789 (reservations only), offers six rooms and suites in three separate, fairly secluded buildings—various configurations with brass beds, private baths, kitchens or mini-kitchens, woodstoves, barbecues, and picnic tables. Rates are $50–100 for two, $10 each extra person. Call between 9 A.M. and 7 P.M. only. For more information on Shelter Cove, try the **Shelter Cove Business Directory,** www.sojourner2000.com.

Eel River Country

North of Fort Bragg, Hwy. 1 continues up the coast until it's deflected inland by the rugged King Range; details on exploring that landscape are included under The Lost (and Found) Coast section of this chapter. The highway ends at Leggett, where it merges into Hwy. 101. Here you can turn south to get back to the wine country (and to a couple of remote nature preserves), or continue north to enter the realm of the coast redwoods. From Leggett north to just beyond Fortuna, the scenic highway winds alongside the aptly named Eel River, past many redwood groves and riverbank beaches.

LEGGETT TO BENBOW

Leggett's big attraction, the **Drive-Thru-Tree Park,** is as schlocky as it sounds, but for some reason humans just love driving through trees. They carved this car-sized hole in the Chandelier Tree in the 1930s, and for a small fee people can "drive thru" it (RVs won't make it). For more information, call 707/925-6363 or 707/925-6446.

The **Standish-Hickey State Recreation Area** is 1.5 miles north of Leggett, this 1,000-acre forest supports second-growth coast redwoods, firs, bigleaf maples, oaks, and alders. It's also thick with ferns and, in spring, water-loving wildflowers. Camp at any of the three developed campgrounds here ($11–14, reservations necessary in summer) or at one of the hike-and-bike campsites ($10), then go fishing, swimming, or on a hike to the 225-foot-tall **Miles Standish Tree,** a massive mature redwood that somehow escaped the loggers. The trail to the tree continues on to a waterfall. The **Mill Creek** trail is a steeper, rugged five-mile loop. Park day use is $4. For more information, contact the park at 69350 Hwy. 101 in Leggett, 707/925-6482. For campground reservations, necessary in summer, contact ReserveAmerica, 800/444-7275, www.reserveamerica.com.

Four miles north of Leggett on Hwy. 101, the lovely Frank and Bess Smithe Grove of redwoods at **Smithe Redwoods State Reserve** can be reached only from the west side of the highway, though most of the 665-acre park's protected trees are to the east. A quarter-mile hike here, once a private resort with cabins and restaurant, will take you to a 60-foot waterfall. For more information, call the park at 707/247-3318.

Nearby is **Confusion Hill,** 707/925-6456, one of those places where gravity is defied and water runs uphill, etc. Open year-round. You can also take the kids on a train ride through the redwoods (summers only) and view the world's largest redwood chainsaw sculpture. A logging museum, petting zoo, gift shop, and snack bar round out the facilities.

North of Leggett in Piercy, at last report the historic lodge at the former Hartsook Country Inn, 900 Hwy. 101—part of 33 acres purchased by the Save-the-Redwoods League to prevent logging—was serving as a summers-only visitor center. Piercy's **World Famous Tree House,** 707/925-6406, is a living redwood with a rotted-out hollow that's home to the "the world's tallest single room." Just south of Piercy along the Eel River is the state's 400-acre **Reynolds Wayside Camp,** offering picnicking and 50 unimproved campsites. For details, call Humboldt Redwoods State Park, 707/946-2409.

Richardson Grove State Park south of Benbow Lake, with more than 800 acres of fine redwoods, was named for 1920s California governor Friend W. Richardson, noted conservationist. Richardson Grove is popular and crowded in summer, though few people hike the backcountry trails. The Richardson Grove Nature Trail is fully accessible. Picnic near the river or camp at any of three developed campgrounds (Huckleberry/Madrone is open all year). Developed campsites are $12–15, and the park's day-use fee is $4. Hike-and-bike campsites are also available ($2), and environmental camps $7–10. The **Seven Parks Natural History Association,** in the visitor center at Richardson Grove Lodge, 1600 Hwy. 101, 707/247-3318 (if no answer, call 707/946-2311), offers a variety of redwood-country publications (open summers only). For more information, contact Humboldt Redwoods State Park, 707/946-2409. For camping reservations, contact ReserveAmerica, 800/444-7275, www.reserveamerica.com. Reservable summer-only.

Benbow Lake State Recreation Area

This state recreation area in the midst of open woodlands two miles south of Garberville is aptly named only in the summer, when a temporary dam goes up on the Eel River's south fork to create Benbow Lake. The lake itself is great for swimming, sailing, canoeing, and windsurfing, with pleasant picnicking and hiking in the hills nearby. No fishing. It's also the scene of several summertime events, including the annual **Jazz on the Lake** festival, **Shakespeare at Benbow Lake,** and the **Summer Arts Fair.** For more lake information, call 707/247-3318 in summer or Humboldt Redwoods State Park, 707/946-2409.

The lake may disappear at summer's end, but the campground remains open all year. It's popular in summer, so reserve campsites ($12–15, or $17–20 with hookups) through ReserveAmerica, 800/444-7275, www.reserveamerica.com. The private **Benbow Valley RV Resort & Golf Course,** 7000 Benbow Dr., 707/923-2777 or 866/236-2697, www.benbowrv.com, which offers 112 sites with full hookups, $25–40 (discounts available), as well as a golf course.

Benbow Inn

Also open year-round is the elegant four-story Tudor-style Benbow Inn, 445 Lake Benbow Dr., 707/923-2124 or 800/355-3301, www.benbowinn.com. Designed by architect Albert Farr, the Benbow Inn first opened its doors in 1926 and over the years has welcomed travelers including Herbert Hoover, Charles Laughton, and Eleanor Roosevelt. A National Historic Landmark, the inn has been restored to a very English attitude. Complimentary scones and tea are served in the lobby every afternoon at 3 P.M., mulled wine at 4 P.M. when the weather is cold, and hors d'oeuvres in the common rooms between 5 and 7 P.M. The inn's dining room serves a good breakfast, lunch during the summer only, and staples like steak-and-kidney pie for dinner. Full bar. The inn is closed from early January until late March.

In addition to the summer activities staged at the lake, the Benbow Inn hosts a Teddy Bear Tea and Luncheon in May, special Thanksgiving festivities, a theme Christmas party, and a New Year's Eve Champagne Dinner Dance to the bigband tunes of Tommy Dorsey and Glenn Miller. Most rooms are $150–250 but some are $100–150; garden cottages are over $250 (starting at $325). Ask about off-season specials, which include three-nights-for-two and $99 main building room rates.

GARBERVILLE AND VICINITY

A former sheep ranching town, Garberville is *not* an outlaw enclave paved in $100 bills by pot-growing Mercedes Benz owners, as media mythology would have it. The town was once considered the sinsemilla cultivation capital of the world, an honor most locals are fed up with. The general belief today is that the big-time Rambo-style growers have gone elsewhere. But don't expect people here to share their knowledge *or* opinions on the subject, pro or con. With annual CAMP (Campaign Against Marijuana Production) invasions throughout the surrounding countryside, discretion is the rule of tongue when outsiders show up.

Not far north of Garberville is **M. Lockwood Memorial Park,** a popular rafting departure point also offering good fishing. Two small southerly outposts of Humboldt Redwood State Park are just north of Redway; **Whittemore Grove** and **Holbrook Grove** are both dark, cool glens perfect for picnicking and short hikes. Another area attraction is the famous **One Log House,** associated with Bear Meadow Espresso, 705 Hwy. 101, 707/247-3717, the hollowed-out "house" relocated here from Phillipsville and remodeled.

In June, the annual **Rodeo in the Redwoods and Bull-O-Rama** is the big to-do in these parts, followed in July or early August by the West Coast's largest and usually most impressive reggae festival—the **Reggae on the River** concert—which attracts top talent from Jamaica and America. For concert and other events information, contact the **Mateel Community Center** in Redway, 707/923-3368, www.mateel.org.

For more area information, contact the **Garberville-Redway Chamber of Commerce,** 773 Redwood Dr. in Garberville, 707/923-2613 or 800/923-2613, www.garberville.org, open daily 9 A.M.–5 P.M. in summer, and weekdays 9 A.M.– 5 P.M. in winter.

Practicalities

Just about everything in Garberville is on Business 101, called Redwood Drive. The 76-room **Best Western Humboldt House Inn,** 701 Redwood Dr., 707/923-2771, has rooms with air-conditioning, color TV, movies, and phones. Some rooms have kitchens. Other extras here include a coin-op laundry, heated pool, whirlpool, and complimentary continental breakfast. Rates are $100–150. The smaller **Sherwood Forest Motel,** 814 Redwood Dr., 707/923-2721, www.sherwoodforestmotel.com, is quite a find, with abundant amenities. Rates are $50–100.

For farm-fresh fruit, veggies, flowers, and herbs, show up at the **Southern Humboldt Farmers Market,** 707/923-9209, held June–Oct. in Garberville at Locust and Church on Fridays, 11 A.M.–3 P.M., and in "uptown Redway," Tuesdays 3–6 P.M. The laid-back **Woodrose Café,** 911 Redwood, 707/923-3191, is beloved for its fine omelettes, tofu specials, good vegetarian sandwiches, and like fare, everything locally and/or organically grown. Open daily for breakfast, for lunch only on weekdays. A good choice for wheat-bread-and-sprouts-style Sunday champagne brunch. For straight-ahead Italian food and pizza, not to mention impressive quantities of Mexican and American fare, try **Sicilito's,** 445 Conger St. (behind the Humboldt House Inn), 707/923-2814, open Fri.–Tues. for lunch and dinner, and Wed.–Thurs. for dinner only. For fresh fish in season and good family-style Italian and American fare, the place is the **Waterwheel Restaurant,** 924 Redwood Dr., 707/923-2031, open daily for breakfast, lunch, and dinner.

Just northwest of Garberville, across the highway in Redway, is the **Mateel Cafe,** 3342-3344 Redwood Dr., 707/923-2030, a fine-food mecca serving everything from Thai tofu to seafood linguine and stone-baked pizza. Vegans, carnivores, low-protein or high-protein dieters—there's something for everyone on the eclectic menu. And check out that Jazzbo Room. Open Mon.–Sat. for lunch and dinner.

HUMBOLDT REDWOODS STATE PARK

This is the redwood heart of Humboldt County, where more than 40 percent of the world's redwoods remain. The Save-the-Redwoods League and the state have added to the park's holdings grove by grove. Most of these "dedicated groves," named in honor of those who gave to save the trees, and many of the park's developed campgrounds are along the state-park section of the Avenue of the Giants parkway.

Humboldt Redwoods State Park is one of the largest state parks in Northern California and the state's largest redwood park, with more than 51,000 acres of almost unfrequented redwood groves, mixed conifers, and oaks. The park offers 35 miles of hiking and backpacking trails, plus 30 miles of old logging roads—and surprising solitude so close to a freeway. Down on the flats are the deepest and darkest stands of virgin redwoods, including Rockefeller Forest, the world's largest stand of stately survivors. The rolling uplands include grass-brushed hills with mixed forest. Calypso orchids and lilies are plentiful in spring, and wild blackberries and huckleberries ripen July–September.

As is typical of the north coast, heavy rainfall and sometimes dangerously high river conditions are predictable Nov.–Apr. But the rampaging Eel River shrinks to garter snake size by May or June, its emerald water fringed by white sand beaches good for swimming, tubing, fishing, and for watching the annual lamprey migration. The wild and scenic stretches of the Eel are also known for early-in-the-year white-water rafting and kayaking. The **Avenue of the Giants Marathon** run through the redwoods happens in early May.

Humboldt Big Trees

At almost 13,000 acres, **Rockefeller Forest** is the main grove here and among the most valuable virgin stands of redwood remaining on the north coast (yes, donated by the John D. Rockefeller family). In **Founder's Grove,** the Founder's Tree was once erroneously known as the World's Tallest Tree; the park's Dyerville Giant is—or was—actually the park's tallest at 362 feet, when last measured in 1972 (the Giant toppled over in a 1991 storm and now lies on the forest floor), and even taller trees reach skyward in Redwood National Park north of Orick. But the Founder's Tree and Dyerville Giant are two mindful monuments to the grandeur of the natural world. After exploring Founder's Grove, consider the nearby **Immortal Tree,** which has withstood almost every imaginable onslaught from both nature and humanity—a testament to this tree's tenacity, and perhaps the forest's.

Not the largest tree or most martyred but a notable one nevertheless is the ***Metasequoia,*** which you can see near Weott (and south down the highway at Richardson Grove State Park). It's a dawn redwood native to China, kissing cousin of both species of California redwoods.

Avenue of the Giants

This scenic 33-mile drive on the old highway, a narrow asphalt ribbon braiding together the eastern edge of Humboldt Redwoods, the Eel River, and Hwy. 101, weaves past and through some of the largest groves of the largest remaining redwoods in Humboldt and Del Norte Counties. Get off the bike (the avenue's very nice for cycling, but wear bright clothing) or out of the car and picnic, take a short walk, and just *appreciate* these grand old giants.

The part-private, part-public Avenue is dotted with commercial attractions—tourist traps offering redwood knickknacks and trinkets manufactured overseas and trees transformed into walk-in or drive-through freaks of nature. But the curio shops and commercial trappings barely distract from the fragrant grandeur of the dim, dignified forest itself, sunlit in faint slivers and carpeted with oxalis and ferns.

Among the tiny towns dwarfed still more by the giants along the Avenue are **Phillipsville, Meyers Flat,** and **Redcrest.** Phillipsville is home to the **Chimney Tree,** 707/923-2265, open 8 A.M.–8 P.M. from May to mid-October, and the Tolkienesque **Hobbitown U.S.A.** Meyers

Flat boasts one of the state's oldest tourist attractions, the **Shrine Drive-Thru-Tree & Gift Shop,** 707/943-3154. Wagon-train travelers heading up and down the Pacific coast once pulled *their* vehicles through it. The tree stands 275 feet tall, measures 21 feet in diameter, and people can see the sky if standing inside the eight-foot-wide tree tunnel. These days, though, everyone worries every time a storm blows in, because most of the Shrine tree is dead and the behemoth is seriously listing. Visitors can also sample the **Step-Thru Stump** and (the SUVers favorite) **Drive-On Tree.** Food is available at the **Drive-Thru-Tree Cafe,** 707/943-1665. In Redcrest you'll find the **Eternal Tree House,** a 20-foot room inside a living tree, 707/722-4262 (gift shop) or 707/722-4247 (café).

Camping

Camping is easy at Humboldt Redwoods, which offers hundreds of campsites and four picnic areas. **Burlington Campground** near Weott is fully developed (hot showers, restrooms, tables—the works for outdoor living), $12–15. Ditto for the **Albee Creek Campground** not far to the south, and **Hidden Springs Campground** near Miranda. All three of these campgrounds are popular, so make advance reservations in summer through ReserveAmerica, 800/444-7275, www.reserveamerica.com.

Unusual at Humboldt Redwoods State Park are five backcountry backpackers' camps, reservable in advance (first-come) at park headquarters. These camps each have piped spring water (but no fires are allowed, so bring a campstove). Only one of the five—**Bull Creek Trail Camp**—is easily reached by nonhikers. Closest to the road but an uphill climb are **Johnson Trail Camp,** a collection of four backwoods cabins used from the 1920s to 1950s by "tie hacks" (railroad tie makers), and the **Whiskey Flat Trail Camp,** a tent camp named for the Prohibition moonshine still once tucked among these massive old-growth redwoods. **Grasshopper Trail Camp** is among the grasshoppers and deer on the meadow's edge below Grasshopper Peak (great view from the fire lookout at the top), and **Hanson Ridge Trail Camp** is tucked among firs and ferns.

In addition to the outback pleasures of these backcountry camps, the park features two walk-in environmental campgrounds: **Baxter** and **Hamilton Barn** (pick apples in the old orchard), both with convenient yet secluded campsites ($7–10); sign up at park headquarters, where you can get the particulars). Group camps and horse camps are also available, $54–81. Should all the state facilities be full, the area also includes a number of private campgrounds and RV parks.

Practicalities

The day-use fee at Humboldt Redwoods is $4 per car. For maps and more information about the park, stop by or contact: Humboldt Redwoods State Park headquarters (at the Burlington Campground), also the district office, at 707/946-2409. Alternatively, call 707/946-1807 or 707/946-1814. The **Humboldt Redwoods Interpretive Association Visitor Center,** between headquarters and Burlington Campground, 707/946-2263, www.humboldtredwoods.org, is open daily 9 A.M.–5 P.M. in summer, Thurs.–Sun. 10 A.M.–4 P.M. in winter, and offers excellent natural history exhibits. In summer park rangers offer guided nature walks, campfire programs, and Junior Ranger activities for kids.

Staying near Humboldt Redwoods

The **Miranda Gardens Resort,** 6766 Ave. of the Giants, 707/943-3011, www.mirandagardens.com, is tops in the condo/cabin department, offering comfortable single or duplex cabins—some with two bedrooms, some with kitchens (all cookware and essentials supplied), several with fireplaces, two with whirlpool tubs. Heated pool, continental breakfast, onsite grocery. Most rates are $100–150, but some units are as low as $65 (one double bed), some as high as $175 and $225.

The **Myers Country Inn,** 12913 Ave. of the Giants in Myers Flat, 707/943-3259 or 800/500-6464, www.myersinn.com, is an 1860-vintage two-story hotel now functioning as a country-style 10-room bed-and-breakfast. Amenities include private baths, separate entrances, a fireplace

in the lobby, and complimentary continental breakfast. Rates are $100–150.

Another best bet for cabins, on the north side of Humboldt Redwoods, is pet-friendly **Redcrest Resort** in Redcrest at 26459 Ave. of the Giants, 707/722-4208. Most cabins are $50–100; RV sites are also available.

Eating near Humboldt Redwoods

Great for a quick all-American meal, from biscuits and gravy to homemade pies, the place is the **Eternal Treehouse Café,** 26510 Avenue of the Giants in Redcrest, 707/722-4247, open daily for breakfast, lunch, and dinner. For American

HEADING FOR HEADWATERS

So intense was public interest in visiting the 7,500-acre Headwaters Grove after its 1999 purchase by California and the U.S. that state officials decided to limit initial access. Only those willing to hike a rugged 10 miles got an early look. Botanists feared—and still fear—that tourism will threaten the fragile old-growth redwood ecosystem.

No trail leads into the reserve's 3,000-acre core, but visitors can drive to the north edge of the forest, just south of Eureka, via Elk River Rd., then hike in some five miles along an abandoned logging road to reach an overlook into the unperturbed heart of the Headlands. Plan to be hiking all day. Limited visitor access is also available from southeast of Fortuna; guided half-day, four-mile roundtrip hikes are offered from mid-May to mid-November.

For current information on Headwaters access and to make reservations for guided hikes, contact the U.S. Bureau of Land Management's **Arcata Field Office,** 1695 Heindon Rd., 707/825-2300, www.ca.blm.gov/arcata. The website includes basic maps of the area. For background information on the battle to protect the Headwaters Grove, updates on current skirmishes, and details on other regional environmental activism, contact: **Environmental Protection Information Center (EPIC)** in Garberville, 707/923-2931, www.wildcalifornia.org.

and international cuisine and fine wines, head toward Myers Flat and **Knight's Restaurant,** 12866 Ave. of the Giants, 707/943-3411. Worthwhile within driving distance are the restaurants in Garberville-Redway and at the Benbow Inn (see above) and the Scotia Inn in Scotia (below).

SCOTIA AND VICINITY

Scotia is a neat-as-a-pin town perfumed by the scents of apple pie, family barbecues, and redwood sawdust. A company town built (to last) from redwood and founded on the solid economic ground of sustained-yield logging, picture-perfect Scotia is one of California's last wholly owned company towns. Generations of children of Pacific Lumber Company (PALCO) loggers happily grew up in Scotia, then went to work in the mills—or went away to college on PALCO-paid scholarships before returning to work as middle managers in the mill offices.

Scotia's serenity has been obliterated, to a large degree, by major economic and political events. One round of trouble started in 1985, when PALCO was taken over in a Michael Milken–related stock raid by the Maxxam Group. Environmentalists loudly mourned the passing of the old PALCO—friend of the Save-the-Redwoods League and sympathetic to conservationist thought, opposed to clearcutting as a forestry practice. Maxxam's Charles Hurwitz began his tenure at PALCO by clearcutting old-growth redwoods on the company's land. When Hurwitz directed his chainsaws toward the Headwaters Grove—in the midst of PALCO's 60,000-acre Headwaters Forest, one of the last privately held stands of virgin redwoods left in the country—it sparked an environmental and political battle that has taken a decade to resolve, to less than unanimous satisfaction. (For more details, see Story Without End: The Politics of Harvesting Redwoods elsewhere in this chapter.) The agreement, among PALCO and the federal and state governments, saved the core groves of redwoods—for which PALCO received a hefty sum from the taxpayers—but left PALCO free to harvest the rest of its holdings, under what environmentalists contend are token environmental restrictions.

As if such stresses weren't enough, the town's business district was lost in April 1992, when fires started by a massive north coast earthquake destroyed the entire business district and damaged many area homes. (The mill was saved.) The quake's total regional price tag: somewhere in the neighborhood of $61 million. In this millennium, two sawmills tooled for now-rare old-growth logs stand idle, and local layoffs have begun.

Still, the big event in Scotia is taking a tour of the **Pacific Lumber Company redwood sawmill** and manufacturing facility, 125 Main St., 707/764-2222, www.palco.com, the largest in the world. The company's self-guided tour (free) is offered weekdays 8 A.M.–2 P.M., year-round except the weeks of July 4th and Christmas. Also stop by the **Scotia Museum** and visitor center on Main, a storehouse of local logging history housed in a stylized Greek temple built of redwood, with logs taking the place of fluted columns. (Formerly a bank, the building's sprouting redwood burl once had to be pruned regularly.) Open summer and early fall only, weekdays 8 A.M.–4:30 P.M.

About five miles south of town is the company's **demonstration forest,** open daily in summer (also free), and a picnic area with restrooms. **Rio Dell** across the Eel River is a residential community, its main claim to fame being good fossil hunting on the shale-and-sandstone Scotia Bluffs along the banks of the Eel.

The town holds a **Wildwood Days** festival in August. The **Rio Dell/Scotia Chamber of Commerce** is at 715 Wildwood Ave. in Rio Dell, 707/764-3436.

Practicalities

While in Scotia, consider a meal or a stay at the spruced-up **Scotia Inn,** directly across from the mill at 100 Main St. (at Mill), 707/764-5683, www.scotiainn.com, a classic 1923 redwood hotel now served up bed-and-breakfast style. The hotel includes a very good restaurant—the **Redwood Room,** serving very American and more worldly fare—plus a separate café and several bars, one known as the **Steak and Potato Pub.** With its second story remodeled and reopened, the Scotia Inn now features 18 rooms rich with antiques and four suites, all with private baths and classic claw-footed bathtubs. Continental breakfast included. Rates for most rooms are $100–150; for some rooms and suites, $150–250. **Cinnamon Jack's Bakery,** 341 Wildwood in Rio Del, 707/764-5858, is a coffee stop locally famous for its cinnamon rolls and muffins. Rio Dell's relaxed **Al's Diner,** 337 Second Ave., 707/764-3445, serves fabulous fresh fish, chops, steaks, and other wood-fired specialties.

FORTUNA AND HWY. 36

The largest city in southern Humboldt County, Fortuna was originally called Springville and established in 1875. Logging is officially the major industry in these parts, but tourism is catching up fast. Come in late March for the **Spring Daffodil Show,** one of the state's three major daffodil shows, and in early April for the **Paddle to the Headwaters** Eel River canoe, kayak, and outrigger marathon and race, 877/837-0902, www.paddletotheheadwaters.com, fun for fiends and casual paddlers alike. Try July for the long-running **Redwood Fortuna Rodeo,** the oldest rodeo in the West; October for the **Apple Harvest Festival;** and December for the **Christmas Music Festival.**

The **Fortuna Depot Museum,** in Rohner Park at 4 Park St., 707/725-7645, occupies the old 1893 rail depot and exhibits the history of the Eel River Valley—everything from logging memorabilia and barbed wire to high school yearbooks and fishing lures. It's open in summer, daily 10 A.M.–4:30 P.M.; the rest of the year, Wed.–Sun. noon–4:30 P.M. Admission is free (donations appreciated).

Area motels have rooms $50–100, some higher. Overnighters can choose from the **Best Western Country Inn,** close to the snazzy River Lodge conference center at 2025 Riverwalk Dr., 707/725-6822 or 800/679-7511, www.bwcountryinnfortuna.com, with an indoor heated pool and Jacuzzi; **Fortuna Super 8,** 1805 Alamar Way, 707/725-2888 or 800/800-8000; and **Holiday Inn Express,** 1859 Alamar Way, 707/725-5500 or 800/465-4329.

For fresh regional produce, show up for the **Fortuna Certified Farmers Market,** 707/768-3342, held May–Oct. at 10th and L Streets, on

Tuesday, 3:30–6 P.M. Otherwise, **Clendenen's Cider Works,** 96 12th St. (next to the freeway), 707/725-2123, open daily Aug.–Feb., is *the* place for half-gallons of homemade apple cider and fresh local produce. The **Eel River Brewing Company,** 1777 Alamar Way, 707/725-2739, offers around half a dozen homemade beers, including Ravensbrau Porter and Climax Amber. Order from a fine menu of steaks (organic Black Angus beef) and seafoods, pastas, and burgers.

For more information about Fortuna and vicinity, contact the **Fortuna Chamber of Commerce,** 735 14th St., 707/725-3959, www.sunnyfortuna.com.

Van Duzen County Park

Humboldt's largest county park, Van Duzen harbors four groves of nearly undisturbed redwoods along the Van Duzen River east from Hwy. 101 via Hwy. 36. Georgia-Pacific donated these groves, as well as Cheatham Grove farther west, to the Nature Conservancy in 1969, a very large corporate conservation gift. The land was subsequently deeded to the county and the Save-the-Redwoods League. You can hike, swim, fish, picnic, and camp ($12) at both **Pamplin** and **Swimmer's Delight** groves. **Humboldt Grove** is pristine old-growth forest open only for hiking. **Redwood Grove** was severely damaged by windstorms in 1978, but hikers can still walk the old roads. Day-use fee $3. For more information, contact Humboldt County's Parks and Recreation Division in Eureka, 707/445-7651.

Grizzly Creek Redwoods State Park

Gone but not forgotten is the now-extinct California grizzly bear, exterminated here by the late 1860s. The smallest of all the redwood parks, Grizzly Creek Redwoods State Park, 35 miles southeast of Eureka, was once a stagecoach stop. It's surrounded by mostly undeveloped forests along the Van Duzen River (visited now by an occasional black bear), among which are a few redwood groves. The main things to do: hike the short trails, swim, and fish for salmon, steelhead, and trout in winter when the river's raging. "Grizz Creek" (as the locals say) also has a natural history museum inside the restored stage stop.

The campground here (30 campsites, 30 picnic sites) is open year-round. Developed campsites are $12–15. ReserveAmerica reservations, 800/444-7275, www.reserveamerica.com, are a good idea in summer. Bring quarters for the hot showers. Grizz Creek also features environmental campsites ($10). The park day-use fee is $4 per car. For more information, contact: Grizzly Creek Redwoods State Park, 16939 Hwy. 36 in Carlotta, 707/777-3683. A few miles beyond the park is the tiny town of **Bridgeville,** sold on EBay at the end of 2002 for $1.77 million.

FERNDALE AND VICINITY

Ferndale (pop. 1,400) is a perfect rendition of a Victorian village, the kind of place Disneyland architects would create if they needed a new movie set. Ferndale, however, is the real thing, a thriving small town where people take turns shuttling the kids to Future Farmers of America and 4-H meetings, argue about education at PTA meetings or ice-cream socials, and gossip on street corners.

The town was first settled in 1864 by Danish immigrants; at that time, the delta plain was heavily forested. The Danes were followed by Portuguese and Italians. Today, quaint and quiet Ferndale values its streets of colorfully restored Victorians.

For more information, contact the **Ferndale Chamber of Commerce** 707/786-4477, www.victorianferndale.org/chamber.

Seeing and Doing Ferndale

Lovers of Victoriana, take the walking tour; for a free guide to historic buildings (almost everything here qualifies), pick up the souvenir edition of the *Ferndale Enterprise* at the Kinetic Sculpture Museum or elsewhere on Main Street. Or take a Victorian-paced carriage ride. The horses and carriages of the **Ferndale Carriage Co.,** 707/786-9675, pick up guests at Main and Washington daily in summer, weekends only otherwise. To fully appreciate the town's history, visit the small **Ferndale Museum,** 515 Shaw Ave. (just off Main at the corner of Third), 707/786-4466, which also includes an Oral History Library, written histories, and old *Ferndale Enterprise* newspaper archives

Ferndale's Gingerbread Mansion

on microfilm. The museum is closed the entire month of January but otherwise open Wed.–Sat. (also Tuesday in summer) 11 A.M.–4 P.M. and Sunday 1–4 P.M. Small admission.

Most of Ferndale's historic commercial buildings are concentrated on three-block-long Main St., including the Roman-Renaissance **Six Rivers National Bank** building at 394 Main, originally the Ferndale Bank. The **Kinetic Sculpture Museum,** in the Ferndale Art & Cultural Center at 580 Main St. (no phone) displays a decidedly eclectic collection of survivors of the annual kinetic sculpture race, as well as works in progress. The Kinetic Sculpture Museum is usually open weekdays 10 A.M.–5 P.M., shorter hours on weekends. In the same building, along with various other galleries, is the **Ferndale Arts Cooperative Gallery,** 707/786-9634, with its impressive array of watercolors, wood work, pottery, sculpture, paper art, and jewelry. Open daily. Worth a stop, too, is the 1892-vintage **Golden Gait Mercantile,** 421 Main St., 707/786-4891, a squeaky-floored emporium of oddities and useful daily items, from sassafras tea and traditional patent medicines to butter churns, bushel (and peck) baskets, and treadle sewing machines. There's a museum on the second floor.

While touring the town—probably the best-preserved Victorian village in the state—travelers will be relieved to find that Ferndale has public restrooms (next to the post office on Main). Once off Main, most people head first to the famous **Gingerbread Mansion,** a Victorian built in a combination of Queen Anne, Eastlake, and stick styles. Tucked into its formal English gardens at 400 Berding and virtually dripping with its own frosting, the Gingerbread is one of the most photographed and painted buildings in Northern California.

Take the scenic drive to small **Centerville County Park & Beach** at the end of Ocean, which provides access to the 10 miles of beaches between False Cape and the Eel River lagoon: good beachcombing, driftwood picking, and smelt fishing in summer. On the way you'll pass **Portuguese Hall,** a popular event venue, and also the historic 1865 Victorian **Fern Cottage,** family farmhouse of state Senator Joseph Russ,

open for tours by appointment only, 707/786-4735 or 707/786-4835. On the short drive along Ocean in the opposite direction from Main, on the way to 110-acre **Russ Park** (trails, forest, bird-watching), you'll pass **Danish Hall** (built in the late 1800s, still used for community events); Ferndale's striking **pioneer cemetery;** and the former **Old Methodist Church,** built in 1871, at the corner of Berding.

Arts and Events

The **Ferndale Repertory Theatre,** 447 Main St., 707/786-5483, offers weekend performances by both its adult and youth troupes most of the year—everything from *Blithe Spirit* and *Our Town* to *One Flew Over the Cuckoo's Nest.* In March, come for the big **Foggy Bottoms Milk Run,** when whole families and serious runners alike participate in a footrace around the farm and back to Main Street. The Portuguese **Holy Ghost Festival** is in May, with a parade, dancing, feasts. Also in May is the annual **Tour of the Unknown Coast Bicycle Ride,** which starts at the county fairgrounds and can be ridden in 10- to 100-mile increments. On Memorial Day, the **Kinetic Sculpture Race** from Arcata ends on Main St., the surviving sculptures proudly paraded through town. Some also take up residence at the Kinetic Sculpture Museum here (for more information about the race, see Arcata and Vicinity). Come in June for the children's **Pet Parade,** in July for Ferndale's all-American **July 4th Parade and Picnic.** In August, the **Humboldt County Fair** and horse races come to the fairgrounds.

In September, **Tastes of Ferndale & Friends** bring a food and music sampler to Main Street. The annual **Victorian Village Oktoberfest & Harvest Day** is the main event in October. In December, come for the town's month-long **Victorian Christmas** celebrations, which include lighting up the world's tallest living Christmas tree (the 165-foot Sitka spruce on Main), a lighted-tractor parade, and the arrival of Santa Claus by horse and carriage. For more events information, contact the chamber office.

Practicalities

Camp at the handsome **Humboldt County Fair-**

grounds, 1250 Fifth St. (off Van Ness), 707/786-9511, www.humboldtcountyfair.org, available for both tent camping and RVs, $15. Water and electricity hookups are available, along with access to restrooms and hot showers.

In the B&B department, the local star is the unabashedly luxurious 1899 **Gingerbread Mansion Inn,** 400 Berding St., 707/786-4000 or 800/952-4136, www.gingerbread-mansion.com, which offers 11 truly unique, antique-rich rooms in a refurbished 1899 Victorian mansion. Amenities include generous full breakfast and afternoon tea. Most rooms and suites are $150–250, for are $250 and up. Also quite fabulous is the **Victorian Inn,** 400 Ocean Ave. (at Main), 707/786-4949 or 888/589-1808, www.a-victorian-inn.com, 12 B&B rooms in a gorgeous downtown 1890 Victorian. All rooms feature private baths and extra amenities, from cable TV and CD players to in-room phones. Full breakfast Most rooms are in the very reasonable $100–150 range, several are $175. Curley's Grill and Silva's Fine Jewelry are other Victorian Inn jewels.

Ferndale offers other Victorian B&Bs, including the romantic **Shaw House Inn,** 703 Main, 707/786-9958 or 800/557-7429, www.shawhouse.com, an 1854 Carpenter Gothic Victorian with three parlors and eight guest rooms, all with private baths. Fabulous full breakfast included. Room rates are $100–150, suites $155 and $185. There are also some very small motels, including the **Francis Creek Inn** on Shaw Ave., 707/786-9611, the **Fern Motel** on Ocean, 707/786-5000, and **Ferndale Motel & Laundromat** on Main, 707/786-9471.

Picnickers can stop in at the **Ferndale Meat Company,** 376 Main, 707/786-4501, to pick up sandwiches, handmade smoked sausages (and other meats from the two-story stone smokehouse), and fine cheeses. For a sit-down meal, try immensely popular, family-friendly **Curley's Grill** downstairs in the Victorian Inn, 400 Main St., 707/786-9696, a California-style tavern open daily for lunch and dinner and also breakfast on weekends. Menu ranges from grilled portobella mushrooms or jumbo prawns to pasta primavera and grilled rib-eye steak, and the daily pasta and

seafood specials are always worth a look. Stop by **Sweetness & Light,** 554 Main next to the post office, 707/786-4403, for truffles and other traditional chocolates.

Fernbridge

Between Eureka and Ferndale is Fernbridge, the name for both a community and a stately seven-arch Romanesque bridge called "the queen of bridges" up here in the north. Caltrans once nearly started a local armed rebellion when it announced plans to tear the bridge down. Fernbridge is home to the **Humboldt Creamery** dairy co-op, 572 Fernbridge Dr., 707/725-6182, as well as **Angelina Inn,** 281 Fernbridge Dr., 707/725-3153, locally loved for its Italian dinners and prime rib, steaks, and seafood. Open daily for dinner, full bar, live music on weekends.

Loleta

Dairies account for nearly half of Humboldt County's agricultural income. Since the pasturelands near Loleta are among the richest in the world, it's only natural that the region's first creamery was established here in 1888. Because of difficult shipping logistics, much of the milk produced here is processed into butter, cheese, and dried-milk products. Big doin's here is the **Loleta Antique Show** in October, not to mention **Swauger Station Days** in July. For more information about these and other events, call the **Loleta Chamber of Commerce,** 707/733-5666.

Loleta today is still a bucolic village of wood-frames and old brick buildings. Most of the action in town is at the award-winning **Loleta Cheese Factory,** 252 Loleta Dr., 707/733-5470 or 800/995-0453, famed for its natural Jersey milk cheeses, tasting room, and retail sales of cheese and wine. Step inside to sample and buy cheese right out of the display case. The company's famous creamy jack cheese comes in garlic, green chili, caraway, jalapeño, and smoked salmon variations. The cheddars also tease the palate—try the salami or smoked salmon versions. Watch the cheesemaking, too. The Loleta Cheese Factory is open Mon.–Fri. 9 A.M.–5 P.M., Sat. 9 A.M.–4 P.M., Sunday noon–4 P.M. Call to request a mail-order catalog.

If you decide to spend the night, try the four-room **Southport Landing Bed and Breakfast,** 444 Phelan Rd., 707/733-5915. This 1890s colonial revival mansion overlooks the Humboldt Bay National Wildlife Refuge. Guests have use of kayaks, bicycles, pool table, and a nature library. Rates, $50–100 and $100–150, include full breakfast and evening beverages/hors d'oeuvres.

Eureka

When James T. Ryan slogged ashore here from his whaling ship in May of 1850, shouting (so the story goes) *Eureka!* ("I have found it"), what he found was California's largest natural bay north of San Francisco. Russian-American Fur Company hunters actually entered Humboldt Bay earlier, in 1806, but the area's official discovery came in 1849 when a party led by Josiah Gregg came overland that winter seeking the mouth of the Trinity River (once thought to empty into the ocean). Gregg died in the unfriendly forests on the return trip to San Francisco, but the reports of his half-starved companions led to Eureka's establishment on "Trinity Bay" as a trading post and port serving the far northern inland gold camps.

While better than other north coast harbors, Humboldt Bay was still less than ideal. The approach across the sand bar was treacherous, and dozens of ships foundered in heavy storms or fog—a trend that continued well into this century. In 1917, the cruiser USS *Milwaukee,* flagship of the Pacific fleet, arrived to rescue a grounded submarine and ended up winching itself onto the beach, where it sat until World War II (when it was scrapped and recycled). But ever-imaginative Eureka has managed to turn even abandoned boats into a community resource. Before the Humboldt Bay Nuclear Power Plant was built here in 1963, the city got most of its energy from the generators of the salvaged Russian tanker *Donbass III,* towed into the bay and beached in 1946.

Oddly expansive and naked today, huge Humboldt Bay was once a piddling puddle at the edge of the endless redwood forest. Early loggers stripped the land closest to town first, but the bare Eureka hills were soon dotted with reincarnated redwoods—buildings of pioneer industry, stately Victorians that still reflect the community's cultural roots.

No matter how vibrant the colors of the old homes here, at times it seems nothing can dispel the fog in these parts. When the fog does finally lift, in wet years the rains come, washing away hillsides and closing roads, trapping the locals behind what they refer to affectionately as the Redwood Curtain. That sense of being isolated from the rest of the human world—something harried visitors from more urban locales long for—and the need to transform life into something other than *gray* may explain why there are more artists and performers per capita in Humboldt County than anywhere else in the state. Sunshine is where one finds it, after all.

SEEING AND DOING EUREKA
Humboldt Bay
Eureka's 10-mile-long Humboldt Bay was named for the German naturalist Baron Alexander von Humboldt. So it's fitting that the extensive, if almost unknown, **Humboldt Bay National Wildlife Refuge** was established on the edge of the bay's South Jetty to protect the black brant, a small migratory goose, and more than 200 other bird species. (Some 36,000 black brants showed up in 1951; some 10,000 come now, up from a recent low of 1,000, and their numbers are still increasing.) Other harbor life includes sea lions, harbor seals, porpoises, and gray whales, seen offshore here in winter and early spring. Humboldt Bay's **Egret Rookery** and other refuge features are best observed from the water. The Humboldt refuge administers the offshore **Castle Rock NWR,** a 14-acre island which serves as rookery for the largest breeding population of common murres in California and offers a migratory roost for Aleutian Canada geese, and also includes the **Lanphere Dunes** near Arcata. The new refuge headquarters and visitor cen-

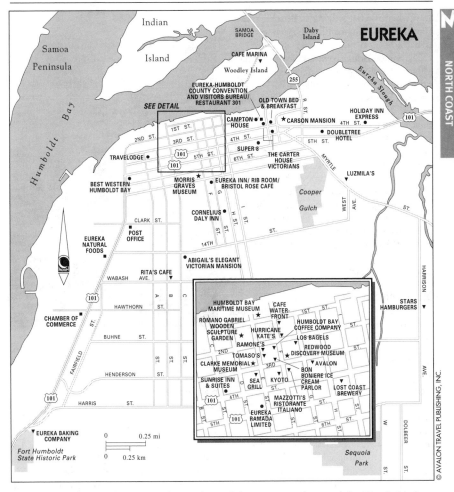

ter, 1020 Ranch Rd. (off Hookton Rd.) in Loleta, 707/733-5406, pacific.fws.gov/humboldtbay, was named in memory of Richard J. Guadagno, former refuge manager, who was aboard United Airlines Flight 93 on September 11, 2001. Interpretive trails include the three-mile (round-trip) **Hookton Slough Trail,** and the seasonal 1.75-mile **Shorebird Loop Trail.**

To get a look at the refuge from the bay, take the **Humboldt Bay Harbor Cruise** or sign on for a kayak tour with **Hum-Boats** (see Eureka Getting Around, below). Human wildlife includes

fishing crews, sailors, and the Humboldt State University crew teams out rowing at dusk (the best bird's-eye view is from the Cafe Marina on Woodley Island).

Fields Landing, where the last Northern California whaling station operated until 1951, is the bay's deep-water port, the place to watch large fishing boats unload their daily catch; the rest of the fleet docks at the end of Commercial St. in downtown Eureka. Fields Landing is also the place to pick up fresh Dungeness crab, usually available from Christmas to February or March.

Stop when the flag's flying at **Botchie's Crab Stand,** 6670 Fields Landing Dr. just off Hwy. 101, 707/442-4134.

The **Samoa Bridge** connects the city of Eureka with the narrow peninsula extending south from Arcata (almost across Humboldt Bay) and the onetime Simpson Lumber Company town of **Samoa,** the name inspired by the bay's resemblance to the harbor at Pago Pago. The entire town was bought in 2000 by locals who plan to spruce things up, and perhaps convert the old manager's mansion into a bed-and-breakfast. (Stay tuned.) Almost the same as always, though, is the **Samoa Cookhouse,** noted rustic restaurant and the last logging camp cookhouse in the West, also a fascinating museum. The **Eureka Municipal Airport** and **U.S. Coast Guard** facilities occupy the fingertip of Samoa Peninsula, near county-owned fishing access (very basic camping, restrooms, boat ramps).

Old Town Eureka

Part of Eureka's onetime skid row—the term itself of north coast origin, referring to the shanty-towns and shacks lining the loggers' "skid roads" near ports—has been shoved aside to make room for Old Town. Most of the fleabag flophouses, sleazy sailors' bars, and pool halls along First, Second, and Third between C and G Streets were razed and others renovated to create this bayside concentration of new cafés, art galleries, and trendy shops. A new phase of waterfront redevelopment was unveiled in early 2002: the $7.9 million, 1,300-foot boardwalk between C and G Streets. A roster of events, from the annual spring **Taste of Main Street** and **Redwood Coast Dixieland Jazz Festival** to the **Old Town Fourth of July Celebration,** also define Old Town.

Most people stop first for a look at the gaudy, geegawed Gothic **Carson Mansion,** 143 M St., at the foot of Second St. (locals say "Two Street"), once the home of lumber baron William Carson. Those in the know say this is the state's—perhaps the nation's—finest surviving example of Victoriana. Now home to the exclusive all-male (how Victorian) Ingomar Club, even unescorted men are not welcome inside or in the club's palatial gardens. So be happy with a look at the ornate

© ROBERT HOLMES/CALTOUR

the elaborately decorated Carson Mansion, home of a males-only club

turrets and trim of this three-story money-green mansion built of redwood. Inside are superb stained-glass works, handworked interiors of hardwoods imported from around the world, and fireplaces crafted from Mexican onyx.

Better, though, and much more accessible despite the protective plate glass, is the fabulous folk art at the **Romano Gabriel Wooden Sculpture Garden** just down the street at 315 Second St., a blooming, blazing, full-color world of delightful plants, people, and social commentary, crafted from packing crates with the help of a handsaw. This is "primitive art" (snobs say "poor taste") on a massive scale, one of two pieces of California folk art recognized internationally (the other is Watts Towers in Los Angeles). Gabriel, a gardener who died in 1977, said of his work: "Eureka is bad place for flowers—the salty air and no sun. So I just make this garden." He worked on this garden, which includes likenesses of Mussolini, the Pope, nosy neighbors, and tourists amid the fantastic flowers and trees, for 30 years. After Gabriel's death, it was restored, then transplanted downtown from his front yard.

Well worth it, too, is a stop at the fine and friendly **Clarke Memorial Museum,** 240 E St. (at Third), 707/443-1947, where you'll feel as though you're stepping into a 19th-century parlor. The museum was founded in 1960 by Cecile Clarke (a history teacher at Eureka High 1914-50), who personally gathered most of the collection. This is the place for a look at various Victoriana, including toys and dolls; glassware and jewelry; pioneer relics, including antique guns and other frontier weaponry, even a signed first edition of *The Personal Memoirs of General Grant;* and the incredible, nationally noted Nealis Hall collection of Native American artifacts, basketry, and ceremonial dance regalia. The museum building, the Italian Renaissance onetime **Bank of Eureka,** is itself a collector's item with its stained-glass skylight and glazed terra-cotta exterior. The building is listed on the National Register of Historic Places. Open Tues.–Sat., noon–4 P.M. Admission is free.

Eureka's family-friendly **Discovery Museum,** Third and F Sts., 707/443-9694, explores science, art, culture, and technology, with interactive exhibits and displays appealing to children of all ages. The big exhibit in 2003 was the *Whole Tooth.* Open Tues.–Sat. 10.am.–4 P.M., Sunday noon–4 P.M. Admission $4.

The **Humboldt Bay Maritime Museum,** 423 First St., 707/444-9440, chronicles the area's contributions to Pacific seafaring heritage with original photographs, ship models, maritime artifacts and library, even an old Fresnel lens from the Table Bluff lighthouse and a refurbished Coast Guard lifeboat. Open daily 11 A.M.–4 P.M. Admission is free (donations welcomed).

The museum also owns and runs the **MV Madaket,** a former Humboldt Bay passenger ferry now providing sightseeing tours of the bay, daily May–Oct. Built in 1910, the *Madaket* is the oldest passenger vessel in continuous use in the United States, with the smallest bar. The harbor cruises depart from 122 I St. in Old Town. For more information, call **Humboldt Bay Harbor Cruise** at 707/445-1910.

Fort Humboldt and Sequoia Park

Reconstruction continues at Eureka's **Fort Humboldt State Historic Park,** 3431 Fort Ave., 707/445-6567. This outpost of the U.S. military's 1850s Indian Wars was onetime stomping grounds of the young U.S. Grant. As depressed in Eureka as he was elsewhere in California, Grant spent six months here then resigned his commission to go home and farm in Missouri. The fort museum tells the story. Also here: an excellent (and wheelchair-accessible) indoor/outdoor museum display of early logging technology, along with picnic tables (good view of Humboldt Bay) and restrooms. Guided tours available on request. Park admission is free. From May through September, "Steam Ups" of historic steam-powered logging equipment are held on the third Saturday of the month. Come in April for the Dolbeer Donkey Days. Get here via Highland Ave. off Broadway. (Call for actual directions—it's tricky to find.)

There's something a little sad about Sequoia

MORRIS GRAVES MUSEUM OF ART

Dazzling new star in Humboldt County's fine arts galaxy is the Morris Graves Museum of Art, at home in the historic, newly restored Carnegie Library. The completely accessible museum, also headquarters for the county arts council, features fine arts galleries, courtyard sculpture garden, a performance rotunda, and a young artists' academy. **Saturday Nights at the Morris Graves,** a performance series offered from September through May, offers everything from jazz, folk, gospel, and accordion concerts to poetry, dance, and theater. The Graves Museum is open to the public Wed.–Sun., noon–5 P.M., and during special Saturday night events.

The Humboldt Arts Council office is inside the museum, located in Eureka at 636 F St., 707/442-0278, www.humboldtarts.org. Pick up the arts council's annual magazine *The Palette* (free) wherever you find it around town, or at www.thepalette.com. To learn more about Morris Graves, the artist who endowed the museum, visit www.morrisgraves.com.

Park, the last significant vestige of the virgin redwood forest that once fringed Humboldt Bay. The park is situated southeast of downtown at Glatt and W Streets, 707/443-7331, and is open Tues.–Sun. 10 A.M.–8 P.M. May–Oct., until 5 P.M. the rest of the year. Enjoy the peaceful melancholy of these dark woods laced with walking paths, a rhododendron dell, and duck pond. The five-acre **Sequoia Park Zoo,** 3414 W St., 707/441-4263, is home to animals from six continents, though the native river otters are best. The zoo is open Tues.–Sun. 10 A.M.–5 P.M. (until 7 P.M. in summer). Admission is free. In summer there's also an immensely popular seasonal petting zoo, open 11:30 A.M.–3:30 P.M.

STAYING IN EUREKA

Camping

Camping throughout Humboldt County is best in the wilds, but in a pinch, campers can head to **Redwood Acres Fairgrounds,** 3750 Harris St. (south off Myrtle), 707/445-3037, www.redwoodacres.com, full hookups and showers $15; the **Eureka KOA,** 4050 N. Hwy. 101 (a few miles north of town), 707/822-4243 or 800/562-3136, with facilities including "kamping kabins" ($40–50), tent and trailer spaces ($20–30), laundry room, rec room, showers, heated pool, and playground; or the **E-Z RV Park & Marina,** 1875 Buhne Dr. (south of town on Humboldt Bay) at King Salmon Resort, 707/442-1118, $19 with all hookups (RVs only).

Motels

Broadway is "motel row," and you'll also find reasonable motels on Fourth Street. Most Eureka motels offer substantially cheaper rates Oct.–Apr., and even the cheapest places usually have color TV and cable and/or free HBO.

There are decent motels for $50–100, including (at the low end of that range) the ubiquitous **Motel 6,** 1934 Broadway, 707/445-9631 or 800/466-8356, www.motel6.com; Eureka's **Travelodge,** 4 Fourth St. (at B St.), 707/443-6345 or 800/578-7878, with a pool and cable TV with HBO; and **Sunrise Inn & Suites,** 129 Fourth St., 707/443-9751. Options at the high end of the $50–100 range include **Days Inn,** 4260 Broadway, 707/444-2019 or 800/329-7466, which has an indoor pool and Jacuzzi. Some rooms have kitchenettes; all have cable TV with HBO. Among others are the **Eureka Ramada Limited,** 270 Fifth St., 707/443-2206 or 800/233-3782, with sauna and indoor Jacuzzi; the **Holiday Inn Express,** 2223 Fourth St., 707/442-3261, with indoor pool, exercise room, and continental breakfast buffet; and the **Eureka Super 8,** 1304 Fourth St., 707/443-3193 or 800/235-3232, with indoor pool, sauna, Jacuzzi, and cable TV with HBO.

Motels in the $100–150 range include the **Best Western Humboldt Bay,** 232 W. Fifth St. (at Broadway), 707/443-2234 or 800/521-6996, with spacious rooms, large outdoor pool, whirlpool, and rec room. The large and attractive **Red Lion Inn,** 1929 Fourth St. (between T and V Sts.), 707/445-0844 or 800/733-5466, features amenities such as a swimming pool and spa, laundry and valet service, business center, and good onsite restaurant. The **Best Western Bayshore Inn,** 3500 Broadway (Hwy. 101), 707/268-8005 or 888/268-8005, offers an indoor/outdoor pool and spa, Jacuzzi suites, and a Marie Callender's restaurant. **Quality Inn Eureka,** 1209 Fourth St. (between M and N Streets), 707/443-1601 or 800/772-1622, features an outdoor heated pool and an indoor sauna and Jacuzzi.

Noteworthy Lodgings

Very "old Eureka" is the excellent **Eureka Inn,** 518 Seventh St. (at F St.), 707/442-6441 or 800/862-4906, www.eurekainn.com. First opened in 1922, this imposing 1920s Tudor-style hotel is listed on the National Register of Historic Places. Among the luminaries who have wandered its halls and dined at its famous **Rib Room**—the locals' favorite seafood-and-steak restaurant—are Sir Winston Churchill, Bobby Kennedy, Mickey Mantel, Steven Spielberg, Ronald Reagan, and Shirley Temple. In addition to its spectacular clear-heart redwood interiors, the Eureka Inn features abundant amenities, including a sauna, whirlpool, year-round heated pool, three restaurants (including the **Bristol Rose Café**), three bars, "live hot jazz," a shoe-shine stand, and free transportation to and from the airport. New owners have started renovations. Rates for rooms and suites are $100–150, lower in the off season. Or stay at the Eureka Inn's associated **Downtowner Motor Inn,** across the street.

Definitely "new Eureka" but full of Victorian charms are the **Carter House Inns,** 301 L St., 707/444-8062 or 707/445-1390, or 800/404-1390, www.carterhouse.com. What has become known at The Carter House is actually a complex of four properties—The Hotel Carter, The Carter House Inn, The Carter Cottage, and Bell Cottage—under unified management. The hotel and inn are vintage-1980s facsimiles, while the later cottages are renovations of the original 19th-century structures.

It all began with the 1981 construction of three-story **The Carter House,** built of fine rustic redwood following the very authentic (and very exacting) original design specifications of Carson Mansion architects Samuel and Joseph Newsom. Structurally, The Carter House is a stately re-creation of an 1884 "stick" Victorian home built in San Francisco and lost in the 1906 earthquake and fire. But otherwise it's quite modern, with very un-Victorian sunny rooms and suites (one with fireplace and whirlpool) and an uncluttered, almost contemporary air. That Carter House synthesis of "contemporary good taste with the elegance of a bygone era" extends also to still more luxurious **The Carter Hotel** across the street, and to the two inviting cottages. Homey **Bell Cottage** features three rooms and shared common areas, perfect for a small group traveling together. Romantic and sunny, **The Carter Cottage** is also known as "the love shack." Most high-season rates at the Carter House Inns are $150–250, though there are a handful of pricier suites. The Carter Cottage is about $500. In any accommodation, expect luxurious amenities, a breathtaking full breakfast, evening wine and hors d'oeuvres, and before-bed cookies and tea.

The outstanding restaurant at the Carter House Inns, **Restaurant 301,** is a 1998 recipient of the coveted *Wine Spectator* magazine Grand Award. Restaurant 301 is supported by the extensive, organic **301 Gardens**—guests can help

harvest vegetables, fruits, and herbs before dinner—and the **301 Wineshop.** Quite special, too, are the **Winemakers Dinners at Restaurant 301.** To get you there in style, at last report Mark Carter's 1958 Bentley was still available for limo service to and from the airport.

Bed-and-Breakfasts

Eureka's showplace inn, a destination in its own right for connoisseurs of high-Victorian style, is the award-winning **Abigail's Elegant Victorian Mansion,** 1406 C St., 707/444-3144, www.eureka-california.com. This elegant Victorian mansion offers more than four comfortable rooms, two with private baths (the other two share three baths and a Finnish sauna), fabulous breakfasts, and vintage auto tours. Guided by the inn's irrepressible innkeepers, Doug ("Jeeves") and Lily Vieyra, visitors could easily spend an entire day just touring *this* eclectic place, which is a spectacular de facto museum of authentic Victorian substance and style. Old movies and music add yet another delightful dimension to a stay here. Don't miss the Victorian gardens and croquet field. Rates are $150–250.

The 1905 **Daly Inn,** 1125 H St., 707/445-3638 or 800/321-9656, www.dalyinn.com, offers three inviting antique-rich rooms (two share a bath) and two suites in a 1905 colonial revival. Guests enjoy a spectacular full breakfast, afternoon tea, phones, TV, a library, and gardens with a fish pond. Be sure to peek into the third-floor Christmas Ballroom. Rates are $100–150, though Miss Martha's room, with two antique twin beds, is $80.

The **Old Town Bed and Breakfast Inn,** 1521 Third St., 707/443-5235 or 888/508-5235, was the original redwood home of William Carson (of Carson Mansion fame), built in 1871. The hot tub came later. Rates for most rooms are $100–150. The **Campton House,** 305 M St. in Old Town, 707/443-1601 or 800/772-1622, is managed by the Quality Inn Eureka. The 1911 Arts & Crafts-style house features redwood interiors and abundant antiques. One room has a private bath, others share (two rooms are typically rented as a suite). Guests can use the pool, sauna, and Jacuzzi at the Quality Inn. Rates include

BLUE OX MILLWORKS

Endlessly compelling, Eureka's time-honored Blue Ox Millworks complex is located at the foot of X St., 707/444-3457 or 800/248-4259 (for tour reservations), www.blueoxmill.com. The antithesis of all things high-tech, the Blue Ox pays hands-on homage to the beauty of craftsmanship, and particularly the craft of old-fashioned woodworking. In this going concern—a de facto living history environment, the only mill of its kind remaining in the U.S.—the machines date from 1850 to the 1940s. (Blue Ox recently acquired the late 19th-century Barnes Equipment Company Human-Powered Tool Collection, which includes the only complete and original mortising machine in existence.) There's an aromatic whirl of sawing, chipping, turning, grinding, and sanding as custom orders are filled.

Customers include the National Park Service—which once ordered 400 custom planters for the White House—and endless couples in the midst of Victorian restorations. Victorian replication is the specialty here, though the Blue Ox can duplicate or restore just about anything. The stunning Eureka Trolley built for Old Town merchants is a Blue Ox creation.

Self-guided tours of the mill—visiting the main shop, sawmill, moulding plant, blacksmith shop, "logging skid camp," and more—and the adjacent Blue Ox Craftsman's Village are offered Mon.–Sat. 9 A.M.–4 P.M. Weekday tours are usually more action-packed, if you want to see the craftsmen at work, and Saturday tours more personally guided. Admission is $7.50 adults, $6.50 seniors, $3.50 children 6–12, under 5 free.

continental breakfast and afternoon tea. Rooms are $50–100; the whole house can be rented for $250–400.

Quite special at the waterfront is **Upstairs at the Waterfront,** 102 F St., 707/444-1301 or 888/817-5840, www.upstairsatthewaterfront.com. Listed on the National Register of Historic Places and a recipient of the 1994 Governor's Award for Excellence in Design, "Upstairs" was once a brothel. These days it's a more sedate Victorian, offering two elegant, period styled bed-and-breakfast suites (yet with all the modern comforts) above the popular Café Waterfront (full breakfast included in a stay). Rachel's Room is $125, Sophie's Suite $175; combine the two for a great getaway apartment.

EATING IN EUREKA
Casual Fare

Eureka hosts two certified farmers' markets, both held June–Oct. Fresh veggies, fruit, and other local products abound at the **Eureka Old Town Certified Farmers Market,** Second and F Sts., held on Tuesday 10 A.M.–1 P.M. The **Eureka Certified Farmers Market** at the Henderson Center on Henderson St. (at F), is held Thursday 10 A.M.–1 P.M. For details on both, call 707/441-

9999. **Eureka Natural Foods,** 1626 Broadway, 707/422-6325, is a year-round supply, veggie, fruit, and sandwich stop.

Everyone will tell you that **Stars,** 2009 Harrison Ave., 707/445-2061, is the best bet for burgers. **Luzmila's** at 946 West Ave., 707/444-2508, serves great Mexican, from chiles rellenos to papas con chorizo. Or try immensely popular **Rita's Café & Taqueria,** 107 Wabash Ave., 707/268-0700.

Otherwise, Old Town offers just about everything. For the best bagels anywhere—infused, here, with Mexican flavors and traditions—try **Los Bagels,** 403 Second St. (at E), 707/442-8525, open daily for breakfast and lunch. (The original Los Bagels is in Arcata.) The **Eureka Baking Company,** 108 F St. and also 3562 Broadway (Hwy. 101), 707/445-8997, is wonderful for croissants, muffins, sourdough baguettes, and other fresh-baked fare. **Ramone's Bakery & Cafe,** 747 13th St., 707/826-1088, is excellent for pastries and fresh breads, light lunch, handmade truffles, and exquisite desserts, not to mention espresso and other good coffees. Ramone's has another location in Eureka, at 2225 Harrison, and outlets also in McKinleyville and Arcata. A great choice, too, for fresh-ground coffees (by the pound or by the cup) is **Humboldt Bay Coffee Company,** 211 F St., 707/444-3969, which offers live music on Friday and Saturday nights and outdoor seating in good weather. Another good stop for soup and sandwiches—and quite possibly the best ice cream anywhere on the north coast—is **Bon Boniere Ice Cream Parlor,** 215 F St. in Old Town, 707/268-0122.

More Old Town Draws

Artsy, minimalist **Hurricane Kate's,** 511 Second St., 707/444-1405, serves up some great wood-fired pizzas, "world fusion," and meat-and-potatoes specialties, most everything served tapas style. Full bar. Open Tues.–Sat. for lunch and dinner. **Avalon,** Third and G Sts., 707/445-0500, offers "Old World Food" with quite contemporary style, from the grilled rib-eye steak and local lamb chops to the cedar-planked salmon. Jazz on Saturday nights. Open for dinner only, Tues.–Sun. nights. Hugely popular **Lost Coast Brewery,** in the historic Knights of Pythias Hall at 617 Fourth St., 707/445-4480, is the place to go for eccentric decor and original art by Duane Flatmo, locally handcrafted ales like Alley Cat Amber and 8-Ball Stout, and good pub fare, served until midnight. Specialties include Lost Coast Vegetarian Chili, Stout Beef Stew, and Chicken Lips (really).

Justifiably famous (especially among lovers of the stinking rose) for its tomato and spinach pies, calzones, and other straightforward selections—one slice of the Sicilian pizza makes a meal—**Tomaso's,** 216 E St. (between Second and Third), 707/445-0100, is open for lunch and dinner weekdays and Saturday. Expect a wait—and however long that is, it'll be worth it. For something a bit dressier, the best Italian for miles around is served at **Mazzotti's Ristorante Italiano,** 301 F St., 707/445-1912, where specialties include linguini and white clam sauce, pasta Florentine, and Al Capone Calzone. Kid's menu, too. **Café Waterfront,** 102 F St., 707/443-9190, everybody's favorite for Sunday brunch, also features a small bed-and-breakfast upstairs—the aptly named Upstairs at the Waterfront, 707/444-1301. Other Old Town hot spots include **Kyoto** Japanese restaurant, 320 F St., 707/443-7777, and **Roy's Club Italian Seafood Restaurant,** 218 D St., 707/445-2511.

The longtime "old Eureka" choice for dress-up dining is the **Rib Room** at the Eureka Inn, Seventh and F Streets, 707/442-6441, noted for its steaks, seafood, and great wine list. For breakfast or lunch, try the inn's **Bristol Rose Café.**

Real-Deal Seafood

The hands-down favorite for dress-up seafood is the Victorian **Sea Grill** in Old Town, 316 E St., 707/443-7187, where you'll find sophisticated selections like salmon with garlic wine butter sauce as well as hearty clam chowder. Many other local restaurants—above and below—also offer seafood specialties. Now that the beloved Old Eureka standard, the Eureka Seafood Grottohas closed for good, you have to actively seek real-deal seafood stupor. The **Cafe Marina** on Woodley Island, 707/443-2233, is a popular local fish house, open daily for breakfast, lunch, and dinner. The only place to buy fresh crab is **Botchie's Crab Stand,** 6670 Fields Landing Dr. just off Hwy. 101, 707/442-4134, open for business when the white flag (with orange crab) is flying. Crab season usually runs Dec.–Mar., weather permitting.

Samoa Cookhouse

Everyone should eat at the Samoa Cookhouse on the Samoa Peninsula, 707/442-1659, at least once. The Samoa is a bona fide loggers' cookhouse oozing redwood-rugged ambience. The phrase "all you can eat" takes on new meaning here: portions are gargantuan. No cuisine here, just good ol' American food—platters of thickly sliced ham, beef, turkey, and spare ribs (choices change daily), plus potatoes, vegetables, fresh-baked bread—all passed around among the checkered oilcloth–covered tables. Soup and salad are included in the fixed-price dinner ($12.95 when last we checked), not to mention home-made apple pie for dessert. Come early on weekends, particularly in summer, and be prepared to wait an hour or so. Equally hearty are breakfasts and lunch; a leisurely breakfast here is the best. No reservations are taken but all major credit cards are accepted—and there's a gift shop. To get to the cookhouse, head west from Eureka over the Samoa Bridge, turn left, then left again at the town of Samoa (follow the signs).

Restaurant 301

The Hotel Carter's elegant and small Restaurant 301, 301 L St., 707/444-8062, is open nightly for candlelight, classical music, and quality dining. In fact, Restaurant 301 has become something of an international dining destination since it won *Wine Spectator* magazine's coveted Grand Award in 1998. Fewer than 100 restaurants in the world have been so honored. According to *Wine Spectator,* Restaurant 301 is a "wine-and-food oasis. . . where a superb wine list is complemented by the culinary talent of Chef Rodger Babel." Menus here are created from fresh, local ingredients, from Humboldt Bay seafood to the fresh vegetables, fruits, and herbs harvested daily from the restaurant's own extensive organic gardens. Entrées might include marinated and grilled quail breast medallions with fresh corn waffles, pecan-crusted Pacific salmon, or fennel-roasted sturgeon. The exceptional wine list features "unusually fine and reasonably priced wines," including treasured California wines and rare French wines. The cellar here boasts more than 23,000 bottles. Reservations are a must. The Hotel Carter also offers a famous four-course breakfast. To take the experience home with you, pick up a copy of the *Carter House Cookbook,* available for sale at the hotel.

ARTS AND ENTERTAINMENT

Come in January for the unique **Almost-Annual Humboldt Pun-Off,** a delightful display of tasteless humor, benefit for Easter Seals (immensely popular, so get your tickets early). March brings **A Taste of Main Street** and the **Redwood Coast Dixieland Jazz Festival.** Fog or no fog, almost everybody crawls out in April for the annual **Rhododendron Festival.** In May, over Memorial Day weekend, comes the famous **Kinetic Sculpture Race,** starting in nearby Arcata. From June to August, count on **Summer Concerts in the Park,** at Clarke Plaza in Old Town. Come in June for the **Old Town Cattle Drive** At the top of the lengthy regional calendar of July 4 events is the annual **Humboldt Bay Festival.** Also in July: **Blues by the Bay.** Later in July, rodeo fans can head north to the annual **Orick Rodeo** or east to the **Fortuna Rodeo.**

In July and August, the **Humboldt Arts Festival** keeps the area jumping with concerts, plays, exhibits, even special museum displays. August is hot for history, what with **Fort Humboldt Days** living history and **Steam-Up** (the monthly cranking up of ancient logging locomotives) at Fort Humboldt State Park and the **Civil War Days** reenactments in Fortuna. The annual **Humboldt County Fair** also comes in August, held in Ferndale. But there's also **Blues by the Bay.** In September, come for the **Festival on the Bay** and **Sights, Sounds & Tastes of Humboldt.** In December, the **Eureka Inn Christmas Celebration** is quite the shindig. But so is the **Trucker's Christmas Convoy** parade. For a detailed events calendar, contact local visitor bureaus.

Eureka was listed as number one in John Villani's *The 100 Best Small Art Towns in America.* Popular arts events include the monthly **First Saturday Night Arts Alive!** in the galleries and shops of Old Town and Downtown, the **Eureka Summer Concert Series** in Clarke Plaza at Third and E Sts., and the annual October **Maskibition** international competition of handmade art and performance masks. For information about what's happening arts-wise, stop by the new **Morris Graves Museum of Art,** also performance arts and gallery venue as well as headquarters for the Humboldt Arts Council at 636 F St., or try 707/442-0278, www.humboldtarts.org. **The Ink People Center for the Arts,** 411 12th St., 707/442-8413, www.inkpeople.org, is another arts locus. The Eureka chamber of commerce offers an extensive list of local galleries.

The most comprehensive source of information on the local music scene is **HumboldtMusic.com,** www.humboldtmusic.com. Among good bets for live music are local coffeehouses, the art-deco **Ritz Club,** 240 F St. in Old Town, 707/445-8577; **Club West,** 535 Fifth St. (at G St.), 707/444-2582; and the **Palm Lounge** at the Eureka Inn. The **Eureka Symphony Orchestra,** 1437 Russ St., 707/444-2889, presents several concerts each year; call for schedule and ticket information.

For something more theatrical, try **Redwood Curtain,** 800 W. Harris St., 707/443-7688, www.redwoodcurtain.com, or the **North Coast**

ALL WORK AND NO PLAYS?

The **Redwood Curtain,** a program of the Ink People Center for the Arts, promotes itself with this simple justification: Because Life Shouldn't Be All Work and No Plays. Indeed it shouldn't, especially when those plays are so good. Past Redwood Curtain plays include *Scotland Road* by Jeffrey Hatcher, *The Cripple of Inishmaan* by Martin McDonagh, *Crumbs from the Table of Joy* by Lynn Nottage, and *Two Rooms* by Lee Blessing.

Redwood Curtain's curtain goes up at the Eureka Mall, 800 W. Harris St., behind Staples and next to Six Rivers Bank, on the mall's Henderson St. side. Performances are usually scheduled Thurs.–Sun.; evening performances begin promptly at 8 P.M., Sunday matinees promptly at 2 P.M. Order advance tickets online at www.redwoodcurtain.com, or call the theater at 707/443-7688 for day-of-performance tickets.

Repertory Theatre, 300 Fifth St., 707/442-6278. Also look for performances of the renowned **Dell' Arte Players,** 707/668-5663, www.dellarte.com.

INFORMATION AND SERVICES

Find out what's going on from the **Northcoast Journal Weekly,** www.northcoastjournal.com, which includes a good calendar. The **HumGuide,** www.humguide.com, is a great online general information source for Humboldt County. The **Greater Eureka Chamber of Commerce,** 2112 Broadway, 707/442-3738 or 800/356-6381, www.eurekachamber.com, is the best stop for visitor information. Pick up Old Town information (including a listing of local antique shops) and the free Victorian walking tour guide. (*Really* taking the Victorian tour, though, means getting some exercise, since Eureka boasts well over 100 well-preserved Victorian buildings and homes, and more than 1,000 "architecturally significant" structures.) Or stop by the **Eureka Main Street Information Bureau,** 123 F St. #6, 707/442-9054, www.eurekamainstreet.com. The **Eureka-Humboldt County Convention and Visitors Bureau,** 1034 Second St., 707/443-5097, 800/346-3482, www.redwoodvisitor.org, is the central source for countywide visitor information. Nature appreciation resources, for example, include the free *Humboldt Bay Beaches and Dunes Map and Guide* and, for an introduction to the plants and animals of the local dune ecosystem, the laminated pocket *Beach and Dune Field Guide* ($6).

For books, head to the **Booklegger** in Old Town, 402 Second St., 707/445-1344. Eureka's main **post office** is at 337 W. Clark St., 707/442-1768, though a convenient downtown branch is located at the corner of Fifth and H Streets, 707/442-1828. **Eureka General Hospital,** 2200 Harrison Ave., 707/445-5111, offers 24-hour emergency medical care (707/441-4409). The local **California Dept. of Fish and Game** office is at 619 Second St., 707/445-6493, and provides regulations and licenses. Headquarters for **Six Rivers National Forest** is at 1330 Bayshore Way, 707/442-1721, www.r5.fs.fed.us/sixrivers, a good place to stop for camping information and forest maps. The regional **California Dept. of Parks and Recreation** office is at Fort Humboldt, 3431 Fort Ave., 707/445-6547.

GETTING AROUND

Get around town on the Humboldt Transit Authority's **Eureka Transit Service,** 133 V St. (catch most buses at Fifth and D Sts.), 707/443-0826, which runs Mon.–Sat.; regular fare is $1. The V St. station is also headquarters for **Humboldt Transit Authority,** same phone, www.hta.org, which serves the area from Scotia north to Trinidad Mon.–Sat. (including bicycle transport—call for details) with **Redwood Transit Service** buses. **Greyhound,** 1603 Fourth St. (at P St.), 707/442-0370, runs north to Crescent City and beyond, also south on Hwy. 101 to San Francisco. To fly into the area, the **Arcata-Eureka Airport** actually lies north of Arcata, in

McKinleyville, at 3561 Boeing Ave., 707/839-1906. Rental cars are available there.

Tour the bay on the **Humboldt Bay Harbor Cruise MV** *Madaket* (once the Eureka-Samoa ferry); call 707/445-1910 for information. Rent a sailboat or kayak from **Hum-Boats,** 707/444-3048, www.humboats.com, or join a guided tour with Jay Dottle ("Captain Jay"). Local historian Ray Hillman, 800/400-1849, offers various **guided history tours.** The walking tour explores the waterfront historic district ($18 for two); the three-hour driving/walking tour ranges from an island in Humboldt Bay and Victorian wonders around Eureka to the antique logging equipment at Fort Humboldt; and the redwood park day trips (heading erther north or south) include a picnic lunch created from all-local products. Per-person rates are $9–60.

Arcata and Vicinity

Arcata is Eureka's alter-ego, no more resigned to the status quo than the sky here is blue. In 1996, Arcata made national news when a majority of Green Party candidates was elected to the city council. Environmental activism is an everyday concern here, and far-from-the-mainstream publications are available even at the visitor center. In addition to Arcata's world-famous **Cross-Country Kinetic Sculpture Race** on Memorial Day weekend, popular annual events include April's **Godwit Days Spring Migration Bird Festival;** the **April Fools Income Tax Annual Auction,** a benefit for the North Coast Environmental Center; and the September **North Country Fair,** one of the West Coast's premier craft fairs. A relaxed and liberal town, Arcata is determined to make a difference.

It would be easy to assume that the genesis of this backwoods grass-roots activism is the presence of academia, namely Humboldt State University, the only university on the north coast. But the beginnings of the Arcata *attitude* go back much further. When Arcata was still a frontier trading post known as Union Town, 24-year-old writer Bret Harte set the tone. An unknown underling on Arcata's *The Northern Californian* newspaper between 1858 and 1860, an outraged Harte—temporarily in charge while his editor was out of town—wrote a scathing editorial about the notorious Indian Island massacre of Wiyot villagers by settlers and was summarily run out of town, shoved along on his way to fame and fortune. Besides activism, general community creativity, and education, farming and fishing are growing concerns. Appropriately enough, the popular semipro baseball team, a proud part of the community since 1944, is called the Humboldt Crabs.

SEEING AND DOING ARCATA

The presence of **Humboldt State University** keeps things in Arcata lively. Humboldt State, east of town on Fickle Hill near 14th St. and Grant Ave., 707/826-3011, www.humboldt.edu, emphasizes the study of forestry practices, fisheries and wildlife management, and oceanography. On campus, worthwhile sights include the arboretum, fish hatchery, and art gallery. Off campus, the **HSU Natural History Museum,** 1315 G St., 707/826-4479, features local natural history displays, an impressive fossil collection, and lots of hands-on exploration. Open Tues.–Sat. 10 A.M.–5 P.M. Admission is free (donations appreciated).

Phillip's House Museum, Seventh and Union Sts., is one of Arcata's oldest buildings, offering great views of Humboldt Bay and, inside, a peek into 19th- and early 20th-century life. The local Historical Sites Society, 707/822-4722, www.arcatahistory.org, offers tours every Sunday 2–4 P.M. and by appointment.

Arcata's downtown **Arcata Plaza,** with its memorial statue of President McKinley and out-of-place palm trees, is custom-made for watching people come and go from surrounding cafés and shops, or for resting up after a tour of local Victorian homes—if you don't mind hangin' out with the hang-out crowd. Several of the historic buildings framing the plaza are worth a look, including the **Jacoby Storehouse** on the south

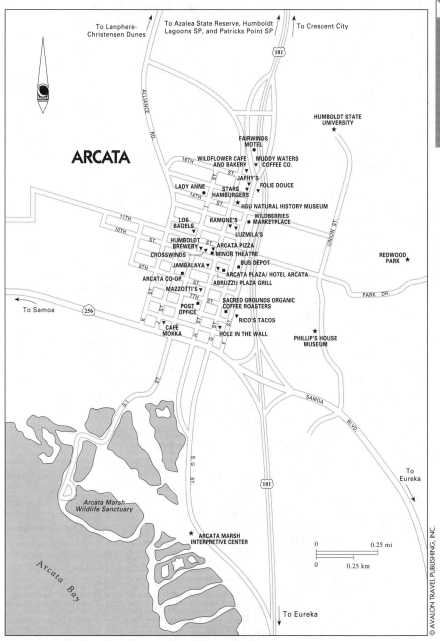

ARCATA

To Lanphere-
Christensen Dunes

To Azalea State Reserve, Humboldt
Lagoons SP, and Patricks Point SP

To Crescent City

101

ALLIANCE RD.

HUMBOLDT STATE
UNIVERSITY

FAIRWINDS
MOTEL

16TH

WILDFLOWER CAFE
AND BAKERY

MUDDY WATERS
COFFEE CO.

JAPHY'S

FOLIE DOUCE

LADY ANNE

STARS
HAMBURGERS

14TH

HSU NATURAL HISTORY MUSEUM

UNION ST.

11TH

LOS
BAGELS

RAMONE'S

WILDBERRIES
MARKETPLACE

10TH

LUZMILA'S

HUMBOLDT
BREWERY

ARCATA PIZZA

CROSSWINDS

MINOR THEATRE

REDWOOD
PARK

8TH

JAMBALAYA

BUS DEPOT

ARCATA CO-OP

ARCATA PLAZA/ HOTEL ARCATA

MAZZOTTI'S

ABRUZZI/ PLAZA GRILL

7TH

PARK DR.

POST
OFFICE

SACRED GROUNDS ORGANIC
COFFEE ROASTERS

To Samoa

256

RICO'S TACOS

CAFÉ
MOKKA

HOLE IN THE WALL

PHILLIP'S HOUSE
MUSEUM

K ST.

J ST.

H ST.

G ST.

F ST.

E ST.

SAMOA BLVD.

S.G. ST.

To
Eureka

101

Arcata Marsh
Wildlife Sanctuary

ARCATA MARSH
INTERPRETIVE CENTER

0   0.25 mi

0   0.25 km

Arcata Bay

© AVALON TRAVEL PUBLISHING, INC.

To Eureka

side at 791 Eighth St., 707/822-2434, a stone-and-brick beauty with iron shutters that now houses a railroad museum, restaurants, shops, and bank. Also admire the striking **Hotel Arcata** on Ninth and the restored 1914 **Minor Theatre** at 10th and H Streets, 707/822-3456 and 707/822-5177, www.minortheaters.com, the nation's oldest operating movie theater built specifically for feature films—and still *the* place to catch art-house, classic, and current films.

Many local businesses exemplify Arcata's fairly elevated and imaginative environmentalism, such as **Fire & Light,** 45 Ericson Crt., 707/825-7500 or 800/844-2223, www.fireandlight.com, which produces hand-poured, hand-pressed recycled glass—dinnerware, glassware, dipping dishes, footed candlestands, and more—in a translucent rainbow of "green" colors, from aqua and cobalt to celery, citrus, and copper. The amount of recycled clear glass in each piece varies by color but averages 85 percent. Tours by appointment.

To get away from the crowds, visit Arcata's parks. Arcata's pretty 20-acre **Redwood Park** is off Park (head east on 11th Street). Just beyond is the town's beloved 600-acre **Arcata Community Forest**, with its second-growth redwoods, educational **Historic Logging Trail,** hiking and mountain-biking trails, and picnicking. For more information and maps, contact or stop by the city Environmental Services Department, in City Hall at 736 F St., 707/822-8184. To get to **Mad River Beach County Park** in the Arcata Bottoms, with its beach, miles of dunes at the mouth of the Mad River, and good ocean fishing, take Alliance Rd. from K St. to Spear Ave., turn left onto Upper Bay Rd., then left again.

Azalea State Reserve

This 30-acre preserve just north of Arcata on North Bank Rd. (Hwy. 200) is famous for its cascading, fragrant pinkish-white western azalea blooms (good in April and May, usually best around Memorial Day) and other wildflowers, all in the company of competing rhododendrons. Good steelhead fishing can be found in the area along North Bank Rd. near Hwy. 299's Mad River bridge. Open daily for day use only, sunrise to sunset. For more information, call 707/488-2041.

Arcata Bay and Marsh

Walk along Arcata Bay to appreciate the impromptu scrap wood sculptures sometimes in bloom. The most fascinating bayside sights, though, are at the Arcata Marsh and Wildlife Preserve at the foot of I Street. This was one of the first wildlife preserves in the U.S. to be created from an old landfill dump and "enhanced" by treated sewage water. The aesthetic settling ponds offer excellent bird-watching. In fact, more than 200 bird species, river otters, muskrats, and pond-raised trout and salmon can all be viewed here. Facilities are well-designed for nature voyeurs, featuring trails, benches, interpretive displays, and bird blinds. Central to the reclaimed marsh's success is the Arcata Wastewater Aquaculture Project, which hatches and raises steelhead trout, coastal cutthroat trout, chinook salmon, and sturgeon. The project's T-shirt logo, Flush with Pride, depicts a fish jumping out of a toilet. For more information—and to get your T-shirts—stop by or call the **Arcata Marsh Interpretive Center,** 600 S. G St., 707/826-2359, open daily 1–5 P.M. The Redwood Region Audubon Society, 707/826-7031, offers guided walks of the preserve at 8:30 A.M. every Saturday morning, rain or shine, leaving from the end of I St.; Friends of the Arcata Marsh offers guided walks every Saturday at 2 P.M., leaving from the interpretive center. Birders can call the Birdbox hotline, 707/822-5666, for information on recent sightings.

The Lanphere-Christensen Dunes Preserve

Just east of Arcata, on the Samoa Peninsula near the Mad River Slough, is the 300-acre Lanphere-Christensen Dunes Preserve, managed by the U.S. Fish and Wildlife Service. It's open to the public by permit, obtained from the office at 6800 Lanphere Rd., 707/822-6378. No camping is permitted.

The Wiyot people once camped in summer on the pristine dunes and beach here, gathering berries in the coastal pine and spruce forest, and clamming, fishing, and hunting. Settlers later grazed cattle in this fragile ecosystem, which today is noted for its many well-preserved plant communities, from vernal pools and salt marsh to forest.

SCULPTURE RACE: A MOVING TRIBUTE TO "FORM OVER SUBSTANCE"

If you're in the area for Memorial Day weekend, don't miss the exuberant 38-mile, three-day transbay **World Championship Great Arcata to Ferndale Cross-Country Kinetic Sculpture Race.** Founded in 1969 by Ferndale artists Hobart Brown and Jack Mays, the race is a moving display of "form over substance." It's an almost-anything-goes tribute to unbridled imagination, but it does have a few rules. The mobile "sculptures" must be people-powered (though it is legal to get an assist from water, wind, or gravity); amphibious; and inspired by the event's high moral and ethical standards—such as "cheating is a privilege, not a right." (Kinetic cops patrol the course and interpret the rules.) Otherwise, anything goes—and rolls, floats, and flounders, through sand, saltwater, and swamp slime—in this ultimate endurance contest, also known at the Triathlon of the Art World.

Coming in first, even dragging in last, is not the point of this race. The contest's most coveted award is the Aurea Mediocritas, for the entry finishing closest to dead center—because, as the founders explain, winning and losing are both extremes, therefore "perfection lies somewhere in the middle." However, losing has its virtues, too, so the much-coveted Loser Award has been reinstated. Even spectators are part of the competition, thanks to the Most Worthy Fanatical Spectator Award.

Favorite recent entries have included the the Worry Wart, Grape Balls of Fire, Prince of Tides, Megasoreass, and Duane Flatmo's six-person Tide Fools. Some race survivors are on display at the sculpture museum in Ferndale. Prerace festivities include the **Kinetic Kickoff Party** and the **Rutabaga Queen Pageant** at Eureka's Ritz Club. For information about the race, now managed by the **Humboldt Kinetic Association,** call 707/845-1717 or see www.kineticsculpturerace.org. Honorable former sculptures are exhibited at the **Kinetic Sculpture Museum,** 580 Main St. in Ferndale, open daily.

First purchased and protected in the 1940s by the Lanpheres, biologists at the university, the area is unique for another reason. At this latitude, the northern and southern dune floras overlap, meaning rare and typical plantlife from both are present as well as more than 200 species of birds and other animals. The best dune wildflowers come in June, but every season holds its attractions. From April to September, bring mosquito repellent. Rain gear is wise during the rest of the year, and always wear soft-soled shoes.

Friends of the Dunes leads nature tours at the dunes and sponsors environmental projects there. Tours begin at the Pacific Union School parking lot, 3001 Janes Road. For more information and to receive the organization's quarterly *Dunesberry* newsletter, call 707/444-1397.

STAYING IN ARCATA

Camp at Patrick's Point if at all possible. If not, the **Mad River Rapids RV Park,** 3501 Janes Rd. (north of town at the Giuntoli Ln./Janes Rd. exit), 707/822-7275 or 800/822-7776, www.madriverrv

.com, is thoroughly civilized full-service facility offering paved sites with full hookups and cable TV, heated pool and spa, restrooms, showers, a laundry, minimart, video arcade, fitness room, tennis and basketball courts, playground, and fish-cleaning station. Each site has a patio, picnic table, and lawn. Rates are $29 and up.

Very nice—and right on the plaza, close to everything—is the refurbished and welcoming 1915 **Hotel Arcata,** 708 Ninth St., 707/826-0217 or 800/344-1221, www.hotelarcata.com, with most rooms $50–100, two-bedroom suites $100–150. If you'd prefer a B&B, equally affordable just a few blocks' stroll from Arcata Plaza is the **Lady Anne,** 902 14th St., 707/822-2797, an 1888 Queen Anne Victorian which features five guest rooms and the Writers Retreat suite, some with fireplaces, all with abundant antiques and plush guest robes. Full breakfast, bikes to borrow, too. The modest **Fairwinds Motel,** 1674 G St., 707/822-0568, $50–100, also offers easy access to campus.

Most local motels are fairly inconveniently located along Valley West Blvd., off Hwy. 101 north of town; take the Giuntoli Ln./Janes Rd. exit and turn right. All offer rooms in the $50–100 range, though some also have higher-priced options. Reliable choices include **Arcata Super 8,** 4887 Valley West, 707/822-8888 or 800/800-8000, and good ol' **Motel 6,** 4755 Valley West, 707/822-7061 or 800/466-8356, www.motel6.com. Solid and somewhat pricier options, and all featuring a heated indoor pool and whirlpool spa, include the pet-friendly **Best Western Arcata Inn,** 4827 Valley West, 707/826-0313 or 800/528-1234; **Comfort Inn,** 4701 Valley West, 707/826-2827 or 888/411-2827, www.comfortinnredwoods.com; the **Howard Johnson Express Inn** across the way at 4700 Valley West, 707/826-9660 or 800/446-4656, www.hojocalifornia.com; and the **North Coast Inn,** 4975 Valley West, 707/822-4861 or 800/406-0046. Across the highway is the **Quality Inn Arcata,** 3535 Janes Rd., 707/822-0409 or 800/549-3336, www.qualityinnarcata.com, which has an outdoor heated pool and Jacuzzi, tennis court, fitness and game rooms, and laundry facilities, and is adjacent to the Denny's Diner & Sports Bar.

EATING IN ARCATA

First stop for those just passing through should be **Arcata Co-op,** Eighth and I Streets, 707/822-5947, a natural-foods store, bakery, and deli with an abundance of organic everything, open 9 A.M.–9 P.M. (until 8 P.M. on Sunday). Healthy groceries, vitamins, and health-care products, as well as a juice bar, deli/café, and a Ramone's Bakery outpost, are all available at **Wildberries Marketplace,** 747 13th St. (at the top of G), 707/822-0095, open daily 7 A.M.–11 P.M. Wildberries is also the site of the **Arcata Certified Farmers Market,** held June–Oct. on Tuesday, 3–6 P.M. The **Arcata Plaza Certified Farmers Market** is held May through November at the Arcata Plaza (Eighth and G Sts.) on Saturday, 9 A.M.–1 P.M., For details on both, call 707/441-9999.

Standards

Los Bagels, 1061 I St., 707/822-3150, is largely a student hangout but every bit as popular as the Eureka shop, serving mostly coffee, bagels,

and bread items with south-of-the-border flair. The **Wildflower Cafe and Bakery,** 1604 G St., 707/822-0360, has fresh bakery items, veggie food, homemade soups and salads, and "macrobiotic night" every Wednesday. **Café Mokka,** 495 J St. (at Fifth), 707/822-2228, serves decadent, incredibly good pastries, good coffee, excellent espresso, and—this is different—Finnish Country Sauna and Tubs out back, private outdoor hot tubs and sauna cabins for rent. Another great java joint, serving a variety of "organic varietals" and special blends, is **Muddy Waters Coffee Co.** at 1603 G Street, 707/826-2233, www.ilovemud.com, also an immensely popular local jazz, blues, and bluegrass venue. But don't miss **Sacred Grounds Organic Coffee Roasters,** 686 F St., 707/822-0690, www.sacredgroundscoffee.com.

Immensely popular for breakfast and lunch and everyone's favorite for brunch is **Crosswinds,** 860 10th St., 707/826-2133. If you're in the mood for coffee and some spectacular dessert, head for **Ramone's Bakery & Café,** 600 F Street, 707 826-9000.

Frequent winner of local Best Burrito awards is **Rico's Tacos,** 686 F St., 707/826-2572, a best bet for inexpensive lunch. An all-around Mexican favorite is **Luzmila's,** 1288 G St., 707/822-5200. Immensely popular near the Minor Theatre is the **Arcata Pizza & Deli,** 1057 H St., 707/822-4650, which features a good variety of vegetarian choices among its pizza, sandwich, soup, and salad selections. Other lunch hotspots include the **Hole in the Wall** sandwich shop, Sixth and G Sts., 707/822-7407, open daily 10 A.M.–6 P.M., and **Japhy's Soup and Noodles,** 1563 G St., 707/826-2594.

Best burger bet is **Stars Hamburgers,** 1535 G St., 707/826-1379. For homegrown brew and good basic pub fare (a bit heavy on the grease) along with pool tables and Oakland Raiders football memorabilia, try the **Humboldt Brewing Co.,** 856 10th St., 707/826-1734, www.humbrew.com, owned and operated by Super Bowl champ Mario Celotto and his brother, Vince.

Special Restaurants

Abruzzi in Jacoby's Storehouse, facing the plaza

at 791 Eighth St., 707/826-2345, is a long-running slice of real Italiana here in the foggy north. Fresh daily are the baguettes, breadsticks, and tomato-onion-and-fennel-seed bread, along with Humboldt-grown veggies and seafood specialties. Good calzones, wonderful pastas. And do try the 14-layer torte. Now, however, Arcata also boasts a stylish branch of beloved **Mazzotti's** on the plaza at 733 Eighth St., 707/822-1900, featuring everything from Sicilian pizzas to pasta primavera with bay shrimp and scallops. For friendly, family-style Italian and fabulous fresh pastas, those in the know head for **La Trattoria,** 30 Sunny Brae Centre, 707/822-6101. How will you ever choose?

Another relative newcomer is super-sophisticated **Jambalaya** American bistro, 915 H St., 707/822-4766, www.thejambalaya.com, an open-kitchen setup serving up fresh seafood and regionally raised meats, fresh vegetables, and organic local produce in dishes such as portobella Napoleon and fresh Humboldt Bay oysters with smoky chipotle aioli. Open weekdays only for lunch, Mon.–Sat. for dinner (extended hours in summer). Kids menu too. Dinner-only **Folie Douce,** 1551 G St., between 15th and 16th, 707/822-1042, www.holyfolie.com, is regionally famous for its exotic and stylish wood fire-baked pizzas—everything from Thai chicken to green coconut curried prawns with fresh mango, jalapeño, and cilantro. Reservations wise.

INFORMATION AND SERVICES

The helpful **Arcata Chamber of Commerce** is in the new California Welcome Center at 1635 Heindon Rd. (near the Hwy. 101.Hwy. 299 junction), 707/822-3619, www.arcatachamber.com, open weekdays 10 A.M.–5 P.M. in tourist season, shorter hours in winter (call for current schedule). Stop to find out about special events, such as the **Bebop & Brew** jazz and microbrew festival and the **Arcata Bay Oyster Festival,** both held in June. Among the free publications available here are the *Tour Arcata's Architectural Past* brochure, *Arcata Outdoors,* and the free *Welcome to Arcata* map, in addition to a tidal wave of free local newsletters and newspa-

pers. The very good annual *Humboldt Visitor* and the monthly *North Coast View* are particularly worthwhile for travelers. The Bureau of Land Management's **Arcata Field Office** is nearby at 1695 Heindon Rd., 707/825-2300, www.ca.blm.gov/arcata, a worthwhile stop for information on exploring Samoa Dunes, camping in the King Range, or hiking the Headwaters. Local semipro ball games are held at the **Arcata Ballpark,** Ninth and F Sts., in June and July. For details and tickets, contact **Humboldt Crabs Baseball,** 707/839-1379, www.crabsbaseball.org.

Like most college towns, Arcata has a decent supply of bookstores. A good place to start exploring them is **Northtown Books,** 957 H St., 707/822-2834, www.northtownbooks.com. In addition to various local publications, keep an eye out for copies of the **Arcata Eye,** headquartered in Jacoby's Storehouse, www.arcataeye.com, "America's most popular obscure small-town newspaper," which often boasts headlines such as "Some Moron Burned Down the Porta-Potty at the Marsh." Pretty darned profound.

Arcata & Mad River Transit System, 707/822-3775, bases its buses at the Transit Center, 925 E St. (between Ninth and 10th). Fare is $1, certain discounts available. The Transit Center is also the local stop for **Greyhound,** 707/825-8934 or 800/231-2222, which offers service to and from Eureka as well as points north and south.

NORTH FROM ARCATA
Blue Lake

In the Mad River Valley just northeast of Arcata on Hwy. 299 is Blue Lake, a tiny town in farm, dairy, and timber country. One thing *not* in Blue Lake is a lake, due to the Mad River changing its course some time ago—the original lake is now a marsh.

Among things that are here: the **Mad River Fish Hatchery,** on Hatchery Rd., 707/822-0592, where a million or more salmon eggs (not to mention steelhead and rainbow trout) become fish each year, and the **Blue Lake Museum,** 330 Railroad Ave. (in the old Arcata and Mad River Railroad Depot), 707/668-4188, which is stuffed with historic memorabilia and open limited hours (Apr.–Sept., Sun.–Tues.–Wed., 1–4 P.M.) or by appointment. The old railroad itself—known locally as the Annie and Mary Railroad, after two company bookkeepers—was originally called the Union Wharf and Plank Walk Company and boasted 7.5 total miles of track. Plank Walk employees proudly declared: "We're not as long as other lines, but we're just as wide." Local fundraising efforts aim to transform the old railbed into a hiking and biking trail. Also on Railroad Ave. are the town's roller skating rink, the **Blue Lake Roller Rink** at Perigot Park, 707/668-5656, and the unique **Logger Bar,** 707/668-5000, quite the Wild West saloon.

Come in July or August (call the chamber for exact date) for **Annie & Mary Day,** with a parade, barbecue, music, and theater. Summer also brings the fabulous **Dell'Arte Mad River Festival,** performances of physical theater, music, comedy, storytelling, clowning, puppetry, and more, hosted from mid-June through July by Blue Lake's famed **Dell'Arte International School of Physical Theatre,** 707/668-5663, www.dellarte.com, at its two local theatres and other area venues. Come in early October for the annual **Humboldt Hoptoberfest,** a festival of live music, "hoppy" people, and ales, lagers, pilsners, and stouts produced by Humboldt County breweries.

For more information on the area, contact the **Blue Lake Chamber of Commerce,** 431 First St. in Blue Lake, 707/668-5345. Come to Blue Lake

East and Northeast

Willow Creek, east from Blue Lake on Hwy. 299, is perhaps most noted as the high-country hamlet coast folks escape to when the summer fog finally becomes unbearable. It can get hot here in the heart of Bigfoot country. The town has basic accommodations and some eateries—such as **Cinnabar Sam's** downtown, 530/629-3437, serving steaks, fajitas, burgers, and more—plus summer repertory theater and the **Big Foot Golf and Country Club,** 530/629-2977. Though Bigfoot may actually be dead—see the Northern Mountains chapter for a discussion of that question—here the legendary man-ape is everywhere. Stop in at the **Willow Creek-China Flat Museum,** on Hwy. 299 at Hwy. 96, 530/629-

2653, to see historical exhibits and a Bigfoot Center, with casts of Bigfoot footprints, literature about the mythic creature, and other Bigfoot memorabilia. Open Fri.–Sun. 10 A.M.–4 P.M. Continue east on Hwy. 299 to follow the Trinity River back to its source near Weaverville and the Trinity Alps. If the turbulent Trinity looks too inviting to pass up, arrange to raft it with **Bigfoot Rafting Company,** Hwy 299 (at Willow Way), 530/629-2263 or 800/722-2223, www.bigfootrafting.com, or with **Aurora River Adventures,** 530/629-3843 or 800/562-8475, www.rafting4fun.com. Both companies run other northstate rivers as well. Bigfoot also offers guided drift fishing trips on the Trinity and Klamath Rivers. For more information on the area, contact the **Willow Creek Chamber of Commerce,** Hwy. 299 and Hwy. 96, 530/629-2693, www.willowcreekchamber.com.

Continue east on Hwy. 299 to follow the Trinity River back to its source near Weaverville and the Trinity Alps. Alternatively, from Hwy. 299 head north along Hwy. 96, passing through the **Hoopa Valley Indian Reservation** and continuing down the lower Klamath River through the **Yurok Indian Reservation.** These reservations, set aside as a single entity in 1864 and since split into two, were the first California lands granted to Native Americans by post-gold-rush civilization. The original land grant was more of a refugee camp for regional peoples than a reservation—since it was established and expanded by orders of Presidents Pierce, Grant, and Harrison rather than by treaty between sovereign nations as was more typical elsewhere in the United States. These days, the town of Hoopa boasts **high-stakes bingo** and the attractive and comfortable **Tsewenaldin Inn,** on Hwy. 96 overlooking the Trinity River at the Tsewenaldin Shopping Center, 530/625-4294, $50–100, where amenities include a heated pool and Jacuzzi. Rates $100–150. Also at the shopping center is the **Hoopa Tribal Museum,** 530/625-4110, with exhibits on the cultural traditions of the Hupa people, from basketry and feather arts to weaponry, as well as Yurok and Karuk artifacts. It's open Mon.–Fri. 8 A.M.–5 P.M. (also Sat. 10 A.M.–4 P.M. in summer). Admission is free.

Up the Coast

Heading north from Arcata on Hwy. 101, the first wide-spot-in-the-road is **McKinleyville,** something of an Arcata suburb "where horses still have the right of way." Stop in for pub grub and a frothy pint of Black Bear Stout at **Six Rivers Brewing Co.,** 1300 Central Ave., 707/839-7580. The town lies adjacent to the Azalea State Reserve and offers good whale-watching from **McKinleyville Vista Point.** For more information on the area, contact: **McKinleyville Chamber of Commerce,** 2196 Central Ave. 707/839-2449.

Farther north off Hwy. 101 via Clam Beach Dr. is **Clam Beach County Park,** a good place for collecting agates and moonstones; camping is available for $8 a night. Adjacent is **Little River State Beach,** where Josiah Gregg and company arrived from Weaverville in December 1849, exhausted and near starvation. Little River has broad sandy beaches backed by dunes, and offers clamming in season and good surf fishing. For more information, call 707/488-2041.

TRINIDAD AND VICINITY

A booming supply town of 3,000 in the early 1850s and later a whaling port, Trinidad is now a charming coastal village recognized as the oldest incorporated town on California's north coast. Impressive **Trinidad Head** looms over the small bay, with a white granite cross at the summit replacing the first monument placed there by Bodega y Cuadra for Spain's Charles III.

The **Trinidad Memorial Lighthouse** on Main St. was the village's original light tower and was relocated to town as a fishermen's memorial. It features a giant two-ton fog bell. The **Trinidad Museum,** 529-B Trinity St., 707/677-3883, offers displays about the region's natural and cultural history. It's open in summer, Fri.–Sun. 1–4 P.M. Humboldt State University's **Fred Telonicher Marine Laboratory,** 570 Ewing St., 707/826-3671, has an aquarium open to the public, as well as a touch tank for getting intimate with intertidal invertebrates. It's open year-round, weekdays 9 A.M.–5 P.M.,

© ROBERT HOLMES/CALTOUR

Trinidad Memorial Lighthouse

and also weekends 10 A.M.–5 P.M. when school is in session.

Besides solitary beachcombing on **Trinidad State Beach,** 707/677-3570 (good for moonstones and driftwood, day-use only, no day-use fee); surfing at rugged **Luffenholtz Beach** two miles south of town; and breathtaking scenery, the area's claim to fame is salmon fishing. Commercial and sport-fishing boats, skiffs, and tackle shops line Trinidad Bay.

For more information on the area, contact the **Trinidad Chamber of Commerce,** Main St. and Patrick's Point Dr., 707/677-1610.

Staying in Trinidad

For the most reasonable accommodations, head north on Patrick's Point Dr. to the state park and its excellent camping (see below). A lovely alternative is **Azalea Glen RV Park & Campground,** 3883 Patricks Point Dr., 707/677-3068, http://azaleaglen.com, a serene, lush garden-like setting complete with lily ponds, azaleas, and ducks. RV and tent sites are $24–30 in summer. No generators. Quite nice for cabins (most have kitchens) is the recently refurbished **Bishop Pine Lodge,** 1481 Patrick's Point Dr., 707/677-3314, www.bishoppinelodge.com, also featuring two-bedroom units and cottages with hot tubs. Most are $50–100. Playground area, well-equipped exercise room. Pet friendly, too. The new **View Crest Lodge,** 3415 Patrick's Point Point Dr., 707/677-3393, www.viewcrestlodge.com, also offers comfortable cabins with all the modern comforts; some have Jacuzzis; most are $100–150. RV and tent camping are available, $16–20.

In town, across from the lighthouse, the **Trinidad Bay Bed and Breakfast,** 560 Edwards St., 707/677-0840, www.trinidadbaybnb.com, is a Cape Cod–style home circa 1950. It offers two standard rooms and two suites, all with king or queen beds and private baths (one suite with fireplace). Closed Dec.–Jan. Most rates are $150–250. About five miles north of Trinidad proper and adjacent to the state park is the **Lost Whale Bed and Breakfast Inn,** 3452 Patrick's Point Dr., 707/677-9105 or 800/677-7859, www.lostwhaleinn.com, a contemporary Cape Cod with eight guest rooms (all with private baths, most with great ocean views), full breakfast, hot tub, and afternoon refreshments. Rates are $150–250. Ask about the Farmhouse, a two-bedroom house on five acres, also available for rent. Nearby is the very nice **Turtle Rocks Inn B&B,** 3392 Patrick's Point Dr., 707/677-3707, www.turtlerocksinn.com, which offers six guest rooms on three oceanfront acres. Each room has a private bath, private deck, and modern amenities. Rates, $150–250 (lower rates in the off-season), include a gourmet hot breakfast.

Eating in Trinidad

In April or May each year, the town hosts a massive **crab feed** at Town Hall. Otherwise, *the* place to eat in Trinidad is the very relaxed and rustic **Seascape Restaurant** (once the Dock Cafe) at the harbor, 707/677-3762, which serves hearty breakfasts, excellent omelettes, and seafood specialties (good early-bird specials). Open 7 A.M.–9 P.M. daily. Reservations are a good idea at dinner. Other dining choices include the **Trinidad Bay Eatery & Gallery,** at Trinity and Parker, 707/677-3777, open Wed.–Sun. for breakfast and lunch. But best of all, just north of town, is the excellent **Larrupin Cafe,** 1658 Patrick's Point Dr., 707/677-0230, a friendly and fine place noted for things like barbecued cracked crab, barbecued oysters, steamed mussels, and chicken breast wrapped up with artichokes and cream cheese in phyllo dough. Or try the mesquite-grilled portobello mushroom on slices of Spanish cheeses and potato bread. Excellent desserts, too. No credit cards. Open Thurs.–Tues. nights.

Patrick's Point State Park

The Yuroks who for centuries seasonally inhabited this area believed that the spirit of the porpoises came to live at modern-day Patrick's Point State Park just before people populated the world—and that the seven offshore sea stacks that stretch north to south like a spine were the last earthly abode of the immortals. Most impressive of these rugged monuments is **Ceremonial Rock,** nicknamed "stairway to the stars" by fond rock climbers. Fine forests grew here until the area was logged and cleared for farming and grazing. Now the surrounding meadows are spectacular with wildflowers every spring, and the parks people are holding forest succession at bay.

Elsewhere, though, the Port Orford cedars, Sitka spruce, shore pines, azaleas, and abundant berry bushes are returning. Both here and just north at Big Lagoon, you'll be in the right place for those "fungus among us" jokes. During the rainy season, duff from spruce trees produces delicious mushrooms—also fantastically fatal ones, so be sure you're an expert (or in the company of one) before you go rooting through forest detritus for dinner. Take the easy, self-guided **Octopus Grove** nature trail near Agate Beach Campground for an introduction to life's hardships from a spruce tree's viewpoint.

Old trails once walked by native peoples lead to and beyond rocky **Patrick's Point,** one of the finest whale-watching sites along the coast. "Patrick" was Patrick Beegan, the area's first white settler and a warrior after Indian scalps. Stroll the two-mile **Rim Trail** for the views, but stay back from the hazardous cliff edge. Sea lions are common on the park's southern offshore rocks near **Palmer's Point.** The short trail scrambling north from near the campground (steep going) leads to long, sandy, and aptly named **Agate Beach,** noted for its many-colored, glasslike stones.

For all its natural wonders, Patrick's Point is also fine for people (good picnicking). Except for mushroomers and whalewatchers, best visiting weather is late spring, early summer, and fall. **Whale-watching** from Ceremonial Rock or Patrick's Point (weekend ranger programs offered in January and February) is best from November to January but also good on the whales' return trip, February to May. Dress warmly and bring binoculars. Call the park for current whale-watching information. The **museum** here features natural history and native cultural exhibits. The park's day-use fee is $4. The park's **Sumêg Village** is a reconstructed traditional Yurok village, with native plant garden adjacent.

Patrick's Point has three developed campgrounds: **Agate Beach, Abalone,** and **Penn Creek** (west of the meadows), with 124 naturally sheltered tent or trailer sites and hot showers ($12–15 per night). ReserveAmerica reservations, 800/444-7275, www.reserveamerica.com, are mandatory during the summer. In addition, there are two group camps (complete with covered picnic areas and propane barbecues) also reservable for day use and 20 hike-and-bike campsites ($10). For more information, call the park at 707/677-3570.

Humboldt Lagoons State Park

The community of **Big Lagoon** just off the highway north of Patrick's Point is also the site of Big Lagoon County Park with its dirty sand beaches and camping. Humboldt Lagoons State Park includes Big Lagoon itself and the miles-long barrier beach separating it from the sea, along with three other lagoons, a total of 1,500 beachfront acres best for beachcombing, boating, fishing, surfing, and windsurfing (swimming only for the hardy or foolhardy).

Next north is freshwater **Dry Lagoon,** five miles of sandy beach and heavy surf particularly popular with agate fanciers and black jade hunters. Camp beside this marshy lagoon at one of six environmental campsites: outhouse, no water, no dogs. Ocean fishing is possible in winter only, but there's no fishing at Dry Lagoon, which lives up to its name most of the year. **Stone Lagoon** two miles north is prettier but smaller, with boat-in primitive campsites. A half mile farther north is part-private, part-public **Freshwater Lagoon,** planted with trout for seasonal fishing (no official camping here, though RVs are a permanent fixture along the highway). The **Harry A. Merlo State Recreation Area,** 800-plus acres named for a noted Louisiana-Pacific executive, entwines throughout the lagoon area. Boat-in campsites are $10, hike-in sites $3. There is no day-use fee. The small **Humboldt Lagoons Visitors Center** is at Stone Lagoon, open summers only. For more information and to reserve campsites, contact **Humboldt Lagoons State Park,** 15336 Hwy. 101, 707/488-2041.

Redwood National Park and Vicinity

Pointing north to Oregon like a broken finger is Redwood National Park, California's finest temple to tree hugging. Although well-traveled Hwy. 101 passes through the park, away from the highway much of the park is remote and often empty of worshippers. Those visitors just passing through to the Trees of Mystery are likely unaware that they're witnessing a miracle—forests being raised (albeit slowly) from the dead. Redwood National Park is complete, yet unfinished. Standing in the shadow and sunlight of an old-growth redwood grove is like stepping up to an altar mindful only of the fullness of life. But elsewhere in the park—out back toward the alley, looking like remnants of some satanic rite—are shameful scars of sticks and scabbed-over earth, the result of opportunistic clearcutting during the political wrangling that accompanied the park's formation. Today, these areas are still in the early stages of healing. Yet Redwood National Park features some magnificent groves of virgin old-growth redwood. Three of the world's 10 tallest trees grow here—one of the reasons for UNESCO's 1982 declaration of the area as a World Heritage Site, the first on the Pacific coast. Redwood National Park is also an international Man in the Biosphere Reserve.

But other people call it other things. When the sawdust finally settled after the struggle to establish this national park—the costliest of them all, with a total nonadministrative pricetag of $1.4 billion—no one was happy. Despite the park's acquisitions to date, purists protest that not enough additional acres of old-growth redwoods have been preserved. Philistines are dismayed that there is so little commercial development here, so few gift shops and souvenir stands. And some locals are still unhappy that prime timber stands are now out of the loggers' reach, and that the prosperity promised somewhere just down the skid roads of Redwood National Park never arrived—or, more accurately, never matched expectations.

Though federal and state lands within the boundaries of Redwood National Park are tech-nically under separate jurisdictions, as a practical matter the national and its three associated state parks—the Prairie Creek Redwoods, Del Norte Coast Redwoods, and Jedediah Smith Redwoods State Parks—are cooperatively managed. In general, the visiting weather is best in late spring and early autumn. August and September are the busiest times here (the salmon fishing rush), but September after Labor Day offers fewer crowds and usually less fog.

FLORA AND FAUNA

Some of the lush terrain included within the borders of Redwood National Park is so strange that filmmaker George Lucas managed to convince much of the world it was extraterrestrial in his *Return of the Jedi*. The park's dominant redwood forests host more than 1,000 species of plants and animals. Sitka spruce, firs, and pines grow on the coast. Leather-leaved salal bushes, salmonberries, and huckleberries control the forest's understory. Rhododendrons and azaleas bloom in May and June, followed by flowering carpets of oxalis or redwood sorrel, whose tiny leaves fold up like umbrellas when sunlight filters down to the forest floor. Mushrooms, various ferns, lacy bleeding hearts, and other delicate wildflowers also flourish here. In the meadows and along coastal prairies are alders, bigleaf maples, hazels, and blackberries.

Roosevelt elk, or wapiti, survive only here and in Washington's Olympic National Park, though they once roamed from the San Joaquin Valley north to Mt. Shasta. Black bears, mountain lions, bobcats, deer, beavers, raccoons, and porcupines are fairly common. Offshore are gray whales, seals, sea lions, porpoises, and sea otters, and you'll find creatures large and small in the tidepools. Trout and salmon are abundant in all three of the park's rivers.

The park is also home to 300 species of birds, including Pacific Flyway migrants, gulls, cormorants, rare brown pelicans, raptors, and songbirds. Redwood-loving birders listen for the

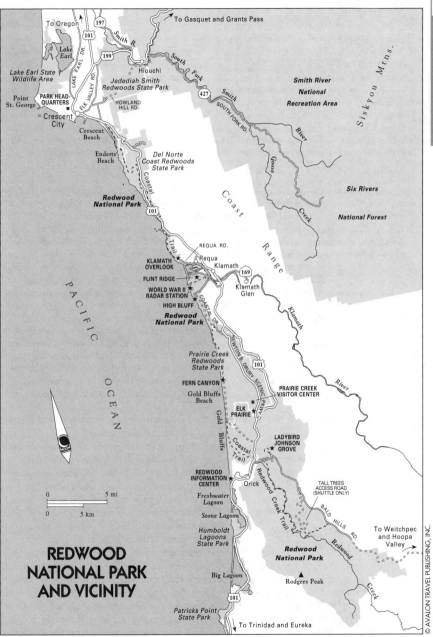

REDWOOD
NATIONAL PARK
AND VICINITY

COASTAL REDWOODS

Though they once numbered an estimated two million, the native population of coastal redwood trees has been reduced through logging and agriculture to isolated groves of virgin trees. The tallest trees in the state but only the fourth oldest, *Sequoia sempervirens* are nonetheless ancient. Well established here when dinosaurs roamed the earth, redwood predecessors flourished throughout the Northern Hemisphere 60 million years ago. Isolated from the rest of their kind by thick ice sheets a million years ago, the redwoods made their last stand in California.

The elders among today's surviving coastal redwoods are at least 2,200 years old. These trees thrive in low, foggy areas protected from fierce offshore winds. Vulnerable to both wind and soil erosion, shallow-rooted redwoods tend to topple over during severe storms. Redwoods have no need for deep taproots since fog collects on their needle-like leaves, then drips down the trunk or directly onto the ground, where the equivalent of up to 50 inches of rainfall annually is absorbed by hundreds of square feet of surface roots.

Unlike the stately, individualistic Sierra big trees or *Sequoiadendron giganteum*, the comparatively scrawny coastal redwoods reach up to the sky in dense, dark-green clusters—creating living, breathing cathedrals lit by filtered flames of sun or shrouded in foggy silence. The north coast's native peoples religiously avoided inner forest areas, the abode of spirits (some ancestral). But in the modern world, the sacred has become profane. A single coast redwood provides enough lumber for hundreds of hot tubs, patio decks, and wine vats, or a couple of dozen family cabins, or a hefty school complex. Aside from its attractive reddish color, pungent fragrance, and water- and fire-resistance, redwood is also decay-, insect-, and fungus-resistant—and all the more attractive for construction.

Despite the fact that downed trees are being floated overseas to Japan and Korea for processing as fast as the ships can load up, coast redwoods never really die. Left to their own devices, redwoods are capable of regenerating themselves without seeds. New young trees shoot up from stumps or from roots around the base of the old tree, forming gigantic woodland fairy rings in second- or third-growth forests. And each of these trees, when mature, can generate its own genetically identical offspring. Sometimes a large, straight limb from a fallen tree will sprout, sending up a straight line of trees. In heavily logged or otherwise traumatized forest areas, tiny winged redwood seeds find room to take root, sprout, and eventually flourish, blending into a forest with stump-regenerated trees.

---

mysterious marbled murrelet, a rare black-and-white seabird often seen but seldom heard and believed to nest in the treetops. If it can be established unequivocally that murrelets nest in old-growth forests (like the now-famous spotted owl), then their habitat will have to be protected from logging.

THE POLITICS OF PARK PRESERVATION

Before settlement, the land here was home to the Yurok, Tolowa, and Chilula peoples. These native residents thrived on an acorn-based diet supplemented by abundant deer, salmon, shellfish, berries, seaweed, and the occasional beached whale. The settlers who later arrived appreciated the landscape not as an intricate web of life, but as a resource ripe for harvest.

Logging in areas now included within Redwood National Park began in the 1850s but peaked after World War II, when annual harvests of more than one million board feet were the rule. By the early 1960s, the redwoods' days were clearly numbered. Lumber mills were closing and only 300,000 of the state's original two million acres of pristine coast redwood forest remained. Just one-sixth of that total was protected, thanks to persistent urging and financial contributions from the Save-the-Redwoods League, the Sierra Club, and other environmental organizations. As demands for redwood lumber increased, it was also increasingly clear that the time to save the remaining old-growth redwoods and their watersheds was now—or never.

One Park, Two Compromises

The establishment of Redwood National Park by Congress in 1968 consolidated various federal, state, and private holdings along the coastline from Crescent City south to the Redwood Creek watershed near Trinidad. The park totalled only 58,000 acres, half of which was already protected within the Prairie Creek, Del Norte, and Jedediah Smith Redwoods State Parks. Included were only a small portion of the Mill Creek (Del Norte Redwoods) area and less than half of the important Redwood Creek watershed (including the Tall Trees Grove). This unsatisfactory settlement cost almost $200 million, more than the U.S. government had ever spent on land acquisition in one place.

In August 1969, President Richard Nixon, former president Lyndon B. Johnson and his wife, Lady Bird, California governor Ronald Reagan, and other bigwigs bunched together for dignified dedication ceremonies in the Lady Bird Johnson Grove. But even then, the shortsightedness of the compromise was all too obvious; bulldozers and logging trucks were making clearcut hay on the ridgetops and unprotected watersheds beyond. Despite adequate bureaucratic procedures, the Reagan administration didn't believe in regulating the timber companies.

With devastation of even the protected groves imminent due to the law of gravity—the onrushing impact of rain-driven erosion from clearcut sites on areas downhill and downstream—environmentalists initiated another long round of legal-and-otherwise challenges. "Think big" U.S. Congressmember Phil Burton of San Francisco proposed an additional acquisition of 74,000 acres, countered by the National Park Service's think-small suggestion of just 21,500 acres. A final compromise, this one engineered by the Carter administration in 1978, added a total of 48,000 acres of new parklands (much of it already clearcut and in desperate need of rehabilitation) at a cost of $300 million more, not to mention $33 million for resurrecting the destroyed slopes of Redwood Creek or the millions set aside to compensate out-of-work lumber-industry workers. In addition, the compromise included a political coup of sorts, giving the National Park Service regulatory authority in a 30,000-acre Park Protection Zone upstream from Redwood National Park proper.

For good war stories from the environmental camp, read the Sierra Club's *The Last Redwoods and the Parkland of Prairie Creek,* by Edgar and Peggy Wayburn, and the definitive *The Fight to Save the Redwoods,* by historian Susan Schrepfer. The logging industry position can be read any day of the week on the devastated slopes around the park, especially in Six Rivers National Forest.

The Park Today

Redwood National Park's regional influence, if not the park itself, continues to grow. Save-the-Redwoods League and other groups consistently seek to arrange or encourage the purchase of essential new redwood parklands. Witness the establishment of the Smith River National Recreation Area in 1990, for example, a preserve for more than 300,000 acres of Six Rivers National Forest. And in 2002, more than 25,000 acres of the Mill Creek watershed were purchased by the State of California in conjunction with Save-the-Redwoods League for $60 million, providing permanent protection for some of the state's healthiest watersheds. The Mill Creek property, the size of San Francisco, links Jedediah Smith and Del Norte Coast Redwood state parks and also connects coastal and inland forests.

The rehabilitation of clearcut lands remains a top park priority—more important than recreational development. Because of the immensity of the task and the slow healing process, Redwood National Park will probably not be "finished" for decades. Nonetheless, the park attracts some 400,000 visitors per year, and park facilities and private-sector developments related to park use (accommodations, restaurants, and recreation-related companies) are slowly growing.

SEEING AND DOING REDWOOD NATIONAL PARK

The main thing to do in Redwood National Park is simply *be* here. Sadly, "being here" to many area visitors means little more than pulling into the parking lot near the 49-foot-tall Paul Bunyan and Babe the Blue Ox at Klamath's Trees of Mystery, buying big-trees trinkets, or stopping for a slab or two at roadside redwood burl stands in Orick.

Though fishing, kayaking, surfing, and rafting are increasingly popular, nature study and hiking are the park's main recreational offerings. For those seeking views with the least amount of effort, take a drive along Howland Hill Rd. (one-lane dirt road) through some of the finest trees in Jedediah Smith Redwoods State Park. (Howland Hill Rd. transects the park and can be reached via South Fork Rd. off Hwy. 199 just east of the park or via Elk Valley Rd. south of Crescent City.) Or try a sunny picnic on the upland prairie overlooking the redwoods and ocean, reached via one-lane Bald Hills Rd., eight miles or more inland from Hwy. 101.

Hiking

The together-but-separate nature of the park's interwoven state and federal jurisdictions makes everything confusing, including figuring out the park's trail system. Pick up a copy of the joint *Trails* brochure published by the Redwood Natural History Association available at any of the state or national park information centers and offices in the area. *Trails* divides the collective system north and south, provides corresponding regional trail maps, describes the general sights along each trail, and classifies each by length and degree of difficulty. Fifty cents well spent.

Among the must-do walks is the easy and short self-guided nature trail on the old logging road to **Lady Bird Johnson Grove.** Near the grove at the overlook is an educational logging rehabilitation display comprised of acres of visual aids—devastated redwood land clearcut in 1965 and 1970 next to a forest selectively logged at the end of World War II. At the parking lot two miles up steep Bald Hills Rd. (watch for logging trucks) you'll find a picnic area and restrooms.

The traditional route for true tree huggers, though, is the long (but also easy) 11.5-mile roundtrip hike (at least five hours one-way, overnight camping possible with permit) along **Redwood Creek Trail** to the famous **Tall Trees**

Grove. The grove's **Howard Libby Redwood** was once 368 feet tall and claimed the title of the world's tallest tree. But in 1999, a storm blew off the top 10 feet, and the tree lost its tallest-tree crown, as it were, to another redwood (unmarked, for its own protection) in Montgomery Woods State Reserve in Mendocino County. The easy way to reach the grove involves taking a shuttle from the information center near Orick; buses leave four times a day in summer, otherwise thrice-daily (small fee). For those shuttled in, the guided tour includes a ranger-led discussion of logging damage and reforestation techniques. Another possibility is coming in via the shuttle, then walking back out on the longer trail.

The longest and most memorable trek in Redwood National Park is the 30-mile-long **Coastal Trail,** which runs almost the park's entire length (hikable in sections) from near Endert's Beach south of Crescent City through Del Norte Redwoods State Park (and past the HI-USA hostel there), inland around the mouth of the Klamath River, then south along Flint Ridge, Gold Bluffs Beach, and Fern Canyon in Prairie Creek Redwoods State Park. A summers-only spur continues south along the beach to the information center.

If the entire coast route is too much, the **Flint Ridge Trail** section from the east end of Alder Camp Rd. to the ocean (primitive camping) is wild and wonderful, passing beavers and beaver dams at Marshall Pond. Easy and exquisite is the short **Fern Canyon Trail,** just off the Coastal Trail in Prairie Creek Redwoods State Park; it's less than a mile roundtrip through a 60-foot-high "canyon" of ferns laced up the sides of Home Creek's narrow ravine. To get there by car, take Davison Rd. from near Rolf's west over the one-lane bridge—watch for cattle being herded home—for six miles to the Gold Bluffs Beach Campground, then continue 1.5 miles to the parking lot. Even better is the four-mile hike west on the **James Irvine Trail** from the visitor center (or via the **Miners Ridge Trail,** which connects to Irvine by means of the **Clintonia Trail**). However you get there, the trip is worth it for the jeweled greenery—sword, deer, five-fingered, chain, bracken, lady, and licorice ferns—clinging to the canyon's ribs along the chuckling stream.

The **Revelation Trail,** just south of the visitor center in Prairie Creek Redwoods State Park, is a short self-guided nature trail for blind and sighted people, with rope and wood handrails the entire length and "touchable" sights. Trailside features are described on signs, in brochures also printed in Braille, and on cassette tapes available at the visitor center. Also special, rarely visited, and especially rich in rhododendrons is the short **Brown Creek Trail,** east of Hwy. 101 and north of the Prairie Creek visitor center.

Orick and Vicinity

The privately owned wide-spot-in-the-road of Orick, mostly a strip of souvenir stands and supply stops (including a good little grocery), is the first outpost of civilization north of the park's excellent **Thomas H. Kuchel Visitor Center** at the mouth of Redwood Creek, 707/464-6101 ext. 5265. The center features a massive relief map of the park, wildlife and cultural displays, an excellent bookstore, plenty of videos, and complete information about the national park and the three state parks. It's wheelchair accessible and open daily 9 A.M.–5 P.M., closed Thanksgiving, Christmas, and New Year's Day. "Patio talks" and coast walks are offered in summer.

For more information on Orick, contact the **Orick Chamber of Commerce,** 707/488-2602, www.orick.net.

PRAIRIE CREEK REDWOODS STATE PARK

An almost dangerous feature at Prairie Creek is the permanent and photogenic herd of Roosevelt elk usually grazing in the meadow area right along Hwy. 101. Whether or not a loaded logging truck is tailgating, drivers tend to screech to a halt at the mere sight of these magnificent creatures—which, despite their technically wild status and correspondingly unpredictable behavior, have that bemused and bored look of animals all too familiar with humankind. A separate herd of elk grazes in the coastal meadows along 11-mile **Gold Bluffs Beach,** also noted for its excellent whale-watching, sand dunes car-

peted in wild strawberries, and a primitive campground with solar showers.

Elsewhere in 14,000-acre Prairie Creek Redwoods State Park, heavy winter rainfall and thick summer fog produce rainforest lushness. Redwoods rub elbows with 200-foot-tall Sitka spruce, Douglas fir, and Western hemlock above an amazing array of shrubs, ferns, and groundcover, not to mention 800 varieties of flowers and 500 different kinds of mushrooms. **Fern Canyon** is unforgettable. Also particularly worthwhile at Prairie Creek: beachcombing, surf fishing, nature walks and photography, picnicking, and camping. Prairie Creek's **Revelation Trail** loop, which includes a rope guide for the blind, has been proposed as the national standard for trail accessibility.

Near the visitor center/museum are some fine family campsites with flush toilets and hot showers. (See Practical Redwood National Park below for details.) The more primitive beach campsites are first-come, first-camped, as are the adjacent hike-and-bike sites. Walk-in campsites are available at **Butler Creek Primitive Camp.** Register first with the office at Prairie Creek.

The park day-use fee is $4. For more park information, contact the **Prairie Creek Visitor Center** here, 707/464-6101 ext. 5300, open 9 A.M.–5 P.M. March through October 31, until 4 P.M. otherwise.

KLAMATH AND VICINITY

This area was once the traditional fishing and hunting territory of the Yurok people. But when settlers arrived, the Yuroks were doomed; the native people were hunted by miners for sport, their villages burned, their fisheries ruined.

In 1964, when 40 inches of rain fell within 24 hours in the Eel and Klamath River basins, the entire town of Klamath was washed away—and not as easily replaced as the gilt grizzlies on the remnants of the Douglas Memorial Bridge outside town. The grizzlies' gold cement den mates, frequently defaced by graffiti artists, decorate the new Klamath River Bridge.

The 263-mile-long Klamath River—California's second-largest—drains 8,000 square miles and is fed by more than 300 tributaries, including the Salmon, Scott, and Trinity Rivers. Despite the shocking die-off of 33,000 salmon along the river's lower reaches in 2002, the Klamath is still one of the world's finest fishing streams. Anglers line the Klamath and the lagoon from late fall through winter for the salmon run, though fishing for cutthroat trout downstream from town is good year-round.

Among sights along the primarily unpaved **Coastal Drive,** which starts on the south side of the Klamath River—great views on a sunny day—is a World War II-vintage early-warning radar station cleverly disguised as a farmhouse (with false windows and dormers) and barn.

In late June, Klamath's **Salmon Festival** attracts mostly locals for an unforgettable salmon barbecue, traditional Yurok dances, singing, basketry displays (not for sale), stick games, and logging skills contests. For more information about the area, contact the **Klamath Chamber of Commerce,** 800/200-2335, www .klamathcc.org.

© KIM WEIR

Paul Bunyan and Babe the Blue Ox at Trees of Mystery in Klamath

Trees of Mystery

The site of old Klamath is now overgrown with blackberries. New Klamath is dominated by the Trees of Mystery, 5500 Hwy. 101, 707/482-2251 or 800/638-3389, www.treesofmystery.net, made famous by Robert Ripley's *Believe It or Not!* Chainsawed redwood characters are the featured attraction along Mystery's Trail of Tall Tales. The free End of the Trail Indian Museum is worth some time, though, with its end-of-the-line artifacts from everywhere in the U.S. and Canada. New and definitely different—a new way to explore a forest—is the **Sky Trail** aerial gondola. The gondola ride begins halfway along the walking trail and glides through the forest for 8 to 10 minutes, climbing to an elevation of almost 750 feet and allowing visitors to get the "big picture" of oceans, mountains, and forest. Some transfer assistance may be required for visitors in wheelchairs; a motorized cart is available for transport to the gondola loading site; call for details. Trees of Mystery admission is $17 adult, $10 kids age 4–10 (under 3 free), Sky Trail included.

Just south of Klamath is the **Tour-Thru-Tree,**

430 Hwy. 169, 707/482-5971, this one some 700 years old and chainsawed in 1976. To tour thru, take the Terwer Valley exit off Hwy. 101 and go east a quarter mile on Hwy. 169. The tree is open year-round. Admission is $2 per car, 50 cents for walk-ins and bike-ins.

Requa

This tiny settlement on the Klamath's north bank was once an important Yurok village. It later became a booming mining supply camp, then a mill town and lumber port. Aside from the wonderful four-mile walk north from the end of the road along the Coastal Trail (to the accompaniment of barking sea lions on the rocks below), most notable in Requa is the restored Historic Requa Inn, a bed-and-breakfast with a good restaurant (see below).

DEL NORTE COAST REDWOODS STATE PARK

Del Norte is a dense and foggy coastal rainforest comprised of 6,400 acres of redwoods, meadows, beaches, and tidepools. It's so wet here in winter that the developed campgrounds close. The **Damnation Creek Trail,** crossing Hwy. 1 en route, leads through magnificent old-growth *Sequoias,* spruce, Oregon grape, and seasonal wildflowers to a tiny beach with offshore sea stacks and tidepools. Or, take the **Coastal Trail** from Wilson Creek to the bluffs. Easier is the short walk to the north coast's finest tidepools (and the Nickel Creek Primitive Camp) at the end of **Enderts Beach Trail,** accessible from Enderts Beach Rd. south of Crescent City. To see the park's second-growth redwoods, and for exceptional bird-watching, take the almost four-mile **Hobbs Wall Trail.** Beyond Del Norte Coast Redwoods as the highway descends to Crescent City is the **Rellim Demonstration Forest,** which offers a well-maintained self-guided nature trail and a comfortable lodge for fireplace-warming after your hike. For more information about Del Norte Redwoods State Park, contact the **Redwood National and State Parks Information Center,** 1111 Second St. in Crescent City, 707/464-6101.

JEDEDIAH SMITH REDWOODS STATE PARK

Though the competition is certainly stiff even close by, this is one of the most beautiful places on earth—and almost unvisited. Few people come inland even a few miles from Hwy. 101 near Crescent City.

Once Tolowa tribal territory, the Smith River, which flows through the park, was crossed by mountain man Jedediah Smith on June 20, 1828, after his grueling cross-country effort to reach the Pacific. The subsequent arrival of trappers, miners, loggers, fishermen, and farmers led to changes in the landscape and the rapid destruction of native populations. Yet this 10,000-acre stand of old-growth redwoods, Douglas fir, pines, maples, and meadows seems almost unscathed.

Historic **Howland Hill Rd.,** once a redwood-paved thoroughfare, is now graveled and meanders like a summer river through the quiet groves. The **National Tribute Grove,** a 5,000-acre memorial to veterans of World Wars I and II, is the

park's largest. Tiny **Stout Grove** includes the area's largest measured redwoods. For an easy two-mile loop, walk both the **Simpson** and **Peterson Trails** through primeval redwoods and ferns. Even shorter is the combined walk along the **Leiffer** and **Ellsworth Trails,** something of a Jedediah Smith sampler. The 30-minute **Stout Grove Trail** offers trees and access to some of the Smith River's excellent summer swimming holes (complete with sandy beaches). Take the **Hiouchi Trail** for rhododendrons and huckleberries. More ambitious are hikes along both forks of the **Boy Scout Tree** and **Little Bald Hills Trails.** Also among the Smith River redwoods are excellent developed campsites.

For more park information, contact the **Jedediah Smith Visitor Center** on Hwy. 101 in Hiouchi, 707/464-6101 ext. 5113, open from late May through September, 9 A.M.–5 P.M., or the **Hiouchi Information Center** on Hwy. 199 in Hiouchi, 707/464-6101 ext. 5067, which offers area natural history exhibits.

STAYING AT THE PARKS

Camping

Each of the three state parks in the area offers developed family-type camping, with hot showers and other very basic comforts ($12–15). Disposal stations for RVs are available but hookups are not. These campgrounds are popular in summer, so advance reservations are advised; contact ReserveAmerica, 800/444-7275, www.reserveamerica.com. Though the Del Norte Campground is closed off-season due to very wet conditions (sometimes washouts), winter drop-in camping at the other campgrounds is usually no problem.

Primitive sites are also available at **Nickel Creek,** Endert's Beach; **Flint Ridge,** west of Klamath; **DeMartin,** between Damnation and Wilson Creeks along the Coastal Trail; and along the **Redwood Creek Trail.** Obtain the required permits at information centers or at park headquarters in Crescent City. Primitive camping at the national park sites is free, though there is a small fee for environmental campsites within the state parks.

STORY WITHOUT END: THE POLITICS OF HARVESTING REDWOODS

Along the north coast, the politics of logging are as universally explosive as the issue of off-shore drilling. The battle to preserve redwoods, especially the remaining first-growth stands, has been going on for decades. So strong are the economic forces in support of logging and related industry that without the untiring efforts of the private Save-the-Redwoods League, Sierra Club, and other environmental organizations, most of the coast redwood groves now protected from commercial "harvesting" would be long gone. The fact that Redwood National Park north of Eureka was established at all, even if late, is something of a miracle. And the recent battle over the old-growth Headwaters Forest echoes all the wars that came before.

Environmentalists adamantly oppose the accelerating practice of clearcutting, the wholesale denuding of hillsides and entire watersheds in the name of efficiency and quick profits. "Tree huggers" have argued for years that anything other than sustained yield timber harvesting—cutting no more timber than is grown each year—not only destroys the environment by eliminating forests, wildlife habitat, and fisheries but ultimately destroys the industry itself. Someday, they've been saying for several decades, the forests will be gone and so will logging and lumber mill jobs. "Someday" has ar-

rived. The timber business has harvested its own industry into oblivion.

The failure of both the 1990 "Green" and Forests Forever initiatives, statewide ballot propositions in favor of forest protection, has only served to increase local furor. Earth First! and other activist groups subsequently took on Pacific Lumber Company and other timber firms—taking the battle into the forests and surrounding communities, as in 1990's "Redwood Summer." Timbermen and truckers also took to the streets defending their traditional livelihoods with community parades and other events accented by yellow solidarity ribbons. The fight became so intense, philosophically, that the Laytonville school board was publicly pressured to ban *The Lorax* by Dr. Seuss because of the book's anti-clearcutting sentiments. (The book banning failed, ultimately.)

A further blow to business as usual came with a 1990s admission by the California Board of Forestry that the state has allowed timber companies to cut down so many mature trees—old growth and otherwise—that there now looms a serious "timber gap," a substantial reduction in future forest harvests. The "statewide emergency" is due to "past failure" to regulate industrial timberlands and "has resulted in long-term overharvesting, drastically reducing both the productive capability

---

Mystic Forest RV Park, about five miles nouth of Klamath at 15875 Hwy. 101, 707/482-4901, offers both grassy and wooded sites for RVs and tenters, $14–20. Abundant amenities, from hot showers and laundry to grocery and gift shop. At the north end of the Klamath River Bridge is the **Camper Corral,** 707/482-5741, offering 100 pull-through sites, most with full hookups and about half with cable TV (RV and tent sites, $14–23). Other amenities include heated swimming pool, hot showers, a Laundromat, rec hall, shuffleboard courts, and other recreation facilities. The **Chinook RV Resort,** 17465 Hwy. 101, 707/482-3511, $18 per night, is another angler's favorite.

OTHER ACCOMMODATIONS

Accommodation prices in and around Orick are reasonable, partly because Redwood National Park is too far north for most visitors to California, but also because it's foggy here during peak tourist season. Most people follow the sun. Within national park boundaries but right on the coast—about 12 miles south of Crescent City at the Hwy. 101 junction with Wilson Creek Rd.—is the fabulous HI **Redwood National Park Hostel,** 14480 Hwy. 101 N. (at Wilson Creek Rd.), 707/482-8265 or 800/909-4776 #74 for reservations, www.norcalhostels.org, known locally as the De-Martin House. This is the grandly restored one-time home (circa 1908) of one of Del Norte

of the land and maintenance of adequate wildlife habitat." This new crisis has further shocked the California timber industry, long accustomed to the board's regulatory sympathies.

The most recent chapter in the redwood wars began when the north coast's Pacific Lumber Company (PALCO) was acquired in a junk bond-financed deal by Maxxam Corporation. The original PALCO was well regarded by environmentalists as a responsible, sustained-yield logger, but with Maxxam CEO Charles Hurwitz at the helm, PALCO began clearcutting on its 202,000 acres in Humboldt County, for the first time in its history—to pay the price of Hurwitz's purchase. Among PALCO's holdings: the 60,000-acre Headwaters Forest, the largest remaining stand of privately owned old-growth redwoods in the world.

When the PALCO chain saws threatened to fell the roadless 3,000-acre Headwaters Grove at the heart of the vast old-growth redwood forest, environmentalist activists went to war with Hurwitz. For more than 10 years, Earth First! and other environmental groups stopped at nothing—public protests, guerrilla theater, tree-sitting, lawsuits—to prevent the harvesting of the Headwaters Forest. After years of forest warfare and hot tempers in nearby north coast communities, a deal brokered in 1998 by U.S. Senator Dianne Feinstein seemed destined to provide the political solution. Feinstein's compromise allowed the federal and state governments to purchase the core Headwaters acreage and a surrounding watershed buffer—a total of 7,500 acres—and required a "habitat conservation plan" for the remaining PALCO acreage, in an attempt to balance logging and wildlife protection.

But Hurwitz balked. The federal funding authorization was set to expire, negotiations were stalled, and the Headwaters' future looked grim. Yet on March 1, 1999—with just *seven minutes* left on the funding clock—the deal was struck and signed, and the Headwaters Forest became public property—for a hefty price tag of $480 million.

After the dramatic conclusion to the Headwaters conflict, most area residents were relieved. At least some of the Headwaters Forest is now preserved, the state and federal governments will regulate logging and wildlife habitat protection on the remaining acreage, and PALCO loggers can return to work.

Some environmentalists, though, say it was a bad deal—not going far enough to protect the Headwaters ecosystem as a viable whole. They are particularly concerned about the probable loss of several pristine old-growth groves, and the threat to the Coho salmon run due to damage to the Elk River watershed.

The saga continues.

County's pioneer families. The 30-bed hostel is perfect even for small group retreats, with a dining room, small dorm rooms, a common room cozied up with a woodstove, outdoor redwood decks with fine views, and good kitchen facilities. The hostel is wheelchair accessible. Couple and family rooms are available with adequate advance notice. The rate is $16 per night adults, $8 children.

Choice in area accommodations may seem meager, but the price is definitely right. Expect tariffs in the $50–100 range. One possibility is **Prairie Creek Motel,** next to Rolf's Park Café in Orick, Hwy. 101 at Davidson Rd., 707/488-3841. The **Motel Trees,** 15495 S Hwy. 101 (across from Trees of Mystery) in Klamath, 707/482-3152 or 800/848-2982, offers amenities including a tennis court, in-room color TV with movies, and an adjacent restaurant. Or try the comfortable **Ravenwood Motel** in Klamath at 151 Klamath Blvd., 707/482-5911 or 866/520-9875. The **Historic Requa Inn,** 451 Requa Rd., 707/482-1425 or 866/800-8777, www.requainn.com, is nothing fancy on the outside but quite appealing—an English country-style inn first opened in 1885. Some rooms have great views. The inn's **dining room** is open to guests for breakfast and dinner, to nonguests for dinner only (by reservation). **Rhodes End Bed & Breakfast,** 115 Trobitz Rd. in Klamath Glen, 707/482-1654, www.rhodes-end.com, offers three romantic rooms, great food, and an outdoor hot tub. Massage available, too.

EATING AT THE PARKS

Most people camp, and bring their own provisions—the Eureka-Arcata area being the last best supply stop before heading north. Supplies are also available in Crescent City, just north of the park.

Best bet for a fascinating meal in Orick, not to mention friendly people, is **Rolf's Park Café,** 123664 Hwy. 101, 707/488-3841, on the highway north of Orick proper (take the Fern Canyon exit), open only in spring and summer Tables are set in the solarium and (weather permitting) outside on the deck. Rolf Rheinschmidt is known for his exotic dinner specialties, like wild turkey, elk and buffalo steaks, wild boar and bear roasts, even antelope sausage, plus chicken and pasta dishes, vegetarian dishes, and forest fare like fiddlehead ferns and wild mushrooms. Rolf also cooks up some great breakfasts, including the house specialty German Farmers Omelette—a creation of eggs with ham, bacon, sausages, cheese, mushrooms, potatoes, and pasta topped with salsa and sour cream—as well as fine and filling pancakes. Lunch features Rolf's special clam chowder, grilled German sausage sandwiches, smoked salmon and sweet onions on rye, hot chicken and mushrooms, burgers, and salads. Wash it down with beer or wine, and have some linzertorte for dessert. Great place.

Other possibilities include the basic diner fare, giant cinnamon rolls, and good cream pies at the **Palm Cafe** in Orick, 121130 Hwy. 101, 707/488-3381, or a quick grocery stop at the **Orick Market,** 121175 Hwy. 101, 707/488-3501. Or try the **Historic Requa Inn,** 451 Requa Rd. in Klamath, 707/482-1425 (reservations advised). Ask locally for other possibilities.

INFORMATION AND SERVICES

In addition to the national park proper, three state parks—Prairie Creek, Del Norte, and Jedediah Smith, all covered above—are included within the larger park boundaries, protecting more redwoods (160,000 acres total for the four parks) and offering additional recreation and camping possibilities. Distinct though they are, the state

and national parks are managed cooperatively. The centralized information source for all the parks is the **Redwood National and State Parks Information Center,** 1111 Second St. (at K St.) in Crescent City, 707/464-6101, www.nps.gov/redw. The center's telephone number includes recorded information on each of the individual parks in the system, and you can also reach a human during office hours; to contact each state park directly, dial the given extensions listed below. There is no fee for admission to Redwood National Park, but the day-use fee for the state parks is $4. Park headquarters and other visitor centers are closed on Thanksgiving, Christmas, and New Year's Day.

The **Thomas H. Kuchel Visitor Center,** near Orick at the old lumber mill site at the mouth of Redwood Creek (north of Freshwater Lagoon and west of the highway), 707/464-6101 ext. 5265, is an imposing, excellent interpretive museum. The enthusiastic staff is very helpful. Open daily 9 A.M.–5 P.M. Pick up a map for the park's trail system. Members of the Yurok tribe occasionally demonstrate the traditional brush dance; call for current information.

Other centers include the **Hiouchi Information Center,** on Hwy. 199 west of Hiouchi, 707/464-6101 ext. 5067, open 9 A.M.–5 P.M. mid-June to mid-September, where members of the Tolowa tribe sometimes offer a renewal dance demonstration, and the **Jedediah Smith Visitor Center** on Hwy. 101 in Hiouchi, 707/464-6101 ext. 5113, with history and natural history exhibits as well as campfire programs, junior ranger activities, and ranger-guided walks, open 9 A.M.–5 P.M. mid-May–Sept. The **Prairie Creek Visitor Center,** 127011 Newton B. Drury Scenic Parkway in Prairie Creek State Park, 707/464-6101, ext. 5300, open 9 A.M.–5 P.M. (4 P.M. in winter), features a natural history museum as well as a nature store.

Park Field Seminars

Redwood National Park Field Seminars, sponsored by the College of the Redwoods Del Norte campus, 883 W. Washington Blvd. in Crescent City, 707/464-9150, include kayak instruction for both the Smith and Klamath Rivers and workshop topics such as local Native American culture, birdlife, freshwater stream ecology, astronomy, and basic outdoor photography. Most field seminars are offered in summer.

Getting Here

Most people drive—and the immense size of the park makes a personal vehicle quite handy. **Greyhound,** 1603 Fourth St. in Eureka, 707/442-0370, or 500 E. Harding in Crescent City, 707/464-2807, stops on its way between those two cities at the Shoreline Deli just south of Orick, at Paul's Cannery in Klamath, and at the Redwood National Park Hostel north of Klamath. To fly into the area, nearest is the **Arcata-Eureka Airport** in McKinleyville, 3561 Boeing Ave., 707/839-1906. Rental cars are available there.

SMITH RIVER NATIONAL RECREATION AREA

California's only completely undammed river system, the three-fork Smith River and its tributaries are the focal points of the Smith River National Recreation Area, a 305,337-acre preserve including 118,000 acres of old-growth forest. Though the environmental protections aren't as strict under NRA status as they would be under national park status, establishment of this reserve means that the Smith River will remain undammed, that no new mining claims will be allowed, and that logging will be strictly limited. Fishing, river play, hiking, and camping are the primary pleasures here.

Since the Smith River National Recreation Area abuts the western edge of Jedediah Smith Redwoods, another possibility is setting up camp at Jed Smith. Basic supplies and reasonable motels (some motor-court style) are available in Crescent City, but Gasquet and Hiouchi may be closer. The **Hiouchi Cafe,** 2095 Hwy. 199, 707/458-3415, serves up hearty breakfasts and lunch. The restaurant at **Patrick Creek Lodge,** 13950 Hwy. 199, 707/457-3323, is famous for its prime rib dinners and also puts on a nice Sunday brunch.

Campsites are $8–15; only Panther Flat Campground is open year-round, others are summer-only. Reserve through the National Park Reservation Service, 877/444-6777, www.reserveusa.com. For maps and other information, contact Six Rivers National Forest headquarters (see below) or the forest's **Smith River NRA/Gasquet Ranger District** office on Hwy. 199 in Gasquet, 707/457-3131, open weekdays 7 A.M.– 5 P.M., until 4:30 P.M. in winter.

SIX RIVERS NATIONAL FOREST

Abutting much of Redwood National Park are almost one million acres of other public forest lands, extending in a long, fairly narrow block from the Oregon border to southeast of Garberville and included within Six Rivers National Forest (just west of the Klamath and Trinity National Forests). Six Rivers' six rivers are the Smith, Klamath, Trinity, Mad, Van Duzen, and Eel. Fall colors are outstanding, with alders, maples, oaks, Oregon grape, and poison oak splashing the dark pine, fir, and cedar forests. Hawks and hummingbirds, ravens and robins, woodpeckers and warblers are among the birds here.

Official campsites throughout the forest are plentiful—there are 15 major campgrounds, at least one in each area open year-round on a first-come basis—and campers can pitch a tent almost anywhere, trailside or roadside, with a permit. Also available and free are "rustic camps" and seasonal hunting camps throughout the area; ask at any ranger station.

Backpackers have privacy and a long season since winters in many areas are mild. The **South Kelsey Trail** and **Horse Ridge Trail** are good backpacking routes. The **North Fork Wilderness,** most accessible from Alderpoint or Covelo near Garberville, has poor trails and is best suited for experienced woodspeople. River fishing, white-water rafting, and hunting are the other main recreational activities here.

For a forest map—definitely advisable—and current river, trail, and camping information, contact **Six Rivers National Forest Headquarters,** 1330 Bayshore Way in Eureka, 707/442-1721, www.fs.fed.us/r5/sixrivers/recreation/smith-river, or any of the ranger district offices: **Smith River NRA/Gasquet Ranger District** on Hwy. 199 in Gasquet, 707/457-3131; **Orleans Ranger District** on Hwy. 96 in Orleans,

530/627-3291; **Lower Trinity Ranger District** on Hwy. 96 in Willow Creek, 530/629-2118; or **Mad River Ranger District,** on Hwy. 36 in Bridgeville, 707/574-6233.

CRESCENT CITY AND VICINITY

Most of the world's Easter lilies, that ultimate modern-day symbol of resurrection, are grown north of Crescent City, the only incorporated city in Del Norte County. A proud if historically downtrodden town laid out in 1853 along the crescent moon harbor, Crescent City is a grim weatherbeaten gray, pounded so long by storms it has become one with the fog. Grim, too, is life for prisoners locked up just outside town at **Pelican Bay State Prison,** the state's largest maximum-security prison. The prison primes the community's economic pump with some $40 million per year and was the focus of California senator Barry Keene's Name That Prison contest. Among the unselected but otherwise superior suggestions from clever north coast minds: The Big Trees Big House, Camp Runamok, Dungeness Dungeon, Saint Dismos State (a reference to the patron saint of prisoners), and Slammer-by-the-Sea.

Crescent City still suffers from the 1964 tsunami that tore the town off its moorings after the big Alaska earthquake, as well as a freak typhoon with 80-mile-an-hour winds that hit in 1972. Life goes on, however; the once devastated and denuded waterfront is now an attractive local park and convention center. Crabbing from the public **Citizens' Wharf,** built at Crescent Harbor with entirely local resources and volunteer labor when government rebuilding assistance fell through, is especially good. The French-design harbor breakwater is unique, a system of interlocking, 25-ton concrete "tetrapods."

Come in February for Crescent City's **World-Championship Crab Races,** an event that includes a world-class crab feed, Dungeness crab races, children's games, and an art fair. March brings the annual **Aleutian Goose Festival,** with more than 80 events, workshops, and guided wilderness excursions celebrating area nature reserves, birding, and cultural heritage. Crescent

City's **July 4th** festivities include everything from cribbage and kite flying to sandcastle sculpting. At Smith River just north, the local **Easter in July Lily Festival** celebrates the lily bloom, the festivities including sunrise church services, a lily float contest, and food and crafts booths decked out with you-know-what. Also fun the last weekend in July is the two-mile **Gasquet Raft Race** on the Smith River, with contestants limited to rafts and other crafts paddled only by hand. The local pronunciation is "GAS-key," by the way, in the same vein as "Del-NORT" County.

Seeing and Doing Crescent City

See the **Battery Point Lighthouse** near town, originally known as the Crescent City Lighthouse and first lit in December of 1856. Weather and tides permitting walk out to it on a path more than 100 years old and visit the island museum, 707/464-3089, open Wed.–Sun. 10 A.M.–4 P.M. (small donation); call for the April–Sept. tour schedule. Decommissioned in 1953, though it was 12 more years before they turned the light out, the Battery Point Lighthouse was restored in 1981 by Craig Miller, with local donations of materials. The Del Norte Historical Society has operated the light as a private navigational aid since 1982. Spend some time in the **Del Norte County Historical Society Museum,** 577 H St., 707/464-3922, to appreciate its collection of Native American artifacts, quilts and kitchenware, and logging and mining paraphernalia—and to get the local lighthouse story. Open Mon.–Sat. 10 A.M.–4 P.M. (admission by donation). Notable at the museum is the first-order lens—over 18 feet tall—taken from the **St. George's Reef Lighthouse,** the town's second and known as the nation's most expensive, built after the tragic loss of the sidewheeler SS *Brother Jonathan* at North Seal Rock in 1865. Restoration of the now-retired St. George's, one of the most dangerously situated lighthouses anywhere, is now beginning; helicopter tours will one day be offered. Stop by the historic **McNulty House** nearby, 710 H St., 707/464-5186, to take in exhibits of antiques, old clocks, and works of area artists.

Another place to find just the right memento is the gift shop at the **Northcoast Marine Mam-**

mal Center in Beachfront Park, 424 Howe Dr., 707/465-6265, www.northcoastmarinemammal.org, a nonprofit rescue and rehabilitation center (donations always appreciated).

Smith River

North of Crescent City, just shy of the Oregon border, is the town of Smith River, where the river flows to the sea. If you wind up here at the end of the day, check out the Ship Ashore Resort, 12370 Hwy. 101 N, 707/487-3141 or 800/487-3141, www.ship-ashore.com, with motel rooms $50–100, or its popular steak and seafood restaurant, the Captain's Galley. The bizarre Ship Ashore Museum and Gift Shop by the highway—a 160-foot-long ship beached in the parking lot—clues diners in to the turnoff. Campers can stay at the Ship Ashore's RV park.

Camping in Crescent City

Nothing in Crescent City beats camping at Jedediah Smith Redwoods State Park, though four national park or national forest campgrounds lie northeast of town near Gasquet, others are to the southeast via Southfork Rd., and still more are scattered through the Smith River/Six Rivers region.

Expect rates of $15–30 at private RV campgrounds. Options in town include the Harbor RV Anchorage, 159 Starfish Way, 707/464-1724, paved parking right on the beach at the north end of town; the Bayside RV Park near the boat harbor, 750 Hwy. 101 N., 707/464-9482; and the Crescent City Redwoods KOA, 4241 Hwy. 101 N., 707/464-5744 or 800/562-5754, www.koa.com, with both tent and RV sites as well as cabins. Another attractive possibility, a 20-acre wooded site, is the Village Camper Inn RV Park, 1543 Parkway Dr., 707/464-3544. You can also park the Winnie at the Del Norte County Fairgrounds, 421 Hwy. 101 N., 707/464-9556, where facilities include showers and a covered driving range ($8–10 per night).

Staying in and near Crescent City

Motel rates in Crescent City drop markedly in winter. Otherwise decent rooms can be found for $50–100. The only motel on the beach is the aptly named Crescent Beach Motel, next to the Beachcomber restaurant at 1455 Hwy. 101 N, 707/464-5436, www.crescentbeachmotel.com, with appealing refurbished rooms—almost all of them opening out onto the beach. Appealing in a more introverted way is the Curly Redwood Lodge, 701 Hwy. 101 S (a half mile south of town on the highway, near the marina), 707/464-2137, www.curlyredwoodlodge.com, a definite blast from the past—1957, to be exact. That was the year the motel first opened, built from the wood of one massive "curly" redwood; the spectacular wood grain is still proudly exhibited throughout. The motel also features large rooms, color TV with cable, and coffee available in the lobby.

The Crescent City Travelodge, 353 L St., 707/464-6124 or 800/578-7878, www.travelodge.com, offers 27 rooms, TV (with HBO, ESPN, and CNN), a sauna, and complimentary continental breakfast. The Super 8, 685 Hwy. 101 S, 707/464-4111 or 800/800-8000, offers inroom coffee makers, cable TV with HBO, a coin-op laundry, and fax service (incoming faxes free). The Best Value Inn, north of town at 440 Hwy. 101 N, 707/464-4141, features both a sauna and indoor hot tub. Econo Lodge, 725 Hwy. 101 N, 707/464-6106, also offers a sauna and hot tub, as well as complimentary breakfast.

Just south of town and also across from the marina is the Best Western Northwoods Inn, 655 Hwy. 101 S, 707/464-9771 or 800/557-3396. Amenities here include in-room hair dryers, irons, and coffee makers, along with high-speed Internet service, a guest laundry, and spa. Good onsite restaurant, free breakfast. Nearby is the fairly new Anchor Beach Inn, 880 Hwy. 101 S at Anchor Way, 707/464-2600 or 800/837-4116, with microwaves and refrigerators, coffee makers, hair dryers, free continental breakfast.

The historic 18-room Patrick Creek Lodge 13950 Hwy. 199 east of Gasquet, 707/457-3323, www.patrickcreeklodge.com, offers fabulous Smith River trout fishing in summer, salmon and steelhead fishing from fall through spring, and rooms with antiques year-round.

The Victorian White Rose Mansion Inn in Smith River near the Oregon border, 149 S. Fred

Haight Dr., 707/487-9260, www.whiterosemansion.com, offers something for bed-and-breakfast fans—specifically, seven nicely decorated guest rooms, including a cottage suitable for families with children. Most are $100–150. Two rooms with two-person Jacuzzi are $150–250. There's also a three-bedroom beach house, $150–250.

Eating in and near Crescent City

Standard grocery chains, like Safeway, exist in Crescent City. Better for replenishing the picnic basket, though, is a stop (and plant tour) at the north coast's noted **Rumiano Cheese Company,** 511 Ninth St. (at E St.), 707/465-1535 or 866/328-2433.

Some restaurants here don't take credit cards, so bring cash. A basic for breakfast is **Glen's Bakery & Restaurant,** 722 Third St., 707/464-2914, where you can get a sticky bun for breakfast and a mean bowl of clam chowder or fresh fish dishes for lunch. **Thai House,** 105 N St., 707/464-2427, is the place for noodle dishes and spicy seafood. The **China Hut Restaurant,** 928 Ninth St., 707/464-4921, serves Cantonese, Mandarin, and Szechuan. **Da Lucianna Ristorante,** 575 Hwy. 101 S., 707/465-6566, is elegant for Italian.

For seafood, head for the **Beachcomber Restaurant,** 1400 Hwy. 101 S. (at South Beach), 707/464-2205, right on the beach. **Harbor View Grotto,** 150 Starfish Way, 707/464-3815, offers no-frills "view dining" along with fresh seafood and steaks.

For hearty prime rib, seafood, and fabulous Sunday brunch served up with a scenic drive, head for the **Patrick Creek Lodge** on Hwy. 199 east of Gasquet, 707/457-3323. North along the coast in Gold Beach, Oregon, and offering the most sophisticated dining for miles around is **Chives,** 29212 Hwy. 101, 541/247-4121.

Information and Services

The **Crescent City-Del Norte County Chamber of Commerce Visitor Center** is at 1001 Front St., 707/464-3174 or 800/343-8300, www.northerncalifornia.net. **Greyhound,** 500 E. Harding St., 707/464-2807, has two buses heading north and two heading south daily. The **post office** is at 751 Second St. (at H St.), 707/464-2151. The **public library** is at 190 Price Mall, 707/464-9793. For medical care and emergencies, contact **Sutter Coast Hospital,** 800 E. Washington Blvd., 707/464-8511 (information) or 707/464-8888 (emergency room).

Northern Mountains and Modoc

The northern mountains are too far north for most travelers, and despite the economic benefits of tourism, most people living here prefer it that way. Here in the Klamaths and Cascades, mountains tower like monuments to the gods, and lava badlands pocked with mudpots and fumaroles create nightmare scenes from hell. Here is "the heart of the great black forests" described by badman poet Joaquin Miller, remnants of the virgin old-growth forests that once defined the land from here to Canada. Here also are craggy mountain peaks under cobalt blue skies, rushing rivers, crystal-clear lakes, and delicate meadows where dainty wildflowers bloom during very short summers. The glacial high-country terrain is as spectacular as the Sierra Nevada. Attention, hikers and backpackers: Bigfoot (or Sasquatch), that legendary hairy but harmless 600-pound man-ape of Northwest lore, has been spotted here from time to time.

Almost as wild as the land is the area's history, a stream of rebellions, secessions, and regional wars. Trappers first came to the northern mountains in the late 1820s, traversing the territory from Oregon to San Francisco via the Siskiyou Trail until the 1840s. In 1842, English pirates discovered gold at Sailors Bar on the Trinity River, and in 1849 one of Frémont's men, Maj.

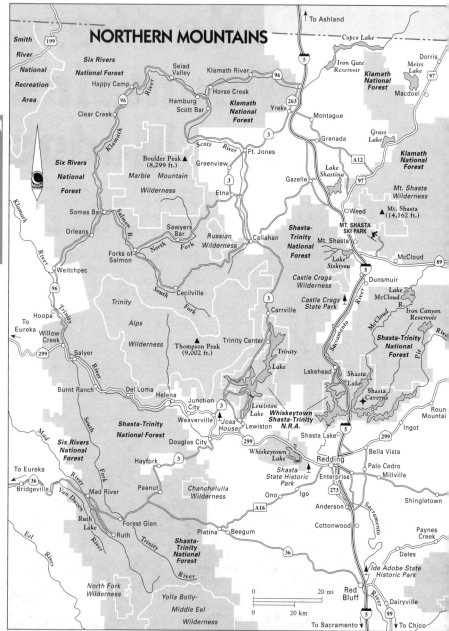

NORTHERN MOUNTAINS

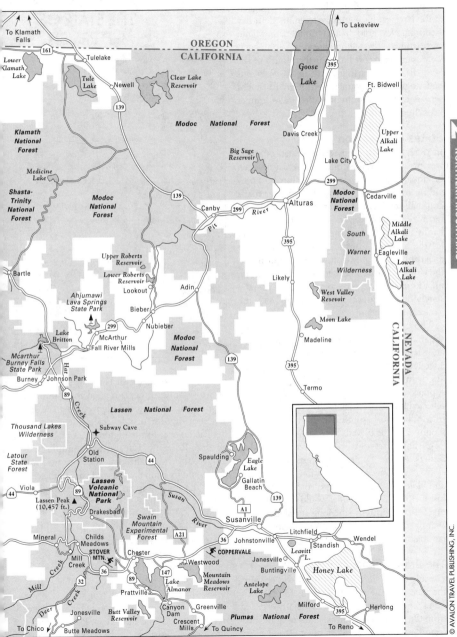

To Klamath
Falls

Lower
Klamath
Lake

161

Tulelake

OREGON
CALIFORNIA

To Lakeview

395

Goose
Lake

Ft. Bidwell

Tule
Lake

Newell

Clear Lake
Reservoir

139

Klamath
National
Forest

Modoc   National   Forest

Davis Creek

Upper
Alkali
Lake

Medicine
Lake

Shasta-
Trinity
National
Forest

Modoc
National
Forest

139

Canby

Pit

299

River

Alturas

Big Sage
Reservoir

Lake City

299

Modoc
National
Forest

Cedarville

Middle
Alkali
Lake

Bartle

Upper Roberts
Reservoir

Lower Roberts
Reservoir

Lookout

Adin

Likely

395

South

Warner

Wilderness

Eagleville

Lower
Alkali
Lake

Ahjumawi
Lava Springs
State Park

Bieber

West Valley
Reservoir

NEVADA
CALIFORNIA

Lake
Britton

299

Nubieber

Moon Lake

McArthur

Mcarthur
Burney Falls
State Park

Fall River Mills

Modoc
National
Forest

139

Madeline

Hat

Creek

Burney

Johnson Park

89

Termo

395

Lassen   National   Forest

Thousand Lakes
Wilderness

Subway Cave

Latour
State
Forest

Old
Station

44

Spaulding

Eagle
Lake

Gallatin
Beach

139

44

Viola

89

Lassen
Volcanic
National
Park

Lassen Peak
(10,457 ft.)

Drakesbad

Susan

River

A1

Susanville

Litchfield

Wendel

Mineral

Childs
Meadows

STOVER
MTN.

Swain
Mountain
Experimental
Forest

A21

36

Johnstonville

Standish

Leavitt
L.

Mill
Creek

36

Chester

COPPERVALE

Westwood

Janesville

Buntingville

Honey Lake

89

147

Lake
Almanor

Mountain
Meadows
Reservoir

32

Prattville

Antelope
Lake

Milford

Herlog

Mill

Deer

Creek

Jonesville

Butt Valley
Reservoir

Canyon
Dam

Greenville

Crescent
Mills

Plumas   National   Forest

395

To Chico

Butte Meadows

To Quincy

To Reno

© AVALON TRAVEL PUBLISHING, INC.

NORTHERN MOUNTAINS

Pierson Barton Reading, likewise found nuggets at Big Bar near his namesake town, modern-day Redding. New gold dreams brought a new gold rush, and the fever soon spread north; nuggets were found at Scott Bar near the mouth of the Scott River and farther north in the Siskiyous and Rogue River country. But if gold brought settlers to these mountains, the lure of lumber kept them here.

States of Rebellion

In 1852, a bill to form the separate State of Shasta was introduced in the California legislature, then headquartered in Vallejo, with the intent of providing more military protection, better roads and mail service, and lower taxes for northstate territory. That bill died in committee, but it was hardly the end of the idea. In 1853 came the call for the formation of the State of Klamath, an area running roughly from Cape Mendocino to the Umpqua River. The following year, a meeting in Jacksonville, Oregon, was convened to plan the statehood convention for Jackson; in 1855, the issue came up again.

Those who sought separate statehood during the mid-1800s did so because they felt isolated and victimized, complaining about the area's inadequate roads and lack of protection against angry, militant native peoples. The widespread support among settlers toward secession was also reflected locally, resulting in the eventual creation of Modoc and Lassen Counties from Siskiyou County and the Nevada Territory, respectively.

Organized acts of rebellion weren't confined to settlers. Attacks by native warriors were expressions of their rage over decimation due to disease and violence. Most famous of these "unwritten histories," as Joaquin Miller would call them, was one actually written—the long-running Modoc War of "Captain Jack" and his band, among the last major Indian Wars fought by U.S. troops.

The State of Jefferson

Possibly only half seriously during this century, the issue of secession came up again. On Nov. 27, 1941, the State of Jefferson officially seceded from Oregon and California. Citizens of the new "state" put up roadblocks on Hwy. 99 and stated

their intent "to secede each Thursday until further notice"—or until they got good roads into the copper belt between the highway and the sea. The short-lived state of Jefferson extended from the Pacific over to the high plateau in Nevada, north to Roseburg, Oregon, and south to Redding, California. The new state's capital was Yreka, and its symbol was a gold pan. In the center of the state seal was "XX," indicating just how the people here felt about California and Oregon: double-crossed.

On December 4, Judge John L. Childs of Crescent City was selected as acting governor of the new U.S. state, and his inauguration ceremony took place on the lawn of the courthouse in Yreka. "Our roads are not passable, barely jackassable; if our roads you would travel, bring your own gravel" read signs posted for the benefit of *Time*, *Life*, and film crews. Plans to release film footage of that event, the formation of what was to be America's 49th state, were foiled on December 8 by the greater news of Japan's attack on Pearl Harbor the day before. If it weren't for World War II, California travelers today would cross Jefferson on the way to Oregon. But the rebellion wasn't ineffective. Roads *were* finally paved in the far north, the construction of a major interstate freeway was inspired, and Stanton Delaplane of the *San Francisco Chronicle* won a Pulitzer Prize for his news coverage.

Klamath Mountains

"Klamath Mountains" is the collective name for several separate ranges in northwestern California reaching 6,000-9,000 feet in elevation and oriented in all different directions. Extending into Oregon, the **Siskiyou Mountains** are one of several California coastal ranges milking moisture from storms headed inland. The Siskiyous, averaging 5,000-6,000 feet in elevation, run mostly east-west along the Oregon border from the Pacific Ocean to the Rogue River Valley. But the western end runs north-south, forming the divide between the Smith and Klamath Rivers.

South of the Siskiyous are the towering peaks, meadowlands, and glacial lakes of the rugged **Marble Mountains,** laced by interconnecting trails, and the nearby **Russian Mountains.** The **Salmon** and **Scott Mountains** (to the south and southeast, respectively) form the northerly fringe of the **Trinity Alps,** which include the Trinity Wilderness and the easterly Trinity Mountains. Most notable in the Trinities is evidence of ancient glacial activity: scoured mountain lakes, serrated ridges, and high, sloping meadows. One glacier remains on Thompson Peak, the highest point in northwestern California. The **Yolla Bolly Mountains** (named from the Wintu Yo-la Bo-li, meaning "high, snow-covered peak") include the **Yolla Bolly-Middle Eel Wilderness** and are the most southerly of the Klamaths. Near Mt. Shasta, the **Castle Crags** area (now a state park) is technically part of the Klamath range, forming its eastern boundary.

The Klamaths include some of the wildest, least-known, and most fragile wilderness areas in California. The fresh, clear streams are still important for salmon and steelhead spawning because few roads cut into these areas. And the timber industry hasn't yet cut out all the heart of the wilds here.

Geology

The Klamath Mountains, a northwestern extension of the Sierra Nevada, are older and more geologically complex than the surrounding northern California terrain. They began as an "upwarp" or arc of ancient igneous and metamorphic rock plunging downward under younger adjacent landforms. Pleistocene glaciers slowly sculpted the granite and other resistant ridges into the jagged peaks of Castle Crags, the Marble and Salmon Mountains, and the Trinity Alps. U-shaped valleys were formed where advancing alpine glaciers encountered serpentine and other soft rock. Concave cirques and lakes were scoured out by glaciers and are most noticeable today on north-facing slopes above 5,500 feet. Moraines—piles of sand and gravel deposited along the sides of glacial troughs—are also evident in the Klamaths.

In the past 10,000 years, some of the glacial landforms here have been modified by stream erosion, forest succession, and rock weathering. Hundreds of tributaries from three major rivers—the Klamath, Trinity, and Scott—make this the most naturally divided landscape of its size in the state. Adding to the area's geological interest is evidence of nearby volcanism; the area once connecting the Klamaths and the Sierra Nevada was buried long ago by lava flows from the southern Cascades.

Well written and worthwhile for information on regional natural history is *The Klamath Knot* by David Rains Wallace (Sierra Club Books).

Climate

The area is cold and snowy in winter and generally cool in summer, though summer days can sometimes get hot at lower elevations. Rainfall averages 50–70 inches per year, with about 35 inches in Weaverville and 100-125 inches in the

HIGHWAYS AND BYWAYS

Far Northern California isn't as remote as it used to be. Still, the region does offer some of the state's most appealing scenery. The **Volcanic Legacy Scenic Byway,** recently declared an All-American Roadway, is one spectacular route—a 360-mile stretch of Shasta-Cascade landscapes. (There are only 28 All-American Roadways in the nation, and only one other—the Big Sur Coast Highway—in California.) Anchoring the byway at the southern end is a multi-highway loop circling Lassen Volcanic National Park. Zig northwest along Hwy. 89 from Lassen, roll by miles-high Mt. Shasta on I-5, then zag northeast on Hwy. 97 toward Klamath Falls; at the Oregon border, the route connects with the 140-mile route celebrating Crater Lake's scenery. For details, see www.volcaniclegacybyway.org.

Northern California boasts many other scenic byways, however, and serious visitors can at least sample them all. Most make good use of two-lane paved highways, like Lassen National Forest's **Lassen Scenic Byway** and (foundation loop of the volcanic legacy route) and the Hwy. 299 **Trinity River Scenic Byway** stretching from Redding to Arcata, south of the Trinity Alps, and traversing both Shasta-Trinity and Six Rivers National Forests. Similarly, the stunning **Feather River Scenic Byway** follows Hwy. 70 from the North Fork of the Feather River's deep canyons up into the Sierra's Plumas National Forest, passing through Portola on the way to Hallelujah Junction at Hwy. 395. But some, like Modoc National Forest's **Modoc Volcanic Scenic Byway** and **Surprise Valley National Back Country Byway,** make good use of unpaved roads. For more information about far northern scenic byways, contact the relevant national forest and see www.byways.org.

western Siskiyous and some parts of the Trinities. Summer thunderstorms are fairly common.

Flora and Fauna

The Klamaths are like an open-air botanical museum—about 1,300 plant species, many rare and endemic, thrive here. Lush growth is the rule for forests nearer the Pacific, which are dense with mosses, fungi, and thick mantles of wildflowers. Big-leaf maple, dogwood, other deciduous trees, and vine maple add brilliant fall colors to the pines, Douglas firs, incense cedars, and the occasional Pacific yew and Port Orford cedar. Higher up, mixed evergreens blend with white fir and chinquapin; Shasta fir, lodgepole pine, western white pine, and mountain hemlock are common only at highest elevations. Rare here is the weeping or Brewer's spruce, a gnarly veteran that grows on north slopes at 7,500-7,600 feet and is found only in the Siskiyous and Trinities. Also here is the Alaska yellow cedar. On dry slopes are vast expanses of almost impassable mountain chaparral: oaks, manzanita, and snowbrush.

Some areas of the Klamaths have serpentine soil, which is toxic to many plant species. As a result, vegetation is quite distinct; look for scattered Jeffrey pines, lodgepoles, and western white

pines in these areas. On those rare serpentine spots where water seeps to the surface, the insectivorous cobra lily can occasionally be found.

Among the rare and endangered animals living largely undisturbed in the Klamaths are wolverines, fishers, mountain lions, bald eagles, peregrine falcons, spotted owls, and pileated woodpeckers. Deer abound. Bears are present but rarely seen; nonetheless, poaching is a problem, fueled by the demand for dried bear gallbladders used in exotic health remedies.

TRINITY MOUNTAINS

There's not a single parking meter or traffic signal in Trinity County. *Wild* is the word in this landscape of rugged, glacier-carved peaks and rounded, scoured-out valleys, steep canyons, and dramatic waterfalls. White-water rafting is good on the Trinity River, as are salmon and trout fishing along quieter stretches. Early in summer, before hot days take their toll, mountain wildflowers are everywhere. In the Trinities, the ultimate destination is the Trinity Alps Wilderness to the north, though there's plenty to see and do elsewhere. Few people live here, but watch out for the area's plentiful cattle (open rangeland) and deer while driving on narrow backcountry highways. Also watch for logging trucks. For information on area attractions and events, including river rafting and pack guides, see Weaverville information below.

Trinity Alps Wilderness

Revel in these glacier-gouged goliaths looming over sapphire lakes. Though not as tall as major Cascade or Sierra Nevada peaks, these mountains, likened to the Swiss Alps, are snow-covered even in summer and thickly forested on lower slopes. The Trinity Alps are rocky and rugged, intimate and close; moist meadows hug crystal-clear streams. Depending upon snowpack and trail conditions, late June to late July is generally the ideal hiking time here. Wildflowers are best in July and early August, but the Trinity Alps are especially nice for hiking in fall, when crowds are absent.

With passage of the Wilderness Act of 1984, the old Salmon-Trinity Alps Primitive Area became California's Trinity Alps Wilderness, second in size only to the John Muir Wilderness in the Sierra Nevada. The area takes in more than a half-million acres, the headwaters of both the Salmon and Trinity Rivers, and more than 400 miles of trails, including a stretch of the Pacific Crest Trail and the New River area to the west. Once ruled by occasionally armed pot growers, New River has since been declared "safe for public use"—but don't count on that; the New River town of Denny has been called the most lawless place in the state. A good overall guide to the area is Wilderness Press's *The Trinity Alps: A Hiking and Backpacking Guide* by Luther Linkhart. Before planning even a day trip into the wilds here, however, check locally on current conditions.

Hiking

Current information about area hiking and backpacking is available through the county chamber of commerce and regional Forest Service offices. There's something here for everyone. Short treks include the 10-minute hike to **Lake Eleanor** near Trinity Center (from the Swift Creek Rd. trailhead), and the three-mile hikes to **Stoddard Lake** (from the Eagle Creek Loop off Hwy. 3), to

Tangle Blue, at the base of Scott Mountain, and to **Deadfall Lakes** (from Parks Creek Road). From Deadfall Lakes you can also reach this region's stretch of the 2,600-mile **Pacific Crest Trail,** which intersects Parks Creek Rd. and Hwy. 3 at the crest of Trinity Dr.

Cycling and Mountain Biking

Trinity County's rollicking backcountry roads make for great cycling. Popular routes include the 30-mile **Trinity–Lake Lewiston Loop** out of Lewiston; the fun 45-mile **Hayfork-Peanut-Wildwood** loop starting in Hayfork (park at the county fairgrounds); and the challenging 100-mile **Mad River–Wildwood** route starting at Ruth and skirting the Yolla Bolly–Middle Eel Wilderness.

Mountain bikers have their day at mid-June's annual **La Grange Cross-Country Classic.** Otherwise, popular fat-tire treks are plentiful and various, due to the area's many abandoned logging roads. Especially challenging is the 22-mile **South Fork Trail** along the South Fork of the Trinity River from Wildwood Rd. to Scotts Flat Campground (saner with a car shuttle).

Trinity Lake

Once officially known as **Clair Engle Lake** in honor of the senator behind the damming of the Trinity here, locals have long refused to recognize that name. The hard feelings of those whose land was taken for this reservoir at the foot of the Trinity Alps have only solidified with time. People here call the lake "Trinity," after the river that once roared through the valley past the gold rush towns of Minersville and Stringtown (now underwater). With 150 miles of forested shoreline, the lake is warm enough for swimming in summer. Fishing for catfish, bass, trout, and salmon is popular, as are all types of boating.

Trinity Center, the main town near the lake, was founded in the 1850s and named for its original location at the center of the Shasta-Yreka Trail; the town was relocated to its present site due to dam construction. **Treasure Creek,** near Trinity Center, was named for a stray Wells Fargo strongbox rumored to still sleep with the fishes. Visit the **Scott Museum** in Trinity

UNHOLY TRINITY

In early 2003 the Bush administration effectively reversed an earlier decision to restore Trinity River flows by reducing water diversions to the Central Valley Project. Nudging the Trinity River closer to its natural state would have helped protect the river's salmon and steelhead runs and enhanced area recreation. Staying the course might also have helped prevent the massive Klamath River fish die-off that shocked the nation in 2002. (For details on that disaster, see Killer Dilemma: Fish or Farms? elsewhere in this chapter.)

Since the 1960s, up to 90 percent of the Trinity River has been diverted at Lewiston Lake, via a tunnel under Trinity Mountain, to Whiskeytown Reservoir and the Central Valley Project; from Whiskeytown the diverted water is routed to Keswick Reservoir and also released down Clear Creek. Without the dams, and the water diversions they allow, the Trinity River would flow west into the Klamath River and, just north of Eureka, into the Pacific Ocean.

The federal law creating the interconnected Trinity and Lewiston system requires that "in-basin needs" for Trinity River Water be met before diversions can be allowed. Significant declines in salmon and steelhead populations begin in the 1960s, after Trinity River water was first diverted.

Results of a comprehensive, 15-year, multiagency state and federal study were released in June 1999 by the U.S. Fish and Wildlife Service. To protect native fisheries and other wildlife and to support the recreation-related local economy, the study recommended that downstream flows from the Trinity and Lewiston Dams be increased from an average of 340,000 to 595,000 acre-feet per year.

So in late 2000 came the U.S. Department of Interior decision to do just that—keeping roughly 48 percent of the Trinity's water "at home" and shipping 52 percent south.

But agricultural water users roared in protest, claiming that their industry would be put at risk. (With CVP water, developed and paid for with U.S. tax dollars, now being sold by some CVP growers—at a tidy personal profit—to Southern California water districts for residential use, such claims seem increasingly dubious.) In late 2002 a sympathetic U.S. District Court judge sided with the San Joaquin Valley's litigious Westlands Water District, which suggested that the Trinity River's fisheries be restored instead by mechanical means—using bulldozers to restore salmon gravel beds, for example—rather than by returning water to its natural course.

As has been its practice in other environmental disputes, the Bush administration failed to challenge the judge's decision within the prescribed 120-day period, and the fate of the Trinity River and its fisheries was sealed. For now.

Center (free admission) for its outstanding collection of historical material, including 500 types of barbed wire. The museum is on Airport Rd. and open June 1 to mid-September, Tues.–Sat. 1–5 P.M.; it shares space with a branch of the **Trinity County Library,** 530/266-3242, open year-round Monday and Wednesday 11:30 A.M.–2:30 P.M. and 4–7 P.M. **Alpen Cellars Winery** on East Fork Rd., 530/266-3363 or 530/266-9513, produces white riesling, gewürztraminer, chardonnay, and pinot noir.

Lewiston Lake

Just south of Trinity Lake, Lewiston Lake is a cold lake just below the dam. The cooler water means excellent fishing for rainbows and browns in the upper channels. Picnicking is good here, and since boat speeds are restricted to 10 mph, you won't hear any roaring engines. Camping is also good, and often less crowded than at Trinity. The most automated salmon and steelhead hatchery anywhere, worth seeing (to believe), is the California Department of Fish and Game's **Trinity River Fish Hatchery,** just south of the Lewiston Dam, 530/778-3931. Steelhead fishing is good along this stretch of the Trinity River.

The town of **Lewiston,** south of the lake and

about five miles from Hwy. 299 via Rd. 105, is just three miles upriver from where the first gold dredger was built. The town's Sons of Temperance meeting hall was erected in 1862 and still stands as **Old Lewiston Schoolhouse Library and Museum** and de facto city hall on Schoolhouse Rd. (near Turnpike), 530/778-0111, www.oldlewistonschoolhouse.org, open Tues. 10 A.M.–2 P.M., Sat. 10 A.M.–5 P.M., and Sun. 2–5 P.M. (Call to arrange tours at other times.) Among other shops, a real find for antique lovers—and a good stop for finding out what's going on—is **The Country Peddler,** 530/778-3325, along Deadwood Rd. in historic downtown. Near Lewiston, **Limekiln Gulch** was once an active gold-mining area, now mostly visited by river-runners, hunters, and hikers. A restored cabin here was built in a style reminiscent of the French Colonial architecture common in the Mississippi River delta.

WEAVERVILLE AND VICINITY

This friendly little city of around 4,000 at the base of the Trinity Alps is the county seat. It's almost a miracle that this charming mountain town is still here, after a wind-whipped, late-summer wildfire roared through the area in 2001 and took with it a number of homes. In Weaverville, still, cottages and old brick or wood-frame homes are corralled by picket fences and covered with creeping vines. Notable here are the gold rush–era buildings with exterior spiral staircases. An inventory of local historic buildings and sights is included in the free walking tour brochure, available at the chamber of commerce.

The **Weaverville Drug Store,** 219 Main St., 530/623-4343, is the oldest drugstore in California—a 1950s-feeling Rexall that's been in business since 1852. Inside you'll find a veritable pharmacological museum, with exhibits including extraction percolators, druggists' mortars and pestles, and pill-rolling machines. Across the street is the old *Trinity Journal* newspaper office, 218 Main, 530/623-2055, home of one of the state's oldest newspapers. To see how they put out fires in the old days, stop by the free **Weaverville Firefighters Museum,** 100 Bremer St. (in the Weaverville Volunteer Fire Station), 530/623-6156, which has a hand pumper, a hose cart, and other old equipment on display. Open Mon.–Thurs. 8 A.M.–noon and 1–5 P.M. In the 1850s, half the town's population was Chinese, so it's not surprising that the old firehouse is a Chinese rammed-earth adobe.

On the south side of Trinity Lakes Blvd. between Washington and Main (near the school) is **Five-Cent Gulch,** site of the local Chinese Tong War of 1852. Cheering miners watched from the sidelines as 800 members of two rival tongs (gangs) met in battle. The Ah Yous were outnumbered and soon badly defeated by the Young Wos; the last two opposing warriors calmly stabbed each other with crude iron pitchforks for 15 minutes until one finally fell dead. (The victor died two weeks later.) There were no other casualties—perhaps only because whites didn't allow the Chinese to have firearms. A marvelous monument to the Chinese presence in Weaverville, the historic **joss house** downtown on Main St. is the oldest Chinese temple in continuous use in California (see listing below for more details). Another tribute is the 1918 **Lee Family Ranch House Folk Art Center,** also on Main, onetime home of the Chinese pioneer Lim-Lee family and now gallery space and headquarters for the Trinity County Arts Council.

Also worth a stop downtown are the **Hays Bookstore,** 106 Main St., 530/623-2516, offering new and used volumes (as well as fax and UPS service); the **Highland Art Center,** 503 Main, 530/623-5111, a complex of galleries showing off the works of local artists; and **Mamma Llama** coffeehouse, 208 Main, 623-6363, www.mammallama.com, which offers an audience for underappreciated singer/songwriters and other musicians whenever possible.

Come to Weaverville in late February for the **Blacksmiths Annual Hammer-In** at the J.J. Jackson Museum, in April for the **Trinity River Freestyle Rodeo,** and in May for the **Bigfoot Gemboree.** Usually in June, Lewiston hosts the **Old Lewiston Peddler's Faire,** and Hyampom the **Hyampom Good Times Fair and Festival.** Come in August for the **Ruth Lake Summer Festival** in Ruth, and the **Trinity County Fair** in Hayfork.

Joss House

A fine old Taoist temple is the focal point at **Weaverville Joss House State Historic Park.** ("Joss" is a corruption of the Spanish word *dios,* meaning "god.") Originally built in 1853, then torched 20 years later, the temple was rebuilt in 1874 and has since been in continuous use. Inside the brightly painted wood-frame (the red interior beyond the "spirit screens" symbolizes happiness) are three ornately carved wooden canopies. The ancient altar, more than 3,000 years old, offers candles, incense, an oracle book and fortune sticks, and glass-painted pictures of Immortals. In front are a table and an urn for food and alcohol (usually whiskey) offerings to the gods. Adjacent to the temple is an unpainted lean-to, once a conference room and temple attendant's quarters. Mysteriously returned in 1989 was one of the temple's guardian "devil dogs," one of four missing since World War II (replica only on display).

The joss house, known as "The Temple of the Forest Beneath the Clouds," located downtown on Main at Oregon St., is closed to the public when Taoists come to worship. Otherwise, tours (small fee) are scheduled on the hour when the park is open. For a current schedule of operating hours and more information, contact Weaverville Joss House State Historic Park, 530/623-5284 or 530/225-2065.

J.J. Jackson Museum

Across the parking lot from the joss house is the county historical society's excellent J.J. "Jake" Jackson Memorial Museum, 508 Main St., 530/623-5211, a handsome brick building with an extensive collection of firearms, mining equipment, Native American basketry, Chinese artifacts, and other documentation of California's development. Also on the grounds of this "historical park" are an original miner's cabin from La Grange; a facsimile blacksmith and tin shop; a fitch tender's cabin; and the working two-stamp Paymaster Stampmill, the only active steam-operated stamp mill in the country. The stamp mill, fired up several times a year to demonstrate how miners crushed rock to extract gold, is housed in a replica of the original building. Open May

1–Oct. 31, daily 10 A.M.–5 P.M.; April and Nov., daily noon–4 P.M.; Dec.–Mar., Tues. and Sat. noon–4 P.M. Admission is free but donations are much appreciated.

West on Hwy. 299

Junction City, known as Milltown, was once a booming trade center for ranchers and miners. North of Junction City along Canyon Creek was the town of **Canyon City,** aka Raggedy Ass. Just one mile farther north, where the Little East Fork branches from Canyon Creek, is **Dedrick.** Here were the Bailey, Silver Gray, and Globe mines—the territory's major gold producers. Settled in 1849 by French Canadian prospectors, **Helena** once had a hotel and boardinghouse. The economy here peaked in 1855 when there were more than 200 acres of fruit orchards. Some old fruit trees and a few brick buildings are all that remain now, though the area was once wild enough to earn the nickname "Baghdad of the Frontier." **Big Bar** was one of about nine gold rush-era spots of the same name in California. The most notorious local resident was "Commodore Ligne," who sold mining claims to the Chinese and then shooed them off the land with a shotgun and sold the sites again. (Justice was eventually served when the commodore was shipped out to San Quentin.) The name **Burnt Ranch** comes from the torching of farmhouses here in 1853 during an Indian raid.

South of Trinity

Old **Douglas City** was once a big placer and hydraulic mining area and is still scarred. All that remains of the historic town is the water tower just above Reading's gold site on the Trinity River near the mouth of Reading's creek. (Reading was responsible for naming the region "Trinity," mistakenly believing that the river led into Trinidad Bay on the coast.)

From Hwy. 3, a 22-mile road follows Brown's Creek to the mineral springs, store, and campground at **Deer Lick Springs.** Beyond the springs, the road eventually leads into the Chanchelulla Wilderness (see below).

Head out of Douglas City on Steiner Flat Rd. (or take Wildwood Rd. off Hwy. 3), then turn onto Bridge Gulch Rd. to see the 200-foot lime-stone **Kok-Chee-Shup-Chee Natural Bridge,** site of the Bridge Gulch Massacre of March 1852. Here some 150 Wintu men, women, and children were knifed or shot to death by a sheriff's posse of miners in revenge for the killing of one of their own. A half-mile self-guided trail runs through the area.

Nearby is **Hayfork,** once called Kingsberry Hay Town, Trinity County's second-largest town and a farming and ranching community. As incongruous as it seems, Hayfork was "attacked" by the Japanese during World War II. The attack was impersonal; one of 6,000 or so unmanned balloons sent up by the Japanese landed here. The 70-foot-tall, bomb-carrying balloons were supposed to hit the ground and explode, setting American forests afire and thereby diverting resources from the war effort. But at least one flaw in the plan was the fact that all 300 bombs known to have reached the U.S. got here in the middle of a cold, wet winter.

Ruth, once known as White Stump, was built where old-timers say a bolt of lightning struck a pine tree. **Ruth Reservoir,** Trinity County's second-largest lake, provides Mad River water to Humboldt County, and is surrounded by lush, remote countryside. **Ruth Lake Community Services,** 707/574-6332, www.saber.net/-ruthlakecsd, offers a marina (boat rentals) and campgrounds; basic services are available in town. From the lake, it's a thrilling trip over to the coast.

Nearby Wilderness

The lonely, heavily forested **Yolla Bolly-Middle Eel Wilderness** is lush and green early in the season, but turns hot and dry in summer. The terrain is steep, but less rugged than the Trinity Alps. Yolla Bolly, all 153,841 acres of it, is open for hiking by late May; Bigfoot was last spotted here in 1970, so watch for hairy hikers. To get here from Weaverville, head east on Hwy. 36 (look for the shadows of logging trucks before blind curves), then south. You can also come in

IS BIGFOOT DEAD?

Bigfoot, the half man–half ape who has haunted the forests of Northern California and the Pacific Northwest for 50 years, is dead. Indeed, Bigfoot was never alive—except in the imagination of Ray L. Wallace, the late Humboldt County man whose "evidence" proved the existence of the creature. Or so claims his family following Wallace's death in 2002.

According to family members, in August 1958 Wallace had a friend carve huge humanoid feet out of alderwood. He and his brother Wilbur then used the feet to leave impressions in the dirt about contractor Jerry Crew's bulldozer on a construction site near Bluff Creek. The timing couldn't have been better for the prank to fuel the public's imagination. Rumors of Bigfoot (aka Sasquatch) had circulated in the region since 1886, and in the late 1950s the nation was fascinated by exotic tales of Abominable Snowmen in the Himalayas. Wallace's story and photos of his "discovery" stirred up considerable interest, hitting the front page of the *Humboldt Times* in Eureka. Over the years Wallace kept the hoax alive, by offering to sell Bigfoot to a Texas millionaire and filming and photographing the creature in the wild as it ate frogs, elk—even breakfast cereal.

Even if the first and original Bigfoot has passed on to that happy primate playhouse in the sky, does that mean the legend will also die? Not necessarily. True believers point to other evidence, including a grainy 1967 film by Roger Patterson and casts of 40 to 50 alleged Bigfoot footprints.

For more information about Bigfoot's heritage in the far northern mountains, be sure to visit Willow Creek on Hwy. 299, which considers itself the Gateway to Bigfoot Country. Since 1998 the **Willow Creek/China Flat Museum** has featured a special Bigfoot wing, based on the private collection of Bigfoot/Sasquatch research material donated by the estate of the late Bob Titmus, a good friend of Jerry Crew. Bigfoot information can also be found online: **Bigfoot Field Researchers Organization,** www.bfro.net; the **Texas Bigfoot Research Center,** www.texasbigfoot.com; and the **Bigfoot Museum,** www.bigfootmuseum.com.

from Red Bluff. Call or obtain a wilderness map in advance for more specific directions, since they differ from trailhead to trailhead. Also in the area are the **North Fork Wilderness,** taking in most of the Middle Eel River's headwaters; and the **Chanchelulla Wilderness,** which includes Chanchelulla Peak (6,399 feet) and features trails up through thickly forested hillsides and across meadows sweet with wildflowers.

For information about the Yolla Bolly-Middle Eel Wilderness, contact: **Mendocino National Forest,** 825 N. Humboldt Ave. in Willows, 530/934-3316, www.r5.fs.fed.us/mendocino; **Six Rivers National Forest,** 1330 Bayshore Way in Eureka, 707/442-1721, www.r5.fs.fed.us/sixrivers; or **Shasta-Trinity National Forest,** 2400 Washington Ave. in Redding, 530/244-2978, www.r5.fs.fed.us/shastatrinity. For information on Chanchelulla Wilderness, contact Shasta-Trinity National Forest (above) or the **Hayfork Ranger District** office, 530/628-5227. For information on the North Fork Wilderness, contact Mendocino National Forest (above).

Camping

In summer, camping is the first choice, and there's lots of choice here. The numerous U.S. Forest Service campgrounds throughout the area feature more than 400 campsites. Some of these are free, but most are $8–15 a night, or around $20 for multiple family units. Most are first-come, first-camped, with a stay limit of two weeks. A few of the more popular campgrounds are reservable; to reserve, call 800/280-2267 or go to www.reserveusa.com. The following listed campgrounds are all Forest Service sites.

The large and popular **Tannery Campground** on the west side of Trinity Lake is reservable. **Alpine View Campground,** under the Trinity Alps at the north end of the eastern reach of the Stuart Fork arm, has 64 campsites and a nature trail. Just across the water is the large **Hayward Flat Campground,** which has a nice swimming beach; reservable. **Eagle Creek Campground,** about 12 miles north on Hwy. 3, then four miles on a dirt road (sign), is a good spot for swimming and fishing.

Around Trinity Lake, free public campgrounds include: **Horse Flat Campground,** 1.5 miles beyond the Eagle Creek turnoff (same road), with pit toilets and good swimming, open May–Oct.; and **Jackass Springs,** in an isolated spot on the east side of the lake, open year-round.

At Lewiston Lake, **Ackerman Campground** is open year-round, $11, and tiny **Cooper Gulch,** $12, is open Apr.–Nov. For private camping options, get information in Weaverville at the chamber office.

Motels

A motor-court motel with classic mountain ambience is the **Red Hill Motel & Cabins** on Redhill Rd. right across from the U.S. Forest Service office, 530/623-4331, www.redhillresorts.com, 14 one- and two-bedroom cabins under the pines. Housekeeping units available. Covered fish-cleaning station. The large **Best Western Weaverville Victorian Inn,** 1709 Main St. (Hwy. 299), 530/623-4432, is actually a contemporary motel with modern conveniences ranging from satellite TV to in-room spas (suites only). You can't go too far wrong at either the **49er Motel,** 718 Main, 530/623-4937, or the knotty-pine paneled **Motel Trinity,** 1112 Main, 530/623-2129 or 877/623-5454. For a genuinely local experience, less expensive than most, the **Weaverville Hotel,** 203 Main St., 530/623-3121, features old-fashioned rooms (no phones) with private baths (either tubs or showers). It's clean and pleasant, and rates include complimentary morning coffee. Quite a find, if nothing fancy. With any luck at all, someday the New York Saloon and Hotel downtown will be renovated and open again as a hostelry. All of these are $50–100.

Bed-and-Breakfasts

The casually elegant **Carrville Inn Bed & Breakfast** on Carrville Loop Rd. just off Hwy. 3 north of Trinity Lake, 530/266-3511, www.carrville-inn.com, is just about the area's most popular phenomenon since the arrival of paved roads. Once a stage stop, this refurbished historic hostelry features five upstairs guest rooms (two share a bath), a lacy two-tiered front veranda that serves as unofficial social hall, an eclectic game room, and a formal sitting room with fireplace. The separate Carr Creek Cabin is also available, a better option for families with children. The pastoral grounds adjoin a vast mountain meadow and include roses, fruit trees, a full-sized swimming pool, and a small menagerie of barnyard animals. Other pluses include a full country-style breakfast and genial hosts. The inn is open mid-April through November; advance reservations are strongly advised. Rooms $100–150, cabin more.

In the historic sector of Lewiston—and complete with prime fishing frontage along the Trinity River near the old bridge—is the **Old Lewiston Inn Bed and Breakfast,** 530/778-3414 or 800/286-4441, www.theoldlewistoninn.com. This completely refurbished tin-roofed gold rush–era building is "as romantic as all get out," as the innkeepers say. Its four comfortable rooms have private baths, separate entrances, and individual decks overlooking the river. Adjacent Baker House is also available, with three additional rooms; President Herbert Hoover once slept there. All rooms feature "local" antiques, refrigerators, and cable TV. A hot tub overlooks the river. Rates include full breakfast, $50–100.

Cabins and Retreats

Most cabins are $50–100, some near the bottom of that range, some near the top. Unique among the Weaverville area's more outdoorsy lodging options are the **Ripple Creek Cabins** on the Eagle Creek loop off Hwy. 3 in Trinity Center, 530/266-3505 or 510/531-5315, www.ripplecreekcabins.com, open year-round. The seven beautifully restored cabins (with both woodstoves and electric heat) are casually scattered through the woods near a meadow, and lie along Ripple Creek and the Trinity River. Cabins vary in size and capacity—one is wheelchair accessible and can also accommodate group meetings and seminars. Each cabin features "basics" like garlic presses, colanders, corkscrews, and wineglasses, not to mention barbecues and picnic tables. There's even a playground. Children and pets welcome.

Also open year-round and good for the budget-conscious are the cabins at **Lakeview Terrace Resort** in Lewiston, 530/778-3803, www.lakeviewterrance.com, each featuring a fully equipped

kitchen, barbecue, bed linens (bring your own towels); kids love the heated swimming pool. "Value season" (mid-Sept.–mid-June) prices are a particularly good deal, as low as $378 per week. Other nice area choices include the one- and two-bedroom housekeeping units at the **Old Garrett Ranch Cabins** along the South Fork of the Trinity River in Hyampon, 530/628-4569, where kids and pets are welcome, and the one-bedroom cabin at **Butter Creek Ranch,** 530/628-4890.

Fully furnished private vacation homes offer even more seclusion. Try **Coffee Creek Chalet** in Trinity Center, 530/266-3235, www.coffeecreekchalet.com.

Traditional Rustic Resorts

Most of the area's truly rustic accommodations are veritable family-vacation traditions, usually booked at least a year in advance with one-week minimum stays during the peak summer season. (Call for the possibility of cancellations.) Weekly cabin rates are $525–650 for four in summer (lower in spring and fall), though full-service resorts, which provide all meals and dude ranch-style amenities, may run $1,000 per person per week.

The 1920s-style **Trinity Alps Resort,** 1750 Trinity Alps Rd. in Trinity Center, 530/286-2205, www.trinityalpsresort.com, is the oldest resort around, with 40 rustic housekeeping cabins along the Stuart Fork starting at $595 per week. The cabins come in various sizes, sleeping anywhere from four to 10 people. Activities here include good fishing and river rafting, horseback riding, a pool hall and game room, and bingo and Ping-Pong at the resort's General Store. Dine onsite at the Bear's Breath Bar & Grill. Open mid-May through September, the resort books one-week minimum stays from Memorial Day weekend through Labor Day, and a three-night minimum the rest of the season.

Small **Bonanza King Resort,** 530/266-3305, www.bonanzakingresort.com, is three miles from upper Trinity Lake on Coffee Creek (near a pack station, if you're literally hoofing it into the Alps). It offers seven fully furnished, comfortable, porched cabins with kitchens. Some cabins feature fireplaces or woodstoves. Other amenities include a laundromat with solar dryer, a sandy beach and swimming hole, and good fishing. One-week minimum stays from mid-June through Labor Day; two-night minimum the rest of the year. Snowmobiling, cross-country skiing, and snowshoeing are popular winter pastimes. No pets.

Coffee Creek Ranch, 530/266-3343 or 800/624-4480, www.coffeecreekranch.com, generally open from Easter to Thanksgiving, is another good choice—especially if you liked the movie *City Slickers.* Also on Coffee Creek Rd., right on the creek, the guest ranch offers a private cabin, all meals, a heated pool, private pond, square dancing, evening bonfires, horseback riding and pack trips, a steak feast on weekends, stream fishing, and every imaginable dude ranch amenity.

Eating in Weaverville

Absolutely organic eaters don't need to starve in Trinity County. The **Trinity Organic Growers Association** sponsors certified farmers markets in Weaverville and Hayfork. The **Hayfork CFM** is held May–Oct. on Friday, 4–7 P.M. on Main. The **Weaverville CFM,** also May–Oct., is held on Wednesday next to the art center, Main and Mill Sts., 4:30–7:30 P.M. For information on both, call 530/623-5947. The **Mountain Marketplace Natural Foods Grocery,** 222 Main St., 530/623-2656, sells organic fruits, vegetables, and bulk grains.

The place for the most creative yet comforting local cuisine—pretty darned sophisticated, from pastas and poultry to fish, game, and the signature tri-tip steak combo—is the **La Grange Cafe,** now at home in a larger, historic brick building at 216 Main St., 530/623-5325. Nice wine list. For dessert, try the blackberry cobbler. Open for lunch and dinner daily, except winter when the café closes on Sunday.

Quite popular is the **Pacific Brewery,** 401 S. Main (across from the joss house in the 1855 Pacific Brewery building), 530/623-3000, as appreciated for its food—everything from chicken fajitas to lasagna, seafood, and steaks—as its great selection of microbrews on tap and eclectic decor.

An old horse buggy hangs from the ceiling, a mannequin masquerades as a dancehall girl, and the old stove shares space with beer kegs and whiskey jugs. Open daily for breakfast, lunch, and dinner. Or try cheery **Noelle's Garden Café,** 252 Main St., 530/623-2058, where the Austrian strudel is a specialty.

For breakfast burritos, sandwiches, homemade cookies, and the occasional Comedy Night, try the **Trinideli** on Hwy. 3 near Main St., 530/623-5856. For those of you who have never had the experience, the onetime A&W burger stand here, **Miller's Drive-In** on the highway, 530/623-4585, still features carhops.

Way out there—north of Trinity Center at the intersection of Hwy. 3 and Coffee Creek Rd.—is the popular, year-round **Forest Cafe,** 530/266-3575, known for its great breakfasts, burgers, and home-style dinner specials.

The **Bear's Breath Bar & Grill** at the Trinity Alps Resort on Trinity Alps Rd. (off Hwy. 3), 530/286-2205, is justly proud of its riverside deck dining—American standards plus pastas and almost adventurous items like "Joss House chicken" marinated in soy sauce and honey then stir-fried with vegetables.

Home to the only traffic signal in Trinity County—and this one is in the bar, to control wait staff traffic between the dining room and kitchen—is the **Lewiston Hotel,** on Deadwood Rd. in Lewiston, 530/778-3823, another local favorite. The dining room here is famous for homemade soups and daily specials as well as additive-free steaks and other cuts of beef. Do spend some time appreciating the decor, perhaps best described as country eclectic with accents of urban humor. Open for dinner Wed.–Sun. from 5 p,m., bar open daily from 3 P.M. Also popular is **Mama's Place,** a country café on Trinity Dam Blvd. (Lewiston's main drag), 530/778-3177, open Fri.–Wed. for breakfast, lunch, and dinner (closed Thurs.). Another possibility, if you're willing to backtrack along Hwy. 299 toward Redding, is the attractive and historic **French Gulch Hotel,** 530/359-2112, usually open Thurs.–Sat. nights for dinner and Sunday for brunch; for more information, see Redding and Vicinity.

INFORMATION

For information and campfire permits for the Trinity, Lewiston, and Whiskeytown Lakes areas (all part of the Whiskeytown-Shasta-Trinity National Recreation Area), contact the U.S. Forest Service **Weaverville Ranger District,** 210 Main St. (Hwy. 299), 530/623-2121, open weekdays 8 A.M.–5 P.M. (daily in summer), or the **Coffee Creek Fire Station** at the north end of Trinity Lake on Hwy. 3, 530/266-3211, open in summer Thurs.–Mon. 8 A.M.–4:30 P.M. (Highway 3 past this point, eventually leading to Yreka, is twisting and treacherously narrow—not recommended for trailers or the fainthearted.)

Wilderness permits for the **Trinity Alps Wilderness Area,** national forest maps ($6), Marble Mountains ($7) and Yolla Bolly ($6) wilderness maps, and other regional camping and recreation information are available at both the Weaverville and Coffee Creek Stations, as well as at historic **Big Bar Ranger Station** in Big Bar, 530/623-6106. Though open weekdays 8 A.M.–5 P.M., these places will leave a permit outside for campers arriving after hours, with advance notice. Other area Forest Service offices: **Hayfork Ranger Station,** on Hwy. 3 in Hayfork, 530/628-5227, and **Yolla Bolly Ranger Station,** 2555 Hwy. 36 in Platina, 530/352-4211.

For more information about the Trinity Alps area and its attractions, including community events and lake recreation, contact the **Trinity County Chamber of Commerce,** 211 Trinity Lakes Blvd. (Hwy. 3, about a block off Main near Alps Lock & Key and the Trinideli), 530/623-6101 or 800/487-4648, www.trinity-county.com. In addition to the downtown walking-tour brochure, ask for the *Trinity Heritage Scenic Byway* auto-tour pamphlet and map of the Hwy. 299 corridor; it's jam-packed with useful details. For local arts information, contact the **Trinity County Arts Council,** 206 Main St., 530/623-2760, www.tcarts.com.

This is fishing country. Trout season opens in late April. California fishing permits are available at local sporting goods stores and bait shops. The **Trinity Fly Shop** in Lewiston, 530/623-6757, www.trinityflyshop.com, offers instruc-

tion as well as guided fishing trips. Other possibilities include and **Trinity River Adventures,** 530/623-4179, www.trinityriveradventures.com, also in Lewiston, and **Trinity River Outfitters** headquartered in the Douglas City Store, 530/623-6376, www.trinityriveroutfitters.com.

For general wilderness experience, packing companies and backcountry guides include the local institution **Coffee Creek Ranch** in Trinity Center, 530/266-3343 or 800/624-4480, www.coffee-creekranch.com. **Como Say Llamas** of Sacramento, 916/923-0408, www.llamapacker.com, offers a popular guided trip into the Trinity Alps; reserve well in advance.

This is also white-water country. **Trinity River Rafting,** 530/623-3033 or 800/307-4837, www.trinityriverrafting.com, specializes in Trinity River runs, including Class II to Class V runs. **Bigfoot Rafting Company,** 530/629-2263 or 800/722-2223, www.bigfootrafting.com, offers local river runs as well as guided drift-fishing trips. Accommodating **Turtle River Rafting Company** 530/926-3223 or 800/726-3223, www.turtleriver.com, organizes trips to suit your travel plans—on the Trinity, Salmon, Klamath, Upper Sacramento, and other rivers—plus kayaking and a white-water rafting school. **Aurora River Adventures,** 530/629-3843 or 800/562-8475, www.rafting4fun.com, offers everything from easy float trips to Class V white-water thrill rides on the Trinity, Klamath, Salmon, and many other rivers, plus a kayaking school, river-rescue classes, and special trips for organized youth groups.

SALMON RIVER

The Salmon Mountains snaggle toward the southeast from the Siskiyous; part of the range is included in both the Trinity Alps and Marble Mountain Wildernesses. The Scott Mountains snake down from the north, the two ranges never quite intersecting but coming close just south of the Marble Mountains. The north and south forks of the wild, undammed Salmon River flow west to their confluence at Forks of Salmon, then northwest to Somes Bar, where they merge with the Lower Klamath River. The headwaters of the Scott River start just miles from the Salmon's,

NORTHERN MOUNTAINS

joining the North Fork near Callahan before flowing north, then northwest to join the Upper Klamath River just east of Hamburg. The two rivers, separated only by a finger of mountains, create a wide mountain valley like a sliver of moon arching south from the lower Klamath, then northwest to its headwaters.

There aren't many people in these parts, but there is plenty to see and do: fishing, white-water rafting, kayaking and canoeing, short hikes, weeklong backpack trips, historical reconnaissance. Travel along the Salmon River is via a one-lane gravel road etched into steep granite.

On the way to Forks of Salmon, a sign marks the site where the town of Somes Bar once stood; now the spot is popular year-round for fishing and camping (king salmon and steelhead are the prized catches here). It's also the starting point for western trails to the Marble Mountains Wilderness. The general store at Forks of Salmon was built in the early 1800s. Secluded camping nearby includes **Hotelling Gulch,** a small campground (five sites) on Cecilville Rd. three miles southeast of the store. (Boil your water.) Seven miles farther, on the Salmon River's south fork, is **Matthews Creek Campground** (12 sites, piped water). For other campgrounds and more area information, contact the **Salmon River and Scott River Ranger Districts** on Hwy. 3 in Fort Jones, 530/468-5351.

Otter Bar Lodge Kayak School

Not for budget travelers, except those willing to save up for a supreme white-water experience, Otter Bar Lodge is a world-class kayaking school and wilderness resort near Forks of Salmon on the banks of the river. Though nothing here is particularly fancy or fussy, to describe Otter Bar as "rustic" is to suggest that Hearst Castle is a tract home. But it is 100 miles from any place you've ever heard of, and more than two hours from the nearest store.

Accommodations (shared) are available in three cabins and a four-bedroom lodge with a library. All rooms have down comforters, and antiques are peppered throughout the complex. Other amenities include an organic garden and great food (raved about in *Bon Appetit*) and an

outdoor sauna and hot tub. When you're not kayaking, borrow a mountain bike to explore local trails, or go fishing—particularly pleasant in fall. The standard program is a weeklong stay including everything—kayak instruction, use of equipment, lodging, and food—for $1,890 per person (early season "playboating" is discounted). Adult classes are grouped by experience, from beginners to advanced; beginning and intermediate kids' kayaking camp is also offered for ages 10–14 ($650–750). For current information or reservations, contact: Otter Bar Lodge, 14026 Salmon River Rd., Forks of Salmon, CA 96031, 530/462-4772, www.otterbar.com.

Marble Mountain Ranch

A family-oriented resort, Marble Mountain Ranch at Somes Bar, 530/469-3322 or 800/552-6284, www.marblemountainranch.com, is a fine yet rustic vacation spot—the kind of place where children have the chance to *act* like children without getting into too much trouble. Because of the resort's remoteness—just off Hwy. 96 about halfway between Happy Camp and Willow Creek, a site near the Klamath River surrounded by a million acres of national forest—electrical power here is generated by a gold rush–style Pelton waterwheel. The flume that supplies the ranch's running water was built by Chinese laborers in the 1800s. Completely stocked housekeeping cabins come in various sizes, one to three bedrooms; three cabins have kitchens. Also available are two luxurious houses. Family-style meals (not included in the rates) are served in the lodge.

White-water rafting is the specialty of the ranch's affiliated company, Access to Adventure, which offers runs on the Trinity, Klamath, Salmon, and Scott, as well as rivers farther afield. The ranch also has some of the finest swimming holes anywhere, access to great hiking, plus basketball, volleyball, and horseback riding. Fishing expeditions are offered from spring through fall, as are horse-pack trips into the wilderness (*you* walk, the horses carry the load). Rates are in the $150–250 range, per person, all meals ("gourmet home-style") and activities included.

MARBLE MOUNTAIN WILDERNESS

With the best hiking and backpacking north of the Trinity Alps, the Marble Mountain Wilderness is a quarter-million acres of thick forests teeming with wild things: bears and mountain lions (though you'll rarely spot either), ever-abundant deer, grouse, quail, and chipmunks. Alpine wildflowers cascade from rocks and meadows and peek out from beneath the forest canopy and snow-covered peaks. The wilderness, named for the two giant "marbles" that mark the juncture of the Salmon and Marble Mountain ranges, Marble and Black Marble Mountains, was first set aside as a primitive area in 1931, thanks in large part to President Herbert Hoover, who had enjoyed Wooley Creek in the 1920s. Fishing is excellent in hundreds of miles of streams, and backpackers can explore about 50 crystal lakes, most to the north in the Marble Mountains proper. The **Pacific Crest Trail** eventually enters the wilderness south of Seiad Valley. If backpacking sounds too strenuous, hire a packer.

Bryan & Sherman Packing, 530/467-3261 or 530/459-5417, based in Etna, offers guided horseback trips as well as supply drops.

Also within Klamath National Forest is the tiny (12,000-acre) **Russian Wilderness,** a few miles southeast of the Marble Mountain Wilderness. The Russian takes in the Klamath's Russian Mountains, a tall granitic ridge with prominent peaks and U-shaped valleys. The area ranges in elevation from 5,000 to more than 8,000 feet (atop Russian Peak).

A worthwhile and well-written book about the region's natural history is *The Klamath Knot* by David Rains Wallace (Sierra Club Books). For more information, contact **Klamath National Forest** headquarters in Yreka (see below) or any of its ranger district offices.

YREKA

Yreka is the only city to speak of in the central far north. People here (all 7,200 of them) are proud of their pioneer history. The town boasts a good local-history museum, a gold nugget display (in

Yreka

the courthouse), well-preserved old Victorians and brick gold-rush buildings, and a historic steam railroad.

The gold rush gave birth to Yreka. Nuggets found at Scott Bar in 1851 brought 2,000 miners here within six weeks. The local legend goes like this: Abraham Thompson stopped to spend the night here and was astonished when grazing pack mules pulled up flecks of gold, tangled in grass roots. Named variously Thompson's Dry Diggings, Shasta Butte City, Wyeka, Wyreka, then Yreka, the town gradually grew, boasting 27 saloons before churches began to gain ground. A big fire on July 4, 1871, demolished one-third of the town in an hour. "Indian Peggy," a Modoc woman, is credited with saving the townspeople from slaughter by warning of an impending Klamath raid in the 1850s; the town eventually gave her a pension.

As capital of the State of Jefferson, in 1941 Yreka garnered considerable publicity for its secessionist demands—issued to protest the area's unpaved roads and general abandonment by California politicians. Every Thursday, members of the State of Jefferson Citizens Committee (Yreka 20-30 Club) barricaded the north-south road to make their point. The short-lived State of Jefferson also generated its own social commentary, with lines such as "The Promised Land: Our Roads Are Paved With Promises." The area has generated unique "color" all along, certainly since the days of old Humbug, a wild mining town Joaquin Miller described as having "neither the laws of God nor man" in a setting "out of sight of everything—even the sun." (The saloon in Humbug was called the Howlin' Wilderness.) Nearby, where McAdams and Cherry Creeks converge, was the mining town of Deadwood, second in stature only to Yreka among mid-1850s boomtowns. Miller wrote his first poem here, an epitaph commemorating the marriage of a local cook. He then recited it at the couple's wedding reception—and a literary career was launched.

Seeing and Doing Yreka

Most of the town's gold rush-vintage buildings, included on the National Register of Historic Places, are concentrated between Oregon and Main, and W. Lennox and Miner Streets. Many of the buildings on Miner St. were built up from the walls left standing after the 1871 fire. Below street level are the remains of tunnels and mine shafts honeycombing the area. Above ground, horsehead hitching posts rear up out of modern-day sidewalks. Also appreciate local murals and the striking sculptures of Ralph Starrit—including the amusing *Moodonna* giant metal cow in a field south of town. (Pick up a walking guide to Yreka's historic district at the chamber of commerce, as well as heritage home tour.) Eye-opening are the gold displays in the foyer of the **Siskiyou County Courthouse,** 311 Fourth St., 530/842-8340. The exhibit shows off a fortune in gold nuggets (the largest such collection south of Anchorage, Alaska) taken from local mines and placers. The museum is open Mon.–Fri. 8 A.M.–5 P.M. (free).

The **Siskiyou County Museum,** 910 S. Main St., 530/842-3836, is an indoor-outdoor collection of historical relics and paraphernalia left behind by trappers and pioneers. The building itself resembles the old Callahan Ranch Hotel stage stop. (Ask for admittance to the outdoor area, a collection of five original buildings, open in summer.) The impressive Native American Gallery represents the Karuk, Shasta, Konomihu, Okwanuchu, Achomawi, and Modoc peoples and their arts and histories. Historical publications are available during normal museum hours, Tues.–Sat. 9 A.M.–5 P.M. Small admission. Worth a stop, too, is the **Klamath National Forest Interpretive Museum,** part of the headquarters complex at 1312 Fairlane Rd., 530/842-6131. Here you'll find an extensive collection of historical and natural history exhibits—one of the most impressive offered at any U.S. Forest Service outpost. Step into the lookout and check out the "firefinder." Admission is free.

For a relaxed, scenic drive to the coast, head west on the **State of Jefferson Scenic Byway,** Hwy. 96, which becomes the **Bigfoot Scenic Highway** beyond Happy Camp.

Blue Goose

Yreka's pride and joy is the Yreka Western Railroad (YWR) and its *Blue Goose* steam excursion train. When the Goose is in full flight,

ANOTHER SCULPTURE FOR PEACE: A LIVING VETERANS MEMORIAL

Dennis Smith was already an artist before serving 13 months as a Marine in Vietnam, but when he returned stateside he discovered that his subject matter had changed forever. The results of that transformation are there for all to see at the **Living Memorial Sculpture Garden** rising up out of the sage and manzanita in the northern shade of Mt. Shasta, some 13 miles north of Weed on Hwy. 97. Situated on the west side of the highway, one mile north of the County Rd. A12 connector to I-5, the "living" part of the memorial includes 58,022 pine trees—a tree planted in remembrance of each of the American dead in Vietnam. Another key part of the memorial is sculptor Smith himself, who lives onsite in a modest one-room cabin/studio.

Most evocative, though, are the stylized, silent yet plaintive metal sculptures, from *The Why Group* (Why me? Why not me? Why war? Why not?),

Those Left Behind, and *The Nurses* to the chilling *POW—MIA.* A visitor can easily spend an hour or more strolling the sculpture garden and quietly contemplating its fruits; the pathways are reasonably accessible, and benches are scattered throughout.

To the surprise of some, after Sept. 11, 2001 the memorial's tone suddenly shifted toward more pro-American recollections. As a result its most powerful sculpture, *The Refugees,* depicting Bru tribesmen, Vietnamese allies abandoned by the U.S. and tragically forced to fend for themselves, was replaced by *The Greatest Generation,* a stylized version of the oft-depicted scene of World War II–era veterans raising the flag atop Mt. Suribachi on Iwo Jima. The latter sculpture, according to the memorial's new brochure, honors Smith's father and that generation's veterans. *Hot LZ,* or "Landing Zone Under Fire," was also modified, its more haunting meanings stripped away.

the 1915 black Baldwin Mikado locomotive pulls the art deco–vintage cars and an open-air passenger flatcar on a sightseeing trip through the Shasta Valley to Montague and back, about 15 miles roundtrip. Special events, such as dinner trains and "The Wild Goose Chase" 5K and 10K race, are also scheduled. Owned by the nonprofit Rocky Mountain Mining and Railway Museum of Denver, Colorado, the YWR operates May–Sept.; steam excursions run weekends and holidays only (at last report) and the diesel engine is scheduled for Wed.–Fri. Fares are $14 adults, $11 seniors (60 and older), $7 children ages 3–12, with special runs (dinner rides and the like) slightly higher. There is also limited space available for passengers to ride in the locomotive ($25–40 per person) and caboose ($8–16). Funds generated by the onsite gift shop and the railroad's unique "steam mail service" help support the *Blue Goose.* For current details, drop by the depot (jog east from I-5's Central Yreka exit) or contact: **Yreka Western Railroad,** 300 E. Miner St., 530/842-4146 or 800/973-5277, www.yrekawesternrr.com.

Camping

On the south side of Yreka, **Waiiaka Trailer Haven,** 240 Sharps Rd., 530/842-4500, is a good bet for those who want to be close to town. Both RV and tent sites, $23. Those who prefer the wilds can head to one of the 26 Klamath National Forest campgrounds in the surrounding area; get information at forest headquarters here, 1312 Fairlane Rd., 530/842-6131. The Forest Service **Tree of Heaven Campground** along Hwy. 96 not far north of Yreka, $10, is easily accessible from I-5. Reservable. For more information, call 530/468-5351. **Iron Gate** and **Copco Lakes** are administered by Pacific Power & Light and fed by the Klamath River. Camping is possible, though some sites have no water; cabins are available at Lake Copco. No motorboats are allowed at Iron Gate, but you can enjoy great fishing in the river, as well as swimming and hiking. For details, contact the **Pacific Power & Light** Recreation Department in Portland, Oregon, at 503/813-6666, www.pacificpower.net.

Staying in Yreka

Top of the mark for Yreka-area motels are

Amerihost Inn Yreka, 148 Moonlight Oaks Ave. (take the Fort Jones Rd. exit), 530/841-1300 or 800/434-5800, www.amerihostinn.com, and the **Best Western Miner's Inn,** 122 E. Miner (near I-5), 530/842-4355 or 800/528-1234, www.bestwestern.com. The attractive **Wayside Inn,** 1235 S. Main St. (about a mile south of town), 530/842-4412 or 800/795-7974, offers a few units with kitchens, as well as one deluxe suite with amenities including a whirlpool bath and fireplace. Others choices include **Economy Inn,** 526 S. Main, 530/842-4404; **Days Inn,** 1804 Fort Jones Rd., 530/842-1612; and **Klamath Motor Lodge,** 1111 S. Main, 530/842-2751.

Eating in Yreka

Charming **Nature's Kitchen** inside the old Bottling Works Mall at 412 Main St., 530/842-1136, is a good choice for simple breakfast fare—try the "Dutch babies" oven-baked pancakes. It features both organic bakery and health-food restaurant (salads, soups, both hot and cold sandwiches); beverages include espresso, smoothies, and carrot juice. **Grandma's House,** 123 E. Center, 530/842-5300, has good breakfasts and lunch specials. For Chinese food, try **Ming's,** 210 W. Miner, 530/842-3888, offering Cantonese, Mandarin, and Szechuan cuisine; or **China Dragon Restaurant,** 520 S. Main, 530/842-3444.

Lalo's, 219 W. Miner, 530/842-2695, is popular at lunch and dinner for its Mexican fare. Quite good, too, is the continental-American **Old Boston Shaft Restaurant,** 1801 S. Main, 530/842-5768, where the menu features seafood, beef, and wonderful Old World desserts. Reservations are a good idea. hose in the know say downtown's **Rex Club,** 111 S. Main, 530/842-2659, is the best local bar.

Information

Pick up the *Siskiyou Daily News* to find out what's going on. Just for fun—and to fully inform yourself—check out the **State of Jefferson website,** www.jeffersonstate.com. Tourist information, maps, and walking-tour brochures are available at the **Yreka Chamber of Commerce,** 117 W. Miner St., 530/842-1649 or 800/669-7352 (recorded message), www.yrekachamber .com, which shares space with the Scoops ice cream and sandwich parlor. Chamber staff can fill you in on upcoming local events, from the **Humbug Hurry Up** and the **Motorcycle Poker Run Rally & Cruise Night** in July to the **Siskiyou Century** in September and the **Northern Siskiyou Brewfest** in October. Travelers sans cars, stop here for a bus schedule for the **Siskiyou S.T.A.G.E.,** 530/842-8295 or 800/247-8243, which goes just about everywhere (weekdays only). At **Klamath National Forest** headquarters, 1312 Fairlane Rd. (at Oberlin), 530/842-6131, www.r5.fs.fed.us/klamath, pick up camping, recreation, and wilderness information plus topo maps and wilderness and campfire permits. Ranger district offices are: **Happy Camp,** 530/493-2243; **Salmon River and Scott River** on Hwy. 3 in Fort Jones, 530/468-5351; **Goosenest** in Macdoel, 530/398-4391; and **Ukonom** on Ishi-Pishi Rd. in Orleans, 530/627-3291.

For information on camping and recreation along and beyond the Oregon border, contact **Rogue River National Forest** headquarters in Medford, 541/858-2217, www.fs.fed.us/r6/rogue, and the new **Cascade-Siskiyou National Monument,** also headquartered in Medford, 541/618-2200, www.or.blm.gov/csnm.

If you're continuing north, take the short trip to Ashland for its famed **Oregon Shakespeare Festival,** 541/482-4331 (box office) or 541/482-2111 (administration), www.orshakes .org, whose season runs from late Feb.–Oct. and features Shakespearean, classical, and contemporary plays.

Mt. Shasta and Vicinity

"Lonely as God and white as a winter moon"— so Joaquin Miller described California's most majestic mountain in the 1800s. And so it still is. Mt. Shasta is California's sixth-highest peak but more awesome than any other—perpetually snow-covered, glowing orange, pink, and purple at sunset, casting shadows on the lava lands below. Area Indians revered Shasta as the abode of the Great Spirit. Others, too, attribute special influences to this peak. French mountaineer Rene Daumal, author of the unfinished cult classic *Mount Analogue: a Novel of Symbolically Authentic Non-Euclidian Adventures in Mountain Climbing,* which chronicles the great mountain climb to God, somehow also describes Shasta:

> *In the mythic tradition the Mountain is the bond between Earth and Sky. Its solitary summit reaches the sphere of eternity, and its base spreads out in manifold foothills into the world of mortals. It is the way by which man can raise himself to the divine and by which the divine can reveal itself to man.*

Sometimes clearly visible from as far away as 150 miles, close up Shasta is more mysterious and obscure. The origin of the name Shasta is unclear, though it's a name shared by a vanished Indian tribe, a dam, a lake, some fascinating caverns, a national forest, and (in slightly modified form) Shastina, Shasta's sister peak. The newest Shastas—Shasta Dam and Shasta Lake, both about an hour south of the mountain—are main features of California's Central Valley Project, a massive feat of water engineering.

First and Sudden Impressions

Mt. Shasta is the highest point in California's Cascades. Though Mt. Whitney is taller by 332 feet and other mountains are bigger by different degrees of measurement, their grandeur is lost among ranks of lofty peaks. Not so Shasta, which stands alone at 14,162 feet and towers 10,000 feet above the surrounding countryside. But height isn't everything. Shasta is the largest volcano in the contiguous 48 states, and with a

diameter of more than 20 miles, it is perhaps in sheer volume the largest mountain as well. There is always snow on Shasta. Hikers and backpackers walk up into it via forest trails from June or July to early September, but only fit and fairly serious hikers and climbers get to the top. Nonclimbers, take the highway up the mountainside to where the road ends. From there, 8,000 feet up, enjoy the view of the entire north end of the Sacramento Valley, Burney Falls, Lassen Park, the Trinity Alps, Castle Crags, the Sacramento River canyon, and Lake Siskiyou below.

THE LAND
Formation of the Cascades

Every rock in California's northeastern volcanic wonderland was once part of a river of molten lava sometime within the past 30 million years. Once an ocean, then a flat plateau, finally a faulted mountain range roped in on the west by a string of volcanoes, the Cascades and Modoc Plateau are the southernmost tip of landforms that dominate the entire Pacific Northwest. Volcanically the Cascades form part of the Pacific Ring of Fire, the eastern half of which burns from Alaska's Aleutian Islands to South America.

The Sierra Nevada and Klamath Mountains separated some 140 million years ago, creating a 60-mile-wide alley for the Cascades. Andesite volcanoes, like all those in the Cascades, typically develop into long chains parallel to the coast in areas also characterized by active earthquakes. Geologists believe these strings of volcanoes are pushed upward when the sea floor collides with the North American continental plate and plunges deep into the earth's molten lava. Cascade lavas, then, were once part of the Pacific Ocean floor before being transformed some three million years ago.

Shasta Geology

Shasta is classified as extinct, though the term "dormant" is probably more prudent. Those boiling sulphur springs near Shasta's summit (among

© ROBERT HOLMES/CALTOUR

Mt. Shasta

other indicators) mean there's still volcanic life below. Despite the fact that Shasta looks like a single volcanic mountain, it's actually a volcanic system, one that has become increasingly complex over time. The main cone, once 200-300 feet higher than it is today but ground down by glaciation, is the result of three separate vents. The tallest, Steep Rock, or "Hotlum" in the native vernacular, appears to be Shasta's peak. The geologically recent "parasitic" cone, Shastina, is 12,433 feet tall and forms a vent on Shasta's west flank. Shastina's volcanic crater is obvious, while Shasta's is buried in ice and snow. Seven glaciers cluster on the mountain's north and east sides.

Despite substantial snowmelt and constant glacial shrinkage, little water pours off Shasta in summer. Instead, most runoff percolates through the porous surface rock and soil then gushes forth near the base of the mountain, most notably north of Dunsmuir at Shasta Springs, where bubbly Shasta mineral water was once bottled and marketed worldwide. (The closest thing to it these days is Castle Rock mineral water, bottled in Dunsmuir.) Invisible runoff from Mt. Shasta flows into the Sacramento River and, eventually, Shasta Lake.

When Will Shasta Erupt Again?

Locals blew their stacks when a booklet published by the U.S. Geological Survey predicted that Shasta will erupt every 250–300 years. Though people aren't overly concerned about the volcano (the last eruption, a minor event, was in 1786, though sister peak Mt. Lassen erupted in a big way in 1915), many *are* worried about scaring away retirees and new businesses; the government has since added an insert stating that there are no indications that Mt. Shasta is about to blow.

However, based on knowledge of the area's geological past, it's likely that some time in the next century a flutter of earthquakes will sound some advance warning. Then an explosion of ash, rock, and gases will announce Shasta's awakening, or—if the eruption is nonexplosive—a lava dome will form inside the crater and searing rivers of hot lava will flow down the mountainside.

Climate

It's frigid here in winter, and always cool but sometimes cold in summer. The weather at the summit is changeable and often severe. Even in summer, sudden storms—wicked icy winds, thunderstorms, sometimes snow or hail—are possible, so always be prepared. Shasta, in a sense, creates its own weather and affects the Sacramento Valley as well, blocking the wet Canadian north winds in winter and turning the north valley into a summertime oven—the primary reason Redding is often among the hottest spots in the nation.

Nothing about Mt. Shasta weather is stranger, though, than the sudden flying saucer-shaped cloud formations generating intense greenish-blue beams of light—evidence, to many, of UFOs or celestial spirit-beings of one sort or another. Scientists, however, explain it like this: cold, fast-moving northerly winds push cold dry air over the top of Shasta and also around and up the mountain's sides. Wind shear is created where these winds meet and, between 6,500 and 10,000 feet, icy, almond-shaped lenticular clouds form. The sun's reflection off the miniscule ice particles creates the mountain light show.

HISTORY

Native peoples believed Mt. Shasta to be the abode of the Great Spirit and out of respect never ascended past the timberline. Fur trader Peter Ogden passed through Shasta Valley in 1827 and noticed Mt. Shasta, which he dubbed "Sastise" after the local Indians. But some believe Father Narciso Duran noted the mountain on a Spanish expedition 10 years earlier and called it "Jesus Maria"—one holy name for each peak. The Russians who settled along the Northern California coast could see Shasta clearly, and some say they named it Tshastal, "White and Pure Mountain."

But Shasta's history is primarily one of mountaineering conquests. A Yreka merchant, E.D. Pearce, is credited with first ascending Shasta, in August 1854. Scientists first braved the mountain in 1862, when Josiah Whitney led a Geological Survey party to the summit. When they got to the top, they found tin cans, broken bottles, a Methodist hymnbook, a newspaper, a pack of cards, "and other evidences of bygone civilization."

John Muir on Shasta

Founder of the Sierra Club and its president until his death in 1914, John Muir first climbed Shasta on Nov. 1, 1874, and was enchanted. Waking up the next day he saw:

> . . . a boundless wilderness of storm clouds of different degrees of ripeness. . . congregated over all the lower landscapes for thousands of square miles, colored gray, and purple, and pearl, and deep-glowing white, amid which I seemed to be floating, while the great white cone of the mountain above was all aglow in the free, blazing sunshine.

The storm Muir watched forming soon hit, forcing him to shelter in a spruce grove for five days.

The following year Muir made two trips up Shasta: the first (uneventful) on April 28, and the second (nearly fatal) just two days later. Caught in a savage snowstorm, he and his guide kept from freezing by burrowing into the hot mud of the sulfur springs at the summit—each alternately scalding one side of his body and losing all sensation in the other. Black Butte, near I-5, was once called Muir Peak in the mountain man's honor.

RECREATION

Hiking

Get current hiking information at the ranger district office in town. Among Shasta sights are virgin stands of rare Shasta red firs—some 300 years old, untouched by loggers—mountain hemlocks, secluded lakes, alpine meadows, clear streams, and open valleys. Few hiking trails surround Mt. Shasta, and the popular mountain trails within the **Mt. Shasta Wilderness,** particularly near Avalanche Gulch, Horse Camp, and Lake Helen, are overused. To get up the mountain to these areas from Mt. Shasta City, head east on Alma St. to the flashing red light and turn left onto Everitt Memorial Highway. The road continues on to Sand Flat, Bunny Flat, Panther Meadow, and the old Mt. Shasta Ski Bowl area.

From Bunny Flat or Sand Flat, it's a short hike through red fir forests and ferns to **Avalanche Gulch** and **Horse Camp,** where the Sierra Club's historic 1922 lodge stands. This small stone hut is a traditional starting point for hikes to Mt. Shasta's summit; visitors from around the world have stayed here and recorded their impressions in the logbook. (Nowadays, too many people make the trip, so the hut is for day use and emergencies only—otherwise camp outside.)

From Panther Meadows Campground, the **Grey Butte Trail** heads uphill along the stream. Another trail begins at Old Ski Bowl and heads east past red fir forests, mountain hemlock, meadows, and summer pools on its way through "The Gate" to Squaw Meadows. The short 1.5-mile **Clear Creek/Mud Creek Trail** (access via Mc-Cloud) is good for a whole day's exploration; highlights along the way include mysterious Sphinx Rock, views of small Konwakiton and Wintun Glaciers, plus a miniature Grand Canyon and waterfalls. Or take the nearby (and higher) **Brewer Creek Trail** to Ash Creek Falls and good views of Wintun and Hotlum Glaciers. Several other Shasta trails are accessible from Weed and Hwy. 97; ask at the ranger station for details.

To the Summit

In summer, as many as 100 hikers ascend Mt. Shasta daily. The Forest Service charges a $5 per vehicle per day parking fee at three of the most popular trailheads—North Gate, Brewer Creek, and Clear Creek (Bunny Flat is still free, so far)—and you'll also need to buy a summit pass to climb above 10,000 feet ($25 for an annual pass that includes parking and climbing, or $15 for a three-day pass that doesn't include parking). Passes are available at the ranger station and at The Fifth Season in Mt. Shasta City; you can self-register for the parking passes and the three-day summit passes outside the ranger station after hours and at most trailheads.

Thousands try to get to Shasta's summit each year, but only half make it. Except for those who purposely make it harder on themselves (choosing more difficult routes up or racing against the clock), reaching the summit is possible for most people who are reasonably fit and sensible. But despite this fact, an average of two people each year die climbing Mt. Shasta, thanks to avalanches, falling rocks, hypothermia, or falls

(caused by wearing unsafe shoes, being unprepared for ice and snow, or climbing recklessly). Many more have been hurt.

Experienced mountaineers ascend Shasta from all directions, but many routes are technical climbs requiring expertise and special equipment (inquire at local sports shops). Mountain hikers, however, can scale Shasta from any of three primary routes. June and July are prime time. In June, snow is common above 8,000 feet; by September, it's loose rock almost the whole route.

The popular and traditional trip to the summit via **Horse Camp/Avalanche Gulch** takes an average of eight hours from the Sierra Club hut, or five hours from Lake Helen. Horse Camp is a popular starting point; climbers and hikers often stay the night here to acclimate and get an early start on the summit. Fill your water bottles at the natural spring next to the lodge—at last report, its delicious water was still free of giardia. Also from Horse Camp, you can climb due north and up **Shastina.**

To get to the summit from the old Ski Bowl, hike to Green Butte, contour over to Lake Helen, then head up Shasta via one of the two main **Avalanche Gulch** routes. Set out at daybreak on any ascent to improve your odds of getting off the mountain before dark, and bring a headlamp or flashlight just in case. (Note that in snow season, the access road to the Ski Bowl isn't plowed past Bunny Flat, which is the primary trailhead for the popular Avalanche Gulch routes).

Hiking Safety and Tips

Sign in at the U.S. Forest Service office in Mt. Shasta City before heading out. Never hike or climb alone, and always check the weather; call the **Forest Service avalanche advisory and mountain condition report** at 530/926-9613 to get the latest update or see www.shastaavalanche.org. Know the symptoms of altitude sickness and hypothermia. Get started early, go slowly, watch your footing (especially on the mountain's east side, where crevasses may be covered with snow), and be alert for falling rocks. Rest frequently. Bring crampons and ice axes for climbing hard snow and ice fields.

Necessary basic equipment for summer climbs

includes good hiking boots or shoes, extra wool socks, high-energy food, adequate water for the day (at least two quarts per person), sunglasses, sunscreen, a headlamp or flashlight, and first-aid supplies including moleskin or bandages for blisters. It's always a good idea to bring an ice axe and know how to use it; though crampons may seem like overkill in summer, depending on the weather you may encounter ice on early morning ascents. In addition, since weather can change, bring layerable clothing and a light-weight waterproof poncho.

Because of the flood of climbers on the mountain, the old "kybo" at Lake Helen has been removed, and all climbers must now pack out all human waste in special bags provided by the forest service (available at the ranger station and at the Bunny Flat Trailhead). And remember: whatever else you pack in, pack it out. For even slightly off-season climbs, more preparation is prudent; contact the Forest Service office for guidance.

Adventuring

The Mount Shasta Book by Andy Selters and Michael Zanger (Wilderness Press) is a valuable resource. **The Fifth Season Sports,** 300 N. Mt. Shasta Blvd., 530/926-3606, www.thefifthseason.com, is equipment central, for skiers, snowboarders, and climbers—new equipment and repairs as well as rentals, including ice axes and crampons. In warmer weather, stop for mountain biking and camping gear. For Fifth Season's **24-hour climbing report,** call 530/926-5555. The best online avalanche and mountain conditions report is available from the Forest Service **Mt. Shasta Wilderness Avalanche and Climbing Advisory** site, www.shastaavalanche.org.

Shasta Mountain Guides, 1938 Hill Rd., 530/926-3117, www.shastaguides.com, offers winter and summer climbs—mountaineering, ice and rock climbing, and glacier travel instruction—and leads guided Shasta and Castle Crags climbs. Among popular nontechnical Shasta climbs is the two-day "Traditional John Muir Route." Custom climbs are easily arranged. Women's trips and free Avalanche Awareness Clinics are also offered.

Turtle River Rafting Company in Mt. Shasta, 530/926-3223 or 800/726-3223, www.turtleriver.com, offers a tremendous selection of fun runs (inflatable kayaks and rafts) spring through fall, on the Klamath, Upper Sacramento, Scott, Salmon, and Trinity Rivers. Turtle River has an exceptional safety record, is fully insured, leaves its schedule "open" to a remarkable degree (to accommodate travelers' particular needs), and happily works with schools, churches, and other groups. Many raft trips are appropriate for children ages 4 and up; families are welcome. Contact the company for current rates, reservations, and further information. Mt. Shasta's **River Dancers Rafting & Kayaking Adventures,** 530/926-3517 or 800/926-5002, www.riverdancers.com, offers Shasta "views" trips on the Upper Sacramento River, Northern California's nearby Salmon, Scott, and Trinity Rivers, and the Upper Klamath River. Rivers. Family and children's trips, white-water and kayak school, and yoga retreats are also offered.

For an aerial view of the mountain aboard a hot-air balloon, contact **Hot Air Balloons USA,** 530/926-3612, www.hot-airballoons.com. Four-hour excursions are offered Fri.–Mon. and include a dawn launch, one-hour flight, open-air brunch, and a champagne toast; $160 per person. For an earthier perspective, **Shasta Cove Stables,** 530/938-3392 or 800/662-3529, offers day trips and overnights as well as hourly horseback rides.

Shastice Park on the outskirts of Mt. Shasta City (see below) now features the **Siskiyou Ice Rink,** a National Hockey League–size ice rink, the largest in northern California. An outdoor facility—a roof may be added one day soon—the rink is open as weather permits, generally from late November through February (skate rentals available onsite). For current details, call 530/926-1702 (rink information line) or the Mt. Shasta Recreation District, 530/926-2494, or see www.visitmtshasta.org/icerink.

Cross-Country Skiing

In addition to the beginners' **Bunny Flat** and **Sand Flat** cross-country ski trails and the intermediate **Overlook Loop Trail,** experienced Nordic skiers often chart their own course on (and up) Shasta for some of the finest cross-country skiing in the state. For more information and suggested routes, contact **The Fifth Season Sports** in Mt. Shasta City, 530/926-3606, www.thefifthseason.com, which also offers avalanche seminars and ski-touring clinics and races. Those who like manicured trails can head to Mount Shasta Board & Ski Park (below), which has a beautiful groomed and tracked Nordic ski area.

Mount Shasta Board & Ski Park

Shasta's downhill ski area has three triple-chair lifts for novice to advanced skiers, a poma lift for beginners, and 425 acres (27 trails) of excellent skiing. A snowmaking system offers protection against drought years. Snug in a valley at lower el-

evations and protected from wicked winter winds, the Ski Park is family-oriented and friendly, reached via Hwy. 89 near McCloud. Lift tickets run around $33 for adults, $17 for juniors 8–12 and seniors over 65, and $5 for kids under age 8. Half-day rates ($26 adults) are available starting at noon, and night skiing is offered Wed.–Sat. 4–10 P.M. Multiday passes are available. "Learn to ski" packages including equipment and either one or two lessons are available. Disabled skiers and snowboarders are welcome. Lifts run daily 9 A.M.–4 P.M. Other facilities include a lodge, cafeteria, rental shop, and an adjacent Nordic ski school and ski area with miles of machine-groomed trails (all-day trail passes: $14 adults, $10 juniors/seniors, $3 kids under 8).

In the off-season, visitors can take snowless

SPIRITUAL SHASTA

In 1987, spiritualists of all stripes converged on Mt. Shasta for the media-hyped Harmonic Convergence of international meditators dedicated to a new era of worldwide peace. Of the seven "power centers" in the world due to harmonically converge that August weekend, Shasta was the only peak chosen in the continental U.S.

Local native people, as well as those farther afield, respect the mountain's spiritual presence. An old Hopi legend says that ancient lizard people once built 13 underground cities, one beneath Mt. Shasta, to escape a major Pacific coast meteor shower. (As recently as 1972, a visitor to Shasta reported seeing a reptile person clad in pants, trousers, and—presumably—good boots, hiking near here.) Bigfoot has been spotted on Shasta too, of course, but rangers maintain that plaster casts of oversized footprints are actually smaller critter prints naturally enlarged as the snow melts.

Some students of the occult believe that descendants of the once-great continent of Lemuria live within Mt. Shasta, a Rosicrucian theory widely circulated during the 1930s. As the story goes, Lemuria (continent of Mu, the world's oldest civilization, preceding even Atlantis) was once to the west of California. Because of great geological changes, Lemuria began listing into the Pacific. That continent's eastern shore became the modern-

day Cascade Range (then separated from the North American continent by an inland sea), where the white-robed Lemurians, both physically and psychically gifted, live secretly to this day. In 1930 Guy Ballard, a paperhanger-cum-government surveyor from Chicago, met up with "a majestic figure, God-like in appearance, clad in jeweled robes, eyes sparkling with light and love," none other than St. Germain. Inspired, Ballard wrote *Unveiled Mysteries* and spawned the I AM group of believers who still have a retreat in the mountain's shadows. The Old Ones, Space Brothers, or Ascended Masters, ageless astral vegetarians, contact only those with synchronistic spiritual vibrations. (To improve your vibrations, there is an I AM Reading Room in Mt. Shasta City, 600 S. Mt. Shasta Blvd., 530/926-2525, open whenever it's open—typically daily 1:30–5:50 P.M.)

Don't despair if the Old Dudes fail to recruit you for the team. Someone or something else may want you. At **The Crystal Room,** "Mt. Shasta's Middle Earth" at 107 W. Castle St., Ste. B, 530/918-9108, www.crystalsmtshasta.com, the right crystal will choose *you.* Area bookstores also feature ample metaphysical guidance and supplies. For other information and options, poke into other shops around town and see the **Shasta Spirit** website, www.shastaspirit.com.

rides on the ski lift for hiking access, or partake in nature hikes and mountain bike tours. Increasingly popular is the park's ever-expanding calendar of events, including full-moon ski tours, summer mountain bike events, and the annual **State of Jefferson Microbrewery Festival** in August or early September. For more information, contact: Mount Shasta Board & Ski Park, 530/926-8610 (lodge), 530/926-8686 (snow and weather conditions), 530/926-8600 (business office), or 800/754-7427 (outside Shasta and Siskiyou Counties), www.skipark.com.

MT. SHASTA CITY

Perpetually in the mountain's shadow, this tiny town popped up in the 1850s and was first called Sisson after J.H. Sisson, John Muir's friend and guide (also the local postmaster and innkeeper). With the growth of tourism here in the 1920s came the more marketable moniker. The town's walkable shopping district boasts increasingly sophisticated shops and smart restaurants.

Taste the mountain's (and the town's) pure sweet water at the public water fountain downtown. Or visit the source, as in the headwaters of the Sacramento River. The mighty Sacramento begins officially at **Mt. Shasta City Park,** N. Mt. Shasta Blvd. and Nixon Rd., 530/926-2494—acres of lawn, paths, and picnic tables perfect for a rest stop. Just outside town is the **Mt. Shasta Fish Hatchery,** 1 N. Old Stage Rd., 530/926-2215, the oldest hatchery west of the Mississippi still in operation. Located here because of the pure water and the railroad (for fish transport), the century-old hatchery spawns new generations of rainbow and brown trout for planting as far afield as New Zealand. The facility is capable of producing millions of fish per year. On the grounds are a well-manicured park (with oaks, cedars, and 50 ponds for the small fry) and the **Sisson Museum,** 530/926-5508, depicting early Shasta mountaineering exploits and other aspects of local history. The museum includes a new major exhibit each year and is open daily, in summer 10 A.M.–4 P.M., in winter 1–4 P.M. (closed January and February).

Coming soon to Mt. Shasta—construction is scheduled to begin in 2004—is the **Volcanic Legacy Discovery Center,** to be located at the old Roseburg Mill site. The interpretive center will highlight the history, culture, ecology, geology, and recreational resources along the new Volcanic Legacy Scenic Byway (for information on the byway, see www.volcaniclegacybyway.org).

Still, no visit to Mt. Shasta is quite complete without spending time on the mountain. For the big picture, drive to treeline on the **Everitt Memorial Highway.** Mountain climbers get higher—ascending from various routes year-round—but the local ranger station can also recommend less challenging area "view" hiking or snowshoe routes. For more ideas, see Shasta Recreation above.

Camping

On Shasta, summertime camping is available at the 10-site Forest Service **McBride Springs Campground** ($6; 14-day limit) and smaller **Panther Meadows Campground** (free; three-night limit). Both are first-come, first-camped. The **Mt. Shasta City KOA,** 900 N. Mt. Shasta Blvd., 530/926-4029 or 800/562-3617, www.koa.com, has both trailer and tent sites; hot showers; a rec room; volleyball, basketball, and shuffleboard courts; laundry facilities; and a small pool. Basic sites are $24–29, cabins $40–55. Camping at **Lake Siskiyou Camp-Resort,** 4239 W.A. Barr Rd. (five miles south of town via Old Stage Rd.), 530/926-2618 or 888/926-2618, www.lakesis.com, both RV and tent camping, includes hot showers, a coin-operated laundry, and recreational diversions galore; $18–25. (Lakeside cabins are available, too.) In addition, more than 100 public campgrounds dot the Shasta-Trinity National Forest; most are open from May to mid-September. Particularly nice is camping at **Castle Lake** (primitive, free) about 10 miles west of town. For other suggestions, ask at the ranger station.

You'll find an undeveloped county campground at Lake Shastina—a locally popular spot for swimming, sailing, boating, water-skiing, and fishing. Or try the U.S. Forest Service **Shafter Campground** ($6) just down the road; for information, contact **Goosenest Ranger District** in Macdoel, 530/398-4391. On winter

Sundays in Macdoel proper are the Cal-Ore Chariot and Cutter Racing Association **chariot drag races** across the ice. Ask about it in town.

Motels and Resorts

Most motels are in the $50–100 range. At the popular **Swiss Holiday Lodge,** 2400 S. Mt. Shasta Blvd. (beyond downtown, near the junction of I-5 and Hwy. 89), 530/926-3446, facilities include a community kitchen, lounge with fireplace, heated pool, covered Jacuzzi, and one apartment with a kitchen and fireplace. Other choices include the **Evergreen Lodge,** 1312 S. Mt. Shasta Blvd., 530/926-2143; the **A-1 Choice Inn** nearby at 1340 S. Mt. Shasta Blvd., 530/926-4811; **Strawberry Court Motel,** 305 Old McCloud Rd., 530/926-4704, which is off the main drag and usually has rooms available; and **Mountain Air Lodge,** 1121 S. Mt. Shasta Blvd., 530/926-3411, which has a Jacuzzi and a free community kitchen.

The Best Western **The Tree House Inn,** 111 Morgan Way (next to I-5 at the Central Mt. Shasta exit), 530/926-3101 or 800/545-7164 for reservations, www.bestwesterncalifornia.com, offers Best Western amenities, here including an indoor heated pool, onsite restaurant (free breakfast), and in-room hair dryers and irons. Rooms $50–100 and $100–150. New and "uptown" is **Mt. Shasta Inn & Suites,** 710 S. Mt. Shasta Blvd., 530/918-9292, www.mtshastainn.com, with most rooms $100–150 (lower in the winter/spring low season).

The **Mount Shasta Resort,** 1000 Siskiyou Lake Blvd., 530/926-3030 or 800/958-3363 (530/926-3052 for golf information), www.mountshastaresort.com, has particular appeal for golfers, with its 6,100-yard course designed in 1993 by Sandy Tatum and Jim Summers. The resort also offers a pro shop, restaurant and lounge, outdoor dining in summer, tennis courts, a spa, lodge rooms, and one- and two-bedroom chalets, each with kitchen, fireplace, and deck. Most rooms are $100–150, chalets $150–250. Special events are another draw.

Bed-and-Breakfasts

Quite wonderful in town is the **Strawberry Valley Inn,** 1142 S. Mt. Shasta Blvd., 530/926-2052, fax 926-0842, www.strawberryvalleyinn.com, a onetime motor court transformed into a welcoming 15-room inn with plenty of privacy, attractive gardens, and oak trees. Wander into the lovely stone home that serves as the inn's lobby—the fireplace is particularly inviting in winter—and either partake of a generous buffet breakfast or load up a tray to take back to your room. Most rooms are $100–150, though in-season prices range to $250.

The **Mt. Shasta Ranch Bed and Breakfast,** 1008 W.A. Barr Rd., 530/926-3870, www.stayinshasta.com, is also something special—a classic in the Dutch Gambrel tradition. Some people would say it's a barn, albeit a barn with covered veranda and unobstructed views of Mt. Shasta. But the atmosphere here is actually like a 1920s lodge—tasteful, almost formal, from the 1,500-square-foot living room with original oak floors and stone fireplace to the huge upstairs suites ($100–150). Five rooms in the separate Carriage House ($50–100) share two bathrooms. The "cottage" is a completely equipped two-bedroom home with woodstove and electric heat ($100–150). Unusual for B&Bs these days, children are genuinely welcome.

For an exceptional overnight, consider a stay at the grand and historic **McCloud Hotel** on the other side of the mountain (see McCloud, below). North of Weed, in Gazelle, is inviting **Edson-Foulke Guest Ranch Bed and Breakfast,** 18705 Old Hwy. 99, 530/435-2627, www.efguestranch.com, a charming stone farmhouse also serving up spectacular views of Mt. Shasta (not to mention pet and horse accommodations). Both the Sunroom Suite and Guesthouse are $50–100. Train fanatics, head south to Castle Crags and the **Railroad Park Resort,** 100 Railroad Park Rd. (just off I-5), Dunsmuir, 530/235-4440 or 800/974-7245 (motel, main office), www.rrpark.com. In keeping with area history, this unique establishment is a modern motel composed almost entirely of refurbished railroad cars (there are also a few cabins), all $50–100. The good American-style dinner house and bar here, 530/235-4611, is a successful meshing of nine separate railroad cars. Campers can stay at the resort's RV park and tent campground, 530/235-0420, $18–25.

Eating in Mt. Shasta

A traditional post-Shasta-climb stop is **Willy's Bavarian Kitchen,** 107 Chestnut (in the flatiron-shaped lot where Chestnut and Mt. Shasta Blvd. split), 530/926-3636. Here you can sit out in the sun slurping a pint of good German beer with the local hip-oisie, and if you're hungry, get German and vegetarian food to go with it. **Lalo's,** 520 N. Mt. Shasta Blvd., 530/926-5123, serves decent Mexican food and in summer has outdoor dining. Very good and reasonable is **Michael's,** 313 N. Mt. Shasta Blvd., 530/926-5288, locally famous for its homemade pastas (including *pelemy,* or Russian ravioli), sauces, and soups. A big hit at lunch is Michael's "rancho burger," a half-pound slab of fresh hamburger cooked to order and served on french bread with good fries on the side.

Lily's, across the street from the Strawberry Valley Inn at 1013 S. Mt. Shasta Blvd., 530/926-3372, is fabulously popular for its ethnically spiced California cuisine at breakfast, lunch, and dinner. Mexican entrées are available at every meal, and the menu features abundant vegetarian choices. Morning fare includes unusual omelettes, *huevos rancheros, machaca,* a very good breakfast burrito, plus eggs Benedict (the eggs Arnold substitutes avocado for the ham, the eggs Benedict Arnold combines the two). Other breakfast fare: malted waffles, French batter pancakes, and Danish pancakes. At lunch, expect fascinating salads, the Quesadilla Pacifica (with several cheeses and shrimp), and sandwiches such as the exceptional eggplant hoagie. Dinner selections include fresh seafood (like scallops in Thai sauce), pastas (jalapeño pasta is a house specialty, served with various sauces), chicken Debra, roasted pork loin, and standards such as prime rib. Open daily. Full bar. For coffee and bakery goods, a **Has Beans Coffee & Tea Company** outlet is nearby in a striking stone storefront at 1011 S. Mt. Shasta Blvd., 530/926-3602.

Sophisticated as all get out and definitely Californian, everybody's favorite new place, the **Trinity Cafe** at 622 N. Mt. Shasta Blvd., 530/926-6200, offers a fresh, seasonally changing menu along with great microbrew and wine selections. In summer, dine out on the deck. Open for dinners Wed.–Sun., reservations advised.

The place for classical French is **Serge's Restaurant,** located a block east of Mt. Shasta Blvd. at 531 Chestnut, 530/926-1276. Serge's, which got its start at Stewart Mineral Springs, offers a seasonally changing menu accented with a few Thai, Cajun, and vegetarian dishes, and finished with wonderful house-made desserts. Closed Mon. and Tues.

Events and Information

The area events calendar is packed. Come in March for the annual **Coyote Classic Ski Race,** in late April for the **Dunsmuir River Festival & Fishing Season Opener,** in June for the huge **McCloud Flea Market** and **Dunsmuir Railroad Days,** in July for the **Siskiyou Art Council's Faire Devine.** Head to nearby McCloud in July or early August for the annual **Civil War Days** reenactment, in August for **McCloud Heritage Days.** Also in August, the **State of Jefferson Microbrewery Festival** pours forth at Mt. Shasta Board & Ski Park.

Very helpful for events and visitor information is the **Mt. Shasta Convention and Visitors Bureau** at the local chamber office, 300 Pine St. (at Lake), 530/926-4865 or 800/926-4865, www.mtshastachamber.com. Equally useful for county-wide information is the **Siskiyou County Visitors Bureau,** 530/926-3850 or 877/747-5496, www.visitsiskiyou.org.

A special treat in Mt. Shasta are the historic Forest Service buildings, included on the National Register of Historic Places. The brown and green wooden buildings of Shasta-Trinity National Forest's **Mt. Shasta Ranger District,** 204 W. Alma (a block and a half west of Mt. Shasta Blvd., across the railroad tracks), 530/926-4511, are the 1930s originals, built by unemployed carpenters and the Civilian Conservation Corps during the Great Depression. At the office stop for camping and climbing information, fire permits, forest maps ($6–7), the Mt. Shasta–Castle Crags Wilderness Map ($7), some topo maps, wilderness permits, trailhead parking and summit-climb passes (which can be self-issued after hours and at the trailheads), and friendly advice. A climber's guide to Mt. Shasta is usually available for $3. Open in summer, daily 8 A.M.–4:30 P.M.;

in winter, Mon.–Fri. 8 A.M.–4:30 P.M.; spring and fall hours may vary, but will at least be Mon.–Fri. 8 A.M.–4:30 P.M. Outside you'll find water to fill your bottles and a bulletin board with posted information. Alternatively, for Mt. Shasta information contact the **McCloud Ranger District** office in McCloud, 530/964-2184.

The **Sisson Fish Hatchery Museum** (see above), has a decent selection of books on the Mt. Shasta region. So does full-service **Village Books,** 320 N. Mt. Shasta Blvd., 530/926-1678, www.villagebooks-mtshasta.com, which also features a nice selection of books by local authors and an awesome quantity of metaphysical books. Downtown's **Golden Bough Books,** 219 N. Mt. Shasta Blvd., 530/926-3228, www.golden-boughbooks.com, is also the place to go for tales of Lemuria and general Shasta strangeness, as well as an eclectic selection of used books. Mt. Shasta has its own movie theater, **Coming Attractions** at the Mt. Shasta Shopping Center, 530/926-1116. Head north to **Weed,** www.weed-chamber.com, home of Siskiyou Community College, to go bowling. **Cedar Lanes** is downtown at 137 Main St., 530/938-3278.

NEAR MT. SHASTA CITY

The trouble with climbing Mt. Shasta is that you can't see it if you're on it. So hike up nearby **Mt. Eddy** (elev. 9,025 feet) and along adjacent stretches of the **Pacific Crest Trail** for majestic Mt. Shasta views. Remote is the **Grayrock Lakes** area (excellent primitive campsites and fair fishing for brook trout) about 11 miles west of town via a logging road paralleling the South Fork of the Sacramento River.

Lake Siskiyou is a reservoir in Mt. Shasta's morning shadows, an easy 4.5 miles southwest from Mt. Shasta City, with sandy swimming beaches, fishing, boating, and paddleboat and canoe rentals. Trout fishing along the **Sacramento River** is generally good from below Box Canyon Dam (Lake Siskiyou) south to Shasta Lake, with favorite spots for anglers at **Ney Springs Creek** and lush **Mossbrae Falls** north of Dunsmuir (also nice for picnicking). The fishing along this stretch of the river was once world-

class, and no doubt will be again—but the area has had some bad luck. No sooner had the fish populations started to recover from a major pesticide spill in July 1991, then floods scoured out the river in 1996 and '97. The upside of all this, local guides say, is that while there may not be as many fish in the river as there once were, the fish that *are* here are big, strong, and wily.

Castle Lake is tucked away behind Castle Crags and accessible only from the north, about eight miles out of Mt. Shasta City via Ream Avenue. The lake offers crystal water, swimming, fishing, picnicking, and a few campsites.

Stewart Springs and Vicinity

Scenic **Stewart Mineral Springs Therapeutic Mountain Retreat,** seven miles north of Weed, was founded in 1875 by the near-dead Henry Stewart, who was brought here by local Indians and healed by the waters. Facilities include a bathhouse with 13 individual mineral baths, three massage rooms (separate fee for massage), a sauna, sun deck, and gift shop. Fee for mineral baths is $20, shower included ($15 for guests), $10 for sauna, shower included. On most Saturday nights, you can join a ceremonial Karuk Indian purification sweat. (Call for details.)

Accommodations at the retreat include cabins and motel rooms ($50–100) as well as tepees ($24), RV and tent campsites ($15), and a three-level A-frame for large groups. For more information, contact: Stewart Mineral Springs Therapeutic Mountain Retreat, 530/938-2222, www.stewartmineralsprings.com. To get there from I-5 north of Weed, take the Edgewood Exit and head west four miles on Stewart Springs Road. Near Stewart Springs is the trail to the **Deadfall Lakes,** some of the prettiest on the Trinity Divide.

McCLOUD

Just north of Dunsmuir, head east on Hwy. 89 into McCloud country. The McCloud River is an excellent trout fishing stream, but only short stretches are open to the public (lots of lumbering, difficult access). The carnivorous Dolly Varden char, a relict species no doubt more at home during the Pleistocene, survived in California only here—until recently, when the local population was declared extinct.

Good fishing areas for Shasta rainbows include **Fowlers Camp, Lakin Lake, Big Springs,** and **McCloud Reservoir.** Fowlers Camp, a U.S. Forest Service campground about six miles east of town (paved sites), is a particularly nice place to set up the tent ($12). The upper, middle, and lower falls of the McCloud River are all spectacular; the picnic area at Lower Falls makes a good lunch stop. For more information about camping and area recreation, stop by the office of the **McCloud Ranger District,** 2019 Forest Rd., 530/964-2184.

Aside from fishing, historically McCloud was most famous for the 60,000-acre Wyntoon estate, a private retreat designed by architect Julia Morgan for mythic American media magnate William Randolph Hearst. The estate's buildings still stand after being charred in a 1992 fire, but the retreat is (and always has been) closed to the public. Otherwise, even today the town reflects its more humble milltown history, from the general store to the variations on camptown architecture. Get McCloud's story at the **Heritage Junction Museum** downtown on Main, 530/964-2604, open May–Oct. 11 A.M.–3 P.M. Mon.–Sat., and 1–3 P.M. Sunday. Stop by the massive **Mercantile Building** to sample the wares at the **McCloud General Store;** the place for a thick old-fashioned milkshake is the **McCloud Soda Shoppe and Café,** adjacent. Also poke into the **Milky Way Trading Company.**

For more information about the area, contact the **McCloud Chamber of Commerce,** 205 Quincy St., 530/964-3113, www.mccloud-chamber.com.

McCloud Reservoir

Ringed by pine trees and rocky shores, McCloud Reservoir is a fine place to linger awhile, with ever-present Mt. Shasta looming over your shoulder. The lake itself belongs to PG&E (which built the dam in 1965), but the surrounding land is owned by The Nature Conservancy and the Hearst Corporation (the family retreat, designed by architect Julia Morgan, is nearby at

the mouth of Mud Creek). The lake is about nine miles east of McCloud; take Squaw Valley Rd. south from town. Camping is available at the U.S. Forest Service **Ah-Di-Na Campground** ($8) and at unimproved campsites (with toilets) at **Star City Creek.** Historic Ah-Di-Na, adjacent to the Lower McCloud River, was once a private fishing retreat.

McCloud River Preserve

The private, nonprofit Nature Conservancy operates this preserve along seven miles of the McCloud River. Though the Conservancy's single mission is preserving species diversity, visitors are welcome to hike here without reservations (no camping) from sunrise to sunset any day of the week; a three-mile trail passes a good swimming hole and there's a one-mile self-guided nature trail. An autumn hike is a stroll into timelessness, the last colored leaves frosted by the first snows along the sleepy river. In winter, visitors have to ski in. By spring, the runoff-rejuvenated river is a rushing torrent again. Fishing is strictly controlled, all catch-and-release with artificial lures, single barbless hooks. Half of the daily 10 fishing "spots" may be reserved through the Conservancy's office in San Francisco, and the rest are first-come, first-cast.

To get to the preserve, from McCloud Reservoir turn right on the dirt road and continue for about eight miles (veering always to the right) until the road dead-ends at the preserve. For more information—and to reserve fishing—call 415/777-0487 and see www.tnccalifornia.org.

McCloud Railway Company Train Rides

The McCloud Railway Company, 530/964-2142 or 800/733-2141, www.shastasunset.com, offers the opportunity to relive the glory days of rail onboard the **Shasta Sunset Dinner Train,** a white linen–and–fine china ride through the area's magnificent mountain scenery. The immaculately restored vintage rail cars feature enough deep mahogany and polished brass to satisfy even the most earnest woulda-been rail barons; modern comforts have been added. Whippersnappers with no appreciation for history will still enjoy the constant clickety-clack of the cars over the track, the scrumptious grub, and the million-dollar views. (Dress as if you were dining with the Hearsts, if you'd like, but most folks are reasonably casual.) Dinner trains leave from the McCloud station on Main St. year-round. The fare is $80 per person (plus tax and tip). Wine tasting and mystery trains ($90) and other special-event trains are also offered; see the website for current details.

For a less ostentatious train tour of Mt. Shasta, opt instead to jostle with the masses on a diesel locomotive day trip for just $12 adults, $8 children (under age 12); the occasional steam-locomotive excursion is slightly higher. The ride lasts a little over an hour and the views are just as priceless.

Staying in McCloud

The painstaking restoration of the old 1915 **McCloud Hotel** has created quite a buzz in the neighborhood. The three-story restored hostelry, now an exceptional bed-and-breakfast listed on the National Register of Historic Places, offers 14 "standard" guest rooms—all exquisitely decorated in 1930s style to achieve an appropriately woodsy English estate ambience—and four Jacuzzi-equipped suites, all with private bath. After the complimentary full breakfast in the lobby, get out and enjoy the mountain scenery— the *Shasta Sunset* departs from the small public park across the street—or relax and read a book by the fireplace in the beautiful lobby. Picnicking tours available. Rooms are $100–150 and $150–250 in season, April–Sept., as low as $84 at other times; ask about specials and packages. For more information and to make reservations, contact: McCloud Hotel, 530/964-2822 or 800/964-2823, www.mchotel.com.

For something more intimate, the five-room **McCloud River Inn Bed and Breakfast,** 325 Lawndale Ct., 530/964-2130 or 800/261-7831, www.riverinn.com, is at home in a remodeled 1900s Victorian office building. All rooms are furnished with antiques and have private baths. Most rooms are $100–150 in season; ask about specials. A luxurious suite, with Jacuzzi tub for two, is pricier.

Something of an alternative B&B, the **Stoney Brook Inn,** 309 W. Colombero, 530/964-2300 or 800/369-6118, www.stoneybrookinn.com, is a "bed with breakfast" retreat and conference center with some fully equipped kitchen suites, therapeutic massage (by appointment), hot tub, and sauna. All rooms and suites are $50–100; some rooms share a bath. Full non-meat breakfast, outdoor hot tub, Finnish sauna. Also here: the Kiva Retreat Center. For groups, catering service is available.

CASTLE CRAGS AND DUNSMUIR

A foreboding granite formation created by volcanic forces some 170-225 million years ago, Castle Crags towers over I-5 40 miles north of Redding. Marking the southeastern edge of the Klamath Mountains, the Crags offer challenging rock climbing, easy and difficult hikes, good camping (but within earshot of the freeway), and picnicking. The first settler here was "Mountain Joe" Doblondy, one of Frémont's guides, who had troubles with angry gold miners (the rush here was short-lived) and native peoples disturbed by the encroaching chaos of civilization. Joaquin Miller chronicled several versions of the infamous 1855 Indian slaughter here.

Castle Crags State Park

Castle Crags is 6,000 acres of dogwoods, oaks, cedars, pines, firs, and rare Brewer's spruce. In summer, tiger lilies, orchids, azaleas, and columbine brighten the granite trailsides. Mountain lions and bobcats prowl the park but are rarely seen. The **Pacific Crest Trail** swings through the park, making this a good spot for trekkers to arrange a supply drop and pick up mail.

The impressive silver-gray crags snaggle upward at an elevation of 6,000 feet. Rock climbing here is only for the experienced. The strenuous **Crags/Indian Springs Trail** to Castle Dome (which resembles Yosemite's Half Dome) is worthwhile for hikers, especially with the side trip to the springs. Easier is the one-mile **Root Creek Trail,** which offers views of the crags and picnicking at Root Creek (soak your feet). High-country hikers, don't wander off the trail: cliffs have sudden 2,000-foot drop-offs and no warn-

Castle Crags State Park

ROBERT HOLMES/CALTOUR

NORTHERN MOUNTAINS

ing signs. The pleasant, one-mile **Indian Creek Nature Trail** loops over the creek and passes old mining paraphernalia. Near Castle Crags is the **Seven Lakes Basin** area of the Trinity Divide, with lakes from two to 13.5 acres in size (good trout fishing). To get there, take the Castella exit from I-5 (at Castle Crags State Park), follow Whalen Station Rd. 10 miles to the trailhead, then hike in 3.5 miles.

Park headquarters is at the park's entrance in Castella (follow the signs from I-5), 20022 Castle Creek Rd., 530/235-2684. The Castle Crags state campground offers attractive campsites, including some large enough for 21-foot trailers. Facilities include tables, barbecue grills, food lockers, hot showers, and flush toilets; reserve in summer through ReserveAmerica, 800/444-7275, www.reserveamerica.com. In the off-season, campsites are first-come, first-camped. Trailside camping is permitted in surrounding Shasta-Trinity National Forest (campfire permit required), but not in the park. Camping fees are $11–14 for standard campsites (reservable); pack-in sites and "bikers and hikers" sites are also available. The park day-use fee, for hikers and

picnickers (the picnic area is on the other side of the Sacramento River, and the freeway) is $4.

Dunsmuir

Six miles to the north, Dunsmuir is a charming mountain town and good supply stop. Waterfalls are the main local attractions, and include **Mossbrae Falls** and **Hedge Creek Falls.** The 10-acre botanical garden in **Dunsmuir City Park,** complete with butterfly and hummingbird gardens, is a delight. Just wandering town around can be a surprise, from **Dunsmuir Hardware** and the **Ted Fay Fly Shop** on Dunsmuir Ave. to stylish **Brown Trout** gallery on Sacramento Ave. and the **Gandy Dancer Café** espresso parlor. The **California Theater** shows first-run flicks as well as art and classic films.

But the most powerful presence in Dunsmuir is the Sacramento River, which has made a spectacular recovery following the much-publicized 1991 toxic spill. River rafting or fly-fishing are good ways to introduce yourself, but so is a stop at the **Upper Sacramento River Exchange Center,** a hands-on museum and watershed information/education center located at 5819 Sacramento Ave., 530/235-2012—winner of the 1998 Governor's Environmental and Economic Leadership Award.

Dunsmuir also offers some great restaurants, including the tiny dinner-only **Café Maddalena,** 5801 Sacramento Ave. (a block west of Dunsmuir Ave.), 530/235-2725. Open only Thurs.–Sun. nights from April to mid-December, Café Maddalena serves fresh Southern Italian fare with the Sardinian accent of proprietor Maddalena Sera. The **Cornerstone Bakery Café,** 5759 Dunsmuir Ave., 530/235-4677, is good for breakfast or lunch. A fairly new local light is **Senthong's Blue Sky** Thai, Laotian, and Vietnamese restaurant at 5853 Dunsmuir Ave., 530/235-4770, kin to famed Senthong's of Etna (now closed). Sengthong's is open for dinner Tues.–Sun. 5–8 P.M. (until 8:30 on weekend nights).

In addition to Dunsmuir's **Railroad Park Resort** (see Mt. Shasta City listings), local accommodations options include the four stone cottages at the **Castlestone Cottage Inn** in Castella, 530/235-0012, with rates $50–100. Another good choice is **Cedar Lodge Motel,**

4201 Dunsmuir Ave. in Dunsmuir, 530/235-4331, with rooms $50–100.

For area information, contact the **Dunsmuir Chamber of Commerce and Visitors Center**, 4118 Pine St., 800/386-7684, www.dunsmuir .com. For guided area white-water rafting, see the local firms listed above under Shasta Recreation. Rather than drive, you can get here on Amtrak; the railyard is a block from downtown.

SHASTA DAM

The Sacramento River is one of the most channelized, diverted, and dammed rivers in the world, and Shasta Dam is its ultimate diversion. The mainstay of the federally funded Central Valley Project (CVP), Shasta Dam was constructed between 1938 and 1945. Flooding the canyons and holding back the waters of the Sacramento, Pit, and McCloud Rivers in addition to Squaw Creek, Shasta Dam is the second-largest concrete dam in the country. Enough concrete to build a three-foot-wide sidewalk around the world created this backwater behemoth, which is 602 feet high, 3,460 feet long, and 883 feet across at its base. The cost of construction: $182 million (in World War II–era dollars), 14 workers' lives, and the taming of the northstate's most impressive river. Public discussion of a possible expansion of Shasta Dam—increasing its height in an effort to store more water and quench the state's endless thirst—began in 1997.

Seeing and Doing Shasta Dam

Security is substantial following the terrorist attacks on Sept. 11. It's no longer possible to walk or drive across the top of the dam for a close-up view of this technological tour de force, or the lake it has created. But for some idea of the dam's size: The **Pit River Bridge** spanning Shasta Lake is the world's tallest double-decker, a north-south aerial artery carrying both I-5 and Southern Pacific Railroad's main line. To the east is the lake, an endless five-armed expanse of blue-green water, a sight often accompanied by the roar of water crashing down the spillway. From here and from the vista point, you can see "the three Shastas" at once: dam, lake, and mountain. **Tours of**

Shasta Dam are available year-round, on the hour from 9 A.M.–4 P.M. in summer and at 10 A.M., noon, and 2 P.M. in winter, though it's not always possible to get a guided tour of the dam itself; guided walks from the visitor center cover much of the same information, however, just not as "up close." The **visitor center** tells at least some of the story, with exhibits and a short film. It's open 7:30 A.M.–4 P.M. daily Apr.–Oct. (closed weekends in winter).

For more information about Shasta Dam, contact the **U.S. Bureau of Reclamation** Northern California Area Office, 16349 Shasta Dam Blvd in Shasta Lake, 530/275-4463 or 530/275-1554. To reach the dam, from I-5 take the Shasta Dam Blvd. exit (about 10 miles north of Redding).

SHASTA LAKE

When full, super-size Shasta Lake has around 370 miles of shoreline—one-third more than San Francisco Bay—and a surface area of 30,000 acres. Despite its gigantic girth, Shasta is not always the best place for those seeking complete solitude; two million or so people come here each year to camp, picnic, fish, swim, sail, and water-ski. And those in search of natural beauty might be disappointed in drought years or at other times when the lake's water level is down—the ugly swath of bare-naked red dirt above the water line looks like a giant-sized bathtub ring. But when the lake is full, Shasta is dazzling.

By virtue of its sheer size, Shasta Lake is water-skiing heaven. Houseboating is particularly popular here, too; with so much lake (and so many coves and inlets to tie up in), houseboaters either party Shasta-style or drift off alone for some peace and quiet. Shasta's rental houseboat fleet is probably the state's finest, some units featuring every amenity imaginable. Warm-water fishing is another big draw (spring is best), with anglers going primarily after small and largemouth bass, but also casting for crappie, and brown and rainbow trout.

All this recreational opportunity has had its price, however, including the flooding of several small towns upstream from the dam site. The old copper mining town of Kennett is gone for good, along with an Indian burial site and miles of salmon spawning grounds—a loss requiring the construction of special fish hatcheries below the dam.

Lake Shasta Caverns

If you've got the time, tour these ancient caves. Only the out-and-out adventurous had access to the caverns until 1964, when a tunnel was driven into the mountain below the original entrance. Now, even armchair adventurers visit these beautiful wonders where California's Coast and Cascade Ranges, Sierra Nevada, and Klamath Mountains come together. The 60-foot-wide, 20-foot-tall drapolite "draperies" of the Cathedral Room were formed from calcium carbonate crystals in a stalactite waterfall. Elsewhere, stalagmites reach up from the cave floor and, fusing with stalactites, create multicolored fluted columns. In the **Spaghetti Patch**, gravity-defying masses of straw-thin helictites seem to swirl and swarm. Though the tour route itself is well lighted, with concrete steps and guardrails, fit purists can still go spelunking through the dank darkness and primal ooze (by reservation only).

Two-hour tours of Lake Shasta Caverns start at **O'Brien** across the lake and cost $18 for adults, $9 for children 4–12 (under age 3 free). Spelunking tours are four hours long. Either way, it's a 15-minute ferry trip by catamaran, then a thrilling bus ride up an 800-foot hill to the lower cave entrance. Bring a sweater or sweatshirt even in summer: the temperature inside is a constant cool 58° F. Open year-round, with tours offered 9 A.M.–4 P.M. every half-hour in summer; hourly 9 A.M.–3 P.M. April, May, and Sept.; and Oct.–March at 10 A.M., noon, and 2 P.M. Special school, group, and spelunking tours are available by advance reservation only. For more information, contact: Lake Shasta Caverns, 20359 Shasta Caverns Rd. in O'Brien, 530/238-2341 or 800/795-2283, www.lakeshastacaverns.com.

Hiking

Pick up a current Shasta Lake Trails Guide at the visitor center (see below). Most trails around and near Shasta Lake provide fishing access, including **Sugarloaf Creek Trail** from the Sugarloaf Creek crossing on Lakeshore Dr. (Lakehead) and, in the Packers Bay area, **Waters Gulch Trail,** which offers a view of the lake's Sacramento arm. The lake's most developed is **Clikapudi Trail,** which begins at the end of Bear Mountain Road. Interpretive trails include the half-mile **Hirz Bay Trail,** which explores the territory of the long-gone McCloud River Wintu (starts at the Hirz Bay Amphitheater), and the slightly longer **Samwel Cave Trail** from Point McCloud Campground (boat access only), which leads to the cave and explains its relationship with both the Wintu and regional prehistoric animals. Ask about Samwel Cave at the Shasta Lake Visitor Center.

Practicalities

Shasta Lake has five recreation areas connected to its arms: **Jones Valley** (near the Pit and Squaw arms), **Gilman Rd.** (upper McCloud River arm), **O'Brien** (lower McCloud River arm), **Salt Creek** (Salt Creek inlet off the Sacramento arm), and **Lakehead** (upper Sacramento River arm). Dozens of public campgrounds are scattered throughout, including reservable developed campgrounds (running water, some with flush toilets and showers), $26–26, to more primitive shoreline and boat-in sites. Group camps, $65–90, are available only by reservation. Popular at Shasta are the primitive boat-in campgrounds as well as walk-in campsites (free-$8). Campgrounds along Gilman Rd. to the north and at backcountry sites near the Squaw and Pit arms near Jones Valley on the southeast are quietest. These areas have more campsites (and more bears too—keep food well out of reach) and are popular with fishing enthusiasts. In addition to public camping, most resorts offer tent and RV campsites with amenities like hot showers.

For information on all U.S. Forest Service campgrounds at Shasta Lake, call the **Shasta Recreation Company** at 530/238-2824; for reservations, call 877/444-6777. Only group campgrounds are reservable, the rest are first-come, first-camped.

Jones Valley and Lakehead are particularly popular with water-skiers. **Jones Valley Resort,** 22300 Jones Valley Marina Dr., 530/275-7950 or 800/223-7950, www.houseboats.com, offers the easiest access from the lake's south side, along with a well-run marina and spanking new houseboats.

Pleasant motel rooms are available at tiny **Fawndale Lodge & RV Resort,** just south of the lake at 15215 Fawndale Rd., 530/275-8000, $50–100.

O'Brien is the major marina-resort center, the hub of hubbub. Above the fray is the **O'Brien Mountain Inn** bed-and-breakfast, 530/238-8026 or 888/799-8026, www.obrienmtn.com, its music-themed rooms—Folk, World Beat, Classical, Jazz—all serene and appealing. Great full breakfast. Two rooms are $100–150; others (including suites and the very private "tree house") are $150–250.

Information

The helpful **Shasta Lake Visitor Information Center** and ranger station is about eight miles north of Redding and just south of the lake (off I-5) at 14250 Holiday Rd. in Mountain Gate, 530/275-1589, open daily in summer 8 A.M.–5 P.M. For other information about Shasta Lake and vicinity, from restaurants and accommodations to houseboat rentals, also contact the excellent **California Welcome Center** and Shasta-Cascade Wonderland Association, 1699 Hwy. 273 (in the Anderson Prime Outlets mall, I-5 at Deschutes Rd.), 530/365-1180 or 800/474-2782, www.shastacascade.org, or the **Redding Convention and Visitors Bureau,** 777 Auditorium Dr. (off Hwy. 299) in Redding, 530/225-4100 or 800/874-7562, www.visitredding.org.

Redding and Vicinity

A boomtown that never busted, this is The City of the northern mountains, with a total metropolitan-area population of 165,000—and counting, in recent years, as new housing developments boom. Redding perches just beyond the northern edge of the Sacramento Valley on the banks of the Sacramento River, which is joined here by 14 tributaries. Early explorer John C. Frémont described the Redding area as "fertile bottom lands watered by many small streams." Still watered by streams, the fertile bottomlands have become housing subdivisions and malls. Intersected by I-5 and Highways 44 and 299, well served by bus and even Amtrak, Redding is the northern getaway gateway. The Shasta County seat was established here in 1888, one year after the torching of Chinatown City and the forced exodus of its residents. Evidence of the once prominent Chinese population is still preserved in nearby Old Shasta, however.

Though it's got its share, Redding still isn't widely known for cultural attractions—with the possible exception of community events such **Redding Rodeo Week** in May and the **Shasta Dixieland Jazz Festival** in September—and it's easy to understand why. The breathtaking landscape surrounding the town tends to draw people away, into nearby mountains and beyond. Entering or leaving the wilderness, stop here for supplies and almost-urban sustenance.

How Reading Became Redding

Major Pierson Barton Reading, paymaster for Frémont's California Batallion, was Shasta County's first white settler. His home, the county seat when Shasta became one of California's original 27 counties in 1850, was built on the site of an old native village, part of Reading's 26,633-acre Mexican land grant. In 1872, the arrival of the first Central Pacific Railroad line signaled the end for the booming town of Shasta a few miles west but the beginning for Redding. The new town became a flourishing trade center, outfitting ranchers, miners, timber companies, and even U.S. Army troops during the Modoc Wars. But Reading was somehow christened "Redding," after a land agent for the Central Pacific Railroad. Though state legislation changed Redding back to "Reading" in 1874, the railroad prevailed again in 1880, making it Redding once and for all.

SEEING AND DOING GREATER REDDING

Turtle Bay Exploration Park

This multimillion-dollar museum and outdoor education complex along the Sacramento River west of I-5 (and just east of the Redding Convention Center), 530/243-8850 or 800/887-8532, www.turtlebay.org, is an impressive work in progress, and will eventually grow to some 300 acres in size—and perhaps into one of the state's finest museums. New in 2002 was the marvelous, and marvelously "green," 35,000-square-foot **Turtle Bay Museum,** emphasizing the area's art, history, and natural science. Once past the inviting concrete turtles outside the park's visitor center, the world of Redding and vicinity (past and present) opens wide its doors. At the museum itself, reached after a long, pleasing stroll through the oak-woodland wetlands as experienced from an elevated boardwalk, visitors are greeted by a striking leafless oak tree, its roots visible below the surface of a thick glass "pond." Adjacent is a Wintu bark house; elsewhere is an impressive basketry collection. Natural history exhibits begin with a walk-through replica of a Shasta Caverns–like limestone cave, and a 22,000-gallon open-air viewing tank, a fish-eye Sacramento River slice of life. Redding's Merle Haggard gets some extra radio play in the 1957 Chevy truck; visitors can also ride a "Zap bike," and find out about the 1816 solar-powered Stirling engine. There's a great little café, too—the **Glass Café,** serving fresh, wholesesome fare and indoor/outdoor views of the spectacular, harp-shaped, $19.7 million **Sundial Bridge** spanning the Sacramento River. Designed by Spanish architect Santiago Calatrava, the Sundial will connect the museum complex with the 220-acre **McConnell Arboretum at Turtle Bay** and the hiking trails, botanical gardens, native bird center, and otter ponds that will one day complete the park, on the other side of the river. At last report the Sundial pedestrian and bike bridge was scheduled for completion in 2004, but there have been delays before; call for current details.

Turtle Bay also includes **Paul Bunyan's Forest Camp,** a replica of a logging camp and interactive children's center complete with a model of Mt. Shasta and the Sacramento River. The seasonal **Butterfly House** at the Forest Camp, cooled with misters, features 1,000 butterflies of some 25 native North American species.

Admission to Turtle Bay is $11 adults, $9 seniors (over 65), and $6 children 4–11 (3 and under free). In summer the park is open daily, 9 A.M.–6 P.M.; from October through May,, Tues.–Sun. 10 A.M.–5 P.M. The arboretum (enter from N. Market St.) is open daily, dawn to dusk. To get here, take Hwy. 299 west off I-5 and exit at Auditorium Dr.; turn right on Auditorium.

Other Attractions

The great outdoors is attractive even *in* Redding, so take a hike. The **Sacramento River Trail,** designed for pedestrian and bike traffic, starts at a parking lot on Court St., slips across the unique concrete stress-ribbon pedestrian footbridge at Keswick Dam, continues under the Deschutes and Lake Redding Bridges, then rolls on to Caldwell Park; it links into the McConnell Arboretum Perimeter Trail (at last report, still blocked construction of the Sundial Bridge; inquire locally) before ending at Hilltop Drive. The **Sacramento River Rail Trail** begins near the town of Keswick at Iron Mountain Rd. and ends near the base of Shasta Dam. In 2002 the two trails, which eventually will connect, were designated as a National Recreation Trail by the National Park Service. For route details, stop by the visitor bureau.

Often worth a stop, depending on what's "playing," is the Shasta County Office of Education's **Schreder Planetarium & Science Learning Center,** 1644 Magnolia St., 530/225-0295, www.schrederplanetarium.com, which offers changing public shows such as **The Cowboy Astronomer** narrated by humorist Baxter Black.

Headquarters for the **Shasta County Arts Council** is the **Old City Hall Arts Center** and art gallery, 1313 Market St., 530/241-7320, www.shastaartscouncil.org. Gallery hours are Tues.–Fri. 9 A.M.–5 P.M. and (during exhibitions) Sat. 11 A.M.–3 P.M. Coming soon: the unveiling of the 1935 art-deco **Cascade Theatre** at 1731 Market St., 530/243-8787, www.cascadetheatre.org, now being restored by Jefferson Public Radio, www.jeff.net, as a new performing arts venue. (Dig that dazzling neon!) Stay tuned. To take a self-guided tour of other notable local architecture, pick up a copy of Redding's *Historic Architecture* brochure at the visitor bureau.

Of course you can always shop. Mainstream

shop ops include the **Mt. Shasta Mall** just off I-5 at Hilltop Dr., 530/223-3575, www.mtshastamall.com where you'll find Macy's, Gottschalks, JCPenney, and more. There are some genuinely unique "local" shops around, too, such as **Bernie's Guitar,** 3086 Bechelli Ln., 530/223-2040, which also offers folk and bluegrass acts on its small stage—shows such as John Reischman and The Jaybirds, the marvelous mandolinist and acclaimed bluegrass band. For current info, contact the **Oaksong Society for the Preservation of Way Cool Music,** 530/472-3065, www.oaksongs.com. *Way* cool.

Shasta State Historic Park

About three miles west of Redding is the town of Shasta, in its heyday the leading gold mining center of the northstate and "Queen City of the Northern Mines." Originally known as Reading Springs (named for Redding's Reading, who found gold here in 1848), Shasta in the early 1850s was a lively little city by all accounts, with up to 100 freight wagons, 2,000 pack mules, and countless drunken miners in the streets on any day of the week. Old Shasta became an overnight ghost town when area mines played out and it

was bypassed by both stage and rail routes, but it was remembered again in 1950 with its designation as a state historic monument.

The **Old Courthouse of Shasta** has been beautifully restored and is now a fine museum. Particularly impressive is the California art collection. Downstairs is the jail, with representative Shasta lawbreakers. Early California writer Joaquin Miller, who'd been living among Indians noted for horse theft and was considered guilty himself, had the good fortune to escape from the original log jail. (Miller "smoked three cigars at once and bit the ankles of English debutantes" while on tour of London's literary salons, according to *Benet's Reader's Encyclopedia*.) Out back, to remind visitors to behave themselves, is a reconstructed double gallows, complete with gallows poetry. Farther back behind the public restrooms in the park area is a **Pioneer Barn,** reassembled here to display old farm implements and technologies. The brick **Masonic Hall** just down the highway (Main St.) from the museum is the state's oldest, built in 1853 and still in use; Peter Lassen brought the charter here from Missouri by ox train.

The **Litsch General Store,** another brick

Shasta State Historic Park

© ROBERT HOLMES/CALTOUR

building across the highway, has also been restored; inside is a cornucopia of 19th-century essentials. Explore Shasta's iron-doored crumbling brick ruins along the highway here, or between the old Trinity and Boell Alleys, via the short **Ruins Trail.** The **Blumb Bakery** has also been restored. The park and its two museums are open Wed.–Sun. 10 A.M.–5 P.M., though visitors can still wander the grounds at other times; admission to the museum is $2 adults (17 and older), children free. Come to town in May for the **Shasta Arts and Crafts Faire** and **Oldtime Fiddlers' Jamboree.** In December, Shasta hosts an old-fashioned **Christmas Celebration.** For more information, contact: Shasta State Historic Park, 530/243-8194 or 530/244-1848.

Whiskeytown National Recreation Area

Miners on the trail to Oregon settled the original Whiskeytown near Whiskey Creek, so christened when a mule fell off a cliff and spilled its precious cargo. That town is now underwater, but its spirit lives on in the brick store north of Hwy. 299 in the new Whiskeytown. The **Whiskeytown Dam,** connecting the waters of the Trinity River with the Sacramento, is another link in the Central Valley Water Project's chain of reservoirs. John F. Kennedy dedicated the dam in 1963. A monument (turn at the information center) marks the spot with a tape recording of his speech. A little farther down the road are the **Whiskeytown Cemetery** and old **Mount Shasta Mine** (an easy hike). On the northwest end of the lake is the **Judge Francis Carr Powerhouse** (good fishing, picnic area). Rangers occasionally lead tours or sponsor special events at the **Tower House Historic District,** on Hwy. 299 eight miles east of the visitor center, including **Camden House** and the **El Dorado Mine.**

Whiskeytown Lake is pretty but packed in summer, subject to water levels. Recreation is the big attraction: boating, water-skiing, swimming, scuba diving, horseback riding, hiking, gold panning, fishing, and deer and duck hunting in season.

Whiskeytown's day-use fee is $5. Camp in backcountry areas ($10 per night, including park day-use fee; get required wilderness permits at the information center) or at **Oak Bottom Campground,** 14 miles west of Redding on Hwy. 299, which has abundant campsites (no hookups, and generally occupied by more tents than RVs) and hot showers ($14–18). Sites at Oak Bottom are reservable; call 800/365-2267. **Oak Bottom Marina,** 530/359-2269, rents boats and has a small store with incidentals, but stock up on supplies in Redding.

For more information, contact: Whiskeytown National Recreation Area, 14412 Kennedy Memorial Dr., 530/246-1225 (visitor information) or 530/242-3400 (park headquarters), www.nps.gov/whis; the lake's visitor center is open 9 A.M.–6 P.M. in summer, 10 A.M.–4 P.M. otherwise.

French Gulch

A short jog north from Whiskeytown Lake is the sleepy gold-rush town of French Gulch, named for the French Canadian miners who staked their claim here in 1849. Located on the California Oregon Trail and smack dab in the middle of the most productive far northern goldfields, French Camp once boasted four hotels, two mercantiles, a post office, and countless blacksmithies and livery stables. Starring attraction on Main Street these days is the 1885 **French Gulch Hotel,** 530/359-2112, originally known as the Feeney Hotel, now listed on the National Register of Historic Places. A comfortable and friendly bed-and-breakfast Mar.–Dec.—most rooms are in the $50–100 range (some lower), which includes full breakfast for two—the French Gulch Hotel also serves hearty dinners on Thursday, Friday, and Saturday nights, brunch on Sunday. Call for reservations. To get here, take the French Gulch exit (north) from Hwy. 299, about one mile west of Whiskeytown Lake.

Shingletown and the Wild Horse Sanctuary

Western culture fans, come rendezvous with mustangs. At this preserve near Manton (southeast of Redding, northeast of Red Bluff), get up close and personal with the wildest of free-ranging horses. Dianne and Jim Clapp started adopting "unadoptable" mustangs more than a decade ago. At the time, their effort was the only private project in America dedicated to protecting wild horses from domestication or destruction. Today, the herds here number around 150 horses, as well as dozens of wild burros. The sanctuary opens to the public on Wednesday and Saturday; visitors are welcome to hike the horse trails. Most exciting are guided horseback trips and two- or three-day overnight rides, complete with hearty campfire fare and a sleeping-bag stay in rustic kerosene-lit cabins. Fall trail rides in Modoc National Forest and a roundup and cattle drive at the Carey Ranch are also offered. Mustang lovers: you can even "adopt" a wild horse, through regular financial contributions. For more information, contact: Wild Horse Sanctuary, 530/222-5728 (recording) or 530/335-2241, www.wildhorsesanctuary.org. The sanctuary office is open Tuesday and Wednesday 10 A.M.–4 P.M.

Shingletown also offers a couple of stores and, for sit-down meals, the **Big Wheels Loggers Lounge & Cookhouse,** 32776 Hwy. 44, 530/474-3131. Open daily 7 A.M.–8 or 9 P.M., bar open until 2 A.M. If roughin' it in and around Lassen National Park has left you (or will soon leave you) a tad rough around the edges, the perfect place to ease the transition back into polite society is the hilltop **Weston House** bed-and-breakfast, 530/474-3738, www.westonhouse.com, which offers six rooms and suites (one with a private entrance); most have private bathrooms, some feature wood stoves and balconies. Swimming pool, fruit trees, vineyard, gardens—and a great view from the pool. Rates are at the low end of $150–250.

STAYING IN REDDING

Under $50–100

To camp in town, head to **Marina RV Park,** 2615 Park Marina Dr., 530/241-4396, a Good Sam park right on the Sacramento River. Sites have full hookups, and amenities include hot showers, plenty of shade, boat ramps, and a swimming pool. **Premier RV Resorts** is just off Lake Blvd. East at 280 N. Boulder Dr., 530/246-0101, and in the same area is **Redding RV Park,** 11075 Campers Ct., 530/241-0707. **Fawndale Lodge RV Resort** about a mile south of Shasta Lake, 15215 Fawndale Rd., 530/275-8000, is another best bet. Public campgrounds are available at surrounding parks and national forests; see above and below.

Most motels in Redding are clustered along Hwy. 299 or Hilltop Dr., but some cheaper places are available south of town on Market St. (Hwy. 273). Redding has three **Motel 6** locations to choose from. The original is at 1640 Hilltop Dr. (Hwy. 44 exit from I-5), 530/221-1800; another is north of town off I-5 at 1250 Twin View Blvd. (take exit of the same name), 530/246-4470; and the last is to the south at 2385 Bechelli Lane (take the Cypress Ave. exit west to Bechelli), 530/221-0562. To make reservations at any Motel 6, call 800/466-8356 or see www.motel6.com.

Redding's **Super 8 Motel** is at 5175 Churn Creek Rd. (at I-5), 530/221-8881, with rates $50–100. Other options on Hilltop Dr. in the same price range include **Best Western Hospitality House,** 532 N. Market St., 530/241-6464 or 800/700-3019; **Best Western Ponderosa Inn,** 2220 Pine St., 530/241-6300; and **Comfort Inn,** 2059 Hilltop Dr., 530/221-6530.

Seven miles north of Redding proper in Shasta Lake is the **Shasta Dam Motel,** 1529 Cascade Blvd. (take the Shasta Dam-Central Valley exit from I-5), 530/275-1065, with a/c, TV, and plenty of shade.

$100–150

Redding, a northstate convention center, also has a number of nice, higher-priced motels, most of these along Hilltop Dr. and including the **Red Lion Hotel,** 1830 Hilltop Dr., 530/221-8700 or 800/733-5466, www.redlion.com; **Best Western Hilltop Inn,** 2300 Hilltop Dr., 530/221-6100 or 800/336-4880 (full breakfast included); **Grand Manor Inn,** 850 Mistletoe Lane (just off Hilltop), 530/221-4472 or 800/626-1900, www.meyercrest.com; **La Quinta Inn,** 2180 Hilltop Dr., 530/221-8200 or 800/531-5900, www.lq.com; and **Oxford Suites,** 1967 Hilltop Dr., 530/221-0100 or 800/762-0133, www.oxfordsuites.com.

Bed-and-Breakfasts

Redding's gabled, hilltop **Tiffany House Bed & Breakfast Inn,** 1510 Barbara Rd., 530/244-3225, is the town's first showplace inn, with enticing views of the area, spacious living areas and deck, and four appealing rooms complete with namesake Tiffany-style lamps and private baths. One of the rooms is a private cottage with its own hot tub. Other amenities include a swimming pool, deck, and full gourmet breakfast. Most rooms are $100–150.

For something fantastically escapist and serene, **Brigadoon Castle,** 9036 Zogg Mine Rd. in Igo, 530/396-2785 or 888/343-2836, www.brigadooncastle.com, is about 15 miles southwest from Redding off Placer Rd. (County Rd. A16) and holds down the fort on 86 acres of forest and meadow. The two guest rooms and Feona's Suite inside the ivy-draped castle are all unique, while the separate turret-like Cottage guesthouse sits streamside and features a fireplace, four-poster bed (with a view), and private hot tub. Midweek, rates include breakfast; on weekends, rates include breakfast and dinner. Rooms are in the $150–250 range (closer to the high end); the suite and cottage are $250 and Up.

Highly recommended, for a comfortable stay off the well-trampled tourist track, is the **Weston House** in Shingletown; for information, see above.

EATING IN REDDING

Casual

Get good fresh seafood at way cool **Buz's Crab Seafood Restaurant, Market & Deli,** 2159 East St., 530/243-2120, "Redding's own Fisherman's Wharf"—a fabulous fish market and popular cheap eatery where you can get everything from snapper and Dungeness crab (in season) with Buz's famous sourdough bread to fish and chips to charbroiled swordfish, seafood burritos, wraps, and pockets. And much more. Beefeaters, don't despair: Redding has its fair share of burger joints, including three different **Bartels Giant Burgers**—at 75 E. Lake Blvd., 2640 Bechelli Ln., and 2475 Eureka Way—and an **In-N-Out Burger,** 1275 Dana Dr. at the Mt. Shasta Mall.

Started as a home-based wholesale cheesecake enterprise, **Cheesecakes Unlimited & Cafe,** 1344 Market St. (just north of the Downtown Redding Mall), 530/244-6670, is a cozy café serving lunch Mon.–Fri., everything simple and fresh. And don't miss the cheesecake, everything from lemon or lime to Dutch chocolate almond and mocha Baileys.

Family-friendly and fun for all-American breakfasts, from biscuits and house-made Italian sausage to omelettes and the-real-deal corned beef hash, is the **Black Bear Diner,** 2605 Hilltop Dr., 530/221-7600. Comfort-food dinners—most under $10—include generous portions of pot roast, homemade meatloaf, and roast turkey. Another all-around good choice for breakfast, lunch, or dinner is **The Italian Cottage,** 1630 Hilltop Dr. (right in front of Motel 6), 530/221-6433; open 6 A.M.–11 P.M. At dinner, try the tasty calzone or pasta dishes, pizzas, the decent chef salad, or vegetarian choices. For Sunday brunch, locals just love **Corina's,** 1630 Hilltop Dr., 530/221-6433. For Mexican food and good margaritas, try **Tortilla Flats,** 2800 Park Marina Dr., 530/244-3343, open for lunch and dinner daily.

Fancier Fare

Chocolat de Nannette Market Street Cafe & Grill, just south of the Cascade Theatre at 777 Market St. (at Sacramento), 530/241-4068, is open Mon.–Sat. for breakfast and lunch. Morning fare ranges from fruit and scones to flapjacks, breakfast burritos, and eggs Benedict. At lunch expect surprising soups, salads, and sandwiches, along with such things as salmon and goat cheese croissants and Mexicali black bean crepes. Microbrews and wine served as well as good coffee, espresso, and fabulous milkshakes—and, of course, great pastries and chocolates. Go ahead, try the Noogie.

Popular at breakfast but also a best bet for lunch is the **Déjà vu Restaurant & Bakery,** a class act in the old Lorentz Hotel, 1590 California St., 530/244-4344 (bakery), 530/244-4272 (restaurant), open daily 7 A.M.–3 P.M.

For elegant ambience and good food, the place is **De Mercurio's,** 1647 Hartnell Ave., Ste. 21,

530/222-1307, which offers fine French, Italian, and American fare nightly. Specialties include gourmet preparations of veal, duck, rack of lamb, and fresh seafood, but De Mercurio's "special event" nights—with Chef Cal cooking up everything from Thai cuisine to St. Patrick's Day surprises—are always fun. De Mercurio's won a gold medal in the 1996 Culinary Olympics in Berlin. Open nightly for dinner (senior specials, too).

Another local legend is **Nello's Place,** 3055 Bechelli Ln. (at Hartnell), 530/223-1636, a very fine Italian restaurant that probably really belongs in Herb Caen's San Francisco. The food here is superb and, like the wine list, the selection impressive. Though Nello's is pricey by local standards, the early-bird dinner special is a remarkable bargain. Be sure to leave room for dessert, since this place is famous for its crepes Suzette, cherries jubilee, and bananas à la crema.

For the best steaks in town, head downtown to legendary **Jack's Grill,** 1743 California St., 530/241-9705, a funky 1930s tavern where people start lining up outside at 4 P.M. in order to get a table. (Closed Sunday.) Another favorite destination of serious carnivores seeking shameless steak: **Cattlemens,** 2184 Hilltop Dr, 530/221-6295, "where the Code of the West is still the Law of the Land." What that law means here is Harris Ranch grain-fed natural beef, from the specialty sizzling prime rib to the two-pound Porterhouse.

EVENTS AND INFORMATION

This town has a full events calendar. Come in September for the **Turtle Bay Arts and Crafts Fair,** the **Stillwater Pow Wow,** the **Trinity Tribal Stomp** world music festival in Hayfork, and **Blues by the River.** October boasts the **Big Bike Weekend** and the annual **Return of the Salmon Festival.** Unique in December is the **Lighted Boat Parade** on Shasta Lake. Come spring, **Kool April Nites** and all kinds of cool classic cars come to town. In the merry, merry month of May, come to Anderson River Park for the **Shasta Highlands Renaissance and Celtic Faire.** Other May events include huge **Redding Rodeo and Rodeo Week,** the **Shasta Art Faire and Fiddle Jamboree,** and the **Civil War Days** reenactment

in Anderson. June brings the **Shasta District Fair,** and usually the beginning of the Thursday **MarketFest** farmers market and crafts fair, 4:30–8:30 P.M. at Library Park. The annual summer **Mosquito Serenade** outdoor concert series also begins in June, at Anderson River Park, and runs through August. Redding celebrates its fiery Fourth of July at its annual **Freedom Festival** and fireworks show on the lawn at the Redding Convention Center.

The **Redding Record Searchlight,** www.redding.com, is the local newspaper of record. The **Redding Convention and Visitors Bureau,** 530/225-4100 or 800/874-7562, www.visitredding.org, is well-situated at 777 Auditorium Dr.; take Park Marina Dr. east, then turn north on Auditorium or, from I-5, follow the signs. Very helpful, also a ticket outlet for regional events, the visitors bureau is open Mon.–Fri. 8 A.M.–5:00 P.M., Sat.–Sun. 9 A.M.–5 P.M. A substantial new reason to stop off at shop-happy **Anderson Prime Outlets** south of Redding just off I-5, 530/378-1000 or 800/414-0490—home to **Pendleton, Tommy Hilfiger,** and dozens of other outlets—is the **California Welcome Center,** also headquarters for the **Shasta-Cascade Wonderland Association,** 530/365-7500 or 800/474-2782, www.shastacascade.org. Useful visitor publications include *An Adventure Around Every Corner: A Guide to the Shasta Cascade's Backcountry Roads.* Open Mon.–Sat. 9 A.M.–6 P.M., Sun. 10 A.M.–6 P.M.

Headquarters for **Shasta-Trinity National Forest** is at Redding's new USDA Service Center, 3644 Avtech Parkway, 530/226-2500, www.fs.fed.us/r5/shastatrinity. he office offers information about regional recreation areas—from Whiskeytown and Trinity Lakes to the Trinity Alps Wilderness Area and the Mt. Shasta Wilderness—and supplies the necessary permits. The national forest's **Shasta Lake Main Office,** 14225 Holiday Rd., 530/275-1587, is just south of the lake at the Mountain Gate exit off I-5. Best bet for local (and lake-oriented) camping and regional recreation information is the **Shasta Lake Visitor Center** across the way at 14250 Holiday, 530/275-1589. The **BLM Redding Resource Area** office, 355 Hemsted Dr., 530/224-2100, has information about recreation on BLM lands.

Lassen Volcanic National Park and Vicinity

Visitors to Lassen Volcanic National Park and its backcountry wilderness should cultivate a better sense of direction than the park's namesake, Danish immigrant and intrepid traveler Peter Lassen. According to a journal entry by his friend, Gen. John Bidwell, Lassen "was a singular man, very industrious, very ingenious, and very fond of pioneering—in fact, of the latter, very stubbornly so. He had great confidence in his own power as a woodsman, but, strangely enough, he always got lost." This almost led to his lynching on at least one occasion, when he confused Lassen and Shasta peaks while guiding a party of immigrants westward, inadvertently taking them more than 200 miles out of their way. More recently, one of the best-known seasonal residents of the Lassen area was Ishi, "the last wild man in North America." In 1916, the year Ishi died and a year after Lassen Peak finished blasting its way into the 20th century, Lassen was designated a national park.

THE LAND

Native peoples knew Lassen Peak by various names: Little Shasta, Water Mountain, Broken Mountain, Fire Mountain, and Mountain-Ripped-Apart. The Atsugewi people tell the story of a warrior chief who burrowed into Lassen Peak to rescue his abducted lover. The mountain spirits, impressed by his audacity, invited him to marry his beloved and live with them inside the peak; storm clouds above the volcano are explained as smoke from the warrior's peace pipe. The Atsugewi also have an earthquake story, possibly connected to the great avalanche that formed the area's Chaos Jumbles about 300 years ago. The Maidu explained earthquakes mythically and quite simply: the earth is anchored in a great sea by five ropes. When the gods get angry, they give these ropes a good tug.

Geology

Lassen is the southernmost outpost of the Cascade Range, which runs almost due north from here to British Columbia. Much of Lassen Peak is cradled within a huge caldera formed by the volcano's collapse 300,000 years ago. Of the four types of volcanoes found in the world, Lassen Park has three: cinder cones, shield volcanos, and dome volcanos. (An example of the fourth type of volcanic mountain, a composite or stratovolcano—and a classic Cascades version, at that—is Mt. Shasta.)

Lassen's unimaginatively named Cinder Cone is also a classic one, composed entirely of pyroclastic, or "fire-broken," rock (molten fragments that solidify before they hit the ground). Prospect Peak is a shield volcano, formed from lava flows. Lassen Peak itself is a dome volcano formed by a "plug," a single, solid mass of rock squeezed up through the vent of a previous volcano. Relatively recent volcanism here—pumice showers, lava flows, and mudflows—has buried most evidence of earlier glacial action, but the scouring of the Warner, Blue Lake, and Mill Creek valleys suggests ancient ice sheets more than 1,000 feet thick.

Climate

The most hospitable season here is summer, roughly mid-June to October. Summer in Lassen is like spring at lower elevations; expect sunny cool days and cold nights. Pacific storms are usually blocked by high-pressure areas off the coast, so summer weather is generally dry except for occasional surprise thunderstorms (and rare snowstorms).

The rest of the year is like one long winter. About 400-700 inches of snow fall each year (an average 30-foot snowpack), and Lassen's winter temperatures are extremely invigorating. Gale winds, subzero temperatures, and blinding snow flurries are expected in winter and can come unpredictably the rest of the year. In years with unusually heavy snowfall, the road through the park may open in July and close in September; call ahead if planning to visit either early or late in the season. Those serious about getting to know Lassen might enjoy a winter visit—for skiing, snowshoeing, or simply appreciating winter vistas.

NORTHERN MOUNTAINS

FINDING LASSEN

If Peter Lassen got disoriented in his time, contemporary travelers could easily do the same if they fall prey to the common-sense notion that Lassen Peak should be located within Lassen County. It's not. When plotting your journey, look for Lassen Peak, and much of Lassen Volcanic National Park, in Shasta County. The usual routes to Lassen are east on Hwy. 44 out of Redding (to the park's north entrance) or east from Red Bluff on Hwy. 36 or from Chico on Hwy. 32 (to enter the park from the south). If the weather is bad in winter, Hwy. 36 is safer than Hwy. 32. Westbound travelers can get to Lassen only via Hwys. 89 and 44 from the north, or Hwys. 44 or 36 out of Susanville.

Like most worthwhile backwaters in California, Lassen isn't easy to reach by public transportation. Bicyclists with a sturdy 10-speed or mountain bike and all necessary gear for emergencies will find the trip up any of these highways invigorating and breathtaking (in more ways than one). A combined mail and passenger service runs daily (except Sundays and holidays) from Red Bluff to Susanville and back, stopping at Mineral; from there, you can hitch into the park. For information, contact: **Mt. Lassen Motor Transit,** 22503 Sunbright Ave. in Red Bluff, 530/529-2722. Buses leave the Greyhound Station in Red Bluff (at the 5 Star Convenience Store, 782 Antelope Blvd. at the Hwy. 36 junction) for Mineral Mon.–Sat. (except holidays) at 8:45 A.M.; call for current fares, and consult with the driver about the return schedule.

Flora

Lassen Volcanic National Park is alive with alpine wildflowers during summer—balsam root, monkey flowers, blue stickweed, corn and fawn lilies, larkspur, lupine, monkshood, mountain heath, pennyroyal, pussypaws, shooting stars, skyrocket gilia, snow plant, wallflowers, and white rain orchids. Trees here as well as other plants are separated into fairly distinct vegetation zones influenced by elevation, exposure, soil type, and moisture. Common Lassen trees include incense cedar, white fir, ponderosa pine, and even sugar pine—a species usually found at lower elevations—on southwestern (warmer) exposures. Lodgepole pines and quaking aspens thrive in the Devastated Area, healing the scars created by Lassen Peak's most recent eruptions. In time, these trees will be replaced by climax forests of red fir. The gnarly whitebark pine grows only at higher elevations and is usually found near droopy-topped mountain hemlocks.

Fauna

Both mule deer and the black-tailed subspecies are found in the park, though the mules (with only a tip of black on their tails) are the minority. Signs everywhere declare that feeding animals is *not* in their survival interests. Some insensitive vis-

itors disregard these pleas, since remarkably tame deer often approach picnickers to beg. Various rodents also hang around campgrounds looking for a handout; people feeding the golden-mantled ground squirrel usually get bitten. Also common throughout the park is Clark's nutcracker; a gregarious relative of jays and crows, it looks like a stubby-tailed mockingbird and is partial to the nuts of the whitebark pine. Large numbers of waterfowl, including Canada geese and the exotic wood duck, stop off at Manzanita Lake in the fall on their way south. You might also see sharp-shinned hawks, peregrine falcons, and rare bald eagles gliding low over mountains, lakes, and streams in search of dinner.

History

Don Luis Arguello, one of the early governors of Spanish California, called Lassen "San Jose." Jedediah Smith anglicized this to "St. Joseph," which was altered to "Mt. St. Joseph" by Charles Wilkes on his 1841 map. Then Peter Lassen, a Danish blacksmith lured to the area by immigrant fever, appeared on the scene. Mexican officials gave him a large tract of land east of the Sacramento River where he established a ranch and put out his "immigrant guide" shingle. (His "Lassen's Cutoff," running south of Lassen Peak

© ROBERT HOLMES/CALTOUR

Lassen Peak

and treacherous for laden wagon trains, was used only a short while.)

The demand for lumber increased as more settlers moved into the region. By 1907, lumberjacks threatened Lassen's magnificent forests, and in an effort to protect the area, Lassen Peak and Cinder Cone were declared national monuments. Lassen's volcanic eruptions of 1914-15 created such a national stir that the area was granted full national park status in 1916—at first in name only, since funding for actual park protection was delayed for years.

LASSEN'S VOLCANIC HISTORY

In the early 1900s, area residents, including the "experts," believed Lassen to be extinct. The naked 10,457-foot peak had stood mute for eons. Though the immediate area was pocked with volcanic scars and various thermal sinks, Lassen as an *event* was considered a thing of the past.

But in late May 1914, preceded by a small earthquake, columns of steam and gases began spewing forth, littering Lassen's upper slopes with small chunks of lava. During the next year, Lassen blew more than 150 times, spitting dust

and steam and spraying the surrounding area with cinders and small boulders. Curious spectators were thrilled but generally unconcerned.

Blasting into the 20th Century

Following an unusually heavy snowfall during the winter of 1914-15, the volcanic activity intensified. Snow in the crater melted almost instantly and, seeping into the earth, contributed large volumes of liquid to the volcanic brew. Then, on May 19, 1915, molten lava bubbled up to the rim of the crater, spilled over on the southwestern side, and flowed 1,000 feet down the mountain slope before cooling into a solid mass. On the peak's north side, lava poured over the rim, steam shot from a vent near the peak, and chunks of lava fell like hard spring rain. Boiling mud flows peeled off tree bark 18 feet above ground and submerged meadows with six feet of debris as the ooze flowed into the valleys of Hat and Lost Creeks.

But the Big One came three days later, when billowing smoke shot five miles into the air, catapulting five-ton boulders skyward. Steam blasted out again, this time horizontally, flattening trees and anything else in its path. After a few more minor eruptions in following years, Lassen was officially declared asleep (again) in 1921, after seven years of volcanic activity.

The Sisters Sleep

Lassen, the world's largest "plug" volcano, today offers relatively subtle reminders of its fiery nature. Hot springs, hot lakes, fumaroles or steam vents, and boiling mudpots are found in seven thermal areas within Lassen Volcanic National Park. Though no one is comfortable predicting when, or even if, Lassen will wake up again, another volcanic eruption—perhaps from an entirely new volcano created from the churning magma below—will probably occur in the general vicinity and in the fairly near geological future (measured in hundreds of years).

NATIVE PEOPLES

Four groups of Indians inhabited the area, their respective summer territories radiating outward from the peak like spokes. The permanent villages of the Atsugewi to the north, the mountain Maidu to the south and southeast, and the westerly Yana and Yahi were at lower elevations, but as deer migrated annually to higher elevations, so did the Indians. They lived in temporary summer camps and hunted, fished, and gathered wild foods.

Life was fairly harmonious, despite occasional intertribal conflicts. The various local cultures were surprisingly similar, considering these four groups sprang from two different tribal families and three language groups. Basketweaving was the outstanding art; women of the Maidu and Atsugewi tribes specialized in intricate, coiled willow baskets of all shapes and sizes, while the Yana and Yahi made mostly twine types. Acorns, leached of bitter tannic acid, then pounded into flour for cakes, were the dietary mainstay. Roots, bulbs, and bugs were dug from the ground (hence the derogatory term "digger Indians"). Hunters wore or carried deer head decoys and sometimes bushes as camouflage. They hunted California grizzlies (now extinct) by building simple stick traps outside dens, then cautiously enticing the bears out.

According to guesstimates, the four Lassen peoples together numbered 4,025 in 1777, 1,080 in 1910, and just 385 by 1950. Here as elsewhere in California, native peoples were virtually wiped out by waves of settlers, introduced diseases, and starvation.

In Search of Ishi

For years it was believed that the last of the Yahi people were wiped out in a massacre by settlers at Kingsley Cave in Tehama County. But in 1908, power-company surveyors in the Deer Creek foothills south of Lassen came across a naked Indian man standing near the stream, poised with a double-pronged fishing spear. The next day a stone-tipped arrow whistled through the underbrush past other members in the same party. The surveyors pushed on and stumbled onto the camp of a middle-aged Yahi woman and two elders, a man and a woman. To prove their find, the interlopers carried off blankets, bows, arrows, and food supplies. They returned

ISHI COUNTRY

The best way to get into Lassen National Forest's **Ishi Wilderness** is from the Lassen area, near the headwaters of Mill and Deer Creeks (ask at national park headquarters). You can also access trailheads from roads connecting to Hwy. 32, and from unpaved Ponderosa Way off Hwy. 36 at Paynes Creek—both routes offer good side trips through the Sierra-Cascade foothills if you're heading down to the valley. Once you get here, you'll understand how Ishi and his family could so successfully shun "civilization," even into the 20th century: steep ravines separated by sharp ridges, dense brush, scattered foothill pine and black oaks, small plateaus with stands of ponderosa pine. The Tehama deer herd, California's largest migratory herd, winters in the area; most of the Ishi Wilderness is also a state game refuge (hunting is not permitted). Yet where once there were only deer trails, there are now lots of jeep and foot trails.

Spring and fall are the best times to visit Ishi Wilderness. Even then, be prepared for extreme weather. Ishi's climate is relatively mild in winter, with little snow, but on some days the temperature drops below freezing; recent rainstorms mean muddy conditions. Summers can be shockingly hot. Carry plenty of water, along with compass and maps, hat, sunscreen, insect repellant, and toilet tissue. Except on the shortest of hikes, given the area's remoteness you may also want to bring first aid kit, flashlight, waterproof matches, candle, pocketknife, extra food, extra clothing, space blanket, and poncho. Backpackers, come prepared for no-trace camping (if you pack it in, pack it out) and camp at least 100 feet from trails and water sources; camp stoves are suggested, and campfire permits are required.

Pick up a trail guide from the Almanor Ranger District office in Chester, 530/258-2141, or Lassen National Forest headquarters in Susanville, 530/257-2151, www.r5.fs.fed.us/lassen.

the next day (reputedly to make reparations), but the camp and the Yahi were gone. Anthropologists searched the area to no avail.

Ishi's Journey

But in August 1911, butchers at a slaughterhouse in Oroville were awakened by barking dogs at the livestock corral. There they found a near-naked man crouched in the mud, surrounded by snarling dogs. The man's only clothing was a piece of dirty, torn canvas hanging from his shoulders. He was emaciated and suffering from severe malnutrition. His skin was sunburned a copper brown, his hair burnt close to his skull (a Yahi sign of mourning). But the oddest thing was the man's speech, a language no one in the area had ever heard. People tried to communicate with him in English, Spanish, and several local Native American dialects, to no avail. Finally, for lack of a better place to put him, the sheriff locked him in a cell usually reserved for mental cases.

The "Wild Man of Oroville" made good newspaper copy, but news of his appearance caused even more excitement in the anthropology department at the University of California. Befriended by anthropologist Alfred L. Kroeber and others, Ishi (as he was called, though he never revealed his true Yahi name) soon moved to San Francisco, where he lived for almost five years in the old UC Museum of Anthropology. On trips through his people's lands with Kroeber and others, Ishi shared his knowledge of his own and other tribes' beliefs, customs, crafts, and technology. *Ishi in Two Worlds: A Biography of the Last Wild Man in North America* by Theodora Kroeber tells this fascinating story. Ishi died of tuberculosis in 1916 but not before sharing with a friend his observation that whites were "smart but not wise, knowing many things including much that is false."

Ishi Comes Home

Illustrating Ishi's astute perception was the scandalous discovery in the late 1990s that not only was his body autopsied after death, against his express wishes, but Ishi's brain was removed, stored in a jar of formaldehyde, and shipped by Alfred Kroeber and the University of California to the Smithsonian Institution, where it was stored for years at a Maryland facility. The University of California had long insisted that Ishi's brain was cremated following the autopsy, along with the rest of his remains. But an investigation launched by the Butte County Native American Cultural Committee, aided by UC San Francisco medical historian Nancy Rockafellar and Duke University professor Orin Starn, traced Ishi's brain to the Smithsonian. As it turns out, the Smithsonian knew all along that it possessed the brain; it just didn't seem to know anyone was looking for it. But people were looking, and quite seriously, since many Native Americans—including those now considered Ishi's closest relatives, Yahi-Yana descendants—believe that a person's spirit is not free unless his or her remains are all buried together. In May 1999, the Smithsonian announced that it was repatriating the brain to the Redding Rancheria and the Pit River Tribe—which both claim Yana descendants, determined to be Ishi's closest kin—so it could be reunited with Ishi's bodily remains for a proper burial in his homeland. As a result, Ishi is finally free—and freed from association with the whites who had befriended him. Ishi's legacy is also freed from the notion that he was the last of his kind, since as a Yana (Ishi means "man" in Yana), or a Yahi-Yana, he has 100–200 living relatives.

SEEING AND DOING LASSEN

Unlike other wilderness areas, many of Lassen's more notable features—including major volcanic peaks and glacial lakes like **Emerald** and **Helen**—are easily visible and/or accessible from the one paved road that traverses the park—making a tour of Lassen enjoyable for families with small children as well as for anyone with physical limitations. See examples of Lassen's explosive personality at **The Sulphur Works, Little Hot Springs Valley, Bumpass Hell** (where the unfortunate Mr. Bumpass lost a leg to a mudpot), **Devil's Kitchen, Boiling Springs Lake, Terminal Geyser,** and **Drakesbad.**

The *Road Guide to Lassen Park* (available at park headquarters and visitor centers) gives a useful overview of what you'll see along the park road, whether walking, biking, or driving.

Hiking

Lassen's 150 miles of interconnecting hiking trails (including 19 miles of the Pacific Crest Trail) offer both short easy strolls and rigorous backcountry treks. Bring water on all walks, and pack a lunch or high-energy snacks on longer hikes. (Mountain bikes are not allowed on any trails. Neither are dogs.)

Among the less strenuous Lassen hikes are those to the volcanic "hot spot" **Bumpass Hell** and to **Paradise Meadows,** the best place to see midsummer wildflowers. The mostly downhill hike from Kings Creek Meadows to impressive **Kings Creek Falls** is not difficult (though what goes down does have to come back up). Extend the hike by continuing to Cold Boiling Lake and eventually Bumpass Hell, or to Crumbaugh Lake and the Sulphur Works. Two trails—the quarter-mile **Devastated Area Interpretive Trail** (wheelchair accessible) and the mile-long **Lily Pond Nature Trail** into the Chaos Jumbles area—offer public access to remnants of Lassen's disruptive past. Or try the three-mile **Devil's**

Kitchen Trail, which begins and ends at the Warner Valley Picnic Area and explores thermal features. (Hikers can get closer to the volcanic action here than at Bumpass Hell, so stay on the trail and keep a close watch on the kids.) The trail to **Boiling Springs Lake** starts from the same spot and offers contrasts of forest, meadow, and a lake fringed with mudpots and steam plumes. Special guided hikes (including **wildflower and nature walks,** and trips to **Forest Lake** and **Mill Creek Falls** in Ishi country) led by park rangers and naturalists are scheduled at regular intervals.

More challenging trips include the steep switchback climb up **Lassen Peak** on the wide and well-graded trail. Bring water and a jacket or sweater. From the summit, see majestic Mt. Shasta to the north, Brokeoff Mountain to the southwest, and Lake Almanor ("Little Tahoe") just south. On a clear day (most likely in spring or fall), the broad Sacramento Valley and the Sutter Buttes are also visible. A hike up **Brokeoff Mountain,** the park's second-highest peak, affords good views of Lassen plus strolls through thick woods and blooming meadows. In ancient times, Brokeoff was the southwestern peak of

Bumpass Hell

mighty Mt. Tehama before most of that ancient mountain collapsed into a caldera.

To hike the Lassen stretch of the **Pacific Crest Trail,** which traverses Drakesbad and Twin Lakes, start at Little Willow Lake at the park's far southern border. Less challenging is the 1.5-mile loop from Summit Lake to the Bear and Twin Lakes areas. Less difficult (but a trudge through loose volcanic cinders followed by a corkscrew climb) is the five-mile roundtrip from Butte Lake on the **Cinder Cone Nature Trail.** After skirting the **Fantastic Lava Beds,** the panoramic views and close glimpses of the **Painted Dunes** lava flow make the unsteady going worthwhile.

Backpacking

Three-fourths of the park is designated wilderness. Instead of hiking in from the main park road, enter the park's wilderness areas from the southeast or northeast and backpack. Reach the **Juniper Lake** area and adjacent **Caribou Wilderness** via Chester-Juniper Lake Rd., and the **Warner Valley** via Chester-Warner Valley Rd.; both roads originate near the town of Chester south of the park. To get to **Butte Lake** area wilderness, take a well-marked turnoff from Hwy. 44.

Overnight outings within the park's 106,000 acres can be a chilling experience early in the season, especially before July 1 or in early fall. Unmelted snow is common through June, and the first snowstorms of winter usually arrive by the end of September. "Winter" can occur anytime in the high country, however, so never hike alone and always bring equipment and apparel suitable for abrupt weather changes. Wilderness permits are required for backcountry camping, and no campfires are allowed in wilderness areas, so pack a campstove and fuel. Remember also that backcountry camping is a privilege; leave the area as clean as you found it (if not cleaner).

Ski Touring and Snowshoeing

Only the southwestern part of the road into Lassen is snowplowed in winter and only as far as the old ski area chalet. (The highway *to* the park at Manzanita Lake is also plowed in

CLIMBING LASSEN

Lassen is tops for rock climbing, and it's a short hike to the best climb sites, on Raker and Eagle Peaks in Lassen's shadow. *Lassen Volcanic National Park: A Climber's Guide* by John Bald is out of print, but it's still the local climbers' bible—if you can beg a copy off somebody, or be lucky enough to find it in a library, used bookstore, or online. Many of the routes at Lassen were established in the 1980s, and there's something for everyone—technical climbs ranging from 5.0 to 5.14 and above. More information and guidance is available at Redding climb shops, including **Hermit's Hut Base Camp 1,** 3184 Bechelli Ln., 530/222-4511, and **Sports Ltd.,** 950 Hilltop Drive, 530/221-7333.

winter, allowing northern park access for Nordic skiers and snowshoe hikers.) Most of the park's main snowshoe and ski-touring routes start from the unplowed road and are well marked during the season. **Lassen Peak, Brokeoff,** and **Bumpass Hell** are difficult treks, but trips from the chalet to **Lake Helen, Kings Creek Meadows,** and **Summit Lake** are possible even for beginners. The entire main road through Lassen Park is available in winter for cross-country ski touring (stunning views). For safety reasons, registration is necessary for both day and overnight trips. Day-trippers can sign in at trail registers outside the chalet or the Manzanita Lake office, as can overnighters. **Ranger-guided cross-country ski tours** are offered from January to early April. Park naturalists also lead free **guided snowshoe hikes,** emphasizing snow ecology, to various areas in winter. Also typically on the park's winter activity schedule: programs on **wilderness survival** and **minimum impact camping.** Call headquarters or see the website for current winter recreation information. Snowmobiles are not allowed in the park.

In addition, winter camping is allowed at the **Southwest Campground** near the chalet. Overnight campers can also register at park headquarters in Mineral (see Information below).

NEAR LASSEN

Lake Almanor

Lovely Lake Almanor is a manmade reservoir, one of the largest in California, but otherwise like a tiny Tahoe—a very pretty deep blue—adjacent to the mountain town of Chester. Almanor is still surprisingly lonely, despite being so close to major valley cities. Its attractions include clean cool air, clear water at a near-perfect 65–70° F in summer, good fishing, swimming, sailing, and water-skiing. Almanor is superb for trout fishing, since the cold water on the bottom (52° F) is ideal for rainbow trout. On rare days not a single outboard motor disturbs the waters, though sailboats appear quickly whenever the wind's up. The lake's west side is more rustic and relaxed; the paved, 10-foot-wide **Lake Almanor Recreation Trail,** for walkers, bikers, skateboarders, winds along Almanor's west side. The lake's east side is newer, mostly private subdivisions and upscale resorts.

In April, come for the popular **Bass Fishing Tournament** here (the lake is home also to trout and salmon). In mid-June, cyclists come for the **Mile High Century Ride.** Get area information in adjacent Chester. Most people get here via Hwy. 32 from Chico, then Hwy. 89 (good road), though a trip on the Old Red Bluff Rd. (Hwy. 36) to Chester is quite scenic—squeezing through steep-walled Deer Creek Canyon, where dogwood and redbud bloom in early summer (nice campgrounds along the way, too). Another way to go is up Hwy. 70 from Oroville through scenic Feather River Canyon.

Chester and Westwood

A rustic logging town in the shadow of Lassen Peak on Almanor's north shore, Chester is fast becoming a recreation and retirement community. Peter Lassen led immigrants through this little valley on his infamous Oregon Trail shortcut. The town has some reasonably priced motels, fast-food joints, decent restaurants, gas stations, and various places to pick up sporting goods and outdoor equipment. It also has a genuine old-time soda fountain—one of the best anywhere—inside the **Lassen Drug Co.** on Main, where the soda jerks err on the side of generosity. The best place to get miscellaneous outdoor supplies and sundries is fascinating **Ayoob's Department Store,** 201 Main St., 530/258-2628, a general store with a quirky array of merchandise. A best bet for cycling and canoeing supplies in summer and snowshoe and cross-country ski rentals in winter is **Bodfish Bicycles & Quiet Mountain Sports,** 152 Main St., 530/258-2338. Stop at Bodfish, too, for suggested local trails and tips. The **Chester/Lake Almanor Museum,** 200 First Ave., 530/258-2742, which shares space with the local library, displays historical photographs of the area, as well as artifacts from the area's early Maidu people and later pioneer industry. Open Mon.–Sat. year-round; call for hours. Another tribute to local history is **Dinky,** displayed on Main, right across from the chamber office—the little Porter engine that could help build Lake Almanor and Butt Lake, and also could survive some 70 years of abandonment underwater. In 1996, when PG&E crews drained Butt Lake in order to reinforce the dam, there was Dinky—a bit worse for the rust and weeds but otherwise intact. Now shiny and black, with Eureka lettered in gold on her cab, Dinky has a home.

Annual Chester events include the August **Almanor Art Show** and the **Bidwell Art & Crafts Show** at Bidwell House, and the September **Annual Street Rod Extravaganza Car Show.** Come in February for the **Winterfest Sled Dog Races** at the Chester Airport. For more information about the area, contact the **Chester/Lake Almanor Chamber of Commerce,** 529 Main St., 530/258-2426 or 800/350-4838, www.chester-lakealmanor.com.

In Westwood, the **Westwood Museum,** 315 Ash St., 530/256-2233, tells the story of the old Red River Lumber Company, which is credited with creating the story of **Paul Bunyan and Babe the Blue Ox** as a promotional gimmick. So it's only appropriate that a carved statue of both mythic figures stands near the western end of the nearby Bizz Johnson Trail. (For trail details, see Susanville, below.) For information on the annual **Paul Bunyan Mountain Festival,** held the weekend after July 4th, call the **Westwood Chamber of Commerce** at 530/256-2456, or see www.westwoodchamber.com. Events include the "giant" parade, lumberjacks and jills in competition, Brimstone Bill's Carnival, Blue Ox bingo, an arts and crafts show, and an all-day blues festival.

The area's future is likely to be less folksy. Coming soon—after some local controversy—is the year-round **Dyer Mountain Resort** development, 530/256-3227, www.dyermt.com, to be located between Westwood and Clear Creek on Hwy. A21, just off Hwy. 36. When the three 18-hole golf courses are snowed under, serious downhill ski facilities—3,000 skiable acres and five lifts to start, including a high-speed gondola—will draw the crowds.

Coppervale Ski Hill

The tiny but steep and surprisingly challenging Coppervale Ski Hill 14 miles west of Susanville and just a few miles east of Westwood, 530/257-9965 or 530/257-6181, is used primarily by Lassen College ski classes, but the public is wel-

come—worth it if you're in the area, come winter. Lift tickets—a poma lift takes you to the top—are $15 per day, $10 half-day fee. Open in winter, Saturdays, Sundays, and holidays (any day school is not in session).

Stover Mountain Ski Area

With just a rope tow—one of the longest in the U.S.—the small Stover Mountain Ski Area overlooking Lake Almanor is strictly local and open weekends and holidays only, when it's open at all—a status that depends on sufficient snow and community interest. Stover Mountain has no facilities aside from a tiny warming hut—and packaged food and bottled water for sale—but much of the downhill terrain is "advanced" and challenging. Snowboarders are welcome. Full-day tickets $15 adults, $10 children under 12. From Hwy. 36 west of Chester, take the county road turnoff to Stover Mountain (Rd. 316A), which is just across from the intersection of Hwys. 36 and 89. For more information, call 530/258-3987.

Feather River Scenic Byway

For a pleasant side trip or alternate route to the Sacramento Valley from Chester or Almanor, head west on Hwy. 89 and then take Hwy. 70 down the rugged, steep canyon of the North Fork of the Feather River, a route now known as the Feather River Scenic Byway. (To trace the entire route, start or finish at Hwy. 395 on the Sierra's eastern flank.) Autumn colors through the canyon can rival those of Vermont. The Southern Pacific "Y" railroad trestle over the Feather River at **Keddie** is the only one of its kind in the world. Farther west, cross the narrow bridge and stop in **Belden Town** for a snack and a look around, admiring the old stamp mill (across the highway, near public restrooms). For a dose of riverside relaxation, stop off farther down the canyon at **Woody's**, 29186 Hwy. 70 in Twain, 530/283-4115, where

---

WORDS STAY

Ishi country. Cold. Our lungs make the words stay in the air long enough for us to watch them drift off. We're eyeing each other as if we were strangers, as if we came from different cultures. The striations in the granite become a game we must play, not to break our mothers' backs. Deer Creek could do this to any being, but it does it best to those who love.

You can't be more alone, and not crazy, than Ishi. I couldn't dream up a game that would come close. And when the crazy came too near, he walked out, away from his women's deaths, into the Oroville streets. And into the California he went to his grave knowing was not Deer Creek, and therefore, was not the world. There were two Yana languages: a man's and a woman's. Ishi's had the flavor of the woman's, his new friend said. Two worlds. Two stubborn hearts.

Our shoes drag over Ishi land, and we don't bother about cracks. Words float. It is sacred, right now, this not-touching. It is enough to get ourselves lost, as Ishi would want, to give Our trust over to this place—Deer Creek—that will be its own story for longer than even Ishi can tell it.

—*Gary Thompson*

you'll find hot springs-fed hot tubs, cabins, RV sites, and a restaurant serving three meals a day.

STAYING IN AND NEAR LASSEN
Camping in Lassen Park

Lassen now has "bear boxes" at every campsite—which means park rangers expect you to use them, to store all food and personal items. Preventing bears' inevitable attraction to the "easy pickin's" provided by human visitors also prevents their inevitable corruption (and sometimes destruction) as a result of human contact.

Campsites are abundant in the park. Because Lassen is the most "unvisited" of all national parks, campground reservations aren't taken. But there *is* a 14-day limit (seven days only at popular **Lost Creek Group Campground** and at both **Summit Lake** campgrounds). The Summit camping fee is $14–16 per night (no showers but swimming allowed). The spacious and more private campground at **Manzanita Lake** ($16; facilities include hot showers) is considered "out of the line of fire" should Chaos Crags ever shake loose in an earthquake or volcanic explosion. The park's overflow, **Crags Campground** ($10), is five miles from Manzanita Lake near Lost Creek. It's basic and open only after Manzanita Lake is full. The tiny **Southwest Campground** is an easily walked-into area adjacent to the Lassen Chalet parking lot at the park's southwestern entrance ($14 in summer, $10 after late Sept.).

More remote campgrounds include **Butte Lake** ($14), open again now that the water treatment plant has been finished, **Juniper Lake** ($10; 13 miles from Chester, primitive), and **Warner Valley** ($14 in summer, $10 from Oct. until the snow flies; 17 miles from Chester, pit toilets, piped water). Neither Juniper Lake nor Warner Valley is recommended for trailers since access is via rough dirt roads.

The best way to land a campsite within Lassen Park is to arrive early in the day, preferably midweek but otherwise early Friday for weekend camping, and Sunday for the following week.

Group campgrounds, by contrast—at **Butte Lake** ($50); **Juniper Lake** ($30); and **Lost Creek**

($50)—are available by reservation only. Call 530/335-7029.

Camping in Lassen National Forest

If the park's campgrounds are full, many fine campgrounds throughout Lassen National Forest often have room for one more; the region's 43 U.S. Forest Service campgrounds include a total of about 1,000 campsites. Most are open May 1–Nov. 1 and are fairly primitive; none currently have showers, but many are near streams and lakes fine for fishing, swimming, and boating. Currently all but three (Butte Creek, Little Grizzly, and South Antelope) charge a fee of $8–12.50 for single family sites, $18.50 for larger group sites. The campgrounds are free if/when no safe water source is available.

Nearest Lassen to the south, popular and easily accessible are **Battle Creek,** on Hwy. 36 just west of Mineral (flush toilets, fee); **Gurnsey Creek,** on Hwy. 36 near Fire Mountain, north of Hwy. 32; and **Almanor Campground,** near Chester on the lake's west side (spacious, private, close to the beaches and hiking trails).

North of Lassen and easy to get to are **Big Pine,** a half mile off Hwy. 44/89 and five miles south of Old Station; **Hat Creek,** just south of Old Station; **Cave Campground,** just north; and **Rocky, Bridge,** and **Honn Campgrounds** along Hat Creek and Hwy. 89 farther north.

Along Deer Creek and Hwy. 32 toward the valley are the **Elam Creek, Alder Creek,** and verdant **Potato Patch Campgrounds.** Farther west, **Soda Springs,** accessible via two miles of dusty roads, and **Butte Meadows** are best reached on the way to or from the valley. In the beautiful Feather River Canyon along Hwy. 70 west from Greenville or Quincy are various Plumas National Forest campgrounds.

Of the campgrounds listed above, reservations are available at Gurnsey, Almanor, and Hat Creek; call 877/444-6777 or go to www.reserveusa.com. For more information on national forest camping, contact area ranger district offices; see Lassen Area Information, below.

Camping Elsewhere
A nonpublic camping alternative is the **Mt.**

Lassen/Shingletown KOA, 14 miles outside Lassen Park's northern entrance, 7749 KOA Rd. (at Hwy. 44) in Shingletown, 530/474-3133 or 800/562-3403, www.koa.com (tent campers also welcome). Tent and RV sites are $20–35; "kamping kabins" and cottages also available. There are various private campgrounds with RV hookups in and around Chester, including fun and funky **Wilson's Camp Prattville Resort,** 2932 Almanor Dr. West on the lake's west shore, 530/259- 2267, www.camp-prattville.com, which also includes a pleasant lake-view front lawn, picnic area, grocery store, cabins, and restaurant. RV sites are $20–23. There are four private **Pacific Gas & Electric campgrounds** in the area, too—at Lake Almanor, Last Chance Creek north of Chester (for groups), Butt Valley Reservoir, and Canyon Dam on Hwy. 89. All are open to the public and are first-come, first-camped (advance reservations required for group camps). For information, call 800/743-5000; for group reservations, call 530/386-5164. For a complete listing of Almanor area camping facilities, public and private, contact the chamber of commerce (see above and below).

Cabin Resorts: $50–100

Though you'll find motels and other accommodations in the Chester/Lake Almanor area, numerous reasonably priced, often rustic "resorts" with cabins ring Lassen. Ever popular on the north side of Lassen Park is **Adams' Hat Creek Resort,** 13 miles north of Manzanita Lake on Hwy. 44, Old Station, 530/335-7121, with both cabins and motel units. Weekly rates available. Under new ownership and now a year-round resort, **Childs Meadow Resort,** southwest of Lassen Park on Hwy. 36, Mill Creek, 530/595-3383, offers motel units and housekeeping chalets, RV sites, tent camping, and amenities including Laundromat, bathhouse, group picnic facilities, and regulation tennis courts. Nice, too, are the 10 cabins at **Mill Creek Resort,** in the woods along Hwy. 172 just a few miles off Hwy. 36/89, 530/595-4449—rustic but comfortable, and prices are consistent year-round. Cabins have kitchens and one or two bedrooms. Some have sitting rooms, and one sleeps six and has a cozy fire-

place. Other facilities include RV spaces, campsites, a small grocery store, and a restaurant with a breakfast and sandwich menu. **Fire Mountain Lodge,** on the west side of Hwy. 36/89, just north of the Hwy. 32 junction, 530/258-2938, features motel rooms and cabins (one, two, or three bedrooms, some with kitchens). A big draw here is the main lodge and its huge stone fireplace, featuring a bar and restaurant.

Bidwell House Bed-and-Breakfast

Close to Lake Almanor and Lassen, the historic Bidwell House country inn at 1 Main St. in Chester, 530/258-3338, www.bidwellhouse.com, was once the summer home of noted California pioneers John and Annie E.K. Bidwell. When the Bidwells first started retreating in summer to the cool mountain meadow below Mt. Lassen, the trip took three days (one-way) by wagon caravan, and "home," once they arrived, was a massive circus tent. But after 30 years of this summertime tradition, Annie apparently tired of the tent and insisted upon a cabin. John built this lovely two-story home instead. First located in a meadow along the Feather River, the house was rolled into town on logs in 1919.

As perfect now as ever for summer retreats—and a great choice in winter, too, given the area's exceptional cross-country skiing and other attractions—the impressive, completely renovated Bidwell House offers a total of 14 guest rooms, most with private baths, some with in-room Jacuzzis, and three with woodstoves. A separate cottage is perfect for two couples or families. Scrumptious full breakfast is included. Most rooms are $100–150; Jacuzzi rooms and cottage slightly higher. With advance reservations for breakfast (daily) and dinner (Thurs.–Sat.), you can eat here even if you don't stay here.

Drakesbad

Comfortably rustic simplicity at its finest, but only for those with the urge (and resources) to splurge, the unusual **Drakesbad Guest Ranch** complex sprouts up seemingly out of nowhere in the Warner Valley, actually part of Lassen Volcanic National Park. The resort is named for trapper and guide Edward Drake, who claimed to be a descendant of Sir Francis. An eccentric who valued his privacy, Drake and his sheep lived alone here for 15 years.

Drake sold the land to Alex Sifford in 1900, and the Sifford family operated Drake's Hot Springs and Ranch (shortened to "Drake's baths" or Drakesbad, *bad* being German for "spa") as a family resort that catered mostly to San Franciscans and was noted for the health-giving properties of the springs. In the 1950s, the U.S. government bought the place as an addition to Lassen Park. Sifford Mountain, south of Drakesbad, is named in the family's honor, since much of their land was given to the park.

Now a 19-room guest ranch that could pass for a laid-back B&B, Drakesbad offers a unique resort *experience*. Soak in the ancient hot springs, now a crystal-clear 116° F swimming pool, and snuggle under quilts in kerosene-lit rooms in the simple pine lodge or cabins (no electricity, though a generator runs the kitchen). In addition to "country basic" lodge rooms, bungalows and other units with private baths are available. Rates are on the American plan, and meals (announced with a clang of the chow bell) are generous. Enjoy big ranch breakfasts, hot lunches (sack lunches for hikers are available with advance notice), and full dinners with fine wines and beers (alcohol extra). Vegetarian meals are available by request. Open usually from the last Friday in June to early October (varies depending on the length of winter); reservations are often booked a year in advance. Rates for lodge and cabin rooms are $100–150 per person per day, up to $890 weekly; children ages 2–11 are $75 per day, $449 weekly. Rates for bungalows and the Northeast Annex are somewhat higher.

Drakesbad is accessible by car only via the Chester–Warner Valley Rd. from Chester (heading east on Hwy. 36, turn left at the firehouse, then left again when the road forks), about 17 miles. For a special treat, hike in—from the Pacific Crest Trail, from Bumpass Hell, Kings Creek Meadows, or from the Summit Lake area. All routes are basically downhill.

Even if you don't stay at Drakesbad, hike through the area. Call ahead to arrange a meal or two, or a guided horseback tour (open to nonguests, space permitting). Otherwise, ranch facilities are open only to Drakesbad guests. For more information and to make reservations, contact: Drakesbad Guest Ranch, 2150 N. Main St., Ste. 5, Red Bluff, CA 96080, 530/529-1512 ext. 120, fax 530/529/4511 (winter), or Warner Valley Rd., Chester, CA 96020 (June to October). To call Drakesbad directly, in season, contact an AT&T long-distance operator and ask to be connected to Area Code 530, Drakesbad Toll Station No. 2. For more information, see www.drakesbad.com.

EATING NEAR LASSEN

Architecturally famous in Chester is the **Timber House Lodge** restaurant at 1010 Main St. (at First St.), an anomaly built into an enigma. Sam Harrell's creation was built from huge quarried stone and "forest duff and storm fall," massive timbers hauled into town in the back of an old Studebaker. Inside, tree trunks (cut into sections, then reassembled with cement), carved wooden bars, bar stools, tables, and even light fixtures suggest a cave-dweller ambience. Also venerable, just the place to pull up a stool to enjoy a real ice cream milkshake or sundae, is the old-fashioned fountain at the **Lassen Drug Co.,** 220 Main St., 530/258-2261.

Cynthia's: A Hand-Made Bakery & Café, 278 Main in Chester, 530/258-1966, is quite contemporary, beloved for its pizzas, artisan breads, and box lunches, and probably also serves the best pastas around. Good coffee, tea, and treats, too, and delightful dinners are served on weekends. Distinctive dinners are also served Thurs.–Sat. at **The Bidwell House,** 1 Main, 530/258-3338; reservations essential.

Popular meat-and-potatoes options include **Carol's Café** in Prattville on Almanor's west shore, 2932 Almanor Dr. West), 530/259-2464, a local tradition. Open daily for all-American but updated breakfast, lunch, and dinner, Carol's serves up fresh-baked homemade pies, and an old-fashioned soda fountain. Or try the **Boathouse Grill** nearby, 530/259-2282, or the seasonal **Osprey's Landing** at Almanor West Golf Course, 111 Slim Dr. (off Hwy. 89), 530/259-4955. Popular on the other side of the lake is **Sam and Ami's,** 449 Peninsula Dr., 530/596-6231.

Bucks Lake Lodge, at Bucks Lake, 530/283-2262, has crepes and buttermilk pancakes for breakfast, burgers and sandwiches at lunch, and seafood and steaks at dinner. Prime rib, the house specialty, is served Thurs.–Sun. nights.

INFORMATION

A park admission pass, good for one week, costs $10 for cars, $5 for hikers or bikers. Pick up the pass and a free *Peak Experiences* tabloid guide (with calendars of seasonal park activities and other pertinent information) upon arrival at the north or south park entrance, or at **Lassen Park Headquarters,** 38050 Hwy. 36 East in Mineral, 530/595-4444, www.nps.gov/lavo, open Mon.–Fri. 8 A.M.–4:30 P.M. year-round. Visitor information is also available at the Southwest Information Station (SWIS), 530/595-3308 (summer only), a booth in the parking lot of the chalet. (A new $9.5 million visitor center, complete with museum exhibits, will replace the old ski chalet; construction is scheduled to begin as soon as snow melts in 2004, and be completed by summer 2005.) The SWIS booth is open 9 A.M.–4 P.M. weekends from Memorial Day weekend to mid-June; daily through Labor Day; then weekends only through the rest of September.

The **Loomis Museum** at Manzanita Lake features natural history and geology exhibits, and also sells books and other publications about the area. The museum is open 9 A.M.–5 P.M. on weekends from Memorial Day weekend to mid-June, then daily through the end of September. Loomis Museum Association publications are also available at park headquarters. Adjacent is the similarly intriguing stone home of B.F. Loomis, the photographer who captured on film Lassen Park's extraordinary early-1900s explosions.

Free wilderness permits, required for backcountry trekking in Lassen, can be obtained at park headquarters in Mineral, at the park entrance stations, at the seasonal SWIS visitor center, or by mail (contact park officials at least 14 days before you plan to arrive).

For information about camping and recreation in surrounding **Lassen National Forest,** contact forest headquarters at 2550 Riverside Dr. in Susanville, 530/257-2151, www.r5.fs.fed.us/lassen, or any of the individual ranger district offices: **Almanor** in Chester, 530/258-2141; **Eagle Lake** on Eagle Lake Rd. near Susanville, 530/257-4188; and **Hat Creek** in Fall River Mills, 530/336-5521. A visitor's guide (including information on campgrounds and the Thousand Lakes and Caribou Wildernesses) and maps ($6–8) are available. Visitors can also contact the Almanor Ranger District to rent **McCarthy Point Lookout,** overlooking Mill Creek Canyon, a large, two-room restored fire lookout—spectacular views—built in 1936 by the Civilian Conservation Corps (under $50 Sun.–Thurs. night, $50–100 on weekends).

For regional visitor information, contact the **Chester/Lake Almanor Chamber of Commerce,** 529 Main St., 530/258-2426 or 800/350-4838, www.chester-lakealmanor.com, and the **Plumas County Visitors Bureau,** located a half-mile west of Quincy on Hwy. 70 (next to the airport), 530/283-6345 or 800/326-2247, plumascounty.org.

EAGLE LAKE

Bordering Lassen National Forest, five miles wide and 14 miles long, Eagle Lake is no jewel at first glance. Its deep waters are fed from below by hundreds of springs. A basin lake on the southern tip of the Modoc Plateau, the lake is fringed by large and small rocks and—at least in some places—ponderosa, Jeffrey, and sugar pines as well as incense cedars, junipers, and white firs. The seven-mile **South Shore Trail** is suited to both bikers and hikers.

Eagle Lake is noted for its excellent fishing—especially for the unusual Eagle Lake trout (very good eating). Uniquely capable of surviving in highly alkaline waters, the Eagle Lake trout is evolutionary testament to the area's isolation over the eons.

Another special thrill here: watching birds of prey fishing; take the **Osprey Overlook Trail.** Bald eagles (most numerous in winter) remain remote even while fishing and hunting, but ospreys also fish here and in greater numbers. It's humbling to watch one of these awesome birds work the waters, scooping prey from the lake and winging homeward, trout writhing in its talons.

The ospreys nest along the lake's west shore, rearing their young high atop huge platform nests built on old telephone poles. Don't bother them—the ospreys are protected here, which is why they still come—but observe them from a distance with binoculars. Brown pelicans and other waterfowl are also abundant at Eagle Lake. For another sight, try **Antelope Mountain Lookout,** 15 miles west of the lake via gravel road (Rd. A-1) and open 8 A.M.–5 P.M. daily during the fire season—great views.

For more information, contact the **Eagle Lake Ranger District** office, 477-050 Eagle Lake Rd., 530/257-4188, or **Lassen National Forest headquarters** in Susanville, 530/257-2151. To get to Eagle Lake, turn north on Rd. A-1 two miles west of Susanville. The turnoff is marked.

Camping

Among the plentiful campsites at Eagle Lake, those at the **Christie** and **Merrill** areas are the quietest. **Eagle Campground** is forested, pretty, and popular with fishing fans. Reservations are available at Christie and Merrill, and are mandatory at Eagle. Campsites are $14; some require two-day minimum stays on weekends. For reservations call 877/444-6777, or see www.reserveusa .com. Food, supplies, and gas are available at Spaulding Tract nearby, but it's cheaper to stock up in Susanville. The boat launch at **Gallatin** is suitable even at low lake levels; an associated breakwater provides fishing access for the disabled.

SUSANVILLE AND VICINITY

On the dry eastern slope of the Sierra Nevada, Susanville is the Lassen County seat and a rough 'n' tumble lumber town full of history, lumber mills, loggers, and cowboys. Pioneer Isaac Roop built the first home here in 1854, naming the town and the river after his daughter Susan. Roop's cabin became **Fort Defiance,** capital of Nataqua ("woman") Territory and headquarters for the Sagebrush War of the early 1860s. Peter Lassen struck gold here, though area mining quickly pe-

tered out. Cattle and timber have dominated the local economy for years; one lumber mill and a door factory are still in operation, survivors of recent hard times. But the biggest employer in Susanville is the California Department of Corrections, providing well over 1,000 jobs at the two minimum-security prisons just outside town.

For more information, contact the **Lassen County Chamber of Commerce,** 84 N. Lassen St., 530/257-4323, www.lassencountychamber.org, and the **Historic Uptown Susanville Association,** 530/257-6506.

Seeing and Doing Susanville

Forget about the prisons and all those stir-crazy prisoners. Susanville can be a fun place. For example: The Historic Uptown Susanville Association sponsors the unique annual two-day **Susan's Birthday Celebration** in late June, www.susansbirthday.org, in remembrance of Susan Roop—daughter of town founder Isaac Roop, and the "Susan" for whom Susanville was named. But Susan's Birthday celebrates *all* Susans and their birthdays—with the annual **Susan Parade,** chocolate festival, sidewalk sales, live music and entertainment, and old-time barbecue and dance. So rename yourself Susan—at least for one weekend—and get on up to Susanville.

Other big events include the **Eagle Lake Bicycle Challenge** in June, an omnium including time trials as well as road and circuit races. Then comes **Lassen County Fair** in early July, and the **Main Cruise** in late July/early August, a family-friendly, 1950s-style event featuring everything from bubble gum blowing, hula hoop, limbo, and trike wheelie contests to a spotlight cruise, muscle car exhibit, slow drags, and **A Taste of Susanville.** Or head to Doyle, south of Susanville, for the famed **Lizard Races.** The "Old West" Susanville Rodeo comes in late August, the annual **Rails to Trails Festival** in October.

Stop off at Susanville's **Historic Railroad Depot,** 601 Richmond Rd., 530/257-3252, now a visitor center and local-history museum. The depot also marks the start of the **Bizz Johnson Trail,** a scenic 25.4-mile path to Westwood via the old Fernley & Lassen Railroad route through Susan River canyon. The trail is open to hikers, mountain bikers, and horseback riders, and makes a great cross-country ski trip in winter. The railroad depot is open May to mid-October, Fri.–Sun. 9 A.M.–5 P.M.

The **Lassen Historical Museum,** 75 N. Weatherlow, 530/257-3292, features historical photographs plus Native American and lumbering artifacts. Next door is **Roop's Fort,** a small log cabin originally constructed in 1854, now storage for furniture, tools, and miscellany.

Practicalities

The **Grand Café,** 730 Main St. (near Gay St.), 530/257-4713, has been a local institution since the 1920s. Slide into a smooth wooden booth or belly up to the Formica counter for buckwheat hotcakes at breakfast, all-American burgers or soup and fresh bread at lunch. Open Mon.–Sat. for breakfast and lunch. The **Daily Grind** café and ice cream parlor, 1002 Main St., 530/251-0511, serves simple breakfasts and lunch specials. The place for dinner is the **Champion Steakhouse** at the St. Francis Hotel, 830 Main (at Union), 530/257-4820, which pays proud homage to the area's cattle ranching heritage. Prime rib—get here early on weekend nights—and hefty New York steaks are specialties. Open Mon.–Sat. for lunch and dinner.

The pleasant **Roseberry House** bed-and-breakfast, 609 North St., 530/257-5675, www .roseberryhouse.com, occupies a 1902 country Victorian rich with antiques, offering four rooms with private bath. Full breakfast. Rooms $50–100. Because there's a local housing shortage in conjunction with the recent boom in state correctional employment, many local motels have become de facto boardinghouses; call ahead to make sure there's room at the inn. Two best bets include the **High Country Inn,** 3015 E. Riverside Dr. (just east of town, off Hwy. 36), 530/257-3450, and the **Best Western Trailside Inn,** 2785 Main St. (east of town, on Hwy. 36), 530/257-4123. Rates at both are $50–100. Or check out the recently redecorated "old-fashioned rooms" at the historic 1914 **St. Francis Hotel,** 830 Main, 530/257-4820. Campsites are available at Eagle Lake (see above).

For area recreation and camping information,

contact **Lassen National Forest headquarters,** 2550 Riverside Dr. in Susanville, 530/257-2151 (TDD 530/257-6244), www.r5.fs.fed.us/lassen, or the forest's **Eagle Lake Ranger District** office at 477-050 Eagle Lake Rd., 530/257-4188. At the **BLM Eagle Lake Field Office** here, 2950 Riverside Dr., 530/257-0456, ask about petroglyph sites in Rice Valley.

NORTH AND WEST OF LASSEN

Latour Demonstration State Forest

These 9,000 acres on the west side of Lassen National Forest, part of the Cascade Range and not far from Thousand Lakes Wilderness, are frequented mostly by hunters. Latour has no hiking trails but does have miles of forest roads and free primitive campgrounds. Area mammals include black bears, mountain lions, bobcats, pikas, and mountain beavers. Birds include the sharp-shinned hawk and goshawk, blue grouse, mountain quail, screech owls, and woodpeckers. Pines, firs, mountain shrubs, and delicate water-loving wildflowers abound.

High winds, extreme cold, and wet snow are the norm here in winter and spring, so come from early July to late October. To get here, at Millville take Whitmore Rd. northeast to Bateman. For more information, contact the forest at 1000 Cypress Ave. in Redding, 530/225-2508.

Old Station

Old Station is the closest thing to a town you'll find immediately north of Lassen. Gas is available, though famed **Uncle Runt's Place** is closed, at last report. Across Hwy. 44/89 from the Hat Creek Campground, a half mile west of Old Station, is the **Spattercone Trail,** a free 1.5-mile self-guided trail through lava tubes and domes, volcanic blowholes, and spattercones. It can get hot here in summer, so hike in the early morning—and bring water.

One mile north of Old Station (across from the Cave Campground) is **Subway Cave,** a 2,000-year-old lava tube you can walk through for one-third mile. A self-guided-tour brochure is available at area national forest offices; for more about the lava flows in Hat Creek Valley, stop off at the **Old Station Information Center** (open Apr.–Dec.) a half mile south of the cave on Hwy. 89. The cave is dark as doom inside and always cool, so bring a powerful flashlight, a sweater, and sturdy shoes.

Hat Creek

Considered one of the best trout-fishing streams in the U.S., Hat Creek is a destination in its own right. The season usually opens May 1, but the two-trout 18-inch-length limit is meaningless to many fishing enthusiasts here, as most throw their catch back. At Cassel—consisting of a general store and PG&E campground (toll-free 800/743-5000)—Hat Creek is joined by Rising River. Heading downstream, you'll pass the **Crystal Lake Fish Hatchery,** Crystal Lake, and Baum Lake. Farther on, below the Hat Creek II Powerhouse and before the creek empties into Lake Britton, are the Lower Hat Creek waters of the **Hat Creek Wild Trout Project,** with big, wily fish (catch-and-release only). From Hat Creek proper, take Doty Rd. for four miles to the **Hat Creek Radio Astronomy Observatory,** a computer-controlled 85-foot-diameter radiotelescope designed to track objects in space—a project of the Berkeley Illinois Maryland Association (BIMA) consortium, http://bima.astro.umd.edu.

Clearwater House

A comfortable, full-service anglers' inn, in the style of an English fishing lodge, Clearwater House is especially appropriate for fly-fishing aficionados. Tucked into the town of Cassel (between Burney and Fall River Mills), on the banks of Hat Creek, a premier wild-trout stream, the inn's location is heaven for fly-fishers. Hat Creek is internationally renowned for its stream-bred and wily wild trout, but it's not alone here; five designated wild-trout streams are all within minutes of the inn, and the expert guide staff takes guests to all of them. Clearwater offers an extensive array of fishing programs, from private guiding and weekend instruction (at all levels) to five-day "Mastering the Art of Fly Fishing" and "Big Trout Tactics" courses ($1,050–1,150).

Though Clearwater caters to fly-fishers, nonanglers are welcome and will find much to do in the area—from mountain biking and wilderness exploration to excellent golfing at Fall River. A tennis court is on the property. The inn's decor is relaxed yet tasteful, from the fish and game prints on the walls to the oriental

E.T., PHONE CALIFORNIA!

Coming soon to Hat Creek and the SETI (Search for Extra-Terrestrial Intelligence) Institute radio observatory site: the **Allen Telescope Array** (ATA), named for Microsoft co-founder Paul Allen and technology officer Nathan Myhrvoid, who jointly contributed $12.5 million to its creation. The 350-dish array, expected to debut in 2005, will be the largest radio telescope anywhere, devoted to listening 24/7 for signs of intelligent life thousands of light years away.

Installed on public as well as adjacent private land, the ATA—also known as the One Hectare Telescope—may ultimately consist of 1,000 6.1-meter offset Gregorian dishes scattered densely, like mushrooms, on a 2.5 acre site, their sheer number along with the large "primary beam" size offering unprecedented flexibility in observing. Once installed, the synchronized radio scope will focus first on receiving radio waves from 1,000 sunlike stars relatively close to "home," or Earth. Next the project will "listen in" on 100,000 stars, then 1 million such stars in the Milky Way, which is estimated to contain some 400 billion stars.

With a total price tag of $25 million, the ATA is cosponsored by the nonprofit SETI Institute of Mountain View (www.seti.org) and the University of California at Berkeley Radio Astronomy Lab (RAL; http://astron.berkeley.edu/ral). For more information about the project, see http://bima.astro.umd.edu. For more information about the area, contact the Hat Creek Ranger District office on Hwy. 299 in Fall River Mills, 530/336-5521.

rugs over hardwood floors—a natural expression of proprietor Dick Galland's experience as a wilderness and fishing guide.

Clearwater House opens to the public from late April through mid-November (but available for private groups in the off-season). Rates are on the American plan; accommodations and three meals are $185 per person per day ($335 with a full day of guiding). Reservations mandatory. For information and reservations, contact: Clearwater House on Hat Creek, 530/335-5500 (phone and fax), www.clearwatertrout.com. In midwinter, call 415/381-1173 in Muir Beach.

BURNEY FALLS AND VICINITY
McArthur–Burney Falls Memorial State Park

Halfway between Lassen Peak and Mt. Shasta, 15 miles northeast of Burney, is one of the state's oldest parks, 910-acre McArthur–Burney Falls Memorial State Park. This is heavily forested northern lava country at about 3,000 feet. Birdlife

Burney Falls

is abundant, including great blue herons, Canada geese, a variety of ducks and grebes, owls, evening grosbeaks, and sometimes bald eagles.

That Teddy Roosevelt called Burney Falls "The Eighth Wonder of the World" is a notorious and lingering misattribution; Roosevelt actually said the waterfall here was a "wonder." Wonder that it still is, Burney Falls is fed by spring flows of 100 million gallons daily and thunders down a moss-covered 129-foot cliff into emerald-green water before flowing into Lake Britton. The porous volcanic basalt makes for some fascinating water action. Delicate plants thrive here in the cool moisture. Rare black swifts (normally seabirds) build nests of lichens on cliffs near the falls from spring until the first frosts and dart after insects, erratically, through the mists. Another fascinating bird near Burney Falls is the wrenlike water ouzel, which dives into the creek and walks along the streambed looking for larvae and other delicacies, then shoots up out of the water like a space shuttle launch.

Easy walks here include the half-mile **Headwaters Trail** to Burney Creek above the falls (for the best view), and the 1.2-mile self-guided **Nature Trail** circuit into the gorge. For a longer trip, follow the **Burney Creek Trail** all the way down to Burney Creek Cove (and beach) at Lake Britton, then climb back up on the **Rim Trail.**

The park is especially popular in summer but open year-round, including the two state park campgrounds—a total of 128 sites with hot showers ($12–15); make reservations for the busy summer months through ReserveAmerica, 800/444-7275, www.reserveamerica.com. The day-use fee is $4 per car. For more information, call the park at 530/335-2777.

Fall River Mills and Burney

Highway-straddling Burney is making a comeback after years of declines in the timber industry (and in local fortunes). Local businesses have spruced up and expanded; downtown has sprouted wall murals, planter boxes, and a flower garden—everything a labor of love and community pride. So slow down a bit and be neighborly. Nearby Fall River is noted for its outcroppings of white diatomaceous rock; its attractions include the four-building **Fort Crook Museum,** 530/336-5110, and the noted **Fall River Valley Golf Course,** 530/336-5555. For more information on the area, contact the **Burney Basin Chamber of Commerce,** 37477 Main St. in Burney, 530/335-2111.

Intriguing for an overnight is the stunning historic 1921 craftsman-style **Pit River Lodge** midway between Burney and Fall River Mills, on the banks of the Pit River. Originally built by PG&E during construction of the Pit One Powerhouse, the lodge was owned and maintained by the utility until the current owners purchased it in 1998. On-site accommodation options are six double rooms in the lodge including a large suite with private bath, four cottages (two two-bedroom and two three-bedroom), a sleeping annex (six bedrooms with shared baths and a cozy common area), and RV parking (no hookups yet). The furnished cottages all feature fully equipped kitchens. Accommodations are available individually or as a complete package for conferences, family reunions, and other large gatherings. Facilities also include a billiards room and spacious dining room serving dinner seven nights a week, breakfast and lunch Saturday and Sunday only. Rooms in the Annex, which share two bathrooms, are $50–100. Lodge rooms and the corner suite (private baths) are $100–150, and cottages are $150–250. Reservations suggested, essentially during major holidays such as Christmas. Currently, the lodge is open Apr.–Dec. For information, contact: Pit River Lodge, Pit 1 Powerhouse Rd. in Fall River Mills, 530/336-5005, www.pitriverlodge.com.

For something literally uptown, head for the 1936 **Fall River Hotel** in Fall River proper, 24860 Main St., 530/336-5550, www.fallriverhotel.com, a local variation on the bed-and-breakfast theme with 17 Victorian-style rooms, most with private baths, and downstairs restaurant and saloon. There are also a number of decent motels in the area, including the **Hi-Mont Motel** on Hwy. 299 (at Bridge St.) in Fall River Mills, 530/336-5541, and, in Burney, both the **Burney Motel,** 530/335-4500, and the **Shasta Pines Motel,** 530/335-2202. Rates for all are $50–100.

In addition to McArthur–Burney Falls, you can camp at nearby **Ahjumawi Lava Springs**

State Park (accessible only by boat) and at PG&E's **Lake Britton Campground,** which offers good swimming (but steep drop-offs from shore) and bass and trout fishing. Lake Britton Campground is also a natural stopover for hikers passing through on the nearby Pacific Crest Trail. Facilities at the lake are usually open May 1–Oct. 31. Six national forest campgrounds are within easy driving distance.

Ahjumawi Lava Springs State Park

A lovely lava springs area of pine, juniper, and chaparral, Ahjumawi ("Where the rivers meet") is a good place to get away from it all—especially since you can only get there by boat. This remote state park is 6,000 acres of wilderness fringing the lakes at the north end of Fall River Valley. Park highlights include fascinating basalt formations, many freshwater springs, and incredible views. Facilities include tent campsites (30-day maximum stay), tables, and an outhouse. Waterfowl and bald eagles nest here.

To get there, from McArthur head north on Main St. past the Intermountain Fairgrounds and turn onto Rat Ranch Rd. (dirt road, unlocked gate—please close) and continue four miles through PG&E's McArthur Swamp (known locally as "the Rat Farm") to the boat launch area. For more information, including suggestions about where to rent boats or canoes and where to camp, contact the rangers at McArthur–Burney Falls State Park.

Big Bend Hot Springs and Iron Canyon

To get far, far from the madding crowds, head out Big Bend Rd. (past the town of Montgomery Creek) and continue past Wengler, through Big Bend, then over the Pit River to little Iron Canyon Reservoir in the Shasta-Trinity National Forest. Forest Service camping is available at Deadlun Creek, and another 10 PG&E campsites are at Hawkins Landing. Back on Hwy. 299, stop where the bridge crosses Hatchet Creek, a half mile from Big Bend Road. Hike upstream a quarter mile through thick brush to **Hatchet Falls** and an isolated pool ideal for swimming.

Modoc County

One of those rare places in California where local folks still wave to strangers passing on back roads, the Modoc Plateau is dramatic in its desolation. Even in the thick of winter's tule fog, accompanied by the lonely musings of migrating waterfowl, cowboys still ride the range here and belly up to the bar in local saloons on Saturday nights. Here in Modoc country, California's outback and site of one of the last major Indian wars in the United States, distrust between native peoples and settlers still lingers. The hundreds of lava caves and craggy outcroppings at what is now Lava Beds National Monument enabled charismatic "Captain Jack" and his Modoc warriors to hold out against hundreds of U.S. Army troops (with superior arms) for more than three months before being starved into defeat in 1873. A 19th-century domestic Vietnam, the Modoc War cost U.S. taxpayers $40,000 for every Native American killed. The other costs cannot be counted.

Despite the deep sadness that seems to seep up from the lava caves and obsidian cliffs, there is great beauty here. On a clear day from the flat-topped, blue, and brooding Warner Mountains, majestic Mt. Shasta to the west seems so close that one can imagine reaching out for a handful of snow. And the view east to the alkaline lakes of Surprise Valley and across the Great Basin is nothing short of spectacular.

Yet even getting to Modoc takes gumption. It's a haul, from almost everywhere. (Without a car—better yet, a pickup truck—forget it.) Highway 139 from Klamath Falls in Oregon provides the most direct access, rolling across the plateau

NORTHERN MOUNTAINS

APOLOGIES TO WATER BIRDS

Industry in Modoc County is agriculture: cattle, sheep, horses, and crops including barley, clover, oats, wheat, potatoes, apples, apricots, and plums, plus the finest alfalfa hay and seed. Recreation (primarily hunting) is a seasonal economic boon. Beyond the grain and hayfields, endless shades of gray-green and yellow are the subtle colors of these rolling sagebrush grasslands. Higher, from the plateau to the mountains, chaparral and junipers blend into pine forests, and glacial meadows abloom with wildflowers.

But what *is* nature is not necessarily natural. The Modoc Plateau is a heavily "managed" environment. Most modern-day wetlands are artificial, timber is second-growth, and the endless expanses of sage and bitterbrush have replaced native perennial grasses. In the Devil's Garden area of Modoc National Forest grows the most generous jumble of juniper in any U.S. national forest—but juniper would not thrive in this plant world without the competitive edge provided by cattle grazing. As the writer William Kittredge (who grew up a rancher in the shadow of the Warner Mountains) observed in his 1988 *Harper's* article, "Who Won the West? Apologies to the Water Birds and Ranch Hands":

Maybe we should have known the world wasn't made for our purposes, to be remodeled into our idea of an agricultural paradise, and that Warner Valley wasn't there to have us come along and drain the swamps, and level the peat ground into alfalfa land. No doubt we should have known the water birds would quit coming. But we had been given to understand that places we owned were to be used as we saw fit. The birds were part of that.

So, where did otherwise good people go wrong, Kittredge asks, using other people (as well as the land and its natural inhabitants) as tools to build our version of a greater destiny? Was it cold-heartedness, crass commerce, and/or stupidity in the face of the sacred? Imagining a world where "in the end all of us would be able to forgive ourselves and care for ourselves," he answers: "We would have learned to mostly let the birds fly away, because it is not necessarily meat we are hunting."

NORTHERN MOUNTAINS

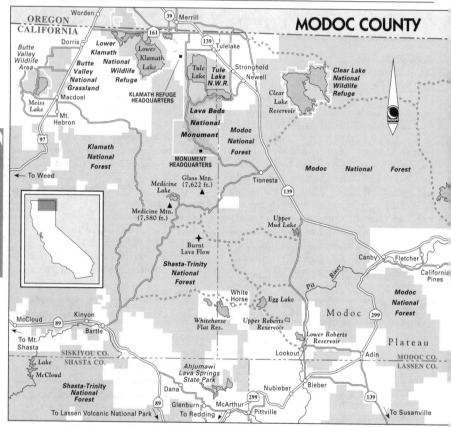

MODOC COUNTY

OREGON
CALIFORNIA

Worden
Merrill
Dorris
Tulelake
Butte Valley Wildlife Area
Lower Klamath Lake
Lower Klamath National Wildlife Refuge
Butte Valley National Grassland
Macdoel
Meiss Lake
Mt. Hebron
KLAMATH REFUGE HEADQUARTERS
Tule Lake
Tule Lake N.W.R.
Stronghold
Newell
Clear Lake Reservoir
Clear Lake National Wildlife Refuge
Lava Beds National Monument
Modoc National Forest
To Weed
Klamath National Forest
MONUMENT HEADQUARTERS
Modoc National Forest
Glass Mtn. (7,622 ft.)
Medicine Lake
Tionesta
Medicine Mtn. (7,580 ft.)
Upper Mud Lake
Burnt Lava Flow
Shasta-Trinity National Forest
Canby
Fletcher
California Pines
Pit River
Modoc National Forest
White Horse
Egg Lake
Modoc
McCloud
Kinyon
Bartle
Whitehorse Flat Res.
Upper Roberts Reservoir
Lower Roberts Reservoir
Plateau
To Mt. Shasta
SISKIYOU CO.
SHASTA CO.
Lake McCloud
Shasta-Trinity National Forest
Ahjumawi Lava Springs State Park
Dana
Lookout
Adin
MODOC CO.
LASSEN CO.
Glenburn
McArthur
Nubieber
Bieber
To Lassen Volcanic National Park
To Redding
Pittville
To Susanville

between the Lava Beds/Klamath wildlife area and Clear Lake. Also get here from the south via Hwy. 299 from Red Bluff, Hwy. 139 from Eagle Lake (then Hwy. 299), or Hwy. 395 as it winds north from Susanville and the farthest reaches of the Sierra Nevada.

THE LAND

Native peoples called the high Modoc Plateau area "the smiles of God," a strangely fitting name for this rugged remnant of the Old West. To the west, mysterious Mt. Shasta presides over the lava-topped tableland. Sister volcano Lassen Peak, the southernmost sentry of the Cascade Range, looms up from the south. By virtue of their *presence,* Shasta and Lassen stand out visually, but the dividing line between the Cascades and the Modoc Plateau is obscure. Defining the area's plateau-ness is also difficult; this high country is both the southern tip of the vast Columbia Plateau and part of the Great Basin, which extends from the Sierra Nevada through Nevada and into Utah, Idaho, Oregon, and Washington.

Compared to the Klamaths and the Cascades, this region has few rivers, lakes, or forests. The Pit River, the only major Modoc County waterway, originates in the Warners and cuts diagonally through the lava plateau and mountains before entering the Sacramento River via Shasta Lake. Modoc lakes are landlocked rem-

Land and Climate

Violent volcanism was the great creator of regional landforms. The Cascades and the Modoc Plateau are the only places in California almost completely created from young basaltic lavas and extrusive igneous rocks like those seen at Lava Beds National Monument. Belying the "softness" of its name, the black moonscape of Lava Beds offers harsh but impressive examples of basalt pahoehoe (smooth) lava formations. Throughout the plateau, mineral springs and hot springs abound (most of the latter, unfortunately for travelers, are on private property). The geology of the Warner Mountains and adjacent Surprise Valley to the east—visible from the road on the way to Cedarville from Alturas—results from the interaction of a double fault through the area.

Relatively dry, with an average precipitation of 12.6 inches annually, Modoc County experiences cold winters and hot summers. Snow is erratic but never extremely heavy, usually four to six inches. Tule fog creates the more common type of white Christmas in these parts.

Pacific Flyway Fauna

In fall and spring, the region's national wildlife refuges become home to a million shorebirds and waterfowl migrating each year along the Pacific Flyway. Though much diminished by extensive "reclamation" of wetlands for agricultural uses, the migrations are still impressive. Snow geese, Canada geese, mallards and other ducks, cormorants, and snowy egrets touch down for the annual interspecies flutter, along with pheasants, great blue herons, marsh hawks, meadowlarks, and other songbirds. Many species nest and raise their young here and are present until summer. In winter, most amazing are the large numbers of bald eagles; hundreds of bald eagles winter in the great Klamath Basin, where they feed on carcasses of the less fortunate waterfowl. The year-round resident bird population includes many species typical of Northern California: quail, pheasants, hawks, golden eagles, woodpeckers, jays, and various songbirds. Not so typical is the spectacular strutting sage grouse.

Mule deer are common, as are coyotes,

© AVALON TRAVEL PUBLISHING, INC.

nants of ancient glacial runoff. Lower Klamath Lake, Tule Lake, Clear Lake Reservoir, and Goose Lake are all major refuges for migratory geese, ducks, and swans. During the past two million years, immense seas covered much of the area. Along the remote far-north section of Hwy. 395, ancient sand dunes, layered sedimentary rocks, and beach terraces suggest a very different long-ago landscape. During the Pleistocene era, the plateau's lava formations trapped water runoff from the Cascades to create Tule Lake. Now little more than an impressive pond among radish and potato fields, the lake was 185,000 acres of water, marshes, and wildlife until post–World War II reclamation turned three-quarters of it into farmland.

smaller mammals and rodents, and rattlesnakes. Mountain lions, bobcats, and pronghorn are rarer. But the small and sleek, tan, white-rumped pronghorn are making a comeback here. They run in the largest numbers among the juniper and sage of remote Devil's Garden between the Warners and Tule Lake, in the company of browsing mustangs. When Europeans first reached California, a half-million or more pronghorn roamed throughout the state. Now fewer remain, most of these in Modoc County, though the total U.S. population is near the half-million mark. Also here, primarily in the South Warner Wilderness, are California big-horn sheep, though this introduced population has been decimated by pneumonia.

Lava Beds and Vicinity

Technically part of Siskiyou County, the 72 square miles of **Lava Beds National Monument** are dry, inhospitable, and rugged—a tumble of lava caves, craggy volcanic chimneys, and cinder cones dusted by sagebrush and tumbleweed. Fog is common, especially in winter, adding to the landscape's eeriness. Somehow this desolate patch of plateau became the perfect staging ground for the most expensive war ever launched against native peoples by the U.S. government—the only full-blown Indian war ever waged in California. During the presidency of U.S. Grant, the U.S. government spent more than a half-million dollars in a relentless six-month war against Chief Kentipoos (or Kentapoos or Keintpoos) and his mixed band of freedom fighters. Known also as "Captain Jack," Kentipoos gained notoriety both for his strategic shrewdness and his style, particularly the brassy habit of wearing brass buttons and military insignia. The Modoc Indian War was not only costly in money and human lives, it also caused cultural disintegration when the surviving Modocs were shipped off to a reservation in the Midwest.

Fascinating background reading is *Life Amongst the Modocs: Unwritten History* by Joaquin Miller, written at the time of the Modoc War. This visionary 1873 based-on-fact fiction is drawn from Miller's personal experiences in Shasta and Siskiyou Counties during the gold rush, among settlers and native peoples alike. His protagonist eventually learns that at the edge of the frontier, that all-American symbol of democratic hope and justice, treachery and self-betrayal are just as likely.

The Modocs

The Modocs' enemies to the north—Oregon's Klamath tribe—named the Modocs *moa*, meaning "southerner," and *docks*, "near." A small group of people even before their systematic destruction during California's settlement, the Modocs are something of a mystery today; little is known about their culture. The Klamath and Tule Lake basins were first inhabited 7,500-9,000 years ago. Unusual petroglyphs carved in sandstone cliffs near Tule Lake feature characters never painted or carved by any other western people. Remains of ancient dwelling sites have been discovered near Lower Klamath Lake, though anthropologists suspect that volcanic activity made the area largely unsuitable for human habitation until the 1400s, when ancestors of the closely related Klamath and Modoc clans first arrived.

Fragile, incredibly intricate pottery has been unearthed in Klamath-Modoc territory in recent years, but the Modocs were primarily basketweavers. They dressed in buckskin, furs, bark, and tule cloth, and also used tule reeds from the lakes to build boats and homes. The Modoc people subsisted primarily on game—the deer, pronghorn, and mountain sheep once so plentiful in the Lava Beds area—and stalked fur-bearing animals, including the now-extinct pine marten. With more tribal solidarity than most California native peoples, the Modocs were considered "the model tribe" by early northern Californian settlers because they were peaceable and helpful. The characterization of the Modocs as inherently warlike was (and is) unfortunate and untrue but a common belief based on later history.

Aside from the Modocs and occasional marauding Klamaths, northern Paiutes or Toloma (a Shoshone people) lived to the east in and around Surprise Valley. Virtually nothing is known about the native people of Surprise Valley, though a Nevada Paiute inspired the great but doomed Ghost Dance movement of the late 1800s—a spiritual doctrine passed on first to Modoc and Achomawi tribes, then to the Shasta, Karuk, Yurok, and others in Northern California. Ritual remnants of this yearning for the Old Ways remain in modern-day Native American ceremonies. The Achomawi lived throughout Pit River country, their villages usually on streambanks (except near Burney and Hat Creeks, where the Atsugewi lived). Deer weren't overly abundant, so the Achomawi developed a unique trapping system—concealing pits six to nine feet deep in the middle of deer paths so their prey would just fall in. This practice, considered a nuisance by settlers who later banned it, gave the Pit River its name.

THE MODOC INDIAN WAR

Not until the mass migrations of whites during the California gold rush (and the rush to settle fertile Oregon Territory) did local native peoples begin attacking settlers in warfare—except in northeastern California, where the Modocs and Paiutes lived. The Modoc Plateau became known as "the dark and bloody ground of the Pacific," center stage for the 30-year struggle between whites and Native Americans that took place throughout California's Lassen, Siskiyou, and Modoc Counties; Oregon's Klamath and Lake Counties; and western Nevada. From the start, wagon trains of settlers frightened away the game so necessary to survival, and a smallpox epidemic in 1847 wiped out infants and tribal elders. Young warriors raided settling parties for survival and in retaliation. The "facts" are unreliable, but an estimated 300 whites had been killed by 1852 and another 112 by 1858.

Captain Jack and His "Hothead" Warriors

Pressure intensified to solve "the Indian problem" by relocating the Modocs. In 1864, the U.S. Bureau of Indian Affairs negotiated a peace treaty with the Modocs, who agreed to leave their ancestral homeland and settle at the Klamath Reservation in Oregon in exchange for money and supplies. But animosity between the Modocs and the Klamaths was great and the threat of starvation real. Because the Klamaths considered the reservation and its resources theirs alone, the Modocs were forced to slaughter their horses for food. When there were no more horses, they began drifting back to their Lost River fishing grounds. Kentipoos gradually emerged as leader of the young Modocs characterized as "hotheads." Angered over being forced off their ancestral lands, he and his band left the reservation at will to raid and steal. Eventually, Captain Jack openly asserted that his people were back on their tribal lands to stay, and that he could lead his band into the lava beds south of Tule Lake and never be dislodged—an almost prophetic statement.

The War Begins

The war, variously considered "farce tragedy" and "a comedy of errors" by observers, began in late November 1872, three years before Custer fell at Little Bighorn. United States soldiers dispatched to herd the Modocs back to the reservation ended up on the run, carrying off 13 dead or wounded. Then the Modocs, who had vowed to kill off every man in Tule Lake Valley if attacked by soldiers, did so. (Captain Jack, not in favor of all-out war or the valley murders, was outvoted by a more militant Modoc faction.) The band retreated to the crumpled lava plateau south of Tule Lake and climbed into its subterranean trenches to await the inevitable Army pursuit.

On Jan. 12, 1873, 175 regular soldiers, 20 Klamath Indian scouts, and 104 volunteers headed by Lt. Col. Frank Wheaton, the Army's district commander (in all, about 300 rifles and two howitzers), moved into position outside what came to be known as Captain Jack's Stronghold.

The Modocs were excellent marksmen and good strategists. The battle at dawn the next morning was disastrous for the U.S. Army. Fog blanketed the battlefield. Wheaton's cold, confused troops fired at phantoms all day—dodging bullets from nowhere, unnerved still more by the Modocs' derisive comments—and retreated all night, leaving behind enough rifles and ammunition to fight another war. They carried off nine dead and 28 wounded; there were no Indian casualties. As the siege wore on, media-conscious Captain Jack gave interviews to various newspaper reporters, a shrewd move that won broad public support for his band, 52 Modocs holding a thousand soldiers at bay.

The War Ends

Then, suddenly, whatever sympathy the Modocs had won through the media was lost. On April 11, militant Modocs killed two members of the Army's Peace Commission negotiating team and half-scalped a third. Furious soldiers forgot their fear and renewed their attack on the stronghold. Army mortars rained missiles for two nights. When soldiers finally reached the Indian command post, it was deserted. The retreating band, on foot and short of water, finally surrendered on May 27. All except Kentipoos. But in a cruel irony, the very warriors who against their leader's wishes had incited the group to murder, helped the government track down Captain Jack. He was captured on June 1, then tried, convicted, and hung at Fort Klamath. Afterward, his head was hacked off and shipped to the Army Medical Museum in Washington, D.C.

"This is vengeance, indeed," wrote an appalled *San Francisco Chronicle* correspondent. "Captain Jack said that he would like to meet the Great White Chief in Washington face to face. The government evidently intends that his dying wish shall be respected." Captain Jack's skull eventually arrived at the Smithsonian but was later returned to tribal members.

LAVA BEDS NATIONAL MONUMENT AND VICINITY

This is where it all happened, the bleak scene of Captain Jack's last stand. Especially when the black lava and death-gray sagebrush are shrouded in drifts of tule fog, unquiet ghosts seem to dwell here. Scrambling into lava caves and up cinder cones, it's apparent how clever the Modocs were.

Captain Jack's battlements were perfect: a lava fortress surrounded by deceptively "easy" terrain almost impossible to cross without being vulnerable to sniper fire.

Even those uninterested in the bloody march of history will enjoy Lava Beds National Monument, however. Two separate, high-desert wilderness areas (no fires, bring water, camping by permit only) offer hiking and some arid vistas. Outside the park to the northeast is an area rich in ancient petroglyphs. (Vandalism has been a problem, so ask for directions and more information at park headquarters.) Also near Lava Beds, in forest clearings along the highway between the towns of Alturas and Tulelake, are three huge U.S. Air Force "backscatter" radar antennae linked to military installations in Mountain Home, Idaho, and NORAD.

Volcanoes and Lava Tubes

At Lava Beds, the area's volcanic history (and the area is still considered volcanically active) is everywhere apparent. Cinder cones, spatter cones, stratovolcanoes, shield volcanoes, chimneys, flows of both smooth pahoehoe and rough and chunky a'a lava, and lava tubes abound. Lava tubes, formed when the outer "skin" on streams of superheated magma cools and hardens, are not unusual in volcanic areas, but the sheer quantity found at Lava Beds is. In fact, there are more lava tube caves here (435, at last count) than anywhere else in North America.

Caves and Cones

Mushpot Cave, in the Indian Well parking lot, is lighted and comes complete with good interpretive displays and a film—all in all, a good place to start. A loop road from Indian Well toward the south offers access to most of the other park caves—altogether, some 300 "wilderness caves"—that can be visited without passes. But don't set out without current information and cautions; stop by the visitor center for guidance. To a large extent, cave names describe what visitors see: Blue Grotto, Sunshine, Natural Bridge, and Catacombs (where spelunkers must crawl to get through). **Crystal Ice Cave,** accessible only on ranger-led tours, Dec.1–March 31, features red lava walls and frost crystals that flash like jewels. Best of all, though, are the **Labyrinth** and **Golden Dome Caves.** Not far south of the loop group, near Caldwell Butte, is **Valentine Cave,** a locals' favorite.

Not a human graveyard, **Skull Ice Cave** was named for the many pronghorn and bighorn sheep skulls found here. The cavern itself is enormous—the domed roof in the main chamber 75 feet high—and the floor below is a solid sheet of ice. (But visitors have been loving Skull and smaller **Merrill Ice Cave** to death, so both have been closed temporarily to protect and clean up their ice floors.) **Big Painted Cave** has fascinating Indian pictographs; others are faintly visible on the bridge at **Symbol Bridge Cave** nearby.

Schonchin Butte above, named for a Modoc chief, is the largest of the area's 11 scoriaceous cinder cones. (A three-quarter-mile trail climbs to the fire tower on the summit, where you'll get great views of the monument.) Other cones—Mammoth, Hippo, Bearpaw, Modoc, and Whitney—are across the road in the wilderness area. **The Castles** are two large groups of fumaroles or chimneys of gas-inflated lava, similar to the fire fountains on Kilauea in Hawaii. Off on a side road farther north are the **Boulevard** and **Balcony Caves.** (To visit more remote caves, ask at park headquarters, then sign in—required, just in case you don't come back.)

Modoc War Sites

About a mile past Boulevard and Balcony Caves, between Black Crater and Hardin Butte, is the **Thomas-Wright Battlefield.** Here, on April 26, 1873, two-thirds of Capt. Evan Thomas's troops met their maker during the Modoc War. The park road crosses over it, then continues past Gillem's Bluff for four miles to **Gillem's Camp,** which was the U.S. Army's field headquarters during the six-month Modoc War. **Canby's Cross,** a white wooden marker erected by U.S. troops, marks the spot where General Canby, the U.S. Army's field operations commander, was gunned down during the last session of the Peace Commission negotiations. At the park's northeast corner near Tule Lake Sump is the complex maze of caves, lava trenches, and natural rock battlements of **Captain Jack's Stronghold,** the center of the war zone. Wounded U.S. Army soldiers were sheltered at **Hospital Rock,** another natural fortification nearby where the cavalry camped in 1873.

Practicalities

Come with a full tank of gas and bring food and containers for water as well as hard-soled shoes and warm- and cool-weather clothes. It can snow here any season, though it can also get quite hot in summer. (But even in summer heat, it stays cool in the lava caves.) The park's northeast entrance is about eight miles from Tulelake. The southeast entrance is 30 miles south of Tulelake (or 58 miles from Klamath Falls) and 47 miles north from Canby on Hwy. 139; then take Tionesta Rd. (follow the signs from the highway). Major airlines serve Medford and Klamath Falls, where rental cars are available.

For basic information and a map, contact **Lava Beds National Monument,** 530/667-2282, www.nps.gov/labe. Park headquarters is near Indian Well, reached most easily via the park's southeast entrance. The day-use fee at Lava Beds is $5 (good for seven days). The park's new visitor center, just up the road and around the corner from the previous one at Indian Well, was scheduled to open by summer's end, 2003. The park is always open to visitors; the visitor center is open 8 A.M.–5 P.M. in winter (closed Thanksgiving and Christmas), until 6 P.M. in summer. Free publications include plant and animal species checklists and pamphlets about Captain Jack's Stronghold, the self-guided walk at Petroglyph Point, and local geology. In addition to cultural and historical museum exhibits, the visitor center offers a good selection of books on area history and natural history. During summer (Memorial Day weekend to Labor Day), ranger-led interpretive programs include morning walks, afternoon cave tours, and evening campfire programs; get current details at the visitor center. If you plan to explore the caves, bring two flashlights (in case one dies in the darkness), or get flashlights (free, but they must be returned) and buy protective hardhats (required) at headquarters.

The 43 campsites at **Indian Well,** near park

BAD MEDICINE AT MEDICINE LAKE

In late 2002 the Bush administration abruptly reversed a previous decision that blocked construction of a geothermal power plant at Telephone Flat near Medicine Lake, on lands considered sacred by Native Americans. In making its decision, the administration rejected the recommendation of the federal Advisory Council on Historical Preservation, which had urged the preservation of Medicine Lake for cultural and historical reasons. (In 1999 some 24 square miles known as the Medicine Lake Highlands were declared a "traditional cultural district," eligible for inclusion on the National Register of Historic Places.) The administration also betrayed a previous geothermal development compromise, in the view of project opponents.

Medicine Lake has been at the center of controversial new "green energy" geothermal development proposals because underlying the area is a massive underground reservoir of 450-degree water and steam, created by a natural hot plate of molten rock.

One controversial Medicine Lake facility was a $120 million, 48-megawatt plant proposed by Calpine of San Jose. Both the U.S. Bureau of Land Management and the U.S. Forest Service gave preliminary approval to the Calpine plant—approval that was subsequently blocked by the Clinton administration due to concerns about that plant's proximity to Medicine Lake, considered a center of healing by Native Americans. Yet when that proposal was rejected, another Calpine geothermal complex was approved nearby, outside the lake's most sacred area at Fourmile Hill. The Pit River tribe abandoned its protests over Fourmile in exchange for a five-year moratorium on additional power projects.

According to the *New York Times,* Calpine subsequently sued the federal government for $100 million, for rejecting its first proposed plant—but agreed to drop the suit if the Bush administration reconsidered. The problem with geothermal development, according to representatives of the Pit River, Modoc, and other area tribes, is that Medicine Lake is sacred ground, a venerated ritual site. At last report the best overall summary on geothermal development at Medicine Lake was provided online by the Earth Island Institute's Sacred Land Film Project, www.sacred-land.org; that site also provides links to relevant newspaper articles.

headquarters, are open year-round ($10). Campgrounds feature picnic tables, fire rings, and running water year-round (in winter, use inside taps). Freestyle camping in nearby national forest areas is free (permit necessary for motorized vehicles). A quiet meadow campground is at **Howard's Gulch,** 30 miles south on Hwy. 39 ($6). Or camp at the **Medicine Lake Highlands** ($7) to the south, reached via 20 miles of gravel road.

The town of **Tulelake** is not much of a destination—weary storefronts in a summertime dustbowl and cold as frozen tules in winter. But if you're bone-tired or just sick of the great outdoors, you can get a motel room there; try the **Ellis Motel** north of town on the highway, 530/667-5242. With extra time, stop by the **Tulelake–Butte Valley Fair Museum of Local History** at the fairgrounds, 800 Main St., 530/667-5312. Small fee. Come to town in Sep-

tember for Tulelake's big fair. Just north across the Oregon border is the small town of **Merrill,** which offers accommodations and services.

MEDICINE LAKE HIGHLANDS

About 14 miles south of the monument by gravel road, the Medicine Lake region truly qualifies for the "lunar landscape" label so often used to describe volcanic areas. In 1965, astronauts from the Manned Spacecraft Center in Texas came here to study the highlands in preparation for the first moon landing. In late 1988, the rumble of earthquakes beneath Medicine Lake attracted the attention of geologists, who believe an eruption from one of the state's most powerful volcanoes is due. Snows close this national forest area for general use from November to mid-June, though the popular "trail" from Mammoth

Crater, 26 miles roundtrip, provides off-season access for cross-country skiers and snowmobilers. **Medicine Lake,** its deep crystal-blue water filling an old volcanic crater, is fringed with lodgepole pines and has sandy beaches and good swimming, picnicking, and camping. The area also offers birding opportunities, good fishing, and water-skiing. "Big medicine" rites were traditionally held here—and still are—by various Native American peoples.

Above the lake is the black jumble of **Burnt Lava Flow,** a "virgin area" because virgin forests form islands within these 14 square miles of very young (300-500 years old) lava. Five miles northeast just off Medicine Lake Rd. is **Medicine Lake Glass Flow,** a square mile of stone-gray dacite formations 50–150 feet tall. **Glass Mountain** is a 1,400-year-old flow of black obsidian and glassy dacite, ending suddenly in a stark contrast of white pumice. Pumice rock is so light an average person could toss huge boulders with ease. (But don't: all of the area's natural features and any artifacts or archaeological sites within the area are protected.) Otherwise, wear proper shoes and be careful here. Native peoples used these flint-edged obsidian stones for making arrowheads, and a fall can cause puncture wounds and lacerations.

If all this close-up volcanism isn't enough, the panoramic view of the Cascades and the Modoc Plateau from the seldom-used lookout tower on Mt. Hoffman is worth a little huffing and puffing.

The three developed camping areas at Medicine Lake (elev. 6,700 feet)—**Hemlock, Medicine Lake,** and **Headquarters**—boast a total of 72 sites; all campsites are $7 per night, with a 14-day limit. All campgrounds close by October 15. (To get away from it all, head to **Bullseye Lake, Blanche Lake,** or **Paynes Springs;** campfire permits required.) For Medicine Lake information and permits, contact the Modoc National Forest's **Doublehead Ranger District** office in Tulelake, 530/667-2246, or **Modoc National Forest headquarters,** 800 W. 12th St. in Alturas, 530/233-5811. Shasta-Trinity National Forest's **McCloud Ranger District** office in McCloud, 530/964-2184, can also answer general questions about the Medicine Lake area.

KLAMATH BASIN WILDLIFE REFUGES

The Klamath Basin was once an almost endless expanse of shallow lakes and marshes. But things have changed. Reclamation has vastly diminished the region's wetlands, and the onetime autumn bird population of 10 million or more dropped to six or seven million by the 1960s and has since been reduced to one or two million. Central to the decline of this, the hub of the Pacific Flyway, is an ongoing war over water between environmentalists and Native Americans on one side of the issue, and farmers and algae growers on the other. This water war continues to boil because, in the latter days of the 20th century, the basin's Tule Lake—once centerpiece of the Klamath Basin refuges—has become little more than an agricultural wastewater sump, and increased water alkalinity due to low water levels and agriculture runoff threatens the ecological health of the entire refuge system. The Nature Conservancy, beginning with the Williamson River Delta Preserve, has started to buy up farmland within the Klamath Basin for wetlands restoration. Despite such positive local intervention, the area remains deeply troubled—as witnessed recently in the nation's newspaper headlines. (Regional farmers were outraged by federal limits imposed on agricultural use of Klamath River water; those original limits were lifted by Secretary of the Interior Gale Norton; and some 30,000 salmon subsequently died, downstream.) Still a critical habitat for most of North America's migratory birds and one of the top birding spots in the nation, as things stand the Klamath Basin may not continue to be.

Bird-Watching

Since hunting is as close to big business as Tulelake and like towns ever get—and also because the battle between the refuges and farmers over scarce water (farmers have first dibs) is increasing in rancor—birdwatchers aren't as popular as hunters in these parts. That could change, though, here as elsewhere, once beleaguered rural economies realize the positive local-business benefits of birding and other low-impact outdoor activities. Spring (early March through early May) is good for birders, but fall is the best—usually phenomenal, in fact, when the largest concentration of migrating waterfowl in North America converges on the Klamath Basin. Until the refuge crisis of the 1990s, Lower Klamath and Tule Lakes in particular were famous for their bird populations. For birding here, the best observation blind is your car (while traveling the dike-road tour routes); there are also blinds for

photographers. But if there's enough water to float a canoe, lake canoe routes offer the chance to get up-close and personal.

The Klamath Basin National Wildlife Refuges include six separate refuge areas. Farthest north is the **Klamath Forest** area; also in Oregon, just south of Crater Lake and north of Klamath Falls, is the **Upper Klamath.** Newest, established in 1978, is the **Bear Valley** refuge between the Oregon towns of Keno and Worden; it's a winter

KILLER DILEMMA: FISH OR FARMS?

Meandering down the backroads of the Klamath River Basin and exploring its small towns, particularly on the picturesque Oregon side of the border, make it clear what farmers and their families have been fighting for, in waging recent water wars. Everything's on the line as they struggle to preserve a relaxed, rural, and modest American way of life that has all but disappeared elsewhere in the West.

Yet a similar sense of wistful woe greets visitors to the Klamath, Modoc, Hoopa, and Yurok nations, to fishing villages along the California and Oregon coasts, and to recreation-dependent communities along the Klamath, Trinity, Scott, and Salmon Rivers. All fear that diverting too much water to the Klamath Project for irrigating potatoes and alfalfa will irreparably harm salmon and steelhead fisheries. As it turns out, everyone has reason to worry.

Roiling conflict over the use of scarce Klamath River water, between farmers on one side and Native Americans, environmentalists, fisherfolk, and white-water rafters on the other, reached a horrifying climax in late September 2002, when 33,000 fall-run adult Chinook salmon suddenly died along the river's lower stretches. Many of those fish were returning to spawn upstream in the Trinity River, which flows west into the lower Klamath.

Area newspapers soon trumpeted the news that the California Department of Fish and Game (DFG) "blamed" farmers in the Klamath River Basin's agricultural midsection for the unprecedented disaster, though that wasn't entirely true. What the DFG did say, in its preliminary report, was that the third-lowest Klamath River flows combined with the third-highest fall salmon run in modern history to kill the largest numbers of adult salmon ever

recorded. Low river flows impeded fish in their upstream migrations and forced them into close contact, causing fatal disease outbreaks. The DFG specifically blamed the U.S. Bureau of Reclamation, which in 2002 authorized full deliveries of irrigation water from both the Klamath and Trinity Rivers despite severe drought conditions.

As National Marine Fisheries Service biologist and whistleblower Michael Kelley revealed, the actual culprit was politics—specifically, political appointees of the Bush administration.

In May 2002, Kelley's draft biological opinion declared that agricultural water diversions would wipe out endangered salmon—a decision that jeopardized the Bush administration's 10-year irrigation plan. Then, in direct violation of the Endangered Species Act, Kelley says he was ordered to change his opinion, to help justify Interior Secretary Gale Norton's decision to divert water to farmers for irrigation.

Making national headlines the previous year were angry Klamath farmers protesting an April 2001 Bureau of Reclamation decision to cut off all Klamath Project agricultural allotments, due to drought and Endangered Species Act requirements. Farmers engaged in acts of civil disobedience, punching holes in dikes and illegally opening headgates on irrigation canals; they marched on Washington, clearly achieving their aims.

Yet no one wants the salmon to die, just as no one wants to destroy the wildlife refuges so essential to the Pacific Flyway. More optimistic locals believe that cooler heads will ultimately prevail—and fish protection and feasible water allocations will be achieved—once government agencies agree to follow their own rules and broker an honest solution.

nighttime roosting area for bald eagles. Straddling the California-Oregon border is the large **Lower Klamath** refuge, the first U.S. waterfowl refuge, created by President Teddy Roosevelt in 1908. Just east are the **Tule Lake** and **Clear Lake** refuge areas.

Seventy to eighty percent of the birds on the Pacific Flyway come together here—more than 250 species. Among them: snow, white-fronted, cackling, Canada, and Ross geese; avocets and egrets; swans and sandhill cranes; grebes and herons; pelicans, ospreys, and eagles. In addition, ducks abound. Redhead, gadwall, cinnamon teal, canvasback, shoveler, mallard, and pintail ducks nest near the lakes, hatching tens of thousands of ducklings each year. (The duck population usually peaks in late October, geese two to three weeks later.) Besides wintering bald eagles and hawks, many shorebirds, songbirds, falcons, and owls can also be spotted here.

The cold dead of winter, when the lakes freeze over and ice forms on the tules, is peak time for observing hundreds of migrating American bald eagles, the largest population on the North American continent outside Alaska. Though bald eagles are present year-round, in winter hundreds may be spotted in one place, usually congregating around unfrozen patches of ice on the lakes. Access restrictions to protect bird populations vary from refuge to refuge; Upper Klamath, for example, is closed from spring through fall.

Another spot with sometimes excellent, easy opportunities for observing migrants, especially geese, is the state's **Ash Creek Wildlife Area,** in Big Valley Marsh near Bieber, east of town, then north three miles on the Bieber-Lookout Highway. For information on the Big Valley area, contact the U.S. Forest Service **Big Valley Ranger District** office, 508 Main St. in Adin, 530/299-3215, and the **Adin Chamber of Commerce,** 530/299-3249.

Information

The Klamath Basin refuges are open to the public during daylight hours only. Birders: bring warm (and water-resistant) clothing, comfortable walking shoes, extra wool socks, and binoculars. For current information about refuge access and the natural rhythms of bird migration, contact: **Klamath Basin National Wildlife Refuges,** 4009 Hill Rd. in Tulelake, 530/667-2231, www.klamathnwr.org. The **visitor center** at refuge headquarters (at the Tule Lake reserve, reached via Hill Rd. from Hwy. 61 or from Lava Beds National Monument) has excellent wildlife exhibits and a museum, as well as information on birding, hunting, upcoming events, and road and weather conditions. Ask for information on the annual **Bald Eagle Conference,** www.eaglecon.org, a three-day celebration (usually in mid-February) of field trips (to the refuge here), photography workshops, and speakers sponsored by the Audubon Society and held at the Oregon Institute of Technology in Klamath Falls.

Warner Mountains

The Warner Mountains were named for William H. Warner, who was killed here by Paiutes while mapping the upper reaches of the Pit River. Widespread lava flows containing quartz crystals (now called Warner basalt) oozed up from the earth several million years ago and covered much of the Modoc Plateau. The later Warner Mountains, a remote spur of the Cascades but technically part of the plateau, are typical of ranges in the Great Basin that are "fault-bounded." As a result of double faulting, the mountains rose and Surprise Valley dropped. Pine forests, clear blue glacial lakes, and good fishing streams are characteristic of the Warners at higher elevations, with chaparral and juniper below. Most of the Warner Range is included in Modoc National Forest, which also contains the South Warner Wilderness Area. Eagle Peak is almost 10,000 feet tall, but most of the range stands at half that height—a green, gently rolling highland area wonderful for walking.

SOUTH WARNER WILDERNESS

The South Warner Wilderness Area is possibly the finest summer hiking spot in the state—70,000 acres of streams, natural springs, some small lakes, and very few people. Relatively few trails cross the flat-topped ridge. The trail along the narrow crest offers awesome views of sunken Surprise Valley and Nevada to the east, the entire Modoc Plateau to the west, and Mt. Shasta beyond. In the Warners you'll find exotic Cascade wildflowers plus more typical summer blooms: buttercups, monkeyflowers, paintbrush, and shooting stars. Pronghorn, coyote, raccoons, beavers, and wide-ranging mustangs are fairly common. Bald and golden eagles, ospreys, and hawks soar overhead; seabirds including gulls and terns are common.

Summit Trail

The 26-mile Summit Trail offers easy walking along the mountains' crest and is especially scenic along the trailhead to the cirque lake. This is an ideal introduction to the Warners and perfect for a weekend backpack. (A longer loop around to the east, coming or going via North Owl Creek and other trails, is also possible for a longer backpack.) Hiking from the south, the trail (sometimes vague and marked by cairns) winds up to the summit through white fir, then levels off, with splendid views on both sides. As you walk, avoid disturbing the vegetation and other features of this delicate tundra area. Dark basalt flows, tilting westward, created the immense cliffs along the way.

Within the state game refuge, down below are lovely campsites along a spring-fed creek near the trail. Or continue to the Patterson Lake area, where fishing is usually excellent for brook, brown, and rainbow trout. (The first reliable water source, a tasty spring, is at Pepperdine Pack Station near Porter Reservoir, about 4.5 miles past this point.) From here, you can veer to the west and follow the official trail or descend via switchbacks on the Squaw Peak connector trail, crossing the lake's outlet a few times and also Cottonwood Creek below the spectacular falls. Then, heading north,

skirt the east side of 8,646-foot Squaw Peak before reconnecting with the Summit Trail at Pepperdine.

To reach the north end of the Summit Trail from Alturas, head east on Road 56. A half mile after it becomes good dirt road, turn left at the Pepperdine-Parker Creek sign onto Parker Creek Rd., continuing another seven miles to the trailhead sign. Turn right and go another two miles. You can park your car here or car-camp farther up (if you can make it up the rocky, steep road) before heading out the next morning. The trailhead in the clearing is just past the campground. Reach the southern end of Summit Trail from Likely in the south: turn right on Jess Valley Rd., travel past Jess Valley on West Warner Rd. to Mill Creek Springs, then follow these trails to Summit Trail.

Information

From **Blue Lake Campground,** just south of the wilderness boundary (paved road access; $7), the **Blue Lake National Recreation Trail** circles west and around the lake's perimeter. Farther north, right on the wilderness boundary, is **Mill Creek Campground** ($6), where trails lead up to beautiful **Mill Creek Falls** and **Clear Lake.** The campground is also the trailhead for the trail to Poison Flat. **Soup Springs Campground** ($6) is at the **Slide Creek** trailhead. On the north side of the wilderness, **Summit Trail** is reached from the **Pepperdine Pack Station** (five sites; free) and **Porter Reservoir Area.** Tiny **Emerson** and **Patterson Campgrounds** (both free) are reached via dirt or gravel roads from south of Eagleville and offer steeper access to South Warner Wilderness trails.

Hiking and backpacking are best from late June to Labor Day, with peak wildflowers in late July and August. When exploring the remote Warners, bring water or water-purification tablets/filter and a backpacking stove and fuel, since firewood is in short supply. Also bring a topo map and good compass; trails sometimes seem to disappear. Otherwise, come prepared for anything.

Predictable for the South Warner Wilderness is its unpredictable weather, with freezing temperatures, thunderstorms, and brutal winds possible anytime, though less likely in July and August. Wilderness permits are necessary for backcountry camping. Camp away from moist meadow areas and well away from streams and lakes. As always, if you pack it in, pack it out. Summer lightning storms are possible; if lightning bolts strike, seek shelter in low forested areas or between rocks in boulder jumbles, *never* in open areas near an isolated boulder or tree.

For wilderness permits and more information, including forest, wilderness, and trail maps, contact **Modoc National Forest** headquarters (also the Devil's Garden Ranger District), 800 W. 12th St. in Alturas, 530/233-5811, www.r5.fs.fed.us/modoc, or Modoc's **Warner Mountain Ranger District,** 385 Wallace St. (just one block north and west of the main intersection) in Cedarville, the eastern slope's main town, 530/279-6116. Wilderness maps and Modoc National Forest maps are $6 each. Winter activities in the South Warners are limited, but snowshoeing, cross-country skiing, and ice fishing at Clear Lake are becoming popular.

ALTURAS

With several thousand people, a few restaurants and motels, and the county's only two traffic lights, Alturas is the biggest city around. Situated in the dry, sparsely vegetated landscape in the western shadow of the Warners, Alturas is predictably hot in summer and cold in winter. The roads in town weren't even paved until 1931, about the same time talking pictures arrived. Some crotchety old buildings still stand, among them a fine museum and the **Elks Hall,** 619 N. Main, onetime headquarters of the old Narrow, Cantankerous, and Ornery Railroad and now on the National Register of Historic Places. The center of social life here is the once wild and woolly Old West **Niles Hotel & Saloon** on Main, something of a museum in its own right. Yet the Old West isn't what it once was, even in Modoc County. Perspective changes—which is why, these days, you can come to Alturas in July for performances of the Lost River: Story of the Modoc Indian War pageant.

Seeing and Doing Greater Alturas

Pick up a free **historic tour** guide and Modoc County historic homes brochure at the **Alturas/Modoc County Chamber of Commerce** office, 522 S. Main St., 530/233-4434. Next door to the chamber is the **Modoc County Museum,** 600 S. Main, 530/233-2944, housing 400 vintage firearms and other antiques; a collection of arrowheads, knives, and spears; 500 woven baskets and other Native American artifacts; and photo and oral-history archives. Open May–Oct. (and two weeks at Christmas).

Check out the works of local artists at the Alturas **Art Center,** 317 S. Main St., 530/233-2574, which occupies a vintage 1877 or '78 building fashioned of locally quarried stone. Another worthwhile stop, especially if you're staying a while, is the **Modoc County Arts Council** office, 212 W. Third St., 530/233-2505, which is also the place to inquire about performances of **Lost River: Story of the Modoc Indian War,** lostriver.org. The **Niles Theatre,** 127 S. Main, 530/233-5454, hosts movies, community events, and live drama.

The 7,000-plus-acre **Modoc National Wildlife Refuge**—100 years old in 2003—extends for miles along Hwy. 395 south of Alturas proper, with access via County Roads 56 and then 115 (follow the signs to the headquarters visitor center). Part and parcel of the semiarid landscape surrounding Dorris Reservoir and open during daylight hours Mar.–Sept., the refuge hosts migrating waterfowl in fall and spring, and is a major summer nesting area. Bird-watching is especially good near headquarters, where a general map/guide, bird list, and hunting brochures are available. The best times for diverse birding: April through May and September through October. For more information, contact: Modoc National Wildlife Refuge headquarters in Alturas, 530/233-3572, http://modoc.fws.gov.

Staying in Alturas

No public campgrounds are nearby, but you can try the **Brass Rail Campground,** on Hwy. 299 adjacent to the Brass Rail Basque Restaurant, 530/233-4185, complete with laundromat and hot showers; around $15 per night. The **Cedar**

Pass Campground, at Cedar Pass (12 miles northeast of Alturas, 8 miles west of Cedarville) is free, as is **Stough Reservoir Campground** (also "Stowe") a few miles farther east. South of town try **Likely Place RV Resort,** 2.5 miles off Hwy. 395 and Jess Valley Rd. in Likely, 530/233-4466 or 888/350-3848, www.likelyplace.com; open mid-April through October, tent sites $8, RVs $20. Amenities include a nine-hole golf course, showers, Laundromat, even horseshoes.

Alturas boasts a number of motels, most of these on Main St. Best bets include the **Super 8,** 511 N. Main, 530/233-3545 or 800/800-8000, www.super8.com, which boasts the onsite **Black Bear Diner,** and **Best Western Trailside Inn,** 343 N. Main, 530/233-4111 or 888/829-0092, where a few units have kitchens; heated pool. Rates for both are typically $50–100. The venerable **Niles Hotel,** 304 S. Main, 530/233-3261 or 877/233-5510, www.nileshotel.com, has been restyled into a Wild West–style country inn. Rooms and suites are $50–100.

Just outside town the **Dorris House** bed-and-breakfast on Parker Creek Rd. in Alturas, 530/233-3786, borders Modoc Wildlife Refuge on the shores of Dorris Reservoir (and even offers accommodations for horses). Rates include expanded continental breakfast, $50–100.

Eating in Alturas

Alturas has fast food restaurants and coffee shops, but the best thing going is at home in a former burger palace—**Nipa's California Cuisine,** 1001 N. Main, 530/233-2520, which actually serves Thai food. What could be better after a brutal weekend backpack than a plate of pad Thai and a tall Thai iced tea? Open daily for lunch and dinner. Good for Basque food at lunch or dinner is the **Brass Rail,** on Lakeview Hwy. (Hwy. 299 a few blocks east of the intersection with Hwy. 395), 530/233-2906. Closed Monday. Locals highly recommend the **Niles Hotel and Saloon,** 304 S. Main, 530/233-3261, for American fare, open for lunch Wed.–Fri. and for dinner nightly; look for good meat-and-potatoes meals and a veritable Buffalo Bill Cody Wild West Show atmosphere. *Don't* miss the saloon. (Rooms are also available at the Niles.)

Events and Information

Come for the **Western Cow Dog Challenge** in June; **Fandango Days,** the town's main event, in July; the **Modoc County Fair** (in Cedarville) every August; and the wildlife refuge's **Migratory Bird Festival** and the **Alturas Century Bike Ride,** held in conjunction in September.

For information about events, sights, and accommodations, stop in at the **Alturas/Modoc County Chamber of Commerce,** 522 S. Main St. (next to the historical society museum), 530/233-4434. Open 9 A.M.–4:30 P.M. weekdays. For additional information, including details about "Sage Stage" transit, contact the **City of Alturas,** 200 W. North St., 530/233-2512, www.cityof-alturas.org. Public lands offices are clustered. **Modoc National Forest,** almost two million acres of volcanic plateaus, lakes, and mountains, offers recreational opportunities for hikers, backpackers, hunters, photographers, and rockhounds. Many campgrounds are free, as are picnic areas. Forest headquarters and the ranger district office share space at 800 W. 12th St. (on the main highway, on the way into town), 530/233-5811, www.r5.fs.fed.us/modoc. (Other ranger district offices are in **Adin,** 530/299-3215; **Tulelake,** 530/667-2246; and **Cedarville,** 530/279-6116.) Available publications include forest and off-road vehicle maps, camping and recreation listings, and brochures/maps for Modoc National Forest, the South Warner Wilderness, and the Medicine Lake Highlands areas. Very helpful and friendly staff. Nearby is the **U.S. Bureau of Land Management Alturas Field Office,** 708 W. 12th, 530/233-4666. (There's another branch in Cedarville, the **BLM Surprise Field Office**—great name, you have to admit—at 602 Cressler St., 530/279-6101.) The Alturas **post office** is at 240 N. Main St., 530/233-2410. The newspaper of record is the weekly **Modoc County Record,** www.modocrecord.com.

NEAR ALTURAS

Goose Lake is the largest of several lakes clustered on both sides of Hwy. 395 north of Alturas near Oregon. Up here you'll find high mountain conifers, abundant game and fish, and few people. **Cave** and **Lily Lakes,** reached via the **Highgrade National Recreation Trail** (rough road), are pristine, with good fishing for rainbow and eastern brook trout. **Cedar Pass Ski Area** is friendly and fun for Alpine and Nordic skiers— a small day-use ski area 20 miles northeast of Alturas near Cedar Pass with a bunny hill for beginners, T-bar lifts, more challenging downhill runs, and cross-country skiing on groomed tracks or through uncharted areas. Snowboarding OK. For more information, call 530/233-3323 (ski lodge, connected only if there's been snow) or 530/233-4882.

Surprise Valley

Now you've arrived, at the farthest reaches of outback California. It's a surprise this place is even here—a rich little valley on the parched eastern side of the Warners, with Nevada's Hayes Canyon still farther to the east. About 80 miles long and 10 miles wide with an average elevation of 4,700 feet, the valley is an agricultural area producing mostly cattle and alfalfa; the alfalfa seed grown here produces hay exceptionally high in protein. The entire area was once submerged under a small sea now reduced to three alkaline lakes. From the valley, don't plan on zipping into Nevada via Hwy. 299—the businesslike paved road dries up in the desert just across the border.

Cedarville and Vicinity

Except for pickup trucks, the gas station, and the one pay phone, Cedarville could inhabit the 19th century: Rangeland, U.S.A. The town's sleepy facade is shattered only on Saturday nights, when ranch hands come from miles around to quench their thirst at local watering holes. In Cedarville Park, the **Cressler-Bonner Trading Post** was built in 1865 and is a state historic landmark. Visit **Louisville** at the Modoc County Fairgrounds, a collection of preserved pioneer buildings.

Tiny **Sunrise Motel** is three miles east of the Cedar Pass ski hill on the highway, 54889 Hwy. 299, 530/279-2161, with rooms $50–100 (RV hookups too). In town is the historic **J.K. Metzker Bed & Breakfast,** 520 Main St., 530/279-2650, with three upstairs guest rooms with private baths, full country breakfast, $50–100. An

intriguing option is **Surprise Valley Hot Springs,** a restyled motel four miles east of Cedarville, 530/279-2040 or 877/927-6426, www.svhotsprings.com. All 10 villas feature theme decor, either a kitchenette or full kitchen, and a private outdoor patio with hot tub fed by warm mineral water. Regular rooms are $50–100, deluxe (twice as large) $100–150. Also available: onsite massage, a Fly-n-Soak pilot package. Culture junkies for whom star-gazing from hot tubs isn't thrilling enough, this place *does* have movie night every night, thanks to its 500-plus video library.

Even farther out is **Soldier Meadows Guest Ranch and Lodge,** the site of the U.S. Army's Civil War–era Camp McGarry, now a working cattle ranch in the Nevada desert along the historic Lassen-Applegate Emigrant Trail. Bunkhouse rooms are under $50 (per person), suite $50–100, and RV sites $10 (no hookups). Cookhouse fare is available for $10 per meal. Revel in private hot springs, take a hike, or do ranch work. Special events (extra fee) include a late May cattle drive, wildflower and other tours, heritage and horseback rides, and Cowboy Christmas weekends. The ranch is located well east of Cedarville (last 30 miles on dirt road) on Soldier Meadows Rd. in Gerlach, NV, 530/233-4881, www.soldiermeadows.com.

For a meal back in town, try the **Country Hearth Restaurant & Bakery,** 551 Main St., 530/279-2280, open daily for breakfast, lunch, and dinner, or the **Tumbleweed Cafe,** 415 Main St., 530/279-6363, open Mon.–Sat. for three meals (both Mexican and American fare) and Sunday for brunch.

Eagleville, 15 miles south of Cedarville, was named for the Warners' Eagle Peak soaring above. It's a sleepy collection of aging farmcountry wood-frames, a handful of homes, a general store, and livestock loading chutes. Just a few miles south, across the road from the turnoff to Middle Fork Spring and Patterson, is **Menlo Baths,** a hot springs area on private land (often used by locals).

For more information about the area, contact the **Greater Surprise Valley Chamber of Commerce,** 519-B Main St. in Cedarville, 530/279-2012.

Fort Bidwell

The farthest northeast town in the far northeastern corner of California, Fort Bidwell was named after Chico's Gen. John Bidwell, who never saw or visited the area but was the territory's most prominent citizen in the mid-1800s. Get here from Cedarville via Hwy. 20, or drive east over the Fandango Pass Rd. (dirt) to Surprise Valley, then head north. Built in 1865, Fort Bidwell began as an important military post protecting settlers from Indian attacks and was later converted into an Indian school. The fort's only original building still standing is the hospital, but fascinating is the 100-year-old **Fort Bidwell General Store,** just a block off Main, which is something of a museum and the town's unofficial information center. Consider a soak in the **Fort Bidwell Hot Springs** just outside of town. **Fee Reservoir,** just to the east of Fort Bidwell, is noted for its large rainbow trout.

Hot Springs

Several private hot springs are in this area. Heading seven miles east of Cedarville, take the dirt road north; four miles ahead is the remnant of **Leonard Hot Springs,** with primitive pools and a natural underground spring. Just two miles farther is **Glen Hot Springs,** consisting of shallow pools on the east side of Upper Alkali Lake. No facilities, no address, no phone, no fax machines, no restrictions, no worries. For more information about regional and area hot springs, stop by or call the Cedarville ranger station, 530/279-6116. True aficionados should check out the quarterly **Hot Springs Gazette,** www.hotspringsgazette.com.

Sierra Nevada

Though the many ancient peoples who once shared California's vast Sierra Nevada territory would surely be puzzled by his comparative historical prominence, John Muir has become California's preeminent mountain man. Long before his fame as freedom fighter for the wilderness and Great White Father of the modern American conservationist ethic, Muir began to act on his then-heretical belief that the orderly beauty of nature was the highest revelation of the One Mind. Unyoked from his heavy sense of social duty by an industrial accident that temporarily blinded him, Muir finally set out to see God. His decade-long, 19th-century wanderings led him to the Sierra Nevada's "sunbursts of morning among the icy peaks," to its "noonday radiance on the trees and rocks and snow," and to its "thousand dancing waterfalls." But the solitary naturalist, by then also a Civil War draft dodger, renamed the mountains even before personally meeting them, as he looked upward from Pacheco Pass. "Then it seemed to me the Sierra should be called not the Nevada, or Snowy Range, but the Range of Light. . . . the most divinely beautiful of all the mountain chains I have ever seen."

The young run-amok Mark Twain, too, was smitten with these mountains and their magic: "Three months of camp life on Lake Tahoe would restore an Egyptian mummy to his pristine

drive-through tree in Giant Forest, Sequoia National Park

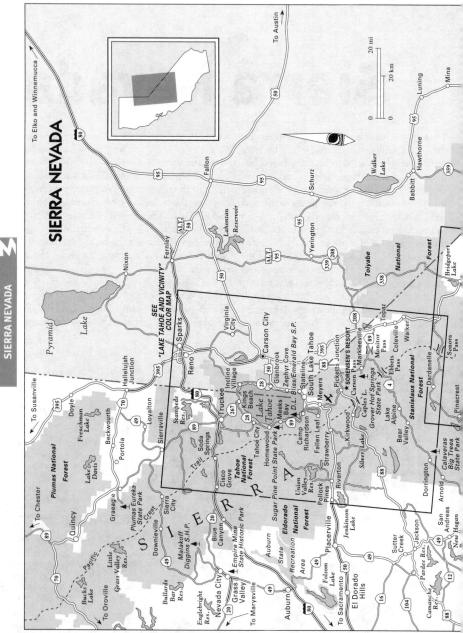

SIERRA NEVADA

SEE "LAKE TAHOE AND VICINITY" COLOR MAP

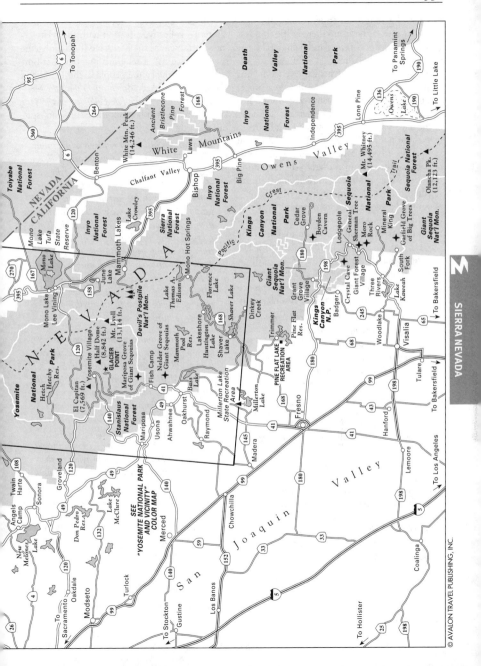

SIERRA NEVADA

vigor, and give him an appetite like an alligator," he wrote. "The air up there in the clouds is very pure and fine, bracing and delicious. . . the same the angels breathe."

Yet something about his experience in this near-vertical expanse of the Old West upset Twain's otherwise refined sense of common humanity. Starting with the acceptable sanctimony of the day—"If we cannot find it in our hearts to give these poor naked creatures our Christian sympathy and compassion, in God's name let us at least not throw mud at them"—he then flung invective with both hands. In *Roughing It,* Twain rejected the "mellow moonshine of romance" about noble red men, whom he found "treacherous, filthy, and repulsive." And though he derided one tribe in particular, he managed, by inference, to include all Native Americans. His comments reflect perfectly the prejudices of his time—precursors to the cultural cataclysm that occurred when gold seekers and settlers swept into California—which was, perhaps, Twain's point:

[They are] a silent, sneaking, treacherous looking race; taking note of everything, covertly. . . and betraying no sign in their countenances; indolent, everlastingly patient and tireless. . . . prideless beggars—for if the beggar instinct were left out of an Indian he would not "go," any more than a clock without a pendulum; hungry, always hungry, and yet never refusing anything that a hog would eat, though often eating what a hog would decline; hunters, but having no higher ambition than to kill and eat jackass rabbits, crickets and grasshoppers, and embezzle carrion from the buzzards and cayotes [sic]; savages who, when asked if they have a common Indian belief in a Great Spirit, show a something which almost amounts to emotion, thinking whiskey is referred to. . . .

Cataclysm or no, the Old Spirits, some of the Old Ways, even some of the Old Ones survive still in the secrecy of lost and lonely places. Among the survivors, there are now new traditions. Followers of the Tipi Way, scattered members of the Washoe Nation from the eastern slopes

of the Sierra Nevada, worship the Great Spirit and seek collective salvation with the relatively new sacrament of the Medicine (hallucinogenic peyote buttons), a religious practice first borrowed from the Paiute people in the 1920s and '30s. Warren L. Azevedo's *Straight with the Medicine: Narratives of Washoe Followers of the Tipi Way* shares the truth about these survivors' spiritual depth:

How can an Indian pray like a white man? The white man gets his prayers out of books. . . old books about things maybe thousands of years ago. He don't even have to think about it. He just says it and it is supposed to do him some good. He can be a drunk bum for a long time, do all kinds of no good thing, think all kinds of bad thoughts about people. But then he can walk right into that Church and pray one of them prayers and he gets away with it. Anybody can go into them Churches anytime and walk out without anything happening to him. . . .

The way a man sing shows you what kind of person he is. If he sings good, he can help people. His song goes through them and the Medicine is working. Singing is like praying. . . it's the same thing. When we sing here it is for a reason. . . . So when I sing, it ain't like on the radio or to pass the time. I'm trying to get myself up good as I can. I don't just sing a song. . . I'm taking a trip. When I'm singing I'm praying in the Tipi and going on that trip over that Road.

Many who visit California's astounding Sierra Nevada come for essentially the same purpose: to take a dose of the mountains' Medicine, to sing praises to the spirits, to get "up good as I can," to embark on a seriously joyous trip.

THE LAND

A massive block of granite some 450 miles long and 60 to 80 miles wide, the Sierra Nevada range starts in the north, just south of Lassen Peak, shimmies down to the southeast toward Walker

Pass east of Bakersfield, then dribbles off into the desert where it meets the Tehachapis. Tilting gracefully to the west, the range's underlying rock foundation gives the broad western side its very gradual slope. Most of the mountains' drama is reserved for the eastern ascent—where spectacular peaks rise in dizzying degrees from the flat high-desert plateaus—and for the range's craggy high country, natural anarchistic architecture of the highest order.

From average elevations of 6,000-8,000 feet near the Feather River in the north, Sierra Nevada summits increase in altitude toward Yosemite, Sequoia, and Kings Canyon National Parks. Mt. Whitney, the tallest mountain in the continental U.S. (excluding Alaska) and the range's triumph, pierces the sky at 14,495 feet. Near Mt. Whitney almost a dozen other peaks stand taller than 14,000 feet, and more than 500 throughout the Sierra Nevada exceed 12,000 feet. But the High Sierra, technically speaking, refers to the 150-mile-long, 20-mile-wide stretch of near-naked glaciated granite peaks, icy blue alpine lakes, and relatively level highlands above treeline from just north of Yosemite south to Cottonwood Pass.

Fire and Earth

The calm, cool facade of the Sierra Nevada range almost succeeds in hiding the region's deep fiery nature—almost, but not quite. Ancient calderas, old volcanic rock formations (basalt and andesite), young volcanoes, and quite contemporary earthquakes and hot springs—all common throughout the eastern Sierra—verify the fire below. Some say the region's abundant hot springs are evidence of decreasing volcanic vigor along the eastern Sierra Nevada; others suggest that the earth's fire is merely sleeping.

Though the greenstone, marble, and slate common to westerly foothills are some 200 million years old, these early, well-eroded formations sank and were submerged by the sea during the late Paleozoic era. After eons of Mesozoic underwater sedimentation and sporadic volcanic activity (creating marine sediment layers interspersed with solidified lava flows), pressure from the superheated magma swirling below pushed these heat-hardened rocks upward in folds, cre-

ating the general outlines of today's mountain ridges and valleys.

Not yet finished with the Sierra Nevada, the earth's volcanic violence surged forth again starting 100 million years ago during the Cretaceous period and "injected" molten granite under, into, and around the undulating rock formations on the surface. These massive granite intrusions were gradually exposed and "peeled" by the erosive forces of nature, creating the granitic domes characteristic of the High Sierra. Found few other places in the world, the best examples of these rounded and unjointed rock formations crop up in the Yosemite region—among them, awesome and enormous Half Dome, which dominates Yosemite Valley's eastern end.

Granite intrusion is also responsible for the Sierra Nevada's mineral wealth. As the hot rock boiled and bubbled up through the earth's crust, it became "contaminated" and transformed by liquified concentrations of surrounding minerals. Mountain and foothill deposits of gold, copper, tungsten, aluminum, and other valued minerals have all caused some excitement during the course of California history.

But in 1986, the discovery of a previously uncharted, 150-mile-long band of tungsten-rich "true granite" on the western slopes of the Sierra Nevada created a stir among geologists, challenging earlier assumptions about granite formation as well as the accepted simplicity of the Sierra Nevada's creation.

According to long-standing scientific opinion, the embryonic mountains were still gently rolling and covered in deep clays when erosion began to expose the range's underlying rock formations. During the Eocene Epoch some 60–70 million years ago, California's coast ranges "folded up" into existence and the Sierra Nevada tilted to the west. Another long period of mountain uplift followed until, about 12 million years ago, the eastern mountains had reached a height of 3,000 feet above sea level. Toward the end of the Pliocene Epoch, the Sierra Nevada's most dramatic and final upward surge took place. Most of the glacial scouring and earthquake faulting responsible for the range's spectacular scenery occurred during the past one million years.

Research by the prestigious Southern Sierra Continental Dynamics project, first published in *Science* in 1996, turned earlier conclusions upside down. According to this "countercultural" view, some 70 million years ago the southern Sierra Nevada already stood as tall as the Andes, a massive mountain range looming above the dying dinosaurs. Its stature has been steadily eroding ever since. Uplift of the ever-lighter mountain range has continued as well, though erosion is ongoing—and on balance erosion stays ahead, ever so slightly.

In modern times, a very active 400-mile-long fault zone shakes, rattles, and rolls along the eastern base of the Sierra Nevada. The area from Mono Lake south to Lone Pine and the now dry Owens Lake area (parallel to Mt. Whitney) has been hardest hit in recent history. A massive quake, perhaps the most powerful in U.S. history, flattened Lone Pine in 1872 and, in a matter of seconds, elevated a vast section of the range by 13 feet.

Water and Ice

The creative fire underlying these massive mountains is usually unseen, but water, the other great shaping force, is everywhere. Like John Muir, everyday mortals are overwhelmed here by the aesthetics of this elixer of life: the crystalline mountain rivers and streams, waterfalls crowned with misty rainbows, and 1,500 or so lakes (including the breathtaking "lake of the sky," Lake Tahoe) in glacier-ground basins. Most rivers and streams flow to the southwest. Many of the west side's 11 major river systems—from the Feather and Yuba Rivers in the north to the Kings, Kern, and Kaweah Rivers in the south—flow first through glacier-scoured gorges, then through V-shaped unglaciated canyons before reaching California's great central valley. On the Sierra Nevada's steep eastern flank, the waters of the few major rivers—among them the Truckee, Carson, and Walker—fly downhill in liquid freefall before settling into alkaline lakes or drying up in the desert. Dramatic waterfalls, though, are more common in western river valleys with glacier-created "hanging valleys," especially in Yosemite National Park and vicinity.

Over the eons, water has played its erosive part in shaping the Sierra Nevada, but frozen

ROCKY MOUNTAIN WARM

The effects of global warming will profoundly change the precipitation patterns and ecosystems of both the Sierra Nevada and the Cascade Range, say scientists at the Lawrence Livermore Laboratory and the University of California, Santa Cruz. According to a 2002 study published in the peer-reviewed journal *Geophysical Research Letters,* the critical February snowpack of both mountain ranges will shrink as much as 82 percent—essentially eliminating the "delayed release" of water (from melting snows) that has been key in California's water storage system. Higher elevations, where average temperatures will increase by as much as 16.5 degrees Fahrenheit, will be hit the hardest. Where snowpack now last well into June, snow will be gone entirely by the end of April, when summer will come to the mountains.

water has exerted even more power. Seeping into cracks, then freezing and expanding, veins of ice eventually break boulders down into stones and gravel- or sand-sized particles. More dramatic, though, is the work of ice sheets and glaciers, which—as they accumulate rock debris on their downslope route—slowly gouge and scour the landscape. During three separate periods of the ice age or Pleistocene Epoch until about 10,000 years ago, glaciers and ice fields worked hardest, particularly in the area from Lake Tahoe to Yosemite. The magnificent U-shaped Yosemite Valley is perhaps the most dramatic example of nature's persistent, always-unfinished sculpture.

Climate

Sierra Nevada weather patterns are dictated by the land; the region's wide latitude and altitude shifts, in addition to local landforms, create innumerable distinct microclimates. To *really* find out about local weather, ask locals.

The range's usually impressive snowpack starts to melt during April and May, and in general, summer is springtime in the Sierra Nevada—those few short months when snow flows as water and snow melt turns mountain meadows into marshy bogs thick with wildflowers. Summer

winter in Yosemite

A LAND UNDER SEIGE

The Sierra Nevada is in serious trouble. Its beauty and utility have bred a familiar plague—popularity with humans—that threatens its very survival. According to an exhaustive three-year environmental study released in 1996 by a 100-member scientific consortium that prepared the report for the U.S. Congress, the region's human population will treble by the year 2040—it doubled between 1970 and 1990—and will far outpace the state's overall growth. That estimate doesn't take into account the millions just visiting each year.

Population growth, with its development pressures, has had a direct impact on the Sierra Nevada's decline, along with overgrazing, logging, mining, soil erosion, water projects, and increasing air and water pollution. In a sense, the cities are making themselves at home in the wilderness. Subdivisions and strip malls are popping up all over, and software firms are the latest Sierra Nevada industry.

At last count, according to the Sierra Nevada Ecosystem Project Report, 69 species of wildlife are now considered "at risk," the predominant cause the loss of essential habitat—particularly foothill woodland, riparian, and late successional forests. If present trends continue, the extinction of many Sierra Nevada fish species and all amphibians is predicted within the next 50 years.

The report also challenged common California forestry practices and beliefs—especially the belief that logging "mimics" the ecological functions of fire—and stated that logging has increased the risk and severity of forest fires. The Sierra Nevada's remaining 15 percent of old-growth forests—the oldest, largest trees, which support a complex community of other plants and animals—represent the last stand of a once-healthy ecosystem. And unregulated grazing has created "widespread, profound and, in some places, irreversible ecological impacts."

Urban-class air pollution plagues highly populated areas, including Truckee and Mammoth in winter, due to the twin scourges of vehicle exhaust and wood-burning stoves. The Sierra Nevada also suffers from environmental damage that

temperatures are relatively cool (often cold at night), especially at higher elevations, but locally variable. Though little rain falls during the summer, sudden thunderstorms and occasional freak snow flurries aren't that unusual, especially at higher elevations. Be prepared for anything.

Following the frosty temperatures and flaming colors of fall, winter settles in to stay, often into May. Most precipitation (rain and snow) falls from January through March, though early and late major storms can close many Sierra Nevada passes from Labor Day through Memorial Day. Especially in low precipitation years, cloud-seeding is a fairly common practice in various Sierra Nevada watersheds, to increase the annual snow-pack and to fatten up downslope reservoirs. Naturally or otherwise, most rain and snow falls on the range's western slopes—the amount increasing with altitude until about 6,500 feet, then decreasing dramatically on eastern slopes, the Sierra Nevada "rainshadow." Latitude also influences precipitation patterns, with substantially more rain and snow falling in northern and central regions than in the south.

originates elsewhere, particularly ozone pollution blown in from Los Angeles, the San Francisco Bay Area, and the great Central Valley. Jeffrey and ponderosa pines on west-facing slopes are increasingly debilitated and dwarfed, as ozone settles onto their leaves and accelerates both defoliation and vulnerability to insects and fire. (Scientists from the U.S. Geological Survey say mountain yellow-legged frogs—the Sierra's "canaries in the coal mine"—are disappearing due to pesticide drift eastward into the Sierra from the central valley.) Drifting pollution is also partially responsible for clouding the waters at Lake Tahoe, which loses about one foot of its once-mythic transparency each year—and will resemble a fairly typical, murkier lake in about 40 years.

Remedies to the Sierra Nevada's problems are available, however, according to the report's authors—assuming that there is sufficient political will. Air pollution could be reduced almost instantaneously, and forest complexity could be restored within a century. Revitalizing degraded watersheds would take considerably longer.

bristlecone pine

FLORA

Wildflower season arrives in late spring and summer, when unusual and unusually delicate plants peek up from forest duff and marshy meadows. Though visitor centers in the national parks and elsewhere offer various good localized natural history guides, one of the better books for Sierra Nevada wildflower identification is *California Mountain Wildflowers* by Philip A. Munz, co-author of *A California Flora,* until quite recently the California botanists' bible (now sharing those honors with *The Jepson Manual*).

Like wildflowers, Sierra Nevada trees and shrubs thrive in fairly specific environments. Though regional plant distribution depends on altitude and latitude, other local environmental factors (such as availability of water and sunlight, soil type, and whether a particular place is on a north- or south-facing slope) also influence the development of plant communities. In general, though, chaparral and drought-adapted foothill pines and oaks dominate the vegetation of the Sierra Nevada's lower western slopes, from elevations of 500 to 5,000 feet (the range generally lower in the north, higher in the south). Next in the vertical progression of plant life comes the transition zone (and predominant timber region) of yellow and sugar pines, Douglas and white firs, incense cedar, and various broadleaf trees such as cottonwoods, oaks, and maples—a broad botanical band ranging from 1,200 feet in the north to nearly 9,000 feet in the southern Sierra Nevada.

Still higher is the lower boreal belt so popular with winter sports fans, characterized by lodgepole pines and red firs but also home to Jeffrey and silver pines, Sierra junipers, aspens, and various mountain chaparral shrubs. (On the range's drier eastern slopes, this zone may consist primarily of Jeffrey pines with scattered drought- and snow-adapted species typical of the higher "sagebrush belt": Utah juniper and mountain mahogany.)

Higher still comes the Sierra Nevada's subalpine belt, an area with heavy snow and long, severe winters "above timberline," where some lodgepole, whitebark, and foxtail pines grow (often in beautifully contorted and weather-twisted forms) in the company of mountain hemlock and heathers. In alpine areas, where slopes and summits are typically bare of vegetation, one dwarfed but sturdy survivor is the alpine willow, which branches out along the ground. Unique in the White Mountains southeast of Mono Lake are specimens of the world's oldest living trees—the Great Basin's ragged and rugged bristlecone pines—including the Methuselah Tree, estimated to be more than 4,600 years old.

Sierra Big Trees

Also ancient and unique is the Sierra Nevada's "big tree" or *Sequoiadendron giganteum,* a species of redwood quite distinct from California's coastal redwoods and surviving in substantial numbers only in Yosemite and neighboring national parks and at Calaveras Big Trees State Park. Also called giant sequoias, these massive forest monarchs are botanical dinosaurs, living relics that first evolved some 160 million years ago—15,000 times older than Yosemite Valley.

Sierra Nevada big trees are indeed big—so gigantic that few people can escape an overwhelming feeling of awe when looking (up) at them. The everyday, garden-variety giant sequoia measures 10 to 15 feet in diameter at maturity and stands some 250 feet tall. The true giants, including the most massive trio, the General Sherman, General Grant, and Boole trees in or near Sequoia and Kings Canyon National Parks, are almost 30 feet across well above ground level. The lowest limb branching off from General Sherman is seven feet thick and would create a canopy for a 12-story office building. During California's pioneer past, people hollowed out big trees for cabins or barns. Though they live to a ripe old age (the oldest verified mature tree is about 3,200 years old), they also grow vigorously and rapidly throughout their life spans. Theoretically, Sierra big trees could live forever, but sooner or later, too-heavy winter snow and brutal winds topple otherwise healthy elders.

Adapted to fire, insect pests, and just about every other natural scourge, the Sierra Nevada big trees were at first unable to escape loggers' saws. Not counting John Muir's advocacy on their behalf and the accompanying public outcry, one major difference between coast and mountain redwoods eventually saved the big trees' skins: the wood of the giant sequoia is brittle and weak. After a big tree is toppled—a task that once took four men sawing by hand up to a month to achieve—it tends to shatter. Though industrious lumber crews still managed to market giant sequoias as shingles, fenceposts, and such, the difficulty of felling big trees and hauling them off to lumber mills slowed the destruction of old-growth groves. Unfortunately, government protection of today's 70 surviving groves of Sierra Nevada sequoias still came too late to save most of California's ancient big trees.

FAUNA

Since animals also require specific conditions in order to survive and thrive, the range of many species coincides with particular climates and types of vegetation. A wide variety of small mammals and birds thrives year-round throughout Sierra Nevada foothill areas, but seasonal migrants—including mule deer and black bears—are more common at lower elevations in winter; in summer, when the living is easier, they mosey back up into the wooded mountains. A fairly common predator, but nocturnal and rarely seen, is the ringtail or big-eyed civet cat, actually a small, sleek cousin of both raccoons and bears. Common, too, are raccoons and spotted and striped skunks, which also range at much higher elevations.

The Sierra Nevada's major timber zones provide food and shelter for larger mammals, including cougars, bobcats, foxes, coyotes, and the ever-busy beaver, whose handiwork can be found along mountain waterways. Native to the foothills, beavers are considered "exotic" where now found. Among other rodents common throughout the range's mid-elevations are the porcupine, or "quill pig," northern flying squirrel, western gray squirrel, golden-mantled ground squirrel, chipmunk, woodrat, and various mice species. Rare is the nocturnal mountain beaver, which looks like a muskrat but has no tail.

THE DEMISE OF THE SIERRA BIGHORN?

The ragged beauty and rugged agility of Sierra Nevada bighorn sheep, John Muir's "bravest of all Sierra mountaineers" and Native Americans' "white buffaloes," can still sometimes be appreciated firsthand by mountain visitors. Though bighorn hunting was banned in California in 1878, the law provided little real protection from domestic sheep ranchers, who viewed bighorn as grazing competition, and from diseases transmitted by domestic herds, particularly bacterial pneumonia. The state's Sierra Nevada bighorn population dropped off steadily until the 1970s, when new bighorn reserves were established and relocation efforts began in earnest, to increase the population. The Sierra bighorn sheep may still be spared the fate of California's wolves and grizzly bears, both extinct.

But no one's too sure. Now numbering as few as 250, this genetically distinct bighorn population has been all but wiped out. In early 1999, both the state and federal governments officially listed the Sierra Nevada bighorn as an endangered species. In 2003 the U.S. Fish and Wildlife Service estimated that restoring the population—by boosting herd sizes, further dispersing herds, and fending off mountain lions as well as domestic sheep—would cost $21 million and take at least two decades to accomplish.

As alive, alert, and independently ingenious as domestic sheep are simple and herd-bound, these magnificent creatures historically have taken in stride whatever tough territory the Sierra Nevada offers. Bands of bachelor rams or small family groups of ewes and lambs, watched over by a wary old ram with massive curved horns, can sometimes be spotted in spring and summer in Lee Vining Canyon west of Mono Lake, scrambling up impossibly steep and unstable inclines or leaping across ravines.

Yet Lee Vining Canyon is the last viable range of the Sierra bighorn. Due to the recent harsh winters, mountain lion predation, mountain lion population increases—which have forced the bighorn to winter (and die) in high elevations—and disease transmitted by contact with domestic sheep grazing on wild lands, even these sheep are under great stress. Several other bighorn populations, relocated elsewhere in the Sierra Nevada in the hopes of increasing total numbers, have virtually disappeared.

As a last-resort effort to guard against species extinction until range management and other political decisions can be made to protect more effectively the surviving wild populations, state biologists plan to capture at least some Sierra Nevada bighorn sheep, pen them, and begin a captive breeding program. Based on the successful captive breeding of Peninsular bighorn near Palm Springs—those sheep quick to revert to their wild ways upon release from captivity—the hope is that the numbers of Sierra Nevada bighorn can be increased fairly rapidly, to establish new relocated populations in the wild.

Among birds common to Sierra Nevada mixed yellow pine forests are pygmy owls and rare spotted owls. (The latter have become targets for the wrath of lumber companies, since old-growth forests and the potential board-feet of these areas are theoretically protected as the owl's habitat.) Also teetering on the edge of extinction in California is the mysterious and reclusive great gray owl, sometimes called "the phantom of the northern forest," an impressive predator with night vision one million times keener than human sight.

Few birds are common to the Sierra Nevada's sparse subalpine forests, but the rosy finch, pine grosbeak, and three-toed woodpecker fly through it; very few mammals make their home near timberline. Aside from fair-weather migrants from lower elevations, including marmots and ground squirrels, jackrabbits and pikas live in the high country year-round.

Less common but quite impressive are High Sierra predators. Sworn enemy of self-respecting squirrels and songbirds is the pine marten, an agile and top-notch treetop hunter with a savage temperament. The ferocious wolverine or "skunk bear" (elusive and now endangered) shares this disposition problem. Territorial loners known for their diabolical cunning, apparent maliciousness, and brute strength, wolverines will attack anything they can overpower—even bears or cougars—in the serious high-country competition for food. Also aggressive and good hunters are weasels and the very rare mink. Rarer still is the elusive fisher, or "fisher cat," a nonfishing fox-sized hunter and member of the weasel family now found only in the southern Sierra Nevada and in remote northwestern areas of the state. Grizzly bears have long been extinct in the Sierra Nevada, but black bears (which are often brown) and mountain lions are increasingly common.

Most impressive of all, to visitors fortunate enough to spot them in the near-perfect camouflage of their pale rocky climbing grounds, are the seriously endangered Sierra bighorn sheep, surviving only in remote areas in and around Yosemite and Sequoia National Parks.

SEEING AND DOING THE SIERRA NEVADA

Those who truly fear and loathe the great outdoors can still appreciate the Sierra Nevada by car. Even the highest mountain passes are usually snow-free and open all summer—often into autumn, when colorful quaking aspens light up the summits. The most spectacular show of fall color occurs along snakelike Sonora Pass and the canyons and high roads to the south.

Among the historic thoroughfares challenging the Sierra Nevada's heights is the I-80 freeway. Descendant of the old Lincoln Highway—the first transcontinental highway in the U.S., a 1912 string of mostly unpaved cowpaths promoted by auto companies to help sell their rolling stock—modern I-80 follows much of the original route, but the exciting hairpin-turn and mudrut thrill is gone.

Before the Lincoln Highway was built, a section of the **Emigrant Trail** threaded over difficult Donner Pass. At the summit (just off the old Hwy. 40), park at the Mary Lake trailhead for the Pacific Crest Trail and hike a couple of miles to the Roller Pass alternate route, where emigrant wagons were hauled up over the crest between 1846 and 1852. (A third route was Coldstream or Middle Pass.) For help tracing these paths of early California settlers, stop for information at **Donner Memorial State Park** adjacent to Donner Lake (ranger-guided walks sometimes offered).

The **Pacific Crest Trail,** which weaves north-south through the Sierra Nevada, is itself something of a historical accomplishment: it's the longest trail in America, 2,665 miles of footpath climbing mountains and crossing deserts between Canada and Mexico, still not quite completed after more than 60 years of labor. (For current trail information or to help out, contact the nonprofit Pacific Crest Trail Association at the website: www.pcta.org.)

But all passes over the Sierra Nevada are "historic," since all routes were once commonly used by bighorn sheep, deer, native peoples, and finally California pioneers. Fredonyer Pass on Hwy. 36 west of Susanville marks the range's far northern reach. Beckwourth Pass on Hwy. 70, northwest of Hallelujah Junction, was named for black mountaineer and trailblazer Jim Beckwourth. Next south are Yuba Pass on Hwy. 49 east of Bassetts; Donner Summit west of Truckee on I-80; Echo Summit on Hwy. 50; Luther Pass northwest of Picketts Junction on Hwy. 89; Carson Pass on Hwy. 88 east of Kirkwood; and Monitor Pass southeast of Markleeville on the way to Nevada. Ebbetts Pass slinks over the summit on Hwy. 4 between Bear Valley and the Hwy. 89/Monitor Pass junction. Very narrow Sonora Pass on Hwy. 108 (trailers and RVs definitely inadvisable) is next south, then Tioga Pass just outside the eastern border of Yosemite National Park on Hwy. 120, which looms up over the vast basin near Mono Lake.

The High Sierra passes south of Tioga cut through the tallest, most rugged terrain in the state and still defy the road builders. Even now these routes are open only in summer and used only by hikers, backpackers, and horseback adventurers. Walker Pass east of Bakersfield and Lake Isabella on Hwy. 178, where the Sierra Nevada starts drifting off into the desert as low, rolling mountains and plateaus, is open to travelers year-round.

Hiking, Backpacking, and Biking

To personally experience the breathtaking beauty of the Sierra Nevada, get out of that car. Throughout its vast range, the Sierra Nevada offers outdoor opportunities for people of all ages and inclinations—from short, easy self-guided nature trails and day hikes along sections of major trails to challenging climbs over peaks and summits. For those who are physically able, backpacking through remote areas of the range is truly a "peak" experience. Maniacal mountain climbers often breeze into the high country, set up base camp, then *really* set out to see (and cling to and clamber over) the Sierra Nevada. Bicycling—again, only for the fit and fatalistic—is another great way to experience California's snowy mountains. See the Gold Country chapter for more information on regional cycling guidebooks.

Guided Pack Trips

For first-timers to the Sierra Nevada outback, or for those who will never warm up to the physical exertion necessary for backpacking and bicycling, a guided pack trip—far from cheap but very enjoyable—is the easy way to go. Yet it's an increasingly controversial option. Some environmental and hiker groups contend that commercial packers don't face the same Sierra Nevada wilderness access limitations that hikers and backpackers do, and that horses and strings of pack animals cause unnecessary environmental damage. Packers—flag bearers for a time-honored Western tradition—bristle at the criticism, saying that though there have been a few problem companies, most packers follow all regulations and are as conscientious about protecting the land as they are about safety. Increasingly, though, the U.S. Forest Service and National Park Service are restricting access to packers.

To cover the same territory backpackers do but without carrying the necessities of life oneself, consider llama packing. California's largest llama packer is **Trailhead & Co. Llama Treks,** 30002 Chihuahua Valley Rd., Warner Springs, CA 92086, 909/767-0172, www.llamahikes.com,

which offers Southern California treks as well as numerous treks in and around Yosemite, Kings Canyon, and Sequoia National Parks. Day hikes, customized overnight trips, and special menus are available, too. Others operating in the Sierra Nevada include **Highland Llama Trekkers** in Grass Valley, 916/273-8105, and **Potato Ranch Packers** in Sonora, 209/588-1707. Some High Sierra packers offer similar burro trips and/or the option of packing in supplies at prearranged destinations and times, so backpackers can travel farther with a lighter load.

Most Sierra Nevada packers and guides offer horseback trips (summer only) and dunnage (a guide and horses or mules to pack one's camping equipment and provisions); many also offer day rides and spring and summer horse or cattle drives and other special events. For a complete current listing of reputable firms (federal permits required), contact the relevant national forest headquarters or ranger districts, and/or local chambers of commerce. Packers in Yosemite and at Sequoia and Kings Canyon National Parks' Cedar Grove, Mineral King, and Wolverton Pack Stations operate under concession contracts.

Pack outfits are located on both the eastern and western slopes of the Sierra Nevada, though most depart from major trailheads along the range's east side—the closest access to the highest high country. For fairly complete listings, contact the **Eastern High Sierra Packers Association,** c/o Bishop Chamber of Commerce, 690 N. Main St., Bishop, CA 93514, 760/873-8405, fax 760/873-6999, www.bishopvisitor.com, and the **Western High Sierra Packers Association,** 8314 Santa Fe Dr., Chowchilla, CA 93610, www.sierranet.net/web/highsierrapackers.

Recommended near Bridgeport is the **Virginia Lakes Pack Outfit,** 702/867-2591 in winter, 760/937-0326 in summer, www.virginialakes.com; near June Lakes, **Frontier Pack Train,** 760/648-7701 (summer), 760/873-7971 (winter). Pack outfits near Mammoth Lakes include **Agnew Meadows Pack Train** and **Red's Meadow Pack Station,** 760/934-2345 or 800/292-7758 for both, and **Mammoth Lakes Pack Outfit,** 760/934-2434, fax 760/934-3975 in summer, and fax 916/495-2569 in winter, www.mammothpack

.com. Closer to Crowley Lake is **McGee Creek Pack Station**, 760/935-4324 in summer, 760/878-2207 in winter, www.mammothweb.com/recreation/McGee.

Packers near Bishop include **Rock Creek Pack Station**, 760/935-4493 (summer), 760/872-8331 (winter), www.rockcreekpackstation.com; **Pine Creek Pack Station**, 760/387-2797 or 800/962-0775, www.395.com/berners; **Bishop Pack Outfitters**, or fax 760/873-4785 or 800/316-4252; and **Rainbow Pack Station**, 760/873-8877, fax 760/873-3479. Near Big Pine is **Glacier Pack Train**, 760/938-2538.

Sequoia Kings Pack Train, 760/387-2797 or 800/962-0775, operates out of Onion Valley west of Independence. West of Lone Pine is **Cottonwood Pack Station**, 760/878-2015. Also serving the Sequoia–Kings Canyon National Parks area, and Golden Trout Wilderness, is **Mt. Whitney Pack Trains**, jointly operated by Red's Meadow and Rock Creek (see above).

The dozen or so packers on the west side include the **Kennedy Meadows Resort & Pack Station**, 209/965-3900 in summer, 209/532-9663 in winter; **Minarets Pack Station** at Miller Meadow, 559/868-3405; and **Yosemite Trails Pack Station** in Fish Camp, 559/683-7611 in summer, 559/665-1123 in winter.

Fishing and Water Recreation

From about May until whenever the lakes freeze over, the fishin' is easy in the Sierra Nevada. For premier trout fishing, head north of I-80 and on into the Feather and Yuba River watersheds. Stampede and Prosser Reservoirs are quiet and quite popular fishing lakes, though others are also excellent. Stream and river fishing can be good, too, but the persistent construction of dams in Northern California means good trout streams are harder to find. Most major reservoirs offer some type of water recreation, from sailing or water-skiing to swimming, but even in summer, Lake Tahoe and most High Sierra lakes are too cold for swimming by most people's standards—though a quick dip *is* invigorating and washes away that trail dust. For various reasons, but primarily because near their sources even the wildest rivers are small and shallow, white-water

rafting on the Sierra Nevada's western slope is better a ways downstream. See The Gold Country chapter for information on rafting in rivers that originate in the Sierra Nevada.

Winter Sports and Recreation

Downhill skiing is big-time fun in these parts and a major economic boon for the Sierra Nevada. Many world-class ski resorts are within easy reach of I-80 and the Lake Tahoe area, from Sugar Bowl and Squaw Valley (host of the 1960 Winter Olympics) to Alpine Meadows and Kirkwood, but keep sledding south to other worthwhile ski spots: Dodge Ridge, June Mountain, and Mammoth Mountain. Most ski resorts are fully accessible to snowboarders; many also offer groomed cross-country ski trails.

The peak "out there" experience for some downhillers is heli-skiing—catching a lift by helicopter to high, otherwise inaccessible powder—but challenging enough for many is Nordic or cross-country skiing. Backcountry skiing is

Heavenly Valley in South Lake Tahoe

© ROBERT HOLMES/CALTOUR

SIERRA NEVADA

EDUCATIONAL ADVENTURES IN THE SIERRA NEVADA

Among the many groups in California offering educational experiences and seminars in the Sierra Nevada is the University of California at Berkeley's **Cal Adventures,** 5 Haas Clubhouse, Strawberry Canyon Recreation Area, Berkeley, CA 94720, 510/642-4000, fax 510/642-3730, www.strawberry.org. This outdoor education program is largely tailored to Bay Area residents, but some programs—particularly its summer backpacking, white-water rafting, and white-water guide school workshops—are held in the Sierra Nevada. Call for a current program. Registration is strictly first-come, first-served, so either call in your registration or fax it after downloading the form from the website. **Field Studies in Natural History,** San Jose State University, One Washington Square, San Jose, CA 95192, 408/924-2625, offers interdisciplinary natural history field seminars, open to the public, as part of its continuing education program. Some focus on the Sierra Nevada. Check with other UC and CSUC campuses for similar programs.

A particular boon for adventurous seniors (age 55 and older) is **Elderhostel,** 75 Federal St., Boston, MA 02110, 877/426-8056, www.elderhostel.org, which offers an abundance of low-cost environmental and educational adventures in California's Sierra Nevada, many of these sponsored by various state colleges and universities. A recent summer schedule, for example, included programs based at the Lost Valley Pack Station (for burro backpacking), Mammoth Lakes, Meadow Valley near Quincy, Oakhurst near Yosemite, Sierra National Forest, and Wonder Valley Ranch near Sequoia and Kings Canyon National Parks. Most trips cost less than $500 per week.

The **Yosemite Association,** P.O. Box 230, El Portal, CA 95318, 209/379-2646, www.yosemite.org, sponsors a variety of excellent college-level field seminars, from bird studies and botany weekends to backpacks and family day hikes. Even specialized day hikes are offered, such as On the Trail of Gourmet Delights. Seminars on Yosemite in winter, basketry, geology, and ecology are also offered, along with photography, poetry, writing, painting, and drawing. Most seminars are in the $150-and-up range.

The **Mono Lake Committee** in Lee Vining, 760/647-6595, www.monolake.org, sponsors naturalist-led tours and seminars on an endless variety of topics. A typical year's roster of courses might include Prehistoric Peoples and Their Environments, Mono-Bodie Historical Tour, Mono Basin Photography, Geology of the Mono Basin, Survival of the Sierra Nevada Bighorn, Birds of the Mono Basin, California Gull Research, High Country Wildflowers, and the Paoha Island Kayak Tour. Usually starting in June, guided Mono Lake canoe tours are also offered. Volunteers are needed, too, for ongoing bird counts and environmental restoration work. Most weekend workshops are $75–150.

At the group, chapter, and national level, the Sierra Club and the Audubon Society also offer hikes and treks—some free, some almost free (like working wilderness outings), and some guided trips with fees. For bird-watching trips, typically offered at the chapter level, contact **Audubon California,** 555 Audubon Place, Sacramento, CA 95825, 916/481-5332, www.audubon-ca.org. (For eastern Sierra Nevada bird-watching in particular, try the chapter website: lnr.dragonfire.net/ESAS.) For information about all Sierra Club trips, including those in and near the Sierra Nevada, contact: **Sierra Club Outing Dept.,** 85 Second St., San Francisco, CA 94105, 415/977-5630 (24-hour voice mail), www.sierraclub.org/outings. Be sure to inquire, too, about current—and very affordable—hikes, outings, and educational programs offered at the Sierra Club's **Clair Tappaan Lodge** near Lake Tahoe.

The **Nature Conservancy of California,** 201 Mission St., San Francisco, CA 94105, 415/777-0487, www.tnc.org/infield/State/California, offers no-cost or low-cost natural history expeditions and restoration work parties throughout the state, though that information is typically only available at the local or regional levels. (Ask for a list of preserves open to the public, and contact these directly.) Inquire for current schedules—and also ask about major trips and tours, which have included expeditions tracing the footsteps of John Muir and Ishi.

increasingly popular, with more private and public tracks and marked trails available every year. Ski mountaineering (using shorter, wider skis than Nordic varieties) combines cross-country and downhill skiing for wide-ranging backcountry adventure and exploration. Snow camping may or may not be included. Snowshoe hiking, sledding, tobogganing, "tubing," ice fishing, ice skating, and just plain snow play are other enjoyable winter pastimes.

State of California **Sno-Park** sites are legal, snow-cleared parking areas scattered throughout the Sierra Nevada that provide easy access to major winter recreation areas without risking a parking ticket or burial by a passing snowplow. Sno-Park permits ($5 for a one-day parking pass, $25 for a season ticket at last report) can be purchased at winter sports equipment outlets and snow-country state parks. For more information or to request a free Sno-Park site map, call the **Sno-Park hotline** at 916/324-1222. Season permits are good from whenever the snow first flies (usually by November 1) until May 30.

HEALTH AND SAFETY

All Sierra Nevada travelers—backpackers, cyclists, day hikers, even car campers and those who plan no outdoor trips—should be reasonably prepared for anything, for despite the Sierra Nevada's recreational popularity, there may be no one around to help if something goes wrong. Though snowstorms are common in winter, these and other freak storms also occur in summer. Drivers should always carry tire chains, blankets, and some water and food in case they become stranded. To help avoid that possibility, have some sort of itinerary and get current destination and road information before setting out.

Even casual hikers need to remember that the air is thin at high elevations and it takes a day or two to adjust. Plan outdoor excursions and exertions accordingly; altitude sickness and hyperventilation are not fun.

Even in the most pristine backcountry areas, drinking water also poses a problem. Sadly, because of the widespread presence of a single-celled intestinal parasite called *Giardia lamblia,* it's no longer safe to dip that tin Sierra Club cup into marshy mountain meadows for a drink of the world's best-tasting water. Backpackers and hikers far from water faucets should boil all drinking water (for at least five minutes), carry water purification tablets, or invest in a portable purification pump—by far the best option. Whatever your choice, also bring a container or containers adequate to the task and a couple of good-sized canteens to help avoid the temptation of drinking unpurified water when suddenly thirsty.

Symptoms of giardiasis include the sudden onset of nausea, stomach cramps, and debilitating diarrhea. Though rarely life-threatening even without treatment, becoming weak or sick from giardia contamination in the Sierra Nevada is no joke, since any physical ailment also increases the possibility of falls and serious injury. Sometimes, too, the malady's symptoms are delayed (average incubation period: one to three weeks) and people fail to connect the sickness with its original cause, suffering unnecessarily for months. To prevent further giardia contamination in the Sierra Nevada, camp well back from lakes and streams, and—with the help of one of those cute little plastic shovels—always bury fecal and other wastes at least six to eight inches deep and at least 100 feet from water.

Adequate food is the next most important necessity. Always bring more than you think you'll need (avoid canned or bottled items if backpacking), including high-energy trail snacks, but not so much that you can't carry the load comfortably. Hikers and backpackers need good, broken-in, and waterproofed hiking boots; plenty of cotton and wool socks (packed accessibly); long pants; cold-weather clothing (including hat and mittens); and rain and wind gear—including a tarp or small waterproof tent, a poncho large enough to keep most of one's body and pack dry, and waterproof matches. (Even for day hikes, a handy item is an inexpensive and lightweight mylar "space blanket," to help stay dry and warm if lost or unexpectedly stranded. A big plastic garbage bag is less effective but even cheaper.) A whistle, good compass, and topographic maps are also wise. It's not uncommon for even experienced woodspeople to accidentally stray from established trails; be sure to learn how to use your compass and topo map before setting out. Insect repellent is another essential (voracious mosquitos are usually worse in marshy meadow or lake areas) as are sunscreen, sun hat, and sunglasses. Other basics include a flashlight or headlamp (extra batteries can't hurt) and a first-aid kit.

Necessities for backcountry camping include a good, well-insulated sleeping bag and pad as well as cooking utensils, cookstove, and fuel. Campfires are not allowed in many wilderness areas—and even if they are, downed and dry firewood is not always available. Also bring sturdy nylon cord and extra stuff sacks to stow food (and any garbage or clothes smelling like food) high in the trees and well away from sleeping areas—to help prevent midnight encounters with bears. A good flashlight, pocketknife, and first-aid and snakebite kits are essential on longer treks, and not a bad idea even on short hikes.

Snow Safety

Special precautions are prudent in winter. If driving, always carry tire chains, blankets, and extra food if storms are possible (and in winter, they always are). Check weather forecasts and snow conditions before setting out. On snowshoes or skis, allow extra travel time if snow is soft. Always take along at least one extra day's food, extra clothing, shelter, and a portable stove—whatever's necessary for an unplanned overnighter—plus extra bindings, ski tips, and other emergency repair supplies.

If caught in a storm, wait it out in an avalanche-safe area. If you become lost or injured, safety experts advise you to STOP—**stay put** (the farther you wander, the longer it will take searchers to track you; **think** (evaluate your options); **observe** (look around to see what's available to help the situation); and **plan** (come up with a plan of action, which will help control fear and prevent panic). Signal your location—with crossed skis and poles, and by stamping "SOS" into the snow (any symbol in threes signifies an emergency)—and light fires, to create smoke in the daytime and light at night. If possible, improvise a snow shelter—scooping out a shallow cave from a snow-

bank or, if in deep snow near trees, burrowing under tree branches away from the wind.

Avoiding Avalanches

Never snowshoe or ski alone—few caught in avalanches survive without help from others—and carry an avalanche probe and snow shovel. High-tech aids include electronic avalanche beacons and transceivers.

About 80 percent of avalanches occur during or after storms. Even a tiny avalanche is no joke if one becomes "one" with it, so pay attention to weather changes. And know your terrain: learn to recognize avalanche-prone topography. Most avalanches occur on mountainsides where the slope is 30 degrees or greater, for example. Lightning may never strike the same place twice, but avalanches often do. Avoid open slopes. Evidence of recent avalanches, or snowballs rolling downslope, means the area's probably unstable.

If crossing a bad spot is unavoidable, go one at a time and stay near the top, avoiding fracture lines. If going up or down, go *straight* up or down—no traversing. If you're caught in an avalanche, try to dart to the side of the slide—and if at all possible, grab a tree. If you can't avoid the slide, swim with the avalanche. As the slide comes to a stop, dig a large air pocket around your head.

PRACTICALITIES

Public and private campgrounds abound throughout the Sierra Nevada. Most national forest service campgrounds are strictly first-come, first-camped, rarely feature hot showers, and may or may not have flush toilets and other amenities. Running water, fire rings, and picnic tables are the norm, however. Most mountain campgrounds are available in summer and early fall only, open as soon as snows melt enough to allow access but closed before the first frosts (when the water is turned off, to avoid burst pipes). Sometimes, early and late high-country bivouacs are possible—campgrounds may be open, and free, though drinking water is unavailable. Contact regional forest service offices for current camping, picnicking, and outdoor recreation information.

State-run campgrounds like those at Tahoe's

Sugar Pine Point State Park (open year-round, snow or no snow) and Grover Hot Springs State Park farther south (also open all year but especially nice in early spring) are quite popular, with ReserveAmerica reservations necessary in summer, 800/444-7275, www.reserveamerica.com. Almost too popular are Yosemite National Park campgrounds; in general, camping is less crowded at redwood-rich Sequoia and Kings Canyon National Parks farther south. Campsites at reservable national park campgrounds—not all are—can be secured in advance through the National Park Reservation Service, 800/365-2267 (outside U.S. and Canada: 301/722-1257), 800/436-7275 for Yosemite, TDD 888/530-9796, http:// reservations.nps.gov. For reservable national forest campgrounds, contact the National Recreation Reservation Service at 877/444-6777 or TDD 877/833-6777 (international: 518/885-3639), www.reserveusa.com. To really get away from it all, try snow camping. Summer or winter, free permits are necessary for backcountry camping on public lands.

For those who never pine for nights spent sleeping under dazzling Sierra Nevada stars, a variety of more civilized accommodations—from motels to hotels and bed-and-breakfasts—is available year-round in "urban" mountain areas like Lake Tahoe and Yosemite Valley, and in more remote areas near downhill ski facilities. Rustic accommodations, from knotty pine-paneled cabins to old stage-stop hotels and hunting lodges, are scattered throughout the mountains. Sit-down dining comes close to city dwellers' expectations only in and around Tahoe, Yosemite, and Mammoth Mountain, though standards elsewhere are definitely trending toward more trendy. But most tiny towns have some sort of grocery store and/or café. If traveling long distances in remote areas of the Sierra Nevada, always carry some groceries and basic cooking utensils—just in case you discover, when hungry for a hot meal, that the town you roll into after dark rolls up its sidewalks at 5 or 6 P.M.

ENTERTAINMENT AND EVENTS

It's hard to imagine anything more rewarding after a day of sweat and trail dust than slipping into a High Sierra hot spring or plunging hot, swollen feet into an icy stream. But, even in God's country, some people prefer casinos and nightlife, après-ski lodges, and the bar scene. The best Sierra Nevada bars, though, are those that spring up like mushrooms in the middle of nowhere—hometown bars in small mountain communities. Once astride a barstool, and after the shock of being a stranger wears off, the experience can be unforgettable. If you're lucky, you just might strike up a friendly conversation with some of the old-timers, the craggy people who have lived the hard life of the mountains so long they now resemble them.

Events

Events in the Sierra Nevada run the gamut from transplanted urban entertainment to dog sled races and hoedowns. In January comes June Lake's **Winterfest**, ski, snowmobile, and other freezing fun centered around June Lake village. Pinecrest's **Mother Lode Classic** ski race is also scheduled in January, followed in February by the **Sonora Pass Classic**. More out of the ordinary are the **Sierra Sweepstakes Dog Sled Races** in Truckee, where they harness the hounds and go for the gold ($5,000 purse) with distance and sprint races, and Markleeville's annual **Canine Connection** sanctioned dog sled races.

In late February or early March, at both Truckee and North Lake Tahoe, is **Snofest,** one of the country's most ambitious winter carnivals, complete with parades, ski races, dances, and fireworks. March is usually prime time for Sierra Nevada ski races, including the **Great Ski Race** from Tahoe to Truckee, California's largest cross-country skiing competition benefiting the Tahoe Nordic Search and Rescue Team; the **Rossignol 5-K Night Race** at Tahoe Donner; and the annual **Echo-to-Kirkwood Race.** In April, try the **Sierra Mountain Race and Relay,** a winter triathlon.

Different in early March is the **Owens River Trout Derby** at Bishop, a "blind bogey" tournament on the open waters of Pleasant Valley Reservoir and along 25 miles of the Owens River; Lone Pine's **Early Trout Opener** usually takes place simultaneously. Also in March comes **Wagon Wheel Race Days,** a 68-mile cycling road race and 24-mile criterium. In April is Bishop's **Rainbow Day,** with awards for best opening-day trout catches, and the **Wild West Marathon** run at Lone Pine.

In May, the **World Championship Cribbage Tournament** in Quincy is quite the showdown, with 400 or more participants and big prize money. Or hang around Lone Pine to see what's left of the **Death Valley to Mt. Whitney Bike Race** contestants when they roll into town. But don't miss **Mule Days** in Bishop, when the self-proclaimed Mule Capital of the World honors the heroic hybrid by holding its World Championship Packing Team contest, as well as a barbecue, parade, and dance.

June's the month for the **Truckee-Tahoe Air Show,** complete with aerobatics, fly-bys, hot air balloon rallies, and parachute drops. Come in June for the annual **Valhalla Renaissance Festival** held at Camp Richardson in South Lake Tahoe—a two-day costumed Elizabethan country fair. Also in June is the three-day **Bear Valley Bike Trek** that starts in the Sierra Nevada above Calaveras Big Trees, rolls through the gold country, and ends in Oakdale. In July come plenty of Fourth of July fireworks—at Donner Lake, Mono Lake, and Lake Almanor far to the north near Chester—plus festivities at Mammoth Lakes, including dancing in the streets, good barbecue, and a chili cook-off. At Graeagle, the holiday is celebrated with swimming in the Old Mill Pond, a parade, barbecue, and more. Also in July: toe-tapping, hand-clapping, thigh-slapping fun at Quincy's **Old Time Fiddling Championships,** a hoedown with square dancing and barbecue, and a 50-K endurance run during **Trailblazer Days** at Walker and Coleville.

Serious cyclists shouldn't miss Markleeville's **Death Ride Tour of the California Alps,** a very fast, almost vertical tour of Sierra Nevada mountain passes, usually held in July. Also in July (at last report), the **Tahoe Fat Tire Festival** at Northstar offers an orgy of events for mountain bikers, from bicycle polo and rodeo to backroads tours and downhill races, in conjunction with a Saturday night Brew Festival. Another species of fun is the **Western States 100/Tevis Cup** cross-country horse race, covering the 100 miles be-

tween Squaw Valley and Auburn. Then comes the **Tri-County Fair** in Bishop, the annual family fun fest for Alpine, Inyo, and Mono Counties. The **Truckee Rodeo** is held in August, as is the **Lake Tahoe Shakespeare Festival** at Sand Harbor and Bishop's **Huck Finn River Festival,** with canoeing, kayaking, and rubber rafting on the Owens River. The town's **Homecoming and Labor Day Rodeo** means cowboys converge for two rodeos, and old-timers return for the parade and western dance.

INFORMATION

At least one good regional visitor bureau or chamber of commerce exists in each of the Sierra Nevada's major travel regions. Also helpful are the visitor centers at state and national parks. Usually best for current backcountry conditions and other information (including topographic maps) are national forest headquarters or ranger district offices. The topo maps "of record" are those put out by the U.S. Geological Survey; they do show elevations and essential features of the terrain, but Sierra Nevada trail enthusiasts say they don't always accurately reflect current routes. So, serious hikers and backpakers should also invest in the various relevant maps and/or trail guides published by Wilderness Press, updated frequently.

Sierra Club Books also publishes some helpful titles, but the best all-around companion volume to tote is *Sierra Nevada Natural History: An Illustrated Handbook* by Tracey I. Storer and Robert L. Usinger, a classic, easy-to-carry guide to plants and animals published by the University of California Press.

Getting Here

Because distances are long, populations sparse, and terrain treacherous in the Sierra Nevada, few public transportation options exist (except in urbanized Mammoth Lake, Tahoe, and Yosemite Valley). Greyhound buses provide limited but regular service along both the eastern and western sides of the Sierra Nevada crest, but buses transect the mountains only via I-80 and Hwy. 50. Though some hardy souls explore the range on foot, by bicycle, on horseback, on skis, or take their chances hitchhiking (best in and around Yosemite and the Tahoe area), most people drive. Of the Sierra Nevada pioneer trails that have since become highways, many are as impassable in winter as they ever were. Only sometimes-snow-snarled I-80 and

Highways 70 and 50 are kept open year-round; Hwy. 395 along the eastern side of the range is also usually open in winter. For regional road conditions, call CalTrans at 916/445-7623 or within the state at 800/427-7623, or consult the website: www.dot.ca.gov/hq/roadinfo.

Lake Tahoe and Vicinity

Like a vast oval mirror laid across the California-Nevada border reflecting both states back on themselves, sapphire-blue Lake Tahoe is North America's largest alpine lake. Mark Twain described Lake Tahoe as "a noble sheet of blue water. . . walled in by a rim of snow-clad mountain peaks. . . . As it lay there with the shadows of the mountains brilliantly photographed upon its still surface I thought it must surely be the fairest picture the whole earth affords." If you ignore modern-day condo-to-condo encroachments and the area's unsightly strip development, the lake is still some picture.

Lake Tahoe exists by the grace of geologic accident. Despite the area's later glacial scouring, the Tahoe Basin was created by the earth's faulting; as the land sank, the Sierra Nevada rose on the west and the Carson Range on the east. Over the eons, snow melt and rain filled this great basin, and kept on filling it: volcanic lava flows then glacial debris plugged the lake's original outlets. (Today, Tahoe's only outlet is the Truckee River, which begins at Tahoe City and flows north and east to Reno and Nevada's Pyramid Lake.) Surface measurements alone—Tahoe is 22 miles long, 12 miles wide, and has a 72-mile shoreline—still don't do the great lake justice. Tahoe's depth averages 989 feet; it plunges down 1,645 feet at its deepest point. And the lake usually contains 122 million acre-feet of water, enough to cover the entire state of California to a depth of about 14 inches.

More important than quantity is the *quality* of the lake's waters. Even today, though there are water quality problems, Lake Tahoe water is some of the purest in the world, with dissolved gases, salts, minerals, and organic matter rivaling the ratios found in distilled water. Tahoe water is so clear that, despite measurable increases in algae

growth and sedimentation during the past 30 years, objects can be spotted to depths of 75 feet or so. One of the lake's stranger characteristics is that, because of its great depth, it never freezes. As surface water gets colder it sinks, forcing warmer, lighter water upwards. Though Emerald Bay—a natural beauty created by glacial moraine—and other shallow inlets may occasionally freeze over, the lake itself is ice free because of its own gentle temperature-controlled dance.

HISTORY

The area's first recorded residents were the Da-ow people, or Washoes, peaceable regional nomads who gathered each spring at Tahoe's Taylor Creek to fish, hunt, and conduct tribal rituals. Some speculate that the Da-ow word *tahoe*, which means "big water" or "high water," may have come via the Spanish *tajo*, "steep cliff area" or "chasm." Though others disagree, George Wharton James, who wrote the definitive guide to Tahoe in 1915, contended that the correct pronunciation is similar to the one-syllable *tao*, "like a Chinese name."

Life as native people had known it changed drastically after explorer John C. Frémont and his guide Kit Carson first spied the great lake in 1844. The wave of westward migration that washed over the Sierra Nevada passed near Tahoe. But even during the gold rush, the difficult Tahoe-area terrain was avoided by most migrants—a tide that turned after the Comstock Lode silver discovery in Nevada. Johnson's Cutoff, the old "Bonanza Road" and now the Hwy. 50 route up from Placerville, swung up and over the Sierra Nevada and through the Tahoe Basin, a treacherous mountain-clutching route for people and products on the move from California's goldfields to the new diggin's near Virginia City. Subsequent chiseling of the Central Pacific Railroad route over the Sierra Nevada by California's hardworking Chinese made access even easier.

The timber demand created by the silver rush led to large-scale logging of Tahoe forests between 1860 and 1890, but once the Comstock Lode petered out by the turn of the century, Lake Tahoe slowly became a resort area for the rich, who were transported from one gala party to another via the lake's steamship fleet. During the 1930s, when roads throughout the Tahoe Basin were finally paved, the middle class began to arrive in California's sky-high vacation land. But modern times have taken their toll on Tahoe. In the 1950s, only 2,500 people lived in the Tahoe Basin year-round, though the area was becoming increasingly popular. Then, when the 1960 Winter Olympics were held at Tahoe's Squaw Valley ski resort, Lake Tahoe became part of the world's vocabulary, setting off an avalanche of commercial and residential development. The concentration of California wealth that came with the dotcom boom has stimulated still more construction. More than 60,000 permanent residents now call the area home, not to mention the millions of summer and winter part-timers and passersby.

Lured by the climate—brisk invigorating winter temperatures, pleasant days and cool nights in summer—the area's natural beauty, and manmade attractions, everyone loves Tahoe. To avoid all this affection, come in late spring when the snowpack is waning or during fall—usually quite nice, depending upon the weather, from mid-September into November.

The Fate of the Donner Party

The Tahoe region's most chilling and most familiar California-bound migration story is that of the Donner Party, an ill-fated group of wagon train travelers who split off from the main train in Utah in the spring of 1846 to try the more southerly, supposedly easier, and shorter Hastings Cutoff to California. But the shortcut, which passed through the alkaline deserts of Utah and Nevada and over difficult mountain ranges, was much too long. Nevertheless, led by George and

monument to the ill-fated Donner Party, at Donner Memorial State Park near Truckee

© ROBERT HOLMES/CALTOUR

Jacob Donner, the group decided to cross the rugged Sierra Nevada in late October. Despite some early snows, the Donner Party almost made it up and over the California Emigrant Trail pass—almost, but not quite. Having found the pass and prepared for the passage, the group decided to sleep and then set out at sunup, and this delay of one day sealed their fate. New snowfall during the night obliterated the trail, and a decision to wait for a break in the weather meant still more snow.

Most of the groups's oxen were lost in the ensuing storms, due to carelessness and panic, and the Donner Party—without adequate provisions and huddled in flimsy tents, makeshift cabins, and snow caves along Alder Creek—settled in for a horrible winter. As the elderly and babies started to sicken and die, the Donner Party's "forlorn hope" group of men and women set out on foot toward the Sacramento Valley to get help. Thirty-two days later, after great privation and misery, the survivors (who cannibalized their fallen travel companions and killed and ate their

Indian guides) finally reached Wheatland, and a rescue party of expert mountaineers immediately set out to save the others. Several successive rescue parties carted out those most capable of making the trip, but only about half of those who set out from the eastern side of the Sierra Nevada—reduced to eating mice, sticks, shoes, and even their own dead just to survive—ever made it to the west side. An 1840s medallion found recently on the archaeological excavation site of Murphy's Cabin contained the inscription: "Blessed Virgin Mary Pray for Us." Even more recent excavations suggest that the actual "last camps" of both George and Jacob Donner have finally been found.

For the most evocative human account of the story, read the powerful *The Donner Party*, a lyrical book-length poem by California writer George Keithley—perhaps not coincidentally, considering the lasting American fascination with this story, the only poetry book ever featured as a Book-of-the-Month Club selection.

Modern Times, Modern Troubles

Lake Tahoe's tremendous popularity with summer vacationers and winter sports fans has brought increasing problems—traffic congestion, air pollution, construction-related erosion, pollution of the lake's pristine waters, and ever-more-limited public access to the lake. Damage to the lake itself is the primary concern. Most famous for its crystal-clear blue waters, Lake Tahoe has already lost about one-third of its fabled clarity, with visibility declining from a depth of 102 feet in 1968 to 67 feet by 1995. Lake Tahoe's water quality continues to decline—losing clarity at a rate of over a foot a year, due primarily to accelerated algae growth caused by phosphorous and nitrogen pollution from fertilizers, septic runoff, and other sources. Changes for the better, if things do start to turn around—experts say we have only a decade to make that happen—will be quite slow. And if they don't turn around, Lake Tahoe will be green in about 40 years.

For more than 20 years, development interests, environmentalists, and hot-under-the-collar citizens—on both the California and Nevada sides of the lake—openly warred over what to do to save Lake Tahoe. Skirmishes were usually waged over various decisions of the two-state Tahoe Regional Planning Agency (TRPA), which has had ultimate control over most Tahoe planning issues since its establishment in 1969.

But the decades-long battle over how to save the lake from its own loveliness has finally simmered down some, with the final acceptance, in the late 1980s, of a new 20-year master plan restricting additional home construction to just 300 per year and controlling commercial development even more tightly. No construction of any kind is now permitted on the lake's more environmentally sensitive areas—including remaining marshlands, which naturally filter the water flowing into Lake

ARE YOU SKIING GREEN?

Most people coming to Tahoe for a ski escape don't know which resorts are most environmentally responsible. Many wouldn't think to ask—or wouldn't know how to ask. But the Ski Area Citizens' Coalition (SACC) *does* ask, and regularly rates large resorts in the 10 western states. The Ski Area Environmental Scorecard is necessary, SACC says, to tally the environmental costs of a sport that cuts down trees, uses precious energy and water in snowmaking, creates traffic jams, and builds virtual cities in the wilderness.

Resorts are graded on 10 criteria, from Avoiding Terrain Expansion on Undisturbed Land to Traffic/Emissions Reduction. For the record, resorts earn as many points for using biodiesel in snowcats as for supporting the Kyoto Treaty or otherwise addressing the issue of climate change. But many, many more points are earned by resorts that don't expand onto new terrain, particularly undisturbed land, wetlands, or wilderness—one reason actively expanding resorts flunk, and then disparage the ratings. Scores are dynamic, though, and can rise or fall with new or better information.

In addition to the overall resort reviews, SACC also issues its "Best in the West" and "Worst in the West" top- and bottom-10 lists. For 2002–03, for example, Alpine Meadows earned an A, and made the Top 10. To study the surprisingly thorough environmental evaluations, go to the website: www.skiareacitizens.com.

Tahoe. In addition, various public and private agencies—the U.S. Forest Service, the California Tahoe Conservancy, The Nature Conservancy, and the Trust for Public Lands—have been buying up much of Tahoe's undeveloped land, to guarantee its permanent protection.

When U.S. President Bill Clinton arrived at Lake Tahoe in July 1997 to convene a presidential forum on the fate of Lake Tahoe—a significant symbolic step in calling the nation's attention to Tahoe's troubles—local efforts had already reached unprecedented levels of cooperation and political harmony. But President Clinton offered more than eloquent talk. He also committed substantial new federal funding to the cause, including $7 million to replace South Lake Tahoe's tired sewage system. In July 2001 the U.S. Senate passed a $20.4 million environmental restoration bill for Tahoe.

Increased attention paid to Lake Tahoe by federal agencies, including the U.S. Environmental Protection Agency and the U.S. Geological Survey, has stimulated new research. (For a stunning bathymetric illustration of Lake Tahoe's underwater geography—and links to all manner of other current research—visit the U.S. Geological Survey's Lake Tahoe Data Clearinghouse website at the website: blt.wr.usgs.gov.) The recent discovery of the fuel ingredient MTBE at a depth of 100 feet, for example, led to the decision to ban all polluting watercraft—these specifically defined as carbureted two-stroke engines over 10 horsepower, both powerboats and jet ski-style personal watercraft—as of June 1999. By 2001 the standards tighten to include engines under 10 horsepower, and auxiliary sailboat engines. At that point, the only allowable two-stroke engines will be those with direct fuel injection.

Even with such relentless efforts to save Tahoe it's too soon to declare success, or declare a reversal in the lake's decline. Yet in early 2003 the lake's clarity was measured to a depth of 78 feet—meaning the lake was clearer than it had been in the previous 10 years.

Redevelopment

Determined to upgrade visitor facilities while improving environmental protections, even be-

fore Clinton's visit to Tahoe the city of South Lake Tahoe launched a massive $236 million redevelopment project. The first phase (completed) created parklike areas where older motels once stood, the reclaimed open land near the lake serving as filtration basins to purify water runoff. New construction projects often reflect a contemporary variation of the "Old Tahoe Style" combination of Tudor and Alpine architecture favored here in the early 1900s. (For every new hotel room added as part of South Lake Tahoe's redevelopment, 1.31 old rooms are being "retired.") A second Park Avenue redevelopment phase, this one with a $200 million-plus price-etag and including a 509-room hotel, timeshare apartments, and a gondola to the ski lifts at Heavenly, was approved in 1996. A third, allowing for a $200 million convention center, another huge hotel, a remodeled marina, and a small hotel with a two-acre replica of Lake Tahoe, got the nod in 1998.

Pricier, more upscale accommodations and shopping/entertainment complexes are the most obvious effect of this immense redevelopment effort. But essential environmental changes are also being made. New "loop roads" now reroute Hwy. 50 around the casino area. Other improvements include a "linear park" along Hwy. 50, for hiking and biking, and other pedestrian-friendly planning. And concerted efforts to coordinate a more effective public transportation system—including a city-owned mass-transit facility—are underway.

SEEING TAHOE

Lake Tahoe has a monster, people say. This is a modern phenomenon, swimming along with Tahoe's trend toward cable TV, condos, and casinos. But so many people claim to have seen the Unidentified Swimming Object now casually referred to as Tahoe Tessie, that in 1984 a USO Hotline was set up to take the flood of calls. The more scientifically oriented suggest that those who spot Tahoe's monster are actually seeing a "standing wave," a phenomenon that occurs when separate boat wakes traveling miles and miles across the lake's still surface finally cross

THUNDERBIRD THUNDERS ON

If you have a little extra time and cash come summer, tour the stunning 16,000-square-foot stone **Thunderbird Lodge** on the Nevada side of Lake Tahoe, just south of Incline Village—and sample how the other one percent lived, even during the Great Depression. Known otherwise as George Whittell's Castle, the real estate magnate's three-story French chateau (with associated boathouse, dungeon, and "card house") is the stuff of local legend. Baseball great Ty Cobb was famous for his all-night poker games at Whittell's summer playhouse, events sometimes also attended by Howard Hughes and all those showgirls. If nothing else impresses you, the fabulous lake views will. And thanks to Whittell, the surrounding 40,000-plus acres of forest is almost untouched as then, most of his holdings included in U.S. Forest Service and Nevada state parks. If not for Whittell's largesse (he left his wealth to animal rights organizations), this side of the lake would be as choked with development as the California side.

In 2003, docent-guided "land tours" were offered from May 1 through September 30, on Wednesdays and Thursdays between 9 A.M. and 3 P.M. (after July 4, also on Friday). To reserve for 1.5-hour docent-led tours, call the Incline Village Visitors Center, 800/468-2463. Meet at the center, and

park in the designated lot before the shuttle ride to the castle. (Arrive at least a half-hour before your tour time.) At last report the cost for the "land tour" was $25 adults, $10 for students (with valid ID) and children age 11 and younger (under 2 free). Shuttle tours from Squaw Valley were available on Monday afternoons at 10:45 and 11:45 A.M. For details and reservations, call 530/581-6610 or 530/581-6628.

Or, come by water, though boat tours are considerably more expensive. In 2003 the 55-foot catamaran *Sierra Cloud* sallied forth from the Hyatt Regency Lake Tahoe for Thunderbird Lodge tours on summer Sunday and Monday mornings at 8 and 9:30 A.M., beginning in June. For details and reservations, call the Hyatt at 775/832-1234 or 800/553-3288. Tours in 2003 also embarked from Zephyr Cove on *The Tahoe* on Sunday at noon and Tuesday at 10:30 A.M., beginning in May, and from the Tahoe Keys on the *Safari Rose* on Sunday at 10 and 11:30 A.M., beginning in June. For details and reservations for both departures, call Caravel Charters at 888/867-6394.

Thunderbird Lodge tours have been immensely popular, consistently selling out, so make reservations well in advance. For current information, contact the Thunderbird Lodge Preservation Society, 775/832-8750, www.thunderbirdlodge.org.

each other and collide. Tessie is described as a 10-foot-long (or longer) dark humpbacked creature, undulating along the water's surface fast enough to leave a wake of its own. Old-timers hope the monster is at least some sort of mutant sturgeon—though no one's ever seen one here— or giant trout.

One definite place to *see* gigantic trout, though—except in drought years when the river has died—is at **Fanny Bridge** on the Truckee River in Tahoe City, named for the fascinating collection of derrieres on display as fish fans lean over to get a good look. (No fishing allowed.) In 1995, the U.S. Fish and Wildlife Service stocked the Truckee River with Lahontan cutthroat trout—a species that hasn't been seen in its native waters here for more than 50

years, when introduced brown and rainbow trout eliminated them.

Most sights on Lake Tahoe proper are easily accessible, even for bicyclists enjoying the bike lanes that help keep cyclists off the highway (50 miles paved). Along Hwy. 28 just northeast of Tahoe City, on the lake, is tiny **Tahoe State Recreation Area,** 530/583-3074 or 530/525-7982, popular for summer camping and beach fun. Farther on, near the Nevada border, is dayuse-only **Kings Beach State Recreation Area,** 530/546-7248, popular in summer for swimming, sunning, and volleyball. In the mountains directly north of Tahoe City is 2,000-acre **Burton Creek State Park,** 530/525-7232, which offers forested hikes and (in winter) short cross-country ski trails.

In Tahoe City is the **Gatekeeper's Museum/ Marion Steinbach Basket Museum,** 130 W. Lake Blvd., 530/583-1762, a reconstruction of the original log cabin—once the residence of the dam's attendant—at Lake Tahoe's Truckee River outlet, part of a several-acre park with picnic area and restrooms. Museum displays include local geology and fossils, Washoe and Paiute artifacts (including arrowheads and grinding stones more than 8,000 years old), and some 800 baskets from the late artist Marion Steinbach's lifetime collection. A real hit with most folks is the dachshund-sized dog sled. Also popular: special film and lecture programs. Usually open April 30–Oct. 1 (daily 11 A.M.–5 P.M. from mid-June through Labor Day, otherwise Wed.–Sun. only). Also worth a peek in Tahoe City is the 1909 **Watson Cabin Museum,** 530/583-8717, the oldest building in town.

North from Tahoe City via Hwy. 89 (or via Hwy. 237) is the down-home community of Truckee, a relaxed old railroading town. South from Tahoe City are houses and condominiums and a string of fine state parks: Sugar Pine Point between Tahoma and Meeks Bay, and the run-together D.L. Bliss and Emerald Bay farther south—all filled to the gills in summer; see below for more information on all of these parks. The young **Tahoe Maritime Museum,** now in a permanent location at 5205 W Lake Blvd. in Homewood, 530/525-9253, www .tahoemaritimemuseum.org, features some classic Tahoe watercraft, engines, and artifacts, and showcases area boating history in photos and videos. A current project is restoring the *Shanghai,* a late-1800s excursion launch recently recovered from the lake. The museum is located on the south side of Homewood Mountain Resort's parking lot and open in summer Friday through Monday 11 A.M.–5 P.M. Still farther south is the Pope-Baldwin Recreation Area and Tallac Historic Site near Camp Richardson and Fallen Leaf Lake.

Worth a stop in South Lake Tahoe is the **Lake Tahoe Historical Society Museum,** 3058 Hwy. 50, 916/541-5458, containing the area's best collection of native cultural artifacts and Tahoe area pioneer relics; call for current days and hours. Rel-

atively new is the year-round **South Tahoe Ice Center** (STIC), 1180 Rufus Allen Blvd., a professional-size facility for recreational skaters, figure skaters, and ice hockey leagues. South Lake Tahoe's **Lake Valley State Recreation Area,** 530/525-9523, offers an 18-hole golf course in summer and snowmobiling and cross-country skiing in winter. (For golf course information, call 530/577-0788.) Adjacent are the undeveloped forests and meadows of 620-acre **Washoe Meadows State Park** on Lake Tahoe Blvd., 530/694-2248.

Truckee and Vicinity

The once wicked tin-roofed town of Truckee, which grew up here during construction of the transcontinental railroad, also once had a thriving Chinatown. The Wild West ambience, still intact today despite galloping growth and gentrification, inspired Charlie Chaplin to film *The Gold Rush* here. Even during Prohibition, Truckee's saloons did a blatantly brisk business, and Truckee's red-light district lasted well into this century—not cleaned up, locals say, until the 1960 Olympics in Squaw Valley. The shops, restaurants, and bars along block-long Commercial Row (off I-80) is where most of Truckee's action is these days, though "new Truckee" boasts shopping centers, a Starbucks, and astounding levels of development. The combination of tourists rolling down off I-80, minimal parking, train traffic, and Truckee's famous southern-right-of-way, three-way stop downtown always made for some exciting local traffic jams. Some of that problem has been rerouted with the late 2002 opening of the $33.5 Truckee Bypass, which links I-80 and Hwy. 267 and bridges downtown, the railroad tracks, and the Truckee River. Yet here and there you can glimpse how it once was. Peek into the Truckee-Donner Historical Society's **Truckee Jail Museum,** 530/582-0893, for example, open on weekends in summer 11 A.M.–4 P.M. or by special arrangement. Or take the society's "online history tour" at http://truckeehistory.tripod.com. Historical society photos are for sale at the **Donner Trading Company,** 11073 Donner Pass Road. To request more community information, see Tahoe Area Information below.

Donner Memorial State Park, 12593 Donner

Pass Rd. (at Donner Lake south of Truckee, just two miles off I-80 via old Hwy. 40), 530/582-7892, is a choice summertime spot for picnicking, camping, short hikes, and water recreation. Notable here, though, is the park's **Emigrant Trail Museum,** which tells the stories of the Donner Party's nightmarish winter of 1846–47, the construction of the Central Pacific Railroad, and the Sierra Nevada's natural history. Open daily 10 A.M.–noon and 1–4 P.M., small admission fee (but free to campers and picnickers who show their receipts). Rangers often offer free guided hikes to interpret the Donner story. Or come in October for the annual commemorative **Donner Party Hike** weekend, which features two days of educational hikes and lectures (extra fee). Call the park for current details. Day-use fee for the park is $5. The park's campground is open late May–Oct. ($16; 10-day camping limit) and quite popular, so reservations are essential. For campsites, call ReserveAmerica, 800/444-7275, www.reserveamerica.com. In the works along the ridges above appealing Donner Lake is the 22-mile **Donner Lake Rim Trail,** which will connect with the Pacific Crest Rail atop Donner Summit. The addition of key Schallenberger Ridge and other acreage has tripled park size, and all but guaranteed the trail's eventual completion.

Worthwhile is the **Western Ski Sport Museum,** 19865 Boreal Ridge Rd., off I-80 at Boreal, 530/426-3313, operated by the Auburn Ski Club and open Sat. and Sun. 10 A.M.–4 P.M. Also worthwhile in the vicinity, southeast of Cisco Grove: the challenging hike to **Loch Leven Lakes,** about a 10-mile roundtrip to see all three glacial lakes. The trailhead is at the Big Bend exit off I-80, across from the Big Bend ranger station west of the Rainbow Tavern.

Sugar Pine Point State Park

A main attraction at Tahoe's Sugar Pine Point State Park is the baronial **Ehrmann Mansion,** probably Tahoe's finest example of a rich person's summer home, built here in 1903 by San Francisco banker Isaias W. Hellman. An amazing shoreline fortress of all-native stone and fine woods—Hellman called the place Pine Lodge—

the mansion-cum-interpretive center is open only in summer for tours, but poke around the estate's spacious grounds anytime. Worth a look, too, are the old icehouse and the Phipps cabin. Down by the lake, at one of the estate's boat-houses, peek through the window for a bit of local boat racing history. Boathouses are usually open to the public over the July 4th weekend.

Also at Sugar Pine Point: almost two miles of mostly rocky lake frontage for sunbathing and swimming, plus hiking and biking trails, picnicking, good year-round camping at the **General Creek Campground** (175 very nice campsites, hot showers only in summer), and the **Edwin L. Z'Berg Natural Preserve** (walk to the point here to see Tahoe's only operating lighthouse). In winter, cross-country skiing is popular, and the heated restrooms serve as de facto warming huts. The park day-use fee is $5. For more information, stop by the area's state park headquarters at D.L. Bliss or call 530/525-7982. To reserve campsites, contact ReserveAmerica, 800/444-7275, www.reserveamerica.com.

D.L. Bliss and Emerald Bay State Parks

Managed as one unit, these two contiguous state parks on Lake Tahoe's southwest shoreline offer camping—268 family campsites, 20 accessible only on foot or by boat—and swimming, fishing, boating, and hiking (day-use fee is $5). Sandy **Lester Beach** at Bliss is packed by noon on summer weekends. Even if you're not up for the longer haul south to Emerald Bay, hike to **Rubicon Point** to get a good, deep look into Tahoe's clear waters. Or take the short **Balancing Rock Nature Trail.**

Emerald Bay offers one of Tahoe's best brief hikes—a very scenic one-mile downhill scramble to 38-room **Vikingsholm,** a Scandinavian-style summer mansion on the bay's fjordlike shore. (People claim it's at least two or three miles climbing back out, however.) The trail heads downhill from the Emerald Bay overlook, where there's a fairly small parking lot, so arrive early. You can also get here the long way, via the easy 4.5-mile Rubicon Trail from D.L. Bliss State Park just north. Considered the Western Hemisphere's

SIERRA NEVADA

© ROBERT HOLMES/CALTOUR

Emerald Bay

finest example of Scandinavian architecture, Vikingsholm seems inspired by all things Norwegian and Swedish—11th-century castles, churches, forts, even sod-roofed homes—and was built in 1928–29; its half-million-dollar original price tag included the now-ruined stone teahouse on tiny Fannette Island. Access to Vikingsholm is by guided tour only ($3 adult, $2 children). In summer—mid-June through Labor Day—tours are offered daily 10 A.M.–4 P.M., every half-hour; tours are usually also offered in spring and fall, on weekends only. Call the park at 530/525-7277 for further details, or see www.vikingsholm.com.

Worthwhile, too, is the short hike up to **Eagle Falls** overlooking the bay (picnicking, also the trailhead to Eagle Lake and the Desolation Wilderness). Even from this far away, you can hear the blaring loudspeakers of tourist-loaded paddlewheelers heading in and out of Emerald Bay. Unusual is the **Emerald Bay Underwater Park,** established here to allow scuba divers a chance to explore the bay's boat boneyard.

Also unique is the 20-site **Emerald Bay Boat Camp,** at the onetime site of the Emerald Bay Resort on the north side of the bay ($10 per night; first-come, first-camped). To reserve other campsites, contact ReserveAmerica at 800/444-7275, www.reserveamerica.com.

For more information about these two parks, contact the California State Parks, Sierra District office in Tahoma, 530/525-7232. Or stop by the central state parks headquarters off the highway at D.L. Bliss. For information about the state parks' excellent year-round schedule of guided hikes, send a self-addressed, stamped business envelope to the address above.

Tallac Historic Site

An enclave of peace preserving the past, the Tallac Historic Site is a 74-acre monument to Tahoe's social heyday, when Lake Tahoe was the elite retreat for California's rich and powerful. Though the Tallac Hotel Casino is long gone, undergoing gradual restoration here under U.S. Forest Service supervision are several impressive summer estates featuring distinct architectural affectations, including "Mr. Santa Anita" Lucky Baldwin's **Baldwin Estate** (now an educational center) and the lavish **Pope-Tevis** and pine-pillared **Valhalla** Mansions (summers-only interpretive center and community events center, respectively). **Thursday**

Night Jazz and other events at Valhalla take full advantage of the great hall downstairs, most notable for its massive stone fireplace. With a boost from the nonprofit Tahoe Tallac Association, a cultural arts organization that also raises funds for restoration, the estate boathouse has now opened its doors as the **Valhalla Boathouse Theatre.**

And that's the point about Tallac. Though it is indeed a monument to Tahoe's past, the complex is fast becoming a cultural and fine arts center. The Tallac Association's "Artists in Action" program, for example, showcases local artists and their talents in various on-site open studio settings, including various guest cottages and the Dextra Baldwin Cabin, the Anita Gibson Cabin, and the Honeymoon Cabin. The twin cabins near Valhalla house the **Cultural Arts Store,** featuring (for sale) arts and fine crafts created by Tallac artists. Almost all summer long, Tallac hosts a refreshingly uncommercial arts and music festival (see Events), well worth several trips, and other creative culture.

The Tallac Historic Site is part and parcel of the Pope-Baldwin Recreation Area near Camp Richardson and popular southwestern Tahoe beaches. Just north of Tallac is a **picnic area, a multiagency visitors center** open only in summer, 530/541-5227, and some **self-guided nature trails.** Particularly worthwhile is the **Rainbow Trail,** which dips down below Taylor Creek into a glass-walled "stream profile chamber" for observing creek life, particularly the October run of Kokanee salmon. For a longer walk, take the trail to **Fallen Leaf Lake.**

Summer tours of Tallac are conducted by the U.S. Forest Service. If you come here just to wander—and the dock at the boathouse is often empty, a great spot for sunbathing—there is no onsite parking, though visitors can park just north at the Kiva Picnic Area or south at Camp Richardson. For more information about the area, contact: **Tahoe Tallac Association,** 530/542-4166 or 888/631-9153 most of the year, 530/541-4975 or 888/632-5859 during the summer festival season (June–Aug.), www.valhalla-tallac.com.

Nevada-Side Sights

Across the state line on the lake's northern end is Incline Village, for Nevada-style diversions and Ben Cartwright's tourist-trampled **Ponderosa Ranch** movie set, 100 Ponderosa Ranch Rd., 775/831-0691, www.ponderosaranch.com, open mid-April through October. More worthwhile but some 25 miles northeast is the entire town of **Virginia City,** 775/847-0311, www.virginiacity-nv.org, "capital" of the historic Comstock Lode, now boasting museums, tours of old silver mines and hard-luck cemeteries, and endless eateries, saloons, and shops. Also intriguing (and closer) is Carson City, Nevada's capital.

The Nevada side of the lake offers a number of worthwhile outdoor destinations. One is **Lake Tahoe Nevada State Park,** 775/831-0494, which includes popular Cave Rock (shore fishing and boating), very popular Sand Harbor (sandy beaches and boating, plus an excellent summer drama and music festival), and Spooner Lake (good backcountry access). There are also scenic diversions, including the historic George Whittell "castle," the **Thunderbird Lodge** just south of Sand Harbor; for tour details, see "Thunderbird Lodge Thunders Along." The 46-acre **Dreyfus Estate** and its mile-long lake frontage just north of Zephyr Cove, until recently owned by New York mutual fund tycoon John Dreyfus, is now public property managed by the U.S. Forest Service. The estate, mired in scandal after a secret three-way, $38 million land swap, will one day be open to public access.

Straddling the border on the lake's south side is the flushed flash and flutter of Stateline, with slot machines and more sophisticated gaming as well as top popular entertainment acts year-round at Caesars Tahoe, Harrah's Tahoe, Harvey's, and Del Webb's High Sierra casino hotels. Interestingly, gambling is on the decline at Tahoe, as high-stakes gamblers migrate to Las Vegas and other gambling hotspots, and Tahoe visitors increasingly prefer spending time—believe it or not—outdoors.

For more suggestions about what to see and do in Nevada, the best guide available is Avalon Travel Publishing's *Moon Handbooks Nevada* by Deke Castleman. Or, contact the region's Nevada visitors bureaus, listed below.

SIERRA NEVADA

SKIING

Purists have always come to Tahoe just for the ride—straight down some of the finest downhill slopes in North America. That's been changing for some time, though, as serious money and corporate style have started reshaping the landscape. In this avalanche of new money skiing has become just part of the state-of-the-art infotainment now being packaged and sold on the slopes. High-speed ski lifts, ice rinks, art galleries, trendy shops and boutiques, movie theaters, nightclubs, stylish restaurants, not to mention "ski-in, ski-out" townhomes, luxury condos, and vanity mansions decked out with all the latest techie accessories—these and similar developments make up the new, endlessly upscale Tahoe.

In the late 1990s California became the top U.S. destination for overnight skiing and snowboarding getaways, surpassing Colorado. Thanks to international marketing efforts, the world now knows that the Sierra Nevada offers world-class skiing—and the "Aspenization" of Tahoe seems destined to roar ahead. Real estate agents are thrilled. Others who love Tahoe are not. The last time Tahoe such unabashed, unapologetic displays of wealth came during the Roaring 1920s, just before the Great Depression. Whether or not current trends will continue is anyone's guess. Still, if it all careens downhill tomorrow there have been lasting area benefits from the recent infusions of cash—like the new sidewalks and streetlights in Tahoe City, making it possible (at last) to walk around town. And—megabucks or no—Tahoe still offers some folksy, friendly resorts with fine skiing. Old Tahoe still exists, alongside New Tahoe.

As a result of increasing national and international popularity, Tahoe-area resorts have seriously upgraded their setups and services in recent years. Snowboarding and snow tubing are among the new trends. Almost all resorts offer ski schools and ski shops, equipment rentals, day lodges, and some sort of accommodations and food. Truly spectacular facilities are increasingly common. Many also provide children's ski instruction and good programs for disabled skiers. Also popular here are private Nordic ski resorts—

sometimes affiliated with downhill facilities—offering great cross-country ski access and/or groomed trails, and low-key but much-appreciated amenities like trailside warming huts.

Due to the possibility of extended drought in California, and the desire to augment nature's gifts as needed, most resorts have invested in snowmaking equipment—so good skiing is possible even when the weather refuses to cooperate.

Alas for thrift-conscious skiers, discounted midweek skiing is a thing of the past. But you can find special bargains if you're willing to hunt them down (often as easy as checking in with the relevant website), from frequent skier programs and family packages to free lessons, two-for-one days, and other special bargain-ticket days or half-days. With money getting tighter all the time, reading online reviews and doing some comparison shopping can be well worth the trouble.

Donner Summit and North Tahoe Resorts

Closest and most accessible to San Francisco and the Bay Area are the four major ski resorts along Donner Summit and two others near Truckee. Farthest west and just off I-80 is small, family-oriented **Soda Springs Ski Area,** open to the public weekends and holidays but otherwise rentable by groups on an advanced-reservation-only basis. Often uncrowded and oriented to beginners and intermediates, advanced skiers still get a good workout on the upper slopes. Snowboarding is allowed and snowshoeing and sledding are also fun, but snow tubing is the thing here. In fact, Soda Springs is a snowtubing showcase—California's largest snow tubing resort—an experience helped along by lifts and groomed runs. Four lifts (two for tubers), 16 runs—and mini-snowmobiles are available for the kiddies. Located on old Hwy. 40, one mile off I-80 via the Norden/Soda Springs exit. For more information, contact: Soda Springs Ski Area, 19455 Boreal Ridge Rd., 530/426-1010 (in season) or 530/426-3666 (snowphone and off season), www.skisodasprings.com. Next east and affiliated with Soda Springs is **Boreal Mountain Resort** (named for Boreas, Greek god of the north

SKI TOURING AND WINTER MOUNTAINEERING

Among instructors and guides offering backcountry ski trips in the Sierra Nevada are **Alpine Skills International (ASI)**, on Donner Summit near Truckee and North Lake Tahoe, P.O. Box 8, Norden, CA 95724, 530/426-9108, www.alpineskills.com; **Sierra Ski Touring,** serving the South Lake Tahoe area, P.O. Box 176, Gardnerville, NV 89410, 775/782-3047; and **Yosemite Mountaineering School,** Yosemite National Park, Yosemite, CA 95389, 209/372-1244, www.yosemitepark.com. Alpine Skills International offers a full range of mountain-climbing, rock-climbing, ice-climbing, and other special outdoor skills instruction. Sierra Ski Touring leads ski trips and also offers avalanche seminars and dog sled trips. Yosemite Mountaineering offers backcountry ski instruction, as well as the world's finest "office" for rock-climbing instruction.

wind), 530/426-3666, www.borealski.com, an intermediate-advanced resort with plenty of beginners' opportunities—and Friday Night Expression Sessions for snowboarders. They also make snow at Boreal when nature won't cooperate. Nine lifts, 38 runs. Located just off I-80 via the Castle exit.

Three miles off I-80 via the Norden/Soda Springs exit is **Donner Ski Ranch,** an unpretentious place by Tahoe standards, with a cozy down-home lodge, inexpensive dormitory-style accommodations, and impressive terrain most suited to intermediate and advanced Alpine skiers (beginners' slopes too). Snowboarders enjoy three terrain parks and a halfpipe. Six lifts, 45 runs. With so much corporate consolidation among Tahoe ski areas determined to become luxury visitor destinations, Donner Ski Ranch is just about the last holdout for pure, relatively inexpensive skiing. It's still fairly uncrowded here. Enjoy it while it lasts. For more information, contact: Donner Ski Ranch, 19320 Donner Pass Rd. in Norden, 530/426-3635, www.donnerskiranch.com.

Nearby, charming 1,500-acre **Sugar Bowl** offers some of California's best Alpine skiing, emphasizing advanced slopes more than any other resort along I-80—though intermediates and beginners also have plenty to do here: Sugar Bowl is nothing if not family-friendly. When necessary, resort-made snow is available on at least main runs. Twelve ski lifts and quad chairs, 80 runs. Sugar Bowl also features a new 20,000-square-foot main lodge, at the base of the Mt. Judah and Jerome Hill Quads. For more information, contact: Sugar Bowl Ski Resort, 11260 Donner Pass Rd. in Norden, 530/426-9000 (snowphone: 530/426-1111), www.sugarbowl.com.

Small **Tahoe Donner,** northwest of Truckee on Northwoods Blvd. off Donner Pass Rd. (take Donner State Park exit from I-80), is primarily for beginners and intermediates, excellent for first-timers and children, with a special Snowflakes Ski School for children ages 3–6. Just six kids per class, too. Four lifts, 14 runs. For more information, contact: Tahoe Donner, 530/587-9400, www.tahoedonner.com.

Northstar-at-Tahoe, between Truckee and Lake Tahoe on Hwy. 267, has always been a convenience- and family-oriented resort, with abundant creature comforts, excellent advanced and intermediate Alpine skiing, and cross-country skiing. Fairly new at Northstar are snow tubing and night skiing, the latter at Polaris Park, at the base lodge. Now owned by Booth Creek Resorts, Northstar is busy expanding, determined to become a year-round resort and become a player in the Swank Sweepstakes (like Squaw Valley). In the works: an outdoor ice rink, conference center, spa, more shopping and restaurants, 2,000 more lodging units, a planned community of 600 homes, and two golf courses. The result will sprawl from Truckee to Tahoe City. Other priorities include adding more lifts (including a "chondola," part chairlift, part gondola) and expanding snowmaking capacities. For more information, contact: Northstar-at-Tahoe, 530/562-1010 (snowphone: 530/562-1330) or 800/466-6784, www.skinorthstar.com.

Not far across the Nevada border is small **Diamond Peak Ski Resort,** 1210 Ski Way in Incline Village, 775/832-1177 (snowphone: 775/831-3211), www.diamondpeak.com, also noted for its snowboarding, cross-country skiing, moonlight tours, sleigh rides, and special kids' area. Six lifts, 30 runs, two natural glades (for advanced skiers). **Mt. Rose—Ski Tahoe** on the way to Reno via Hwy. 431, 11 miles from Tahoe's north shore, boasts Tahoe's highest base, with lodge facilities at 8,260 feet. Six lifts, two terrain parks, 43 trails, endless glades, and room to roam—about 1,000 acres, in fact. For more information, call 775/849-0704 or 800/754-7673 (outside Nevada) or see www.mtrose.com.

Close to the lake and the locals' favorite is 2,000-acre **Alpine Meadows** off Hwy. 89 (via Alpine Meadows Rd.), still one of the West's best ski resorts, now owned by Utah-based Powdr Corp. (which also owns Boreal and Soda Springs). And in 2002–03, Alpine Meadows was the only Tahoe area resort to earn an A on the Ski Area Environmental Scorecard. (For more information, see "Are You Skiing Green?" in this chapter.) With six bowls, steep glades, and exceptional runs and views, Alpine is expansive yet low-key, a fine family-oriented alternative to Squaw Valley. Alpine Meadows is excellent for spring skiing, and also offers one of the state's superior disabled ski programs. The well-respected **Tahoe Adaptive Ski School** here, the winter program of Disabled Sports USA Far West, "is dedicated to the development of lifetime skills for persons with disabilities and their families by providing affordable, quality sports and recreation experiences." Alpine Meadows offers 13 lifts, 100-plus runs. For snowboarders, Alpine offers two terrain parks (one just for children), one halfpipe, and a Superpipe. For more information, contact: Alpine Meadows, 530/583-4232 (snowphone: 530/581-8374) or 800/441-4423, www.skialpine.com.

Still most famous of all Tahoe ski resorts, offering some of the world's finest, most challenging alpine skiing, is **Squaw Valley USA,** 1960 Squaw Valley Rd. (off Hwy. 89 northwest of Tahoe City), 530/583-6985 or 888/766-9321, www.squaw.com. Despite its negative reputation in environmental circles due to its ongoing legal skirmishes over attempts to develop Shirley Canyon—popular with hikers—for still more ski runs, Squaw Valley is still heaven—especially for truly competitive skiers. Squaw Valley's 4,000 acres of skiable terrain include some of the steep-est steeps in the West. It's also one of the most popular and crowded resorts around—a ski-oriented city in its own right. Squaw Valley offers slopes for advanced, intermediate, and beginning skiers; night skiing; snowboarding; and restricted access for disabled skiers. Thirty lifts, open-bowl terrain. Snowboarding options include two terrain parks and two halfpipes (one of each is lighted) and a boardercross facility.

Even nonskiers show up just to ride the Cable Car tram up the mountain for the views—a year-round pleasure, especially now that the cabins are heated. A **climbing wall** in the tram building, 530/583-0150, offers fun and exercise while you wait. An increasing array of recreational opportunities includes the astounding **Bath and Tennis Club** atop the mountain at High Camp, which features the stunning **Olympic Ice Pavilion,** spas, a swimming lagoon, tennis courts (heated for winter play), and restaurants. If that's not enough excitement, sign up for a 75-foot freefall with **Bungee Squaw Valley,** 530/583-4000, also at High Camp and open year-round. Opened in late 1998 at Squaw Valley is its $20 million **Funitel,** a double-cable gondola running from the base up to Gold Coast, Squaw Valley's other mid-mountain facility—a ride that's all but immune to high winds that otherwise shut down the mountain. The six-passenger **High Camp Pulse** shuttles back and forth between High Camp and Gold Coast.

Debuting in late 2002 was the first phase of Squaw Valley's $250 million pedestrian-friendly **Village at Squaw**—north Lake Tahoe's largest development to date, a 13-acre complex of lodging, restaurants (including an outpost of the Balboa Café, the High Sierra Grille, Starbucks), entertainment venues, and shops done in "California alpine" architectural style. For accommodations information—a stay here is $250 and up—contact the Village at 866/818-6963 or visit www.thevillageatsquaw.com.

Relatively new in the valley is the deluxe **Resort at Squaw Creek,** a hotel and conference/convention center with three restaurants, fitness center, shopping, cross-country skiing (golf in summer), and a winter-only outdoor ice rink—more urban luxury in the middle of the wilderness. For more information, contact: Resort at Squaw Creek, 400 Squaw Creek Rd., 530/583-6300 or 800/403-4434, www.squawcreek.com. For special events, call 530/581-6686.

North Tahoe Ski Packages

So you want to do it all? Maybe you can. The north shore's "interchangeable ticket" Ski Tahoe North voucher program and ticket/ski packages offer good deals for multiday ski vacations. One voucher gets you into Squaw Valley USA, Northstar-at-Tahoe, Alpine Meadows, Sugar Bowl, Diamond Peak (two adults on one voucher any day), Homewood Mountain Resort (two adults on one voucher Mon.–Thurs. and nonholidays), and Mt. Rose ("skills and drills" clinic with lift ticket). The price in 2002–2003 was $150 for three days; $200, four days; $250, five days; and $300, six days. For Alpine skiers, the three nights' lodging/three days' ski option (accommodations plus voucher) started at $90 per person per day (double occupancy). Such a deal. For more information and to make reservations, contact the **North Lake Tahoe Resort Association,** 888/434-1262, www.tahoefun.org.

West Shore Resorts

Skiing-as-consumerism hasn't yet arrived here. More resort than ski area is **Granlibakken** just south of Tahoe City (off Hwy. 89 via Tonopah Rd., at the end of Granlibakken Rd.), mostly a beginners' hill perfect for families. One of Tahoe's first snowplay areas, opened in 1928, one of the country's best ski jumps was built here in 1930— allowing Granlibakken to host the National and Olympic Trial Jumping Championships. For more information, contact: Granlibakken Resort and Conference Center in Tahoe City, 530/583-4242 or 800/543-3221, www.granlibakken .com. Far from the madding weekend crowds but so close to the lake it looks like you'll end up water skiing, **Homewood Mountain Resort,** is six miles south of Tahoe City at 5145 W. Lake Blvd., 530/525-2992 (snowphone: 530/525-2900), www.skihomewood.com, is unassuming and small—homey—with stunning Tahoe views. *Outside* magazine has declared Homewood the best tree-skiing resort in the United States. Slopes

are perfect for intermediate skiers but there are also good advanced runs, even a few beginner and family ski possibilities (and a child care center). Kids age 10 and under ski free, yet rates are otherwise quite reasonable—up to $20 less than Alpine or Squaw Valley. Snowboarders enjoy the "Shredwood Forest" terrain park. Good spring skiing. New in 2002–03: Senior Moment Mondays. Don't forget, now.

South Shore Resorts

Heavenly, "America's Largest Ski Resort," on the California-Nevada border near South Lake Tahoe, is geared toward advanced and high-intermediate skiers. Its 20 square miles of ski terrain offers great opportunities—and views—for intermediates. A children's ski center and a reasonable number of beginners' slopes make Heavenly heavenly for families, too. Courageous skiers head for Motts Canyon, Killebrew's, and the legendary Gunbarrel. Snowboarders enjoy a half-pipe on each side, a permanent boardercross trail, and additional terrain. Heavenly, now owned by Colorado's respected Vail Resorts, has expanded ambitiously during the last decade—and that expansion is destined to continue, in conjunction with South Lake Tahoe redevelopment plans. A grand, $23 million, high-speed gondola from urban South Lake Tahoe up to the slopes is already in place; 138 eight-person cabins make the trip along 2.4 miles of cable in 12 minutes. The **Marriott Timber Lodge Hotel** and the **Marriott Grand Residence Club** anchor the pedestrian complex—with shopping, restaurants and bars, multiplex movie theater, outdoor ice rink, transit center—near the gondola's base, a setup that allows people to hit the slopes without driving. Souped-up resort restaurants, more high-speed lifts, and new trails are all on the way. Vail has promised $40 million in improvements as part of its own five-year plan. At last count Heavenly sported 27 lifts and 82 runs. In relatively dry years, snowmaking saves the day. For more information, contact Heavenly Ski Resort in Stateline, Nevada, 775/586-7000 or 800/2-HEAVEN, www.skiheavenly.com.

A few miles west of Echo Summit off Hwy. 50 is impressive **Sierra-at-Tahoe Ski & Snowboard**

Resort, sister resort to Northstar-at-Tahoe, offering something for everyone: open bowls and tree-lined runs for experts and intermediates, snowboarding, also plenty of fun for beginners and families—including a tubing hill with a lift. The emphasis here on better access and options for beginning skiers continues, but Sierra-at-Tahoe also offers free lessons for intermediates and above. The Ranchhouse restaurant up top is a worthy destination, just for the views. For more information, contact: Sierra-at-Tahoe Ski & Snowboard Resort in Twin Bridges, 530/659-7453 (snowphone: 530/659-7475), www.sierratahoe.com. South of Tahoe via Hwy. 89 then Hwy. 88, but close enough for Tahoe skiers, are Iron Mountain and Kirkwood (see Near Tahoe below).

Nordic Skiing: Public Trails

Fun is the three-mile **Castle Peak Trail,** a Sno-Park site near Boreal (exit I-80 at Castle Peak/Boreal), which also offers unmarked backcountry cross-country access and a nearby ski hut. (There are other backcountry huts in the area as well.) A variety of other marked and unmarked Nordic ski trails near Tahoe are maintained in winter by the U.S. Forest Service, including those at Donner Memorial State Park (easy), Martis Lookout (moderate), and Tahoe Meadows (easy). Cross-country ski trails along the lake's west shore include Five Lakes (strenuous), Paige Meadows and Blackwood Canyon (both moderate), Sugar Pine Point State Park and Meeks Creek (both easy), and McKinney/Rubicon (moderate).

The **most strenuous Nordic trails** near the south shore are at Angora Lookout and Trout Creek/Fountain Place. The Taylor Creek/Fallen Leaf trail is **moderately difficult** but good for beginners. There are **moderate trails** at the Echo Lakes area (which also offers good ski camping access into Desolation Wilderness), Benwood Meadows, and Big Meadow/Round Lake. The **easiest trails** are at the Lake Tahoe Visitor Center and at Grass Lake and Hope Valley.

For more information about the area's national forest ski trails, and to find out about ranger-led interpretive ski tours—usually scheduled January through mid-March—contact the U.S. Forest Service (see Tahoe Area Information below).

South and southwest from Tahoe are other good public Nordic ski areas, including the Loon Lake area north of Hwy. 50 (reached via Ice House Rd.) and Strawberry Canyon near Strawberry and Twin Bridges; the invigorating Leek Springs Loop and Winnemucca Lake Loop off Hwy. 88; various sites along Hwy. 4 (including—a good workout—skiing the highway beyond Bear Valley's Hwy. 4 closure gate to Ebbetts Pass); and Pinecrest (24 miles of trails) above Sonora on Hwy. 108.

Nordic Skiing: Private Resorts

Nordic skiing is big news at Tahoe ski resorts. Adult all-day rates are $15–30. Closest to Sacramento (off I-80 at Yuba Gap) is **Eagle Mountain Nordic,** offering 86 km of trails groomed for both skating and striding, both a day lodge and a wilderness lodge, lessons, and special events. The resort becomes a mountain-biking mecca in summer. For more information, call 530/389-2254 or 800/391-2254, www.tahoebest.com/skiing/eaglemtn.htm.

Among the best in the country—and largest, most complete in the nation—is immensely popular, 9,000-acre **Royal Gorge** in Soda Springs, with 88 trails and 204 miles of track, warming huts, day lodge, cafés, and rental-retail ski shops. Royal Gorge's lifts offer easier access to upper slopes; steeper slopes are good for practicing downhill cross-country. Guided snowshoe hikes and ski clinics are also offered. And there are hot tubs, for soaking those screaming muscles. The historic Wilderness Lodge at Royal Gorge Cross-Country (the lodge actually owned by Boy Scouts, who use it in the summer as Camp Pahatsi) burned down in early November 2003, cause unknown. An identical, three-story log lodge will be built to replace it, completion date as yet uncertain. For more information, contact: Royal Gorge Cross-Country Ski Resort, 530/426-3871 or 800/500-3871, www.royalgorge.com. The Sierra Club's volunteer-built 1934 **Clair Tappaan Lodge,** 19940 Donner Pass Rd. in nearby Norden, 530/426-3632—one of the best inexpensive places to stay near Tahoe, any time of year—offers cross-country lessons, rentals, and a few miles of track (free for lodge guests). (Discounts offered for Sierra

Club members.) The **Tahoe Donner Cross Country Center,** 11509 Northwoods Blvd., 530/587-9484, www,tahoedonner.com, features 39 trails and 56 miles of track (with some night Nordic skiing). **Northstar-at-Tahoe,** 530/562-2475 or 530/562-1010, www.skinorthstar.com, has 38 trails and 40 miles of cross-country and telemarking track. The **Resort at Squaw Creek Cross-Country Ski Center,** 530/583-6300 or 800/403-4434, www.squawcreek.com, offers 18 trails and a scenic 400-acre setup for even entry-level skiers, with protection from high winds. See listings above for more information on both Northstar and Squaw Valley. Popular for beginners at **Diamond Peak at Ski Incline,** 1210 Ski Way in Incline Village, Nevada, 775/832-1177, www.diamondpeak.com, is the Vista View Loop, which offers sweeping Tahoe views.

The nonprofit educational **Tahoe Cross Country,** 925 Country Club Dr., 530/583-5475, www.tahoexc.org, offers more than 65 km of set trails. Seniors over 70 and children under 10 ski free. Dogs can play, too; with a dog pass ($3) Fido is welcome on five miles of trail, Mon.–Fri. 8:30 A.M.–5 P.M. and also 3–5 P.M. on weekends and holidays. This is also the starting point for **The Great Race,** the annual 18-mile adventure over Starrett's Pass to Truckee. every year, annual The **Lakeview Cross Country Ski Area,** 938 Country Club Dr. near Tahoe City, 530/583-3653, offers 18 trails and plenty of track, moonlight ski tours, daytime tours, warming hut, rest areas, and clinics. Resort areas south of Tahoe also offer good cross-country skiing opportunities. Just south of the airport is the **Lake Tahoe Winter Sports Center,** 3071 Hwy. 50, 530/577-2940, with many miles of groomed trails. The center also offers snowmobiling on groomed tracks adjacent to its cross-country ski trails.

To really get away from them all at Tahoe, consider Spooner Lake at 14,000-acre Lake Tahoe Nevada State Park, located on the lake's east side, about halfway between Incline Village and South Lake Tahoe. **Spooner Lake Cross Country Ski Area,** 775/887-8844 (state park: 775/831-0494, www.spoonerlake.com, offers 80 km of groomed trails, from easy to challenging, along with lessons and rentals. Special at Spooner Lake are the two wilderness cabins—truly private. Hand-built in Scandinavian style, the Wild Cat and Spooner Lake log cabins have no electricity or running water but are otherwise quite civilized, with propane cook stove, wood stove for heat, composting toilet, and comfy furnishings. Peak snow season rates are $150–200 per night (weekdays lower), "dirt season" weekend rates are less than $100. No pets. To reserve wilderness cabins, call 775/749-5349 or 888/858-8844.

On the other side of the lake is the **Cross Country Ski Center at Camp Richardson,** 530/541-1801, www.camprich.com, which offers 15 km of easy, scenic groomed trails and 35 km of spectacular intermediate "view" trails.

Exceptional south of Tahoe proper are **Hope Valley Cross Country** on Hwy. 88, 530/694-2266, www.sorensensresort.com, with 60 km of wilderness trails, and **Kirkwood Cross Country** at Kirkwood, 209/258-7248 or 209/258-6000, www.kirkwood.com, with 80 kilometers of safe and scenic groomed backcountry trails, kiddie trail, warming hut, and lodge.

RECREATION

Ski Resorts in Summer

As elsewhere, ski resorts in and around the Tahoe area have been transformed into year-round vacation destinations. Formerly winter-only resorts now offer everything from guided hikes (sometimes with llamas), mountain biking, mountain boarding, and horseback riding to tennis and fly-fishing.

Lift-assisted hiking, in which a chairlift, cable car, or gondola ferries hikers to higher elevations, is available at Northstar, Squaw Valley, Heavenly, and Kirkwood. During summer months, for example, **Northstar-at-Tahoe** near Truckee, 530/562-1010 or 800/466-6784, www.skinorthstar.com, offers hiking and mountain biking (rentals available) on 1,700 acres of diverse trails, not to mention full use of its recreation center with swimming pool, tennis courts, exercise room, and hot tubs. Golfing—including golf school—and horseback riding available, too, as well as organized programs for children. Special events in summer are almost endless. Vacation packages, featuring rodeos to romance, can be very good deals. Nearby **Squaw Valley,** 530/583-6985 or 888/766-9321, www.squaw.com, also dedicates itself to endless summers, offering everything from a full roster of special events to alpine hiking, mountain biking, ice skating, tennis, horseback riding, bungee jumping, and swimming at its **High Camp Bath & Tennis Club** (elev. 8,200 feet).

Near Tahoe, in the off-season **Kirkwood** on Hwy. 88, 209/258-6000 or 800/967-7500, www.skikirkwood.com, offers private tennis courts, golf, a mountain bike park (open weekends and holidays), mountain bike trails, a climbing wall, a disc golf course, hiking, horseback riding (and pony rides for children), nearby fly-fishing, and occasional special events. **Sorensen's Resort** on Hwy. 88, 530/694-2203 or 800/423-9949 for reservations (see Hope Valley and Sorensen's under Southeast from Picketts Junction, below, for more information on the resort), is perhaps the epitome of resort creativity any time of year, with summer activities including fly-fishing instruction, historical hikes, stargazing, photography workshops, and other educational adventures.

Hiking

Local state parks offer nature trails and longer hikes, plus sponsor a full schedule of guided hikes—including winter snowshoe and Nordic ski treks—throughout the Tahoe area. Popular short hikes include the trip to seasonably swimmable **Five Lakes** (the trailhead is two miles off Hwy. 89 on Alpine Meadows Rd.), a steep six-mile roundtrip with great scenery. Or take the **Shirley Lake** hike from the Squaw Valley tram building, a five-mile roundtrip of granite and waterfalls.

The **Donner Summit** area offers exceptional hiking, some routes quite challenging (and therefore least traveled). A complete listing of longer trails in the Tahoe National Forest, including lonely routes like the **Hawley Grade** trek from near Meyers, and the **Tucker Flat** and **Duck Lake-Lost Lake** hikes, are available locally from national forest headquarters. Also try out the **Tahoe Rim Trail,** now completed.

For more information about long hikes and

SKY-HIGH TAHOE RIM TRAIL

It finally happened. Tahoe's sky-high circle is unbroken. In late 2001 the dedicated 25-year effort of locals, visitors, and various public and private organizations finally completed the 165-mile Tahoe Rim Trail. And in June 2003 the Tahoe trail was designated as a National Recreation Trail, one of the West's best.

The Tahoe Rim Trail is open to mountain bikers and equestrians as well as hikers, though wilderness stretches are strictly for hikers and horses, and the Tahoe Meadows segment is closed to bikes on odd days. Some sections are wheelchair accessible. Gaze down on North America's largest alpine lake from 10,000 feet, stroll through meadows wild with wildflowers, silently watch the sun slip away at the end of day. Maybe you can even join the 165 Mile Club.

The trail boasts nine trailheads—located at Brockway Summit, Tahoe City, Barker Pass, Echo Lake, Echo Summit, Big Meadow, Kingsbury Grade, Spooner Summit, and Tahoe Meadows—many of them hard to find, each with parking area and information kiosk. Unless you're backpacking the entire trail, which takes about two weeks, for one-way day hikes you'll want to arrange a shuttle system or an end-of-day pick-up.

For more information, contact the Tahoe Rim Trail Association (TRTA), 775/588-0686, www.tahoerimtrail.org. An essential companion is *The Tahoe Rim Trail* guidebook by Tim Huaserman (Wilderness Press), endorsed by the TRTA and jam-packed with useful information.

Tahoe area backpacking, contact U.S. Forest Service headquarters for the Lake Tahoe Basin Management Unit year-round (see Information below) or, in summer, stop by the visitors center on the highway near Camp Richardson.

The best available guidebook to Tahoe area hiking and backpacking is *The Tahoe Sierra* by Jeffrey P. Schaffer, published by Wilderness Press, though Schaffer's *Desolation Wilderness and the South Lake Tahoe Basin* and Thomas and Jason Winnett's *Sierra North: 100 Back-Country Trips* (also published by Wilderness Press) are also good.

With its glaciated High Sierra scenery, the **Des-**

olation **Wilderness** straddling the Sierra Nevada divide on Tahoe's southwestern side is far from desolate. In fact, this rugged 63,475-acre wonderland is so popular that the wilderness permit system is actually a quota system to minimize human impact in the wild. Permits are required for both day-use and overnight trips. Half of all wilderness permits for the backpacking season (mid-June through early September) are issued up to 90 days in advance of planned trips, the other half reserved for entrance dates. At last report, permits were $3 for day use, $5 for one night, and $10 each for two or more nights; 80 percent of the revenues stay at Tahoe, to pay for maintenance and new services. To obtain advance permits to enter from the east, contact the U.S. Forest Service office in South Lake Tahoe (see Information below). To enter from the west, contact the Eldorado National Forest Information Center, 3070 Camino Heights Dr. in Camino, 530/644-6048, www.r5.fs.fed.us/eldorado.

Usually better for privacy on backpacks and longer hikes is the **Granite Chief Wilderness** to the west of Tahoe City, established in 1984 to protect the headwaters of the American River. Also not yet subject to visitor rationing and within easy reach of Tahoe is the 105,165-acre **Mokelumne Wilderness** between Hwy. 88 and Hwy. 4—meadows, lakes, and mountains dominated by Mokelumne Peak and the canyon of the Mokelumne River. Farther south still but almost adjacent to Mokelumne is the **Carson-Iceberg Wilderness** between Hwy. 4 and Hwy. 108 and—south of Hwy. 108—the 112,000-acre **Emigrant Wilderness** on the edge of Yosemite, another glaciated lakes-and-meadows volcanic landscape, quite accessible. The Sierra Nevada stretch of the Pacific Crest Trail either skirts (on other national forest lands) or climbs through all of these wilderness areas.

Cycling and Mountain Biking

The Tahoe area, particularly the west shore, is perfect for fat-tired bike enthusiasts. (Mountain bikes aren't allowed in wilderness areas, though other national forest areas are accessible.) Come in September for Tahoe's annual **Fat Tire Festival,** a mountain biking blowout. If

you don't tote your own, rent bikes at **Porter's Ski and Sport,** 501 North Lake Blvd. in Tahoe City, 530/583-2314, or **CyclePaths,** 1785 West Lake Blvd. (two miles south of town on Hwy. 89), 530/581-1171 or 800/780-2453, also a great stop for trail maps and suggestions, including guided half-day or full-day mountain bike tours of the area. Information about more ambitious mountain bike routes, including old area logging roads, is also available through national forest headquarters and local ranger district offices (see Information below).

An unusually scenic and far from lonely bike route is the **Flume Trail** from the trailhead at Spooner Lake (a loop if you return, a fun one-way if you arrange a car shuttle from Incline Village). Fairly challenging is the 12-mile **Paige Meadows/Truckee River** loop, starting from Fanny Bridge in Tahoe City and heading south then west, ending up back in Tahoe City after cruising several miles along the Truckee River bike path. Much easier: the six-mile **Blackwood Canyon** loop or the six-mile loop through undeveloped sections of **Sugar Pine Point State Park.** Many major ski resorts offer mountain biking trails, rentals, and even tote-your-bike lift rides to quite challenging high-altitude terrain and trails.

Other Summer Diversions

In spring, summer, and fall, **North Tahoe Cruises** in Tahoe City, 530/583-0141 or 800/218-2464, www.tahoegal.com, offers tours of Emerald Bay, sunset jazz cruises, and a west shore scenic tour taking in historical sites and astounding private estates (just about the only way most folks will ever see them) onboard the *Tahoe Gal.* **Lake Tahoe Cruises,** 900 Ski Run Blvd. in South Lake Tahoe, 530/541-3364 or 800/238-2463, is noted for its endless variety of charters and cruises (popular with tour groups) aboard the glass-bottomed sternwheeler *Tahoe Queen,* including runs to Emerald Bay. In winter, the *Tahoe Queen* also serves as a south-to-north shuttle service for skiers. Also popular for tours is the **MS *Dixie II*** paddlewheeler, which schedules a breakfast cruise along the lake's eastern shore, served up with local history. For all three, call or write for current schedule and rates.

Kayakers with lake-sized appetites can shove off on a **Tahoe Paddle and Oar** kayak brunch tour, departing from the North Tahoe Beach Center. For more information about the brunch bunch and other kayak-tour options, contact Paddle and Oar at 530/581-3029, www.tahoepaddle.com. Quite popular, for rentals, tours, and instruction, is **Kayak Tahoe**, 3411 Lake Tahoe Blvd. (Hwy. 50), 530/544-2011. For another unique take on Tahoe water touring, try **Woodwind Sailing Cruises**, P.O. Box 1375, Zephyr Cove, NV 89448, 775/588-3000 or 530/542-2212.

Seaplane tours are the specialty of **Commodore Seaplanes**, based at Tahoe City Marina, 530/583-1039. Both **Balloons Over Lake Tahoe**, P.O. Box 7797, South Lake Tahoe, CA 96158, 530/544-7008, and **Lake Tahoe Balloons**, 530/544-1221 or 800/872-9294, offer hot-air balloon flights right out over the lake, with a boat landing and a cruise back to shore. Also silent and soaring is a glider ride over the Sierra Nevada; for information or reservations, contact **Soar Minden** at the Douglas County Airport in Nevada, 775/782-7627 or 800/345-7627.

Horseback riding is much more down to earth. Many resorts offer guided rides and/or horse rentals. For other stables, contact area visitors bureaus. **Golfing** is even closer to the ground. There are eight courses in the North Lake Tahoe/Truckee area—two designed by Robert Trent Jones—and five courses in South Lake Tahoe, including nationally recognized **Tahoe Edgewood** and **Glenbrook.**

For other area recreation information—on everything from parasailing, sailboarding, jet-skiing, fishing charters, scuba diving, and boat rentals to the best places to go rollerblading or wildflower hiking—contact local visitors bureaus (see Information below).

STAYING AT NORTH TAHOE
Camping
State park campgrounds at Lake Tahoe are popular. Reservations through ReserveAmerica, 800/444-7275, www.reserveamerica.com, are necessary May–early Sept.—though all campgrounds may be open considerably later in the

year, weather permitting, on a first-come, first-camped basis—and Sugar Pine Point is open to campers year-round. Nearby state parks with campgrounds include Donner Memorial State Park and Grover Hot Springs State Park, the latter also open year-round. Most U.S. Forest Service campgrounds—there are plenty near the lake, and dozens throughout the greater Tahoe area—are first-come, first-camped, but popular campgrounds like **Fallen Leaf** can be reserved in advance ($12–14 per night) through the National Recreation Reservation Service, 800/280-2267, www.reserveusa.com. One of the area's best-kept camping secrets is near South Lake Tahoe across the Nevada border, at **Nevada State Beach,** with open, pine-shaded lake frontage camping just a stone's throw from the beach and an easy walk to Safeway and other signposts of civilization. Ask about other regional campground choices at ranger stations, chambers of commerce, or visitors centers.

Clair Tappaan Lodge and Rainbow Lodge
The Sierra Club's **Clair Tappaan Lodge,** 19940 Donner Pass Rd. in Norden, 530/426-3632, www.sierraclub.org, is a time-honored skiers' tradition—rustic dormitory-style rooms, family rooms, and tiny two-person rooms in a rambling (all with bunk beds) cedar shake-sided three-story lodge complete with hot tub, library, kitchen, and dining facilities. Three family-style meals per day are included in the rates—as is the necessity to do at least one simple housekeeping chore each day. Inexpensive (five- and seven-day rates available). Extra fee for cross-country ski rentals, ski school, and hot tub. But Clair Tappaan is a year-round treat, also popular with hikers and those who just need to get away for a while. Weekend and summer programs include Donner Rim Trail work days, the Fourth of July barbecue and open hike, folk dancing, fly-fishing, fort-building for kids, and instruction in technical rope skills, rock climbing, and mountain biking. Call to request a current brochure.

Also a particular pleasure, but more of the simple-but-comfort-conscious variety, is the **Rainbow Lodge,** about six miles west of Soda

Springs on old Hwy. 40 (take the Rainbow Rd. exit from I-80), Soda Springs, 530/426-3871, or 800/500-3871, websites: www.royalgorge.com and www.rainbowlodge.net. Now affiliated with the Royal Gorge Nordic ski resort, Rainbow Lodge was originally built in the late 1800s of granite and hand-hewn timbers, then expanded in 1928. It features a log-beamed ceiling and knotty pine interiors, 31 homey rooms, 20 with private baths, the rest sharing bathrooms down the hall. The Rainbow Lodge also features a ghost named Mary, who lives on the third floor; according to lodge lore, she was shot to death here when her husband found her with another man. Rates are $150 and up, breakfast included. The fine **Engadine Cafe,** 530/426-3661, is on the premises—serving breakfast, lunch, and dinner daily—as well as a tavern with bar menu and live weekend entertainment.

Truckee and Donner Summit

Get complete accommodations listings from local visitors bureaus. Most ski resorts in and around the Tahoe-Truckee area and elsewhere offer restaurants and various accommodations options, but unusually interesting inns are also scattered throughout the greater Tahoe area.

A real treat in downtown Truckee is the **Truckee Hotel** at Commercial and Bridge Streets, 530/587-4444 or 800/659-6921, an old 1868 lumberjack hotel spruced up to suit the modern world, with 37 rooms (but only eight with private bath). Bargain basement rooms are $50–100; rooms with private baths are $150 and up. Includes continental breakfast buffet, and features a good restaurant, **Passages,** and bar downstairs.

Motels in the Truckee area include the **Donner Lake Village Resort Hotel & Marina,** 15695 Donner Pass Rd. (about six miles west of town on old Hwy. 40 at the west end of Donner Lake), 530/587-6081 or 800/621-6664, www.donnerlakevillage.com, with studios and one- and two-bedroom units. Rates are $150 and up. The simple, small, and quiet **Loch Leven Lodge** on Donner Lake, 13855 Donner Pass Rd., 530/587-3773, features eight motel-style units with kitchens and queen beds, also a townhouse that sleeps eight, complete with fireplace. Extras here include a 5,000-square-foot redwood deck, rowboat, barbecue, picnic tables, and spa. Rates are $100–150.

SIERRA NEVADA

TRUCKIN' ON THE EMIGRANT TRAIL

A road by any other name would serve travelers as well. And so the original Emigrant Trail over Donner Pass—"the damndest, rockiest and roughest road I ever saw," according to 1849 traveler John Markle—later became a passable toll road then by turns a graveled and a paved highway and a multilane freeway. A new transportation museum at the Tahoe National Forest **Big Bend Visitor Center,** 49685 Hampshire Rocks Rd. (Old Hwy. 40, 530/426-3609, commemorates the ancient Washoe Indian trade route in all its transformations.

Situated on the winter campsite of the Stephen-Townsend-Murphy party, the first to cross the Sierra Nevada by wagon train, the museum also offers up artifacts from the trail's well-traveled incarnation as the Dutch Flat–Donner Lake Wagon Road; from 1864 to 1868 this toll road was also a secret haul road delivering construction materials needed for the transcontinental railroad. In 1913 the wagon road was graveled, an improvement that created the Lincoln Highway, the nation's first cross-country, all-weather automobile highway. In 1928 came Highway 40—still in use near Donner Summit, known as Old Highway 40—and in the 1950s the construction of Interstate 80 began.

The visitor center is open daily 8:30 A.M.–4:30 P.M., making this a handy information and rest stop. Guided Emigrant Trail walks are offered on weekends (call for details); seasonal activities include wildflower walks and star gazing. To get there: if heading east on I-80, take the Big Bend exit at Donner Summit, about 45 miles east of the Foresthill exit; if heading west, take the Big Bend/Rainbow Road exit about 20 miles west of Truckee.

(No credit cards.) Just over a mile outside town is the **Best Western Truckee Tahoe Inn,** 11331 Hwy. 267, 530/587-4525 or 800/824-6385. Rates are $150 and up.

Overlooking Truckee is the elegant 1881 Victorian **Richardson House** bed-and-breakfast, 10154 High St. (at Spring), 530/587-5388 or 888/229-0365, www.richardsonhouse.com, with period decor and abundant amenities. Wonderful breakfast; rates $150 and up.

North and West Shores

Overall best bets for travel bargains are seasonal vacation packages—suited to all interests and income levels—offered in the north shore area (including Truckee) through the North Lake Tahoe Resort Association, 950 North Lake Blvd., Tahoe City, 530/583-3494 or 888/434-1262, www.tahoefun.org. The visitors bureau will also recommend (and make) lodging reservations based on budgetary and other preferences.

The **Cedar Glen Lodge,** 6589 North Lake Blvd. (Hwy. 28), just a few miles west of the Nevada border, 530/546-4281, 800/500-8246 or 800/341-8000, www.cedarglenlodge.com, has motel rooms, housekeeping cottages, sauna, whirlpool, pool, and playground. Rates are $50–150. Farther from the madding crowds as well is the **Charmey Chalet Resort** (pronounced shar-MAY) in Tahoe Vista at 6549 N. Lake Blvd., 530/546-2529, where the highway widens into four lanes. A hot tub, pool, and other relatively recent renovations have jazzed up this hill-climbing motel with tall trees and outdoor patios, sliding glass doors, in-room refrigerators, TV, and phones. Coffee and sweet rolls at breakfast. Rates are $100. Nearby are other decent midrange motels.

In Tahoe City, the **Tahoe City Inn,** 790 N. Lake Blvd., 530/581-3333 or 800/800-8246 for reservations, has rooms with waterbeds and in-room spas; $100 and up. Also an off-season bargain, especially for AAA members, is the **Tahoe City Travelodge,** 455 N. Lake Blvd., 530/583-3766, comfortable and attractive, near the lake, with golfing adjacent.

About a mile from Royal Gorge and less than five miles from Sugar Bowl is charming **Ice Lakes Lodge,** on the shores of Donner Summit's Serene Lakes at 1111 Soda Springs Rd., 530/426-7660, www.icelakeslodge.com. The 26-room, two-story lodge is something of a neighborhood project, to provide pleasant, convenient area accommodations. All have private bathrooms, king or queen beds, telephones, and TV with cable. Rates are $100–200, off-season rates much lower.

Cabins, Motels, and Lodges

Homey as all get out, from the homemade chocolate chip cookies and video library to the horsehoe pit, are the historic **Rustic Cottages** in Tahoe Vista, 7449 North Lake Blvd., 888/778-7842, www.rusticcottages.com. The 18 cottages, originally the Brockway Lumber Company sawmill and labor camp, were converted into a cottage "court" in 1926. Cottages vary in size and configuration, but all include coffeemaker, microwave, refrigerator, TVs with HBO and video players, porch, outdoor patio furniture; some have kitchenettes and/or fireplaces. Most rates are $50–150, though some are as high as $199. Extras include croquet, guest bikes, and (in winter) snowshoes, discs, and sleds.

Always a best bet among area motels is the **Franciscan Lakeside Lodge,** 6944 N. Lake Blvd. (Hwy. 28), 530/546-6300 or 800/564-6754, which also features lakefront cottages. The simple rooms and cottages are either one- or two-bedroom and include full kitchens. The lodge offers a private beach and pier, swimming pool, volleyball, croquet, horseshoes, and children's play area. Rates are $100 and up.

A popular après-ski spot, fun in summer for riverside dining, and a great choice year-round for lodgings is the **River Ranch Lodge** on the Truckee River just off Hwy. 89 at Alpine Meadows Rd., 530/583-4264 or 800/535-9900, www.river-ranchlodge.com. Originally established in 1888 as the Deer Park Inn, the old building was replaced in 1950 with this woodsy shingle-sided lodge overlooking the Truckee River. All 19 rooms feature antiques and modern amenities, and some offer private river-view balconies. Continental breakfast; $150 and up. Another attraction here is the very good **River Ranch Lodge Restaurant.** For top-knotch music, head for the River Ranch Bar—

also famous for the River Ranch Heater, a hot buttered rum concoction.

For updated Old Tahoe ambience, a great choice is the refurbished 1908 **Sunnyside Lodge,** 1850 W. Lake Blvd., 530/583-7200 or 800/822-2754, www.sunnysideresort.com, on the lake south of town. Some of the 23 rooms feature stone fireplaces, and many have lake views. Luxury, continental breakfast included. For good California-style fare, try Sunnyside's restaurant. Among cabin choices, those at the **Tahoma Lodge,** 7018 W. Lake Blvd., 530/525-7721, are quiet and comfortable. Three-night minimum; $150 and up.

Upscale Resorts

Particularly appealing to skiers are the many area resorts, which also offer options in the summer. For a complete listing of the possibilities, see the Resorts sections above. San Francisco–style upscale is the 60-room **Plumpjack Squaw Valley Inn,** 1920 Squaw Valley Rd., 530/583-1576 or 800/323-7666, www.plumpjack.com, a sophisticated and stylish hotel offering all the understated urban comforts, great views, swimming pool, spas, and room service from the excellent on-site **Plumpjack Café.** Otherwise, swankest of the swank in the north shore area is the nine-story, 450-room **Resort at Squaw Creek,** 400 Squaw Creek Rd. in Squaw Valley, 530/583-6300 or 800/403-4434, website www.squawcreek.com, which, from the outside, resembles Darth Vader's corporate headquarters. The superluxury resort offers every imaginable amenity, with extras including children's programs, shopping promenade, three excellent restaurants, three swimming pools, fitness center and spa, ice-skating rink, cross-country ski trails, and ski-in, ski-out access to Squaw Valley lifts. In summer, there's the Robert Trent Jones Jr. 18-hole golf course, equestrian center, and Peter Burwash International Tennis Center. An oddity here is that all the rooms, suites, and penthouses are in one building and all the other attractions and front desk are in the other. Some people are stunned—particularly in the midst of a winter gale—to have to walk through nature to get back and forth. $200 and up, but ask about midweek packages—sometimes a good deal.

Return to the luxurious Roaring 20s at the **Hyatt Regency Lake Tahoe** resort and casino in Incline Village just across the Nevada border, 111 Country Club Dr., 775/832-1234 or 888/899-5019, www.laketahoehyatt.com, now completing a major renovation and expansion. "The Lodge" is the spectacular $60 million beginning—stone, rough timbers, leather, a sky-high sense of luxury, all very Old Tahoe. Guest rooms and suites are stylish and comfortable, with all the amenities, though the lakeside cabins (one- and two-bedroom) are most appealing of all. The new terrace wing will feature tiers of swimming pools. Rates are $200 and up, suites and cabins higher, though spring and fall rates can be relative bargains. Complete spa facilities, a full-service bar, three restaurants, and a casino round out the facilities. For more information on Nevada-side accommodations, as well as suggestions on condominium and cabin rentals, contact the visitors bureau.

Bed-and-Breakfasts

The north shore boasts B&B accommodations in addition to those near Donner Pass and Truckee. All rates are about $150 and up.

A popular lakefront newcomer is **The Shore House at Lake Tahoe,** 7170 N. Lake Blvd., 530/546-7270 or 800/207-5160, www.tahoeinn.com, where all nine refreshingly outdoorsy rooms feature custom-built log furniture, Scandia down comforters and feather beds, and gas fireplaces. All have private bathrooms, private outdoor entrances and unique features. Private pier. Wonderful breakfast.

An excellent choice, and a Tahoe classic, is the 15-cabin **Cottage Inn,** 1690 W. Lake Blvd. (Hwy. 89, just south of town), 530/581-4073 or 800/581-4073, www.thecottageinn.com, a cluster of cozy knotty-pine bed-and-breakfast cabins; full breakfast is served in guest rooms or in the dining room. Beach access and sauna.

A half mile north of the Hwy. 28/89 intersection and just blocks from the lake, the **Mayfield House** bed-and-breakfast inn, 236 Grove St., 530/583-1001, www.mayfieldhouse.com, is the former cottage home of Norman Mayfield, a contractor who worked closely with architect

Julia Morgan. Five rooms plus a cottage, all with private bath; full breakfast served.

Five miles south of Tahoe City proper, the lakefront **Chaney House** bed-and-breakfast in Homewood at 4725 W. Lake Blvd., 530/525-7333, www.chaneyhouse.com, is a striking 1920s-vintage stone house complete with Gothic arches and massive fireplace, four rooms or suites with private baths, private beach and pier, wonderful full breakfast. Quite popular (two-week notice required for cancellations). An elegant choice nearby is the **Rockwood Lodge** bed-and-breakfast, 5295 W. Lake Blvd., 530/525-5273 or 800/538-2463, www.rockwoodlodge.com, which offers antique furnishings in a plush, 1930s-vintage Tahoe rock-and-pine home. Full breakfast.

Quite reasonable and welcoming is the **Tahoma Meadows Bed & Breakfast,** 6821 W. Lake Blvd. in Tahoma, 530/525-1553 or 866/525-1553, www.tahomameadows.com, where the 11 cabins all feature private baths, comfortable beds—king, queen, or twin—TV, and framed watercolors. One cabin sleeps six—perfect for families. Full breakfast is served in the main lodge, which is upstairs from the separate Stoneyridge Cafe. Also near Sugar Pine Point State Park is the **Norfolk Woods Inn,** 6941 W. Lake Blvd., Tahoma, 530/525-5000, www.norfolkwoods.com, a collection of five self-contained cottages with full breakfast, pool, and whirlpool.

STAYING AT SOUTH TAHOE

The **Lake Tahoe Visitors Authority,** 1156 Ski Run Blvd. (at Tamarack), South Lake Tahoe, CA 96150, 530/544-5050 or 800/288-2463 (reservations only), www.virtualtahoe.com, maintains a current listing of South Lake Tahoe accommodations and is happy to help with reservations. Also helpful is the **South Lake Tahoe Chamber of Commerce,** 3066 Lake Tahoe Blvd., 530/541-5255.

Ski bums on a budget can try the **Monaco Blu-Zu Hostel,** 4140 Pine Blvd., South Lake Tahoe, 530/542-0705, where dorm bunks go for $16 per day, $80 per week. Two good motels outside town are both great bargains. The **Lazy S Lodge,** 609 Emerald Bay Rd., 530/541-0230, is a quiet find,

featuring quaint cottages with kitchens and Swedish wood-burning fireplaces or motel-style rooms, as well as barbecues, picnic tables, lots of lawn, pool, and deck. Rates are $50 and up. Closer still to Sierra Ski Ranch and Kirkwood is the **Ridgewood Inn,** 1341 Emerald Bay Rd., 530/541-8589, a small motel (12 units), some adjoining rooms perfect for families; $50 and up.

Motels clog the artery of Hwy. 50 toward South Lake Tahoe and Stateline. Inexpensive and predictable is **Motel 6,** 2375 Lake Tahoe Blvd. (Hwy. 50, just east of the Hwy. 89 junction), 530/542-1400. The usual amenities are offered; $50 and up.

Cabins, Motels, and Lodges

A time-honored rustic retreat on U.S. Forest Service land across the border is the **Zephyr Cove Resort,** 760 Hwy. 50, 775/588-6644, with choices of lodge rooms, bungalows, cabins, and chalets. Good restaurant.

The 83-acre **Camp Richardson Resort,** 1900 Jameson Beach Rd., 530/541-1801 or 800/544-1801, www.camprichardson.com, is a wonderful 1930s-style rustic respite among the pines located a few miles south of Emerald Bay on Hwy. 89. The circa-1923 lodge includes a rugged stone fireplace, log rafters, and 30 rooms with private baths. Out back are Camp Richardson's 42 cabins, complete with kitchens and bathrooms, available by the week in summer. The resort's campground across the highway features 112 campsites with amenities like hot showers for $17–22 per night. Camp Richardson also offers a beach, marina, and other recreational attractions, including Nordic skiing in winter. For just the basics in summer—cabins with electricity—the place is **Camp Concord** at Fallen Leaf Lake, 925/671-3273 for information, operated by the city of Concord. Moderate; three cafeteria-style meals included.

South on Hwy. 50, the granite-and-log **Echo Chalet,** 9900 Echo Lakes Rd., 530/659-7207, is quiet and isolated, with 10 rustic, woodsy summer cabins that sleep two to four. (Take the chalet's water taxi service across the lake to Desolation Wilderness). Also special, winter or summer, is the refurbished **Strawberry Lodge** roadhouse, 17510 Hwy. 50 in Strawberry, 530/659-7200, www.strawberry-lodge.com. Tucked under the granite cliffs beyond Echo Summit, about 20 miles west of South Lake Tahoe via Hwy. 50, it's the first genuine ski lodge in the Sierra Nevada, originally built in the 1850s. Smack dab in the middle of the popular Strawberry Canyon cross-country ski area, lodge rooms—either in the main lodge or the annex across the highway—are Inexpensive-Premium (shared or private bath). Also here: a dining hall with stone fireplace, hearty restaurant fare (open-air deck dining in summer), even an ice cream shop. Open only Fri.–Sun. in winter. Great bar, too. If you won't be driving, be sure to sample a drink served here that definitely reflects these times—the Knuckle-Dragger.

Upscale Resorts

South Lake Tahoe has a seemingly endless supply of motels and hotels—with more on the way— but is still short on bed-and-breakfasts. However, upscale resorts—with rates in the $200 range—abound. **The Christiania Inn** ("The Chris" to its fans), 3819 Saddle Rd. (off Ski Run Blvd.), 530/544-7337, www.christianiainn.com, has been around just about forever—a European-style country inn almost under Heavenly's main chairlift. Two rooms and four unique suites—popular with honeymooners—all with private baths, plus lounge and excellent continental restaurant. Continental breakfast. Two-night minimum on weekends.

Also right on the California-Nevada border, near the base of Heavenly's gondola, is the **Embassy Suites Resort,** 4130 Lake Tahoe Blvd., 530/544-5400 or 877/497-8483, www.embassytahoe.com, an example of South Tahoe's new redevelopment style—a modern take on the traditional early-1900s architecture on display at Tallac and elsewhere. Luxury. Another nice hotel close to the casinos (which are also housed in four-star hotels) is the **Best Western Station House Inn,** 901 Park Ave., 800/822-5953, www.stationhouseinn.com. Luxury. Another best bet, if you want to stay condo-style, is **Lakeland Village Beach & Ski Resort,** 3535 Lake Tahoe Blvd., 530/544-1685

or 800/822-5969, www.lakeland-village.com, a townhouse resort where the appeal includes the lakefront beach, two swimming pools, and tennis courts.

Top-flight farther up the hill is the **Tahoe Seasons Resort** at Heavenly Valley, 3901 Saddle Rd. (at Keller), 530/541-6700 or 800/540-4874, www.tahoeseasons.com, featuring comfortable suites with in-room spas, kitchenettes (refrigerators, sink, microwave), TVs and VCRs, and fold-out sofa bed in a sitting room, all with adequate privacy for families or two couples traveling together. Valet parking. Exceptionally elegant and with every imaginable resort amenity is **The Ridge Tahoe,** 400 Ridge Club Dr., Stateline, NV, 775/588-3553 or 800/334-1600, www.ridge-tahoe.com, a resort complex at an elevation of 7,300 feet—just a gondola lift to the slopes.

EATING AT NORTH TAHOE

Truckee

Most everything is along Commercial St. or within a block or two. For cheap eats in Truckee, try the **Squeeze In,** 10060 Donner Pass Rd. (Commercial Row), 530/587-9814, noted for its 22 kinds of sandwiches, 57 varieties of omelettes, and city-style pizzas with toppings like artichoke hearts and prosciutto. Open for breakfast and lunch daily. After lunch, stop off at **Bud's Fountain,** 10043 Donner Pass Rd. (inside the sporting goods store), 530/587-3177, for that old-fashioned ice cream soda. **Andy's Truckee Diner,** 10144 W. River St. (at Hwy. 267), 530/582-6925, does a good job with all the American standards at breakfast, lunch, and dinner. For casual California-style Italian, the place is **Truckee Trattoria,** in the Safeway shopping center, 11310 Donner Pass Rd., 530/582-1266, where fresh pastas star. But to open up those nostrils—to fully take in the alpine air—start with a bowl of garlic soup.

A relative newcomer, offering "dining on a higher level," is sophisticated, friendly, and high-flying **Dragonfly,** upstairs at 10118 Donner Pass Rd. downtown, 530/587-0557, fast becoming famous for its largely pan-Asian fusion. The weekly changing menu features everything from sweet-and-sour eggplant stirfry and Asian-cured pork tenderloin roulade to grilled Moroccan spiced lamb sirloin. Weather permitting, try for a table out on the balcony. Open daily for both lunch and dinner. Stylish art-deco **Moody's Bistro** in the Truckee Hotel, 10007 Bridge St., 530/587-8688, serves hearty Northern California fare, from roasted venison loin to red wine–braised Niman Ranch short ribs. Open for lunch and dinner, and for weekend brunch. Bar menu available, too, in speakeasy-style Moody's Lounge. There can be unpredictable pluses being far from the madding crowds. The newlywed Paul McCartneys stayed (incognito) here at the Truckee Hotel in early 2003 for part of their skiing honeymoon. Late one night, though, Paul himself sang a few numbers for the folks in the bar. Imagine that.

Also quite wonderful is dinner—any meal, actually—at the Rainbow Lodge's exceptional **Engadine Cafe,** on Rainbow Rd. in Soda Springs, 530/426-3661, featuring pastas, seafood, and more eclectic selections. You won't go wrong at lunch with the chicken Waldorf salad, or the baked French baguettes—tasty hot sandwiches. Open daily, if the roads are open.

North and West Shores

A local favorite for breakfast and lunch in Carnelian Bay is the **Old Post Office Cafe,** 5245 N. Lake Tahoe Blvd., 530/541-0630. The casual **Boulevard Café & Trattoria** in Tahoe Vista at 6731 N. Lake Blvd., 530/546-7213, serves great house-made pastas and breads, filet mignon, and changing seafood specials. Beer and wine. Open daily for dinner. Fun and quite good for hot and spicy Cajun food in Tahoe Vista is **Colonel Claire's,** 6873 N. Lake Blvd., 530/546-7358. *The* breakfast and lunch place in Kings Beach is the **Log Cabin Caffe,** 8692 N. Lake Blvd., 530/546-7109, where everything is fresh and tasty—from the Belgian waffles to the turkey, cranberry, and cream cheese sandwiches.

For something fresh to load up the daypack, head to Tahoe City's farmers' markets, held June–Oct. at the Watermelon Patch, Dollar Hill and Hwy 28, 530/823-6183. The **Tahoe City Sunday Certified Farmers Market** runs 3–7 P.M., and the **Tahoe City Thursday Certified Farmers Market** runs 8 A.M.–1 P.M. Much-loved is **Rosie's Cafe,** 571 N. Lake Blvd. in Tahoe City, 530/583-8504, for reasonably priced and tasty American favorites like ham and eggs for breakfast, burgers at lunch. *The* thing for dinner in ski season is the Yankee pot roast, though the Southern-fried chicken holds its own. Open daily for breakfast, lunch, and dinner. Full bar.

Very "Tahoe" and a genuine locals' hot spot is the **Fire Sign Cafe** two miles south of Tahoe City at 1785 W. Lake Blvd. in Tahoe Park (near the Cottage Inn), 530/583-0871—wholesome home-style cooking in a casually eclectic atmosphere, fabulous for a morning meal—fresh-squeezed juices, homemade muffins and coffeecake, omelets, eggs Benedict, and other hearty fare—and open seven days a week (until 3 P.M.) for both breakfast and lunch. In good weather, sun yourself out on the deck. But expect a wait on weekends. Another local hangout, **Hacienda del Lago,** 760 N. Lake Blvd., 530/583-0358, is open daily for lunch and dinner—*the* place for Mexican food and great margaritas.

Especially at lunch, another good spot to soak up local atmosphere is the **Bridgetender,** at 65 W. Lake Blvd., 530/583-3342, located across the street from its eccentric, onetime biker-bar beginnings on the south side of Fanny Bridge—now even better for burgers (including veggie burgers) and fabulous garlic fries. Not far away is the northshore outpost of **Izzy's Burger Spa,** 100 W. Lake Blvd., 530/583-4111. Best bet for pizza and Italian is tiny, casual **Za's,** 395 N. Lake Blvd., 530/583-1812, open daily for dinner. For seafood and steaks on the lake, the place is **Jake's on the Lake,** downtown at 780 N. Lake Blvd., 530/583-0188. Open for dinner daily year-round, and in summer for lunch Mon.–Sat. and Sun. brunch. Full bar. The **Tahoe House** restaurant and bakery, 625 W. Lake Blvd. (a half-mile south of Tahoe City's "Y" on Hwy. 89), 530/583-1377, serves European fare (specializing in Swiss-German and Swiss-French entrées at dinner), also pastas and fresh seafood specials. Children's menu, takeout available.

In Tahoma, cool **Stony Ridge Café,** 6821 W. Lake Blvd, 530/525-0905, serves great breakfasts—everything from sourdough french toast to Asian scramble—as well as hearty, homey—felafels and fish tacos—and dinner Wed.–Sun. nights. The weekly changing menu includes such things as roasted vegetable gnocchis and blackened Pacific salmon. And Wednesday is sushi night. The place for pizza is **Angela's,** 7000 Emerald Bay Rd. (W. Lake Blvd.), 530/525-4771, where everything is homemade from scratch.

North Shore

Casual but sophisticated, the place for "New American cooking, Sierra style" is the **Sunnyside Resort,** right on the lake at 1850 W. Lake Blvd., 530/583-7200, just the place for everything from locally famous cheddar burgers and crispy zucchini to corn tamale salmon and beef tenderloin. Full bar, grand view from the deck.

Area resorts are starting to outdo themselves in the foodie destination sweepstakes. At Squaw Valley alone you can enjoy a midday meal at top-of-the-tram **Alexander's,** 530/583-1742, and an exceptional dinner at the urbane New American **PlumpJack Café**—sister restaurant to the one in San Francisco—at the new PlumpJack Squaw Valley Inn, 1920 Squaw Valley Rd., 530/583-1576 or 800/323-7666. The PlumpJack is open for breakfast, lunch, and dinner, though, so take your pick. Nothing will disappoint. The frequently changing menu features hearty fare—such things as scallops and sweetbreads and braised Kobé beef short ribs. Great wine list, some wines from the PlumpJack Winery in Napa Valley. Bar menu, too. Or head to Squaw Valley's Resort at Squaw Creek, 530/583-6300, for any of its three restaurants—the exceptional contemporary French-American **Glissandi** (brought to you by the former La Cheminée folks), the continental **Cascades,** and the **Ristorante Montagna** Italian bistro.

For more fine dining—reservations always recommended—North Tahoe choices include very romantic, very expensive **Christy Hill** in the Lakehouse Mall, 115 Grove St. in Tahoe City, 530/583-8551, noted for its California cuisine, views, and fireplace. Also quite famous in Tahoe City—and unforgettable for its excellent if high-priced vegetarian fare—is **Wolfdale's,** 640 N. Lake Blvd. in Tahoe City, 530/583-5700,

noted for Japanese-flavored California cuisine. Everything served here is made here. Good wine list, full bar. Still considered one of the best French restaurants in the West is **Le Petit Pier** in Tahoe Vista at 7238 N. Lake Blvd., 530/546-4464, where the sunset views are part of the fixed-price experience. Open nightly for dinner in summer, more limited days the rest of the year. Impressive wine list, full bar. Also time-honored in the high-priced dinner category, truly special, is the classical French **Swiss Lakewood Restaurant,** 5055 W. Lake Blvd., 530/525-5211, unstuffy yet elegant (dining room dress code), at home in a remodeled 1920 chalet. Full bar. Open Tues.–Sun. for dinner. Stylish **Sunsets on the Lake** in Tahoe Vista, 7320 N. Lake Blvd., 530/546-3640, serves exceptional California-style Northern Italian and, yes, sunsets. Heated outdoor deck. Full bar. Open for dinner nightly, for lunch daily in summer.

EATING AT SOUTH TAHOE

The cheapest eats of all are available in the casinos in Nevada's Stateline; the big hotels are happy to serve breakfast for a couple of bucks just to get folks within reach of those one-armed bandits. In South Lake Tahoe, fast-food eateries, small cafés, and some very decent restaurants manage to coexist.

This is a good breakfast town, though you'll have to elbow your way into the more well-known places, including generous **Red Hut Waffles,** 2723 Hwy. 50 (Lake Tahoe Blvd.), 530/541-9024, noted for its huge waffles and good omelettes. (There's another Red Hut across the border in Nevada, on Kingsbury.) A treat for fans of Tyrolean kitsch is **Heidi's,** 3485 Hwy. 50, 530/544-8113, famous for its hearty, day-at-the-slopes breakfasts—everything from pancakes, fruit crepes, and Belgian waffles to the famed, ever-changing "kitchen sink omelet." An excellent choice is **Carina's Café,** in the Bijou Shopping Center at 3469 Lake Tahoe Blvd., 530/541-3354, serving Swedish-style American fare at lunch and dinner. Spinach lovers, try the Florentine omelet. And such a deal.

Locally beloved, quite casual in the lunch and dinner fast food tradition, is **Izzy's Burger Spa,**

2591 Hwy. 50, 530/583-4111. Immensely popular **Sprouts Natural Foods Café,** 3123 Harrison St., 530/541-6969, offers some great burger alternatives, from turkey and tuna-veggie sandwiches to burritos and fruit smoothies. For fun-in-the-sun Tahoe party atmosphere, consider at-the-beach-priced **Beacon Bar & Grill** at Camp at 1900 Jameson Beach Rd., 916/541-0630, where you can order up the beefy Beacon burger, prime rib sandwich, Buffalo wings, and steamed clams.

For fancier fare, **Nephele's,** 1169 Ski Run Blvd., 530/544-8130, has excellent daily specials, also pastas, baby back ribs, and scampi. Private hot tubs on the premises. **Scusa! on Ski Run,** 530/542-0100, features imaginative pizzas and calzones, great pastas (try one of the specialties) and select chicken, fish, seafood, and steak entrées, all in an inimitable Tahoe atmosphere. Also raved about: the exceptionally fine dining room at the **Christiania Inn,** 3819 Saddle Rd., 530/544-7337. Romantic Italian **Café Fiore,** 1169 Ski Run Blvd. #5, 530/541-2908, features just seven (inside) tables; eat on out the deck, too, when weather permits. Fiore serves up such things as eggplant and salmon crepes, fresh lobster fettuccini, and tarragon Dijon pork tenderloin.

Popular for European cuisine (mostly German and Swiss) and fairly casual is the **Swiss Chalet Restaurant,** four miles west of Stateline at 2540 Tahoe Blvd. (Hwy. 50 at Sierra Blvd.), 530/544-3304. Probably the best for American-style seafood is **The Dory's Oar,** 1041 Fremont, 530/541-6603, a New England–style restaurant and lounge with fresh seafood from both coasts plus a selection of steaks, though the Japanese **Samurai,** 2588 Hwy. 50, 530/542-0300, is the best bet for sushi and other seafood specialties.

The Edgewood Terrace at the Edgewood country club, 775/588-2787, offers great food and good views. Sometimes a meal here is a real bargain, too, with two-for-one coupons available in winter and at other slower times. The **Zephyr Cove Resort** is also quite good, the dining room cozied up in winter by wood heat. Worth it, Nevada-side, is **Primavera,** the Italian restaurant at Caesars Tahoe, 55 Hwy. 50,

775/588-3515. Also exceptional is **Llewelyn's,** on the 19th floor at Harvey's on Hwy. 50 at Stateline, 775/588-2411. The wonderful view is unveiled, on sunny days, by light-sensitive electronic shades that raise automatically at sunset.

For fine dining, *the* place to eat in South Lake Tahoe is still eclectic **Evan's American Gourmet Cafe,** 536 Emerald Bay Rd., 530/542-1990, a tiny restaurant (just 12 tables) raved over by repeat guests—and by *Bon Appetit.* Great wine list. Reservations essential. Open nightly for dinner.

EVENTS

For both major and minor area events, contact local chambers and visitors bureaus for current information (see Information below).

In winter, most of the action centers around the ski resorts and—Nevada-side—the casino scene. South Lake Tahoe's **Lake Tahoe Winter Festival** in January is some show, with Heavenly Valley ski events (some televised) combined with community events like the torchlight parade down the mountain and ice-carving contests. North Tahoe's **Snowfest** comes in late February or early March. This cold-weather fun-fest is considered the largest in the western U.S., events and activities including ski racing and films and concerts but also offbeat antics such as the Polar Bear Swim, Diaper Derby, Napkin Hat Contest, and the Dress Up Your Dog Contest. Come back in April for North Lake Tahoe's **Tahoe International Film Festival.**

Come summer, activities and events spin by. Fun for everyone in June: the **Truckee-Tahoe Air Show,** with hot air balloons, daredevil aerialists, and more. Fun for some: the **Western States 100 Mile Run** from Squaw Valley to Auburn. Fun for cyclists is **America's Most Beautiful Bike Ride,** a fully supported one-day tour around Tahoe's 72-mile shoreline (with shorter and longer mileage options) starting and ending at Zephyr Cove near South Lake Tahoe. Fun for brewski fans is the **Blues and Brews Festival** at Northstar. Also come in June for the annual **Valhalla Renaissance Festival** held at Camp Richardson in South Lake Tahoe—a two-day costumed Elizabethan country fair. The annual

Tahoe ARTour, usually scheduled for mid-July, showcases the art and artists of North Lake Tahoe and Truckee in a self-guided open studios tour.

The don't-miss Tahoe event, though, is the **Valhalla Summer Arts & Music Festival** at the Tallac Historic Site near South Lake Tahoe, a multifaceted experience that runs from late June or early July into September. Galleries and working exhibits showcasing fine artists and their craft are open to the public Fri.–Wed., 11 A.M.–3 P.M. Exhibits and events change weekly. Increasingly prominent is the annual **Wa She Shu Edeh** ("Washoe People's Hand") **Native American Fine Arts Festival & Celebration,** usually held late July/early August and featuring basketry and other cultural contributions from the Da-ow people. Other events are musical, ranging from bluegrass and mariachi performances to **Thursday Evening Jazz** in Valhalla—great music and a mellow crowd—and **Sunday Afternoon Chamber Music** at Tallac. The phenomenally popular **Starlight Jazz Series,** usually held on consecutive weekends in early September at the Lake of the Sky Amphitheatre (at the Forest Service visitor center adjacent to Tallac), presents major jazz artists like Johnny Otis, Queen Ida, Zachary Richard and the Bon Ton Boys, and the Dirty Dozen Brass Band. For more information about the Valhalla Arts & Music Festival, contact the Lake Tahoe Visitors Bureau or: the **Tahoe Tallac Association,** P.O. Box 19273, South Lake Tahoe, CA 96151, 530/541-4975 (year-round), 530/542-2787 (summer only), or 530/542-4166 (winter only). Also held at Tallac: the **Great Gatsby Festival.**

Fireworks are hot here on July 4th—including a truly spectacular South Lake Tahoe display sponsored by casinos and area radio stations, launched over the lake from a floating dock near the casinos, and visible from Nevada Beach to Camp Richardson. The show usually begins at dusk, about 9:45 P.M., and can be seen from Nevada Beach to Camp Richardson. People really crowd onto the beaches, so arrive early. (There are other fireworks shows, too, elsewhere around the lake.) Also hot in July: the **Isuzu Celebrity Golf Championship** at South Lake Tahoe's Edgewood Tahoe Golf Course and the north shore's

Music at Sand Harbor festival held at Nevada State Beach in Nevada. The **Lake Tahoe Summer Music Festival** runs from mid-July to mid-August and includes everything from pops, classical, and children's music to jazz and highland bagpipes. Concerts are held at a wide variety of venues all around the lake. In the same vein: **Tahoe Mountain Musicals,** usually held in August at Tahoe Vista's Lakeview Amphitheatre, and the **Lake Tahoe Shakespeare Festival** (website: www.laketahoeshakespeare.com) at Sand Harbor. Quite the draw for the cowboy set is August's **Truckee Championship Rodeo.** But only the truly intrepid show up in late August to participate in Lake Tahoe's **World's Toughest Triathlon,** which those in the know say is indeed more difficult than Hawaii's legendary Ironman. One of four events now included in the Lake Tahoe Summer Sports Festival, the World's Toughest is now a qualifying event for the Ironman.

The Great Reno Balloon Race, with more than 100 hot-air balloonists in hot competition, and the **Virginia City International Camel Races** offer some oddball fun on the Nevada side come September. **Truckee Railroad Days** also arrive in September, festivities complete with parade, trains and locomotives on display, and stiff competition in the U.S. National Handcar Races. In October comes the **Kokanee Salmon Festival** near South Lake Tahoe (sometimes, but not often, the salmon show up late) as well as **Oktoberfest** at Alpine Meadows and the **Lake Tahoe Harvest Festival** in North Lake Tahoe. To hike in the path of history, also come in October for the annual **Donner Party Hike** along the Emigrant and Donner Trails. With or without nature's cooperation, ski season officially starts in November, kicking off an endless parade of **ski races** and other snow-related celebrations—including the latest ski flicks, showcased at the annual **Squaw Valley Film Festival.**

INFORMATION

To get current information on the entire Tahoe area and its attractions, contact *all* area visitors bureaus, since each represents a limited geographical area.

SIERRA NEVADA

The best source for South Lake Tahoe information is the **Lake Tahoe Visitors Authority,** 1156 Ski Run Blvd. (at Tamarack), 530/544-5050 or 800/288-2463 (reservations only), www.virtualtahoe.com. Request a copy of the annual *Lake Tahoe Travel Planner* and, if you stop by, be sure to pick up the *Tahoe Resource Brochure,* an all-around Lake Tahoe-at-your-fingertips guide produced in conjunction with the Nevada Commission on Tourism and the Tahoe-Douglas Chamber of Commerce. Another helpful option is the **South Lake Tahoe Chamber of Commerce,** 3066 Lake Tahoe Blvd., 530/541-5255, www.tahoeinfo.com.

The **North Lake Tahoe Resort Association,** 950 North Lake Blvd.in Tahoe City, 530/583-3494 or 800/824-6348 (for accommodations, rates, special package information, and reservations), www.tahoefun.org, shares office space with the **Greater North Lake Tahoe Chamber of Commerce,** 530/581-6900. Visitors arriving after business hours can use the light-up "locator map" and free reservations phone for lining up last-minute lodgings, plus rifle the racks for brochures and free local publications. To take advantage of Tahoe North's aggressive marketing of vacation packages, from ski weekends to honeymoon and wedding specials, advance planning is necessary—and usually well worth it.

For more regional information, contact the **Truckee-Donner Chamber of Commerce,** 10065 Donner Pass Rd. (inside the train station) in Truckee, 530/587-2757 or 800/548-8388 (central reservations), www.truckee.com, and the **Lake Tahoe Incline Village/Crystal Bay Visitors Bureau,** 969 Tahoe Blvd. in Incline Village, 775/832-1606 or 800/468-2463, www.gotahoe.com. For Reno visitor information and assistance, contact the **Reno-Sparks Convention and Visitors Bureau,** 800/367-7366, website www.renotahoe.com.

Headquarters for the U.S. Forest Service's **Lake Tahoe Basin Management Unit** are at 870 Emerald Bay Rd., P.O. Box 8465, South Lake Tahoe, CA 96158, 530/573-2600, www.fs.fed.us/r5/ltbmu, and open year-round. Regional ranger district offices are another good source for camping, hiking, recreation, and other national forest information. Local outdoors and recreation stores are always good sources for information, as well as rental equipment. Summers-only information centers, at the Pope-Baldwin visitor center and at the west shore's William Kent campground, can be useful. Stop by or contact the local state parks headquarters (see the D.L. Bliss and Emerald Bay State Parks listing, above) for current information about state parks camping, hiking, and other activities. Another helpful resource is the Forest Service **Truckee Ranger District** office, 10342 Hwy. 89 N. in Truckee, 530/587-3558

One of the most useful publications around is the *Lake of the Sky Journal* published jointly by the U.S. Forest Service and California and Nevada state parks offices. Another great free publication is *North Tahoe/Truckee Week,* available everywhere around the north shore. For very comprehensive and updated regional tourist information, everything from recreation and sightseeing to area accommodations and select restaurant menus in magazine-style, buy *The Guide to Lake Tahoe,* available locally for around $5.

If you really want to know Tahoe, invest in a copy of *Moon Handbooks Tahoe* by Ken Castle.

GETTING HERE AND AROUND

At last report, the **South Lake Tahoe Airport,** 530/542-6180, www.laketahoeairport.com, wasn't served by private carriers (but check to see if that's changed). Closest major airport is **Reno/Tahoe International Airport** (RNO), 775/328-6400, served by nine major carriers (including American, Southwest, and United). Either rent a car and drive from Reno or take a van ride. The **No Stress Express,** 888/474-8885, www.nostressexpress.com, offers roundtrip van trips to Tahoe for $72–82, depending on destination, $43 per person one way. For $19 per person one-way ($34 roundtrip), the **Tahoe Casino Express** bus, 775/785-2424 or 800/446-6128, www.tahoecasinoexpress.com, offers nonstop transportation to and from the Reno airport and south shore destinations (skiers and non-casino guests welcome, with room for ski gear and luggage). Contact local visitor bureaus for transportation updates.

Avoid the nightmare of trying to drive—and park—in increasingly congested Tahoe. If you're staying in Truckee—or just want to visit for a few hours—climb aboard the **Truckee Trolley,** 530/587-7451, which connects Truckee and Tahoe City (fare is $1, $2 all day). The **Tahoe Trolley** ($1.25, $3 all day) also offers a fun transportation alternative day and night, connecting north and west shore towns and resorts. **TART** (Tahoe Area Regional Transit) buses run year-round, serving northwest Placer County and the Incline Village area, stopping only at TART signs ($1.25 per ride, commuter passes available). For current schedule information on both, call 530/550-1212 or 800/736-6365, or see the website: www.mytahoevacation.com. **STAGE** (South Tahoe Area Ground Express) buses, 530/542-6077, provide 24-hour service around South Lake Tahoe, more limited routes elsewhere, fare $1.25 (a 10-trip pass is $10). The summer-only **Nifty 50 Trolley,** 530/542-6328, $3 for narrated tour (all-day pass), connects Zephyr Cove and Emerald Bay (including Vikingsholm) and all points in between, 10 A.M.–11 P.M. In winter, major ski resorts provide shuttle service to and from major hotels and motels.

To take a taxi ride anywhere around the lake, any time of day or night, call **Yellow Cab,** 775/831-8294 (Incline Village area), 530/546-9090 (North Lake Tahoe), or 775/588-5555 (South

Lake Tahoe). An unusual Tahoe-style transportation option is the sternwheeler. Take a paddle-wheel boat tour onboard the **M.S.** *Dixie II* or the *Tahoe Queen,* 800/238-2463, www.laketahoecruises.com. The *Queen* runs from South Lake Tahoe to the north shore regularly and—in combination with a bus shuttle system—even carries skiers to Northstar, Squaw Valley, and Alpine Meadows ski slopes in winter. Tour prices for adults begin at $25.

If you're not cycling, driving, flying, or hitchhiking, **Greyhound,** 800/231-2222, can get you to Lake Tahoe. Buses leave daily from South Lake Tahoe (1000 Emerald Bay Rd.) to San Francisco and Los Angeles, also to Las Vegas, Reno, and other Nevada destinations. (Or connect with Greyhound in Truckee at the train station, 10065 Donner Pass Rd.)

Best bet for sights and serenity, though, is riding the rails on **Amtrak,** which stops at Truckee's restored train depot. There's no office or ticket sales here, however; call 800/872-7245 for fare and route information, or see the website: www.amtrak.com. Coming from Oakland, Amtrak's *California Zephyr* rolls through Berkeley backyards, over the Benicia-Martinez Bridge, through the Suisun Marsh (good bird views in winter and a look at the Mothball Fleet), then across farmland and fields to Sacramento. From there to Tahoe, riders are treated to some fine, rare views: a cliff-hanging peek into the yawning canyon of the American River's north fork, the Yuba River, Sugar Bowl's slopes, then through the Judah Tunnel and Coldstream Valley to Truckee.

South from Tahoe

Instead of heading east to the South Lake Tahoe strip and the Stateline casino wilderness, jog due south into the rock-hard heart of true wildness. Highway 50 veering west toward Placerville and Sacramento is a major mountain thoroughfare that shoots past pretty little Echo Lake (fishing, picnicking, and boating; no camping but good access to the Desolation Wilderness) and up and over Echo Summit for some fine high-mountain scenery.

Off in the other direction from just south of Meyers, Hwy. 89 leads into big-sky country, including both the Mokelumne and Carson-Iceberg Wilderness Areas. Heading west on Hwy. 88 from Picketts Junction leads to Carson Pass and its gorgeous granite high lakes. South of fun and funky Markleeville and nearby Grover Hot Springs State Park, Hwy. 4 also cuts west, this time over Ebbetts Pass and the Pacific Grade Summit, dipping slightly into the Bear Valley–Lake Alpine high country before sliding down the Sierra Nevada's western slope to Calaveras Big Trees State Park, then Angels Camp and vicinity. And here's a thought, while you admire the scenery: Archaeologists working near Ebbetts Pass have unearthed evidence of a Native American campsite some 10,000 years old—one of the oldest ever found in the Sierra Nevada—and the clay floor and hearth of an ancient hunting hut, the oldest prehistoric structure ever found in North America.

Southeast from the Hwy. 4 junction, Hwy. 89 heads up and over Monitor Pass—special in autumn, with fiery fall-colored aspens and an unusual autumn fishing season at Heenan Lake for rare Lahontan cutthroat trout (strict limits, current fishing license necessary). At Hwy. 395, the eastern Sierra Nevada's only major roadway, head north to windy Topaz Lake straddling the California-Nevada border for trophy-sized trout, camping, and (once across the state line) that omnipresent casino scene. Or roll south past the lonely towns of Topaz, Coleville, and Walker to Sonora Junction, then on into Bridgeport, the nearby Mono Lake Basin, and the breathtaking beauty of the Sierra Nevada as experienced from the backside (see Mono Lake and Vicinity). But heading west on Hwy. 108, past the U.S. Marine Corps' Mountain Warfare Training Center, then up and over incredible Sonora Pass (closed in winter), can prove equally enticing.

NEAR CARSON PASS

Hwy. 88 from Picketts Junction—where a roadside monument marks the old Pony Express route—climbs to an elevation of 8,573 feet at Carson Pass. From the vista point downslope to the east, often muddy **Red Lake** below offers surprisingly good fishing for brook and rainbow trout. More aesthetic, some distance south of the pass, and accessible via Blue Lakes Rd., are the **Blue Lakes** (which include Granite, Meadow, Tamarack, and Twin Lakes), for fishing, swimming, picnicking, and camping at PG&E campgrounds, also good access into the Mokelumne Wilderness via the Pacific Crest Trail, which traverses the area.

Caples Lake Area and Kirkwood

Also quite serene, with fine national forest campgrounds (some operated by concessionaires) open in summer, are the alpine lakes just off the highway west of Carson Pass. Small **Woods Lake** a couple of miles south of Hwy. 88 offers a quiet wooded campground (water, no showers), nice lakeside picnicking (wheelchair accessible), fishing, also a nice hike to the old Lost Cabin Mine. Large **Caples Lake** farther west and right on the highway, like tiny **Kirkwood Lake** nearby, also offers good camping, picnicking, swimming, fishing, and boating. (No motorboats are allowed at Kirkwood; larger RVs also discouraged.) From near the dam at Caples Lake, hike south into the Mokelumne Wilderness. Near the highway maintenance station close to Caples Lake is the trailhead for **Round Lake** and relatively remote **Meiss Lake.** For more information about these lakes, trails, and campgrounds, contact the **Amador Ranger District** office in Pioneer, 209/295-4251.

Popular here in winter is the excellent **Kirkwood Mountain Resort,** 209/258-6000 or 800/967-7500, 209/258-3000 for ski conditions, and 209/258-7000 for resort lodgings, www.kirkwood.com, a modern ski complex once beloved for its frontier feel and relative lack of urban-style amenities. The degree of upscale, dotcom-fueled development in the area is shocking—and just hints at what's to come, now that the Telluride Ski and Golf Co. owns a hunk of Kirkwood. But that hasn't changed the fact that this area receives Tahoe's driest winter powder and biggest snowfalls. Kirkwood's steep slopes are necessary for skiers to plow through all that powder. There are tame slopes here, too, which makes for a good family resort. Adding a bit of luxury is the 43,000-square-foot **Lodge at Kirkwood,** a four-story condominium hotel—phase one of Kirkwood Village, a ski-in, ski-out complex located at the base of the lifts. A 4,000-square-foor Children's Center, Snowboard Center, condominium developments, and the **Mountain Club** condominum hotel are recent additions in Kirkwood's ongoing $250 million expansion. More shopping, an outdoor ice skating rink, and a swimming center are coming soon. Also on the menu here are sleigh rides, not to mention endless summer activities.

The 1860s **Kirkwood Inn** and bar, 1.5 miles down the road from the lifts, is now home base for ever-popular **Kirkwood Cross Country** for Nordic skiers, 209/258-7248, 80 km of excellent track with warming huts (lessons and tours also offered). Five miles east of Kirkwood Cross Country, at an elevation of 8,600 feet, is the **Carson Pass Sno-Park**—one of the most popular public-access ski tour trailheads near Tahoe. Pick up a topo map and tips at Kirkwood. You'll need a Sno-Park permit to park there.

Silver Lake and Vicinity

About six miles west of the Caples Lake-Kirkwood area is Silver Lake, another popular granite-and–blue water recreation lake along Kit Carson's trail. Good camping at both national forest and PG&E campgrounds as well as **Plasse's Resort** at the lake's south end, 209/258-8814. Rent cabins at **Kay's Silver Lake Resort** on the highway, 209/258-8598; or try the wonderful, knotty-pine-and-Naugahyde **Kit Carson Lodge,** in Kit Carson, 209/258-8500 and 530/676 1370, for motel rooms or cabins (by the week). Kit Carson is open fully from June 1 to October 31, but one cottage—the aptly named Polar Bear Cottage, sleeping up to six people and reachable on foot, snowshoes, or cross-country skis—is open from November 1 to May 31.

For more information about Silver Lake and vicinity, contact the **El Dorado National Forest Information Center,** 3070 Camino Heights Dr., Camino, 530/644-6048, or **forest headquarters,** 100 Forni Rd. in Placerville, 530/622-5061.

About 10 miles west of Tragedy Springs just southwest of Silver Lake, where members of the Mormon Battalion were killed in 1848 (the original tree blaze is on display at Marshall Gold Discovery State Park in Coloma) is the Bear River Rd. turnoff to **Upper and Lower Bear River Reservoirs.** Lower Bear River Reservoir often gets quite low in late summer and fall—the reason lazy fishing enthusiasts get such good catches here. Most of the year, though, there's plenty of water—enough for water-skiing and good swimming (especially south of the dam near the campgrounds) in summer, ice skating and snowmobiling across the frozen lake in winter. The U.S. Forest Service campgrounds are first-come, first-camped, and have water. Camping (with hot showers and RV hookups) as well as lodging are available at the **Bear River Lake Resort,** 40800 Hwy. 88, Pioneer, 209/295-4868, www.bearriverlake.com. Bear River becomes a Nordic ski center in winter. For more information about the Bear River reservoir area, contact the Forest Service **Lumberyard Ranger District** office in Pioneer, 209/295-4252.

SOUTHEAST FROM PICKETTS JUNCTION
Hope Valley and Sorensen's

The **Hope, Charity,** and **Faith Valleys** near the Hwy. 88 and Hwy. 89 junction are great for picnics. Due to massive land purchases by the Trust for Public Lands, developers shoveled out of the

Tahoe Basin have also been held at bay here. With any luck, Hope Valley will remain a peaceful mountain valley where camping, fishing, hiking, and Nordic skiing are the main attractions. **Sorensen's Resort** on Hwy. 88/89 south of Lake Tahoe (a half mile east of Picketts Junction) is *the* local institution, with a café, cozy cabins, and roadside serenity far removed from the Stateline casino scene. Most cabins have kitchens and woodstoves; all have gas heaters and bathrooms. Otherwise, each cabin is unique, with distinct features. General amenities include a sauna (small fee) and wedding gazebo. Rates are complicated (two-night minimum on weekends), calculated on a per-cabin basis, some rates lower midweek, everything higher in winter. Two bed-and-breakfast rooms share a bath. (To make an enlightened choice, contact Sorensen's well in advance and request the current brochure/rate card.)

Besides good food (breakfast, lunch, and dinner served at the café) and reasonably priced lodging, Sorensen's also offers a variety of special events, from historical tours of the Mormon Emigrant Trail over Carson Pass to river rafting on the East Fork of the Carson River, from watercolor painting and photography workshops to cross-country ski tours and sleigh rides. In the works: plans for a new bed-and-breakfast lodge and dozens more cabins. For more information and to get on the mailing list for Sorensen's seasonal newsletter, contact: Sorensen's Resort, 14255 Hwy. 88, Hope Valley, CA 96120, 530/694-2203 or 800/423-9949, www.sorensensresort.com. The **Hope Valley Cross-Country Ski Center,** with 60 miles of trails, is also affiliated with Sorensen's.

Markleeville and Vicinity

Except for a few memorable bar brawls and an occasional natural disaster here in Pleasant Valley, the biggest thing to happen for decades in the tiny onetime timber town of Markleeville was the news in 1988 that Bank of America was getting out of town. County seat and social center of rugged Alpine County (total population: around 1,200), Markleeville residents were—and are—insulted. So when you come to Markleeville, bring cash.

The next biggest thing to happen in Markleeville: the annual **Death Ride Tour of the California Alps,** website: www.deathride.com, considered one of the top 10 cycling challenges in America (and one of the top five toughest). This is a *tour,* not a race—a fact most participants are probably eternally grateful for, since just finishing is an accomplishment. Cyclists can pick their poison, climbing one high mountain pass (a distance of 48 miles) or up to five (about 130 miles). All tours start and end at Turtle Rock Park, halfway between Markleeville and Woodfords. This adventure is limited to the first 2,500 prepaid applicants. Or come for the annual **Markleeville Motorcycle Arts Festival** in late June. For more information on area events, contact the Alpine County Chamber of Commerce.

Up on the hill above town is the **Alpine County Historical Museum** complex, Markleeville, 530/694-2317, open Thurs.–Mon. 11 A.M.–4 P.M. from Memorial Day through October (free, but donations greatly appreciated). Here stands the white clapboard **Old Webster School,** restored to its one-room 1882 ambience, and the county's unusual **Old Log Jail,** with hand-riveted iron jail cells imported north from the original Silver Mountain City building in 1875. Also here: miscellaneous farming, mining, and lumbering artifacts. The modern museum itself has an impressive display of local historical memorabilia, including some beautiful Washoe basketry used for gathering then winnowing pine nuts, a dietary staple.

On the west side of town, in the new Webster School, is the **Alpine County Library and Archives,** 530/694-2120, a collection of everything from mining and property records to voting registrations.

A fascinating feature in downtown Markleeville is the redneck **Cutthroat Bar** inside the Alpine Hotel and Cafe. Typical are the D.A.M.M. (Drunks Against Mad Mothers) bumper sticker on the pool table, brand-name beer mirrors, and animal heads on the walls. Unusual, though, are the "trophies" hanging from the ceiling—an impressive but somehow empty collection of women's bras. The standing deal is that any "gal" can trade in her bra for a free Cutthroat Saloon T-shirt, as long as she makes the trade right then and there. Despite the lingerie on display, there aren't that many takers.

Markleeville Practicalities

To stay awhile, camp at Grover Hot Springs State Park four miles west of town. If there's no room at Grover, try the BLM's **Indian Creek Reservoir** campground for tents and RVs a few miles north of Markleeville off the highway—no swimming but fishing, picnicking, hikes with good views, also the Curtz Lake Environmental Study Area to explore. (Call the BLM office in Carson City, Nevada, at 775/882-1631 for information.) Or camp at the county's **Turtle Rock Park** midway between Markleeville and Woodfords; first-come, first-camped. National forest campgrounds are also good choices; inquire at regional ranger district offices or the local chamber of commerce.

There are accommodations options aside from camping. The 1920s-vintage **J. Marklee Toll Station,** on Main across from the chamber office, 530/694-2507, offers decent food and clean motel rooms. Also good for a meal—enter from the side door to avoid the bar scene up front—is the **Alpine Cafe** behind the Cutthroat Bar (in the same building). *The place* for a great meal, however, is **Villa Gigli,** 145 Hot Springs Rd., 530/694-2253, where the menu is limited but reasonably priced and just about everything is house-made. Beer and wine. Usually open only on weekends for dinner, but call ahead. The family also operates **Grandma's House** downtown, as a guest rental, but sometimes rents out individual rooms. Other good possibilities for an area stay include the **Carson River Resort,** 12399 SR 89, 877/694-2229, and the **Woodfords Inn,** 20960 Hwy. 89, 530/694-2410.

For more information about the area, contact: **Alpine County Chamber of Commerce/U.S. Forest Service office,** at the corner of Main and Webster in Markleeville, 530/694-2475 (chamber) or 530/694-2911 (Forest Service), www.alpinecounty.com. Trail and recreation information is also available at Grover Hot Springs.

Grover Hot Springs State Park

Just west of Markleeville via Hot Springs Rd. is Grover Hot Springs State Park, the perfect hot-soak antidote for weary high-country hikers. Tucked into a mountain meadow near the northeastern edge of the Mokelumne Wilderness, the hot and cool natural spring-fed pools at Grover Hot Springs aren't particularly aesthetic (caged with cement and nonclimbable fence like public swimming pools, but complete with changing rooms and presoak showers—bathing suits required). Yet who cares? The water feels so *good.* (Mineral purists, walk up the hill to the spring's source to find out the water's exact mineral content.)

Except for two weeks in September when the pools are closed for their annual cleaning, Grover Hot Springs is open all year—if you can get here—and popular in winter for hardy souls hankering for a hot soak and a roll in the snow. The small pool-use fee is good all day, so you can leave and come back. During the high season, Apr.–Sept., the pools are open daily 9 A.M.–9 P.M., but otherwise more limited hours (call for current schedule). The park, including campground, is open year-round.

Most developed campsites, just outside the valley, are in an open forested area, none too private—but tired muscles first tightened by the trail then suddenly soak-stretched into relaxation rarely complain. Campsites are $16. ReserveAmerica reservations, 800/444-7275, are usually necessary in summer. The park day-use fee is $5. For more information, contact: Grover Hot Springs State Park, P.O. Box 188, Markleeville, CA 96120, 530/694-2248 or 530/525-7232.

EBBETTS PASS AND BEAR VALLEY

Another impressive after-the-snows climb is up and over Ebbetts Pass via Hwy. 4 (toward the top, on very narrow roads with hairpin turns) and down the other side to Bear Valley, Calaveras Big Trees, Murphys, and ultimately Angels Camp in the Sierra Nevada foothill gold country. The **Highland Lakes** area off the highway just west of Ebbetts Pass offers good trout fishing and primitive camping (no drinking water), as do the tiny,

east of Ebbetts Pass

very picturesque **Mosquito Lakes** beyond Hermit Valley on the Pacific Grade Summit.

Lake Alpine and Vicinity

The sky-high Lake Alpine area northeast of Bear Valley features backpacking trailheads into both Mokelumne and Carson-Iceberg Wilderness Areas, spring and early summer white-water rafting on the North Fork of the Stanislaus River (usually from Sourgrass to Calaveras Big Trees downriver), and lake recreation: canoeing, kayaking, and sailing (motorboats: 15 mph speed limit) in addition to fishing for rainbows, swimming, picnicking, and casual hiking.

National forest campgrounds at Lake Alpine include Lake Alpine, Pine-Marten, Silver Tip, and Silver Valley, all "full-service" (but no hot showers), open only in summer. Nearby and free are other **lake and riverside campgrounds,** including Boards Crossing, Highland Lakes, Sand Flat, and Sourgrass. The newly renovated, previously primitive **Spicer Reservoir** area at Spicer Meadows also offers lake recreation and campgrounds.

The noncamping alternative, open only mid-June to September, is the 1920s-vintage **Lake Alpine Lodge,** 209/753-6358, which features eight fully equipped cabins (most have kitchens) with showers and lake-view decks, along with three tent cabins. And you can get three squares at the **Lake Alpine Lodge Café.**

For more information about Lake Alpine and vicinity, contact the **Calaveras Ranger District,** 5314 Hwy. 4 in Hathaway Pines, 209/532-3671, or stop by the ranger station on the north side of the highway just west of the Silver Tip and Lodgepole (overflow) campgrounds.

Seeing and Doing Bear Valley

Though Hwy. 4 is closed just east of Bear Valley by winter snows, the **Bear Valley Ski Area,** 209/753-2301 or 209/753-2308 (snow conditions), www.bearvalley.com, is accessible from the gold country even in winter. Limited winter access may be what's saved Bear Valley from the relentless onslaught of style and related developments, though it also helps that the ski area is surrounded by Stanislaus National Forest. Surrounded by a walkable, low-rise condominium city complete with mall, Bear Valley is otherwise a medium-sized mellow alternative to the Tahoe ski scene. The resort offers an uncrowded but top-notch downhill ski slope with comfortable Cathedral Lodge; good beginning, intermediate, and advanced ski runs; the excellent Creekside Dining Room (complete with French chef); and a well-developed program for disabled skiers. Bargain prices on weekdays, when it's especially quiet here, and for groups.

The resort's affiliated **Bear Valley Cross Country Ski & Adventure Company,** 1 Bear Valley Rd., 209/753-2834, www.bearvalleyxc.com, offers impressive Nordic-ski facilities, from trails to warming huts, in winter. In summer, come here to rent canoes and two-person kayaks for touring nearby alpine lakes, or to rent a mountain bike for exploring the region's trails. Ask about mountain-bike tours, clinics, and lodging/biking packages. Come in March for the long-running annual **Bjornloppet** two-day cross-country ski festival and race.

For rustic elegance, the place to stay is **The Lodge at Bear Valley,** 3 Bear Valley Rd., 209/753-2327, www.bearvalleylodge.com, especially in the new fourth-floor luxury suites. You'll find the lodge on the left side of Hwy. 4, about a quarter of a mile down Bear Valley Road. Features swimming pool, hot tubs, spa facilities, and on-site restaurant. Inquire about packages and specials. From here, skiers can practically slide out the door to the groomed Ebbetts Pass trails.

Other accommodations in the area include **Red Dog Lodge,** 148 Bear Valley Rd. in town, 209/753-2344, with shared-bath rooms and a sauna, perfect for hotdoggers, and family-friendly **Tamarack Pines Inn** B&B, 18326 Hwy. 4, 209/753-2080, www.tamarackpinesinn.com, where most of the six rooms have private baths and a couple have kitchens (microwaves and refrigerators otherwise available). Kids (all ages) welcome, but no pets. Rates are $50–150 in the winter high season (holidays higher), otherwise $50–100. The affiliated **Tamarack Lodge** nearby features lodge rooms with shared bathrooms, family units with kitchens, a private cottage, and a three-room chalet. For family-style Italian, head downslope for the 1860 **Dorrington Hotel,** 3431 Hwy. 4, 209/795-5800. Back in Bear Valley proper, a great café alternative to the Lodge is the **Headwaters Coffee House** in the village, 209/753-2454.

Bear Valley Events

For some musical Ebbetts Pass rambling in summertime, come to Bear Valley and the tent pavilion set up outside the Bear Valley Lodge for the annual **Bear Valley Music Festival** concert series—a long-standing tradition usually scheduled from late July through mid-August, featuring everything from classical music and opera to Rodgers and Hammerstein and pop. For more information, contact: Bear Valley Music Festival, 209/753-2574 or 209/753-2334, www.bearvalleymusic.org. Season tickets and single-event tickets are available. You can also arrange accommodations with ticket purchase, but plan well ahead.

Another musical attraction is the four-day Bear Valley **High Sierra Music Festival,** 510/420-1529, www.hsmusic.net, held in early July. Featured artists in the past have included Leftover Salmon, Living Daylights, the Tony Furtado Band, and Keller Williams.

SONORA PASS AND VICINITY

Though the old Sonora & Mono Toll Rd. has been a state highway since 1901, the stomach-churning, switchback slither over shoulderless Sonora Pass, where the granite meets the clouds above timberline at an elevation of 9,626 feet, is unforgettable. Assuming he or she survives, anyone attempting the pass in an RV or pulling a trailer of any kind up this lonely stringlike stretch of Hwy. 108, onetime film location of *For Whom the Bell Tolls,* should check into the nearest mental health clinic immediately. But otherwise, don't hesitate—especially if you're cycling. It's beautiful, and literally breathtaking. Stop near the top for a picnic or to camp.

Sliding down the western slope from Sonora Pass, just south of the Carson-Iceberg Wilderness and north of the 107,000-acre Emigrant Wilderness of alpine meadows, high lakes, and granite adjacent to Yosemite National Park, the road leads to **Kennedy Meadows** (trailhead and pack station) and **Dardanelle,** with a string of national forest campgrounds between the two. (For off-highway camping, head northeast on Clark Fork Rd. west of Dardanelle to the campgrounds on the way to **Iceberg Meadow** just outside the wilderness area.) The volcanic peaks known as the Dardanelles were named by the Whitney Survey Party in the 1860s, based on their resemblance to mountains in Turkey overlooking the entrance to the Sea of Marmora.

Pinecrest Lake and Dodge Ridge

About 20 miles southwest beyond Dardanelle are the tiny towns of Strawberry and Pinecrest near **Pinecrest Lake,** quite popular in summer for lake recreation—swimming, canoeing, and boating (no water-skiing) to fishing and horseback riding—and family camping.

Also at Pinecrest is the casual, gold rush-flavored **Dodge Ridge** ski and snowboarding resort, with exceptional but underrated downhill skiing for beginner, intermediate, advanced, and skiers with disabilities, as well as a ski school—all the more vast after a $3.5 million terrain expansion. In summer, mountain biking is a draw. For more information, contact: Dodge Ridge, 209/965-3474, www.dodgeridge.com.

Some area U.S. Forest Service campsites are reservable, others are first-come, first-camped. To reserve campsites at the Forest Service **Pinecrest Family Campground** and the **Pioneer Trail Group Campground,** contact the National Forest Reservation System, 877/444-6777, www.reserveusa.com. Summer or winter, the **Pinecrest Lake Resort,** 421 Pinecrest Lake Rd., 209/965-3411, www.pinecrestlakeresort.com, has motel rooms, rustic cabins, and condos for rent ($80 and up), also a restaurant. Another possibility (for housekeeping cabins) is pet-friendly **The Rivers Resort,** 28635 Herring Creek Ln. in Strawberry, 209/965-3278 or 800/514-6777, www.gorrr.com. Rates are $100–200 for one- to four-bedroom cabins. Weekly rates available. The **All Seasons Sugar Pine Resort** in Sugar Pine at 19958 Middle Camp Rd., 209/586-2007 or 800/788-5212, www.allseasonssugarpineresort .com, is the place for B&Bers, offering imaginative

takes on historical themes—from the John Muir and Wells Fargo Wagon suites to the amazing Confidence Mine. Abundant amenities, Most rates are $100–200; the downstairs Sierra Railway Room is $85, and the Confidence Mine Room is $225. Ski-season weekends are higher.

Get local camping, hiking, horseback riding, and nature trail information, national forest and wilderness maps, as well as wilderness permits, topo maps, and updates on trail conditions for both Emigrant and Carson-Iceberg Wilderness Areas at the **Summit Ranger Station** at the "Y" on Hwy. 108 near Pinecrest, 1 Pinecrest Lake Rd., Pinecrest, CA 95364, 209/965-3434. Various natural history and campfire programs and tours are offered by Pinecrest rangers in July and August. You can even check out free audio tour tapes for the Hwy. 108 route (from Pinecrest to Sonora Pass) at the ranger station. For information on Brightman and Lake Alpine Campgrounds, call 209/795-1381.

Mono Lake and Vicinity

Calling it "one of the strangest freaks of Nature found in any land," Mark Twain was particularly impressed by his mid-1800s visits to Mono Lake, then commonly referred to as the Dead Sea of California:

Mono Lake lies in a lifeless, treeless, hideous desert. . . . This solemn, silent, sailless sea—this lonely tenant of the loneliest spot on earth—is little graced with the picturesque. It is an unpretending expanse of grayish water, about a hundred miles in circumference, with two islands in its centre, mere upheavals of rent and scorched and blistered lava, snowed over with gray banks and drifts of pumice-stone and ashes, the winding sheet of the dead volcano whose vast crater the lake has siezed upon and occupied.

Mono Lake's water was so alkaline, Twain quipped, that "the most hopelessly soiled garment" could be cleaned simply by dipping it in

the lake then wringing it out. He also noted the peculiarity of a sky full of seagulls so far from the sea, and the region's predictable two seasons: "the breaking up of one winter and the beginning of the next."

While some characteristics of modern-day Mono Lake are still as Twain described them, the depth, size, and very nature of this high-desert sea have changed greatly. Mono Lake today is the victor in one of the hardest-fought environmental wars of the century, a preeminent political hot potato pitting Los Angeles water consumers against lovers of the land and landowners in the eastern Sierra Nevada.

SEEING AND DOING MONO LAKE

To understand what all the fuss has been about, visit Mono Lake. For the best "big picture" view, head to the top of the Black Point fissures near the county park, reached via Cemetery Rd. northwest of the lake off Hwy 395. No trail—also no shade or water—so come prepared and pick your way carefully up the volcanic-cinder terraces to the top, defined by solid red rock, about a 45-minute meandering climb. Stop, afterward, at the park and **Mono Basin Historical Society Museum** in the restored 1922 schoolhouse, open in summer Thurs.–Tues. 10–5 P.M., Sun. noon–5 P.M.

Despite the craters-of-the-moon look, highly alkaline waters, and surrounding day-old stubble of sage, life abounds at 750,000-year-old Mono Lake, now protected as both the **Mono Basin National Forest Scenic Area** and the **Mono Lake Tufa State Reserve.** Though early settlers considered the lake "dead," since it was too salty to support even fish life, native peoples knew better. They observed the huge seagull populations nesting here in spring—85 percent of the total California gull population—and some 300 other bird species, including migrants like phalaropes and eared grebes, and knew they depended on lake shrimp and brine flies for survival. (The word *mono* means "fly" in Yokut. The Kutzadika'a Paiutes who lived near Mono Lake harvested the brine fly grubs, a protein-rich delicacy, and traded them to the Yokuts for acorns.)

When spring winds stir the lake's waters, algae grows to support increased new populations of both brine flies and brine shrimp. The delicate cycle of life at Mono Lake can easily be observed in spring and summer, anywhere around the lake's shoreline. By mid-summer it peaks, when some four-trillion brine shrimp reach maturity and become the birds' second major food source, about the time fledgling gulls and other birds first take flight and go foraging.

Still a vast gray-blue inland sea despite Los Angelos' long-term water predation, Mono Lake's saline waters make for fun, unusually buoyant swimming. Old-timers claim a good soak in Mono Lake's medicinal waters will cure just about anything. (One of the best beaches is **Navy Beach** along the south shore; avoid salt in the eyes or open wounds.) But Mono's most notable features are its surrounding salt flats and peculiar tufa formations—strangely beautiful salt-white pillars of calcium carbonate (limestone). Naturally created underwater when salty lake water combines with calcium-rich fresh spring water bubbling up from below, these 200- to 900-year-old "stone" spires are now more exposed due to receding water levels. (Since 1941, the first year that water from four

© ROBERT HOLMES/CALTOUR

Mono Lake, South Tufa area

THE WAR WAGED FOR MONO LAKE

The war of politics and power waged on behalf of Mono Lake and its water has been so contentious, convoluted, and long-running, and has involved so many public agencies and public hearings, so many lawsuits and compromises, that the simple facts are virtually impossible to separate from the details.

Central to the saga, though, is the Los Angeles Department of Water and Power. "If we don't get the water," said self-taught engineer and water czar William Mulholland in 1907, "we won't need it." To get water to the L.A. desert—necessary to fulfill his vision of a lush southstate paradise, only incidentally profitable to real estate interests secretly connected to the plan—Mulholland and his DWP proposed an aqueduct that would carry the eastern Sierra Nevada's water south from the Owens Valley (and the towns of Bishop, Big Pine, Independence, and Lone Pine) to Los Angeles. To gain support (and municipal bond funding) for "Mulholland's ditch," even the *Los Angeles Times* helped fudge on the facts—convincing the public in the early 1900s that a drought existed, a deception unchallenged until the 1950s.

After buying up nearly all private land in the Owens Valley (usually dishonestly, by condemning the land and water rights by lawsuit to drive down the price), Mulholland and his water people had their finest day in November 1913, when the first Owens Valley water flowed into the aqueduct: 30,000 people showed up for the event.

Commenting on the subsequent, permanent desolation of the once lush, quarter-million-acre Owens Valley, the cowboy comedian Will Rogers said soberly: "Los Angeles had to have more water for its Chamber of Commerce to drink more toasts to its growth."

As L.A.'s thirst grew ever more unquenchable—by 1930, the city's population had grown from 200,000 to 1.2 million—violence over eastern Sierra Nevada water rights became commonplace. Denied use of the land as abruptly as their forebears had denied the native Paiutes, outraged ranchers "captured" and controlled the aqueduct on many occasions, and dynamited it 17 times. But urban growth was seemingly unstoppable, and in 1930, L.A. voters approved another bond issue—to extend the aqueduct north into the Mono Lake Basin.

Following completion of this northern stretch in 1941, runoff from Rush, Lee Vining, Walker, and Parker Creeks was diverted into the ditch-tunnel drilled under the Mono Craters and into the Owens River and aqueduct. Even worse for Mono Lake—with its water level dropping and its delicate aquatic ecology suffering almost instantaneously—Los Angeles completed a second aqueduct in 1970, to "salvage" runoff otherwise lost to the lake. Until quite recently, Mono Lake had been shrinking ever since. In 1990, it was estimated that about 17 percent of Los Angeles water came from Mono Lake. California's Dead Sea had nearly died as a direct result.

Central to the present-day chapter of Mono Lake's story is David Gaines, longtime Lee Vining resident, biologist, and founder of the Mono Lake Committee—killed, along with committee staffer Don Oberlin, in a January 1988 car accident near Mammoth Lakes. Though he surely would have loved to see Mono Lake's waters rise again, at the time of his death, Gaines had already made major progress toward that eventual result. Starting in the 1970s, he and his growing, loosely organized band of Mono Lake lovers began taking on the Los Angeles Department of Water and Power and anyone else involved, even through passive inaction. From guerrilla theater and educational "events"—such as public picketing, protests, and volunteer bucket brigades hand-carrying water from Lee Vining Creek to Mono Lake—to press conferences and political confrontations, the Mono Lake Committee was untiring in its war against water diversions.

As a result, the Interagency Mono Lake Task Force—including representatives from Mono County, the L.A. Department of Water and Power, the California Departments of Water Resources and Fish and Game, the U.S. Forest Service, the U.S. Fish and Wildlife Service, and the federal Bureau of Land Management—was convened. The group agreed, by 1980, that the only way to protect the natural resources of the Mono Basin was by curtailing water diversions and raising the lake's level. An almost endless round of lawsuits against the DWP and state and federal regulatory agencies (along with countersuits) in both the state and federal court systems has subsequently helped implement the task force recommendations.

A state Supreme Court decision in 1983—specifically related to Mono Lake but setting the California legal precedent that now protects all state waters—declared that lakes, rivers, and other natural resources are owned by all the people and must be protected by the state for the public trust. Though competing needs are undeniable, the right to divert water from any ecosystem depends upon that system's continued health—and if harm occurs, water rights must be adjusted accordingly, throughout time.

But though the tide finally turned in Mono Lake's favor, at least legally, skirmishes have continued over how much water must be released into the Mono Lake Basin to ensure the health of that ecosystem—how much water will protect island-nesting gulls from coyote predation, how much water will protect the lake's brine shrimp, how much water will protect the region's stream fisheries. Needless to say, the opinions of Mono Lake Committee members and other environmentalists differ from those of L.A.'s Department of Water and Power. Actual cutbacks in diversions—under court order—didn't begin until 1989.

Political pundits contend that recent state legislation to make peace at Mono Lake merely pays the city of Los Angeles, with public funds, to strike a rather vague deal with the Mono Lake Committee—and encourages L.A. to increase groundwater pumping from Inyo County's Owens Valley, all at California taxpayers' expense. "If this is what peace looks like for Mono Lake and the Owens Valley," commented the *Sacramento Bee*'s Bill Kahrl, "it's hard to understand what anyone thought was worth fighting for in the first place."

Members of the Mono Lake Committee answered that even successful lawsuits have not yet protected Mono Lake, and that state legislative action at least opens the door for a lasting peace. The committee also noted that new state and federal water reclamation and conservation projects would more than compensate for L.A.'s loss of Mono Lake water.

Events of immediate, and lasting, benefit to Mono Lake continued through the 1990s. In 1994, the State Water Resources Control Board promised that Mono Lake's water level would rise to 6,392 feet above sea level (it was 6,417 feet in 1941, when water diversions began)—an accomplishment expected to take some 20 years—and supported the restoration of the lake's watershed streams and wetlands. The lake continues to rise, to 6.382.3 feet in 2003. The DWP now has two annual meetings with the Mono Lake Committee to coordinate efforts and improve communication, sessions described by the committee as "collegial" and a "testament to the progress made in opening up communication. . . and building a promising working relationship." The Mono Lake Committee now offers tours of DWP facilities.

But despite L.A.'s impressive progress in water conservation, the city's Department of Water and Power has indeed increased its groundwater pumping in the Owens Valley, directly south, to the great detriment of that environment—a crisis without a committee to speak on its behalf.

The war over eastern Sierra Nevada water goes on.

of Mono Lake's feeder streams was shipped south to L.A., the lake's level dropped an average of 18 inches per year, a total drop of about 45 feet. In the 1990s, however, with area streams now flowing into the lake once again, that trend is reversing. By Memorial Day 2003 the lake level had risen almost eight feet, to 6,382.3 feet about sea level.) The best place to see and wander through these fantastic tufa formations—no climbing or souvenir-taking allowed—is in the **South Tufa Area** off Hwy. 120 ($3 admission), which features basic visitor facilities, including flush toilets. Here and elsewhere, due to deceptively soft pumice "sand," heed warnings about driving on less-traveled roads—particularly on the lake's east side—without a four-wheel-drive vehicle.

Mono Lake has two major islands: the yin-yang twins of white **Paoha** and black **Negit;** until recently the latter was the gulls' preferred nesting spot. (The islands, and the lake itself within one mile of them, are closed to the public from April through July to protect nesting birds.) Environmentalists fighting for Mono Lake's right to life pointed out that L.A.-bound water diversions, made worse by natural disasters like drought, created the land bridge that connected the islands to the mainland, allowing coyotes and other bird and egg predators to reach nesting seagull colonies on Negit Island. But lack of fresh water also increased the lake's salt levels by two or three times, threatening both Mono Lake's brine shrimp and brine fly populations—a more subtle but long-term threat to gulls and other bird species dependent on these creatures for food.

Other problems as well may have affected area life. Long-term measurements of the levels of radioactive carbon in Mono Lake, for example, showed notable increases in the 1950s and 1970s. For a time there was worry that nuclear waste may have been dumped here, but more recent information suggests that the carbon increase came from U.S. Navy munitions testing (carbon 14 was used as a tracer element).

Now the lake's future—and future water levels—are less clouded by human politics. But in a sense, life had already "returned" to the Mono Lake Basin by 1985, when bald eagles came back to the area's stream canyons.

Nearby Sights

Just south from Mono Lake's bitter waters are the **Mono Craters,** a dozen dove-colored volcanoes tinged with black. These explosion pits, domes, and lava flows with light-colored slopes of ash and pumice are volcanic infants, ranging in age from 640 to 40,000 years; most are around 12,000 years old. Despite Mt. St. Helens's recent performance, volcanologists still rate these hot-blooded babies at the top of the list of continental American volcanoes most likely to blow any day. Most accessible from Mono Lake is 640-year-old **Panum Crater** (trailhead reached via dirt road heading south from just west of the South Tufa Area turnoff), an easy climb for a great view. To get to **Devils Punchbowl** at the Mono Craters' southern end, head south on Hwy. 395 from Lee Vining for 12 miles, then east for 1.75 miles on unpaved Punchbowl Road. As elsewhere, avoid pumice soils and stay on the roads—if signs say travel is unsafe for ordinary vehicles, believe them.

STAYING NEAR MONO LAKE

Camping

No developed camping is available at Mono Lake, but independent camping—"dispersed camping"—is allowed in certain areas near Mono Lake, so long as campsites are staked out above the 1941 waterline. For more information, ask at the Mono Basin National Forest Scenic Area Visitor Center or the Mono Lake Committee Information Center (see below). In town, **Murphey's RV Park,** 760/647-6358, and the **Mono Vista RV Park,** 760/647-6401, both offer RV and tent sites. But the best place around is back up Hwy. 120 at the U.S. Forest Service **Big Bend Campground** along Lee Vining Creek—a beautiful but basic creekside setting (complete with small waterfall) reached via a gravel and dirt road from the highway. Amenities include chemical-flush pit toilets and piped-in untreated creek water (no showers, 14-day limit). Usually open mid-April through October (weather permitting).

Farther east, and closer to the highway, are the county-run **Aspen Grove** and **Lee Vining Campgrounds** in a creek meadow setting. Many other public campgrounds are within 15 miles of Lee Vining. Free and low-fee camping is available at **Saddlebag Lake** north of Hwy. 120 and just outside the Hoover Wilderness. Also at Saddlebag is a summers-only resort, at the highest California lake accessible by public road, reached via narrow, steep Saddleback Lake Road.

Motels and Lodges

Lee Vining is "town" for Mono Lake, a pleasant roadside collection of motels, gas stations, and supply stops on Hwy. 395 just north of the junction with Tioga Rd./Hwy. 120 from Yosemite. Before Hwy. 120 begins its straight-ahead descent just east of Yosemite through desert-dry rock to Mono Lake—look for Sierra bighorn on the unstable shale slopes above the road—is the rustic **Tioga Pass Resort,** P.O. Box 307, Lee Vining, CA 93541, winter reservations phone only, 209/372-4471 (Oct. 15–May 1), reservations@tiogapass.com. Lodge accommodations and cabins are available by advance reservation; open year-round.

For noncampers, usually the cheapest motel around (pets allowed) is the **King's Inn,** two blocks off the highway at 45 Second St., 760/647-6300, with small, cozy rooms, kitchen units extra. $50–150. Also reasonable and small-pet friendly is **Murphey's Motel,** on the highway, 760/647-6316. The **Gateway Motel,** 85 Main St. (Hwy. 395), 760/647-6467, has comfortable rooms with queen beds, coffee, and TV. $100–150 (rates lower from November through mid-May). Pretty uptown in this town is the **Best Western Lake View Lodge,** 30 Main St., 760/647-6543, complete with coin-op laundry and putting green. $100–150.

The **Tioga Lodge,** just north of Lee Vining, overlooking the lake from the east side of Hwy. 395, 760/647-6423 or 888/647-6423, www.tiogalodge.com, started out as the Hammond Station stagestop on the old toll road here in 1897. The successful resort and restaurant that sprouted on the spot was all but wiped out by a flood in the 1950s. Yet the Tioga Lodge has risen again, rebuilt thanks to the tireless efforts of Walt and Lou Vint. The lodge offers gussied-up, western-themed cabins, with private bathrooms and en-

trances. Rates are $50–100. There's also an onsite restaurant and saloon. In summer, Tioga Lodge offers 90-minute Mono Lake boat tours.

EATING NEAR MONO LAKE

Folks here will tell you *the* place to eat in town is **Nicely's Restaurant** ("real nicely people") on Main, 760/647-6477, open daily for good café fare—breakfast, lunch, and dinner. Another option, just north of town about four miles in the otherwise long-gone town of Mono Lake, is the exquisitely restored 1920s **Mono Inn** restaurant and bar, 760/647-6581, What you'll get here in addition to the elegantly rustic Arts and Crafts farmhouse ambience and great California-style American fare (be sure to save room for the chocolate pecan pie) are some great lake views. Entrées range from vegetarian and pasta specials to broiled filet mignon, with spicy peanut sauce. The Mono Inn is open for dinner 5–9 P.M., Wed.–Sun. in summer (May through October) and Thurs.–Sun. in winter (Nov.–Apr.; closed Jan. and Feb.). Or try the **Tioga Lodge** (see above). The Virginia Creek Settlement near the turnoff to Bodie (see below) is worth the drive, if what you're hungry for is whole wheat-crust pizza and other wholesome yet reasonably sophisticated fare.

INFORMATION AND SERVICES
Mono Lake Committee

Stop by the **Mono Lake Committee Information Center and Bookstore** (a onetime dance hall, now renovated) on Hwy. 395 at Third St., P.O. Box 29, Lee Vining, CA 93541, 760/647-6595, www.monolake.org. The Mono Lake Committee headquarters also houses the **Lee Vining Chamber of Commerce,** www.leevining.com, making this the all-purpose Lee Vining visitor center—providing the latest information on Mono Lake politics (including educational slide show); schedules of lake hikes, tours, and canoe trips; suggestions about what else to see and do in the area—including where some of the best hot springs are—and practical guidance on visiting the eastern Sierra Nevada.

The ***Mono Lake Guidebook*** by David Gaines

and the Mono Lake Committee is quite useful, plus you'll find other intriguing, informative books here. Even a small donation in support of the committee's work will yield a subscription to the group's quarterly *Mono Lake Newsletter,* the best information source for the ongoing politics of water and power in the eastern Sierra Nevada, also for keeping abreast of current ecological research and Mono Lake activities and events. For a good solid background on relevant California water politics, also read *Water and Power* by William Kahrl. And watch the movie *Chinatown.*

Among the many fundraising/educational activities organized by the Mono Lake Committee are the annual **Mono Basin Bird Chautauqua** and the annual mileage-sponsored **High Sierra Fall Century** bike ride in September. Other events have included **Restoration Days** in September, and the **Living Lakes International Conference: Stream and Lake Restoration.** In addition, many educational field seminars are held annually by the Mono Lake Foundation, primarily from late spring to early fall. Sample topics include: Birds of the Mono Basin; High Country Birds; High Country Wildflowers; Natural History Canoe Tours; Geology of the Mono Basin; Mono-Bodie Historical Tour; and Writing of the Eastern Sierra. Most weekend workshops run $75–150.

General Information

Easy **naturalist-guided walks** of Mono Lake are offered year-round, daily in summer—usually at 10 A.M., 1 A.M., and 6 P.M.—and every Saturday and Sunday from mid-September through mid-June, in the South Tufa Area, 10 miles southeast of Lee Vining via Highways 395 and 120. Off-season hikes usually meet at 1 P.M. There's no charge for the walk, but there is a $3 admission fee for the South Tufa Area. Even if you've hiked the lake before, be sure to come again; now that Mono Lake's water level is rising, the landscape is surprisingly *different.*

For guided walk details and more Mono Lake information, stop by the impressive **Mono Basin National Forest Scenic Area Visitor Center** just north of town off the highway, 760/873-2408 or 760/647-3045 TDD, www.fs.fed.us/r5/

inyo/vc/mono, open daily 9 A.M.–4:30 P.M. most of the year. Call for winter days and hours. An impressive contemporary museum overlooking the lake, it features an information center (the introductory video *Of Ice and Fire* is shown every half hour in summer), a good bookstore, and very well-done natural history exhibits. Many are of the interactive "hands-on" variety, like the Guess Your Weight in Brine Shrimp display. (An average-sized adult weighs 450,000 shrimp, for example, roughly equivalent to 150 pounds.) Particularly amusing, though—since we humans consider ourselves the world's most discriminating cultural connoisseurs—is the display of "gull juju," odd treasures scavenged by seagulls and incorporated into their nests. Birds here have collected everything from Styrofoam cups and cocktail-sized American flags to decapitated toy soldiers, plastic cowboys, and a Daryl Strawberry baseball card—all in all, a fairly insightful representation of U.S. society—though the display changes to reflect current gull preferences. Once you're done with the museum, enjoy the spectacular lake views from the patio.

The Mono Basin Visitor Center is also a good source for general U.S. Forest Service information, including area day hikes, forest and wilderness maps ($6–10), topo maps, wilderness permits, and regional campground information. Ask too about surrounding national forest areas—including the eastern Sierra Nevada's Hoover Wilderness adjacent to Yosemite north of Hwy. 120 and the Ansel Adams Wilderness south of the highway.

Services

For AAA emergency road service, call 800/400-4222. Hospital and **medical care** is available in Bridgeport at the Bridgeport Medical Clinic, 760/932-7011, or in Mammoth Lakes at Mammoth Hospital, 760/934-3311, but for medical emergencies call 911, or contact the **Mono County Sheriff's Office** in Bridgeport, 760/932-7549.

BODIE AND VICINITY

Evocative even these days is the published 19th-century response of a young girl when told her

© ROBERT HOLMES/CALTOUR

Bodie was the wickedest Old West mine camp of them all, locals boasted, but there were a few churches in town.

family was moving to this bad, brawling, desolate frontier town on the lonely, wind-sheared plateau: "Goodbye, God, we are going to Bodie." In defense of this godless Gomorrah, a gold mining town with a population of more than 10,000 employed at 30 mines in its heyday, a Bodie newspaper editor claimed the child had been misquoted—that what she actually said was: "Good, by God, we are going to Bodie." But the town's own citizenry boasted that Bodie had the widest streets, wickedest men, and worst climate and whiskey in the West. Fisticuffs and murders were daily events. (Another local newspaper editor observed: "There is some irresistible power that impels us to cut and shoot each other to pieces.") Virgin Alley and Maiden Lane in Bodie's redlight district boasted neither, and a local minister described the community as "a sea of sin lashed by tempests of lust and passion."

What remains of the busted boomtown of Bodie—California's largest ghost town, which actually persisted as a town until 1942—is now protected as part of **Bodie State Historic Park.**

A strangely silent place still standing (more or less) in the shadow of the old Standard Mine, where the whistling sage winds speak loudest of days gone by, Bodie still somehow evokes the spirit of the truly wild Wild West. Preserved in its entirety in a state of arrested decay, what's here is certainly worth at least a half-day's exploration, but only about five percent of Bodie's well-weathered 1860s and 1870s wood-frames still stand, the rest destroyed over the decades by fire and the elements. Pick up a self-guided tour brochure at the small museum (in the old Miner's Union Hall) or at the ranger's office/residence on Green St., one of the few occupied buildings in town.

Visitors are free to wander at will through godless, lawless, treeless Bodie. Peek through tattered lace curtains into the Boone Store and Warehouse, Wheaton & Hollis Hotel and Bodie Store, Sam Leon's bar, and other restaurants, saloons, livery stables, and miners' shacks abandoned for more than a century, and peer into dusty rooms furnished with cracked and peeling wallpaper and woodstoves, sprung bedframes, banged-up wash basins, even battered old shoes and clothing. Inside the Henry Metzger and Lester E. Bell homes are wicker baby carriages; the morgue features three child-sized coffins. Most poignant of all, though, is the time-twisted, rusted child's wagon abandoned in the middle of the street. Done with town, head for the hillside cemeteries for an introduction to some of Bodie's colorfully memorialized former residents. (The fenced-in cemetery was set aside for local decent folk; most bad Bodie boys were buried on Boot Hill.)

Bodie State Historic Park doubled in size with the addition of 520 acres, at a price of $5 million, in late 1997—the result of successful public advocacy to eliminate the threat to the Bodie experience from open-pit gold mining on Bodie Bluff and Standard Hill above town. And in September 2002, Governor Gray Davis designated Bodie as California's official gold rush–era ghost town.

Practicalities

For obvious reasons, beyond the parking lot no smoking is allowed in Bodie. Camping is also prohibited, but picnicking is okay (no shade, just tables and pit toilets). Pack a lunch and bring your own drinking water—Bodie is a ghost town, with no stores or services. The small museum is open daily 9 A.M.–6 P.M.; if you didn't BYOW, bottled drinking water is available at the museum. The park is open daily 8 A.M.–7 P.M. in summer, closing as early as 4 P.M. the rest of the year—hours strictly enforced (the rangers close and lock the road gates). A great self-guiding tour brochure ($1) is available just beyond the parking lot. Day-use fee: $2 per person per car ($1 age 17 and under). For more information and to volunteer time and/or money to help The Friends of Bodie preserve the town, contact: Bodie State Historic Park, 760/647-6445, www .bodie.net. Guided tours of the Standard Stamp Mill are available in summer and early fall, $5 adults, $3 children (12 and under). Photography walks and workshops (reservations required) are also offered. Call for current hike, tour, and history talk schedules.

Most Bodie visitors come anytime but winter, via 13-mile Hwy. 270/Bodie Rd. (paved most of the way) from Hwy. 395, the turnoff about seven miles south of Bridgeport and 20 miles north of Lee Vining. Even when Bodie Rd. is closed by winter snows (usually November through mid-April), technically the park is still open. The truly intrepid sometimes snowmobile or ski in, but this isn't advisable. If you insist, do call ahead and tell rangers you're coming—just in case you don't make it. (It's lonely out here, and winter storms can be brutal, with winds up to 100 miles per hour.) Alternate good-weather routes include (from Mono Lake) the washboard-style dirt and gravel Cottonwood Canyon Rd. from Hwy. 167 and (from Bridgeport) the narrow Aurora Canyon–Masonic back roads.

Bridgeport

A middle-of-nowhere supply stop and center of local social action, such as it is, Bridgeport is the place to get extra food, parts for emergency car repairs, and outdoor equipment—as well as to rest one's head in a real bed. Bridgeport attracts an eclectic array of visitors, and events. On the last weekend in June, the entire western U.S. chapter of organized Harley-Davidson enthusiasts—some 5,000-6,000 bikers—convenes here for the annual **Bridgeport Motorcycle Jamboree.** The town's **July 4th celebration** is one of the nation's oldest Independence Day parties, locals say, complete with real-deal rodeo. But perhaps Bridgeport's most notable party is the **Big Mountain Man Rendezvous** in August, like stepping 150 years back into the past (no cars allowed). Participants dress in period frontier attire; competitions and friendly rivalries include everything from black-powder shooting contests to bake-offs. Fun, too, is "Trader's Row," a frontier-style marketplace where everything is historically authentic, from trading beads to children's toys.

Motels line the highway. The very nice **Walker River Lodge,** on the East Walker River at 100 Main St., 760/932-7021 or 800/688-3351, fax 760/932-7914, has the usual amenities—including smoke-free rooms and suites—plus satellite TV, heated pool, whirlpool, and fish cleaning and freezing facilities. $100–150. Pets okay. Open year-round. The **Best Western Ruby Inn,** 333

WILL YOUR HONEY TAKE YOU TO HUNEWILL?

Horse fanatics who are also fans of the grand Sierra Nevada landscape may want to ask themselves that very question. The **Hunewill Guest Ranch** (pronounced "Honeywill") may be the ideal destination for an equine-oriented family vacation.

A 4,500-acre working cattle ranch on the eastern flanks of the Sierra Nevada near Bridgeport, the Hunewill Ranch was founded by Napoleon Bonaparte Hunewill and his wife Esther in 1861; LeNore and Stanley Hunewill started the guest ranch in the 1930s. To this day the ranch is very much a Hunewill family affair, the current owners being the sixth generation of Hunewills to occupy the Victorian ranch house.

Guests sometimes arrive with visions of *City Slickers* dancing in their heads—perfectly understandable, since cattle work is available. Several special cattle events are featured, such as a cattle working week, ranch roping clinic, and the traditional fall cattle drive to the winter ranch in Nevada, a 60-mile journey.

Most people, though, come to ride. (Bring your own horse for a slight discount.) Wranglers quite knowledgable about the ranch lead all rides, and may even tell jokes or recite cowboy poetry. Beginners sign on for easy-going "buckaroo" rides. Advanced riders can gallop across meadows and jump ditches (just like in the movies) or play equestrian "games," like splashing through large puddles of water. If a fast-slow combination ride seems a better fit, that's possible, too. There's a group,

and a pace, for everyone. (Children must be at least 6 years old to ride. A baby-sitter is provided for smaller children.) In addition to regular daily rides Hunewill offers an optional all-day trail ride, a breakfast ride, even a Horseback Play Day.

There's plenty else to do besides ride, including barbecue, talent show, and family dance nights. There is also excellent hiking and catch-and-release fishing nearby (and at the ranch's own pond), or simply relax back at the ranch and take in spectacular views.

Comfortable cabins and three daily buffet-style meals—hearty and homemade—are included in a stay at Hunewill Guest Ranch, which is open to guests from late May into early October. Prices vary depending on when you come; the high season runs from about mid-June to mid-August. At last report the basic seven-day package was $1,215 per person (double occupancy) for adults,: $1,130 single occupancy, $799.75 per child 10–12, $532.75 per child under 10, and $260 per child under 2. Special packages (for more advanced riders) are offered for the Fall Color Ride, Spring and Fall Cattle Work, the Annual Cattle Drive, and the Buckeye Canyon Cattle Gather.

For more information, contact Hunewill Guest Ranch, winter: 200 Hunewill Ln., Wellington, NV 89444, 775/465-2201; summer: P.O. Box 368, Bridgeport, CA 93517, 760/932-7710, www .hunewillranch.com.
—*Melanie Weir*

Main St. (north of downtown, across from the courthouse), 760/932-7241, fax 760/932-7531, offers the same basic features (no pool, but whirlpool) and even more comfort. $100–150. Equally nice and quite unusual is **The Cain House,** a country inn at 340 Main St., 760/932-7040 or 800/433-2246, fax 760/932-7419, www.cainhouse.com. This restored historical home features seven elegant but distinctly Western bed-and-breakfast rooms, all with private baths, and serves full breakfast. $150 and up. Rustic lodges, cabins, and campgrounds abound at nearby lakes (see below).

Get basic food supplies at area groceries. Locals

recommend the **Bridgeport Inn** on Main, 760/932-7380, for breakfast, lunch, and dinner (open Mar.–Nov.). A better choice for dinner, also an option for an overnight stay, is Virginia Creek Settlement about five miles south of town (see below).

For more information about the area, contact **Bridgeport Chamber of Commerce,** 85 Main St. (the highway), P.O. Box 541, Bridgeport, CA 93517, 760/932-7500, www.ca biz.com/bridgeportchamber or bridgeportchamber.com. Another good information source, especially for national forest maps, wilderness permits, and area campground and hiking information, is the

Toiyabe National Forest's **Bridgeport Ranger Station,** P.O. Box 595, 760/932-7070.

Lee Vining Area Recreation

Ask in Bridgeport for directions to the primitive **Big Hot Warm Springs** just south of town and east one-half mile off the highway. Nearby **Bridgeport Reservoir** (sometimes little more than a massive mud puddle) and **Kirman Lake** are popular for trout fishing. Excellent for rainbow and brown trout fishing are the pretty, high-altitude **Twin Lakes** southwest of Bridgeport via Twin Lakes Rd., which also offer trailhead access into the Hoover Wilderness.

In addition to eight national forest campgrounds along Robinson Creek, the area also offers picnicking, lake recreation, and several popular private resorts (closed in winter). The **Hunewill Guest Ranch** between Bridgeport and the lakes, 760/932-7710, is a working cattle ranch complete with comfortable accommodations, good food, and guided horseback trips into the wilderness. **Doc & Al's** resort on the way to Lower Twin Lake, 760/932-7051, is a time-honored fishing retreat. And at the end of the road, at the far-western edge of Upper Twin Lake, is the rustic **Mono Village** resort, 760/932-7071, with cabins and private camping.

About halfway between Bridgeport and Lee Vining on the south side of Conway Summit is the turnoff to **Virginia Lakes,** a cluster of 10 small lakes (no swimming) in the high country (elevation 9,700 feet) just six miles west of Hwy. 395 and perfect for camping. There's a national forest campground at Trumbull Lake, along with various undeveloped creekside campsites. Also here: the summers-only **Virginia Lakes Resort,** Bridgeport, CA 93517, 760/647-6484, virginialakesresort.com, with cabins, small grocery, restaurant, and public bathhouse.

Close to both Bodie and Mono Lake is **Lundy Lake,** reached via Lundy Lake Rd., which heads west at the Hwy. 395/Hwy. 167 intersection. Trailhead into the Twenty Lakes Basin area, the aspen-and-pine fringed lake is also noted for its fishing, beaver ponds, out-of-the-way camping—there are 100 primitive county campsites along Mill Creek below the dam—and the relaxed rustic charms of the **Lundy Lake Resort,** P.O. Box 550, Lee Vining, CA 93541, with housekeeping cabins, RV and tent camping, as well as grocery, Laundromat, and hot showers.

Virginia Creek Settlement

The best little dinner house (and overnight stop) for miles around is the Virginia Creek Settlement on Hwy. 395 five miles south of Bridgeport, just a half-mile north of the turnoff to Bodie. A windmill out front marks the spot. The settlement was once part of Dogtown, the region's first gold-rush mining camp, though nearby Bodie surpassed it in reputation and longevity. These days, Virginia Creek Settlement, 760/932-7780, serves a variety of good American-style dinners and nightly specials, from steaks and chicken to pastas, but the real prize here is the pizza. Choose either whole wheat or white, then ponder the toppings—everything from Canadian bacon and garlic to artichoke hearts and jalapeño peppers. The restaurant is open for dinner Wed.–Sat. in spring and fall, Tues.–Sun. in summer.

An equally great deal is a stay in the large suite directly above the restaurant, the only historically authentic rooms remaining from the building's past as a boardinghouse for Bodie miners. The two bedrooms have iron bed frames and country-style floral decor plus a shared sitting room. The rooms can also be rented separately. Moderate.

Behind the restaurant and well back from the highway are a few log cabin-style motel units with knotty-pine walls, iron bed frames, and in-room brewed coffee. They're clean and comfortable, and sleep up to four people. Moderate. Even more intriguing is an overnight in one of Virginia Creek's wood cabins. Each looks like an Old West storefront, complete with tongue-in-cheek business shingle (like "Dewey, Cheatam & Howe" for the law office). Inside are a table and chair plus beds with bare mattresses (bring your own sleeping bags or rent linens and blankets, $4.50 per bed). Most sleep four. $50–100. Outside is a barbecue and picnic table. You can also camp at Virginia Creek, right along the creek, $12 for two, $2 each additional person. Some sites have electricity, but no RV sewer hookups are available. (RVers might want to check in at Willow Springs Resort just up the highway toward Bridgeport, which has full facilities—and extra rooms, if Virginia Creek is full.) Though no rooms at Virginia Creek Settlement have telephones, there *is* a pay phone. Just step into the outhouse up by the highway and see for yourself.

THE JUNE LAKE LOOP

About five miles south of Lee Vining off Hwy. 395 is Hwy. 158, the northern end of the June Lake Loop, leading to a high-country collection of lakes and summer cabins eerily shadowed in late afternoon by the saw-toothed snowy peaks looming up from the Ansel Adams Wilderness just to the west. Particularly worthwhile in summer is the short hike to **Obsidian Dome,** a poetically poised mountain mass of once-molten black- and color-streaked glass; the trailhead is reached via dirt road 1.5 miles south of June Lake Junction. In October, this is leaf peepers' paradise; quaking aspen groves fringe area lakes. Worth it in winter is the excellent, usually uncrowded **June Mountain Ski Area** (now owned by Mammoth Mountain, which is now partially owned by Intrawest), 760/648-7733 or 888/586-3686, www.junemountain.com. June Mountain often has better snow and ski conditions than Mammoth—and is more sheltered—but year after year the big guy gets all the glory. Terrain is the big news these days. Expect to see the pros at June's **JM2Unbound,** with one superpipe, three parks, a snowskate park, and a "progressive skate influenced pipe." June Mountain also offers cross-country skiing.

The stunning subalpine scenery here includes four lakes—Grant, Silver, Gull, and June—popular for fishing and water recreation (water-skiing allowed at Grant Lake only) and a multitude of U.S. Forest Service campgrounds. Perhaps prettiest are the campgrounds near Silver Lake, but the **Oh! Ridge Campground** is accessible for the disabled, and **Hartley Springs,** not far south of June Lake Junction, is free. For noncamping accommodations, try **Silver Lake Resort,** 760/648-7525, which offers housekeeping cabins, RV and tent camping, restaurant, store, gas station, and rental boats and launch ramp. Other possibilities include the **Fern Creek Lodge,** 760/648-7722 or 800/621-9146, motel units plus housekeeping cabins (some with fireplaces), and the **Boulder Lodge,** 2282 Hwy. 158, 760/648-7533, for cabins and motel units plus swimming pool and tennis courts.

Good places to eat include the **Sierra Inn,** 2588 Hwy. 158, 760/648-7774, open daily for breakfast, lunch, and dinner, and the exceptional **Carson Peak Inn,** also on Hwy. 158, 760/648-7575, serving Australian lobster tail and other seafood, chicken, pork, ribs, steaks, and other well-prepared American fare nightly for dinner. For more information about local accommodations and restaurants, contact the **June Lake Chamber of Commerce,** 760/648-7584.

SIERRA NEVADA

Mammoth Lakes and Vicinity

The Mammoth Lakes area offers surprising contrast to the sagebrush scrub along the main highway—and good summer hiking among the geological wonders, mountain lakes, hot springs, and cool conifers of this otherwise hotshot winter ski area.

One thing not immediately apparent, however, is the fact that the Mammoth Lakes area lies near the southwestern edge of the massive Long Valley Caldera—stretching north to near Obsidian Dome and east to beyond Lake Crowley—one of the biggest, most powerful volcanoes in the West yet essentially invisible to the eye. Only its crater, and a new, emerging volcanic dome at its center, remain after the original volcanic peak was blasted to the four winds some 700,000 years ago during a monstrous eruption. At that time, ash and pumice spewed for at least 50 miles in all directions; no other volcanic event in recorded history, volcanologists say, has approached that level of volcanic fury. Despite a resurgence in area volcanic activity—with one earthquake a minute during a particularly jittery 1,000-quake period in late 1997—scientists don't believe the Big One will hit, here at least, any time soon. Odd byproducts of area volcanism include 170 acres of forest suffocated by carbon dioxide gas, on Mammoth Mountain, and temporary geysers at Hot Creek.

MAMMOTH LAKES AND BASIN

Aside from the area's lovely lakes and streams, the star attraction of the Mammoth Lakes Basin is **Devils Postpile National Monument,** a seemingly pile-driven vertical collection of three- to eight-sided basalt columns formed by slowly cooling lava flows (getting there involves an easy day hike, after a national forest shuttle ride). Nearby is colorful **Rainbow Falls,** complete with mountain pools for invigorating swimming. Near Devils Postpile is **Fish Creek Hot Springs,** with no facilities, no fees, no restrictions, reached from Reds Meadow by hiking south on the Fish Creek Trail past the Sharktooth Creek Trail (about 100 yards along the path beyond the campground).

But the area's all-time favorite hot soak is at **Hot Creek,** three miles east of Hwy. 395 via Long Valley Airport Rd. Officially "not recommended" for swimming or soaking by the Forest Service, people happily hop in nonetheless. The steaming Hot Creek experience is created by a *very* hot spring bubbling into an ice-cold stream—so the trick is finding a spot that's not so hot that you'll get scalded. (Most people manage.) Swimsuits required. Open daily from sunrise to sunset, free.

Do explore some of the area's 100-plus lakes. The only one noted for swimming is **Horseshoe**

© KIM WEIR

Devils Postpile National Monument

Lake, also the trailhead for the Mammoth Pass Trail. For shorter hikes, there are many ways to get to **Lake George.** Picture-perfect for picnicking is **Lake Mamie.** Diehard trout fishing enthusiasts may want to visit **Lake Crowley,** some 15 miles south of Mammoth Lakes.

To get an eagle's-eye view of the area, in summer take a tram ride up **Mammoth Mountain** and stop halfway for a snack or cup of coffee. The mammoth Mammoth ski resort boasts other summer attractions, from mountain biking (with a "lift" from the Eagle Express chair) and 80 miles of track for fat-tire bikers to mountain climbing, trout fishing with Mammoth's Orvis-approved fly-fishing school, and golfing at 18-hole Sierra Star Golf Club.

For more Mammoth-area recreation ideas, from hot-air ballooning and golfing in summer to sleigh rides and dogsledding in winter, contact the **Mammoth Visitor Center and Ranger Station,** on Hwy. 203 on the way into town (three miles west of Hwy. 395), 760/924-5500, TDD 760/924-5531, www.fs.fed.us/r5/inyo. Also contact the **Mammoth Lakes Visitor Bureau,** 760/934-2712 or 888/466-2666, www.visitmammoth.com.

Winter Sports

The area's natural features have enduring star power, but the profit's in development—skiing, shopping, restaurants, golf courses, and condos. IntraWest, Mammoth's new owner, is pumping $1 billion into mountain's facilities and associated development. It all adds up to the "biggest resort makeover in the history of skiing," according to *Ski* magazine. As a result property values tripled from 1999 to 2003, a speculative explosion not everyone celebrates. At the center of this increasingly upscale international ski scene is **Mammoth Mountain Ski Area** just past town, 760/934-2571 or 800/626-6684, www.mammothmountain.com, where the big news includes The Village at Mammoth—retail, restaurants, accommodations, and more, like IntraWest's similar Squaw Valley village—the Village Gondola, But the skiing's the thing. Mammoth Mountain receives an average of 385 inches of snow per year, which means people are often on the slopes well into summer. (In a bad year, Mammoth makes snow.)

The resort serves up variety, with 3,500 acres of varying terrain, 27 lifts, and three terrain parks. To avoid the parking crunch at Mammoth Mountain's slopes, take the shuttle from the village. If the crowds seem unbearable, head north to smaller June Mountain.

Mammoth also offers good cross-country skiing. The **Tamarack Cross-Country Ski Center** at Tamarack Lodge, 760/934-2442 or 800/626-6684, www.tamaracklodge.com, offers extensive backcountry trails (children under age 12 free), telemarking, tours, rentals, and lessons. The **Sierra Meadows Ski Touring Center** at Sherwin Creek Rd. off Old Mammoth Rd., P.O. Box 2008, Mammoth Lakes, CA 93546, 800/626-6684, has groomed trails and set track plus lessons, rentals, and warming hut.

Forest Service cross-country ski trails include the **Obsidian Dome Trail,** which begins at the junction of Hwy. 395 and Glass Flow Rd. (south of June Lake Junction), as well as several near Mammoth Lakes, such as the **Earthquake Fault Trail** to Inyo Craters. Winter camping is available, too, at the national forest's Shady Rest campgrounds.

STAYING AT MAMMOTH

Camping

The best bet in summer is camping. There are numerous **Inyo National Forest campgrounds** in the Mammoth Lakes Basin, including sites at Twin Lakes, Lake Mary, and Lake George, as well as some near town—including **Pine City** (tents only), **Coldwater** (near the trailhead into the John Muir Wilderness), **Pine Glen** (wheelchair accessible), and **New Shady Rest** and **Old Shady Rest Campgrounds.**

Forest Service campgrounds can also be found at crystal-clear Convict Lake south of Mammoth Lakes and at Rock Creek Lake halfway between Mammoth Lakes and Bishop. Some of the national forest campsites can be reserved in advance through the National Recreation Reservation Service, 877/333-6777, or online at reserveusa.com. For complete listings of regional camping choices, contact the Mammoth Ranger Station (see Events below).

Camp High Sierra just west of New Shady Rest, operated by the L.A. Department of Recreation, 760/934-2368, has nice tent sites, rustic cabins, hot showers, even a lodge.

Motels

Surprising for such an elite retreat, in winter and summer Mammoth does offer other reasonably priced accommodations, generally most appropriate for travelers on their own. Most inexpensive are lodges that provide dorm-style bunks for around $15–25 per person (lower summer rates). These include the homey, smoke-free **Davison St. Guest House** (formerly the Asgard Chalet), 19 Davison St., 760/924-2188, fax 760/544-9107, which also rents rooms or the entire lodge, and **Ullr Lodge,** on Minaret Rd., 760/934-2454.

Motel 6 is at 3372 Main St. (Hwy. 203), 760/934-6660 or 800/466-8356, www.motel6.com. The **Travel Lodge** is at 54 Sierra Blvd., 760/934-8892, $50–100. The **White Stag Inn** is west of town on the highway, 760/934-7507. $50–100. Other midrange motels include the **Econolodge Wildwood Inn,** 3626 Main St., 760/934-6855 ($50–100); and the **Swiss Chalet Motel,** 3776 Viewpoint Rd., 760/934-2403 ($50–100).

Bed-and-Breakfasts

The **Rainbow Tarns** bed-and-breakfast, 888/588-6269, www.rainbowtarns.com, is south of Mammoth Lakes at 505 Rainbow Tarns Rd. (off Crowley Lake Dr., a mile north of Tom's Place). The Rainbow offers three B&B rooms, unusual serenity, access to cross-country skiing, hiking, and horseback trails, and a full country breakfast. Rates are $100–150, lower in winter. No credit cards.

There are other good choices, though. Near town is the **White Horse Inn Bed & Breakfast,** 2180 Old Mammoth Rd., 760/924-3656, which offers several theme rooms in a private home. The Emperor's Room, for example, paying homage to the area's mining-era Chinese influence, features as a centerpiece an heirloom antique Chinese bed. All rooms (except one kids' room) have private baths; a full breakfast is served every morning, wine and cheese in the afternoon. Two-night minimum stay required.

The **Mammoth Country Inn** bed-and-breakfast, 75 Joaquin St., 760/934-2710 or 866/934-2710, www.mammothcountryinn.com, has a VCR and goose-down comforter in every room, a shared lounge with huge stone fireplace and indoor diversions, and an upstairs guest kitchen. Seven themed rooms, one with private bath. Another good choice is the **Cinnamon Bear Bed & Breakfast,** downtown at 113 Center St., 800/845-2873, www.cinnamonbearinn.com, famous for its teddy bears. The Cinnamon Bear offers three separate buildings with a hot tub, 14 rooms with New England Colonial decor (some with four-poster beds), weekly rates, and packages. Most rooms are $100–150, with higher rates on weekends; there are several cozy "single" rooms, $50–100.

Hotels

People who plan to stay awhile often opt for comfort on the group living plan—renting condominiums, cabins, or homes by the week and cooking most meals "at home." For information on reputable area rental agencies, contact the Mammoth Lakes Visitors Bureau (see below) or stop by the visitor center.

The **Sierra Lodge,** 3540 Main, 760/934-8881 or 800/356-5711, www.sierralodge.com, is a completely nonsmoking, contemporary hotel. Rooms include kitchens and microwaves, refrigerators, TV and cable, access to spa. Children under age 12 stay free. Free breakfast, covered parking provided. Rates are $100–150. Nice, too, is the **Alpenhof Lodge,** 6080 Minaret Rd. (a mile west of town on Hwy. 203), 760/934-6330 or 800/828-0371 (reservations only), www.alpenhof-lodge.com. Mini-suites (some with fireplaces) close to the slopes, with spa, sauna, and pool in summer. Rates are $50–100 in summer, $100–150 in winter. Another good choice is the **Quality Inn,** 3537 Main St. (just west of town on the highway), 760/934-5114; $100. The all-suites **Shilo Inn,** 2963 Main (on the highway east of Old Mammoth Rd.), 760/934-4500, has rooms with kitchens, refrigerators and wet bars, continental breakfast, free access to complete fit-

ness center and sauna, whirlpool, indoor pool, and steam room. Rates are $100–150.

Time-honored and very traditional, though, for a ski-in, ski-out stay on the slopes is the ski resort's bustling, and mammoth **Mammoth Mountain Inn,** 1 Minaret Rd., 760/934-2581. Rooms feature the usual amenities and somewhat thin walls, but skiers and summer mountain bikers can't get much closer to the action. Rates start at $100–150. All rooms are less expensive during midweek in winter, and substantially less in summer. Ask about special packages and off-season deals. Mammoth also offers snazzy new hotel-style condo accommodations on the slopes at its new **Juniper Springs Lodge,** adjacent to the new Eagle Express chair lift at 4000 Meridian Blvd., 760/924-1102. One- to three-bedroom units feature TV, VCR, telephone, gas fireplace, full kitchen, and amenities such as in room humidifiers. The resorts **Sunstone Lodge, Eagle Run Lodge, The Village,** and (eventually) the grand **Grand Sierra Lodge** offer other options. Other pluses include heated outdoor pools, Jacuzzis, workout facilities, onsite restaurants, and 24-hour bell service. Rates start at $150–250. To make reservations at any resort accommodation, call 800/626-6684 or see the website: www.mammothmountain.com.

Resorts

Now an adjunct to the Mammoth Mountain resort, the special **Tamarack Lodge** a few miles beyond town on Lake Mary Rd. (the extension of Hwy. 203), 760/934-2442 or 800/626-6684, www.tamaracklodge.com, is a 1920s mountain lodge on Twin Lakes at the foot of Mammoth Mountain. Fish for trout in summer, try Nordic skiing in winter—also ice skating, when the lakes freeze over. Tamarack features a fine restaurant— the Lakefront—and a fireplace-anchored lobby, plus knotty pine–paneled lodge rooms (only four have private baths). Outlying housekeeping cabins—studios and cabins with one, two, or three bedrooms—are more rustic but nice, and feature kitchens, bathrooms, some fireplaces. Some have been remodeled, and five new cabins have been built, to add modern amenities; one of the new cabins fully meets federal Americans with Disabilities Act requirements. Rates are $100–150 for smaller rustic cabins, $150 and up (as high as $425 per night) for larger cabins.

Also recommended in the area: the rustic summers-only **Red's Meadow Resort** near Devils Postpile and Rainbow Falls, next door to a hot springs and practically in the middle of the Pacific Crest Trail. Trout fishing is popular here, but so is hiking: the Ansel Adams Wilderness is one mile away, and the John Muir Wilderness is two miles away. Facilities include lodging, café, and store, also a large string of horses and mules for wilderness rambling. Open mid-June to the end of September. Under $50 (two motel rooms)-$50–100 (cabins). For more information and reservations, contact: Red's Meadow Resort, Mammoth Lakes, 760/934-2345 or 800/292-7758, www.mammothweb.com/redsmeadow. Bob Tanner's affiliated pack station offers horseback excursions, parent-child trips, fishing trips, pack trips, and special events including the three-day Horse Drive (offered in spring and fall) and the four-day Bishop to Bodie Horse and Wagon Ride, offered in late May.

Rock Creek Lodge, 7497 Rock Creek Rd. in Little Lakes Valley, halfway between Mammoth Lakes and Bishop (take the Rock Creek Rd. turnoff at Tom's Place on Hwy. 395), heaven for anglers and the outdoorsy, features good fishing and access to excellent high country hiking. A home-style restaurant is close to the small rustic cabins; two-bedroom cabins have completely equipped kitchens (but no bathrooms: showers and flush toilets a short walk away), or rent two-story A-frames with the works. In winter, when getting here involves a two-mile snowmobile trek for you and your gear, cross-country skiing and guided tours are offered—with the extra added attraction of a backcountry trailside hut available for overnights. In summer rates are $50–100 for camp-style rustic cabins with kitchenettes (shared bathrooms and showers) and $100–150 for modern, A-frame, and larger cabins with kitchens, private bathrooms, and hot showers. In winter, dorm-style accommodations are $70 per person per night (you ski in), $95 for rustic cabins, and $120 for modern cabins. For more information and to make reservations, contact:

Rock Creek Lodge, 760/935-4170 or 877/935-4170, www.rockcreeklodge.com.

Another area classic is **Convict Lake Resort** south of Mammoth Lakes, 760/934-3800 or 800/992-2260, www.convictlakeresort.com. Some cabins are rustic, some quite deluxe (one of the newer ones sleeps up to 32), and rates start at $95 per night. The excellent Restaurant at Convict Lake, 760/934-3803, serves country French fare.

Another great choice, in lush meadows and Jeffrey pine forests along the Owens River, is the **Alper's Owens River Ranch** near Mammoth Lakes, 760/648-7334 in summer, 760/647-6652 in winter, a collection of simple cabins on a one-time cattle ranch.

EATING AT MAMMOTH

Though fast-food stops have popped up in this forested town like mushrooms after the first fall rains (there's a Safeway here, too), Mammoth Lakes' attractions include its restaurants, a better selection of good eateries than anywhere else along the Sierra Nevada's eastern slope. Excellent is **Blondie's Kitchen**, 3599 Main St., 760/934-4048, noted for its exceptional breakfasts—including breakfast burritos—and daily specials.

Berger's on Minaret Rd. (at Canyon) on the way to the slopes, 760/934-6622, has good burgers and other American fare, excellent fries, and great homemade desserts. **Perry's Pizza and Italian Cafe** in the Village Center West on Main, 760/934-6521 or 760/934-3251, serves it Sicilian style, along with good all-you-can-eat specials Tuesday and Wednesday nights.

Whiskey Creek on Hwy. 203 (Main at Minaret), 760/934-2555, is the locals' choice for steaks, prime rib, and barbecued ribs. Just as good, others say, smaller and usually less crowded, is **Mogul**, 1528 Tavern Rd., 760/934-3039.

The **Ocean Harvest** restaurant, just south of Hwy. 203 on Old Mammoth Rd., 760/934-8539, is noted for its fresh mesquite-grilled seafood. **Restaurant Skadi,** in Sherwin Plaza on Old Mammoth Rd. (at Chateau Rd.), 760/934-3902, serves upscale California/Alpine cuisine, along with fine California wines, champagnes, and a full bar. Open for dinner nightly except Wed. and Sun.

The very small (10-table) **Lakefront Restaurant** at Tamarack Lodge Resort at Twin Lakes, 760/934-3534 or 760/934-2442, serves salmon and other fresh fish plus such classics as rack of lamb and beef Wellington, "excellent meals that will satisfy both the heartiest of appetites and the most finicky," according to *Bon Appétit*. At the top of the local food chain is lively American **Nevados** on Minaret Rd. at Main St., 760/934-4466, open nightly for dinner. Reservations recommended.

EVENTS AND INFORMATION

Ski events large and small dominate the local events calendar in winter when, after dark, local bars and lodges are the main event. In addition, the year-round events calendar is usually full. Fun in mid-July is the annual **Mammoth Lakes Jazz Jubilee,** and in late July, the **Children's Fishing Festival.** Another of the year's major events is the **Sierra Summer Festival,** sierra-summerfestival.org, an excellent music festival (from pops to classical) usually held the first half of August, conveniently overlapping the **Mammoth Lakes Fine Art Festival.** Cycling events, fishing derbies, even roller blade and tennis and volleyball tournaments round out summer events.

For more information about Mammoth Lakes and vicinity, contact the **Mammoth Visitor Center and Ranger Station,** on Hwy. 203 as you come into town, 760/924-5500, TDD 760/924-5531, www.fs.fed.us/r5/inyo, where you can pick up information on the town as well as surrounding national forest lands, wilderness maps ($6–10), wilderness permits, and current information on hiking, backpacking, and camping (the *Mammoth Trails Hiking Guide,* available for $3, is worth the investment if you're staying awhile). Also contact the **Mammoth Lakes Visitor Bureau,** 760/934-2712 or 888/466-2666, www.visitmammoth.com, which is helpful for phone queries but is no longer set up as a walk-in visitor center. Another good source for Mammoth Lakes information is the website: www.mammothweb.com, an online visitor's guide including many useful topics such as lodging, food, weather, attractions, events, road conditions, and more.

GETTING AROUND

For AAA emergency road service, call 800/400-4222. Those with private planes can fly in to the **Mammoth Lakes Airport,** 760/934-3813.

The Mammoth Lakes area is so popular in winter that public transit is almost mandatory. The **Mammoth Shuttle System,** 760/934-3030, is a taxicab company operating year-round. **Mammoth Area Shuttle,** 760/934-0687, is Mammoth Mountain ski area's local shuttle-bus service, which operates only during the ski season; the "red line" connects the main lodge and the village, another line serves Tamarack (760/934-2442) in winter for cross-country skiing, and other lines connect to base chairlifts.

In summer, it's almost necessary to take the Forest Service shuttle to reach the Agnew Meadows, Red's Meadow, and Devils Postpile areas beyond Mammoth Lakes. Backpackers *must* ride the shuttle, because wilderness permits prohibit driving into the valley or parking at trailheads. Car campers, however, *can* drive in—assuming they first get a camping permit—but during the summer high season, anyone opting to drive must do so either before 7:30 A.M. or after 5:30 P.M. Board shuttles at the Mammoth Mountain Inn near the ski slopes; buses leave every half hour between 8 and 10 A.M., between 3:30 and 5 P.M., and every 15 minutes from 10 A.M. to 3:30 P.M. (Returning to Mammoth Mountain, the last bus leaves Red's Meadow at 6:15 P.M.) Roundtrip fare: $7 adults, $4 children ages 3–15, age 2 and under free.

BISHOP AND VICINITY

Some 40,000 people descend on Bishop over the Memorial Day weekend for kick-over-the-traces celebrations of native mulishness—mule races, mule-drawn chariot races, and braying contests for people who (apparently) would rather be mules—during the town's annual **Mule Days Celebration.** The next biggest community party comes on Labor Day weekend, during the **Eastern Sierra Tri County Fair.** For the Lion's Club pancake breakfast, followed by rodeo, chili cook-offs, western-style dinner, and street dancing, come on home to Bishop. Other events also well worth showing up for include April's **kick-off for the eastern Sierra fishing season** (trout) and the **Millpond Bluegrass Festival** in late September. Come in October for **The Owens Valley Cruisers Annual Fall Colors Car Show,** with hundreds of classy cars, pancake breakfast, parade, and poker run.

Seeing and Doing Bishop

Bishop itself is pleasant in the neon-and-highway category, with a few parks and swimming pools scattered among the markets, motels, and cowboy cafés. But who needs more? From anywhere, just look up—and there they are, those amazing mountains. Look around, too. Bishop also has its share of around-town vistas, thanks to the Bishop Mural Society and its history-themed murals. Also remarkable here is the **Mountain Light Gallery** at 106 S. Main St., 760/873-7700, www.mountainlight.com, which showcases the spectacular work of photographer Galen Rowell and his wife Barbara Cushman Rowell, both tragically killed in a plane crash while returning home to Bishop in August 2002. Some of their legacy shines forth here—as photographs, posters, books, calendars, and greeting cards. Worth a stop just outside town on the reservation is the **Paiute-Shoshone Indian Cultural Center and museum,** where traditional gambling "stick games" are sometimes played at night. The **Paiute Palace Casino,** http://paiutepalace.com, offers more contemporary gambling, including bingo poker and video gaming.

About 25 miles north of Bishop and east of the highway is **Crowley Lake,** where thousands of anglers swarm on opening day of trout season (the last Saturday of April)—quite the human zoo. Some of the big German browns hooked here weigh in at 25 pounds or so (until recently, California's record for trophy trout). Nearby, to the west, is more serene **Convict Lake,** named for a bloody attempted roundup of 29 escaped convicts in 1871. More beautiful still, and providing entry points for fine high-country hiking on the backside of the John Muir Wilderness and Kings Canyon National Park, are **Lake Sabrina, North Lake,** and **South Lake** in Bishop

Creek Canyon. Locals can give directions to the area's wildest and woolliest out-there hot springs.

Laws Railroad Museum

About five miles outside town on Hwy. 6 is the Laws Railroad Museum, 760/873-5950, the old Laws Station railroad depot complete with the *Slim Princess* narrow gauge train and a collection of historic buildings with indoor and outdoor museum displays. (Across the road is the newly old Drover's Cottage, built in 1966 for the Steve McQueen movie *Nevada Smith.*) Like the rest of the Owens Valley, death came to the Carson & Colorado Railroad by the 1930s, when Los Angeles's groundwater pumping decimated local ranching and farming, leaving nothing left to ship. The Laws Station railroad-history complex is open daily 10 A.M.–4 P.M. (except Thanksgiving, Christmas, and New Year's Day).

Chalfant Valley Petroglyphs

From Laws, keep going northeast on the 50-mile **Petroglyph Loop Trip** through the sagebrush tableland of Chalfant Valley, earthquake country in the shadow of the stone-faced White Mountains. A total of six stops offer up-close looks at unusual (and unusually varied) ancient rock drawings predating the Paiute people. Due to increasing problems with vandalism, the BLM office in Bishop now "screens" those interested in seeing local petroglyphs. If you pass muster and get directions, look but do not touch.

Staying in Bishop

Camp almost in town (just south) at **Brown's Town** (complete with free museum), Hwy. 395 at Schober Ln., 760/873-8522, at the city of Los Angeles campgrounds at Crowley Lake, 213/485-4853, or (better yet) try the national forest campsites at Convict Lake.

Motels abound in Bishop, where most people are either going fishing or just passing through on the way to someplace else. Most accommodations are quite reasonable, often with cheaper off-season rates. Off the highway (one block east, near the Best Western Westerner) is the **Elms Motel,** 233 E. Elm St., 760/873-8118. Amenities here (and at many other motels in town) include fish cleaning and freezing facilities, under $50. Pleasant **El Rancho Motel** sits off the highway at 274 Lagoon St., 760/872-9251 ($50–100), and the very nice **Comfort Inn** is at 805 N. Main St., 760/873-4284 or 800/576-4080 ($50–100). The **Best Western Holiday Spa Lodge,** 1025 N. Main, 760/873-3543, features a coin laundry, pool, whirlpool—and fish cleaning and freezing facilities. Quite nice is the **Mountain View Motel,** 730 W. Line St., 760/873-4242, with heated pool and attractive grounds. ($50–100).

The historic **Matlick House Bed and Breakfast,** 1313 Rowan Ln. (north of town), 760/873-3133 or 800/898-3133, provides pleasant and peaceful rooms far removed from motel-style accommodations. $50–100. (Weekly rates also available; lunch, too, by reservation only.) Also a good choice is the very Victorian **Chalfant House,** just west of the highway at 213 Academy St., 760/872-1790, www.chalfanthousebb.com, featuring eight rooms in the onetime home of Owens Valley's first newspaper publisher; $50–100, with full breakfast and evening ice cream sundaes.

For a more rustic yet special stay, try updated **Parchers Resort** near South Lake, 2100 South Lake Rd., 760/873-4177, a time-honored trout-lovers' collection of cabins and RV campsites (full hookups available) now also featuring a fine restaurant and weekend seminars on natural history, mountaineering skills, and photography. Open from the start of fishing season through summer only. The associated **Bishop Creek Lodge,** 760/873-4484, features rustic cabins—no TV, no phones but all the essential comforts. Cabins are $50–100. For more details about both, see www.bishopcreekresorts.com. Also unusual, and unusually inviting, is the **Rainbow Tarns** bed-and-breakfast inn just south of Mammoth Lakes, with waterfalls, solitude, and great hiking and ski access. For more information, see Mammoth area Bed-and-Breakfasts above.

Eating in Bishop

The **Bishop–Eastern Sierra Certified Farmers Market,** 760/873-1038, is held July-Oct. on Sat., 9 A.M.–noon, on Hwy. 395 at Sierra Street. The **Inyo Country Store,** 177 Academy St., 760/872-2552, open for breakfast and lunch Mon.–Sat., for

dinner Thurs.–Sat. nights, is *the* place for fine coffee, cappuccino, and espresso, not to mention American bistro fare and gourmet picnic items. For a truly fine sit-down dinner, head for **The Restaurant at Convict Lake** at Convict Lake, 760/934-3803, where the seasonal menu might include fresh-caught local trout and beef Wellington. Full bar. Open daily for dinner. Other decent out-of-town dining choices include **Parchers** (see above), and the homey **Bishop Creek Lodge** nearby, 760/873-4484.

Otherwise, a good bet among possible chow stops in Bishop is **Whiskey Creek,** 524 N. Main, 760/873-7174, for hearty omelets and other breakfast choices, a variety of sandwiches and salads at lunch, good ol' American fare at dinner. Locally popular is **Jack's Waffle Shop,** 437 N. Main, 760/872-7971, 6am-9pm. **Erick Schat's Bakkerÿ** ("Home of the World-Famous Sheepherder Bread") at 763 N. Main, 760/873-7156, is also a local institution not to be missed. Traditional dinner houses—steaks and such—include the **Firehouse Grill** north on the highway, 760/873-4888.

Information

An excellent book to tote along is *Sierra South: 100 Back-Country Trips* by Thomas Winnett and Jason Winnett, published by Wilderness Press. Also worthwhile, especially if you'll be staying awhile (or returning often) are *John Muir Trail Country* and *Sequoia-Mt. Whitney Trails,* both by Lew and Ginny Clark and published by Western Trails Publications.

For more information about Bishop and vicinity, stop by the **Bishop Chamber of Commerce & Visitors Center** at City Park, 690 N. Main St., 760/873-8405, www.bishopvisitor.com. The **Inyo National Forest headquarters** (also the Bishop area BLM office), is in a new location, 351 Pacu Ln., Ste. 200, 760/873-2400 or TTY 760/873-2538, www.fs.fed.us/r5/inyo, though the national forest's **White Mountains Ranger Station** at 798 N. Main, 760/873-2500 or TDD 760/873-2501, is actually better for national forest and wilderness maps ($6–10), wilderness permits, and information on area hikes, sights, and campgrounds. Bookstore and gift shop, too. The

RETURN TO MANZANAR

The land itself says little about it, the devastating experience of Japanese Americans imprisoned during World War II at Manzanar some six miles south of Independence. Now as then, Manzanar is bleak and desolate, dust and sagebrush surrounded by barbed wire and remnants of chain-link fencing. Two pagoda-style stone guardhouses, sans doors and windows, stand near what was once the entrance to the internment camp; remnants of building foundations seem like skeletons exposed by shifting sands. A few buildings, gnarled fruit trees, a cemetery, and a monument—the white and austere Soul Consoling Tower, or Buddhist "tower of memory"—honor those who lived here during the post–Pearl Harbor days of the war.

Executive Order 9066, signed in 1942 by President Franklin Roosevelt, created Manzanar and nine other isolated Pacific Coast internment camps. That decree meant that some 120,000 men, women, and children of Japanese descent were immediately removed from their communities and imprisoned by the U.S. Army. Ten thousand people, most of these U.S. citizens, many with sons in the military, were herded into tarpaper shacks at Manzanar ("apple orchard" in Spanish). The name of the place seemed inappropriate, but not for long. Allowed irrigation water and the opportunity to work the land, internees soon transformed their arid section of valley into lush, productive farm acreage and a tight-knit community. In addition to its orchards, gardens, and hog and chicken ranches, Manzanar once boasted a Bank of America branch, an orphanage, a Boy Scout troop, baseball teams, pools, a nine-hole golf course (with oiled sand for greens), and a swing band called the Jive Bombers.

The U.S. Supreme Court struck down Roosevelt's executive order in 1944, ruling it unconstitutional, and Manzanar was closed. Its legacy lived on, however. Upon returning to their hometowns, former internees often found themselves facing blatant racism and discrimination from former neighbors—and, this time, facing it largely alone.

Every year, camp survivors and their families and friends make the pilgrimage to Manzanar, to remember. In April 1992, the Owens Valley **Manzanar Pilgrimage** attracted some 1,500 people, to formally celebrate the establishment of the **Manzanar National Historic Site** by the U.S. Congress. (In the hope that we'll all remember.) And restoration has begun, albeit slowly, on this vast and empty monument to a nightmarish political past. Various "lost" elements of Manzanar's history are being found and returned, including the camp's original mess hall. The old high school auditorium is open as a visitor center, after a $5.2 million renovation.

Explore the site. Take the 3.2-mile self-guided auto tour (route description and map available at the entrance), or take a walk. From the stone guardhouses stroll Manzanar's old roads and orchards. A walking tour takes one or two hours; at last report guided tours were offered in summer and fall.

For more information about this place and its history, contact: Manzanar National Historic Site in Independence, 760/878-2194 (visitor information) or 760/878-2932 (headquarters), www.nps.gov/manz. The collected photographs of both Ansel Adams and Dorothea Lange tell more. Revealing on a deep level too is the book *Farewell to Manzanar* by Jeanne Wakatsuki Houston.

© KIM WEIR

SIERRA NEVADA

ranger station is open daily from mid-June to mid-September, otherwise only on weekdays.

FROM BISHOP TO INDEPENDENCE

Heading south from Bishop, it's hard to notice anything except the awesome Sierra Nevada looming ever higher. But in this long, lonely country, watch out for gray dust devils rising up from long-dead Owens Lake—stormy clouds of flourlike, alkali dust creating driving and health hazards, some of the highest levels of dust ever recorded on the continent, as much as 11 tons per day. Also watch out for elk, which may suddenly spring up near the highway from their sagebrush and charcoal-colored stone camouflage. With any luck at all, the elk will abide and the dust will soon be gone. In 1998 the city of Los Angeles, whose long-running regional water predation caused the disappearance of Owens Lake and the resulting dust plague, agreed to return enough water to permanently soak parts of the lake bed to a depth of a few inches; other areas will be sown with salt-tolerant grasses, and still others will be covered with dust-taming gravel.

Ancient Bristlecone Pine Forest

Anthropologists have recently retrieved some 24,000 artifacts from two peoples who lived, from 1300 B.C. to the 14th century, high in the White Mountains. But today's most notable old-timers are the gnarled and gristly *Pinus longaeva* trees, still thriving here in the Ancient Bristlecone Pine Forest, apparently unperturbed by summer drought and heat, severe winters, or the passage of time—though smog may now be doing them in.

Bristlecones growing in this stark, dry, and dramatic mountain range have been alive longer than anything else on earth, many for more than 4,000 years. Studies of these austere, graceless, scruffy ancients have revolutionized traditional understanding about the origins of human civilization.

Starting in the 1950s, Edmund Schulman of the University of Arizona began his tree-ring studies of the bristlecone pines here, discovering that the oldest among them are 4,600 years or older (nearly twice as old as any redwood). But conflicts between his dendrochronological data and that derived by the then-unquestioned carbon-14 dating techniques of Willard F. Libby led to C-14 testing corrections. The corrections resulted in a shake-up of the accepted time frames of world history—eliminating the theory of Greek and Roman cultural diffusion to explain the astronomical accuracy of Stonehenge and other peculiarities of early European society, among other revelations.

Along the **Schulman Grove**'s short **Pine Alpha Trail** and 4.5-mile **Methusaleh Trail,** home turf of the Methusaleh Tree, the planet's oldest living being (unidentified for its own protection), there's a strange sense of timelessness. Life and death, past and future, are almost indistinguishable.

These dwellers on the threshhold—storm-sculpted abstractions in wood—are dead and alive simultaneously, with naked trees sometimes bursting forth with just enough contorted, curved branchlets of pine needles to sustain life and produce resin-covered red cones ripe with fertile seeds. Eleven miles and 40 minutes farther up the road, another 1,000 feet higher in elevation, the moonscape at the **Patriarch Grove** (home of the biggest known bristlecone) is even bleaker, with just scattered specimens of firm-rooted, living driftwood.

A visit to the White Mountains' Bristlecone Pine Forest is at least an all-day journey—and one usually not possible in winter, when the road is closed. Start out with a full tank of gas and bring food, water (none is available, even at campgrounds and picnic areas), good walking shoes, and sun protection as well as warm clothing, since even in summer it's cool at higher elevations and the weather changes constantly. To get here, head northeast on Hwy. 168 from Big Pine to near Westgard Pass, about 13 miles, then head north on White Mountain Rd.—the highest auto route in California, reaching an elevation of 10,500 feet. Picnic near the fossil area beyond Cedar Flat; family campsites are available in summer at **Grandview Campground** on the way to Schulman Grove.

To get oriented to these trees and their significance, pick up a brochure/map at the Cedar Flat entrance station. Better yet, spend some time at the handsome new **Ancient Bristlecone Pine Visitor Center** at Schulman Grove, open from mid-June to Nov. 1, and study the interpretive displays. The Schulman Grove center also hosts other visitor programs and is the starting point in summer for naturalist-led hikes.

For more information about the 100-million-year-old White Mountains—home also to ghosts of mining history, mustangs, and golden eagles—stop by or call the **White Mountains Ranger Station** at 798 N. Main in Bishop, 760/873-2500 (recorded info after hours). There you can also find out about special summer events like mountain bike racing, and off-season possibilities including cross-country skiing and snow camping. Another valuable resource is the Ancient Bristlecone Pine website, www.sonic.net/bristlecone.

Big Pine

The Palisade Glaciers looming above Big Pine Canyon to the west and looking down on the town of Big Pine are small but distinguished, being the continent's southernmost "living" glaciers (which means they melt, break off, and otherwise diminish at the low end while new snowpack-turned-to-ice replenishes them on the high side). Big Pine itself offers no comparable experiences or sights.

Camp in Big Pine Canyon or, for a real bed, try either the **Big Pine Motel**, 370 S. Main, 760/938-2282 (under $50), or the **Starlite Motel,** 511 S. Main St., 760/938-2011. The historic **Glacier Lodge** near the Palisades at Big Pine Creek, built in 1917, was a popular dining destination until it burned to the ground some years back. The rustic, fully equipped cabins are still in fine fettle, though. No phones, no TV, no swimming pool, and—since Glacier Lodge generates its own electricity—absolutely no extra appliances (hair dryers, etc.) are allowed. Rates are $50–100. Also at Glacier: a general store (takeout meals available with advance notice), RV and tent camping, and overnight parking for hikers. For more information, contact Glacier Lodge, 760/938-2837, www.jewelofthesierra.com.

Independence

The next town south is Independence, the Inyo County seat, once a trading post called Putnam's (or Little Pine, after the creek), which grew in stature and significance when gold was discovered in the Inyo Mountains to the east. The striking 1920s classical revival **Inyo County Courthouse,** 168 N. Edwards St., was designed by architect William R. Weeks. Worth a side trip just north of Independence is the **Mt. Whitney Fish Hatchery,** 760/878-2272, possibly the most beautiful in the world—an Old World-style fish monastery with a Tudor tower, built in 1917 of native stone. (Pleasant pond, park, and picnic facilities.) Near the turnoff are the ruins of old **Fort Independence.** The World War II-vintage **Manzanar Relocation Center** stood southeast of Independence, one of California's internment camps, temporary "home" to 10,000 Japanese Americans (see Return to Manzanar).

Stop for a look at the **Mary Austin Home** in town (follow the signs), designed and built under the supervision of the very independent author of *Land of Little Rain,* an ode to the once-beautiful Owens Valley. Also worthwhile is time spent at the modern, wheelchair-accessible **Eastern California Museum,** 155 N. Grant St., 760/878-0258 or 760/878-0364, with its excellent displays of Paiute and pioneer artifacts, including a yard full of old farming implements, photo archives, books, and publications. Open daily except Tuesday, 10 A.M.–4 P.M. (Free, but donations always appreciated.)

Practicalities

The 1926 **Winnedumah Hotel** on the highway in Independence, 211 N. Edwards St., 760/878-2040, www.qnet.com/-winnedumah/, has been transformed into a creative bed-and-breakfast perfect for fans of affordability—folks without SUVs full of cash but who'd still like to stay long enough to revel in the wonders of the eastern Sierra Nevada. Though the hotel's style has changed considerably since the 1920s, this venerable hostelry actually has quite a history. It was once a popular place to stay for movie stars and film crews during the region's Hollywood heyday, and a favorite stopover for that desert myth-maker, Death Valley

SIERRA NEVADA

Scotty. These days the Winnedumah features a fireplace in the casual lobby, lots of colorful over-stuffed furniture, a grand piano, plenty of games and books, classical music, and a relaxed Western-outdoors ambience that invites adventurers. The 24 guest rooms are simple but charming and eclectic, furnished with original handpainted 1920s furniture and handmade quilts. Some share baths. There's even air-conditioning when the weather gets hot—and a lovely garden to enjoy balmy evenings. Rates are on the low end of $50–100, and ask about the off-season Three for Two special. Usually a sweet deal at the Winnedumah Hotel are its **Winnedumah Weekends** special-events packages, ranging from mountain-biking tours and Manzanar photography to watercolors.

Especially a find if you've stumbled straight out of Death Valley—civilization at last!—the star in town is the artful **Still Life Café**, 135 S. Edwards St., 760/878-2555 which started its climb to fame as a stylish roadhouse in Olancha, some 20 miles south of Lone Pine. The modest menu here is French with a North African accent—everything from roast chicken and lamb stew with couscous to filet mignon. Tiny wine list, at least a few decadent desserts.

MT. WHITNEY

A climb up Mt. Whitney, California's highest point, is not an experience for solitude seekers. It seems everyone wants to do it—though it's a strenuous vertical walk, most people can—and they all want to hike the 10-mile trail at the same time, during the snow-free period from mid-July (sometimes as early as mid-May) into early October. Mt. Whitney is the most frequently climbed peak in the Sierra Nevada—and possibly the United States. For this simple reason, a trail quota is in effect May 22–Oct. 15. Ascending Mt. Whitney requires a permit. (Plan ahead, and contact the local Wilderness Reservation Service.) Because parking can be such a problem at the trailhead—and parking tickets are expensive—contact the chamber office in Lone Pine and ask if the shuttle system is up and running.

Savvy hikers can put quick distance between themselves and the crowds, however, by continuing on from the summit along the John Muir Trail—but again, plan ahead, as permits are required for all back-country travel in Sequoia and Kings Canyon National Parks and associated wilderness areas.

Among other thoughts to ponder while here in God's country: Mt. Whitney is the highest point in the Lower 48, but quite nearby is the lowest. Southeast from Lone Pine via Hwy. 136 is Death Valley National Monument, dramatic, endless desert that boasts the lowest elevation in the continental U.S.—and often the highest summer temperatures.

For those cycling or driving up and back via 13-mile Whitney Portal Rd., take the dirt-road detour through the area's Alabama Hills (follow the signs), a sparse desert sage landscape most people have seen before as the jumbled, round-bouldered granite backdrop for countless movies (*High Sierra, Red River, Bad Day at Black Rock,* and *They Died with their Boots On*) and TV westerns including *Bonanza, Have Gun—Will Travel,* and *Tales of Wells Fargo.*

Hiking

Due to the immense popularity of hiking Mt. Whitney, trail quotas for both overnight and day hikes during peak season (May 1 through November 1) have been in place since 2000 for the main Mt. Whitney Trail. It's a lottery system. This lottery offers fairly high odds of success—particularly if you include a number of alternate dates. For each day during "quota season," 60 overnight permits and 115 day hike permits are issued; in the recent past, 90-plus percent of day-hike applicants received permits, and 57 percent of applicants for overnight permits. Permits are free, technically, but there is a $15 "request fee," refunded for those who don't win a permit. Applications may be faxed or mailed to the permit office only in February; those received during the first two weeks in February will be processed first; others will be added to the ongoing lottery as they are received. For more information, contact the Inyo National Forest **Wilderness Permit Office** (former forest headquarters) at 873 N. Main St. in Bishop, 760/873-2485, www.fs.fed .us/r5/inyo. Download permit forms, in several different formats, directly from the website. For the possibility of last-minute cancellations and additional information, contact the **Mt. Whitney Ranger Station** next to the high school in Lone Pine, 760/876-6200, staffed only May 1 through November 1.

The Mt. Whitney permit system applies only to day hikes and overnight trips undertaken during the peak hiking season, May through October; come earlier or later, and a wilderness permit from any ranger station will suffice. In addition, if you approach Mt. Whitney via any other trail (Shepherd Pass, Kearsarge Pass, etc.), lottery applications are *not* required.

For additional regional wilderness travel and permit and trip-planning information, try the National Park Service website, www.nps.gov/seki, which covers Sequoia and Kings Canyon National Parks as well as Mt. Whitney.

Camping

Camp at the scrub-shrouded national forest **Lone Pine Campground** on the way to Mt. Whitney, with water, picnic tables, and stoves (but not showers) for $12 per night—with the extra free thrill of waking up at dawn to see Mt. Whitney bathed in the orange glow of morning's first light. Or try the **Whitney Portal Campground,** $14. For a reservation at either, call 877/444-6777 or see www.reserveusa.com. If you feel lucky, try the **Whitney Portal Trailhead** campground—just 11 walk-in sites, one-night limit—near the trailhead to the top of California. (Trailers are not recommended on this narrow, steep road). In addition to other nearby U.S. Forest Service campgrounds, other camping possibilities include the county's **Portagee Joe** campground just outside town (off Whitney Portal Rd.); the **Diaz Lake county campground** south of Lone Pine, with 300 campsites; and the BLM's free **Tuttle Creek Campground.** For a list of available L.A. Dept. of Water and Power campsites, see www.395.com/dwpland.htm.

Lone Pine and Vicinity

Lone Pine, below Mt. Whitney, has abundant motels, restaurants, and other services. It also has a Hollywood past and presence. More than 300 movies have been shot near here, including *High Sierra, Gunga Din,* and *Star Trek V.* Movie stars and their antics are also an important part of local lore. Stop by the **Indian Trading Post,** 137 S. Main St., 760/876-4641, to see "the wall"—even movie stars have tried to buy it, or steal it, for the priceless autographs. For more information about the area's cinematic history, pick up *The Movies of Lone Pine* brochure at the chamber of commerce, or point your browser to the chamber's website. To really celebrate, show up in October for the annual **Lone Pine Film Festival,** www.lonepinefilmfestival.org, a three-day celebration of eastern Sierra Nevada cinema—from Fatty Arbuckle in the 1920 classic *The Round Up* to Hopalong Cassidy and his trusty steed Topper.

About 20 miles southeast of Lone Pine via Hwy. 136 and (rough-dirt) Cerro Gordo Rd. is the tumbled-down silver-mining ghost town of **Cerro Gordo,** which overlooks the Owens Valley. The town is now being slowly resurrected and offers a small museum, guided town tours, and area hiking, mountain biking, horseback riding, and rockhounding. For day use, a $5 donation is requested. Accommodations—basic bunkhouse rooms with shared baths, and eventually rooms in the 1868 Belshaw House and the restored American Hotel—start in the Expensive category. Call ahead before you come for any reason, 888/446-7888, since the town is privately owned.

For more information about Lone Pine and vicinity, including events and activities sponsored by the Inyo County Arts Council, contact the **Lone Pine Chamber of Commerce,** 126 S. Main St., 760/876-4444 or 877/253-8981, www.lonepinechamber.org. Especially fun, and free, is the chamber's *Southern Inyo Self-Guided Tours* brochure (with map). If available, also pick up the *Campground Guide* put out by the Inyo County Parks and Recreation office. For wilderness permits and other national forest recreation information, contact the **Mt. Whitney Ranger Station** (see Hiking Mt. Whitney above) or the excellent **Eastern Sierra Interagency Visitor Center** just south of Lone Pine at the Hwy. 395/Hwy. 136 junction, 760/876-6222, which offers in-depth information about hikes, sights, and practicalities; wonderful books; and public bathrooms and picnic area.

Staying and Eating in Lone Pine

Most people who climb Mt. Whitney also spend some time in Lone Pine. For an overnight, sometimes the best deal around is the **Mt. Whitney Motel,** 305 N. Main St., 760/876-4207 or 800/845-2362, with pool, a/c, color TV (even a movie channel), and in-room coffee; $50–100. Also open year-round, quite comfortable and reasonable, are the **National 9 Trails Motel,** 633 S. Main, 760/876-5555 ($50–100), and the **Portal Motel,** 425 S. Main, 760/876-5930 ($50–100), both with abundant amenities.

Quite nice and reasonably priced is the **Best Western Frontier Motel,** 1008 S. Main St., 760/876-5571 or 800/231-4071 (in California), fax 760/876-5357. Rooms are attractively furnished, with in-room coffee and refrigerators; some are rather spacious, with in-room Jacuzzis. The attractive grounds include a heated pool. Continental breakfast. $50–100. But don't overlook the **Dow Villa Hotel** and motel at 310 S. Main St., 760/876-5521 or 800/824-9317 (in California), built in the 1920s to house the movie stars; the modern 42-unit motel was added later; $50–100.

For groceries, a good stop is **Joseph's Bi-Rite Market,** 1195 Main (at Mountain View), open daily 8:30 A.M.–9 P.M. The **Frosty Stop,** 701 S. Main, 760/876-5000, has the best cheeseburgers around. **Bo-Bo's Bonanza** (also known as the Bonanza Restaurant), 104 N. Main, on the highway at the south end of town, 760/876-4768, is the town's most popular spot for pre- and post-backpack gluttony. For reasonable 24-hour home-style cooking, including wonderful pies, try **the Modern Sierra Cafe,** 446 S. Main, 760/876-5796. Small **Margie's Merry-Go-Round,** 212 S. Main, 760/876-4115, specializes in barbecue and charbroiled steaks (reservations advised).

The place for tiki lamps out on the patio is the family-friendly **Totem Café** next to the Trading Post at 131 S. Main, 760/876-1120, open daily for breakfast, lunch, and dinner and famous for its baby back ribs, steaks, and seafood. Still popular these days is the casual but stylish dinner-only **Seasons Restaurant** at 206 S. Main St., 760/876-8927, where pastas, seafood, chicken, and steaks star on a health-conscious menu. Full bar. Still big news in these parts, at last report, was the sophisticated North African and French **Still Life Café,** originally a roadhouse south of town in Olancha, now a stylish restaurant just north, in Independence. Well worth the drive.

Yosemite

Somewhere in Yosemite National Park there should be a placard that reads: "This is the spot where John Muir fell in love with life" because this *is* the spot. When Muir found Yosemite (from the native *uzumati,* or "grizzly bear"), he found his spiritual home, a place where even this notable traveler was "willing to stay forever in one place like a tree." He also found himself. His passion for this high holy place became the impetus behind a lifelong commitment to preserving this and other great works of wildness. Though even John Muir couldn't save Hetch Hetchy Valley (from the native *hatchhatchie,* or "grass," since seeds were an important native food source) from the water engineers acting on behalf of urban thirst, he did manage to achieve

U.S. National Park protection for most of his beloved Yosemite country.

Despite the chiselings of progress, Yosemite is still a wild wonder of granite, gorges, and silent godlike peaks with names that only hint at their true presence: El Capitan, Half Dome, Royal Arches, Cathedral Rock, Clouds Rest, Three Brothers. Even the trees, the ancient giant sequoias, are larger than life. The sky itself can barely keep the area's grandness down to earth. But the laws of gravity hold true even in Yosemite—witness the waterfalls. Cascading from a height of 2,425 feet, Yosemite Falls is the highest waterfall in North America and the fifth highest in the world. Other park waterfalls—which often seem to shoot out from nowhere, sometimes right off the edge of glacier-scoured hanging valleys—include Yosemite Valley's equally famous Bridalveil, Vernal, and Nevada Falls, plus many of the park's lesser-known liquid gems. The abundance of water in Yosemite also sustains the subtle, flower-rich summer lushness of its meadows, the mountain-fringed and massive Tuolumne Meadows still among the loveliest in the Sierra Nevada.

The pitfalls of John Muir's enthusiastic promotion of Yosemite Valley and vicinity are all too apparent these days. Once word of its wonders got out, people from around the world started coming to see Yosemite for themselves, and what was once a tourist trickle has now become a rampaging torrent. In summer, a virtual city—complete with rush-hour traffic, litter, overflowing garbage cans, smog, juvenile delinquency, and crime—sprawls out across the valley floor. Despite the Park Service's commitment to "de-develop" Yosemite for the sake of saving the place from its own overwhelming popularity, congestion is still the rule. Visitors who relish even some semblance of solitude in the wilds should plan a Yosemite visit in early spring, late fall, or winter—and anytime of year, come on weekdays if at all possible.

Preservation and Popularity

Yosemite National Park is now completing—and revising—its master planning, a process that's been in progress for more than 20 years. Park planners are trying to find practical ways to protect the park's unique character and natural features while managing the large number of visitors who love Yosemite. Park attendance dropped to 3.2 million visitors in 2002—down from an all-time high of 4.2 million in 1996—but that's still a large number of people to accommodate in any wilderness. Now as then, most park visitors are categorized as day-use visitors—and most of that day use takes place in summer, in overcrowded Yosemite Valley.

The politics of park preservation also teeter between civilized and wild. Former Yosemite Park Superintendent David A. Mihalic, appointed in October 1999, was obliged to carry the banner of a master-planning process that had

stalled out due to some ideas not enthusiastically embraced by nearby communities dependent on Yosemite tourism. Among these: plans to close campgrounds and otherwise reduce low-end overnight lodging in overcrowded Yosemite Valley, and a Yosemite Valley mass-transit proposal to limit the number of cars in the park by providing outside-the-park public parking and shuttle bus "staging" areas.

Lawsuits and other political fisticuffs had ensued by the time current Superintendent Michael Tollefson arrived in 2003, and preservation issues were more muddled. Park visitation—and the seasonal pressures of human population in Yosemite Valley—were down sharply, in part due to bad press related to fires, floods, and murders but also due to changing economic and travel patterns and a park entrance fee increase from $5 to $20. The related loss of regional tourism dollars had ratcheted up opposition to many elements of the park's master plan. As a result the mass transit proposal was quickly shelved (the idea is not expected to

Yosemite Falls in spring

A THREATENED NATURAL COMMUNITY

Though native plant and animal life is, to some extent, naturally adapted to forest fires, uncontrolled blazes are nonetheless a hazard to mountain ecosystems. California's success in controlling all types of forest fires, to protect lumber, residential, and recreational lands, has allowed unnatural quantities of tinder-dry forest duff and deadwood to accumulate throughout the Sierra Nevada. As a result, when fires do occur, they're devastating—burning too high and too hot for most fire-adapted trees to survive. And after major mountain fires, not to mention clearcutting and other controversial forestry practices, soil erosion and downslope flooding become serious problems as well.

It would be naive to assume that the wild granite-and-tree spirit of the Sierra Nevada, so far removed from city life, is otherwise unaffected by faraway humanity. Ozone pollution, a byproduct of automobiles and fossil fuel–burning industries, presents a clear and present danger. More than half the trees in Yosemite National Park and more than 90 percent of those in nearby Sequoia and Kings Canyon National Parks have been damaged by high concentrations of ozone in the air. Acid rain and acid snow are other human-caused plant predators, and these now affect the Sierra Nevada's delicate lake ecosystems as well. Due to increasing evidence that salt sprinkled on Sierra highways is at least partially responsible for killing miles of roadside trees, CalTrans has rescinded its "bare pavement policy" in most areas; mountain travelers on winter roads must now stop and put chains on their vehicles much more frequently.

Not all damage to Sierra Nevada forests is directly due to human influence, however. Nearly all pines and cedars in and around Yosemite Valley will eventually die from root rot, while tussock moths (now being fought with bacterial sprays) and voracious beetles have taken their toll elsewhere, most successfully attacking forests of trees weakened by drought and pollutants.

be dusted off again for at least a decade), and the notion of building a parking structure in the valley was dropped altogether.

Changes are underway, however, from ongoing meadow restoration and building a new trail network to adding back some of the campgrounds lost to 1996 flooding. Striking in spring 2003 was the spruced-up parking complex, designed by landscape architect Lawrence Halprin, and rebuilt trails at the foot of Yosemite Falls. A variety of valley construction and remodeling projects have been completed, and a new Native American cultural center will soon be among them. A dam on the Merced River will be removed. New shuttle buses have been purchased. The voluntary Yosemite Area Regional Transportation System (YARTS) of shuttle buses has been up and running since May 2000 (for details, see below). Other changes won't happen overnight. Assuming all practical and political differences are eventually resolved, park officials expect full implementation to take 10 or more years.

HIKING AND BACKPACKING

Like its campgrounds, the overall level of activity on Yosemite trails relates directly to the distance traveled from Yosemite Valley. Some of the short, easily accessible trails to the valley's most famous sights can resemble pedestrian freeways in summer and on peak visitor weekends. The best way to avoid the crowds, on any hike, is to start out very early in the morning. Except on the park's shortest strolls, bring water on all excursions.

For casual short-distance hikers, the Park Service's trail map is adequate for getting oriented. For backcountry hiking and backpacking, more detailed maps (including topo maps), a compass, and a good guidebook are advisable. Wilderness permits are required for overnight camping in the Yosemite outback (see below). Those planning an extensive backpacking trip should inquire, too, about access into adjacent and nearby federal wilderness areas—including the Emigrant, Hoover, Ansel Adams, and John Muir wildernesses—also limited by national forest permit. There are many good books of use to Yosemite-area hikers and backpackers. Among the best: the *Tuolumne Meadows* hiking guide by Jeffrey B. Schaffer and Thomas Winnett; Schaffer's *Yosemite National Park;* and *Sierra North* by Thomas Winnett and Jason Winnett, all published by Wilderness Press.

Shorter Trails

Among Yosemite's most popular trails are the easy half-mile, half-hour hikes to Lower Yosemite Fall and to Bridalveil Fall, called Pohono or "puffing wind" by native people. Also fairly easy, and noted for its magnificent view of Half Dome, is the two-mile roundtrip to Mirror Lake (trailhead accessible only by shuttle), though you can make the walk longer by circling the lake. With some assistance, all the paved trails are wheelchair accessible. Along Glacier Point Rd. is the one-mile trail to **Sentinel Dome,** a fairly easy "view" hike, the last 200 yards strenuous. The nearby Taft Point Trail offers great views of El Capitan and Yosemite Falls—mountain climbers' vistas without all that extreme effort. (To avoid doubling back on both trails, see both on a seven-mile loop via the Pohono Trail from Sen-

tinel.) Though often quite crowded, the stroll to the scenic splendor of Glacier Point should not be missed. Near Wawona, it's a half-mile hike uphill from the parking lot to the lower reaches of Chilnualna Fall. For a strenuous hike, keep climbing; several more miles of trail leads to small pools and more cascading waterfall.

Longer Trails

Strenuous but short is the Inspiration Point Trail that starts at the park's **Wawona Tunnel,** offering good views. For a panoramic view of Yosemite Valley, the seven-mile roundtrip hike to **Upper Yosemite Fall** starts from Sunnyside Campground—a steep trail with many switchbacks, hot in summer; quite a vigorous workout, allow an entire day. The **Vernal Fall** hike from Happy Isles via the Vernal Fall Mist Trail (closed in winter) is less strenuous but a three-mile, half-day roundtrip nonetheless. It's a seven-mile hike up and back on the Nevada Fall Horse Trail to take in both **Vernal and Nevada falls,** a day's outing for most people.

But unforgettable—and only for the determined and fit—is the 10–12 hour "hike" from

© ROBERT HOLMES/CALTOUR

Half Dome in winter

Happy Isles up the back side of **Half Dome,** a 17-mile roundtrip with hang-on-for-dear-life assistance at the end from steel cables anchored in granite (the cables are usually taken down in mid-October).

Also challenging: the five-mile Four Mile Trail from the valley up to **Glacier Point** (trail closed in winter), easily a full-day roundtrip. Easier but longer is the 8.5-mile, half-day (one way) downhill route from **Glacier Point to Yosemite Valley** via the park's Panorama Trail. (A popular all-day excursion is hiking up via the Four Mile Trail then back down on the Panorama route.) Another option entails starting from Glacier Point and taking the all-day, 13-mile (one way) Pohono Trail hike to Wawona Tunnel—well worth it for the rim-hugging views.

Backcountry

The best way to get away from it all is to head into the Yosemite backcountry for camping, long-distance hiking, and backpacking. Because of the popularity of this option, and to protect the park from overuse, access to each trailhead is by wilderness permit only. Permits are free, and wilderness-conscious camping is permitted anywhere along the trail (beyond a minimum radius away from Yosemite Valley). Reserve Yosemite wilderness permits well in advance—or

take your chances come summer. Half of the season's permits are issued by mail Feb.–May ($5 processing fee), the others are available in person up to 24 hours in advance from visitor centers and ranger stations (free). For advance reservations, write to **Yosemite Wilderness Center,** P.O. Box 545, Yosemite National Park, CA 95389. Call 209/372-0200 for general information, 209/372-0740 for reservations. You can also visit www.nps.gov/yose/wilderness.

OTHER RECREATION

Yosemite manages to offer something for just about everyone. Dedicated people-watchers can have a field day in Yosemite Valley. Guided **horseback rides** (either from Yosemite Valley, Tuolumne Meadows, or Wawona) are available for time periods of two hours, a half-day, or a full day; call 209/372-8348 (Valley), 209/372-8427 (Tuolumne), or 209/375-6502 (Wawona) for information and reservations. **Bike rentals** are available April–Oct. at Curry Village, 209/372-8319, or year-round at Yosemite Lodge, 209/372-1208. A two-hour open-air **tram tour** of Yosemite Valley, leaving from Yosemite Lodge, costs $20.50, and several other tours—to Mariposa Grove, Glacier Point, and elsewhere, as well as a hikers' shuttle to Tuolumne Meadows—also

YOSEMITE MOUNTAINEERING

Yosemite is a natural magnet for rock-climbers, ice-climbers, and mountaineers of every persuasion. The **Yosemite Mountaineering School,** Yosemite National Park, CA 95389, 209/372-8344, www.yosemitepark.com, is the place to leave behind one's fear and scale the heights.

Headquartered in Yosemite Valley with a summers-only outpost on the highway at Tuolumne Meadows, this mountaineers' mountaineering school offers exceptional training and outings for beginners, intermediates, and the expert let's-go-hang-off-the-edge-of-the-world granite-hugging Yosemite subculture. All climbing students must be at least 14 years of age.

Basic and intermediate rock-climbing classes

are offered daily from April to mid-October. Spring and fall classes are held in Yosemite Valley, and summer sessions adjourn to the heights near Tuolumne Meadows. The basic class starts off with ground school followed by some hands-on experience in bouldering and rappelling. Also available are advanced seminars and private guiding, big walls included. (Even amateur mountaineers must be "in reasonably good condition" and need to bring lunch and water.) Reservations are advisable, though drop-ins sometimes find space available. Yosemite Mountaineering also offers backpacking instruction and guided backpack trips, and rents outdoor equipment—the obvious plus backpacks, sleeping bags, and ski mountaineering necessities.

depart from the Lodge. For more information, call the Lodge Tour Desk at 209/372-1240.

Other entertaining diversions include free classes offered spring through autumn and over Thanksgiving and Christmas holidays (painting, photography, sketching), sponsored by the **Art Activity Center** in Yosemite Village. Next to the Valley Visitor Center are the **Museum Gallery,** where bits and pieces of Yosemite's history are on display in rotating exhibits, and the **Indian Cultural Museum,** featuring excellent exhibits on the Miwok and Paiute peoples as well as native arts demonstrations. (Behind the visitors center is a self-guided trail through a reconstructed native village.) Also worth exploring is the revitalized **Happy Isles Nature Center,** complete with nature shop, open daily in summer (through September).

At the park's south end on Hwy. 41 is the **Pioneer Yosemite History Center,** a walk-through collection of historic buildings (self-guiding trail), which includes an introduction to U.S. national parks history. The charming 1878 **Wawona Covered Bridge** spanning the Merced River's south fork is the only covered bridge in the national park system; situated at an elevation of 4,000 feet, the country's "highest" covered bridge; and the oldest still standing in California. In 2000, the Wawona bridge was repaired and restored using historically authentic techniques. For a 10-minute thrill, take a summer-through-September stagecoach ride from the Gray Barn near the covered bridge (fare $3 adults, $2 children). The center's buildings are open daily 9 A.M.–5 P.M., usually from June through Labor Day, but you can wander around outside anytime.

In the same general neighborhood, from summer into early fall, the **Big Trees** open-air tram ride into the Mariposa Grove leads to Grizzly Giant (considered the oldest surviving Sierra big tree) and on to the Mariposa Grove Museum, the old Wawona drive-through tree (now toppled and known as the Fallen Tunnel Tree), and Wawona Point. Tram fare is $8.50 adults, reduced fare for seniors and children.

Just outside the park's south gate near Fish Camp is the **Yosemite Mountain Sugar Pine Railroad,** 56001 Hwy. 41, 559/683-7273, which offers four-mile scenic steam and "Model A"-powered rail rides into Sierra National Forest daily from late March through October (call for winter schedule), $9.50 adults, $4.75 children 3–12. Special Saturday-night moonlight tours include steak dinner late May through early October, $36 adults, $20 children 3–12.

Skiing

Winter in Yosemite is the hot new trend for park visitors, though it's not *really* new, since Badger Pass was California's first ski area. Skiing, snowshoe hiking, ice skating in the rink at Curry Village, and just plain snow play are popular. For those who want to get around and see the sights without too much winter exercise, inquire about open-air snow-cat tours. Ranger-led snowshow tours are popular, with a token equipment maintenance fee.

A half-hour drive up from Yosemite Valley via the park highway then Glacier Point Rd. is **Badger Pass Ski Area,** 209/372-8430 (year-round information), 209/372-1000 (ski conditions and park activities), noted for its emphasis on beginning and intermediate downhill skiing—especially fun for families. Badger Pass features four chairlifts and one cable tow. Skiers with disabilities are welcome at Badger Pass (call for particulars). Babysitting is available in the **Badger Pups Den,** and children can also have a good time participating in the park's various naturalist-led wintertime children's programs. Special Badger Pass events include the 17-km **Nordic Holiday Race** in March, April's **Yosemite Springfest,** and the **Ancient Jocks Race,** for antique skiers (over age 30). The Badger Pass Midweek Ski Package is usually a good deal, but see if the Ski Free offer is still on—one free day's skiing for every night you stay at either the Ahwahnee or Yosemite Lodge. Yosemite's ski season runs from Thanksgiving through Easter Sunday, daily 9 A.M.–4:30 P.M.

The **Yosemite Cross-Country Ski School** at Badger Pass offers telemarking and Nordic ski instruction, overnight ski trips to the Glacier Point Hut, instructional snow-camping trips, and trans-Sierra ski excursions. Use of the groomed track from Badger Pass to Glacier Point and the park's 90 miles of marked cross-country ski trails (map available) is free. (To avoid the parking crunch at Badger, and to enjoy Yosemite's winter views without worrying about the adequacy of one's winter driving skills, take the free park service shuttle from Yosemite Lodge.)

Yosemite boasts two ski huts for cross-country skiers, in the European tradition. Beyond Badger Pass—available only on guided cross-country ski tours—is the hip new **Glacier Point Hut.** With its cathedral ceiling, timber beams, and impressive stone fireplace, the hut stands on the site of the original Glacier Point Hotel as positive testament to the park's recent $3.2 million Glacier Point restoration. In summer, it's a snack bar and gift shop. But in winter, out go the shelves and in go the bunk beds—and voilà, the hut becomes a cozy overnight lodge. Deeper into the wilderness, some nine miles from Badger Pass—the last four miles definitely uphill—is Yosemite's rustic 25-bunk **Ostrander Hut,** built in 1940 of oak and stone, and a favorite destination for intermediate to advanced cross-country skiers. Visitors (selected by lottery) pack in their own food (by tradition, gourmet fare), stoves, and sleeping bags. The cost is $20 per night. For more information, contact: **Ostrander Reservations,** P.O. Box 545, Yosemite, CA 95389, 209/372-2646.

Just outside Yosemite's eastern entrance—and reached after a one- to six-mile uphill ski to Tioga Pass on Hwy. 120, depending on the year's snow levels—is the **Tioga Pass Winter Resort,** P.O. Box 307, Lee Vining, CA 93541, 209/372-4471, where cozy heated log cabins and hearty lodge fare support spectacular back-country skiing into Yosemite's high country.

STAYING IN YOSEMITE
Camping

Why come to God's country if you refuse to introduce yourself? Sleeping under the stars is one way to say hello. Camping possibilities abound in Yosemite—but to come even close to a spiritual rendezvous, it's necessary to get far from those we-brought-along-everything-but-the-kitchen-sink RV encampments that dominate Yosemite Valley. Except for backcountry tent pitching—see Yosemite Hikes and Backpacks

above—camping outside designated campgrounds is not allowed.

Hundreds of Yosemite Valley campsites, almost half of the original 849 sites, were destroyed in the 1997 Merced River floods. Local tourism interests are lobbying hard to get at least 200 campsites added back into Yosemite Valley. Reservations for developed year-round valley campgrounds are advisable from April into November. Most Yosemite National Park campsites can be reserved through the National Park Reservation Service's Yosemite-only number, 800/436-7275, or through the website, http://reservations.nps.gov, up to three months in advance. In the mid-September through May off-season, the maximum campground stay is 30 days, but the summertime limit is seven days for Yosemite Valley campgrounds, 14 days for camping outside the valley. Yosemite also has five group campgrounds, reservable in advance through the National Park Reservation Service.

One problem with camping for any length of time at Yosemite is that campgrounds here have no showers. To get cleaned up, from spring into fall, buy yourself a shower at Curry Village in the valley, at Curry's housekeeping cabin complex, or at the lodges at White Wolf and Tuolumne Meadows in summer.

For those committed to a stay in the valley, the **Lower Pines, Upper Pines,** and **North Pines** campgrounds a mile and a half east of Yosemite Village, are urban zoos in summer, with water and flush toilets, open May through mid-October, $18 per night. Lower Pines is open year-round, Upper Pines is open Apr.–Oct., and North Pines is open May–Oct.

More peaceful in general is the very basic walk-in **Backpackers Camp** behind North Pines, open summer through mid-October, with running water and toilets, $3 per person per night, available without reservation but only to campers carrying wilderness permits, two-night limit. The year-round **Sunnyside** walk-in campground (also known as Camp Four) near Yosemite Lodge is also $3 per person, no reservations, with a seven-day limit in summer. Sunnyside is *the* rock climbers' camp, collecting climbers from around the globe in season. Contention has been hot over the park's plans to close the campground for the construction of Yosemite Lodge accommodations, to replace units lost in disastrous recent flooding. Such a fate seems unlikely now that Sunnyside has been listed on the National Register of Historic Places.

In general, the quantity of peace available while camping out is directly proportional to distance removed from Yosemite Valley. One exception to this rule, though, is the **Tuolumne Meadows Campground** about 55 miles northeast on Tioga Rd., with 314 family campsites, $18 per night. The campground is usually open from early June to mid-October; half the campsites are reservable through the National Park Reservation Service, the others are first-come, first-camped. The walk-in campsites here are strictly for backpackers with wilderness permits, one-night limit, $3 per person.

Both **Porcupine Flat** and **Yosemite Creek Campgrounds** farther west are peaceful and primitive—no drinking water, pit toilets only, but cheap at just $6 per night. The **White Wolf Campground** a few miles west of Yosemite Creek, does have water, and thus a higher price: $10.

The year-round **Hodgdon Meadow Campground** is close to Yosemite's Big Oak Flat entrance on Big Oak Flat Rd., $18 per night for the usual amenities, limited facilities in winter, National Park Reservation Service reservations required through October. The **Crane Flat Campground** is spread out and fairly serene, open late May–Sept., and reservable through the National Park Reservation Service's Yosemite number, 800/436-7275, $15 per night. More remote and more primitive in the same general vicinity is **Tamarack Flat Campground,** reached via Old Big Oak Flat Rd. heading south from Tioga Rd., $6 per night.

Heading south from Yosemite Valley, very nice for a summer stay is the **Bridalveil Creek Campground** halfway to Glacier Point on Glacier Point Rd., with the usual facilities, $10 per night. The **Wawona Campground** on Old Wawona Rd. north of the park's south entrance is open all year, $15.

Ahwahnee Hotel

In a setting like the Yosemite Valley, even a peek out the window of a Motel 6 would be inspirational. But Yosemite's Ahwahnee Hotel, just a stone's throw from Yosemite Fall under the looming presence of the Royal Arches, is *the* place to bed down in Yosemite. The Ahwahnee is as much a part of the changeless Yosemite landscape as the surrounding stone, sky, and water—and quite possibly the most idyllic (and most popular) hotel in all of California.

Open to the public since 1927, except for a short two-year commission as a U.S. Navy hospital during World War II, this plush six-story hotel handcrafted of native stone combines art deco and Native American flourishes with that Yosemite sense of *vastness.* The impressive fireplace in the ruggedly comfortable Great Lounge, the downstairs floor-to-ceiling windows, and the 130-foot-long dining hall with open-raftered ceiling trussed with unpeeled sugar pine logs all reinforce the idea that at the Ahwahnee, the outdoors is welcome even indoors. For an extra taste of the hotel's ambience, try the Awahnee Bar. Other diversions include a swimming pool and—at least for a while—tennis.

Stay either in the palatial stone lodge, with its large, comfortable public rooms, guestrooms, or in the cottages. During a $1.5 million makeover in 1997, rooms were restyled and refurnished, with unique, specially made headboards, armoires, and storage chests. Fabrics, designs, and colors reflect the hotel's original Native American motif. Make reservations early; unless there are cancellations, the hotel will be booked. Reservations are accepted a year and a day in advance; $350.

Even if a stay here is a bit steep for the family budget, do eat at least one meal at the Ahwahnee, 209/372-1489. The dining room looks out on one of the most spectacular settings imaginable, though the food is expensive and usually far from extraordinary. (Dress code at dinner—no jeans—and during most of the year, reservations are a must.) The Sunday buffet breakfast is a good bet. The hotel's "special event" meals, like the annual Bracebridge Dinner at Christmas, are also fun—if you can get tickets (see Events below).

For more information about the Ahwahnee Hotel—and all other concessionaire-operated accommodations at Yosemite—and to make reservations, contact: Yosemite Concession Services, 559/252-4848, TTY 559/255-8345, fax 559/456-0542, www.yosemitepark.com. To contact hotel guests, call 209/372-1407.

Wawona Hotel

Set amid the lush summer meadowlands of one-time Clark Station near the park's southern entrance, the wood frame Wawona Hotel is the Ahwahnee's rustic kissing cousin. Here, at the main hotel and its adjacent wings (known as "cottages"), sit out on the veranda and imagine that the next stagecoach full of tourists will be arriving any minute. Time seems forgotten, judging from some interior touches, too. Rooms (half have private baths) feature brass doorknobs, push-button light switches, steam radiators, and clawfoot bathtubs. Other pleasures here include the swimming pool, golf course, and tennis court—all these in season—and the dining room and lounge. You can go on a guided horseback ride from the stables. Or wander through the **Pioneer Yosemite History Center,** explore the **Mariposa Grove** of big trees nearby, or hike to Chilnualna Falls. Rates are $100–200. Open year-round. For reservations, call 559/252-4848.

Cabins and Motels

At **Curry Village,** two miles east of park headquarters, you can choose from among canvas tent cabins (no food or cooking allowed;); basic back-to-back cabins, with or without private bath ($50–100); or a standard room ($100–150). Summer-only tent cabins are also available at **White Wolf Lodge** on Tioga Rd. and at **Tuolumne Meadows Lodge,** just a half-mile from the visitor center at Tuolumne Meadows. Rates: $50–100.

The rapidly upgrading facilities at **Yosemite Lodge** near the foot of Yosemite Fall, on the site of the U.S. Army Cavalry's Fort Yosemite, now include standard and deluxe motel rooms—deluxe rooms including a deck or patio—and European-style rooms with a central shared bath.

HIGH SIERRA HIKERS' CAMPS

Definitely plan ahead for one of Yosemite's finest pleasures—an overnight or longer "luxury" camping trip with stays at backcountry hikers' **High Sierra Camps**—a trail-connected loop of tent cabins complete with two-person bunks, clean sheets, and showers (breakfast and dinner also included). The trip is not necessarily a piece of cake, though, even without the burden of a heavily laden pack: the route is strenuous, and hikers must cover up to 10 miles of ground each day to get to camp.

Most people start at the Tuolumne Meadows Lodge (one of the "camps") and loop either north or south, but you can start and end elsewhere.

Getting to **Glen Aulin** beside the White Cascades and near Waterwheel Falls (spectacular in spring) involves leaving Tuolumne Meadows into the Grand Canyon of the Tuolumne. The climb to **May Lake** to the southwest offers good views of Mt. Hoffman, and the camp is a good base for climbers. **Sunrise** is in the high-lake Sunrise Lakes country south of Tenaya Lake, a splendid setting. From there, it's downhill back into the forest and **Merced Lake**—then either a further descent to Yosemite Valley alongside the Merced River or a climb up to **Vogelsang,** the highest of the high, rooted in an alpine meadow, the last stop before trekking back to Tuolumne Meadows.

Yosemite's High Sierra Camps are usually open from late June through Labor Day, but the actual dates vary from year to year, depending on snowpack and weather conditions. Not surprisingly, they're immensely popular. Reservations are booked by lottery. Submit your request for an application anytime, either by phone or on the website; applications are mailed out in September for the following year's hiking season. Backpackers following the same camp loop but sleeping under the stars can lug substantially less food and gear by arranging for meals (breakfast and dinner) at the encampments.

For more information, contact: High Sierra Reservations, Yosemite Concession Services, 5410 E. Home Ave., Fresno, CA 93727, 559/454-2002, www.yosemitepark.com.

Yosemite Lodge cabins, damaged in the floods of 1997 along with some of the motel rooms, are temporarily closed and may be relocated. Rates are $50–100.

Accommodations not affiliated with Yosemite Concession Services include **Yosemite West Condominiums** six miles from Badger Pass, 209/372-4240. **The Redwoods,** 8038 Chilnualna Falls Rd., 209/375-6666, reservations only 866/875-8456, www.redwoodsinyosemite.com, are very nice, fully equipped one- to five-bedroom cabins (houses, actually) with picture windows, fireplaces, and cable TV. Quite comfy, laundry facilities available, close to the Merced River. Rates are $150 and up.

Nearby Family Camps

The tradition of city-run family camps offers some rustic options near Yosemite. **Camp Tuolumne** between Groveland and Yosemite's west entrance, 510/981-5140 for info and reservations, has been here since 1922, run by the city of Berkeley. The very basic accommodations include beds in tent cabins with decks (bring your own bedding), three family-style meals included. Rates are $150–200. The city of San Francisco's **Camp Mather** (once a labor camp known as the Hog Ranch), also on Hwy. 120 near Yosemite's west entrance, 415/831-2715 for details, offers 90 cabins with beds and electricity (bring your own bedding). Rates start at about $300 per week, with meals available separately. Also in the same vicinity is **San Jose Family Camp,** 408/277-4666, with 60 tent cabins. Rates are $50–100; three meals included. All are open mid-June to late August. Residents of sponsoring cities pay discounted rates.

Nearby Motels, Lodges, and Hotels

Just outside the park's southern entrance is the very nice cottage-style **Apple Tree Inn,** 1110 Hwy. 41, 559/683-3200 or 888/683-5111, www.appletreeinn-yosemite.com. The 53 cheerful yellow units, a collection of two-story duplexes and triplexes scattered in the woods, feature a fireplace, microwave, refrigerator, coffee maker, and TV with VCR; kitchenettes are available. Also here: an indoor pool, spa, and racquetball court.

Great breakfast buffet; rates $150–250. Another good choice in Fish Camp, a couple miles west, is **The Narrow Gauge Inn,** 48571 Hwy. 41, 559/683-7720 or 888/644-9050, www.narrowgauge-inn.com, especially for fans of railroading nostalgia. Families and "well-behaved pets" welcome, open Apr.–Oct. Rates $100–150.

Also in Fish Camp is the **Tenaya Lodge at Yosemite,** 1122 Hwy. 41, 559/683-6555 or 888/514-2167, www.tenayalodge.com, an outpost of urban-style rusticity with heirloom and antique accents and all the amenities (including workstations and in-room movies and Nintendo). Includes three onsite restaurants, swimming pools, fully equipped fitness center, and full-service spa. Full conference facilities available. $150 and up, with rates usually substantially lower in the spring, fall, and nonholiday winter seasons.

Barely more than a mile from Yosemite and just off Hwy. 41 in Fish Camp is two-story **Karen's Yosemite Bed and Breakfast,** 1144 Railroad Ave., 559/683-4550 or 800/346-1443, where all three rooms have private baths and rates include full breakfast and afternoon tea or refreshments with homemade pastries and such. Rates are $100–150.

Less exciting accommodations options in El Portal include the **Cedar Lodge,** 9966 Hwy. 140, 209/379-2612 ($100–150), and five miles east the **Yosemite View Lodge,** 11136 Hwy. 140, 209/379-2681 ($150–250). For reservations at both, call 888/742-4371 or see www.yosemite-motels.com. Other good choices are available in Mariposa and vicinity—an area overflowing with bed-and-breakfasts these days. Budget travelers of all ages will appreciate the lively HI-USA **Yosemite Bug Hostel, Lodge, & Campgrounds,** 6979 Hwy. 140 in Midpines, 209/966-6666, www.yosemitebug.com, just 25 miles from Yosemite Valley on the way to Mariposa, and just $16 a night ($13 HI) for a dorm-style bunk. Private cabins (private or shared bath) are $50–100; canvas tent cabins are under $50; campsites are $17. The fun and camaraderie center around the great onsite café. Most dinner entrées are under $10, including vegetarian moussaka and pecan-encrusted trout. Both the Bug Brew coffee and Guinness are on tap. The Bug is open year-round, and offers a year-round roster of people's activities too. Excellent choice. At the other end of the scale is the very elegant, very pricey **Chateau du Sureau** farther south in Oakhurst, 559/683-6860, www .chateaudusureau.com ($250 and up), also noted for its very high-end restaurant. Accommodations are also available in Groveland, Coulterville, Jamestown, Sonora, and Columbia. See the Gold Country chapter for some possibilities reasonably close to Yosemite. Another option in summer, for high-country enthusiasts, is staying in Lee Vining (see Mono Lake and Vicinity in this chapter) and entering the park from the east.

EATING IN YOSEMITE

If you're backpacking, camping, staying in tent cabins, or otherwise trying to do Yosemite and vicinity on the cheap, bring your own food. Groceries are available in Yosemite Village at the **Village Store,** open daily 8 A.M.–9 P.M. in summer, just 9 A.M.–7 P.M. otherwise, but it's more expensive to stock up at the park than in a major town en route. (Some groceries are also available, summer into early fall, at White Wolf, Tuolumne Meadows, Crane Flat, and the valley's Housekeeping Camp.)

The **Village Grill** next door to the Village Store is just a snack bar serving basic breakfasts and burgers, the most inexpensive place around. The village's **Degnans Deli,** fast-food stand, and ice cream parlor are other options, but **Degnan's Pasta Palace** is the place to carbo-load.

The **Yosemite Lodge** features a **cafeteria** open for breakfast, lunch, and dinner (they put together box lunches here for picnickers if you remember to order the day before); the new family-friendly **Garden Terrace** restaurant—an all-you-can-eat, serve-yourself buffet with soups, salads, pastas, and hand-carved meats; and the all-new, dinners-only **Mountain Room Restaurant,** a striking rough-sawn-cedar-walled restaurant featuring fantastic views of Yosemite Fall. In addition to steaks, seafood, and poultry, the menu includes pastas, salads, and such things as duck quesadillas.

Curry Village has a **cafeteria** (closed in winter) and a seasonal hamburger deck, coffee and ice cream corners, and the **Terrace Meadow** deck for lunch, pizza, and light dinner. There's also a seasonal snack stand at **Happy Isles.** Both **Tuolumne Meadows Lodge**—there's also a separate grill— and **Whitewolf Lodge** serve meals (breakfast and dinner) until the snow flies. Sandwiches, salads, pizza, and such are available at **Badger Pass Lodge** (open winters only), and in summer, the new **Glacier Point Hut** serves as a snack stand.

TAKE A PHOTOGRAPHY WALK WITH ANSEL ADAMS

Some of the bets things in life are still free, including photography walks in Yosemite National Park with Ansel Adams. OK, not *with* Ansel Adams, but with his spirit, the spirit that infused his spectacular black and white landscape photography. In the 1940s Adams himself offered small Sierra Nevada photography classes. These days staff photographers from Yosemite's Ansel Adams Gallery—originally an art gallery known as Best's Studios, owned by Adams's father-in-law—carry on the tradition, leading shutterbugs on leisurely, two-hour walks that include vantage points made famous in some of the photographer's most noted work.

Photographers of all abilities, with all types of equipment, are welcome on the gallery's free camera walks. Dates and times change seasonally. Reservations are required—space is limited— and can be made no more than 10 days in advance. The photo walks usually begin at the Ansel Adams Gallery, located in Yosemite Village between the visitor center and the post office.

A full schedule of Sierra Nevada photography workshops—from digital imaging, platinum printing, and large format photography to black and white and color photography—is also offered. Daily rates start at about $100. For current details and more information about free camera walks as well as photography workshops, see the gallery website, www.anseladams.com.

For a good breakfast and decent lunch in Yosemite Valley's priciest price range, or for those who simply must dress for dinner (no jeans allowed), try the **Ahwahnee Hotel Dining Room,** 209/372-1488 or 209/372-1489 (dinner reservations), open 7–10:30 A.M. for breakfast, 11:30 am.–3:00 P.M. for lunch, and 5:30–9 P.M. for dinner. (Hours may change slightly from season to season.) Less expensive and more casual is the Victorian-style dining room in the **Wawona Hotel** near the park's southern entrance, open 7:30–10 A.M. for continental and American breakfasts, 11:30–1:30 P.M. for lunch, and 5:30–9 P.M. for dinner. Sunday brunch is a special treat here, 7:30 A.M.–1:30 P.M.

For a truly fine meal, set out for **Erna's Elderberry House** in Oakhurst or other nearby destinations. See the Gold Country chapter and Mono Lake and Vicinity, in this chapter, for more information about restaurants within reasonable reach of Yosemite.

ENTERTAINMENT

Park rangers sponsor a wide variety of guided nature walks and campfire programs year-round (current schedule of events listed in *Yosemite Guide*). Come nightfall, the visitor center auditoriums become center stage for **Yosemite Theater** performing arts programs, including music, films, and live drama like *An Evening with John Muir: A Conversation with a Tramp*—an acclaimed one-man show starring Lee Stetson—and its sequel, *Another Evening with John Muir: Stickeen and Other Fellow Mortals*. Nominal admission.

The stone-and-wood Tudor-style **LeConte Memorial Lodge,** built by the Sierra Club to honor geologist Joseph LeConte and staffed in summer by club members, also marks the northern terminus of the John Muir Trail. The lodge sponsors a variety of free summer programs on natural history, conservation issues, and outdoor adventure, usually several evenings each week, starting at 8 P.M. Also at LeConte: a very good bookstore, including a wide range of Sierra Club titles, books by and about John Muir, and a children's nature literature section. Ask here and at the visitors center about park programs sponsored by the **Yosemite Institute,** a nonprofit organization offering environmental education programs and campouts for schoolchildren and families.

The **Yosemite Association** offers a year-round schedule of natural history and field seminars, everything from Native American basketry, botany, and bird-watching to photography and photo history courses, special hikes and backpacks, and winter ski tours. For more information about the association, see below.

Near the visitor center in Yosemite Village is the **Ansel Adams Gallery,** with a breathtaking collection of prints, posters, postcards, and books commemorating the life's work of Yosemite's most renowned photographer. (John Muir may have described the Sierra Nevada as the "Range of Light," but Ansel Adams managed to capture the same truth without words—on film.) Special activities and events include photography workshops, camera walks, and free screenings of the one-hour documentary film *Ansel Adams: Photographer.* Rent camera equipment here, too.

EVENTS

A mythic event in Yosemite Valley is the annual Christmas season **Bracebridge Dinner** in the Ahwahnee Hotel, the 1927 brainchild of photographer Ansel Adams and cohorts. Modeled after the Yorkshire feast of Squire Bracebridge as portrayed in *The Sketch Book of Geoffrey Crayon, Gent.* by Washington Irving, the three-hour medieval pageant includes a full-dress, seven-course processional English feast of fish, "peacock pie," boar's head, baron of beef, and more, accompanied by music, song, and great merriment. The Lord of Misrule and his pet bear provide still more entertainment. Because of the event's great popularity, there are five dinner seatings these days, but even so, it's almost impossible to get tickets—and those who get them (by lottery) find it quite an expensive experience.

Also incredibly popular is Yosemite's other great holiday tradition, the **New Year's Eve Dinner-Dance.** To attend either event, contact Yosemite Concession Services (see Information and Services below) in November to request ticket-lottery applications. A separate application is necessary for each event. Applications—for the *following* year's festivities—are accepted Dec. 15–Jan. 15.

Other Ahwahnee-centered events include the very popular **Vintners' Holidays,** wines-among-the-pines appreciation offered from November into December, and the equally popular **Chefs' Holidays** offered from January into February. During Yosemite's Vintners' Holidays, some 30 California winemakers are invited to bring their best to these special tastings, seminars, and dinners, which are usually scheduled Sun.–Thurs. Chefs' Holidays feature some of California's most innovative chefs sharing their culinary secrets, food demonstrations, and banquet finales. For more information, contact Yosemite Concession Services, www.yosemitepark.com.

Not park-sponsored but a great party nonetheless is the **Strawberry Music Festival,** www.strawberrymusic.com, held at Camp Mather, usually over Memorial Day and Labor Day weekends. Expect a parking lot full of VWs with fading Grateful Dead bumper stickers along with BMWs and Volvos, everyone assembled for a long weekend of folk music, bluegrass, and big-time good times. Plan ahead if you're going—the event often sells out well in advance due to headliners such as Asleep at the Wheel, Natalie MacMaster, and Laurie Lewis. Other Yosemite-centered events are sponsored by surrounding communities, including February's family-friendly **Yosemite Sierra Winterfest** weekend, 559/683-4636, www.sierrawinterfest.com, two days of snowplay, skiing, snowshoeing, and photography and history tours sponsored by the Yosemite Sierra Visitors Bureau.

INFORMATION AND SERVICES

The $20-per-car park entry fee is good for one week, though the fee is only $10 for walk-in and bike-in visitors and those who arrive by bus. Except hiking, backpacking, and free park-sponsored activities, almost everything else in Yosemite—camping and other lodging, food, and park-related services of all kinds—is extra.

Tracking down information about Yosemite is an adventure in itself, considering the number of separate agencies involved. The all-purpose clear-

WASH THOSE PAWS AND TIRES

To safeguard local flora from a fast-spreading botanical plague, the state of California and Yosemite National Park have imposed a quarantine on "host materials" for the pathogen now causing outbreaks of sudden oak death in some 10 Bay Area and northern coastal counties. Firewood (and any other wood pieces), soil, and plants from affected counties are now banned from the park.

Sudden oak death, caused by the pathogen *Phytophthora ramorum,* infects and kills live oaks, black oaks, maples, bay laurel, tan oak, bay laurel, azaleas, and California buckeye—all significant species in Yosemite forest, woodland, and valley areas.

To protect Yosemite from exposure to the bacteria that causes sudden oak death, park visitors who live in affected California areas are asked to take special precautions. Don't bring firewood into the park from infested areas, for example; buy firewood locally instead. Also remove soil and mud from shoes, pets' paws, bikes and bike tires, vehicles, and vehicle tires—a proscription considerably harder to achieve.

inghouse for information about the park itself and about current activities is the National Park Service. For general information, contact: **Yosemite National Park,** 209/372-0200 or 209/372-0264, TTY 209/372-4726, www.nps.gov/yose.

Though the current edition of the *Yosemite Guide* tabloid and a park map are included in the "package" passed out to visitors at all park entrances, the **Yosemite Valley Visitors Center** in Yosemite Village (at the west end of Yosemite Village Mall), 209/372-0200, open 8:30 A.M.–5 P.M., is the place to get oriented. The displays here are good, also the various park-sponsored special programs, but the visitors center also offers maps, hiking and camping information, do-it-yourself trip planning assistance, and wilderness permits. Foreign-language pamphlets and maps are also available.

Next to the visitor center in Yosemite Valley is the park's **Valley Wilderness Center,** 209/372-

0745 for wilderness information, 209/372-0740 for reservations—the essential stop for those seriously setting out to see Yosemite. Other park visitor information centers are at **Big Oak Flat** near Crane Flat, and at **Wawona.**

A good selection of books about Yosemite, including *Yosemite Wildflower Trails* by Dana C. Morgenson, *Birds of Yosemite, Yosemite Nature Notes,* and other titles published by the Yosemite Association, is available in the visitor center bookstore. Worth it, especially for first-time visitors, is the *Yosemite Road Guide,* a key to major sights throughout Yosemite. To get a publications list and/or to obtain books and pamphlets in advance, contact: **Yosemite Association,** 209/379-2646, www.yosemite.org. A portion of the proceeds from an introductory 50-minute video widely available throughout the park, *Tour Yosemite Ahwahnee Style,* supports the Yosemite Association. For information on ongoing park restoration projects—or to make a contribution—contact: **The Yosemite Fund,** 155 Montgomery St., Ste. 1104, San Francisco, CA 94104, 415/434-1782, www.yosemitefund.org.

For information about noncamping accommodations and most other facilities and services available at Yosemite, contact the concessionaire's headquarters: **Yosemite Concession Services,** 5410 E. Home Ave. in Fresno, 559/252-4848, fax 559/456-0542, www.yosemitepark.com. The company's general in-park phone number is 209/372-1000.

For **Yosemite Area Traveller Information,** brought to you by a consortium of surrounding counties also via touch-screen kiosks, message signs, and highway radio advisories, the website is www.yosemite.com.

As an urban outpost in a wilderness setting, Yosemite National Park offers most of the comforts of home. The main post office (open even Saturday mornings) is next to the visitors center in Yosemite Village. There's another at Yosemite Lodge, and a stamp vending machine at Curry Village. To contact the local lost-and-found bureau, call 209/372-4357 or 209/379-1001. For both regular appointments and 24-hour emergency care, the **Yosemite Medical Group,** 209/

372-4637, is located near the Ahwahnee Hotel in Yosemite Village. Other valley services include the laundry facilities at Housekeeping Camp, an auto repair garage, 24-hour tow service, even warm-weather-only dog kennels. The gas station in Yosemite Valley has closed permanently—be sure to gas up outside the park—though gas is available at Wawona, Crane Flat, and (in summer only) Tuolumne Meadows.

GETTING HERE AND AROUND

Coming from most places in Northern California, Hwy. 140 through Merced and Mariposa is usually the best route into Yosemite—especially in winter—though Hwy. 41 from Fresno is more convenient when coming from the south. The only trans-Yosemite road, Hwy. 120 or Tioga Rd., is usually open between Groveland and Yosemite Valley (via New Big Oak Flat Rd.), but the high-country stretch from beyond Crane Flat to Mono Lake and the eastern Sierra Nevada is closed in winter. When driving Yosemite roads in spring, fall, and winter, come prepared for frosty road conditions (use snow tires or chains).

You can't get to Yosemite by train, but **Amtrak,** 800/872-7245, www.amtrak,com, does come close. From the Amtrak stop in Merced, buses take you the rest of the way. Greyhound doesn't serve the park directly either, but family-owned **Yosemite Via,** 300 Grogan Ave. in Merced, 209/384-1315, www.via-adventures.com, makes daily bus trips year-round between Merced (stops include the Greyhound Station) and Yosemite via Mariposa and Midpines, $20 one-way (or $11 from Mariposa). Guided bus tours and overnight packages also available.

More significantly, in the summer peak season a voluntary shuttle bus system along the same Hwy. 140 route has been in place for the benefit of all park visitors since 2000, in keeping with the park's ongoing efforts to welcome Yosemite fans yet discourage the congestion and pollution associated with their cars. The **Yosemite Area Regional Transportation System** (YARTS), 209/388-9589 or 877/989-2787, www.yarts.com, also offers a Hwy. 120 route over Tioga Pass,

SIERRA NEVADA

connecting Mammoth Lakes and Yosemite Valley in summer. Roundtrip fares on the Hwy. 140 Merced-to-Yosemite route are $7 to $20, depending on where you start and end your trip. (From Mariposa to Midpines, the fare is $1, and riders pay the driver directly.) For each adult fare, one child (under 16) rides free. Multiuse (two- or three-day) fares and commuter passes are also available. The YARTS PDF-format route and fare schedules, for both Hwy. 140 and Hwy. 120 E., are available online. Shuttles also connect with The Bus in Merced, 209/384-3111, and Mariposa County Transit buses, 209/966-7433. For those visiting Yosemite entirely without access to a car, contact the California Welcome Center in Merced, 209/384-2791, and other YARTS ticket vendors for details.

Most people drive to Yosemite. Gas stations are available on the way. (Be sure to fill the tank, too, because there are no longer any gas stations in Yosemite Valley.) Yet because of the park's immense popularity, getting around on the park's free **shuttle bus system** is the best option during summer and other "peak" popularity periods; this holds true, to avoid slick snowy and icy roads, for getting to Badger Pass and elsewhere in winter. And the only way to get to Mirror Lakes Junction and Happy Isles is via shuttle. Though the shuttle schedule changes with the seasons, in summer buses run every five minutes 9 A.M.–10 P.M.

The Southern Sierra Nevada

To most California mountain lovers, the "Southern Sierra" means Mt. Whitney and other eastern slope destinations. But the term technically refers to all the range south of Yosemite, including places most accessible from the western slope. Sierra National Forest fills in most of the gaps between Yosemite National Park and Sequoia and Kings Canyon National Parks farther south. The national forest's Bass Lake area directly south of Yosemite is popular for lake and forest recreation, as are both Huntington and Shaver Lakes. Other popular recreation areas include Dinkey Lakes—named after a beloved dog killed by a bear—and Pine Flat Reservoir on the Kings River.

SIERRA NATIONAL FOREST

Truly worth it for back-roaders is the hair-raising climb up from Huntington Lake and over Kaiser Pass via a one-lane paved cowpath—possible only in summer (honk your horn on the hairpin turns) and impossible anytime for trailers or RVs—to reach Mono Hot Springs between Lake Thomas A. Edison and Florence Lake in the morning shadows of the John Muir Wilderness. A summer stay here is almost as memorable as the trip in.

Another don't-miss pleasure is the 90-mile **Sierra Vista Scenic Byway** route up the San Joaquin River Canyon from either Oakhurst or North Fork; some 16 miles of this back-roads tour are on gravel roads. (Free pamphlet available from Sierra National Forest headquarters or area ranger district offices; see below.) Especially worth the slight detours required are the short hike to **Fresno Dome** and a stroll through the 1,500-acre **Nelder Grove** of big trees, which includes the Bull Buck Tree. The true marvels of the Sierra National Forest and vicinity, after all, are its wilderness areas.

Southern Sierra Nevada Wilderness Areas

The spectacular **Ansel Adams Wilderness** nearest to Yosemite (once known as the Minarets Wilderness, then doubled in size and renamed with the passage in 1984 of the California Wilderness Act), headwaters for San Joaquin River's middle and north forks, is known for its glaciers, gorges, and alpine granite. Adjacent just south, crossing the crest into Inyo National Forest and practically surrounding Kings Canyon National Park, is the **John Muir Wilderness,** a wild array of snow-crowned peaks, meadows, and hundreds of lakes.

Immediately north of Huntington Lake is the **Kaiser Wilderness**—red fir and Jeffrey pine forest, the alpine Kaiser Ridge area, and small mountain lakes. To the west of the John Muir

Wilderness and just north of Courtright Reservoir is the **Dinkey Lakes Wilderness,** a 30,000-acre land of lodgepole pines, lakes, meadows, and rocky outcroppings.

Just west of Kings Canyon National Park and south of John Muir is the **Monarch Wilderness,** which stretches into Sequoia National Forest and straddles the Kings River Canyon—very rugged and difficult terrain but not completely unfriendly. Also in Sequoia National Forest are the **Golden Trout** and **Jennie Lakes Wilderness Areas,** the former named for the trout originally found only in the Kern River watershed—the official state fish since 1947—and the latter known for its lakes.

The **South Sierra Wilderness** bordering Golden Trout is shared by both Sequoia and Inyo National Forests—meadows and meandering streams, rolling hills, forested ridges, and high-country granite. The almost-unknown **Domeland Wilderness** just south reaches up to heights of 9,000 feet, though the predominant vegetation is sagebrush and piñon pine. Real road access to most of these areas, especially the Kern River and Kern Plateau, is quite recent. Here there is little granite, so typical of the rest of the Sierra Nevada, but abundant timberland, even magnificent redwoods along the Tule River.

For more information, including national forest and wilderness maps ($6–10 each), and to obtain backcountry wilderness permits, contact local ranger stations or U.S. Forest Service headquarters: **Sierra National Forest,** 1600 Tollhouse Rd. in Clovis, 559/297-0706, www.fs.fed.us/r5/sierra; **Sequoia National Forest,** 900 W. Grand Ave. in Porterville, 559/784-1500, www.fs.fed.us/r5/sequoia; and **Inyo National Forest,** 351 Pacu Ln., Ste. 200 in Bishop, 760/873-2400, www.fs.fed.us/r5/inyo.

Winter Recreation

Just south of Yosemite off Hwy. 41 in Sierra National Forest (access road one mile north of Fish Camp) are the 18 miles of marked **Goat Camp** cross-country ski trails, including a three-mile trek into Yosemite's Mariposa Grove. Some trails are perfect for beginners, others adequate for advanced Nordic skiers. Trail map available; for more information, contact the **Bass Lake Ranger District,** 57003 Rd. 225 in North Fork, 559/877-2218; the **Mariposa Visitor's Bureau,** 209/966-3638; or the **Yosemite/Sierra Visitor's Bureau** in Oakhurst, 559/658-7588.

The **Sierra Summit Mountain Resort** on Hwy. 168 at Huntington Lake, 559/233-2500 or 559/893-3316 (office), 559/233-3330 or 559/893-3311 (snow conditions), www.sierrasummit.com, is designed for expert and advanced skiers, though there are beginner and intermediate runs here, too. Sno-Park snowplay areas, including cross-country ski trails, are also nearby (see this chapter's introduction, above, for more information on the state's Sno-Park program). Other national forest Nordic trails include several at **Hume Lake** near Kings Canyon National Park. To obtain a free trail map, contact Sequoia National Forest's **Hume Lake Ranger Station,** 35860 E. Kings Canyon Rd. in Dunlap, 559/338-2251.

Huntington and Shaver Lakes

Both mountain recreation lakes are popular in summer. When the water level's up, Shaver Lake is a boater's paradise, with some 2,000 surface acres of clear blue water perfect for water-skiing, houseboating, and fishing. From Shaver, head south 12 miles on Rock Creek Rd. for hiking access into the Dinkey Lakes Wilderness. No-frills Huntington Lake (also actually a reservoir) is higher and prettier, particularly popular for sailing and windsurfing, surrounded by resorts, marinas, and summer cabins—also very nice campgrounds and picnic areas. It's a good hike (and five-mile climb) from the D & F Pack Station near here to College Rock. Then again, you can always pack it in—summers only, advance planning advisable—with the help of area pack outfits: **D & F Pack Station,** 559/893-3220 (rental horses also available); **High Sierra Pack Station,** 559/285-7225 (summer) or 559/299-8297 (off-season); **Lost Valley Pack Station,** 559/855-8261 or 559/855-6215.

National forest camping and picnicking are available at both Huntington and Shaver Lakes—both are popular and crowded in summer—and elsewhere throughout Sierra National Forest and at nearby Bass Lake. For more information about the area, contact Sierra National Forest head-quarters (see above); the **Pineridge Ranger District,** 29688 Auberry Rd. in Prather, 559/855-5360; the U.S. Forest Service **Eastwood Visitor Center at Huntington Lake,** 559/893-6611; or see www.sierragatewaymap.com. For advance reservations at popular regional national forest campgrounds—at Shaver, Huntington, and Bass Lake to the north—contact the National Recreation Reservation Service, 800/280-2267, www.reserveusa.com.

Lodging choices are limited (book well ahead) but classic. At Huntington Lake they include the rustic 1922 **Lakeshore Resort** and outlying cabins, 61953 Huntington Lake Rd. at Lakeshore, 559/893-3193, www.lakeshoreresort.com, where cabins start at $77 but most (for two to four people) are $100–150; the 11 still more venerable summers-only **Lakeview Cottages** at Big Creek, 562-6976-5566, from $340 per week; and the vintage cabins, tent cabins, and RV campsites at **Cedar Crest Lodge,** 61011 Cedar Crest Ln., 619/927-6115, where cabins start at $84. Other area options include the **Shaver Lake Lodge,** 44185 Hwy. 168, 559/841-3326. Basic services are available at both lakes; ask around for locally recommended restaurants. For more information about the area, contact the **Shaver Lake Chamber of Commerce,** 41930 Hwy. 168 in Shaver Lake, 559/841-3350, www.shaverlakechamber.com.

Mono Hot Springs and Vicinity

Not much could beat a summer stay at the rustic cobblestone housekeeping cabins ($50–100) at summers-only **Mono Hot Springs Resort and Bathhouse,** 559/325-1710, www.monohot-springs.com with a hot mineral soak available (swimsuits required) a few steps from your front door. Massage is usually available too, the total experience quite tonic for backpackers stumbling down out of the wilderness. Weekends at Mono Hot Springs are often booked well in advance, though, so plan ahead—or plan to call for possible midweek openings and/or cancellations. You can camp nearby at the **Mono Creek Campground.** Groceries and grub are available at the tiny store and post office; drivers, please note, no gas is available here; last gas before Mono is at

After the exciting trip via paved cowpath over Kaiser Pass, a summer stay at rustic Mono Hot Springs is quite refreshing.

Huntington Lake. For a real good time, head on up to the hiker-friendly **Vermilion Valley Resort** on Lake Thomas A. Edison, 559/259-4000, www.edisonlake.com. A popular supply drop and stop along the Pacific Crest Trail, open from late spring to fall, Vermilion Valley features tent cabins and cabin-style motel units (most with kitchens) and a good restaurant, famous for BBQ, vegetarian fare, and Pat's pies. Another exceptional "high" is camping at the U.S. Forest Service campgrounds at nearby **Ward** and **Florence Lakes.** For information on all of these public campgrounds, contact the Forest Service **Pineridge Ranger District** in Prather, 559/855-5360.

SEQUOIA AND KINGS CANYON NATIONAL PARKS

Separate but equal, contiguous Sequoia National Park and Kings Canyon National Park are Yosemite's less-popular redwood country cousins—which means privacy seekers can more easily find what they're looking for here. Connected by the big tree-lined, closed-in-winter Generals Hwy., both parks offer limited winter access—via Hwy. 198 from Visalia, Sequoia's southern entrance, and via Hwy. 180 from Fresno into Kings Canyon's Grant Grove Village area. But because of the ruggedness and haughty height of eastern Sierra Nevada peaks, including Mt. Whitney, no road connects west to east—so vast areas of both parks are inaccessible to casual sightseers, perfect for hiking and backcountry trekking. The Pacific

GIANT SEQUOIA NATIONAL MONUMENT

An ancient yet new presence on the western flanks of Sequoia–Kings Canyon National Park is 328,000-acre Giant Sequoia National Monument, created by executive order of President Bill Clinton in April 2000. This new national monument, created from lands previously included within Sequoia National Forest, protects 34 groves of ancient sequoias. Giant Sequoia National Monument and nearby national parks together encompass the area first identified by naturalist John Muir in 1901 as crucial for adequate protection of these massive trees.

Though these groves were already protected from logging, national monument status ends commercial timber harvest within the groves' respective watersheds. Environmentalists have long contended that logging within the big trees' watersheds is detrimental to their survival. Off-road vehicles and motorcycles are banned from trails in the new national minument, but hiking, backpacking, horseback riding, fishing, river rafting, and camping are all permitted.

Giant Sequoia National Monument, which is managed by Sequoia National Forest, contains two separate units. The **northern section** straddles Hwy. 180 just west of the national parks. Of particular note is **Converse Basin,** logged in the late 1800s and early 1900s. The basin's **Stump Meadow** is something of a big tree graveyard. For maps and other information, contact the **Hume Lake Ranger District** office in Dunlap, 559/338-2251.

The monument's **southern section,** reached from Hwy. 190 east of Porterville, borders the national parks on the south. Highlights include the half-mile **Trail of the 100 Giants** loop and the more challenging **Freeman Creek Trail.** For more information and maps, contact the **Tule River Ranger District** office in Springville, 559/539-2607.

For more information about Giant Sequoia National Monument and surrounding national forest lands, contact headquarters for **Sequoia National Forest,** 900 W. Grand Ave. in Porterville, 559/784-1500, www.fs.fed.us/r5/sequoia.

Crest Trail threads its way north through both parks, and through adjacent wilderness areas, to Yosemite. The new Giant Sequoia National Monument and surrounding areas of Sequoia National Forest definitely augment the area's recreational possibilities.

Seeing and Doing Kings Canyon

The **Grant Grove** trails are easiest, pleasant strolls through Kings Canyon's impressive giant sequoias; most trails start near campgrounds. Also easy are fairly short trails to waterfalls, including the very easy one-mile roundtrip River Trail on the way to Zumwalt Meadow, the longer Hotel Creek Trail, and the lovely Sunset Trail. The Paradise Valley Trail offers a fairly easy day trip to **Mist Falls** and back, a longer (and more challenging) journey to Paradise Valley.

Indeed, Kings Canyon National Park, which includes most of the deep middle and south fork canyons of the Kings River, celebrates the height and majesty of the High Sierra and its rushing waters to the same degree that Sequoia honors its

trees. Most of this park is true wilderness, seemingly custom-made for the customs of backpacking and backcountry camping, with more than 700 miles of trails. The Copper Creek Trail is one of the park's most strenuous day hikes, quickly leading into the Kings Canyon backcountry. Also beginning at Roads End is the 43-mile, one-week roundtrip trek to Rae Lakes, a lake basin as lovely as any in the Sierra Nevada. For suggestions on other good backcountry routes (wilderness permit required), contact park headquarters or any visitor information center.

Boyden Cavern between Grant Grove Village and Cedar Grove on Hwy. 180, 209/736-2708, www.caverntours.com, offers a 45-minute guided tour of crystalline stalactites and stalagmites (fee).

Seeing and Doing Sequoia

No tree cathedral on earth is as awesome as the **Giant Forest** in Sequoia National Park, a silent stand of big trees threaded with some 40 miles of footpaths. Visitor cabins and other high-intensity visitor uses have been relocated, leaving just

SUBTERRANEAN SEQUOIA

Caverns, secret streams, stalactites, and other subterranean surprises are fairly common in (or under) Sequoia National Park. Guided tours of **Crystal Cavern,** just off Generals Highway between the Ash Mountain entrance and Giant Forest, offer an intriguing introduction to what usually remains unseen at Sequoia.

Three different tours are provided by the Sequoia Natural History Association: the 45-minute general tour; the two-hour geology and wildlife tour; and the Wild Cave Tour, featuring four to six hours of off-trail crawling and climbing. Tour tickets, which start at $9 adults, are not sold at the cave entrance; they must be purchased in person at either the Foothill or Lodgepole visitor centers. Call visitor centers or see the national park website for current schedule information. For more cave information, pick up *A Guidebook to the Underground World of Crystal Cave,* published by Sequoia Natural History Association.

Temperature in the cave is a constant 48 degrees F (9 degrees C), so bring a sweater or jacket. No strollers, baby backpacks, or camera tripods are allowed in Crystal Cave. The cave is not wheelchair accessible, and it's a half-mile stroll from the parking lot to the cave. Trailers or RVs longer than 22 feet are not allowed on the winding paved access road.

nature, the 2,700-square-foot **Giant Forest Museum,** and the **Beetle Rock Educational Center** to accommodate human curiosity. Self-guiding nature trails offer an introduction to forest history and features, from delicate meadow flora to towering giant sequoias

The Giant Forest's easy nature trails tell the story of the giant sequoias, but the two-mile Congress Trail loop leads to the famous **General Sherman** and other trees strangely honored with military and political titles (General Lee, Lincoln, McKinley, House, Senate, etc.). The National Park Service stopped naming trees after presidents and politicians after 1940, when what was once General Grant National Park became Kings Canyon National Park, but Sequoia's statesmen still make the news. In 2000, for example,

came word that though General Sherman is the world's largest tree—at 275 feet tall, 83 feet around, and 30 feet in diameter—it's not really all that old. The general was originally declared to be 6,000 years old, an estimate trimmed to 3,500 years in the 1960s. Scientists now believe the gentle giant to be no more than 2,100 or 2,200 years young, and still growing at a constant rate. According to new understandings of forest ecology, even the largest sequoias are middle-aged at most. General Sherman has also been cloned, as part of the national Champion Tree Project. It's hard to say where he'll turn up next.

Sequoia National Park's newest grove is 1,540-acre **Dillonwood** along the Tule River's north fork, donated in 2001 by the Save-the-Redwoods League and newly attached to the park's southernmost reaches.

Tried and true for hikers are some of the longer, more lyrical trail loops: the moderately challenging, six-mile Trail of the Sequoias and Circle Meadow trip through the eastern forest (some of the finest trees) and adjacent meadows; the five-mile Huckleberry Meadow journey into the heart of the redwoods; and the Crescent Meadow and Log Meadow walk around the forest's fringe—since sometimes a view of these giants from afar is the best way to really *see* them. Near Giant Forest Village is the Moro Rock and Soldier's Loop Trail to the impressive granite dome **Moro Rock**—famous for its views of the Kaweah River's grand middle fork canyon.

Hiking in the park's impressive **Mineral King** area—all trails start at an elevation of near 7,500 feet—is only for fit fans of fantastic scenery. Steep but very scenic is the White Chief Trail, a four-mile roundtrip through luscious summer meadow flowers to and from the old White Chief Mine. (Mineral King was named for the Nevada-generated silver mining mania that stormed through the area in the 1870s.) For unforgettable views of the southern Sierra Nevada, take the Monarch Lakes Trail to Sawtooth Pass, a challenging roundtrip of just over four miles. Other worthwhile trails lead through dense red fir forests to Timber Gap; to the alpine granite of Crystal Lake; to sky-high Franklin Lake; and to Eagle and Mosquito lakes.

Most spectacular, though, are Sequoia's high-country trails, some of the finest in the nation and the only way to appreciate the land's grandeur once the park's big trees have been honored. Most popular is the High Sierra Trail, which connects with the John Muir (Pacific Crest) Trail and eventually arrives at hiker-congested Mt. Whitney.

Montecito

Winter is wonderful. Ranger-led snowshoe hikes (snowshoes provided) and cross-country ski trips are offered on winter weekends. Marked ski trails are available throughout Sequoia and Kings Canyon National Parks; pick up a map at any visitor center.

Winter is also a fine time to try one of the area's true treasures. The private, family-owned **Montecito-Sequoia Nordic Ski Center and Family Vacation Camp** between Sequoia and Kings Canyon on Hwy. 180, nine miles south of Grant Grove, offers fabulous access to miles and miles of marked and groomed national forest ski trails (trail map available), warming huts, also private and group lessons and equipment rentals. Fun too in winter are dog sled rides—and the naturally frozen skating rink with Zamboni grooming, where at night you can skate to music under the stars then warm yourself with hot chocolate in front of the bonfire. Teachers, check out the Winter Outdoor Education Camp. Also welcoming are the old-fashioned lodges, offering cozy accommodations (private baths) and very good home-style food (buffet meals). Moonlight photo tours, ski football, igloo building, adult and senior mixers, and endless other activities are also sponsored.

With other seasons come equally impressive programs—spring and fall getaways and special events, weeklong summer camps for families (singles and couples welcome, too), horseshoes, canoeing, tennis, heated pool, and almost anything else you can think of. Rates vary considerably, depending on the season and the dates you select, but for adults start at $69–99 per person per night, meals included. For more information, contact: **Montecito-Sequoia Lodge,** 8000 Generals Hwy., 559/565-3388 or 800/843-8677, www.mslodge.com. For reservations, call 650/967-8612 or 800/227-9900.

Staying and Eating in Sequoia–Kings Canyon

If you'll be camping or backpacking, the best bet is to bring your own food, though small grocery stores and restaurants are available. Campgrounds at Sequoia and Kings Canyon are reservable through the National Park Reservation Service, 800/365-2267, http://reservations.nps.gov. Both parks have a 14-day camping limit (in summer). Among the most popular in Sequoia is **Lodgepole Campground,** an enclave with its own visitor center and organized activities; **Dorst Creek** is a good choice. Popular Kings Canyon campgrounds cluster near Grant Grove: **Azalea, Sunset, Swale,** and **Crystal Springs.** Camping options abound in nearby **Sequoia National Forest,** 559/784-1500, www.fs.fed.us/r5/sequoia. You can also rent remote ("pack in, pack out") U.S. Forest Service cabins, including the hilltop 1933 **Poso Guard Station** near Poso Creek, the **Mountain Home Guard Station,** and the **Frog Meadow Guard Station** managed by the Tule River Ranger District, 559/539-2607, and the **Big Meadow Guard Station** and **Camp 4 1/2 Cabin** managed by the Hume Lake Ranger District, 559/338-3222. Most cabin permits are under $50 per night.

For information and reservations on lodging options in Kings Canyon National Park, contact: **Sequoia–Kings Canyon Park Services Company,** 559/335-5500 or 866/522-6966, www.sequoia-kingscanyon.com. The company's offerings include **Cedar Grove Lodge,** about 30 miles north of Grant Grove at the end of Hwy. 180, a small 18-room lodge open only from late May into September, $100–150; the impressive new 30-room **John Muir Lodge,** offering stylish motel-style rooms and suites in Grant Grove, $150–250, lower in "value" seasons; **Grant Grove Cabins,** which range from tent and rustic ($30 and $55, respectively) to "deluxe" (with electricity, heat, and private bathrooms, $100–150); and **Stony Creek Lodge,** between Giant Forest and Grant Grove in the new Giant Sequoia National Monument, $100–150.

In Sequoia, the attractive timber-and-stone **Wuksachi Lodge,** with 102 rooms in three separate buildings, 559/253-2199 or 888/252-5757, www.visitsequoia.com for information and reservations, has replaced Giant Forest Village as the center of park lodging—so the trampled forest area can take a rest and return to a more natural state. Rooms are quite nice, with contemporary mission-style decor, telephones with data ports, in-room refrigerators, and coffeemakers, though sound-proofing could be better. Wuksachi is six miles north of Giant Forest, offers no TV, and is open year-round. Rates are $150–250, though much lower in the winter/early spring "value season." Very nice casual restaurant, too, serving such things as pasta, vegetarian entrées, and baked trout.

Sequoia's **Bearpaw Meadow High Sierra Camp** offers tent cabins and clean sheets, hot showers, and home-style meals. It's an 11.3-mile hike in (figure anywhere from four to eight hours, depending on your speed). Bearpaw is usually open from some time in June to early September, depending on weather and snowpack. Rates are $160 per person per day for one adult, $75 per day additional adult or child under 12, including breakfast and dinner. Each of six tents accommodates a maximum of three people.Reservations are taken beginning at 7 A.M. January 2 for the following summer, and the camp is usually booked out for the whole season by 7:30 A.M. If you snooze, your only hope is a subsequent cancellation. For more information, call 559/253-2199 or 888/252-5757, or visit www.visitsequoia.com.

If entering the park via Hwy 198, the **Gateway Restaurant and Lodge,** 45978 Sierra Dr. (Hwy. 198) in Three Rivers, 559/561-4133, serves good café-style meals, champagne breakfasts on Saturday and Sunday, and fine dinners. Motel, too. (While in Three Rivers, do stop at **Reimer's Candies,** 42375 Sierra Dr.—a fantasyland of sweets along the Kaweah River.) From Hwy. 180, a particularly cozy choice in winter is the Montecito-Sequoia Lodge and cross-country ski resort about nine miles south of Grant Grove Village; for more information, see Montecito in the Mountains. Other nice area lodgings—these all in three Rivers—include the **Buckeye Tree Lodge,** 559/561-5900; the **Lazy J Ranch Motel,** 559/561-4449; and the **Best Western Holiday Lodge,** 559/561-4119.

Information

The $10-per-car entrance fee is good for one week, in either park. (If you walk, cycle, or arrive by motorcycle or bus, it's $5.) For more information, contact: **Sequoia and Kings Canyon National Parks,** Ash Mountain, 47050 Generals Hwy. in Three Rivers, 559/565-3341 or 559/335-2856, www.nps.gov/seki. For road and weather information, call 559/565-3341, then press 4 (message updated after 9 A.M. daily). Informational brochures, maps, and other information are available in foreign languages at the visitor centers. The park newspaper, *Sequoia Bark,* provides current information on activities, events, and services. Bicycles aren't allowed on park trails. Also, RVers should note that Hwy. 180 from Fresno is the best route in. Generals Highway from Hwy. 198 to Giant Forest is narrow and steep; trailers and vehicles longer than 15 feet are advised not to travel beyond Potwisha Campground during business hours on summer weekends and holidays.

For area natural history, contact the **Sequoia Natural History Association** in Three Rivers, 559/565-3759, www.sequoiahistory.org, which sponsors a variety of activities and programs, including the **Beetle Rock Education Center,** 559/565-4251, and **Sequoia Field Institute** field trips, seminars, and natural history hikes. The nonprofit association also offers an impressive online roster of books for sale. Stop by the parks' visitor centers for current information—especially regarding trail status—and a good selection of trail maps, guidebooks, and natural history titles. (To obtain complete publications lists in advance, contact the natural history association directly.) The *Kings Canyon Country* hiking guide by Lew & Ginny Clark is worthwhile, and the Sierra Club and Wilderness Press publish various excellent, useful titles. The best overall guide for backpacking in and around the region is *Sierra South: 100 Back-Country Trips* by Thomas Winnett and Jason Winnett.

The **Grant Grove Visitor Center,** 559/565-4307, is the main information stop in Kings Canyon, open daily 9 A.M.–4:30 P.M. Area parks information is also available at the new **Giant**

Forest Museum, 559/565-4480, in Giant Forest Grove. In Sequoia National Park, the former Ash Mountain Visitor Center near the park's southern entrance has been expanded into the **Foothills Visitors Center,** 559/565-3135, still the best stop for books, maps, wilderness permits ($10), and information, along with natural history exhibits. Bear-proof canisters ($3) are available at Sequoia's Wilderness Office, 559/565-3766. Tickets for Crystal Cave are sold here (summer only) and at Lodgepole until 3:45 P.M. The **Lodgepole Visitor Center,** 559/565-3782, is now open year-round, and features history and natural history exhibits.

Gold Country

When James Marshall found flakes of gold in the tailrace of Sutter's sawmill on the American River, hundreds of thousands of fortune hunters—a phenomenal human migration—set sail for California. Some came by boat, making either the brutal voyage around South America or a shorter two-leg sailing involving a treacherous overland crossing at the Isthmus of Panama. Others chose to lurch across the North American plains in landlubbing prairie schooners. The money-hungry hordes who soon arrived swept aside everything—native populations, land, vegetation, animals—that stood between them and the possibility of overnight wealth. The California gold rush was largely responsible for the Americanization of the West.

Though the region's native peoples were obliterated by the gold rush, the wildness of the life and land they loved lived on through a colorful cast of characters who came pouring in from around the world. In search of adventure, freedom, and overnight wealth, the stampeding gold seekers also unwittingly created a new collective cultural identity; without the old social restraints that once bound them, men and women in the gold camps made up new rules. From principled bandits like Black Bart and Joaquin Murrieta to literary scalawags like Mark Twain, from the gambling Madame Moustache to the railroad barons who controlled

Empire Mine State Historic Park, Grass Valley

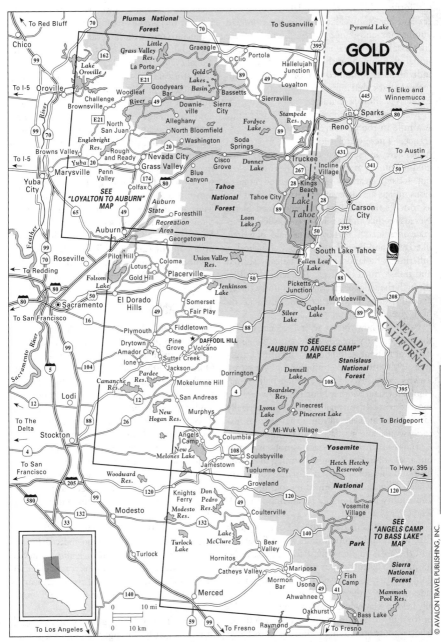

GOLD
COUNTRY

GOLD COUNTRY

California politics, from scandalous Lola Montez and her "spider dancing" to her innocent young song-and-dance protégé Lotta Crabtree (the first U.S. entertainer ever to become a millionaire)—somehow these and other creative individualists combined into one great psychological spark that became the essence of the modern California character.

Mark Twain wryly observed that "a gold mine is a hole in the ground with a liar at the entrance." There were, and still are, many gold mines here, and some say there's at least as much gold remaining in the ground as has been taken out. Today, recreational goldpanners and more serious miners are increasingly common. And just as tourists flooded into the gold-laced Sierra Nevada foothills in the mid- to late 1800s (the literate ones lured in part by the tall tales of writers like Twain and Bret Harte), so they come today, inheritors of a landscape systematically scarred and transformed by greed. But while strolling through the relics of an era, gold country travelers can witness the evidence that some scars do heal, given a century or two.

No matter how you go, several separate trips to the gold country are advisable, since the abundance of museums, old hotels, and other attractions is almost overwhelming on one long trip. Towns along Hwy. 49, the much-ballyhooed "Golden Chain Mother Lode Highway," are the most touristy. If you're allergic to commercially tainted quaint, keep in mind that there *is* historic, scenic, and actual gold to be mined here.

Travel off the beaten track is not easy without a car or bicycle. If you're planning to explore most of the gold country's major towns on wheels, take the interconnecting old highways and county roads roughly paralleling Hwy. 49 whenever possible.

Bicycle tours of the Mother Lode are great fun; towns and campgrounds aren't far apart, and the area's many scenic back roads are too narrow and harrowing for most autophiles. The gold country also boasts some fine organized rides, including the annual Sierra Century, usually held in May, which winds through 100 miles of foothill wine country and climbs 6,800 feet (shorter route options make the ride accessible to cyclists of all abilities, however). In the June 1998 issue of *Bicycling* magazine, the Sierra Century was named one of the 50 great rides in the United States. For information and to register, contact regional cycling shops.

Historical exploration, gold seeking, hiking, camping, fishing, swimming and tubing, boating, and water-skiing are other popular gold country pursuits. In many areas, with the recent rise of recreation and retirement developments, golf and gold share top billing. River-running offers even more thrills, since most rivers that begin in the Sierra Nevada flow westward—and down through the gold county's foothills on their way to the valley. April and May are usually the "high water" months, though in some years even June is wet and wild. Summer and fall offer a tamer experience. Pick up a copy of *California Whitewater* by Fryar Calhoun and Jim Cassady—a worthwhile investment for fans of the inland wave.

THE LAND

The Mother Lode, or "La Veta Madre," is the name often given to California's gold country, though purists say this generality is incorrect. Only the Southern Mines, those from the Placerville area south, comprise the mythical Mother Lode—the never-found vein from which all foothill gold was thought to derive. The gold territories from Auburn and Grass Valley north to the Oroville area and northeast to Loyalton and Vinton make up the Northern Mines. But "Mother Lode" is still a convenient and poetic name for the entire region of rolling, rounded foothills on the western slope of the Sierra Nevada. Some 135 million years ago, these granite mountains pushed up from the sea, transforming sedimentary and volcanic rock into metamorphic rock. Rich veins of gold, silver, tungsten, and molybdenite formed at the places where ancient rock and the newer, upward-pushing granitic magma connected. Eons of erosion gradually exposed the gold-bearing quartz, freeing the nuggets and flakes later plucked from streams.

For the most part, the gold country's foothill terrain is gently sloping, ranging in elevation from about 1,000 to 3,000 feet. These red-dirt hills and flat-topped rock ridges are defined by gullies and steep ravines carved by year-round rivers and countless seasonal streams. Flowing downslope to the west, the region's major rivers include the Feather, Yuba, American, Bear, Cosumnes, Mokelumne, Stanislaus, Tuolumne, and Merced. Soils are generally poor, and variously volcanic, granitic, or serpentine. Iron, leached out of rock over the ages by rain, creates the soil's reddish color.

Climate

Hot, dry, 100-degree summers lasting well into October are typical for the lower foothill areas, with cooler temperatures at higher elevations. Rain, 20 to 40-plus inches annually, comes from late fall through spring, though Sierra summer storms occasionally bring surprise thundershowers. In winter, snow isn't uncommon down to 2,500 feet, in cold years falling at elevations of 2,000 feet or lower. Fingers of valley fog can creep up through river canyons to the hills in winter, though most of the gold country soaks up the sun on winter days while flatlanders shiver in the bone-chilling mists below.

Flora

The best time to explore the hills of the gold country is spring, particularly March and April, when the wildflowers are (almost) the most colorful characters around. Wild mustard, a European import, grows everywhere, but natives like valley goldfields, yellow monkeyflowers, buttercups, and Mariposa lilies add ephemeral, natural gold to the hillsides. Also abundant are lupine, blue dicks, the poisonous nightshade, larkspur, baby blue-eyes, meadowfoam, shooting stars, pink bell-blossomed manzanita bushes, and the lovely redbud (a shrub related to the common garden pea). Fritillarias are rarer. The native California poppies—the state's flower and the "gold" that once carpeted miles and miles of the great central valley—are among the latest to bloom, popping up along roads and on hillsides in May and June. By the start of summer, once-green flowers usually become fields of gold-brown grass, little more than tinder for wildfires. In the autumn, the searing summer heat softens and the area's golden grasses and blazing fall foliage look like the backdrop of an impressionist painting.

Climbing in elevation—always watch for poison oak in shady areas below 5,000 feet—rangy

PIKE NOT YET BLOWN AWAY

California is still fishing for a solution to the problem of predatory northern pike in Lake Davis near Portola, a nationally noted trout fishing lake. The pesky non-native fish persist despite relentless eradication efforts—from attempts to poison, net, and hook them to trying to blow them away with detonation cord. The harder California has tried to eliminate the pike, the faster the population has grown. By spring 2003 officials from the California Department of Fish and Game (DFG) were afraid the population of the voracious, unbelievably fecund fish would reach one million.

When and how the state's efforts to eliminate the northern pike will conclude is anyone's guess, particularly since the desire is to protect the area ecology, including native salmon and other fisheries. The years-long process of draining the lake has emerged as the most likely final solution, despite the fact that such a move would devastate the local economy.

Not that economic devastation is anything new to Lake Davis and nearby Portola. In 1994 Fish and Game discovered the northern pike, probably planted from nearby Frenchman Lake (where they were eradicated in 1991). Motivated by the fear that if the fish weren't quickly eradicated they would spread into surrounding watersheds, via Big Grizzly Creek, which feeds into the Feather River's middle fork, the DFG decided to poison Lake Davis with rotenone, a "natural" insecticide and fish control agent derived from tropical and subtropical plants. Fish and Game also proposed using Nusyn-Noxfish, a chemical compound containing cancer-causing tricholoroethylene (TCE). Many area citizens—who rely on the water in Lake Davis for drinking and for generating tourism revenues—protested loud and long. The DFG ultimately prevailed, and poisoned Lake Davis in 1997. Yet in June 1999 four fingerling pike were found in the lake; some 25,000 pike were fished from the lake in the following few years. For an update on the DFG's current plans—and to comment—check the website at www.dfg.ca.gov.

---

gray-green foothill pines and small oaks stand guard above fire-resistant chaparral scrub. Even in early summer, the peculiar habit of the California buckeye catches the eye: the round, pear-shaped white "fruits" and desiccated orange-tan leaves announce early dormancy. Usually not far from the maples, oaks, and streamside cottonwoods, alders, and sycamores is the flashy dogwood. Higher up, heat-seeking vegetation eventually bows to forests of pine, fir, and deciduous trees.

Fauna

Black bears (which are either black or cinnamon-colored) aren't unusual, especially near campgrounds, but bobcats and mountain lions are rare. Deer are most abundant in the foothills during winter and spring. Gray foxes slink through the underbrush, seeking cottontails, black-tailed jackrabbits, California gray and ground squirrels, and other smaller mammals for dinner. Skunks are plentiful, as are opossums and raccoons—both usually seen at night. Visitors may not see "pack-rats," but may find their caches of shiny trinkets stashed in logs or tree trunks.

One of the bold busybodies of the bird world, the California or scrub jay seems to enjoy snooping and yammering; the jays comment at length on current events (such as your flat tire or miserly lunch crumbs). Travelers might also spot gregarious yellow-billed magpies and, rarely, chaparral-loving California thrashers. Along steep-walled rock valleys in spring, listen for canyon wrens; to spot them, look for their striking red backs and white throats. They usually live in barren canyons but can also be found near cabins. If you want to see wrentits (found only in California), crawl under chaparral brush and "screep" out loud; they (or curious locals) may come to investigate. Keep an eye out for the rare red-legged frogs near stream pools, lakes, and ponds. Most of the Mother Lode's rivers have abundant rainbow and brown trout, steelhead, and salmon.

HISTORY

The Maidu, who did not value gold, had long used gold-laced quartz for ceremonial purposes and for spear tips, knives, and mortars. They inhabited the northern reaches of the gold country south to the Placerville and Coloma areas. Nearby, in the valley now cradling Coloma Rd., lived the Cullooma. The peaceable, quiet Miwok ranged throughout the broad central foothill area, roughly from El Dorado County south to Mariposa. And fringe groups of Yokut lived in the southern reaches of the Mother Lode.

Like Maidu and Yokut (and many other Native American "tribal" names), *miwok* means "people." The interior Miwok were true foothill people, rarely inhabiting the valley and moving into the mountains only to hunt or escape the summer heat. Untouched by early Spanish missionaries but brutally eliminated by gold rush immigrants, the Miwok numbered only in the hundreds by 1910. Little is known about their civilization, but they were hunters and gatherers who shared the spiritual bent of the Maidu, dressing in unusual costumes for varied rituals and spirit impersonations enacted in half-underground ceremonial dance houses and sweat lodges.

The Rush Is On

In the fall of 1847, Sacramento businessman John Sutter sent his carpenter James Marshall up the American River to build a sawmill for his expanding agricultural empire. The mill was all but complete on January 28, 1848, when Marshall strolled into Sutter's office with the news that there was gold in them thar hills. It was the beginning of the end for Sutter, who lost his work force, then his empire, to the ensuing gold rush. "What a great misfortune was this sudden gold discovery for me!" Sutter wrote in 1857 in *Hutchings' California Magazine.* "Had I succeeded with my mills and manufactories for a few years before the gold was discovered, I should have been the richest citizen on the Pacific shore." He died a poor, unhappy man.

Marshall fared no better, for all the excitement and glory of his discovery. He had little success himself as a miner and tried blacksmithing, growing grapes, lecturing, even selling autographed photos of himself. He died penniless in 1885 at Kelsey, but was buried in Coloma, overlooking the site of his momentous find.

If James Marshall and John Sutter died pau-

pers, others did well. Levi Strauss started his blue jeans empire by manufacturing trousers for miners. Philip Armour started another empire selling meats. And it was in the mines that Leland Stanford (of Stanford University fame) made his first fortune, the foundation for his railroad investments and other political exploits. John Studebaker started manufacturing wheelbarrows, and bandits like Joaquin Murrieta and Black Bart raked it in as highway robbers.

By July 1848, 4,000 feverish miners worked the river above and below Sutter's Mill in Coloma. That winter, shiploads of would-be prospectors, enthralled by the possibility of bringing home some of the "one thousand millions" in gold said to be waiting for them in the Mother Lode, set sail from the eastern U.S.; stories of disasters at sea, disease, Indian attacks, and starvation did nothing to slow the flow.

The '49ers

The main wave of miners, the '49ers, began to pour in the following year. Mostly the young sons of middle-class and well-to-do American families, they were well-educated, could pay the passage to the distant California frontier, and sought adventure as much as wealth. True adventure or not, life in the California goldfields was rough. Most of the year the '49ers labored 12–16 hours a day in icy water, though the century-mark summer heat was scorching. When clothing wore out it was seldom replaced, and these hardscrabblers paid little attention to their health. Meals consisted of beef jerky and stale bread, usually supplemented with copious amounts of hard liquor. Ironically, the miners knew nothing of the medicinal plants and natural tonics that kept the native peoples healthy. Malnutrition, scurvy, cholera, and typhus were common ailments. While a few became millionaires, many returned to their family homes broken men.

A rougher breed, men determined to share the wealth by whatever means available and described by Scotsman Hugo Reid as "vagabonds from every quarter of the globe, scoundrels from nowhere. . . assassins manufactured in Hell for the express purpose of converting highways and byways into theaters of blood," arrived in

California's gold country by the early 1850s. Others in the new gold rush towns, once decent men, sunk to new lows, spurred on by poverty, bad company, and the devil's brew. The opening of the Concord Stage line, which connected the mines to San Francisco, Stockton, Marysville, and other valley cities, kept the hopeful coming.

Respectability, Then Decline

By the peak year of 1852, more than 100,000 miners were tromping through the Sierra Nevada foothills in search of fortune. Towns sprang up overnight near productive finds, each with an almost predictable life cycle. They started as supply towns for serious miners, became drunken boomtowns, gradually gave way to respectability, then collapsed almost overnight upon failure of the mines. But during the 10 major years of California's gold rush, more than $600 million (in 1850 dollars) was carried off from the Mother Lode and the more far-flung Northern Mines—

wealth accumulated more successfully by financiers and merchants than by the hardworking miners themselves, very few of whom ever realized their dreams of riches.

By the late 1850s, along with shipments of goods from the East came the influences of civilization and the possibility of "respectable" family life. That development, plus the emergence of hydraulic and hardrock mining, brought more stable wealth and "community" to the foothills. Fear of wildfires fostered the formation of volunteer fire brigades, local governments, and the construction of solid adobe, stone, and brick-and-iron buildings.

But by the time civilization arrived, the gold rush was all but over. The miners, young men still, began to migrate toward San Francisco, Sacramento, Stockton, and other new cities that had flourished on the profits from gold mining and related commerce. As gold mining declined, so did the foothill towns created by the gold rush. Some were all but abandoned when the last mines closed during World War II; the rest became backwater burgs with declining populations, crumbling old buildings, and weed-grown ruins.

E CLAMPUS VITUS

Members of a gold rush fraternity established in 1857, the Clampers were and are a parody of brotherhoods like the Masons and Odd Fellows. The organization's stated purpose was assisting and comforting orphans and "widders"—especially the latter. In addition to this vital public service, and the many worthwhile community activities the group actually *did* support, Clampers spent most of their time holding drunken initiation ceremonies and thinking up overblown titles to recognize all members' equality. Throughout the gold country, E Clampus Vitus met in their "Halls of Comparative Ovations" (the Latin motto over the door meaning "I believe because it is absurd").

Revived in San Francisco in 1931 by historian Carl Wheat, E Clampus Vitus thrives today, its primary modern mission marking historical sites and otherwise bringing early California history to life. But the order's debauched traditions continue to this day, with drunken annual celebrations still sometimes causing consternation for Sierra City citizenry.

MINING TECHNIQUES

The first gold hunters merely scratched the surface of California's gold country, sloshing through foothill streams and rivers to pan for that telltale color. Later they created their own large-scale erosion. Placer miners scooped up dirt, gravel, and sand, and using broad, finely woven Native American baskets or shallow metal pans like pie tins, swirled the watery slurry round and round, looking for the gold already mined by the forces of nature. ("Bars," on the convex side of bends in rivers and creeks, usually yielded rich finds and were the sites of the first mining camps and towns.)

In their search for wealth, the lustful legions whittled and blasted away entire hillsides, dug up and rerouted rivers, and dynamited their way into the earth. Miners quickly discovered they could hit pay dirt faster if they used larger rockers and cradles to process the murky gold-rich slurry. Another early innovation was the "long tom," or small version of the later sluice box, a shallow wooden trough 12 to 24 feet long connected at the lower end to a sieve-covered "ripple-box" where the gold collected. The long tom's upper end was usually inserted into a dam, ditch, or flume, to take advantage of gravity. At the end of the day, miners panned the contents of the ripple-box.

Sluicing meant greater productivity but also required steady supplies of water, not naturally available during summer or autumn. So massive wooden flumes—seen everywhere throughout the gold country today—were built to deliver water to dry areas from year-round mountain streams. Construction of these flumes required considerable capital investment and encouraged the formation of mining companies, then corporations.

Hydraulic Mining

By the early 1850s, foothill rivers and streams had been picked clean. Hydraulic mining, using huge rawhide firehoses and one-ton iron nozzles called "monitors" to blast pressurized water against hillsides, exposed placer gravel and gold but destroyed the land and created muddy runoff that killed streamlife and ruined downstream farmland. (The technique created the weirdly beautiful landscape preserved today at Malakoff Diggins near Nevada City and the scoured rocks near Columbia.) The sediment or "slickens" from big-time gold mining made its way to the lower reaches of both the Sacramento and San Joaquin Rivers and filled in about one-third of San Francisco Bay during a 10-year period. Outraged downstream landowners, including California's powerful railroad lobby, petitioned the courts for relief and won. Hydraulic mining was banned in 1883, marking the first major U.S. political victory on behalf of the environment.

Hardrock Mining

When the surface gold was gone, the search went deeper. Fortune hunters, like monstrous moles, burrowed into hillsides with machinery to bleed ancient veins of gold-bearing quartz. Hardrock mining, with shafts hammered into and under mountains, was another later development. One factor that delayed it was the assumption by early miners that all gold, like placer gold, came from rivers and streams. Also, the dynamite necessary for such massive earthmoving enterprises wasn't invented until 1860. As hardrock mining was only feasible with large infusions of capital, this method and big business arrived hand in hand.

Mining crews working down below with pickaxes and shovels separated the gold-bearing quartz ore from bedrock and hauled it to the surface in mule-driven carts. To crush the rock and free the gold, the mule-powered Mexican *arrastra*, a device similar to a giant mortar with a drag-stone pestle, was first used. More efficient, though, were the deafening stamp mills that loomed up like two-story hotels around gold rush towns. The pistonlike stamps quickly pulverized the stone, then the gold was separated through amalgamation with mercury; at temperatures of 2,600° F, the mercury vaporized and the molten gold was ready for pouring into 80- to 90-pound ingots.

Dredging for Dollars

The effects of later large-scale gold dredging, popular in the 1890s, are all too apparent more than a century later. Gasoline-powered dredges mounted on barges turned river and streambeds upside down and inside out, sucking up loads of river-bottom rock, gravel, and sand for sluicing, then dumping the tailings along creek banks and farther afield, burying entire areas with mounds of rock, choking off natural vegetation, and permanently changing the courses of rivers and creeks. Serious contemporary gold seekers face restrictions unheard of in the past. Small-scale dredging, with portable pumps, is restricted to only a few months in summer, to avoid permanent damage to the fisheries and other creek life.

Nevada City

In this small, sophisticated mountain town near the beloved San Juan Ridge of poet Gary Snyder, ghost-white Victorians cling to the hillsides. Most streets are little more than paved crisscrossing cowpaths, and the creek running along the downtown area blazes with New England color in autumn. Officially populated by only a few thousand these days, Nevada City once competed with Sonora for recognition as California's third-largest city. It was first called Deer Creek Dry Diggins and Caldwell's Upper Store, but after the particularly brutal winter of 1850, the Spanish *nevada* ("snow covered") seemed more fitting. When the state of Nevada stole that name about 15 years later, the town took today's name of Nevada City.

History

Nevada City began as a placer mining camp. But due to only seasonal natural water supplies, local miners soon developed unique mining techniques allowing them to work year-round; the long tom, ground sluice, and hydraulic mining were all Nevada City "firsts." More than $400 million in gold was unearthed in the area.

Bold and brazen women were (and still are) a fact of life in and around the town; the lives of Nevada City's infamous gambler, Eleanor "Madame Moustache" Dumont, as well as precocious Lotta Crabtree and outrageous Lola Montez of Grass Valley, all intersected here. Appropriately enough, the U.S. senator who introduced legislation eventually leading to women's suffrage lived in Nevada City. Other famous Nevada City natives included world-class soprano Emma Nevada and cable car inventor Andrew Hallidie.

Nevada City's Baptist church stands on the site of a joint session of the Congregational Association of California and the San Francisco Presbytery, a meeting that eventually led to the establishment of the University of California. Water barons created by the conglomeration of capital necessary for mining-related water engineering also met here to create Pacific Gas and Electric Company (PG&E), the world's largest utility.

Not so successful was the railway connecting Nevada City and Grass Valley, built in 1901; service on the notoriously unreliable "Never Come, Never Go" railroad stopped for good after a harsh 1926 snowstorm.

SEEING AND DOING NEVADA CITY

Though the town nestles into steep hills, downtown Nevada City, primarily along Broad and Commercial Streets, is fairly level. Start exploring at the **Nevada City Chamber of Commerce,** 132 Main St. (the old office of the South Yuba Canal Company), 530/265-2692 or 800/655-6569, www.nevadacitychamber.com, where you can pick up guides and maps (including the walking tour guide and a terrific area mountain biking guide), almost endless information on arts, entertainment, and New Age happenings, and a copy of the exhaustive *Compleat Pedestrian's Partially Illustrated Guide to Greater Nevada City.* Next door is **Ott's Assay Office,** now an antique store.

Stroll up the hill to Firehouse No. 1, now the small **Nevada County Historical Society Museum,** 214 Main, 530/265-5468. Inside the tall, thin gingerbread you'll find a dusty collection of Donner Party relics, fine Maidu basketry, and the altar from Grass Valley's original Chinatown joss house. Open daily 11 A.M.–4 P.M. in summer, Wed.–Sun. the rest of the year. Small fee. On gaslamp-lit Broad St. is the handsome stone-and-brick **Nevada Theatre,** 401 Broad, 530/265-6161, where Mark Twain launched his career as a lecturer. One of the oldest theaters in the state, it was built in 1865 and renovated a century later. Nearby, you can stroll through the lobby of the green and white **National Hotel,** 211 Broad St., 530/265-4551. Open continuously since 1856, despite a few fires, the National is one of several gold rush hotels claiming to be the state's oldest hostelry. Not content with just that honor, it also claims to be the oldest hotel in continuous operation west of the Rockies. The old **New York**

Hotel at 408 Broad was built in 1853, then rebuilt four years later after burning to the ground. Right next door is the redbrick **Firehouse Number 2,** still in operation as a firehouse.

A quarter mile west on E. Broad lies a stone monolith known locally as Nevada City's first hospital; the area's early Maidu people, believing the sun healed all, climbed atop this impressive sunning rock and nestled into the hollow to take the cure.

Museums

The **Miners Foundry Cultural Center,** 325 Spring St., 530/265-5040, is the town's de facto arts center. It occupies the meandering old Miners Foundry building, built in 1856 to make machinery for the mines and other industries. Part of the building is devoted to a mining museum with historical displays. The center's huge freespan Old Stone Hall features a large pipe organ and a stage, making it a popular venue for local drama and music performances, occasional banquets, and other events. Docent-led tours are available by appointment, but a thorough self-guided-tour pamphlet is always available.

The **Searls Historical Library,** 214 Church St., 530/265-5910, operated by the Nevada County Hisorical Society, houses a curious collection of historical Nevada County manuscripts, books, photographs, and genealogical materials; open Mon.–Sat. 1–4 P.M.

Railroad buffs will enjoy taking the short ride on the narrow-gauge railway of the **Nevada County Traction Company,** 402 Railroad Ave. (next to the Northern Queen Inn), 530/265-0896. A joint project of the Northern Queen Inn and the local historical society, the narrated rail tour winds through woods to the old Chinese cemetery and back. Along the way, guides detail many facets of local history. In summer the depot is open daily; trains depart at noon and 2 P.M. on weekdays, more frequently on weekends. Fare is $8 adults, $5 children. Call for off-season hours and schedule. The new **Nevada County Narrow Gauge Railroad and Transportation Museum** at 5 Kidder Court (off Bost Avenue), 530/470-0902, www.ncngrrmuseum.org, exhibits rolling stock and otherwise tells the story of Nevada City's notorious "Never Come, Never Go" railroad. Dolled-up Engine No. 5 will take your breath away. Also note the Jeffery Steam Automobile on display, another Nevada City original. The museum is open Fri.–Tues. 10 A.M.–4 P.M. in summer and weekends only in winter. Things change, so call before you go. Free, though donations are greatly appreciated.

Wineries

Wine drinkers can sample the wares at the **Nevada City Winery,** 321 Spring St., 530/265-9463, www.ncwinery.com, open daily 11 A.M.–5 P.M. (from noon on Sunday), where award-winning

ELEANOR DUMONT, "MADAME MOUSTACHE"

Eleanor Dumont arrived in Nevada City in 1854, a 25-year-old woman with a vague past and a French accent. Within 10 days of her arrival, she held a gala opening for her new gambling house, the ultimate in respectability by gold camp standards. She was an overnight sensation and fabulously successful. Miners, all dusted off for the occasion, came from far and wide to bask in her genteel presence and lose their hard-earned gold dust.

But, almost as suddenly, her fortune faded. After a business partnership soured and before hardrock mining took hold, she grew restless and drifted out of Nevada City in 1856 into less amiable gold camps. Twenty-one years later she turned up in Eureka, Nevada—a harder, stouter, and older woman nicknamed "Madame Moustache" by a California wit. Dumont's new establishment in Eureka offered entertainments other than gambling, and though the Wild West was fast becoming tamed, mining camps had become Dumont's life.

In September 1879, in the desolate High Sierra town of Bodie, she committed suicide and was buried and forgotten. The last line of her obituary, printed in the 1880 *History of Nevada County, California,* read: "Let her many good qualities invoke leniency in criticising her failings."

zinfandel, cabernet sauvignon, and merlot are the starring attractions. Or savor Penn Valley's **Indian Springs Vineyard** wines at the local tasting room, 303 Broad St., 530/478-1068, www.indianspringsvnyrds.com, open daily 11 A.M.–5 P.M. Half a mile east of downtown up Boulder is **Pioneer Park,** good for Frisbee tossing, picnics, or cooling your toes in the creek.

STAYING IN NEVADA CITY
Camping

Among tent-pitching and RV possibilities near Nevada City is private **Scotts Flat Lake Recreation Area,** 23333 Scotts Flat Rd. (second gate), 530/265-5302 or 530/265-8861. To get there, head five miles east on Hwy. 20, then four miles south on Scotts Flat Road. This very nice campground offers year-round campsites in the pines near the lake, as well as a beach, swimming, fishing, a playground, hot showers, and a coin laundry. Rates are $16–18 for up to four persons. Reservations advisable in summer. Farther east off Hwy. 20 in Washington near the Yuba River is the private **River Rest Resort,** 530/265-4306. The resort offers tent sites, RV sites, and hot showers. Another option is the U.S. Forest Service **White Cloud Campground,** 11.5 miles east on Hwy. 20, open late May–Sept. ($10, no showers). For information, call the Tahoe National Forest headquarters in Nevada City, 530/265-4531.

If you're heading northeast of town via Hwy. 49, basic but clean and pleasant camping is available in the **South Yuba Campground** about a mile from the river in the South Yuba River Recreation Area ($5; contact the BLM office in Folsom, 916/985-4474, for information and map). Or consider an overnight at remote **Malakoff Diggins State Historic Park,** 23579 N. Bloomfield Rd., 530/265-2740. Malakoff is open all year ($10 a night, no showers); cabins are also available for rent at $18 a night. Make reservations through ReserveAmerica, 800/444-7275, www.reserveamerica.com.

Closer to Downieville and Sierra City, camp at **Bullards Bar Reservoir** in the foothills north of North San Juan, accessible via Marysville Rd. just south of Camptonville. For information,

contact the Yuba County Water Agency, 530/692-2166, or Emerald Cove Resort and Marina, 530/692-3200. Campsites at Emerald Cove cost $14 a night plus a $5 reservation fee. The marina can also rent you a houseboat to "camp" on the water in style; rates range anywhere from $550 for three days on a small houseboat in the off-season to around $3,500 for a week onboard a floating palace in peak season.

Meditation Retreat

For a unique stay, try **The Expanding Light,** the nearby Ananda Village meditation retreat of Swami Sri Kriyananda and his followers. Ananda is off Tyler Foote Crossing Rd. (14618 Tyler Foote Rd.) near North San Juan, 530/478-7518 or 800/346-5350, www.expandinglight.org. A wide variety of yoga and personal retreats are available, and surprising choice in accommodations—everything from tent and RV camping to shared cabins, European-style inn rooms (shared baths), and air-conditioned B&B-style rooms with private baths. Sign up for a retreat or call in advance to work out lodging and food arrangements, including possible labor exchange.

Hotel, Motels, and Cabins

Staying at the **National Hotel,** 211 Broad St., 530/265-4551, can be something of a disappointment, considering the hotel's illustrious past. But it's not so bad if you land in a spacious room with balcony. Amenities include a saloon, restaurant, pool, soft beds, and clean Victorian rooms with hand-painted (if tired) old wallpapers. Newly gussied up is the 1853 **U.S. Hotel,** 233-B Broad St., 530/265-7999 or 800/525-4525, www.ushotelbb.com, featuring seven rooms with private baths and full breakfast. Rates are $150–200.

If you're in the area to enjoy the great outdoors—kayaking, rock climbing, mountain biking, or whatever—you'll love the concept behind the **Outside Inn,** 575 E. Broad St., 530/265-2233, www.outsideinn.com. Manager and inveterate outdoorswoman Natalie Karwowski has taken an old motor court–style motel and turned it into an outdoor-lover's home away from home. Each of the 11 rooms has been remodeled in a specific outdoor/sport theme, and Natalie and the staff can tell you all the best local places to pursue your particular passion. Two cabins (one two-bedroom) are also available. Very fun, and a good value. Pets and kids OK. Rooms are $50–100, cool cabins $100–150. Other cabin possibilities include the **Nevada City Inn,** 760 Zion St., 530/265-2253 or 800/977-8884, www.nevadacityinn.com, which offers seven Victorian cottages and 27 guest rooms. Rates are $100–200.

The **Northern Queen Inn,** 400 Railroad Ave., 530/265-5824 or 800/226-3090, www.northernqueeninn.com, offers modern and clean motel rooms as well as cottage units, all on 34 wooded acres. Amenities include a pool, spa, restaurant, and an affiliated **narrow-gauge railroad.** Rooms are $50–100, cottages $100–150. For more information on the railroad, contact **Nevada County Traction Company,** 402 Railroad Ave., 530/265-0896.

Historic Bed-and-Breakfasts

Most B&Bs require a two-night minimum stay. Some charge higher holiday rates. **Grandmere's Inn,** 449 Broad St., 530/265-4660, www.grandmeresinn.com, is generally considered Nevada City's downtown showplace inn. This grand dame Colonial Revival was built in 1856 by former U.S. senator Aaron Sargent and his wife, Ellen. He was a political mover and shaker also involved in establishing the transcontinental railroad. She was a suffragette and an early champion of women's rights; Susan B. Anthony and other feminists were guests here. That her husband authored the U.S. legislation that eventually allowed women to vote seems no coincidence. Dignified still, the house today only hints at its past. The three rooms and three suites are homey in an elegant country style, and some are quite spacious. All have private baths and luxurious touches. Full breakfast served downstairs. Rooms and suites are $150–250.

Nearby is **The Parsonage Bed & Breakfast Inn,** 427 Broad St., 530/265-9478 or 877/265-9499, www.theparsonage.net, once parsonage of the Nevada City Methodist Church. The historical emphasis only begins there, however, since innkeeper Deborah Dane is the great-granddaughter of California pioneer (and Mark Twain's editor) Ezra Dane. The Parsonage is proper, like a living museum, from the tasteful selection of family antiques and other period pieces to the line-dried and handpressed linens. It's peaceful here yet far from stuffy. All six rooms have private baths; the two toward the back of the house also have an extra sofa bed or daybed. Full breakfast is served in the formal dining room or, weather permitting, out front on the veranda. Rates are $110–125.

The 1856 **Emma Nevada House,** 528 E. Broad St., 530/265-4415 or 800/916-3662, www.emmanevadahouse.com, is the childhood home of opera star Emma Nevada—painstakingly restored and transformed into a romantic six-room inn; all rooms feature private baths, two have Jacuzzis. Scrumptious full breakfast. Rates are $130–200.

Also artistically, architecturally, and historically fascinating, in a more eclectic sense, is the wonderful **Red Castle Inn,** 109 Prospect St. (on the south side of the highway and up the hill; call for directions), 530/265-5135 or 800/761-4766, www.historic-lodgings.com. This towering four-story brick home, painted barn red and dripping with white icicle trim, is one of only two genuine Gothic Revival mansions on the West Coast. And the Red Castle has been in business since 1963—well in advance of America's bed-and-breakfast trend—making this perhaps the oldest U.S. hostelry of its type. Despite apparent propriety and genuine antique treasures—a Bufano cat guards the Gold Room and its Renaissance Revival Victorian bed—this place is friendly and sometimes downright funny, from the antique mannequin arms doing duty as towel racks in the bathroom of the Garden Room to the fishing creels dispensing tissues in the child-scale suites on the former nursery floor. Though it's quite a climb up—the stairs are steep and narrow, and the shared bathroom is down one floor (bathrobes provided)—the fourth-floor garret suite offers the finest possible view of Nevada City from its veranda. The Forest View Room, four floors down and very secluded, with a separate entrance and private garden, is perfect for honeymooners. All rooms come with a private veranda or garden area. And all guests get to experience at least one Red Castle breakfast—a full meal and a feast, everything homemade. (Vegetarians are easily, and happily, accommodated, as is anyone with specific dietary needs.) Most rooms are $120–170.

The **Deer Creek Inn,** on the creek downtown at 116 Nevada St. (at Broad), 530/265-0363 or 800/655-0363, www.deercreekinn.com, is an inviting Queen Anne Victorian with six feminine but unfussy guest rooms with details such as Waverly print wallpaper, private verandas, and private baths (some with clawfoot tubs). Delightful and elegant full breakfast, complimentary wine and hors d'oeuvres every evening. Rates are $150–200.

For a current listing of the region's historic bed-and-breakfasts or a referral, contact **Historic Bed and Breakfast Inns of Grass Valley & Nevada City,** 530/477-6634 or 800/250-5808, www.goldcountryinns.net.

Other Bed-and-Breakfasts

Are you the kind of person who would love to stay at a B&B if you didn't have to happytalk with strangers? Nevada City's **Two Room Inn** might be just the place you've dreamed of. Supremely private, tucked into the gabled "Teddy Bear Castle" right downtown at 431 Broad St., 530/265-3618, the inn offers just two generous rooms—one upstairs, one down—with verandas and views, a shared, well-stocked kitchen, and private outdoor hot tub. Rates are $150–200, with midweek specials sometimes available.

Piety Hill Inn, 523 Sacramento St., 530/265-2245 or 800/443-2245, www.pietyhillcottages.com, consists of restyled motor court-style cottages converted into very nice bed-and-breakfast units decorated in Early American, Victorian, or 1920s furnishings. Some units are small, others are larger two-room suites; the three-bedroom cabin has complete kitchen and other features making it a good choice for families and other large group events. All units include a kitchen or kitchenette; the units in back are quietest. There's a spa in the gazebo out back (open seasonally), plus a small garden area for barbecuing, picnicking, lawn games, or just sitting around. Children are genuinely welcome here; there's room to play outdoors, and a school playground is adjacent. Most cottages are $100–150 with continental breakfast (higher with full breakfast); two cabins are $85.

The eclectic, carefully tended **Flume's End Bed & Breakfast Inn,** 317 S. Pine St. (on Gold Run Creek across the one-car-at-a-time bridge), 530/265-9665 or 800/991-8118, www.flumesend.com, was once a quartz mill, then, until the 1950s, a brothel. Like the gardens and decks, the building is terraced to "fit" the hillside. Down the steep spiral staircase are two rooms (the Garden Room and spectacular "view" Creekside Room) that share a sitting/living room and refrigerator, wet bar, and TV—a good set-up for two couples traveling together. Among other rooms, the Master Bedroom has its own Jacuzzi; the Garrett has a spacious sitting room and bedroom, and a wonderful clawfoot bathtub that soaks up morning sun. The Cottage, perched above the creek near the roadside parking area, comes complete with kitchenette and woodstove. Most rooms are $150–200; the smallish Stained Glass Room, $125.

EATING IN NEVADA CITY
Basics

Find fresh regional produce at the **Nevada City Certified Farmers Market,** held July–Sept. every Tuesday 3–6 P.M., Argall at Zion. Any time of year you'll find yourself wondering: how can a town with barely 3,000 people have so many restaurants, most of them very good? **Cowboy Pizza,** 315 Spring St., 530/265-2334, is the locals' favorite for fast food and quite a find. Cowboy's slogan—"Small children cry for it, mothers ask for it by name"—becomes believable once you pass the "Free Tibet" bumpersticker and open the door. The aroma of garlic is almost overwhelming—garlic blended with traditional gourmet pizza toppings and some very untraditional ones (like Danish feta cheese, spinach, pine nuts, and onions). Pizzas here take a while, so either call ahead or sit down and enjoy some of California's best microbrews (Red Tail, Sierra Nevada, St. Stan's) while studying the oddball collection of decorative cowboy kitsch, from the Gene Autrey: Singing Cowboy poster to the official emblem of Manure Movers of America. For something light, or maybe just a sinful dessert and espresso, try **Cafe Mekka,** 237 Commercial St., 530/478-1517. There are a number of other worthy cafes in town, including **Broad Street Books & Café,** 426 Broad St., 530/265-4204.

Harder to find (not a tourist joint) but worth it for all-American café fare is the **Northridge Inn,** 773 Nevada St., 530/478-0470. On the menu are fabulous burgers and home fries, café standards like BLT and grilled-cheese sandwiches, *real* milkshakes, and more than 100 beers to choose from, including local Nevada City brews. Dinner entrées include barbecued chicken or ribs, fresh trout, and daily specials. The Northridge is a few minutes' drive from downtown, off Uren at the Hwy. 49/20 junction; ask locally for directions.

Back in town and trendier is the **Posh Nosh** pub, 318 Broad St., 530/265-6064, a casual gourmet restaurant with a fine wine and brew selection and an outdoor patio. At lunch, look for huge sandwiches and good pasta dishes. At dinner, you'll be tempted by a variety of steaks (try the delectable house-made steak sauce) and such ambitious delights as chicken breast stuffed with Danish bleu cheese and prosciutto, grilled and topped with sun-dried tomato pesto. Open for lunch daily, and for dinner Wed.–Sun.

Beer lovers, head straight for the **Stonehouse Brewery & Restaurant,** 107 Sacramento St., 530/265-3960, for tasty handcrafted lagers and ales. Open for lunch and dinner daily, the Stonehouse serves upscale pub grub—burgers, sandwiches, salads, pastas, and seafood.

The **Nevada City Bakery Cafe,** 316 Commercial St., 530/470-0298, offers great morning pastries, potent coffee, sandwiches and hot specials for lunch, and creative entrées for dinner. East Indian influences are evident—the eclectic dinner menu includes curry dishes, lamb, chicken, and veggie specials—and the white walls and bright decor provide something of a Mediterranean feel. At lunch, try the stuffed portobello mushroom sandwich. Good wine selection. Sister restaurant to the Downieville Bakery & Café, the Nevada City sibling is open for lunch Tues.–Sun. 11 A.M.–2:30 P.M. and open nightly

for dinner from 5–8:30 P.M. (9:30 P.M. on weekends). The **Country Rose Cafe,** 300 Commercial (at Pine), 530/265-6248, is a country French-style bistro with wonderful lunch specials. (If the weather's nice, ask to sit outside in the garden patio.) The Country Rose features a daily-changing dinner menu with an emphasis on seasonal fresh fish and seafood plus standards like rack of lamb and filet mignon. Open for lunch and dinner Tues.–Sun.

Cirino's, downtown at 309 Broad St., 530/265-2246, is a local institution, famous for its hearty Italian fare. Gold brocade walls and garish red accents liven up the dark wood decor. Cirino's is open Fri.–Sun. for lunch and daily for dinner. Reservations advised. For more down-home cooking, head two miles west of town on Hwy. 49 to **The Willo,** 16898 Hwy. 49, 530/265-9902, an unpretentious restaurant and bar where you grill your thick steak yourself, baked potato and green salad included. Open for dinner only, 5–9 P.M. daily.

Fancier Fare

Nevada City's latest culinary star is **Citronée Bistro & Wine Bar,** 320 Broad St., 530/265-5697, beloved for its sunny, zesty American regional fare where classical French techniques are as apparent as other Mediterranean accents. The menu changes seasonally, specials daily, though expect such delights as braised chuck roast in red wine sauce, black cod with pistachio crust and fruit sherry sauce, and sautéed halibut with curry sauce. Impressive wine list (wine and beer). Open for lunch and dinner (closed Sunday). Reservations strongly suggested.

Peter Selaya's **New Moon Cafe,** 203 York St., 530/265-6399, Nevada City's bright-eyed bistro, is sure to please even citified connoisseurs. Serving imaginative California-style Mediterranean for the most part—such things as grilled duck and smoked salmon—the New Moon also offers lighter choices, including some outstanding vegetarian fare. For an appetizer, try the shiitake mushrooms with cashew garlic butter. For pasta, choose Selaya's "market ravioli," usually exceptional, with different ingredients daily depending upon what's freshest. Also wonderful is the Tuscany salad, with radicchio, Belgian endive, red peppers, and a sundried tomato vinaigrette. And everything's fresh—even the breads and ice cream served here are house-made. Open Tues.–Fri. for lunch and Tues.–Sun. for dinner. Reservations advised.

Romantic creekside atmosphere is the trademark of **Kirby's Creekside Restaurant & Bar,** 101 Broad St., 530/265-3445, one of the best restaurants for miles around. Specializing in international fare—pastas, seafood, steaks, and more—Kirby's is open daily for lunch (brunch on Sunday) and dinner.

A major shock in September 2002 was the devastating fire that destroyed the venerable downtown building that housed Friar Tuck's restaurant and a handful of other businesses. The owners no doubt contemplated escape to some desert island, at least for a few seconds. But given the restaurant's centrality to Nevada City life, no one would allow it. So **Friar Tuck's Restaurant & Bar,** 111 N. Pine St., 530/265-9093, is open again, in newly rebuilt digs. The good friar's bill of fare includes creative seafood and steak variations—such as cedar-planked salmon and Sherwood Forest–style charbroiled New York steak—and is beloved for its fondue, from cheese or meat fondue dinners to chocolate fondue for dessert. Full wine bar; warm brick-and-beam setting. Reservations are wise. Open nightly for dinner at 5 P.M.

ENTERTAINMENT AND EVENTS

Nevada City is more *event* than destination, so some people tend to get bored if they arrive without the right attitude. To get with the program, you must participate. Nevada City's rich local cultural life—besides the rugged Yuba River backcountry, attractive town, and good restaurants—is the main reason for coming here and/or staying a while. For an overview, get a complete listing of current goings-on from the **Nevada County Arts Council** (see Grass Valley) or inquire at the Nevada City chamber office.

Entertainment

For information about year-round local musical events, from pop music and cabaret to the classics—and especially the three-week summer festival in nearby Grass Valley—contact **Music in the Mountains,** 530/265-6173 (business office), or 530/265-6124 or 800/218-2188 (box office), www.musicinthemountains.org. Tickets can also be purchased online. For hot music on the saloon circuit, the place is **Coopers Saloon,** 235 Commercial St., 530/265-0116, serving up everything from blues, jazz, bebop, and swing to bluegrass, electric country, art rock, and California surf tunes.

A variety of first-rate plays—usually including some Shakespeare—are performed at the Miners Foundry or at the Nevada Theatre by the award-winning **Foothill Theatre Company,** 401 Broad St., 530/265-8587 or 888/730-8587, www.foothilltheatre.org, on most Thurs.–Sat. nights during the season. Tickets are in the $12–21 range ($10 on preview nights). The long-running film series at the **Nevada Theatre,** 401 Broad St., 530/265-6161 (theater) or 530/274-3456 (film series information), www.nevadatheatre.com, offers foreign and offbeat movies on Sundays—high local turnout. Also popular for fine film buffs is **The Magic Theatre,** 107 Argall Way, 530/265-8262.

Events

Every January at the Miners Foundry, a **Robert Burns Dinner and Celebration** is sponsored by the Gold Country Celtic Society, featuring Scotch whiskey, haggis, bagpipers and other traditional music, and Romantic verse in honor of Scotland's famed poet (who never slept, slummed, or spoke here). Come to town in February for **Mardi Gras Nevada City** (formerly Joe Cain Days), complete with masquerade ball at the Miners Foundry Cultural Center, in March for the annual **Psychic Fair,** and April for the annual **Teddy Bear Convention.** About 10,000 people line the streets in June for the Father's Day **Tour of Nevada City Bicycle Classic,** 530/265-2692, which draws some of America's best cyclists and Olympic hopefuls.

Come in September for the living-history **Constitution Days Celebration.** The parade, a local tradition since 1967, features such unforgettable highlights as the Ophir Prison Marching Kazoo Band and the Marching Presidents of

BOOKTOWN

There's something distinctly literary about Nevada City and environs, and this has been true since the day Mark Twain took the stage at the Nevada Theatre on Broad Street to speechify. Biggest of local literary bigwigs these days is Gary Snyder, winner of the Pulitzer and the Böllingen poetry prizes. Come in October for the annual **Wordslingers Festival** authors' readings and check out *Wild Duck Review*, the local literary mag, to see who else is appreciated.

People in and around Nevada City are notably well read. It's also true that the area boasts more impressive independent, used, and specialty bookstores and unique library collections than many large cities—at least 30, by most accounts. Which came to town first, books or book lovers, remains an enduring chicken-or-egg mystery, though the phenomenon has clearly been noticed. The Nevada City–Grass Valley area's bookish tendencies have earned the official designation "booktown," one of only several U.S. and a dozen international destinations so honored. Hay-on-Wye in Wales was the first and is still the original booktown, opened in 1961.

Broad Street Books & Espresso Café, 426 Broad St. in Nevada City, 530/265-4204, offers a cuppa joe to go with your travel plans—a broad range of options encouraged here, from local hikes to international escapades. **Mountain House Books,** 418 Broad, 530/265-0241, specializes in Mark Twain, California, and the West, including rare and out-of-print titles. **Brigadoon Books** and **Toad Hall Books,** together at 108 N. Pine St., 530/265-3450, specialize in Scotland, the American West, California, novels, and children's classics, the selection including rare and unique used

books. But there's more, such as the **Original Cannibal Bookshop** tucked into a corner, serving up tongue-in-cheek appreciations such as *To Serve Man: A Cookbook for People.*

You can buy books after hours, on the honor system, at **Moonshine Books,** 108 S. Pine, 530/470-0790. Specializing in used books—literature, art, nature, history, and children's books, as well as metaphysics and spirituality—Moonshine has well-laden shelves out on the front porch. Peruse and choose then slip your cash through the mail slot. Also comfortably New Agey, **Harmony Books,** 231 Broad St., 530/265-9564 offers a metaphysical mix but also impressive sections on California and the gold country. Tiny **Main Street Antiques & Books,** 214 1/2 Main St., serves up some fabulous Americana. Astonishing rarities are surprisingly common at **Mountain House Books,** 418 Broad, 530/265-0241, back in Brigadoon's neighborhood. Across the street is **Gold Cities Book Town,** 421 Broad, 530/265-3490, proof—if any should be needed—that this is indeed a booktown.

Done with Nevada City, you're just warming up. Humongous **Ames Bookstore** in Grass Valley at 309 Neal St. (but sprawling through five buildings), 530/273-9261, is stuffed to the rafters with some 300,000 used books. What's *not* here? **The Book Seller,** 107 Mill St., 530/272-2131, features 75,000 titles and the Children's Cellar, an entire floor of children's books. **Booktown Books,** 11671 Maltman Dr. #2, 530/273-4002, is nine stores in one—the booktown co-op, with shops such as **Lost Town Books,** featuring horse books galore, and **Tomes,** literature, history, and philosophy. Also something different in Grass Valley: **Bud Plant Comic Art,** 13393 Grass Valley Ave., 530/273-2166.

Nevada City. The party also includes a Civil War battle reenactment in Pioneer Park and a big band dance downtown. Nevada City's October bookfest, held at the Miners Foundry, is the **Wordslingers Literary Festival,** www.litalive.org, featuring writers and poets, readings and recitations, book signings and storytelling.

The long-running **Victorian Christmas** celebration takes place here in December (they close down the streets for it), with boutique Christmas

shopping, period costumes, caroling, and sometimes even snow-frosted windows.

INFORMATION AND SERVICES

The **Nevada City Chamber of Commerce,** 132 Main St., 530/265-2692 or 800/655-6569, www.nevadacitychamber.com, is staffed by helpful and friendly folks and offers dozens of pamphlets and promotions. Pick up free publications like the Nevada County Art Council's monthly *Art Matters,* KVMR radio's program guide, and North San Juan's *Local Endeavor: Planetary News Advocating Personal Involvement.* Of particular assistance for visitors are brochures including *Insider's Guide to Parking in Nevada City,* the *Nevada City Walking Tour,* and *Nevada County Calendar of Events.* The post office is at 200 Coyote St. and is open Mon.–Fri. 8:30 A.M.–5 P.M. **Tahoe National Forest headquarters** is at 631 Coyote St. (by the Hwy. 49/20 junction), 530/265-4531, www.fs.fed.us/r5/tahoe; stop by for forestwide recreation and camping information, including maps. The nonprofit **Nevada County Land Trust,** 530/272-5994, www.nevadacountylandtrust.org, offers a variety of area hikes.

Greyhound has abandoned the area, making public transportation to and from the area all but impossible—except for the Amtrak bus connecting to Sacramento's Capitol trains. (For details, see the Sacramento chapter.) You can get to Grass Valley and back on the local **Gold Country Stage** bus, 530/477-0103, with arrivals and departures at the National Hotel (and elsewhere). Basic fees start at $1, longer trips are $2. Call for current details. Rent bikes at **Tour of Nevada City Bicycle Shop,** 457 Sacramento St., 530/265-2187, www.tourofnevadacity.com, which also offers bicycle tours.

To play tourist to the hilt, take a carriage tour with **Nevada City Carriage Company,** 431 Uren, 530/265-8778, boarding in front of the National Hotel and in front of Friar Tuck's. Options include a short saunter downtown ($25 for up to four adults), custom taxi rides to and from dinner, and various tours. One of these— the Carriage House and Stable Tour—heads out to the stunning company stable at the east end of town, home to the company's 20-some draft horses. The carriage house really is something— a 12,000-square-foot replica of a 19th-century gentleman's stable, complete with cobblestone floors and ornate stall dividers. Free walking tours of the carriage house are offered Monday, Friday, and Saturday at 10 A.M. sharp.

North of Nevada City

Six miles north of Nevada City, before the Hwy. 49 South Yuba River crossing and along Rush Creek, is the nation's first wheelchair accessible wilderness trail—**Independence Trail,** constructed *in* a hill-hugging flume, the old Excelsior Canal. You can hike downstream (west) 2.5 miles, with an optional 4.3-mile loop added on, or upstream (east) 2.5 miles. Wheelchair accessibility extends about 1.5 miles in either direction. The trail provides a nice view of the canyon, and along the way you'll see waterfalls and, in spring, wildflowers. There's even a ramp, with seven switchbacks, leading down to a fishing pool. Sequoya Challenge, the same local group that worked to preserve the covered Bridgeport Bridge, bought the land here and sold it back to the state, but continues to repair and maintain the trail. Guided nature walks are occasionally offered. Donations and support are always welcome. For more information, call 530/273-9458

About 7 miles east of Nevada City on Hwy. 20 is the **Rock Creek Nature Study Area,** a small picnic area with pit toilets (no treated water) and a one-mile self-guided nature trail with an explanatory brochure. For details, inquire at the Nevada City chamber office (see above) or contact Tahoe National Forest, 530/265-4531. If you're on the way to Tahoe via Hwy. 20, the mile-long PG&E **Sierra Discovery Trail** loop offers more nature study opportunities. To get there: Just before the I-80 turnoff, turn left onto Boman Lake Rd.

SAN JUAN RIDGE
Yuba River

The Yuba River, called Rio de las Uvas ("River of the Grapes") by the Spanish for the vines woven along its rocky banks, squeezes rugged San Juan Ridge from both sides. During and since the gold rush, the Yuba and its tributaries have yielded more gold than any other U.S. river system. Miners blasted away at the San Juan hillsides during the peak years of greed, when the area's population boomed to 10,000. About $5 million was spent just on the 300 miles of elaborate, interconnecting flumes and canals necessary for hydraulic mining on the ridge. Some estimate that $200 million in gold remains in the earth, but ridge people arm themselves (at least verbally) and go after every new corporate mining proposal. Enough is enough, after all.

Despite the historically recent devastation here, there's a wild, untouched feeling about this stretch of northern mine country—steep, rocky ridges, dramatic gorges, dense pine and oak forests, thick underbrush. A strong spirit never dies. Gary Snyder, California's poet laureate under former Governor Jerry Brown, lives, chops wood, and writes here.

And there is regeneration culturally, too. The **North Columbia Schoolhouse Cultural Center** on San Juan Ridge hosts plays, concerts, and storytelling and folk-music festivals.

North San Juan

A spot in the road worth a wander, North San Juan mixes gold rush memorials with new accomplishments like the lovingly handcrafted **North San Juan School** built by local people and parents. The long-running Ananda commune near North San Juan, fairly well accepted even by redneck mountain folk, is a notable presence. To the southwest (via Pleasant Valley Rd.) is what's left of **French Corral**, the oldest town on San Juan Ridge, named after a mule pen. The 1878 long-distance telephone line from here to French Corral was the state's first, connecting hydraulic mining centers. That service saved lives in the 1880s, when the upstream English Dam broke after heavy rains and siltation; phone calls spread the warning. Other technological "firsts" here were electric arc lamps and the Burleigh drill. The **North San Juan Certified Farmers Market** convenes every Saturday at 29190 Hwy. 49, 9 A.M.–noon.

To the north is **Bullards Bar Reservoir,** a lovely, steep-sided recreation lake with campsites reached from this area via either Moonshine or Marysville Roads. Wandering the narrow back roads from here into the far northern gold camps is only for those with time to get thoroughly lost. Most campsites (at Madrone Cove, Schoolhouse, Dark Day, and Bullards Shoreline campgrounds) are $14; group sites also available. For more campground information, contact the Tahoe National Forest's **Downieville Ranger District** office on Hwy. 49 in Camptonville, 530/288-3231 or 530/478-6253.

If you have the time and inclination, head out in search of 365-acre **Renaissance Vineyard & Winery,** 12585 Rices Crossing in Oregon House (northwest of Nevada City and northeast of Marysville), 800/655-3277, www.renaissance-winery.com, sponsored by the Fellowship of Friends, devotees of P.D. Ouspensky and George Gurdjieff. Renaissance's 1985 Special Select Late Harvest Riesling was ranked among the world's top 10 dessert wines by the *Gault Millau* wine journal, and the 1986 won a gold medal in the 1995 American Wine Competition. The awards have been rolling in. The wide-open hilltop setting is enhanced by the individually terraced vineyard rows. The Renaissance grounds also feature a lovely formal rose garden, a 250-seat theater for symphony and choir performances, and the spectacular fine arts museum, with its ever-changing collection of cultural riches. French arts are the current emphasis—such items as a Louis XVI gilt bronze clock, a rococo Louis XV gilt console table, and Salvator Rosa's 1660 painting *St. Peter Delivered by the Angel*—though past exhibits included Ming Dynasty furniture and European Masters. Tours and tasting are offered by appointment only. Also on the property is **French Bistro** restaurant, which offers gourmet lunches paired with wine tastings. For details and reservations, call 530/692-8231.

Oregon Creek

Just north of the bridge over the Yuba River is the turnoff to the Oregon Creek Day Use Area, nice for picnicking, swimming, and some shallow wading. The area is popular with nude sunbathers. There's a wrong-way covered bridge here, too. When the English Dam upstream failed in the 1880s, the Oregon Creek Covered Bridge broke loose but didn't break up, whirling around instead in the backwater. When workers hitched it back up to the road, they got it backward.

MALAKOFF DIGGINS

North and then east of Nevada City (about 26 miles) is 3,000-acre Malakoff Diggins State Historic Park, an unforgettable, ecologically horrifying, yet strangely seductive monument reminding one that positive thinking may move mountains, but greed can do it too. Here's the proof—a ghoulish moonscape created by 1870s "high-tech" hydraulic mining.

The Malakoff Mine

Hydraulic mining scoured the area into barren, colorful spires haunted by the lonely spirit of Utah's Bryce Canyon. You can wander below San Juan Ridge along 16 miles of trails that cut through otherworldly terrain. The mine pit itself, once an ancient riverbed, is about one square mile in size and 600 feet deep in places; it produced about $5 million in gold. The elements have weathered Malakoff's sharp edges, tinting the exposed rock in soft natural tones. A 1.5-mile-long tunnel here, now buried by mud at the bottom of the pit, was once the world's longest "sluice box," separating gold from the gravel and sludge. But you can explore the much smaller Hiller Tunnel it replaced, off to the left near the entrance to North Bloomfield. Other trails in the area include the Humbug, Rock Creek, and South Yuba Trails, generally easy walks through grassy hills and forests.

The North Bloomfield mining case finally eroded hydraulic mining. Outraged farmers in the valley below banded together in 1873 to protest the monumental quantities of silt that alternately clogged downstream waterways in summer and buried their croplands and communities after winter floods. The town of Marysville was flooded due to mining siltation in 1875, and even San Francisco Bay turned as brown and murky as a cup of coffee. Backed by the Southern Pacific Railroad, a powerful valley landowner, the farmers and flatlanders finally won their war. The Federal Anti-Debris Act—banning sediment dumping, not hydraulic min-

ing per se—was passed in 1883, followed in the next year by a sympathetic California Supreme Court opinion that effectively ended water-nozzle land rape in California. After this, the first major legal victory on behalf of the environment in the U.S., the Malakoff Mine closed.

North Bloomfield

North Bloomfield is a ghost town on the site of old Humbug City, so named and then abandoned by disgusted miners (though rich claims were later found). The town, including its large 1872 schoolhouse outside North Bloomfield proper, is now part and parcel of the park. Old **Cummins Hall** is the park's interpretive center, with an impressive display of simulated gold plus a working hydraulic mine model and other exhibits. The saloon is right next to the drugstore—note the appropriate popular gold rush-era home remedies on display in the window. The old mine office and machine shop, where nuggets were melted down and molded into gold bars weighing up to 500 pounds (a typical month's yield) before transport, are also included in the park. Among the spiffed-up wood-frame homes and shops here is a weathered wooden meeting hall display and monument to the anarchistic men of the mining camps, E Clampus Vitus.

Practicalities

Camp at **Malakoff Diggins State Historic Park,** which features 30 individual sites ($10) plus a group camp, but no showers; sinks with running water in the bathrooms make sponge baths feasible, though. Or stay in one of three restored, original cabins "in town"—rustic, historically evocative, and only $18 per night (reservations required at least five days in advance). To reserve campsites or cabins year-round, contact ReserveAmerica, 800/444-7275, www.reserveamerica.com. The park's interpretive center and other exhibits are open daily 10 A.M.–4 P.M. in summer, but in other seasons you may have to track down the ranger to get in. Come in June for Malakoff's **Homecoming** celebration. For information, call the park at 530/265-2740.

INTO THE SIERRA NEVADA

Past North San Juan and the intriguing dance of light and shadow on the canyon walls, Hwy. 49 starts climbing to the northernmost reaches of the gold country, up past Loyalton. **Camptonville,** just off the highway, with its old-fashioned flower gardens, was once a booming way station. Lester Alan Pelton, the millwright who invented the tangential waterwheel, lived here before moving to Nevada City. Stop by the **North Yuba Ranger Station** (Tahoe National Forest) on the highway here, 530/288-3231 or 530/478-6253, for camping and recreation information. Special in Camptonville is the cowboy continental **J.R.'s Historic Saloon & Restaurant,** 15315 Cleveland Ave. (the town's main street) with creatively prepared soups, salads, and entrées served in a vintage Western saloon. Open for lunch Mon.–Sat., for dinner Wed.–Sat., and for brunch on Sunday.

From Camptonville, head into the mountains on Henness Pass Rd., once an immigrant trail connecting Marysville and Nevada's Comstock Lode. This scenic paved road, though narrow, is much less frightening than the Foote Crossing route from Malakoff. Along the way you can picnic by the river, camp at one of several campgrounds, and explore a few old gold towns. If you keep going, you'll eventually connect up with Hwy. 89 north of Truckee and Lake Tahoe. Or, from Alleghany head back toward Downieville and Sierra City on Ridge, Pliocene Ridge, and Gallaway Roads. Another possibility: take treacherous Mountain Ranch Rd. down into the ravine, then snake up to Goodyear's Bar at the confluence of Goodyear's Creek and the north fork of the Yuba River. Today, just a handful of houses whisper the names of long-gone mining camps like Cutthroat Bar, Hoodoo, and Ranse Doddler.

Alleghany

Alleghany's original Sixteen-to-One Mine, www.origsix.com, was the last old-time working gold mine in California. It closed in the 1960s when a fire almost destroyed the town. Today the mine is again back in business, on a small scale. Or might be. Recent insolvency and a spate of lawsuits have clouded the picture.

Tours of both the historic and present mine operations are available by reservation only in May through Oct. and the museum is open only when tours are scheduled. Contact the **Underground Gold Miners Museum,** 356 Main St., 530/287-3330 for details. Alleghany's other buildings (and collections of decrepit cars) are tucked into terraced hillsides with winding streets.

DOWNIEVILLE

A tidy, tiny brick-and-tin-roof town is squeezed into the cool canyon at the confluence of the Yuba (north fork) and Downie Rivers. Locals sit on storefront porches and watch the tourists go by. Downieville is sleepy these days (with about 350 of Sierra County's total 3,500 souls), but was colorful and crazy during the placer boom days after William Downie and his multiracial mining crew panned upriver riches. Nuggets weighing up to 25 pounds were found here in Slug Canyon, so named because gold just sat atop the stream gravel as if waiting to be found, like coins on a street. A bad, bustling city far from the mainstream, miners had to pay high prices in exchange for their seclusion: eggs were $3 each, whiskey $16 a bottle, and medicinal pills $10 each without advice ($100 with). Prices are a bit more reasonable nowadays. During the gold rush, Downieville was known for its spontaneous sense of justice. One collective citizen action earned national headlines. In 1851, a local dancehall girl fatally stabbed a Scottish miner—in self-defense, she said, since he "pressed his attentions" on her. She was summarily convicted of her crime and lynched from a bridge over the Yuba River—the first woman in California executed by hanging.

Seeing and Doing Downieville

Downieville Heritage Park (aka Lions Park), near the river forks downtown, has picnic tables and a rusty outdoor collection of mining mementos; you can pan for gold here, right in town. In the trees near the jailyard of the **Sierra County Courthouse** is the state's only remaining original gallows, used for the first and last time in 1885 to hang convicted murderer James O'Neal. Rescued from oblivion with help from the state and the county sheriff and his Friends of the Gallows (seriously), the refurbished and restored **Downieville Gallows** is now a state historic monument. You can also stroll past Major Downie's cabin. Imagine other local histories studying headstones at the **Downieville Cemetery.** To get there, head northeast on Upper Main then north at Gold Bluff Road. The 1852 **Downieville Museum,** 330 Main St., 530/289-3423, is a homey hodgepodge of pioneer and mining memorabilia housed in a former Chinese store, gambling hall, and opium den. Open daily in summer 11 A.M.–4 P.M., weekends only at the beginning and end of the travel season. (Free, but donations appreciated.) Downieville's 1852 **Foundry** on Pearl Street, 530/289-1020, boasts a tiny turn-of-the-century Downieville model and logging and mining exhibits. Newspaper hounds take note: the town's *Mountain Messenger* has been published since 1853.

On weekends Downieville is transformed into a mountain biking mecca, thanks in large part to the area's challenging and steep trails (some say "brutal" and "gnarly"), definitely not for beginners. **Downieville Outfitters,** next to the Yuba Theater at 208 Main St., 530/289-0155, www .downievilleoutfitters.com, www.downieville-outfitters.com, is a full-service bike shop (mechanics on duty every day) offering Specialized and custom bikes, guides, and shuttles (climb aboard the Bad Bus). **Yuba Expeditions,** "purveyors of fine singletrack" at 105 Commercial St., 530/289-3010, www.yubaexpeditions.com, also offers bike rentals and repairs, guided rides, and shuttle service. Come in early September for the **Downieville Classic Mountain Bike Festival,** www.downievilleclassic.com, with cross-country and downhill races, river jump, bicycle expo, live music, and more. Nonbikers, come in June for **Downieville Gold Rush Days.**

For more information about Downieville and the rest of Sierra County, contact the **Sierra County Chamber of Commerce,** 800/200-4949, www.sierracounty.org.

Staying in Downieville

Camp at the public U.S. Forest Service **Union Flat Campground** ($16, no showers), about six miles east on Hwy. 49, 530/288-3231, or at any of the Forest Service campgrounds near Sierra City and the Gold Lakes area.

Or backtrack to the Forest Service campgrounds clustered near the highway midway between Camptonville and Downieville. In this area are the **Upper and Lower Carlton Flat camping areas** (one just a mile north of the bridge at Indian Valley, the other on Cal Ida Rd.), **Fiddle Creek, Rocky Rest, Indian Valley,** and **Ramshorn Campgrounds.** All cost $16 a night, except Ramshorn, which is $10. Also in the area are the tiny **Convict Flat** and **Indian Rock picnic areas** (purify water before drinking).

Downieville has a few motels. The pet-friendly **Downieville River Inn & Resort,** 121 River St. (along the river at the end of the street; cross the Nevada Street Bridge, then turn right), 530/289-3308 or 800/696-3308, www.downievilleriverinn.com, is a good bet. The main building is over a century old, and the rest stretch out in all directions. Accommodations include rooms in the country inn, as well as some housekeeping cottages and a small travel trailer with front porch and snow roof. A heated pool is available late spring through early fall. (In winter, it's enough just to keep the pipes from freezing.) Most rates are $75–100, two- and three-bedroom units are $150–200.

Top of the line in local cabin competition is secluded **Sierra Shangri-La,** 12 Jim Crow Canyon Rd., 530/289-3455, www.sierrashangrila.com, 2.5 miles east of Downieville along Hwy. 49. Perched on a rugged rock ledge above the foaming North Yuba River, the resort offers clean cabins with potbellied woodstoves and kitchenettes, some with decks jutting right out over the water, as well as three bed-and-breakfast units in an updated pre-World War II fieldstone lodge. In summer, the cabins rent by the week and are available by the night only if space is available (unlikely); regular visitors usually reserve cabins for summer a year in advance, but call for possible cancellations. The B&B units, however, are often available on limited notice in summer. Great off-season specials. Peak-season daily cabin rates are $100–200 (La Siesta is $80), bed-and-breakfast rooms around $100. If there's no room in

Shangrila, try the **Lure Resort,** 100 Lure Bridge Ln., 530/289-3465 or 800/671-4084, www.lure-resort.com, which offers well-appointed housekeeping cottages and just-the-basics riverfront log "camping cabins" with separate (shared) bathroom/shower building. Most cottages are $85–215, cabins $55.

Eating in Downieville
On the Downie River, the **C & J's Diner,** 322 Main St., 530/289-3616, is the best place around for breakfast—omelettes, homemade muffins, Texas toast (French toast made with thick American-style white bread)—and a darn good choice for hearty lunch and early dinner. Salads, homemade soups, and sandwiches share the bill of fare with dinner entrées such as Southern fried chicken, chicken fried steak, New York steaks, and roast beef. Open Tues.–Sun. for breakfast and lunch, 7 A.M.–2 P.M. and for dinner on weekends only. If you can manage it, try a decadent Downieville Diner dessert, like the Kahlua mocha mousse pie ("as if you've died and gone to chocolate"). Another possibility on Main is **Riverview Pizzeria,** 530/289-3540. For a shot or two to wash it all down, try **Double Shot,** 530/289-0746, where lattes, espresso, and java shakes share top billing with Italian sodas and fruit smoothies.

SIERRA CITY

Another tiny mountain town, Sierra City is the kind of place where fathers play football with their small sons right on the highway on a Saturday morning in autumn. It's also the reputed birthplace of The Ancient and Honorable Order of E Clampus Vitus, hog Latin meaning "from the handshake comes life." In the 19th century, avalanches were the main hazard in Sierra City; crushing snow slides flattened the town in 1852, 1888, 1889, and 1952. Otherwise, the steep rocky cliffs have been kind to the local economy. The Sierra Buttes Mine was richly veined with high-grade gold; one nugget found here weighed 141 pounds.

Old Kentucky Mine
Definitely stop by **Kentucky Mine Park and Museum,** at the Kentucky Mine just north of town. Thanks to the efforts of Sierra County citizenry, the old Kentucky Consolidated Gold Mining Co. hardrock mine is now a beautifully restored historical park, its original machinery still intact. Note the modern amphitheater, then step into the excellent museum (small admission), a rebuilt version of Sierra City's old Bigelow House hotel. Best of all are the mine itself—these days being painstakingly cleared of old rock and debris that has blocked it since the 1950s—which produced some $8 billion in its day, and the six-story stamp mill, the only original, fully operable one available for tours. The system here included a Pelton wheel, an air compressor for dynamite drilling, and a mammoth mill operation with jawlike ore crushers and stamps. New and well attended are summer concerts and performances, from cowboy poetry and opera to jazz and swing. The park is open Wed.–Sun. 10 A.M.–5 P.M., from Memorial Day through September, then on weekends only in October; tours of the stamp mill are usually offered at 11 A.M., 1 P.M., and 3 P.M. Closed the rest of the year. For information, call the Sierra County Historical Society, 530/862-1310.

Practicalities
Two miles west of town is the U.S. Forest Service **Loganville Campground,** while just east of (and closest to) town is the larger **Wild Plum Campground,** off Hwy. 49 on Wild Plum Rd. along Haypress Creek. Both campgrounds have water but no showers ($16 per site). Past the Gold Lakes turnoff on the way to Sierraville are the Forest Service **Sierra, Chapman Creek,** and **Yuba Pass Campgrounds,** along the north fork of the Yuba River, open mid-June until mid-October. Sierra is $10 a night, and Chapman and Yuba are $16; no reservations. For more information, contact the Tahoe National Forest's **North Yuba Ranger District** office in Camptonville, 530/288-3231.

Dog lovers, you and your pooch may discover heaven at **Herrington's Sierra Pines Lodge,** 101 Main St., 530/862-1151 or 800/682-9848, www.herringtonssierrapines.com. Herrington's also offers a decent restaurant, famous for fresh trout (catch your own) as well as homemade bread and other baked goods. Also popular for its pet-friendliness, most of the 21 motel-style rooms here have decks and river views. Rates are $50–100. Apartment-style units with full kitchens, two double beds, and a Franklin stove are also available. Open for breakfast and dinner daily mid-May–mid-Oct.; lodgings are usually available Apr.–Oct. The historic **Buckhorn Restaurant & Tavern,** 225 Main, 530/862-1171, is another best bet.

Sierra City's Victorian **Holly House,** 119 Main, 530/862-1123, www.hollyhouse.com, offer five charming rooms with private baths, featuring either clawfoot or Jacuzzi tubs. Most rooms are $85–135; two smaller rooms can be combined into a suite. Open June–Sept.

The **High Country Inn,** 100 Greene Rd. (some distance north of town at Bassetts and the junction with Gold Lakes Rd.), 530/862-1530 or 800/862-1530, www.hicountryinn.com, is a modern mountain home in an astounding setting—complete with private trout pond. From the deck and some of the rooms—particularly the second-story suite, which also features a wood-stove and spacious vanity and bathroom with huge antique tub—the view of the Sierra Buttes is spectacular, and the sound of rushing river water and wind in the aspens is almost hypnotic. The folks here are well informed about the area and happy to share their knowledge. The food is fabulous, gourmet fare in every respect. Rooms all feature private baths and cozy, homey features, and guests also enjoy lolling around in front of the downstairs family room fireplace. All in all, it's a great escape. The inn is open year-round; the area is increasingly popular for mountain biking and winter cross-country skiing and usually accessible even in severe weather, since Hwy. 49 is open when I-80 is not. Rates are $100–150.

LAKES BASIN

Beyond the Kentucky Mine, turn north at Bassetts onto Gold Lakes Highway. The dramatic Sierra Buttes stand guard above an intimate, seemingly unspoiled glacial landscape popular for fishing, camping, swimming, hiking, backpacking, and mountain biking in summer, cross-country skiing and snowshoeing in winter. On the way to Gold Lake proper you'll pass **Sand Pond** (good swimming), **Sardine Lake,** and others; more than 45 alpine lakes add to the region's charm. **Gold Lake** is a reminder of Donner Party guide Caleb Greenwood's tall tale of a lake in the Sierra with nuggets so large and plentiful that pioneer children played with them like marbles. Modern-day Gold Lake is easy to reach via Old Gold Lake Road and a gem in its own right, like nearby **Frazier Falls** (a short, easy hike). From the Gold Lakes area, head to Graeagle and nearby Johnsville (turn at Rd. A14), part of **Plumas-Eureka State Park** (see below), a ghost town mining camp in steep canyon country.

Practicalities

You can't camp at most of the lakes, but campgrounds are nearby. The public **Sardine Lake Campground** is 1.5 miles north of Bassetts along Gold Lake Hwy., then a half mile southwest along Sardine Lake Rd. ($16, no showers). Some supplies are available at the **Sardine Lake Resort** and marina, 530/862-1196.

Two miles north of Bassetts is **Salmon Creek Campground** ($16, no showers). A few miles farther north is **Snag Lake Campground** (camp free, undesignated sites, purify your drinking water). Two other campgrounds—**Diablo Camping Area** and **Berger Campground** (both $8)—as well as **Packsaddle Camping Area** ($16; as the name suggests, pack and saddle animals permitted), all at about 6,000 feet, are a short distance west along Packer Lake Road. For information, call the Tahoe National Forest's **North Yuba Ranger District** office in Camptonville, 530/288-3231.

An all-time favorite stay is the **Gray Eagle Lodge,** 5000 Gold Lake Rd., 530/836-2511 or 800/635-8778, www.grayeaglelodge.com. Cabins along Gray Eagle Creek are basic but comfortable. Gray Eagle's pine-log-walled **Firewoods** restaurant elevates campfire fare to cuisine status. Presided over by California Culinary Academy graduate Heather Strandberg, Firewoods is noted at dinner for fresh fish, prime rib, and fine wines (reservations necessary). And don't miss the s'-mores. Daily rates for most of the charming one- and two-bedroom cabins—no phones, no TV—

are $200–250, breakfast and dinner included. Popular, semirustic resort-style stays in the area include the circa-1912 **Gold Lake Lodge,** 530/836-2350 or 530/836-2751, www.lakesbasin.com/gold, with 11 charming cabins (portable heaters), some with shared exterior baths. Listed on the National Register of Historic Places, Gold Lake also includes a homey lodge and restaurant serving a limited but impressive menu. Rates for two are $150–200 per day, breakfast and dinner included (weekly rates available). Or simply plan to eat at the pleasant restaurant (call ahead for reservations if you're not a resort guest). There are other great accommodations options in the area; see below for more choices.

Information

For a map and guide to the Lakes Basin area, as well as recreation and other information, contact the **Eastern Plumas Chamber of Commerce,** 424 E. Sierra Ave. (Hwy. 70) in Portola, 530/831-1811 or 800/995-6057, www.easternplumas-

chamber.com, or the **Plumas County Visitors Bureau,** located in Quincy a half-mile west of town on Hwy. 70 (next to the airport), 530/283-6345 or 800/326-2247, www.plumascounty.org. Another good source for recreation information is the **Tahoe National Forest** office in Sierraville (see below). For guided llama backpack trips in the area, contact **Highland Llama Trekkers,** in Grass Valley, 530/273-8105. The **Reid Horse & Cattle Co., Inc.,** headquartered in Quincy, 530/283-1147, www.reidhorse.com, offers guided trail rides, pack trips, horse boarding, riding lessons, and children's camp; call or email for more information. The company also operates **Gold Lake Stables,** 530/836-0940, and **Graeagale Stables,** 530/836-0430.

SIERRA VALLEY

Sierra Valley is the largest alpine valley in the Sierra Nevada, and one of the largest in the continental U.S. Despite development pressures already being felt in the region due to its location,

GOLD COUNTRY GOLF

California's historic gold country is famous for its priceless, golf ball–sized gold nuggets, but these days golf balls are increasingly prized. As the region's museum-quality Wild West scenery is transformed into upscale retirement enclaves, regionally associated words like "gold," "greenhorn," "camp," and "saddle" are more apt to be associated with golf course developments than cowboys and more traditional prospectors. Historians may cringe but many among the legions of retired and pre-retired are thrilled.

The 18-hole Dick Bailey–designed course **Whitehawk Ranch** near Clio in eastern Plumas County's Mohawk Valley, 530/836-0394 or 800/332-4295, www.golfwhitehawk.com, comes with grand practice facilities, clubhouse, and exclusive residential community.

The **Dragon at Gold Mountain** course at the Nakoma Resort and Spa near Graeagle and Portola, 530/832-4887, 800/368-7786, or 877/418-0880 (resort), www.dragongolf.com, comes with luxury

homes and accommodations, fine dining, and a unique perk—a chance to check out Nakoma. The fabulous Nakoma clubhouse and restaurant, originally designed in the 1920s by Frank Lloyd Wright for a golf course near Madison, Wisconsin, was never built. Wright's soaring, steep-roofed octagonal vision is now a California treasure.

Greenhorn Creek just south of Angels Camp, 209/736-8111 or 888/736-5900 (resort) www .greenhorncreek.com, offers 18 holes (redesigned by Robert Trent Jones II), clubhouse, pool, fitness and spa facilities, hiking trails, luxury cottages, and housing developments. Fabulous Camps restaurant is another draw. About 10 miles south near Copperopolis is **Saddle Creek Golf Club,** 209/785-3700, 888/852-5787, or 800/611-7722 (bungalows), www.saddlecreekgolf.com, where exceptional golf is served up with inviting clubhouse, golf shop, the Copper Grille, and an equally great night's sleep. To dig up more gold country golf information, contact area visitor bureaus.

GOLD COUNTRY

dangerously close to Tahoe, hopes are high that much of the valley, grazing land and prized habitat for migrating birds, will be preserved. Conservationists were buoyed in 2002 by the news that the 13,000-acre Bar One Ranch will be preserved through California Rangeland Trust conservation easements. It's expected that other ranchers will follow suit.

Sierra Valley Lodge

Quite a treat just minutes north on Hwy. 89 is the Sierra Valley Lodge, 103 Main St. in Calpine, 530/994-3367, a log-cabin restaurant serving good seafood and great steaks and prime rib, and featuring a decent wine list. Sit out on the deck for a cocktail before dinner, or head to the bar—which has a great jukebox and a trophy case displaying the illustrious history of the Calpine Marching Band (mostly members of the local volunteer fire brigade, including a saxophonist, kazoo players, and hummers). On summer weekends, plan on some square dancing in the back room. Hotel rooms here are small, basic, and very down-home, as is the hallway with its three-dimensional western memorabilia (even a full-size saddle) coming out of the wall. The lodge is open year-round, but most of the rooms are closed in winter, due to lack of insulation.

Sierraville

A tiny town beyond Yuba Pass in the fertile Sierra Valley, Sierraville was first "discovered" by the legendary black mountain man Jim Beckwourth. The valley later became a breadbasket for the mines. The **Sierraville Ranger Station** of Tahoe National Forest is located here; stop by, 317 S. Lincoln St., or call 530/994-3401 for area camping and recreation information. You can camp about five miles southeast at either **Cottonwood Campground** or **Cold Creek Campground,** or head toward Truckee from Sierraville and the **Upper** and **Lower Little Truckee Campgrounds.** All are $14 per night and can be reserved through the National Recreation Reservation Service, 877/444-6777, www.reserveusa.com.

Sierraville's historic, clothing-optional **Sierra Hot Springs,** 530/994-3773, www.sierrahot-springs.org, is sister resort to Harbin Hot Springs,

a nonprofit retreat center operated by the New Age Church of Being. Facilities include the geodesic copper Temple Dome, with a hot and two cooling pools; an outdoor medicine bath; private baths; swimming pool and sundeck; an 1860s lodge with private and dorm rooms; and the Globe Hotel in downtown Sierraville. Access to both facilities is for members only, but a membership is just $5 for 30 days and is honored at both locations.

From Sierraville, head northwest on Hwy. 89 to Graeagle, Quincy, and the volcanic wonders of Lassen National Park, or south to Truckee and Lake Tahoe.

Loyalton

Stop in this mountain ranching town for a picnic at **Loyalton City Park,** which offers tennis courts, playgrounds, and barbecues. Visit the **Sierra Valley Museum** to see an eclectic display of memorabilia from 19th-century farms, Depression-era glassware, even Odd Fellows vestments from an early local temple. The museum is open from just before Memorial Day through mid-October, Wed.–Sun. noon–4:30 P.M. (free, but donations are appreciated). Call 530/993-6754 for information. The **Country Cookin' Cafe,** downtown at 820 Main St. (Hwy. 49), 530/993-1162, serves up just what the sign says—steak and eggs and omelettes for breakfast, good burgers, soups, and sandwiches for lunch, and the extra treat of local artwork (for sale) displayed on the walls. **Clover Valley Mill House,** 225 Railroad Ave. (at S. First St.), in Loyalton, 530/993-4819, is a surprising find in the midst of wilderness. This 1906 Colonial B&B has three rooms sharing a bath-and-a-half, as well as one suite with a private bath and sitting room. Full breakfast is served inside or out on the deck. The proprietors can give you good advice on what to do and see in the area.

PORTOLA, GRAEAGLE, AND VICINITY

Portola

"New" in Portola is the 1931 **Williams House Museum** at the city's eastern portal, 424 E. Sierra

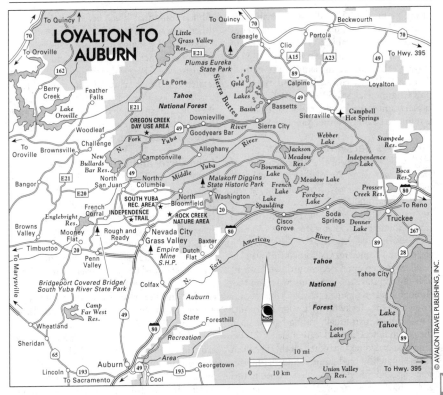

LOYALTON TO AUBURN

Ave. (Hwy. 70), 530/832-0671, onetime residence and gas station that tells family and local mining, lumbering, and railroading histories with photos, documents, quilts, and more. This is also the new home of the **Eastern Plumas County Chamber of Commerce,** 530/831-1811 or 800/995-6057, www.easternplumaschamber.com, so stop by to find out what's up.

In Portola proper the most popular attraction is the **Portola Railroad Museum** (cross the river and follow the signs), an all-volunteer effort sponsored by the Feather River Rail Society, 530/832-4131. The quantity and quality of in-process and already-restored iron stock on display at the one-time Western Pacific railway yard here is impressive. At last report there were nearly 40 locomotives and more than 100 passenger and freight cars. Unlike other museums, here you can climb all over the collected relics—really get a feel for how

they work. Admission is free, but donations are greatly appreciated. A successful ongoing fundraiser here is the Run-a-Locomotive program, wherein visitors rent a diesel locomotive and drive it around the yard (with guidance from an onboard instructor). Much more affordable are family-friendly caboose rides along a one-mile balloon track, offered in the summer. Be sure to show up in August for **Feather River Railroad Days.** For more museum information, call 530/832-4532.

Stop by **The Fat Cat Café,** 150 Commercial, 530/832-4595, for deli sandwiches and espresso drinks. The **Beckwith Tavern** dinner house, 81037 Hwy. 70 at Clover Valley Rd. in Beckwourth, 530/832-5084, features good ol' American food, fireplace, bar, and dance floor. Open Thurs.–Sun., reservations recommended.

Charming **Sleepy Pines Motel,** 74631 Hwy. 70, 530/832-4291, www.sleepypinesmotel.com, offers rooms for $50–100, some with kitch-enettes. All rooms feature refrigerator, microwave, drip coffee maker, cable TV, and phones. Some pets allowed. Cabins (for up to four) are $110. Close to the railroad museum is the railroad-themed **Pullman House Bed and Breakfast,** 256 Commercial St., 530/832-0107, with six casual country rooms (all private baths) in what was once a boardinghouse. Rates are $50–100.

The James Beckwourth Legacy

Highway 70 east from the Blairsden-Graeagle area passes through Portola before lurching up over Beckwourth Pass, then hooking up with Hwy. 395 at Hallelujah Junction in the high desert—the official end of the Feather River National Scenic Byway that starts some 130 miles away in Oroville. Mt. Ina Coolbrith south of the pass was named for California's first poet laureate, who met James Beckwourth while an 11-year-old girl traveling westward by wagon train through his same-named pass, on what became known as the Beckwourth Emigrant Trail. A dark-skinned man usually riding bareback and dressed in moccasins and leather jacket, his two long braids tied up in colored cloth, the adventurer apparently made quite an initial impression on Coolbrith. Beckwourth described himself as a Crow Indian war chief, trapper, trader, and explorer; today he is also credited with being an African-American pioneer and trailblazer.

A once dilapidated two-story cabin believed to be Jim Beckwourth's 1852 hotel and trading post, on Rocky Point Rd. east of Portola near the town of Beckwourth (old maps carry the distorted "Beckwith"), has been painstakingly restored by volunteers and is now known as **Beckwourth's Cabin,** 530/832-4888, open only by appointment. In 1992, Governor Pete Wilson honored the project with a state historic preservation award. Controversy lingers, however, over whether this impressive building was actually Beckwourth's. No one disputes that Beckwourth built a cabin in 1851 on what was known as Beckwourth's Ranch, and replaced it with another when the original burned down. But a 1937 newspaper account by Quincy historian E.C. Kelsey disputed accepted local oral history about this particular cabin, stating that it was actually built by two other men in 1861 or 1862—four years after Beckwourth left Plumas County. Locals, however, are still convinced that this was, and is, Beckwourth's cabin, largely due to the building's own "statement" in the matter. Quite unusual for a California log cabin, Beckwourth's was built in the V-notched style, with deep cuts made in square logs, a practice peculiar to the area of Virginia where Jim Beckwourth was born.

Lake Davis and Other Area Lakes

Just north of Portola via Davis Road is Lake Davis, 530/836-2575, long noted for its very fine trout fishing—some call it the premier trout lake in the western U.S.—as well as boating, swimming, fishing, and camping. But in recent years Lake Davis and surrounding communities have been at the center of an environmental nightmare caused by the discovery here of northern pike, an aggressive non-native predator species, and the state's subsequent equally aggressive efforts to eradicate it. (For details, see Pike Not Blown Away.) Still, at last report the trout fishing at Lake Davis was still fine. To get acquainted with the area, try **Lake Davis Resort** on the lake's south side near the Grizzly Store, 530/832-1060, www.lakedavisresort.com, which offers well-stocked housekeeping cabins and motel rooms starting at $50–100. As of late, the motel was being posted for sale, so call ahead. For boat rentals call the store, 530/832-0270.

The shores of **Frenchman Lake** reservoir, headwaters of the Feather River just north of Chilcoot, are studded with sage and pine; there's good fishing and camping April through October. Deer hunting is popular in season. Notable among the campgrounds here is Big Cove—now remarkably welcoming for people in wheelchairs, with a paved walking trail all the way to the lake and 11 fully accessible campsites (hardened surfaces, raised tent pads, accessible water hydrants and bathrooms). But come early; even in good years the water level takes quite a dive by late summer and fall. For other regional water recreation, just north of I-80 and the Tahoe-Truckee area are **Prosser Creek Reservoir,** quiet and popular for canoeing, sailing, and fishing, with both primitive and developed U.S. Forest Service campsites; **Boca Reservoir,** a powerboat lake with excellent sailing, free campsites, and a more stable water level; and **Stampede Reservoir,** a very large lake with excellent westerly winds for sailors—though the water drops severely by the end of summer, mainly through diversions to Pyramid Lake to save two rare trout species— and hundreds of Forest Service campsites.

See www.ucampwithus.com for information about campgrounds at Lake Davis and French-man Lake; for reservations, call 877/444-6777 or see www.reserveusa.com. For information about camping ($12–15) and other recreation at Prosser Creek, Boca, and Stampede Reservoirs, contact the **Truckee Ranger District** of Tahoe National Forest, 10342 Hwy. 89 in Truckee, 530/587-3558, www.fs.fed.us/r5/tahoe.

Graeagle, Clio, and Blairsden

Think 18-hole golf courses (there were six in the area, at last count, most championship caliber)

along with glorious pine-scented scenery and charming barn-red cabins and shops. That's Graeagle. A onetime mill town with rough-edged beginnings—the California Fruit Exchange started manufacturing fruit boxes here in 1920— Graeagle these days is downright uptown. Show up in July for the **Mohawk Valley 4th of July Celebration,** complete with parade and fire-works; the **Great American Craft Fair** continues from July through August. Expect jazz and other concerts all summer long. For more information about Greagle and vicinity, see the **Graeagle Merchants** website, www.graeagle.com.

The charming 1915 **Feather River Inn** in Blairsden, with its 26-room European chalet-style lodge, cabins, and onsite restaurant, 530/836-2623 or 888/324-6400, www.feather-riverinn.com, was recently renovated and re-opened as a camp and conference center. Such a deal, when space is available: Comfy one-bed-room cabins are $50–100; two-bedroom cab-ins, lodge rooms, and suites are $100–150; and

---

WRIGHT THIS WAY: NAKOMA AT GOLD MOUNTAIN

Portola is becoming a prosperous leisure-oriented outpost in the northern Sierra Nevada, thanks to legendary American architect Frank Lloyd Wright (1867–1959). Centerpiece of the nearby Gold Mountain development is Nakoma, Wright's dramatic 1924 clubhouse design, planned for the Nakoma Country Club in Madison, Wisconsin, but never built. The stunning 23,000-square-foot **Nakoma Resort and Spa** is a mountain of cobbled stone with five soaring, teepee-style spires, wooden roofs strung with multicolor "beads," and Native American–inspired art glass windows. Most spectacular inside is the Wigwam restaurant, with its 45-foot-high, open-beamed ceiling. Being seated near the four-sided central stone fireplace feels like snuggling up next to a massive tree trunk in a storm, certain that the grand canopy will offer shelter.

Now that Nakoma (a Chippewa word said to mean "I do as I promise") has fulfilled its orig-inal promise, an entire community of Wright-inspired architecture is taking root in the neigh-borhood. Many of these multimillion-dollar homes were designed by the Frank Lloyd Wright Foundation's Taliesin Architects.

If permanent shelter here seems prohibitive, perhaps an overnight is possible. Or a round of golf at the resort's challenging Robert Nelson–designed **Dragon** 18-hole course, or some-thing special from the pro shop. Maybe even an afternoon at the full-service spa, which offers massage and aroma and herbal therapies as well as sauna, steam room, indoor pool, Jacuzzis, "monsoon showers," and a cardio fitness center.

For more information, contact the Nakoma resort at 877/418-0880, www.nakomare-sort.com. To cash in on the success of Wright-inspired golf developments, the city of Portola is now going ahead with another—**Spirit Mountain,** which will include a nine-hole golf course, another Wright-designed clubhouse, and homes and apartments.

midweek and off-season specials can be even better. Lodge rooms and suites, all newly renovated, feature dataports, TV, and air-conditioning. Also on the grounds: conference and wedding facilities, theater, golf course, swimming pool, stocked trout pond, hiking trails, volleyball and tennis courts, picnic grounds, horseshoes.

Near Graeagle is **White Sulfur Springs Ranch,** 2200 Hwy. 89 (just south of Clio proper), 530/836-2387 or 800/854-1797.Once an old stage stop on the meadow edge of Mohawk Valley, White Sulphur Springs is a very special place in an idyllic setting—a bed-and-breakfast with antiques in the attic and, outdoors, a spring-fed swimming pool. Now that cattle ranches are being supplanted by exclusive western-style golf communities, a more recent Mohawk Valley star is **The Lodge at White-hawk Ranch,** 985 Whitehawk Dr. in Clio, 530/836-4985 or 877/945-6343, www.lodgeat-whitehawk.com, where the stylish one- and two-bedroom cabins are $150–250, breakfast and other perks included.

There are so many great restaurants in the area, including **Firewoods** at the **Graeagle Lodge** (see above) and both **Loggia** and the **Wigwam Room** at **Nakoma Resort and Spa** (see Wright This Way: Nakoma at Gold Mountain elsewhere in this chapter). For something light and simple, stroll the highway in Graeagle and see what's new in local café society. But don't miss delightful, decidedly upscale **Grizzly Grill Restaurant & Bar** in Blairsden, 250 Bonta St., 530/836-1300, www.grizzlygrill.com, serving classical California cuisine with understated mountain style. Grizzly specialties included the cassoulet, pastas, fresh fish, and expertly prepared meat selections. Early-bird dinners, a limited menu served 5:30–6:30 P.M., are a real deal—entrées such as grilled sirloin or salmon filet for about $15, soup, salad, and dessert included. Children's menu, too. The Grizzly Grill is open daily in summer for dinner from 5 P.M.–9 P.M. (reservations strongly suggested), limited days in winter.

Plumas-Eureka State Park

One of those almost-undiscovered outdoor gems, Plumas-Eureka State Park is crowned by thick pines and firs, and offers good hiking, fine camping, a ski-tour trail in winter, and even limited, low-key downhill ski facilities. When the land was owned by the Sierra Buttes Mining Co., in the 19th century, one of the area's old mining trams served as the world's first ski lift when snowbound miners organized, promoted, and wagered on high-speed downhill ski competitions.

At Plumas-Eureka proper, the old Mohawk Mill and other mining outbuildings have been restored. Nearby is the park's excellent interpretive center and museum, a former miners' bunkhouse featuring displays on mining technology, natural history, and skiing history. Open daily in summer, when docent-led tours are offered—destinations including **Moriarty House,** restored and furnished to reflect 1890s mining camp domesticity. **Living History Day** is scheduled once a month in summer, with "lifestyle" demonstrations including blacksmithing, mining techniques, and ice cream making.

The park features several short hiking trails (good views from the top of Eureka Peak) plus access to the backcountry; in late spring and early summer, trout fishing is good in Madora and Eureka Lakes, as well as Jamison Creek. The campground is about a mile downhill from the interpretive center via a narrow, winding paved road. Open only seasonally (usually May 1 through October), the campground offers 67 campsites, hot showers, tables, and fire rings ($12–15, first-come, first-camped). For more information, contact Plumas-Eureka State Park, 310 Johnsville Rd. in Blairsden, 530/836-2380.

Plumas-Eureka is increasingly popular in winter for cross-country skiing (bring your own everything). The small Plumas-Eureka Ski Bowl facilities include 20 trails, two lifts, two poma lifts, a snowtubing area, snowboarding, and a rustic lodge with a café and a warm fire. Come on the third Sunday of January, February, and March (snowy weather permitting) for the **Historic Longboard Revival Series** races. The mountain is open in the winter (when there's snow on the ground) Friday through Sunday and also on holidays, 9:30 A.M.–4 P.M. Full-day tickets are $24 adults, $16 seniors (65 and older), and youths 13–18, $12 children 7–12; half-day rates are available. Contact the Plumas travel center for more information: 800/995-6057, www.easternplumaschamber.com.

Recreation

Speaking of downhome downhill: A worthwhile side adventure, at least when you've got plkenty of time and the roads are passable, is the back-road (dirt) route from Plumas-Eureka to **Little Grass Valley Reservoir** and the onetime mining town of La Porte, which shares the distinction of inventing the sport of downhill ski racing. The Alturas Ski Club, founded here in 1866, was the country's first organized ski society; its first racing tournament was held the following February. The **Frank C. Reilly Museum** on Main St., 530/675-1922 or 530/675-2841, open weekends and holidays in summer, tells the story of La Porte's mining and longboard skiing days. The 1906 **Union Hotel,** 530/675-2860, www.laporteunion.com, serves "mountain cuisine," including famous Mercer Family sourdough pancakes, and offers 21 rooms with private baths, most $85–125. You'll find plenty of campsites (six campgrounds) at the little lake, where swimming, water-skiing, hiking, and fishing are popular in warm weather. In winter, the road around the reservoir is great for cross-country skiing; more challenging, though, is Lexington Hill a few miles south of town off Quincy/La Porte Road. Trails are unmarked and ungroomed, and snowmobilers like the area, too. For more information about the area, contact Plumas National Forest's **Feather River Ranger District** office, 875 Mitchell Ave. in Oroville, 530/534-6500, www.fs.fed.us/r5/plumas.

QUINCY AND VICINITY

The northernmost reaches of the Sierra Nevada are well north of Lake Tahoe and I-80—scattered forested lakes, reservoirs, and rivers among still more scattered small towns. Quincy, on Hwy. 70/89 south of Lake Almanor and Indian Valley, is a picturesque mountain town with a long-time lumber history. Hiking is great in the neighborhood, area trails all but empty. Still, some say Plumas County hasn't been the same since Quincy put in the county's first stoplight, in 1993.

Stop by the **Plumas County Art Gallery** at 372 Main St., 530/283-3402, www.plumasarts.com, to see what's up with regional artists. Come in late June or early July for the annual **High Sierra Music Festival,** 510/420-1590, www.highsierramusic.com, a four-day world music celebration featuring the likes of Steve Winwood, John Scofield, the Del McCoury Band, Kaki King, and the Lil Rascals Brass Band. Otherwise the main attraction here is the impressive indoor-outdoor **Plumas County Museum,** 500 Jackson St., 530/283-6320, open weekdays 8 A.M.–5 P.M., on weekends and holidays 10 A.M.–4 P.M. ($2 admission). Museum exhibits rotate periodically yet typically include area natural history, Maidu basketry, cultural and home art displays, and pioneer weaponry. New since 1999, with the museum's expansion, is the Industrial History Wing, which offers exhibits on gold mining, railroading, and early logging. Outdoors, explore a blacksmith shop, miner's cabin, miscellaneous mining and logging equipment, and a carriage house complete with a meticulously restored buggy.

If you're here May–Sept., consider a tour of the historic **Variel Home** adjacent to the museum (same phone), a three-story Victorian built by Joseph Variel in 1878 and furnished in turn-of-the-20th-century middle-class style from the museum's collection. Call for the current tour schedule—or to arrange a tour by appointment—but the house is also open during the museum's annual Summertime Open House and Christmas "Wassail Bowl" festivities.

Practicalities

If you're not here to partake of the wassail bowl, find refreshment otherwise at mountain-bohemian **Morning Thunder Cafe,** 557 Lawrence, 530/283-1310, open 7 A.M.–2 P.M. daily for breakfast and lunch, veggie omelettes and such as well as beefy burgers. Beer and wine, espresso bar too. For organic vegetarian, another possibility is **Pangaea,** 56 Harbison St., 530/283-0426. Stock up on organic this and that at **Quincy Natural Foods,** 30 Harbison St. (at Main), 530/283-3528. **Sweet Lorraine's,** 384 Main St., 530/283-5300, is the place for fresh California-style fare. **Moon's,** 497 Lawrence, 530/283-0765, serves

Italian-American food, from hand-spun gourmet pizzas and pasta to poultry, seafood, and steaks.

Snazziest stay in town is the **Feather Bed** bed-and-breakfast, 542 Jackson St. (near the courthouse), 530/283-0102 or 800/696-8624, www.featherbed-inn.com, with seven cozy rooms and cottages (all with private baths), full breakfast, even bikes to borrow. Rates are $100–150. A motel option is the **Lariat Lodge**, 2370 E. Main St., 530/283-1000 or 800/999-7199, which has a pool (seasonal), king and queen beds, and cable TV with HBO. Rates are $50–100.

Fun for a rustic family-oriented stay—platform tents and cabins—is **Feather River Camp** on Hwy. 70, 530/283-2290. Open mid-June to mid-August. A tad fancier and also family-friendly is the **Greenhorn Creek Guest Ranch** in Spring Garden, 530/283-0930 or 800/334-6939 ("33-HOWDY"), www.greenhornranch.com, a ranch-style resort with modern cabins, motel units, and a full-on schedule of "dude" activities—from horseshoes, horseback riding, and riding lessons to frog races and line dancing. Swimming pool and Jacuzzi too. Rates are $200–250 per adult per day in peak summer season, family-style meals and all activities included, but dip to $60–100 (accommodations only) in the off season. Weekly rates are available. More rustic, a bit of a drive, but much cheaper even in summer are the 11 rustic lakefront housekeeping cabins (one, two, or three bedrooms) at pet-friendly **Bucks Lake Lodge**, 10206 Bucks Lake Rd. (at Bucks Lake west of town), 530/283-2262 or 800/481-2825 for reservations, open year-round. Motel units (no dogs) are also available. Rates start at $75–115; weekly rates available. The onsite restaurant serves breakfast, lunch, and dinner daily—but prime rib is the specialty, served Thurs.–Sun. nights. Considerably more luxurious is the six-room **Haskins Valley Inn**, 16860 Bucks Lake Rd., 530/283-9667, www.haskinsvalleyinn.com, a striking two-story inn built specifically as a B&B (thus the Jacuzzi tubs). Rates are $110–150, and in winter they'll snowmobile you in for $25.

Cheaper is camping at **Antelope Lake** southeast of Greenville near Taylorsville, 530/284-7126, a beautiful recreation lake with very nice national forest campgrounds (Boulder Creek, Lone Rock, Long Point), $13–15. For more information, see www.ucampwithus.com; for reservations, call 877/444-6777 or see www.reserveusa.com. The **Indian Valley Museum** east of Taylorsville in the Mt. Jura Gem & Mineral Society Building at Cemetery and Portsmouth Roads, 530/284-6511, chronicles regional history and also offers minerals for sale. Open Memorial Day to Labor Day on weekends and holidays, 1–4 P.M., or by appointment. Small fee.

Information

For more information about Quincy and vicinity, contact the **Plumas County Visitors Bureau**, located a half-mile west of town on Hwy. 70 (next to the airport), 530/283-6345 or 800/326-2247, www.plumascounty.org. Folks here offer an array of very useful information, from good county activity guides (hiking, mountain biking, etc.) to the intriguing *Plumas Country Backcountry Drives* brochure series. Area camping, hiking, and other recreation information is also available at **Plumas National Forest** headquarters, 159 Lawrence St., 530/283-2050, www.fs.fed.us/r5/plumas. For Plumas County campground information specifically, see www.ucampwithus.com. For more information about the Indian Valley area, contact the **Indian Valley Chamber of Commerce**, 410 Main St. in Greenville, 530/284-6633. For information about the nearby Lake Almanor area, contact the **Chester/Lake Almanor Chamber of Commerce**, 529 Main St. in Chester, 530/258-2426 or 800/350-4838, and also see The Northern Mountains chapter.

Grass Valley

Some people, including many who live here, think of Grass Valley as a redneck alternative to the effete egghead ambience of neighboring Nevada City. It's hometown working-class America, complete with fast food, tire-repair shops, and other ungainly development. But Grass Valley has a charm all its own, especially downtown, where a sidewalk stroll takes you straight into the '50s—the 1950s as well as the 1850s. Increasingly, though, Grass Valley and Nevada City are affluent siblings struggling to accept their fairly new identities as gold-city sophisticates.

History

In 1850, George McKnight discovered gold-laced quartz here, and Grass Valley, a company town of former copper miners and their kin from England's Cornwall, quickly became a hardrock mining capital. It's estimated that nearly a billion dollars in gold was deep-mined in and around Grass Valley during the gold rush. The high cost of underground mining meant capital investment and consolidation: the Idaho-Maryland, North Star, and Empire Mines soon became the area's main operations. The Empire Mine, now a state park but once the largest of these 19th-century mining conglomerates—some say the richest gold mine in the U.S.—operated profitably until the 1950s. In 2003 Canada's Emgold Mining Corp. was gearing up to reopen the Idaho-Maryland Mine, expecting to extract some 1.3 million ounces of gold. Some look forward to the prospect of new jobs, others dread the impact of heavy equipment and trucks on narrow local streets. With permits and financing still to finesse, it's too soon to know whether the Idaho-Maryland will once again go for the gold.

Among Grass Valley's famous and infamous was Amos Delano, a Wells Fargo agent and very funny writer better known as "Old Block," a descendant (he said) of the Block-Head family. Also creative: inventor and early amateur aeronautical engineer Lyman Gilmore, who locals say launched a successful airplane here over a year prior to the Wright brothers' first flights.

Isaac Owen, the Methodist minister who preached Grass Valley's first sermon, later moved on to the Santa Clara Valley, where he founded the College of the Pacific. Josiah Royce was born in Grass Valley, attended Harvard University, studied philosophy with William James, and later became James's academic successor.

William Bourn of Empire Mine fame survived the boom and bust years to become one of the wealthiest men in California. He also owned the Spring Valley Water Company in San Francisco and the San Francisco Gas Company; besides his stone lodge and expansive estate in Grass Valley, he built beautiful homes in San Francisco's Pacific Heights district, the Fioli estate in Woodside, and the huge stone winery in Napa Valley later owned by the Christian Brothers and now occupied by the Culinary Institute of America.

SEEING AND DOING GRASS VALLEY

None of the boomtown's original buildings survived the hellish two-hour fire of 1855—one of the gold country's worst—but the surrounding hillsides were quickly clearcut for lumber to rebuild the town. Take a walk around town for a glimpse of the colorful past: brick buildings, wooden awnings, old gas streetlamps. The **Lola Montez House,** 248 Mill St. (a replica of the original building condemned and demolished in 1975), now houses the chamber of commerce and a small one-room museum displaying some of Lola's belongings. The town's first election was held here in November 1850. Two doors down at 238 Mill is **Lotta Crabtree's House** (now private apartments), where Lola Montez taught the six-year-old redhead to dance and sing.

Down the street, the **Grass Valley Public Library,** 207 Mill St., 530/273-4117, was built in 1916 with Carnegie funds on the site of Josiah Royce's birthplace. Mark Twain slept at the impressive **Holbrooke Hotel,** 212 W. Main Street. The site originally held two separate buildings, but both were later destroyed by fire. The saloon was rebuilt immediately (gold country priorities) and the later hotel incorporated it, so now the hotel has two separate bars. Behind the Holbrooke, the **Purcell House,** 119 N. Church St., was once living quarters for the adjacent livery stable. At the end of Main St. is Lyman Gilmore's airfield (now a school), where he reportedly flew his 20-horsepower steam-powered aircraft on or before May 15, 1901—more than a year and a half before the Wright brothers took off from Kitty Hawk.

At the **Alta Sierra Biblical Gardens** seven miles south of Grass Valley at 16343 Auburn Rd., 530/272-1363, you'll find picnic tables, steep hills (wear walking shoes), and a bit of botany with a biblical theme. The self-guided tour takes about 90 minutes. Open year-round, 9 A.M. to sunset, weather permitting. Admission by donation.

Empire Mine State Historic Park

English miners from Cornwall, called "cousin Jacks," worked this mine complex on Gold Hill, one of the oldest and most profitable hardrock mines in the state. In business for more than 100 years, the Empire's 367 miles of tunnels reluctantly yielded millions of ounces of gold; it's estimated that four times as much is still there, too expensive to dig out. The mine closed in 1956 and is now a 800-acre state park at 10791 E. Empire St., 530/273-8522, www.empiremine.org. It's easy to find by following the signs around town.

Near the park's entrance is a model of the underground tunnel maze. The **Bourn "Cottage"** on the hill, an elegant epistle to wealth tucked into the estate's impressive gardens, was designed by San Francisco architect Willis Polk for mine owner William Bowers Bourn II. It was built from mine tailings and stone, paneled inside with hand-rubbed heart redwood, and finished with leaded stained-glass windows. Take the tour and appreciate the original furnishings. The fragrant roses in the formal garden outside are pre-1929 varieties. Also on the grounds are a gardener's cottage, a carriage house, and a shingled clubhouse built in 1905 for use by guests.

See the mining and geology displays at the **visitors center** and museum, which also includes a small book and gift shop. On your way in or out, stop for a look at the Rowe Mine headframe near the parking lot—a gallows-like contraption used as an elevator to ferry men and minerals up and down mine shafts. Down the hill are the well-preserved mine offices, machine shop, retort room and furnaces, and hoist house. Most of the mine shafts are now flooded, so forget about an underground hike. You can get a feeling for life in the tunnels by taking the stairs down into the one open shaft as far as it goes. The **Hardrock Trail,** a two-mile walk through the forest past mining relics and old shafts, loops up into the hills for a peek at the remains of the Betsy, Daisy Hill, and Prescott Mines.

The park is open daily year-round, 10 A.M.–5 P.M. (9 A.M.–6 P.M. May–Aug.). Films and slide shows are offered regularly, tours of the "cottage" and grounds usually depart at 1 P.M., and tours of the mineyard typically start at 2 P.M. Additional tours are offered in summer; open house and living history events are also offered. Hours and schedules for all events vary considerably with the seasons, so call ahead. Small admission.

North Star Mining Museum

The mine's old power station on Allison Ranch Rd., near the intersection of Mill St. and Mc-Courtney Rd., is now a local historical museum (530/273-4255). On display here is a 30-foot-diameter, 10-ton Pelton wheel, the world's largest, which was used to harness water power and later to generate power for the mines with air compressors. Also here are displays of changing mine technology, mine models, old photos, and dioramas. You can pick your way down to Wolf Creek for a picnic on the rocks, then take a look at the Cornish water pump, a device that made pit mining possible. The museum is open May–mid-Oct., daily 10 A.M.–5 P.M.; admission by donation. The docents do an exceptional job. Farther down Allison Ranch Rd. are the massive, eerie ruins of a 60-stamp mill, part of North Star Mine Number 2.

Grass Valley Museum

A restored 1863 convent, orphanage, and school behind imposing brick walls, the Old Mount St. Mary's Academy (and St. Joseph's Chapel), 410 S.

NOTORIOUS LOLA MONTEZ AND LITTLE LOTTA CRABTREE

Most fascinating of all Grass Valley's characters were two women: Lola Montez and Lotta Crabtree. The infamous Lola Montez was a charming Irish actress from Galway who reinvented herself as a Spanish dancer. The mistress of pianist Franz Liszt, but pursued by Honoré de Balzac, Alexandre Dumas, and Victor Hugo, Montez (née Liza Gilbert) was eventually run out of Europe and came to California during the gold rush, where she single-handedly created more excitement than the completion of the transcontinental railroad. Montez's notorious "spider dance" (the arachnids may have been imaginary, but the kick-off-your-knickers dance routine was real) was too popular in sophisticated San Francisco. After about three days in any city venue, the fire department had to be called in to hose down the overheated all-male crowd.

Finally run out of the city, Lola moved to the goldfields, where her spider dance was jeered by miners. So Montez retired to Grass Valley with her husband, a bear, and a monkey. She stayed long enough to scandalize respectable women, send her hubby packing after he shot her bear, and encourage the career of schoolgirl Lotta Crabtree before setting sail for Australia, where she continued her career and lectured in theosophy.

Little Lotta Crabtree sang and danced her way into the hearts of California's miners and later the world. The darling of the gold camps, Lotta began her career at age six and was the first entertainer ever to become a millionaire. When she died in 1924 at age 77, she left $4 million to charity.

Church St. (at Chapel), 530/273-5509, is home to the Grass Valley Museum. Museum exhibits include period memorabilia, a music room, parlor, doctor's office, some fine old lace, and a collection of glass slippers, all on the convent's second floor. Downstairs is a thrift shop, and the grounds themselves are inviting. Also here are the **Gold Country Fine Arts Center** and the **Pacific Library,** which houses a collection of 10,000 old scientific and historical books dating from the 16th century. Call owner Peter Vander Pas for an escorted look at the library; books can't be checked out. The museum is open June 1–Oct. 1, Tues.–Fri. 12:30–3:30 P.M., the rest of the year Tues.–Fri. only. Admission is free, though donations are appreciated.

Video History Museum

This museum, run by the Nevada County Historical Society, serves as an archive of historical video footage shot in the county. Some clips are available for public viewing. Also here are displays of local historical artifacts. The museum is at 415 Central Ave. (in the middle of Memorial Park, at Race and Colfax Aves.), 530/274-1126, and is open May–Oct.; call for hours. Admission is free, but donations are appreciated.

STAYING IN GRASS VALLEY

Camping

For something unique, consider the **Sivananda Ashram Yoga Farm,** 530/272-9322 or 800/469-9642, www.sivananda.org, where outdoor options include tent camping and teepees, and farmhouse choices include both dorm and private rooms. (Dorms are $35, double cabins are $45–50, and private cabins are $70–90. All prices include yoga classes and meals.) RVers can camp at the **Nevada County Fairgrounds,** 11228 McCourtney Rd., www.nevadacountyfair.com, 530/273-6217 ($20–25, group rates are available). Otherwise, the closest camping is at **Scotts Flat Lake** to the northeast (see Nevada City above), a very pretty area but crowded in summer (call ahead for reservations). Another possibility is Rollins Lake, about 11 miles south on Hwy. 174. Here you'll find **Greenhorn Campground,** 15000 Greenhorn Access Rd., 530/272-6100, where facilities include 48 campsites, pit toilets, coin-op showers, a general store/video arcade, barbecue pits, and picnic tables ($18–24), and **Peninsula Camping & Boating Resort,** 21597 You Bet Rd., 530/477-9413, which offers 78 campsites and similar facilities ($25–30). Other campgrounds at the lake include **Long**

GOLD COUNTRY

Ravine, 530/346-6166, and **Orchard Springs,** 530/346-2212. Or camp at **Englebright Reservoir,** near Penn Valley north of Smartville, off Hwy. 20 heading west ($10). Englebright is mostly a lowland boating lake and—unless you're packing your own—to reach the campsites you'll need to rent a skiff at Skippers Cove Marina, 13104 Marina in Smartville, 530/639-2272. For information about the lake, call the U.S. Army Corps of Engineers at 530/639-2342.

Motels

Grass Valley has most of the area's motels, though most cheaper ones have essentially become low-income public housing. A couple of miles south of town, the **Golden Chain Resort Motel,** 13363 Hwy. 49, 530/273-7279, has the usual amenities plus a putting green ($50–100). Or try the **Best Western Gold Country Inn,** 11972 Sutton Way, 530/273-1393 or 800/247-6590, which has a pool and spa, kitchens and kitchenettes, and a location close to the local bus stop. Rates are $100–150 and about 10 percent less than that in the off-season.

The Holbrooke

Top of the mark is the fine **Holbrooke Hotel,** downtown at 212 W. Main St., 530/273-1353 or 800/933-7077, www.holbrooke.com, where rich green colors and fine wood interiors create an atmosphere of seasoned elegance. The 28 authentic gold rush-era rooms have been completely restored and are named for luminaries and famous lunatics who once snored here, including roustabouts like Mark Twain and Ulysses S. Grant. This historic landmark is one of a few truly fine gold country hotels, and its rates are remarkably reasonable. Most rooms are around $100, suites and rooms with verandas higher; all rates are lower in the Jan.–March "value season." Because Main Street is Grass Valley's main drag, and because the hotel's Golden Gate Saloon downstairs is the best bar in town, light sleepers should request accommodations away from both.

Bed-and-Breakfasts

For casual artsy surroundings, try the **Swan-Levine House,** 328 S. Church St., 530/272-1873, www .swanlevinehouse.com, an 1867 Queen Anne Victorian once a local hospital and now a home away from home for the artistic soul (both owners are artists). Fellow printmakers can arrange use of studio space. Pets welcome (fee). Rates are about $100. Considerably more Victorian is the 1892 **Elam Biggs Bed and Breakfast,** 220 Colfax Ave., 530/477-0906, www.elambiggs.com, featuring five rooms with private baths, gracious gardens. Most rooms are about $100.

EATING IN GRASS VALLEY

Basics

Grass Valley has the certified farmers markets. The **Grass Valley Friday Market** is held downtown at Mill and Main Streets on Friday, July–Oct. 5:30–9 P.M. The **Grass Valley–Nevada County Certified Farmers Market** convenes at the Nevada County Fairgrounds (Gate #4), 11228 McCourtney Rd., May–Oct. 9 A.M.–noon.

A modest local landmark and legendary in Grass Valley is cozy brick-and-oak **Tofanelli's** bistro, 302 W. Main St., 530/272-1468; open daily for breakfast, lunch (brunch on weekends), and dinner. Every breakfast you can imagine is on the menu, or dream up your own egg specialty with their design-your-own omelettes. At lunch, you'll find sandwiches, salads, lots of burger choices (including veggie burgers), and a nice selection of teas and desserts. Good dinner specials and even more reasonable "early-bird" dinners. **Charlie's Angels Café,** 145 S. Auburn, 530/274-1839, is another possibility, a best bet for biscuits and gravy.

If you're heading south, stop off at **Happy Apple Kitchen,** 10 miles down Hwy. 174 in Chicago Park, 530/273-2822, for great salads, sandwiches, burgers, and other simple lunches. On a cold day, cozy up to the fireplace for some unforgettable desserts, or get a treat for takeout.

Pasties: Historical Fast Food

In Grass Valley, sample the local specialty: Cornish pasties. These hot turnover-like pies with various spicy meat and vegetable fillings were favored by early miners. A good place to start is **Marshall's Pasties,** 203 Mill St., 530/272-2844;

good pasties that are less spicy—"like eating a piece of heaven," according to one fan.

Fine Dining

The **212 Bistro** at the Holbrooke Hotel, 212 W. Main St., 530/273-1353, is excellent for continental and American lunches and dinners, as well as a famous weekend brunch. The Holbrooke is popular on weekends (reservations a must). Lunch features pasta, salads, some exceptional sandwiches, and unusual choices like chicken pesto and a spinach omelette. If you pass up the onion rings, you might have room for a piece of the Holbrooke's locally famous Chocolate Hazelnut Cake. Dinner entrées are dressed up with some unique sauces and garnishes, and include salmon, prawns, rack of lamb, pork tenderloin, steaks, chicken dishes, blackened prime rib, and vegetarian pastas. Weather permitting, dine out on the patio.

Just across the street from the Holbrooke is another contender in the fine food sweeps: the **Main Street Saloon & Eatery,** 213 W. Main, 530/477-6000. Contemporary and casual, Main Street offers steaks, pastas, and fresh seafood for lunch and dinner daily. Try the house specialty mussels, sautéed with leeks, tomato, garlic, white wine, and fresh basil.

EVENTS

Come in May for the family-friendly **Sierra Festival of the Arts** downtown on Mill Street, an all-day juried art show and street festival; call the chamber for current dates and details. Show up weekends May–Oct. for **Living History Days** at Empire Mine State Park, 530/273-8522. In June, for four days over Father's Day weekend, is the large and long-running California Bluegrass Association (CBA) **Father's Day Bluegrass Festival** at the Nevada County Fairgrounds here, virtually nonstop music from the nation's bluegrass bluebloods.

Incidentally, most of Nevada City's famous three-week **Music in the Mountains** June-into-July tune festival (see Nevada City above) actually happens here in Grass Valley, at the fairgrounds and at St. Joseph's Hall at Church and Chapel

Streets. The event features orchestras, chamber music, and an outdoor "pops" concert. Considerably hipper is July's **California Worldfest** at the fairgrounds, 530/891-4098 for information, www.worldfest.net, where you can expect the likes of 2003's Laura Love, Alasdair Fraser, the Waifs, the Robert Cray Band, the John Cowan Band, Mumbo Gumbo, Incendio, and the Palm Wine Boys. Also in July, the Empire Mine State Historic Park hosts the annual **Cornish Miners' Picnic,** 530/273-8522.

In August, head to the fairgrounds for the **Nevada County Fair,** bringing on the Logger's Olympics, country-western music till your ears bleed, a rodeo, and a destruction derby. In late September, hoof it back to the fairgrounds to see Percherons, Clydesdales, Shires, and more compete in the annual **Draft Horse Classic,** the top draft-horse show in the western United States. For information on either event, call the fairgrounds at 530/273-6217. In November and December, the **Cornish Christmas Street Faire** is good Friday-evening fun, especially if it's been snowing.

For up-to-the-minute information about goings-on in Grass Valley's arts and entertainment scene, contact the **Nevada County Arts Council** 251 S. Auburn St., Ste. C, in Grass Valley, 530/271.5955, www.artmatters-ncac.org.

INFORMATION AND SERVICES

The **Grass Valley/Nevada County Chamber of Commerce,** 248 Mill St., 530/273-4667, www.grassvalleychamber.com, occupies the rebuilt Lola Montez home. The staff is very helpful, providing maps, a walking-tour guide, and information on current events, accommodations, and eateries; the chamber office is open 9 A.M.–5 P.M. weekdays, 10 A.M.–3 P.M. Sat. For additional information, contact the **Grass Valley Downtown Association,** 151 Mill St., 530/272-8315. For guided area historical tours ($20) stop by or call the Holiday Lodge at 1221 E. Main St., 530/273-4406 or 800/742-7125, www. holidaylodge.biz.

If you need diversion for the kiddos, possibilities include the **49er Family Fun Park** at 314 Railroad Ave., 530/272-4949, featuring miniature golf, go-cart racing, even batting cages, and 18-lane **Prosperity Lanes Bowling,** 420 Henderson St., 530/274-6484.

NEAR GRASS VALLEY

Rough and Ready

Once a wild mining camp founded by Mexican War veterans remembering Gen. Zachary "Old Rough and Ready" Taylor, this town seceded from the Union during the Civil War to protest a miners' tax. But the "Great Republic of Rough and Ready," population 3,000, lasted only from April 7, 1850, until the 4th of July—when latent patriotism erupted and Old Glory waved once again. The town is now bypassed by Hwy. 20, so head west on W. Main St., which becomes the Rough and Ready Highway.

Center of community activity is the Rough and Ready Grange Hall, built in 1854. The old school and blacksmith shop still stand, as does the Old Toll House, now an antique shop. The post office, once in the old Rough and Ready Hotel, now has its own building. On the last Sunday in June is the town's **Secession Day** revival, and October brings a **Chili Cook-Off** sanctioned by the International Chili Society. For information, contact the volunteer-staffed **Rough and Ready Chamber of Commerce,** 530/272-4320, www.roughandreadychamber.com.

Bridgeport Covered Bridge

Just south of Grass Valley, head north from Hwy. 20 via Pleasant Valley Rd. (head south on Pleasant Valley from North San Juan) to reach the shingle-sided Bridgeport Covered Bridge stretched across the South Fork of the Yuba River. (Good swimming below the bridge, near the trail.) This is one of the longest single-span covered bridges in the U.S., a 229-foot length of timber, iron bolts, and braces. In regular use from 1862 to 1971, the bridge is now a state historic monument and part of **South Yuba River State Park** (SYRSP). California's first river-corridor state park, the SYRSP takes in 20 miles of the Yuba's south fork, from the edge of Tahoe National Forest near Nevada City to Bridgeport on the west. The park also offers hiking trails, including the Point Defiance Trail that runs beside the river down to

© ROBERT HOLMES/CALTOUR

There's great swimming below the Bridgeport Covered Bridge.

Englebright Lake. For more information, contact South Yuba River State Park, 17660 Pleasant Valley Rd. in Penn Valley, 530/432-2546. Guided hikes are sometimes offered by the **Nevada County Land Trust,** 530/272-5994, www.nevadacountylandtrust.org.

Smartville, named not for the locals' collective intelligence but after the proprietor of the town's old hotel, was a vigorous burg during the days of hydraulic mining. Ruins of the old Wells Fargo building are just about all that remain of **Timbuctoo.** The **Penn Valley** area, once called the "pantry of the mines," is still primarily small farm and ranch land; there's a big rodeo here in mid-June, and **Wild, Wild West Days** come in late August. For information, contact the **Penn Valley Area Chamber of Commerce,** 530/432-1802, www.pennvalleycoc.org.

Auburn and Vicinity

Hill-hugging Auburn, once a tent city called North Fork Dry Diggins, then Wood's Dry Diggins, was one of the first towns in the gold country. In the spring of 1848, Frenchman Claude Chana, a friend of James Marshall, found three gold nuggets here while panning in the north fork of the American River. Auburn today has a small Old Town, a homey downtown, shady old streets lined with Victorian homes, and some fine restaurants. The Auburn *Journal* has published regularly since 1872, though the Rocklin-Loomis *Placer Herald* has been a media mainstay since 1852; the newspaper's longevity (and the town's) was assured by the construction of the transcontinental railroad through here.

One of the big construction issues these days is the controversial proposal to complete the long-stalled Auburn Dam on the American River. (We need the jobs, say some locals, and more water and down-river flood protection. It's a boondoggle and ecological travesty, say environmentalists, determined to save the North Fork of the American River.) The project appears to be stalled, but Republican Congressman John Doolittle has been unrelenting in his attempts to "do a lot" and get the dam built in these otherwise budget-challenged times. The odds are slim, or at least they have been for the century or so the idea's been in political play. Still, stay tuned. Another issue is suburbia. Sacramento-style sprawl is fast approaching and, as elsewhere throughout the gold country, the area's population and home prices are surging.

SEEING AND DOING AUBURN

Downtown Auburn, the business district along Lincoln Way, is distinctly Midwestern; visitors feel more like neighbors than suckered tourists. Old Town, a national landmark, is nearby but separate, a five-square-block area at the intersection of Lincoln and Sacramento Streets. The stately **Placer County Courthouse** on Lincoln, its impressive arcaded dome looming above Old Town, was built in 1849, entirely

Placer County Courthouse

© ROBERT HOLMES/CALTOUR

GOLD COUNTRY

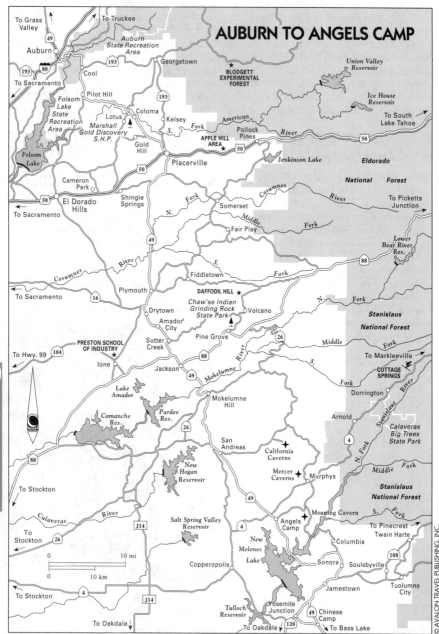

AUBURN TO ANGELS CAMP

of local materials. The town's volunteer fire department, established in 1852, is the state's oldest. But the odd four-story, red-and-white **Hook and Ladder Company Firehouse** in Old Town was built in 1893. Inside is California's first motorized fire engine. Antique hunters like the area for its antiquities and junk shops. Take a peek inside the **Shanghai Bar,** 289 Washington St., Auburn's oldest bar and almost a museum.

Museums

The fine **Gold Country Museum** is at the fairgrounds, 1273 High St., 530/887-0690, in a log-and-stone building that is itself a WPA project. Inside you'll find an elaborate model of the old courthouse crafted from leaded and stained glass, an aged doll collection, and artifacts from the town's former Maidu and Chinese communities. Gold-related exhibits include gold rush memorabilia, a walk-through hardrock mining tunnel, and a display of quartz crystals and gold. Open Tues.–Sun 11 A.M.–4 P.M., closed holidays (small fee). Nearby is the **Bernhard Museum Complex,** 291 Auburn-Folsom Rd., 530/888-6891, actually an annex of the main museum (same hours, one ticket admits you to both). Originally the Traveler's Rest Hotel, the museum is now an old Auburn family home furnished with Victorian antiques typical of the 1800s middle class. And do stop by the grandly domed, meticulously restored **Placer County Courthouse,** 101 Maple, on a rise above Old Town. Now home to the free **Placer County Museum,** 530/889-6500, displays emphasize local history, including the Placer County Gold Collection (inside the gift shop; open Tues.–Sun. 11 A.M.–4 P.M.). Added in September 2001, the museum's new communications history exhibit includes the original *Placer Herald* printing press. Then appreciate the courthouse itself—its fine wood, marble stairways, and terrazzo floors. The prettiest picture of all, though, may be from outside at night.

Diehard museum fans may want to visit some smaller local samples of the species, including the **Griffith Quarry Museum and Park,** 7504

FEATS OF CLAY

In 1874 Charles Gladding and partners Peter McBean and George Chambers established a company to manufacture sewer pipe for fast-growing San Francisco and other cities throughout the state. In the late 1800s Gladding, McBean Pottery began making architectural terracotta and roof tile for many of the country's landmark buildings—including the Wrigley Building in Chicago and Carnegie Hall in New York. Now a subsidiary of Pacific Coast Building Products located in Lincoln, just northwest of Auburn, Gladding, McBean recently reintroduced its historical glazed terracotta collection—hand-formed, made-to-order "architectural garden pottery," from oil jars, decorative planters, and urns to fountains, benches, and birdbaths. More than 130 Gladding, McBean pots were created for the new Getty Center in Los Angeles.

Still, there's plenty of clay remaining in Lincoln, judging from the impressive annual **Feats of Clay** national ceramics competition and juried exhibition sponsored by Lincoln Arts and held every spring (late April through May) at the Gladding, McBean factory, Seventh and F Sts. Admission is on guided tours only ($5), offered Wed.–Sun. 9 A.M.–noon. Reservations are required.

For more information about Feats of Clay, contact Lincoln Arts, 916/645-9713, www .lincolnarts.org. For more information about Gladding, McBean Pottery, see www.gladding-mcbean.paccoast.com.

Rocks Springs Rd. (at Taylor) in Penryn, 530/663-1837 (park open daily during daylight hours; museum open only weekends noon–4 P.M.); the **Forest Hill Divide Museum,** 24601 Harrison St. (in Leroy Botts Memorial Park) in Foresthill, 530/367-3988, with exhibits on gold rush and area logging history (open in summer, weekends noon–4 P.M.); and the one-room miner's cabin **Golden Drift Museum,** 32820 Main St. in Dutch Flat (Alta), 530/389-2126 (open in summer on Wednesday and weekends, noon–4 P.M., and by appointment at other times). All of these museums are free.

STAYING IN AUBURN

Camping

The **Auburn KOA,** 3550 KOA Way (exit I-80 at Hwy. 49 or Bell Rd.), 530/885-0990 or 800/562-6671, www.koa.com, has all the usual KOA amenities, and in this location a pool, pond, and playground. Tent sites (all prices for two people) are $25–27, RV spots $29–37. "Kamping kabins" are $45. In town, a good deal for tent campers is **Bear River Park** on Plum Tree Rd., 530/886-4900 ($10 per night per vehicle). Another choice is **Auburn State Recreation Area,** some 42,000 acres surrounding the North and Middle Forks of the American River and generally south on Hwy. 49 toward Placerville. There are five different campgrounds ($11–14); boat-in sites at the Lake Clementine campground are reservable through ReserveAmerica, 800/444-7275, www.reserveamerica.com; and the others are first-come, first-camped. For more information, contact the office at 501 El Dorado St. (at Old Foresthille Rd.) in Auburn, 530/885-4527.

If you're aching for more hill-country solitude, head out Foresthill Divide Rd. 18 miles past Foresthill to Tahoe National Forest's large **Sugar Pine Reservoir,** which offers two family campgrounds, **Shirttail Creek** and **Giant Gap Campgrounds,** both $12; to reserve sites call 877/444-6777 or see reserveusa.com. At smaller Big Reservoir nearby, popular **Big Reservoir/Morning Star Campground** (elevation 4,000 feet) includes 100 sites, piped water, pit toilets, and a beach ($18–25); call 530/367-2129 for reservations. The larger Six miles farther on a treacherous, unpaved road is the primitive **Secret House Campground** (just two sites, no water, pack garbage out), and after another eight miles, six-site **Robinson Flat Campground,** also primitive.

For real mountain camping, 35 miles beyond Foresthill via Mosquito Ridge Rd. is **French Meadows Reservoir** (no gas here). Abundant campsites are available at the U.S. Forest Service **Ahart** ($10) and **French Meadows** and **Lewis Campgrounds** (both $12), but the lake level gets very low in late summer and fall. (To reserve sites at French Meadows call 877/444-6777 or see reserveusa.com.) On the way you'll pass near the tiny **Placer Grove of Big Trees,** the northernmost grove of Sierra redwoods (picnic tables, flush toilets, nature trail). For more information about the area, call the **Foresthill Ranger Station,** 22830 Foresthill Rd., 530/367-2224.

Motels

Most of Auburn's motels line the I-80 freeway north of town near the Foresthill turnoff. There are plenty to choose from. You probably won't go wrong at **Super 8 Motel,** 140 E. Hillcrest Dr., 530/888-8808 or 800/800-8000, www.super8.com, or **Motel 6,** 1819 Auburn Ravine Rd., 530/888-7829 or 800/466-8356, www.motel6.com, but a better bet may be the **Best Western Golden Key Motel,** off I-80 at 13450 Lincoln Way, 530/885-8611 or 800/201-0121, www.bestwesterncalifornia.com. Rates at all three are $50–100.

Bed-and-Breakfasts

Auburn's showplace inn, the **Powers Mansion Inn** downtown at 164 Cleveland Ave., 530/885-1166, is a luxurious, pastel pink Victorian beauty built by gold rush millionaire Harold T. Powers at the turn of the century. It offers 15 unique rooms with antique touches yet with modern private baths. The suites are something special, with a heart-shaped Jacuzzi big enough for two in the Honeymoon Suite. Breakfast is served in the dining room downstairs. Most rooms are $100–200. Quite special north along I-80 in Colfax is the very Victorian **Rose Mountain Manor,** 233 Plutes Way, 866/444-7673, www.rosemountainmanor.com, offering peace, quiet, three gorgeous rooms, spacious grounds, and delicious home-style breakfast. Rates are $100–150. In-room day spa services and afternoon high tea are also available (extra charge).

Other choices in the area include two B&Bs in Loomis: the charming **Old Flower Farm,** 4150 Auburn-Folsom Rd., 916/652-4200 or 800/870-1104, www.oldflowerfarm.com, offering three rooms plus a country cottage ($100–150), and elegant **Emma's,** 3137 Taylor Rd., 916/652-1392 or 800/660-5157, with four suites and a cottage ($100–200) with abundant amenities, from in-room refrigerators to two-person Jacuzzi tubs.

EATING IN AUBURN

The **Auburn Certified Farmers Market** convenes every Saturday, 8 A.M.–noon, at the intersection of Lincoln Way and Auburn-Folsom Rd.; for information, call 530/823-6183. But if you're not here on a Saturday, stop instead at family-owned and -operated **Ikeda's** just off I-80 at 13500 Lincoln Way, 530/885-4243, a wonderful full-service food emporium that's been an Auburn institution, in one form or another, since 1950. Ikeda's includes a dynamite burger bar, espresso bar, fresh-fruit pie shop, fruit smoothie counter, and impressive fresh produce and gourmet food shop. If coming from Sacramento, take the Foresthill exit from I-80; from Tahoe/Reno, take the Bowman exit. Fast fooderies line the freeway frontage. Best of the bunch is **In-N-Out Burger,** located close to downtown at the junction of I-80 and Hwy. 49.

Old Town and downtown offer decent cafés and fine-dining establishments. **Mary Belle's,** 1590 Lincoln Way, 530/885-3598, serves American standards at breakfast and lunch. One of the better Asian eateries in the gold country is the **Shanghai Restaurant,** 289 Washington (in Old Town's former American Hotel), 530/823-2613. Open Thurs.–Mon. for lunch and dinner, lunch only on Wed. Full bar. **Bootleggers Old Town Tavern & Grill,** at home in Auburn's old-brick original city hall, 210 Washington St., 530/889-2229, looks something like a boardinghouse cum barn, yet the food here is far from bumpkin fare—great ribeye steak and barbecued baby back ribs, sure, but also grilled shrimp, fried oysters, vegetarian spring rolls, Indonesian satays, chicken strudel, baked Brie—everything surprisingly consistent. Wine and beer are available, including some 50 bottled beers, both imported and domestic; here you can also get a whole "boot" full of nine on-tap brews, a daunting 128 ounces worth. Open Tues.–Sat. for lunch, Tues.–Sun. for dinner.

Exceptional **Latitudes,** in the White House at 130 Maple (across from the county courthouse in Old Town), 530/885-9535, serves healthful and intriguing international cuisine in serene historic surroundings. Much of the fare here is vegetarian—a flavorful and risk-taking,

ever-changing "world cuisine" menu, from chilled fruit soups, spicy curried tofu, and fettuccine Alfredo to gingered prawns and filet of salmon. Full bar downstairs, with plentiful beer—including Sierra Nevada Pale Ale and Deschutes' Obsidian Stout on tap—and wine selections. Open for lunch and dinner Wed.–Sun., and serves brunch on Sunday.

French-country regional fare in these parts means a reservation at tiny **Le Bilig French Cafe,** 11750 Atwood Rd. (look for the Bail Bonds sign), 530/888-1491, which features a changing menu of hearty dishes—baked salmon, lobster in white butter sauce, lamb shanks roasted with fennel, ham hocks with lentils, and buckwheat or whole-wheat crepes. Beer and wine only. Open Wed.–Sun. for dinner. But for something truly special, reserve a dinner table on Wed. or Thurs.—a $25 fixed-price three-course feast.

Nearby

Madonna's Classic Kitchen up I-80 in Colfax, 42 N. Main St., 530/346-8213, is a sunny, unassuming breakfast and lunch stop by day, a classy Eurostyle Californian on weekend nights. The menu of classic and contemporary dishes changes frequently but you may discover beer-battered coconut prawns, Jamaican jerk chicken, and beef Wellington. Beer and wine only.

Worth a stop even if it weren't for the good brews and great food, **Beermann's Restaurant and Beerwerks** in Lincoln, 645 Fifth St., 916/645.2377, is housed in the town's grand brick 1864 Odd Fellows Hall, all gussied up as a gregarious Victorian-era beerhall. The charming Wild West ambience is a match for the well-muscled "cowboy cuisine," from steaks to ribs and back. Tuesday night is All-You-Can-Eat Ribs and Sides Night. (Vegans, fear not: there are other possibilities here.) The brewpub also serves Beermann's award-winning beers, including Rip Roarin' Red, Lincoln Lager, Industrial Stout, and Bourbon Barrel Barley-Wine Ale. Open Tues.–Sun. 11:30 A.M.–10 P.M. Some of the other "rooms" here, reservable for meetings and special events, are quite special—including the Victorian Roof Garden and the Empire Ballroom.

Another great choice is the **Horseshoe Bar**

Grill in Loomis at 3645 Taylor Rd., 916/652-2222, "an American bistro" serving contemporary, seasonally changing fare, from oysters "salsafeller" and other seafood selections to blackened red snapper, pan-roasted herbed chicken, and pastas. Open Tues.–Fri. for lunch, nightly for dinner, and Sun. for brunch.

EVENTS

The **Auburn Wild West Stampede** comes in April, bringing pro rodeo and a parade to town. Wild and wet in early June is the annual **American River Confluence Festival** on the river just a few miles south of town via Hwy. 49—a day of ecology hikes, children's nature and art activities, kayaking demonstrations, and music. In late June, stand downtown and watch people drop at the finish line of the **Western States Endurance Run,** a one-day, 100-mile run so popular that runners are selected by lottery for the privilege of brutalizing their bodies on the horse trail between here and Squaw Valley. Horses and riders undergo the same ordeal in July during the **Western States Trail Ride,** also known as the Tevis Cup 100 Miles One Day cross-country endurance race. In September, come for the **Gold Country Fair,** a round-up of all the best food, fun, and festivities the gold country has to offer. The **Auburn Air Fair** comes in October, and December brings a **Festival of Lights Parade and Celebration,** as well as **Country Christmas** festivities (in Old Town).

Always fun, and within reasonable reach of Auburn, is the annual, world-class **Feats of Clay** national ceramics competition and exhibition usually held from April into May at the Gladding McBean factory at Seventh and F Streets in Lincoln, and sponsored by Lincoln Arts. For current information, call 916/645-9713 or see www.lincolnarts.org.

INFORMATION AND SERVICES

The **Auburn Area Chamber of Commerce,** 601 Lincoln Way, 530/885-5616, www.auburnchamber.net, is housed in the attractive and restored railroad depot, open weekdays 9 A.M.–5 P.M. Stop by to pick up the local walking-tour brochure and other visitor information. The helpful **Placer County Visitor Information and California Welcome Center,** 13411 Lincoln Way (Foresthill exit from I-80), 530/887-2111 or 866/752-2371, http://visitplacer.com, is open daily 9 A.M.–3 P.M.—though you can peruse the racks outside at other times. Here, you'll find info on just about everything. To get current state camping and recreation information for the area, contact the **Auburn State Recreation Area** (see Camping above). For white-water rafting, hiking, and other camping options, contact the U.S. Forest Service **Foresthill Ranger District** office, 22830 Foresthill Rd. in Foresthill, 530/367-2224.

"AUBURN DAM" AND VICINITY

What outraged environmentalists couldn't stop—a massive dam construction project destined to create a two-fingered, 25-mile-long lake in these canyons of the American River—nature did. In 1975, an impressive earthquake with its epicenter at Oroville Dam 60 miles to the north revealed a major, previously unrecognized fault line directly beneath the Auburn Dam site.

The first calls in support of dam construction came in response to potential downstream flooding problems—and also in response to the state's occasional prolonged droughts and ever-increasing demand for energy. (A major dam, the argument went, would create some balance between the dangers of either too much or too little water, plus generate hydroelectricity.) But the costs of such a dam, and lack of unanimity about the genuine need for it, has led to great acrimony, and to a variety of scaled-down proposals. One possibility, proposed by the U.S. Army Corps of Engineers, called for a smaller yet expandable 498-foot-high dry dam for flood control—a project since scaled down to a height of 430 feet. That proposal was subsequently attacked by independent consultants because downstream levees along the American River may not withstand the calculated high-water river flows, and because the environmental consequences of a "dry" dam—which would create a substantial lake—were significantly underestimated.

Though the U.S. Congress has approved the dam, in some form, it has yet to authorize funding for it—and, with the exception of local Congress member John Doolittle, area political support is fairly tepid. Locals say the project is on hold indefinitely, much to the relief of environmentalists and white-water rafting enthusiasts, but with Republicans in control of Congress, these days all bets are off.

Foresthill Bridge

East of Auburn near the confluence of the American River's north and middle forks, the half-mile-long Foresthill Bridge is hard to miss, pulled taut across the canyon like a giant concrete clothesline. Built to connect Foresthill to the outside world if and when the Auburn Dam ever inundates the canyon, the $1.5 million bridge is a solution without a problem, though it has created problems of its own. Looming almost 800 feet above the chasm, the span is a temptation for thrill-seeking (if stupid) parachutists, hang gliders, and (sadly) the suicidal. If you don't mind heights and speeding traffic, walk across for a spectacular vista. To get to the big bridge, head north from Old Town on Lincoln Way, then turn south on Foresthill Rd.

Cool

The best thing about the horseshoe-shaped town of Cool is the sign announcing the town's existence and—if you're from around these parts—being able to say "I'm from Cool." How *cool.* Once a stage stop, Cool's now just a semicommercial spot in the road where Hwy. 49 joins Hwy. 193. A handful of shops plus 1880s-vintage general store, gas station, deli, bar, and feedstore are Cool's main attractions. Limestone quarries operate north of here, and the area supports cattle ranching and pear orchards.

Pilot Hill

"Pilot" fires were lit on the tallest hill near here to guide one of Frémont's parties into the Sierra, hence the name. There's not much to see here except a unique gold country phenomenon, the only Southern-style plantation around. The 22-room, 10,000-square-foot "Bayley's Folly" is an 1862 red-brick Greek revival–style railroad roadhouse doomed when the "Big Four" routed the Central Pacific Railroad tracks near Auburn instead. Next to the old hotel is the first California grange hall, built in 1880; by 1860 wheat was a more valuable commodity here than gold. In 1989 the Georgetown Divide Recreation District bought the Bayley House (now listed on the National Register of Historic Places) for $1, and still seeks restoration funds. To help out, see www.thebayleyhouse.com.

COLOMA

Coloma was the site of a former Cullooma Maidu village but is most notable for its historic role as birthplace of the California gold rush. In 1849, more than 10,000 miners populated this tiny valley, but just two years later the town was "gold-dry" and dull (at least by miners' standards). Most of Coloma is now part of the 240-acre **Marshall Gold Discovery State Historic Park.**

You could spend a lazy day wandering through Coloma's scattered buildings and exhibits, especially pleasant in spring when sweet peas, poppies, and blackberry bushes bloom, or in fall when the leaves turn gold in honor of the town's historic beginnings. Plan a pleasant picnic by the river, go for a swim or wade in the American River's south fork—watch for rampaging rafts—and hike foothill trails.

In summer, the park is inundated with waves of river rafters, up to 1,800 people a day on weekends. Expect bumper-to-bumper traffic, trash problems, quarrels over parking spaces, theft, and hearty partying. Serious rafters should leave Coloma, at least in summer, to the partiers.

The park is open 8 A.M.–sunset year-round. The day-use fee is $5 per vehicle ($4 for seniors). For information on the park or special events, contact: Marshall Gold Discovery State Historic Park, 530/622-3470. For more information about the area, contact the **Coloma-Lotus Chamber of Commerce,** www.colomalotus.com.

Seeing and Doing Coloma

The park's main attraction, with summer tourists buzzing around it like wasps, is the full-size

24-KARAT WHITE WATER

The Sierra Nevada white-water so essential to river rafting, and so refreshing to the active imagination, is actually a gold country phenomenon. Waterways that begin as mere springs fed by High Sierra snowmelt are raging torrents by the time they race down through the western foothills. River conditions can change dramatically from year to year, depending on snowpack and rainfall, so it pays to pay for guidance. Get a listing of the region's many reputable local rafting companies from chambers of commerce or national forest offices. Offerings vary widely in price and level of adventure. Midweek rates are often cheaper, and group plans are usually available.

Many of the companies listed below also offer river trips in the state's far northern mountains, along the north coast, or elsewhere in California. Some even offer trips in other parts of the U.S. and the world. To gather complete and current information, with plenty of time to make an informed choice (and reservations), contact any of the companies listed below in early fall and request a current expeditions catalog for the following winter/spring season. Most trips include rafts, guides, meals, and beverages, and the rafting companies will state specifically what you'll need to bring. Most companies accept credit cards. For information on other worthwhile river trips and rafting

companies in Northern California, see in particular The Northern Mountains chapter.

In business since 1969, Outdoor Adventure River Specialists or **O.A.R.S., Inc.** of Angels Camp, 209/736-4677 or 800/346-6277, www.oars.com, is noted for its white-water guide and kayaking school as well as its excellent trips, including the Jawbone Canyon run on the upper Tuolumne River and the spectacular North Fork of the Stanislaus. Its spring Merced River run makes the most of a Yosemite trip. Or try special wine-tasting tours, considerably tamer. Intriguing, too, is the O.A.R.S. Family Friendly program, which offers fun (and safe) river float or kayak trips in California and elsewhere (Wyoming, Utah, Idaho, Oregon), the adventure including tent-pitching, and hiking excursions designed for parent and child, Or you might be interested in the company's Senior Program, which includes whale-watching in Mexico, a cruise to Alaska, Utah Canyonlands excursions, and a Grand Canyon Five-Day Sampler. You can book reservations for any trip online, too.

Whitewater Connection, 7170 Hwy. 49 (near Marshall Gold Discovery State Park and a stone's throw from the American River) in Coloma, 530/622-6446 or 800/336-7238 in the U.S., www .whitewaterconnection, is a popular concern offering everything from placid family float trips to Class

replica of **Sutter's Mill** near the river. Demonstrations and lectures about how it works are held daily at 2 P.M. Adjacent is a restored miners cabin.

The park's **Gold Museum** and visitors' center, across the highway from the mill, is first-rate and a good place to start exploring. Here are a rare collection of Maidu artifacts, history exhibits, some of James Marshall's memorabilia, plus dioramas and films. Open daily 10 A.M.–4:30 P.M., except on major holidays.

The stone-and-shuttered **Wah Hop Store and Bank** is a revivified Chinese general store; on display are herbs and animal parts for medicinal potions, an altar and ancestral portraits, business desk, tea cups, and rice bowls. Another store—and you can shop at this one—is the **Arg-

onaut,** a soda fountain and candy shop with home-brewed root beer.

Farther south, note the freestanding steel jail cell and crumbling old stone jailhouse ruins. Nearby is the new **Papini House Museum,** a turn-of-the-20th-century home complete with antique garden tools. Other sights and activities include mining technique demonstrations, stagecoaches, and the old "Mormon Cabin" (a reconstruction of Marshall's cabin, downhill from his final resting place near the Catholic church). Art lovers should peek into the 1855 **Friday House,** the gallery home of the late artist George Mathis. On the hill behind Coloma is a monumental statue of James Marshall, erected in belated gratitude by the state after his death.

On the American River across from Sutter's

VI white-water adventures designed "for those with suicidal tendencies." Great for parents of children too young for rafting are the reasonably priced Shared Parenting Trips, which allow each parent a day out on the water while the other tends to the tykes. The company emphasizes runs on the American, including challenging Class III–IV Middle Fork and North/South Fork combination runs, as well as Class IV North Fork trips (experience and wetsuits required). For a similar challenge, sign on for White-water Connection's Kaweah River run, an eight-mile rush through the redwoods of Sequoia National Park. Still, this business is not all fun and games; all Whitewater Connection trip prices include a contribution to the American River Coalition, the American River Land Trust, and the Friends of the River.

Other firms offering American River raft and white-water trips include **Adventure Connection** in Coloma, 530/626-7385 or 800/556-6060, www .raftcalifornia.com; **All-Outdoors Whitewater Rafting** 800/247-2387, www.aorafting.com; **EarthTrek Expeditions** in Lotus (near Coloma), 530/642-1900 or 800/229-8735, www.earthtrekexpeditions .com; **Mother Lode River Center** in Lotus, 800/427-2387, www.malode.com; and **Tributary Whitewater Tours** of Grass Valley, 530/346-6812 or 800/672-3846, www.whitewatertours.com, which also runs the Yuba, Truckee, Carson, and other rivers.

Ahwahnee Whitewater Expeditions in Columbia, 209/533-1401 or 800/359-9790, www.ah-wahnee.com, is a small firm offering some big rides within reach of both Tahoe and Yosemite. The one- to three-day trips include easy floats on the Carson River in the High Sierra and more challenging plunges down the Tuolumne (one of the state's best), Merced, and Stanislaus Rivers as well as Cherry Creek near Yosemite. Sister raft outfit **Zephyr River Expeditions, Inc.,** 209/532-6249 or 800/431-3636, www.zrafting.com, offers reasonably priced runs on the American and wilder rivers, including the Kings, Merced, and the almost unrunnable Upper Tuolumne (experts only). Zephyr also offers charter group "gourmet" trips and contributes a pass-through fee to river conservation and relevant environmental groups. **Sierra Mac River Trips, Inc.** of Sonora, 209/532-1327 or 800/457-2580, www.sierramac.com, also comes highly recommended—particularly for expert Class IV and V runs on the Tuolumne River.

Women-owned **Mariah Wilderness Expeditions,** 510/233-2303 or 800/462-7424, www.mari-ahwe.com, offers one- or two-day trips on the Merced, Kings, and Tuolumne Rivers and the south, middle, and north forks of the American River. Some trips, designed especially for families, take a storyteller along.

Mill is the **Coloma Outdoor Discovery School,** 6921 Mt. Murphy Rd., 530/621-2298, offering three-day "experiential learning" natural history and environmental education programs for children Oct.–May.

Gold Hill

About a mile north of the old Vineyard House is the ghost town of Gold Hill. Here in the 1860s, a German immigrant who'd spent most of his life in Japan started the first Japanese settlement in California. The Wakamatsu Tea and Silk Colony brought bamboo, tea seeds, grape cuttings, and mulberry trees here from Japan in hopes of starting a major tea and silk plantation. Despite the favorable climate, unhealthy stock and damaging incursions by miners prevented

the venture from becoming a success. The school here includes a lovely Japanese garden and shrine.

Practicalities

The fine and friendly **Coloma Country Inn,** 345 High St. (just a two-block stroll from Sutter's Mill), 530/622-6919, www.colomacountryinn .com, is a Cape Cod–style home with sitting porch and gardens. Painstakingly restored, the inn offers four quilt-cozied guest rooms (in the main house, all with private baths, and one separate suite (sleeps up to four) in the carriage house. Rooms are $100–150, suite $250.

Area campgrounds include **Camp Lotus,** 530/622-8672, www.camplotus.com, with hot showers, picnic tables, barbecues, volleyball, and horseshoes. Rates are $18–24 per campsite per

© ROBERT HOLMES/CALTOUR

Marshall Gold Discovery State Historic Park, Sutter's Mill

night, or $6 per person midweek ($8 on weekends), kids eight and under free. Lotus is sometimes packed with rowdy river rafters, so call ahead for weekend reservations. The **Coloma Resort & RV Park,** right on the river at 6921 Mt. Murphy Rd., 530/621-2267 or 800/238-2298, www.colomaresort.com, offers fishing, gold panning, and camping rates of $30–32 for two people. Tent cabins, bunkhouses, and group camps also available.

Adam's Red Brick Restaurant at the Golden Lotus Bed and Breakfast, 1006 Lotus Rd., 530/621-4562, is an eccentric Coloma dining destination, an 1855 general store—just the place for discovering spicy beef vindaloo with mango chutney or beef bourgignon or pork Madeira. Dinners are served Friday and Saturday nights only, at a price of $25 per couple. Specialty desserts—including lemon tart, triple chocolate mousse pie, and pear-raspberry and other cobblers—are extra, as are appetizers. Last checked, the restaurant was for sale, so call ahead for information. Or try the **Coloma Club Cafe,** on Hwy. 49 at Marshall Rd. (the road to Georgetown), 530/626-6390, where you'll get Western humor and generous helpings (the lasagna is particularly good). The club is

open daily, with live C&W music on Saturday nights. If it's pizza you crave, head to **Yosum's Pizza,** 7312 Hwy. 49, 530/622-9277.

Events

In May, Coloma hosts its **Art in the Park** weekend arts and crafts festival in conjunction with El Dorado County's Celebrate the Arts week. For drama and melodrama on weekend nights (May–Sept.), try the Crescent Players' performances at the **Olde Coloma Theatre,** 380 Monument Trail (just up the hill off Cold Springs Road). Tickets are $10 ($5 for children 12 and under); call 530/626-5282 for reservations. Come in mid-June for **Coloma Fest,** something of a historic demonstration day, when costumed docents display all kinds of period arts, crafts, and trade skills, from ropemaking to pine-needle basketry. But there's more—everything from river float trips and classic car show to the Highway 50 Wagon Train. **Gold Rush Days** and the **U.S. National Goldpanning Championship** (in some years Coloma hosts the World Goldpanning Championships) are scheduled concurrently in late September/early October, a tent-city circus including also goldpanning lessons, a market, parade, live music, and living history demonstrations. Come in October for the **49er Family Festival.** Big doings here in winter include the **Christmas in Coloma** festivities each December and **Discovery Day,** January 24. Tours of the town's **Pioneer Cemetery** are offered on weekends, subject to the availability of docents. For current information on local events, contact the state park office. For current river-rafting information, see 24-Karat White Water in this chapter.

Georgetown and Vicinity

"Mr. Gold Rush" James Marshall, reclusive blacksmith, lived in **Kelsey** from 1848 until he died, penniless, in 1885. His blacksmith shop still stands just outside town, though most of Marshall's memorabilia is in the museum at Coloma. Mining-camp names near here (except self-evident Fleatown) reflected miners' ethnic origins: Irish Creek, Louisville (French), Elizatown (English), American Flat, Spanish Flat. Take Rock Creek Rd., then Reservoir Rd. to pretty **Finnon Lake,** where you can camp, picnic, fish, and hike. There's even a restaurant. Or, take Marshall Rd. back down toward the river and Coloma.

Here in the far north of the mythic Mother Lode on the divide between the American River's north and south forks, **Georgetown** is like a tiny New England hill town with pretty Victorians and fragrant rose gardens. It was once called Growlersburg, because the nuggets found here were so large they "growled" in the gold pans. The 1859 **Balzar House,** now the Odd Fellows Hall, was originally a three-story dance hall and was later used as an opera house. The **Shannon Knox House,** like a few other gold country structures, was constructed from lumber shipped around the Horn. Near Georgetown is the 3,000-acre **Blodgett Experimental Forest,** a UC Berkeley outdoor laboratory where computer models help create U.S. commercial forests of the future. From Georgetown, head west on Wentworth Springs Rd. to **Stumpy Meadows Reservoir,** a pretty 320-acre lake with clear, cold water, and plentiful pines and firs. Good camping.

Center of local social life is the balconied **Georgetown Hotel & Bar,** 6260 Main St., 530/333-2848. Even if you're just passing through, peek in to appreciate the rough stone bar and fireplace, rich woodwork, and eclectic furnishings: tractor seat barstools, decorative farm equipment, cowboy boots dangling from the ceiling. Karaoke on Sat. and Mon. nights. (Yep. It gets rowdy here.) Quite good for café fare is the **Corner Kitchen** across the street at the onetime Wells Fargo stage stop, 6265 Main St., 530/333-1630. The 1853 **American River Inn** at Main and Orleans, 530/333-4499 or 800/245-6566, www.americanriverinn.com, was once a Wells Fargo office and a mining camp boardinghouse. Today it offers nothing but elegant country-style Victorian luxury, with a pool, spa, lovely gardens, an aviary, and yes, an antique shop. Breakfasts here are fabulous. And how about that eight-person jetted Victorian hot tub? Rates are $85 for rooms with shared baths, $95 for private baths. Suites are around $100.

Placerville and Vicinity

Hangtown and Oak Tree Justice

Known at one time or another as Dry Diggins, Ravine City, and Hangtown—in honor of the locals' enthusiastic administration of oak tree justice—Placerville was a wild town in bygone days. Today the seat of El Dorado County and the historical heart of the gold country, Placerville was strategically located on the old Overland Trail (now Hwy. 50) and the road to Coloma. The town prospered during the rush to Nevada's Comstock Lode; it was a chief way station en route, boasting telegraph, Pony Express, and Overland Mail service.

A few industrial kingpins got their start here. Railroad magnate Mark Hopkins set up shop on Main St., peddling groceries from Sacramento. Canned meat king Philip Armour ran a small butcher shop here. John Studebaker built wheelbarrows for miners, one-wheeled predecessors of his later automobiles. And Leland Stanford, progenitor of Stanford University, ran a store in nearby Cold Springs. These days, Placerville is losing much of its charm to progress and is often crowded to overflowing with a fast-growing local population and Tahoe traffic.

SEEING AND DOING PLACERVILLE

The town's pride and joy is the 60-acre **Gold Bug Mine** in Gold Bug Park (about a mile north of town on Bedford Ave.), 530/642-5207, www .goldbugpark.org, the only city-owned gold mine in the country. Take a guided tour of the well-lit Gold Bug, one of 250 gold mines once active within the park's perimeter; bring a sweater. Also tourable: the Hendy Stamp Mill and the Priest Mine on the hill above the Gold Bug. Open daily 10 A.M.–4 P.M. mid-Apr.–Oct., and only on weekends noon–4 P.M. (weather permitting) otherwise. Small admission.

The **El Dorado County Historical Museum,** 104 Placerville Dr. at the county fairgrounds two miles west of town, 530/621-5865, is worth a stop. Exhibits in the yard full of aged vehicles and equipment include a restored Concord stagecoach, one of Studebaker's wheelbarrows and several Studebaker Brothers wagons, Pony Express paraphernalia, and a pair of Snowshoe Thompson's skis. Open Wed.–Sun. 10 A.M.–4 P.M. Admission free. Also operated by the El Dorado Historical Society is downtown's **Fountain-Tallman Historical Museum,** 524 Main St., 530/626-0773, located in the town's original 1852 soda works and today serving up period furnishings and other exhibits on local history. Open Mar.– Oct. Fri.–Sun. noon–4 P.M. and Nov.–Feb. on weekends only, noon–4 P.M.

Downtown

Downtown Placerville has other attractions, and is worth a stroll. At 305 Main is the spot where Hangtown's old hangin' tree once grew; a doomed dummy strung up from the second story of the Hangman's Tree Bar offers graphic testimony to the reality of the bad ol' days. (Inside there's a swell jukebox stocked with an ever-changing array of genuine 45 rpm records, spinning tunes from Guy Lombardo's *Hot Time in the Old Town Tonight* and Bing Crosby's *My Blue Heaven* to

Funky New Year by the Eagles.) Hangtown's old fire bell, used to summon both vigilantes and volunteer firefighters, also hangs—from an 1898 steel tower up the street at Main and Center. The narrow, rugged old firehouse is now **Placerville City Hall,** at Main and Bedford Streets. The local **courthouse,** circa 1912, is flanked by two Civil War cannons. The classic brick **Cary House,** which replaced the old Raffles Hotel at 300 Main, is worth a look-see; today it's an elegant hostelry also housing professional offices. Also peek into the **Placerville News Company,** 409 Main, a genuine old general store-style newsstand, and **Placerville Hardware,** 441 Main.

STAYING IN PLACERVILLE
Camping

For clean, close-in camping with hot showers (RVs only, unfortunately), head to the **El Dorado County Fairgrounds,** 100 Placerville Dr., 530/621-5860, www.eldoradocountyfair.org ($15, but not available when a big event is going on). In nearby Shingle Springs, is the attractive **KOA Placerville Campground,** 4655 Rock Barn Rd., 530/676-2267 or 800/562-4197 (reservations only), www.koa.com; tent sites are $22–25, RV sites $30–45, and "kabins" $45–60. Primitive campgrounds are scattered throughout El Dorado National Forest, but most are well into the Sierra Nevada; for information, contact the **ENF Information Center,** 3070 Camino Heights Dr. in Camino, 530/644-6048, www.fs.fed.us/r5/eldorado. At Jenkinson Lake, **Sly Park Recreation Area,** 4771 Sly Park Rd. in Pollock Pines, 530/644-2545 (general information) or 530/644-2792 (reservations), is RV paradise; to get here, drive 17 miles east on Hwy. 50 to Pollock Pines, then turn south on Sly Park Rd./County Rd. E16. The campground offers swimming and fishing, but no showers ($16 per night per vehicle).

Cary House and B&Bs

For a sense of local history stay at the refurbished and cheerful 19th-century **Historic Cary House Hotel,** downtown at 300 Main St., 530/622-4271, www.caryhouse.com, with fresh but simple rooms, each uniquely decorated with antiques, all with private baths, TV, phone, even air-conditioning, many with kitchenettes. Rates are $100–150. If you happen to be here for the inn's reception on Friday or Saturday night, behave yourself; you'll probably meet up with the Hangtown Marshalls.

The Seasons, a block off main street at 2934 Bedford Ave., 530/626-4420, www.theseasons .net, is an exquisitely restored, artfully decorated 1859 redbrick and stone home with vast gardens. The Gardener's Cottage hosts both the Pomegranate and the Dreamer rooms; the Cottage was once seamstress "Miss Jo's" home, as befits the cheering quilts and other colorful fabrics dressing up the white wrought-iron bed. Inside the house, with a private entrance off the flagstone terrace, the Plumado Suite is suitable for couples traveling together or a family of four, though the two rooms can be let separately. Rooms are $100–150, $240 for both Plumado rooms.

The elegant **Chichester-McKee House,** 800 Spring St., 530/626-1882 or 800/831-4008, www.cabbi.com, is an 1892 Victorian featuring four upstairs guest rooms with private baths, fireplaces, a parlor, library, conservatory, and large porches. A full breakfast is served in the dining room. Rates are $100–150. The **Combellack-Blair House,** 3059 Cedar Ravine Rd., 530/622-3764, is another lovely local Victorian with three rooms, all with private bath. The porch swing adds to the old-days ambience, as do the gardens; a three-story spiral staircase climbs to the cupola. Rates are $100–150. North of town near Chili Bar, the **River Rock Inn,** 530/622-7640, has four rooms all opening onto the deck (with hot tub) above the American River. Two rooms have half baths. Children are genuinely welcome, and a full breakfast is served. Rooms are $100–150. For a current bed-and-breakfast brochure, contact **Historic Country Inns of El Dorado County,** 877/262-4667, www.goldcountrylodging.com.

EATING IN PLACERVILLE

The **Placerville Certified Farmers Market** convenes May–Oct. on Sat., 8 A.M.–noon, at Main St. and Cedar Ravine Rd. For information, call 530/622-1900. The **Placerville Coffee House and Pub,** 594 Main St., 530/642-8481, is just the place for latte and a tour of the abandoned mining tunnel just behind.

Placerville is the hometown of "Hangtown fry," a surprisingly tasty creation of oysters and bacon wrapped up as an omelette or scramble, first concocted during the days of the gold rush. Two places to try Hangtown fry are **Chuck's Restaurant,** 1318 Broadway, 530/622-2858, where it's served all day and included as an omelette on the American menu (not the Chinese menu); and the **Hangtown Grill,** 423 Main, 530/626-4431, where it's served as a scramble and only until 4 P.M. A favorite breakfast and lunch spot on the road to Tahoe is the **Apple Café,** a few miles past town at 2740 Hwy. 50 E., 530/626-8144, where people have been known to stop just for the homemade apple strudel. Otherwise a good bet at breakfast is **Sweetie Pies,** 577 Main, 530/642-0128, where coffee and a pecan roll (or two) will sweeten you up at breakfast. At lunch, order quiche and a green salad or house-made soup and sourdough bread. Don't miss the olallieberry pie.

Z Pie, 3182 Center St., 530/621-2626, is another place for pie, in this case, fresh, house-made pot pies—11 kinds, from Mediterranean salmon, Italian sausage, and steak and cabernet to Thai chicken and tomatillo stew. Healthy fare, organic coffees, smoothies, and microbrews are on tap at **Cozmic Café,** 594 Main St. in the striking Pearson's Soda Works, 530/642-8481. For seafood, including tasty clam chowder and cioppino, try **Powell Brothers Steamer Co.,** 425 Main St., 530/626-1091. Still a local culinary star in town is inventive **Café Luna,** on the creek at 451 Main, 530/642-8669, where the fare often takes on a European accent. The menu changes weekly, but expect everything from vegetarian fusion and pastas to marinated flank steak.

Sequoia, 643 Bee St., 530/622-5222, occupies the striking 1853 Bee-Bennett House, an imposing, rambling Victorian setting for its French-accented New American meals. At lunch and dinner Sequoia offers entrées such as rack of lamb chop, flank steak Chimichurri, prime rib, and Southwestern grilled salmon.

Eating near Hangtown

A fine-dining find east of Diamond Springs just south of Placerville is the exceptional **Zachary Jacques,** 1821 Pleasant Valley Rd., 530/626-8045, noted for its seasonal country French wonders, from roast rack of lamb and cassoulet to king salmon in puff pastry. Wine and beer only (excellent wine list, earning the *Wine Spectator* Award of Excellence for 10 years and counting). Full dinners are served Wed.–Sun., with a light menu also available in the wine bar after 4:30 P.M. Winemakers' dinners are also scheduled. Reservations advised, especially on weekends. The special, weekly-changing "Sunday in the Country" menu for Sunday dinner is a fixed price ($24 at last report).

For barbecue lovers, and considerably more casual, **Poor Red's** bar and restaurant, 6221 Pleasant Valley Rd. (the main street) in El Dorado, 530/622-2901, is material for legendary. Somewhat unsavory looking—a stark institutional-green stucco building with metal door and neon on the blink—this is the town's 1858 Wells Fargo building and the perfect place to hide decent down-home food: oakwood pit-broiled ribs, chicken, ham, and steak. People here and elsewhere swear Red's barbecue is the best in the West, but expect a wait for a table on weekends. While you wait, sample Red's secret-recipe alcoholic concoction, the "golden cadillac," which takes its color from Galliano—and Poor Red's buys more of it from its Italian maker than anyone else in the world. Here, you can stuff yourself at dinner plus walk out with that unmistakable golden glow for about $15. To beat the weekend wait for tables, try takeout (at least on the food). Open every day except Thanksgiving and Christmas.

EVENTS

Starting in January, come any month for downtown's **Third Saturday Night Artwalk,** 6–9 P.M., when merchants and galleries stay open late. Major in early April are the El Dorado Winery Association's **Passport Weekends,** special tours of area wineries that typically sell out many months in advance. Coolest thing going in late April is the annual, family-friendly **American River Festival,** www.americanriverfestival.org, which includes a white-water rodeo and races, live music, dinner, and more. Come to the El Dorado County Fairgrounds in June for the annual **John M. Studebaker Championship Wheelbarrow Races,** an event founded in 1939. From June through October, free **Jazz and Blues in the Plaza** concerts are offered on Sat. 2–5 P.M. in Fountain Plaza (behind the Cary House) downtown; jazz is offered on the first and third Saturdays of each month, blues on the second and fourth Saturdays. The **El Dorado County Fair** takes place in mid-June at the county fairgrounds. Late in June, the **Pioneer Days Festival** coincides with the high point of the annual wagon train trip overland from Carson City, Nevada, to Sacramento.

At the end of August, the annual **Mother Lode Antique Show and Sale** comes to the fairgrounds. On Labor Day weekend, 45 area farms open their gates for apple picking (see Apple Hill below). Also come midmonth for the **El Dorado County Harvest Faire, Logging Days, and Wine Festival,** www.atasteofeldorado.com, and in late September for downtown's **Antique Street Faire.** In October downtown Placerville hosts the **Art & Wine Festival.**

INFORMATION

Placerville has a huge, free parking garage downtown. The **Placerville Downtown Association,** 530/672-3436, www.placerville-downtown.org, organizes multiple events in historic downtown, and offers other downtown information. Stop by the **El Dorado County Chamber of Commerce,** 542 Main St., 530/621-5885 or 800/457-6279, www.eldoradocounty.org, for information about what's going on farther afield, too, plus free maps and guides. Also under the same roof is the **El Dorado County Visitors Authority,** www.visit-eldorado.com. Across the street in Town Hall is the city's **parks and recreation office,** 549 Main, 530/642-5232.

The county boasts about 35 wineries, most of these near Placerville. A complete list of them is available at the chamber office; from the **El Dorado Wine Grape Growers Association,** www.edwgga.org, and from the **El Dorado Winery Association,** 800/306-3956, www.eldoradowines.org.

APPLE HILL AND VICINITY

On the ridge east from Placerville to near Camino, the Apple Hill "tour" follows a path originally blazed by Pony Express riders—a great bike ride when the roads aren't choked with cars. It's hard to believe that half a million people visit this suburban ranch region each autumn, but they do; weekend traffic then is a nightmare. The reason for the influx? In late summer and fall, farms along the way sell tree-fresh apples and delectable, decadent homemade treats: apple pies and strudel, cheesecake, other fine baked goods, apple cider, spicy apple butter, and even caramel and fudge apples. Earlier in the year you can get cherries, strawberries, plums, peaches, and pears; natural honey is available year-round.

What can beat fresh, crisp homegrown apples themselves, especially some of the rare varieties you'll find here, from Arkansas Black, Empire, King David, and Northern Spy to Paula Red and Winesap? Mmm-mmm. **Denver Dan's** in the Quonset hut at 4354 Bumblebee Ln., 530/644-6881, offers well over 30 kinds of apples—many not available until later in the fall, when the crowds drop off—plus all kinds of applesauces and at least 20 apple vinegars. A good year-round produce (and gift) stop is **Boa Vista Orchards,** 2952 Carson Rd., 530/622-5522, where you'll also find apple wine, great traditional pie, and apple turnovers. Country store–style **Grandpa's Cellar,** 2360 Cable Rd., 530/644-2153, offers all kinds of apple pie, from fabulous apple turnovers to raspberry cream-cheese apple pie. But don't miss the "walkin' pie" with hot cider sauce at **Kid's Inc.,** 3245 N. Canyon Rd., 530/622-0184, where the apple crisp and French apple pie are also quite good. **Rainbow Orchards,** 2569 Larsen Dr., 530/644-1594, serves killer apple-cider doughnuts, fabulous apple crisp, and incredible caramel apples. The Larsens of **Larsen Apple Barn,** 2461 Larsen Dr., 530/644-1415, have roots on Apple Hill that reach back to 1860, so the clan definitely knows its apples—and apple turnovers. An-

other long-running favorite is **High Hill Ranch,** 2901 High Hill Rd., 530/644-1973, something of an apple-themed funhouse complete with arts and crafts booths and kiddie fishing pond. **Abel's Apple Acres,** 2345 Carson Rd., 530/626-0138, offers 20 varieties of apple pie, consistently good; try the buttermilk apple pie. Especially fun for the kiddos: pony rides and a hay maze.

Hometown-style Apple Hill hoedowns include the June **Father's Day Cherry Festival** and the **Blueberry Festival** in July. The **Harvest Festival** is really more like "Harvest Season," taking place from Labor Day through the end of the year. ("We have a *lot* of apples up here," locals say.) People also come up to Apple Hill in October, November, and December for pumpkins and gourds, late-ripening apples, and to cut their own locally grown yule trees. Get a free Apple Hill growers map and other information at the **Apple Hill Visitor Center,** 2461 Larsen Dr. in Camino, 530/644-7692, or see the **Apple Hill Growers Association** website, www.applehill.com. If you're packing off pecks of farm-fresh apples, you may also want to pick up the official *Apple Hill Growers Cookbook.*

Just a half block from Apple Hill's visitors center is the **Camino Hotel Bed and Breakfast,** downtown at 4103 Carson Rd., 530/644-7740 or 800/200-7740, www.caminohotel.com, a charming, fully renovated historic hotel (The Seven Mile House) along the old Carson Trail. The nine guest rooms here are intimate and as cheery as the parlor; several have private baths, and the others share two hall baths. Enjoy breakfast, fresh coffee, and dessert (in the evening) on the sun porch or inside by the woodstove. Special events, such as the annual Camino Art Show, are sometimes scheduled here, too. Room rates are $50–100.

Wineries and Brewery

Fruit of the vine is also a hot item around Apple Hill. The biggest establishment is **Boeger Winery,** 1709 Carson Rd. (at Schnell School), 530/622-8094, www.boegerwinery.com, which offers a fine 1872 stone cellar and tasting room open daily 10 A.M.–5 P.M.—try some Hangtown Red table wine—as well as picnicking near a stream.

Boeger was one of California's first producers of a varietal merlot—and is still a varietal innovator. Free tours are available on Wednesdays and weekends. Among the many other area wineries offering tasting and picnicking are **Coulson Winery,** 3550 Carson Rd., 530/644-2854, www.coulsonwinery.com, "home of the happy grapes"; **Lava Cap Winery,** 2221 Fruitridge Rd., 530/621-0175, www.lavacap.com; and **Madroña Vineyards,** on High Hill Rd. (off Carson Rd.) in Camino, 530/644-5948, www.madronavineyards.com. Call for tasting times and other details.

If what you need is a *beer*, though, head for the **Jack Russell Brewing Co.,** 2380 Larsen Dr. (off Carson Rd.), 530/644-4722, www.jackrussellbrewing.com. This microbrewery doggedly produces British-style ales using finishing hops grown right here on the farm. Tours, tasting, and picnicking are available. Open daily 11 A.M.–5 P.M.

Somerset and Fair Play Wineries

Southeast of Placerville in Pleasant Valley (reached via Pleasant Valley Rd. off Hwy. 49) is the **Sierra Vista Winery,** 4560 Cabernet Way (end of Leisure Ln.), 530/622-7221, sierravistawinery.com, specializing in Northern Rhône varietals and open for tasting daily 10 A.M.–4 P.M. Good wineries in the Fair Play/Somerset areas farther south include **Granite Springs Winery,** 5050 Granite Springs Winery Rd., 530/620-6395 or 800/638-6041, www.latcham.com, affiliated with nearby **Latcham Vineyards,** 2860 Omo Ranch Rd. in Mt. Aukum, 530/620-6642 or 800/750-5591 (same website). Interested in organic wines and warm, earth-friendly ambience? Then find the celebrated **Fitzpatrick Winery and Lodge,** 7740 Fairplay Rd., 530/620-3248 or 800/245-9166, www.fitzpatrickwinery.com, which also offers a very welcoming five-room B&B lodge ($100–150) already famous for its Irish hospitality. The lodge serves a worthy ploughman's lunch on weekends, wood-fired pizzas on Friday nights.

Other worthwhile stops include **Oakstone Winery,** 6440 Slug Gulch Rd., 530/620-5303, www.oakstone-winery.com, and large **Perry Creek Vineyards** near Fair Play at 7400 Perry Creek Rd., 530/620-5175 or 800/880-4026, www.perrycreek.com. The star of 20-acre **Charles**

B. Mitchell Vineyards, 8221 Stoney Creek Rd., 530/620-3467 or 800/704-9463, www.charlesbmitchell.com, is a signature cabernet sauvignon blend. Enjoy an oak-shaded picnic. Affiliated with Charles B. Mitchell is the nearby **Barkley Historic Homestead,** 8320 Stoney Creek Rd, 530/620-6783 or 888/708-4466, www.barkleyhomestead.com, a historic 3000-square-foot lodge and separate Lake House. Rooms are $100–200, gourmet breakfast included. Winemakers' dinners are sometimes offered.

PLYMOUTH AND VICINITY

Heading south from Placerville on Hwy. 49 toward Jackson, the rolling foothills become the steep canyon sides of the Cosumnes River—the Sierra Nevada's only undammed river—and Amador County visitor information becomes useful. Plymouth, formerly Pokerville then Puckerville, was a late-in-the-game but lucrative mining center. A short walk along Main St. takes you by most of the historic sites. Stop at the **Pokerville Market,** 18170 Hwy. 49, 209/245-6986, for picnic supplies and deli fare. The last weekend in July, stop by for the **Amador County Fair and Rodeo** here. Other big parties at the fairgrounds have included the **Sierra Showcase of Wines** in May, the **Wine Festival** in June, the **Bluegrass Festival** in August, and **Plymouth 49er Days** in September. Call the Amador County Chamber of Commerce, 209/223-0350, for more information.

Wineries

From Plymouth, travel east into a cluster of old mining and lumber camps—River Pines, Mt. Aukum, Fair Play, Grizzly Flat, Cole's Station, Somerset—in and beyond the Shenandoah Valley, which again flourishes with foothill vineyards and winemakers. Today this is impressive California zinfandel country. But it's been California zin country for more than 150 years; the region's winemaking history reaches back to the days of the gold rush. Most wineries can be reached from Plymouth via Plymouth-Shenandoah Rd. (Rd. E-16). To get oriented, pick up free wine-tour pamphlets locally or contact

Amador Vintners Association, 209/267-2297, www.amadorwine.com, and **Amador County Wine Grape Growers' Association,** 209/245-4910, www.amadorwinegrapes.com. (For wineries located near Somerset and Fair Play, see Apple Hill above.) Come celebrate local winemaking heritage and tour the wineries in mid-February, at the annual **Amador County Vintners' Barrel Tasting,** which usually starts at the Shenandoah Valley Schoolhouse on Shenandoah School Rd. just outside Plymouth. Come back the first weekend in October for the **Harvest Festival.**

Most famous for a taste and a tour is the Sobon family's **Sobon Estate,** just northeast of town at 14430 Shenandoah Rd., 209/245-6554, www.sobonestate.com, previously the old D'Agostini winery, the fourth-oldest winery in California and a state historic landmark. The **Sobon Valley Museum** here offers free self-guided tours that include the vintage (1856) stone cellar, old casks made from local oak, coopering equipment, old farm equipment, and old-fashioned household items—something like a historical overview of the entire area. The winery and museum are open daily 10 A.M.–5 P.M. except major holidays. Just as fascinating, though, is Sobon's newest tradition—organic farming. Nearby is the Sobon family's award-winning **Shenandoah Vineyards,** 12300 Steiner Rd., 209/245-4455, open year-round, daily 10 A.M.–5 P.M., which also offers a fine art gallery. Impressive **Renwood Winery,** 12225 Steiner Rd., 209/245-6979, www.renwood.com, is famed for its varietal zinfandels.

Deaver Vineyards, 12455 Steiner Rd., 209/245-4099, www.deavervineyard.com, is open for tasting Thurs.–Mon. 11 A.M.–5 P.M. Also here is the **Amador Harvest Inn,** 209/245-5512, the only bed-and-breakfast in the Shenadoah Valley. An excellent newcomer in the zinfandel sweeps and a pioneer in California sangiovese is the modern **Amador Foothill Winery,** 12500 Steiner Rd., 800/778-9463, www.amadorfoothill.com. Pleasing to the eye as well as the palate is the Mediterranean **Montevina,** 20680 Shenandoah School Rd., 209/245-6942, www.montevina.com, noted for its barbera, zinfandel, sangiovese, and syrah.

Dobra Zemlja Winery (Croation for "good earth") at 12505 Steiner Rd., 209/245-3183, www.dobrazemlja.com, specializes in zinfandel, syrah, sangiovese and viognier. A surprise here is the winery itself, a 19th-century barn hiding a 1,800-square-foot cave excavated into the hillside. Picnic grounds and tasting room open daily. **Charles Spinetta Winery & Wildlife Art Gallery,** 12557 Steiner Rd., 209/245-3384, www.charlesspinettawinery.com, specializes in red wines, framed wildlife art, ceramics, and sculptures. The 3,000-square-foot gallery features work by a number of noted artists, including Gary Burghoff, Corporal "Radar" O'Reilly from the *M*A*S*H* TV series. Art by Joe Garcia and Sherrie Russell Meline appears on Charles Spinetta wine labels. Also exceptional in the region are **Karly Wines,** 11076 Bell Rd., 209/245-3922, www.karlywines.com, which offers zin and Mediterranean varietals, and **Domaine de la Terre Rouge,** 10801 Dickson Rd., 209/245-3117, www.terrerougewines.com, which also produces award-winning **Easton** wines. Best for wines with a mountaintop view is family-operated **Story Winery,** 10525 Bell Rd., 209/245-6208, www.zin.com, which makes zinfandel and "mission wines"; some of the old vines here date to the early 1900s. Story's tasting room is open daily, noon–4 P.M. on weekdays, 11 A.M.–5 P.M. weekends. Plan to picnic here, if at all possible, where rounded, oak-dotted hillsides dip down into the Cosumnes River Canyon.

FIDDLETOWN AND DRYTOWN

Fiddletown

Bret Harte immortalized this rowdy placer mining town in "An Episode of Fiddletown," though today it's considerably calmer. A friendly, slightly down-at-the-heels spot in the road, Fiddletown was reportedly named by a Missourian who noted the townspeople's fondness for "fiddlin'" (though what he meant is still a matter of speculation, since he didn't mention violins). Center of social life here is the old **Fiddletown General Store,** where locals loiter on the front porch and gossip. Note the shiny new 20-foot fiddle atop the community center. Rest or play a while at the community's green and well-groomed **Ostrom-McLean Park,** with its picnic tables, playground, and basketball and tennis courts. Come in May for the town's annual celebration—more fiddlers are always welcome.

Walk down Oleta Rd. to see most of the town's older buildings. Rare in California is the 1850s Chinese rammed-earth adobe **Chew Kee Store** on Main Street. A medicinal herb shop run by the doctors Yee (father and son), it was in remarkably good shape even before its relatively recent restoration. Now a museum displaying many rare items, Chew Kee exhibits include a private altar and oddities like paper good luck charms, ginger jars, and rubber stamps with Chinese characters. The tiny museum is open Saturday noon–4 P.M. from April through October, or by appointment (209/223-4131 or 209/367-0696). During the gold rush, Fiddletown was home to the state's largest Chinese population outside San Francisco. Nearby is the brick-and-stone Chinese "gambling hall," next to the old blacksmith shop (complete with original forge).

Drytown

Once noted for its 27 saloons—they called it "dry" for the diggins here—Drytown today is mostly noted for its antique and other shops. Near Drytown are some more colorfully named remnants of mining sites: Blood Gulch, Murderer's Gulch, Rattlesnake Gulch. The **Old Well Motel and Grill,** 15947 Hwy. 49, 209/245-6467, is a good burger and sandwich stop with rustic "cabin" rooms, a swimming pool, picnic area, and gold panning in the creek.

AMADOR CITY

Amador City straddles the Mother Lode. Mines along the "Amador strip" between here and Plymouth produced half the $300 million in gold yielded by Southern Mines. The Keystone Mine was most famous, yielding about $40,000 the first month and $24 million or so between 1853 and the 1940s. The state's smallest incorporated city, Amador City today is just one block long, but it's as pretty as Sutter Creek. The town's main events are strolling up and down the block, dodging cars while trying to cross the highway, and poking into shops. While you're strolling, peek

into the **Amador Whitney Museum** on Main Street, a biannually changing exhibit recognizing women's contributions to the "Mother" Lode.

Imperial Hotel

You can't miss this reincarnated red brick gold-rush hotel, the one boldly embracing the big curve as Hwy. 49 snakes through Amador City— a delightful surprise upstairs and down. Take a few moments to appreciate the weight-bearing construction of the building itself, a thickness of 12 bricks at the base tapering to four at the roofline. Inside, the striking **Oasis Bar** and small lounge area adjoins the open dining area. At dinner (served seven days a week), the weekly changing menu might feature entrées like poached salmon in mandarin orange dill sauce, cinnamon roasted pork loin, and grilled filet of beef with shallot tarragon sauce. At least consider dessert—creations like chocolate orange torte and hazelnut praline cheesecake—everything house-made by the hotel's pastry chef. (Lunch is served only on a special-event basis.) Or come for Sunday brunch, served 10 A.M.–2 P.M., with choices from Kahlua French toast and fruit crepes to omelettes or quiche.

Upstairs, the six guest rooms are all artistically eclectic, some with a fun, almost folk-art feel. All

the Imperial Hotel in Amador City

© KIM WEIR

feature modern private bathrooms (with "extras" like hair dryers and heated towel racks); several have balconies or access to the back upstairs patio. Best of all, though, a stay here also includes a full breakfast. Rates are $100–150. For more information and to make reservations, contact Imperial Hotel, 14202 Hwy. 49, 209/267-9172 or 800/242-5594, www.imperialamador.com.

Practicalities

For unapologetic comfort, though, there's another choice. Once the office for the Keystone Mining Company, the **Mine House Inn,** 14125 Hwy. 49, 209/267-5900 or 800/646-3473, www.minehouseinn.com, is a fully restored bed-and-breakfast inn. The rooms are named after their original purpose—the Mill Grinding Room, the Retort Room, the Vault Room—and are quite comfortable, furnished in gold rush antiques. Eight rooms are available in the 1870 main building ($100–150), and three romantic suites with whirlpool tubs and fireplaces occupy the refurbished 1930 former mine superintendent's home ($150–200). An affiliated Victorian home offers two luxurious suites, the Louis XV–style **French Romance** and **Oriental Gardens** ($200–250). All rooms have private baths, and the inn has a pool and spa.

The venerable **Buffalo Chips Emporium,** 14175 Hwy. 49, 209/267-0570, occupies what was once the old Wells Fargo Bank. Sporting offbeat ice cream parlor decor, it offers a juke box, good breakfast and lunch, and decadent ice cream and soda fountain treats. You can sit out front on the time-polished benches and watch the world buzz by.

SUTTER CREEK

John Sutter passed up this area as a possible site for his lumber mill, but he did set up a lumber camp along the creek, hence the name. Never much of a placer mining town, though Leland Stanford started amassing his fortune by means of the hardrock Lincoln Mine here, Sutter Creek grew slowly as a supply center. The area's Central Eureka Mine became one of the state's richest, finally shutting down in 1958, leaving behind a legacy of toxic wastes.

A tiny town still, Sutter Creek is among the most attractive and authentic gold rush towns, its cheerful, spiffed-up Main Street a blend of aged wood-frames and solid brick-and-stone buildings. A favorite pastime here is browsing through the excellent antique and other shops. To imagine 1900s Sutter Creek, peek into the **Monteverde General Store** on Randolph Street at Boston Alley, 209/267-1344 or 209/267-1431, open Thursday and Friday 11 A.M.–4 P.M., Saturday and Sunday noon–5 P.M. Small admission. For a proper introduction to Sutter Creek, pick up a walking-tour guide at the Knight Foundry on Eureka Street, also the local visitors center. Still something of a touchy subject in these parts is the **Sutter Gold Mining Co.** between Amador City and Sutter Creek, which many locals believe undermines the community's charms. Others, however, see the gold mine tours as a worthy visitor attraction. One-hour family trips feature an underground shuttle tour; "deep mine" tours, gold panning, and gemstone mining are also offered. For more information, call 866/762-2837 or see www.caverntours.com. Touchier still is the issue of the new Hwy. 49 bypass which, perhaps as soon as 2005, will direct the merciless traffic away from both Amador City and Sutter Creek. Life here will be less hectic, but will people still stop to shop? For more information, call the **Sutter Creek Business and Professional Association** at 209/267-1344 or 800/400-0305, www.suttercreek.org, or call the city at 209/267-5647.

Knight & Co., Ltd. Foundry and Machine Shop

Sutter Creek's 1872 Knight Foundry, on the creek just east of Main at 81 Eureka St., has been rescued at last from the vagaries of fate—or so the community hopes. A state historical landmark also included on the National Register of Historic Places, the Knight Foundry is the only water-powered foundry in the nation. For quite some time it was the largest foundry in the U.S. outside San Francisco. Considered by some to be "the Jurassic Park of metallurgy," thanks to the efforts of dedicated volunteers this astonishing and unique facility seems destined to live on—continuing to operate as a historic foundry, to preserve historic industrial skills, and also to serve as a living history environment for public information and education.

An active metal-working facility until quite recently, all of the foundry's original metal-making and machine-shop equipment is still here, and still functional—fully capable of the complicated pouring and fabrication required for historic preservation projects, including the restoration of ships and locomotives. Preserving the hands-on metalworking skills necessary for such critical work—including work with large-cast iron, bronze, and brass—is another reason it was so important to save the foundry. In addition to its other programs, the foundry plans to offer apprenticeships and weekend workshops to teach the almost-lost craft of metal making. Public education is the resurrected foundry's other primary purpose. Of particular interest to visitors are its monthly metal pourings, guided tours, and special living history events. Regular tours are offered from 10 A.M. to 4 P.M. Saturday and Sunday, group and midweek tours by request.

For other current information and more details, contact the **Knight Foundry Preservation Society,** also known as the Samuel Knight Chapter of the Society of Industrial Archeology, 209/267-0201. Fundraising for foundry renovation is ongoing.

Staying in Sutter Creek

Motels are *out* in Sutter Creek—fine bed-and-breakfasts are definitely in. The pick of the litter is probably **The Foxes Inn,** 77 Main St., 209/267-5882 or 800/987-3344, www.thefoxesinn.com, which boasts elegant surroundings and exquisite Victorian antiques. Seven guest rooms, four with fireplaces, all with private baths. Full breakfasts are cooked to order and served in your room. Rates are $150–250. **Hanford House,** 61 Hanford St., 209/267-0747 or 800/871-5839, www.hanford-house.com, offers both elegance and romance in its strylish rooms and suites—from the British Bankers Room to the Roof Top Suite. Full wheelchair access, gourmet full breakfast. Rates are $100–250. At the rambling Victorian **Grey Gables Inn,** nearby at 161 Hanford St., 209/267-1039 or 800/473-9422, www.greygables.com,

the eight guest rooms are named after British literary lights, from Brontë (a favorite) and Byron to Tennyson. Casual afternoon tea and evening wine and cheese are served, in addition to generous breakfasts. Rates are $150–250, with midweek and other discounts available.

Fans of the Arts and Crafts movement will particularly appreciate the "bones" of the Craftsman-era **Eureka Street Inn,** near the Knight Foundry at 55 Eureka St., 209/267-5500 or 800/399-2389, www.eurekastreetinn.com. Rooms, some dressed up Victorian style, are $100–150, with the lowest rate on weekdays.

Eating in Sutter Creek

The **Sutter Creek Certified Farmers Market** is held June–Oct. Sat. 8–11:30 A.M., at the intersection of Eureka St. and Hwy. 49.; for information, call 209/296-5504. **Susan's Place Wine Bar & Eatery,** just off Main at 15 Eureka St., 209/267-0945, offers indoor and (shaded) outdoor seating, is a best bet both at lunch and dinner—homemade soups, salads, sandwiches, and pastas along with beef, chicken, and seafood entrées. Taste your way through local wines. Beer and wine only. Open Wed.–Sun. for lunch, and Friday and Saturday for dinner. **Zinfandels,** 51 Hanford St. (Hwy. 49), 209/267-5008, has filled-in admirably for long-gone Pelargonium—pouring out contemporary California-style cuisine, its monthly-changing menu from pastas and risotto to charbroiled chicken and filet mignon, in wine country-inspired surroundings. The wine list emphasizes regional wines, and the chef pairs a wine with each dish. Open Thurs.–Sun. for dinner only. Monthly wine dinners too. Another possibility is the **Sutter Creek Palace,** 76 Main St., 209/267-1300, offers Wild West-style Victorian decor and continental cuisine—fish, pastas, seafood, all fresh as fresh can be. Prime rib is available on Friday and Saturday nights, and patio dining is available whenever the weather cooperates. Open for lunch and dinner Fri.–Tues.

You can get à la carte items or just a burger at the **Bellotti Inn,** 53 Main, 209/267-5211, but the main reasons to come here are the huge, family-style Italian meals (don't miss the minestrone) and reasonable prices (no credit cards).

Entertainment and Events

The big bash in town is the **Italian Benevolent Society Picnic and Parade,** a community festival steeped in well over a century of tradition, held on the first Sunday in June—food, music, dancing, bingo, and a spectacular parade down Hwy. 49 on Sunday morning. The night before, don't miss the All-You-Can-Eat Spaghetti and Chicken Feed. In August the **Ragtime Festival,** and in September the **Blues & Brew Fest.** The 1919 art-deco **Sutter Creek Theatre** at 44 Main St. (Hwy. 49), 209/267-1070 (events), www.suttercreektheatre.com, offers near-perfect acoustics for its dramas, musicals, and other live entertainment and events. To find out what else is going on, contact the **Amador County Arts Council,** 209/267-9038, www.acaconline.com. For some fun (and exercise) after stuffing yourself, go bowling at the **Gold Country Lanes,** 81 W. Ridge Rd., 209/223-3334; the setup here includes video games plus live music and dancing on weekends.

Jackson and Vicinity

Though it wasn't the wildest of the gold rush settlements, Jackson was nonetheless a rambunctious place on the Sacramento-Stockton branch of the old Carson Pass Emigrant Trail. Not a classic boomtown—Jackson had a surprisingly stable population for more than 100 years—the town has remained lively even in recent times, with local bordellos and gambling halls operating until the 1950s and card parlors still dotting Main Street. Plan on spending some time in and around Jackson if you're not already museumed, ghost-towned, Victorian gingerbreaded, and gift "shoppe"ed out.

In the political-karma-can-be-serious department: Jackson's citizens literally stole the county seat—archives, seals, assorted legalistic paraphernalia, and all—out from under Double Springs in 1851, the apparent final round in a dispute that included the judge gunning down the county clerk. But this battle for power and prestige wasn't over yet. When nearby Mokelumne Hill won the political prize (honorably, through the electoral process) and held it for two terms, stubborn Jacksonians, determined to maintain their collective clout, voted to create a new county—Amador County, one of the state's smallest. Despite the much-improved electoral odds, Jackson barely maintained its status as county seat when challenged by nearby Volcano.

Placer mining started it all, but Jackson's real wealth came from hardrock mines like the mile-deep Kennedy and Argonaut (at one time the world's deepest mines). Both these consolidated conglomerates closed briefly during World War I and again, finally, during World War II. One of the gold country's biggest disasters happened here in 1922, when 47 miners died in the Argonaut Mine fire.

SEEING AND DOING JACKSON

Walking Tour

Get a walking-tour map from the **Amador County Chamber of Commerce,** 125 Peek, Ste. B (at the southern juncture of Highways 49 and 88, next to the Chevron gas station), 209/223-0350, www.amadorcountychamber.com. (The entire town is better for walking than either biking or driving, and parking is just about impossible.) Stone buildings with iron doors and shutters are the architectural rule in downtown Jackson. Main Street, with its high wooden sidewalks, is narrow, crooked, and intersected by hill-climbing alleylike streets. Many intriguing old homes are sprinkled around town, easily enjoyed on foot.

Tucked in between trees and terraced tombstones, the tiny white **St. Sava Serbian Orthodox Church,** 724 N. Main St., 209/223-2700, is the "mother church" of the Serbian Orthodox faith in the United States. Note the stained-glass work, and peek into the sanctuary on Sundays before services to appreciate the stars on the church's "sky dome."

The imposing **National Hotel,** 2 Water St. (down at the end of Main), 209/223-0500, is another California hostelry claiming the oldest-in-continuous-operation title. A peek into the National's saloon is almost like peering into a black hole—but one with brassy crystal light reflected from the bar mirror and absorbed by the honky-tonk piano and fake red velvet wallpaper. This is a lively place on weekend nights.

Amador County Museum

The best thing to see in town is the museum, 225 Church St., 209/223-6386, which occupies an 1850s redbrick house at the top of the hill. Out back, scale models of several historic local mining structures—the (working) North Star Stamp Mill, the Kennedy Mine headframe, a tailing wheel—provide a clear explanation of what gold mining was and is. Tours of the model Kennedy Mine are offered 11 A.M.–3 P.M. on weekends. Also worth appreciation: the shiny black *Hooterville Cannonball,* on display near the street, and a cool shady garden holding mining paraphernalia and a few picnic tables. The museum is open Wed.–Sun. 10 A.M.–4 P.M. (admission by donation). For more Amador County history, see www.amadorarchives.org.

Kennedy Mine

To get to what remains of the storied Kennedy Mine, from the highway turn onto Kennedy Mine Road and follow it to the end. The Kennedy "tailing wheels" were built in 1912 to lift mine tailings into flumes, then over two hills to a holding dam. The system theoretically solved mining-related environmental problems—stream erosion, siltation, water pollution—caused by dumping tailings into streams and rivers. Only one of the original four wheels is still standing, though another lies just downhill in pieces. Docent-guided mine tours tell the rest of the story—from the mine office building, where ore samples were processed and flakes of gold melted into bricks, to the stamp mill, steam boiler, and massive steel head frame. Here miners traded in their "brass" for a full day's work deep underground. At the miners' changing house, now a small museum and gift shop, watch a short, silent, 1914 movie of the mine in action. Also here is a modest city park where you can stop for a picnic—especially pleasant in spring before the heat descends and hillside grasses turn to straw. Don't miss the gold rush–era **Chichizola Store** complex at 1316–1330 Jackson Gate Rd., now listed on the National Register of Historic Places.

Kennedy tailing wheel in Jackson

© KIM WEIR

The Kennedy Mine is open March through October for 90-minute guided tours and self-guided tours every Saturday, Sunday, and holiday. Admission is $9 adult (age 13 and up), $5 children (under age 6 free). Group tours are available, by reservation, all year. For more information, contact the **Kennedy Mine Foundation,** 209/223-9542 www.kennedygoldmine.com.

STAYING IN JACKSON
Camping

Head toward **Indian Grinding Rock State Park** near Volcano (see below) or camp at one of three reservoirs just west of Jackson. Closest is tiny **Lake Amador,** where you can also fish and sail. There's a separate one-acre swimming pond with sandy beaches, a playground, and about 150 campsites ($20–25). For information: Lake Amador Resort, 7500 Lake Amador Dr. in Ione, 209/274-4739, www.lakeamador.com. Or try either **Camanche** or **Pardee,** two reservoirs slaking the thirst of San Francisco's East Bay area. You can't swim in these waters, but you can boat, fish, and camp here (1,100 campsites altogether) and hike on trails through 15,000 acres. Cheapest is **Lake Pardee Resort,** 4900 Stony Creek Rd., 209/772-1472, www.lakepardee.com, with hot showers, flush toilets, and some RV hookups ($17–23). At Camanche, **Lake Camanche Recreation,** 2000 Camanche Rd. outside Ione, www.camancherecreation.com, offers two camping areas with showers and flush toilets, $19–26. The north campground, 209/763-5121 or 866/763-5121, has a coffee shop and sites with no hookups. The south campground, 209/763-5178 or 866/763-5178, has sites both with hookups and without. Both areas also include a Laundromat, cabins, a market, and gas station.

Motels and Inns

El Campo Casa Resort Motel, 12548 Kennedy Flat Rd., 209/223-0100, is a pleasant, middle-aged Spanish-style establishment northwest of town near the intersection of Hwys. 49 and 88. Amenities include a pool and wonderful gardens. Noticeable downtown, near the southern Hwy. 48/49 junction, is the **Best Western Amador Inn,** 200 S. Hwy. 49, 209/223-0211 or 800/543-5221, a modern red brick affair with the usual motel amenities, including a pool and restaurant. Rates at both are $50–100.

A noted Jackson hostelry is the elegant, largely original Queen Anne **Gate House Inn,** 1330 Jackson Gate Rd., 209/223-3500 or 800/841-1072, www.gatehouseinn.com, included on the National Register of Historic Places. The Gate House offers four rooms in the main house, plus a cottage and a two-room summer house. Rates are $100–200, full breakfast included. The **Windrose Inn,** 1407 Jackson Gate, 209/223-3650 or 888/568-5250, www.windroseinn.com, is an authentic Victorian farmhouse with four guest rooms (private baths), koi pond, fruit trees, flowers, and full breakfast. Wine aficionados, get to know local wines at the hosted wine hour every afternoon;

winery tours and winemaker dinners also available, by reservation. Rates are $100–200. Another possibility is the **Wedgewood Inn,** tucked into the woods at 11941 Narcissus Rd., 209/296-4300 or 800/933-4393, www.wedgewoodinn.com, with five Victorian-style guest rooms (private baths, antiques, woodstoves) with all the modern comforts; some rooms have two-person Jacuzzis. Full breakfast. Rooms are $150–200, the Carriage House Suite is $200–250.

EATING IN JACKSON

Jackson has its downhome aspects. A local hotspot is **Mel and Faye's Drive-in,** 205 N. Hwy. 49, 209/223-0853, which serves chili, "moo-burgers," and daily specials (takeout). Not bad for Chinese food (eat-in or takeout) is the **Great Wall of China,** 12300 Martell Rd., 209/223-3474; open daily for lunch and dinner. **Rosebud's Classic Café,** 26 Main, 209/223-1035, is a good American-style café open daily for breakfast and lunch.

Jackson's getting fairly uptown too—which means, in most cases, a unique combination of old and new. At **Cafe Max Swiss Bakery,** 140 Main St., 209/223-0174, every morning they pop the fresh-baked pastries out of the shop's original 1865 brick oven. The **Upstairs Restaurant and Sidestreet Bistro,** 164 Main, 209/223-3342, offers a contemporary dining experience both upstairs and downstairs in a narrow, gold rush-era brick and stone building. Lunch is downstairs (Streetside Bistro), a creative selection of soups, salads, sandwiches, and some surprisingly sophisticated entrées. The real adventure starts upstairs in the 12-table restaurant, where the weekly changing dinner menu trots the globe. Entrées might include roasted New Zealand lamb chops in merlot and licorice sauce, grilled flank steak spiced with peppers and Caribbean rum, or Moroccan vegetarian stew in honey sauce. Good fixed-price special, too. Beer and wine only. Desserts are delightful; try the banana wontons or the Key lime tart with coconut and ginger crust. Out of town a bit is **Teresa's Place,** 1235 Jackson Gate Rd., 209/223-1786, a fixture since World War II—serving hearty home-style Italian-American fare ("boardinghouse Italian"). These days the plaster has been chipped away to reveal the fabulous old rock walls, and the dinner menu includes such things as bisteca Florentina and braised swordfish in pinenut-basil cream sauce. But show up on Friday, Saturday, and Sunday night for Teresa's traditional family-style dinners—a real deal, from the antipasto, French bread, salad, minestrone, and pasta platter to the generous entrées. Teresa's serves its own desserts, too, including memorable chocolate cake and tasty pies.

IONE

First called Bedbug, then Freeze Out, the town's new name—honoring one of the characters in Edward Bulwer-Lytton's *The Last Days of Pompeii*—came with the arrival of the post office. The dark "castle" outside town was the state's first reform school, the **Preston School of Industry.** It's now a historic monument surrounded by the modern-day Preston complex. The Preston Castle Foundation, 209/274-6082, www.prestoncastle.com, welcomes contributions to help renovate the castle. Country-western singer Merle Haggard, tennis player Pancho Gonzales, movie star Rory Calhoun, and Eddie "Rochester" Anderson of the Jack Benny radio show all grew up at Preston. (Haggard later described the place as "something out of a Frankenstein movie.") Sometimes bad boys do okay after all. And sometimes they don't: Ione is also home to **Mule Creek State Prison.** Downtown has some historic restoration—notably the restored 1910 **Ione Hotel,** restaurant, and saloon at 24 W. Main St., 209/274-6082—but mostly this is a reform school-and-prison company town, the county's largest city. Come to Ione the first weekend in May for **Ione Homecoming,** first celebrated during the nation's centennial celebration in 1876 and held every year since.

At the intersection of Lancha Plana-Buena Vista and Jackson Valley Roads south of Ione is the **Buena Vista Saloon and Store,** all that's left of the town of the same name. This old fieldstone store was originally in Lancha Plana, one of the historic sites now underwater at Camanche Reservoir. Chinese laborers carried the building, stone by stone, seven miles uphill and rebuilt it. The buttes here were a protective citadel for the thousands of Miwok people who once lived throughout Jackson Valley. Take Jackson Valley Road then Camanche Road to get to the buttes. To stay near here, cheapest is camping at nearby Lake Amador or either Camanche or Pardee Reservoirs farther south (see Jackson above).

Wine tasting is a possible diversion in these parts. The **Clos du Lac Cellars/Greenstone Winery,** 3151 Hwy. 88 (at Jackson Valley Rd.), 209/274-2238, www.closdulac.com, has a picnic area plus tasting and tours. Open Wed.–Sun. 10 A.M.–4 P.M. The **Argonaut Winery,** 13825 Willow Creek Rd. (between Ione and Plymouth), 209/245-5567, www.argonautwinery.com, invites tasters to try its wines—including old-vine Barbera and Syrah. Picnicking available. Open for tasting Saturday and Sunday 10 A.M.–5:30 P.M.

INDIAN GRINDING ROCK STATE HISTORIC PARK

Tucked into the foothills east of Jackson and just north of Pine Grove on the road to Volcano, Indian Grinding Rock State Historic Park is a grassy meadow with clusters of oaks and more than 1,100 ancient mortar holes *(chaw'se)* and petroglyphs on a flat limestone plateau. Miwok women used the holes as mortars in which to grind acorns and other seeds. This is the largest grinding rock in the U.S.; a replica is on display at the Smithsonian Institution. Also here: a reconstructed native village, with roundhouse, or *hun'ge*, bark tepees, a granary, and a Miwok ball field (the traditional game was similar to soccer). The **Chaw'se Regional Indian Museum** features a good collection of artifacts from 10 area tribes plus other displays (open daily except holidays).

On the last weekend in September, the **Native American Big Time Celebration**—sponsored by the Amador Tribal Council—brings an acorn harvest ceremony, traditional festival, and the **Chaw'se Association Art Show** to the park. Two short hiking trails meander through the foothills here (watch out for poison oak and rattlers). Day-use fee is $3 a car ($2 seniors). For information, contact Indian Grinding Rock State Historic Park, 14881 Pine Grove–Volcano Rd., Pine Grove, CA 95665, 209/296-7488.

The state park includes 23 year-round campsites ($12, coin-op showers, no reservations). Or live like the Miwok in one of five bark houses—an "environmental camping" experience with a seven-day limit. Each house, built of cedar poles interwoven with wild grapevines, then covered with cedar bark, holds up to six people. Facilities for the houses include outside tables, fire rings, and pit toilets, but bring your own water or tote it from the main campground. Also bring firewood. You can reserve a bark house separately (or all five together as a group camp), but plan ahead as prices and availability vary. To make a reservation, get an application and return it to: *U'Macha'tam'ma' Environmental Campground,* in care of the park, or call 209/296-7488.

VOLCANO AND VICINITY

Not a volcano in sight, but early settlers thought the landscape resembled a crater and abandoned the original name, Soldier's Gulch. Because the town sits in a little dale atop limestone caves, it's fairly green here year-round. Sleepy Volcano is a ghost town that wouldn't die, refreshingly free of tourist lures and alive with history, including a number of cultural "firsts." The **Miner's Library Association** here was the state's first lending library. California community theater was born here, too, with the formation of the 1845 **Volcano Thespian Society** and the subsequent construction of two local theaters. The state's first literary and debating society also thundered up from Volcano. On **Observatory Hill** two miles away sat California's first observatory. Volcano also once had a law school. The trip from Volcano to Sutter Creek on the Sutter Creek-Volcano Rd. is lovely any time, but especially in spring and fall. There are no fences, a rarity in these parts, so you can stop along the way for an unimpeded picnic.

Come in December for the annual **Mother Lode Scots' Christmas Faire and Walk,** which ends with a candle-lit parade—accompanied by bagpipers—through town.

A local secret since the days of the gold rush and now a new area attraction is **Black Chasm Cavern** on Volcano-Pioneer Road, declared a National Natural Landmark in 1976. The first public tours of Black Chasm, featuring at least three underground lakes and three deep chambers, were offered in September 2000. Foot-long crystals, stalactites, stalagmites, columns, draperies, and spectacular, gravity-defying helictites are among the notable formations. Anyone who can climb 150 stairs can manage the tour. (Wear shoes with good traction and dirt-friendly clothes—some walls are muddy—and also bring a sweater; it's chilly down below.) First stop is the Colossal Room, a vast chamber with high rock bridges and deep, dark lakes; the domed Landmark Room is famous for its swarms of rare helictite crystals, some as large as VW bugs. Black Chasm's giant Hall of Arches is a maze of wall-to-wall marble arches which weave over and under each other. The cavern is open daily May–Oct. 9 A.M.–5 P.M. and Nov.–Apr. 10 A.M.–4 P.M. for 50-minute tours. Landmark tours are $12 adult, $6 children (ages 3–13). Gemstone "mining," in onsite flumes, is available for the kiddos. Adventurers, ask about spelunking expeditions. For more information, call 209/736-2708 or 866/762-2837, or see www.caverntours.com.

A Volcano Stroll

The Odd Fellows and Masonic Halls here were the state's first (outside town is the Masonic Cave, where the brotherhood met before the lodge was built). On one side of Main Street near the park is a block of crumbling stone ruins, including the **Cobblestone Theater,** once the old assay office. (The **Volcano Theatre Company,** 209/223-4663, www.volcanotheatre.org, offers productions both here and at the outdoor amphitheater from spring through fall.) Note the "Old Abe" **Volcano Blues Cannon** in the middle of town. Without ever firing a shot, Abe helped the Yanks win the Civil War, then was smuggled from San Francisco to Volcano, where it was occasionally used for Saturday-night crowd control. Speaking of crowds: See what's happening at the **Happy Union Blues Bar.** Whether you stay or not, the venerable St. George Hotel is worth a stop.

The St. George Hotel

If you're not inclined to fuss over every little creature comfort, treat yourself to a stay at the charming and venerable brick St. George Hotel, 16104 Main St., 209/296-4458, www.stgeorgehotel.com. Included on the National Register of Historic Places, these days the three-story St. George is dressed up in lace curtains, comfortable Victoriana. Once the most elegant hotel in the gold country, now an architectural elder, the St. George is still quite a character. (On a good day, you'll find plenty of other characters in the hotel's saloon.) At last report all 14 rooms in the hotel—recently redecorated, named for gold rush towns—shared five bathrooms. (Due to steep stairs, balcony access, and other details, the hotel isn't safe for young children.) Expect things to continue to improve under the hotel's new owners, who have added a conference center and made other major improvements—like the onsite art salon, www.salon-of-art.com, and the massage room on the hotel's second floor—since 1997. Hotel rates are still a genuine bargain, and include continental breakfast. Quieter lodgings are available in the "bungalow rooms" (named for Volcano streets) in the onetime motel annex next door, where all rooms have private bathrooms and other modern amenities. One annex room is completely accessible. Rates for most rooms are $50–100. The St. George is usually at the center of Volcano's events calendar, too. Come in August, for example, for the annual Volcano Scholarship Golf Invitational.

Even if you're just passing through, *definitely* plan to eat here. The St. George is one of Amador County's best restaurants. The Sunday brunch menu includes the St. George Scramble and Volcano Burrito as well as salmon Florentine. At dinner, served Thurs.–Sun. 5:30–9 P.M., expect creative California-style and Mediterranean fare—everything from spinach and chicken ravioli to New York steak in mushroom sauce or pork Cancun with peach and jalapeño salsa. Seasonally changing menu. Great desserts, included a famed crème brûlée. Reservations strongly advised.

Daffodil Hill

The McLaughlins started planting daffodils here in 1887, when the area was a stage stop; their descendants have continued the tradition to this day. Daffodil Hill is a private six-acre

Daffodil Hill near Volcano

© ROBERT HOLMES/CALTOUR

farm with some 400,000 plantings—daffodils (300 varieties) plus crocuses, tulips, hyacinths, lilacs, violets, and a few almond trees—an entire blooming hillside, free for the looking. The daffodils are best from mid-March through mid-April—call 209/296-7048 for blossom updates—but it's nice to come here any time to picnic (tables available) and to visit with the farm animals. Usually open daily 10 A.M.–4 P.M.; free, but donations are accepted. To get here, take Ramshorn Grade north from Volcano. Ramshorn eventually intersects with Shake Ridge Rd.; you can shake on down to Sutter Creek, or head east, then turn west onto Fiddletown Rd. at Lockwood Junction.

MOKELUMNE HILL

Known affectionately as Mok Hill, this block-long town perches on the divide between the Mokelumne and Calaveras Rivers. So rich were gold claims at Mokelumne Hill, they were limited in size to 16 square feet. Destroyed by fires in 1854, 1864, and 1874, the town was best known for its gold rush wars. One was between miners and a Chilean doctor accused of using slaves to work his claims. Another involved sudden patriotic fervor: Yanks jumped the claim of some French miners—a particularly rich claim, incidentally—allegedly because the Frenchmen had raised their own country's flag over it.

Poke around the saloon, eat in the restaurant, or perhaps stay at the historic **Hotel Leger,** 8304 Main St., 209/286-1401, www.hotelleger.com (most rooms $100–150). Peek into the museum at Main and Center. Or enjoy the small quiet park on the downhill end of Main. Just across the street is the dusty and seemingly decrepit **Adams and Co. Genuine Old West Saloon and Museum and Less** in the old I.O.O.F. hall on W. Center St., 209/286-1331, usually open only Friday and Saturday from 3:30 P.M. until whenever the bartender feels like going home. It's all but impossible to describe. "You just have to experience it," locals say. The casual restaurant at the Hotel Leger serves casual burgers, pizzas, soups, and the like at dinner (Thurs.–Sun.) and offers dining alfresco. For lunch, try the deli across the street.

BLACK BART

South across the Mokelumne River, the infamous Black Bart tossed and turned at least a little while in the San Andreas jail (now a museum). The "gentleman bandit" robbed 28 stagecoaches of their gold shipments, on foot and with the aid of an unloaded shotgun, before his capture in 1883. Black Bart (aka Charles Bolton or Charles Boles of San Francisco), a lover of the finer things in life, was characteristically polite, if commanding, and left quaint rhyming poetry with his unhappy victims. One of his finer efforts read: "I've labored hard and long for bread, for honor and for riches. But on my corns too long you've tred, you fine haired sons of bitches. Let come what will, I'll try it on, my condition can't be worse. And if there's money in that box, 'tis munney in my purse." Black Bart was something of a New World Robin Hood, since he stole nothing from the passengers—just money from Wells Fargo.

As successful as he was, the "PO8" of the placers violated the never-return-to-the-scene-of-the-crime rule of criminology and was finally undone. Wounded in a holdup at Funk Hill near Copperopolis, the scene of his first and last known robberies, Black Bart dropped a handkerchief before he fled. Wells Fargo detective Harry Worse traced the hankie's laundry mark to an apartment house on Bush St. in San Francisco, and Charles Bolton's days of highway robbery were over. Arrested and returned to San Andreas, the county seat, Black Bart confessed to only the Funk Hill holdup and was sentenced to six years in San Quentin. Freed for good behavior after four years, Bolton then disappeared. An old rumor has it that Wells Fargo pensioned him in exchange for his promise to cease his stage (robbing) career, a suggestion dismissed by historians.

SAN ANDREAS AND VICINITY

Once a Mexican town with a few adobes, San Andreas is now the Calaveras County seat, a bustling metropolis with a touristy downtown. The block-long historically interesting part of town is perpendicular to the highway. Still standing: both the courthouse where Black Bart finally faced justice and the jailhouse cell he called home before doing time in San Quentin. A walk through the pioneer cemetery west of town is sobering—so many young men, such short lives. Since San Andreas never had a daily newspaper, tradition dictated that obituaries be posted on the traditional "death tree" outside the former post office—now office space for the weekly *Calaveras Enterprise.*

Calaveras County Museum

The brick county Hall of Records complex, beautifully restored, now houses the outstanding Calaveras County Museum and Archives, 30 N. Main St., 209/754-3918. Also a de facto visitors center, the museum's exhibits include a Miwok bark tepee, artifacts, and basketry; you can even try your own skill at grinding acorns into meal. Study the legal papers, including a black-bordered public hanging invitation signed and sealed by the sheriff. The mining displays include a tip of the hat to early Spanish prospectors and Depression-era miners. Full-size room displays include a typical miner's cabin and a gold rush-era general store. The jail is downstairs in the courtyard, which is planted with native flora. This little stone-walled garden provides a shady, pleasant respite from highway traffic and hot sun. The museum is open daily 10 A.M.–4 P.M.; small admission fee.

Practicalities

To camp, head west on Hwy. 12 to **New Hogan Lake,** 2713 Hogan Dam Rd. in Valley Springs, 209/772-1343. Of the four Army Corps of Engineers campgrounds at the lake, one is a boat-in only campground ($8 per night) and several are reservable ($10–16 per night) through ReserveUSA, 877/444-6777 or www.reserveusa.com for reservations. Call the lake for more details.

In town, the **Black Bart Inn,** 55 W. St. Charles, 209/754-3808, www.blackbartinn.com, offers rooms in both an old-time brick hotel and a motel. Rates are $50–100. Nine-room **Robin's Nest,** a spacious Queen Anne Victorian downtown at 247 W. St. Charles, 209/754-1076, www.robinest.com, features romantic and attractive rooms, grand gardens, generous breakfasts. Most rooms are $100–150.

California Cavern

The onetime resort town of Cave City has long since bitten the dust, but the California Cavern (reached from Mountain Ranch Rd.; follow the signs) is still going strong. Now a state historic landmark but first opened in 1850—John Muir wrote about his spelunking here in *The Mountains of California*—the cavern ain't what it used to be, due to visitor overload and vandalism. But it's still worth a peek. The easy "trail of lights" tour ($12 adults, $6 ages 3–13) is suitable for the whole family. More adventurous are the two-hour Mammoth Cave trip ($99) and the half-day, muddier Middle Earth Expedition ($130, guide, rafts, hardhats, and coveralls included). The cavern is open daily, 10 A.M.–5 P.M. May–Dec., until 4 P.M. otherwise. For current details, contact California Caverns, 9565 Cave City Rd., 209/736-2708 or 866/762-2837, www.caverntours.com.

Near California Caverns

Near the caverns are some fascinating back roads and ghost towns to explore. **Sheep Ranch** was once a former quartz-mining camp where William Randolph Hearst's dad started the family fortune. Beautiful San Antonio Falls is nearby. **Mountain Ranch,** an early tourist destination once called El Dorado, supported two separate mining camps. Here today you'll see typical gold rush buildings, most still in use. The Domenghini Store was once a saloon and has been a general store since 1901.

Calaveritas, closer to San Andreas, was another alleged outpost for Joaquin Murrieta. There's not much to see here except a few old buildings, including the 1852 adobe store built by Luigi Costa. But the countryside whispers of bygone travelers and long-dead dreamers. If you're heading south from San Andreas, take Dogtown Rd. from Mountain Ranch Rd. to Calaveritas and across a few creeks to Angels Camp—the old miners' route.

Angels Camp and Vicinity

Originally a simple trading post—and officially named City of Angels, though no one calls it that—Angels Camp became a jumping mining camp after Bennagar Rasberry accidentally shot the ground while cleaning his muzzleloader, murdering a manzanita bush and revealing an impressive chunk of gold-seamed quartz dangling from its roots. Placer gold was found here by either Henry Angel or George Angell, depending on the story, but the pans soon came up empty. The town boomed again, though, with help from later hardrock mining companies.

SEEING AND DOING ANGELS CAMP

Mark Twain once hung out in the Hotel Angels bar and pool hall here, where he first heard the miners' tall tale about the jumping frogs—inspiration for his first successful story, "The Celebrated Jumping Frogs of Calaveras County," published in 1864. When the roads in Angels Camp were finally paved in 1928, someone jokingly suggested holding a jumping frog contest to commemorate the fictional athletic humiliation of that now-famous toady, Dan'l Webster. And so the town's **Jumping Frog Jubilee** was hatched.

The event is now staged for tourists every May at Frogtown (the fairgrounds just south of Angels Camp) in conjunction with the Calaveras County Fair. Rental frogs are available. It's all considered serious sport by some—so don't kiss or otherwise distract the frogs until after the $1,500 prize has been awarded.

Among other annual celebrations staged at the fairgrounds is the **Calaveras Celtic Faire** in March, two days of bagpipe bands, Irish harpists, Highland dancers, step dancing, jousting, competitive games, a Celtic marketplace, and live music, and the three-day **Sierra Nevada World Music Festival** in June. Come to town in September for the **Wild West Days and Film Festival.** For current information about these and other local events, stop by the Angels Camp Museum on Main (see below). Or contact the **Calaveras County Visitors Bureau,** 1192 S. Main St.,

Jumping Frog Jubilee

© ROBERT HOLMES/CALTOUR

GOLD COUNTRY

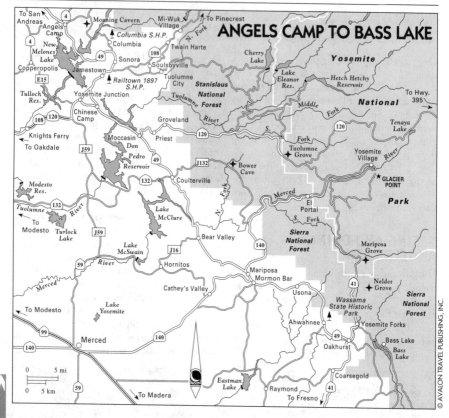

ANGELS CAMP TO BASS LAKE

© AVALON TRAVEL PUBLISHING, INC.

209/736-0049 or 800/225-3764, www.visit-calaveras.org, which publishes the useful ***Calaveras County Visitor's Guide*** and serves as a reservations and information service for lodging, skiing and other recreation, and area events. For information on the jumping frog contest and other events at the fairgrounds, contact the **Calaveras County Fairgrounds,** 209/736-2561.

Though not exactly a vintage gold rush town these days, Angels Camp is also not yet overrun by corporate America. But it does seem to be an amphibian's paradise. Frogs leap from store windows, perch atop monuments, hang from balconies, swing from shop signs, and decorate sidewalks. The **Angels Camp Museum & Carriage House** buildings, 753 S. Main, 209/736-2963, are just part of a three-acre complex open 10 A.M.–3 P.M.,

daily from March through December, weekends only in January and February (small fee). Stop by if you're especially interested in mining equipment, horse-drawn wagons, buggies, and rock collections. At one time, many Chinese lived in town, but only two brick Chinatown buildings remain. The redbrick **Altaville School** at 125 N. Main has been restored and is open to visitors daily. The 1924 **Angels Theatre,** 1228 S. Main, 209/736-6768 complete with handpainted interior murals, is open for business again, now showing art-house and first-run movies.

South of town, just off Main between Angel and Altaville, is **Utica Park,** which includes picnic tables and a playground. The low spot here is a permanent reminder of the 1889 mine cave-in directly below, a disaster that killed 16 men. The

MARK TWAIN

After staying for a time in Carson City, Nevada, with his brother Orion, the governor's secretary, Samuel Clemens wandered through western Nevada in the early 1860s, suffering from a severe case of gold fever. Deeply in debt after his prospecting attempts repeatedly failed, in 1862 he walked 130 miles from Aurora to Virginia City to accept a $25-a-week job as a reporter on the *Territorial Enterprise*. Later, in San Francisco, Twain became part of the city's original Bohemia, mixing with Prentice Mulford, Ina Coolbrith (California's first poet laureate), Cincinnatus Heine "Joaquin" Miller, and Bret Harte. He defamed the city police in print, then decided to leave town after another bad turn of affairs, escaping in 1865 to the Mother Lode and an isolated cabin on the Stanislaus River's Jackass Hill near Angels Camp.

Surrounded by a few remaining pocket miners, Twain was content with wandering through the abandoned town and nearby settlements, symbols of the vagaries of fate and fortune. Most of the locals bored him, but he enjoyed the company of his more well-read cabin mates. Twain's laziness was legendary—his unwillingness to draw one more bucket of water later meant his friend lost out on a $20,000 gold find—but the period here was productive nonetheless. Many of the stories shared by his imaginative friends ended up in Twain's later books, and it was here that he first heard the miner's tale of a local frog-jumping competition. "The Celebrated Jumping Frog of Calaveras County" was an overnight success with the Eastern literary establishment.

---

model undershot waterwheel resembles the one that once powered the Utica Mine's ore-crushing mill. The park's Mark Twain statue was a gift to the town in 1945 from a movie company doing the story of Mark Twain (played by Frederick March).

STAYING IN ANGELS CAMP

For camping, try **Frogtown** (at the county fairgrounds) just south of town, 209/736-2561 ($13–15 for decent tent or RV sites, including hot showers). Or head to the **Angels Camp RV and Camping Resort,** 3069 Hwy. 49 (two miles south), 209/736-0404 or 888/398-0404, where you'll find RV sites with varying hookups ($30 for two people) as well as camping cabins ($46 and up). Amenities include a pool and playground. Also close is **New Melones Reservoir.** Up into the Sierra Nevada but worth the trip is **Calaveras Big Trees State Park.** For details on the latter two, see below.

There are a number of good motels in Angels Camp, including the pet-friendly **Best Western Cedar Inn & Suites,** 444 S. Main St., 209/763-4000 or 800/767-1127, www.bestwesternangelscamp.com, with large, well-appointed rooms with all the contemporary comforts—in-room refrigerator, microwave, coffeemaker, hairdryer, iron and ironing board; extras including Jacuzzis, fireplaces, and balconies are available. Outdoor pool,

spa, exercise room. Rooms are $100–150, suites are $150–250. Decidedly "uptown" west of town at the golf course development—an 18-hole Robert Trent Jones II–redesigned course—are **The Cottages at Greenhorn Creek,** 711 McCauley Ranch Rd., 209/736-6201 or 888/736-5900, www.greenhorncreek.com—actual houses with complete kitchens, "great rooms" with cathedral ceilings and fireplaces, patios or decks, and multiple bedrooms. If a whole house is more than you'll need, a cottage can be divided into a multi-room suite with separate motel-style room. "Extras" here include access to resort recreational facilities. Rates are $100–200 for suites, $200–400 for cottages.

EATING IN ANGELS CAMP

Dave's Diner, 451 Hwy. 49, 209/736-8080, does a mean breakfast and lunch. Dave's vies for local favor with **Sue's Angel's Creek Cafe,** 1246 S. Main St., 209/736-2941. The **Pickle Barrel,** 1225 S. Main, 209/736-4704, is a deli offering sandwiches and other light fare, along with patio and "pet" dining (so you can bring Fido to lunch with you). For Mexican, try **La Hacienda Restaurant** at the Hwy. 4/49 junction, 209/736-6711.

Crusco's Ristorante, 1240 S. Main St., 209/736-1440, at home in a venerable, stone-walled gold rush–era building, serves up very good Italian fare, both contemporary and classic. (Dig that Venetian mural.) Harder to find but fancier still is **Camps** restaurant, star of the Lodge at Greenhorn Creek, 676 McCauley Ranch Rd., 209/736-8181. Camping out at Camps means appreciating Sierra-style Pacific Rim fare prepared with classical French techniques. Fresh local ingredients, organic veggies. The wine list has earned the *Wine Spectator* Award of Excellence. Open daily for lunch and dinner.

AROUND ANGELS CAMP

Gold Rush Towns

Altaville was officially annexed to Angels Camp in 1971. First called Forks in the Road, then Winterton, then Cherokee Flat, this is where Bret Harte set his play *To the Pliocene Skull.* **Copperopolis,** which produced most of the copper for Civil War armaments, now has its few historic buildings fenced off to discourage vandalism. Once-rich **Carson Hill** is now a ghost town, though the biggest U.S. gold nugget ever found (195 pounds) was unearthed here in 1854.

New Melones Reservoir

Despite a bitterly fought campaign by environmentalists to save this wild stretch of the Stanislaus River, the New Melones Reservoir has flooded the river's ruggedly lovely canyon, the 1840s stage crossing at Parrott's Ferry, and much of the landscape familiar to Mark Twain and his cohorts. Limestone caves, once enclaves for native peoples, are now mostly underwater, as is the early mining camp of Melones ("melons" in Spanish). One of California's roughest, toughest gold camps, Melones was first called Slumgullion after the slimy riverbank mud. It took its later name from the melon-shaped gold nuggets found here by Mexican miners. **Funk Hill,** where Black Bart staged his first and last holdup, is still above water. The reservoir, California's fourth largest, offers no-fee day use for picnicking, lake launch ramps, fishing, and hiking and mountain bike trails. Primitive camping is available in the area; entrance gate closed 11 P.M.–4 A.M. For more information, contact the **New Melones Visitor's Center** on Hwy. 49 just south of the Stevenot Bridge, 209/536-9543, open

10 A.M.–4 P.M. daily, which includes gold rush and natural history exhibits and offers a year-round administrative complex.

Jackass Hill

Though old-timers claim that Mark Twain never slept in the crumbling cabin that bears his name on Jackass Hill, it was here that he reportedly spent five months as a guest of miners Bill and Jim Gillis. The cabin, reached by a well-marked side road, was rebuilt in 1922, though at least the chimney is original, folks say. The hill itself didn't take its name from Twain's loud mouth or lazy habits. The area was a nighttime stopover for mine suppliers, whose braying pack animals (up to 2,000 a night during peak years) grazed there.

MURPHYS

Nice place to stay put awhile, old Murphys. Known affectionately as "Mountain Queen" and "Queen of the Sierra" by locals and only recently discovered by the tourist trade, this one-street town is shaded by locust trees, cottonwoods, sycamores, and elms. Down-home Murphys has hosted its share of Hollywood outsiders filming Westerns. The restored **Murphys Hotel** on Main Street was once considered the state's finest lodging outside of San Francisco, despite its Wild West reputation (genuine bullet holes decorate the doorway). The 1860 **Murphys Elementary School** was once called Pine Grove College, so locals could claim they'd been to college. Particularly intriguing is the **Murphys Olde Timers Museum,** 470 Main, 209/728-1160, an eclectic collection of Murphys history and artifacts dating to the gold rush open Fri.–Sun. 11 A.M.–4 P.M. Most memorable of all is the E. Clampus Vitus **Wall of Comparative Ovations,** a testment to human modesty. To get the real lowdown on the town, sign on for a **Murphys Historical Walking Tour,** usually offered every Saturday at 10 A.M. Tour information is usually posted at the museum.

The **Murphys Creek Theatre** company, 209/728-8422, www.murphyscreektheatre.org, produces the beloved "Theatre Under the Stars" summer theatre festival at the Stevenot Winery amphitheatre. ntriguing local events include the annual **Calaveras Grape Stomp and Gold Rush Street Faire** held the first Saturday in October.

Wineries

Family-owned wineries are big in Murphys. A few scenic miles north of town is the **Stevenot Winery** tasting room and deli, located in the 1870 Shaw family ranch house, 2690 San Domingo Rd., 209/728-0638 or 209/728-3436, www.stevenotwinery.com, offering chardonnay, merlot, and old vine zinfandel. A big buzz these days is Stevenot's Tempranillo, a Spanish varietal that combines the flavors of pinot noir and syrah. Open daily 10 A.M.–5 P.M. Stevenot also has a tasting room on Main (at Sheep Ranch Rd.), 209/728-0148, open Wed.–Mon. 11 A.M.–5 P.M.

There are multiple downtown tasting opportunities, starting with the small **Milliaire Winery,** in town inside the old Flying A gas station at 276 Main, 209/728-1658, www.milliairewinery.com. **Malvadino Vineyards** offers old-vine mission wine, zinfandel, and more at its downtown tasting room, 457-C Algiers St. (off Main), 209/728-9030, www.malvadino.com. **Black Sheep Winery,** on Main at French Gulch Road, 209/728-2157, www.blacksheepwinery.com, specializes in zinfandel (try the True Frogs Lily Pad Red, a cinsault blend) and is open for tastings on weekends noon–5 P.M. (weekdays by appointment). Also tastable downtown are wines (as well as cheese and chocolate fondues) from Vallecito's **Zucca Mountain Vineyards,** the tasting room situated underground at 425-E Main (across from the hotel), 209/728-1623, www.zuccawines.com. Try the Sorprendere (Italian for "surprise"), a 50-50 blend of zinfandel and syrah. Open daily noon–5 P.M. Two miles west of town on Hwy. 4 is the **Chatom Vineyards** tasting room, 209/736-6500, www.chatomvineyards.com, the place to taste the finished fruit of the vineyards' 14 grape varietals. Picnic grounds, too.

Opulent **Kautz Ironstone Vineyards** about a mile from town at 1894 Six Mile Rd., 209/728-1251, owns the largest cabernet franc acreage in the nation. Visit the stamp mill-styled winery complex with plush tasting room—and visit everything else. Ironstone has it all, and has become something of a regional cultural center. The free **Mother Lode Heritage Museum and Gallery** exhibits include the 44-pound "Crown Jewel" gold nugget dug from the ground by the Sonora Mining Co. in 1992—the largest specimen of its kind (crystalline leaf gold) in the world. The **Ironstone Gallery** showcases nationally known artists working in various media, and the **Alhambra Music Room** (home to Silent Movie Night) boasts a rare 1927 Robert Morton theater pipe organ. The winery also sponsors an astonishing array of events throughout the year, from Civil War battle reenacts and winemaker dinners to concerts in the amphitheater featuring luminaries such as the Laurie Lewis Trio, Los Lobos, and Willie Nelson. Open daily for tasting 10 A.M.–5 P.M. Free tours are offered daily at 11:30 A.M. and 1:30 and 3:30 P.M. For a complete list of area wineries, contact the **Calaveras Wine Association,** 800/225-3764 ext. 25, www.calaveraswines.org.

Staying in Murphys

The 1856 **Murphys Historic Hotel and Lodge,** 457 Main St., 209/728-3444 or 800/532-7684, www.murphyshotel.com, is a national historic monument and a hot night spot to boot. Good literary and financial vibes: Black Bart, U.S. Grant, Will Rogers, Mark Twain, Daniel Webster, Horatio Alger, and J.P. Morgan have all slept here. Rooms have been updated, yet (in the tradition of the Wild West) some share bathrooms. The Murphys Hotel also has a wonderful Western bar, the noise from which rises into the rooms overhead; to guarantee a good night's sleep, light sleepers should opt for the more mundane but quiet motel units next door. Rates are $50–100. Another good choice is the **Murphys Inn Motel,** 76 Main (at Hwy. 4), 209/728-1818 or 888/796-1800, www.cloud9inns.com, with all the modern amenities—from swimming pool, exercise room, and videos to inroom coffee and hairdryers—served up with with B&B attitude. Most rooms are $50–150.

Nearby is the grand **Dunbar House 1880** bed-and-breakfast inn, 271 Jones St., 209/728-2897 or 800/692-6006, www.dunbarhouse.com, one of the best around. This 1880 Italianate Victorian, surrounded by lush gardens, offers

JOAQUIN MURRIETA: ROBIN HOOD OF THE PLACERS

The notorious bandit Joaquin Murrieta reportedly ranged from San Andreas to Murphys and beyond, but may have been more legend than reality, a composite of many "Joaquins" forced into crime by the racism of the day. There's hardly a town in the gold country without tunnels, cellars, or caves supposedly frequented by him, or nearby hills where he gunned someone down. According to some versions, Murrieta was a bright, handsome young man who settled on the Stanislaus River with his bride and his brother. Primarily interested in farming, the Murrietas nonetheless took the liberty of panning for a little gold, ignoring the prohibition against Mexican miners until accosted by drunken whites. His brother was gunned down (or lynched), his wife assaulted or killed. Horsewhipped and left for dead, Murrieta survived and assembled a bandit band, and one by one, those who had murdered his wife and brother eventually met death at Joaquin's hands.

Settling just north of Marysville, Murrieta and his men became accomplished horse thieves and stagecoach robbers. According to legend, much of Joaquin's booty went to poor Mexican families, who considered him a modern-day Robin Hood. (Others claim that Murrieta committed nearly 30 murders, usually victimizing unarmed men, including many Chinese.) Pursued by vigilantes, he moved farther north to Mt. Shasta (where writer "Joaquin" Miller borrowed the name for his nom de plume), then south to San Jose and various San Joaquin Valley towns. Turned in by a former lover, Murrieta was eventually tracked down in the Tehachapis by bounty hunters and state rangers—or so at least one version of the story goes.

exquisite accommodations (down to the imported English towels and 350-thread-count Egyptian cotton sheets) warmed with tasteful décor, heirlooms, and gas fireplaces. Every imaginable contemporary comfort, too—from central heat/air, two-person Jacuzzi or clawfoot tub, and personal refrigerator (stocked with local wine, water, and appetizer plate) to hair dryer, irons, and TV/VCR with classic movies. Generous gourmet breakfasts. Most rooms are $200–250.

Eating in Murphys

Stop for a picnic or just a rest at **Murphys Town Park,** just off Main near the creek. (While you're here poke into the Murphys Pokey, the town's old jailhouse.) Justifiably popular **Grounds** coffeehouse and café, 402 Main St., 209/728-8663, is open daily for breakfast and lunch—great coffee, omelettes made from free-range eggs, fresh-baked bread, enticing sandwiches—and Wed.–Sun. for very good dinners, fresh seafood and pastas to pork tenderloin. Or see what's cooking at **Biga Murphys Bakery,** 458 Main, 209/728-9250. The **Pick & Shovel Café,** 419 Main, 209/728-3779, is perfect for something quick

and simple like fruit smoothies and sandwiches. **Firewood,** 420 Main, 209/728-3248, serves good wood-fired pizzas.

Murphy's Grille, 380 Main, 209/728-8800, serves fairly sophisticated San Francisco-style fare—from steaks and chicken to veggie entrées and pasta—at both lunch and dinner, not to mention that nice selection of Amador and Calaveras County wines. Closed Wednesday. More than a dinner house and surprisingly good is the **Murphys Hotel Restaurant,** 457 Main, 209/728-3444, which offers American-continental fare at dinner, as well as a great breakfast and lunch. And the hotel serves the **Murphys Brewing Company**'s great Murphys Red, on tap.

Mercer Caverns and Moaning Cavern

About one mile north of Murphys, the **Mercer Caverns,** 1665 Sheep Ranch Rd., 209/728-2101, www.mercercaverns.com, were formed from an earthquake-caused fissure. Note the unusual aragonite crystals in these limestone formations. Nowadays, the experience is a bit flashy, with colored lights, but offers good examples of "flowstone," stalagmites, and stalactites. The Mercer caves were called Calaveras Caverns at one time (*calaveras* means skulls in Spanish) because human bones were found here; the Miwok lowered bodies into caves as part of their traditional burial rites. Open daily year-round, 10 A.M.–4:30 P.M. (expanded hours in summer). The 45-minute tours climb down (and back up) the equivalent of 16 flights of stairs and are $10 adults, $6 children (ages 5–12).

More pristine is **Moaning Cavern,** 5350 Moaning Cave Rd. (off Hwy. 4 between Vallecito and Douglas Flat), 209/736-2708 or 866/762-2837, www.caverntours.com, reportedly California's largest hidden hole in the ground. Don't be put off by the hype. Local Native Americans were said to hold this spot in awe because of the voices calling out from the cave's mouth. Moaning Cavern is really a vertical cave with a main cavity large enough to hide the Statue of Liberty (if anyone could ever figure out how to get it down the staircase). Thrill-seekers (over age 12) can rappel down into darkness; a three-hour "adventure" is also available. Admission for the family-friendly walking tour is $12 adults, $6 children. Open daily 9 A.M.–6 P.M. (10 A.M.–5 P.M. in winter).

CALAVERAS BIG TREES STATE PARK

The first grove of *Sequoiadendron giganteum,* or Sierra redwoods, ever spied by white explorers was noted by members of the Joseph Walker party in 1833; northstate pioneer John Bidwell recorded his first observations in 1841. Yet word didn't spread until 1852, when Augustus T. Dowd discovered what became known as the **Discovery Tree** here; the following year someone felled the giant and shipped pieces to New York City for public exhibition. Though 6,500-acre Calaveras Big Tree State Park wasn't established until 1931, big trees have been a major California tourist attraction since Dowd's discovery. Once widespread, these trees now grow only on the western slopes of the Sierra Nevada and are more plentiful in the Yosemite, Sequoia, and Kings Canyon areas to the south. Here, about four miles east of Arnold, there are relatively few "big

trees," and these grow in isolated groves among mountain yew, sugar pine, white fir, and flowering dogwood. But Calaveras Big Trees is a good spot for a summer escape (it's cool up here). It's also nice for fall color, uncrowded autumn campouts, and wintertime snowshoe hikes or cross-country skiing.

Start your exploration at the **Big Trees Visitor Center,** with a nod to the wooden grizzly outside, for a good orientation to the area's natural and cultural history. An easy one-mile **nature trail** winds through the park's **North Grove.** A brochure is available in Braille for the 600-foot **Three Sense Trail,** where you can touch, smell, and hear the forest. The North Grove area near the highway is most accessible and therefore most visited, but the **South Grove** has about 1,000 big trees in a nearly primeval setting. It's only a mile to the southern group of trees from the parking lot, up the **Big Trees Creek Trail** to the self-guided loop. The longer **Lava Bluffs Trail** winds through ancient lava formations and natural springs. Great swimming in the Stanislaus River. The trail to the **Bradley Grove**—a 2.5-mile loop through a redwood grove planted (in a logged-over area) in the 1950s—starts on the left side of the South Grove trail, just past the Beaver Creek Bridge.

Practicalities

Day use is $4 per vehicle. You can camp at the **North Grove Campground** or at **Oak Hollow.** The pleasant campsites have wonderful hot coin-op showers (not available in winter) and piped drinking water, $12–15. Reservations are a must in summer: ReserveAmerica, 800/444-7275, www.reserveamerica.com. Otherwise, here it's first-come, first-camped. There's a seven-day limit, and no more than eight people are allowed per site. The park also offers environmental campsites, $7–10. Or just come for the day to picnic and hike on trails and fire roads. For more information, contact **Calaveras Big Trees State Park,** 209/795-2334, or see www.bigtrees.org.

If the campgrounds at Calaveras are full, try the splendid new U.S. Forest Service **Wa Ka Luu Hep Yoo Campground.** (The name means "wild river" in the Miwok language.) The campground offers hot showers, running water, an extensive interpretive program emphasizing local Native American history, and a commercial rafting facility and public put-in. Campsites are $13 (no reservations). To get to the campground, usually open June–Oct., take Hwy. 4 about four miles east from Arnold to the town of Dorrington; make the first right onto Board's Crossing Rd., and follow the winding road about five miles down to the Stanislaus River—the campground will be on your left. For more information, contact the Stanislaus National Forest's **Calaveras Ranger District** office in Hathaway Pines, 209/795-1381, www.fs.fed.us/r5/stanislaus.

For a historic nonpark stay, try the 1852 **Dorrington Hotel,** 3431 Hwy. 4 in Dorrington, 209/795-5800 or 866/995-5800, www.dorringtonhotel.com, which offers five gussied-up hotel rooms (brass beds, homemade quilts, antiques, lace curtains, shared bathrooms) and a separate cabin with Jacuzzi tub. Rates are $100–150. Good restaurant, too, serving Northern Italian fare. Another possibility is the nearby **Dorrington Inn,** 3450 Hwy. 4, 209/795-2164 or 888/874-2164, www.dorringtoninn.com, where amenities include small refrigerator, microwave, wet bar, and cable TV with VCR. Most pine-paneled cottages (chalets) are $100–200. Arnold, just west of Calaveras Big Trees, has its charms too—particularly **Tallahan's Café,** 1225 Oak Circle, 209/795-4005, serving imaginative, sophisticated fare. Open Fri.–Tues. for lunch and dinner.

Columbia

Drunken bar brawls, shady ladies, and muddy, manure-filled streets once defined daily life in Columbia. The "Gem of the Southern Mines," Columbia served as capital city to an area population of more than 15,000 in its prime. But in 1854, the town lost the sensitive scuffle for state capital to Sacramento by just two legislative votes. It was a devastating political loss for the biggest, richest, and wickedest gold town of them all. When the mines declined in the 1870s, more than $87 million in gold had been stripped from the earth. Much of the land near Columbia has been laid waste by hydraulic mining.

Even before its painstaking restoration, the former American Camp was the most beautifully preserved of all gold country towns. Quite a few Westerns, including *High Noon* and scenes from Clint Eastwood's *The Unforgiven,* have been filmed here. Now a state historic park, downtown Columbia is a fine outdoor "museum"; no cars are allowed in the historic sector, only tourists—about a half million each year. Most of the town's attractions and shops are open daily 10 A.M.–5 P.M.

To get oriented, pick up a free guide at the visitors center, then wander through blocks of fire-resistant brick and iron buildings in the Greek-revival style, built following devastating fires in 1854 and 1857. Main Street today is only half the length it once was; the northern arm was never reattached to the town. Push the "talking buttons" outside various buildings to hear tape-recorded "guides" explain what you see as you peer into old windows and doors.

For more information about the area, contact **Columbia State Historic Park,** 209/532-0150, and the **Columbia California Chamber of Commerce,** 209/536-1672, www.columbia-california.com.

SEEING AND DOING COLUMBIA

The tiny **William Cavalier Museum** at Knapp's Corner, Main and State Sts., makes a good first stop. The museum's collection includes real gold and plentiful Western paraphernalia. Displays chronicle the massive townwide restoration, and slide shows and films add historical context. Guided walking tours (check for current schedule) depart from the museum. The **Museum of the Gold Rush Press** is a cast-iron Palmer & Rey sharing space with Columbia Booksellers & Stationers in the reconstructed *Columbia Gazette* building, along with a collection of old-time newspapers and a rogue's gallery of gold rush journalists. The two-story red brick **Columbia**

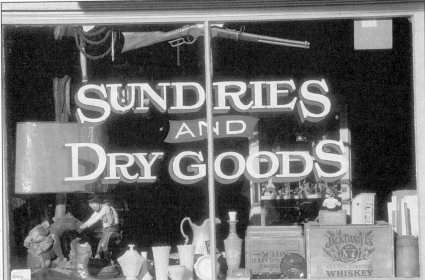

store window in Columbia State Historic Park

Grammar School on Kennebec Hill (at the top of School Street) was used from 1860 to 1937 and is in excellent condition. Inside you'll see old desks with inkwells, dusty books, writing slates, tobacco-can lunchboxes, and wood-burning stoves. And if your kids still think milk and eggs come from the grocery store, make sure they get historical perspective and some agricultural awareness at the park's **Chicken Coop.** They can even buy banty eggs at the **Columbia Mercantile.**

The seedy **miner's cabin** at the end of Main is a bleak, definitely unromantic reminder of prospectors' real lives. About $55 million in gold bullion and nuggets passed through the authentically furnished **Wells Fargo office** here. Notice the beautiful scales. The **D.O. Mills Building** next door was one of the first branches of the later Bank of California. Another authentic touch is the town's ample supply of saloons; before the first big fire, about one-fifth of Columbia's business establishments were bars.

The fine **Fallon Hotel,** 11175 Washington St., with its elegant theater and restaurant, has been righteously restored. No matter what else you do, stop here to appreciate the careful craftsmanship. The **City Hotel,** on Main St., is less ostentatious but still impressive. Also in Columbia are the state's oldest barbershop (need a haircut?), a dentist's office, Chinese herb shop, smithy, carpenter shop, tintype photography studio, ice house, and livery stable. **Papeete,** Columbia's first and most extravagant fire pumper (originally destined for the Society Islands), is now just for show, used only during the annual Firemen's Muster festivities.

With the right attitude—and here, there's nothing wrong with being one more tourist among the multitude—anyone can enjoy Columbia's family-focused emphasis. Climb aboard the **A.N. Fisher & Co. Stage Line,** 209/588-0808, for a stagecoach ride ($5) or sign on at the stable for a horseback ride ($30). Get a glimpse of gold-bearing quartz on a guided tour of a nearby working gold mine (daily in summer, otherwise usually on weekends only). Gold panning, too. For information contact **Matelot Gulch & Hidden Treasure Gold Mine,** 209/532-9693. If you're going down into the mine, bring a sweater. In the Fallon Hotel the **Fallon House** theater hosts stage performances by Sonora's **Sierra Repertory Theatre,** 209/532-3120, www.sierrarep.com.

About a mile southwest of Columbia is **Springfield Trout Farm,** 21980 Springfield Rd., 209/532-4623, a fun place offering family fishing from the stocked pond. When you catch your rainbow trout—raised here just for that purpose, in spring water—the folks even clean it for you and pack it on ice. Tackle and bait are part of the deal, but you can also buy fresh-dressed trout to go. Or just wander and watch the fingerlings grow. Open daily 10 A.M.–6 P.M. in summer; 10 A.M.–5 P.M. the rest of the year.

For adults who've had enough of everything else, there's always winetasting. Try attractive **Yankee Hill Winery,** 11755 Coarsegold Ln. (just off Yankee Hill Rd.), 209/533-2417, where you can also picnic and at least peek into the production facility, and the **Gold Mine Winery and Old Stamp Mill Brewery,** 22265 Parrotts Ferry Rd., 209/532-3089, www.goldminewinery.com.

STAYING IN COLUMBIA

Both tent campers and RVers are welcome at the **'49er RV Ranch,** 23223 Italian Bar Rd., 209/532-4978, www.49rv.com ($29.50 per night for two). Facilities include hot showers, picnic tables, barbecues, a laundromat, nightly campfire, and a square-dance center. Or try the nearby **Marble Quarry RV Resort,** 11551 Yankee Hill Rd., 209/532-9539 or 866/677-8464, www.marblequarry.com ($22–33 for two), which features a swimming pool, Laundromat, picnic tables, barbecues, and RV hookups.

The clean, old-fashioned **Columbia Gem Motel,** 22131 Parrotts Ferry Rd., 209/532-4508 or 866/436-6685, www.columbiagem.com, is pleasant, offering tiny barn-red-and-white 1940s-style cottages with mini sitting porches, plus a few standard motel rooms. (This "gem" has just a handful of units, so be sure to reserve in advance.) Rates are $50–150.

The once-opulent **City Hotel,** on Main St. (between Jackson and State Streets), 209/532-1479 or 800/532-1479, www.cityhotel.com, has regained its gloss. Period furniture and marble-topped tables accent the authenticity of the Victorian parlor. The 10 guest rooms have half-baths and share showers down the hall (bathrobes, slippers, and toiletries provided). Rates ($100–150) include generous continental breakfast, served in the central parlor. Before it became a hotel in the 1870s, the building was used as an assay office, opera house, stagecoach office, and newspaper headquarters.

The ornate lobby of the **Fallon Hotel,** 11175 Washington St. (just off Broadway), 209/532-1470 or 800/532-1479, also on the web at www.cityhotel.com, features almost-too-perfect vintage wallpapers, green velvet drapes, oak furnishings, and Oriental rugs—all in all an overstatement of Old West luxury; when this was a miners' lodging house, the accommodations were much more spartan. (No wandering through the elegant hallways unless you're a paying customer.) The 14 exquisitely redone Victorian rooms—quite small, excepting the balconied rooms—feature chain-pull toilets and porcelain basins in the half-baths (showers are shared here, too). Continental breakfast. Rates are $70–125; rooms without bathrooms are cheapest ($60). Hotel management students from the local junior college, dressed in 1850s attire, assist staff in attending to your every need at both the City and Fallon Hotels.

EATING IN COLUMBIA

Eat, at least once, at the **City Hotel** dining room, 209/532-1479 or 800/532-1479, another community college "project" and *Wine Spectator* Award of Excellence winner since 1986. Expect contemporary American regional cuisine with classic French touches: light sauces, intriguing appetizers—smoked salmon and dill cheesecake, grilled potato flatbread, and that '49er favorite, oysters on the half shell—crisp linen and fresh flowers, and fine service. Seasonally changing menu might include entrées such as grilled chicken and Asian vegetables with fresh udon noodles; pan seared salmon with teriyaki glaze, basmati rice, and grilled pineapple and toasted coconut sauce; and filet of beef tenderloin crowned with Dungeness crab. Open Tues.–Sun. 5–9 P.M. for dinner, and also

Sunday 11 A.M.–2 P.M. for a spectacular brunch. Reservations are necessary. Also in the hotel is the **What Cheer Saloon,** an historic bar with a comfortable Western atmosphere.

The **St. Charles Saloon,** 209/533-4656, is a beer and wine bar for adults (kids can order a sarsaparilla). More unnecessary calories are available at **Nelson's Columbia Candy Kitchen,** 380 Main St., 209/728-2820, a third-generation family operation featuring old-recipe specialties like rocky road, almond bark, peppermint or horehound candies, even genuine licorice whips, plus decadent hand-dipped truffles. Another treat: good ice cream in fresh-baked waffle cones at the **Fallon Ice Cream Parlor,** 11175 Washington, 209/532-1470.

ENTERTAINMENT AND EVENTS

Local historian Carol Biederman offers a popular **Ghost Walk** of the City Hotel and other haunted local venues, $8 per person, reservations strongly advised. For details about this and other popular hotel-sponsored events, contact the City Hotel (see above). Show up on Easter Sunday for the town's **Victorian Easter Parade,** quite the mobile display of bonnie bonnets. Usually in late April, the City Hotel **Wine Festival** benefit shares—and demonstrates—the history of area wine-

making. The **Firemen's Muster** here in May is a major event; volunteer fire brigades from around the state, dressed in period costumes, haul their antique engines to Columbia to compete in pumping contests and otherwise join in the general jolliness. The **Columbia Diggins living history weekend** takes place in early June, offering a gold rush tent-town reenactment. The inhabitants, dressed in period clothes, discuss only "current" events (go ahead, try to trip them up) and ply their trades: panning for gold, preaching to the heathen hordes, and running for political office.

Also big in Columbia is the Americana-filled **Fourth of July Celebration.** Other events include the **Poison Oak Show** in late September and the **Christmas Lamplight Tour** on the first Saturday in December—part of the two-weekend **Miner's Christmas,** which also include the **Las Posadas** nativity pageant and candlelight procession down Main Street. Quite special at the City Hotel each December is the annual **Victorian Christmas Feast,** an unforgettable four-course meal preceded by a champagne reception in the parlor and accompanied by carolers and other entertainment. The feast ($85 per person, at last report) is usually offered Tues.–Fri. and Sun. nights from Dec. 1 until just before Christmas; call the hotel well in advance to make reservations because it books up fast every year.

Sonora

Mexican miners founded the town during a particularly nasty period of Yankee us-firstism. Greedy gringos eventually forced the first Sonorans off their claims here, too, creating considerable outlaw backlash. The novel *The Last Californian* by modern-day Sonora resident and schoolteacher Feliz Guthrie spins the story of the infamous Rancheria Massacre, a telling tale about racism in the Mother Lode. After the Latino "lawbreakers" were eliminated, the rich placer fields near Sonora harvested, and the pocket mines turned inside out and emptied, lumber became the area's main industry, spurred by the arrival of the railroad in 1898. Orange crates for packaging California citrus were manufactured here by the millions.

Sonora, the "Queen of the Southern Mines" and old-time Columbia rival, is today something of a suburban octopus, its tentacles of one-acre ranchettes flailing out in all directions. No wonder people want to live here: this *is* a pretty town (downtown).

The helpful **Tuolumne County Visitors Bureau,** 542 W. Stockton St., 209/533-4420 or 800/446-1333, www.thegreatunfenced.com, dispenses information on just about everything. There's even a photograph flipbook on area bed-and-breakfasts, so you can see how they look. Public camping, trail, and outdoor recreation information and permits are available at the **Stanislaus National Forest** headquarters, 19777

GOLD COUNTRY

Greenley Rd. (across from the fairgrounds), 209/532-3671, www.fs.fed.us/r5/stanislaus.

SEEING AND DOING SONORA

Washington is the town's main street, an identity shared with Hwy. 49 and Hwy. 108 as both squeeze through Sonora's central ravine. Travelers flow in fits and spurts through a mother lode of boutiques, specialty shops, and eateries, all tucked into and around some noteworthy architecture. Pick up a free local guides at the county museum and elsewhere around town. After a sightseeing stroll, simply rest and read by Sonora Creek in **Coffill Park** downtown at S. Washington and Theall.

The elegant and unusual red **Saint James Episcopal Church** at Washington and Snell is still a place of worship, but also maintains a museum (in the rectory). Open weekdays 9 A.M.–5 P.M. Next door is the **Bradford Building,** complete with copper doors and an elaborate dome. It was constructed by local lumber baron S.S. Bradford, who also built the impressive, very San Francisco **Street-Morgan Mansion,** across from the church at 23 W. Snell.

The original 1850 **Gunn Adobe,** 286 S. Washington, later grew a balcony and new wings, becoming the Hotel Italia and today a motel. The **Tuolumne County Courthouse,** 2 S. Green St., is a bizarre yet stately building constructed from local materials: green sandstone, yellow pressed bricks, Columbia marble, and Copperopolis copper (for the Byzantine clock tower and doors). Inside, the **County Recorder's office** features a pre-dam photo of Hetch Hetchy Valley—second only to Yosemite Valley in natural beauty, according to John Muir—and a good collection of old newspapers.

At home in the town's former jailhouse, the Tuolumne County Museum and History Center, 158 W. Bradford Ave., 209/532-1317, www .tchistory.org, is worth some time. Inside are paintings by William West and some fascinating Western photography. The jailhouse setting itself lends an intriguing atmosphere, with local

The historic red Saint James Episcopal Church

gold rush relics and other historical items exhibited in a "cell by cell" arrangement. Picnic in the jailyard. Open daily 10 A.M.–3:30 P.M. year round.

STAYING IN SONORA

Camping

Far from wilderness but close to town are the **Mother Lode Fairgrounds,** 220 Southgate Dr. (off Hwy. 49 south of town), 209/532-7428, www.motherlodefair.com ($20 per night). This place is nothing fancy—just a basic RV setup with hot showers and picnic tables—but you can pitch tents on the lawn. Camp at **New Melones** (see Angels Camp above), or head east up into the Sierra Nevada high country on Hwy. 108 and pitch your tent at **Fraser Flat Campground** ($13) past Long Barn (take the Spring Gap turnoff north; steep, winding road). You'll find other possibilities near Pinecrest. For seclusion and scenery, take Cottonwood Rd. from Tuolumne to remote **Cherry Valley Campground** at Cherry Lake just outside Yosemite ($12 per night). For more information, contact the Stanislaus National Forest's **Miwok Ranger District** office, 24695 Hwy. 108 in Miwuk Village, 209/586-3234, or stop by forest headquarters here in town (see below). If you're heading into Yosemite via Hwy. 120 from the gold country, you'll find wonderful primitive campsites near the wild Tuolumne River (see Groveland below).

Motels and Hotels

Right downtown (and worth it for the "feel" of local history) is the **Sonora Days Inn,** 160 S. Washington, 209/532-2400 or 800/580-4667, www.sonoradaysinn.com, previously the Sonora Inn—a beige Spanish California beauty with tile roof, pool, hot tub, onsite saloon, and steakhouse. Newly remodeled rooms feature all the modern comforts, including private bathrooms; annex rooms offer in-room refrigerators and microwaves. Rates are about $100. Across from the fairgrounds, just southwest of town along Hwy. 49/108, the **Gold Lodge,** 480 W. Stockton St., 209/532-3952 or 800/363-2154, is a settled-in motel with big shade trees. Rates are $50–100.

Several miles east of downtown via Hwy. 108 is the deluxe **Best Western Sonora Oaks Motor Hotel,** 19551 Hess Ave., 209/533-4400 or 800/532-1944 (reservations), www.bestwesterncalifornia.com. Rates are $50–100.

Bed-and-Breakfasts

The surprisingly Parisian **Barretta Gardens Inn,** 700 S. Barretta St., 209/532-6039 or 800/206-3333, www.barrettagarden.com, overlooks the town from an acre of lovely lawns and gardens. Four gorgeous guest rooms (two can be combined) and one suite feature private baths and various little luxuries, from fresh flowers and terrycloth-lined robes to two-person Jacuzzis and TV with VCR (large video library). Fully stocked guest refrigerator, and the owners' onsite boulangerie creates the luscious, all-natural French pastries. Rates are about $100–150, full breakfast included. A particularly good deal for a couple with small child is the very pink Chantal, $95, with a private bathroom across the hall. Another great choice is the **Bradford Place Inn,** 56 W. Bradford St., 209/536-6075 or 800/209-2315, www.bradfordplaceinn.com, featuring four striking rooms and suites with abundant comforts, from dataports and TV/VCR to in-room coffeemakers; two rooms have microwaves and refrigerators, one has a two-person Jacuzzi. Luscious breakfasts. Rates are $100–200.

For a current regional bed-and-breakfast brochure, reservations, and referrals, contact **Gold Country Bed and Breakfast Inns of Tuolumne County,** 888/465-1849, www.goldbnbs.com.

EATING IN SONORA

The **Sonora Certified Farmers Market** is held May–Oct. on Sat., 8 A.M.–noon, at Theall and Stewart Streets. For information, call 209/532-7725. **Wilma's Café & Flying Pig Saloon** downtown at 275 S. Washington, 209/532-9124, is locally famous for its hickory-smoked barbecue. But it's also one of those down-home American-style cafés where most everyone can find something good to eat. Great breakfast specials, wonderful homemade pies, microbrews. Wilma the Flying Pig sits by the cash register; other pig statues and oddities are everywhere. Open daily.

More sophisticated, in the culinary sense, is **Banny's,** 83 S. Stewart St., 209/533-4709, where dinner entrées include marinated lamb chops with spicy Morrocan sauce, grilled chicken ragout, and grilled eggplant. At lunch there are many choices, from juicy burger to vegetarian wrap of the day. Open for lunch Mon.–Sat., for dinner nightly; senior menu, 4:30–6 P.M.

Stylish newcomer **One Twenty-Four** restaurant, in a grandly restyled Victorian at 124 N. Washington, 209/533-2145, serves up sublime California-style coastal Mediterranean, from wild mushroom ravioli and Greek grilled chicken to trout almondine. Many inviting, intimate dining areas, and great patio dining in season. Regional wineries and microbreweries are well represented in the restaurant as well as the bar. Open Wed.–Sun., reservations advisable.

ENTERTAINMENT AND EVENTS

The **Sierra Repertory Theatre,** 13891 Mono Way (Hwy. 108), 209/532-3120, www.sierrarep.com, offers a year-round schedule of comedies, dramas, and musicals at both its East Sonora Stage (address above) and at the Fallon House in Columbia. There's no lack of other nightlife otherwise—the bar scene, live music, dancing—around town, either, especially on weekends. Find out about current arts events from the **Central Sierra Arts Council,** 208 S. Green St., 209/532-2787, www.centralsierraarts.org.

Trout and salmon fishing are popular throughout nearby mountain areas. White-water rafting on the Tuolumne River is passionately pursued from spring to fall. (Get a list of commercial rafting companies at the visitors bureau or the forest service office, and see this chapter's introduction.) If you go on your own—no beginners—you'll need a permit, available at the Forest Service office here or in Groveland, where you can also pick up hiking and camping information.

In early April, Sonorans have their annual **Sonora Smoke Polers** festival, an early Western shoot-'em-up, with flintlocks and muzzle-loading rifles, even mountain men in animal skins living in tepees. Come on Mother's Day weekend in May for the **Mother Lode Roundup** and associated parade, one of California's oldest and largest. Show up in June for Sonora's annual **Dixieland Festival,** in July for the **Mother Lode Fair,** and in August for the **Fire on the Mountain Blues Festival.** More blues arrive in September, for the **Fire on the Mountain Blues & Brews Festival.** Fun for fiddlin' types in October is the annual **Fiddle and Banjo Contest.** During the annual **Christmas Craft & Music Festival,** there is a commercial cornucopia of quality handicrafts.

Other local events—chili cook-offs, pancake breakfasts, charity brunches, fashion shows, rummage sales, square dances, musical extravaganzas—tend to stitch Columbia, Sonora, Jamestown, and even Dodge Ridge and other mountain areas together into a countywide patchwork of activity; get a current events calendar at the visitors bureau.

VICINITY OF SONORA

The trip south on Hwy. 49 toward Jamestown is hideous—unattractive helter-skelter construction, heavy traffic, cars wheeling onto the highway from every which way—so go on back roads if at all possible. A worthwhile excursion is up Hwy. 108 (nice autumn colors) to explore the onetime logging town of Standard, Soulsbyville, Tuolumne, and the area from Twain Harte to Long Barn. Don't be fooled by the name **Twain Harte,** which doesn't have any connection with either Mark Twain or Bret Harte. The town's name comes from a 1920s effort to promote Mother Lode tourism through its literary legacy. To find out what is and isn't happening in these parts, contact the **Twain Harte Chamber of Commerce,** 22997 Joaquin Gully Rd., 209/586-4482, www.twainhartecc.com. **Mi-Wuk Village** is a subdivision named after the Miwok people, though none live here, and the long barn that **Long Barn** was named for burned to the ground, but before that the town was a way station for oxen teams and their drivers en route across the Sierra Nevada. Quite special is the friendly, three-story **McCaffrey House Bed & Breakfast Inn,** 23251 Hwy. 108, 209/586-0757 or 888/586-

0757, www.mccaffreyhouse.com, with every imaginable comfort, handmade Amish quilts, amazing breakfasts. Rates are $100–150. For steaks, eat at **Diamond Jim's,** 24535 Hwy. 108, 209/586-3561.

This old mining camp of **Soulsbyville** north of Tuolumne City was settled by Cornish miners and their families and was noted for its tranquility even in the gold rush heyday. Ben Soulsby was a farmer and lumberman who became a hardrock miner (and mine owner) when his son, Little Ben, stumbled over a large gold nugget on a cowpath.

Approaching **Tuolumne City,** bear in mind that "Tuolumne" comes from a Miwok word meaning "those who live in stone houses," a possible reference to native people who fled with the arrival of the Spanish and became Stanislaus Canyon cave dwellers. Tuolumne today is a pretty, crisp-aired mountain town with some charming homes, a playground, and a public swimming pool. In September, the annual **Acorn Festival** is held at the Sierra Miwok roundhouse on the nearby **Tuolumne Rancheria** (one of the last remaining Miwok reservations) on Miwok Road. In keeping with the times, these days there's considerably more interest in the Tuolumne band's Black Oak Casino. **Cover's Apple Ranch,** 19200 Cherokee Rd., 209/928-4689, www.coversappleranch.com, has delicious apples in season, also apple-nut bran muffins, "mile-high" pies, jams, and other goodies.

From Tuolumne City you can drive east all the way to Hetch Hetchy Reservoir in Yosemite; Buchanan Rd. connects up with Cottonwood Rd., a winding but well-paved mountain path through magnificent countryside.

Jamestown and Vicinity

Once a supply station for area mines and now pretty as a tintype photograph, Jamestown (also known as Jimtown) gained attention as the site of the Crocker family's Sierra Railroad Company, the main line running from here through Sonora and on to the mill at Fasler—rails you can still ride today, now part of Railtown 1897 State Historic Park. Countless movies, including *High Noon, The Virginian, Dodge City,* and *My Little Chickadee,* not to mention TV westerns like *The Lone Ranger, Tales of Wells Fargo,* and *Little House on the Prairie,* have been filmed at least partially in Jamestown.

SEEING AND DOING JAMESTOWN

Main Street is a bustling quarter-mile-long cowboy alley lined with pickup trucks. Hold down a bench in Jamestown Park on Main and just watch the summer sideshow pass by, or brave the streets and explore the stores. Gold rush–oriented stores and jewelry shops abound. If you're a serious gold-lover, try finding some of your own. **Gold Prospecting Expeditions,** in the old livery stable at 18170 Main, 209/984-4653, can tell you how to go about it. Kids pan for free in a trough outside, but basic placer mining, "rafting for riches," high-tech helicopter gold trips, and classes for grownups cost money. An hour of basic panning instruction costs $30, and you can "rent" a gold mining claim, too. The possibilities are almost endless.

For a different type of risk—in this case, legal high-stakes California gambling—check out the red-hot bingo games (and they *do* get hot when the purse reaches five figures) out at the **Chicken Ranch Bingo & Casino** on the Miwok reservation, 16929 Chicken Ranch Rd. (about one mile west of Jamestown), 209/984-3000.

Worth a stop is **Jamestown's Railtown 1897 State Historic Park,** headquartered at the old Sierra Railway Depot on Fifth at Reservoir (just above Main, off the highways), 209/984-3953 (main office), www.csrmf.org. With its expanse of cool green lawn, tables, barbecues, and running water, the park is pleasant for picnics. The 26-acre site includes a collection of venerable railroad cars—be sure to see the parlor car from the *California Zephyr*—and the Sierra's massive old roundhouse, still in use for locomotive and railroad car repairs and restorations. Guided

GOLD COUNTRY

roundhouse tours, which include movie arti-facts and props, are offered daily (small fee).

On weekends Apr.–Oct. (and weekends only in November), you can take a 45-minute, six-mile trip on the steam-powered Mother Lode Cannon Ball, which departs hourly 11 A.M.–3 P.M. (get tickets at the depot). Trains also run on Memorial Day, Independence Day, and Labor Day. The fare is $6 youths and adults, $3 children 6–12 (age 5 and under free). Please call ahead to make sure trains are running. Special runs are offered peri-odically, too, including Gold Rush, Murder Mys-tery, Wine and Cheese, and Santa trains.

Now managed in conjunction with the Cali-fornia State Railroad Museum in Sacramento, Railtown 1897 sponsors other special events throughout the year, including its **Movie Rail-road Days** in autumn; call to request a com-plete calendar of events. The park is open year-round, daily 9:30 A.M.–4:30 P.M. (closed Thanksgiving, Christmas, and New Year's Day). Small admission.

STAYING IN JAMESTOWN

The closest campgrounds are at unattractive **Don Pedro Reservoir** near La Grange, 209/852-2396, www.donpedrolake.com; both RV and tent sites are available, $12–25. Considerably farther south are **Lake McClure** and **Lake Mc-Swain**, reservoirs with ample campsites (see Coulterville below).

The **Jamestown Railtown Motel,** 10301 Wil-low St. (just up from Main), 209/984-3332, of-fers rooms at $40–60. Most "hotels" in Jimtown are actually bed-and-breakfasts. The elaborate, eye-catching balcony and wooden boardwalk at the exquisitely restored **1859 Historic National Hotel,** 18183 Main St., 209/984-3446 or 800/894-3446, www.national-hotel.com, are like frosting on a luscious cake. This authentic gold rush relic, now a bed-and-breakfast with some original furnishings and pull-chain toilets, of-fers nine nicely decorated rooms with modern comforts (private bathrooms, TV, dataports, hairdryers). Continental breakfast, great onsite restaurant and saloon open to the public. Most rooms are $100–150, and pets are welcome ($10)

with advance arrangements. The equally historic **Jamestown Hotel,** 18153 Main St., 209/984-3902 or 800/205-4901, www.jamestownho-tel.com, is now a red-brick country inn featuring 11 delightfully decorated rooms named for no-table women, including gold rush figures such as spider-dance star Lola Montez and her protégé, Lotta Crabtree. Most rooms are $100–200. Here, too, the remodeled bar and contemporary coun-try-style restaurant are open to the public.

EATING IN JAMESTOWN

At **Kamm's Chinese Restaurant,** 18208 Main St., 209/984-3105, you can get a five-course Cantonese meal for next to nothing. Another possibility is the **Smoke Cafe,** 18191 Main St., 209/984-3733, which serves good margaritas and decent Mexican dinners, such as *chile verde* and *pollo de poblano,* in a tin-walled Western at-mosphere. The specials are usually enticing. For something decidedly uptown, **Michelangelo** downtown at 18288 Main, 209/984-4830, serves a fine array of area wines along with some tanta-lizing Italian, from fabulous pastas to prosciutto-wrapped chicken.

AROUND JAMESTOWN

Take Rawhide Rd. north, the starting point for worthwhile hikes to 40-mile-long **Table Moun-tain** and colorful displays of spring wildflowers. The half-mile walk to **Peppermint Falls** starts at the end of Peppermint Falls Rd., or hike to vol-canic **Pulpit Rock.** The main road continues on to Rawhide Flat, where you'll see remnants of the 1890s **Rawhide Mine** and the long-gone town of **Jefferson.** A jaunt up Jamestown Rd. toward Shaw's Flat also leads to the gracefully decaying gold rush-era **Mississippi House** hotel. From Jamestown, Jacksonville Rd. runs toward Quartz Mountain, site of the once-prosperous Heslit-App Mine and the remains of old **Quartz.** Nearby **Stent** was called Poverty Hills during the gold rush because the pickin's were so poor.

Just 12 miles west of Jamestown toward the valley, **Knights Ferry,** with a historic district of old brick and pine-frame buildings along the banks of the Stanislaus River, is a haven for swimmers, picnickers, and campers in summer. Appreciate the Knights Ferry Covered Bridge, reportedly the longest of its type in the U.S., designed by U.S. Grant; there's also a fine small museum and visitors' center.

Chinese Camp

Near the junction of Hwy. 49 and Hwy. 120 and east of Yosemite Junction is Chinese Camp, today consisting of a volunteer-staffed **visitor information center,** post office, a combination store/bar/restaurant/gas station, aged adobes, creaky wood-frames, and crumbling brick buildings hidden by trees of heaven along Main Street. There's obviously not much happening here today, but this was once one of the largest U.S. Asian settlements. In September 1856, 2,000 Chinese from rival tongs battled after one group was excoriated in print by the other as "perfect worms" who "ought to be exterminated." Onlookers were disappointed when only four warriors were dead and a few dozen wounded after it was all over several hours later.

Groveland

Past Moccasin Creek Fish Hatchery and the brutal climb up Hwy. 120 to Priest (locals say the old road was worse) is Groveland. Once called Garrote and founded by the gold rush, Groveland boomed again during the construction of Hetch Hetchy Reservoir. The town is now a pine-woodsy, pleasant resort community.

A real '49er old-timer, the gracious 1849 adobe **Groveland Hotel,** 18767 Main St., 209/962-4000 or 800/273-3314, www.grovelandhotel.com, was modeled after the famed Larkin House in Monterey and was itself one of the state's first grand hostelries. With its new conference center and saloon, the Groveland is still quite stylish and accommodating, its 17 refurbished rooms and suites (all with private baths) plush with Old World atmosphere, attractive antiques, and abundant contemporary comforts. Continental breakfast. The gracious Victorian Room serves dinner nightly; the spectacular saloon serves forth award-winning wines and microbrews. Most rooms are around $150, suites $250; ask about packages. If you're traveling to or from Yosemite, a time-honored stop for a country-style breakfast is **Buck Meadows Lodge,** 7647 Hwy. 120, 209/962-5281, with restaurant, saloon, and motel.

For information about nearby camping in Stanislaus National Forest, contact the **Groveland Ranger District** office, 24545 Hwy. 120, 209/962-7825, www.fs.fed.us/r5/stanislaus. From near Yosemite are the U.S. Forest Service **The Pines, Lost Claim, Sweetwater,** and (on Evergreen Road) **Diamond-O Campgrounds** ($10–13, first-come, first-camped, open Apr.–Oct.). Also in the area but accessible by rugged dirt road are the Forest Service **Lumsden, Lumsden Bridge,** and **South Fork Campgrounds** (turn north at Buck Meadows), all free.

Or head north to **Cherry Valley Campground,** for camping near Cherry Lake outside Yosemite National Park ($12), open Apr.–Oct.; the turnoff is a few miles past Buck Meadows. Take the Camp Mather turnoff from Hwy. 120 just outside Yosemite to enjoy a spectacular drive to Hetch Hetchy, a lovely vista even with the dam. To stay, take a cabin at summers-only **Evergreen Lodge** near Camp Mather, Star Rte. 160, 209/379-2606, www.evergreenlodge.com. Rates are $50–100. Be warned on major holiday weekends: bluegrass festivals book out the rooms here every Memorial Day and Labor Day weekend.

COULTERVILLE

Coulterville is unpocked by progress and is, in its entirety, a state historic landmark; Main Street is included on the National Register of Historic Places. The second-largest town in Mariposa County, fringed by barren oak and chaparral slopes, Coulterville is safe (so far) from the stylized rusticity that's raking in the tourists elsewhere. From Coulterville, take J132 past Greeley Hill; the main road becomes Smith Station Road and connects to Hwy. 120 outside Yosemite. Alternatively, head east on Greeley Hill Road (J20) then follow F.R. 2S01, Old Yosemite Road—the locals' route, "the John Muir Corridor"—to F.R. 20 and on into **Yosemite National Park.**

Along the latter route is **Bower Cave,** called *Oo-tin* or "Home of the Evening Star" by the

Miwok people, a once-popular 1800s tourist destination with a down-deep dance floor. The cave was technically closed to the public in the 1950s, after an accidental death, and was acquired in 1990 by the U.S. Forest Service. (You can't go inside the cave, and just to go look at the outside you'll need to pick up a permit from the Forest Service office in Groveland, 209/962-7825.) Or head west to the valley on Hwy. 132 to La Grange, south to Snelling, then east to **Hornitos, Mt. Bullion,** and John C. Frémont's **Mariposa.**

Contact the **North County Visitor Center,** 5007 Main St. in Coulterville, 209/878-3074, for current visitor information, or stop by the Northern Mariposa County History Center (see below).

Coulterville started as a Mexican village called Banderita, named, some say, after the miners' red bandanas. Others claim the name comes from the perennially tattered American flag that flew above founding merchant George Coulter's blue tent. Like clockwork, during the booming 1800s the new town of Coulterville burned to the ground at 20-year intervals. When gold fever finally broke, the Yosemite Turnpike toll road from here offered the only vehicle access to the park (and tourist-related business opportunities for local merchants) into the early 1900s.

Seeing and Doing Coulterville

First stop by the visitor center, or pick up a free map and guide to local sights and services on the counter just inside the door at the museum. Since most of the town's old saloons, cafés, storehouses, and homes have neither been restored nor vandalized, you can peer in windows and see original, faded wallpapers, heavy old doors with ancient handles, and miscellaneous old-time oddities.

Intriguing is the **Coulterville General Store,** seemingly tossed into the middle of a six-way junction of highways and streets. (Note the tiny jail nearby, next to the volunteer fire department.) Two original buildings still stand in Chinatown just off Main, one of them the old adobe **Sun Sun Wo Company Store** (not open to the public). Next door is the town's time-honored wood-frame whorehouse, **Candy's Place.** The ancient rosebush out front was harvested by Candy, who handed out the blooms to "gentlemen callers."

Most imposing of all, though, is the tin-sided, pine-green-and-tan **Hotel Jeffery,** 1 Main St., 209/878-3471 or 800/464-3471, a natural summer hideout with thick original adobe walls built in 1851. Legend has it that, among others, Ralph Waldo Emerson, Teddy Roosevelt, and Carrie Nation once slept here. There's no air-conditioning, but with adobe walls and ceiling fans, summer heat rarely poses a problem. European-style rooms (four shared baths down the hall) and some rooms with private bathrooms are around $100; suites are $100–200. Continental breakfast. Just swing open the batwing doors of the **Magnolia Saloon & Grill** downstairs and step into another century, one dressed up with tintype photographs, mineral collections, dusty memorabilia, even a genuine wooden Indian. There's one obvious concession to life in the 20th century: a jukebox. Lunch and dinner are served Wed.–Sun. year-round, breakfast only in summer. (Come by Saturday nights for live music.) Also next to the Jeffery is a cool and pleasant park hosting local events like barbecues, bluegrass festivals, and the annual **Coyote Howl** and **Gunfighters Rendezvous.**

The **Northern Mariposa County History Center,** 10301 Hwy. 49, 209/878-3015, is definitely worth a stop. Enter this aged stone museum complex, the old Wells Fargo and McCarthy's Store buildings, through the roofless shell of an open-air "courtyard" with cascading vines and flowers. Inside are well-done displays of Victorian Americana, the apothecary's art, surface mining, Wells Fargo boxes and gold scales, a well-preserved antique gun collection, and the old Studebaker buckboard Grace Kelly graced in *High Noon.* Nice, too, is the attention paid to "women's work," the wicked wooden washboard, flat iron, and butter churn all telling the truth about hard work. The center is open Wed.–Sun. 10 A.M.–4 P.M. except in January.

Outside by the town's hangin' tree is a small steam engine locals call *Whistling Billy.* Bill once pulled ore carts to the stamp mills from the nearby **Mary Harrison Mine** along a snaking, nearly vertical route.

Practicalities

If you don't stay at the Hotel Jeffery, consider the **Penon Blanco Lookout Bed and Breakfast,** 209/878-0146 or 888/257-4397, which offers many comforts and views once shared by naturalist John Muir. Or why not camp? McClure and McSwain Lakes are at the bottom of the long Hwy. 132 grade down into the valley from Coulterville. Most campsites ($15–22) are at **Lake McClure,** 209/378-2521 (information) or 800/468-8889 (reservations), www.lakemcclure.com, which spreads out over old mines and the onetime town of Bagby. **Lake McSwain** is McClure's forebay (cold water, good fishing, no powerboating).

AROUND COULTERVILLE

To Bear Valley

The stretch of "highway" between Coulterville and Bear Valley is beautiful but brutal, with hairpin turns, steep ascents, and sudden descents—a reminder of the demanding terrain challenged daily by hardscrabblers forced to traverse Merced River Canyon (nicknamed "Hell's Hollow"). You'll notice many closed mines along the way, but resist the temptation to go exploring; abandoned mineshafts are dangerous, each for different reasons.

John C. Frémont, intrepid explorer, militarist, and California's first U.S. senator, established his empire's headquarters in Bear Valley. He once owned the entire area from Mariposa to Bagby (fudging on the eastern boundary by about 50 miles when gold was discovered outside his original holdings). Frémont's scout Kit Carson discovered the first gold at the main Mariposa Mine and made strikes at other Bear Valley sites. But high overhead, lawyers' fees, and claim jumpers (Frémont had the governor call in the state militia to forcibly oust them) gradually nibbled away at the mines' potential profits. In his later years,

weeds and weather-beaten wood near Coulterville

© KIM WEIR

Frémont bragged ruefully that he came to California penniless, "but now I owe $2 million!"

Today, note the ruins of **Frémont's house,** poke into the **Oso House** museum (actually the old Odd Fellows Hall—the original Oso, Frémont's headquarters, was lost to fire), visit the jail, explore the graveyard. There's not much else here.

Hornitos

Hornitos was once Mariposa County's only incorporated city until the state Legislature took even that status away. A wild place in its day, the town was named after outdoor Mexican bread ovens, or *hornos,* though some say the oddly shaped gravestones in the cemetery are the eponymous inspiration. Today Hornitos is becoming a ghost town; its central plaza is empty, its sad cemetery more populous than the town. Among the buildings here are an old fandango hall, a two-story hotel, and the ruins of the red-brick **Ghirardelli Store** (the San Francisco chocolate king's humble beginnings, now a de facto garbage dump). From Hornitos, take the Hornitos-Old Toll Road east to **Mt. Bullion** (named after John Frémont's father-in-law, Thomas Hart "Old Bullion" Benton—a Republican senator adamantly opposed to paper money), the site of the Princeton Mine.

Mariposa to Bass Lake

MARIPOSA AND VICINITY

Mariposa (Spanish for "butterfly"), a woodsy town of 1,500 with old homes and wide, peaceful streets, was named by General John C. Frémont during his sneaky land grab. It's the southernmost of the major gold camps and one of the southern gateways to Yosemite. (The highway from here into the park is almost always open, even in winter.) The hills near here—like half of California, if you believe all the stories—were once Joaquin Murrieta's stomping grounds. Also in these hills are the remains of many ghost towns, most not marked by so much as a stone. Good luck.

To get oriented, stop by the **Mariposa County Chamber of Commerce** office and visitors center, 5158 Hwy. 140 (at Hwy. 49), 209/966-2456 or 866/425-3366, www.mariposa.org.

Frémont's old **Mariposa Mine,** the first steam-powered quartz mining operation in California, is at the end of Bullion, though visitors aren't exactly encouraged. Nearby is the white-steepled landmark, **St. Joseph's Catholic Church,** at 4985 Bullion. The grizzled granite **Old Mariposa Jail,** on Bullion between Fourth and Fifth, has natural rock walls more than two feet thick and was used until 1960. The office building of the *Mariposa Gazette* has burned to the ground twice, but the paper has never missed an issue since 1854.

Mariposa County Courthouse

Mariposa boasts California's oldest courthouse in continuous use. Built in 1854 with local white pine, it has original furnishings on the second floor, including a potbellied woodstove and simple wooden benches. As elsewhere in the gold country, mineral wealth seems to be the holy grail. There's a large rock collection here, and a mineral collage monument outside. Since Mariposa County has no incorporated cities, this is where the governmental action—such as it is—is. The courthouse sits on Bullion between Ninth and 10th Streets.

Mariposa Museum and History Center

Just one block off Hwy. 140 at Jessie and 12th Streets, the Mariposa Museum and History Center, 209/966-2924, is an excellent museum sharing space with the local library. In the outdoor courtyard, note the mule-powered Mexican *arrastra* used to grind ore (as well as corn for tortillas) and the full-scale model of a five-stamp mill. Push the button on the miniature version inside, and you'll see how gold-rich rocks were pulverized. Also here are displays of printing and mining equipment, an old-time apothecary, school rooms, Miwok dwellings and sauna, a lady's boudoir, a sheriff's office, and a miner's cabin—altogether a thoughtfully tended historical record. The museum is open daily 10 A.M.–4 P.M., open only in weekends in January. Small admission (by donation).

California State Mining and Mineral Museum

Also in Mariposa is the excellent California State Mining and Mineral Museum, 5005 Fairgrounds Dr. (at the county fairgrounds), 209/742-7625. Displays include a re-created assay office and mine tunnel, as well as some fine examples of the state's mineral riches—including the famed Fricot Nugget, the largest gold nugget found during the California gold rush—201 ounces of crystalline gold. Open daily May–Sept., 10 A.M.–6 P.M.; the rest of the year, Wed.–Mon. 10 A.M.–4 P.M. Small admission.

Wineries

Like so many other places in the gold country, the Mariposa-Oakhurst area has its boutique wineries. Inquire at the chamber of commerce for information on new ones. **Butterfly Creek Winery,** 4063 Triangle Rd., 209/966-2097, most accessible from just north of town, offers some award-winning chardonnay, cabernet sauvignon, white riesling, pinot blanc, and merlot. Open Friday and Saturday 10 A.M.–4 P.M. in summer, or by appointment. Nearby **Silver Fox Vineyards,** 4683 Morningstar Ln., 209/966-4800, is open for tasting and picnicking by appointment.

Camping

In a pinch, pitch your tent or park your RV at the **Mariposa County Fairgrounds** all year (except Labor Day weekend, when the fair is underway), just two miles south of town on Hwy. 49, 209/966-2432, www.mariposafair.com. Facilities include hot showers, hookups, dump station, picnic tables, and barbecues ($18). Various private campgrounds can be found in and around Mariposa; ask locally for suggestions.

Or sleep under the stars (first-come, first-camped) at nearby U.S. Forest Service sites. The free Forest Service **Jerseydale Campground** is about five miles north on Hwy. 140, then another nine miles on county roads (open from mid-May until October 1), and primitive **Summit Campground,** about 8 miles east on Hwy. 49, then seven miles northeast on a county road (4WD-only), is open June 1 to mid-October. There are two new campgrounds 30 miles east of Mariposa on Hwy. 140 toward Yosemite; take the Foresta Rd. turnoff before El Portal, turn left just over the bridge, and follow along the river about two miles. None of these has showers. Jerseydale has potable water, and the new campgrounds will at some point, but bring your own just in case. Last checked, they still did not have water. For more information about area camping, hiking trails, and other recreational possibilities—and for Forest Service permits—stop by the **Mariposa Visitors Bureau,** 209/966-2456, or contact **Sierra National Forest** headquarters, 1600 Tollhouse Rd., 559/297-0706, www.fs.fed.us/r5/sierra.

Yosemite Bug Hostel

All travelers—and particularly budget travelers—will appreciate the HI-USA **Yosemite Bug Hostel,** Lodge, Cabins, Tent Cabins, & Campground, 6979 Hwy. 140 in Midpines, 209/966-6666, www.yosemitebug.com, beyond Mariposa and just 25 miles from Yosemite Valley. It's an experience, not just a pleasant place to stay. Rates start at $16 per night for a dorm-style bunk; $30 for tent cabins; $40 for a private room with a shared bath; and $55 for a private room with private bath. Campsites ($17) are also available. The camaraderie begins but hardly ends at the impressive onsite bistro, where the fare is healthy, fresh, and

very reasonably priced—from buckwheat pancakes at breakfast to the vegetarian moussaka and pecan-encrusted trout at dinner. Guinness on tap, live entertainment, and a year-round calendar of special events and activities—swimming at local swimming holes, rafting, kayaking, hiking, mountain biking, cross-country skiing, snowshoeing—are also offered. Open year-round.

Bed-and-Breakfasts and Motels

The renovated 1901-vintage **Mariposa Hotel Inn,** right downtown at 5029 Hwy. 140 (at Sixth St.), 209/966-4676 or 800/317-3244, www.yosemitehotel.com, is a bed-and-breakfast-style inn with generously sized rooms with queen beds and exceptional Victorian detail. Amenities include completely modern private baths, and in-room TVs, tape players, radios, and coffee or tea. Plus, there's a wonderful "roof garden" area perfect for coffee or continental breakfast in the morning. Rates are around $100–150. Closed in January. Halfway to Oakhurst, the friendly and very secluded **Meadow Creek Ranch,** 2669 Triangle Rd. (at S. Hwy. 49), 209/966-3843, www.meadowcreekranch-bnb.com, was originally a stage stop and cattle ranch headquarters. These days, Meadow Creek offers one guest room (private bath, separate entrance) adjacent to the main house with antiques and Early American décor and a separate "country cottage," a stylishly rehabilitated chicken coop. Generous country breakfast. Rates are around $100. Usually closed in winter.

Visitors could spend an entire vacation just trying to count all of the area's bed-and-breakfast inns, which are sprouting up in these parts like spring wildflowers. Some favorites are listed below. For more information, at least about member inns, stop by or call the Mariposa County Chamber of Commerce (see above) or request a current brochure from the **Yosemite-Mariposa Bed and Breakfast Association,** 209/742-7666, www.yosemitebnbs.com.

Most other lodgings in town provide the usual motel ambience for $50–100. (Except during slow times, scouting around for bargain discoveries in areas so close to Yosemite is almost a fruitless effort.) Some of Mariposa's better choices include the imposing **Miners Inn,** 5181 Hwy. 40 N, 209/742-7777 or 888/646-2244; the **Best Western Yosemite Way Station,** 4999 Hwy. 140 (at S. Hwy. 49), 209) 966-7545 or (for reservations) 800/321-5261; and the nearby **Comfort Inn-Mariposa,** 4994 Bullion, 209/966-4344 or 800/321-5261.

Eating in Mariposa

There are two **Mariposa Certified Farmers' Markets**—both held May–Oct., one on Sunday, 9:30–11 A.M., at Darrah and Triangle, the other on Wednesday, 5–6:30 P.M., at Mariposa Park on Sixth Street. For information, call 209/742-5097. A find for Mexican food—everything quite tasty, served in humongous portions—is inexpensive, been-there-forever **Castillo's** up the hill from the highway at 4995 Fifth St., 209/742-4413. Open daily after 10 A.M. for lunch and dinner. The local choice for Chinese food is **China Station,** 5004 Hwy. 140, 209/966-3889. Good for breakfast and lunch as well as steaks and seafood at dinner is **The Red Fox,** 5114 Hwy. 140 (at 12th St.), 209/966-7900. Family-friendly **Grizzly Grill,** 5024 Hwy. 140 is another possibility.

One of the area's finer dining salons is the **Charles Street Dinner House,** 5043 Hwy. 140, 209/966-2366, which serves American fare with inimitable Old West flair. The well-prepared fare—portobello ravioli parmesan, honey-glazed chicken, and "scallone," a blend of abalone and scallops sautéed with toasted almonds in lemon butter—is served up in an appealing period dining room by a wait staff also dressed for the part. For foodies, well worth tracking down is **Ocean Sierra,** at home in an old farmhouse at 3292 Westfall Rd. (at Triangle), 209/742-7050, where entrées range from vegetarian Alfredo to chicken mushroom fettuccini, New York pepper steak, and lemon grilled prawns. Beer. Open Fri.–Sun. for dinner only. Reservations strongly suggested.

For incredibly good coffee—the "handmade" gourmet roast variety—stop by the **Mariposa Coffee Company** at 2945 Hwy. 49 S, 209/742-7339.

Vicinity of Mariposa

Mormon Bar predates the gold rush. Its first residents were Mormons determined to establish the state of Deseret (capital: Salt Lake City)—an application denied by the federal government. The **Dexter Museum** here, once a newspaper office, is worth a peek. Andrew Cathey grew fruits and vegetables in **Cathey's Valley** and marketed them in the gold camps, with Chinese laborers clearing the land and building characteristic stone fences. (Locals pronounce the name "Ca-THAYS," though that's not how Cathey said it.) The **Guadalupe Mountains** nearby are the first foothill "step" up into the Sierra.

OAKHURST

Oakhurst, a scrubby little foothill town in Madera County, is the tail end of the southern Mother Lode and the southernmost official route into Yosemite. The talking grizzly statue downtown at the intersection of Hwy. 41 and Rd. 426 is an unusual monument to extinction. The historical society's **Fresno Flats Historical Park,** 49777 Rd. 427 (on School Rd., just off Crane Valley Rd.), 559/683-6570, www.fresnoflatsmuseum .org, is a park complex with a museum contained in two old schoolhouses and displaying old lace, quilts, and "Yosemite Sam" guns and memorabilia. There's also a jail, blacksmith shop, double "dog-trot" log cabin, and several wagons and stagecoaches—everything here collected, restored, and maintained by local volunteers. Open Mon.–Fri. 10 A.M.–3 P.M. for self-guided tours, and on Saturday and Sunday noon–4 P.M. for guided tours. Small admission (by donation). Two miles north of town, Oakhurst's **Golden Chain Theatre,** 559/683-7112, offers old-time melodramas in summer; reservations advised.

For other local information, contact the **Eastern Madera County Chamber of Commerce,** 49074 Civic Circle Dr., 559/683-7766, www .oakhurstchamber.com, or the **Yosemite Sierra Visitors Bureau** just north of town at 41969 Hwy. 41, 559/683-4636, www.go2yosemite.net, which can provide Forest Service permits (call for details).

Practicalities

The hautest place around to eat—and stay—is the elegant Estate by the Elderberries, www.elderberryhouse.com, just west of town, both excellent restaurant and sophisticated country inn. Famed **Erna's Elderberry House,** a Mediterranean-style villa at 48688 Victoria Ln. (at Hwy. 41), 559/683-6800, serves up the region's ultimate foodie feast—French- and European-influenced cuisine with a California sensibility. The fixed-price dinners (about $80 per person) change daily and are offered nightly 5:30–8:30 P.M. Brunch is offered Saturday and Sunday 11 A.M.–1 P.M. Eat outside on the terrace, or inside in one of three elegant, Old World dining rooms. Reservations are all but essential, though passersby may luck out at slow times. Guest chefs and a variety of special events year-round—including the annual **Valentine's Epicurean Dinner** in February—keep Estate by the Elderberries fans coming back for more, year after year. Still, unbelievable meals are only half the point here. Lodgings offered up the hill at the acclaimed, elegantly European **Chateau du Sureau,** 559/683-6860, more than match the exceptional quality of the food. Rooms, each uniquely decorated and featuring every imaginable comfort, start at $350. The chateau's adjacent two-bedroom, 2,000-square-foot **Villa du Sureau,** which comes complete with private butler, has its own private entrance and rents for $2,800.

Much more affordable for most of us are the charming, very private cottages at **The Homestead,** 41110 Rd. 600 in nearby Ahwahnee, 559/683-0495 or 800/483-0495 (U.S. only), www.homesteadcottages.com, each with fully equipped kitchen, separate bedroom, spacious bathroom (with hairdryer), and outdoor gas barbecue. Rates are $100–200. Excellent equine overnight facilities (for up to five horses) are also available.

If Erna's is too rich for your pocketbook, head instead for sophisticated yet relaxed **Three Sisters,** 40291 Junction Dr. (near the bowling alley), 559/642-2253, named after the owners' three charming pot-bellied pigs: Barbie-Q, Carnita, and Sade. In honor of the sisters, you might start with the oysters Rocksisters with creamed spinach. The lengthy list of pastas includes fettucine Alfredo with prawns and smoked salmon as well as spaghetti with Italian sausage and basil. Entrées are also a surprise, from the chicken and

walnut crepes, Navajo buffalo stew, and lamb curry Bombay to prime rib. Such a deal at dinner: the prix-fixe tasting menu for two is $25–36, depending on the number of courses you choose. Breakfast, lunch, and weekend brunch also served. Hours can be a bit quirky, so call ahead to make sure the Three Sisters will be there. Open Wed.–Sun., reservations advised.

VICINITY OF OAKHURST

A valley excursion from Oakhurst: take Raymond Rd. west for about 10 miles, then veer left on Rd. 606 to **Knowles,** where most of the granite needed to rebuild San Francisco after the 1906 quake was quarried. Turn right on Rd. 600 and travel north to **Raymond,** the hillside farm country here stitched together with 100-year-old stone fences built by the Chinese.

The **Wassama ("leaves falling") Round House** northwest of Oakhurst, is a state historic site. The house was constructed in the mid-1970s, though the original structure dated to the 1860s. **Gathering Day,** held the second Saturday in July, includes demonstrations of dancing, basket weaving, and crafts. Other special events are sometimes scheduled; call before going since Native American ceremonies aren't always open to the public. Call 209/742-7625 for more information. To get to Wassama, head north from Oakhurst on Hwy. 49 for 5.5 miles to Ahwahnee, then turn right on Round House Rd. (Rd. 628) and continue for half a mile.

Northeast of Oakhurst, heading toward Yosemite, a variety of nondescript Sierra National Forest roads eventually arrive at Yosemite's Mariposa Grove of Sierra big trees—usually quite crowded. This route is scenic and uncrowded—the locals' favorite. Nearby is the Nelder Grove of *Sequoiadendron giganteum* (giant sequoias), near John Muir's Fresno Dome. To appreciate these and other area delights, take the spectacular 90-mile **Sierra Vista Scenic Byway** tour up into the San Joaquin River Canyon (16 miles on unpaved gravel) via Mammoth (sometimes called Minarets) and Beasore Roads. Call the Sierra National Forest headquarters in Clovis, 559/297-0706, www.fs.fed.us/r5/sierra, or the **Bass Lake**

Ranger District office in North Fork (see below) for information. The **Lewis Creek National Recreation Trail** offers a scenic 3.7-mile trail with waterfalls that parallels a section of the historic Madera Sugar Pine Lumber Co. flume; near Sugar Pine, access the trailhead from Sugar Pine Road off Hwy. 41.

More of a classic gold camp than Oakhurst (a $15,000 gold nugget was unearthed here in 1890), **Coarsegold** was mostly a farm and timber town when it went by the poetic name of Fresno Flats. One of the largest rodeos in the state is held here on the first weekend in May.

BASS LAKE

Hunter S. Thompson immortalized Bass Lake's days as stomping grounds for bad-boy motorcyclists in his 1965 book *Hell's Angels*. But the scene these days is comparatively tame, the main draw being reservoir recreation amid evergreens and summer homes. Other action includes bike races, classic car shows, and a Coors marathon (running, not drinking); **Jazz on the Lake** at Ducey's is a big summer draw. The lake, an irrigation reservoir managed by California Land Management, is usually best in late spring and summer; pick up a parking pass (required for picnic areas) and a map at their office on Rd. 222, 559/642-3212. For current area camping, picnicking, hiking, and other recreation information, contact the **Bass Lake Ranger District** office, 57003 Rd. 225 in North Fork, 559/877-2218. For more information, contact the **Bass Lake Chamber of Commerce,** 54432 Rd. 432, 559/642-3676, www.basslakechamber.com.

The **Sierra Mono Indian Museum,** between Oakhurst and North Fork via Rd. 247 (off Rd. 222), 559/877-2115, holds an eclectic collection of basketry, beadwork, and natural history organized by the local Mono people. Open Tues.–Sat. 9 A.M.–4 P.M.; small fee. If you make it as far as North Fork, stop by **La Cabana** for tasty, inexpensive Mexican fare. For more information about the area, contact the **North Fork Chamber of Commerce,** 33045 Main St. (Rd. 222), 559/877-2410, www.north-fork-chamber.com.

Practicalities

Popular lakeside campgrounds in summer include **Wishon Point, Spring Cove, Lupine,** and **Forks** (all $18–20); for reservations, contact the National Recreation Reservation Service, 877/444-6777 or www.reserveUSA.com. More remote campgrounds (tables, fire rings, no safe drinking water, no reservations) are found along a mostly unpaved route east of Hwy. 41 between Bass Lake and Yosemite. (Only **Chilkoot** on Rd. 434 is accessible via paved road.) Among these, **Nelder Grove** campsites are unique—near an impressive, isolated grove of Sierra big trees. To the southwest there's a mile-long, self-guided interpretive walk, The Shadow of the Giants, along Nelder Creek on the National Recreation Trail. To get to Nelder Grove, take Sky Ranch Rd. (Rd. 632) from Hwy. 41 (north of the turnoff to Bass Lake), then turn left on California Creek Road.

Plush lodge suites at **The Pines Resort,** 39255 Marina Dr., 559/642-3121 or 800/350-7463 (U.S. and Canada only), www.basslake.com, were built on the site of classic Ducey's Bass Lake Lodge, which burned down in 1988. The Pines also offers chalet-style condos. Resort rates are $150–250 (and up). Open all year. The resort's **Ducey's on the Lake** serves the most stylish meal around, though the Pines also offers **Ducey's Bar & Grill.**

Great Valley and the Delta

When John Muir wandered west out of the Sierra Nevada in the late 1800s, he was overwhelmed by California's great central valley. "When California was wild," he wrote, "it was one sweet bee garden throughout its entire length. . . so marvelously rich that, in walking from one end of it to the other, a distance of more than four hundred miles, your foot would press about a hundred flowers at every step." As if in Kansas, early immigrants to California's great valley gazed out upon green waves of vegetation washed clean by April rains but burnished to a golden

brown by August. The *tulares,* or marshes, and shallow lakes rippled with birdsong, and ancient rivers meandered through woodland jungles of deciduous trees, riverside thickets that were home to the valley's most complex web of wildlife. Grass-land prairies, stretching to the distant foothills on every horizon, buzzed with life.

Millions of ducks, geese, swans, and other wa-terfowl once flocked here in feathery winter clouds so thick that amazed explorers claimed their flight blotted out

the California State
Capitol in Sacramento

the sun. Vast herds of tule elk, pronghorn, and deer browsed through woodlands and prairies. Even grizzly bears galloped across valley grasslands just over a century ago. Supported by the land's natural richness, California's great valley was also home to one of the continent's densest native populations, the Maidu, Miwok, Wintu, and Yokut peoples. To the native Maidu who populated much of the north, California's great valley was the source of life itself.

The Great Valley

California's great central valley forms a 50-mile-wide, 400-mile-long plain between the rugged Sierra Nevada and the gentler Coast Ranges, stretching north to near Redding and south to the Tehachapis. There is no other flatland area of comparable size in the U.S. west of the Rocky Mountains. The great valley is the state's primary watershed basin, collecting almost half of California's precipitation.

Most of the valley today is slightly above sea level, excepting the delta area near San Francisco's Bay Area, which is *below* sea level and dry only due to an extensive system of levees and dikes. But more than 140 million years ago, the area was an inland sea complete with swimming dinosaurs. Geologists speculate that this great trough started to fill with sediments when it became an isolated oceanic arm; sedimentation accelerated when the newborn Sierra Nevada range was carved by glaciers. Though flecks of gold still wash down through the foothills to the valley, the region's real wealth is its rich loamy topsoil, up to thousands of feet deep. The only interruption of the steady soil- and valley-building process occurred about three million years ago, when a series of volcanic eruptions near what is now Yuba City and Marysville created a large volcano. Today its remains are the handsome and heavily eroded Sutter Buttes, the world's smallest mountain range and the only peaks on California's vast interior plain.

As recently as 200 years ago, great shallow lakes covered the southern San Joaquin Valley, and when Sierra Nevada snow melt transformed creeks into raging rivers, the entire central valley became an inland sea once more, this time with fresh water lapping against the Sutter Buttes and the valley's encircling foothills.

Though the central valley has long been considered "stable ground," recent geological discoveries suggest that the western edge of at least the Sacramento Valley is webbed with numerous earthquake faults, capable of producing a tremor above magnitude 6 on the Richter scale. The 6.4 magnitude quake in Coalinga in 1982 suggests that this phenomenon is also applicable to the San Joaquin Valley farther south.

Taming the Watershed

Water is life in California's great valley, a fact reflected in the words on the sign arched across the old highway in Modesto: Water Wealth Contentment Health. But land is likewise necessary for economic wealth—for cities, local industries, and agriculture—and during the past 150 years, the valley's marshes and lakes have been drained and "reclaimed" to obtain that land. Converting California's vast central valley to farmland has also meant taming the rivers within its watershed. All major rivers have been dammed, redirected, or "channelized." The Central Valley Project and other 20th-century feats of water

IN A FOG

When driving in valley fog—don't, if it's possible to avoid it—always use the car's low-beam headlights, avoid panic, and never stop suddenly, even in surprise "zero-visibility" situations. Multiple-car accidents involving drivers who freeze up due to fog blindness are an all-too-common occurrence in the valley and delta areas. If the fog becomes so thick you can't see, pull off onto the road's shoulder, *then* stop. The same rules apply to dust storms, which can occur suddenly along I-5 and Hwy. 99 in the San Joaquin Valley.

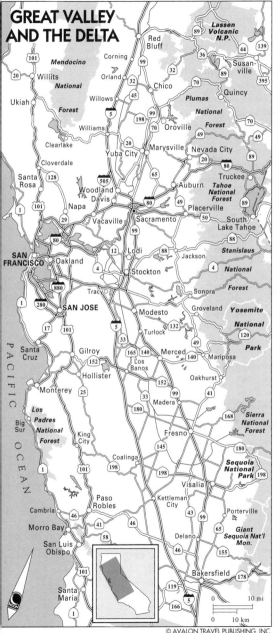

GREAT VALLEY
AND THE DELTA

engineering have made it possible to transport water from the rain-soaked north to the arid San Joaquin Valley in the south, transforming inland deserts into gardens—truck gardens.

Despite its almost complete re-modeling by water engineers, the largest and longest California river is still the Sacramento, which flows south from near Mt. Shasta to its confluence with the Pit and McCloud Rivers at Shasta Lake, then snakes south through the Sacramento Valley, where it is joined by the American, Feather, and Yuba. The San Joaquin River, which lends its name to the southern reaches of the great valley, once flowed westward until pushed north by the Coast Ranges, fed along the way by the Merced, Tuolumne, Stanislaus, Mokelumne, and Cosumnes Rivers. Due to agricultural water diversions, the San Joaquin River has been dry since the 1940s. What remains of the valley's two dominant river systems converge in the delta region, now a predominantly unnatural maze of canals, sloughs, islands, and levees, before flowing through the Carquinez Strait into San Pablo and San Francisco Bays.

Climate

John Muir noted that in California's great valley "there are only two seasons—spring and summer," which just goes to show he wasn't right about everything. Summers are long and hot, and the transitional seasons of spring and fall are often mild. Winter in the valley, often foggy and cold, coincides with the state's rainy season—the only time of year this part of the Golden State is green without the assistance of irrigation. If less than hospitable for humans, the valley's climate is perfect for crops. In most areas, characteristic 100-degrees-plus summertime tem-

GREAT VALLEY & THE DELTA

peratures are unforgettable and virtually unlivable, but worse throughout the valley in summer is air pollution. (In fall, the valley's otherwise crisp, clear air is often colored by smoke and airborne detritus from field burning.)

The rainy season usually begins in November, with little or no precipitation after April or May. Though nothing is really typical due to the state's increasingly erratic weather patterns, 20–40 inches of rain falls in the north valley during the rainy season, and less than seven inches in the desert-like plains farther south near Bakersfield.

Thick, ground-hugging tule fog is common between winter storms, insulating the valley from most winter freezes. (Sacramento is derisively known as the Tule Fog Capital of the World by its bone-chilled residents.) On clear nights after a good rain, blankets of mist form that the weakened winter sun can't burn through for days, sometimes weeks. When it settles in for a stay, California's valley fog creates one of the world's largest ground clouds, a moist, ghostly shroud often going the distance between Redding and Bakersfield and stretching across the farmland between the Coast Ranges and the Sierra Nevada foothills; fog ceilings usually reach 1,000 feet or more above the valley floor.

Without fog, valley winters become even colder, with subfreezing temperatures no surprise December through February. A phenomenon colloquially known as "false spring" sometimes occurs in late January or February—unseasonally balmy weather that encourages people to believe, albeit briefly, in the promise of spring. To experience California's heartland at its best, try a sparkling day in early spring when snowcapped coastal mountains and Sierra Nevada peaks seem just within reach beyond the wildflower-thick foothills.

FLORA

The tule marshes, the prairies of perennial grasses, and the riverside woodlands—each of these three ecosystems dependent on different soil types and moisture levels—once covered the land, forming a vast marshland prairie. Due to the demands of agriculture and the reclamation projects that have made possible California's phenomenal agricultural productivity, all of these natural environments are now rare. In modern times, fields of cotton, alfalfa, and vegetables; vast expanses of watery rice acreage; and orchards and vineyards now take their place.

Unusual in the valley but typical of its bone-dry southern reaches are salt-tolerant desert plants and salt marsh species like pickleweed. Even in the desert areas, spring carpets of wildflowers

THE LESSON OF BIRDS: SIX

Canada Geese
on the wing on the flyway
above our house
in Spring. V
after V stars the day sky
in a straight-line journey
home. The ah-honks
of their joy are like haunting
jazz solos—
"wings of meaning"
Stevens sort of said.
One blue afternoon
I watched a lead goose
lose its way (the wingless
can't say why), drop,

and circle—
its well-taught flock
strung behind.
Each new skein joined
the confusion, and soon
thousands of geese were swirling,
wildly honking.
I felt scared
hearing those birds. We know
so little about home,
let alone the world,
and there's so much wing
up there.

—*Gary Thompson*

once stretched to every horizon: blooming fields of orange poppies, blue dicks and other *Brodaeia* species, lupines, native grasses, and cream cups, goldfields, and endless other tiny "vernal pool" plants. These slight depressions in valley hardpan areas—called vernal pools because they catch winter rainfall that slowly evaporates come spring—host a unique array of annual wild-flowers where the pattern of bloom succession can be observed with the changing fairy rings of flowers. Rare now, threatened by overgrazing and encroaching development, vernal pools nonetheless remain in some grazing areas on the valley's fringe and in areas protected by the Nature Conservancy. (Tread lightly while visiting.)

The valley's hardy native bunchgrasses and many native wildflowers have been replaced by introduced pasture grasses and flowers that turn to straw by May. Agriculture and housing de-velopments have replaced wild vegetation alto-gether in sprawling urban and suburban areas.

Ecologically rich riparian woodlands once cov-ered vast areas of the great central valley: dense, tall forests of oaks, sycamores, willows, ash, alders, maples, and cottonwoods entwined with wild roses, berry vines, and wild grapes, and fringed with tules and cattails. The sheer volume of ri-parian loss is staggering: less than two percent of the valley's original riparian habitat remains. In the northern Sacramento Valley alone, an esti-mated 800,000 acres of riparian forest have dwin-dled to about 12,000. Surviving, scattered remnants of California's riparian vegetation still represent the state's most diverse ecosystem, home to 60-odd species of birds (including the rare western yellow-billed cuckoo) and seasonal stopover for more than 200 others.

Of all the tree species native to the region, most impressive—for its sheer size and gnarled grace—is California's valley oak, *Quercus lobata,* now endangered partly because early farmers soon realized that the most fertile and deepest soils (along with high natural water tables) were found wherever it grew. The largest oaks in North America, these light-barked, gray-green giants can grow to more than 100 feet in height, with a trunk diameter of up to eight feet. In addition to agriculture and the woodcutter's ax, encroach-ing development projects also threaten the valley oak. For reasons still incompletely understood (though livestock grazing, reduction of river flooding, and competition from introduced grasses are among the suspected problems), for decades valley oaks have not been successfully reproducing. This fact alone presents the most permanent threat to the species' survival, since many remaining trees are now dying of old age.

FAUNA

Though many ducks and other species are year-round residents, 92 percent of the valley's four million acres of wetlands have disappeared for-ever. But to the federal and state wildlife refuges established on former marshes and lakes (now productive grain fields) come the migrating win-ter waterfowl common in the valley, including whistling swans and Canada, white-fronted, and snow geese. Visiting shorebirds include avocets, curlews, egrets, sandpipers, and stilts. In sum-mer, blue-winged and cinnamon teals are fairly common. Black-crowned, night, green, and great blue herons also thrive in the valley. The region's rich native grasslands once supported vast herds of prairie grazers: deer, the exclusively Californian tule elk, and the now-rare pronghorn. The only remaining species of its family (related to nei-ther deer nor European antelopes), the prong-horn has almost vanished in the state, surviving only in restricted ranges.

In rapidly vanishing native riverside forests is a wildlife wonderland: songbirds and waterfowl, cottontails and jackrabbits, beavers, raccoons, striped skunks, coyotes, and gray foxes. Turtles and salamanders thrive near the river rapids, but salmon and steelhead attract more human at-tention. Threatened by water diversion projects and river pollution are the spring- and winter-run chinook salmon, whose numbers once nearly choked the Sacramento River and its tribu-taries—particularly "wild-strain" fish not de-scended from fish hatchery stock.

Where there are valley oaks there are also acorn woodpeckers, mischievous red-capped birds that store acorns and seek insect larvae in carefully bored holes in trees and telephone poles. Bold scrub jays abound in bottomland forests—where they "plant" new oaks by burying their acorn booty in the ground—though they also thrive in cities and towns throughout the valley.

Though the valley's elderberry longhorn beetle, one of only 13 U.S. insects on the nation's endangered species list, is at home only in the valley's vanishing riparian forests, more noticeable in this environment is the complex relationship of oak and insect embodied in light-as-a-ping-pong-ball oak galls. Female wasps lay their eggs on oak stems, then the hatched-out larvae feed on plant tissue and secrete an irritant that stimulates the oak to produce the light-colored, apple-sized galls—actually benign "tumors" that protect and nourish the larvae.

THE LAND AS FARMLAND

Given the region's rich loam soils and abundant water, it's no surprise that immigrants came—and still come—to the valley primarily to farm or work in the fields. The valley's first landed gentry were recipients of Mexican land grants who transformed wildlands into ranchos dedicated first to livestock grazing, then to more diversified agricultural enterprises. Disillusioned fortune hunters from California's goldfields, attracted to the fertile heartland and its more predictable wealth, were followed by generations of farmers from around the country and the globe.

Almost from the beginning, helped along by the completion in 1869 of the transcontinental railroad, California agriculture developed to suit the interests of large landholders. Though foreign immigrants still find their way to the central valley—about one in every 10 new valley residents was born outside the U.S.—most are destined to become manual laborers on corporate farms. Modern-day farm communities include produce patches tended by Hispanics, Sikhs, and Hmong refugees, but in California, Thomas Jefferson's ideal of the yeoman democrat and the romance of the family farm have primarily been fiction.

Agriculture in California is agribusiness, and it's big business. The enormous holdings of corporate agriculture dominate both the landscape and

local economies. Even the University of California historically has dedicated its agricultural research to the high-yield, chemically enhanced, and mechanically harvested farming styles typical of California agribusiness. The state's agricultural production, a $17 billion-a-year industry, includes one-fourth of all food consumed in the United States, most of the country's raisin and wine grape production, and massive cotton, rice, and orchard crops.

Trouble in Paradise

If the world began here, as the Maidu believed, California at least may soon end here. Nothing fails like success, and success has come to the valley. Massive publicly funded water-engineering projects coupled with corporate agricultural expansion have eliminated most of the valley's native beauty, vegetation, and wildlife, and now directly threaten the region's economic and environmental health.

The valley is one of the richest, most productive agricultural areas on earth, but the price of that productivity climbs higher every year—a price paid in ongoing economic and social injustice, large-scale ecological disruptions, and escalating environmental contamination. California's great central valley is fast becoming the state's toxic waste sump—and since rivers draining the valley flow to sea via the delta and San Francisco Bay, these environments, too, are becoming increasingly polluted. Experts also predict that millions of acres of farmland, particularly in the naturally arid San Joaquin Valley, will soon be abandoned due to increasing costs of irrigation as well as accumulated salt deposits and other contamination, a side effect of irrigating poorly drained desert soils.

Urban and suburban growth also threaten agriculture. Thousands of acres of prime farmland are paved over each year for shopping malls, parking lots, and new subdivisions as the San Francisco Bay Area expands into the San Joaquin Valley and as farm towns become cities committed to creating their own suburbs. With the region's human population growing more rapidly than the state as a whole, California's country is quickly disappearing.

THE NEW GRAPES OF WRATH:
THE KESTERSON STORY

To some degree, pesticides and herbicides pollute most rivers draining valley agricultural land, and river-dumping of toxic wastes and sewage only compounds the problem. In the San Joaquin River, residues of DDT and other pesticides banned in the early 1970s are still present—at levels hundreds of times higher than those the federal government says are safe for fish and wildlife. In many agricultural communities, nitrate contamination of groundwater has become an increasing problem, and pesticides and other environmental contaminants are the suspected culprits of unusual childhood cancers and cancer "clusters" in the farm towns of Rosamond, Fowler, McFarland, and Earlimart. Even air pollution has become a problem, particularly in the San Joaquin Valley, where it also damages field crops and trees in the adjacent Sierra Nevada.

Yet the most widely publicized disaster of them all is the story of the Kesterson National Wildlife Refuge and reservoir near Los Banos, an area set aside to preserve and protect migrating waterfowl populations but offering instead silent and deadly testimony to the dark side of modern agriculture.

By 1995 Kesterson—now known as the San Luis National Wildlife Refuge, Kesterson Unit—was declared "cured" of its ills. But the sighs of relief may have come too soon.

It must have seemed so sensible, and simple, when the U.S. Bureau of Reclamation (USBR) agreed to build a concrete-lined channel to drain San Joaquin Valley fields of subsurface Central Valley Project irrigation water. Without such drainage, standing water (due to impermeable clay soils) would essentially drown field and orchard crops. So the USBR purchased 5,900 acres of valley grasslands and by the early 1970s had built an 82-mile-long channel leading to 12 evaporation ponds on 1,280 acres—the foundation of Kesterson National Wildlife Refuge, which was intended to eventually cover. Wintering waterfowl began to flock to the area were observed on the water-filled ponds with many more on the surrounding habitat. The pond refuge system of the San Luis Drain was planned to expand over 4,700 acres area, with the used irrigation water eventually discharged into the San Joaquin River. Refuge expansion never occurred.

The first signs, in 1983, that something had gone wrong at Kesterson were hideous ones: dead and deformed wildlife, including the most severe examples of bird deformities ever recorded in the wild. Even cattle and other livestock in the vicinity were suffering horrible, slow deaths, and vegetation was dying for no apparent reason. The cause was toxic levels of selenium, a naturally occurring trace mineral so potent that levels over 10 parts per billion (ppb) in drinking water are considered unsafe. At Kesterson, selenium was measured at levels of 236 ppb and higher in the water alone; concentrations increased exponentially as the poison moved up the food chain.

How did the selenium get there? Tainted agricultural drainage water produced by heavy "soil washing," which involves adding gypsum to the soil, then irrigating to eliminate undesirable minerals and salts, flowed via the unfinished San Luis Drain into evaporation ponds at the refuge. The rest is history—the history of an ongoing environmental nightmare.

The first response to the problems at Kesterson was a program designed to "scare away" birds and other wildlife from the contaminated refuge—a solution that failed, as animals continued to arrive and rates of death and reproductive deformity climbed. After government cover-ups of the circumstances were revealed in a series of excellent *Sacramento Bee* articles published in 1985, earnest efforts to remedy the situation began.

(continued on next page)

GREAT VALLEY & THE DELTA

THE NEW GRAPES OF WRATH:
THE KESTERSON STORY (cont'd)

Initial proposals to "clean up" Kesterson by dumping tainted refuge waters into the San Joaquin River (already a selenium "hot spot," especially the stretches alongside but parallel to Merced and Bakersfield) and repeatedly flushing the refuge with fresh water, created an uproar. Why, critics argued, spread the contamination still further? Following much government wrangling, a solution was finally arrived at: after the surface water evaporated, dig up all contaminated soil and mud at Kesterson and treat it like the toxic waste it was by reburying it in a sealed on-site dump. This plan was finally underway in 1988.

Estimates of what it will really cost to clean up the Kesterson Wildlife Refuge range from $25 million to $100 million or more. Because groundwater supplies beneath the refuge ponds are tainted with selenium, it was necessary to add topsoil to the refuge ponds to prevent upward seepage of selenium when groundwater levels rise in winter. In addition, no one has yet estimated the cost of new waterfowl and wildlife habitat. Critics of federal water-management practices argue that the economic costs are much higher than most people realize, since the public subsidizes the delivery of low-cost water to agricultural users growing federally subsidized crops, then ends up footing the bill for the resulting pollution.

But there are other, more horrifying costs. Ducks with selenium levels higher than those at Kesterson have been found in adjacent wildlife marshes, and scientists are also concerned that migrating birds are carrying selenium north to contaminate nesting grounds. Even scientific detachment falters at the possibility that the dramatic decline in Pacific Flyway duck populations (a 20 percent decrease from 1984 to 1985 alone) has been caused by selenium toxicity and other environmental poisons created by agricultural practices and water-development policies.

Equally nightmarish are the recent discoveries of "mini-Kestersons" elsewhere throughout the San Joaquin Valley and toxic levels of selenium in groundwater supplies—raising fears that drinking water is affecting the health of humans and livestock as well as wildlife. Even eating produce (particularly green leafy vegetables) irrigated with selenium-contaminated groundwater, or meat from animals whose food and water supplies have been contaminated, may pose serious threats to human health. In 1991, toxic mushrooms—of the otherwise edible variety—were discovered in "clean" Kesterson soil used to fill drained ponds at the refuge. With selenium levels measured at 320-660 parts per million, eating just a few ounces could prove fatal.

In 1995, the general consensus was that Kesterson's pollution problems were over, or at least contained. Some even stated that the disastrous bird die-off in the 1980s was the best thing that ever happened to the refuge—because the land is now managed by the U.S. Fish and Wildlife Service (rather than the Bureau of Reclamation), and the refuge has grown to 10,000 acres as part of its rehabilitation. The Grasslands, which represents one-third of all central valley wetlands, now totals 160,000 acres. But selenium levels are still high at Kesterson. And in 1999, researchers discovered that large numbers of mice and moles (four different species) at Kesterson had both male and female sex organs. Other researchers have found sexual abnormalities in fish in the San Joaquin River near Kesterson.

The nightmare seems destined to continue, with taxpayers destined to pay the price for making things right. Since the Kesterson disaster the Westlands Water District has sought to retire 200,000 acres of poisoned land from agricultural use—farm land that could not be drained once the San Luis Drain was closed at Kesterson. In February 2003, a federal judge approved a deal in which Westlands agreed to assume ownership (including water rights) of about 32,000 acres, and the U.S. Bureau of Reclamation agreed to pay $107 million in damages to 150 prominent landowners.

Can Paradise Lost Be Regained?

There is still hope that solutions can be found for most of the valley's serious environmental problems—problems only exacerbated by water shortages in California, and by the resulting wars over possession of lake, river, and groundwater supplies. Small but dedicated armies of volunteers are determined to save—and even expand, through habitat acquisition and restoration—native plant communities and waterways essential to threatened and endangered wildlife. Regional environmental disasters, such as selenium poisoning at Kesterson Wildlife Refuge, have stimulated still more awareness about the price of agricultural productivity. Business as usual, it has become clear, won't last for long.

Though almost unimaginable even a decade ago, the serious study and promotion of agricultural practices emphasizing water conservation, including the fairly simple technology of drip irrigation, is now underway. Solar-powered desalination plants, designed on the Israeli model to clean up agricultural wastewater *and* generate electricity, are one promising alternative. An experimental plant of this type is now operated by the state's Department of Water Resources near Los Banos.

Sacramento and Vicinity

People have long poked fun at Sacramento, California's capital city. Mark Twain himself was among the first. In Sacramento, he observed, "It is a fiery summer always, and you can gather roses, and eat strawberries and ice cream, and wear white linen clothes, and pant and perspire at eight or nine o'clock in the morning." Comparing it to New York, the Big Apple, some people have affectionately dubbed Sacramento the Big Tomato—a wry reference to the area's agricultural heritage. (Those who dismiss Sacramento as an overgrown cowtown may have confused it, linguistically, with Vacaville down the road—vaca meaning "cow" in Spanish.) A sure sign that the city is outgrowing its rural roots is the fact that Sacramentans no longer laugh at the jokes.

This rural hub of commerce and political wheeling and dealing, the nation's 15th largest economy, is now a real city around which the county's nearly two million people revolve. Sacramento has a winning professional basketball team—the Sacramento Kings—and hopes to lure a pro football franchise, meanwhile dreaming still about major league baseball. (The city loves its Pacific Coast League Sacramento River Cats, a Triple-A baseball team affiliated with the Oakland A's.) It has one of the state's finest newspapers, a skyscraping skyline visible from nearby rice fields, and reverberating rings of suburbs. It also has traffic congestion, air pollution, and the seemingly hopeless problem of human homelessness, though from a distance the city glitters and glows.

What's more, lately Sacramento has set its more personal sights on bodily fitness, stylish possessions, and "lifestyle." Writer Cob Goshen protests this trend toward trendiness. "It's as if we've packed up and moved to the remotest suburbs of Eliot's Wasteland," he suggests, "[and] exchanged lives of quiet desperation for those of cheerful inconsequence. No more long hot days. No life and death struggle. It finally happened. We're in California now." Well, perhaps not quite yet. Despite its big-city ways, Sacramento is still somehow uniquely lovable. The town is stuffed with good restaurants, sparkles with unpretentious arts and entertainment, and still offers some evidence of its friendlier but wilder past at the edge of the gold rush frontier.

Unique in Sacramento is the opportunity to observe the antics of the state legislature up close and personal, as if at the zoo. There's nothing quite like sitting in on committee hearings or other wrangles to appreciate the absurd beauty of political fisticuffs, California style. Try exploring the Capitol building during the final days of budget battles before legislative recess in summer, when hallways are crowded with arm-twisting lobbyists, and exhausted politicians are most likely to call each other names in public or slip up and tell the truth to the press. All in all it's great fun—but only for those with strong constitutions.

GREAT VALLEY & THE DELTA

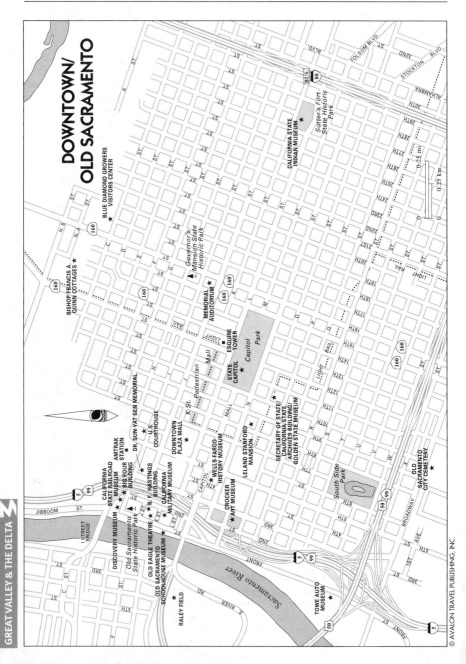

DOWNTOWN/ OLD SACRAMENTO

Sacramento River

GREAT VALLEY & THE DELTA

© AVALON TRAVEL PUBLISHING, INC.

HISTORY

The Spanish claimed much of California's heartland from the 1540s until the early 1800s but never settled it. The first Europeans to see the Sacramento River were members of the Pedro Fages expedition of 1772, who discovered the confluence of the San Joaquin and Sacramento while exploring San Francisco Bay. Russian and Canadian fur trappers followed in the 1820s and '30s. First here, of course, were the Maidu and Miwok peoples. In 1839, when Johann August Suter (John Sutter) and his Hawaiian crew moored his ships near the future site of Sacramento's city dump on the American River, the native population had already been laid low by introduced diseases. Well before the end of the century, they were all but eradicated by cultural displacement and straight-ahead slaughter.

Though native peoples had long navigated the region's rivers in tule-reed boats, the valley's great waterways became commercial transportation arteries only with the arrival of the gold rush. The crush of gold-crazed '49ers initiated the shipping and inland port industries that still thrive on the fringes of the Sacramento-San Joaquin Delta. New gold dreams, the area's water transport potential, the transcontinental railroad, and the valley's amazing agricultural productivity quickly created the city of Sacramento.

John Sutter: King of Sacramento

John Sutter arrived at a fortunate time when he put down roots here in 1839. California's Mexican government was fretting over territorial invasions by trappers and mountain men, and Governor Alvarado happily granted the Swiss immigrant 50,000 acres—a move partially intended to thwart General Vallejo, his political rival. Sutter's fortunes increased again when the Russians abandoned Fort Ross and Alvarado's successor gave him still more land. Sutter's dream was to "civilize" the entire valley, and he set out to attract other European immigrants to Nueva Helvetia, his New Switzerland. Together with his small band of fellow travelers and native peoples, he built his adobe outpost, the center of his short-lived agricultural empire. By 1845, with

fur trapping all but exhausted by the near extinction of both beavers and otters, Sutter had become the undisputed king of Sacramento.

The official arrival of the United States presence the next year, however, virtually ended his rule. Even then, Sutter managed to land on his feet, and he became a delegate for the task of writing the new state's constitution. Though essentially a blundering businessman, Sutter's empire was nonetheless becoming so large that his only limitation was lack of lumber. So, in 1848, he sent carpenter and wagon builder James Marshall to a site 40 miles east of Sacramento on the American River to build a lumber mill. With Marshall's discovery of gold, the end of Sutter's reign soon followed.

Sutter became financially solvent for the first time in his life in 1849, with the assistance of his son, John A. Sutter Jr., who founded the city of Sacramento in 1848 (naming it after the river). But neither could hold the empire together against the forces of Sutter's alcoholism or the dirty-dealing march of California history. Within five years, more than a half-million people arrived in the Sacramento area to seek their fortunes. Asians, Pacific Islanders, Central and South Americans, Europeans, and migrants from all regions of the U.S. flooded into the eastern foothills. Gambling and gambolling thrived in Sacramento, de facto capital of the gold rush and the new Wild West.

But gold seemed to line everybody's pockets except Sutter's. Largely victimized by his own excess, he saw things differently. "I was the victim of every swindler that came along," he said. "These swindlers made the cornerstone of my ruin." In Washington, D.C., where he went to beg a pension for the services he rendered America prior to the gold rush, John Sutter died a bitter and broken man in 1880. His body was buried in the Pennsylvania Dutch town of Lititz; former adversary Gen. John C. Frèmont gave the eulogy. Buried next to Sutter is his wife Anna, who died seven months later.

Railroad Ties

The valley's first railroad, completed in 1856, ran the 22 miles between Folsom and Sacramento.

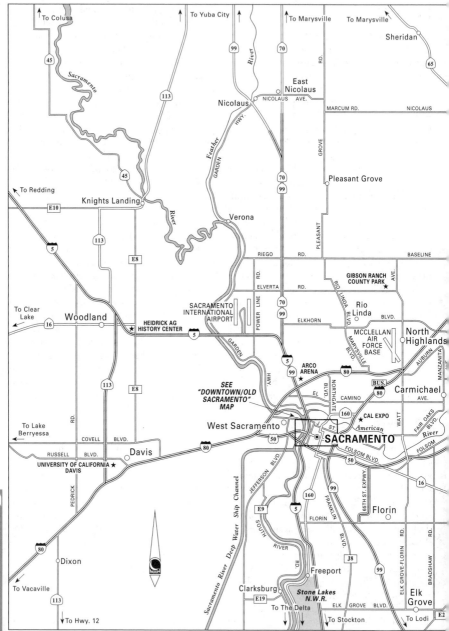

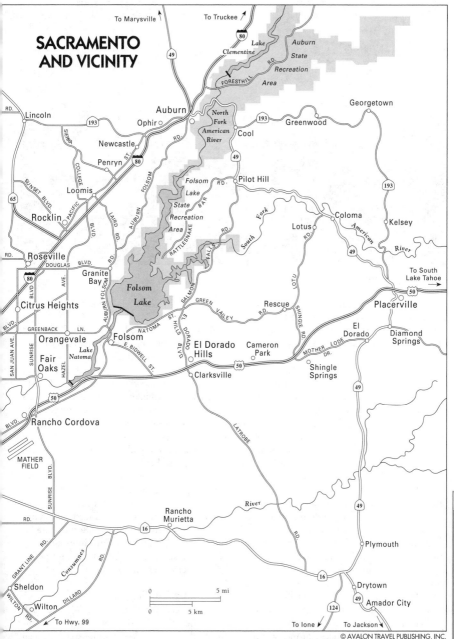

SACRAMENTO
AND VICINITY

To Marysville

To Truckee

80

Lake
Clementine

Auburn
State
Recreation
Area

FORESTHILL   RD.

49

Georgetown

RD.   Lincoln

193

Auburn

Ophir

North
Fork
American
River

Cool

193

Greenwood

Newcastle

80

Penryn   ST.

SIERRA

COLLEGE

PACIFIC

49

Pilot Hill

193

Loomis

Folsom
Lake
State
Recreation
Area

RD.

AUBURN

FOLSOM

RATTLESNAKE   BAR

South   Fork

Coloma

American   River

Kelsey

Lotus   RD.

65

Rocklin

LAIRD   RD.

BLVD.

RD.   Roseville

DOUGLAS   BLVD.

80

Granite
Bay

BLVD.

AVE.

AUBURN FOLSOM

Folsom
Lake

SALMON   FALLS   RD.

GREEN   VALLEY

Rescue   RD.

LOTUS

49

To South
Lake Tahoe

50

Placerville

Citrus Heights

BLVD.

GREENBACK   LN.

Orangevale

Lake
Natoma

Folsom

E. BIDWELL ST.

NATOMA   ST.

EL DORADO   HILLS   BLVD.

El Dorado
Hills

Cameron
Park

SHINGLE   RD.

MOTHER   LODE   DR.

El
Dorado

Diamond
Springs

SAN JUAN AVE.

SUNRISE

Fair
Oaks

HAZEL

50

Clarksville

50

Shingle
Springs

49

BLVD.   Rancho Cordova

MATHER
FIELD

SUNRISE   BLVD.

LATROBE

RD.

River

49

GRANT LINE   RD.

Consumnes   RD.

DILLARD   RD.

WILTON   RD.

Sheldon

Wilton

To Hwy. 99

Rancho
Murietta

16

Plymouth

16

124

Drytown

49

Amador City

To Ione   To Jackson

0   5 mi

0   5 km

© AVALON TRAVEL PUBLISHING, INC.

GREAT VALLEY & THE DELTA

Sacramento riverfront

But the railroad's engineer, Theodore Judah, dreamed of a transcontinental railroad connecting California growers and merchants to the rest of the nation. Judah convinced four Sacramento business leaders that this east-west link over the treacherous Sierra Nevada could be built. With the help of California's "Big Four"—Charles Crocker, Mark Hopkins, Collis Huntington, and Leland Stanford—he founded the Central Pacific Railroad Company, which soon began lobbying the U.S. Congress for federal construction loans. In 1862, legislation finally authorized loans to construct a railroad route over Donner Pass—with the proviso that no money would be lent until 40 miles of track were laid.

Central Pacific's plans to sell stock in its speculative venture failed, so the company's founders financed much of the first-phase work with their own resources. The Big Four made money even during this difficult construction phase by convincing Congress that the Sierra Nevada started 12 miles farther west than it actually did, then pocketing the extra cash. For almost seven years, thousands of Chinese workers, seasoned in the California goldfields, picked tunnels through mountains of solid rock and hand-graded the railroad beds.

In the spring of 1869, the Central Pacific and Union Pacific railroads were ceremoniously joined at Promontory Point, Utah. As Oscar Lewis noted in *The Big Four,* the slogan of the day was: "California Annexes the United States." Half in arrogance and half in the spirit of play, the wildest of the western colonies, he noted, "prepared to take its place (near the head of the table) with the family of states."

Soon after, railroad feeder lines connected Sacramento to Benicia and Oakland, and links were planned to Southern California and Oregon. As portrayed in the novel *The Octopus* by Frank Norris, Southern Pacific's tracks became tentacles reaching out in all directions to control the state's economy and political climate for more than 40 years, and Theodore Judah's financial backers became the richest, most politically powerful men in the state.

Becoming the Capital

After Benicia, San Jose, and Vallejo had each taken their turn, by 1854 Sacramento was influential enough to become the state's official capital. During the late 1850s when California's gold fever had subsided, people still came to Sacramento, drawn by dreams of business success and landed wealth. Growth meant jobs and opportunities; the most important field of opportunity was agriculture.

By the 20th century, valley farming expanded far beyond rain-watered winter wheat fields to embrace big-time irrigation and an endless array of field and orchard crops, from beans and tomatoes to cotton and rice, from peaches and pears to almonds and walnuts. Institutions like the California Packing Corporation (later to become Del Monte) and the Libby Cannery became symbols of the community's economic backbone.

During and after World War II, people still came to Sacramento for the jobs at Mather and McClellan Air Force bases and the Sacramento Signal depot. In the 1950s with Aerojet's expansion into the space program, engineers and rocket scientists arrived—Sacramento's first but far from last big taste of high-tech industrial development. While the U.S. military offers scant local job security these days, what with the closure of Mather and McClellan, government bureaucracy and politics here are growth industries. (It's too soon to say whether that will change as part of California's current fiscal crisis.) And in Sacramento as elsewhere in the state, orchards and productive farms have given way, and are still giving way, to business and industrial development and suburban housing projects.

SEEING OLD SACRAMENTO

The original gold rush boomtown of Sacramento boomed first as a tent city on the mudflats along the river, an area more or less defined these days by the intersection of Front and J Streets downtown, just west of I-5. Mark Twain wrote here, Lola Montez danced here, and William Fuller painted here. These eight city blocks, appropriately called Old Sacramento and now both a state historic park and national landmark, almost capture the ambience of the Old West—especially during **Gold Rush Days** over Labor Day weekend, when suddenly the streets are dusty again and only horse-drawn vehicles are

allowed. Old Sacramento's Embarcadero tent city thrives, again, just as it did in 1849; you can peek into authentic gold rush shops, play period games, and encounter genuine 19th-century characters. Yet despite the careful restoration of the area's old buildings, most of the time that freeway looming overhead and the all-too-modern commercialism of the hundreds of shops and restaurants detract from the illusion.

Most worthwhile in Old Sacramento are the excellent history museums; plans are in the works for still more museums and an old-fashioned waterfront park. Another unusual attraction is the five-story *Delta King,* the last of California's original steam paddle-wheelers and a 1920s Prohibition-era pleasure palace. The *King,* now a floating luxury hotel and restaurant/saloon, faithfully delivered passengers between San Francisco and Sacramento until the 1940s and World War II, when he and sister ship *Delta Queen* dressed up in battleship gray and transported Navy troops. (The *King* is docked these days. To paddle-wheel up and down the river, other boats are available. See Touring Old Sacramento below.) While wandering through Old Sacramento, note the elevated boardwalks and original streetside curbing, reminders of the days when neighborhood rivers regularly rampaged through town in winter.

Less obvious, now that Old Sacramento is all spruced up and spit-shined, is the fact that it was until recently a fairly typical urban slum. When the unwanted old buildings once again became desirable, the addicts, homeless, and mentally ill were shoved aside. They now mix and mingle throughout downtown, rubbing elbows with politicians, lobbyists, office workers, and tourists.

Tours

Showing yourself the town is easy here, so pick up a current visitor guide at the visitor information center, 1004 Second St. (next to the Wells Fargo History Museum); an Old Sacramento walking tour is included. Or, let the horses do the walking and hail a **horse-drawn carriage** (various concessionaires, $10 and up), available daily except in bad weather. Rent bikes at **Bike Sacramento,** Front and J Streets,

GOVERNOR ARNOLD: TERMINATOR OR TOTAL RECALL?

Governor Arnold Schwarzenegger is the shock of the century in California, though of course the new age is still young. Thoughtful observers are still in awe. The surprise is not so much that Schwarzenegger pulled off the first gubernatorial recall in California history, only the second in U.S. history. Nor is it all that surprising that the whole affair cast California in such an unflattering, narcissistic light. Before the spotlight focused exclusively on Schwarzenegger the recall circus included 135 contenders, from infamous smut publisher Larry Flynt and a porn queen to a bounty hunter. Some who live in California—home of Hollywood, after all—love to call attention to themselves, to pursue adulation for its own sake. They're almost always ready for their close-up.

It isn't even that surprising that Californians would explode in what seemed to be a sincere populist revolt, since social earthquakes and other eruptions shake the status quo here quite frequently. Only time and the historians ever settle things, ever determine whether a particular political upheaval was truly heroic, a necessary if violent act of creative passion on behalf of the greater good, or mere brutish petulance. California voters have a history of both great generosity and mean-spirited tantrums.

No, the surprise of California's 2003 recall election is that even politically moderate and liberal Californians would stand up, cheer, and vote for a Hummer-driving Hollywood action hero whose handlers had so carefully scripted his low-content, high-concept campaign. In the end Schwarzenegger's election is a testament to the awesome and slightly frightening power of celebrity. "Hasta la vista, baby!" was the taunt the Terminator repeatedly hurled at his target, Governor Gray Davis, but he was also terminating any expectation that California politics will be predictable any time soon.

In a time when the fantasy of filmmaking is achieved with ever more realistic technique, many people seem to believe that the character an actor inhabits on the big screen is a portrayal of real life. They imagine a larger-than-life personal relationship with fictional characters and stars about whom, in actuality, they know almost nothing.

Yet stardom is, and always has been, a sales job, another form of advertising. And what was being advertised during the recall election was Schwarzenegger the he-man action hero, no questions asked—or answered. It wasn't until after the election, after the Terminator had terminated Gray Davis, that any details of Schwarzenegger's plan were revealed. Will Californians ultimately like what they've been sold?

It is ironic that Schwarzenegger would so handily win a campaign dubbed, in some quarters, as The Revenge of Pete Wilson, Schwarzenegger's mentor and California's previous Republican governor. Wilson was a political pariah, even in his own party, since he was unceremoniously dumped by voters in 1998 in apparent reaction to Wilson's rabid support of Proposition 187, an initiative designed to deny

---

916/444-0200, to enjoy the **Jedediah Smith Memorial Trail** along the American River.

With time and a little cash to spare, consider a one-hour paddle-wheel tour (spring, summer, and fall only) or a lunch or dinner cruise. Channel Star Excursions offers two boats: the very large *Spirit of Sacramento,* onetime star of the John Wayne movie *Blood Alley* (all cleaned up now), and the smaller *Matthew McKinley.* Sightseeing tours as well as brunch, lunch, happy hour, dinner, and dinner theater cruises are offered; private parties and charters are also possible. The company's office is at 110 L St., 916/552-2933 or 800/443-0263, http://spiritofsacramento.com,

but trips depart from the L Street Landing, across the way. Another possibility is **Exodus Boat Cruises** at 1115 Front St., Ste. 9, 916/447-0266, which offers steam paddle-wheel tours and a delta cruise to San Francisco.

Fairly new in the neighborhood but already immensely popular is the **River Otter Taxi Company,** part shuttle, part pleasure cruise. River Otter's happy yellow tug-like boats resemble river-size bathtub toys, albeit toys assigned the grown-up task of connecting Old Sac with marinas and waterfront restaurants just to the north along the Sacramento River and destinations across the way in West Sacramento. The River

public benefits to illegal immigrants—a wedge issue devised by Republicans to galvanize older white voters. Yet that Republican campaign was perceived as race-baiting and anti-immigrant, and the voter reaction swept Wilson and every other top-level Republican from statewide office, and kept them swept. Until Arnold, that is.

A further irony is that the "unfair car tax" Schwarzenegger railed against during his campaign, a steep jump in car registration fees triggered by the state's budget woes, was actually ushered in during Republican Governor Pete Wilson's watch.

Still another irony is that the anti-tax Republican stalwarts supporting Schwarzenegger would also support putting a $15 billion bond issue before the voters—effectively taxing into perpetuity the citizens of succeeding generations—to solve the state's structural budget problems. These same politicos would gleefully eviscerate any Democrat who dared promote a fiscal-salvation-through-taxation message.

Most strikingly ironic, though, is that Schwarzenegger's victory is perceived as a populist victory. California's new governor ran as an outsider even though his campaign was executed from start to finish by the pros—skilled Republican strategists all too happy to take advantage of Gray Davis's monumental unpopularity to grab again at the reins of government. Not surprisingly, the hot air that blew the new governor into office came largely from right-wing radio. During the recall campaign,

Schwarzenegger attacked Gray Davis's "pay-to-play" politics, suggesting that his own personal wealth would shield him from the demands of special interests. But in two short months he collected millions and millions in campaign contributions from real estate, energy, and other business interests, industries in a position to profit substantially from changes in California public policy.

So the question remains: Is Arnold Schwarzenegger more than just another politically ambitious corporate bootlicker? Does he have solutions for California's seeming intractable social, environmental, and financial problems?

Even fictional California history suggests that the voter outrage that carried the new governor into office can easily take him out. Nathaniel West, in the "bedlam scene" of his 1939 novel *The Day of the Locust,* described disgruntled fans congregating in the streets, bathed in the sickly neon light of a Hollywood movie premiere:

"He could see a change come over them as soon as they had become part of the crowd. . . . [T]hey turned arrogant and pugnacious. They were savage and bitter, especially the middle-aged and the old, and had been made so by boredom and disappointment. . . . Their boredom becomes more and more terrible. . . . They have been cheated and betrayed." In West's California bedlam, the fans prove themselves to be fickle, violently so— perhaps a cautionary real-life tale for any actor, and any politician.

Otter water taxis, which hold a maximum of 24 people, make regular runs from around noon to 9 P.M. all summer long; charters are also available. Rides to River Cats games are also offered (free for ticket holders). At last report, taxi fare was $5 adults, $3 for children under 42" tall. Get tickets at the waterfront booth near the Rio City Café, open daily 10:15 A.M.–7:15 P.M. For more information call the booth, 916/446-7704, or see www.riverotter.com.

Full-steam-ahead train fans, take a ride on the **Sacramento Southern Railroad,** affiliated with the California State Railroad Museum. These 40-minute steam-powered excursions ($6 adult,

$3 children) start from the railroad museum's reconstructed freight depot and public market on Front Street and head south to the delta town of Hood. Trips run Apr.–Sept. on Saturday and Sunday only, with trains departing on the hour, 11 A.M.–5 P.M. "Theme" and dinner trains are also scheduled, on special weekends Oct.–Dec. For current information, call 916/445-6645.

If that's not enough train time, there's always the **Yolo Shortline Railroad Company.** On selected Saturdays May–Oct., steam train fans climb aboard the "Clarksburg Special" near the intersection of Jefferson Blvd. and S. River Rd. (there's no depot) across the river in West Sacramento

the skyline of Sacramento old and new

and relax for a three-hour ride through surrounding farmland. In season all trains stop at Uncle Ray's Fruit Stand, so passengers can load up on fresh fruits and vegetables. Or sign on for a barbecue run. (Watch out for those train robbers!) The basic fare is $15 adult, $10 children. Trips run from Woodland to West Sacramento on a more frequent schedule. Special holiday and "theme" trips are also offered. For more information, call 916/372-9777 (800/942-6387 for reservations) or see www.yslrr.com.

California State Railroad Museum

Situated at the old terminus of Southern Pacific, the huge California State Railroad Museum at 111 I Street in Old Sacramento warehouses an exceptional collection of locomotives and railway cars that once rode the rails "over the hump," connecting California with more civilized areas of the United States. Stop just to appreciate the painstaking restoration of these fine old machines, among them Central Pacific's first locomotive. Exceptional is the North Pacific Coast Railroad's *Sonoma,* the finest re-

stored American Standard locomotive in the nation, all brass and elegant beauty. Also fine is *The Gold Coast* private car, an updated 1890s business suite. *Santa Fe Number 1010* was "Death Valley Scotty" Walter Scott's iron steed during his high-speed 1905 L.A.-to-Chicago run. *Southern Pacific Number 4294* is the last of the behemoth cab-forwards that formerly scaled Sierra Nevada summits. Ever-popular is the *St. Hyacinthe,* a restored 1929 sleeping car that rocks and rolls in simulated nighttime travel. A relative newcomer is the elegant 1940s-style stainless steel *Cochiti* dining car, where a selection of Mary Colter's stunning 1937 Mimbre dinnerware (designed specifically for this car) is on display. Selections from the recently donated **Thomas W. Sefton Collection of Toy Trains** are usually exhibited. Expect special changing exhibits, too. The railroad museum's walk-through introductory diorama is well done, as are the films and interpretive exhibits. Docent-led tours are available daily. And don't miss the museum store.

Part of the museum complex is the reconstructed **Central Pacific Railroad Passenger Station** at Front and J, point of departure for steam train excursions and also home to the **Old Sacramento Public Market.** The museum's **Silver Palace Café,** 916/448-0151, is also housed at the passenger depot.

The railroad museum is open daily 10 A.M.– 5 P.M. At last report admission was $4 adults, youths and children under 17 free (prices may increase as a result of the state's budget crisis). The same all-day ticket is good for admission to the passenger station. For more information, stop by the museum or call 916/445-6645 (recorded). For details on museum memberships, which allow unlimited one-year admission, call 916/445-7387. For information on upcoming events, including occasional **Thomas the Tank Engine** visits and the exciting **National Handcar Races,** see the website, www.csrmf.org. To contact the museum store, call 916/324-4950.

Coming one of these days, if the budget crisis is ever resolved and if the state legislature ever plumps up the state parks' purse, is the California State Railroad Museum's new **Museum of Rail-**

Beautifully restored locomotives, the stars of the California State Railroad Museum, chronicle the state's railroad history.

road **Technology,** a 114,000-square-foot facility planned for a site along the Sacramento River at Front and R Streets. It is hoped that the museum's next **Railfair** will celebrate the new museum's unveiling, perhaps in 2007 or 2008.

Sacramento Museum of History, Science, Space, & Technology

Also worth a stop is Old Sac's **Discovery Museum** near the waterfront at 101 I St., 916/264-7057, www.thediscovery.org, more formally known as the Sacramento Museum of History, Science, Space, and Technology—a merger of the original Sacramento History Museum with the Sacramento Science Center. Its exhibits emphasize education and fun. Local history is the first focus here, explored via artifacts, photos, and hands-on activities, but expect surprising special exhibits, too. The museum is open daily 10 A.M.–5 P.M. Admission is $5 adults, $4 seniors and youth (13–17), $3 children ages 4–12 (under age 4 free). Group tours are available. Call for information about the museum's Learning Center science exhibits and activities.

California Military Museum

Among historical attractions in Old Sacramento is the four-story California Military Museum at 1119 Second St., 916/442-2883, www.military-museum.org. Exhibits chronicle the early days of the California Militia, and the long-running history of the state's National Guard—first headquartered in the Pacific Stables building across the street. At home here are more than 30,000 military relics, many genuine blasts from the past, from rifles, World War I machine guns, and Civil War muskets and bayonets to uniforms predating the Civil War—even the sword that Major General Zachary Taylor carried into battle during the Mexican War. Military-oriented gift shop, too. Open Tues.–Sun. 10 A.M.–4 P.M. Admission is $3 adults, $1.50 seniors, $1 children ages 10–17 (under age 10 free) and military with ID.

Other Sights

The **B.F. Hastings Building** at Second and J Streets was once the original Wells Fargo office, rebuilt in 1852 after a fire destroyed most of the city. The small communications museum downstairs

GREAT VALLEY & THE DELTA

© ROBERT HOLMES/CALTOUR

Old Sacramento

honors Sacramento's importance in Old West information flow. This was the end of the line for the original Alta Telegraph Company and the western terminus of the Pony Express, the place where trail-weary horses and dog-tired riders laid down their mailbag burdens after the last leg of the 10-day, 1,966-mile cross-country relay race against time. (From here, correspondence went on to San Francisco via steamboat.) Upstairs are the original chambers of the **California Supreme Court,** dignified courtroom and dark justices' chambers, the quality of pioneer jurisprudence perhaps polished by the passage of time.

The **Big Four Building** at 113 I St. between Front and Second, Central Pacific's original headquarters, actually stood on K St. when Theodore Judah made his bold pitch to the Big Four of California railroading fame; the building was moved to its present site to make way for the I-5 freeway. Downstairs these days is an open-for-business re-creation of the original 1880s **Huntington & Hopkins Hardware Store** (where visitors can gain recognition for themselves by correctly identifying samples of 19th-century hardware). Upstairs is the railroad museum's library/reading

room, 916/323-8073, open Tues.–Sat. 1–5 P.M., and a replica of Central Pacific's boardroom.

The tiny, tin-roofed **Old Eagle Theatre** at 925 Front St. is a canvas reconstruction of the 1849 original, a venerable venue offering docent-guided tours and video program to school groups. Expect to see vintage gold-rush theater during Labor Day weekend's Gold Rush Days celebration. Stop by the **Old Sacramento Schoolhouse Museum** at Front and L Streets, 916/483-8818, to contemplate the romantic minimalism of one-room schools.

In the very early years of the 20th century, two prominent architects—Charles Cheney and Lewis Hobart, who had designed both San Francisco's Bohemian Club and Grace Cathedral—proposed that West Sacramento be designed as "Paris on the West Bank," Sacramento's dazzling twin city. Those plans never made it off the drawingboard, and Sacramento and West Sacramento have been trying to get together again ever since.

Making the entire riverfront more visitor-friendly is a major local priority, along with reconnecting Old Sac more effectively with downtown and with increasingly appealing West Sacramento across the river. Back in 1999 the riverfront promenade, stretching from Capitol Mall just south of Old Sacramento to O Street near the Crocker Museum, was completed, as was the riverside bike path from O south to Miller Park. Those were followed in short order by the **Embassy Suites Hotel** looming up just south of the Tower Bridge, and the bridge's new gold paint job. Across the way in West Sacramento is a public park, **Raley Field** for Sacramento's Triple-A Pacific Coast League **River Cats**, 916/376-4700, www.rivercats.com, and the onetime Money Store headquarters "pyramid," actually a golden ziggurat restyled as office space for the state Department of General Services.

With all these improvements, there's still the problem of how to get people *to* them—particularly pedestrians and cyclists—given that I-5 neatly separates downtown from the riverfront. One proposed solution, usually dismissed as grandiose, is to "deck" I-5—the section that already dips down well below ground level—and create a pedestrian walkway and park between downtown and the Sacramento River. Whether or not the deckway ever materializes, urban planners are proposing three new bridges to span the Sacramento River. Two of these are for pedestrians only—one at Richards Boulevard, just south of Discovery Park, the other at R Street, connecting to West Sacramento near the site of a proposed amphitheater. The third proposed bridge, for cars as well as people, would extend Broadway into West Sacramento.

Shopping

Established in late 1996 and still struggling to make its mark with locals is the open-air **Old Sacramento Public Market,** a slice of foodie heaven located in the Central Pacific depots along Front St., near K Street. Open Tues.–Sun. 10 A.M.–6 P.M., the market features a variety of produce, flower, and specialty food vendors— such as **Apodaca Natural Foods** and **Laszlo's Gourmet Smoked Fish** for human food, and **My Best Friend's Barkery** for Fifi and Fido.

Of the 100-plus other shopping possibilities in the neighborhood, offering the kitschy to the truly creative, personal favorites include the **Artists' Collaborative Gallery** at 1007 Second St., 916/444-

3764, an artist-run co-op offering locally crafted pottery and ceramics, glass, game boards, fabric art, even eclectic earrings, all at surprisingly reasonable prices. For serious bibliophiles, also in the neighborhood is the **Bookmine,** 1015 Second, 916/441-4609, www.bookmine.com, featuring first editions, Western Americana, children's literature, and many rare and unusual books, not to mention a free book search service. Head downstairs, by appointment, to appreciate the fruit crate art collection. Down the street (across from the railroad museum) is **Capital Crimes Mystery Bookstore,** 906 Second, 916/441-4798.

If the kids are getting restless, herd them into **Old City Kites** at 1201 Front St., 916/446-7565, a shop also chock-full of windsocks, flags, frisbees, yo-yos, and hand puppets. **Sacramento Cotton, Etc.,** across from the public market at 1031 Front, 916/441-7099, features an impressive selection of colorful and affordable women's separates. The pricier and hip **Hemp in the Heartland** at 125 K St., 916/447-4367, sports wearable and otherwise useful (not smokable) cannabis.

The place for hilarious cards and outrageous gifts is **Evangeline** at 119 K, 916/443-2181 or 916/448-2594. For arts, crafts, dolls, children's clothing, and other items handcrafted by Sacramento area seniors, stop by the nonprofit **Elder Craftsman** at 130 J St., 916/264-7762. **Stage Nine Entertainment,** 102 K St., 916/447-3623, www.stagenine.com, offers an impressive array of animation, movie, and TV memorabilia—including original cell art, limited edition hand-inked Disney prints, and Charles Schulz classics.

Information

Historical purists disdain this fact but parking *in* Old Sacramento proper is often possible, especially with the addition of parking spaces along Front Street and elsewhere. Metered parking (90-minute limit; 25 cents for 45 minutes) is more suitable for shoppers or lunchers than students of history, and may be phased out. There's plenty of convenient parking, in any event. The large public lots just to the east (under the freeway) and south are ample; from either, it's an easy stroll straight into the olden days. Most shops and restaurants validate. Or, if you'll be exploring

BIG NEWS FOR THE BIG TENT

Every summer a big blue and green canvas tent pitched downtown on H Street served as summer home of Sacramento's popular Music Circus. That tent is now gone, along with its sweltering ambience and uncomfortable old folding canvas chairs. In its stead stands the new Wells Fargo Pavilion, a permanent "tent" constructed of Teflon-coated fiberglass that preserves the much-loved **Music Circus** "theater in the round" experience. The new Music Circus tent also boasts major technological improvements (lighting, sound, actor facilities), luxurious upholstered seats, improved lobby and restrooms—and air-conditioning. No more sweating along to *The Sound of Music*. Music Circus attendance is better than ever, even with the new $4-per-ticket surcharge.

The new pavilion is centerpiece of the H Street Theatre Project, a cooperative effort including the Sacramento Theatre Company, www.sactheatre.org, which stages plays onsite from September to May.

To find out what's up under the tent at the Music Circus, contact California Musical Theatre, 1510 J St., Ste. 200, 916/446-5880, www.californiamusicaltheatre.com. For tickets for both California Musical Theatre and Sacramento Theatre Company productions, stop by the box office at the Wells Fargo Pavilion, 1419 H St., call 916/557-1999, or see the websites.

mento.com. Since Old Sacramento is as much event as destination—from the renowned Memorial Day weekend **Sacramento Jazz Jubilee** to **Gold Rush Days** over Labor Day weekend, among the proliferating possibilities—find out what's going on by calling both organizations and the Old Sacramento events line (recorded) at 916/558-3912.

If you're short on cash yet enticed by local shops and restaurants, there's a 24-hour ATM at the Old Sacramento Public Market on Front at K, the section of the depot just south of the *Delta King*.

SEEING DOWNTOWN
California State Capitol

Painstakingly restored in the 1980s to its early 1900s ambience, California's spectacular state Capitol is hard to miss in its central Capitol Park location at 10th St. and the Capitol Mall (between L and N Streets). Its construction begun in 1860 and completed in 1874, the Capitol and its magnificent gold-domed rotunda, bronze and crystal chandeliers, rich walnut woods, "Eureka tile," and marble mosaic floors speak of an era when buildings represented material yet high-flying ideals. The red-hued Senate and soft green Assembly chambers on the second floor hint at Greco-Roman governmental tradition. Official declarations of these respective political bodies—"It is the duty of a Senator to protect the liberty of the people" and "It is the duty of the Legislators to pass just laws"—are inscribed in gold leaf but in Latin, perhaps so most citizens (including politicians) can't decipher them. Worth seeing, too, are the individual county displays, which offer intriguing perspective on official self-perceptions. The **Capitol Museum** displays in Room 124 are historically authentic 1906 recreations of Governor Pardee's anteroom and offices plus the offices of the secretary of state, treasurer, and attorney general.

The Capitol also includes a fairly decent cafeteria serving short-order meals and snacks (in the basement, home also to a gift shop and museum headquarters), but more enjoyable is a picnic outside in **Capitol Park.** This elegantly landscaped 40-acre

downtown too, from the Downtown Plaza stroll into Old Sac (or vice versa) via the K Street Tunnel—a wide public walkway under the freeway—which typically isn't too scary during daylight hours. Or take the downtown shuttle buses.

The Sacramento Convention & Visitors Bureau operates the **Old Sacramento Visitor Information Center** at its newest location, 1004 Second St. (next to the Wells Fargo History Museum), 916/442-7644, www.discovergold.org, and offers countless brochures, maps, and personable assistance. For more information about Old Sacramento shops and merchants, contact **Old Sacramento Management,** 1111 Second St., Ste. 300, 916/264-7031, www.oldsacra-

© ROBERT HOLMES/CALTOUR

Be sure to step in for a peek at the elegantly decorated Capitol.

park of impressive and unusual trees—many planted in the 1870s, three the largest known specimens of their kind—includes a redwood grown from a seed that circled the moon aboard Apollo 13 in 1970 and a Civil War memorial grove started with saplings collected from major battlefields. (Many of Capitol Park's trees are aging, however, rapidly reaching the end of their normal lifespans; don't be surprised to see tree removal crews on the grounds.) The **Vietnam Veterans Memorial** honoring California's war dead has been added near the rose garden at the east end of the park: 22 black granite panels with the final roll call, weeping cherry trees, and a statue of a 19-year-old soldier reading a letter from home. A 28-foot-tall black granite obelisk is centerpiece of the new **California Veterans Memorial,** unveiled in late 1998 to honor the five million Californians who have served in the U.S. armed forces since 1850. The new heart-centered **International World Peace Rose Garden** has replaced the Capitol's previous rose garden. Not far away is the most expensive art yet commissioned by the city of Sacramento, the million-dollar *Golden State* by artist Lita Albuquerque installed along the original Capitol Avenue route between 15th and 17th

Streets to soften the domineering granite-and-glass East End Project, the neighborhood's new office megolith. The sculpture locates California in the universe, metaphorically speaking, the 54 "star sculptures" representing the exact alignment of the sun, five planets, and the stars on the day California enetered the union (September 9, 1850).

The Capitol itself is open 9 A.M.–5 P.M. daily except Thanksgiving, Christmas, and New Year's Day. Free guided tours focus separately on the Capitol building's restoration, its history, the legislative process, and Capitol Park (weather permitting). Get oriented in a more general way by watching the 10-minute film shown in the basement (Room B-27). From Memorial Day through Labor Day, tours are offered daily, on the hour, from 9 A.M.–5 P.M. (last tour leaves at 4). Capitol Park tours are scheduled only from spring through fall. Sign-language and foreign-language tours are available. On weekends and holidays, use the entrance at 11th and L Streets. For more information, call 916/324-0333. For individual or group reservations, call ReserveAmerica at 866/240-4655, at least two weeks in advance. To take a virtual tour, see www.capitolmuseum.ca.gov. To get tickets for the visitors galleries of the state

GREAT VALLEY & THE DELTA

Legislature, contact individual Assembly or Senate representatives or call 916/445-5200.

Golden State Museum

Open since summer 1998, the $10.8-million Golden State Museum tells the story of California since statehood through the themes of place, people, promise, and politics. (How could anyone launch a museum so near the Capitol *without* dabbling in politics?) But the perspective offered by this first-class museum, the brainchild of former Secretary of State March Fong Eu, is far from bureaucratic or institutional. Exhibits have been created from the paperwork of people's everyday lives, though the displays represent only a few file folders' worth of the 120 million documents collected in the State Archives. Just inside the entry gates is the five-story **Constitution Wall**, composed of words from the preamble of the 1879 Constitution (a revision of the 1849 original, which was written on animal hide). Note the approval of house sparrows, which have already built nests within some of the more protective aspects of the alphabet.

Once inside the 3,500-square-foot museum—the entrance is on the first level, but exhibits start on the second—grab a headset and audio guide. For the full program, punch in the posted guide numbers at each exhibit; there is much more info, too, when you add in the various video and audio presentations. For a fast-paced, intense tour, just let the audio program run and try to keep up. The museum's **Place** gallery explores the diversity of California's natural landscape—including notable instabilities due to earthquakes, fires, and floods—as well as the land's radical transformation by the gold rush and subsequent economic and social forces. In addition to the voices of resource management, a holographic ghost of John Muir also speaks. **People** introduces the astonishing diversity of new Californians, how and why they came as well as what it took to create a new collective homeland. Climb aboard the dissected 1949 school bus for a multimedia tour of California immigration history. Back downstairs, the overarching ceiling mural in the **Promise** gallery amplifies the historic and mythic themes that attracted

settlers from around the globe. And, given the immense differences of experience and opinion that have characterized Californians since statehood, a peek into the facsimile Posey's Cafe (complete with original phone booth, still scented with smoke and stale beer) and **Politics** makes one marvel that we've managed to pull it off this long. Since Sacramento's newest museum is self-supporting, be sure to seriously explore the stylish gift shop before strolling on.

Congratulations, California. The grand experiment continues.

Special changing exhibits, such as *A Walk in the Woods* and *Through My Father's Eyes,* are also regularly added; call or see the website for current information. Occupying the first two floors of the California Archives building at 1020 O St. (10th and O, just one block south of the state Capitol), 916/653-7524, www.goldenstatemuseum.org, the Golden State Museum is open Tues.–Sat. 10 A.M.–5 P.M. and Sunday noon–5 P.M. Guided tours are available on weekdays, 9:30 am-3:30 pm.; call for details. To schedule a group tour, call 916/653-3476 at least two weeks in advance. Admission is $5 adults, $4 seniors, $3.50 children ages 6–13 (under age 6 free). For something to eat, try the **Gold Rush Grille** on the second floor, on the Secretary of State's side of the building (other side of the courtyard), open weekdays until 2:30 P.M.

California State Indian Museum

Not far from the Capitol and sharing a city block with Sutter's Fort is the refurbished and updated California State Indian Museum at 2618 K St., 916/324-0971, open 10 A.M.–5 P.M. daily except Thanksgiving, Christmas, and New Year's Day. With its fine collection of artifacts and exhibits, selected and approved by Native American elders, the museum chronicles the material, social, and spiritual development of California native culture. Particularly fascinating is the significance of basketry, a sacred survival art in which the basketmaker first offers thanks to the plant world for the materials gathered, then becomes part of that world and the basket itself, thereby guaranteeing abundant future harvests.

California Indian Days in October attracts

Native Americans from around the state for the festivities. Call for current information on other special programs. Admission to the museum is $2 adults (age 17 and older). Metered parking for both the museum and Sutter's Fort is available on K, L, 26th, and 28th Streets nearby.

Sutter's Fort State Historic Park

Sutter's Fort, around the corner at 2701 L St., 916/445-4422, was Sacramento's—and the valley's—first nonnative settlement, the center of John Sutter's attempted agrarian empire. Among other cross-country travelers who shared Sutter's hospitality were rescued survivors of the ill-fated Donner Party. Many of Sutter's original furnishings and implements actually came from Fort Ross, which Sutter bought from the Russians in 1841. During the gold rush, unruly, rampaging '49ers plundered Sutter's storehouses, gardens, and fields, squatted on his territory, and even shot his cattle for food and sport. The "fort" was all but destroyed before restoration began in 1891, though the original adobe brick walls of the central building somehow survived.

Exhibits at the fort complex re-create the feel of daily life in 1846—an experience quite popular with school and tour groups. Take a self-guided audio tour. Special events at Sutter's Fort include **Living History Days** (usually held in March, April, June, September, and November), when docents and volunteers dressed in 1846 fashions reenact life at the fort and demonstrate the settlers' survival arts, everything from candlemaking and weaving to blacksmithing and musket drills. **Pioneer Demonstration Days** in spring and early fall focus even more specifically on survival skills. Even more fun for schoolchildren, parents, and teachers is the fort's day-long (24-hour) **Environmental Living Program,** which allows fourth-to-sixth graders the opportunity to live and work as early settlers did. Call for information on special events and programs. Sutter's Fort is open daily 10 A.M.–5 P.M. except Thanksgiving, Christmas, and New Year's Day (gift shop open till 4:30 P.M.). Admission is $4 adults (17 and older), $1 children ages 6–16, free for age 5 and under; the price of admission increases on special-event days. During the warmer months of the school year the

place swarms with schoolchildren Tues.–Thurs., but on weekends expect fellow travelers.

Governor's Mansion State Historic Park

Now part of the state park system, this 1877 Victorian home at 16th and H Streets, 916/323-3047, was one of the first houses in California to feature indoor plumbing, central heating, and other niceties of modern life. Other more elegant touches include seven unique marble fireplaces from Italy, gold-framed mirrors, and impeccably handcrafted doorknobs and hinges. Home to 13 California governors—including Ronald Reagan, though he and Nancy moved out in 1967—the Governor's Mansion is now furnished with an eclectic collection of items including a 1902 Steinway piano owned by Governor George Pardee's family, Hiram Johnson's 1911 plum-colored velvet sofa and chairs, the state's official 1950s china, and a clawfoot bathtub off the master bedroom with each toenail painted red by former Governor Jerry Brown's younger sister Kathleen (more recently noteworthy as state treasurer) during their father Pat Brown's term in office. Special events held at the Governor's Mansion include **Living History Day** (usually in summer), depicting the life and times of particular gubernatorial families, and the **Victorian Christmas Celebration** in early December. The mansion is open daily 10 A.M.–5 P.M. for guided tours only (last tour leaves at 4 P.M.). General admission is $2 adults (age 17 and older); fees are higher on special-event days. Tours start at the two-story Carriage House, now a gift shop and visitors center. Public parking is available in the lot at 14th and H Streets if street parking is impossible.

Leland Stanford Mansion

That stunning presence at 800 N St. downtown (on the southeast corner of Eighth and N) was once the home of Leland Stanford, one of California's "Big Four" railroad barons and Stanford University's founder. A fairly straightforward two-story house when Governor Stanford bought the place in 1861, as the Stanford Mansion it was destined to become the Golden State's de facto capitol and "the most perfect specimen of a

CALIFORNIA'S HOMELESS GOVERNORS

One of California's official peculiarities is the fact that the state has had no official governor's residence since 1967, when the old mansion was added to the state park system. It's a somewhat typical tale of California political throat-tearing.

In a way, it's all Ronald Reagan's fault. Preceding former Governor Edmund G. "Pat" Brown's last campaign in the 1960s, land for a new governor's mansion had been cleared—at substantial expense—across from the Capitol near 14th, 15th, O, and N Streets, all part of the Capitol Master Plan. Mansion construction was delayed by design disagreements, however. Ultimately, a statewide contest was launched, and the winning Spanish-modern architectural design came from the San Francisco firm of Campbell & Wong. Though the mansion was privately estimated to cost less than $800,000, the official state estimate was $1.2 million. And the Ronald Reagan gubernatorial campaign suddenly had a hot populist issue—"Pat Brown's Million Dollar Mansion"—though Pat Brown had nothing to do with it.

Once elected governor in 1966, Reagan probably regretted his success in derailing mansion construction. The old governor's mansion had been good enough for Pat Brown and family for all those years, but Ron and Nancy Reagan refused to live there. It was probably time for the old residence to retire. In case of fire, for example, the Reagans would have had to shimmy down a rope ladder to escape its upper floors, which is why Nancy called it a "fire trap." California's new first family instead quietly moved into a private home on 45th Street, in East Sacramento's Fabulous Forties.

In the early 1970s, the idea of an official governor's residence reemerged. A group of influential businesspeople the Reagans counted as friends and political allies, including a number of lobbyists, bought an isolated 11-acre lot along the American River in Carmichael—way out in the suburbs, adjacent to a golf course—for a new governor's mansion, and donated it to the state. After considerable partisan wrangling (Democrats felt coerced by the Republican land contribution), the state eventually paid $1.3 million to build an ostentatious but otherwise fairly ordinary home on the site. The *Los Angeles Times* described it as a giant roof suspended on poles; other critics compared its architecture to Safeway.

The mansion was not completed in time for the Reagans' benefit, however. Reagan's successor, then-Governor Jerry Brown—picking up on the same issue that had pilloried his father, Pat Brown—pointedly called the place a "Taj Mahal," partly to embarrass the Republicans, and refused to move into it.

Although Brown's successor, Republican Governor George Deukmejian, wanted to occupy California's Taj Majal, the Democrat-dominated Legislature defied him—and in 1984 auctioned the house off to the highest bidder. During his term, Deukmejian, and subsequently both Republican Governor Pete Wilson and Democrat Governor Gray Davis, lived in another fairly nondescript suburban home provided by a private foundation chaired by Republican anti–affirmative action activist Ward Connerly.

Yet California's governors may not be homeless forever.

Until he was unceremoniously booted out of office by California voters in the infamous recall election of October 2003, Governor Davis was committed to building an official California governor's mansion to house his successors. The most recent site under consideration was in West Sacramento, just across the river from the Capitol—an isolated 40-acre bluff overlooking the confluence of the Sacramento and American Rivers yet still within sight of the Capitol. When that site was selected, however, no one knew that Arnold Schwarzenegger would be California's next governor. Despite his populist posturings, Schwarzenegger is foremost a celebrity of major stature—with equally pumped-up security needs—and a luxurious life established elsewhere. As he suggested immediate after his election, he could easily commute from his Pacific Palisades mansion (or his Sun Valley, Idaho mansion) in his personal Gulfstream IV jet.

house in all of California." Said specimen soon grew from a fairly modest 1,700 to an astonishing 19,000 square feet. The original house was hoisted up off the ground to allow for construction of a new first floor and grand entrance stairway; on top of other additions came a new mansard-roofed fourth floor. A grab bag of architectural styles, including Italianate and federalist, the Stanford Mansion is both a state and national historic landmark featuring many of its original furnishings. At last report major restoration work was underway, and weekly public tours had been suspended. For current details, call 916/324-0575.

In lieu of a Stanford Mansion tour, consider taking a peek at the beautifully restored 1928 **Julia Morgan House and Gardens,** 3731 T St., owned by California State University, Sacramento and used as a special events venue. To make an appointment to see it, call 916/227-5527.

Crocker Art Museum

Among the oldest public art museums in the West, the Crocker Art Museum at 216 O St. (on the corner of Third and O, a short walk from Old Sacramento), 916/264-5423, www.crockerartmuseum.org, is very Victorian, and one of Sacramento's finest features. Built in 1869 by banker B.F. Hastings and later sold to E.B. Crocker (Charles "Big Four" Crocker's brother), the museum is listed on the National Register of Historic Places and is itself a work of art—High Italianate art, with twin curving stairways, ornate painted plaster, elaborate woodwork, and inlaid polychromed tile floors. The interiors echo San Francisco's early Nob Hill nuance. The Crocker family's original collection of predominantly 19th-century European paintings and drawings has been generously supplemented with new works over the years, including samples of Victorian decorative arts, Asian ceramics, and California landscapes and photography. A collector's coup came in late 1995, with Sacramento artist Wayne Thiebaud's gift of 68 original works; some of Thiebaud's legacy is usually on display.

Yet even with two expansions over the years, at present the Crocker can exhibit only a miniscule portion of its collection. The museum's new

$75 million addition will debut in late 2006, tripling the museum's size and expanding its gallery and "cultural event" space.Already events are a Crocker claim to fame, from lectures to musical programs. Come every month for Third Thursday Jazz, and on Saturdays for hands-on Artblast events. Major social events include the annual **Crocker Ball** and **Crocker Uncorked** gourmet feast and wine auction.

In addition to extra hours for special events and activities, the museum is open Tues.–Sun. 10 A.M.–5 P.M., until 9 P.M. on Thursday, closed Mondays and major holidays. Docent-guided tours are offered; call for current details or see the website. The museum is free every Sunday 10 A.M.–1 P.M. Otherwise admission is $6 adults, $4 seniors, $3 students (with valid ID), free for age 6 and under. Wheelchair accessible. Metered parking.

Towe Museum of Automotive History

The onetime Towe Ford Museum is now the Towe Museum of Automotive History, following the traumatic 1997 car-by-car sale of the fabulous Towe Ford collection, to satisfy the Internal Revenue Service. Located just a few blocks south of the Crocker Art Museum, 2200 Front St. (corner of Front and V), 916/442-6802, www.toweautomuseum.org, the Towe (rhymes with "cow") was once the most complete collection of antique Fords anywhere—a stable of more than 100 of Ford's horseless carriages including Henry Ford's first successful production model, a rare 1906 Model N Runabout, which miraculously survived the IRS auction slaughter and is still on display. But for classic car enthusiasts the new collection is still quite fine, showcasing some 150 venerable vehicles in themed American "dream car" exhibits, including "The Dream of Cool" and "The Dream of Speed." The Hall of Technology offers a hands-on study in significant mechanical design change. Special monthly car club meets and other events are also scheduled. The Towe auto museum is open daily 10 A.M.–6 P.M.; admission is $7 adults, $6 seniors, $3 high school students, $2 grade school students. Gift shop. Free parking. Come for "Show & Sell" the first Saturday of every month.

© ROBERT HOLMES/CALTOUR

Towe Museum of Automotive History

Other Sights

Attractions downtown include an impressive number of newer government buildings and office complexes adding still more vertical lift to the skyline. Most striking is the grand 16-story **U.S. Courthouse** at Sixth and I Streets. Inside there's an oval atrium and, if you take the elevator up, some spectacular views; outside, near the entrance, there's some intriguing interpretive art (do look down to appreciate the judicial aphorisms). Inspiring, too, is the **Secretary of State/California State Archives Building** at 11th and O Streets. (Considerably less thrilling: the **Department of Justice** and **California EPA** buildings on I Street.) But the state's not done yet. The mother of all government building booms is just beginning, the **East End Project** near Capitol Park's east end—five new state office buildings and three parking garages between L and O and 14th and 17th Streets, 1.5 million square feet in all.

Downtown offers striking historical architecture, too, including the 1927 **Westminster Presbyterian Church** at 13th and N Streets. Housing the California State Library and a world-class collection of books and historic materials, the **Library and Courts Building,** 914 Capitol Mall (on the circle), is also a de facto Maynard Dixon center. Four panels the artist painted for the home of Lucky Baldwin's daughter are on the second floor; his western *Pageant of Tradition* is on the third floor, in the Gillis Hall reference room.

The 1923 **Public Market** building at 1230 J St., designed by architect Julia Morgan, has been incorporated into the new Sheraton Grand Hotel. Nearby are two of the city's earliest skyscrapers, the office tour at 926 J St. and the 1926 **Elks Building,** 921 11th Street. Both the 1918 **Central Library** at 828 I St. and the 1933 **Post Office** across the street at 801 I feature terra cotta trim from Gladding, McBean. And don't miss the city's stunning 1911 beaux arts **City Hall,** 915 I St., with its elaborate cornucopia ornamentation—fruits and vegetables, homage to the city's agricultural heritage.

Fascinating at N. A and 15th Streets, near the railroad tracks, are the 60 tiny **Bishop Francis A. Quinn Cottages,** each just 375 square feet, one attempted local solution to the persistent problem of homelessness. Tenants have two-year leases, and pay one-third of their incomes for rent. The cottages were unveiled in mid-1998, and already there's a hopelessly long waiting list. Not far away, the modern brick **Blue Diamond Growers Visitors Center** of the California Almond Growers Exchange—the world's largest almond processing plant, whose nuts get around on Air Force One and the space shuttles—is located at 1701 C St., 916/446-8439, www.bluediamond.com, and offers a 20-minute informational video, free almond tasting, and onsite sales. Open Mon.–Fri. 10 A.M.–5 P.M., Saturday 10–4 P.M.

Another unique downtown attraction is the **Dr. Sun Yat Sen Memorial** and museum honoring the "Father of China," in the Chinatown Mall near I-5, between Third and Fifth and J and I Streets, open Tues.–Sat. 1–3 P.M. The mall stands on the site of Sacramento's **Old Chinatown**, "Yee Fow," and is notable for its Chinese language school, association halls, and shops.

For some high-test consumerism and rocking cultural contrast, from here stroll south to K Street then east to the vast **Downtown Plaza** mall, where the **Hard Rock Cafe** is a main attraction. From the mall, stroll east along K Street, downtown's central boulevard. The impending "K Street Comeback" seems well underway—there's the new **Esquire Tower**, very cool Esquire Grill, and IMAX theater at 13th and K, near the convention center. New in 2003: an outpost of upscale Pyramid Alehouse, which serves several strictly Sacramento brews, including the memorable K Street Nitro Stout. Adding a new CinéArts complex (art-house theater, bistro, and full bar) in K Street's old Woolworth building is under consideration—a development that might undermine the success of dazzling, historic **Crest Theatre,** an established asset.

The Wells Fargo Center nearby at 400 Capitol Mall includes a **Wells Fargo History Museum,** 916/440-4161, in its five-story lobby. Exhibits range from an authentic Concord Stagecoach—imagine how nine passengers actually managed to fit—and a facsimile 19th-century Wells Fargo agent's office to a collection of gold ore samples from the Grass Valley area and a set of Howard & Davis gold balance scales, one of the museum's hottest attractions. Well worth a stop if you're in the neighborhood. Free. Open during regular business hours, Mon.–Fri. 9 A.M.–5 P.M., closed on bank holidays.

But for those with deep historical interests, the best museum in town could well be the vast **Old Sacramento City Cemetery** (once poetically known as the City of the Dead) founded by John Sutter in 1849 at Broadway and Riverside, where 20,000 pioneers from around the globe take their final rest; these marble monuments make good reading. Some of the city's most scandalous tales are also memorialized here, though to get the dirt you'll have to sign on for a weekend tour (free, but donations happily accepted). Regular tours are offered March to mid-November, weather permitting, on the second and fourth Saturday of the month. Themed evening tours are also quite popular; private tours can be arranged. Most tours depart from 10th St. and Broadway. For current details, contact the Old City Cemetery Committee, 916/448-0811, www.oldcitycemetery.com.

Tangentially related, just beyond downtown in East Sacramento, is the Sierra Sacramento Valley Medical Society's **Museum of Medical History,** housed in the former Guttman Medical Library, 5380 Elvas Ave., 916/452-2671, offering a sometimes frightening look at the evolution of western medicine and technology. Consider the Diathermy Machine, used to treat patients with cancer, gallstones, or pneumonia. Open daily 9 A.M.–4 P.M., docent usually available Thursday 10 A.M.–2 P.M.

Nearby Attractions

The military at onetime McClellan Air Force Base (now McClellan Park) has cleared out, but the **McClellan Aviation Museum** is still going strong. The impressive collection here—"the finest collection of aircraft and aviation memorabilia in the West"—includes 33 aircraft dating back to World War II (including a MiG-21 Soviet fighter and an F4-C Phantom II jet), a veritable Air Force fashion show of uniform and insignia changes over the years, and historical displays. Open Mon.–Sat. 9 A.M.–3 P.M., Sunday noon–4 P.M. Admission free, though donations are greatly appreciated. The museum was located at 3204 Palm St. (directly west of the Peacekeeper Gate) in North Highlands, most easily reached via Watt Ave. (from I-80). As of fall 2003, however, the museum was in the process of moving to Freedom Park, at the edge of McClellan Park. By mid-2004 the attractive, new 15,500-square-foot wing-shaped permanent museum was expected to open; it will be some years yet before the massive adjacent hangar is finished. Financial contributions and other assistance greatly appreciated. For current information, call 916/643-3192 or see www.mcclellanaviation-museum.org. Equally fascinating at McClellan are its historic art deco buildings, most located quite near the old museum on WPA-era Mc-Clellan Mall. At last report, 51 were listed on the National Register of Historic Places. Among the most striking: the 1938 Headquarters building (Building 1), where inside there's a multi-colored floor map of North America done in terrazzo; Building 250, with its very-deco propeller and aviation-themed concrete castings; the Officers Club; and the commander's house, among others.

If you've got restless kids in tow, consider a stop at the **Discovery Museum Learning Center** at 3615 Auburn Blvd., 916/575-3940 (recorded) or 916/575-3941, www.thediscovery.org, affiliated with Old Sac's Discovery Museum. The northstate's first Challenger Learning Center, a planetarium, science and history programs, nature trails, and hands-on exhibits are among its notable attractions. At last report open daily in summer 10 A.M.–5 P.M., otherwise Tues.–Fri. noon–5 P.M. and weekends 10 A.M.–5 P.M. To play it safe, call ahead for current schedule, program, and admission information.

A relief for kids and heat-stunned adults come summer is the **Waterworld USA Family Waterpark** at Cal Expo, 1600 Exposition Blvd., 916/924-3747 or 916/924-0556, www.sixflags.com, with massive waterslides, rides including Shark Attack, and Breaker Beach, the northstate's largest wave pool. The hillside Hook's Lagoon here, new in 1997, is something of an aquatic jungle gym. Adjacent **Paradise Island Family Fun Park,** 916/924-3595, is raucous fun without the water, featuring attractions from a dragon roller coaster and bumper boats to 36-hole miniature golf and video and arcade games. For more kid-friendly possibilities, parks, and playgrounds, keep reading.

SPORTS AND RECREATION

Spectator Sports

The Maloof brothers' **Sacramento Kings** NBA basketball squad, 916/928-6900, www.nba.com/kings, are Sacramento's pride and joy these days, finally making their play for national recognition as nearly full-time rivals of the L.A. Lakers. Home games are scheduled Nov.–May at the Arco Arena, just north of town via I-5. At last report, Sacramento was also home to the Maloofs's **Sacramento Monarchs** WNBA women's team, 916/928-8499, www.wnba.com/monarchs, their season running June–Aug. Almost as big in Sacramento as professional basketball is Triple-A baseball—the Pacific Coast League's **Sacramento River Cats** (affiliated with the Oakland A's), to be more specific. For current information, call 916/376-4700 or see www.rivercats.com. Games are played at Raley Field in West Sacramento, 400 Ballpark Dr.

Greenspace

The greater Sacramento area is a neighborhood recreation wonderland, with almost endless public parks, pools, tennis courts, and recreational programs, plus amusement centers, bowling alleys, and skating rinks. For more information on city parks, call Parks and Recreation North, 916/566-6581, or Parks and Recreation South, 916/277-6060, or see www.cityofsacramento.org/parksandrecreation. For more information on Sacramento County parks (including golf courses), call 916/875-6961 or see www.sacparks.net. For information on organized area hikes, contact the Mother Lode Chapter of the Sierra Club, 1414 K St., Ste. 500, 916/557-1100 ext. 108, http://motherlode.sierraclub.org.

The 5,000-acre **American River Parkway** is Sacramento's outdoor gem, a riverside stretch of public parklands set aside for river lovers, cyclists, runners, walkers, horseback riders, and just plain nature lovers. The river itself is popular for fishing, rafting, and swimming, but the parkway corridor is perfect for spring bird-watching, as are the oak woodlands surrounding Folsom Lake near the end of the line. The parkway starts on the west at the American's confluence with

PAWS TO THE RESCUE

Where do hard-working pachyderms go to pack it in? Fortunate retired elephants and other exotic animals end up at a **Performing Animal Welfare Society** (PAWS) refuge—the original 30-acre sanctuary in Galt, the affiliated 100-acre **Amanda Blake Memorial Wildlife Refuge** (ABMWR) for hooved animals at Rancho Seco Park in Herald, or the new 2,300-acre **Ark 2000** foothill refuge and education facility near San Andreas.

Hollywood animal trainer Pat Derby and partner Ed Stewart founded PAWS to offer sanctuary to abandoned or abused performing animals. In her work with exotic animals on popular Disney movies and numerous TV shows (*Flipper, Daktari, Gunsmoke, Lassie*), Derby developed revolutionary training methods based on non-dominance, or "love instead of fear."

For more information—and to find out about special events, like the Animals' Christmas Open House in December—contact PAWS, 1435 Simmerhorn Rd. in Galt, 209/745-2606, www.paws-web.org. The museum and visitor center at the Amanda Blake Museum and Visitors Center at the Rancho Seco Park refuge, southeast of Sacramento at 14440 Twin Cities Rd., is open to visitors every Sat. 10 A.M.–3 P.M. or by special appointment; $5 park admission. Blake, who played Miss Kitty on *Gunsmoke,* befriended Pat Derby on the set of that TV show. When Blake died in 1989, she left her entire estate to PAWS, and the museum here offers an eclectic collection of celebrity memorabilia and some of her African wildlife photography.

Not open to the public, Ark 2000 is among the nation's largest "free-range" exotic animal sanctuary—designed to allow elephants and (eventually) lions, tigers, and other animals to live in near-natural conditions. Once the visitor center is constructed, Ark 2000 will educate the public about keeping and breeding wildlife in captivity—a practice opposed by PAWS. The facility will also serve as a training and observation site for wildlife behaviorists and veterinarians. At last report unique three-day/two-night **See the Elephant** "nature experience" getaways were offered once a month. Contact PAWS for details.

the Sacramento River, near Old Sacramento at **Discovery Park,** and continues east, ending near Folsom Dam. Though it's sadly unsafe for women alone even during the daylight hours, with the general crime rate increasing, the parkway's 23-mile **Jedediah Smith Memorial Bicycle Trail** starts near Discovery Park (usually closed in winter due to flooding) just north of Downtown, once a Depression-era shantytown. Passing restrooms and clusters of picnic tables along the way, the bike trail (equally popular with hikers and runners) heads east along the American River's north bank, then crosses the river to Goethe Park and continues on to Beals Point at Folsom. River rafting (Apr.–Sept.) is popular along the parkway stretch of the American, with most trips shoving off from rental places near Sunrise Boulevard. **American River Raft Rentals** along the river in Rancho Cordova, 916/635-6400 or 888/338-7238, www.raftrentals.com, has been paddling these waters since 1974 and is active in various American River Parkway Foundation events.

In addition to Goethe and multiple other parks, the parkway passes through **Ancil Hoffman Park** in Carmichael, noted for its self-guided nature trails along the American River and the educational exhibits and live animals at its **Effie Yeaw Nature Center,** 6700 Tarshes Dr., 916/489-4918, www.effieyeaw.org, open daily 10 A.M.–5 P.M. (9:30 A.M.–4 P.M. Nov.–Feb.). Free, but a $4 parking fee if you drive.

The **Gibson Ranch County Park** near Watt Ave. and Elverta Rd. in Elverta, 916/875-6961, www.gibson-ranch.com, is particularly fun for children, with its farm setting and petting zoo of domestic animals, sheepdog demonstrations, and more. The park also features shaded picnic areas, swimming, fishing, and horseback trails. Open daily 7 A.M.–dusk. Free. *Not* free but fun are horse and pony rides (hayrides available, too); for horse or pony reservations, "horse camp," and other current equestrian information, call 916/991-7592.

Strange as it seems, Sacramento's notoriously troubled (and now defunct) **Rancho Seco Nuclear Power Plant** south of town has recreational value. Hiking, biking, swimming, kayaking, windsurfing, even pedal boating and RV and tent camping are available on or near the shores of **Rancho Seco Regional Park**'s fish-stocked lake— all in the long shadows of the plant's cooling towers. Day use is $5. To get here: Head south from Sacramento on Hwy. 99, take the Twin Cities exit, then head east. For current information, call the Sacramento Municipal Utilities District (SMUD) at 209/748-2318 (recording); for additional information and reservations for RV, tent, or group camping and picnicking, call 916/732-4913.

Land Park and Vicinity

William Land Park, a few miles south of the Capitol in the midst of one of the city's most appealing older neighborhoods, is home to the 15-plus-acre **Sacramento Zoo**, 3930 W. Land Park Dr. (Sutterville Rd. at Land Park Dr.), 916/264-5888, www.saczoo.com, which is itself home to hundreds of exotic animals, including 23 endangered species. Attractions include the Lake Victoria flamingos, a quarter-acre summer butterfly and hummingbird garden nearby, and the golden-headed lion tamarin monkeys. Plans for the zoo's $40 million expansion program—changes limited to the zoo's current boundaries—include a new animal hospital, a completely redesigned entry, and new and refurbished animal habitats. Open daily in summer 9 A.M.–4 P.M., 10 A.M.–4 P.M. otherwise, though closing times vary. On weekdays admission is $6.75 adults, $4.50 children ages 3–12, free for babies and toddlers; on weekends the fees are $7.75 and $5, respectively. Free parking. Among Land Park's other attractions are a nine-hole golf course, athletic fields, picnic areas, the **FairyTale Town** kiddie playground (closed Dec.–Jan.), 916/264-5223, and the **Funderland Amusement Park** and pony rides also near the zoo, 916/456-0115.

Stone Lakes National Wildlife Refuge

The 18,200-acre Stone Lakes refuge, flanking I-5 near the Sacramento River just south of the town of Freeport, is home to an astonishing assortment of birds—egrets, great blue herons, double-crested cormorants, grebes, geese, ducks, hawks, and some 150 species of perching birds—

not to mention muskrats, beavers, coyotes, raccoons, foxes, snakes, lizards, bullfrogs, and insects. From fall through spring, expect to see the full range of migrating waterfowl. Regular public access is allowed on the second and fourth of every month (except summer). The meandering self-guided trail begins at the Elk Grove Boulevard Gate, at the west end of the boulevard and I-5, and ends at a 12-foot viewing platform tucked into the tree canopy. The refuge is also open to the public for special events, tours, and guided walks. Come in May, for example, for the **Walk on the Wildside Festival.** For current information, call 916/775-4420 (recorded) or 916/775-4421, or see www.stonelakes.org.

Cosumnes River Preserve

The Nature Conservancy also has been quite busy in southern Sacramento County, particularly in the 1990s—determined to protect and preserve the Cosumnes River floodplain from development. The result is the massive (and ever-expanding) 37,000-acre Cosumnes River Preserve, one of The Nature Conservancy's 75 "last great places," designed to protect the entire Cosumnes River watershed—wetlands, grasslands, woodlands, and agricultural lands—as safe haven for native plants and wildlife. The last undammed river originating in the Sierra Nevada, the Cosumnes River still nourishes flood-dependent valley oaks, which require deep alluvial soils; the oak stands here are among the most impressive remaining in California. In addition to significant recent land acquisitions, including the 4,300-acre Valensin Ranch and 12,362 acres of Howard Ranch adjacent to Rancho Seco, The Nature Conservancy and state, federal, and private agencies hope to protect the entire 1,200-square-mile watershed through cooperative land management agreements. An example of this approach came in spring 1999 when the 9,200-acre M&T Staten Ranch on the delta's Staten Island southeast of Walnut Grove, between the north and south forks of the Mokelumne River, was added to the preserve—extending its total reach to well south of Isleton. (Agriculture will continue here, so don't go wandering around uninvited.)

However, you can take a walk along the preserve's 3.3-mile **Willow Slough Nature Trail** loop (naturally enough, the trail typically floods in winter) or the easier, mile-long **Lost Slough Trail,** where the boardwalk section is wheelchair accessible. Birdwalks are scheduled monthly. Ask at headquarters about the new **Howard Ranch/ Rancho Seco Trail,** a 4.7-mile trail that starts at the lake in Ranch Seco Park and extends several miles into Howard Ranch. Kayaking is an increasingly popular preserve activity. The river's calmest in summer, though plan your trip around the tide tables (avoid putting in or taking out at low tide). Getting around by boat, in fact, is the best way to see the preserve, particularly now that old levees are being breached and the waterway is expanding in all directions. Free guided boat tours (BYOB) are sometimes scheduled. Plus there's work to do. Habitat restoration work is ongoing throughout the preserve; volunteers and donations of supplies and materials are always needed. You can also kayak the Cosumnes on naturalist-led tours offered by **Blue Waters Kayaking,** 415/669-2600; **Current Adventures,** 530/642-9755; and **Outdoor Adventures** at UC Davis, 530/752-4362. The website includes a driving tour.

For more information about the preserve and current activities, call 916/684-2816, see www.co-sumnes.org, or stop by the visitor center, on the east side of Franklin Blvd. about 1.7 miles south of Twin Cities Rd., open most weekends 10 A.M.–4 P.M. (8 A.M.–noon in summer).

STAYING IN SACRAMENTO

Sacramento offers a good selection of accommodations in all price ranges. The listings below are convenient to Old Sacramento, Downtown, and Midtown, though there are accommodations options flanking major freeways and thoroughfares throughout the greater metropolitan area. For a fairly complete and current listing, contact the Sacramento Convention and Visitors Bureau (see Capital Information below). Camping is possible at various city-style RV campgrounds in the area—particularly at the **Sacramento Metro KOA** in West Sacramento, 916/371-6771, and at the **Cal Expo RV Park,** 916/263-3187—but for those without wheels the nearest public camping (to

the east, at Folsom Lake, and south of town at Rancho Seco) is too far away for convenience.

Finding suitable accommodations in and around Sacramento is usually no problem, except when a large convention, the Jazz Jubilee, or other major event is underway. The incorporated warehouse district of West Sacramento, just across the Sacramento River from Downtown and Old Sacramento, also offers reasonably priced lodgings.

Old Sacramento

Most tourists are attracted to the big hotels downtown, but there is a local secret—the selection of inexpensive and moderately priced motels located along Richards Boulevard and Jibboom Street, close to I-5 just north of Old Sacramento (Jibboom is west of the freeway, the extension of Richards). The neighborhood isn't all that special, decorated with overhead freeway, gas stations, and quick-stops, but the location is quite good—practically *in* Old Sacramento and Downtown, at the confluence of the Sacramento and American Rivers, yet the last stop before both Arco Arena and the airport. Being able to gas up here is a plus, by the way, if you'll be returning a rental car to Sacramento International; there's only one gas station at the airport.

Closest to Old Sacramento is the **Best Western Sandman Motel** at 236 Jibboom St., 916/443-6515, fax 916/443-8346, always a best bet. (Look for the Perko's restaurant—and the huge carved bison and other redwood sculptures outside.) Rooms are quite spacious and clean, with basic amenities plus HBO, in-room refrigerators, hair dryers, continental breakfast, swimming pool, and restaurant adjacent. Rooms are $50–100. Other good mid-range choices in the neighborhood include **Governors Inn** at 310 Richards Blvd., 916/448-7224 or 800/999-6689, www.governorsinn.net; **Super 8 Executive Suites,** 216 Bannon St. (off Richards), 916/447-5400 or 800/800-8000 (national), where all rooms have microwaves and refrigerators; and the nice **Days Inn Discovery Park,** 350 Bercut Dr. (off Richards), 916/442-6971 or 800/952-5516. Most have swimming pools and other amenities, with rates $50–100.

Even closer to the Sacramento River is the **Delta King River Boat Hotel** in Old Sacramento, 1000 Front St., 916/444-5464 or 800/825-5464, www.deltaking.com. The real draw here is location, location, location—*in* Old Sacramento. Rooms are pleasant, if a bit small—but how often do you get the chance to sleep *on* a river? Beyond the onboard Pilothouse restaurant—even if you don't dine here, explore the stunning wood and brass decor—the shops and restaurants of Old Sac beckon. Rooms go as low as $100–150, with AAA, AARP, and other discounts available Sun.–Thurs. nights, but you'll usually find standard weekend rates at the high end of $150–200. Dinner/theater hotel packages are the big push, most running $200–250 per night. For a truly swank stay, sign on for a night in the "Captain's Quarters," $550.

Overlooking Old Sacramento from father south, adjacent to Tower Bridge, is the new, 242-room **Embassy Suites Hotel Riverfront Promenade,** between I-5 and the Sacramento River at 100 Capitol Mall, 916/326-5000 or 800/362-2779. Not all that unique on the outside, the hotel offers some surprises inside—from the soaring, skylit atrium lobby to an abundance of locally commissioned artwork. (At the hotel entrance *Camellia Ladies,* by Camille Vanden-Berge, welcomes guests.) The two-room suites feature private bedroom, refrigerator, microwave, coffeemaker, two phones (with data ports), and two TVs. Suites are $150–200, with lower rates on weekends.

Downtown

Quite convenient among Downtown motels and a good visitor choice when conventions aren't booked is the comfortable, ivy-covered **Clarion Hotel** at 700 16th St. (Hwy. 160), 916/444-8000 or 800/443-0880. On-site restaurant and bar. Across the street is the historic Governor's Mansion, and in summer the Music Circus convenes next door. Room are $50–100, with AAA and other discounts and specials available. Other best bets, also close to the Capitol, include the 98-room **Best Western Sutter House Motel** at 1100 H St. (between 11th and 12th), 916/441-1314 or 800/830-1314, and **Quality Inn** at 818 15th

St., 916/444-3980 or 800/228-5151. Since summer in Sacramento can be sizzling, all have swimming pools.

Special downtown is the elegant 16-room **Sterling Hotel** at 1300 H St. (13th and H), 916/448-1300 or 800/365-7660, www.sterling-hotel.com. Once known as the Hale Mansion, the sophisticated boutique-style Sterling opened following an extensive renovation. During the week, the Sterling caters to business travelers—thus the new ballroom and other meeting facilities—but weekends are prime time for pleasure travelers. All rooms feature Italian marble bathrooms with Jacuzzis, understated yet exquisite furnishings, and little extras like fresh flowers, bathrobes, hairdryers, CD players, and voicemail. In addition to the good Chanterelle restaurant on-site, the Sterling also features a small bar in the lobby. Rates are $100–250.

New among the city's crop of large hotels and close to the convention center is the **Sheraton Grand Hotel Sacramento,** 1230 J St. (at 12th), 916/447-1700, www.sheratongrandsacramento.com, which incorporates the historic, Julia Morgan–designed Public Market Building as its atrium lobby. Rooms have all the essential comforts plus in-room coffee, iron and ironing board, hairdryer, bathrobes, dual-line cordless phone, data port, high-speed Internet access (by request), and voicemail. In addition to the on-site restaurants and bar, facilities include full fitness center and outdoor heated pool. Rooms are $150–250.

Still top drawer is the towering 500-room **Hyatt Regency Sacramento** right across from Capitol Park at 1209 L St. (12th and L), 916/443-1234 or 800/233-1234. The Mediterranean-style Hyatt can be crowded with conventioneers on weekdays—inquire, if it matters—but weekends are usually slow, a plus for vacationers. Swimming pool, two on-site restaurants, full business services, airport transportation. Most rooms are $100–250.

Bed-and-Breakfasts

These days, Sacramento's accommodating bed-and-breakfast inns are a mainstream lodging option, for business and pleasure. In general, prices compare favorably with much less personal hotels

BACK TO THE FUTURE: A CAPITAL HOSTEL

Aside from being an inexpensive and safe choice to hang one's hat, the HI-USA **Sacramento Hostel,** is an unusually elegant place to hang out in. There's no hostel quite like it anywhere in the United States.

Open since 1995, the hostel is housed in the historic Llewellyn-Williams mansion (also known locally as Mory's Place, after previous owner Mory Holmes), and sleeps up to 70 guests in its bunk-style dorms and private rooms. Meticulously restored to its 1885 Italianate Victorian grandeur at a cost of $2.1 million, thanks to financial support from American Youth Hostels, the National Trust for Historic Preservation, and the Sacramento City Council, the hostel features original stained glass, hand-carved oak staircases and decorative detail, parquet floors, original chandeliers, embossed wallpapers, period-style carpeting, and elegant marble

fireplaces. Facilities also include modern shared baths and a sleek Euro-style kitchen.

In an odd quirk of fate, the hostel—relocated some years back, in its pre-hostel days, due to imminent high-rise construction—has been *re*-relocated. Turns out the city needed the land adjacent to City Hall (where the hostel was relocated and rehabilitated) for its own construction plans. Since that skyscraper wasn't so imminent after all, the hostel has been moved back to its original site. (Don't ask how much all that cost.) The Sacramento Hostel is still downtown, though, more or less at its original address near city hall at 925 H St. (at 10th), 916/443-1691 or 800/909-4776 #40, www.norcalhostels.org, and is open daily (for checkout and check-in) 7:30–9:30 A.M. and 5–10 P.M. Rates for a hostel bed are $20 adult, $10 children (plus $3 guest fee for nonmembers).

and motels. Inquire about weekday special rates and seasonal bargains.

A particularly fine Midtown choice is **Amber House Bed and Breakfast Inn,** actually three Craftsman houses headquartered at 1315 22nd St. (between Capitol Ave. and N St.), 916/444-8085 or 800/755-6526, www.amberhouse.com. Amber House started out as just one striking 1905 Craftsman under the elms, today's romanticized Poets' Refuge; the five rooms pay homage to Lord Byron, Chaucer, Dickinson, Longfellow, and Wordsworth. Then came the neighboring 1913 bungalow, Artists' Retreat, its four rooms dedicated to Monet, Degas, Renoir, and Van Gogh. The most recent addition is the colonial revival Musician's Manor across the street, its five rooms dedicated to some classics: Bach, Brahms, Vivaldi, Beethoven, and Mozart (and yes, expect appropriate musical accompaniment). Rooms at Amber House are exquisitely decorated with antiques and appropriate artistic touches. Each is unique. Emily Dickinson, for example, is light and airy, with white wicker and 22 etched glass windows; a heart-shaped Jacuzzi cozies up to an antique fireplace that can also be appreciated from the bed. Rooms boast abundant amenities; some rooms feature two-person

Jacuzzis, and all have private marble bathrooms with plush robes on hand. Cable-connected TVs with VCRs, CD players, and private phones with voice mail are also provided. Full gourmet breakfast, scrumptious cookies, and just plain hospitality make it feel like home (if not a tad better). Most rates are in the $150–250 range. The corporate weekday rate here is reasonable, certainly comparable to many high-end hotels (all comforts included) for a solo traveler—and the service is incomparable.

Also reasonably close to the Capitol and the Sacramento Convention Center is the federalist **Capitol Park Bed and Breakfast,** 1300 T St., 916/414-1300 or 877/753-9982, www.capitolparkbnbinn.com, where the four suites are named for the Central Pacific Railroad's "Big Four": Crocker, Hopkins, Huntington, and Stanford. Breakfast is made to order, from "eggs your way" to French toast. Rates are $150–200.

A pleasant find in East Sacramento, particularly for fans of Gilbert and Sullivan, is the **Savoyard Bed and Breakfast,** 3322 H St., 916/442-6709 or 800/772-8692, www.savoyard.com. Located right across from McKinley Park and its rose gardens, Savoyard is a 1925 Italian Renaissance home serving up gracious guest rooms (private baths) and full breakfast. Choose from the appropriately costumed Penzance, Mikado, Iolanthe, and Pinafore rooms. Rates are $100–150.

The seven-room **Inn at Parkside** near Southside Park at at 2116 Sixth St., 916/658-1818 or 800/995-7275, opened as a bed-and-breakfast since 1994. Under new ownership, the exquisite 1936 Fong Mansion was built for Nationalist China's ambassador to North America—a role that helps explain the art deco ballroom, complete with spring-loaded maple dance floor, and other surprising features. These days the home's decor has returned to British Empire style, though the sensibility otherwise is contemporary and very Californian. All seven rooms feature private baths, including the large, loft-style Happiness Suite, with its spectacular marble bathroom and spa tub, two fireplaces, and kitchenette. All rooms feature private baths. The basics here include full breakfast, luxury kimono robes, and TV, VCR, and telephone (with data ports) in every room; irons, ironing boards, and hairdryers are available. Another inn feature is its art gallery. Gourmet three-course breakfast can be served in your room. Most weekday rates are $100–150 ($175 for Olympus), while weekend rates are $150–300; Jazz Jubilee prices are even higher.

Once known as the Driver Mansion Inn, **Vizcaya** on the edge of Midtown at 2019 21st St. (between T and U Sts.), 916/455-5243 or 800/456-2019, www.sterlinghotel.com, is a study in luxurious Italian marble and Victorian propriety, brought to you by the folks who own the stylish Sterling Hotel. Catering to business execs during the week and hopeless romantics on weekends, Vizcaya features seven rooms and two suites—six in the main house, three in the carriage house—many with fireplaces and/or Jacuzzis. Full breakfast (small, private tables) and all the amenities. A fairly recent addition is Vizcaya's adjacent New Orleans–style events palace, quite appealing for weddings and other special events. Rooms are $150–200.

QUICK BITES

The elderly homes and Victorians of Midtown Sacramento have some pretty hip company these days. "Midtown" is the city's hottest, most happening, and diverse dining and nightlife district, a neighborhood tucked neatly between Downtown and high-rent East Sacramento. People quibble over Midtown's actual territory, but you'll surely find it if you head for the area just east of downtown's skyscrapers, bounded by 28th Street (and the Capital City Freeway soaring overhead) on the east, 16th Street on the west, P Street on the south, and H Street on the north. If you're veering off the freeway specifically in search of a good meal, just head for J Street, which serves as Midtown's unofficial main drag.

Sacramento's "gourmet gulch," however, would have to be in upscale East Sacramento, particularly on or near Fair Oaks Boulevard—the extension of H Street east of the Capital City Freeway, just beyond CSU Sacramento—on the east side of the American River, more or less between Howe and Munroe Avenues.

As the neighborhood listings below also reflect, Downtown and Old Sacramento also have a respectable selection of restaurants of all stripes, as do outlying Folsom and Davis. That's as far as this book goes, though there are many more worthy selections throughout the greater Sacramento region. Even if you find yourself at some mall or minimall in the vast suburban jungle, remember that good food is rarely far away. Ask around.

Produce and Picnic Fixings

With Sacramento smack dab in the middle of a rich agricultural region, certified farmers' markets (CFM) abound. Show up, in season, for farm-fresh fruit, vegetables, baked goods, flowers, and memorable cheap eats, such as homemade tamales. Most accessible for most visitors are those in and around central Sacramento, held from May through October, including the **Sacramento Roosevelt Park Certified Farmers Market** at Ninth and P Streets, held on Tuesday 10 A.M.–2 P.M.; the **Sacramento Chavez Plaza CFM** in downtown's César Chavez Plaza (still shown on some maps as Plaza Park) at 10th and J Streets, held Wednesday 10 A.M.–2 P.M.; and the **Downtown Plaza CFM** at Fourth and K Streets (between the mall and the Holiday Inn), held Friday 10 A.M.–2 P.M. The **Sacramento**

Central Certified Farmers Market convenes every Sunday year-round, 8 A.M.–noon, beneath the Capital City Freeway at Eighth and W Streets. Another year-round possibility is the Country Club Plaza Certified Farmers Market on Butano Drive behind Macy's (Watt and El Camino) 8 A.M.–noon. For information on these and other area farmers' markets, call 916/688-0100 or see www.california-grown.com.

Otherwise, cheapest and best for organic groceries is the recently remodeled Sacramento Natural Foods Co-op, 1900 Alhambra Blvd. (at S Street), 916/445-2667, www.sacfood-coop.com, with an incredible selection of herbs and teas, a grand selection of organic produce, and natural foods in bulk. "Sac Natch" has a decent deli, too, serving such wonders as Kung Pao tofu, smoked tofu or roasted eggplant sandwiches, and various rice dishes, soups, and salads, including a very tasty Asiago cheese, basil, and chicken pasta salad. (Yes, veggie purists, chicken and turkey *are* served here. Beef and pork, too.) Open daily 7:30 A.M.–10 P.M. Much to the chagrin of co-op members, a 37,000-square-foot branch of the Texas-based Whole Foods chain opened in 2003, 4315 Arden Way (at Eastern Avenue), 916/488-2800.

Greater Sacramento is also full of ethnic markets and nifty neighborhood groceries. If you're heading to the zoo or are otherwise in the Land Park neighborhood, *the* place for essentials is been-there-forever Taylor's Market at 2900 Freeport Blvd., 916/443-6881, with fresh fish, meats, and poultry at the in-house butcher shop, a fairly impressive wine selection, and sundry grocery and deli items. (Safety note: It's hazardous getting into the parking lot here if you're heading north on Freeport; the easiest and safest way is to continue north until the first possible left turn over the railroad tracks, make the turn, then double back.) While you're in the neighborhood, don't miss the fabulous French-style Freeport Bakery just a few doors to the south, 2966 Freeport Blvd., 916/442-4256, a popular neighborhood pastry-and-coffee hangout and bakery famous for its rustic bread, French pastries, and fresh fruit tarts and cakes. Another great artisan bread stop, nearby in Midtown, is New Roma

Bakery, 1800 E Street, 916/443-2346, beloved for its French, sourdough, Italian, and rye breads.

In specialty food shops, some say the ultimate in upscale is served up at David Berkley Fine Wines & Specialty Foods at 515 Pavillions Ln., on the north side of Fair Oaks Blvd. between Howe and Fulton, 916/929-4422, a deli with 20 cut-above sandwiches, and a number of popular take-out dinner items (menu changes weekly). Others swear by Corti Brothers at 5810 Folsom Blvd., 916/736-3800 (kitchen 916/736-3801, deli 916/736-3802, wine 916/736-3803), which carries every gourmet menu item imaginable, excellent meats, fine produce, cheeses and deli items, and a wide selection of fine wines. Deli selections abound, everything from roast beef sandwiches to carrot and raisin salad. Sacramento also has Trader Joe's, the first at 2601 Marconi (at Fulton) in the Town and Country Village shopping center, 916/481-8797—much cheaper for eclectic staples and gourmet fare. Closer to downtown in East Sacramento is the new Trader Joes's in East Sacramento, 50th St. and Folsom Blvd., next door to Burr's Fountain and across from Long's Drugs.

Burgers and Road Food

Picture yourself speeding through town, racing to or from Tahoe, San Francisco, L.A., and suddenly in need of serious fuel—road food, a truly good hamburger, say, or memorable pizza. Sacramento has some exceptional pit-stop possibilities, none all that far from a major freeway.

Probably the best burger stop around is Ford's Real Hamburgers at 1948 Sutterville Rd. (just a few blocks east of I-5, on the south side of Land Park near the zoo, at Freeport Blvd.), 916/452-6979. Since everything's cooked to order (or medium, if you don't specify otherwise), you may have to sit down on the patio and wait awhile. The toasted sourdough buns are slathered in Ford's sweet special sauce. Depending on your cholesterol count, choose between the humongous one-pound burger, hefty third-pound burger, and kid-sized burger. All are a bit pricey but worth the money; cheese (Swiss, cheddar, or American) and other additions (such as bacon) cost extra. And here, even a small order of fries is pretty large. Open daily (for lunch only on Sunday). There's another Ford's at 6092 Garfield Ave., 916/944-4810.

Also locally beloved, if you find yourself anywhere near Broadway and the Tower Records neighborhood (just north of Land Park), is **Willie's Hamburgers** at 2415 16th St. (on the alley, a half-block north of Broadway), 916/444-2006, something of a stylistic River City hybrid of L.A.'s legendary Tommy's Original World Famous Hamburgers (noted for its dripping chiliburgers) and the In-N-Out chain. Naturally enough, the simple menu features flavorful burgers, chiliburgers, hot dogs (actually seasoned sausages), and fries. Prices here are quite reasonable. You'll know these juicy, cooked-to-order burgers (hammers), chiliburgers (slammers), and killer fries mean business once you see the napkin dispensers—actually, industrial-strength paper towel holders—on the walls. Also on display and ever popular, particularly with adults, are the "No Whining" T-shirts available as vacation souvenirs. The way it works at Willie's: You order your meal at the cash register, pay up, then move down to the other end of the counter to pick up the goods. (Be sure to grab the right bag.) Indoor seating, a few outdoor tables, and limited alley parking (or park out on the street, where you're more likely to find shade). Open daily 10 A.M. to at least midnight (until 2:30 the next morning on Friday and Saturday nights). If you'll be in Folsom, there's another Willie's there—at 823 Wales Dr., 916/983-6755—but gussied up, what with the wine bar, juice bar, and brie appetizers.

Another reasonably well-kept local secret is **Nation-Wide Freezer Meats** at 20th and H Streets, 916/444-3287, famous for its ground steakburgers, served up on hefty Muzio Bakery rolls. Open Tues.–Sat. until 7 P.M. A beloved burger hotspot in midtown is **Hamburger Mary's**, 1630 J St., 916/441-4340, where the menu includes the Meaty Mushroom Burger and the Hawaiian Burger. If downtown and looking to get malled, head for the Downtown Plaza and the retro-style **Johnny Rockets** at Downtown Plaza, 916/444-3404, just upstairs from the River City Brewing Company and next to the United Artists theater complex. It's hard to miss

with the burgers here—the St. Louis, with Swiss cheese, bacon, and grilled onions, is ever popular—but there's more, from veggie burgers to egg salad sandwiches. An even more entertaining sit-down burger scene is at the other end of the mall. For that glittery and boisterous rock-star fantasy, the place is Sacramento's own **Hard Rock Cafe** at Seventh and K Streets, 916/441-5591.

If nothing but an **In-N-Out** burger will do, at last report greater Sacramento featured several outposts—one at 3501 Truxel Rd., another at 2475 Sunrise Blvd. in Rancho Cordova (east of Sacramento proper via Hwy. 50), and the third in Elk Grove (south of Sacramento via I-5), at 9188 E. Stockton Boulevard. New In-N-Outs are popping up all over Northern and Central California now, however, so for an up-to-date list, call 800/786-1000 or see www.in-n-out.com.

Sacramento's legendary Merlino's Orange Freeze, particularly popular on sizzling summer days for its fresh-squeezed fruit freezes, is no more. The secret family recipe has been resurrected, however, at **Merlino's Freeze**, 3200 Folsom Blvd. (extension of Capitol Avenue), 916/731-4000. Orange may have disappeared from the title but there's plenty on Merlino's walls—and in Merlino's signature freeze flavor. Sacramentans from all walks of life also line up to slurp down lemon, strawberry, pineapple, and black raspberry freezes (plus the flavor of the month). Great deli sandwiches (including veggie), soups, and salads are available, too. In summer, you can get Merlino's freezes at River Cats ball games and (at last report) at an outpost in Old Sac, too.

Pizza

A local pizza hot spot, typically at or near the top of the annual "Best of Sacramento" lists, is **Original Pete's** in Midtown at 2001 J St. (20th and J), 916/442-6770, popular for its thick-crust pizzas. (There's another Original Pete's in Elk Grove at 8785 Center Pkwy., 916/689-3300.) Also a Midtown classic is **Zelda's Original Gourmet Pizza** at 1415 21st St., 916/447-1400, *the* place for fantastic Chicago-style pizza accompanied by abundant attitude and somewhat bizarre charm. South of Land Park and the Sacramento Zoo you can get the real thing—New

York–style—at **Giovanni's** in the South Hills shopping center, 5924 S. Land Park Dr., 916/393-7001. Also immensely popular: **Steve's Place Pizza,** 813 Howe Ave., 916/920-8600. Stylish wood-fired pizzas also star at upscale local eateries around town, including Paragary's.

Coffee

Just about the coolest place around is Midtown's **Naked Lounge,** snuggled downstairs in a restored Victorian-era grocery at 15th and Q Streets, 916/442-0174. There's no physical nakedness here, though, except for some of the art. With any luck at all, though, souls may be bared from time. The lounge is stuffed with overstuffed furniture and art, serves the best espresso in town (and other well-brewed, fair trade-certified coffees), and is open daily 7 A.M.–11 P.M. Also unique in Midtown is the **True Love Coffeehouse,** 2406 J St., 916/492-9002, a late-night art and music scene (open until 2 A.M. on weekends) that welcomes even boomer-aged geezers. Show up at midnight on Friday or Saturday for Waffle Time, when you can order big Belgian waffles with your choice of a couple dozen toppings. Like IHOP, only cool.

Midtown's original hip coffee hangout, **Java City,** 1800 Capitol Ave., 916/444-5282, has gone corporate (owned by an Irish company, at last report) but it's still endlessly popular. You'll find Java Citys all over the place. Another established see-and-be-seen scene in Midtown is the time-honored and low-key **Weatherstone Coffee & Tea Company,** also owned by Java City, 812 21st St., 916/443-6340. Whether anybody sees you or not, try those chocolate-dipped macaroons and Key West bars. There are Starbucks all over the place, of course—more than 20, at last count—and a surprising number of java drive-throughs. If you find yourself craving caffeine in Gourmet Gulch, Sacramento even has a **Peet's,** Berkeley's fabled java joint, at 2580 Fair Oaks Blvd. (near Blockbuster) between Watt and Howe, 916/485-7887.

Desserts and Treats

Wonderful desserts are available all around town. See restaurant listings above—including the Black Cat Café—for possibilities. A classic destination for ice cream in Sacramento, **Gunther's,** 2801 Franklin Blvd., 916/457-6646, is beloved for its 1940s neon and other old-timey affectations. Just like the good ol' days, Gunther's is unconcerned about cholesterol and proud of it, serving 16 percent butterfat ice cream, shakes, sundaes, and banana splits. Open until 10 P.M. in summer. Also in East Sacramento, **Artie's Star-Lite Fountain,** at 3839 J St. (39th and J), 916/457-1155, offers "the galaxy's best" ice cream plus the *real* real thing—Coca-Cola from a fountain—along with more classics, like cherry and vanilla Cokes, banana splits, and hot fudge sundaes. And for a dime, the kids can ride the rocket ship. Near Land Park and the Sacramento Zoo, **Vic's** at 3199 Riverside Blvd., 916/448-0892, is the place for sundaes, shakes, summer cones, and people-watching. People line up for seasonal specials, too, like fresh cranberry sorbet and peppermint stick ice cream during the holiday season.

At family-run **Fog Mountain Candy Company,** 2019 Q Street, 916/448-4140 or 800/719-9889, www.fogmountaincandy.com, the gourmet goodies include the handmade white toffee, almond toffee slathered with white chocolate then coated with chopped almonds. Nummy. Other wonders: peanut brittle, chocolate peanut crunch, dark or white chocolate peanut butter squares, traditional English toffee, triple-chocolate toffee chip cookies, and candied walnuts and pecans. Sprectacular sandwiches served, too. Open weekdays 10 A.M.–5:30 P.M.

Rick's Dessert Diner, 2322 K St., 916/444-0969, offers truly decadent desserts in a 1950s-retro atmosphere—apple and other fresh-baked pies, carrot cake, and the infamous midnight torte. If you find yourself near the Sacramento Zoo or anywhere near the Land Park neighborhood, don't miss fabulous French-style **Freeport Bakery** just south of the Freeport Market at 2966 Freeport Blvd. (Hwy. 160), 916/442-4256, a popular daytime neighborhood coffee-and-pastry hangout where the fresh fruit tarts—if they still have any—are a starring attraction. Nice fresh-baked bread selection, too.

GREAT VALLEY & THE DELTA

EATING IN OLD SAC AND DOWNTOWN

Old Sacramento

Pleasant for a quick cuppa and scones or a light lunch is **Steamers Coffee Roasting Co.** at 101 K. St. (Front and K Streets), 916/448-9404, where a few tables outside offer great people-watching. For good, fresh Mexican, try **Ramona's Comida Mexicana** inside the Sidelines Sports Bar, 1023 Front St., 916/447-9227. Try the chile verde super burrito or the flautas.

Something of a neighborhood old-timer and immensely popular for pre–River Cats chow downs, **California Fat's Asia Grill & Dim Sum Bar** at 1015 Front St., 916/441-7966, still makes a major splash. The indoor waterfall remains, but in the new millennium every other aspect of the restaurant's interior has been dramatically transformed. The kitsch is gone, replaced by gold rush–era brick, seasoned timbers, wood floors, and forests of bamboo and palms. The menu is more traditionally Asian, too, from the dim sum sampler and spicy fried calamari to honey walnut prawns (a family specialty). The signature dish here, though, is rack of lamb. All entrées are served family-style. Great desserts, full bar, value-conscious California wine list. The **Fat City Bar and Cafe** next door, 1001 Front (at J St.), 916/446-6768, is a more relaxed relative with casual Victorian café style, housed in the 1849 building once home to Sam Brannan's general store. Some classic Fat family recipes show up on the menu, but here you can also get a South-western veggie wrap, chicken pot pie, old-fashioned meatloaf, and the Fat City Hamburger. Open for lunch and dinner daily, also for brunch on Saturday and Sunday.

Feeling crabby? New along the waterfront is campy, family-friendly **Joe's Crab Shack,** 1210 Front St., 916/553-4249, predictably famous for its crab. "Rug rat" menu, too. Still a star in Old Sacramento is **Rio City Cafe** near the Tower Bridge, housed in an open, airy, and inviting replica of a gold rush–era freight warehouse on the river at 1110 Front St., 916/442-8226. South-western entrées have been replaced by California-style Mediterranean—everything from Rio City's beloved, diet-busting sourdough cheese loaf to "drunken" ribeye and linguine with prawns and chicken-apple sausage. Wonderful house-made desserts. Full bar, sophisticated California wine list. Weather permitting, try to get a table out on the deck—perfect for Huck Finn fantasies. Open for lunch Mon.–Sat., dinner nightly, and brunch on Sunday. Reservations wise.

Still fine for fine dining Old Sac–style is **The Firehouse,** a local landmark at 1112 Second St., 916/442-4772. Known for decades as the place to go for rococo atmosphere and rich, heavy American and French fare, the Firehouse does somehow resemble a museum. But lately this particular brick Victorian, once home to Sacramento's Engine Company No. 3, has lightened up all the way around, in keeping with changing tastes and attitudes. Some of its classics are still on the menu—crab cakes, steak Diane—but so are more contemporary and light-hearted continental selections. From a variety of continents. Dungeness crab (in season) is big, or try lavender salmon, almond-encrusted chicken breast, or pan-roasted sea bass. At lunch, sample the cheeseburger with smoked bacon and caramelized red onions. Drop in 3–7 P.M. weekdays for happy hour, and specialties such as sweet Dungeness crab cakes with a Thai chili butter sauce. Open for dinner Tues.–Sat. (reservations advised), for lunch week-days only; lunch in the inviting patio courtyard when the weather's balmy. The very romantic **Pilothouse** restaurant onboard Old Sacramento's *Delta King,* 1000 Front St., 916/441-4440, once served traditional French, but these days the menu runs to regional American, both traditional and contemporary. Seafood, shellfish, and fish are often the best bets here. Full bar, wine list. Open Mon.–Sat. for lunch, daily for dinner, and Sunday for brunch. Valet parking available, but you can also park on the street or try the public lots near the Tower Bridge.

Yet these days true Kings fans—Sacramento Kings, that is—will probably head to long, narrow **Tunel 21,** 926 Second St., 916/447-7577 a dark, fairly loud restaurant and club scene owned by Ana Divac (wife of Vlade Divac, the Kings' No. 21), where the food plays second fiddle to the club atmosphere, celebrity seekers, and all those

TVs, overstuffed couches, and red velvet-covered pool table. Fabulous desserts, though. Head for the quiet outdoor patio to enjoy them.

To appreciate some truly eclectic decorative touches—typically without the celebrity scene—for a nightcap stroll over to **Fanny Ann's Saloon** at 1023 Second St., 916/441-0505. Stuff hangs everywhere, or lurches out from the walls—everything from a circa-1925 fire department pumper truck, the fish tank fashioned from a gas pump, and a rhinoceros head to baseball memorabilia, license plates, and washboards. (And you thought *your* place was getting cluttered.) Or try the **Hogshead Brewery & Pub,** Sacramento's oldest in the genre, at 114 J St., 916/443-2739. At last report the beloved local Cajun rockers, the Beer Dawgs, were still howlin' here, acoustically speaking; expect live entertainment Wed.–Sat. nights (small cover).

Over the River

If you crave culinary adventure in West Sacramento, just across the river, the best place anywhere for garlic steak sandwiches (filet mignon on a roll) is **Club Pheasant,** 1822 Jefferson Blvd., 916/371-9530, a folksy family-style Italian restaurant (and unofficial community center) two miles south of I-80 on Jefferson Boulevard. The Pheasant is famous for its ravioli, too. There are other menu choices on this side of the river, too, including family-owned **Carol's** near Raley Field at 1201 W. Capitol Ave., 916/372-4631, where breakfast—French toast, blueberry pancakes, omelettes, and bacon and eggs—is the best part of the day (breakfast and lunch served), and **Emma's Taco House,** "the House of 36 Combination Dinners" at 1617 Sacramento Ave., 916/371-1151, where the beef tamale, posole, and chicken enchilada in tomatillo sauce are all best bets. There's another Emma's in downtown Sacramento, at 723 K Street.

Also in West Sacramento, featured in the May/June 2003 issue of *Saveur* magazine, is Laotian/Thai **Vientiane,** 2480 W. Capitol Ave., 916/373-1556—just the place for green chicken curry, stuffed chicken wings, beef or pork laap, and Thai-style green papaya salad. Very good, very reasonable. Open Mon.–Sat. for lunch and dinner. Another surprise is Austrian/German **Café Vienna,** at home in a strip mall, 1229 Merkley Ave. (off Jefferson), 916/371-9560, where the buffet lunch is such a deal. Dig into an astonishing selection—all kinds of sausages, chicken in wine sauce, potato dumplings, garlic mashed potatoes, breaded pork cutlets—for under $10. Don't miss the desserts, including unbelievable lemon squares and chocolate Amaretto mousse. Open weekdays for lunch (11 A.M.–2 P.M.), Mon.–Sat. for dinner.

Just a hop, skip, and a jump north from Old Sac via I-5 and the Garden Highway takes you to the Sacramento River Complex—a hard-partyin' collection of riverside restaurants, bars, and barges, including Cajun-flavored, river-themed **Crawdad's River Cantina,** 1375 Garden Hwy., 916/929-2268, and the **Virgin Sturgeon,** 1577 Garden Hwy., 916/921-2694. The onetime foodie fish palace Jammin' Salmon is now Tokyo Fro's **Sushi on the River,** 1801 Garden Hwy., 916/929-2525, a rockin' river scene that nonetheless treats fish and seafood with care and courtesy.

Near Downtown

There's a bit of everything south of downtown. Beyond Broadway, the old Hereford House steakhouse (near the south end of the City Cemetery) is running with a new herd. Even the landmark fiberglass Hereford over the entrance has been "redecorated." Stylish as all get out, the **Riverside Grill,** 2633 Riverside Blvd., 916/448-9988, showcases a cowhide-lined horsehoe bar and a postmodern patio complete with a copper-sheeted wall of water and fascinating three-level fireplace. Just about everything at the Riverside is hearty, from the delectable roasted baby back ribs in espresso barbecue sauce to the BLT with apple-smoked bacon, the lobster ravioli, and the spit-roasted chicken with fried lemons. For dessert, try crème brûlée cheesecake or the spectacular individual Key lime pie.

Sacramento's only Indonesian restaurant is **Balinesia Asian Bistro,** 3071 Freeport Blvd., 916/447-8388, serving a fascinating combination of Malaysian, Thai, Chinese, Filipino, Indian, and Pakistani flavors and cuisines. Start with something reasonably familiar, like chicken satay or the Indonesian egg rolls, then sample the *rijstaffel* (Dutch for "rice table"), rice served with a variety of distinctive side dishes. Intriguing desserts, too.

On the way to Sacramento Executive Airport is another real find—immensely popular **Jumbo Seafood Restaurant,** 5651 Freeport Blvd. (near Claudia), 916/391-8221, which serves authentic Chinese seafood—everything from seafood hot and sour soup and salt-baked prawns to clams in black bean sauce. Nonseafood lunch specials are about $5. Another treat, for fans of Irish pubs, is **Brownie's Lounge,** still father south at 5858 S. Land Park Dr., 916/424-3058, where the steaks are famous and the specials are *special*—hand-crafted sausages and sauerkraut or baby back ribs on Wednesday, corned beef (with cabbage or on a sandwich) on Thursday, seafood on Friday.

If you find yourself hungry in the Sierra-Curtis neighborhood (just northeast of Land Park and the Sacramento Zoo), consider a stop at **Cafe Melange,** at 2700 24th St. (at Second Ave.) 916/451-2312, open daily 6:30 A.M.–11 P.M. This cool neighborhood coffee house and bakery, which started life as sibling to Midtown's New Helvetia, is also a great little café, serving quiche, salads, sandwiches, and various specials. A bit farther afield, **El Novillero** at 4216 Franklin Blvd., 916/456-4287, is a popular, attractive local restaurant serving authentic Mexican specialties.

Tower Cafe, 1518 Broadway, 916/441-0222, next to the movie theater and otherwise a prominent part of the "trendy triangle" of Towers at Land Park and Broadway, isn't really a fine dining spot. It's a very good restaurant, though, with coffeehouse style (evening dress and dreadlocks okay) and globetrotting cuisine, from unforgettable Jamaican jerk chicken to Crouching Towers, Hidden Dragons (pan-seared halibut and tiger prawns with stir-fried veggies, ginger rice cakes, and black bean sauce). Unhurried breakfast and leisurely late-night dessert are pure pleasure, too. People come here to people-watch, grab a bite, and talk—about films (note art-house Tower Theater next door), about ideas, about what's going on. That's the concept, anyway, and the staff, menu, and decor reflect a one world/global

village attitude. Cultural artifacts and oddities are prominent. During decent weather, the patio outside is packed until the wee hours—the better to take in all those Broadway traffic fumes.

Despite the proliferation of good Chinese restaurants well south, Broadway is still considered Sacramento's Little Asia, *the* place to go for very good, usually inexpensive meals. A long-running local favorite for Vietnamese is **Andy Nguyen's** at 2007 Broadway (20th and Broadway), 916/736-1157, where rice noodle soup, five-spice chicken, and sautéed clams star. Lots of veggie choices. Open daily for lunch and dinner, 10 A.M.–10 P.M. There's a small parking lot out back, accessible from the alley; otherwise, jockey for a spot on a side street. Even more venerable, here for more than 30 years, is the wonderful Japanese **Fuji** at 2422 13th St. (at Broadway), 916/446-4135, where the lunch specials—bento boxes available—are a particularly good deal. Lunch served weekdays only, dinner every night (holidays included). **Fortune House** a block away at 1211 Broadway, 916/443-3128, is popular for inexpensive Cantonese, seafood specialties. Family-owned **Kamon Japanese Restaurant,** 2210 16th St. (north of Broadway, near W Street), 916/443-8888, serves a number of authentic dishes (including *tonkatsu,* breaded pork cutlet in delectable sauce) and quite respectable sushi.

The Mall

Sacramento's own **Hard Rock Cafe** is at Downtown Plaza (Seventh and K Streets), 916/441-5591—just look for the 36-foot-tall revolving neon guitar out front. The Hard Rock is a major draw at the mall these days, so don't be too surprised if there's a line to get in. The 78th link in the hard-rockin' Hard Rock chain, this one is decked out in memorabilia including an Elton John patchwork denim overcoat, one of Elvis Presley's knit shirts (embroidered with peacocks), and one of Bob Dylan's harmonicas, complete with holder. Not to mention the World War I German/Prussian iron cross once worn by Jimi Hendrix. Beyond the ubiquitous merchandise and catalogs, the point here is the museum-like atmosphere—an inimitable, ear-splitting commercial homage to rock 'n' roll. If you're here to eat, expect mostly meat-and-potatoes diner fare, from burgers and ribs to chicken and T-bone steaks. There are a few culinary alternatives, though, such as the veggie burger, grilled fajitas, and Chinese chicken salad. But who really comes here for the food, eh? For more burgers and such, there's **Johnny Rockets** at the west end of the mall.

Also at the mall, immensely popular, and quite good, is the semi-industrial **River City Brewing Co.** near the west end, 916/447-2739, serving eclectic European-influenced fare along with its sandwiches, salads, and oak-oven-fired pizzas. Favorites inspired by the American Southwest include the Santa Fe snow crab cakes. Great desserts, too, along with a bevy of award-winning brews. (Beer enthusiasts, please note that the Pyramid Alehouse and the Fox & Goose pub are also downtown; for details, see below.) Open for lunch and dinner daily, late-night menu available at the bar. Early birds, River City also opens for coffee and pastries in the A.M. Definitely high end for dinner at the mall is **Morton's of Chicago** (see Top Drawer Downtown below).

Inexpensive and Midrange

Pennisi's Deli, 1237 J St., 916/448-5610, started way back when as a neighborhood grocery. With its cold cases stuffed with quality salads, pastas, cheeses, and meats, there's no place better for a deli lunch. Typically some two dozen sandwich selections—from a house-made chicken salad san to genuine New Orleans–style muffuletta—fill out the sandwich board, and there are daily specials, too. Open weekdays 7:30 A.M.–5:30 P.M., Saturday 9 A.M.–4 P.M. Also been-there-forever **Amarin Thai Cuisine** at 900 12th St. (12th and I Streets), 916/447-9063, features an amazingly varied menu with such things as spicy eggplant and angel wings. Open 11 A.M.–9 P.M. on weekdays, from noon on weekends. Closer to Midtown but equally wonderful for vegetarian lunch—Middle Eastern, this time—is long-running **Juliana's Kitchen** at 1401 G St. (14th and G), 916/444-0966, also open weekdays only, 11 A.M.–3 P.M. Falafel sandwiches (or pita with fried cauliflower, fried zucchini, or hummus) and the combination plate are best bets, but don't pass up the soups and salads. For the less adven-

turous, mainstream deli-style sandwiches are available. **Texas Mexican Restaurant,** 1114 Eighth St., 916/443-2030, serves the real thing, from the handmade flour tortillas and horchata to tasty chiles relleno. Open weekdays 8 A.M.–3 P.M.

The homegrown **Fox & Goose Public House,** housed in the onetime Fuller Paint and Glass building at 1001 R St. (a few blocks south of downtown proper at 10th and R), 916/443-8825, is also a venerable downtown destination—and the closest thing to a British pub you'll find in these parts. Bangers and mash? Ploughman's lunch? Cornish pasties? Welsh rarebit? It's all here (and all very reasonably priced) along with an impressive selection of European and English beers (13 on tap). Open weekdays for breakfast and lunch; Mon.–Sat for dinner (bar menu) and live entertainment; and weekends for brunch. No reservations, so at peak times be prepared to wait.

There's a new pub in town, right downtown in the old Ransohoff department store building on the K Street Mall. This slick and shiny yet quite casual sibling of Seattle's **Pyramid Alehouse, Brewery & Restaurant,** close to both the Capitol and the convention center at 1029 K St., 916/498-9800, offers beer scenester bliss. About 15 beers are on tap; if you're undecided, start with a five-beer sampler. "Local" Alehouse beers—brewed and served only in Sacramento—include K Street Nitro Stout (aerated with nitrogen instead of carbon dioxide), Capitol Park Porter, and River Town Belgian White. The menu otherwise features pizzas, burgers and meaty "brewer's plates," ribs, and more. Open from 11 A.M. daily. Brewery tours available. Sacramento also has an outpost of **Il Fornaio Cucina Italiana** on the ground floor of the Wells Fargo Building, 400 Capitol Mall, 916/446-4100, open for lunch and dinner weekdays, for dinner nightly.

If you're downtown looking for politicians in their native habitats—hey, it happens—don't overlook stunning, museum-like **Frank Fat's,** 806 L St., 916/442-7092, a local political showplace almost as revered as the Capitol itself. State lawmakers once lived here, wheeling, dealing, and shoveling down New York steaks, upscale Cantonese, and scotch. (Open for lunch on weekdays only, for dinner every night. Full bar, California wine list. Reservations advised.) These days, though, most politicos are more harried, health conscious, culturally diverse, and violently partisan, so it's rare to see them schooling or otherwise congregating in large numbers anywhere. Still, according to those in the know you're likely to spot California politicians and lobbyists at **Tootsie's,** a yogurt shop at 11th and L Streets, 916/443-6494, at nearby **Chops,** and at the sophisticated **Esquire Grill** just a block from the Capitol; see below for details on the latter two.

Parking can be a challenge downtown. There are a number of public parking structures, including one under the Downtown Plaza mall and another at 10th and L Streets.

Top Drawer

Look for the sky-high blue neon spire and you'll find sizzling, cosmopolitan **Esquire Grill,** down below on the ground floor of the 26-story Esquire Plaza Building, 1213 K St., 916/448-8900, at the east end of the K Street Mall. The classic American fare served up from the open kitchen of this supper club–style steakhouse is contemporary and accomplished: succulent spit-roasted ribeye, grilled Niman Ranch pork chops with cider glaze, and spectacular seafood, such as grilled yellowtail in red pepper sauce and seared ahi with soy vinaigrette and toasted sesame seeds. Full bar, classic cocktail menu, good California wine list, grand desserts (including banana cream pie). Children's menu too. Open for lunch weekdays, for dinner nightly.

Quite good nearby is **Chops Steak, Seafood & Bar,** 1117 11th St. (at L Street), Sacramento 916/447-8900, which serves prime-grade, aged beef—note the custom glass and steel aging vault—including thick prime rib and a juicy T-bone, not to mention a wonderful rack of lamb and well-prepared seafood. Impressive housemade desserts. Open weekdays for lunch, Mon.–Sat. for dinner. For pricey men's-clubby fine dining and still more unabashed meat consumption, Sacramento has its own **Morton's of Chicago** at Downtown Plaza, 521 L St. (between Fifth and Sixth), 916/442-5091. Steaks and chops are the featured attractions—select

SOMEONE'S IN THE KITCHEN

A unique Sacramento foodie experience is **The Kitchen** at 2225 Hurley Way, Ste. 101 (north of Fair Oaks Blvd., east off Howe Ave.), 916/568-7171, www.thekitchenrestaurant.com, which is certainly not guilty of false advertising. More kitchen and catering business than restaurant, here you show up and practically participate in the demonstration four-course dinners so marvelously staged by Randall Selland and Nancy Zimmer. Performance art for the palate.

What's served is never the same; each week's New American menu determined by what's best and freshest. One summer menu started with heirloom tomato soup, Dungeness crab–crispy bread salad, and 'lite' herbed goat cheese. Entrees included wood-roasted organic chicken with pasta, apple, walnuts, ricotta, lemon, and grilled-duck consommé; local halibut with lobster-infused sticky rice, sashimi-grade bay scallops, mushrooms, and a lemongrass-kaffir lime broth; and buffalo tenderloin with fingerling potatoes, bacon, baby red onions and squash, and bernaise and cabernet reduction. Dessert choices included farm-fresh fruit; a peach tart with bittersweet chocolate; house-made sorbets; and caramel tuiles.

The Kitchen offers one seating per night, with a maximum 48 guests, three or four nights each week. Reservations are taken up to six months in advance, and new opportunities open up daily. Call or show up in person early (9 A.M.). The evening's many pleasures will cost you—$115 per person, at last report, plus tax and tip. Wine list and retail-priced wines available, or bring your own ($18 per bottle corkage). On Wine & Dine Wednesday, recommended wines are included for $35 extra.

your own, from the presentation tray—along with lobster, swordfish, and chicken. Full bar, California wine list. Open nightly for dinner. Also clubby and long a romantic favorite Downtown is **Dawson's** at the Hyatt Regency, 1209 L St., 916/321-3600, a chop house, bistro, and martini bar. Full bar, California wine list. Open weekdays only for lunch, Mon.–Sat. for dinner. Valet parking advisable.

EATING IN MIDTOWN

Inexpensive

Midtown has some great inexpensive Mexican restaurants, quite popular. For contemporary, good-for-you Mexican—great flavor without so many unhealthy fats—try **Tres Hermanas** at 2416 K St. (at 24th), 916/443-6919, beloved for its posole and pork tamales as well as health-conscious selections. At **Taqueria Taco Loco,** 2326 J St. (at 23rd), 916/447-0711, people go crazy for chile verde burritos and generous tacos (try the carnitas, or charbroiled chicken). Another best bet is **Una Mas Mexican Grill** at 19th and J Streets, 916/448-2900, where the fish tacos, steak tacos, chicken tostadas, and hefty burritos are among the shining stars. Wash 'em down with a glass of strawberry lemonade. Part of the same small chain is **Pescado's** at 2801 P St. (28th and P Streets), 916/452-7237, beloved for its shrimp and fish tacos and its machaco burrito, not to mention burritos, tostadas, and veggie and other specials. The combination plates here are a real treat. Wildly popular for more mainstream Mexican fare—a perfect place to take mom and dad—is **Ernesto's Mexican Food** teetering on the edge of Midtown at 16th and S Streets, 916/441-5850. For a special treat with your combo plates, try a margarita with 100-percent agave tequila—something you definitely won't find everywhere. Lunch and dinner served daily, brunch on Sunday beginning at 9 A.M.

Casual **Cafe Bernardo** at 2726 Capitol Ave. (at 27th), 916/443-1180, part of the Paragary's local restaurant empire, is not the unbelievably cheap, tasty, and hip counterculture hot spot it used to be. But it's still Eurostyle Californian, still inexpensive, and still pretty darn good, open both early and late for coffee and lighter fare. Winners here include the potato-red pepper soup, the grilled salmon BLT, and well-prepared salads. Open daily 7 A.M.–10 P.M. (until 11 P.M. on weekend nights). There are CBs in Roseville and Davis, too. Inside the café, on the corner or 28th and Capitol, is Paragary's incredibly cool **Monkey Bar,** 916/442-8490, open until the wee hours.

Ever popular for burgers and good brewskis—always packed at lunch, and most other times—is the **Rubicon Brewing Co.** at 2004 Capitol Mall, 916/448-7032. Everybody comes here. Before or after sampling local favorites on the beer menu—watch the brewing process through the glass walls—chow down on Rubicon wings, chicken fajitas, fish and chips, crisscross fries, sandwiches, or any of the daily specials. Breakfast served on weekends. If you really like the beer, you can get a Rubicon "box"—a full gallon (refillable) to go. Good food and lots of it is what you'll get at hip, hofbrau-style **Jack's Urban Eats,** 1230 20th St. (at Capitol Ave.), 916/444-0307, from the grand sandwiches—the roasted turkey, chicken, and flank steak are cooked and carved here—and unbeatable fries to veggie selections and big, bouncing salads. Most everything is $5–7.

The affordable late-night menu at **Ink,** the tattoo-art café on the corner once anchored by super-starched Twenty-Eight, across from Paragary's at 28th and N, 916/456-2800, includes comfort foods such as breakfast burritos, Texas toast, and grilled ham sandwiches. Also popular with latenighters is the **Black Pearl Oyster Bar,** 2724 J St. (27th and J), 916/440-0214, which offers a late menu (until 1 A.M.) most nights and a very late menu (11 P.M.–3 A.M.) on Friday and Saturday nights. There are plenty of Midtown pizza joints, too. For suggestions, see Capital Pizza above.

Midrange

Sliding slightly up the affordability scale on the Midtown food chain—though here as elsewhere, the tab depends on what you order—at hot **Tapa the World,** 2115 J St. (at 21st), 916/442-4353, Spanish tapas are the main attraction, natch, from grilled organic vegetables, steamed mussels, or filet mignon to *quesos español del dia* (Spanish cheeses of the day) and *calamares fritos* (fried cala-mari). *paella mixta,* empañada specials, and oc-casional flamenco guitar add to the menu. Open daily 11:30 A.M.–midnight. For Nuevo Latino there's also **Habañero Cava Latina** (also at 2115 J, a kind of a minimalist Midtown minimall), 916/492-0333, a cavelike wine cellar believably "of Havana." Here, you can get the wonderful spices, sauces, and citrus-based dressings of life in the far south with a lighter, contemporary touch—and without all that artery-hardening lard, since olive and other cooking oils are used in-stead. Marvelous chicken mole, very imaginative tamales, and other hearty selections star on the en-trée menu. But don't neglect the starters, which alone could make a memorable meal. Beer and wine; takeout available. Street parking. Open Mon.–Fri. from lunch until late (11 P.M. or mid-night), and on weekends from 5 P.M. An older sibling to Habañero is **Aioli Bodega Española** at 1800 L St. (at 18th), 916/447-9440, which serves wonderful regional Spanish in stylish surround-ings—such things as seafood stew, ribeye steak with anchovy glaze, and vegetarian paella. Or make a meal out of the exceptional tapas, both hot and cold. Full bar. Lunch served Mon.–Sat., din-ner nightly. Street parking; reservations wise.

Centro Cocina Mexicana, 2730 J St., 916/442-2552, is another Paragary creation, this one serving imaginative, California-chic Mexican fare blended with some of the loud local seeing-and-being-seen scene (a big reason for Centro's popularity). On a hot day people suck down Cocina's first-rate margaritas, made with various fresh fruit juices, like mineral water—and they hardly ever complain about paying good money for chips and salsa. The food is worth it, though, starting with appetizers such as the Michoacan *uchepos,* tortilla soup, and unforgettable que-sadillas. Daily seafood specials, wonderful desserts—including coconut pie. And Centro's style can spice up slow table conversation. The marvelous guacamole here, for example, is served in a *molcajete,* a three-legged stone mortar used in Mexico for grinding spices. Full bar too, with plenty of stylish tequilas on hand. Open weekdays for lunch, nightly for dinner. If you seek some post-feast fun among Sacramento sophisticates,

head upstairs to Paragary's **Blue Cue,** 916/442-7208, an unbelievably cool pool hall.

Glittering **City Treasure Restaurant** at 1730 L St., 916/447-7380, started out as a relaxed deli and has evolved into a sophisticated eatery—a city treasure indeed, all decked out in local art, hand-painted fabrics, and fresh flowers. The long global menu features tortilla prawn salad, jam-balaya, smoked salmon fettucini, pad Thai, and meatloaf—choice enough for anyone. Desserts are delightful, from the crème brûlée to the chocolate bread pudding. Exciting California wine list. Open weekdays for lunch, nightly for dinner. Reservations wise.

Then there's cheerful **Celestin's Caribbean Restaurant & Voodou Lounge** happily at home in new digs at 1815 K St., 916/444-2423. Ce-lestin's celebrates—you guessed it—bold French-Caribbean fare, from sea scallops in creamy coconut lime sauce—almost 30 different gumbos are available here—to lambi (conch) or shrimp Creole, chicken curry, and grio. Wonderful grilled snapper. Waistline- or budget-conscious vegetarians, dig right in to the low-fat peasant plate. For dessert, how 'bout some coconut or Key lime pie? Open Tues.–Fri. for lunch at last report, Tues.–Sun. for dinner.

How 'bout a Californian with New York atti-tude? One of the best places in town for hefty, homestyle meatloaf, pot roast, lasagna and other upscale comfort food is **Moxie,** inside the one-time Burger Basket at 2028 H St. (between 20th and 21st Streets), 916/443-7585, named after a tangy late 1800s soft drink marketed in Maine as nerve medicine, to prevent softening of the brain. The brain won't go soft here, whether you go with the homey entrées or the bold California-style selections. Daily specials at lunch and dinner, good desserts. Beer and wine. Open weekdays for lunch, Tues.–Sun. for dinner (reservations essential on weekend nights). There's a Moxie Jr. hidden away in East Sacramento at 3440 C St., 916/341-0905. For homemade European and Hungarian comfort food, try **Café Marika,** 2011 J St., 916/442-0405.

A best bet in Midtown for a quick, tasty meal is fun **Michelangelo's Italian Art Restaurant** at 1725 I St., 916/446-5012, where one of the first things you'll notice is a Sacramento version of *The Creation of Adam*. The fare here runs to muscular East Coast–style Italian, from spaghetti and meatball (yes, just one, quite large) and spinach ravioli to steak Michelangelo. Full bar. Open weekdays for lunch, nightly for dinner.

Top Drawer

The onetime brick machine shop at 2000 Capitol Ave. (20th and Capitol), previously the popular Italian restaurant Americo's, is now a sunnier, more stylish bistro, though the muralistic monument to Bacchus remains. **The Waterboy,** 916/498-9891, adjacent to the Rubicon Brewing Co., cheerfully serves up sophisticated provincial French and American fare. One of Sacramento's best restaurants, the Waterboy is beloved for its pizzettas, daily fish and seafood specials, entrées such as chicken pot pie (or chicken with prosciutto and chard), and desserts including chocolate meringue roulade cake. Exceptional service. Monthly changing menu, beer and wine only.

Beloved **Paragary's Bar & Oven** at 1401 28th St. (28th and N), 916/457-5737, is known for its exceptional California-style northern Mediterranean entrées—pastas, seafood, grilled meats, brick-oven pizzas—and relaxed yet sophisticated atmosphere. The entrée menu changes regularly. A star here is the Starlight Courtyard, a onetime parking area transformed into a Mediterranean paradise, complete with fountains and olive trees—a truly marvelous patio dining setup. Lunch served weekdays only, dinner nightly. Full bar, good wine list. Free valet parking (plenty of lots nearby).

Still, the most elegant and extravagant night out for Sacramento residents is dinner at exceptional **Biba,** 2801 Capitol Ave. (28th and Capitol), 916/455-2422, noted for its Tuscan tilt but also quite respectful to Southern Italian traditions—and easily the most cosmopolitan restaurant for many miles around. The menu changes with the seasons, and proprietor Biba Caggiano—she of the popular *Biba's Italian Kitchen* cooking show on The Learning Channel, and the author of a multitude of Italian cookbooks—is always introducing new wonders. Specialties include gnocchi, tortelloni (giant tortellini) in cream tomato sauce, smoked-salmon fettucine, and carefully prepared (in-house) desserts. Full bar, excellent wine list. Open weekdays for lunch, Mon.–Sat. for dinner. Reservations all but mandatory. Public parking adjacent.

EATING IN EAST SACRAMENTO
Inexpensive

Casual neighborhood eateries are quite popular throughout East Sacramento. Even if you arrive at beloved **Queen of Tarts Bakery & Cafe** in the McKinley Park neighborhood, 3608 McKinley Blvd. (at 36th St.), 916/451-3102, with the intention of limiting yourself to a savory salad or soup and sandwich at lunch, in no time you'll be drooling over the delectable sweets on display. So you may as well give in and order a lemon tart, some shortbread, or a cinnamon roll to go. Great stop for coffee and breakfast pastries, too. Open weekdays 6:30 A.M.–7 P.M., weekends until 3 P.M.

Otherwise, just about everyone's casual favorite is cool **Black Cat Café,** 5140 Folsom Blvd. (at 52nd Street), 916/451-9100, where the food is fast, top quality, and reasonably priced. Savory meat, cheese, and vegetable crepes ("Paris street-corner crepes") are the menu's mainstay; if you order before 11 A.M. they come served with breakfast potatoes, after 11, with a salad of mixed field greens. Or choose from the panini selections, including chicken with mozzarella cheese, marsala mushrooms, roasted peppers, and pesto sauce. There are also dessert crepes, the 10 choices including cherry and ricotta, apples in caramel sauce, and Nutella. The quiche, crème brûlée, chocolate mousse, banana-coconut tarts, and other spectacular desserts are made on-site by Casey Hayden, acclaimed pastry chef. Open 7 A.M.–2 P.M. daily (from 8 A.M. on weekends). For pizzas and pastas, try unpretentious **Café Milazzo,** 4818 Folsom Blvd., 916/454-3400, serving California-style Sicilian. Also quite European, **Rolle French Gourmet Food** at 5357 H St., 916/455-9140, is strong on seafood and fish—seafood salad, shrimp cakes, smoked salmon sandwiches—and surprisingly reasonable.

Tiny neighborhood **Nopalitos Southwest Cafe** near CSU Sacramento at 5530 H St. (near 55th St.), 916/452-8226, is open weekdays only for breakfast and lunch; show up early for lunch, or plan on takeout. For lots of food at a fair price, try the taco plate, the smothered burrito—six kinds to choose from, including veggie, swimming in either green chile or ranchero sauce—or the chile verde, which is served up in various incarnations, including "tamale in a bowl." Java City coffee, great chocolate chip cookies.

Midrange

Right across the street from Rolle French Gourmet (see above) is **Selland's Market-Café,** 5340 H St., 916/736-3333, its "handcrafted quality foods" (organic, hormone-free) served up by the talented Sacramento food lovers better known for The Kitchen (see Someone's in the Kitchen elsewhere in this chapter). You'll probably spend money here, because the seasonally changing selection is so good. Sandwiches might include marinated mushrooms and goat cheese on foccacia; leg of lamb with salsa; or citrus-and-curry marinated turkey with curry mayo, caramelized onions, and brie. There are also salads, "plates" (a selection of hot entrées with vegetables), and an unbelievable selection of hot and cold deli delights, from wood-fired teriyaki chicken wings and roast chicken stuffed with thyme to the weekly cheese plate. But save some room: there are desserts, too. Open Tues.–Sun. 10:30 A.M.–8 P.M.

East Sacramento's **33rd Street Bistro** at 3301 Folsom Blvd. (the extension of Capitol Ave., separated from Midtown by the freeway), 916/455-2233, is bright, bold, relaxed, and natural, specializing in reasonably priced seafood, heman sandwiches, and impressive salads, though you'll find Sacramento scenesters also digging into other contemporary cuisine styles. Unlike most restaurants in town, 33rd Street is open daily for breakfast, lunch, and dinner. Breakfast means omelettes and egg dishes, cracked hazelnut waffles with whipped cream and fruit, or berry griddlecakes with maple syrup. For lunch and dinner expect wood-fired pizzas, wild mushroom ravioli, shellfish chowder, coconut-crusted prawns, Uncle Bum's jerk ribs, and roasted meatloaf blend of lamb and pork sausage. Full bar, California and Oregon wine list. Reservations aren't taken, so muscle your way in.

Shining forth from the sunnied-up former site of Gallagher's Bar & Grill, **Three Sisters,** 5100 Folsom Blvd., 916/452-7442, is sister restaurant to Midtown's Tres Hermanas. Rather than duplicate everyone's favorite Hermanas' fresh traditional Mexican, here the three also serve contemporary Southwestern—rock-shrimp quesadillas, chicken chipotle, chicken tequila hornitos, steak chalupa, and more. But don't miss the chicken mole poblano, a family recipe. Full bar, Mexican beers, killer margaritas. Open for lunch and dinner daily, for breakfast (starting at 8:30 A.M.) on weekends.

Definitely doing right by its historic locale, cosmopolitan and fun **East End Bar & Grill,** 5641 J St., (at 57th), 916/452-7511, is at home in the original Shakey's Pizza Parlor. Pizza, though, is one of the choices you *won't* find on the uptown New American menu, which includes Dungeness crab sandwiches, fettucine pesto, grilled pork chops, and cedar-planked oven roasted salmon. The weekend brunch menu ranges from brie-stuffed French toast and crab cakes Benedict to soba noodles chicken salad. Full bar. Open Mon.–Sat. for lunch and dinner, on weekends for brunch.

Immensely popular and justifiably so is the **California Cafe Bar & Grill,** kissing cousin to the Blackhawk Grille and other upscale links in its chain, just a stroll from Nordstrom inside the Arden Fair mall, 1689 Arden Way, 916/925-2233. The fare here is very creative and well-executed Californian—the menu changes daily—from rock shrimp spring rolls to pancetta and portobello pizza and grilled lamb sirloin. Impressive house-made desserts. Full bar, lengthy and largely Californian wine list. Open daily for both lunch and dinner. Reservations advisable.

Inexpensive and Midrange in Gourmet Gulch

If you're on a budget but craving something spectacular from Gourmet Gulch, try **Ettore's** at 2376 Fair Oaks Blvd., 916/482-0708, a European-style bakery café well worth it for marvelous soups, salads, wood-fired pizzas, and sandwiches (including panini), everything under $10. The menu changes monthly, though the burger is so popular it never changes: hamburger with Swiss cheese and sautéed mushrooms on a cheddar scallion bun. Dinner entrées (available after 5 P.M.) are $10–15. But the real claim to fame here is dessert—elaborate and exceptional cakes, fruit tarts, and other bakery items. Don't leave without a bag-full. Open most days 6 A.M.–9 P.M. (until 10 P.M. Fri.–Sat.), and Sunday 8 A.M.–2 P.M. Also quite good and reasonably affordable is **Danielle's Creperie** at Arden Town Center (Fair Oaks and Watt), 916/972-1911, where the famous French onion soup, crepe Normande, ham and artichoke crepe, and some half-dozen veggie crepes are worth serious consideration. Danielle's is dog-friendly, too, so you can dine with well-behaved Fido at outdoor tables. Open most days 9 A.M.–9 P.M., Sun.–Mon. 9 A.M.–3 P.M.

Affordable at Loehmann's Plaza, cafeteria-style **Jack's Urban Eats 2**, 2535 Fair Oaks Blvd., 916/481-5225, offers the same substantial fare as the original Jack's on 20th Street, including great custom salads and sandwiches built from hand-carved meats.

Chinois City Cafe in the Arden Town Center, 3535 Fair Oaks Blvd., 916/485-8690, is a casual but sophisticated "fusion" descendant of Sacramento's Chinois East/West. Particularly beloved here: honey-walnut prawns with crisp red and green peppers, prawn pot stickers, the "phoenix and dragon" stir-fry, and the Mongolian beef "laughing buns." Takeout available. At dinner-only **Bandera** in University Village, 2232 Fair Oaks Blvd., 916/922-3524, hearty regional American stars—Southwestern standards such as black-bean chicken chili and chicken enchiladas (a real treat at Bandera is the spit-roasted chicken) as well as meaty entrées like tenderloin and beef ribs. Reservations not taken. Full bar.

A long-running vegetarian favorite way out there in Fair Oaks Village is the **Sunflower Natural Food Drive-In** at 10344 Fair Oaks Blvd., 916/967-4331, where the specialty nutburgers, nutty tacos, and falafels have kept folks coming for two decades and counting. And do try the yogurt shakes. Open just 11 A.M.–3 P.M. on Monday and 11 A.M.–5 P.M. Sunday, but otherwise 11 A.M.–8 P.M.

Top Drawer in Gourmet Gulch

Classy **Lemon Grass Restaurant** at 601 Munroe St. (just north of Fair Oaks Blvd., near Loehmann's Plaza), 916/486-4891, is Sacramento's reigning Vietnamese-Thai restaurant—not to mention one of the region's best, period. Particularly wonderful for vegetarians here is the monk's curry—tofu and veggies bathed in a sweet and sour coconut-milk curry garnished with fresh basil. Other signature entrées keep everyone coming back for more, including Mom's catfish in clay pot. Indeed, these days the menu tilts toward Vietnamese selections—such as pan-seared salmon with roasted shallots, tomatoes, and Vietnamese sweet and sour sauce—which is a grand thing for adventurous foodies. And quite reasonable, really, considering that chef Mai Pham of Lemon Grass is already a culinary superstar. Full bar, good wine list. Open for lunch on weekdays only, for dinner nightly. Find out more about the chef, her cooking, and her life in her two books: *Pleasures of the Vietnamese Table* and *The Best of Vietnamese and Thai Cooking*. There's a **Scott's Seafood Grill & Bar** nearby, in Loehmann's Plaza at 545 Munroe St. (at Fulton), 916/489-1822, where diners people-watch while digging into an internationally accented array of seafood specialties. Full bar, California wines (heavy on the Chardonnays). Open nightly for dinner, Mon.–Sat. for lunch.

One fine Sacramento restaurant that doesn't get nearly enough attention—most people would be hard pressed to find it, in fact—is **Bravo Ristorante Italiano**, 2333 Fair Oaks Blvd., 916/568-0494, flanked by swank Pavilions yet effectively hidden behind Swanson Cleaners. Delightful Northern Italian entrées include chicken breasts stuffed with ricotta, garlic, and spinach. House-made desserts, full bar, Californian wine list.

The onetime Paragary's at 2384 Fair Oaks Blvd. is now **Zinfandel Grille**, 916/485-7100, named after "California's own varietal" and still hip, fun, and one of the best restaurants in town. The seasonally changing menu emphasizes California-style Italian—such things as lemon risotto and prawns; braised beef short ribs; and Dungeness crab, mushroom, or eggplant and goat cheese lasagna—though the wood-fired pizzas and salads are reliable standards year-round. And how about some lemon mascarpone cheesecake or chocolate lava cake for dessert? Reservations advisable (taken for any group at lunch but only for six or more at dinner). Full bar, good California wine list. Open for lunch and dinner daily.

At white-tablecloth, colonial empire-themed **Mace's** at the Pavilions shopping center, 501 Pavilions Ln., 916/922-0222, Cal-Italian New American still stars—from the house-made ravioli and jambalaya to bacon-wrapped sea bass. Desserts are typically all-American, from the apple and coconut cream pies to the fudge brownie sundae. Lunch is served weekdays only, dinner nightly, and Sunday brunch 10 A.M.–2 P.M. Sophisticated **La Boheme** at 9634 Fair Oaks Blvd., 916/965-1071, proudly serves duck a l'orange, steak Diane, cherries jubilee, crepes Suzette, baked Alaska, and other continental classics. European and California wine list. Full bar. Open weekdays for lunch, Mon.–Sat. for dinner. Reservations wise.

EATING IN GREATER SACRAMENTO

Almost everyone's favorite for romantic ambience is landmark **Slocum House** at 7992 California St. in Fair Oaks, 916/961-7211. Once beloved for its French fare, Slocum House has gone regional American—with global accents from Asia and the Caribbean as well as Italy and France. Southwestern American and Caribbean specialties dominate, from the "high-five" tortilla soup to jerk prawns and stacked New Mexican enchiladas with chicken and red chili sauce. Or try roasted Indonesian pork chops, and wood-fired filet mignon. Vegetarians will prefer the shiitake mushroom linguine with veggies, ginger, and Chinese pesto, or the baked rigatoni gratin with mushrooms and grilled eggplant. People say Slocum House still serves the best crab cakes around, and a memorable Caesar salad. Full bar, predominantly California wine list. Open Tues.–Sun. for dinner, Tues.–Fri. for lunch, and Sunday for brunch. Reservations strongly advised.

Fast suburbanizing Elk Grove south of Sacramento also has its treasures. **Silva's Sheldon Inn,** a onetime stage stop at 9000 Grant Line Rd., 916/686-8330, attracts local cowboy hats as well as more urban fine-food fanatics with a preference for low-key class—one of the region's finest restaurants. Silva's specializes in family-style American (as in heartland) classics, from filet mignon, ribeye, and pork chops stuffed with apples to a lengthy list of fresh seafood and other specials. Desserts, like the marionberry cobbler, are worth the trip. Full bar. Open Tues.–Sun. for dinner. Other area notables include **Sunnyrose Café,** in old town Elk Grove at 9007 Elk Grove Blvd., 916/685-2233, serving impressive heartland fare—omelettes and granola, grand sandwiches, chicken-fried steak, Colorado lamb chops, well-prepared seafood, homemade pies—and nearby **Mel Dog's Café,** 9766 Waterman Rd., 916/686-4615, with a great grilled veggie sandwich—avocado, tomato, sautéed mushrooms, and Swiss cheese on Parmesan sourdough—burgers such as bleu cheese and the nitro cheddar burger (with "triple-X" hot sauce), and killer chocolate shakes. Brewpub fans flock to the award-winning **Elk Grove Brewery Restaurant,** 9085 Elk Grove Blvd., 916/685-2537, housed in the 1885 Elk General Store.

Enotria Café & Wine Bar north of Hwy. 160 at 1431 Del Paso Blvd. (at Arden Way), 916/922-6792, is a combination wine shop and sunny Mediterranean café that still somehow blends well, along with new neighborhood galleries, into this rough-edged northern Sacramento neighborhood. Possibilities on the seasonally changing menu include spinach and ricotta ravioli, pan-roasted salmon with sweet-corn succotash, and black pepper-encrusted pork tenderloin. Winner of the *Wine Spectator* grand award. Full bar, largely California wine list. Garden patio, too. Open Tues.–Sat. for dinner, for prix-fixe lunch on Friday.

ARTS AND ENTERTAINMENT

To find out what's going on while you're in town, the *Sacramento Bee*'s "Ticket" section, included in the Friday edition, is quite comprehensive. Or see www.sacbee.com. Also check out the free weekly *Sacramento News & Review* for its calendar section and current reviews. Cultural events and entertainment scheduled at **UC Davis** and **CSU Sacramento,** as well as **Sacramento City College,** are usually included in all of these listings.

Art Galleries

Second Saturday, 916/264-5558 weekdays, www.sacramento-second-saturday.org, is Sacramento's gallery crawl, scheduled on the second Saturday evening of each month and showcasing current shows at galleries primarily concentrated in the artsy Downtown-Midtown area and the new "uptown" art district on and near Del Paso Blvd., on both sides of Arden Way. In addition to the pleasures of art, refreshments and entertainment are also on tap at participating galleries. Folsom galleries also do Second Saturday, and galleries in nearby Davis have a Second Friday program—so come for the whole weekend and try to visit them all.

Central Sacramento galleries often included on Second Saturday include the contemporary **Thomas Oldham** at 1729 L St., 916/444-9624, and **Excentrique Art Gallery** at 1409 R St., 916/446-1786, specializing in functional art and whimsy. Perhaps the most gorgeous gallery space around is the very impressive **b. sakata garo,** 923 20th St., 916/447-4276. The imaginative inaugural show here, "Generations," in late 1998, featured the work of well-known local artists—Wayne Thiebaud, Sandra Shannonhouse, Jimi Suzuki, Bob Brady, and Clayton Bailey—alongside the work of respective children and grandchildren. Many shows are similarly thoughtful.

Midtown's **La Raza Galeria Posada** long housed inside the old Heilbron Mansion at 704 O St., 916/446-5133, www.galeriaposada.org, celebrates Latino and Native American cultures. It will soon be celebrating a brand new gallery, too. Galeria Posada is scheduled to move (in late 2003) into new space in Paragary's Empire nightclub and restaurant complex in a former warehouse near 15th and R Streets—a very auspicious move. With its soaring ceilings and white walls, downtown's **Exploding Head Gallery,** 924 12th St. (at I Street), 916/442-8424, www.explodingheadgallery.com, exhibits contemporary paintings, ceramics, and other art.

Del Paso venues usually include the non-profit **MatrixArts** at 1518 Del Paso Blvd. (at Hawthorne), 916/923-9118, featuring the work of women artists, predominantly, and the **Center for Contemporary Art,** 1516 Del Paso, 916/927-2278. Always intriguing **Gallery Horse Cow,** 1409 Del Paso, 916/922-9142, displays self-taught art, from contemporary Southern folk art, outsider art, and "art brut" to art and artifacts from Burning Man. **Doiron Gallery,** in new space at 1819 Del Paso, 916/564-4433, www.doirongallery.com, showcases contemporary art and crafts, from original oils, acrylics, and watercolors to metal sculptures and wearable art.

If you're hankering to spend $10,000 on a cutting-edge couch, be sure to stop by the **LIMN** furniture showroom, 501 Arden Way, 916/564-2900, the Sacramento outpost of the famous South of Market shop in San Francisco. Keep an eye out, too, for **Phantom Galleries** along Del Paso—exhibitions and performance art popping up in various venues (including abandoned buildings and storefront window installations). For current Phantom info, call Uptown Arts at 916/922-2787.

Always well worth the trip is **Solomon Dubnick Gallery,** just north of the Howe Ave./Fair Oaks Blvd. intersection at 2131 Northrop Ave., 916/920-4547, www.sdgallery.com, which exhibits the paintings, sculptures, and photography of both established and up-and-coming Northern California and national artists. In Old Sacramento, always worth a stop is the **Artists' Collaborative Gallery** at 1007 Second St., 916/444-3764, www.artcollab.com, showcase for the long-running, 40-artist co-op. For art on the cheap—from $20 to $300—there's an overwhelming room full of "art from the street" at **Toyroom Gallery** in Curtis Park, a converted barn in an alley south of Sloat Way and north of Second Avenue, just east of 24th Street, 916/457-5269, www.toyroomgallery.com.

Movie Theaters

The city's virtual year-round film festival is staged at the **Tower Theater** at 16th and Broadway, 916/443-1982, noted as much for its fabulous neon and good movie food as for its foreign, art, and cult film schedule. Grab a bite before or after at the adjacent Tower Cafe—but allow plenty of time, because the wait staff is sometimes on some other (international) clock. The area is hangout heaven, too, what with Tower Records, Tower Books, and Tower Video right across the street. For more unusual movies (including documentaries), see what's playing at the elegant **Crest Theatre** downtown at 1013 K Street Mall, 916/442-7378, www.thecrest.com, a three-screen art movie house and community events magnet. Quite striking here, now that the Crest has been restored to much of its art-deco glory, are the dramatic gold-leaf ceilings; one local writer described taking in a show here as akin to sitting inside a Fabergé egg. Not only that, there's a glowing neon tower and marquee outside, too. In addition to showing movies, the Crest sponsors concerts and other special events, like the Trash Film Orgy and Mr. Lobo's Japanese Sci-Fi Supershow. Not far away is the new, improved Esquire Theater, adjacent to the Sacramento Convention Center at 13th and K Streets, 916/443-4629, unveiled in the summer of 1999 as an **Esquire IMAX Theater,** showing both 2-D and 3-D films on a screen 59 feet tall and 81 feet wide. For mainstream movie fare, there are theaters throughout greater Sacramento. Convenient for visitors is the **Downtown Plaza** theater, originally located at Fourth and J Streets, 916/442-7000, though the mall's owners are proposing a new 16-screen version near Morton's of Chicago on the mall's L Street side. Call for current details.

Performing Arts

Among local theatrical groups is the professional **Sacramento Theater Company,** 1419 H St., 916/443-6722, www.sactheatre.org, which stages challenging contemporary plays, such as Tom Stoppard's *Arcadia* and David Sedaris's *Santaland Diaries.* Sac Theatre offers a "mainstage season" in its 300-seat McClatchy Mainstage theater, mid-September to mid-May, plus performances in 90-seat Stage Two. For professional staging of new works, from *Copenhagen* to *Christmastime,* the place is **B Street Theatre** at 2727 B St., 916/443-5300, founded by actor Timothy Busfield and his brother Buck. B Street's new **Children's Theatre of California** produces professional theater for children in "B-2" at 2711 B St., 916/442-5635, and will soon occupy new

digs in Midtown near Café Bernardo, between 27th and 28th Streets.

Sacramento's historic 1915 **Guild Theater** in Oak Park, 2828 35th St. (at Third Avenue and Broadway), 916/736-1185, www.guildtheater .com or www.sthope.com, offered its first dramatic performance, Richard Broadhurst's one-act *Inside,* in August 2003. Centerpiece of NBA star Kevin Johnson's 40 Acres redevelopment project, the attractive brick theater has become a state-of-the-art performance and movie venue as well as multicultural community center for lectures and special events.

Special in summer is the annual **Sacramento Shakespeare Festival,** 916/558-2228, with performances held outdoors in the William A. Carroll Amphitheatre in William Land Park. For liberal entertainment, don't miss the **Studio Theatre** at 1028 R St., 916/446-2668, www .thestudiotheatre.net, where the musical *Six Women with Brain Death (or Expiring Minds Want to Know)* has been a big hit since the late 1990s. Other intriguing troupes abound around town, so check local events calendars to see what's playing.

California Musical Theatre, 1419 H St. (box office), 916/557-1999, www.calmt.com, offers the **The Broadway Series** of nationally touring shows and musicals during its Sept.–May season—the likes of *Flower Drum Song* and *The Producers*—with performances staged in the Community Center Theater, 1301 L Street. Then CMT's **Music Circus,** 916/557-1999, takes over during the off-season, its theater-in-the-round summer stock musicals (*Cats, Ragtime, Damn Yankees*) staged inside the new, improved circus tent on H Street—the permanent Wells Fargo Pavilion, complete with commodious seating and air-conditioning. Way cool.

Other performing arts have fallen on hard times in recent years—a trend now slowly reversing itself with increased attention from the city and local businesses. The Sacramento Symphony is no more, alas, felled by bankruptcy, though the region is filling the void. Among worthy contributors: the **California Wind Orchestra,** 916/489-2576, www.cawinds.com, a 38-piece professional "wind" ensemble (wood-

BOOMING B STREET

Ever since it mounted the stage in a downtown warehouse next to the railroad tracks, Sacramento's **B Street Theatre** has been strictly Manhattan basement, complete with subway-like rumble. Highly professional but nothing posh. The emphasis at B Street is on the plays, all new works, and the performance. *Content.* The address will change—B Street Theatre and its new children's theater program are included in Sutter Hospital's midtown expansion plans—but the innovation and professionalism will surely continue.

B Street is an outgrowth of actor Timothy Busfield's touring Fantasy Theatre for children. Busfield, better known to many as reporter Danny Concannon on *The West Wing* and (especially to aging boomers) Elliot Weston, the red-headed ad agency guy from *Thirtysomething*, started B Street with his brother Buck in the early 1990s. These

days Buck Busfield runs the show. In 2003 the theater schedule included *Rounding Third* by Richard Dresser; *Just the Guy* by stand-up comedian Jack Gallagher; the whodunit *Red Herring* by Michael Hollinger; and Kira Obolensky's *Lobster Alice,* which imagined Walt Disney's 1946 film collaboration with surrealist Salvador Dalí. Also in 2003 Busfield launched B Street's professional **Children's Theatre of California,** which stages two-hour, two-act plays appropriate for children and their parents, such as *Lilly's Purple Plastic Purse, The Hardy Boys,* and *The Boxcar Children.*

At last report the B Street Theatre was still located at 2711 B St., 916/443-5300, www.bstreettheatre.org, with ticket prices in the $17.50–21.50 range. The Children's Theatre of California stages most performances nearby at "B2," 2727 B St., 916/448-9707.

---

wind, brass, and percussion), and the critically acclaimed **Camellia Symphony Orchestra,** 916/929-6655, www.camelliasymphony.org, a volunteer troupe performing new works as well as classical compositions that are too rarely presented. Performances are usually staged in the breathtaking Westminster Presbyterian Church downtown at 13th and N Streets. Always worth the drive out to campus are performances by the **Chamber Music Society of Sacramento,** staged on Sunday evenings in fall at the CSU Sacramento Recital Hall, 916/443-2908, www.cmssacto.org. Expect both classics and modern chamber music, performed by master local musicians. Usually in mid-November, CSU Sacramento sponsors its free, decades-strong **New American Music Festival,** 916/278-5155, celebrating 20th-century music.

Typically more staid, the **Sacramento Philharmonic,** 916/732-9045 (season tickets), sacramentophilharmonic.org, offers "home" performances at the Community Center Theater downtown, though Memorial Auditorium and the new Mondavi Center at UC Davis are other venues. Tickets for single performances are available through the Community Center Theater Box Office, 1301 L St., 916/264-5181,

or Tickets.com, 916/766-2277, www.tickets.com. Also performing in the Community Center are the **Sacramento Opera Association,** 916/737-1000 or 916/264-5181 (tickets), www.sacopera.org, which stages at least two professional operas per season, one in fall, one in spring, and the **Sacramento Ballet,** 916/552-5800, www.sacballet.org, whose regular season typically includes two fall and two spring performances, traditional as well as contemporary. Sac Ballet also offers a dazzling December full of *Nutcracker* performances, with a live symphony orchestra and sets made in St. Petersburg, Russia, by French artist Alain Vaës.

In addition to the **Crest Theatre,** the **Community Center Theater** (best acoustics), and the massive **Arco Arena** just north of Downtown via I-5, memorable Sacramento concerts and other events are staged at the venerable **Memorial Auditorium** at 1515 J St. in Midtown—a local landmark now seismically safe, restored, and reopened since 1996, thanks to the tireless efforts of local activists and dedicated craftspeople. The maple floors here hark back to the big band era; note the gold-leaf trim and the building's other design subtleties. Following a three-year renovation, the Memorial Auditorium's classical concert organ—

a 1926 Estey—was unveiled in 1999. Given the Memorial's august local heritage, baby boomers are most likely to gush over favorite concerts here—from the Rolling Stones (the concert in which Keith Richards fainted on stage due to electrical shock, when his electric guitar bashed into a mike), Bob Dylan, Joan Baez, and The Who to The Beachboys, Mahalia Jackson, and Janis Joplin. But Marian Anderson, Paul Robeson, Spike Jones, Frank Sinatra, Hank Williams, and Barbra Streisand also performed here. Since its reopening, Sheryl Crow, Sarah McLachlan, John Fogerty, and Kevin Sharp have played the Memorial. Everyone in town has a best-concert story, despite the fact that the Memorial has the worst acoustics in town. So, go ahead, go there—and make up one of your own.

Still, there's now serious competition in the Cool Venue Sweepstakes with the debut of the world-class **Mondavi Center for the Performing Arts,** 530/754-2787 or 866-2787, www.mondaviarts.org, on the UC Davis campus, not far beyond Sacramento via I-80. For more information, see Mondavi's High Culture elsewhere in this chapter.

Nightlife

Making the scene—the dance scene, the singles scene, or whatever—requires some effort, if only because "the scene" here changes faster than the political roster at the Capitol. To find out what's latest and greatest, ask around, eavesdrop on the conversations of interesting strangers, and check local newspapers.

A cool surprise in "Uptown" (North) Sacramento is the **Stoney Inn Bar & Grill,** 1320 Del Paso Blvd., 916/927-6023, where you might hear the likes of Little Charlie and the Nightcats, Bonnie Rait, Freddy Fender, Elvin Bishop, Leon Russell, Norton Buffalo, and Tommy Castro along with loads of local talent. Cheap drinks, too. Also pretty cool is the **Blue Lamp Lounge** in East Sacramento, 1400 Alhambra Blvd. (at N Street), 916/455-3400, affiliated with the Blue Lamp on Geary in San Francisco and famous here for its awesome audience participation, regular bands like the Blues Jam with Kentucky Slim, and occasional big gigs like the Hackensaw

Boys and their ramped-up bluegrass. If you're up for a little drive, there's also the famous **Palms Playhouse,** relocated from its original ramshackle barn in Davis to 13 Main St. in Winters, 530/795-1825, but still hosting touring singer-songwriters and national country, blues, Cajun, and worldbeat talent.

Otherwise, much of what's going on is conveniently located for visitors—in Downtown and Midtown. One thing you'll probably discover is that the R Street Corridor just south of the Capitol is suddenly happening—an area becoming chockablock with loft apartments, art galleries, and restaurants, all just a stroll from the 13th and 16th Street Light Rail Stations. By now Randy Paragary's local restaurant/entertainment empire should have launched his dance club for geezers, a venue purported to be suitable for baby boomers and others over age 30. The onetime Wonder Bread factory at 15th and R Streets now includes Paragary's 10,000-square-foot **Empire,** a thousand-person club (multiple bars) that books hot touring bands. Home also to **Sammy Chu's** Asian restaurant, the complex heads upstairs to **La Raza Galeria Posada** Latino art gallery.

Yet not everything in the neighborhood is new and improved. Been-there-forever **Fox and Goose,** in a refurbished old brick warehouse at 10th and R, 916/443-8825, is comfortably dark and British publike, with a bustling bar—impressive national and international beer selection—and live music, everything from bluegrass, country-western, and folk to blues and jazz. **Old Ironsides** at 1901 10th St. (10th and S), 916/443-9751, is one of the most diverse venues in town, featuring everything from avant-garde jazz, rock, and punk to swing bands, both well-established locals and new regional acts. Tuesday night is Lipstick, a dance club starring 1960s British pop and indie rock. Wednesday is Open Mic Night. For information on upcoming shows, call 916/442-8832.

There's plenty going on along the K Street Mall, too, where the **Crest** and **Esquire IMAX Theatres** hold forth (a new art house movie venue has been proposed), and the clean-cut Capitol crowd crowds into the **Pyramid Ale-**

house brewery and restaurant, 1029 K St., 916/498-9800. Across from swank Esquire Grill and right behind the Hyatt is Paragary's sleek, small **KBar**, 1200 K St. (at 13th), 916/669-5762, with DJed dancing Thursday, Friday, and Saturday nights (Sunday is "Service Industry Night"), plasma video monitors, and state-of-the-art lights and sound. Considerably more diverse and unassuming, **Marilyn's @ 12th & K,** 916/446-4361, offers cover bands and R&B on weekends. And there are more options at Downtown Plaza, from the Hard Rock Café to River City Brewing. Farther downtown is **815 L St.,** once Sam's Hof Brau, 815 L St., 916/443-8155, Sacramento's "best singles scene" and good for frenetic dancing and occasional live music, in a seedy section of Downtown near the Greyhound station.

A lively nightlife district is also developing near the Sacramento Theatre Company/Music Circus and Memorial Auditorium, along 15th between H and K Streets. There are restaurants and pubs, such as **Lucca Restaurant & Bar** for loud Mediterranean, inside the 1924 redbrick C.J. Hastings Public Garage, 1615 J St., 916/669-5300; the **Melting Pot** fondue restaurant, 814 15th St., 916/443-2347; and the **Brew it Up** brewpub on the ground floor of the parking structure at 14th and H Streets, 916/441-3000, serving 23 brews and plenty of pub grub. And there are clubs. The **Torch Club,** across the street from the Memorial Auditorium at 904 15th St. (between I and J), 916/443-2797, www.thetorchclub.com, is "Sacramento's premiere blues club," offering blues and jazz nightly. Self-consciously chic **Elements Nightclub,** in the onetime Veterans of Foreign War post at 805 15th St., 916/325-0056, features the Mercury Lounge, Titanium Bar, and a 3,000-square-foot dance floor (techno, house, Hip Hop, R&B) plus vast outdoor patio.

Otherwise, the intersection of 20th and K Streets in Midtown is *the* club scene. Mainstay here is the gay and lesbian dance club **Faces,** 2000 K St., 916/448-7798—everyone's favorite dance club, grandly expanded—and friendly competitor **The Depot** video bar across the street at 2001 K St., 916/441-6823. Affiliated with Faces and scheduled to open in late 2003 (along with other new venues in the immediate neighborhood): **Head Hunters Video Lounge & Grille** nearby at 1930 K St., a sleek, semi-industrial bar and coffeehouse in a onetime auto shop.

A different scene altogether but not far away is the small **Press Club** at 21st and P Streets, 916/447-7625, a onetime dive bar that's spiffed up a bit and now offers dancing, too, but eclectic and cool—not the same-old sound you'll find all over town. Another Midtown option is postmodern deco-style **Harlow's Restaurant and Nightclub** at 2708 J St., 916/441-4693, where the surviving stained glass window from the old Alhambra Theater still stars. Historically, Harlow's serves "modern American" for dinner and just about everything else on the dance floor—from electronic funk and Motown to salsa and disco. Upstairs is the superhip **MoMo Lounge and Cigar Bar,** 916/441-4693, smokin' with jazz, blues, and swing.

The under-18 nightclub scene is complicated and ever-changing. Many local dance clubs accommodate the younger crowd, at least certain nights or times. Some venues, like downtown's **Capitol Garage,** 1427 L St., 916/444-3633, are mild-mannered restaurants by day, all-ages clubs for new and touring bands by night. And just about everybody, young and old, loves alcohol-free **True Love Coffeehouse,** 2406 J St., 916/492-9002, which offers live music on Friday and Saturday nights (get tickets in advance), a relaxed, arty atmosphere, and board games out on the patio.

Brewpubs

Sometimes beer's the main attraction. Always a winner at award-winning **Sacramento Brewing Company,** way out there in Town & Country Village at 2713 El Paseo Ln., 916/485-4677, is River Otter Ale, a copper-colored British-style ale that helps raise funds for Sacramento River's popular River Otter Taxi. Other brews include Miner's Extra Pale Ale, Red Horse Ale, Celtic Amber, Imperial Stout, and Hefe Weizen, an unfiltered wheat beer. Good food, too, from apple walnut gorgonzola salad and fish and chips to tequila-marinated ribeye steak. There's another Sac Brewing outlet, a surprisingly good restaurant and stylized ancient Egyptian **Oasis** in Citrus Heights at Sunrise Village Center, 7811 Madison Ave., 916/966-6274—just the place to sample Sac Brewing's Pharaoh's Liquid Gold India pale ale.

Otherwise, Sacramento's **Rubicon Brewing Co.** in Midtown, 2004 Capitol Ave., 916/448-7032, may be the city's favorite brewpub, with brews including Summer Wheat and Irish Red. Worthy newcomers include **Brew It Up** in the parking structure at 14th and H Streets, 916/441-3000, serving pub grub, 23 impressive brews, and Music Circus views. Another new kid in town is **Pyramid Alehouse, Brewery, & Restaurant** tucked into the K Street Mall at 1029 K St., 916/498-9800. Poke your snout into a glass of K Street Nitro Stout and a few other strictly local brews. Relaxed, convivial, British pub–style **Fox and Goose,** just south of the Capitol in a warehouse at 10th and R Streets, 916/443-8825, offers what may be the West coast's largest selection of English and European beers. On the way to Old Sacramento, a worthy beer stop is **River City Brewing Company** at the Downtown Plaza mall, 916/447-2739. The **Hogshead Brewpub** down in the basement at 114 J St. in Old Sac, 916/443-2739, is Sacramento's oldest brewpub, a no-frills rock and blues bomb shelter with Old Sac's only pool table.

Hoppy Brewing in East Sacramento at 6300 Folsom Blvd., 916/451-4677, serves its own special "hoppy" brews, the get-happy theme underscored by the happy-face-with-legs beer label art on the Hoppy Face Pale Ale, Stony Face Red Ale, and Total Eclipse Black Ale bottles. Draft pints are $2 during daily "hoppy hour," 3–6 P.M. For genuine German-style lagers, get on I-80 and drive west to famous **Sudwerk Brewery & Grill.** (See Davis and Vicinity below.)

EVENTS

Things happen year-round in Sacramento. Thanks to the delta breeze summer evenings are often balmy—perfect for bike rides and baseball—but even withering heat barely slows the local pace. Icy winter fogs can, however. For information about area events, contact the Convention and Visitors Bureau or refer to local newspapers (see Capital Information below).

It's obvious enough come spring that this is a camellia city—just look around Midtown, East Sacramento, and Land Park neighborhoods—but it's official: the camellia is Sacramento's flower. The **Camellia Show** comes in early March, usually held at the Sacramento Community Convention Center, a pruned-down version of the long-running Camellia Festival. Even without the Camellia Luncheon, Camellia Parade, and Camellia Ball, the event attracts some 10,000 people each year. Anyone can bring camellias from home to exhibit. Unusual camellia varieties are available for sale, too. Also usually in March: the **Sacramento Home and Garden Show** and the **Sacramento Boat Show.**

The **Festival de la Familia,** usually scheduled in late April, is an ambitious cultural festival celebrating Latin American heritage and featuring folk art, music, dancing, and storytelling, plus fabulous food from everywhere (homemade tamales, fish tacos, *carimanolas, hallacas, tequenos,* Spanish roasted corn on the cob, Mexican and Cuban desserts, Cuban-style coffee, and much more). Headliners have included major international entertainers such as Jose Feliciano and Sergio Mendes.

In late April or early May look for the local **Highland Scottish Games and Gathering,** with most events open to the public. The gathering includes Scottish Clan and Family Society tents, native foods, bagpipes, and events such as "tossing" the caber, the hammer throw, and more sedate performances by Highland dancers.

Cinco de Mayo, celebrated throughout the city, is a major event on and around May 5 each year. The entire month of May is Asian Pacific-American Heritage Month, but head for Old Sacramento in mid-May for the Saturday **Pacific Rim Street Festival,** which includes storytelling, face-painting, and games for the kiddos, historical exhibits and cultural presentations, intriguing entertainment—from martial arts to the Chinese lion dance—arts, crafts, and fabulous food. Also in May: the **Sacramento County Fair** at Cal Expo and the **Pacific Coast Rowing Championships** at Lake Natoma. Over the Memorial Day weekend in late May is the city's famous **Sacramento Jazz Jubilee** (for more information, see below).

The best family fun around in May or June comes with the day-long **Sacramento Children's Festival,** held in Old Sacramento and at the Downtown Plaza—an endless parade of school bands, international dance, puppeteers, theater, and hundreds of displays and exhibits. Events are busting out all over the place in June, from the Crest Theatre's **Sacramento Film Arts Festivals** to the **Croatian Extravaganza** and the **Jewish Food Faire and Craft Sale.**

Early in July comes the **Folsom Championship Rodeo.** Just to be weird, people in Old Sacramento celebrate **Independence Day** on July 3rd instead—still no fireworks at last report, alas, because the immense popularity of the riverside pyrotechnics attracted up to 300,000 people each year, a safety nightmare. But that could change one day soon. Then on the 4th, Independence Day festivities get under way in Capitol Park with a parade, a classic car exhibition, bands, live entertainment, and good food—not to mention all the fireworks and fun at Cal Expo and Folsom Lake. Impressive, too, are the throngs of ironpeople participating in **Eppie's Great Race,** a running, cycling, and kayaking competition billed as "the world's oldest triathlon." Usually held late in July, the four-day **Strauss Festival** in Elk Grove south of Sacramento honors Johann Strauss the Younger, "the Waltz King," with symphonic performances of "The Blue Danube," "The Emperor Waltz," choreographed Viennese waltzes, and more.

Festa Italiana arrives in August, as does the **Japanese Cultural Bazaar** at the Sacramento Buddhist Church—a noncommercial, neighborhood-style celebration complete with kimono fashion show, dancing to koto music, and calligraphy and Kabuki makeup demonstrations. Also come in August for the **River Otter Amphibious Race** (ROAR), Sacramento's kinetic art challenge, inspired by the similar event held in Arcata. The race starts in Old Sacramento, crosses the American River at Discovery Park, churns through the sandbars and mudflats, crosses the Sacramento River, and ends near the ziggurat in West Sacramento.

The area's biggest commercial event is the **California State Fair** at the California Exposition grounds (Cal Expo), a bigger-than-life bash starting in August and lasting through Labor Day. The fair offers bushels of California-style cultural activities, from cowboy poetry, fiddling contests, and top-name country-western, swing, rock, and pop concerts to grape-stomping, cow-milking, and pie-eating contests. But there's more, from livestock and produce shows, wine-tasting, quiltmaking, and bake-offs to horse and pig races, rodeos, and destruction derbies. Don't miss the Insect Pavilion. The Magnificent Midway here is a class act, more amusement park than carnival, with spectacular rides. For more information about the current fair, call 916/263-3000 or try www.bigfun.org. Also a big deal over Labor Day weekend: Old Sacramento's family-friendly **Gold Rush Days,** a four-day festival of gold rush–era authenticity when streets are "paved" with dirt again and only pedestrians, equestrians, horse-drawn vehicles, and steam-train travel are allowed. Spicing up the 1850s' street drama are actors and other characters, period musicians, dancers, saloons, miners' tents, ethnic villages, arts and crafts, and exhibits

Come in September for the **Greek Food Festival** and the **Chalk it Up to Sacramento!** sidewalk chalk festival. Usually scheduled for the last weekend in September is the impressive but friendly **Sacramento Reads** literary festival, normally held at Crocker Museum, which features a variety of reading- and book-related events, from readings to guest author panel discussions on various topics.

In October, of course, comes **Oktoberfest,** two days of beer, food, music, and traditional German and Swiss dancing sponsored by the local Turn Verein, the oldest western chapter of the venerable German Athletic Club. Also big in October: the **Sacramento Festival of Cinema, Art on the River** in Old Sacramento, the **Sacramento Arts Festival** at the convention center, and the **Crocker Art Museum Antique Show and Sale.**

November highlights include the **Sacramento Parade of Lights** and the **Santa Parade.** Come to Old Sacramento throughout the holiday season for the **Hertitage Holidays.** December is known for the **California International Marathon** run from Folsom Dam to the state Capitol.

Most winter events are of the huddle-inside-and-dream-of-spring variety, from January's **International Sportsmen's Expo** to February's **Autorama** and **Sacramento Sports, Boat, and RV Show.**

Sacramento Jazz Jubilee

Sacramento's original Dixieland Jazz Jubilee is now the Sacramento Jazz Jubilee, held each year over the Memorial Day weekend and attracting 100,000 or more often outlandishly dressed but friendly fans and 100 or more bands from around the country and the world—from big-name performers (Joanne Castle, Pete Barbutti, and Mr. Emperor in 2003) to less famous groups with unforgettable names, such as Eight Misbehavin', The Boondockers, Juggernaut Jug Band, Igor's Jazz Cowboys, Chuck Taylor & the Dixie Squid, the Night Blooming Jazzmen, and Paco Gatsby. Bridging the cultural divide between twentysomethings and their grandparents, swing bands joined the mix in 1999.

As the Jazz Jubilee has grown—it started out as a predominantly local event, staged in Old Sacramento—so has its need for space. These days, there are four additional event centers beyond Old Sacramento and miscellaneous venues nearby. Closest of these is the Sacramento Convention Center, but largest is Cal Expo (site of the annual state fair); various hotels complete the roster. Most concert and cabaret sites are clustered in and around Old Sacramento (from I to L Streets between the river and I-5). The "satellite" centers are linked to Old Sac by free shuttle buses. Wear walking shoes and dress for comfort (and temperature extremes, from blistering outdoor heat to ice-like air-conditioning), and consider a sun hat, sunscreen, and a flashlight if you plan to party till the cows come home.

At last report (2003), ticket badges for the entire four-day weekend were $92 adults and $46 children and youths ages 7–17 (age 6 and under free). One-day adult badges were $38, and other badges—half-day, evening only, etc.—were $17–27 adults ($8–13 for children/youth). Usually free, though, is all that jazz played at private local clubs, theaters, and watering holes throughout the weekend. Buy tickets online or at various local venues. For current details, contact the **Sacramento Traditional Jazz Society,** 2787 Del Monte St. in West Sacramento, 916/372-5277, www.sacjazz.com.

Unlimited transportation is available on concert shuttles, which run 10–15 minutes apart, as well as Regional Transit's light rail system. Almost the only way to survive and/or know what's going on amid the merry madness is to buy a program ($5 or so), though on the Friday kicking off the weekend's party, the *Sacramento Bee* publishes a free and very useful jubilee guide in its regular "Ticket" section.

SHOPPING

Not to be missed on a Sacramento-area excursion is been-there-forever **Denio's Roseville Farmers Market and Auction, Inc.** on the wrong side of the railroad tracks in Roseville at 1551 Vineyard Rd., 916/782-2704, www.denios.org, something of a down-home shopping city sprawling out over 70 acres and usually open Saturday and Sunday 7 A.M.–5 P.M. every week of the year (open-air bazaar on Friday, 8 A.M.–2 P.M.). On weekends—the main event—expect more than 1,000 vendors, selling everything from auto parts and birdhouses to kitchen appliances and toys. And talk about one-stop shopping: People even set up their own yard sales here. Small admittance, parking fees.

Shopaholics, ask at the visitor center downtown for a current rundown on the area's major department stores, shopping centers, and smaller, more specialized shops. Big-league venues include the Australian-owned **Westfield Shoppingtown Downtown Plaza,** located between Fourth and Seventh and J and L Streets, 916/442-4000, already home to the Hard Rock Café, Macy's, and dozens of shops and eateries and scheduled for a $40 million makeover and expansion. For Nordstrom and other upscale pleasures, head for **Arden Fair** just off the Capital City Freeway at Arden Way; an easy, "backdoor" way to get there from Downtown involves heading north on Hwy. 160

(follow the signs). While you're in the neighborhood, visit Sacramento's 25,000-square-foot **Virgin Megastore** at nearby **Market Square,** 1715 Arden Way (at the Fair's east end), 916/564-0414. (But don't forget Tower Records, a Sacramento original; see below.) Tony possibilities include **Pavillions Shopping Plaza** on Fair Oaks between Howe and Fulton, 916/925-4463, and farther east in Roseville the **Westfield Shoppingtown Galleria at Roseville,** 1151 Galleria Blvd., 916/787-2000, a shopping palace (1.07 million square feet) that made its debut in 2000. For outlet shopping, head east to Folsom and the **Folsom Premium Outlets** at 13000 Folsom Blvd., Ste. 309, 916/985-0312, where you'll find London Fog, Donna Karan, and the Off 5th–Saks Fifth Avenue Outlet among the 60-plus choices. Antiquers will find fascinating shops in Midtown, on Sutter St. in Folsom, and elsewhere, but a big draw these days is the 75,000-square-foot **Antique Plaza** at 11395 Folsom Blvd. in Rancho Cordova, 916/852-8517, www.antiqueplazaonline.com, California's largest antique mall. Shops for the 300-plus dealers here open daily 10 A.M.–6 P.M.

Discriminating shoppers will also do quite well in the trendier shops and boutiques in **Old Sacramento** and scattered throughout **East Sacramento** and **Midtown Sacramento.** If you're looking for a unique gift or souvenir, don't forget that museum gift shops often offer unique, sometimes decidedly "Sacramento" selections. Sales also support museum survival, always a worthwhile cause.

If you're in the mood for record shop nostalgia, on the way to or from Land Park, stop at the humble beginnings of the now-national **Tower Records** chain at the corner of Land Park Drive and Broadway, 916/444-3000, open 9 A.M.–midnight. Though the empire has been troubled lately, at last report all the neighboring Towers—bookshop, video store, movie theater, and café—still kept the neighborhood interesting.

INFORMATION

If you're Downtown, find out what you need to know at the **Sacramento Convention and Visitors Bureau** at 1303 J St., Ste. 600, 916/264-7777, www.sacramentocvb.org. To book a room, call the bureau at 800/359-3653. The visitors bureau is open Mon.–Fri. 8 A.M.–5 P.M. If you're down by the river, the **Old Sacramento Visitor Information Center** at 1004 Second St. (next to the Wells Fargo History Museum), 916/442-7644, also offers brochures, maps, and personable assistance—and is open on weekends as well as during the week.

The best all-around source of local information is the award-winning *Sacramento Bee,* www.sacbee.com, main link in the McClatchy newspaper chain, noted for its solid political coverage, reasonably enlightened editorials, and engaging features. Still the new kid in town after all these years is the free weekly *Sacramento News & Review,* www.newsreview.com, especially strong on news features and entertainment coverage and attracting aging boomers and sometimes the younger crowd. Crowded out by the *New & Review's* nascent success, alas, was *The Suttertown News,* gone but still not forgotten. Check out the coolest local coffeeshops and cafes for the latest alternative and indie rags. The local lifestyle mag is *Sacramento Magazine,* www.sacmag.com, with local features, restaurant reviews, and golf guide.

GETTING HERE

Traditionally, Sacramento's "formal entrance" has been from the Bay Area: over the Tower Bridge and up Capitol Mall, passing blocky business buildings and federal then state office buildings. The valley's great transportation hub, Sacramento is now served by an impressive maze of freeways and major highways converging in unusual and confusing ways. Downtown Sacramento is defined by two rivers—the American to the north, the Sacramento to the west—and by some of these similarly meandering thoroughfares. To the west of downtown, fronting the Sacramento River, is I-5, in tandem with Hwy. 99 (the valley's other major north-south roadway). South of downtown, Hwy. 99 splits off, heads east, and comes together with the Capital City Freeway (formerly known as Business 80, a name changed in 1996 to avoid confusion with I-80) and the beginning of Hwy. 50. The Capital City

© ROBERT HOLMES/CALTOUR

Tower Bridge at night

Freeway then jogs northward, creating the Downtown area's eastern boundary, and joins I-80. (I-80 is the "straight-line" connection between San Francisco and Lake Tahoe/Reno, a route just north of Sacramento proper.) Highway 50 arrows eastward toward Placerville (Hwy. 16 is another route from Sacramento into the gold country), and Hwy. 99 continues south through the San Joaquin Valley. Highway 160 shoots out from Downtown from both ends of 15th or 16th Streets. Heading north on 160 provides an easy route to Arden Way shopping and Cal Expo. Heading south (via 15th St.) leads to Broadway; Hwy. 160 then becomes Freeport Blvd. (21st St. if you're going north) and eventually leads to William Land Park and the Sacramento Zoo.

However one arrives, central Sacramento itself (comprised of Downtown and Midtown) is fairly easy to navigate. From west to east, streets are numbered one to 28. From north to south, streets are "lettered" A to W (with the Capitol Mall taking the place of M St. between Third and Ninth, and becoming Capitol Ave. between 16th and 29th Streets). With a street address, it's fairly simple to derive the exact location of anything Downtown or in Midtown (400 Third St., for ex-

ample, would be at the intersection of D St., the fourth letter of the alphabet). Many streets are one-way, so pay attention.

Another potential source of visitor consternation (as for locals) is the city's aggressive new "traffic calming" program in Midtown and East Sacramento—a combination of new stop signs, stoplights, intersection traffic circles, half-street closures, and diverters intended to re-create a more neighborly ambience otherwise threatened by excess traffic, excess speeds, noise, and pollution.

Even with traffic calming, be aware that Sacramento drivers have a notable penchant for running red lights. Everyone's in such a *hurry.* Shockingly bad "neighborhood" accidents occur throughout the region as a result. Aggressive law enforcement hasn't been enough to turn this trend around; it's hoped that the installation of video cameras at particularly bad intersections—to catch culprits in the act—may help. In the meantime, look both ways (and listen for oncoming hotrodders) before entering any intersection.

By Air

Sacramento International Airport (SMF), 12 miles northwest of town via I-5, 916/929-5411, www.sacairports.org, is served by major airlines plus a few connector services. Airport traffic has definitely picked up since no-frills Southwest Airlines carved out a major slice of Sacramento airspace. In fact, business has been brisk here even since September 11, 2001: four new carriers have been added. The airport's name change (adding the "International") preceded a dramatic choice—the decision to build toward adding nonstop flights to both Mexico and Canada—Mexicana Airlines is already here, and Canada should arrive soon—and then the East Coast and Europe. The first step in that airport building program was completed in 1998, when the airport's size was doubled with the addition of new $58 million Terminal A, dominated by Southwest Airlines but also including Hawaiian, Continental, Delta, and America West. An interim terminal serves international arrivals.

Visitor facilities in light, airy Terminal A include a snazzy new food court—with Java City, Starbucks, Cinnabon, and California Pizza, among others—plus retail shops selling everything from golf duds and luggage to gourmet California food items. Sacramento's Art in Public Places project has been busy here, too. Brian Goggin's *Samson* sculptures near the baggage claim area are particularly amusing in an airport setting—two towers of luggage from around the world piled high—some 23 feet tall—as if holding up the ceiling. The changes keep coming. Wireless Fidelity (Wi-Fi) Internet access is also available in both terminals, $6.95 per day. And Terminal A already needs a retrofit, to accommodate bulky new security equipment. A multilevel 4,500-space parking garage directly across from Terminal A, complete with connector bridge, is scheduled to open in summer 2004.

Terminal B (once known as Terminal B and C, and now designated B1 and B2) has had a makeover—everything from new carpets and ceilings, remodeled snack bars, and renovated elevators to improved restrooms, lighting, heating, air-conditioning, and security systems. Major airlines housed here include Alaska, American, Northwest, TWA, and United. Other substantial airport improvements include traffic flow—directing airport arrivals into lots designated for either Ter-

minal A or B—and parking lots for each terminal that include both hourly and daily parking. Near the rental car terminal (well south of the flight terminals) is an overflow lot (served by shuttle).

The bad news is, even with recent expansion the airport is barely adequate to handle current use, let alone anticipated future growth in air travel—which means it's still hectic and crowded here; further expansion is already on the drawing board. Looming large in future plans is a new, improved Terminal B with double-deck roadway, associated multilevel parking garage, and a new hotel. Lengthening an existing runway and adding a new one are also on the wish list, along with improving concessions and shops, particularly to emphasize shopping and add more local brands and flavors.

As you can judge from the airport parking lots, most Sacramentans drive to catch their flights. Day/overnight parking is $7–10 per day in the daily lots, $1 per hour ($24 per day for poor planners) in the short-term lots. The first half-hour at hourly lots is free, though. At last report SMF was served by seven national car-rental agencies—Alamo, Avis, Budget, Dollar, Enterprise, Hertz and National—plus there's a Rent-a-Wreck downtown. After a long hiatus, there is once again a gas station (Arco) at the airport, so rental cars can be topped off here rather than back in Sacramento.

Sacramento Regional Transit does not provide bus service to the airport, but **Yolobus,** 530/661-0816, www.yctd.org, does; see the website for information on Route 42, which runs between Sacramento and West Sacramento to Davis and Woodland. Another viable alternative is **Supershuttle Sacramento,** the airport's exclusive on-call van service, headquartered at 520 N. 16th St., 916/557-8370 or 800/258-3826, www.supershuttle.com. Several other companies offer van transport only with advance reservations: **Airport Transportation Service,** 530/891-1219 or 800/832-4223, www.buttecounty.com, serving Marysville, Oroville, Chico, and Paradise; **Davis Airporter,** 530/756-6715 or 800/565-5153, www.davisairporter.com, serving Yolo County; and **Foothill Flyer,** 530/878-0808 or 800/464-0808, www.foothillflyer.com, serving Auburn, Grass Valley, Colfax, and Weimar. Better regional hotels and motels also offer airport transport. Cab service is available, too, through a variety of companies including **Yellow Cab** at 900 Richards Blvd., 916/444-2222, which has been here since 1917 and offers computerized dispatch, and **Sacramento Independent Taxi,** an association of independents contracted by the airport and headquartered at 555 Capitol Mall, Ste. 1440, 916/457-4862.

By Train

The **Amtrak** depot, in the shadow of the I-5 freeway at Fifth and I Streets, is a wonderful remnant of Sacramento's railroading heyday. Built in the 1920s, the depot was designed by Bliss and Faville, architects of San Francisco's St. Francis Hotel. It features a lofty ceiling, similarly arched floor-to-ceiling windows, welcoming back-to-back oak benches with heaters, a classy California marble floor, and terra cotta embellishments made by the Gladding, McBean Company. A wall-length mural titled *Breaking Ground at Sacramento January 8, 1863 for First Transcontinental Railroad* commemorates the day California got serious about connecting its fate to the rest of the nation. The Amtrak depot is now owned by the city and destined to be the historic focal point of its 10-acre multiagency railway hub. At present the depot is point of departure and arrival for Amtrak trains, including the regional Capitol trains connecting to the Bay Area. It will also soon be a link in the local light-rail line, connecting to Folsom and eventually Natomas (North Sacramento) and the Sacramento International Airport.

Well worth it on Amtrak is the climb over the Sierra Nevada to Reno (ultimately Chicago) onboard the **California Zephyr,** a particularly appropriate opportunity to honor the unimaginable difficulty of building the nation's first transcontinental railroad. Amtrak's **Coast Starlight** also connects here, to Seattle/Vancouver in the north and Los Angeles/San Diego in the south. Amtrak passengers can also get from Sacramento to Bakersfield (and points in between)—without having to first take a bus to Stockton—now that several **San Joaquin** trains are routed directly to Stockton daily (call for details).

Now more viable, too, are train connections between Sacramento and the Bay Area—thanks to the **Capitol** trains, a system initiated by Amtrak but now managed by the Capitol Corridor Joint Powers Authority and operated by the Bay Area Rapid Transit District. Capitol trains run daily in both directions between Auburn and San Jose. Each weekday 12 westbound trains connect Sacramento with Emeryville and Oakland, passing through Davis, Fairfield, Martinez, and Richmond on the way. From Oakland, a "feeder" bus links to San Francisco; another motorcoach route continues on to Hayward, Fremont/Centerville, Santa Clara/Great America, San Jose/Caltrain, and Mountain View/Caltrain. Motorcoaches also connectAuburn, in the foothills east of Sacramento, to Colfax, Truckee, and ultimately Reno/Sparks in Nevada. Other links include the far northern Sacramento Valley (an area also served by a separate Amtrak route); the Napa Valley; and Santa Cruz and Monterey. Capitol trains also connect to the Bay Area's San Joaquin trains, which run from Oakland to Stockton, then south through the San Joaquin Valley to Bakersfield (with bus connections onward to just about everywhere). In summer, Amtrak buses also connect to Yosemite National Park from Merced or Fresno.

As of summer 2003—this is a fast-growing route, with more trains added all the time—the first westbound Capitol train departed Sacramento for the Bay Area on weekdays at 4:25 A.M., the last at 8:45 P.M. First and last departure times for the reverse trip (from Oakland) were 5:25 A.M. and 8:15 P.M., respectively. On weekends, there are nine trains, the earliest leaving Sacramento for Oakland at 7:40 A.M., the last at 8:10 P.M.; in reverse, the earliest train departs Oakland at 7:15 A.M., the latest at 8:55 P.M. At last report the one-way fare between Sacramento and Oakland was $18. (See the website for current fare information.) One-way and roundtrip tickets can be purchased at any staffed station or at Quik Trak vending machines (Sacramento offers both options) and on the Amtrak website (www.amtrak.com). Discounted fares are offered to children and seniors. Ten-ride (45-day limit) and unlimited monthly ticket are available by

GREAT VALLEY & THE DELTA

mail; to order either, call Amtrak or visit the website (see below) at least nine days in advance.

For more information on Amtrak's Capitol Corridor train service, contact Amtrak at 800/872-7245 (USA-RAIL), www.amtrak.com, or see the websites www.amtrakcapitols.com or www.511.org. A current route map, fare schedule, and weekday and weekend/holiday train schedules can be downloaded or printed from the websites.

By Bus and Car

The **Greyhound Bus** terminal in downtown Sacramento, 715 L St. between Seventh and Eighth Streets, 916/444-7270 or 800/231-2222 for route and fare information, www.greyhound.com, is open 24 hours and centrally located in a dicey part of Downtown. From here, buses head out to Reno, L.A., San Francisco, Portland, and just about everywhere in between and beyond. In addition to its regular routes, Greyhound also offers Quikline commuter bus service to and from San Francisco's financial district. Though Greyhound has improved its downtown facilities and beefed up security, plans are in the works to relocate Greyhound to the "intermodal hub" transit center the city is developing near the train depot at Fifth and I Streets.

Since this is California, most people drive. Traffic throughout the greater Sacramento area can be hellish—particularly during peak weekday commute hours—though it's usually not that bad in central Sacramento. See Getting Oriented, above, for a general rundown on regional freeways and the ins and outs of getting around in the central city. To keep abreast of traffic snarls (usually worse during the morning commute), tune in to local radio stations or watch morning TV news broadcasts. To rent a car for delta or gold country day trips and other adventures afield, contact the visitors bureau for a listing of reputable local companies.

GETTING AROUND
By Bus

Quite popular Downtown and in Midtown, since their routes expanded recently, are the vivid orange, violet, and yellow **Downtown Area Shuttle** (DASH) buses, operated by Sacramento Regional Transit, which travel in a loop linking Old Sacramento, the Downtown Plaza, and the Sacramento Convention Center on J St. with CSU Sacramento in East Sacramento. The loop runs east on J St.—passing major attractions in Midtown—and returns to Downtown on L Street. Shuttle stops are signed with the same bright colors, and if you miss the bus, another will be along in 10–15 minutes. Depending on how far you're going, the fare is 50 cents to $1.50. Regular shuttle operating hours are weekdays 5–11 A.M.–10:05 P.M., Saturday and Sunday noon–6 P.M. Other public transit bus routes link Downtown with other destinations and provide service 5 A.M.–10 P.M. daily.

By Light Rail

Always fun, though, especially to get out into the northeastern and eastern suburban sectors, is the city's new **RT Metro light rail** trolley system. Two separate links (roughly paralleling I-80 and Hwy. 50) connect Downtown with the suburbs, primarily to get people to work without their cars. As of 1999, the light rail system extended only as far as Watt Ave. on the I-80 route and to Mather Field (past CSU Sacramento) on the Hwy. 50 route. A new link, extending from downtown through the Land Park neighborhood near Freeport Boulevard to Meadowview Road, was scheduled to open in late 2003; this route will eventually extend all the way to Elk Grove. The Folsom line is expecting to be up and running by 2004.

Likely future extensions will reach to Roseville, to Davis, and to Natomas (North Sacramento) and Sacramento International Airport. The light rail system runs 4:30 A.M. A.M.–1 A.M. daily with trolleys every 15 minutes during the day, every half-hour in the evening. The Art in Public Places program is behind the eclectic, often amusing artwork at each trolley station, where tickets are dispensed from vending machines (directions given in both English and Spanish). The central city fare—good on both light rail and city buses—is 50 cents, good for one ride within the city's central area. Otherwise, the basic light-rail and bus fare is $1.50 (75 cents senior, disabled, or student), and a daily pass is $3.50 ($1.75 senior, disabled, or student).

To buy a light rail ticket, (1) select the appropriate fare (push button), (2) deposit the exact change required (change machines are available, though the maximum change given is $9.75), and (3) take your ticket, which you'll have to show to RT fare inspectors. If you bought your ticket in advance, you'll have to validate it in the ticket machine before boarding. Discounted ticket books and various monthly passes, good for both light rail and bus transit, must be purchased in advance.

For more information on DASH shuttles and bus and light rail routes, stops, and fares, contact Regional Transit headquarters at 1400 29th St. (at N Street), 916/321-2877 or 916/321-2800, or see www.sacrt.com. Or stop by the RT Downtown Service Center at 818 K Street (on the K Street Mall), open weekdays only, 9:30 A.M.–4:30 P.M. (closed weekends and holidays). Purchase passes and tickets by telephone (with a major credit card) by calling 916/321-2849 or by mail; to request mail order forms, call 916/321-2877. Pick up a copy of the *Regional Transit Bus & Light Rail Timetable Book* for $1 at Raley's or Bel Air markets and at area newsstands.

FOLSOM AND VICINITY

Sprawling, high-tech Folsom was a technology center even in the early days of California statehood. Folsom was eastern endpoint for the West's first railroad, in fact—Theodore Judah's Sacramento Valley Railroad, which launched its first Sacramento-to-Folsom run in September 1856. Overnight Folsom became a transportation hub essential for supplying nearby gold mines and miners; both stage and freight lines met the train in Folsom. From July 1860 until July 1861, Folsom also served as western terminus for the Pony Express. The West's first commercial facility capable of transmitting electricity long-distance, the 1895 Folsom Powerhouse—now a state historic park and a national historic landmark—was in use here until 1952. It was replaced in 1956 by Folsom Dam and its new powerhouse,

central to huge Folsom State Recreation Area. Yet some local traditions, such as the 1856 *Folsom Telegraph* newspaper and 1880 Folsom Prison, made famous by singer-songwriter Johnny Cash and his *Folsom Prison Blues,* are still going strong.

The closure of Folsom Dam Road in 2003 due to national security concerns caused traffic havoc in Folsom's charming historic **Sutter Street** business district, with its wrought iron and old-brick storefronts, antique outlets, and unique shops including **Clouds,** the **Fire & Rain Gallery,** and the **Sutter Street Emporium.** Which is all the more reason to make the extra effort. (Perhaps by now experiments to resolve the problem and support local businesses will have succeeded.) To get to and from central Folsom without using the dam road, take Folsom Boulevard, Prairie City Road, or Scott Road. Coming soon (2004, they say): a Folsom connection to greater Sacramento's light-rail system, offering a convenient way to get here without a car.

The tiny **Folsom City Zoo Sanctuary,** in Folsom City Lions Park at the corner of Natoma and Stafford Streets, 916/351-3527, is open Tues.–Sun. 10 A.M.–4 P.M., admission $3. Sometimes called "the misfit zoo," the sanctuary provides a home for unreleasable wild animals but the emphasis is on education—teaching responsible human behavior toward all animals. Some creatures protected here even provide valuable public service, such as Fisher, the black bear who tests purported "bear-proof" camping and backpacking containers for the National Park Service. Also something of a surprise in Folsom is the **Gekkeikan Sake U.S.A.** sake brewery and tasting room at 1136 Sibley St., 916/985-3111, complete with Japanese gardens and koi ponds (group tours available, open weekdays only). Museums in Folsom include the **Folsom History Museum,** 823 Folsom St., 916/985-2707, and the original Folsom Powerhouse, now **Folsom Powerhouse State Historic Park,** on Riley Street near the Rainbow Bridge, 916/988-0205 or 916/985-4843 (tour information), www.folsompowerhouse.com, open for tours Wed.–Sun. noon–4 P.M. The original dam at Folsom Lake hosted this, the nation's first viable hydroelectric plant, which first supplied power 22 miles west to Sacramento in 1895 via what were then the world's longest electrical lines. Also in the neighborhood is **Folsom Prison,** the well-sung slammer immortalized by Johnny Cash, where the small museum, 916/985-2561 ext. 4589, is oddly inviting. (Cash may have spent time behind bars, by the way, but never in a state or federal prison—a fact that, strangely, deeply disappoints some visitors.) Prison artifacts and records are intriguing. See the seven-foot-tall motorized Ferris wheel made entirely of matchsticks—inmates do have a lot of time on their hands—and admire that shockingly realistic carved wooden semiautomatic pistol. Shudder at the canvas and leather straitjacket finally banned in 1912, as well as the similarly horrifying "Iron Claw" restraint.

Come to Folsom in April for the **Annual Antique Fair,** in May for the **Annual Arts and Crafts Fair,** and every Thursday evening in summer for the **Thursday Night Market.** For more events and other area information, contact the **Sutter Street Merchants Association** at 724 Sutter St., 916/985-7452 (info and events hotline), http://historicfolsom.net, or contact the **Folsom Chamber of Commerce and Visitor Center** inside the old Southern Pacific train depot at 200 Wool St., 916/985-2698 or 800/377-1414, www.folsomchamber.com. The chamber office is open during weekday business hours, the visitor center also on weekends 11 A.M.–4 P.M.

Folsom Lake and Lake Natoma

At the edge of the gold country is the 18,000-acre **Folsom Lake State Recreation Area,** the Sacramento area's biggest outdoor draw. It begins some 20 miles east of Sacramento where the American River Parkway ends near sprawling Folsom and its antique shops and old-brick downtown. The oak woodlands surrounding Folsom Lake and its campgrounds and picnic areas are threaded with hiking and horseback-riding trails, but the area's main attraction is summertime water recreation, everything from sailboarding to jetskiing. The 150 campsites are quite popular during summer (reserve well in advance). For current Folsom Lake information, contact: **Folsom Lake State Recreation Area,** 7806 Folsom-

Auburn Rd., 916/988-0205. For camping reservations ($12–15), necessary from Memorial Day to Labor Day, contact ReserveAmerica, 800/444-7275, www.reserveamerica.com.

Tiny **Lake Natoma** behind Nimbus Dam is Folsom's forebay—more idyllic for rowing and sailing because the speed limit prohibits speedboats and water-skiing. Just downriver from Natoma's Nimbus Dam is the **Nimbus Fish Hatchery** in Rancho Cordova, 916/358-2820, a salmon and steelhead farm adjacent to the **American River Trout Hatchery** at 2001-2101 Nimbus Rd., 916/358-2865. Both hatcheries attempt to compensate for blocked access to upriver spawning grounds, and both offer tours. Salmon spawn here from late October to December—come in October for the **American River Salmon Festival**—and steelhead January to mid-March. To get here from Hwy. 50, head north on Hazel Ave., then turn left on Gold Country Boulevard.

Eating in Folsom

The breakfast place is the wonderfully homey **Lake Forest Cafe** in a venerable old house at 13409 Folsom Blvd. (at Park Shore), 916/985-6780. Stars here include the pecan and cinnamon rolls, some 40 omelettes, Mike's potatoes, even lox, eggs, and onions. But don't miss the wholesome oatmeal or applesauce and honey whole-wheat pancakes. Open just Wed.–Sun., for breakfast and lunch only—and be sure to show up early on weekends. For burgers, think Stephen King but sink your teeth into **Redrum Burger** inside the Folsom Hotel, 703 Sutter St., 916/985-8553, a branch of the famed Davis stop, serving the best around. For decent Mexican in a kid-friendly environment, head for **Chico's Tecate Grill,** 1008 E. Bidwell St., 916/984-1370, where the roasted pasilla burrito and the three-taco plate (choose fish, chicken, or steak) are make-a-meal deals.

The **Bidwell Street Bistro,** 1004 E. Bidwell St. (at Montrose), 916/984-7500, is a warm, welcoming French bistro serving fabulous country-style fare—roasted salmon sandwiches or ham and gruyère quiche at lunch, roasted polenta with portobello mushrooms, grilled ribeye, and roasted rack of New Zealand lamb at dinner. It's worth a trip for the house-made desserts alone, including crème brûlée and tart tatin. Open weekdays for lunch, Mon.–Sat for dinner.

Excellent for Thai is tiny **Thai Siam,** in The Lakes shopping center, 705 Gold Lake Dr., Ste. 360, 916/351-1696, serving specialties literally fit for royalty. That's because the proprietor lived in the royal palace for several years, when her grandmother served as an aide to Thailand's queen mother. Ask for royal family favorites, including a Thai fish soup, or stick to tried-and-true Thai standards, from spicy and sour or coconut milk chicken soup to panang curry. Open nightly for dinner, Mon.–Sat. for lunch. **Zinfandel's** (previously Paragary's) adjacent (Ste. 380), 916/985-3321, serves such things as poached salmon and panzanella; bacon, arugula, and tomato sandwiches on grilled sourdough; roasted eggplant and goat cheese lasagna; lemon risotto and prawns; and grilled flatiron steak. The wood-fired pizzas (most around $15) are hot day and night, from chicken-pesto and smoked ham–artichoke to Italian sausage and peppers. Full bar, impressive California wine list. Open daily for lunch and dinner.

Just above Lake Natoma on the west side of Folsom is popular **Scott's Seafood Grill & Bar,** on the onetime site of Woody's Grill & Bar at 9611 Greenback Ln., 916/989-6711. Dig into such things as lobster with filet mignon, pan-seared scallops, macadamia nut–crusted halibut, blackened Cajun-style snapper, and a variety of tasty steaks. Impressive oyster bar. Weather—and crowds—permitting, dine out on the deck. Full bar, predominantly California wine list. Open for dinner daily, lunch Mon.–Sat., brunch on Sunday.

Still first-rate for French fine dining is **Christophe's,** 2304 E. Bidwell St., 916/983-4883, where entrées range from Hereford ribeye to roast Sonoma duck and wild king salmon. The three-course prix fixe dinner is $35, four-course $45 (wine flights extra); the pricier chef's tasting menu is available upon request. For dessert, try the three-chocolate tart with Strauss organic chocolate ice cream. Full bar, impressive French and California wine list. Christophe's is a dinner-only restaurant, open Tues.–Sun. nights. Patio dining available in summer. Reservations advisable.

If you're in a rockin' mood after dinner, power on in to the **Powerhouse Pub** downtown at 614 Sutter St., 916/355-8586, the local blues, rock, and funk club famous for its shockingly large drink specialty, the Tease Freeze. Do not drink this and drive.

DAVIS AND VICINITY

Northwest of Sacramento via I-80 but close enough to be socially connected is Davis, primarily home to the University of California, Davis, and its student body. People in self-consciously casual Davis, the self-proclaimed Bicycle Capital of the World and an intellectual oasis amid the fields of beans and tomatoes, are quite conscious of their environmental and global responsibilities—this despite the fact that some in California still dismiss the campus as strictly an agricultural school. Among its many other distinctions, UC Davis is one of the top 25 research universities in the nation. The scramble for corporate cash has been immensely successful, with Davis raking in some $300 million for research in 2001. A $95 million Genome and Biomedical Center was set to be unveiled in 2004.

Yet Davis does shine in agriculture. Its veterinary school is renowned. A $42 million new Plant and Environmental Sciences Building opened in 2002. Wine lovers should note that UC Davis has the largest enology department in the nation, with hundreds of students dedicated to the study of winemaking, and a distinguished program in viticulture. Coming soon: a new institute for wine and science. Davis supports less glamorous crops, too—including tomatoes. These "love apple" aphrodisiacs, all but banned by the Puritans, are a specialty in and around Davis—and more publicly since the local biotech firm, Calgene, Inc. (now owned by Monsanto) debuted its "Flavr Savr" variety in 1994. Ready or not, Calgene has also patented red and blue cotton varieties.

But Davis is more than agriculture, which is surely why UC Davis's unofficial poet-in-residence Gary Snyder, who won the Pulitzer Prize in 1975, was awarded the prestigious Bollingen Prize in Poetry in 1997. Davis offers other sur-

MONDAVI'S HIGH CULTURE

Talk about spectacular acoustics and unimpeded sightlines. Talk about soaring, inspired architecture, down to stunning interior touches such as the "recycled" 500-year-old Douglas fir veneer, from seasoned, "lost" old-growth logs recently fished up from the depths of Canada's Ruby Lake. Talk about green attitude in general, from the intentional east/west orientation of the building (for optimal passive solar heating and cooling) and nontoxic paints, wood sealers, and adhesives to landscape plants that are either California natives or drought-tolerant species. Talk about a world-class roster of performers—from Yo-Yo Ma and Itzhak Perlman to Herbie Hancock and Bobby McFerrin, from the Bavarian Radio Symphony Orchestra to the Lincoln Center Jazz Orchestra.

Whatever the topic, the new $61 million, 104,000-square-foot **Mondavi Center for the Performing Arts** at the University of California at Davis campus, just west of Sacramento via I-80, is the talk of the town.

Its seed funding provided by Robert and Margrit Mondavi of the Napa Valley's Robert Mondavi Winery fame, the dramatic sandstone and glass Mondavi Center features a see-and-be seen lightbox lobby for the beautiful people yet plenty of warmth and substance for everyone else. Designed by Stanley Boles and BOORA Architects of Portland, Oregon, the Mondavi Center includes 1,800-seat Jackson Hall, the main performance venue, and the 250-seat Studio Theatre. Mondavi wines and other refreshments are served at the facility's snack bars. Call the Mondavi Center at 530/754-2787 or 866/754-2787 for tickets (530/754-5000 for non-ticket questions) or see www.mondaviarts.org.

The Mondavi Center is a prominent feature of what UC Davis officials call the university's "new front door," a prominent public access point now in development just off I-80 at Old Davis Road. There's another Mondavi monument in the works there, just west of the Mondavi Center. Groundbreaking for the **Robert Mondavi Institute for Wine and Food Science** is set for 2004. Along with the existing Buehler Alumni and Visitors Center, the new UC Davis front door will also include a hotel with restaurant and pub, a conference facility, and a visual arts center.

prises, including the 110-acre **UC Davis Arboretum,** along Putah Creek on the south side of the campus, home to numerous trees and a wide variety of native and other plantlife well adapted to the valley's Mediterranean climate. More intriguing to most people, though, are the five on-campus "egghead sculptures" of UC Davis alumnus **Robert Arneson.** Personal favorites include **Bookhead** outside Shields Library, **See no Evil—Hear no Evil** outside the law school's King Hall, and **Stargazer** near the main campus quadrangle. And the art just keeps on coming: A new campus luminary is the stunning $61 million **Mondavi Center for the Performing Arts** at the university's entrance, which hosted the Alvin Ailey American Dance Theater, cellist Yo-Yo Ma, the London City Opera, and the Stuttgart Ballet in its 2002–03 inaugural season. Forthcoming projects include a hotel, restaurant, and visual arts gallery.

For more information about UC Davis, and to arrange a campus tour, contact the **UC Davis Visitor Services** at the Walter A. Buehler Alumni and Visitors Center, corner of Mrak Hall Drive and Old Davis Road, 530/752-8111 or see www.ucdavis.edu. For more information about the larger community, contact the **Davis Chamber of Commerce,** 130 G Street in Davis, 530/756-5160, www.davischamber.com, or the associated **Davis Conference and Visitors Bureau,** 530/297-1900 or 877/713-2847, www.davisvisitor.com.

Doing Davis and Vicinity

A community fueled these days by good food, good ideas, and a fairly creative cultural atmosphere, Davis's biggest event of all nonetheless dates back to the early 1900s. **Picnic Day** in April attracts up to 80,000 people each year for the academic open house plus parade, partying, picnicking, and participatory sports like Ozz Ball (volleyball played in ankle-deep mud) and the traditional Cow Chip Flip. Earthy in a different way is the long-running **Whole Earth Festival** in early May, its focus on appropriate environmental values enforced by the Karma Patrol. Also famous in Davis are the town's long-distance bicycle races, among them the semisuicidal **Double Century Bike Tour** in May, a 200-mile roundtrip from Davis to Clear Lake, and the July 4th **Criterium Bicycle Races.** The big deal in mid-February, though, and quite appropriate here in the middle of the Pacific Flyway, is the weekend-long **California Duck Days** wetlands festival. Duck Days events include regional wildlife sanctuary field trips, bird-watching, and workshops on topics such as tule boat making, Native American uses of wetlands plants, gardening for wildlife, fly fishing, even birddog demonstrations.

If you're in town with the kids, explore hands-on **Explorit Science Center,** 3141 Fifth St., 530/756-0191, www.explorit.org, with changing exhibits such as "Count On It: Numbers In Nature," exploring snowflakes, honeycombs, tree rings, tidal currents, and other mathematical patterns in nature. Explorit is usually open Tues.–Fri. 2–4:30 P.M. and Saturday and Sunday 11 A.M.–4:30 P.M. Admission is $3, free for everyone on the fourth Saturday of each month. A long-running Davis tradition, the eclectic **Palms Public Playhouse** has moved to Winters. (See Adventuring near Davis.) But this being a university town, beer alone is a big draw. Notable is **Sudwerk Privatbraueri Hubsch,** the first computerized U.S. microbrewery, at home in what looks like an office complex at 2001 Second St., 530/758-8700, www.sudwerk.com, beloved for its Bavarian lager beers and German-style pub fare. (Try the chicken-apple sausage, or the Cajun-style andouille.) The outdoor beer garden here is particularly inviting during the hazy days of summer.

Otherwise, the best way to appreciate Davis is to do like the students do—just hang out. A walking tour of public art is worth it; ask for guidance at the chamber office. And art galleries, like bookstores, abound. Come for **Second Friday** evening gallery receptions each month. Also keep in mind that Davis is a grand jumping-off point for the Bay Area—especially if you don't want to drive. Catch the Amtrak Capitol trains to Oakland here at Davis's train station, 840 Second St., 530/758-4220 (information only), www.amtrak.com.

There are worlds worth exploring near Davis, too. Historic **Woodland** just to the north features some fine 19th- and 20th-century architecture, including the **Woodland Opera House,** and the unique **Hays Antique Truck Museum** and the **Heidrick Ag History Center.** South of **Dixon,** home of the annual spring **Lambtown U.S.A. Festival,** and southeast of Fairfield is the **Western Railway Museum,** which offers daytrip excursions on "wildflower trains" to the **Jepson Prairie Reserve** as well as "Santa trains" at Christmas. For more information, see Adventuring near Davis. Also quite unique near Davis is **DQ University** (short for Deganawidah-Quetzalcoatl University), the nation's oldest Indian-controlled college not housed on a reservation, founded in 1971.

Eating in Davis

For the freshest possible fresh food, try to arrive for the famous **Davis Certified Farmers Market** in Central Park (Fourth and C Streets), 530/756-1695, scheduled year-round on Saturday 8 A.M.–noon and on Wednesday 4:30–8:30 P.M. (May–Sept.) or 2–6 P.M. (Oct.–Apr.). Otherwise, the member-owned **Davis Food Co-op** in flashy remodeled quarters at the onetime Safeway at Sixth and G Streets, 530/758-2667, is a good stop for nonmembers, too, offering organic produce, bulk foodstuffs, and more standard grocery items. Of architectural note: Though numerous locals were outraged when the co-op unveiled its new look, a combination of corrugated steel, vividly painted exposed plywood, and oddball shapes, the design won a prestigious award from the California Council of the American Institute of Architects in 1998. For bread, nothing beats **Village Bakery,** next to the Amtrak station at 814 Second St. (at H), 530/750-2255, which supplies artisan breads to regional restaurants and markets—asiago and garlic Parmesan to challah, ficelle, Kalamata, and more. But the Village also sells some bread here retail—and also bakes unforgettable pizzas in its brick oven. Open weekdays 6 A.M.–8 P.M., Saturday until 7 P.M.

Another essential foodie stop—you can easily gather up the fixings here for a bang-up picnic or rolling lunch—is the **Nugget Market** in the Oaktree Plaza at 1414 E. Covell Blvd., 530/750-3800, where the food court boasts a burrito bar, a Chinese buffet, and a cold case full of delightful surprises, from Hawaiian pasta or Sicilian bean salad to shrimp ceviche, chipotle chicken wings, chicken picadillo enchiladas. Nugget offers specialty olives, too, and (at last count) more than 200 cheeses. Marvelous produce, seafood, meat, and wine departments.

Davis also boasts a branch of Auburn's beloved **Ikeda's,** 26295 Mace Blvd., 530/750-3379, where you can load up on regional fruit and vegetables, home-style pies, real ice cream shakes, and teriyaki burgers with fries.

This being a university town, there's lots of good food and in all price ranges. Local coffeehouses and cafes serve inexpensive fare appropriate to student budgets. Popular **Pluto's,** 500 First St., 530/758-8676, serves up all kinds of fresh, fairly inexpensive food—grilled eggplant sandwiches, buffalo wings, you name it—and does it cafeteria-style. Open daily for lunch and dinner. Wildly popular **Sophia's Thai Kitchen,** inside the shaded food court at 129 E St. (between First and Second), 530/758-4333, is a best bet for curries, seafood dishes, and vegetarian specialties such as *sri da chom,* chunks of tofu and fresh spinach in red curry and peanut sauce. Always popular nearby is the Davis branch of Sacramento's popular **Cafe Bernardo** bistro, here at home inside the Palm Court Hotel at Third and D Streets, 530/750-5101, open for breakfast, lunch, and dinner. Favorites here include omelettes, turkey burgers, stir-fry, and pizzas. Due to some legal technicalities, beloved Murder Burgers ("Burgers so Good, They're to Die For") has now gone Stephen King, as in **Redrum Burgers.** Redrum, still located at 978 Olive Dr., 530/756-2142, serves pretty good burgers—not necessarily worth dying for—and fries. Nearby, at 1020 Olive, Davis also has an **In-N-Out Burger.**

A bit more refined at lunch is **The Mustard Seed** café downtown at 222 D St., 530/758-5750, where the menu runs to New American. Very Davis. Open Mon.–Sat. for lunch and din-

ner. Reservations advised. Quite good for flavorful Mediterranean is stylish **Soga's** nearby at 217 E. St. (at Second), 530/757-1733, where you can savor favorites such as grilled New York steak, pork chops with pear and mint chutney, and pistachio-crusted salmon with coconut-mango rice and red Thai curry. Great California wine list. Open weekdays for lunch, Mon.–Sat. for dinner, reservations strongly suggested.

A real find in Davis is been-there-forever, family-run **Symposium,** tucked away in a shopping complex at 1620 E. Eighth St., 530/756-3850, a sophisticated Greek restaurant serving 23 kinds of exceptional "spicy Greek pizza," exceptional broiled lamb chops, homemade moussaka, and a variety of seafood specialties normally caught considerably closer to the Aegean Sea. Open for dinner Mon.–Sat., for lunch weekdays only. Though this is the kind of place one happily lingers over a meal, takeout is available. For downhome Czechoslovakian, the place is **Little Prague Bohemian Restaurant** at 330 G St., 530/756-1107, where the Viennese pastries—eclairs, cream puffs, napoleons, tortes, marzipan, and astonishing cakes—shine forth daily. Before you indulge that sweet tooth, sample the hearty fare—beef stroganoff; pork schnitzel; several goulashes; roast duck; pork tenderloin stuffed with apples, bacon, and red onions; and salmon in saffron sauce. Beer and wine only. Pastries are served whenever the restaurant is open, but otherwise Little Prague is open Tues.–Fri. for breakfast and lunch; Saturday and Sunday for brunch; and daily for dinner.

If time and waistline elastic allow, the most delectable postdinner destination around is **Ciocolat,** 301 B St., 530/753-3088, locally famous for its extraordinary desserts, including French and Italian mousse cakes. Also stop for breakfast pastries or afternoon "high tea," served Thurs.–Sat. 2–4:30 P.M. Open Tues.–Sat. 7:30 A.M.–10 P.M. Nearby and almost as sinful for dessert: **Crepeville,** 330 Third St., 530/750-2400, featuring fruit and Nutella dessert crepes. Crepeville's lunch and dinner varieties are tasty, too.

Adventuring near Davis

Get out and into nature. Notable between West Sacramento and Davis is the Yolo Bypass floodway, including the 16,500-acre **Vic Fazio Yolo Wildlife Area,** federally protected wetlands, an essential migratory bird stop along the Pacific Flyway, and the largest public/private restoration project west of the Florida Everglades. An auto tour route and walking trails offer public access. Monthly field trips are offered, often led by Yolo Audubon Society members. To visit: From I-80 just east of Sacramento, exit at Mace Boulevard and turn south. Turn left onto Chiles Road and continue 1.5 miles to the Department of Fish and Game Yolo Bypass Wildlife Area Headquarters, 45211 Chiles Road. The Vic Fazio Yolo Wildlife Area is another two miles to the east. For information on field trips ($3 donation) call the Yolo Basin Foundation at 530/758-1018 or see www.yolobasin.org. Closer to the Bay Area, hike the Marsh Trail at the 2,000-acre **Rush Ranch** Suisun Marsh preserve, two miles south of Fairfield on Grizzly Island Road, 707/432-0150, also noted for its birding.

The **Jepson Prairie Reserve** near Dixon, purchased for protection in 1980 by The Nature Conservancy and now managed by the Solano County Farmlands and Open Space Foundation, includes 1,556 acres of native bunchgrass— grasslands that have never been tilled. Spectacular on a small scale at Jepson is the concentric-ring bloom progression of vernal pool wildflowers that grow in rainwater-collecting "hog wallows." Starting in early spring, the subtle show changes almost weekly. Other stars of the vernal pool ecosystem protected here include three species of fairy shrimp protected under the U.S. Endangered Species Act. There's a short self-guided nature trail at Jepson Prairie, but otherwise access is offered only on guided tours—offered every Saturday and Sunday during peak wildflower season, mid-March to mid-May (small donation requested). For more information see www.vernalpools.org. For groups of five or more, call 707/432-0150 to make a reservation. To get to Jepson Prairie, head south on Hwy. 113 from Dixon, then dogleg left onto Cook Ln. (dirt road). Cross the railroad tracks and continue on to the parking area.

Another way to get to Jepson Prairie is by train—the Spring Wildflower Train offered by Solano County's **Western Railway Museum,** lo-cated between Suisun and Rio Vista, 707/374-2978, www.wrm.org. The railroad's new Visitors and Archives Center, 5848 Hwy. 12, includes the Depot Café, where you can grab a snack. The museum itself, a project of the Bay Area Electric Railroad Association, offers unlimited rides on its rickety streetcars and "interurbans." The museum is always open weekends, 10:30 A.M.–5 P.M., and in summer Wed.–Sun. (same hours). Admission is $8 adults, $7 seniors, $5 children. But for the Jepson Prairie excursion, it enlists a diesel locomotive and Pullman parlor car coaches. Call for additional information and reservations (required) for the **Spring Wildflower Train** to Jepson Prairie and the holiday **Pumpkin Patch Train** and **Santa Train.**

The **Yolo Shortline Railroad,** 341 Industrial Way in Woodland, 916/372-9777 (recorded information), 530/681-1031 or 800/942-6387 (reservations), www.ysrr.com, offers a great train ride along the original Sacramento Northern route, with trains departing variously from Woodland, Raley's Landing, and West Sacramento on Saturday and Sunday from May through December. The refurbished 1940s-vintage trains are fun for family outings; basic fare is $15 adults, $10 children. Murder Mystery, Great Train Robbery, Haunted Halloween, Polar Express trains and other special events are also scheduled. On the third weekend of the month, the railroad usually gives its diesel weekend off—and conscripts its World War I-vintage steam engine for all trips. Private charters also available.

Woodland itself, just north from Davis via Hwy. 113, was once a sleepy farm town but is now a fast-growing commercial center with little of its honorable hayseed history intact. Or so it seemed true until 1997, when the 130,000-square-foot **Heidrick Ag History Center** opened at 1962 Hays Ln. (just off I-5 adjacent to the County Road 102 offramp), 530/666-9700, www.aghistory.org. Stars of this collection of more than 170 farm machines include a number of Fordson tractors—not to mention the 150 trucks of the **Hays Antique Truck Museum,** all-American trucks from more than 100 manufacturers (like Graham Brothers, Old Reliable, and Oshkosh), also collected here. Open most days 10 A.M.–5 P.M. (until 6 P.M. Sat., 4 P.M. Sun.), admission $6 adults, $5 seniors, and $4 children under age 12. A real attention-getter immediately adjacent, open late September until early November, is the amazing **MAiZE**—a 10-acre field of corn shaped and pruned into a very challenging maze (you need the map to get out). Admission $5–7. For current information, see www.cornfieldmaze.com.

Also worth a look in Woodland is its architecture, given the town's impressive record of preserving its old-timers. The Gibson House at 512 Gibson Rd., 530/666-1045, a restored 1872 farmhouse with gardens, prime for picnicking, now the **Yolo County Museum** and open Monday and Tuesday 10 A.M.–4 P.M., weekends noon–4 P.M. Admission $2. John Phillip Sousa and Sidney Greenstreet once performed at the imposing redbrick **Woodland Opera House,** 340 Second St. (at Main), 530/666-9617, www.wohtheatre.org, the only 19th-century theater in California to survive without being put to other uses. Come for plays like *The Rainmaker,* and Young People's Theatre performances such as *Alice in Wonderland.* To fully appreciate local architecture, though, come for the annual **Stroll Through History** in September. For details about the area and its events and attractions, contact the **Woodland Chamber of Commerce,** 307 First St., 530/662-7327 or 888/843-2636, www.woodlandchamber.com. Worthy local restaurants include **Ludy's Main Street BBQ,** 667 Main St., 530/666-4400, chock full of old-timey touches, and fancier **Morrison's Upstairs** downtown on First Street, 530/666-6176. Just northwest of Woodland in Yolo, off I-5, is **Gorman's Fine Food and Provisions,** 37380 Sacramento St., 530/662-6889, the onetime Gorman's Fine Food Fountain transformed into an outpost of fresh regional American—sautéed golden trout, braised beef ribs with Parmesan polenta, lamb with tongues-of-fire beans. Good wine list, full bar.

South of Davis via Hwy. 113 is **Dixon,** once known as the sheep capital of the world. At the **Dixon May Fair,** www.dixonmayfair.com, an annual rite of spring, sheep are still big, what with the international sheep-shearing competition and sheepdog trials as well as concerts, car-

nival games, and rides. Or come in July for the annual **Lambtown Festival,** www.lambtown.com, with its Sheep to Shawl contest, more sheepdogs, and lamb cookoff. In recent years there's been serious talk about building Dixon Downs, a $150 million horse-racing facility, on the north side of town near I-80.Many locals oppose the project and the crowds and congestion it would bring, but others welcome the prospect of more jobs.

Since *vaca* in Spanish means "cow," impolite passersby have attached the literal "cowtown" to **Vacaville** as a modern epithet, though the community is one of the valley's oldest and was actually named for the area's original landowner, Don Manuel Vaca. The California Medical Facility at Vacaville is the place mass murderer Charles Manson now calls home, but the town itself was most noted as that stretch of freeway perfumed by the overpowering aroma of onions. Now that the local dehydrating plant has closed its doors, even Vacaville's annual Onion Festival is defunct. And so is **The Nut Tree,** Vacaville's famous restaurant—originally a humble roadside fruit stand when it opened for business in the 1920s. People still hope someone will buy the Nut Tree and resurrect it. In the meantime, alternative rest stops include the **Vacaville Museum,** 213 Buck Ave., 707/447-4513, www.vacavillemuseum.org, open Wed.–Sun., 1 P.M.–4:30 P.M.The **Animal Place** animal sanctuary at 3448 Laguna Creek Trail, 707/449-4814, www.animalplace.org, home to abused and discarded farmed animals, offers occasional farm tours. For a bite (including veggie options), try the **Old Post Office Seafood & Grill,** at 301 Main St., 707/447-1858, Vacaville's grand old post office, now a California-style French restaurant.

Though new subdivisions are popping up among the tomato fields and fruit and nut orchards, **Winters** on Hwy. 128 (near Lake Berryessa as you head north off the 505 cutoff) is still an outpost of California's Western ethos. Winters' attractions include one of California's last working blacksmith shops (Anderson Iron Works); the elegant white terra-cotta First Northern Bank of Dixon, with its antique opaque glass and marble floors and counters; and a well-known trout stream, Putah Creek, running right through town. Something of a reluctant transplant from Davis, the famed **Palms Playhouse** is now at home in the 1875 Winters Opera House, 13 Main St. (near Railroad Avenue), 530/795-1825, www.palmsplayhouse.com, a surprisingly comfortable yet offbeat venue for showcasing the likes of the Laura Love Band, Rodney Crowell, Mumbo Gumbo, Peter Rowan and Don Edwards, the Waybacks, and the Austin Lounge Lizards. The location may be new—and who can adjust to central heating and air-conditioning?—but you can still buy Cracker Jacks and pretzels by the cup.

Within a block or two are all kinds of great little shops and restaurants, including **Chuy's Taqueria,** 208 Railroad Ave., 530/795-9811. Killer for breakfast and lunch is **Putah Creek Café,** 1 Main St., 530/795-2682, where the cool comfort food includes blueberry pancakes, banana-caramel-walnut waffles, and the Putah Creek scramble. House specialties include the Santa Fe Mexican corn pie, Moroccan lamb stew, and char-roast sirloin sandwiches. Open daily from 6 A.M. for lunch and dinner, with lunch starting at 11 or 11:30 A.M. Dinner served too, Thurs.–Sat. nights, until 9 P.M. And why not try an apricot bar for dessert? Across the street is Putah Creek's sibling, the **Buckhorn Steak & Roadhouse** inside the onetime DeVilbiss Hotel at 2 Main St., 707/795-4503, decorated with a mountain lion pelt over the bar and omnipresent mounted heads everywhere: bucks, rams, goats, antelopes, even a moose. Without reservations, it's a long wait playing liar's dice at the mahogany bar or sitting on "the horny bench" built of bullhorns and cowhide. The food is vegetarian nightmare fare—three kinds of prime rib, excellent steaks, and combos—though the daily specials usually offer some worthy alternatives. Full saloon, too.

The Delta

The ancient tule marshes created by the confluence of the Sacramento and San Joaquin Rivers are long gone in California's great delta. The Sacramento–San Joaquin Delta is the largest estuary on the West Coast, and the second largest in the country, overshadowed only by Chesapeake Bay. But by contemporary California standards there's really nothing to *do* in the delta—no world-class sights, amusement parks, or zoos, no big-name entertainment, nightclubs, coffeehouses. This fact is the main attraction of this lazy labyrinth of backwater sloughs, canals, lakes, lagoons, and meandering rivers and streams. The personality and pace of the Deep South seep up throughout the delta; no one here was surprised when Samuel Goldwyn Jr. picked it as the filming location for *Huckleberry Finn.* People come here to drive along the levees and count great blue herons, to watch drawbridges go up and down, and ferries and freighters pass, to windsurf and sail and water-ski, or to houseboat like modern-day Huck Finns down unknown waterways in search of nothing in particular.

THE LAND

Since the last ice age and until the last century, the delta was a jungle of oaks, sycamores, willows, and vines punctuated by thickets of tules and teeming with life: herds of tule elk, pronghorn, and deer; beavers, river otters, and foxes; migrating waterfowl and songbirds; rivers of fish and the grizzlies who fished for them. Life went on, eon after eon, and however much water flowed through the delta—and then, as now, the mighty Sacramento River contributed 70–80 percent—it was always enough. But the situation soon changed, beginning in the 1860s when California leaders urged settlers to come and save the delta from its own wildness, to "reclaim" it for productive use. The wetlands were sold off for $1 an acre to anyone willing to dike and drain them.

The land in California's great delta—whether agricultural or recreational—isn't really *land,* not in the usual sense of the word. Before completion of the delta's complex system of levees and dredged canals, the annual winter-spring flooding of the area was as predictable as rain and

WHEN THE LEVEE BREAKS

Like the lyrics from a traditional blues song—"When the levee breaks I'll have no place to stay"—in an area dependent on its dikes and levees for its very existence, what happens when this system becomes unreliable? No one knows. But one of these days we'll probably find out.

For one thing, the levees themselves never were strong. Built of the area's loose peat soils and vulnerable even to gophers, they break when floodwaters threaten—more frequently all the time, despite increasing water diversions. During the past 100 years, each of the delta's 70 major islands and tracts has flooded at least once, and since 1930, some have flooded several times. Meanwhile, delta islands have been steadily "sinking" at a rate of three to five inches per year. As they do, internal water pressure against the levees increases. When a break occurs under these circumstances, ocean water from the Bay Area flows into the resulting water-pressure vacuum, adding salinity to the delta's freshwater ecosystem and, potentially, all interconnected federal and state water projects. Also, delta levees—in an area with five separate known fault lines—are unusually vulnerable to earthquakes. The peat soil itself is a particular problem, since it tends to amplify quake vibrations.

These problems are compounded by others, such as soil erosion. Since 1976, the dollar value of delta crops has plummeted; the fact that agricultural islands have the weakest levees has also affected agricultural productivity. And new housing developments for Bay Area commuters are bringing growth related problems, including more polluted runoff and displacement of wetlands. Estimates of how much it will cost to repair or rebuild the Sacramento–San Joaquin levee system range to $4–10 billion or more. For some reason, no one wants to pick up that tab.

Delta restoration may move forward when California's water wars end—a reality many felt was close at hand in 2000. That year, as a result of the complicated CalFed (state and federal) negotiations, environmentalists, large-scale agricultural interests, and urban water users reached a restoration agreement. The solution lacked—and lacks—only legislative approval and funding from the U.S. Congress and the state legislature.

Sierra Nevada snowmelt. Some islands emerged in summer and fall, or appeared only in dry years—a fact acceptable to the 30,000 or so native people who once lived off the region's natural bounty but too unpredictable for settlers determined to stake their ownership claims.

The delta is the largest water engineering network in the world, its century-old levee system built by Chinese laborers just finished with the transcontinental railroad. Before the advent of the clamshell dredge in the 1930s, hundreds of windmills once dotted the landscape, powering the pumps that first drained the area. Almost all Northern California river water eventually arrives in the delta; today up to 85 percent is channeled, diverted, and pumped south to irrigate farmland and to provide drinking water for some 20 million urbanites in the Bay Area and Los Angeles.

But even with levees and modern water-pumping stations in place, the struggle to control life and water here is difficult.

Out of that struggle has come innovation, such as snowshoe-like horseshoes for draft animals to keep them from sinking into mushy delta soils. With the arrival of agricultural machinery, the same problem called for an equally novel solution. Thus delta resident Ben Holt devised the caterpillar tread tractor shortly after the turn of the century, just in time for the British to buy the idea and convert it to military use, producing tanks that would roll ahead with ensuing world wars, mucky ground or no.

SEEING AND DOING THE DELTA

Only five of the delta's 70 major islands feature sizable development or towns. These include Bethel Island and its namesake subdivision; Byron Tract, home to Discovery Bay; Brannan-Andrus Island,

GREAT VALLEY & THE DELTA

with Brannan Island State Recreation Area and the town of Isleton; New Hope Tract and the town of Thornton; and Hotchkiss Tract and Oakley.

Many of the area's tiny towns and attractions are scattered around the delta's edges. The port city of Stockton, itself missable, is nonetheless a major jumping-off point for the southern delta. Rio Vista (via Hwy. 12) is a good place to start from in the north, Sacramento (via scenic Hwy. 160) in the east, and Antioch (over the Antioch Bridge via Hwy. 160) in the west.

Locke

The Chinese community of Locke sprang to life in 1915 shortly after nearby Walnut Grove's Chinatown burned to the ground. America's last rural Chinatown and listed on the National Register of Historic Places, today Locke has the look of a faded frontier town and consists of little more than levee-bound Main St., one block long, with weatherbeaten wood frames leaning out over the narrow, pickup-lined street. But Locke in its prime was home to 2,000 or so Chinese and had general stores, herb shops, fish markets, a hotel, a dozen boardinghouses, even the Star Theatre, where Chinese opera was performed. In the roaring twenties and through the Depression, Locke was also known for its Caucasian brothels and speakeasies, and Chinese gambling houses and opium dens—attractive to both bone-tired field workers seeking escape from their dismal lives and big-city sophisticates out slumming.

Open on weekends only, the **Dai Loy Museum** on Main St. is a former gambling house that was in business from 1916 to 1950. Dai Loy, which means "big welcome," displays gamblers' artifacts, old photos, and gaming tables set up for fan-tan and flying bull, as well as testimony to the vital role of the Chinese in delta development. The museum is usually open Thurs.–Sun. 11 A.M.–4:30 P.M.; for more information, call the **Sacramento River Delta Historical Society** at 916/776-1661.

Almost a museum is **Al the Wop's** bar and restaurant, 13936 Main St., 916/776-1800, exuding delta cultural history (and crammed with farmers, ranch hands, and tourists), with local wisdom behind the bar and jars of peanut butter

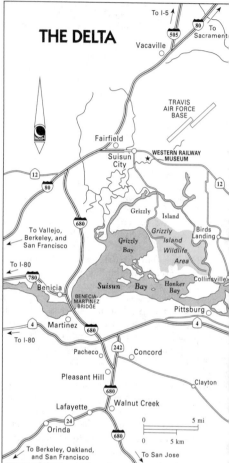

THE DELTA

and jelly on every table. The question people always ask: How *do* they get all those dollar bills up there on the ceiling? Check out the works of local artists at **River Road Art Gallery,** 13944 Main St., 916/776-1132; open Fri.–Sun. 11 A.M.–5 P.M.

Locke, itself a museum, is the center of various commercial-development proposals that preservationists fear will destroy its historic Chinese character. An excellent book about Locke is *Bitter Melon: Stories from the Last Rural Chinese Town in America* by Jeff Gillenkirk and James Motlow, published by The University of Washington Press.

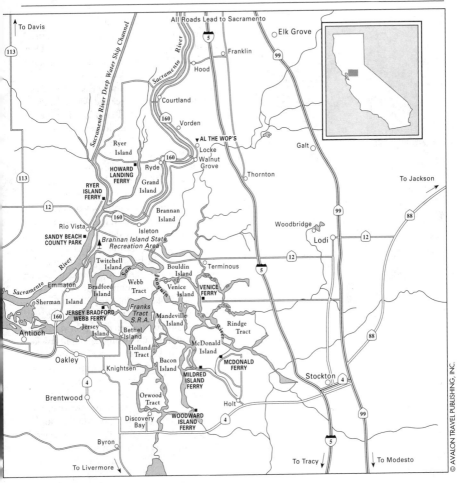

Near Locke is **Delta Meadows River Park,** a portion of California's everglades—tule marshes and shady sloughs with water hyacinths and pond lilies, particularly popular with houseboaters for overnight anchorage. To get there from Locke head south, turn left off Hwy. 160 at the Ti-Gas Company (onto Twin Cities Road).

Walnut Grove

Three miles from Ryde and a hop across the Delta Cross Channel from Locke is tiny Walnut Grove, the only town south of Red Bluff to

occupy both banks of the Sacramento River. Reputed to be a lair for riverboat bandits in its early days, for decades the town has been serene and sleepy, a farm community with little left of its Japanese and Chinese past except a block-long strip of boarded-up bareboard buildings. One of Walnut Grove's newer attractions is the **Walnut Grove Dock,** which has spurred a mini-boom in local business improvements.

Isleton

Another delta town with a Chinatown past is

Locke, the last rural Chinatown in America

Isleton on Andrus Island, today a tin-sided shadow of its former self. In the 1930s, Isleton billed itself as The Asparagus Center of the World, since 90 percent of the world's canned asparagus was grown and processed in the area. During post-fire rebuilding in the 1920s and '30s, Japanese-Americans also became an integral part of the community. Gambling and prostitution once flourished along today's boarded-up Main Street. During World War II, the population declined when residents of Japanese descent were shipped off to California internment camps; after the war, the decline continued as asparagus canneries, which were once king in the area, largely relocated elsewhere. The **Isleton Historical Museum,** 60 Main St., offers exhibits on the town's history, and staff can answer your questions about the area. Open May–Sept., weekends 1–4 P.M. For more information, call the Isleton Chamber of Commerce, 916/777-5880.

Isleton only really comes to life these days during the community's **Crawdad Festival** in June—if you miss that, there's an annual **Rodeo on the River** in September—but there's a mix of old and new businesses scattered among abandoned storefronts and two decent local restaurants. A good place to picnic just north of Isleton is **Hogback Island County Park** (free). To get there, from Hwy. 160 take Poverty Rd. north to its intersection with Walker Landing Rd., then turn left and continue on to the levee and Walker Landing's intersection with Grand Island Rd.; facilities include barbecues, picnic tables, and restrooms.

Rio Vista

Rio Vista, a small town astride Hwy. 12 just across the drawbridge from Brannan-Andrus Island, is most famous for a 45-ton celebrity humpback whale named **Humphrey,** who swam into the delta and up the Sacramento River in the fall of 1985, apparently determined to become the first whale to live in the community. Lost for weeks in nearby backwaters and sloughs after taking a wrong turn through the Golden Gate on his way to Mexico, Humphrey was an endangered individual of an endangered species.

His official rescuers at first maintained a hands-off policy, hoping the whale would realize his error, turn around, and swim the 55 miles back to sea. When it became clear that Humphrey couldn't or wouldn't make the trip on his own, marine biologists attempted to herd him with boats, lure him back to sea with recorded sounds of whales eating, or scare him downriver with killer whale sounds and by pounding on underwater pipes. But Humphrey the wrong-way whale didn't budge until he was good and ready—which was after he was treated to the sounds of whales mating—and even then he kept changing his mind and swimming back upriver. Prodded almost all the way out to the ocean, at one point Humphrey was the focus of 11 Navy vessels included in a flotilla of 30 boats determined to keep him going through San Pablo Bay. The world cheered when Humphrey finally swam—this time in the right direction—under the Golden Gate Bridge. Humphrey made it home, and has survived.

A short poem by 12-year-old Rio Vista resident Richard Fonbuena, inscribed on the town's monument to Humphrey, summarizes the event for all time:

Humphrey the Humpback whale, a mighty whale was he.

He swam into the Delta to see what he could see.

The people stood and stared. The fish was scared.

He was famous across the nation until they ended his vacation.

Sightseeing humans might peek into the **Rio Vista Museum,** 16 N. Front St., 707/374-5169, open 1:30–4:30 P.M. weekends only—a onetime blacksmith shop with several rooms of area memorabilia telling the story of Rio Vista. One wall is covered with old license plates and newspaper front pages.

From May to October, world-class **windsurfing** is possible—and quite popular—in the open expanses of the Sacramento River near Rio Vista, at the **Sherman Island Public Access** just south of town via Hwy. 160. Other local diversions include the Bay Area Electric Railroad Association's **Western Railway Museum** at the Hwy. 12—Rio Vista Junction, 707/374-2978 featuring more than 100 streetcars and railroad cars, also a small looping track for 15-minute rides. Open Wed.–Sun. and holidays 10:30 A.M.–5 P.M. in summer, 10:30 A.M.–5 P.M. weekends only the rest of the year; admission is $7 adults, $6 seniors, $4 children 3–12. Special rail excursions are frequently scheduled; call for information.

From Rio Vista, head north for a free ride on one of the delta's few remaining ferries, this one an authentic passenger ship requiring a licensed navigator at the helm. The **Ryer Island Ferry** *Real McCoy* navigates Cache Slough from Ryer Island Rd. off Hwy. 160 to Ryer Island. For another down-home delta crossing, turn right and follow the levee road to Steamboat Slough and the *J-Mack* cable-driven ferry, which runs to Grand Island and its landmark 1917 **Grand Island Mansion,** a four story, 58-room Italian Renaissance villa, 916/775-1705.

Brannan Island State Recreation Area

Not a natural environment by any means, open, often wind-blown Brannan Island State Recre-ation Area three miles south of Rio Vista nonetheless makes an ideal spot for picnicking, year-round camping, and recreational pursuits from boating and windsurfing to fishing and swimming. Flanked on three sides by the Sacramento River, Seven Mile Slough, and Three Mile Slough and accessible via Hwy. 160, Brannan Island's facilities include two family camping areas (the Willow and Cottonwood camp-grounds); six group camps; 32 boat-in campsites with boat berths; boat-launching ramps; a public swimming beach and picnic area; a rally site for RVs; a sanitation station (but there are only water hookups). Learn more about area history and wildlife at the park's interpretive center.

Accessible only by boat across Piper Slough from Bethel Island, **Franks Tract State Recreation Area** five miles southeast of Brannan Island is now largely underwater due to levee breakage. The large "lake" here offers exceptional fishing. **Little Franks Tract** is a marsh area rich in natural vegetation and wildlife (no hunting, no fires) and still protected by the levees.

Camping is popular at Brannan Island ($16, cold showers only). Reservations through ReserveAmerica, 800/444-7275 or www.reserve-america.com, are usually necessary Mar.-Oct. The day-use fee for Brannan Island is $5. To help celebrate National Fishing Week in June, the park sponsors a children's fishing derby. For more information, contact: Brannan Island/Franks Tract State Recreation Areas, 17645 Hwy. 160 in Rio Vista, 916/777-6671.

Grizzly Island Wildlife Area

Adjacent to privately owned portions of Solano County's Suisin Marsh is Grizzly Island Wildlife Area. Now only semivast after a century of reclamation but still one of the world's richest estuarine marshes, the marsh has no grizzlies these days, but tule elk, "the little elk of the prairie," have come home again. Believed extinct more than 100 years ago, California's tule elk population is making quite a comeback everywhere the species has been reintroduced. (March and April are the best months for observing the matriarchal tule elk during calving season, also for watching river otters.)

Corraled by delta levees, the Grizzly Island area includes 1,887-acre Joice Island near the on-site headquarters and 8,600-acre Grizzly Island proper. Waterfowl hunting (by permit only, these issued at the headquarters) is popular here, as is fishing. With more than a million birds wintering here, birdwatchers and hikers rule the roost when hunters aren't afield.

The reserve is closed for extended periods each year. For exact dates and more information, contact: Grizzly Island Wildlife Area, Department of Fish & Game, 2548 Grizzly Island Rd. in Suisun, 707/425-3828, or Department of Fish & Game, Region 3 Headquarters, 7329 Silverado Trail in Napa, 707/944-5500.

Lower Sherman Island Wildlife Area

This state reserve at the confluence of the Sacramento and San Joaquin Rivers is also popular with waterfowl hunters and fisherfolk. It's a delta island reclaimed by the forces of nature, with boat access only beyond the parking lot—fun to explore by canoe outside hunting season but only with great care, due to the area's strong tidal currents and sudden high winds (usually in the afternoon). For more information, call the Department of Fish & Game, Region 2 Headquarters at 916/358-2900 during regular business hours.

STAYING IN THE DELTA

Most popular for overnights in the delta is houseboating. The cost for houseboat rentals is almost reasonable for groups and families when calculated per person, and summer reservations are necessary many months in advance. (Count on better rates and less advance planning, depending on weather trends, in the spring and autumn off-season.) For houseboat rental sources, see Delta Information below.

Camping at **Brannan Island State Recreation Area** (see above) for both boaters and landlubbers is another popular option, though campers can also try **Sandy Beach Regional Park,** on Beach Dr. in Rio Vista, 707/374-2097 or 800/396-7275, which offers tent and RV sites (with water and electric hookups), barbecue grills,

restrooms, and hot showers; $15. Day-use fee: $4 per car. The delta is dotted with private campground-cabin complexes as well, with motel accommodations also available at some local resorts. For local listings, refer to Hal Schell's *Delta Map and Guide,* available at marinas, stores, information centers, and the Brannan Island State Recreation Area visitor center.

Among the delta's most historically notorious stops is the **Ryde Hotel,** 14340 Hwy. 160 in Ryde, 916/776-1318, which housed a password-only speakeasy casino and dancehall in its basement during Prohibition. Later a popular bikers' bar and flophouse, the old Ryde Hotel was restored to its grand 1920s art-deco style—when people like Al Jolson and Herbert Hoover used to arrive by paddle wheeler for parties—and renamed the Grand Island Mansion. Today the peach-colored 1928 hotel is fully restored and again named the Ryde, featuring a range of accommodations-from European style with shared bath, doubles with private bath, to theme suites. There's a popular restaurant and river-view patio. Rooms are $100–150, the European style (shared bath) a little less, suites $150–250.(The summer season books early). Rooms at the **Delta Daze Inn** bed-and-breakfast, 20 Main St. in Isleton, 916/777-7777, all feature private baths—and a parlor for afternoon tea. Rates $50–100.

EATING IN THE DELTA

Especially in smaller areas, even popular restaurants are open only seasonally, spring through fall. Just south of Sacramento in Freeport, on the edge of the delta, is **Freeport Bar & Grill,** 8259 Freeport Blvd., 916/665-1169, serving chicken, seafood, steaks, pasta, pot roast, and more for lunch and dinner daily.

The place to stop in Locke is **Al the Wop's,** 13936 Main St., 916/776-1800, noted for its very good grilled-steak sandwiches, music video jukebox, and stuffed moose heads and ostrich. A small bribe may be all it takes to get the bartender to share the secret of how all those dollar bills got thumbtacked to the ceiling. (Hint: experiment origami-style with a dollar bill, a silver dollar, and a thumbtack.) Once a year, management cleans the money off the ceiling to finance employee vacations *and* the world-famous Al the Wop's free liver-and-onions feed (usually held in February).

Popular and quite good in Walnut Grove is **Tony's Place,** 14157 Market St., 916/776-1317, which serves lunch on weekdays, and dinner—three entrées only (20-ounce grilled New York steaks, chicken Mornay, or breaded veal Mornay)—with all the trimmings on weekends. Outside Walnut Grove, near the Miller's Ferry Bridge over the north fork of the Mokelumne River, is **Giusti's,** 14743 Walnut Grove–Thornton Rd., 916/776-1808, one of Erle Stanley Gardner's favorite places and fine for country-style Italian fare. (Note the hundreds of baseball and tractor caps on the walls.) Excellent California wine list. Reservations usually necessary weeks in advance for weekends. Open seasonally.

Just east of Giusti's is **Wimpy's,** 14001 W. Walnut Grove Rd., Thornton, 209/794-2544, a homey American café with coffeecake and apple pie, hearty breakfasts and burgers, and an excellent fried chicken dinner.

The **Ryde Hotel,** 14340 Hwy. 160, Ryde, 916/776-1318, offers dinners (full bar) including California country-style entrées like pan-fried catfish and Cajun-spiced pork tenderloin. Breakfast, lunch, and Sunday brunch also served.

Rogelio's, 32 Main St. in Isleton, 916/777-6606, is popular for both Chinese and Mexican fare. Lunch and dinner daily, plus a 24-hour card room. Also here is the **Pineapple Restaurant,** 22 Main St., 916/777-6294, offering Mandarin and Cantonese cuisine for lunch and dinner daily. **Ernie's,** 212 Second St., 916/777-6510, a venerable café and saloon going upscale but still specializing in asparagus and crawdads, is also open for breakfast, lunch, and dinner. Well south of Isleton is **Moore's Riverboat II Restaurant,** 106 W. Brannan Island Rd., on the Mokelumne River at Riverboat Marina, 916/777-4884, serving up some of the area's best crawdads (plastic bibs provided) and other seafood specialties like grilled calamari and baked red snapper. Live rock 'n' roll on weekend nights. Open weekends only in the off-season.

Wild in Rio Vista is the nonvegetarian **Foster's**

Bighorn, 143 Main St., 707/374-2511, noted for its 250 big-game "trophies," including a 13-foot-tall bull elephant, part of one of the world's largest private collections (reputed to be worth $1.5 million and reputed to be for sale). **The Point Restaurant,** 120 Marina Dr., 707/374-5400, a half-mile south of Hwy. 12 and Rio Vista proper via Main then Second St., offers American fare and riverside views at lunch, dinner, and Sunday brunch. Open daily except Monday and the week between Christmas and New Year's. Reservations wise at dinner. For Mexican food in Rio Vista, head to **Maria's,** 646 Hwy. 12, 707/374-5359, open daily for breakfast, lunch, and dinner, or **Taqueria Mexico,** 133 Main St., 707/374-2680.

STOCKTON

Billing itself as both "cosmopolitan and country," Stockton is mostly a bit strange, a hodge-podge of comfortable subdivisions and depressed ethnic neighborhoods, modern shopping centers, and a harbor district and partially devastated downtown now undergoing commercial redevelopment. But Stockton has its history. This place, after all, was the inspiration for the baseball poem "Casey at the Bat," first published in the *San Francisco Examiner.* Poetically speaking, this is Mudville. Whether or not that historic fact had anything to do with it, Stockton is now home to the San Francisco 49ers summer football training camp.

Once known as Tuleberg, Stockton is also home to the University of the Pacific—summer headquarters for the 49ers—which shares a campus with Delta College. The city is justifiably proud of its recently refurbished **Fox Theatre,** 242 E. Main, now drawing big-name entertainment downtown, and the multimillion-dollar Weber Point Events Center, 211 N. Center St., 209/937-8958. In addition to its community ballet, civic theater, chorale group, opera, symphony, and art galleries, the city also boasts the fine art-and-history **Haggin Museum,** 1201 N. Pershing Ave. in Victory Park, 209/462-4116, www.hagginmuseum.org, which has an excellent collection of late 19th-century landscape paintings, including works by Albert

Bierstadt, famous for his paintings of Yosemite, and displays on local historical figures, including Ben Holt, inventor of the caterpillar-type tractor, and Tillie Lewis, the "Tomato Queen." Hours are Tues.–Sun. 1:30–5 P.M. Small admission fee. **Victory Park** surrounding the museum, is a park with a lake and duck ponds. Free evening band concerts held here in summer. Tykes will also like **Pixie Woods,** a kiddie park with train and boat rides and a merry-go-round, in Louis Park, west of I-5 at the Monte Diablo exit, 209/937-8220. Small admission fee.

Odd but fun is **Pollardville,** 10464 N. Hwy. 99 (between Stockton and Lodi), 209/931-0272, a somewhat garish decades-old "ghost town" with a "chicken kitchen" restaurant—you can't miss the huge rooster on the sign—and the **Palace,** a country dance bar. Inveterate stargazers can check out **Clever Planetarium and Earth Science Center** at San Joaquin Delta College, 5151 Pacific Ave., 209/954-5051, which hosts star parties of the Stockton Astronomical Society as well as rock music laser-light shows (209/954-5110).

A complete listing of area attractions and events—including the big Stockton Asparagus Festival the fourth weekend in April and Lodi's Vines to Wines shindig in May—plus accommodations, restaurants, and nightclubs, is available through the local visitors bureau. A series of area brochures, about antique shops, the delta, the greater Stockton area, and San Joaquin County gold-rush stops, is especially worthwhile.

For more information about Stockton and vicinity, contact the **Stockton-San Joaquin Convention and Visitors Bureau,** 46 W. Fremont St., 209/943-1987 or 800/350-1987, www.visitstockton.org.

Lodi

The nearby farming town of Lodi is noted for its vineyards-local farmers have been growing grapes here since 1850. Today area vintners produce 600,000 tons of grapes annually. The **Discover Lodi Wine and Visitor Center** near downtown at 2545 W. Turner Rd., 209/365-1195, www.lodiwine.com, offers tasting advice and educational displays on grape growing and winemak-

ing, as well as a virtual tour of the region. Visitors can sample local wines at the tasting bar, and pick up maps of the new **Lodi Wine Trail.** The tour is a clearly marked 30-mile loop that leads to destination tasting rooms. Lodi is also noted for Micke Grove Regional Park, and the indoor-outdoor **San Joaquin County Historical Museum** (largely an ode to agriculture), 11793 N. Micke Grove Rd., 209/331-2055 or 209/953-3460 (open Wed.–Sun. 10 A.M.–3 P.M.). Also at the park: a Japanese garden; the **Micke Grove Zoo,** 209/953-8840 or 209/331-7270; and **Funderwoods,** 209/369-5437 or 209/469-9654, a small children's amusement park (open daily May–September).

Staying in Stockton

In the under $50 range, Stockton has three **Motel 6** choices: 817 Navy Dr., 209/946-0923; 6717 Plymouth Rd., 209/951-8120; and 1625 French Camp Turnpike Rd. (west of town just off I-5 at Hwy. 4/Charter Way), 209/467-3600. To make reservations at any Motel 6, call 800/466-8356 or visit www.motel6.com.

Comfort Inn is at 3951 E. Budweiser Ct., 209/931-9341 or 800/228-5150. $50–100. Also in that neighborhood is the very nice **Best Western Stockton Inn,** 4219 E. Waterloo Rd., 209/931-3131 or 800/528-1234, with large rooms, some suites, whirlpool, and pool. Rooms are $50–100.

North of Stockton proper are the **Holiday Inn,** 111 E. March Ln. (at El Dorado), 209/474-3301 ($50–100); the **Radisson Hotel,** 2323 Grand Canal Blvd. (off March Ln.), 209/957-9090 or 800/333-3333 ($50–100); and the **La Quinta Inn,** 2710 W. March Ln., 209/952-7800 or 800/531-5900 ($50–100).

At the upscale **Residence Inn by Marriott,** 3240 W. March Ln., 209/472-9800 or 800/331-3131, all rooms have kitchens, $100–150. Quite nice north of Stockton is the **Wine and Roses Country Inn,** 2505 W. Turner Rd. in Lodi, 209/334-6988 or 877/310-3358, www.winerose.com, an elegant country-style bed-and-breakfast in an early 1900s home on five acres. Accommodations are in 10 guest rooms in the historic main building, or in 40 luxury guest rooms in the expanded building. Rates include afternoon wine and breakfast, and the inn's restaurant also serves lunch Tues.–Fri., dinner Wed.–Sat., and Sunday brunch; $150–250.

Eating in Stockton

Well worth a stop for early risers is the **Stockton Certified Farmers Market,** 209/943-1830, held downtown under the Crosstown Freeway at Washington and El Dorado Streets every Sat. morning 6–11:30 A.M. (though the show's really over by 9 A.M. or so), an amazing multicultural convention of San Joaquin Valley farmers and international produce (some varieties with no name in the English language). Other certified farmers' markets are held on Fri. year-round, and on Thurs. and Sun. May–Dec.; call for current information. Stockton even offers some ethnic variety in its restaurants, from **Joe's Mexico City Cafe,** 311 E. Weber Ave., 209/462-5637, and **Mi Ranchito Cafe,** 425 S. Center St., 209/946-9257, for Mexican food, to **De Parsia's,** 3404 N. Delaware, 209/944-9196, for Italian cuisine and **Yasoo Yani,** 326 E. Main St., 209/464-3108, for Greek. Time-honored in Stockton (since 1898) for reasonable Cantonese fare is **On Lock Sam** downtown at 333 S. Sutter St., 209/466-4561, full bar, reservations wise.

Another local tradition is the popular **Ye Olde Hoosier Inn,** 1537 N. Wilson Way, 209/463-0271, a family restaurant serving American standards daily for breakfast and lunch, and Fri.–Sun. for dinner. Part of the popular chain, **La Boulangerie,** 324 Grand Canal Blvd., 209/478-4780, is a French bakery-style establishment with excellent coffee, croissants (try the raisin custard), and sandwiches such as Swiss cheese with pesto. (Another branch is at 5308 Pacific Ave., 209/472-0995.) **Albert's,** 8103 N. Hwy. 99 (at E. Hammer Lane), 209/476-1763, is refined and unusual, serving primarily Portuguese fare. Dress code; reservations.

Continental and French, excellent, and upscale by Stockton standards is **Le Bistro,** 3121 W. Benjamin Holt Dr. (north of town in the Village Square Shopping Center), 209/951-0885, specializing in seafood and open for lunch on weekdays and for dinner nightly. Opera performances seasonally.

Microbrew lovers will sniff out the **Bull 'n Bear Pub,** 2301 Pacific Ave., 209/937-0228, which features lots of micros and imports (including Guinness on tap) and Tex-Mex cuisine; and **Valley Brewing Co.,** 157 W. Adams St., 209/464-2739, which brews its own ales and offers pastas, steaks and seafood, and veggie items for accompaniment (open for lunch and dinner daily).

For on-the-water dining, head to **Garlic Brothers,** 6629 Embarcadero Dr. (one mile west of I-5), 209/474-6585, which specializes in wood-fired-grill pizzas, as well as pastas, seafood, and more. Ribs fans will note an outpost of **Tony Roma's** at 2671 W. March Ln., 209/957-7662.

EVENTS

The **Frozen Bun Run** water-skiing challenge on New Year's morning at Boyd's Harbor on Bethel Island is (they say) unforgettable, though those who miss it due to hangovers can participate in the similar **Polar Freeze** at Windmill Cove, usually held on the first Sunday of the new year. Also in January comes the next best thing to Christmas for delta folks: Stockton's annual **Ag Expo,** with row upon row of agricultural equipment, products, and services on display.

In early March, Isleton hosts a colorful **Asian Festival** to celebrate Chinese New Year, with a parade, lion dancers, and dragons. The **Lodi Spring Wine Show** also takes place in March at the Lodi Grape Festival grounds, with 50 Northern California wineries in attendance, hors d'oevres, music, and cooking demonstrations. The artsy-craftsy **Stockton Asparagus Festival** in Oak Grove Regional Park usually comes in late April. May's traditional **Portuguese Festa** in Clarksburg includes an auction, dances, food, and a parade. In May, Stockton hosts the **San Joaquin County Spring Festival** celebration of ethnic diversity, as well as its annual **Arts Festival,** but the big deal is the Lodi **Vines to Wines** weekend passport event in the Lodi wine country in May.

An even bigger draw, though, is Isleton's June **Crawdad Festival,** a weekend-long shindig

UNIQUE DELTA ENTERTAINMENT: POKER RUNS

Entertainment in the delta falls into two basic categories: outdoor recreation and barhopping. Ever ingenious, delta residents have long combined the two into periodic "poker runs," unique barhopping-by-boat events where up to 500 or so boaters stop off at participating waterside watering holes to pick up playing cards for "the game." Among locally favorite runs is **Wimpy's Poker Run** in July and the **Big Dog Poker Run** in September. Poker run or no, a perennially popular delta-style bar is **Lost Isle** at the Lost Isle Marina, a thatched-roof hideout accessible only by boat that hosts the **Lost Isle Luau** in August. For more information, call Lost Isle at 209/948-4135.

featuring crawdads (also known as crayfish and crawfish) boiled alive and spiced Louisiana Cajun style, a fairly new food fest attracting upwards of 125,000 people. In June, too, are the **San Joaquin County Fair** in Stockton, and the **Bethel Island Boat Show,** a showcase also featuring crawdad races and other entertainment. (Boat shows, parades, and regattas abound year-round.) Celebrating Independence Day is also a major event in the delta, with Venice Island July 4th fireworks the most impressive. In late July comes Courtland's **Delta Pear Fair,** with pear-peeling and pear pie-eating contests, and the crowning of the community's much-admired Queen of the Pears. In August come the **Alligator Races** at Haven Acres Resort, where inflatable reptiles ply the waters in good-natured competition, not to mention the **Tracy Dry Bean Festival** and the **Filipino Barrio Festival.** In fall (usually the first week in October) is the famous four-day **Rio Vista Bass Derby,** billed as California's oldest bass-fishing competition. Come December, don't miss the **Oxbow Marina Lighted Boat Christmas Parade.**

INFORMATION AND SERVICES

Fans of Perry Mason might poke around in delta-area stores, old bookshops, and libraries for copies of the three books Erle Stanley Gardner wrote about his delta experiences. Though good books, maps, and pamphlets are locally available, the best basic source of information about what to do and where to go in the delta—with everything from houseboat rental listings and tour boat information to ferry facts; from anchorage, marina, and fishing tips to tide corrections and water depths—is *Hal Schell's Delta Map and Guide,* available at marinas, stores, information centers, and the Brannan Island State Recreation Area visitor center.

For more detailed local information, contact the **Stockton Visitors and Convention Bureau** (see Stockton above) or any of the chambers of commerce from the following locales: **Bethel Island,** 925/684-3220; **Byron,** 925/634-0917; **Isleton,** 916/777-5880; **Rio Vista,** 707/374-2700; **Sacramento,** 916/443-3771; and **Tracy,** 209/835-2131. Or, for the sake of efficiency, try the **California Delta Chambers,** 916/777-5007.

The Sacramento Valley

SUTTER BUTTES

Heading north from Sacramento through the rice fields and orchards, up ahead near Yuba City loom the unusual midvalley mountains known as the Sutter Buttes, the world's smallest mountain range. The sacred, spiritual center of the world to the Maidu, the place where woman and man were created, the buttes were included in John Sutter's original New Helvetia land grant and also provided safe haven for Gen. John C. Frémont and his ragtag ruffians before they launched their Bear Flag Republic invasion of Sonoma to the southwest.

The Sutter Buttes were known by many names before Sutter's name was attached in 1949. The Wintu people called them Ono Lai Tol (the Middle Mountain), the native Maidu knew them as Histum Yani (Middle Mountains of the Valley or Spirit Mountain); the Spanish named them Los Picachos (the Peaks) or Los Tres Picos (the Three Peaks); and early American settlers called them either the Marysville or Sacramento Buttes. The area was valued highly by early settlers, who homesteaded here to avoid valley flooding. Small farms, cattle and sheep ranches, coal mines, rock quarries, natural gas wells, communications towers, and even a 1950s Titan missile base have since changed the Sutter Buttes landscape. Despite the incursions of civilization something about the land has refused to be shaped by human hands. That may soon change. Housing developments encroach, a reality no one likes. Yet current state Department of Parks and Recreation plans to buy acreage for a public park are also deemed dubious in these parts, since neighboring landowners fear that hikers, mountain bikers, and picnickers will stray onto their lands. The Sutter Buttes have been on the state's acquisition wish list since 1929.

The Land

Rising like some natural fortress from the surrounding flatlands, the circular Sutter Buttes include 20 or so separate peaks anchored by deep volcanic roots to the bedrock below. The formation is almost completely circular, about 10 miles in diameter. In the 1920s, UC Berkeley geologist Howel Williams first likened the buttes to a castle, with the surrounding low hills the ramparts, the small interior valleys the moat, and the cluster of peaks and rocky spires at the center the castle itself. Because the buttes aren't connected to either the Sierra Nevada or California's coastal ranges, some geologists speculate that the Sutter Buttes are a volcanic extension of the Cascade Range (especially since similar but below-ground buttes lie near Colusa).

True or not, about 2.5 million years ago streamers of hot magma surged up through the soggy sediments to create a rounded rhyolite dome eight miles across and up to 2,500 feet tall. Cracks created during this process of volcanic uplift broke the tilted layers into blocks subsequently worn down into small mounds by the forces of nature. Some half-million years later, another burst of volcanic violence disrupted the watery sediments with steam explosions and spewed rock. Molten magma again reached the surface, and this outer ring of domes created an inner lake basin that gradually filled with rock debris and mudflows. Andesite domes created by still hotter lava thrust up from the center and tumbled the lake's contents outward to the "ramparts" region. These brittle new mountains (including today's Twin Peaks and North, South, and West Buttes) split into craggy spires and slabs, sometimes crashing down in avalanche trails of rough-hewn boulders.

The plant and animal life of the Sutter Buttes is almost typical of the valley's foothill oak woodland areas, with lizards and rattlesnakes sunning themselves on rocks while golden eagles and red-tailed hawks soar over grasses, chaparral, and gnarled oaks. In the Sutter Buttes the population density of ringtails, nocturnal cousins of raccoons, is among the highest ever documented. In the buttes' wetland fringes, red-winged blackbirds bob from their high-grass perches while nonnative ring-necked pheasants dart out from

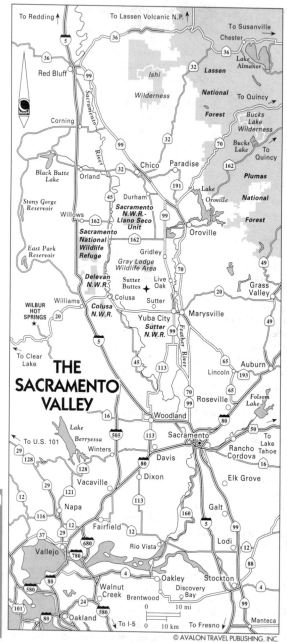

THE
SACRAMENTO
VALLEY

the brush. Since genetic isolation here has never been complete (or, if it was, didn't last long), there are no native animals or plants that exist only in the Sutter Buttes. Unlike the surrounding valley, a dozen different types of ferns thrive here. Also among the region's unusual vegetation are the rock gooseberry, otherwise found in Alameda and Tuolumne Counties and farther south; the narrowleaf goldenbush, a coastal shrub; and the Arizona three-awn, generally ranging east from Southern California and south to Guatemala. Also fascinating is the fact that many plants common throughout the valley and its foothills *aren't* here, including the foothill pine, three types of oak, California buckeye, and meadowfoam.

Touring by Bike or Car

For a general orientation to the Sutter Buttes, not to mention a fabulous bike ride or leisurely car trip, circle these middle mountains via an interconnecting 39-mile loop of county roads. From Hwy. 99 just west of Yuba City, head west on Hwy. 20 then, after about six miles, turn right (toward the tiny town of Sutter) onto Acacia Ave. and head north just over a mile to Acacia's junction with Butte House Rd.—the journey's official starting point. (To get off the highways as soon as possible, an alternate approach to Sutter is taking Butte House Rd. all the way from just north of the Hwy. 20-Hwy. 99 intersection.) From the Acacia-Butte House junction, head west onto Pass Rd., which climbs past the **Frémont Monument** near where Frémont and company camped in 1846 (good views of

MAIDU CREATION MYTH

There was no sun, no moon, no stars. All was dark, and everywhere only water. A raft floated down from the north, carrying Turtle and Father of the Secret Society. Then a rope of feathers was let down from the sky, and down came Earth Initiate. When he reached the end of the rope, he tied it to the bow of the raft and stepped in. His face was never seen, but his body shone like the sun.

Earth Initiate wanted to make land so there could be people. Turtle said he would dive for some, then was gone for six years. When he came back, Earth Initiate scraped out the dirt from under Turtle's fingernails, rolled it into a ball the size of a pebble, then looked at it until it was as big as the world and they had run aground on it. All around it were mountains. Father of the Secret Society shouted loudly and the sun came up. Then he called out the stars, each by name. Then he made a giant tree with 12 different types of acorns. Earth Initiate called the birds from the sky and made all the trees and animals. Later, Coyote and Earth Initiate were at E'stobusin Ya'mani (the Sutter Buttes). Earth Initiate decided to make people, mixing dark red earth with water to make two figures, the first man and woman, Ku'ksu and Morning-Star Woman.

---

the buttes' interior), past the Kellogg Rd. turnoff into Moore Canyon, then past Potato Hill and a good view of South Butte, the minuscule mountain range's tallest peak. At the crest, rows of large rocks mark the old wagon route through the Sutter Buttes.

At the intersection with West Butte Rd., turn right and continue northward, skirting the western flanks of the Sutter Buttes and the triangular **Goat Rocks** just south of jagged **West Butte.** To the west, almost as far as the eye can see, is the **Butte Sink** area, which hosts one of the north valley's largest populations of migrating waterfowl. Turn right again at the intersection with North Butte Rd. and continue on, past the well-paved road to the old Titan missile base (private property) and through the almond orchards. (Heading north at the intersection with Pennington Rd. leads you straight into the state's Gray Lodge waterfowl refuge.) Continue east to what's left of the town of Pennington; shortly thereafter, the road jogs sharply south (becoming Powell Rd.) then east again (as Pennington Rd.). Just west of Live Oak, turn south onto Township Rd., then west onto Clark Rd., which becomes East Butte Rd. when it turns south. East Butte Road eventually connects with Butte House Rd.—thus completing the circle.

Hiking

Though it's possible to see the Sutter Buttes from near and far, the buttes themselves are privately owned and off-limits to the public. The only way to explore the area is on a guided tour conducted with the cooperation of landowners. The nonprofit Middle Mountain Foundation, "A Sutter Buttes Land Trust," offers interpretive hikes from fall through spring. Though every trip has a particular emphasis—from spring wildflowers, wildlife, geology, or full-moon strolls to more challenging excursions, such as a hike in Brockman Canyon—each also shares the story of the Sutter Buttes' human and natural history. A day in the Buttes typically begins at 9 A.M. and ends around 3 P.M. Hikes proceed as scheduled except in severe weather conditions; most cost $30 per person (additional donations appreciated). For more information and for trip reservations, contact the **Middle Mountain Foundation,** 530/671-6116, www.middlemountain.org.

TWIN CITIES: YUBA CITY AND MARYSVILLE

Yuba City seems to sprawl like a fast-food jungle beyond the southeastern edge of the Sutter Buttes. The town has been the butt of north valley humor since 1985, when mapmaker Rand McNally, in its *Places Rated Almanac,* listed the town as the worst place to live in the entire United States. Community leaders decided to sidestep the notoriety Yuba City had accidentally earned for all it doesn't have by focusing attention on one thing it *does* have—prunes, about two-thirds of the nation's $200 million crop. So in 1988 Yuba City launched its annual September Prune Festival (more recently known as the Dried Plum Festival) to celebrate Yuba City's uniqueness. At first the festival only seemed to make things worse, since the idea of 30,000 people sampling pitted and whole prunes, prunes dipped in chocolate, prune-spiced chili and hamburgers, and chicken barbecued in prune sauce inevitably generated scatological "regularity" jokes. The new public relations effort definitely improved Yuba City's place in the world. The Prune/Dried Plum Festival is no more, alas, during to declines both in attendance and volunteer enthusiasm—related in part to sudden prune oversupply, globally, and precipitous price drops. Prune acreage has been bulldozed, too, thanks to federal tree-buyout subsidies. This is Prune City USA nonetheless.

Just across the Feather River from Yuba City is Marysville, a gold rush–era town founded by Chilean miners and named after Mary Murphy, a survivor of the Donner Party disaster. If most people in Yuba City work in the prune orchards or at the Sunsweet processing plant, most people in Marysville are somehow affiliated with Beale Air Force Base, an aerial reconnaissance facility home to the U-2, the new Global Hawk, and the now-decommissioned SR-71 spy planes.

For more information about Marysville and Yuba City, contact the **Yuba-Sutter Chamber of Commerce,** 429 10th St. (10th and E), 530/743-6501, http://yubasutterchamber.com.

Yuba City

Stock up on T-shirts and sample dried plums and other specialty dried fruits at the Growers Store for **Sunsweet,** 901 N. Walton Ave., 530/674-5010, www.sunsweet.com, one of the nation's largest food co-ops; tours are available by reservation. There's more to Yuba City, of course, than prunes, or ribald prune-related repartee. Fascinating, for example, is the large Sikh community living here, transplants from the Punjab region of India and Pakistan. Some have become successful rice farmers and ranchers since immigrating to the U.S. at the turn of the century, though most make a living working in someone else's fields and processing plants. Though there are three Sikh temples in the area, all of which welcome respectful visitors for worship services, the **Tierra Buena Sikh Temple,** 2468 Tierra Buena Rd. west of Yuba City (call 530/673-9918 or 530/673-8623 for permission to visit), is the largest and most architecturally authentic. Tour the grounds, discuss the Sikh religion, even share a meal. Visitors are asked to wear a scarf or other appropriate head covering and to remove their shoes while touring the temple. Stopping in at the **Punjab Bazaar,** 1190 Stabler Ln. in Yuba City, 530/673-4503, is also like taking a side trip to India, with everything from incense, Indian silks, and perfumed hair oils to pickled mango slices and every imaginable herb and spice available for sale. Closed Tuesday.

Considerably more mundane is the annual **Yuba-Sutter County Fair,** held in late summer at the fairgrounds, 442 Franklin Ave., 530/674-1280. Among other community events held at the fairgrounds is February's **Sutter North Chili Cook Off** and May's **American Punjabi Festival.** More slices of everyday life are served up at the county-run **Community Memorial Museum of Sutter County,** 1333 Butte House Rd., 530/822-7141, open Tues.–Fri. 9 A.M.–5 P.M. and weekends noon–4 P.M. Free. Also head downtown to the **Second Street historical district** (south of Bridge Street to the Garden Highway and also along B and C Streets) to appreciate the 1870s Victorians as well as Craftsman and Prairie architecture. In addition to a Julia Morgan–designed house, note the classical revival 1899 Sutter County Courthouse, and the 1891 Romanesque-style Sutter County Hall of Records. Just west and extending north to Highway 20 is **Plumas Street,** downtown's heart, boasting 1920s-vintage retail shops.

Marysville

Hey, even Marysville has dried plums. Sample the Japanese take on the subject at **Shoei Foods,** one of Japan's largest food companies. Here you'll find a food museum and various products (prunes, chocolates, and candy) for sale. The Shoei plant is

SAVING THE BOK KAI

Prominent on the Trust for Historic Preservation's 2001 list of America's Most Endangered Historic Places—spectacular recognition indeed—Marysville's 1880 **Bok Kai Temple** is in need of up to $1 million worth of repairs. Built near the confluence of the Yuba and Feather Rivers following a devastating flood, this Taoist temple is the only one of its kind outside Asia that pays homage to Bok Eye, God of Water (also known as the God of the Dark North), an ancient Chinese engineer who achieved deity status after saving China from great floods. Since Bok Kai was built, nearby areas have occasionally been inundated by rampaging rivers, but Marysville has been spared, proof positive in these parts that Bok Eye is still on the job. Congenial celestial circumstance may have been helped along by the fact that Marysville's earthly community relationships were also good. Marysville is one of the rare California gold-rush towns that never sacked and burned its Chinatown or otherwise terrorized Chinese residents.

Though it looks like a goner from the outside, Bok Kai remains an active place of worship as well as a site of pilgrimage for art historians and perservationists from the National Trust for Historic Preservation and L.A.'s J. Paul Getty Museum. Among the treasures are 19th-century artwork and antiques, including a gilt sedan chair, rod puppets, and the golden parade dragon Moo Lung. The temple's murals are quite rare, difficult to find even in China due to the Cultural Revolution.

With major restoration underway, Bok Kai tours are available by appointment only. It is located a few buildings down from the Silver Dollar Saloon at First and D Streets (there's no street address). To contribute to Bok Kai's cause, sign up for a tour, and otherwise do your part for Bok Eye, contact the City of Marysville Bok Kai Temple, P.O. Box 1844, Marysville, CA 95901. The local chamber of commerce may also have current tour information. For in-depth history and other details about the temple, see www.bokkaitemple.org.

Every bit as unique as the temple itself is the annual **Bok Kai Festival,** traditionally also known as Bomb Day (for the 100 "bombs" and enclosed good fortune rings that are shot into the air), the only event of its kind in the northern hemisphere and California's oldest parade. Officially scheduled for the second day of the second month of the lunar New Year, a date that changes every year, the two-day Bok Kai Festival is typically held on a weekend as close as possible to that date. Booming gongs and thundering drums kick off the parade as lion dancers and the festival dragon prance down Marysville's D Street. The festival also features a pancake breakfast, Bok Kai fun run, arts and craft vendors, good food, live entertainment, kite flying, and children's activities. For current details, see www.bokkaifestival.com.

---

located at 1900 Feather River Blvd., the two-story farmhouse-style **Honda Food Cultural Museum** at 1744 Feather River Blvd., 530/749-0568; the museum is open on 10 A.M.–4 P.M. on weekends. For more company information, call 530/742-7866. Tours are available.

Stop in at the two-story brick **Mary Aaron Museum** downtown, 704 D St. (at Seventh), 530/743-1004, to see historical furniture, art, photographs, and artifacts from late 19th- and early 20th-century Marysville; open Tues.–Sat. 1–4 P.M. and by appointment. The 1856 Gothic revival house was designed by noted local architect William P. Miller and served as the Aaron family residence from 1874 until 1935. Also

worthwhile is the **Bok Kai Temple,** on the levee at the foot of D St., built to honor the Chinese river god of water and good fortune (see Saving the Bok Kai for details). Also destined for salvation, at long last, is downtown's boarded-up 1920s-vintage **Hotel Marysville.** Plans are underway to restore the aging brick beauty as apartments and retail space.

Particularly pleasing downtown is tiny **Ellis Lake,** a piece of peace, relative quiet (picnic with the ducks and geese), and pedal bikes amid the traffic threading through downtown via the somewhat confusing conjunctions of Highways 20 and 70. (Highway 20 heading east is a pretty route to Grass Valley and Nevada City.) Get picnic fixings locally or stop by the popular burger stand just to the north of the lake for takeout—then enjoy the park. Originally unwanted wetlands, the area was transformed into Ellis Lake thanks to plans presented in 1924 by John McLaren, designer of San Francisco's Golden Gate Park.

Marysville rocks, though. In 1999 Bill Graham Presents began work on a $20 million, 20,000-seat open-air amphitheater nearby, about five miles north of Wheatland via Hwy. 65. That facility, now owned by Clear Channel and most recently known as the **Sleep Train Amphitheatre,** www.sleeptrainamphitheatre.com, attracts big-name talent—from Bob Dylan to Britney Spears.

Staying in the Twin Cities

Motels abound. Central in Marysville is the **Travelodge,** 721 10th St. (Hwy. 20 between Maple and H Streets), with the basics plus swimming pool, $50–100. A best bet on the other side of the Feather River is the downtown **Best Western Bonanza Inn,** one block north of Hwy. 20 at 1001 Clark Ave., 530/674-8824 or 800/562-5706, $50–100 ($100–150 for rooms with Jacuzzis). Bed-and-breakfast fans, the **Harkey House,** 212 C St. (downtown across from the courthouse), 530/674-1942, www.harkeyhouse.com, a striking 1864 Victorian Gothic once home to the local sheriff. All four rooms feature queen beds, private baths, antiques, and pleasingly eclectic style. Particularly nice, upstairs, is the spacious Harkey Suite, with its paisley attitude, woodstove, and adjoining library/sitting room. Equally inviting, with more feminine sensibilities, is the Empress Room, a study in soft gray and green and a reminder of the town's deep Chinese roots. Supreme for privacy is French-country Camilla's Cottage. Harkey House amenities include phones, color TVs with cable and VCR, CD players, full breakfast, in-room coffee and tea, robes, and two-person spa. Rates are $100–200.

Eating in the Twin Cities

The summer-only **Marysville Certified Farmers Market,** 530/674-0252, is held in at 10th and E Streets every Wednesday, 3–6 P.M. For farm-fresh produce on the other side of the river, the **Yuba City CFM** (same phone) is held at Center and Plumas Streets from May to mid-October on Saturday, 8 A.M.–noon.

In terms of putting fresh local produce to superb use, top of the local food chain is **The City Café** in Yuba City, 667 Plumas St., 530/671-1501, a stylish and inviting Californian. Lunch options include focaccia-bread panini, such as grilled eggplant with spinach and feta, other creative sandwiches and burgers, house "pizza," salads, and daily specials. Dinner is far-ranging, from grilled chicken in Gorgonzola sauce on spinach fettuccine to duck and rice timbale and grilled Southwestern-style rack of pork. House-made breads and desserts. Beer and wine. Open weekdays for lunch, Tues.–Sat for dinner, reservations wise.

Also locally loved is **Ruthy's Bar and Oven** at the Hillcrest Plaza minimall, 229 Clark Ave. (east of Hwy. 99, south of Franklin), 530/674-2611. Ruthy's is a local breakfast favorite, serving everything from homemade whole-wheat and buttermilk pancakes to French toast (made with Ruthy's own cinnamon raisin bread) and scampi omelettes. If you're just passing through, stop for a bag of fresh-baked bagels, cinnamon rolls, and blueberry or English tea muffins. At lunch, try the homemade soup and a pass or two at the exceptional salad bar. At dinner, show up for veggie stir-fry, chicken quesadillas, smoked salmon fettuccine Alfredo, Cancun chicken, or teriyaki beef brochettes. Friendly and attentive service. Open Tues.–Sat for breakfast, lunch, and dinner, Sunday for brunch. Full bar.

Yuba City is clearly more than a fast-food jungle—though in that genre, get off the highway and try **Margie's Deli & Diner,** 728 Forbes Ave., 530/673-2203, with booths like the back of a customized '57 Chevy, golden oldies on the jukebox, and other '50s affectations. Open Mon.–Sat. for breakfast and lunch. Also down-home for breakfast: the **Cook N' Pot,** 408 Bell Ave. (off Garden Highway), 530/673-9895. A grand alternative in the midst of the jungle is **Taste of India** just west Hwy. 99 in a minimall, 1456 Bridge St., 530/751-5156. Another Yuba City eating option is **The Refuge,** 1501 Butte House Rd., 530/673-7620, where the Rotary Club meets every Friday. The most obvious draw here is the building itself, the outdoorsy aesthetic quite appropriate. For an American-style dinner house, the food is quite imaginative. Open for lunch Mon.–Fri., and for dinner daily.

Notable in Marysville, particularly popular with the cowboy and cowgirl set is the **Silver Dollar Saloon,** 330 First St. (between C and D Streets), 530/743-0507. Contributing to its ambience are a genuine frontier relic wooden Indian just inside the door, country-western music on the jukebox, a massive Old West bar—and one wild time on Friday or Saturday night. The former brothel upstairs—now rooms reservable for meetings, private dinners, or other special events—is a veritable museum of Western memorabilia, including "artifacts" from Nevada's Mustang Ranch. Downstairs, place your lunch or dinner order at the counter behind the indoor open-pit grill—great steaks, steak sandwiches, half-rack of barbecued ribs, some good pastas. Open Mon.–Sat. for lunch and dinner.

Other good choices in the same general area, downtown east of Hwy. 70, include the **Four Seasons Deli** at 423 B St., 530/743-8221, for lunch or picnic supplies; **Casa Carlos** for Mexican, 413 Sixth St. (at High), 530/742-7793; and **Daikoku** for Japanese, 301 C St. (at Third), 530/742-6503.

North of Yuba City—near the slow S-curve over the railroad tracks, about five miles south of the stoplight in Live Oak—is **Pasquini's,** 6241 Live Oak Hwy., 530/695-3384, a warm and sometimes raucous roadhouse restaurant and bar attracting "regulars" from surrounding farm towns and from as far away as San Francisco. The dinner menu here is as thick as a magazine, offering an endless selection of steaks, seafood, chicken, and veal, along with Basque lamb and smoked lambchops, pastas, crepes, and eggplant Parmesan. Come Monday or Wednesday for Pasquini's specials—selections like blackened prime rib, beef ribs, or lasagna on Monday, or all kinds of pastas on Wednesday. Pasquini's has a full bar—the best one for miles around, and quite the scene on weekend nights—and is open daily for dinner. Look for the neon martini glass and swizzle stick, and a herd of pickups in the gravel parking lot.

Also within reach of Yuba City is the **El Rio Club** in Meridian, 530/696-0900. It's just off Hwy. 20 east of the Meridian Bridge, between Yuba City and Colusa. The club offers good food and interesting ambience—especially in the bar, where animal heads and eclectic clutter are everywhere. Open Tues.–Sat. for lunch and Tues.–Sun. for dinner.

NORTH VALLEY WILDLIFE REFUGES

Every winter, 44 percent of the Pacific Flyway's migratory waterfowl winter in the Sacramento Valley. Unless the tule fog is thick, even beginning birders will have little trouble spotting ducks, geese, cranes, egrets, ibises, swans, and raptors—a total of 236 identified species—at the state's 9,150-acre **Gray Lodge Wildlife Area** just west of Gridley. In part to distract birds from surrounding rice and grain fields, Gray Lodge intensively farms crops attractive to Pacific Flyway migrants and also "creates" appealing wetlands for a million or more ducks, hundreds of thousands of geese, and rarer birds like sandhill cranes and tundra swans. On hunting days (three days a week during the season) up to a half-million birds huddle together at one end of the reserve while hunters hunker down in the cold water and mud elsewhere. Named for the old gray duck club once on the property, Gray Lodge is open daily to birdwatchers. The best winter bird show is from late November into February; as the waterfowl depart in spring, shorebirds and neotropical birds arrive. A day pass is $2.50/person (16 and older) or free with a valid California hunting, trapping, or fishing license. Take the auto tour loop or walk other roads; 60 miles of dirt roads and trails meander along the edge of the wetlands. There's also a wheelchair-accessible viewing platform with attached spotting scope. Photographers can reserve a special photo blind on weekends and Wednesdays during the winter waterfowl season.

For more information, contact Gray Lodge Wildlife Area, 3207 Rutherford Rd. in Gridley, 530/846-3315. To get there, from Hwy. 99 in Gridley head west on Sycamore Road about six miles to Pennington Road; turn south and continue a few more miles to Rutherford Road; head

THE LESSON OF BIRDS: SEVEN

Egrets, delicate and pure
white, are more

like a Chinese poet's
precise and intricate

words about his sullied
impure world

gone mad,
than birds.

—*Gary Thompson*

largest concentration of waterfowl in the world. The complicated new Sacramento River National Wildlife Refuge includes 26 separate properties totaling about 10,000 acres (at last report) along the Sacramento River, from Red Bluff south to Princeton.

Though birds are present at all refuges year-round, the best time to come is in winter, usually November and December. Areas available for public use are open daily during daylight hours, though these access hours are sometimes modified during hunting season. The **Sacramento National Wildlife Refuge,** flanking I-5 between Willows and Maxwell, is refuge headquarters and offers a two-mile hiking trail, a photography blind for birders, and a six-mile auto-tour route with a multi-level viewing platform halfway. Day-use fee here is $3. The refuge visitor center is open daily 7:30 A.M.–4 P.M. October through March, otherwise weekdays only. To the northeast between Glenn and Chico is the Llano Seco unit of the new **Sacramento River NWR,** the only part of the refuge currently offering public access. Visitor facilities (restrooms, information kiosk), a short walking trail, and two multilevel viewing platforms are located at Llano Seco, on Seven Mile Lane two miles south of Ord Ferry Road. Come in fall to watch the sandhill cranes. The 4,626-acre **Colusa NWR** (entrance south off Hwy. 20, just west of town) features a three-mile auto tour, a one-mile trail, and abundant ducks and geese. The 2,600-acre **Sutter NWR** offers limited wildlife viewing and photography along Hughes Road, which bisects the refuge, and is open seasonally to hunters and fisherfolk. The **Delevan NWR,** with more than 5,800 acres of marsh and croplands, is another prime waterfowl wallow.

With advance notice, special programs and guided tours of all federal north valley wildlife refuges are available for clubs, schools, and other groups. For more information—including current fishing and hunting regulations and schedules—contact headquarters at Sacramento National Wildlife Refuge, 752 County Road 99 in Willows, 530/934-2801 or 530/934-7774 (recorded information), http://sacramentovalleyrefuges.fws.gov.

west on Rutherford for two miles to reach the reserve's headquarters. Adjacent to and managed in conjunction with Gray Lodge is a major portion of the old Schohr Ranch, which was purchased by the Trust for Public Lands and the State of California Wildlife Conservation Board. The result of a complicated multiagency land swap, two additional parcels totalling 750 acres were added to Gray Lodge in 1997.

Scattered to the south, north, and west of the Sutter Buttes are six separate areas that make up the 35,000-acre **Sacramento National Wildlife Refuges Complex.** Of these, five are open to the public. The largest, Sacramento National Wildlife Refuge in Willows, includes 10,783 acres first set aside in 1933 to provide feeding and resting areas for migrating waterfowl. (Today some 80 percent of the valley's migratory waterfowl make their winter home here.) As valley farming expanded and the natural wetlands disappeared, waterfowl damage to crops increased—the reason behind creating the smaller Colusa and Sutter Refuges (named after the nearby towns to the east and north, respectively) toward the end of World War II. In 1962, the Delevan Refuge was established southwest of Princeton and east of Maxwell. The small Butte Sink NWR, just east of Colusa and west of the Sutter Buttes, and associated, privately owned, 18,000-acre Butte Sink Wildlife Management Area—both closed to the public—protect the

GRIDLEY, COLUSA, AND WILLIAMS

Gridley, on Hwy. 99 north of Yuba City, claims the title of Kiwi Capital of the World; come in August for the **Butte County Fair.** Just west of town is the Gray Lodge Wildlife Area (see above). Stop for magnificent mandarin oranges at area roadside stands, usually from December into February. You know you're not in San Francisco anymore when you stop for coffee at **Lasso a Latte,** 1804 Hwy. 99, 530/846-3629. For more community information, contact the **Gridley Area Chamber of Commerce,** 613 Kentucky St., 530/846-3142.

Across the valley is **Colusa,** a rice-farming center with some stunning old homes on its tree-shaded streets. Just west of town is the **Colusa National Wildlife Refuge** (see above), and north of town on Hwy. 45 is the Wintun **Colusa Indian Bingo** palace, www.colusacasino.com, open 24 hours daily (21 and older only) and featuring high-stakes legal bingo, blackjack, pai gow, video slots, and more. In town but almost invisible is the small **Colusa-Sacramento River State Recreation Area,** 530/458-4927, once the city dump and now a tangle of riparian vegetation fine in spring, summer, and fall for fishing, swimming (beach at the end of trail from parking lot), picnicking, and camping. Developed campsites (with hot showers) are $9–12; reserve through ReserveAmerica, 800/444-7275 or www.reserveamerica.com. The park usually floods in winter, and mosquitos torture visitors in spring and summer (bring repellent). To get there, head east over the levee from the Hwy. 20/Hwy. 45 intersection. Colusa itself is a bit short on amenities. But just southeast of town, off Hwy. 20 near the Meridian Bridge, is the marvelous **El Rio Club,** 1198 Third St., 530/696-0900, which serves decent dinners in a moosehead-decorated bar. For more area information, contact the **Colusa Area Chamber of Commerce,** 258 Main St., Ste. 213, 530/458-5525.

West of Colusa, in Williams, is **Granzella's,** 451 Sixth St., 530/473-5496 or 800/759-6104 (for orders), www.granzellas.com, a regional produce wonderland featuring marinated olives to go—almond-stuffed, garlic-flavored, spicy Greek, martini olives, and more—good deli fare, bakery, and a decent down-home American restaurant serving straightforward meals for breakfast, lunch, and dinner. (Try the pesto veggie pizza.) There's a sports bar, too. The unveiling of the **Granzella's Inn** motel ($50–100, 800/643-8614 for reservations) has transformed this family enterprise into the city's largest single employer, the second largest in Colusa County. If you're here at the right time, check out the wonderful **Sacramento Valley Museum** in the old Williams High School at 1491 E St., 530/473-2978, typically open Friday and Saturday 10 A.M.–4 P.M.

Wilbur Hot Springs

West from Colusa and past Williams, an overgrown I-5 rest stop, Hwy. 20 winds up into the eastern foothills of the coast range. A surprise pleasure for bone-tired travelers there is Wilbur Hot Springs, 530/473-2306 (10 A.M.–8 P.M.), www.wilburhotsprings.com, a relaxed resort and spa tucked back in the hills, clothing-optional behind the screening. To get there the official way, turn north at the intersection of Hwy. 20 and Hwy. 16 (onto an unpaved old stage road) and continue for four miles, then turn left at the silver bridge; the elegant old Victorian hotel and spa are about a mile farther. There's no on-the-grid electricity, no traffic (park in the lot and walk the quarter mile in), and no particular concern with the concerns of the outside world. When you get here, take your shoes off—once inside the lodge, no shoes are allowed. Strip off everything else at the bathhouse.

Wilbur Hot Springs offers massage, yoga classes, volleyball, the option of sleeping under the stars, and a community kitchen (bring your own food; cooking and eating utensils supplied). Still, the main attraction is the rustic bathhouse itself. The three covered mineral-water pools run warm to hot. Outside are a hot mineral sitting pool; a larger, cool mineral pool; and a dry sauna. Overnight guests can stay in the solar-lit hotel. The 17 private rooms are $150–200, use of all facilities included, and a stay in the 11-bed dormitory is $75 per person. Day use (10 A.M.–5 P.M.) is $40. Children are welcome ($17.50), pets are not. Advance reservations required.

Chico and Vicinity

Though the up-valley university town of Chico has been on the map for quite some time, it took the late *San Francisco Chronicle* columnist Herb Caen to remind the rest of California. Caen's original 1970s comment on Chico, that it was "the kind of place where you find Velveeta in the gourmet section at the supermarket," didn't offend anyone. In fact, good-humored locals started sending him similar examples of high culture, Chico-style—enough to keep Caen busy printing punchy one-liners for well over a decade.

Chico is equally famous for the local university's onetime ranking by *Playboy* magazine as the nation's number-one party school, a dubious honor indirectly connected to the drunken debauchery of CSU Chico's now-dead Pioneer Days celebration. Over the years, the students' "fun" ceased to amuse the rest of the community, concerned with increased alcohol-related deaths and violence. When notified in 1987 of yet another round of national party-school notoriety, former university president Robin Wilson—a onetime CIA operative and part-time writer—said he was "appalled, horrified, disgusted." Trying to make the best of a bad situation, he added: "It's nice to be number one at something." But Wilson's most quoted remark was his warning that if Pioneer Days continued true to form he would personally "take it out in the backyard and shoot it in the head." He kept his word. Mission accomplished, he retired in 1993.

THE BIDWELL LEGACY

Bidwell Mansion, onetime home of John and Annie E.K. Bidwell and now a state historic park at 525 Esplanade, 530/895-6144, was the center of valley social life from the 1860s until the turn of the century. (To understand the couple's prominence in California history, see The Bidwells: High-Minded Mavericks.) An elegant three-story Victorian designed in the style of an Italian villa by Henry W. Cleveland (later architect of San Francisco's Palace Hotel), it was outfitted in the finery of the day and boasted newfangled technology, including the first indoor bathroom ever installed in California. Open only for guided tours, the mansion is well worth a stop; the original kitchen has been restored, and is now included on the tour. The visitor center adjacent features exhibits about native peoples, the women's suffrage movement, the temperance movement, Chico's Chinese community, gold mining, agricultural history, and the mansion's most famous guests. At last report 50-minute docent-led tours were offered on the hour Wed.–Fri. noon–5 P.M. (last tours leave at 4 P.M.) and Saturday and Sunday 10 A.M.–5 P.M. Tours are $2 adults, free for age 16 and under. A worthy reminder of the Bidwell era, just five blocks south of the mansion, is the **Stansbury Home** at 307 W. Fifth St. (at Salem), 530/895-3848, open Saturday and Sunday 1–4 P.M., $1 adults. Closer to the mansion, just one block behind (west) on Mansion Avenue, is the university's onetime President's Mansion, the classical revival **Albert E. Warrens Reception Center,** built in 1923 as a private home and designed by architect Julia Morgan.

Every bit as impressive as Bidwell Mansion is 3,600-acre **Bidwell Park,** one of largest city parks in the nation following a recent 1,380-acre land acquisition. World famous while it lived was the magnificent old **Hooker Oak,** a majestic valley oak believed to be 1,000 years old and named after the famed British botanist Sir Joseph Hooker, who declared it the world's largest. Hooker Oak was felled by the fates in 1977 during a spring storm, whereupon it was discovered that the tree was actually two fused together and only a few centuries old. But the Hooker Oak was just one feature of wooded Bidwell Park that prompted Warner Brothers to come to town in 1937 to film *The Adventures of Robin Hood,* starring Errol Flynn and Olivia de Havilland. Many of the backdrops for 1939's classic *Gone with the Wind* were also filmed in Bidwell Park. (Other films shot at least in part in Butte County include the 1944 war film *Thirty Seconds over Tokyo;* John Houston's 1951 *The Red Badge of*

THE BIDWELLS: HIGH-MINDED MAVERICKS

That Chico has been known for its bad behavior and beer consumption is quite the irony, since city founders General John Bidwell and Annie E.K. Bidwell were politically progressive, active prohibitionists. It's no accident that Lincoln and Frances Willard—the latter a well-known prohibitionist, suffragette, and friend of the Bidwells—are among the streets laid out directly west of the adobe-pink Bidwell Mansion. Chico's founding couple was also civic-minded on the local level: they laid out the city's streets and gave lots away to anyone who wanted one. To start a teacher's college, they donated land for the Chico Normal School (now California State University, Chico). And they preserved the most beautiful creekside acres of their massive landholdings in a natural state, land Annie deeded to the city as a park after John's death. Even Chico's abundant street trees are part of the Bidwells's legacy.

Among the first party of overland settlers to arrive in California in 1841, John Bidwell first worked for John Sutter as his bookkeeper and business manager (leaving temporarily to join Frémont and the bear flaggers at Sonoma). He then helped confirm the Sutter's Mill gold find, later discovering gold himself on the Feather River. With his gold rush earnings, Bidwell started a new career as an innovative farmer and horticulturist on his 28,000-acre Rancho del Arroyo Chico—the most admired agricultural enterprise in the state—where he grew wheat and other grains, nuts, olives, raisins, and more than 400 varieties of fruit.

Always active in politics yet considered a high-minded maverick, Bidwell met the serious-minded Annie Ellicott Kennedy while serving a term in the U.S. Congress from 1865 to 1867. Bidwell's first bid for the California governorship was derailed by the state's powerful railroad lobby, and despite his incredible public popularity, he lost again in the 1870s. The Bidwells's farsighted beliefs, including support for election reforms, control of business monopolies, and women's rights, were quite controversial during the 19th century but have proved their worth to subsequent generations. Some of John Bidwell's biographical reminiscences (including "Life in California before the Gold Discovery," first published in 1890 in *The Century Illustrated* magazine) are available in the state parks' facsimile reprint, *Echoes of the Past.* A new biography, *John Bidwell and California: The Life and Writings of a Pioneer, 1841–1900,* by Michael J. Gillis and Michael F. Magliari (A.H. Clark, 2003) is worth the hefty investment.

Courage; and Clint Eastwood's *The Outlaw Josie Wales.*) The small **Chico Museum,** downtown at 141 Salem St. (at Second, in the lovely old Carnegie library), 530/891-4336, sometimes features movie memorabilia, along with other locally focused rotating exhibits; open Wed.–Sun. noon–4 P.M.

In the narrow creekside section known as Lower Park, closest to downtown, are both the **One-Mile** and **Five-Mile** Chico Creek public swimming areas, with shade trees, cool lawns, picnic tables, playground facilities, and miles of walking, biking, and equestrian trails. (These distances are measured from the Bidwell Mansion.) Thanks to a 1920s-vintage Works Progress Administration (WPA) project, the creekbed here was redesigned as a pool; the creek is dammed for swimming during summers only. Dogs allowed on leashes only. Also in Lower Park (most accessible from the south side) is the **Chico Creek Nature Center,** 1968 E. Eighth St. (just east of Parkview Elementary School), 530/891-4671, http://now2000.com/naturecenter, a nonprofit organization that serves as park nature center, natural history museum, and visitor information center. The center is open Tues.–Sun. 11 A.M.–4 P.M. (closed Monday) and also for special events. A full schedule of guided naturalist walks is offered on Saturdays year-round—from Sssssssssnakes Alive and the night-time Owl Prowl to Maidu Medicine (medicinal plants)—along with a full calendar of children's nature workshops, field trips, and "summer camp."

The popular municipal **Bidwell Park Golf**

John and Annie Bidwell's mansion boasted the first indoor bathroom ever installed in California.

Course, 530/891-8417, is in the otherwise undeveloped foothill wildness of Upper Park, known for its fine natural (sometimes *au naturel*) swimming holes and trails for hiking and mountain biking. New in 2001: the free **Chico Community Observatory** at Horseshoe Lake (at the golf course turnoff), a project of the Greater Chico Kiwanis Club, open to the public Thurs.–Sun. for three hours, beginning at twilight (longer hours for special celestial events); for information, see www.chicoobservatory.com. Except for golfing fees, access to Bidwell Park, upper and lower, is free. The park is locked up at night—after 11 P.M.—so don't even think about camping there. For more information about Bidwell Park, stop by the Chico Creek Nature Center (see address above), which also serves as the park's visitor information center, or call the city parks department at 530/895-4972.

STAYING IN CHICO

Since Chico is no tourist town, finding a motel room is easy most times of the year—exceptions being homecoming (October) and graduation celebrations (May) at CSU Chico. Not particularly convenient to downtown but reasonably priced ($50–100) are **Motel 6,** 665 Manzanita Court (just off Hwy. 99 next to the Holiday Inn), 530/345-5500 or 800/466-8356, www .motel6.com, and **Super 8,** right next door at 655 Manzanita Court, 530/345-2533 or 800/ 800-8000, www.super8.com. The **Holiday Inn,** 685 Manzanita Court, 530/345-2491 or 800/

310-2491, www.holiday-inn.com, has more amenities (including whirlpool and exercise room) and somewhat higher rates. In the same general area is the **Best Western Heritage Inn,** 25 Heritage Ln. just off Cohasset Rd. (near K-Mart), 530/894-8600 or 800/446-4291, www.best-westerncalifornia.com, with outdoor pool and Jacuzzi. South of town near the Chico Mall is the equally box-like but comfortable all-suite **Oxford Suites,** 2035 Business Ln., 530/899-9090 or 800/870-7848, www.oxfordsuites.com. The basics here include two-room suites with in-room refrigerators, microwaves, and VCRs, as well as heated pool, spa, and guest laundry. Rates are $100–150. There are also a few motels downtown on Main and Broadway, more north of town on the Esplanade.

Winning the Best B&B Name contest, hands down, is the **Grateful Bed,** close to Enloe Hospital and not far from downtown at 1462 Arcadian Ave., 530/342-2464, with four gracious guest rooms (all with private baths) in a restored early 1900s Tudor-style Victorian. Rates, $100–150, include full breakfast and evening beverages. Still closer to downtown is Craftsman-style **The Esplanade Bed & Breakfast,** a 1915 Craftsman bungalow at 620 Esplanade, 530/345-8084, with a convenient location right across from Bidwell Mansion (look for the icicle lights after dark). The only disadvantage to the location is that Esplanade is a main drag and can be noisy. All five rooms here have private baths and cable TV. One has a Jacuzzi tub. Rates include full breakfast and evening wine. Most rooms are $50–100; Kelsey's Room, which can sleep three, is $120.

Quite special, tucked into the orchards on the west side of town, is **Johnson's Country Inn,** 3935 Morehead Ave., 530/345-7829—all the modern comforts within bicycling distance of downtown. All four rooms, tastefully decorated with family-themed furnishings, artwork, and memorabilia, have private baths. Three are $50–100. The Harrison Room, all decked out in Eastlake furnishings, pampers guests with a fireplace and private Jacuzzi and is $125. Rates include gourmet breakfast and complimentary wine, sweets, and coffee.

Well worth the drive to Orland, both for the

ANIMAL FARM

At the 300-acre **Farm Sanctuary** refuge near Black Butte Lake just west of Orland, all animals are created equal—every bit the equal of Fido or Fluffy or other pets. And they're definitely the lucky ones.

Farm Sanctuary's mission is to rescue, rehabilitate, and lovingly care for hundreds of animals rescued from abuse and neglect suffered at stockyards, factory farms, and slaughterhouses. Cows, pigs, sheep, goats, chickens, ducks, geese, and other farm animals saved by Farm Sanctuary find themselves snoozing in spacious, clean barns and roaming acres of green, sunny pastures. Farm Sanctuary also coordinates a national **Farm Animal Adoption Network,** and places hundreds of rescued animals into loving, vegetarian homes.

See it all for yourself on a sanctuary visit. Guided tours are offered on Saturdays from April through November, every hour on the hour from 10 A.M. until 3 P.M. Coming or going, stop at the visitor center to take in the informational displays and browse the cruelty-free gift shop.

Farm Sanctuary was started in 1986 by Gene and Lorri Bauston, who were horrified to find a very ill but still-living sheep abandoned on a stockyard "deadpile." They rescued that sheep—they named her Hilda—and nursed her back to health. To raise money to rescue and care for other farm animals, the Baustons started selling veggie dogs at Grateful Dead concerts. Farm Sanctuary now has more than 100,000 members, who help support the California sanctuary as well as a farm in upstate New York. For more information, contact Farm Sanctuary, 530/865-4617, www.farmsanctuary.org.

---

price and the genuine country quiet, is **The Inn at Shallow Creek Farm,** about three miles west of I-5 at 4712 County Road DD, 530/865-4093. Shallow Creek is a small ivy-covered farmhouse surrounded by orchards and fields—and an impressive flock of poultry. Rooms are restful and tastefully decorated. The suite in the main house is large, with private bath; the two upstairs rooms share a bath. Downstairs there's a sunporch, a roomy living area with well-worn leather sofas in front of the fireplace, and a welcoming formal country dining room. Perhaps the best escape of all, though, and a real bargain by B&B standards, is The Cottage near the barn—the onetime groundskeeper's quarters with four rooms, fully equipped kitchen, sunporch, and wood-burning stove. Breakfast menus emphasize regional fruits, nuts, and other produce. Ask about Shallow Creek's special literary weekends. Room rates are $50–100.

EATING IN CHICO

Chico's Velveeta cheese connection is a myth, since the city has more excellent, reasonably priced food choices per capita than most places in the state. The freshest local produce, of course, is available through the local **Chico Certified Farmers' Markets,** held here year-round on Saturday at the public parking lot downtown at Second and Wall Streets, 7:30 A.M.–1 P.M., and June–Sept. on Wednesday at the North Valley Plaza Mall (same hours), on East Avenue outside Mervyn's. For current information, call 530/893-3276. For an excellent natural foods grocery selection year-round, head for **Chico Natural Foods,** a top-notch community cooperative located downtown at 818 Main St. (at Eighth Street), 530/891-1713, or **S&S Produce and Natural Foods** at 1924 Mangrove Ave. (at Ninth Avenue), 530/343-4930.

Breakfast, Lunch, and Coffee

Truly loved downtown for its decadent pastries, baked goods, and good coffees is the **Upper Crust,** 130 Main St., 530/895-3866, consistently rated Chico's best bakery but also great for a light lunch—roast turkey and chipotle chutney or California vegetable sandwiches, say, and homemade soups, and deli salads including Thai peanut tofu, ginger sesame slaw, and citrus wild rice. **Cory's Sweet Treats & Gallery,** 230 W. Third St. (between Broadway and Salem), 530/345-2955, serves good coffee, wonderful pastries, and breakfast entrées, from Belgian waffles to veggie scramble. The simple lunch menu

GREAT VALLEY & THE DELTA

includes unbelievable lumberjack-size sandwiches built from thick slices of fresh-baked bread and house-baked ham, smoked turkey, or vegetarian fillings. Also hearty and homestyle are the soups, salads, quiches, and daily specials. "Gallery" refers to the fine local artwork on the walls; once each month, Cory's usually hosts an evening reception for the artist and current show. Open Tues.–Sat. 6 A.M.–4 P.M.

An easy stroll from downtown (head east on Second Street and over the Chico Creek bridge) is **Morning Thunder Cafe,** 352 Vallombrosa Ave. (near Christian & Johnson), 530/342-9717, by far the most popular sit-down breakfast place in town. On weekends, get there early or expect to wait outside for a while. The menu is pancakes, waffles, and creative eggs and potatoes fare; try the scrumptious vegetaters, a half order of which will satiate all but the most porcine diners.

Equally beloved for breakfast is the very cool **Sin of Cortez,** north of downtown at 2290 Esplanade (at Rio Lindo), 530/879-9200, where the killer pancakes, breakfast burritos, pesto scramble, and tasty rosemary potatoes all star. An eccentric Sin favorite is the Bohemian Breakfast, which offers the choice of a cigarette or vitamins at the end of your meal. For lunch, try the great blue cheese and walnut salad or the black bean and chicken nachos. But Sin of Cortez coffee is the real art—the best, very well prepared. Open daily, 6:30 A.M.–2 P.M., breakfast served until closing. Also pretty darn cool, on the other end of town, is artful **Café Flo,** 365 E. Sixth St., 530/892-0356, just around the corner from the art-house Pageant Theater. Famous for its creative sandwiches—wasabi lime tuna, roasted red pepper hummus, herbed natural cream cheese and artichoke—Flo's muffins and other baked goods aren't to be missed. The Hostess Flo Cakes are just what you think, only better. Open Mon.–Wed. 7 A.M.–4 P.M., Thurs.–Sat until 10 P.M.

Shockingly popular for breakfast, particularly on weekends, is the **Italian Cottage,** where you can order up everything from Belgian waffles, pancakes, and French toast to an endless array of omelettes. And dig that sawdust on the floor. There are two Chico locations—the original, a couple of blocks from Sin at 2234 Esplanade (near Cohasset Rd.), 530/343-7000, and 2525 Dominic Dr. (at E. Park Ave.), 530/342-7771. Both are open daily for breakfast, lunch, and dinner.

As for coffee places—well, there are *dozens,* if you count the surprising number of drive-through java joints. Genuine coffeehouses are a much rarer breed. Unbelievably hip: the **Naked Lounge,** 118 W. Second St., 530/895-0676, which exhibits local art, displays furniture made by local artisans, and serves top-drawer coffee, tea, and chai. Relaxed **Moxie's Café & Gallery,** 128 Broadway, 530/345-0601, with its local art on the walls and live music at night, is another cool community hangout. **The Bean Scene Coffeehouse and Gallery,** 1387 E. Eighth St., 530/898-9474, serves art, espresso, food, wine, and ice cream. Proof that Chico has finally arrived, in terms of California coffee cachet, is that outpost of Berkeley's own **Peet's** downtown on the corner of Second Street and Main, 530/894-6716. There's a **Starbucks** downtown, too, at 246 Broadway (at Third), 530/343-7469. More uniquely "Chico," and not far north from downtown and Bidwell Park, is **Bidwell Perk,** 1058 Mangrove Ave. (at First Avenue), 530/899-1500, a cheery place that draws a roster of regulars, including students and the over-30 crowd. It features all the usual espresso drinks, light and delicious breakfast and lunch fare, and occasional live acoustic music in the evening. Farther east, for killer chai the place is **Higher Ground Coffee House,** 1288 E. First Ave., 530/343-3336 (closed Sunday).

More Lunch, Simple Dinners, Sweets

Everybody's new favorite for inexpensive, tasty, and wholesome "slow food" is **Grilla Bites,** downtown between Main and Broadway at 119 W. Second St., 530/894-2691. The simple menu stars "grilla" grilled sandwiches—such things as turkey and cranberry, organic tofu with pesto and avocado, pastrami on rye, and ginger-teriyaki tempeh on organic breads from the local Tin Roof Bakery. Sandwiches were $3.73 each, at last report. The Grilla also serves a tasty organic vegetarian minestrone, and boast Chico's only organic salad bar. And don't miss the best-ever lemon bars. Free trade coffees and teas served. Hey, ya gotta love a place determined to navigate by Wendell Berry's 17 Points to a Successful Community. Open weekdays 11 A.M.–9 P.M., on Saturday until just 5 P.M.

Another good, inexpensive choice with lots of vegetarian options is hole-in-the-wall **Sultan's Bistro,** inside the red-brick Morehead Building at Third and Broadway, 530/345-7455, great for quick and inexpensive Greek salads, gyros, falafel, shish kebobs, moussaka, and more. Beer and wine. Open Mon.–Sat. 11 A.M.–9 P.M., Sunday noon–7 P.M. Also serving good vegetarian fare in addition to its meat-eater selections is the **Kramore Inn,** south of downtown at 1903 Park Ave., 530/343-3701, which specializes in crepes—more than 20 different kinds. The chocolate mousse dessert crepe is its own reason for crammin' more in. Open for dinner after 5:30 P.M. and Sunday brunch.

Carnivores have choices, too. "Just Say Mo!" is the motto at **Smoking Mo's BBQ,** 131 Broadway, 530/891-6677, definitely downtown's red-hot meat palace. Order up a hickory-smoked tri-tip or shredded chicken sandwich, and plates including Mo's Memphis Pork Ribs and Philthy Phil's Pork Ribs. Across the way at 100 Broadway (on the corner of First Street) is **Tres Hombres Long Bar & Grill,** 530/342-0425, grand for fish tacos and fajitas—not to mention 50 premium tequilas and countless margarita options. For inexpensive, real-deal Mexican, there are a number of authentic taco wagons and tin-roofed restaurants around town. One of the first has now become a sit-down restaurant—**Tacos Cortes,** 1110 Dayton Rd., 530/342-4189. A favorite in the second category is **El Grullo,** well north of town on The Esplanade, two blocks south of East Avenue across from Winchell's Donuts (no phone), where the Super Burrito ($4.75) could easily feed two.

For pizza—and Chico is full of pizza palaces—try **Woodstock's,** 166 E. Second St., 530/893-1500, featuring homemade sauce and fresh ingredients on hand-thrown pizzas with either whole wheat or white crust. Another top choices downtown include **Celestino's Live from New York Pizza,** 101 Salem St. (at W. First Street),

530/896-1234, and **Jasco's California Cafe** upstairs at 300 Broadway (at Third), 530/899-8075, where Caesar salad and intriguing sandwiches round out the menu. Great, too, is **Gashouse Pizza,** north of downtown at 2359 Esplanade, 530/345-3621. **Caffé Malvina,** 234 W. Third St., 530/895-1614, serves light lunches (including pizza by the slice), Italian dinners, and fine coffees.

The **Gen Kai Japanese Restaurant & Sushi Bar** in the small Almond Orchard mall, 2201 Pillsbury Rd., 530/345-7226, is quite good. If you find yourself downtown and hungry for Thai, the place is **Chada Thai** downstairs at 117 W. Second St., 530/342-7121. Better by far, though, is nondescript **Grayatip Thai,** sharing space with an adjacent locals' bar at 2574 Esplanade (just north of East Avenue), 530/899-1055. Particularly wonderful here is the Tom Ka Kai, coconut milk soup with chicken and mushrooms, though many other entrées—from the curries to the Panang beef—are unforgettable. Lunch here is a real deal, too, with rice plates about $6 per person. For dessert, try a fried banana. Grayatip is open Monday and Wed.–Fri. for both lunch and dinner, on weekends for dinner only.

A memorable student-style burger scene is **Madison Bear Garden,** 316 W. Second St. (right next to the CSU Chico campus), 530/891-1639, a somewhat bizarre beer hall with decor literally hanging from the ceiling. A bit north of downtown at Ninth and Esplanade is old-fashioned **Big Al's,** 530/342-2722, home of the Happy Burger, another local favorite. True Burger aficionados shouldn't miss Chico's own **Burger Hut,** though, a gem in the genre. The original is located close to downtown at 933 Nord Ave. (near W. Sacramento Ave.), 530/891-1418, open daily for both lunch and dinner. There's another Hut in the sprawling suburban hinterlands near the Chico Mall, 2451 Forest Ave., 530/891-1430. Chico also has an In-N-Out Burger, in a somewhat difficult location just off the freeway (near the Chico Mall) at 2050 Business Lane.

If you're heading toward Upper Bidwell Park for a hike and need a quick sandwich to pack along, stop in at **Port of Subs** in the Safeway Marketplace at 1354 East Ave., 530/899-8312. A few blocks west, **Yummy's Homemade Ice**

Cream & Deli at 2500 Floral Ave., 530/893-2663, serves real ice cream, malts, sundaes, banana splits, and real fruit freezes (nonfat, nondairy). Still, for house-made candies and ice cream the local tradition (since 1938) is **Shubert's Ice Cream and Candy** downtown at 178 E. Seventh St., 530/342-7163, near the Pageant Theater, where you can get one or two scoops in a sugar cone, waffle cone, or dish. Closer to campus is the **Coldstone Creamery,** W. Second Street and Broadway, serving everybody's favorite milkshakes and malts—including chocolate black cherry malts made with fresh black cherries. Yum.

Fancier Fare

Lots of people hike into the **Redwood Forest,** 121 W. Third St., 530/343-4315, for casual lunch—and for very good homemade food, from famous Forest enchiladas, quiche specials, fresh soups, and homemade chicken pot pies to sandwiches (even egg salad and a vegetarian Dagwood) and great salads (try the poppy seed dressing). Not to mention the excellent wine bar. In fact, the Redwood Forest has earned the *Wine Spectator* Award of Excellence for a number of years now. To fully appreciate the significance of that fact, try dinner, too—and entrées such as fettuccine alfredo with smoked salmon, filet mignon, and tenderloin Florentine. Open Mon.–Sat. for lunch, Wed.–Sat. for dinner (other nights for special events or by advance arrangements).

The **Black Crow Grill & Taproom,** 209 Salem St. (at W. Second Street), 530/892-1391, is a casual yet urbane restaurant offering contemporary California cuisine in the dining room and fine beers, wines, and cocktails in the adjoining bar—a bright place looking out on a busy corner downtown. You can make quite a meal by sampling a little of this—angry prawns, say, or garlic fries, or Fuji apple salad—and digging into a little of that, be it baby back ribs, pan-roasted chicken, or grilled salmon. A casual, considerably noisier relative is the **Raw Bar,** serving sushi from the grand central sushi bar as well as a variety of delectable small plates at 346 W. Third St., 530/897-0626.

Everybody's favorite for white-tablecloth, California-style Mediterranean bistro fare—great

UPSTAIRS AT THE BLUE ROOM

Chico is an artsy place—and that's official, now that the city is included in John Villani's *100 Best Small Arts Towns in America.* A notable presence in Chico's arts community is the **Blue Room Theatre,** located upstairs (above Collier Hardware) at First and Broadway. Started as the infamous Butcher Room by Denver and Dylan Latimer in their parents' backyard then later dubbed the Cosmic Travel Agency, the Blue Room has maintained its edgy theatrical attitude over the years while also reaching a broader audience.

The Blue Room stages at least 10 plays—including original works and premieres—and countless eccentric late-night dramas and comedies during its two-season, year-round schedule. A typical Blue Room season would include plays such as *The Real Thing* by Tom Stoppard (of *Shakespeare in Love* fame), *Big Love* by Charles Mee, an adaptation of Jane Austen's *Northanger Abbey,* and maybe even a world premiere, such as David Davalos' *Darkfall.* Scary fare, such as *Dracula* and Jeffrey Hatcher's adaption of *The Turn of the Screw,* is usually served up during October, for the Halloween season, along with a special *War of the Worlds* radio play. Come in May for the Blue Room's Fresh Ink new works festival, and in June for its renowned Bloomsday celebration (usually sold out weeks in advance).

Admission to most plays is $12, but only $6 if you come on a Thursday; special events prices vary. For more information contact the Blue Room Theatre, 139 W. First St., 530/895-3749, www.blueroomtheatre.com, where the box office is open Wed.–Sat. noon–5 P.M.

crab cakes, house-made pastas and risotto, coq au vin, fresh seafood, local produce—is **Christian Michael's,** 192 E. Third St. (at Wall), 530/894-4005, open weekdays for lunch, Sunday for brunch, and nightly for dinner. Full bar.

Another dress-up dinner opportunity is offered by the **Red Tavern** at 1250 Esplanade (between Second and Third Avenues), 530/894-3463, where the seasonally changing menu might include such things as Red Tavern gazpacho, upside-down eggplant tart, and garlic-coriander crusted pork loin with Amish corn pudding, roasted plums, and summer green beans. Or pale ale-braised pork shoulder. Or wood-smoked ribeye steak. Open Mon.–Sat. for dinner, reservations suggested. Special fixed-price three-course seasonal dinners are offered on Tuesday, Wednesday, and Thursday nights ($22.50 per person at last report).

Chico's famous local beer is brewed and served at casual but top-drawer **Sierra Nevada Brewing Co. Taproom & Restaurant,** 1075 E. 20th St. (just west of Hwy. 99 via the 20th St. exit), 530/345-2739. This respectable brewpub is light and airy, with a contemporary spit-polished brass, copper, stained glass, and hand-rubbed wood decor. The seasonally changing menu features good sandwiches and salads at lunch and home-made, wholesome entrées at dinner—everything from eggplant parmesan and wood-fired pizzas to pasta, chicken, and steak selections. Of note in the what-goes-around-comes-around department: truckloads of the select hops used in Sierra Nevada's brewing process are "recycled" as feed for cattle raised out at the college farm, and that or-ganically raised beef is eventually served here in the restaurant. Of course the taproom always serves up the chance to sample Sierra Nevada's brews, including some available only here. In nice weather, eat and drink outside in the *bier-garten,* well-supplied with misters and usually comfortable even in Chico's wilting summer heat. Open Tues.–Sun. for lunch and dinner (closed Monday).

ENTERTAINMENT

The Chico arts and entertainment scene is lively and diverse—even in summer, when the student population thins out. For a current overview, see http://chicoart.com, which includes fairly com-plete listings of public murals and sculptures. In the latter category, everybody's favorite downtown near city hall is the *Dancing Trout* fountain.

Unless it's hideously hot outside, quite fun is summer-only **Shakespeare in the Park,** an evening program staged in a faux castle tem-porarily nestled into a glen in Bidwell Park. The short summer performance schedule, from mid-

July into August, typically includes one Shake-speare play and one contemporary work. For in-formation on tickets and shows, call 530/891-1382. Year-round, dramatic productions in Chico's top-knotch **Blue Room Theatre,** located upstairs above Collier Hardware at 139 W. First St., 530/895-3749, www.blueroomtheatre.com, are well worth the modest ticket price. Blue Room presentations range from classic and con-temporary drama and comedy—including some premieres of original works—to eccentric late-night programs Come in May for the Blue Room's innovative New Works Festival. **Chico Cabaret** dinner theater, 2201 Pillsbury Rd., 895-0245, http://chicocabaret.com, presents fare such as **The Wizard of Oz** and **I Love You, You're Perfect, Now Change,** plus the **Rocky Horror Show Live!** from mid-October into November and an annual holiday special. The newly formed **Chico Theater Company,** 166 Eaton Rd., 894-3282, www.chicotheatercompany.com, offers musicals, from **Seven Brides for Seven Borthers** to **big, the musical.**

The university also offers a full theatrical sched-ule. Through its performing arts programs and other sponsors, CSU Chico attracts fairly big mu-sical acts, from rock 'n' roll to country-western and folk, from classical, jazz, and blues to world beat, not to mention prominent writers and lecturers and other special events. The university also spon-sors excellent film series. To find out what's going on at the university, see www.chicoperformances .com and www.csuchico.edu. Talented local mu-sicians, in ever-evolving new combinations or in long-running bands, still take the stage in bars and clubs all over town. In that category, don't miss the **Big Room** upstairs at the Sierra Nevada Brewing Co. on 20th Street, www.sierra-nevada .com, which serves a special $10 pub dinner with every show (optional). For more information on current shows—from Capercaillie and The Way-backs to Norton Buffalo & Friends—see the web-site. For tickets, call 530/345-2739. All shows are family-friendly.

Funky and fun for foreign and avant-garde films is the casual **Pageant Theater,** 351 E. Sixth St., 530/343-0663. You'll know you're in for an art house experience, Chico style, when you see the

BIG NAMES, BIG ROOM

Definitely a big deal upstairs at Chico's Sierra Nevada Brewing Company is the **Big Room,** a midsize nightclub with superb acoustics and sound, two bars, graceful ascending tiers (no bad seats in this house), and spare-no-expense details such as handrubbed custom mahogany tables and chairs and spit-shined brass fixtures. Wow.

Eventually Big Room patrons stop admiring the cool setting and turn their attention to the still cooler music. An impressive roster of genuine American talent has graced the Big Room stage since it opened early in the new millennium—from blues legend Charlie Musselwhite and honky-tonk piano player Marcia Ball to bluegrass queen Rhonda Vincent and the Rage, the Celtic Tim O'Brien Band and Capercaillie, and

acoustic artists including Tommy Emmanuel and The Waybacks.

The Big Room seats 300 for shows with table seating, 400 without. Concerts are held on Sunday evenings and other weeknights. An optional full dinner ($10) is served from the time doors open (usually 6 or 6:30 P.M.) until the beginning of the evening's entertainment (7 or 7:30 P.M.). All ages are welcome at Big Room shows, to encourage family enjoyment of live music. Cameras, video or audio recorders, and controlled substances are not welcome. For current and future show information, see the Sierra Nevada website, www.sierra-nevada.com, or contact Bob Littell, boblittell@sierranevada.com. For tickets, typically $15–20, call the Sierra Nevada pub (credit card at the ready) at 530/345-2739. Most shows do sell out, well in advance.

row of overstuffed couches down in front—not to mention that Godzilla mural on the wall. To find out what's coming up at the Pageant, pick up a flyer from the rack at the door. A good cinema downtown is the large, single-screen **El Rey,** 230 W. Second St., 530/342-2727. At the North Valley Plaza mall north of downtown is the 14-screen **Tinseltown,** 801 East Ave., 530/879-9612.

A good place to start if you're doing the galleries is the **Chico Art Center,** exhibiting work from an impressive roster of local artists in the old railroad depot, 450 Orange St., Ste. 6 (south of CSU Chico, between Fourth and Fifth), 530/895-8726, www.chicoartcenter.com, open Wed.–Sun. noon–4 P.M. **Dovetail Design** is a sophisticated new art and furniture gallery a few blocks north of downtown at 173 E. Third Ave. (at the Esplanade), 530/345-7500, www.dtdesign.net. Definitely worth a stop downtown is the **Vagabond Rose,** 236 Main, 530/343-1110. The eclectic and award-winning **1078 Gallery,** 738 W. Fifth St. (near Ivy), 530/343-1973, www.1078gallery.org, which got its start at 1078 Humboldt Road.

Don't miss the galleries at CSU Chico, including the fine **Turner Print Collection and Gallery,** located in the mezzanine of Laxson Auditorium (First and Salem Streets), 530/898-4476, which

displays some of the artist's spectacular collection as well as changing exhibits. Open weekdays 11 A.M.–4 P.M., during auditorium events, or by appointment. Also see what's up at the **University Art Gallery** in nearby Taylor Hall (First Street between Salem and Mornal), 530/898-5864, open weekdays 10 A.M.–4 P.M. and Sunday 1–5 P.M.; the **Third Floor Gallery** upstairs at the Bell Memorial Student Union building, CSU, Chico, 530/898-6002; and the **Humanities Center Gallery** across the way in Trinity Hall, 530/898-4642.

For a current rundown on what's going on and where, any time of year, pick up a free copy of the weekly *Chico News & Review* for its calendar section or see www.newsreview.com. The *Chico Enterprise-Record's* weekly *Buzz* and the independent *Synthesis* are other good info sources. Also contact the local chamber of commerce.

EVENTS

On Thursday evenings from spring into fall, downtown closes off a few streets for the **Thursday Night Market,** a low-key community festival built around fresh produce stands, good food, and entertainment. On Friday nights in summer, eclectic and free community **Concerts in the Park** were traditionally staged at the Downtown

Plaza Park (between Broadway and Main), showcasing local musical talent and attracting just about everyone in town. But since 2003, when the towering elms in the plaza were chopped down due to disease, Friday concerts have been held instead in the shady Children's Playground area between Bidwell Mansion and downtown, adjacent to Bidwell Memorial Presbyterian Church.

Come in January for the **Snowgoose Festival,** celebrating the birds of Butte County with workshops (building bird nest boxes, butterfly gardening) and field trips to area wildlife refuges, including Gray Lodge and the Sacramento National Wildlife Refuge. Chico is big on bicycling, which is why *Bicycling* magazine named Chico "America's greatest bicycling town" in 1997. Notable among local cycling celebrities are mountain bike pioneer Jeff Lindsay of Mountain Goat Cycles; innovative parts-maker Paul Price; renegade off-roader Bob Seals, who also invented the Cool Tool; and cycling columnist Maynard Hershon. Though there are plenty of bike shops in town, best of the bunch and hub of the local biking hubbub is **Pullins Cyclery** downtown at 801 Main St. (at Eighth), 530/342-1055. That's the place to stop to find out about local cycling events including the Chico Velo bicycle club's **Tour of the Unknown Valley, Gourmet Century,** and **Wildflower Century** rides in March and April. But runners also have their day, particularly during the **Bidwell Classic** half-marathon, usually scheduled in March. A major fundraiser for the local chapter of the nonprofit California Native Plant Society is the annual **Wildflower Show & Plant Sale,** a stunning exhibit of some 200 species usually held in late April. Unusual, oddly inspiring, and fun for the whole family—quite the eclectic interspecies celebration—is the annual **Endangered Species Faire** held near Cedar Grove in Bidwell Park each May.

Still the big local event over Memorial Day weekend is the long-running **Silver Dollar Fair** held at the fairgrounds in south Chico over Memorial Day weekend; call 530/895-4666 for information. The Silver Dollar is noted for family- and farm-style fun: carnival rides, car races, country-western headliners, 4-H livestock competitions, and rodeo.

Summer high life, Chico style, is climbing into a well-inflated tractor tire inner tube with a six-pack of beer and floating slowly down the Sacramento River to Scotty's Landing. This thrill isn't free anymore, either, now that state park rangers charge a "launch fee" at Irvine Finch Park, a popular starting point.

In September comes **A Taste of Chico,** bringing samples of local food and drink from more than 40 local restaurants and more than 20 wineries and breweries, plus live music and a party atmosphere to the downtown streets, which are blocked off to traffic for the event. Then there's the world-class two-day **Chico World Music Festival** in September, now staged at CSU Chico and featuring headliners such as the Laura Love Band, Tim O'Brien, and Kelly Joe Phelps. For more information see www.chicoperformances.com; for tickets, call the University Box Office at 530/898-6333 for tickets. In October, big events include downtown's **Fall Harvest Fair** and the **CSU Chico Homecoming** celebration and parade, downtown and on campus. Not to mention the **National Yo-Yo Contest** staged by Bob Malowney of Bird in Hand, where the world's largest yo-yo is ceremonially dropped from atop a 70-foot crane. The annual weekend-long Chico Art Center **Open Studios Art Tour** usually comes in early November

SHOPPING

Also worth particular note in Chico is the accomplished creativity of its business community. Thanks to the university's downtown location and the substantial consumer power of its students, Chico is one of those rare valley towns that still has an economically viable downtown business district, one not yet choked off by the California shopping mall syndrome. Downtown (more or less defined by Wall and Salem Streets to the east and west, respectively, and by First and Sixth Streets to the north and south) are contemporary cafés, coffeehouses, restaurants, and unusual shops, like **Grace Jr.,** 331 W. Fifth St., 530/342-1369, wonderful for unique jewelry, eccentric crafts, and odd greeting cards; **Cotton Party** at 337 Broadway, 530/893-4923, a tasteful selection of relaxed natural-fiber fashions; and **Bird in Hand** at 320 Broadway, 530/893-1414, an eclectic gift shop and yo-yo museum. For unique and stylish homewares, don't miss **Zucchini & Vine** at Second and Main, 530/345-3551. **Made in Chico** at 232 Main, 530/894-7009, is the authoritative source for local arts, crafts, and mementos, *the* place to find Chico's own Christmas **Woof & Poof** angels, elves, reindeer, Santas, and more. A fabulous used bookstore, especially if you have time to rummage through the shelves, is **The Bookstore,** 118 Main, 530/345-7441. And remember when you could buy just one nut, bolt, or nail, if that's all you needed? Those days still exist in downtown Chico, where you'll find one of the best old-time hardware stores anywhere, helpful and friendly **Collier Hardware,** 105 Broadway (First St. and Broadway), 530/342-0195. Collier's sells just about every useful doodad imaginable—and provides friendly personnel to help you find it. The housewares section is also a delightful surprise. If downtown doesn't do it for you, Chico's major shopping center, the **Chico Mall,** is on E. 20th Street, just south of town on the east side of the freeway (Hwy. 99).

A surprising number of local businesses are actually at the top of their respective art or craft nationally and/or internationally. Since these *are* businesses, call first before dropping by. Most widely recognized is **Orient and Flume Art Glass,** 2161 Park Ave., 530/893-0373, www.orientandflume.com, its handblown glasswares sold in places like Gump's, the Corning Museum of Glass, and the Smithsonian's National Museum of American History. Just across the railroad tracks, a showroom fronts the large warehouse studio. Open Mon.–Sat. 10 A.M.–5 P.M. Also hot for art glass is **Satava,** Richard Satava's art glass gallery, 819 Wall St. (between Eighth and Ninth Streets, east of Main), 530/345-7985, www.satava.com, where petroglyph and nature themes predominate (jellyfish, harvest moon, iris). Here and in England, industry leader **AVL Looms & Weaving School,** 3851 Morrow Ln., Ste. 9, 530/893-4915, www.avlusa.com, manufactures exceptional dobby looms for worldwide cottage industries as well as home weavers. Its computer-interfaced models

("compu-dobby" looms) are popular with fabric designers. **Cruces Classic Cars** downtown at 720 Main, 530/345-9779, is the streetside showroom for the restored (and unrestored) classic cars that are Cruces's passion. Renowned worldwide for his work, Cruces displays some of these beauties in his walk-through museum of old cars. Most people just look, but some buy.

With its no-expense-spared expansion finished just before the new millennium, famed **Sierra Nevada Brewing Company** just west of the Hwy. 99 freeway at 1075 E. 20th St., 530/893-3520 (brewery office), 530/345-2739 (taproom/restaurant), or 530/896-2198 (gifts/tours), www.sierranevada.com, is now the ninth-largest brewing company in the country. If you'd like a close-up look at the facilities, free tours are scheduled daily, Sun.–Fri. at 2:30 P.M., and on Saturday every half-hour from noon to 3 P.M. (Self-guided tours are available 10 A.M.–6 P.M.; pick up a brochure in the gift shop.) No tastings are offered on tours, so kids can come, too. Call to arrange large group tours. All tours begin at the gift shop, where you can buy Sierra Nevada T-shirts, baseball caps, and other clothing bearing the company logo. If you didn't sample Sierra Nevada's wares before the tour, make sure you do so afterward. At the company's impressive restaurant and taproom you'll find all the beers bottled by the company—pale ale, porter, stout, brown ale, Bigfoot barleywine ale, not to mention a German-style lager and various seasonal and special-event brews—as well as some available only here, on draught. Samplers are available. The pub (closed Monday) also serves some of the best food in town, from wood-fired pizzas, pastas, and fish and chips to rotisserie chicken and steaks. Music lovers, upstairs from the gift shop is Sierra Nevada's amazing new **Big Room,** a San Francisco-quality performance venue (blues, jazz, bluegrass) with great acoustics and tiered risers with tables—a vision of hand-finished woods and brass, another Sierra Nevada class act.

Almonds are also locally famous. The Chico area produces a hefty portion of California's annual $1 billion crop, the state's largest food export. To sample some of Chico's finest—blanched, sliced, diced, honey roasted, dry roasted, smokehouse flavor, and Jordan almonds, even Nut Thins crackers and Almond Breeze almond "milk"—stop by the **Blue Diamond Nut & Gift Shop,** in a converted farmhouse at 703 Miller Ave. (just off W. Fifth Street/Chico River Road), 530/895-1853, www.bluediamond.com, open weekdays 10 A.M.–5 P.M. Blue Diamond is the world's largest tree-nut processing company, a grower's co-op founded in 1910. Another great choice is cheery **Maisie Jane's California Sunshine Products,** 116 W. 12th St. (just west of Park Avenue), 530/899-7909, www.maisiejanes.com. The quality products sold here include flavored dry-roasted almonds—from cinnamon-glazed and coffee-glazed to Cowboy BBQ and Country Herb and Garlic—all grown by the local Bertagna clan. But there's more, including almond butter, caramel corn and almonds, chocolate-covered almonds, mint chocolate almonds, and chocolate-almond butter cups. Maisie Jane Bertagna, who started this business as a Future Farmers of America (FFA) project when she was 17, hires her workers from the local Work Training Center, thereby providing jobs to local adults with disabilities.

Fisherfolk won't want to miss the **Chico Fly Shop** 1154 W. Eighth Ave. (not Street) near the railroad tracks, 530/345-9983, a business descendant of Chico's own Powell Fly Shop, the original home of Powell & Company fishing rods—once famous as the world's best bamboo and graphite rods. Powell rods featured prominently in the Robert Redford film *A River Runs Through It.* That company is now owned by stockbroker Charles Schwab and his son Sandy, who moved the manufactory to Rancho Cordova; no Powells are now involved in that company. But at last report Press Powell was still hand-crafting innovative rods here.

INFORMATION

The **Chico Chamber of Commerce** office downtown, just two blocks south of the CSU Chico campus at 300 Salem St., 530/891-5556 or 800/852-8570, www.chicochamber.com, is a good source for maps and brochures, open weekdays 9 A.M.–5 P.M. Particularly worth picking up are the chamber's *Butte County Spring Blossom Tour* and *Winter Migratory Waterfowl Tour* brochures. An-

THE VINA CEMETERY

This is only cultural
I tell myself
as we walk from marker to marker,
hands held.
She's an archaeologist,
of sorts, a meticulous eye
working a startling new find—
this graveyard.
We move from stone
to weather-cracked stone
that must be touched
and catalogued in her memory
of gravestones.
She is an archaeologist
with a gentle touch and gentle
step, as we move
over this soil that will mother
us, too, into the next
millennium,
hands held.

—Gary Thompson

other good information source is the ***Chico News & Review,*** www.newsreview.com, published on Thursdays and available free in distribution racks all over town. The local daily, the ***Chico Enterprise-Record,*** offers a daily calendar plus the weekly *Buzz* entertainment insert.

Public transportation is fairly limited in Chico, which is big on bicycling—but bigger on cars. The community's **Chico Area Transit System (CATS)** buses (also linked to county transit), 530/342-0221, www.bcag.org, provide get-around-town service to major destinations (like shopping centers and hospitals) during the day and into early evening on weekdays and Saturdays. At hideous hours in the middle of the night, **Amtrak** stops in Chico at the depot at 450 Orange St. (at Fifth), with one train north to Seattle and another south to Los Angeles daily. (Women, do not wait for the train alone.) There's no ticket office locally (though any travel agency can issue Amtrak tickets); call Amtrak at 800/872-7245 for schedule information or see www.amtrak.com. **Greyhound,** 800/231-2222 or www.greyhound

.com, also stops at the Amtrak depot (four or five north-south buses per day).

The **Chico Municipal Airport** is served by United Express. To connect with cheaper flights out of Sacramento, you can take the **Airport Transportation Service** van shuttle, 354 E. Fifth St., 530/891-1219 or 800/832-4223, which runs from Paradise, Oroville, Chico, and Marysville-Yuba City south to the Sacramento Metropolitan Airport (and the same trip in reverse) on a regular schedule. Reservations required.

BEYOND CHICO

South of town are almond orchards, scattered rice fields, and farm communities, including down-home Durham, founded as a 1931 California Land Act colony. A surprise in Durham is the **Barry R. Kirshner Wildlife Foundation** and its "big cats" refuge, on Laura Lane behind Durham Park, 530/345-1700, www.kirshner.org, open daily 9 A.M.–4 P.M. by appointment. Animals at home here include leopards, a Bengal tiger, two white Bengal tigers, a Sumatran tiger, two African lions, two servals, a caracal, and a snow leopard. Donations always appreciated. In nearby Richvale, the north valley's unofficial rice-growing capital, the **Richvale Café** at 5285 Midway, 530/882-4421, is the de facto seat of government. The town itself owns the restaurant, usually open just for breakfast and lunch. Civic leaders wait tables and do dishes. **Lundberg Family Farms** in Richvale, 5370 Church St., 530/882-4551, www.lundberg.com, is famous for its sustainable agricultural practices and organic, specialty, and brown rices. Farther east is the boom-and-bust town of Oroville, with its own unique sights (see listing below).

Closer to Chico and pleasant for picnicking is the restored 1887 **Honey Run Covered Bridge** in Butte Creek Canyon to the southeast, restored by local volunteers and reached via Humbug Road (nice bike ride for the brave—narrow road, fast traffic) from the Skyway. This bridge is unique primarily because of its trilevel roofline, one roof for each interconnected span. From the bridge, snaking Honey Run Road climbs almost vertically up the craggy canyon walls, the hair-

raising back-door route to **Paradise,** a large ridgetop retirement and residential community. Humbug Road, which forks to the left from the covered bridge, continues up the canyon to the remains of old Centerville and the small **Colman Museum,** next to the Centerville School and pioneer cemetery at 13548 Centerville Rd., 530/893-9667 (open weekends 1–4 P.M.), displaying Native American and pioneer artifacts.

Past the municipal airport north of town via Cohasset Road is the onetime luxury mineral springs spa and resort of Richardson Springs, now privately owned. Just southwest of the Richardson Springs turnoff, almost visible from Cohasset Road, are remnants of the old Titan Missile Base built here in the 1950s but never actually operational (though an explosion in one of the missile silos brought national media attention). It's a pleasant drive on to Cohasset, a foothill town with a general store and church but most famous for **Vose's Shopping Center,** 9145 Cohasset Rd., 530/342-5214, in actuality a fabulous funky antique store with great bargains on refurbished furniture. Continuing on past Cohasset proper, soon the paved road disappears. With any luck, adventurers who press on might end up in the Ishi Wilderness Area.

About 13 miles north of Chico via Hwy. 99 is The Nature Conservancy's **Vina Plains Preserve,** a private ranch noted for its native grasslands and fine springtime display of vernal pool wildflowers. For more information on seasonal guided tours, contact: **The Nature Conservancy**'s California Regional Office at 201 Mission St. (Fourth Floor) in San Francisco, 415/777-0487, www.tnccalifornia.org.

The Cistercian **Abbey of New Clairvaux Trappist Monastery** and farm along the Sacramento River 17 miles north of town near Vina, on part of Leland Stanford's onetime vineyard and ranch, has some guest facilities for spiritual seekers (individuals as well as married couples); retreatants are asked to make reservations (two days or longer) at least one month in advance. For reservations call 530/839-2434 or email trappist@maxinet.com. An amazing project now underway at New Clairvaux is the complete reconstruction of a 12th-century Spanish Cis-

RELIVE AG HISTORY AT PATRICK RANCH

Just south of Chico on the Midway is the 27-acre remnant of the once vast **Patrick Ranch,** now a new historic park affiliated with the Chico Museum. Listed on the National Register of Historic Places, the centerpiece 1875 brick English renaissance Patrick Mansion was built by William Northgraves, a man who had come to California in 1845 with James Marshall (who made the historic gold discovery at Sutter's Mill in 1849) and later partnered with John Bidwell in gold mining ventures.

A variety of treasures are now on display in the house, from period furniture and clothing to Bea Compton's historic bell collection. Future plans include an onsite visitor center, blacksmith shop, Chinese gardens, and a replica Maidu village, exhibiting the old Wright Hotel, constructed on what was originally the north end of the ranch, may also be relocated here.

Summer 2003 brought the first annual Historic Threshing Bee and Antique Farm Equipment Display at Patrick Ranch, an astonishing exhibit of antique farm equipment still in good working order—everything from the surprisingly quiet grain threshers to the mule-powered mechanical hay balers.

For current information about the Patrick Ranch, including special events and dates and times for guided tours, contact the Chico Museum, 530/891-4336, open Wed.–Sun. noon–4 P.M., or check the website for updated information, www.chicomuseum.com.

tercian monastery chapter house dismantled by newspaper mogul William Randolph Hearst in 1930—"sacred stones" shipped to the U.S. but never reconstructed, as he'd intended, at Hearst Castle. When the historic chapter house is rebuilt here, a similarly styled new abbey church and a pastoral center will be built nearby.

If you happen to be in the Los Molinos vicinity on a Sunday in April or May, and if you happen to be a miniature or steam train aficionado, call ahead to find out if the **Humann Ranch** on Holmes Road near Gerber, 530/385-1389, still offers public tours of its genuine blast from the past. Located in Godfrey Humann's farmhouse basement is the amazing **South Shasta Model Railroad Museum,** a remarkably detailed model of the steam-train era route of the *South Shasta* between Gerber and Dunsmuir in the 1940s. You can also take a ride on a wood-fired German-built steam locomotive. At last report admission was $4 adults, $3 children. From Hwy. 99E in Los Molinos, turn onto Aramayo Way and follow the signs—or call ahead for directions.

OROVILLE

The first thing most people notice about Oroville is the assortment of desolate gravel heaps surrounding the town—remaining dredge piles from placer miners who literally stripped away the fertile Feather River floodplain in search of gold. Still something of a rough-and-tumble foothill town, Oroville's historic boom-and-bust economic cycle has hounded the community into this century. When Oroville got a 20th-century boost in the form of state money and jobs for constructing the massive earth-filled Oroville Dam that created Lake Oroville, things were almost rosy for a while. When the job was done, though, the town was busted flat again. Even the recreational possibilities of the lake and surrounding areas have done little to help Oroville break its bad-luck streak, mostly because of the state's failure to fulfill its promises. Now the state is shipping Northern California water once stored in Lake Oroville way south—to Hemet, in the desert—to fill the Metropolitan Water District's brand-new Diamond Valley Lake and support its new southstate recreational fishery. That hush-hush move has implications far beyond Oroville. So—especially now—give Oroville a break, and stop and take a look around.

Attractions cluster near historic downtown, including the **Butte County Pioneer Memorial Museum,** 2332 Montgomery St., 530/538-2497 for tours, a 1932-vintage replica miner's cabin stuffed with memorabilia (including a Donner Party doll), Native American basketry, and more; open Fri.–Sun. noon–4 P.M., small fee. The Victorian Gothic revival **Lott Home** at 1067 Montgomery, 530/538-2497, collects more decorative pioneer memorabilia, and appealing Sank Park, an old-fashioned Victorian garden with gazebo, roses, herbs, and picnic tables tucked into what remains of the orange grove. Home tours ($2) are offered Sunday, Monday, and Friday 11:30 A.M.–3:30 P.M., and the park is open daily. The colonial revival **Ehmann Home** at the corner of Lincoln and Robinson, "the house that olives built," is now headquarters for the Butte County Historical Society but is open for tours on Fridays 1:30–4 P.M. Freda Ehmann launched the ripe olive packing industry, after perfecting the curing process. The **Butte County Historical Society Museum** at Baldwin and Spencer, 530/533-9418, open Saturday 11 A.M.– 3 P.M., exhibits gold scales, the door to Ishi's jail cell, and historic photos; buy Ehmann brand olives in the gift shop.

Spectacular in spring is the lava cap wildflower display on flat-topped **Table Mountain,** near the onetime mining town of Cherokee just north of Oroville. Most of Table Mountain is privately owned, however, and public access is tricky, so inquire locally before heading out for a hike. The tiny **Cherokee Museum,** 4226 Cherokee Rd. (off Hwy. 70), 530/533-1849, is in the old boardinghouse there, offering historical photos and mining exhibits; open weekends 11 A.M.–2 P.M. and by appointment. Especially in spring, visit the historic Cherokee cemetery.

Good-time events in the area include the **California State Old Time Fiddler's Association** regional championship competition in March, **Bidwell Bar Day** in May, and the **Wild Mountain Faire** in nearby Concow, a full day of mountain music and merriment usually taking place in June. Come in September for the huge **Oroville Salmon Festival** in September,

Oroville has its motels and its fast fooderies, and if you're staying a while the local chamber can fill you in. Most intriguing for a meal is **Checkers,** a local Employment Development Department food service "training restaurant" at the

onetime Table Mountain Tavern, 109 Table Mountain Blvd. (at Grant), 530/538-2007. The training here tends toward Italian bistro fare, though at last report no wine or beer was served. Still, how can you complain when the food's so good—and so inexpensive? Produce is organic and locally grown, all pastas are house-made, and at lunch you can expect to spend $3.50 for a lunch entrée—like tasty mushroom ragout with polenta—and $3 for sandwiches (panini) or salad. Lunch (cash only) is served weekdays 11:30 A.M.–1:30 P.M. But you can break out the credit cards on Friday and Saturday nights, whether you opt for rustic fare (such as penne portobello, mushrooms with sausage, grilled chicken, and cream sauce) or fancier entrées, such as grilled salmon served with sautéed spinach and orzo pasta.

For more information about the area, contact the **Oroville Chamber of Commerce,** 1789 Montgomery St., 530/538-2542 or 800/655-4653, www.orovillechamber.net.

Temple of Assorted Deities

A reminder that many of those who created California's Old West were non-Western is Oroville's **Liet Sheng Kong,** the Temple of Assorted Deities (or "Many Gods"), 1500 Broderick St. (off First, at Elma), 530/538-2496. The temple was built by local Chinese (with financial support from the Chinese emperor) in 1863 for worshippers of three different faiths: Confucianism, Buddhism, and Taoism. A state historic landmark also listed on the National Register of Historic Places, Oroville's Chinese temple is both a place of worship and a museum. It's rich with artifacts throughout, from the Oroville Chinese Opera Theater puppets to the parade parasols and tapestries. On the main temple's altar sit the Queen of Heaven and Goddess of the Sea and Travel (Sing Moe or Tien How); God of Literature and Courage (Kwan Kung or Kuan Yu); and Guardian of the Monastery and Protector of the Law of Buddhism (Wei T'o). Call for current hours. Small fee.

Lake Oroville State Recreation Area

Completed in 1967, the **Oroville Dam** supplies water to local farmers, the San Joaquin

Valley, and Southern California. It also provides some flood control and generates electricity. The dam's construction—and this is the nation's tallest earth-filled dam—created a large, many-fingered lake plus the necessity for the state's downstream **Feather River Fish Hatchery,** 5 Table Mountain Blvd., 530/538-2222, to artificially perpetuate the salmon and steelhead spawn. (The best time to watch the salmon and steelhead run, throwing themselves in vain against the below-dam barrier, is in the fall, especially during the Oroville Salmon Festival.) In addition to good views from the 47-foot observation tower, the **Lake Oroville Visitor Center and Museum,** atop Kelly Ridge at 917 Kelly Ridge Rd., 530/538-2219, offers films and exhibits on gold rush history, natural history, and the development of the California Water Project. Open daily 9 A.M.–5 P.M. New at Lake Oroville: the 41-mile **Bradford B. Freeman Mountain Bike Trail** across Oroville Dam and around the Thermalito Forebay, the Thermalito Afterbay, and the Oroville Wildlife Area. The **Dan Beebe Trail** is dedicated to hikers and equestrians.

The lake itself, with a receding summertime waterline, is popular for boating, fishing, and houseboating. New in 2001: the Lime Saddle Campground off Pentz Road (between Oroville and Paradise), offering a small (six-tent) group site and 45 family and RV campsites with views of the lake's North Fork. Camping facilities at Loafer Creek include picnic tables and outdoor stoves plus flush toilets, laundry tubs, and hot showers. Bidwell Canyon Campground has RV hookups. Also available: a "horse camp" at Loafer Creek; more than 100 boat-in campsites and group camps; and boat-in "environmental floating campsites"—open, two-deck anchored pontoon boats with barbecue grills—available for $67 per night (up to three boats). One site features a wheelchair-accessible restroom. Fees for the other campsites are $10–20. From April 1 through September, reserve campsites through ReserveAmerica, 800/444-7275, www.reserveamerica.com. At other times camping is first-come, first-camped. For more information, contact: Lake Oroville State Recreation Area, 400 Glen Dr. in Oroville, 530/538-2200.

Feather Falls

Feather Falls, just above Lake Oroville in Plumas National Forest, is fabulous for a day hike. The highest waterfall in California (outside Yosemite) and the sixth highest in the continental U.S., 640-foot Feather Falls is best from March through May, when Sierra Nevada snowmelt surges through the middle fork of the Feather River, then plummets over the steep granite precipice into the Fall River, creating roaring white-water and rainbow mist. The firs, ferns, and wildflowers are best in spring, too. (In January and February, snow may line the trail; in summer, the trip is surprisingly hot.) The new 9.8-mile **Feather Falls National Recreation Trail**—about a mile in, take the right fork—is flatter and wider, more shaded, definitely an improvement; this route, which skirts the canyon, is about 1.2 miles longer than the original trail but travel time is about the same. But wear good walking shoes and layered clothing; bring plenty of drinking water, a picnic lunch, and any valuables (since vandalism and theft are an occasional problem in the parking lot). Walking at a moderate pace, with time out for a picnic, a short commune at the overlook to observe the rivers' confluence, and a longer stay at the viewing platform, the roundtrip takes about six or seven hours. (The original Frey Creek switchback trail—the left fork—is shorter but more daunting on the climb back out; the route follows the creek down then back up and around a ridge to the falls, offering views of Bald Dome.) Mountain bikes and dogs are allowed. For more information, contact Plumas National Forest's **Feather River Ranger District,** 875 Mitchell Ave. in Oroville, 530/534-6500, www.fs.fed.us/r5/plumas.

To get to Feather Falls from Hwy. 70 in Oroville, exit onto Oro Dam Boulevard (Hwy. 162) and continue east a couple miles to Olive Hwy.; turn right and continue (still Hwy. 162) 6.5 miles to Forbestown Road; turn right and continue 6 miles. Turn left on Lumpkin Road, then left again after about 11 miles (at the sign for Feather Falls Trail); the trailhead is just 1.6 miles more.

GREAT VALLEY & THE DELTA

CHEROKEE: ROMANCING THE STONE

About 12 miles northeast of Oroville as you head up Hwy. 70 a battered sign suddenly announces the turnoff to Cherokee. A side trip on the narrow, curving road mosies straight into this old Table Mountain mining town's gold- and diamond-studded past.

Two-laned Cherokee Road loops for 16 miles, branching once at Oregon Gulch Road—a wooded, six-mile mini-loop that takes in Oregon City and its old covered bridge—but otherwise meandering along the plateau's rim before plunging back down into Oroville at Table Mountain Blvd. Despite Cherokee's sparsely inhabited first impression, countless unimproved side roads lead to private residences guarded, more often than not, by ill-tempered dogs and even the occasional shotgun.

During the Miocene age, Table Mountain was actually a river system, and the area around the present-day ghost town an ancient valley. Table Mountain pushed itself up along with the Sierras, but besides the more geologic commonplaces you'd expect to find-quartz, sand, gravel and coal-petrified mastodon bones dug up here attest to a very different ecological zone than the tough foothill scrub that survives today.

A band of Christianized Cherokees became the mountain's first permanent settlers. Led there by an East Coast schoolteacher during the 1840s, the group sought a peaceful outpost in which to farm and prospect. History, however, overran them a few years later, after one of them unearthed a good-sized gold nugget and word got out. Within 10 years all but the utopia's name had disappeared, and in its place had mushroomed the usual boom-town—including eight hotels, two churches, a brewery, and 17 saloons. At its height in 1975, Cherokee's population topped 1,000; all but a hundred of these enterprising souls worked at the mine.

Hopeful prospectors included Welsh miners, who've left examples of their stonework, notably the **assay office** ruin a mile up from the Hwy. 70 turnoff. Across the street from it, another building from the period houses the funky (and usually closed) **Cherokee Museum.** Less than a hundred yards farther along on the museum side stands the old white clapboard **schoolhouse,** refurbished and now a meeting hall. A half-mile from there and across the road is the marked entrance to **Cherokee Cemetery,** where many of the headstones reflect the international mix that comprised the old town.

The mine itself, run by the Spring Valley Hydraulic Gold Company, the largest hydraulic outfit in the world and one of the last, sprawled to the east of town and concentrated on Sugar Loaf Peak. Standing at the assay office and facing back the way you came, you can see what's left of the peak. Using high-pressure monitors to hose the mountainside away, the mine during its 25-year existence hauled away $15 million in nuggets. Much of this went to pay for the Civil War; in 1880 a grateful President Hayes, with General William Tecumseh Sherman in tow, showed up to congratulate the town.

Although Cherokee's gold drew most people's attention, the area also held diamonds (aside from a mine in Arkansas, it's the only place in the country that does). Welsh miner Mike Maher found the first stone in 1859, and most of the thousand or so gems discovered by others found their way onto ladies' necks and dignitaries' pinkies. General John Bidwell himself sported a Cherokee diamond ring, while Oroville jeweler and then-city treasurer Harry Jacoby spent much of the gold-boom years fash-

RED BLUFF AND VICINITY

Named for the color of the riverbanks, Red Bluff often gains national notoriety in summer for being the hottest spot in the nation—with an all-time high temperature of 121 degrees in 1981. Besides the heat, the town is famous locally for the annual **Red Bluff Bull and Gelding Sale** in January, and the **Red Bluff Round-Up** parade and rodeo in April—one of the largest three-day rodeos on the professional rodeo circuit. The rodeo attracts hundreds of world-champion cowboys and cowgirls competing in saddle bronco riding, steer wrestling, calf roping, bareback riding, team roping, and barrel racing. The larger nine-day celebration includes an International Chili Society-sanctioned chili cook-off, parade, cowboy poetry, and the running of the bucking horses down Main Street. Mechanical big buckers are featured at the **West Coast Monster**

ioning jewelry. Even Tiffany's in New York undertook to cut and set 10 diamonds into a necklace for the wife of David Gage, a co-owner of the Spring Valley mine. In 1884, as the diamond news reached interested ears, Gardner F. Williams, the mine's superintendent, was lured away by diamond baron Cecil Rhodes to manage his emerging monopoly in South Africa.

One semiserious attempt to profit from Cherokee diamonds was undertaken by Michael J. Cooney, an Irishman familiar with Nevada mines and who'd taken a look around Rhodes' empire shortly before Gardner arrived there. Cooney showed up in Oroville in 1907, established the United States Diamond Mining Company, sold 2,500,000 shares at $1 apiece, then sunk a couple of shafts. The first was at Thompson's Flat near the cemetery, the other some eight miles south. Cooney, believing that a diamond-bearing kimberlite pipe ran deep under Table Mountain, figured he could save himself time and money by approaching it farther downslope.

And indeed, 200 feet into the second shaft, his miners discovered "blue ground" with what looked like diamonds in it. Away in Forbestown at the time, Cooney was summoned to take a look, and on the strength of what he saw invited a couple of consultants up from San Francisco for their opinions.

Here the story makes a sudden about-face. In his *Days of Old, Days of Gold,* area historian Bill Talbitzer vividly captured the excitement: "For the next two days, an air of mystery cloaked the office and armed guards suddenly appeared at the mine to keep everybody except a few workmen at a distance. . . . The next day two strangers got off the train and vanished into the office building. They

emerged in time to catch the next train out without any of the citizenry learning their identity. The day after that, Cooney ordered the mine closed and the entrance boarded up." Investors, understandably irate, called the venture a confidence trick. Others said Cooney had sold out to Rhodes' cartel heavies.

Though Cooney himself died broke in 1929 and is buried in Oroville cemetery, diamond rumors continue to sparkle, kept polished by aerial surveys conducted in 1990 by the Kennecott Mining Company as well as by an ongoing and vigorously contested bid to reopen Spring Valley mine.

Beyond Cherokee "town," Table Mountain gives little indication of its gold-dominated past and today supports small ranches and homes for the country-minded. To see what sort of people have replaced the miners, gandy dancers and saloonkeepers, time your visit to one of the seasonal events held here.

In spring, usually in early May, the **Wildflower Century** draws cyclists, who whiz through on their hundred-mile route; check out specifics at www.chicovelo.org. **Wildflowers** hit their peak about this time as well; drive five or so miles past the town to the multicolored flats and feast your eyes. On July 4th, the very local holiday **parade** features 4Hers, bedecked horses, classic cars, an anti-mine float, and some years even the county supervisor. The parade ends at the schoolhouse, where a barbecue and booths encourage folks to linger. You'll find the museum open then, as well as during **President Hayes Days,** a weekend barbecue and mammoth community yard sale also held at the schoolhouse, usually the third weekend in September.
—*Taran March*

Truck Nationals in October. Also come in October for the annual **Antique Street Faire.**

Stop by the free **Red Bluff Round-Up Museum,** just east of the entrance to the Tehama County Fairgrounds, 530/528-1477, for a quick ride through local rodeo history. Open Thurs.–Sat. 1–5 P.M. The **Kelly-Griggs House Museum,** 311 Washington, 530/527-1129, offers historical exhibits of local interest in an 1880s Italianate Victorian. Open Thurs.–Sun. 1–4 P.M.

Taking the local Victorian House walking tour is also worthwhile.

Down by the Sacramento River, which bisects town, controversy is brewing over the U.S. Fish and Wildlife Service's plan to deep-six the Red Bluff Diversion Dam, which creates the summers-only Lake Red Bluff every summer. In the meantime you can visit the **Salmon Viewing Plaza,** 530/527-3043, located along the east bank, daily 6 A.M.–8 P.M. May through September, and watch salmon via TV monitors. Better yet, try the interpretive trails at the **Sacramento River Discovery Center,** 530/527-1196.

The small **William B. Ide Adobe State Historic Park** is two miles northeast of town on the Sacramento River, 21659 Adobe Rd., 530/529-8599, and features remnants of the rustic adobe homestead of the first (and only) president of the Bear Flag Republic plus picnic tables and fishing. Open 8 A.M.–sunset daily. Free. **Ide Adobe Day** in August includes demonstrations of adobe brick-making, candle-making, and old-time log sawing.

The 37,000-acre **Gray Davis-Dye Creek Ranch Preserve** bordering the Tehama Wildlife Area east of Hwy. 99 and 10 miles southeast of Red Bluff on Cone Grove Rd. is an award-winning working cattle ranch and cooperative "habitat enhancement" venture uniting ecologists, ranchers, and hunters. Jointly managed by The Nature Conservancy and Multiple Use Management, Inc., the goal is improving wildlife habitat and encouraging healthy deer, duck, and other wildlife populations. Guided nature talks and walks into Dye Creek Canyon and the heart of Ishi country are offered periodically, from fall into spring. For information and reservations, contact **The Nature Conservancy**'s California Regional Office in San Francisco, 201 Mission St., Fourth Fl., 415/777-0487, www.tnccalifornia.org.

For more information about Red Bluff and about the north valley's hotspots, particularly recreation opportunities, contact the **Red Bluff-Tehama County Chamber of Commerce,** 100 Main St. in Red Bluff, 530/527-6220 or 800/655-6225, www.redbluffchamberofcommerce.com.

The San Joaquin Valley

Californians may make fun of Sacramento, but they dismiss and demean the San Joaquin Valley. Here, truly, is the Other California. The Kingston Trio started the public insults decades ago with: "How many of you are from San Francisco? How many are from someplace else? How many are from Modesto and don't understand the first two questions?" More recently, a San Francisco newspaper columnist quipped that Fresno is "just like Modesto but without all the glitter," a meaningless insult except to those who have searched for Modesto nightlife. Former late-night talker Johnny Carson did it too, referring to Fresno as "the Gateway to Bakersfield." So most people travel through the long, hot landscape between Los Angeles and parts north with barely a blink.

Yet people in Modesto, Fresno, and Bakersfield enjoy life in California's salad bowl. By way of explanation, Fresno's most famous son, William Saroyan, says, "We made this place of streets and dwellings in the stillness and loneliness of the desert." And Sacramento native Joan Didion says: "Valley towns understand one another, share a peculiar spirit." But the best explanation to date is still inscribed on the Modesto Arch stretched across the old highway: Water Wealth Contentment Health.

MODESTO AND VICINITY

The biggest thing in Modesto is giant **Gallo Winery,** which produces millions of gallons of wine each year. But this is also the town that inspired George Lucas's film *American Graffiti,* which explains the bronze monument to Saturday night cruising at George Lucas Plaza. Nearby Turlock is most famous for its longtime "Turkeys from Turlock" slogan, a radio advertising jingle stuffed into California's consciousness decades ago, though Livingston is Foster Farms headquarters. Livingston is also famous as the site of the last stoplight on the San Joaquin stretch of Hwy. 99—a distinction recently removed by progress.

Despite the jokes, there *is* high culture in and around Modesto, including Modesto Civic Theatre performances, Central West Ballet productions, and concerts by the Modesto Symphony and the Townsend Opera Players. Increasingly popular is the annual **International Festival** held each year in October in Graceada Park. More typical of the area, though: the **Modesto**

Model A's Swap Meet at the fairgrounds in January, the **Ripon Almond Blossom Festival** in February, and the **Oakdale Rodeo** in April, followed in late May or early June by the **Patterson Apricot Fiesta.** The May **Chocolate Festival** in Oakdale includes—you guessed it—chocolate, inspired by the proximity of the local Hershey factory, as well as entertainment, classic car show, tennis tournament, 5K run, children's games, and arts and crafts. But don't miss the **Stanislaus County Fair** in Turlock every August, the **Delicato Vineyards Grape Stomp** in late August or early September, and the **Manteca Pumpkin Fair** in October.

Once arrived in Modesto, stop for a tour of the **McHenry Mansion,** 906 15th St. (at I St.), 209/577-5341, www.mchenrymuseum .org, an astounding restoration of the 1883 Italianate Victorian home of local banker Robert McHenry and his pioneering family. To achieve period authenticity, and the Anglo-Japanese style popular at the time, wallpapers here have been reproduced to exacting artistic specifications—some stenciling done by hand—and the carpets were woven on 19th-century looms by Stourvale Mills in England. Very unusual is the rose brass chandelier in the parlor, still lit by gas. Though restoration funds have been collected and administered by the McHenry Mansion Foundation, the home itself was purchased in 1976 by the Julio Gallo Foundation and presented to the city of Modesto. Open Sun.–Thurs. 1–4 P.M., Friday noon–3 P.M.; admission is free (donations appreciated). For information on

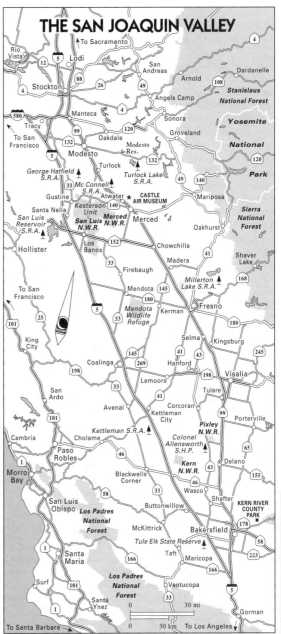

THE SAN JOAQUIN VALLEY

© AVALON TRAVEL PUBLISHING, INC.

renting the facility for luncheons, weddings, and other group functions, contact the city's **Recreation and Neighborhoods Department,** 209/577-5344.

The art-deco **State Theatre,** 1307 J St. (at 13th), 209/527-4697, designed by noted architect S. Charles Lee, has been a local institution since it opened in 1934 with a premiere of the film *Flirtation Walk*. Restored in the 1990s, the 480-seat theater offers indie films, plays, live music shows, and other events nightly. Also downtown, the **McHenry Museum,** 1402 I St. (at 14th), 209/577-5366, www.mchenrymuseum.org, offers a look at local history. It's free, and open Tues.–Sun. noon–4 P.M. In the museum's basement, the **Central California Art League Gallery,** 209/529-3369, displays California arts and crafts. The **Great Valley Museum of Natural History** at Modesto Junior College, 1100 Stoddard Ave., 209/575-6196, features exhibits, many interactive, on Central Valley animals, plants, and natural ecosystems. Open Tues.–Fri. noon–4:30 P.M., Sat. 10 A.M.–4 P.M., closed in August; small admission.

With extra time on your hands, taste your way around town, at places such as **Nick Sciabica & Sons Olive Oil Gift Shop,** 2150 Yosemite Blvd. (at Mitchell Rd.), 209/577-5067, www.sciabica.com, offering a selection of California olive oils, tomato products, and local honey. Or take a trip to Oakdale and indulge yourself, starting at the **Bloomingcamp Apple Ranch,** 10528 Hwy. 120, 209/847-1412, open July through late December, and continuing on to the ever-popular **Hershey's Visitors Center,** 120 S. Sierra Ave., 209/848-8126, www.hersheys.com, where you can view a 15-minute video of the chocolate-making process and sample sweets at the gift shop, and **Oakdale Cheese & Specialties** at 10040 Hwy. 120, 209/848-3139, www.oakdalecheese.com, noted also for its European bakery goods and low-calorie "Quark" cheesecake. Almond lovers, head to Salida and the **Blue Diamond Growers Store,** 4800 Sisk Rd. (near Pelandale Ave.), 209/545-3222, www.bluediamond.com.

For a complete listing of accommodations, activities, and restaurants (also a current copy of the local harvest trails guide), contact the **Modesto Convention & Visitors Bureau,** 1150 Ninth St., Suite C, 209/526-5588 or 800/266-4282, www.modestocvb.org. Another good source of local information is the daily *Modesto Bee* newspaper.

Camping

Camp at nearby **Modesto Reservoir,** 18139 Reservoir Rd. in Waterford, 209/874-9540, or at **Turlock Lake State Recreation Area** farther south, 22600 Lake Rd. in La Grange, 209/874-2008. **Caswell Memorial State Park,** to the west along the banks of the Stanislaus River, 28000 S. Austin Rd. in Ripon, 209/599-3810, is more noted for its 138-acre stand of valley oak forest and nature trail than for its swimming. The fee for day use is $4 per vehicle. Good campsites with hot showers, $12–15; reserve through ReserveAmerica, 800/444-7275, www.reserveamerica.com. Another possibility, just west of Santa Nella and I-5 via Hwy. 152, is the **San Luis Reservoir State Recreation Area,** 209/826-1197. For current park information, call the hotline at 800/346-2711; for wind conditions (can be hair raising) and weather, call 800/805-4805.

Staying in Modesto

Modesto offers at least some accommodation options under $50, including **Motel 6** just off Hwy. 99 at 1920 W. Orangeburg Ave. (Briggsmore exit), 209/522-7271 or 800/466-8356, www.motel6.com, with pool and a/c, and nearby **Vagabond Inn,** 2025 W. Orangeburg, 209/577-8008 or 800/854-1744, www.vagabondinns.com, with free continental breakfast and a pool. Motel row in Modesto proper is McHenry Avenue, so also look around there. Modesto offers more $50–100 options. A good choice close to downtown is the **Best Western Town House Lodge,** next to the McHenry Mansion and across from the library at 909 16th St. (at I St.), 209/524-7261, www.bestwesterncalifornia.com.

Slightly more upscale ($100–150) is the recently remodeled **Courtyard by Marriott,** just off the highway at 1720 Sisk Rd. (near Briggsmore), 209/577-3825 or 800/294-4040, www.marriott.com. Rooms are generous, with queen

INTO THE SUNSET

Following the tracks of the old Sierra Railroad, the diesel-powered **Golden Sunset Dinner Train** rolls east from Oakdale to Cooperstown, passing through locations for some famed Hollywood Westerns—from *The Long Riders* and *Dodge City* to *High Noon*.

Though "California's Golden Shortline" still offers freight service between Oakdale and Standard, just east of Sonora, outings and excursions aboard the train's luxurious 1940s and 1950s art deco-style cars are the Sierra Railroad's main attractions. Some, like the Golden Sunset and Starlight dinner trains and the Friday night Murder Mystery whodunnit, include full five-course meals and "libations." Wild West outings (complete with gunfights) and lunch and brunch trips are also offered, along with special "theme" excursions, including the Great Pumpkin Express and the Christmas Train. Summer season Rail and Raft trips end with a two-hour float down the Stanislaus River. Day and evening excursions also depart from Sonora, in the gold country foothills.

The modern Sierra Railroad Depot is located at the junction of Highways 108 and 120 in Oakdale, "Cowboy Capital of the World," one block south of the Hershey Chocolate Visitors Center at 220 S. Sierra Street. For schedule and price information, call 209/848-2100 or see www.sierrarailroad.com.

beds and vanities, in-room brewed coffee and refrigerator, hair dryer, irons and ironing board, two phone with data ports, TV, and HBO. Some suites available. Other amenities include a pool, spa, and onsite restaurant. Weekend rates can be lower—great deal for pleasure travelers. In the same price range Modesto also has a **Red Lion,** 1612 Sisk Rd. (off Hwy. 99 between Carpenter and Briggsmore), 209/521-1612 or 800/334-2030, www.redlion.com, with two pools, a whirlpool, sauna, putting green, and lighted tennis courts, and the big **Doubletree Hotel** downtown at Convention Center Plaza, 1150 Ninth St., 209/526-6000 or 800/222-8733, www.doubletree.com, with a rooftop pool, fitness center, Jacuzzi, and all modern amenities.

Eating in Modesto

If you're in farm country, you must sample the wares. The **Modesto Certified Farmers Market,** 209/632-9322, www.modestofarmersmarket.com, convenes May–Nov. every Thursday and Saturday next to the public library at 16th and H Streets, 7 A.M.–noon.

Downtown Modesto has undergone massive revitalization, with the addition of the Tenth Street Plaza entertainment/restaurant complex and open pedestrian plaza near the intersection of 10th and J Streets. Nearby is a Gallo-sponsored performing arts center, scheduled for completion in 2005. After some lean decades downtown is beginning to thrive, so if you have time, poke around and see what's new.

Restaurant Fifteen O-Five, 1505 J Street. (at 15th St.), 209/571-1505, occupies a stylishly converted flower shop. Subdued lighting and intimate, modern decor establish a cool, soothing atmosphere. The creative new American cuisine features organic meats and produce from local farms. The iceberg wedge, accompanied by a tangy blue cheese dressing, makes a salad big enough for two. Lightly seared scallops are a memorable warm up for a perfect pork chop, or the 20-oz porterhouse steak popular with local ranchers. Its bar, known for some serious cocktails, is popular on Friday and Saturday nights.

Four blocks away on J Street, the Gallo-owned **Galletto Ristorante,** at 1101 J St. (at 11th St.), 209/523-4500, is clubby and old-school, with deep leather booths and starched white tablecloths. The food is Northern Italian—delicate antipasto misto, a perfect risotto, and traditional seafood and meat dishes prepared with a creative twist. The side courtyard, with outdoor seating, a full bar, even a bocce ball court, adds pizzazz. Across the street **Tresetti's World Caffe,** 927 11th St., 209/572-2990, was an early pioneer in downtown's renaissance—a lively bar and restaurant with adjacent wine shop serving world-flavored fare at lunch and dinner (the motto here is "Think globally, eat locally") and also offering wine tastings every Tuesday 5–7:30 P.M. It's small, just 12 tables, and romantic for dinner. Also around awhile and still locally recommended is elegant **Hazel's,** 431 12th St. (at E), 209/578-3463,

GREAT VALLEY & THE DELTA

which serves divine seven-course meals. Reservations are advisable most nights.

Modesto also has an **A & W Root Beer,** 14th and G Streets, 209/522-7700, that's been here since 1957, complete with carhops on roller skates. Try **Deva** downtown at 1202 J St. (at 12th), 209/572-3382, for good strong coffee, simple pastries, salads, and healthful sandwiches.

St. Stan's Brewery, Pub, & Restaurant, 821 L St., 209/524-2337 or 209/524-4782, spins out basic pub fare over the counter, open daily for lunch and dinner. The main attraction at St. Stan's is the "alt bier," or old-style (pre-lager) beer, brewed and served right here. (Since St. Stan's brews are high in alcohol content, in California they're considered malt liquors.) The Black Forest bar ambience includes 15-foot-tall faux fir trees. Upstairs is the elegant yet relaxed dining room. On the menu: plentiful pasta choices and dinner entrées from baked stuffed eggplant and Belgium beef stew to broiled New York steak. Jazz and dinner theater, too.

Worth searching for is **P. Wexford's** at 3313 McHenry, a cozy old Irish-style pub with a neighborhood vibe—a truly down-to-earth option in the midst of strip mall development. Pub fare includes Harp-battered fish and chips, bangers and mash, and Shepherd's pie. Guinness and Newcastle Brown Ale on tap.

MERCED AND VICINITY

Highway 140, which meets Hwy. 99 in Merced, is a popular route to Yosemite National Park and open year-round, making Merced a useful "last stop" for travelers headed to Yosemite. The big news in Merced these days is that this is the chosen site for the University of California's 10th campus. When development is complete—and construction has been delayed, due to the state's budget crisis—the $750 million **University of California, Merced** campus will serve 20,000 students.

Castle Air Museum

The area's current pride and joy, Castle Air Museum is adjacent to the former Castle Air Force Base just north of town in Atwater, on Santa Fe Drive (at Buhach Road), 209/723-2178, www .elite.net/castle-air. Castle's indoor museum features an impressive collection of wartime mementos,

the Castle Air Museum in Atwater

THE CARRIZO PLAIN: CALIFORNIA'S SERENGETI

Remote **Carrizo Plain National Monument,** sometimes referred to as California's Serengeti, was established in 2001 to protect the 250,000-acre plain, the largest remaining tract of virtually untouched San Joaquin Valley grassland prairie. The monument provides habitat for many endangered, threatened, and rare plant and animals species—the latter including the San Joaquin kit fox, the blunt-nosed leopard lizard, the San Joaquin antelope squirrel, and the giant kangaroo rat. The Carrizo Plain is "critical habitat" for endangered California condors, and was the first region in California to reintroduce both pronghorn antelope and tule elk, native ungulates that had been hunted to the brink of extinction by the late 1800s. Winter birding is fine. Raptors thrive here, along with wintering sandhill cranes and mountain plovers. To the east of the Carrizo Plain is the Temblor Range—and the best aerial view of the famed San Andreas Fault, which resembles the long-buried spinal column and scraggly skeleton of some giant dragon or other ancient beast. To the west are the rolling hills of the Caliente Range, velvet green and embroidered with wildflowers in spring but sparse and spare in the searing summer heat. Yet the rains make their mark here as well; roads maybe impassable in winter.

Centerpiece of the Carrizo Plain, is **Soda Lake,** a 3,000-acre seasonal alkali lake that fills with rainwater in winter then disappears in the sere summer, its receding shoreline marked by crunchy white carbonate and sulfate crusts. **Painted Rock,** a sacred site to native Chumash people, features abstract pictographs of humans and animals between 200 and 2,000 years old. Visits to Painted Rock are restricted, and dogs are not allowed.

Serving as Carrizo's de facto visitor center is the **Guy L. Goodwin Education Center,** 805/475-2131, located a half-mile west of the junction of Painted Rock and Soda Lake Roads. Exhibits explain the uniqueness of the Carrizo and adjoining Elkhorn Plain landscapes, where "the closer you look, the more you see." The center is typically open December through May, Thurs.–Sun. 9 A.M.–5 P.M., though maps and brochures are available at the front door when it's closed. The Goodwin Center also boasts an expanded native plant garden, a convenient "classroom" for studying Carrizo Plain botany.

Come to Carrizo in spring for docent-guided tours, available on weekends by reservation. (Special group tours can also be scheduled for weekdays.) Free docent-led Painted Rock tours are offered on Saturdays—in spring the area is accessible by tour only, and access may be restricted at other times—and guided Wallace Creek (San Andreas Fault) walks are scheduled for Sundays. You can also visit Wallace Creek without a guide; there's a new interpretive trail along the creek and a portion of the San Andreas Fault. Self-guiding brochures are available at the trailhead or at the Goodwin Center. To explore Carrizo Plain geology on your own, purchase a booklet featuring two self-guided auto tours at the Goodwin Center or through the BLM Bakersfield Field Office.

Before you come, keep in mind that this is a remote area with minimal facilities; start out with a full tank of gasoline. There is no drinking water available, so bring your own. Handicapped-accessible restrooms are located at the Goodwin Center and at Painted Rock; portable toilets are available in several locales. The nearest public phone is in California Valley, 15 miles north of the Goodwin Center on Soda Lake Road. (Forget cell phones on the Carrizo Plain.) Emergency services are also available in California Valley, at the California Division of Forestry fire station.

Originally protected as a Nature Conservancy preserve, the Carrizo Plain is now jointly managed by the U.S. Bureau of Land Management, the California Department of Fish and Game, and the Nature Conservancy. For more information, contact the **BLM Bakersfield Field Office,** 3801 Pegasus Dr. in Bakersfield, 661/391-6000, www.ca.blm.gov/bakersfield, or the Goodwin Education Center, 805/475-2131, from December through May.

from vintage military uniforms and a Congressional Medal of Honor to a once-top-secret Norden Bomb Site. The big show's outside, though—a meticulously restored open-air collection of World War II, Korean War, and Vietnam War aircraft, among them: a B-17 Flying Fortress, a B-24 Liberator (one of only 15 still in existence), a B-25 Mitchell Bomber, a B-29 Superfortress (like the one that dropped the atomic bomb on Hiroshima), and an SR-71 spy plane. Quite an aviary of war birds. Also here, in the air base's onetime chapel, is the **Challenger Learning Center,** 209/726-0296, a space-and-science exhibit offering a two-hour space mission via simulator.

The museum complex also includes the Flights of Fancy cafeteria, which offers the basics—the "bomber burgers" are impressive examples of American culinary art. Special events at the museum include **Open Cockpit Day,** the Sunday of Memorial Day weekend, when the planes' interiors are open for viewing; and the two annual culinary fundraisers: the **Strawberry Waffle Brunch** in May, and the **Omelette Brunch** in October.

The museum is open daily 9 A.M.–5 P.M. May–Sept., 10 A.M.–4 P.M. the rest of the year; closed major holidays. Admission is $7 adults, $5 seniors and children age 12 and older. Guided tours are available with advance notice. Aviation buffs can also plan to show up for area air shows, including the **Antique Fly-In** in early June, held at the Merced Municipal Airport.

Other Sights

Quite impressive is the **Merced Multicultural Arts Center,** 645 W. Main St., 209/388-1090, www.artsmerced.org, three floors of sculpture, paintings, photography, and performance space open weekdays 9 A.M.–5 P.M., Sat. 10 A.M.–2 P.M., and otherwise on weekends for special events. With extra time on your hands, take the tour of the **Old Courthouse,** now the Merced County Courthouse Museum, at 21st and N Streets, 209/723-2401, www.mercedmuseum.org, a striking 1875 Italianate renaissance revival building designed by A. A. Bennett (also architect of the state capitol) and open to the public Wed.–Sun. 1–4 P.M. Note the statues up top, all handcarved

from redwood. The three on the sides of the roof represent Justica, the Roman Goddess of Justice (without blindfold). Above them, on the cupola, is Minerva, Goddess of Wisdom. The free **Merced Agricultural Museum** at 4498 E. Hwy. 140, 209/383-1912, displays old-time farm equipment, horse-drawn buggies, and a working blacksmith shop. Open Tues.–Sun. 8 A.M.–5 P.M.

Notable in the valley southeast of Merced is **The Grasslands,** a 200-square-mile, 25,000-acre grassland prairie containing multiple national wildlife refuges—including what was once the notorious Kesterson National Wildlife Area—160 hunt clubs, and altogether about one-third of the state's remaining wetlands (160,000 acres), essential to the survival of migrating waterfowl. The California Nature Conservancy is working to preserve some 60,000 acres threatened both by "incompatible agriculture" and the relentless construction of new housing developments. The **San Luis National Wildlife Refuge** complex, 209/826-3508, http://sanluis.fws.gov, includes three separate national wildlife refuges and a national wildlife area, also popular for bird-watching and hunting (peak season: Oct.–Apr.). Ask for directions and current information; some refuges are more accessible from the other side of the valley.

Practicalities

The **Original Merced City Certified Farmers Market** convenes Apr.–Dec. every Saturday at N and 18th Streets, 7 A.M.–noon, 209/667-2916. As much community party as market—they close Main St. for this event—is the **Merced Certified Farmers Market,** held May–Oct. on Thursday nights, 6–9 P.M., downtown at Main and Canal Streets, 209/722-8820. Another area tasting opportunity is the impressive **Hilmar Cheese Company** and deli in Hilmar, 209/667-6076, www.hilmarcheese.com, complete with picnic grounds, not to mention the **Buchanan Hollow Nut Co.** on Minturn Road in LeGrand, 209/389-4594 or 800/532-1500, www.bhnc.com, which specializes in organic pistachios and almonds.

For a grand sandwich and delectable housemade quiche in the general vicinity of the Castle Air Museum, try **Out to Lunch** in Atwater (take the Applegate exit), 1301 Winton Way, 209/357-1170. Yum. The **Mansion House Restaurant** in Merced proper, 455 W. 20th St. (at Canal), 209/383-2744, offers citified cuisine in a graceful but casual Victorian with multiple downstairs dining rooms and upstairs banquet rooms. Open Mon.–Fri. for lunch, Mon.–Sat. for dinner, and Sunday for a popular brunch. Very Merced is the **Branding Iron,** 640 W. 16th St. (at M St.), 209/722-1822, with local brands dominating the decor. Open for lunch weekdays, for dinner daily. The **Eagles Nest** at the Ramada Inn, 2000 E. Childs Ave., 209/723-1041, serves fish, pasta, and meateater's classics in a family atmosphere (children's menu), open daily for breakfast, lunch, and dinner. The associated **Ramada Inn,** 209/723-3121, www.ramada.com, is as good a place as any to stay, by the way (exit Hwy. 99 at Childs Avenue). Rooms ($50–100) are quiet and there's an outdoor pool (and a bowling center with arcade next door). Other similarly priced stays include the **Sequoia Inn,** 1213 V St. (at Hwy. 140), 209/723-3711, and the **Best Western Inn,** 1033 Motel Dr., 209/723-2163.

For more information about the area, contact the **Merced Convention and Visitors Bureau,** 690 W. 16th St., 209/384-7092 or 800/446-5353, www.yosemite-gateway.org.

FRESNO AND VICINITY

Johnny Carson may consider Fresno the gateway to Bakersfield, but the city prefers being recognized as the gateway to three Sierra Nevada national parks: Yosemite, Sequoia, and Kings Canyon. California's sixth-largest city, larger than Sacramento, Fresno has become much more than the Raisin Capital of the World. Though it sprawls out in all directions, the city has a distinct and walkable downtown where the newer, taller buildings haven't yet crowded out the old. Fresno also boasts a full cultural calendar, a state university and a city college, worthwhile sights, and culinary diversions. Certainly appropriate to its agricultural roots, Fresno now boasts the largest population of Hmong in the U.S., more than 30,000.

For more area information, contact the **Fresno City & County Convention and Visitors Bu-** reau, 808 M St. in Fresno, 559/233-0836 or 800/788-0836, www.fresnocvb.org. Or stop by the new tourist attraction and visitor information center, Fresno's historic **Water Tower**—at 2430 Fresno St., 559/237-0988, where you can tour the inside of the tower and pick up information on Fresno attractions, dining, and lodging. The 100-foot-tall structure, designed to hold 250,000 gallons of water, was patterned after a medieval German water tower by Chicago architect George Washington Maher in 1894.

Seeing and Doing Fresno

The **Fresno Metropolitan Museum of Art, History, and Science** in the old *Fresno Bee* building, 1555 Van Ness (at Calaveras), 559/441-1444, www.fresnomet.org, features a permanent exhibition based on (former Fresnoan) William Saroyan entitled A Life in the World: Fresno's William Saroyan; the permanent collection also contains a comprehensive antique puzzle collection and an Asian Gallery. The Fresno Met has built its reputation with special rotating exhibits on local culture and natural history, success in securing major touring exhibits such as a life-sized T-Rex replica "Sue," and world-class retrospectives, such as Edward Hopper on loan from the Whitney Museum in New York. The museum's Reeves Exploration Center offers 50 hands-on science exhibits. Open Tues.–Fri. 11 A.M.–5 P.M. Admission $7 adults, $4 seniors, $3 children 3–12, children under 3 free. Every Thursday 5–8 P.M. is "dollar night," when admission is $1 (age 3 and up).

Among other local sights is the exceptional **Fresno Art Museum,** 2233 N. First St. (between McKinley and Clinton), 559/441-4221, www.fresnoartmuseum.com, which each year features multiple exhibits—Mexican, American, French impressionist—in its contemporary galleries. Museum facilities also include a gift shop and an auditorium for films and plays. Handicapped accessible. Open Tues.–Fri. 10 A.M.–5 P.M., weekends noon–5 P.M. Small admission fee, free for children under age 15. Guided group tours are available upon request. Other intriguing local arts museums include the **African American Historical and Cultural Museum,** 1857 Fulton St. (at Divisadero St.), 559/268-7102, and

Kearney Mansion

the Hispanic **Arte Americas,** 1630 Van Ness (at Calaveras), 559/266-2623.

The **Discovery Center,** 1944 N. Winery Ave. (between Clinton and McKinley), 559/251-5533, www.thediscoverycenter.net, is a hands-on museum offering exhibits on physical science and natural history. The center is surrounded by a six-acre park with picnic area and a pond filled with turtles and goldfish. Open Tues.–Sat. 10 A.M.–4 P.M. Small admission fee.

The **Shin-Zen Japanese Friendship Gardens** in Woodward Park (Audubon Dr. and Friant Rd.), 559/498-1551, are a wonderful respite for the road weary, with three acres of gardens, koi ponds, bridges, Japanese sculptures representing the four seasons, and a Japanese teahouse (open only on special occasions). Docent-led tours are available. Call for current hours. More mainstream and quite popular is Fresno's 157-acre **Roeding Park,** 894 W. Belmont Ave., a cool and green park that's also home to **Chaffee Zoological Gardens** (aka the Fresno Zoo), 559/498-2671 or 559/498-4692, www.chaffeezoo.org, as well as Playland (559/233-3980) and Storyland (559/264-2235) for the kiddies.

The Fresno Historical Society's marvelous

Kearney Mansion Museum in Kearney Park seven miles west of downtown, 7160 W. Kearney Blvd., 559/441-0862, http://valleyhistory.org, was once the center of M. Theo Kearney's Fruit Vale Estate. This early 1900s mansion, listed on the National Register of Historic Places, has been lovingly restored—down to exact replicas of original wallpapers and carpets—and now honors the memory of "The Raisin King of California." Small admission fee. (No fee to use the surrounding 225-acre park if you tour the mansion.) Open for tours Fri.–Sun. 1 P.M., 2 P.M. and–3 P.M. Pick up the local *Guide to Historic Architecture—Tower District* (available in the gift shop) to more fully appreciate the community's architectural heritage.

Back in town, the **Meux Home Museum,** 1007 R St. (at Tulare), 559/233-8007, occupies the last remaining example of the Victorian homes built earlier in Fresno's settlement history. Former residence of Dr. Thomas R. Meux and family, built circa 1889, the house is now restored and authentically furnished. Guided tours are offered Fri.–Sun. noon–3:30 P.M. Small admission fee.

Other worthwhile stops in and around Fresno

WILLIAM SAROYAN: THE TIMES OF HIS LIFE

Known for the human reach of his writings, Fresno's own William Saroyan won the Pulitzer Prize in 1940 for his play *The Time of Your Life: A Comedy in Three Acts.* And the Academy of Motion Picture Arts and Sciences awarded Saroyan an Academy Award for *The Human Comedy.* Justifiably proud of Saroyan, Fresno named its convention center after him. There's also an exceptional permanent Saroyan exhibit at the Fresno Metropolitan Museum. Still, the biggest commemoration comes each year at the **William Saroyan Festival,** usually held during April and May—a celebration featuring guided historical walks through Old Armenian Town, writers' conferences and contests, dramatic presentations—both on radio and on stage—and other events. For current details contact the William Saroyan Festival, 559/221-1441.

include the **Mennonite Quilt Center,** 1012 G St. in Reedley, 559/638-3560, with free demonstrations and displays on the folk art of quilting; **Sun-Maid Growers** raisin-processing plant and store, 13525 S. Bethel Ave. in Kingsburg, 559/888-2101 or 559/896-8000; **Simonian Farms,** 2629 S. Clovis Ave. in Fresno, 559/237-2294, which offers bushels and bushels of everything in season (more than 100 varieties of fruits and vegetables) and also displays an impressive collection of antique farm equipment (hayrides offered in October); and **Sierra Nut House,** 3034 E. Sierra Ave., 559/299-3052, (also at 788 W. Bullard, 559/439-7707, and at 7945 N. Blackstone in Riverpark, 559/432-4023), which sells all sorts of nutty products—raw nuts, roasted nuts, chocolate-covered nuts, nut butters—as well as fruits, seeds, honey, coffee, tea, and gourmet food items.

Tower District

Fresno's Tower District, on Olive between Palm, Wishon, Fulton, and Van Ness Avenues, is anchored by Fresno's beautifully restored 1939 **Tower Theater,** 815 E. Olive, 559/485-9050, with its mural of *Leda and the Swan* and glass

bas-relief of *The Huntsman,* a fabulous venue for local theater and other performances. Fresno's hip district, magnet for bohemian and alternative everything, the Tower District is the best place to escape the town's sprawling patchwork of chain stores. Used-clothing and record stores, coffeehouses, and restaurants are all within easy walking distance. Weekend nights are especially frisky, with live music, festivals, and art events at various venues throughout the neighborhood. For more information, see Eating in Fresno and Eventful, Entertaining Fresno below.

Forestiere Underground Gardens

Sicilian immigrant Baldasare Forestiere started his underground domestic sculpture, the beginnings of a somewhat fantastic underground retreat, in 1906. Determined to beat the heat of Fresno's searing summers, and utilizing the tunneling techniques he learned while working on New York subway construction, he worked steadily for 40 years—carving out for himself a two-bedroom home with kitchen and library, and a multitude of patios, grottos, a fish pond, even an amazing glass-bottomed "walk-under" aquarium. But he didn't stop there. Forestiere's 10-acre underground labyrinth ultimately included more than 50 underground rooms, a ballroom complete with stage, a chapel, and interconnecting tunnels, arches, and stonework patterned after the catacombs of ancient Rome. To meet the needs of his changing world, he also added an 800-foot automobile tunnel, a "car corridor" for patrons of the underground restaurant and hotel Forestiere was building. Open in places to the sunlight above, the complex also included lush and exotic gardens with Moroccan grapevines, Chinese date trees, loquats, and citrus trees bearing multiple varieties of fruit.

Situated in the midst of strip development, only about 4.5 acres of Baldasare Forestiere's original domain remains. The Forestiere Underground Gardens, now a National Historic Landmark, are located two blocks east of Hwy. 99 at 5021 W. Shaw Avenue. Weekend tours depart on the hour from noon to 2 P.M. in spring (weather permitting), Wed.–Sun. in summer. Admission is $8 adults, $7 seniors and teenagers,

$5 children (children under 4 not permitted). For more information, call 559/271-0734.

Institute for Japanese Art

Do make the side trop to charming Hanford, some 45 miles south of Fresno and home to the spectacular **Ruth and Sherman Lee Institute for Japanese Art,** 15770 10th Ave. (about six miles south of Hwy. 198), 559/582-4915, www .shermanleeinstitute.org, one of the finest collections of Japanese art in the country. This well-designed museum, tucked into a walnut orchard, houses at least some of this growing and distinguished collection of Japanese arts from the 10th into the 21st centuries—including exquisite folding screens, Buddhist sculptures, and paintings. Only a small part of the collection is exhibited at any one time.

For special exhibits are offered each year. Museum hours are Tues.–Sat. 1–5 P.M., with docent-guided tours scheduled every Saturday at 1 P.M., except in August, when the gallery is closed. For more information about the area, contact the **Hanford Chamber of Commerce/Visitor Agency,** 200 Santa Fe Ave., Ste. D in Hanford, 559/582-5024 or 559/582-0483, www.hanfordchamber.com.

Staying in Fresno

Camp at **Millerton Lake State Recreation Area,** 5290 Millerton Rd. in Friant, 559/822-2225 or 559/822-2332. Reserve campsites through ReserveAmerica, 800/444-7275, www.reserveamerica.com. For information about camping in nearby **Sierra National Forest,** stop by headquarters at 1600 Tollhouse Rd. in Clovis, 559/297-0706, www.fs.fed.us/r5/sierra.

Motel 6 offers three area locations, with prices usually Under $50—at 4245 N. Blackstone Ave. (south of Shaw Avenue and just north of the Hwy. 99-Hwy. 41 intersection), 559/221-0800; 4080 N. Blackstone Ave. (just south of Ashlan), 559/222-2431; and 1240 N. Crystal Ave. (in west Fresno), 559/237-0855. For reservations at any Motel 6, call 800/466-8356.

There are many decent hotels with rooms in the $50–100 range, including the **Best Value Water Tree Inn** at 4141 N. Blackstone, 559/222-

4445. The lushly landscaped **Sheraton Four Points Hotel,** 3737 N. Blackstone Ave., 559/226-2200, offers quiet rooms and an outdoor pool. Piccadilly Inns are well represented, with the **Piccadilly Inn—Shaw,** 2305 W. Shaw Ave., 559/226-3850; the **Piccadilly Inn—University,** 4961 N. Cedar Ave. (northeast of town), 559/224-4200; and the **Piccadilly Inn—Airport,** 5115 E. McKinley Ave., 559/251-6000.

For information about other accommodations, contact the accommodating Fresno Convention and Visitors Bureau, 848 M St., 559/233-0836 or 800/788-0836, www.fresnocvb.org. Besides providing current motel and hotel rates, the bureau will book and reserve rooms.

You could also get away from the madding crowds. A nice place to stay in Hanford is the 1890 **Irwin Street Inn,** originally a boardinghouse downtown at 522 N. Irwin Street, now a cheery bed-and-breakfast with private bathrooms and all the other modern comforts. For more information or reservations, call 559/583-8000 or 866/583-7378, or see www.irwinstreetinn.com. Pets welcome. Some rooms are $50–100, topping out at $125, but ask about special packages.

Eating in Fresno

Worth a stop for fresh local produce is the **Fresno Pavilion Certified Farmers Market,** every Saturday 10 A.M.–2 P.M. at Pavilion West Shopping Center, at W. Bullard and N. West Avenues, 559/439-8389. On Tuesday, head for the **Fresno Tuesday CFM** in River Park at Blackstone and Nees (same phone), 5–9 P.M. in summer, 4–7 P.M. in winter. Or check out the outdoor **produce market** convention on Tues., Thurs., and Sat. 7 A.M.–3 P.M. at the corner of Merced and N Streets.

For inexpensive ethnic food, mostly Japanese and Mexican, head to old Chinatown, west of the railroad tracks in the vicinity of Kern and G streets. **George's,** 2405 Capitol St. (at Tulare), 559/264-9433, has that California-cuisiney look but in fact dishes up wonderful Armenian authenticity, from peasant soup to shish kebab. Quite reasonable. Another George's is at 3045 W. Bullard (at Marks), 559/449-0100.

The Tower District's **Butterfield Brewing Co.**

TULARE'S WORLD OF AGRICULTURE

The San Joaquin Valley is agribusiness country. Fresno County has been the nation's top-producing farm region from the Eisenhower administration. Now that Fresno is losing much of its prime ag land to development, its neighbor—dairy-rich Tulare County—grabbed the title in 2001 with a crop value of $3.5 billion.

If you're not fully aware of California's presence as the overall top U.S. agricultural producer, come to the city of Tulare and the **International Agri-Center**, 4450 S. Laspina St., www.farmshow.org, during the second week in February and see how it's done. Attracting a half million or more people and 1,600 or more equipment and technology exhibitors, the **World Ag Expo** is an agribusiness fantasyland, the largest agricultural trade show in the world. Area agricultural tours are also offered. Event admission is $7. For more information or advance tickets, call 559/688-1751 or 800/999-9186 or see www.worldagexpo.org. Come to the center in April for the two-day annual **California Antique Farm**

Equipment Show, 559/688-1030, www.antiquefarmshow.org, which showcases antique equipment, collectors, and craftsmen from throughout the United States.

Also on the agri-center grounds is its **Heritage Complex,** 4500 S. Laspina St., 559/688-1030, www.heritagecomplex.org, with an impressive Farm Equipment Museum and an agricultural Learning Center. The complex also offers a picnic area, deli, and (to walk it off) a self-guided tree tour.

Across the street is Southern California Edison's **Agricultural Technology Application Center** (AgTAC), 4175 S Laspina St., 800/772-4822, an industry-focused agricultural education center (open weekdays) emphasizing technological innovation and offering exhibits and displays as well as classes and workshops.

Also within walking distance of the agri-center is Tulare County Agriculture Commissioner's office, the county office of University of California Cooperative Extension, and the UC Veterinary Teaching & Research Center.

Bar & Grill, 777 E. Olive, 559/264-5521, is open for lunch and dinner daily, serving its award-winning handcrafted Bridalveil, Tower Dark, and San Joaquin Ales, plus specialty beers. A restaurant more than a pub, at lunch Butterfield offers salads and sandwiches, "stout" chili, and barbecued ribs or chicken. Dinner entrées include more of the same plus pastas, the brewhouse platter (an assortment of sausages to complement the beer), and a good selection of chicken, beef, and seafood. Brunch features quiche, specialty omelettes, scrambles, and classic eggs Benedict. Specialty coffees available, too. A few blocks away, California-style **Echo Restaurant,** 609 E. Olive Ave., 559/442-3246, has achieved national acclaim serving up the best available produce, simply and elegantly—surprisingly affordable with the nightly fixed-price menu. Style-wise, the **Daily Planet** 1211 N. Wishon, 559/266-4259, is out of this world—art deco and delightful, with a weekly changing menu featuring contemporary American cuisine, starting with lobster quesadillas for appetizers.

Also good at lunch and dinner is **Livingstone's Restaurant and Pub,** 831 E. Fern, 559/485-5198. For French country classics with a San Joaquin touch, the place is the **Ripe Tomato,** 5064 N. Palm Ave. (at Shaw), 559/225-1850.

Famous in Fresno is the **Basque Hotel,** 1102 F St. (at Tulare), 559/233-2286, with inexpensive and incredibly generous portions of peasant fare served up family-style; entrées change nightly. Traditional in Fresno is the family-style Basque fare at the **Santa Fe Basque Restaurant,** 3110 N. Maroa (at Shields), 559/266-2170. Plenty of good food at a fair price. To get the true flavor of this town, try other local ethnic offerings, too, from Vietnamese and Japanese to Mexican and Russian-German.

For a quick meal, try burgers at **Colorado Grill,** 46 E. Herndon (at Blackstone), 559/439-2747, or head to the nation's first franchised **McDonald's** restaurant, with golden arches built into the sides, on the corner of Blackstone and Shields Avenues, 559/229-0539.

Out there in Hanford southeast of Fresno is

another surprise, the impeccable **Imperial Dynasty,** adjacent to the Taoist Temple at 2 China Alley, 559/582-0196. The Dynasty is in the middle of nowhere, and not a Chinese restaurant (expect continental); people jet in from everywhere for the gourmet fare. You can drop in for regular dinners but reservations are necessary well in advance for the daily changing seven-course dinners that run from $75 (food only). The **Superior Dairy** ice cream parlor in Hanford, 559/582-0481, is worth a stop for its real ice cream, milk shakes, sodas, and sundaes. Try the S-O-S, truly excessive! And if you have the time, take in a movie or a show at the fabulous **Hanford Fox Theatre,** 559/584-7423, worth the price of admission just to see the interior.

Entertainment and Events

If you're in the area between February and May, you'll be just in time to take in the spring blossoms. Pick up a map to the 62-mile **Blossom Trail Driving Tour** at the water tower visitor center at 2430 Fresno St., 559/237-0988 or 800/788-0836. The self-guided tour takes you through the county's colorful orchards and past picnic spots and historic sites. Perhaps the best time to come is March, when the **Blossom Days Celebration** takes place in Sanger.

Fresno attracts some big-league entertainment, so the local events calendar constantly changes. The annual **"Carnival" Mexican Music Festival** is held at the convention center in March. The two-day **Clovis Rodeo** in April includes bronc and bull riding plus a barbecue and dance. A completely different crowd attends the April/May **William Saroyan Festival,** honoring Fresno's own Pulitzer Prize winner with films, exhibits, walking tours, and Armenian food and dancing. Also in May, in nearby communities: the **Selma Raisin Festival** and the **Kingsburg Swedish Festival.** In late May or early June comes Selma's **Portuguese Festival.** In July, Fresno hosts the **Obon Odori Festival.** But if you like county fairs, don't miss the **Big Fresno Fair** in October, one of the world's largest, lasting more than two weeks.

For Fresno nightlife, head for the Tower District. The restored 1939 **Tower Theater,** 815 E.

Olive, 559/485-9050, is a fabulous venue for local theater, touring bands, and other performances. The Good Company Players hold forth, theatrically, from their **Second Space Theatre,** 928 E. Olive, 559/266-0660. The same troupe performs Broadway musicals for dinner theater at **Roger Rocka's Music Hall,** 1226 N. Wishon (at Olive), 559/266-9494. Cost for dinner and a show: $32 and up.

For something more highbrow, consider the **Fresno Ballet,** 559/233-2623. The **Fresno Philharmonic Orchestra,** 559/261-0600, performs a season of subscription concerts (with occasional guests like Claudio Arrau, Roberta Peters, and Isaac Stern), at the William Saroyan Theatre in the city's Convention Center complex (box office at 700 M St., 559/498-4000). For current events and nightlife, pick up a copy of the *Fresno Bee.*

VISALIA

This, officially, is Middle America. Not only is Visalia (like Fresno) located near the state's geographic center, market researchers have discovered that the likes and dislikes of Visalians are a microcosm of West Coast consumer preference. For more information about what's going on in Middle America, contact the **Visalia Convention & Visitors Bureau,** 301 E. Acequia Ave., 559/713-4000 or 800/524-0303, www.cvbvisalia.com.

Practicalities

Next to the airport, the **Holiday Inn Plaza Park** at 9000 W. Airport Dr., 559/651-5000 or 800/465-4329, has rates of $50–100, as does the **Visalia Radisson Hotel** at 300 S. Court St. (at Mineral King), 559/636-1111 or 800/333-3333. For something a bit different, consider Visalia's **The Spalding House** downtown at 631 N. Encina St., 559/739-7877, www.the-spaldinghouse.com, an elegant, lovingly restored historic home with three lovely bed-and-breakfast suites (one once an aviary), $50–100 each. Such a deal. At the historic 1876 **Ben Maddox House** across the way at 601 N. Encina St. downtown, 559/739-072 or 800/401-9800, www.benmaddoxhouse.com, you can stay in the water tower room—any of the five rooms, in fact—for $100–150.

For Visalia's homegrown, ask at the visitors bureau for a copy of the current *Tulare County Harvest Trail Guide,* which also lists locations of area Certified Farmers' Markets. **Mearle's Drive-In,** 604 S. Mooney Blvd., 559/734-4447, no longer has carhops, but just hop inside for the 1950s ambience and burgers, fries, milkshakes, and 15 flavors of ice cream. A classic in the genre. Among the area's Mexican restaurants, **Colima** 111 E. Main, 559/733-7078, is locally favored for its jumbo-sized burritos and traditional dinner plates, which are served with handmade tortillas. For Visalia-style fine dining the place is **Vintage Press,** 216 N. Willis St., 559/733-3033, a *Wine Spectator* favorite, with daily specials (predominantly seafood) and glorious desserts.

BAKERSFIELD

Bakersfield is still prime agricultural country (grapes, citrus, and cotton are the top three crops), but it's also the center of the southern San Joaquin's oilfield development. Pumpjacks march across the valley's landscape like industrial-age scarecrows.

The city and its environs feature a symphony orchestra, theater troupes, country-western music and rodeos, and agricultural festivals celebrating everything from cotton and grapes to tomatoes and potatoes. The two-week-long **Great Kern County Fair** takes place here from late September into October. If that's too overwhelming for you, there's always the April **Iris Festival** in Porterville, to the north, centered on the world's largest re-blooming iris garden.

Contact the **Kern County Board of Trade,** 661/861-2367 or 800/500-5376, www.visitkern.com, for information on Kern County parks, wildlife, and arts events. Or contact the **Greater Bakersfield Convention and Visitors Bureau,** 661/325-5051, www.bakersfieldcvb.org

Seeing Bakersfield

The **Bakersfield Museum of Art,** 1930 R St. (between 19th and 21st Sts), 661/323-7219,

www.bmoa.org, is surrounded by a small park and sculpture garden. Stop here to get a feel for the complexity of that adventure into temporary contemporary outdoor art—and to appreciate current shows, which emphasize Southern California artists. Hours are Tues.-Sat. 10 A.M.–4 P.M.; small admission fee.

Other diversions include the **Kern County Museum,** 3801 Chester Ave., 661/852-5000, www.kcmuseum.org, part of a complex that includes 14-acre **Pioneer Village** (an excellent outdoor "museum" of buildings and other history from the 1860s) and the hands-on **Lori Brock Children's Discovery Center.** To better understood the local landscape, check out the new Black Gold exhibit. The museum is open Mon.-Sat. 10 A.M.–5 P.M., Sunday noon–5 P.M. Admission (tickets sold until 3 P.M.) is $7 adults, $6 students and seniors, $5 children (under 3 free). Kids big on dinosaurs will particularly enjoy the **Buena Vista Museum of Natural History,** 2018 Chester Ave. (20 th and 21 st), 661/324-6350, http://sharktoothhill.com, the largest private collection of Sharktooth Hill Miocene fossils in the world, which also offers rock and mineral exhibits, a black light room, and taxidermied animals. Open Thurs.-Sat 10 A.M.–5 P.M., small admission fee. Family-oriented, too, is the 13-acre **California Living Museum (CALM),** 10500 Alfred Harrel Hwy., 661/872-2256, www.calmzoo.org, home to Central Valley indigenous fauna (animals all unreleasable into the wild for one reason or another) and also open for up-close examination of native flora Tues.–Sun. 9 A.M.–5 P.M., some Monday holidays. Small admission fee.

Country-western music fans will want to check out **Buck Owens' Crystal Palace,** 2800 Buck Owens Blvd., off Hwy. 99 at the Rosedale Hwy./24th St. exit, 661/328-7560 or 888/855-5005, www.buckowens.com, a shrine to Buck Owens and the "Bakersfield sound" he invented. Local and touring bands take the stage every night. The club features a $1.5 million sound system, several bars, and a restaurant serving huge platters of steak and chicken for around $15. Merle Haggard and Dwight Yoakum stop by when they're in town. Please note that Buck hisself

CALIFORNIA'S GRAPES OF WRATH

During the Great Depression of the 1930s, California's fertile valley was flooded with the down-and-out from the Midwest's dust bowl. Almost overnight, the valley, which historically relied on migrant farm labor, became center stage for a real-life drama of human abuse and exploitation in the fields and squalid migrant labor camps. The story was best told by John Steinbeck in his Pulitzer Prize–winning *The Grapes of Wrath;* Steinbeck researched the novel while working as a journalist for the *San Francisco News.* Befriended by government worker Tom Collins, the two wandered up and down the valley, tending to people living in unimaginable poverty and despair. Steinbeck's many articles, illustrated by the wrenching photographs of Dorothea Lange, are now collected in Heyday Books' *The Harvest Gypsies: On the Road to the Grapes of Wrath.*

Thus, in California we find a curious attitude toward a group that makes our agriculture successful. The migrants are needed, and they are hated. . . for the following reasons, that they are ignorant and dirty people, that they are carriers of disease, that they increase the necessity for police and the tax bill for schooling in a community, and that if they are allowed to organize they can, simply by refusing to work, wipe out the season's crops. . . . Wanderers in fact, they are never allowed to feel at home in the communities that demand their services.

Despite the surprising popularity of Steinbeck's work, salvation for the migrants came only with the arrival of World War II. Most Dust Bowl refugees moved into the cities, getting well-paying jobs in munitions factories and other war-related industry. Desperate for cheap labor once again, California farmers turned to Mexico with the aid of the federal government's *bracero* (laborer) program. With Anglo workers removed from the picture, most Americans remained unconcerned about worsening agricultural labor conditions until 1965, when the Delano Strike, César E. Chávez and his fledgling United Farm Workers union, and long-running lettuce and table grape boycotts began to focus worldwide attention on the same story Steinbeck had told—illustrated now with different faces.

There have been some improvements in the lives, wages, and working conditions of at least some farm laborers since the 1960s, but abuses continue. In 1975, the California Legislature acted on one of Steinbeck's ideas and established its strife-torn Agricultural Labor Relations Board, though critics contend it's ineffective and politically stacked in favor of growers. Yet no matter what legal protections exist for farm workers, the continuing flood of illegal aliens into California's fields almost guarantees exploitation at the hands of the unscrupulous, since those avoiding deportation rarely speak out about even the most basic human rights (such as drinking water and sanitation facilities). Growers insist that workers' rights are being protected, but all evidence suggests that this is no truer now than it ever was.

Though few people even in California were paying attention, at the time of his death in 1993, Chávez and his supporters were still boycotting table grapes, this time primarily over the issue of worker protection against pesticide poisoning. Some former supporters contend the union has become ineffective, beset by infighting and not seriously concerned about the welfare of farm workers, and embittered growers claim the UFW has become "a boycott looking for an issue." But almost no one else is speaking out on behalf of farm workers.

ponied up the $175,000 required to rescue the historic but rusty 40-ton welcome sign that once stretched over Union Avenue. Bakersfield's famous sign now adorns Sillect Avenue, across from the Crystal Palace.

Near Bakersfield

An economically famous if somewhat frumpy outpost of oil history is **Taft,** home of the **West Kern Oil Museum,** 1168 Wood St. (west of Hwy. 33), 661/765-6664, www.westkern-oil-museum.org, open Tues.-Sat. 10 A.M.–4 P.M., Sunday 1–4 P.M. (Free, but donations always welcome.) Farther north—to the east of I-5 and across the valley from Visalia, and just as significant for its role in California's oil development since the 1890s—is **Coalinga,** where the **R.C. Baker Memorial Museum,** 297 W. Elm Ave., 559/935-1914, www.coalingachamber .com, tells a more detailed story about the area's cultural, economic, and geologic history. Coalinga hosts the longest-running hot air balloon rally in the United States. If you're anywhere near Coalinga (Hwy. 198) and I-5, stop at **Harris Ranch,** 559/935-0717, noted for its brand-name beef, decent American food, and very comfortable accommodations.

On the way to Taft, a slight detour off Hwy. 33 via Stockdale and Morris Roads leads to the well-intentioned but disappointing **Tule Elk State Reserve,** 8653 Station Rd. near Buttonwillow, 661/764-6881 or 661/248-6692, with herds of native tule elk confined in protective pastures since their native grassland range is now under the plow. The elk roam 975 acres; human viewing access is restricted to a five-acre area (wheelchair accessible). The visitor center area (small fee) is open daily 8 A.M.–sunset and offers picnic areas with barbecue pits, shade ramadas and restrooms, a viewing platform with spotting scope, and a small museum. A favorite exhibit in the museum: the skulls and locked antlers of two bulls that died fighting each other. View a 26-minute movie on the history of the herd.

Lakes and Preserves

To the east in the Sierra Nevada foothills is **Lake Isabella** in the Kern River Valley, 760/

379-5236 or 866/KRV4FUN, www.kernriver-valley.com, popular for camping, fishing, and water sports. If heading through the area in mid-February, stop off in **Kernville** for Whiskey Flat Days, a celebration of the area's ripsnorting gold rush history.

Other campable recreation lakes closer to Bakersfield proper include **Lake Webb** and adjacent, smaller Lake Evans just southeast of town, as well as **Ming Lake** and **Hart Lake** in Kern River Park to the northeast. They're all part of the Kern County Park system, headquartered at 1110 Golden State Ave., 661/868-7000.

The best outdoor destination around is the huge, BLM-managed **Carrizo Plain Natural Monument,** 805/475-2131 or 661/391-6000, west of Taft and Maricopa. (For detailed information, see The Carrizo Plain: California's Serengeti.) Other smaller preserves are near Bakersfield; many originally purchased by The Nature Conservancy are now under new management. The **Kern River Preserve,** along the South Fork of the Kern River 60 miles northeast of the city, is a nesting area for the rare yellow-billed cuckoo and now managed by the Audubon Society. Open sunrise to sunset. Come in late September for the **Kern Valley Turkey Vulture Festival.** For information, contact the preserve at 760/378-3044. Also see www.valleywild .org. Farther north near Visalia is the 311-acre **Kaweah Oaks Preserve,** now managed by the Sequoia Riverlands Trust. For information, call 559/738-0211 and see www.sequoiariverlands .org. Also see www.kaweahoaks.com. Four additional San Joaquin Valley preserves near Bakersfield—the 3,000-acre **Lokern Preserve** to the west, the 41-acre **Pixley Vernal Pools Preserve** and the 3,085-acre **Semitropic Ridge Preserve** (sometimes known as the Paine Wildflower Preserve) to the northwest, and the 261-acre **Sand Ridge Preserve** to the east—are managed by the **Center for Natural Lands Management,** 661/387-9453 or 760/731-7790, www .chlm.org. For more information about its ongoing habitat preservation work, contact **The Nature Conservancy**'s California Regional Office in San Francisco, 415/777-0487, www.tnc-california.org.

GREAT VALLEY & THE DELTA

Colonel Allensworth State Historic Park

This park north of Bakersfield (west of Hwy. 99 near Earlimart) preserves the remnants of the only town in California founded, financed, and governed by African Americans. Determined to develop a pragmatic yet utopian community, one dedicated to the values of education and economic independence and to the idea that blacks could live in equality with whites, Col. Allen Allensworth (a former slave who won his freedom during the Civil War) arrived in the area in 1908 to stake a claim to a piece of the American dream. As the community grew, its early farming and other successes attracted more residents. In addition to the community schoolhouse (like some of the other buildings, beautifully restored), Allensworth dreamed of starting a major technical institute for black students—a proposal rejected by the state legislature. Soon after his accidental death in L.A. in 1914, Allensworth's dreams turned to dust, as agricultural development elsewhere in the valley created a water shortage that choked off community progress.

In May, come to the park for its annual **Allensworth Old Time Jubilee,** complete with living history programs, historic games, and special guided tours. The park's annual rededication ceremony is held in October. Camping is available; $6. For more information, call the park at 661/849-3433. The visitor center is open daily 10 A.M.–4 P.M. To get there from Earlimart, turn right on J22 and take it five miles to Hwy. 43 (heading south)—two miles to Allensworth.

Staying in Bakersfield

Abundant camping possibilities are available in the general area; contact the Kern County Board of Trade, 2101 Oak St. in Bakersfield, 661/861-2367 or 800/500-5376, www.visitkern.com, for a comprehensive current listing of campgrounds and other recreation information.

For lodgings under $50, there's always **Motel 6,** and in Bakersfield there are a number to choose from, including one near downtown at 1350 Easton Dr. (California Ave. exit), 661/327-1686, and another south of town at 2727 White Ln. (just off Hwy. 99), 661/834-2828. To make

the schoolhouse at Colonel Allensworth State Historic Park

reservations at any Motel 6, call 800/466-8356 or see www.motel6.com. Another good choice under $50: the **Royal Oak Inn** at 889 Oak St., 661/324-9686.

Plusher is the **Best Western Crystal Palace Inn,** 2620 Buck Owens Blvd., 661/327-9651 or 800/424-4900, www.bestwesterncalifornia.com, with many amenities—hair dryers, in-room refrigerators, coffeemakers, irons, ironing boards—plus pool, spa, restaurant, and lounge. **Best Western Hill House,** 700 Truxtun Ave., 661/327-4064 or 800/300-4230, is also quite comfortable, with complimentary coffee and continental breakfast. Rooms at both are $50–100. Parked near the business parks is Bakersfield's **Four Points by Sheraton,** 5101 California Ave., 661/325-9700 or 866/223-9330, boasting all the amenities, The Bistro restaurant, and rates $150–250.

Eating in Bakersfield

Don't miss out on the local produce. Year-round Bakersfield offers just two possibilities—the **Bak-**

ersfield **Wall Street Alley Certified Farmers Market,** 661/345-5735, held Thursday 5–9 P.M., and the **Bakersfield Saturday CFM,** 661/319-9108, held at 30th and F Streets every Saturday 8 A.M.–noon.

Bakersfield has a notable Basque heritage, a fact reflected in its restaurants. One popular place for Basque fare is the **Wool Growers Restaurant,** 620 E. 19th St., 661/327-9584. Excellent but more expensive is **Chalet Basque,** 200 Oak St. (one block east of Hwy. 99 between Brundage and California), 661/327-2915, featuring seven-course dinners—choose from seafood, beef, chicken, or lamb—including wonderful sourdough bread, pink beans and salsa, well-spiced green beans, fabulous French fries (the potatoes peeled by hand), and Basque pudding for dessert. **Maitia's Basque Cafe,** 4420 Coffee Rd. (in Vons Shopping Center), 661/587-9055, is a relaxed, low-key Basque restaurant with a menu leaning more toward the contemporary than the traditional. Then

there's the **Noriega Hotel,** 525 Sumner St., 661/322-8419, another good choice for family-style Basque dining. Everyone waits in the bar—fascinating place in its own right—until the dining room doors open and dinner begins. Call for current seating time.

For fine Italian food, good choices include **Mama Tosca's,** 9000 Ming Ave., 661/831-1242, and **Uricchio's Trattoria,** 1400 17th St., 661/326-8870. Another local favorite, for Mediterranean and California cuisine, is **Cafe Med,** 4809 Stockdale Hwy., 661/834-4433, which also offers a martini bar and live jazz. If you're just flying by on the freeway, for good American fare try **Hodel's,** 5917 Knudsen Dr. (Olive exit off Hwy. 99), 661/399-3341; for pizza, visit **John's Incredible Pizza** at the Hwy. 178 (Rosedale) exit off Hwy. 99, 661/859-1111.

Dewar's, 1120 Eye St. (south of California and west of Chester Avenues), 661/322-0933, is a candy and ice cream shop attracting people from far and wide, a Bakersfield tradition since 1909.

Monterey Bay and Big Sur

The only remembered line of the long-lost Ohlone people's song of world renewal, "dancing on the brink of the world," has a particularly haunting resonance around Monterey Bay. Here, in the unfriendly fog and ghostly cypress along the untamed coast, the native "coast people" once danced. Like the area's vanished dancers, Monterey Bay is a mystery: everything seen, heard, tasted, and touched only hints at what remains hidden.

The first mystery is magnificent Monterey Bay itself, almost 60 miles long and 13 miles wide. Its offshore canyons, grander than Arizona's Grand Canyon, are the area's most impressive (if unseen) feature: the bay's largest submarine valley dips to 10,000 feet, and the adjacent tidal mudflats teem with life.

A second mystery is how cities as different as Carmel, Monterey, and Santa Cruz could take root and thrive near Monterey Bay. The monied Monterey Peninsula is fringed by

Mission San Antonio De Padua, near San Luis Obispo

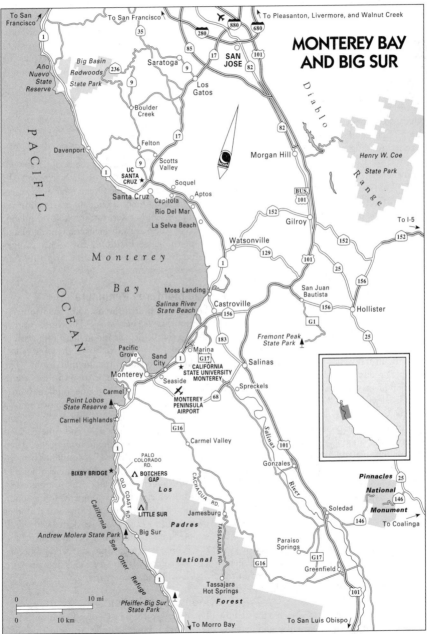

MONTEREY BAY AND BIG SUR

shifting sand dunes and some of the state's most ruggedly wild coastline. Carmel, or Carmel-by-the-Sea, is where Clint Eastwood once made everybody's day as mayor. (Inland is Carmel Valley, a tennis pro playground complete with shopping centers. The Carmel Highlands hug the coast on the way south to Big Sur.) Noted for its storybook cottages and spectacular crescent beach, Carmel was first populated by artists, writers, and other assorted bohemians who were shaken out of San Francisco following the 1906 earthquake. Yet the founding of Carmel would have to be credited to Father Junípero Serra and the Carmelite friars of the Carmel Mission, built here in 1771, the second Spanish mission in California.

The original version of the Carmel mission was built the previous year, however, near the Spanish presidio in what is now Monterey. The cultured community of Monterey would later boast California's first capital, first government building, first federal court, first newspaper, and—though other towns also claim the honor—first theater. Between Carmel and Monterey is peaceful Pacific Grove, where alcohol has been legal only since the 1960s—and where the annual Monarch butterfly migration is big news.

Just inland from the Monterey Peninsula is the agriculturally rich Salinas Valley, boyhood stomping grounds of John Steinbeck. Steinbeck's focus on Depression-era farm workers unleashed great local wrath—all but forgotten and almost forgiven since his fame has subsequently benefited area tourism. South of Salinas and east of Soledad is Pinnacles National Monument, a fascinating volcanic jumble and almost "the peak" for experienced rock climbers. Not far north, right on the San Andreas Fault, is Mission San Juan Bautista, where Jimmy Stewart and Kim Novak conquered his fear of heights in Alfred Hitchcock's *Vertigo*. Nearby are the headwaters of San Benito Creek, where lucky rockhounds might stumble upon some gem-quality, clear or sapphire-blue samples of the state's official gemstone, benitoite, found only here. Also in the neighborhood is Gilroy, self-proclaimed garlic capital of the world.

Once working-class Santa Cruz has the slightly seedy Boardwalk, sandy beaches, good swim-ming, surfers, and—helped along by the presence of UC Santa Cruz—an intelligent and open-minded social scene. Nearby are the redwoods, waterfalls, and mountain-to-sea hiking trails of Big Basin, California's first state park, plus the Año Nuevo coastal area, until recently the world's only mainland mating ground for the two-ton northern elephant seal.

LAND AND SEA

Much of the redwood country from San Francisco to Big Sur resembles the boulder-strewn, rough-and-tumble coast of far Northern California. Here the Pacific Ocean is far from peaceful; posted warnings about dangerous swimming conditions and undertows are no joke. Inland, the San Andreas Fault menaces, veering inland from the eastern side of the Coast Ranges through the Salinas Valley and on to the San Francisco Bay Area.

The Monterey Peninsula

Steinbeck captured the mood of the Monterey Peninsula in *Tortilla Flats*—"The wind. . . drove the fog across the pale moon like a thin wash of watercolor. . . . The treetops in the wind talked huskily, told fortunes and foretold deaths." The peninsula juts into the ocean 115 miles south of San Francisco and forms the southern border of Monterey Bay. The north shore sweeps in a crescent toward Santa Cruz and the Santa Cruz Mountains; east is the oak- and pine-covered Santa Lucia Range, rising in front of the barren Gabilan ("Sparrow Hawk") Mountains beloved by Steinbeck. Northward are the ecologically delicate Monterey Bay Dunes, now threatened by off-road vehicles and development. To the south, the piney hills near Point Pinos and Asilomar overlook rocky crags and coves dotted with wind-sculpted trees; farther south, beyond Carmel and the Pebble Beach golf mecca, is Point Lobos, said to be Robert Louis Stevenson's inspiration for Spyglass Hill in *Treasure Island*.

Monterey "Canyon"

Discovered in 1890 by George Davidson, Monterey Bay's submerged valley teems with sealife:

SEA OTTERS DECLINING AGAIN

Sea otters range north along the coast to Jenner in Sonoma County, and south to Cambria (and beyond). Watching otters eat is quite entertaining; to really see the show, binoculars are usually necessary. Carrying softball-sized rocks in their paws, sea otters dive deep to dislodge abalone, mussels, and other shellfish, then return to the surface and leisurely smash the shells and dine while floating on their backs, "rafting" at anchor in forests of seaweed. The playful sea creatures feed heartily, each otter consuming about two and a half tons of seafood per year—much to the dismay of commercial shellfish interests.

Such scenes are still fairly common, yet the California sea otter, listed as a threatened species under the federal Endangered Species Act, is declining again—and scientists aren't quite sure why. Infectious disease; parasitic disease such as toxoplasma, introduced by cat feces flushed into sewage systems; other coastal pollution and toxins, which contaminate food supplies as well as the water;

and entrapment in wire fishing pots are all suspected reasons. In 1995, the U.S. Fish and Wildlife Service counted 2,377 sea otters. By 1998, the population had dropped to 1,937—and some 200 dead otters washed ashore on area beaches, for reasons unknown. The population decline continues at the rate of about one to two percent per year.

In centuries past, an estimated population of almost 16,000 sea otters along the California coast was decimated by eager fur hunters. A single otter pelt was worth upward of $1,700 in 1910, when it was generally believed that sea otters were extinct here. But a small pod survived off the coast near Carmel, a secret well guarded by biologists until the Big Sur Highway opened in 1938.

Until the 1990s, the sea otters seemed to be making a comeback; their range had expanded widely up and down the coast. Much to the chagrin of the south coast commercial shellfish industry, sea otters had even started moving south past Point Conception into shellfish waters.

bioluminescent fish glowing vivid blue to red, squid, tiny rare octopi, tentacle-shedding jellyfish, and myriad microscopic plants and animals. This is one of the most biologically prolific spots on the planet. Swaying with the ocean's motion, dense kelp thickets are home to sea lions, seals, sea otters, and giant Garibaldi "goldfish." Opal-eyed perch in schools of hundreds swim by leopard sharks and bottom fish. In the understory near the rocky ocean floor live abalones, anemones, crabs, sea urchins, and starfish.

Students of Monterey Canyon geology quibble over the origins of this unusual underwater valley. Computer-generated models of canyon creation suggest that the land once used to be near Bakersfield and was carved out by the Colorado River; later it shifted westward due to plate tectonics. More conventional speculation focuses on the creative forces of both the Sacramento and San Joaquin Rivers, which perhaps once emptied at Elkhorn Slough, Monterey Canyon's principal "head."

However Monterey Canyon came to be, it is now centerpiece of the 5,312-square-mile **Mon-**

terey Bay National Marine Sanctuary which extends some 400 miles along the coast, from San Francisco's Golden Gate in the north to San Simeon in the south. Established in 1992 after a 15-year political struggle, this federally sanctioned preserve is now protected from offshore oil drilling, dumping of hazardous materials, the killing of marine mammals or birds, jet skis, and aircraft flying lower than 1,000 feet. As an indirect result of its federal protection, Monterey Bay now boasts a total of 18 marine research facilities.

Big Sur

The Big Sur land itself is unfriendly, at least from the human perspective. The indomitable, unstable terrain—with its habit of sliding out from under whole hillsides, houses, highways, and hiking trails during winter rains and otherwise at the slightest provocation—has made the area hard to inhabit. But despite its contrariness, the central coast, that unmistakable pivotal point between California's north and south, successfully blends both.

Though the collective Coast Ranges continue

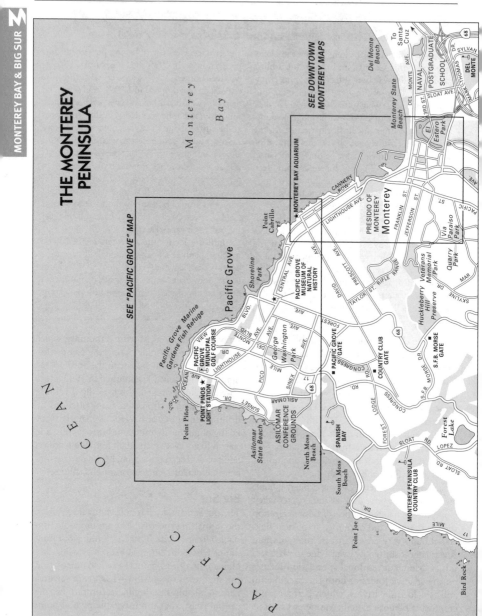

THE MONTEREY PENINSULA

SEE DOWNTOWN MONTEREY MAPS

SEE "PACIFIC GROVE" MAP

Monterey Bay

PACIFIC OCEAN

Point Piños

Pacific Grove Marine Gardens Fish Refuge

Pacific Grove

Shoreline Park

Point Cabrillo

MONTEREY BAY AQUARIUM

CANNERY ROW

LIGHTHOUSE AVE

PRESIDIO OF MONTEREY

Monterey

PACIFIC GROVE MUSEUM OF NATURAL HISTORY

CENTRAL AVE

OCEAN VIEW BLVD

MONTE BLVD

LIGHTHOUSE

PICO

SINEY AVE

DEL MONTE

MILE

17 MILE

ASILOMAR

PACIFIC GROVE MUNICIPAL GOLF COURSE

POINT PIÑOS LIGHT STATION

Asilomar State Beach

ASILOMAR CONFERENCE GROUNDS

SUNSET DR

North Moss Beach

South Moss Beach

SPANISH BAY

George Washington Park

FOREST AVE

PACIFIC GROVE GATE

CONGRESS AVE

COUNTRY CLUB GATE

68

S.F.B. MORSE GATE

DAVID AVE

PRESCOTT AVE

TAYLOR ST. RIFLE RANGE

FRANKLIN ST

JEFFERSON ST

PACIFIC ST

Via Paraiso Park

Quarry Park

MAR

SKYLINE DR

Huckleberry Hill Preserve

Veterans Memorial Park

Forest Lake

S.F.B. MORSE DR

FOREST LODGE RD

CONGRESS RD

SLOAT RD

LOPEZ RD

MONTEREY PENINSULA COUNTRY CLUB

17 MILE DR

Point Joe

Bird Rock

Del Monte Beach

To Santa Cruz

68

POSTGRADUATE SCHOOL

NAVAL

DEL MONTE AVE

SYLVAN DR

MARK THOMAS DR

DEL MONTE

3RD ST

SLOAT AVE

Monterey State Beach

El Estero Park

Estero

PACIFIC OCEAN

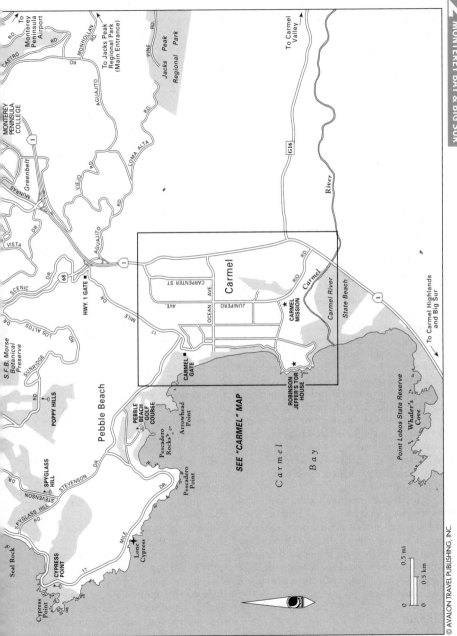

SEE "CARMEL" MAP

© AVALON TRAVEL PUBLISHING, INC.

south through the region, here the terrain takes on a new look. Northern California's redwoods begin to thin out, limiting themselves to a few large groves in Big Sur country and otherwise straggling south a short distance beyond San Simeon, tucked into hidden folds in the rounded coastal mountains. Where redwood country ends, either the grasslands of the dominant coastal oak woodlands begin or the chaparral takes over, in places almost impenetrable. Even the coastline reflects the transition—the rocky rough-and-tumble shores along the Big Sur coast transform into tamer beaches and bluffs near San Simeon and points south.

Los Padres National Forest inland from the coast is similarly divided into two distinct sections. The northernmost (and largest) Monterey County section includes most of the rugged 100-mile-long Santa Lucia Range and its Ventana Wilderness. The southern stretch of Los Padres, essentially the San Luis Obispo and Santa Barbara backcountry, is often closed to hikers and backpackers during the summer due to high fire danger.

Another clue that the north-south transition occurs here is water or, moving southward, the increasingly obvious lack of it. Though both the North and South Forks of the Little Sur River, the Big Sur River a few miles to the south, and other northern waterways flow to the sea throughout the year, as does the Cuyama River in the south (known as the Santa Maria River as it nears the ocean), most of the area's streams are seasonal. But off-season hikers, beware: even inland streams with a six-month flow are not to be dismissed during winter and spring, when deceptively dinky creekbeds can become death-dealing torrents overnight.

Major lakes throughout California's central coast region are actually water-capturing reservoirs, including Lake San Antonio, known for its winter bald eagle population, Lake Nacimiento on the other side of the mountains from San Simeon, and Santa Margarita Lake east of San Luis Obispo near the headwaters of the Salinas River.

Climate

The legendary California beach scene is almost a fantasy here—almost but not quite. Surfers can be seen here year-round, though often in wetsuits. Sunshine warms the sands (between storms) from fall to early spring, but count on fog from late spring well into summer. Throughout the Monterey Bay area it's often foggy and damp, though clear summer afternoons can get hot; the warmest months along the coast are August, September, and October. (Sunglasses, suntan lotion, and hats are prudent, but always bring a sweater.) Inland, expect hotter weather in summer, colder in winter. Rain is possible as early as October, though big storms don't usually roll in until December.

FLORA AND FAUNA

Flora

California's central coast region, particularly near Monterey, exhibits tremendous botanic diversity. Among the varied vascular plant species found regionally is the unusually fast-growing Monterey pine, an endemic tree surviving in native groves only on hills and slopes near Monterey, Cambria, and Año Nuevo, as well as on Guadalupe and Cedros Islands off the coast of Baja, Mexico. It's now a common landscaping tree—and the world's most widely cultivated tree, grown commercially for its wood and pulp throughout the world. The unusual Monterey cypress is a relict, a specialized tree that can't survive beyond the Monterey Peninsula. The soft green Sargent cypress is more common, ranging south to Santa Barbara along the coast and inland. The Macnab cypress is found only on poor serpentine soil, as are Bishop pines, which favor swamps and the slopes from "Huckleberry Hill" near Monterey south to the San Luis Range near Point Buchon and Santa Barbara County.

Coastal redwoods thrive near Santa Cruz and south through Big Sur. Not as lusty as those on the north coast, these redwoods often keep company with Douglas fir, pines, and a dense understory of shade-loving shrubs. Other central coast trees include the Sitka spruce and beach pines. A fairly common inland tree is the chaparral-loving knob-cone pine, with its tenaciously closed "fire-climax" cones. Other regional trees include the

TOO MUCH FUNGUS AMONG US

Two new plant plagues have sprouted in California, and nowhere have they had more profound effects—so far—than in the greater San Francisco region, and in areas near Monterey Bay.

Newest is a disease known as **sudden oak death,** or *Phytophthora ramorum,* a shockingly sudden, fast-moving fungus-like primitive brown alga that afflicts native California oak, madrone, and bay trees. First identified in the mid-1990s near Mt. Tamalpais in Marin County and now found as far south as Big Sur and as far north as southern Oregon, the disease is most prevalent along California's central coast regions. Trees in their death throes have large, weeping cankers that "bleed" dark red viscous fluid; they also host swarms of beetles and the *Hypoxylon* fungus, evidence that tree tissues are dying. (There was some confusion about this fungal infection when sudden oak death was first identified. It's now believed that the fungus is a symptom rather than cause—already present in trees, harmlessly, breaking out and growing rapidly only where sapwood is dying.) Sudden oak death is similar to a pathogen that has afflicted forests in the Pacific Northwest since the 1960s. Perhaps ominously, it has also been found in redwood trees. There is no known effective treatment or cure.

So far sudden oak death has been spreading within the coastal "fog belt." The disease spreads through soil and root systems, and probably also through water. The cooperation of hikers, mountain bikers, and even casual visitors is required to avoid spreading sudden oak death. Preventive steps include thoroughly washing one's shoes and tires before leaving infected areas, as well as prohibiting the export of wood products and plants. Complicating the problem further is the fact that a variety of other plants serve as "hosts" and spreaders of sudden oak death. These include coffeeberry, huckleberry, and California buckeye, though the two dominant sources of ongoing infection are rhododendrons and California bay laurels.

For current information about sudden oak death, including quarantines and preventive measures, see the California Oak Mortality website: www.suddenoakdeath.org.

Then there's the fate of Monterey pines. Eons ago, Monterey pines blanketed much of California's coastline. Today, only a few native stands remain in California—and within a decade at least 80 percent of these trees will be gone, done in by a fungus. That fungus, known as **pine pitch canker,** was first discovered in Alameda and Santa Cruz Counties in the mid-1980s. Since then, it has spread throughout California, via contaminated lumber and firewood, Christmas trees, infected seedlings, pruning tools, insects, birds, and wind; there is no known cure. Afflicted trees first turn brown at the tips of their branches, then erupt in pitchy spots; within the tree, water and nutrients are choked off. The open infections attract bark beetles, which bore into tree trunks and lay eggs, an invasion that hastens tree death. Usually within four years, an infected tree is completely brown and lifeless. The United Nations has declared the Monterey pine an endangered species.

Enjoy the majestic groves of Monterey pine near Monterey while they still stand, endangered as they are both by disease and further development plans. Also take care to avoid being an unwitting "carrier" for the disease; don't cart home any forest products as souvenirs. Pine pitch canker has been found in at least eight other species, including the Ponderosa pine, sugar pine, and Douglas fir, though it appears the Monterey pine is most susceptible. The California Department of Forestry is justifiably concerned that the disease will soon spread—or is already spreading—into the Sierra Nevada and California's far northern mountains.

the Lone Cypress at Pebble Beach

California wax myrtle, the aromatic California laurel or "bay" tree, the California nutmeg, the tan oak (and many other oaks), plus alders, big-leaf maples, and occasional madrones. Eucalyptus trees thrive in the coastal locales where they've been introduced.

Whales and Sharks

The annual migration of the California gray whale, the state's official mammal, is big news all along the coast. From late October to January, these magnificent 20- to 40-ton creatures head south from Arctic seas toward Baja (pregnant females first). Once the mating season ends, males, newly pregnant females, and juveniles start their northward journey from February to June. Females with calves, often traveling close to shore, return later in the year, between March and July. Once in a blue moon, when the krill population mushrooms in winter, rare blue whales will feed in and around Monterey Bay and north to the Farallon Islands.

A wide variety of harmless sharks are common in Monterey Bay. Occasionally, 20-foot-long great white sharks congregate here to feed on sea otters, seals, and sea lions. Unprovoked attacks on humans do occur (to surfers more often than scuba divers) but are very rare. The best protection is avoiding ocean areas where great whites are common, such as Año Nuevo Island at the north end of the bay; don't go into the water alone and never where these sharks have been recently sighted.

Seals and Sea Lions

Common in these parts is the California sea lion; the females are the barking "seals" popular in aquatic amusement parks. True seals don't have external ears, and the gregarious, fearless creatures swimming in shallow ocean waters or lolling on rocky jetties and docks usually do. Also here are northern or Steller's sea lions—which roar instead of bark and are usually lighter in color. Chunky harbor seals (no ear flaps, usually with spotted coats) more commonly haul out on sandy beaches, since they're awkward on land. Less common but rapidly increasing in numbers along the California coast—viewable at the Año Nuevo rookery during the winter mating and birthing season—are the massive northern elephant seals, the largest pinnipeds (fin-footed mammals) in the Western Hemisphere. One look at the two- or three-ton, 18-foot-long males explains the creatures' common name: their long, trunklike noses serve no real purpose beyond sexual identification, as far as humans can tell.

Pelicans and Other Seabirds

The ungainly looking, web-footed brown pelicans—most noticeable perched on pilings or near piers in and around harbors—are actually incredibly graceful when diving for their dinners. A squadron of 25 or more pelicans "gone fishin'" first glide above the water then, one by one, plunge dramatically to the sea. Brown pelicans are another back-from-the-brink success story, their numbers increasing dramatically since DDT (highly concentrated in fish) was banned. California's pelican platoons are often accompanied by greedy gulls, somehow convinced they can snatch fish from the fleshy pelican pouches if they just try harder.

Seabirds are the most obvious seashore fauna; besides brown pelicans you'll see long-billed curlews, ashy petrels nesting on cliffs, surf divers like grebes and scooters, and various gulls. Pure white California gulls are seen only in winter here (they nest inland), but yellow-billed western gulls and the scarlet-billed, white-headed Heermann's gulls are common seaside scavengers. Look for the hyperactive, self-important sandpipers along the shore, along with dowitchers, plovers, godwits, and avocets. Killdeers—so named for their "ki-dee" cry—lure people and other potential predators away from their clutches of eggs by feigning serious injury.

Tidepool Life

The twice-daily ebb of ocean tides reveals an otherwise hidden world. Tidepools below rocky headlands are nature's aquariums, sheltering abalone, anemones, barnacles, mussels, hermit crabs, starfish, sea snails, sea slugs, and tiny fish. Distinct zones of marine life are defined by the tides. The highest, or "splash," zone is friendly to creatures naturally protected by shells from desiccation, including black turban snails and hermit crabs. The intertidal zones (high and low) protect spiny sea urchins and the harmless sea anemone. The "minus tide" or surf zone—farthest from shore and almost always underwater—is home to hazardous-to-human-health stingrays (particularly in late summer, watch where you step) and jellyfish.

HISTORY

Cabrillo spotted Point Piños and Monterey Bay in 1542. Sixty years later, Vizcaíno sailed into the bay and named it for the viceroy of Mexico, the count of Monte-Rey. A century later came Portolá and Father Crespi, who, later joined by Father Junípero Serra, founded both Monterey's presidio and the mission at Carmel.

The quiet redwood groves near Santa Cruz remained undisturbed by civilization until the arrival of Portolá's expedition in 1769. The sickly Spaniards made camp in the Rancho de Osos section of what is now Big Basin, experiencing an almost miraculous recovery in the valley they called Cañada de Salud (Canyon of Health). A Spanish garrison and mission were soon established on the north end of Monterey Bay.

By the end of the 1700s, the entire central California coast was solidly Spanish, with missions, pueblos, and military bases or presidios holding the territory for the king of Spain. With the Mexican revolution, Californio loyalty went with the new administration closer to home. But the people here carried on their Spanish cultural heritage despite the secularization of the missions, the increasing influence of cattle ranches, and the foreign flood (primarily American) that threatened existing California tradition. Along the rugged central coast just south of the boisterous and booming gold rush port of San Francisco, the influence of this new wave of "outsiders" was felt only later and locally, primarily near Monterey and Salinas.

Monterey

In addition to being the main port city for both Alta and Baja California, from 1775 to 1845 Monterey was the capital of Alta California—

BEACHCOMBING BY THE BAY

Beachcombing is finest in February and March after winter storms—especially if searching for driftwood, agates, jasper, and jade— and best near the mouths of creeks and rivers. While exploring tidepools, refrain from taking or turning over rocks, which provide protective habitat for sea critters (the animals don't like being molested, either). Since low tide is the time to "do" the coast, coastwalkers, beachcombers, and clammers need a current tide table (useful for a range of about 100 coastal miles), available at local sporting goods stores and dive shops. Also buy a California fishing license, since a permit is necessary for taking mussels, clams, and other sea life. But know the rules: many regulations are enforced to protect threatened species, and others are for *human* well-being. There's an annual quarantine on mussels, for example, usually from May through October, to protect omnivores from nerve paralysis caused by the seasonal "red tide."

and naturally enough, the center of much political intrigue and scheming. Spared the devastating earthquakes that plagued other areas, Monterey had its own bad times, which included being burned and ransacked by the Argentinean revolutionary privateer Hippolyte Bouchard in 1818. In 1822, Spanish rule ended in California, and Mexico took over. In 1845, Monterey lost part of its political prestige when Los Angeles temporarily became the territory's capital city. When the rancheros surrendered to Commodore Sloat in July 1846, the area became officially American, though the town's distinctive Spanish tranquility remained relatively undisturbed until the arrival of farmers, fishing fleets, fish canneries, and whalers. California's first constitution was drawn up in Monterey, at Colton Hall, in 1849, during the state's constitutional convention.

Santa Cruz

Santa Cruz, the site of Misión Exaltación de la Santa Cruz and a military garrison on the north end of Monterey Bay, got its start in 1791. But the 1797 establishment of Branciforte—a "model colony" financed by the Spanish government just across the San Lorenzo River—made life hard for the mission fathers. The rowdy, quasi-criminal culture of Branciforte so intrigued the native peoples that Santa Cruz men of the cloth had to use leg irons to keep the Ohlone home. And things just got worse. In 1818, the threat of pirates at nearby Monterey sent the mission folk into the hills, with the understanding that Branciforte's bad boys would pack up the mission's valuables and cart them inland for safekeeping. Instead, they looted the place and drank all the sacramental wine. The mission was eventually abandoned, then demolished by an earthquake in 1857. A small port city grew up around the plaza and borrowed the mission's name—Santa Cruz—while Branciforte, a smuggler's haven, continued to flourish until the late 1800s.

Carmel

Carmel-by-the-Sea was established in 1903 by real estate developers who vowed to create a cultured community along the sandy beaches of Carmel Bay. To do this they offered to "creative people" such incentives as building lots for as little as $50. As the result of such irresistible inducements Carmel was soon alive with an assortment of tents and shacks, these eventually giving way to cottages and mansions.

Tourism grew right along with the art colony; the public had a passion for travel during those early days of automobile adventuring. Quaint Carmel, home to "real Bohemians," also offered tourists the chance to view (and buy) artworks—a prospect cheered by the artists themselves. Carmel's commitment to the arts and artists was formalized with the establishment of the Carmel Art Association in 1927. Still going strong, with strict jury selection, this artists' cooperative is a cultural focal point in contemporary Carmel.

Santa Cruz

Still in tune with its gracefully aging Boardwalk, Santa Cruz is a middle-class tourist town enlightened and enlivened by retirees and the local University of California campus. It's possible to live here without a lot of money, though it's getting harder, with the advent of Silicon Valley commuters. Still, Santa Cruz is quite a different world from the affluent and staid Monterey Peninsula.

The Santa Cruz attitude has little to do with its name, taken from a nearby stream called Arroyo de Santa Cruz ("Holy Cross Creek") by Portolá. No, the town's relaxed good cheer must be karmic compensation for the morose mission days and the brutishness of nearby Branciforte. The Gay Nineties were happier here than anywhere else in Northern California, with trainloads of Bay Area vacationers in their finest summer whites stepping out to enjoy the Santa Cruz waterfront, the Sea Beach Hotel, and the landmark Boardwalk and amusement park. The young and young at heart headed straight for the amusement park, with its fine merry-go-round, classic wooden roller coaster, pleasure pier, natatorium (indoor pool), and dancehall casino. More decadent fun lovers visited the ships anchored offshore to gamble or engage the services of prostitutes.

Santa Cruz still welcomes millions of visitors each year, yet it somehow manages to retain its dignity—except when embroiled in hot local political debates or when inundated by college students during the annual rites of spring. A tourist town it may be, but some of the best things to do here are free: watching the sun set from East or West Cliff Drive, beachcombing, bike riding (excellent local bike lanes), swimming, surfing, and sunbathing.

"People's Republic of Santa Cruz"

Old-timers weren't ready for the changes in community consciousness that arrived in Santa Cruz along with the idyllic UC Santa Cruz campus in the 1960s. More outsiders came when back-to-the-landers fled San Francisco's Haight Ashbury for the hills near here, and when Silicon Valley electronics wizards started moving in. The city's boardwalk-and-beach hedonism may be legendary, but so are the Santa Cruz City Council's foreign policy decisions opposing contra aid, proclaiming the city a "free port" for Nicaragua, and calling for divestiture of South African investments. In October 2000 Santa Cruz passed its own "living wage" law, mandating a minimum pay rate of $11 per hour ($12 without benefits) for city workers and companies that contract with the city.

Though there's always some argument, the city's progressive politics are now firmly entrenched, as are other "dancing-on-the-brink" attitudes. The "People's Republic of Santa Cruz" is also a way station for the spiritually weary, with its own unique evangelical crusade for higher consciousness. Dreams and dreamers run the show.

History

The charming Santa Cruz blend of innocence and sleaze has roots in local history. The area's earliest residents were the Ohlone people, who avoided the sacred redwood forests and subsisted on seafood, small game, acorns, and foods gathered in woodland areas. Then came the mission and missionaries, a Spanish military garrison, and the den-of-thieves culture of Branciforte; the latter community posed an active threat to the holy fathers' attempted good works among the heathens. Misión Exaltación de la Santa Cruz declined, was abandoned, then collapsed following an earthquake in 1857.

GREATER SANTA CRUZ

Just east of Santa Cruz, along the south-facing coast here, are the towns of Soquel, Capitola, and Aptos—the Santa Cruz burbs. High-rent **Soquel**, once a booming lumber town and the place where Portolá and his men were all but stricken by their first sight of coastal redwoods, is now noted for antiques and oaks.

The wharf in **Capitola** has stood since 1857, when the area was known as Soquel Landing. The name "Camp Capitola" was an expression of Soquel locals' desire to be the state capital—the closest they ever came. The city was, however, the state's first seaside resort. Nowadays, Capitola is big on art galleries and fine craft shops—take a stroll along Capitola Avenue from the trestle to the creek—but it's still most famous for its begonias. The year's big event is the **Begonia Festival,** usually held early in September. Stop by **Antonelli Bros. Begonia Gardens,** 2545 Capitola Rd., 831/475-5222, to see a 10,000-square-foot greenhouse display of begonias, best in August and September.

Aptos, on the other side of the freeway, is more or less the same community as Capitola but home to Cabrillo College and the **World's Shortest Parade,** usually held on the July 4th weekend and sponsored by the Aptos Ladies' Tuesday Evening Society.

Heading north on Hwy. 9 from Santa Cruz will take you through the Santa Cruz Mountains and the towns of Felton, Ben Lomond, and Boulder Creek before winding down the other side of the mountains into Saratoga on the flank of Silicon Valley. This route is the gateway to several beautiful redwood state parks, including Henry Cowell, Fall Creek, Big Basin, and Castle Rock.

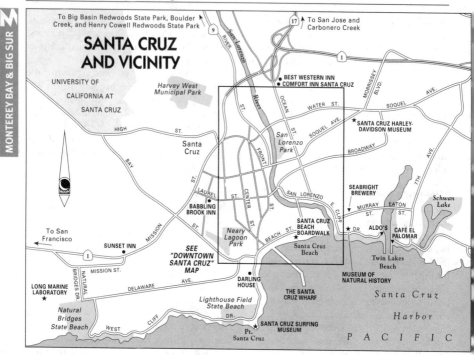

SANTA CRUZ
AND VICINITY

To Big Basin Redwoods State Park, Boulder
Creek, and Henry Cowell Redwoods State Park

To San Jose and
Carbonero Creek

UNIVERSITY OF
CALIFORNIA AT
SANTA CRUZ

Harvey West
Municipal Park

BEST WESTERN INN
COMFORT INN SANTA CRUZ

SANTA CRUZ HARLEY-
DAVIDSON MUSEUM

Santa
Cruz

San
Lorenzo
Park

SEABRIGHT
BREWERY

Schwan
Lake

BABBLING
BROOK INN

Neary
Lagoon
Park

SANTA CRUZ
BEACH
BOARDWALK

ALDO'S
CAFÉ EL
PALOMAR

To San
Francisco

SUNSET INN

SEE
"DOWNTOWN
SANTA CRUZ"
MAP

Santa Cruz
Beach

Twin Lakes
Beach

LONG MARINE
LABORATORY

DARLING
HOUSE

MUSEUM OF
NATURAL HISTORY

Santa Cruz

Lighthouse Field
State Beach

THE SANTA
CRUZ WHARF

Harbor

Natural
Bridges
State Beach

SANTA CRUZ SURFING
MUSEUM

Pt.
Santa Cruz

P A C I F I C

A small trading town, borrowing the mission's name, grew up around the old mission plaza in the 1840s. The town supplied whalers with fruits and vegetables. Nearby Branciforte became a smugglers' haven, hosting bullfight festivals and illicit activities until 1867. The "education" and excitement imported by foreigners proved to be too much for the Ohlone; the only traces of their culture today are burial grounds. Branciforte disappeared, too, absorbed as a suburb when loggers and "bark strippers" (those who extracted tannin from tan oaks for processing leather) arrived to harvest the forests during the gold rush.

By the late 1800s, Santa Cruz was well established as a resort town. Logging continued, however. In the early 20th century, the local lumber industry was ready to log even majestic Big Basin. But those plans were thwarted by the active intervention of the Sempervirens Club, which successfully established California's first state park.

THE BOARDWALK

The Santa Cruz Beach Boardwalk may be old, but it's certainly lively, with a million visitors per year. This is the West Coast's answer to Atlantic City. The original wood planking is now paved over with asphalt, stretching from 400 Beach Street for a half mile along one of Northern California's finest swimming beaches. A relatively recent multimillion-dollar facelift didn't diminish the Boardwalk's charms one iota. Open daily from Memorial Day to Labor Day and on weekends the rest of the year, the Boardwalk is an authentic amusement park, with dozens of carnival rides, odd shops and eateries, good-time arcades, even a big-band ballroom. Ride the **Sky Glider** to get a good aerial view of the Boardwalk and beach scene—and, across the street, the **Boardwalk Bowl** bowling alley at 115 Cliff St. (at Beach), 831/426-3324.

None other than *The New York Times* has declared the 1924 **Giant Dipper** roller coaster here

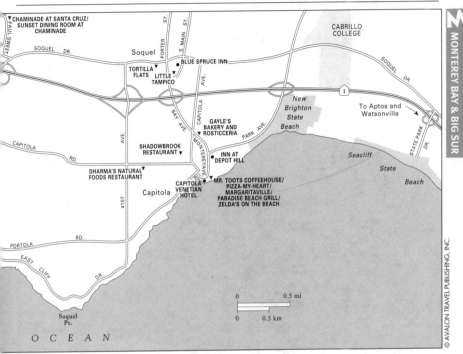

one of the nation's 10 best. A gleaming white wooden rocker 'n' roller, the Dipper is quite a sight anytime, but it's truly impressive when lit up at night. The 1911 **Charles Looff carousel,** one of a handful of Looff creations still operating in the United States, has 70 handcrafted horses, two chariots, and a circa-1894 Ruth Band pipe organ—all now lovingly restored to their original glory. (Both the Dipper and the carousel are national historic landmarks.)

New rides feature more terror, of course. The **Cliff Hanger** offers spins and hang gliding–likethrills, and the pendulum-like **Fireball** serves up fiery upside-down spins. The bright lights and unusual views offered by the Italian-made **Typhoon** are just part of the joys of being suspended upside down in midair. The **Hurricane** is the Boardwalk's modern high-tech roller coaster, providing a two-minute thrill ride with a maximum gravitational force of 4.7 Gs and a banking angle of 80 degrees. There's only one other coaster of its kind in the United States. Also state of the art in

adrenaline inducement at the Boardwalk is the **Wave Jammer**—not to mention **Chaos, Crazy Surf, Tsunami,** and **Whirl Wind.**

The antique devices in the penny arcades at the Boardwalk's west end cost a bit more these days, but it's worth it to Measure the Thrill of Your Kisses or Find Your Ideal Mate. Playing miniature golf at the new, two-story, $5.2 million **Neptune's Kingdom** amusement center—housed in the Boardwalk's original "plunge" building, or natatorium—is a nautical-themed adventure in special effects, with an erupting volcano, firing cannons, and talking pirates. It's the perfect diversion for the video-game generation and their awestruck parents. Though the rest of the Boardwalk's attractions are seasonal, Neptune's Kingdom and the arcade are open daily year-round. Nearby is the esteemed **Cocoanut Grove** casino and ballroom, a dignified old dancehall that still swings with nostalgic tunes from the 1930s and '40s at special shindigs. Sunday brunch in the Grove's Sun Room, with its Victorian-modern

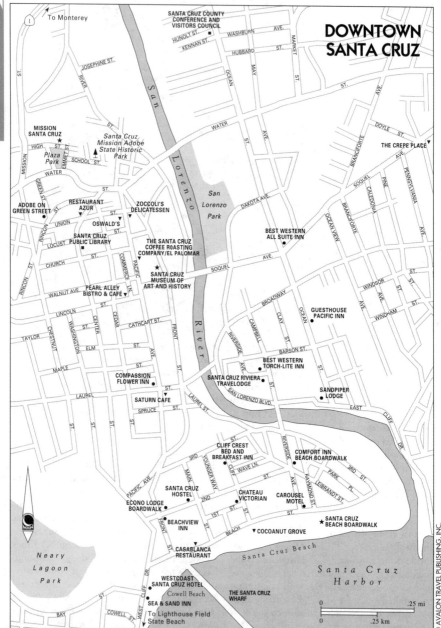

DOWNTOWN SANTA CRUZ

© AVALON TRAVEL PUBLISHING, INC.

© ROBERT HOLMES/CALTOUR

Santa Cruz Beach Boardwalk

decor and galleria-style retracting glass roof, is a big event.

To fully appreciate the Boardwalk then and now, pick up the *Walking Tour of the Historical Santa Cruz Boardwalk* brochure, as well as a current attractions listing/map. Both will help you locate yourself, then and now. Annual events held at the Boardwalk include the **Clam Chowder Cook-Off and Festival** in late February; the **Central Coast Home & Garden Expo** in early April; the **Santa Cruz Band Review** in October, a fundraiser for local high school bands; and the **Santa Cruz Christmas Craft and Gift Festival** held at the Cocoanut Grove during Thanksgiving weekend. On Friday nights in summer, starting in June, come for free **Summertime, Summer Nights** concerts.

Admission to the Boardwalk is free, though enjoying its amusements is not. If you'll be staying all day, the best deal is usually the all-day ride ticket, $24.95 at last report, or Unlimited Rides Plus, $29.95, which offers unlimited rides plus two other attractions. During **1907 Nights**, on certain Monday and Tuesday evenings in summer, ride prices revert to 1907 equivalents— $.50 per ride. Season passes are available. Height,

age, and chaperone requirements are enforced. For current complete information, contact the **Santa Cruz Seaside Company,** 400 Beach St., Santa Cruz, CA 95060-5491, 831/423-5590, www.beachboardwalk.com. While you're at it, inquire about special vacation packages, including accommodations at the Sea & Sand Inn or the Carousel Motel.

For current Boardwalk hours, call 831/426-7433. For information on special Boardwalk activities, call 831/423-5590. To find out what's happening at the Cocoanut Grove, call 831/423-2053.

The Wharf

The pier at the western end of Santa Cruz Beach, once a good place to buy cheap, fresh fish, did booming business during the state's steamship heyday. Today, the place is packed instead with tourists, and most fish markets, restaurants, and shops here charge a pretty penny. Still, the wharf's worth a sunset stroll. (Peer down into the fenced-off "holes" to watch the sea lions.) A few commercial fishing boats still haul their catches of salmon and cod ashore in summer, doubling as whale-watching tour boats in winter. Worth a look, too, are the kiosk displays on wharf and fishing history.

OTHER SIGHTS

If you're over- or underwhelmed by the Board-walk, take the Santa Cruz **walking tour.** This expedition is a lot quicker than it used to be—since many of the city's unusual Victorians—with frilly wedding-cake furbelows and "witch's hat" towers on the Queen Annes—departed to that great Historical Register in the Sky during the 1989 earthquake. But some grande dames remain. To find them, stop by the visitors center and pick up the *Historic Santa Cruz Walking Tours and Museum Guide* brochure. Most houses are private homes or businesses, so don't trespass. **Ocean View Avenue** is so perfect in terms of period authenticity that it took only a few loads of topsoil (to cover the asphalt street with dirt) to successfully transform the neighborhood into the cinematic setting for John Steinbeck's *East of Eden*. A good example of the Colonial Revival style is **Villa Perla** at the head of Ocean View. Near the Santa Cruz Mission are other notables, including the **Stick Villa** at 207 Mission Street; the **Schwartz Mansion** at 222 Mission; and the saltbox-style **Willey House** on the corner of Mission and Sylvar.

To find out more about area history, stop by the Santa Cruz Museum of Art and History. In particular, the museum staff can fill you in on regional historical sites under their care, including the Davenport Jail (1917), up the coast in Davenport, though no longer open to the public, and the Evergreen Cemetery (established 1850) at Evergreen and Coral Streets, one of the oldest Protestant cemeteries in California. Next door to the museum is the visitors center.

Santa Cruz Museum of Art and History

A sure sign that downtown Santa Cruz is almost done digging out from the rubble of the devastating 1989 earthquake is the Museum of Art and History at the McPherson Center, 705 Front St. (Front and Cooper), 831/429-1964, www.santacruzmah.org. Traveling exhibits and local artists get prominent play. Recent shows include 2001's

Art Undercover: Tom Killion, Gay Schy, Peter and Donna Thomas, an examination of "small press art," and *The Home Front: Santa Cruz County's War Front During World War II.* The museum is open Tues.–Sun. 11 A.M.–5 P.M. (until 7 P.M. on Friday); a small admission fee is charged. Adjacent to the museum is The Octagon, an eight-sided 1882 brick building relocated here, now the museum store. Inside is an intriguing collection of gift and art items, including—at least sometimes—the marvelously whimsical work (including greeting cards) of Santa Cruz artist James Carl Aschbacher.

Santa Cruz Mission Adobe State Historic Park

Restored and open to the public is the Santa Cruz Mission Adobe, a state historical park just off Mission Plaza at 144 School St., 831/425-5849. This is one of the county's last remaining original adobes, built by and for Native Americans "employed" at Mission Santa Cruz. It was later a 17-unit "home for new citizens." Only seven units remain, these now comprising a Cal-

ALL HAIL THE SANTA CRUZ SLUGS

Refreshingly out of step with the period's college careerism, the UC Santa Cruz student body convinced then-Chancellor Robert Sinsheimer in 1986 to declare the noble banana slug—a common on-campus companion—their school mascot (instead of the more acceptable sea lion) after a hard-fought, five-year campaign. When the chancellor declared the Santa Cruz Sea Lions the official choice in 1981, students protested that the banana slug would more appropriately be "a statement about the ideology of Santa Cruz," a philosophy with no room for football teams, cheerleaders, fraternities, and sororities.

Finally acceding to the students' preference for a slimy, spineless, sluggish, yellow gastropod—defended as "flexible, golden, and deliberate" by one professor—Sinsheimer said that students should have a school mascot "with which they can empathize." He also proposed genetic engineering research on slugs to "improve the breed" because "the potential seems endless."

ifornia history museum circa the 1840s. Restored rooms illustrate how Native American, Californio, and Irish American families once lived. Call for current information about guided tours and "living history" demonstrations (usually offered on Sundays, the latter just in March). School groups are welcome on Thursdays and Fridays—by advance reservation only. Plan a picnic here anytime (bring your own water). The park is open Thurs.–Sun. 10 A.M.–4 P.M. A small admission fee is charged.

Mission Santa Cruz

Nearby, at 126 High St., is what's left of the original mission: just a memory, really. The original site of the **Misión de Exaltacion de la Santa Cruz** was at High and Emmet Streets, too close to the San Lorenzo River, as it turned out. The move to higher ground left only the garden at the lower level. The original Santa Cruz mission complex was finished in 1794 but was completely destroyed by earthquakes in the mid-19th century. The replica church, scaled down by half and built in 1931 on the upper level, seems to have lost more than just stature. It's open Tues.–Sat. 10 A.M.–4 P.M., Sun. 10 A.M.–2 P.M.; call 831/426-5686 for more information.

Santa Cruz City Museum of Natural History

At least for now, the city's natural history museum is at home in Tyrell Park above Seabright/Castle Beach, east of the Boardwalk at 1305 E. Cliff Drive. The onetime 1915 Carnegie Library that anchors the park's southern edge, overlooking Monterey Bay, features exhibits and displays on the Santa Cruz area's natural and cultural history. There's a Tidepool Touch Tank and a Fossil Sand Dollar Dig—and the kids also dig that big cement gray whale on the lawn. The museum is open Tues.–Sun. 10 A.M.–5 P.M. A small admission fee is charged. The museum also sponsors a year-round schedule of classes and events. For more information, call 831/420-6115 or see website: www.santacruzmuseums.org.

Santa Cruz Harley-Davidson Museum

The local Harley-Davidson shop, 1148 Soquel Ave., 831/421-9600, www.santacruzharley.com, is something of a "destination dealership." Among the exquisitely restored Harleys on display are an H-D bicycle, first introduced in 1917, a 1929 JDH two-cam twin, and a stylish 1930 VL. Historical photos, posters, and memorabilia round out the collection, which is available for public viewing Tues.–Sun.

Santa Cruz Mystery Spot

The much bumper-sticker–ballyhooed Mystery Spot is a place where "every law of gravitation has gone haywire." Or has it? Trees, people, even the Spot's rustic shack and furnishings seem spellbound by "the force"—though people wearing slick-soled shoes seem to have the hardest time staying with the mysterious program. Hard-core tourists tend to love this place—Mom, Dad, and the kids can *literally* climb the walls—but others leave wondering why they spent the $5 to get in.

The Mystery Spot is located at 465 Mystery Spot Rd., 831/423-8897, www.mysteryspot.com. To get there, follow Market Street north from Water Street for a few miles. Market becomes Branciforte; Mystery Spot Road branches left off Branciforte—you can't miss it. Open daily 9 A.M.–7 P.M. (last tour at 7) in summer, 9 A.M.–4:30 P.M. (last tour at 4:20) the rest of the year.

Santa Cruz Surfing Museum

Cowabunga! Instead of cutting a ribbon, they snipped a hot pink surfer's leash when they opened the world's first surfing museum here at **Lighthouse Field State Beach** in May 1986. This historical exhibit reaches back to the 1930s, with displays on the evolution of surfboards and equipment—including the Model T of boards, a 15-foot redwood plank weighing 100 pounds, and an experimental Jack O'Neill wetsuit made of nylon and foam, the forerunner to the Neoprene "short john." Some say two Polynesian princes introduced surfing to Santa Cruz in 1885. True or not, by 1912 local posters announced the surfing exploits of Olympic swimmer and "Father of Surfing" Duke Kahanamoku. Come at Christmas for the popular **Caroling under the Stars** annual event.

The museum's location on the ground floor of

© ROBERT HOLMES/CALTOUR

Santa Cruz Surfing Museum

the brick lighthouse on West Cliff Drive, northwest of town near Steamer's Lane—prime surf turf—seems the most fitting place for official homage to life in pursuit of the perfect wave. The lighthouse was built by the family of Mark Abbott, a surfer killed nearby. The museum is open noon–4 P.M. Wed.–Mon. in summer, Thurs.–Mon. in winter; admission is free. For more information, call 831/420-6289. For beach information, call 831/420-5270.

Santa Cruz now has two functioning lighthouses. The **Santa Cruz Harbor Light** on the rock jetty at the entrance to the Santa Cruz harbor, also known as Walton's Lighthouse in honor of Derek Walton, was officially dedicated in June 2002.

Spiritual/Supernatural Attractions

Perhaps more interesting even than the Mystery Spot are two other oddball attractions, located at the **Santa Cruz Memorial Park & Funeral Home,** 3301 Paul Sweet Rd., 831/426-1601. Here you'll find a wax interpretation of *The Last Supper,* plus displays attempting to rekindle the controversy over the Shroud of Turin—that renowned piece of linen purported to show Christ's

after-death visage—by challenging the conclusions of carbon tests declaring the shroud a fake.

An interpretation of Da Vinci's famous painting in life-sized wax figures, *The Last Supper* is the original work of two Katherine Struberghs (mother and daughter) from Los Angeles. The women spared themselves no trial or trouble in this endeavor. (Each hair on every wax head was implanted by hand—that task alone requiring eight months.) But after some 40 years' residence at the Santa Cruz Art League, Jesus and his disciples were in a sad state of disrepair. That was before the funeral home and local Oddfellows Lodge took on the task of financing something of a resurrection. The job involved patching the cracks in the figures' heads, washing and setting their hair and beards, replacing fingers (and fingernails and toenails), and polishing their glass eyeballs.

Visitors can see both attractions Mon.–Fri. by appointment. Contributions are appreciated.

University of California at Santa Cruz

The city on the hill just beyond town is the UC Santa Cruz campus, planned by architect John Carl Warnecke and landscape architect Thomas Church—a total of 10 clustered colleges and as-

SURF'S UP AT O'NEILL'S

A Santa Cruz phenomenon with considerable worldwide renown is **O'Neill Surf Shop,** the legendary business legacy of Jack O'Neill, a local surfer who in the 1950s created a wetsuit that protected surfers from Northern California's chilling waters. The business grew and flourished, becoming the world's number-one wetsuit manufacturer. O'Neill also sells popular surfing-styled sportswear. There are four O'Neill shops in Santa Cruz County, including one at the beach, 222 E. Cliff Dr.; one at the Boardwalk, 400 Beach St.; and one downtown at 110 Cooper St., Ste. 100-D. The fourth is in Capitola at 1115 41st Avenue. For more information, call the company at 831/475-4151 or see the website: www.oneill.com.

O'Neill's legacy is broader and deeper, however. The slogan "It's always summer on the inside" is not just a marketing slogan but a life philosophy. Come to Santa Cruz in February for a literal test of the summer-inside lifestyle at the famed O'Neill Cold Water Classic, a contest that attracts top surfers from around the world. On land, check out the **Stylin' Recyclin'** thrift shop in Capitola at 1095 41st Ave. (next to the railroad tracks), 831/477-2893, a venture started to support **O'Neill Sea Odyssey,** website: www.oneillseaodyssey.org, an ocean-going environmental education program offered free for grammar school children onboard the 65-foot Team O'Neill catamaran.

bers of California's moneyed upper classes have attended UC Santa Cruz that it has been playfully dubbed "California's public finishing school." The university's student body has so far remained relatively small (more than 12,000 currently), though growth is on the agenda. A sign that the times they are a-changin' at Santa Cruz came in February 2000, when the faculty voted overwhelmingly to eliminate the university's founding "no required grading" policy.

The University of California regents set about transforming the redwood-forested rangeland here, once the Henry Cowell Ranch, into California's educational Camelot in 1961. Designs ranged from modern Mediterranean to "Italian hill village" (Kresge College). The official explanation for the Santa Cruz "college cluster" concept was to avoid the depersonalization common to large UC campuses, but another reason was alluded to when then-Governor Ronald Reagan declared the campus "riot-proof."

To truly appreciate this place, wander the campus hiking trails and paths (but not alone). Some of the old converted ranch buildings are worth noting: the lime kilns, blacksmith's shop, cookhouse, horse barn, bull barn, slaughterhouse, cookhouse, workers' cabins, and cooperage. On a clear day, the view of Monterey Bay (and of whales passing offshore in winter and spring) from the top of the hill on the 2,000-acre campus is marvelous. For information and guided campus tours, stop by the wood-and-stone Cook House near the entrance. You can also contact UCSC Admissions Office, Cook House, Santa Cruz, CA 95064, 831/459-4008, slugvisits@cats.ucsc.edu.

Long Marine Laboratory

Well worth a stop for nature lovers, the Joseph M. Long Marine Laboratory is just off Delaware Avenue near Natural Bridges State Beach on the western edge of town. A university research and education facility, the lab is affiliated with the on-campus Institute of Marine Sciences, established in 1972. Research conducted here ranges from marine biology and marine geophysics to paleoceanography and coastal processes—from plankton to blue whales, from cold water ecology to tropical coral reefs. Associated facilities include

sociated buildings overlooking the Pacific Ocean. Campus buildings were designed by noted architects including Charles Moore, William Wurster, Joseph Esherick, Ernest Kump, Antoine Predock, Hugh Stubbins, Ralph Rapson, William Turnbull, and Kathy Simon. When the doors of UC Santa Cruz opened in the 1960s, few California students could gain admission to the close-knit, redwood-cloistered campus. The selection process (complete with essay) was weighted in favor of students with unusual abilities, aptitudes, and attitudes—those not likely to thrive within the traditional university structure. So many children of movie stars and other mem-

CIRCLE OF ENCHANTMENT

Tour the eclectic scenery of Santa Cruz green-belt areas on the area's Circle of Enchantment Trail, also known as the Circle Trail. The 23-mile trail is actually two separate loops; each segment can be hiked in a half day.

Begin either loop in downtown Santa Cruz at the San Lorenzo River pedestrian bridge, just off Front Street.

The circle's western loop, about a 12-mile hike, follows the river down to the Boardwalk. It then climbs to the bayside recreation trail along W. Cliff Drive and continues on to Natural Bridges State Park and the Long Marine Lab before angling inland. The route then follows Delaware Avenue into wooded Arroyo Seco Canyon, then up the hill to the UC Santa Cruz campus—redwoods and fabulous views—and the Pogonip grasslands before circling back to the river levee.

The eastern loop is more urban, yet it eventually leads to the "Top of the World" lookout, Arana City Park, Santa Cruz Yacht Harbor, and along E. Cliff Drive and the Pleasure Point area before returning to Lorenzo Park downtown.

A general route map and detailed directions are available at www.ecotopia.org.

mourcenter. For additional information about Long Marine Lab programs and facilities, see www.natsci.ucsc.edu.

To get here from Santa Cruz, take Highway 1 (Mission Street) north, turn left on Swift Street, then right on Delaware Avenue. Continue on Delaware to the Long Marine Lab entrance at the end of the road.

BEACHES

Most of the outdoor action in Santa Cruz proper happens at local beaches; swimming, surfing, and fishing are all big, as are tamer pastimes like beachcombing, sandcastle building, and sunbathing. The in-town **Santa Cruz Beach** at the Boardwalk, with fine white sand and towel-to-towel baking bodies in summer, is "the scene"—especially for outsiders from San Jose, locals say. For more privacy, head east to the mouth of the San Lorenzo River. Southwest of the pier, **Cowell Beach** is a surfing beach, where Huey Lewis and the News filmed one of their music videos. Just before **Lighthouse Field State Beach** on West Cliff is the Santa Cruz Surfing Museum, an eclectic lighthouse collection of surf's-up memorabilia keeping watch over the hotdoggers in churning Steamer Lane.

Natural Bridges State Beach

Located farther southwest, at the end of West Cliff Drive, Natural Bridges attracts the mythic monarch butterflies each year from October to May. Though Pacific Grove near Monterey proudly proclaims itself the destination of choice for these regal insects, Santa Cruz claims to get the most monarchs. This is the only state-owned monarch butterfly preserve in California. One of the sandstone "natural bridges" here collapsed in 1980, under assault from a winter storm. The other still stands, though. To the north are some great tidepools, available for exploration (don't touch) at low tide. Leathery green fields of Brussels sprouts fringe the fragile sandy cliffs.

Monarch butterfly tours (wheelchair accessible) are offered on weekends from mid-October

an 18,000-square-foot California Department of Fish and Game Marine Wildlife Veterinary Care and Research Center, the nation's largest and most advanced, and a state-of-the-art National Marine Fisheries Service laboratory, which conducts fisheries research and houses the nation's first National Science Center for Marine Protected Areas. Under construction, at last report: the UC Santa Cruz Center for Ocean Health and a seabird/raptor facility.

To help interpret the lab's work and to educate future generations of marine biologists, the new **Seymour Marine Discovery Center** is open to the public Tues.–Sat. 10 A.M.–5 P.M., Sunday noon to 5 P.M. Admission is $5 adults; $3 students, seniors, and youths 6 to 16; free for children 5 and under. Docent-led tours of the lab's other marine research facilities are available. For information contact 831/459-3800 or www2.ucsc.edu/sey-

through February. For information on guided butterfly walks and tidepool tours, stop by the visitors center or call 831/423-4609. For additional parks information, see the websites: www.santacruzstateparks.org and www.scpark-friends.org. Come in October for **Welcome Back Monarchs Day** and again in February for the annual **Migration Festival** sendoff, a park fundraiser cosponsored by Friends of Santa Cruz State Parks. (The monarchs may be leaving, but the gray whales offshore are just arriving in February; migrants come and go all year.) The parking fee at Natural Bridges is $5 per car; walk-ins and bike-ins are free. Natural Bridges is open daily 8 A.M.–sunset.

Locals' Beaches

Along East Cliff Drive are **Tyrell Park** and more inaccessible sandy beaches. **Twin Lakes State Beach,** near the Santa Cruz Yacht Harbor on the eastern extension of East Cliff before it becomes Portolá, is a popular locals' beach, usually quite warm. Beyond the Santa Cruz Yacht Harbor, various small, locally popular beaches line East Cliff Drive. The unofficially named **26th Street Beach** (at the end of 26th Street, naturally enough) is probably tops among them. Hot for local surfing is the **Pleasure Point,** East Cliff at Pleasure Point Drive.

North of Town

Davenport Beach, at Davenport Landing up the coast toward Año Nuevo, is a hot spot for sailboarders and is often relatively uncrowded. **Red White and Blue Beach,** 5021 Coast Rd., just south of Davenport, 831/423-6332, is a popular, privately operated nude beach (too popular, some say; women shouldn't go alone). It costs $5 per day for an all-over tan. Camping is also available. Nearby is **Bonny Doon Beach,** up the coast from Santa Cruz at the intersection of Highway 1 and Bonny Doon Road south of Davenport. It's free, and even wilder for sunbathing sans swimsuit. It's also popular with surfers.

East and South of Town

About six miles down the coast from Santa Cruz City Beach and just south of the Capitola suburbs is **New Brighton State Beach,** 1500 Park Ave., 831/464-6330. Its 93 often-sunny acres are protected by wooded headlands that offer a great family campground (campsites $13–16), nature trails, good bird-watching, and a dazzling nighttime view of Monterey Bay. The day use fee is $5.

Several miles farther south, two-mile-long **Seacliff State Beach,** on Park Drive in Aptos, 831/685-6500 or 831/685-6442 (recorded information), or 831/685-6444 (visitors center), is so popular you may not be able to stop. It's nice

---

FOREST OF NISENE MARKS STATE PARK

Forest of Nisene Marks is definitely a hiker's park. Named for the Danish immigrant who hiked here until the age of 96 and whose family donated the land for public use, Nisene Marks is an oasis of solitude. (This was also the epicenter of the 1989 earthquake that brought down parts of Santa Cruz.) You'll have lots to see here but little more than birdsong, rustling leaves, and babbling brooks to listen to. The park encompasses 10,000 acres of hefty second-growth redwoods on the steep southern range of the Santa Cruz Mountains, six creeks, lovely Maple Falls, alders, maples, and more rugged trails than anyone can hike in a day. Also here are an old mill site, abandoned trestles and railroad tracks, and logging cabins.

To get here from the coast, take the Aptos-Seacliff exit north from Hwy. 1 and turn right on Soquel Drive. At the first left after the stop sign, drive north on Aptos Creek Rd. and across the railroad tracks. (Bring water and food for day trips. No fires allowed.) The park is open daily 6 A.M.–sunset. Day use is $2. For information and a trail map, contact: Forest of Nisene Marks State Park, Aptos Creek Rd. in Aptos, 831/763-7063, www.santacruzstateparks.org. Call to reserve the trailside campsites—a six-mile one-way hike, just six sites, primitive, first-come, first camped, $2 per night.

for hiking, pelican-watching, fossil spotting, swimming, and sunbathing. The wheelchair-accessible pier reaches out to the pink concrete carcass of the doomed World War I–vintage *Palo Alto,* sunk here after seeing no wartime action and now a long-abandoned amusement pier (not open to the public). Birds live in the prow these days. People enjoy the pier's more mundane pleasures: people-watching, fishing (no license required), and strolling. Guided walks are occasionally offered; call the visitors center for schedules and reservations. The day use fee is $5. Campsites here are for RVs only, $21–23.

As the name suggests, **Rio del Mar** beach is where Aptos Creek meets the sea. Here you'll find restrooms, miles of sand, and limited parking. It's free.

To reserve campsites—absolutely essential in summer—contact *ReserveAmerica,* 800/444-7275, www.reserveamerica.com. For more information on regional state beaches and parks, see www.santacruzstateparks.org. For beaches farther south, see Watsonville and Vicinity.

WATER RECREATION
Sailing

For an unusual view of the Boardwalk and the bay, take a boat ride. One of the best going—definitely not just any boat—is the *Chardonnay II,* a 70-foot ultralight sailing yacht offering special-emphasis cruises. Choose from astronomy, fireworks, "gourmet on the bay," marine ecology, wine-tasting, and whale-watching (winter and spring) cruises. There's even a Wednesday night Boat Race Cruise in the company of almost every other boat from the Santa Cruz Yacht Harbor. At last report, per-person fare for most scheduled trips was $43.50. This sleek albino seal of a sailboat can hold up to 49 passengers and features every imaginable amenity, including a CD player, a TV/VCR, cellular phones, a built-in bar, and plenty of below-deck space, making it fun as a private group charter for personally designed adventures. There's a two-hour minimum rental for departures from Santa Cruz, a three-hour minimum from Monterey. Private charter rates are

sailing on Monterey Bay near Santa Cruz

$550–800 per hour. For more information and to make reservations (required), call **Chardonnay Sailing Charters** at 831/423-1213 or inquire online at www.chardonnay.com.

Other boat and charter companies at or near the city's yacht harbor include **Pacific Yachting,** 790 Mariner Park Way, 831/423-7245 or 800/374-2626, www.pacificsail.com, which offers similar boat rides on smaller yachts as well as sailing lessons and a six-day seagoing instruction vacation. Probably the best deal going, though, is through the University of California at Santa Cruz Boating Club. In summer, UCSC sailing and boating courses are open to the public. For information, call 831/425-1164, ucscboat@cats.ucsc.edu, or see www.ucsc.edu/opers/boating. If you qualify for membership—as a student or alumnus—you can use the boats all year. The local **Coast Guard Auxiliary,** 432 Oxford Way, 831/423-7119, also offers sailing, boating skills, seamanship, and coastal navigation courses.

Other Water Sports

For more traditional boat tours, whale-watching trips, and fishing charters, contact **Stagnaro's Fishing Trips** at the municipal wharf, 831/427-2334, or **Scurfield's Landing/Shamrock Charters** at the yacht harbor, 831/476-2648.

Kayaking is great sport in these parts. **Venture Quest,** 125 Beach St., 831/427-2267, and at the municipal wharf, 831/425-8445, www.kayak-santacruz.com, sells kayaks and accessories and offers lessons and guided tours. **Kayak Connection** at the Santa Cruz Yacht Harbor, 413 Lake

Ave., 831/479-1121, www.kayakconnection.com, also rents and sells equipment, in addition to offering guided bird-watching, fishing, and moonlight tours.

Several full-service dive shops in town can provide complete information on local diving conditions, as well as instruction, rentals, and sales. Try **Aqua Safaris Scuba Center,** 6896-A Soquel Ave., 831/420-5270, www.aquasafaris.com, or **Adventure Sports Unlimited,** 303 Potrero St., 831/458-3648, www.asudoit.com.

Club Ed, on Cowell Beach (on the right side of Santa Cruz Wharf, in front of the WestCoast Santa Cruz Hotel), 831/459-9283 or 800/287-7873, rents surfboards, boogie boards, skim boards, and sailboards, and offers lessons in riding all of the above. Find out more about their surf camps on the Web at www.club-ed.com.

CAMPING IN SANTA CRUZ

Beaches

Best for nearby tent camping is **New Brighton State Beach,** 1500 Park Ave. in Capitola, 831/464-6330 or 831/464-6329. "New Bright" features 115 developed campsites (especially nice ones on the cliffs), some sheltered picnic tables, and a small beach. It's a good base camp for the entire Santa Cruz area. You can get here via local bus—take number 58 or the Park Avenue route. This area was once called China Beach or China Cove, after the Chinese fishermen who built a village here in the 1870s. Developed family campsites cost $13–16. The campground is popular, so reserve (see below) for summer at least six months ahead.

Near Aptos, **Seacliff State Beach,** 831/685-6500 or 831/685-6444, has a better beach than New Brighton, but camping is a disappointment. Strictly an RV setup, the park has 26 sites (with hookups) that cost $21–23 (less for overflow campsites).

For more information about the area's beach parks, contact the state parks office in Santa Cruz, 600 Ocean St., 831/429-2850 www.santacruzstateparks.org. For state campground reservations, contact ReserveAmerica at 800/444-7275 or website: www.reserveamerica.com.

Redwoods

Big Basin Redwoods State Park, 21600 Big Basin Hwy. in Boulder Creek, 831/338-8860, www.bigbasin.org, offers 146 family campsites, group camps, and horse camps. Family campsites cost $13–16. Tents-only trail campsites are $10; hiker/biker campsites $2 per person. The park also boasts 41 year-round "tent cabins," each with two double beds, a camp lamp, and a woodstove. Tent cabins sleep four comfortably but can house up to eight. Rates are $49, two-night minimum on weekends, three-night minimum on holidays. (Add $10 for linen and blanket rental in lieu of sleeping bags.) You can also arrange "hassle-free" tent camping—all you have to pack is kids and clothes. For cabin reservations, call 800/874-8368. To reserve trail camps, call Big Basin headquarters, 831/338-8860.

Henry Cowell Redwoods State Park, just north of the UC campus on Highway 9 in Felton, 831/335-4598 (administration) or 831/438-2396 (campground), offers 150 sites, 105 of them developed ($13–16). Sites in the developed areas are quite civilized, with amenities including hot showers, flush toilets, tables, barbecues, and cupboards. Primitive hike-in backpacking campsites are available at Castle Rock State Park, 15000 Skyline Blvd. in Los Gatos, $10; to reserve, call Big Basin at 831/338-8861.

Family and group campsites at both Big Basin and Henry Cowell Redwoods State Park are sometimes available at the last minute, even in summer and on warm-season weekends. But make reservations—up to seven months in advance—to guarantee a space. Reserve through ReserveAmerica, 800/444-7275, www.reserveamerica.com.

Elsewhere

Private campgrounds and trailer parks are always a possibility; a complete current listing is available at the local chamber of commerce. Possibilities include **Cotillion Gardens,** 300 Old Big Trees Rd. in Felton, 831/335-7669; **Carbonero Creek,** 917 Disc Dr. in Scotts Valley, 831/438-1288; and the **Santa Cruz KOA,** 1186 San Andreas Rd. in Watsonville, 831/722-0551 or 831/722-2377.

STAYING IN SANTA CRUZ

Hostel

The **HI-USA Santa Cruz Hostel,** 321 Main St., 831/423-8304, www.hi-santacruz.org, occupies the historic 1870s Carmelita Cottages downtown. The hostel is open year-round, is wheelchair accessible, and features an on-site cyclery, fireplace, barbecue, lockers, and rose and herb gardens. Family rooms and limited parking available (extra fee for both). Reservations strongly suggested. Under $50.

Motels and Hotels

As a general rule, motels closer to the freeway are cheaper, while those on the river are seedier. There are some fairly inexpensive motels near the beach (some with kitchens, Jacuzzis, pools, cable TV, etc.). Off-season rates in Santa Cruz are usually quite reasonable, but prices can sometimes mysteriously increase in summer and on weekends and holidays—so verify prices before you sign in.

All of the following have rates of $50–100. The **Beachview Inn,** less than a block from the beach at 50 Front St., 831/426-3575 or 800/946-0614, features all the essentials plus air-conditioning and direct-dial phones, with rooms $65 and up in the high season. The **Econo Lodge Santa Cruz,** just a block from the Boardwalk and the Wharf at 550 Second St., 831/426-3626 or 800/553-2666, offers rooms for $75 and up. Close to downtown, **Travelodge Santa Cruz,** 525 Ocean St., 831/426-2300 or 800/578-7878, offers rooms for $79 and up.

Rates at the following are $100–150. Endlessly convenient for Boardwalkers is the Boardwalk's own **Carousel Motel,** 110 Riverside Ave., 831/425-7090 or 800/214-7400, www.santacruzmotels.com. Also a best bet is the attractive **Best Inn & Suites,** 600 Riverside Ave., 831/458-9660 or 800/527-3833, where standard rooms include two queen beds. Other options are available—including two-story suites and "evergreen" rooms with air, water, and shower filtration. The inn also features a heated pool and hot tubs, a pleasant garden courtyard, and a picnic area with barbecues, plus complimentary ex-

panded continental breakfast. The appealing **Comfort Inn Beach Boardwalk,** 314 Riverside Ave., 831/471-9999 or 800/228-5150, offers 28 rooms with color TV and cable, a complimentary breakfast bar, and a heated pool and hot tub. Suites are available. Though they can range higher in the high season, reasonably priced rooms can also be found at the **Best Western Inn,** 126 Plymouth St., 831/425-4717 or 800/528-1234, and the **Best Western All Suites Inn,** 500 Ocean St., 831/458-9898 or 800/528-1234, an all-suites setup that offers rooms with whirlpool tubs and microwaves, plus some with gas fireplaces. Other amenities include a heated pool, lap pool, and sauna. Some rooms at the pleasant **Sunset Inn,** close to UC Santa Cruz and Natural Bridges at 2424 Mission St., 831/423-7500, also fit this price category. Amenities include microwaves, refrigerators, some in-room Jacuzzis, free local phone calls, breakfast, a hot tub, and a sauna.

Close to the wharf and overlooking the bay is the Boardwalk's small **Sea & Sand Inn,** 201 W. Cliff Dr., 831/427-3400, www.santacruzmotels.com. All 20 rooms boast an ocean view; suites have abundant amenities. Rates: $150–250.

All of the following have rates of $250 and up. Adjacent to the wharf and across from the Santa Cruz Beach Boardwalk, the imposing **WestCoast Santa Cruz Hotel,** 175 W. Cliff Dr., 831/426-4330 or 800/325-4000, www.westcoasthotels.com, is right on the beach (the only beachfront hotel in Santa Cruz), not far from the lighthouse. It features 163 rooms and suites with balconies and patios, in-room coffeemakers, modern amenities, satellite TV, a heated pool, and a whirlpool.

For value and views, nothing beats **Chaminade at Santa Cruz,** up on the hill and overlooking Monterey Bay at 1 Chaminade Lane (just off Paul Sweet Rd.), 831/475-5600 or 800/283-6569, www.chaminade.com. Occupying the old Chaminade Brothers Seminary and Monastery, this quiet resort and conference center offers a wealth of business amenities—but also personal perks such as a health club (with massage and men's and women's therapy pools), jogging track, heated pool, saunas, and whirlpools. There are lighted tennis courts, too. Rooms and suites are scattered around the 80-acre grounds in 11 "villas" that include shared parlors with refrigerators, wet bars, and conference tables. Rooms feature king or queen beds, in-room coffeemakers, irons and ironing boards, and two direct-line phones. Valet parking and airport transportation are available. Chaminade also boasts two good restaurants and a bar (with meal service), all open to the general public.

Bed-and-Breakfasts

The stylishly renovated oceanfront **Pleasure Point Inn** at 2-3665 E. Cliff Dr. (at 37th Ave.), 831/469-6161 or 877/577-2567, www.pleasurepointinn.com, is indeed a pleasure. The inn offers four fresh, uniquely decorated rooms, each with abundant amenities—from in-room refrigerator, microwave, coffee maker, and digital safe to gas-burning fireplace and private patio. Fresh fruit platter and continental breakfast every morning, and a "welcome basket" on arrival. And, oh, those views—especially from the hot tub and the rooftop deck. Most rooms are $150–250; the second-story Coral Room is $265. Ask about specials and packages.

One of the loveliest newer B&Bs in Santa Cruz is actually the nation's first "BB&B"—Bed, Bud, and Breakfast. The **Compassion Flower Inn,** 216 Laurel St., 831/466-0420, www.compassionflowerinn.com, opened in March 2000 with the express purpose of being a hemp- and medical marijuana–friendly bed-and-breakfast. The establishment is "named for both the beauty of the passionflower and the compassion of the medical marijuana movement" to which the owners have dedicated themselves. If you come, don't expect to find some tie-dyed, weed-happy scene reminiscent of San Francisco's Haight-Ashbury district during the Summer of Love. The proprietors have impeccably restored this gothic revival Victorian, at a cost of a half-million dollars. Tastefully and creatively decorated with antiques, hand-painted furniture, and custom tilework, the Compassion Flower Inn instead harks back to its historical roots as the onetime home of Judge Edgar Spalsbury, who made regular trips to a pharmacy downtown to buy opium as a pain medication for his tuberculosis. Rooms range from the fairly simple **Hemp Room** and **Passionflower Room,** "twin"

accommodations tucked under the eaves (these two share a bath), to the first-floor, fully wheelchair accessible **Canabliss Room** and the elegant **Lovers' Suite.** Particularly striking in the suite is its bathroom, where exquisite tiled hemp designs wrap the two-person sunken tub. Rates, $100–250, include full organic breakfast, with fresh-baked bread (two-night minimum stay).

Quite inviting and a perfect stay downtown is **The Adobe on Green Street,** 103 Green St., 831/469-9866 or 888/878-2789, www.adobeongreen.com. This historic yet unfrilly adobe features four uniquely decorated guest rooms—Adobe, Courtyard, Mission, and Ohlone—that marry elements of Native American, Mexican, and Arts and Crafts style. Amenities include private baths, in-room Jacuzzis, cable TV, and VCRs. Rates run $150–250.

Other Santa Cruz inns tend to cluster near the ocean. Tastefully decorated is the **Cliff Crest Bed and Breakfast Inn,** just blocks from both downtown and Main Beach at 407 Cliff St., 831/427-2609, www.cliffcrestinn.com, a Queen Anne by the beach and Boardwalk. Full breakfast is served in the solarium. Rates fall in the $150–250 range, starting at $220. The **Chateau Victorian,** 118 First St., 831/458-9458, www.chateauvictorian.com, offers seven rooms a bit more on the frilly side, with queen-sized beds, private tiled bathrooms, and wood-burning fireplaces. Local Santa Cruz Mountains wines are served, as are generous continental breakfasts. Rates run $100–150.

For something more formal, the 1910 **Darling House** seaside mansion at 314 W. Cliff Dr., 831/458-1958 or 800/458-1988, www.darling-house.com, is an elegant 1910 Spanish Revival mansion designed by architect William Weeks. In addition to spectacular ocean views, Darling House offers eight rooms (two with private baths, two with fireplaces), telephones, and TV on request. There's a hot tub in the backyard; robes are provided. If you loved *The Ghost and Mrs. Muir,* you'll particularly enjoy the Pacific Ocean Room here—complete with telescope. Rates, including breakfast and evening beverages, are $100–250.

Legendary is the been-there-forever local landmark, the **Babbling Brook Inn,** 1025 Laurel St.,

WILDER RANCH STATE PARK

Open to the public since mid-1989, Wilder Ranch State Park is best summed up as "a California coastal dairy-farm museum," a remnant of the days when dairies were more important to the local economy than tourists. Before it was a dairy farm, this was the main rancho supplying Mission Santa Cruz. Though damaged by the 1989 earthquake, the old Victorian ranch house is open again, decked out in period furnishings. The grounds also include an elaborate 1890s stable, a dairy barn, and a bunkhouse/workshop with water-driven machinery. Seasoned vehicles and farm equipment, from a 1916 Dodge touring sedan to seed spreaders and road graders, are scattered throughout the grounds.

Almost more appealing, though, are the park's miles of coastline and thousands of acres of forest, creeks, and canyons (not to mention the Brussels sprouts). To help visitors take in the landscape, 7,000-acre Wilder Ranch features 34 miles of hiking, biking, and equestrian trails. Restoration of these coastal wetlands is ongoing.

General ranch tours, led by docents dressed in period attire, are offered every Saturday and Sunday, usually at 1 P.M. Historical games are played on the lawn—hoop 'n' stick, bubbles, stilts—on weekends as well. A variety of other history- and natural history-oriented events are sponsored throughout the year, from demonstrations on making corn-husk dolls or quilts to mastering cowboy-style roping, plus guided hikes and bird walks. Usually on the first Saturday in May is the park's annual open house, a full day of old-fashioned family fun (and fundraising, for future park restoration work).

Wilder Ranch is two miles north of Santa Cruz on the west side of Hwy. 1 at 1401 Coast Rd., about a mile past the stoplight at Western Drive. For more information, call 831/423-9703 or 831/426-0505 or see the websites: www.santacruzstateparks.org and www.scparkfriends.org. The ranch is open for day-use ($5 per car) and for equestrian camping ($12). The park's new interpretive center is open daily in summer, only Fri.–Sat. 10 A.M.–4 p.m. in winter. To get here by bus, take Santa Cruz Metro No. 40 and ask the driver to drop you at the ranch.

831/427-2437 or 800/866-1131, www.cacoastalinns.com. Once a log cabin, this place was added to and otherwise spruced up by the Countess Florenzo de Chandler. All 13 rooms and suites are quite romantic, with private bathrooms, phones, and TVs. Most are decorated to suggest the works of Old World artists and poets, from Cézanne and Monet to Tennyson. Most also feature a fireplace, private deck, and outside entrance. Two have whirlpool bathtubs. Full breakfast and afternoon wine and cheese (or tea and cookies) are included. Also here: a babbling brook, waterfalls, and a garden gazebo. Rates run $150–250.

For more bed-and-breakfast choices in the greater Santa Cruz area, see the listings below.

STAYING OUTSIDE SANTA CRUZ
Hostels

In additional to the Hostelling International hostel in downtown Santa Cruz, the region boasts other exceptional budget choices—including the **Pigeon Point** and **Point Montara Lighthouse Hostels** up the coast toward San Francisco, both unique and incredibly cheap for on-the-beach lodgings—if you don't mind bunk beds or spartan couples' rooms. Or try the **Sanborn Park** hostel just over the hills in Saratoga, 408/741-0166 or 408/741-9555, www.sanbornparkhostel.org. If you're heading south, another best bet is the new **Carpenter's Hall Hostel** in Monterey, at 778 Hawthorne St. Rates at all are under $50.

Davenport

If you're heading up the coast from Santa Cruz, consider a meal stop or a stay at the **Davenport Bed and Breakfast Inn,** 31 Davenport Ave. (Hwy. 1), 831/425-1818 or 800/870-1817, www .davenportinn.com. The 12 comfortable rooms are upstairs, above the New Davenport Cash Store and Restaurant, where the food is very good at breakfast, lunch, and dinner. Rates, including full breakfast, are $100–150. Some of the pastries served here are made just up the road at **Whale City Bakery Bar & Grill,** 831/423-9803 or 831/429-6209, where the wide variety of homemade treats and very good coffee are always worth a stop.

Ben Lomond and Felton

Nothing fancy, but fine for pine-paneled cabin ambience just five miles north of Santa Cruz, the **Fern River Resort Motel,** 5250 Hwy. 9, Felton, 831/335-4412, www.fernriver.com, offers 14 cabins with kitchens or kitchenettes, fireplaces, cable TV, and a private beach on the river. Rates are $50–150.

For a bed-and-breakfast stay in Ben Lomond, consider the lovely and woodsy **Fairview Manor,** 245 Fairview Ave., 831/336-3355 or 800/553-8840, www.fairviewmanor.com, which features five rooms with private baths as well as a big deck overlooking the San Lorenzo River. Rates run $100–150. For a super-stylish (and expensive) stay, there's the elegant **Inn at Felton Crest,** 780 El Solyo Heights Dr., Felton, 831/335-4011 (also fax) or 800/474-4011, www.feltoncrest.com, featuring just four guest rooms—each on a separate floor—with in-room Jacuzzis, cable TVs and VCRs, and private baths. Rates: $250 and up.

Soquel

The **Blue Spruce Inn,** 2815 S. Main St. in Soquel, 831/464-1137 or 800/559-1137, www.bluespruce.com, is a romantic 1875 Victorian farmhouse just a few miles from downtown Santa Cruz. Its six rooms—three in the house, three garden rooms—all feature private baths and entrances, queen-sized featherbeds, and unique antique decor color-keyed to handmade Lancaster County quilts. Five rooms have private spas; two have gas fireplaces. Great breakfasts. Rates start at $100.

Capitola

A long-standing Capitola jewel is the **Capitola Venetian Hotel,** 1500 Wharf Rd., 831/476-6471 or 800/332-2780, www.capitolavenetian.com, California's first condominium complex, built in the 1920s. These clustered, Mediterranean-style stucco apartments are relaxed and relaxing, and close to the beach. In various combinations, rooms have kitchens with stoves and refrigerators, in-room coffeemakers, color TV with cable, and telephones with voicemail and data ports; some have separate living rooms, balconies, ocean views, and fireplaces. Rates are $150–250, with real deals available in the off-season.

Almost legendary almost overnight, Capitola's **Inn at Depot Hill,** 250 Monterey Ave., 831/462-3376 or 800/572-2632, www.cacoastalinns.com, is a luxurious bed-and-breakfast (essentially a small luxury hotel) housed in the onetime railroad depot. Each of the eight rooms features its own unique design motif, inspired by international themes (the Delft Room, Stratford-on-Avon, the Paris Room, and Portofino, for example), as well as a private garden and entrance, fireplace, telephone with modem/fax capability, and state-of-the-art TV/VCR and stereo system. The private white-marble bathrooms feature bathrobes, hair dryers, and other little luxuries. Bathrooms have double showers, so two isn't necessarily a crowd. The pure linen bed sheets are hand washed and hand ironed daily. Rates include full breakfast, afternoon tea or wine, and after-dinner dessert. Off-street parking is provided. Rates are $150 and up, though ask about winter specials (up to 40 percent off rack rates) and off-season packages.

Aptos

The apartment-style **Rio Sands Motel,** 116 Aptos Beach Dr., 831/688-3207 or 800/826-2077, www.riosands.com, has a heated pool, spa, and decent rooms not far from the beach. The "kitchen suites" feature full kitchens and a separate sitting room and sleep up to four. "Super rooms" sleep up to six and include a refrigerator and microwave. All rooms have two TVs. Extras include the large heated pool, spa, picnic area with barbecue pits, and expanded continental breakfast. Peak-season rates are $150–250, with real deals ($100–150) available in winter.

Also a pleasant surprise is the **Best Western Seacliff Inn,** just off the highway at 7500 Old Dominion Court, 831/688-7300 or 800/367-2003. It's a cut or two above the usual motel and an easy stroll to the beach. The rooms are large and comfortable, with private balconies. They cluster village-style around a large outdoor pool and Jacuzzi area. Suites have in-room spas. But the best surprise of all is the restaurant, **Severino's,** 831/688-8987, which serves good food both inside the dining room and outside by the koi pond. Great "sunset dinner" specials are served Sun.–Thurs. 5–6:30 P.M. Rates are $150–250.

On the coast just north of Manresa State Beach is the condo-style **Seascape Resort Monterey Bay,** 1 Seascape Resort Dr., 831/688-6800 or 800/929-7727, www.seascaperesort.com. Choices here include tasteful studios and one- and two-bedroom villas. You'll also find a restaurant, golf course, tennis courts, and on-site fitness and spa facilities. Two-night minimum stay, late May through September. Rates are expensive, $250 and up.

For a bed-and-breakfast stay, the historic **Sand Rock Farm** at 6901 Freedom Blvd., 831/688-8005, www.sandrockfarm.com, offers a huge, exquisitely restored, turn-of-the-20th-century Craftsman-style home—complete with original push-button light switches. The 10-acre setting includes country gardens, walking trails, and the ruins of the old Liliencrantz family winery. Open since fall 2000, Sand Rock features five guest rooms and suites with in-room Jacuzzis, cable TV, VCRs, and private baths, plus a lounge, fireplace, hot tub, and room service. Well-informed foodies will make a beeline to Sand Rock strictly for the wondrous breakfasts created by famed Chef Lynn Sheehan. Rates are $150–250.

Historic Victoriana in Aptos includes the **Apple Lane Inn,** 6265 Soquel Dr., 831/475-6868 or 800/649-8988, www.applelaneinn.com. Rates are $100–250. Also quite nice, and near Forest of Nisene Marks State Park, is the newly restored and redecorated **Bayview Hotel Bed and Breakfast Inn,** 8041 Soquel Dr., 831/688-8654 or 800/422-9843, www.bayviewhotel.com, an 1878 Italianate Victorian hotel with new owners and 12 elegant guest rooms, all with private baths and some with fireplaces and two-person tubs. Rooms also feature TVs, telephones, and modem hookups. Rates are $100–150.

Another possibility is the **Aptos Beach Inn,** once known as the Inn at Manresa Beach, 1258 San Andreas Rd. in La Selva Beach, 831/728-1000 or 888/523-2244, www.aptosbeachinn.com,

built in 1897 as a replica of Abraham Lincoln's home in Springfield, Illinois. One grass and two clay courts are available for tennis, and guests can also play badminton, croquet, or volleyball on the lawn. The eight rooms and suites here feature king or queen beds, fireplaces, private bathrooms (most with two-person spa tubs), two-line phones, cable TV, VCRs, and stereos. From here amid the strawberry and calla lily fields, it's an easy walk to both Manresa and Sand Dollar State Beaches. Rates are $150–250.

EATING IN SANTA CRUZ
Farm Trails and Farmers Markets

To do Santa Cruz area farm trails, pick up a copy of the *Country Crossroads* map and brochure, a joint venture with Santa Clara County row-crop farmers and orchardists. It's the essential guide for hunting down strawberries, raspberries, apples, and homegrown veggies of all kinds. Or head for the local farmers' markets. The **Santa Cruz Community Certified Farmers Market,** 831/335-7443, is held downtown at Lincoln and Cedar every Wednesday from 2:30 to 6:30 P.M. There are many other markets in the area; inquire at the visitors center for a current listing.

Near the Beach

Unforgettable for breakfast or lunch is funky **Aldo's,** 616 Atlantic Ave. (at the west end of the yacht harbor), 831/426-3736. The breakfast menu features various egg and omelet combinations. Best of all, though, is the raisin toast, made with Aldo's homemade focaccia bread. Eat outdoors on the old picnic tables covered with checkered plastic tablecloths and enjoy the sun, sea air, and seagulls. At lunch and dinner, look for homemade pastas and fresh fish.

The Boardwalk alone features about 20 restaurants and food stands. The best Sunday brunch experience around is also here, at the historic **Cocoanut Grove,** 400 Beach, 831/423-2053, a veritable feast for the eyes as well as the stomach. In good weather, you'll enjoy the sunny atmosphere created by the sunroof. Nearby, along streets near the beach and Boardwalk, are a variety of restaurants, everything from authentic and casual ethnic

NEWMAN'S OWN SANTA CRUZ

Nell Newman, Cool Hand Luke's daughter, is the farm-loving Santa Cruz resident posing with the actor on all those tongue-in-cheek, stylized *American Gothic* Newman's Own Organics product labels.

Formerly a biologist with the Ventana Wilderness Sanctuary Research and Education Center down the coast in Big Sur, Nell Newman is an accomplished cook who in 1993 was inspired by the Santa Cruz area's love affair with whole food to add an organics division to her father's popular company, Newman's Own.

The point of Newman's Own Organics is producing "good tasting food that just happens to be organic." So far the brand has focused on what might be considered the inessentials—snack foods including chocolate bars, tortilla chips, pretzels, Pop's Corn, and several cookie varieties, from Fig Newmans to Oreo-like Newman-O's.

Like the first generation of Newman's Own, Newman's Own Organics—the second generation—donates 100 percent of after-tax profits to charitable causes. To date these have included the University of California Santa Cruz Farm and Garden Project, the Organic Farming Research Foundation, the Henry A. Wallace Institute for Alternative Agriculture, and the Western Environmental Law Center in Taos, New Mexico. For more information, see www.newmansownorganics.com.

eateries to sit-down dining establishments. Head to the municipal wharf to see what's new in the fresh-off-the-boat seafood department.

For romantic California-style and continental cuisine, the place is **Casablanca Restaurant,** 101 Main St. (at Beach), 831/426-9063, open for dinner nightly and brunch on Sunday. Lively for worldly American—and a surprising selection of vegetarian—options is **Blacks Beach Café,** E. Cliff at 15th, 831/475-2233, open Tues.–Sun. for dinner, on weekends for brunch.

Veggie Fare and Cheap Eats

The Crepe Place, 1134 Soquel Ave., 831/429-6994, offers inexpensive breakfasts, dessert crêpes (and every other kind), good but unpretentious lunches, and dinners into the wee hours—a great place for late-night dining. Open daily for lunch and dinner, on weekends for brunch. The **Saturn Cafe,** downtown at 145 Laurel St., 831/429-8505, has inexpensive ($8 or less) and wonderful vegetarian meals for lunch, dinner, and beyond. Open daily for lunch and dinner, until late for desserts and coffee (Sun.–Thurs. 11:30 A.M.–3:00 A.M., Fri. and Sat. 11:30 A.M.–4 A.M. Theme days here can be a scream. During Monday Madness, Chocolate Madness sells at two for the price of one. Random Tuesdays, on random Tuesdays, feature local live music. On Wig-Out Wednesday, just wear a wig and you'll get 20 percent off your tab. Such a deal.

A vegetarian visit to Santa Cruz wouldn't be complete without feasting at the **Whole Earth Restaurant** on the UC Santa Cruz campus (Redwood Blvd. next to the library), 831/426-8255. A quiet, comfortable place, this very fine organic eatery was the inspiration and training ground for Sharon Cadwallader's well-known *Whole Earth Cookbook* and its sequel. After all these years, the food is still good and still reasonable.

For "natural fast foods," don't miss **Dharma's Natural Foods Restaurant,** in Capitola at 4250 Capitola Rd., 831/462-1717, where you can savor a Brahma Burger, Dharma Dog, or Nuclear Sub sandwich (baked tofu, guacamole, cheese, lettuce, olives, pickle, and secret sauce on a roll).

The **Seabright Brewery** brewpub, 519 Seabright Ave., Ste. 107, 831/426-2739, is popular for its Seabright Amber and Pelican Pale—not to mention casual dining out on the patio. If you're heading toward Boulder Creek, beer fans, stop by the **Boulder Creek Brewery and Cafe,** 13040 Hwy. 9, 831/338-7882.

The **Santa Cruz Coffee Roasting Company** at the Palomar Inn, 1330 Pacific Ave., 831/459-0100, serves excellent coffee and a bistro-style café lunch. Not far away and absolutely wonderful is **Zoccoli's Delicatessen,** 1534 Pacific Ave., 831/423-1711, where it's common to see people lining up for sandwiches, salads, fresh homemade pastas, and genuine "good deal" lunch specials, usually under $5. Open Mon.–Sat. 9 A.M.–5:30 P.M.

Best Bets Downtown

Downtown Santa Cruz is getting pretty uptown these days. A case in point: Eccentric India Joze, 1001 Center St., serving up affordable Southeast Asian and Middle Eastern food since 1971—and responsible for launching the famed Santa Cruz **International Calamari Festival**—has been replaced by the sophisticated San Francisco-style Mediterranean **Restaurant Azur,** 831/427-3554, which opened in late 2000. Enjoy such things as seafood gazpacho, pizzas, and spit-roasted chicken at lunch, similar fare plus braised salmon, roast leg of lamb, pork rib chops, and New York steak at dinner (veggie selections always available). There's a tasting menu, too, and a nice patio. Naturally raised meat and organic local produce are served at Azur, along with wines by the glass; $10 corkage fee. Open Tues.–Fri. noon to 10 or 11 P.M., Sat. from 4:30 P.M., Sun. 11 A.M.–3 P.M. for brunch and 3 to 9 P.M. for dinner.

Intimate **Oswald's**, 1547 Pacific Ave. (near Cedar), 831/423-7427, is another stylish local favorite, serving the best California cuisine around—starting with only the freshest seafood, meats, and local produce. Fashionable yet eclectic for ethnic fare is the fun, fairly affordable **Pearl Alley Bistro & Café,** 110 Pearl Alley (at Cedar), 831/429-8070, open daily for lunch (until 5 P.M.) and dinner. Full bar. Less fun but everybody's favorite for sophisticated Chinese is **Omei**, 2316 Mission St. (at King), 831/425-8458.

El Palomar at the Pacific Garden Mall, 1336 Pacific Ave., 831/425-7575, is a winner for relaxed Mexican meals—especially seafood. For about a decade now, it's been just about everybody's top choice for south-of-the-border fare. Open daily for breakfast, lunch, and dinner. Full bar. (At the yacht harbor, you'll find **Café El Palomar**, 2222 E. Cliff Dr., 831/462-4248, open 7 A.M.–5 P.M. daily.)

Chaminade

The old Chaminade Brothers Seminary and Monastery, 1 Chaminade Lane (just off Paul Sweet Rd.), 831/475-5600, fell into the hands of developers and is now Chaminade Executive Conference Center and Resort. As part of the deal, the new owners had to include a public restaurant in their development plans. The **Sunset Dining Room at Chaminade** is the place to come on Friday nights for no doubt the best seafood buffet in Santa Cruz County—15 types of fish and seafood, an outdoor grill, and a spectacular view of Monterey Bay. It's worth every penny of the (fairly high) price. The Sunset Room also serves appetizing breakfast, lunch, and dinner buffets and a popular Sunday brunch. Outdoor dining is available, weather permitting. Open daily; reservations advised. You can also sign on for a stay here (see Staying in Santa Cruz, above).

EATING NEAR SANTA CRUZ

Felton, Ben Lomond, and Boulder Creek

The **White Raven** bookshop in Felton, 6253 Hwy. 9, 831/335-3611, is also a cool coffee and pastry stop. Best bet for wholesome, hearty sit-down breakfast and lunch is the **Blue Sun Café** down the road in Boulder Creek, 13070 Hwy. 9, 831/338-2105. For pub fare, the place is the **White Cockade Scottish Pub** nearby at 18025 Hwy. 9, 831/338-4148. For Italian, backtrack to **Ciao Bella** in Ben Lomond, 9217 Hwy. 9, 831/336-9221, where the singing fish and waitstaff are just part of the show. Ben Lomond's **Tyrolean Inn**, 9600 Hwy. 9, 831/336-5188, serves very good traditional German fare.

Soquel

The **Little Tampico,** 2605 Main St., 831/475-4700, isn't exactly inexpensive. A real bargain, though, is the specialty Otila's Plate: a mini-taco, enchilada, tostada, and taquito, plus rice and beans. Another good choice: nachos with everything. (Various Tampico restaurant relatives dot the county.) Another popular Mexican restaurant is **Tortilla Flats**, 4616 Soquel Dr., 831/476-1754. Open daily for lunch, dinner, and Sunday brunch.

Capitola

Dharma's Natural Foods Restaurant, a Santa Cruz institution at 4250 Capitola Rd., 831/462-1717, is purported to be the oldest completely vegetarian restaurant in the country. Open daily for breakfast, lunch, and dinner. Also classic in

Capitola is **Mr. Toots Coffeehouse,** upstairs at 221-A Esplanade, 831/475-3679, where you can get a cup of joe until late, and **Pizza-My-Heart,** 209-A Esplanade, 831/475-5714.

Casual, in more upscale style, and unbeatable for pastries and decadent desserts is **Gayle's Bakery and Rosticceria,** 504 Bay Ave., 831/462-1200. The rosticceria has a wonderful selection of salads and homemade pastas, soups, sandwiches, pizza, spit-roasted meats—even dinners-to-go and heat-and-serve casseroles. But the aromas drifting in from Gayle's Bakery are the real draw. The bakery's breakfast pastries include various cheese Danishes, croissants, chocolatine, lemon tea bread, muffins, pecan rolls, apple nut turnovers, and such specialties as a schnecken ring smothered in walnuts. The apple crumb and ollalieberry pies are unforgettable, not to mention the praline cheesecake and the two dozen other cakes—chocolate mousse, hasselnuss, raspberry, poppy seed, mocha. . . (All pies and cakes are also served by the slice.) For decadence-to-go, try Grand Marnier truffles, florentines, éclairs, or Napoleons. Gayle's also sells more than two dozen types of fresh-baked bread. The Capitola sourdough bread and sour baguette

would be good for picnics, as would the two-pound loaf of the excellent Pain de Compagne. Gayle's is open daily 7 A.M.–7 P.M. (If you're heading toward the bay or San Jose the back way via Corralitos, stop by the **Corralitos Market and Sausage Co.,** 569 Corralitos Rd. Watsonville, 831/722-2633, for homemade sausages, smoke-cured ham and turkey breast, or other specialty meats—all great with Gayle's breads.)

Near the beach, on or near the Esplanade, you'll find an endless variety of eateries. **Margaritaville,** 221 Esplanade, 831/476-2263, serves appetizers and sandwiches along with its margaritas. Open for lunch and dinner daily and for brunch on weekends. The **Paradise Beach Grill,** 215 Esplanade, 831/476-4900, offers California cuisine as well as a variety of international dishes. Great views. Open for lunch and dinner daily. Also serving California cuisine is **Zelda's on the Beach,** 203 Esplanade, 831/475-4900, which features an affordable lobster special on Thursday night.

The most famous restaurant in Capitola is the **Shadowbrook Restaurant,** 1750 Wharf Rd. (at Capitola Rd.), 831/475-1511, known for its romantic garden setting—ferns, roses, ivy outside, a Monterey pine and plants inside—and the

SANTA CRUZ WINERIES

The coastal mountains near Santa Cruz are well known for their redwoods. But since the late 1800s, they have also been known for their vineyards. Regional winemaking is back, helped along since 1981 by the official federal recognition of the Santa Cruz Mountain appellation for wine grapes grown in the region defined by Half Moon Bay in the north and Mount Madonna in the south. More than 40 wineries now produce Santa Cruz Mountain wines.

The eclectic **Bonny Doon Vineyard,** north of Santa Cruz at 10 Pine Flat Rd., 831/425-4518, www.bonnydoonvineyard.com, specializes in Rhône and Italian varietals, though wine lovers and critics are also smitten with the winery's worldly, witty, and wildly footnoted newsletter (also available online). Open 11 A.M.–5 P.M. daily for tastings, except major holidays.

Nearby in Felton is the award-winning and historic **Hallcrest Vineyards,** 379 Felton Empire Rd. (call for directions), 831/335-4441, noted for its cabernet sauvignon, chardonnay, merlot, and zinfandel. Hallcrest is also home to **The Organic Wine Works,** producing the nation's first certified organic wines. Made from certified organically grown grapes, the winemaking process is also organic, without the use of sulfites. Open daily 11 A.M.–5:30 P.M. Also in Felton and open only by appointment is the small **Zayante Vineyards,** 420 Old Mount Rd., 831/335-7992.

For more information about Santa Cruz area wineries, including a current wineries map, contact: **Santa Cruz Mountains Winegrowers Association,** 7605 Old Dominion Ct., Ste. A in Aptos, 831/479-9463, www.wines.com/santa_cruz_mountains.

tram ride down the hill to Soquel Creek. The Shadowbrook is open for "continental-flavored American" dinners nightly. The wine list is extensive. Brunch, with choices like apple and cheddar omelettes, is served on weekends. Reservations recommended.

Aptos

The **Bittersweet Bistro,** 787 Rio Del Mar Blvd., 831/662-9799, offers Mediterranean-inspired bistro fare featuring fresh local and organic produce—everything from Greek pizzettas and seafood puttanesca to garlic chicken and grilled Monterey Bay king salmon. Open Tues.–Sun. for "bistro hour" (3 to 6 P.M.)—half-priced pizzettas and drink specials—and for dinner. The best place around for Thai food, locals say, is **Bangkok West,** 2505 Cabrillo College Dr., 831/479-8297, open daily for lunch and dinner. For stylish and fresh Mexican food, the place is **Palapas** at Seascape Village on Seascape Boulevard, 831/662-9000, open daily for lunch and dinner, brunch on Sunday.

For a romantic dinner, splurge at the **Cafe Sparrow,** 8042 Soquel Dr., 831/688-6238, which serves pricey but excellent country French cuisine at lunch and dinner daily. Family friendly. Open Mon.–Sat. for lunch, daily for dinner. Extensive wine list.

ARTS AND ENTERTAINMENT

For an introduction to local galleries, at the visitors council request the self-guided **Gallery Walk** tour map of downtown Santa Cruz, which will also guide you to coffeehouses and unusual shops. Santa Cruz has more than its fair share of good movie theaters and film series. The historic 1936 **Del Mar Theatre,** 1124 Pacific Ave., 831/469-3220, has been lovingly renovated and now shows great art house and independent films. If it's not playing at the Del Mar, then it's probably at the associated **Nickelodeon Theatre,** 210 Lincoln St., 831/426-7500. For what's playing at both, see www.thenick.com. Pretty darned hip for flicks too is the **Rio Theatre for the Performing Arts,** 1205 Soquel Ave., 831/423-8209, www.riotheatre.com, which also stages live performances.

For what's playing where at a glance, scan local entertainment papers and/or pick up a current copy of the free bimonthly **Santa Cruz Movie Times.**

Nightlife

If you're into big-band swing, check out **Cocoanut Grove** dances (call 408/423-5590 for information); tickets run $15 and up. **The Kuumbwa Jazz Center,** 320-2 Cedar St. #2, 831/427-2227, www.kuumbwajazz.com, is a no-booze, no-cigarettes, under-21-welcome place with great jazz (often big names), and it's rarely packed. Most shows are Monday and Friday at 8 P.M.; ticket prices vary and are often low. The **Catalyst,** 1011 Pacific Ave., 831/423-1336, is legendary for its Friday afternoon happy hour in the Atrium—seems like *everybody's* here from 5 to 7 P.M., drinking beer, making the scene, and sometimes tapping their toes to the house band: Wally's Swing World. The 700-seat theater (massive dance floor) hosts good local bands or national acts nightly (cover charge). Local coffeehouses from Santa Cruz to Capitola also offer casual, relaxed, and sometimes highbrow entertainment (like poetry readings).

Performing Arts

On a smaller scale, local performing arts are always an adventure. The **Santa Cruz Chamber Players** specialize in both traditional and modern chamber music, with an emphasis on the unusual. For a performance schedule, call 831/425-3149. The **Santa Cruz County Symphony,** 200 Seventh Ave. #225, 831/462-0553, schedules performances year-round at both the Santa Cruz Civic Auditorium and Watsonville's Mello Center.

The noted **Tandy Beal & Company** dance troupe, 740 Front St. #300B, 831/429-1324, performs locally when not touring internationally. The **Santa Cruz Ballet Theatre,** 2800 S. Rodeo Gulch Rd., Soquel, 831/479-1600, is a good bet for a year-end production of *The Nutcracker.* **Actors' Theatre,** 1001 Center St., 831/425-1003 (administration) or 831/425-7529 (tickets and reservations), schedules live stage productions year-round. In Capitola, the Quonset hut–housed Capitola Theater is now the **Bay Shore Lyric**

Opera Company and Theater for the Performing Arts, 831/462-3131.

For information on what's going on at UCSC, pick up a copy of the quarterly **UCSC Performing Arts Calendar,** available around town, or call 831/459-ARTS. (Other useful campus numbers include Arts and Lectures, 831/459-2826; Theatre Arts, 831/459-2974; and the Music Department, 831/459-2292). To order tickets by phone ($2 service charge), call the UCSC Ticket Office at 831/459-2159.

EVENTS

For an up-to-date quarterly calendar of city and county events, contact the local visitors council (see Information and Services, below). Bike races have prominent local appeal, and professional volleyball competitions are also held year-round. Whale-watching in winter is another popular draw.

For wine lovers, mid-January features the countywide **Wineries Passport Program,** offering tours, tastings, and open houses at Santa Cruz Mountains wineries (also held in mid-April, mid-July, and mid-November). Mid-month, Santa Cruz celebrates its **Fungus Fair,** always fun for mushroom lovers.

Cold and very cool in February is the **O'Neill Cold Water Classic** surfing competition, sponsored by Santa Cruz–based O'Neill, Inc. and its legendary founder, Jack O'Neill, inventor of the wetsuit. Also in February, the **Migration Festival** at Natural Bridges State Beach celebrates many migrants, from monarch butterflies and the gray whale to salmon, salamanders, elephant seals, and shorebirds. The decades-long tradition of the **Santa Cruz Baroque Festival** starts in February and continues until May, offering concerts of early music masterworks. For information, call 831/457-9693 or see www.scbaroque.org. Head for the Boardwalk in late February for the annual **Clam Chowder Cook-Off.**

Come in March for the free annual **Jazz on the Wharf** festival, which serenades Monterey Bay from the Santa Cruz Municipal Wharf and its restaurants, and for the **Santa Cruz Kayak Surf Festival,** the world's largest. In mid- to late March,

Felton holds its **Great Train Robberies** festival, followed by the **Amazing Egg Hunt** in April (usually). Memorial Day weekend brings the annual **Civil War Reenactment** at Roaring Camp.

May is big for art, wine, and music, starting with **Celebrate Santa Cruz Art, Wine & Jazz** in downtown Santa Cruz and continuing with the **Boulder Creek Art, Wine & Music Festival.** Come in mid-May for the popular **Industrial Hemp Expo,** a celebration of hemp products from soaps to backpacks and hammocks. A fashion show is included. Also fun in May: **Bug Day** at Henry Cowell Redwoods State Park in Felton. Come in June for the **We Carnival Street Parade and World Music Festival.** Come on July 4 for Aptos's **World's Shortest Parade.**

The acclaimed and innovative **Shakespeare Santa Cruz** festival runs mid-July through August in an outdoor theater in the redwoods at UCSC. For information call 831/459-2121, for tickets 831/459-2159, or see www.shakespearesantacruz.org. The very fast **Santa Cruz to Capitola Wharf-to-Wharf Race** in late July is a major event for runners, with more than half the applicants turned away due to the event's immense popularity—a popularity fueled by the $12,000 total prize purse. For information, call the race hotline, 831/475-2196.

After 20-some years, the famed August **Cabrillo Music Festival** (described by *The New Yorker* as one of the most adventurous and attractive in America) is still going strong, with performances at UC Santa Cruz, Mission San Juan Bautista, and Watsonville. For information—and do make your plans well in advance—contact the Cabrillo Music Festival, 831/426-6966, www.cabrillomusic.org. To reserve tickets, call 831/420-5260, beginning in late June.

The first couple of weeks in September, Capitola's **Begonia Festival** includes several big events, including a sandcastle contest and nautical parade. It's followed (and nearly overshadowed) in mid-September by the city's annual **Art & Wine Festival,** which has become incredibly popular. The second and third weekends in October, come for the countywide artists' **Open Studios,** with open-house art shows held everywhere, from private homes and studios to galleries and museums. It's wonderful exposure for artists and great pleasure for aficionados.

In late November, look for Felton's **Mountain Man Rendezvous** and the **Christmas Craft and Gift Festival** at the Boardwalk's Cocoanut Grove. In December, Felton sponsors its **Holiday Lights Train** Christmas festivities.

For more information on many of the above festivals, contact **Santa Cruz County Conference and Visitors Council,** downtown at 1211 Ocean St., 831/425-1234 or 800/833-3494, www.santacruzca.org.

SHOPPING

Clothing shops abound along Pacific Avenue, places such as **The Vault** at 1339 Pacific Ave., 831/426-3349, noted for unique jewelry and clothing, and **Eco Goods** at 1130 Pacific Ave., 831/429-5758, "an alternative general store offering organic, recycled, and non-toxic products at affordable prices"—everything from organic cotton underwear and hemp backpacks to handcrafted maple bedroom sets. **Madame Sidecar** at 907 Cedar St., 831/458-1606, offers distinctive style in quality women's clothing, lingerie, jewelry, and accessories—inspired by flattering 1930s and 1940s fashions.

MADE IN SANTA CRUZ

I t should surprise no one that the Santa Cruz area's creativity is also expressed in fine arts and crafts. **Lundberg Studios** in Davenport is noted for its luminescent blue "worldweights"—globe-styled paperweights that have been presented to various luminaries. Another star is **Annieglass** handcrafted sculptural glass dinnerware designed by artist Ann Morhauser—everyday, dishwasher-safe "art for the table" sought out by celebrities including Barbra Streisand and Oprah Winfrey. **West Coast Weather Vanes** is famed for its custom handcrafted American folk art copper and brass weather vanes. The **Santa Cruz Guitar Co.** is at the forefront of modern guitar making, famous for its acoustic guitars.

Downtown also boasts thrift and vintage clothing shops. **Ample Annies,** 717 Pacific Ave., 831/425-3838, is the vintage destination for larger sizes. **Cognito,** 821 Pacific, 831/426-5414, offers such things as swing dance fashions, two-toned panel shirts, and Hawaiian shirts. Other best bets include **Moon Zoom Endangered Clothing,** 813 Pacific, 831/423-8500; **Volume!,** 803 Pacific, 831/457-9262; and **The Wardrobe,** 113 Locust St., 831/429-6363.

There are plenty of bookstores, too, including the classic **Bookshop Santa Cruz,** 1520 Pacific Ave., 831/423-0900, a community institution that offers a full calendar of author and reader events. Downtown also draws music fans, to **Rhythm Fusion,** 1541 Pacific, 831/423-2048, and **Union Grove Music,** 1003 Pacific, 831/427-0670.

Santa Cruz County is marvelous for locally made wares—some almost affordable. Barbra Streisand and Oprah Winfrey are among the national fans of Santa Cruz's **Annieglass,** which has a shop downtown at 109 Cooper St., 831/427-4260. Translucent sculptural glass dinnerware with fused metal rims, Annieglass comes in various styles, including Roman antique gold or platinum. Also check out **Strini Art Glass** at the Pacific Garden Mall, 103 Locust, 831/462-4240. **Artisans Gallery,** 1368 Pacific Ave., 831/423-8183, features handcrafted leather, wood, pottery, and other wares, with an emphasis on local craftspeople. For a large selection of strictly local wares, head for the Santa Cruz Wharf and **Made in Santa Cruz,** 831/426-2257 or 800/982-2367, www.madeinsantacruz.com, where you'll find everything from art glass, ceramics, and sculpture—check out the struttin' teapots—to soap, salsa, and jewelry.

For a truly unique housewarming gift, head for **West Coast Weather Vanes** in Bonny Doon, 831/425-5505 or (U.S.) 800/762-8736, a company whose artisans carefully craft—without molds—copper and brass weather vanes in the Victorian tradition. Visitors are welcome by appointment.

For more shopping ideas, contact the **Downtown Association of Santa Cruz,** 831/429-1512, www.downtownsantacruz.com, and the

Santa Cruz County Conference & Visitors Council, 831/425-1234 or 800/833-3494, www .santacruzca.org.

INFORMATION AND SERVICES

The best all-around source for city and county information is the **Santa Cruz County Conference and Visitors Council,** downtown at 1211 Ocean St., 831/425-1234 or 800/833-3494, www.santacruzca.org, open Mon.–Sat. 9 A.M.–5 P.M., Sun. 10 A.M.–4 P.M. Definitely request the current accommodations, dining, and visitor guides. If you've got time to roam farther afield, also pick up a current copy of the *County Crossroads* farm trails map and ask about area wineries. Cyclists, request the *Santa Cruz County Bikeway Map.* Antiquers, ask for the current *Antiques, Arts, & Collectibles* directory for Santa Cruz and Monterey Counties, published every June— not a complete listing, by far, but certainly a good start. If you once were familiar with Santa Cruz and—post-1989 earthquake—now find yourself lost, pick up the *Downtown Santa Cruz Directory* brochure.

A valuable source of performing arts information, focused on the university, is the *UCSC Performing Arts Calendar,* published quarterly and available all around town. The excellent UC Santa Cruz paper, *City on a Hill,* is published only during the regular school year. *Santa Cruz Good Times* is a good, long-running free weekly with an entertainment guide and sometimes entertaining political features. The free *Student Guide* comes out seasonally, offering lots of ads and some entertaining reading about Santa Cruz.

The *Santa Cruz County Sentinel* and the *Watsonville Register-Pajaronian* are the traditional area papers. The **Santa Cruz Parks and Recreation Department** at Harvey West Park, 307 Church St., 831/429-3663, open weekdays 8 A.M.–noon and 1–5 P.M., usually publishes a *Summer Activity Guide* (especially useful for advance planning).

The Santa Cruz post office is at 850 Front St., 831/426-5200, and is open weekdays 8 A.M.– 5 P.M. The **Santa Cruz Public Library** is at 224 Church St., 831/420-5700. (If you want to hob-

nob with the people on the hill, visit the **Dean McHenry Library** on campus, 831/459-4000.) For senior information, stop by the **Senior Center,** 222 Market, 831/423-6640, or 1777 Capitola Rd., 831/462-1433.

GETTING HERE AND AROUND
Getting Here

If you're driving from the San Francisco Bay Area, the preferred local route to Santa Cruz (and the only main alternative to Hwy. 1) is I-280 or 880 south to San Jose, then hop over the hills on the congested and treacherously twisting Highway 17.

The **Greyhound** bus terminal is at 425 Front

THE ROARING CAMP AND BIG TREES RAILROAD

F Norman Clark, the self-described "professional at oddities" who also owns the narrow-gauge railroad in Felton, bought the Southern Pacific rails connecting Santa Cruz and nearby Olympia, to make it possible for visitors to get to Henry Cowell Redwoods State Park and Felton (*almost* to Big Basin) by train. During logging's commercial heyday here in the 1900s, 20 or more trains passed over these tracks every day.

Today you can still visit Roaring Camp and ride the rails on one of two different trips. Hop aboard a 100-year-old steam engine and make an hour-and-fifteen-minute loop around a virgin redwood forest ($15 general, $10 kids 3–12), or take a 1940s-vintage passenger train from Felton down to Santa Cruz (roundtrip fare $16.50 general, $11.50 kids 3–12). The year-round calendar of special events includes October's **Harvest Faire** and the **Halloween Ghost Train,** the **Mountain Man Rendezvous** living history encampment in November, and December's **Pioneer Christmas.**

The railroad offers daily runs (usually just one train a day on nonsummer weekdays) from spring through November and operates only on weekends and major holidays in winter. For more information, contact: Roaring Camp and Big Trees Narrow-Gauge Railroad, 831/335-4484, www.roaringcamp.com.

St., 831/423-1800, open weekdays 7:30 A.M.–8 P.M. Greyhound provides service from San Francisco to Santa Cruz, Fort Ord, and Monterey, as well as connections south to L.A. via Salinas or San Jose. From the East Bay and South Bay, take Amtrak, now also offering bus connections from Salinas. You can get *close* to Santa Cruz by plane. The **San Jose International Airport,** 408/501-7600, www.sjc.org, the closest major airport in the north and not far from Santa Cruz, is served by commuter and major airlines. Or fly into Monterey.

Getting Around

Bicyclists will be in hog heaven here, with everything from excellent bike lanes to locking bike racks at bus stops. But drivers be warned: Parking can be impossible, especially in summer, especially at the beach. There's a charge for parking at the Boardwalk (in lots with attendants) and metered parking elsewhere. Best bet: Park elsewhere and take the shuttle. Second best: Drive to the beach, unload passengers and beach paraphernalia, then park a mile or so away. By the time you walk back, your companions should be done battling for beach towel space.

You can usually find free parking on weekends in the public garage at the county government center at 701 Ocean Street, conveniently also a stop for the **Santa Cruz Beach Shuttle** on summer weekends. The shuttle—a great way to avoid parking nightmares—provides regular service between the county government center, downtown, and the wharf area, weekends only Memorial Day through Labor Day. The fare is $1.

The **Santa Cruz Metro,** 230 Walnut Ave., 831/425-8600, www.scmtd.com, provides superb public transit throughout the northern Monterey Bay area. The Metro has a "bike and ride" service for bicyclists who want to hitch a bus ride partway (bike racks onboard). Call for current route information or pick up a free

copy of the excellent *Headways* (which includes Spanish translations). Buses will get you anywhere you want to go in town and considerably beyond for $1 ($3 for an all-day pass)—exact change only.

You can rent a car from **Enterprise Rent-A-Car,** 1025-B Water St., 831/426-7799 or 800/325-8007; **Avis,** 630 Ocean St., 831/423-1244 or 800/831-2847; or **Budget,** 919 Ocean St., 831/425-1808 or 800/527-0700. **Yellow Cab** is at 131 Front St., 831/423-1234, also home to the **Santa Cruz Airporter,** 831/423-1214 or in California 800/223-4142, which provides shuttle van service to both the San Francisco and San Jose Airports, as well as to *Caltrain* and the Amtrak station in San Jose.

For some guided assistance in seeing the sights, contact **Earth, Sea and Sky Tours,** P.O. Box 1630, Aptos, CA 95001, 831/688-5544.

Getting Away

Metro buses can get you to Boulder Creek, Big Basin State Park, Ben Lomond, Felton, north coast beaches, *almost* all the way to Año Nuevo State Reserve just across the San Mateo County line, and to south coast beaches and towns. (**Monterey-Salinas Transit** from Watsonville provides good service in Monterey County.) For ridesharing out of town, check the ride board at UC Santa Cruz and local classifieds.

Another way to get out of town is via Santa Cruz Metro's **Caltrain Connector** buses to the San Jose train station—more than 10 trips daily on weekdays (fewer on weekends and holidays)—which directly connect with **Caltrain** (to San Francisco) and **Amtrak** (to Oakland, Berkeley, and Sacramento). The fare is just $6. For information on the Connector, call 831/425-8600. For **Caltrain** fares and schedules, call 650/508-6200 or 800/660-4287 (in the service area). For Amtrak, contact 800/872-7245 or website: www.amtrak.com.

North of Santa Cruz

Travelers heading north toward San Francisco via Highway 1 will discover Año Nuevo State Reserve, breeding ground for the northern elephant seal—quite popular, so don't expect to just drop by—and two delightful hostels housed in former lighthouses. Not far from Año Nuevo, as the crow flies, is spectacular Big Basin Redwoods State Park, California's first state park, and other spectacular redwood parks.

AÑO NUEVO STATE RESERVE

About 20 miles north of Santa Cruz and just across the county line is the 4,000-acre Año Nuevo State Reserve, breeding ground and rookery for sea lions and seals—particularly the unusual (and once nearly extinct) northern elephant seal. The pendulous proboscis of a "smiling" two- to three-ton alpha bull dangles down like a fire hose, so the name is apt.

At first glance, the windswept and cold seaward stretch of Año Nuevo seems almost desolate, inhospitable to life. This is far from the truth, however. Año Nuevo is the only place in the world where people can get off their bikes or the bus or get out of their cars and walk out among aggressive, wild northern elephant seals in their natural habitat. Especially impressive is that first glimpse of hundreds of these huge seals nestled like World War II torpedoes among the sand dunes. A large number of other animal and plant species also consider this area home; to better appreciate the ecologically fascinating animal and plant life of the entire area, read *The Natural History of Año Nuevo*, by Burney J. Le Boeuf and Stephanie Kaza.

Survival of the Northern Elephant Seal

Hunted almost to extinction for their oil-rich blubber, northern elephant seals numbered only 20 to 100 at the turn of the 20th century. All these survivors lived on Isla de Guadalupe off the west coast of Baja California. Their descendants eventually began migrating north to California. In the 1950s, a few arrived at Año Nuevo

Island, attracted to its rocky safety. The first pup was born on the island in the 1960s. By 1975 the mainland dunes had been colonized by seals crowded off the island rookery, and the first pup was born onshore. By 1988, 800 northern elephant seals were born on the mainland, part of a total known population of more than 80,000 and an apparent ecological success story. (Only time will tell, though, since the species' genetic diversity has been eliminated by the swim at the brink of extinction.) Though Año Nuevo was the first northern elephant seal rookery established on the California mainland, northern elephant seals are now establishing colonies elsewhere along the state coastline.

Mating Season

Male northern elephant seals start arriving in December. Who arrives first and who remains dominant among the males during the long mating season is important because the alpha bull gets to breed with most of the females. Since the males are biologically committed to conserving their energy for sex, they spend much of their time lying about as if dead, in or out of the water, often not even breathing for stretches of up to a half hour. Not too exciting for spectators. But when two males battle each other for the "alpha" title, the loud, often bloody nose-to-nose battles are something to see. Arching up with heads back and canine teeth ready to tear flesh, the males bellow and bark and bang their chests together.

In January the females start to arrive, ready to bear offspring conceived the previous year. They give birth to their pups within the first few days of their arrival. The males continue to wage war, the successful alpha bull now frantically trying to protect his harem of 50 or so females from marauders. For every two pounds in body weight a pup gains, its mother loses a pound. Within 28 days, she loses about half her weight, then, almost shriveled, she leaves. Her pup, about 60 pounds at birth, weighs 300 to 500 pounds a month later. Although inseminated by the bull before leaving the rookery, the emaciated female

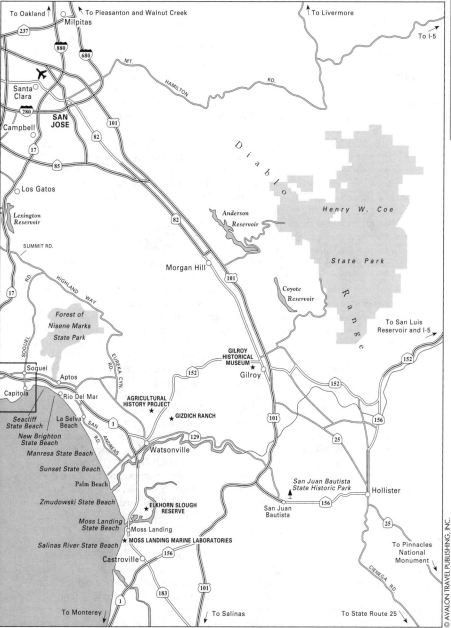

is in no condition for another pregnancy, so conception is delayed for several months, allowing the female to feed and regain her strength. Then, after an eight-month gestation period, the cycle starts all over again.

Etiquette

The Marine Mammal Act of 1972 prohibits people from harassing or otherwise disturbing these magnificent sea mammals, so be respectful. While walking among the elephant seals, remember that the seemingly sluglike creatures *are* wild beasts and can move as fast as any human across the sand, though for shorter distances. For this reason, keeping a 20-foot minimum distance between you and the seals (especially during the macho mating season) is important. No food or drinks are allowed on the reserve, and nothing in the reserve may be disturbed. The first males often begin to arrive in November, before the official docent-led tours begin, so it's possible to tour the area unsupervised. Visit the dunes without a tour guide in spring and summer also, when many elephant seals return here to molt.

The reserve's "equal access boardwalk" across the sand makes it possible for physically challenged individuals to see the seals.

Information and Tours

Official 2.5-hour guided tours of Año Nuevo begin in mid-December and continue through March, rain or shine, though January and February are the prime months, and reservations are necessary. The reserve is open 8 A.M.–sunset; the day-use parking fee is $5 (hike-ins and bike-ins are free, but you still must pick up a free day-use permit). Tour tickets ($4 plus surcharge for credit card reservations) are available only through ReserveAmerica's Año Nuevo and Hearst Castle reservations line, 800/444-4445. For international reservations, call 916/638-5883. Reservations cannot be made before November 1. To take a chance on no-shows, arrive at Año Nuevo before scheduled tours and get on the waiting list. The reserve offers a 1,700-foot-long wheelchair accessible boardwalk for seal viewing. There's also a van equipped with a wheelchair lift, to transport visitors from the parking lot to

the boardwalk; accessible restrooms; and guided walks offered in American Sign Language (by advance reservation). For wheelchair access reservations, December 15 through March 15, call 650/879-2033, 1 to 4 P.M. only on Monday, Wednesday, and Friday.

Organized bus excursions, which include walking tour tickets, are available through **San Mateo County Transit,** 800/660-4287 or 650/508-6441 (call after November 1 for reservations), www.samtrans.com, and **Santa Cruz Metro**. The HI Pigeon Point Hostel, near Año Nuevo, sometimes has extra tickets for hostelers. For more information, contact Año Nuevo State Reserve, New Year's Creek Rd. in Pescadero, 650/879-2027 (recorded information) or 650/879-2025.

BIG BASIN REDWOODS STATE PARK

California's first state park was established here, about 24 miles up canyon from Santa Cruz on Highway 9. To save Big Basin's towering *Sequoia sempervirens* coast redwoods from loggers, 60-some conservationists led by Andrew P. Hill camped at the base of Slippery Rock on May 15, 1900, and formed the Sempervirens Club. Just two years later, in September 1902, 3,800 acres of primeval forest were deeded to the state, the beginning of California's state park system.

Flora and Fauna

Today, Big Basin Redwoods State Park includes more than 18,000 acres on the ocean-facing slopes of the Santa Cruz Mountains, and efforts to protect (and expand) the park still continue under the auspices of the Sempervirens Fund and the Save-the-Redwoods League. (Donations are always welcome.) Tall coast redwoods and Douglas fir predominate. Wild ginger, violets, and milkmaids are common in spring, also a few rare orchids grow here. Native azaleas bloom in early summer, and by late summer huckleberries are ready for picking. In the fall and winter rainy season, mushrooms and other forest fungi "blossom."

At one time, the coast grizzly (one of seven bear species that roamed the state's lower regions) thrived between San Francisco and San Luis

Obispo. The last grizzly was spotted here in 1878. Common are black-tailed deer, raccoons, skunks, and gray squirrels. Rare are mountain lions, bobcats, coyotes, foxes, and opossums. Among the fascinating reptiles in Big Basin is the endangered western skink. Predictably, rattlers are fairly common in chaparral areas, but other snakes are shy. Squawking Steller's jays are ever-present, and acorn woodpeckers, dark-eyed juncos, owls, and hummingbirds—altogether about 250 bird species—also haunt Big Basin. Spotting marbled murrelets (shorebirds that nest 200 feet up in the redwoods) is a birding challenge.

Seeing and Doing Big Basin

The best time to be in Big Basin is in the fall, when the weather is perfect and most tourists have gone home. Winter and spring are also prime times, though usually rainier. Road cuts into the park offer a peek into local geology—tilted, folded, twisted layers of thick marine sediments. Big Basin's **Nature Lodge** museum features good natural history exhibits and many fine books, including *Short Historic Tours of Big Basin* by Jennie and Denzil Verado. The carved-log seating and the covered stage at the amphitheater attract impromptu human performances (harmonica concerts, freestyle softshoe, joke routines) when no park campfires or other official events are scheduled.

Also here: more than 80 miles of hiking trails. (Get oriented in the Sempervirens Room adjacent to park headquarters.) Take the half-mile **Redwood Trail** loop to stretch your legs and to see one of the park's most impressive stands of virgin redwoods. Or hike the more ambitious **Skyline-to-the-Sea** trail, at least an overnight trip. It's 11 miles from the basin rim to the seabird haven of Waddell Beach and adjacent **Theodore J. Hoover Natural Preserve**, a freshwater marsh. There are trail camps along the way (camping and fires allowed only in designated areas). Hikers, bring food and water, as Waddell Creek flows with reclaimed wastewater. Another popular route is the **Pine Mountain Trail.** Thanks to recent land acquisitions along the coast north of Santa Cruz, the new 1.5-mile **Whitehouse Ridge Trail** now joins Big Basin with Año Nuevo State Reserve; call ahead or inquire at either park for directions.

Most dramatic in Big Basin are the waterfalls. **Berry Creek Falls** is a particularly pleasant destination, with rushing water, redwood mists, and glistening rocks fringed with delicate ferns. Nearby are both **Silver Falls** and the **Golden Falls Cascade.**

Information

For park information, contact Big Basin Redwoods State Park, 21600 Big Basin Way in Boulder Creek, 831/338-8860, www.bigbasin.org. Big Basin has family campsites ($12) plus five group camps. Reserve all campsites through ReserveAmerica, 800/444-7275, www.reserveamerica.com, up to seven months in advance. An unusual "outdoor" option: the park's tent cabins. For more information, see Santa Cruz Camping. To reserve backpacker campsites at the park's six trail camps ($5), contact park headquarters. Big Basin's day-use fee is $3 per vehicle (walk-ins and bike-ins are free), and a small fee is charged for the map/brochure showing all trails and major park features. To get oriented to the town, pick up a copy of the Boulder Creek Historical Walking Tour, available at most area merchants and at the **San Lorenzo Valley Historical Museum,** now at home in a onetime church built with local old-growth redwood at 12547 Hwy. 9, 831/338-8382, at last report open on Wednesday, Saturday, and Sunday afternoons. Call for current details.

Henry Cowell Redwoods State Park

The Redwood Grove in the dark San Lorenzo Canyon here is the park's hub and one of the most impressive redwood groves along the central coast, with the Neckbreaker, the Giant, and the Fremont Tree all standouts. You can camp at Graham Hill, picnic near the grove, or head out on the 15-mile web of hiking and horseback trails. New in the summer of 1999 was the **U-Con Trail** connecting Henry Cowell to Wilder Ranch State Park on the coast—making it possible to hike, bike, or horseback ride from the redwoods to the ocean on an established trail. For information about Henry Cowell Redwoods State Park, off Highway 9 in Felton, call 831/335-4598 or 831/438-2396 (campground). Henry Cowell has 150 campsites;

reserve through ReserveAmerica, 800/444-7275 or website: www.reserveamerica.com.

Other Parks off Hwy. 9

Between Big Basin and Saratoga is **Castle Rock State Park**, 15300 Skyline Blvd., Los Gatos, 408/867-2952, an essentially undeveloped park and a hiker's paradise. Ask at Big Basin for current trail information. Primitive campsites are $7 per night. **Highlands County Park,** 8500 Hwy. 9 in Ben Lomond, is open daily 9 A.M.–dusk. This old

estate, transformed into a park with picnic tables and nature trails, also has a sandy beach along the river. Another swimming spot is at **Ben Lomond County Park** on Mill Street, which also offers shaded picnic tables and barbecue facilities. Free, open daily in summer. Closer to Big Basin is **Boulder Creek Park** on Middleton Avenue east of Highway 9 in Boulder Creek; also free. The swimming hole here has both shallows and deeps, plus there's a sandy beach. Other facilities include shaded picnic tables and barbecue pits.

South of Santa Cruz

MOSS LANDING AND VICINITY

Near the mouth of Elkhorn Slough on the coast, Moss Landing is a crazy quilt of weird shops and roadside knickknack stands, watched over by both a towering steam power plant (formerly under PG&E [Pacific Gas & Electric] control and now owned and recently expanded by Duke Energy), built circa 1948, the second largest in the world, and a Kaiser firebrick-making plant. All of which makes for an odd-looking community.

First a Salinas Valley produce port, then a whaling harbor until 1930, Moss Landing is now surrounded by artichoke and broccoli fields. The busy fishing harbor and adjoining slough are home to hundreds of bird and plant species, making this an important center for marinelife studies.

These days the area is also noted for its indoor recreational opportunities, with more than two-dozen antique and junk shops along Moss Landing Road. Show up on the last Sunday in July for the annual **Antique Street Fair,** which draws more than 350 antiques dealers and at least 12,000 civilian antiquers. October brings the **Monterey Bay Bird Festival.**

For more information about the area, contact the **Moss Landing Chamber of Commerce,** P.O. Box 41, Moss Landing, CA 95039, 831/633-4501, www.monterey-bay.net/ml.

Moss Landing Marine Laboratories

The laboratories here, at 895 Blanco Circle, 831/755-8650, are jointly operated by nine cam-

puses of the California State Universities and Colleges system. Students and faculty study local marinelife, birds, and tidepools, but particularly Monterey Bay's spectacular underwater submarine canyons, which start where Elkhorn Slough enters the bay at Moss Landing. Stop for a visit and quick look around, but don't disturb classes or research projects. Better yet, come in spring—usually the first Sunday after Easter—for the big open house, when you can take a complete tour; explore the "touch tank" full of starfish, sea cucumbers, sponges, snails, and anemones; and see slide shows, movies, and marinelife dioramas.

Elkhorn Slough Reserve

Most people come here to hike and bird-watch, but the fishlife in this coastal estuary, the second largest in California, is also phenomenal. No wonder the Ohlone people built villages here some 5,000 years ago. Wetlands like these, oozing with life and nourished by rich bay sediments, are among those natural environments most threatened by "progress." Thanks to the Nature Conservancy, the Elkhorn Slough (originally the mouth of the Salinas River until a 1908 diversion) is now protected as a federal and state estuarine sanctuary and recognized as a National Estuarine Research Reserve—California's first. Elkhorn Slough is managed by the California Department of Fish and Game.

These meandering channels along a seven-mile river are thick with marshy grasses and wildflowers beneath a plateau of oaks and eucalyptus.

In winter an incredible variety of shorebirds (not counting migrating waterfowl) call this area home. Endangered and threatened birds, including the brown pelican, the California clapper rail, and the California least tern, thrive here. The tule elk once hunted by the Ohlone are long gone, but harbor seals bask on the mudflats, and bobcats, gray foxes, muskrats, otters, and black-tailed deer are still here. Come in fall for the annual **Monterey Bay Bird Festival.**

Though this is a private nature sanctuary, not a park, the public can visit. Some 4.5 miles of trails pass by tidal mudflats, salt marshes, and an old abandoned dairy. The reserve and visitors center, which offers a bird-watchers map/guide to the Pajaro Valley, are open Wed.–Sun. 9 A.M.–5 P.M. There's a small day-use fee to use the trails. Docent-led walks are offered year-round on Saturday and Sunday at 10 A.M. and 1 P.M. On the first Saturday of the month, there's also an Early Bird Walk at 8:30 A.M. Still, there's no better way to see the slough than from the seat of a kayak. Stop by the visitors center at the entrance to arrange a guided tour or contact the **Elkhorn Slough Foundation,** 1700 Elkhorn Rd., P.O. Box 267, Moss Landing, CA 95039, 831/728-2822 or 831/728-5939, www.elkhornslough.org. Arrange kayak tours through **Monterey Bay Kayaks,** 693 Del Monte Ave., Monterey, 831/373-5357 or 831/633-2211, or **Kayak Connections,** 831/724-5692. For a guided tour aboard a 27-foot pontoon boat, contact **Elkhorn Slough Safari** in Moss Landing, 831/633-5555, www.elkhornslough.com.

Practicalities

Time-honored people's eateries abound, particularly near the harbor. Most serve chowders and seafood and/or ethnic specials. Quite good, right on the highway, is **The Whole Enchilada,** 831/633-3038, open for lunch and dinner daily and specializing in Mexican seafood entrées. (The "whole enchilada," by the way, is filet of red snapper wrapped in a corn tortilla and smothered in enchilada sauce and melted cheese.) The Enchilada's associated **Moss Landing Inn and Jazz Club,** 831/633-9990, is a bar featuring live jazz on Sunday 4:30–8:30 P.M. Hit **Haute Enchilada,** 7902-A Sandholdt Rd., 831/633-5843, A best

bet for fish is **Phil's Fresh Fish Market and Eatery** on Sandholdt, 831/633-2152. (To get there from Moss Landing Road, take the first and only right-hand turn and cross the one-lane bridge; it's the wooden warehouse just past the research institute.) Stop for fresh fruit smoothies and generous deli sandwiches at the associated **Phil's Snack Shack,** 7921 Moss Landing Road. For seafood with a view, try dinner at **Maloney's Harbor Inn** a half-mile north along the highway, 831/724-9371.

"En route camping" for self-contained RVs is available at **Moss Landing State Beach.**

Castroville

The heart of Castroville is Swiss-Italian, which hardly explains the artichokes all over the place. Calling itself "Artichoke Capital of the World," Castroville grows 75 percent of California's artichokes, though that delicious leathery thistle grows throughout Santa Cruz and Monterey Counties. Come for the annual **Artichoke Festival** and parade every May; contact 831/633-6545 or website: www.artichoke-festival.org for information. It's some party, too, replete with artichokes fried, baked, mashed, boiled, and added as colorful ingredients to cookies and cakes. Nibble on french-fried artichokes with mayo dip and artichoke nut cake, sip artichoke soup, and sample steamed artichokes. Sometimes Hollywood gets in on the action: In 1947 Marilyn Monroe reigned as California's Artichoke Queen. If you miss the festival there are other artichoke options, including **Giant Artichoke Fruits and Vegetables** at 11261 Merritt St., 831/633-3501, and the **Thistle Hut,** just off Highway 1 at Cooper-Molera Road, 831/633-4888. The **Franco Restaurant,** 10639 Merritt, 831/633-2090, sponsors a Marilyn Monroe look-alike contest in June. But come by otherwise just to grab a burger—some say the best in the county—and to ogle the Marilyn memorabilia. The Italian **Ristorante La Scuola** is housed in Castroville's first schoolhouse, 10700 Merritt, 831/633-3200.

WATSONVILLE AND VICINITY

Watsonville, an agriculturally rich city of over 25,000, is the mushroom capital of the United

States, though the town calls this lovely section of the Pajaro Valley the Strawberry Capital of the World and Apple City of the Ives. Farming got off to a brisk clod-busting start during the gold rush, when produce grown here was in great demand. Among the early settlers were Chinese, Germans, Yugoslavs, and immigrants from the Sandwich Islands and the Azores. None gained as much notoriety as Watsonville stage driver Charley Parkhurst, one of the roughest, toughest, most daring muleskinners in the state—a "man" later unveiled as a woman, the first to ever vote in California.

Watsonville made history still earlier. Nothing remains today to commemorate the site of the 1920s "Mother House" of California's Vallejo clan, yet the **House of Glass** once stood about 2.5 miles southeast of Watsonville near Highway 1. General Mariano Guadalupe Vallejo was one of five sons and eight daughters born to his parents there, in a house with 20-inch-thick walls and hand-hewn redwood window frames and joists. It was called the House of Glass for its completely glassed-in second story veranda. Legend has it the veranda got its unique fishbowl design when Don Ignacio Vincente Ferrer Vallejo mistakenly received a shipment of 12 dozen windows instead of one dozen. It was from the Vallejo ranch that Jose Castro, Juan Bautista Alvarado, and their rebel troops launched their 1835 attack on Monterey to create the free state of Alta California. The victorious single shot (fired by a lawyer who consulted a book to figure out how to work the cannon) hit the governor's house, and he surrendered immediately.

Seeing and Doing Watsonville

For the local *Country Crossroads* farm trails map and other visitor information, contact the **Pajaro Valley Chamber of Commerce,** 444 Main St. in Watsonville, 831/724-3900, www.pvchamber.com. Or stop by Country Crossroads headquarters at the farm bureau office, 141 Monte Vista Ave., 831/724-1356. Get up to speed on local agricultural history at the **Agricultural History Project** at the Santa Cruz County Fairgrounds, 831/724-5898. Museum exhibits and demonstrations are open to the public on Fri. and Sat. noon–4 P.M. An almost mandatory stop, from May through January, is **Gizdich Ranch,** 55 Peckham Rd., 831/722-1056, www.gizdichranch.com, fabulous from late summer through fall for its fresh apples, homemade apple pies, and fresh-squeezed natural apple juices. Earlier in the season, this is a "Pik-Yor-Sef" berry farm, with raspberries, olallieberries, and strawberries (usually also available in pies, fritters, and pastries). Another best bet is **Emile Agaccio Farms,** 4 Casserly Rd., 831/728-2009, known for its you-pick raspberries and chesterberries (a blackberry variety). Also worth seeking in Watsonville are Mexican and Filipino eateries, many quite good, most inexpensive. Watsonville has its share of motels, too, in addition to camping at Pinto Lake (see below) and at the Santa Cruz KOA.

Beaches

At **Manresa State Beach,** 400 San Andreas Rd., 831/724-3750, stairways lead to the surf from the main parking lot and Sand Dollar Drive; there are restrooms and an outdoor shower. No camping here, but camping is available one mile south at Manresa Uplands Campground. Rural San Andreas Road also takes you to **Sunset State Beach,** 201 Sunset Beach Rd., 831/763-7062 or 831/763-7063, four miles west of Watsonville in the Pajaro Dunes (take Bus No. 54B from Santa Cruz). Sunset offers 3.5 miles of nice sandy beaches and tall dunes, with the historic Van Laanen farm as backdrop. Sunset also features a wooded campground with 90 campsites (tents and RVs, but way too many RVs and not much privacy), group campsites, and 60 picnic sites. After sunset the beach is open only to campers. Day use at both is $5, camping $13–16. For more on area state parks, see www.santacruzstateparks.org. To reserve family campsites at all state beaches and parks, contact ReserveAmerica, 800/444-7275, www.reserveamerica.com.

Parking for pretty **Palm Beach** near Pajaro Dunes—a great place to find sand dollars—is near the end of Beach Street. Also here are picnic facilities, a par course, and restrooms. **Zmudowski State Beach** is near where the Pajaro River reaches the sea. You'll find good hiking and surf fishing. The beach is rarely crowded. Next, near Moss Landing, are **Salinas River State Beach** on Potrero Road, 831/384-7695, and **Jetty State Beach.**

Recreation

Just a few miles northwest of Watsonville is tiny **Pinto Lake City Park,** 451 Green Valley Rd., 831/722-8129, www.pintolake.com, where you can go swimming, sailing, pedal-boating, sailboarding, fishing, or RV camping (28 sites with full hookups, $24; no tent camping) or enjoy a 180-acre urban nature refuge and picnic area.

The **Ellicott Slough National Wildlife Refuge,** a 180-acre ecological reserve of coastal uplands for the Santa Cruz long-toed salamander, is four miles west along San Andreas Road. To get there, turn west off Highway 1 at the Larkin Valley Road exit and continue west on San Andreas Road to the refuge, next to the Santa Cruz KOA. For information about the reserve, call 510/792-0222.

Events

The area also offers unusual diversions. The biggest event here is the annual **West Coast Antique Fly-In** in May (Memorial Day weekend), when more than 50,000 people show up to appreciate hundreds of classic, antique, and homebuilt airplanes on the ground and in the air. Originally held over Memorial Day weekend but now usually scheduled for early August is the annual **Monterey Bay Strawberry Festival,** www.mbsf.com. Come in mid-September for the **Santa Cruz County Fair.**

Monterey

In his novel by the same name, local boy John Steinbeck described Monterey's Cannery Row as "a poem, a stink, a grating noise, a quality of light, a tune, a habit, a nostalgia, a dream," and also as a corrugated collection of sardine canneries, restaurants, honky-tonks, whorehouses, and waterfront laboratories. The street, he said, groaned under the weight of "silver rivers of fish." People here liked his description so much that they eventually put it on a plaque and planted it in today's touristy Cannery Row, among the few Steinbeck-era buildings still standing.

Local promoters claim that the legendary writer would be proud of what the tourist dollar has wrought here, but this seems unlikely. When Steinbeck returned in 1961 from his self-imposed exile, he noted the clean beaches, "where once they festered with fish guts and flies. The canneries that once put up a sickening stench are gone, their places filled with restaurants, antique shops, and the like. They fish for tourists now, not pilchards, and that species they are not likely to wipe out."

A Dream "Under Siege"

An early port for California immigrants—California's first pier was built here—and now a bustling tourist mecca, Monterey (literally, "the King's Wood") is trying hard to hang onto its once-cloistered charm. The justifiably popular Monterey Bay Aquarium is often blamed for the hopeless summer traffic snarls, though tourism throughout the Monterey Peninsula is the actual culprit. *Creative States Quarterly* editor Raymond Mungo once described Monterey as a city "under siege," asking rhetorically: "How do you describe the difference a tornado makes in a small town, or the arrival of sudden prosperity in a sleepy backwater?" How indeed?

During peak summer months you can avoid feeling under siege yourself—and worrying that you're contributing unduly to the city's siege state—by using Monterey's public WAVE shuttles whenever possible.

MONTEREY BAY AQUARIUM

The fish are back on Cannery Row, at least at the west end. Doc's Western Biological Laboratory and the canneries immortalized by Steinbeck may be long gone, but Monterey now has an aquarium that the bohemian biologist would love.

Just down the street from Doc's legendary marine lab, the Monterey Bay Aquarium on Cannery

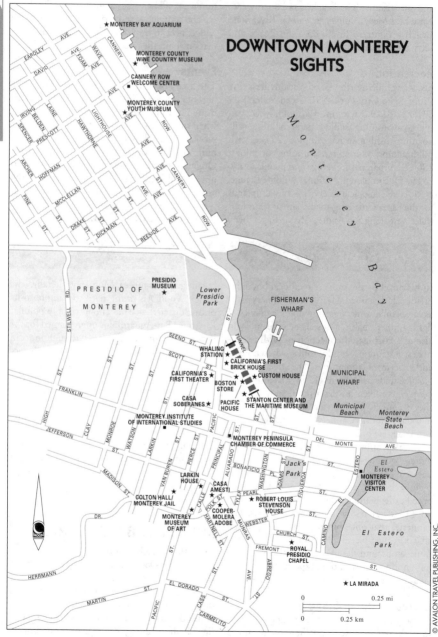

DOWNTOWN MONTEREY SIGHTS

★ Monterey Bay Aquarium

Monterey County Wine Country Museum

Cannery Row Welcome Center

Monterey County Youth Museum

EARDLEY AVE.
DAVID
WAVE AVE.
FOAM AVE.
CANNERY AVE.
IRVING
BELDEN
SPENCER
PRESCOTT
LAINE
HAWTHORNE
LIGHTHOUSE AVE.
ROW ST.
ARCHER
HOFFMAN
MCCLELLAN
DRAKE ST.
PINE ST.
DICKMAN ST.
REESIDE AVE.
CANNERY ROW AVE.

Monterey Bay

STILWELL RD.

PRESIDIO OF MONTEREY

PRESIDIO MUSEUM ★

Lower Presidio Park

FISHERMAN'S WHARF

FRANKLIN
HIGH
CLAY
MONROE
WATSON
LARKIN
PIERCE ST.
JEFFERSON

SEENO ST.

SCOTT

TUNNEL ST.

WHALING STATION ★
★ CALIFORNIA'S FIRST BRICK HOUSE
CALIFORNIA'S FIRST THEATER ★
BOSTON STORE ★
★ CUSTOM HOUSE
CASA SOBERANES ★
PACIFIC HOUSE
STANTON CENTER AND THE MARITIME MUSEUM

MONTEREY INSTITUTE OF INTERNATIONAL STUDIES

MUNICIPAL WHARF

Municipal Beach

Monterey State Beach

MONTEREY PENINSULA CHAMBER OF COMMERCE

DEL MONTE AVE.

VAN BUREN
MADISON ST.
CALLE
PRINCIPAL
ALVARADO
BONAFACIO
WASHINGTON
ADAMS
FIGUEROA
PEARL
TYLER
WEBSTER
MUNRAS
ESTERO ST.

Jack's Park

El Estero

MONTEREY VISITOR CENTER

LARKIN HOUSE ★
CASA AMESTI ★
COLTON HALL/MONTEREY JAIL ★
★ COOPER-MOLERA ADOBE
★ ROBERT LOUIS STEVENSON HOUSE

DR.

MONTEREY MUSEUM OF ART

HARTNELL ST.
CHURCH ST.
FREMONT
ABREGO
CAMINO
CASS
IS

El Estero Park

ROYAL PRESIDIO CHAPEL

HERRMANN
MARTIN
EL DORADO ST.
PACIFIC
CARMELITO

★ LA MIRADA

0   0.25 mi

0   0.25 km

MOON

Row is a world-class cluster of fish tanks built into the converted Hovden Cannery. Luring 2.35 million visitors in 1984, its first year, Monterey's best attraction is the brainchild of marine biologist Nancy Packard and her sister, aquarium director Julie Packard. Much help came from Hewlett-Packard computer magnate David Packard and wife, Lucile, who supported this nonprofit, public-education endeavor with a $55 million donation to their daughters' cause. Not coincidentally, Packard also personally designed many of the unique technological features of the major exhibits here. Through the aquarium's foundation, the facility also conducts its own research and environmental education and wildlife rescue programs. The aquarium's trustees, for example, have allocated $10 million for a five-year unmanned underwater exploration and research project in the bay's Monterey Canyon.

The philosophy of the folks at the Monterey Bay Aquarium, most simply summarized as "endorsing human interaction" with the natural world, is everywhere apparent. From a multi-level view of kelp forests in perpetual motion to face-to-face encounters with sharks and wolf eels, from petting velvety bat rays and starfish in "touch pools" to watching sea otters feed and frolic, here people can observe the native marine plants and wildlife of Monterey Bay up close and personal. More than 300,000 animals and plants representing 571 species—including fish, invertebrates, mammals, reptiles, birds, and plant life—can be seen here in environments closely approximating their natural communities. Volunteer guides, dressed in rust-colored jackets, are available throughout the aquarium and are only too happy to share their knowledge about the natural history of Monterey Bay.

The engineering feats shoring up the amazingly "natural" exhibits in the 322,000-square-foot Monterey Aquarium are themselves impressive. Most remarkable are the aquatic displays, concrete tanks with unbreakable one-ton acrylic windows more than seven inches thick. The exhibits' "wave action" is simulated by a computer-controlled surge machine and hidden water jets. In the Nearshore Galleries, more than a half-million gallons of fresh seawater are pumped through the various aquarium

tanks daily to keep these habitats healthy. During the day, six huge "organic" water filters screen out microorganisms that would otherwise cloud the water. At night, filtration shuts down and raw, unfiltered seawater flows through the exhibits—nourishing filter-feeders and also carrying in plant spores and animal larvae that settle and grow, just as they would in nature. The Outer Bay Galleries operate as a "semi-closed" system, with water from the main intake pipes heated to 68° F and recirculated through the exhibits. Wastes are removed by biological filters and ozone treatment, and a heat-recovery system recaptures energy from the water (cools it) before it is discharged into the bay.

In the event of an oil spill or other oceanic disaster, the aquarium's 16-inch intake pipes can be shut down on a moment's notice and the aquarium can operate as a "closed system" for up to two weeks.

Seeing and Doing the Aquarium

Just inside the aquarium's entrance, serving as an introduction to the **Nearshore Galleries,** is the 55,000-gallon, split-level **Sea Otter Tank.** These sleek aquatic clowns consume 25 percent of their body weight in seafood daily. If they're not eating or playing with toys, they're grooming themselves—and with 600,000 hairs per square inch on their pelts, it's easy to understand why otters were so prized by furriers (and hunted almost to extinction). To spot an occasional otter or two slipping into the aquarium over the seawall, or to watch for whales, head for the outdoor observation decks, which include telescopes for bay watching. The **Outdoor Tidepool** is surrounded by the aquarium itself on three sides, on the fourth by artificial rock. It is home to sea stars, anemones, small fish—and visiting sea otters and harbor seals that occasionally shimmy up the stairs for a better look at the people. Also here are telescopes for bay watching.

The three-story-tall **Giant Kelp Forest** exhibit, the aquarium's centerpiece and the first underwater forest ever successfully established as a display, offers a diver's-eye view of the undersea world. "Dazzling" is the only word for the nearby **Anchovies** exhibit, a cylindrical tank full of darting silver shapes demonstrating the "safety in

ABOUT DOC RICKETTS

Marine biologist Edward F. Ricketts (Steinbeck's character "Doc") was, according to Richard Astro, the writer's "closest friend and his collaborator on *Sea of Cortez*—his most important work of nonfiction, a volume which contains the core of Steinbeck's worldview, his philosophy of life, and the essence of a relationship between a novelists and a scientist. . . . " Much of the novelist's success, he says, is due to Ricketts's influence on Steinbeck's thinking.

According to Steinbeck himself: "He was a great teacher and a great lecher—an immortal who loved women. . . . He was gentle but capable of ferocity, small and slight but strong as an ox, loyal and yet untrustworthy, generous but gave little and received much. His thinking was as paradoxical as his life. He thought in mystical terms and hated and mistrusted mysticism."

To explore the world according to both Steinbeck and Ricketts, pick up a copy of *The Log from the Sea of Cortez*, published in a paperback edition by Penguin Books.

numbers" group-mind philosophy. The 90-foot-long hourglass-shaped **Monterey Bay Habitats** display is a simulated underwater slice of sea life. Sharks roam the deep among colorful anemones and sea slugs, bat rays glide under the pier with the salmon and mackerel, accompanied by octopi and wolf eels. The craggy-shored, indoor-outdoor **Coastal Stream** exhibit has a steady rhythm all its own and provides a small spawning ground for salmon and steelhead. In the huge **Marine Mammals Gallery**, you'll see models of a 43-foot-long barnacled gray whale and her calf, plus killer whales, dolphins, sea lions, and seals.

Unusual among the predominantly bay-related exhibits, but popular, is the live chambered nautilus in the **Octopus and Kin** exhibit. Also exciting here, in a spine-tingling way, is watching an octopus suction its way across the window. But to really get "in touch" with native underwater life, visit the **Bat Ray Petting Pool**, the **Touch Tidepool** of starfish and anemones, and the **Kelp Lab.** Visitors can stroll through the **Sandy Shore** outdoor aviary to observe shorebirds.

New exhibits are continually added to the Monterey Bay Aquarium. The stunning and relatively new, $57 million **Outer Bay Galleries** nearly doubled the aquarium's exhibit space when it opened in early 1996. Devoted to marine life "at the edge," where Monterey Bay meets the open ocean, the centerpiece exhibit is a million-gallon "indoor sea," housing a seven-foot sunfish, sharks, barracudas, stingrays, green sea turtles, and schooling bonito—all seen through the largest aquarium window yet built, an acrylic panel some 15 feet high, 54 feet wide, and 78,000 pounds. Quite visually arresting in the **Drifters Gallery** is the orange and deep-blue **Sea Nettles** jellyfish exhibit, where one might stand and watch the show—something like a giant, pulsing lava lamp—for hours. Equally mesmerizing, on the way into the Outer Bay, is the swirling, endlessly circling stream of silvery mackerel directly overhead. The best way to watch—you'll notice that young children, not yet socially self-conscious, figure this out immediately—is by lying flat on your back. The **Mysteries of the Deep** exhibit studies the often-bizarre creatures that inhabit the murky depths. Seldom seen in an aquarium environment, the deep-dwelling species in this exhibit include mushroom soft coral, the predatory tunicate, the spiny king crab, and many others—a total of 40 to 60 species at any one time. In addition, daily video programs present live broadcasts from a remote submersible vehicle exploring the depths of Monterey Bay.

Debuting at the Monterey Bay Aquarium in spring 2000 was the **Splash Zone: Rock and Reef Homes** exhibit, designed particularly for families with small children. On display: some 50 species, from leafy sea dragons to black-footed penguins. An interactive tour leads through two different shoreline habitats. Special activities include crawl-through coral reef structures, "make a wave" water play, dress-up costumes, and sea creature puppets. New exhibits in 2001 included **Saving Seahorses**, exploring the survival challenges of these unique fish that are so popular in traditional Asian medicine, and **Mysteries of the Deep,** an exhibit of more than 40 species of animals collected from the depths of submarine Monterey Canyon just offshore. Recent exhibits included Jellies: Living Art. Throughout the aquarium, also expect several rotating special exhibits each year.

Information

Advance tickets are highly recommended, especially in summer. Call 831/648-4937 or, from within California, 800/756-3737. You can also order tickets via Ticketweb at www.mbayaq.org. If you purchase tickets more than 10 days in advance, they can be mailed to you. Otherwise, you can order tickets online as late as 7 A.M. on the day you arrive (assuming they're available); at the aquarium, you won't need to wait in line. Simply present your email confirmation receipt at the will call/group entrance window and walk on in. You also can come on a just-show-up-and-take-your-chances basis—not advisable in summer.

The aquarium is open daily except Christmas, 10 A.M.–6 P.M. (from 9:30 A.M. in summer). At last report, admission was $15.95 for adults; $13.95 for youths age 13 to 17, students with college ID, seniors, and active-duty military; $7.95 for children ages 3 to 12 and disabled visitors; and free for tots under 3.

Free self-guided tour scripts with maps, also available in Spanish, French, German, and Japanese, are available at the aquarium's information desk, along with current "special event" details, including the exhibit feeding schedule. All aquarium facilities and exhibits are accessible to the disabled; an explanatory brochure is available at the information desk. Taped audio tours are available for rent (for a small fee). Docent-guided aquarium tours and tours of the aquarium's research and operations facilities are also available for a fee. (Guided tours for school groups are free, however.) For group tour information and reservations, call 831/648-4860.

The aquarium's restaurant and gift/bookstores are worthwhile. The **Portola Café and Restaurant** has very good food and an oyster bar—the very idea surely a shock to the aquarium's permanent residents—and is fine for a glass of wine at sunset (open 10 A.M.–5 P.M.). Along with good books, educational toys, and nature art, the aquarium gift shops have some touristy bric-a-brac and forgettable edibles like chocolate sardines.

For additional information, contact Monterey Bay Aquarium, 886 Cannery Row, in Monterey, 831/648-4800 or 831/648-4888 (24-hour recorded information). Or visit the "E-Quarium" anytime for virtual tours and information, www.mbayaq.org. For more information about the bay, the **Monterey Bay National Marine Sanctuary** headquarters and information center is near the aquarium at 299 Foam St. (at D St.), 831/647-4201, www.mbnms.nos.noaa.gov.

Avoid the worst of the human crush and come in the off-season (weekdays if at all possible). If you do come in summer, avoid the traffic jams by riding Monterey's WAVE shuttle, which operates from late May into September.

CANNERY ROW AND FISHERMAN'S WHARF

Today the strip is reminiscent of Steinbeck's Cannery Row only when you consider how tourists are packed in here come summertime: like sardines.

Of all the places the Nobel Prize–winning author immortalized, only "Doc's" marine lab at 800 Cannery Row still stands unchanged—a humble brown shack almost as unassuming as it was in 1948, the year marine biologist Ed Ricketts met his end quite suddenly, his car smashed by the Del Monte Express train just a few blocks away. Today the lab is owned and preserved as a historic site by the city and is open for guided public tours from time to time.

Wing Chong Market, Steinbecked as "Lee Chong's Heavenly Flower Grocery," is across the street at 835 Cannery Row and now holds a variety of shops. The fictional "La Ida Cafe" cathouse still survives, too, in actuality the most famous saloon on the Monterey Peninsula, **Kalisa's,** at 851 Cannery Row, 831/644-9316. Billed as "A Cosmopolitan Gourmet Place," Kalisa's, since the 1950s, has really been an eclectic people's eatery. Steinbeck personally preferred the beer milkshake.

Nowadays along Cannery Row, food and wine are becoming attractions in their own right. The new, 10,000-square-foot **Culinary Center of Monterey,** 625 Cannery Row, Ste. #200, 831/333-2133, www.culinarycenterofmonterey.com,

© ROBERT HOLMES/CALTOUR

Cannery Row

bills itself as a "Fantasy Land for Foodies." Here food lovers will find a complete food and wine center offering classes in just about everything—from Artisan Breads, Chocolate Desserts, and Cooking with Beer to Heart Healthy Cuisine and Sushi Party. The latter might be particularly inspiring after a tour through the Monterey Bay Aquarium. (Think about it.) Gourmet takeout is also available, the choices including an in-house bakery, appetizer bar (including local wines and microbrews), and cheese market. Inside the old Monterey Canning Company cannery, 700 Cannery Row, wine enthusiasts can enjoy the **Monterey County Wine Country Museum** and perhaps follow their museum visit with wine tasting, either at **A Taste of Monterey,** 831/646-5446, which offers tastings of regional wines as well as local produce, **Bargetto Winery** downstairs, 831/373-4053, or **Baywood Cellars** across from the Monterey Plaza Hotel, 831/645-9035.

Wine tasting or no, adults might escort the kids to the nearby **Monterey County Youth Museum** (M.Y. Museum), 601 Wave St., 831/649-6444 or 831/649-6446, www.mymuseum.org, a hands-on adventure full of interactive exhibits on science, art, and more. The museum is open Mon., Tues., Thurs., Fri., and Sat. 10 A.M.–5 P.M., Sunday noon to 5 P.M. Admission is $5.50.

For more information about Cannery Row, or to seriously trace Steinbeck's steps through the local landscape, check in at the Cannery Row Foundation's **Cannery Row Welcome Center** in the green railroad car at 65 Prescott Ave., 831/372-8512 or 831/373-1902. Guided tours of Cannery Row can also be arranged there. The free and widely available ***Official Cannery Row Visitors Guide*** is well done, historically, and quite helpful. For other information, see www.canneryrow.com.

Fisherman's Wharf

Tacky and tawdry, built up and beat up, Fisherman's Wharf is no longer a working wharf by any account. Still, a randy ramshackle charm more honest than Cannery Row surrounds this 1846 pier, full of cheap shops, food stalls, decent restaurants, and stand-up bars indiscriminately frosted with gull guano and putrid fish scraps (the latter presumably leftovers from the 50-cent bags tourists buy to feed the sea lions). Built of stone by enslaved natives, convicts, and military deserters when Monterey was Alta California's capital, Fisherman's Wharf was origi-

SEAFOOD WATCH

Much of the work done by the **Monterey Bay Aquarium** is not necessarily visible to visitors. Since the mission of the aquarium is to "inspire conservation of the oceans," public education and scientific research are high priorities.

Particularly useful for seafood fans, and accessible via the aquarium's website, www .mbayaq.org, is its **"Seafood Watch—A Guide for Consumers,"** a regularly updated listing designed to help us all make enlightened choices about the fish and seafood we eat. On the aquarium's "avoid" list at last report, for example, were bluefin tuna from the Atlantic and the Pacific; Chilean seabass; Atlantic cod; lingcod; orange roughy; Pacific red snapper and other rockfish; all sharks; and all farmed salmon, shrimp, and prawns. Consumer guidance in support of sustainable fisheries worldwide is available as a wallet-sized card—to order, call 831/647-6873—which can also be downloaded from the website as a PDF file.

Specific research initiatives sponsored by the Monterey Bay Aquarium include the Sea Otter Research and Conservation Program (SORAC) and the Tuna Research and Conservation Center (TRCC), the latter in conjunction with Stanford University's Hopkins Marine Station. The Monterey Bay Aquarium Research Institute (MBARI) at Moss Landing initiates dozens of bay-related projects each year and is also a full research partner in the Monterey Bay National Marine Sanctuary's Research Program. More information on all of these is available via the website.

nally a pier for cargo schooners. Later used by whalers and Italian American fishing crews to unload their catches, the wharf today is bright and bustling, full of eateries and eaters. Come early in the morning to beat the crowds, then launch yourself on a summer sightseeing tour of Monterey Bay or a winter whale-watching cruise.

MONTEREY STATE HISTORIC PARK

Monterey State Historic Park, with headquarters at 20 Custom House Plaza, 831/649-7118, www.mbay.net/-mshp, protects and preserves some fine historic adobes, most of which were surrounded at one time by enclosed gardens and walls draped with bougainvillea vines. Definitely worth seeing are the Cooper-Molera, Stevenson, and Larkin homes, as well as Casa Soberanes.

The park is open daily 10 A.M.–4 P.M. (until 5 P.M. in summer) and closed Christmas, Thanksgiving, and New Year's Day. A small all-day admission fee ($5 adults) gets you into all buildings open to visitors. Guided tours of particular buildings are offered, as are general guided walking tours. Schedules vary, so ask about current tour times. You can also design your own tours or organize group tours; call for details. It's also pos-

sible to reserve regular guided tours; reservations must be made at least 15 days in advance. To reserve or to change plans, see the park's website or call 831/649-7118 on Mon. 9 A.M.–5 P.M. or on Wed. or Fri. 9 A.M.–2:30 P.M. Reservations are "confirmed" only when approved by the park office; call to check. Fees must be paid at least 24 hours in advance of the tour. To poke around on your own, pick up the free *Path of History* self-guided walking tour map before setting out. Available at most of the buildings, the brochure details the park's adobes as well as dozens of other historic sights near the bay and downtown. Also stop by the Monterey State Historic Park Visitor Center at the Stanton Center.

Stanton Center and the Maritime Museum

A good place to start any historic exploration is the colossal Stanton Center at 5 Custom House Plaza. Inside you'll find the new **Maritime Museum Visitor Center,** where staff can answer questions about the park. They'll also direct you to the center's **theater,** which screens a 17-minute park-produced film about area history—a good way to quickly grasp the area's cultural context. Most walking tours of the park (led by state park staff) also leave from the Stanton Center. Buy guided walking tour tickets here, as well as tickets for the adjacent maritime museum. The Stanton Visitor Center is open seven days a week, 10 A.M.–5 P.M. For state historic park information, call 831/649-7118 or try the web at www.mbay.net/-mshp. For visitor information, call 831/649-1770.

Don't miss the Monterey History and Art Association's **Maritime Museum of Monterey,** 831/372-2608, www.mntmh.org, which houses an ever-expanding local maritime artifact collection—compasses, bells, ship models, the original Fresnel lens from the Point Sur lighthouse, and much more—as well as the association's maritime research library, an acclaimed ship photography collection, and a scrimshaw collection. The museum's permanent exhibits, many interactive, cover local maritime history, from the first explorers and cannery days to the present. Recent special exhibits included World War II: The Pacific Theatre and the Sites and Citizens exhibition of 109 black-and-white Robert Lewis photographs from the 1950s. The museum is open Tues.–Sun. 11 A.M.–5 P.M., closed Thanksgiving, Christmas, and New Year's Day. Admission is $5 adults, $2.50 seniors and youth, free for children under 12. Guided group tours are available by reservation.

Custom House and Pacific House

On July 7, 1846, Commodore John Drake Sloat raised the Stars and Stripes here at Alvarado and Waterfront Streets, commemorating California's passage into American rule. The Custom House Building is the oldest government building on the West Coast—and quite multinational, since it has flown at one time or another the flags of Spain, Mexico, and the United States. Until 1867, customs duties from foreign ships were collected here. Stop by to inspect typical 19th-century cargo.

Once a hotel, then a military supply depot, the building at Scott and Calle Principal was called Pacific House when it housed a public tavern in 1850. Later came law offices, a newspaper, a ballroom for "dashaway" temperance dances, and various small shops. Today the newly renovated Pacific House includes an excellent museum of Native American artifacts (with special

attention given to the Ohlone people) upstairs and interactive historical exhibits covering the city's Spanish whaling industry, pioneer/logging periods, California statehood, and more. The Pacific House museum is wheelchair accessible, with Braille interpretive materials and video and audio recordings available. The museum's Memory Garden connects, via wheelchair accessible gate and pathway, to the city's Sensory Garden.

Larkin House and Others

Built of adobe and wood in 1835 by Yankee merchant Thomas Oliver Larkin, later the only U.S. consul in the territory during Mexican rule, this home at Jefferson and Calle Principal became the American consulate, then later military headquarters for Kearny, Mason, and Sherman. A fine pink Monterey adobe and the model for the local Colonial style, Larkin House is furnished with more than $6 million in antiques and period furnishings.

The home and headquarters of William Tecumseh Sherman is next door; it's now a museum focusing on both Larkin and Sherman. Around the corner at 540 Calle Principal, another Larkin building, the **House of the Four Winds,** is a small adobe built in the 1830s and named for its weathervane. The **Gutierrez Adobe,** a typical middle-class Monterey "double adobe" home at 580 and 590 Calle Principal, was built in 1841 and later donated to the state by the Monterey Foundation.

Cooper-Molera Adobe

The *casa grande* (big house) at 508 Munras Avenue, a long, two-story, Monterey Colonial adobe, was finished in pinkish plaster when constructed in 1829 by Captain John Bautista Rogers Cooper for his young bride, Encarnación (of California's influential Vallejo clan). The 2.5-acre complex, which includes a neighboring home, two barns, gardens, farm animals, and visitor center, has been restored to its 19th-century authenticity. Downstairs rooms in all buildings are wheelchair accessible, as are restrooms and the Victorian garden picnic area. Stop by the **Cooper Store** here, run by the nonprofit Old Monterey Preservation Society, to sample the wares—unique books, antique reproductions, and other specialty items representing the mid-1800s.

Robert Louis Stevenson House

The sickly Scottish storyteller and poet lived at the French Hotel adobe boardinghouse at 530 Houston Street for several months in 1879 while courting his American love (and later wife) Fanny Osbourne. In a sunny upstairs room is the small portable desk at which he reputedly wrote *Treasure Island.* While in Monterey, Stevenson collected *Treasure* material on his convalescing coast walks and worked on "Amateur Immigrant," "The Old Pacific," "Capital," and "Vendetta of the West." He also worked as a reporter for the local newspaper—a job engineered by his friends, who, in order to keep the flat-broke Stevenson going, secretly paid the paper $2 a week to cover his wages. The restored downstairs is stuffed with period furniture. Several upstairs rooms are dedicated to Stevenson's memorabilia, paintings, and first editions. Local rumor has it that a 19th-century ghost—Stevenson's spirit, according to a previous caretaker—lives upstairs in the children's room.

Casa Soberanes

Also known as the House of the Blue Gate, this is an 1830 Mediterranean-style adobe with a tile roof and cantilevered balcony, hidden by thick hedges at 336 Pacific. Home to the Soberanes family from 1860 to 1922, it was later donated to the state. Take the tour—the furnishings here are an intriguing combination of Mexican folk art and period pieces from China and New England—or just stop to appreciate the garden and its whalebone-and-abalone-bordered flowerbeds, some encircled by century-old wine bottles buried bottoms up.

California's First Theater

First a sailors' saloon and lodging house, this small 1844 weathered wood and adobe building at Scott and Pacific was built by the English sailor Jack Swan. It was commandeered by soldiers in 1848 for a makeshift theater, and it later—with a lookout station added to the roof—became a whaling station. Wander through the place and take a trip into the bawdy past, complete with the requisite painting of a reclining nude over the bar, brass bar rail and cuspidor, oil lamps, ancient booze bottles, and old theatrical props and paraphernalia. A modern postscript is the garden out back.

Today, the Troupers of the Gold Coast present melodramas here year-round on Friday and Saturday nights and Wednesday through Saturday in July and August; for information and reservations, call 831/375-4916.

Boston Store

Built by Thomas Larkin at the corner of Scott and Olivier as part of his business empire, this two-story chalk and adobe building once known as Casa del Oro (House of Gold) served a number of purposes. At one time or another it was a barracks for American troops, a general store (Joseph Boston & Co.), a saloon, and a private residence. Rumor has it that this "house of gold" was also once a mint or that (when a saloon) it accepted gold dust in payment for drinks—thus the name. These days it's the Boston Store once more, operated by the nonprofit Historic Garden League and themed as if in the 1850s. Antiques and reproductions, including handcrafted Russian toys and games, are on sale here. The garden league also operates the **Picket Fence** shop. For more information, call 831/649-3364.

Whaling Station

The old two-story adobe Whaling Station at 391 Decatur Street near the Custom House, now maintained and operated by the Junior League of Monterey County, was a flophouse for Portuguese whalers in the 1850s. Tours are sometimes available (call the main state park number for information) and include access to the walled garden. The junior league also makes the house and gardens available for weddings and other special events; call 831/375-5356 for details. Whale lovers, walk softly—the sidewalk in front of the house is made of whalebone.

California's First Brick House

This building nearby at 351 Decatur was started by Gallant Duncan Dickenson in 1847, built with bricks fashioned and fired in Monterey. The

MONTEREY'S DISTINCTIVE ARCHITECTURE

Monterey State Historic Park's **Larkin House,** a two-story redwood frame with low shingled roof, adobe walls, and wooden balconies skirting the second floor, and the **Cooper-Molera Adobe** are both good examples of the "Monterey colonial" architectural style—a marriage of Yankee woodwork and Mexican adobe—that evolved here. Most traditional Monterey adobes have south-facing patios to absorb sun in winter and a northern veranda to catch cool summer breezes. On the first floor were the kitchen, storerooms, dining room, living room, and sometimes even a ballroom. The bedrooms on the second floor were entered from outside stairways, a tradition subsequently abandoned. Also distinctive in Monterey are the "swept gardens"—dirt courtyards surrounded by colorful flowers under pine canopies—which were an adaptation to the originally barren home sites.

That so many fine adobes remain in Monterey today is mostly due to genteel local poverty; until recently, few developers with grandiose plans came knocking on the door. For an even better look at traditional local adobes and their gardens, come to the **Monterey Historic Adobe and Garden Tour** in April, when many private adobes are open for public tours.

---

builder left for the goldfields before the house was finished, so the home—the first brick house in California—and 60,000 bricks were auctioned off by the sheriff in 1851 for just over $1,000.

MUSEUMS AND HISTORIC SITES

Colton Hall

The Reverend Walter Colton, Monterey's first American alcalde, or local magistrate, built this impressive, pillared "Carmel Stone" structure at 351 Pacific (between Madison and Jefferson), 831/646-5640, as a schoolhouse and public hall. Colton and Robert Semple published the first American newspaper in California here, cranking up the presses on August 15, 1846. California's constitutional convention took place here during September and October of 1849, and the state constitution was drafted upstairs in Colton Hall. Now a city museum, Colton Hall is open daily 10 A.M.–noon and 1–5 P.M. Closed Thanksgiving, Christmas, and New Year's Day.

Next door is the 1854 **Monterey jail** (entrance on Dutra Street), a dreary, slot-windowed prison once home to gentleman-bandit Tiburcio Vasquez and killer Anastacio Garcia, who "went to God on a rope" pulled by his buddies.

Monterey Museum of Art

The fine Monterey Museum of Art at the Civic Center, across the street from Colton Hall at 559 Pacific, 831/372-5477, www.montereyart.org, offers an excellent collection of Western art, including bronze cowboy-and-horse statues by Charles M. Russell. The Fine Arts collection includes folk art, high-concept graphics, photography, paintings, sculpture, and other contemporary art in changing exhibits. Open Wed.–Sat. 11 A.M.–5 P.M., Sun. 1–4 P.M., closed holidays. Admission $5.

An impressive Monterey-style adobe, the amazing **La Mirada,** the onetime Castro Adobe and Frank Work Estate at 720 Via Mirada, 831/372-5477, is now home to the museum's Asian art and artifacts collection. The home itself is exquisite, located in one of Monterey's oldest neighborhoods. The original adobe portion was the residence of Jose Castro, one of the most prominent citizens in California during the Mexican period. Purchased in 1919 by Gouverneur Morris—author/playwright and descendant of the same-named Revolutionary War figure—the adobe was restored and expanded, with the addition of a two-story wing and huge drawing room, to host artists and Hollywood stars. The Dart Wing, added in 1993, was designed by architect Charles Moore.

These days, the 2.5-acre estate overlooking El Estero still reflects the sensibilities of bygone eras. The house itself is furnished in antiques and early California art, and the gardens are perhaps even more elegant, at least in season, with a walled rose garden (old and new varieties), traditional herb garden (medicinal, culinary, fragrant, and "beautifying"), and a rhododendron garden with more than 300 camellias, azaleas, rhododendrons, and other flowering perennials and trees. Changing exhibits are displayed in four contemporary galleries that complement the original estate. La Mirada is open Wed.–Sat. 11 A.M.–5 P.M., Sun. 1–4 P.M. Admission is $5.

Monterey Institute of International Studies

This prestigious, private, and nonprofit graduate-level college, headquartered at 425 Van Buren, 831/647-4100t, www.miis.edu, specializes in foreign-language instruction. Students here prepare for careers in international business and government, and in language translation and interpretation. Fascinating and unique is the school's 200-seat auditorium, set up for simultaneous translations of up to four languages. Visitors are welcome Mon.–Fri. 8:30 A.M.–5 P.M., and most of the institute's programs—including guest lectures—are open to the public.

Presidio of Monterey

One of the nation's oldest military posts, the Presidio of Monterey is the physical focal point of most early local history, though the original complex, founded by Portolá in 1770, was located in the area now defined by Webster, Fremont, Abrego, and El Estero Streets. History buffs, note the commemorative monuments to Portolá, Junípero Serra, Vizcaíno, and Commodore Sloat, plus late-in-the-game acknowledgement of native peoples. (When Lighthouse Avenue was widened through here, most of what remained of a 2,000-year-old Rumsen village was destroyed, leaving only a ceremonial rain rock, a rock mortar for grinding acorns, and an ancient burial ground marked by a tall wooden cross.) Also here: incredible panoramic views of Monterey Bay.

The new **Presidio Museum,** in Building 113, Cpl. Ewing Rd., 831/646-3456, once a tack house, is now filled with cavalry artifacts, uniforms, pistols, cannons, photos, posters, and dioramas about local history, beginning with Native Americans and the arrival of the Spanish and continuing into Monterey's Mexican then American periods. The museum is open Thurs.–Sat. 10 A.M.–4 P.M. and Sun. 1–4 P.M. Call for driving directions. Pick up a copy of the Presidio's *Walk Through History* brochure at the Command Historian's Archives office, 1759 Lewis Rd., Ste. 209, 831/242-5536, to visit the earthen ruins and cannons of the **Fort Mervine** battlements; they were built by Commodore Sloat and dismantled in 1852. Fort Mervine's log huts were built during the Civil War.

The Presidio's main gate at Pacific and Artillery Streets leads to the **Defense Language Institute,** 831/242-5000, http://pom-www.army.mil.

Royal Presidio Chapel

Originally established as a mission by Father Junípero Serra in June 1770, this building at 555 Church Street near Figueroa became the Royal Presidio Chapel of San Carlos Borromeo when the mission was relocated to Carmel. The chapel was rebuilt from stone in 1791, and after secularization in 1835, it became the San Carlos Cathedral, a parish church. The cathedral's interior walls are decorated with Native American and Mexican folk art. Above, the upper gable facade is the first European art made in California, a chalk-carved Virgin of Guadalupe tucked into a shell niche. To get here, turn onto Church Street just after Camino El Estero ends at Fremont—a district once known as Washerwoman's Gulch.

RECREATION

Beaches and Parks

The 18-mile **Monterey Peninsula Recreation Trail** is a spectacular local feature—a walking and cycling path that stretches from Asilomar State Beach in Pacific Grove to Castroville. Scenic bay views are offered all along the way, as the trail saunters past landmarks including Point Pinos Lighthouse, Lovers Point, the Monterey Bay Aquarium, Cannery Row, Fisherman's Wharf, Custom House Plaza, and Del Monte Beach. The 14-acre **Monterey Beach** is not very impressive (day use only), but you can stroll the rocky headlands on the peninsula's north side without interruption, traveling the Monterey

the Monterey Bay Recreation Trail

Peninsula Recreation Trail past the **Pacific Grove Marine Gardens Fish Refuge** and **Asilomar State Beach,** with tidepools, rugged shorelines, and thick carpets of brightly flowered (but non-native) ice plants.

For ocean swimming, head south to **Carmel River State Beach,** which includes a lagoon and bird sanctuary, or to **China Cove** at Point Lobos. **El Estero Park** in town—bounded by Del Monte Avenue, Fremont Boulevard, and Camino El Estero—has a small horseshoe-shaped lagoon with ducks, pedal boat rentals, picnic tables, a par course, hiking and biking trails, and the **Dennis the Menace Playground,** designed by cartoonist Hank Ketcham. (Particularly fun here is the hedge maze.) Also at El Estero is the area's first **French Consulate,** built in 1830, moved here in 1931, and now the local visitor information center. The **Don Dahvee Park** on Munras Avenue (one leg of local motel row) is a secret oasis of picnic tables with a hiking/biking trail.

For information on local parks and beaches, contact the **Monterey Peninsula Regional Park District,** 831/372-3196, www.mprpd.org.

Jacks Peak County Park

The highest point on the peninsula (but not *that* high, at only 1,068 feet) and the focal point of a 525-acre regional park, Jacks Peak offers great views, good hiking and horseback trails, and picnicking, plus fascinating flora and wildlife. Named after the land's former owner—Scottish immigrant and entrepreneur David Jacks, best known for his local dairies and their "Monterey Jack" cheese—the park features

marked trails, including the self-guided **Skyline Nature Trail.** Almost 8.5 miles of riding and hiking trails wind through Monterey pine forests to breathtaking ridge-top views. From Jacks Peak amid the Monterey pines, you'll have spectacular views of both Monterey Bay and Carmel Valley—and possibly the pleasure of spotting American kestrels or red-shouldered hawks soaring on the currents. The park's first 55 acres were purchased by the Nature Conservancy, and the rest were bought up with county, federal, and private funds. To get here, take Olmstead County Road (from Highway 68 near the Monterey Airport) for two miles.

Biking

Get some fresh air and see the sights by bicycle. Either bring your own or rent one at any of several local outfits. Or tool around on a moped, available for rent through **Monterey Moped Adventures,** 1250 Del Monte Ave., 831/373-2696, which also rents bikes—tandem bikes, bikes with child trailers, and beach cruisers, plus the standards—and offers ample parking and easy access to the bayside bike/hike trail. Bike rentals are also the specialty of **Bay Bikes,** 640 Wave St., 831/646-9090, which has 21-speed, fat-tire bikes. You can rent in-line skates here, too, for around $15 a day. For more on bike rentals, see below.

Water Sports

Another way to "see" Monterey Bay is by getting right in it, by kayak. **Monterey Bay Kayaks,** 693 Del Monte Ave., 831/649-5357, offers tours—bay tours and sunset tours, even trips into Elkhorn Slough and along the Salinas River—as well as classes and rentals of both open and closed kayaks. Wetsuits, paddling jackets, life jackets, water shoes, and a half-hour of on-land instruction are included in the basic all-day rental price of $30 or so. **AB Seas Kayaks,** 32 Cannery Row #5, 831/647-0147 or 888/371-6035, www.montereykayak.com, offers similar services at similar prices, including guided wildlife and birding tours. **Adventures by the Sea** also offers kayak rentals and tours—in addition to bike rentals (bikes de-

MONTEREY PENINSULA GOLFING

Golfers from around the globe make a point of arriving on the Monterey Peninsula, clubs in tow, at some time in their lives. The undisputed golf capital of the world, the Pebble Beach area between Carmel and Pacific Grove is the most famous, largely due to "The Crosby," which is now the AT&T Pebble Beach National Pro Am Golf Tournament. Making headlines in 1999 was news that the Pebble Beach Company and its four world-class courses had been sold to an investor group—Clint Eastwood, Richard Ferris, Arnold Palmer, and Peter Ueberroth—for $820 million.

It may cost a pretty penny—the greens fee at Pebble Beach Golf Links, for example, is more than $350—but the public is welcome at private **Pebble Beach Golf Links,** the **Links at Spanish Bay, Spyglass Hill Golf Course,** the **Peter Hay Par 3,** and the **Del Monte Golf Course** (in Monterey), all affiliated with The Lodge at Pebble Beach on 17 Mile Dr., 831/624-3811 or 831/624-6611, or 800/654-9300, www.pebblebeach.com. (Fees at Del Monte are $90 plus cart.) Also open to the public are the **Poppy Hills Golf Course,** 3200 Lopez Rd. (just off 17 Mile Dr.), 831/624-2035, designed by Robert Trent Jones, Jr.; the **Pacific Grove Municipal Golf Links,** 77 Asilomar Ave., 831/648-3177, great for beginners and reasonably priced; the **Bayonet** and **Black Horse Golf Courses** on North-South at former Fort Ord, 831/899-7271; and the Robert Trent Jones (Sr. and Jr.) **Laguna Seca Golf Club** on York Rd. between Monterey and Salinas, 831/373-3701 or 888/524-8629.

Though Pebble Beach is world-renowned for its golf courses and golf events, Carmel Valley and vicinity has nearly as many courses—most of them private in the country-club model, most recognizing reciprocal access agreements with other clubs. The **Rancho Cañada Golf Club,** about a mile east of Hwy. 1 via Carmel Valley Rd., 831/624-0111 or 800/536-9459, is open to the public, however. As part of accommodations packages, nonmembers can golf at **Quail Lodge Resort & Golf Club,** 8000 Valley Greens Dr., 831/624 2888, and at **Carmel Valley Ranch,** 1 Old Ranch Rd. in Carmel, 831/625-9500, which features an 18-hole Pete Dye course.

---

livered to your hotel room and picked up again at no charge), bike trips (including a Point Pinos Lighthouse tour), in-line skate rentals, and custom-prepared beach parties. Offices are located at 299 Cannery Row, 831/372-1807 or 831/648-7236.

Carrera Sailing, 66 Fisherman's Wharf (at Randy's Fishing Trips), 831/375-0648, offers the comfortable 30-foot sloop *Carrera* for nature tours, sunset cruises, and chartered sails. **Scenic Bay Sailing School and Yacht Charters,** 831/372-6603 or 831/625-6394, offers sailing lessons and is also willing to sail off into the sunset.

Other boating companies also offer bay tours (including cocktail cruises), winter whale-watching, and fishing trips (discount coupons often available at local visitor information centers). Good choices include **Monterey Sportfishing & Whale Watching Cruises,** 96 Fisherman's Wharf No. 1, 831/372-2203 or

800/200-2203; **Randy's Fishing Trips,** 66 Fisherman's Wharf #1, 831/372-7440 or 800/251-7440, which also offers Point Sur fishing charters; and **Chris' Fishing Trips,** 48 Fisherman's Wharf #1, 831/375-5951, which offers a fleet of four big boats, including the 70-foot *New Holiday.* **Sanctuary Cruises** at Fisherman's Wharf, 831/917-1042, www.sanctuarycruises.com, offers whale-watching aboard the *Princess of Whales,* a double-decked power catamaran that holds up to 149 people.

Another way to see the bay is to get a fish-eye view. An excellent assistant is the **Monterey Dive Center,** 225 Cannery Row, 831/656-0454 or 800/607-2822, www.mbdc.to, which offers rentals and lessons, chartered dive trips, guided dives and snorkeling, and night dives. The **Aquarius Dive Shop,** at two Monterey locations—32 Cannery Row, 831/375-6605, and 2040 Del Monte Ave., 831/375-1933, www.aquariusdivers.com—is another best bet for rentals, instruction, equipment, and repairs. Aquarius also offers guided underwater tours (specializing in photography and video) and can provide tips on worthwhile dives worldwide. If you primarily need a ride out into the bay, **Monterey Express Diving Charters,** 32 Cannery Row, 831/659-3009 or 888/422-2999, www.montereyexpress.com, will take you there.

Adrenaline junkies can get a bird's-eye view of the bay by throwing themselves out of an airplane with **Skydive Monterey Bay,** 3261 Imjin Rd. in Marina, 831/384-3483 or 888/229-5867, www.skydivemontereybay.com. No experience is necessary; after a bit of instruction, you'll make a tandem jump harnessed to a veteran skydiver. The cost is $199. The company is open daily, year-round.

SAND DUNE CITIES

The sand-dune city of **Marina** was once the service center supporting Fort Ord. The U.S. Army base is now closed, replaced by the fledgling campus of California State University at Monterey Bay. So Marina, the peninsula's most recently incorporated city (1975), is also being transformed. Marina now boasts a new municipal airport, sports arena, and state beach popular for hang-gliding and surfing. On the ground, explore the nearby dunes; they're serene in a simple, stark way, with fragile shrubs and wildflowers. Some are quite rare, so don't pick. The new **Fort Ord Dunes State Park,** 831/649-2836, once part of Fort Ord, features a four-mile stretch of beachfront. Head out to the Marina Municipal Airport to visit the two-acre **Sculpture Habitat at Marina,** 711 Neeson Rd., 831/384-2100, a collection of original sculptures by both local and world-renowned artists scattered throughout the grasslands, live oaks, and chaparral shrubs. Handicapped accessible. Check it out at www.sculpturepark-atmarina.org.

Seaside and **Sand City,** to Marina's north, share "ownership" of former Fort Ord and the new CSU Monterey campus—and all three cities, the peninsula's traditionally low-rent neighborhoods, are still feuding with more affluent Mon-

terey, Pacific Grove, and Carmel over future development plans. Opponents contend that proposed new hotels, golf courses, conference and shopping centers, and housing developments will adversely affect limited area water supplies, roads and other public infrastructure, and the environment.

But no one seems to object to the new **California State University Monterey** campus—the school's mascot is the sea otter—which has to date taken over some 2,000 acres at Fort Ord (of the 13,065 set aside for it) and is expected to grow to a student population of 13,000 to 15,000 by 2015. The emphasis at California's 21st state university campus is fairly unconventional. The focus here is on mastering subjects, rather than simply amassing course credits. Students are expected to become fluent in a second language as well as fully computer literate and to engage in community service work, along with mastering more than a dozen other essential skills. For information about and reservations (required) for 45-minute individual tours of campus, usually offered Mon.–Fri. at 10 A.M. and 2 P.M. and Saturday at 10 A.M., call 831/582-3518. Also worth exploring are some 50 miles of trails open to the public—now known as **Fort Ord Public Lands.** The 16,000 acres, administered by the U.S. Bureau of Land Management, are just about the last truly wild areas remaining on the Monterey Peninsula. Two fishable lakes and picnic areas are also available. As fun as it is to be out and about in these wide-open spaces, hikers, bikers, and horseback riders should take care to stick only to authorized trails; military explosives and other hazards are found in still-restricted areas, and habitat restoration is underway. Some 35 rare and endangered species inhabit Fort Ord Public Lands. For current trail information, contact the BLM field office in Hollister, 831/630-5000, www.ca.blm.gov/hollister.

Head inland on Canyon del Rey Road to **Work Memorial Park** and the nearby **Frog Pond Natural Area** (entrance in the willows near the Del Rey Oaks City Hall), a seasonal freshwater marsh home to birds and the elusive inch-long Pacific tree frog. Or take Del Monte

SUCH A DEAL: SEASIDE AND MARINA

The secret may no longer be much of a secret, but just in case: People who live on the Monterey Peninsula know that prices for both food and lodging can be considerably lower in the "sand dune cities" of Seaside and Marina.

Ethnic eateries abound, most of them quite good. In Seaside, the wonderful **Fishwife Seafood Cafe,** 789 Trinity (at Fremont), 831/394-2027, is everyone's favorite for seafood. The Fishwife offers quick and interesting seafood, pastas, and other California cuisine standards with a Caribbean accent, fresh Salinas Valley produce, and housemade desserts. (There's another Fishwife in Pacific Grove near Asilomar.) For more exceptional seafood, consider the Salvadoran **El Migueleño,** also in Seaside at 1066 Broadway, 831/899-2199. The house specialty, Playa Azul, combines six different kinds of seafood with ranchera sauce, white wine, and mushrooms, served with white rice and beans. Yum.

But there are more nationalities to sample in Seaside. For Chinese food, there's **Chef Lee's Mandarin House,** 2031 N. Fremont St., 831/375-9551. Or head for University Plaza at 1760 N. Fremont, not all that aesthetic but something of a haven for ethnic eateries. Best bets include **Fuji Japanese Restaurant and Sushi Bar,** 831/899-9988, with good lunch specials; **Orient Restaurant,** 831/394-2223, for Chinese and Vietnamese specialties, notably an abundance of soup and noodle dishes; and **Barn Thai,** 831/394-2996, where a great lunch goes for about $5.

Marina offers restaurant possibilities, too, including **Café Pronto! Italian Grill,** 330-H Reser-

vation Rd., 831/883-1207, where pastas, pizzas, and seafood specialties star.

In accommodations, less expensive choices in Seaside include the **Thunderbird Motel,** 1933 Fremont Blvd., 831/394-6797, fax 831/394-5568, with some rates under $50. Good rooms are available for $50–100 at the **Best Western Magic Carpet Lodge,** 1875 Fremont Blvd., 831/899-4221, fax 831/899-3377; the **Pacific Best Inn,** 1141 Fremont, 831/899-1881, fax 831/392-1300; the **Seaside Inn,** 1986 Del Monte Blvd., 831/394-4041, fax 831/394-2806; and the **Sandcastle Inn,** 1101 La Salle Ave., 831/394-6556, fax 831/394-1578.

For something more stylish, nestled in next to two fine golf courses, try Seaside's **SunBay Suites,** 5200 Coe Ave., 831/394-0136, fax 831/394-0221, with most apartment-style suites $100–150; weekly and monthly rates are available.

The newest resort on the Monterey Peninsula is in Marina—the plush 30-room **Marina Dunes Resort** in the dunes just west of Hwy. 1 at 3295 Dunes Dr., 831/883-9478 or 877/944-3863, fax 831/883-9477, www.marinadunes.com. Rooms and suites in these beachfront bungalows feature California King beds, oversized furnishings, gas fireplaces, fully tiled baths with pedestal sinks, and either a private patio or balcony. Extras include heated pool, lap pool, hydrotherapy, and complete spa services—plus the opportunity to stroll on the beach, for miles in either direction. Rates are $150 and up. The lodge building offers meeting facilities and the **A.J. Spurs** restaurant and tapas bar.

Avenue off Highway 1 to **Del Monte Beach,** one of the least-bothered beaches of Monterey Bay (no facilities).

Del Monte Avenue also takes you past the **U.S. Naval Post-Graduate School,** 831/656-2441, www.nps.navy.mil, a navy preflight training school during World War II and now a military university offering doctorates. It's housed on the grounds of the stately 1880 Spanish-style **Del Monte Hotel.** The state's oldest large resort and queen of American watering holes for California's nouveau riche, the

Del Monte was built by Charles Crocker and the rest of the railroading Big Four. You can tour the grounds from 8 A.M.–4:30 P.M. daily. Downstairs in the old hotel is the school's **museum,** with memorabilia from the Del Monte's heyday (open Mon.–Fri. 11 A.M.–2 P.M., closed on major holidays).

Worth stopping for in Seaside is the tranquil **Monterey Peninsula Buddhist Temple,** 1155 Noche Buena, 831/394-0119, surrounded by beautiful Asian-style gardens and carp-filled ponds. Come in May for the bonsai show.

For the present at least, accommodations are considerably less expensive here than elsewhere on the Monterey Peninsula. For example, RVers can hole up at **Marina Dunes R.V. Park,** 3330 Dunes Dr. in Marina, 831/384-6914, which has sites with full hookups as well as tent sites. It's just nine miles from Monterey, making it a good potential base of operations for your visit. And the new **Marina Dunes Resort,** 831/883-9478, www.marinadunes.com, is the first new resort hotel built in the greater Monterey area in 20 years. For more information about the sand dune cities, contact the **Marina Chamber of Commerce,** 211 Hillcrest, Wagner Hall, 831/384-9155, www.marinachamber.com, and the **Seaside/Sand City Chamber of Commerce,** 505 Broadway in Seaside, 831/394-6501, www.seaside-sandcity.com.

CAMPING

Right in downtown Monterey, RV campers can plug in at **Cypress Tree Inn,** 2227 N. Fremont St., 831/372-7586 or 800/446-8303 (in California), www.cypresstreeinn.com. This pleasant motel also features amenities for RVers, including water and electric hookups, showers, restrooms, a hot tub, and sauna. Rates are under $50. Also in Monterey, if you're desperate, try pitching a tent in year-round **Veterans Memorial Park** on Via del Rey adjacent to the presidio, 831/646-3865. First-come, first-camped. Hikers and bikers pay a small fee; rates are under $50 for others, including restrooms and hot showers. No hookups. (Arrive before 3 P.M. and get a permit from the attendant.)

Outside town on the way to Salinas is **Lake Laguna Seca,** at the Laguna Seca Raceway just off Highway 68, with 93 tent sites and 87 spots for RVs (under $50). The park is not recommended for light sleepers when the races are on. For information and reservations, contact Laguna Seca County Recreation Area in Salinas, 831/422-6138 (information), 831/647-7799 (reservations), or 888/588-2267, www.co.monterey.ca.us/parks.

For other camping options, head south to Carmel.

HOSTELS

It's happened at last: Monterey's onetime Carpenter's Union Hall, now the town's long-awaited 45-bed hostel, is finally open. Thanks to the Monterey Hostel Society, travelers can now bunk in separate women's and men's dorms (shared bathrooms) just four blocks from Cannery Row. Among its other features, the **Carpenter's Hall Hostel** offers the latest in water conservation technology—token-operated showers, metered faucets, ultra-low-flow half-gallon Microphor toilets, and water-saving appliances. Rates are under $50. The price includes a pillow, sheets, and a blanket; bring your own sleep sack for $1 discount (no sleeping bags allowed). Family and private group rooms (for up to 35) are available. For groups, discounts on overnight fees are available for youths and children. Given the area's popularity, advance reservations are usually essential. Reserve with personal check or Visa/MasterCard. Free on-site parking. To avoid adding to local traffic woes, leave your vehicle here and take public transportation. For more hostel information contact Carpenter's Hall Hostel, 778 Hawthorne St., 831/649-0375, www.montereyhostel.org. The office is open 8 to 10 A.M. and 5 to 10 P.M.

Now that there is genuinely affordable accommodation available in Monterey, there are debts to be paid. Please express your gratitude by sending an extra contribution to the Monterey Hostel Fund, in care of the hostel.

If you'll be continuing on, excellent HI hostels are available in Santa Cruz, just north, and also farther north along the San Mateo County coastline. If you're heading south, there's also a great hostel in San Luis Obispo. For current details on these and other hostels in California, see http://hostelweb.com/california.htm.

MOTELS AND HOTELS

Current complete listings of accommodations (including prices) and restaurants in Monterey proper are available free from the convention and visitors bureau. Discounts of 50 percent or more are available at many inns, hotels, and motels during off-season promotions.

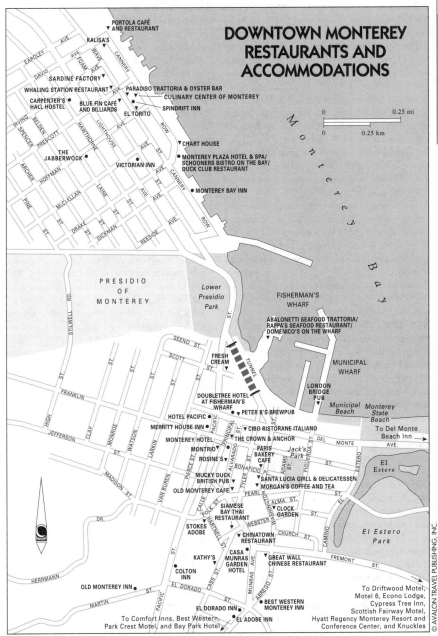

MONTEREY BAY & BIG SUR

DOWNTOWN MONTEREY
RESTAURANTS AND
ACCOMMODATIONS

© AVALON TRAVEL PUBLISHING, INC.

Monterey has a reasonable supply of decent motels, with most rooms in the $100 to $150 range, but many much higher. Most offer all modern amenities, and many establishments provide complimentary breakfast and other extra services. If you're here for the Jazz Festival, plan to stay at a motel in Marina or Seaside and vicinity, or on Fremont Street (motel and fast-food row) just a block from the fairgrounds. Motels on Munras are generally pricier. Be on the lookout, especially during high season, for "floating" motel rates, wherein the price may double or triple long *after* you've made your reservation. When in doubt, request written reservation and price confirmation.

For assistance in booking midrange to high-end accommodations in and around Monterey, contact **Resort II Me Room Finders**, 800/757-5646, www.resort2me.com, a firm with a good track record in matching peninsula visitors with appropriate local lodgings. Or try **Monterey Peninsula Reservations**, 831/655-3487 or 888/655-3424, www.monterey-reservations.com.

$50–100

Not many motel choices in Monterey are truly inexpensive. You might try the 15-room **Driftwood Motel**, 2362 N. Fremont, 831/372-5059, where pets are allowed, or the **Econo Lodge**, 2042 Fremont St., 831/372-5851, with its pool and spa, free continental breakfast, and some rooms with kitchenettes. Both are basic but pleasant, comfortable enough for anyone sticking to the family budget, with better deals in the off-season.

Other motels with lower-priced rooms include the pleasant **El Adobe Inn**, 936 Munras Ave., 831/372-5409, www.El-Adobe-Inn.com, where amenities include in-room coffeemakers and refrigerators. Another possibility is the **Motel 6**, 2124 N. Fremont, 831/646-8585, which is clean, has a pool, and isn't far from the downtown action—reachable on any eastbound bus (take number 1). It's popular, so make reservations six months or more in advance or stop by at 11 A.M. or so to check for cancellations. There's another Motel 6 in the same price range (a bit less expensive) just outside Monterey proper, at 100

Reservation Rd. in Marina, 831/384-1000. For reservations at any Motel 6, call 800/466-8356 or try website: www.motel6.com.

Quite nice, quite reasonably priced, and surprisingly homey are the locally owned Comfort Inns on Munras Avenue. **Comfort Inn-Carmel Hill**, 1252 Munras Ave., 831/372-2908, features 30 cheery rooms with the usual amenities and electronic door locks. Adjacent is the **Comfort Inn-Munras**, 1262 Munras, 831/372-8088. Both are close enough—but not too close—to local attractions, especially if you're looking forward to some vigorous walking. The best thing about the location, which is quite close to Highway 1 and the Del Monte Shopping Center, is its walkability. Directly across the way, flanking Munras all the way back downtown to its junction with Abrego, is long, narrow **Dan Dahvee Park**, with its pleasant trees, flowers, birds—and walking paths.

Other motels with at least some lower-priced rooms include the 15-room **El Dorado Inn**, 900 Munras Ave., 831/373-2921, and the very nice **Best Western Park Crest Motel**, 1100 Munras, 831/372-4576 or 800/528-1234, where rooms include in-room coffeemakers and refrigerators, and extras include TVs with free HBO, a pool, a hot tub, and free continental breakfast. There are also a number of good motels off Fremont.

$100–150

Most of the area's less expensive motels, including those listed above, also offer pricier rooms. Centrally located, near Highway 1 and within easy reach of all area towns, is the **Bay Park Hotel**, 1425 Munras Ave., 831/649-1020 or 800/338-3564, www.bayparkhotel.com, featuring in-room coffeemakers, refrigerators, and hair dryers, plus on-site extras including a restaurant, pool, and hot tub. The nonsmoking **Best Western Monterey Inn**, 825 Abrego, 831/373-5345 or 877/373-5345, www.montereyinnca.com, is quite pleasant, with 80 spacious rooms—some with fireplaces, all with in-room coffeemakers and refrigerators. The motel also has a heated pool and hot tub. Best bets on Fremont include the **Scottish Fairway Motel**, 2075 Fremont St., 831/373-5551 or 800/373-5571, www.scottishfairway.com, where kitchens and kitchenettes are available.

$150–250

With a delightful Old World ambience, right downtown, the refurbished and fashionable **Monterey Hotel,** 406 Alvarado St., 831/375-3184 or 800/727-0960 (reservations), www.montereyhotel.com, comfortably combines the best features of a hotel with a bed-and-breakfast feel. This graceful 1904 Victorian is classic yet contemporary. The large breakfast room downstairs is reserved for complimentary breakfast (you can watch morning news programs on the TV). Just outside the cozy lobby is a wonderful small garden where wine and cheese are served every afternoon from 5 to 7:30 P.M., and cookies and milk are served 8 to 11 P.M. Rooms feature custom-made armoires (with TV sets), telephones, private baths with tub showers, antiques, queen-sized beds, and tasteful yet subtle decorating touches, all individualized. Only two rooms, smaller than standard, feature double beds. One suite (Room 217) features two separate entrances, a featherbed in the bedroom, a sofa bed in the sitting area, and an interior garden plot between. The street-facing suites feature fabulous fan-shaped windows, fireplaces, wet bars, refrigerators, Jacuzzi-style tubs, and queen-sized beds with down comforters. Back-landing suites include many of the same amenities, plus special touches like marble countertops and antique sinks. Every floor features an outdoor landing and deck area, and the third-floor interior landing boasts an intimate atrium parlor lit by a skylight. The only inconvenience is a lack of on-site parking, but an inexpensive city lot (rarely full) is nearby.

Offering good value in comfortable accommodations on acres of lovely landscape is the **Casa Munras Garden Hotel,** 700 Munras, 831/375-2411 or 800/222-2446 in California, 800/222-2558 nationwide, www.casamunras-hotel.com, conveniently located close to historic downtown. A restaurant is on-site.

Another good deal, right downtown, is the attractive and accommodating **Colton Inn,** 707 Pacific, 831/649-6500 or 800/848-7007, www.coltoninn.com, where extras include a sauna and sundeck. The comfortable **Doubletree Hotel at Fisherman's Wharf,** 2 Portola Plaza (adjacent to the Convention Center downtown at Pacific and Del Monte), 831/649-4511 or 800/222-8733 (reservations), www.doubletreemonterey.com, boasts a full-service fitness center and 370 rooms—all stylishly redecorated by fall 2002—and is convenient to just about everything.

$250 and Up

For definite bayside luxury, head for the 290-room, Craftsman-style **Monterey Plaza Hotel & Spa,** 400 Cannery Row, 831/646-1700 or 800/368-2468, www.woodsidehotels.com. The Monterey Plaza's fine accommodations include Italian Empire and 18th-century Chinese furnishings, every convenience (even a complete fitness center with six Nautilus stations), and exceptional food service, including the Duck Club, one of the area's finer restaurants. The 15 Grand Suites feature grand pianos. Great on-site restaurants, rental bikes, and kayaks are available. Recently, the Monterey Plaza added a $6 million, 10,000-square-foot, Euro-style rooftop full-service spa and three spa-level suites. Coming soon to the neighborhood is a new IMAX theater.

Also deluxe and downtown is the contemporary, faux-adobe-style **Hotel Pacific,** 300 Pacific, 831/373-5700 or 800/554-5542, www.innsofmonterey.com. All rooms are suites and feature hardwood floors, separate sitting areas, balconies or decks, fireplaces, wet bars, honor bars, in-room coffeemakers, irons, ironing boards, two TVs, two phones, and terrycloth bathrobes. The tiled bathrooms have a separate shower and tub. Some rooms have a view. Continental breakfast, afternoon tea, and free underground parking are also available.

Surprisingly appealing is the **Spindrift Inn,** a onetime bordello at 652 Cannery Row (at Hawthorne), 831/646-8900 or 800/841-1879, www.innsofmonterey.com. Rooms feature hardwood floors, wood-burning fireplaces, TVs with VCRs, second telephones in the tiled bathrooms, marble tubs, featherbeds (many canopied) and goose-down comforters, all-cotton linens, and terry bathrobes. In the morning, continental breakfast and the newspaper of your choice is delivered to your room. With a rooftop garden and sky-high atrium, the Spindrift also offers a luxurious lobby with Oriental rugs and antiques.

The huge (575-room) **Hyatt Regency Monterey Resort and Conference Center,** 1 Old Golf Course Rd., 831/372-1234, 800/824-2196 (in California), or 800/233-1234 (central reservations), www.montereyhyatt.com, is definitely a resort. The spacious grounds here include an 18-hole golf course, six tennis courts (extra fee for both), two pools, whirlpools, and a fitness center—the works. The sports bar here, **Knuckles,** offers 200 satellite channels and 11 TV monitors.

Other upscale stays include the **Monterey Bay Inn,** 242 Cannery Row, 831/373-6242 or 800/424-6242, www.innsofmonterey.com, offering contemporary accommodations right on the bay (many view rooms with balconies). Near the Row is the 68-room **Victorian Inn,** 487 Foam St., 831/373-8000 or 800/232-4141, www.innsofmonterey.com, where gas fireplaces, complimentary continental breakfast, and afternoon wine and cheese are among the amenities. Concierge-level rooms include featherbeds and robes; some feature whirlpool tubs. Two family suites are available.

BED-AND-BREAKFASTS

Monterey's showcase country inn is the gorgeous ivy-covered 1929 English Tudor **Old Monterey Inn,** 500 Martin St., 831/375-8284 or 800/350-2344, www.oldmontereyinn.com, featuring 10 elegant rooms and suites, most with fireplaces. All have sitting areas, featherbeds, CD players, a Jacuzzi for two, and special touches such as skylights and stained glass. As if the inn itself isn't appealing enough, it is shaded by a specimen oak amid stunning gardens. Buckeye, the inn's rescued golden retriever, will probably greet you when you arrive. You'll also enjoy marvelous full breakfasts and a sunset wine hour. Rates are $250 and up.

The Jabberwock, 598 Laine St., 831/372-4777 or 888/428-7253, www.jabberwockinn.com, is a seven-room "post-Victorian" with a Victorian name and an Alice-through-the-looking-glass sensibility. Some rooms share baths. Rates include full breakfast (imaginative and good) plus cookies and milk at night. Rates are $100 to $250.

A classic in inimitable Monterey style is the historic **Merritt House Inn,** downtown at 386 Pacific St., 831/646-9686 or 800/541-5599, www.merritthouseinn.com. The original adobe, built in 1830, features three suites with 19th-century sensibility and modern bathrooms. Rates are $250 and up. The 22 surrounding motel-style rooms are more contemporary. Rates are $150 to $250.

At the European-style **Del Monte Beach Inn,** 1110 Del Monte Ave., 831/649-4410, most of the rooms share baths—which means this place is affordable for people who don't normally do B&Bs. Rates, including continental breakfast, are $50 to $100.

EATING IN MONTEREY

In Monterey, eating well *and* fairly inexpensively is easier than finding low-cost lodgings. Hard to beat is picnicking at the beaches or local parks. Happy hour—at the wharf, on the Row, and elsewhere—is a big deal in the area. In addition to cheap drinks, many bars serve good (free) food from 4 to 7 P.M. Due to an abundance of reasonably priced (and generous) breakfast places, an inexpensive alternative to three meals a day is skipping lunch (or packing simple picnic fare), then shopping around for early-bird dinners, a mainstay at many local restaurants. Do-it-yourselfers can pick up whatever suits their culinary fancy at the open-air **Old Monterey Marketplace Certified Farmers Market** on Alvarado Street at Pearl, held every Tuesday 3 to 8 P.M. year-round (until 7 P.M. in winter). Great food, great fun. For more information, call 831/665-8070. On Thursday, head for the **Monterey Bay Peninsula College Certified Farmers Market,** 831/728-5060, held 2:30 to 6 P.M. year-round at Fremont and Phisher.

No doubt helped along by the abundance of fresh regional produce, seafood, cheese and other dairy products, poultry, and meats, the Monterey Peninsula has also become a sophisticated dining destination. Some of the area's great restaurants are listed below (in various categories). But to get a true "taste" of the Monterey Peninsula, consider dining as well in nearby Pacific Grove and Carmel.

haggling over fresh strawberries at the farmers market on Alvarado Street

Standards

By "standard," we mean places people can happily—and affordably—frequent. The **Old Monterey Cafe**, 489 Alvarado, 831/646-1021, serves all kinds of omelettes at breakfast—try the chile verde—plus unusual choices like calamari and eggs, lingüiça and eggs, and pigs in a blanket. Just about everything is good at lunch, too, from homemade soups, hearty shrimp Louie, and the Athenian Greek salad (with feta cheese, Greek olives, shrimp, and veggies) to the three-quarter-pound burgers and steak or calamari sandwiches. Fresh-squeezed juices and espresso and cappuccino are featured beverages. Open daily for breakfast and lunch, 7 A.M.–2:30 P.M.; breakfast served until closing.

Rosine's, nearby at 434 Alvarado, 831/375-1400, is locally loved at breakfast, lunch, and dinner. In addition to good pancakes, waffles, and other standards, at breakfast here you can get veggie Benedict (with avocado, sautéed mushrooms, and tomatoes instead of Canadian bacon). Lunch features homemade soups, salads, sandwiches, and burgers. Pasta, chicken, seafood, and steak appear on the menu at dinner, with prime rib available on Friday and Saturday nights.

Still reasonable (and delicious) is **Kathy's,** 700 Cass St., 831/647-9540. Pick any three items for a fluffy omelette. Your meal includes home fries, cheese sauce, bran muffins, and homemade strawberry jam for around $5. Sandwiches, similarly priced, are best when eaten on the patio.

For a casual lunch, dinner, or Sunday jazz brunch, the **Clock Garden,** 565 Abrego, 831/

375-6100, is a popular place. Guests sit outside amid antique clocks planted in the garden, weather permitting. Closed Sunday evening.

Thai food fanatics should try **Siamese Bay Thai Restaurant,** 131 Webster St., 831/373-1550. You can make a meal of the appetizers—such things as veggie tempura with plum sauce and crushed peanuts. The **Great Wall Chinese Restaurant,** 724 Abrego St., 831/372-3637, has wonderful soups and an extensive vegetarian menu. At **Chinatown Restaurant,** close to downtown at 600 Munras St., 831/375-1111, arrive early for the $5 lunch buffet. The food goes fast.

Wonderful for lunch and takeout is the **Santa Lucia Grill & Delicatessen,** downtown at 484 Washington St., 831/333-1111, which serves memorable sandwiches—chicken pesto, chicken Malaysian—and thin-crusted brick oven pizza. Santa Lucia is also a full-service breakfast and dinner house. Or stop in at **Morgan's Coffee and Tea** next door, 498 Washington, 831/373-5601, for superb coffees as well as organic green, black, and herb teas—not to mention sweets like mixed nut cake and pear tarts. Unusual sandwiches and a great $4.95 pizza are available at lunch. Morgan's and Santa Lucia share pleasant outdoor street seating, complete with tables, chairs, and umbrellas. One block away, at 271 Bonifacio Place, is another pleasant, quite reasonable breakfast or lunch stop, **Paris Bakery Café,** 831/646-1620. The lunch menu includes sandwiches, salads, and soups, and the breads and pastries are wonderful.

Pubs

For fans of British pubs, the real deal in Monterey is **The Crown & Anchor,** 150 W. Franklin St., 831/649-6496, dark and inviting with a brassy seagoing air. The full bar features 20 beers on tap, and the food is pretty darn good and reasonably priced—from the fish and chips or bangers and mash to spicy meatloaf, curries, cottage pie, and steak and mushroom pie. You'll also find salads and sandwiches and a special menu for the "powder monkeys" (Brit sailor slang for kids). Open for lunch and dinner daily. Also consider the **London Bridge Pub,** Municipal Wharf (north of Fisherman's Wharf),

831/655-2879, which specializes in authentic British cuisine and pours more than 60 different beers to wash it down with, and the **Mucky Duck British Pub,** 479 Alvarado, 831/655-3031, Monterey's original British pub.

With a logo depicting a one-eyed jack doing the proverbial 12-ounce curl, **Peter B's Brewpub,** 2 Portola Plaza (in the alley behind the Doubletree Hotel), 831/649-4511, offers 10 different Carmel Brewing Company microbrews on tap and good pub grub.

At the Wharf

Named for tender squid breaded and then sautéed in butter, TV chef John Pisto's **Abalonetti Seafood Trattoria,** 57 Fisherman's Wharf, 831/373-1851, offers relaxed lunch and dinner—primarily seafood and standard Italian fare. The restaurant is fairly inexpensive with a nice view. Out on the end of the secondary pier at the wharf is **Rappa's Seafood Restaurant,** Fisherman's Wharf #1, 831/372-7562, an ocean-side oasis with outdoor dining, reasonable prices, good food, and good early-bird dinners.

Domenico's on the Wharf, another Pisto outpost, 50 Fisherman's Wharf #1, 831/372-3655, is famous for its Southern Italian accent. The menu features fresh seafood, homemade pasta, chicken, steak, and veal dishes and a long, very California wine list. An oyster bar is open from 10 A.M. daily.

Cannery Row

If you're spending most of the day at the Monterey Aquarium, try the **Portola Café and Restaurant** there. Or head out onto the Row. Many of the places along Cannery Row offer early-bird dinners, so if price matters, go deal shopping before you get hungry.

Get your margarita fix and decent Mexican fare at **El Torito,** 600 Cannery Row, 831/373-0611. For something simple, an interesting choice for "views, brews, and cues" is the **Blue Fin Café and Billiards,** 685 Cannery Row, 831/375-7000. In addition to salads, sandwiches, and full dinners, the Blue Fin boasts a full bar emphasizing bourbons and scotches and also serves some 40 beers, including 22 ales and lagers on tap. There's plenty to

do besides eat and drink, too, thanks to 18 pool tables, snooker, foosball, darts, and shuffleboard.

Naturally enough, seafood is the predominant dinner theme along the Row. The **Chart House,** 444 Cannery Row, 831-372-3362, brings its trademark casually elegant, nautical-themed decor to the Row, serving primarily seafood, steaks, and prime rib—predictably tasty. A bit inland but still looking to the sea for inspiration is TV chef John Pisto's casual **Whaling Station Restaurant,** 763 Wave, 831/373-3778, another locally popular dinner house offering everything from seafood and house-made pastas to mesquite-grilled Black Angus steaks. Open daily. Pisto's newest outpost is right on the Row: **Paradiso Trattoria & Oyster Bar,** 654 Cannery Row, 831/375-4155, open daily for lunch and dinner, serving fresh California-style Mediterranean food. You'll enjoy a full bar and an extensive Monterey County wine list.

The exceptional, semiformal **Sardine Factory,** 701 Wave St., 831/373-3775, serves California-style regional fare, from seafood and steaks to pasta and other specialties. Full bar. Open daily for dinner.

Another upscale Row restaurant going for the nautical theme is **Schooners Bistro on the Bay,** 400 Cannery Row (at the Monterey Plaza Hotel), 831/372-2628, specializing in California cuisine at lunch and dinner. If a bistro isn't chi-chi enough for you, consider the hotel's renowned but still casual **Duck Club Restaurant,** 831/646-1706, which serves outstanding bay views and superb American regional cuisine for breakfast and dinner daily.

Stylish Dining

Fresh Cream, across from Fisherman's Wharf and upstairs at 100-C Heritage Harbor, 99 Pacific St., 831/375-9798, has wonderful French country cuisine lightened by that fresh California touch. One of the Monterey Peninsula's best restaurants, it's more formal than most. Great views of Monterey Bay are served, too. Meals are expensive, but even travelers light in the pocketbook can afford dessert and coffee. Open for dinner only; menu changes daily. Call for information and reservations.

Still popular is the relaxed all-American bistro **Montrio,** 414 Calle Principal (at Franklin), 831/648-8880, at home in a onetime firehouse. You might start with fire-roasted artichokes, terrine of eggplant, or Dungeness crab cakes, then continue with grilled gulf prawns, lamb tenderloins, or Black Angus New York steak. Vegetarians can dig into the oven-roasted portobello mushroom over polenta and veggie ragout. At last report, Monday was still cioppino night. You'll also enjoy marvelous sandwiches at lunch, exquisite desserts, a full bar (good bar menu), and a great wine list. Open Mon.–Sat. for lunch, daily for dinner.

Equally stylish is the historic 1833 **Stokes Adobe,** 500 Hartnell St. (at Madison), 831/373-1110, its exteriors—including the gardens—preserving that Monterey Colonial style, its interiors beautifully recast with terra-cotta floors, plank ceilings, and a light, airy ambience. But the food is the thing. On the menu here is rustic, refined, and reasonably affordable California-style Mediterranean fare, from savory soups, salads, and tapas to seafood, chicken, lamb, and beef. Small plates might feature choices such as housemade mozzarella and ciabatta bread served with herbed olive oil and oven-roasted spinach gratin with mussels and herbed breadcrumbs. Large plates might include pasta tubes with housemade fennel sausage, manila clams, and spinach aioli; seared hanger steak with spinach cheese tart; or perhaps grilled lavender pork chops with leek-lemon bread pudding. Full bar, good wines. Open for lunch Mon.–Sat.; dinner daily.

Other Mediterranean possibilities include **Cibo Ristorante Italiano,** 301 Alvarado, 831/649-8151, serving rustic but stylish Sicilian fare—plenty of pastas and pizzas, house specialties, and house-made desserts.

Serving up stylish "American country" fare, **Tarpy's Roadhouse,** inside the historic stone Ryan Ranch homestead three miles off Highway 1 on Highway 68 (at Canyon del Rey), 831/647-1444, is not to be confused with some cheap-eats-and-beer joint. The culinary challenge here is reinterpreting American classics—and that's no inexpensive task. Dinner includes such things as Indiana duck, Dijon-crusted lamb loin, baby back ribs, and grilled vegetables with succotash. Great desserts; salads and sandwiches at lunch; full bar. Open for lunch and dinner daily; brunch on Sunday.

For other high-style dining in Monterey, consider some of the choices on Cannery Row and at Fisherman's Wharf, listed above.

EVENTS

Visitors have a whale of a time at January's free **Whalefest** weekend, held at Fisherman's Wharf. Come in February for **A Day of Romance in Old Monterey**—"living history" storytelling, with 19th-century Monterey characters holding forth from the Cooper-Molera and Diaz Adobes, Larkin House, and Sherman Quarters. In late February come for the **Steinbeck Cannery Row Birthday Celebration** and **Mardi Gras on Cannery Row.** In early March, **Dixieland Monterey** brings three days of Dixie and swing to various venues around town. Later in March, come for the **Taste of Old Monterey** food and entertainment fest and the **Sea Otter Classic,** one of the world's best cycling parties. Mid-April, show up for the **Monterey Wine Festival,** when more than 200 California wineries strut their stuff. Traditionally, though, April is adobe month in Monterey, with the popular **Adobe Tour** through public and private historic buildings toward the end of the month. Monterey's **Historic Garden Tours,** beginning at the Cooper-Molera Adobe and including the Stevenson and (usually) Larkin Houses, continue into September. Come in May for the **Marina International Festival of the Winds,** which includes the annual **Tour de Ford Ord** bike ride and the free Memorial Day weekend **Red, White & a Little Blues** music festival, staged at Custom House Plaza and along Alvarado Street in Monterey. In late May, the **Great Monterey Squid Festival** is a chic culinary indulgence for those with calamari cravings, plus arts, crafts, and entertainment.

June brings the acclaimed **Monterey Bay Blues Festival.** The **Fourth of July** celebration here is fun, with fireworks off the Coast Guard Pier, music in historic Colton Hall, and living history in Old Monterey. Come mid-month for the **Old Monterey Sidewalk Art Festival.** There's almost always something going on at nearby Laguna Seca, too, including July's **Honda International Superbike Classic.** In August, the **Monterey County Fair** comes to the fairgrounds, bringing amusement rides, livestock shows, and young faces sticky with cotton-candy residue. Also come in August for the annual **Winemaker's Celebration** and the **Downtown Celebration Sidewalk Sale.**

In early September, race car fans zoom into town for the three-day **Monterey Sports Car Championships** at Laguna Seca. Come mid-September, it's time for the city's most famous event of all: the **Monterey Jazz Festival,** the oldest continuous jazz fest in the nation. Not as daring as others, it nonetheless hosts legendary greats and up-and-coming talent. This is the biggest party of the year here, so get tickets and reserve rooms well in advance (four to six months). Birders, come in October for the annual **Monterey Bay Bird Festival** in nearby Elkhorn Slough. Other October possibilities include the annual **Old Monterey Seafood & Music Festival** and the **California Constitution Day** reenactment of California's 1849 constitutional convention. In mid-November comes the **Robert Louis Stevenson Un-Birthday Party** at the Stevenson House, as well as the **Great Wine Escape Weekend,** when area wineries all hold open houses, and the **Cannery Row Christmas Tree Lighting.** The **Christmas in the Adobes** yuletide tour in mid-December is another big event, with luminaria-lit tours of 15 adobes, each dressed up in period holiday decorations. Festivities are accompanied by music and carolers. Also come in December for the annual **Cowboy Poetry & Music Festival.** Celebrate New Year's Eve through the arts at **First Night Monterey.**

SHOPPING

Cannery Row is the obvious starting point for most visiting shoppers. Wander the Row's shops on the way to and from the Monterey Bay Aquarium. Intriguing possibilities include the Monterey satellite of the **National Steinbeck Center Museum Store** at 700 Cannery Row, just off Steinbeck Square, 831/373-3566, where you'll find most of the writer's works. The **Monterey Soap & Candle Works,** 685 Cannery Row Ste. 109, 831/644-9425, offers natural, handmade coconut, glycerin, and specialty soaps as well as beeswax candles. Don't overlook the gift and book shop at the nonprofit **Monterey Bay Aquarium,** 886 Cannery Row, 831/648-4800, which offers good books and a wonderful selection of educational and "eco" items. Proceeds support the aquarium and its educational and research mission.

Shopping is good in adjacent Pacific Grove, too—starting right next to Cannery Row at the **American Tin Cannery Premium Outlet** mall, 125 Ocean Ave., 831/372-1442, where shops include Carole Little, Carter's Children's Wear, Nine West, and Woolrich. **The First Noel,** 562 Lighthouse Ave., 831/648-1250, specializes in all things Christmas, with other holidays thrown in for good measure.

The Monterey area boasts its fair share of antique and "heritage" shops. But consider actively supporting the preservation of local history. A few shops within downtown's Monterey State Historic Park actually operate out of park buildings—to help generate funds for historic preservation, garden development, and other improvements. Worth a look along Monterey's Path of History is the **Cooper Shop** in the Cooper-Molera Adobe at Polk and Munras Sts., 831/649-7111, operated by the nonprofit Old Monterey Preservation Society, which offers quality 1800s-vintage reproductions, from toys to furniture. The **Boston Store** or Casa del Oro at the corner of Scott and Olivier, 831/649-3364, is run by the nonprofit Historic Garden League and offers antiques, collectibles, and reproductions. The garden league also operates the **Picket Fence,** an upscale garden shop.

There are many great shops downtown, and just wandering around is an enjoyable way to find them. Typically a best bet for previously loved clothing is **Nice Twice,** 397 Calle Principal, 831/373-5665. **Avalon Beads** at 490 Alvarado St., 831/643-1847, features beads from around the globe as well as imported jewelry. The unique **California Views Historical Photo Collection,**

469 Pacific St., 831/373-3811, offers more than 80,000 historical photographs of California and Monterey. For "a superb collection of gourmet cheeses, fine wines, and gifts," the place is **Monterey Bay Vintage,** 481 Tyler St., 831/375-5087.

A first stop for books and magazines is **Bay Books,** 316 Alvarado St., 831/375-1855, with a nice selection of Steinbeck and titles of local or regional emphasis. Used-book aficionados will have a field day at places such as **Book End,** 245 Pearl St., 831/373-4046; **The Book Haven,** 559 Tyler St., 831/333-0383; and the Craftsman-style **Old Monterey Book Company,** 136 Bonifacio Place, 831/372-3111. **Carpe Diem Fine Books** at 502 Pierce St., 831/643-2754, specializes in rare and out-of-print books and is open only by appointment.

In addition to gathering up fresh produce and bakery items, head for downtown's Tuesday **Old Monterey Market Place** on Alvarado Street and Bonafacio Place (4 to 7 or 8 P.M.) for quality crafts.

For more shopping ideas and other visitor information, contact the **Monterey County Convention & Visitors Bureau,** 831/649-1770 (recorded) or 888/221-1010, www.montereyinfo.org, and the **Old Monterey Business Association,** 321 Alvarado St. Ste. G, 831/655-8070, www.oldmonterey.org.

INFORMATION

The **Monterey Visitor Center,** 401 Camino El Estero, is staffed by the Monterey County Convention & Visitors Bureau and offers reams of flyers on just about everything in and around the region. It's open April–Oct., Mon.–Sat. 9 A.M.–6 P.M., Sun. 9 A.M.–5 P.M.; Nov.–March, Mon.–Sat. 9 A.M.–5 P.M., Sun. 10 A.M.–4 P.M. The Visitor & Convention Bureau also cosponsors the new **Maritime Museum Visitor Center** at 5 Custom House Plaza (near Fisherman's Wharf), open daily 10 A.M.–5 P.M. For additional area information, including a current *Monterey County Travel & Meeting Planner,* contact **Monterey County Convention & Visitors Bureau,** 831/649-1770 or 888/221-1010, www.montereyinfo.org. For answers to specific questions, driving directions, and hotel reservations assistance, call

ON MONTEREY FOG

I t is the Pacific that exercises the most direct and obvious power upon the climate. At sunset, for months together, vast, wet, melancholy fogs arise and come shoreward from the ocean. From the hilltop above Monterey the scene is often noble, although it is always sad. The upper air is still bright with sunlight; a glow still rests upon the Gabelano Peak; but the fogs are in possession of the lower levels; they crawl in scarves among the sand-hills; they float, a little higher, in clouds of a gigantic size and often of a wild configuration; to the south, where they have struck the seaward shoulder of the mountains of Santa Lucia, they double back and spire up skyward like smoke. Where their shadow touches, color dies out of the world. The air grows chill and deadly as they advance. The trade-wind freshens, the trees begin to sigh, and all the windmills in Monterey are whirling and creaking and filling their cistern with the brackish water of the sands. It takes but a little while till the invasion is complete. The sea, in its lighter order, has submerged the earth. Monterey is curtained in for the night in thick, wet, salt, and frigid clouds; so to remain till day returns; and before the sun's rays they slowly disperse and retreat in broken squadrons to the bosom of the sea. And yet often when the fog is thickest and most chill, a few steps out of town and up the slope the night will be dry and warm and full of inland perfume.

Excerpted from Robert Louis Stevenson's "The Old Pacific Capital," Fraser's Magazine, *1880*

the MCCVB Call Center at 877/666-8373 or inquire via email to info@mccvb.org. Another resource is the **Monterey Peninsula Chamber of Commerce,** 380 Alvarado St. in Monterey, 831/648-5360, www.mpcc.org.

The *Monterey County Herald* is the mainline community news source. For an alternative view of things, pick up the free *Coast Weekly,* 831/394-5656, www.coastweekly.com, also offering entertainment and events information. Other free local publications detail dinner specials and current activities and entertainment.

GETTING HERE AND AROUND

Hitching into, out of, and around the Monterey Peninsula is difficult. Even getting around by car is a problem; finding streets is confusing due to missing signs, complex traffic signals, and one-way routes. Local traffic jams can be horrendous; save yourself some headaches and avail yourself of local public transportation. Drivers, park at the 12-hour meters near Fisherman's Wharf—the cheapest lots are downtown—and walk or take the bus. For more specific parking advice, pick up the free *Smart Parking in Monterey: How to Find Affordable Legal Public Parking* brochure at area visitors centers.

By Bicycle

Bicycling is another way to go. The local roads are narrow and bike paths are few, but you can get just about everywhere by bike if you're careful. Rent bikes at **Bay Bikes,** 640 Wave St. (on Cannery Row), 831/646-9090, where you can opt for mountain bikes, touring bikes, or four-wheel covered surreys known as pedalinas. Other bike rental firms include **Monterey Moped Adventures,** 1250 Del Monte Ave., 831/373-2696, and **Adventures by the Sea,** 299 Cannery Row, 831/372-1807, www.adventuresbythesea.com. For more about both, which also offer information on scheduled rides with the local **Velo Club Monterey,** see Outdoor Monterey, above.

By Shuttle and Bus

Once parked, from Memorial Day through Labor Day you can ride Monterey's **WAVE**—Waterfront Area Visitor Express—a free shuttle bus system connecting the Tin Cannery shopping center (at the edge of Pacific Grove), the Monterey Bay Aquarium, Cannery Row, Fisherman's Wharf, and the town's historic downtown adobes with the downtown conference center, nearby motels and hotels, parking garages, and the Del Monte Shopping Center. WAVE's Monterey-Salinas transit buses are identified by a wave logo. Buses run north every 10 to 12 minutes and south every 30 minutes from 9 A.M.–7:30 P.M. See a Monterey-Salinas Transit guide—or MST's website—for a route map.

To get around on public buses otherwise, contact **Monterey-Salinas Transit,** 1 Ryan Ranch Rd., 831/899-2555 or 831/424-7695 (from Salinas), www.mst.org. "The Bus" serves the entire area, including Pacific Grove, Carmel, and Carmel Valley, from Watsonville south to Salinas. Local buses can get you just about anywhere, but some run sporadically. Pick up the free Rider's Guide schedule at the downtown **Transit Plaza** (where most buses stop and where Alvarado, Polk, Munras, Pearl, and Tyler Streets converge) or at motels, the chamber of commerce, and the library. The standard single-trip fare (one zone) is $1.75; exact change required; free transfers. Some longer routes traverse multiple zones and cost more. Seniors, the disabled, and children can ride for $.85 with the transit system's courtesy card. Children under age 5 ride free. A regular adult day pass costs $3.50, and a super day pass (valid on all routes and all zones) is $7; seniors and students pay half price. From late May through mid-October, bus 22 runs south to famous Nepenthe in Big Sur (two buses per day in each direction; $3.50 one way).

Greyhound is at 1042 Del Monte Ave., 831/373-4735 or 800/231-2222 (system-wide information and reservations), www.greyhound.com, open daily 8 A.M.–10 P.M.

By Train

Amtrak's Coast Starlight runs from Los Angeles to Seattle with central coast stops in Oxnard, Santa Barbara, San Luis Obispo, Salinas, and Oakland. If you'll be heading to the San Francisco Bay Area from the Monterey Peninsula, keep in mind that Amtrak also connects in San Jose with the San Francisco-San Jose **Caltrain,** 650/817-1717 or 800/660-4287 (in the service area), www.caltrain.com. For help in figuring out the way to San Jose—and how to get around the entire Bay Area by rapid transit—see www.transitinfo.org.

Monterey-Salinas Transit buses can get you to and from the **Amtrak** station in Salinas, 11 Station Place. Contact 831/422-7458 (depot), 800/872-7245, or website: www.amtrak.com for reservations and schedule information, including information on Amtrak's Thruway bus connections from Monterey and vicinity, a service included in some fares.

By Air

Not far from Santa Cruz, the **San Jose International Airport,** 408/501-7600, www.sjc.org, is the closest major airport served by commuter and major airlines. To get to Monterey from the airports in San Jose or San Francisco—or vice versa—you can take **Monterey-Salinas Airbus,** based at Marina Municipal Airport, 791 Neeson Rd., Marina, 831/883-2871. The buses shuttle back and forth up to 10 times daily.

You can fly directly into the Monterey Peninsula area. The **Monterey Peninsula Airport,** 200 Fred Kane Dr. #200, 831/648-7000, www.montereyairport.com, offers direct and connecting flights from all domestic and foreign locales—primarily connecting flights, because this is a fairly small airport. **United Airlines/ United Express,** 800/241-6522; **American/ American Eagle Airlines,** 800/433-7300; and **America West Airlines/America West Express,** 800/235-9292, are all allied with major domestic and/or international carriers. You can fly directly into Monterey from San Francisco, Los Angeles, or Phoenix.

The newest peninsula airport is the **Marina Municipal Airport,** north of Monterey proper on Neeson Road in Marina, 831/582-0102, www.airnav.com/airport/OAR. Another possibility is the **Salinas Municipal Airport,** 831/758-7214, www.salinasairport.com, a mecca for private pilots and charters, helicopter tours, and flight training companies.

Tours

An unusual thrill: cruising town in a facsimile Model A or Phaeton from **Rent-A-Roadster,** 229 Cannery Row, 831/647-1929, www.rent-a-roadster.com. The basic rate is about $30–35 an hour, but you can arrange half-day and full-day tours, too—and head south to Big Sur and San Simeon in style.

Ag Venture Tours in Monterey, 831/643-9463, www.whps.com/agtours, specializes in winery tours in the Salinas Valley, Carmel Valley, and Santa Cruz Mountains. A typical daylong tour includes tasting at three different wineries, a vineyard walk, and a picnic lunch.

Otter-Mobile Tours & Charters, based just south of town in Carmel, 831/649-4523 or 877/829-2224, www.otter-mobile.com, offers van tours of local sights ("Peninsula Highlights") as well as trips to Point Lobos, Big Sur, San Simeon and Hearst Castle, and wineries in the Salinas Valley. The company designs personalized tours around specific interests, from nature hikes to hunting down Steinbeck's haunts.

Almost a local institution, and particularly popular as an adjunct to corporate meetings and conventions, is **California Heritage Guides,** 535 Polk St., 831/373-6454, which organizes large group tours, teas, and shopping expeditions.

Salinas and Vicinity

The sometimes bone-dry Salinas River starts in the mountains above San Luis Obispo and flows north through the Salinas Valley, much of the time underground, unseen. Named for the salt marshes, or *salinas,* near the river's mouth, the Salinas River is the longest underground waterway in the United States. The 100-mile-long Salinas Valley, with its fertile soil and lush lettuce fields, is sometimes referred to as the nation's Salad Bowl. To the west is the Santa Lucia Range; to the east are the Gabilan and Diablo Mountains. Cattle graze in the hills.

No longer such a small town, Salinas is the blue-collar birthplace of novelist John Steinbeck, who chronicled the lives and hard times of California's down-and-out. Some things don't change much. More than 60 years after the 1939 publication of Steinbeck's Pulitzer Prize–winning *The Grapes of Wrath,* the United Farm Workers (UFW) are still attempting to organize the primarily Hispanic farm laborers and migrant workers here. The idea of a unionized agricultural labor force has never been popular in the United States, and certainly not with Salinas Valley growers. In 1936, during a lettuce workers' strike, Salinas was at the center of national attention. Reports to the California Highway Patrol that communists were advancing on the town—"proven" by red flags planted along the highway, some of which were sent as evidence to politicians in Sacramento—led to tear gas and tussling between officers, growers, and strikers. The state highway commission later insisted that the construction warning banners be returned to the area's roadsides.

SEEING AND DOING SALINAS

A Salinas tradition (since 1911) is the four-day **California Rodeo,** held on the third weekend in July. It is one of the world's largest rodeos, with bronco busting and bull riding, roping and tying, barrel racing, and a big western dance on Saturday night. The rowdiness here—cowboy-style, of course—rivals Mardi Gras. For information, contact the California Rodeo, 1034 N. Main St. in Salinas, 831/775-3100 (office), 831/775-3113 (event information), or 831/775-3131 (advance ticket sales), www.carodeo.com. There's western high art, too. See the massive triptych sculpture by Claes Oldenberg, titled *Hat in Three Stages of Landing,* on the lawn of the nearby Salinas Community Center, 940 N. Main St. The series of 3,500-pound yellow hats appear to have been tossed from the nearby rodeo grounds.

The **Boronda Adobe,** 333 Boronda Rd. (at W. Laurel), 831/757-8085, is an outstanding example of a Mexican-era Monterey Colonial adobe. Built between 1844 and 1848 by Jose Eusebio Boronda and virtually unaltered since, the tiny structure has been refurbished and now features museum displays and exhibits, including a few handsome original furnishings. Note the wood shingles, a considerable departure from traditional red-clay tiles. Open Mon.–Fri. 10 A.M.–2 P.M. and Sun. 1–4 P.M. for tours (donation requested). Also here is the one-room 1897 **Old Lagunita School House** and a turn-of-the-20th-century home designed by architect William H. Weeks.

Toro Park, on the way to Monterey via Highway 68, is a pleasant regional park with good hiking, biking, and horseback trails. For an invigorating walk and views of both Monterey Bay and Salinas Valley, take the 2.5-mile trail to Eagle Peak. The park is open daily 8 A.M.–dusk. The day-use fee is $3 on weekdays, $5 on weekends and holidays. For information call 831/484-1108.

A satellite community southeast of Salinas, the town of **Spreckels** was developed by Claus Spreckels in the late 1890s to house employees of his sugar beet factory. This is a genuine "company town," down to the sugar beet architectural motifs in the roof gables of many historic homes. **Natividad** is a onetime stage station about seven miles north of Salinas and the site of the 1846 **Battle of Natividad,** where Californios attacked Yankee invaders herding 300 horses to Frémont's troops in Monterey.

STEINBECK'S LEGACY

The Grapes of Wrath didn't do much for John Steinbeck's local popularity. Started as a photojournalism project chronicling the "Okie" Dust Bowl migrations to California during the Depression, Steinbeck's *Grapes* instead became fiction. The entire book was a whirlwind, written between June and October 1938. After publication, it became a bestseller and remained one through 1940. Steinbeck was unhappy about the book's incredible commercial success; he believed there was something wrong with books that became so popular.

Vilified here as a left-winger and Salinas Valley traitor during his lifetime, Steinbeck never came back to Salinas. (The only way the town would ever take him back, he once said, was in a six-foot wooden box. And that's basically how it happened. His remains are at home at the local Garden of Memories Cemetery.) Most folks here have long ago forgiven their local literary light for his political views, so now you'll find his name and book titles at least mentioned, if not prominently displayed, all around town.

National Steinbeck Center

Some people have long been trying to make it up to Steinbeck. After all, he was the first American to win both the Pulitzer and Nobel Prizes for literature. Efforts to establish a permanent local Steinbeck center finally succeeded, and in summer 1998 the doors of the $10.3 million National Steinbeck Center opened to the public. Billed as a "multimedia experience of literature, history, and art," the Steinbeck Center provides at least one answer to the question of how to present literary accomplishment to an increasingly non-literary culture. And that answer is—ta da—high-tech interactivity. In addition to changing exhibits, seven themed permanent galleries—incorporating sights, sounds, and scents—introduce Steinbeck's life, work, and times, in settings ranging from Doc Rickett's lab on Cannery Row and the replica boxcar of "ice-packed" lettuce to the (climbable) red pony in the barn. Seven theaters show clips from films derived from Steinbeck's writings. But some appreciations are strictly literal, including John Steinbeck's trusty green truck and camper Rocinante (named after Don Quixote's horse), in which the writer sojourned while researching *Travels with Charley.* The **Art of Writing Room,** with literary exhibits and all kinds of technical interactivity, explores the themes of Steinbeck's art and life. The 30,000-piece **Steinbeck Archives** here, open only to researchers by appointment, was originally housed in the local John Steinbeck Library on Lincoln Avenue. The archival collection includes original letters, first editions, movie posters, and taped interviews with local people who remember Steinbeck. Some of the barbed remarks, made decades after the publication of *The Grapes of Wrath,* make it clear that local wrath runs at least as deep as the Salinas River.

Other attractions include the sunny **Steinbeck Center Café** and the **museum store,** which features a good selection of books in addition to gift items. (To visit some of the actual places Steinbeck immortalized in his fiction, be sure to pick up the 24-page *Steinbeck Country: A Guide to Exploring John Steinbeck's Monterey County.* Also see if you can find a used copy of *The John Steinbeck Map of America,* now out of print.) A 6,500-square-foot wing, the **Salinas Valley Agricultural History and Education Center,** opened in 2000 and showcases the Salinas Valley's agricultural heritage; another wing, Valley of the World, opened in September 2003.

The center is open daily 10 A.M.–5 P.M., but is closed on Easter, Thanksgiving, Christmas, and New Year's Day. Admission is $7.95 adults, $6.95 seniors (over age 62) and students with ID, $5.95 youths (ages 13 to 17), $3.95 children (age 6 to 12), free for age 5 and under. For more information about the center and its events and activities, contact National Steinbeck Center, 1 Main St. in Salinas, 831/775-7240 or 831/796-3833, www.steinbeck.org.

Other Steinbeck Attractions

On the first weekend in August, come for the annual **Steinbeck Festival**—four days of films, lectures, tours, and social mixers. And in late February or early March, the town throws a Piscean **Steinbeck Birthday Party.** For information on either event, call 831/796-3833. The **Western Stage** performs occasional Steinbeck works, other dramatic productions, and popular concerts on the Hartnell College campus, 156 Homestead Ave. For information and reservations call 831/755-6816 or 831/375-2111.

Steinbeck described the family home—a jewel-box Victorian, located just two blocks from the National Steinbeck Center—as "an immaculate and friendly house, grand enough, but not pretentious." And so it still is, as both a dining and historic destination. The Salinas Valley Guild serves up gourmet lunches for Steinbeck fans and literary ghosts alike, featuring Salinas Valley produce and Monterey County wines and beer, at **Steinbeck House,** the author's birthplace and "a living museum" at 132 Central St., open Mon.–Sat. 11 A.M.–2:30 P.M. The menu changes weekly, served by volunteers dressed in period Victorian costumes. Call 831/424-2735 for information and reservations (suggested but not required). The house is also open for guided tours (call for information), and there's a "Best Cellar" book and gift shop in the basement, 831/757-0508. All proceeds maintain and support the Steinbeck House and local charities.

STAYING IN SALINAS

Camp at the **Laguna Seca Raceway** facility near Monterey (see Monterey chapter). **Fremont Peak State Park,** on San Juan Canyon Road (southeast from San Juan Bautista), 831/623-4255, has some first-come, first-camped primitive campsites.

In the Soledad and King City areas, **Arroyo Seco** features several U.S. Forest Service campgrounds; take Arroyo Seco Road west off Highway 101, just south of Soledad, or take Carmel Valley Road south to its end and turn right. Or camp at **Los Coches Wayside Camp,** just south of Soledad, or **Paraiso Hot Springs,** nearby on Paraiso Springs Road, 831/678-2882. **San Lorenzo County Park,** on the Salinas River near King City, 831/385-5964, boasts some 200 campsites with hot showers and picnic tables; call 831/385-1484 for information and reservations. The **Monterey County Agricultural & Rural Life Museum** in San Lorenzo Park at 1160 Broadway, 831/385-8020, features Spreckels farmhouse, a barn with antique farm equipment, a cook wagon, a schoolhouse, and a historic railroad depot. Continuing south toward San Luis Obispo, both **Lake San Antonio** (north and south shore, call 831/385-8399 for information) and **Lake Nacimiento** have abundant campsites. All camping options are under $50.

For something a tad more uptown, Salinas has two **Motel 6** locations: 140 Kern, 831/753-1711, and 1257 De La Torre Blvd., 831/757-3077. Both feature the basics plus a pool and in-room color TV. Rates are under $50. For reservations at any Motel 6, contact 800/466-8356 or website: www.motel6.com. Most other motels lining Highway 101 are a bit more upscale. Rooms at the **Comfort Inn,** just off the freeway at 144 Kern St., 831/758-8850 or 800/888-3839, feature in-room coffeemakers; some have microwaves and refrigerators. Rates are $100 to $150.

For something different, head for casual **Barlocker's Rustling Oaks Ranch Bed & Breakfast,** off River Road at 25252 Limekiln Rd., 831/675-9121. There are five guest rooms. Extras include horseback trails, a swimming pool, a pool table, and a genuine country breakfast. Rates are $100 to $250.

EATING IN SALINAS

Get up to speed on the local politics of food production, then sample that famed Salinas Valley produce. The **Old Town Salinas Certified Farmers Market** is held downtown along the 200 block of Main Street (near Alifal Street) every Wednesday from 3 to 7 P.M. (until 8 P.M. in summer). Call 831/758-0725 for details. If you're here on the weekend, head for the **Salinas Certified Farmers Market** at the Northridge Mall, 796 Main St., 831/728-5060, held on Sunday from 8 A.M.–noon. Another possibility is **The Farm,** on Highway 68 just west of Salinas off the Spreckels exit, 831/455-2575—just look for the giant murals—featuring certified organic fruits and vegetables, specialty products, agricultural memorabilia, and the opportunity to get out in the fields and commune with the vegetables. Open Mon.–Sat. 10 A.M.–6 P.M. Farm tours are available by reservation.

A wonderful coffee stop just a couple blocks from the Steinbeck Center is the **Cherry Bean Gourmet,** 332 Main St., 831/424-1989. (And if you're really in a hurry—just passin' through—Salinas has an **In-N-Out Burger,** at 151 Kern Street.) For breakfast downtown, try the breakfast specialists at **First Awakenings,** 171 Main, 831/784-1125, where the pancakes are reputedly the best in the county. Open daily 7 A.M.–2:30 P.M. Cheap and good is the locally popular **Rosita's Armory Cafe,** 231 Salinas St., 831/424-7039. Always a best bet for literary lunch, especially for Steinbeck fans, is the historic **Steinbeck House,** just two blocks from the National Steinbeck Center at 132 Center St., open Mon.–Sat. 11 A.M.–2:30 P.M., 831/424-2735 (see above for more information).

The **Salinas Valley Fish House,** 172 Main St., 831/775-0175, offers various "fresh catches" plus an oyster bar. For Italian food try **Spado's,** 66 W. Alisal, 831/424-4139, featuring fresh pastas, a daily stew, and lamb dishes. **Smalley's Roundup,** 700 W. Market, 831/758-0511, is locally famous for its oak-wood barbecue and other cowboy-style fine dining. (Reservations advised at dinner.)

INFORMATION

The **Salinas Valley Chamber of Commerce,** 119 E. Alisal, 831/424-7611, www.salinaschamber.com, offers information on accommodations and sights, as well as a great little brochure: *Steinbeck Country Starts in Salinas.* The Salinas chamber is also a county-wide visitors center, so stop here for any Monterey County information. Open 8:30 A.M.–5 P.M. Mon.– Fri., 9 A.M.–3 P.M. on Sat. (closed Sun.). **Amtrak** is at 11 Station Place; contact 831/422-7458 or 800/872-7245, or website: www.amtrak.com for fare and schedule information. There's no train station in Monterey, but you can connect from there to Salinas via **Monterey-Salinas Transit** bus 20 or 21 (or via the Amtrak Thruway bus as part of your train fare). For more information, contact Monterey-Salinas Transit, 1 Ryan Ranch Rd., Monterey, 831/424-7695 or 831/899-2555, www.mst.org. **Greyhound** is at 19 W. Gabilan St., 831/424-4418 or 800/231-2222. The **Salinas Municipal Airport** is on Airport Boulevard, 831/758-7214.

SOLEDAD

Soledad, a sleepy town where no one hurries, is the oldest settlement in the Salinas Valley. Stop by the local bakery *(panaderia)* on Front Street for fresh Mexican pastries and hot tortillas. **Misión Nuestra Señora de La Soledad** was founded here in 1791 to minister to the Salinas Valley natives. Our Lady of Solitude Mission three miles southwest of town was quite prosperous until 1825. But this, the 13th in California's mission chain, was beset by problems ranging from raging Salinas River floods to disease epidemics before it crumbled into ruin. The chapel was reconstructed and rededicated, and another wing has since been restored. The original 1799 mission bell still hangs in the courtyard of this active parish church. Outside is a lovely garden. The mission, 831/678-2586, which also offers a museum and gift shop, is open daily 10 A.M.–4 P.M. Just three miles south of Soledad (west at the Arroyo Seco interchange from Highway 101) is another historic survivor, the 1843 **Richardson Adobe**, at Los Coches Rancho Wayside Campground.

Paraiso Hot Springs

Nestled in a grove of lovely palm trees, with a sweeping valley view, this 240-acre old resort a few miles southwest of Soledad has an indoor hot mineral bath (suits required), outdoor pools, picnic tables and barbecues, campgrounds, and Victorian cabins—all rarely crowded. Weekly and monthly rates are available. Most people fancy day use, a bit pricey at $35. For more information and reservations, contact Paraiso Hot Springs, 34358 Paraiso Springs Rd. west of Soledad, 831/678-2882.

PINNACLES NATIONAL MONUMENT

Exploring these barren 24,000 acres of volcanic spires and ravines is a little like rock climbing on the moon. The weird dark-red rocks are bizarrely eroded, unlike anywhere else in North America, forming gaping gorges, crumbling caverns, terrifying terraces. Rock climbers' heaven (not for beginners), this stunning old volcano offers excellent trails, too, with pebbles the size of houses to stumble over. Visitors afraid of earthquakes should know that the Pinnacles sit atop an active section of the San Andreas Fault. Spring is the best time to visit, when wildflowers brighten up the chaparral, but sunlight on the rocks creates rainbows of color year-round. Rock climbing is the major attraction, for obvious reasons. Climbers come during the cool weather. But you can also hike, and in winter watch the raptors: golden eagles, red-shouldered hawks, kestrels, and prairie falcons.

Though it was Teddy Roosevelt who first utilized presidential decree on behalf on the Pinnacles—protecting it as a national monument in 1906—in early 2000 President Bill Clinton announced plans to expand the park by some 5,000 acres. Some of that acreage, when acquired, may encourage gentler, more family-oriented recreation.

Hiking

Of Pinnacles' existing (pre-expansion) 24,000-plus acres, nearly 16,000 are protected as wilderness. Only hiking trails connect the park's east and west sides. Some trails are fairly easy, while others are rugged. Pinnacles has four self-guided nature trails; the **Geology Hike** and **Balconies Trail** are quite fascinating. The short **Moses**

Spring Trail is one of the best. Longest is the trek up the **Chalone Peak Trail,** 11 miles round-trip, passing fantastic rock formations (quite a view of Salinas once you get to the top of North Chalone Peak). Less ambitious is the **Condor Gulch Trail,** an easy two-mile hike into Balconies Caves from the Chalone Creek picnic area. Various interconnecting trails encourage creativity on foot. The best caves, as well as the most fascinating rock formations and visitors center displays, are on the park's east side. The fit, fast, and willing can hike east to west and back in one (long) day. Easiest return trip is via the Old Pinnacles Trail, rather than the steep Juniper Canyon Trail. Pack plenty of water.

Practicalities

As lasting testament to the land's rugged nature, there are two districts in the Pinnacles—west and east—and it's not possible to get from one to the other by road. Within the monument, bicycles and cars may only be used on paved roads. If coming from the west, get visitor information at the **Chaparral Ranger Station,** reached via Highway 146 heading east (exit Highway 101 just south of Soledad). For most visitors, Pinnacles is most accessible from this route, but it's a narrow road, not recommended for campers and trailers. If coming from the east, stop by the **Bear Gulch Visitor Center,** reached via Highway 25, then Highway 146 heading west. From Hollister, it's about 34 miles south, then about five miles west to the park entrance. Pinnacles is open for day use only; the vehicle entry fee is $5, the walk-in fee is $2; valid for seven days. An annual pass costs $15. Within the monument, bicycles and cars may only be used on paved roads. For additional information, contact Pinnacles National Monument, 5000 Hwy. 146in Paicines, 831/389-4485, www.nps.gov/pinn.

Good rules of thumb in the Pinnacles: Carry water at all times and watch out for poison oak, stinging nettles, and rattlesnakes. Spelunkers should bring good flashlights and helmets. Pick up guides to the area's plantlife and natural history at the visitors centers, and also topo maps. Rock climbers can thumb through old guides there for climbing routes.

No camping is offered (or allowed) within the park. The closest private camping is **Pinnacles Campground, Inc.,** near the park's entrance on the east side, 2400 Hwy. 146, 831/389-4462, www.pinncamp.com. The campground is quite nice, featuring flush toilets, hot showers, fire rings, picnic tables, a swimming pool, some RV hookups, and group facilities. Under $50. Basic supplies and some food are available at the campground's store.

SAN JUAN BAUTISTA AND VICINITY

The tiny town of San Juan Bautista is charming and charmed, as friendly as it is sunny. (People here say the weather in this pastoral valley is "salubrious." Take their word for it.) Named for John the Baptist, the 1797 Spanish mission of San Juan Bautista is central to this serene community at the foot of the Gabilan Mountains. But the historic plaza, still bordered by old adobes and now a state historic park, is the true center of San Juan—rallying point for two revolutions, onetime home of famed bandit Tiburcio Vasquez, and the theatrical setting for David Belasco's *Rose of the Rancho.* Movie fans may remember Jimmy Stewart and Kim Novak in the mission scenes from Alfred Hitchcock's *Vertigo,* which were filmed here.

One of the most colorful characters ever to stumble off the stage in San Juan Bautista was one-eyed stagecoach driver Charley Parkhurst, a truculent, swaggering, tobacco-chewing tough. "He," however, was a woman, born Charlotte Parkhurst in New Hampshire. (Charley voted in Santa Cruz in 1866, more than 50 years before American women won the right to vote.)

In addition to history, San Juan Bautista has galleries, antiques and craft shops, and an incredible local theater troupe. To get oriented, pick up a walking tour brochure at the **San Juan Bautista Chamber of Commerce,** 1 Polk St., 831/623-2454, www.sanjuanbautista.com. In June experience mid-1800s mission days at **Early Days in San Juan Bautista,** a traditional celebration complete with horse-drawn carriages, period dress, music, and fandango. The barroom at the Plaza Hotel is even open for card games.

Also fun in June is the **Peddler's Faire and Street Rod Classic Car Show,** one of the biggest street fairs anywhere, the chamber's annual fund raiser. The **Flea Market** here in August, with more than 200 vendors, is one of the country's best. Later in the month, **San Juan Fiesta Day** is the most popular venue of the wandering **Cabrillo Music Festival.** But the event of the year is *La Virgen del Tepeyac* or *La Pastorela* (they alternate yearly), traditional Christmas musicals that attract visitors from around the world. (For details, see El Teatro Campesino, below.) Christmas chorale music is also offered at the mission.

History

Partly destroyed by earthquakes in 1800 and 1906 (the San Andreas Fault is just 40 feet away), **Mission San Juan Bautista** has been restored many times. The 15th and largest of the Franciscan settlements in California, the mission here is not as architecturally spectacular as others in the Catholic chain. Visitors can tour sections of the mission—which still features an active parish church—though it's not really part of the adjacent state historic park. After visiting the small museum and gardens, note the old dirt road beyond the wall of the mission cemetery. This is an unspoiled, unchanged section of the 650-mile El Camino Real, the "royal road" that once connected all the California missions. Archaeological excavations at the mission by CSU Monterey, Hartnell College, and Cabrillo College students unearthed the foundations of the mission's original quadrangle, tower, well, and convent wing (which many historians previously believed had never existed). Students also cleared the 1799 Indian Chapel of debris and restored it; inside is an ornate altar built in the 1560s and moved to the chapel for the Pope's visit in 1987. Many of the students' other discoveries are on display in the mission's museum.

San Juan Bautista's oldest building is the **Plaza Hotel** at Second and Mariposa Streets on the west side of the plaza, originally barracks built in 1813 for Spanish soldiers. In horse and buggy days, San Juan Bautista was a major stage stop between San Francisco and Los Angeles, and the hotel was famous statewide. (Note the two-story outhouse

out back.) Also fascinating are the stable—with its herd of fine old horse-drawn vehicles and the "Instructions for Stagecoach Passengers" plaque out front—and the restored blacksmith shop. Also worth a peek: the jail, washhouse, and cabin.

Above the town of San Juan Bautista is **Pagan Hill.** Today a giant concrete cross stands where mission fathers once put up a wooden one, intended to ward off evil spirits supposedly summoned by Indian neophytes secretly practicing their traditional earth religion. The park is open daily 9:30 A.M.–4 P.M., in summer until 5 P.M. For information, contact San Juan Bautista State Historic Park, 19 Franklin St., 831/623-4881.

El Teatro Campesino

Don't pass through San Juan Bautista without trying to attend a performance by San Juan Bautista's El Teatro Campesino. Chicano playwright Luis Valdez founded this small theater group as guerrilla theater on the United Farm Workers' picket lines more than two decades ago. But Valdez's smash hits *Zoot Suit* and *Corridos* have since brought highly acclaimed nationwide tours and the birth of other Chicano *teatros* throughout the American Southwest. El Teatro's Christmas-season *La Pastorella*, the shepherd's story that alternates with the miracle play *La Virgen del Tepeyac,* is a hilarious and deeply poetic spectacle, a musical folk pageant about shepherds trying to get past comic yet terrifying devils to reach the Christ child. Besides Spanish-language plays, concerts, and film festivals, the company also presents contemporary and traditional theater in English. El Teatro Campesino's permanent playhouse is at 705 Fourth St., 831/623-2444. For a current calendar of events, call or see the website: www.elteatrocampesino.com.

Practicalities

A few tent sites and 165 RV hookups are available at the private **Mission Farm Campground and RV Park,** in a walnut orchard at 400 San Juan–Hollister Rd., 831/623-4456. Under $50. Motel accommodations are available at the **San Juan Inn,** Hwy. 156 and The Alameda, 831/623-4380, rates $50–100, and the **Posada de San Juan Hotel,** a mission-style motel at 310 Fourth

St., 831/623-4030, with fireplace and whirlpool tubs in every room. Rates $100–150.

For farm-fresh produce, pick up a copy of the free guide to nearby family farms and ranches. (Fresh cherries are available in June; apricots in July; and apples, walnuts, and kiwis in the fall.) The **Mission Cafe,** 300 Third St., 831/623-2635, is good for families at breakfast and lunch. Try **Felipe's,** 313 Third St., 831/623-2161, for Mexican and Salvadoran food.

La Casa Rosa, 107 Third St., 831/623-4563, is famous for its butter lettuce salads with fresh herb dressing, fresh rolls, and hearty Peruvian-style casseroles (a Californio favorite). **Doña Esther,** 25 Franklin, 831/623-2518, serves Mexican fare—and the best margaritas in town. More upscale is **Jardines de San Juan,** 115 Third St., 831/623-4466, where you can get *pollos borachos* (drunken chickens) at lunch and dinner daily. For Italian, try either **Don Ciccio's,** 107 The Alameda, 831/623-4667, or the **Inn at Tres Pinos** south of Holliuster in Tres Pinos at 6991 Hwy. 25, 831/628-3320.

For steaks with plenty of giddyup, locals single out the very Western, dinner-only **The Cutting Horse** at 307 Third St., 831/623-4549. People say this is the best steakhouse around. Despite the ominously accurate name, well worth a stop for continental-style lunch and dinner (and the view of the San Juan Valley) is the **Fault Line Restaurant** nearby at 11 Franklin, 831/623-2117.

Fremont Peak State Park

In March 1846, Gen. John C. Frémont and Kit Carson built a "fort" here in defiance of the Mexican government, unfurled their flags on Gabilan Peak (now Fremont Peak), and waited for the supposedly imminent attack of Californio troops. When no battle came, they broke camp and took off for Oregon. Fremont Peak State Park, a long, narrow, isolated strip in the Gabilan Mountains northeast of Salinas, has rolling hills with oaks, madrones, Coulter pines, and spring wildflowers that attract hundreds of hummingbirds. The park offers good hiking in spring and good views from the top of Fremont Peak. Another attraction at Fremont Peak is an observatory with a 30-inch Challenger reflecting

telescope, open to the public at least twice monthly for free programs including lectures and observation; call 831/623-2465 for details (recorded) or see www.fpoa.net.

Camping is available in about 25 primitive campsites (some in the picnic area) and a group camp. To get to the park from Highway 156, head 11 miles south on San Juan Canyon Road (County Road G1)—paved but very steep and winding (trailers definitely not recommended). For information, contact Fremont Peak State Park, 831/623-4255.

Hollister

If Gilroy is the garlic capital of the world, then Hollister is the earthquake capital. Because of the region's heavy faulting, some say this San Benito County town moves every day, however imperceptibly. (A small 1985 quake shook loose a 20,000-gallon oak wine cask and flooded the Almaden Winery just south of town.) Agricultural Hollister is as historic as San Juan Bautista, but the "feel" here is straight out of the Old West. Stop by the **San Benito County Historical Society Museum,** 498 Fifth St. (at West), 831/635-0335 (open Sat.– and Sunday 1 to 3 P.M.; other times by appointment), then wander through Old Town (particularly along Fifth) to appreciate Hollister's old Victorians.

Traditional cowboy events and some unique competitions are the name of the game during June's **San Benito County Rodeo,** an event dedicated to the vaquero. The **Fiesta-Rodeo** in July dates back to 1907, when it was first held to raise funds for rebuilding Mission San Juan Bautista after the big quake in 1906. Up-and-coming on the events scene here is a big motorcyclists gathering (à la Sturgis, South Dakota) on the **Fourth of July** weekend.

GILROY AND VICINITY

Will Rogers supposedly described Gilroy as "the only town in America where you can marinate a steak just by hanging it out on the clothesline." But Gilroy, the "undisputed garlic capital of the world," dedicates very few acres to growing the stinking rose these days. The legendary local gar-

© ROBERT HOLMES/CALTOUR

lic farms have been declining due to soil disease since 1979—ironically, the first year of the now-famous and phenomenally successful Gilroy Garlic Festival. Gilroy now grows housing sub-divisions—former *San Francisco Chronicle* columnist Herb Caen defined modern Gilroy as the place "where the carpet ends and the linoleum begins"—and the San Joaquin Valley grows most of California's garlic. Nonetheless, that unmistakable oily aroma still permeates the air in summer, since more than 90 percent of the world's garlic is processed or packaged here.

Other attractions in Gilroy include Goldsmith Seeds' seasonal six-acre **Field of Dreams** experimental flower seed garden. Call 408/847-7333 for tour information. Downtown Gilroy has its historic attractions, too. The best place to start exploring is the **Gilroy Historical Museum** at Fifth and Church, 408/848-0470, open weekdays 9 A.M.–5 P.M.

For more information about what's cookin' in and around Gilroy, contact the **Gilroy Visitor Bureau,** 7780 Monterey St., 408/842-6436, www.gilroyvisitor.org, and the **Gilroy Chamber of Commerce,** 7471 Monterey, 408/842-6437, www.gilroy.org.

Gilroy Garlic Festival

It's chic to reek in Gilroy. On the last full weekend in July, 150,000 or more garlic lovers descend on the town for several dusty days of sampling garlic perfume, garlic chocolate, and all-you-can-eat garlic ice cream (for some reason, just a few gallons of the stuff takes care of the entire crowd). Who wouldn't pay the $10 admission for belly dancing, big bands, and the crowning of the Garlic Queen? For more information, contact the **Gilroy Garlic Festival Association,** 7473 Monterey, 408/842-1625, www.gilroygarlicfestival.com. If you're looking for garlic gifts and accessories at other times, Gilroy boasts a number of garlic-themed shops; get a current listing from the city's website, www.gilroy.org.

Wineries

Besides sniffing out local Italian scallions, tour the Gilroy "wine country." Most of the area's wineries are tucked into the Santa Cruz Mountain foothills west of the city, seven of these along Highway 152's Hecker Pass. The hearty, full-flavored red wines produced here are still made by hand. **Solis Winery,** 3920 Hecker Pass Rd., 408/847-6306, offers tastings of its chardonnay and merlot Wed.–Sun. 11 A.M.–5 P.M. (tours by appointment). Come by **Sarah's Vineyard** Sat. noon–4 P.M. (otherwise by appointment only), 4005 Hecker Pass Rd., 408/842-4278, to meet delightful proprietor Marilyn Otteman, who refers to her fine white wines as "ladies," or visit the nearby **Thomas Kruse Winery,** 4390 Hecker Pass Rd., 408/842-7016, with its eclectic collection of antique equipment, presided over by philosopher-winemaker Thomas Kruse. His Gilroy Red and other wines sport handwritten, offbeat labels. Open for tasting and tours most days noon to 5 P.M. The **Fortino Winery,** 4525 Hecker Pass Rd., 408/842-3305, and **Hecker Pass Winery,** 4605 Hecker Pass Rd., 408/842-8755, are both run by the Fortino family and specialize in hearty old-country red wines.

For more information about these and other regional wineries, contact the **Santa Clara Valley Wine Growers Association** in Morgan Hill, 408/778-1555 or 408/779-2145, www.scvwga.com.

Bonfante Gardens

The region's most amazing new visitor attraction, Gilroy's glorious, $100 million Bonfante Gardens Theme Park, reopened in May 2002 after a brief hiatus.

The appeal of 75-acre Bonfante Gardens is rooted in its inspired horticultural ambience. That's right—*horticultural.* Trees and shrubs, in particular. Some 23 years were spent planning and developing the park's unique landscape before Bonfante Gardens finally opened its gates in June 2001. Botanical oddities abound, from the five themed gardens to the 25 wonderful "circus trees" created by the late Axel Erlandson—wonders created by grafting and pleaching, feats that have never been successfully duplicated. Kids are equally impressed by the Monarch Garden's immense greenhouse with a monorail, train, and river running through it.

Though the pace here is relaxed and the thrills understated, traditional theme park attractions haven't been neglected. Bonfante Gardens includes 40 family-friendly rides and attractions, from the cheerful 1927 Illions Supreme Carousel and the Quicksilver Express roller coaster to the very cool antique car ride. The latter allows you to "tour" either the 1920s or 1950s—dig those old gas stations—depending on where you climb on. Still, encouraging people to appreciate trees is the main point of Bonfante Gardens. All attractions are literally woven into the landscape.

The not-for-profit Bonfante Gardens closed in late September 2001—just days after the World Trade Center and Pentagon disasters—in order to "conserve capital, concentrate on future funding requirements, and complete additional attractions rather than deplete resources by keeping the park open during times of economic uncertainty," according to founder Michael Bonfante. During its first three months of operation the park attracted 28,000 visitors; hopes are high that the park will again flourish, now that it has reopened.

At last report, park admission was $29.95 adults, $26.95 seniors, and $19.95 children ages 3–12 (age 2 and under free); parking, $7 per vehicle. For current details, contact: Bonfante Gardens, 3050 Hecker Pass Hwy. (Hwy. 152 West in Gilroy, 408/840-7100, www.bonfantegardens.com.

Casa de Fruta and Coyote Reservoir

Unforgettable is one word for Casa de Fruta on Pacheco Pass Highway, 831/637-0051, www.casadefruta.com. The sprawl of neon-lit, truck stop–type buildings is complete with trailer park and swimming pool, motel, petting zoo, merry-go-round, and miniature train and tunnel. Stop off at the Casa de Fruta Coffee Shop (open 24 hours) and read about the Casa de Fruta Country Store, Casa de Fruta Gift Shop, Casa de Fruta Fruit Stand, Casa de Burger, Casa de Sweets Bakery and Candy Factory, Casa de Choo-Choo, and Casa de Merry-Go-Round on the "mail me" souvenir paper placemats. (To see the coffee cups "flip," ask the coffee shop staff for a show.)

Coyote Reservoir, eight miles north of Gilroy, is great for sailboarding, sailing, and fishing. Open year-round 8 A.M.–sunset for day use; 75 campsites. For information, contact **Coyote Lake Park,** 10840 Coyote Lake Rd. in Gilroy, 408/842-7800. To get to Coyote Lake, take the

CASA DE RENAISSANCE

To experience the Middle Ages modern-style, head for the long-running **Renaissance Pleasure Faire.** Held almost forever in Novato's Black Point Forest just off Hwy. 37, of late the Faire has been on the move—looking for a new permanent home. In 2002, the Faire's 36th year, it settled into Casa de Fruta, near Gilroy and is held on weekends from September through mid-October, 10 A.M.–6 P.M.

During the Faire, life in the local shire features an authentic return trip to 16th-century England, on the world's largest stage—a mile-long Elizabethan village with 16 separate neighborhood villages inhabited by thousands of corporate executives, computer programmers, housewives, and other amateur medievalists (including paying guests) dressed and acting in historical character and speaking only "Basic Faire Accent."

In keeping with Northern California history, Sir Francis Drake himself presides over each day's opening ceremonies; the queen leaves the shire by late afternoon. But in between, the activity never ends. There are madrigal groups and musical processions; games, juggling, singing, and dancing; full-contact fighting and jousting; feasts of broiled beef, beer, and fresh-baked bread, mixed inimitably with other aromas—incense and herbs and flower essence—in the air. At last report, admission was $17.50 adults, $15 seniors and students with current ID, and $7.50 children ages 5–11 (under 5 free). Call for current details and directions. For more information, call 800/523-2473 or see the website: www.renfair.com.

Leavesley Road/Highway 152 exit east from Highway 101; after two to three miles, head north on New Avenue then east on Roop Road to Gilroy Hot Springs Road. The Coyote Reservoir Road turnoff is about a mile farther, the campground two miles more.

Pacific Grove

Pacific Grove began in 1875 as a prim, proper tent city founded by Methodists who, Robert Louis Stevenson observed, "come to enjoy a life of teetotalism, religion, and flirtation." No boozing, waltzing, zither playing, or reading Sunday newspapers was allowed. Dedicated inebriate John Steinbeck lived here for many years, in the next century, but had to leave town to get drunk. Pacific Grove was the last dry town in California: Alcohol has been legal here only since 1969. The first Chautauqua in the western states was held here—bringing "moral attractions" to heathen Californians—and the hall where the summer meeting tents were stored still stands at 16th and Central Avenues.

Nicknamed Butterfly City U.S.A. in honor of migrating monarchs (a big fine and/or six months in jail is the penalty for "molesting" one), Pacific Grove sparkles with Victorians and modest seacoast cottages, community pride, a rocky shoreline with wonderful tidepools, and an absolutely noncommercial Butterfly Parade in October. Also here is Asilomar, a well-known state-owned conference center with its own beautiful beach.

The town also offers some great bargains, especially for secondhand shoppers. Trendy **Time After Time,** 301 Grand Ave., 831/643-2747, and **Encore Boutique,** 125 Central Ave., 831/375-1700, are good places to start.

Pacific Grove is well served by Monterey-Salinas Transit buses (see Monterey section). For events, accommodations, restaurants, and other current information, contact the **Pacific Grove Chamber of Commerce** at Forest and Central, 831/373-3304 or 800/656-6650, www.pacificgrove.org. Another interesting web portal is www.93950.com. The **Pacific Grove Public Library,** 550 Central (at Fountain), 831/648-3160, is open Mon.–Thurs. 10 A.M.–8 P.M., Fri.–Sat. 10 A.M.–5 P.M.

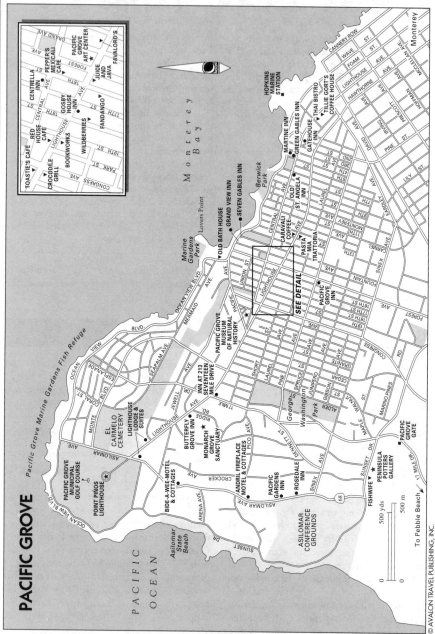

PACIFIC GROVE

Pacific Grove Marine Gardens Fish Refuge

Monterey Bay

PACIFIC OCEAN

Asilomar State Beach

Point Pinos Lighthouse

Pacific Grove Municipal Golf Course

El Carmelo Cemetery

Lighthouse Lodge & Suites

Bide-A-Wee Motel & Cottages

Butterfly Grove Inn

Monarch Grove Sanctuary

Inn at 213 Seventeen Mile Drive

Andril Fireplace Motel & Cottages

Rosedale Inn

Pacific Gardens Inn

Asilomar Conference Grounds

Fishwife

Peninsula Potters Gallery

Pacific Grove Gate

Pacific Grove Museum of Natural History

Marine Gardens Park

Lovers Point

Old Bath House

Grand View Inn

Seven Gables Inn

Berwick Park

Martine Inn

Green Gables Inn

Gatehouse Inn

Thai Bistro

Hopkins Marine Station

Tillie Gort's Coffee House

Old St. Angela Inn

Caravali Coffee

Pasta Mia Trattoria

Pacific Grove Inn

SEE DETAIL

Cannery Row

Monterey

SEE DETAIL (inset):

Pacific Grove Art Center

Pepper's Mexicali Cafe

Favaloro's

Juice and Java

Centrella Inn

Gosby House Inn

Fandango

Wildberries

Bookworks

Red House Cafe

Crocodile Grill

Toastie's Cafe

To Pebble Beach

500 yds
500 m

© AVALON TRAVEL PUBLISHING, INC.

SEEING AND DOING PACIFIC GROVE

From Pacific Grove, embark on the too-famous 17-Mile Drive in adjacent Pebble Beach. But better (and free), tour the surf-pounded peninsula as a populist. The city of Pacific Grove is one of few in California owning its own beaches and shores, all dedicated to public use. Less crowded and hoity-toity than 17-Mile Drive, just as spectacular, and absolutely free, is a walk, bike ride, or drive along Ocean View Boulevard. Or take the Monterey Peninsula Recreation Trail as far as you want; this path for walkers, joggers, bicyclists, skaters, and baby-stroller-pushers runs all the way from Marina to Pebble Beach. It's paved in places (right through downtown Monterey, for example), dirt in others. Or cycle from here to Carmel on the Del Monte Forest ridge via Highway 68 (the Holman Highway) for a spectacular view of the bay, surrounding mountains, and 17-Mile coastline to the south.

The "Three-Mile Drive"—or Walk

Along the Ocean View route are Berwick Park, Lovers Point, and Perkins Park; altogether, Pacific Grove boasts 13 community parks. These areas (and points in between) offer spectacular sunsets, crashing surf, craggy shorelines, swimming, sunbathing, and picnicking, plus whale-watching in season, sea otters, sea lions, seals, shorebirds, and autumn flurries of monarch butterflies. Stanford University's **Hopkins Marine Station** on Point Cabrillo (China Point) is also along the way, the crystal offshore waters and abundant marinelife attracting scientists and students from around the world. This is the first marine laboratory on the Pacific coast. (An aside for Steinbeck fans: This was the location of Chin Kee's Squid Yard in *Sweet Thursday.*) As for **Lovers Point,** the granite headland near Ocean View Boulevard and 17th Street, there is considerable disagreement over whether Pacific Grove could have been *sexual* in Methodist days, when it was named. The popular local opinion, still, is that the name was originally Lovers of Jesus Point. But conscientious researchers have established that the reference is to romance—and was, at least as

far back as 1890. (For help in divining other arcane area details, pick up a copy of *Monterey County Place Names: A Geographical Dictionary* by Donald Thomas Clark and its companion *Santa Cruz County Place Names.*) Trysting place or no, Lovers Point is not a safe place to be during heavy weather; entirely too many people have been swept away to their deaths. Picnic at **Perkins Point** instead, or wade or swim there (safe beach). **Marine Gardens Park,** an aquatic park stretching along Ocean View, with wonderful tidepools, is a good spot for watching sea otters frolic in the seaweed just offshore.

Pacific Grove Museum of Natural History

Pacific Grove's Museum of Natural History at Forest and Central showcases *local* wonders of nature, including sea otters, seabirds (a huge

MONARCH BUTTERFLIES

Pacific Grove is the best known of the 20 or so places where monarch butterflies winter. Once partial to Monterey pine or cypress trees for perching, monarchs these days prefer eucalyptus introduced from Australia. Adults arrive in late October and early November, their distinctive orange-and-black Halloweenish wings sometimes tattered and torn after migrating thousands of miles. But they still have that urge to merge, first alighting on low shrubs, then meeting at certain local trees to socialize and sun themselves during the temperate Monterey Peninsula winter before heading north to Canada to mate in the spring and then die. Their offspring metamorphose into adult butterflies the following summer or fall and—mysteriously—make their way back to the California coast without ever having been here. Milkweed eaters, the monarchs somehow figured out this diet made them toxic to bug-loving birds, who subsequently learned to leave them alone.

Even when massed in hundreds, the butterflies may be hard to spot: with wings folded, their undersides provide neutral camouflage. But if fog-damp, monarchs will spread their wings to dry in the sun and "flash"—a priceless sight for any nature mystic.

collection with more than 400 specimens), rare insects, and native plants. A fine array of Native American artifacts is on rotating display. Particularly impressive is the relief map of Monterey Bay, though youngsters will probably vote for *Sandy,* the gray whale sculpture right out front. Besides the facsimile butterfly tree, the blazing feathery dried seaweed exhibit is a must-see. Many traveling exhibits visit this museum throughout the year, and the annual **Wildflower Show** on the third weekend in April is excellent. For information, contact the museum at 165 Forest Ave., 831/648-5716, www.pgmuseum.org. Open Tues.–Sun. 10 A.M.–5 P.M. Admission is free (donations greatly appreciated).

Point Piños Lighthouse

Built of local granite and rebuilt in 1906, this is the oldest operating lighthouse on the Pacific coast. The beacon here and the mournful foghorn have been warning seagoing vessels away from the point since the 1850s. The original French Fresnel lenses and prisms are still in use, though the lighthouse is now powered by electricity and a 1,000-watt lamp instead of whale oil. The lighthouse and the **U.S. Coast Guard Museum** inside

are free and open Thurs.–Sun. 1–4 P.M. **Doc's Great Tidepool,** yet another Steinbeck-era footnote, is near the foot of the lighthouse.

Across from the lighthouse parking lot is fascinating **El Carmelo Cemetery,** a de facto nature preserve for deer and birds. (For more bird-watching, amble down to freshwater **Crespi Pond** near the golf course at Ocean View and Asilomar Boulevards.) The Point Piños Lighthouse is two blocks north of Lighthouse Avenue on Asilomar Boulevard. For information about the lighthouse and Coast Guard Museum, call 831/648-5716, ext. 13.

Asilomar

The Young Women's Christian Association's national board of directors coined this Spanish-sounding non-word from the Greek *asilo* ("refuge") and the Spanish *mar* ("sea") when they established this facility as a YWCA retreat in 1913. **Asilomar State Beach** has tidepools and wonderful white-sand beaches, shifting sand dunes, wind-sculpted forests, spectacular sunsets, and sea otters and gray whales offshore. Inland, many of Asilomar's original buildings (designed by architect Julia Morgan, best known

© ROBERT HOLMES/CALTOUR

Pacific Grove painter

for Hearst's San Simeon estate) are now historical landmarks.

Primarily a conference center with meeting rooms and accommodations for groups, Asilomar is now a nonprofit unit of the California state park system; subject to room availability, the general public can also stay here. Guest or not, anyone can fly kites or build sandcastles at the beach, stop to appreciate the forest of Monterey pine and cypress, and watch for deer, raccoons, gray ground squirrels, hawks, and owls. For information, contact: Asilomar Conference Center, 800 Asilomar Blvd. in Pacific Grove, 831/372-8016 or 831/642-4242 (reservations for leisure travelers), www.visitasilomar.com. You can book online. To stay here, make reservations up to 90 days in advance, or call (not more than a week in advance) to inquire about cancellations. Rates are $100–150—full country-style breakfast included. Children ages 3–12 can stay (in the same room with an adult) for $5 more.

The 17-Mile Drive

The best place to start off on the famed 17-Mile Drive (technically in Pebble Beach) is in Pacific Grove (or, alternatively, the Carmel Hill gate off Hwy. 1). Not even 17 miles long anymore, since it no longer loops up to the old Del Monte Hotel, the drive still skirts plenty of ritzy digs in the 5,300-acre, privately owned Del Monte Forest in the four-gated "town" of Pebble Beach. Note the Byzantine castle of the banking/railroading Crocker family. Believe it or not, the estate's private beach is heated with underground pipes.

From **Shepherd's Knoll,** there's a great panoramic view of both Monterey Bay and the Santa Cruz Mountains. **Huckleberry Hill** does have huckleberries, but botanically more fascinating is the unusual coexistence of Monterey pines, Bishop pines, and Gowen and Monterey cypress. **Spanish Bay,** a nice place to picnic, is named for Portolá's confused land expedition from Baja in 1769; Portolá was looking for Monterey Bay, but he didn't find it until his second trip. **Point Joe** is a treacherous, turbulent convergence of conflicting ocean currents, wet and wild even on calm days. ("Joe" has been commonly mistaken by mariners as the entrance to Monterey Bay, so

countless ships have gone down on these rocks.) Both **Seal Rock** and **Bird Rock** are aptly named. **Fanshell Beach** is a secluded spot good for picnics and fishing, but swimming is dangerous.

Most famous of all is the landmark **Lone Cypress**—the official (trademarked) emblem of the Monterey Peninsula—at the route's midpoint. No longer lonely, this craggy old-timer is visited by millions each year; it's now "posed" with supporting guy wires, fed and watered in summer, and recovering well from a recent termite attack. At **Pescadero Point,** note the cypress bleached ashen and ghostlike by sun, salt spray, and wind.

From Pacific Grove (or from other entrances), it won't cost you a cent to travel the 17-Mile Drive by bike—the only way to go if you can handle some steep grades. (On weekends, cyclists must enter the drive at the Pacific Grove Gate). By car, the drive costs $7.75, which is refundable if you spend at least $25 on food or greens fees at The Lodge at Pebble Beach. A map is available at any entrance. The drive is open for touring from sunrise to 30 minutes before sunset year-round. For more information, call Pebble Beach Resort at 831/649-8500 or 800/654-9300 or see website: www.pebblebeach.com.

Pebble Beach

Very private Pebble Beach has seven world-class golf courses made famous by Bing Crosby's namesake tournament. The Crosby, now called the **AT&T Pebble Beach National Pro Am Golf Tournament,** is held each year in late January or early February. For golfing information or reservations, contact 800/654-9300 or website: www.pebblebeach.com. Only guests at the ultra-upscale resort accommodations can reserve more than 24 hours in advance. And some guests book their stays one to two years in advance. Other facilities are open to the public, including jogging paths and beautiful horse trails. Just about everything else—country clubs, yacht clubs, tennis courts, swimming pools—is private (and well guarded), though the public is welcome for a price. If you're here in August, join in the **Scottish Highland Games** or see how the rich get around at the **Concours d'élégance** classic car fest at The Lodge.

© ROBERT HOLMES/CALTOUR

Events

Pacific Grove boasts more than 75 local art galleries, enough to keep anyone busy. The **Peninsula Potters Gallery,** 2078 Sunset Dr., 831/372-8867, is the place to appreciate the potter's art; open Mon.–Sat. 10 A.M.–4 P.M. Also worth stopping for is the **Pacific Grove Art Center,** 568 Lighthouse, 831/375-2208.

There are hometown-style events year-round. The renowned Pacific Grove **Wildflower Show** is in mid-April, with more than 600 native species (150 outdoors) in bloom at the Pacific Grove Museum of Natural History. In March or April, the **Good Old Days** celebration brings a parade, Victorian home tours, and arts and crafts galore. In late July, come for the annual **Feast of Lanterns,** a traditional boat parade and fireworks ceremony that started when Chinese fishermen lived at China Point (their village was torched in 1906).

Pacific Grove's biggest party comes in October with **Welcome Back Monarch Day.** This native, naturalistic, and noncommercial community bash heralds the return of the migrating monarchs and includes the **Butterfly Parade,** carnival, and bazaar, all to benefit the PTA. Not coincidentally, from October to February the most popular destination in town is the **Monarch**

Grove Sanctuary on Ridge Road (just off Lighthouse), where docent-led tours are offered daily; for reservations, call 831/375-0982 or 888/746-6627. Otherwise, come in October for the **Pacific Grove Victorian Home Tour** or in November for the **State Championship High School Marching Band Festival.** In December, check out **Christmas at the Inns,** when several local B&Bs, decorated for the holidays, hold an open house and serve refreshments.

STAYING IN PACIFIC GROVE

To maintain its "hometown America" aura, Pacific Grove has limited its motel development. The local chamber of commerce provides accommodations listings. Bed-and-breakfast inns are popular in Pacific Grove—see separate listings, below—and these comfortable, often luxurious home lodgings compare in price to much less pleasant alternatives elsewhere on the peninsula.

$50–100

Especially if the monarchs are in town, consider a stay at the **Butterfly Grove Inn,** 1073 Lighthouse Ave., 831/373-4921 or 800/337-9244, www.butterflygroveinn.com. Butterflies are partial to some of the trees here. The inn is quiet, with a pool, a spa, some kitchens, and fireplaces. Choose rooms in a comfy old house or motel units. Closest to the beach are the 1930s-style cottages at **Bide-a-Wee-Motel & Cottages,** near Asilomar at 221 Asilomar Blvd., 831/372-2330. Some of the cottages have kitchenettes. Also comfortable is woodsy **Andril Fireplace Motel & Cottages,** 569 Asilomar Blvd., 831/375-0994, www.andrilcottages.com (the cottages have the fireplaces).

$100–150

The state-owned **Asilomar Conference Center,** 800 Asilomar Ave. in Pacific Grove, 831/372-8016 or 831/642-4242 (reservations for leisure travelers), fax 831/372-7227, www.asilomarcenter.com, enjoys an incredible 60-acre setting on the Pacific Ocean, complete with swimming pool, volleyball nets, horseshoe pits, and miles of beaches to stroll. When it's not completely booked with businesspeople, conferences, and other groups, it can be a reasonably priced choice for leisure travelers. Adding to the earthy appeal: architect Julia Morgan designed many of the resort's pine lodges. Cheapest are the older, rustic cottages. Some units have kitchens and fireplaces. Call ahead for reservations, up to 90 days in advance, or hope for last-minute cancellations. Rates are $100–150, full country breakfast included. Children ages 3–12 stay (in same room with adult) for $5 more.

Near Asilomar is the **Pacific Gardens Inn,** 701 Asilomar Blvd., 831/646-9414 or 800/262-1566 in California, www.pacificgardensinn.com, where the contemporary rooms feature wood-burning fireplaces, refrigerators, TVs, and phones—even popcorn poppers and coffeemakers. Suites feature full kitchens and living rooms. Complimentary continental breakfast and evening wine and cheese are offered. Very nice. Right across from Asilomar is the all-suites **Rosedale Inn,** 775 Asilomar Blvd., 831/655-1000 or 800/822-5606, www.rosedaleinn.com, where all rooms have a ceiling fan, fireplace, large Jacuzzi, wet bar, refrigerator, microwave oven, in-room coffeemaker, remote-control color TV and VCR, even a hair dryer. Some suites have two or three TVs and/or a private patio.

$150 and Up

The **Lighthouse Lodge and Suites,** 1150 and 1259 Lighthouse Ave., 831/655-2111 or 800/858-1249, www.lhls.com, are two different properties close to one another. The 31 Cape Cod–style suites feature abundant amenities—king beds, large Jacuzzi tubs, plush robes, mini-kitchens with stocked honor bars—and are the most expensive. The 64 lodge rooms feature basic motel-style comforts and are family friendly, with extras including breakfast and a complimentary poolside barbecue in the afternoon (weather permitting). Lower rates in the off-season; two-night minimum on summer weekends.

Three super-swank choices in adjacent Pebble Beach are definitely beyond the reach of most people's pocketbooks. At the **Inn at Spanish Bay,** 2700 17 Mile Dr. (at the Scottish Links Golf Course), 831/647-7500, rooms are definitely deluxe, with gas-burning fireplaces, patios, and balconies with views. Amenities include beach access, a pool, saunas, whirlpools, a health club, tennis courts, and a putting green. Also an unlikely choice for most travelers is **The Lodge at Pebble Beach,** another outpost of luxury on 17 Mile Drive, 831/624-3811. (If you don't stay, peek into the *very* exclusive shops here.) A recent addition are the elegant, estate-style cottages at the 24-room **Casa Palmero,** near both The Lodge and the first fairway of the Pebble Beach Golf Links. For still more pampering, the **Spa at Pebble Beach** is a full-service spa facility. For reservations at any of these Pebble Beach Resort facilities, contact 800/654-9300 or website: www.pebblebeach.com.

Bed-and-Breakfasts

Victoriana is particularly popular in Pacific Grove. The most famous Victorian inn in town is the elegant **Seven Gables Inn,** 555 Ocean View Blvd., 831/372-4341, www.pginns.com, which offers ocean views from all 14 rooms and an abundance of European antiques and Victorian finery. Rates include fabulous full breakfast and afternoon tea. Sharing the garden and offering equally exceptional, if more relaxed, Victorian style is the sibling **Grand View Inn** next door, 557 Ocean View Blvd., 831/372-4341. The view from all 11 rooms, with their antique furnishings and luxurious marble bathrooms, is indeed grand. Full breakfast, afternoon tea. Rates at both are $150 and up.

Another Pacific Grove grande dame is the pretty-in-pink, 23-room **Martine Inn,** 255 Ocean View Blvd., 831/373-3388 or 800/852-5588, www.martineinn.com, a study in Victorian refinement and propriety masquerading, on the outside, as a Mediterranean villa. Full breakfast here is served with fine china, crystal, silver, and old lace. Also enjoy wine and hors d'oeuvres in the evening, a whirlpool, spa, game room, library, and a baby grand piano in the library. Rates are $150 and up.

The lovely **Green Gables Inn,** 104 Fifth St., 831/375-2095 or 800/722-1774, www.foursisters.com, is a romantic gabled Queen Anne. The seaside "summer house" offers marvelous views, five rooms upstairs, a suite downstairs, and five rooms in the carriage house. Of these, seven feature private bathrooms. Rates include continental breakfast. The Green Gables, a Four Sisters Inn, was named the number one bed-and-breakfast inn in North America in 1997, according to the Official Hotel Guide's survey of travel agents. Rates are $150 and up.

The **Gosby House Inn,** 643 Lighthouse Ave., 831/375-1287 or 800/527-8828, www.foursisters.com, is another of the Four Sisters—this one a charming (and huge) Queen Anne serving up fine antiques, a restful garden, homemade food, and fresh flowers. All 22 rooms boast great bayside views, and most feature private bathrooms. Some have fireplaces, Jacuzzi tubs, and TVs. Rates are $100 and up.

The 1889 **Centrella Inn,** 612 Central Ave., 831/372-3372 or 800/233-3372, www.centrellainn.com, a national historic landmark, offers 20 rooms plus a Jacuzzi-equipped garden suite and five cottages with wood-burning fireplaces and wet bars. The cottage-style gardens are quite appealing, especially in summer. Rates include complimentary morning newspaper, full buffet breakfast, and a social hour in the afternoon (wine and hors d'oeuvres). Rates are $100 to $250.

The **Gatehouse Inn,** 225 Central Ave., 831/649-8436 or 800/753-1881, offers nine rooms in an 1884 Victorian that's strolling distance from the Monterey Bay Aquarium. Rates include full gourmet breakfast and afternoon wine and hors d'oeuvres. The property's comely sister inn is the Cape Cod–style **Old St. Angela Inn,** 321 Central Ave., 831/372-3246 or 800/748-6306, a converted 1910 country cottage featuring eight guest rooms decorated with antiques, quilts, and other homey touches. Amenities include a garden hot tub, solarium, living room with fireplace, complimentary breakfast, and afternoon wine or tea and hors d'oeuvres. For a virtual preview, visit www.sueandlewinns.com. Rates at both are $100 to $250.

The historic three-story (no elevator) **Pacific Grove Inn** is at 581 Pine (at Forest), 831/375-2825. Some rooms and suites in this 1904 Queen Anne have ocean views, most have fireplaces, and all have private baths and modern amenities like color TVs, radios, and telephones. Breakfast buffet every morning. Rates are $150 to $250.

Not every choice in Pacific Grove is Victorian. Perfect for aquatic sports fans—the proprietors can paddle you out to the best sea kayaking—is the **Inn at 213 Seventeen Mile Drive,** 981 Lighthouse Ave. (at 17 Mile Dr.), 831/642-9514 or 800/526-5666, www.innat213-17miledr.com. Guest rooms in this restored 1928 Craftsman home and affiliated cottages, all named for seabirds, feature king or queen beds and essentials like down comforters, TVs, and phones. All rooms have private baths. Generous buffet at breakfast; hors d'oeuvres and wine in the evening. Rates are $100 to $250.

EATING IN PACIFIC GROVE
Breakfast

Great for imaginative and very fresh fare at breakfast, lunch, and dinner is the **Red House Café,** a cozy cottage-style restaurant, tea salon, and tea shop at 662 Lighthouse Ave., 831/643-1060. You can get marvelous crêpes for breakfast or lunch, as well as good waffles and homemade soups, at **Toastie's Cafe,** 702 Lighthouse Ave., 831/373-7543, open daily 7 A.M.–2 P.M. Or try the vegetarian dishes and cheesecake at **Tillie Gort's Coffee House** and art gallery at 111 Central, 831/373-0335.

For lattes, cappuccinos, espressos or just a good cuppa joe, head to **Caravali Coffee,** 510 Lighthouse Ave., 831/655-5633; **Juice and Java,** 599 Lighthouse Ave., 831/373-8652; or the dual-purpose **Bookworks,** 667 Lighthouse Ave., 831/372-2242, where you can sample the wares in the bookstore as well as the coffeehouse. Great for vegetarian fare as well as a wild cup or two is the college hangout-style **Wildberries,** 212 17th St., 831/644-9836.

Lunch and Dinner

Thai Bistro, 159 Central Ave., 831/372-8700, is the place to go for outstanding Thai food. Those with a fireproof palate will love the restaurant's spicy dishes, and vegetarians will appreciate the large number of meatless entrées. Open for lunch and dinner daily. (There's another Thai Bistro in Carmel Valley at 55 W. Carmel Valley Rd., 831/659-5900.)

The **Crocodile Grill,** 701 Lighthouse Ave. (at Congress), 831/655-3311, offers eclectic and exotic decor along with fresh California-style Caribbean and Central-South American cuisine. Seafood is the specialty here—such as red snapper Mardi Gras—and for dessert, don't miss the house-made Key lime cheesecake with mango syrup. Beer and wine are served. Open for dinner nightly except Tuesday.

Popular with locals (and a favorite of the late, great Ansel Adams) is **Pablo's,** 1184 Forest Ave., 831/646-8888, featuring *real* Mexican food, including *mariscos.* Open 11 A.M.–9 P.M. Locals say the homemade *chiles rellenos* at immensely popular **Peppers MexiCali Cafe,** 170 Forest Ave., 831/373-6892, are the best on the peninsula, but you won't go wrong with the tamales, seafood tacos, or spicy prawns. Beer and wine are served. Closed Tuesday, but otherwise open weekdays and Saturday for lunch, nightly for dinner. Also popular for seafood is the relaxed and family-friendly **Fishwife** in the Beachcomber Inn, 1996-1/2 Sunset Dr., 831/375-7107, where such things as Boston clam chowder and grilled Cajun snapper fill out the menu. Beer and wine

served. Open for lunch and dinner every day but Tuesday; brunch on Sunday.

Allegro Gourmet Pizzeria, 1184 Forest (near Prescott), 831/373-5656, offers innovative pizzas and exceptional calzones—people come from far and wide for the latter—but you can also enjoy pasta and risotto dishes, Italian-style sandwiches, and salads.

Favaloro's, 542 Lighthouse (at Fountain), 831/373-8523, is popular for traditional Italian, served in a bright location at street level in the Holman's Building. Try the gourmet specialty pizzas or the house-made pastas. Open for lunch Tues.–Sat. and for dinner Tues.–Sun. Friendly **Pasta Mia Trattoria,** 481 Lighthouse Ave. (near 13th), 831/375-7709, open nightly for dinner, serves exceptionally creative and good house-made pastas. Beer and wine served.

For boisterous Basque food, try **Fandango,** in the stone house at 223 17th St. off Lighthouse Ave., 831/372-3456. The restaurant serves up wonderful Mediterranean country fare—from mesquite-grilled seafood, steak, and rack of lamb to tapas, pastas, and paella—in several separate dining rooms warmed by fireplaces. Try the chocolate nougatine pie or *vacherin* for dessert. Sunday brunch here is superb. Formal dress prevails at dinner in the smaller dining rooms, but everything is casual in the Terrace Room. Open for lunch and dinner daily and for brunch on Sunday. Lunch is fairly inexpensive; dinners a bit pricier.

Upscale in more traditional continental style is gracious **Gernot's Victoria House,** at home in the 1892 Victorian Hart Mansion, 649 Lighthouse Ave., 831/646-1477, where fine Austrian and European fare stars. Beer and wine served. Open Tues.–Sun. after 5:30 P.M. (reservations advised). Still one of the best restaurants on the entire Monterey Peninsula, some say, is the **Old Bath House** at Lovers Point, 620 Ocean View, 831/375-5195. It's elegant, expensive, and quite romantic, featuring lively Northern Italian and French fare, exceptional desserts, and appetizing views. Full bar, extensive wine list. Open nightly for dinner.

MONTEREY BAY & BIG SUR

Carmel

Vizcaíno named the river here after Palestine's Mount Carmel, probably with the encouragement of several Carmelite friars accompanying his expedition. The name Carmel-by-the-Sea distinguishes this postcard-pretty, almost too-cute coastal village of 5,000 souls from affluent Carmel Valley 10 miles inland and Carmel Highlands just south of Point Lobos on the way to Big Sur. Everything about all the Carmels, though, says one thing quite loudly: money. Despite its bohemian beginnings, these days Carmel crankily guards its quaintness while cranking up the commercialism. (Shopping is the town's major draw.) Still free at last report are the beautiful city beaches and visits to the elegant old Carmel Mission. Almost free: tours of Robinson Jeffers's **Tor House** and fabulous **Point Lobos** just south of town.

Carmel hasn't always been so crowded or so crotchety. Open-minded artists, poets, writers, and other oddballs were the community's original movers and shakers—most of them shaken up and out of San Francisco after the 1906 earthquake. Upton Sinclair, Sinclair Lewis, Robinson Jeffers, and Jack London were some of the literary lights who once twinkled in this town. Master photographers Ansel Adams and Edward Weston were more recent residents. But, as often happens in California,land values shot up and the original bohemians were priced right out of the neighborhood.

Carmel-by-the-Sea is facing trying times. Sinclair Lewis predicted the future in 1933 when he said to Carmelites: "For God's sake, don't let the Babbits run the town. You've got every other city in the country beat." Growth—how much and what kind—has always been the issue here. Tourists who come here to stroll and shop (locals sometimes refer to them as "the T-shirt and ice cream people") are both loved and hated.

In summer and on most warm-weather weekends, traffic on Highway 1 is backed up for a mile or more in either direction by the Carmel "crunch." Sane people take the bus, ride bikes, or walk. The overly quaint community is so congested that parking is usually nonexistent. (Even if you do find a parking spot in downtown Carmel, you won't get to dawdle; parking is limited to one hour, and you'll risk a steep fine if you're late getting back.) Other scarce items in Carmel: streetlights, traffic signals, street signs, sidewalks, house numbers, mailboxes, neon signs, and jukeboxes.

SEEING AND DOING CARMEL

To get oriented, take a walk. Carmel has a few tiny parks hidden here and there, including one especially for walkers—**Mission Trails Park,** featuring about five miles of trails winding through redwoods, willows, and wildflowers (in season). Finding it is challenging since Carmel doesn't believe in signs. To do the walk the easy way, start at the park's cleverly concealed Flanders Drive entrance off Hatton Road (appreciate the **Lester Rowntree Memorial Arboretum** just inside) before strolling downhill to the Rio Road trailhead near the mission. Then visit the mission or head downtown. Carmel's shops and galleries alone are an easy daylong distraction for true shoppers, but local architecture is also intriguing. The area between Fifth and Eighth Streets and Junipero and the city beach is packed with seacoast cottages, Carmel gingerbread "dollhouses," and adobe-and-post homes typical of the area.

Carmel Walks, 831/642-2700, www.carmel-walks.com, offers a great two-hour guided walk, with highlights including the town's original fairytale cottages, architecture by Bernard Maybeck and Charles S. Greene, onetime homes of bohemians, the local doings of photographers Edward Weston and Ansel Adams, and oddities such as a house made entirely of doors and the one built from pieces of old ships. The tour also visits Doris Day's pet-friendly hotel, includes tales of locally famous dogs, and notes local restaurants where dogs are permitted to dine with the family out on the patio. At last report, walks—$20 per person—were offered Tues.–Fri. at 10 A.M. and Sat. at 10 A.M. and 2 P.M. Reservations required.

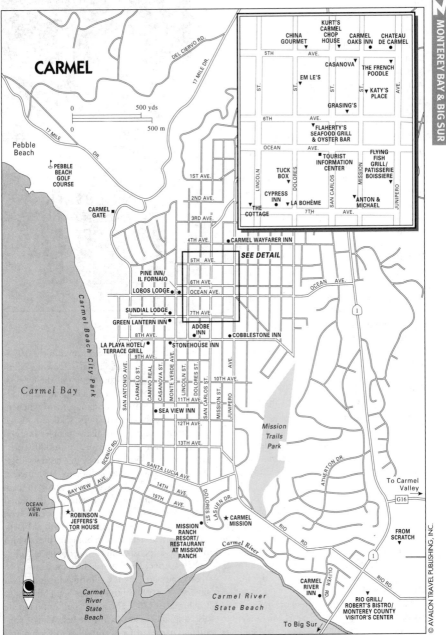

MONTEREY BAY & BIG SUR

CARMEL

Pebble
Beach

PEBBLE
BEACH
GOLF
COURSE

CHINA
GOURMET

KURT'S
CARMEL
CHOP
HOUSE

CARMEL
OAKS INN

CHATEAU
DE CARMEL

5TH   AVE.

CASANOVA   THE FRENCH
POODLE

EM LE'S   KATY'S
PLACE

GRASING'S

6TH   AVE.

OCEAN   AVE.

FLAHERTY'S
SEAFOOD GRILL
& OYSTER BAR

TOURIST
INFORMATION
CENTER

FLYING
FISH
GRILL/
PATISSERIE
BOISSIERE

TUCK
BOX

CYPRESS
INN   LA BOHÊME

ANTON &
MICHAEL

THE
COTTAGE   7TH   AVE.

CARMEL
GATE

1ST AVE.

2ND AVE.

3RD AVE.

4TH AVE.   CARMEL WAYFARER INN

5TH AVE.   SEE DETAIL

PINE INN/
IL FORNAIO   6TH AVE.

LOBOS LODGE   OCEAN AVE.

OCEAN   AVE.

SUNDIAL LODGE   7TH AVE.

GREEN LANTERN INN

8TH AVE.   ADOBE
INN   COBBLESTONE INN

LA PLAYA HOTEL/
TERRACE GRILL   9TH AVE.   STONEHOUSE INN

Carmel Bay

SEA VIEW INN   10TH AVE.

11TH AVE.

12TH AVE.

13TH AVE.

Mission
Trails
Park

SANTA LUCIA AVE.

BAY VIEW   AVE.

14TH   AVE.

15TH   AVE.

OCEAN
VIEW
AVE.   ROBINSON
JEFFERS'S
TOR HOUSE

MISSION
RANCH
RESORT/
RESTAURANT
AT MISSION
RANCH   CARMEL
MISSION

Carmel River

To Carmel
Valley

G16

FROM
SCRATCH

Carmel
River
State
Beach   Carmel River
State Beach

CARMEL
RIVER
INN   RIO GRILL/
ROBERT'S BISTRO/
MONTEREY COUNTY
VISITOR'S CENTER

To Big Sur

© AVALON TRAVEL PUBLISHING, INC.

0   500 yds
0   500 m

Beaches

The downtown crescent of **Carmel Beach City Park** is beautiful—steeply sloping, blinding-white sands and aquamarine waters—but too cold and dangerous for swimming. It's also a tourist zoo in summer. (A winter sunset stroll is wonderful, though.) A better alternative is to take Scenic Road (or Carmelo Street) south from Santa Lucia off Rio Road to **Carmel River State Beach,** 831/649-2836, fringed with eucalyptus and cypress and often uncrowded (but dangerous in high surf). This is where locals go to get away. The nearby marsh is a bird sanctuary providing habitat for hawks, kingfishers, cormorants, herons, pelicans, sandpipers, snowy egrets, and sometimes flocks of migrating ducks and geese. Beyond (and almost a secret) is **Middle Beach,** a curving sandy crescent on the south side of the Carmel River and just north of **Monastery Beach** at San Jose Creek. Middle is accessible year-round by taking Ribera Road from Highway 1; in summer or fall you can also get there by walking across the dry riverbed and following the trail. Safety note: Middle Beach is hazardous for swimming and sometimes even for walking, due to freak 10-foot waves. Monastery Beach is popular for scuba diving, but its surf conditions are equally treacherous.

Carmel Mission

The Carmel Mission, properly called Mission Basilica San Carlos Borromeo del Rio Carmelo, is wonderful and well worth a visit. California's second mission, it was originally established at the Monterey Presidio in 1770, then moved here the following year. It is the onetime headquarters and favorite foreign home of Father Junípero Serra, whose remains are buried at the foot of the altar in the sanctuary. The mission's magnificent vine-draped cathedral is the first thing to catch the eye. The romantic Baroque stone church, one of the state's most graceful buildings, complete with a four-bell Moorish tower, arched roof, and star-shaped central window, was completed in 1797.

Most of the buildings here are reconstructions, however, since the Carmel Mission fell to ruins in the 1800s. But these "new" old buildings,

Carmel Mission

painstakingly rebuilt and restored in the 1930s under the direction of Sir Harry Downie, fail to suggest the size and complexity of the original bustling mission complex: an odd-shaped quadrangle with a central fountain, gardens, kitchen, carpenter and blacksmith shops, soldiers' housing, and priests' quarters. The native peoples attached to the mission—a labor force of 4,000 Christian converts—lived separately in a nearby village. More than 3,000 "mission Indians" are buried in the silent, simple cemetery. Most graves in these gardens are unmarked, but some are decorated with abalone shells. The gardens themselves, started by Downie, are fabulous, with old-fashioned plant varieties, from bougainvillea to bird of paradise, fuchsias, and "tower of jewels."

The Carmel Mission has three museums. The "book museum" holds California's first unofficial library—the 600 volumes Padre Serra brought to California in 1769. The silver altar furnishings are also originals, as are the ornate vestments, Spanish and native artifacts, and other mission memorabilia. Serra's simple priest's cell is a lesson by contrast in modern materialism.

The mission is just a few blocks west of Highway 1 at 3080 Rio Rd., 831/624-3600 (gift shop) or 831/624-1271 (rectory), and is open for self-guided tours Mon.–Sat. 9:30 A.M.–4:30 P.M., Sun. 10:30 A.M.–4:15 P.M. Admission is free, but donations are appreciated.

Robinson Jeffers's Tor House

A medieval-looking granite retreat on a rocky knoll above Carmel Bay, Tor House was built by family-man poet Robinson Jeffers, who hauled the huge stones up from the beach below with horse teams. The manual labor, he said, cleared his mind, and "my fingers had the art to make stone love stone." California's dark prince of poetry, Jeffers was generally aloof from the peninsula's other "seacoast bohemians." On the day he died here, January 20, 1962, it snowed—a rare event along any stretch of California's coast.

You can only begin to appreciate Tor House from the outside (it's just a short walk up from Carmel River Beach, on Ocean View Avenue

ROBINSON JEFFERS MEETS UNA

If William Hamilton Jeffers [his father] was the archetypal wise old man in Robinson's life, then Una Call Kuster was, in Jungian terms, his anima ideal. Robinson met Una the first year he attended USC [the University of Southern California], in 1906. They were in Advanced German together, reading *Faust*. Una was strikingly beautiful and very intelligent. She was also three years older than Robinson and married. Nevertheless, a friendship developed that was nurtured by a mutual love for literature and ideas. She gave him Arthur Symons' *Wordsworth and Shelley* to read, and the two spent many hours discussing this and other essays, books, and poems.

When Jeffers left USC for the University of Zurich, he sent her an occasional note. When he returned to begin medical studies, the friendship resumed and deepened.

At this time in her life, Una was struggling to define her own identity. Several years before, at eighteen, she had left Mason, Michigan, in order to enter the University of California at Berkeley. She met a young attorney there, Edward ("Teddie") Kuster, whom she promptly married. When they moved to the Los Angeles area, she lived the life of a successful lawyer's wife—with golf at the San Gabriel Country Club, social events, even road races in big, expensive cars taking up most of her time. But something was missing. . . .

Inevitably, her marriage fell apart. Her husband, trying to explain to an interested public what had happened, blamed the breakdown on Una's unconventional ideas. As he says in an interview that appeared in the February 28, 1913, edition of the

Los Angeles Times, "my wife seemed to find no solace in the ordinary affairs of life; she was without social ambition, and social functions seemed a bore to her. Her accomplishments are many, and she sought constantly for a wider scope for her intelligence. She turned to philosophy and the school of modern decadents, and she talked of things beyond the ken of those of us who dwelt upon the lower levels."

Though Teddie could not understand his wife, he knew there was someone who could—a "vile poetaster" named Robinson Jeffers.

From the first time they met, Robinson had listened to Una and shared her enthusiasms. His own extensive background in languages, philosophy, religion, and literature made him a perfect conversation partner. Moreover, he was a handsome man, rugged, poetic, melancholy, and intense.

And Una listened to Robinson. She was perhaps the only person he had ever known who could understand and appreciate the complex thoughts he brooded on. Moreover, she was unconventional and passionate. While the fashionable women wore their hair in high pompadours topped by large hats, Una often wore hers in a braid that fell loose down her back.

In time, their casual friendship grew more rich. "Without the wish of either of us," says Una, "our life was one of those fatal attractions that happen unplanned and undesired."

Excerpted with permission from the literary biography Robinson Jeffers: Poet of California *by James Karman (Ashland, OR: Story Line Press, 1995)*

between Scenic Road and Stewart Way). Jeffers built the three-story Hawk Tower, complete with secret passageway, for his wife, Una. The mellow redwood paneling, warm oriental rugs, and lovely gardens here soften the impact of the home's bleak tawny exterior—the overall effect somehow symbolizing Jeffers's hearth-centered life far removed from the world's insanity. Almost whimsical is the collection of 100-plus unicorns the poet gathered. Now a national historic landmark, Tor House is still a family-owned retreat, so don't go snooping around. Small-group guided tours are offered Friday and Saturday, advance reservations required. Adults pay $7, full-time college students $4, high school students $2. No children under 12 allowed. For more information and reservations contact Tor House, 26304 Ocean View Ave. in Carmel, 831/624-1813, www.torhouse.org. Make reservations by phone or via the website.

The Tor House Foundation also offers a full schedule of events, from its annual poetry prize and sunset garden parties to the Robinson Jeffers Seminars, Jeffers Country Bus Tour (of Big Sur), and Jeffers Poetry Walk.

STAYING IN CARMEL

Camping

Mary Austin's observation that "beauty is cheap here" may apply to the views, but little else in the greater Carmel area—with the exception of camping.

Carmel by the River RV Park, 27680 Schulte Rd. (off Carmel Valley Rd.), 831/624-9329, is well away from it all. Some 35 attractively landscaped sites sit right on the Carmel River, with full hookups, cable TV, a Laundromat, a rec room, and other amenities. Nearby **Saddle Mountain Recreation Park,** also at the end of Schulte Rd., 831/624-1617, offers both tent and RV sites (reservations accepted for weekends only), restrooms, showers, picnic tables, a swimming pool, a playground, and other recreational possibilities—including nearby hiking trails. Another possibility is **Veterans Memorial Park** (see Monterey Camping and Hostels). In the primitive-and-distant category, you

can camp southeast of Carmel Valley at the U.S. Forest Service **White Oaks Campground,** which has seven sites, or **China Camp,** with six sites; both are first-come, first-camped and best suited for wilderness trekkers. Farther on you'll find **Tassajara Zen Mountain Center,** offering camping (and other accommodations) in summer by advance reservation—call 415/865-1899 after April 1, or try www.sfzc.com. The nearby Forest Service **Arroyo Seco Campground** has 46 sites. Camping is also plentiful to the south in Big Sur (see below). The Forest Service sites require purchase of a daily (or annual) Adventure Pass, available at Forest Service ranger stations and many sporting goods stores and other vendors. For more information on local Forest Service campgrounds, contact the Monterey District of Los Padres National Forest at 831/385-5434, www.r5.fs .fed.us/lospadres.

$100–150

Wonderful is the only word for the historic **Pine Inn,** downtown on Ocean between Monte Verde and Lincoln, 831/624-3851 or 800/228-3851, www.pine-inn.com. This small hotel offers comfortable "Carmel Victorian" accommodations and fine dining at the on-site **Il Fornaio** restaurant and bakery; there's even a gazebo with a rollback roof for eating alfresco, fog permitting. Even if you don't stay, sit on the terrace, act affluent, and sip Ramos fizzes.

The **Carmel River Inn,** 26600 Oliver Rd. (south of town on Hwy. 1 at the Carmel River Bridge), 831/624-1575 or 800/882-8142, www .carmelriverinn.com, is a pleasant 10-acre riverside spread with a heated pool, 24 cozy, family-friendly cottages and duplexes (some with wood-burning fireplaces and kitchens), and 19 motel rooms. Two-night minimum stay on weekends. Pets welcome for a $25-per-pet fee.

Other above-average Carmel accommodations—and there are plenty to choose from—include the **Carmel Oaks Inn,** Fifth and Mission, 831/624-5547 or 800/266-5547, attractive and convenient and a bargain by local standards, and the **Lobos Lodge,** Monte Verde and Ocean, 831/624-3874, fax 831/624-0135.

$150–250

The **Sundial Lodge,** Monte Verde and Seventh, 831/624-8578, www.sundiallodge.com, is a cross between a small hotel and a bed-and-breakfast. Each of the 19 antique-furnished rooms has a private bath, TV, and telephone. Other amenities include lovely English gardens and a courtyard, continental breakfast, and afternoon tea.

The **Adobe Inn,** downtown at Dolores and Eighth, 831/624-3933 or 800/388-3933, www .adobeinn.com, features just about every motel comfort. Rooms include gas fireplaces, wet bars and refrigerators, patios or decks, color TVs, and phones; some have ocean views. Other amenities include a sauna and heated pool. Another option is the recently upgraded, 19-room Victorian-style **Chateau de Carmel** at Fifth and Junipero, 831/624-1900 or 800/325-8515, www.chateaudecarmel.com.

The landmark 1929 **Cypress Inn,** downtown at Lincoln and Seventh, 831/624-3871 or 800/ 443-7443, www.cypress-inn.com, is a charming, gracious, and intimate place—another small hotel with a bed-and-breakfast sensibility, recently updated. Pets are allowed—invited, actually—since actress-owner Doris Day is an animal-rights activist. Dog beds provided. And when hotel staff place a mint on your pillow at turn-down, they'll also leave a treat for your dog or cat. How's *that* for service? Continental breakfast included.

Très Carmel, and a historic treasure, is the Mediterranean-style 1904 **La Playa Hotel,** Camino Real and Eighth, 831/624-6476 or 800/582-8900, www.laplayahotel.com, where lush gardens surround guest rooms and cottages on the terraced hillside. Recently remodeled, rooms at La Playa feature evocative Spanish-style furnishings. The five cottages ($250 and up) feature fireplaces, ocean-view decks, and separate living areas. Especially enjoyable when the gardens are in their glory is the on-site **Terrace Grill.**

Mission Ranch Resort

Long the traditional place to stay, just outside town, is the Mission Ranch, 26270 Dolores (at 15th), 831/624-6436 or 800/538-8221. A quiet, small ranch now owned by Clint Eastwood, Mission Ranch overlooks the Carmel River and features views of the Carmel River wetlands and Point Lobos. And the mission *is* nearby. With Eastwood ownership, the Victorian farmhouse and its outbuildings have had an expensive makeover and together now resemble a Western village. The 31 guest rooms are decorated here and there with props from Eastwood movies. Lodgings are available in the main house, the Hayloft, the Bunkhouse (which has its own living room and kitchen), and the Barn. The newer Meadow View Rooms feature, well, meadow views. Rates are $100 to $250. Another attraction is the casual on-site **Restaurant at Mission Ranch,** 831/625-9040, which serves make-my-day American fare complete with checkered tablecloths and a wood-burning stove that starred in *The Unforgiven.*

Bed-and-Breakfasts

Local inns offer an almost overwhelming amount of choice. (But keep in mind, what with the B&B craze, that "inn" in Carmel may be a revamped motel.) Local bed-and-breakfast inns are comparable in price to most Carmel area motels, and they're usually much homier.

A Carmel classic is the ivy-draped **Stonehouse Inn,** Eighth and Monte Verde, 831/624-4569 or 877/748-6618, www.carmelstonehouse.com, constructed by local Indians. All six rooms here are named after local luminaries, mostly writers, and all but two share bathrooms. Rates include full breakfast, wine and sherry, and hors d'oeuvres. Rates are $100 to $250. The **Cobblestone Inn,** on Junipero near Eighth, 831/625-5222 or 800/833-8836, www.foursisters.com, is a traditional Carmel home now transformed into a Four Sisters inn—complete with a cobblestone courtyard, gas fireplaces in the guest rooms, and English country-house antiques. Rates include a full breakfast buffet, complimentary tea, and hors d'oeuvres. Rates are $150 to $250.

The **Green Lantern Inn,** Eighth and Casanova, 831/624-4392 or 888/414-4392, www .greenlanterninn.com, offers 18 rustic multiunit cottages, some with lofts, others with fireplaces or sunset-viewing porches, not far from town and beaches. A generous continental breakfast with fresh-squeezed juices is served in the morning, wine and cheese in the afternoon. Rates are $100 to $250. The Victorian **Sea View Inn,** on Camino Real between 11th and 12th, 831/624-8778, www.seaviewinncarmel.com, is three blocks from the beach and offers eight rooms, six with private baths, and antique-filled decor. Rates include continental breakfast as well as afternoon tea and cookies or sherry. Rates are $100 to $250.

The pleasant **Carmel Wayfarer Inn,** Fourth Ave. at Mission St., 831/624-2711 or 800/533-2711, is now a bed-and-breakfast. Some rooms feature ocean views and kitchens, and most have gas fireplaces. Rates include breakfast and are $100 to $250.

Carmel Highlands

The swank and well-known 1916 **Highlands Inn,** along Highway 1 four miles south of Carmel, 831/620-1234 or 800/233-1234 (Hyatt central reservations), www.hyatt.com, is indeed beautiful, though many people would have to forfeit their rent or house payment to stay long. That may not be a problem much longer, though, since the Highlands Inn is now beginning to sell off its luxurious rooms and suites as timeshares—a reality not too popular with long-time guests. Quite luxurious, with some of the world's most spectacular views, some suites feature wood-burning fireplaces, double spa baths, fully equipped kitchens, and all the comforts. Rates are $250 and up. Even those of more plebeian means can enjoy a stroll through the Grand Lodge to appreciate the oak woodwork, twin yellow granite fireplaces, gorgeous earth-toned carpet, leather sofas and chairs, and granite tables. Or stay for a meal—the exceptional **Pacific's Edge** features stunning sunset views and was a top 10 winner in *Wine Spectator* magazine's 1998 Reader's Choice Awards. Open for lunch, dinner, and Sunday brunch. The more casual **California Market** is open daily 7 A.M.–10 P.M.

The nearby **Tickle Pink Inn,** just south of the Highlands Inn at 155 Highlands Dr., 831/624-1244 or 800/635-4774, www.ticklepink .com, offers equally spectacular views and 35 inviting rooms and suites, an ocean-view hot tub, continental breakfast, and wine and cheese at

sunset. Two-night minimum stay on weekends. Rates are $250 and up.

Carmel Valley

Robles del Rio Lodge, 200 Punta Del Monte, 831/659-3705 or 800/883-0843, www.robles-delriolodge.com, perches atop a hill overlooking Carmel Valley and is reached via winding back roads—a bit hard to find the first time. Scheduled to reopen in 2004 following an extensive remodeling, Robles del Rio is destined to become a 59-room "luxury boutique spa"—no longer the deluxe yet rustic down-home 1920s wonder it once was. Affiliated with the lodge is the excellent **The Ridge** restaurant, 831/659-0170. Call for current details and rates.

A popular local tradition is the historic **Los Laureles Country Inn,** 313 W. Carmel Valley Rd., 831/659-2233, www.loslaureles.com, once part of the Boronda Spanish land grant and later a Del Monte ranch. Rooms here used to be horse stables for Muriel Vanderbilt's well-bred thoroughbreds. The inn has an excellent restaurant (American regional), pool, and conference facilities. Golf packages are available. Rates are $100 to $250.

A great choice, too, is the **Carmel Valley Lodge** on Carmel Valley Rd. at Ford, 831/659-2261 or 800/641-4646 (reservations only), www.valley-lodge.com. After all, who can resist "Come listen to your beard grow" as an advertising slogan? The lodge features rooms fronting the lovely gardens plus one- and two-bedroom cottages with fireplaces and kitchens. Other amenities include a pool, sauna, hot tub, and fitness center. Dog friendly. Rates are $150 to $250. Two-bedroom, two-bath cottages are $250 and up.

If you must see how the other 1 percent lives, head for the five-star **Quail Lodge Resort & Golf Club** at the Carmel Valley Golf and Country Club, 8205 Valley Greens Dr., 831/624-2888, www.peninsula.com, now part of the Peninsula Group of international hotels. The lodge features elegant contemporary rooms and suites, some with fireplaces, plus access to private tennis and golf facilities and fine dining at **The Covey** restaurant. Rates are $250 and up.

Pricey, too, in the same vein is Wyndham Ho-

© ROBERT HOLMES/CALTOUR

Carmel Valley

tels's **Carmel Valley Ranch Resort,** 1 Old Ranch Rd. (off Robinson Canyon Rd.), 831/625-9500, www.wyndham.com, a gated resort with 100 suites, all individually decorated, with wood-burning fireplaces and private decks. Some suites feature a private outdoor hot tub. Recreation facilities include a private golf course, 12 tennis courts, pools, saunas, and whirlpools. Rates are $250 and up.

Luxurious but still something of a new concept in Carmel Valley accommodations is the **Bernardus Lodge,** 831/659-3247 or 888/648-9463, www.bernardus.com, a luxury resort affiliated with the Bernardus Winery and open since August 1999. Crafted from limestone, logs, ceramic tiles, and rich interior woods, the nine village-style buildings feature 57 suites for "discriminating travelers" and offer endless luxury amenities, including a different wine-and-cheese tasting every night at turn-down, a full-service spa, and special educational forums on gardening, the culinary arts, and viticulture. On-site ballroom and restaurants. Outdoor recreation options include tennis and bocce ball, croquet, swimming, hiking and

horseback riding on adjacent mountain trails, and golfing at neighboring resorts. Rates are $250 and up.

Otherwise, for a super-luxury stay—and to avoid the country clubs and other "too new" places—the choice is the 330-acre **Stonepine Estate Resort,** 150 E. Carmel Valley Rd., 831/659-2245, www.stonepinecalifornia.com, once the Crocker family's summer home. A Carmel version of a French chateau, Stonepine features luxury suites in the manor house, Chateau Noel, and others in Briar Rose Cottage, the Gate House, and—for horse lovers—the Paddock House. Rates are $250 and up.

EATING IN CARMEL
Breakfast

For a perfect omelette with home fries and homemade valley pork sausage, try **The Cottage,** on Lincoln between Ocean and Seventh, 831/625-6260. Another good choice for breakfast is **Katy's Place,** on the west side of Mission between Fifth and Sixth, 831/624-0199, another quaint cottage, this one boasting the largest breakfast and lunch menu on the West Coast. Great eggs Benedict— 10 different varieties to choose from! Open daily. Also cozy and crowded is **Em Le's,** Dolores and Fifth, 831/625-6780. Try the buttermilk waffles, available for lunch or dinner. The **Tuck Box** tearoom, on Dolores near Seventh, 831/624-6365, inspires you to stop just to take a photograph. It was once famous for its pecan pie, shepherd's pie, and Welsh rarebit, as well as great cheap breakfasts. New owners have changed the menu—and prices.

Lunch and Dinner

The **Rio Grill,** 101 Crossroads Blvd. (Hwy. 1 at Rio Rd.), 831/625-5436, is a long-running favorite for innovative southwestern-style American fare. Everything is fresh and/or made from scratch, and many entrées are served straight from the oak wood smoker. Try the ice-cream sandwich. Open for lunch and dinner daily, great Sunday brunch. Interesting, too, is the inexpensive **From Scratch** restaurant at The Barnyard Shopping Center, 831/625-2448, a casual and eclectic place—with local art on the walls—serving up an abundant, ambitious, and very "local" breakfast menu, from fresh-squeezed orange and grapefruit juice to smoothies and pancakes and huevos rancheros. Look for soups, salads, pastas, and sandwiches at lunch and such things as seafood pasta with shrimp, crab, and scallops or pork chops glazed in honey-mustard sauce at dinner. Open for breakfast and lunch daily, for dinner Tues.–Sat., and for brunch on Sunday.

Beloved in Carmel Valley is the **Corkscrew Café,** sibling to Carmel's Casanova at 55 W. Carmel Valley Rd., 831/659-8888, serving up local wines, the café's own organic garden produce, and great things at lunch—from the grilled portabella mushroom sandwich and black-bean chicken and cheese enchiladas to salmon niçoise salad. And check out the Corkscrew Museum. Friendly, quite reasonable **Café Rustica,** 10 Delfino Place, 831/659-4444, is brought to you by the same people who launched the Taste Café & Bistro in Pacific Grove. The fare here covers vast continental territory, so at lunch you can enjoy an egg salad sandwich on a baguette, a

small pizza, or a grilled vegetable salad with creamy balsamic vinaigrette. Try the Pasta Rustica at dinner.

The dinner specialty at the **Flying Fish Grill** at the Carmel Plaza shopping center, on Mission between Ocean and Seventh, 831/625-1962, is Pacific Rim seafood—from yin-yang salmon to peppered ahi tuna served with angel hair pasta. Beer and wine only. Another possibility for seafood is **Flaherty's Seafood Grill & Oyster Bar,** on Sixth between Dolores and San Carlos, 831/625-1500 (grill) or 831/624-0311 (oyster bar), an excellent two-in-one enterprise—one of Northern California's best—that offers just-off-the-boat–fresh catches of the day, great chowders, and cioppino.

Fine for takeout pastries and desserts or a light French-country lunch is **Patisserie Boissiere,** on Mission between Ocean and Seventh, 831/624-5008. **China Gourmet,** on Fifth between San Carlos and Dolores, 831/624-3941, specializes in Mandarin and Szechuan cuisine (takeout available).

Fine Dining

All the Carmels are crowded with "cuisine," some possibilities mentioned previously. Ask around if you're looking for the latest special dining experience. Some of that cuisine is pretty relaxed. Immensely popular **Grasing's** at the corner of Sixth and Mission, 831/624-6562, for example, serves "coastal cuisine." At lunch this translates into sandwiches such as grilled eggplant with roasted peppers, onions, and mushrooms, as well as a Bistro Burger with apple-wood smoked bacon, avocado, and cheddar cheese. At dinner, fish is the big deal. Dig into bronzed salmon with portabella mushrooms, roasted garlic, and Yukon golds, or try the petite filet mignon with shallot marmalade, baby carrots, asparagus, and potato cakes. Vegetarians won't starve, with choices such as lasagna with artichokes, tomatoes, spinach, Asiago cheese, and lemon vinaigrette. Somewhat less "fishy" is upbeat **Kurt's Carmel Chop House,** Fifth and San Carlos, 831/625-1199, a true steak house featuring the Chop House Caesar salad and corn-fed meat. Every entrée is served with potatoes and veggies.

Among other local stars is **Robert's Bistro,** an outpost of French-country atmosphere in the Crossroads Shopping Center, 217 Crossroads Blvd., 831/624-9626, brought to you by the chef behind Monterey's Fresh Cream. The stylish bistro fare includes sautéed red snapper, roast duckling with sweet wild cherry sauce, and cassoulet à la Robert. Open for lunch on weekdays, dinner daily. **The French Poodle,** Junipero and Fifth, 831/624-8643, gets rave reviews for its light, award-winning French cuisine. The wine list is extensive.

Casanova, Fifth and Mission, 831/625-0501, serves both country-style French and Italian cuisine in a landmark Mediterranean-style house (complete with heated garden seating for you temperature-sensitive romantics). House-made pastas here are exceptional, as are the desserts. Impressive wine list. Open daily for breakfast, lunch, and dinner. Sophisticated yet simple is excellent **La Bohême,** Dolores and Seventh, 831/624-7500, a tiny, family-style place with French cuisine and European peasant fare for dinner. No reservations; call for the day's menu or pick up the monthly calendar when you get to town. Open daily for dinner. Beer and wine are available. Elegant **Anton & Michel,** in the Court of the Fountains on Mission between Ocean and Seventh, 831/624-2406, isn't really that expensive considering the setting and good continental fare.

Even if you can't afford to stay there, you can probably afford to eat at the Highlands Inn, on Highway 1 south of Carmel. The inn's **California Market** restaurant, 831/622-5450, serves California regional dishes with fresh local ingredients. You'll enjoy ocean-view and deck dining, plus fabulous scenery. Open for breakfast, lunch, and dinner daily. In the considerably pricier category at the Highlands is the elegant and renowned **Pacific's Edge** restaurant, 831/622-5445, open for lunch, dinner, and Sunday brunch.

More marvelous hotel dining is offered at California-French **Marinus** at Bernardus Lodge, 415 Carmel Valley Rd., 831/658-3400 or 888/648-9463, a recipient of *Wine Spectator*'s Excellence Award, and at **Covey** at Quail Lodge Resort, 8205 Valley Greens Dr., 831/620-8860.

ENTERTAINMENT AND EVENTS

Entertainment

Sunsets from the beach or from craggy Point Lobos are entertainment enough. But the **Sierra Club** folks above the shoe store, on Ocean near Dolores, 831/624-8032, provide helpful information on hikes, sights, and occasional bike rides. Open Mon.–Sat. 12:30–4:30 P.M.

For live drama, the outdoor **Forest Theater,** Santa Rita and Mountain View, 831/626-1681, hosts light drama and musicals, Shakespeare, and concerts. (There's also an *indoor* **Forest Theater,** 831/624-1531.) The **Pacific Repertory Theatre Company** presents a variety of live stage productions at the Golden Bough Theatre, on Monte Verde between Eighth and Ninth; for information, call 831/622-0100 (Tues.–Sat. noon–4 P.M.).

Carmel proper has laws prohibiting live music and leg-shaking inside the city limits. **Mission Ranch,** in the county 11 blocks out of town at 26270 Dolores, 831/625-9040, has a piano bar. Otherwise, you'll have to head into rowdy Monterey for dancing and prancing. But you can always go bar-hopping locally.

Events

Come on New Year's Day for the annual **Rio Grill Resolution Run** and in February for the annual **Masters of Food & Wine.** Come in May for the **Jeffers Tor House Garden Party,** the annual fundraiser, and June for the Carmel Valley **California Cowboy Show.** June also kicks off the theater season in Carmel. Right around the first of the month (or slightly before), the Pacific Repertory Theatre troupe opens its performance season, part of which is devoted to the **Carmel Shakespeare Festival,** with plays presented from August into October. Plays are presented at the Golden Bough Playhouse and other venues. The entire season runs through mid-October. For information, call 831/622-0100. The **Films in the Forest** theater series also gets underway in June at the outdoor Forest Theatre; call 831/626-1681 for information.

Johann Sebastian Bach never knew a place like Carmel, but his spirit lives here nonetheless. From mid-July to early August, Carmel sponsors its traditionally understated **Bach Festival,** honoring J. S. and other composers of his era, with daily concerts, recitals, and lectures at the mission and elsewhere, sometimes including the Hotel Del Monte at the Naval Postgraduate School in Monterey. If you're going, get your tickets *early.* For information, contact 831/624-2046 or website: www.bachfestival.org. Closer to performance dates, stop by the festival office at the Sunset Cultural Center, San Carlos at Ninth, to check on ticket availability.

At Carmel Beach, usually on a Sunday in late September or early October, the **Great Sandcastle Building Contest** gets underway. Events include Novice and Advanced Sandbox. (Get the date from the Monterey Chamber of Commerce, as Carmel locals generally "don't know," just to keep the tourists away.) Also in October, the **Tor House Festival,** the annual **Carmel Performing Arts Festival,** and the annual **Taste of Carmel** event, in recent years held at the Bernardus Lodge. In December, the **Music for Christmas** series at the Carmel Mission is quite nice. And special events take place from early in the month right up through Christmas Eve during the **Carmel Lights Up the Season** festival. For more information on special events, contact the Monterey County Visitors Center or Carmel Valley Chamber of Commerce.

SHOPPING

For something different to tote home as a souvenir, **It's Cactus** on Mission between Ocean & Seventh, 831/626-4213, offers colorful indigenous folk art from Guatemala, Indonesia, and other places around the globe. For candles, candlesticks, and oil lamps, try **Wicks & Wax** in the Doud Arcade, Ocean at San Carlos, 831/624-6044. For fine soaps, other bath products, and home scents, head for the **Rainbow Scent Company,** on Lincoln between Ocean and Seventh, 831/624-6506. **Nature's Bounty** on Lincoln between Ocean and Seventh, 831/626-0920, is a gem and mineral "gallery" featuring jewelry, sculptures, and more.

You'll find plenty of antique shops in and around Carmel. For old toys and memorable

memorabilia try **Life In The Past Lane,** 24855 Outlook Court, 831/625-2121. **Sabine Adamson Antiques & Interiors,** on Dolores between Fifth and Sixth, 831/626-7464, specializes in fine European antiques and accessories. **Conway of Asia,** Seventh and Dolores, 831/624-3643, offers antiques and oriental rugs from Myanmar (Burma), India, Tibet, and Thailand. **Vermillion** in the Crossroads Shopping Center (Rio Road and Highway 1), 831/620-1502, emphasizes museum-quality Japanese items, both antique and contemporary.

For all its antique finery, Carmel has even more art galleries—dozens of them. A great place to start is the **Carmel Art Association Gallery** on Dolores between Fifth and Sixth, 831/624-6176, founded here in 1927. The art association features more than 120 local artists and regularly presents an impressive selection of their painting, sculpture, and graphic arts. The **Weston Gallery, Inc.,** on Sixth between Dolores and Lincoln, 831/624-4453, offers 19th- and 20th-century photographs by namesake local photographers Edward Weston and Brett Weston as well as Ansel Adams, Michael Kenna, Jeffrey Becom, and Jerry Uelsmann.

The **Chapman Gallery and Frame Shop,** on Seventh between San Carlos and Mission, 831/626-1766, showcases regional California artists. Wonderful for local art is the **Lyonshead Art Gallery,** 12 Del Fino Place in Carmel Valley, 831/659-4192, and **Savage Stephens Contemporary Fine Art** at Su Vecino, Dolores between Fifth and Sixth, 831/626-0800. The bronze and stone sculptures by Sharon Spencer are standouts. The impressive **Highlands Sculpture Gallery,** on Dolores between Fifth and Sixth, 831/624-0535, is Carmel's oldest contemporary art gallery.

Carmel's also no slouch when it comes to personal fashion, most of it on the pricey side. Definitely upscale is **Girl Boy Girl** at the Court of the Fountains, Mission and Seventh, 831/626-3368, featuring contemporary fashions from more than 50 designers. Worth exploring at Carmel Plaza, Ocean and Mission, are classic **Ann Taylor,** 831/626-9565, and trendier **Chico's,** 831/622-9618. Always fun for something more exotic is **Exotica** at the Crossroads

Shopping Center, 831/622-0757, where you'll find handpainted and batiked natural fiber fashions along with Laurel Burch, other interesting jewelry, and folk art.

Carmel being a pet-pampering town, Fido generally fares well. The place to shop for canine and feline fashion, for example, is **Fideaux,** Ocean and Monte Verde, 831/626-7777. Buy gently used clothing, jewelry, art, books, collectibles, and antiques at the **SPCA Benefit Shop** (Society for the Prevention of Cruelty to Animals), Su Vecino Court between Fifth and Sixth, 831/624-4211 or 831/373-2631 ext. 224, to help less fortunate creatures.

For current shopping information and more suggestions, contact the **Carmel Business Association** Visitor & Information Center on San Carlos between Fifth and Sixth, 831/624-2522 or 800/550-4333, www.carmelcalifornia.org.

INFORMATION

The *Carmel Pine Cone* newspaper covers local events and politics. The **Carmel Business Association** is upstairs in the Eastwood Building on San Carlos between Fifth and Sixth, 831/624-2522 or 800/550-4333, www.carmelcalifornia.org. Its annual *Guide to Carmel* includes information on just about everything—from shopping hot spots to accommodations and eateries. The **Tourist Information Center** at Ocean and Mission, 831/624-1711, is quite helpful and provides assistance with lodging reservations. The **Carmel Valley Chamber of Commerce** is in the Oak Building at 71 W. Carmel Valley Rd. in Carmel Valley, 831/659-4000, www.carmelvalleychamber.com. For countywide information, contact the **Monterey County Visitors Center,** 137 Crossroads Blvd. (in the Crossroads Shopping Center, off Hwy. 1 and Rio Rd.), 831/626-1424 or 888/221-1010, www.montereyinfo.org. The center is open daily 10 A.M.–6 P.M. in summer; Mon.–Sat. 10 A.M.–5 P.M. and Sun. 11 A.M.–4 P.M. the rest of the year.

To get to Carmel from Monterey without car or bike, take Monterey-Salinas Transit bus 52 (24 hours), 831/899-2555.

Near Carmel

POINT LOBOS

One of the crown jewels of California's state parks, Point Lobos State Reserve is a 1,250-acre coastal wonderland about four miles south of Carmel. Pack a picnic; this is the best the Monterey area has to offer. The relentless surf and wild winds have pounded these reddish shores for millennia, sculpting six miles of shallow aquamarine coves, wonderful tidepools, aptly named Bird Island, and jutting points: Granite, Coal, Chute, China, Cannery, Pinnacle, Pelican, and Lobos itself. From here, look to the sea, as Santa Cruz poet William Everson has, "standing in cypress and surrounded by cypress, watching through its witchery as the surf explodes in unbelievable beauty on the granite below." Local lore has it that Point Lobos inspired Robert Louis Stevenson's Spyglass Hill in *Treasure Island*. The muse for Robinson Jeffers's somber "Tamar" definitely lived (and lives) here.

Seeing and Doing Point Lobos

From the dramatic headlands, watch for whales in winter. Many other marine mammals are year-round residents. Brown pelicans and cormorants preen themselves on offshore rocks. Here, the sea otters aren't shy: They boldly crack open abalone and dine in front of visitors. (The entire central coast area, from San Francisco south to beyond Big Sur, is protected as part of the **Monterey Bay National Marine Sanctuary.** And by order of former President Bill Clinton, the state's entire coastline is now protected as the California Coastal National Monument.) If you're heading south into Big Sur country, watch offshore otter antics—best with binoculars—from highway turnouts. Harbor seals hide in the coves. The languorous, loudly barking sea lions gave rise to the original Spanish name Punta de los Lobos Marinos ("Point of the Sea Wolves"). Follow the crisscrossing reserve trails for a morning walk through groves of bonsai Monterey cypress and pine, accented by colorful seasonal wildflowers (300 species, best in April). Watch for poison oak, which thrives here, too. Whalers Cove near the picnic and parking area was once a granite quarry, then a whaler's cove—the cabin and cast-iron rendering pot are still there—and an abalone cannery. It's something of a miracle that the Point Lobos headland exists almost unscarred, as cattle grazed here for decades. Fortunately for us all, turn-of-the-20th-century subdivision plans for Point Lobos were scuttled.

Head for Whalers Cove to bone up on local history. **Whalers Cabin Museum,** "the shack" overlooking Whalers Cove, built by Chinese fishermen, tells the story of Point Lobos and vicinity. The adjacent **Whaling Station Museum,** once a garage, features displays about shore whaling along California's central coast—everything from harpoons and whale-oil barrels to historic Monterey Peninsula whaling photos. Guided hikes are also offered at Point Lobos; see the monthly schedule posted at the park's entrance. Curious students of history and natural history can also get an impressive area introduction via the park's website, below.

Safety

Point Lobos is considered one of the state's "underwater parks," in recognition of its aquatic beauty. Scuba and free diving are popular but allowed by permit only; call 831/624-8413 for reservations or see the website. Diver safety is a major concern of park staff. Get permits and current information about what to expect down below before easing into the water. People aren't kidding when they mention "treacherous cliff and surf conditions" here, so think first before scrambling off in search of bigger and better tidepools. Particularly dangerous even in serene surf is the Monastery Beach area, near San Jose Creek just beyond the reserve's northern border; there's a steep offshore drop-off into submarine Carmel Canyon and unstable sand underfoot. Children should be carefully supervised, and even experienced divers and swimmers might think twice before going into the water.

Practicalities

Point Lobos is beautiful—and popular. It can be crowded in summer and sometimes on spring and fall weekends. Since only 450 people are allowed into the park at one time, plan your trip accordingly and come early in the day (or wait in long lines along Highway 1—not fun). Open for day use only (sunrise till sunset in summer; until 5 P.M. in winter); $5 per car, but free for walk-ins and bike-ins. Trail brochures are $1. Bikes must stay on pavement in the park—no trail riding.

You can also get to Point Lobos on Monterey-Salinas Transit's bus 22 (to Big Sur). From Carmel, it's a fairly easy bike ride. The weather can be cold, damp, and windy even in summer, so bring a sweater or jacket in addition to good walking shoes (and, if you have them, binoculars). The park's informative brochure is printed in five languages. Guided tours are offered daily. To better appreciate local flora and the 200-plus species of birds spotted at Point Lobos, pick up the plant and bird lists at the ranger station. In May, the Department of Fish and Game's **Marine Resources and Marine Pollution Studies Laboratory** at Granite Canyon sponsors an open house. For more information, contact Point Lobos State Reserve, 831/624-4909, http://ptlobos.parks.state.ca.us.

CARMEL VALLEY

The sunny (and warmer) sprawling "village" of Carmel Valley stretches some 14 miles inland via Carmel Valley Road, a well-designed but hellacious highway, at least between Carmel and these affluent suburbs and golf and tennis farms (including John Gardiner's Tennis Ranch). Locals curse tourists and others who drive the speed limit.

The village area has definite diversion value for the wealthy and the wannabes—note the shopping centers—but the valley has always been the one Carmel's just plain folks were most likely to inhabit. In 1939 Rosie's Cracker Barrel on Equiline Road became the valley's general store and soon the unofficial community center. Though Rosie's was always the place to pick up picnic supplies and whatnot, there was also a bar out back where locals held forth—definitely not a tourist joint. Rosie's is closed now; plans to re-open it as a museum are in the works. Still, some notable before-the-wealthy Carmel Valley traditions remain—like wide-open spaces. Outdoorsy types will appreciate **Garland Ranch Regional Park,** north of town at 700 W. Carmel Valley Rd., 831/659-4488. The park offers hiking trails on 4,500 hilly acres; you'll get an astounding view from the top of Snively's Ridge.

For more information about Carmel Valley and vicinity, contact the **Carmel Valley Chamber of Commerce,** 91 W. Carmel Valley Rd., 831/659-4000, www.carmelvalleychamber.com.

Wineries

Not surprising in such a moderate Mediterranean climate, vineyards do well here. So do wineries and wines, recognized as eight distinct appellations. To keep up with them all, pick up the free *Monterey Wine Country* brochure and map at area visitor centers or contact the **Monterey County Vintners & Growers Association,** 831/375-9400, www.montereywines.org. Wine-related events well worth showing up for include the **Annual Winemakers' Celebration** in August and the **Great Wine Escape Weekend** in November. If you're short on touring time this trip, many Monterey County wines are available for tasting at **A Taste of Monterey,** 700 Cannery Row in Monterey, 831/646-5446, www.taste-monterey.com, open daily 11 A.M.–6 P.M.

The very small **Chateau Julien Winery,** 8940 Carmel Valley Rd., 831/624-2600, www.chateau-julien.com, is housed in a French-style chateau and is open daily for tasting, for tours by reservation. The winery's chardonnay and merlot have both been honored as the best in the United States at the American Wine Championships in New York. Southwest of Carmel Valley and bordering Los Padres National Forest is the remote spring-fed "boutique" **Heller Estate/Durney Vineyards,** originally owned by the late William Durney and his wife, screenwriter Dorothy Kingsley, and still noted for its award-winning organic wines. The winery is not open to the public, but the organic wines are available for tasting in Carmel Valley Village at 69 W. Carmel Valley

Rd., 831/659-6220 or 800/625-8466, www.durneywines.com or website: www.hellerestate.com, and are also widely available in Carmel, Monterey, and vicinity.

Bernardus Winery, 5 W. Carmel Valley Rd., 831/659-1900 or 800/223-2533, www.bernardus.com, has a tasting room open 11 A.M.–5 P.M. daily. Also look around for other premium, small-production wineries, such as **Joullian Vineyards Ltd.,** with cabernet sauvignon, sauvignon blanc, merlot, zinfandel, and chardonnay. Joullian's new tasting room in Carmel Valley at 2 Village Dr., Ste. A, 831/659-8100, www.joullian.com, is open for tasting and sales Mon.–Fri. 11 A.M.–3 P.M., excluding holidays. The winery is occasionally open for special Saturday open house events; for details call 877/659-2800.

Between Greenfield and Soledad along the inland Highway 101 corridor are a handful of good wineries. The 1978 private reserve cabernet sauvignon of **Jekel Vineyards,** 40155 Walnut Ave. in Greenfield, 831/674-5522 or 800/625-2610, www.usawines.com/jekel, washed out Lafite-Rothschild and other international competitors in France in 1982. Tastings daily 10 A.M.–5 P.M., tours by appointment. **Hahn Estates/Smith & Hook Winery,** 37700 Foothill Blvd. in Soledad, 831/678-2132, www.hahnestates.com, is known for its cabernet sauvignon—also for the amazing view across the Salinas Valley to the Gabilan Mountains. Open daily 11 A.M.–4 P.M.; tours by appointment. Also in the area: **Chalone Vineyard** on Stonewall Canyon Rd. (Hwy. 146), 831/678-1717, www.chalonewinegroup.com, the county's oldest vineyard and winery, known for its estate-bottled varietals; and noted **Paraiso Springs Vineyard,** 38060 Paraiso Springs Rd., 831/678-0300, website:www.usawines.com/paraiso, open for tasting Mon.–Fri. noon–4 P.M., Sat. and Sun. 11 A.M.–5 P.M. (tours by appointment).

Farther north is small Salinas-area **Cloninger Cellars,** 1645 River Rd., 831/675-9463, www.usawines.com/cloninger, which offers chardonnay, pinot noir, and cabernet sauvignon in its tasting room. Open for tasting Mon.–Thurs. 11 A.M.–4 P.M., Fri.–Sun. 11 A.M.–5 P.M. Not open to the public (no tasting room) but well worth visiting during special events is **Morgan**

Winery in Salinas at 590 Brunken Ave., 831/751-7777, www.morganwinery.com, which has garnered a glut of gold medals and other recognition for its chardonnays. Winners here, too, are the cabernet, pinot noir, and sauvignon blanc.

True wine fanatics must make one more stop—at America's most award-winning vineyard, **Ventana Vineyards,** 2999 Monterey-Salinas Hwy. (near the Monterey Airport just outside Monterey on Hwy. 68), 831/372-7415, www.ventanawines.com. Open daily 11 A.M.–5 P.M., until 6 P.M. in summer.

JAMESBURG EARTH STATION

The 10-story, 34-ton AT&T Jamesburg Earth Station is a popular stop for space technology fans. The impressive parabolic COMSAT dish antenna here transmits information to and from an orbiting communications satellite more than 22,000 miles away. The visitor program includes a movie, lecture, and chance to peek into the control room. Call 831/659-6100 to arrange a tour. To get here, head southeast into the hills on Carmel Valley Road (20 miles east of Highway 1), which becomes Tularcitos Road. About 10 miles from Carmel Valley Village, turn right on Cachagua Road and hold onto your hat (and/or head) for the next five miles.

After (or instead of) the Jamesburg tour, continue on Tularcitos until it joins Arroyo Seco Road, then jog southwest toward the backside of Big Sur and the Arroyo Seco River canyon. There you can enjoy camping, picnicking, and hiking. Backpackers can head west on a long but rewarding trek to remote, undeveloped **Sykes Hot Springs,** near Horse Bridge Camp.

TASSAJARA ZEN MOUNTAIN CENTER

Not far beyond the COMSAT station is one-time Tassajara Hot Springs, a respected old resort established in 1869. (The Tassajara Road turnoff is off Cachagua Road near the southward intersection with Tularcitos.) According to Native American legend, these curative springs first flowed from the eyes of a young chief seeking help for his dying sister. Offering himself as a sacrifice to the sun, he turned to stone, and his tears became the hot springs.

Now the monastic Tassajara Zen Mountain Center, affiliated with the **San Francisco Zen Center,** Tassajara is the first Soto Zen monastery outside of Asia, open to the general public from May 1 until early September. Most people come here for the hot springs (bathing suits required), but fabulous wilderness access and marvelous vegetarian meals are also available. A wide variety of accommodations—most fairly simple and in the $100 to $150 price category—are available. Dorm accommodations are $50 to $100. A stay here includes three vegetarian meals per day and use of all facilities. You can even camp here. Advance reservations are a must. With confirmed reservations, the center will send a map and directions. Also here: serene surroundings, a swimming pool, and picnicking. Feel free to join in the monastery's prayers and meditations.

For current details, try the Zen Center's website, www.sfzc.com. For reservations, after April 1 call 415/865-1899. For information and help in planning your stay, especially if you haven't visited Tassajara before, first call 415/865-1895. There is no phone at Tassajara—and no cell phones, radios, tape players, TVs, or cars allowed.

MIRA OBSERVATORY

If for some reason you decide to drive the last six miles of unpaved Tassajara Road, this is where you'll end up. Not officially open to the public, the MIRA Observatory, built by the Monterey Institute for Research in Astronomy (MIRA), is a barrel-shaped, roll-top professional observatory 12 miles inland from Big Sur. MIRA's earth-tone, two-story corrugated Oliver Observing Station—named after a retired Hewlett-Packard vice president who kicked in some cash, some advanced electronics, and a 36-inch telescope—includes office and living space. It has earned design awards from the American Institute of Architects. For information, contact: MIRA, 200 Eighth St. in Marina, 831/883-1000, ext. 58, www.mira.org.

Big Sur

The poet Robinson Jeffers described this redwood and rock coast as "that jagged country which nothing but a falling meteor will ever plow." It's only fitting, then, that this area was called Jeffers Country long before it became known as Big Sur. Sienna-colored sandstone and granite, surly waves, and the sundown sea come together in a never-ending dance of creation and destruction. Writer Henry Miller said Big Sur was "the face of the earth as the creator intended it to look," a point hard to argue. Still, Big Sur as a specific *place* is difficult to locate. It's not only a town, a valley, and a river, but the entire coastline from just south of Carmel Highlands to somewhere north of San Simeon (some suggest the southern limit is the Monterey County line) is considered Big Sur country.

Once "in" Big Sur, wherever that might be, visitors notice some genuine oddities—odd at least by California standards. Until recently, most people here didn't have much money and didn't seem to care. (This situation is changing as the truly wealthy move in.) They built simple or unusual dwellings—redwood cabins, glass tepees, geodesic domes, even round redwood houses with the look of wine barrels ready to roll into the sea—both to fit the limited space available and to express that elusive Big Sur sense of *style*.

Because the terrain itself is so tormented and twisted, broadcast signals rarely arrive in Big Sur. In the days before satellite dishes, there was virtually no TV; electricity and telephones with dial service have been available in Big Sur only since the 1950s, and some people along the south coast and in more remote areas still have neither.

Social life in Big Sur consists of bowling at the naval station, attending a poetry reading or the annual Big Sur Potluck Revue at the Grange Hall in the valley, driving into "town" (Monterey) for a few movie cassettes, or—for a really wild night—drinks on the deck at sunset and dancing cheek to cheek at Nepenthe. Big Sur is a very *different* California, where even the chamber of commerce urges visitors "to slow down, meditate," and "catch up with your soul."

It's almost impossible to catch up with your soul, however, when traffic is bumper-to-bumper. Appreciating Big Sur while driving or, only for the brave, bicycling in a mile-long coastline convoy is akin to honeymooning in Hades—a universal impulse but entirely the wrong ambience. As it snakes through Big Sur, California's Coast Highway (Highway 1), the state's first scenic highway and one of the world's most spectacular roadways, slips around the prominent ribs of the Santa Lucia Mountains, slides into dark wooded canyons, and soars across graceful bridges spanning the void. Though its existence means that a trip into Monterey no longer takes an entire day, people here nonetheless resent the highway that brings the flamed out and frantic.

To show some respect, come to Big Sur during the week, in balmy April or early May, when wildflowers burst forth, or in late September or October to avoid the thick summer fog. Though winter is generally rainy, weeks of sparkling warm weather aren't uncommon. In April, Big Sur hosts the annual **Big Sur International Marathon,** with 1,600 or more runners hugging the highway curves from the village to Carmel.

HISTORY

The earliest Big Sur inhabitants, the Esselen people, once occupied a 25-mile-long and 10-mile-wide stretch of coast from Point Sur to near Lucia in the south. A small group of Ohlone, the Sargenta-Ruc, lived from south of the Palo Colorado Canyon to the Big Sur River's mouth. Though most of the area's Salinan peoples lived inland in the Salinas Valley near what is now Fort Hunter-Liggett, villages were also scattered along the Big Sur coast south of Lucia. Little is known about area natives, since mission-forced intertribal marriages and introduced diseases soon obliterated them. It is known, though, that the number of Esselens in Big Sur was estimated between 900 and 1,300 after the Spanish arrived in 1770 and that the Esselen people lived in the Big Sur valley at least 3,000 years ago.

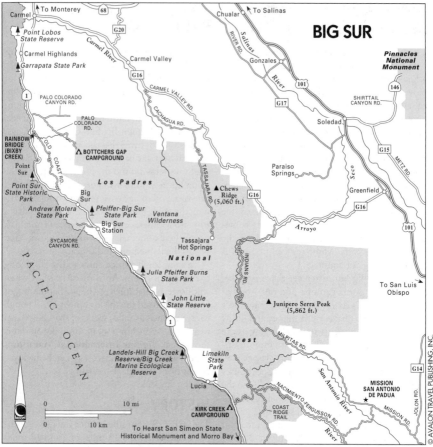

The Esselen people were long gone by the time the first area settlers arrived. Grizzly bears were the greatest 18th-century threat to settlement, since the terrain discouraged any type of travel and the usual wildlife predation that came with it. The name Big Sur ("Big South" in Spanish, a reference point from the Monterey perspective) comes from Rio Grande del Sur, or the Big Sur River, which flows to the sea at Point Sur. The river itself was the focal point of the 1834 Mexican land grant and the Cooper family's Rancho El Sur until 1965.

In the early 1900s came the highway, a hazardous 15-year construction project between Big Sur proper and San Simeon. Hardworking Chi-

nese laborers were recruited for the job along with less willing workers from the state's prisons. The highway was completed in 1937, though many lives and much equipment were lost to the sea. Maintaining this remote ribbon of highway and its 29 bridges is still a treacherous year-round task. Following the wild winter storms of 1982–83, for example, 42 landslides blocked the highway; the "big one" near Julia Pfeiffer Burns State Park took 19 bulldozers and more than a year to clear.

Big Sur's Semi-Civil Wars and Big Surbanization

Today only 1,300 people live in Big Sur country—just 300 more than in the early 1900s. Yet "Big Surbanization" is underway. Land not included in Los Padres National Forest and the Ventana Wilderness is largely privately owned. Plans for more hotels, restaurants, and civilized comforts for frazzled travelers continue to come up, and the eternal, wild peace Robinson Jeffers predicted would reign here forever has at last been touched by ripples of civilization. Nobody wants the character of Big Sur to change, but people can't agree on how best to save it.

As elsewhere in California, some Big Sur landowners believe that private property rights are sacrosanct, beyond the regulation of God or the government. Others argue that state and local land-use controls are adequate. Still others contend that federal intervention is necessary, possibly granting the region scenic area or national park status—an idea fought sawtooth and nail by most residents. The reason Big Sur is still ruggedly beautiful, they say, is because local people have kept it that way. A favorite response to the suggestion of more government involvement: "Don't Yosemitecate Big Sur." In March 1986, both of California's senators proposed that the U.S. Forest Service take primary responsibility for safeguarding Big Sur's scenic beauty—with no new logging, mining claims, or grazing privileges allowed. The final plan, which limits but doesn't eliminate new development, seems to please almost everyone—except when new controversies arise.

Some proposed changes create no controversy, such as the late 2000 acquisition by Los Padres National Forest of 784 acres along San Carpoforo Creek and the 2001 purchase of the 1,226-acre Bixby Ocean Ranch by the Trust for Public Land for eventual inclusion in the national forest. The Bixby Ranch, once owned by the late Allen Funt, host of TV's *Candid Camera*, was prime Big Sur property otherwise slated for development. In May 2002, The Nature Conservancy and The Big Sur Land Trust bought the 10,000-acre Palo Corona Ranch, the "gateway to Big Sur" beginning a block south of Carmel. That property, most of which will be managed as state park land and accessible to the public, connects 13 other parks and preserves.

Other proposals, though, raise quite a ruckus, such as the Hearst Corporation's 1998 plan to build a luxury golf result just south of Big Sur near San Simeon and the famed Hearst Castle. Negotiations to sell development rights for the corporation's 83,000-acre Piedra Blanca Ranch, or White Rock Ranch, which surrounds Hearst's castle, were continuing, at last report.

SEEING BIG SUR
Garrapata State Park

Garrapata State Park stretches north along the coast for more than four miles from Soberanes Point, where the Santa Lucia Mountains first dive into the sea. Southward, the at-first unimpressive **Point Sur** and its lighthouse beacon stand out beyond 2,879-acre Garrapata State Park and beach, the latter named after the noble wood tick and featuring a crescent of creek-veined white sand, granite arches, caves and grottos, and sea otters. Ticks or no ticks, the unofficial nude beach here is one of the best in Northern California. Winter whale-watching is usually good from high ground. On weekends in January, ranger-led whale-watch programs are held at Granite Canyon. Or, if it's not foggy, take the two-mile loop trail from the turnout for the view.

For more information about the park, call 831/624-4909, or call the **Big Sur Station** joint State Parks/U.S. Forest Service office at 831/667-2315.

South of Garrapata and inland is private **Palo Colorado Canyon,** reached via the road of the same name. Dark and secluded even in summer, the canyon is often cut off from the rest of the world when winter storms stomp through. The name itself is Spanish for "tall redwood." About eight miles in at the end of the road is isolated **Bottchers Gap Campground,** complete with restrooms, picnic tables, and multiple trailheads into the Ventana Wilderness. A few miles farther south on the highway is the famous **Rainbow Bridge** (now called Bixby Creek Bridge), 260 feet high and 700 feet long, the highest single-arch bridge in the world when constructed in 1932 and still the most photographed of all Big Sur bridges.

© ROBERT HOLMES/CALTOUR

Point Sur State Historic Park

Up atop Point Sur stands the Point Sur Light-station, an 1889 sandstone affair still standing guard at this shipwreck site once known as the Graveyard of the Pacific. In the days when the only way to get here was on horseback, 395 wooden steps led to the lighthouse, originally a giant multi-wick kerosene lantern surrounded by a Fresnel lens with a 16-panel prism. The Point Sur Lightstation is now computer-oper-ated and features an electrical aero-beacon, radio-beacon, and fog "diaphone." This 34-acre area and its central rocky mound (good views and whale-watching) is now a state park, though the Coast Guard still maintains the lighthouse. Guided three-hour lighthouse walk-ing tours are offered five or six times a week in summer, three times weekly in winter. Full moon tours are also offered monthly, spring through fall. Tours are $5 adults, $3 teens, $2 children. Current tour information is posted throughout Big Sur. For details,contact the park at 831/625-4419, www.lighthouse-point-sur-ca.org. For information about winter whale-watching programs here and at both Garrapata and Julia Pfeiffer Burns State Parks, call 831/667-2315.

Andrew Molera State Park

Inland and up, past what remains of the pio-neering Molera Ranch (part of the original Ran-cho El Sur), is marvelous Andrew Molera State Park, 2,100 acres first donated to the Nature Conservancy by Frances Molera in honor of her brother, then deeded to the state for manage-ment. There's no pavement here, just the pio-neer family's home, now the Molera Cultural and Natural History Center; a dirt parking lot; and a short trail winding through sycamores, maples, and a few redwoods along the east fork of the Big Sur River to the two-mile beach and ad-jacent seabird sanctuary-lagoon below. (The big breakers cresting along the coast here are created by the Sur Breakers Reef.) The trail north of the river's mouth leads up a steep promontory to Garnet Beach, noted for its colorful pebbles.

The new, improved Andrew Molera Trail Camp opened in April 2003—a primitive yet peaceful walk-in campground with 24 environ-mental campsites (first-come, first-camped, three-night limit, no RVs, four people maximum per site, $7). New restrooms. Dogs allowed only with a leash and proof of current rabies vacci-nation—and not beyond beyond the picnic area. Day use at Andrew Molera is $5. For more information about the park, contact Andrew Molera State Park, 831/667-2315.

Also at the park: **Molera Horseback Tours,** 831/625-5486 or 800/942-5486, www.molerahorsebacktours.com, which offers regularly scheduled one- to three-hour rides along the beach and through meadows and redwood groves. Guides explain the history, flora, and fauna of the area. Private rides are also available by appointment. Rates are $25 to $35 an hour.

Pfeiffer–Big Sur State Park

Inland, on the other side of the ridge from Andrew Molera State Park, is protected, sunny Big Sur Valley, a visitor-oriented settlement adjoining the Ventana Wilderness and surrounding picnic, camping, and lodge facilities at 821-acre Pfeiffer–Big Sur State Park. Take the one-mile nature trail or meander up through the redwoods to **Pfeiffer Falls,** a verdant, fern-lined canyon at its best in spring and early summer, then to **Valley View** for a look at the precipitous Big Sur River gorge below. Redwoods, sycamores, bigleaf maples, cottonwoods, and willows hug the river, giving way to oaks, chaparral, and Santa Lucia bristlecone fir at higher elevations. There's abundant poison oak, and raccoons can be particularly pesky here, like the begging birds, so keep food out of harm's way.

To hike within the Ventana Wilderness, head south on the highway one-half mile to the U.S. Forest Service office, 831/667-2315, for a permit and current information (trails begin here). About a mile south of the entrance to Pfeiffer-Big Sur is the road to Los Padres National Forest's **Pfeiffer Beach** (take the second right-hand turnoff after the park) and its cypresses, craggy caves, and mauve and white sands streaked with black. It's heaven here on a clear, calm day, but the hissing sand stings mercilessly when the weather is up. On any day, forget the idea of an ocean swim. The water's cold, the surf capricious, and the currents tricky; even expert divers need to register with rangers before jumping in. Pfeiffer Beach is open to the public from 6 A.M.–sunset; $5 fee.

The outdoor amphitheater at Pfeiffer-Big Sur State Park (which hosts many of the park's educational summer campfires and interpretive programs) and lagoons were built by the Civilian Conservation Corps during the depression. The large developed year-round campground features 214 family campsites with picnic tables and hot showers; rates are $13–16 and $17–20 (premium) per night. Group campsites are $45. To make camping reservations—essential in summer, when the park is particularly crowded, and on good-weather weekends—contact ReserveAmerica, 800/444-7275, www.reserveamerica .com. The day-use fee for short park hikes and picnicking is $5. For more information, contact Pfeiffer–Big Sur State Park, 831/667-2315.

Urban Big Sur

Nowhere in Big Sur country are visitors really diverted from the land, because there are no bigtime boutiques, gaudy gift shops, or even movie theaters. But urban Big Sur starts at Big Sur Valley and stretches south past the post office and U.S. Forest Service office to the vicinity of Deetjen's Big Sur Inn. This "big city" part of Big Sur includes the area's most famous and fabulous inns and restaurants: the Ventana Inn, the Post Ranch Inn, Nepenthe, and Deetjen's. (For more on all of these, see Practical Big Sur, below). Fascinating about Nepenthe is that although cinematographer Orson Welles was persona non grata just down the coast at San Simeon (for his too-faithful portrayal of William Randolph Hearst in *Citizen Kane*), when he bought what was then the Trails Club Log Cabin in Big Sur for his wife Rita Hayworth in 1944, he was able to haunt Hearst from the north. Welles's place became Nepenthe ("surcease from sorrows" in the *Odyssey*) shortly after he sold it in 1947. More or less across the street from Nepenthe is the **Hawthorne Gallery,** 48485 Hwy. 1, 831/667-3200, www.hawthornegallery.com, something of a Hawthorne family enterprise also offering Albert Paley forged metal sculptures, Max DeMoss bronze castings, Jesus Bautista Moroles granite sculptures, and the landscape creations of Frederick L. Gregory, among others.

North of Deetjen's is the **Henry Miller Memorial Library,** a collection of friendly clutter about the writer and his life's work, located on the highway about one mile south of the Ventana

Inn but almost hidden behind redwoods and an unassuming redwood double gate. Henry Miller lived, wrote, and painted in Big Sur from 1944 to 1962. The library is housed not in Henry Miller's former home but in that of the late Emil White. A good friend of Miller's, White said he started the library "because I missed him." Now a community cultural arts center, the library sponsors exhibits, poetry readings, concerts, and special events throughout the year. Original art and prints, posters, and postcards are available in the gallery. Miller's books, including rare editions, are also available. In summer the library is often open daily, but year-round it is typically open Wed.–Sun. 11 A.M.–6 P.M. and for special events. For current information, contact the Henry Miller Library, 831/667-2574, www.henrymiller.org.

South of Deetjen's is the noted **Coast Gallery** at Lafler Canyon (named for editor Henry Lafler, a friend of Jack London), 831/667-2301, www.coastgalleries.com, open daily 9 A.M.–5 P.M. Rebuilt from redwood water tanks in 1973, the Coast Gallery offers fine local arts and crafts, from jewelry and pottery to paintings—including watercolors by Henry Miller—plus sculpture and woodcarvings.

Julia Pfeiffer Burns State Park

Partington Cove is about one mile south of Partington Ridge, the impressive northern boundary of Julia Pfeiffer Burns State Park. To get to the cove, park on the east side of the highway and head down the steep trail that starts near the fence (by the black mailbox) on the west side of the road. The branching trail leads back into the redwoods to the tiny beach at the stream's mouth, or across a wooden footbridge, through a rock tunnel hewn in the 1880s by pioneer John Partington, and on to the old dock where tan bark was once loaded onto seagoing freighters. A fine place for a smidgen of inspirational solitude.

There's a stone marker farther south at the park's official entrance, about seven miles south of Nepenthe. These spectacular 4,000 acres straddling the highway also include a large underwater park offshore. Picnic in the coast redwoods by McWay Creek (almost the southern limit of their range) or hike up into the chaparral and the Los Padres National Forest. After picnicking, take the short walk along McWay Creek (watch for poison oak), then through the tunnel under the road to **Saddle Rock** and the cliffs above **Waterfall Cove,** the only California waterfall that plunges directly into the sea. The cliffs are rugged here; it's a good place to view whales and otters. Only experienced scuba divers, by permit, are allowed to dive offshore.

The park also features limited year-round camping at walk-in environmental sites and group campgrounds. The two hike-in environmental campsites (up to eight people each) offer spectacular views, $11–14 per night. For more information about the park, including winter whale-watching programs on weekends, contact Julia Pfeiffer Burns State Park, 831/667-2315.

The still-raw, 1,400-foot-wide slash of earth just north of Julia Pfeiffer Burns State Park, which stopped traffic through Big Sur for more than a year, has earned the area's landslide-of-all-time award (so far). Heading south from the park, the highway crosses Anderson Creek and rugged Anderson Canyon, where an old collection of highway construction cabins for convicts sheltered such bohemians as Henry Miller and his friend Emil White in the 1940s. A few human residents and a new population of bald eagles now call Anderson Canyon home.

The Esalen Institute

The Esselen and Salinan peoples frequented the hot springs here, supposedly called *tok-i-tok,* "hot healing water." In 1939, Dr. H. C. Murphy (who officiated at John Steinbeck's birth in Salinas) opened Slate's Hot Springs resort on the site. The hot springs were transformed by grandson Michael Murphy into the famed Esalen Institute, where human-potential practitioners and participants including Joan Baez, Gregory Bateson, the Beatles, Jerry Brown, Carlos Castaneda, Buckminster Fuller, Aldous Huxley, Linus Pauling, B.F. Skinner, Hunter S. Thompson, and Alan Watts taught or learned in residential workshops.

Esalen is the Cadillac of New Age retreats, according to absurdist/comedian/editor Paul Krassner. Even writer Alice Kahn who, before arriving at Esalen, considered herself the "last psycho-virgin in

California" and "hard-core unevolved," eventually admitted that there was something about the Esalen Institute that defied all cynicism.

Esalen's magic doesn't necessarily come cheap. The introductory "Experiencing Esalen" weekend workshop runs $405–545 or so, including simple but pleasant accommodations and wonderful meals ($260 if a sleeping bag is all you'll need). Five- to seven-day workshops are substantially more—in the $740–990 and $1,145–1,535 ranges, respectively. But Esalen tries to accommodate the less affluent with scholarships, a work-study program, senior citizen discounts, family rates, and sleeping bag options. You can also arrange just an overnight or weekend stay (sans enlightenment) assuming space is available.

Esalen offers more than 400 workshops each year, these "relating to our greater human capacity." Topics cover everything from the arts and creative expression to "intellectual play," from dreams to spiritual healing, from martial arts to shamanism. Moving in a more intellectual and philosophical direction these days, Esalen increasingly offers programs such as "Psyche and Cosmos in the 21st Century: The Return of Soul to the World"; "Sure Enough: Getting Comfortable with Irreducible Uncertainty"; and "Applied Wisdom: Enduring Truths of the World's Wisdom Traditions."

Equally elevated are Esalen's baths. In February 1998 a mudslide roared down the hill to demolish the previous bathhouse facilities. The new, improved Esalen baths now open, include a geothermally heated swimming pool and a handicapped-accessible hot tub and massage area—at a cost of $5.3 million. Designed by architect Mickey Muennig, the new baths "float" above the ocean, thanks to an engineering feat that required driving 34 piers and horizontal anchors into 25 feet of rock. Note the outdoor massage deck, tile work, fountain, and the "living roof," planted in native coastal grasses. Esalen satisfies the California Coastal Commission's public access requirement by allowing the general public access to the hot tubs (at the fairly unappealing hours of 1–3 A.M. daily). Call for details. The massages at Esalen are world-renowned, from $50 an hour. Nudity is big at Esalen, particularly in the hot tubs, swimming pool, and massage area, though not required.

Entrance to Esalen and its facilities is strictly by reservation only. For information on workshops and lodgings and to request a copy of Esalen's current catalog, contact: Esalen Institute, 831/667-3000, www.esalen.org. The website's online *In the Air* magazine offers a good sense of what Esalen is all about and also includes a complete current workshop catalog (which you can download). To make workshop reservations, call 831/667-3005 or fax completed registration forms to 831/667-2724.

Nature Reserves

Just south of the Esalen Institute is the **John Little State Reserve,** 21 acres of coast open to the public for day use (frequently foggy). For information, call the state parks Monterey District office (weekdays only), 831/649-2836. About five miles south of Esalen, beyond the Dolan Creek and dramatic Big Creek bridges, is the entrance to **Landels-Hill Big Creek Reserve,** more than 4,200 acres owned by the University of California. Adjacent is the 1,200-acre **Big Creek Marine Ecological Reserve.** The two are co-managed as the Big Creek Reserve. Safe behind these rusted cast-iron gates are 11 different plant communities, at least 350 plant species, 100 varieties of birds, and 50 types of mammals. A 10-acre area is open as a public educational center; groups are welcome. Access is by permit only (in advance or sign in at the entrance), for educational field trips and research. Camping is available. For more information, contact **Big Creek Reserve,** 831/667-2543, www.redshift.com/-bigcreek.

Lucia and the New Camaldoli Hermitage

The tiny "town" of Lucia is privately owned, with a gas station and a good down-home restaurant, open from 7 A.M. until dark, when they shut off the generator. Try the homemade split pea soup. Different, too, is a stay in one of the 10 rustic coastal cabins at **Lucia Lodge.** Rates are $100 to $150. Come nightfall, kerosene lanterns provide the ambience. A simple yet spectacular spot. Call 831/667-2391 for current information (no reservations).

South of Lucia (at the white cross), the road to

the left leads to the New Camaldoli Hermitage, a small Benedictine monastery at the former Lucia Ranch. The sign says that the monks "regret we cannot invite you to camp, hunt, or enjoy a walk on our property" due to their customary solitude and avoidance of "unnecessary speaking." But visitors *can* come to buy crafts and homemade fruitcake and to attend daily mass.

In addition, the hermitage is available for very serene retreats of up to two weeks, though few outsiders can stand the no-talk rules for much longer than a few days. Simple meals are included. The suggested offering is $60 per day for the retreat rooms, $70 per day for trailer hermitages. For more information, contact the New Camaldoli Hermitage in Big Sur, 831/667-2456, www.contemplation.com.

Limekiln State Park

About two miles south of Lucia is the newest Big Sur state park, open since 1995. It encompasses 716 acres in an isolated and steep coastal canyon, preserving some of the oldest, largest, and most vigorous redwoods in Monterey County. Named for the towering wood-fired kilns that smelted quarried limestone into powdered lime—essential for mixing cement—here in the late 1800s, Limekiln State Park offers a steep one-mile round-trip, creekside hike through redwoods to the four kilns, passing a waterfall (to the right at the first fork), pools, and cascades along the way. The park includes a day-use area for picnicking ($5 fee) and a very appealing 43-site family campground with minimal amenities but abundant ambience. Campsites are $13–16; extras include hot showers and laundry facilities. To get there, take the signed turnoff (on the inland or landward side of the highway) just south of the Limekiln Canyon Bridge. For more information, contact Limekiln State Park, 63025 Hwy. 1 in Big Sur, 831/667-2403. See also Public Camping in Big Sur, below.

DOING BIG SUR

The ultimate activity in Big Sur is just bumming around, scrambling down to beaches to hunt for jade, peer into tidepools, or scuba dive

Bixby Bridge

© ROBERT HOLMES/CALTOUR

or surf where it's possible. Cycling, sight-seeing, and watching the sunset are other entertainments. Along the coastline proper there are few long hiking trails, since much of the terrain is treacherous, and most of the rest privately owned, but the Big Sur backcountry offers good hiking and backpacking.

Ventana Wilderness

Local lore has it that a natural land bridge once connected two mountain peaks at Bottchers Gap, creating a window (or *ventana* in Spanish) until the 1906 San Francisco earthquake brought it all tumbling down. The Big Sur, Little Sur, Arroyo Seco, and Carmel Rivers all cut through this 161,000-acre area, creating dramatic gorges and wildland well worth exploring. Steep, sharp-crested ridges and serrated V-shaped valleys are clothed mostly in oaks, madrones, and dense chaparral. Redwoods grow on north-facing slopes near the fog-cooled coast; pines at higher elevations. The gnarly spiral-shaped bristlecone firs found only here are in the rockiest, most remote areas, their total range only about 12 miles wide and 55 miles long.

Most of all, the Ventana Wilderness provides a great escape from the creeping coastal traffic (a free visitor permit is required to enter) and offers great backpacking and hiking when the Sierra Nevada, Klamath Mountains, and Cascades are still snowbound—though roads here are sometimes impassible during the rainy season. Hunting, fishing, and horseback riding are also permitted. Crisscrossing Ventana Wilderness are nearly 400 miles of backcountry trails and 82 vehicle-accessible campgrounds (trailside camping possible with a permit).

The wilderness trailheads are at Big Sur Station, Carmel River, China Camp, Arroyo Seco, Memorial Park, Bottchers Gap, and Cone Peak Road. The Ventana Wilderness recreation map, available for $4 from ranger district offices, shows all roads, trails, and campgrounds. Fire-hazardous areas, routinely closed to the public after July 1 (or earlier), are coded yellow on maps.

Trail and campground traffic fluctuates from year to year, so solitude seekers should ask rangers about more remote routes and destinations. Since the devastating Marble Cone fire of 1978 (and other more recent fires), much of what once was forest is now chaparral and brush. As natural succession progresses, dense undergrowth obliterates trails not already erased by erosion. Despite dedicated volunteer trail work, lack of federal trail maintenance has also taken its toll.

Backcountry travelers should also heed fire regulations. Because of the high fire danger in peak tourist season, using a camp stove or building a fire outside designated campgrounds requires a fire permit. Also, bring water—but think twice before bringing Fido, since flea-transmitted plague is a possibility. Other bothersome realities include ticks (especially in winter and early spring), rattlesnakes, poison oak, and fast-rising rivers and streams following rainstorms.

For more Ventana Wilderness information, contact the Big Sur Station office (see above) or **Los Padres National Forest** headquarters, 6755 Hollister Ave., Ste. 150 in Goleta, 805/968-6640, www.r5.fs.fed.us/lospadres. Additional information is available from the **Ventana Wilderness Society,** 831/455-9514, www.ventanaws.org, and the **Ventana Wilderness Alliance,** 831/423-3191, www.ventanawild.org. For guided trips on horseback, contact **Ventana Wilderness Guides and Expeditions,** 38655 Tassajara Rd. in Carmel Valley, 831/659-2153, www.nativeguides.com, operated by members of the Esselen tribe.

Hiking

The grandest views of Big Sur come from the ridges just back from the coast. A great companion is *Hiking the Big Sur Country* by Jeffrey P. Schaffer (Wilderness Press). The short but steep **Valley View Trail** from Pfeiffer-Big Sur State Park is usually uncrowded, especially midweek; there are benches up top for sitting and staring off the edge of the world. Those *serious* about coastal hiking should walk all the way from Pfeiffer-Big Sur to Salmon Creek near the southern Monterey County line. The trip from Bottchers Gap to Ventana Double Cone via **Skinner Ridge Trail** is about 16 miles one way and challenging, with a variety of possible campsites, dazzling spring wildflowers, and oak and pine forests.

Otherwise, take either the nine-mile **Pine Ridge Trail** from Big Sur or the 15-mile trail from China Camp on Chews Ridge to undeveloped Sykes Hot Springs, just 400 yards from Sykes Camp (very popular these days). Another good, fairly short *visual* hike is the trip to nearby Mount Manuel, a nine-mile round trip. The two-mile walk to **Pfeiffer Beach** is also worth it—miles from the highway, fringed by forest, with a wading cove and meditative monolith.

Back Roads

For an unforgettable dry-season side trip and a true joy ride, take the **Old Coast Road** from just north of the Bixby Bridge inland to the Big Sur Valley. You'll encounter barren granite, a thickly forested gorge, and good views of sea and sky before the road loops back to Highway 1 south of Point Sur near the entrance to Andrew Molera State Park. **Palo Colorado Road,** mostly unpaved and narrow, winds through a canyon of redwoods, ferns, and summer homes, up onto hot and dry Las Piedras Ridge, then down into the Little Sur watershed.

EYEING E-SEALS

Everyone knows that massive northern elephant seals lumber ashore every winter at Año Nuevo north of Santa Cruz, much as the swallows come back to Capistrano. Yet most people don't know that if you can't get reservations to see the "e-seals" at the Año Nuevo preserve, you can come observe them from a vista point just south of Piedra Blancas, about 4.5 miles north of Hearst Castle.

The northern elephant seal colony here began in November 1990, when a handful of seals hauled ashore at the small cove just south of the Piedras Blancas lighthouse; the following spring, almost 400 seals came ashore to molt; and in 1992 the first pup was born. By 2002, the total Piedras Blancas population of northern elephant seals was estimated at 8,500, including 2,150 new pups. More than 2,600 pups were born during the 2002–2003 pupping season. The seals'

breeding and pupping season begins in December and lasts into March. (Keep your distance at all times, and never come between an e-seal and the ocean, their natural escape route. These are wild animals that will react to provocation and perceived threats.) From April to August the e-seals molt, a natural phenomenon that looks like an outbreak of disease as old fur is shed and shiny new skin emerges. Docents at the designated viewing area explain the natural history and habits and life cycles of the northern elephant seal. Tours can be arranged.

For more information, stop by the **Friends of the Elephant Seals** office in the Plaza del Cavalier in San Simeon, 250 San Simeon Ave., Ste. 3B (next door to the San Simeon Chamber of Commerce), or contact the Friends at 805/924-1628, www.elephantseal.org.

Marvelous for the sense of adventure and the views is a drive along the **Nacimiento-Fergusson Road** from the coast inland to what's left of old Jolon and the fabulous nearby mission, both included within the Fort Hunter-Liggett Military Reservation. (Taking this route is always somewhat risky, particularly on weekends, since all roads through Hunter-Liggett are closed when military exercises are underway.) Even more thrilling is driving rough-and-ready **Los Burros Road** farther south, an unmarked turnoff just south of Willow Creek and Cape San Martin that leads to the long-gone town of Manchester in the Los Burros gold mining district. An indestructible vehicle and plenty of time are required for this route, and it's often closed to traffic after winter storms.

Big Sur back roads leading to the sea are rarer and easy to miss. About one mile south of the entrance to Pfeiffer-Big Sur State Park is **Sycamore Canyon Road,** which winds its way downhill for two exciting miles before the parking lot near Pfeiffer Beach. At Willow Creek there's a road curling down from the vista point to the rocky beach below, and just south of Willow Creek a dirt road leads to Cape San Martin (good for views any day but especially fine for whale-watching).

STAYING IN BIG SUR
Public Camping

In the accommodations category, nothing but camping is truly inexpensive in Big Sur, so to travel on the cheap, make campground reservations *early* (where applicable) and stock up on groceries and sundries in Monterey up north or in San Luis Obispo to the south. All the following options are Under $50. The U.S. Forest Service **Bottchers Gap Campground** on Palo Colorado Canyon Road has primitive, walk-in tent sites (first-come, first-camped). Rough road, no drinking water. The Forest Service **Kirk Creek Campground** is far south of urban Big Sur and just north of the intersection with Nacimiento-Fergusson Road. It consists of 33 first-come, first-camped sites ($16), picnic tables, and grills, all situated on a grassy seaside bluff. Inland, halfway to Jolon, are two small creekside campgrounds managed by Los Padres National Forest. They are free, since there's no reliable drinking water, and are popular with deer hunters. Also run by the Forest Service and even farther south, north of Gorda, is the 43-site **Plaskett Creek Campground,** $16.

For more information on the area's national

forest campgrounds and for free visitor permits, fire permits, maps, and other information about Los Padres National Forest and the Ventana Wilderness, stop by the **Big Sur Station** State Parks/U.S. Forest Service office at Pfeiffer-Big Sur State Park, open daily 8 A.M.–4:30 P.M., 831/667-2315, or the **Monterey Ranger District** office at 406 S. Mildred Ave. in King City, 831/385-5434.

At state park facilities, for secluded camping try **Andrew Molera State Park,** with walk-in tent sites not far from the dusty parking lot, three-night maximum; or **Julia Pfeiffer Burns State Park,** with two separate environmental campsites (far from RVs). More comforts (including flush toilets and hot showers) are available at the attractive family campground at **Pfeiffer–Big Sur State Park.** It has 214 campsites, group campgrounds, plus a regular summer schedule of educational and informational programs. There are no hookups. Another possibility, just south of Lucia, is the postcard-pretty **Limekiln State Park,** 63025 Hwy. 1, 831/667-2403, which takes up most of the steep canyon and offers some good hiking in addition to attractive tent and RV sites (no hookups, but water, hot showers, and flush toilets are available). For information about any of the area's state park campgrounds, stop by the office at Pfeiffer-Big Sur State Park or call 831/667-2315. For ReserveAmerica reservations (usually necessary May through early September and on warm-weather weekends) at Pfeiffer–Big Sur and Limekiln, call 800/444-7275 or reserve online at website: www.reserveamerica.com.

Private Camping

Not far from the state campgrounds at Pfeiffer–Big Sur State Park is the private riverside **Big Sur Campground,** Hwy. 1, 831/667-2322, with tent sites and RV sites including hookups. Tent cabins and cabins are also available, as well as hot showers, laundry facilities, a store, telephone access, and a playground. Also on the Big Sur River, with similar facilities and prices, is the **Riverside Campground,** Hwy. 1, 831/667-2414, with tent or RV sites plus cabins. The private **Ventana Campgrounds,** managed by the Ventana Inn, Hwy. 1, 831/667-2712, www.ven-tanabigsur.com, has 80 very private, pretty sites in a scenic 40-acre redwood setting along Post Creek. There are some RV hookups, hot showers (three bathhouses), fireplaces, and picnic tables. Rates for all the above are Under $50.

Affordable Accommodations

Always a best bet for cabins and affordable for just plain folks is the charming **Ripplewood Resort,** about a mile north of Pfeiffer-Big Sur, 831/667-2242, www.ripplewoodresort.com. The primo units, most with fireplaces and kitchens (bring your own cookware), are down by the Big Sur River (and booked months in advance for summer). Rates are $100–150. Convenient on-site café, too; open for breakfast and lunch. At last report there were still several nice, private cabins at **Mill Creek Ranch,** 64955 Hwy. 1 (at Nacimiento Road), 831/667-2757, website: bigsurmillcreek.com, set up for weekly or monthly rentals (call for other possibilities). The one-bedroom Kiwi Cabin is $600/week; the two-bedroom, two-story Bay Tree House is $800/week; and the striking, redwood and stone Wisteria House is $1,250/week. Winter weekend rates are quite reasonable.

Other Big Sur options include the adobe **Glen Oaks Motel,** 831/667-2105, www.glenoaksbigsur.com, and the **Fernwood Resort,** 831/667-2422, both on Highway 1 and both with rates of $50–150. The **Big Sur River Inn,** on Highway 1 in Big Sur Valley, 831/625-5255 or 800/548-3610, is a motel-restaurant-bar popular with locals and featuring views of the river and live music most weekends. The 61-room **Big Sur Lodge** nearby, just inside the park's entrance at 47225 Hwy. 1, 831/667-3100 or 800/424-4787, www.bigsurlodge.com, is quiet, with a pool, sauna, restaurant, and circle of comfy cabins, each with its own porch or deck. Some rooms feature wood-burning fireplaces or fully stocked kitchens. Rates start at $50. A lodge stay includes a complimentary pass to all area state parks.

Deetjen's Big Sur Inn

Just south of the noted Nepenthe restaurant and the Henry Miller Library is the landward Norwegian-style Deetjen's Big Sur Inn in Castro

Canyon, 831/667-2377, a rambling, ever-blooming inn with redwood rooms—now listed on the National Register of Historic Places. *Very Big Sur.* The 20 eccentric, rustic rooms and cabins—one's named Chateau Fiasco, after the Bay of Pigs invasion—are chock-full of bric-a-brac and feature thin walls, front doors that don't lock, fireplaces, books, and reasonably functional plumbing. No TVs, no telephones. Forget about trendy creature comforts. People love this place—and have ever since it opened in the 1930s—because it has *soul.* Private or shared baths. Reservations advised because rooms are usually booked up many months in advance. Rooms are $100 and up. Eating at Deetjen's is as big a treat as an overnight. Wonderfully hearty, wholesome breakfasts are served 8 to 11:30 A.M., and dinner starts at 6:15 P.M. Reservations are also taken for meals.

Ventana Inn & Spa

Perhaps tuned into the same philosophical frequency as Henry Miller—"There being nothing to improve on in the surroundings, the tendency is to set about improving oneself"—the Ventana Inn didn't provide distractions like TV or tennis courts when writer Lawrence A. Spector first built the place in 1975. Though it's still a hip, high-priced resort, and there are still no tennis courts, things have changed. Now the desperately undiverted *can* phone home, if need be, or watch in-room TV or videos. But the woodsy, world-class Ventana high up on the hill in Big Sur, 831/667-2331 or 800/628-6500, www.ventanainn.com, still offers luxurious and relaxed contemporary lodgings on 240 acres overlooking the sea, outdoor Japanese hot baths, and heated pools. Rates are $250 and up; reservations usually essential; two-night minimum stay on weekends. Children are discouraged at Ventana, which is not set up to entertain or otherwise look after them.

This rough-hewn and hand-built hostelry comprises 12 separate buildings with rooms featuring unfinished cedar interiors, parquet floors, and down-home luxuries like queen- or king-sized beds with hand-painted headboards, handmade quilted spreads, and lots of pillows. All rooms are reasonably large and have in-room refrigerators;

NEPENTHE

Nepenthe, about a mile south of the Ventana Inn, was built almost exactly on the site of the cabin Orson Welles bought for Rita Hayworth. So it's not too surprising that the restaurant is almost as legendary as Big Sur itself. A striking multilevel structure complete with an arts and crafts center, the restaurant was named for an ancient drug mentioned in Homer's *The Odyssey,* taken to help people forget their grief. Naturally enough, the bar here does a brisk business.

As is traditional at Nepenthe, relax on the upper deck (the "gay pavilion," presided over by a sculpted bronze and redwood phoenix) with drink in hand to salute the sea and setting sun—surreal views. The open-beamed restaurant and its outdoor above-ocean terrace isn't nearly as rowdy as all those bohemian celebrity stories would suggest. Nonetheless, thrill-seekers insist on sitting on the top deck, though there's often more room available downstairs at the Café Kevah health food deli and deck, open Mar.–Dec. for brunch and lunch. The fare at Nepenthe is good, but not as spectacular (on a clear day) as the views. Try the homemade soups, the hefty chef's salad, any of the vegetarian selections, or the world-famous Ambrosia burger (an excellent cheeseburger on French roll with pickles and a salad for a hefty price) accompanied by a Basket o' Fries. Good pies and cakes for dessert.

To avoid the worst of the tourist traffic and to appreciate Nepenthe at its best, come later in September or October. And although Nepenthe is casual any time of year, it's not *that* casual. Local lore has it that John F. Kennedy was once turned away because he showed up barefoot. Nepenthe is open for lunch and dinner daily, with music and dancing around the hearth at night. For more information or reservations, call 831/667-2345. To reach Café Kevah, call 831/667-2344.

And if at the moment you can't be here in person, you can be here in spirit—much easier now that Nepenthe has an online weather camera pointing south over the back deck. To "see" what's happening along Nepenthe's coastline, try www.nepenthebigsur.com.

most have fireplaces. Rooms and suites with both fireplaces and hot tubs are at the top of the inn's price range. The Ventana Inn also has a library, not to mention hiking trails and hammocks. Complimentary group classes—so very *California*—include Native American tai chi, Chi Gong, guided meditation, yoga, and hiking. Complimentary continental breakfast is served (delivered to your room by request), and in the afternoon from 4 to 5:30 P.M. you can enjoy the complimentary wine and cheese buffet in the main lodge.

Ranked number two of the 25 "Best Small Hotels in the World" in the 1998 *Travel & Leisure* reader survey, the Ventana Inn became the Ventana Inn & Spa with the 1999 debut of its full-service spa. For a price, expect world-class massage, wraps, facials, scrubs, and other body therapies.

If a stay here or a self-pampering spa session seems just *too rich,* try drinks with a view or a bite of enticing California cuisine served in the inn's lovely two-tiered **Cielo** restaurant overlooking the ocean, a pleasant stroll through the woods. The Ventana Inn is located 0.8 miles south of Pfeiffer–Big Sur State Park; look for the sign on the left.

Post Ranch Inn

For good reason, new Big Sur commercial development has been rare in the 1990s. If further coastal development must come, the environmentally conscious Post Ranch Inn offers the style—if not the price range—most Californians would cheer. All the upscale travel mags rave about the place, open since 1992, calling it "one of the best places to stay in the world" *(Condé Nast Traveler)* and "the most spectacular hotel on the Pacific Coast" *(Travel & Leisure).* This place is something special. Developer Myles Williams, of New Christy Minstrels folksinging fame, and architect Mickey Muennig took the Big Sur region's rugged love of the land to heart when they built the very contemporary Post Ranch Inn. They also acknowledged the community's increasing economic stratification and took other real-world problems into account, adding 24 housing units for workers (affordable housing is now scarce in these parts) and donating land for Big Sur's first fire station.

Perched on a ridge overlooking the grand Pacific Ocean, the Post Ranch Inn is a carefully executed aesthetic study in nature awareness. The 30 redwood-and-glass "guest houses" are designed and built to harmonize with—almost disappear into—the hilltop landscape. The triangular "tree houses" are built on stilts, to avoid damaging the roots of the oaks with which they intertwine; the spectacular sod-roofed "ocean houses" literally blend into the ocean views; and the gracious "coast house" duplexes impersonate stand-tall coastal redwoods. Absolute privacy and understated, earth-toned luxury are the main points here. Each house includes a wood-burning fireplace, a two-person spa tub in the stunning slate bathroom, a good sound system, in-room refrigerators stocked with complimentary snacks, a private deck, a king-sized bed—and views. Extra amenities include plush robes, in-room coffeemakers and hair dryers, even walking sticks. Priced for Hollywood entertainment execs and Silicon Valley survivors, rates are $250 and up, continental breakfast included.

Guests can also enjoy the **Post Ranch Spa**—offering massage, wraps, and facials—and the exceptional California-style **Sierra Mar** restaurant, where the views are every bit as inviting as the daily changing menu. Full bar. Open for lunch and dinner.

The Post Ranch Inn is 30 miles south of Carmel on Highway 1, on the west (seaward) side of the road. As at Ventana, children are discouraged here. For more information, contact Post Ranch Inn in Big Sur, 831/667-2200, www.postranchinn .com. For inn reservations, call 800/527-2200. For restaurant reservations, call 831/667-2800.

EATING IN BIG SUR

Look for fairly inexpensive fare in and around the Big Sur Valley. Good for breakfast is the **Ripplewood Resort** just north of Pfeiffer-Big Sur near the tiny Big Sur Library, 831/667-2242, where favorites include homemade baked goods and French toast. Another local find is the **Big Sur Bakery & Restaurant** near the post office, 831/667-0520. **Deetjen's,** 831/667-2377, is special for breakfast—wholesome and hearty fare served in the open-beamed, hobbit-style dining

JULIA MORGAN:
LETTING THE WORK SPEAK FOR ITSELF

Julia Morgan, San Simeon's architect, supervised the execution of almost every detail of Hearst's rambling 165-room pleasure palace. This 95-pound, teetotaling, workaholic woman was UC Berkeley's first female engineering graduate, and the first woman to graduate from the École des Beaux-Arts in Paris. She was credited only after her death for her accomplishments, but if acclaim came late for Morgan, it was partly her preference. She loathed publicity, disdained the very idea of celebrity, and believed that architects should be like anonymous medieval masters and let the work speak for itself.

Morgan's work with Hearst departed dramatically from her belief that buildings should be unobtrusive, the cornerstone of her brilliant but equally unobtrusive career. "My style," she said to those who seemed bewildered by the contradiction, "is to please my client." Pleasing her client in this case was quite a task. Hearst arbitrarily and habitually changed his mind, all the while complaining about slow progress and high costs. And she certainly didn't do the job for money, though Hearst and her other clients paid her well. Morgan divided her substantial earnings among her staff, keeping only about $10,000 annually to cover office overhead and personal expenses.

The perennially private Morgan, who never allowed her name to be posted at construction sites, designed almost 800 buildings in California and the West, among them the original Asilomar in Pacific Grove; the Berkeley City Club; the Oakland YWCA; and the bell tower, library, social hall, and gym at Oakland's Mills College. She also designed and supervised the reconstruction of San Francisco's Fairmont Hotel following its devastation in the 1906 earthquake. Other Hearst commissions included the family's Wyntoon retreat near Mt. Shasta as well as the *Los Angeles Herald-Examiner* building.

---

rooms. Dinner is more formal (fireplace blazing to ward off the chill mist, classical music, and two seatings, by reservation only), with entrées including steaks, fish, California country cuisine, and vegetarian dishes. Tasty home-baked pies are an after-meal specialty at the casual and cheery **Big Sur Lodge Restaurant** at the Big Sur Lodge, 831/667-3111, overlooking the river and also known for red snapper and California-style fare. Beer and wine. Another draw is the lodge's **Espresso House,** perfect for coffee, tea, or a quick snack.

Everyone should sample the view from famed **Nepenthe,** 831/667-2345, at least once in a lifetime; just below Nepenthe is **Café Kevah,** 831/667-2344, open March through December for brunch and lunch. A culinary hot spot is the locally popular **Bonito Roadhouse** (previously the Glen Oaks Restaurant) at the Glen Oaks Motel, next door to the Ripplewood Resort, 831/667-2264. It is diverse, low-key, and likable à la Big Sur. Entrées emphasize what's local and fresh and include crêpes, good vegetarian dishes, seafood gumbo, and chicken pot pie.

Open for dinner Wed.–Mon. nights. The roadhouse also serves a fine Sunday brunch, with omelettes, eggs Benedict, and cornmeal hotcakes. A quarter-mile north of Palo Colorado Rd. on Highway 1 is the **Rocky Point Restaurant,** 831/624-2933, a reasonably well-heeled steak and seafood place overlooking the ocean. Open for lunch, dinner, and cocktails daily.

The finest of local fine dining is served at the area's luxury-hotel restaurants—at **Cielo** at the Ventana Inn & Spa and **Sierra Mar** at the Post Ranch Inn—which both serve lunch and dinner daily. For information, see listings above.

INFORMATION, SERVICES, AND TRANSPORTATION

For general information about the area, contact the **Big Sur Chamber of Commerce,** 831/667-2100, www.bigsurcalifornia.org. (Send a stamped, self-addressed legal-sized envelope for a free guide to Big Sur, or download it from the website.) Combined headquarters for area state parks and the U.S. Forest Service is **Big Sur Station** on the south side of Pfeiffer-Big Sur on Hwy. 1, 831/667-2315. Open daily 8 A.M.–4:30 P.M., this is the place to go in search of forest and wilderness maps, permits, and backcountry camping and recreation information. There's a **laundromat** at Pfeiffer-Big Sur State Park in the Big Sur Lodge complex.

Bicycling Big Sur can be marvelous, except when you're fighting RVs and weekend speedsters for road space. Forewarned, fearless cyclists should plan to ride from north to south to take advantage of the tailwind. (Driving south makes sense, too, since most vistas and turnouts are seaward.) It takes *at least* five hours by car to drive the 150 miles of Highway 1 between Monterey and San Luis Obispo.

Hitchhiking is almost as difficult as safely riding a bicycle along this stretch of road, so don't count on thumbs for transportation. More reliable is **Monterey-Salinas Transit** Bus 22, which runs to and from Big Sur daily mid-April to October, stopping at Point Lobos, Garrapata State Park, the Bixby Creek Bridge, Point Sur Lightstation, Pfeiffer-Big Sur and the River Inn, Pfeiffer Beach, the Ventana Inn, and Nepenthe; call 831/899-2555 for information.

San Simeon and Vicinity

HEARST CASTLE: PLEASURE HE COULD AFFORD

The **Hearst San Simeon State Historic Monument** just south of Big Sur ranks right up there with Disneyland as one of California's premier tourist attractions. Somehow that fact alone puts the place into proper perspective. Media magnate William Randolph Hearst's castle is a rich man's playground filled to overflowing with artistic diversions and other expensive toys, a monument to one man's monumental ego and equally impressive poor taste.

In real life, of course, Hearst was quite a wealthy and powerful man, the man many people still believe was the subject of the greatest American movie ever made, Orson Welles's 1941 *Citizen Kane.* (These days even Welles's biographers say the movie was about the filmmaker himself.) Yet there's something to be said for popular opinion. "Pleasure," Hearst once wrote, "is worth what you can afford to pay for it." And that attitude showed itself quite early; for his 10th birthday little William asked for the Louvre as a present. One scene in the movie, in which Charles Foster Kane shouts across the cavernous living room at Xanadu to attract the attention of his bored young mistress, endlessly working jigsaw puzzles while she sits before a fireplace as big as the mouth of Jonah's whale, won't seem so surreal once you see San Simeon.

Designed by Berkeley architect Julia Morgan, the buildings themselves are odd yet handsome hallmarks of Spanish Renaissance architecture. The centerpiece La Casa Grande alone has 100 rooms (including a movie theater, a billiards room, two libraries, and 31 bathrooms) adorned with silk banners, fine Belgian and French tapestries, Norman fireplaces, European choir stalls, and ornately carved ceilings virtually stolen from continental monasteries. The furnishings and art Hearst collected from around the world complete the picture, one that includes everything but humor, grace, warmth, and understanding.

The notably self-negating nature of this rich but richly disappointed man's life is somehow fully expressed here in the country's most ostentatious and theatrical temple to obscene wealth. In contrast to Orson Welles's authentic artistic interpretation of either his own or Hearst's life, William Randolph's idea of hearth, home, and humanity was full-flown fantasy sadly separated from heart and vision.

Tours

In spring when the hills are emerald green, from the faraway highway Hearst Castle appears as if by magic up on the hill. (Before the place opened for public tours in the 1950s, the closest view commoners could get was from the road, with the assistance of coin-operated telescopes.) One thing visitors *don't* see on the tour shuttle up to the

© ROBERT HOLMES/CALTOUR

Hearst Castle

enchanted hill is William Randolph Hearst's 2,000-acre zoo—"the largest private zoo since Noah," as Charles Foster Kane would put it— once the country's largest. The inmates have long since been dispersed, though survivors of Hearst's exotic elk, zebra, Barbary sheep, and Himalayan goat herds still roam the grounds.

The four separate tours of the Hearst San Simeon State Historic Monument take approximately two hours each. Theoretically you could take all the San Simeon tours in a day, but don't try it. So much Hearst in the short span of a day could be detrimental to one's well-being. A dosage of two tours per day makes the trip here worthwhile yet not overwhelming. Visitors obsessed with seeing it all should plan a two-day stay in the area or come back again some other time. Whichever tour, or combination of tours, you select, be sure to wear comfortable walking shoes. Lots of stairs.

The **Experience Tour,** or Tour One, is the recommended first-time visit, taking in the castle's main floor, one guesthouse, and some of the gardens—a total of 150 steps and a half mile of walking. Included on the tour is a short showing in the theater of some of Hearst's "home movies." Particularly impressive in a gloomy Gothic way is the dining room, where silk Siennese banners hang over the lord's table. The poolroom and mammoth great hall, with Canova's *Venus,* are also unforgettable. All the tours include both the Greco-Roman Neptune Pool and statuary and the indoor Roman Pool with its mosaics of lapis lazuli and gold leaf. It's hard to imagine Churchill, cigar in mouth, cavorting here in an inner tube. The Experience Tour also includes the National Geographic movie, *Hearst Castle—Building the Dream.*

Tour Two requires more walking, covering the mansion's upper floors, the kitchen, the libraries, and Hearst's Gothic Suite, with its frescoes and rose-tinted Venetian glass windows (he ran his 94 separate business enterprises from here). The delightfully lit Celestial Suite was the nonetheless depressing extramarital playground of Hearst and Marion Davies. **Tour Three** covers one of the guesthouses plus the "new wing," with 36 luxurious bedrooms, sitting rooms, and marble bathrooms furnished with fine art.

Gardeners will be moved to tears by **Tour Four** (offered April–Aug. only), which includes a long stroll through the San Simeon grounds but does not go inside the castle itself. Realizing that all the rich topsoil here had to be manually carried up the hill makes the array of exotic plantlife, including unusual camellias and about 6,000 rosebushes, all the more impressive—not to mention the fact that gardeners at San Simeon worked only at night because Hearst couldn't stand watching them. Also included on the fourth tour is the lower level of the elegant, 17-room Casa del Mar guesthouse (where Hearst spent much of his time), the recently redone underground Neptune Pool dressing rooms, the never-finished bowling alley, and Hearst's wine cellar. David Niven once remarked that, with Hearst as host, the wine flowed "like glue." Subsequently, Niven was the only guest allowed free access to the castle's wine cellar.

Fairly new at San Simeon are the **Hearst Castle Evening Tours,** two-hour adventures featur-

CITIZEN HEARST

The name San Simeon was originally given to three Mexican land grants—40,000 acres bought by mining scion George Hearst in 1865. George, the first millionaire Hearst, owned Nevada's Comstock Lode silver mine, Ophir silver mine, and the rich Homestake gold mine in South Dakota, and also staked-out territory in California's goldfields. George Hearst later expanded the family holdings to 250,000 acres (including 50 miles of coastline) for the family's "Camp Hill" Victorian retreat and cattle ranch. With his substantial wealth, he was even able to buy himself a U.S. Senate seat.

But young William Randolph had even more ambitious plans—personally and for the property.

The only son of the senator and San Francisco schoolteacher, socialite, and philanthropist Phoebe Apperson, the high-rolling junior Hearst took a fraction of the family wealth and his daddy's failing *San Francisco Examiner* and created a successful yellow-journalism chain, eventually adding radio stations and movie production companies.

Putting his newfound power of propaganda to work in the political arena, Hearst (primarily for the headlines) goaded Congress into launching the Spanish-American War in 1898. But unlike his father, William Randolph was unable to buy much personal political power. Though he aspired to the presidency, he had to settle for two terms as a congress member from New York.

---

ing the highlights of other tours—with the added benefit of allowing you to pretend to be some Hollywood celebrity, just arrived and in need of orientation. (Hearst himself handed out tour maps, since newcomers often got lost.) Guides dress in period costume and show you around. It's worth it just to see the castle in lights. At last report, evening tours were offered on Friday and Saturday nights March–May and Sept.–Dec., but call for current details. December **Christmas at the Castle** tours are particularly festive.

To make reservations for **physically challenged/wheelchair-accessible tours,** call Hearst Castle directly at 805/927-2070, 10 days or more in advance. Wheelchair-accessible tours, which explore the ground floor only, take about two hours and are offered at least three times daily. Wheelchairs are available for lending, at no extra charge. Chairs brought by visitors need to be able to get through doorways 28 inches wide. Someone strong enough to maneuver an occupied chair up and down narrow ramps and steep inclines must accompany visitors requiring wheelchairs.

Practicalities

San Simeon is open daily except Thanksgiving, Christmas, and New Year's Day, with the regular two-hour tours leaving the visitor center area on the hour from early morning until around dusk. Tour schedules change by season and day of the

week. Reservations aren't required, but the chance of getting tickets on a drop-in, last-minute basis is small. For current schedule information and reservations, call ReserveAmerica at 800/444-4445 and have that credit card handy. You can also book online via the website: www.hearst-castle.org. For cancellations and refunds, in the U.S. call 800/695-2269. (To make ticket reservations from outside the U.S., call 916/414-8400 ext. 4100.) Wheelchair-access tours of San Simeon are offered on a different schedule; call 805/927-2070 for reservations and information. The TDD number is 800/274-7275.

Admission to Tour One is $18 adult, $9 youth (ages 6–17). Each of the other three San Simeon day tours is $12 adults, $7 youth. Evening tour rates are $24 adults, $12 children. A special brochure for international travelers (printed in Japanese, Korean, French, German, Hebrew, Italian, and Spanish) is available. With a little forethought—head for Cambria or the town of San Simeon—visitors can avoid eating the concession-style food here.

Adjacent to the visitor center is the Hearst Castle's giant-screened **National Geographic Theater,** 805/927-6811, where at last report the larger-than-life *Hearst Castle—Building the Dream* and *Everest* were showing on the 70-foot by 52-foot screen. Call for current times and details (no reservations required).

For other information, contact: Hearst San Simeon State Historic Monument, 750 Hearst Castle Rd. in San Simeon, 805/927-2020 (recorded) or 805/927-2000, www.hearstcastle.org. The Experience Tour, recommended for first-time visitors, includes the movie *Hearst Castle: Building the Dream.* For more information about the San Simeon area, contact the **San Simeon Chamber of Commerce,** 250 San Simeon Dr., Ste. 3B in San Simeon, 805/927-3500, and the **Cambria Chamber of Commerce,** 767 Main St. in Cambria, 805/927-3624.

SOUTH FROM SAN SIMEON

Done with the display of pompous circumstance on the hill, sample San Simeon proper. The area's serene sandy beaches are heavenly for a long coast walk—just the thing to clear out all the clutter. Good ocean swimming, too, and picnicking. (Stop for picnic supplies and sandwiches at **Sebastian's General Store,** 805/927-4217, a state historic monument in the red-roofed village of San Simeon, built by Hearst for his laborers.) Another picnicking possibility, ar area especially appealing for winter whalewatchers, is **Piedras Blancas Lighthouse** just up the coast. There's good tidepooling at nearby **Twin Creeks Beach** but public access may be restricted, as the area is now seasonal home for a northern elephant seal colony. Docent tours are available. For current details call 805/924-1628 or see www.elephantseal.org.

Its borders blending into San Simeon Acres motel row about eight miles south of Hearst castle, the artsy coastal town of **Cambria** now bears the Roman name for ancient Wales but was previously called Rosaville, San Simeon, and (seriously) Slabtown. In some ways, Cambria is becoming the Carmel of southern Big Sur, with its galleries and come-hither shops—and so far without the crowds. Several of the area's historic buildings remain, including the 1877 Squibb-Darke home, the Brambles restaurant on Burton Drive in Old Town to the east, and the restored Santa Rosa Catholic Church on Bridge Street (across Main, past the library and post office). Just outside Cambria proper in Cambria Pines is Arthur Beal's beautifully bizarre **Nit Wit**

Ridge, 881 Hillcrest Dr., 805/927-2690, something of a middle-class San Simeon built from abalone shells, glass, discarded car parts, toilet seats, beer cans and more, a state historical monument since 1981. Guided tours are available.

For more information about the area, including events, accommodations, and restaurants, contact the **San Simeon Chamber of Commerce,** on the highway just south of the Sands Motel in the Cavalier Plaza, 9255 Hearst Dr., 805/927-3500, or the **Cambria Chamber of Commerce,** 767 Main St., 805/927-3624, www.cambriachamber.org.

The biggest city immediately south from San Simeon is **San Luis Obispo,** a convenient stop halfway between L.A. and San Francisco along Hwy. 101 and most famous for creating both the word and the modern-concept "motel," a contraction of "motor hotel." The town's (and the world's) first motel, the Motel Inn on Monterey Street, still stands, at last report slated for complete renovation. Agriculture is big business around here, a fact reflected in the prominent presence of the well-respected **California State Polytechnic University,** also known as Cal Poly or (snidely) "Cow Poly." Pick up an "Ag's My Bag" bumpersticker as a souvenir or—if you can time your trip appropriately—roll into town on a Thursday evening to enjoy the **Higuera Street Farmers' Market,** one of the best anywhere (cancelled only in the event of rain). To get more of the San Luis Obispo story, stop by **Mission San Luis Obispo de Tolosa** downtown on Mission Plaza, 751 Palm St., and the **Museum & History Center of San Luis Obispo County** in the old Carnegie library at 696 Monterey Street. For current city and county information, stop by the **San Luis Obispo County Visitors & Conference Bureau** downtown at 1037 Mill St., 805/781-2531 or 800/634-1414, www.sanluisobispocounty.com.

Speaking of missions and old California stories: Well worth going out of your way for—inland from the coast and north of San Luis Obispo— is **Mission San Antonio de Padua,** smack-dab in the middle of Fort Hunter-Liggett (expect a security check at the base gate), not the grandest or most spruced-up but among the the most evocative of all the California missions. From here, take narrow, unpaved Nacimiento-Fergusson Rd. back over the coastal mountains to Big Sur. Nearby **Lake San Antonio** is popular in winter for guided bald eagle-watching tours.

Off in the other direction, via Hwy. 58, is the new **Carrizo Plain National Monument,** earthquake territory once sacred to the Chumash people. The native grasses and scrub lands surrounding Soda Lake offer refuge to some of the state's most endangered animal species. (For details, see the San Joaquin Valley section of this book.) And if you head east from Paso Robles via Hwy. 46, you'll come to the shrine marking (almost) the spot where actor **James Dean** (*Rebel Without a Cause, Giant,* and *East of Eden)* died in a head-on car accident in 1955. **Paso Robles** itself and nearby **Templeton** are the center of an increasingly popular—and increasingly impressive—wine region. For area information, contact the **Paso Robles Visitor & Conference Bureau,** 1225 Park St., 800/406-4040, www.pasorobleschamber.com.

Near San Luis Obispo along the coast is Morro Rock, California's own little Gibraltar, spotted by Cabrillo in 1542—the first thing people notice at **Morro Bay.** Worthy of a gaze downtown: the Morro Bay Chess Club's **giant outdoor chessboard,** though **Morro Bay State Park, Montana de Oro State Park,** and area parks and beaches offer more varied scenery. For more area information, contact the **Morro Bay Visitors Center & Chamber of Commerce,** 880 Main St. in Morro Bay, 805/772-4467 or 800 231-0592, www.morrobay.org, and the **Cayucos Chamber of Commerce,** 158 N. Ocean Ave. in nearby Cayucos, 805/995-1200 or 800/563-1878, www.cayucoschamber.com.

Still heading south, **Santa Maria** is most noted for its unique culinary heritage, this one preserved since the days of the vaqueros. This is the hometown of Santa Maria Barbecue, a complete meal that traditionally includes slabs of prime sirloin barbecued over a slow red-oak fire then sliced as thin as paper, served with *salsa cruda,* pinquito beans, salad, toasted garlic bread, and dessert. Near town is the **Guadalupe-Nipomo Dunes Preserve,** a coastal wildlife and plant preserve also protecting the remains of Cecil B. DeMille's *The Ten Commandments* movie set, buried under the

sand here once filming was finished. **Lompoc** is noted for its blooming flower fields—this is a major seed-producing area—and is home to **Vandenberg Air Force Base** as well as **Mission La Purisima State Historic Park** four miles east of town, California's only complete mission compound. For more detailed area information, contact the **Santa Maria Visitor & Convention Bureau,** 614 S. Broadway in Santa Maria, 800/ 331-3779, www.santamaria.com, and the **Lompoc Valley Chamber of Commerce,** 111 S. I St. in Lompoc, 805/736-4567 or 800/240-0999.

Farther south, **Solvang** is an authentic Danish-style town founded in 1911 and now a well-trod tourist destination. If you've got time, worth exploring nearby are the towns of **Los Olivos** and **Los Alamos,** center of northern Santa Barbara County's impressive wine country. For area information, contact the **Solvang Visitors Bureau,** 1639 Copenhagen Dr., 805/688-6144 or 800/468-6765, www.solvangusa.com.

Technically speaking, Point Conception just below Vandenberg marks the spot where California turns on itself—that pivotal geographical point where Northern California becomes Southern California. The subtle climatic and terrain changes are unmistakable by the time you arrive in **Santa Barbara,** a richly endowed city noted for its gracious red-tile-roofed California Spanish-style buildings—for the most part an architectural affectation subsequent to the 1925 earthquake that was so devasting here. Even if you have time for nothing else, stop to see the **Santa Barbara County Courthouse** one block up from State Street at Anapamu and Anacapa, an L-shaped Spanish-Moorish castle that is quite possibly the most beautiful public building in all of California. Other attractions are abundant, from **Mission Santa Barbara,** "Queen of the Missions," to the **Santa Barbara Museum of Natural History** and the **Santa Barbara Botanic Gardens.** Despite the presence of offshore oil wells, public beaches in the area are sublime. In the harbor area don't miss **Stern's Wharf,** for serene sunsets and other attractions, and the new **Santa Barbara Maritime Museum.** For more information about Santa Barbara and vicinity, contact the **Santa Barbara Conference & Visitors Bureau,** 1601

Anacapa St. in Santa Barbara, 805/966-9222 or 800/549-5133, www.santabarbaraca.com.

For less expensive yet equally satisfying coastal adventures continue south from Santa Barbara to **Ventura** and **Oxnard.** From here set off on whalewatching trips and guided boat tours of California's **Channel Islands,** a national park equally visible but often less accessible from Santa Barbara. For more area information, contact the **Ventura Visitors & Convention Bureau,** 89 S. California St., Ste. C, 805/648-2075 or 800/333-2989, www.ventura-usa.com, and the **Oxnard Convention & Visitors Bureau** inside Connelly House at Heritage Square, 200 W. Seventh St., 805/385-7545 or 800/269-6273, www.oxnardtourism.com.

Resources

Suggested Reading

The virtual "publisher of record" for all things Californian is the **University of California Press,** 510/642-4247 or 800/777-4726, www.ucpress.edu, which publishes hundreds of titles on the subject—all excellent. Stanford University's **Stanford University Press,** 650/723-9434, www.sup.org, also offers some books of particular interest to Californiacs—especially under the subject categories of American Literature, California History, and Natural History—though in general these are books of academic interest.

Other publishers offering California titles, particularly general interest, history, hiking, and regional travel titles, include **Heyday Books,** 510/549-3564, www.heydaybooks.com, and the **Foghorn Outdoors** series by Avalon Travel Publishing, 510/595-3664, www.foghorn.com, which publishes a generous list of unusual, and unusually thorough, California outdoor guides, including Tom Stienstra's camping, fishing, and other recreational guides.

Sierra Club Books, 415/977-5500 or 888/722-6657 for orders, www.sierraclub.org/books, offers a few useful titles—such as *Starr's Guide to the John Muir Trail and High Sierra*—but these days **Wilderness Press** is the top publisher of wilderness guides and maps for California. For new titles and to survey the impressive backlist, contact the press directly at 510/558-1666 or 800/443-7227 for orders, www.wildernesspress.com.

The following book listings represent a fairly selective introduction to books about Northern California history, natural history, literature, recreation, and travel. The interested reader can find many other titles by visiting good local bookstores and/or state and national park visitor centers. As always, the author would appreciate suggestions about other books that should be included. Send the names of new candidates—or actual books, if you're either a publisher or an unusually generous person—to: Kim Weir, c/o Avalon Travel Publishing, 1400 65th St., Ste. 250, Emeryville, CA 94608, atpfeedback@avalonpub.com.

COMPANION READING

Austin, Mary, with a foreword by John Walton. *The Ford.* Berkeley: University of California Press, 1997. Appreciating Mary Austin's "bold and original mind" in reviewing this novel for the *New York Times,* Carey McWilliams also said: "Of her novels, *The Ford,* which deals with the battle for the water of the Owens Valley, [is] perhaps the best."

Baldy, Marian. *The University Wine Course.* San Francisco: The Wine Appreciation Guild, 1992. Destined to be a classic and designed for both instructional and personal use, this friendly book offers a comprehensive education about wine. *The University Wine Course* explains it all, from viticulture to varietals. And the lips-on lab exercises and chapter-by-chapter examinations help even the hopelessly déclassé develop the subtle sensory awareness necessary for any deeper appreciation of the winemaker's art. Special sections and appendixes on reading (and understanding) wine labels, combining wine and food, and understanding wine terminology make it a lifelong personal library reference. Definitely "do" this book before doing the California wine country.

Bright, William O. *1,500 California Place Names: Their Origin and Meaning.* A revised version of the classic *1,000 California Place Names* by Erwin G. Gudde, first published in 1949. University of California Press, 1998. Though you can also get the revised edition of Gudde's original masterpiece (see below), this convenient, alphabetically arranged pocketbook is perfect for travelers, explaining the names of mountains, rivers, and towns throughout California.

Buckley, Christopher, and Gary Young, eds. *The Geography of Home: California's Poetry of Place.* Berkeley: Heyday Books, 1999. This contemporary anthology showcases the work of 76 California poets. In addition to multiple selections of each poet's work, the poets also talk about their history in California, and the state's influence on their poetry.

Clappe, Louise Amelia Knapp Smith, with an introduction by Marlene Smithe-Baranzini. *The Shirley Letters from the California Mines, 1851-1852.* Berkeley: Heyday Books, 1998. A classic of California gold rush-era literature, and a vivid portrait of both the exuberance and brutality of life in that time—a tale told from a woman's perspective. An absolutely superb read.

Dana, Richard Henry, Jr. *Two Years Before the Mast.* New York: New American Library, 1990. A classic of early California literature. After recovering from a bout with the measles, young Harvard man Richard Henry Dana sailed off to complete his convalescence—not as a privileged ship passenger but as a sailor. On August 14, 1834, he boarded the *Pilgrim* in Boston Harbor and was underway on what was to be the greatest adventure of his life. This realistic depiction of life on the high seas offers an accurate firsthand account of what it was like to see the California coastline for the first time—and to tie up in San Francisco *before* the gold rush. Some of the earliest written descriptions of California—and still an exceptional read.

Fisher, M.F.K. *The Art of Eating.* Foster City, CA: IDG Books Worldwide, 1990. Reprint ed. John Updike has called her "the poet of the appetites." Often characterized as California's premier food writer, particularly after she settled into the Sonoma County wine country, Mary Frances Kennedy Fisher was actually a *writer*—one who understood that the fundamental human needs are food, love, and security. She wrote about them all, in more than 20 books and countless other essays, letters, and stories. Five of her most beloved book-length essays—*An Alphabet of Gourmets, Consider the Oyster, The Gastronomical Me, How to Cook a Wolf,* and *Serve It Forth*—are all included in this collection.

Gilbar, Steven. *Natural State: A Literary Anthology of California Nature Writing.* Berkeley: University of California Press, 1998. This hefty and dazzling collection includes many of the writers you'd expect—Gretel Ehrlich, M.F.K. Fisher, John McPhee, John Muir, Gary Snyder, and Robert Louis Stevenson—but also a few surprises, including Joan Didion, Jack Kerouac, and Henry Miller.

Gudde, Erwin G. Edited by William O. Bright. *California Place Names: The Origin and Etymology of Current Geographical Names.* Berkeley: University of California Press, 1998. Did you know that *Siskiyou* was the Chinook word for "bobtailed horse," as borrowed from the Cree language? More such complex truths await every time you dip into this fascinating volume— the ultimate guide to California place names (and how to pronounce them). A revised and expanded fourth edition, building upon the masterwork of Gudde, who died in 1969.

Hammett, Dashiell. *The Maltese Falcon.* New York: Vintage Books, 1992. Reissue ed. Sam Spade is Dashiell Hammett's tough-as-nails San Francisco private dick, also central to Hammett's *The Dain Curse* and *The Glass Key.* Spade in this story unravels the enigma of the Maltese Falcon, a solid-gold statuette originally crafted as a tribute to Holy Roman Emperor Charles IV. While trying to find the falcon, Spade's partner is murdered, the coppers blame him for it, and the bad guys are out to get him, too. Then, of course, there's also the beautiful redhead, who appears and just as mysteriously disappears. Whodunnit? And why?

Hansen, Gladys. *San Francisco Almanac.* Second revised ed. San Francisco: Chronicle

Books, 1995. Finally back in print after a too-long hiatus, this easy-to-use source for San Francisco facts was written by the city archivist. Contains a detailed chronology, maps, and bibliography. Also fun: what some famous people have said about San Francisco. Fascinating, too, is the author's *Denial of Disaster: The Untold Story & Unpublished Photographs of the San Francisco Earthquake & Fire of 1906,* co-authored by Emmet Condon, 1989 (Cameron & Co.).

Hart, James D. *A Companion to California.* Berkeley: University of California Press. Revised and expanded, 1987 (OP). Another very worthy book for Californiacs to collect, if you can find it, with thousands of brief entries on all aspects of California as well as more in-depth pieces on subjects such as literature.

Hong Kingston, Maxine. *The Woman Warrior: Memoirs of a Girlhood Among Ghosts.* New York: Vintage Books, 1989. Reissue ed. Fictionalized memoir about growing up Chinese-American in Stockton, California. In China, ghosts are supernatural beings, but in California they become everyone who is not from China. This is an elliptical and powerful story about finding a place in American society, though still raising ire in some quarters for its representations of Chinese culture.

Houston, James D. *Californians: Searching for the Golden State.* Santa Cruz, CA: Otter B Books, 1992. 10th reprint ed. Good prose, good points in this collection of personal essays about Californians in their endless search for the meaning of their own dream.

Jeffers, Robinson. *Selected Poems.* New York: Random House, 1965. The poet Robinson Jeffers died in 1961 at the age of 75, on a rare day when it actually snowed in Carmel. One of California's finest poets, sophisticated yet accessible, many of his poems pay homage to the beauty of his beloved Big Sur coast. Poems collected here are selections from some of his major works, including *Be Angry at the Sun, The Beginning and the End, Hungerfield,* and *Tamar and Other Poems.*

Kahrl, William. *Water and Power: The Conflict over Los Angeles' Water Supply in the Owens Valley.* Berkeley: University of California Press, 1982. Perhaps the best book available for anyone who wants to understand the politics of water and power in California, and how water and political power have transformed the state's economy and land.

Karman, James. *Stones of the Sur.* Stanford: Stanford University Press, 2001. Here's a coffee table book well worth buying a table for—a stunning marriage of the poetry of Robinson Jeffers and the photographs of Morley Baer.

Kerouac, Jack. *Subterraneans.* New York: Grove Press, 1989. Considered by some to be Kerouac's masterpiece and first published in 1958, this is a Beat exploration of life on the fringes, a novel largely set in the San Francisco Bay Area. Others, however, prefer *The Dharma Bums* (1958) and *Big Sur* (1962).

Keithley, George. *The Donner Party.* New York: George Braziller, 1989. The most nightmarish winter of early California settlement is here so tenderly unveiled that we share the determined struggle and wrenching loss.

Kowalewski, Michael, ed. *Gold Rush: A Literary Exploration.* Berkeley: Heyday Books, 1998. This official companion guide to the PBS Special *The Gold Rush* commemorates the 150th anniversary of the California gold rush—and is, in the words of James D. Houston, "an extraordinary read."

Le Guin, Ursula K. *Always Coming Home.* Berkeley: University of California Press, 2001. Unbelievably, this book was out of print for a time. Thanks to UC Press, it's back. *Always Coming Home* is perhaps Le Guin's masterwork, and a special treat for those who love

Suggested Reading

Suggested Reading

California—particularly Northern California, described (and mapped) in this imaginative exploration of "futuristic anthropology." Equally rare sidelong glances into the soul of the northstate come in Le Guin's essay collection *Dancing at the Edge of the World: Thoughts on Words, Women, Places.* And why not? The daughter of UC Berkeley anthropologist Alfred L. Kroeber and Ishi's biographer Theodora Kroeber, Le Guin offers a unique perspective on California as a place—then, now, and in the times to come.

London, Jack, ed. by Gerald Haslam. *Jack London's Golden State: Selected California Writings.* Berkeley: Heyday Books, 1999. The first major U.S. writer to use California as his base, Jack London has finally come home—so California can reclaim him. Included here are some of London's finest works, from *John Barleycorn: or Alcoholic Memoirs* and *Star Rover* to *Valley of the Moon,* along with journalism, short stories, and letters.

McPhee, John. *Assembling California.* New York: Noonday Press (Farrar, Straus and Giroux), 1993. The indefatigable natural history writer here deconstructs California, tectonically speaking, as a cross-section of both human and geologic time.

Michaels, Leonard, David Reid, and Raquel Scherr, eds. *West of the West: Imagining California.* New York: HarperCollins Publishers, 1991. Though any anthology about California is destined to be incomplete, this one is exceptional, offering selections by Maya Angelou, Simone de Beauvoir, and Joan Didion as well as Umberto Eco, Aldous Huxley, Jack Kerouac, and Rudyard Kipling, among many other notables.

Miller, Henry. *Big Sur and the Oranges of Hieronymus Bosch.* New York: W.W. Norton & Co., 1978. First published in 1958, the famed writer shares his impressions of art and writing along with his view of life as seen from the Big Sur coastline—the center of his personal universe in his later years.

Miller, Joaquin. *Life Amongst the Modocs: Unwritten History.* Berkeley: Heyday Books, 1996. First published in 1873, Miller's fierce descriptions of the sublime yet melancholy beauty of California's wild landscape come from his years in the 1850s mining towns and Indian camps of northernmost California. Epic in scope and groundbreaking in its blending of fiction and fact, *Life Amongst the Modocs* gives us an intensely felt and unforgettable portrait of the birth of modern California.

Muir, John, ed. by Frederic Gunsky. *South of Yosemite: Selected Writings of John Muir.* Berkeley: Wilderness Press, 1988. The first collection of Muir's writings to explore what is now the Sequoia and Kings Canyon region fulfills the famed naturalist's dream of a book he intended to title *The Yosemite and the Other Yosemites.* This "Other Yosemite" anthology includes some of Muir's best work. To appreciate his complete works, find *John Muir: His Life and Letters and Other Writings* and *John Muir: The Eight Wilderness Discovery Books.*

Norris, Frank. *McTeague: A Story of San Francisco.* New York: New American Library, 1997. Reissue ed. The basis for the classic silent film *Greed,* Norris's novel is, in a way, the ultimate Western. First published in 1899, a retelling of an actual crime, *McTeague* tells the story of a dimwitted dentist and his greedy wife—all in all a bleak, low-brow tour of life in San Francisco at the turn of the 20th century. Greed is a topic Norris tackled more than once—notably in *The Octopus: A Story of California,* a purported work of fiction that chronicles the struggles of California wheat farmers against rapacious California railroad barons and their relentless campaign for complete economic and political dominion. Now available in a Penguin USA edition with Introduction by California historian Kevin Starr.

Paddison, Joshua, ed. *A World Transformed: First-hand Accounts of California Before the Gold Rush.* Berkeley: Heyday Books, 1999. According to popular California mythology, the Golden State was "born" with the onrushing change that came with the gold rush of 1848. But this collection of earlier California writings gathers together some intriguing earlier observations—from European explorers and visitors, missionaries, and sea captains—that reveal pre-gold rush California.

Rice, Scott, ed. *It Was a Dark and Stormy Night: The Final Conflict.* New York: Penguin, 1992. An anthology of the best of bad fiction from San Jose State University's Bullwer-Lytton fiction contest. And if that's not enough tortured verbiage for you, try the 1984 *It Was a Dark and Stormy Night: The Best (?) from the Bulwer-Lytton Contest.*

Roumieu, Graham. *In Me Own Words: The Autobiography of Bigfoot.* San Francisco: Manic D Press, 2003. You gotta love a book that opens with: "I am not Chewbacca. Me think Chewbacca jerk." Bigfoot abandons the primitive life of a bond trader to start a grunge band. And that's all before the hamster dies.

Russack, Benjamin, ed. *Wine Country: A Literary Companion.* Berkeley: Heyday Books, 1999. This intriguing anthology includes stories from the Wappo Indians and early explorers as well as recognized literary figures—Robert Louis Stevenson, Jack London, Ambrose Bierce, Dorothy Bryant, Jessamyn West, among others—associated with the Napa and Sonoma Valleys.

Saroyan, William. *The Daring Young Man on the Flying Trapeze: And Other Stories.* New York: New Directions, 1997. Known for the *humanness* of his writings, Fresno's own William Saroyan won the Pulitzer Prize for his play *The Time of Your Life: A Comedy in Three Acts.* As befits one of the first writers in the 20th century to explore life in immi-grant communities, the protagonists in "Daring Young Man"—a collection first published in 1934—are African, Armenian, Chinese, Jewish, and Irish immigrants.

Stegner, Wallace Earle. *Angle of Repose.* New York: Penguin USA, 1992. Reprint ed. Wallace Stegner's Pulitzer Prize-winning novel, in which the disenchanted, wheelchair-bound historian Lyman Ward decides to write about the lives of his grandparents on the American frontier.

Stegner, Wallace Earle. Edited and with a preface from the author's son, Page Stegner. *Marking the Sparrow's Fall: Wallace Stegner's American West.* New York: H. Holt, 1998. This brilliant collection of Stegner's conservation writings traces his development as a Westerner—and as a Western writer—starting with his seemingly inauspicious beginnings as an avid reader, hunkered down in small-town libraries in places almost no one's ever heard of. The first collection of Stegner's work since the author's death in 1993, *Marking the Sparrow's Fall* includes 15 essays never before published, his best-known essays on the American West—including *Wilderness Letter*—and a little-known novella.

Snyder, Gary. *Turtle Island.* New York: W.W. Norton & Co., 1974. Titled with a Native American term for the entire North American continent, this Pulitzer Prize-winning 1975 poetry collection honors almost every aspect of that vast landscape. When the poem cycle *Mountains and Rivers Without End* was published in 1996, Snyder was awarded the Böllingen Poetry Prize and the *Los Angeles Times*'s Robert Kirsch Lifetime Achievement Award.

Thompson, Gary. *On John Muir's Trail.* Cohasset, CA: Bear Star Press, 1999. A marvelously accessible and original collection of poetry that pays homage to people and places in Northern California. Includes all of the poems in *Moon Handbooks Northern California.*

Copies are available directly from the publisher: Bear Star Press, 185 Hollow Oak Dr., Cohasset, CA 95973, www.bearstarpress.com.

Twain, Mark. *Roughing It.* New York: Penguin USA, 1994. Reissue ed. What we now recgnize as vintage Twain, as he blunders into California and elsewhere throughout the West, in search of elusive fortune.

WPA Guide to California: The Federal Writers Project Guide to 1930s California. New York: Pantheon Press (an imprint of Random House), 1984. The classic travel guide to California, first published during the Depression, is somewhat dated as far as contemporary sights but excellent as a companion volume and background information source.

HISTORY AND PEOPLE

Atherton, Gertrude. *My San Francisco, A Wayward Biography.* Indianapolis and New York: The Bobbs-Merrill Company, 1946. The 56th book—written at the age of 90—by the woman Kevin Starr has called "the daughter of the elite" whose career of historical fiction "document[ed]. . . itself. . . in a careless but vivid output. . . ." A delightfully chatty browse through the past, filled with dropped names and accounts of Atherton's own meetings with historic figures.

Brands, H.W. *The Age of Gold: The California Gold Rush and the New American Dream.* New York: Doubleday, 2002. Turns out the California gold rush was a turning point in American and world history, and this brilliant new history explains why.

Bronson, William. *The Earth Shook, The Sky Burned: A Photographic Record of the 1906 San Francisco Earthquake & Fire.* San Francisco: Chronicle Books, 1997. Originally published by Doubleday, 1959. A San Francisco classic—just the book to tote home as a memento of your San Francisco vacation. This moving story of the city's devastating 1906 earthquake and the four-day fire that followed includes more than 400 on-the-scene photographs.

Chaffin, Tom. *Pathfinder: John Charles Frémont and the Course of American Empire.* New York: Hill &Wang, 2002. From accounts of Frémont's mapping expeditions topolitical intrigue, a revealing picture of one who carried high the banner of Manifest Destiny.

Didion, Joan. *Where I Was From.* New York: Knopf, 2003. Originally she was from Sacramento, almost part of California. Even in some of these essays Didion reveals doubts about whether she's from here anymore, but she is—and has been ever since her ancestors wandered west with the Donner Party.

Dreyer, Peter. *A Gardener Touched with Genius: The Life of Luther Burbank.* Berkeley: University of California Press, 1985.

Ellison, William Henry. *A Self-Governing Dominion, California 1849-1860.* Berkeley: University of California Press, 1978.

Farquhar, Francis P. *History of the Sierra Nevada.* Berkeley: University of California Press, 1965.

Farquhar, Francis P., ed. *Up and Down California in 1860-1864: The Journal of William H. Brewer.* Berkeley: University of California Press, 2003. Fourth ed., with maps, now in paperback. Brewer's letters to his brother chronicle the first geological survey of California.

Frémont, John Charles. *Memoirs of My Life.* New York: Penguin, 1984. Originally published in Chicago, 1887. The old Bearflagger himself tells the story of early California—at least some of it.

Gutierrez, Ramon A., and Richard J. Orsi, eds. *Contested Eden: California Before the Gold Rush.* Berkeley: University of California Press, 1998. In this first volume of a projected four-part series, essays explore California before the gold rush.

Harlow, Neal. *California Conquered: The Annexation of a Mexican Province, 1846-1850.* Berkeley: University of California Press, 1982.

Heizer, Robert F. *The Destruction of the California Indians.* Utah: Gibbs Smith Publishing, 1974.

Heizer, Robert F., and M.A. Whipple. *The California Indians.* Berkeley: University of California Press, 1971. A worthwhile collection of essays about California's native peoples, covering general, regional, and specific topics—a good supplement to the work of A.L. Kroeber (who also contributed to this volume).

Holliday, J.S. (James). *The World Rushed In: The California Gold Rush Experience: An Eyewitness Account of a Nation Heading West.* Norman, OK: University of Oklahoma Press, 2002. Holliday labored for decades to compile and recast as narrative history diary entries and letters of William Swain, a young man from near Niagara Falls who came to California to pan for gold at Bidwell's Bar

Houston, James, and Jeanne Houston. *Farewell to Manzanar.* New York: Bantam Books, 1983. A good goodbye to California's World War II internment of Japanese immigrants and American citizens of Japanese descent, a nightmarish experience that lives on in the cultural memory of Southern California's large population of Japanese Americans.

Hutchinson, W.H. *California: The Golden Shore by the Sundown Sea.* Belmont, CA: Star Publishing Company, 1988. The late author, known as Old Hutch to former students, presents a dizzying amount of historical, economic, and political detail from his own unique perspective in this analysis of California's past and present. Hutchinson saw the state from many sides during a lifetime spent

as "a horse wrangler, cowboy, miner, boiler fireman, merchant seaman, corporate bureaucrat, rodeo and horse show announcer, and freelance writer."

Irons, Peter. *Justice at War: The Story of the Japanese-American Internment Cases.* Berkeley: University of California Press, 1993. Irons examines the internment of Japanese Americans and noncitizen immigrants in World War II "relocation" camps as historical travesty in a brilliantly researched, beautifully written book.

Jackson, Mrs. Helen Hunt. *Century of Dishonor: A Sketch of the US Government's Dealings (with some of the Indian tribes).* Temecula, CA: Reprint Services, 1988. Originally published in Boston, 1881.

Jackson, Joseph Henry. *Anybody's Gold: The Story of California's Mining Towns.* San Francisco: Chronicle Books, 1970. A lively history back in print after a 30-year hiatus.

Kroeber, Alfred L. *Handbook of the Indians of California.* New York: Dover Publications, 1976 (unabridged facsimile version of the original work, *Bulletin 78* of the Bureau of American Ethnology of the Smithsonian Institution, published by the U.S. Government Printing Office). The classic compendium of observed facts about California's native peoples by the noted UC Berkeley anthropologist who befriended Ishi—but also betrayed him, posthumously, by allowing his body to be autopsied (in violation of Ishi's beliefs) then shipping his brain to the Smithsonian Institution.

Kroeber, Theodora. *Ishi in Two Worlds: A Biography of the Last Wild Indian in North America.* Berkeley: University of California Press, 1961. The classic biography of Ishi, an incredible 20th-century story—illustrating California's location at the edge of the wilderness well into the 20th century—well-told by A.L.

Kroeber's widow and also available in an illustrated edition. Also very worthwhile by Kroeber: *Inland Whale: California Indian Legends*, and, co-written with Robert F. Heizer, *Ishi the Last Yahi: A Documentary History*. That Ishi may not have been the last Yahi after all—see the Northern Mountains chapter for the latest twists in this tale—just makes the story all the more intriguing.

Lapsley, James T. *Bottled Poetry: Napa Winemaking from Prohibition to the Modern Era*. Berkeley: University of California Press, 1997. Though California's Napa Valley is now one of the world's premier wine regions, it was not always thus. This entertaining history explains how a collective post-Prohibition desire for excellence, in combination with promotional savvy, transformed the fate of the region and its wines.

Lewis, Oscar. *The Big Four*. Sausalito, CA: Comstock Editions, 1982. Originally published in New York, 1938.

Margolin, Malcolm. *The Way We Lived*. Berkeley: Heyday Books, 1981. A wonderful collection of California native peoples' reminiscences, stories, and songs. Also by Margolin: *The Ohlone Way*, about the life of California's first residents of the San Francisco-Monterey Bay Area.

McWilliams, Carey, with a foreword by Lewis H. Lapham. *California, the Great Exception*. Berkeley: University of California Press, 1999. Historian, journalist, and lawyer Carey McWilliams, editor of *The Nation* from 1955 to 1975, stepped back from his other tasks in 1949 to assess the state of the Golden State at the end of its first 100 years. And while he acknowledged the state's prodigious productivity even then, he also noted the brutality with which the great nation-state of California dealt with "the Indian problem," the water problem, and the agricultural labor problem—all issues of continuing relevance to California today. McWilliams' classic work

on the essence of California, reprinted with a new foreword by the editor of *Harper's* magazine, is a must-read for all Californians.

Milosz, Czeslaw. *Visions from San Francisco Bay*. New York: Farrar, Straus & Giroux, 1982. Essays on emigration from the Nobel Prize winner in literature. Originally published in Polish, 1969.

Murray, Keith A. *The Modocs and Their War*. Norman, OK: University of Oklahoma Press, 1976.

Nasaw, David. *The Chief: The Life of William Randolph Hearst*. New York: Houghton Mifflin, 2000. Drawing on many new sources, including Hearst's own papers, Nasaw's Hearst emerges as more complex (and accurate) character than the one portrayed in Orson Welles's *Citizen Kane*.

Phillips, Kate. *Helen Hunt Jackson: A Literary Life*. Berkeley: University of California Press, 2003. Finally, someone steps forward to write the definitive biography of this remarkable social reformers and 19th-century novelist, responsible for countless migrations to "Ramona country."

Reisner, Marc. *Cadillac Desert: The American West and Its Disappearing Water*. New York: Penguin Books, 1993. Revised ed. Inspiration for the four-part 1997 PBS documentary, this is the contemporary yet classic tale of water and the unromantic West—a drama of unquenchable thirst and reluctant conservation, political intrigue and corruption, and economic and ecological disasters. How Los Angeles got its water figures prominently—the histories of William Mulholland and the Owens Valley as well as the Colorado River. A must-read book. Reisner's apocalyptic *A Dangerous Place: California's Unsettling Fate*, which he huried to finish before he died, explores the omnipresent danger of earthquakes and California's heedlessness.

Royce, Josiah. *California from the Conquest in 1846 to the Second Vigilance Committee in San Francisco 1856.* New York: AMS Press. Originally published in Boston, 1886.

Sinclair, Upton. *I, Candidate for Governor: And How I Got Licked.* Berkeley: University of California Press, 1994. Reprint of the original edition. This is a genuine treasure of California history—a first-person account of California's liveliest and most notorious gubernatorial race, in which California business employed Hollywood's tools to defeat muckraking journalist and socialist Democratic candidate Sinclair in the too-close-to-call 1934 campaign. Sinclair's platform was EPIC—End Poverty in California—and he almost got the chance to try.

Starr, Kevin. *Americans and the California Dream: 1850–1915.* New York: Oxford University Press, 1973. The first volume in an ever-expanding cultural history, written by a native San Franciscan, historian, and current California State Librarian. The focus on Northern California taps an impressively varied body of sources as it seeks to "suggest the poetry and the moral drama of social experience" from California's first days of statehood through the Panama-Pacific Exposition of 1915 when, in the author's opinion, "California came of age." Starr's 1985 *Inventing the Dream: California Through the Progressive Era,* second in his California history series, and *Material Dreams: Southern California Through the 1920s,* his third, primarily tell the southstate story. Annotations in all three suggest rich possibilities for further reading.

Starr, Kevin. *The Dream Endures: California Enters the 1940s.* New York: Oxford University Press, 1997. This, the fifth volume in Kevin Starr's Americans and the California Dream series, traces the history of the California good life—in architecture, fiction, film, and leisure pursuits—and how it came to define American culture and society. Chosen Outstand-ing Academic Book of 1997 by *Choice,* and one of the best 100 books of 1997 by the *Los Angeles Times Book Review.* Starr's sixth volume, *Embattled Dreams: California in War and Peace, 1940-1950,* published in 2003, chronicles California's part in the vast expansion of the war industry, the state's role as the "arsenal of democracy," and anti-Communist red-baiting and the early career of Richard M. Nixon.

Starr, Kevin. *Endangered Dreams: The Great Depression in California.* New York: Oxford University Press, 1996. "California," Wallace Stegner has noted, "is like the rest of the United States, only more so." And so begins the fourth volume of Starr's imaginative and immense California history, in which the author delves into the Golden State's dark past—a period in which strikes and unions were forcibly suppressed, soup kitchens became social institutions, and both socialism and fascism had their day.

Stevenson, Robert Louis. *From Scotland to Silverado.* Cambridge, MA: The Belknap Press of Harvard University Press, 1966. An annotated collection of the sickly and lovelorn young Stevenson's travel essays, including his first impressions of Monterey and San Francisco, and the works that have come to be known as *The Silverado Squatters.* Contains considerable text—marked therein—that the author's family and friends had removed from previous editions.

Stone, Irving. *Jack London: Sailor on Horseback.* New York: Doubleday, 1986. Originally published in Boston, 1938.

Stone, Irving. *Men to Match My Mountains.* New York: Berkeley Publishers, 1987. A classic California history, originally published in 1956.

Turner, Frederick. *Rediscovering America.* New York: Penguin, 1985. A fascinating cultural history and biography of John Muir—the man in his time and ours—generally more interesting reading than much of Muir's own work.

Walton, John. *Western Times and Water Wars: State, Culture, and Rebellion in California.* Berkeley: University of California Press, 1992. Winner of both the Robert Park and J.S. Holliday Awards, Walton's compelling chronicle of the water wars between Los Angeles and the farmers and ranchers of the Owens Valley is a masterpiece of California history.

NATURE AND NATURAL HISTORY

Alden, Peter. *National Audubon Society Field Guide to California.* New York: Alfred A. Knopf, 1998. A wonderful field guide to some 1,000 of the state's native inhabitants, from the world's smallest butterfly—the Western Pygmy Blue—to its oldest, largest, and tallest trees. Well illustrated with striking color photography.

Alt, David, and Donald Hyndman. *Roadside Geology of Northern & Central California.* Missoula, MT: Mountain Press, 2000. Second edition. The classic glovebox companion guide to the northstate landscape is now revised— and expanded to include central regions.

Bakker, Elna. *An Island Called California: An Ecological Introduction to Its Natural Communities.* Berkeley: University of California Press, 1985. Expanded revised ed. An excellent, time-honored introduction to the characteristics of, and relationships between, California's natural communities. New chapters on Southern California, added in this edition, make *An Island* more helpful statewide.

Barbour, Michael, Bruce Pavlik, Susan Lindstrom, and Frank Drysdale, with a foreword by Pulitzer Prize-winning California poet Gary Snyder. *California's Changing Landscapes: Diversity and Conservation of California Vegetation.* Sacramento: California Native

Plant Society Press, 1993. This well-illustrated, well-indexed lay guide to California's astonishing botanical variety is an excellent introduction. For more in-depth personal study, the society also publishes some excellent regional floras and plant keys.

California Coastal Commission, State of California. *California Coastal Resource Guide.* Berkeley: University of California Press, 1997. This is the revised and expanded fifth edition of the California coast lover's bible, the indispensable guide to the Pacific coast and its wonders—the land, marine geology, biology—as well as parks, landmarks, and amusements. But for practical travel purposes, get the commission's *The California Coastal Access Guide,* listed under Enjoying the Outdoors below.

Collier, Michael. *A Land in Motion: California's San Andreas Fault.* Berkeley: University of California Press, 1999. An intriguing geologic tour of the world's most famous fault, which runs the entire length of western California—and right through the San Francisco Bay Area. Wonderful photographs.

Dunn, Jon L., and the National Geographic Society staff. *National Geographic Society Field Guide to the Birds of North America.* Washington, D.C.: National Geographic Society, 1999. Third ed. One of the best guides to bird identification available.

Duremberger, Robert. *Elements of California Geography.* Out of print but worth searching for. This is the classic work on California geography.

Fagan, Brian. *Before California: An Archaeologist Looks at Our Earliest Inhabitants.* Lanham, MD: Rowman and Littlefield, 2003. Life has always been hard in California—even before it was California. Fagan shows how even the earliest California residents learned to adapt, in order to overcome their survival challenges.

Fix, David, and Andy Bezener. *Birds of Northern California*. Auburn, WA: Lone Pine Publishing, 2000. Already the bible of beginning birders.

Garth, John S., and J.W. Tilden. *California Butterflies*. Berkeley: University of California Press, 1986. At long last, the definitive field guide and key to California butterflies (in both the larval and adult stages) is available, and in paperback; compact and fairly convenient to tote around.

Grinnell, Joseph, and Alden Miller. *The Distribution of the Birds of California*. Out of print but worth looking for; among other places, at last report you could find it online at the University of New Mexico's "elibrary" site, provided by the Coioper Onrnithological Society. This is the definitive California birder's guide—for those interested in serious study.

Hickman, Jim, ed. *The Jepson Manual: Higher Plants of California*. Berkeley: University of California Press (with cooperation and support from the California Native Plant Society and the Jepson Herbarium), 1993. Hot off the presses more than a decade ago but 10 years in the making before that, *The Jepson Manual* is already considered the bible of California botany. The brainchild of both Jim Hickman and Larry Heckard, curator of the Jepson Herbarium, this book is a cumulative picture of the extraordinary flora of California, and the first comprehensive attempt to fit it all into one volume since the Munz *A California Flora* was published in 1959. The best work of almost 200 botanist-authors has been collected here, along with exceptional line drawings and illustrations (absent from the Munz flora) that make it easier to identify and compare plant species. This book is the botanical reference book for a California lifetime—a hefty investment for a hefty tome, especially essential for serious ecologists and botanists, amateur and otherwise. New in 2002: *The Jepson Desert Manual*.

Hill, Mary. *California Landscape: Origin and Evolution*. Berkeley: University of California Press, 1984. An emphasis on the most recent history of California landforms. Also by Hill: *Geology of the Sierra Nevada*.

Johnston, Verna R. *California Forests and Woodlands: A Natural History*. Berkeley: University of California Press, 1994. For beginning botany students, a very helpful general introduction to the plants, animals, and ecological relationships within California's varied types of forests.

Kaufman, Kenn. *Lives of North American Birds*. New York: Houghton Mifflin Co., 1997. Sponsored by the Roger Tory Peterson Institute. A bit bulky for a field guide but already considered a classic, this 674-page hardbound tome focuses less on identifying features and names and more on observing and understanding birds within the contexts of their own lives. Now, there's a concept.

Le Boeuf, Burney J., and Stephanie Kaza. *The Natural History of Año Nuevo*. Santa Cruz, CA: Otter B Books, 1985. Reprint ed. An excellent, very comprehensive guide to the natural features of the Año Nuevo area just north of Santa Cruz.

McMinn, Howard. *An Illustrated Manual of California Shrubs*. Berkeley: University of California Press, 1939. Reprint ed. An aid in getting to know about 800 California shrubs, this classic manual includes keys, descriptions of flowering, elevations, and geographic distributions. For the serious amateur botanist, another title for the permanent library.

Munz, Phillip A., and David D. Keck. *A California Flora and Supplement*. Berkeley: University of California Press, 1968. Until quite recently this was it, the California botanist's bible—a complete descriptive "key" to every plant known to grow in California—but quite hefty to tote around on pleasure trips. More useful for amateur botanists are Munz's *California Mountain Wildflowers* (new ed. 2003) *Shore Wildflowers* (new ed. 2003), and *California Desert Wildflowers,* as well as other illustrated plant guides published by UC Press. Serious amateur and professional botanists and ecologists are more than ecstatic these days about the recent publication of the *new* California plant bible: *The Jepson Manual,* edited by Jim Hickman.

Ornduff, Robert. *Introduction to California Plant Life.* Berkeley: University of California Press, 2003. Second ed. An essential for native plant libraries, this classic offers a marvelous introduction to California's botanical abundance. The new edition includes expanded discussions of changes in California landscape and flora.

Pavlik, Bruce, Pamela Muick, Sharon Johnson, and Marjorie Popper. *Oaks of California.* Santa Barbara: Cachuma Press, 1993. Reissue ed. In ancient European times, oaks were considered spiritual beings, the sacred inspiration of artists, healers, and writers since these particular trees were thought to court the lightning flash. Time spent with this stunning book will soon convince anyone that this truth lives on. Packed with photos and lovely watercolor illustrations, maps, even an oak lover's travel guide, this book celebrates the many species of California oaks.

Peterson, Roger Tory, and Virginia Marie Peterson. *A Field Guide to Western Birds.* Boston: Houghton Mifflin Co., 1998. Reissue ed. The third edition of this birding classic has striking new features, such as full-color illustrations (including juveniles, females, and in-flight birds) facing the written descriptions and arrows to emphasize fie;ld markings. The only thing you'll have to flip around for are the range maps, tucked away in the back. Among other intriguing titles in the Peterson Field Guide series: *A Field Guide to Western Birds' Nests* by Hal Harrison.

Robbins, Chandler, et al. *Birds of North America.* New York: Golden Books Publishing Co., 1983. A good field guide for California birdwatching.

Schmitz, Marjorie. *Growing California Native Plants.* Berkeley: University of California Press, 1980. A handy guide for those interested in planting, growing, and otherwise supporting the success of California's beleaguered native plants.

Schoenherr, Allan A. *A Natural History of California.* Berkeley: University of California Press, 1992. With introductory chapters on ecology and geology, *A Natural History* covers California's climate, geology, soil, plant life, and animals based on distinct bioregions, with almost 300 photographs and numerous illustrations and tables. An exceptionally readable and well-illustrated introduction to California's astounding natural diversity and drama written by an ecology professor from CSU Fullerton, this 700-some page reference belongs on any Californiac's library shelf. Another worthy addition: *Natural History of the Islands of California.*

Sibley, David Allen. *The Sibley Guide to Birds.* New York: Knopf, 2000. Already a birding bestseller, Sibley's guide is a tad unwieldy for some. But it is durable, detailed, profusely illustrated with watercolors, and accurate. More portable and to the point: *The Sibley Field Guide to Birds of Western North America.* A companion: *The Sibley Guide to Bird Life and Behavior.*

Storer, Tracy I., and Robert L. Usinger. *Sierra Nevada Natural History: An Illustrated Handbook.* Berkeley: University of California Press, 1989. The indispensable, all-in-one natural history companion volume, compact and packable, for appreciating and understanding the Sierra Nevada.

Wallace, David Rains. *The Klamath Knot.* San Francisco: Sierra Club Books, 2003. 20th anniversary ed. with new epilogue by author.

Award-winning nonfiction about the botanically rich Klamath Mountains and its relict species—very readable natural history from the perspective of "evolutionary mythology."

Weeden, Norman. *A Sierra Nevada Flora.* Berkeley: Wilderness Press, 1996. Fourth ed. Perhaps *the* definitive field guide to Sierra Nevada plants, this one includes trees, shrubs, and ferns in addition to wildflowers. Complete, accurate, and quite compact, with hundreds of illustrations.

ENJOYING THE OUTDOORS

Bakalinsky, Adah. *Stairway Walks in San Francisco.* Berkeley: Wilderness Press, 2003. Fourth ed. This updated San Francisco classic offers 27 neighborhood walks connecting San Francisco's 200-plus stairways, choreographed by a veteran city walker and walking tour guide.

Blue, Anthony Dias, ed. *Zagat San Francisco Bay Area Restaurant Survey.* New York: Zagat Survey. This annually updated collection, a compilation of "people's reviews" of regional restaurants, is a reliable guide to what's hot and what's not in San Francisco and surrounding Bay Area destinations.

Brown, Ann Marie. *Foghorn Outdoors Northern California Biking.* Emeryville, CA: Avalon Travel Publishing, 2003. First ed. Covers over 150 of the best road cycling and mountain biking routes in Northern California. Also by Brown: *Foghorn Outdoors 101 Great Hikes in the San Francisco Bay Area,* second ed., 2003.

California Coastal Commission, State of California. *The California Coastal Access Guide.* Berkeley: University of California Press, 2003. Sixth ed. According to the *Oakland Tribune,* this is "no doubt the most comprehensive look at California's coastline published to date." A must-have for serious Californiacs.

California Coastal Conservancy, State of California. *San Francisco Bay Shoreline Guide.* Berkeley: University of California Press, 1995. This is it, the definitive guide to the entire 400-mile Bay Trail shoreline route, from its piers to its paths and parks. Comprehensive and user-friendly, with full-color maps and illustrations.

Cassady, Jim, and Fryar Calhoun. *California White Water: A Guide to the Rivers.* Berkeley: North Fork Press, 1995. Third revised ed.

Clark, Jeanne L. *California Wildlife Viewing Guide.* Helena, MT: Falcon Press, 1996. Second ed. This revised and expanded guide tells you where to go for a good look at native wildlife, and what to do once you're there. Color photos, overview maps.

Dirksen, Diane J. *Recreation Lakes of California.* Santa Cruz, CA: Recreation Sales Publishing, 2003. 14th ed. A very useful guide to the multitude of recreation lakes in California, complete with general maps (not to scale) and local contact addresses and phones. A worthwhile investment for boaters and fisherfolk.

Hart, John. *Walking Softly in the Wilderness: The Sierra Club Guide to Backpacking.* San Francisco: Sierra Club Books, 1998. Third ed., revised and updated.

Hauserman, Tim. *The Tahoe Rim Trail: A Complete Guide for Hikers, Mountain Bikers, and Equestrians.* Berkeley: Wilderness Press, 2002. Celebrate the trail's completion by giving it a go.

Hosler, Ray. *Bay Area Bike Rides.* San Francisco: Chronicle Books, 2002. Third ed. More than 50 bike rides throughout the greater Bay Area—all the way to Napa and Sonoma Counties—useful for both mountain bikers and touring cyclists.

Jeneid, Michael. *Adventure Kayaking: Trips from the Russian River to Monterey.* Berkeley: Wilderness Press, 1998. Tired of fighting that freeway traffic around the Bay Area? Try a kayak. Under decent weather conditions—and with an experienced kayaker to clue you in—you can get just about everywhere. If you'll be shoving off a bit farther south, try *Adventure Kayaking: Trips from Big Sur to San Diego*, by Robert Mohle (1998).

Jenkins, J.C., and Ruby Johnson Jenkins. *Exploring the Southern Sierra: East Side*. Berkeley: Wilderness Press, 1992. Third ed. Originally titled *Self Propelled in the Southern Sierra, Volume 1*. This guide includes 150 adventures in one of the state's remaining sanctuaries of solitude. Includes a four-color foldout map. Also by the Jenkins' (also retitled): *Exploring the Southern Sierra: West Side* (1995).

Linkhart, Luther. *The Trinity Alps: A Hiking and Backpacking Guide*. Berkeley: Wilderness Press, 2004. Fourth ed.

Lorentzen, Bob. *The Hiker's Hip Pocket Guide to the Mendocino Coast*. Mendocino, CA: Bored Feet Publications, 2003. Third ed., updated to include Big River State Park. One of the stars in Lorentzen's excellent hiking series, this best-selling, easy-to-follow hiking guide now includes 100 more miles of trails. Coverage includes all Mendocino area state parks, Jackson State Forest, Sinkyone Wilderness State Park, and little-known coastal access points. Also by Lorentzen: *The Hiker's Hip Pocket Guide to the Humboldt Coast* (updated 2001), *The Hiker's Hip Pocket Guide to Sonoma County* (1995), and *The Hiker's Hip Pocket Guide to the Mendocino Highlands* (1992).

McConnell, Doug, with Jerry Emory and Stacy Gelken. *Bay Area Backroads*. San Francisco: Chronicle Books, 1999. Day trips and more throughout the greater Bay Area—and beyond—brought to you by the host of the San Francisco Bay Area's most popular local television show.

McKinney, John. *Coast Walks: 150 Adventures Along the California Coast*. Santa Barbara: Olympus Press, 1999. The new edition of McKinney's coast hiking classic contains plenty of new adventures, from Border Field State Park at the Mexican Border north to Damnation Creek and Pelican Bay. Along the way, you'll also learn about local lore, history, and natural history—a bargain no matter how you hike it. Maps and illustrations.

McKinney, John. *Day Hiker's Guide to California State Parks*. Santa Barbara: Olympus Press, 2000. Second ed. The *Los Angeles Times* travel columnists offers about all you need to know to stretch your legs *and* see the sights in the Golden State's hikable parks and recreation areas. McKinney also offers a national park hiking guide.

Neumann, Phyllis. *Sonoma County Bike Trails*. Second ed. Penngrove, CA: Penngrove Publications, 2001. Third revised ed., updated. The long-running, ever-popular cycling guide to Sonoma County. Also available: *Marin County Bike Trails*.

Ostertag, Rhonda, and George Ostertag. *California State Parks: A Complete Recreation Guide*. Seattle: The Mountaineers, 2001. Second ed. Moving from north to south, this readable companion serves as a good general introduction to the state parks—and guide to what to do while you're there, with an emphasis on hikes. Here California is divided into six regions. Helpful maps, some entertaining photos.

Perry, John, and Jane Greverus Perry. *The Sierra Club Guide to the Natural Areas of California*. San Francisco: Sierra Club Books, 1997. Second ed. A just-the-facts yet very useful guide to California's public lands and parks—a book to tuck into the glovebox. Organized by regions, also indexed for easy access.

Schaffer, Jeffrey. *Hiking the Big Sur Country: The Ventana Wilderness.* Berkeley: Wilderness Press, 1988 (updated 1998). Other good hiking and backpacking guides by this prolific pathfinder include: *The Carson-Iceberg Wilderness; Desolation Wilderness and the South Lake Tahoe Basin; Lassen Volcanic National Park; The Pacific Crest Trail Volume 1: California; The Tahoe Sierra;* and *Yosemite National Park.*

Selters, Andy, and Michael Zanger. *The Mt. Shasta Book: A Guide to Hiking, Climbing, Skiing, and Exploring the Mountain and Surrounding Area.* Berkeley: Wilderness Press, 2001. Second ed.

Soares, John R., and Marc J. Soares. *100 Classic Hikes in Northern California.* Seattle: Mountaineers Books, 2001. Second ed. The brothers Soares show your where to hike—many classic California trips included—and why.

Socolich, Sally. *Bargain Hunting in the Bay Area.* San Francisco: Chronicle Books, 2000. The ultimate shop-til-you-drop guide, now in its 13th (perhaps by now 14th) edition, including discount stores, outlets, flea markets, and the year's best sales.

Stanton, Ken. *Great Day Hikes in & around Napa Valley.* Mendocino, CA: Bored Feet Publications, 2001. Second ed.

Stevens, Barbara, and Nancy Conner. *Where on Earth: A Guide to Specialty Nurseries and Other Resources for California Gardeners.* Berkeley: Heyday Books, 1999. Fourth ed. Ever wondered where to get that unusual color of iris or that exotic azalea, or where to find the state's best native plant nurseries? Wonder no more. California gardeners won't be able to live for long without *this* essential resource, thoroughly revised, expanded, and updated.

Stienstra, Tom. *Foghorn Outdoors California Camping.* Emeryville, CA: Avalon Travel Publishing, 2003. 13th ed. This is undoubtedly the ultimate reference to California camping and campgrounds, public and private. Every single one is in here. In addition to a thorough practical introduction to the basics of California camping—and reviews of the latest high-tech gear, for hiking and camping comfort and safety—this guidebook is meticulously organized by area, starting with the general subdivisions of Northern, Central, and Southern California. Even accidental outdoorspeople should carry this one along at all times. Also by Stienstra and Ann Marie Brown: *Foghorn Outdoors California Hiking,* 2003. Sixth ed.

Wach, Bonnie. *San Francisco as You Like It: 20 Tailor-Made Tours for Culture Vultures, Shopaholics, Neo-Bohemians, Fitness Freaks, Savvy Natives, and Everyone Else.* San Francisco: Chronicle Books, 1998. A hefty helping of more than the usual tourist fare, from The Politically Correct and Avant-Garde Aunts tours to Current and Former Hippies, and Queer and Curious. And a good time will be had by all.

Index

Index

U.S.~ Metric Conversion

To compute Celsius temperatures, subtract 32 from Fahrenheit and divide by 1.8. To go the other way, multiply Celsius by 1.8 and add 32.

1 inch	=	2.54 centimeters (cm)
1 foot	=	.304 meters (m)
1 yard	=	0.914 meters
1 mile	=	1.6093 kilometers (km)
1 km	=	.6214 miles
1 fathom	=	1.8288 m
1 chain	=	20.1168 m
1 furlong	=	201.168 m
1 acre	=	.4047 hectares
1 sq km	=	100 hectares
1 sq mile	=	2.59 square km
1 ounce	=	28.35 grams
1 pound	=	.4536 kilograms
1 short ton	=	.90718 metric ton
1 short ton	=	2000 pounds
1 long ton	=	1.016 metric tons
1 long ton	=	2240 pounds
1 metric ton	=	1000 kilograms
1 quart	=	.94635 liters
1 US gallon	=	3.7854 liters
1 Imperial gallon	=	4.5459 liters
1 nautical mile	=	1.852 km

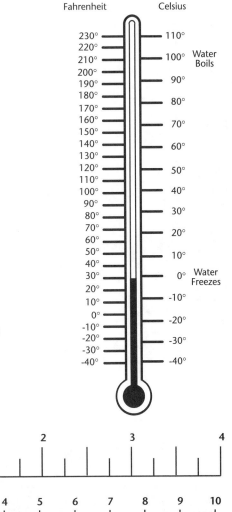

www.moon.com

For helpful advice on planning a trip, visit www.moon.com for the **TRAVEL PLANNER** and get access to useful travel strategies and valuable information about great places to visit. When you travel with Moon, expect an experience that is uncommon and truly unique.

HANDBOOKS • METRO • OUTDOORS • LIVING ABROAD

MO●N

Keeping Current

Although we strive to produce the most up-to-date guidebook humanly possible, change is unavoidable. Between the time this book goes to print and the moment you read it, a handful of the businesses noted in these pages will undoubtedly change prices, move, or even close their doors forever. Other worthy attractions will open for the first time. If you have a favorite gem you'd like to see included in the next edition, or see anything that needs updating, clarification, or correction, please drop us a line. Send your comments via email to atpfeedback@avalonpub.com, or use the address below.

Moon Handbooks Northern California
Avalon Travel Publishing
1400 65th Street, Suite 250
Emeryville, CA 94608, USA
www.moon.com

Editor: Ellen Cavalli
Series Manager: Kevin McLain
Graphics and Production Coordinator: Amber Pirker (cover: Melissa Sherowski)
Cover Designer: Kari Gim
Interior Designers: Amber Pirker, Alvaro Villanueva, Kelly Pendragon
Map Editor: Olivia Solis
Cartographer: Mike Morgenfeld, Kat Kalamaras
Research Assistance: Jenica Szymanski, Samantha Metzger, Miguel Diaz
Indexer: Deana Shields

ISBN-10: 1-56691-555-4
ISBN-13: 978-1-56691-555-7
ISSN: 1524-4148

Printing History
1st Edition—1990
4th Edition— May 2004
5 4 3 2

Avalon Travel Publishing
an imprint of
Avalon Publishing Group, Inc.

Poems by Gary Thompson are © 1999 by Gary Thompson. All rights reserved. All of these poems are included in the collection *On John Muir's Trail* (1999), which is available from Bear Star Press, 185 Hollow Oak Dr., Cohasset, CA 95973, www.bearstarpress.com.

Some photos and illustrations are used by permission and are the property of the original copyright owners.

Front cover photo: © Randy Wells
Table of contents photos: cable car: Susan Snyder; Bay Bridge: © Kim Weir; all other photos: © Robert Holmes/CalTour

Printed in the USA by Worzalla